VOLUME I

THE HANDBOOK OF
SOCIAL PSYCHOLOGY

VOLUME I

THE HANDBOOK OF SOCIAL PSYCHOLOGY

FOURTH EDITION

Daniel T. Gilbert

Harvard University

Susan T. Fiske

*University of Massachusetts
at Amherst*

Gardner Lindzey

*Center for Advanced Study in the
Behavioral Sciences*

The McGRAW-HILL Companies, Inc.

Boston, Massachusetts   Burr Ridge, Illinois   Dubuque, Iowa
Madison, Wisconsin   New York, New York   San Francisco, California   St. Louis, Missouri

*Distributed exclusively by Oxford University Press
New York and Oxford*

McGraw-Hill

*A Division of The **McGraw·Hill** Companies*

THE HANDBOOK OF SOCIAL PSYCHOLOGY
VOLUME I

Acknowledgments appear on page xx and on this page
by reference.

This book is printed on acid-free paper.

1 2 3 4 5 6 7 8 9 0   DOC   DOC   9 0 9 8 7

ISBN 0-19-521376-9

Publisher: *Jane Vaicunas*
Sponsoring editor: *Beth Kaufman*
Marketing manager: *Jim Rozsa*
Project manager: *Ann Morgan*
Production supervisor: *Deb Donner*
Cover and text designer: *Kiera Cunningham*
Project supervision: *The Total Book*
Compositor: *Ruttle, Shaw & Wetherill, Inc.*
Typeface: 9.5/11 Times Roman
Printer: *R. R. Donnelley—Crawfordsville*

Distributed exclusively by
Oxford University Press, Inc.
198 Madison Avenue
New York, NY 10016

With offices in:
Oxford   New York   Toronto   Delhi
Bombay   Calcutta   Madras   Karachi
Kuala Lumpur   Singapore   Hong Kong
Tokyo   Nairobi   Dar es Salaam   Cape Town
Melbourne   Auckland   Warsaw

and associated companies in
Berlin   Ibadan

http://www.oup-usa.org
Telephone: 1-800-732-3120

Library of Congress Cataloging-in-Publication Data

The handbook of social psychology / [edited by] Daniel Gilbert, Susan
    Fiske, Gardner Lindzey. — 4th ed.
       p.   cm.
    Previous ed. edited by Gardner Lindzey and Elliot Aronson.
    Includes bibliographical references and index.
    ISBN 0–19–521376–9 (v. 1 and v. 2)
     1. Social psychology.   I. Gilbert, Daniel.   II. Fiske, Susan T.
  III. Lindzey, Gardner.
  HM251.H224   1998
  302–dc21   97–5436

We dedicate this book
to the memory of Ned Jones—
teacher, scholar, gentleman, friend.

CONTENTS

PREFACE TO THE FOURTH EDITION

When Carl Murchison brought out the first *Handbook of Social Psychology* in 1935, he had never seen a television, never photocopied a letter, never ridden on a jet plane. Neither had anyone else. Almost twenty years later, many things had changed—including social psychology—and Gardner Lindzey saw "an acute need for a source book more advanced than the ordinary textbook in the field but yet more focused than the scattered periodical literature" (Lindzey, 1954, p. ix). With the strong encouragement and assistance of Gordon Allport, the new *Handbook of Social Psychology* appeared in 1954 under Lindzey's editorship, and then again in 1969 and 1985 under the joint editorship of Lindzey and Elliot Aronson. Somewhere on the road from then to now, the *Handbook* stopped being a mere sourcebook and became instead the standard professional reference for the field of social psychology, which it has remained for almost half a century. With each new edition, the *Handbook* gave readers an opportunity to listen as a new generation of scholars pondered social psychology's enduring questions, surveyed its past progress, and set its agenda for the future. *The Handbook of Social Psychology* may well be the field's most venerable institution, and it is thus with a mixture of pride and humility that we offer this, its fourth edition.

For the most part, the fourth edition continues the traditions of previous editions, whose histories are chronicled in the prefaces reprinted on the following pages. But there have been some changes. Elliot Aronson served with such skill as co-editor of the second and third editions that when he retired it took two people to fill his shoes, and Daniel Gilbert and Susan Fiske have now joined Gardner Lindzey on the editorial bench. These changes in editorship mirror similar changes in authorship. In 1993, the editors contacted fifty-seven of the field's most eminent scholars and asked them to nominate both authors and topics for the fourth edition. Their nominations showed surprising consensus, and almost without exception, the authors they nominated accepted invitations to contribute to the *Handbook*. Of the sixty-six authors who have contributed to the current edition, only fourteen contributed chapters to the previous edition—and in many cases, those authors wrote about entirely different topics for the two different editions. The authors of the *Handbook* represent a new and diverse group of men and women who vary in experience (from graduate student to university president), intellectual orientation (from political scientist to evolutionary psychologist), and cultural background (from Ann Arbor to Hong Kong), but who share a keen sense of the history, methods, and phenomena of social psychology. They are by any measure an enormously distinguished group, and we are honored to assemble their insights in these volumes.

But the most important changes from one edition to the next are not in the personnel, but in the contents of the chapters themselves. Each edition's table of contents provides a thumbnail sketch of social psychology's topical concerns, and although a few topics have come and gone in a single edition (one can hardly imagine a modern version of "The Social Life of Bacteria"), on the whole these tables reveal a striking stability at the field's core. Topics rarely appear like miracles in one edition and then drop off the face of the next. Rather, they develop in a life cycle, appearing first as subtopics within chapters, expanding next into full chapters of their own, dividing later into multiple chapters, and finally growing so complex that they pervade the other chapters and defy any single, comprehensive treatment. The "new" topics that appear in this edition—such as self, emotions, automaticity, stigma, memory, evolution, and more—are surely not new to social psychology. Rather, they are topics that have long been central to the discipline, but about which enough has now been learned to warrant independent coverage. At least twenty of the current chapters have no obvious counterpart in the last edition, but the observer who concludes that these new titles signal an abrupt change in social psychology's intellectual mission (or a slavish devotion to fads and trends) has failed to recognize the continuity of the field's intellectual evolution. If the table of contents of this edition has a message for us, it is that the center of social psychology is holding quite well.

This is not to say, of course, that the social psychology of 1997 is—or is even very much like—the social psychology of 1935. Indeed, the field's growth in the past few decades has been remarkable. Since the last edition, social psychology has continued its downward push toward the information-processing and even physiological levels of analysis, while renewing its traditional commitment to the group, organizational, political, and cultural levels. It has developed new scientific methods and new analytic techniques, and has continued fruitful partnerships with other disciplines, such as law, medicine, and political science. Editors attempt to expose the structure of a discipline by clustering chapters in particular ways, and the structure of the fourth edition is meant to highlight the many levels of analysis at which modern social psychologists seem both capable and comfortable. Whether considering the behavior of neurons, nodes, neighbors, or nations, the authors of these chapters share a concern with a fundamental question—how do people think about, feel about, and act toward each other?—as well as a commitment to empirical analysis and a respect for the diverse approaches that con-stitute the science. If the questions have remained the same, the places in which the answers are sought have changed profoundly. Social psychology is, like the rest of the known universe, expanding in all directions at once, and that expansion has led to many of the exciting developments that are detailed in the chapters that follow.

Much has changed since the first *Handbook* appeared in 1935. If its authors were here today, they would be amazed to see that airplanes travel faster than sound, puzzled to hear that people copy and download, and amused to learn that mice now go *click* rather than *squeak*. But as wondrous as these technological advances would undoubtedly seem, we suspect the authors of the first *Handbook* would be just as impressed—and twice as delighted—by the intellectual advances documented in these volumes.

January 1997

D.T.G., *Cambridge*
S.T.F., *Amherst*
G.L., *Stanford*

PREFACE TO THE THIRD EDITION

This is the fourth *Handbook of Social Psychology*—the third involving one or both of the current editors. To examine these four *Handbooks* for constancy and change is a revealing exercise.

In introducing his 1935 *Handbook* Carl Murchison remarked, "The social sciences at the present moment stand naked and feeble in the midst of the political uncertainty of the world. The physical sciences seem so brilliant, so clothed with power by contrast. Either something has gone all wrong in the evolution of the social sciences, or their great day in court has not yet arrived. It is with something akin to despair that one contemplates the piffling, trivial, superficial, damnably unimportant topics that some social scientists investigate with agony and sweat. And at the end of all these centuries, no one knows what is wrong with the world or what is likely to happen to the world" (p. ix). A mere decade later this paragraph already seemed to many observers archaic and poorly informed. Even more remarkable is the fact that more than one-third the chapters in the 1935 *Handbook* dealt with the social psychology of bacteria, plants, and lower animals. Moreover, four chapters dealt with the social history of the negro, the red man, the white man, and the yellow man—labels that if used today would create a wave of revulsion. These chapters and others not mentioned strike no note of resonance with contemporary social psychology.

Are there any traces in Murchison's *Handbook* of what has emerged as social psychology fifty years later? Clearly, the answer is yes, although the number of such continuities is not large. Perhaps the most dramatic example of anticipating the future is Gordon Allport's chapter on attitudes. In the 1954 *Handbook* there were to be two chapters on attitudes—one on measurement, and the other on attitude theory and research—and it was a last-minute withdrawal that led to omission of the chapter on attitude theory and research. In subsequent volumes we have observed a very heavy emphasis on attitude research as a cornerstone of social psychology. A second line of continuity is represented by Esper's chapter on language, which has been reflected

and elaborated on in each of the subsequent editions. Moreover, Dashiell's chapter on human social experiments remarkably anticipates the industrious experimental social psychologists who to date have played an increasingly dominant role in American social psychology. Chapters on gender differences and the behavior of children in social situations are also reflected in subsequent *Handbooks*.

The 1954 edition fell naturally into two volumes: Volume I was devoted to prominent theories and major methods; Volume II dealt entirely with the most active substantive research areas of the time. The theoretical positions represented in the 1954 edition were almost identical to those in the 1968–1969 edition. In 1954, separate chapters were devoted to S–R theory (including reinforcement and contiguity), cognitive theory, psychoanalytic theory, field theory, and role theory. In the 1968–1969 edition each of those theoretical positions was again represented, and in addition, separate chapters were devoted to organization theory and mathematical models. In the current edition we have reverted to five theoretical positions. We retained S–R theory but broadened it to include the wider issues implied by the title "learning theory." Our chapter on cognitive theories acknowledges the continuing development of exciting systematic positions in that area. Similarly, our decision to retain a chapter on organization theory indicates the continued impact of that position. Our chapter on role theory has now been expanded to include symbolic interactionism in order to provide stronger representation of sociological perspectives. Although we have dropped specific chapters on mathematical models and field theory, work in these areas is very much in evidence in our new chapters on decision theory and cognitive theories. Our decision not to include a chapter on psychoanalytic theory was difficult. Although we appreciate the riches that social psychologists have extracted from this particular mine of ideas, it seems clear that over the past two decades very little research by social psychologists has been directly stimulated by this theory.

With regard to methods, we find few changes in chapter

titles over the past thirty years. Social psychologists are still interested primarily in experimentation, attitude and opinion measurement, survey research, systematic observation, and quantitative analysis. Needless to say, the *content* of the chapters has changed dramatically over the years as our colleagues have become increasingly sophisticated in their use of these methods. The one new chapter that has been added concerns evaluation—reflecting a body of techniques that has become increasingly important since the late 1960s and has resulted in a new psychological specialty.

It is particularly interesting to compare the substantive research areas across the three modern editions of the handbook. Some areas have been a major focus of social psychological research since World War II and seem destined to remain so for the foreseeable future. Thus since the war all three handbooks have included chapters on attitude change, leadership, the media, prejudice and racism, anthropological social psychology, psycholinguistics, and political behavior.

Some content areas have undergone a shift in emphasis over the years that has been great enough to require a major change in the title of the chapter. Thus our current chapter on social influence covers some of the same issues and kinds of research contained in chapters from earlier editions on group problem solving, but with a much wider range. Similarly, social psychologists have been interested in the socialization process for a very long time. The title of the current chapter emphasizes that the socialization process is not confined to infants, children, and adolescents, and reflects the increase in research on socialization throughout the life cycle. Likewise, the new chapter on social factors in cognition combines and expands earlier chapters on person perception and social and cultural factors in perception. The current edition also continues some trends that were initiated in the 1968–1969 edition. These include a special emphasis on interpersonal attraction and on the interaction between personality and social psychology.

Finally, there are some substantive chapters that are either totally new to this edition or that bear only slight resemblance to anything that has appeared in previous editions. These include chapters on sex roles, environmental psychology, social deviance, prosocial and antisocial behavior, and applications of social psychology. The chapters on sex roles and environmental psychology reflect issues and interests that were simply not factors in 1954, were barely on the horizon in 1968–1969, but are very much a part of our lives in the 1980s. Social psychologists have been playing a major role in increasing our understanding of these issues. In one sense, the handbook has been involved with applied social psychology throughout its existence. Thus the 1954 edition included a chapter on industrial social psychology; the 1968 edition included a revised

version of that chapter but also included separate chapters on the social psychology of education, social psychological aspects of international relations, the social psychology of mental health, and others. But in another sense, the current chapter is innovative in that its focus is not on "applied social psychology" but on the broader issue of "the application" of social psychological knowledge and methods to a wide variety of contemporary problems such as health care, the legal system, and the classroom.

The only author to appear in all four *Handbooks* is Allport, who has written both on attitudes (1935) and on the history of social psychology (1954, 1968, 1985). His contribution to the present volume appears posthumously and is a slightly abridged version of the chapter that appeared in the last edition. No other author has appeared in more than two editions, although one was involved with four chapters in the 1954 and 1968–1969 editions, and a substantial number (twenty-five) have contributed to two editions. There are forty-five contributors to the current edition only seven of whom contributed to the last edition. As these figures indicate, the current volumes represent a decidedly fresh perspective on the field of social psychlogy. Many of our colleagues continued to find the 1954 edition useful after the appearance of the 1968–1969 edition, and we have little doubt that both the previous editions will continue to be of utility even with the appearance of this revision.

Because the *Handbook* is generally regarded as a kind of "standard," it is sometimes used to gauge current interests in social psychology or even to predict the health and direction of social psychology. For this reason we feel the editors have an obligation to make certain that our decisions (implicit and explicit) are not misinterpreted. For example one reviewer, in noting that the 1954 edition did not contain a chapter on "Attitude Theory and Research," concluded that social psychologists were losing interest in the concept of attitude. As noted earlier, the absence of that chapter was no more meaningful than the delinquency of one of our contributors! A final *Handbook* is almost never a precise reflection of the intentions of the editors and their advisors, and consequently readers should be cautious in interpreting trends or the current state of the field from the contents of the various editions.

With these concerns in mind, it is clearly important to discuss changes we have made in the format of the *Handbook*. The 1954 edition consisted of two volumes. The 1968–1969 edition was expanded to five volumes. For the current edition we decided to return to the two-volume format. A facile (but incorrect) interpretation might be that social psychology reached its peak in the 1960s and is now declining. We do not hold this view. We believe social psychology is as vital today as it was twenty years ago. Our decisions regarding format were based on more mundane issues—utility, convenience, and cost. Specifically, in

1967–1968 we believed that the five-volume format would make it easier for social psychologists interested in specific topics to purchase one or two small volumes rather than the entire set. This proved to be a poor prediction: sales figures indicated that most users purchased all five volumes simultaneously. Moreover, we noted with dismay that the five-volume format changed the way the *Handbook* was being used. Apparently there is a tendency for a work in five volumes to be seen and used as if it were an encyclopedia. That is, our graduate students and colleagues tended to place their *Handbooks* on a shelf and to pull down a volume only when they needed a reference book. This was not the case with the 1954 edition, which was used both as a text and as a portable companion. Moreover, the cost of producing a five-volume set today would place the *Handbook* beyond the financial grasp of all but libraries and the very well-to-do. In short, our decision to return to a two-volume format was made because we believe the *Handbook* is more vital if it is off the shelf and priced at the lowest possible level.

The current volumes had their beginnings in May 1978, when we sent more than 130 letters to well-known social psychologists, including all contributors to the previous edition of the *Handbook*. We enclosed a tentative outline for the current *Handbook* and asked for comments about both topics and potential authors. We also pointed to a reorganization that in both number of volumes and chapters implied a product that would be more like the 1954 volumes than the 1968–1969 *Handbook*. We received more than seventy-five replies. All but one of the respondents felt a revision was timely. All but one respondent also ap-

proved, explicitly or implicitly, the reduction in number of volumes from five to two. Virtually all had suggestions for changes in our outline and roster of potential authors. The outline was substantially altered as a result of these suggestions, and in October 1978 we began to solicit authors. We will not take you through the tortuous path of changing deadlines, authors, and (very slightly) chapters. Actually, of the thirty-two chapters included in our outline, only two have been lost through attrition.

Some readers may be surprised to discover that these volumes have been published by Random House rather than Addison-Wesley. Certainly the editors were surprised when informed in the late stages of production that Addison-Wesley was transferring all of its social science publications to Random House. We were assured that there would be no delay in the appearance of the volumes and that Random House was looking forward eagerly to the production and promotion of the *Handbook*. We see no reason to doubt these statements and look forward to an amicable and rewarding relationship with Random House.

The facilities of the Center for Advanced Study in the Behavioral Sciences played a very significant role in the production of these volumes. In particular, the patience and skill of Joyce McDonald were indispensable and are deeply appreciated.

September 1984

G. L., *Stanford, California*
E. A., *Santa Cruz, California*

PREFACE TO THE SECOND EDITION

In the fourteen years that have elapsed since the last edition of this *Handbook*, the field of social psychology has evolved at a rapid rate. The present volumes are intended to represent these changes as faithfully as possible and at a level appropriate for the beginning graduate student as well as the fully trained psychologist.

The reader familiar with the previous *Handbook* will realize that we have employed the same general outline in the present volumes. The many new chapters reflect the increased quantitative and methodological sophistication of social psychologists, the development of certain specialized areas of research, and the increased activity in a variety of applied areas. In some instances we have attempted to compensate for known deficiencies in the coverage of the previous edition.

One can never be certain of portraying adequately the changes in a large and diverse area of scholarship, but we can be certain that this *Handbook* is very different from its predecessor. It is substantially larger—instead of one million words, two volumes, and 30 chapters, there are now approximately two-and-one-half million words, five volumes, and 45 chapters. We are convinced that our decision to present this material in five volumes will increase its utility for those who have specialized interests linked to either teaching or research activities. But the difference goes beyond mere size. The list of contributors has a decidedly new flavor—of the 45 authors in the previous edition, only 22 have contributed to this volume. Viewed from another vantage, of the 68 authors contributing to the current volume, 46 are represented in the *Handbook* for the first time. Only one chapter is reprinted without a thorough revision, and this, an essay (Hebb and Thompson) presenting a point of view that seems little affected by recent research and formulation. There are 15 chapters that are completely new and, in addition, a number of the replacements bear little resemblance to the chapter of the same, or similar, title that appeared earlier.

Plans for the current revision were begun in January of 1963. By July of that year a tentative chapter outline had been prepared and distributed to an array of distinguished social scientists, including the previous contributors to the *Handbook*. We benefited materially from the advice of dozens of persons in regard to both the chapter outline and the nomination of potential authors; we are grateful for their efforts on behalf of the *Handbook*. By fall of 1963 we had succeeded in constructing a final outline and a list of contributors. Our initial letters of invitation asked that completed manuscripts be submitted by January 1, 1965. We managed to obtain the bulk of the chapters eighteen months and several deadlines later, and the first two volumes were sent to the publishers early in 1967. The final chapters were secured the following July, when the remaining volumes went to press.

In selecting contributors we made every effort, within the general constraints of technical competence and availability, to obtain scholars of diverse professional and institutional backgrounds. Thus we take special pleasure in the fact that almost all areas of the country are well represented, that six of the contributors are affiliated with institutions outside the United States, and that the authors include political scientists, sociologists, and anthropologists as well as psychologists.

We consider it extremely fortunate that of the chapters listed in our working outline, all of those that we regarded as "key" or central chapters are included here. Indeed, there are only three chapters from that list that are not a part of the present volumes; this includes one (attitude change) that was deliberately incorporated within another chapter because such an arrangement seemed to offer a greater likelihood of satisfactory integration and coverage. It should be noted that this success is in marked contrast to the previous *Handbook*, where such essential areas as attitudes and social perception were omitted because of last-minute delinquencies. Although a few invited contributors did withdraw from the present *Handbook* after initially having agreed to prepare a chapter, in all cases we were fortunate in being able to find equally qualified replacements who were willing to take on this assignment on relatively short notice. To these individuals we owe a special debt of gratitude.

We wish to acknowledge the indispensable assistance of Judith Hilton, Shirley Cearley, and Leslie Segner in connection with the final preparation of the manuscript. Finally, we would like to express our gratitude to Mary Jane Whiteside for her tireless efforts in the final indexing of all volumes of the *Handbook*.

February 1968

G. L.
E. A.
Austin, Texas

PREFACE TO THE FIRST EDITION

The accelerating expansion of social psychology in the past two decades has led to an acute need for a source book more advanced than the ordinary textbook in the field but yet more focused than scattered periodical literature. Muchison's *Handbook of Social Psychology* (1935), the only previous attempt to meet this need, is out of date and out of print. It was this state of affairs that led us to assemble a book that would represent the major areas of social psychology at a level of difficulty appropriate for graduate students. In addition to serving the needs of graduate instruction, we anticipate that the volumes will be useful in advanced undergraduate courses and as a reference book for professional psychologists.

We first considered the possibility of preparing a *Handbook* three years ago. However, a final decision to proceed with the plan was not reached until the fall of 1951. During the interval we arranged an outline of topics that represented our convictions concerning the present state of social psychology. We then wrote to a large number of distinguished social psychologists asking them whether they felt our venture was likely to be professionally valuable and asking for criticisms of the outline we had prepared. The response to these letters was immensely gratifying—social psychologists as a group appear sufficiently altruistic to spend large amounts of time criticizing and commenting on a project of which they approve even though they may be unable to participate in it themselves. We also asked for specific recommendations of people who seemed best qualified to prepare the various chapters. After receiving answers we drastically revised our outline and proceeded to invite authors to prepare the various chapters. It was not until the spring of 1952 that we completed our list of contributors and even this list later underwent change. We first suggested (tongue in cheek) that the manuscripts be submitted by September 15, 1952. However, as we secretly expected, we were forced to change this due date to January 1, 1953. This "deadline" we tried hard to meet. But of course we failed and shifted our aspiration to June 15, 1953. Again we failed, although by now we were making

substantial progress. By early in the fall of 1953 we had all the chapters excepting two, and the first volume was completed and in the hands of the publishers. The last two chapters were not received until early in 1954, when the second volume went to press.

Something should be said concerning the basis for the organization of the subject matter of these volumes. It became apparent early that there are many ways to subdivide social psychology but very little agreement concerning just which is best. Although we sought the advice of others, we found for almost every compelling suggestion an equally compelling countersuggestion. Thus, in the end, it was necessary to make many arbitrary decisions. So much for our knowledge that the *Handbook* could have been organized in many different ways. There is no single scheme that would satisfy all readers.

We early discovered that the subject matter was too voluminous to be contained in a single volume. Given this decision it seemed quite natural to present in one volume the chapters that dealt primarily with theoretical convictions or systematic positions, and also the methods and procedures commonly employed in social psychology. Likewise it seemed wise to present in one volume those chapters that focus upon the substantive findings and applications of social psychology. The decision to place the historical introduction, theory, and method chapters in the first volume reflects a bias in favor of investigation that begins with an awareness of the message of the past, an attempt at theoretical relevance, and finally with a full knowledge of the procedural or measurement alternatives. All of the content of the first volume is seen, at least by the editor, as a necessary preparation for good investigation. These are the things the social psychologist should know before he lifts a single empirical finger. The second volume, then, can be seen as a justification of the contents of the first volume. Here are the empirical fruits stemming from the theories and methods summarized in the first volume.

But does this ideal scheme mirror common practice? Are the major empirical advances summarized in the second volume in reality a legitimate by-product of theoretical conceptions and sophisticated method? In fairness to science in action (as opposed to science on the books) we are afraid the answer is No. Social psychology has made its advances largely on the shoulders of random empiricists and naive realists. Inability to distinguish between analytic and synthetic and a tendency toward reification of concepts has accompanied many of the most significant advances in this field. Who would say that those who view an attitude as a "construct" created by the investigator have made more of a contribution to this area of psychology than those who naively view attitudes as real and concrete entities? Thus we sorrowfully admit the organization we have imposed upon the *Handbook* may bear little relation to the path thus far trod in the development of social psychology. Nevertheless, it stands as a suggestion of the manner in which future development may well take place and as a reminder that the powerful weapon of systematic theory is now more nearly within the grasp of the wise psychologist than formerly. Where yesterday the theoretically oriented investigator and the random realist may have been on even terms, recent developments within the field may well have destroyed this equality. An approach efficient in the wilderness may be foolish in a more carefully mapped region. In summary, the precedence we give to theoretical positions reflects our conviction of the importance of theories as spurs to research, but may also represent a program for the future rather than a reflection of the past.

It must be conceded that not all areas of social psychology are covered in these volumes with equal thoroughness. Some gaps are due to the blind spots of the editor while others are the result of contributors failing to cover an area they originally agreed to cover and, in a few cases, to contributors who withdrew altogether. In spite of these shortcomings, the volumes in their present state provide the most comprehensive picture of social psychology that exists in one place today. While deficiencies of the final product are my own responsibility, they exist in spite of a number of advisors who gave their time and energy generously throughout the venture. Of these collaborators none was nearly so important as Gordon Allport. In fairness he should be co-editor of the volume, as he contributed immeasurably both in matters of policy and in matters of detail. I owe a very special debt of gratitude to my wife Andrea for her tolerance, encouragment, and detailed assistance. Likewise of great importance is the contribution of Shirley H. Heinemann, who has been of constant help throughout the editorial process and in preparing the Index. Crucial to the success of this work were various additional colleagues who served as referees, reading individual chapters and suggesting changes and deletions. On this score I express my gratitude to Raymond Bauer, Anthony Davids, Edward E. Jones, Kaspar Naegele, David Schneider, and Walter Weiss. In addition, many of the contributors served as referees for chapters other than their own. I am indebted to E. G. Boring, S. S. Stevens, and Geraldine Stone for many helpful suggestions based on their experience in arranging the *Handbook of Experimental Psychology*. Mrs. Olga Crawford of Addison-Wesley played an indispensable role in final preparation of the manuscripts.

April 1954

G. L

ACKNOWLEDGMENTS

Chap. 4, p. 157, Table 1: Adapted from Schwartz, N., Hippler, H. J., Deutsch, B., & Strack, F. Response scales: Effects of category range on reported behavior and comparative judgments, *Public Opinion Quarterly, 49,* pp. 388–395. Copyright © 1985. Reprinted by permission of The University of Chicago Press.

Chap. 5, p. 185, Figure 2: From Kruskal, J. B., & Wish, M., *Multidimensional scaling,* Figure 8, p. 32. Copyright © 1978. Reprinted by permission of Sage Publications.

Chap. 5, p. 186, Figure 3: From Wainer, H., & Thissen, D., Graphical data analysis. In Rosenzweig, M. R., & Porter L. W. (Eds.), *Annual Review of Psychology, 32,* © 1981, by Annual Reviews Inc.

Chap. 5, p. 197, Figure 10: From van der Ven, A. H. G. S., *Introduction to scaling,* p. 208. Copyright © 1980. Reprinted by permission of John Wiley & Sons, Ltd., Chichester, England.

Chap. 5, p. 221, Figure 14: From Judd, C. M., Jessor, R., & Donovan, J. E., Structural equation models and personality research, *Journal of Personality, 54,* Figure 3, p. 168. Copyright © 1986 by Duke University Press. Reprinted by permission of Duke University Press.

Chap. 7, p. 299, Figure 3: Adapted from Aizen, I., & Fishbein, M., *Understanding attitudes and predicting social behavior,* Figure 7.1, p. 84. Copyright © 1980. Reprinted by permission of Prentice-Hall, Inc., Upper Saddle River, NJ.

Chap. 9, p. 398, Figure 2: From Carlston, D. E., Associated systems theory: A systematic approach to cognitive representations of persons, Figure 1.2, p. 7. In Srull, T. K., & Wyer, R. S. (Eds.), *Advances in social cognition: A dual process model of impression formation* (Vol. 7). Copyright © 1994. Reprinted by permission of Lawrence Erlbaum Associates, Inc.

Chap. 11, p. 499, Figure 1: From Tversky, A., & Kahneman, D., Rational choices and the framing of decisions, Figure 1, p. S259. In *Journal of Business, 59.* Copyright © 1986. Reprinted by permission of The University of Chicago Press.

Chap. 11, p. 506, Figure 2: From Kahneman, D., Knetsch, J. L., & Thaler, R. H., Anomalies: The endowment effect, loss aversion, and status quo bias, *Journal of Economic Perspectives, 5,* Figure 3, p. 201. Copyright © 1991. Reprinted by permission of the American Economic Association.

Chap. 11, p. 507, Table 1: From Tversky, A., Intransitivity of preferences, *Psychological Review, 76,* p. 33. Copyright © 1969. Reprinted by permission of The American Psychological Association.

Chap. 11, p. 534, Figure 5: From Russo, J. E., & Schoemaker, P. J. H., *Decision traps.* Copyright © 1989 by J. Edward Russo and Paul J. H. Schoemaker. Used by permission of Doubleday, a division of Bantam Doubleday Dell Publishing Group, Inc.

Chap. 17, p. 790, Figure 1: From Deaux, K. & Major, B. Putting gender into context: An interactive model of gender-related behavior, *Psychological Review, 94,* p. 372, 1987. Used with permission.

Chap. 17, p. 809, Figure 2: From Eccles, J. S., Understanding women's educational and occupational choices: Applying the Eccles et al. model of achievement-related choices, *Psychology of Women Quarterly, 18,* Figure 1. Developed by Eccles (Parsons), J., Adler, T. F., Futterman, R., Goff, S. B., Kaczala, C. M., Mese, J. L., & Midglevy, C., Expectations, values and academic behaviors. In Spence, J. T., *Perspective on achievement and achievement motivation.* San Francisco: W. H. Freeman, 1983. Copyright © 1994. Reprinted with the permission of Cambridge University Press.

Chap. 27, p. 479, Figure 2: From Carnevale, P. J., & Pruitt, D. D., Negotiations and mediation, Figure 1, p. 563. Reproduced with permission from the *Annual Review of Psychology, 43.* Copyright © 1992, by Annual Reviews Inc.

Chap. 27, p. 481, Figure 3: Adapted from Pruitt, D. G., & Carnevale, P. J., *Negotiations in social conflict.* Buckingham, England: Open University Press, and Pacific Grove, CA: Brooks/Cole.

Adapted from Rubin, J. Z., Pruitt, D. G., & Kim, S. H., *Social conflict: Escalation, stalemate, and settlement,* Figure 3.1, p. 30. Copyright © 1994. Reprinted by permission of The McGraw-Hill Companies.

PART ONE

HISTORICAL PERSPECTIVES

CHAPTER 1

MAJOR DEVELOPMENTS IN FIVE DECADES OF SOCIAL PSYCHOLOGY

EDWARD E. JONES, *Princeton University*

G. W. Allport (1985) sets the stage for the following review of five decades of social psychology (from about 1935 to 1985). We need not recapitulate, then, the celebrated event of Triplett's (1898) experiment, the coincidental publication of social psychology texts by the sociologist Ross and the psychologist McDougall in 1908, or the defining impact on psychology of F. H. Allport's 1924 text. In addition, we accept G. W. Allport's definition of social psychology with its emphasis on "the thought, feeling, and behavior of individuals" as shaped by the "actual, imagined, or implied presence of others." Finally, we concur that social psychology (or at least the field as currently defined) is largely a North American phenomenon. The reasons why this is so will be explored later in this chapter. This chapter will concentrate on American social psychology with only occasional references to European developments. Although European social psychology (at least until quite recently) has been largely derived from American models and methods, it should be noted that many outstanding contributors to the field were European refugees,

Preparation of this chapter was supported in part by the National Science Foundation. Portions of the chapter were written while the author was a Fellow at the Center for Advanced Study in the Behavioral Sciences. The author is indebted to the many readers of early drafts who helped to shape the present version. They are, unfortunately, too numerous (and no doubt in some cases too reluctant) to be mentioned.

Editors' Note: Edward E. Jones died on July 30, 1993. This chapter, which was originally titled "Major Developments in Social Psychology During the Past Five Decades," appeared in the third edition of the Handbook of Social Psychology *in 1985. It has been reprinted here with only minor changes of wording necessitated by the passage of time.*

a fact that led Cartwright (1979) to name Adolph Hitler as the one person who had the greatest impact on the development of social psychology. Without the influence of Lewin, Heider, Lazarsfeld, the Brunswiks, and Katona, and without the upheaval of the Second World War and the political events preceding it, the history of social psychology would be different indeed.

INTERDISCIPLINE OR SUBDISCIPLINE?

Perhaps it is curious that a subject matter focusing on the "thought, feeling, and behavior of individuals" should have strong roots in the field of sociology as well as psychology. G. W. Allport (1985) has noted the lack of clearly defined boundaries among the various social sciences, and social psychology seems like an excellent candidate for an interdisciplinary field. In 1951 Newcomb argued that social psychology is the study of interaction in its own right, and thus requires a field separate from either psychology or sociology.

In general, however, proponents of both the interdisciplinary and the separate disciplinary approaches have failed in their efforts and social psychology has clearly evolved as a subdiscipline of psychology—with some resonating pockets of highly compatible interest in sociology. This judgment is supported by the history of failed interdisciplinary administrative arrangements in U.S. universities, by the increasing domination by psychologists of the social psychology textbook market (and the allied college course market), and by the proportionate volume of social psychological literature in psychological journals.

Undoubtedly the boldest and most celebrated early effort to break down the barriers between social science disciplines was Harvard's formation of the Department of Social Relations in 1946. Here social psychology was to exist as one of four component parts, the other three being clinical psychology, sociology, and cultural anthropology. Though the department was born in an atmosphere of heady exhilaration, it was soon subject to the inexorable pressures of regression toward the parent disciplines of psychology, sociology, and anthropology. This regression may have had more to do with the academic job market, publication opportunities, and internal politics than with intellectual concerns. Nevertheless, for a variety of tangled reasons the study of social relations became increasingly fractionated and the label is now a concession to nostalgia that is attached to a reconstructed psychology department.

An alternative arrangement emerged at the University of Michigan when a joint psychology-sociology doctoral program in social psychology was established in 1946. Psychologists always outnumbered sociologists in this program, however, and it was eventually abandoned in 1967, not without some bitterness on the part of representatives from both departments (Newcomb, 1973). Columbia University exemplified the separate discipline alternative when it authorized the formation of the Department of Social Psychology in 1961. Shortly after its formation, however, the small faculty of this new department worked to re-

establish itself with the psychology department, an endeavor accomplished eight years after the initial split.

Interdisciplinary institutes and research groupings have been more common and more viable. Yale's Institute of Human Relations was an early and important example of such a grouping, lasting from 1929 until its gradual demise in the early 1960s. The University of Michigan's Institute for Social Research, a more durable prototype, still thrives after more than thirty years. Typically, however, such institutes or laboratories or research groups have had more to do with funding and with space than with fundamental intellectual convergence.

If one considers social psychology textbooks, a different kind of case may be made for viewing social psychology primarily as a psychological subdiscipline. In the early 1950s G. W. Allport noted that somewhat more than half of the dozens of social psychology textbooks were written by psychologists. This trend has accelerated, as Fig. 1 clearly shows. Out of seventy-three textbooks appearing between 1947 and 1980 fully 75 percent were written by psychologists, 22 percent were written by sociologists, and 3 percent were collaborative efforts capitalizing on the overlap between the two fields.

Those who question the value of such frequency counts may be somewhat mollified by the realization that text-

FIGURE 1   Introductory Social Psychology Textbooks Published in the United States, 1908–1980, Written by Psychologists and by Sociologists.

Figures for "total" include collaborations by psychologists and sociologists as well as texts authored by neither group.

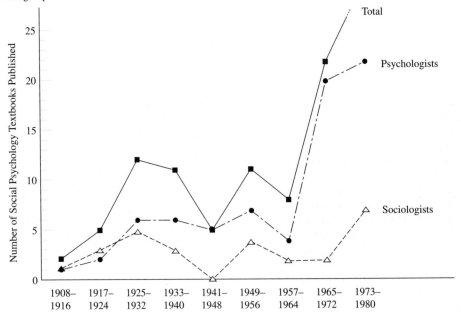

books in social psychology have played a distinctive role in shaping and integrating the field. This has been particularly true of a handful of systematic and original texts written by psychologists. It is hard to think of another field in which textbooks have served as such an important vehicle for theorizing about, and generating influential distinctions within, their subject matter. Two examples suffice to make the point. The highly original textbook of Krech and Crutchfield (1948), with its organizing propositions, influenced a generation of social psychologists and several generations of subsequent textbook authors. Asch's (1952) textbook represents an elegant and articulate advocacy of a neogestalt approach to social psychology, emphasizing humankind's rational capacities and the primacy of the individual's search for understanding. It, too, has had a lasting impact on the field and represents a major contribution to our understanding of social psychological processes.

In addition, empirical journals in social psychology are more likely to be edited by psychologists than by sociologists or to be sponsored by psychological organizations. The following major journals publish almost the entire empirical literature of social psychology in the United States:

- *Basic and Applied Social Psychology*
- *Journal of Applied Social Psychology*
- *Journal of Experimental Social Psychology*
- *Journal of Personality*
- *Journal of Personality and Social Psychology*
- *Journal of Social Issues*
- *Journal of Social Psychology*
- *Personality and Social Psychology Bulletin*
- *Social Cognition*
- *Social Psychology Quarterly*

Of these, only *Social Psychology Quarterly* (formerly *Sociometry*) is edited and sponsored by sociologists (The American Sociological Association), and many of the articles in this journal are written by psychologists.

Despite the quantitative dominance by psychologists and psychological organizations in the conduct of social psychology's intellectual business, it is not surprising that sociologists usually reject Allport's definition of social psychology and the assumption that it is a psychological subdiscipline. Stryker (1977) distinguishes between psychological and sociological social psychologies, arguing that the latter is more explicitly concerned with reciprocity of the society and the individual and with social interaction per se. He points specifically to developments of the symbolic interactionist model, identity theory, and ethnomethodology. House (1977) adds a third face to social psychology, namely, the study of social structure and personality. He notes that each of the three faces of social psychology is associated with a characteristic method: psycho-

logical social psychology with the experimental method, symbolic interactionism with participant observation and informal interviewing, and sociological social psychology (or social structure and personality) with survey methods. Both Stryker and House argue for increased cross-fertilization and interchange among the social psychologies.

Examples of such cross-fertilization can be seen in the impact of Erving Goffman (1959) and other symbolic interactions (Mead, 1934; Manis and Meltzer, 1962), on psychological accounts of self-presentation (cf. Schlenker, 1980), and in how the work of B. F. Skinner (1953) influenced the behavioral sociology approach to interaction (Homans, 1961, 1974; Burgess and Bushell, 1969). Although these instances of interdisciplinary influence are important, it remains the case that the literatures of the social aspects of psychology and of the psychological aspects of sociology are remarkably sealed off from each other. Take, for example, the relatively self-contained literatures of medical sociology and labeling approaches on the one hand and behavioral medicine and attributional approaches on the other. Such mutual isolation and disciplinary inbreeding is not entirely irrational, however, because the central foci and traditions of the two disciplines are quite divergent. For the sociological social psychologist the processes of interaction are viewed largely from a social function or a system maintenance point of view. Processes of conformity, for example, may be viewed by the sociologist in the broader institutional context of social control and normative stability. The psychologist, on the other hand, is more likely to treat conformity as a process of reality definition or a personal adaptation to affiliative pressures.

In conclusion, there is some interweaving between psychological and sociological approaches to interpersonal behavior, but the ultimate interests of the two approaches are distinctive. Therefore much of the overlap in empirical content may reflect superficial similarities that gloss over distinct analytic differences. Moreover, the sheer volume of work on interpersonal processes in psychology relative to sociology sustains our claim that most of social psychology may be treated as a subdiscipline of the field of psychology, though much research by psychologists has some homologous ties to microsociological concerns with the details of social interaction and the processes of social control.

THE SOCIAL PSYCHOLOGY-PERSONALITY INTERFACE

As much of psychology became increasingly austere in the 1930s and 1940s, pushing toward a more refined understanding of molecular learning, sensory, and perceptual processes, a more molar, integrative thrust also evolved into the psychology of personality. Personality theories vied with each other to provide comprehensive accounts of the motivational dynamics of the "whole person."

Many of these theories were heavily influenced by psychoanalysis (e.g., Murray, 1938; Erickson, 1950). Others fused dynamic motivational ideas to strong social psychological concerns (e.g., Horney, 1939; Sullivan, 1947). G. W. Allport (1937) specifically rejected many major psychoanalytic assumptions, formulating a sophisticated trait theory of personality and a conception of motivation that was liberated from infantile fixations. Other personality theories were elaborations of reinforcement and conditioning propositions central to research in learning (Dollard and Miller, 1950; McClelland, 1951; Rotter, 1954).

Although all personality theories focus primarily on more or less stable internal structures and processes, personality theorists have generally acknowledged that a comprehensive view of human action requires some specification of the actor's social environment. Since it is even more generally understood that personality structures reflect individualized social experiences, it is not surprising that personality psychologists and social psychologists have often fallen into symbiotic relationships. One view, at least, is that each needs the other to achieve reasonable precision in the prediction of decisions and choices in the complex natural environment. Without a recognition of individual differences, the social psychologist must be content with low-level actuarial predictions of responses to representative settings. On the other hand, without taking into account the requirements and cue values of situations, the personality psychologist can only talk about the most generalized trans-situational response tendencies. And the existence of such tendencies in other than ability and stylistic domains is highly debatable (Mischel, 1968).

Perhaps some such awareness of mutual dependence prompted Morton Prince to change the name of the publication, *Journal of Abnormal Psychology,* to that of the *Journal of Abnormal and Social Psychology* in 1921 and to invite F. H. Allport to serve as a cooperating editor. In 1965, now under the auspices of the American Psychological Association, a new alignment resulted once again in a revived *Journal of Abnormal Psychology,* and a new *Journal of Personality and Social Psychology.* Another sign of integrative pull is the fact that the Society of Personality and Social Psychology is one of the largest and most active divisions in the American Psychological Association, with a total of more than 4,000 members, fellows, and associates. A journal sponsored by this division is called the *Personality and Social Psychology Bulletin.* Though a 1980 referendum approved a reorganization of the society into sections, 60 percent of the members chose affiliation with the section called "Both Personality and Social Psychology." In addition to this evidence at the organizational level of the integration of personality and social psychology, the independent *Journal of Personality* has published articles

for many years, to use Sechrest's (1976) description, "in the mainstream of social psychology." Finally, the fact that there are many graduate programs labeled "personality and social psychology" across the country suggests at least some consensus regarding an intellectual affinity between the two approaches to molar behavior.

Within the history of psychology, many individuals defy an easy classification as being either a social or a personality psychologist and have theorized about one in such a way as to incorporate the other. The names of G. W. Allport, Gardner Murphy, and Daniel Katz stand out in this regard. Many other self-identified social psychologists have developed dispositional measures to capture important individual difference dimensions. The Authoritarian Personality scales provide one well-known example (Adorno, Frenkel-Brunswik, Levinson, and Sanford, 1950). Others include "Machiavellianism" (Christie and Geis, 1970) and "self-monitoring" (Snyder, 1974).

Undoubtedly there are those who would insist that a comprehensive social psychology must include relevant dispositional constructs as manifested by persistent complaints in the "personality" chapters of recent *Annual Reviews of Psychology* that social psychologists have taken over or at least "dominate" the field of personality. Sechrest (1976), in particular, complains that social psychologists have "nabbed off" a number of personality-relevant concerns that are therefore now identified as parts of the domain of social psychology: for example, attribution, aggression, emotion, obesity. Helson and Mitchell (1978) express similar concerns about the identity of the field of personality, wondering whether parts of the field will disappear and, because of the absence of "a viable center and core problems," whether the field itself will disappear with them.

In addition to the combinatorial, integrationist forces and incorporative, imperialistic forces within social psychology there have also been strong separatist forces. These forces were in part mobilized by the metatheoretical statements of Kurt Lewin, but they have also been strengthened by the methodological distinction between experimental (S–R) and correlational (R–R) approaches (cf. Cronbach, 1957). In his persistent advocacy of the relational or constructive versus the classificatory or taxonomic approach to conceptual development, Lewin argued explicitly against explanations involving individual differences (1951a, p. 61). This argument was part of a more general opposition of Galilean versus Aristotelian science and was no doubt heavily influenced by Cassirer's (1923) distinction between *thing* concepts and *relation* concepts.

An outgrowth of this way of thinking was Lewin's preference for systematic versus historical explanations and his emphasis on contemporaneous, situational causation. Since personality theory has almost invariably included developmental accounts and featured historically flavored determinism, Lewin's "Dynamic Theory of Personality" hardly seems like a theory of personality at all. Though he did have his own ideas of intrapersonal structure, the emphasis of his writings is on the deterministic potency of the concrete situation in which the individual found himself.

Perhaps as a legacy of the strong Lewinian influence on social psychology, many opinion leaders of social psychology have tended to view the inclusion of individual difference variables in experimental research as an unimaginative concession to ignorance or to poor experimental planning. In their view of "personality and social interaction" in the second edition of this handbook, Marlowe and Gergen (1968) distinguish between researchers primarily interested in situational effects who use individual difference measures to account for some of the variance and those researchers concerned with the manifestations within social interaction contexts of single personality dimensions. Those in the former group often treat the interactive or main effects of their individual difference variables with apologetic demurrers, as if conceding that accounting for variance is not necessarily an act of scientific enlightenment. Those in the latter group may wish to dissociate themselves from clinical or psychometric approaches to personality study, but they presumably are comfortable attempting to predict behavior in meaningful social settings from indices based on penciled responses to brief inventories. Their comfort no doubt suggests the absence of a strong Lewinian introject, but it is hard to gainsay the heuristic fruitfulness of the best examples of this approach (Adorno et al., 1950; Christie and Geis, 1970; Snyder, 1974, 1979).

The intellectual, almost ideological, battle between what has been called situationism (Bowers, 1973) and what might be called dispositionism, flared into the open at the beginning of the 1970s. In a series of books and papers, Mischel (1968, 1973, 1977) criticized those trait psychologists who search for trans-situational dispositions, claiming that behavioral consistencies across settings are empirically rare. He also discussed some reasons why the level of consistency is thought to be higher than it really is. The presumption of exaggerated *perceived* consistency resonated with developments in attribution theory was featured in a paper on actor-observer differences by Jones and Nisbett (1971) and later became celebrated as the "fundamental attribution error" (Ross, 1977). The error referred to is the tendency of observers to underestimate the power of situations in shaping a target person's behavior and to overestimate the correspondence between behavior and dispositions.

It can reasonably be argued that the proposal of this particular form of attribution error, along with Mischel's advocacy of a stimulus-oriented social learning view of personality, drove a deeper wedge between the traditionalists in social psychology and those favoring the explo-

rations of systematic individual differences. The "Establishment" social psychologists could now claim that the individual difference approach was not only causally uninformative but also based on an illusory assumption. The reliability of dispositional differences, in this view, was vastly overrated by personality psychologists who were victimized by the fundamental attribution error. It mattered little that some personality psychologists took strong exception to this line of argument (cf. Block 1977; Hogan, DeSoto, and Solano, 1977).

It mattered more, perhaps, that Daryl Bem sought a constructive rapprochement in several papers combining empirical data with theoretical argument. Bem and Allen (1974) take us back to G. W. Allport's advocacy of an idiographic approach to personal consistency. They argue that people are only consistent when the specified dispositional dimensions apply to them or are personally relevant. Bem and Allen contend that individual differences reside primarily in *which* personality traits are important, central, or salient for the individual, and they report a demonstration study that supports this position.

In subsequent papers Bem (Bem and Funder, 1978; Bem, 1980a; Bem, 1980b) has advocated the development of assessment techniques for characterizing both persons and situations in comparable terms. Bem and Lord's study (1979) provides one example of the use of an assessment technique to predict response preferences in a prisoners' dilemma game. Judges provided Q-sort ratings of the kind of person who would adopt competitive, independent, or joint outcome strategies in the game. Roommates' ratings of individual subjects' tendencies to be competitive in the natural environment were found to be significantly related to the strategy actually chosen by the subject. Bem and Lord thus provided evidence for the ecological validity of a particular laboratory setting, that involving a mixed-motive game. The flexibility of what Bem has called the "template matching" approach seems to promise renewed pressures toward the integration of social and personality approaches in predicting behavior.

The question of how best to characterize the interplay between personalities and situations remains a matter of considerable controversy, however. In spite of their general sympathy with idiographic approaches and strong situational influences, Mischel and Peake (1982) criticize Bem's approach as too empirical and produce some evidence to support their contention that "atheoretical approaches yield results that tend to seem promising at first but are notoriously difficult to replicate."

It is not surprising that someone (Endler and Magnusson, 1976) has proposed that the only reasonable position to take with regard to persons and situations is a strong interactionism. The argument is that person, situation, and behavior all affect each other continuously. They are so causally intertwined that it is impossible to separate out the effects of one, the other, or even their statistical interactions by conventional analysis of variance techniques. These and other issues are discussed in Ross and Fletcher (1985) in greater detail, but it is obvious that the relations between social and personality psychology are very much in ferment at the present time.

In summary, no one has ever argued that behavior is entirely determined by the actor's pre-existing dispositions or that all variance in behavior can be accounted for by an analysis of situational cues or requirements. It is both popular and truistic to emphasize the importance of the person-situation interaction term. However, social and personality psychologists have historically placed their bets on different elements in the Lewinian B = f (P,E) equation. Social psychologists not strongly infected by the Field Theory virus have generally emphasized the complementarity of approaches emphasizing settings and approaches emphasizing dispositions. The strong experimental model emerging from the Lewinian camp attached secondary importance, at best, to individual differences. The individual difference approach has been further eroded within social psychology by the emphasis on attributional error that involves assigning too much weight to internal dispositions. In addition, it has been eroded within personality psychology itself by those who favor a social learning approach, since this approach emphasizes distinctive learning histories and current reinforcement contingencies. It seems possible that methods based on idiographic considerations and parallel analyses of perceived situations will revive interest in personality psychology and strengthen its now fragile ties with social psychology. It also seems likely that separatist pressures will be more persistent if personality is conceived exclusively in terms of individual differences than if it is conceived in terms of general cognitive and motivational processes. Social psychological research must invariably include explicit or implicit theorizing about persons, but that theorizing is likely to be strongly oriented to the role of situational or contextual influences, as perceived and interpreted by the person involved.

THE GEOGRAPHY OF SOCIAL PSYCHOLOGY

The field of social psychology grew out of the recognition of human diversity within cultural uniformity. The social psychologist typically seeks a level of generalization that falls between broad cultural abstractions and accounts of individual learning experiences. If personality were merely the subjective side of culture or if uniqueness always overwhelmed the variance attributable to cultural constraints, the concept of a social psychology would hardly be salient. The individual must be seen as the intersection point of a variety of pressures: immediate situational demands, conflicting social expectations, and internalized beliefs and values. It is the social psychologist's task to understand how the conflict among these pressures is resolved. Though social psychologists typically work with samples that are culturally homogeneous and adapt the content of their inquiry to the concerns of the sample members, they hope to uncover relationships that can be stated in general and fundamental terms.

These considerations have some bearing on the "geography" of social psychology's development. It seems to follow from the intersecting pressures model that social psychology would be less prominent, if it existed at all, in more homogeneous and traditional cultures. In such cultures behavior priorities within settings are rather well established by unquestioned cultural norms. Conflict is minimal as everyone more or less follows the traditional ways. The presence of competing normative options may account, in part, for the distinctive flowering of social psychology in the United States, and for the distribution of social psychologists and programs within our states and regions.

The development of social psychology encompasses a very short time span. Cartwright (1979) estimates that 90 percent of all social psychologists who have ever lived are alive at the present time. He also suggests that social psychology truly became a field only after the Second World War when it exploded into prominence in America at a time when European and Asian universities were reeling from the exhausting global struggle. Within the United States, however, the emergence of social psychology was strongly linked to universities in metropolitan regions: Columbia, Yale, Harvard, and the University of Michigan. Until the postwar explosion Cartwright describes, vast areas of the country were innocent of any contact with academic social psychology. Psychology departments in midwestern universities—with the notable exception of the University of Michigan—were almost exclusively involved in "brass instrument" methodology, research on traditional problems of learning and sensory processes, and in the applications of aptitude and interest measurement. This traditionalism was at least as pronounced in the southeastern region of the United States where most prewar psychology departments viewed themselves as closely tied to the natural sciences on the one hand or to philosophy on the other. It is tempting to propose that just as the United States, the melting pot of world cultures, was a natural context for the emergence of social psychology, so for similar reasons within the United States, social psychology emerged most vigorously in the universities of metropolitan urban areas. It was here that problems of intergroup conflict, prejudice, deviance, and attitudinal differences were the most salient. Indeed, a rural social psychology is almost a contradiction in terms, at least in comparison to a psychology based on animal behavior.

Added to this rather benign view of urban versus rural impact is the likelihood that ideology, prejudice, and economics may have also been involved in the distribution of social psychology programs. Cartwright suggests (personal communication) that it was difficult for social psychology to penetrate the Old South because of the volatile conditions of racial ferment that prevailed there from 1930 to 1960. Many administrators (and legislators) probably viewed social psychology as a troublesome disrupter of the status quo. In addition, Cartwright proposes, social psychology may have come sooner to the prosperous schools of the Northeast not because they were urban, but because they could afford this "luxury" of adding a social component to the more traditional areas of learning, sensory processes, and physiological psychology.

Although social psychology was nurtured until the mid 1940s in only a handful of prestigious metropolitan universities, the end of the Second World War clearly accelerated its growth in these universities and in other institutions influenced by them. Nevertheless, the growth of the field was still largely contained in a few universities large enough to support diverse interests within a psychology department. Until well into the 1950s, only a small number of university departments had anything approaching a program of study in social psychology.

During the next fifteen years, however, social psychology spread into every region of the country, and social psychology doctoral programs began to multiply. A proliferation of undergraduate offerings is also apparent in the upsurge in social psychology textbooks in the late 1960s. This striking diffusion of social psychology and social psychologists may be seen as a product of the general academic expansion affecting all academic fields plus an additional impetus stemming from a new perception of social psychology as constructively linked to the experimental method and therefore entitled to a place in the psychological mainstream. This respectability was not universally accorded, but there was enough of an increment to make a difference in an expanding academic economy.

Summary Remarks   In summary, the growth of social psychology has been shaped by the intertwining of accident with broader socio-political events. We have argued that social psychology was, for an important period at least, not only largely confined to the United States but largely an urban phenomenon. This does not explain why Lewin was invited to the Iowa Child Welfare Station in 1934, or why attribution theory flowered in Kansas, to which Fritz Heider moved in 1947. In general, however, social psychology can be accurately described as the understandable intellectual by-product of normative complexity. It is thus not surprising that historically the major urban centers were the spawning ground for social psychology in its early formative years, though the picture now is one of widespread geographical and regional diffusion. It is interesting to speculate whether social psychology will maintain its newly

gained footing in the more traditional, culturally homogeneous regions of the United States when, as seems likely, many universities will be forced to trim their programs and faculty rosters.

THE SOCIAL PSYCHOLOGY OF RESEARCH CONCERNS IN SOCIAL PSYCHOLOGY

This section might be labeled "bandwagons and sinking ships" for it deals with the waxing and waning of research fashions in social psychology. Many social psychologists feel that their field is uniquely or especially vulnerable to faddism. Since the grounds for such feelings are largely matters of definition and involve developments that evade easy documentation, it would be hard to prove that social psychology is unique in this respect. Surely there are bandwagons upon which graduate students and more established scholars climb in all research fields. However, it may be that such labels as "fad" or "fashion" are more easily applied to the social sciences than to the natural sciences because developments in the social sciences tend to be less cumulative and each research concern is therefore more limited by time. In any event, any student of social psychology knows that particular theories or methods or paradigms gain favor, dominate segments of the literature for a period of time, and then recede from view. Taking a look at the history of social psychology, a historical analysis should have something to offer about why the field is vulnerable to faddism.

The "Waxing" of Research Interests

To avoid the pejorative connotations of "fads and fashions," let us speak more neutrally of *dominating research themes* to characterize rather self-contained spurts of interests in a particular topic or in a particular way of looking at an old topic in the research literature. We suspect there would be fairly wide agreement on the following examples: social facilitation effects, prestige suggestion effects, authoritarian personality studies, the forced-compliance paradigm in dissonance research, Asch's conformity research paradigm, the "risky shift" phenomenon, bystander intervention, mixed motive game research, overjustification effects, and actor-observer attribution differences. A consideration of these examples suggests that there is no single determinant of "waxing." Indeed, we can identify six determinants that might reasonably be relevant and important.

The first is the social and political zeitgeist. Social psychology is obviously affected more than most disciplines by the surrounding social milieu. As Cartwright (1961) notes, it depends on society for financial support, it obtains its data from society, and its findings may be used to influence the course of societal events. The data-providing function needs amplification because it is true in so many respects. Society provides not only our subjects but also many of the themes and problems that challenge and instigate the research progress. For example, the study of attitude change received enormous impetus from concerns during the Second World War with propaganda, military morale, and the potential integration of ethnic minorities into established military units. Authoritarian personality research obviously grew out of the Nazi experience as did, in a quite different way, Milgram's later research on obedience. It seems more than a coincidence that the widespread interest in the determinants of peer conformity reached its peak shortly after the rise of Senator McCarthy and associated public concerns with social deviance in the form of "card-carrying Communists" and "fellow travelers." Much of the interest in mixed-motive games derived from concerns about international disarmament negotiations in a nuclear age. While specifically citing the Kitty Genovese murder as its starting point, bystander intervention research was nurtured by a broader public concern with urban alienation, apathy, and anomie. Undoubtedly many other connections between social problems and research themes can be traced but these examples are probably clear enough to make the point without further elaboration.

A more subtle and yet related source of research themes can be found in the personal interests and concerns of the innovating researcher and of others who resonate to the theme he or she introduces. We assume that most researchers work on problems that interest them personally. Though the sources of this interest are undoubtedly numerous, an important determinant may be the motivational dynamics of the researcher. It would be extremely mischievous (and just plain wrong) to assert that all aggression researchers are personally troubled by the management of their own aggressive impulses, that reactance theorists are especially touchy about their personal freedom, that students of bargaining have a deathly fear either of being outmaneuvered in negotiations or of being too ruthlessly exploitative. Nevertheless, a research problem that is endlessly fascinating to one group of psychologists may seem totally trivial to another. It stands to reason that one source of this fascination is the salience of the problem in the researcher's personal life space. If Professor X is totally unconcerned with his own appearance, he is not likely to spend a lifetime doing research on the effects of physical attractiveness. Victims of prejudice are probably more likely than nonvictims to end up as its students. Certainly the number of males who are interested in sex roles and in sexist discrimination is eclipsed by female counterparts. Students of inequity, locus of control, and achievement motivation may also have become involved in these problems because of personal concerns.

Although our intent is not to minimize the complexity that may underlie personal concerns, it is probable that only a very small minority of researchers attempt to resolve their own hidden conflicts or neurotic problems through their own research. More have chosen research problems that are natural and open reflections of their past experiences in the absence of hidden motivational dynamics. Still others, perhaps a definite majority, choose to work on problems bearing no particular relation to their own unique social or personal history. Nevertheless we feel confident in asserting that *sometimes* a cluster of empirical studies is spawned by a researcher attempting to illuminate a personal enigma. In the process, the researcher develops propositions to which a significant group of other researchers resonate.

A second determinant of dominant research themes is theoretical power. The classic or conventional image of scientific deduction embraces a sequence running from assumptions, to theoretical propositions, to experimental tests. Though it has, perhaps, become fashionable to note the many exceptions to this idealized sequence in the real world of social science research, it remains true that a good theory can provide a powerful stimulus for research. Almost by definition, *good* theories are likely to get involved in bandwagon effects as claims, qualifications, and counterclaims dominate a segment of the literature. This involvement ends when the theory becomes part of accepted social science wisdom, is demonstrated to have little or no predictive utility, or is supplanted by a better theory more congruent with existing data. (At appropriate points in this chapter documentation about the role that theories have played in the recent history of social psychology will be presented.)

Convenient research paradigms constitute a third determinant. Unlike the natural sciences where advances are often dependent on technical innovations in measurement or detection, there is no such applicable technology to mark advances in the social sciences. However, there are new measuring instruments that have often facilitated clusters of research because of their convenience and availability. This is particularly obvious in the case of personality measures. We have seen the waxing and waning of research on authoritarianism, need for achievement, social desirability, locus of control, and Machiavellianism. In addition, dominant research themes can also emerge from convenient research designs or experimental scenarios. Some of the attractiveness of Asch's path-breaking studies of impression formation stems from the fact that they involve the extremely simple procedure of giving subjects lists of adjectives and asking them to rate or describe the person characterized by them. Thus it is not surprising that his "warm-cold" study (see page 38) was soon followed by dozens of replications with slight variations. Norman Anderson later gave this paradigm an even more solid footing by developing all-purpose lists of adjectives scaled for evaluative direction and potency. In addition, an argument can be made that one reason for the shift in interest from dissonance research to attribution research in the late 1960s and early 1970s is the fact that much attribution research could be performed without having to construct elaborate scenarios involving complex cover stories. In contrast, research in such areas as personal attraction, social comparison, and aggression has persisted more because of the practical and theoretical importance of these problems than because of the development of convenient research paradigms for their investigation. Elaborate, impactful experiments such as those conducted by Aronson and Linder (1965), Walster (1965), or Milgram (1974) are very costly to replicate and do not readily form the cornerstones of dominating themes.

The fourth determinant is the prestige of the innovator and his institution or laboratory. More than most areas of psychology, social psychology is a personalized subdiscipline. People are often more concerned with "what Arbuthnot is up to" than with the state of knowledge on a particular topic. Prestigious researchers can be very influential in elevating the perceived importance of a research topic or claiming it for social psychology. For example, Schachter's prestige was an important determinant of the sudden upsurge of interest in the effects of birth order that occurred in the 1960s, and the facts that Osgood became interested in attitude change, Kelley in attribution, Freedman in crowding, and Thibaut in procedural justice no doubt enhanced the legitimacy and interest value of these areas for other scholars.

Funding priorities are a fifth important determinant of research themes. Availability of funding surely plays a role in the choice of research area for many people. "Health-related" research is obviously more fundable than research on language usage or on self-presentational strategies. In the middle and late 1970s, those applying for support to do research on alcoholism or drug abuse tended to receive a particularly warm reception. It would be hard if not impossible to calculate the subtle effects of funding priorities on the choice of research area, but it seems reasonable to include such external incentive factors in this list of bandwagon facilitators.

Because funding priorities are not always obvious, researchers must sometimes learn from their own bitter experiences with granting agencies and editors just what fields of study are valued by their peers. They may or may not decide to continue their lonely pursuit of arcane truth, but feedback from peers and powerful gatekeepers can be an important determinant of choices among reasonably intriguing options. The role of students should also not be ignored. The enthusiasm that both undergraduates and graduate students have for some topics and not others has some influence on research directions. It is difficult to persist in one's research when students and colloquium audiences convey nothing but somnolent disinterest.

A sixth determinant is the fact that certain scholars are attracted by the freedom available at the frontiers of unexplored scientific terrain. The researcher who follows up previous work may be performing an important service in the advancement of knowledge, but he or she is necessarily constrained by procedures and by a scholarly literature provided by others. Such a researcher may receive modest commendations for competence displayed but will typically be by-passed when more spectacular kudos are issued. It is perhaps inevitable that those who, through accident or through shrewd forecasting, get in on the problem-posing phases of a research theme, are more likely to reap the accolades of academic success. The accolades for innovation in social psychology may indeed be differentially higher than in better established scientific fields. This might be true because the field is still expectantly waiting for its true intellectual messiah, since there is a common recognition that the field is still in a problem-posing rather than problem-solving phase. In any event, social psychologists appear to have a peculiar penchant for being impatiently critical of their own field. No doubt for very complex reasons, it might be hypothesized that compared to other fields of science, social psychology is unusually oriented toward, and responsive to, new approaches, new conceptualizations, and new openings.

The appeal of working at the frontiers, of course, is not at all specific to social psychology. Work in undercultivated areas is in many ways much easier than work on problems characterized by heavy research traffic. Any contribution, no matter how modest, is likely to seem more of an increment than the result of comparable effort expended on a well-researched problem. Lack of rigor in the design of the research and in the analysis of its data can more readily be excused when one is searching for problem definition, for hypotheses rather than for confirmation of problem solutions. The researcher has more to gain and less to lose when operating in unexplored terrain. No one can be too critical if the researcher fails to make headway on a problem that no one else has addressed or solved. Of course, the terrain may be so ill-chosen that the innovative researcher works in isolation and confronts an indifferent audience when presenting his or her contribution. But at the very least he or she will gain credit for daring to leave the beaten path.

The "Waning" of Research Interests

Dominant research themes wane when the more active and prestigious researchers turn their attention to new problems. Four reasons for the waning of research interests may be identified. The discussion is brief because in many ways "sinking ships" are the opposite of "bandwagons."

The first is the fact that the problem is solved. Though some may think problem solutions are an empty category in the social sciences, there are cases where work on a problem declines because the main outlines of a solution have become clear and a point of diminishing returns has been reached. When this happens the task that remains is to "dot the i's and cross the t's"—that is, to fill in the outline with more detailed information predictable from what already exists. Thus a theory may be extended to new areas where it accounts for some, but not an important amount of the variance. In another case, researchers may test the empirical generality of a finding by using larger and more representative samples than those used in the launching stages. In still another example, mediating variables may be introduced that mute or exaggerate the established effects. All these may be important endeavors, but they are the kinds of efforts that many researchers hope will be done by others. A clean-up hitter in baseball is highly regarded; a clean-up person in research is likely to be tolerated at best with patronizing, supercilious praise. Laborers in the replication vineyard are needed but are not well paid in the coin of academic prestige. Given the existing incentive structure in social psychology, it is very understandable that people move away from a research area when the prestige payoffs loom larger elsewhere. Once the alternatives become more attractive, positive or confirming results in the waning area may add at best a small increment to our knowledge whereas disconfirming results tend to be ignored or attributed to poor research procedures.

Perhaps the best example of this reason for a declining volume of research can be found in the cognitive dissonance area (well summarized in a recent volume by Wicklund and Brehm, 1976). Because the main propositions of dissonance theory have been confirmed with sufficient regularity, there is not a great deal to be gained from further research in this area. Although there is, of course, still room for debate about the mechanisms involved and about the role of dissonance reduction in various naturalistic settings, much is already known about the determinants of dissonance and its various contexts of manifestation. Research on dissonance continues but no longer holds the center stage.

The second reason behind the decline of research in a formerly lively area is the existence of an empirical dead end. Sometimes a promising theory ultimately proves untestable or a dominant research theme becomes stymied in empirical confusion or in failures to replicate. Empirical confusion presumably results when researchers are asking the wrong question, have misidentified the appropriate controlling variables, or have been too inflexible in the application of procedures that are appropriate in one setting but not in another. Some examples of empirical confusion include research on the effects of drawing conclusions from attitude change, order effects and first-impression formation, the role of prior expectancy in response to performance feedback, self-esteem and the response to being liked, postdecisional exposure to relevant information, and aggression as a precursor of catharsis or more aggression. Some of these research problems will be resuscitated when conceptualized in more fruitful ways or when better measurement techniques emerge. At present, however, research in these areas of empirical confusion is relatively quiescent—not because the problems are seen as trivial, but because the evidence refuses to order itself into stable, consistent patterns.

A third reason for declining research interest is the discovery of methodological flaws leading to artifactual re-explanations. Perhaps the most fundamental single advantage of the scientific method is that it is self-correcting. Some may argue that authoritarian personality theory, certainly a dominant research theme in the 1950s, did not really survive the methodological attacks epitomized by the definitive critique of Hyman and Sheatsley (in Christie and Jahoda, 1954). Such a proposition, we believe, overstates the case, but the serious methodological flaws in authoritarian personality research certainly contributed to a decline in research employing the various interrelated scales. Interrelationships among the scales measuring antisemitism, ethnocentrism, and antidemocratic ideology were crucial to theoretical arguments about the nature of the authoritarian personality. When it became apparent that these interrelationships were to some unknown degree inflated by acquiescent response bias (the simple tendency to agree with any statement), many felt that the entire concept of authoritarianism was based on an artifact of scale construction. Other flaws in sampling and content analysis procedures contributed to this pessimistic conclusion. Sophisticated young researchers tended to accept the validity of such criticisms; authoritarian research became a tainted enterprise; and budding social psychologists began to look elsewhere for dissertation topics (cf. Brewster Smith, 1979).

Another fascinating case of the rapid emergence and geometric spread of a research paradigm, followed by an even more rapid decline, is the investigation concerned with group decisions involving risk. Cartwright (1973) offers a discerning discussion of the factors contributing to the compelling attractiveness of this aspect of research for so many experimenters. As early as 1924 F. H. Allport reported that individuals tend to produce more common or popular verbal associations in a group than in an individual context. This and similar findings on conformity and opinion convergence in groups contributed to a widely accepted assumption that group interaction would produce conservative problem solutions and that compromise would lead the group normally to the average or modal final position. Stoner's (1961) observation that group discussion led the members to take a riskier stance on a variety of issues therefore came as a considerable surprise. His study, dealing with hypothetical dilemmas, launched a series of experiments that generally replicated the so-called "risky shift" effect, and it seemed that an important and very general social phenomenon had been discovered. After researchers had accepted the validity of the risky shift, they tried in their research to discriminate among the hypothetical reasons behind the shift. Ironically, it was at this point that they began to find that the phenomenon was not so robust after all. As Cartwright (1973) notes, "Instead of providing an explanation of why 'groups are riskier than individuals,' they in fact cast serious doubt on the validity of the proposition itself. And since this proposition was such a central part of the risky-shift paradigm, they undermined the confidence in the very paradigm that led to their discovery" (p. 225).

Teger and Pruitt (1967), among others, began to notice that for some choice dilemmas the shift was in the cautious or conservative direction. Furthermore, the direction of the shift was found to be a function of the group members' initial position on the item. If they were initially on the risky side, they became riskier after group discussion. If initially conservative, they became more cautious. Thus in spite of the illusion of generality born in the many risky-shift replications, using different subject samples in different experimental contexts, it was belatedly recognized that the standard measure of risk (Kogan and Wallach's [1964] choice dilemma questionnaire) contained a biased sample of dilemmas favoring initial riskiness. If the research had broken away earlier from the choice dilemma questionnaire initially used by Stoner, progress toward a clearer understanding of the complexities involved would have been more rapid. However, the ease of relying on such a readily administered instrument, coupled with the high replicability of results obtained when the scale's total scores were used, proved highly seductive. The rise and fall of this self-contained tradition of risky-shift studies covered a ten-year period. Cartwright's (1973) review of the risky-shift paradigm identified 196 bibliographic items, representing the work of 187 investigators from 8 different countries. Though reaching a realistic conclusion about the complexity of risk-taking behavior took a long time and involved many now forgotten words, the research does represent progress toward greater understanding of how groups function and how they influence individual decision making. At the very least it represents progress in learning about some of the ways in which researchers can be misled by an overly psychometric orientation. Others have salvaged the idea of *group polarization* (Moscovici and Zavalloni, 1969) from the wreckage of risky-shift research, and this endeavor may eventually prove to be an important step forward.

The fourth determinant of "waning" is the possibility that research paradigms may prove vulnerable to changes in ethical standards and the increasing pervasiveness of institutional monitoring of research practices. As already noted, one explanation for the shift from dissonance as a dominant research theme to attribution research may have been the greater appropriateness of straightforward, nondeceptive procedures to explore attributional questions. Part of the appeal of attribution-based research may simply be that experiments in the cognitive realm are easier to conduct and replicate because they lend themselves more naturally to simple paper-and-pencil implementation. In addition, however, it is also probable that attribution-based research tends to involve only the most benign deceptions, if it involves any deceptions at all. Many problems on which dissonance researchers focused, on the other hand, required elaborate staging and convoluted deceptions. The most extreme instance of this, undoubtedly, was the infiltration of a doomsday group to study what happens when strongly held beliefs are dramatically disconfirmed (Festinger, Riecken, and Schachter, 1956). Literature generated by the so-called forced-compliance paradigm within dissonance theory abounds with instances in which subjects were promised rewards that were never actually granted, manipulated into decisions they would have preferred to avoid, and subjected to various forms of stress and suffering in the process of arousing dissonance. Undoubtedly, many of these procedures would be ruled out or severely diluted by contemporary institutional committees designed to protect the welfare of human subjects (cf. Festinger, 1980).

It is even more likely that today experimental investigations involving physically invasive procedures would be proscribed in the ethical review process. Thus Schachter's work involving the injection of epinephrine (1964) would probably fail to pass ethical muster today in many human subjects committees. The decline of stress research involving electric shock is undoubtedly also attributable in part to the difficulty of getting such research past review committees. In discussing this fourth reason for the waning of research, one must mention not only abort the immediate effect of committee decisions in constraining research but also the more insidious ripple effects whereby whole classes of research are not even considered by rising generations of researchers because of the anticipated difficulty of institutional review. Regardless of whether one celebrates or laments this state of affairs, the point is that shifting ethical concerns are clearly important determinants of the kinds of problems tackled as well as the specific procedures used to tackle them.

In summary, there are many factors involved in the rise and fall of particular research paradigms or investigative traditions—whether these are defined narrowly by such self-contained research clusters as the risky-shift studies or more broadly by such comprehensive programs of research as those concerning cognitive dissonance. This discussion has mentioned only the more obvious of these factors and those that are easiest to exemplify. In doing so, reference to prestige and status considerations has been unavoidable. Some bandwagons become bandwagons because they are bandwagons. Just as surely, prestige factors can cause researchers to turn a bandwagon into a sinking ship when the traffic becomes too heavy and the increments to knowledge too slight or improbable. Prestige factors become directly relevant in the choice of research topics and indirectly relevant through the operation of editorial review processes. In addition to such extrinsic motivational factors, however, the research process has its own internal dynamics. Sometimes problems do get solved, and there is little payoff in further research. Sometimes it takes a certain number of studies before it becomes clear that the wrong question is being asked. The study of research innovation, of paradigm development and paradigm shifts, has become an important offshoot of the philosophy of science literature. We have tried to show the specific applicability of the more general determinants to lines of investigation in social psychology.

SOCIAL PSYCHOLOGY AS METHOD

The identity of social psychology in the 1930s was clearly strengthened by the development of distinctive methods. However, the ambitious agenda of a social psychology poses severe methodological problems. Conventional social psychology textbooks have often defined their subject matter as the study of responses made to social stimuli. The definer usually goes on to elaborate on both the independent variable and the dependent variable side. Social stimuli, it is noted, may be and are often "implicit"; the individual's behavior may be conditioned by his or her consideration of how significant others or reference groups might react if they were present. On the response side, the social psychologist is interested in more than "overt behavior." In fact, overt behavior—what a person says or does at a moment in time—often is considered transient and so multiply determined that it is not a reliable basis for psychological understanding. More important and more stable may be the underlying dispositions that guide complex molar behavior; that is, the values, attitudes, and beliefs that persist as influences on the things we say and do in diverse settings.

Thus social psychologists inevitably find themselves dealing with inferred dispositions influencing responses not only to ongoing stimuli but also to implicit or imagined stimuli. Such a state of affairs could lead to the avoidant reductionism of animal experimentation, to the metaphoric syntheses of the humanities, or to methodological invention. The advance of the kind of social psychology celebrated in this chapter was clearly dependent on the latter.

The problem of access to subtle social stimulus values was eventually addressed by the followers of Kurt Lewin, and various solutions to the problem of stimulus identification became triumphant achievements within the experimental movement in social psychology. Historically, however, priority was assigned to the measurement of social responses and their attitudinal underpinnings. In fact, social psychology's progress during much of the 1930s is reflected in the ascendant muscle flexing of attitudinal measurement.

By the end of the 1920s, social psychology had become an area capable of textbook demarcation, but it was a field lacking in relevant theory or distinctive methodology. As for theory, Cottrell and Gallagher (1941) argued, the early "social psychologists conducted a kind of a clearing house for the theoretical output of other social scientists. They battened on the research efforts in other fields but offered little in the way of research return from their own field" (p. 48). The methodology was also derivative. Investigators used quantitative measures of performance or other measures of attention, learning, or forgetting that had been developed in the field of educational testing or in the experimental laboratories of "natural science psychology." It was becoming increasingly clear, however, that the attitude concept was the distinctive domain of social psychology and that the development of reliable and valid attitudinal measures was an important contribution to the growing identity of the field.

Attitude Measurement

In 1929 Thurstone and Chave published a classic monograph, "The Measurement of Attitude." In it they espoused the application of psychophysical methods to the measurement of a person's position along an attitudinal dimension such as pro- or anti-religion. Their adaptation of the law of comparative judgment was ingenious. The purpose of their method was to develop a collection of statements falling at different points along a particular pro-con dimension. The problem was how to determine with any degree of precision what the "scale value" or location of a given statement should be. This was done by applying the logic that the distance between two statements was a function of the number of people who agreed that they were different. If 90 percent of a group of judges rated statement A as more prorelilgion than statement B, whereas 65 percent rated A as more pro than C, then C not only could be placed between A and B but also the distance between these statements could be stated as a conversion of the percentage of judged difference figures. Through variants of this basic method (the most popular being the "method of equal-appearing intervals") a group of statements could be developed by judges to form a scale. This scale could in turn be administered to subjects whose own position on the dimension could be scored as the median scale value of endorsed items or as a similar measure of central tendency.

Thurstone's scaling procedures were essentially rational and required a separation of judges from eventual subjects. It was assumed that a judge's own opinion would not bias his or her relative placement of items, and the method required that the items be straightforward and clearly related to the belief or issue in question. In 1932, however, Likert employed a very different and more clearly empirical approach to the measurement of attitudes. His method was to generate statements about the target issue without any necessary restriction that the statements were on their face related to the issue. The items could then be administered to groups of pretest subjects with instructions to indicate the degree of agreement or disagreement with each one. Total scores for each subject could be gained by scoring each item in terms of degree of agreement (reversing those phrased in the negative) and summing these item scores. Each item could then be evaluated for each pretest subject sample in terms of its contribution to the total score. If the items were concerned with political liberalism, for example, endorsement of some items would correlate more highly with the total score than others. The diagnostic (high correlating) items could then be retained for further use. This procedure could be repeated over several pretest samples until a relatively robust and purified scale resulted, a scale built by the subjects themselves rather than by a group of presumably objective judges. The Likert approach proved to be more suitable than Thurstone's approach for detecting unpopular or prejudiced attitudes because the items did not need an obvious surface relationship to the issue involved. The advantages of this approach were exploited in building the authoritarian personality scales in the early 1950s. For example, the investigators in this project predicted and found that subjects who endorse the item "people were born with an urge to jump from high places" tend to endorse statements reflecting authoritarianism and antisemitism. It is hard to imagine how this finding could have been discovered or confirmed with the Thurstone method.

The 1930s marked the beginnings of a concern with the structure and functioning of attitudes and an accounting of their distribution in different classes or groups. The former emphasis is reflected in Gordon Allport's chapter on attitudes in Murchison's 1935 *Handbook of Social Psychology*. Allport analyzes the history of usage of the terms and considers, for example, whether attitudes have their own motive power (concluding that at least some do) and whether attitudes can be either individual, defying nomothetic measurements, or common and measurable (yes they can be either, he concludes).

A more strictly empirical approach is reflected in many of the chapters of Murphy, Murphy, and Newcomb's *Experimental Social Psychology,* published in 1937 (as a very extensive revision of Murphy and Murphy's 1931 edition). Much of the research described in this book amounts to a mapping of the terrain—a charting of sex, age, and educational level differences in such attitudes as liberalism versus conservatism. The correlates of attitudes toward ethnic and national groups are also extensively reviewed in this useful compendium. Because of the emphasis on straight-

forward description, however, most of the conclusions presented by Murphy, Murphy, and Newcomb are time and context specific. Nevertheless, one has to be impressed with the variety of early approaches to the study of attitudes and the high level of interest in exploring attitudinal correlates. The range of attitude studies reported before the outbreak of the Second World War reflected both a substantive interest in the social determinants of specific attitudes and a flexing of methodological muscles.

Public Opinion Research

Though the academic study of attitudes focused to some extent on the basic questions of dispositional structure raised by Allport in his handbook chapter, a related but separate development focused more directly on the distribution of politically or economically consequential opinion in the society at large. The growth of public opinion studies was in turn highly dependent on the refinement of population sampling techniques. The American Institute of Public Opinion was founded in 1934, the first major practitioner of the form of opinion assessment that is now so commonplace in journalism, campaign strategy, and marketing research. Other survey research operations soon followed. George Gallup, Elmo Roper, and Archibald Crosley each used the sample survey method to forecast correctly the outcome of the 1936 presidential election. This method became widespread not only in the political prediction arena and in the commercial sphere where opinions about consumer products and advertising campaigns were systematically gathered, but also in the U.S. government where bodies such as the Department of Agriculture made extensive use of sample surveys. The public opinion industry has clearly mushroomed during the past twenty years, although the results of many subsidized surveys are used for competitive economic or political advantages and have not become part of the social science literature. There are, of course, many surveys addressed to important theoretical issues. However, the development of appropriate sampling and questioning techniques has had a much greater impact on the growth of empirical sociology than on social psychology itself. This was particularly true when, in the 1950s, the sample survey was wedded to computer processing.

Sociometry

Of somewhat greater relevance for psychology was the introduction of sociometric measurement by J. L. Moreno in 1934. His technique involved the simple questioning of group members regarding those fellow members with whom they would choose to associate in some activity. More generally, the sociometric method is now defined as including any procedure that involves choice, preference, or liking among group members. From such statements of preference certain aspects of group structure can be readily derived. For example, groups can be characterized in terms of the presence of clique cleavages, the degree of mutuality of choice, or the concentration of attraction directed toward a few members. In addition, individuals can be readily identified as sociometric "stars" (heavily chosen by others) or isolates. The addition of dislike dimensions provides many further possibilities of group characterization.

Sociometric measures have become so ubiquitous in social psychology that they are now viewed as one among many measures of attraction or social preference (cf. Kenny, 1985). They have been widely used in applied research on morale and leadership as well as in basic research on such topics as the rejection of opinion deviates (Schachter, 1951), the measurement of in-group cohesion (Sherif et al., 1961), and the study of hysterical contagion (Kerckhoff and Back, 1968).

Systematic Observational Methods

The development of systems for recording and quantifying social behavior has a number of ancient antecedents, certainly including the training of behavioral observation in medicine. In 1933 Dorothy Thomas made the first explicit attempts to systematize and quantify the observation of social behavior. Interestingly enough, the development of systematic observational techniques beginning in the 1930s parallels the development of other measures of complex molar behavior in psychology. First there were competing attempts to develop all-purpose instruments that yielded high observer agreement. Enthusiasm in the early stages was fed by a naive realism that there was something "there" to be measured and observed. The task was to measure that something accurately and without bias. Eventually, however, whether dealing with general attitude measures in which the name of the issue was plugged in or with all-purpose observational systems of group behavior, researchers began to realize that the possible gains of reliability were offset by the empty, formalistic character of the measurement procedures themselves. In the case of systematic observational systems, for example, researchers began to realize how unproductive it was to divorce observer systems from theories of interaction or group functioning.

All such systems clearly involve selection and embody theoretical assumptions whether these are explicit or implicit. The heyday of general observational systems linked to theories about the way in which people behave toward each other was in the 1950s, though many of these systems were inductively derived in part. The best known and most widely used of the observational schemes was Bales's Interaction Process Analysis (1950). Bales wanted to develop a set of categories that could be applied to groups varying in size, composition, and function. The final set of twelve categories was a compromise between pressures of theory and practicality. Bales wanted the category system to be a set of hypotheses about face-to-face interaction, although the categories emerged in part from long and tedious hours of observing ad hoc laboratory groups. The Interaction Process Analysis system instructs the observer to place individual statements or idea units in one of the twelve categories, noting who made the remark and to whom it was directed. The categories are basically divided into expressive social-emotional actions and instrumental task-oriented actions. It was Bales's belief that successful groups moved from defining the situation (orientation), to developing a consensual value system (evaluation), to a phase of mutual influence attempts (control), and hence to a final decision. Along the way there were problems of tension management and group maintenance.

Bales's Interaction Process Analysis system was more influential than other category systems that appeared at about the same time (Steinzor, 1949; Coffey, Freedman, Leary, and Ossorio, 1950; Carter et al., 1951a; 1951b) though its influence has been primarily felt in the sociological literature. In their review of laboratory experimentation featuring sociological investigators, Bonacich and Light (1978) suggest that Bales set the agenda for much current research on group participation rates and role differentiation, although many of his early findings and conjectures about group interaction have since been rejected. The impact of Bales's three-dimensional conceptualization of personality (1970), derived from factor analytic studies of interaction process and intermember perceptions, has been less profound. In general, the approach to systematic observation has changed from a main-force assault into a more sophisticated recognition that observation is merely a part of complex research procedures in the laboratory or field. Thus Weick (1968) stresses the importance of setting selection and of subtle interventions that facilitate reliable and meaningful observations. Perhaps the major holdover in social psychology from the early attempts to quantify social interaction (most particularly Chapple's "interaction chronograph" 1940, 1949) is the work of Darren Newtson (1973, 1976). The basic procedure in his work is to ask subjects to break behavior into units—to observe ongoing action and press a recording button when one meaningful segment of action ends and another begins. Thus far, Newtson has generated some interesting data concerning the high level of agreement over "break points" and the effects of such variables as behavioral predictability on unit size. (When behavior becomes unpredictable, the units recorded become smaller and smaller in duration.) The theoretical significance of Newtson's work is difficult to evaluate at present, but it is clear that his efforts raise some interesting possibilities concerning the perceptual organization of behavioral stimuli.

The Evolution of an Experimental Social Psychology

Though the emphasis on method in the 1930s struck first on the response side with the measurement of social behavior and behavior-linked attitudes, toward the end of the decade there was increasing interest in identifying and manipulating social stimuli. This increasing interest coincided with the vigorous development of experimental approaches to animal learning and undoubtedly borrowed part of its impetus from the dominant concern with discovering the laws of stimulus-response relationships. However, the full implementation of an experimental social psychology depended more directly on a combination of technical and theoretical developments that will be discussed in this and the following section. In order for the idea of an experimental social psychology to take hold, social stimulus variables had to be identified and techniques developed so they could be realized empirically. The main development in social psychology between 1930 and 1945 was movement toward the solution of these two problems. As a consequence, experimentation in the postwar period began to exert a dominant influence on the methodology of the field.

The idea of experimentation in social psychology did not suddenly emerge. By the time of Murchison's *Handbook of Social Psychology* in 1935, there were already a substantial number of studies dealing with the effects on individual performance of the presence of other people—what today we call "social facilitation." As Haines and Vaughan (1979) note, scattered experiments on suggestibility even preceded the Triplett (1898) experiment on the effects of competition. However, the variables chosen were typically restricted to concrete conditions that could be easily (often physically) specified, such as the presence or absence of other people, the difficulty level of the task, or the high versus low prestige of a communicator. The possibilities of creating complex and realistic social situations in the laboratory were essentially ignored until the contributions of Sherif (1936) and Lewin (with Lippitt and White, 1939; with Barker and Dembo, 1941).

If Murchison's *Handbook* can be cited to affirm the antiquity of experimental research in the one area of social facilitation effects, it may also be cited as a clear indication of the status of social psychology as a nonexperimental discipline in the mid 1930s. With the exception of Dashiell's chapter, the remainder of the handbook consists of essays in comparative psychology. It does offer, however, separate treatments concerning the social history of the white man, the yellow man, the black man, and the red man. As Farr (1976) notes (p. 226):

Social psychology was very broadly concerned with the study of social aggregates (whether of birds, insects, or even bacteria) as well as with studying the varieties of human nature resulting from growing up in widely different cultures.

This interest in the cultural variability of psychological states remained a prominent theme in social psychology well into the 1940s as typified by Klineberg's (1940) text.

Murchison's *Handbook of Social Psychology* marked the end of the preexperimental era in social psychology. The development of a distinctive experimental methodology in social psychology was forecast and facilitated by three important landmarks: the social memory studies of F. C. Bartlett (1932), the group influence studies of Sherif (1936, 1947), and the leadership atmosphere studies of Lewin, Lippitt, and White (1939).

Bartlett's "Experimental" Work   In 1932 Frederick C. Bartlett's *Remembering* was published in England. This classic book may be viewed as a major precursor of contemporary cognitive psychology. It specifically set the stage for studies of the role of motivation and expectancy in perception (Bruner and Goodman, 1947), introduced many of the procedures and concepts used by G. W. Allport and Postman in their study of rumor (1947), and even may be credited with an important role in the development of dissonance theory. Festinger (1957) was clearly impressed by the Indian rumor studies of two of Bartlett's students (Sinha, 1952; Prasad, 1950) in developing his theory. In the present context, we emphasize Bartlett's contribution to an experimental orientation in social psychology. This contribution was essentially a liberating one, for Bartlett was intent on resisting "the artificiality which often hangs over laboratory experiments in psychology" (p. 47) and boldly attempted to cope with subjects' verbal accounts of their perceptions, imagery, and memory in all their complexity. His reports of these accounts come across as faithfully accurate descriptions. He moved somewhat reluctantly to inductive generalizations, so impressed was he by the variety and uniqueness of responses to complex verbal and pictorial materials. He was essentially an experimental naturalist.

In Bartlett's best-known study, subjects were asked to read a 300-word folk story containing unfamiliar ideas and obscure connections and then to report on what they had read. In their reproductions, the subjects (who were British) assimilated the story to their own culturally determined cognitive categories, or as Bartlett called them, *schemata.* Bartlett's subjects condensed, highlighted, and rationalized the story to enhance its apparent coherence and consistency. His systematic observations were similar to those that had often been made by students of the psychology of courtroom testimony. As far back as the turn of the century, psychologists had been interested in showing how witnesses assimilate recalled experiences to their own expectations and distort them to agree with their motives. Bartlett, however, brought such considerations into the mainstream of psychological research and provided a number of useful descriptive labels for summarizing common cognitive tendencies.

Today, we readily accept the idea that our recollections and interpretations of events are biased by our cultural history and our current motives, but such a point of view came rather late to a psychology concerned with "pure memory" and therefore concentrating on the remembering of nonsense syllables—supposedly uncontaminated by "meaning." Thus Bartlett's contribution has to be weighed against the constricting earlier work typified by Ebbinghaus (1885) whose influence dominated the approach to the study of memory until the appearance of *Remembering.*

Most of the research listed by Bartlett in Part I of *Remembering,* under the heading "experimental studies," was not experimental at all. The studies typically did not feature the hallmarks of control, comparison, and random assignments that are usually considered the defining criteria of an experiment (cf. Campbell and Stanley, 1966; Carlsmith, Ellsworth, and Aronson, 1976). They did feature procedures in which materials were presented under controlled conditions to subjects in laboratory settings. Responses were faithfully and carefully recorded. There was little or no attempt, however, to compare experimental with control conditions. Although in the experiments on repeated and serial reproduction, successive renderings of recall were compared with each other, in the remainder of the research the only comparisons were between total accuracy and subjects' recollections. Thus statisticians and compulsive methodologists would not refer to Bartlett's work as a model of scientific research. Nevertheless, Bartlett's faithful attention to the rich associative imagery of his subjects left an important legacy for the cognitive psychologist, showing that processes heavily infused with motivational, affective, and experiential variables can be elicited in a laboratory and preserved for scrutiny and reflection.

In his comments on experimental procedure, Bartlett left a more controversial legacy. It was *not* important to him that the same procedural sequences or instructional wordings be followed for each successive subject. The important thing, rather, was to establish comparable conditions for his subjects. Thus, he tells us in introducing the experimental studies (p. 12):

> I have not hesitated to vary [the presentation of material] from person to person, or from time to time, and to adapt the conditions of its presentation, if it appeared to me that by doing so I could best get comparable conditions on the subjective side.

The issue of procedural consistency versus impact comparability is still a matter of debate among experimental social psychologists (e.g., Aronson and Carlsmith, 1968, p. 48). Though his role as an experimenter may be questioned, Bartlett was certainly important methodologically as a spokesman against reductionism on both the stimulus and the response side. He took his subjects seriously and was eager to let them tell their own stories in their own vernacular.

The Group Influence Studies of Sherif   Bartlett argued vigorously that the subjects' cultural backgrounds should be the frames of reference for interpreting events. In an important series of experiments done shortly after Bartlett's book, Sherif (1936) dramatically showed how such frames of reference can be bred in the laboratory. Subjects, either alone or in groups of two or three, were exposed to a stationary light in an otherwise dark room. They were asked to indicate when the light started moving and to estimate how far it moved. It is a common illusion ("autokinetic effect") that such a light will appear to move, but the situation is obviously very ambiguous. When an individual faced the light alone, he or she rather quickly developed a personally characteristic range within which his or her judgments fell. Sherif referred to this as the individual's "norm." When the subject was exposed to the judgments of others (in some cases preinstructed accomplices of the experimenter), his or her judgments converged toward a group norm. When the individual was then re-exposed to the light in isolation, he or she retained the group-established norm, which continued to influence judgments made.

Sherif proposed that "the psychological basis of the established social norms, such as stereotypes, conventions, customs, and values, is the formation of common frames of reference as a product of the contact of individuals" (1947, p. 85). Though this particular generalization may be debatable, his experiments beautifully dramatized the cognitive interdependence of persons confronting an ambiguous situation and set the stage for hundreds of conformity experiments in the following two decades. Sherif's experiments also showed how a social situation could be constructed in the laboratory by the occasional use of experimental confederates. Such deception in the interest of combining impact with control later became a common feature of social psychology experiments.

The Leadership Atmosphere Studies   Both Bartlett and Sherif made imaginative use of laboratory settings to bring crucial features of the natural social environment under experimental control. They championed the idea that experiments do not have to deal only with variables definable in terms of centimeters, seconds, or grams. This idea was more audaciously illustrated by the leadership atmosphere experiments of Lewin, Lippitt, and White (1939), experiments undoubtedly stimulated by Lewin's strong belief in the psychological fruits of democracy. In these experiments, groups of five boys were formed to carry out such extracurricular activities as making masks. The boys were assigned to groups that were as comparable as possible in terms of the personality and level of popularity of each member. Each group was led by an adult who played, initially, one of two carefully constructed roles: he or she was either consistently autocratic or democratic. In subsequent experiments a third leader, who played a laissez-faire role, was added to the design. Unlike the democratic leader who solicited agreement and helped guide the group along its chosen course of action, the laissez-faire leader was a passive resource person available for consultation.

Five observers took continuous notes on the behavior of the leader and the boys in each group. Observation categories were devised so that quantitative indexes of such actions as "hostile criticism," "friendly cooperation," or "giving instructions" could be developed to compare the different leadership atmospheres. Different experimental events were arranged to explore the reactions of the children in the different experimental groups. At times the leader was deliberately late; at other times the leader left the group, and a janitor entered to make standard hostile comments. In order to study out-group scapegoating, groups sometimes met at the same time in adjacent areas.

The autocratic leadership produced both aggressive and apathetic reactions. The democratic leadership was uniformly preferred to both autocratic and laissez-faire styles. Scapegoating and blowing off steam in the absence of the leader were minimal in the democratic groups, but very apparent in the others. Productivity was approximately the same in the democratic and autocratic groups but considerably lower in the laissez-faire group. From the perspective of current experimental designs, the Lewin-Lippitt-White experiments were rather crude and confounded. Many compromises were made in an attempt to get more information from fewer groups than a fully counter-balanced design would require. However, the experiment had a number of features later more generally associated with the Lewinian approach:

1. A complex situational variable, in this case leadership atmosphere, was manipulated, and systematic observations provided a quantitative check on the success of that manipulation. This procedure represented a breaking away from the constraints of purely physical specification of independent variables.

2. Every effort was made to keep the setting as natural as possible and to inhibit self-consciousness in the subjects. One can speculate about the impact of observers, unobtrusive though they tried to be, but the boys apparently did not know that they were experimental subjects. The report suggests that their behavior was quite natural, implying that they adapted readily to the potentially distracting observers.

3. Theoretical considerations led to the initial choice of independent variables, but changes and additions were made in follow-up experiments as a function of initial observations.

4. The detailed observation of social behavior reflected an interest in interpersonal processes rather than merely in the products or outcomes of interaction. Thus there was only an incidental interest in such things as ratings of satisfaction and the number of masks made.

5. Follow-up interviews were conducted to assess each child's phenomenal perceptions of the experience in accord with Sherif's interest in how aware subjects are of their own responses to social influence pressures.

Though it is difficult to assess the actual effects of such an experimental demonstration on subsequent developments, perhaps it is no coincidence that so many experiments in the 1950s, 1960s, and 1970s also involved the use of preinstructed role players, an emphasis on nonreactive behavioral measures, a concern with validation of experimental manipulations, and a retrospective examination of the subject's phenomenal experiences while going through the experiments. In addition, the attempt of Lewin and his colleagues to realize empirically such a nebulous concept as leadership atmosphere may have served to challenge future investigators and to provoke them to think about similar nebulous concepts that might be realized through the construction of creative role-playing scenarios.

Probability Statistics and Experimental Design   The sine qua non of experimentation is comparison—looking at the differential consequences of systematically varied antecedents. Physical scientists of the 1920s and 1930s pressed toward purification of the materials used, the procedures followed, and the measurements made so as to produce unequivocal and uniform effects. In their pure research efforts, they did not have to worry unduly about experimental settings, samples and populations, and individual differences. The prospects of a true experimental science involving reactions to complex social settings must have seemed remote as long as one held up the idea of uniform experimental effects. After all, common sense tells us that the more complex the environment, the greater the likelihood that individuals will differ in their responses to it.

Clinical and personality psychologists converted their recognition of this fact into the search for stable dimensions of individual differences. To some extent, this search represented an ultimate optimism about the development of penetrating measures of predictive dispositions as well as a certain sense of defeat about the specification or measurement of environmental features. Since the ultimate objective of social psychology is to predict behavior in the natural environment and the natural environment is too complicated to control with precision in the laboratory, the personality-clinical approach emphasized a strategy of extrapolating from an individual's standing on a psychometric instrument his response in a meaningful social situation. Insofar as statistical techniques were involved, this approach relied on correlational measures and, in some cases, factor analysis. During the 1930s an alternative approach focused on an increased understanding of the role of situational contexts. The popularity of this alternative was undoubtedly elevated as social psychologists began to understand the relevance of probability statistics to an experimental approach. With the development of the "critical ratio" and the more flexible and sophisticated *t*-test, it became possible to reach consensus about whether an experimental effect was or was not substantial enough to be meaningful. One could concede the inevitable role of individual differences and unmeasured sources of error variance while still being able to tease out the effects of sufficiently powerful experimental variables. Never mind that not all members of condition A give the same uniform response, the central tendency can be assessed and differences in such tendencies can be measured against the degree of noise or variance associated with the condition. The idea that one could accurately assess the probability of a true difference between experimental conditions was enormously important in paving the way for an experimental social psychology. Although well-established correlational techniques were derived from the same model of variance, the particular format of the *t*-test (and similar measures of differences between groups) undoubtedly facilitated its influence in the development of experimental procedures.

Also of great importance, especially since the Second World War, was the increasing use of analysis of variance procedures. The potential of such procedures naturally affected the planning of experiments and decisions about feasible experimental designs. If the *t*-test was liberating in permitting the assessment of group differences in the face of "error," analysis of variance techniques was liberating in permitting the assessment of multiply determined effects. Not only could more than two groups be compared in one analysis, but cross-cutting factorial designs made possible investigations of the effects of one variable at different levels of other variables. Statistical interaction effects, an intriguing yield of analysis of variance procedures, became the hallmark of sophisticated theorizing about nonobvious effects in social psychology. Though lending itself to an almost unlimited potential complexity of experimental design, analysis of variance procedures proved most informative with designs of no more than moderate complexity. In particular, the advent of analysis of variance techniques highlighted the beauties of the four-fold table or the two-by-two design, beauties that had only been hinted at with chi square and tetrachoric correlation approaches. Without the many two-by-two designs developed to test theoretical hypotheses, the literature of social psychology in the 1960s and 1970s would have been considerably thinner.

All this, however, gets ahead of our story. We have tried to isolate certain methodologically important examples of experimentation during the thirties and to acknowledge the role of statistical innovations applied to comparisons of experimentally contrived conditions. One can argue, however, that experimental demonstrations in social psychology would have been isolated and selective without the metatheoretical underpinning provided by Lewinian Field Theory. We turn next to the role of Kurt Lewin in fathering a coherent experimental social psychology.

THE LINKAGE OF THEORY WITH EXPERIMENTATION

To some extent, the development of theory in social psychology awaited the generation of reliable data that needed to be explained and integrated. But the reverse was even more true. Social psychology was very slow to develop indigenous theory, and this fact unquestionably handicapped its emergence as an experimental science. Without some kind of bridging theory of interpersonal process, would-be experimenters were thwarted by what might be called the generalization question. How could an experimenter claim that his findings on thirty male college sophomores were in any important sense generalizable to a broader population of human beings or even to college males? Sociology essentially confronted the generalization question by abjuring the laboratory experiment and constructing or testing theories through survey methods in which sample representativeness was an important consideration. Psychologists, on the other hand, developed and refined experimental techniques that would test the plausibility of general process theories in restricted concrete contexts. In the late 1920s and 1930s this effort increased particularly in studies of animal behavior in which psychologists like Hull and Tolman attempted to theorize about general learning processes from data produced by rats in mazes. Thus there developed a broad context in U.S. psychology nurturing the importance of theory as a bridge between concrete experimental findings. As the experimental tradition developed in social psychology, researchers became more preoccupied with the conceptual generality of their findings than with the representativeness of their samples. Theories were useful to the extent that they predicted superficially different but conceptually similar relations in a variety of contexts. It was Kurt Lewin who, more than anyone else, stimulated and provided the philosophical rationale for this approach.

Lewinian Field Theory

Lewin was a refugee from the Nazis who arrived in this country to stay in 1933, making the rather remarkable shift from Berlin's Psychological Institute to Cornell's Department of Home Economics. He moved shortly thereafter to the Iowa Child Welfare Research Station where he began to apply his basic theoretical predilections to the study of group dynamics and to train a number of students who were to play an important role in social psychology. In 1945 he moved to the Massachusetts Institute of Technology where he organized the Research Center for Group Dynamics. He died prematurely in 1947. Lewin was to an extent influenced by the Gestalt psychology triumvirate Wertheimer, Kohler, and Koffka, but he was by no means a classic Gestaltist. Whereas Gestalt psychologists traditionally emphasized perceptual and cognitive structures, Lewin was much more intrigued with questions of motivation and the dynamics of feeling and action. If a Gestaltist, he was a "hot" Gestaltist.

At least as important as his contact with the leading Gestalt psychologists was Lewin's assimilation of Cassirer's philosophical teachings. These he wove into his own field theory, which is described in a variety of publications appearing from 1937 to 1947. Unlike the usual set of assumptions and propositions from which empirical hypotheses could be deduced, this theory was more like a language or point of view. Lewin himself described the theory as "a method: namely a method of analyzing causal relations and building scientific constructs" (1951a, p. 45, orig. 1943). Lewin did use a terminology borrowed from force-field physics. Instead of behaving or responding, organisms "locomoted" through a field of bounded "regions" impelled by "forces" or drawn by "valences" along power "vectors." Much more important than the specific terminology was Lewin's movement away from conceiving man as a bundle of propensities confronting a structured social system. For certain purposes he conceived of a person as a point in psychological space, constrained to move in certain directions by the field of forces operating in that space. The imagery evoked by this conceptualization offers an invitation to experimentation or at least an invitation to the kind of theorizing that in turn could lead to experimentation. A view of a human being as the product of long developmental history emphasizes the uniqueness and the distinctiveness of his or her responses to a common environment. On the other hand, a view of a human being as a point at the intersection of environmental forces emphasizes the contemporaneous perceptions and related actions he or she shares with others in that same position. Through experimenta-

tion, one hopes that such common action patterns can be determined.

Lewin had glimmerings of an ultimate theory that was highly abstract and expressible in the new mathematics of topology. Of much greater historical importance, however, was his recognition that one must initially proceed with crude approximations, with what he called "quasi-concepts" like hope, expectancy, and frustration. Lewin openly and persistently advocated the experimental method, but at least as important an influence on the evolution of experimental social psychology were the research examples provided by him and his students.

The path-breaking studies of Bluma Zeigarnik (1927), under Lewin's direction, provide excellent examples of the bold use of psychological theory in generating an experimental program. We have already described the impact of the leadership atmosphere studies of Lewin, Lippitt, and White (1939), stressing the innovative methodology. Other influential examples included Lewin's studies of regression with Barker and Dembo (1941), of group decision and social change (1947), and his work with several associates on level of aspiration (Lewin, Dembo, Festinger, and Sears, 1944).

In spite of the interesting substantive issues raised by these examples, Lewin's contribution was basically atmospheric. His mode of conceptualizing fed easily into experimental interventions. He also provided a rationale for theory-based experimentation and for the idea of conceptual generality of a relationship across contexts rather than simple empirical generality across samples. As early as 1926 Lewin said, "the quantitative level most propitious for experimental analysis varies from case to case and laws shift little as a function of this level" (1951b, p. 83). And fourteen years later he made more specific the way to implement conceptual generality (1951a, p. 9, orig. 1940):

> to prove or disprove the theory of tension systems, it seems much more important to find a variety of derivations from this theory which should be as different as possible from each other, and to test as many as possible of these derivations, even if this test should be rather crude quantitatively at the beginning.

In addition to his contribution to an experimental social psychology, Lewin made numerous others to applied social psychology and was himself a consultant to industry, government, and social service organizations. He was the founder of group dynamics, an approach to interactions in groups that laid the ground work for such subsequent movements as T-groups and certain kinds of encounter groups. In addition to writing a variety of influential books and articles, Lewin attracted a distinguished group of students who played a vital role in the evolution of social psychology. Prior to his emigration to the United States, Lewin's students included Dembo, Hoppe, Ovsiankina, and Zeigarnik. His Iowa years were shared with Bavelas, Festinger, Lippitt, and White. The next generation joined the Center for Group Dynamics at the Massachusetts Institute of Technology. Dorwin Cartwright and Leon Festinger helped to form a faculty nucleus for a student group that included Kurt Back, Morton Deutsch, Murray Horwitz, Harold Kelley, Stanley Schachter, and John Thibaut. After Lewin's death and the Center's move to the University of Michigan, a number of students working with Festinger began to tackle the challenges posed by his theory of social comparison processes. Festinger went on to become the dominant figure in social psychology for a period roughly spanning the two decades from 1950 to 1970.

The Theory of Social Comparison Processes

Festinger's first highly influential achievement was the publication of a theory of social comparison processes in 1954. Festinger presented his theory in the form of postulates and corollaries, reminiscent of Hull's earlier theoretical efforts, and probably intended to emphasize that social psychology had "come of age." In addition to offering the most formal theorizing yet to appear in social psychology, Festinger reported the results of many experiments specifically designed to test hypotheses about our sensitivity to others' opinions and our abilities in coming to terms with our own. He proposed that there are large areas of judgment in which "reality" cannot be reliably measured by conventional physical devices. In these areas reality must be socially defined. When a person finds himself or herself in disagreement with others about the nature of this reality, he or she will be motivated to handle the discrepancy in some way. The individual may either change his or her own opinion, persuade others to change theirs, or decide that the others are irrelevant as comparison persons. Festinger spelled out in some detail the independent variables that should affect the resolution of opinion and ability discrepancies. Many of his students conducted experiments manipulating group cohesiveness (the attraction of the group to its members), issue relevance, degree of discrepancy, and other sources of pressure toward uniformity in a group. Most of these studies are included in a bibliography of social comparison studies collected by Radloff and Bard (1966). A more recent volume edited by Suls and Miller (1977) extends and refines many of the theory's hypotheses.

The theory was a tour de force in tying together conformity, rejection of deviates, and instrumental communication and in illustrating the role comparison processes play in evaluating our abilities as well as our opinions. Festinger's theory was generally compatible with previous formulations such as those of James (1890), Cooley (1902), and Mead (1934) in its emphasis on the social derivation

and maintenance of one's self-concept. The form and particulars of the theory, however, seem to have been more specifically influenced by Lewin's (1936) theory about the spread of tension within systems. Festinger's 1950 essay on informal communication was a bridging paper in which he conceived of small groups as systems tending toward equilibrium. Since differences of opinion are disequilibrating, they generate "pressures toward uniformity" and result in influence attempts, opinion change, and/or social rejection (cf. Jones and Gerard, 1967, p. 340). In addition, the ideas of judgmental relativity from level of aspiration theory (Lewin et al., 1944) were prominently carried over into social comparison theory.

Although the pervasive influence of social comparison theory is difficult to document, certainly social comparison ideas have played a prominent role in subsequent research on equity (Adams, 1965), attribution (Kelley, 1967) and social interaction (Thibaut and Kelley, 1959). A specific, closely related offshoot from the theory of social comparison was Schachter's (1959) work on the need for self-appraisal as a determinant of affiliation. In a series of realistic experiments, subjects were threatened with electric shock and given the choice of waiting alone or with others in a similar predicament. Schachter's major finding was that highly anxious subjects preferred to affiliate with others before being given electric shocks (they in fact never were) in order to calibrate through social comparison their own level of fear. Schachter's student Wrightsman found, in addition, that experienced anxiety became more homogeneous in groups of subjects waiting together in anticipation of a drug injection. Thus the effects of social comparison on emotional experience were similar to those predicted for the evaluation of one's own opinions and abilities.

Schachter followed the implications of the Wrightsman finding into a broader theory of emotional experience. He proposed (1964) that emotional states are a combination of physiological arousal and cognitive labeling and showed that vastly different emotional states could result from the same physiological arousal in different social contexts. Schachter's subsequent research into obesity and nicotine addiction has removed him from social psychology proper—in fact he has recently (1980) expressed considerable skepticism about the role of psychological and social factors in addictive patterns. Nevertheless, his approach to emotional experience, as we shall see, played a vital role in the emergence of attributional approaches to social explanation.

Cognitive Dissonance Theory

Although Festinger's theory of social comparison was a dramatic integrative attempt, it did not clearly exemplify the evolution of understanding through the interplay of theorizing and experimenting. The theory certainly spawned research, yet many of its postulates and propositions have proved relatively intractable or exceedingly difficult to confirm. The issues raised by social comparison theory will be with us for a long time, but progress toward their solutions seems sporadic and generally indirect. The theory of cognitive dissonance, on the other hand, comes closer to the prototypic middle-range theory that Lewin idealized. It is generally recognized as Festinger's greatest creative contribution, and research related to dissonance theory dominated the journals of social psychology from the late 1950s to the early 1970s. This period presents the historian with the fruits of a flexible, abstract theory being tested in a variety of socially interesting content domains.

The idea that people are more comfortable with consistent than with inconsistent cognitions has been proclaimed by many psychologists and philosophers. People are not only rational most of the time but also (as Freud especially noted) rationalizers. We want our attitudes and beliefs to support rather than contradict our behavior, and we want our cognitions tied together in a coherent, mutually reinforcing system. Such basic assumptions characterize a variety of consistency theories that appeared in the 1940s and 1950s (Heider, 1946; Lecky, 1945; Newcomb, 1953; Osgood and Tannenbaum, 1955). What Festinger did was to consider the motivational implication of those inconsistencies that are from time to time thrust upon us; the result of his work was the firm establishment of the experimental method in discriminating among theoretical alternatives in social psychology.

Festinger's theory can be very simply stated: two cognitions can be either relevant or irrelevant. If they are relevant, then they must be consonant or dissonant. To say that two cognitions are dissonant is to say that one does not follow from the other or that one follows from the converse of the other. Dissonant cognitions produce an aversive state which the individual will try to reduce by changing one or both of the cognitions. If a heavy smoker is exposed to statistics showing that smoking leads to lung cancer, he or she can change the cognition about how much he smokes ("I'm really only a light smoker") or perceive the statistical data as hysterical environmentalist propaganda and discount it. Festinger went beyond the other consistency formulations in recognizing and exploiting the recognition that some cognitions are more resistant to change than others. Cognitions about behavior, in particular, are resistant to change. It is hard to convince ourselves that we did not just knock over our wine glass when we did, that we did not vote for a particular candidate when we just pulled the lever, and so on. Putting together the combined ideas of inconsistency-generated motivation and the fact that cognitions are differentially resistant to change, Festinger and his students were able to derive a number of diverse and often counter-intuitive propositions.

A sampling of these shows the versatility and power of cognitive dissonance theory in its applications to decision processes, social influence attempts, classic learning phenomena, moral developments, and attitude change:

1. *Postdecision changes in the desirability of alternatives.* Choosing between two equally desirable alternatives creates dissonance, which can be reduced by seeing the chosen alternative as more desirable and the unchosen alternative as less desirable than initially judged (Brehm, 1956).
2. *Bolstering belief through the recruitment of social consensus.* Irrevocable commitment to a belief that is later disconfirmed fosters attempts to persuade others to share the disconfirmed belief (Festinger, Riecken, and Schachter, 1956).
3. *Learning to love that for which you have suffered.* Resistance to extinction by partially reinforced rats may be explained in terms of dissonance reduction. Running in a maze to an empty goal box on nonreinforced trials creates dissonance, which can be reduced by developing an extra attraction for the goal box or other features of the correct paths (Lawrence and Festinger, 1962).
4. *Internalization of prohibitions under insufficient deterrence.* Children who obey a weak injunction not to play with a desirable toy will subsequently like the toy less than those who obey a completely sufficient injunction (Aronson and Carlsmith, 1963).
5. *The energizing quality of cognitive dissonance.* Conditions known to produce dissonance also increase the emission of responses governed by strong habits at the expense of responses governed by weak habits (Cottrell, 1972).
6. *The inducement of attitude change by counter attitudinal behavior.* Cajoling subjects to speak out against cherished beliefs for insufficient justification encourages them to change those beliefs in a moderating direction (Festinger and Carlsmith, 1959; Brehm and Cohen, 1962). The contributions of dissonance theory to our understanding of attitude change are so substantial that we shall return to the "induced compliance paradigm" in a subsequent section.

Much of the more recent research on dissonance theory specifies the precise conditions under which cognitive dissonance is or is not aroused. In particular, research on the role of foreseeability, personal responsibility, and aversive consequences has led to a new emphasis on implications of behavior for the self-concept (Aronson, 1968, 1980). Thus, inconsistency between behavior and attitudes is not sufficient for dissonance arousal unless the attitudes are firmly anchored in the self-concept and the behavior produces aversive consequences that could have been foreseen.

In summary, cognitive dissonance theory and research

not only made a substantive contribution to our understanding of human nature but also served as a clear example of the promise offered by theory-based experimental research in social science. From Festinger's extremely simple, rather vague theoretical statement, the theory evolved with the aid of experimental feedback to include a set of well-articulated systematic relationships. Inherent in this development were many of the features encouraged by Lewin in the construction of a theory of behavior causation: here was a middle-range theory being used to generate testable propositions. Although these findings were conceptually replicable in a variety of superficially different domains, they were not self-evident without the theory to house them. Many of these experiments involved the kind of stage management first noted in the Lewin, Lippitt, and White studies discussed earlier. Although most of the research was done in the laboratory, there were also many excursions into field settings to check on the empirical utility of the developing theory.

Dissonance research aroused considerable controversy in the middle and late 1960s for a variety of complex reasons. The fact that the major terms of the theory (cognition, importance, relevance, obverse implication) were defined in only the most sketchy way did not help matters. Because the theory did not contain specific operational rules, much was left to the imagination and creativity of the researcher. Thus individual experiments purporting to confirm the theory could be dismissed with some justification as triumphs of clever experimental engineering. The presentation of the theory contrasted sharply with the formal elegance of Hullian behavior theory and the detailed empirical linkages of Skinner's formulation. These departures might have gone unnoticed and unlamented by other psychologists if dissonance researchers had restricted their concern to the "soft" domains of cognitive selectivity and attitude change. However, as Aronson (1980) notes, in flexing their theoretical muscles, dissonance researchers took on the conventional wisdom at many points. In particular, dissonance theorists challenged the reigning importance of secondary reinforcement notions in proposing that action to obtain a small reward will stamp in associative cognitions more than actions to obtain a large reward. When Lawrence and Festinger (1962) invaded the domain of animal learning by suggesting that rats possessed something like cognitions and that dissonance theory could explain response persistence and resistance to extinction better than the established learning theories, their claims were challenged.

The methodological style of the dissonance proponents also contributed to the controversy. No one denied the rather bold inventiveness of the early dissonance researchers, but this inventiveness was usually coupled with procedural complexities that made precise replication difficult. Those bred in the tradition of cumulative research in experimental psychology thought they saw serious vulner-

ability in this complexity and in the apparent disregard of standardized dependent variable measurement. Also, almost without exception, dissonance experiments involved deceptive scenarios that often enticed subjects into doing things they would not normally do—presumably a sine qua non for studying adjustments to counter-attitudinal activities. An ethical reaction against deception developed in the late 1960s (e.g., Kelman, 1968) which chose as its target the form of laboratory deception research typical of that deriving from dissonance theory.

Such controversy and criticisms are not entirely a thing of the past (e.g., Fishbein and Ajzen, 1975) and debate still continues about the generality and replicability of dissonance phenomena. Nevertheless, it is probably fair to say that dissonance theory has reached a stage of middle-aged respectability and that most social psychologists accept the fact (however reluctantly in some quarters) that the insights gained through dissonance-related research are important and lasting.

Stimulus-Response (Behavior) Theory

Lewinian metatheory, particularly as a backdrop for Festinger's productive theorizing, was directly instrumental in converting social psychology into a primarily experimental discipline. The impact of stimulus-response (S–R) theory over the past fifty years is more ubiquitous and therefore more difficult to trace. Certainly S–R theorists like Miller and Dollard, Mowrer, Sears, Rotter, Campbell, Aronfreed, Bandura, and Mischel reached out in an attempt to incorporate responses to social stimuli. They did this, by and large, through the expansion of mediational constructs, such as response-produced stimulation. Clearly contemporary approaches that partake of the S–R legacy have increasingly featured complex cognitive, affective, and motivational processes. However, it is probably accurate to say that S–R formulations were extended more naturally and gracefully into the areas of personality and developmental psychology than into social psychology per se. It is worth a little space to speculate on why this might be so.

An important impediment to extending S–R formulations to the social arena is the difficulty in specifying the social stimulus in clear, objective, noncircular terms. The major reference experiments of Thorndike, Pavlov, Guthrie, Hull, Tolman, and Skinner involved animals interacting with various features of the physical environment. This environment could be described objectively in terms of centimeters, grams, or seconds. The everyday social behavior of human beings, of course, defies description in these terms. To extend the S–R analysis to such behavior episodes requires reference to some internal set of mechanisms encompassing attention, perception, memory, and complex cognitive transformations. Almost since its inception, the S–R approach has really been a stimulus-organism-response approach. By elaborating the organism (O) term within the classical S–O–R paradigm, behavior theorists were able to account for complex social behavior—at least after the fact. The problem has always been that of specifying independently of observed behavior the social stimulus conditions of which that behavior is a function. The fact that each organism confronts each social situation with a history of prior learning that is ultimately unique and unrecoverable by the behavior analyst (except, perhaps, in the individualized settings of psychotherapy), makes specification of stimuli very difficult.

There are three basic responses to this dilemma: reductionism (which might take the form of a researcher dealing only with schedules of reinforcement in the pigeon while speculating about analogies to complex human functioning), working with personality differences as intervening variables to predict responses to representative situations, and "bootstrapping" the definition of social stimuli. The latter procedure typically involves creating an experimental situation designed to mean roughly the same thing to different human subjects and checking on the validity of this intended construction by a variety of direct and indirect postexperimental probes. The early behavior theorists traditionally placed great emphasis on an objective, independent stimulus definition. It is not surprising, therefore, that those coming out of this tradition would feel uneasy, to say the least, with complex social stimulus configurations that can only be summarily described and that are specified through some joint combination of experimenter intentions and subject response. Hullians and Skinnerians found the circularity lurking in such definitional bootstrapping disturbing and pseudoscientific.

In comparison, personality approaches involving the exploitation of measurable individual differences have two major advantages. First, personality can be readily conceptualized in terms of learning processes and products—whether the major constructs used are habits, operants, traits, or secondary drives. Second, useful measures of individual differences in personality (learning history?) can be exploited in conjunction with standardized stimulus settings. In Spence's (1944), Kimble's (1953), or Cronbach's (1957) terms, one shifts from S–R laws to R–R laws, from experimental to correlational approaches. In this way the purity of experimentation with independent variables anchored in replicable operations can be supplemented by a differential personality approach in which predictive variance in response can be attributed to measurable differences in learning history.

Whether or not these speculations have any validity, it is our impression that S–R psychologists in the 1950s and 1960s were much less sympathetic to the Lewin-Festinger approach to experimentation than they were to research developments in personality and clinical psychology. Perhaps a rather cruel way to put it is to state that the behaviorist

had a respectable "applied" category for clinicians—they were R&R, correlational psychologists—whereas the experimental social psychologists of that period encroached on the turf of objective science with independent variables that were not truly independent. Thus the experimental social psychologists in the Lewinian tradition seemed to be subverting the rules against subjectivity that had been so laboriously fought for within the behavioristic tradition.

Though the behaviorist tradition has had more of an impact on personality and developmental research than on the central problems of social influence within social psychology, there are many important exceptions. One area where theorizing has historically partaken of (usually liberated) S–R concepts is that of *aggression*. The importance of frustration-aggression theory to social psychology in particular and to the social sciences in general cannot be overestimated. In 1939, Dollard et al., proposed a hypothesis linking aggression with frustration that allegedly was derived from "common sense observation, from clinical case histories, from experimental investigations, from sociological studies, and from the results of anthropological field work" (Miller, 1941, p. 337). However, the hypothesis was clearly couched in the Hullian idiom of the time. Frustration was defined as an "interrupted behavior sequence," and aggression as one of a hierarchy of responses that are instigated by frustration, and so on. The ideas of displacement and catharsis were also heavily influenced, presumably, by psychoanalytic formulations of motivational dynamics, although the theory departed from Freud in avoiding any reference to the instinctual origins of aggression. Frustration-aggression theory has been criticized for the circularity of its major terms and maligned for its apparent invulnerability to disconfirmation. Nevertheless, the theory, when joined to Miller's subsequent theory of conflict and displacement (1944, 1948), represented an important advance that exposed a variety of social problems to experimental attack. Among other things, the approach opened up a much more sophisticated set of possibilities for dealing with the "scapegoat theory of prejudice." Extrapolating from animal maze-running behavior in approach and avoidance learning situations, Miller developed a theoretical basis for predicting the displacement of responses when the most strongly instigated approach response is inhibited by even stronger avoidance tendencies. This conceptual relation offered some promise to those who wanted to predict the conditions under which particular minority group targets would be chosen as scapegoats by members of the majority. In theory, if an aggressive response to life's frustrations must be displaced from more powerful instigating sources to less relevant and less powerful substitutes (e.g., a minority group), this displacement should be a function of the shapes of the instigation and inhibition gradients and of the degree of similarity between instigator and substitute target. Unfortunately, the problems of specifying gradients and sorting out appropriate dimensions of similarity have proved to be insurmountable. Nevertheless, the scapegoat notion lay at the heart of authoritarian personality theory (Adorno et al., 1950), and Miller's work provided a behavior theory underpinning for the looser displacement idea of Freudian psychoanalysis.

In general, more recent theorizing about aggression has underplayed psychoanalytic drive-displacement ideas while placing greater emphasis on a combination of cognitive and attributional considerations within the hospitable confines of contemporary behavior theory. The two most influential spokesmen for a neo-behavioral view have been Berkowitz and Bandura. In particular, Berkowitz has emphasized the combination of emotional arousal (generally because of some form of frustration) with cues that have been previously associated with reinforced aggression. This view has been given some support by several provocative (albeit controversial) experiments in which an experimental frustration occurs in conjunction with cues that either have or have not been associated with aggressive acts in the past (e.g., Berkowitz and Geen, 1966; Berkowitz and LePage, 1967). Bandura's (1973) theoretical account of aggression also emphasizes learned determinants and incentives and takes the position that aggression is one of a number of responses linked to aversive experiences and controlled by anticipated consequences. Bandura's experimental research has focused on the imitation of aggressive models, although his flexible theoretical housing may be more adaptable to therapeutic intervention than to basic experimental research. A basic problem, as Bandura (1973) notes, is that aggression is a complex synthesis of emotion, attitude, and action, each of which can be linked in different ways to instigating conditions. Because our learning histories are so diverse, it is likely that research on aggression will continue to be more promising with young children than with adults. Nevertheless, a considerable amount of experimental research on aggression (both with children and adults) has been spawned within the S–R, reinforcement framework.

Imitation and vicarious learning are two closely related areas where S–R behavior theories have contributed to informative experimental research. Miller and Dollard's (1941) *Imitation and Social Learning* was unquestionably an important book that liberalized S–R theory in proposing that the behavior of a model can serve as a discriminative cue for an observer. (A very similar view was later proposed by Skinner, 1953.) The authors also conducted a number of experiments demonstrating "matched-dependent" learning, in which a rat or a child learns to make the correct (rewarded) response by paying attention to the rewarded response of another rat or child. Bandura and Walters (1963) were later to argue that Miller and Dollard focused on only one form of imitation and a trivial form at

that. They presented many examples of complex imitation going well beyond the simple discriminative learning identified by Miller and Dollard. Nevertheless, from a historical point of view, Miller and Dollard's work was important in distinguishing among different forms of imitation-like behavior, releasing the concept from its instinctual and reflexive origins and showing how empirical progress can be made through a program combining human and animal experimentation.

Vicarious learning phenomena have been distinguished from imitation because they do not necessarily involve any direct reinforcement to the observer. They would include, therefore, the spontaneous and elaborate imitative responses singled out by Bandura and Walters. As is true with his work on aggression, Bandura has made significant contributions to our understanding of imitation, identification, and vicarious learning through a series of complex and ingenious experiments. This work is important in understanding some of the subprocesses of socialization. Yet progress in our understanding of imitation and vicarious learning over the past forty years has been surprisingly modest, given the importance of the topic. One reason may be that even a liberalized S–R approach is too static because it fails to deal with the active role of the model (parent) in shaping the observer's (child's) behavior. The importance of such active shaping has been emphasized by Brown and Bellugi (1964) in their work on language acquisition. Another reason for this lack of progress is that social psychologists have expended more of their energies on processes of social influences and conformity, thus treating many of the phenomena of imitation in a radically different, but quite heuristic, context.

Important aspects of the S–R behavior theory approach have been treated in many other research contexts in social psychology. Hovland and his Yale colleagues' approach to attitude change was initially framed in terms of learned "implicit responses" that may change under the normal conditions of learning, controlled by incentives conveyed by persuasive communications. (This approach will be discussed in greater detail in the next section.) A number of attempts have been made to incorporate social interaction within an S–R framework (most explicitly Homans, 1961, 1974, but also Thibaut and Kelley, 1959). Since many other theoretical elements are also involved in these treatments, they will be dealt with subsequently as separate descriptive frameworks.

Zajonc's (1965) analysis of social facilitation, one of the oldest empirical phenomena in experimental social psychology, is explicitly derived from Hull-Spence behavior theory. The mere presence of others, according to Zajonc, provides a nonspecific drive stimulus that energizes responses. As in Spence's theory (1956) the stronger or more dominant responses in a hierarchy are energized more than the weaker responses. Zajonc and his colleagues present suggestive support for this view by showing that well-learned responses are strengthened by the presence of others, whereas weaker responses are disrupted.

Byrne (1971) has provided a model showing how reinforcements influence evaluations of people and objects. His extensive research relating attraction to perceived similarity in others has produced remarkably stable and consistent results. However, his research has been criticized as being derived from highly restricted and artificial settings, and his theory has been cited as too restricted in its explanatory power (West and Wicklund, 1980).

Finally, researchers within the S–R tradition have raised questions concerning the automatic and "unconscious" operations of reinforcements in dyadic interaction. Sidowski (1957; with Wykoff and Tabori, 1956) investigated the "minimal social situation" in which two physically isolated subjects have the means to provide reinforcing points for each other by pressing a button in their respective booths. In the classic minimal information case, neither subject is aware that he or she controls the outcomes of the other. In fact neither knows that another subject is present in the experiment. Posed with the problem of obtaining the maximum number of points, each subject is free to press the button in his or her booth as often or as seldom as he or she wishes. In these early studies, the authors found that the subjects generally "learned" to reinforce each other whether or not they were aware of the contingency between their button presses and their hidden partner's outcomes. However, later studies by Kelley, Thibaut, Radloff, and Mundy (1962) did show that explicit information about the nature of the subjects' mutual dependence significantly improves learning in a similar, minimal social situation. Comparable issues of "learning without awareness" received considerable attention in the 1960s (e.g., Eriksen, 1962). If one person shapes another's behavior through such subtle reinforcements as head nods and verbal "uh-huhs," does this occur without the target person's awareness? Though this question has never been clearly resolved because of the insurmountable difficulties involved in recapturing awareness after the behavioral fact, similar problems of behavioral decisions without awareness are embedded in contemporary treatments of naive cognition (e.g., Nisbett and Wilson, 1977).

In summary, experimentation without theory presents severe generalization problems. Lewin clearly saw that testing theories of sufficient abstraction in different empirical domains would help to resolve questions of conceptual generality. Festinger became the creative executor of Lewin's metatheoretical estate, first with his theory of social comparison processes and then even more clearly with his theory of cognitive dissonance. In the 1960s and 1970s the clearly dominant paradigm in social psychology became the laboratory experiment in which complex independent variables were embedded in systematically varied,

realistic scenarios designed to eliminate inapplicable theoretical alternatives. Though the idea of theoretical advance through the elimination of alternatives is a very general one in science, the particular style and expression of this goal within social psychology owes much to the exhortations of Lewin and the exemplifications of Festinger.

The traditions of S–R behavior theory, on the other hand, have had a less specific, secondary impact on social psychological research and theory. In the study of the complexity of human social behavior, the pronouncements of reinforcement psychologists can have the banal ring of truisms. The classic behavior theory paradigm emphasized temporal relations between stimuli in restricted settings where relevant incentives could be easily specified in terms of deprivation operations. Sloppy generalizations from such reference experiments to the complex human scene have not been helpful in furthering our understanding. Nevertheless, as behavior theorists have become more sophisticated about internal mediating processes in the human organism, they have had more and more to say to social psychologists. Although the impact of behavior theory has been more apparent in the specific areas of socialization and personality functioning than in social psychology, this area also has benefited in both general and specific ways from the traditional concepts and analytic procedures of behavior theory. At the very least, reinforcement concepts have often provided an ever-present alternative to more subtle, cognitive explanations. In addition, however, behavior theory has advanced our understanding of imitation, vicarious behavior, social interaction decisions, attitude change, attraction, and aggression.

CENTRAL RESEARCH AREAS

Communication and Persuasion: Attitude Change

Social psychologists were remarkably slow to turn their attention to the study of attitude and opinion change. Though the study of attitudes had been almost equated with social psychology by Watson's work in 1925 and even earlier by Thomas and Znaniecki's endeavor in 1918, one finds there were only a handful of studies dealing with the processes of attitude change until the Second World War. Instead, as McGuire (1969) points out, from 1920 to 1945 attitude theorizing had "become top heavy with conceptual elaboration including contentious questions of definition, analysis into components, and distinctions between attitudes and related concepts" (p. 137). Perhaps the reverence for the attitude concept during the 1930s—for the sovereign role of attitudes as crucial determinants of behavior—impeded experimental research into the conditions under which attitudes can and do change.

The Second World War shifted many priorities within social psychology, as it did within the other social sciences.

In particular, the Information and Education branch of the U.S. Army conducted a number of surveys and experimental studies to assess the impact of morale films and internal Army "propaganda" (e.g., concerning the likelihood of a long war with Japan after V. E. day) on soldiers. One psychologist heavily involved in many of these studies was Carl I. Hovland. Prior to the war Hovland had been primarily interested in conditioned generalization and rote learning, though he also played a role in the development of the frustration-aggression hypothesis and had become increasingly receptive to the liberalization of Hullian behavior theory. Hovland became fascinated by the potential of studying the determinants of attitude change with the use of carefully developed experimental designs, and his contributions to *Experiments on Mass Communication* (with Lumsdaine and Sheffield, 1949), a summary of the army research that he directed, alone marks him as a significant figure in the history of social psychology. His contribution to this volume was both substantive and methodological; it clearly showed that it was possible to disentangle experimentally the effects of different components of the persuasion process. Hovland returned to Yale after the war and established a project studying persuasion and attitude change that activated a whole new tradition of empirical research.

The Yale Communication Research Program, as it was officially called, attracted young scholars from a variety of universities and generated a stream of collaborative research under Hovland's general direction. The classic *Communication and Persuasion* (Hovland, Janis, and Kelley, 1953) clearly established the value of an experimental paradigm that Laswell had earlier anticipated by his didactic phrase: "who says what to whom with what effect." Hovland and his colleagues explored a number of communicator variables (such as prestige, expertise, and credibility), communication variables (such as whether or not a conclusion is drawn in the persuasive message), and context variables (whether a particular reference group is made salient) and examined the effects of these variables on changes in opinion. The experiments involved exposing undergraduates to persuasive communications in laboratory or classroom settings, although Hovland later (1959) compared laboratory experiments with field research in an important analysis. The hypotheses of the various experiments derived from diverse theoretical origins. Hovland was clearly most comfortable with a view of attitude change as a special instance of human learning. He was especially interested in the implications for learning and retention of exposure to verbal symbols and made distinctive contributions in his chapters dealing with the organization of persuasive arguments and the retention of opinion change. Janis was a personality psychologist intrigued with the effects on motivation of messages having different arousal potential. His work in *Communication and Persuasion* on fear-arousing messages and the consequences of participative role playing established a research area that is still active thirty years later. Kelley brought to the collaboration the approach of Lewinian group dynamics, contributing research on the role of membership and reference groups in the resistance to persuasive communications. In retrospect, perhaps, the great importance of the Hovland, Janis, and Kelley volume is its emphasis on the importance of theory, the effective use of controlled experimentation, and the example of the friendly coexistence of different viewpoints in shedding light on an important and ubiquitous social phenomenon.

Until his premature death in 1961 Hovland continued to attract gifted young researchers from different theoretical backgrounds to work on problems within the attitude change framework. Jack Brehm, fresh from working with Festinger in the formative stages of dissonance theory, joined the group and soon was collaborating with Arthur R. Cohen on the implications of that theory for attitude change. Their work began to take form as the "induced compliance paradigm" (as labeled by Worchel and Cooper, 1979), and the many subsequent studies within this paradigm represent the central showpiece of dissonance research. The induced compliance paradigm was essential for capturing and portraying the vital switch on common sense: although everyone knows that attitudes affect behavior, it may be more important to realize the circumstances under which behavior affects attitudes. The induced compliance paradigm involved a crucial experimental condition in which subjects were cajoled to engage in some action that would normally be dishonest, embarrassing, or at least counter to their own prior attitudes. However, the induction was subtle enough to leave the subject with a feeling that he or she had a choice and was behaving voluntarily. The experimenters were able to show convincingly that such subtle behavior inductions lead to accommodating changes in belief, attitude, or values. For example, if a subject previously opposed to nuclear war was induced to write an essay favoring it, a subsequent measure would typically show a moderation of the antiwar stand. If, however, he or she was merely assigned such an essay (with no choice), there would be no such attitude change. In theoretical terms, the "freely chosen" behavior would be dissonant with existing attitudes; since perception of behavior is especially resistant to change, a change in attitude would be the most convenient way to reduce dissonance.

Research within the induced compliance paradigm uncovered a number of basic issues concerning the relations between behavioral commitment, motivation, and cognitive processes. On a number of occasions arguments were precipitated between those who were convinced that induced compliance findings could best be explained by dissonance theory and those who held out for the more traditional reinforcement view, patched up with assumptions about "self-persuasion." Janis himself, along with M. Rosenberg and other members of the Yale group, argued for variations of the reinforcement alternative in a number of papers (e.g., Janis and Gilmore, 1965; Elms and Janis, 1965; Rosenberg, 1965). Their former colleague Brehm (1965) remained unconvinced, and the controversy eventually receded as researchers began to identify more clearly the proper domains for the operation of dissonance reduction and secondary reinforcement processes (e.g., Linder, Cooper, and Jones, 1967).

The Yale program provided a vigorous continuing stimulus for the study of attitude change for approximately fifteen years. Following the pathbreaking Hovland, Janis, and Kelley book, the program spawned a series of more specialized volumes dealing with order effects (Hovland, 1957), personality and persuasibility (Hovland and Janis, 1959), cognitive consistency factors (Rosenberg et al., 1960), and the role of assimilation and contrast (Sherif and Hovland, 1961). Research on attitude change through these and many other contributions moved from a strangely neglected area to the center stage of social psychology. By the end of the 1960s, attitude change took more space in social psychology textbooks than any other topic (McGuire, 1969, p. 138, estimates 25 percent).

This turned out, however, to be a high water mark of attitude change research. As the seventies began, the research flow receded into a steady but no longer torrential stream. Perhaps the Laswell flowchart ("who says what to whom with what effect") was too unidirectional, too focused on messages delivered by speakers to an audience, to sustain the interest of psychological researchers indefinitely. In a broader sense, of course, an interest in attitude change is embodied in all studies of socialization, of person perception and attraction, of the self-concept, and of the transformations that take place in personal relationships over time. Studies with a more limited focus on communicator characteristics, message content, or audience features, however, gave way in the 1970s to the vigorous development of a strongly cognitive social psychology. Instead of focusing on communicator characteristics or features of the message, researchers increasingly turned to a consideration of consistency, dissonance, and attributional processes in the communication recipient. Before turning to these developments, we first return in time to discuss the impact of the 1940s and 1950s on investigation and theory dealing with group processes.

Interdependence and Group Dynamics

In a curious way, social psychology has always been ambivalent about the study of groups per se. Some of this ambivalence may be traced to the heated controversies of the 1920s over the conceptualization of group properties. McDougall's 1920 treatment of group processes was dramatically titled *The Group Mind,* even though he later vigorously denied consciousness as a group property. The mystical idea that groups could be characterized by emergent anthropomorphic properties was mercilessly attacked by F. H. Allport and others in the mainstream of behaviorism, a fact that probably channeled subsequent psychological research toward the study of individual responses to group influences and away from the study of groups as groups.

In particular, the tradition of research comparing individual productivity and problem solving with those of the group (to which F. H. Allport was a major contributor) was seen as proper turf for an experimental social psychology. As we have already noted, this tradition was so well established by the 1950s that Kelley and Thibaut could build on Dashiell's chapter in the *Handbook of Social Psychology* (1935) in writing their own for Lindzey's *Handbook of Social Psychology* (1954). However, Kelley and Thibaut correctly noted that a great proportion of the research on group functioning was quite innocent of penetrating theory. The research, though continuous during the 1920s, 1930s, and 1940s, was quite empirical and rarely grappled with the crucial processes in a group's "locomotions" toward a goal. The subtleties of social influence were not laid bare, and little was known or discovered about power strategies and the conditions affecting their successful employment. Conceptions of leadership were basically noninteractive and tended to avoid group dynamics considerations. Investigations in the 1930s and 1940s often involved a search for the personal characteristics of the effective leader. This search was not tied into a broader theory of influence processes.

Part of the problem was remedied by the success of the Lewinian group dynamics movement. Because of the abstract cast of his theorizing, Lewin had no trouble avoiding the anthropomorphic trap that had so bedeviled many of his predecessors. He approached the discussion of groups in a language that facilitated treating the group as a system of interrelated parts, and he personally advocated a concern with microprocesses rather than global descriptions or quantifications of group products. Many of Lewin's students in the Research Center for Group Dynamics at the Massachusetts Institute of Technology developed interesting theories about such different aspects of group process as identification with the group goal, communication as a substitute for mobility, and the dynamics of cooperative interaction.

Influential theoretical accounts of group functioning with a definite psychological flavor were also advanced by sociologists Homans (1950) and Bales (1950). In a tradition established by Barnard in 1938, both of these authors emphasized the distinction between task-oriented (external system) functions and social-emotional (internal system) functions in groups. Theoretical analysis was further advanced by Kelley and Thibaut's (1954) lucid identification of group problem-solving variables and their distinction between group influences on individual solution attempts on the one hand and factors influencing the combination or pooling of these attempts on the other. Their contribution provided a rational framework for organizing those portions of the social interaction literature concerned with group problem solving.

These same authors (Thibaut and Kelley, 1959) made a more basic and general contribution five years later in a book that introduced a framework for looking at the complexities of social interdependence in dyads and other small groups. Essentially, the framework dealt with the outcomes for the interacting parties that are consequences of their actual or potential responses to each other. By the ingenious use of "payoff matrixes" conceptualizing the response repertoires of two or more individuals, Thibaut and Kelley were able to consider the response combinations that would provide the greatest satisfaction to each party and thus locate the most likely drift of the subjects' social behavior. In this way, Thibaut and Kelley developed a taxonomy of interpersonal power relations and provided the prototype of a social exchange model.

In their analyses of power and dependence, they crucially applied the ideas of social comparison. Thus a person's power in a given relationship depended on the attractiveness of alternative relationships into which he or she could conveniently enter. This feature of social comparison was missing in Homans' otherwise similar formulation that appeared two years later (1961). Nevertheless, it is interesting that Homans, Thibaut, and Kelley independently reached almost the same place from rather different origins. Thibaut and Kelley were influenced by Homans' earlier *The Human Group* (1950) and by developments in the economics of game and decision theory (Luce and Raiffa, 1957). They had also both been trained at the Research Center for Group Dynamics and were obviously influenced in a general way by the theorizing of Lewin and Festinger. Homans, on the other hand, was more explicitly influenced by the operant conditioning paradigm of B. F. Skinner. In any case, both formulations emphasized the exchange of reward and punishment in social interaction, and through this vehicle we are better able to understand norms, power, social dependence, and more generally group formation and maintenance. It is interesting, incidentally, that in the 1974 revision of his 1961 book, Homans explicitly incorporates many features of Thibaut and Kelley's analysis, including the exchange or payoff matrix.

In 1978 Kelley and Thibaut produced an extension and refinement of their earlier work in a book called *Interpersonal Relations: A Theory of Interdependence*. It offers a brilliant further analysis of matrix components and the dynamics of matrix transformations over time. The book contains a taxonomy of interdependent relations and could serve as the scaffold for a true social psychology of groups.

It is too early to assess the eventual impact of the Thibaut-Kelley and Kelley-Thibaut works on the transformation of investigative interests within social psychology. In spite of the elegance and originality of their 1959 treatment and the uniform critical acclaim with which both books have been received, there has not been a widespread embrace of mutual interdependence as a research and teaching focus in the United States. There are numerous graduate programs in social psychology where the study of small groups is given little attention, and where neither the students nor the faculty are familiar with the Thibaut and Kelley analysis. Given the elegance and profundity of this analysis, however, there is good reason to assume that its impact will indeed be durable.

The resistance of many social psychologists to full immersion in the study of groups has been noted by Steiner (1974) in his lament: "Whatever happened to the group in social psychology?" Steiner contrasts what he calls the "individualistic orientation" that characterizes most U.S. social psychologists and the "groupy approach." The latter differs from the former in attempting to treat the individual as an element in a larger external system. Individualists may focus on responses to group influence, but they ignore the "mutual responsivity of participants." Even the Lewinian group dynamics approach, Steiner argues, basically concentrated on the viewpoint of individuals confronting ad hoc groups operating under highly controlled and specialized conditions. Rather than deplore the individualists, Steiner calls for complementary pluralism of approaches and, of course, for more attention to the embedding dynamics of mutual interdependence. He links the neglect of group research to relative societal tranquility and predicts that group research will rise again when segments of society diverge or collide. But he also points to a "lack of nourishing theory." In this context, it is all the more surprising that his paper contains no reference to Thibaut and Kelley (1959) or to Homans (1961).

Though full-blown groupy research may have been the victim of relative neglect in the 1960s and 1970s, the same cannot be said for many of the component processes of small group dynamics. Several of these received lavish investigative attention. Two large clusters of experimental work can be singled out for brief review: social conformity and social conflict research. It is perhaps noteworthy and instructive that each of these clusters grew around convenient procedural paradigms, a fact that may well explain the heavy research traffic that brings these areas to our attention.

Social Conformity and Consensual Influence   Since social psychology can almost be defined as the study of social influence, it is hardly surprising that the conditions of this area's influence have received substantial research attention. Attitude change breaks away as one rather distinctive research cluster and judgmental or behavioral compliance as another. The attitude change paradigm exposes an individual (whose attitudes have been premeasured) to a persuasive communication by a source. The conformity paradigm, on the other hand, exposes the individual to a social consensus diverging from his or her presumed perception or judgment, the latter being usually inferred from the reports of control subjects responding in the absence of influence pressures. One of the earliest to exploit this paradigm was H. T. Moore in 1921. He exposed subjects to majority opinions on ethical judgment, language usage, and musical preferences and found these exerted a marked influence on the subjects' subsequent judgments. As noted earlier, Sherif (1936) showed how subjects when reporting their perceptions of a highly ambiguous stimulus situation were strongly influenced by the judgments of others. More than twenty years later the limits of ambiguity were tested in a series of conformity experiments by S. E. Asch (1956). His work established a simple and dramatic paradigm in tapping the conflict between consensus on the one hand and unambiguous perceptions or judgments on the other. Because of their intrinsic interest and the timing of their publication, Asch's studies rapidly became widely known in the social sciences, and their import began to be emphasized routinely in introductory psychology textbooks.

Asch's interests in the effects of social influence on individual cognitive judgments were very much influenced by his senior colleague Max Wertheimer, the eldest of the Gestalt triumvirate. Asch himself was (and remains) a "cold" Gestaltist, very much impressed with our needs to make "reasonable" sense out of experience. Although such influential authors as Fromm (1941) and Riesman (1950) had emphasized modern man's eagerness to hide among the consensus, Asch surmised that if subjects were exposed to several other subjects making unanimously erroneous judgments of unambiguous stimuli, they would reject any inherent pressures toward uniformity and report the correct answer. Thus he set out to study independence, not conformity. Asch was surprised when so many of his college students subjects denied the visual evidence in favor of the unanimous consensus. On the average, subjects made between four and five errors out of a possible twelve. Three-quarters of the subjects made at least one promajority error, and this turned out to be true in a variety of different samples of subjects. Though Asch's faith in the rationality and good sense of his subjects was somewhat shaken, his painstaking analyses of the subjective strain induced by the conformity conflict in many of his subjects inspired a number of investigators to pursue the determinants of conformity and independence.

Basically, this follow-up research established that people conformed either because they thought the majority was correct or because they were so reward- and punishment-oriented that they did not particularly care about accuracy. In fact, the underlying conditions of conformity, in perceptual judgment situations such as those studied by Asch, were essentially the same as those proposed by Festinger in a paper (1950) on informal social communication

that presaged his social comparison theory. Social influence could be based either on considerations of social reality (influence oriented toward accuracy) or on those of group locomotion (influence oriented toward social reward). Under a variety of different labels (cf. Jones and Gerard, 1967) a number of other theorists emphasized this distinction between the individual's dependence on the group for information and his or her dependence on the group for rewards and acceptance.

Research within the Asch paradigm has waned during the past fifteen years, no doubt in part because of the very notoriety of the procedure and the necessary deceptions involved. However, conformity literature is sizable and rich, adding substantially to our understanding of what determines the average person's response when confronted with a conflict between his or her senses, perceptions, or convictions, and a strong contrasting social consensus. Of course, such conflict situations are rarely if ever experienced in anything like the dramatic form contrived by Asch. This line of research provides an excellent example of the value to be gained from procedures low in mundane realism (Aronson and Carlsmith, 1968) but sharply highlighting the issues to be studied.

A dramatic offshoot from the conformity conflict paradigm was the obedience research of Milgram (1963), who was very much influenced by the work of Asch. Milgram did strive for a certain kind of mundane realism in creating a laboratory analogue for the transmission of "totalitarian" orders to commit harmful actions. Subjects were induced to operate a device that they believed was transmitting electric shocks to another subject, ostensibly as part of corrective feedback in a teacher-learner situation. The typical subject, appointed to the teacher-shocker role, expressed extreme discomfort when told to raise the shock level to apparently dangerous heights. Many tried to refuse the order to do so. However, often under extreme and unrelenting pressure from the experimenter, many subjects acted against their own moral feelings in carrying out these potentially harmful commands.

The Milgram experiments generated an unusual amount of controversy. Much of this evolved around the serious ethical issues raised by the conduct of the research. Subjects not only were temporarily deceived but also had to live with the memory of their socially harmful experimental capitulation. There was also considerable disagreement concerning the importance and value of the research. Some of those who were normally critical of the trivial and artificial quality of experiments in social psychology (including a number of sociologists and clinicians) were enthusiastic about the fact that, at last, here was a set of experiments that shed light on something as important as the Nazi holocaust. Others felt that the research was theoretically barren and did not justify the psychological risks entailed. In their view, the findings were overdramatized and overpublicized. The degree of compliance could be readily under-stood once the extremely active role of the experimenter was fully detailed, something that was not at all clear in the earlier experimental reports. The jury is still out concerning the long-range value of the obedience paradigm in shedding new light on conditions controlling what Milgram (1974) has called "the agentic state." In any event, the research brought social psychology an unusual amount of attention in the popular media. The procedures and findings were the topics of feature articles in national magazines and served as the basis for a full-length prime time television drama.

Conflict Resolution in "Mixed-Motive" Settings The early literature on problem-solving in groups concentrated on the social facilitation (and disruption) of individual performance and, to a lesser extent, on the coordination of individual actions to produce a group solution. Coordination studies were generally conducted within a framework of assumed cooperation as researchers posed questions about the relative effectiveness of cooperative groups versus comparable individuals working in isolation. An important development in the 1950s was the recognition that many group activities involved subtle mixtures of cooperation and competition, that the interests of the members generally converge in some respects and diverge in others.

This development was facilitated by two factors discussed together in Thibaut and Kelley's (1959) book. One of these was the matrix representation of interdependence borrowed from game theory (Von Neumann and Morgenstern, 1944). The other was a coordinate commitment to a "social exchange" view of interaction and relationship formation. The term *coordinate* is used because game theory deals in outcomes whose values are determined by the intersection of the responses of two or more persons. This model fit very nicely with a social exchange orientation that stressed the mutual delivery of rewards and punishments within a relationship, for it provided a precise way of defining the reward structure underlying various forms of interdependence.

Added to this promising convergence of a quantitative format and a particular view of interaction was a general concern in the late 1950s with international tension. As Pruitt and Kimmel (1977) note, many of the early users of experimental games were alarmed about world conditions and hoped to find ways of resolving them through laboratory experimentation.

The experimental gaming and peace research movement were closely related at this time, as can be seen in the fact that the *Journal of Conflict Resolution: A Quarterly for the Study of War and Peace,* [founded in 1957] had a special section for articles based on experimental gaming. Hence there was an initial aura of urgency and even

sacredness about the research, which probably contributed to its rapid proliferation (p. 367).

The game approach was especially adaptable to the kinds of mixed-motive situations (Schelling, 1960) that most intrigued social psychologists. There was a whole range of "non-zero-sum games" that lent themselves to the study of interactions featuring both convergent and divergent interests, such as those involved in real world disarmament negotiations and labor-management disputes.

The first social psychologist to exploit the possibilities of mixed-motive matrix games was Morton Deutsch. In his dissertation, published in 1949 (a,b), Deutsch launched a frontal theoretical assault on the process implications of cooperative and competitive goal structures in small groups. As he himself notes (1980), his ideas were influenced by Lewin's theorizing and research on tension systems and by the general atmosphere of the Research Center for Group Dynamics at the Massachusetts Institute of Technology, where the participants spoke of group goals and their interrelationship and of the various possibilities of vicarious gratification and the substitutability of one member's performance for another's. Deutsch's theory of promotive versus contrient interdependence has been widely cited because of the importance of the phenomena it addressed and because it represented a distinct advance over previous conceptions that were more typically focused on narrow issues of work output under the category of cooperation *versus* competition.

Deutsch's interest in the psychological consequences of interdependence made him highly receptive to the experimental possibilities of game theory and especially of the mixed-motive game. He used a version of the prisoner's dilemma game to study the determinants of interpersonal trust and suspicion (1958, 1962). His student Solomon (1960) also used a matrix game to study the development of trust, using a preprogrammed simulated other. Though matrix games had a number of attractive features, not the least of which was procedural convenience, the huge volume of subsequent research using such games has not substantially benefited social psychological understanding. The hundreds of prisoner's dilemma game studies have generated little more than a self-contained set of variations on a convenient procedure. Deutsch (1980) himself describes much of the game research as "mindless." Pruitt and Kimmel (1977) lament the slight impact such studies have had and propose that the lack of relevant theory has made it difficult to generalize from game behavior to important conflict situations in the natural world.

Though matrix games have generated a literature that is largely incestuous, the same cannot be said for other game settings designed to illuminate mixed-motive conflict and its resolution. Shortly after getting involved with matrix games himself, Deutsch (with Krauss, 1960) invented a simulated trucking game in which each of two subjects attempted to move a truck to a destination by manipulating electric switching devices. Since there was only a one-lane common path along the shortest route, the possibilities for confrontation and subsequent stalemate were clear. In some conditions, one or both subjects had control of a gate which could be used to bar access to the common path. The major finding was that the trucks of both subjects reached their destination more often and with higher joint payoffs when one player had control of the gate than when both players did.

This study became an instant classic, or at least it was soon widely cited and won the prestigious AAAS award for social science research. Unlike the relatively sterile setting of a matrix game, played over and over again, the trucking scenario with its associated maps and apparatus posed an intriguing and highly involving dilemma for subjects, a dilemma that could be readily appreciated by the reader of the experimental report. The results seemed to support arguments of unilateral disarmament, though the authors were cautious about pushing their implications too far in that direction. As with most provocative and important studies, however, the specific meaning of the findings later became a subject of considerable dispute. Kelley (1965), in particular, questioned the definition of a gate as a genuine *threat* and suggested several possible alternative explanations for the results obtained. Kelley's student Gallo (1966) demonstrated that the results found by Deutsch and Krauss did not replicate if real money was involved as an incentive. When substantial sums of money were at stake, subjects were basically less competitive, and joint payoffs were higher. Apparently, when only imaginary sums were involved, there were no serious constraints to prevent the subjects from converting the game into a purely competitive one to make the experimental hour more interesting.

The debate over the significance of Deutsch and Krauss' findings highlights the central problem with all game research: how to use game behavior to make meaningful predictions in important naturalistic conflict settings. Obviously the role of stake or incentive may be crucially different in a laboratory situation than at most bargaining tables. In addition, it is easy to imagine the interactive role of many contextual variables in the real world that are typically excluded from the self-contained game situation. Although the problem of generalization is not unique to game research, of course, it is exacerbated here by the very seductiveness of generalization opportunities, coupled with the poverty of theoretical development in this area. Rapoport (1970), a major figure in game research, has argued that we should not extrapolate from laboratory games to situations of real-life conflict. Rather, the results should be conceptualized in their own terms and valued for the perspectives they suggest and the questions

they raise. Although this position has served as one justification for an insular tradition of experimental game research, it has been clearly rejected by many investigators who feel that the only justification for game research is the continuity between the laboratory and the real world (cf. Pruitt and Kimmel, p. 367).

Within social psychology, at least, the trend since the mid-1970s has been a greater concern with processes of negotiation and bargaining, coupled with a turning away from further variations on matrix game themes. The massive international experiment conducted by the committee of U.S. and European social psychologists (Kelley *et al.,* 1970) illustrates how sophisticated and complex the designs in this area have become: at eight laboratories, three in Europe and five in the United States, different investigators conducted essentially the same experiment featuring a complex negotiation game involving the choice of interdependent versus independent action. The negotiation game was played for either points or money, the difficulty level of the problems was varied, and in some conditions one subject was made systematically more dependent on reaching agreement than his or her partner. The major finding that held across the different experimental sites was that increasing the value of the stakes has a beneficial effect on negotiation when cooperation yields clear mutual gain and when exploitation is difficult. (There were also intriguing differences attributed to the meaning of cooperation in the different cultural contexts.)

The study of strategic conflict resolution has many origins, as we have seen, and many ramifications. A number of factors important in conflict resolution are relevant for understanding even the most casual sequences of social interaction. Thus, the social psychology of equity and justice (Berkowitz and Walster, 1976) is clearly involved in the conflict resolution process and remains an active area of theory and research. The study of self-presentation (Schlenker, 1980; Jones and Pittman, 1982) is often couched in power strategy terms and is clearly a crucial aspect of any conflict resolution situation. Finally, contemporary decision theories (Hammond, McClelland, and Mumpower, 1980) may ultimately have much to contribute to the debate on conflict resolution strategies, though as yet the communication links between social psychological and decision theory approaches are fragile and underdeveloped.

In summary, the study of group dynamics, or more generally social interdependence, has produced a voluminous literature of research, only a small portion of which we have mentioned here. The importance of the area is self-evident because most of our lives are conducted in groups and most of our important life decisions occur in contexts of social interdependence. It is easy to become discouraged by the bewildering complexities involved in the study of interdependent relations. As we have noted, useful theory has been difficult to develop, and much research has been inconclusive because the variables have been inadequately conceptualized. Nevertheless, it is clear that we have made substantial progress in organizing the interlocking concerns that influence group functioning and in identifying the crucial issues that merit intensive additional study. The differences between Kelley and Thibaut's two handbook chapters bear dramatic testimony to the growth of our knowledge and conceptual sophistication from 1954 to 1969. Much of the research bearing on problems of group dynamics has, reasonably enough, singled out component processes for intensive study. We have focused on two such areas by summarizing research developments in social conformity and social conflict. In both areas the importance of a convenient procedural paradigm is apparent. The problem of conformity is less complex than the ramified problems of social interdependence and social conflict. Whereas conformity research has waned, perhaps because many of the easy answers have been found, research in the latter area will probably continue to attract the interest of many social psychologists—especially those who are not intimidated by complexity and who are optimistic about extrapolating from experimental simulations to crucial human conflicts and their resolution. Useful framing models and taxonomies of interdependence are available. Perhaps what is most needed now are a series of subprocess theories that generate explicit disconfirmable hypotheses.

THE WAXING OF COGNITIVE SOCIAL PSYCHOLOGY

In a 1980 essay, Zajonc claimed that "cognition pervades social psychology, [that social psychology] has been cognitive for a very long time. It was cognitive long before the cognitive revolution in experimental psychology" (p. 181, 186). He traces the latter to Neisser's liberating treatment, *Cognitive Psychology* (1967) though Broadbent's *Perception and Communication* (1958) is certainly another important precursor along with Miller, Galanter, and Pribram's *Plans and the Structure of Behavior* (1960). Although we agree with this general assessment, we should also note that there have been peaks and valleys in the emphasis on cognitive factors and that, relative to earlier periods, social psychology has been undergoing its own less dramatic cognitive revolution since the ascendance of attributional approaches in the late 1960s. At present, there are abundant signs that a broader cognitive psychology is emerging to blur the boundary between social and nonsocial psychology. Social psychologists have reached out to borrow from, and argue with, cognitive psychologists. And cognitive psychologists have more uniformly come to recognize that *nonsocial* cognition is really a special case of understandings typically incorporating social factors. This section will trace the evolution of this vigorous hybrid.

In order to understand clearly the rise of cognitive psychology and the forms it took, it is necessary to comment briefly on the traditional orientations that served as a backdrop and as a source of resistance to the "cognitivation" of psychology. A positivistic, natural science branch of experimental psychology was the dominant psychology of the U.S. "Establishment" from the 1930s to the 1950s. Basically, the orientation of experimental psychologists in this period was not merely noncognitive but anticognitive. The fear of mentalism was widespread as was the methodological conviction that science must deal only with observable, physically measurable variables. Sensation and perception research and theory were anchored in psychophysics and in the elegant functions relating physical stimulus variations to detection and estimation responses (which, in turn, were *not* treated as indices of thought or judgment). The study of learning was even more behavioristic, concentrating either on the locomotion of animals or on the retention of meaningless lists of rote-learned words, chosen especially because they supposedly had no affective or experiential significance for the subject.

It is commonly assumed that Gestalt psychology was much more receptive to mentalistic or cognitive concepts. To be sure, Koffka and Kohler spoke of pragnanz, of dynamic perceptual fields, of isomorphism, and of other constructs far removed from operational measurement. Both Koffka and Kohler, however, stressed nativistic or quasi-physiological determinants, and neither had much interest in dealing with the shaping of perception and thought by either current motivation or prior experience. The cognitive processes they wished to deal with were closely bound to lawful perceptual processes that were, in turn, linked to (in their terms, isomorphic with) properties of the stimulus environment or of electro-chemical brain fields. This proved to be a rather arbitrary restriction that is not, as we shall later note, fundamental to the Gestalt orientation. Lewin, Asch, and Heider eventually elaborated on the principles of Gestalt psychology in ways that were useful to social psychology. Prior to this elaboration, it was against the firmly established traditions of behaviorism, psychophysics, and classical Gestalt psychology that a cognitive psychology struggled to emerge after the Second World War. A number of other developments, however, were setting the stage for a cognitive social psychology. Most of these had to do with the willingness to assume that the perceived world, and not the objective world, determines behavior.

The Rise of Subjectivism in the 1930s and 1940s

Though the full development of a cognitive approach to social psychology may have been impeded by the conservative traditions of behaviorism and physiological reductionism, the concerns of social psychology inevitably required certain broad assumptions concerning cognitive structure. We have already cited Bartlett's classic work, *Remembering,* and Sherif's work on frames of reference as clear examples of experimentation in social psychology. Both works also exemplified a subjectivist tradition that had already been introduced in the late 1920s by the sociologist, W. I. Thomas. Thomas stressed the role of experience in shaping one's "definition of the situation" and insisted that situations are real if they are perceived as real (Thomas and Thomas, 1928, p. 572). We apply the label of subjectivism in the present context to the general position that events are interpreted in terms of internal information processing structures and that these, in turn, vary as a function of cultural and individual experience. Events are not passively registered on the perceptual apparatus. They are organized in categories shaped by past experiences, and they take on their meaning as part of an active, constructive process in dealing with reality.

Subjectivism was explicit not only in Thomas's concept of the definition of a situation, Bartlett's notion of schema, and Sherif's frame of reference concept, but also in the idea of internal processing structures that was a part of many conceptualizations of attitude (G. W. Allport, 1935). Regardless of which particular processing construct one prefers, it is clear that social psychology was receptive to the relativism of values, motives, and perspectives that was promoted by the work of anthropologists. As Thomson (1968) points out, Margaret Mead's *Coming of Age in Samoa* (1928) and *Growing Up in New Guinea* (1930) "had a striking effect on social psychology in the 1930's" (p. 75). Although he does not provide any further details, the general ideas that personality is shaped by culture and that different cultures produce citizens with different beliefs and orientations were clearly resonant with the early stirrings of a cognitive social psychology. Bartlett's observations on the recall biases of Swazi herdsmen forged an explicit historical linkage between cognitive psychology and cross-cultural comparison.

Kurt Lewin's conceptual approach represented an elaboration of what we have labeled the subjectivist view, though he was less concerned with the origin of cognitive framing structures than with their behavioral consequences. Thus, we take the unusual step of linking the Lewinian approach more to Thomas, Bartlett, and Sherif than to the classical Gestalt triumvirate, though there is no evidence that Lewin was explicitly influenced by these former sources. Still, Lewin is often classified as a Gestalt psychologist because of his early exposure to the Berlin triumvirate and because of some of the structural characteristics of his field theory. Lewin's most fundamental concept was that of the "life space," which is equivalent to the interdependent relationship between the person and his environment (thus, $B = f P, E = fLSp$). It is, therefore, the psychological or the interpreted environment that elicits or guides behavior, an idea that may seem self-evident to us now, but one that was met with considerable skepticism by psychologists in the grip of positivism. W. K. Estes (1954), for example, found Lewinian field theory incapable of *a*

priori prediction and lacking in functional relationship statements that could be anchored in measurable stimuli and observable responses. Nevertheless, Lewin's grand truism $[B = f (PE)]$ and his emphasis on the psychological environment proved peculiarly adaptable to the concerns of social psychology where the most relevant governing stimuli must be defined in terms of their inferred meaning for the actor.

However, the question of how to penetrate an individual's life space, how to know his or her "definition of the situation," is almost overwhelming and partakes liberally of our earlier concern with how social stimuli can be defined independently of responses to them. Phenomenological inquiry seems called for, and indeed it seems reasonable to explain an actor's behavior in terms of his phenomenal world just prior to action. For Lewin, features of the life space need not be represented in consciousness. For him, "the phenomenal properties are to be distinguished from the conditional-genetic characteristics of objects and events, that is, from the properties that determine their causal relationship" (1936, p. 19). Thus the life space is a construct inferred to account for the individual's behavior. As Smith (1950) points out, the approach of directly tapping the actor's phenomenal representation of his current world is only one important kind of information about a subjective frame of reference. This frame may contain effective factors that are distorted or disguised in the subject's awareness. Even MacCleod (1947), in his classic paper advocating a phenomenological approach to social psychology, acknowledges that "the phenomenological method . . . can never be more than an approach to scientific inquiry" (p. 208).

Thus, very early in the development of a cognitive social psychology, it became important to distinguish between an actor's *conscious awareness* of his behavioral determinants and the fact that his behavior is shaped by cognitive structures that define reality for him. Such a distinction has reappeared in many guises in the subsequent decades so that there now seems to be a general consensus that cognitive determinants do not necessarily imply phenomenal awareness. Most would agree that one can gain valuable data about the determinants of an actor's behavior by eliciting his view of those determinants, although such phenomenological reports should not necessarily be taken at face value. Subjectivists, in the Thomas tradition, would argue that we are often unaware that there are perspectives alternative to our own. The world that we at least partially construct is perceived instead as the world given to us. To the extent that our perceptions are shaped by expectancies and other framing cognitions that we cannot explicitly identify, phenomenological accounts can clearly be little more than unwitting rationalizations.

The impact of more transitory motives and moods on cognitive processes has been somewhat more controversial, at least to the extent that one wants to argue for influences on perception itself in addition to influences on thought, interpretation, or memory. However, the "New Look" in perception after the Second World War explicitly argued that perception itself could be affected by motives and prior expectancies. This point of view too was an important line of theory and research that contributed to the development of a cognitive social psychology.

The Effects of Motivation on Perception

Lewinian Field Theory initially developed outside the mainstream of U.S. psychology. Although Clark Hull's theoretical work held a certain morbid fascination for him, Lewin spent little time coming to terms with the theories and research data comprising the psychological literature. Instead, he wove together ideas borrowed from force-field physics and topological mathematics into a complex and highly original structure of terms and diagrammed relations. Both he and his first U.S. students relied mainly on intuition and each other for the ideas they converted into research on group dynamics. For a number of years the *apartheid* feeling was mutual. Although Lewin's contributions to the analysis of conflict and regression had an early impact on the fields of child development and personality, the broader theoretical issues he raised received spotty, belated, and skeptical reception in U.S. academic psychological circles. Social psychologists did not immediately flock to the banner of field theory when they dealt with topics of group psychology, leadership, and social influence. Mathematically inclined psychometricians tended to look upon his venture into topology with bemused derision. Positivistic learning and perception psychologists of the immediate postwar years seldom took Lewin seriously and responded as though whatever contribution he was making was to a discipline unrelated to their own.

In comparison, the new experimental approach to motivational effects on perception grew out of, and was in response to, traditional themes in perception research. Jerome Bruner did more than anyone else to render obsolete the idea that perception involves merely the passive registration of incoming stimulation. In doing so, he adopted a strong functionalistic position, looking at perception as an organismic process in the service of adaptive behavior. Bruner not only issued a verbal challenge to the staid perception establishment but also exploited through his experimental research variations in the classical methods of psychophysics in order to challenge the traditionalists in their very own backyard. The traditionalists fought back and won several local skirmishes; but in the end the research on motivational effects forced reformulations that were of crucial importance to the revolution of cognitive psychology. In this section we shall try to outline these developments.

Before the Second World War there had been suggestions that the study of perceptual processes could shed some light on the workings of personality. Social and personality psychologists generally agreed that people to some extent "see" what they want to see in the environment around them, but what the researchers usually meant was that the environment was *interpreted* differently by different people. Studies of perceptual discrimination, selectivity, and size judgment seldom if ever took social or personality factors into account. In the late 1940s such psychologists as Bruner, Ericksen, Klein, Lazarus, McClelland, McGinnies, Murphy, and Postman advocated a "new look" at the determinants of perception. The resulting volume of studies signified a radical departure in that they explored the effects of personal determinants on the most basic features of perceptual discrimination. Bruner and Postman, especially, wanted to move as far as current experimental methods would allow them from the metaphorical "see" of interpretation to the literal "see" of perception.

The basic argument of the new-look perception psychologists was that perceptions are often erroneous and that the errors bear some systematic relation to such interpersonal variables as expectancies, current motive states, stable value patterns, moods, and preferred defense mechanisms. The strategy was to inject these variables into the traditional settings of perceptual research and to measure the resulting distortions and differential sensitivities. Distortions in the estimation of size, color, and luminance were measured by such standard psychophysical techniques as the classic "method of average error." In addition, standard laboratory instruments, such as tachistoscopes, were routinely used to assess visual thresholds. F. H. Allport (1955) provides an excellent summary of this line of research on "directive state theory," and we shall present only the broadest outlines of the research here.

The new look in perception was really launched by experiments showing the increased salience of positively valued stimuli. A number of studies conducted by Gardner Murphy and his colleagues in the 1940s (e.g., Proshansky and Murphy, 1942; Schafer and Murphy, 1943) had shown that stimuli recently associated with reward were more salient and more readily perceived than stimuli associated with failure. A widely discussed study by Bruner and Goodman (1947) showed that subjects overestimated the size of valuable coins more than those of lower value and presented some data to show that this tendency was exaggerated with poor children. As controversial as some of these studies became, research concerning the perception of negatively valued stimuli generated considerably more controversy. Rather early in his research program, Bruner (with Postman and McGinnies, 1948) introduced the concepts of perceptual defense and vigilance to explain differential perceptual thresholds for value-charged words. The concept of perceptual defense was welcomed by many psychologists who were sympathetic to the psychoanalytic concept of repression and who saw its potential relevance for capturing the dynamics of personality functioning in the laboratory. Many others were both skeptical of the data and concerned about the paradox of having to see something before you can decide not to see it. Bruner and Postman's position was caricatured as involving the super ego, peering through the Judas eye, and scanning incoming percepts in order to decide which shall be permitted into consciousness. Nevertheless, the idea of the selective rating of personally relevant information touched on so many interests in psychology that a voluminous literature on perceptual defense and related issues was generated during the decade of the 1950s. Researchers tracked down artifacts, offered alternative explanations, and debated the Judas eye problem at length. Meanwhile, Bruner extricated himself from the controversy surrounding the perceptual defense idea by becoming more explicitly cognitive in his focus. His first step in this direction was the formulation of an expectancy or hypothesis theory of perception (1951). This theory emphasized the prepared or tuned state of the organism exposed to an informational input. The perceiver has a hypothesis that is either confirmed, or to varying degrees made infirm, by stimulus information. The stronger the hypothesis, the more it is likely to be confirmed by "unreliable" or ambiguous information. Hypothesis strength in turn is a function of both motivational and experiential factors. Thus the tuned organism is biased to perceive that which fulfills its needs, and strong hypotheses can also result from the frequency of past confirmations and the relative absence of alternatives. The reference to past experience was crucial here, for it marked a turn away from emphasis on the effects of motivation to a concern with probabilistic information processing. The idea that one's expectancies, based on the repeated contingencies of past experience, affect one's perceptual thresholds, proved easy to demonstrate in a variety of contexts. Such had not been the case with less stable motivational or attitudinal variables.

The role of the perceiver's personal history was even more heavily emphasized in Bruner's (1957) classic paper "On Perceptual Readiness." Here the language shifts from "hypotheses" to "categories," and this shift is critical because the prepared organism is now prepared with a cognitive structure of shaped expectations about the nature of the world. The cognitive category is for Bruner essentially a set of rules for classifying objects as equivalent. Bruner writes of the conditions affecting the "accessibility" of categories to stimulus input. He emphasizes the similarity between perceptual activity and problem solving in general. Perception always involves a decision process, a placement of incoming information into a network of meaningful categories developed largely from prior learning.

This paper was well ahead of its time, since many contemporary approaches to information processing and psycholinguistics are similarly concerned with category labels and the circumstances under which semantic and other codes produce assimilation to a typical instance or prototype. Bruner's essay can also serve as a useful framework for talking about stereotypes, a topic in which he had a long-term interest because of his early involvement in public opinion research and the study of propaganda. Subsequent to the perceptual readiness paper, Bruner moved on to the study of concept attainment, strategies of information packaging in classroom instruction, and problems of cognitive and linguistic development.

Though Bruner's work had largely stimulated the controversy over motivational effects on perception, that controversy continued in the 1950s without his active involvement in related research. In his very useful review, Erdelyi (1974) cites the year 1958 as a watershed marking the diminishing of publications on the new look. Lengthy critical papers by Ericksen and Goldiamond in that year seemed to take the steam out of the enterprise that had generated more than one thousand research publications. Erdelyi (1974) goes on to argue, convincingly, that "the New Look was to a large extent discredited on the basis of preconceptions about perception that were themselves on the verge of being superceded" (p. 2). In particular, much concern about the paradox of perceiving what not to perceive, inherent in the perceptual defense idea, loses its bite when one views perception as a multistage process. The distinction between perception and response also became usefully complicated as the research on motivational and experiential effects progressed. Since there is general agreement that perception involves going beyond the information given, what is the locus of this organismic elaboration? Do we talk here of internal responses to partial information (which certainly is consistent with perceptual defense ideas), or is it possible to distinguish still between perceptual elaboration and response selection? Bruner had argued (1957) that selective attention is a multiprocess phenomenon and, after Neisser's (1967) book, this view began to be widely accepted as part of an expanded information processing approach to cognitive functioning. This viewpoint is captured by the central theses of Erdelyi's paper, which rests on a view of multiple stages in the processing of information: "Selectivity is pervasive throughout the cognitive continuum, from input to output" (p. 12). Though such a formulation hardly solves the problem of where bias enters in, the casting of new-look-in-perception issues in terms of selective attention and multiple information processing stages brought the problem back to the cognitive fold as a legitimate offspring.

Whereas the motivation and perception research of the 1940s and 1950s developed from traditional views of perception, the study of "person perception" had rather different historical origins. We turn next to review some of the early developments in impression formation research.

Person Perception Research

Motivation and perception research in the early postwar period was often referred to as *social perception,* meaning very generally the study of various social determinants of perceptual processes. This was not an appropriate term because many determinants being studied were not really social and also because the label promoted a confusion between social determinants of perception on the one hand and the perception of social stimuli (persons and groups) on the other. As the latter topic began to emerge as an explicit research focus in the early 1950s, the term *person perception* began to supplant *social perception* in designating research on the formation of first impressions. Person perception research was almost a syllogistic conclusion to the subjectivist premise: If people respond to the perceived environment and if other people are some of the most important entities in that environment, then it is important to study how people are perceived.

Despite the obvious importance to social psychology of knowledge about person perception processes, the development of such knowledge was delayed by a preoccupation with the accuracy of judgments about personality. Insofar as there was a tradition of person perception research before the Second World War, it lay in the literatures dealing with the identification of expressed emotions and with personality rating methodology. The recognition of emotions was seen as basically a side issue, a way of assessing the consistency or diagnosticity of emotional expression. Little attention was given to the process whereby perceivers relate facial expression to situational cues in the resultant perception of an emotion (cf. Bruner and Tagiuri, 1954). In the personality-rating literature, much of which appeared in educational psychology journals, the concern was with biasing proclivities (such as the "halo effect") that interfere with objectively accurate ratings of personality. How can such factors be checked or partialed out? What kinds of judges make accurate raters? What kinds of people and what kinds of traits are easy to rate accurately?

The naivete of this early assessment research was ultimately exposed by Cronbach's elegant critique in 1955. Cronbach showed that accuracy criteria are elusive and that the determinants of rating responses are psychometrically complex. Prior to this pivotal analysis, however, Asch solved the accuracy problem by bypassing it, thus ushering in a new era of impression formation experimentation. In a series of experiments published in 1946, Asch used an ingeniously simple procedure to explore some processes of forming a coherent impression of another person based on minimal, and sometimes conflicting, information about him or her. Asch presented subjects with adjective strings purported to describe a person. One such string, for example, was "The person is intelligent, skillful, industrious, warm, determined, practical, cautious." Subjects were asked to write a brief sketch of the person thus described and to check those traits among a list of additional adjectives that were judged as applicable to the person. Other subjects were confronted with an adjective string identical to the previous example, except that the word *cold* was substituted for the word *warm.* The resulting impressions were dramatically different due to the switch of these particular attributes. The *warm* person was described as much more generous, good-natured, and sociable than the *cold* person, who was generally described more negatively but was nevertheless judged to be slightly more reliable and restrained than the *warm* individual. Asch used these and other experimental results to argue for the dynamic interaction among trait qualities in the impression formation process. The meaning of each trait is modified by the context provided by the other traits, giving rise to a organized Gestalt of the entire person. The classic series of experiments spawned a crucial shift in the person perception area from a concern with judgmental outcome to a concern with perceptual process.

The simplicity of Asch's procedure was so seductive that a rash of impression formation studies followed. The idea that component bits of information are not necessarily additive, that the characteristics of a person are defined in relation to each other, was not initially challenged. Some years later, Wishner (1960) tried to make a refined analysis of the relation between stimulus traits and response lists. In doing so, he succeeded in dispelling much of the mystery generated by Asch's contention concerning emergent meaning. He also succeeded in showing how the centrality of a particular trait in a given context can be predicted on the basis of independent evidence. This was an important advance. Asch had merely argued that some traits are more central than others, without suggesting why this might be so. Shortly thereafter, Anderson (1962) published the first of a series of studies exploring the effects of the order of evaluative adjectives on the favorability of resulting impressions. Anderson sought to discriminate between different models of information processing, and his work is only an indirect contribution to the field of person perception. Nevertheless, he proposed a weighted average model based on the evaluation scale values of the individual traits, and for a time he challenged the Gestalt notion of interactive, emergent meaning. Many of his experiments showed that resultant judgments could be reliably predicted by adding or averaging the separately derived values of component adjectives. Later (with Jacobson, 1965) Anderson retreated somewhat to concede that (p. 539):

> Even though the averaging formulation shows promise in accounting for the impression response data *per se,* it cannot completely account for [the form of differential weighting observed]. In this respect it would appear that the adjectives do interact in forming the impression, a conclusion in harmony with the view of Asch (1946).

As we have intimated, however, Asch's contributions to the person perception area were more fundamental than creating a convenient research procedure to show how trait adjectives interact. By focusing on questions of process, he helped to launch or re-orient a whole field of study that was to become a standard chapter in social psychology textbooks. In the long run, however, the work of Fritz Heider became even more important in shaping the manner in which this chapter was written.

Heider evolved from an aspiring painter into a student of perception as he made the transition to adulthood in his native Austria. After receiving his doctoral degree at Graz in 1920, he moved to Berlin where he began to audit Kohler's and Wertheimer's courses and soon became acquainted with Kurt Lewin with whom he was in continuous contact for the next twenty-six years. Heider certainly absorbed many features of the Gestalt approach, but his first important paper in 1927 ("Thing and Medium") had more of the flavor of functionalism than of Gestalt psychology. In it he anticipated the main thrust of a later cognitive psychology by insisting that information from the external environment (the "thing" that reaches us through "the medium") must be read or interpreted through established organizing processes in the person. The distinction between thing and medium comes close to the distinction Brunswik later (1933) made between distal and proximal stimuli. In reading Heider's (1958) book, certainly his magnum opus, one is impressed with the use of Brunswikian notions in the development of attribution theory. However, the influence was at least mutual, and Heider contends that Brunswik "often said that he was influenced by *my* papers" (Harvey, Ickes, and Kidd, 1976). In any event, the two were close friends, and attribution theory is probably best described as synthesizing the tradition of perceptual functionalism and Gestalt psychology. The latter was more explicitly involved in Heider's development of cognitive balance theory that was clearly influenced by Wertheimer's ideas of unit formation.

Heider left his position in Hamburg, Germany, to visit the United States in 1930 at the request of Kurt Koffka who wanted his help in setting up a research department in a school for the deaf in Northampton, Massachusetts. There he remained, also teaching at Smith College, until

moving to the University of Kansas in 1947. He stayed at the University of Kansas until his retirement some thirty years later. The careers of Heider and Asch have several things in common. Both were born in Europe, though Asch came to New York City as a thirteen-year-old in 1920. They were both heavily influenced by Gestalt psychology and clearly swam against the mainstream of American behaviorism. Neither was a prolific writer, both made each publication count. Because of the similarity of their interests, it is hardly surprising that they remained close freinds who spent much time in each other's company after their retirement from active teaching.

One of Heider's early contributions to person perception research was his effort in 1946 to conceptualize the relations between attitudes (incorporating affect) and cognitive organization. The history of subsequent person perception research reveals the intertwining of inferential and evaluative processes, and Heider's paper presented certain postulates along with a notational system for examining some of these relations. In particular, he argued that we tend to have the same positive or negative feelings about objects or persons who are cognitively associated with each other, who belong together. From such considerations a burgeoning interest in cognitive consistency was derived that was elaborated further in Heider's book (1958), in Newcomb's theorizing about communicative acts (1953), in Osgood and Tannenbaum's concern with the congruity of message source and content (1955), in Cartwright and Harary's elaboration of Heider's earlier notions (1956), and in Festinger's introduction of cognitive dissonance theory (1957).

Heider's formulation of balance theory is an important historical event, and there is no question that a large volume of research subsequently attempted to grapple with the issues he raised. However, contemporary hindsight indicates that the research value obtainable from assumptions of cognitive and affective unit formation was limited. Balance theory did not possess the clear motivational grounding that dissonance theory featured or the crucial ideas of commitment and differential cognitive resistance. In addition, the paradigmatic research (e.g., Jordan, 1953; Morrisette, 1958) was pallid, involving as it did hypothetical paper-and-pencil scenarios. Except for dissonance-related experimental reports, most balance theory publications had begun to subside by the mid 1960s, and the huge compendium edited by Abelson et al. (1968) can almost be viewed as a capstone for this line of research. Nevertheless, the idea of a human preference for cognitive consistency is obviously an important and powerful one. Balance theory, in one form or another, has become a fundamental part of social psychological thinking.

In 1944, actually two years before his paper on attitudes and cognitive organization, Heider published a paper on "phenomenal causality" that became even more important for subsequent theorizing, though it did not have the immediate impact of his cognitive balance paper. In it he approached causal attributions as perceptual Gestalten linking motives or dispositions to action. Action is apprehended in a context that provides immediate meaning, and this meaning is heavily determined by causal attribution. In addition to laying the groundwork for attribution theory (see the following section) this paper directly influenced person perception research in the 1950s, research that further shaped our understanding of how we form impressions of others and interpret their actions. The experimental work of Thibaut and Reicken (1955) and of Jones and de Charms (1957) are examples of Heider's strong influence during this period.

Person perception research and research on the closely related topic of interpersonal attraction continued steadily in the early 1960s. By the end of the decade, however, it was no longer possible even to talk about perceiving persons without coming to terms with attributional considerations. What started as the rather local impact of Heider's phenomenal causality ideas about person perception became a pervasive influence on almost all of social psychology. We now describe the sequence of events that culminated in this pervasive influence.

The Rise of Attributional Approaches

Heider's *The Psychology of Interpersonal Relations* was published in 1958. In active preparation for fifteen years, this book summarized Heider's insights and reflections on social behavior and its cognitive support systems. Specifically, it was an analysis of "common sense psychology" based on the conviction that if we can capture the naive understandings of the person on the street, we can accurately infer from them his other expectations and actions. In addition to this affirmation of functionalist subjectivism, Heider suggested that naive psychology may contain many experience-based truths and that scientific psychology has much to learn from the common sense intuitions of the everyday person. Heider's own approach to naive psychology was to break down the commonly offered reasons for actions, and the actions themselves, into their essential verbal prototypes. Thus, we have analyses of the concepts of *can, ought, try, harm, benefit, like, belong to,* and so on. To an extent, then, Heider presented an interpersonal psycholinguistics that traded on the reader's own understandings of the determinants of social behavior, while attempting to sharpen these understandings. Probably the most crucial distinction Heider drew, as far as future research and theory were concerned, was that between external or situational forces and internal or dispositional forces. People tend to explain human behavior by placing emphasis either on environmental causation or on the causal contri-

butions of the actor's own beliefs, motives, or traits. Unraveling the determinants of internal versus external causal attribution was the central challenge for research. Armed with such information, one could better predict the circumstances of anger and aggression, of information seeking, of social influence, of various mood shifts, of task perseverance, and of many other crucial human states or activities.

Heider not only focused on the cognitions of others but also studiously cultivated the fruits of his own cognitive analyses. Never glib, he assimilated the data of interpersonal relations slowly, over a long and thoughtful lifetime, and carefully mulled their significance. Ambivalent toward laboratory experimentation, he was more comfortable dealing with literary plots and parables as repositories of naive wisdom concerning the drama of interpersonal relations. His book was a tangled skein of rich insights, consistently provocative, but only in the loosest sense programmatic. Its nuances enrich the reader's own naive psychology and its insights contain the sources of a thousand experiments.

Heider must surely be considered the father of attribution theory, though his assumptive framework was shaped by the broad traditions of functionalism, the subjectivism of Lewin, and the themes of cognitive organization and consistency implicit in Gestalt psychology. The attributional approach that became dominant in the 1970s was fed by other ideas as well.

A 1965 paper by Jones and Davis attempted to formalize some of Heider's attributional ideas in a "theory of correspondence inference." Drawing on Jones's early person perception research, which itself was influenced by Heider's paper on phenomenal causality, this essay considered the determinants of dispositional versus situational attributions and suggested that people infer intentions from behavioral effects to the extent that these effects are uniquely associated with the behavior chosen.

Although this paper launched a group of experiments on the attribution of attitudes, abilities, and emotions, it was Kelley's seminal paper two years later (1967) that finally began to generate momentum for the attributional approach. Kelley was able to integrate Heider's idea with Festinger's emphasis on social comparisons. He showed how Schachter's (1964) theory of emotion was basically an attributional account and noted that Bem's work (1967) provided an attributional alternative to dissonance theory. Kelley discussed the conditions under which we confidently attribute our perceptions and judgments to environmental entities. Our perception of such entities will be stable and unbiased to the extent that it is consistent over time, distinctive among entities, and in agreement with the perceptions of others. If not, the perception will be judged to be a function of perceiver dispositions or circumstances.

Self-Perception versus Dissonance Theory   A broad interest in the attributional approach began to emerge in the late 1960s just at the time that dissonance research was starting to wane. In addition to some of the reasons already discussed for this shift of interest from dissonance to attribution, another reason was the hospitality of the attributional approach to empirical phenomena generated in diverse theoretical contexts. The waxing of the attribution approach was due in part to the benign imperialism of attributionists themselves, as they reached out to provide attributional accounts of well-known psychological phenomena. In addition, there were many instances in which researchers starting with a different orientation ended up translating their findings into attributional terms, attempting to endow them with more general significance.

As noted, Schachter's theory of emotional experience, featuring a synthesis of cognitive labeling and physiological arousal, was essentially absorbed into attribution theory by Kelley (1967) and this was later facilitated by Schachter's own students Nisbett, Valins (in Jones *et al.,* 1972), Ross, and Rodin (Ross, Rodin, and Zimbardo, 1969; Rodin, 1976). The incorporation of Schachter's basic ideas as instances of self-attribution took place without a struggle. The attempt to incorporate the phenomena of cognitive dissonance met with considerably more resistance, however. Daryl Bem conducted a series of experiments for his dissertation at the University of Michigan, and the results of these were published in 1965—well before the impact of Heider's book was widely felt. Arguing from a Skinnerian "radical-behaviorist" position, Bem proposed that inferences about the self are fundamentally similar in process to inferences about someone else, that is, they are grounded in the observation of behavior. If our behavior is not "manded" (to use Skinner's term) by external requirements or incentives, we assume that it reflects our attitudes and desires. Thus, turning this around, it is reasonable that we infer our own beliefs (when asked to reflect on them) from observations of our own non-manded behavior. Bem applied this argument to well-established "attitude change" phenomena within the induced-compliance paradigm of dissonance research. He showed that observers could predict the obtained attitude results if informed about the subject's decision to comply and the circumstances under which the decision was elicited. Bem contended that subjects when asked about their attitudes after they had written counter-attitudinal essays for barely sufficient incentives would simply report an attitude that followed from their recent and therefore salient behavior. This alternative considerably reduced the "nonobviousness" of dissonance results and reasserted the relevance of behaviorism. Though Bem did not make the connection at the time, his finding also made dissonance theory a special case of attribution theory: we attribute behavior to dispositions (our own as well as others) when that behavior cannot readily be attributed to environmental forces.

Bem was immediately attacked for ignoring the fact that involved actor-subjects in traditional dissonance experiments brought a previous attitude to the experiment; Bem's observer-subjects were given no previous attitude information (Jones et al., 1968). Bem countered by arguing that actor-subjects are essentially unaware of their previous attitudes by the time they are asked to state their final attitudes in the experiment. Controversy surrounded this issue for several years until a consensus began to emerge that the only grounds for choosing between dissonance theory and Bem's alternative were esthetic.

Since all this controversy was happening while the attributional approach was gathering impressive momentum, Bem began increasingly to describe his position in more cognitive attributional terms. He tired of the arguments with dissonance protagonists and tried to extricate himself with a general presentation of "self-perception" theory in 1972. In this elegant and thoughtful essay, although Bem paid appropriate tribute to Skinner, he essentially brought together the literature of self-knowledge under an attributional framework. In fact, this essay was a very important addition to the attributional literature because Bem raised sharp and well-formulated questions concerning the extent to which, and the conditions under which, attributions mediate behavior.

It is, perhaps, a final irony that the dissonance protagonists used a "misattribution" methodology to prove that Bem's self-attribution account of dissonance phenomena was inadequate. The basic theoretical divergence between dissonance theory and self-perception theory involved the assumption of motivational arousal. Dissonance theory assumed that counter-attitudinal behavior aroused an unpleasant affective state that, in turn, motivated the subject to reduce the dissonance in the most economical way. Self-perception theory argued that such motivational assumptions were superfluous. Zanna and Cooper (1974) showed the relevance of affective arousal in the induced-compliance paradigm. Schachter and Singer (1962) had shown that subjects who were given a drug injection causing autonomic arousal and a correct description of what to expect were least likely to interpret the resulting experience as an emotion. Those who were given the injection and misinformed about the effects or not told there would be any attributed arousal to other features of the situation. Zanna and Cooper (1974) thought that these findings could be exploited to distinguish between the dissonance and the self-perception explanations of why people change their beliefs after compromising them for very little reason. They asked subjects to write a counter-attitudinal essay after participating first in an experiment supposedly dealing with the effect of drugs on memory. In that "prior experiment" subjects were given a placebo and told that the pill either would make them tense, relax them, or have no side-effects. Following the logic of Schachter and Singer, the results showed that post-essay attitude change was reduced when subjects could attribute the arousal presumably caused by writing a counter-attitudinal essay to the pill and enhanced when they thought the pill was supposed to relax them. Bem would have had difficulty incorporating this result into his version of attitude change, although more recent studies (Fazio, Zanna, and Cooper, 1977) have shown that Bem's explanation may be appropriate when the discrepancy between attitudes and behavior is mild, when the behavior is not sufficiently counterattitudinal to create dissonance.

More Examples of Attributional Hospitality   Other examples of the hospitality of an attributional approach are not hard to find. The learned helplessness model of depression (Seligman, 1975) was rather painlessly moved under the attributional rubric (cf. Abramson, Seligman, and Teasdale, 1978) though many questions remain about just how attributional notions should be applied to helplessness phenomena (Wortman and Dintzer, 1978).

Our understanding of intrinsic versus extrinsic motivation has also been enhanced by the attributional framework. Considerable evidence has accumulated that activities performed for high incentives or under high external pressure will not be subsequently seen as enjoyable by the actor. The assumption is that the "overjustification" of a performance leads to an attribution that it would not have occurred in the absence of such external incentives. Therefore, the activity cannot be intrinsically enjoyable. As an elegant experimental demonstration of this point, Lepper, Greene, and Nisbett (1973) showed that children who performed an activity for an expected reward did not freely choose to perform the same activity later in a different setting. Those who were *not* initially rewarded for performing the activity were more likely to engage freely in the activity at a subsequent time.

Weiner and his colleagues have been engaged in a very self-conscious attempt to recast achievement motivation in attributional terms (1974). Weiner's basic argument is that the motivation to perform or to continue to perform an activity is closely linked to the actor's perception of the determinants of success. This reformulation has been very influential as a stimulus for both laboratory and classroom research.

The fact that it is relatively easy to use attributional terms to characterize different social phenomena suggests the importance of distinguishing between attribution theory and an attributional approach. There are attributional theories about inferring dispositions (Jones and Davis, 1965), about achieving stable inferences about the environment (Kelley, 1967), about actor-observer differences in explaining behavior (Jones and Nisbett, 1971), and about schemata used to handle partial data sets (Kelley, 1971). Much of the attributional literature, however, is not addressed to the testing of particular theoretical hypotheses; it can more accurately be described as attribution-based research and deals with diverse social phenomena in terms of various "local" or concrete determinants of causal allocation to persons versus situations. The flexibility of an attributional approach, as distinguished from attribution theory *per se,* is undoubtedly an important factor in its growth and staying power. The empirical literature exploiting this approach has been voluminous. Nelson and Hendrick's survey in 1974 showed that, at that time, attribution-based studies formed by far the largest category in the social psychology research literature. Some decline thereafter was inevitable, but the amount of attributional research remains considerable. In addition, the volumes edited by Harvey, Ickes, and Kidd (entitled *New Directions in Attributional Research,* Volume 1, 1976; Volume 2, 1978; and Volume 3, 1981) were important as forums for the discussion and consolidation of attribution research. And finally, it should be noted that an entire social psychology textbook has been written from an attributional approach (Harvey and Smith, 1977). The fact that the text is not obviously deviant or idiosyncratic is testimony once again to the flexibility of the approach and its basic compatibility with other orientations.

In summary, the attributional approach became dominant in social psychology for a variety of reasons, including the decline of specific interest in dissonance theory, the general momentum of cognitive approaches within psychology at large, the hospitable flexibility of the approach, and its capacity to offer a reasonable alternative explanation for important results generated by other theories. By and large, the waxing of the attributional approach was not an imperialistic putsch engineered by aggressive attribution theorists. In many cases (including those of Bem and Seligman), an attributional approach was adopted by those whose research began under different premises. Once again, the attributional approach is not a theory. In fact, it has become practically synonymous with research based on the premise that people act with reference to their conception of causal forces in the environment. Such a premise covers a very large terrain.

Inference Shortcomings   As far as research specifically relevant to attribution theory is concerned, the formulations of Heider, Jones, Kelley, and Weiner have primarily served as normative models of rational inference that are often honored by real subjects only in the breach. Correspondent inference theory (Jones and Davis, 1965), especially, has been used to identify such pervasive inference biases as the "fundamental attribution error" (Ross, 1977). This is the tendency to overattribute causation to dispositions and/or to underattribute causation to the situation.

The work on bias has been extended recently into the broader domain of general inference processes and judgmental heuristics. Building on the data of attributional biases as well as the work of Tversky and Kahneman (1974), Nisbett and Ross (1980) have identified a variety of human shortcomings in reaching conclusions from available evidence about the self, other persons, and events. Their approach suggests that many processing short cuts that have survived because of their general usefulness can lead to serious errors of understanding when misapplied. This provocative review constructs a wide and inviting bridge between the domains of social and cognitive psychology.

The Role of Affect   The 1970s have been characterized as a period in which cognitive approaches to the understanding of interpersonal relations have become ascendant. Is it likely that "this, too, shall pass?" There are more than a few signs that the cognitive revolution will be at least moderated by an increasing interest in affect and arousal. As long as cognitivists could buy the strong version of Schachter's theory of emotion—that nonspecific, uninformative, autonomic arousal becomes "emotion" when attached to a cognitive label—affect could be confined to glandular subservience. However, any evidence of separate affective systems, operating with some independence of the cognitive sphere, cries for a theoretical orientation that gives affect its own place in the conceptual realm. Tomkins (1981) is convinced that such evidence is abundant in pancultural consistencies of facial response mediation as well as in our own phenomenal experience. He argues that "affect can determine cognition at one time, be determined by cognition at another time, and be independent under other circumstances" (p. 324). Although he hopes that reality confirms the rumors that the next decade or so belongs to affect he fears that affect will continue to be co-opted by "the hypertrophy of cognitive imperialism" (p. 328). Thorough, sensitive reviews like Leventhal's (1980), however, may help to keep such imperialism in its place. Leventhal's formulation provides a comprehensive housing for emotions built around "innate motor scrips" and their separate cognitive representations. However, in emphasizing the enormous complexity of cognitive-affective interactions, his view will perhaps dismay those who would rather cling to a simpler version. Indeed, it is quite possible that more one-sided formulations may prove to be heuristic, even though they are obviously incomplete or even wrong.

An important paper by Zajonc (1980) pleads for the recognition of independent affective and cognitive response systems. Though we normally think of affect as following from cognition (believing that one must identify or discriminate before evaluating or preferring), Zajonc argues persuasively for the temporal primacy of affective response systems and for their relative independence from cognitive recognition response systems. Affect may be generated by the most primitive or minimal discriminations, and the subsequently elaborated cognitions typically incorporate the affective response and are, to an extent, determined by it.

The works of Zajonc and of Nisbett and Ross converge

to raise considerable doubt about the accuracy of self-knowledge in determining our actions, beliefs, and feelings. Although interest in attribution was originally premised on the causal role that attributions play as determinants of behavior, there are increasing signs that, in many important respects, we are out of touch with many determinants of our behavior and are readily seduced into offering salient cultural stereotypes and rationalizations in answer to Why questions. In any event, the precise relations between cognition, affect, and behavior remain very much a mystery—a fact that must certainly have been sensed by both Lewin and Heider, who refused to equate subjectivism with phenomenological validity. It seems reasonable to predict that there will be much more to say in the near future about the complex relations between attributions and behavior, and the role of affect is likely to receive greater attention by social psychologists than has been the case up to now.

THE ANALYSIS OF SOCIAL PROBLEMS

Our discussion thus far has emphasized the major lines of theoretical development in social psychology and the clusters of research (primarily experimental) relating to them. This portrayal presents a distorted picture of the total range of social psychology's contribution, since it omits the extensive literature growing out of, and responding to, social problems. This literature is difficult to characterize historically, since the research tends to be triggered by contemporary circumstances and interpretations of the findings weave together both new and old theoretical trends. One can visualize a continuum ranging from theory-driven research at one extreme to research focused on social problems at the other. Some researchers tend to operate with a theory in search of exemplification, whereas others begin with a phenomenon and try to conceptualize its features, often with reference to one or more existing theories. However, the two approaches are often in various stages of transition so that the distinction between them may become easily blurred.

Social psychology has always straddled the line between theory and application. Many natural science psychologists would no doubt (privately if not publicly) cast most of social psychology in the "applied" camp. On the other hand, those in the applied fields of clinical and organizational psychology often look to social psychology for basic concepts and general principles. To an important extent, what is basic and what is applied are functions of the observer's orientation. Furthermore, the same research can often be titled and described in basic or applied terms. (Presentational format may be at least partly determined by the state of the external reward system in the social sciences.)

No doubt social relevance is always "in," but sometimes it is more "in" than at other times. The Second World War was a clear and obvious stimulus for applied research in the social sciences. It precipitated an urgent need for problem solutions, resources were ample, and the accessibility of large numbers of military subjects was often a researcher's dream. Many social psychologists turned their attention to such things as the analysis of propaganda, methods of inducing attitude change on vital war-related issues, and the determinants of high versus low morale, especially as linked to the concept of relative deprivation (cf. Cartwright, 1948). In the relatively quiet Eisenhower years, the cry for social relevance was muted in favor of the development of basic research paradigms that would separate the conceptual gold from the idiosyncratic complexities of the interpersonal behavior episodes. This was the Rodney Dangerfield era, with social psychology attempting to gain respect as a coherent field with its own powerful theoretical and investigative tools. The Kennedy and King assassinations and our tragic Vietnam involvement were important factors that changed all this as they changed so many other features of our society.

The early 1970s witnessed dramatic shifts in the teaching of undergraduates in psychology courses. Students demanded and generally received larger amounts of relevance in their courses. New courses were added and instructors in the traditional courses turned to textbooks that featured a greater concern with the problems of society. Such textbooks began to be the rule rather than the exception, and it is hard to find a contemporary text without obligatory treatments of the determinants of violence, helping behavior, crowding, environmental psychology, love and attraction, and the psychology of women.

Though textbooks have, quite understandably, reflected the perceived demands for relevance in their packaging of available research data, problem-driven research has itself grown substantially in the past fifteen years. It is a commentary on the nature of the field that problem-focused research articles appear in the same journals with theory-driven research, though it is also true that the *Journal of Applied Social Psychology* was explicitly founded in 1971 as an outlet for the applications of behavioral science research to the problems of society. In order to redress, ever so slightly, the balance of the present chapter, we shall briefly mention some major clusters of social problem research that have received particular attention since the early 1970s.

Prejudice and Stereotypy

Research on ethnic prejudice, stereotypes, and intergroup relations has persistently attracted the attention of social psychologists. LaPiere's classic study in 1934 raised the intriguing and still unanswered question, "When does prejudice toward an out-group lead to discrimination toward individual out-group members?" Many measures of attitudes developed during the 1930s and 1940s focused on social distance preferences toward various ethnic groups (e.g., Hartley, 1946). As early as 1933, Katz and Braly showed the striking consensus of Princeton students concerning their ethnic stereotypes. In *The Nature of Prejudice,* G. W. Allport (1954a) provided a comprehensive view of the patterning and determinants of prejudice, summarizing the state of our knowledge at that point in time. His review gave impetus to the idea that prejudice grows out of normal cognitive processes; thus Allport directed the field away from the emphasis on abnormality and individual differences conveyed by authoritarian personality theory (Adorno et al., 1950) and from the motivated irrationality implied by frustration-aggression theory (Dollard et al., 1939). Interest in the cognitive bases of stereotypy has accelerated in recent years as a natural consequence of the upsurge of interest in cognitive biases of all sorts. Brigham's (1971) useful review marks a convenient starting point for this accelerated interest which, ten years later, was exemplified in a volume edited by Hamilton (1981) on cognitive processes in stereotyping and inter-group behavior.

The affective side of prejudice has also been recently highlighted in Katz's (1981) book, *Stigma,* which presents an analysis of reactions to black or disabled target persons in a series of experiments. Clearly, the study of affective biasing factors in interpersonal relations lies at the heart of the social psychology domain and is likely to remain a topic of research concern.

The Impact of Television Violence

Social psychologists have also participated in the wave of research on the effects of television on its viewers. Much of this research has centered on the role exposure to violence on television plays in the induction of crime and aggressive behavior. Though some researchers (e.g., Feshbach and Singer, 1971) have found that watching violence reduces aggressive behavior, the general consensus, as expressed in the conclusions of the Eisenhower Commission on the Causes and Prevention of Violence, is that "violence on television encourages violent forms of behavior." For the time being, at least, the imitation or modeling approach seems to have won out over catharsis theory.

Helping Behavior

A classic example of phenomena-driven research was the series of studies conducted by Latané and Darley that investigated bystander intervention in emergency situations (summarized in their 1970 book). Undoubtedly, the zeitgeist was an important background factor in alerting them to the social problems that they addressed. Post-assassination years of the 1960s brought an increasing societal concern with alienation and the fragmentation of social bonds.

The urban environment, in particular, was portrayed as an anarchic jungle characterized by a decline in human compassion and in feelings of social involvement. In this general context of concern, the brutal courtyard murder of Kitty Genovese, featuring the failure of thirty-eight witnesses to intervene, became a critical stimulus for launching a program of experimental research. In a series of ingenious and realistic experiments, conducted both in the laboratory and in the field, Latané and Darley were able to show that intervention is the final step in a complex sequence of interpretations. How these interpretations resolve the issue of personal responsibility is a critical feature in the decision process.

The themes of the Latané and Darley research resonated with the heightened concern that social psychology should be more relevant, and a large literature on bystander intervention has developed over the past decade. An even larger literature has developed dealing with more general issues of helping and altruism and touching on the role of perceived equity, the desire for justice, and evocation of the social responsibility norm (cf. Macauley and Berkowitz, 1970). Although the general area of prosocial behavior has long been a concern of social psychologists, the specific twist provided by Latané and Darley accelerated research in the treacherous theoretical briar patch where considerations of morality are tangled with reward-cost calculations, with probability assessments, and with questions of courage and fear.

Crowding and Stress

Reflections on urban life in the late 1960s and 1970s also generated a cluster of research on the relations between crowding and stress. Much of this research was done by social psychologists, and much of it has been rather doggedly empirical. Because useful theoretical formulations have been difficult to develop, the thrust of the research has been to dramatize the lack of any simple connection between crowding and density on the one hand and stress or performance decrements on the other. Indeed, the major conclusion of the most widely known treatment of crowding (Freedman, 1975) is that the destructive effects of high urban density have been vastly exaggerated. According to Glass and Singer (1972), however, the stressful effects of urban noise have not been. In their important and ingenious experimental program, Glass and Singer were able to show that the after-effects of noise pollution can be as debilitating on performance as the concurrent ones. In particular, Glass and Singer stressed the "therapeutic" importance of predictability and of control over the onset of such potential stressors as noise and shock.

The research on crowding, noise, and other factors contributing to urban stress form part of the rapidly developing field of environmental psychology. The relations between

this field and social psychology are not entirely clear. In addition to the work of such social psychologists as Freedman, Glass, and Singer, environmental psychology clearly owes much to the research and intellectual orientation of such pioneers as Roger Barker (e.g., 1968), who prefers the label of "ecological psychology." Many if not most environmental psychologists are also identified as social psychologists, though some would prefer to be called *former* social psychologists, perhaps to strengthen their sense of identification with what they perceive as a new field. In fact, two (former?) social psychologists have expressed their strong disagreement with each other concerning the relationship between social and environmental psychology. Altman (1976) feels that social psychological methods and theories are highly relevant in developing the field of environmental psychology. Proshansky (1976) disagrees and contends that social psychology "broke its promise" and has not really solved the problems it had set out to solve. Its methods, he claims, are too restrictive and violate the "environmental assumption of person-environment integrity." Obviously there are aspects of environmental psychology rather far removed from traditional social psychological concerns, but the historical, if not also the theoretical and methodological, affinity between the two fields is clear.

Health and Medicine

Especially in the wake of developments in attribution theory, social psychologists have devoted considerable attention to the behavioral aspects of health and medicine. Though the label "behavioral medicine" tends to connote a behavior modification approach, the last decade has seen important contributions by social psychologists to such problems as the analysis of doctor-patient relations, reactions to diagnostic information, placebo effects, "illness management" by patients, and some of the relations between causal attribution and the experience of pain (cf. Taylor, 1978). Much of the research in this area centers around the concept of personal responsibility and control in the adjustment of the aged. Other research has dealt with consequences of personal responsibility or control in the prevention of illness as well as in the rehabilitation process.

Social Psychology and Law

Finally, there has been a growing involvement of social psychologists in the study of problems posed by the legal system. This is hardly surprising in view of the general pressure toward relevance and the many easily identifiable social psychological problems embedded in the administration of justice. An interest in the psychology of testimony goes back at least to the turn of the century, and

many experimental studies of selective retention and attitude change have used the jury-trial setting to promote
mundane realism. It is hard to imagine a more fertile setting than jury deliberations for the study of social influence
processes at work. Because the sanctity of such deliberations cannot be directly breached, social scientists have had
to content themselves with simulated jury situations. Perhaps the closest approximation to true jury deliberations
was the study of Strodtbeck, James, and Hawkins (1958) in
which jurors drawn by lot from the regular jury pool of
Chicago and St. Louis courts were exposed to recordings
of two civil trials and then proceeded to discuss each case
as a mock jury. Many other jury simulation experiments
have since been conducted, focusing on the role of juror attitudes and personality factors as well as on different features of case presentation or characteristics of the defendant. As social psychologists have become more familiar
with the kinds of legal issues that recur in the adjudication
process, there has been a shift from using legal contexts in
pursuing general psychological questions to the analysis of
legal procedures themselves. Thus, an issue of the *Journal
of Personality and Social Psychology* (1978, *36,* no. 12)
presents a collection of experimental studies focusing on
such questions as the role of sentencing strategies, plea
bargaining, the severity of prescribed penalties, and the
consequences of adversarial versus inquisitorial procedures. An acceleration of this trend toward law-tailored research may generate findings that begin to have an impact
on judicial decisions as well as on procedural arrangements. Tanke and Tanke (1979) point out, however, that the
actual use of social science findings in courtroom proceedings is rare. They note that the role of social science findings in the historic 1954 Supreme Court desegregation ruling has been highly exaggerated. Following Kalven and
Zeisel (1961), they refer to the citation of social science
work in the *Brown vs. Board of Education* ruling as a peda-
gogical sideshow and argue that these works were not a
moving force in the decision.

Relevance and Funding Priorities

As noted earlier, the flow of research traffic in and out of
various topic areas is partly determined by the funding priorities of foundations and governmental agencies. An important question for the future is the level of specification
these agencies use in defining relevance. Natural scientists
appear to have better control than social scientists over the
setting of relevant research agendas. Perhaps natural scientists, because their procedures and findings are relatively
immune to evaluations by lay overseers, are in a better position to insure that available funds support research on
tractable problems of their own choosing. In contrast, be-

cause their findings and procedures are more open to lay
evaluations, social scientists are likely to be pressed into
working on problems defined as urgent or important by
those outside the profession. Some of these problems may
be much less tractable than others, and yet the lay evaluator
may uniformly expect results in proportion to the money
spent. Not surprisingly, some social scientists have acqui-
esced in, if not promoted, the raising of unrealistic expectations about the potential value for society of social science
research. Failure to fulfill these expectations is then used
by Congress or the administration in power to justify funding restrictions or cutbacks in times of economic distress.
As Homans (1967) has said, "I sometimes think that the
social sciences are criticized as sciences for failing to do
what a respectable physical science would not have ever
tried to do" (p. 96).

Perhaps it is too much to expect that social scientists
will ever approach the degree of control the natural science
community has over its own research priorities, at least not
until the unlikely event that a basic "breakthrough" can be
utilized to support successful social change. In the mean-
time, our best hope may lie in the gradual accumulation of
results on a variety of fronts, results that enter by osmosis
into important forms of social decision making. Indeed,
many definite changes in society brought about by social
science findings quickly become such an integral part of
the cultural background that it is easy to forget their origins. For example, consider the ever-growing number of
social psychological principles currently embedded in political campaigning, industrial management, and mixed
motive negotiations. In any event, quite independently of
funding opportunities and considerations of disciplinary
prestige, many social psychologists were attracted to the
field in the first place because of their interest in understanding and solving social problems, and a large number
of them are members of the Society for the Psychological
Study of Social Issues, a group emphasizing involvement
in contemporary social problems. Undoubtedly a high proportion of social psychological research will continue to be
generated by contemporary social issues, and social psychological findings will eventually work their way into the
solution strategies of some policy and decision makers.

REPRISE AND FORECAST

All behavioral science disciplines share a strong tendency
to examine and criticize themselves periodically. We have
already noted the self-doubts of contemporary personality
psychologists. Elms (1975), among others, has cited the
widespread self-doubts about goals, methods, and accomplishments in developmental and clinical psychology, in
sociology, in anthropology, and in economics. Social psychology has certainly not escaped this tendency toward

self-flagellation, and criticism has taken a variety of forms. Asch (1952) was neither the first nor the last to complain of the reductionistic tendencies of those who would emulate the techniques of the natural sciences without noticing the limits of their applicability. Through the years other internal critics have commented on various theoretical or methodological shortcomings in social psychology. A unique convergence of events in the late 1960s brought about an exacerbation of self-criticism that became identified as "the crisis in social psychology." To some extent, this despairing rhetoric fed on itself. The research literature continued to grow during the 1970s at a fast rate, and it is hard to detect any direct effects of malaise in the journals carrying this prime research. However, enough people were disturbed by developments in their field to organize symposia and generate essays proclaiming social psychology as a field in moral and methodological disarray. The events converging to bring this about generally fell in three areas: ethics, artifacts, and relevance (cf. Rosnow, 1981).

The Rise of Ethical Concern

The linkage of deceptive scenarios with experimentation grew stronger and stronger as social psychology moved into the 1960s. Conformity research, whether in the Asch or the social comparison paradigm, inevitably involved deceptive information about the opinions or judgments of others. It also involved a kind of entrapment of subjects who would later have to deal with the implications on their self-concept of their particular resolution of the conformity conflict. As dissonance research gained momentum in the 1960s, hundreds of experiments were published in which subjects were induced to do things, or to commit themselves to do things, that they would ordinarily avoid doing. The ethical problems inherent in the use of deception were especially highlighted by Festinger, Riecken, and Schachter's (1956) infiltration of a doomsday group and by Milgram's (1963) obedience research. It was perhaps inevitable that the widespread adoption of deception techniques, especially those that embarrassed subjects or lowered their self-esteem, would elicit a chorus of concerned comment. A strong early criticism was voiced by Baumrind (1964) concerning Milgram's research. This resulted in a debate that constituted the first truly public airing of the pros and cons of deception in social psychological research. Kelman (1967) was also an early critic of the unbridled use of deception, and the title and thrust of his subsequent book (*A Time to Speak,* 1968) may have reinforced the picture of social scientists involved in a silent conspiracy to manipulate and humiliate subjects.

Although the full impact of such criticisms is difficult to assess, they undoubtedly sensitized psychologists and the public to the ethical dilemmas inherent in social psychological experimentation and stimulated considerable debate about alternative (i.e., nondeceptive) procedures. In this atmosphere of ethical concern, the federal government began to extend its monitoring of the protection of human subjects from medical to behavioral science research. Under pressure from federal granting agencies—especially the Department of Health, Education and Welfare—universities established or reorganized committees to monitor all human subjects research conducted by their personnel or on their premises. Though there has undoubtedly been considerable variation on how individual committees have viewed deception research, it is fair to say that the range of available procedures has been restricted by ethical concerns enforceable by human subjects committees.

Artifacts and Experimenter Effects

In the rush to consolidate the experimental triumphs of Lewin and Sherif in the 1930s, many investigators lost sight of the fact (first emphasized by Rosenzweig in 1933) that the contact between an experimenter and his subjects involves a complex social interaction. The work of Robert Rosenthal reminded them (even while it was annoying them). As early as 1956, in his doctoral dissertation, Rosenthal suggested that experimenters may exert subtle influence within the experimental setting to confirm their theoretical hypotheses or expectancies. At the time he wrote of "unconscious experimenter bias" to indicate that experimenters might be quite unaware of their contributions to self-fulfilling prophecies in interacting with subjects. Although Rosenthal's research has itself been severely criticized on many grounds (cf. Barber and Silver, 1968), the cumulative impact of his experimenter bias studies was to improve decidedly the methodology of experimentation. His research, combined with Orne's (1962) demonstrations of "experimenter demand" artifacts, were important determinants of the increasing inclusion of sophisticated precautions within experimental designs. In particular, investigators have become much more sensitive to the need to keep experimenters blind to the experimental conditions of the subject being run.

The "Ethogenic Approach"

Whereas the artifact crisis was basically self-corrective, resulting in clear methodological advances, more fundamental and disturbing criticisms raised fundamental doubts about the status of social psychology as a quantitative empirical science. These criticisms have involved a convergence of British linguistic philosophy, micro-sociology (especially, "ethno-methodology"), and good old-fashioned humanism. This convergence is especially apparent in the writings of Harré (with Secord, 1972, 1977), who has tried to urge an "ethogenic approach" on restless, dissatisfied social psychologists. This approach is considerably clearer about what it is against than what it is for. It is against a mechanistic model of man, antipositivistic, and skeptical of the naive determinism implicit in stimulus-response causal models. Experimentation embodies all these evils, according to Harré and his group, and should be replaced by methods appropriate to an anthropomorphic view of humankind, emphasizing the human being's capacity to initiate action, monitor his or her performances, and monitor his or her monitorings. The only method described in detail is "account analysis" defined by Harré (1977) with characteristic opacity (p. 284):

> It is the analysis of both the social force and explanatory content of the speech produced by social actors as a guide to the structure of the cognitive resources required for the genesis of intelligible and warrantable social action by those actors.

Above all else, account analysis involves a reliance on the negotiation of explanations between actors and observers until satisfactory concordance is achieved.

The ethogenic approach has much in common with the "descriptive psychology" approach of Peter Ossorio (1981). Both approaches emphasize structural linguistic features and shared assumptions about the meaning of social behavior. Though they both have raised interesting possibilities about future research formats, neither has yet proved itself as an alternative to the mix of existing empirical approaches. It seems especially unfortunate that the ethogenic approach involves an exclusionary stance, arguing for replacing experimental approaches with a loose assortment of observational techniques and "negotiation" by interview. As Schlenker (1977) points out, social psychologists are not forced to rely exclusively on either a rigorous quantitative or a more sensitive qualitative methodology. Each has its place, and the contributions of a Goffman or a Garfinkel can enrich, without replacing or superceding, the contributions of a Kelley or a Zajonc.

Exclusionary arguments may originate from the misplaced assumption that social psychology's so-called "crisis" is actually a paradigmatic crisis in the sense proposed by Kuhn (1962). Kuhn has argued that major scientific advances emerge only after the normal problem-solving activities have for the time being failed. Thus, crises are healthy; they lead to paradigm shifts. As Elms (1975) notes, however, this may be wishful thinking, based on the fallacious assumption that there is a genuine scientific paradigm in social psychology, a well-developed and widely shared version of normal science. In his view, a crisis of confidence does not necessarily denote a shattering of an old orthodoxy (that in the case of social psychology never existed) in preparation for a new one (that is unlikely to arrive in the near future).

Social Psychology as History?

The most controversial aspect of an experimental approach in social psychology has always been the problem of generalization or ecological validity. How does one proceed from a context-bound finding to a statement about the condition of human nature? Kenneth Gergen (1973, 1976) tackled this problem and produced a sweeping indictment of social psychology's scientific pretensions. First, Gergen argued that the data of human behavior are culturally and historically relative, at best characterizing a particular sample of subjects in a particular setting at a particular time. Second, and with more than a trace of self-contradiction, he stated that social psychological findings enlighten the public and can thus generate oppositional tendencies that render the observed behavior less likely in the future. In a recent book, Gergen (1982) has adumbrated these themes and incorporated them into a sophisticated attack on positivism in general and hypothesis-testing empiricism in particular. In this treatment, Gergen argues for a "sociorationalistic" position that emphasizes collective sources of knowledge as an alternative both to the "exogenous" view of science as a mapping of nature and to the completely "endogenous" view of knowledge as entirely relative to the individual knower. It remains to be seen whether appropriate methods can be developed to implement this orientation and to make it more than a vaguely shimmering promissory note.

Though Gergen is clearly trying in this recent work to sketch the outlines of a paradigm shift, many social psychologists viewed his earlier statements as intellectually irresponsible invitations to despair. Schlenker has provided strong rebuttals not only to Gergen (1973, 1976) but also to Harré (1977).

Putting aside the particular merits of the argument, the response to Gergen's 1973 paper poses interesting problems for this historical review. Since Gergen's pessimistic conclusions are not particularly novel, one can wonder why contemporary social psychologists paid such lavish attention to them. Countless symposia during the 1970s were built around a debate of his thesis. It seems likely that his paper is as widely known as any single essay on the general subject published in the past decade. A widespread need for self-flagellation, perhaps unique to social psychologists, may account for some of the mileage of the Gergen message. It is also the case that the message (especially in this early paper) has the advantage of rhetorical simplicity;

the rejoinders are perforce more complex and therefore more forgettable, partly because it would be difficult simply to stand up for the straw men that Gergen attacks.

It is not too surprising that those who hope to change the ways of social psychologists create such straw men to substitute for the actual heterogeneity of research approaches and objectives within social psychology. Thus there is a tendency to caricature past social psychological research and to consign it to a simple positivistic trash bin along with reductionistic learning experiments. Such a caricature may be easily lampooned to make the experimental approach to the complexities of social behavior appear irrelevant and derivative. Perhaps more attention should be paid to the varieties of experimentation that actually have generated our literature and to the diverse roles that experiments can play in illuminating the nature of a problem and the ways of thinking about it. Perhaps, as Kaplan (1964) has suggested, we do not have to believe that laws exist to believe that they are worth looking for. Even Gergen (1976) acknowledges that "theories of social behavior may play a number of very useful roles other than improving prediction" (p. 375). And even if we concede, along with Gergen (1982), that the main function of research is to lend rhetorical power to theoretical interpretation, this is a vastly important function that hardly deserves belittlement.

The crisis of social psychology has begun to take its place as a minor perturbation in the long history of the social sciences. The intellectual momentum of the field has not been radically affected by crisis proclamations, though some of the broader institutional consequences should be considered and eventually assessed. A case can be made that the severity of the self-doubting criticisms, along with the publicity they received, played into the hands of political and academic forces poised to put social psychology in its place. There is a clear sense in which the apparent malaise affecting social psychology was seen as more devastating by outsiders than by social psychologists themselves. Other psychologists and other social scientists are more likely to know social psychology through its current self-depictions than through its prime research literature. Perhaps it is not surprising that some of them thought the malaise was terminal.

From a long-range perspective, the educational reproduction of social psychologists will ebb and flow with shifts in social and economic priorities. The number of social psychologists will expand rapidly at times and contract at others. Graduate programs will emerge, and others will disappear. But as this handbook testifies, the progress in our understanding has been remarkable in the short period of little more than a decade since the preceding edition. The progress should not be measured either in terms of neat cumulative linear increments or in terms of great reorienting breakthroughs but rather in the increased insights that gradually work their way into our cultural wisdom. It

is a person's very nature to understand himself or herself in relation to others. The future of social psychology is assured not only by the vital importance of its subject matter but also by its unique conceptual and methodological strengths that permit the identification of underlying processes in everyday social life.

REFERENCES

Abelson, R. P., Aronson, E., McGuire, W. J., Newcomb, T. M., Rosenberg, M. J., & Tannenbaum, P. H. (Eds.). (1968). *Theories of cognitive consistency: A source book.* Chicago: Rand McNally.

Abramson, L. Y., Seligman, M. E. P., & Teasdale, J. D. (1978). Learned helplessness in humans: Critique and reformulation. *Journal of Abnormal Psychology, 87,* 49–74.

Adams, J. S. (1965). Inequity in social exchange. In L. Berkowitz (Ed.), *Advances in Experimental Social Psychology.* (Vol. 2). New York: Academic Press.

Adorno, T. W., Frenkel-Brunswik, E., Levinson, D. J., & Sanford, R. N. (1950). *The authoritarian personality.* New York: Harper & Row.

Allport, F. H. (1924). *Social psychology.* Boston: Houghton Mifflin.

Allport, F. H. (1955). *Theories of perception and the concept of structure.* New York: Wiley.

Allport, G. W. (1935). Attitudes. In C. Murchison (Ed.), *A handbook of social psychology.* (pp. 798–844). Worcester, Mass.: Clark Univ. Press.

Allport, G. W. (1937). *Personality: A psychological interpretation.* New York: Henry Holt.

Allport, G. W. (1954a). *The nature of prejudice.* Reading, Mass.: Addison-Wesley.

Allport, G. W. (1954b). The historical background of modern social psychology. In G. Lindzey (Ed.), *The handbook of social psychology.* (Vol. I, pp. 3–56). Cambridge, Mass.: Addison-Wesley.

Allport, G. W. (1985). The historical background of social psychology. In G. Lindzey and E. Aronson (Eds.), *The handbook of social psychology.* (Vol. I, pp. 1–46). New York: Random House.

Allport, G. W., & Postman, L. (1947). *The psychology of rumor.* New York: Henry Holt.

Altman, I. (1976). Environmental psychology and social psychology. *Personality and Social Psychology Bulletin, 2,* 96–113.

Anderson, N. H. (1962). Application of an attitude model to impression formation. *Science, 138,* 817–818.

Anderson, H., & Jacobson, A. (1965). Effect of stimulus inconsistency and discounting instructions in personality impression formation. *Journal of Personality and Social Psychology, 2,* 531–539.

Aronson, E. (1968). Dissonance theory: progress and problems. In R. P. Abelson, E. Aronson, W. J. McGuire, T. M. Newcomb, M. J. Rosenberg, & P. H. Tannenbaum, (Eds.). *Theories of cognitive consistency: A source book.* (pp. 5–27). Chicago: Rand McNally.

Aronson, E. (1980). Persuasion via self-justification: Large commitments for small rewards. In L. Festinger (Ed.), *Retrospections on social psychology.* (pp. 3–21). New York: Oxford Univ. Press.

Aronson, E., Brewer, M., & Carlsmith, J. M. (1985). Experimentation in social psychology. In G. Lindzey & E. Aronson (Eds.), *The handbook of social psychology* (Vol. I, pp. 441–486). New York: Random House.

Aronson, E., & Carlsmith, J. M. (1963). The effect of the severity of threat on the devaluation of forbidden behavior. *Journal of Abnormal and Social Psychology, 66,* 584–588.

Aronson, E., & Carlsmith, J. M. (1968). Experimentation in social psychology. In G. Lindzey and E. Aronson (Eds.), *Handbook of social psychology* (2nd ed., Vol. 2). Reading, Mass.: Addison-Wesley.

Aronson E., & Linder D. (1965). Gain and loss of esteem as determinants of interpersonal attractiveness. *Journal of Experimental Social Psychology, 1,* 156–172.

Asch, S. E. (1946). Forming impressions of personality. *Journal of Abnormal and Social Psychology, 41,* 258–290.

Asch, S. E. (1952). *Social psychology.* New York: Prentice-Hall.

Asch, S. E. (1956). Studies of independence and conformity: a minority of one against a unanimous majority. *Psychological Monographs, 70,* No. 9 (Whole No. 416).

Bales, R. F. (1950). *Interaction process analysis.* Cambridge, Mass.: Addison-Wesley.

Bales, R. F. (1970). *Personality and interpersonal behavior.* New York: Holt, Rinehart and Winston.

Bandura, A. (1973). *Aggression: A social learning analysis.* Englewood Cliffs, N.J.: Prentice-Hall.

Bandura, A., & Walters, R. H. (1963). *Social learning and personality development.* New York: Holt, Rinehart and Winston.

Barber, T. X., & Silver, M. J. (1968). Fact, fiction, and the experimenter bias effect. *Psychological Bulletin,* Monogr. Suppl., 70, 1–29.

Barker, R. (1968). *Ecological psychology: Concepts and methods for studying the environment of human behavior.* Stanford: Stanford Univ. Press.

Barker, R., Dembo, T., & Lewin, K. (1941). Frustration and regression: an experiment with young children. *Univ. of Iowa Studies in Child Welfare, 18,* No. 1.

Bartlett, F. C. (1932). *Remembering.* Cambridge: Cambridge Univ. Press.

Baumrind, D. (1964). Some thoughts on ethics of research: After reading Milgram's "behavioral study of obedience," *American Psychologist, 19,* 421–423.

Bem, D. (1965). An experimental analysis of self-persuasion. *Journal of Experimental Social Psychology, 1,* 199–218.

Bem, D. (1967). Self-perception: an alternative interpretation of cognitive dissonance phenomena. *Psychological Review, 74,* 183–200.

Bem, D. (1972). Self-perception theory. In L. Berkowitz (Ed.), *Advances in experimental social psychology.* (Vol. 6). New York: Academic Press.

Bem, D. (1980a). Assessing situations by assessing persons. In D. Magnusson (Ed.), *Toward a psychology of situations: An interactional perspective.* Hillsdale, N.J.: Erlbaum.

Bem, D. (1980b). Assessing persons and situations with the template-matching technique. In L. Kahle (Ed.), *New directions in the methodology of behavioral research: Methods for studying person situation interactions.* San Francisco: Jossey-Bass.

Bem, D., & Allen, A. (1974). On predicting some of the people some of the time: the search for cross-situational consistencies in behavior. *Psychological Review, 81,* 506–520.

Bem, D. J., & Funder, D. C. (1978). Predicting more of the people more of the time: assessing the personality of situations. *Psychological Review, 85,* 485–501.

Bem, D., & Lord, C. J. (1979). Template matching: a proposal for probing the ecological validity of experimental settings in social psychology. *Journal of Personality and Social Psychology, 37,* 833–846.

Berkowitz, L., & Geen, R. (1966). Film violence and cue properties of available targets. *Journal of Personality and Social Psychology, 3,* 525–530.

Berkowitz, L., & Lepage, A. (1967). Weapons as aggression-eliciting stimuli. *Journal of Personality and Social Psychology, 7,* 202–207.

Berkowitz, L., & Walster, E. (1976). Equity theory: toward a general theory of social interaction. *Advances in experimental social psychology.* (Vol. 9). New York: Academic Press.

Block, J. (1977). Advancing the psychology of personality: paradigmatic shift or improving the quality of research? In D. Magnusson & N. S. Endler (Eds.), *Personality at the crossroads: Current issues and interactional psychology.* Hillsdale, N.J.: Erlbaum.

Bonacich, P., & Light, J. (1978). Laboratory experimentation in sociology. In *Annual Review of Sociology, 4,* 145–170.

Bowers, K. S. (1973). Situationism in psychology: an analysis and critique. *Psychological Review, 80,* 307–336.

Brehm, J. W. (1956). Post decision changes in the desirability of alternatives. *Journal of Abnormal and Social Psychology, 52,* 384–389.

Brehm, J. W. (1965). Comment on "counternorm attitudes induced by consonant versus dissonant conditions of role-playing." *Journal of Experimental Research in Personality, 1,* 61–64.

Brehm, J. W., & Cohen, A. R. (1962). *Explorations in cognitive dissonance.* New York: Wiley.

Brigham, J. C. (1971). Ethnic stereotypes. *Psychological Bulletin, 76,* 15–38.

Broadbent, D. E. (1958). *Perception and communication.* London: Pergamon Press.

Brown, R., & Bellugi, U. (1964). Three processes in the

child's acquisition of syntax. In E. H. Lennenberg (Ed.), *New directions in the study of language.* (pp. 131–161). Cambridge, Mass.: MIT Press.

Bruner, J. S. (1951). Personality dynamics and the process of perceiving. In R. R. Blake and G. B. Ramsey (Eds.), *Perception: An approach to personality.* New York: Ronald Press.

Bruner, J. S. (1957). On perceptual readiness. *Psychological Review, 64,* 123–152.

Bruner, J. S., & Goodman, C. C. (1947). Value and need as organizing factors in perception. *Journal of Abnormal and Social Psychology, 42,* 33–44.

Bruner, J. S., & Tagiuri, R. (1954). The perception of people. In G. Lindzey (Ed.), *Handbook of social psychology.* (Vol. 2, pp. 634–654). Cambridge, Mass.: Addison-Wesley.

Brunswik, E. (1933). Die Zuganglichkeit Von Gegenstanden Fur Vie Wahrnehmung. *Archives of Gestalt Psychology, 88,* 377–418.

Burgess, R. L., & Bushell, D. (1969) *Behavioral sociology: The experimental analysis of social process.* New York: Columbia Univ. Press.

Byrne, D. (1971). *The attraction paradigm.* New York: Academic Press.

Campbell, D. T., & Stanley, J. C. (1966). *Experimental and quasi-experimental designs for research.* Chicago: Rand McNally.

Carlsmith, J. M., Ellsworth, P. C., & Aronson, E. (1976). *Methods of research in social psychology.* Reading, Mass.: Addison-Wesley.

Carter, L., Haythorn, W., Meirowitz, B., & Lanzetta, J. (1951a). The relation of categorization and ratings in the observation of group behavior. *Human Relations, 4,* 239–254.

Carter, L., Haythorn, W., Meirowitz, B., & Lanzetta, J. (1951b). A note on a new technique of interaction recording. *Journal of Abnormal and Social Psychology, 46,* 258–260.

Cartwright, D. (1948). Social psychology during World War II. *Human Relations, 1,* 333–352.

Cartwright, D. (1961). In W. Dennis (Ed.), *Current trends in psychological theory: A bicentennial program.* Pittsburgh: Univ. of Pittsburgh Press.

Cartwright, D. (1973). Determinants of scientific progress: the case of research on the risky shift. *American Psychologist, 28,* 222–231.

Cartwright, D. (1979). Contemporary social psychology in historical perspective. *Social Psychological Quaterly, 42,* 82–93.

Cartwright, D., & Harary F. (1956). Structural balance: a generalization of Heider's theory. *Psychological Review, 63,* 277–293.

Cassirer, E. (1923). *Substance and function, and Einstein's theory of relativity.* Chicago: Open Court.

Chapple, E. D. (1940). Measuring human relations: an introduction to the study of the interaction of individuals. *Genetic Psychological Monographs, 22,* 1–147.

Chapple, E. D. (1949). The interaction chronograph: Its evolution and present application. *Personnel, 25,* 295–307.

Christie, R., & Geis, F. L. (1970). *Studies in Machiavellianism.* New York: Academic Press.

Christie, R., & Jahoda, M. (1954). *Studies in the scope and method of the "authoritarian personality."* Glencoe, Ill.: Free Press.

Coffey, H. S., Freedman, M. B., Leary, T. F., & Ossorio, A. G. (1950). Community service and social research—group psychotherapy in a church program. *Journal of Social Issues, 6,* 1–65.

Cooley, C. H. (1902). *Human nature and social order.* New York: Scribner.

Cottrell, L. S., & Gallagher, R. (1941). Developments in social psychology, 1930–1940. *Sociometry* Monogr. No. 1. New York: Beacon House.

Cottrell, N. B. (1972). Social facilitation. In C. B. McClintock (Ed.), *Experimental social psychology.* (pp. 185–236). New York: Holt, Rinehart, and Winston.

Cronbach, L. J. (1955). Processes affecting scores on "understanding of others" and "assumed similarity." *Psychological Bulletin, 52,* 177–193.

Cronbach, L. J. (1957). The two disciplines of scientific psychology. *American Psychologist, 12,* 671–684.

Deutsch, M. (1949a). A theory of cooperation and competition. *Human Relations, 2,* 129–152.

Deutsch, M. (1949b). An experimental study of the effects of cooperation and competition upon group process. *Human Relations, 2,* 199–232.

Deutsch, M. (1958). Trust and suspicion. *Journal of Conflict Resolution, 21,* 265–279.

Deutsch, M. (1962). Cooperation and trust: some theoretical notes. In M. R. Jones (Ed.), *Nebraska Symposium on Motivation.* Lincoln: Univ. of Nebraska Press.

Deutsch, M., & Krauss, R. M. (1960). The effect of threat on interpersonal bargaining. *Journal of Abnormal and Social Psychology, 61,* 181–189.

Deutsch, M. (1980). Fifty years of conflict. In L. Festinger (Ed.), *Retrospections on social psychology.* (pp. 46–77). New York: Oxford Univ. Press.

Dollard, J., Doob, L. W., Miller, N. E., Mowrer, O. H., & Sears, R. R. (1939). *Frustration and aggression.* New Haven: Yale Univ. Press.

Dollard, J., & Miller, N. E. (1950). *Personality and psychotherapy.* New York: McGraw Hill.

Ebbinghaus, H. (1885). *Memory.* (Trans. H. A. Ruger and C. E. Bussenius) New York: Teachers College (1913). Originally *Uber das Gedachtnis.* Leipzig, Germany: Duncker.

Elms, A. C. (1975). The crisis of confidence in social psychology. *American Psychologist, 30,* 967–976.

Elms, A. C., & Janis, I. L. (1965). Counternorm attitudes induced by consonant versus dissonant conditions of role playing. *Journal of Experimental Research in Personality, 1,* 50–60.

Endler, N., & Magnusson, D. (1976). Toward an interactional psychology of personality. *Psychological Bulletin, 83,* 956–974.

Erdelyi, M. H. (1974). A new look at the new look: perceptual defense and vigilance. *Psychological Review, 81,* 1–25.

Eriksen, C. W., Ed. (1962). *Behavior and awareness.* Durham, N.C.: Duke Univ. Press.

Eriksen, C. W. (1958). Unconscious processes. In M. R. Jones (Ed.), *Nebraska symposium on motivation.* Lincoln: Univ. of Nebraska Press, 169–227.

Erickson, E. H. (1950). *Childhood and society.* New York: Norton.

Estes, W. K. (1954). Kurt Lewin. In W. K. Estes, S. Koch, K. MacCorquodale, P. Muhl, C. G. Mueller, W. N. Schoenfeld, & W. S. Verplanck, *Modern learning theory.* (pp. 317–344). New York: Appleton-Century-Crofts.

Farr, R. M. (1976). Experimentation: a social psychological perspective. *British Journal of Social and Clinical Psychology, 15,* 225–238.

Fazio, R. H., Zanna, M. P., & Cooper, J. (1977). Dissonance and self-perception: an integrative view of each theory's proper domain of application. *Journal of Experimental Social Psychology, 13,* 464–479.

Feshbach, S., & Singer, R. C. (1971). *Televison and aggression: An experimental field study.* San Francisco: Jossey-Bass.

Festinger, L. (1950). Informal social communication. *Psychological Review, 57,* 271–282.

Festinger, L. (1954). A theory of social comparison processes. *Human Relations, 7,* 117–140.

Festinger, L. (1957). *A theory of cognitive dissonance.* Evanston, Ill.: Row-Peterson.

Festinger, L. (1980). Looking backward. In L. Festinger (Ed.), *Retrospections on social psychology.* (pp. 236–254). New York: Oxford Univ. Press.

Festinger, L., & Carlsmith, J. M. (1959). Cognitive consequences of forced compliance. *Journal of Abnormal and Social Psychology, 58,* 203–211.

Festinger, L., Riecken, H. W., & Schachter, S. (1956). *When prophecy fails.* Minneapolis: Univ. of Minnesota.

Fishbein, M., & Ajzen, I. (1975). *Belief, attitude, intention and behavior: An introduction to theory and research.* Reading, Mass.: Addison-Wesley.

Freedman, J. L. (1975). *Crowding and human behavior.* New York: Viking Press.

Fromm, E. (1941). *Escape from freedom.* New York: Rinehart.

Gallo, P. S. (1966). Effects of increased incentives upon the use of threat in bargaining. *Journal of Personality and Social Psychology, 4,* 14–20.

Gergen, K. (1973). Social psychology as history. *Journal of Personality and Social Psychology, 26,* 309–320.

Gergen, K. J. (1976). Social psychology, science, and history. *Personality and Social Psychology Bulletin, 2,* 373–383.

Gergen, K. J. (1982). *Toward transformation in social knowledge.* New York: Springer-Verlag.

Glass, D. C., & Singer, J. E. (1972). *Urban stress.* New York: Academic Press.

Goffman, E. (1959). *The presentation of self in everyday life.* Garden City, N.Y.: Doubleday, Anchor Books.

Goldiamond, I. (1958). Indicators of perceptions: I. subliminal perception, subception, unconscious perception: an analysis in terms of psychophysical indicator methodology. *Psychological Bulletin, 55,* 373–411.

Haines, H., & Vaughan, G. M. (1979). Was 1898 a "great date" in the history of experimental social psychology? *Journal of the History of Behavioral Sciences, 15,* 323–332.

Hammond, K. R., McClelland, G. H., & Mumpower, J. (1980). *Human judgment and decision making.* New York: Praeger.

Hamilton, D. L., Ed. (1981). *Cognitive processes in stereotyping and intergroup behavior.* Hillsdale, N.J.: Erlbaum.

Harré, R. (1977). The ethogenic approach: theory and practice. In L. Berkowitz (Ed.), *Advances in experimental social psychology.* (Vol. 10, pp. 283–314). New York: Academic Press.

Harré R., & Secord, P. F. (1972). *The explanation of social behavior.* Oxford: Blackwell.

Hartley, E. L. (1946). *Problems in prejudice.* New York: King's Crown Press.

Harvey, J. H., Ickes, W. J., & Kidd, R. F. (1976). *New directions in attribution research.* (Vol. 1). Hillsdale, N.J.: Erlbaum. Vol. 2 (1978); Vol. 3 (1981).

Harvey, J. H., & Smith, W. P. (1977). *Social psychology: An attributional approach.* St. Louis: Mosby.

Heider, F. (1944). Social perception and phenomenal causality. *Psychological Review, 51,* 358–374.

Heider, F. (1946). Attitudes and cognitive organization. *Journal of Psychology, 21,* 107–112.

Heider, F. (1958). *The psychology of interpersonal relations.* New York: Wiley.

Helson, R., & Mitchell, V. (1978). Personality. *Annual Review of Psychology, 29,* 555–586.

Hogan, R., DeSoto, C. B., and Solans, C. (1977). Traits, tests, and personality research. *American Psychologist, 32,* 255–264.

Homans, G. C. (1950). *The human group.* New York: Harcourt, Brace.

Homans, G. C. (1961, 1974, Rev.). *Social behavior: Its elementary forms.* New York: Harcourt Brace Jovanovich.

Homans, G. C. (1967). *The nature of social science.* New York: Harcourt, Brace and World.

Horney, K. (1939). *New ways in psychoanalysis.* New York: Norton.

House, J. (1977). The three faces of social psychology. *Sociometry, 40,* 161–177.

Hovland, C. I., Ed. (1957). *The order of presentation in persuasion.* New Haven: Yale Univ. Press.

Hovland, C. I. (1959). Reconciling results derived from experimental and survey studies of attitude change. *American Psychologist, 14,* 8–17.

Hovland, C. I., & Janis, I. L. (1959). *Personality and persuasibility.* New Haven: Yale Univ. Press.

Hovland, C. I., Janis, I. L., & Kelley, H. H. (1953). *Communication and persuasion.* New Haven: Yale Univ. Press.

Hovland, C. I., Lumsdaine, A. A., & Sheffield, F. D. (1949). *Experiments on mass communications.* Princeton: Princeton Univ. Press.

James, W. (1890). *The principles of psychology.* New York: Henry Holt.

Janis, I. L., & Gilmore, J. (1965). The influence of incentive conditions on the success of role playing in modifying attitudes. *Journal of Personality and Social Psychology, 1,* 17–27.

Jones, E. E., & Davis, K. E. (1965). From acts to dispositions: the attribution process in person perception. In L. Berkowitz (Ed.), *Advances in experimental social psychology.* (Vol. II, pp. 219–266). New York: Academic Press.

Jones, E. E., & deCharms, R. (1957). Changes in social perception as a function of the personal relevance of behavior. *Sociometry, 20,* 75–85.

Jones, E. E., & Gerard, H. B. (1967). *Foundations of social psychology.* New York: Wiley.

Jones, E. E., Kanouse, D., Kelley, H. H., Nisbett, R., Valins, S., & Weiner, D. (1971, 1972). *Attribution: Perceiving the causes of behavior.* Morristown, N.J.: General Learning Press.

Jones, E. E., & Nisbett, R. E. (1971–1972). The actor and the observer: divergent perceptions of the cause of behavior. In E. E. Jones, D. Kanouse, H. H. Kelley, R. E. Nisbett, S. Valins, B. Weiner. *Attribution: Perceiving the causes of behavior.* Morristown, N.J.: General Learning Press.

Jones, E. E., & Pittman, T. S. (1982). Toward a general theory of strategic self presentation. In J. Suls (Ed.), *Psychological perspectives on the self.* (Vol. I, pp. 231–262). Hillsdale, N.J.: Erlbaum.

Jones, R. A., Linder, D. E., Kiesler, C. A., Zanna, M. P., & Brehm, J. W. (1968). Internal states or external stimuli: observers' attitude judgments and the dissonance theory—self-persuasion controversy. *Journal of Experimental Social Psychology, 4,* 247–269.

Jordan, N. (1953). Behavioral forces that are a function of attitudes and of cognitive organization. *Human Relations, 6,* 273–288.

Kalven, H., & Zeisel, H. (1961). Science and humanism. In J. Huxley (Ed.), *The humanist frame.* New York: Harper.

Kaplan, A. (1964). *The conduct of inquiry: Methodology for behavioral science.* San Francisco: Chandler.

Katz, D., & Braly, K. W. (1933). Racial stereotypes of 100 college students. *Journal of Abnormal and Social Psychology, 28,* 280–290.

Katz, I. (1981). *Stigma: A social psychological analysis.* Hillsdale, N.J.: Erlbaum.

Kelley, H. H. (1965). Experimental studies of threats in interpersonal negotiations. *Journal of Conflict Resolution, 9,* 79–105.

Kelley, H. H. (1967). Attribution theory in social psychology. In D. Levine (Ed.), *Nebraska symposium on motivation.* Lincoln: Univ. of Nebraska Press, 192–241.

Kelley, H. H. (1971, 1972). Causal schemata and the attribution process. In E. E. Jones, D. Kanouse, H. H. Kelley, R. E. Nisbett, S. Valins, B. Weiner. *Attribution: Perceiving the causes of behavior.* (pp. 151–174). Morristown, N.J.: General Learning.

Kelley, H. H., Shure, G. H., Deutsch, M., Faucheux, C., Lanzetta, J. T., Moscovici, S., Nutting, J. M. Jr., Rabbie, J. M., & Thibaut, J. W. (1970). A comparative experimental study of negotiation behavior. *Journal of Personality and Social Psychology, 16,* 411–438.

Kelley, H. H., & Thibaut J. W. (1954). Experimental studies of group problem solving and process. In G. Lindzey (Ed.), *Handbook of social psychology* (Vol. 2, pp. 735–785). Cambridge, Mass.: Addison-Wesley.

Kelley, H. H., & Thibaut, J. W. (1978). *Interpersonal relations: A theory of interdependence.* New York: Wiley.

Kelley, H. H., Thibaut, J. W., Radloff, R., & Mundy, D. (1962). The development of cooperation in the "minimal social situation." *Psychological Monographs, 76,* No. 19 (Whole No. 538).

Kelman, H. C. (1967). Human use of human subjects: the problem of deception in social psychological experiments. *Psychological Bulletin, 67,* 1–11.

Kelman, H. C. (1968). *A time to speak.* San Francisco: Jossey-Bass.

Kenny, D. A. (1985). Quantitative methods for social psychology. In G. Lindzey & E. Aronson (Eds.), *Handbook of social psychology* (3rd ed., Vol. I, pp. 487–508). New York: Random House.

Kerckhoff, A. C., & Back, K. W. (1968). *The junebug.* New York: Appleton-Century-Crofts.

Kimble, G. A. (1953). Psychology as a science. *Scientific Monthly.* New York, *77,* 156–160.

Klineberg, O. (1940). *Social Psychology.* New York: Henry Holt.

Krech, D., & Crutchfield, R. S. (1948). *Theory and problems of social psychology.* New York: McGraw-Hill.

Kogan, N., & Wallach, N. W. (1964). *Risk taking: A study in cognition and personality.* New York: Holt, Rinehart, Winston.

Kuhn, T. S. (1962). *The structure of scientific revolutions.* Chicago: Univ. of Chicago Press.

LaPiere, R. T. (1934). Attitudes versus actions. *Social Forces, 13,* 230–237.

Latané, B., & Darley, J. M. (1970). *The unresponsive bystander: Why doesn't he help?* New York: Appleton-Century-Crofts.

Lawrence, D. H., & Festinger, L. (1962). *Deterrents and reinforcement: The psychology of insufficient reward.* Stanford: Stanford Univ. Press.

Lecky, P. (1945). *Self-consistency: A theory of personality.* New York: Island Press.

Lepper, M. R., Greene, D., & Nisbett, R. E. (1973). Undermining children's intrinsic interests with extrinsic reward: a test of the overjustification hypothesis. *Journal of Personality and Social Psychology, 28,* 129–137.

Leventhal, H. (1980). Toward a comprehensive theory of emotion. In L. Berkowitz (Ed.), *Advances in experimental social psychology.* (Vol. 13). New York: Academic Press.

Lewin, K. (1936). *Principles of topological psychology.* New York: McGraw-Hill.

Lewin, K. (1947). Group decision and social change. In T. M. Newcomb and E. L. Hartley (Eds.), *Readings in social psychology.* New York: Henry Holt.

Lewin, K. (1951a). *Field theory in social science* (D. Cartwright, Ed.). New York: Harper & Bros.

Lewin, K. (1951b). Comments concerning psychological forces and energies, and the structure of the psyche. In D. Rapaport (Ed.), *Organization and pathology of thought* (pp. 76–94). New York: Columbia Univ. Press. (Orig. Publ. 1926).

Lewin, K., Dembo, T., Festinger, L., & Sears, P. (1944). Level of aspiration. In J. McV. Hunt (Ed.), *Personality and the behavior disorders* (pp. 333–378). New York: Ronald Press.

Lewin, K., Lippitt, R., & White, R. K. (1939). Patterns of aggressive behavior in experimentally created "social climates." *Journal of Social Psychology, 10,* 271–299.

Likert, R. (1932). A technique for the measurement of attitudes. *Archives of Psychology,* No. 140.

Linder, D. E., Cooper, J., & Jones, E. E. (1967). Decision-freedom as a determinant of the role of incentive magnitude in attitude change. *Journal of Personality and Social Psychology, 6,* 245–254.

Luce, R. D., & Raiffa, H. (1957). *Games and decisions.* New York: Wiley.

Macauley, J., & Berkowitz, L. (1970). *Altruism and helping behavior.* New York: Academic Press.

McClelland, D. C. (1951). *Personality.* New York: William Sloane.

MacCleod, R. B. (1947). The phenomenological approach to social psychology. *Psychological Review, 54,* 192–210.

McDougall, W. (1908). *An introduction to social psychology.* London: Methuen.

McDougall, W. (1920). *The group mind.* New York: Putnam's.

McGuire, W. J. (1969). The nature of attitudes and attitude change. In G. Lindzey and E. Aronson (Eds.), *Handbook of social psychology.* (2nd ed., Vol. 3, pp. 136–314). Reading, Mass.: Addison-Wesley.

Manis, J. G., & Meltzer, B. N., Eds. (1962, Rev. 1972). *Symbolic interaction.* Boston: Allyn and Bacon.

Marlowe, D., & Gergen, K. J. (1969). Personality and social interaction. In G. Lindzey and E. Aronson (Eds.), *Handbook of social psychology.* (2nd ed., Vol. 3, pp. 590–665). Reading, Mass: Addison-Wesley.

Mead, G. H. (1934). *Mind, self and society.* Chicago: Univ. of Chicago Press.

Mead, M. (1928). *Coming of age in Samoa: A psychological study in primitive youth for western civilization.* New York: Morrow.

Mead, M. (1930). *Growing up in New Guinea: A comparative education.* New York: Morrow.

Milgram S. (1963). Behavioral study of obedience. *Journal of Abnormal and Social Psychology, 67,* 371–378.

Milgram, S. (1974). *Obedience to authority.* New York: Harper & Row.

Miller, G. A., Galanter, E., & Pribram, K. H. (1960). *Plans and the structure of behavior.* New York: Holt, Rinehart, and Winston.

Miller, N. E. (1941). Frustration-aggression hypothesis. *Psychological Review, 48,* 337–342.

Miller, N. E. (1944). Experimental studies in conflict. In J. McV Hunt (Ed.), *Personality and the behavior disorder* (pp. 431–465). New York: Ronald Press.

Miller, N. E. (1948). Theory and experiment relating psychoanalytic displacement to stimulus-response generalization. *Journal of Abnormal and Social Psychology, 43,* 155–178.

Miller, N. E., & Dollard, J. (1941). *Social learning and imitation.* New Haven: Yale Univ. Press.

Mischel, W. (1968). *Personality and assessment.* New York: Wiley.

Mischel, W. (1973). Toward a cognitive social learning reconceptualization of personality. *Psychological Review, 80,* 252–283.

Mischel, W. (1977). The interaction of person and situation. In D. Magnusson and N. S. Endler (Eds.), *Personality at the crossroads: Current issues in interactional psychology.* Hillsdale, N.J.: Erlbaum.

Mischel, W., & Peake, P. K. (1982). Beyond déjà vu in the search for cross-situational consistency. *Psychological Review, 89,* 730–755.

Moore, H. T. (1921). The comparative influence of majority and expert opinion. *Journal of Psychology, 32,* 16–20.

Morrisette, J. O. (1958). An experimental study of the theory of structural balance. *Human Relations, 11,* 239–254.

Moreno, J. L. (1934). *Who shall survive?* Washington, D.C.: *Nervous and mental disease monograph,* No. 58.

Moscovici, S., & Zavalloni, M. (1969). The group as a polarizer of attitudes. *Journal of Personality and Social Psychology, 12,* 125–135.

Murchison, C., Ed. (1935). *Handbook of social psychology.* Worcester, Mass.: Clark Univ. Press.

Murphy, G., & Murphy, L. B. (1931). *Experimental social psychology.* New York: Harper.

Murphy, G., Murphy, L. B., & Newcomb, T. M. (1937). *Experimental social psychology* (rev. ed.). New York: Harper.

Murray, H. A. (1938). *Explorations in personality.* New York: Oxford Univ. Press.

Neisser, U. (1967). *Cognitive psychology.* New York: Appleton-Century-Crofts.

Nelson, C. A., & Hendrick, C. (1974). Bibliography of journal articles in social psychology. Mimeo. Kent State Univ.

Newcomb, T. M. (1951). Social psychological theory: integrating individual and social approaches. In Rohrer, J. H.,

& M. Sherif (Eds.), *Social psychology at the crossroads* (pp. 31–49). New York: Harper.

Newcomb, T. M. (1953). An approach to the study of communicative acts. *Psychological Review, 60,* 393–404.

Newcomb, T. M. (1954). Sociology and psychology. In J. Gillin (Ed.), *For a science of social man: Convergences in anthropology.* New York: Macmillan.

Newcomb, T. M. (1973). In G. Lindzey (Ed.), *A history of psychology in autobiography.* (Vol. 6). New York: Prentice- Hall.

Newtson, D. (1973). Attribution and the unit of perception of ongoing behavior. *Journal of Personality and Social Psychology, 28,* 28–38.

Newtson, D. (1976). Foundations of attribution: the perception of ongoing behavior. In J. H. Harvey, W. J. Ickes, and R. F. Kidd, (Eds.), *New directions in attribution research.* (Vol. 1). Hillsdale, N.J.: Erlbaum.

Nisbett, R. E., & Ross, L. (1980). *Human inference: strategies and shortcomings of social judgment.* Englewood Cliffs, N.J.: Prentice-Hall.

Nisbett, R. E., & Wilson, T. D. (1977). Telling more than we can know: verbal reports on mental processes. *Psychological Review, 84,* 231–259.

Orne, M. T. (1962). On the social psychology of the psychological experiment: with particular reference to demand characteristics and their implications. *American Psychologist, 17,* 776–783.

Osgood, C. E., & Tannenbaum, P. H. (1955). The principle of congruity in the prediction of attitude change. *Psychological Review, 62,* 42–55.

Ossorio, P. (1981). Foundations of descriptive psychology. In K. Davis (Ed.), *Advances in descriptive psychology.* (Vol. 1, pp. 13–135). Greenwich, Conn.: JAI Press.

Postman, L., Bruner, J. S., & McGinnies, E. (1948). Personal values as selective factors in perception. *Journal of Abnormal and Social Psychology, 43,* 142–154.

Prasad, J. A. (1950). A comparative study of rumors and reports and earthquakes. *British Journal of Psychology, 41,* 129–144.

Proshansky, H. M. (1976). Environmental psychology and the real world. *American Psychologist, 31,* 303–310.

Proshansky, H. M., & Murphy, G. (1942). The effects of reward and punishment on perception. *Journal of Psychology, 13,* 295–305.

Pruitt, D. G., & Kimmel, M. J. (1977). Twenty years of experimental gaming: critique, synthesis, and suggestions for the future. *Annual Review of Psychology, 28,* 363–392.

Radloff, R., & Bard, L. (1966). A social comparison bibliography. *Journal of Experimental Social Psychology,* Supplement *1,* 111–115.

Rapoport, A. (1970). Conflict resolution in the light of game theory and beyond. In P. Swingle (Ed.), *The structure of conflict* (pp. 1–42). New York: Academic Press.

Reisman, D. (1950). *The lonely crowd: A study of the changing American character.* New Haven: Yale Univ. Press.

Rodin, J. (1976). Menstruation, reattribution and competence. *Journal of Personality and Social Psychology, 33,* 345–353.

Rosenberg, M. J. (1965). When dissonance fails: on eliminating evaluation apprehension from attitude measurement. *Journal of Personality and Social Psychology, 1,* 28–43.

Rosenberg, M. J., Hovland, C. I., McGuire, W. J., Abelson, R. T., & Brehm, J. W. (1960). *Attitude organization and change.* New Haven: Yale Univ. Press.

Rosenthal, R. (1956). An attempt at the experimental induction of the defense mechanism of projection. Unpublished doctoral dissertation. University of California, Los Angeles.

Rosenzweig, S. (1933). The experimental situation as a psychological problem. *Psychological Review, 40,* 337–354.

Rosnow, R. L. (1981). *Paradigms in transition.* New York: Oxford Univ. Press.

Ross, E. A. (1908). *Social psychology: An outline and a source book.* New York: Macmillan.

Ross, L. (1977). The intuitive psychologist and his shortcomings: distortions in the attribution process. In L. Berkowitz (Ed.), *Advances in experimental social psychology* (Vol. 10). New York: Academic Press.

Ross, L., Rodin, J., & Zimbardo, P. (1969). Toward an attribution therapy: the reduction of fear through induced cognitive-emotional misattribution. *Journal of Personality and Social Psychology, 12,* 279–288.

Ross, M., & Fletcher, G. J. O. (1985). Attribution and social perception. In G. Lindzey & E. Aronson, (Eds.), *The handbook of social psychology,* (3rd ed., Vol. 2, pp. 73–122).

Rotter, J. B. (1954). *Social learning and clinical psychology.* Englewood Cliffs, N.J.: Prentice-Hall.

Schachter, S. (1951). Deviation, rejection, and communication. *Journal of Abnormal and Social Psychology, 46,* 190–207.

Schachter, S. (1959). *The psychology of affiliation.* Stanford: Stanford Univ. Press.

Schachter, S. (1964). The interaction of cognitive and physiological determinants of emotional state. In L. Berkowitz (Ed.), *Advances in experimental social psychology* (pp. 49–80). New York: Academic Press.

Schachter, S. (1980). Non-psychological explanations of behavior. In L. Festinger (Ed.), *Retrospections on social psychology* (pp. 131–157). New York: Oxford Univ. Press.

Schachter, S., & Singer, J. E. (1962). Cognitive, social, and physiological determinants of emotional state. *Psychological Review, 69,* 379–399.

Schafer, E., & Murphy, G. (1943). The role of autism in a visual figureground relationship. *Journal of Experimental Psychology, 32,* 335–343.

Schelling, T. C. (1960). *The strategy of conflict.* Cambridge, Mass.: Harvard Univ. Press.

Schlenker B. R. (1974). Social psychology and science. *Journal of Personality and Social Psychology, 29,* 1–15.

Schlenker, B. R. (1977). On the ethogenic approach: etiquette and revolution. In L. Berkowitz (Ed.), *Advances in experi-*

mental social psychology (Vol. 10, pp. 315–330). New York: Academic Press.

Schlenker, B. R. (1980). *Impression management.* Monterey, Calif.: Brooks/Cole.

Sechrest, L. (1976). Personality. *Annual Review of Psychology, 27,* 128.

Seligman, M. E. P. (1975). *Helplessness.* San Francisco: Freeman.

Sherif, M. (1936). *The psychology of social norms.* New York: Harper Bros.

Sherif, M. (1947). Group influences upon the formation of norms and attitudes. In T. M. Newcomb & E. L. Hartley (Eds.), *Readings in social psychology* (pp. 77–90). New York: Henry Holt.

Sherif, M., Harvey, O. J., White, B., Hood, W., & Sherif, C. (1961). *Intergroup conflict and cooperation: The robbers' cave experiment.* Norman: Institute of Group Relations, Univ. of Oklahoma.

Sherif, M., & Hovland, C. I. (1961). *Social judgment.* New Haven: Yale Univ. Press.

Sidowski, J. B. (1957). Reward and punishment in a minimal social situation. *Journal of Experimental Psychology, 54,* 318–326.

Sidowski, J. B., Wykoff, L. B., & Tabori, L. (1956). The influence of reinforcement and punishment in a minimal social situation. *Journal of Abnormal and Social Psychology, 52,* 115–119.

Sinha, D. (1952). Behavior in a catastrophic situation: a psychological study of reports and rumors. *British Journal Of Psychology, 43,* 200–209.

Skinner, B. F. (1953). *Science and human behavior.* New York: Macmillan.

Smith, M. B. (1950). The phenomenological approach in personality theory: some critical remarks. *Journal of Abnormal and Social Psychology, 45,* 516–522.

Smith, M. B. (1979). Attitudes, values, and selfhood. In H. E. Howe, Jr. and M. M. Page (Eds.), *Nebraska symposium on motivation* (pp. 305–350). Lincoln: Univ. of Nebraska Press.

Snyder, M. (1974). Self-monitoring of expressive behavior. *Journal of Personality and Social Psychology, 30,* 526–537.

Snyder, M. (1979). Self-monitoring processes. In L. Berkowitz (Ed.), *Advances in experimental social psychology* (Vol. 12) (pp. 86–128). New York: Academic Press.

Solomon, L. (1960). The influences of some types of power relationships and game strategies upon the development of interpersonal trust. *Journal of Abnormal and Social Psychology, 61,* 223–230.

Spence, K. W. (1944). The nature of theory construction in contemporary psychology. *Psychological Review, 51,* 47–68.

Spence, K. W. (1956). *Behavior theory and conditioning.* New Haven: Yale Univ. Press.

Steiner, I. D. (1974). Whatever happened to the group in social psychology? *Journal of Experimental and Social Psychology, 10,* 94–108.

Steinzor, B. (1949). The development and evaluation of a measure of social interaction. *Human Relations, 2,* 103–122.

Stoner, J. A. F. (1961). A comparison of individual and group decisions involving risk. Unpublished M.A. thesis, M.I.T.

Strodtbeck, F. L., James, R. M., & Hawkins, C. (1958). Social status in jury deliberations. In E. Maccoby, T. M. Newcomb, & E. L. Hartley (Eds.), *Readings in social psychology* (3rd ed., pp. 379–388). New York: Henry Holt.

Stryker, S. (1977). Development in "two social psychologies": toward an appreciation of mutual relevance. *Sociometry, 40,* 145–160.

Sullivan, H. S. (1947). *Conceptions of modern psychiatry.* Washington, D.C.: W. A. White Foundation.

Suls, J. M., & Miller, R. L. (Eds.) (1977). *Social comparison processes: Theoretical and empirical perspectives.* New York: Washington Hemisphere Pub. Corp.

Tanke, E. D., & Tanke, T. J. (1979). Getting off the slippery slope: social science in the judicial process. *American Psychologist, 34,* 1130–1138.

Taylor, S. E. (1978). A developing role for social psychology in medicine and medical practice. *Personality and Social Psychology Bulletin, 4,* 515–523.

Teger, A. I., & Pruitt, D. G. (1967). Components of group risk taking. *Journal of Social Psychology, 3,* 189–205.

Thibaut, J. W., & Kelley, H. H. (1959). *The social psychology of groups.* New York: Wiley.

Thibaut, J. W., Riecken, H. W. (1955). Some determinants and consequences of the perception of social causality. *Journal of Personality, 24,* 113–133.

Thibaut, J. W., & Walker, L. (1975). *Procedural justice: A psychological analysis.* Hillside, N.J.: Erlbaum.

Thomas, D. (1933). An attempt to develop precise measurement in the social behavior field. *Sociologus, 9,* 1–21.

Thomson, R. (1968). *The Pelican history of psychology.* Baltimore: Penguin.

Thomas, W. I., & Thomas, D. S. (1928). *The child in America: Behavior problems and programs.* New York: Knopf.

Thomas, W. I., & Znaniecki, F. (1918–1920). *The Polish peasant in Europe and America* (5 vols.). Boston: Badger.

Thurstone, L. L., & Chave, E. J. (1929). *The measurement of attitude.* Chicago: Univ. of Chicago Press.

Tomkins, S. S. (1981). The quest for primary motives: biography and autobiography of an idea. *Journal of Personality and Social Psychology, 41,* 306–329.

Triplett, N. (1898). The dynamogenic factors in pacemaking and competition. *American Journal of Psychology, 9,* 507–533.

Tversky, A., & Kahneman, D. (1974). Judgment under uncertainty: heuristics and biases. *Science, 185,* 1124–1131.

Von Neumann, J., & Morgenstern, O. (1944). *The theory of games and economic behavior.* Princeton: Princeton Univ. Press.

Walster, E. (1965). The effect of self-esteem on romantic liking. *Journal of Experimental Social Psychology, 1,* 184–198.

Watson, J. B. (1925). *Behaviorism.* New York: Norton.

Weick, K. E. (1968). Systematic observational methods. In G. Lindzey and E. Aronson (Eds.), *Handbook of social psychology* (Vol. 2, 2nd ed., pp. 357–451). Reading, Mass.: Addison-Wesley.

Weiner, B. (1974). *Achievement motivation and attribution theory.* Morristown, N.J.: General Learning.

West, S. G., & Wicklund, R. A. (1980). *A primer of social psychological theories.* Monterey, Calif.: Brooks/Cole.

Wicklund, R. A., & Brehm, J. W. (1976). *Perspectives on cognitive dissonance.* Hillsdale, N.J.: Erlbaum.

Wishner, J. (1960). Reanalysis of "impressions of personality." *Psychological Review, 67,* 96–112.

Worchel, S. & Cooper, J. (1979). *Understanding social psychology.* Homewood, Ill.: Dorsey Press.

Wortman, C. B., & Dintzer, L. (1978). Is an attributional analysis of the learned helplessness phenomenon viable?: a critique of the Abramson-Seligman-Teasdale reformulation. *Journal of Abnormal Psychology, 87,* 75–90.

Zajonc, R. B. (1965). Social facilitation. *Science, 149,* 269–274.

Zajonc, R. B. (1980). Feeling and thinking: preferences need no inferences. *American Psychologist, 35,* 151–175.

Zajonc, R. B. (1980). Cognition and social cognition: a historical perspective. In L. Festinger (Ed.), *Retrospections on social psychology.* (pp. 180–204). New York: Oxford Univ. Press.

Zanna, M. P., & Cooper, J. (1974). Dissonance and the pill: an attribution approach to studying the arousal properties of dissonance. *Journal of Personality and Social Psychology, 29,* 703–709.

Zeigarnik, B. (1927). Uber das leehalten von Erledigten und unerleighten Handbegen. *Psycholische Forschung, 9,* 1–85.

CHAPTER TWO

THE SOCIAL BEING IN SOCIAL PSYCHOLOGY

SHELLEY E. TAYLOR, *University of California, Los Angeles*

What is the essence of the social being? This question has been at the core of social psychological theory and research since the inception of the field. The answer to it has varied at different points in time, and those variations reflect fundamental differences in the theories we have articulated, the research we have conducted, and the methodologies we have used. Understanding how social psychologists conceptualize the social being necessitates a historical tour of the field. At each theoretical juncture in the field, the view of the person that has emerged has taken somewhat different form. As such, the person becomes a screen onto which theoretical concerns and tenets are projected.

To illustrate this point, consider the statement, "To understand the person, one must understand———?" At various points in social psychology's history, the majority of researchers might have answered that question somewhat differently. A reader of one of the first social psychology texts in the field (McDougall, 1908) would have completed that blank with the word "instinct." Had one participated in the exciting and dominant group dynamics movement of the late 1940s and 1950s, one might have completed that

The author gratefully acknowledges the helpful comments and suggestions of Jack Brehm, Barry Collins, Susan Fiske, Dan Gilbert, Curtis Hardin, Anne Peplau, and David Sears on an earlier draft. Preparation of this chapter was facilitated by research grants from the National Institute of Mental Health (MH 42152) and the National Science Foundation (SBR-9507642). Correspondence should be addressed to taylors@psych.ucla.edu or to the author at the Department of Psychology, Franz Hall, University of California, Los Angeles, Los Angeles, CA 90095-1563.

sentence with the phrase "the social group." One can imagine filling in the blank with "socialization," had one been a follower of Adorno, Frenkel-Brunswik, and the school of F scale researchers at Berkeley following World War II (Adorno et al., 1950). With the ascendance of the cognitive viewpoint in social psychology, and its effort to identify how people represent themselves and the social world, we might have seen the sentence completed with the phrase "cognitive processes." And, given a plethora of images of the person that predominate in social psychology at the present time, we might expect to see many of these phrase completions, as well as two additional ones: "culture" and "biology." Thus, the vision of the person may assume quite different form, depending upon the metatheoretical lens through which the individual is viewed.

Despite the manifold ways in which social psychology has viewed the person, there are at least two assertions on which we have achieved some consensus. The first is that individual behavior is strongly influenced by the environment, especially the social environment (cf. Ross & Nisbett, 1991). The person does not function in an individualistic vacuum, but in a social context that influences thought, feeling, and action. The second point of consensus is that the individual actively construes social situations. We do not respond to environments as they are but as we interpret them to be. But beyond these two points of near-unanimity—the force of the social environment and the importance of the perceiver's active construction of social experience—there is considerable diversity in the views of the social being that have predominated at different times in social psychology's history.

Understanding conceptualizations of the social being through the history of social psychology necessitates consideration not only of the predominant viewpoints that have ebbed and flowed in response to theoretical developments, but also a recognition of those vantage points that have not held sway in social psychology's view of the person. In particular, two formulations, otherwise highly influential in psychology's history, have had a more limited impact on how social psychologists conceive of the person. First, the psychoanalytic perspective offered by Freud and his disciples has, for the most part, not been a predominant theoretical vision in social psychology. No elaborated view of the individual as reacting to powerful, unconscious motives and influences, the product of early childhood conflicts and experience, has emerged as a formally articulated vision in the field.

This is not to say that Freudian conceptualizations and insights have had no impact. Psychoanalytic principles, such as identification, regression, defense mechanisms, and the unconscious were explicitly incorporated into research on the motivational and defensive processes observed in group life by certain of the group dynamics theorists (e.g., Bach, 1954; Bales, 1970; Scheidlinger, 1952; Stock & Thelen, 1958). Theory and research on the authoritarian personality was heavily influenced by the psychoanalytic perspective (Adorno et al., 1950). Research on aggression drew on psychoanalytic explanatory principles (see Geen, 1998, in this *Handbook*), such as the relation of frustration to aggression (Dollard et al., 1939; Hovland, Janis, & Kelley, 1953). The catharsis hypothesis, which has spawned social psychological work on aggression (e.g., Feshbach, 1955; Konecni & Ebbesen, 1976), and on the effects of physiology on illness (Pennebaker, 1985) owes its origins to psychoanalytic thinking. However, despite the fact that certain concepts from the Freudian tradition have appeared in the exploration of phenomena in social psychology, a formal articulated vision of the person from a psychoanalytic perspective has never taken root within the field.

Likewise, behaviorism (Watson, 1930) that so dominated psychology in the 1920s and 1930s did not find as strong a foothold in social psychology. In identifying overt behavior and not subjective states, such as thoughts or feelings, as legitimate objects of study, the fundamental principles of behaviorism were at odds with the social psychological perspective. With some exceptions (Bem, 1967; see Krech & Crutchfield, 1948; Hovland et al., 1953), social psychology's view of the person has virtually always regarded internal experience and active construal as important forces in how individuals behave in social situations. While one can argue that behaviorism had a methodological impact on the field, by focusing us on observable behavior as opposed to relying on introspective methods, its theoretical impact was more modest. The failure of psychoanalytic theory and of behaviorism to gain precedence in social psychology is not surprising, given the two points on which, as noted earlier, social psychologists have

achieved some consensus. The belief that situational forces strongly determine individual behavior is inherently in conflict with a Freudian analysis, and an emphasis on the person as actively construing the environment virtually precludes the behaviorist perspective.

In this essay, I will trace the historical development of social psychology with an emphasis on the view of the person that has emerged. In so doing, I will suggest that the image of the person has resulted not only from the particular theoretical and metatheoretical positions that have been in ascendance in the field at any given point in time but also from at least two other factors that inadvertently and implicitly shape the view of the person: the research methods in favor at a particular time, and our relation to the other sciences, especially the other social sciences. With these perspectives in mind, I will then turn to the questions, What view of the person do we hold at the present time in social psychology? Are there ways in which our current viewpoint may be incomplete? and How have we progressed beyond the initial visions of the person?

The Ancient Practice of Social Psychology

Many regard Aristotle as the first social psychologist. Whereas Plato maintained that people form social groups because they serve utilitarian functions, Aristotle regarded the person's nature as inherently social. People, he maintained, are by nature gregarious, desiring to affiliate with others and to live collectively. Thus, Aristotle reasoned, to understand human behavior, one must be fundamentally attuned to the social environment and its impact on people.

Breaking with philosophical traditions of the past, Aristotle maintained that personality and other dispositional qualities are inadequate explanations of people's actions. Like other Grecian philosophers of his age, Aristotle had been taught that physical constitution and temperament may be understood with reference to the circulating fluids of the body and their relations to each other. Specific personality types were believed to be associated with bodily states in which different humors predominated. Aristotle questioned the value of such an approach on two grounds. First, he observed that the environment exerts potent effects on individual behavior, a fact not easily explained by the humoral theory of temperament. Second, he noted that individuals show high degrees of both intraindividual and interindividual variability in their behavior. As such, he reasoned that human behavior may best be understood as the product of the joint influence of temperament and situational qualities.

Aristotle may also be credited with being among the first to achieve the second basic insight of social psychology, namely, that how individuals construe situations influences their responses to them. In particular, he emphasized the importance of personal goals in how people construct and behave in situations. He believed that the overarching goal of the human being is the achievement of happiness. Happiness, in turn, Aristotle argued, was achieved by fulfilling our primary life function: to reason. A happy life, according to Aristotle, is a life governed by reason.

In his articulation of the social being, Aristotle foreshadowed several themes that would become important in the view of the person in social psychology. First, he emphasized the importance of the environment, or situational forces, the sine qua non of the field. At the same time, however, he ascribed to the person an active role, rather than a reactive one. He regarded the person not as the pawn of situational forces but as an active participant who sought to achieve goals within the context of a social and physical environment that encouraged or impeded purposeful action. A survey of recent empirical contributions to social psychology reveals that we have returned to a view of the person as fundamentally concerned with goals and the situations that enable him or her to achieve them (Fiske, 1992). The importance Aristotle ascribed to reason is, in important respects, a foreshadowing of the rise of the cognitive perspective within social psychology. As will be seen, such questions as, "Are people rational?" and "Can we understand human thought in terms of its correspondence to and deviations from rational standards of human inference?" have been focal concerns recently in social psychology (Fiske & Taylor, 1991; Nisbett and Ross, 1980); and in the social sciences more generally (*The Economist,* 1994).

With an Aristotelian anchor in place, we now turn to more contemporary origins of social psychology. Although other philosophical traditions have profoundly influenced social psychological thinking, such as the Gestaltists, the German introspectionists, and the writings of Immanuel Kant, we will examine these viewpoints in the context of the particular images of the person that emerged from social psychological theory. We now turn to the explicit formulation of social psychology that began in the 1930s and that shaped itself into a distinct field in the 1940s.

THE INDIVIDUAL IN THE SOCIAL GROUP: LEWIN AND THE GROUP DYNAMICS TRADITION

The father of modern social psychology is generally acknowledged to be Kurt Lewin. The vision that Lewin articulated for the field placed the active social perceiver squarely at the forefront of human behavior. Credited with the statement, "There is nothing so practical as a good theory,"[1] Lewin developed field theory, a quasi-mathematical model of forces in the field designed to predict behavior and behavior change in response to changes in various environmental forces; he was especially concerned with the ways in which people select their goals and go about implementing them.

Although Lewin's initial investigations pursued field theory from the standpoint of individual behavior, he became increasingly intrigued by interpersonal relationships and the developing group dynamics movement. Interest in group dynamics had been brewing within social psychology since the 1930s. Muzafer Sherif's (1936) book, *The Psychology of Social Norms,* which was heavily responsible for this interest, provided a systematic theoretical account of how social norms develop and the ways in which they influence people. According to Sherif, the social norm is a product of social interaction that acts as a social stimulus on individuals who are members of the groups that hold such norms. Drawing upon the importance of the frame of reference that an individual brings to a situation, Sherif suggested that, even in the most ambiguous and unstable of situations, group norms may evolve.

This analysis, in turn, gave rise to his ingenious research on the autokinetic effect: if an individual looks at a stationary point of light in a dark room, he or she will come to see it moving. Sherif first established that individuals vary in the range of movement that they ascribe to such stimuli, achieving a degree of perceptual stability in an unstable environment. He then demonstrated that, with groups of participants, individual ranges of judgment converge to a group range that is distinctive to the particular group. This convergence to a group norm occurs even when an individual's range has been established by prior experience with the phenomenon. And, most important, when returned to an individual state, the group member carries with him or her the established group norm that now dictates individual perceptions imposed on the unstable perceptual situation. By extracting social norms from the social situations in which they usually arise and investigating them in the context of an experiment on perception, Sherif (1936) was able to establish clearly their potency and the fact that they arise in group situations. This observation prompted his view that there is a factual psychological basis to the insight that new qualities that transcend the individual arise from group situations.

Theodore Newcomb's (1943) studies in the late 1930s also investigated the impact of the social group on the individual, using the political and social culture of Bennington College. His exploration of this natural setting demonstrated the important ways in which the college community changed the attitudes of its initially conservative freshmen college students and how such attitude change was implicitly rewarded. Students who most clearly embodied and espoused the liberal attitudes in ascendance at Bennington at the time were most likely to be named to political office and perceived as "most worthy to represent the college at an intercollegiate gathering" by their peers. Thus, Newcomb was able to demonstrate that individual attitudes are strongly determined by the groups to which one belongs or the groups to which one aspires. The degree of group influence on an individual depends on the relation of the individual to that group, and groups evaluate their members based, in part, upon adherence to group norms. These important insights were elaborated upon in naturalistic investigations, such as William F. Whyte's (1943) investigations of the structure, culture, and functioning of gangs and clubs in the "streetcorner society" of Boston in the late 1930s.

Group Dynamics

The field of group dynamics was formalized in the late 1930s and early 1940s, and credit for developing this distinct field of investigation is generally accorded to Lewin (Cartwright & Zander, 1953). Lewin popularized the term, "group dynamics," and in 1945, he helped establish the first research organization explicitly devoted to research on group dynamics at MIT. There he joined forces with Lippett, Cartwright, Festinger, and Yarrow to spawn what was to become a major force in social psychology for two decades. Reflecting this legacy, Lewin's concern with the small face-to-face group represented more than an empirical interest in group processes. It embodied his view of the person. He regarded the group as a potent agent of socialization:

> It is easier to affect deeply the personality of ten people if they can be melded into a group than to affect the personality of any one individual treated separately (Lewin, 1943, p. 115).

He believed that social psychology's mission should be to study small face-to-face groups as the transmitters of social and cultural knowledge and norms. Thus, Lewin's view of the social being placed the individual squarely in a cultural and social context. Focusing on the small group level as his empirical point of departure was, in part, a tactical decision, because he regarded the group level as most promising for enabling one to understand how large-scale cultural forces shape individuals' lives (see Bargal, Gold, & Lewin, 1992).

The impact of the Lewinian vision of the person was substantial. His view that social groups represent the point at which the influence of social forces on individuals may best be viewed was incorporated into research on group dynamics. Reviewed in the classic volume, *Group Dynamics: Research and Theory,* the field of group dynamics was "dedicated to achieving knowledge about the nature of groups, the laws of their development, and their interrelations with individuals, other groups, and larger institutions" (Cartwright & Zander, 1953, p. 4). This highly influential empirical effort was concerned not only with clarifying the nature of social forces on the individual, but of locating social psychology fundamentally within the social sciences as a whole, with the goal of improving the functioning of groups and their consequences for individuals and society. Explicit in this vision were the ties that social psychological work on group dynamics would have, not only to the academic fields of sociology, anthropology, economics, and political science, but to the applied fields of social work, group psychotherapy, education, management science, public health, the military, religion, education, and community organizations, among others.

Lewin's empirical contributions to the group dynamics traditions began with his work with Lippett and White on styles of leadership. Prompted by their rising concern over the emerging, powerful dictatorships taking hold in Europe during the late 1930s and 1940s, these investigators explored the empirical question, What is good leadership? By creating small groups of ten- and eleven-year-old children and assigning leaders who embodied particular leadership styles, this work sought to characterize the impact of democratic, autocratic, and laissez-faire leadership styles on the behavior of followers. A wealth of empirical findings emerged. For example, groups that performed tasks under autocratic leaders tended to show scapegoating and more aggressive, destructive behavior, at least under some circumstances, compared with those in laissez-faire or democratic styles. The goal of the work was "to create setups which would give insight into the underlying group dynamics" (Lewin, 1948, p. 74), to create a body of knowledge that would be useful for understanding family life, work groups, classrooms, committees, military units, and community groups. As such, Lewin recognized the leap that had to be made from the empirical work in his naturalistic laboratory to the settings to which he wished to generalize the leadership style findings. Consequently, he kept his empirical investigations naturalistic and unconstrained, so as to make those links evident. From this early work, Lewin envisioned a coherent body of empirical knowledge about the nature of group life that would apply across a diverse array of settings.

The political origins and implications of the leadership style research were not an incidental aspect of the work. Lewin regarded social psychological research as a set of tools by which the important political and social phenomena of the day could be objectively investigated. The concern he and his colleagues shared over the dictatorships of Hitler and Mussolini was the impetus for seeking to demonstrate that democracy was an inherently superior form of leadership that would produce higher morale and greater productivity than an autocratic style. The findings emerged as predicted, although a close examination of the methodology of the studies suggests that, given the guidelines offered to the democratic and the autocratic leaders, one could not have expected any other results.[2] Nonetheless, the work was a landmark in bringing social science methods to the study of political systems and for producing a coherent pattern of empirical results concerning the impact of leadership style.

Following this initial work were systematic experimental investigations of group membership (e.g., Siegel & Siegel, 1957); group cohesiveness, including the impact of external danger (Cartwright, 1968; Janis, 1963); pressures to uniformity exerted and experienced in group situations (e.g., Festinger, Schachter, & Back, 1953; Schachter, 1951); ways in which power and influence are created and used in group situations (e.g., French & Raven, 1959); motivational processes in groups, including risk-taking (Wallach, Kogan, & Bem, 1962) and cooperation/competition (Deutsch, 1960); and structural properties of groups and their impact on communication and task performance (e.g., Bavelas, 1950).

As already noted, the view of the person that emerged from these investigations was as the recipient of culture mediated by the small groups of which the individual was a member. But what was the essence of the person in the context of the small group? At least two sharply contrasting viewpoints historically characterized the relation between the individual and the social group. One viewpoint maintained that, alone, the person is weak, imperfect, and sometimes evil; social organization is needed both to control individual, aggressive, selfish impulses and to achieve outcomes that a single individual alone cannot achieve. As such, social groups act as a moderating influence on individual nature (Freud, 1930/1961; see Cartwright & Zander, 1953). A contrasting viewpoint conceptualized group life as inherently aggressive and destructive, bringing about the conditions that remove individual concerns about morality and appropriate behavior in favor of a more lawless behavior (e.g., Le Bon, 1896; see also Zimbardo, 1970). This viewpoint owes its origins to Le Bon's (1896) analysis of "the crowd," in which he argued that mob behavior is infectious. According to Le Bon, such social contagion leads people to commit violent and immoral acts that would otherwise be unacceptable to individuals and to society. In both these extreme viewpoints, individual nature and social groups were represented as foils for each other, the one representing the countervailing force against the other. The empirical legacy of the group dynamics tradition helped to put the extreme form of both these viewpoints to rest. It made clear that groups are powerful forces that have important consequences for individual identity and behavior, yet it showed that the group is neither intrinsically good or bad; nor, by implication, is the individual.

The group dynamics tradition in social psychology did more than furnish a view of the individual that derived from his or her membership in social groups. It also established a methodological tradition, exploring group dynamics and their impact on the individual in a wide variety of settings, ranging from naturalistic social groups to the experimental manipulation of variables in laboratory settings. The use of naturalistic settings stemmed from two beliefs: first, a sense that individual behavior can be well understood when it is examined in circumstances that approximate the natural conditions in which it occurs and, second, a guiding belief that the mission of social psychology is to shed light on important social problems of the day, including war, social injustice, and discrimination. Under many conditions, the creation of naturalistic conditions (such as those found in the Lewin, Lippett, and White leadership research) made these extrapolations to social problems clear.

But the reliance on experimental methods was equally important, enabling the scientist to extract phenomena from the real world, manipulate them in the laboratory, and identify general rules of individual and social functioning. In addition to his seminal role in the content of social psychology, Lewin is considered the father of experimentation in social psychology, having written extensively about the value of the experiment as a vehicle for creating the forces one wishes to study in a microcosm. Lewin felt that through laboratory experimentation, it would be possible to establish principles of human behavior scientifically that would, in turn, generalize to a wide variety of situations and subsequently provide the basis for social change. Thus, the group dynamics tradition embodied a richness of methodologies. Converging insights from this diverse array of methodologies were believed to provide the best empirical foundation for an understanding of group life. We will return to this methodological legacy.

Finally, it is useful to make explicit the group dynamics vision of where social psychology fits into the sciences as a whole. Lewin and the other group dynamics researchers clearly saw themselves as social scientists, part of a larger endeavor fed by sociology, anthropology, political science, and economics.[3] In concert, Lewin believed, these disciplines would illuminate the practical workings of social groups, while simultaneously working cooperatively to solve social problems.

Social Comparison Processes

The early group dynamics tradition was concerned primarily with establishing the realities of group life and the impact of that group life on individuals' attitudes and behavior (see Cialdini & Trost, 1998, in this *Handbook*). As Kelley (1952) noted, however, there are two important functions of a group: a normative function that helps to establish personal standards and a comparison function that leads to personal evaluation. This very important insight contributed to the second major empirical legacy of the group dynamics tradition, namely, research on the social bases of self-knowledge. Recognition of the comparative function of social groups established the centrality of group life as a source of self-understanding, as well as a source of guidelines for appropriate behavior.

In 1954, Leon Festinger developed social comparison theory which maintained that people are motivated to have stable, accurate appraisals of themselves, including their abilities, opinions, and outcomes. According to the theory, although generally people prefer to evaluate themselves using objective and nonsocial standards, if such information is unavailable to them, they will compare themselves using social information, namely, information about or from other people. Originally, the theory stipulated that the preferred source for social comparison is a person who is similar to the self on the ability, opinion, or outcome in question. Comparison with a similar other is maximally informative, according to the theory, because it provides an individual with a more precise, stable evaluation than would comparison with someone who is very different.

Early social comparison research was heavily concerned with self-evaluation processes, namely, the ways in which people evaluate the appropriateness of their abilities, opinions, and emotions. This emphasis derived primarily from the fact that the origins of social comparison theory were group processes, and, thus, much of social comparison theory was formulated from the standpoint of a person in a social group attempting to evaluate the self and the appropriateness of his or her behavior (Festinger, 1954). Schachter's (1959) subsequent studies of affiliation, also a product of the group dynamics tradition, further extended the importance of social comparison processes to the understanding of how people interpret their internal states, namely, emotional reactions to situations. In a series of experimental investigations, Schachter was able to show that, under threatening circumstances, among many people, there is a preference to affiliate with similar others in order to compare their own feelings and reactions.

Thibaut and Kelley (1959) took the social nature of the individual a step further in maintaining that the dyad, and not the individual, is the basic unit of social psychology. Their writings also extended the comparison function of social relationships to the understanding of how individuals evaluate their circumstances and choose to remain in them or to leave them as a function of the alternatives available to them. In particular, they specified the importance of comparison level (the nature and quality of outcomes an individual believes he or she deserves) and comparison level for alternatives (the degree to which an individual perceives alternative situations that are better or worse than the current situation). Comparison level enables one to evaluate one's outcomes and determines the satisfaction one experiences in a relationship. The alternative outcomes that one might achieve, the comparison level for alternatives, function as bases for deciding whether to remain in a particular relationship or to abandon a current situation in favor of a more desirable alternative.

The other social sciences were exploring related concepts at the same time. Within sociology, concern with the referent function and knowledge function of social groups led to the development of several important theoretical perspectives (Pettigrew, 1967). These included Hyman's (1942) and Merton's (1957) theory of reference groups, Stouffer's (Stouffer et al., 1949) principle of relative deprivation (see Davis, 1959), and Homans' (1961, 1965) concepts of exchange and distributive justice, among others. These theoretical and empirical traditions clarified when social groups and larger social categories come to be regarded as reference groups and provide bases for evaluations of one's outcomes. For example, Stouffer's (Stouffer et al., 1949) studies of the American soldier established the underlying comparative bases of many important phenomena in Army life. He demonstrated the paradoxical finding that air corpsmen, whose promotions were typically rapid, were less satisfied with their chances for promotion than military police, whose promotions were infrequent. The high aspirations generated by the promotion policy within the Air Corps produced greater frustration than was true among the military police, where there was high morale despite the few individual advances that were achieved. Such findings led to the general principle that it is not one's absolute level of attainment, but the discrepancy between one's socially derived expectations and one's attainments that account for satisfaction with outcomes.

The significance of social comparison processes for the view of the person in social psychology is considerable. Such a perspective makes explicit the fact that the influence of the social environment on the individual is pervasive and substantial. Not only does it largely dictate norms that constitute guidelines for behavior, but it is also an important source of self-knowledge and of knowledge critical to the evaluation of outcomes, emotions, abilities, and opinions. Moreover, social comparison processes help to define parameters of individual change, generating predictions concerning when an individual will abandon a current situation in favor of an alternative one. Finally, by establishing that the social environment provides bases for self-evaluation and evaluation of potential alternatives, research on social comparison and related processes also provides a context for understanding how the individual carries around social groups in the head from situation to situation, without those groups being physically present in face-to-face situations. Thus, only with the articulation of both the referent principle and the comparison principle do we fully appreciate the vision of the social group predominant in social psychology at this time: individual self-knowledge does not exist in a vacuum but is largely a social product.

INDIVIDUAL DIFFERENCES IN SOCIAL PSYCHOLOGY: AN HISTORICAL PERSPECTIVE

While group dynamics theorists were developing their vision of the individual in the social group, a team of researchers at the University of California, Berkeley was articulating an individual difference view of the social being that was to have a profound influence on social psychological investigations during the 1950s, namely, research on the authoritarian personality. On the surface, research on the authoritarian personality could not have been more different from the group dynamics perspective. Originating jointly in the psychoanalytic perspective on the individual and Marxist analyses of the effects of class structure on individual behavior, it put forth a social psychological view of personality that regarded the person's behavior as a result of stable individual differences in behavioral predispositions brought about by stabilities in the social environment. The authoritarian personality (Adorno et al., 1950) was said to be characterized by an exaggerated need to submit to strong authority, rigid adherence to conventional patterns of behavior, a commitment to harsh punishment for deviant behavior, and generalized hostility. It was believed to derive from early personality conflicts and a mystical, superstitious cast of mind. Authoritarianism was measured by a scale (the Fascism or F scale), and individual differences in scores were used to predict behavior in social situations. Despite apparent differences between the authoritarian personality line of work and research on group dynamics, the perspectives are more compatible than might first appear and have become increasingly so over the years (Altemeyer, 1988).

The authoritarian personality was a conceptual analysis developed by Adorno, Frenkel-Brunswik, and their colleagues (Adorno et al., 1950), who had fled from Germany during World War II, ultimately to settle at the University of California, Berkeley. The impetus for their vision of the person was an effort to understand the factors that could lead individuals in a country to embrace an authoritarian political movement like Nazism. Authoritarian personality researchers argued that there are reliable individual differences in authoritarianism that can be traced directly to culture. The lynchpin of their analysis was the socialization practices that exist within a culture and the degree to which they emphasize obedience to authority. Adorno and his colleagues implied that a particular pattern of child-rearing practices, those embodied by German socialization norms of the time, would make for a personality constellation marked by commitment to authority. Over the years, research on authoritarianism has evolved explicitly into viewing this individual difference as a function of socialization (Altemeyer, 1988). That is, social learning from parents and peers and lack of experience with nonconventional people or minorities, it is hypothesized, lead individuals to need to submit to a strong, established, legitimate authority, with the result that their behavior is marked by a high degree of conventionalism and adherence to standard social conventions.

In essence, the analysis of the authoritarian personality

was a social psychological one. It argued that, given culturally based child-rearing practices that lead to natural propensities toward accepting authority, if a situation evolves that is conducive to the rise of an authoritarian figure like Hitler, the personality dynamics would be in place for the development of a scenario like Nazi Germany. This fundamentally interactionist view of the individual difference–environment interface is representative of how social psychologists have historically thought about individual differences, and it contrasts somewhat with a more traditional emphasis on individual differences within personality research. The effects of authoritarianism were regarded as critically moderated by situational factors. In an environment or society in which authoritarianism would have little relevance to expected patterns of behavior, this predisposition might remain latent. But in environmental and societal circumstances that fostered authoritarianism, individual differences in authoritarianism would importantly moderate how individuals construe situations and their behavioral responses to them.

Note how similar this vision of the person is to that articulated by Lewin. Although Lewin emphasized the small group as the transmitter of culture, and F scale researchers emphasized individual differences that evolve in response to socialization, both regarded the individual as embedded in a cultural and social context, with behavior resulting from the joint product of individual predispositions and the evolving environment. There are two additional points of surprising commonality between the group dynamics perspective and research on the authoritarian personality. Like the group dynamics tradition, research employing the F scale made use of a variety of methodological techniques, with a heavy emphasis on behavior in naturalistic settings. And, like the group dynamics tradition, research on the authoritarian personality was concerned with fundamental social problems such as prejudice and discrimination. The view of both traditions was that, together with the other social sciences, social psychology could provide an important perspective, perhaps even a partial solution, to these important social issues.

The impact of research on the authoritarian personality on social psychology was dramatic. Large numbers of Ph.D. dissertations in social psychology completed during the 1950s included the F scale as an individual difference measure. Some of its popularity may have been a direct effect of the zeitgeist that favored such work or a tactical expectation that an individual difference result would emerge, making the dissertation an acceptable product. In so doing, this work somewhat obscured the initial social psychological viewpoint of personality as resulting from the confluence of socialization and cultural forces. Once authoritarianism could be measured via the F scale, investigators fell into more conventional individual difference research, and the social psychological context of the original work and the view that personality predispositions are engaged (or not) by situational conditions faded from view.[4]

LEARNING THEORY APPROACHES IN SOCIAL PSYCHOLOGY

As research on the authoritarian personality implies, the social psychological perspective on socialization has been concerned with how individuals learn and acquire patterns of social behavior through principles elucidated by classical and operant conditioning paradigms. As such, as has been true for virtually all areas of psychology, social psychology has been heavily influenced by learning theory. In its basic form, learning theory maintains that a person's current behavior is determined by prior learning, which occurs by virtue of simple principles of association, repetition, and reinforcement (Lorge, 1936; Hovland et al., 1953). The individual learns certain behaviors which, over time, may become habits. To the extent that this is true, if an individual is presented with the same situation, he or she tends to respond in the same way. In classical conditioning, one acquires attitudes and preferences by virtue of association. For example, if we learn to associate the Ku Klux Klan with hate crimes, then we come to believe that the Ku Klux Klan is bad. The second fundamental learning mechanism, elucidated by operant conditioning research, is the principle of reinforcement: a person learns to perform a particular behavior because it is followed by something pleasurable or need-satisfying. A child may learn to help others because her parents praise her when she shares or helps with family chores.

Where has the learning theory perspective been most influential in social psychology? The earliest and clearest example of a learning theory perspective in social psychology was Hovland, Janis, and Kelley's (1953) analysis of attitudes. The Yale program on attitudes and attitude change, as it was called, was not initially designed to build theory, but rather, largely represented an application of the basic principles and technology of learning theory to attitude research. Attitudes were regarded as subject to the same forces as other habits. Just as other kinds of learning occur as a consequence of association, repetition, and reinforcement, so the learning of attitudes and their change may be similarly understood. The assumption was that attitudes, like other habits, persist unless the individual undergoes some new learning experience, which typically occurs in the form of exposure to a persuasive communication. Depending upon the characteristics of that communication, the individual may or may not accept the new opinion. Acceptance of a counterattitudinal communication was hypothesized to depend upon the source of the communication, the setting in which the person is exposed to the communication, the nature of the communication stimuli,

and the qualities of the target. A substantial empirical legacy that explored these parameters of the attitude change situation resulted from this formulation.

In the original learning theory viewpoint, the person was represented as a relatively passive participant in the persuasion process, exposed to stimuli that vary in particular ways, that subsequently determine whether or not a new attitude is formed or an old attitude is changed. It posits a somewhat mechanistic process with a minimal role of the social perceiver as active in the attitude change process. Despite this view of the person, the empirical conclusions reached by the Yale group stood up remarkably well over time. This may have occurred largely because the program of research generated by the learning theory perspective was strongly empirically based, with individual studies of specific phenomena building incrementally on those that preceded them. The research legacy did not depend upon untested theoretical assumptions.

Nonetheless, the emphasis of learning theory on the individual as a passive recipient of information was inherently limited. Persuasion was conceptualized as something that is done to a person. Attitudes were assumed to be formed or changed through a simple process of transfer of affect by pairing one stimulus, namely, an attitudinal communication, with another already-valenced stimulus, such as an attractive source. Attitude researchers now know that successful persuasion depends in important ways on the involvement of the individual, the types of cognitive responses that an individual generates to an intended persuasive communication (Petty & Cacioppo, 1986), and other, more active processes (see Petty & Wegener, 1998, in this *Handbook*). Another flaw in the learning theory analysis was its emphasis on the importance of retention of a counterattitudinal communication, achieved through repetition. It was assumed that, if information gets into the cognitive system and "sticks," that is, it can be recalled by an individual, there should be enduring effects of persuasive communication. It is now established that explicit memory bears an irregular relation to persuasion. People can often recall the details of an argument quite well and, nonetheless, find it to be unacceptable. Thus, the paradoxical effect of the learning theory perspective in attitude research was to demonstrate that the person, as a target of persuasion, is not a passive participant in the process but an active one.

Learning theory was influential in other areas of social psychological investigation as well. For example, in the arena of interpersonal attraction, Byrne and Clore (Byrne, 1971; Byrne & Clore, 1970; Clore & Byrne, 1974) proposed that attraction largely parallels a process of classical conditioning. They suggested that, when an originally neutral stimulus (e.g., a new roommate) is repeatedly paired with a valenced stimulus (such as a compliment), the neutral stimulus begins to elicit a positive affective response. Moreover, affect should generalize to the circumstances in which the condition occurs. One of the most enduring empirical traditions from the learning theory approach to interpersonal attraction is research on similarity and attraction. Specifically, it was argued that another person's similarity to the self is reinforcing, and thus pairing of similar attitudes with an initially neutral individual will lead to conditioning, such that high levels of similarity will produce positive affective responses; likewise, dissimilarity or high levels of disagreement in opinions will lead to negative reactions to another person. Critics have argued that the learning theory model of interpersonal attraction is too simple to pertain in complex, realistic situations (Murstein, 1971), and research revealed that some of the predictions are importantly moderated by other factors (Aronson & Linder, 1965). Moreover, the learning theory approach failed to take adequate account of the interdependence that exists between individuals in a relationship (Kelley & Thibaut, 1978). Thus, although its empirical legacy was impressive, it created a vision of interpersonal relations that primarily addressed superficial or initial stages of relationships; ultimately, it was at odds with the increasing complexity of the developing view of the person as actively constructing experience and as social in nature.

The failure of traditional learning theory to be an enduring theoretical position within social psychology may derive from three factors. First, learning theory located the causes of individual behavior largely in the learning history of the individual. To a large extent, then, the current situation was deemed less important than the past experience an individual brought to a situation. Such a conceptualization is inherently in conflict with the view that social psychological processes are heavily influenced by the immediate social context. Second, learning theory tended to locate the causes of behavior largely in the external environment or in the internalized traces of the cumulative external environment, and not in an individual's subjective interpretation of it. As just noted, this relatively passive view of the individual is at odds with social psychological conceptualizations of the person. Finally, and related to the second point, the learning theory approach focused largely on overt behavior rather than on psychological or subjective states. As we have noted, this viewpoint ignores an important part of social psychological experience.

Social Learning Theory

Social learning theory (Bandura, 1977; Bandura & Walters, 1963) offered a more compatible orientation for social psychology. It built on the propositions of learning theory but placed special emphasis on how new behavior

is acquired through observational learning. A thorny issue for traditional learning theory had been how to elicit a target behavior from an organism so that it could be reinforced and strengthened. With social learning theory, the behavior need not first occur, nor need it be rewarded. A person can learn simply by watching the behavior of another. The observation of another's actions leads to a cognitive representation for that behavior that can be used as a model when an individual confronts related circumstances. Thus, social learning was thought to require the minimal components of attention to a behavioral sequence, retention of its form, and the ability to reproduce the behavioral sequence.

Social learning theory also introduced the importance of cognition in accounting for learning and behavior, that is, an emphasis on how the person thinks about and interprets his or her experience. The role of motivation was also somewhat different in social learning theory, as compared with the original learning theory formulation. In the original theory, reinforcements were considered to be essential for increasing incrementally the probability of a behavioral sequence. In social learning theory, reinforcements came to be seen instead as motivators, affecting primarily the performance, rather than the learning, of a behavioral sequence. In addition, reward and punishment were considered to have potential secondary effects on learning new behaviors via their influence in enhancing attention and rehearsal of learned sequences of behavior. Thus, social learning theory applied broadly to a wide range of individual and social behavior. It has provided advantages over traditional learning theory for social psychology by extending learning theory principles to self-reward and learning in the absence of direct reinforcement. The theory also gave people a central role in their own behavior, first, through their abilities to learn new action sequences through observation and mental rehearsal, and second, through the cognitive representations and constructions that they brought to situations as guidelines for behavior.

As noted, an important feature of social psychological research from its inception has been a concern with social issues, especially prejudice and discrimination. Social learning theory provided an important theoretical basis for the exploration of these issues. It maintained that prejudiced attitudes toward groups are learned, developing in much the same manner and through the same basic processes as other attitudes. According to this viewpoint, children acquire negative attitudes toward various social groups because they hear such attitudes expressed by parents, teachers, and peers. Moreover, such attitudes are implicitly or explicitly reinforced through praise, approval, or tacit acceptance for expressing them. Thus, the social learning perspective provided an explanation for the persistence of prejudice and discrimination (Sears, 1975).

Research on aggression was also importantly informed by a social learning perspective (see Geen, 1998, in this *Handbook*). From this standpoint, aggression was considered to be largely learned behavior (Bandura, 1973). That is, people learn aggression just as they acquire other forms of social behavior, through direct experience or through vicarious learning by observing the behavior of others. Moreover, individuals learn not only to aggress, but when to aggress and against whom one may aggress. Thus, people learn that appropriate targets for aggression may be minority groups or women and children, and they learn what kinds of provocations are appropriate reasons for an aggressive response (Nisbett, 1993). Through the social learning communicated by socialization practices, individuals come to acquire the norms that govern the expression of aggression and the cultural and social values that surround the expression of aggression and its contextual moderators.

The study of prosocial behavior has been similarly informed by the learning theory perspective, which emphasizes how children are taught to share and to help others (see Batson, 1998, in this *Handbook*). Children learn not only to help by being systematically exposed to rewards and punishments, but also learn to identify the circumstances under which they should help others. In addition, by observing others who help, modeling contributes to the development of prosocial behavior (Piliavin & Charng, 1990).

Subsequent research has not proven the social learning theory perspective wrong but has provided a basis for moving beyond the fundamental processes that social learning theory elucidates. Thus, for example, in current research on prejudice and discrimination, researchers have increasingly come to emphasize the cognitive underpinnings of these phenomena, as well as to elaborate the social contexts in which they occur (Crocker & Major, 1989; Devine, 1989; Gilbert & Hixon, 1991). Research on aggression and on prosocial behavior has moved in a biological direction, emphasing the evolutionary significance of aggression (e.g., Buss, 1995) and helping (Trivers, 1971), while at the same time fleshing out the social context within which aggressive or helpful acts are committed (see Geen, 1998; Batson, 1998, in this *Handbook*).

Currently, the social learning theory viewpoint is most evident in research on attitude change, especially that which examines attitude change in applied contexts such as health. In such studies, it has become evident that changing behavior requires instilling a sense of personal control, a self-efficacy belief that one can actually perform a relevant behavior (Bandura, 1977, 1986). Thus, one of the most enduring principles of social learning theory has been the importance placed on self-control, namely, the processes by which an individual evaluates the self and administers self-rewards or punishments accordingly. Such an emphasis, of course, puts the individual squarely back in the role of the active participant in the construction of experience in response to situational forces.

THE GESTALT TRADITION AND THE VIEW OF THE PERSON

As we have seen, traditional learning theory failed to provide social psychology with an adequate view of the person because of its insufficient emphasis on the role of the person as an active participant in experience. Even the social learning theory perspective, which had far greater explanatory power for addressing the role of the perceiver, has gained only a limited foothold in the field. The reason for this may lie in the important and pervasive influence of the Gestalt tradition on social psychology, which was, in turn, to give rise to two of its major empirical traditions, namely, person perception research and cognitive consistency theory.

The Gestalt perspective of the 1920s and 1930s originated in research on perception. Gestalt psychology was concerned with the manner in which objects and events are perceived to go together. Specifically, Gestaltists explored how people see patterns in stimuli before them and conjoin isolated events into meaningful structures. Literally, in translation, Gestalt means "configuration." Although the German tradition was primarily concerned with the perception of inanimate objects (Koffka, 1935; Kohler, 1947; Wertheimer, 1923), Heider (1946, 1958) brought this configural approach to the understanding of social situations. Gestalt psychology argued for the importance of two factors in perception: proximity and equality. Proximity refers to the fact that we use location information to infer relation. Two elements that are near each other will likely be seen as going together. For example, two dots located together on a page and apart from a single dot alone will be seen as a pair, the solo dot as alone. Equality refers to the fact that elements are perceived as belonging together if they resemble each other in form. Thus, one is more likely to see two dots as belonging together than a dot and an asterisk (Wertheimer, 1923). Gestalt psychologists argued for simple laws of good form or good fit as the basic unit of analysis, an insight first extended to people by Koffka (1935). *Pragnanz* refers to the fact that people tend to organize their perceptual field into coherent wholes. Instead of perceiving isolated elements in the visual field, the perceiver attempts to impose a meaningful structure, balance, and completeness.

The *pragnanz* principle gave rise to the field of person perception, suggesting that we see coherence not only in the object world but within the interpersonal world as well. This insight assumed specific form in the Gestaltist view of person perception developed by Asch (1946). According to Asch, the social perceiver attributes central traits to an object of perception, namely, another person. These central traits act as vehicles for organizing what is known about the person, but more important, they direct the evaluative meaning of the impression, shaping the interpretation of other surrounding traits. When information is encountered that does not obviously relate to those central traits, a "change of meaning" may occur in the surrounding traits so as to make them consistent with the central traits. Thus, for example, in the context of "dishonest," "intelligent" may become "sly" or "cagey," whereas in the context of "kind," "intelligent" may become "wise." Chief among these central traits are general evaluations, such as warm or cold. If we generally think positively of someone, then we tend to regard individual traits in that positive light (Kelley, 1950). Other principles of person perception may be similarly understood from the standpoint of *pragnanz.* The role of physical attractiveness in evoking generally positive reactions from others may be construed as an effort to impose evaluative consistency (Berscheid & Walster, 1978). The just world phenomenon, in which individuals who observe the suffering of another come to assume that the other individual deserved his or her fate, also reflects an underlying tension toward resolving inconsistent perceptions (Lerner, 1980), especially those that challenge the individual's conceptions of justice. Thus, the principle of *pragnanz,* coherence, or consistency may be said to apply to the perception of people (Hastorf, Schneider, & Polefka, 1970), just as it applies in the arena of object perception.

Not content with this simple extrapolation from object perception to person perception, social psychologists pursued the importance of coherence further. *Pragnanz* was to become the cornerstone of research and theory on cognitive consistency. While many in social psychology associate the cognitive consistency era with attitude change research, and in particular, the cognitive dissonance tradition, in fact the consistency principle was pervasive throughout social psychology at this time. As such, it became a truly metatheoretical vision of the person, as actively invested in the process of perceiving and striving to achieve coherence and consistency in social perception and social behavior.

Gestalt-Based Theories of Attitude Change

The influence of Gestalt psychology on the study of social psychological issues was first felt in the 1940s and 1950s in emerging work on attitude change (Heider, 1946; Lorge, 1936), and an especially influential manifestation of this viewpoint was Heider's (1958) *The Psychology of Interpersonal Relations.* Drawing on Koffka (1935), Heider based much of his social psychological theorizing on the Gestalt law of *pragnanz.* However, when it was first published, many of the central ideas in the text attracted relatively little attention, and its influence would not be readily apparent until the early 1970s. Instead, social psychologists were most intrigued at first by Heider's balance theory analysis. In balance theory, Heider was concerned with how people see individuals and objects. He characterized unit relations as a state of belongingness or going-togetherness and liking relations in terms of evaluation (positivenegative). Thus, two individuals may like each other intensely but yet not be a unit, and two people may be a unit, and yet not care for each other. As Heider noted, however, we tend to see liking in unity relations and unity in liking relations, and we tend to assume that the reactions one person has to another are reciprocated. These are, he argued, fundamental principles of interpersonal perception. Of particular concern to Heider and theorists and researchers to follow was the situation of imbalance. How do people manage situations that do not cohere? Helen admires John, but John has only contempt for Helen. Marcia likes Allan, Allan likes Bob, but Bob can't stand Marcia. Balance theory was preeminently concerned with consistency, how people achieve balance and coherence from imbalanced situations.

Although the empirical legacy of balance theory was substantial, the most influential of the Gestalt-based consistency theories was Festinger's (1957) theory of cognitive dissonance. What dissonance theory added to the consistency perspective was first, an extension to selfperception. Festinger's theory implicitly argued that principles of coherence and consistency apply not only to our perceptions of objects, people, and situations in the world but also to an understanding of our own behavior. Thus, *pragnanz* became a principle for understanding not only how people impute structure and order to their external worlds but how they structure their internal worlds as well. This extension gave the Gestaltist principles central status in a conceptualization of the social being that encompassed all life domains.[5]

The second extension that Festinger's theory offered, one that was not without controversy, was the notion of an underlying motivational principle: Dissonance was conceptualized as a state of tension that results from the perception that one's cognitions and/or the relation between one's cognitions and behavior are inconsistent. This motivational principle had not been explicit in the Gestalt position, which had assumed that people impose coherence on elements, largely by virtue of intrinsic cognitive regularities. Dissonance was explicitly regarded as having motivational properties, and to the extent that an individual experiences cognitive dissonance, he or she is believed to be motivated to reduce that state. Subsequent refinements of the theory brought the consistency principle even farther into the social world. Individuals were said to experience cognitive dissonance only to the extent that the outcomes of their decisions were perceived to be freely chosen and foreseeable. Choosing to undertake a behavior or making a decision that is inconsistent with other beliefs should not, according to the theory, produce cognitive dissonance if one is under duress or is externally induced to make a particular decision or adopt a particular stance. Aronson (1968) took this extension farther, arguing that dissonance occurs primarily when the self is involved.

It is beyond the scope of this chapter to review every consistency theory that evolved within social psychology, but it must be noted that a variety of related theoretical endeavors emerged that drew importantly on the principles of *pragnanz* and on the concept of a motivation to reduce inconsistency or incoherence. These included Lorge's (1936) work on transfer of affect, Cartwright and Harary's (1956) elaboration of the balance principle, Abelson and Rosenberg's (1958) psychologic, Osgood and Tannenbaum's (1955) congruity model, and Newcomb's (1953) strain toward symmetry approach. The delineation of these and related theoretical endeavors, their examination in many dozens of empirical investigations, and their subsequent refinements, formed the basis of a study group at the Center for Advanced Studies in the Behavioral Sciences, that later culminated in *Theories of Cognitive Consistency: A Sourcebook,* otherwise known as TOCCAS or simply "the red book" (Abelson et al., 1968).

By far, the most impressive empirical legacy of the consistency principle was cognitive dissonance theory, which has now generated well over 1,200 empirical investigations. But the influence of the Gestalt tradition and the consistency principles that resulted had a pervasive impact on social psychology far beyond these boundaries. In equity theory, the Gestalt principle of *pragnanz* was implicitly extended to perceptions of the relation of self and others (Adams, 1963, 1965). Equity theory proposed a system by which relationships are enacted and evaluated according to rules about what is fair or just (Adams, 1965; Walster, Walster, & Berscheid, 1978). Similar to dissonance, inequity was conceptualized as a motivational state of tension that moves an individual toward attempting resolution, a state that may come about by demanding more outcomes, reducing inputs, demanding that the other change the ratio of outputs to inputs, or abrogating a relationship.

The consistency principle pervaded empirical investigations of other social psychological phenomena as well. For example, Aronson and Carlsmith (1962) used the consistency principle to explain a classic problem in achievement behavior: why some people sabotage their own performance when they are given an opportunity to succeed. They showed that, given a history of poor performance, the sudden experience of a success may be threatening to stable conceptions of the self, and accordingly, an individual

may actively sabotage subsequent performance in such a way that the success is undone. Aronson and Mettee (1968) used the consistency principle to show how individuals in whom low self-esteem has been induced may engage in further self-destructive behavior, such as cheating, because it is consistent with the new salient self-image. Much of the research on group dynamics implicitly or explicitly incorporated the consistency point of view. For example, Siegel and Siegel (1953) explored how one's attitudes come to correspond to those of a group which one joins or to which one aspires. Consistency approaches provided a basis for analyses of social movements in *When Prophecy Fails* (Festinger, Riecken, & Schachter, 1956), the intriguing field study of a doomsday cult whose members became even more committed to the cult's ideology following the disconfirmation of its prophecy of the end of the world. Aronson and Carlsmith (1963) demonstrate the applicability of the consistency principle to socialization in the classic forbidden toy experiment: children given a very gentle prohibition not to play with a particular toy ignored the toy and subsequently internalized the implications of their behavior; when later given the opportunity to play with the toy, they inferred from not having played with it, that they did not like it, and consequently, they left it alone. The ubiquity with which the consistency principle could be documented throughout life domains studied by social psychologists made it the best example of the dictum that there is nothing so practical as a good theory.

The consistency era in social psychology put much emphasis upon a few very basic principles of perception. Perhaps for that reason alone, the endeavor would eventually fall into disfavor. Consistency theories presented numerous empirical difficulties, such as measuring inconsistency and specifying the relations among cognitions or between cognitions and behavior that must exist in order for the consistency principle to be operative. Research progress was impeded by the fact that the perspective generated a plethora of theoretical approaches that did not generate discriminably different testable hypotheses (Kiesler, Collins, & Miller, 1969).

But the larger question was whether consistency is truly as significant a feature of human inner life as the theories had made it out to be. The consistency era had generated a distinct and pervasive view of the social being as motivated by concerns with consistency and coherence that had not only a perceptual but a motivational basis. Empirical evidence that contradicted this view of the social being began to mount. Research revealed that people can tolerate high degrees of inconsistency within their belief systems, and when such inconsistencies are pointed out to them, instead of experiencing states of tension that require resolution, people seem often not to find them aversive. If consistency were such a pervasive perceptual principle or such a potent motivational force, one would not expect to find such high degrees of inconsistency or comfort in the apparent ability to live with inconsistency. The observation that individuals often hold attitudes that are either not realized in behavior or that are actively inconsistent with behavior led to concern about the ubiquity of consistency. Salient empirical examples of discrepancies between attitudes and behavior (e.g., La Piere, 1934) took on symbolic significance as representative of the failure of the consistency approach to explain behavior (Suchman, 1950).

The vision of the person in social psychology was now shifting away from an emphasis on pervasive motivational factors like consistency. The insights afforded by the consistency approach were not lost, but they came to assume a more modest role than had been true in the 1950s and 1960s. The empirical emphasis on consistency as a principle faded from prominence. On the other hand, the view of the individual as actively imposing meaning and structure on social stimuli not only remained but actually gained force, as cognitive views of the person increasingly characterized the field.

THE COGNITIVE REVOLUTION AND THE VIEW OF THE PERSON

The cognitive revolution arrived on the doorstep of social psychology at a receptive moment. There was general dissatisfaction, not only with consistency approaches but with motivationally based theories more generally. Occam's razor had sliced its way through the field, leaving behind a preference for simple, mid-range theories whose principles could be demonstrated and tested. The field was ready for a new metatheoretical vision and a different way of thinking about the social being. Cognitive psychology provided such a vision.

In order to understand why social psychology was so receptive to cognitive theory and research, it is useful to begin with the theoretical contributions of Immanuel Kant, whose reasoning strongly influenced Kurt Lewin and many others in social psychology. Kant's major work, *Critique of Pure Reason* (Kant, 1781/1969), explored the nature of limits of human knowledge. It was written as a direct response to the mainstream philosophical position of his day, which had argued that the regularities of the world are substantial and easily and directly perceived by individuals. According to this viewpoint, we see things as they actually are. Kant argued for a more active constructive role of the social perceiver in the perception and interpretation of experienced objects. In maintaining that the mind actively organizes experience, Kant argued that we do not know people and objects as they are in themselves, we know them as we infer them to be. As we have already seen, this view of the social perceiver as actively involved in the construction

of experience has had a profound impact on social psychology throughout its history. Because this position was embodied in the cognitive viewpoint, the receptivity of the field to the cognitive viewpoint was substantial.

The incorporation of the cognitive viewpoint into social psychology was accompanied by a rejection, or at least a deemphasis of motivational principles. Cognitively oriented social psychologists began to think of the person as a "naive scientist" (Kelley, 1967), one who solves problems much as scientists do, albeit with quasi-scientific approximations to scientific methods. To the extent that motivation assumed importance in perception and inference, it was believed to play two roles. First, motivation was considered an impetus for cognitive processing in the underlying assumption that people are motivated to have good and stable beliefs about themselves and the world. If a situation requires an inference or judgment, with enough time and enough mental capacity, the person should take in available relevant information in reasonably sound manner and combine it into some logical, specifiable, and complex product, making generally good and accurate inferences and decisions. The second way in which motivation was argued to enter into this process was as a disruption, something that gets in the way of rational processing. That is, departures from rational processing were assumed to be due to motivational or emotional factors.

That the vision of the rational person should assume such prominence in social psychology is not surprising. It was a vision shared by many of the other social sciences, and one that persists today in political science and economics, albeit with increasing recognition of its limitations (*The Economist,* 1994; Sears, 1991). From an empirical standpoint, the gold standard against which human behavior was compared consisted of normative models of inference. Empirical questions focused on how closely the social perceiver approximates normative models of problem-solving, including covariation, probability estimation, and sampling theory (Dawes, 1998, in this *Handbook*; Fiske & Taylor, 1984, 1991; Nisbett & Ross, 1980).

Attribution Theory and Research

The cognitive revolution was never imported in pure form from cognitive psychology, but rather, it took on a distinctly social psychological flavor from the outset. The articulation of the cognitive viewpoint in social psychology owes much to Fritz Heider (1958). Initially responsive largely to the balance theory ideas, by the 1960s, the field of social psychology was ready to digest Heider's more complex and previously elusive observations in *The Psychology of Interpersonal Relations*. Heider reasoned that people have the goals to predict and control what goes on around them. In order to do so, he argued, we impute structure to social stimuli and to the environment, draw inferences from those structures, and behave in accordance with them. As such, an underlying awareness of the causal structure of human behavior is essential to the ability to predict and control. This quite simple observation gave rise to a collection of theoretical endeavors known as attribution theory (Jones & Davis, 1965; Kelley, 1967; Weiner, 1986).

Heider argued that we need to study commonsense psychology, that is, the ways in which individuals make sense of the interpersonal environment around them, because such commonsense psychology can tell scientists a lot about how people perceive the intentions of others and impute stability to behavior. In particular, Heider was concerned with the underpinnings of the inferences of ability and motivation. That is, how do we assume that another individual *can* perform a behavior and predict when an individual will *try* to do so? Because ability and motivation must both be present for an attribution of causality, Heider argued, the social perceiver must infer the other's ability and motivation from the cues and circumstances under which behavior occurred. As such, Heider was centrally concerned with what the social perceiver contributes to the perception process, rather than with what the target of observation contributes to inference. Heider's goal in *The Psychology of Interpersonal Relations* was to do more than provide a theory of causal attribution. It was to provide a model of how to use commonsense psychology and normal language to infer how people construct the social world. As a result, he left his theoretical statements about causality at a relatively undeveloped level, but his work provided an important impetus for subsequent theory and research on causal attribution.

Drawing on Heider, Jones and Davis (1965) offered a theoretical account of how we perceive others. The central goal of the social perceiver is, according to Jones and Davis, the ability to draw correspondent inferences about another person's behavior. That is, to what extent can one infer a stable and enduring internal disposition of another person as the cause of a specific behavior? Using logic derived from Heider, Jones and Davis argued that there are some simple cues and processes that enable social perceivers to structure information in a causally relevant manner and to form causal attributions quickly and reliably. For example, the social desirability of an outcome is an important and valuable cue for a social perceiver: behavior that is low in social desirability, assuming it is deliberate, is likely to be attributed to personal dispositions compared with socially desirable behavior, which is assumed to be governed by social norms. Focal in their attribution theory was Jones and Davis' proposal of the analysis of noncommon effects. Basically, they argued that the social perceiver asks the question, "What is this action producing that other actions would not have produced?" To the extent that a chosen action produces distinctive consequences, dispositions reflecting these consequences are assumed to be the underlying cause of the action or behavioral choice.

The theory most allied with the phrase "naive scientist," and indeed, the one that gave rise to this characterization, is Harold Kelley's (1967) attribution theory, which built on Heider's (1958) and Jones and Davis' (1965) earlier observations. Whereas Jones and Davis were primarily concerned with imputed stabilities to others' intentions, Kelley was concerned with a broader range of dispositional properties of entities in the environment, whether people or situational factors. He maintained that our information about the world and ourselves is always incomplete, and when our information level falls below an adequate level, it produces attributional instability. When we encounter some effect we cannot explain, such as an action or an outcome, Kelley argued, we seek information along three dimensions: distinctiveness, namely, whether the effect occurs when the thing is there versus when it is not; consistency over time/modality, namely, whether the effect occurs each time the condition is present; and consensus, namely, whether the effect is experienced by other people in the same way. Kelley argued that, holding other dimensions constant, the social perceiver collects information along each of the dimensions serially and then calculates what amounts to an F ratio in an analysis of variance framework in which one looks for conditions that meet the criteria of high distinctiveness and low variance across time, modality, and persons. Together with his other causal contributions on the discounting principle (Kelley, 1972a) and on causal schemas (Kelley, 1972b), Kelley's proposals, along with those of Heider and Jones and Davis, were to heavily influence the field of social psychology over the next decade.

Students who lack the historical perspective that spawned interest in attribution theory sometimes express surprise that so much attention was devoted to one type of cognition, namely, inferences about causality. To explain the importance of these theoretical positions, one must realize that the causal attribution was seen as a basic and focal type of inference on which many others are predicated. Thus, for example, making a causal attribution for another person's behavior not only addresses the specific question of what caused the behavior but also enables one to estimate with some accuracy whether the behavior was intended, whether it is likely to be repeated, and whether it is otherwise informative regarding an individual's enduring personal characteristics (Jones & Davis, 1965). Causal attributions for one's own behavior, such as why one succeeded or failed on a task, lead to expectations of reward or censure, decisions regarding whether to persist at or abandon a task, and the development of long-term expectations about one's talents and shortcomings (Weiner, 1986). The importance and centrality of the causal attribution to human inference was also assumed to derive from the basic social goals of predicting and controlling the environment (Heider, 1958). This emphasis on prediction and control became a central principle in the emerging field of social cognition and played a role not unlike that played by consistency theories in theoretical formulations of the 1950s and 1960s, albeit a more implicit one. Prediction and control were thought to be achieved by understanding the causes of behaviors, especially enduring causes, that are stable across a wide range of situations.

From the consistency era and its failure to establish broad-based principles of behavior also came a concern with parsimony, the desire to avoid unnecessary theoretical principles. The best example of this trend toward parsimony and effort to explain behavior with reference to a few simple principles was Bem's (1965, 1972) self-perception theory. Bem argued that people explain their own behavior, as well as that of others, with reference to the context and the circumstances in which it took place. If situational constraints are sufficient to explain behavior, then the person is seen as behaving in accordance with those situational pressures. If, however, there are no special situational pressures on the person to engage in a behavior, then the person's behavior will be regarded as reflecting an underlying disposition, such as an attitude or a personality trait. The radical nature of Bem's proposal was in maintaining that individuals draw inferences about their own behavior in much the same way. He argued that, to the extent that internal cues are weak or ambiguous, people infer the meaning of their behavior using a process essentially identical to that of an observer.[6]

Bem's radical behaviorist perspective was significant in attribution theory, not so much for the theoretical insight it provided or for the empirical legacy it generated, as for the metatheoretical and methodological controversy it provoked. Social psychologists found it hard to accept the Bemian perspective and challenged it theoretically and empirically with an intensity rarely witnessed in social psychological controversies (Kiesler, Nisbett, & Zanna, 1969). Although the self-perception–dissonance controversy proved to be unnervingly resistant to empirical resolution,[7] opposition to Bem's position came not so much from empirical evidence as from a deeply ingrained belief that radical behaviorism cannot properly characterize self-perception (or, for that matter, the perception of others as well). Although social psychology had embraced a variety of models of the social being, this was a viewpoint that challenged basic and cherished tenets of the field. Bem's radical behaviorist position implied that the active constructive role of the social perceiver in interpreting experience is quite modest, and that the social perceiver may draw on superficial aspects of observable behavior as a basis for self-inference. It is also implied that individuals

have little special expertise as observers of their own behavior. Bem's (1967) position came perilously close to saying that there is no self there. In attempting to refute Bem, then, social psychologists drew the line concerning what was an acceptable view of the social being.

Social Cognition

Although social psychologists were unwilling to adopt a radical behaviorist view of the person, the willingness to live with a fundamentally cognitive view of the social being, to the relative exclusion of motivational, affective, and behavioral processes took root, at least temporarily. This vision assumed full form in what has come to be known as social cognition (Fiske & Taylor, 1984, 1991). Although the numbers are waning now, at one time, social cognition was believed to account for more than 85 percent of all the empirical submissions to the *Journal of Personality and Social Psychology,* a statistic that bears testimony to the enthusiastic reception of its insights.

In the late 1960s and early 1970s, social psychology went through a self-labeled crisis. Most psychological conventions included a symposium on the decline, despair, or questionable future of the field. Although attribution research had enjoyed an empirical run in the early 1970s, otherwise the field seemed adrift, without a discernable future direction. While a number of factors may have led to the passing of this "crisis," an important one was the advent of social cognition (Fiske & Taylor, 1984; Wyer & Srull, 1984). Social cognition was guided by the belief that cognitive processes account for much of how people understand themselves and others. The specification of mental organization and cognitive processes underlying social psychological phenomena was seen not only as necessary but as potentially tractable because of methodological and empirical developments in cognitive psychology. Receptivity in social psychology to the cognitive revolution, as it came to be known, occurred not only because of social psychology's crisis and consequent willingness to consider a new metatheoretical vision, but also because, unlike other aspects of psychology, social psychology never fully abandoned an emphasis on cognition. Cognitive psychology provided a means for doing what social psychology had not been able to do before, namely, established measures designed to address the psychological processes going on in an individual's head (see, for example, Smith, 1998, in this *Handbook*).

To understand why this constituted such a methodological achievement, a historical note is warranted. Cognition has had a checkered past in psychology. Early empirical psychological work drew heavily on cognitive processes. For example, Wundt's (1897) research methods included trained introspection, and the goal of these methods was clearly cognitive. An emphasis on cognition fell into temporary disfavor when introspection was abandoned as a methodology. It failed to conform to emerging scientific standards deemed appropriate for empirical investigation because its data were not reproducible. There was a movement in favor of studying external, publically observable events instead—a movement that reached its height in the behaviorist tradition that held sway in most areas of psychology.

Beginning in the 1960s, experimental psychologists began to reconsider the importance of cognition. This movement occurred, first, because of controversies within psycholinguistics criticizing behaviorist efforts to account for language. The complex symbolic aspects of language could not easily be explained by behaviorist approaches. A second trend that led to the renewed importance placed on cognition within psychology was the development of the field of information processing that grew out of research on how people acquire knowledge and skills (Broadbent, 1985). Information processing refers to the fact that mental operations can be broken down into sequential stages. It specifies the steps that occur between the appearance of a stimulus and the response made to it. Methodological techniques were developed that permitted cognitive psychologists to trace nonobservable internal processes that were presumed to intervene between the stimulus and the response (Taylor & Fiske, 1981).

Research on social cognition began with the naive psychology of Heider, but it went beyond these insights in providing a fine-grained analysis about how people think about themselves and others. As such, it relied heavily upon the theory and methods of cognitive psychology and upon the comparison of actual behavior against the prediction of detailed normative models from cognitive psychology. Within social cognition, the cognitive emphasis was manifested in two major lines of research. The first was an assessment of the judgment and decision-making capabilities of the social perceiver as compared against normative theory. The second was an exploration of social psychological processes such as person perception, person memory, social schemas, and the like, from the standpoint of internal representations and dynamics.

Normative theories of judgment and decision making provided useful models against which to compare the behavior of the social perceiver, in large part because discrepancies between the two were virtually always assured (see Dawes, 1998, in this *Handbook*). Within attribution research, several key biases received considerable empirical attention. Research on the actor-observer effect (Jones & Nisbett, 1972), for example, revealed that, although people offer dispositional explanations for others' behavior, as Jones and Davis' attribution formulation predicts, they typically offer more situational and unstable explanations for their own behavior. Research on the self-serving attributional bias (Miller & Ross, 1975) showed that people as-

sume credit for the successful outcomes of their efforts (the self-enhancing bias) and, under some circumstances, minimize responsibility for failure (the self-protective bias). By far, the greatest amount of empirical attention was devoted to the fundamental attribution error (Heider, 1958; Ross, 1977), the observation that people generally regard another person's behavior as freely chosen and as representative of the person's stable qualities, instead of recognizing that there are situational forces, such as social norms and social roles, that may fully or partially account for behavior. A large volume of experimental investigations resulted from this interest in judgmental errors and biases, and for the most part, empirical research focused on the question, "Is the error motivational in origin or intrinsic to the cognitive system?"

Research on judgmental errors and biases exposed the many ways in which the social perceiver fell short of the standards embodied in normative models (Dawes, 1998, in this *Handbook*). But much more important was the shift in the view of the social being that arose in the wake of this research. Collectively, research on judgmental errors and biases brought into focus the fact that the underlying view of the person as a rational scientist was flawed (Simon, 1967; see Dawes, 1998, in this *Handbook*). In positing that individuals gather a range of relevant information, weigh it carefully, and integrate it into a social judgment, the implicit assumption was that the time and cognitive capacity of the social perceiver were relatively unconstrained. Belatedly, social psychologists began to recognize intrinsic constraints on human on-line capacity and short-term memory, limitations that had been known to cognitive psychologists for some time (Fishhoff, 1976). On-line processing and short-term memory are very "expensive." People can hold only a few things in short-term memory at a time, processing is time-consuming, and in a busy world where things happen quickly, the goal of the social perceiver may often be to process a lot of information efficiently, rather than to carefully consider more moderate amounts of information thoroughly (Tversky & Kahneman, 1974). In contrast to on-line capacity, long-term memory is virtually boundless. These twin observations—the limitations of short-term memory and on-line processing, and the almost limitless nature of long-term memory—led to the recognition that much of our inferential work must be accomplished through rapid, efficient, even unconscious methods of relating current data to representations stored in long-term memory.

Does this recognition of cognitive limitations and resources constitute a vision of the social being? The collected insights from social cognition research on judgment provided not so much a vision of the person as an assessment of the constraints within which any portrait of the person must exist. In an effort to characterize this shift in thinking about cognitive constraints, Fiske and Taylor

(1984) invented the term "cognitive miser," to reflect the fact that the person, of necessity, is stingy in the allocation of on-line capacity. Such a term, however, reflects only one facet of the cognitive perspective: the person is also an "administrative assistant" who gets the job done efficiently, but who has a lot of file cabinets for storing information that may be needed at a moment's notice. Increasingly, too, researchers began to recognize the limits of studying conscious properties in favor of understanding implicit automatic processes that may account for a lot of inferential work (see Wegner & Bargh, 1998, in this *Handbook*).

The recognition that long-term memory must be significant in social psychological reasoning prompted an important shift in emphasis within several topic areas in social psychology. Whereas previously, research had focused on the active, on-line tasks of the social perceiver, now attention was focused more on the long-term knowledge structures that provide a basis for much social psychological reasoning (see Smith, 1998, in this *Handbook*). Thus, for example, research on person perception, which had previously explored almost exclusively the on-line task of impression formation, moved heavily in the direction of person memory and the representations we hold of people (e.g., Ostrom, 1989; Wyer & Srull, 1984). Attribution theory, which had focused on generic models that posited often elaborate on-line processing for inferring causality, shifted toward emphasizing the role of knowledge structures in causal explanation (e.g., Hilton & Slugoski, 1986). The legacy of research on schemas and its extensions into self-schemas (Cantor & Mischel, 1977; Markus, 1977) must also be regarded as a product of the emerging viewpoint of the person as relatively stingy with on-line capacity but lavish with long-term memory (Fiske & Taylor, 1991). Research on regularities in behavior and their transpersonal stereotyped enactment drew heavily on the script concept (Schank & Abelson, 1977).

The predominance of the cognitive miser perspective was not to last. Critics argued that social psychology was becoming too cognitive. Topics of enduring and passionate interest to social psychologists, such as stereotyping and prejudice, were becoming reduced to little more than byproducts of normal categorization processes, convenient for representing information in long-term memory (see Brewer & Brown, 1998, in this *Handbook*). Critics argued that the study of social cognition was moving in one direction only, namely, toward understanding how cognition influences social inference and behavior. The ways in which social processes determine cognitive phenomena received short shrift (Ostrom, 1984). Perhaps most important, with the implicit vision of the administrative assistant performing tasks in a smooth but dispassionate way, there were only modest roles for emotion, motivation, commitment, and other affective processes. Given its historical origins, it was inevitable that social psychology's theoretical pendu-

lum would swing back toward affective and motivational concerns (Clark & Fiske, 1982; Zajonc, 1998, in this *Handbook*).

Although the vision of the person provided by the cognitive perspective contained several shortcomings, the cognitive perspective did force social psychologists to make an important set of changes in research methodologies. From cognitive psychology, social psychology imported a focus on process models. Research in cognitive psychology posited the exact steps in internal processes and then demonstrated them through methods such as recall protocols and reaction time measures to show that the process was as it had been conceptualized (Taylor & Fiske, 1981; Wyer & Srull, 1984). It was no longer enough to detail a theoretical process model and use the results as confirmation of the model. If one stated what one thought the process was, one had to provide evidence for the intervening steps. But while the cognitive legacy did enable social psychological researchers to make effective use of cognitive techniques in demonstrating process models, it had the unfortunate byproduct of removing much of what is social from the research it generated. The limitations of borrowing methods from cognitive psychology for social psychology became increasingly evident. Nonetheless, even as cognitive methodologies were criticized, the wise message that initially inspired the use of those methodologies was retained: if our theoretical models have an implicit view of the person's internal psychological processes, then we must provide evidence not only of the expected outcomes but of the underlying processes as well.

From a metatheoretical perspective, the shift in the view of the person that derived from the cognitive perspective was significant in social psychology in several respects. First, the representative of the person changed from one characterized as governed primarily by motivational and quasi-irrational principles to one guided primarily by rational principles with a more modest role for motivational and irrational factors. Second, the emphasis on cognition led to increasing interest in internal inferential processes and the social representations held by the social perceiver, rather than on an external social reality. Social psychology increasingly moved from the external environment into the social perceiver's head.

An example of this transition is research on consensus processes. Kelley (1967) had initially argued that consensus of the social group is a major determinant of attributional processes: we believe our causal attributions to the degree that others share them. But empirical research on attribution theory (e.g., McArthur, 1972) suggested that consensus is a relatively weak source of causal attributions or attributional validation. Research, instead, suggested the importance of "false consensus" (Marks & Miller, 1987; Ross, Greene, & House, 1977): that is, individuals' beliefs about what their social network would believe or might believe are often based on their own opinions that overrule actual consensus information that comes from the social environment. This shift in emphasis away from social processes to individual cognitive processes, of which consensus research is but one example, represented a major change in orientation within social psychology.

The active cognitive construction of the social environment represents an important insight from social cognition. But the insight may derived as much from the metatheoretical perspective in vogue at the time as from the underlying truth of the observation. To return to the example of consensus research, there is clear evidence for the importance of real consensus as well as false consensus. Recall that in 1936, Sherif demonstrated that the consensus of a social group could lead an individual to reject such basic perceptions as the movement of light in a darkened space. In a similar vein, Asch (1955) demonstrated that individuals would overrule their own perceptions and report that a clearly shorter line was longer than a comparison line when others in a social group had apparently reached the erroneous judgment. Thus, while research on social cognition implicitly argued that individual beliefs overwhelm social reality, work from group dynamics demonstrated that social reality can overwhelm individual perception. Clearly, both insights must be true. To give either metatheoretical vision precedence over the other is to deny the important realities and insights that the other provides.

The Motivated Tactician

The cognitive miser perspective was based on a fairly narrow literature on social judgments that often examined hypothetical or inconsequential inferences reached by participants in the laboratory. As such, it ignored many powerful influences that typically impinge on people's behavior. These include motivation, emotion, and, for lack of a better phrase, the anticipated and actual consequences of one's actions. Certainly there is a kernel of truth to the cognitive miser view of the person. Sometimes we seek to be efficient, but often we are anything but. Consider the amount of time and attentional capacity a lovesick adolescent can lavish on interpreting the meaning of a neutral comment made by the object of his or her affections. Or consider how much charm and attention a would-be vice president can lavish on someone relevant to his or her personal goals, and how little he or she can spend on someone irrelevant to those goals. Inevitably, the pendulum swung back in the direction of acknowledging the importance of and incorporating affective and motivational processes into social cognition (see Zajonc, 1998 in this *Handbook*). The confluence of these trends gave rise to a view of the social being that has been characterized as a *motivated tactician* (Fiske & Taylor, 1991).

The motivated tactician is neither uniformly stingy with on-line capacity nor uniformly thorough in forming inferences and making decisions. Instead, the motivated tactician is viewed as having multiple information processing strategies available, selecting among them on the basis of goals, motives, needs, and forces in the environment. As such, the motivated tactician exemplifies the pragmatic tradition in social psychology. In 1890, William James maintained that "my thinking is first and last and always for the sake of my doing" (p. 333), a statement that captures the essence of this tradition. Although social cognition theorists had always recognized the functional importance of cognition and cognitive processes, this viewpoint assumed centrality in the motivated tactician perspective. The practical and epistemic functions that govern thought and inference provided the context for interpreting the flexibility of cognitions and cognitive strategies.

According to this viewpoint, sometimes the motivated tactician makes use of strategies that have shortcomings, but that solve problems efficiently (Tversky & Kahneman, 1974). Some of these strategies are well-practiced and virtually automatic, whereas others involve more on-line consideration and computation. At other times, the motivated tactician is fully engaged, and allocates attention and uses inferential strategies that involve extensive consideration of a range of information and careful attention to its implications. Other times, the motivated tactician behaves defensively in the interests of self-esteem: people will often construct theories or use evidence in ways that will make their final inferences come out the way they want them to (Kunda, 1990).

The view of the person as a motivated tactician is perhaps best exemplified in research on attitudes and attitude change processes. Petty and Cacioppo's (1986) work on the elaboration likelihood model using cognitive response analysis reveals that attitude change can occur either via central routes or via peripheral routes. When attitude change occurs via central routes, it involves active, careful thinking and cognitive processing. When it occurs via peripheral routes, it typically occurs without much thought or awareness (cf. Chaiken, 1980; Eagly & Chaiken, 1998, in this *Handbook*; Petty & Wegener, 1998, in this *Handbook*). The decades of research that have followed the elaboration of this and similar models reveal clearly the utility of the approach and the need to consider both characteristics of the person and situational characteristics that foster central versus peripheral processing (see Petty & Wegener, 1998, in this *Handbook*).

Attribution research suggests the importance of a similar continuum: when people's causal interpretations have no consequences for their future behavior, they may make rapid attributions, seizing upon a single, simple, and sufficient explanation, and accept such distorted information as false feedback as a basis for their causal beliefs; when their attributions will have consequences for their future behavior, they lavish more time on their causal attributions, actively refuting the implications of feedback they understand to be flawed (Taylor, 1975). Research on accountability by Tetlock and his associates (Tetlock, 1983) points to the utility of conceptualizing the individual as having a diverse array of capabilities and strategies that may be engaged as a function of individual predispositions or powerful situational forces. Accountability for one's inferences produces more thorough and more elaborate processing that takes account of more information and that is, at least sometimes, more accurate than processing that occurs in the absence of accountability (Chaiken, Liberman, & Eagly, 1989).

Person perception research demonstrates clearly how an individual's goals determine the kind of information that is remembered about another person (and indeed, whether information is remembered at all), the content of the impression that is formed, the way in which it is structured, and its accessibility for future use (e.g., Devine, Sedikides, & Fuhrman, 1989). Social comparison research demonstrates that the comparison of one's abilities, attributes, outcomes, or emotional states occurs not only for purposes of self-evaluation, as Festinger (1954) and Schachter (1959) established, but also to meet self-improvement needs, self-enhancement needs, and needs best understood as social bonding (Helgeson & Mickelson, 1995; Taylor, Wayment, & Carrillo, 1995; Wills, 1981; Wood, 1989; Wood & Taylor, 1991).

The Self

Research on social cognition prompted renewed interest in understanding the self (see Baumeister, 1998, in this *Handbook*). Once an active area of investigation in personality research (e.g., Wylie, 1979), the self was, for many years, a dormant topic within social psychology and in psychology more generally. Early social cognition research, however, revealed a need for understanding the self, because without such an articulation, many phenomena of interest to social cognition researchers were difficult to understand. Self-referencing effects, for example, in which people remember material better if they encode it with reference to the self, virtually demand some theoretical statement regarding the nature of the self. Investigations by Markus and her associates (Markus, 1977; Markus & Nurius, 1986) revealed the importance of long-term knowledge structures that represent the self or what the self may become, and their effects on information processing. An array of research on the working self-concept revealed the ways in which one's self-representations and individual actions are influenced by transient social settings, roles, and the groups within which one enacts one's identities (e.g., McGuire & Padawer-Singer, 1976; Tajfel & Turner, 1986).

The burgeoning literature on the self exemplifies many

of the themes that the term "motivated tactician," was designed to capture. An empirical explosion of research has examined the diverse motives that may govern an individual's thoughts, feelings, and behavior, including self-verification (e.g., Swann, 1983), the need for an accurate sense of self (e.g., Trope, 1975), self-enhancement (e.g., Tesser, 1988; Steele, 1988), the need to belong (Baumeister & Leary, 1995), and the conditions likely to foster the ascendance of any and all of these motives (e.g., Sedikides & Strube, 1996; Stevens & Fiske, 1995). Renewed interest in the affective consequences of cognition led to models such as Higgins' (1987) self-discrepancy theory, showing that discrepancies between the current self and one's ideal self, or between the current self and what one thinks one ought to be are associated with depression and anxiety, respectively. This extended empirical attention to the self has also enabled us to understand how people will actually behave and why they will behave that way (e.g., Fazio, 1987). Because research on the self so clearly embodies many of the important themes raised by social cognition research, it has represented the turf on which many of social psychology's recent controversies have been fought. These include fundamental questions, such as the degree to which people are rational or irrational, motivated by accuracy or self-enhancement, or individual beings or social beings.

Perhaps the most important intellectual achievement of this work on the self has been the articulation of a view of the social being that does not rely on a single principle or kernel of truth as its core. We have successfully moved away from visions of the self that emphasize a single fundamental principle, such as consistency, or a single source of self-knowledge or influence, such as the social group. Instead, we have achieved an appropriately complex vision of the person as actively constructing the social environment but also as responsive to feedback, and as governed by a wide range of motivational and cognitive influences. Thus, the view of the social being as affected by cognitive as well as motivational and emotional concerns achieves a balanced vision of the person that has not previously been evident in social psychology.

As social cognition research has struck a balance between cognition and affect and begun to systematically investigate the multiplicity of motives and forces that impinge upon the self, it has moved more into the mainstream of social psychology. Attention to motivational and affective concerns makes social cognition more relevant to the familiar problems and issues of social psychology's content. Many topics of traditional interest to social psychologists have integrated a cognitive perspective, including interpersonal relationships (e.g., Berscheid & Reis, 1998, in this *Handbook*; Murray & Holmes, 1993), prejudice (see Fiske, 1998, in this *Handbook*), attitudes (e.g., Chaiken, 1980), aggression (see Geen, 1998, in this *Handbook*), intergroup relations (Brewer & Brown, 1998, in this *Hand-*

book), and prosocial behavior (Weiner, 1995; see Batson, 1998, in this *Handbook*). In so doing, each of these research areas has been extended to encompass a broader array of phenomena. In turn, the motivated tactician perspective that has emerged in social cognition research incorporates the flexibility that enables researchers to continue to draw on insights from cognitive psychology and from artificial intelligence without compromising what is social about the social being.

In suggesting that social cognition research has begun to reflect the complexity with which social psychology now views the person, it is also important to consider the shortcomings that may remain in this vision. A first shortcoming concerns the term "motivated tactician." Despite its metaphorical value, the label has proven to be a misnomer, inasmuch as it connotes a strategically oriented social perceiver who makes conscious decisions regarding how to allocate attention and time. In fact, much of this inferential work is accomplished quickly and without awareness, as people respond to situational contingencies with efficient, virtually automatic strategies (e.g., Wegner & Bargh, 1998, in this *Handbook*). The motivation guiding such processing may be tacit, and the tactics, unconsciously employed.

A second shortcoming is that social cognition's vision of the self insufficiently incorporates the centrality of interpersonal relationships and social groups to the self. Progress is being made on this front (e.g., Hardin & Higgins, 1996; Levine & Higgins, 1995; Murray & Holmes, 1993; Shaver & Hazan, 1993; Tesser, 1988). Social identity theory and research on self-categorization are excellent examples of how understanding of social groups has expanded understanding of the self and its dynamics (Tajfel & Turner, 1986). Nonetheless, the ties between the social cognition literature and research on interpersonal and intergroup relationships are not as developed as they could be. As such, there is room for remaining progress in social psychology's view of the person, an issue to which we now turn.

THE PERSON IN PRESENT-DAY SOCIAL PSYCHOLOGY

The breadth of vision of the person in social psychology at the present time reflects a very important development in social psychology as a science. It suggests that, as a field, we may have escaped the fads that dominated the content of social psychological investigations for decades. Frank and thoughtful discussions of the nature of social psychology during the 1960s and 1970s could not avoid the conclusion that social psychologists demonstrated a recurrent bandwagon approach to science, shifting abruptly in topical interests as well as metatheoretical visions. The inevitable run of dissertations and preponderance of journal articles that each empirical fad spawned reflected the fact that what was considered good science was sometimes merely fashionable.

Recent inspection of the content of the field's major journals reveals some important good news: there is no apparent fad in ascendance at the present time. The last discernable lurch in social psychology occurred in the early 1980s, when social cognition imported, in pure form, the observations and methodologies of cognitive science. Since that time, the cognitive perspective has receded, and nothing comparable has occurred since. While there may be no guarantee that our propensity to embrace scientific fads is over, the knowledge base of the field is so large, so wide-ranging, and so theoretically and empirically diverse, that the need for a predominant fad or way of thinking may now have passed. Dare we hope to believe that our science has reached a point of maturity that enables us to embrace new scientific insights without rejecting old ones?

Although some may disagree with this assessment, I believe that we have entered a period of integration and generativity. We have managed to retain what is healthy about our ongoing theoretical and empirical skirmishes without assuming that some existing king or queen must be beheaded before we can crown a new one. In part, the current state of social psychology has come about because theory and research have evolved from studying single effects and single processes to studying multiple effects and multiple processes (Petty, 1996). Whereas in the past, we implicitly assumed that the goal of science is to determine what the effect of some variable is, we have come to recognize that any given variable can produce different, even opposite effects. Whereas in the past, we sought to identify the true process responsible for each effect, we now recognize that multiple processes may underlie patterns of effects among variables. The resulting programs of research have as their goal the development of coherent theories that account for these multiple effects and multiple processes, and specify the conditions under which each effect obtains and each process operates. Persuasion theory is an excellent example of this change in focus (Petty, 1996), and similar integrative efforts characterize research on the self (Sedikides & Strube, 1996) and on interpersonal relationships (Berscheid & Reis, 1998, in this *Handbook*), among others.

The differentiated and complex view of the person that occupies center stage in social psychology at present is matched by developing efforts to address the complexity of the social contexts within which people live, implement their goals, and interact with others. Increasingly, our understanding of individual behavior is informed by research on culture, biology, personality, social development, and social roles, among other influences. In the next sections, I will address some of these themes and the ways in which these approaches represent guiding frameworks for future research. In so doing, I will also attempt to address ways in which we may remain short-sighted or incomplete in our vision of the social being.

The Individual in the Cultural Setting

From its outset, social psychology has been concerned with culture. Indeed, in the first *Handbook of Social Psychology,* Franz Boas defined the field as "the reaction of the individual to culture," arguing that our phenomena are "no more than empty formulas that can be imbued with life only by taking account of individual behavior in cultural settings." Yet since "culture does not 'behave'; only individuals behave" (Boas, 1932, cited in Kluckhohm, 1954, p. 924), individual behavior becomes a cue to cultural regularities, just as cultural regularities manifest themselves in individual behavior. Concern with culture, however, has not consistently translated into cross-cultural or multicultural research, and as a result, whatever insights early social psychology may have achieved regarding the importance of culture for individual experience remained for several decades at a relatively undeveloped level.

Fortunately, culture has now moved to the forefront of social psychological constructions of the social being (e.g., Fiske, Kitayama, Markus, & Nisbett, 1998, in this *Handbook*; Markus & Kitayama, 1991; Pepitone & Triandis, 1988; Peplau & Taylor, 1997). Much current writing explicitly acknowledges and investigates the impact of culture on individual behavior, the ways in which it is transmitted through socialization, and its cumulative effects on how people think, feel, and behave.

Not surprisingly, the first efforts to examine the impact of culture from an empirical standpoint have emphasized the lack of cross-cultural generalizability of many findings. For example, recent research has questioned the cross-cultural generalizability of the fundamental attribution error (Ross, 1977). The tendency to view people's behaviors as originating from their dispositions was, at one time, thought to be universal, in part because it was thought to be wired-in perceptually or cognitively. Current work, however, reveals the important degree to which culture influences whether or not this bias is manifested. Although Western societies tend to view individual behavior as determined by stable individual dispositions, Eastern and Southern European societies are more likely to acknowledge the situation as a potent soure of influence on individual behavior (e.g., Miller, 1987; Morris & Peng, 1994). Similarly, research reviewed by Markus and Kitayama (1991) suggests that such robust phenomena as the false consensus effect and egocentric attribution are not found, and indeed, may be reversed, in other cultures. On first glance, such findings lend a discouraging sense to empirical investigation, inasmuch as the goal of identifying cultural universals seems unachievable and ill-advised. More-

over, the empirical implication is that one must address all social psychological phenomena cross-culturally.

Rather than regarding such qualifications with the rueful acknowledgment of the limitations of any specific investigation, such discrepancies can instead be viewed as enlightening with respect to the meaningful social psychological differences that exist among cultures. As such, cultural discrepancies in social psychological phenomena enable us to see those phenomena within the context of larger cultural themes. As an example, consider several of the biases that social cognition research has identified in social inference, such as the tendency of people to make self-enhancing causal attributions (Miller & Ross, 1975) and the tendency to use false consensus (Marks & Miller, 1987), that is, inferring that other people's beliefs are like one's own to a greater degree than is true. Researchers exploring these diverse phenomena within a single culture have largely explored them in isolation, attempting to identify the parameters and limits around their existence. Cross-cultural investigations, such as that undertaken by Markus and Kitayama (1991), show that such phenomena covary culturally. Thus, for example, self-enhancing causal attributions and false consensus may be seen as components of a large pattern of self-centeredness that varies substantially from culture to culture. In Western societies, individuals tend to be self-serving and self-centered, and they tend to draw on false consensus for forming inferences. In Eastern societies, individuals make more modest causal attributions, inflate the contributions of others to joint products, and do not necessarily believe that their beliefs are widely shared by others.

Thus, an examination of the cultural regularities and discontinuities in social psychological phenomena provide the basis for three important insights for the field. First, such breadth creates the potential to weave together more elemental social psychological phenomena currently studied in isolation to identify their relations to each other (see also Betancourt & Lopez, 1993). Second, cultural investigations enable us to see the cultural basis of errors, biases, and misinterpretations that are documented in the social psychological literature. As Ichheiser notes, "these misinterpretations are not personal errors committed by ignorant individuals. They are, rather, a consistent and inevitable consequence of the social system" (Ichheiser, 1943, p. 152). Third, empirical investigations at the cultural level may enable us to identify how phenomena that covary reflect broader cultural themes, enabling us to articulate the important dimensions of which cultures are composed.

In his writings, Kurt Lewin exhorted social psychology to maintain an emphasis on culture. He would, no doubt, be pleased with the degree to which we have returned to this theme in the past decade. The renewed investigation of culture has provided us with the opportunity to move toward a metatheoretical synthesis of social psychological phenomena previously studied in isolation, which when brought together, have the potential to identify significant cultural themes. In so doing, the view of the person in social psychology has become multifaceted indeed. No longer do we view the person as a constant that moves through the environment. Rather, we have come to realize that the fundamental essence of the person is dependent upon the culture in which the person resides.

The Individual in Biological and Evolutionary Context

An important trend in contemporary social psychology, one largely unanticipated from earlier theory and research, is the degree to which social psychological investigations are moving in a biological direction. Lewin, it will be recalled, emphasized the embeddedness of social psychology in the mission of the social sciences, stressing ties to related academic disciplines such as sociology and anthropology, and to applied social fields such as education and social work. He would no doubt be surprised at the degree to which social psychology has become biologically oriented. Viewed from another angle, however, the movement of social psychological processes in a biological direction is consistent with some of the important themes of our early foundations. Insofar as Lewin and other pioneers in social psychology emphasized our role as exporters of knowledge to applied fields, the role of social psychology in understanding health and illness represents such an approach. Increasingly, we can address such important questions as "Who becomes ill?" "Who recovers?" and "How do biological and psychosocial processes interact to produce varying states of health and illness?" (Adler & Matthews, 1994). Rising interest in the biological foundations and implications of social psychological processes may be attributed to at least three factors.

First, during the past two decades, health psychology has firmly established itself as a major subfield within the discipline of psychology (see Salovey, Rothman, & Rodin, 1998, in this *Handbook*). Social psychologists have played a pivotal role in this developing field since its outset. More important is the fact that we can now see connnections between the basic research that we conduct in the laboratory and the formidable problems in the field to which they are relevant.

What have been some of the intellectual and empirical contributions from health psychology to our understanding of social psychological processes? To begin with, such research has begun to expose the genetic foundations of social behavior. Using the traditional "twin" methodology comparing the incidence, frequency, or strength of a particular process in identical versus fraternal twins raised apart

or together, researchers have increasingly demonstrated a surprisingly high degree of heritability in socially relevant individual differences and processes. For example, dispositional optimism, the robust tendency to regard the future in positive terms and to believe that one's efforts will be successful in bringing about one's desired goals (Scheier & Carver, 1985), appears to have a substantial genetic component (Plomin et al., 1992). The willingness to turn to others and to seek social support under stress also has substantial heritability as does the tendency to engage in active problem solving, as opposed to avoidant coping, in response to stressful life events (Kendler et al., 1991). There even appears to be a genetic basis for the perception that other people are available to provide help during stressful times, reflecting a genetic underpinning either to construe support as available or in the ability to select supportive individuals for one's social network (Kendler et al., 1991). Such studies point to the continued importance of investigating the genetic underpinnings of social processes, especially in response to stress.

Another important tie-in between biological and psychosocial processes has been in establishing links between the stress and coping literature in health psychology and the social cognition literature on self-regulatory processes. The goals of both lines of research are virtually identical but, until recently, they were pursued largely independently. Yet, it is evident that the stress appraisal processes that people go through in determining whether an event is stressful draws fundamentally on principles of social cognition, and the coping responses that people generate as a result of exposure to stress are consistent with basic processes of self-regulation. A closer alliance between these two literatures would put more empirical teeth into the health psychology literature on stress and coping, and at the same time, give the social cognition and self-regulation literatures a vehicle for studying basic processes of cognition and self-regulation in important real-world situations (e.g., Aspinwall & Taylor, in press; Carver & Scheier, 1981).

A similar relationship exists between the social psychological literature on interpersonal relationships and the health psychology literature on social support. These two literatures have evolved largely independently, with the result that the social support literature is heavy on understanding the adaptive and maladaptive aspects of personal relationships, but weak on the origins and development of those relationships; the reverse is true of the interpersonal relationships literature, in which the determinants of attraction are fairly well understood, but the processes by which social relationships have an impact on mental and physical health have, until recently, been largely ignored. These two literatures have the capability of informing each other in ways that will be to their mutual benefit (Stroebe et al., 1996).

Other empirical links between fundamental social psychological processes and biopsychosocial issues in the health psychology literature can be forged. For example, French and Raven's bases of power have been used effectively by Rodin and Janis (1979) to understand how appeals to different aspects of authority may influence individuals' adherence to medical treatments and willingness to obtain follow-up care. Principles of attitude change and persuasion have been used effectively to get people to practice better health behaviors (e.g., Fishbein & Ajzen, 1975; Leventhal, 1970). The recognition and identification of symptoms, the decision to obtain treatment, and the cognitions that one holds about one's illness have all been enlightened by social cognition approaches (Croyle & Barger, 1993; Leventhal, Nerenz, & Strauss, 1982; Pennebaker, 1983). It is fair to say that the field of health psychology would be at a very nascent stage, were it not for the rich empirical tradition of social psychology. As social psychologists have become increasingly interested in health-related problems and as they develop expertise in the biological origins of thought and behavior, health psychology may, in turn, have important effects on how social psychologists conceive of the scope and influence of the field.

A second development that has fostered a biological emphasis within social psychology stems from the fact that all areas of psychology are becoming more biological in orientation, as the field of neuroscience makes empirical progress. Cognitive neuroscience provides the possibility of relating psychological states and functions to underlying structures and events in the brain (Sarter, Berntson, & Cacioppo, 1996). Parallel distributed processing (PDP) models, which have had a significant impact on research in neuroscience, are beginning to be applied in social psychology as well (see Smith, 1998, in this *Handbook*). The relevance of neurotransmitters to mood and to active self-regulation represent fledgling insights that will likely increase in number as the empirical base of neuroscience grows. The importance of neuroscience to social psychology is, at the moment, largely potential, rather than explicit, but it will be a continuing source of influence on the biological bases and concomitants of social psychological processes.

The third basis for biological interests within social psychology has stemmed from sociobiology. The sociobiological perspective is heavily concerned with two issues: the origins of psychological mechanisms that guide social interaction and social relationships and the functions of those mechanisms. As is true for other individual characteristics, sociobiologists suggest that natural selection and sexual selection provide a viable scientific perspective on the origins and functions of social psychological processes. Indeed, it has been suggested that the sociobiological perspective can provide an overarching theoretical framework that has the potential for scientists to see relations among a

broad array of psychosocial processes (Buss, 1995). The sociobiological perspective has already contributed to certain traditional content areas within social psychology. These include the understanding of mating processes in adults (Buss & Kenrick, 1998, in this *Handbook*), helping and altruism (see Batson, 1998, in this *Handbook*), the nature of intergroup relations (Brewer & Brown, 1998, in this *Handbook*), aggression (Buss, 1995), the universality of facial expressions conveying emotions (Ekman, 1982; see DePaulo & Friedman, 1998, in this *Handbook*), and sex differences in gender roles (see Deaux & LaFrance, 1998, in this *Handbook*), as well as certain aspects of attitudes and causal attribution processes (see Buss & Kenrick, 1998, in this *Handbook*).

The sociobiological perspective also provides a basis for thinking about a recurrent problem in social psychology, namely, the domain specificity of many cognitive and affective processes. For example, although early work in artificial intelligence proposed generic models of inference (e.g., Abelson & Rosenberg's [1958] psychological implication), such content-free models ultimately yielded to models that included highly domain-specific world knowledge as a basis of inference, such as the script concept (Schank & Abelson, 1977). Attribution theorists initially proposed generic models of attribution processes, arguing that causality is inferred in much the same way across a broad array of domains. Recently, researchers have taken exception with such a position (e.g., Hilton & Slugoski, 1986), arguing that causal knowledge is domain-specific and that causal attribution may understood as a gap-filling process that occurs when expected occurrences in a specific domain do not go as anticipated. The idea that domain-general cognitive processes can be identified is increasingly being questioned in other areas of psychology as well, including learning, cognitive neuroscience, linguistics, emotion research, motion perception, and reasoning (e.g., Buss, 1995; Pinker, 1994; Tooby & Cosmides, 1992). The response of evolutionary psychology is to argue that individual life domains are defined by the adaptive problems that they pose, and thus, seeking processes that cut across a broad array of domains is not a reasonable undertaking. Whether the sociobiological perspective assumes a mainstream guiding focus within social psychology remains to be seen. What it clearly accomplishes is to alert the field to the need to address the origins of social psychological phenomena, the functions of those phenomena, and their interrelatedness or lack of it.

Biology is undeniably an important aspect of the social being, and to evolve a social psychology without taking into account the great importance of biological processes in social phenomena would be shortsighted. Consequently, the increasing importance that social psychologists have placed on the biological underpinnings and concomitants of social phenomena can be heralded as a significant advance for our field and of our articulation of the view of the person. One area of social psychology, it should be noted, has never lost sight of the importance of biology, and that is the area of social development, an issue to which we now turn.

Social Development

Early empirical efforts in social psychology placed great importance on understanding the development of attitudes, prejudice, and other important social psychological phenomena. As such, social psychologists were fundamentally concerned with social development. For example, as noted earlier, research on the authoritarian personality was explicitly concerned with the socialization practices that led individuals to develop intolerant attitudes. Moreover, this interest in socialization translated directly into a body of knowledge that was deemed of social psychological importance. For example, one of the classic textbooks in social psychology, *Foundation of Social Psychology* by Jones and Gerard (1967), devoted no less than three of its sixteen chapters to this topic.

Social psychological investigations are inherently developmental (Ruble & Goodnow, 1998, in this *Handbook*). Whether a study examines college students' attitudes toward political issues on their campus, a nine-year-old's grasp of social comparison processes, or an adult's efforts to cope with an illness, all investigations focus on some point in social development which implicitly or explicitly influences the nature of the phenomenon studied and the conclusions to be drawn. Maintaining a developmental focus keeps us aware of this fact. Unfortunately, social psychology's concern with social development is only intermittent, occurring in some research areas but not in others. Although there is an active literature on attitudes across the life cycle (Abeles, 1987; Alwin, Cohen, & Newcomb, 1991; Sears, 1983), in other areas of social psychology, such a focus is almost entirely lacking. Moreover, none of the major current social psychology textbooks has a chapter on socialization or social development, and two prominent textbooks do not even have index references to the terms. A defender of this shift might respond that the field of psychology has grown so complex that no one area can cover all topics; development may more properly be the province of developmental psychology, since it is "about children" (Ruble & Goodnow, 1998, in this *Handbook*). As social development research has expanded into adolescence, adulthood, and old age, so the importance of viewing any social psychological phenomenon or a specific empirical result in the context of development becomes evident.

Attention to social development and to the origins of social psychological phenomena has several potential benefits for how we conceptualize phenomena. First, considering the origins of social psychological phenomena enables

us to appreciate their dynamics. In order to understand the factors that promote or undermine social psychological regularities, we need to know how these phenomena developed in the first place. Second, an understanding of the social practices and developmental regularities that produce a social psychological phenomenon can be enlightening with regard to its functions. Charting the evolution of a social psychological phenomenon provides knowledge of why the pattern developed and the several forms it may take. Third, incorporating a social development perspective provides the field with an important historical perspective. Narrowly speaking, it may enable us to identify cohort effects, and more broadly, it enables us to see the historical context within which specific social psychological phenomena emerge and within which they are expressed. Imagine the limited value of research on the authoritarian personality, had the work not been firmly grounded in the study of German socialization practices of the times.

Finally, adding a social development perspective to our field can provide an intellectual enrichment that fosters our ability to develop a truly synthetic psychology. When we ignore social development, we are limited in our ability to integrate work with that of developmental psychology at the very least, and to the extent that we rob ourselves of an understanding of the functions and dynamics of our phenomena by ignoring social development, we impair our ability to make extrapolations to other areas in psychology as well. In short, an understanding of social development, and how social psychological phenomena evolve, provides a more integrative, dynamic, functional, and historical portrait of the social being than we can hope to achieve with a more limited focus that ignores it (Ruble & Goodnow, 1998, in this *Handbook*).

There are corresponding risks to ignoring the importance of social development as well. For example, in his analysis of the social psychological experiment, Sears (1986) pointed to the liabilities of basing a science heavily on empirical studies with college student participants. College students occupy a very special and unrepresentative position in developmental history with respect to many of the topics that social psychologists study heavily. College students have less crystallized attitudes than adults, making their attitudes more subject to change in response to persuasive communications than may be the case with older populations. Most college students have a less well-formulated sense of self than is true for adults, with the result that research on college student participants makes the self-concept appear to be quite malleable in response to feedback, manipulation, and other transient forces. College students are brighter and have stronger cognitive skills when compared with the general population, making social cognitive research on judgment formation and decision-making potentially unrepresentative. College students are more likely to comply with authority figures than are adults, and as a result, social psychological investigations paint a picture of the person as compliant and easily influenced. College students have more unstable peer group relationships, given that their geographic location, occupations, and long-term relationships are still largely in flux. The end result is a vision of the social being as strongly dependent on cognitive processes, with little attention to personality dispositions, material self-interest, emotionally based irrationalities, group norms, and phenomena that are specific to life stage (Sears, 1986). In short, the Sears analysis shows pointedly the important ways in which social psychological knowledge is developmentally based, and it raises the spectre that a truly developmental focus is not only desirable but necessary to ensure that social psychological regularities identified in research are indeed stable and generalizable. Also implicit in the Sears critique is the fact that social psychological investigations also do not typically incorporate sufficient emphasis on social roles, an issue to which we now turn.

Social Roles

Social roles embody the regularities in the environments in which people participate. The overwhelming majority of situations in which people find themselves are not new situations but recurrent ones. We do not negotiate each situation separately, but rather bring to it the insights, knowledge, and behavioral regularities that provide stability and coherence in behavior from situation to situation. Social roles are the product of biological and economic needs and of regularities in social development and culture. It is difficult to imagine how we could achieve a true understanding of social psychological phenomena without a comprehension of social roles. For a chilling example of the power of social roles, one need only consider the Zimbardo (Zimbardo et al., 1973) prison study, in which perfectly normal Stanford undergraduates easily and unnervingly adopted the demeanor and behavior patterns of prisoners and guards, depending upon the role to which they had been assigned.

In the first edition of the *Handbook of Social Psychology,* an entire chapter was devoted to a discussion of social roles, and in addition, several applied chapters dealt with the regularities in behavior that derive from environmental constancies. No chapter on social roles appears in any of the major current social psychological texts, nor will such a chapter appear in this collection. One might respond that social roles are dull, representing the ways in which people enact behavioral sequences in the same ways, as governed by formal and informal rules and norms. Or, one might respond that social roles have become the province of sociol-

ogy and that, as such, their exploration no longer falls to empirical social psychology.

Perhaps because social psychological research increasingly relies on college student subjects whose social role is incidental to their participation in work, family, and community, and whose status as students is only temporary, we have come to pay scant attention to the potent effects of social roles on adult behavior. Yet without an understanding of social roles, there can be little comprehension of such phenomena as obedience to authority (e.g., Milgram, 1963, 1974), crimes of obedience (Kelman & Hamilton, 1989), or the effects of attitudes merely espoused versus those that are internalized (Kelman, 1974; see also Cialdini & Trost, 1998, in this *Handbook*). Eagly (1987) makes a persuasive case that sex differences in social behavior are almost incomprehensible without an understanding of the different social roles and gender roles that men and women occupy. As social psychologists have moved into the study of health-related problems and issues, the need to acknowledge the importance of social roles has become increasingly clear. Without an appreciation of role-related stressors, for example, an understanding of how chronic stress adversely affects health is inconceivable (Lepore, 1995). Without an understanding of social roles, we cannot appreciate the mundane activities of daily life in which social psychological phenomena are embedded. In seeking a multifaceted and complete view of the person in social psychology, our appreciation of social roles and their contextual importance for social psychological phenomena will be essential.

The Interface of Personality and Social Psychology

Although the regularities imposed on individual behavior by social roles have not been fully incorporated into our view of the person, the impact of situational regularities more generally has been acknowledged, and as such, has contributed to a distinctively social psychological approach to the study of personality. In the earlier discussion of the authoritarian personality, it was noted that social psychologists developed a social view of individual difference characteristics, emphasizing socialization as the basis for their development, and situational moderators as determinants of their expression. Thus, for example, as a result of socialization, an individual may have a propensity to behave in an authoritarian manner, but without the environmental circumstances conducive to the expression of these tendencies, they might well remain latent. However, subsequent to these early insights, much individual difference work in personality was confined to employing an individual difference measure as one variable in an experimental design, so as to demonstrate that individuals variously categorized as high or low on some dimension would respond in ways predictable from that dimension in carefully constructed environmental circumstances.

In 1968, Walter Mischel dealt such a simplistic approach a heavy blow. Beginning with his analysis of the Hartshorne and May (1928) studies on moral behavior, he demonstrated that important and presumably highly stable individual differences (such as those involved in moral behavior) may show low cross-situational generalizability. A child might cheat in one situation but refuse to steal in another. A different child might copy a friend's homework but not lie. Across a series of studies, Mischel estimated that the relation between a measured individual difference on a given trait dimension and behavior in a situation that plausibly relates to that trait dimension rarely exceeds 0.3.[8] Mischel's important observations fit comfortably with the situational determinism viewpoint that has historically characterized social psychology (Ross & Nisbett, 1991). As far back as Lewin, social psychologists have argued that patterns of behavior that are often attributed to personality dispositions and preferences may, in fact, be explained by the potency of situational dynamics or by regularities in situational and social contexts.

These beliefs prompted many social psychologists to ignore personality factors altogether. Others, however, questioned the advisability of such a course, inasmuch as ignoring personality belies the individual differences that people see among their acquaintances in everyday life, and provides few opportunities for understanding the role of learning histories or distinctive personal experience in the production of individual behavior. The view that people make their own situations by virtue of their personality, which had given way to the view that situations overwhelm these individual differences, was now yielding to an interactionist viewpoint: truth lies not in the main effect of the person or the situation but in their joint determination of behavior.

The social psychological view that behavior can be explained by the interaction between personality and the situation spawned a new kind of research on personality (Jones, 1985). Researchers began to focus on stabilities in how people construe situations as relevant (or not) for themselves, so as to establish guidelines for their behavior. In this viewpoint, individual differences are believed to manifest themselves in terms of chronically accessible knowledge that leads people to categorize situations in particular ways. The situation, in turn, provides contextual priming, which leads people to categorize it as calling for one or another kind of behavioral response. When situational cues are minimal, individual differences in the propensity to construe situations in particular ways may be used as guidelines for behavior, but when situational variables that demand certain kinds of behavior are clear, or

when certain situation-relevant constructs have been activated, then situational factors may overwhelm individual propensities in construal (Higgins, 1990). The person, then, represents chronic knowledge accessibility and the situation provides contextual priming. Behavior is a function of the knowledge that is primed by these individual differences and by situational parameters (Higgins, 1990).

The interplay of the person and the situation and the recognition that their interaction critically determines the ability to predict behavior has become a guiding insight for social psychological analyses of personality. An example is Snyder's (1979) research on self-monitoring, in which he distinguished between individuals who routinely scan the environment attempting to determine how they can best fit in (high self-monitoring individuals) versus those who look inward to their dispositions in an attempt to establish guidelines for any particular situation (low self-monitoring individuals). Through a program of research manipulating a broad array of situational factors, Snyder and his associates have been able to demonstrate that phenomena such as persuasion and conformity can be altered, even reversed, by framing the situation in ways that differentially engaged the high or low self-monitor (Snyder, 1979). Such a viewpoint has also formed the core of a guiding view of the person for such contributions as Higgins' self-discrepancy theory (1987), Markus' possible selves formulation (Markus & Nurius, 1986), Cantor and Kihlstrom's (1987) work on social intelligence, and research concerning the expression of prejudice (e.g., Devine, 1989).

This social psychological view of personality has several important benefits. First, it provides insights regarding when individuals' dispositional qualities will serve as referents for their personal behavior, and when and why they will not in other circumstances. It also provides insights regarding when and why particular situational factors will be salient, and when and why they will overrule individuals' dispositional qualities. By drawing on the concept of knowledge accessibility, this perspective also suggests that knowledge accessed from either individual differences or situational variables follows the same basic underlying processes, differing simply in their origins (Higgins, 1990). The cognitive processes that determine what knowledge is available, accessible, and activated enables the scientist to predict how an individual will subjectively interpret a social situation and then make use of personal or situational standards to determine the meaning of the situation and to generate behavioral responses to it.

The current state of personality research in social psychology represents an intellectual achievement of considerable stature. Knowledge of the stabilities and instabilities of people, coupled with an understanding of cognitive processes provided by cognitive psychology and social cognition, have merged with a social psychological literature that recognizes the power of situational variables to influence behavior (Ross & Nisbett, 1991). The result has been a synthetic approach to the person that integrates the insights from all these fields in a heuristically useful framework that has advanced our understanding of the person substantially.

Research Methods

Rounding out the portrait of the person in social psychology requires not only attention to the content of the field but also a consideration of its methods. The portrait of the person that emerges from research is necessarily affected by the nature of the subject populations investigated and the methods used to investigate them, often in subtle ways of which we may be unaware (Jones, 1985).

Rereading social psychology's history is rediscovering its rich empirical legacy, its careful attention to levels of analysis, and its explorations of diverse research populations in a dazzling array of settings. For example, the early group dynamics tradition is marked by the use of field studies, natural experiments, field experiments, natural groups in the laboratory, and artificial groups in the laboratory, all converging on the phenomena of group life. Reviewing this work reveals the excitement and optimism that came not only from the sense of discovery but from this very wealth of research techniques that contributed to the accumulating body of knowledge (Cartwright & Zander, 1953, Chapter 2).

Indeed, prior to 1960, as Sears (1986) noted, published research in social psychology was typically based on a wide variety of participant populations and a large number of research sites. After 1960, social psychology increasingly based its empirical foundations on studies of college students, testing in academic laboratories on academic-like tasks. For my course in social psychology, I have repeated the Sears content analysis every other year to determine the extent to which his warnings and concerns have been taken to heart. In two of the *Journal of Personality and Social Psychology*'s subsections, the reliance on college student participant populations has subsided somewhat, with approximately 78 percent of studies in the Interpersonal Relations and Group Processes section and between 65 percent and 70 percent of studies in the Personality Processes and Individual Differences section using only college student participants. Although research settings continue to draw heavily on academic-like tasks in academic settings, there has been a modest increase (20 to 35 percent of studies, depending upon the year and section) in studying human behavior in nonacademic settings using nonexperimental methods and/or in using multiple methods to converge on the phenomena of interest. The Attitudes and Social Cognition section, in contrast, has increased the percentage of articles that use only college student participants, from 80 percent five years ago to approximately 97 percent at present. This trend appears to be due, in part, to the fact that most articles currently include multiple studies (an average of 2.62 per article in a recent analysis), and it may be difficult for researchers to make use of other than college student participants for multiple investigations of a single phenomenon.

The importance of college student participants in laboratory settings is undeniable to progress in our field, enabling us to conduct the precise experimental work that builds knowledge cumulatively. Nonetheless, to utilize these methods, sometimes to the exclusion of other approaches and participant samples, seems unwise. Advances in measurement (Judd & McClelland, 1998, in this *Handbook*) and data analysis (Kenny, Kashy, & Bolger, 1998, in this *Handbook*) illustrate how diverse our tools are for the analysis of social psychological phenomena. Survey methods have been used to address a wide array of empirical questions, ranging from opinions about political, economic, and social issues to the conditions most likely to foster assimilation and contrast effects in social judgment (Schwarz, Graves, & Schuman, 1998, in this *Handbook*). Increasingly, experimentation in social psychology has helped to lend teeth to field experiments and to observational and correlational studies (Aronson, Wilson, & Brewer, 1998, in this *Handbook*).

In an important essay, "In Defense of External Invalidity," Mook (1983) pointed out that, because the goal of many laboratory experiments is to test theory and address questions that assume the form "What can happen and why does it happen?" pleas for them also to be high in external validity are misguided. He argues that field studies may tell us more about "what does happen" in life, answering questions regarding what is usual, typical, frequent, or normal. While such a position is defensible up to a point, to the extent that any program of research must ultimately address both what can happen and what does happen, making use of laboratory experiments to the exclusion of parallel field studies is unwise.

Moreover, field studies, whether experimental, correlational, interview, or survey in nature, do far more than establish the normality of phenomena. They provide valuable insights into the natural contexts in which phenomena occur; they provide information about the strength of the phenomena, given correlated environmental circumstances; they may be helpful in elucidating mediation; and they are extremely important for identifying variables both internal to the person and environmental in nature that moderate the phenomenon. Thus, field investigations can be central to theory development. While Mook's defense of external invalidity is certainly appropriate for individual experiments with particular purposes, over the long term, programs of research that are perched on a pedestal of external invalidity are likely to collapse (see Aronson, Wilson, & Brewer, 1998, in this *Handbook* for a thoughtful discussion of this issue). As Allport (1954) noted, we are a useful science. This can be achieved by preserving the essence of the question in our empirical investigations and moving back and forth between the laboratory and the field.

Are there areas within social psychology at the present time that embody the empirical richness that was a tradition of the field? Social comparison theory has gone from being studied primarily in the laboratory to being studied in both the laboratory and the field (e.g., Buunk et al., 1990; Taylor & Lobel, 1989; Wheeler & Miyake, 1992; Wills, 1981; Wood, 1989). The richness of the research settings and the diverse array of populations studied has provided a wealth of valuable theoretical and empirical insights as a result. Initially focused primarily on self-evaluation within a group context, social comparison research has now demonstrated the importance of multiple self-evaluative motives; it has explored the cognitive as well as social processes underlying comparisons; it has elaborated the importance of a variety of comparison targets, including dissimilar as well as similar ones; it has demonstrated the circumstances under which people choose upward versus downward comparison targets; and it has detailed the emotional and epistemic consequences of different types of comparisons. In short, social comparison theory, always social psychology's second-favorite theory (Thornton & Arrowood, 1966), has become a vibrant, exciting, renewed area, precisely because of the richness of its contemporary methodological foundation.

Initially, research on interpersonal attraction was based heavily on studies of interactions between two college student strangers or between a single college student and a "phantom other" (Bersheid & Walster, 1978). Research on interpersonal relationships, as it is now called, includes naturalistic studies of friendship networks, research on committed and married couples, and longitudinal examinations of the development of interpersonal relationships (Bersheid & Reis, 1998, in this *Handbook*), culminating in such rich theoretical models as attachment theory (Hazan & Shaver, 1994). The increasing attention of studies on interpersonal relationships to the importance of friendship, marriage, and romantic relationships has, in turn, provided insights to other fields, such as the observation that compliance and conformity effects are often best understood in the context of interpersonal goals, such as the desire to develop new relationships or to strengthen existing ones (Cialdini & Trost, 1998, in this *Handbook*). The empirical diversity in participant populations and settings is precisely what has kept this field lively and energetic, even in the face of politically motivated attack (Berscheid, 1994; Berscheid & Reis, 1998, in this *Handbook*).

Intergroup relations has always been a central topic for social psychologists, and it, too, has enjoyed a dynamic resurgence and empirical proliferation in response to a wealth of perspectives and methodologies (see Brewer & Brown, 1998, in this *Handbook*). A combination of precise laboratory experiments and field investigations has revealed the importance of social identity to individual behavior and the interpretation of others' behavior; it has identified the situational parameters that influence when social identity is engaged (Tajfel & Turner, 1979) and when individual identity is engaged, and the consequences of those different conditions (Brewer & Brown, 1998, in this *Handbook*). Classic field investigations, such as Sherif's (Sherif et al., 1961) "Robber's Cave" experiment,[9] as well as highly controlled laboratory investigations have examined the relationship of intergroup orientation to conflict and competition, power, status, and the reduction of prejudice (see Brewer & Brown, 1998, in this *Handbook*). A combination of laboratory and field investigations reveals the importance of optimal distinctiveness, the need for individuals to derive their identity from the social groups to which they belong, while simultaneously establishing their distinctiveness through their intergroup comparisons (Brewer, 1991). Social dominance theory (Pratto et al., 1994; Sidanius, 1993) makes use of survey methods with individuals in established social roles as well as experimental evidence to demonstrate how position in a social hierarchy evokes and maintains beliefs about others that promulgate one's own position, often at the expense of others. Thus, there is ample evidence that throughout our history and in current arenas of investigation, multiple research methods with a broad array of subject populations importantly advanced our understanding of social psychological phenomena.

As we recapture and maintain what has been of value in our research methods historically, the storytelling quality of much social psychological research merits preservation. Some of our most intriguing and insightful social psychological investigations have come from our ability to recognize the larger truth embodied in a poignant story, an important incident, or the dark side of human life. The origins of Stanley Milgram's (1974) experiments on obedience to authority was the Holocaust, based on the observation that guards at the prison camps followed the orders of authorities, often without questioning the terrible acts they were asked to commit (see Aronson, Wilson, & Brewer, 1998, in this *Handbook*). The impetus for the classic "line experiment" on conformity effects by Solomon Asch, in which participants often overruled their own perceptual experience in favor of social consensus, is said to have come from an incident during Asch's early childhood in Poland.

As a boy of seven, he stayed up late for his first Passover night. He saw his grandmother pour an extra glass of wine and asked whom it was for. "For the prophet Elijah," an uncle told him. "Will he really take a sip?," the boy asked. "Oh yes," the uncle replied, "you just watch when the time comes." Filled with the sense of suggestion and expectation, the boy thought he saw the level of wine in the cup drop just a bit (Stout, *New York Times,* February 1996).

Visible and poignant human stories, such as the Kitty Genovese incident, have been the impetus for wide-ranging empirical investigations (e.g., helping behavior) and theoretical formulations (e.g., prosocial behavior) (see Batson, 1998, in this *Handbook*).[10] Lee Ross and his colleagues have been especially adept at turning quirks of human nature into important observations about psychological functioning, such as the capital punishment study that illustrates how people with opposite opinions can become even more polarized following exposure to the same information (Lord, Ross, & Lepper, 1979). In our quest to be more scientific, we may sometimes look askance on the potential psychological importance of individual incidents or stories, preferring instead to draw on the previous literature as the source for our new insights. But these incidents or stories have served a valuable function, alerting us to as-yet-unexplored social psychological phenomena and to insights regarding how people cope with the continually changing world. As such, we can preserve this tradition by being storytellers to our students, in the hopes that they will both pass them on and create new ones for future social psychologists.

CONCLUSION: THE VISION OF THE PERSON IN SOCIAL PSYCHOLOGY

In the 1954 edition of the *Handbook of Social Psychology,* Gordon Allport was charged with the responsibility of writing Chapter 1, the historical background of modern social psychology (Allport, 1954). In his essay, he noted the "spectacular expansion" of social psychological research and influence following World War II. He credited this rapid expansion to the "pragmatic tradition" of the United States, the fact that conditions of social strain and national emergencies provide Americans with incentives to invent new techniques and to strike out for solutions to practical problems. He regarded social psychology as very much an invention of this tradition, a response to the first and second World Wars, the social problems of the Depression, the rise of Hitler, and the genocide of the Jews. Stimuli for all of the social sciences, these forces had a special impact on the social psychological tradition.

This pragmatic emphasis has been in evidence in social psychology throughout its history. The storytelling tradition noted above and its influence on theory and empirical

research is an example of this approach. The phenomenon of mindless violence has spawned insightful and profound social psychological investigations of deindividuation (Zimbardo, 1970), especially in institutional settings (Zimbardo et al., 1973). The social activism of the 1960s led not only to an explosion of research on prejudice and discrimination (Crocker, Major, & Steele, 1998, in this *Handbook*), but to the expansion of the field of social psychology itself, as students came to believe that social psychology might offer solutions to some of the country's serious social problems. Social psychological theory and research provides a valuable perspective for understanding political issues facing nations (Tetlock, 1998, in this *Handbook*).

The challenges facing our current world may not seem as immediately and obviously threatening as those about which Allport wrote, but they may be every bit as troubling. Conservative political times inevitably bring to the fore a view of behavior as determined by reliable differences in personality, intelligence, and other stable characteristics, as well as a resurgence of the viewpoints that individuals create and are ultimately responsible for the conditions under which they live. The fact that situations and economic and political realities heavily shape individuals, their characteristics, and their behavior has receded from the forefront of much current conservative social commentary. *The Bell Curve* (Herrnstein & Murray, 1994), for example, argues that environmental dynamics have less effect on IQ and individual intellectual performance than social science investigators have assumed, and it implies that genetic contributions to intelligence have been understated.

The insights of social psychological investigation are desperately needed (Jones, 1985). Our special expertise has always been an understanding of the impact of the social environment on the individual and how the individual constructs meaning from social situations. We are experts in the comprehension of emergent phenomena, those that cannot be predicted from individuals in isolation, but only from a comprehension of the dynamics of individuals in group situations. Increasingly, we have incorporated cultural understanding and developmental insights into analyses that help explain why individuals may have the inherent capacities to learn and perform at a high level of functioning but are unable to do so (e.g., Steele & Aronson, 1995). Our willingness and ability to contribute to the solution of problems embodied by the social action tradition remains (see Jones, 1985; Levinger, 1986).

Moreover, we are, and always have been, a field that exports knowledge. Several recent analyses of the most-cited psychologists and the most-cited articles shows an overrepresentation of social psychologists, relative to our numbers. Our work currently provides a basis for educational interventions (e.g., Wilson & Linville, 1985), analyses of political behavior, analyses of world politics (Tetlock, 1998, in this *Handbook*), understanding of legal phenomena

(Ellsworth & Mauros, 1997, in this *Handbook*), and analyses of health-related issues (Salovey, Rothman, & Rodin, 1998, in this *Handbook*), among other contributions. Our work is cited not only by other subfields of psychology, such as developmental, cognitive, and clinical, but also by the other social sciences.

Our seemingly disproportionate influence on the rest of psychology and on the social sciences more generally may stem from our status as an interstitial field. We provide an understanding of the person in the social context that can be informative to clinicians about normal behavior, reactions to pathological conditions, and ultimately to pathology itself (e.g., Taylor & Brown, 1988). Our focus on the concerns of adolescent and adult life provide contexts for developmental interest in how cognitive and social understandings evolve that provide the basis for an interpretation of the world. Our examination of cognition in its social context reveals the active nature of thought and how it changes in response to the construal of situations; indeed, many landmark contributions to cognitive psychology are as much social as they are cognitive (e.g., Kahneman & Tversky, 1973). As noted earlier, many social psychologists have moved in a biological direction. Links between social psychology and physiological processes and linkages to the field of behavioral neuroscience are becoming more plentiful (see, for example, Adler & Matthews, 1994; Rodin & Salovey, 1989). The fact that we focus both on the characteristics of the individual and on the bidirectional influences between individual and environment virtually guarantees that basic theoretical observations about human behavior will be useful input to related fields.

As such, it is useful to return to Lewin's borrowed dictum, "There is nothing as practical as a good theory," and make explicit the context within which it was originally voiced. Many have assumed that Lewin regarded theories as practical (or useful, as he has often been misquoted) because they enable a researcher to explore a set of relations among variables in a well-defined problem area in which clear predictions are made. Thus, one can cut through a domain by means of the structure and guidelines provided by the theory. What Lewin (1943) initially meant by the phrase, however, is the fundamental value of using theory to investigate practical problems. As early as 1943, he felt compelled to chide his audience for losing sight of the important relation between theoretical and applied problems, and the fact that they had once shared equal status in the study of psychology. He decried the tendency to look down on applied problems, arguing that we must "watch out that theory never breaks loose from its proper place as a servant, as a tool for human beings" (Lewin, 1943, p. 118) to use for the solution of social problems.

Nostalgia is an easy emotion. In hindsight, the goodness and right-headedness of the past becomes evident and its limitations fade from view. One might argue that an essay that extols the values of the past is inherently nostalgic, and that the progress made by the field should enable us to transcend earlier and more limited visions. While the progress within the field is undeniable, the sheer volume of specific empirical findings we have generated can produce a myopia that comes from focusing on the details rather than the broader themes. The clarity that came from the early vision developed by pioneering social psychologists like Lewin still serves us well.

POSTSCRIPT

From an historical perspective, the field of social psychology has provided a view of the person that resembles Robert J. Lifton's (1993) protean person. With every decade has come the image of a different facet. Over the past seven decades, the field has produced portraits of the individual as a socially derived product of the group; as a being driven by motivational need for consistency; as a manifestation of individual differences that result from stabilities in socialization histories; as the product of social learning; and as governed by cognitive needs, abilities, and constraints. Each viewpoint, in turn, has had considerable heuristic value for research. There is always a risk in assuming that the past has led inevitably to the present, such that present trends culminate in a superior and synthetic view. Despite this caution, it is tempting to conclude that the view of the self that is emerging within social psychological research at present is truly a collaborative and shared vision with the promise to guide the field for decades to come. Its synthetic complexity encompasses, as no vision within social psychology has previously, the manifold phenomena of social life that social psychological investigations have elucidated.

NOTES

1. Students of social psychology may be chagrined to learn that Lewin's actual statement was, "A business man once stated 'there is nothing as practical as a good theory' " (Lewin, 1943, p. 118).
2. For example, the autocratic leader was instructed to be personal in his praise and criticism of group members and to remain aloof from active participation except when demonstrating a task. He was told to dictate steps one at a time, so that future steps would always be largely uncertain to the group members. Whether these characteristics are intrinsic to autocratic leadership is a matter of considerable debate and raises the question concerning whether the operational definition actually manipulated a cold, aloof, critical, and secretive way of dealing with subordinates, rather than an autocratic leadership style per se.
3. It should be noted that Lewin also looked to the natural sciences for guidance in the development of social psy-

chology. He believed that psychological theories should mirror theories in physics in both form and function, a point that is especially evident in his development of field theory. But in terms of the contributions that social psychology would make to knowledge, he saw our ties as being primarily to the social, rather than the natural sciences.

4. As will be seen, this fundamentally interactionist view of personality as the product of and as moderated by situational factors has been much more in evidence from the 1970s onward, as work by Mischel and other personality theorists have further elaborated this vision (e.g., Mischel, 1968).

5. It should be noted that Festinger did not use the language of Gestalt psychology to construct cognitive dissonance theory, but the theory has been viewed by others as implicitly incorporating important principles and insights from Gestalt psychology (see, for example, West & Wicklund, 1980).

6. It should be noted that Bem credits the derivation of self-perception theory to Skinner's radical behaviorism (Bem, 1967). However, the unfolding logic of self-perception theory, especially as embodied in the 1972 theoretical statement, came to resemble more closely attribution theory principles articulated by Heider (1958) and by Jones and Davis (1965), and thereby qualifies more as a cognitively based attribution theory than a manifestation of radical behaviorism.

7. Not until Zanna and Cooper (1974; see also Fazio, Zanna, & Cooper, 1977) was significant empirical light shed on the conditions under which the predictions of each theory could be borne out.

8. It should be noted that Mischel's analyses of the Hartshorne and May studies have been criticized on conceptual and methodological grounds (Rushton, 1980), although his arguments have been convincingly applied to other personality traits as well.

9. The Robber's Cave experiment, conducted by Sherif and coworkers (Sherif et al., 1961), involved two groups of boys at a summer camp. Initially divided into competitive teams, the boys developed so much anger and hostility toward each other that these feelings and the behavior they prompted emerged in noncompetitive situations as well. By inducing the boys to cooperate to solve a common problem, the researchers successfully reduced the hostility.

10. Kitty Genovese, a young New York resident, was stabbed to death on a city street while at least 38 people watched the incident or heard her screams and did nothing.

REFERENCES

Abeles, R. P. (Ed.) (1987). *Life span perspectives and social psychology.* Hillsdale, NJ: Erlbaum.

Abelson, R. P., Aronson, E., McGuire, W. J., Newcomb, T. M., Rosenberg, M. J., & Tannenbaum, P. H. (Eds.) (1968). *Theories of cognitive consistency: A sourcebook.* Chicago: Rand McNally.

Abelson, R. P., & Rosenberg, M. J. (1958). Symbolic psycho-logic: A model of attitudinal cognition. *Behavioral Science, 3,* 1–13.

Adams, J. S. (1963). Toward an understanding of inequity. *Journal of Abnormal and Social Psychology, 67,* 422–436.

Adams, J. S. (1965). Inequity in social exchange. In L. Berkowitz (Ed.), *Advances in experimental social psychology* (Vol. 2, pp. 267–300). New York: Academic Press.

Adler, N. E., & Matthews, K. A. (1994). Health and psychology: Why do some people get sick and some stay well? *Annual Review of Psychology, 45,* 229–259.

Adorno, T. W., Frenkel-Brunswik, E., Levinson, D. J., & Sanford, R. N. (1950). *The authoritarian personality.* New York: Harper.

Allport, G. W. (1954). The historical background of modern social psychology. In G. Lindzey (Ed.), *Handbook of social psychology* (1st ed.). Cambridge, MA: Addison-Wesley.

Altemeyer, B. (1988). *Enemies of freedom: Understanding right-wing authoritarianism.* San Francisco: Jossey-Bass.

Alwin, D. F., Cohen, R. L., & Newcomb, T. M. (1991). *Political attitudes over the life span: The Bennington women after fifty years.* Madison: University of Wisconsin.

Aristotle. *Politics.* (trans. by B. Jowett, 1885). Oxford: Clarendon Press.

Aronson, E. (1968). Dissonance theory: Progress and problems. In R. P. Abelson, E. Aronson, W. J. McGuire, T. M. Newcomb, M. J. Rosenberg, & P. H. Tannenbaum (Eds.), *Theories of cognitive consistency: A sourcebook* (pp. 5–27). Chicago: Rand McNally.

Aronson, E., & Carlsmith, J. M. (1962). Performance expectancy as a determinant of actual performance. *Journal of Abnormal and Social Psychology, 65,* 178–182.

Aronson, E., & Carlsmith, J. M. (1963). Effect of the severity of threat on the devaluation of forbidden behavior. *Journal of Abnormal and Social Psychology, 66,* 584–588.

Aronson, E., & Linder, D. (1965). Gain and loss of esteem as determinants of interpersonal attractiveness. *Journal of Experimental Social Psychology, 1,* 156–171.

Aronson, E., & Mettee, D. M. (1968). Dishonest behavior as a function of differential levels of induced self-esteem. *Journal of Personality and Social Psychology, 9,* 121–127.

Aronson, E., Wilson, T. D., & Brewer, M. (1998). Experimentation in social psychology. In D. T. Gilbert, S. E. Fiske, & G. Lindzey (Eds.), *The handbook of social psychology* (4th ed., pp. 99–142). New York: McGraw-Hill.

Asch, S. E. (1946). Forming impressions of personality. *Journal of Abnormal and Social Psychology, 41,* 258–290.

Asch, S. E. (1955). Opinions and social pressure. *Scientific American, 19,* 31–35.

Aspinwall, L. G., & Taylor, S. E. (in press). A stitch in time: Self-regulation and proactive coping. *Psychological Bulletin.*

Bach, G. R. (1954). *Intensive group psychotherapy.* New York: Ronald Press.

Bales, R. F. (1970). *Personality and interpersonal behavior.* New York: Holt, Rinehart, and Winston.

Bandura, A. (1973). *Aggression: A social learning analysis.* Englewood Cliffs, NJ: Prentice Hall.

Bandura, A. (1977). *Social learning theory.* Englewood Cliffs, NJ: Prentice-Hall.

Bandura, A. (1986). *Social foundations of thought and action: A social cognitive theory.* Englewood Cliffs, NJ: Prentice-Hall.

Bandura, A., & Walters, R. H. (1963). *Social learning and personality development.* New York: Holt, Rinehart, and Winston.

Bargal, D., Gold, M., & Lewin, M. (Eds.) (1992). The heritage of Kurt Lewin: Theory, research, and practice. *Journal of Social Issues, whole issue 48(2).*

Batson, C. D. (1998). Altruism and prosocial behavior. In D. T. Gilbert, S. T. Fiske, & G. Lindzey (Eds.), *The handbook of social psychology* (4th ed., Vol. 2, pp. 282–316). New York: McGraw-Hill.

Baumeister, R. F. (1998). The self. In D. T. Gilbert, S. T. Fiske, & G. Lindzey (Eds.), *The handbook of social psychology* (4th ed., Vol 1., pp. 680–740). New York: McGraw-Hill.

Baumeister, R. F., & Leary, M. R. (1995). The need to belong: Desire for interpersonal attachments as a fundamental human motivation. *Psychological Bulletin, 117,* 497–529.

Bavelas, A. (1950). Communication patterns in task-oriented groups. *Journal of the Acoustic Society of America, 22,* 725–730.

Bem, D. J. (1965). An experimental analysis of self-persuasion. *Journal of Experimental Social Psychology, 1,* 199–218.

Bem, D. J. (1967). Self-perception: An alternative interpretation of cognitive dissonance phenomena. *Psychological Review, 74,* 183–200.

Bem, D. J. (1972). Self-perception theory. In L. Berkowitz (Ed.), *Advances in experimental social psychology* (Vol. 6, pp. 1–62). New York: Academic Press.

Berscheid, E. (1994). Interpersonal relationships. *Annual Review of Psychology, 45,* 79–129.

Berscheid, E., & Reis, H. (1998). Attraction and close relationships. In D. T. Gilbert, S. T. Fiske, & G. Lindzey (Eds.), *The handbook of social psychology* (4th ed., Vol 2, pp. 193–281). New York: McGraw-Hill.

Berscheid, E., & Walster, E. (1978). *Interpersonal attraction* (2nd ed.). Reading, MA: Addison-Wesley.

Betancourt, H., & Lopez, S. R. (1993). The study of culture, ethnicity, and race in American psychology. *American Psychologist, 48,* 629–637.

Brewer, M. B. (1991). The social self: On being the same and different at the same time. *Personality and Social Psychology Bulletin, 17,* 475–482.

Brewer, M. B., & Brown, R. (1998). Intergroup relations. In D. T. Gilbert, S. T. Fiske, & G. Lindzey (Eds.), *The handbook of social psychology* (4th ed., Vol 2, pp. 554–629). New York: McGraw-Hill.

Broadbent, D. E. (1985). *Perception and communication.* London: Pergamon Press.

Buss, D. M. (1995). Evolutionary psychology: A new paradigm for psychological science. *Psychological Inquiry, 6,* 1–30.

Buss, D. M., & Kenrick, D. (1998). Evolutionary social psychology. In D. T. Gilbert, S. T. Fiske, & G. Lindzey (Eds.), *The handbook of social psychology* (4th ed., Vol 2, pp. 982–1026). New York: McGraw-Hill.

Buunk, B. P., Collins, R. L., Taylor, S. E., Van YPeren, N. W., & Dakof, G. (1990). The affective consequences of social comparison: Either direction has its ups and downs. *Journal of Personality and Social Psychology, 59,* 1238–1249.

Byrne, D. (1971). *The attraction paradigm.* New York: Academic Press.

Byrne, D., & Clore, G. L. (1970). A reinforcement model of evaluative responses. *Personality: An International Journal, 1,* 103–128.

Cantor, N., & Kihlstrom, J. F. (1987). *Personality and social intelligence.* Englewood Cliffs, NJ: Prentice-Hall.

Cantor, N., & Mischel, W. (1977). Traits as prototypes: Effects on recognition memory. *Journal of Personality and Social Psychology, 35,* 38–48.

Cartwright, D. (1968). The nature of group cohesiveness. In D. Cartwright & A. Zander (Eds.), *Group dynamics: Research and theory* (3rd ed., pp. 91–109). New York: Harper & Row.

Cartwright, D., & Harary, F. (1956). Structural balance: A generalization of Heider's theory. *Psychological Review, 63,* 277–293.

Cartwright, D., & Zander, A. (Eds.) (1953). *Group dynamics: Research and theory.* New York: Harper & Row.

Carver, C. S., & Scheier, M. F. (1981). *Attention and self-regulation: A control theory approach to human behavior.* New York: Springer-Verlag.

Chaiken, S. (1980). Heuristic versus systematic information processing and the use of source versus message cues in persuasion. *Journal of Personality and Social Psychology, 39,* 752–766.

Chaiken, S., Liberman, A., & Eagly, A. H. (1989). Heuristic and systematic information processing within and beyond the persuasion context. In J. S. Uleman & J. A. Bargh (Eds.), *Unintended thought* (pp. 212–252). New York: Guilford Press.

Cialdini, R. B., & Trost, M. R. (1998). Influence, social norms, conformity, and compliance. In D. T. Gilbert, S. T. Fiske, & G. Lindzey (Eds.), *The handbook of social psychology* (4th ed., Vol. 2, pp. 151–192). New York: McGraw-Hill.

Clark, M. S., & Fiske, S. T. (Eds.) (1982). *Affect and cognition: The 17th Annual Carnegie Symposium on Cognition.* Hillsdale, NJ: Erlbaum.

Clore, G. L., & Byrne, D. (1974). A reinforcement-affect model of attraction. In T. L. Huston (Ed.), *Foundations of interpersonal attraction.* New York: Academic Press.

Crocker, J., & Major, B. (1989). Social stigma and self-esteem: The self-protective properties of stigma. *Psychological Review, 96,* 608–630.

Crocker, J., Major, B., & Steele, C. (1998). Social stigma. In D. T. Gilbert, S. T. Fiske, & G. Lindzey (Eds.), *The handbook of social psychology* (4th ed., Vol. 2, pp. 504–553). New York: McGraw-Hill.

Croyle, R. T., & Barger, S. D. (1993). Illness cognition. In S. Maes, H. Leventhal, & M. Johnston (Eds.), *International review of health psychology* (Vol. 2, pp. 29–49). New York: Wiley.

Davis, J. A. (1959). A formal interpretation of the theory of relative deprivation. *Sociometry, 22,* 280–296.

Dawes, R. M. (1998). Behavioral decision making and judgment. In D. T. Gilbert, S. T. Fiske, & G. Lindzey (Eds.), *The handbook of social psychology* (4th ed., Vol. 1, pp. 497–548). New York: McGraw-Hill.

Deaux, K., & LaFrance, M. (1998). Gender. In D. T. Gilbert, S. T. Fiske, & G. Lindzey (Eds.), *The handbook of social psychology* (4th ed., Vol. 1, pp. 788–827). New York: McGraw-Hill.

DePaulo, B. M., & Friedman, H. S. (1998). Nonverbal communication. In D. T. Gilbert, S. T. Fiske, & G. Lindzey (Eds.), *The handbook of social psychology* (4th ed., Vol. 2, pp. 3–40). New York: McGraw-Hill.

Deutsch, M. (1960). The effects of cooperation and competition upon group process. In D. Cartwright & A. Zander (Eds.), *Group dynamics: Research and theory* (2nd ed., pp. 414–448). Evanston, IL: Row, Peterson, & Company.

Devine, P. G. (1989). Stereotypes and prejudice: Their automatic and controlled components. *Journal of Personality and Social Psychology, 56,* 5–18.

Devine, P. G., Sedikides, C., & Fuhrman, R. W. (1989). Goals in social information processing: The case of anticipated information. *Journal of Personality and Social Psychology, 56,* 680–690.

Dollard, J., Doob, L., Miller, N. E., Mowrer, O. H., & Sears, R. (1939). *Frustration and aggression.* New Haven, CT: Yale University Press.

Eagly, A. H. (1987). *Sex differences in social behavior: A social-role interpretation.* Hillsdale, NJ: Erlbaum.

Eagly, A. H., & Chaiken, S. (1998). Attitude structure and function. In D. T. Gilbert, S. T. Fiske, & G. Lindzey (Eds.), *The handbook of social psychology* (4th ed., Vol. 1, pp. 269–322). New York: McGraw-Hill.

Economist, The. (1994). Rational economic man: The human factor. *The Economist, December 24th, 1995—January 6th, 1995,* 90–92.

Ekman, P. (1982). *Emotion in the human face* (2nd ed.). Cambridge: Cambridge University Press.

Ellsworth, P., & Mauro, R. (1998). Psychology and law. In D. T. Gilbert, S. T. Fiske, & G. Lindzey (Eds.), *The handbook of social psychology* (4th ed., Vol. 2, pp. 684–732). New York: McGraw-Hill.

Fazio, R. H. (1987). Self-perception theory: A current perspective. In M. P. Zanna, J. M. Olson, & C. P. Herman (Eds.), *Social influence: The Ontario symposium* (Vol. 5, pp. 129–149). Hillsdale, NJ: Erlbaum.

Fazio, R. H., Zanna, M. P., & Cooper, J. (1977). Dissonance and self-perception: An integrative view of each theory's proper domain of application. *Journal of Experimental Social Psychology, 13,* 464–479.

Feshbach, S. (1955). The drive-reducing function of fantasy behavior. *Journal of Abnormal and Social Psychology, 50,* 3–12.

Festinger, L. (1954). A theory of social comparison processes. *Human Relations, 7,* 117–140.

Festinger, L. (1957). *A theory of cognitive dissonance.* Palo Alto, CA: Stanford University Press.

Festinger, L., Riecken, H., & Schachter, S. (1956). *When prophecy fails.* Minneapolis: University of Minnesota Press.

Festinger, L., Schachter, S., & Back, K. (1953). Operation of group standards. In D. Cartwright & A. Zander (Eds.), *Group dynamics: Research and theory* (pp. 152–164). New York: Harper & Row.

Fishhoff, B. (1976). Attribution theory and judgment under uncertainty. In J. H. Harvey, W. J. Ickes, & R. F. Kidd (Eds.), *New directions in attribution research* (Vol. 1, pp. 421–452). New York: Wiley.

Fishbein, M., & Ajzen, I. (1975). *Belief, attitude, intention, and behavior: An introduction to theory and research.* Reading, MA: Addison-Wesley.

Fiske, A., Kitayama, S., Markus, H., & Nisbett, R. (1998). The cultural matrix of social psychology. In D. T. Gilbert, S. T. Fiske, & G. Lindzey (Eds.), *The handbook of social psychology* (4th ed., Vol. 2, pp. 915–981). New York: McGraw-Hill.

Fiske, S. T. (1992). Thinking is for doing: Portraits of social cognition from daguerreotype to laserphoto. *Journal of Personality and Social Psychology, 63,* 877–889.

Fiske, S. T. (1998). Stereotypes, prejudice, and discrimination. In D. T. Gilbert, S. T. Fiske, & G. Lindzey (Eds.), *The handbook of social psychology* (4th ed., Vol. 2, pp. 357–411). New York: McGraw-Hill.

Fiske, S. T., & Taylor, S. E. (1984). *Social cognition.* New York: Random House.

Fiske, S . T., & Taylor, S. E. (1991). *Social cognition* (2nd ed.). New York: McGraw-Hill.

French, J. R. P., Jr., & Raven, B. (1959). The bases of social power. In D. Cartwright (Ed.), *Studies in social power.* Ann Arbor, MI: Institute for Social Research.

Freud, S. (1930/1961, trans. J. Strachey). *Civilization and its discontents.* New York: W. W. Norton.

Geen, R. G. (1998). Aggression and antisocial behavior. In D. T. Gilbert, S. T. Fiske, & G. Lindzey (Eds.), *The handbook of social psychology* (4th ed., Vol. 2, pp. 317–356). New York: McGraw-Hill.

Gilbert, D. T. (1998). Ordinary personology. In D. T. Gilbert, S. T. Fiske, & G. Lindzey (Eds.), *The handbook of social psychology* (4th ed., Vol. 2, pp. 89–150). New York: Mc-Graw-Hill.

Gilbert, D. T., & Hixon, J. G. (1991). The trouble of thinking: Activation and application of stereotypic beliefs. *Journal of Personality and Social Psychology, 60,* 509–517.

Hardin, C. D., & Higgins, E. T. (1996). Shared reality: How social verification makes the subjective objective. In R. M. Sorrentino & E. T. Higgins (Eds.), *Handbook of motivation and cognition, Vol. 3: The interpersonal context.* New York: Guilford.

Hartshorne, H., & May, M. A. (1928). *Studies in the nature of character: Vol. 1. Studies in deceit.* New York: Macmillan.

Hastorf, A. H., Schneider, D. J., & Polefka, J. (1970). *Person perception.* Reading, MA: Addison-Wesley.

Hazan, C., & Shaver, P. (1994). Attachment as an organizational framework for research on close relationships. *Psychological Inquiry, 5,* 1–22.

Heider, F. (1946). Attitudes and cognitive organization. *Journal of Psychology, 21,* 107–112.

Heider, F. (1958). *The psychology of interpersonal relations.* New York: Wiley.

Helgeson, V. S., & Mickelson, K. (1995). Motives for social comparison. *Personality and Social Psychology Bulletin, 21,* 1200–1209.

Herrnstein, R. J., & Murray, C. (1994). *The bell curve: Intelligence and class structure in American life.* New York: Free Press.

Higgins, E. T. (1987). Self-discrepancy: A theory relating self and affect. *Psychological Review, 94,* 319–340.

Higgins, E. T. (1990). Personality, social psychology, and cross-situation relations: Standards and knowledge activation as a common language. In L. A. Pervin (Ed.), *Handbook of personality: Theory and research* (pp. 301–338). New York: Guilford Press.

Hilton, D. J., & Slugoski, B. R. (1986). Knowledge-based causal attribution: The abnormal conditions focus model. *Psychological Review, 93,* 75–88.

Homans, G. C. (1961). *Social behavior: Its elementary form.* New York: Harcourt, Brace, & World.

Homans, G. C. (1965). Effort, supervision, and productivity. In R. Dubin, G. C. Homans, F. C. Mann, & D. C. Miller (Eds.), *Leadership and productivity: Some facts of industrial life* (pp. 51–67). San Francisco: Chandler.

Hovland, C. I., Janis, I. K., & Kelley, H. H. (1953). *Communication and persuasion.* New Haven, CT: Yale University Press.

Hyman, H. H. (1942). The psychology of status. *Archives of Psychology,* No. 269.

Ichheiser, G. (1943). Misinterpretations of personality in everyday life and the psychologist's frame of reference. *Character and Personality, 12,* 145–160.

James, W. (1890). *The principles of psychology* (Vol. 2). New York: Henry Holt & Co.

Janis, I. (1963). Group identification under conditions of external danger. *British Journal of Medical Psychology, 36,* 227–238.

Jones, E. E. (1985). Major developments in social psychology during the past five decades. In G. Lindzey & E. Aronson (Eds.), *Handbook of social psychology* (3rd ed., Vol. 1, pp. 47–108). New York: Random House.

Jones, E. E., & Davis, K. E. (1965). From acts to dispositions: The attribution process in person perception. In L. Berkowitz (Ed.), *Advances in experimental social psychology* (Vol. 2). New York: Academic Press.

Jones, E. E., & Gerard, H. B. (1967). *Foundations of social psychology.* New York: Wiley.

Jones, E. E., & Nisbett, R. E. (1972). The actor and the observer: Divergent perceptions of the causes of behavior. In E. E. Jones, D. E. Kanouse, H. H. Kelley, R. E. Nisbett, S. Valins, & B. Weiner (Eds.), *Attribution: Perceiving the causes of behavior* (pp. 79–94). Morristown, NJ: General Learning Press.

Judd, C. M., & McClelland, G. H. (1998). Measurement. In D. T. Gilbert, S. T. Fiske, & G. Lindzey (Eds.), *The handbook of social psychology* (4th ed., Vol. 1, pp. 180–232). New York: McGraw-Hill.

Kahneman, D., & Tversky, A. (1973). On the psychology of prediction. *Psychological Review, 80,* 237–251.

Kant, I. (1781/1969). *Critique of pure reason.* New York: St. Martin's Press. (Originally published, 1781.)

Kelley, H. H. (1950). The warm-cold variable in first impressions of persons. *Journal of Personality, 18,* 431–439.

Kelley, H. H. (1952). Two functions of reference groups. In G. E. Swanson, T. M. Newcomb, & E. L. Hartley (Eds.), *Readings in social psychology* (pp. 410–414). New York: Holt, Rinehart, & Winston.

Kelley, H. H. (1967). Attribution theory in social psychology. In D. Levine (Ed.), *Nebraska symposium on motivation* (pp. 192–238). Lincoln: University of Nebraska Press.

Kelley, H. H. (1972a). Attribution in social interaction. In E. E. Jones, D. E. Kanouse, H. H. Kelley, R. E. Nisbett, S. Valins, & B. Weiner (Eds.), *Attribution: Perceiving the causes of behavior* (pp. 1–26). Morristown, NJ: General Learning Press.

Kelley, H. H. (1972b). Causal schemata and the attribution process. In E. E. Jones, D. E. Kanouse, H. H. Kelley, R. E. Nisbett, S. Valins, and B. Weiner (Eds.), *Attribution: Perceiving the causes of behavior* (pp. 151–174). Morristown, NJ: General Learning Press.

Kelley, H. H., & Thibaut, J. W. (1978). *Interpersonal relations: A theory of interdependence.* New York: Wiley-Interscience.

Kelman, H. C. (1974). Attitudes are alive and well and gainfully employed in the sphere of action. *American Psychologist, 29,* 310–324.

Kelman, H. C., & Hamilton, V. L. (1989). *Crimes of obedience: Toward a social psychology of authority and responsibility.* New Haven, CT: Yale University Press.

Kendler, K. S., Kessler, R. C., Heath, A. C., Neale, M. C., & Eaves, L. J. (1991). Coping: A genetic epidemiological investigation. *Psychological Medicine, 21,* 337–346.

Kenny, D. A., Kashy, D. A., & Bolger, N. (1997). Data analysis in social psychology. In D. T. Gilbert, S. T. Fiske, & G. Lindzey (Eds.), *The handbook of social psychology* (4th ed., Vol. 1, pp. 233–265). New York: McGraw-Hill.

Kiesler, C. A., Collins, B. E., & Miller, N. (1969). *Attitude change: A critical analysis of theoretical approaches.* New York: Wiley.

Kiesler, C. A., Nisbett, R. E., & Zanna, M. P. (1969). On inferring one's beliefs from one's behavior. *Journal of Personality and Social Psychology, 11,* 321–327.

Kinder, D. (1998). Attitude and action in the realm of politics. In D. T. Gilbert, S. T. Fiske, & G. Lindzey (Eds.), *The handbook of social psychology* (4th ed., Vol. 2, pp. 778–867). New York: McGraw-Hill.

Kluckhohn, C. (1954). Culture and behavior. In G. Lindzey (Ed.), *The handbook of social psychology* (Vol. 2, pp. 924–976). Reading, MA: Addison-Wesley.

Koffka, K. (1935). *Principles of Gestalt psychology.* New York: Harcourt Brace Jovanovich.

Kohler, W. (1947). *Gestalt psychology.* New York: Liveright.

Konecni, V. J., & Ebbesen, E. B. (1976). Disinhibition versus the catharthic effect: Artifact and substance. *Journal of Personality and Social Psychology, 34,* 352–365.

Krech, D., & Crutchfield, R. S. (1948). *Theory and problems in social psychology.* New York: McGraw-Hill.

Kunda, Z. (1990). The case for motivated reasoning. *Psychological Bulletin, 108,* 480–498.

La Piere, R. T. (1934). Attitudes versus actions. *Social Forces, 13,* 230–237.

Le Bon, G. (1896). *The crowd: A study of the popular mind.* London: Ernest Benn.

Lepore, S. J. (1995). Measurement of chronic stressors. In S. Cohen, R. C. Kessler, & L. U. Gordon (Eds.), *Measuring stress: A guide for health and social scientists.* New York: Oxford University Press.

Lerner, M. J. (1980). *The belief in a just world: A fundamental delusion.* New York: Plenum.

Leventhal, H. (1970). Findings and theory in the study of fear communications. In L. Berkowitz (Ed.), *Advances in experimental social psychology* (Vol. 5, pp. 120–186). New York: Academic Press.

Leventhal, H., Nerenz, D. R., & Strauss, A. (1982). Self-regulation and the mechanisms for symptom appraisal. In D. Mechanic (Ed.), *Monograph series in psychosocial epidemiology 3: Symptoms, illness behavior, and help-seeking* (pp. 55–86). New York: Neale Watson.

Levine, J. M., & Higgins, E. T. (1995). Social determinants of cognition. *Social Cognition, 13,* 183–187.

Levinger, G. (Ed.). (1986). SSPSI at 50: Historical accounts and selected appraisals. *Journal of Social Issues, whole issue 42*(4).

Lewin, K. (1943). Psychology and the process of group living. *The Journal of Social Psychology, SPSSI Bulletin, 17,* 113–131.

Lewin, K. (1948). *Resolving social conflicts.* New York: Harper.

Lewin, K., Lippitt, R., & White, R. K. (1939). Patterns of aggressive behavior in experimentally created "social climates." *Journal of Social Psychology, 10,* 271–299.

Lifton, R. J. (1993). *The protean self: Human resilience in an age of fragmentation.* New York: Basic Books.

Lord, C. G., Ross, L., & Lepper, M. R. (1979). Biased assimilation and attitude polarization: The effects of prior theories on subsequently-considered evidence. *Journal of Personality and Social Psychology, 37,* 2098–2109.

Lorge, I. (1936). Prestige, suggestion, and attitudes. *Journal of Social Psychology, 7,* 386–402.

Marks, G., & Miller, N. (1987). Ten years of research on the false-consensus effect: An empirical and theoretical review. *Psychological Bulletin, 102,* 72–90.

Markus, H. (1977). Self-schemata and processing information about the self. *Journal of Personality and Social Psychology, 35,* 63–78.

Markus, H., & Kitayama, S. (1991). Culture and the self: Implications for cognition, emotion, and motivation. *Psychological Review, 98,* 224–253.

Markus, H., & Nurius, P. (1986). Possible selves. *American Psychologist, 41,* 954–969.

McArthur, L. A. (1972). The how and what of why: Some determinants and consequences of causal attribution. *Journal of Personality and Social Psychology, 22,* 171–193.

McDougall, W. (1908). *Introduction to social psychology.* London: Methuen & Co.

McGuire, W. J., & Padawer-Singer, A. (1976). Trait salience in the spontaneous self-concept. *Journal of Personality and Social Psychology, 33,* 743–754.

Merton, R. K. (1957). *Social theory and social structure* (rev. ed.). Glencoe, IL: Free Press.

Milgram, S. (1963). Behavioral study of obedience. *Journal of Abnormal and Social Psychology, 67,* 371–378.

Milgram, S. (1974). *Obedience to authority: An experimental view.* New York: Harper & Row.

Miller, D. T., & Ross, M. (1975). Self-serving biases in the attribution of causality: Fact or fiction? *Psychological Bulletin, 82,* 213–225.

Miller, J. G. (1987). Cultural influences on the development of conceptual differentiation in person description. *British Journal of Developmental Psychology, 5,* 309–319.

Mischel, W. (1968). *Personality and assessment.* New York: Wiley.

Mook, D. G. (1983). In defense of external invalidity. *American Psychologist, 38,* 379–387.

Morris, M. W., & Peng, K. (1994). Culture and cause: American and Chinese attributions for social and physical events. *Journal of Personality and Social Psychology, 6,* 949–971.

Murray, S., & Holmes, J. G. (1993). Seeing virtues in faults: Negativity and the transformation of interpersonal narratives in close relationships. *Journal of Personality and Social Psychology, 65,* 707–722.

Murstein, B. I. (1971). Critique of models in dyadic attraction. In B. I. Murstein (Ed.), *Theories of love and attraction.* New York: Springer.

Newcomb, T. M. (1943). *Personality and social change.* New York: Dryden.

Newcomb, T. M. (1953). An approach to the study of communicative acts. *Psychological Review, 60,* 393–404.

Nisbett, R. E. (1993). Violence and U.S. regional culture. *American Psychologist, 48,* 441–449.

Nisbett, R. E., & Ross, L. (1980). *Human inference: Strategies and shortcomings of social judgment.* Englewood Cliffs, NJ: Prentice-Hall.

Osgood, C. E., & Tannenbaum, P. H. (1955). The principle of congruity in the prediction of attitude change. *Psychological Review, 62,* 42–55.

Ostrom, T. M. (1984). The sovereignty of social cognition. In R. S. Wyer, Jr., & T. K. Srull (Eds.), *Handbook of social cognition* (Vol. 1, 1–38). Hillsdale, NJ: Erlbaum.

Ostrom, T. M. (1989). Three catechisms for social memory. In P. R. Solomon, G. R. Goethals, C. M. Kelley, & B. R. Stephens (Eds.), *Memory: Interdisciplinary approaches* (pp. 201–220). New York: Springer.

Pennebaker, J. W. (1983). Accuracy of symptom perception. in A. Baum, S. E. Taylor, & J. Singer (Eds.), *Handbook of psychology and health* (Vol. 4, pp. 189–217). Hillsdale, NJ: Erlbaum.

Pennebaker, J. W. (1985). Traumatic experience and psychosomatic disease: Exploring the roles of behavioral inhibition, obsession, and confiding. *Canadian Psychology, 26,* 82–95.

Pepitone, A., & Triandis, H. C. (1988). On the universality of social psychological theories. *Journal of Cross-Cultural Psychology, 18,* 471–498.

Peplau, L. A., & Taylor, S. E. (Eds.) (1977). *Sociocultural perspectives in social psychology.* Englewood Cliffs, NJ: Prentice-Hall.

Pettigrew, T. F. (1967). Social evaluation theory: Convergences and applications. In D. Levine (Ed.), *Nebraska symposium on motivation* (Vol. 15). Lincoln: University of Nebraska Press.

Petty, R. (1996). The evolution of theory and research in social psychology: From single to multiple effect and process models of persuasion. In C. McGarty & S. A. Haslam (Eds.), *The message of social psychology: Perspectives on mind in society.* Oxford, England: Basil Blackwell, Ltd.

Petty, R. E., & Cacioppo, J. T. (1986). *Communication and persuasion: Central and peripheral routes to attitude change.* New York: Springer-Verlag.

Petty, R. E., & Wegener, D. T. (1998). Attitude change: Multiple roles for persuasion variables. In D. T. Gilbert, S. T. Fiske, & G. Lindzey (Eds.), *The handbook of social psychology* (4th ed., Vol. 1, pp. 323–390). New York: McGraw-Hill.

Piliavin, I. M., & Charng, H. (1990). Altruism: A review of recent theory and research. *Annual Review of Sociology, 16,* 27–65.

Pinker, S. (1994). *The language instinct.* New York: William Morrow.

Plato. *The Republic.* Vol. 3 of *Dialogues of Plato* (5 vols.) (trans. by B. Jowett, 2nd ed., 1975). Oxford: Clarendon Press.

Plomin, R., Scheier, M. F., Bergeman, C. S., Pedersen, N. L., Nesselroade, J. R., & McClearn, G. E. (1992). Optimism, pessimism, and mental health: A twin/adoption study. *Personality and Individual Differences, 13,* 921–930.

Pratto, F., Sidanius, J., Stallworth, L. M., & Malle, B. F. (1994). Social dominance orientation: A personality variable predicting social and political attitudes. *Journal of Personality and Social Psychology, 67,* 741–763.

Rodin, J., & Janis, I. L. (1979). The social power of health-care practitioners as agents of change. *Journal of Social Issues, 35,* 60–81.

Rodin, J., & Salovey, P. (1989). Health psychology. *Annual Review of Psychology, 10,* 533–579.

Ross, L. (1977). The intuitive psychologist and his shortcomings: Distortions in the attribution process. In L. Berkowitz (Ed.), *Advances in experimental social psychology* (Vol. 10, pp. 174–221). New York: Academic Press.

Ross, L., Greene, D., & House, P. (1977). The "false consensus effect": An egocentric bias in social perception and attribution processes. *Journal of Experimental Social Psychology, 13,* 279–301.

Ross, L., & Nisbett, R. E. (1991). *The person and the situation: Perspectives of social psychology.* New York: McGraw-Hill.

Ruble, D. N., & Goodnow, J. J. (1998). Social development in childhood and adulthood. In D. T. Gilbert, S. T. Fiske, & G. Lindzey (Eds.), *The handbook of social psychology* (4th ed., Vol. 1, pp. 741–787). New York: McGraw-Hill.

Rushton, J. (1980). *Altruism, socialization and society.* Englewood Cliffs, NJ: Prentice-Hall.

Salovey, P., Rothman, A. J., & Rodin, J. (1998). Social psychology and health behavior. In D. T. Gilbert, S. T. Fiske, & G. Lindzey (Eds.), *The handbook of social psychology* (4th ed., Vol. 2, pp. 633–683). New York: McGraw-Hill.

Sarter, M., Berntson, G. G., & Cacioppo, J. T. (1996). Brain imaging and cognitive neuroscience: Toward strong inference in attributing function to structure. *American Psychologist, 51,* 13–21.

Schachter, S. (1951). Deviation, rejection, and communication. *Journal of Abnormal and Social Psychology, 46,* 190–207.

Schachter, S. (1959). *The psychology of affiliation.* Stanford, CA: Stanford University Press.

Schank, R. C., & Abelson, R. P. (1977). *Scripts, plans, goals and understanding: An inquiry into human knowledge structures.* Hillsdale, NJ: Erlbaum.

Scheidlinger, S. (1952). *Psychoanalysis and group behavior.* New York: Norton.

Scheier, M. F., & Carver, C. S. (1985). Optimism, coping, and health: Assessment and implications of generalized outcome expectancies. *Health Psychology, 4,* 219–247.

Schwarz, N., Groves, R. M., & Schuman, H. (1998). Survey methods. In D. T. Gilbert, S. T. Fiske, & G. Lindzey (Eds.), *The handbook of social psychology* (4th ed., Vol. 1, pp. 143–179). New York: McGraw-Hill.

Sears, D. O. (1975). Political socialization. In F. I. Greenstein & N. W. Polsby (Eds.), *Handbook of political science* (Vol. 2). Reading, MA: Addison-Wesley.

Sears, D. O. (1983). The persistence of early political predispositions: The roles of attitude object and life stage. In L. Wheeler & P. Shaver (Eds.), *Review of personality and social psychology* (Vol. 4, pp. 79–116). Beverly Hills, CA: Sage.

Sears, D. O. (1986). College sophomores in the laboratory: Influences of a narrow database on social psychology's view of human nature. *Journal of Personality and Social Psychology, 51,* 515–530.

Sears, D. O. (1991). Socio-economics: Challenge to the neoclassical economic paradigm. *Psychological Science, 2,* 12–15.

Sedikides, C., & Strube, M. (1996). *Motivated self-evaluation: To thine own self be good, to thine own self be sure, and to thine own self be true.* Manuscript submitted for publication. University of North Carolina at Chapel Hill.

Shaver, P., & Hazen, C. (1993). Adult romantic attachment: Theory and evidence. In D. Perlman & W. Jones (Eds.), *Advances in personal relationships* (Vol. 4, pp. 29–70). London: Jessica Kingsley.

Sherif, M. (1936). *The psychology of social norms.* New York: Harper.

Sherif, M., Harvey, O. J., White, B. J., Hood, W. R., & Sherif, C. W. (1961). *Intergroup conflict and cooperation. The robber's cave experiment.* Norman, OK: University of Oklahoma Press.

Sidanius, J. (1993). The psychology of group conflict and the dynamics of oppression: A social dominance perspective. In S. Iyengar & W. McGuire (Eds.), *Explorations in political psychology* (pp. 183–219). Durham, NC: Duke University Press.

Siegel, A. E., & Siegel, S. (1957). Reference groups, membership groups, and attitude change. *Journal of Abnormal and Social Psychology, 55,* 360–364.

Simon, H. A. (1967). Motivational and emotional controls of cognition. *Psychological Review, 74,* 29–39.

Smith, E. R. (1998). Mental representation and memory. In D. T. Gilbert, S. T. Fiske, & G. Lindzey (Eds.), *The handbook of social psychology* (4th ed., Vol. 1, pp. 391–445). New York: McGraw-Hill.

Snyder, M. (1979). Self-monitoring processes. In L. Berkowitz (Ed.), *Advances in experimental social psychology* (Vol. 12, pp. 85–128). New York: Academic Press.

Steele, C. M. (1988). The psychology of self-affirmation: Sustaining the integrity of the self. In L. Berkowitz (Ed.), *Advances in experimental psychology* (Vol. 21, pp. 262–302). New York: Academic Press.

Steele, C. M., & Aronson, J. (1995). Stereotype threat and the intellectual test performance of African-Americans. *Journal of Personality and Social Psychology, 69,* 797–811.

Stevens, L. E., & Fiske, S. T. (1995). Motivation and cognition in social life: A social survival perspective. *Social Cognition, 13,* 189–214.

Stock, D., & Thelen, H. A. (1958). *Emotional dynamics and group culture.* New York: New York University Press.

Stouffer, S. A., Lumsdaine, A. A., Lumsdaine, M. H., Williams, R. M., Jr., Smith, M. B., Janis, I. L., Star, S. A., & Cottrell, L. S., Jr. (1949). *The American soldier: Vol. 2. Combat and its aftermath.* Princeton, NJ: Princeton University Press.

Stout, P. (1996, February 29). Solomon Asch is dead at 88: A leading social psychologist. *New York Times, Front Section,* A13.

Stroebe, W., Stroebe, M., Abakoumkin, G., & Schut, A. (1996). The role of loneliness and social support in adjustment to loss: A test of attachment versus stress theory. *Journal of Personality and Social Psychology, 70,* 1241–1249.

Suchman, E. A. (1950). The intensity component in attitude and opinion research. In S. A. Stouffer, L. Guttman, E. A. Suchman, P. F. Lagersfeld, S. A. Star, & J. A. Clausen (Eds.), *Measurement and prediction.* Princeton, NJ: Princeton University Press.

Swann, W. B., Jr. (1983). Self-verification: Bringing social reality into harmony with the self. In J. Suls & A. G. Greenwald (Eds.), *Social psychology perspectives* (Vol. 2, pp. 33–66). Hillsdale, NJ: Erlbaum.

Tajfel, H., & Turner, J. C. (1979). An integrative theory of intergroup conflict. In W. Austin & S. Worchel (Eds.), *The social psychology of intergroup relations* (pp. 33–48). Pacific Grove, CA: Brooks/Cole.

Tajfel, H., & Turner, J. C. (1986). The social identity theory of intergroup behavior. In S. Worchel & W. G. Austin (Eds.), *Psychology of intergroup relations* (2nd ed., pp. 7–24). Chicago: Nelson-Hall.

Taylor, S. E. (1975). On inferring one's own attitudes from one's behavior: Some delimiting conditions. *Journal of Personality and Social Psychology, 31,* 126–131.

Taylor, S. E., & Brown, J. D. (1988). Illusion and well-being: A social psychological perspective on mental health. *Psychological Bulletin, 103,* 193–210.

Taylor, S. E., & Fiske, S. T. (1981). Getting inside the head: Methodologies for process analysis. In J. Harvey, W. Ickes, & R. Kidd (Eds.), *New directions in attribution research* (Vol. 3, pp. 459–524). Hillsdale, NJ: Erlbaum.

Taylor, S. E., & Lobel, M. (1989). Social comparison activity under threat: Downward evaluation and upward comparison. *Psychological Review, 89,* 155–181.

Taylor, S. E., Wayment, H. A., & Carrillo, M. A. (1995). Social comparison and self-regulation. In R. M. Sorrentino & E. T. Higgins (Eds.), *Handbook of motivation and cognition.* New York: Guilford Press.

Tesser, A. (1988). Toward a self-evaluation maintenance model of social behavior. In L. Berkowitz (Ed.), *Advances in experimental social psychology* (Vol. 21, pp. 181–227). New York: Academic Press.

Tetlock, P. E. (1983). Accountability and complexity of thought. *Journal of Personality and Social Psychology, 45,* 74–83.

Tetlock, P. E. (1998). Social psychology and world politics. In D. T. Gilbert, S. T. Fiske, & G. Lindzey (Eds.), *The handbook of social psychology* (4th ed., Vol. 2, pp. 868–912). New York: McGraw-Hill.

Thibaut, J. W., & Kelley, H. H. (1959). *The social psychology of groups.* New York: Wiley.

Thornton, D., & Arrowood, A. J. (1966). Self-evaluation, self-enhancement, and the locus of social comparison. *Journal of Experimental Social Psychology, 2* (Suppl. 1), 40–48.

Tooby, J., & Cosmides, L. (1992). Psychological foundations of culture. In J. Barkow, L. Cosmides, & J. Tooby (Eds.), *The adapted mind* (pp. 19–136). New York: Oxford University Press.

Trivers, R. (1971). The evolution of reciprocal altruism. *Quarterly Review of Biology, 46,* 35–57.

Trope, Y. (1975). Seeking information about one's own abilities as a determinant of choice among tasks. *Journal of Personality and Social Psychology, 32,* 1004–1013.

Tversky, A., & Kahneman, D. (1974). Judgment under uncertainty: Heuristics and biases. *Science, 185,* 1124–1131.

Wallach, M. A., Kogan, N., & Bem, D. J. (1962). Group influence on individual risk-taking. *Journal of Abnormal and Social Psychology, 65,* 75–86.

Walster, E., Walster, G. W., & Berscheid, E. (1978). *Equity: Theory and research.* Boston: Allyn & Bacon.

Watson, J. (1930). *Behaviorism.* New York: Norton.

Wegner, D., & Bargh, J. A. (1998). Control and automaticity in social life. In D. T. Gilbert, S. T. Fiske, & G. Lindzey (Eds.), *The handbook of social psychology* (4th ed., Vol. 1, pp. 446–496). New York: McGraw-Hill.

Weiner, B. (1986). *An attributional theory of motivation and emotion.* New York: Springer-Verlag.

Weiner, B. (1995). *Judgments of responsibility: A foundation for a theory of social conduct.* New York: Guilford.

Werthemier, M. (1923). Untersuchungen zur Lehre von der Gestalt. II. *Psychologische Forschung, 4,* 301–350.

West, S. G., & Wicklund, R. A. (1980). *A primer of social psychological theories.* Monterey, CA: Brooks/Cole.

Wheeler, L., & Miyake, K. (1992). Social comparison in everyday life. *Journal of Personality and Social Psychology, 62,* 760–773.

Whyte, W. F., Jr. (1943). *Street corner society.* Chicago: University of Chicago Press.

Wills, T. A. (1981). Downward comparison principles in social psychology. *Psychological Bulletin, 90,* 245–271.

Wilson, T. D., & Linville, P. W. (1985). Improving the performance of college freshmen with attributional techniques. *Journal of Personality and Social Psychology, 49,* 287–293.

Wood, J. V. (1989). Theory and research concerning social comparisons of personal attributes. *Psychological Bulletin, 106,* 231–248.

Wood, J. V., & Taylor, K. L. (1991). Serving self-relevant goals through social comparison. In J. Suls & T. A. Wills (Eds.), *Social comparison: Contemporary theory and research* (pp. 23–50). Hillsdale, NJ: Erlbaum.

Wundt, W. (1897). *Outlines of psychology.* New York: Stechert. (Translated 1907.)

Wyer, R. S., Jr., & Srull, T. K. (1984). *Handbook of social cognition.* Hillsdale, NJ: Erlbaum.

Wylie, R. (1979). *The self concept.* Lincoln: University of Nebraska Press.

Zajonc, R. B. (1998). Emotions. In D. T. Gilbert, S. T. Fiske, & G. Lindzey (Eds.), *The handbook of social psychology* (4th ed., Vol. 1, pp. 591–632). New York: McGraw-Hill.

Zanna, M. P., & Cooper, J. (1974). Dissonance and the pill: An attribution approach to studying the arousal properties of dissonance. *Journal of Personality and Social Psychology, 29,* 703–709.

Zimbardo, P. G. (1970). The human choice: Individuation, reason and order versus deindividuation, impulse and chaos. In N. J. Arnold & D. Levine (Eds.), *Nebraska symposium on motivation, 1969.* Lincoln: University of Nebraska Press.

Zimbardo, P. G., Haney, C., Banks, W. C., & Jaffe, D. (1973, April 8). The mind is a formidable jailer: A Pirandellian prison. *New York Times Magazine, Section 6,* 36, ff.

PART TWO

METHODOLOGICAL
PERSPECTIVES

CHAPTER 3

EXPERIMENTATION IN SOCIAL PSYCHOLOGY

ELLIOT ARONSON, *University of California, Santa Cruz*
TIMOTHY D. WILSON, *University of Virginia*
MARILYNN B. BREWER, *The Ohio State University*

PROLOGUE

This chapter is aimed primarily at helping the reader to learn to think like an experimental social psychologist. It is both a blessing and (in a sense) a curse to think like an experimental social psychologist. Let us give you one of many possible examples of what we mean by that statement. While we were working on this chapter, we happened to pick up a copy of *The New Yorker* magazine where we read an excellent, highly informative essay by James Kunen about college-level educational programs in our prisons. Kunen (1995) wrote passionately about the effectiveness of these programs and how, in an amendment to the crime bill, a generally punitive, "penny-wise/pound foolish" congressional majority was eliminating these programs after characterizing them as wasteful, and as tending to coddle criminals. The essay contains a few vivid case histories of prisoners who completed a college program and went on to lead productive lives. Any systematic data? You bet. Kunen reports one study released in 1991 by the New York State Department of Correctional Services, which "found that male inmates who completed one or more years of higher education in prison had a recidivism rate, four years after their release, more than twenty percent lower than the average for all male inmates" (Kunen, 1995, p. 36).

The liberal/humanist in us wanted to get excited by the results of this study; it would be terrific to have convincing data proving that prison education really pays off. But alas, the experimental social psychologist in us was far more skeptical than Mr. Kunen. Yes, it *would* be wonderful to have convincing data on this issue, but, unfortunately, these data fall far short of the mark. We must raise at least one vital methodological question: Are the prisoners who were "assigned" to the control condition the same kind of people as those "assigned" to the experimental condition? That is, might it not be the case that the prisoners who signed up for the course of study and completed a year of it were different *to begin with* (say, in motivation, ability, intelligence, prior education, mental health, or what have you) from those who did not sign up for the course—or those who signed up but dropped out early? As you will see, this is not simply nit-picking; if they were different from the general run of prisoners, then it is likely (or, at least, possible) that they would have had a lower rate of recidivism even without having taken the course of study. If so, then it wasn't the prison courses that caused the lower recidivism.

The *curse* of thinking like an experimental social psychologist is that it keeps us from rejoicing. Part of the

This essay is a major revision of a chapter by Elliot Aronson and J. Merrill Carlsmith which first appeared in the 1968 edition of Lindzey and Aronson's Handbook of Social Psychology. *To the best of our knowledge that was the first time an experimental social psychologist attempted a formal and thorough presentation of the so-called tacit knowledge of the experimental method. By "tacit knowledge" we refer to the countless, mundane—but vitally important—details involved in designing and conducting an experiment in this field. Much of this knowledge is considered to be intuitive in that it is difficult to articulate because it is something that experienced experimentalists simply "know"; i.e., this knowledge is almost invariably gleaned from day-to-day experience in the laboratory rather than the classroom.*

It is with a deep sense of gratitude that we acknowledge our indebtedness to Merrill Carlsmith (a very intuitive experimentalist) for the important contributions he made to the original chapter as well as to our current thinking about methodology. His premature death in 1984, at the age of 48, was an irreparable loss to his friends and to the discipline.

blessing is that it keeps us from rejoicing—over potentially meaningless data like those described above. Moreover, as you shall see over and over again throughout this chapter, another part of the blessing is that experimental social psychologists are able to use their knowledge and skill to perform the appropriate research to test hypotheses like these in a solid and more convincing manner. For example, there are some simple but elegant solutions to the methodological shortcomings of the prison data, solutions we will discuss in this chapter.

INTRODUCTION

There are a great many ways of gathering information about social behavior. We can simply observe people; we can interview them about their attitudes, beliefs, intentions, and motivation; we can ask them to fill out questionnaires and rating scales. The list of techniques and variations on these techniques is filled with interesting possibilities. These techniques have provided us with some of our richest and most fascinating data about social phenomena, as described in other chapters in this *Handbook*. In this chapter we hope to convey something about the approach that has been the workhorse of social psychological research, the experimental method. With this method the researcher randomly assigns people to different conditions and ensures that these conditions are identical except for the independent variable (the one believed to have a causal effect on people's responses). Although there is merit in all methods of investigating social behavior, the experiment has been the chief method of choice for social psychology.

We have two main missions in this chapter. First, it is important to discuss why the experiment is the method of choice. What are its advantages and disadvantages? Why is it used so frequently when it has some clear drawbacks? This is a timely question, because it is our impression that the use of the experimental method has become less frequent in many areas of psychology, including social psychology. One reason for this is that social psychologists have ventured into areas in which it is much more difficult to do experiments, such as the study of close relationships and culture. Another reason is that promising new statistical techniques (e.g., structural equation modeling) are now available, allowing more precise tests of the relationships between variables in correlational designs. Although we welcome these advances, we fear that the unique power and value of the experimental method sometimes gets lost in the enthusiasm generated by these new topics and techniques. In the first part of the chapter we will discuss the advantages of experiments in general terms, and then return to these issues at the end of the chapter in a discussion of validity and realism in experiments.

The middle part of the chapter is more of a "how to" manual describing, in some detail, how to conduct an ex-

periment. It is our hope that, during the first part of the chapter, we will have convinced the reader of the continued value of experiments; then, in the middle part, we hope to provide detailed instructions in "how to do it" for those new to this method. We hasten to add that the best way to learn to do an experiment is to do so under the guidance of an expert, experienced researcher. Experimentation is very much a trade, like plumbing or carpentry or directing a play; the best way to learn to do it is by apprenticing oneself to a master. Nonetheless, just as it helps to read manuals explaining how to fix a leaky faucet or stage a production of Hamlet, our "how to do an experiment" manual might prove to be a helpful adjunct to a hands-on apprenticeship.

WHY DO EXPERIMENTS?

Let's begin with an example of a research problem and a discussion of different ways this problem could be addressed empirically. For this purpose, we will use a problem that is dear to the hearts of most social psychologists, including ourselves: prejudice and stereotyping. Perhaps no other social problem has captured the attention of social psychologists as much as this one, from early research by Allport (1954) and Sherif et al. (1961) to modern research on in-group favoritism and the cognitive bases of stereotyping (Abrams & Hogg, 1990; Brewer & Brown, 1998, in this *Handbook*; Fiske et al., 1998, in this *Handbook*; Hamilton & Trolier, 1986; Tajfel, Billig, Bundy, & Flament, 1971; von Hippel, Sekaquaptewa, & Vargas, 1995). One reason for this fascination is that few problems are as prevalent and seemingly ingrained in human nature as discord between social groups. Centuries-old conflicts persist in many parts of the world, such as disputes between Israelis and Arabs, Irish Protestants and Irish Catholics, and Serbians and Croatians. In the United States racism persists decades after the Civil Rights movement of the 1950s and 1960s.

The causes of prejudice and stereotyping have been debated at great length by philosophers, social scientists, politicians, and pundits of all kinds. Social psychology offers a unique perspective by studying prejudice experimentally. Indeed, what sets social psychology apart from most other disciplines is the claim that it can discover the causes of human behavior by conducting scientific research. What sort of research might be done to understand the causes of prejudice?

We often ask our students this question at the beginning of our courses. We find a definite preference for certain types of studies, and these preferences, we believe, are highly instructive, because they reveal a good deal about most people's understanding (or lack thereof) of the experimental method. Consider this response, which is pretty typical of what our students suggest:

The best way to study prejudice, it seems to me, is to go to places where it is most likely to be seen and study what happens. It would be interesting, for example, to hang out at a car dealership and watch how the salespeople treat white versus African American customers. Or maybe you could go to the rental office of an apartment complex in a white neighborhood, and see what happens when an African American comes in and inquires about an apartment. If we see any signs of prejudice we could interview people to see why they acted the way they did.

As we tell our students, valuable insights can be gained by such careful observations of everyday behavior. One might even take this simple observational study a half step further and compare the experience of African Americans with the experience of Caucasians in a variety of situations. For example, the television program *Primetime Live* conducted a study much like the one described above and uncovered some disturbing examples of prejudicial behavior (Lucasiewicz & Sawyer, 1991). Two college-aged middle-class males—one African American, one white—were filmed with a hidden camera as they encountered several everyday situations, including the attempt to buy a car and rent an apartment. In viewing the show, it was clear that the differences in the way the two men were treated were striking. The white man, for example, was offered a better price on the same car by the same salesman than was the African American.

It does not take our students long, however, to recognize that this type of study has many limitations. When journalists report the results of their observations it is difficult to gauge the typicality of what they report. In the *Primetime Live* segment, for example, the reporter (Diane Sawyer) casually mentioned that the two men were not *always* treated differently, but the viewer has no way of determining how often this was the case. The examples of blatant prejudice were undoubtedly more "newsworthy," and thus more likely to be broadcast. All the segments showing the African Americans being treated fairly were left on the cutting-room floor, so to speak. In addition, there is no way of knowing to what extent the different treatment the men received was due to the fact that one was African American and one was white. Undoubtedly the producers attempted to make sure that the two men were similar in some respects; the men dressed similarly, were of similar age, and so on. Who is to say, though, whether other differences in appearance, demeanor, facial expression, or personality contributed to the way they were treated? It is highly likely that race played a role—and perhaps even a major role—but the point is that it is not possible to disentangle the effects of race with other uncontrolled factors.

If social scientists were conducting the study, instead of journalists, these problems would be easy enough to correct. Nothing would have been left on the cutting-room floor; scientists would report precisely how often prejudice was observed and how often it wasn't, rather than presenting only the newsworthy cases. A larger sample of interactions would be observed between many different kinds of people, to make sure that the differences were not skewed by the specific characteristics of one or two individuals. Even so, there would be some drawbacks to such an observational study. Chief among them is the difficulty of discovering the *causes* of prejudice. We might gain insights as to how often prejudiced behaviors occur, and obtain clues to some of its causes by observing when it occurs and when it does not. We could not, however, make any definitive statements about causality.

One solution to this problem would be to question the people we observe. In the *Primetime Live* segment filmed at a car dealership, for example, Diane Sawyer asked the car salesman, who had just been observed treating the African American man more negatively than the white man, to explain his actions. As you can imagine, the salesman did not say, "Well, Ms. Sawyer, let me explain to you the deep-seated causes of my prejudice. It all began when I was three and my father wouldn't let me play with an African American kid down the street. . . ." Instead he was quite defensive and refused to admit that he was biased in any way. Well, you might say, this is because he knew his answers would be broadcast on national television. And you might be right. As we will see, however, there are other deeper reasons to be wary of the answers people give about the causes of their behavior. They often do not want to tell scientists the real causes, out of embarrassment or defensiveness. More fundamentally, they might not even know the causes of their own behavior.

Observational versus Correlational versus Experimental Studies

The observational method is one in which naturalistic behavior is systematically observed and recorded. This was the method suggested by our student, in which people's behavior toward African Americans would be observed in natural settings. As we have noted, this method is often valuable for generating hypotheses about the causes of social behavior, but it is a poor technique for testing causal hypotheses.

As a step closer to understanding the causes of a phenomenon, we could try to uncover variables that predict its occurrence. Questions about prediction are often addressed with the *correlational method,* in which two or more variables are systematically measured, and the relationship between these variables is assessed. If there is a correlation between the variables, then we can predict one from the other (within a given margin of error). The *Primetime Live* segment was more of a correlational study, in that the one variable (the race of the college student) was correlated with another (how the student was treated by people at car dealerships, rental offices, etc.). Correlational studies go beyond observational studies by making systematic observations of at least two variables and correlating these variables with each other, allowing the researcher to estimate the extent to which people's standing on one variable predicts their standing on the other variable. For example, Tumin, Barton, and Burrus (1958) assessed people's level of education and amount of prejudice toward African Americans and found a negative correlation: the more education people had, the lower their prejudice.

Correlational designs are still inadequate, however, in specifying cause and effect. This is nothing more than an elaboration of the old phrase "correlation does not prove causation." Whenever we observe that Variable X is correlated with Variable Y, there are three possible causal relationships: X could be causing Y, Y could be causing X, or some third variable could be causing both X and Y. Consider the correlation between lack of education and prejudice. It could be that there is something about getting an education that causes a reduction in prejudice. Although it may seem implausible, it is equally possible that there is something about prejudice that causes a lack of education (perhaps prejudiced people find it difficult to work with others and this impedes their educational progress). It is also possible that there is absolutely no causal link between education and prejudice. Some third variable, such as intelligence or social class, might cause people both to get more education and to not be prejudiced.

There are many examples of people making unwarranted causal inferences from correlational data with potentially serious consequences. Consider the results of a study in which the type of birth control women used was correlated with whether they had sexually transmitted diseases (STDs). Surprisingly, the researchers found that women whose partners used condoms had more STDs than women who used diaphragms or contraceptive sponges (Rosenberg et al., 1992). This finding was reported widely in the popular press, often with the conclusion that diaphragms and sponges prevented STDs better than did condoms. This conclusion, of course, makes a causal assumption from correlational data—the assumption that the types of birth control (Variable X) had a causal effect on STDs (Variable Y). The study, however, showed nothing of the kind. Perhaps women who had STDs (Variable Y) were more likely to insist that their partners use condoms (Variable X). It is equally possible that some third variable contributed both to the type of contraception women used and their likelihood of getting STDs. The women who relied on condoms might have differed from the other women in any number of ways that contributed to their getting more STDs; perhaps their sexual partners were more likely to be infected, perhaps they had sex more often, perhaps they had more partners (in fact, these women reported having had sex with more partners in the previous month than did

the women who used diaphragms and sponges). The conclusion that condoms protect people less is completely unfounded and could lead to dangerous behavior on the part of women and men who draw this conclusion from the correlational design.

The great advantage of the experimental method is that the causal relationship between variables can be determined with much greater certainty. This is done in two ways: by controlling all factors except the independent variable and by randomly assigning people to condition. We will elaborate on how and why this is done shortly. For now, consider the following laboratory experiment on stereotyping: Gilbert and Hixon (1991) were interested in the conditions under which a stereotype about a social group is activated when a member of that group is encountered. Some theories assume that stereotypes are activated automatically, without any conscious intent on the part of the perceiver. According to this view, when we encounter a member of a stereotyped group our stereotype comes to mind, even if we don't want it to. In contrast, Gilbert and Hixon (1991) argued that, at least under some circumstances, it takes cognitive effort to bring a stereotype to mind. If people are distracted or preoccupied, the stereotype will not be activated.

Gilbert and Hixon (1991) tested this hypothesis as follows: white college students were asked to watch a videotape of a woman holding up a series of cards with word fragments on them, such as P_ST. The participants' job was to make as many words from these fragments as they could within fifteen seconds, such as POST or PAST. Unbeknownst to the participants there were two versions of the videotape. In one the woman holding up the cards was Caucasian, whereas in the other she was Asian. This was one of the *independent variables,* which is a variable that the researcher varies to see if it has an effect on some other variable of interest (the *dependent variable*). The other independent variable in this study was how "cognitively busy" or distracted people were while watching the videotape. People in the "busy" condition were asked to remember an eight-digit number, which made it difficult for them to think carefully about what they were doing. People in the "nonbusy" condition were not asked to remember any numbers. Gilbert and Hixon (1991) predicted that people who had to remember the eight-digit number would not have the cognitive resources to activate their stereotype of Asians, and thus should judge the Asian woman no differently than the Caucasian women. Not busy participants, however, should have the resources to call to mind their stereotype, and thus should judge the Asian woman differently than the Caucasian woman.

The way in which the activation of stereotypes was measured was as follows: it just so happened that five of the word fragments on the cards people saw could be completed to form words that were consistent with American college students' stereotypes about Asians (as established in pretesting). For example, the fragment "S_Y" could be completed to make the word "SHY," and the fragment "POLI_E" could be completed to form the word "PO-LITE." The measure of stereotype activation was the number of times people completed the fragments with the words that reflected the Asian stereotype. The results were as predicted: people who were not busy and saw the Asian woman generated the most stereotypic words. People who were cognitively busy did not generate any more stereotypical words for the Asian as opposed to the Caucasian woman. In a second study, Gilbert and Hixon (1991) distinguished between the activation and the application of a stereotype, and found that the people's ratings of the Asian woman's personality were most stereotypic when they were not busy while viewing the videotape (allowing their stereotypes to be activated) but cognitively busy while listening to the assistant describe her typical day (allowing the stereotype to be applied to the woman with no inhibition).

The Gilbert and Hixon (1991) experiment differs in many ways from the other studies of prejudice we have considered (the observational study proposed by our student, the *Primetime Live* "study," and the correlational study by Tumin et al. (1958) on level of education and amount of prejudice). We suspect that some readers will find it unsatisfactory: How can stereotyping be studied in the confines of the laboratory, on such artificial tasks as asking people to complete word fragments? What can be learned about prejudice in a study in which people never actually interacted with anyone but only watched videotapes?

There *are* drawbacks to laboratory experiments that we will consider at some length. For now we point to the main advantage of experiments: their ability to determine causality. To illustrate this point, imagine the following hypothetical study that tested Gilbert and Hixon's hypotheses about stereotype activation with a correlational design. At a large state university, the researchers attend the first day of classes that are taught by graduate student teaching assistants—some of whom happen to be Caucasian and some of whom happen to be Asian. The researchers take advantage of the fact that some of the classes are held in a building that is being renovated, such that the high-pitched whine of power saws and drills intrudes into the classrooms. Students in these rooms are assumed to be cognitively busy, because the noise makes it difficult to pay close attention to the instructor. Other classes are held in buildings in which there is no construction noise, and these students are assumed to be relatively "nonbusy."

At the end of each class the researchers ask the students to rate their instructor on various trait dimensions, including some that are part of the Asian stereotype (e.g., shyness). Suppose that the results of this study were the same as Gilbert and Hixon's: students in the "nonbusy" (quiet) classrooms rate Asian instructors more stereotypically than students in the "busy" (noisy) classrooms (e.g., they think

the instructors are more shy). There is no difference between busy and nonbusy students in their ratings of Caucasian instructors.

To many readers, we suspect, this study seems to have some definite advantages over the one conducted by Gilbert and Hixon (1991). The measure of stereotyping—students' ratings of their TA—seems a lot more realistic and important than the word fragments people complete after watching a videotape in a psychology experiment. On the other hand, the limitations of this study should by now be clear: it would demonstrate a correlation between cognitive busyness and stereotypic ratings of Asians (at least as these variables were measured in this study), but there would be no evidence of causal relationship between these variables. For example, there is no way of knowing how students who took classes in the noisy building differed from students who took classes in the quiet building. Maybe some departments offer classes in one building but not the other, and maybe students interested in some subjects have more stereotypic views of Asians than other students do. If so, the differences in ratings of the Asian instructors might reflect these differences in endorsement of the stereotype and have nothing to do with cognitive busyness. Second, there is no way of knowing whether the instructors who teach in the different buildings have similar personalities. Perhaps the Asian instructors teaching in the noisy building really were more shy than the Asian instructors teaching in the quiet building. In short, there is simply no way of telling whether students' ratings of the Asian instructors in the different buildings were due to (a) differences in their level of cognitive busyness; (b) the fact that different students took classes in the different buildings, and these students differed in their endorsement of the Asian stereotype; or (c) the fact that different instructors taught in the different buildings, and these instructors had different personalities.

One of the great advantages of an experiment is the ability to control variation to insure that the stimuli in experimental conditions are similar. The fact that Gilbert and Hixon showed all participants the same videotape of an Asian or Caucasian woman solved one of the problems with our hypothetical correlational study: personality differences between the instructors of the courses. The fact that people who were nonbusy showed more evidence of stereotyping than people who were busy cannot be attributed to differences in the personality of the Asian women they saw on the videotape, because participants in both conditions saw the same woman.

But how do we know that this difference was not due to the fact that the students in the nonbusy condition happened to be more prejudiced toward Asians? Gilbert and Hixon (1991) solved this problem with the most important advantage of experimental designs: the ability to randomly assign people to conditions. Unlike the correlational study, people did not "self select" themselves into the busy or nonbusy condition (i.e., by deciding which courses to take). Everyone had an equal chance of being in either condition, which means that people who were especially prejudiced against Asians were as likely to end up in one condition as the other. Random assignment is the great equalizer: as long as the sample size is sufficiently large, researchers can be relatively certain that differences in the personalities or backgrounds of their participants are distributed evenly across conditions. Any differences that are observed, then, are likely to be due to the independent variable encountered in the experiment, such as their different levels of cognitive busyness.

Our discussion of the limits of correlational designs—and the advantage of experiments—is similar to that in any introductory course in statistics or research methodology. As straightforward and obvious as these points may seem, however, they are often overlooked, by both lay people and professional researchers. To understand why, consider the following two (fictitious) investigations of the same problem.[1] In the first, a team of researchers finds that school performance in a group of inner-city children is related to the frequency with which they eat breakfast in the morning. The more often the kids eat breakfast, the better their school performance, with a highly significant correlation of 0.30 (this means that the relationship between eating breakfast and school performance is moderately strong and highly unlikely to be due to chance). As far as you can tell the researchers used good measures, and the study was well-conducted. What do you think of this finding? Does it make you more confident that programs that provide free breakfasts for underprivileged children are having positive effects on their academic performance? If you were reviewing a report of this study for a journal, how likely would you be to recommend publication? Most of us, we suspect, would find this to be an interesting and well-conducted study that should be in the literature.

Now consider this study: a team of researchers conducts an experiment with a group of inner-city children. Half the kids are randomly assigned to a condition in which they receive free breakfasts at school every morning, whereas the other half are in a control group that does not receive this intervention. Unfortunately the researchers introduced a confound into their design: while the kids in the first group eat their breakfast, teachers read to them and help them with their homework. After a few months, the researchers assess the kids' school performance and find that those in the breakfast condition are doing significantly better than the controls. The measure of academic performance is the same as in the previous study and the magnitude of the effect is the same. What do you think of this experiment?

How likely would you be to recommend that it be published? The confound in the design, we would guess, is likely to be apparent and appalling to most of us. Is it eating breakfast that improved the kids' performance, or the reading and extra attention from the teachers? Many of us would feel that the design of this study is so flawed that it should not be published.

But let's compare the two studies more carefully. The key question is how confident can we be that eating breakfast causes improved academic performance. The flaw in the experiment is that we cannot be sure whether eating breakfast or extra attention from a teacher or both were responsible for the improved performance. But how confident can we be from the correlational study? Kids who eat breakfast probably differ in countless ways from kids who do not. They may come from more functional families, get more sleep—or, for that matter, have parents or teachers who are more likely to help them with their homework! The experimental study, despite its flaw, rules out every single one of these alternative explanations except for one. Admittedly this is a serious flaw; the researchers did err by confounding breakfast eating with extra attention from the teachers. But the fact remains that the correlational study leaves the door open to the same confound, and dozens or hundreds of others besides. If the goal is to reduce uncertainty about causality, surely the correlational study is much more flawed than the experimental one.

Why, then, does it seem like more can be learned from the correlational study? One reason may be that the flaw in the experiment is an act of commission (the researchers erred by introducing a confound), whereas the flaw in the correlational study was more an act of omission (the researchers erred by failing to consider the natural confounding of breakfast eating with any number of other variables). The correlational study was done poorly, by the standards of correlational designs; whereas the experimental study was done poorly, by the standards of experimental designs. Our point is that the same standard should be applied to both types of studies: How much do they reduce uncertainty about causality?

The ability to determine relationships between variables in correlational designs has improved, we should add, with the advent of sophisticated statistical techniques such as structural equation modeling. These methods allow researchers to test complex relationships between several variables. For example, suppose a researcher measured three variables: teachers' expectations about how well their students will perform, the children's academic achievement, and the educational level of the children's parents. Do the teachers' expectations predict the children's academic achievement independently of the third variable? Or, does the educational level of the parents predict both teacher expectations and children's academic achievement, with no relation between these latter two variables? Several

---

1. We have adapted this example from Mook, Wilson, and DePaulo (1995).

different relationships between these variables might exist and structural equation modeling is a useful technique for distinguishing between competing models.

We do not have the space to review all the pros and cons of structural equation modeling (for excellent reviews see Kenny, Kashy, & Bolger, 1998, in this *Handbook*; and Reis, 1982). Our point is that as useful as this technique is, it cannot, in the absence of experimental manipulations with random assignment, determine causal relationships. One of the main reasons for this is obvious but sometimes overlooked: it is impossible to measure all variables in a correlational design, and the researchers might have omitted one or more crucial causal variables. Thus, although there may be a direct path between two variables in a structural model (e.g., between teacher expectations and children's academic performance), one can never be sure whether this is because one variable really causes the other, or whether there are unmeasured variables that are the true causes and happen to correlate highly with the measured variables (e.g., perhaps the children's performance on standardized tests influences both academic performance and teachers' expectations). The only way to definitely rule out such alternative explanations is to use experimental designs in which people are randomly assigned to different experimental conditions (as Rosenthal, 1994, did in his seminal, experimental work on expectancy effects).

We hope we have convinced the reader of the great advantage of the experiment—its ability to answer causal questions. Some, however, might still be a little uncomfortable with our conclusions, in that there is one way in which experiments are often inferior to observational and correlational studies: they are often done in the "artificial" confines of a psychology laboratory and involve behaviors (e.g., forming words from word fragments, remembering eight-digit numbers) that seem to have little to do with the kinds of things people do in everyday life. This is, perhaps, the most common objection to social psychological experiments—they seem "artificial" and "unrealistic." How can we generalize from such artificial situations to everyday life? We will consider this question at length when we discuss external validity later in the chapter. To set the stage for this discussion it is useful to discuss some basic distinctions between different types of research.

Field versus Laboratory Research

Many observational and correlational studies are conducted in the field, such that people are unaware that they are being studied or observed. Laboratory research is true to its name: it is conducted in a laboratory, usually in such a way that people know they are being observed or that they are in a scientific investigation. When we ask students how they would study prejudice, they almost always propose field over laboratory studies. Their (quite reasonable)

assumption is that behavior is best understood if it is observed in the context in which it naturally occurs. It is more difficult to generalize when people are observed in an artificial setting that they usually do not encounter in everyday life, such as in a laboratory in the psychology department of a university. It is unlikely, for example, that many people are asked to observe videotapes of people holding up cards with word fragments, and to generate words from these fragments.

Why, then, did Gilbert and Hixon (1991) conduct their study in the laboratory? We discussed the answer earlier: to gain enough control over the situation to be able to make causal inferences. In the hypothetical correlational study we discussed, in which students rated their instructors on the first day of class, there was no way to ensure that students in the different buildings had instructors with similar personalities. By showing people the same videotape of an Asian or Caucasian woman, Gilbert and Hixon (1991) solved this problem. Differences in ratings of the woman were likely to be due to the independent variable (cognitive busyness), and not to differences in who people were rating. A critical feature of experimental designs is that the situation is identical for all people except for the independent variables of interest. This is more difficult in naturalistic settings, in which the experimenter is often unable to control extraneous variables that can contaminate the results.

The distinction between field and laboratory research, however, is not always so clear-cut. One common misconception is to confuse it with the difference between experimental and correlational designs. True enough, most correlational studies are conducted in the field, and most experiments are conducted in the laboratory. As seen in Fig. 1, however, the two distinctions are not identical. It is sometimes possible to conduct experiments in naturalistic settings; we will discuss some classic field experiments later in this chapter. It is also possible to do correlational studies in the laboratory. The most common example of correlation laboratory studies is the attempt to develop a new measure of personality, in which people are given a battery of personality tests in a laboratory session, to see how much the new measure correlates with existing measures. Nonetheless, it is true that social psychological studies are not evenly distributed across the four cells in Fig. 1. The majority of studies are laboratory experiments. Increasingly, however, social psychologists are conducting research in naturalistic settings, and we will discuss both laboratory and field experiments later in the chapter.

In general, the laboratory makes it easier to accomplish the random assignment of people to conditions. In addition, a laboratory setting permits the researcher to manipulate independent variables more precisely and to eliminate or minimize the intrusiveness of "extraneous" variables. Advocates of laboratory experiments believe that the world is a complex place consisting of a great many noisy vari-

	Laboratory Settings	**Field Settings**
Experimental Designs	Laboratory Experiments	Field Experiments
Correlational Designs	Correlational Studies Conducted in the Laboratory (e.g., Personality Research)	Correlational Studies Conducted in the Field

FIGURE 1   Experimental versus Correlational Designs in Field versus Laboratory Settings.

ables, a condition that impedes the chances of obtaining a pure indication of the effect of one variable upon another. If the experimenter wants to discover the effects of an event on the behavior, attitudes, or feelings of participants, the laboratory provides the sterility that enables observation of those effects unencumbered by extraneous variables that could confound interpretation. Conversely, the field is generally regarded as being more "real." In the real world the event in question always occurs in context; it is that very context that might have important but extraneous effects upon the behavior, feelings, or attitudes of the individual. Critics of the laboratory setting have suggested that it is silly to eliminate contextual variables in the interest of precision if those variables are always present in the world. We will elaborate on this distinction later in the chapter. For now we focus on another distinction concerning the focus of an experiment.

Problem-Oriented versus Process-Oriented Research: Studying the Phenomenon versus Studying the Process

In some experiments the researcher is mainly interested in studying a phenomenon that he or she wants to understand and possibly change, such as prejudice. In others, the researcher is interested in the underlying mechanisms responsible for the phenomenon. This distinction may seem a little odd, in that it probably seems that these goals are interdependent—and they are. To understand and change a phenomenon, it is necessary to understand the mechanisms that cause it. How can we reduce prejudice, for example, without understanding the psychological mechanisms that

produce it? In practice, however, there is a distinction to be made between research that focuses on the problem itself and research that focuses on mechanisms.

Part of this distinction involves still another one: the difference between *basic* and *applied* research. With basic research, investigators try to find the best answer to the question of why people behave the way they do, purely for reasons of intellectual curiosity. No direct attempt is made to solve a specific social or psychological problem. In contrast, the goal in applied research is to solve a specific problem. Rather than investigating questions for their own sake, constructing theories about why people do what they do, the aim is to find ways of alleviating such problems as racism, sexual violence, and the spread of AIDS. Thus, the basic researcher is more likely to be interested in the mechanisms underlying an interesting phenomenon than the applied researcher. If applied researchers find something that works they might not be as concerned with why. In medicine, for example, there are many examples of cures that work for unknown reasons, such as the effects of aspirin on body temperature.

The distinction between problem-oriented and process-oriented research, however, involves more than the distinction between applied and basic research. To illustrate this, consider two basic researchers who are equally interested in understanding the causes of prejudice and racism. (As with many social psychological topics this is, of course, an eminently applied one as well, in that the researchers are interested in finding ways of reducing prejudice.) One researcher conducts a field study in which members of different races interact under different conditions (e.g., cooperative versus competitive settings), to study the conditions under which reductions in prejudicial behavior occur. The other conducts a laboratory experiment on automatic processing and categorization, or the way in which people categorize the physical and social world immediately, spontaneously, and involuntarily. The stimulus materials, however, have nothing to do with race per se; in fact, the issue of race never comes up in this experiment. Participants judge a white stimulus person, under conditions thought to trigger automatic evaluations and conditions thought to trigger more controlled, thoughtful evaluations (e.g., Bargh, 1989; Brewer, 1988; Uleman, 1989).

Which study is a better investigation of prejudice and racism? Most people, we suspect, would say the former study. What does the second study have to do with prejudice? How can you possibly study racism, one might argue, without looking at behavior and attitudes of one race toward another? Herein lies our point: for researchers interested in process and mechanisms, the study of a phenomenon (such as prejudice) can involve the study of basic, psychological processes that are several steps removed from the phenomenon itself. In our view both types of studies are important: those that study the phenomenon (e.g., racism) itself and work backward to try to discover its causes, and those that study the basic mechanisms of human perception, cognition, motivation, emotion, and behavior, and then work forward to apply these concepts to important problems (e.g., racism).

Like our earlier distinctions, we hasten to add that this one is not entirely clear-cut. Sometimes research is both problem- and process-oriented; it explores a problem and the mechanisms responsible for it simultaneously. Often, however, the focus of research on a particular problem changes as research on it progresses. As noted by Zanna and Fazio (1982), initial investigations of a problem tend to explore "is" questions: What is the phenomenon? Does it exist? These studies are, in our terms, very much problem-oriented; they establish the existence of a particular phenomenon (e.g., whether there is a stereotype based on physical attractiveness). When this question is answered researchers typically move on to questions that have more to do with the underlying mechanisms, namely, studies exploring variables that moderate or mediate the effect. Interestingly, these process-oriented studies sometimes do not study the original problem at all, focusing instead on general mechanisms that produce many different effects (as in our example of basic research on categorization and impression formation that do not study interactions between people of different races, but which are quite relevant to stereotyping and prejudice).

Our position is that to understand the causes of social psychological phenomena, it is often necessary to conduct experimental rather than correlational or observational studies, with process-oriented rather than problem-oriented approaches. Again, we do not intend to demean or devalue

other approaches; any problem is best understood with a variety of techniques, and we have used other methods ourselves (e.g., correlational designs). To really get at the heart of a problem, however—namely, to understand its causes—experimental, process-oriented studies are often the method of choice, usually conducted in the laboratory instead of the field.

Interestingly, this assertion runs against the grain of the layperson's view of how research should be conducted. Think back to our early example of the student's suggestion about how to study prejudice: it was an observational study, it was conducted in the field, and it was problem-oriented rather than process-oriented. In general, we find that many people new to the field of social psychology believe that a problem should be studied in as natural a context as possible (i.e., in the field), often using correlational or observational techniques. Further, there is a definite preference for problem-oriented research. If the goal is to understand prejudice then the topic of the study should be prejudice. We have never heard a student new to the field say, "Prejudice should be studied by doing laboratory studies on automaticity or cognitive dissonance theory!"

Because of this (understandable) bias, students are sometimes dismayed to encounter so many studies that are just the opposite: experimental, laboratory, process-oriented studies. We hope the reader is at least somewhat convinced that in addition to studying a phenomenon such as prejudice in naturalistic settings, it is critical to study its underlying mechanisms in the laboratory, so that the causal relationships between intervening variables can be established more definitely. Sometimes, as we will see, this involves studying fundamental psychological processes, such as cognitive dissonance, attitude change, and social cognition in the laboratory, even if such studies do not directly investigate prejudice.

We will return to a discussion of the limits of laboratory research later in the chapter, when we discuss such issues as how the results obtained in the laboratory can be generalized to everyday life. Given the clear advantages of laboratory experiments—namely, the ability to determine causal relationships between variables—we turn now to a detailed discussion of how to do a laboratory experiment. In discussing the nuts and bolts of experimentation we will not lose sight of these important questions about the advantages or disadvantages of experiments and will in fact return to these issues frequently.

PLANNING AND CONDUCTING A LABORATORY EXPERIMENT

The best way to describe how to conduct an experiment is to take a real study and dissect it carefully, examining how it was done and why it was done that way. We have chosen for illustrative purposes a classic laboratory experiment by

Aronson and Mills (1959). We use this experiment for several reasons. First, it illustrates clearly both the advantages and the challenges of attempting to do experimental research in social psychology; we did not select it for its purity as a model of experimental efficiency. Second, we discuss it as an example of basic, process-oriented research that is applicable to many different phenomena, including the one already mentioned—prejudice. At first glance this might be difficult to see, in that the Aronson and Mills (1959) study investigated the effects of the severity of an initiation on liking for a discussion group—a topic which seems far removed from the kinds of prejudice and racism we see around us today. Indeed, some aspects of the Aronson and Mills study might even seem old-fashioned; it was, after all, conducted nearly forty years ago. Nonetheless it deals with basic issues that are as fresh and important today as they were in 1959: What happens when people invest time and effort in something, such as joining a social group, that turns out to be much less enjoyable than they thought it would be? Can the psychological processes that are triggered add to our understanding of why people in contemporary society tend to be attached to their own groups to an extreme degree, and why they derogate members of other groups? The fact is that a laboratory experiment—even one conducted four decades ago—because it illuminates basic psychological processes does have a lot to say about a variety of current real-world phenomena, including prejudice.

Aronson and Mills set out to test the hypothesis that individuals who undergo a severe initiation in order to be admitted to a group will find the group more attractive than they would if they were admitted to that group with little or no initiation. To test this hypothesis, they conducted the following experiment. Sixty-three college women were recruited as volunteers to participate in a series of group discussions on the psychology of sex. This format was a ruse in order to provide a setting wherein people could be made to go through either mild or severe initiations in order to gain membership in a group.

Each participant was tested individually. When a participant arrived at the laboratory, ostensibly to meet with her group, the experimenter explained to her that he was interested in studying the "dynamics of the group discussion process" and that, accordingly, he had arranged these discussion groups for the purpose of investigating these dynamics, which included such phenomena as the flow of communications, who speaks to whom, and so forth. He explained that he had chosen as a topic "The Psychology of Sex" in order to attract volunteers, as many college people were interested in the topic. He then went on to say that, much to his dismay, he subsequently discovered that this topic presented one great disadvantage; namely, that many volunteers, because of shyness, found it more difficult to participate in a discussion about sex than in a discussion about a more neutral topic. He explained that his

study would be impaired if a group member failed to participate freely. He then asked the participant if she felt able to discuss this topic freely. Each participant invariably replied in the affirmative.

The instructions were used to set the stage for the initiation that followed. The participants were randomly assigned to one of three experimental conditions: a severe-initiation condition, a mild-initiation condition, or a no-initiation condition. The participants in the no-initiation condition were told, at this point, that they could now join a discussion group. It was not that easy for the participants in the other two conditions. The experimenter told these participants that he had to be absolutely certain that they could discuss sex frankly before admitting them to a group. Accordingly, he said that he had recently developed a test that he would now use as a "screening device" to eliminate those students who would be unable to engage in such a discussion without excessive embarrassment. In the severe-initiation condition, the test consisted of having people recite (to the male experimenter) a list of 12 obscene words and two vivid descriptions of sexual activity from contemporary novels. In the mild-initiation condition, the women were merely required to recite words related to sex that were not obscene.

Each of the participants was then allowed to "sit in" on a group discussion that she was told was being carried on by members of the group she had just joined. This group was described as one that had been meeting for several weeks; the participant was told that she would be replacing a group member who was leaving because of a scheduling conflict.

To provide everyone with an identical stimulus, the experimenter had them listen to the same tape-recorded group discussion. At the same time, the investigators felt it would be more involving for participants if they didn't feel that they were just listening to a tape recording but were made to believe that this was a live-group discussion. In order to accomplish this and to justify the lack of visual contact necessitated by the tape recording, the experimenter explained that people found that they could talk more freely if they were not being looked at; therefore, each participant was in a separate cubicle, talking through a microphone and listening in on headphones. Since this explanation was consistent with the other aspects of the cover story, all the participants found it convincing.

Needless to say, it was important to discourage participants from trying to "talk back" to the tape, since by doing so they would soon discover that no one was responding to their comments. In order to accomplish this, the experimenter explained that it would be better if she did not try to participate in the first meeting, since she would not be as prepared as the other members who had done some preliminary readings on the topic. He then disconnected her microphone.

At the close of the taped discussion, the experimenter returned and explained that after each session all members were asked to rate the worth of that particular discussion and the performance of the other participants. He then presented each participant with a list of rating scales. The results confirmed the hypothesis. The women in the severe-initiation condition found the group much more attractive than did the women in the mild-initiation or the no-initiation conditions.

At first glance, this procedure has some serious problems. As with the Gilbert and Hixon (1991) study we discussed earlier, the experimenters constructed an elaborate scenario bearing little relation to the "real-life" situations in which they were interested. The "group" which people found attractive was, in fact, nothing more than a few voices coming in over a set of earphones. The participant was not allowed to see her fellow group members nor was she allowed to interact with them verbally. This situation is a far cry from group interaction as we know it outside the laboratory. In addition, reciting a list of obscene words is undoubtedly a much milder form of initiation to a group than most actual initiation experiences outside the laboratory (e.g., a college fraternity or into the Marine Corps). Moreover, the use of deception raises serious ethical problems as well as more pragmatic ones such as whether or not the deception was successful.

The reasons why Aronson and Mills (1959) opted to do a laboratory experiment should be clear from our earlier discussion of experimental versus correlational methods and laboratory versus field research: the ability to control extraneous variables and the ability to randomly assign people to the different conditions. They could have opted to study real groups, such as fraternities and sororities, measuring the severity of their initiations and the attractiveness of each group to its members. Though such a study would have some advantages, we trust its disadvantages are by now clear: the inability to determine causality. Because of the inability to control extraneous variables (i.e., the actual attractiveness of the different fraternities and sororities) and the inability to randomly assign people to condition (i.e., to groups with mild or severe initiations), there would be no way of knowing whether severe initiations caused more attraction to the group. For example, it may be that desirable fraternities are inundated with applicants; because of this, they set up severe initiations to discourage people from applying. Once word gets around, only those who are highly motivated to join those particular fraternities are willing to subject themselves to severe initiations. If this were the case, it is not the severity of the initiation that caused people to find the fraternities attractive; rather, it is the attractiveness of the fraternities that produced the severity of the initiation!

Choosing the Type of Experiment to Perform

Let us assume that you are a novice researcher with a terrific idea for an experiment. The first decision you would want to make is whether to design your experiment for the laboratory or the field. While this is an important individual decision for the novice, it is our position that all experiments should be conducted in a variety of settings. Thus, we advocate that, ideally, all experimentally researchable hypotheses should be tested in both the laboratory and the field. As we have mentioned, and will discuss in detail later, each approach has its advantages and disadvantages. There is no logical reason, however, for starting in one domain or the other nor is there any reason for assuming that particular hypotheses lend themselves more easily to the laboratory or the field. The decision is frequently dictated by such factors as the momentary availability of resources, idiosyncratic preferences of the experimenter, and so on.

Suppose you decide to bring the experiment into the laboratory. The next decision you must make is whether the experiment is to be an *impact* or a *judgment* type. In impact experiments people are active participants in an unfolding series of events and have to react to these events as they occur. Often, these events have a substantial impact on their self-views and people thus become deeply involved in the experiment. In judgment experiments participants are more like passive observers; they are asked to recognize, recall, classify, or evaluate stimulus materials presented by the experimenter. Little direct impact on participants is intended, except insofar as the stimulus materials capture people's attention and elicit meaningful judgmental responses. Thus, the crucial distinction between an impact experiment and a judgment experiment is whether or not the event in question is happening to the participant. In the Aronson and Mills experiment, for example, the embarrassment produced by reciting obscene words was happening to the participants themselves. It is the effect of that embarrassment that is the major interest of the experimenter. In a judgment study the event might be important and dramatic, but it is not happening to the participant. For example, I (the participant) might read about or witness (via film) an aggressive or violent act (which might sicken or outrage me), but the violent act is not happening to me.

There are ideas that can be tested by either technique; for example, the investigation of equity. In some of these experiments, people are simply handed a description of the effort expended and product produced by individuals, given a distribution of the relative rewards or payments to the individual, and asked to evaluate the equity of the distribution. In other experiments, a person's own effort or output is rewarded in a more or less equitable way, and he or she is allowed to respond.

Some hypotheses, however, can only be tested with one type of experiment. A researcher who was interested in the effects of sexual arousal on persuasibility would be in the domain of the impact study. It would be absurd to conduct an experiment on the effects of sexual arousal without doing something aimed at affecting the degree of sexual arousal among some of the participants. On the other hand, some hypotheses are judgmental in nature. For example, as we saw, Gilbert and Hixon (1991) hypothesized that stereotypes are more likely to be activated when people are not cognitively busy. They pointed out that interacting with a member of a stereotyped group can itself make people "busy," in that people have to think about their own actions and the impressions they are making at the same time they are forming an impression of the other person. Thus, to see whether stereotypes are more likely to be triggered when people are *not* cognitively busy, it was important to have people judge a member of a stereotyped group but not to interact with this person—in short, to make it more of a judgment than an impact study. They accomplished this by showing people a videotape of an Asian or Caucasian woman, instead of having them actually meet and interact with the woman.

The point is that researchers should tailor their method to their hypothesis. Judgment experiments are usually easier to do, because they require a less elaborate "setting of the stage" to involve the participants in an impactful situation. If researchers are interested in what happens when a person's self-concept is engaged by a series of events that happen to that person, however, there is no substitute for the impact experiment.

The Four Stages of Laboratory Experimentation

The process of planning a laboratory experiment consists of four basic stages: (1) setting the stage for the experiment, (2) constructing the independent variable, (3) measuring the dependent variable, and (4) planning the postexperimental follow-up. In this section we will suggest ways of developing a sensible and practical *modus operandi* for each of those stages. We will be looking at both the impact experiment and the judgment experiment. It should be mentioned at the outset that the four phases listed above apply to both types of laboratory experiment. Almost without exception, however, the impact experiment is much more complex and involves a wider scope of planning than does the judgment experiment. In effect, the judgment experiment is a "bare bones" operation. Although the design of both types requires attention to similar issues (e.g., random assignment, the order of presentation of the stimulus materials, and the context in which these materials are presented), the impact experiment entails a more elaborate scenario. Accordingly, much of our discussion will be devoted to the high-impact type of study, not because we consider such experiments as necessarily more important but because we consider them more complex.

Setting the Stage   In designing any laboratory experiment, a great deal of ingenuity and invention must be directed toward the context, or stage, for the manipulation of the independent variable. Because of the fact that our par-

ticipants tend to be intelligent, adult, curious humans, the setting must make sense to them. It not only must be consistent with the procedures for presenting the independent variables and measuring their impact but also can and should enhance that impact and help to justify the collection of the data.

Many experiments involve deception; if deception is used, the setting must include a sensible, internally consistent pretext or rationale for the research as well as a context that both supports and enhances the collection of the data and reduces the possibility of detection. This false rationale is often referred to as a *cover story.*

In a judgment experiment, the cover story is typically less elaborate and more straightforward than in an impact experiment. Although deception is frequently used in a judgment experiment, it is usually minimal and aimed primarily at increasing the interest of the participants and providing a credible rationale for the data collection procedures and judgment task. For example, Aronson, Willerman, and Floyd (1966) performed a judgment experiment to test the hypothesis that the attractiveness of a highly competent person would be enhanced if that person committed a clumsy blunder—because the clumsy blunder would tend to humanize the person. To provide an adequate test of the hypothesis, it was necessary to expose people to one of four experimental conditions: (1) a highly competent person who commits a clumsy blunder, (2) a highly competent person who does not commit a clumsy blunder, (3) a relatively incompetent person who commits a clumsy blunder, and (4) a relatively incompetent person who does not.

What would be a reasonable context that would justify exposing people to one of these stimulus persons and inducing them to rate the attractiveness of that person? The experimenters simply informed the participants (who were students at the University of Minnesota) that their help was needed in selecting students to represent the university on the *College Bowl,* a television program pitting college students from various universities against one another in a test of knowledge. They told the participants that they could evaluate the general knowledge of the candidates objectively, but that this was only one criterion for selection. Another criterion was judgments from the participants concerning how much they liked the candidates. The experimenter then presented the participant with a tape recording of a male stimulus person being interviewed. This stimulus person answered a number of questions either brilliantly or not so brilliantly and either did or did not clumsily spill a cup of coffee all over himself. The participants then rated the stimulus person on a series of scales. The cover story in this experiment was simple and straightforward and did succeed in providing a credible rationale for both the presentation of the stimulus and the collection of the data.

Providing a convincing rationale for the experiment is almost always essential, since participants do attempt to make sense of the situation and to decipher the reasons for the experiment. A good cover story is one that embraces all the necessary aspects of the experiment in a plausible manner and thus eliminates speculation from a participant about what the experimenter really has in mind. It also should capture the attention of the participants so that they remain alert and responsive to the experimental events. This is not meant facetiously; if a cover story strikes the participants as being a trivial or silly reason for conducting an experiment, they may simply tune out. If the participants are not attending to the independent variable, it will have little impact on them.

The setting may be a relatively simple one, or it may involve an elaborate scenario, depending on the demands of the situation. Obviously, the experimenter should set the stage as simply as possible. If a simple setting succeeds in providing a plausible cover story and in capturing the attention of the participants, there is no need for greater elaboration. A more elaborate setting is sometimes necessary, especially in a high-impact experiment. For example, suppose one wants to make people fearful. One might achieve this goal by simply telling the participants that they will receive a strong electric shock. Yet the chances of arousing strong fear are enhanced if one has set the stage with a trifle more embellishment. This can be done by providing a medical atmosphere, inventing a medical rationale for the experiment, having the experimenter appear in a white laboratory coat, and allowing the participant to view a formidable, scary-looking electrical apparatus as in Schachter's (1959) experiments on the effects of anxiety on the desire to affiliate with others. One might go even further by providing the participant with a mild sample shock and implying that the actual shocks will be much greater.

The point we are making here is that in a well-designed experiment, the cover story is an intricate and tightly woven tapestry. With this in mind, let us take another look at the Aronson and Mills (1959) experiment. Here we shall indicate how each aspect of the setting enhanced the impact and/or plausibility of the independent and dependent variables and contributed to the control of the experiment. The major challenge presented by the hypothesis was to justify an initiation for admission to a group. This was solved, first, by devising the format of a sex discussion, and second, by inventing the cover story that the experimenters were interested in studying the dynamics of the discussion process. Combining these two aspects of the setting, the experimenter could then, third, mention that because shyness about sex distorts the discussion process, it was, fourth, necessary to eliminate those people who were shy about sexual matters by, fifth, presenting the participants with an embarrassment test.

All five aspects of the setting led directly to the manipu-

lation of the independent variable in a manner that made good sense to the participants, thereby allaying any suspicions. Moreover, this setting allowed the experimenter to use a tape-recorded group discussion (for the sake of control) and at the same time to maintain the fiction that it was an ongoing group discussion (for the sake of impact).

This fiction of an already formed group served another function in addition to that of enhancing the involvement of the participants. It also allowed the experimenter to explain to the participant that all the other members had been recruited before the initiation was made a requirement for admission. This procedure eliminated a possible confounding variable, namely, that participants might like the group better in the severe-initiation condition because of the feeling that they had shared a common harrowing experience.

Finally, because of the manner in which the stage had been set, the dependent variable (the evaluation of the group) seemed a very reasonable request. In many experimental contexts, obtaining a rating of attractiveness tends to arouse suspicion. In this context, however, it was not jarring to the participant to be told that each member stated her opinion of each discussion session, and therefore it did not surprise the participant when she was asked for her frank evaluation of the proceedings of the meeting. Ultimately, the success of a setting in integrating the various aspects of the experiment is an empirical question: Do the participants find it plausible? In the Aronson-Mills experiment only one of sixty-four participants expressed any suspicions about the true nature of the experiment.

The testing of some hypotheses is more difficult than others because of their very nature. But none is impossible; with sufficient patience and ingenuity a reasonable context can be constructed to integrate the independent and dependent variables regardless of the problems inherent in the hypothesis.

Constructing the Independent Variable   The independent variable is the experimental manipulation. It is, ideally, a variable that is independent of all sources of variation except those specifically under the control of the experimenter. One of the most important and difficult parts of experimental design is constructing an independent variable that manipulates only what you want it to manipulate. The experimenter begins with what we will call the *conceptual variable,* which is a theoretically important variable that he or she thinks will have a causal effect on people's responses. In the Aronson and Mills study, for example, the conceptual variable might be thought of as cognitive dissonance caused by an embarrassing initiation. There are many ways to translate an abstract conceptual variable such as this into a concrete experimental operation. One of the most important parts of experimental design is to devise a procedure that "captures" the conceptual variable perfectly without influencing any other factors. If we have our participants recite a list of obscene words and then listen to a boring group discussion, how can we be sure that this is, in fact, an empirical realization of our conceptual variable? Sometimes this is very difficult, and after an experiment is done, the researcher realizes that whereas participants in Conditions A and B were thought to differ only in one conceptual variable (the amount of cognitive dissonance people experienced), they also differed in some other way.

Controversy over the correct interpretation of the results obtained in the Aronson and Mills initiation experiment discussed earlier provides an example of this problem. The complex social situation used by Aronson and Mills has many potential interpretations, including the possibility that reading obscene materials generated a state of sexual arousal that carried over to reactions to the group discussion. If that were the case, it could be that transfer of arousal, rather than effort justification, accounted for the higher attraction to the group.

A replication of the initiation experiment by Gerard and Mathewson (1966) ruled out this interpretation. Their experiment was constructed so as to differ from the Aronson and Mills study in many respects. For example, Gerard and Mathewson used electric shocks instead of the reading of obscene words as their empirical realization of severe initiation (and the dissonance it produced); the shocks were justified as a test of "emotionality" rather than as a test of embarrassment; the tape recording concerned a group discussion of cheating rather than of sex; and the measure of attractiveness of the group differed slightly. Thus sexual arousal was eliminated as a concomitant of the experimental procedures. The results confirmed the original findings: people who underwent painful electric shocks in order to become members of a dull group found that group to be more attractive than did people who underwent mild shocks. Such a confirmation of the basic initiation effect under quite different experimental operations supports, at least indirectly, the idea that it was cognitive dissonance produced by a severe initiation, and not some other conceptual variable, that was responsible for the results. A considerable amount of research in social psychology has been motivated by similar controversies over the valid interpretation of results obtained with complex experimental procedures.

We will return to this issue later in the chapter, when we discuss different kinds of validity of experiments. We return now to a discussion of independent variables and how they should be administered. Recall that the essence of an experiment is the random assignment of participants to experimental conditions. For this reason, it should be obvious that any characteristics that the participants bring to the experiment cannot be regarded as independent variables in the context of a true experiment. Although such characteristics as prejudice, intelligence, self-esteem, and socioeco-

nomic class can be measured and taken into account or ignored, they should not be regarded as independent variables of an experiment. It is not infrequent to find an "experiment" purporting to assess the effects of a participant variable (like level of self-esteem, for example) on some behavior in a specific situation. It should be clear that although such a procedure may produce interesting results, it is not an experiment because the variable was not randomly assigned.

Nonrandom assignment of participants to experimental conditions is not confined to the use of personality measures in lieu of experimental treatments. It usually takes place in more subtle ways. One of the most common occurs when the experimenter is forced to perform an "internal analysis" in order to make sense out of his or her data.

The term "internal analysis" refers to the following situation. Suppose that an experimenter has carried out a true experiment, randomly assigning participants to different treatment conditions. Unfortunately, the treatments do not produce any measurable differences on the dependent variable. In addition, suppose that the experimenter has had the foresight to include an independent measure of the effectiveness of the experimental treatment. Such "manipulation checks" are always useful in providing information about the extent to which the experimental treatment had its intended effect on each individual participant. Now, if the manipulation check shows no differences between experimental treatments, the experimenter may still hope to salvage his or her hypothesis. That is, the manipulation check shows that for some reason the treatments were unsuccessful in creating the internal states in the participants that they were designed to produce. Since they were unsuccessful, one would not expect to see differences on the dependent variable. In this case, the experimenter may analyze the data on the basis of the responses of the participants to the manipulation check, resorting participants into "treatment" according to their responses to the manipulation check. This is an internal analysis.

For example, Schachter (1959) attempted to alter the amount of anxiety experienced by his participants by varying the description of the task in which the participants were to engage. However, in some of the studies, many participants who had been given the treatment designed to produce low anxiety actually reported higher anxiety levels than some who had been given the treatment designed to produce high anxiety. From the results of an internal analysis of these data, it does seem that anxiety is related to the dependent variable. Again, these data can be useful and provocative, but since the effect was not due to the manipulated variable, no causal statement can be made. Although many of the "highly anxious" participants were made anxious by the "high-anxiety" manipulation, many were highly anxious on their own. Since people who become anxious easily may be different from those who do not, we are dealing with an implicit personality variable. This means that we can no longer claim random assignment—and, in effect, we no longer have an experiment.

Another situation in which the treatments are assigned nonrandomly occurs when the participants assign themselves to the experimental conditions. That is, in certain experimental situations the participant, in effect, is given a choice of two procedures in which to engage. The experimenter then compares the subsequent behavior of participants who choose one alternative with those who choose the other. For example, in one study, Wallace and Sadalla (1966) placed participants in a room with a complex machine and had a confederate tempt them to press a conspicuous button on the front of the machine. When a participant pressed the button, the machine exploded. Unfortunately, whether or not a participant chose to press the button was determined by the participant and not by the experimenter. Since there may be important differences between those who choose to press and those who do not, the experimenters in this kind of situation relinquish control to the participant and are left with a nonexperimental study.

The problem of free choice is a particularly sticky one because, if the hypothesis involves the effect of choice, it is obviously important to give the participant a perception of clear choice. Yet this perception must remain nothing more than a perception, for as soon as the participant takes advantage of it, we are beset with the problems of nonrandom assignment. One solution to this problem is to conduct a pilot test of the variable until a level is found for it that is just sufficient enough to inhibit participants from actually choosing the "wrong" behavior. For example, in an experiment by Aronson and Carlsmith (1963), children were given either a mild or severe threat to prevent them from playing with a desirable toy. In order for this experiment to work, it was critical to make the mild threat strong enough to ensure compliance. On the other hand, it could not be too strong, for the experimental hypothesis hinged upon the child's not having a terribly good reason for declining to play with the toy. The situation had to be one in which the child was making a choice whether to play or not to play with the specific toy and was bothered by the lack of a good reason to avoid playing with that toy. It is sometimes possible to find such a level by elaborate pretesting. As an alternative, in some experimental situations a solution can be effected through the use of instructions that give a strong perception of choice, although little choice is actually present.

Between- versus within-subject designs   Another decision facing the experimenter is whether to manipulate the independent variable on a between-subject or within-subject basis. In a between-subject design people are randomly assigned to different levels of the independent variable, as in the Aronson and Mills study, in which different groups of people received different levels of initiation. In a within-subject design all participants receive all levels of the independent variable. For example, in the literature on detecting deception, participants are typically shown a videotape of another person and are asked to judge whether that person is lying or telling the truth. A number of factors have been manipulated to see how easy it is to tell whether the person is lying, such as whether the person on the tape is saying something good or bad about another person, and whether the person had the opportunity to think about and plan the lie before delivering it (e.g., DePaulo, Lanier, & Davis, 1983). These factors are often manipulated on a within-subject basis. In the DePaulo et al. (1983) study, for example, participants watched people make four statements: a planned lie, a spontaneous lie, a planned true statement, and a spontaneous true statement. The participants did not know which statement was which, of course; their job was to guess how truthful each statement was. As it turned out, people were able to detect lies at better than chance levels, but spontaneous lies were no easier to detect than planned lies.

Within-subject designs are often preferred, because fewer participants are required to achieve sufficient statistical power. Imagine that DePaulo et al. (1983) has used a between-subject design, such that four separate groups of participants saw statements that were either planned lies, unplanned lies, planned truthful statements, or unplanned truthful statements. They probably would have had to include at least 15 people per condition, for a total of 60 participants. By using a within-design in which every participant was run in each of the four conditions, fewer people were needed (there were only 24 people who judged the statements in this study).

One reason fewer participants are needed is because each participant serves as his or her own control; each person's responses in one condition are compared to that same person's responses in the other conditions. This controls for any number of individual difference variables that are treated as error variance in a between-subject design. Suppose, for example, that one participant has a very suspicious view of the world and thinks that people are lying most of the time. Another participant is very trusting and thinks that people seldom lie. Suppose further that a between-subject design was used, and the distrustful and trusting people are randomly assigned to different conditions. In this design, it would be difficult to separate the effects of the independent variable (e.g., whether the person on the tape was lying or telling the truth) from how suspicious participants are in general. With random assignment, of course, individual differences are averaged across condition; the number of suspicious versus trusting people should be roughly the same in all conditions. Nonetheless the "noise" produced by personality differences makes it difficult to detect the "signal" of the effects of the independent variable, and a large number of participants often have to be run to detect the "signal." In a within-subject design this problem is solved by running every person in every condition. The suspicious person's responses to the lies are compared to his or her responses to the nonlies, thereby "subtracting out" his or her tendency to rate everyone as deceptive.

If a within-subject design is used it is important, of course, to vary the order of the experimental conditions, to make sure that the effects of the independent variable are not confounded with the order in which people receive the different manipulations. This is referred to as "counterbalancing," whereby participants are randomly assigned to get the manipulations in different orders. In the DePaulo et al. (1983) study, for example, the presentation of the deceptive versus nondeceptive statements and planned versus unplanned statements was counterbalanced, such that different participants saw the statements in different orders.

In many social psychological experiments within-subject designs are not feasible, because it would not make sense to participants to evaluate the same stimulus more than once under slightly different conditions. For example, in the experiment by Aronson, Willerman, and Floyd, once a participant was exposed to a tape recording of a competent person spilling coffee, it would have been ludicrous to present that same participant with an otherwise identical tape of a competent person who doesn't spill coffee. Who would believe that there are two people in the world who are identical in all ways except for their coffee-spilling behavior? By the same token, in the vast majority of impact experiments, the nature of the impactful manipulation precludes utilization of the same participants in more than one condition. For example, in the Aronson and Mills experiment, once the experimenters put a participant through a severe initiation in order to join a group and then asked her to rate the attractiveness of that group, it would have been silly to ask her to start all over and go through a mild initiation! Thus, within-subject designs are preferable if at all possible, but in many studies—especially impact experiments—they are not feasible.

Avoiding participant awareness biases It is arguably more challenging to perform a meaningful experiment in social psychology than in any other scientific discipline for one simple and powerful reason: in social psychology, we are testing our theories and hypotheses on adult human beings who are almost always intelligent, curious, and experienced. They are experienced in the sense that they have spent their entire lives in a social environment and—because of their intelligence and curiosity—they have formed their own theories and hypotheses about precisely the behaviors we are trying to investigate. That is to say, everyone in the world, including the participants in our experiments, is a social psychological theorist.

In a nutshell, the challenge (and the excitement) of doing experiments in social psychology lies in the quest to find a way to circumvent or neutralize the theories that the participants walk in with so that we can discover their true behavior under specifiable conditions—rather than being left to ponder behavior that reflects nothing more than how the subjects think they should behave in a contrived attempt to confirm their own theory.

One special form of participant awareness is closely related to the idea of "demand characteristics" as described by Orne (1962). Demand characteristics refers to features introduced into a research setting by virtue of the facts that it *is* a research study and that the participants know that they are part of it. As aware participants, they are motivated to make sense of the experimental situation, to avoid negative evaluation from the experimenter, and perhaps even to cooperate in a way intended to help the experimenter confirm the research hypothesis (Sigall, Aronson & Van Hoose, 1970). Such motivational states are likely to make participants highly responsive to any cues—intended or unintended—in the research situation that suggest what they are supposed to do to appear normal or "to make the study come out right." This problem can present itself in both impact and judgment experiments, particularly those in which each participant is exposed to more than one variation of the stimulus. Such a procedure, by its very nature, increases the probability that the participant will begin to guess which aspects of the experiment are being systematically varied by the experimenter. This is less of a problem in most impact experiments where participants are presented with only one variation of a given independent variable. But, of course, manipulations with high impact may also create problems of participant awareness. It is for this reason that experimenters frequently employ deception, elaborate cover stories, and the like.

Another aspect of the problem of demand characteristics and participant awareness is the possibility that the experimenter's own behavior provides inadvertent cues that influence the responses of the participants. In our experience novice researchers often dismiss this possibility; they smile knowingly and say, "Of course I wouldn't act in such a way to bias people's responses." Decades of research on expectancy effects, however, show that the transmission of expectations to participants is subtle and unintentional, and that this transmission can have dramatic effects on participants' behavior. It can occur even between a human experimenter and an animal participant; in one study, for example, rats learned a maze quickly when the experimenter thought they were good learners and slowly when the experimenter thought they were poor learners (Rosenthal & Lawson, 1964; Rosenthal, 1994).

Therefore steps must be taken to avoid this transmission of the experimenter's hypotheses to the research participants. One way of doing so is to keep the experimenter unaware of the hypothesis of the research. The idea here is that if the experimenter does not know the hypothesis, he or she cannot transmit the hypothesis to the research participants. In our judgment, however, this technique is inadequate. One characteristic of good researchers is that they are hypothesis-forming organisms. Indeed, as we mentioned earlier, this is one characteristic of all intelligent humans. Thus, if not told the hypothesis, the research assistant, like a participant, attempts to discover one. Moreover, keeping the assistant in the dark reduces the value of the educational experience. Since many experimenters are graduate students, full participation in an experiment is the most effective way of learning experimentation. Any technique involving the experimenter's ignorance of the hypothesis or a reduction in contact with the supervisor is a disservice to him or her. A more reasonable solution involves allowing the experimenters to know the true hypothesis but keeping them ignorant of the specific experimental condition of each participant. In theory, this is a simple and complete solution to the problem and should be employed whenever possible.

In a study by Wilson et al. (1993), for example, the independent variable was whether people were asked to think about why they felt the way they did about some art posters, to examine the effects of introspection on attitude change and satisfaction with consumer choices. Participants were told that the purpose of the study was to examine the different types of visual effects that people like in pictures and drawings, and that they would be asked to evaluate some posters. The critical manipulation was whether people wrote down why they felt the way they did about each poster (the reasons condition) or why they had chosen their major (the control condition). To assign people to condition randomly, the experimenter simply gave them a questionnaire from a randomly ordered stack. To make sure the experimenter did not know whether it was the reasons or control questionnaire an opaque cover sheet was stapled to each one. The experimenter left the room while the participant completed the questionnaire, and thus throughout the experiment was unaware whether the participant was in the reasons or control condition.

In other types of experiments the experimental manipulations cannot be delivered simply by having people read written instructions, making it more difficult to keep the experimenter unaware of condition. In studies on intrinsic motivation, for example, the critical manipulation is the level of reward people believe they will get for performing a task. This could be conveyed in written form, but there is a risk that participants will not read the questionnaire carefully enough, missing the crucial information about the reward. A frequently used solution to this problem is to tape record the instructions and to keep the experimenter unaware of which recorded instructions each participant receives (e.g., Harackiewicz, Manderlink, & Sansone, 1984).

In other studies, however—particularly high-impact ones—the experimenter must deliver the independent variable in person, making it more difficult for him or her to be unaware of participant's experimental condition. In the Aronson and Mills experiment, for example, people's condition was determined by which list of words they had to read aloud to the experimenter. The experimenter could have given people a questionnaire and asked them to read the list to themselves, but this obviously would have reduced the impact of the manipulation considerably. In studies such as these, where it is necessary for the experimenter to "deliver" the independent variable, several steps can still be taken to avoid demand characteristics, participant awareness biases, and experimenter expectancy effects. First, the experimenter should be kept ignorant of people's condition until the precise moment of crucial difference in manipulations. That is, in most studies, the experimenter need not know what condition the participants is in until the crucial manipulation occurs. When the choice point is reached, a randomizing device can be used, and the remainder of the experiment is, of course, not carried out in ignorance. For example, in the Aronson and Mills study, it would have been easy to delay assignment of participants to condition until the point of initiation; by reaching into a pocket and randomly pulling out one of three slips of paper, the experimenter could determine whether the participant would recite the obscene words, the mild words, or no words at all. Thus, all the premanipulation instructions would be unbiased.

This is only a partial solution because the experimenter loses his or her ignorance midway through the experiment. However, if the experimenter left the room immediately after the recitation and assigned a different experimenter (unaware of the participant's experimental condition) to collect the data, this solution would approach completeness. The use of multiple experimenters, each ignorant of some part of the experiment, offers a solution that is frequently viable. For example, Wilson and Lassiter (1982) were interested in whether prohibiting people from engaging in unattractive activities would increase the appeal of those activities; that is, whether the Aronson and Carlsmith (1963) "forbidden toy" effect would apply when the prohibited activity was undesirable at the outset. The participants were preschool children who were seen individually. In one condition the experimenter showed the child five toys and said that he or she could play with any of them but a plastic motorcycle, which was known to be unattractive to children. In the control condition the children were allowed to play with all five toys. As we have discussed, the experimenter randomly assigned people to condition at the last possible moment, namely, after he had shown the children all the toys and demonstrated how they worked.

To assess children's subsequent interest in the toys the children were seen again a week later, and given two of the toys to play with—the plastic motorcycle and another, attractive toy. At this session the same experimenter could not be used, however, because he was no longer unaware of the child's experimental condition. Further, his presence might cause children to base their choice on factors other than their liking; for example, they might be concerned that he still did not want them to play with the motorcycle. Thus, a different experimenter (unaware of the child's condition) was used, and the children were not told that this session was part of the same study as the first session. As predicted, the children who were prohibited from playing with the motorcycle in the first session played with it significantly more at the second session than did people in the control condition.

Returning to the more general issue of demand characteristics, it should be clear that the most effective type of deception in an impact experiment involves the creation of an independent variable as an event that appears not to be part of the experiment at all. Creating such an independent variable not only guarantees that the participant will not try to interpret the researcher's intention but also that the manipulation has an impact on the participant. Several classes of techniques have been used successfully to present the independent variable as an event unrelated to the experiment. Perhaps the most effective is the "accident" or "whoops" manipulation, in which the independent variable is presented as part of what appears to be an accident or unforeseen circumstance. Wilson, Hodges, and LaFleur (1995) used a variation on this procedure to influence people's memory for behaviors performed by a target person. These researchers showed people a list of positive and negative behaviors the target person had performed, and then wanted to make sure that people found it easiest to remember either the positive or negative behaviors. They did so by simply showing people either the positive or negative behaviors a second time. The danger of this procedure, however, is that it would be obvious to people that the researchers were trying to influence their memory. If Wilson et al. had said, "OK, now we are going to show you only the positive (negative) behaviors again," participants would undoubtedly have wondered why, and possibly figured out that the point was to influence their memory for these behaviors. To avoid this problem, Wilson et al. told people that they would see all of the behaviors again on slides. After only positive (or negative) ones had been shown, it just so happened that the slide projector malfunctioned. The projector suddenly went dark, and after examining it with some frustration the experimenter declared that the bulb was burned out. He searched for another for awhile, unsuccessfully, and then told participants that they would have to go on with the study without seeing the rest of the slides. By staging this "accident," the researchers ensured that people were not suspicious about why they saw only positive or negative behaviors a second time.

Another way to make the independent variable seem like a spontaneous, unrelated event is to have a confederate, apparently a fellow participant, introduce the manipulation. For example, Schachter and Singer (1962) attempted to manipulate euphoria by having a confederate waltz around the room shooting rubber bands, play with hula hoops, and practice hook shots into the wastebasket with wadded paper. Presumably, this behavior was interpreted by the participant as a spontaneous, unique event unrelated to the intentions of the experimenter. A third method is to use the whole experimental session as the independent variable and to measure the dependent variable at some later time. For example, in the Wilson and Lassiter (1982) study mentioned earlier, the independent variable (whether people were constrained from playing with an unattractive toy) was assessed at another session a week later. It is unlikely that the participants realized that what happened in the first study was the independent variable of interest. Even within the same experimental session it is possible to convince people that they are taking part in separate, unrelated experiments. A common ruse is the "multiple study" cover story, in which people are told that for reasons of convenience several unrelated mini-experiments are being conducted at the same session. This ruse is commonly employed in priming experiments, in which it is very important that people not connect the independent variable (the priming of a semantic category) with the dependent variable (ratings of a target person whose standing on that category is ambiguous). Higgins, Rholes, and Jones (1977), for example, had people memorize words related to adventurousness or recklessness as part of an initial, "Study 1" concerned with perception and memory, and then had people rate a stimulus person, whose behavior was ambiguous as to whether it was adventurous or reckless, as part of a "Study 2" on impression formation.

Of course, if one is primarily concerned with eliminating participant awareness, the ultimate strategy is to induce the independent variable in such a manner that the participants are oblivious to the fact that any experiment is taking place at all. This strategy is best implemented in field settings, which we will discuss shortly.

Optimizing the impact of the independent variable   As we mentioned, one problem with keeping experimenters unaware of condition, by delivering the independent variable in written form, is that the impact of the independent variable will be reduced. One of the most common mistakes the novice experimenter makes is to present instructions too briefly; consequently, a large percentage of the participants fail to understand some important aspects of the instructions. To ensure that all participants understand what is going on in an experiment (especially one as complicated as most social psychological experiments), the instructions should be repeated in different ways.

More important than simple redundancy, however, is ensuring the instructions are expressed precisely so that each participant fully understands them and the events that occur in the experiment. This can be accomplished by a combination of written and verbal instructions, in which the experimenter repeats or paraphrases key parts of the instructions until satisfied that the participant is completely clear about all of them. Although the point seems obvious, it has been our experience that many experiments fail precisely because the instructions were never made clear enough to become understandable to all the participants.

The experimenter also must ensure that the participants attend throughout the course of the experiment to the relevant stimulus conditions that constitute the independent variable. In judgment research this aspect of impact is particularly critical. All the care and effort devoted to careful and systematic stimulus control are wasted if the participant because of boredom or inattention fails to perceive the critical variations in the stimuli presented. Increasingly, stimuli in social psychological experiments are being presented in carefully controlled ways on computers, and it is interesting to note that this can be a two-edged sword with respect to keeping people's attention. Some participants find working on a computer more novel and interesting than working with the usual paper-and-pencil instruments, and thus pay more attention to the information that is presented. Other participants, however, find computer presentations to be a less engaging social exchange than a real-life interaction, and quickly become bored. The differences between communication over computers and direct communication between people is an interesting topic of research in its own right (e.g., Kiesler & Sproull, 1987). For present purposes the point is that researchers should be careful that their task is engaging to keep people's attention, whether it is presented over a computer or in the "old-fashioned way."

In the well-designed impact experiment, there is less likely to be a question about whether the participant is paying attention to the relevant stimulus conditions. Nonetheless the experimenter should be as certain as possible that the complex bundle of stimuli constituting the independent variable produces the intended phenomenological experience in the participants. For this purpose, there is no substitute for the thorough pretesting of the manipulation. During the pretesting, the experimenter can conduct long, probing interviews with the participant after the test run of the experiment is completed or, better yet, after the manipulation of the independent variable.

One of the most frequently misunderstood aspects of experimentation is the amount of pretesting that is often required to make sure that the independent variable is having the desired impact. When students read published experiments in psychological journals, they often have the impression that the researchers had an idea, designed a study,

collected the data in a few weeks, analyzed the data, and presto, found exactly what they predicted. Little do they know that in most cases the experiment was preceded by a good deal of pretesting, whereby different versions of the independent variable were "tried out." For example, in the Wilson, Hodges, and LaFleur (1995) study mentioned earlier, in which the researchers staged a malfunction of a slide projector, a good deal of pretesting was required to "fine tune" this manipulation. Different versions of the manipulation were tried before one was found that worked convincingly.

This might seem to be misleading, in that the researchers ended up reporting only the version of the independent variable that had the desired effect. It is important to note, however, that there are two meanings of the phrase "desired effect": (a) whether the researchers manipulated what they intended to manipulate and (b) whether the independent variable had the predicted effect on the dependent variable. An experiment cannot test a hypothesis unless the independent variable manipulates what it is supposed to manipulate. For example, in the Wilson, Hodges, and LaFleur (1995) study, the point was to see what happens when people analyze the reasons for their impressions of a person and either positive or negative thoughts about that person are accessible in memory. The hypotheses of the study could only be tested if the manipulation of people's memory succeeded in making positive or negative thoughts more accessible. If the slide projector malfunction did not influence people's memory, the hypotheses could not be tested. The ability to play with a design so that the manipulations change the right variables is a skill similar to that of a talented director who knows exactly how to alter the staging of a play to maximize its impact on the audience. This is where some of the most important work in experimental design occurs, but it is rarely reported in published articles, because it would not be very informative or interesting to begin the methods section by saying, "We will first tell you about all the ways of manipulating the independent variable that didn't work. The first mistake we made was. . . ."

It is another matter, however, if the manipulation works as intended but does not influence the dependent variable in the predicted manner. Another reason that a manipulation can fail to have an effect is because the researcher's hypothesis is wrong. The manipulation might work exactly as intended (as indicated, for example, on a manipulation check) but have a different effect on the dependent variable than predicted. This *is* informative, because it suggests that the hypothesis might be wrong. The catch is that it is often difficult to tell whether an experiment is not working because the manipulation is ineffective or because the hypothesis is wrong. The answer to this question often becomes clear only after extensive tinkering and restaging of the experimental situation.

Once it becomes clear that the manipulation is working as intended but the hypothesis is off the mark, a second talent comes into play: the ability to learn from one's mistakes. Some of the most famous findings in social psychology did not come from reading the literature and deducing new hypotheses, or from "aha" insights while taking a shower. Rather, they came about from the discovery that one's hypotheses were wrong and the data suggest a very different hypothesis—one that is quite interesting and worth pursuing faithfully.

Choosing the number of independent variables   We have been talking thus far of the independent variable in the social psychological experiment as if it were a simple two-level variation on a single dimension. Yet many, if not most, experiments conducted in the area involve procedures that simultaneously manipulate two or more variables. Once one has taken the time and trouble of setting up a laboratory experiment, recruiting participants, and training research assistants, it seems only efficient to take the occasion to assess the effects of more than one experimental treatment.

There are no pat answers to the question of how many independent variables can or should be manipulated at one time, but our own rule of thumb is that an experiment should be only as complex as is required for important relationships to emerge in an interpretable manner. Sometimes it is essential to vary more than one factor because the phenomenon of interest appears in the form of an interaction. Petty, Cacioppo, and Goldman (1981), for example, hypothesized that the way in which people process information in a persuasive communication depends on the personal relevance of the topic. When the topic was highly relevant people were predicted to be most influenced by the strength of the arguments in the communication, whereas when it was low in relevance people were predicted to be most influenced by the expertise of the source of the communication. To test this hypothesis the authors had to manipulate (a) the personal relevance of the topic, (b) the strength of the arguments in the message, and (c) the expertise of the source of the message. Only by including each of these independent variables could the authors test their hypothesis, which was confirmed in the form of a three-way interaction.

Measuring the Dependent Variable   The basic decision facing the researcher in planning the measurement of dependent variables is whether to rely on participants' self-reports or observations by others as the means of assessing a person's responses to the experimental situation. Actually, it is not that simple, for it is possible to imagine a continuum ranging from behaviors of great importance and consequence for the participant down to the most trivial paper-and-pencil measures about which the participant has no

interest. At one extreme the experimenter could measure the extent to which participants actually perform a great deal of tedious labor for a fellow student (as a reflection of, say, their liking for that student). At the other extreme one could ask them to circle a number on a scale entitled "How much did you like that other person who participated in the experiment?" Close to the behavioral end of the continuum would be a measure of the participant's commitment to perform a particular action without actually performing it. We call this a "behavioroid" measure.

It is a fair assumption to say that most social psychologists care the most about social behavior: how people treat each other and how they respond to the social world. The goal is not to explain and predict which number people will circle on a scale or which button on a computer they will press, but people's actual behavior toward another person or the environment. Thus, the first choice of a dependent measure in a social psychological experiment is usually overt behavior. The ideal measure of prejudice is the way in which members of different groups treat each other, the ideal measure of attitude change is behavior toward an attitude object, and the ideal measure of interpersonal attraction is affiliative behaviors between two individuals. If you pick up a copy of a recent social psychological journal, however, you will find that measures of actual behavior are hard to come by (de la Haye, 1991). The dependent measures are more likely to be such things as questionnaire ratings of people's thoughts, attitudes, emotions, and moods; their recall of past events; the speed with which they can respond to various types of questions; or, as we saw in the Gilbert and Hixon (1991) study, the ways in which people complete word fragments.

There are three main reasons why social psychologists often measure things other than actual behavior. The first is convenience: it is much easier to give people a questionnaire on which they indicate how much they like a target person, for example, then to observe and code their actual behavior toward the target person. Of course, convenience is no excuse for doing poor science, and the assumption that questionnaire responses are good proxies for actual behavior should not be taken on faith. In the early years of attitude research, for example, it was assumed that people's questionnaire ratings of their attitudes were good indicators of how they would actually behave toward the attitude object. It soon became apparent that this was often not the case (e.g., Wicker, 1969), and many researchers devoted their energies to discovering when questionnaire measures of attitudes predict behavior and when they do not. A large literature on attitude-behavior consistency was the result, and it is now clear that self-reported attitudes predict behavior quite well under some circumstances but not others (e.g., Fazio, 1990; Wilson, Dunn, Kraft, & Lisle, 1989).

Needless to say, there are some situations in which obtaining a direct measure of the behavior of interest is not simply inconvenient, it is virtually impossible. For example, Aronson and his students conducted a series of laboratory experiments aimed at convincing sexually active teenagers to use condoms as a way of preventing AIDS and other sexually transmitted diseases (Aronson, Fried, & Stone, 1991; Stone et al., 1994). The ideal behavioral dependent variable is obvious: whether the participants in the experimental condition actually used condoms during sexual intercourse to a greater extent than participants in the control condition. Think about it for a moment: How would you collect those data? Even experimental social psychologists feel obliged to stop short of climbing into bed with their subjects in order to observe their sexual behavior directly. Aronson and his students were forced to use proxies. In some of their studies, they used self-report as a proxy. In others, in addition to self-report, they set up a situation where, at the close of the experiment, the experimenter while leaving the room, indicated that the participants, if they wanted, could purchase condoms (at a bargain price), by helping themselves from a huge pile of condoms on the table—and leaving the appropriate sum of money. Although the participants had no way of suspecting that their behavior was being monitored, as soon as they left the laboratory, the experimenter returned and recounted the condoms on the table to ascertain exactly how many they had purchased. Admittedly, the number of condoms *purchased* is not quite as direct a measure as the actual *use* of the condoms, but especially given the fact that this measure was consistent with self-report measures it seems like a reasonable proxy.

A second reason behavioral measures are sometimes avoided has to do with our earlier distinction between problem-oriented and process-oriented research. If the research is problem-oriented then the dependent measures should correspond as closely to that phenomenon (e.g., prejudice, consumer behavior, condom use) as possible. If it is process-oriented, however, the goal is to understand the mediating processes responsible for a phenomenon, and the dependent measures are often designed to tap these processes and not the phenomena they produce. For example, to understand when people will act in a prejudiced manner toward a member of a social group, it is important to know when their stereotype of that group is activated. As we saw earlier, Gilbert and Hixon (1991) addressed this question by showing people a videotape of a woman holding up cards with word fragments on them, and asking people to complete the fragments to make as many words as they could. The main dependent measure was the number of times people completed the fragments with words that were consistent with Caucasians' stereotypes of Asians, to see if this differed according to whether the woman on the tape was Asian and whether people were under cognitive load. Note that the researchers never measured people's behavior toward Asians—participants never interacted with anyone except the experimenter. How, then, can this be an experiment on stereotyping and prejudice? It is by studying some of the psychological processes (stereotype activation) hypothesized to mediate prejudicial behavior.

As another example, consider the Aronson and Mills (1959) study on initiation into a group. The major goal of this study was to investigate some of the conditions and consequences of cognitive dissonance. The main dependent variable was people's ratings of the attractiveness of the group they listened to. Again, there were no measures of actual behavior. The assumption was that people's questionnaire ratings of the group were a good proxy of actual behavior toward a group, an assumption that has been borne out in other studies (see, for example, Aronson & Osherow, 1980). Considered even more broadly, however, the Aronson and Mills study can also be viewed as an investigation of some of the processes responsible for prejudice: developing favoritism for one's own group due to self-justification needs, and, possibly, derogating other groups as a result. Superficially, it seems odd to suggest that a laboratory study in which people listened to a boring group discussion about sexual behavior in animals might have anything to do with prejudice. True, the researchers did not investigate the end product of prejudice: negative manner toward an individual because of his or her group membership. Nevertheless, it seems perfectly reasonable to view this experiment as a study of some of the psychological processes *responsible* for prejudice.

Occasionally, the researcher is interested in both problem and process simultaneously. For example, in the condom research (mentioned above), Aronson and his students were interested in persuading sexually active teenagers to use condoms as a way of safeguarding against AIDS. That's problem-oriented research. They were also interested in testing their new theory of hypocrisy induction. Specifically, they were testing the hypothesis that a change in behavior could be brought about by making people mindful of the fact that they were not practicing what they were preaching—in this case, that the participants were urging others to practice safer sex, while they, themselves, were falling far short of the mark. In this instance, the investigators felt it was important to test the process in a manner that came as close to addressing the problem as they could reasonably get. If they had been primarily interested in the process, they would have chosen a different problem—one where a meaningful dependent variable would be easier to measure (see, for example, Dickerson, Thibodeau, Aronson, & Miller (1992).

A third (and related) reason why nonbehavioral measures are often used is that, in many situations, they can be a more precise measure of intervening processes than overt behavior. Behavior is often complex and multidetermined, making it difficult to know the exact psychological processes that produced it. For example, suppose in an experiment a confederate (posing as a fellow participant) either praises the participant, implying that he or she is brilliant, or insults the participant, implying that he or she is stupid. Suppose our dependent variable is how much the participant likes the confederate. We can measure it by handing participants a rating scale and asking them to rate their liking for the confederate, from +5 to –5. Or, on a more behavioral level, we can observe the extent to which the participant makes an effort to join a group to which the confederate belongs. This latter behavior seems to be a reflection of liking, but it may reflect other things instead. For example, it may be that some participants in the "insult" condition want to join the group in order to prove to the confederate that they are not stupid. Or it may be that some want an opportunity to see the insulting person again so that they can return the favor. Neither of these behaviors reflects liking, and consequently, may produce results different from those produced by the questionnaire measure.

Nonetheless it is important to note some limitations of questionnaire measures. Most fundamentally people may not know the answer to the questions they are asked. This is especially true of "why" questions, whereby people are asked to report the reasons for their behavior and attitudes. Rather than reporting accurately, people might be relying on cultural or idiosyncratic theories about the causes of their responses that are not always correct (Nisbett & Wilson, 1977; Wilson & Stone, 1985).

In recent years techniques have been developed to avoid some of the problems of reports about one's own cognitive processes; for example, Ericsson and Simon (1993) advocate the use of verbal protocols, in which people "think aloud" into a tape recorder, verbalizing whatever thoughts they happen to have. This technique can be a valuable means of assessing the contents of consciousness, avoiding the kinds of interpretations and distortions that occur when people attempt to reconstruct, after the passage of time, what they had been thinking (Fiske & Ruscher, 1989). Even when thinking aloud, however, people cannot report cognitive processes that are inaccessible to consciousness. Ericsson and Simon (1993) acknowledge this problem but are of the opinion that nonconscious processing is rare. In contrast, a good deal of recent research has found evidence for widespread nonconscious processing of many types (e.g., Higgins & Bargh, 1992; Jacoby, Lindsay, & Toth, 1992; Kihlstrom, 1987; Wegner, 1994).

Assuming that verbal protocols tap all aspects of cognitive processing is a dangerous enterprise, and whenever possible, researchers should check the validity of the reports (Wilson, 1994). Further, there is some evidence that verbal protocols can be reactive, by changing the nature of people's thought processes (Schooler, Ohlsson, & Brooks, 1993; Wilson, 1994). More generally, any type of self-report instrument should not be taken on faith; its relation to

the criterion variable of interest, which is usually overt behavior, should be tested.

There are several more mundane problems to be considered in making concrete decisions about what the dependent variable should be. One constantly recurring question is the extent to which the behavior of the participant should be constrained. This takes several forms. First, should one attempt to block most possible alternative behaviors so as to maximize the likelihood of observing changes in the specific variable of interest? For example, in a dissonance study, should the experimenter attempt to rule out all possible methods of reducing dissonance except the one he or she has decided to study? Clearly doing this will maximize the likelihood of observing differences in the behavior studied. This is a perfectly sound and reasonable technique. Indeed, it is part of our definition of experimental control. However, we do this only when we ask a certain kind of question, namely: "Is there dissonance in this situation and does it get reduced?" If this is the question, the experimenter should attempt to construct the experiment in order to be ready and able to measure the effects of the independent variable as powerfully as possible.

The investigator, however, may have a different question in mind. He or she may want to find out how people typically reduce dissonance. If this is the question, the preceding technique will almost certainly obscure what the participant really is likely to do in a situation of this sort and present the experimenter with an artificial relationship. The same concern arises when a researcher tries to decide whether to use open-ended questions or a rigidly constrained measure. Although the more quantitative measure may increase the likelihood of observing differences between experimental treatments, it also may obscure what the behavior of the participant would normally be. Any experimenter who has seen many participants close at hand has experienced the feeling that a given person is "really" showing many interesting effects, although the measures are too constrained to be sensitive to them. One answer to this problem is to use more qualitative methods, which are open-ended interviews with participants without a prior set of questions or hypotheses; trying to understand the world as participants see it, without imposing the researchers' world view.

Disguising the measure   Even if people know the answer to a question, they may not answer truthfully. As previously mentioned, people might distort their responses due to self-presentational concerns, or because they have figured out the hypothesis and want to tell the experimenters what they want to hear. It is thus often important to disguise the fact that a particular collection of data is actually the measurement of the dependent variable. This presents problems very similar to those involved in attempting to disguise the independent variable, as discussed in the earlier section on guarding against demand characteristics. Again, there are several classes of solutions that can be applied to the problem of disguising the dependent variable.

One approach is to measure the dependent variable in a setting that participants believe is totally removed from the remainder of the experiment. For example, in research on intrinsic motivation it is common to assess people's interest in an activity by observing how much time they spend on that activity during a "free time" period. Participants believe that this time period is not part of the experiment and do not know that they are being observed. Lepper, Greene, and Nisbett (1973), for instance, measured children's interest in a set of felt-tip pens by unobtrusively observing how much time they spent playing with the pens during a free-play period of their preschool class.

Another example of how the dependent measure can be disguised comes from the study by Wilson et al. (1993) mentioned earlier, in which people either analyzed why they liked some posters or did not. One hypothesis of this study was that people who analyzed reasons would change their minds about which posters they preferred the most and would thus choose different types of posters to take home than people in the control condition. To test this hypothesis the experimenter told people, at the end of the study, that as a reward for their participation they could choose one poster to take home. Asking people to make that choice in front of the experimenter would have been problematic, because self-presentational biases might have come into play, whereby people chose a poster on the basis of how this made them look to the experimenter, rather than on the basis of which one they really liked the best (DePaulo, 1992; Baumeister, 1982; Schlenker, 1980). The posters were of different types; some were reproductions of classic paintings, whereas others were more contemporary, humorous posters. Participants might have thought, "I would prefer one of the humorous posters but this might make me look shallow and inane, so I will go ahead and take the one by Monet."

To minimize self-presentational biases Wilson et al. took the following steps to make the choice of poster as private as possible: after telling the participant that she could choose a poster to take home, the experimenter said that she had to go get the explanation sheet describing the purpose of the study. She told the participant to pick out a poster from bins that contained several copies of each poster, and then left the room. The participant expected the experimenter to return shortly, and thus may still have been concerned that the experimenter would see which poster she chose. To minimize such a concern the researchers placed multiple copies of each poster in each bin. Further, all the posters were rolled up so that only the reverse, blank side was showing, making it impossible (in the minds of the participants) for the experimenter to tell which poster she had chosen. (After the participant had left the experi-

menter was able to tell which poster people chose by counting the number left in each bin.) It is possible that despite these rather elaborate precautions some participants were still motivated to choose posters that would make them look good rather than ones they really liked. It is important to minimize such self-presentational concerns, however, as much as possible. As it happened, Wilson et al.'s predictions were confirmed: people who analyzed reasons chose different types of posters than people who did not.

A similar approach is to tell participants that the dependent variable is part of a different study than the one in which the independent variable was administered. As mentioned earlier the "multiple study" cover story can be used, in which participants think they are taking part in separate studies (e.g., Higgins, Rholes, and Jones, 1977).

If the independent and dependent variables are included in the same study, steps are often taken to disguise the purpose of the dependent measure. For example, there is a family of techniques for measuring a dependent variable that is parallel to the "whoops" procedure for manipulating an independent variable. The most common member of this family involves claiming that the pretest data were lost so that a second set of measures must be collected. In attitude-change experiments, the most typical solution is to embed the key items in a lengthy questionnaire that is given to the participant. One may have some qualms about the extent to which this always disguises the measurement from the participant; yet it has been used effectively in some instances.

Dependent measures that are uncontrollable   All of the above ways of disguising the dependent measure make the assumption that if people knew what was being measured, they might alter their responses. The prototypical example of such a measure is the questionnaire response; if people are asked on a seven-point scale whether they would help someone in an emergency, they might indicate how they would like to respond, or how they think they should respond, instead of according to how they really would respond. There is another way of avoiding this problem: use dependent measures that by their very nature are uncontrollable, such that people could not alter their responses even if they wanted to—obviating the need to disguise the measure. Controllability is a matter of degree, of course; it is more difficult to control one's heart rate than one's response on a seven-point scale, but even heart rate can be controlled to some degree (e.g., by holding one's breath). Social psychologists have broadened their arsenal of dependent measures considerably in recent years, and for present purposes it is interesting to note that many of these measures are more difficult for people to control than questionnaire responses, and less susceptible to demand characteristics or self-presentational concerns. Consider the following examples.

1. As we have seen, one of the most important topics in social psychology is prejudice and stereotyping. Measuring how prejudiced someone is is very difficult, however, for the reasons we have been discussing: people do not want to admit their prejudice. As a way around this problem, researchers are increasingly relying on indirect measures of prejudice, rather than self-report instruments (e.g., Brewer, Dull, & Lui, 1981; Crosby, Bromley, & Saxe, 1980; Dovidio & Fazio, 1992; Fazio, Jackson, & Williams, 1995). For example, in the Gilbert and Hixon (1991) study reviewed earlier, the extent to which people used an Asian stereotype was measured by giving people a word completion task, and counting the number of times they came up with words that were consistent with the stereotype (e.g., saying "polite" instead of "police" when given the fragment "poli_e"). The more indirect and uncontrollable a measure of prejudice is, the more confident we can be that it is tapping how people really feel and not the feelings they want to display publicly.

2. In recent years it has become clear that some responses occur automatically, in the sense that they are uncontrollable, occur without conscious intention or awareness, and do not require processing resources. Automaticity is not an either-or phenomena, but occurs in degrees (Bargh, 1989). Research on automaticity was initially studied by cognitive psychologists interested in motor behavior and relatively "low level" responding, but it quickly became apparent that many kinds of interesting social behaviors are also automatic—which means that people cannot easily control these responses according to self-presentational concerns or demand characteristics. A number of recent researchers have taken advantage of this fact, including measures of automaticity to explore a number of fascinating mental phenomena (e.g., Bargh, 1990; Gilbert, 1991; Greenwald & Banaji, 1995; Wegner, 1994).

Social psychologists have borrowed a number of other dependent variables from cognitive psychology as well. Attitude researchers have long regarded differential or biased attention to, and memory for, pro versus con attitudinal statements as a measure of an individual's attitudinal position. Recently, more sophisticated measures of recognition, reaction time, and accuracy of recall have been applied to other aspects of social perception. Again, assuming people exercise less control over memory than they do over verbal self-reports, such measures may reveal phenomena that otherwise may be suppressed—as in our example of prejudice.

For instance, it may no longer be socially desirable for subjects to admit that they think physicians should be men rather than women. Thus, a direct measure might fail to reveal such biased expectations even if they existed in subjects' minds. Suppose instead that a researcher presented people with a picture of a man or a woman dressed like a physician and surrounded by medical paraphernalia. The participants could then be asked to identify the person's profession as quickly as possible. If it requires more time to identify correctly the female picture than the male picture, this differential recognition may be taken as an indication of a continuing propensity to think of the "ideal" doctor as a male. Similarly, suppose people are able to recall information about a pattern that fits social stereotypes to a greater extent than information that is unrelated to the stereotype (e.g., Hamilton & Rose, 1980; Brewer, Dull, & Lui, 1981). This would provide indirect but reasonably conclusive evidence of the presence of stereotyping, where a more direct measure may have revealed none. The use of all such measures presupposes some hypothetical mechanism linking biases in information processing and recall with underlying cognitive structures or beliefs.

3. The study of nonverbal communication has included measures of behavior that are difficult to control. When someone is trying to deceive someone else, for example, he or she is actively trying to control or mask their nonverbal responses in such a way that the other person is unaware that they are lying. Some nonverbal channels (e.g., facial expressions) are easier to control than others (e.g., tone of voice), thus some channels are more likely to "leak" a person's true feelings. By including such measures, researchers can more easily bypass people's attempts to control or suppress how they really feel (DePaulo, 1992).

4. The use of physiological measures, such as galvanic skin response or heart rate, is increasing. An obvious advantage of such measures is that they are difficult for people to control. A drawback is that often there is no single, physiological response that is a precise measure of the psychological state the researcher wants to measure. There is no physiological measure, for example, that is a perfect correlate of anxiety or fear or happiness. The use of such measures is becoming increasingly sophisticated, however, and shows promise for measuring psychological states. For example, some researchers are using measures of electromyographic activity over facial muscles to assess both the valence and intensity of people's affective reactions (Cacioppo, Petty, & Tassinary, 1989). In addition, sometimes physiological responses are of interest in their own right, as indicants of people's health and responses to stress (e.g., Pennebaker, 1983). Rodin and Langer (1977) and Schultz and Hanusa (1978), for example, were interested in the effects of perceived control on the health of nursing home residents and found that changes in perceived control had effects on the residents' health, as assessed by such things as the number of medications they took and ratings by the staff. In addition, these studies included what can be considered the ultimate dependent measures: mortality rates. Interestingly, changes in the residents' perceptions of control and predictability influenced how soon residents died.

An interesting variation on the true physiology measure was devised by Jones and Sigall (1971). Their technique, dubbed the "bogus pipeline," consists of convincing the participants that the experimenter has an accurate physiological measure of their attitudes. This is accomplished by the use of an electrical apparatus rigged so that, before the experiment, the participants receive a striking demonstration: the electrodes attached to their arm affect a needle on a dial in a manner consistent with their actual feelings on a number of issues. Actually, the dial is surreptitiously manipulated by the experimenter. Subsequently, the participants are asked to state their true attitudes while attached to the electrodes (although they themselves cannot view the dial). Since the participants believe that the experimenter can read the dial and that the dial reflects their real feelings, they are motivated to respond as accurately as possible. This device has proved particularly useful in measuring socially sensitive attitudes. For example, Sigall and Page (1971) found that white participants connected to the "bogus pipeline" expressed attitudes toward blacks that were more stereotypically negative than did participants in a "no pipeline" control condition.

Planning the Postexperimental Follow-up   The experiment does not end when the data have been collected. Rather, the prudent experimenter will want to remain with the participants to talk and listen in order to accomplish four important goals:

1. To ensure that the participants are in a good and healthy frame of mind.
2. To be certain that the participants understand the experimental procedures, the hypotheses, and their own performance so that they gain a valuable educational experience as a result of having participated.
3. To avail themselves of the participant's unique skill as a valuable consultant in the research enterprise; that is, only the participants know for certain whether the instructions were clear, whether the independent variable had the intended impact on them, and so on.
4. To probe for any suspicion on the part of the participants, such as whether they believed the cover story.

It is impossible to overstate the importance of the postexperimental follow-up. The experimenter should never conduct it in a casual or cavalier manner. Rather, the experimenter should probe gently and sensitively to be certain that all the above goals are accomplished. This is especially and most obviously true if any deception has been employed. In this case, the experimenter needs to learn if the deception was effective or if the participant was suspicious in a way that could invalidate the data based on his or her performance in the experiment. Even more important, where deception was used, the experimenter must reveal the true nature of the experiment and the reasons why deception was necessary. Again, this cannot be done lightly. People do not enjoy learning that they have behaved in a

naive or gullible manner. The experimenter not only must be sensitive to the feelings and dignity of the participants but also should communicate this care and concern to them. We have found that people are most receptive to experimenters who are open in describing their own discomfort with the deceptive aspects of the procedure. Then, in explaining why the deception was necessary, the experimenter not only is sharing his or her dilemma as an earnest researcher (who is seeking the truth through the use of deception) but also is contributing to the participants' educational experience by exploring the process as well as the content of social psychological experimentation.

Although it is important to provide people with a complete understanding of the experimental procedures, this is not the best way to begin the postexperimental session. In order to maximize the value of the participants as consultants, it is first necessary to explore with each the impact of the experimental events. The value of this sequence should be obvious. If we tell the participants what we expected to happen before finding out what the participants experienced, they may have a tendency to protect us from the realization that our procedures were pallid, misguided, or worthless. Moreover, if deception was used, the experimenter before revealing the deception should ascertain whether or not the participant was suspicious and whether or not particular suspicions were of such a nature as to invalidate the results.

This should not be done abruptly. It is best to explore the feelings and experiences of the participants in a gentle and gradual manner. Why the need for gradualness? Why not simply ask people if they suspected that they were the victims of a hoax? Subjects may not be responsive to an abrupt procedure for a variety of reasons. First, if a given person *did* see through the experiment, he or she may be reluctant to admit it out of a misplaced desire to be helpful to the experimenter. Second, as mentioned previously, since most of us do not feel good about appearing gullible, some participants may be reluctant to admit that they can be easily fooled. Consequently, if participants are told pointedly about the deception, they might imply that they suspected it all along, in order to save face. Thus, such an abrupt procedure may falsely inflate the number of suspicious participants and may, consequently, lead the experimenter to abandon a perfectly viable procedure. Moreover, as mentioned previously, abruptly telling people that they have been deceived is a harsh technique that can add unnecessarily to their discomfort and, therefore, should be avoided.

The best way to begin a postexperimental interview is to ask the participants if they have any questions. If they do not, the experimenter should ask if the entire experiment was perfectly clear—the purpose of the experiment as well as each aspect of the procedure. The participants should then be told that people react to things in different ways and it would be helpful if they would comment on how the experiment affected them, why they responded as they did, and how they felt at the time, for example. Then each participant should be asked specifically whether there was any aspect of the procedure that he or she found odd, confusing, or disturbing.

By this time, if deception has been used and any participants have any suspicions, they are almost certain to have revealed them. Moreover, the experimenter should have discovered whether the participants misunderstood the instructions or whether any responded erroneously. If no suspicions have been voiced, the experimenter should continue: "Do you think there may have been more to the experiment than meets the eye?" This question is virtually a giveaway. Even if the participants had not previously suspected anything, some will probably begin to suspect that the experimenter was concealing something. In our experience, we have found that many people will take this opportunity to say that they did feel that the experiment, as described, appeared too simple (or something of that order). This is desirable; whether the participants were deeply suspicious or not, the question allows them an opportunity to indicate that they are not the kind of person who is easily fooled. The experimenter should then explore the nature of the suspicion and how it may have affected the participant's behavior. From the participant's answers to this question, the experimenter can make a judgment as to how close a participant's suspicions were to the actual purpose of the experiment and, consequently, whether or not the data are admissible. Obviously, the criteria for inclusion should be both rigorous and rigid and should be set down before the experiment begins; the decision should be made without knowledge of the participant's responses on the dependent variable.

The experimenter should then continue with the debriefing process by saying something like this: "You are on the right track, we *were* interested in exploring some issues that we didn't discuss with you in advance. One of our major concerns in this study is. . . ." The experimenter should then describe the problem under investigation, specifying why it is important and explaining clearly exactly how the deception took place and why it was necessary. Again, experimenters should be generous in sharing their own discomfort with the participant. They should make absolutely certain that the participant fully understands these factors before the postexperimental session is terminated.

It is often useful to enlist the participant's aid in improving the experiment. Often the participant can provide valuable hints regarding where the weaknesses in the manipulation occurred and which one of these caused competing reactions to the one the experimenter intended. These interviews can and should, of course, be continued during the time the experiment is actually being run, but it is usually during pretesting that the most valuable information is obtained.

Finally, whether or not deception is used, the experimenter must attempt to convince the participants not to discuss the experiment with other people until it is completed. This is a serious problem because even a few sophisticated participants can invalidate an experiment. Moreover, it is not a simple matter to swear participants to secrecy; some have friends who may subsequently volunteer for the experiment and who are almost certain to press them for information. Perhaps the best way to reduce such communication is to describe graphically the colossal waste of effort that would result from experimenting with people who have foreknowledge about the procedure or hypothesis of the experiment and who thus can rehearse their responses in advance. The experimenter should also explain the damage that can be done to the scientific enterprise by including data from such participants. It often helps to provide participants with some easy but unrevealing answers for their friends who ask about the study (e.g., "it was about social perception"). If we experimenters are sincere and honest in our dealings with the participants during the post-experimental session, we can be reasonably confident that few will break faith.

To check on the efficacy of this procedure, Aronson (1966) enlisted the aid of three undergraduates who each approached three acquaintances who had recently participated in one of his experiments. The confederates explained that they had signed up for that experiment, had noticed the friend's name on the sign-up sheet, and wondered what the experiment was all about. The experimenter had previously assured these confederates that their friends would remain anonymous. The results were encouraging. In spite of considerable urging and cajoling on the part of the confederates, none of the former participants revealed the true purpose of the experiment; two of them went as far as providing the confederates with a replay of the cover story, but nothing else.

What if the participant *has* been forewarned before entering the experimental room? That is, suppose a participant does find out about the experiment from a friend who participated previously. Chances are, the participant will not volunteer this information to the experimenter before the experiment. Once again, we as experimenters must appeal to the cooperativeness of the participant, emphasizing how much the experiment will be compromised if people knew about it in advance. We cannot overemphasize the importance of this procedure as a safeguard against the artifactual confirmation of an erroneous hypothesis because of the misplaced cooperativeness of the participant. If the participants are indeed cooperative, they will undoubtedly cooperate with the experimenter in this regard also and will respond to a direct plea of the sort described.

We would like to close this section by emphasizing our recommendation that a thorough explanation of the experiment should be provided *whether or not deception or stressful procedures are involved.* The major reason for this recommendation is that we cannot always predict the impact of a procedure; occasionally, even procedures that appear to be completely benign can have a powerful impact on some participants. An interesting example of such an unexpectedly powerful negative impact comes from a series of experiments on social dilemmas by Dawes and his students (Dawes, McTavish, & Shaklee, 1977). In these experiments, typically, the participant must make a decision between cooperating with several other people or "defecting." The contingencies are such that if all participants choose to cooperate, they all profit financially; however, if one or more defect, defection has a high payoff, and cooperation produces little payoff. Each person's response is anonymous and remains so. The nature of the decision and its consequences are fully explained to the participants at the outset of the experiment. No deception is involved.

Twenty-four hours after one experimental session, an elderly man (who had been the sole defector in his group and had won nineteen dollars) telephoned the experimenter trying to return his winnings so that it could be divided among the other participants (who, because they chose to cooperate, had each earned only one dollar). In the course of the conversation, he revealed that he felt miserable about his greedy behavior and that he had not slept all night. After a similar experiment, a woman who had cooperated while others defected revealed that she felt terribly gullible and had learned that people were not as trustworthy as she had thought. In order to alleviate this kind of stress, Dawes went on to develop an elaborate and sensitive follow-up procedure.

We repeat that these experiments were selected for discussion precisely because their important and powerful impact could not have been easily anticipated. We are intentionally not focusing on experiments that present clear and obvious problems like the well-known obedience study (Milgram, 1974), or the Stanford prison study (Haney, Banks, & Zimbardo, 1973). We have purposely selected an experiment that involves no deception and is well within the bounds of ethical codes. Our point is simple but important. No code of ethics can anticipate all problems, especially those created through participants discovering something unpleasant about themselves or others in the course of an experiment. However, we believe a sensitive postexperimental interview conducted by a sincere and caring experimenter not only instructs and informs, but it also provides important insights and helps reduce feelings of guilt or discomfort generated by such self-discovery (see Holmes, 1976a, 1976b; Ross, Lepper, & Hubbard, 1975).

Moving into the Field

We have gone into considerable detail discussing the features and conduct of laboratory experiments because we believe it provides the prototypic (if not necessarily modal) case of social psychological experimentation. Certainly the four stages of research associated with the lab experiment—setting the stage, constructing the independent variable, measuring the dependent variable, and debriefing—are in some form common to all experimental research endeavors.

As we mentioned earlier, one big advantage of conducting an experiment in the laboratory is that the researcher has more control over the situation, which allows for a "cleaner" manipulation of the independent variable. In field experiments it is more likely that unforeseen, uncontrolled events will occur that will compromise the integrity of the experimental design. Nonetheless there are big advantages to field experiments as well, such as the fact that people are less likely to know that they are in an experiment and the setting will be more like ones people encounter in their everyday lives. A number of extremely important and clever field experiments have been done in social psychology, and in this section we will focus on the ways in which the conduct of field experiments is most likely to differ from that of the prototypic lab study.

Control over the Independent Variable   The amount of control an experimenter has over the independent variable is a matter of degree. In some cases, the researcher constructs experimental situations from scratch, creating the background context as well as experimental variations. In other cases, the experimenter controls less of the setting but introduces some systematic variation into existing conditions, as in the field experiment by Piliavin, Rodin, and Piliavin (1969) in which the behavior of an experimental accomplice was varied in the largely uncontrolled context of a New York subway train in order to study bystander helping in that setting.

In other field research, the experimenter does not manipulate the stimulus conditions but instead selects among naturally occurring stimulus situations those that embody representations of the conceptual variable of interest. Here the line between experimental and correlational research becomes thin indeed, and the distinction depends largely on how standardized the selected field conditions can be across participants. One good illustration of the use of selected field sites in conjunction with laboratory research comes from the literature on mood and altruism. A variety of mood-induction manipulations have been developed in laboratory settings, such as having participants read affectively positive or negative passages (e.g., Aderman, 1972). After the mood state induction, participants are given an opportunity to exhibit generosity by donating money or helping an experimental accomplice. Results generally show that positive mood induction elevates helping behavior (Salovey, Mayer, & Rosenhan, 1991). Despite multiple replications of this effect in different laboratories with different investigators, the validity of these findings has been challenged both because of the artificiality of the setting in which altruism is assessed and because of the potential demand characteristics associated with the rather unusual mood-induction experience.

To counter these criticisms, researchers in the area took advantage of a natural mood-induction situation based on the emotional impact of selected motion pictures (Underwood et al., 1977). After the pilot research in which ratings were obtained from moviegoers, a double feature consisting of *Lady Sings the Blues* and *The Sterile Cuckoo* was selected for its negative affect-inducing qualities, and two other double features were selected to serve as neutral control conditions. A commonly occurring event—solicitation of donations to a nationally known charity with collection boxes set up outside the movie theater lobby—was chosen as the vehicle for a measure of the dependent variable of generosity.

Having located such naturally occurring variants of the laboratory mood-induction operation and altruism measure, the major design problem encountered by the researchers was that of participant self-selection to the alternative movie conditions. Whereas random assignment of volunteer moviegoers was a logical possibility, the procedures involved in utilizing that strategy would have created many of the elements of artificiality and reactivity that the field setting was selected to avoid. Therefore, the investigators decided to live with the phenomenon of self-selection and to alter the research design to take its effect into consideration. For this purpose, the timing of collection of donations to charity at the various theaters was randomly alternated across different nights so that it would occur either while most people were entering the theater (before seeing the movies) or leaving (after seeing both features). The rate of donations given by arriving moviegoers could then be a check on preexisting differences between the two populations apart from the mood induction. Fortunately, there proved to be no differences in initial donation rates, as a function of type of movie, whereas post-movie donations differed significantly in the direction of lowered contribution rates following the sad movies. This pattern of results, then, preserved the logic of random assignment (initial equivalence between experimental conditions) despite the considerable deviation from ideal procedures for participant assignment.

Two points should be emphasized with respect to this illustration of field research. First of all, the field version of the basic research paradigm was not—and could not be— simply a "transplanted" replication of the laboratory operations. The researchers had considerably less control in the field setting. They could not control the implementation of the stimulus conditions or extraneous sources of variation. On any one night a host of irrelevant events may have occurred during the course of the movies (e.g., a breakdown of projectors or a disturbance in the audience) that could have interfered with the mood manipulation. The researcher was not only helpless to prevent such events but would not have been aware of them if they did take place. In addition, as already mentioned, in the field setting the experimenters were unable to assign participants randomly to conditions and had to rely on luck to establish initial equivalence between groups.

The second point to be emphasized is that the results of the field experiment as a single isolated study would have been difficult to interpret without the context of conceptually related laboratory experiments. This difficulty is partly due to the ambiguities introduced by the alterations in design and partly to the constraints on measurement inherent in the field situation where manipulation checks, for example, are not possible. The convergence of results in the two settings greatly enhances our confidence in the findings from both sets of operations. Had the field experiment failed to replicate the laboratory results, however, numerous alternative explanations would have rendered interpretation very difficult.

Random Assignment in Field Settings   Subject self-selection problems plague field experimentation in multiple forms. In the field experiment of mood and helping behavior cited previously, random assignment to experimental conditions was not even attempted. Instead, the effects of potential selection factors were handled in other ways that involved an element of risk taking. The premovie data collection served as a check on the assumption that people who attend sad movies are not inherently different from people who attend other movies in their propensity to give to charities. But what if that assumption had proved false and there had been an initial difference in the rate of donations between attendants at the different types of movie? Such previous differences in behavior would have made interpretation of any differences in donations after exposure to the movies hazardous at best. In this case, the researchers were taking a gamble in counting on the absence of initial population differences. The logic of their experimental design required that the premovie data collection sessions be interspersed with postmovie data collection in order to control for timing effects. As a consequence, the investigators could not know until after the experiment had been completed whether the data supported their assumption of initial equivalence. Had they been wrong, the experimental design would have been undermined, and any effort expended would have been wasted.

In other settings, too, the research may rely on the essentially haphazard distribution of naturally occurring events as equivalent to controlled experimental design. Parker, Brewer, and Spencer (1980), for instance, undertook a study on the outcomes of a natural disaster—a devastating brush fire in a southern California community—

on the premise that the pattern of destruction of private homes in the fire constituted a "natural randomization" process. Among homes in close proximity at the height of the fire, only chance factors—shifts in wind direction and velocity, location of fire fighting equipment, and traffic congestion—determined which structures were burned to the ground and which remained standing when the fire was brought under control. Thus, homeowners who were victims of the fire and those who were not victimized could be regarded as essentially equivalent before the effects of the fire, and any differences in their attitudes and perceptions following the fire could be attributed to that particular differential experience. When comparisons are made between such naturally selected groupings, the burden of proof rests on the investigator to make a convincing case that the groups are not likely to differ systematically in any relevant dimensions other than the causal event of interest.

In other field research efforts, the researcher may be able to assign participants randomly to experimental conditions. However, once assigned, some participants may fail to participate or to experience the experimental manipulation. If such self-determined "de-selection" (also known as "participant mortality") occurs differentially across treatment conditions, the experimental design is seriously compromised. One way of preserving the advantages of randomization in such cases is to include participants in their assigned experimental conditions for purposes of analysis regardless of whether they were exposed to the treatment or not (assuming, of course, that one is in a position to obtain measures on the dependent variable for these participants). This was the solution applied in the two field experiments conducted by Freedman and Fraser (1966) to test the effectiveness of the "foot-in-the-door" technique for enhancing compliance.

In these studies the dependent variable was whether individuals contacted in their homes would agree to a rather large, intrusive request from the researcher (e.g., to permit a five-person market survey team to come into the home for two hours to classify household products). Of primary interest was the rate of compliance to this large request by participants who had been contacted previously with a small request (e.g., to respond to a very brief market survey over the telephone), in comparison to that of the control participants who were contacted for the first time at the time of the large request.

The purpose of the manipulation in the Freedman and Fraser studies was to test the effect of actual *compliance* to the initial small request on response to the later request. However, the operational experimental treatment to which potential participants could be randomly assigned was exposure to the request itself. Approximately one-third of those who were given the initial small request refused to comply; hence they failed to complete the experimental

manipulation. If these participants had been excluded from the study, the comparability between the remaining experimental participants and those randomly assigned to the no-initial-contact condition would have been seriously suspect. To avoid this selection problem, the researchers decided to include measures from all participants in the originally assigned treatment groups, regardless of their response to the initial request. With respect to testing treatment effects, this was a conservative decision, since the full treatment was significantly diluted among those classified in the experimental group. As it turned out, the initial compliance effect was powerful enough to generate a significant difference between treatment groups (of the order of 50 percent versus 20 percent compliance rates) despite the dilution of the experimental condition. Had the results been more equivocal, however, we would have been uncertain whether to attribute the absence of significant differences to lack of treatment effects or to failure to achieve the experimental manipulation. When the experimental treatment condition is diluted even more seriously than in the present illustration, comparisons between intact treatment groups become meaningless, and more sophisticated techniques for correcting for participant self-selection must be adopted (Brewer, 1976).

When full random assignment cannot be implemented in field settings, various forms of "quasi experiments" (cf. Cook & Campbell, 1979) can be creatively employed to preserve the logic of experimental design and control without rigid adherence to specific procedures. It should be kept in mind, however, that loss of control over stimulus conditions or participant assignment inevitably carries with it some measure of risk. Assumptions upon which the quasi-experimental design rests (such as initial equivalence of different groups) may prove untenable, or uncontrolled environmental inputs may "swamp" the stimulus conditions of interest to the researcher. In such cases, the costs in terms of wasted effort are high; thus decisions to take risks in undertaking field studies must be made sensibly. It would be foolish not to adjust the features of one's research design to the practical realities of a given field setting. But it is even more foolish to proceed with an expensive study that, from the start, has a high probability of resulting in uninterpretable outcomes.

Assessment of Dependent Variables in Field Settings
In many field contexts, the design and evaluation of dependent measures is parallel to that of laboratory experiments. In the guise of a person-on-the-street interview or a market research survey, for example, the field researcher may elicit self-reports of relevant attitudes, perceptions, or preferences. Or behavioroid measures may be designed that assess the willingness of the participants to engage in relevant acts such as signing a petition or committing themselves to some future effort. Finally, situations may be

constructed so as to elicit the type of behavior of interest to the experimenter, such as providing participants with opportunities to donate to charity (Underwood et al., 1977), to help a stranger who has collapsed (Piliavin et al., 1969), or to trade in a lottery ticket (Langer, 1975). One advantage of experimentation in field settings is the potential for assessing behaviors that are, in and of themselves, of some significance to the participant. Instead of asking participants to report on perceptions or intentions, we may observe them engaging in behaviors with real consequences. In such cases, our dependent measures are much less likely to be influenced by demand characteristics or social desirability response biases. In laboratory settings participants may check a particular point on a liking scale in order to please the experimenter or to look good; however very few people would choose someone as a roommate for the entire year unless there were more powerful reasons.

In some field settings, the kinds of dependent measures typically employed in laboratory studies would be exclusively intrusive in ways that would destroy the natural flow of events characteristic of the setting. Field experimenters have to be particularly sensitive to the issue of "reactivity" discussed by Campbell and Stanley (1963). This concept refers to the possibility that the measurement of the dependent variable reacts with the independent variable or related events in such a way that effects are found that would not have been present otherwise. For example, suppose some people have seen a movie designed to reduce prejudice. They may be completely unaffected by this movie *until* they are asked to fill out a questionnaire that clearly deals with prejudice. As a result of seeing this questionnaire, the moviegoers may realize for the first time that the movie was about prejudice and may reflect on the movie in a new way that now has an influence. In effect, the introduction of the dependent measure has served as a kind of independent variable in combination with the originally intended treatment variable. Note that this kind of effect is conceptually different from experimental artifacts generated by demand characteristics or experimenter bias effects. We are not postulating that the respondent changes the expression of prejudicial attitudes in order to please the experimenter but only that no change would have taken place without the intrusion of a very obvious measurement.

In order to prevent or minimize the occurrence of reactivity, field researchers may devise a variety of techniques to make unobtrusive measurements of the dependent variable of interest (see Webb et al., 1981). Some unobtrusive measures are based on observations of ongoing behavior, utilizing methods of observation that interfere minimally or not at all with the occurrence of the behavior. For instance, voluntary seating aggregation patterns have been used as an index of racial attitudes under varied conditions of classroom desegregation; observational studies of conformity have recorded public behaviors such as pedestrians crossing against traffic lights or turn signaling by automo-

bile drivers, and studies of natural language often resort to eavesdropping on conversations in public places. Cialdini et al. (1976) used naturalistic observation of clothing and accessories to study what they call the "Basking in Reflected Glory" phenomenon. They recorded the wearing of T-shirts and other apparel bearing the school name or insignia by students in introductory psychology classes at seven universities each Monday during football season. The proportion of students wearing such apparel at each school proved to be significantly greater on Mondays following a victory by that school's team than on Mondays following defeat. A simple monitoring of public displays provided quantitative confirmation of the hypothesized tendency to identify with success.

Other observational techniques may rely on the use of hidden hardware for audio or video recording of events outside the experimenter's control, such as physical traces left after an event has occurred or archival records that are kept for administrative or economic purposes (police files, school absenteeism records, and sales figures). One interesting illustration of the use of unobtrusive physical trace measures is provided in the previously mentioned Langer and Rodin's (1976) field experiment testing the effects of responsibility inductions on the well-being of residents of a nursing home. The major outcome of interest in that study was the general alertness and activity level of the residents following introduction of the experimental treatment. This level was assessed not only by the traditional methods of self-report and the ratings of nurses but also by various specially designed behavioral measures. One measure involved covering the right wheels of patients' wheelchairs with two inches of white adhesive tape, which was removed after twenty-four hours and analyzed for the amount of discoloration as an index of patient-activity level. Alas, clever ideas do not always work; the amount of dirt picked up by the tape turned out to be negligible for patients in all conditions.

The results of the Langer and Rodin nursing home study serve to illustrate some of the problems of reliance on unobtrusive measures in field settings. The adhesive tape index did not produce any detectable treatment effect; other, more direct and experimenter-controlled, self-report, and behavioral measures demonstrated significant impact of the experimental treatment. Had the researchers been forced to limit their assessment of effects to the least intrusive measure, they would have missed a great deal. The validity of dependent variable measures—the extent to which they measure what they are supposed to measure—is of concern in any research endeavor. However, the farther removed the actual measure is from the variable of interest, the more reason there is for concern. For instance, consider the number of steps involved in going from the dependent variable of patient-activity level of the measurement of discoloration of white adhesive tape in the nursing home study. First patient activity had to be translated into distance traveled in the wheelchair, which in turn had to be related to the amount of dirt picked up by different sections of the tape, which in turn had to produce measurable differences in discoloration. In such a chain, many intervening processes can reduce the correspondence between the initial variable (activity) and the measured outcome—the speed with which the wheelchair traveled, how often the floors were cleaned, whether the patients' movement was self-propelled or passive, and so on. Reliance on a single measure affected by so many irrelevant factors would have been treacherous indeed.

Sometimes indirect, unobtrusive measures do prove sensitive to experimental treatments but still turn out to be measuring the wrong thing. For example, the residents of Portland, Oregon, participated in an experimental attempt to decrease automobile use by lowering bus fares for a trial period (Katzev & Backman, 1982). Bus-rider records provided evidence that the goals of the study were being met during the experimental period: bus ridership was way up. Unfortunately, however, the use of bus-rider records as an indirect (an unobtrusive) measure of reduction in automobile use proved to be misleading. The researchers kept careful odometer records of cars before and during the study and found there was no decrease in average miles driven. One possible explanation is that people felt so virtuous riding to work on the bus every day that they treated themselves to long recreational car trips on weekends! Reliance on bus ridership alone as a measure of the program's success would have led to an inappropriate conclusion.

VALIDITY AND REALISM IN EXPERIMENTS

To this point we have discussed in some detail how laboratory and field research is conducted. It is important to return to a fundamental question: Given the advantages of field experiments, why are laboratory studies conducted at all? Indeed, it seems to us that the perfect social psychological study would be one that was conducted in a naturalistic setting, in which people were randomly assigned to experimental conditions, the independent variable was one that was impactful and involving, and all extraneous variables were controlled. Sounds good, doesn't it? Unfortunately, such a study is like a Platonic ideal that can rarely be achieved. For reasons we have already discussed, experimentation almost always involves a trade-off between competing goals: control and realism. It is worth discussing this trade-off in more detail, in terms of precisely what is meant when we say an experiment is "well-controlled" or "realistic."

Types of Validity

Campbell and his colleagues (Campbell, 1957; Campbell & Stanley, 1963; Cook & Campbell, 1979) distinguished

among different types of validity. In Campbell's taxonomy, the interpretation of research results may be assessed with respect to at least three different kinds of validity—internal validity, external validity, and construct validity.

The meaningfulness of experimental research rests first of all on *internal validity*. Basically, internal validity refers to the confidence with which we can draw cause and effect conclusions from our research results. To what extent are we certain that the independent variable, or treatment, manipulated by the experimenter is the sole source or cause of systemic variation in the dependent variable? Threats to the internal validity of research results arise when the conditions under which an experiment is conducted produce systematic sources of variance that are irrelevant to the treatment variable and not under control of the researcher. The internal validity of a study is questioned, for instance, if groups of participants exposed to different experimental conditions are not assigned randomly and are different from each other in some important ways before the research operations. In the field study of mood and altruism cited earlier, had it happened that the moviegoers who attend sad films differed from attendees at other movies in their propensity to contribute to charities even before exposure to the movies themselves, that difference would have constituted a threat to the internal validity of the study. In that case, any differences obtained between groups in donations following the movies could be interpreted either as an effect of the movie mood induction or of personality differences unrelated to the treatment. Other factors that can undermine internal validity include the occurrence of events during the course of the research that are unrelated to the treatment variable and that produce different effects in the various experimental groups.

Internal validity is the sine qua non of good experimental research. The procedures for standardizing treatments, avoiding bias, and assuring comparability of participant groups discussed in our earlier section on planning and conducting laboratory experiments are all addressed to internal validity concerns. The essence of good experimental design is to control the assignment of participants to treatment groups and the conditions of treatment delivery in such a way as to rule out or minimize threats to the internal validity of the study. Thus any differences obtained on outcome measures can be traced directly to the variations in treatment introduced by the experimenter.

One major limitation on internal validity is the extent to which unmeasured individual differences may obscure the results of an experiment. The ideal of an experiment is to take two identical units (corn plants, rocks, rats, children, or fraternities) and to apply different experimental treatments to them. Although it is a philosophical truism that no two units are ever precisely identical, the experimenter must strive to make them as close to identical as possible. One can approximate this idea much more satisfactorily in most sciences, and even in most of psychology, than is possible in social psychology. Our participants differ from each other genetically, in learned personality characteristics, in values and attitudes, in abilities, and in immediate past experiences. Any and all of these differences may have a large impact on the way in which participants respond to our experimental treatments. This is one reason why it is important in most social psychological experiments to have large sample sizes; through random assignment and large numbers, the differences between individuals are "averaged out." It is also the reason, as we saw earlier, that a within-subject manipulation of the independent variable, when feasible, is advantageous. In a within-subject design, each participant serves as his or her own control, which controls for any number of individual difference variables that would be treated as error variance in a between-subject design.

As we have seen, it is usually much easier to maintain high internal validity in a laboratory experiment, because the researcher has much more control over extraneous variables that might compromise the design. Even when internal validity is high, however, there may be questions about the validity of interpretations of causal effects obtained in any given study. It is here that the distinction between external validity and construct validity becomes relevant. *External validity* refers to the robustness of a phenomenon—the extent to which a causal relationship, once identified in a particular setting with particular research participants, can safely be generalized to other times, places, and people. Threats to external validity arise from potential interaction effects between the treatment variable of interest and the context in which it is delivered or the type of participant population involved. When laboratory experimentation in social psychology is criticized as being "the study of the psychology of the college sophomore," what is being called into question is the external validity of the findings. Because so many laboratory experiments are conducted with college students as participants, the truth of the causal relationships we observe may be limited to that particular population (Sears, 1986). If it happens that college students—with their youth, above-average intelligence, and nonrepresentative socioeconomic backgrounds—respond differently to our experimental treatment conditions than other types of people, then the external (but not internal) validity of our findings would be low.

The issue is actually a little more subtle. No one would seriously deny that Princeton students might respond differently to a particular experimental treatment than would a sample of fifty-year-old working-class immigrants. External validity refers to the extent to which a particular causal relationship is robust across populations or settings. Thus, if we were interested in the effects of lowered self-esteem on aggression, we might have to use different techniques to lower self-esteem in the two populations. Being informed that one had failed a test of creative problem-solving might

lower self-esteem more for Princeton sophomores than for working-class immigrants. But if we can find another technique of lowering self-esteem among that second sample, we still must ask whether this lowered self-esteem will have the same effects on aggression in both samples.

External validity is related to settings as well as to participant populations. The external validity of a finding is challenged if the relationship between independent and dependent variables is altered if essentially the same research procedures were conducted in a different laboratory or field setting or under the influence of different experimenter characteristics. For example, Milgram's (1974) initial studies of obedience were conducted in a research laboratory at Yale University, and a legitimate question is the extent to which his findings would generalize to other settings. Because participants were drawn from outside the university and because many had no previous experience with college, the prestige and respect associated with a research laboratory at Yale may have made the participants more susceptible to the demands for compliance that the experiment entailed than they would have been in other settings. To address this issue Milgram undertook a replication of his experiment in a very different physical setting. Moving the research operation to a "seedy" office in the industrial town of Bridgeport, Connecticut, adopting a fictitious identity as a psychological research firm, Milgram hoped to minimize the reputational factors inherent in the Yale setting. In comparison with data obtained in the original study, the Bridgeport replication resulted in slightly lower but still dramatic rates of compliance to the experimenter. Thus, setting could be identified as a contributing but not crucial factor to the basic findings of the research.

To question the external validity of a particular finding is not to deny that a cause and effect relationship has been demonstrated in the given research study but only to express doubt that the same effect could be demonstrated under different circumstances or with different participants. Similarly, concerns with *construct validity* do not challenge the fact of an empirical relationship between an experimentally manipulated variable and the dependent measure but rather question how that fact is to be interpreted in conceptual terms. Construct validity refers to the correct identification of the nature of the independent and dependent variables and the underlying relationship between them. To what extent do the operations and measures embodied in the experimental procedures of a particular study reflect the theoretical concepts that gave rise to the research in the first place? Threats to construct validity derive from errors of measurement, misspecification of research operations, and, in general, the complexity of experimental treatments with numerous stimulus features. As we discussed earlier, one of the most difficult parts of experimental design is constructing a concrete independent variable (e.g., reciting a list of obscene words) that is a good instantiation of the conceptual variable (cognitive dissonance produced by undergoing an embarrassing initiation to a group). This is essentially an issue of construct validity: How well does the independent variable capture the conceptual variable?

The same issue holds for the dependent variable. When we devise an elaborate rationale for inducing our participants to express their attitudes toward the experiment or toward some social object in the form of ratings on a structured questionnaire, how can we be sure that these responses reflect the effect variable of conceptual interest rather than (or in addition to) the myriad of other complex decision rules our participants may bring to bear in making such ratings? And how do we know that the functional relationships observed between treatment and effect, under a particular set of operations, represent the conceptual processes of interest?

We can now see that the experimenter is faced with a daunting task: designing a study that is well-controlled (high in internal validity), has independent and dependent variables that are good reflections of the conceptual variables of interest (high in construct validity), and is generalizable to other settings and people (high in external validity). Internal validity may be considered a property of a single experimental study. Our confidence in the validity of cause and effect results from a particular experiment may be enhanced if the finding is repeated on other occasions. However, the degree to which a study has internal validity is determined by characteristics intrinsic to the study itself. With sufficient knowledge of the conditions under which an experiment has been conducted, of the procedures associated with assignment of participants, and of experimenter behavior, we should be able to assess whether the results of that study are internally valid.

Issues involving construct validity and external validity, on the other hand, are more complicated. A researcher does the best that he or she can in devising independent and dependent variables that capture the conceptual variables perfectly. But how can external validity be maximized? How can researchers increase the likelihood that the results of the study are generalizable across people and settings? One way is to make the setting as realistic as possible, which is, after all, one point of field research: to increase the extent to which the findings can be applied to everyday life by conducting the study in real-life settings. The issue of realism, however, is not this straightforward. There are several different types of realism with different implications.

Mundane Realism versus Experimental Realism versus Psychological Realism

Aronson and Carlsmith (1968) distinguished broadly between ways in which an experiment can be said to be real-

istic. In one sense, an experiment is realistic if the situation is involving to the participants, if they are forced to take it seriously, if it has impact on them. This kind of realism they called *experimental realism*. In another sense, the term "realism" can refer to the extent to which events occurring in the research setting are likely to occur in the normal course of the participants' lives, that is, in the "real world." They called this type of realism *mundane realism*. The fact that an event is similar to events that occur in the real world does not endow it with importance. Many events that occur in the real world are boring and unimportant in the lives of the actors or observers. Thus, it is possible to put a participant to sleep if an experimental event is high on mundane realism but remains low on experimental realism.

Mundane realism and experimental realism are not polar concepts; a particular technique may be high on both mundane realism and experimental realism, low on both, or high on one and low on the other. Perhaps the difference between experimental and mundane realism can be clarified by citing a couple of examples. Let us first consider Asch's (1951) experiment on perceptual judgment. Here the participants were asked to judge the length of lines and then were confronted with unanimous judgments by a group of peers that contradicted their own perceptions. For most participants this experiment seems to have contained a good deal of experimental realism. Whether participants yielded to group pressure or stood firm, the vast majority underwent a rather difficult experience that caused them to squirm, sweat, and exhibit other signs of tension and discomfort. They were involved, upset, and deeply concerned about the evidence being presented to them. We may assume that they were reacting to a situation that was as "real" for them as any of their ordinary experiences. However, the experiment was hardly realistic in the mundane sense. Recall that the participants were judging a very clear physical event. In everyday life it is rare to find oneself in a situation where the direct and unambiguous evidence of one's senses is contradicted by the unanimous judgments of one's peers. Although the judging of lines is perhaps not important or realistic in the mundane sense, one cannot deny the impact of having one's sensory input contradicted by a unanimous majority.

On the other hand, consider an experiment by Walster, Aronson, and Abrahams (1966) that, although high on mundane realism, was low indeed on experimental realism. In this experiment, participants read a newspaper article about the prosecution of criminal suspects in Portugal. In the article, various statements were attributed to a prosecuting attorney or to a convicted criminal. The article was embedded in a real newspaper and hence, the participants were doing something they frequently do—reading facts in a newspaper. Thus the experiment had a great deal of mundane realism. However nothing was happening to the participant. Very few U.S. college students are seriously affected by reading a rather pallid article about a remote situation in a foreign country. The procedure did not have a high degree of experimental realism.

Aronson, Wilson, and Akert (1994) introduced a third type of realism that they termed *psychological realism*. This is the extent to which the psychological processes that occur in an experiment are the same as psychological processes that occur in everyday life. It may be that an experiment is nothing like what people encounter in everyday life (low in mundane realism) and fails to have much of an impact on people (low in experimental realism). It could still be high in psychological realism, however, if the psychological processes that occur are similar to those that occur in everyday life. Consider the Gilbert and Hixon (1991) study we described at the beginning of the chapter. This study was low in mundane realism; in everyday life people rarely, if ever, watch a videotape of a woman holding up cards with word fragments on them and think of words to complete the fragments. It was also relatively low in experimental realism, in that the study was not very impactful or engaging. Watching the woman was probably of mild interest, but surely the study was less impactful than the Milgram or Asch studies. The study was very high in psychological realism, however, to the extent that the psychological processes of stereotype activation and application were the same as those that occur in everyday life. It is common to encounter a member of a group and for a stereotype of that group to come to mind automatically. To the extent that this psychological process is the same as what occurred in Gilbert and Hixon's (1991) study, they succeeded in devising a situation that was high in psychological realism.

There is some overlap between experimental and psychological realism, in that many of the psychological processes of interest to psychologists are ones that occur when people are reacting to impactful events in their environments. Thus, the situations in everyday life in which cognitive dissonance, prejudice, or aggression occur are usually ones in which people are quite engaged. Thus, when studying these phenomena, it is imperative to devise experimental settings that are equally impactful. Such studies would be high in both experimental and psychological realism (although not necessarily high in mundane realism). Increasingly, however, social psychologists have become interested in psychological processes that occur when people are not actively engaged or motivated to process information carefully. Examples include the study of automatic processing (as in the Gilbert & Hixon study), peripheral or heuristic processing of persuasive messages (Chaiken, 1987, Petty & Cacioppo, 1986), or "mindlessness" (Langer, 1989). To study these phenomena it is important to devise experimental settings that are high in psychological realism but low in experimental realism.

For example, Langer (1989) has conducted a number of

studies on "mindlessness," or what happens when people are in a state of reduced attention. People are hypothesized to be on "automatic pilot," following well-learned rules rather than actively attending to what is happening in their environment. To study this mode of processing, Langer, Blank, and Chanowitz (1978) sent a nonsensical memo to a sample of secretaries that asked them to return the memo immediately to the sender. If people thought about the request they probably wouldn't return the memo; after all, if the sender wanted the memo, why didn't he just keep it in the first place? In some conditions Langer et al. attempted to mimic everyday situations in which people are not processing information very carefully and thus mindlessly do rather silly things. In one condition, for example, the memo was made to look like the ones the secretaries got most of the time: it was unsigned and was phrased more in terms of a request ("I would appreciate it if you would return this paper immediately to Room 238") than a demand ("This paper is to be returned immediately to Room 238"). In this condition almost everyone returned the memo to its sender. When the memo was unusual, however—such as when it was phrased in terms of a demand—people were predicted to think about it more carefully, recognize its absurdity, and fail to return it—which is exactly what happened. For our purposes, the point is that the critical experimental condition—the one in which people were predicted to respond mindlessly—was one that was the lowest in experimental realism, but high in psychological realism.

External Validity: Is It Always a Goal?   Before leaving this topic it is important to make one more point about external validity and generalizability. It is often assumed (perhaps mindlessly!) that all studies should be as high as possible in external validity, in the sense that we should be able to generalize the results as much as possible across populations and settings and time. Sometimes, however, the goal of the research is different. Mook (1983) published a provocative article entitled, "In defense of external invalidity," in which he argued that the goal of many experiments is to test a theory, not to establish external validity. Theory-testing can take a variety of forms, some of which have little to do with how much the results can be generalized. For example, a researcher might construct a situation in which a specific set of results should occur if one theory is correct, but not if another is correct. This situation may be completely unlike any that people encounter in everyday life, and yet, the study can provide an interesting test of the two theories.

Mook (1983) gives the example of Harlow's classic study of emotional development in rhesus monkeys (Harlow & Zimmerman, 1958). Infant monkeys were separated from their mothers and placed in cages with wire-covered contraptions that resembled adult monkeys. Some of the wire monkeys were covered with terry cloth and were armed with a light bulb, whereas others were bare and un-inviting. Nourishment (in the form of a baby bottle) was sometimes available from one type of monkey and some-times from the other. Harlow found that the monkeys clung to the terry cloth "mother," regardless of whether or not it contained the bottle of milk. These results were damaging to drive-reduction theories that argued that the monkeys should prefer nourishment over emotional comfort. Was this study high in external validity? Clearly not. There was no attempt to randomly select the monkeys from those reared in the wild, or to simulate conditions that monkeys encounter in real-life settings. Nonetheless, if theories of drive reduction that were prevalent at the time were cor-rect, the monkeys should have preferred the nourishment, regardless of which "monkey" it came from. The re-searchers succeeded in devising a situation in which a spe-cific set of actions should have occurred if a particular the-ory was right—even though the situation was not one that would be found in everyday life.

Mook also points out that some experiments are valu-able because they answer quesitons about "what can hap-pen," even if they say little about "what does happen" in everyday life. Consider Milgram's experiments on obedi-ence to authority. As we've seen, there was little attempt to simulate any kind of real-life setting in these studies; out-side of psychology experiments, people are never asked to deliver electric shocks to a stranger who is performing poorly on a memory test. The results were very informa-tive, however, because it was so surprising that people would act the way they did under *any* circumstances. The fact that people *can* be made to harm a complete stranger, because an authority figure tells them to, is fascinating (and frightening) despite the artificiality of the setting.

Mook's (1983) position is persuasive, and we heartily agree that the goal of many experiments is to test a theory, rather than to establish external validity. This is especially true of basic research, of course; the point of applied re-search is to find solutions to problems that will work in everyday life. Nonetheless, we believe that even if external validity is not the main goal of study, it should never be completely forgotten. The importance of a theory, after all, depends on its applicability to everyday life. The reason Harlow's study is so important is because the theories it ad-dresses—drive-reduction and emotional attachment—are so relevant to everyday life. The theories apply to humans as well as monkeys and to many situations beyond cages and wire mothers. It is precisely because the *theories* are generalizable (i.e., applicable to many populations and set-tings) that a test of those theories is important. Thus, a spe-cific study might test a theory in an artificial setting that is low in external validity, but why would we conduct such a study if we didn't believe that the theory was generaliz-able? Similarly, Milgram's results are so compelling be-cause we can generate important, real-life examples of

times when similar processes occurred. Indeed, the inspira-tion for Milgram's study was the Holocaust, in which seemingly normal individuals (e.g., guards at prison camps) followed the orders of authority figures to the point of committing horrific acts. Thus, if we were to conclude that the psychological processes Milgram uncovered never occur in everyday life, we could justifiably dismiss his findings. The fact that these processes appear to be similar to those that occurred at some of humankind's darkest mo-ments, such as the Holocaust, is what makes his results so compelling.

We are essentially reiterating the importance of psycho-logical realism in experimentation. To test a theory it may be necessary to construct a situation that is extremely arti-ficial and low in mundane realism. As long as it triggers the same psychological processes as occur outside of the laboratory, however, it can be generalized to those real-life situations in which the same psychological processes occur. Of course, as discussed earlier, claims about psycho-logical realism cannot be taken completely on faith; only by replicating a study in a variety of settings can external validity be firmly established.

The Basic Dilemma of the Social Psychologist

It should be clear by now why our perfect experiment—one conducted in a naturalistic setting, in which people were randomly assigned to experimental conditions, the inde-pendent variable was one that was impactful and involving, and all extraneous variables were controlled—would be ex-tremely difficult to perform. It is next to impossible to de-sign an experiment that is high in both internal and external validity. We see this as the basic dilemma of the experimen-tal social psychologist. On the one hand we want maximal control over the independent variable, to maintain internal validity. We want as few extraneous differences as possible between our treatments. We want a precise specification of the treatment we have administered and of its effect on the participant. These desires lead us to try to develop manipu-lations that are highly specifiable, in which the differences between treatments are extraordinarily simply and clear and in which all manipulations are standardized—in short, to an approximation of something like a verbal learning ex-periment. On the other hand, if the experiment is controlled to the point of being sterile, it may fail to involve partici-pants, have little impact on them, and therefore may not af-fect their behavior to any great extent. It might be quite low in psychological realism, limiting the extent to which we can generalize the results to other settings.

Programmatic Research A solution to the basic dilemma of the social psychologist is to not try to "do it all" in one experiment. Instead, a programmatic series of studies can be conducted in which different experimental procedures are used, in different settings, to explore the same conceptual relationship. It is in this realm of conceptual replication with different scenarios that the interplay between lab and field experimentation is most clear. However, in considering these interrelationships, the trade-off mentioned earlier between control and impact in different experimental settings becomes especially salient. In order to be defensible, weaknesses in one aspect of experimental design must be offset by strengths or advantages in other features, or the whole research effort is called into question. This dictum is particularly applicable to field experiments in which inevitable increases in cost and effort are frequently accompanied by decreases in precision and control that can be justified only if there are corresponding gains in construct validity, impact, or the generalizability of findings.

Essentially, there are two properties that we demand of a series of experiments before we are convinced that we understand what the conceptual interpretation should be. First, we ask for a number of empirical techniques that differ in as many ways as possible, having in common only our basic conceptual variable. If all these techniques yield the same result, then we become more and more convinced that the underlying variable that all techniques have in common is, in fact, the variable that is producing the results. For example, the construct of cognitive dissonance has been operationalized in a wide variety of ways in both laboratory and field studies, including having people read lists of obscene words, write counterattitudinal essays, eat unpleasant foods, and make a difficult choice between which horse to bet on at a racetrack.

Second, we must show that a particular empirical realization of our independent variable produces a large number of different outcomes, all theoretically tied to the independent variable. Again, we point to research on cognitive dissonance, in which a wide array of dependent variables have been used. For example, asking people to engage in unpleasant activities, under conditions of high perceived choice, has been found to influence their attitudes, their galvanic skin response while receiving electric shocks, and how hungry they are.

When it comes to interpretation, there is a fundamental asymmetry between positive and negative results of replications. If proper techniques have been employed to preclude bias, successful replications speak for themselves; failures to replicate are ambiguous and therefore require supplementary information. For these reasons, good programmatic research involves replication with systematic differences and similarities in procedures and operations so that differences in results are potentially interpretable. In many cases, including exact replication along with conceptual variations is useful. Suppose, for example, that Jones, a hypothetical psychologist at the University of Illinois, produces a specific experimental result using Illinois undergraduates as participants. In addition, suppose that

Smith, at Yale University, feels that these results were not a function of the conceptual variable proposed by Jones but rather were a function of some artifact in the procedure. Smith then repeats Jones's precedure in all respects save one: he changes the operations in order to eliminate this artifact. He fails to replicate and concludes that this demonstrates that Jones's results were artifactual. This is only one of many possible conclusions. Smith's failure to replicate has several possible causes and is, therefore, uninterpretable. It may be a function of a change in experimenter, a different participant population (Yale students may be different on many dimensions from Illinois students), or countless minor variations in the procedure such as tone of voice. Most of this ambiguity could be eliminated by a balanced design that includes an "exact" replication of the conditions run by the original experimenter. That is, suppose Smith's design had included a repeat of Jones's conditions with the suspected artifact left in, and his results approximated those of Jones's experiment. If, as part of the design, Smith changed the experiment slightly and produced no differences, or differences in the opposite direction, one could then be sure that this result was not merely a function of the change in the procedure. If he failed even to replicate Jones's basic experiment, we would have to conclude that there was some important factor in the variables used in the original experiment, that the results are limited to a particular population, that either Jones or Smith (or both) had unconsciously biased their data, that Smith was simply incompetent, and so on.

In many situations it is difficult to modify the particular operational definition of the independent variable without changing the entire experimental setting. This is most dramatically true when conceptual replication involves a shift from laboratory setting to field setting. The potential complementary aspects of different research paradigms is best exemplified when operations of independent and dependent variables in laboratory procedures are significantly modified to take advantage of field settings so as to embed them appropriately in this altered context. Such modifications often involve fundamental rethinking about the conceptual variables; it is "back to square one," with attendant costs in time and effort. If the result is a successful conceptual replication, the effort has paid off handsomely in enhanced validity for our theoretical constructs. But what if the replication fails to confirm our original findings? In this case, the multitude of procedural differences that could have increased our confidence (with a successful replication) now contributes to the ambiguity.

Field Experimentation and Application

Conceptual replication highlights the advantages of combining laboratory and field experimentation for purposes of theory-building. In addition, the interplay between laboratory and field research is also critical to the development of an effective applied social psychology. Basic process-oriented experimental research may isolate important causal processes; however, convincing demonstrations that those processes operate in applied settings are essential before theory can be converted into practice.

The research literature on psychological responsibility and control provides a particularly good example of how a synthesis between field and laboratory experiments can work at its best. It began with animal research in the laboratory (Brady, 1958), extended to field studies of stress in humans (e.g., Janis, 1958; Egbert, Battit, Tundorf, & Becker, 1963), then moved to laboratory analogues (e.g., Glass & Singer, 1972; Kanfer & Seidner, 1973), and returned to the field (e.g., Johnson & Leventhal, 1974; Langer & Rodin, 1976). Results from both settings repeatedly demonstrated the potent effect of the perception of control or responsibility on an individual's ability to cope with stressful events. Even the illusion that one has control over the onset or the consequences of potential stressors is apparently sufficient to increase tolerance for stress and reduce adverse effects. As a result of these findings, procedures developed for inducing actual or perceived personal control are applicable in medical practice and in the administration of health-care institutions. At the same time, the fact that field applications permit testing research hypotheses in the presence of severe, noxious, or potentially life-threatening situations has contributed substantially to our theoretical understanding of the role of psychological factors in physiological processes.

Another good example of the creative interplay between laboratory and field experimentation is the work of Aronson and his colleagues on the effects of cooperative learning (Aronson & Bridgeman, 1979; Aronson & Osherow, 1980; Aronson, Stephan, Sikes, Blaney, & Snapp, 1978). The research began as an experimental intervention in response to a crisis in the Austin (Texas) school system following its desegregation. Aronson and his colleagues observed the dynamics of the classroom and diagnosed that a major cause of the existing tension was the competitive atmosphere that exacerbated the usual problems brought about by desegregation. They then changed the atmosphere of existing classrooms by restructuring the learning environment so that some students were teaching one another in small, interdependent "jigsaw" groups, while others continued to study in more traditional classrooms.

The results of this and subsequent field experiments showed that the cooperative classroom atmosphere decreased negative stereotyping, increased cross-ethnic liking, increased self-esteem, improved classroom performance, and increased empathic role taking. At the same time, Aronson and his colleagues were able to enhance their understanding of the underlying dynamic of this cooperative behavior by closer scrutiny under controlled laboratory conditions. For example, in one such laboratory experiment, they showed that, in a competitive situation,

individuals make situational self-attributions for failure and dispositional self-attributions for success, while making the reverse attributions to their opponent. However, in a cooperative structure, individuals gave their partners the same benefit of the doubt that they gave to themselves, that is, dispositional attributions for success and situational attributions for failure (Stephan, Presser, Kennedy, & Aronson, 1978).

Field experimentation in applied settings often provides an opportunity for impact and involvement of research participants that vastly exceeds any ever achieved in the laboratory. However, the focus of such research also tends to be more limited than the general tests of theory underlying most laboratory research efforts, because they are forced to deal only with variables found in the particular applied context under study. If the distinctive contribution of experimental social psychology to the general body of knowledge is ever to be realized, an optimal integration of theory-oriented laboratory research with applied field experimentation will be required.

At present we are concerned because the alternative research modes in social psychology seem, for the most part, to be functioning in isolation from each other. What is needed now is a new attempt at synthesis, that is to construct a more limited (and perhaps closer to the original) version of the Lewinian model of the interplay between laboratory and field reseach. Such a synthesis will require a concern with discovering more specifiable relationships rather than with attempts to find sweeping general theories of human social behavior. It will require an emphasis on assessing the relative importance of several variables, which all influence an aspect of multiply-determined behavior, rather than on testing to see if a particular variable has a "significant" impact. And it will require a sensitivity to the interaction between research design and research setting and the benefits of multiple methodologies.

ETHICAL CONCERNS IN EXPERIMENTATION

In our discussion of the postexperimental follow-up, we touched on the topic of ethics. Experimental social psychologists have been deeply concerned about the ethics of experimentation for a great many years precisely because our field is constructed on an ethical dilemma. Basically, the dilemma is formed by a conflict between two sets of values to which most social psychologists subscribe: a belief in the value of free scientific inquiry and a belief in the dignity of humans and their right to privacy. We will not dwell on the historical antecedents of these values or on the philosophical intricacies of the ethical dilemma posed by the conflict of these values. It suffices to say that the dilemma is a real one and cannot be dismissed either by making pious statements about the importance of not violating a person's feelings of dignity or by glibly pledging allegiance to the cause of science. It is a problem every social psychologist must face squarely, not just once, but each time he or she constructs and conducts an experiment, since it is impossible to delineate a specific set of rules and regulations governing all experiments. In each instance the researcher must decide on a course of action after giving careful consideration to the importance of the experiment and the extent of the potential injury to the dignity of the participants.

It should be emphasized, of course, that ethical problems arise even in the absence of either deception or extreme circumstances. We refer again to the experiment by Dawes, McTavish, and Shaklee (1977) as one of many possible examples of a benign-appearing procedure that can profoundly affect a few participants in ways that could not easily have been anticipated even by the most sensitive and caring of experimenters. Obviously, some experimental techniques present more problems than others. In general, experiments that employ deception cause concern because of the fact that lying, in and of itself, is problematical. Similarly, procedures that cause pain, embarrassment, guilt, or other intense feelings present obvious ethical problems. In addition, any procedure that enables the participants to confront some aspect of themselves that may not be pleasant or positive is of deep ethical concern. For example, many of Asch's (1951) participants learned that they could confirm in the face of implicit group pressure; many of Aronson and Mettee's (1968) participants learned that they would cheat at a game of cards; and many of Milgram's (1974) participants learned that they could be pressured to obey an authority even when such obedience involved (apparently) inflicting severe pain on another human being. Even more imposing are the findings of the Stanford prison study in which college students learned that, even in the absence of direct explicit commands, they would behave cruelly and even sadistically toward fellow students (Haney et al., 1973).

It can be argued that such procedures are therapeutic or educational for the participants. Indeed, many of the participants in these experiments have made this point. But this does not, in and of itself, justify the procedure primarily because the experimenter could not possibly know in advance that it would be therapeutic for all participants. Moreover, it is arrogant for the scientist to decide that he or she will provide people with a therapeutic experience without their explicit permission.

The use of deception, when combined with the possibility of "self-discovery," presents the experimenter with a special kind of ethical problem. In a deception experiment it is impossible, by definition, to attain informed consent from the participants in advance of the experiment. For example, how could Milgram or Asch have attained informed consent from their participants without revealing aspects of the procedure that would have invalidated any results they obtained? An experimenter cannot even reveal in advance

that the purpose of an experiment is the study of conformity or obedience without influencing the participant to behave in ways that are no longer "pure." Moreover, we doubt that the experimenter can reveal that deception *might* be used without triggering vigilance and, therefore, adulterating the participant's response to the independent variable.

It could be argued that the results are good or useful for society even though the procedure may be harmful to some of the participants. Again, this does not, in and of itself, justify the procedure unless the participants themselves are in a position to weigh the societal benefits against the possibility of individual discomfort. It should also be clear that an ex post facto defense is not adequate. That is, suppose one finds after running the experiment that all participants attest that they are glad they participated and would still have agreed to participate if they had been properly informed in advance. This is not adequate because many participants who might have agreed to participate in advance might attempt to justify their participation after the fact as an ego protective device or as a way of helping the experimenter save face. Once the experiment is over, an ex post facto endorsement is ambiguous at best.

During the past several years, moral philosophers have entered the controversy and have suggested some solutions to the problem of informed consent which, while creative enough, strike us as being impractical in the extreme. One example might suffice. Sable (1978) has suggested a technique called "Prior General Consent Plus Proxy Consent." In this technique, the experimenter first obtains the general consent of the subject to participate in an experiment that may involve extreme procedures. The participant then empowers a friend to serve as a proxy; that is, to examine the details of the specific procedure in advance and to make a judgment as to whether the participant would have consented to it if given the choice. If the proxy says yes, then the experimenter may proceed. While this technique may be ethical in the most technical sense, it has some obvious flaws both ethically and methodologically. First, the participants are still agreeing to something that they cannot fully understand—the proxy can be wrong. Second, it is reasonable to assume that most proxies will probably make conservative errors; that is, they will try to protect the welfare of the participant by being more cautious than the participant would have been. If that is the case, and a substantial number of proxies say no, we may have a sample of extreme and unknown bias.

In recent years, a number of guidelines have been developed to protect the welfare of research participants. In 1973 the American Psychological Association (APA) published a set of guidelines for the conduct of research involving human participants, which have since been revised and updated a number of times. Recent APA ethical guidelines include these principles (American Psychological Association, 1992):

1. Investigators must take steps to protect the rights and welfare of their participants. Because individual researchers might not be objective judges of the ethical acceptability of their studies, they should seek ethical advice from others.

2. As much as possible, the researcher should describe the procedures to participants before they take part in a study and obtain informed consent from participants that documents their agreement to take part in the study as it was described to them. Participants must be informed that they are free to withdraw from the study at any point.

3. If the participant is legally incapable of giving informed consent (e.g., he or she is a minor), the investigator must obtain permission from a legally authorized person (e.g., the participant's parent).

4. Deception may be used only if it is "justified by the study's prospective scientific, educational, or applied value" and only if "equally effective alternative procedures that do not use deception are not feasible" (American Psychological Association, 1992, p. 1609). After the study, participants must be provided with a full description and explanation of all procedures, in a postexperimental interview. Participants in all studies should be given the opportunity to learn about the nature and results of the study.

x All information obtained from individual participants must be held in strict confidence, unless the consent of the participant is obtained to make it public. Investigators must inform participants how their data will be used, and how it will be shared with others.

We have only summarized the guidelines here; we urge the reader to study the American Psychological Association guidelines carefully before undertaking the difficult task of ethical decision making. Further, as the guidelines state, this decision should not be made alone. Researchers may not always be in the best position to judge whether their procedures are ethically permissible. Because of this fact, all research using human subjects that is funded by the federal government, or conducted at colleges and universities, must receive approval from an Institutional Review Board (IRB). This is a panel of scientists and nonscientists who judge whether the risks to participants outweigh the potential gains of the research. It is not uncommon for an IRB to ask researchers to revise their procedures to minimize risks to participants.

It is worth noting that there have been some empirical investigations of the impact of deception experiments on participants. These studies have generally found that people do not object to the kinds of mild discomfort and deceptions typically used in social psychological research (e.g., Christensen, 1988; Sharpe, Adair, & Roese, 1992; Smith & Richardson, 1983). If mild deception is used, and

time is spent after the study discussing the deception with participants and explaining why it was necessary, the evidence is that people will not be adversely affected. Nonetheless, the decision as to whether to use deception in a study should not be taken lightly, and alternative procedures should always be considered.

Ethical Issues in Field Research In many ways the nature of field research places even more responsibility on the researcher to weigh research needs against ethical principles. Whatever the ethical compromises of laboratory experiments may be, at least the laboratory setting assures that participants are aware in some sense that they are participating in research. Even if the consent to participate is not fully informed (or is actively *mis*informed) there is the presence of an "implicit contract" between participant and experimenter that reflects their mutual expectations about the conduct of research. The researcher's contractual obligation is partially fulfilled at the time of the debriefing and postexperimental interview, where any deceptions are unveiled, participants are informed about the goals and purposes of the research, and people's responses to the research procedures are assessed. Thus, even if the participants enter the experimental session ignorant of the researcher's intent, they do so in the expectation of being fully informed by the time it is all over. The postexperimental session also provides an opportunity for subject feedback to correct errors of judgment on the part of the experimenter. If the researcher misjudged the amount of distress or embarrassment the experimental procedure will cause people, information from the first few participants can provide a basis for altering those procedures before the research has gone too far.

When experiments are conducted in field settings where participants are *unaware* at the time that they are participating in research, the basic ethical dilemma is magnified. In such cases, there is not even an implicit contract to be adhered to, and decisions regarding ethical considerations rest solely with the experimenter. There are two different versions of participation without awareness: cases in which the participants are not informed that they had been involved in a research study until after their data have been collected, and cases in which participants are never informed. When participants are contacted and debriefed at the end of the field research, the goals and conduct of the postexperimental interview are essentially the same as those in a laboratory study, although there is one important difference, namely, the fact that the participants had no previous opportunity to decline participation. Hence not even an implicit obligation to cooperate can be assumed. Special sensitivity on the part of the researcher is required to avoid embarrassing people and to ensure that mechanisms are available for refusal to be included in the study after the fact. Again, however, postexperimental contact allows for participant feedback and participation in judgments about legitimacy and appropriateness of the research procedures.

When participants are never told about the research, the opportunity for corrective feedback is greatly reduced. Under such circumstances, the researcher has the full obligation and responsibility of ensuring that the privacy of participants has not been violated, that they have been protected from undue embarrassment or distress, and that their lives have not been altered in any significant way by the nature of the research procedures. This obligation places the researcher in an essentially parental role that many find uncomfortable. To avoid this stance, some have suggested that ethical principles should proscribe the observation or recording of behavior for research purposes unless every person included in the study can be fully informed. This position strikes us as misguided. There are clearly cases of innocuous observation in public places (or the use of public records for research purposes) where the necessity to contact individual participants would destroy the anonymity that makes the procedures innocuous in the first place. Where data are recorded with no possibility of identifying information being available on the persons observed, postexperimental debriefing could produce more participant embarrassment than any effects associated with the observation itself. In such cases it is probably better that the research is conducted in ways that maximize anonymity rather than informed consent.

Of course, the mere fact that the participants (or the experimenter) may be embarrassed by disclosure of the research purpose does not by itself justify a decision to forego informing participants of their research participation. Such decisions should be closely restricted to situations involving high frequency behaviors in public places where only aggregate data are needed for research purposes. The decision becomes especially delicate when the researcher has intervened in the setting in any direct way that alters the situation beyond the normal range of events. In such cases, the experimenter must be sensitive to any possibility that participants may have been affected by the intervention in ways that warrant disclosure of the experimental setup. Finally the conscientious researcher should not rely on his or her judgment alone to make such determinations but should consult widely among people who may bring different perspectives to bear on the decisions to be made.

CONCLUDING COMMENTS

We began this chapter with a defense of the experimental method. For most social psychologists, this defense is, doubtless, unnecessary. For, although those who have been in the discipline for a while have a reasonably clear understanding of the difficulties and drawbacks of this approach, most also have developed an experience-based appreciation of its enormous advantages. For beginning students of social psychology, however, we are convinced that it is vital to take a very close look at precisely why a tightly controlled experiment, with random assignment of subjects to conditions, remains the method of choice. We hope this chapter has succeeded in doing just that, and that the student is now as convinced as we are as to the viability of the experimental method.

At the same time, it is of great importance that experimentalists (both veterans and novices) avoid complacency. As we have indicated earlier, research methodologies are not static but are continually evolving. As we continue to fine-tune the experimental method, we must meet a myriad of challenges by, for example, remaining sensitive to the situation—to determine precisely how our research design interacts with the research setting that interests us. We must also maintain a continued deep concern with ethics and, at the same time, attempt to ensure that this concern does not strangle creativity. We should continue to address serious and important social psychological questions in unique ways with equally serious and important experimental interventions both inside and outside the laboratory.

REFERENCES

Abrams, D., & Hogg, M. A. (Eds.) (1990). *Social identity theory: Constructive and critical advances.* London: Harvester Wheatsheaf.

Aderman, D. (1972). Elation, depression, and helping behavior. *Journal of Personality and Social Psychology, 24,* 91–101.

Allport, G. (1954). *The nature of prejudice.* Reading, MA: Addison-Wesley.

American Psychological Association. (1992). Ethical principles of psychologists and code of conduct. *American Psychologist, 47,* 1597–1611.

Aronson, E. (1966). Avoidance of inter-subject communication. *Psychological Reports, 19,* 238.

Aronson, E., & Bridgeman, D. (1979). Jigsaw groups and the desegregated classroom: in pursuit of common goals. *Personality and Social Psychology Bulletin, 5,* 438–446.

Aronson, E., & Carlsmith, J. M. (1963). Effect of the severity of threat on the devaluation of forbidden behavior. *Journal of Abnormal and Social Psychology, 66,* 583–588.

Aronson, E., & Carlsmith, J. M. (1968). Experimentation in social psychology. In G. Lindzey and E. Aronson (Eds.), *The handbook of social psychology* (Vol. 2, pp. 1–79). Reading, MA.: Addison-Wesley.

Aronson, E., Fried, C. B., & Stone, J. (1991). Overcoming denial and increasing the intention to use condoms through the induction of hypocrisy. *American Journal of Public Health, 81,* 1636–1637.

Aronson, E. & Mettee, D. (1968). Dishonest behavior as a function of differential levels of induced self-esteem. *Journal of Personality and Social Psychology, 9,* 121–127.

Aronson, E., & Mills, J. (1959). The effect of severity of initiation on liking for a group. *Journal of Abnormal and Social Psychology, 59,* 177–181.

Aronson, E., & Osherow, N. (1980). Cooperation, prosocial behavior, and academic performance: Experiments in the desegregated classroom. *Applied Social Psychology Annual, 1,* 163–196.

Aronson, E., Stephan, C., Sikes, J., Blaney, N., & Snapp, M. (1978). *The jigsaw classroom.* Beverly Hills: Sage Publications.

Aronson, E., Willerman, B., & Floyd, J. (1966). The effect of a pratfall on increasing interpersonal attractiveness. *Psychonomic Science, 4,* 227–228.

Aronson, E., Wilson, T. D., & Akert, R. M. (1994). *Social psychology: The heart and the mind.* New York: HarperCollins.

Asch, S. (1951). Effects of group pressure upon the modification and distortion of judgment. In H. Guetzkow (Ed.), *Groups, leadership, and men* (pp. 177–190). Pittsburgh: Carnegie Press.

Back, K. W. (1951). Influences through social communication. *Journal of Abnormal and Social Psychology, 46,* 9–23.

Bargh, J. A. (1989). Conditional automaticity: Varieties of automatic influence in social perception and cognition. In J. S. Uleman & J. A. Bargh (Eds.), *Unintended thought* (pp. 3–51). New York: Guilford Press.

Bargh, J. A. (1990). Auto-motives: Preconscious determinants of social interaction. In E. T. Higgins & R. M. Sorrentino (Eds.), *Handbook of motivation and cognition* (Vol. 2, pp. 93–130). New York: Guilford.

Baumeister, R. F. (1982). A self-presentational view of social phenomena. *Psychological Bulletin, 91,* 3–26.

Brady, J. (1958). Ulcers in "executive monkeys." *Scientific American, 199,* 95–100.

Brehm, J. W., & Cole, A. H. (1966). Effect of a favor which reduces freedom. *Journal of Personality and Social Psychology, 3,* 420–426.

Brewer, M. B. (1976). Randomized invitations: One solution to the problem of voluntary treatment selection in program evaluation research. *Social Science and Research, 5,* 315–323.

Brewer, M. B. (1988). A dual process model of impression formation. In T. K. Srull & R. S. Wyer, Jr. (Eds.), *Advances in social cognition* (Vol. 1, pp. 1–36). Hillsdale, NJ: Erlbaum.

Brewer, M. B., & Brown, R. (1998). Intergroup relations. In D. T. Gilbert, S. T. Fiske, & G. Lindzey (Eds.), *The handbook of social psychology* (4th ed., Vol 2, pp. 554–629). New York: McGraw-Hill.

Brewer, M. B., Dull, V., & Lui, L. (1981). Perceptions of the elderly: stereotypes as prototypes. *Journal of Personality and Social Psychology, 41,* 656–670.

Brunswik, E. (1956). *Perception and the representative design of psychological experiments* (2nd ed.). Berkeley: Univ. of California Press.

Cacioppo, J. T., Petty, R. E., & Tassinary, L. G. (1989). Social psychophysiology: A new look. In L. Berkowitz (Ed.), *Advances in experimental social psychology* (Vol. 22, pp. 39–91). San Diego: Academic Press.

Campbell, D. T. (1957). Factors relevant to validity of experiments in social settings. *Psychology Bulletin, 54,* 297–312.

Campbell, D. T., & Stanley, J. C. (1963). Experimental and quasi-experimental designs for research. In N. L. Gage (Ed.), *Handbook of research on teaching* (pp. 171–246). Chicago: Rand McNally.

Chaiken, S. (1987). The heuristic model of persuasion. In M. P. Hanna, J. M. Olson, & C. P. Herman (Eds.), *Social influence: The Ontario Symposium* (Vol. 5, pp. 3–39). Hillsdale, NJ: Erlbaum.

Christensen, L. (1988). Deception in psychological research: When is its use justified? *Personality and Social Psychology Bulletin, 14,* 664–675.

Cialdini, R. B., Borden, R. J., Thorne, A., Walker, M. R., Freeman, S., & Sloan, L. R. (1976). Basking in reflected glory: three (football) field studies. *Journal of Personality and Social Psychology, 34,* 366–375.

Cook, T. D., & Campbell, D. T. (1979). *Quasi-experiments: design and analysis issues for field settings.* Skokie, IL.: Rand McNally.

Crosby, F., Bromley, S., & Saxe, L. (1980). Recent unobtrusive studies of black and white discrimination and prejudice. A literature review. *Psychological Bulletin, 87,* 546–563.

Dawes, R. B., McTavish, J., & Shaklee, H. (1977). Behavior, communication, and assumptions about other people's behavior in a common dilemmas situation. *Journal of Personality and Social Psychology, 35,* 1–11.

de la Haye, A. (1991). Problems and procedures: A typology of paradigms in interpersonal cognition. *Cahiers de Psychologie Cognitive, 11,* 279–304.

DePaulo, B. M. (1992). Nonverbal behavior and self-presentation. *Psychological Bulletin, 111,* 203–243.

DePaulo, B. M., Lanier, K., & Davis, T. (1983). Detecting the deceit of the motivated liar. *Journal of Personality and Social Psychology, 45,* 1096–1103.

Dickerson, C., Thibodeau, R., Aronson, E., & Miller, D. (1992). Using cognitive dissonance to encourage water conservation. *Journal of Applied Social Psychology, 22,* 841–854.

Dovidio, J. F., & Fazio, R. H. (1992). New technologies for the direct and indirect assessment of attitudes. In J. M. Tanur (Ed.), *Questions about questions: Inquiries into the cognitive bases of surveys* (pp. 204–237). New York: Russel Sage Foundation.

Egbert, L. D., Battit, G. E., Tundorf, H., & Becker, H. K. (1963). The value of the preoperative visit by an anesthetist. *Journal of the American Medical Association, 185,* 553–555.

Ericsson, K. A., & Simon, H. A. (1993). *Protocol analysis: Verbal reports as data* (Rev. ed.). Cambridge, MA: MIT Press.

Fazio, R. H. (1990). Multiple processes by which attitudes guide behavior: The MODE model as an integrative framework. In M. P. Zanna (Ed.), *Advances in experimental social psychology* (Vol. 23, pp. 75–109). San Diego: Academic Press.

Fazio, R. H., Jackson, J. R., & Williams, C. J. (1995). Variability in automatic activation as an unobtrusive measure of racial attitudes: A bona fide pipeline? *Journal of Personality and Social Psychology, 69,* 1013–1027.

Fiske, A. P., Kitayama, S., Markus, H. R., & Nisbett, R. E. (1998). The cultural matrix of social psychology. In D. T. Gilbert, S. T. Fiske, & G. Lindzey (Eds.), *The handbook of social psychology* (4th ed., Vol 2, pp. 915–981). New York: McGraw-Hill.

Fiske, S. T., & Ruscher, J. B. (1989). On-line processes in category-based and individuating impressions: Some basic principles and methodological reflections. In J. N. Bassili (Ed.), *On-line cognition in person perception* (pp. 141–173). Hillsdale, NJ: Erlbaum.

Freedman, J. L., & Fraser, S. C. (1966). Compliance without pressure: The foot-in-the-door technique. *Journal of Personality and Social Psychology, 4,* 195–202.

Gerard, H. B., & Mathewson, G. C. (1966). The effects of severity of initiation on liking for a group: A replication. *Journal of Experimental Social Psychology, 2,* 278–287.

Gergen, K. J. (1973). Social psychology as history. *Journal of Personality and Social Psychology, 26,* 309–320.

Gilbert, D. T. (1991). How mental systems believe. *American Psychologist, 46,* 107–119.

Gilbert, D. T., & Hixon, J. G. (1991). The trouble of thinking: Activation and application of stereotypic beliefs. *Journal of Personality and Social Psychology, 60,* 509–517.

Glass, D., & Singer, J. (1972). *Urban stress.* New York: Academic Press.

Greenwald, A. G., & Banaji, M. R. (1995). Implicit social cognition: Attitudes, self-esteem, and stereotypes. *Psychological Review, 102,* 4–27.

Gross, A. E., & Fleming, I. (1982). 20 years of deception in social psychology. *Personality and Social Psychology Bulletin, 8,* 402–408.

Hamilton, D., & Rose, T. L. (1980). Illusory correlation and the maintenance of stereotypic beliefs. *Journal of Personality and Social Psychology, 39,* 832–845.

Hamilton, D. L., & Trolier, T. K. (1986). Stereotypes and stereotyping: An overview of the cognitive approach. In J. Dovodio & S. Gaertner (Eds.), *Prejudice, discrimination and racism* (pp. 127–164). New York: Academic Press.

Haney, C., Banks, C., & Zimbardo, P. (1973). Interpersonal dynamics in a simulated prison. *International Journal of Criminology and Penology, 1,* 69–97.

Harackiewicz, J. M., Manderlink, G., & Sansone, C. (1984). Rewarding pinball wizardry: Effects of evaluation and cue value on intrinsic interest. *Journal of Personality and Social Psychology, 47,* 287–300.

Harlow, H. F., & Zimmerman, R. R. (1958). The development of affectional responses in infant monkeys. *Proceedings of the American Philosophic Society, 102,* 501–509.

Higgins, E. T., & Bargh, J. A. (1992). Unconscious sources of subjectivity and suffering: Is consciousness the solution? In L. L. Martin & A. Tesser (Eds.), *The construction of social judgments* (pp. 67–103). Hillsdale, NJ: Erlbaum.

Higgins, E. T., Rholes, W. S., & Jones, C. R. (1977). Category accessibility and impression formation. *Journal of Experimental Social Psychology, 13,* 141–154.

Holmes, D. S. (1976a). Debriefing after psychological experiments: I. Effectiveness of postdeception dehoaxing. *American Psychologist, 31,* 858–867.

Holmes, D. S. (1976b). Debriefing after psychological experiments: II. Effectiveness of postexperimental desensitizing. *American Psychologist, 31,* 868–875.

Jacoby, L. L., Lindsay, S. D., & Toth, J. P. (1992). Unconscious influences revealed: Attention, awareness, and control. *American Psychologist, 47,* 802–809.

Janis, I. L (1958). *Psychological stress.* New York: Wiley.

Johnson, J. E., & Leventhal, H. (1974). Effects of accurate expectations and behavioral instructions on reactions during a noxious medical examination. *Journal of Personality and Social Psychology, 29,* 710–718.

Jones, E., & Sigall, H. (1971). The bogus pipeline: A new paradigm for measuring affect and attitude. *Psychological Bulletin, 76,* 349–364.

Kanfer, F. H., & Seidner, M. L. (1973). Self control: Factors enhancing tolerance of noxious stimulation. *Journal of Personality and Social Psychology, 25,* 281–389.

Katzev, R., & Bachman, W. (1982). Effects of deferred payment and fare rate manipulations on urban bus ridership. *Journal of Applied Psychology, 67,* 83–88.

Kenny, D. A., Kashy, D. A., & Bolger, N. (1998). Data analysis in social psychology. In D. T. Gilbert, S. T. Fiske, & G. Lindzey (Eds.), *The handbook of social psychology* (4th ed., Vol 1, pp. 233–265). New York: McGraw-Hill.

Kiesler, S. B., & Sproull, L. S. (1987). (Eds.). *Computing and change on campus.* New York: Cambridge.

Kihlstrom, J. F. (1987). The cognitive unconscious. *Science, 237,* 1445–1452.

Kunen, J. S. (1995, July 10). Teaching prisoners a lesson. *The New Yorker,* 34–39.

Landy, D., & Aronson, E. (1968). Liking for an evaluator as a function of his discernment. *Journal of Personality and Social Psychology, 9,* 133–141.

Langer, E. J. (1975). The illusion of control. *Journal of Personality and Social Psychology, 32,* 311–328.

Langer, E. J. (1989). Minding matters: The consequences of mindlessness-mindfulness. In L. Berkowitz (Ed.), *Advances in experimental social psychology* (Vol. 22, pp. 137–174). San Diego, CA: Academic Press.

Langer, E. J., & Rodin, J. (1976). The effects of choice and enhanced personal responsibility for the aged: A field experiment in an institutional setting. *Journal of Personality and Social Psychology, 34,* 191–198.

Langer, E. J., Blank, A., & Chanowitz, B. (1978). The mindlessness of ostensibly thoughtful action: The role of "placebic" information in interpersonal interaction. *Journal of Personality and Social Psychology, 36,* 635–642.

Lepper, M. R., Greene, D., & Nisbett, R. E. (1973). Undermining children's intrinsic interest with extrinsic reward: A test of the overjustification hypothesis. *Journal of Personality and Social Psychology, 28,* 129–137.

Lucasiewicz, M., & Sawyer, D. (1991, Sept. 26). *True Colors: Primetime Live.* New York: American Broadcasting Company. (Available from MTI Film & Video.)

Milgram, S. (1974). *Obedience to authority: An experimental view.* New York: Harper & Row.

Mook, D. G. (1983). In defense of external invalidity. *American Psychologist, 38,* 379–388.

Mook, D. G., Wilson, T. D., & DePaulo, B. M. (1995). *Shortcomings of research on important social problems.* Unpublished manuscript, University of Virginia, Charlottesville.

Nisbett, R. E., & Wilson, T. D. (1977). Telling more than we can know: Verbal reports on mental processes. *Psychological Review, 84,* 231–259.

Orne, M. (1962). On the social psychology of the psychological experiment. *American Psychologist, 17,* 776–783.

Parker, S. D., Brewer, M. B., & Spencer, J. R. (1980). Natural disaster, perceived control, and attributions to fate. *Personality and Social Psychology Bulletin, 6,* 454–459.

Pennebaker, J. (1983). Physical symptoms and sensations: Psychological causes and correlates. In J. T. Cacioppo & R. E. Petty (Eds.), *Social psychophysiology: A sourcebook* (pp. 543–564). New York: Guilford.

Petty, R. E., & Cacioppo, J. T. (1986). *Communication and persuasion: Central and peripheral routes to attitude change.* New York: Springer-Verlag.

Petty, R. E., Cacioppo, J. T., & Goldman, R. (1981). Personal involvement as a determinant of argument-based persuasion. *Journal of Personality and Social Psychology, 41,* 847–855.

Piliavin, I. M., Rodin, J., & Piliavin, J. A. (1969). Good samaritanism: An underground phenomenon? *Journal of Personality and Social Psychology, 13,* 289–299.

Reis, H. T. (1982). An introduction to the use of structural equations: Prospects and problems. In L. Wheeler (Ed.), *Review of personality and social psychology* (Vol. 3, pp. 255–287). Beverly Hills, CA: Sage.

Rodin, J., & Langer, E. J. (1977). Long-term effects of a control-relevant intervention with the institutional aged. *Journal of Personality and Social Psychology, 35,* 897–902.

Rosenberg, M. J., Davidson, A. J., Chen, J., Judson, F. N., & Douglas, J. M. (1992). Barrier contraceptives and sexually transmitted diseases in women: A comparison of female-dependent methods and condoms. *American Journal of Public Health, 82,* 669–674.

Rosenthal, R. (1994). Interpersonal expectancy effects: A 30-year perspective. *Current Directions in Psychological Science, 3,* 176–179.

Rosenthal, R., & Lawson, R. (1964). A longitudinal study of the effects of experimenter bias on the operant learning of laboratory rats. *Journal of Psychiatric Research, 2,* 61–72.

Ross, L., Lepper, M. R., & Hubbard, M. (1975). Perseverance in self perception and social perception: Biased attributional processes in the debriefing paradigm. *Journal of Personality and Social Psychology, 32,* 880–892.

Sable, A. (1978). Deception in social science research: Is informed consent possible? *Hastings Center Report, 8,* 40–46.

Salovey, P., Mayer, J. D., & Rosenhan, D. L. (1991). Mood and helping: Mood as a motivator of helping and helping as a regulator of mood. In M. S. Clark (Ed.), *Prosocial Behavior: Review of Personality and Social Psychology* (Vol. 12, pp. 215–237). Newbury Park, CA: Sage.

Schachter, S. (1959). *The psychology of affiliation: Experimental studies of the sources of gregariousness.* Stanford: Stanford University Press.

Schachter, S., & Singer, J. E. (1962). Cognitive, social and physiological determinants of emotional state. *Psychological Review, 69,* 379–399.

Schlenker, B. R. (1980). *Impression management.* Monterey, CA: Brooks-Cole.

Schooler, J. W., Ohlsson, S., & Brooks, K. (1993). Thoughts beyond words: When language overshadows insight. *Journal of Experimental Psychology: General, 122,* 166–183.

Schulz, R., & Hanusa, B. H. (1978). Long-term effects of control and predictability-enhancing interventions: Findings and ethical issues. *Journal of Personality and Social Psychology, 36,* 1202–1212.

Sears, D. O. (1986). College sophomores in the laboratory: Influences of a narrow data base on social psychology's view of human nature. *Journal of Personality and Social Psychology, 51,* 515–530.

Sharpe, D., Adair, J. G., & Roese, N. J. (1992). Twenty years of deception research: A decline in subjects' trust? *Personallity and Social Psychology Bulletin, 18,* 585–590.

Sherif, M., Harvey, O. J., White, J., Hood, W., & Sherif, C. (1961). *Intergroup conflict and cooperation: The robber's cave experiment.* Norman: University of Oklahoma, Institute of Intergroup Relations.

Sigall, H., Aronson, E., & Van Hoose, T. (1970). The cooperative subject: Myth or reality? *Journal of Experimental Social Psychology, 6,* 1–10.

Sigall, H., Page, R. (1971). Current stereotypes: A little fading, a little faking. *Journal of Personality and Social Psychology, 18,* 247–255.

Smith, S. S., & Richardson, D. (1983). Amelioration of deception and harm in psychological research: The important role of debriefing. *Journal of Personality and Social Psychology, 44,* 1075–1082.

Stephan, C., Presser, N. R., Kennedy, J. C., & Aronson, E. (1978). Attributions to success and failure after cooperative or competitive interaction. *European Journal of Social Psychology, 8,* 269–274.

Stone, J., Aronson, E., Crain, A. L., Winslow, M. P., & Fried, C. B. (1994). Inducing hypocrisy as a means for encouraging young adults to use condoms. *Personality and Social Psychology Bulletin, 20,* 116–128.

Tajfel, H., Billig, M., Bundy, R., & Flament, C. (1971). Social categorization and intergroup behavior. *European Journal of Social Psychology, 1,* 149–178.

Tumin, M., Barton, P., & Burrus, B. (1958). Education, prejudice, and discrimination: A study in readiness for desegregation. *American Sociological Review, 23,* 41–49.

Uleman, J. S. (1989). A framework for thinking intentionally about unintended thoughts. In J. S. Uleman & J. A. Bargh (Eds.), *Unintended thought* (pp. 425–449). New York: Guilford Press.

Underwood, B., Berenson, J., Berenson, R., Cheng, K., Wilson, D., Kulik, J., Moore, B., & Wenzel, G. (1977). Attention, negative affect, and altruism: An ecological validation. *Personality and Social Psychology Bulletin, 3,* 54–58.

von Hippel, W., Sekaquaptewa, D., & Vargas, P. (1995). On the role of encoding processes in stereotype maintenance. In M. Zanna (Ed.), *Advances in experimental social psychology* (Vol. 27, pp. 177–254). San Diego: Academic Press.

Wallace, J., & Sadalla, E. (1966). Behavioral consequences of transgression: I. The effects of social recognition. *Journal of Experimental Research in Personality, I,* 187–194.

Walster, E., Aronson, E., & Abrahams, D. (1966). On increasing the persuasiveness of a low prestige communicator. *Journal of Experimental Social Psychology, 2,* 325–342.

Webb, E. S., Campbell, D. T., Schwartz, R. D., Sechrest, L., & Grove, J. (1981). *Nonreactive measures in the social sciences.* Boston: Houghton Mifflin.

Wegner, D. M. (1994). Ironic processes of mental control. *Psychological Review 101,* 34–52.

Wicker, A. W. (1969). Attitudes versus actions: The relationship between verbal and overt behavioral responses to attitude objects. *Journal of Social Issues, 25,* 41–78.

Wilson, T. D. (1994). The proper protocol: Validity and completeness of verbal reports. *Psychological Science, 5,* 249–252.

Wilson, T. D., Dunn, D. S., Kraft, D., & Lisle, D. J. (1989). Introspection, attitude change, and attitude-behavior consistency: The disruptive effects of explaining why we feel the way we do. In L. Berkowitz (Ed.), *Advances in experimental social psychology* (Vol. 19, pp. 123–205). Orlando, FL: Academic Press.

Wilson, T. D., Hodges, S. D., & LaFleur, S. J. (1995). Effects of introspecting about reasons: Inferring attitudes from accessible thoughts. *Journal of Personality and Social Psychology, 68,* 16–28.

Wilson, T. D., & Lassiter, D. (1982). Increasing intrinsic interest with the use of superfluous extrinsic constraints. *Journal of Personality and Social Psychology, 42,* 811–819.

Wilson, T. D., Lisle, D., Schooler, J., Hodges, S. D., Klaaren, K. J., & LaFleur, S. J. (1993). Introspecting about reasons can reduce post-choice satisfaction. *Personality and Social Psychology Bulletin, 19,* 331–339.

Wilson, T. D., & Stone, J. I. (1985). Limitations of self-knowledge: More on telling more than we can know. In P. Shaver (Ed.), *Review of personality and social psychology* (Vol. 6, pp. 167–183). Beverly Hills, CA: Sage.

Zanna, M. P., & Fazio, R. H. (1982). The attitude-behavior relation: Moving toward a third generation of research. In M. P. Zanna, E. T. Higgins, & C. P. Herman (Eds.), *Consistency in social behavior: The Ontario Symposium* (Vol. 2, pp. 283–301). Hillsdale, NJ: Erlbaum.

CHAPTER 4

SURVEY METHODS

NORBERT SCHWARZ, *University of Michigan*
ROBERT M. GROVES, *University of Michigan and Joint Program in Survey Methodology, University of Maryland*
HOWARD SCHUMAN, *University of Michigan*

INTRODUCTION

This chapter provides an introduction to the logic of survey research and reviews the current state of the art in survey methodology. In selecting the material to be covered, we were guided by the assumption that most social psychologists will be users rather than producers of survey data. Moreover, when social psychologists undertake a major survey, they are likely to draw on the services of a professional survey center to conduct the data collection. Accordingly, we pay more attention to components of the survey process in which social psychologists who embark on a survey are likely to be involved (such as questionnaire construction) than to components (such as drawing a probability sample) that are better left to professionals from other disciplines. Finally, we do not address aspects of data analysis, which are covered in other chapters.

MAJOR COMPONENTS OF A SURVEY

In its most general meaning, the term *survey* refers to systematic data collection about a sample drawn from a specified larger population. If data are obtained from every member of the population, the study is called a *census*. The final product of surveys are survey statistics, that is, percentages, means, measures of association and the like. A common approach within the field of survey methodology, labeled the *total survey error* perspective, encourages an

integrated concern with all the sources of quality (and error properties) of survey statistics. The various errors inherent in survey statistics arise from the individual steps of a survey. Figure 1 shows the major components of a survey.

Starting from a set of research objectives, researchers specify the population of interest and draw an appropriate sample. The research objectives further determine the con-

FIGURE 1 Major Elements of a Survey.

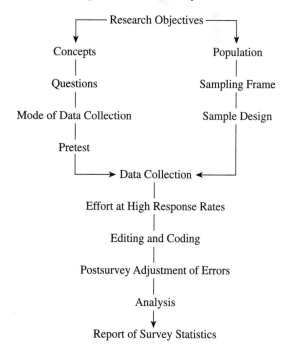

We thank Susan Fiske, Daniel Gilbert, Bärbel Knäuper, Gardner Lindzey, Eleanor Singer, Stanley Presser, and Seymour Sudman for helpful comments on a previous draft.

cepts to be investigated, which need to be translated into appropriate questions. Ideally, sampling design and question construction should proceed hand in hand, both guided by the problem to be investigated. When these stages are not well integrated—a rather common failing—one ends up with questions that do not fit part of the sample or with a sample that provides too few cases for a key analysis. Note that neither the sample nor the specific question asked is what the researcher is primarily interested in. Rather, investigators use the one (sample, question) to make inferences about the other (population, concept), with the latter being what one is primarily interested in. Sampling populations and operationalizing concepts are each intended to allow us to go from the observed to the unobserved.

The nature of the sample and of the questions to be asked, as well as the budget available, determine the choice of administration mode, i.e., the use of face-to-face or telephone interviews, or of self-administered questionnaires, which may be mailed to respondents. Following pretesting, the survey is administered to collect relevant data.

If interviews are conducted, the questions written by the researcher need to be appropriately delivered by the interviewer at this stage. To answer a question, respondents have to understand its meaning, which may or may not match the meaning that the researcher had in mind. Next, they have to retrieve relevant information from memory to form a judgment, which they then need to adapt to fit the response alternatives provided to them. Moreover, they may want to edit their answer before they convey it to the interviewer, due to reasons of social desirability and self-presentation concerns. Finally, the interviewer needs to understand the respondent's answer and to record it for subsequent processing.

At the post-survey stage, the interviewer's questionnaire may need editing and coding prior to data processing. Finally, data analysis, interpretation, and dissemination of the findings complete the research process.

The total survey error perspective notes that the accuracy of a survey statistic (e.g., a mean, a regression coefficient) is a function of four principle sources of error: *coverage error,* weaknesses in the statistic because of failure to include some persons in the definition of the relevant population from which any sample might be selected; *sampling error,* inaccuracies in the estimates because only a specific subset of the defined population was actually sampled; *nonresponse error,* due to failure to obtain responses from some of those sampled; and *measurement error,* deviations between the attributes of the respondents and what they report. Measurement error is often separated into components due to the questionnaire, the interviewer, the respondent, and the mode of data collection. This terminology may appear foreign to psychologists trained in notions of reliability and validity (see Groves, 1989, for a more detailed discussion); these psychometric terms refer to com-

ponents of measurement error in the present terminology. In the subsequent sections of this chapter, we address the key components of the survey process in more detail.

DETERMINING WHOM TO ASK

Sample surveys developed as means to produce quantitative descriptions of large populations (e.g., the proportion female, the number of college graduates in a country) more cheaply than complete enumerations of the population. The use of surveys for descriptive purposes exploded in the United States in the early 1940s after the introduction of probability sampling techniques.

A *probability sample* is one that assigns to each member of a population a known, nonzero chance of selection. In the late 1930s basic statistical theorems were completed that demonstrated that with probability samples, survey statistics could be shown to be unbiased (i.e., over replications using the same sample design, the average result will equal the result obtained if one did a full census) and to have sampling variances that can be calculated from the sample itself.

The calculatability of *sampling variance,* or *sampling error,* is crucial for inferences from the sample to a finite population. Sampling error is often referred to as the *margin of error* when survey results are reported. Suppose that a survey based on simple random sampling (to be explained below) indicates that 70 percent of the sample would vote for candidate A. With a sample size of $N = 500$ and a desired confidence interval of 95 percent, sampling error would be around 4 percent. Hence, one may conclude that between 66 percent and 74 percent of the population would vote for candidate A. Sampling error decreases with increasing sample size, but the decrease is nonlinear. For the above example, sampling error declines from 9 percent for a sample of 100 to 4 percent for a sample of 500. But doubling the sample size from 500 to 1,000 further decreases sampling error only modestly to 3 percent, and to reduce sampling error to 1 percent one would need a sample of approximately 10,500. Because sampling error depends on sample size, the sampling error for any subgroup, e.g., 18–20-year-olds or residents of a particular state, is much larger than the sampling error for the sample as a whole. If it is important to obtain accurate estimates for specified subgroups, one needs to increase their representation through oversampling.

Importantly, sampling variability can only be calculated for probability samples, rendering *nonprobability samples* of limited use. Because probability sampling is expensive, for reasons that will become apparent below, nonprobability samples are nevertheless used in some studies. The main type of nonprobability sampling is *quota sampling,* where a sample is selected based on a set of characteristics in the population. For example, if the population of interest contains 40 percent married people, 18 percent African American and 35 percent over the age of 45, one can select a sample that will conform to these characteristics. To accomplish this, interviewers are not given a specified list of respondents or addresses but are provided with the quota criteria and are free to select any respondent who fits these criteria. Because the selection of respondents within the quota specifications is left to the interviewers' discretion, the members of the population do not have an equal likelihood of being selected, rendering it impossible to draw strong conclusions about the population. These problems are compounded when *convenience samples* are used, that is, samples which are readily available or comprised solely of volunteers. Such samples, be they college students who voluntarily sign up for a study or readers who respond to a questionnaire printed in a magazine, do not allow inferences to any population because their representativeness is unknown.

Accordingly, we only address probability sampling in the present chapter. For probability samples, one can demonstrate through the application of statistical theorems the properties of unbiasedness and measurability of sampling variability. These properties affect inference from the sample to the finite population and are not important if one were interested only in describing the characteristics of the sample respondents themselves. However, surveys by their very nature are oriented toward this inference—in psychometric terms they excel in external validity rather than internal validity. Hence, any property of a sampling technique affecting its ability to describe the full population is important.

As with any observational data, surveys can also be used for analytic purposes—to address issues of causes and consequences of human behavior and thought. Much of the use of surveys in the academic sector is of this ilk. Here, the typical assumption of the multivariate models used is that the observations are the products of a consistent process (i.e., the right-side or independent variables) producing independent and identically distributed outcomes (i.e., the left-side or dependent variables). The inference in these models is generally to the process itself, which is often viewed to go on indefinitely (e.g., the process by which intention to purchase a car at time 1 impacts on the behavior at time 2 for different types of consumers). When survey data are used for analytic purposes, concerns about internal validity arise. Here sample surveys are notoriously ill-controlled relative to randomized experiments, though in some research, randomized experiments are built into surveys for substantive as well as methodological purposes.

Designing and Drawing Probability Samples

The first step in probability sampling is choice of the *sampling frame:* a listing of all the members of the population. Sampling frames can be simple listings of individual members or complex procedures that have the theoretical property of a complete listing of persons. Whereas some countries (like Denmark or Sweden) have population registers with individual records for each person in the country, equivalent registers are not available in the United States. Hence, common sampling frames for U.S. persons are telephone numbers (assign each person in the United States to a telephone) and areas of land along with their housing units (assign each person to a unit). Large-scale face-to-face surveys use sampling of counties, census tracts within sampled counties, blocks within census tracts, and housing units within blocks in successive stages, thus relying on several frames simultaneously.

A perfect sampling frame is one that contains one and only one listing for each population member. The fact that not all persons are attached to a frame is a source of *undercoverage,* an error of nonobservation in surveys. This is the most common error in frames for human populations. Area frames, where persons are assigned to the housing unit that is their residence, miss persons with marginal attachment to households (Fay, 1989). Telephone number frames miss persons who live in households without telephones, resulting in an underrepresentation of poor, small, and rural households (Thornberry & Massey, 1988).

As with all survey errors, there are ways to reduce coverage errors prior to the survey and ways to statistically adjust estimates to reduce coverage error effects after the data have been collected. Errors of undercoverage are a function of two characteristics—the proportion of the full population not covered by the frame and the differences on the survey statistic between those covered by the frame and those not covered by the frame. Increasing the proportion covered is achieved by checks at the time of data collection to include those not covered (e.g., the half-open interval, Kish, 1965; multiplicity approaches, Sirken, 1970). Attacking the problem of repairing the frame for particular types of persons, the simultaneous use of multiple frames is attractive (e.g., Lepkowski & Groves, 1986). In the absence of improvements in the coverage rate, different groups in the sample can be weighted by their proportions in the full population, provided that appropriate population counts are available. When the groups are homogeneous on the survey variables of interest (whether or not they appear on the frame), this *poststratification* reduces the errors of undercoverage.

After a sampling frame is identified, the next step in sampling is the creation of a *sample design.* There are three dimensions of probability sampling that affect the quality of survey statistics. The first noteworthy dimension of probability sampling is *stratification,* the separation of the sampling frame into separate groups from which independent samples are drawn. To the extent the different strata contain persons with different values on the survey variables, the stratified design assures representation of the different groups in each sample drawn. Thus, stratification acts to reduce variability in survey estimates across different samples and thus lowers standard errors of estimates.

The second major characteristic of probability samples is *clustering,* the selection into the sample of groups of persons rather than individuals. For example, it is common in face-to-face surveys to sample blocks of housing units and to include in the survey many people from the same block. Typically persons who live on the same block resemble one another on residential lifestyle, income, education, and a host of other demographic and socioeconomic variables. For a given number of persons in the sample, therefore, cluster samples run the risk of more instability—variation in sample statistics depending on what clusters are selected. This means that clustered samples usually have larger standard errors on statistics than unclustered designs.

A third characteristic pertains to whether equal probabilities of selection are assigned to each element or unequal probabilities of selection. *Simple random samples* are ones giving an equal chance of selection to each element, equal chances to each pair of distinct elements, equal chances to each triplet, etc. In the absence of knowledge about how the phenomenon distributes itself over the population, assigning equal probabilities of selection is a desirable property. When unequal probabilities of selection are arbitrarily assigned to different elements in the population the relative efficiency of the design is reduced (i.e., the sampling variance is higher for the same sample size). Larger probabilities of selection assigned to groups of specific analytic interest, however, can assure sufficient sample sizes in those groups to permit separate analyses of them, at desired levels of sampling error. Survey data arising from unequal probability samples require the use of selection weights assigned to each data record for sample estimates to reflect the full population more accurately. These weight up the cases given small probabilities of selection and weight down those oversampled.

Many common sample designs combine stratification, clustering, and unequal probabilities of selection, thus departing from simple random samples in many ways. Such survey data cannot correctly be analyzed using many statistical software packages (e.g., SPSS, SAS, BMDP) because the computations do not reflect the sample design. Although many statistical software packages permit the use of case-level weights (to reflect unequal probabilities of selection), they do not correctly reflect the effects of stratification and clustering on standard errors. To do this other packages are needed (e.g., SUDAAN, WESVAR, CENTAB, and others).

In summary, probability samples are needed to draw reliable inferences from a sample to a specifiable population. Drawing a probability sample, however, is a complex task that is best left to trained professionals. Readers interested in a more detailed treatment are advised to consult Kalton (1983) or Sudman (1976). Next, we turn to a factor that may threaten the representativeness of a probability sample, namely, the inability to contact sample persons or once contacted their refusal to be interviewed.

Causes and Consequences of Nonresponse in Sample Surveys

A sample drawn to be a perfect microcosm of the target population will be of no inferential value to the researcher if members of the sample cannot be measured. However, nonresponse is a feature of virtually all surveys of human populations. Since nonresponse has implications not only for the quality of the survey statistics, but also for the cost of data collection, it is of concern to both users and producers of survey data.

Nonresponse creates error in survey statistics as a function of the proportion of sample cases not measured and the differences on the survey statistic between those measured and those not measured on the survey. With most surveys, there is little information available about the nonrespondents and, hence, no way to speculate on the nature of nonresponse bias.

Over time in most developed countries of the world, response rates for surveys using interviewers seem to have declined—and when an ongoing survey has maintained its response rate over time, it appears to have done so with greater effort. Speculations about the causes of this phenomenon include a saturation of the population with survey requests, practices of selling or fund-raising under the guise of a survey (Schleifer, 1986), increased women's labor force participation, yielding more frequent absences from sample housing units, and fear of crime (House & Wolf, 1978). In addition, it is currently more common to use telephone surveys than face-to-face surveys, and these have routinely been found to achieve lower response rates (Groves & Kahn, 1979).

Methods to increase response rates include advance letters (e.g., Dillman, Gallegos, & Frey, 1976), payment to respondents (e.g., James & Bolstein, 1990), persuasive interviewer scripts, different strategies of timing calls on sample households, and repeated callbacks to reluctant respondents (see Groves, 1989, for a review). Much of the work in this area is based on randomized experiments, permitting strong causal inference, but does not show consistent effects across all survey conditions.

Some efforts to increase participation through persuasion and inducement strategies begin to threaten the informed consent principles of modern science and, increasingly, are nonefficacious. Sole attention to maximizing response rates may in the long run erode the legitimacy of the method among the population. In addition to the scientific and ethical issues arising from such efforts to reduce nonresponse, there are practical issues involving the costs of scientific research. Any reluctance of the population to participate in surveys increases the costs of the method.

Cost and ethical issues both serve to limit the usefulness of efforts to reduce the extent of survey nonresponse.

Causes of Nonresponse   There are two types of nonresponse, failure to deliver the survey request to the sample person (often termed "noncontacts") and refusals. *Noncontacts* arise as a rather simple function of how much effort was expended to contact the sample person and what barriers exist to that contact (e.g., limited time at home in telephone and face-to-face surveys, inadequate address information in mail questionnaires).

Refusals, on the other hand, appear to stem from a more complex set of causes (see Figure 2). The concepts on the left side of the figure, "Social Environment" and "Householder," describe factors that are out of the control of the researcher. Those on the right side of the figure, "Survey Design" and "Interviewer," are determined in large part by the researcher.

The characteristics on the left side of Figure 2 include both current social and economic conditions that may affect perceived needs for information, as well as public opinion and visibility of debate on issues of privacy and confidentiality of information provided for research and administrative uses (Lyberg & Dean, 1992). In addition, attributes of the neighborhood and the urbanicity of the residential location of the householder can influence reactions to survey requests from strangers. The likelihood of survey participation is also directly influenced by various attributes of the persons sampled. These include knowledge of the survey topic, which may determine the cognitive burden of answering survey questions; prior experience as a survey respondent; and affective states extant at the time of the survey request.

Researchers generally manipulate the characteristics on the right side of Figure 2 to minimize nonresponse rates. Surveys with different length of interviews, respondent selection procedures, and mode of data collection tend to vary in cooperation rates, depending on the characteristics of the population studied. Similarly, the survey design, through recruiting, training, and supervision of interviewers, leads to a set of interviewers whose sociodemographic and attitudinal characteristics can influence the likelihood of cooperation of the sample persons they contact.

The influences of survey design and interviewer characteristics may or may not manifest themselves in the interaction between interviewer and sample person, depending on the nature of the conversation between the two. In the brief contacts that characterize the initial interactions between interviewers and householders, that subset of factors in Figure 2 deemed by the householder most relevant to the decision to participate is evoked and forms the basis of the judgment to accept or refuse the survey request.

When the interviewer first makes contact, the sample person is actively engaged in an effort to comprehend the intent of the interviewer's visit. The concepts inherent in cognitive script theory (Abelson, 1981) are useful here. These would assert that the words, behavior, and physical appearance of the interviewer will be used to identify possible "stories" or scripts that are potential explanations of the interviewer's purpose. These scripts are used as heuristic devices that quickly help the householder anticipate the next steps in the interaction and the ultimate goals of the visitor. Past experience with similar situations will dictate behavior (e.g., if this is a sales encounter, then be reluctant or uninterested).

Experienced interviewers often report that they adapt their approach to characteristics of the sample unit (Groves, Cialdini, and Couper, 1992). Which statement they use to begin the conversation is the result of observations about the housing unit, the neighborhood, and immediate reactions upon first contact with the person who answers the door. The reaction of the householder to the first statement dictates the choice of the second statement to use. With this perspective, all features of the communication are relevant—not only the words used by the interviewer, but the inflection, volume, pacing (see Oksenberg, Coleman, and Cannell, 1986), as well as physical movements and demeanor of the interviewer.

In summary, respondents' refusal to be interviewed can threaten the representativeness of even the most carefully drawn probability sample. At present, the determinants of survey nonresponse are still poorly understood, although current research suggests that the initial interaction between interviewer and respondent may play a crucial role. Understanding the dynamics of these initial interactions provides a promising avenue for social psychological research into social influence processes.

Post-Survey Adjustment for Nonresponse

No effort at nonresponse reduction will be completely successful, and some nonresponse remains in almost all sample surveys. There are two approaches to adjusting survey statistics to reduce the effects of nonresponse. In the last ten years the survey literature has witnessed a significant increase in attention to nonresponse error in surveys, stimulated by the U.S. National Academy of Sciences Panel on Missing and Incomplete Data (Madow, Nisselson, & Olkin, 1983). There are five common statistical procedures for nonresponse adjustment: population-based weighting class adjustments, sample-based weighting class adjustments, propensity model weighting, full case imputation, and selection model adjustments.

Population-based weighting (also called *poststratification*) is limited to those cases in which there are known distributions for the full population for some variable measured in the survey (Kish, 1965). For example, national household surveys often form weighting classes of respondents by age, gender, and race, and then use national population counts in those classes from the U.S. Census Bureau

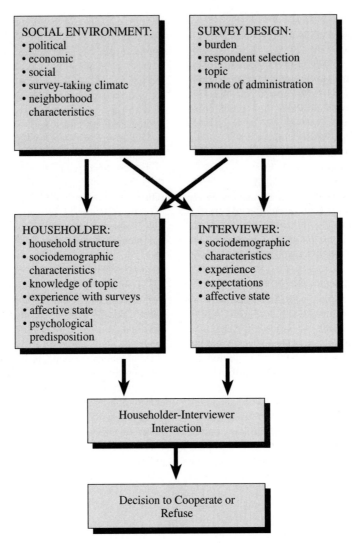

FIGURE 2 **Factors Affecting Survey Participation.**

to adjust the respondent distribution to conform to those counts. For example, if an age-gender-race class formed 10 percent of the national population but 5 percent of the respondent pool from a national sample, respondents in that class would be weighted by a factor of 2.0, other things being equal.

Sample-based weighting class adjustments use the same procedures, but adjust the respondent data to known distributions on the selected sample, not the full population. Thus, the weighting classes must be based on variables known for both respondent and nonrespondent sample cases. Sample based weighting class adjustments generally produce weighted statistics with higher standard errors than those with population-based weighting class adjustments (Kalton, 1983b).

Both types of weighting class adjustments can be viewed as weighting each respondent case by the reciprocal of the response rate of its weighting class. *Propensity model weighting* takes that adjustment to the individual case level instead of a set of cases. That is, weights are assigned as the reciprocal of the expected propensity to respond for a respondent case. Typically logit or probit models are fit to data, using variables available on both respondent and nonrespondent cases and related to the likelihood of contact or cooperation (Ekholm and Laaksonen, 1991). With a powerful set of predictors, propensity model adjustments can theoretically be more effective in reducing nonresponse bias but suffer from the same problems of increased standard errors as sample-based weighting class adjustments.

Imputation essentially uses information on respondent cases to substitute for the data missing from nonrespondent cases. It is most useful when a large set of predictor variables for key dependent variables is available on both respondent and nonrespondent cases (e.g., from earlier waves in a longitudinal survey). Imputation techniques vary from ad hoc to ones requiring specific models and complex estimation routines (see Kalton, 1983a, for a review). Multiple imputation (Rubin, 1987; Little & Rubin, 1987) replaces each missing case with several respondent cases, each appropriately weighted, and permits estimation of the component of standard errors affected by the imputation.

Selection bias modeling is an adjustment technique designed for use in structural modeling with survey data. In this context the analyst builds a "selection model" similar to those used in propensity model weighting schemes, but then uses a function of the expected value for the model as an added predictor variable in the structural model. The utility of the technique appears to vary by the nature of the structural model, distributions of the selection model and structural model variables, and the fit of the two models.

Within the research of the past few years there appears to be growing acceptance of the perspective that nonresponse is a phenomenon subject to stochastic properties; that is, all persons have some tendencies to participate and to fail to participate in surveys. This is in contrast to earlier perspectives (see the review by Holt & Elliot, 1991) that viewed nonresponse as a fixed attribute of a sampled unit (e.g., person). The view that the decision to participate or not to participate is a process that has random components to it has led even those most attached to design-based estimation to contemplate the use of models for the adjustment process. It is, however, at the model specification level that the field currently has its limitations. For the most part the practical use of adjustment procedures has been post hoc to survey design, the application of a statistical adjustment using whatever information happened to be available at the estimation stage. There has been very little discussion about the proper specification of post-survey adjustment models, in contrast to analytic and empirical demonstrations of adjustment effects and little attention to how survey designs might be altered to improve the quality of post-survey adjustments.

Panel Surveys

We noted above that one weakness of sample surveys is the largely descriptive and correlational nature of the produced data, rendering it difficult to identify causal relationships. In many cases, however, knowing the temporal ordering of events helps to substantiate causal interpretations. In these cases, the use of longitudinal designs, often referred to as *panel surveys,* becomes attractive. In a longitudinal design, a sample of persons is repeatedly measured over time, and data from several waves of interviewing are combined at the analysis phase. Longitudinal measurement reveals patterns of phenomena that cannot be seen with cross-section samples, even cross-section samples repeated over time. For example, the percentage of families living in poverty remains rather stable over time in cross-sectional studies, although spells of poverty for individual families are transient and connected to life experiences like the death of a spouse or loss of employment—and these dynamics are best captured by longitudinal designs. A *fixed panel* longitudinal design is one in which a sample drawn at one point of time is followed over repeated waves. This permits inference about the experiences of the population that was present at the time when the original sample was drawn, but not about the population alive at the time of the last wave of the panel (reflecting that any changes in the population are not reflected in the previously drawn sample). To permit both analysis of change over time and inference to the population existent at multiple time points, the sample must be refreshed with new sample members at each wave for which cross-section inference is desired. Thus, many government surveys have *rotating panel* designs, which interview each sample member for a fixed number of times (say, six) but add fresh sample cases in each interviewing wave.

There are distinctive methodological and statistical problems with panel surveys. First, there are problems of attrition over waves of the panel from persons who initially provide data but then fail to do so in later waves. This affects the ability to study change, especially when those who leave the panel do so for reasons connected with the survey variables (e.g., in an epidemiological study of depression, the more severely depressed respondents may be more likely to refuse participation in later waves). Kasprzyk et al. (1989) provide an extensive review of attrition problems in longitudinal surveys.

Second, repeated measurement may systematically affect measurement error. For example, if reporting some life event extends the length of the interview through follow-up questions, respondents may learn this in the first wave, resulting in declined reports over successive waves in a panel survey (e.g., Cantor, 1989). Moreover, where change in reports over time may be expected, later waves of a panel survey tend to find this change to a larger degree than cross-sectional surveys (e.g., repeated measurement of unemployment status tends to show lower employment rates in later waves, beyond that exhibited by fresh cross-section samples).

Third, there is even evidence that measurement of a phenomenon at time 1 can affect true values at time 2. For example, asking respondents about their intention to vote (e.g., Greenwald, Carnot, Beach, & Young, 1987) or to buy certain consumer products (Morwitz, Johnson, & Schmittlein, 1993) has been found to influence actual behavior, an issue to which we return in our discussion of respondents' tasks.

Fourth, longitudinal surveys reveal measurement errors that are probably also present in cross-sectional data, although unobservable. For example, quarterly panel surveys that ask respondents to report income sources for each of the previous three months (say, January-February-March and April-May-June), observed smaller reported change across adjacent months within the three-month reference period (e.g., February-March) than between adjacent months forming the boundary between the reference periods of adjacent waves (e.g., March-April) (see Kalton & Miller, 1986). This phenomenon has been labeled the *seam effect* and is related to within period estimation and anchoring procedures. The repeated measurement of longitudinal surveys exposes this effect, but it is problematic but invisible in retrospective recall tasks in cross-section surveys.

As this discussion indicates, panel surveys extend the researcher's ability to draw causal inferences and to assess change over time. However, panel surveys are subject to specific problems of measurement error that require careful attention (see Groves, 1989, for a more detailed discussion). Having addressed the complexities of "whom to ask," we next turn to "how to ask."

ASKING AND ANSWERING SURVEY QUESTIONS: COGNITIVE AND COMMUNICATIVE PROCESSES

Quite obviously, survey estimates are only as meaningful as the answers that respondents provide. In the total survey error framework the questionnaire is one of the sources of measurement error (deviations between answers of respondents and some average or "true" value of the measured attribute). Although this fact has been recognized since the early days of survey research (see Payne, 1951, for an early review), survey methodology has long been characterized by rigorous theories of sampling on the one hand, and the so-called "art of asking questions" on the other hand. Despite a tradition of carrying out split-sample experiments within surveys in order to address practical problems of question form, wording, and context (see Schuman & Presser, 1981, for reviews and extensions of much of this early experimentation), it has only been recently that the cognitive and communicative processes underlying question answering in surveys have received sustained theoretical attention from psychologists. Drawing on theories of language comprehension, memory, and judgment, psychologists and survey methodologists have begun to formulate explicit models of the question answering process and have tested these models in tightly controlled laboratory experiments and split-sample surveys. Several recent volumes reflect the progress made in this area (Hippler, Schwarz, & Sudman, 1987; Jabine et al., 1984; Jobe & Loftus, 1991; Schwarz & Sudman, 1992, 1994, 1996; Sudman, Bradburn, & Schwarz, 1996; Tanur, 1992). Below, we introduce respondents' tasks and subsequently address implications for behavioral reports and attitude measurement.

Respondents' Tasks

Answering a survey question requires that respondents perform several tasks, as first emphasized by Cannell and his colleagues (Cannell, Marquis, & Laurent, 1977). Subsequent researchers built on their model (Strack & Martin, 1987; Tourangeau, 1984; Tourangeau & Rasinski, 1988). Not surprisingly, the first task of respondents consists of interpreting the question to understand what is meant. If the question is an attitude question, they may either retrieve a previously formed attitude judgment from memory, or they may "compute" a judgment on the spot. To do the latter, they need to retrieve relevant information from memory to form a mental representation of the target that they are to evaluate. In most cases, they will also need to retrieve or construct some standard against which the target is evaluated.

If the question is a behavioral question, respondents need to recall or reconstruct relevant instances of this behavior from memory. If the question specifies a reference period (such as "last week" or "last month"), they must also determine if these instances occurred during this reference period or not. Similarly, if the question refers to their "usual" behavior, respondents have to determine if the recalled or reconstructed instances are reasonably representative or if they reflect a deviation from their usual behavior. If they cannot recall or reconstruct specific instances of the behavior, or are not sufficiently motivated to engage in this effort, respondents may rely on their general knowledge or other salient information to compute an estimate.

Once a "private" judgment is formed in respondents' minds, they have to communicate it to the researcher. To do so, they may need to format their judgment to fit the response alternatives provided as part of the question, and in many instances the offered alternatives may both suggest and constrain what is retrieved from memory. Moreover, respondents may wish to edit their response before they communicate it, due to influences of social desirability and situational adequacy.

Accordingly, interpreting the question, generating an opinion or a representation of the relevant behavior, formatting the response, and editing the answer are the main psychological components of a process that starts with respondents' exposure to a survey question and ends with their overt report.

Question Comprehension   The key issue at the question comprehension stage is whether the respondent's understanding of the question does or does not match what the researcher had in mind: Is the attitude object, or the behavior, that the respondent identifies as the target of the question the one that the researcher intended? Does the respondent's understanding tap the same facet of the issue and the same evaluative dimension?

From a psychological point of view, question comprehension reflects the operation of two intertwined processes (see Clark & Schober, 1992; Strack, 1994; Strack & Schwarz, 1992). The first refers to the semantic understanding of the utterance. Comprehending the *literal meaning* of a sentence involves the identification of words, the recall of lexical information from semantic memory, and the construction of a meaning of the utterance, which is constrained by its context (see Mitchell, 1994; Simpson, 1994, for reviews). Not surprisingly, survey textbooks urge researchers to write simple questions and to avoid unfamiliar or ambiguous terms. Sudman and Bradburn's (1983) *Asking Questions* provides much useful advice in this regard.

However, understanding the words is not sufficient to answer a question. For example, if respondents are asked, "What have you done today?", they are likely to understand the meaning of the words. Yet, they still need to determine what kind of activities the researcher is interested in. Should they report, for example, that they took a shower? Hence, understanding a question in a way that allows an appropriate answer requires not only an understanding of the literal meaning of the question but involves inferences about the questioner's intention to determine the *pragmatic meaning* of the question.

To understand how respondents infer the intended meaning of a question, we need to consider the assumptions that govern the conduct of conversation in everyday life. These tacit assumptions were systematically described by Paul Grice (1975), a philosopher of language (see Clark & Schober, 1992; Schwarz, 1994; Strack, 1994; Strack & Schwarz, 1992, for applications to survey research and experiments). According to Grice's analysis, conversations proceed according to a cooperativeness principle, which can be expressed in the form of four maxims. A *maxim of quality* enjoins speakers not to say anything they believe to be false or lack adequate evidence for, and a *maxim of relation* enjoins speakers to make their contribution relevant to the aims of the ongoing conversation. In addition, a *maxim of quantity* requires speakers to make their contribution as informative as is required, but not more informative than is required, while a *maxim of manner* holds that the contribution should be clear rather than obscure, ambiguous, or wordy. In other words, speakers should try to be informative, truthful, relevant, and clear. As a result, "communicated information comes with a guarantee of relevance" (Sperber & Wilson, 1986, p. vi) and listeners interpret the speakers' utterances "on the assumption that they are trying to live up to these ideals" (Clark & Clark, 1977, p. 122). These tacit assumptions have important implications for question wording.

Response Alternatives Suppose, for example, that respondents are asked in an open response format, "What have you done today?" To give a meaningful answer, respondents have to determine which activities may be of interest to the researcher. In an attempt to be informative, respondents are likely to omit activities that the researcher is obviously aware of (e.g., "I gave a survey interview") or may take for granted anyway (e.g., "I took a shower"). If respondents were given a list of activities that included giving an interview and taking a shower, most respondents would endorse them. At the same time, however, such a list would reduce the likelihood that respondents report activities that are not represented on the list (see Schuman & Presser, 1981; Schwarz & Hippler, 1991, for reviews). Both of these question form effects reflect that response alternatives can clarify the intended meaning of a question, in the present example by specifying the activities the researcher is interested in. Moreover, the response alternatives may serve as reminders, bringing behaviors or opinions to mind that may otherwise not have been accessible. These processes result in pronounced differences between questions that use an *open* versus a *closed* response format (see Schuman & Presser, 1981, for examples).

Whereas the notion that response alternatives may clarify the meaning of a question may seem rather obvious in the above example, more subtle influences are frequently overlooked. Suppose that respondents are asked how frequently they felt "really irritated" recently. To answer this question, they again have to determine what the researcher means by "really irritated." Does this term refer to major or to minor annoyances? To identify the intended meaning of the question, they may consult the response alternatives provided by the researcher. If the response alternatives present low frequency categories, e.g., ranging from "less than once a year" to "more than once a month," respondents may conclude that the researcher has relatively rare events in mind and that the question cannot refer to minor irritations, which are likely to occur more often. Supporting this assumption, Schwarz, Strack, Müller, and Chassein (1988) observed that respondents reported examples of differentially extreme irritations, depending on the frequency range of the response alternatives presented to them.

Similarly, Schwarz et al. (1991) observed that respondents may use the specific numeric values provided as part of a rating scale to interpret the meaning of the scale's labels. A representative sample of German adults was asked, "How successful would you say you have been in life?" This question was accompanied by an 11-point rating scale, ranging from "not at all successful" (combined with the numeric values 0 or –5) to "extremely successful" (10 or +5). The results showed a pronounced impact of the numeric values of the rating scale. Whereas 34 percent endorsed a value below the midpoint of the 0 to 10 scale, only 13 percent endorsed one of the formally equivalent values on the –5 to +5 scale. Subsequent experiments indicated that this difference reflects differential interpretations of the term "not at all successful." When this label was combined with the numeric value of "0," respondents interpreted it to reflect the absence of success. However, when the same label was combined with the numeric value "–5," and the scale offered "0" as the midpoint, they interpreted it to reflect the presence of failure. In general, rating scales that use only positive numeric values suggest that the researcher has a unipolar dimension in mind (pertaining to the extremity of a single attribute, e.g., success), whereas a combination of negative and positive numeric values suggests that the researcher has a bipolar dimension in mind (pertaining to the presence of a given attribute or its opposite, e.g., success vs. failure).

Such findings demonstrate that respondents use the response alternatives in interpreting the meaning of a question. In doing so, they proceed on the tacit assumption that every contribution is relevant to the aims of the ongoing conversation. In the survey interview, as in laboratory experiments, these contributions include apparently formal features of questionnaire design, such as the numeric values given on a rating scale. Hence, identically worded questions may acquire different meanings, depending on the response alternatives by which they are accompanied (see Schwarz, 1996; Schwarz & Hippler, 1991, for more extended discussions).

Question Context Respondents' interpretation of a question's intended meaning is further influenced by the context in which the question is presented. Not surprisingly, this influence is more pronounced, the more ambiguous the wording of the question is. As an extreme case, consider research in which respondents are asked to report their opinion about a highly obscure—or even completely fictitious—issue, such as the "Agricultural Trade Act of 1978" (e.g., Bishop, Oldendick, & Tuchfarber, 1986; Schuman & Presser, 1981). Questions of this type reflect public opinion researchers' concern that the "fear of appearing uninformed" may induce "many respondents to conjure up opinions even when they had not given the particular issue any thought prior to the interview" (Erikson, Luttberg, & Tedin, 1988, p. 44). To explore how meaningful respondents' answers are, survey researchers introduced questions about issues that don't exist. Presumably, respondents' willingness to report an opinion on a fictitious issue casts some doubt on the reports provided in survey interviews in general. In fact, about 30 percent of a sample do typically provide an answer to issues that are invented by the researcher, although the percentage of such answers can be reduced by including an explicit "Don't Know" alternative as part of the question, thus providing more legitimacy to the admission of ignorance (see Schuman & Presser, 1981).

From a conversational point of view, however, the answers provided to fictitious issues may be more meaningful than has often been assumed. The sheer fact that a question about some issue is asked presupposes that the issue exists—or else asking a question about it would violate every norm of conversational conduct. Respondents, however, have no reason to assume that the researcher would ask a meaningless question and hence will try to make sense of it. If the interviewer does not provide additional clarification, they are likely to turn to the wording and context of the ambiguous question to determine its meaning, much as they would be expected to do in any other conversation. Once respondents have assigned a particular meaning to the issue, thus transforming the fictitious issue into a better defined issue that makes sense in the context of the interview, they may have no difficulty reporting a subjectively meaningful opinion. Even if they have not given the particular issue much thought, they may easily identify a broader set of issues to which this particular one apparently belongs, using their general attitude toward the broader set of issues to determine their attitude toward this particular one. Supporting this reasoning, Strack, Schwarz, and Wänke (1991, Experiment 1) observed that German university students favored the introduction of a fictitious "educational contribution" when a preceding question pertained to fellowships for students, but opposed it when it pertained to tuition. Open-ended responses confirmed that they used the content of the preceding question to determine the nature of the fictitious issue.

As the preceding examples illustrate, question comprehension is not primarily an issue of understanding the literal meaning of an utterance. Rather, question comprehension involves extensive inferences about the speaker's intentions to determine the pragmatic meaning of the question. To make these inferences, respondents draw on the nature of preceding questions as well as the response alternatives. Accordingly, survey methodologists' traditional focus on using the "right words" in questionnaire writing needs to be complemented by a consideration of the conversational processes involved in the question-answering process (see Bless, Strack, & Schwarz, 1993; Hilton, 1995; Schwarz, 1994, for a related discussion of psychological experiments).

Recalling Information and Computing a Judgment
Once respondents determined what the researcher is interested in, they need to recall relevant information from memory. In some cases, respondents may have direct access to a previously formed relevant judgment that they can offer as an answer. In most cases, however, they will not find an appropriate answer readily stored in memory and will need to compute a judgment on the spot. The processes involved in doing so are somewhat different for behavioral questions and attitude questions, and are discussed in the respective sections below.

Formatting the Response Having formed a judgment, respondents cannot typically report it in their own words. Rather, they are supposed to report it by endorsing one of the response alternatives provided by the researcher. This requires that they format their response in line with the options given. Accordingly, the researcher's choice of substantive response alternatives, and the order in which they are presented, may strongly affect survey results (see Schwarz & Hippler, 1991, for a review). We address some of these issues in more detail in the section on attitude measurement.

From a theoretical point of view, however, it is important to note that the influence of response alternatives is not limited to the formatting stage and that response alternatives are likely to influence other steps of the question-answering sequence as well, as we have seen in the section on question comprehension. The only effects that seem to occur unequivocally at the formatting stage pertain to the anchoring of rating scales (e.g., Ostrom & Upshaw, 1968; Parducci, 1983). As numerous studies demonstrate, respondents use the most extreme stimuli to anchor the endpoints of a rating scale. As a result, a given stimulus will be rated as less extreme if presented in the context of a more extreme one, than if presented in the context of a less extreme one. In Parducci's range-frequency model, this impact of the range of stimuli is referred to as the "range effect." In addition, if the number of stimuli to be rated is sufficiently large, respondents attempt to use all categories of the rating scale about equally often to be maximally informative. Accordingly, the specific ratings given also depend on the frequency distribution of the presented stimuli, an effect that is referred to as the "frequency effect" in Parducci's model (see Daamen & de Bie, 1992, for an application to survey research).

Editing the Response Finally, respondents may want to edit their response before they communicate it, reflecting considerations of social desirability and self-presentation (see DeMaio, 1984, for a review of the survey literature on this topic). Not surprisingly, editing on the basis of social desirability is particularly likely in response to threatening questions (DeMaio, 1984) and is more pronounced in fact-to-face interviews than in self-administered questionnaires, which provide a higher degree of confidentiality (e.g., Krysan et al., 1994; Smith, 1979). All methods designed to reduce socially desirable responding address one of these two factors.

A question is considered threatening when it pertains to a highly desirable or undesirable behavior or opinion. Respondents may find it embarrassing to admit that they did not engage in the desirable behavior or did engage in the undesirable one, resulting in over- and underreporting, respectively. Note that what is considered desirable or undesirable may often depend on the specific nature of the social situation: while admitting that one has tried drugs may seem threatening to a teenager when interviewed by an adult, admitting that one has never tried drugs may seem as threatening when interviewed by a peer. To reduce question threat, researchers often embed threatening questions among less threatening ones (e.g., by presenting the target behavior on a list with more innocuous ones). Moreover, one may try to normalize the undesirable behavior along the lines of, "As you know, many people have been killing their wives these days. Do you happen to have killed yours?" (see Barton, 1958, for amusing examples). To reduce overreporting of voting (a desirable behavior), for example, a question may read, "We know a lot of people aren't able to vote in every election. Do you happen to remember for certain whether you voted . . . ?" (Parry & Crossley, 1950).

More promising than these attempts, however, are strategies designed to guarantee the *privacy* of respondents' answers. In the simplest case, the threatening question may be presented in writing and the respondent may return the answer in a sealed envelope. A particularly elaborate version of this theme is known as the randomized response technique (e.g., Greenberg et al., 1969; Horvitz, Shaw, & Simmons, 1967; Warner, 1965). In one variant of this technique, the respondent is given a card with two questions, one innocuous ("Were you born in April?") and one threatening ("Have you ever taken heroin?"). Both of these questions can be answered "yes" or "no" and which question the respondent is to answer is determined by a probability mechanism, such as drawing a colored bead from a box. The interviewer and researcher remain unaware which color the respondent drew, thus making it impossible to determine which question a particular respondent answered. Knowledge of the proportion of different color beads in the box, however, allows researchers to estimate the proportion of respondents who answered "yes" to the heroin question. As a result, this procedure permits estimates for the sample as a whole but limits more detailed analysis because the responses cannot be linked to specific characteristics of the respondents. Sudman and Bradburn (1983, chap. 3) provide detailed advice on the use of different question wording and confidentiality techniques, and we encourage readers to consult their suggestions.

Although socially desirable responding is undoubtedly a threat to the validity of survey results, many of the more robust findings commonly cited as evidence of socially desirable response editing may be overdetermined and may reflect the impact of several distinct processes. For example, white respondents have frequently been found to mute negative sentiments about African Americans when the interviewer is black rather than white (e.g., Hatchett & Schuman, 1976; Williams, 1964). From a social desirability perspective, the answers they provide to the interviewer are assumed not to reflect their "true" attitude. However, the friendly conversation with a middle-class African American interviewer may itself serve as input into the attitude judgment, resulting in (temporary) "real" attitude change, much as exposure to liked African Americans has been found to affect attitudes towards the group in experimental studies (e.g., Bodenhausen, Schwarz, Bless, & Wänke, 1995). Hence, the impact of social desirability per se is often difficult to isolate in survey data. Furthermore, since considerations of social desirability certainly affect everyday behavior (for example, ordinary interactions between whites and blacks), social desirability should not be regarded as simply an artifact of survey interviewing, nor is it obvious that it should be entirely eliminated in a survey if the goal is to predict such everyday behavior.

Self-generated Validity: Consequences of Survey Participation   Although the question-answering sequence ends with the respondent's report, it is worth noting that the cognitive processes involved in question answering may change respondent's attitudes, intentions, and behaviors (see Feldman & Lynch, 1988; Feldman, 1992, for reviews). For example, Greenwald et al. (1987) demonstrated that asking respondents whether they intended to vote increased their actual participation in the election and Morwitz et al. (1993) observed that a single question about one's intention to buy a car increased the likelihood of actual purchases over the following six months. Throughout, the data suggest that such behavioral effects, if they occur, confirm the response provided in the survey, resulting in what Feldman and Lynch (1988) have termed self-generated validity.

Summary   This section reviewed what respondents must do to answer a question. For ease of exposition, respondents' tasks were presented in a sequential order. Although this order is plausible, respondents may obviously go back and forth between different steps, revising, for example, their initial question interpretation once the response alternatives suggest a different meaning. In any case, however, they have to determine the intended meaning of the question, recall relevant information from memory, form a judgment, and format the judgment to fit the response alternatives provided to them. Moreover, they may want to edit their private judgment before they communicate it.

Next, we turn to specific considerations that pertain to retrospective reports of behaviors and events and to reports of attitudes and opinions. Historically, questions about behaviors and events have been considered as pertaining to objective phenomena, reflecting that what actually happened could, at least in principle, be verified by independent observers, which does not hold for subjective phenomena, such as a person's attitudes or feelings. But "however clear the distinction between objective and subjective phenomena may be in principle, there is much blurring in practice" (Turner & Martin, 1984, p. 9). If one believes one has been a victim of a criminal act, or self-labels as "Black" or "Hispanic," for example, it is partially a

function of subjective definitions (see Turner & Martin, 1984). Moreover, many apparently factual reports are based on complex judgmental processes, thus blurring the distinction between presumably memory-based behavioral reports and presumably judgment-based attitude reports, which themselves require complex retrieval processes.

Asking Questions about Behaviors

Many survey questions about respondents' behavior are frequency questions, pertaining, for example, to how often the respondent has bought something, has seen a doctor, or has missed a day at work during some specified period of time. Survey researchers who ask these questions would ideally like the respondent to identify the behavior of interest; to scan the reference period; to retrieve all instances that match the target behavior; and to count these instances to determine the overall frequency of the behavior. This, however, is a route that respondents may infrequently take.

In fact, except for rare and very important behaviors, respondents are unlikely to have detailed representations of numerous individual instances of a behavior stored in memory. Rather, the details of various instances of closely related behaviors blend into one global representation (Linton, 1982; Neisser, 1986). Thus, many individual episodes become indistinguishable or irretrievable, due to interference from other similar instances (e.g., Baddeley & Hitch, 1977; Wagenaar, 1986), fostering the generation of knowledge-like representations that "lack specific time or location indicators" (Strube, 1987, p. 89). The finding that a single spell of unemployment is more accurately recalled than multiple spells (Mathiowetz, 1986), for example, suggests that this phenomenon does not apply only to mundane and unimportant behaviors, but also to repeated experiences that profoundly affect an individual's life. Accordingly, a "recall-and-count" model does not capture how people answer questions about frequent behaviors or experiences. Rather, their answers are likely to be based on some fragmented recall and the application of inference rules to compute a frequency estimate (see Bradburn, Rips, & Shevell, 1987; Pearson, Ross, & Dawes, 1992; Schwarz, 1990; Sudman et al., 1996, chap. 7–10, for reviews and the contributions in Schwarz & Sudman, 1994, for research examples). Below, we review strategies that facilitate recall and subsequently turn to the estimation strategies that respondents are most likely to use.

Recall Cues   If researchers are interested in obtaining reports that are based on recalled episodes, they may simplify respondents' task by providing appropriate recall cues and by restricting the recall task to a short and recent reference period. There are, however, important drawbacks to both of these strategies. Although the quality of recall will generally improve as the retrieval cues become more specific, respondents are likely to restrict their memory search to the particular cues presented to them, reflecting that the cues constrain the meaning of the question. As a result, respondents are likely to omit instances that do not match the specific cues, resulting in underreports if the list of cues is not exhaustive. Moreover, using a short reference period may result in many "zero" answers from respondents who rarely engage in the behavior, thus limiting later analyses to respondents with a high behavioral frequency.

If one decides to provide specific recall cues, one has to be aware that different cues are differentially effective. The date of an event is the poorest cue, whereas cues pertaining to what happened, where it happened, and who was involved have been found to be more effective (Wagenaar, 1986, 1988). In addition, recall will improve when respondents are given sufficient time to search memory. Recalling specific events may take up to several seconds (e.g., Reiser, Black, & Abelson, 1985), and repeated attempts to recall may result in the retrieval of additional material, even after a considerable number of previous trials (e.g., Williams & Hollan, 1981). Unfortunately, respondents are unlikely to have sufficient time to engage in repeated retrieval attempts in most research situations (and may often not be motivated to do so even if they had the time). This is particularly crucial in the context of survey research, where the available time per question is usually less than one minute (Groves & Kahn, 1979).

Moreover, the direction in which respondents search memory has been found to influence the quality of recall, in particular when the sequence of events does not have a natural temporal order (in contrast to one's educational history, for example). Specifically, better recall is achieved when respondents begin with the most recent occurrence of a behavior and work backward in time than when they begin at the beginning of the reference period (e.g., Loftus & Fathi, 1985; Whitten & Leonard, 1981). This presumably occurs because memory for recent occurrences is richer and the recalled instances may serve as cues for recalling previous ones. If the material has an inherent temporal order, however, this advantage may not be observed.

Even under optimal conditions, respondents will frequently be unable to recall an event or some of its critical details, even if they believed they would "certainly" remember it at the time it occurred (e.g., Linton, 1975; Thompson, 1982; Wagenaar, 1986). In general, the available evidence suggests that respondents are likely to underreport behaviors and events, which has led many researchers to assume that higher reports of mundane behaviors are likely to be more valid. Accordingly, a "the more the better" rule is frequently substituted for external validity checks, a rather risky assumption when extended to less mundane areas where there are pressures in both directions (for example, self-reports of sexual activity).

Dating Recalled Instances After recalling or reconstructing a specific instance of the behavior under study,

respondents have to determine if this instance occurred during the reference period. This requires that they understand the extent of the reference period and that they can accurately date the instance with regard to that period.

Reference periods that are defined in terms of several weeks or months are highly susceptible to misinterpretations. For example, the term "during the last twelve months" has been found to be construed as a reference to the last calendar year, as including or excluding the current month, and so on (Bradburn, Rips, & Shevell, 1987). Similarly, anchoring the reference period with a specific date, e.g., "Since March 1, how often . . .?" is not very helpful because respondents will usually not be able to relate an abstract date to meaningful memories. A more efficient way to anchor a reference period is the use of salient personal or public events, often referred to as temporal "landmarks" (Loftus & Marburger, 1983). Without a chance to relate a recalled event to a well-dated landmark, time dating is likely to reflect both "forward" and "backward" telescoping." That is, distant events are assumed to have happened more recently than they did, whereas recent events are assumed to be more distant than they are (see Bradburn, Huttenlocher, & Hedges, 1994; Sudman, Bradburn, & Schwarz, 1996, chap. 8, for reviews and a theoretical model).

Respondents' Estimation Strategies Given the difficulties of a "recall-and-count" strategy, it is not surprising that respondents rely on inference strategies to arrive at an estimate (see Sudman, Bradburn, & Schwarz, 1996, chap. 9). The most important strategies involve the decomposition of the recall problem into subparts, reliance on subjective theories of stability and change, and the use of information provided by the response alternatives.

Decomposition Strategies Many recall problems become easier when the recall task is decomposed into several subtasks (e.g., Blaire & Burton, 1987). To estimate how often she has been eating out during the last three months, for example, a respondent may determine that she eats out about every weekend and had dinner at a restaurant this Wednesday but apparently not the week before. Thus, she may infer that this makes 4 times a month for the weekends, and let's say twice for other occasions, resulting in about "eighteen times during the last three months." Estimates of this type are likely to be accurate if the respondent's inference rule is adequate and if exceptions to the usual behavior are rare.

In the absence of these fortunate conditions, however, decomposition strategies are likely to result in overestimates. People tend to overestimate the occurrence of low frequency events and to underestimate the occurrence of high frequency events (see Fiedler & Armbruster, 1994). As a result, asking for estimates of a global, and hence frequent, category (e.g., "eating out") may elicit an underestimate, whereas asking for estimates of a narrow, and hence rare, category (e.g., "eating at a Mexican restaurant") may elicit an overestimate. The observation that decomposition usually results in higher estimates therefore does not necessarily reflect better recall.

Subjective Theories   A particularly important inference strategy is based on subjective theories of stability and change (see Ross, 1989, for a review). In answering retrospective questions, respondents often use their current behavior or opinion as a benchmark and invoke an implicit theory of self to assess whether their past behavior or opinion was similar to, or different from, their present behavior or opinion. The resulting reports of previous opinions and behaviors are correct to the extent that the implicit theory is accurate.

In many domains, individuals assume a rather high degree of stability, resulting in underestimates of the degree of change that has occurred over time. Accordingly, retrospective estimates of income (Withey, 1954) or of tobacco, marijuana, and alcohol consumption (Collins, Graham, Hansen, & Johnson, 1985) were found to be heavily influenced by respondents' income or consumption habits at the time of interview. On the other hand, when respondents have reason to believe in change, they will detect change, even though none has occurred (see Ross, 1989). For example, respondents who participated in a study skills training (that did not improve their skills on any objective measure), subsequently recalled their skills prior to participation as considerably poorer than they had indicated in an earlier assessment. Presumably, they used their belief in the effectiveness of the training program to infer what their skills must have been before they "improved" (Conway & Ross, 1984).

Quantitative Response Alternatives   Another source of information that respondents use in arriving at an estimate is provided by the questionnaire itself. In many studies, respondents are asked to report their behavior by checking the appropriate alternative from a list of response alternatives of the type shown in Table 1. While the selected alternative is assumed to inform the researcher about the respondent's behavior, it is frequently overlooked that a given set of response alternatives may also constitute a source of information for the respondent, as we have already seen in the section on question comprehension. Specifically, respondents assume that the range of the response alternatives provided to them reflects the researcher's knowledge of, or expectations about, the distribution of the behavior in the "real world"—values in the middle range of the scale presumably reflect the "average" or "usual" behavioral frequency, whereas the extremes of the scale correspond to the extremes of the distribution. Given this assumption, respondents can use the range of

the response alternatives as a frame of reference in estimating their own behavioral frequency.

This strategy results in higher estimates along scales that present high rather than low frequency response alternatives, as shown in Table 1. In this study (Schwarz, Hippler, Deutsch, & Strack, 1985), only 16.2 percent of a sample of German respondents reported watching television for more than 2 1/2 hours a day when the scale presented low frequency response alternatives, whereas 37.5 percent reported doing so when the scale presented high frequency response alternatives. Similar results have been obtained for a wide range of different behaviors (see Schwarz & Hippler, 1991, for a review). As may be expected, the impact of response alternatives is more pronounced the more taxing the estimation task is (e.g., Bless, Bohner, Hild, & Schwarz, 1992) and the less episodic information is available (e.g., Schwarz & Bienias, 1990). In contrast, the impact of response alternatives is weak or absent when the question pertains to highly regular behaviors, for which respondents can draw on rate-of-occurrence information (e.g., "once a week"; Menon, 1994; Menon, Rhagubir, & Schwarz, 1995).

In addition to affecting respondents' behavioral reports, response alternatives may also influence subsequent comparative judgments. For example, a frequency of "2 1/2 hours per day" constitutes a high response on the low frequency scale, but a low response on the high frequency scale shown in Table 1. A respondent who checks this alternative may therefore infer that her own television consumption is above average in the former case, but below average in the latter. As a result, Schwarz et al. (1985) observed that respondents were less satisfied with the variety of things they do in their leisure time when the low frequency scale suggested that they watch more television than most other people (see Schwarz, 1990, for a review). Moreover, such comparison effects may even be obtained under conditions where the behavioral report itself is not influenced by the response alternatives (e.g., Menon et al., 1995).

To avoid systematic influences of response alternatives, it is advisable to ask frequency questions in an open response format, such as "How many hours a day do you watch TV? ___ hours per day." Note that such an open format needs to specify the relevant units of measurement (e.g., "hours per day") to avoid nonnumeric answers.

Vague Quantifiers   As another alternative, researchers are often tempted to use vague quantifiers, such as "sometimes," "frequently," and so on. This, however, is the worst possible choice (see Pepper, 1981, for an extensive review). Most importantly, the same expression denotes different frequencies in different content domains. Thus, "frequently" suffering from headaches reflects higher absolute frequencies than "frequently" suffering from heart attacks.

TABLE 1
Reported Daily Television Consumption as a Function of Response Alternatives

Reported Daily Television Consumption			
Low Frequency Alternatives		**High Frequency Alternatives**	
Up to $^1/_2$ h	7.4%	Up to $2^1/_2$ h	62.5%
$^1/_2$ h to 1 h	17.7%	$2^1/_2$ h to 3 h	23.4%
1 h to $1^1/_2$ h	26.5%	3 h to $3^1/_2$ h	7.8%
$1^1/_2$ h to 2 h	14.7%	$3^1/_2$ h to 4 h	4.7%
2 h to $2^1/_2$ h	17.7%	4 h to $4^1/_2$ h	1.6%
More than $2^1/_2$ h	16.2%	More than $4^1/_2$ h	0.0%

Note: N = 132. Adapted from Schwarz, N., Hippler, H. J., Deutsch, B., & Strack, F. (1985). Response scales: Effects of category range on reported behavior and comparative judgments. *Public Opinion Quarterly, 49,* 388–395. Reprinted by permission.

Moreover, different respondents use the same term to denote different objective frequencies of the same behavior. For example, suffering from headaches "occasionally" denotes a higher frequency for respondents with than without a medical history of migraine. Accordingly, the use of vague quantifiers reflects the objective frequency relative to respondents' subjective standard, rendering vague quantifiers inadequate for the assessment of objective frequencies, despite the popularity of their use.

Proxy-reports: Questions about Other Household Members The difficulties associated with retrospective behavioral reports are compounded when the questions pertain to the behavior of other household members rather than to the respondent's own behavior. Such *proxy-reports* are routinely collected in major government surveys when the other household members are not available for an interview, thus eliminating the need of return visits or repeated calls to the same household. Survey researchers usually assume that self-reports are more complete and accurate than proxy-reports and the available literature is compatible with this assumption (see Moore, 1988, for a review). Many of the available comparisons of self- and proxy-reports, however, are seriously flawed because proxy-reports are only accepted when the target person is not available, thus introducing possible selection biases.

Experimental studies, based on the collection of self- and proxy-reports from two members of the same household, obtained moderate degrees of agreement between self- and proxy-respondents (e.g., Mingay, Shevell, Bradburn, & Ramirez, 1994; Skowronski, Betz, Thompson, Walker, & Shannon, 1994; Sudman, Bickart, Blair, & Menon, 1994). Not surprisingly, agreement is highest for

behaviors in which both household members participated (reaching $r = 0.8$ for frequency reports in some cases) and lowest for individual behaviors that are rarely discussed in the household (with r's hovering around 0.4). Frequently discussed individual behaviors fall in between these extremes (with r's around 0.6).

Note that self-reports are reports of an actor about his or her own behavior, whereas proxy-reports are reports of an observer about a (well-known) other's behavior. Accordingly, we may bring basic research on actor-observer differences in social perception (Jones & Nisbett, 1971) to bear on these tasks. As experimental research in social psychology demonstrated (see Watson, 1982, for a review), observers are more likely to draw on the actor's disposition in explaining his or her behavior than is the actor him- or herself. Hence, proxy-respondents may derive their reports to a larger degree from their assumptions about the actor's disposition, a tendency that is further facilitated by their lack of situational knowledge when they did not themselves participate in the respective behavior. Consistent with this assumption, several experiments indicated the proxy-reports are more likely to be derived from dispositional information than self-reports, which are more likely to be based on episodic information (Schwarz & Wellens, in press).

As a result of these different strategies, proxy-reports on related issues show a higher internal consistency than self-reports, since related judgments are derived from the same dispositional information. Hence, the internal consistency of proxy-reports should not be taken as evidence for their accuracy. Moreover, proxy-respondents underestimate the variability of the actor's behavior over time. Accordingly, proxy-reports and self-reports of behavioral frequencies show low convergence for short and recent reference periods, for which the actor can draw on episodic information in providing a self-report. As the actor's access to episodic information decreases due to longer or more distant reference periods, however, the actor has to rely on dispositional information as well. As a result, the convergence of self- and proxy-reports increases, although this increase presumably reflects reliance on the same inference strategies rather than higher accuracy (Schwarz & Wellens, in press).

Summary   The findings reviewed in this section emphasize that retrospective behavioral reports are rarely based on adequate recall of relevant episodes. Rather, the obtained reports are to a large degree theory driven: respondents are likely to begin with some fragmented recall of the behavior under study and to apply various inference rules to arrive at a reasonable estimate. Moreover, if quantitative response alternatives are provided, they are likely to use them as a frame of reference, resulting in systematic biases. Although researchers have developed a number of strategies to facilitate recall, it is important to keep in mind that the best we can hope for is a reasonable estimate, unless the behavior is rare and of considerable importance to respondents.

Asking Questions about Attitudes

The goal of many surveys is to learn about the distribution and correlates of attitudes in a population by collecting reports from a representative sample. The extent to which the collected data do indeed inform us about the attitudes held in the population depends crucially on the research instrument used. As we have seen in the discussion of respondents' tasks, respondents' interpretation of a question, or the information they draw on in forming a judgment, may be strongly influenced by the specific wording of the question or by the content of other questions. As a result, the research instrument may draw respondents' attention to aspects they may otherwise not consider or may bring information to mind that would otherwise go unnoticed. Survey researchers refer to all such influences of the research instrument as *response effects*.

From a total survey perspective, response effects are a component of measurement error. However, this is a somewhat misleading term in the case of attitude measurement. Whereas reports about behaviors or events can—at least in principle—be verified, attitude reports always reflect subjective evaluative judgments. Human judgment, however, is always context dependent. If we want to talk of "errors" in attitude measurement at all, we can only do so relative to what we were trying to measure in the questionnaire, not relative to any objective standard that reflects respondents'

"true" attitudes. In fact, the assumption that there exist attitudes entirely independent of how they are assessed can itself be seen as a version of the well-known fundamental attribution error, the tendency to overestimate the importance of personal and dispositional factors relative to situational influences (Ross, 1977). In survey research, this error manifests itself in taking marginals too seriously as indicators of the dispositions of the general public (see Schuman, 1983). For example, if 10 percent of a sample say spontaneously that they have "no opinion" on an issue, this does not imply that the other 90 percent do have firm opinions— simply introducing a "no opinion" response alternative is likely to raise that 10 percent two-fold or more. Hence, to interpret answers as representing in a literal way the inner dispositions of a population is to forget the extent to which survey responses are shaped by situational influences.

The psychology of response effects is essentially the psychology of human judgment, with which social psychologists are familiar. Below, we address issues of question wording and question order, focusing on some classic examples and recent applications of social cognition theorizing to survey measurement. Comprehensive reviews of the survey literature, including issues not addressed here, are provided by Bradburn (1983) and Schuman and Presser (1981). In addition, the classic volumes by Cantril (1944) and Payne (1951) have lost none of their original importance. For a more detailed discussion of recent cognitive research see Sudman et al. (1966, chap. 4–6).

Question Wording   Textbooks typically urge researchers to write attitude questions that are "fair" and "unbiased." Although sound in principle, this advice is difficult to implement because the social issues addressed in attitude questions are usually complex, whereas survey questions necessarily need to be kept simple. Hence, survey questions typically tap only one facet of an issue and the obtained results may look rather different if a different facet had been addressed. Accordingly, many researchers have cautioned against reliance on a single item measure and have urged researchers "to ask a sufficient number of different questions to permit an assessment of the effects of question wording" (Turner & Martin, 1984, p. 77; see also Schuman, 1986). Due to time and budget constraints, however, this advice is more often offered than heeded.

Studies that explored different question wordings have repeatedly demonstrated that apparently minor changes in the exact wording of a question can lead to major changes in the obtained responses (see Bradburn, 1983; Schuman & Presser, 1981, for reviews), though exactly what is a minor and what is a major change in wording is not always obvious (Schuman, 1986). These findings reflect differences in question meaning as well as differences in the constraints imposed upon respondents.

Question Meaning　Survey researchers usually distinguish between *substantive* and *nonsubstantive* changes in question wording (e.g., Schuman & Presser, 1981), although this distinction may be problematic, as will become apparent below. Substantive differences reflect that different questions on the same issue may tap different aspects, such as when a question about gun control asks, "Would you favor or oppose a law that would require a person to obtain a police permit before he or she can buy a gun?" versus "Would you favor or oppose a law that would ban possession of guns, except by police and military authorities?" Although both questions pertain to the issue of "gun control," it is not surprising—and not problematic for the validity of survey data—that the different aspects emphasized by these questions elicit different opinions (see Schuman & Presser, 1981; Turner & Martin, 1984, for additional examples). Such findings emphasize, however, that users of survey data must be careful not to misinterpret responses to one facet of an issue as responses to the issue in general. What is called an issue is often a constellation of issues, and its specific components (e.g., gun permits versus banning of guns) may be of more interest than the overall rubric. Furthermore, an attempt to finesse the problem by asking an overall summary question (for example, "Do you favor or oppose gun control?") invites quite different interpretations of the term "gun control," which may in turn be based on variations in context or personal predisposition.

Other changes in question wording may affect responses by eliciting differently loaded associations, thus affecting respondents' construal of the issue. For example, introducing a reference to "communist" activities has frequently been found to increase Americans' support for their country's military operations (e.g., Mueller, 1973; Schuman & Presser, 1981), presumably because the term "communist" brings information to mind that is otherwise not considered. For this reason, textbook knowledge urges researchers not to use "loaded" terms. Note, however, that not using loaded terms that are common in public discourse, but are considered inappropriate by the researcher, may also elicit responses that deviate from respondents' spontaneous reasoning about the issue. Thus, it may not be the use of loaded terms per se, but the match between the wording of the question and the terms spontaneously used by respondents that is likely to be the crucial issue.

Other changes in question wording, however, seem less substantive in nature, although closer inspection reveals that they may change respondents' cognitive task. The best known of these so-called nonsubstantive wording changes, and the one that produced probably the largest wording effect documented in the literature, is the forbid-allow asymmetry originally reported by Rugg (1941; see Schuman & Presser, 1981, for replications and extensions). Respondents are either asked whether something should be "allowed" (yes or no) or whether it should be "forbidden" (yes or no). The general finding is that respondents are more likely to say that the behavior under investigation should not be forbidden than that it should be allowed, and are more likely to say that it should not be allowed than that it should be forbidden. In essence, respondents are more likely to say "no" rather than "yes" to each form of the question. In Rugg's data, for example, only 25 percent of the respondents were willing to allow "speeches against democracy," but 46 percent were against forbidding such speeches.

An analysis of the cognitive processes underlying this phenomenon (Hippler & Schwarz, 1986) suggests that respondents define their task differently depending on the form of the question. Most importantly, respondents focus on the implication of doing what they are asked about, namely, forbidding or allowing something, rather than on the implications of not doing it. For this reason, indifferent respondents respond "no" to both question forms because they neither want to support the issue by allowing something, nor do they want to oppose the issue by forbidding something. Accordingly, a majority of 73.3 percent of the respondents who were considered "indifferent" on the basis of previous questions preferred not to "allow" the behavior under investigation when asked the allow version of the question, whereas a majority of 81.2 percent preferred not to "forbid" the behavior when asked the forbid version of the question (Hippler & Schwarz, 1986). Thus, a "nonsubstantive" change in question wording focused respondents' attention on the implications of different acts, namely, forbidding or allowing. Moreover, respondents apparently missed the implications of the absence of these acts, namely, that not forbidding amounts to allowing and vice versa, thus exhibiting a well-known cognitive bias termed the "feature positive effect" (e.g., Fazio, Sherman, & Herr, 1982).

As these examples illustrate, minor changes in question wording may result in different construals of question meaning, resulting in markedly different responses. Moreover, the meaning of a question may not only change as a function of changes in the question stem, but also as a function of changes in apparently formal features, such as the numeric values of a rating scale (e.g., Schwarz, Knäuper, et al., 1991), as discussed in the section on question comprehension.

There is an important qualification to the sensitivity of survey results to apparently minor changes in wording. Although the original forbid/allow difference discovered by Rugg (1941) was replicated some 35 years later by Schuman & Presser (1981), the latter researchers found that both versions of the question showed similar substantial change over time. Thus an investigator using either version and keeping it constant at both time points would have concluded that American tolerance for dissent had increased significantly over the intervening decades. This finding reflects a common assumption and typical finding in survey research: correlational results are less sensitive to response effects than are single item distributions or "marginals" (Stouffer & DeVinney, 1949). This assumption is not without exceptions, however, as later examples will indicate.

Question Constraint　　The observation that respondents ordinarily accept the framework provided by a question and try to answer within it is referred to as *question constraint*. Although the concept of question constraint has typically been applied to response alternatives, it is worth noting that every question imposes a perspective that is usually taken for granted by respondents (see Clark & Schober, 1992). For example, in 1980, British respondents were asked, "The government believes that in the interest of fighting inflation, local authority [municipal] workers should get no more than a 6 percent pay raise this time. Do you agree with this view or do you think they should get more?" As Turner and Martin (1984, p. 80) noted, this question introduces the presupposition that a ceiling on increases in pay will fight inflation, yet this presupposition is not the subject matter of the question. However, respondents are likely to work within the constraints of the question presented to them, selecting one of the response alternatives rather than questioning the entailed presupposition. Researchers therefore need to keep in mind that it is they, not the respondents, who are determining the framework within which survey answers are given.

Respondents' tendency to work within the constraints imposed by the question is particularly apparent with regard to "*don't know*" (DK) or "*no opinion*" responses. Standard survey questions usually omit "no opinion" as an explicit option, but instruct interviewers to accept this response when volunteered. Experimental studies (e.g., Bishop, Oldendick, & Tuchfarber, 1983; Schuman & Presser, 1981) have consistently found that respondents are more likely to report not having an opinion when a DK option is explicitly offered (see Schwarz & Hippler, 1991, for a review). Similarly, many respondents prefer a *middle alternative* between two extreme positions when offered, but endorse one of the extremes when the middle alternative is omitted (e.g., Bishop, 1987; Kalton, Collins, & Brook, 1980; Schuman & Presser, 1981). Thus, most respondents assume that the rules of the game call for working within the categories offered, even though a desire to answer otherwise is evident when more choice is provided. As Clark and Schober (1992) noted, however, acceptance of the constraints imposed by the questioner is not unique to survey interviews but characterizes question answering in more natural contexts as well, although its effects may be less apparent in daily conversations.

The extent to which question constraint can affect answers has been demonstrated in two experiments on open and closed questions (Schuman & Scott, 1987). The first experiment showed that when a widely used open-ended question about "the most important problem facing this country today" was converted into a closed question listing four specific problems, the listed responses rose dramatically ("quality of public schools" increased from 1 percent to 32 percent), while almost none of the common responses to the open question (e.g., "unemployment") were offered much despite the encouragement for "other" answers. Lest this suggest that the solution to avoiding question constraint is to ask open questions, a second experiment showed that an open inquiry about important events of the past half century elicited only a few mentions of "the invention of the computer," but when the invention of the computer was included as an alternative in a closed question, it was the most frequently chosen answer, exceeding even World War II which had been the leading mention to the open question. In this case, other evidence suggested that the computer response was indeed highly important to respondents, but that the open question had unintentionally limited the scope of thinking to events of a political nature. Thus, there is no purely formal way to avoid question constraint entirely in survey questioning, and investigators need to constantly be aware of the limits they are themselves imposing on their respondents.

Summary　　Our selective discussion of issues of question wording indicates that apparently minor changes in the specific wording of the question stem, or in the response alternatives presented, may have a pronounced impact on the obtained responses. Whereas some observers concluded from such findings that respondents provide relatively meaningless answers, or else their opinions wouldn't change as a function of minor wording changes (e.g., Crossen, 1994), we prefer a more optimistic summary. In our reading, these findings indicate that respondents pay close attention to the question asked, treating the specifics of the wording and the response alternatives offered as relevant contributions to the ongoing conversation. As noted earlier, this is, indeed, what they are entitled to on the basis of the tacit norms that govern the conduct of conversation. Moreover, respondents draw on these specifics in their efforts to infer the meaning intended by the questioner, much as the tacit rules of conversational conduct would want them to (see Schwarz, 1994, 1996, for a more detailed discussion). Hence, the apparent artifacts of question wording are likely to reflect regularities of normal conversational conduct, except that we as researchers often fail to take these regularities into account in writing questions and interpreting answers.

Question Order: The Emergence of Context Effects

Survey researchers have long been aware that the order in

which questions are asked may strongly influence the obtained results, as numerous studies illustrate (see Bradburn, 1983; Schuman & Presser, 1981; Sudman et al., 1996; Tourangeau & Rasinski, 1988, for reviews and the contributions in Schwarz & Sudman, 1992, for recent examples). From a theoretical point of view, it is important to emphasize that *question order* is a technical aspect of a questionnaire and does not constitute, by itself, a meaningful psychological variable. Rather, the content of preceding questions may affect any of the steps of the question-answering process that we outlined above, involving a number of different psychological processes. Moreover, any given order effect may reflect the impact of several of these processes. Disentangling the relative contribution of different processes in a given case presents a difficult task and some of the more robust "classic" context effects are likely to be overdetermined. In addition, we can only speak of *order effects* in the strict meaning of the term when the questions are presented in a face-to-face or telephone interview. In mail surveys and other self-administered questionnaires, respondents may potentially read subsequent questions before answering preceding ones, or may backtrack and change previous responses, thus obliterating the impact of presentation order. In that case, subsequent questions may influence responses to preceding ones, as has been observed in several studies (e.g., Schwarz & Hippler, 1995). Hence, we prefer the term *context effect* in the present chapter.

What, however, are the processes that underlie the emergence of context effects? Below, we review the key candidates following the sequence of respondents' tasks introduced above (see Sudman et al., 1996, chap. 3–6, for a more detailed discussion).

Question Comprehension   As a first possibility, the content of preceding questions (or subsequent ones, if presented in a self-administered questionnaire) may influence respondents' interpretation of later questions, resulting in context effects at the comprehension stage, as already seen in the section on respondents' tasks. These influences may reflect the operation of relatively automatic semantic priming processes as well as the operation of relatively deliberate pragmatic inferences (see Strack, 1992a). Thus, respondents may automatically encode an ambiguous question in terms of an applicable concept rendered accessible by a preceding question (see Higgins, 1989; Wyer & Srull, 1989, for reviews), or they may deliberately refer to preceding questions to infer the intended meaning of the ambiguous one.

Note in this regard that the situation of survey respondents differs from the situation of subjects in psychological priming experiments (e.g., Higgins, Rholes, & Jones, 1977). In these experiments, the priming episode is usually disguised and separated from the judgment episode, and

both are often introduced as separate experiments. Hence, subjects who are aware that a certain piece of information may come to mind because it was part of the preceding, presumably unrelated, experiment are likely to correct for undue influences, resulting in contrast effects (e.g., Lombardi, Higgins, & Bargh, 1987; Martin, 1986; Strack, Schwarz, Bless, Kübler, & Wänke, 1993). Survey respondents, on the other hand, may see little reason to disregard previously used information. Based on the assumption that different contributions to an ongoing conversation build on one another, they may deliberately draw on the content of preceding questions to infer the question's intended meaning, which usually results in an assimilation to the meaning of preceding questions.

An important exception is worth noting, however. Rules of conversational conduct request speakers to provide information that is new to the recipient, rather than to reiterate information that has already been given (see Clark & Haviland's, 1977, given-new contract). Application of this rule to the survey interview may lead respondents to interpret a subsequent question as a request for new information, thus inducing them to disregard information that they have already provided, as the following example may illustrate. Schwarz, Strack, and Mai (1991; see also Strack, Martin, & Schwarz, 1988; Tourangeau, Rasinski, & Bradburn, 1991) first asked respondents to report their happiness with their marriage and subsequently their satisfaction with their life as a whole. When these questions were presented on different pages of the questionnaire, respondents included the highly accessible information about their marriage when answering the general life-satisfaction question, resulting in a correlation of $r = 0.67$. For other respondents, however, both questions were placed in the same conversational context by a joint lead-in that read, "We now have two questions about your life." Under this condition, the correlation dropped to $r = 0.18$. Apparently, these respondents interpreted the general life-satisfaction question as if it were worded, "Aside from your marriage, which you already told us about, how satisfied are you with *other* aspects of your life?" Consistent with this assumption, a condition in which this reworded general question was presented resulted in a highly similar correlation of $r = 0.20$.

In summary, respondents are likely to draw on the content of preceding questions in interpreting subsequent ones. This will usually result in an assimilation of question meaning, unless this renders the second question redundant, thus violating conversational norms of nonredundancy.

Recall and Judgment   Most context effects at the judgment stage reflect the increased accessibility of information that was used to answer preceding questions. However, they may take different forms depending on whether the information rendered accessible pertains to features of the target of judgment or a general norm. We address these possibilities below. In addition, the process of answering a question may elicit subjective experiences, such as whether it is easy or difficult to answer a given question, and these experiences may themselves provide information that is used in making subsequent judgments (see Clore, 1992, for a review of that literature, which we do not address here).

General Norms   A context effect that reflects the activation of a general norm was first reported by Hyman and Sheatsley (1950). In 1948, they asked Americans if "the United States government should let Communist reporters from other countries come in here and send back to their papers the news as they see it." When this question appeared in the first position, only 36 percent of the American sample supported freedom of press for communist reporters. However, when respondents were first asked if "a Communist country like Russia should let American newspaper reporters come in," a proposition that most respondents endorsed, support for communist reporters in the United States increased to 73 percent. Endorsing freedom of the press for American reporters in Russia apparently made respondents aware that the same principle should hold reciprocally for communist reporters in the United States. In subsequent research, Schuman and colleagues (Schuman & Ludwig, 1983; Schuman & Presser, 1981) traced this and related findings to the operation of a norm of "reciprocity" or "even-handedness." Moreover, this is a case where holding context constant over time may not lead to unequivocal conclusions about change. When the Hyman and Sheatsley (1950) experiment was replicated three decades later, the condition that implicitly elicited the norm of reciprocity showed no change at all (i.e., the force of the norm of reciprocity had not altered over time). However, the condition that emphasized the attitude object (communist reporters) revealed substantial change (fear of communists had evidently declined from its 1950 level).

Although the empirical evidence is currently limited to the impact of reciprocity norms, we may expect that any question, or question sequence, that draws respondents' attention to a general norm is likely to elicit an application of this norm in making subsequent judgments to which the norm is applicable.

Features of the Target: Conditions of Assimilation and Contrast   Most question order effects discussed in the survey literature occur because preceding questions increase the cognitive accessibility of aspects of the target that respondents may draw on in forming subsequent judgments. The underlying processes have been conceptualized in several models that are consistent with current theorizing in social cognition (Feldman, 1992; Feldman & Lynch, 1988; Schwarz & Bless, 1992a; Schwarz & Strack, 1991;

Strack, 1994, Strack & Martin, 1987; Tourangeau, 1987, 1992; Tourangeau & Rasinski, 1988). Our selective discussion draws on the inclusion/exclusion model proposed by Schwarz and Bless (1992a), which is highly similar to Tourangeau's (1992) belief-sampling model in its conceptualization of assimilation effects, but has the advantage of offering an explicit conceptualization of contrast effects, which is absent in other models.

Mental representations   Schwarz and Bless (1992a) assume that evaluative judgments require a representation of the target (i.e., the object of judgment), as well as a representation of some standard against which the target is evaluated. Both representations are context dependent and include information that is chronically accessible as well as information that is only temporarily accessible, for example, because it was used to answer a preceding question. How accessible information influences the judgment depends on how it is used. Information that is *included* in the temporary representation that respondents form of the target results in *assimilation effects*. The size of assimilation effects increases with the amount and extremity of temporarily accessible information and decreases with the amount and extremity of chronically accessible information included in the representation of the target.

For example, Schwarz, Strack, and Mai (1991) asked respondents to report their marital satisfaction and their general life-satisfaction in different question orders. As noted earlier, the correlation between both questions increased from $r = 0.32$ in the life-marriage order to $r = 0.67$ in the marriage-life order, reflecting that marital information rendered accessible by the preceding question was included in the representation formed of one's life in general (provided that conversational norms did not prohibit its use). This increase in correlation was attenuated, $r = 0.43$, when questions about three different life-domains (job, leisure time, and marriage) preceded the general question, thus bringing a more diverse range of information to mind.

However, the same piece of accessible information that may elicit an assimilation effect may also result in a *contrast effect*. This is the case when the information is *excluded* from, rather than included in, the cognitive representation formed of the target. As a first possibility, suppose that a given piece of information with positive (negative) implications is excluded from the representation of the target category. If so, the representation will contain less positive (negative) information, resulting in less positive (negative) judgments. This possibility is referred to as a *subtraction based* contrast effect (see Bradburn, 1983; Schuman & Presser, 1981, for related suggestions). The size of subtraction based contrast effects increases with the amount and extremity of the temporarily accessible information that is excluded from the representation of the target, and decreases with the amount and extremity of the information that remains in the representation of the target.

For example, happily married respondents in the Schwarz, Strack, and Mai (1991) study, discussed above, reported lower general life-satisfaction when the operation of conversational norms induced them to disregard their happy marriage, whereas unhappily married respondents reported higher life-satisfaction under this condition. These diverging effects reduced the correlation from $r = 0.67$ to $r = 0.18$ when the same questions, asked in the same order, were introduced by a joint lead-in, as discussed earlier. Such subtraction based contrast effects are limited to the specific target, reflecting that merely "subtracting" a piece of information only affects this specific representation.

As a second possibility, respondents may not only exclude accessible information from the representation formed of the target but may also use this information in constructing a standard of comparison or scale anchor. If the implications of the temporarily accessible information are more extreme than the implications of the chronically accessible information used in constructing a standard or scale anchor, they result in a more extreme standard, eliciting contrast effects for that reason. The size of *comparison based* contrast effects increases with the extremity and amount of temporarily accessible information used in constructing the standard or scale anchor, and decreases with the amount and extremity of chronically accessible information used in making this construction. In contrast to subtraction based comparison effects, which are limited to a specific target, comparison based contrast effects may generalize to all targets to which the standard is applicable.

As an example, consider the impact of political scandals on assessments of the trustworthiness of politicians. Not surprisingly, thinking about a politician who was involved in a scandal, say Richard N., decreases trust in politicians in general, reflecting that the exemplar can be included in the representation formed of the political class. If the trustworthiness question pertains to a specific politician, however, say Bill C., the primed exemplar cannot be included in the representation formed of the target—after all, Bill C. is not Richard N. In this case, Richard N. may serve as a standard of comparison, relative to which Bill C. seems very trustworthy. An experiment with German exemplars confirmed these predictions (Schwarz & Bless, 1992b): thinking about a politician who was involved in a scandal decreased the trustworthiness of politicians in general, but increased the trustworthiness of all specific exemplars assessed. In general, the same information is likely to result in assimilation effects in evaluations of wide target categories (which allow for the inclusion of a variety of information), but is likely to result in contrast effects in evaluations of narrow target categories. These judgmental processes are reflected in a wide range of discrepancies between general and specific judgments in public opinion research. For example, Americans distrust congress in gen-

eral but trust their own representative (e.g., Erikson, Luttberg, & Tedin, 1988), and they support capital punishment in general but are less likely to apply it in any specific case (e.g., Ellsworth & Gross, 1994). Moreover, members of minority groups consistently report high levels of discrimination against their group, yet also report that they personally have experienced much less of it. In each case, these patterns are to be expected when we take into account that recalling extreme and vivid instances drives the general and the specific judgments in opposite directions, as predicted on theoretical grounds.

Determinants of inclusion/exclusion Schwarz and Bless (1992a) assume that the default operation is to include information that comes to mind in the representation of the target. This suggests that we should be more likely to see assimilation rather than contrast effects in survey research. In contrast, the exclusion of information needs to be triggered by salient features of the question-answering process. In principle, *any* variable that affects the categorization of information is likely to affect the emergence of assimilation and contrast effects, linking the model to cognitive research on categorization processes in general. The most relevant variables can be conceptualized as bearing on three implicit decisions that respondents have to make with regard to the information that comes to mind.

Some information that comes to mind may simply be irrelevant, pertaining to issues that are unrelated to the question asked. Other information may potentially be relevant to the task at hand and respondents have to decide what to do with it. The first decision bears on why this information comes to mind. Information that seems to come to mind for the "wrong reason," e.g., because respondents are aware of the potential influence of a preceding question, is likely to be excluded (e.g., Lombardi et al., 1987; Strack et al., 1993). This exclusion condition may be more likely to be met under laboratory conditions, where the priming phase and the judgment phase are deliberately separated, than under survey interview conditions, as noted above. The second decision bears on whether the information that comes to mind "belongs to" the target category or not. The content of the context question (e.g., Schwarz & Bless, 1992a), the width of the target category (e.g., Schwarz & Bless, 1992b), the extremity of the information (e.g., Herr, 1986), or its representativeness for the target category (e.g., Strack, Schwarz, & Gschneidinger, 1985) are relevant at this stage. Finally, conversational norms of nonredundancy may elicit the exclusion of previously provided information (e.g., Schwarz, Strack, & Mai, 1991; Strack et al., 1988), as discussed in the section on question comprehension.

Whenever any of these decisions results in the exclusion of information from the representation formed of the target, it will elicit a contrast effect. Whether this contrast effect is limited to the target, or generalizes across related targets, depends on whether the excluded information is merely subtracted from the representation of the target or is used in constructing a standard or scale anchor. Whenever the information that comes to mind is included in the representation formed of the target, on the other hand, it results in an assimilation effect. Hence, the model predicts the emergence, direction, size, and generalization of context effects in attitude measurement.

A caveat needs to be added, however. Although researchers can reliably produce the theoretically predicted effects when the questions are written to clearly operationalize the relevant variables, it is often impossible to predict the effects of a given question that has been written with other goals in mind. Hence, the applied utility of the theoretical models in this area is more limited than survey practitioners may hope for. Nevertheless, social cognition theorizing has provided a useful framework for understanding context effects at the judgment stage. Next, we turn to issues of formatting and editing.

Formatting   At the formatting stage, the content of preceding questions may affect how respondents anchor a rating scale. As discussed in our review of respondents' tasks, this may result in shifts in the obtained ratings as predicted by Ostrom and Upshaw's (1968) perspective theory and Parducci's (1983) range-frequency model.

Editing   Finally, preceding questions may draw respondents' attention to issues of social desirability and self-presentation, resulting in biases in responses to subsequent questions to which these concerns may be relevant. This seems particularly likely when the issue is not sufficiently sensitive to elicit these concerns spontaneously. We would expect different responses to questions about tranquilizer consumption, for example, depending on whether the context questions pertain to medical issues or to issues of drug abuse. However, we are not aware of systematic investigations of context dependent desirability effects, despite the considerable attention that socially desirable responding has received in the survey literature (see DeMaio, 1984, for a review).

The Role of Attitude Strength   Survey researchers have long assumed that attitudes vary in their degree of "strength," "centrality," or "crystallization" and that context effects are limited to attitudes that are weak and not (yet) crystallized (e.g., Blankenship, 1940, 1943; Cantril, 1944; Converse, 1964; see Krosnick & Abelson, 1992; Schuman, 1995, for reviews). The data bearing on this proposition are mixed.

The concept of attitude strength has been found to be difficult to operationalize (e.g., Scott, 1968) and the various measures used—including the intensity of respondents' feelings about the object, the certainty with which

they report holding the attitude, or the importance they ascribe to it—are only weakly related to one another (Krosnick & Abelson, 1992). Moreover, the widely shared hypothesis that context effects in survey measurement "are greater in the case of weaker attitudes has clearly been disconfirmed" (Krosnick & Abelson, 1992, p. 193). In the most comprehensive test of this hypothesis, based on more than a dozen experiments and different self-report measures of attitude strength, Krosnick and Schuman (1988) found no support for it, except for the not surprising finding that respondents with a weak attitude are more likely to choose a middle alternative.

In contrast, measures of attitude strength have proven useful as predictors of the malleability of attitude judgments in other domains of research. Most importantly, strongly held attitudes have been found to be more stable over time, less likely to change in response to persuasive messages, and to be better predictors of behavior than weak attitudes (see Krosnick & Abelson, 1992, for a review). Addressing the measurement of attitude strength, Bassili (1993, 1996) suggested that "meta-attitudinal" measures of attitude strengths, based on self-reports of intensity, importance, and related properties of one's attitude, may be less useful than "operative" measures of attitude strength, most notably measures of response latency. Drawing on Fazio's (e.g., 1986) work on attitude accessibility, Bassili observed that response latencies were better predictors of resistance to attitude change and attitude-behavior consistency than self-report measures of attitude strength. Whether highly accessible attitudes are less likely to show context effects in survey measurement, however, remains an open issue.

In our reading, the analysis of the role of attitude strength in the emergence of context effects has been hampered by a lack of attention to the different sources of context effects in the first place. Many context effects reflect context dependent differences in respondents' inferences about the specific meaning of the question, resulting in answers to somewhat different questions. These effects should be unlikely to be influenced by attitude strength or attitude accessibility. Other context effects reflect differences in the accessible information used in forming a judgment. These effects should be limited when a previously formed judgment is highly accessible in memory, suggesting that attitude accessibility should play a moderating role. Moreover, the influence of temporarily accessible information decreases as the amount or extremity of chronically accessible information increases, as discussed above (Schwarz & Bless, 1992a). If we assume that more information is chronically accessible on topics that individuals consider more important, we should observe weaker context effects under this condition.

As the latter prediction illustrates, the assumption that

"strong attitudes" are more resistant to change is not incompatible with a construal model of attitude judgment: the attributes tapped by self-report measures of attitude strength (such as importance, centrality, and extremity) are likely to covary with the chronic accessibility of relevant information. If so, a construal model predicts limited influences of temporarily accessible information under these conditions. Hence, the exploration of attitude strength has a limited bearing on the basic issue of whether people "have" attitudes or "construct" attitudes on the spot because the expected influences are compatible with either assumption.

Summary   As our selective review illustrates, the order in which attitude questions are asked can profoundly affect the obtained responses. The underlying processes can be coherently conceptualized in the framework of recent social cognition theorizing that emphasizes the constructive nature of attitude judgments (e.g., Feldman & Lynch, 1988; Schwarz & Bless, 1992a; Wilson & Hodges, 1992). From a theoretical point of view, the emergence of context effects reflects the general context dependency of human judgment, in daily life as well as in surveys, and does not constitute an "artifact." Nevertheless, context effects pose a major challenge for survey research, reflecting that we usually collect attitude reports from a sample to make inferences about the attitudes held in a population. To the extent that the judgments obtained from the sample reflect the specific context created by the questionnaire, inferences to a population that has not been exposed to this context are fraught with more uncertainty than is reflected in sampling error.

For investigators who wish to use surveys for substantive purposes the main implication of context effects, and of response effects more generally, is the need to keep clearly in mind that answers to survey questions are always problematic in meaning. There is no simple way around this fact, but there are several strategies that can help the investigator avoid being misled by response effects. One already mentioned is to use more than a single or small number of questions; to vary their format and wording in order to minimize, or at least become aware of, the impact of a particular type of effect; and to look at the responses independently, not simply as interchangeable components in a scale (see Mueller, 1973, 1994, for good examples). A second is to employ the kind of split-sample experimentation exemplified in earlier pages when addressing substantive issues, so that variations due to form, wording, and context can be exploited for theoretical purposes and in unconfounded form (Schuman & Bobo, 1988, and Sniderman, Brody, & Tetlock, 1991, offer examples of substantively motivated survey experimentation). Finally, careful multivariate analysis of survey data can often yield insights

into the meanings of responses that are not evident in the responses themselves (e.g., Zaller, 1992).

Pretesting Survey Questions: Recent Developments

An area of survey practice that has seen rapid improvements as a result of cognitive research is the pretesting of questionnaires, where cognitive methods—initially employed to gain insight into respondents' thought processes—are increasingly used to supplement traditional field pretesting (see Sudman et al., 1996, chap. 2, and the contributions to Schwarz & Sudman, 1996, for reviews and research examples). These methods have the potential to uncover many problems that are likely to go unnoticed in traditional field pretests, which essentially consist of administering the survey to a small number of respondents. This is particularly true for question comprehension problems, which are only discovered in field pretesting when respondents ask for clarification or give obviously meaningless answers. In contrast, asking pretest respondents to paraphrase the question, or to think aloud while answering it, provides insights into comprehension problems that may not result in explicit queries or recognizably meaningless answers. Moreover, these procedures reduce the number of respondents needed for pretesting, rendering pretests more cost efficient—although this assertion may reflect psychologists' potentially misleading assumption that cognitive processes show little variation as a function of sociodemographic characteristics (see Groves, 1996, for a critical discussion). At present, a variety of different procedures are routinely used by major survey organizations (see Forsyth & Lessler, 1991, for a review).

The most widely used method is the collection of *verbal protocols,* in the form of concurrent or retrospective think-aloud procedures (e.g., Groves, Fultz, & Martin, 1992; Willis, Royston, & Bercini, 1991). Whereas concurrent think-aloud procedures require respondents to articulate their thoughts as they answer the question, retrospective think-aloud procedures require respondents to describe how they arrived at an answer after they provided it. The latter procedure is experienced as less burdensome by respondents but carries a greater risk that the obtained data are based on respondents' subjective theories of how they would arrive at an answer. In contrast, concurrent think-alouds are more likely to reflect respondents' actual thought processes as they unfold in real time (see Ericsson & Simon, 1980, 1984).

Related to these more elaborate techniques, respondents are often asked to paraphrase the question, thus providing insight into their interpretation of question meaning (see Nuckols, 1953, for an early example). Incorporating such strategies into ongoing surveys, Schuman (1966) suggested that closed questions may be followed by a "random probe" (administered to a random subsample of a national sample), inviting respondents to elaborate on their answers in response to follow-up requests to explain them further. The use of such probes provides a fruitful way to extend research into question comprehension beyond the small set of respondents used in laboratory settings.

A procedure that is frequently applied in regular survey interviews (often called "production interviews" to distinguish them from pretests) is known as *behavior coding* (e.g., Cannell, Miller, & Oksenberg, 1981; see Fowler & Cannell, 1996, for a review). Although initially developed for the assessment of interviewer behavior, this procedure has proven efficient in identifying problems with questionnaires. It involves tape-recording interviews and coding behaviors such as respondent requests for clarification, interruptions, or inadequate answers. Much as regular field pretesting, however, this method fails to identify some problems that surface in verbal protocols, such as misunderstanding what a question means. Recent extensions of this approach include automated coding of interview transcripts, for which standardized coding schemes have been developed (e.g., Bolton & Bronkhorst, 1996).

Based on insights from verbal protocols and behavior coding, Forsyth, Lessler, and Hubbard (1992; see also Lessler & Forsyth, 1996) have developed a detailed coding scheme that allows cognitive experts to identify likely question problems in advance. At present, this development represents one of the most routinely applicable outcomes of the knowledge accumulating from cognitive research. Other techniques, such as the use of sorting procedures (e.g., Brewer, Dull, & Jobe, 1989; Brewer & Lui, 1996) or response latency measurement (see Bassili, 1996, for a review), are more limited in scope and are not yet routinely employed in pretesting.

Presser and Blair (1994) carried out a systematic comparison of four pretest methods: conventional informal pretesting in the field, behavior coding, cognitive interviews (concurrent and retrospective think-alouds with follow-up probes), and panels of experts. They found the expert panels to be most productive, as well as least expensive, in terms of overall number of problems identified. Moreover, experts, along with cognitive interviewing, were especially able to spot specific types of problems likely to occur during later analysis. Conventional pretesting and behavior coding were particularly good at identifying problems involving the interviewer. However, the ultimate test of "Does it make a difference in analytic outcome?" is still missing. Any set of survey data is bound to include some errors (including some due simply to data entry), but with large samples a fair amount of (potentially) more or less random error is unlikely to have much effect on the substantive results of interest to survey users. It is the discovery of substantial systematic error that is

particularly important and that most merits investigation in the future.

MODES OF DATA COLLECTION

Survey data may be collected in face-to-face interviews, telephone interviews, or through self-administered questionnaires. The choice of administration mode is determined by many factors, with cost and sampling considerations usually being the dominant ones (see Groves, 1989, for a discussion). We now summarize the key differences between modes of data collection.

Key Differences Between Modes of Data Collection

Coverage, Nonresponse, and Self-selection   For surveys of household populations the sampling frames and sample designs for the three modes might differ. Moreover, the use of interviewers permits more control over who actually completes the questionnaire when specific persons within a household are sampled, while mailed questionnaires may be completed by other household members. However, the use of interviewers in face-to-face and telephone surveys generally raises the cost of those surveys, relative to a mailed self-administered questionnaire. The cost of interviewer travel from sample housing unit to sample housing unit typically makes face-to-face surveys the most expensive of the three, with telephone surveys falling in between.

Nonresponse differences among the modes vary by population and topic. There is consistent evidence that less literate persons tend to be nonrespondent to self-administered questionnaires (e.g., Dillman, 1978), presumably because of the higher burdens they face in completing the instrument. The elderly appear to have lower cooperation rates on telephone surveys, perhaps because of larger prevalence of hearing problems, but also, with the current cohort of the elderly, less tendency to use the telephone for extended conversations with strangers.

In addition, the different modes are differentially susceptible to respondent self-selection. Respondents in mail surveys have the opportunity to preview the questionnaire before they decide to participate (Dillman, 1978). In contrast, respondents in face-to-face or telephone surveys have to make this decision on the basis of the information provided in the introduction (and are unlikely to revise their decision once the interview proceeds). As a result, mail surveys run a considerably higher risk of topic-related self-selection than face-to-face or telephone surveys. Although topic-related nonresponse becomes less problematic as the response rate of mail surveys increases, self-selection problems remain even at high response rates. Suppose that a mail and a telephone survey both obtain an 80% response rate. In the telephone survey, the 20 percent nonresponse includes participants who refuse because they are called at a bad time, are on vacation, and so on. However, it does not include respondents who thought about the issue and decided it is not worth their time. In contrast, mail respondents can work on the questionnaire at a time of their choice, thus potentially reducing nonresponse due to timing problems. On the other hand, however, they have the possibility to screen the questionnaire and are more likely to participate in the survey if they find the issue of interest. As a result, an identical nonresponse rate of 20 percent under both modes is likely to be unrelated to the topic under interview conditions but not under mail conditions. Hence, similar response rates under different modes do not necessarily indicate comparable samples.

Moreover, the variable that drives nonresponse under mail conditions is respondents' interest in the topic, which may be only weakly related to sociodemographic variables. Accordingly, topic driven nonresponse may be present even if the completed sample seems representative with regard to sociodemographic variables like age, sex, or income. To address the potential problem of topic related self-selection, future research will need to assess respondents' interest in the topic and its relationship to substantive responses under different administration modes.

Cognitive Variables   In addition, different modes of data collection differ in the cognitive and communicative tasks they pose, which affects the emergence of response effects (see Schwarz, Strack, Hippler, & Bishop, 1991, for a review). The most obvious difference is the *sensory channel* in which the material is presented. In self-administered questionnaires, the items are visually displayed to the respondent who has to read the material, rendering research on visual perception and reading highly relevant to questionnaire design (see Jenkins & Dillman, 1997). In telephone interviews, as the other extreme, the items and the response alternatives are read to respondents, whereas both modes of presentation may occur in face-to-face interviews, where interviewers may present visual aids.

Closely related to this distinction is the *temporal order* in which the material is presented. Telephone and face-to-face interviews have a strict sequential organization and respondents have to process the information in the temporal succession and the pace in which it is presented by the interviewer. They usually cannot go back and forth or spend relatively more or less time on some particular item. Even if respondents are allowed to return to previous items should they want to correct their responses, they rarely do so, in part because tracking one's previous responses presents a difficult memory task under telephone and face-to-face conditions. In contrast, keeping track of one's responses, and going back and forth between items, poses no difficulties under self-administered questionnaire condi-

tions. As a result, self-administered questionnaires render the sequential organization of questions less influential and subsequent questions have been found to influence the responses given to *preceding* ones (e.g., Bishop, Hippler, Schwarz, & Strack, 1988; Schwarz & Hippler, 1995).

Different administration modes also differ in the *time pressure* they impose on respondents. Time pressure interferes with extensive recall processes and increases reliance on simplifying processing strategies (Krosnick, 1991; Kruglanski, 1980). The greatest time pressure can be expected under telephone interview conditions, where moments of silent reflection cannot be bridged by nonverbal communication that indicates that the respondent is still paying attention to the task (Ball, 1968; Groves & Kahn, 1979). If the question poses challenging recall or judgment tasks, it is therefore particularly important to encourage respondents to take the time they may need under telephone interview conditions. The least degree of time pressure is usually induced by self-administered questionnaires that allow respondents to work at their own pace, though in some cases respondents may rush through a self-administered questionnaire to get it done quickly. Face-to-face interviews create intermediate time pressure, due to the possibility of bridging pauses by nonverbal communication.

Social Interaction Variables   While social interaction is severely constrained in all standardized survey interviews, the modes of data collection differ in the degree to which they restrict *nonverbal communication*. While face-to-face interviews provide full access to the nonverbal cues of the participants, participants in telephone interviews are restricted to paraverbal cues, whereas social interaction is largely absent under self-administered conditions. Psychological research has identified various functions of nonverbal cues during face-to-face interaction (see Argyle, 1969, for a review). Most importantly, nonverbal cues serve to indicate mutual attention and responsiveness and provide feedback as well as illustrations for what is being said (in the form of gestures). Given the absence of these helpful cues under self-administered questionnaire conditions, particular care needs to be taken to maintain respondent motivation in the absence of interviewer input and to render the questionnaire self-explanatory.

Further contributing to the need of self-explanatory questionnaires, respondents have no opportunity to elicit additional *explanations* from the interviewer under self-administered conditions. In contrast, interviewer support is easiest under face-to-face conditions, where the interviewer can monitor the respondent's nonverbal expressions. Telephone interview conditions fall in between these extremes, reflecting that the interviewer is limited to monitoring the respondent's verbal utterances. Even though any additional information provided by the interviewer is usually restricted to certain prescribed feedback, it may help respondents to determine the meaning of the questions. Even the uninformative—but not unusual—clarification, "whatever it means to you," may be likely to shortcut further attempts to screen question context in search for an appropriate interpretation. Under self-administered questionnaire conditions, on the other hand, respondents have to depend on the context that is explicitly provided by the questionnaire to draw inferences about the intended meaning of questions—and they have the time and opportunity to do so. This is likely to increase the impact of related questions and response alternatives on question interpretation (Strack & Schwarz, 1992).

Whereas self-administered questionnaires are therefore likely to increase reliance on contextual information (although potentially independent of the order in which it is presented), they have the advantage to be free of interviewer effects. In general, *interviewer characteristics* are more likely to be noticed by respondents when they have face-to-face contact than when the interviewer cannot be seen, as is the case under telephone interview conditions, where the identification of interviewer characteristics is limited to characteristics that may be inferred from paralinguistic cues and speech styles (such as sex, age, or race). Under self-administered questionnaire conditions, of course, no interviewer is required, although respondents may infer characteristics of the researcher from the cover letter or the person who dropped off the questionnaire. While respondents' perception of interviewer characteristics may increase socially desirable responses, it may also serve to increase rapport with the interviewer, rendering the potential impact of interviewer characteristics on responses complex.

Impact on Data Quality

There is a substantial methodological literature documenting and attempting to explain differences in survey results obtained in the three different modes of data collection (e.g., Groves & Kahn, 1979; Groves et al., 1988; Körmendi & Noordhoek, 1989; Sykes & Collins, 1988). Because the relevant comparisons are based on well-executed mail, telephone, and face-to-face surveys, however, all of the above differences between modes are confounded, rendering it difficult to identify which of the many differences is responsible for an observed mode effect (for an exception see Bishop et al., 1988). Moreover, the effects of different variables may cancel one another, rendering most of the available findings utterly nondiagnostic for the hypotheses offered above. Clearly, more carefully controlled experimental research is needed in this area before any strong conclusions can be drawn.

Below, we provide a short summary of the results of an extensive meta-analysis and then turn to the issue of interviewer effects.

Results of Mode Comparison   In a meta-analysis of 52 studies, deLeeuw (1992) found only small differences among the modes in reliability, consistency, and susceptibility to social desirability. The largest differences were observed between self-administered (mail) questionnaires and the interviewer-administered modes, with the latter not differing much from one another. Specifically, mail surveys tended to have the lowest response rates and the highest rates of unanswered questions (item missing data)—but when answered there was evidence of more self-disclosure on sensitive items, higher reliability, and consistency. Hence, self-administered questionnaires may be preferable when sensitive questions are asked. However, this advantage may also be achieved in face-to-face surveys, which are likely to foster higher response rates, where the respondent may return a self-administered questionnaire in a sealed envelope. Finally, face-to-face interviews had somewhat higher response rates than telephone interviews, as well as a slightly lower rate of unanswered questions. In general, however, all obtained differences between modes were small, both on univariate comparisons and multivariate models.

These findings suggest that researchers will usually arrive at similar conclusions independent of the mode of data collection used, provided that the respective mode is competently implemented. In fact, Groves (1989) had previously concluded that the most consistent finding in comparisons of face-to-face and telephone interviews is the lack of major differences. While this is encouraging, experimental research (see Bishop et al., 1988) has documented mode-dependent differences on questions specifically designed to explore likely mode effects. Examples include the order dependency of context effects in face-to-face and telephone interviews, but not in self-administered questionnaires (Schwarz & Hippler, 1995) and the differential emergence of response order effects under visual and oral presentation conditions (Krosnick & Alwin, 1987; Sudman et al., 1996, chap. 6). Clearly, more research under tightly controlled conditions is needed.

Interviewer Effects   Interviewer-assisted surveys are subject to one error source that doesn't appear in self-administered surveys—interviewer effects. There are several methodological literatures on interviewer effects, looking at demographic characteristics of the interviewers, interviewer expectations, and effects of training. The research on interviewer expectations flowed from the same concerns as that on experimenter expectations (see Rosenthal, 1976). Hyman (1954/1975) was the first to hypothesize that interviewers carried with them an expectation of the population distribution on each survey question, and unconsciously tended to achieve that distribution during their interviewing. Studies that measured interviewers' individual beliefs about the sensitivity and difficulty of questions (e.g., Singer & Kohnke-Aguirre, 1979; Sudman et al., 1977), however, obtained little support for this hypothesis and tended to find only small relationships between these prior assessments and missing data rates.

Methodological studies in the United States have found that the reports of racial attitudes are affected by the racial mix of interviewer and respondent (e.g., Schuman & Converse, 1971; Hatchett & Schuman, 1976) and that reports of attitudes toward feminist issues are affected by gender of interviewer (e.g., Ballou & Del Boca, 1980). This is consistent with a perspective that these attributes of the interviewer are relevant pieces of information used by the respondent in judging the intent and social context of the questioning.

Much of the methodological literature on interviewer training effects is associated with efforts to reduce interviewer variability and to set up a conversational mode that facilitates thoughtful and open responses to survey questions. Cannell and his associates (e.g., Cannell, Miller, & Oksenberg, 1981) obtained higher reports of autobiographical events and socially undesirable behaviors through altering the training and scripting of interviewers. Under their experimental regimen, interviewers obtained a respondent commitment to work hard at the response task, provided instructions regarding the intent of questions, and provided feedback on adequate and inadequate effort to respond.

The component of interviewer effects receiving the greatest research attention is *interviewer variance,* a loss of precision because different interviewers induce different response patterns in respondents. Many studies, using randomized assignment of interviewers to respondents, have measured the component of variance in response associated with interviewers (for a review see Groves, 1989). In general the interviewer variance estimates are small among surveys using trained interviewers. They tend to be higher for responses to open questions, but there are no substantial differences for attitudinal versus factual questions, and, to the disappointment of field managers, no large differences across interviewers judged to be better or worse by their supervisors.

In summary, most of the available research suggests that interviewer characteristics and expectations exert a minor influence in face-to-face and telephone surveys. The exception are questions to which the specific interviewer characteristic is particularly relevant, such as questions pertaining to race. Moreover, different modes of data collection do not typically result in major differences in the obtained results, provided that the respective mode is competently implemented. Experimental research suggests, however, that a small number of specific question charac-

teristics may interact with the mode of data collection (see Schwarz, Strack, Bishop, & Hippler, 1991), although more research is needed in this domain. Overall, the available findings confirm Sudman and Bradburn's (1974) conclusion that the major source of response effects in surveys are characteristics of the question, rather than characteristics of the interviewer, respondent, or administration mode. Next, we turn to a specific issue related to administration mode, namely, the quickly growing use of computers in survey administration.

COMPUTER ASSISTANCE IN SURVEYS

Over the last few years computers have been used by researchers to assist in the collection of survey data. This first occurred in telephone surveys, where centralized interviewing facilities equipped with computer terminals administered the sample and presented the questionnaire to interviewers question by question. This general area is labeled CASIC, computer assisted information collection. At this point, small microcomputers are being used to assist the interviewers in face-to-face surveys; to assist the respondent in self-administered surveys; and to present the questions orally to the respondent using digitized speech capabilities of microcomputers. Survey respondents are using touchtone data entry to communicate numeric data over telephone lines, and survey organizations are using voice synthesis and recognition software to conduct interviews without interviewers.

These developments have altered the design of large-scale surveys, with potential effects on survey quality. The most obvious change is that the computer software controls the presentation of the survey questions, skipping from one question to another based on answers provided, forcing some response entry at each question. This feature has been found to reduce item missing data (Groves & Mathiowetz, 1984; Tortora, 1985). Other changes induced by computer assistance include the constraint of the visual presentation of questions to a 20 line by 80 character display, thus inhibiting certain gridlike presentations of questions; the restricted visibility of the whole set of questions to the interviewer (or the respondent in self-administered computer assisted instruments); the use of automatic changes in question wordings to tailor questions to the circumstances of the respondent (e.g., "When your SON, CHRIS, first entered school, what age was HE?"); and range checks on answers (e.g., a respondent reporting that he is 18 years old but is currently retired). In addition, these developments have facilitated the integration of experimental elements into large-scale surveys, allowing researchers to experiment with different question wordings, question orders, and the like without increasing the burden on the interviewer. Finally, CASIC software directs the next time for the interviewer to call on a case not yet contacted and compiles administrative data on the progress of the survey administration, thus facilitating survey administration.

So far, the research literature evaluating the impact of computer assistance on the quality of survey data has not kept pace with the adoption of the technology by survey organizations. There is some evidence of reduction of inconsistency through programmed checks (Tortora, 1985). In methodological examinations using comparison of records (assumed to be accurate) and survey responses, there are few recorded net effects of computer assistance (Grondin & Michaud, 1994); similarly there appears to be few if any differences found in studies of interviewer effects by mode (see Nicholls, Baker, & Martin, 1997, for a review of these developments).

DATA EDITING AND ANALYSIS

Kenny, Kashy, and Bolger (1998, in this *Handbook*) review recent developments in statistical data analysis and we restrict our remarks to those features of data editing and analysis more common with survey data than other data sources. Thus we ignore the editing and coding problems of translating verbal responses to quantitative codes, the construction of multi-item scales, and the host of statistical modeling and analysis procedures common to all quantitative data.

The term *editing* is used to refer to procedures for detecting erroneous and/or questionable survey data with the goal of correcting it prior to analysis. Editing includes both checking for answer codes recorded outside of legal range (e.g., a reported age of 197 years) or inconsistent with prior information (e.g., reported age of 18 years and an answer that the respondent fought in the Korean war). Range checks apply to all survey data, but consistency checks apply only to those with logical contingencies. Such contingencies are rare in attitudinal data but common in behavioral data.

The use of computer assistance in survey data collection has integrated much of the data editing step with the data collection step, with edit checks made by the computer immediately upon entry of the response. This has led to new measurement issues in surveys—effective methods of alerting the interviewer and respondent to potential logical inconsistencies in answers without damaging the relationship between interviewer and respondent.

We have already reviewed the use of case-level weighting and poststratification in survey statistics to reduce errors of nonresponse of sample persons (called *unit nonresponse*). The survey analyst must also be alert to problems of *item nonresponse,* the failure of a respondent to provide usable answers for one or more questions in an otherwise complete interview. Most of the same logic applies to unit and item nonresponse with regard to their impact on the quality of survey statistics. That is, the item nonresponse error is a function of the proportion of cases missing a datum and the differences between those providing answers and those not.

Data collection methods to reduce item missing data have concentrated on reducing the burden of reporting. For example, when a respondent is asked to report total family income in the last year and fails to be able to report an exact figure, coarsened follow-up questions are asked (e.g., "Could you tell me whether it was more or less than $35,000?"). This has been found to reduce item missing data rates.

In the presence of item missing data, the survey analyst is forced into some assumption as part of the data analysis. The default assumption (taken by ignoring cases with missing data on an item) is that those with missing data are identical to those with complete data. There is often evidence from methodological research that such an assumption is false (e.g., those failing to report whether they voted in the last election tend not to have voted). In the last few years there has been substantial progress in handling item missing data in surveys through statistical imputation, filling in missing data with answers based on models of the response process. These statistical imputation models are beyond the scope of this chapter (see Kalton & Miller, 1986; Little & Rubin, 1987; Rubin, 1987) but have been found to be desirable methods of improving the quality of survey estimates.

ETHICAL PROBLEMS BEARING ON SURVEY RESEARCH

In addition to the ethical problems that attend all science—the integrity of the scientific process and the uses of the knowledge obtained—survey research shares with other behavioral and biological sciences the additional problem of treating human beings as objects of investigation. This problem is especially acute for survey research because it cannot rely on self-selected volunteers: the goal of generalizing to natural populations makes it important to try to obtain responses from all members of a selected sample. Yet survey investigators recognize that in principle they should not—and in practice they cannot—require individuals to take part in a survey or force them to answer particular questions within it. We previously discussed this tension between the scientific needs of survey research and the obligation to respect the right of people to decline to participate at all, or decline to answer particular questions, as an essential aspect of the issue of unit and item nonresponse.

A closely related dilemma arises from the principle of informed consent: the right of respondents to know ahead of time the content and purpose of a survey. Desirable as informed consent may be in the abstract, it can threaten the validity of a survey by leading individuals to refuse to participate because of the specific nature of the questions. For example, if potential respondents are told that a standard question on personal income is to be included in the survey, some who are especially sensitive about providing such information may decide not to take part at all. Nonresponse, always a problem, becomes even more so when such content-related bias occurs. Likewise, if the sponsorship or primary purpose of the survey is revealed initially, this may affect both decisions about participating and the answers of those who do choose to participate (Presser, 1994). A related problem pertains to guaranteeing the confidentiality of respondents' answers, especially as surveys include more and more questions that might once have been taboo, for example, inquiries about use of illegal drugs, exotic forms of sexual behavior, or sources of income not likely to have been reported for tax purposes. It is only by taking exceptional steps, such as destroying all identifying information, that survey investigators can really make guarantees of confidentiality stick. Paradoxically, explicit guarantees of confidentiality can backfire by drawing respondents' attention to the dangers of candor. While this may be a minor problem when the questions are sensitive enough to raise these concerns anyway, research indicates that guarantees of confidentiality provided at the beginning of an interview lead respondents to anticipate sensitive questions, thus decreasing participation (Singer, Hippler, & Schwarz, 1992).

Fortunately for most surveys, respondents do not seem terribly worried ahead of time about breaches in confidentiality, nor are they greatly impressed by promises of it. Thus, few respondents believe that the Census Bureau—which is trusted more than nongovernment survey organizations—really protects individual records from non-Census use (National Research Council, 1979). Those most concerned doubtless contribute one component to nonresponse rates, though the size of this component is difficult to establish.

An ethical problem that is not intrinsic to scientific surveys, but must nonetheless be contended with, is the increasing number of efforts to influence people under the guise of a survey. This occurs in good part because the survey is an all-purpose tool, attractive not only to social scientists in pursuit of knowledge but also to commercial firms in pursuit of sales, politicians seeking votes, newspapers trying to attract readers, and all manner of other organizations. Unlike the social psychological experiment, the survey method has never been restricted to any one discipline or even to academicians as such. This can be seen as a mark of its versatility and success in obtaining useful information, as Davis (1975) concludes, but it also gives rise

to a range of problems that extend well beyond those involving use and misuse by academic researchers.

Finally, it is worth noting an ethical problem that has rarely been addressed by survey researchers, namely, the potential impact of participating in a survey interview on respondents' subsequent attitudes and behaviors, which we reviewed under the heading of "self-generated validity." At present, survey practitioners are rarely aware of the pronounced impact their questions may have and hence do not attempt to reinstate the status quo ante by "putting respondents back where they were," in contrast to what is occasionally attempted in social psychological experiments. Note a crucial difference, however: in social psychological experiments, subjects may be exposed to false feedback, extensive mood manipulations, and similar procedures, placing some burden on the experimenter to undo adverse effects after completion of the experiment. In contrast, deliberately misleading information is rarely introduced in legitimate surveys (although deliberate attempts to change respondents' mind are part of so-called "push polls" used by political candidates, which we consider part of campaigning rather than survey research). In general, survey respondents are "only" asked to answer questions, e.g., to report whether they intend to buy a car during the next six months (Morwitz et al., 1993). While thinking about this intention may increase the likelihood that respondents go out and do buy a car (as discussed earlier), it is less clear under which conditions this possibility requires the researcher to take steps that counteract the intentions respondents form: when is a researcher to take responsibility for the thoughts that a question elicits? Admittedly, we do not have an answer to this thorny issue.

SUMMARY

As our review of the major components of a survey indicates, a sample survey is the result of a host of individual decisions that affect coverage, nonresponse, sampling, the cognitive tasks presented to respondents, as well as respondents' opportunity to solve these tasks in a meaningful way. Unfortunately, these decisions are taken in a context where each one has cost implications for the research: using methods to increase the coverage of difficult-to-locate persons in the sampling frame reduces coverage error but increases costs; increasing sampling size reduces sampling error, but again increases costs; making repeated callbacks on persons who are difficult to contact, and attempting persuasion efforts on the reluctant respondents often reduces nonresponse errors, but inflates the amount of interview hours on the survey; using multiple indicators for constructs usually improves the precision of survey estimates but lengthens the questionnaire and increases costs.

Because of these tradeoffs of costs and errors, every survey is a compromise measurement tool. It is difficult if not impossible to assess whether a particular tradeoff decision was optimal. It is generally easy for a post hoc assessment to identify weaknesses in individual questions or batteries of measures, especially on grounds of inadequate reflection of different dimensions of a construct. Especially in multipurpose surveys, measuring many constructs simultaneously, single items may be used when multiple items might be preferable in the absence of any cost constraint. And given the high costs of a survey, one cannot usually redo it when major problems are detected after completion, in contrast to the flexibility provided by low-cost laboratory experiments.

Our review further indicates that survey methodology profits from contributions from many disciplines, including statistics, computer science, sociology, psychology, and psycholinguistics. Improvement in the practice of surveys is increasingly arising from research on the interface of these various disciplines. For example, with increasing difficulty with obtaining high response rates, statistical models for the adjustment of estimates in the presence of nonresponse are more important. These models require insights into the social psychology of compliance and helping, as well as statistical sophistication in their parameterization. Similarly, we have reviewed the cognitive and communicative processes that underlie survey responding, an interdisciplinary area that has seen particular progress over the last decade and has resulted in the development of theoretical frameworks that may guide questionnaire construction. Finally, we have noted the increasing uses of computer assistance in survey data collection, with attendant human-machine interface issues affecting data quality. These and other areas of survey methodology are ripe for the attention of social and cognitive psychologists and will profit from their collaboration with survey methodologists and practitioners. At the same time, psychological research is likely to benefit from the access to a broader population and the theoretical and methodological challenges that such a collaboration can provide.

REFERENCES

Abelson, R. P. (1981). The psychological status of the script concept. *American Psychologist, 36,* 715–729.

Arglye, M. (1969). *Social interaction.* London: Methuen.

Baddeley, A. D., & Hitch, G. J. (1977). Recency reexamined. In S. Dornic (Ed.), *Attention and performance.* (Vol. 6, pp. 647–667). Hillsdale, NJ: Erlbaum.

Baddeley, A. D., Lewis, V., & Nimmo-Smith, J. (1978). When did you last . . . ? In M. M. Gruneberg, P. E. Morris, & R. N. Sykes (Eds.), *Practical aspects of memory* (pp. 77–83). London: Academic Press.

Ball, D. W. (1968). Toward a sociology of telephones and telephoners. In M. Truzzi (Ed.), *Sociology and everyday life* (pp. 59–75). Englewood Cliffs, NJ: Prentice-Hall.

Ballou, J., & Del Boca, F. K. (1980, May). Gender interaction effects on survey measurement in telephone interviews. Paper presented at the meetings of the American Association for Public Opinion Research, Mason, Ohio.

Banaji, M., Blaire, I., & Schwarz, N. (1996). Implicit memory, subjective experiences and survey measurement. In N. Schwarz & S. Sudman, (Eds.), *Answering questions: Methodology for determining cognitive and communicative processes in survey research* (pp. 347–372). San Francisco: Jossey-Bass.

Barton, A. J. (1958). Asking the embarrassing question. *Public Opinion Quarterly, 22,* 271–278.

Bassili, J. N. (1993). Response latency versus certainty as indexes of the strength of voting intentions in a CATI survey. *Public Opinion Quarterly, 57,* 54–61.

Bassili, J. N. (1996). The how and why of response latency measurement in telephone surveys. In N. Schwarz & S. Sudman (Eds.), *Answering questions: Methodology for determining cognitive and communicative processes in survey research* (pp. 319–346). San Francisco: Jossey Bass.

Berk, M., Mathiowetz, N., Ward, E., and White, A. (1987). The effect of prepaid and promised incentives: Results of a controlled experiment. *Journal of Official Statistics, 3,* 449–457.

Bishop, G. F. (1987). Experiments with middle response alternatives in survey questions. *Public Opinion Quarterly, 51,* 220–232.

Bishop, G. F., Hippler, H. J., Schwarz, N., & Strack, F. (1988). A comparison of response effects in self-administered and telephone surveys. In R. M. Groves, P. Biemer, L. Lyberg, J. Massey, W. Nicholls, and J. Waksberg (Eds.), *Telephone survey methodology* (pp. 321–340). New York: Wiley.

Bishop, G. F., Oldendick, R. W., & Tuchfarber, A. J. (1983). Effects of filter questions in public opinion surveys. *Public Opinion Quarterly, 47,* 528–546.

Bishop, G. F., Oldendick, R. W., & Tuchfarber, A. J. (1986). Opinions on fictitious issues: The pressure to answer survey questions. *Public Opinion Quarterly, 50,* 240–250.

Blair, E., & Burton, S. (1987). Cognitive processes used by survey respondents to answer behavioral frequency questions. *Journal of Consumer Research, 14,* 280–288.

Blankenship, A. B. (1940). The influence of the question form upon the response in a public opinion poll. *Psychological Record, 3,* 345–422.

Blankenship, A. B. (1943). *Consumer and opinion research.* New York: Harper.

Bless, H., Bohner, G., Hild, T., & Schwarz, N. (1992). Asking difficult questions: Task complexity increases the impact of response alternatives. *European Journal of Social Psychology, 22,* 309–312.

Bless, H., Strack, F., & Schwarz, N. (1993). The information functions of research procedures: Bias and the logic of conversation. *European Journal of Social Psychology, 23,* 149–165.

Bodenhausen, G. V., Schwarz, N., Bless, H., & Wänke, M. (1995). Effects of atypical exemplars on racial beliefs: Enlightened racism or generalized appraisals? *Journal of Experimental Social Psychology, 31,* 48–63.

Bodenhausen, G. V., & Wyer, R. S. (1987). Social cognition and social reality: Information acquisition and use in the laboratory and the real world. In H. J. Hippler, N. Schwarz, & S. Sudman (Eds.), *Social information processing and survey methodology* (pp. 6–41). New York: Springer Verlag.

Bolton, R. N., & Bronkhorst, T. M. (1996). Questionnaire pretesting: Computer assisted coding of concurrent protocols. In N. Schwarz & S. Sudman (Eds.), *Answering questions: Methodology for determining cognitive and communicative processes in survey research* (pp. 37–64). San Francisco: Jossey-Bass.

Bradburn, N. M. (1983). Response effects. In P. H. Rossi, J. D. Wright, & A. B. Anderson (Eds.), *Handbook of survey research* (pp. 289–328). New York: Academic Press.

Bradburn, N. M. Huttenlocher, J., & Hedges, L. (1994). Telescoping and temporal memory. In N. Schwarz & S. Sudman (Eds.), *Autobiographical memory and the validity of retrospective reports* (pp. 203–216). New York: Springer Verlag.

Bradburn, N. M., Rips, L. J., & Shevell, S. K. (1987). Answering autobiographical questions: The impact of memory and inference on surveys. *Science, 236,* 157–161.

Bradburn, N. M., & Sudman, S. (1988). *Polls and surveys: Understanding what they tell us.* San Francisco: Jossey-Bass.

Brewer, M. B., Dull, V. T., & Jobe, J. B. (1989). A social cognition approach to reporting chronic conditions in health surveys. *National Center for Health Statistics. Vital Health Statistics.* 6(3).

Brewer, M. L., & Lui, L. N. (1996). Use of sorting tasks to assess cognitive structures. In N. Schwarz & S. Sudman (Eds.), *Answering questions: Methodology for determining cognitive and communicative processes in survey research* (pp. 373–387). San Francisco: Jossey-Bass.

Campbell, A. (1981). *The sense of well-being in America.* New York: McGraw-Hill.

Cannell, C. F., Miller, P. V., and Oksenberg, L. (1981). Research on interviewing techniques. In S. Leinhardt (Ed.), *Sociological Methodology 1981.* San Francisco: Jossey-Bass.

Cannell, C. F., Marquis, K. H., & Laurent, A. (1977). A summary of studies of interviewing methodology. *Vital and Health Statistics,* Series 2, No. 69 (DHEW Publication No. HRA 77-1343). Washington, DC: Government Printing Office.

Cantor, D. (1989). Substantive implications of selected operational longitudinal design features: The National Crime Survey as a case study. In D. Kasprzyk, G. J. Duncan, G. Kalton, and M. P. Singh (Eds.), *Panel surveys* (pp. 25–51). New York: John Wiley & Sons.

Cantril, H. (1944) *Gauging Public Opinion.* Princeton, NJ: Princeton University Press.

Clark, H. H., & Clark, E. V. (1977). *Psychology and language.* New York: Harcourt, Brace, Jovanovich.

Clark, H. H., & Haviland, S. E. (1977). Comprehension and the given-new contract. In R. O. Freedle (Ed.), *Discourse production and comprehension* (pp. 1–40). Hillsdale, NJ: Erlbaum.

Clark, H. H., & Schober, M. F. (1992). Asking questions and influencing answers. In J. M. Tanur (Ed.), *Questions about questions* (pp. 15–48). New York: Russel Sage.

Clore, G. L. (1992). Cognitive phenomenology: Feelings and the construction of judgment. In L. L. Martin & A. Tesser (Eds.), *The construction of social judgment* (pp. 133–164). Hillsdale, NJ: Erlbaum.

Collins, L. M., Graham, J. W., Hansen, W. B., & Johnson, C. A. (1985). Agreement between retrospective accounts of substance use and earlier reported substance use. *Applied Psychological Measurement, 9,* 301–309.

Converse, P. E. (1964). The nature of belief systems in the mass public. In D. E. Apter (Ed.), *Ideology and discontent* (pp. 206–261). New York: Free Press.

Conway, M., & Ross, M. (1984). Getting what you want by revising what you had. *Journal of Personality and Social Psychology, 47,* 738–748.

Crossen, C. (1994). *Tainted truth. The manipulation of fact in America.* New York: Simon & Schuster.

Daamen, D. D. L., & deBie, S. E. (1992). Serial context effects in survey items. In N. Schwarz & S. Sudman (Eds.), *Context effects in social and psychological research* (pp. 97–114). New York: Springer-Verlag.

Davis, J. A. (1975). On the remarkable absence of nonacademic implications in academic research: An example from ethnic studies. In N. J. Dermath, III., O. J. Larsen, & K. Schuessler (Eds.), *Social policy and sociology.* New York: Academic Press.

DeLeeuw, E. D. (1992). *Data quality in mail, telephone, and face to face surveys.* Ph.D. dissertation, Free University Amsterdam. The Hague: CIP-Gegevens Koninklijke Bibliotheek.

DeMaio, T. J. (1984). Social desirability and survey measurement: A review. In C. F. Turner & E. Martin (Eds.), *Surveying subjective phenomena* (Vol. 2, pp. 257–281). New York: Russel Sage.

Dillman, D. A. (1978). *Telephone and mail surveys: The total design method.* New York: Wiley.

Dillman, D. A., Gallegos, J. G., and Frey, J. H. (1976). Reducing refusal rates for telephone interviews, *Public Opinion Quarterly, 40:1,* pp. 66–78.

Ekholm, A., & Laaksonen, S. (1991). Weighting via response modeling in the Finnish household budget survey. *Journal of Official Statistics, 7,* 325–337.

Ellsworth, P. C., & Gross, S. R. (1994). Hardening of attitudes: Americans' views of the death penalty. *Journal of Social Issues, 50,* 19–52.

Ericsson, K. A., & Simon, H. (1980). Verbal reports as data. *Psychological Review, 8,* 215–251.

Ericsson, K. A., & Simon, H. A. (1984). *Protocol analysis: Verbal reports as data.* Cambridge, MA: MIT Press.

Erikson, R. S., Luttberg, N. R., & Tedin, K. T. (1988). *American public opinion* (3rd ed.). New York: Macmillan.

Fay, R. (1989). An analysis of within-household undercoverage in the current population survey. *Proceedings of the Bureau of the Census Fifth Annual Research Conference, U.S. Bureau of the Census* (pp. 156–175). Washington, DC: U.S. Bureau of the Census.

Fazio, R. H. (1986). How do attitudes guide behavior? In R. M. Sorrentino & E. T. Higgins (Eds.), *Handbook of motivation and cognition: Foundations of social behavior* (Vol. 1, pp. 204–243). New York: Guilford Press.

Fazio, R. H., Sherman, S. J., & Herr, P. M. (1982). The feature positive effect in self-perception process: Does not doing matter as much as doing? *Journal of Personality and Social Psychology, 42,* 404–411.

Feldman, J. M. (1992). Constructive processes in survey research: Explorations in self-generated validity. In N. Schwarz & S. Sudman (Eds.), *Context effects in social and psychological research* (pp. 49–61). New York: Springer-Verlag.

Feldman, J. M., & Lynch, J. G. (1988). Self-generated validity and other effects of measurement on belief, attitude, intention, and behavior. *Journal of Applied Psychology, 73,* 421–435.

Fiedler, K., & Armbruster, T. (1994). Two halfs may be more than one whole: Category-split effects on frequency illusions. *Journal of Personality and Social Psychology, 66,* 633–645.

Forsyth, B. H., & Lessler, J. T. (1991). Cognitive laboratory methods: A taxonomy. In P. Biemer, R. Groves, N. Mathiowetz, & S. Sudman (Eds.), *Measurement error in surveys* (pp. 393–418). Chichester: Wiley.

Forsyth, B. H., Lessler, J. L., & Hubbard, M. L. (1992). Cognitive evaluation of the questionnaire. In C. F. Turner, J. T. Lessler, & J. C. Gfroerer (Eds.), *Survey measurement of drug use: Methodological studies.* Washington, DC: DHHS Publication No. 92-1929.

Fowler, F. J. (1991). Reducing interviewer-related error through interviewer training, supervision, and other means. In P. Biemer, R. Groves, N. Mathiowetz, & S. Sudman (Eds.), *Measurement error in surveys* (pp. 259–278). Chichester: Wiley.

Fowler, F. J., & Cannell, C. F. (1996). Using behavioral coding to identify cognitive problems with survey questions. In N. Schwarz & S. Sudman (Eds.), *Answering questions: Methodology for determining cognitive and communicative processes in survey research* (pp. 15–36). San Francisco: Jossey-Bass.

Frey, J. H. (1983). *Survey research by telephone.* Newbury Park, CA: Sage.

Greenberg, B., Abul-Ela, A., Simmons, W., & Horvitz, D. (1969). The unrelated questions randomized response model theoretical framework. *Journal of the American Statistical Association, 64,* 421–426.

Greenwald, A. G., Carnot, C. G., Beach, R., & Young, B. (1987). Increased voting behavior by asking people if they expect to vote. *Journal of Applied Social Psychology, 72,* 315–318.

Grice, H. P. (1975). Logic and conversation. In P. Cole & J. L. Morgan (Eds.), *Syntax and semantics, Vol. 3: Speech acts* (pp. 41–58). New York: Academic Press.

Grondin, C., & Michaud, S. (1994). Data quality of income data using computer assisted interview: The experience of the Canadian survey of labour and income dynamics. *Proceedings of the Survey Research Methods Section, American Statistical Association, 1994,* 838–844.

Groves, R. M. (1989). *Survey errors and survey costs.* New York: John Wiley.

Groves, R. M. (1996). How do we know that what we think they think is really what they think? In N. Schwarz & S. Sudman (Eds.), *Answering questions: Methodology for determining cognitive and communicative processes in survey research* (pp. 389–401). San Francisco: Jossey-Bass.

Groves, R. M., Biemer, P., Lyberg, L., Massey, J., Nicholls, W., & Waksburg, J., (Eds.) (1988). *Telephone survey methodology.* New York: John Wiley and Sons.

Groves, R. M., Cialdini, R. B., & Couper, M. P. (1992). Understanding the decision to participate in a survey. *Public Opinion Quarterly, 56,* 475–495.

Groves, R. M., Fultz, N. H., & Martin, E. (1992). Direct questioning about comprehension in a survey setting. In J. M. Tanur (Ed.), *Questions about questions* (pp. 49–61). New York: Russel Sage.

Groves, R. M., & Kahn, R. L. (1979). *Surveys by telephone: A national comparison with personal interviews.* New York: Academic Press.

Groves, R. M., & Mathiowetz, N. A. (1984). Computer assisted telephone interviewing: Effects on interviewers and respondents. *Public Opinion Quarterly, 48,* 356–369.

Hatchett, S., & Schuman, H. (1976). White respondents and race of interviewer effects. *Public Opinion Quarterly, 39,* 523–528.

Haviland, S. E., & Clark, H. H. (1974). What's new? Acquiring new information as a process of comprehension. *Journal of Verbal Learning and Verbal Behavior, 13,* 512–521.

Herr, P. M. (1986). Consequences of priming: Judgment and behavior. *Journal of Personality and Social Psychology, 51,* 1106–1115.

Higgins, E. T. (1989). Knowledge accessibility and activation: Subjectivity and suffering from unconscious sources. In J. S. Uleman & J. A. Bargh (Eds.), *Unintended thought* (pp. 75–123). New York: Guilford Press.

Higgins, E. T., Rholes, W., & Jones, C. (1977). Category accessibility and impression formation. *Journal of Experimental Social Psychology, 13,* 141–154.

Hilton, D. J. (1995). The social context of reasoning: Conversational inference and rational judgment. *Psychological Bulletin, 118,* 248–271.

Hippler, H. J., & Schwarz, N. (1986). Not forbidding isn't allowing: The cognitive basis of the forbid-allow asymmetry. *Public Opinion Quarterly, 50,* 87–96.

Hippler, H. J., Schwarz, N., & Sudman, S. (Eds.) (1987). *Social information processing and survey methodology.* New York: Springer Verlag.

Holt, D., & Elliot, D. (1991). Methods of weighting for unit non-response. *The Statistician, 40,* 333–342.

Horvitz, D. G., Shaw, B. V., & Simmons, W. R. (1967). The unrelated question randomized response model. *Proceedings of the American Statistical Association* (pp. 65–72). Washington, DC: American Statistical Association.

Hox, J. J., de Leeuw, E. D., & Kreft, I. G. G. (1991). The effect of interviewer and respondent characteristics on the quality of survey data: A multilevel model. In P. Biemer, R. Groves, N. Mathiowetz, & S. Sudman (Eds.), *Measurement error in surveys* (pp. 393–418). Chichester: Wiley.

House, J., & Wolf, S. (1978). Effects of urban residence and interpersonal trust and helping behavior. *Journal of Personality and Social Psychology, 36,* 1029–1043.

Hyman, H. H. (1975 [1954]). *Interviewing in social research.* Chicago: University of Chicago Press.

Hyman, H. H., & Sheatsley, P. B. (1950). The current status of American public opinion. In J. C. Payne (Ed.), *The teaching of contemporary affairs* (pp. 11–34). New York: National Education Association.

Jabine, T. B., Straf, M. L., Tanur, J. M., & Tourangeau, R. (Eds.) (1984). *Cognitive aspects of survey methodology: Building a bridge between disciplines.* Washington, DC: National Academy Press.

James, J. M., & Bolstein, R. (1990). The effect of monetary incentives and follow-up mailings on the response rate and response quality in mail surveys. *Public Opinion Quarterly, 54,* 346–361.

Jenkins, C. R., & Dillman, D. A. (1997). Towards a theory of self-administered questionnaire design. In L. Lyberg, P. Biemer, M. Collins, E. DeLeeuw, C. Dippo, & N. Schwarz (Eds.), *Survey measurement and process quality.* (pp. 165–196) Chichester, UK: Wiley.

Jobe, J., & Loftus, E. (Eds.) (1991). Cognitive aspects of survey methodology [Special issue]. *Applied Cognitive Psychology, 5.*

Jones, E. E., & Nisbett, R. E. (1971). *The actor and the observer: Divergent perceptions of the causes of behavior.* Morristown, NJ: General Learning Press.

Kalton, G. (1983a). *Compensating for missing survey data.* Ann Arbor: Institute for Social Research, The University of Michigan.

Kalton, G. (1983b). *Introduction to survey sampling.* Beverly Hills, CA: Sage.

Kalton, G., Collins, M., & Brook, L. (1980). Experiments in wording opinion questions. *Journal of the Royal Statistical Society, C., 27,* 149–161.

Kalton, G., and Miller, M. E. (1986). Effects of adjustments for wave nonresponse on panel survey estimates. *Proceedings of the section on survey research methods, American Statistical Association* (pp. 194–199).

Kasprzyk, D., Duncan, G., Kalton, G., & Singh, M. (1989). *Panel surveys,* New York: John Wiley & Sons.

Kenny, D. A., Kashy, D. A., & Bolger, N. (1998). Data analysis in social psychology. In D. Gilbert, S. T. Fiske, & G. Lindzey (Eds.), *Handbook of social psychology* (4th ed., Vol. 1, pp. 233–265). New York: McGraw-Hill.

Kish, L. (1965). *Survey sampling.* New York: John Wiley & Sons.

Körmendi, E., & Noordhoek, J. (1989). *Data quality and telephone interviews.* Copenhagen: Danmarks Statistik.

Krosnick, J. A. (1991). Response strategies for coping with the cognitive demands of attitude measures in surveys. *Applied Cognitive Psychology, 5,* 213–236.

Krosnick, J. A., & Abelson, R. P. (1992). The case for measuring attitude strength. In J. M. Tanur (Ed.), *Questions about questions* (pp. 177–203). New York: Russel-Sage.

Krosnick, J. A., & Alwin, D. F. (1987). An evaluation of a cognitive theory of response order effects in survey measurement. *Public Opinion Quarterly, 51,* 201–219.

Krosnick, J. A., & Schuman, H. (1988). Attitude intensity, importance, and certainty and susceptibility to response effects. *Journal of Personality and Social Psychology, 54,* 940–952.

Kruglanski, A. W. (1980). Lay epistemologic process and contents. *Psychological Review, 87,* 70–87.

Krysan, M., Schuman, H., Scott, L. J., & Beatty, P. (1994). Response rates and response content in mail versus face-to-face surveys. *Public Opinion Quarterly, 58,* 381–399.

Lepkowski, J. M., & Groves, R. M. (1986). A mean squared error model for dual frame, mixed mode survey design. *Journal of the American Statistical Association, 81,* 930–937.

Lessler, J. T., & Forsyth, B. H. (1996). A coding system for appraising questionnaires. In N. Schwarz & S. Sudman (Eds.), *Answering questions: Methodology for determining cognitive and communicative processes in survey research* (pp. 259–292). San Francisco: Jossey-Bass.

Linton, M. (1975). Memory for real-world events. In D. A. Norman & D. E. Rumelhart (Eds.), *Explorations in cognition* (pp. 376–404). San Francisco: Freeman.

Linton, M. (1982). Transformations of memory in everyday life. In U. Neisser (Ed.), *Memory observed: Remembering in natural contexts* (pp. 77–91). San Francisco: Freeman.

Little, R. J. A., & Rubin, D. B. (1987). *Statistical analysis with missing data.* New York: John Wiley & Sons.

Loftus, E., & Fathi, D. C. (1985). Retrieving multiple autobiographical memories. *Social Cognition, 3,* 280–295.

Loftus, E. F., & Marburger, W. (1983). Since the eruption of Mt. St. Helens, has anyone beaten you up? *Memory and Cognition, 11,* 114–120.

Lombardi, W. J., Higgins, E. T., & Bargh, J. A. (1987). The role of consciousness in priming effects on categorization: Assimilation and contrast as a function of awareness of the priming task. *Personality and Social Psychology Bulletin, 13,* 411–429.

Lyberg, L., & Dean, P. (1992, May). *Methods for reducing nonresponse rates: A review.* Paper presented at the annual meeting of the American Association for Public Opinion Research, St. Petersburg, FL.

Madow, W., Nisselson, H., & Olkin, I. (1983). *Incomplete data in sample surveys* (Vols. 1–3). New York: Academic Press.

Martin, L. L. (1986). Set/reset: Use and diuse of concepts in impression formation. *Journal of Personality and Social Psychology, 51,* 493–504.

Martin, L., & Harlow, T. (1992). Basking and brooding: The motivating effects of filter questions in surveys. In N. Schwarz & S. Sudman (Eds.), *Context effects in social and psychological research* (pp. 81–96). New York: Springer-Verlag.

Martin, L. L., Seta, J. J., & Crelia, R. A. (1990). Assimilation and contrast as a function of people's willingness to expend effort in forming an impression. *Journal of Personality and Social Psychology, 59,* 27–37.

Mathiowetz, N. A. (1986, June). *Episodic recall and estimation: Applicability of cognitive theories to survey data.* Paper presented at the Social Science Research Council Seminar on Retrospective Data, New York.

Menon, G. (1993). The effects of accessibility of information in memory on judgments of behavioral frequencies. *Journal of Consumer Research, 20,* 431–440.

Menon, G. (1994). Judgments of behavioral frequencies: Memory search and retrieval strategies. In N. Schwarz & S. Sudman (Eds.) (1994). *Autobiographical memory and the validity of retrospective reports* (pp. 161–172). New York: Springer-Verlag.

Menon, G., Raghubir, P., & Schwarz, N. (1995). Behavioral frequency judgments: An accessibility-diagnosticity framework. *Journal of Consumer Research, 22,* 212–228.

Mingay, D. J., Shevell, S. K., Bradburn, N. M., & Ramirez, C. (1994). Self and proxy reports of everyday events. In N. Schwarz and S. Sudman (Eds.), *Autobiographical memory and the validity of retrospective reports* (pp. 235–250). New York: Springer-Verlag.

Mitchell, D. C. (1994). Sentence parsing. In M. A. Gernsbacher (Ed.), *Handbook of psycholinguistics* (pp. 375–410). San Diego, CA: Academic Press.

Moore, J. C. (1988). Self/Proxy response status and survey response quality. *Journal of Official Statistics, 4(2),* 155–172.

Morwitz, V., Johnson, E., & Schmittlein, D. (1993). Does measuring intent change behavior? *Journal of Consumer Research, 20,* 46–61.

Mueller, J. E. (1973). *War, presidents and public opinion.* New York: Wiley.

Mueller, J. E. (1994). *Public opinion in the Gulf War.* Chicago: University of Chicago Press.

National Research Council (1979). *Privacy and confidentiality as factors in survey response.* Washington, DC: National Academy of Sciences.

Neisser, U. (1986). Nested structure in autobiographical memory. In D. C. Rubin (Ed.). *Autobiographical memory* (pp. 71–88). Cambridge: Cambridge University Press.

Nicholls, W., Baker, R., & Martin, J. (1997). The effect of new data collection technologies on survey data quality. In L. Lyberg et al. (Eds.), *Survey measurement and process quality* (pp. 221–248). New York: John Wiley & Sons.

Nisbett, R. E., & Wilson, T. D. (1977). Telling more than we know: Verbal reports on mental processes. *Psychological Review, 84,* 231–259.

Nuckols, R. (1953). A note on pre-testing public opinion questions. *Journal of Applied Psychology, 37,* 119–120.

Oksenberg, L., Coleman, L., & Cannell, C. F. (1986). Interviewers' voices and refusal rates in telephone surveys. *Public Opinion Quarterly, 50,* 97–111.

Ostrom, T. M., & Upshaw, H. S. (1968). Psychological perspective and attitude change. In A. C. Greenwald, T. C. Brock, & T. M. Ostrom (Eds.), *Psychological foundations of attitudes.* New York: Academic Press.

Ottati, V. C., Riggle, E. J., Wyer, R. S., Schwarz, N., & Kuklinski, J. (1989). The cognitive and affective bases of opinion survey responses. *Journal of Personality and Social Psychology, 57,* 404–415.

Parducci, A. (1965). Category judgments: A range-frequency model. *Psychological Review, 72,* 407–418.

Parducci, A. (1983). Category ratings and the relational character of judgment. In H. G. Geissler, H. F. J. M. Bulfart, E. L. H. Leeuwenberg, & V. Sarris (Eds.), *Modern issues in perception* (pp. 262–282). Berlin: VEB Deutscher Verlag der Wissenschaften.

Parry, H. J., & Crossley, H. M. (1950). Validity of responses to survey questions. *Public Opinion Quarterly, 14,* 61–80.

Payne, S. L. (1951). *The art of asking questions.* Princeton: Princeton University Press.

Pearson, R. W., Ross, M., & Dawes, R. M. (1992). Personal recall and the limits of retrospective questions in surveys. In J. Tanur (Ed.), *Questions about questions* (pp. 65–94). New York: Russell-Sage.

Pepper, S. C. (1981). Problems in the quantification of frequency expressions. In D. W. Fiske (Ed.), *Problems with language imprecision* (New Directions for Methodology of Social and Behavioral Science, Vol. 9). San Francisco: Jossey-Bass.

Presser, S. (1994). Informed consent and confidentiality in survey research. *Public Opinion Quarterly, 58,* 446–459.

Presser, S., & Blair, J. (1994). Survey pretesting: Do different methods produce different results? In P. Marsden (Ed.), *Sociological Methodology 1994*. Oxford: Blackwell.

Reiser, B. J., Black, J. B., & Abelson, R. P. (1985). Knowledge structure in the organization and retrieval of autobiographical memories. *Cognitive Psychology, 17,* 89–137.

Rosenthal, R. (1976). *Experimenter effects in behavioral research* (Enl. ed). New York: Irvington Publishers.

Ross, L. (1977). The intuitive psychologist and his shortcomings: Distortions in the attribution process. In L. Berkowitz (Ed.), *Advances in experimental social psychology* (Vol. 10, pp. 173–220). New York: Academic Press.

Ross, M. (1989). The relation of implicit theories to the construction of personal histories. *Psychological Review, 96,* 341–357.

Rubin, D. B. (1987). *Multiple imputation for nonresponse in surveys*. New York: John Wiley & Sons.

Rugg, D. (1941). Experiments in wording questions. *Public Opinion Quarterly, 5,* 91–92.

Schleifer, S. (1986). Trends in attitudes toward and participation in survey research. *Public Opinion Quarterly, 50,* 17–26.

Schuman, H. (1966). The random probe. A technique for evaluating the validity of closed questions. *American Sociological Review, 31,* 218–222.

Schuman, H. (1983). Survey research and the fundamental attribution error. *Personality and Social Psychology Bulletin, 9,* 103–104.

Schuman, H. (1986). Ordinary questions, survey questions, and policy questions. *Public Opinion Quarterly, 50,* 432–442.

Schuman, H. (1995). Attitudes, beliefs, and behavior. In K. S. Cook, G. A. Fine, & J. S. House (Eds.), *Sociological perspectives on attitudes* (pp. 68–89). Boston: Allyn & Bacon.

Schuman, H., & Bobo, L. (1988). Survey-based experiments on white racial attitudes toward residential integration. *American Journal of Sociology, 94,* 273–299.

Schuman, H., & Converse, J. (1971). Effects of black and white interviewers on black responses in 1968. *Public Opinion Quarterly, 35,* 44–68.

Schuman, H., & Kalton, G. (1985). Survey methods. In G. Lindzey & E. Aronson (Eds.), *Handbook of social psychology* (Vol. 1, pp. 635–697). New York: Random House.

Schuman, H., & Ludwig, J. (1983). The norm of even-handedness in surveys as in life. *American Sociological Review, 48,* 112–120.

Schuman, H., & Presser, S. (1981). *Questions and answers in attitude surveys*. New York: Academic Press.

Schuman, H., & Scott, J. (1987). Problems in the use of survey questions to measure public opinion. *Science, 236,* 957–959.

Schwarz, N. (1990). Assessing frequency reports of mundane behaviors: Contributions of cognitive psychology to questionnaire construction. In C. Hendrick & M. S. Clark (Eds.), *Research methods in personality and social psychology* (Review of Personality and Social Psychology, Vol. 11, pp. 98–119). Beverly Hills, CA: Sage.

Schwarz, N. (1994). Judgment in a social context: Biases, shortcomings, and the logic of conversation. In M. Zanna (Ed.), *Advances in experimental social psychology* (Vol. 26). San Diego, CA: Academic Press.

Schwarz, N. (1995). What respondents learn from questionnaires: The survey interview and the logic of conversation. *International Statistical Review, 63,* 153–177.

Schwarz, N. (1996). *Cognition and communication: Judgmental biases, research methods, and the logic of conversation*. Hillsdale, NJ: Erlbaum.

Schwarz, N., & Bienias, J. (1990). What mediates the impact of response alternatives on frequency reports of mundane behavior? *Applied Cognitive Psychology, 4,* 61–72.

Schwarz, N., & Bless, H. (1992a). Constructing reality and its alternatives: Assimilation and contrast effects in social judgment. In L. L. Martin & A. Tesser (Eds.), *The construction of social judgments* (pp. 217–245). Hillsdale, NJ: Erlbaum.

Schwarz, N., & Bless, H. (1992b). Scandals and the public's trust in politicians: Assimilation and contrast effects. *Personality and Social Psychology Bulletin, 18,* 574–579.

Schwarz, N., & Hippler, H. J. (1991). Response alternatives: The impact of their choice and ordering. In P. Biemer, R. Groves, N. Mathiowetz, & S. Sudman (Eds.), *Measurement error in surveys* (pp. 41–56). Chichester: Wiley.

Schwarz, N., & Hippler, H. J. (1995). Subsequent questions may influence answers to preceding questions in mail surveys. *Public Opinion Quarterly, 59,* 93–97.

Schwarz, N., Hippler, H. J., Deutsch, B., & Strack, F. (1985). Response categories: Effects on behavioral reports and comparative judgments. *Public Opinion Quarterly, 49,* 388–395.

Schwarz, N., Hippler, H. J., & Noelle-Neumann, E. (1992). A cognitive model of response order effects in survey measurement. In N. Schwarz & S. Sudman (Eds.), *Context effects in social and psychological research* (pp. 187–201). New York: Springer-Verlag.

Schwarz, N., Knäuper, B., Hippler, H. J., Noelle-Neumann, E., & Clark, F. (1991). Rating scales: Numeric values may change the meaning of scale labels. *Public Opinion Quarterly, 55,* 570–582.

Schwarz, N., & Strack, F. (1991). Context effects in attitude surveys: Applying cognitive theory to social research. In W. Stroebe & M. Hewstone (Eds.), *European Review of Social Psychology* (Vol. 2, pp. 31–50). Chichester: Wiley.

Schwarz, N., Strack, F., Hippler, H. J., & Bishop, G. (1991). The impact of administration mode on response effects in survey measurement. *Applied Cognitive Psychology, 5,* 193–212.

Schwarz, N., Strack, F., & Mai, H. P. (1991). Assimilation and contrast effects in part-whole question sequences: A conversational logic analysis. *Public Opinion Quarterly, 55,* 3–23.

Schwarz, N., Strack, F., Müller, G., & Chassein, B. (1988). The range of response alternatives may determine the meaning of the question: Further evidence on informative functions of response alternatives. *Social Cognition, 6,* 107–117.

Schwarz, N., & Sudman, S. (Eds.). (1992). *Context effects in social and psychological research.* New York: Springer-Verlag.

Schwarz, N., & Sudman, S. (Eds.). (1994). *Autobiographical memory and the validity of retrospective reports.* New York: Springer-Verlag.

Schwarz, N., & Sudman, S. (Eds.). (1996). *Answering questions: Methodology for determining cognitive and communicative processes in survey research.* San Francisco: Jossey-Bass.

Schwarz, N., & Wellens, T. (in press). Cognitive dynamics of proxy responding: The diverging perspectives of actors and observers. *Journal of Official Statistics.*

Scott, W. A. (1968). Attitude measurement. In G. Lindzey & E. Aronson (Eds.), *Handbook of Social Psychology* (2nd ed., Vol. 2, pp. 204–273). Reading, MA: Addison-Wesley.

Simpson, G. B. (1994). Context and the processing of ambiguous words. In M. A. Gernsbacher (Ed.), *Handbook of psycholinguistics* (pp. 359–374). San Diego, CA: Academic Press.

Singer, E., Hippler, H. J., & Schwarz, N. (1992). Confidentiality assurances in surveys: Reassurance or threat? *International Journal of Public Opinion Research, 4,* 256–268.

Singer, E., & Kohnke-Aguirre, L. (1979). Interviewer expectation effects: A replication and extension. *Public Opinion Quarterly, 43,* 245–260.

Sirken, M. (1970). Household surveys with multiplicity. *Journal of the American Statistical Association, 65,* 257–266.

Skowronski, J. J., Betz, A. L., Thompson, C. P., Walker, W. R., & Shannon, L. (1994). The impact of differing memory domains on event-dating processes in self and proxy reports. In N. Schwarz & S. Sudman (Eds.), *Autobiographical memory and the validity of retrospective reports* (pp. 217–234). New York: Springer-Verlag.

Smith, T. W. (1979). Happiness. *Social Psychology Quarterly, 42,* 18–30.

Smith, T. W. (1992). Thoughts on the nature of context effects. In N. Schwarz & S. Sudman (Eds.), *Context effects in social and psychological research* (pp. 163–185). New York: Springer-Verlag.

Sniderman, P. M., Brody, R. A., & Tetlock, P. E. (1991). *Reasoning and choice: Explorations in political psychology.* New York: Cambridge University Press.

Sperber, D., & Wilson, D. (1986). *Relevance: Communication and cognition.* Cambridge, MA: Harvard University Press.

Steeh, C. (1981). Trends in nonresponse rates. *Public Opinion Quarterly, 45,* 40–57.

Stouffer, S. A., & DeVinney, L. C. (1949). How personal adjustment varied in the army—by background characteristics of the soldiers. In S. A. Stouffer, E. A. Suchman, L. C.

DeVinney, S. A. Star, & R. M. Williams, (Eds.), *The American soldier: Adjustment during army life.* Princeton, NJ: Princeton University Press.

Strack, F. (1992a). Order effects in survey research: Activative and informative functions of preceding questions. In N. Schwarz & S. Sudman (Eds.), *Context effects in social and psychological research* (pp. 23–34). New York: Springer-Verlag.

Strack, F. (1992b). The different routes to social judgment: Experiential versus informational strategies. In L. L. Martin & A. Tesser (Eds.), *The construction of social judgments* (pp. 249–276). Hillsdale, NJ: Erlbaum.

Strack, F. (1994). *Zur Psychologie der standardisierten Befragung.* Heidelberg, FRG: Springer-Verlag.

Strack, F., & Martin, L. (1987). Thinking, judging, and communicating: A process account of context effects in attitude surveys. In H. J. Hippler, N. Schwarz, & S. Sudman (Eds.), *Social information processing and survey methodology* (pp. 123–148). New York: Springer-Verlag.

Strack, F., Martin, L. L., & Schwarz, N. (1988). Priming and communication: The social determinants of information use in judgments of life-satisfaction. *European Journal of Social Psychology, 18,* 429–442.

Strack, F., & Schwarz, N. (1992). Implicit cooperation: The case of standardized questioning. In G. Semin & F. Fiedler (Eds.), *Social cognition and language* (pp. 173–193). Beverly Hills, CA: Sage.

Strack, F., Schwarz, N., Chassein, B., Kern, D., & Wagner, D. (1990). The salience of comparison standards and the activation of social norms: Consequences for judgments of happiness and their communication. *British Journal of Social Psychology, 29,* 303–314.

Strack, F., Schwarz, N., & Gschneidinger, E. (1985). Happiness and reminiscing: The role of time perspective, mood, and mode of thinking. *Journal of Personality and Social Psychology, 49,* 1460–1469.

Strack, F., Schwarz, N., Bless, H., Kübler, A., & Wänke, M. (1993). Awareness of the influence as a determinant of assimilation versus contrast. *European Journal of Social Psychology, 23,* 53–62.

Strack, F., Schwarz, N., & Wänke, M. (1991). Semantic and pragmatic aspects of context effects in social and psychological research. *Social Cognition, 9,* 111–125.

Strube, G. (1987). Answering survey questions: The role of memory. In H. J. Hippler, N. Schwarz, & S. Sudman (Eds.), *Social information processing and survey methodology* (pp. 86–101). New York: Springer-Verlag.

Sudman, S. (1976). *Applied sampling.* New York: Academic Press.

Sudman, S., Bickart, B., Blair, J., & Menon, G. (1994). The effect of level of participation on reports of behavior and attitudes by proxy reporters. In N. Schwarz & S. Sudman (Eds.), *Autobiographical memory and the validity of retrospective reports* (pp. 251–266). New York: Springer-Verlag.

Sudman, S., & Bradburn, N. M. (1974). *Response effects in surveys: A review and synthesis.* Chicago: Aldine.

Sudman, S., & Bradburn, N. M. (1983). *Asking questions.* San Francisco: Jossey-Bass.

Sudman, S., Bradburn, N. M., & Schwarz, N. (1996). *Thinking about answers: The application of cognitive processes to survey methodology.* San Francisco, CA: Jossey-Bass.

Sykes, W., & Collins, M. (1988). Effects of mode of interview: Experiments in the U.K. In R. Groves, P. Biemer, L. Lyberg, J. Massey, W. Nicholls, & J. Waksberg (Eds.), *Telephone survey methodology* (pp. 301–320). New York: Wiley.

Tanur, J. M. (Ed.). (1992). *Questions about questions.* New York: Russel Sage.

Thompson, C. P. (1982). Memory for unique personal events: The roommate study. *Memory & Cognition, 10,* 324–332.

Thornberry, O., & Massey, J. (1988). Trends in United States telephone coverage across time and subgroups. In R. Groves, P. Biemer, L. Lyberg, J. Massey, W. Nicholls, & J. Waksberg, *Telephone survey methodology* (pp. 25–50). New York: John Wiley & Sons.

Tortora, R. D. (1985). CATI in an Agricultural Statistical Agency. *Journal of Official Statistics, 1,* 301–314.

Tourangeau, R. (1984). Cognitive science and survey methods: A cognitive perspective. In T. Jabine, M. Straf, J. Tanur, & R. Tourangeau (Eds.), *Cognitive aspects of survey methodology: Building a bridge between disciplines* (pp. 73–100). Washington, DC: National Academy Press.

Tourangeau, R. (1987). Attitude measurement: A cognitive perspective. In H. J. Hippler, N. Schwarz, & S. Sudman (Eds.), *Social information processing and survey methodology* (pp. 149–162). New York: Springer-Verlag.

Tourangeau, R. (1992). Attitudes as memory structures: Belief sampling and context effects. In N. Schwarz & S. Sudman (Eds.), *Context effects in social and psychological research* (pp. 35–47). New York: Springer-Verlag.

Tourangeau, R., & Rasinski, K. A. (1988). Cognitive processes underlying context effects in attitude measurement. *Psychological Bulletin, 103,* 299–314.

Tourangeau, R., Rasinski, K. A., & Bradburn, N. (1991). Measuring happiness in surveys: A test of the subtraction hypothesis. *Public Opinion Quarterly, 55,* 255–266.

Turner, C. F., & Martin, E. (Eds.). (1984). *Surveying subjec-*

tive phenomena (Vol. 1). New York: Russel Sage.

Van der Zouwen, J., Dijkstra, W., & Smit, J. H. (1991). Studying respondent-interviewer interaction: The relationship between interviewing style, interviewer behavior, and response behavior. In P. Biemer, R. Groves, N. Mathiowetz, & S. Sudman (Eds.), *Measurement error in surveys* (pp. 419–438). Chichester: Wiley.

Wagenaar, W. A. (1986). My memory: A study of autobiographical memory over six years. *Cognitive Psychology, 18,* 225–252.

Wagenaar, W. A. (1988). People and places in my memory: A study on cue specificity and retrieval from autobiographical memory. In M. M. Gruneberg, P. E. Morris, & R. N. Sykes (Eds.), *Practical aspects of memory: Current research and issues* (Vol.1, pp. 228–232). Chichester: Wiley.

Warner, S. L. (1965). Randomized response: A survey technique for eliminating error answer bias. *Journal of the American Statistical Association, 60,* 63–69.

Watson, D. (1982). The actor and the observer: How are their perceptions of causality divergent? *Psychological Bulletin, 92,* 682–700.

Williams, J. A. (1964). Interviewer-respondent interaction: A study of bias in the information interview. *Sociometry, 27,* 338–352.

Williams, M. D., & Hollan, J. D. (1981). The process of retrieval from very long term memory. *Cognitive Science, 5,* 87–119.

Willis, G., Royston, P., & Bercini, D. (1991). The use of verbal report methods in the development and testing of survey questions. *Applied Cognitive Psychology, 5,* 251–267.

Wilson, T. D., & Hodges, S. D. (1992). Attitudes as temporary constructions. In L. L. Martin & A. Tesser (Eds.), *The construction of social judgments* (pp. 37–65). Hillsdale, NJ: Erlbaum.

Whitten, W. B., & Leonard, J. M. (1981). Directed search through autobiographical memory. *Memory and Cognition, 9,* 566–579.

Withey, S. B. (1954). Reliability of recall of income. *Public Opinion Quarterly, 18,* 31–34.

Wyer, R. S., & Srull, T. K. (1989). *Memory and cognition in its social context.* Hillsdale, NJ: Erlbaum.

Zaller, J. R. (1992). *The nature and origins of mass opinion.* Cambridge: Cambridge University Press.

CHAPTER FIVE

MEASUREMENT

CHARLES M. JUDD, *University of Colorado*
GARY H. MCCLELLAND, *University of Colorado*

INTRODUCTION

In the practice of social psychology, in the research and teaching we do, most of us pay relatively little attention to the issue of measurement. We design our studies, we collect and analyze our data, and we write and submit our papers, taking much for granted about how we measure and how we should measure the phenomena of interest. So, if we are interested in attitudes, we generally know how to ask attitude questions. If we are interested in person perception or stereotyping, we know how to ask subjects about social perception. And if our focus is on groups, we can proceed to code the sorts of decisions groups make and how they operate without worrying unduly about measurement issues.

By and large, this lack of attention to measurement issues works fairly well for the individual researcher and for the conduct of his or her research. Only rarely does it seem that reviewers criticize a manuscript on the grounds of inadequate measurement. Almost never does it seem that we get called to task for failing to provide evidence in support of our measurement goals.

So why, one might ask, do we need a *Handbook* chapter on measurement, and why should one read it? The answer, we suggest, is that our discipline's lack of attention to mea-surement is a common dilemma. While the individual researcher can ignore measurement issues for the most part without consequence, the discipline as a whole suffers when the theories and methods underlying measurement are undeveloped and unscrutinized. Conceptual advances in science frequently follow measurement advances. The everyday practice of normal science can successfully operate without much attention to measurement issues. But for the discipline as a whole to advance and develop, measurement must be a focus of collective attention.

We have at least two goals in writing this chapter. On the one hand, we simply want to provide practical advice for constructing and evaluating measures and scales in social psychology. Accordingly, much of this chapter is concerned with the *how* of measurement. But we also have a much broader goal of encouraging social psychologists to self-consciously reflect on what they measure, how they measure, and the implicit theories that they use in constructing measures and scales. We hope to encourage reflection on the *why* of measurement and the *what* of measurement. And we hope that this reflection ultimately will lead to advances in measurement and in the theory of measurement for social psychology.

The What and the Why of Measurement

Most books and chapters on measurement jump to the how-to without considering what measurement really is, why we are interested in it, and what its benefits are. There are of course some notable exceptions. Torgerson (1958), Coombs (1964), Messick (1989), and Michell (1990), for instance, consider the role and benefits of measurement and scaling within the larger context of the goals of sci-

Preparation of this chapter was partially supported by NIMH Grant R01 MH45049 to Charles M. Judd and Bernadette Park. We thank Sara Culhane, Robyn Dawes, Bruce Dehning, Reid Hastie, David Kenny, and Carol Nickerson for helpful comments and other assistance. Correspondence should be addressed to either author at the Department of Psychology, University of Colorado, Boulder, CO 80309-0345 or via the Internet to charles.judd or gary.mcclelland both @colorado.edu.

ence. The material in this section is heavily influenced by these sources.

The raw data of social psychology, and of the social and behavioral sciences in general, potentially consist of infinitely minute observations of ongoing behavior and attributes of individuals, social groups, social environments, and other entities or objects that populate the social world. Measurement is the process by which these infinitely varied observations are reduced to compact descriptions or models that are presumed to represent meaningful regularities in the entities that are observed.

This definition is rather different from the classic definition of measurement offered by Stevens in 1951 (p. 22). He defined measurement simply "as the assignment of numerals to objects or events according to rules." Like Torgerson (1958) and Dawes and Smith (1985), we take issue with this definition on at least two grounds. First, not all measurement involves numbers. As we illustrate later on, compact descriptions of observations can be well represented non-numerically. Second, and more importantly, rules for assigning numbers constitute measurement only if the subsequent numbers ultimately represent something of meaning, some regularity of attributes or behaviors that permits prediction. Dawes and Smith (1985, p. 511) nicely make the point:

> Consider, for example, the number of rules that could be used to assign numbers to beauty contestants or politicians (e.g., cube the distance between the candidate's chin and left forefinger when he or she is standing at attention; then divide by the time of his or her birth). Few of these rules would tell us anything worth knowing (e.g., who will win). The assignment of numbers not only must be orderly if it is to yield measurement but must also represent meaningful attributes and yield meaningful predictions.

The compact model or description that we construct of observations through measurement we will call a scale or a variable. The meaningful attribute or regularity that it is presumed to represent we will call a construct. Accordingly, measurement consists of rules that assign scale or variable values to entities to represent the constructs that are thought to be theoretically meaningful.

The entities to be measured typically consist of individuals or social groups in social psychology. But in fact, many other sorts of objects can be measured. For example, the entities to be measured might be attitude statements, cookies made with varying amounts of sugar and salt, archaeological sites, political candidates, or automobiles. Likewise, the constructs to be measured may include a wide array of attributes thought to be meaningful within the context of some theory about the entities. Potential constructs or attributes to be measured about these entities might be (in order of the above entity ex-

amples) political liberalness, taste appeal, age, honesty, or fuel efficiency.

A bit more abstractly, assume that $a, b, c. . .$, represent different entities and we want to measure one or more constructs or attributes of these entities. We will say that $s()$ is a scale if it assigns values to all the entities under consideration, with $s(a), s(b), s(c), . . .$, being the respective values. This scale will then constitute a measurement of the entities if in fact it adequately models or represents the construct that we wish to measure.

As an example consider the following specific rule for assigning numbers to attitude statements to represent how "liberal" they are.

> *Assignment Rule.* The number assigned to attitude statement a will be larger than the number assigned to statement b, that is, $s(a) > s(b)$ if and only if a majority of a panel of 15 randomly selected students judges that statement a is more liberal than statement b.

This assignment rule is a sufficient example of measurement according to Stevens (1951) definition. According to ours, it is not. Further conditions of measurement are that there is in fact an attribute "liberalness" that can be assessed and that the assigned scale values actually capture or adequately model this construct. In essence, for a variable or scale to be a valid measure, the scale values of the entities must resemble the true but unknown standings of the entities on the construct that is of theoretical interest. The variable or scale is then said to possess "construct validity" (Cronbach & Meehl, 1955).

The defining conditions of measurement necessitate that measurement and theory are inextricably linked. Measurement presupposes a theory that defines the important constructs to be measured and that provides a motivation for the rule for assigning scale values to entities. Theory in turn depends on measurement, for confidence in a set of theoretical hypotheses increases by showing empirical relationships among measured variables. And theoretical disconfirmation only occurs if the relationships posited by theory are empirically contradicted.

Good measurement then can lead to a disconfirmation of theoretical expectations. This can happen in two ways. The first way is the most obvious: empirical relationships among measured variables may show inconsistencies with theoretical expectations. This then leads to theoretical modifications or elaborations and further empirical work. The second way in which theoretical disconfirmation can happen is that the measurement model itself may fail. For instance, the theory may lead one to believe that there is in fact a construct to be measured or scaled, but the scaling procedure itself may reveal inconsistencies that suggest that a unidimensional construct is untenable. A good scaling or measurement model, thus, is one that provides the possibility of theoretical disconfirmation. It allows measurement inconsistencies to suggest that constructs do not exist as theoretically defined.

Two different measurement traditions exist within psychology as a whole and these have influenced contemporary approaches to measurement in social psychology. As we shall see, the two traditions differ in the sort of evidence that they rely upon in order to disconfirm a measurement model. We follow the lead of Dawes and Smith (1985) and others in referring to these two different traditions as the representational approach and the psychometric approach. In the sections that follow we briefly define these two approaches. The subsequent organization of the chapter is based on the distinction between the two approaches. Thus, following this introduction, we first discuss in some detail representational measurement and its approach to model disconfirmation. We then turn to the psychometric tradition, outlining how it assesses measurement adequacy. Each of these sections can be read by itself once the definitions in this introduction have been covered. In writing this chapter, it was striking for us to note the extent to which these two traditions speak different languages and have, as a result, failed to communicate with each other. Accordingly, in the concluding section of the chapter we attempt to build bridges between them.

Representational Measurement

Representational measurement is the assignment of numbers to entities so that properties of the numbers (e.g., greater than, addition, subtraction, multiplication) *represent* empirical relationships. The rule for assigning scale values to attitude statements as mentioned earlier provides an example: the greater-than property of numbers represents or corresponds to the empirical observation that a majority of the panel judged one statement to be more liberal than another. Or, as another example, consider the physical measurement of length. If rod a is 5 centimeters and rod b is 15 centimeters, then placing the two rods end to end will produce a rod 20 centimeters long. In this case, the additive property of numbers represents the physical concatenation of the two rods. In effect, numbers along with their specified properties become a model for our observations.

An important feature of numerical representations is that they can be used to make predictions about the empirical observations. For example, if statement c has a scale value of 9 and statement d a scale value of 2, we would predict that a majority of the panel would judge statement c to be more liberal than statement d. Similarly, we can predict that concatenating rods of lengths 3 and 5 would produce exactly the same length as concatenating rods of lengths 2 and 6 because $3 + 5 = 2 + 6$. Note that we must be careful in each instance to specify the properties of numbers that are supposed to apply to the empirical observations. For example, our assignment rule for attitude

statements only involved the order property of numbers. We would have no basis, given this particular assignment rule, for predicting that someone who agreed with two attitude statements with scale values of 3 and 4 was more liberal than someone who agreed with a statement with a scale value of 6 even though $3 + 4 > 6$. The assignment rule simply does not imply that addition is meant to represent such empirical observations.

It is usually not obvious which numerical properties ought to apply to a given set of observations. At this point, it might not even be clear why the additive property should not apply in the example of the attitude statements. That is why we need theories of measurement to tell us the conditions or relationships that must be true for our observations before we can represent them with numbers and specified numerical properties. Representational measurement theory is concerned with the specification and testing of those conditions for a variety of data types (Coombs, 1964). Later in this chapter, we consider examples of these conditions for several data types.

For now, note that the ability to make predictions about the set of entities whose properties we are measuring provides us with an internal consistency check of the particular scaling model we are using. For example, if statement a is judged more liberal than statement b (which we will denote by $a > b$ for a dominates b) and $b > c$, then clearly the number assigned to a ought to be higher than the number assigned to c. After assigning numbers to a, b, and c we could then predict an observation that has not yet been used in the measurement process: namely, a should be judged to be more liberal than c. If it is, then we have a bit more confidence in our measurement and scaling; if it is not, then we have a serious problem with our measurement model because an internal consistency check has been violated. The implications of violations are discussed more thoroughly in later sections. The important point here is that a defining characteristic of representational measurement is that it is always possible to derive internal consistency checks to assess the validity of the measurement model being used to represent the observations.

Psychometric Measurement

The other approach to measurement relies on external and aggregate patterns of data to evaluate the adequacy of a measurement model rather than on internal consistency checks on the behavior of individual entities. The most common example of the nonrepresentational approach to measurement in the social sciences is the ubiquitous rating scale. For example, in a typical attitude scale (sometimes called a Likert scale), respondents indicate whether they agree very strongly, agree strongly, agree, neither agree nor disagree, disagree, disagree strongly, or disagree very strongly with each attitude statement in the questionnaire.

It is common to associate the numbers +3, +2, +1, 0, –1, –2, and –3 with those categories, respectively. The respondent's scale score is simply the sum of his scores for each item with a prior multiplication by –1 for items that run in the opposite "direction."

Unlike the representational approach to measurement, in psychometric measurement there are no strong checks of internal consistency that can be applied at the level of the individual entity and that could lead to a conclusion that the measurement model was violated. For example, knowing that someone *agreed strongly* with, say, attitude item *a* or that someone's total score on the attitude questionnaire is 36, provides no logical basis for predicting that person's response to, say, attitude item *b*. To be sure, given the way such scales are constructed, we would expect responses to items *a* and *b* to be correlated statistically across respondents. However, there is no way for a single individual to behave *inconsistently* with respect to the scale items. For example, we can make the following claim without any knowledge of the content of items *a* and *b*: it is not inconsistent for someone to agree strongly with item *a* and to disagree very strongly with item *b*. We can perhaps say that such a situation is unlikely or statistically improbable, but there is no internal logic that renders such a pattern inconsistent for any pair of items.

The psychometric approach to measurement relies on procedures for evaluating a scale or a measure at the aggregate level because the approach presumes that there is a huge amount of noise or error at the level of the individual entity response and so only aggregate consistency checks make sense. In other words, the psychometric approach doesn't care very much that rating scales, for instance, provide no logical basis for predicting a person's response to one item, given his or her response to another. This lack of concern derives from the presumption that the magnitude of errors in individual responses is such that a consistency check at this level is unlikely to be informative. Rather, the expectation at the aggregate level is that there should be a correlation between items if they are measuring the same thing. Thus, psychometric measurement does not rely on internal consistency checks at the level of the individual because it starts with the assumption of considerable error in responses. Instead it relies on patterns of variances and covariances that can be evaluated only at the aggregate level and only probabilistically.

Representational versus Psychometric Measurement

Some measurement theorists have suggested that nonrepresentational measurement is an oxymoron. For example, Pfanzagl (1968) referred to measurement in the Likert scale tradition as "measurement by fiat." Such measurement theorists believed that representational measurement as expounded in the three-volume *Foundations of Measurement* (Krantz et al., 1971; Suppes et al., 1989; and Luce et al., 1990) would allow psychology to replace measurement by fiat with more defensible measurement procedures. However, more recently, Dawes (1994), who championed the representational approach to measurement in his chapter (Dawes & Smith, 1985) in the previous edition of the *Handbook of Social Psychology,* and Cliff (1992) have referred to representational measurement theory as the revolution that "failed" outside psychophysics or that "never happened," respectively. Dawes and Cliff individually speculate about the reasons the revolution failed, including the difficulty of the underlying abstract mathematics, the lack of demonstrated empirical power, the apparently intractable problems of dealing with error, and the conflict with traditional research styles in psychology. Dawes (1994, p. 280) sums up: "the revolution outside psychophysics may have failed because the investigators too seldom managed to relate representational scale values . . . to anything else of importance."

While there are some success stories in psychophysics for representational measurement, successful applications of representational measurement in social psychology are difficult to find. Dawes (1994; see also Dawes & Smith, 1985) cites Coombs, Coombs, and McClelland (1975) as a successful application in which representational measurement procedures (a) resolved a theoretical problem that had stumped demographers trying to measure preferences for family size and composition and (b) created scales that had generality over a wide range of cultures. However, when these same techniques were applied to the study of other fertility-related topics such as the choice among contraceptive alternatives (Nickerson, McClelland, & Petersen, 1991), the results were less satisfactory.

While the revolution of representative measurement was sputtering, psychometric measurement was faring better in its ability to make predictions and was making progress at getting its own house in order with respect to being able to test its measurement scales. We describe those developments, especially the use of confirmatory factor analysis, in later sections.

If the revolution represented by representational measurement has failed, then why discuss it in this chapter? First, not everyone agrees that it has failed. Marley (1992, p. 96), for example, believes that the revolution is still in its early stages and that recent work on representational measurement represents "the foundations of measurement upon which future generations of theoreticians and experimentalists can build to test theories. . . ." We suspect there is some wisdom in this prediction. Second, even if they are not used for actually constructing scales, representational measurement models can often provide theoretical insights not available if we rely exclusively on traditional rating scale measures. We emphasize such insights in our quick tour of representational methods. Third, we do think that there is a potential difficulty in the psychometric approach's exclusive reliance on statistical patterns of covariation to evaluate the adequacy of a measurement model. The problem arises because patterns of variance and covariance are used not only for this purpose but also to evaluate theoretical predictions about the relationships between different constructs. As a result, it can be difficult to know when covariation (or its absence) reflects the adequacy of a measurement model and when it reflects relationships between constructs predicted by theory. Suppose we find that two measures are highly correlated. When do we conclude that they are alternative measures of the same construct and when do we conclude that the relationship represents a theoretically meaningful association between different constructs?[1] This question would be less likely to arise if there were internal and logical consistency checks that could be conducted, independent of aggregate patterns of covariation, to assess the adequacy of the measures.

Alternatives to Numerical Representations of Scales

The field of measurement and scaling is replete with metaphors and analogies. Our word "scale" has its origins in two analogies—"scale" as a ladder with rungs or ranks and "scale" as a pan balance. Before proceeding to the *how* of representational and psychometric measurement, we digress briefly to consider geometrical and other nonnumerical methods for depicting numerical scale values. These alternative depictions often have important practical advantages in terms of communicating information about observations effectively.

Geometric Representations   Measurement and scaling are often associated with geometric depictions of data. For example, scale values are sometimes thought of as points on a line as in Figure 1. Such geometric representations show the location of each entity on a single dimension or continuum and so such scales are often called "unidimensional."

The ubiquity of geometrical representations in measurement and scaling means that other geometrical concepts are often employed as convenient metaphors. One particularly pervasive metaphor is the geometrical concept of dis-

tance. Many social psychologists employ the concept of "psychological distance." The use of the adjective "psychological" to modify "distance" indicates that it is not real distance that is meant but rather the psychologically effective distance between two entities. The distance between the location of two entities on a scale or dimension then represents this psychological or subjective distance. For example, if the scale in Figure 1 represents liberalness and the entities are attitude statements, then the psychological distance between items *a* and *b* is greater than the psychological distance between items *b* and *c* in terms of liberalness. Somewhat more general than psychological distance is the metaphor "functional distance," representing the functional effect of the entity, in terms of whatever dimension is being scaled.

Multidimensional Geometric Representations   Often we will measure more than one attribute of each entity so that a vector of scale values will be assigned. For example, in research using the semantic differential (Osgood, Suci, & Tannenbaum, 1957) we might want to assign three scale values to each noun to represent its evaluation (good-bad), its potency (strong-weak), and its activity (active-passive).

When more than one scale value is assigned to each entity, the entities can be represented as points in a multidimensional space with each dimension corresponding to a different type of scale value. For example, Figure 2 displays a two-dimensional scaling from Wish (1971) for twelve nations, based on their similarity ratings. Just as was the case for unidimensional measurement, we will sometimes be able to refer to the distance between points in multidimensional space as the functional distance between the corresponding entities.

Nongeometrical Representations   We also can use depictions which are nongeometrical, but still visual. For example, we might want to assign different shades of blue to be the scale values for the attitude statements with deeper shades of blue representing the more liberal statements and lighter shades the more conservative statements. Or we might want to assign a line drawing of a face to each census tract with the degree of the smile representing the average per capita income of the census tract (Chernoff, 1973).

Nongeometrical depictions would certainly not be very useful for some purposes—they would be difficult to input into statistical computer programs, for example. However, such depictions do have at least two important advantages. First, they can often be understood more readily. Many innovative methods for displaying information have been proposed (e.g., Cleveland, 1993b; Tufte, 1990), and there is active research and theoretical development about the intelligibility of visual displays and colored graphs (e.g., Cleveland, 1993a; Cleveland & McGill, 1987; Kosslyn, 1989;

FIGURE 1   Geometric, Unidimensional Representation of a Scale.

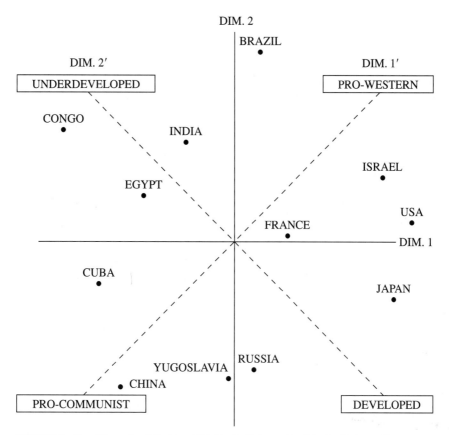

FIGURE 2   Two-Dimensional Scaling of Similarity Judgments of Twelve Nations. (*Source:* Kruskal & Wish, 1978, Figure 8, p. 32.)

Shah & Carpenter, 1995; Simkin & Hastie, 1987; Tversky & Schiano, 1989; Wainer & Theissen, 1981) and on the presentation of complex multivariate tables by means of faces such as the one described for census tracts (Chernoff & Rizvi, 1975). If the scales are to serve as input to a human computer instead of an electronic one, then nonnumerical depictions may well be preferred to confusing numerical tables.

A second advantage of nonnumerical scale values within the representational framework is that with a careful choice we can be sure that the depictions represent just the empirical relationship we observe. With numbers, on the other hand, there can be some ambiguity unless we are very careful to specify just which properties of numbers are meant to apply. For example, we might assign 6 to attitude statement *a* and 2 to attitude statement *b* with the intention of only meaning that statement *a* is more liberal than statement *b*. Even if we are careful to state that only the ordering of the numbers is meaningful, some subsequent user of our scale might overlook that restriction and wonder whether *a* is three times more liberal than *b* be-

cause the scale value of *a* is three times that of *b*'s. Such confusions are prevented if shades of color or some other nonnumerical depictions are assigned.

There is of course no reason why more than one nonnumerical depiction cannot be assigned to each entity. In fact, Chernoff's (1973) FACES were designed primarily for multivariate rather than univariate data. All that is required is a careful specification of what properties are to be represented by which characteristics. For example, Wainer and Theissen (1981) constructed the map of faces in Figure 3 to represent various observed properties of states that might be related to the quality of life by using the following assignment rules:

- Population: number of faces/state. (The number of faces is proportional to the log of the population.)
- Literacy Rate: size of the eyes (bigger = better).
- % HS Graduates: slant of the eyes (the more slanted the better).
- Life Expectancy: the length of the mouth (the longer the better).

FIGURE 3   Example of Chernoff's FACES for Displaying Multivariate Data. (*Source:* Wainer & Thissen, 1981, Figure 24, p. 230.)

- Homicide Rate: the width of the nose (the wider the nose the lower the homicide rate).
- Income: the curvature of the mouth (the bigger the smile the higher the income).
- Temperature: the shape of the face (the more like a peanut the warmer, the more like a football the colder).
- Longitude and Latitude: the position of the face on the coordinate axes of the paper.

Figure 3 nicely illustrates the two advantages of non-numerical depictions previously discussed. First, a number of interesting comparisons and observations are almost immediate. For example, (a) it is striking that North and South Dakota are virtually identical on all the characteristics except for a dramatic difference in per capita income favoring North Dakota; (b) the greater population in the East is obvious; and (c) the faces in the South appear homogeneously grim reflecting a low quality of life with respect to these variables (see Wainer & Theissen, 1981, pp. 227–231, for a discussion of many other observations based upon visual inspection of this map). Second, note how Wainer and Theissen controlled the kinds of comparisons that could be made

by their choice of features. For those characteristics for which a natural preference ordering is obvious (e.g., higher literacy is more desirable), a feature was chosen so that more of it was better (e.g., bigger eyes meant higher literacy) and so that the overall effect of more of the desirable characteristics was to create a happy, cheerful face. In contrast, for those characteristics for which there is not a natural preference ordering (e.g., temperature—some people want to ski and some want to swim), they chose a feature of the face (e.g., shape) which did not have a natural ordering and which did not make the face either more or less cheerful.

REPRESENTATIONAL MEASUREMENT

Ordinal Measurement

We begin with ordinal measurement because it is the simplest example of representational measurement. As such, it provides a good introduction to the basic ideas. Researchers in the social and behavioral sciences frequently want to assign scale values so that higher numbers represent more of the property being measured. The resulting scales are called ordinal scales because only the ordering of the numbers is important. A classical ordinal scale from outside the social sciences is the Mohs' scale used in geology. Rock *a* is harder than rock *b* if and only if *a* can scratch *b*, in which case it is assigned a higher numerical scale value. The "if and only if" means that if rock *c* has a higher scale value than rock *d*, then we can be assured that *c* will scratch *d*.

The hardness scale illustrates the key component for ordinal scaling: the existence of a well-defined empirical relationship (in this case, *a* scratches *b*) that is to be represented by the greater-than relationship of real numbers. For example, the entities might be a set of attitude statements, the property to be scaled might be degree of liberalness, and the empirical relationship might be a pairwise majority vote of a panel of fifteen randomly selected students. We will use $\geqslant$ to represent an empirical greater-than relationship between entities ("$a \geqslant b$" can be read as "*a* dominates *b*" or "*a* is at least as great as *b*"), and we will restrict the use of $\geq$ to comparisons between numerical scale values. For example, in the case of the attitude statements and the specified empirical comparison, $a \geqslant b$ would mean that a majority of the panel voted that statement *a* was more liberal than statement *b*, and $s(a) \geq s(b)$ would mean that the numerical scale value assigned to *a* is higher than that assigned to *b*.

Axioms for Ordinal Measurement   In measurement theories, axioms state the empirical conditions which must be satisfied before it is possible to construct a scale. In effect the axioms tell us the internal consistency checks which need to be tested. For the case of ordinary scaling, if the numerical relationship $\geq$ is to represent the empirical relationships $\geqslant$, then the latter must behave exactly like the former. For example, for any two specific scale values it is always possible to determine either that they are tied or that one is larger than the other—either $s(a) \geq s(b)$ or $s(b) \geq s(a)$ or both (in which case $s(a) = s(b)$). So we should expect to observe this same property when we examine the empirical relationship $\geqslant$. Thus, we have the following necessary axiom.

Connectedness. Either $a \geqslant b$ or $b \geqslant a$ or both.

Connectedness simply means that it must be possible to compare all the entities with one another. It is important to note that this does not rule out ties; both $a \geqslant b$ and $b \geqslant a$ may be true (in which case we will write $a \approx b$, meaning *a* and *b* are equivalent). Connectedness simply means that some decision can be made for every *a* and *b*.

Another basic ordering property of numbers and hence a property of our ordinal scale values is transitivity. If $s(a)$

$\geq s(b)$ and $s(b) \geq s(c)$, then it must be true that $s(a) \geq s(c)$. For example, if $3 \geq 2$ and $2 \geq 1$, then of course $3 \geq 1$. Requiring this same property for the empirical relation $\geqslant$ yields the corresponding axiom which follows.

Transitivity. If $a \geqslant b$ and $b \geqslant c$, then $a \geqslant c$.

An empirical relationship $\geqslant$ on a set of entities is said to be a *weak order* if and only if it satisfies the two properties of connectedness and transitivity. It is generally simple to test these two empirical properties in a given context. For example, if attitude statement *a* had been judged to be more liberal than attitude statement *b* and attitude statement *b* had been judged to be more liberal than attitude statement *c*, it would be easy to check whether or not statement *a* was judged to be more liberal than statement *c* as predicted by the transitivity axiom. Although these two axioms seem almost trivial, there is certainly no assurance that they will be satisfied for the sets of entities and empirical relationships we might want to study in social psychology. For example, in the case of attitude statements, the panel might balk and refuse to compare two statements because they appeared to pertain to different topics; that would violate the connectedness axiom. Transitivity can also easily be violated. There is no assurance, as economists and political scientists have known since the publication of Arrow's (1951) famous Possibility Theorem, that majority pairwise votes by the attitude panel will produce a transitive ordering even if everyone votes transitively. For example, if five students think the order of liberalness is $a \geqslant b \geqslant c$, five think it is $c \geqslant a \geqslant b$, and five think it is $b \geqslant c \geqslant a$, then *a* "wins" over *b* ten votes to five and *b* wins over *c* ten votes to five. By transitivity, it should be the case that *a* would win over *c* but instead it loses five votes to ten. If that were to occur, then it would mean that the transitivity axiom was violated and because transitivity is a necessary property for ordinal scale values that would mean in turn that no ordinal scale for those attitude statements could possibly be constructed using that empirical definition of "more liberal than." The importance of the connectedness and transitivity axioms is that it can be proved (see Krantz, Luce, Suppes, and Tversky, 1971, p. 15) that an ordinal scale, a representation of the data, is possible if and only if those two axioms are satisfied in the data. This is an important and surprisingly powerful result because it tells us that if we want to construct an ordinal scale, connectedness and transitivity are the only empirical properties that need be checked in the data. If those axioms are satisfied then we may proceed with the actual construction of an ordinal scale.

Constructing an Ordinal Scale   Testing the axioms and constructing an ordinal scale is very simple. The process is most readily understood in the context of a real example. Table 1 contains a subset of the data from a study by Clark

TABLE 1
Subset of Residential Location Preference Data from Clark (1982)

		a	b	c	d	e	f	g	h	i	j	Count
Locations (header)												
	a	X	1	1	1	1	1	1	1	1	1	9
	b	0	X	1	0	0	1	0	1	1	0	4
	c	0	0	X	0	0	0	0	1	0	0	1
	d	0	1	1	X	1	1	0	1	1	1	7
	e	0	1	1	1	X	1	1	1	1	1	8
	f	0	0	1	0	0	X	0	1	1	0	3
	g	0	1	1	1	0	1	X	1	1	1	7
	h	0	0	0	0	0	0	0	X	0	0	0
	i	0	0	1	0	0	1	0	1	X	0	3
	j	0	1	1	0	0	1	0	1	1	X	5

Note: A "1" in row i, column j means that location i was preferred to location j by at least 50 percent of the movers who could have moved to either location i and j and who did move to either i or j.

(1982) which investigated preferences for residential location within the Milwaukee area. In this table, a 1 in row i and column j means that $i \succeq j$. Clark used the following empirical definition. If from among those movers who moved to either location i or j and who could have moved to either, a majority moved to location i, then location i is presumed to be more preferred than location j and a 1 is entered in the appropriate row and column (see Clark, 1982, for more details).

The first step is to test the two axioms. Connectedness is easy—there is an entry in every cell of the data matrix so every comparison has been made. That is, either $a \succeq b$ and/or $b \succeq a$ for every pair of locations. Transitivity can be checked by testing each subset of three locations in each possible ordering of the three. For example, $a \succeq e$ and $e \succeq h$ so we can check if $a \succeq h$ as it should be if transitivity is satisfied. In this case, it is. However, testing each individual transitivity separately would amount to 720 tests of transitivity in this instance. An easier and mathematically equivalent approach is to seek a permutation or reordering of the rows and columns so that the 1's form a triangular pattern above the diagonal. It is an easy exercise to verify that such a triangular pattern will result if and only if transitivity is satisfied. A useful heuristic is to sum the entries within each row. The top row in the triangle must have the greatest number of 1's so it should have the greatest count. Similarly, the bottom row should contain no 1's (i.e., it is not greater than anything else). The other rows should be ordered similarly between these two extremes according to their counts. The necessary counts are displayed in Table 1.

These counts imply the order

$$a \succeq e \succeq g \succeq d \succeq j \succeq b \succeq i \succeq f \succeq c \succeq h$$

although we note that there are some ties which will make it difficult to obtain a perfect triangular pattern. The same data matrix with the rows and columns permuted according to the above order is displayed in Table 2.

Any 1's below the diagonal in Table 2 indicate a potential violation of transitivity; there are two such instances involving the location pairs (d,e) and (f,i). Both of these result from equivalence relationships; that is, both $d \succeq e$ and $e \succeq d$ so $d \approx e$, and both $f \succeq i$ and $i \succeq f$ so $f \approx i$. The (f,i) pair poses no problems because they are adjacent in the ordering. This simply means that locations f and i are functionally equivalent so that they can be combined into a single row and column. However, that is not the case for the (d,e) pair; locations d and e cannot be combined because the data indicate that location g is between them. This is a violation of transitivity because $g \succeq d$, $d \succeq e$, but g is not $\succeq e$. This means that an ordinal scale cannot be constructed for these data. If we want to construct a scale anyway, then one of the locations d, e, or g must be eliminated or one of the empirical observations changed. In general, whether it will be wise to do so depends on other information such as the reliability of the empirical comparison. A return to the raw data reveals that the observation that $d \succeq e$ was due to the fact that exactly 50 percent of the movers choose d and exactly 50 percent choose e. There would be no problem with transitivity had the pro-

T A B L E 2
The Data of Table 1 Rearranged to an Approximate Triangular Pattern

		a	*e*	*g*	*d*	*j*	*b*	*i*	*f*	*c*	*h*	Count
						Locations						
Locations	*a*	X	1	1	1	1	1	1	1	1	1	9
	e	0	X	1	1	1	1	1	1	1	1	8
	g	0	0	X	1	1	1	1	1	1	1	7
	d	0	1	0	X	1	1	1	1	1	1	7
	j	0	0	0	0	X	1	1	1	1	1	5
	b	0	0	0	0	0	X	1	1	1	1	4
	i	0	0	0	0	0	0	X	1	1	1	3
	f	0	0	0	0	0	0	1	X	1	1	3
	c	0	0	0	0	0	0	0	0	X	1	1
	h	0	0	0	0	0	0	0	0	0	X	0

portion choosing *d* over *e* been 49 percent. While Clark does not provide sufficient information to conduct a statistical test, it is unlikely that the difference between 50 percent and 49 percent is statistically reliable. Hence, we will eliminate the observation of $d \geqslant e$. The resulting matrix is displayed in Table 3. The scaling is now complete because the count for each row can be the scale value for that row's location.

Summary of Ordinal Scaling   We now have everything we need to construct ordinal scales for any entities which

may be of interest to us. We have axioms or consistency checks which specify the empirical conditions that must be satisfied in order to construct a scale, and we have a scaling algorithm for actually constructing the scale. As will often be the case, the scaling algorithm is intimately linked with checking the properties of the representation theorem. Rearranging the data into a form that facilitates checking the axioms will often be equivalent to constructing the scale if it is possible to do so.

There are many instances in the social and behavioral sciences where an ordinal scale is all that is required and in

T A B L E 3
The Data of Table 2 Modified
(Two Locations Combined and One Observation Switched)
to Create a Perfect Triangular Pattern

		a	*e*	*g*	*d*	*j*	*b*	*f,i*	*c*	*h*	Count
						Locations					
Locations	*a*	X	1	1	1	1	1	1	1	1	8
	e	0	X	1	1	1	1	1	1	1	7
	g	0	0	X	1	1	1	1	1	1	6
	d	0	0	0	X	1	1	1	1	1	5
	j	0	0	0	0	X	1	1	1	1	4
	b	0	0	0	0	0	X	1	1	1	3
	f,i	0	0	0	0	0	0	X	1	1	2
	c	0	0	0	0	0	0	0	X	1	1
	h	0	0	0	0	0	0	0	0	X	0

some cases is to be preferred. A test of ordinal scaling is preferred, for example, when our goal is to reject a particular theory. If a substantive theory, which we would like to test, predicts at least an ordinal scaling of a set of entities, then finding that the data did not satisfy the axioms for ordinal scaling would constitute a powerful rejection of the theory. For example, Tversky (1969) considered alternative models of how people might make choices between entities described by several dimensions. Additive models, in which an overall evaluation is formed by adding together separate evaluations of the components of each entity, were rejected because those models predicted an ordinal scale, but the data showed clear violations of the transitivity axiom necessary for an ordinal representation. Measurement and scaling theories are just like any other theories, so we always have more confidence in their rejection than in their confirmation.

In other situations where an actual scale is required, an ordinal scale may be sufficient. For example, if the task is to select the three best candidates from among a pool of applications, then an ordinal scale of the applicants provides all the information that is necessary. Furthermore, in practice, ordinal scales are just as reasonable to be used in statistical analyses as most of the variables used by social psychologists. For example, it would be informative to correlate the ordinal scale from Table 3 with census tract information to identify possible bases for neighborhood preferences. The simplicity, transparency, and usefulness of ordinal scales suggest that they should be used much more in social psychology than they are.

Thurstone and Fechnerian Scaling

With an ordinal scale one, of course, does not know how large the differences are between adjacent entities. For example, although we know from our ordinal scale that location a is a more desirable location than e, we do not know whether there is a large or small difference in preference between the two. Thurstone (1927) saw how to transfer ideas from psychophysics to the scaling of social stimuli. Psychophysicists had created scales by assuming that just noticeable differences were subjectively equal. Thurstone substituted equally-often noticed differences for just noticeable differences. That is, if in a number of trials, either within or across respondents, the empirical relation $a \geqslant b$ was observed 85 percent of the time and the relation $c \geqslant d$ was also observed 85 percent of the time, then Thurstone created scales by assuming the psychological distance between a and b equaled the psychological distance between c and d. This was a significant breakthrough because it meant that scaling could be accomplished without starting with physical measurements of the stimuli as required in psychophysical scaling. To construct scale values, Thurstone based a model on the normal distribution. Subse-

quent work in measurement theory has revealed that assumptions about a particular probability distribution are not crucial. We first present Thurstone's model because it is the most practical way to obtain scale values, and then we consider the internal consistency checks implied by the notion that equally-often noticed differences are equal.

Thurstone's Model Thurstone argued that simuli, whether they be lights in the psychophysicist's lab or attitude statements in a survey, never strike us in exactly the same way because of all the usual things that contribute to error in psychological processes. He assumed that on some undefined scale of psychological intensity in the head, each stimulus would have a normal distribution of possible ways in which it might strike the observer. We would expect the impression of a given stimulus to be near the mean on average, but the normal distribution implies that sometimes, but infrequently, that impression could be a considerable distance from the mean. We will let $\psi(a)$ be the particular impression experienced when stimulus a is presented; $\psi(a)$ is modeled as a normal random variable with mean μ_a and variance σ_a^2. When a judge is asked which, for example, of two attitude statements a or b is more liberal, then, according to Thurstone, two impressions $\psi(a)$ and $\psi(b)$ are obtained. The judge then reports that "a is more liberal than b," which we record as $a \geqslant b$. From these assumptions it is straightforward to derive what Thurstone referred to as the *law of comparative judgment,* although it really is just a theoretical model and not a law, namely,

$$s(a) - s(b) = z_{ab} \sqrt{\sigma_a^2 + \sigma_a^2 - r_{ab}\sigma_a\sigma_b}$$

where z_{ab} is the z-score corresponding to the probability of $a \geqslant b$ and r_{ab} is the correlation between the respective normal distributions. Only z_{ab} is observed, so this model has far more parameters than observations. Simplifying assumptions are needed to reduce the number of parameters. Thurstone identified five cases corresponding to different sets of assumptions. By far the most commonly used is Case V, which makes the strong assumption that the underlying normal distributions are independent of one another, so that $r_{ab} = 0$, and that they have the same variance, which can be fixed at 1 without loss. With these assumptions, the model simplifies to

$$s(a) - s(b) = z_{ab}.$$

If all possible comparisons are made among k entities, then there are k scale values to be estimated from $k(k-1)$ z-scores. Standard regression programs can provide the estimated scale values; the least-squares estimate for an entity is simply the average of all the z-scores in which that entity is involved.

In theory, enough data could be collected from individual respondents to do the scaling for each respondent. How-

TABLE 4

Affirmative Action Attitude Statements and Probability that Row Item Was Judged More Liberal than Column Item

a In college admissions, at least 15 percent of all openings should be reserved for blacks.

b Blacks should be given a special break in college admission decisions regardless of their qualifications.

c If two candidates are equally qualified for college admission, a slight preference should be given to the black candidate.

d I'm all for affirmative action admissions, but that shouldn't mean that a qualified white candidate gets turned down in favor of a less qualified black candidate.

e Only merit, rather than any affirmative action considerations, should determine college admissions.

f Affirmative action programs in college admissions only result in underprepared students being admitted.

	a	*b*	*c*	*d*	*e*	*f*
a	—	0.58	0.73	0.71	0.78	0.80
b	0.42	—	0.73	0.76	0.76	0.84
c	0.27	0.27	—	0.69	0.71	0.87
d	0.29	0.24	0.31	—	0.67	0.73
e	0.22	0.24	0.29	0.33	—	0.71
f	0.20	0.16	0.13	0.27	0.29	—

ever, in practice, due to the practical problems of obtaining enough repeated judgments of paired comparisons of memorable items, such as attitude statements, most researchers present each pair comparison to each respondent only once. Thus, probabilities are computed across respondents. This adds the assumption that, except for error, respondents are replicates of one another; in particular, they must be viewing all attitude statements from the same perspective. While such an assumption might be appropriate for, say, liberalness judgments, it is clearly not appropriate for preference judgments because respondents are likely to have many different perspectives with respect to preference.

We illustrate the construction of a Thurstone scale using data collected for this chapter. Forty-five students saw all possible pairs of six attitude statements and judged which statement in each pair they believed was the more liberal statement. The statements and the probability with which the row statement was judged more liberal than the column statement are listed in Table 4.

Table 5 displays the probabilities of Table 4 converted to *z*-scores, with the average *z*-score in the last column representing the estimated scale value. In addition to information about the ordering of the items on liberalness, the Thurstone scale also provides information on the relative spacing of the attitude statements. This relative spacing is easier to see when points representing the items are arranged on a line as in Figure 4. Clearly, students did not judge much difference in the liberalness of items *a* and *b*, while they did judge a large difference between the liberalness of items *e* and *f*.

The Thurstone scaling model is indeed a model, so the scale values can be inverted to generate predictions. That is, once we have the scale values from Table 5, we can use the model equation

$$s(a) - s(b) = z_{ab}$$

to derive predicted *z*-scores, which in turn lead to predicted probabilities. For example, $s(a) = 0.5$ and $s(c) = 0.15$ so $z_{ac} = 0.5 - 0.15 = 0.35$. Converting this *z*-score to a probability yields a prediction that the probability that *a* is judged more liberal than *c* ($a \succcurlyeq c$) is 0.63. All the predicted *z*-scores and probabilities are displayed in Table 6.

The Thurstone scaling model can then be tested by comparing the observed and predicted probabilities. For example, the predicted probability of 0.63 for $a \succcurlyeq c$ was

TABLE 5
z-scores for Probabilities of Table 4

	a	*b*	*c*	*d*	*e*	*f*	Average = Scale Value
a	0	0.20	0.62	0.56	0.76	0.84	0.50
b	−0.20	0	0.62	0.69	0.69	1.01	0.47
c	−0.62	−0.62	0	0.49	0.56	1.11	0.15
d	−0.56	−0.69	−0.49	0	0.43	0.62	−0.11
e	−0.76	−0.69	−0.56	−0.43	0	0.56	−0.31
f	−0.84	−1.01	−1.11	−0.62	−0.56	0	−0.69

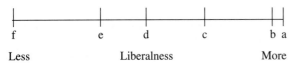

f   e   d   c   b a

Less   Liberalness   More

FIGURE 4   Liberalness Scale Values Depicted on a Line.

observed to be 0.73. Standard procedures can be used to compare the observed and predicted probabilities. In this case, $\chi^2(10) = 15.84$, $p = 0.10$. Hence, the Thurstone scaling model is not rejected for these data. Had the model been rejected, this omnibus test would not tell us which aspects of the Thurstone model were incorrect: the specific Case V assumptions, the normal distribution assumption, and/or the basic idea that equally-often noticed differences are subjectively equal.

Fechnerian Scaling   Since Thurstone's pioneering work, measurement theorists have made much progress in identifying the key properties of Thurstonian scaling. First, it was noted by Burke and Zinnes (1965) and Yellott (1977) that subsequent scaling models attributed to Bradley and Terry (1952), Luce (1959), and Dawkins (1969) make very similar predictions even though those models have very different assumptions, especially different implicit assumptions about the underlying probability distribution. This

suggested that it should be possible to distill the more basic principles underlying Thurstone scaling and similar models. The essence of the idea that equally-often noticed differences are equal can be represented by

$$P(a \geqslant b) = F\,[s(a) - s(b)]$$

where P represents the probability of $a \geqslant b$ and F is any monotonically-increasing function. For Thurstone scales, F is the cumulative normal probability function. Scales consistent with the above equation which allow F to be any increasing function are often referred to as generalized Thurstone scales or Fechnerian scales in honor of the source of the psychophysical scaling ideas that Thurstone extended. Although the Fechnerian scaling model represented by the above equation avoids making any assumptions about an underlying probability distribution, it makes surprisingly strong predictions. One such prediction is

Independence. $P(a \geqslant c) \geq P(b \geqslant c) \Leftrightarrow P(a \geqslant d)$
     $\geq P(b \geqslant d).$

In other words, as Tversky and Russo (1969, p. 3) state, "if two stimuli [(a,b)] are ordered according to their choice probabilities relative to some fixed standard then, . . . the ordering is independent of the particular standard." This implies that it should be possible to reorder the rows and columns of a matrix of probabilities so that the probabilities decrease within each column and increase within each row. Examining the rows and columns of the probabilities in Table 4 we see that this is generally, but not completely, true. Notably, if the order of the attitude statements on the scale is indeed a to f, then the greatest difference between scales values ought to be between $s(a)$ and s(f) so that the largest probability in the matrix ought to be $P(a \geqslant f)$, but in fact its probability is only 0.80 which is less than the probability of 0.87 for $P(c \geqslant f)$. Rearranging the row and columns so that c and f would be the furthest apart leads to even more serious inconsistencies of the orderings within rows and columns. Hence, the ordering from a to f is the best ordering, but it violates a necessary condition for constructing a Fechnerian scale. Unfortunately, the Achilles heel of measurement theory models such as this is that it is difficult to decide whether the discrepancy between 0.80 and 0.87, which is not statistically significant, and the other discrepancies in Table 4 are large enough to invalidate the Fechnerian scaling model. Luce et al. (1990, p. xiii) admit, "The [planned] chapter on statistical methods was not written, largely because the development of statistical models for fundamental measurement turned out to be very difficult."

    If independence and other related necessary conditions (e.g., see Michell, 1990, for details) are satisfied, then it is possible to solve the system of inequalities generated from

$$P(a \geqslant b) \geq P(c \geqslant d) \Leftrightarrow s(a) - s(b) \geq s(c) - s(d)$$

TABLE 6

Predicted *z*-scores and Probabilities Derived from Thurstone Scale Values of Table 5

Predicted *z*-scores

	a	b	c	d	e	f
a	0	0.03	0.35	0.61	0.81	1.2
b	−0.03	0	0.32	0.58	0.78	1.2
c	−0.35	−0.32	0	0.27	0.47	0.84
d	−0.61	−0.58	−0.27	0	0.20	0.57
e	−0.81	−0.78	−0.47	−0.20	0	0.37
f	−1.2	−1.2	−0.84	−0.57	−0.37	0

Predicted Probabilities

	a	b	c	d	e	f
a	—	0.51	0.63	0.73	0.79	0.88
b	0.49	—	0.62	0.72	0.78	0.88
c	0.37	0.38	—	0.61	0.68	0.80
d	0.27	0.28	0.39	—	0.58	0.72
e	0.21	0.22	0.32	0.42	—	0.65
f	0.12	0.12	0.20	0.28	0.35	—

to provide rather precise estimates of the scale values. It is surprising how strongly the ordinal relationships constrain the possible scale values (Lehner & Noma, 1980; McClelland & Coombs, 1975; Roskam, 1992). However, the algorithms for solving the system of inequalities will only be successful if there is not a single violation of any of the necessary conditions.

Coombs' Unfolding Model

The Thurstone scaling method, when used with data collected from many individuals, assumes that everyone is viewing the entities from the same perspective. For example, the assumption for the affirmative action attitude statements is that everyone, except for some random error, agrees on the ordering of the items with respect to liberalness. While that assumption may or may not be correct for liberalness judgments, it is certainly not correct for preferences. A very liberal person and a very conservative person might well agree on the ordering of the attitude statements from conservative to liberal, but their preference orderings might be exactly opposite. Coombs (1950, 1964) formalized such a situation in his unfolding model. In addition to scaling the items, the unfolding model also adds a scale value for each individual's "ideal" point on the same scale as the items. Figure 5 illustrates the unfolding model. The notion is that individuals, when confronted by a choice between two items, prefer the item which is closer to their ideal point. For example, in Figure 5, individual i's ideal point is closest to item b, which would be his or her first choice, next closest is a, and so on; thus, i's preference ordering would be

$$b \succcurlyeq a \succcurlyeq c \succcurlyeq d.$$

While for individual j, the preference ordering would be

$$c \succcurlyeq d \succcurlyeq b \succcurlyeq a.$$

Formally, we can state Coombs' unfolding model as

$$a \succcurlyeq_i b \Leftrightarrow |s(a) - s(i)| \le |s(b) - s(i)|$$

which means that we would observe that individual i has a preference for a over b, if and only if the scale values for a

and i's ideal point are closer together than the scale values for b and i's ideal point. Just as for Thurstonian and Fechnerian scaling, this model generates predictions that can be tested in the data. For example, if the ordering, but not necessarily the spacing, of the items is as in Figure 5, then the least preferred alternative for every individual must be either a or d. The model also implies less obvious predictions. For example, if there is an individual i for whom we observe

$$c \succcurlyeq b \succcurlyeq a \succcurlyeq d,$$

then we can infer that the distance between $s(a)$ and $s(b)$ is smaller than the distance between $s(c)$ and $s(d)$. If that is the case, then Coombs' model predicts that there should *not* be an individual with the preference ordering

$$b \succcurlyeq c \succcurlyeq d \succcurlyeq a$$

which would imply the opposite ordering of the distances. If a set of preference orderings is consistent with the Coombs' unfolding model, then it is possible to solve the resulting system of inequalities derived from the formal model (e.g., McClelland & Coombs, 1975). However, the procedures are sufficiently complex (cf., Michell, 1990) and the problems of error sufficiently difficult that it seems unlikely that many social psychologists will use the full unfolding model. Nevertheless, there are important insights to be gained by considering the model and even some simple and useful scaling techniques based on a partial unfolding model. We turn to those now.

Second Choices When given a choice in a survey among several options, respondents seldom select an extreme alternative. Instead, many respondents, sometimes a majority, select the same alternative. In such cases, the choice provides little discrimination among the respondents. In those situations, Coombs' unfolding model suggests it would be useful to ask respondents for their second and perhaps third choices. The second choice reveals the option that the individual is subjectively next most closest to and will necessarily be towards one extreme or the other. For example, most young couples in the United States say they would prefer to have two children. Attempts to correlate preferences for family size with actual behavior fail because there is so little variance in the preference measure. However, additional variance in the predictor can easily be obtained by asking for second and third choices. For example, we would expect, on average, larger actual family sizes for couples whose preferences are $2 \succcurlyeq 3 \succcurlyeq 4$ than for couples whose preferences are $2 \succcurlyeq 1 \succcurlyeq 0$, even though they share the same first choice (see Coombs, 1974, for an empirical confirmation of this prediction). And in this context the ordering $2 \succcurlyeq 0 \succcurlyeq 1$ would reveal a strong bias against only children.

As another example of the usefulness of second

FIGURE 5 Ideal Points for Individuals on the Same Scale as for Items.

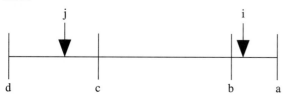

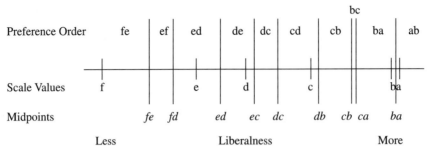

FIGURE 6   Scale of Midpoints and Predicted Preferences for Two Choices.

choices, consider the Thurstone scaling of affirmative action statements from Figure 4. Figure 6 illustrates the response patterns predicted for the ordering and spacing of the items from the Thurstone scaling. For example, an individual whose ideal point on the affirmative action scale is to the right of the dc midpoint (who therefore is closer to c than d), but to the left of the db midpoint (and therefore closer to d than b) would have the first two choices c, then d. Note that six items have the potential of discriminating respondents into ten ordered categories from most favorable to least favorable towards affirmative action. Such discrimination is often sufficient for many social psychological studies.

Obtaining only the first and second choices does not provide enough information for the full set of internal consistency checks afforded by the complete unfolding model. However, there are some inconsistencies that can be detected. For example, if the affirmative action statements are ordered on liberalness as indicated by the Thurstone scaling, then there should be no respondents whose first two choices included nonadjacent items. Having a number of respondents with nonadjacent preferences would suggest that their preferences with respect to affirmative action programs could not be represented on a liberal/conservative dimension.

The same students who made the liberalness pair comparison judgments for the Thurstone scaling also indicated their first and second preferences among the six attitude statements. There were few instances of choice pairs including nonadjacent items. There were not enough preferences at the less liberal end of the scale to discriminate items e and f, so they were combined. Figure 7 shows the frequency distribution of the preference orderings. Note that most everyone included statement b ("Blacks should be given a special break in college admission decisions regardless of their qualifications") as either the first or second choice. The discrimination among respondents is then produced largely by the more liberal statement a or the less liberal statement c. Using second choices to enhance differentiation among respondents and to provide light testing

of preference models would be a useful addition to many studies in social psychology.

Interpreting Survey Responses   The unfolding model, especially the notion that it is the midpoints between items that determine choices, is useful for understanding responses to simple questions often used in surveys. For example, suppose an opinion pollster asks a random sample of respondents how good a job the President is doing with response categories "very poor," "fairly poor," "neither good nor poor," "fairly good," and "very good." Assuming those response categories could be ordered along a continuum of approval, it would be the midpoints between items that would determine the responses. For example, according to the unfolding model, someone would select the category "fairly good" only if their opinion of how good a job the President was doing was closer to "fairly good" than "very good" and also closer to "fairly good" than "neither good nor poor." If a different category had been used for the top end, say, "good" instead of "very good," then we would expect the proportion choosing "fairly good" to change because the midpoint between "fairly good" and the top category would have changed.

Failure to realize that it is the midpoints and not the labels of the response categories that determines choices can lead to confusion. For example, consider the hypothetical results in Table 7 from two polls A and B which asked how good a job the President is doing. The results seem quite different. Pollster A concludes that over half (50.5 percent) of the people are satisfied with the job the President is doing, while only 22 percent are definitely dissatisfied. Pollster B, on the other hand, concludes that only 35.5 percent are satisfied, while an almost equal proportion (34.5 percent) are dissatisfied. Note that in Poll A 37.5 percent chose the "fairly good" category, but only 17.5 percent selected that category in Poll B. Such disparate results might prompt us to question their sampling methods or even to suspect skullduggery. However,

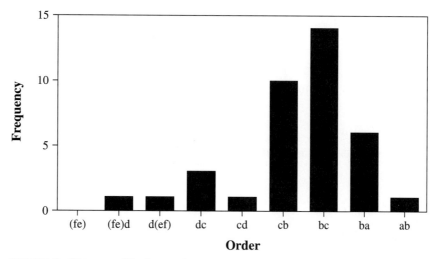

FIGURE 7 Histogram of Preferences from Two Choices for Affirmative Action Items.

both polls are completely consistent with a common underlying distribution of ideal points. The two polls just divide the distribution differently. Figure 8 illustrates the consistency of the two polls. The line in Figure 8 represents the underlying dimension of approval of the job the President is doing. The midpoints for Poll A are depicted above the line and those for Poll B below the line. The proportion between each pair of midpoints (i.e., the proportion choosing each alternative as in Table 7) is displayed above and below the line, respectively, for Polls A and B. The combined midpoints divided the distribution of ideal points into the proportionate categories indicated on the line. The key difference in the two polls is that the middle or "neutral" category in Poll A ("neither good nor bad") is viewed as more negative (in this hypothetical

example) than the middle category in Poll B ("just OK"). With the position of the middle category being more negative in Poll A, the midpoint between that middle label and the "fairly good" label is also necessarily more negative. Thus, some respondents (15 percent) who selected the middle category in Poll B would select "fairly good" instead of the middle category had they responded to Poll A. An unscrupulous pollster wanting the President to look good would select a "neutral" category label that was as negative as possible while one wanting the President to look bad would select a "neutral" category that was as positive as possible.

It is at first counterintuitive that using different middle categories can have such a dramatic impact on the proportion of respondents selecting more positive responses; however, it makes perfect sense in terms of the unfolding model. Finally, note that the dramatic difference in the proportions of each poll choosing "fairly good" is due to the large difference in neighboring midpoints, both above and below. In Poll B, the "fairly good" category is squeezed by a closer middle category than in Poll A and a closer more positive category ("good" rather than "very good" in Poll A).

Conflict and Social Choice The unfolding model has interesting implications for the understanding of conflict, a topic of long-standing interest in social psychology. Here is one simple example. Suppose there are three individuals X, Y, and Z who have the following preferences for alternatives *a, b,* and *c*. (These alternatives might be political candidates or movies the group of three might go see or anything else they might be trying to agree about).

TABLE 7

Hypothetical Results for Two Polls Asking the Same Question with Different Response Categories

Poll A		Poll B	
Category	Percent	Category	Percent
Very poor	4.5	Poor	12.0
Fairly poor	17.5	Fairly poor	22.5
Neither good nor poor	27.5	Just OK	30.0
Fairly good	37.5	Fairly good	17.5
Very good	13.0	Good	18.0

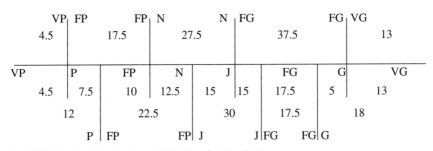

FIGURE 8   Combined Scale and Midpoints for Two Polls.

X: $a > b > c$

Y: $b > c > a$

Z: $c > a > b$

If we ask this group whether they prefer a or b, there would be two votes for a and one for b, so we would conclude that for the group

$$a >_g b$$

And similarly, when we ask about b versus c, there would be two votes for b and only one for c, so we would conclude that for the group

$$b >_g c$$

Transitivity would then imply that

$$a >_g c$$

However, when we ask this group whether they prefer a or c, there would be two votes for c and only one for a. Thus, in fact,

$$c >_g a$$

which violates transitivity. A group with intransitive preferences (even though each individual has transitive preferences) will have much difficulty making decisions and is likely to have a great deal of conflict among group members. The above illustration is the famous example that Condorcet (1785) used to demonstrate that majority voting is not guaranteed to be transitive (i.e., it is not guaranteed of producing even an ordinal scale).

Interestingly, a group will not face this sort of intransitive conflict if everyone's preferences can be represented by the unfolding model on a common unidimensional scale (Arrow, 1951). Further insight is gained by considering ordinal preference functions. Figure 9 depicts the preferences of the three individuals as ordinary functions over the three alternatives. The spacing of the alternatives in Figure 9 is only ordinal and the preferences are represented only as ranks. If the data meet the axioms for the

unfolding model, then it is always possible to represent everyone's preferences as a single-peaked ordinal preference function. In Figure 9 it is clear for the alphabetical ordering of alternatives that individuals X and Y both have single-peaked preference functions, but Z has a single-dipped preference function. If we tried other orderings of the alternatives on the abscissa, we would find that at least one of these three individuals did not have a single-peaked preference function.

Presume for the moment that the correct ordering of the alternatives on an underlying dimension is indeed alphabetical so that it is Z who has a single-dipped instead of a single-peaked ordinal preference function. The problem is clearly that Z likes either extreme better than the middle. In other words, a prescription for creating group conflict is for some members of the group to prefer an extreme alternative no matter in what direction those alternatives are extreme.

A famous example of group conflict created by preferring extreme alternatives occurred when the U.S. Congress considered major civil rights legislation in the 1960s. Let b represent the proposed civil rights legislation, let a represent an amended version of that legislation with many strengthening provisions added, and, finally, let c represent the status quo (no new legislation). The preferences of liberals corresponded to those of X above (i.e., they wanted the strongest possible legislation), and the preferences of moderates corresponded to those of Y (i.e., they wanted some legislation, but not if it were too strong). The Southern Democrats did not want any new legislation so their preferences were

$$c > b > a$$

However, the Southern Democrats realized that if they voted in this way, then the proposed legislation would pass. So, in order to produce conflict in the group decision, they *pretended* to have preferences corresponding to Z above. That is, they pretended to prefer either the status quo or a strongly amended bill to the more moderate proposed legislation. In terms of the unfolding model, they were pretending to have preferences that could not be represented on the same unidimensional scale as those of the other two

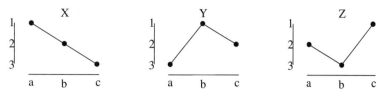

FIGURE 9   Ordinal Preference Functions for Three People across Three Alternatives.
The abscissa represents alternatives, and the ordinate is rank-order preference with "1" being most preferred.

groups. In particular, they joined with the liberals to vote for strong amendments to the proposed legislation in the hope that the bill would become so radical that it would no longer appeal to the moderates. This plan was foiled when the liberals realized that voting according to their true preferences would produce a bill that was too strong to pass. So, they *pretended* that their preferences were

$$b > a > c$$

The possibility of group intransitivity was then eliminated because the pretend preferences of the liberals and the pretend preferences of the Southern Democrats are again exactly opposite. Note that the preferences of all three groups can still not be represented on the same unidimensional scale; however, the possibility of group intransitivity is still eliminated. This demonstrates that single-peaked preference functions on a common scale is a sufficient, but not necessary, condition for group transitivity.

In the end, the civil rights legislation passed because so many congresspersons misrepresented their preferences! However, it is simple to understand what happened in the context of an unfolding scaling model for preferences. Coombs and Avrunin (1988) develop a number of other implications about conflict from the unfolding model and related ideas. Thus, even if representational measurement is not used to construct scales, the associated models still are often useful for understanding social phenomenon.

Multidimensional Unfolding   So far we have assumed that the entities can be arrayed on a single dimension. There is of course no reason why entities cannot be distinguished in terms of multiple dimensions. A multidimensional unfolding model then applies. Figure 10 illustrates the location of four entities in a two-dimensional configuration. The lines divide the plane midway between each pair of entities. Again, the presumption is that people will prefer those entities that are closest to their ideal points. Thus, the lines separate the plane into preference regions; anyone with an ideal point within the same region should have the same preference ordering. The resulting preference orderings for each region are indicated in Figure 10.

Recovering the configuration—determining the number of dimensions and locating each entity on those dimen-

sions—solely from knowing which preference patterns occur can be excruciatingly difficult (see Bennett & Hays, 1960; Coombs, 1964; Hays & Bennett, 1961) and little is known about the necessary and sufficient conditions for multidimensional unfolding. In practice, multidimensional scaling programs, which conduct iterative searches to maximize some goodness-of-fit measure (Young, 1984), are used to find a multidimensional configuration. At the end of the chapter, we explore some implications of the multidimensional unfolding model in terms of the psychometric approach.

Conjoint Measurement

The most important example of representational measurement is additive conjoint measurement. Indeed, Fechnerian scaling, Coombs unfolding, and many other representative measures are in some sense special cases of conjoint measurement (Michell, 1990). We do not have space within a

FIGURE 10   Multidimensional Unfolding of Four Items in Two Dimensions. (Source: Van der Ven, 1980, Figure 12.5, p. 208.)

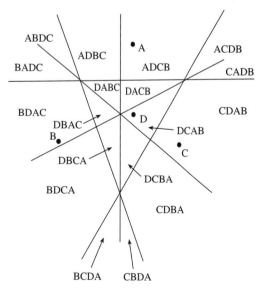

chapter to present anything close to a complete treatment of this important topic. Instead, we present a brief explanation of the major ideas and again focus on broader implications of those ideas, implications that apply whether or not one is using conjoint measurement. Accessible and more complete coverage is available elsewhere (e.g., Michell, 1990; van der Ven, 1980).

Conjoint measurement is based on an empirical combination operation or concatenation. That is, each stimulus is a combination of several components. In the same way that one would put two weights in the same pan of a balance or would put two measuring rods end-to-end, the empirical combination operations in conjoint measurement put, say, two colored lights together or two attitude statements attributed to the same person. For example, we might ask respondents to judge whether someone who made statement a about affirmative action and statement p about abortion is more or less liberal than someone who made statements b and q. Empirical combinations (a,p) and (b,q) are arranged by the researcher and form the basis for constructing the additive conjoint measures. The respondent's task is to judge whether:

$$(a,p) \geqslant (b,q)$$

The key idea underlying conjoint measurement is to measure one variable in the empirical combination against another, and vice versa. Doing so conjoins the resulting two scales. For example, in a psychophysical context, suppose that we want to assess uncomfortableness as a function of subjective scales for temperature and humidity. Suppose further that we discovered that a person felt equally uncomfortable when the temperature was 80° with 93 percent humidity as when the temperature was 90° with 75 percent humidity. Then we could infer that increasing the temperature from 80° to 90° is exactly compensated psychologically by decreasing the humidity from 93 percent to 75 percent. In other words, the change in the uncomfortableness scale values for the temperatures must exactly equal the change in uncomfortableness scale values for the humidity levels. Then, if we observe that a person felt equally uncomfortable at the combination (80°, 75 percent) as at (90°, 51 percent), we would know that the change from 80° to 90° is also exactly compensated by decreasing the humidity from 75 percent to 51 percent. This establishes that the difference in uncomfortableness scale values between 75 percent and 93 percent humidity is equal to the difference in uncomfortableness scale values between 51 percent and 75 percent. That is,

$$H(93\%) - H(75\%) = H(75\%) - H(51\%)$$

where H represents the uncomfortableness scale for humidity. By equating intervals it seems obvious, and the

measurement theorems of conjoint measurement confirm this (Krantz et al., 1971; Luce & Tukey, 1964), that we are building an interval[2] scale from such equivalences. If we let $H(51\%) = 1$ and $H(75\%) = 2$, in order to fix the origin and unit for the interval scale, then $H(93\%)$ must equal 3. Also, we know that

$$T(90°) - T(80°) = H(93\%) - H(75\%) = 1$$

This is the conjoint part; once the unit of measurement is chosen for one scale, the same unit of measurement applies to the other scale. Scale construction would continue by finding the temperature that would make the equivalence (80°, 75%) ~ (?, 93%), in terms of uncomfortableness. Let's say that temperature were 72°; then the equivalence would establish that

$$T(80°) - T(72°) = T(90°) - T(80°) = 1$$

which would put us on the road to developing an interval scale for the subjective uncomfortableness of temperature, an interval scale that is linked to the interval scale for the subjective uncomfortableness of humidity. More importantly, we would also have the testable prediction that (80°, 51%) ~ (72°, 75%). If the subjective scales for humidity and temperature (not humidity and temperature themselves) did not combine additively, then this equivalence prediction would not hold and an inherent interaction between subjective humidity and temperature would be established.

Seldom do social psychologists use variables like temperature and humidity that are quantitative and infinitely divisible in practice, nor are equivalences practical. However, this is not a difficulty because it is possible to utilize conjoint measurement when only ordinal information is available and for arbitrary entities. Let $A = \{a,b,c,...\}$ be one set of entities and let $P = \{p,q,r,...\}$ be another set. For example, A and P might be sets of attitude statements, one set about affirmative action and another set about abortion. We might ask respondents to order pairs of statements according to how liberal they would judge a person to be who endorsed both statements. Or, we could ask respondents to order the pairs of statements according to how favorable they would be to a political candidate who made both statements.

Conjoint measurement specifies the conditions that must be satisfied for an ordering of all pairs (a,p) to be represented by the addition of the respective scale values. That is,

$$(a,p) \geqslant (b,q) \Leftrightarrow f(a) + g(p) \geq f(b) + g(q)$$

where $f()$ and $g()$ are the respective scale values for the two sets of entities. Necessary conditions that can be tested in the data are easily derivable.

Independence. $(a,p) \succcurlyeq (a,q) \Leftrightarrow (b,p) \succcurlyeq (b,q)$

and

$$(a,p) \succcurlyeq (b,p) \Leftrightarrow (a,q) \succcurlyeq (b,q)$$

Simply, if fixing the first component at some entity *a* implies that $p \succcurlyeq q$, then fixing the first component at any other entity *b* must also yield $p \succcurlyeq q$. Similarly, the ordering of entities from the first set must be the same no matter at which entity the second component is fixed. Figure 11 depicts the independence condition graphically. The condition requires the ordering of the columns within rows to be the same, regardless of row, and the ordering of the rows within columns to be the same, regardless of column.

Double Cancellation.

If $(b,p) \succcurlyeq (a,q)$ and $(c,q) \succcurlyeq (b,r)$, then $(c,p) \succcurlyeq (a,r)$

The unusual name and the seemingly nonintuitive condition are best understood from the simple derivation of the double cancellation property. First, restate the two conditions in terms of the additive representation of the scale values:

$$(b,p) \succcurlyeq (a,q) \Leftrightarrow f(b) + g(p) \geq f(a) + g(q)$$

$$(c,q) \succcurlyeq (b,r) \Leftrightarrow f(c) + g(q) \geq f(b) + g(r)$$

Then, add the two inequalities to obtain:

$$\boldsymbol{f(b)} + f(c) + \boldsymbol{g(p)} + \boldsymbol{g(q)} \geq f(a) + \boldsymbol{g(q)} + \boldsymbol{f(b)} + g(r)$$

Canceling the common terms (bolded) on both sides of the inequality, (the double cancellation) yields the conclusion:

$$f(c) + g(p) \geq f(a) + g(r) \Leftrightarrow (c,p) \succcurlyeq (a,r)$$

Figure 12 depicts the double cancellation condition graphically.

With more than three entities in a set, there are tests of higher-order cancellation (triple, quadruple, etc.). How-

FIGURE 11   The Independence Condition.
The arrow tip represents the ordinally greater cell; the small arrow implies the large arrow.

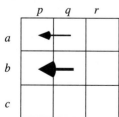 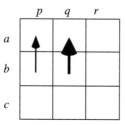

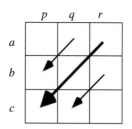

FIGURE 12   Double Cancellation.
The two small arrows imply the large arrow.

ever, the antecedents for those conditions become so complicated that the higher-order cancellation conditions are seldom violated. In practice, if independence and double cancellation are satisfied, one then tries to solve the system of inequalities generated by the ordering of the pairs (Lehner & Noma, 1980; McClelland & Coombs, 1975; Roskam, 1992). A solution results, producing scale values, if and only if all the necessary conditions are satisfied. If a system of inequalities does not have a solution, then one can look for the violations of the higher-order cancellation conditions. Alternatively, some researchers use iterative algorithms such as MONANOVA (Kruskal, 1965), ADDALS (de Leeuw, Young, & Takane, 1976), PROC TRANSREG (SAS Institute, 1990), and generalized additive models (Hastie 1992; Hastie & Tibshirani, 1990) to find a best-fitting additive solution. Such methods have been popular in marketing (Green & Srinivasan, 1990; Wittink & Cattin, 1989). Anderson (1981, 1982, 1991) and colleagues use techniques based on analysis-of-variance for essentially the same purpose.

As with other representational measures, there are few successful applications of conjoint measurement in social psychology. In most cases, the axioms or consistency checks are violated so that scales cannot be successfully constructed. A particularly pernicious type of violation is illustrated by Tversky, Sattath, and Slovic (1988) who show that choice and matching (setting equivalences) can produce different preference orders. A representational analysis, which we briefly describe, was key to reaching that conclusion. Suppose that when presented the choice between two options, a respondent's choice is

$$(a,p) \succcurlyeq (b,q)$$

In an equivalence or matching task, the respondent fills in a missing value for one of the components to make the two options equivalent. For example, what value of the first component of the second option would make the two options equivalent in this representation:

$$(a,p) \succcurlyeq (?,q)$$

Obviously, the value of the second option needs to be increased so the missing value ought to be greater than the value of *b*. However, in this matching task, which is perhaps akin to the rating tasks of psychometric measurement, there are many empirical instances (e.g., Lichtenstein & Slovic, 1971; Tversky et al., 1988) in which respondents often fill in the missing value with something that they value *less* than *b*. Tversky et al. (1988) suggest that the preference weighting of the different components of the empirical combination depends on the response—choosing induces a different weighting than matching. As they argue, this raises fundamental questions concerning the nature, the meaning, and the assessment of preference.

Coombs, Coombs, and McClelland (1975) provide an instructive example of the successful application of conjoint measurement in social psychology. They modeled the family composition preferences (i.e., the desired number of boys and girls). The additive model in terms of the number of boys and girls,

$$\text{Pref}[B,G] = f(B) + g(G),$$

where *B* and *G* represent the number the number of boys and girls, respectively, was unambiguously rejected by substantial violations of independence in data from several different countries. Clearly, and not surprisingly, preferences for the ideal number of boys depended on the number of girls in the family, and vice versa. However, most violations of independence and double cancellation disappeared when the model was reexpressed as

$$\text{Pref}[T,D] = f(T) + g(D)$$

where $T = B + G$ and $D = B - G$. Although it seemed reasonable to try to model preferences in terms of *B* and *G*, the obvious way in which family compositions vary, the conjoint measurement analysis revealed that total number of children and the difference in the number of boys and girls were the appropriate psychological variables.

Hammond, McClelland, and Mumpower (1980) show that other methodological approaches capable of detecting configurality or interactions, such as Social Judgment Theory (Hammond, Stewart, Brehmer, & Steinmann, 1975) or Information Integration Theory (Anderson, 1981, 1982, 1991) would also likely have detected the failure of the additive model in terms of the number of boys and girls and the superiority of the additive model in terms of total number of children and the gender difference. Thus, the lesson of the Coombs et al. example is that the value of the representational approach may not be in the specific testing of the conjoint measurement axioms. Instead, it illustrates the importance of specifying a model in sufficient detail that it can be tested and also the importance of collecting enough data to be able to test the model at the level of the individual.

Interpretating Interactions   Conjoint measurement has implications not just for measurement in social psychology but also for data analysis in general. Conjoint measurement distinguishes between noninteractive models and inherently interactive models (Michell, 1990). Figure 13 illustrates both types of models in terms of graphs of data that might be obtained in a two-way design. In neither graph are the lines parallel; the question is whether there might be a monotonic transformation (i.e., one that preserves order) of the response variable that would make the lines parallel, and hence noninteractive.[3] If a monotonic transformation would make the lines parallel, then any conclusions about an interaction would depend on the assumption that the response variable had been measured on an interval scale. However, if no monotonic transformation could be found to make the lines parallel, then the interaction is inherent. Conjoint measurement provides a definitive answer as to whether such a transformation exists.

The data values for the noninteractive model, the left panel of Figure 13, satisfy the axioms of additive conjoint measurement. Independence is clearly satisfied (each line is monotonically increasing and no lines intersect) and double cancellation is satisfied vacuously because the antecedent condition is not true (there is a double cancellation implication only if the two dotted arrows both point down or both point up). Thus, there exists a monotonic transformation of the response variable that would make the lines parallel. In contrast, the data values for the inherently interactive model, the right panel of Figure 13, fail the axioms of additive conjoint measurement. Although independence is satisfied, double cancellation is violated (if the two small arrows both point up or both point down, then the large arrow must point in the same direction). Thus, there is no monotonic transformation that could make the lines parallel; the interaction is essential or inherent and a claim for the interaction does not depend on having measured the response on an interval scale.

An implicit assumption underlying additive conjoint measurement is that noninteractive models are preferred. Luce (1995, p. 21) states this explicitly:

> . . . evidence of interactions is usually a signal of trouble. . . . All too often, in my opinion, the interactions are treated as a finding and not as evidence of a lack of understanding of the combining rule for measures of the independent variables.

A lot of current work in social psychology emphasizes interactions. Perhaps many of these interactions are not inherent and would disappear with appropriate scale transformations. Hence, the perspective of conjoint measurement suggests that it might be more fruitful to identify fundamental variables that combine noninteractively to influence social behavior.

Noninteractive   Inherently Interactive

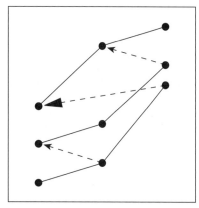

FIGURE 13   Noninteractive and Inherently Interactive Data.
Small arrows indicate antecedents of double cancellation test; if both small arrows point up or both point down, then the large arrow must point in the same direction.

The Future of Representational Measurement   While the theoretical developments in representational measurement have not had as much impact on empirical science as its developers may have envisioned and while throughout this section we have noted that successful applications of representational measurement in social psychology are rare, we would be remiss in closing this section without pointing to the dramatic success of representational measurement in the study of individual decision making. We provide a brief summary and refer interested readers to more complete overviews (Lopes, 1995; Luce, 1996; Luce & von Winterfeldt, 1994). The specification of formal models of expected utility and subjective expected utility, along with sets of necessary and sufficient axioms for those models, provided the grounds for empirical challenges to those models. Numerous empirical studies, mostly conducted by psychologists, identified a number of flaws in the expected utility models. For a time, it seemed as if no model would emerge to replace the shattered expected utility model and that we would be left with no more than a disparate collection of empirical violations. However, decumulative weighting function and rank-dependent utility function models are now seen to integrate a vast research on individual decision making and to include important concepts omitted from the earlier models of decision making, including such social psychological concepts as aspirations, hopes, and fears. The new integrative models and their axioms are now being challenged (see Luce, 1996) as one would hope. With persistence, even more sophisticated representational models of individual decision making are likely to emerge. Perhaps this same process will be repeated for

representational measurement in other areas of social psychology.

PSYCHOMETRIC MEASUREMENT

Representational measurement has much to recommend it, since the quality of measurement or the scalability of the measures can be examined through the sort of internal consistency checks we have reviewed. Nevertheless, most measurement in social psychology has not adopted the representational approach in spite of repeated admonitions to do so (e.g., Dawes & Smith, 1985). Most measurement in social psychology consists of questionnaire and observational measures whose validity is established not by a set of axiomatic consistency tests but rather by the observed patterns of variances and covariances that they display.

In general, we want to measure the attributes of some set of objects. Most typically in social psychological research, these objects consist of subjects and groups of subjects. And the set of attributes includes their traits, dispositions, attitudes, preferences, aptitudes, performances, and so forth. We collect data with the goal of ordering subjects on the measured variable or variables so that this observed ordering is the same as the unknown ordering on the true or latent construct that we wish to measure. A variable is said to possess high construct validity if these two orderings are highly similar.

The data that we use to order subjects on variables comes from a variety of sources, and each of these sources makes certain assumptions about the subjects. Most typically, we ask subjects to report on themselves. They indicate their preferences, their values, their attributes by responding to questionnaire and interview items. So the attitude researcher directly asks subjects for their evaluation of the attitude object. The researcher who studies stereotypes and intergroup relations asks subjects to provide descriptions of how they perceive various target groups. Someone interested in intimate relationships asks couples to report on the quality of their relationships. All of these ways of gathering data make the strong assumptions that a) subjects have access to the psychological property that the researcher wishes to measure, and b) subjects are willing to report that property.

Other, less direct measures assume that subjects have access to what we wish to measure but may be unwilling to provide accurate self-reports. Thus, these approaches attempt to minimize or otherwise overcome self-presentational concerns, typically through deception. Examples include: a) the bogus-pipeline approach to attitude measurement (Aguinis, Pierce, & Quigley, 1995; Jones & Sigall, 1971) in which subjects are led to believe that they might as well respond truthfully since the researcher has direct access to his or her emotional response to the stimulus object; and b) randomized responding procedures, again in attitude measurement (Dawes & Moore, 1979; Greenberg, Abdula, Simmons, & Horvitz, 1969; Warner, 1965), in which the subject knows that the researcher is unaware of the content of specific questions being asked but, unbeknown to the subject, the researcher is nevertheless able to infer attitudes from patterns of responses across multiple questions that have been sampled with some known probability from a universe of questions.

Other measurement approaches assume that there exists a psychological attribute to measure but that subjects may not have access to it and are unable, for whatever reason, to provide accurate self-reports. Unobtrusive observations of behavior, and inferences about attitudes and attributes from those behaviors, fall into this class of data collection approaches (Webb et al., 1981). Thus, to measure ethnocentrism, we observe how closely subjects are willing to sit to an outgroup member (Macrae, Bodenhausen, Milne, & Jetten, 1994); to measure interpersonal intimacy, we might examine whether individuals adopt similar and synchronous nonverbal gestures (Bernieri & Rosenthal, 1991); and to measure alcohol consumption, we count bottles and cans in garbage containers (Webb et al., 1981). Measures in this category may also assess responses over which subjects presumably have little or no control, assuming that these responses are indicators of underlying psychological attributes or states. Thus, interest or attention might be measured by pupil dilation (Petty & Cacioppo, 1983; Woodmansee, 1970), arousal by galvanic skin response (Cook & Selltiz, 1964; Rankin & Campbell, 1955), and attraction or revulsion by minute movements in relevant facial muscles (Cacioppo & Petty; 1979; Petty & Cacioppo, 1983). Response

latency measures, widely used in social cognition research (e.g., Dovidio, Evans, & Tyler, 1986; Fazio, Sanbonmatsu, Powell, & Kardes, 1986; Wittenbrink, Judd, & Park, 1997), also fall into this class.

Regardless of the assumptions that one makes about the willingness and ability of subjects to provide accurate reports, the validity of all these measures must ultimately be demonstrated by confirmation of expected covariance patterns in the data. Appeals to the face validity of a variable ("It certainly seems to ask appropriate questions given our measurement goals") are insufficient. Interestingly, in our opinion, such appeals seem somewhat more likely with less direct measurements. Thus, for instance, one may be more likely to encounter validity and reliability information (in the form of appropriate correlations and covariances) in the case of questionnaire measures than in the case of response latency data. In both cases, of course, the validity and reliability information is necessary.

The central question in measurement concerns the construct validity of measured variables. Each variable is assumed to be only an imperfect indicator of the underlying theoretical construct that one wishes to measure (Cook & Campbell, 1979; Cronbach & Meehl, 1955). According to traditional test theory, measures are imperfect because they necessarily contain some degree of random error or unreliability. According to more recent and comprehensive approaches, measures are imperfect indicators of constructs of interest not only because of random errors of measurement but also because they measure unintended constructs, systematic error, or what we will call constructs of disinterest. Thus, the latent reality of any measured variable is that the scores reflect three potentially distinguishable things: the construct that we would like to be measuring, a variety of constructs that we would rather not be measuring (i.e., constructs of disinterest), and random error or unreliability.

One argues for the construct validity of a variable by showing that its observed covariances and correlations with other variables provide evidence of 1) convergent validity, 2) discriminant validity, and 3) reliability. These three components of construct validity can be mapped on to the three categories of the latent reality underlying the variable. Thus convergent validity amounts to the demonstration that the variable reflects the construct of interest. Discriminant validity is the demonstration that constructs of disinterest are not in fact being measured. And reliability amounts to the demonstration that random errors of measurement are not large. Again, each of these demonstrations relies solely upon observed variance/covariance patterns rather than the sort of internal consistency checks found in the representational approach to measurement.

Only relatively recently in the psychometric tradition has it been recognized that the central measurement question is that of construct validity (Messick, 1989, 1995). If one surveys older measurement texts (e.g., Anastasi, 1961; Cronbach, 1960) or testing and measurement standards as set forth by the American Psychological Association (1966), one finds references to additional criteria that must be satisfied to establish measurement quality. Thus, in addition to construct validity, these sources identify content validity, predictive validity, and concurrent validity as additional considerations that must be satisfied. More recently, however, the literature has recognized that these different forms of validity really can be subsumed under the general heading of construct validity and that the differences among them amount to differences in the sort of evidence used to establish construct validity. Thus, for instance, predictive validity is established by showing that a given measure predicts subsequent standing on other criterion measures. Concurrent validity examines covariances with other criterion measures taken simultaneously. We concur with others in the field (Cronbach, 1984; Messick, 1989, 1995) that these simply amount to alternative sources of evidence from which one gathers information about the construct validity of a variable. Covariance patterns with a variety of different other variables can be informative for different aspects of construct validity. The fundamental question is whether the variable measures what we want it to measure and not what we don't want it to measure.

To know where to look for evidence of construct validity requires that the construct that one wants to measure be theoretically defined. Thus, as we argued earlier, measurement once again presupposes theory. It is from theory that expectations are derived about observed patterns of variance and covariance that the measured variable ought to exhibit. The construct that is measured is embedded in a theoretically defined "nomological net" (Cronbach & Meehl, 1955), and the pattern of covariances that one expects with other measured variables is the manifestation of this net.

Finally, this approach to measurement relies upon patterns of linear association among variables. Linear associations are not, however, scale-invariant. Nonlinear transformations of variables (e.g., log or inverse transformations) can affect the pattern of covariances that are observed. Given that the psychological metric of a variable may not be the same as the measured metric, one needs to attend to whether the appropriate metric has been used in examining the construct validity of a variable. Most importantly, one needs to be sensitive to reasonable transformations and their effects on observed variance/covariance patterns. Fortunately, nonlinear but monotonic transformations tend to have small effects on observed correlations. But there are occasions when one ought to be invoking a strongly nonlinear and nonmonotonic model of association, such that more moderate scores on one variable ought to be associated with higher scores on another, for instance. Unless one realizes that one is confronting this situation, traditional approaches to construct validity are unlikely to yield informative results.

The remainder of this section is organized as follows. We begin with the classic psychometric approach to reliability estimation and, in this context, briefly discuss what is known as item response theory. We then turn to a more general approach to the issue of reliability, involving the computation of components of variance and intraclass correlations. We then turn to a consideration of convergent and discriminant validity. First, we consider the general approach to these topics and demonstrate the utility of the multitrait-multimethod correlation matrix (Campbell & Fiske, 1959). Second, we return to a discussion of variance components in multifaceted designs, where systematic error components are manipulated and their contributions estimated (Cronbach, Gleser, Nanda, & Rajaratnam, 1972). Third, we discuss in some detail a more general approach to construct validity that relies on confirmatory factor analysis. We illustrate its utility in examining multitrait-multimethod matrices and show its relationship to the variance components approach.

Classic Test Theory and Reliability Estimation

As we have already noted, the classic approach to measurement assumes that each observed variable has two underlying components: true score and random error

$$X_i = T_i + E_i$$

At a later point, we will expand this model to include systematic error or constructs of disinterest, but for present purposes we can use this simpler model to motivate traditional approaches to reliability estimation. Recall that reliability is a component of construct validity. In theory it tells us about the relative amount of random errors of measurement in a variable. As such, it places an upper limit on the construct validity of the variable, since the more random error in it, the less it can be measuring the construct of interest.

From the above equation and the assumption that errors of measurement are random and therefore uncorrelated with true scores, it follows that the variance of the measured variable can be broken into two components: variance due to the true score and error variance

$$\sigma_X^2 = \sigma_T^2 + \sigma_E^2$$

From this, we can define the reliability of a measured variable as the proportion of its total variance that is true score variance:

$$\rho_{XX} = \frac{\sigma_T^2}{\sigma_X^2} = \frac{\sigma_T^2}{\sigma_T^2 + \sigma_E^2}$$

The square root of the reliability is the correlation between the measured variable and the true score.

It is important to realize that this is the theoretical definition of reliability. Reliability can be estimated in a variety of ways, as we will describe below. The important point, however, is that any estimate of reliability only approximates what we mean theoretically by the notion of reliability.

To derive estimates of the reliability of a variable, we begin by assuming that we have what are called "parallel forms" of the variable. That is, we have two items, X_1 and X_2, each of which contains the true scores and each of which contains random errors of measurement to the same degree. Note that since the errors are assumed to be random, we are not assuming identical errors in the two variables. Rather we are assuming equal error variances. Under these assumptions, the correlation between the two variables estimates the reliability of each:

$$r_{X_1 X_2} = \rho_{X_1 X_1} = \rho_{X_2 X_2}$$

With k parallel items, each of the $k(k-1)/2$ bivariate correlations estimates this same reliability. Additionally, since the errors in each item are random, they tend to cancel each other out when we form a single measure by summing scores on the set of k items. The extent to which this is true is given by the Spearman-Brown Prophecy Formula for the reliability of the sum of k parallel items:

$$\rho_{\text{sum}} = \frac{k r_{ij}}{1 + (k-1) r_{ij}}$$

where r_{ij} is the average of the $k(k-1)/2$ bivariate correlations between pairs of items.[4]

The assumptions of parallel items are strong. One might want, for instance, to allow unequal error variances in the various items, but still estimate the reliability of the sum of the items. This can be done by realizing that the variance of a sum equals the sum of the variances of the individual items plus two times the sum of all the item covariances. Since errors of measurement are assumed to be random, they contribute to the magnitude of the item variances but not to the magnitude of item covariances. Hence, the greater the relative contribution of the item covariances to the variance of the sum, the more reliable the sum. Equivalently, the more the variance of the sum exceeds the sum of the individual item variances, the higher the sum's reliability. This rationale lies behind the derivation of coefficient alpha (Cronbach, 1951), estimating the reliability of a composite score made by summing individual items:

$$\alpha = \left(\frac{k}{k-1} \right) \left(1 - \frac{\Sigma \sigma_i^2}{\sigma_{\text{sum}}^2} \right)$$

This formula is equivalent to the Spearman-Brown Prophecy Formula given above if one standardizes all variables and computes the sum of standardized scores, thus

forcing them to have equal variance. In essence, a composite score based on the simple sum of the variables weights the variables according to their variance. A sum of standardized variables weights them equally.

Although social psychologists frequently report coefficient alpha for a composite score, they are more likely to conduct a factor analysis or principal components analysis of the individual items and then form a composite or sum of the measures weighted by their factor loadings. In essence, this approach relaxes the assumptions made by the parallel forms in a different way, weighting the individual items in computing the sum neither equally nor according to their variance but according to the magnitude of their relationship with the true score. Thus, we no longer are assuming equal true score variance in each of the items.

In general, the principal components approach to reliability estimation involves the following steps. One takes a set of items presumed to have a single underlying construct or factor in common. One performs a principal components analysis, with the resulting factor loadings on the first unrotated principal component estimating the correlation between each item and the single underlying construct. The sum of these squared loadings is the component's eigenvalue or latent root, which should be large relative to the number of items if a strong argument is to be made that the items tap a single underlying construct. Next, a composite or weighted-sum score is computed for each individual, summing standardized scores that are weighted by the item's factor loading. The reliability of this composite score is given as:

$$\alpha = \left(\frac{k}{k-1} \right) \left(1 - \frac{1}{\lambda} \right)$$

where λ is the eigenvalue of the first principal component. This has been shown to be the maximum possible alpha for any weighted linear combination of the component items (Bentler, 1968). Extensions of this approach have also been made for the case where the set of items is not single-factored and where multiple composite scores are derived from a rotated factor solution (Armor, 1974).

Numeric Example   In Table 8, hypothetical data are given representing the scores of six subjects (A through F) on three alternative items ($X1$, $X2$, and $X3$). Also given are

1. the means and variances of the three items;
2. the simple sum of the three items for each subject and its mean and variance;
3. the item intercorrelations and covariances; and
4. the loadings of the three items on their first principal component and its eigenvalue.

We have included only six subjects in these data to keep the example simple. Many more subjects would be needed

TABLE 8
Hypothetical Data for Reliability Estimation

Item	A	B	C	D	E	F	Mean	Variance
X1	5	3	6	5	2	2	3.833	2.967
X2	6	3	9	5	3	4	5.000	5.200
X3	9	6	7	5	5	3	5.833	4.167
Sum	20	12	22	15	10	9	14.667	28.667

Correlation (Covariance) Matrix

	X1	X2	X3
X1	1.000 (2.967)		
X2	0.866 (3.400)	1.000 (5.200)	
X3	0.673 (2.367)	0.516 (2.400)	1.000 (4.167)

Principal Components Analysis: 1st Component Only

	Loadings
X1	0.958
X2	0.902
X3	0.805
Eigenvalue:	2.380

to assess reliability and construct validity of the three items with confidence.

The reliability of the simple sum of the items using the formula for coefficient alpha based on the simple sum is:

$$\alpha = \left(\frac{3}{2}\right)\left(1 - \frac{2.967 + 5.200 + 4.167}{28.667}\right) = 0.855$$

The average intercorrelation among the three items equals 0.685. We can use the Spearman-Brown Prophecy Formula to find the reliability of the sum of the standardized items:

$$\alpha = \frac{(3)0.685}{1 + (2)0.685} = 0.867$$

Equivalently, the formula for alpha can be used, forcing the three items to have equal variance by standardizing them. Thus the variances of the standardized items equal 1.00 and the variance of the sum of the standardized items equals the sum of the variances plus 2 times the sum of the three intercorrelations:

$$\alpha = \left(\frac{3}{2}\right)\left(1 - \frac{1 + 1 + 1}{1 + 1 + 1 + 2(0.866 + 0.673 + 0.516)}\right) = 0.867$$

The reliability of the optimally weighted sum, weighting the three items according to their loadings on the first principal component is

$$\alpha = \left(\frac{3}{2}\right)\left(1 - \frac{1}{2.380}\right) = 0.870$$

Note that all three methods of weighting the three items yield quite similar reliabilities. This will generally be the case when the variances of the items are similar and their intercorrelations are high and relatively uniform. The three weighting methods can give radically different results, however, if the items have substantially different variances. This is particularly likely to be the case when the measures are in different metrics (e.g., using income [in dollars] and job prestige [on a nine-point rating scale] as indicators of socioeconomic status). In such a case, the standardized or principal components weighting should be used instead of the simple sum, since items with larger variance are weighted more heavily in the simple sum and, in the case of the use of different metrics, this would amount to weighting by a variable's metric.

Assuming that items are all positively and uniformly intercorrelated (or that some have been reversed to accomplish this), it is typically the case that the principal components weighting will produce a reliability estimate only slightly higher than the reliability of the sum of the standardized scores. Since there exists sampling variability in the optimal weights (or factor loadings) used in deriving the principal components estimate, it may frequently be preferable to use the simple sum of the standardized measures (Green, 1977; Wainer, 1976).

When the measured intercorrelations are quite variable in magnitude, the principal components approach can yield a more reliable composite than the standardized sum. One needs to be careful in interpreting the composite score from a principal components analysis in such a case however, since very unequal weights will be used and the composite may end up reflecting only some of the items.

When some of the intercorrelations are negative, items need to be reverse-scored unless the principal components weighting is used. Finally, the reliability of an index based on the average of the items (whether standardized or not) is equal to the reliability of an index based on summing the items. The advantage of averaging the items rather than summing them is that resulting index scores are not dependent on the number of items in the index.

Item Response Theory   Although not widely used in social psychology, in the last twenty-five years there have been significant extensions of the classic test theory model in the case of items with dichotomous responses (e.g., correct versus incorrect, yes versus no). These extensions permit one to assess characteristics of individual items beyond their reliability. Specifically, depending on the complexity of the underlying item response model, one can estimate both the difficulty and discrimination of an item. These are defined as follows, in the context of ability testing where responses are either correct or incorrect:

Item difficulty: the point on the underlying ability continuum where the item maximally discriminates. A very easy item is one that everyone, even those of lowest ability, gets correct. A moderately difficult item is one that separates those with lower ability from those with higher levels of ability. A more difficult item discriminates best at the high end of the ability spectrum.

Item discrimination: at the point of the item's maximum discrimination (i.e., its difficulty level) how discriminating is it? Some items may more clearly separate those with small ability differences while others may discriminate less precisely.

The primary strength of item response theory is that it permits one to select items for inclusion in a test or a scale based on more complete information than simply the extent to which the item correlates with the total score and the other items. That is, one can select items with differing difficulty levels to insure that the complete test is capable of discriminating at a variety of levels of ability. Additionally, if the complete test is to be used for selection purposes, one can select items that are most discriminating at the desired selection point on the underlying ability dimension.

The significant extensions of the classic test theory model in cases such as these merit attention by social psychologists, particularly those interested in more applied measurement issues. Introductions to the relevant literature can be found in Hambleton (1989), Hambleton and Swaminathan (1985), and Weiss and Yoes (1990).

Components of Variance and Intraclass Correlations

An alternative approach to reliability estimation partitions the variability in a subject by items matrix of scores into its various components, following the rules of analysis of variance. Returning to the data in Table 8, one can use analysis of variance procedures to calculate the following values for sums of squares and mean squares due to subjects, items, and residual or error:

Source	Sum of Squares	df	Mean Square
Between subjects	47.778	5	9.556
Between items	12.111	2	6.056
Residual	13.889	10	1.389

These mean squares have expected values that are functions of the variance due to subjects, items, and error (Cornfield & Tukey, 1956). Once these functions are specified, one can estimate these unknown variance components and from them derive reliability estimates. These reliability estimates are, in their most general form, ratios of the component of variance of interest to the sum of that component plus component(s) of error variance. They are known as intraclass correlations (Shrout & Fleiss, 1979), and we illustrate their computation in the following paragraphs.

The exact functions that relate the expected mean squares due to subjects, items, and error to the variance components depend on whether subjects and items are treated as random or fixed effects. In essence, a random effect involves a sample of levels from a population of levels to which one wishes to generalize. A fixed effect is one in which all levels to which generalization is sought are included in the data collection design. We will return to this distinction in a bit and clarify its meaning for interpreting the intraclass correlations that we compute from the mean squares. We routinely treat subjects as a random effect since it is rarely the case that we wish to confine generalization to only the subjects from whom data have been collected. Whether items should be treated as a fixed or random effect is a more difficult choice and depends on the design of anticipated future studies about which inferences are sought. Again, further discussion on this topic follows.

In general, in this two-way design, the three variance components, due to subjects, items, and error, can be estimated as follows from the mean squares:

$$S_S^2 = \frac{MS_S - MS_E}{k}$$

$$S_I^2 = \frac{MS_I - MS_E}{n}$$

$$S_E^2 = MS_E$$

where S_S^2, S_I^2, S_E^2 are the estimated variance components associated with subjects, items, and error or residual, respectively, MS_S, MS_I, MS_E are the computed mean squares due to subjects, items, and error, and k and n are the number of items and subjects. For the data of Table 8, the estimated values of the variance components are:

$$S_S^2 = 2.722$$

$$S_I^2 = 0.778$$

$$S_E^2 = 1.389$$

If items are considered fixed, then their variance is considered to be constant in the current and future studies, since in all future studies the same items will be included. To estimate the reliability of the subjects' scores on these individual items, we want to compare the component of variation due to subjects with the total variation due to subjects and error, excluding the fixed item variance. Expressed as a function of mean squares, this ratio equals:

$$\frac{S_S^2}{S_S^2 + S_E^2} = \frac{MS_S - MS_E}{MS_S + (k-1)MS_E} = \frac{9.556 - 1.389}{9.556 + (2)1.389} = 0.662$$

This value is the estimated reliability of a single item. It is called the intraclass correlation with measures fixed, ICC(3,1) in the notation of Shrout and Fleiss (1979). Note that it is similar in value, although not identical to the average intercorrelation between the three items computed earlier, i.e., 0.685. Actually it is the reliability of a single measure not assuming standardization. One can compute it directly from the variances and covariances of the items given in Table 8, by dividing the sum of the three covariances by the sum of the three variances:

$$\frac{3.400 + 2.367 + 2.400}{2.967 + 5.200 + 4.167} = 0.662$$

Thus, rather than averaging the three correlations, one pools the three covariances and the three variances and computes a single correlation from these pooled values.

The relationship between this intraclass correlation and what we earlier computed as coefficient alpha is further clarified by noting that if we use the intraclass correlation for the value of r_{ij} in the Spearman-Brown Prophecy Formula, we get a value for the reliability of the sum of the three items that is equivalent to coefficient alpha for these three items, allowing differences in their variances:

$$\alpha = \frac{kr_{ij}}{1 + (k-1)r_{ij}} = \frac{(3)0.662}{1 + (2)0.662} = 0.855$$

This is identical to the value that we computed previously using the formula for coefficient alpha. In other words, the intraclass correlation in this case can be seen as another way of computing the intercorrelation among the items and this value can then be used to estimate the reliability of the sum or average of the items, assuming in future studies that the exact same items will be used.

If items are considered random, then the specific ones included in the current study are only a sample of items and different samples of items are presumably to be used in future studies. As a result, subjects' scores may contain error in part because we employ different items or subsets of items with different subjects. Accordingly, item variance should be considered a component of error variance. Hence, we want to compare the component of variation due to subjects in the current study with the total variation due to subjects, items, and error. We can express this also as a function of the mean squares:

$$\frac{S_S^2}{S_S^2 + S_I^2 + S_E^2} = \frac{MS_S - MS_E}{MS_S + (k-1)MS_E + k(MS_I - MS_E)/n}$$

$$= \frac{9.556 - 1.389}{9.556 + 2(1.389) + 0.5(4.667)} = 0.557$$

This is also an intraclass correlation that estimates the reliability of a single item, ICC(2,1) in the notation of Shrout and Fleiss (1979). But this time, we are estimating the reliability of an item allowing for the fact that different subjects may receive different items so that variation between items becomes a part of the error variation.

Again, this intraclass correlation can be seen as an estimate of the item intercorrelation, allowing future studies to include different items sampled from the same population of items. Accordingly, if we want to estimate the reliability of the sum or average of three items, we can substitute this intraclass correlation for the average item intercorrelation in the Spearman-Brown formula to estimate the reliability of the sum of the three items, allowing different samples of three items in future studies:

$$\alpha = \frac{kr_{ij}}{1 + (k-1)r_{ij}} = \frac{(3)0.557}{1 + (2)0.557} = 0.790$$

To clarify the difference between the two intraclass correlations, imagine two future studies. In the first, we use the same three items for all subjects as used in the current study. Then the appropriate item reliability to be computed from the current data is the intraclass correlation with items fixed (i.e., 0.662). And the reliability of the sum or average of the three items is 0.855. In the second future study, however, different samples of items are used so that some of the differences from subject to subject are due to item differences as well as to true subject differences and error. If that is the future study to which we want to generalize, then the intraclass correlation that treats items as a random factor is the appropriate reliability estimate (i.e., 0.557). And the estimated reliability of the sum of the three items is now 0.790. The two intraclass correlations (and hence the two reliabilities for the sums) will differ to the extent that the variance component due to items is large or, equivalently, to the extent that differences among means of the items are relatively large.

An Alternative Estimation Approach An alternative procedure for estimating the variance components and intraclass correlation has recently been outlined by Kenny and Judd (1996). The advantage of this procedure is its flexibility. For instance, it handles randomly missing data with relative ease.

Consider the eighteen scores in Table 8. The overall variance of these eighteen scores can be expressed as a function of the sum of the squared differences between all possible pairs of scores. However, some of these pairs of scores involve two scores from the same subject. They thus are dependent because they come from the same subject. Other pairs are dependent because they come from the same measure or item. Only pairs of scores that come from different subjects and different items are independent of each other.

In Table 9, we present a matrix of all possible pairs of the eighteen scores, indicating which pairs are independent (O), which share a common subject (S), and which share a common item (I). If two scores are dependent because of a common subject or a common item, then we would expect their squared difference on average to be smaller than the squared difference between pairs of scores that are independent, to the extent that subject and item dependencies are large. More formally, it can be shown that the expected value of the squared difference between independent pairs

TABLE 9
Dependencies Among Pairs of Scores in Table 8

	A1	A2	A3	B1	B2	B3	C1	C2	C3	D1	D2	D3	E1	E2	E3	F1	F2	F3
A1																		
A2	S																	
A3	S	S																
B1	I	O	O															
B2	O	I	O	S														
B3	O	O	I	S	S													
C1	I	O	O	I	O	O												
C2	O	I	O	O	I	O	S											
C3	O	O	I	O	O	I	S	S										
D1	I	O	O	I	O	O	I	O	O									
D2	O	I	O	O	I	O	O	I	O	S								
D3	O	O	I	O	O	I	O	O	I	S	S							
E1	I	O	O	I	O	O	I	O	O	I	O	O						
E2	O	I	O	O	I	O	O	I	O	O	I	O	S					
E3	O	O	I	O	O	I	O	O	I	O	O	I	S	S				
F1	I	O	O	I	O	O	I	O	O	I	O	O	I	O	O			
F2	O	I	O	O	I	O	O	I	O	O	I	O	O	I	O	S		
F3	O	O	I	O	O	I	O	O	I	O	O	I	O	O	I	S	S	

equals $2\sigma_O^2$, where σ_O^2 is the variance of independent scores. The expected value of the squared difference between pairs that share a common subject equals $2\sigma_O^2(1 - \rho_S)$. If pairs share the same measure, then the expected squared difference equals $2\sigma_O^2(1 - \rho_I)$. In these expressions, ρ_S and ρ_I are the correlations or dependencies in the data due to common subjects or items. From these expressions we can estimate the values of σ_O^2, ρ_S, and ρ_I from the computed averages of the squared differences between independent and dependent pairs of scores. Let U equal the average of the squared differences computed between pairs of scores that are independent of each other (i.e., those pairs designated O in Table 9). Let L_S equal the average squared difference between pairs that have a common subject, and let L_I equal the average squared difference between pairs that have a common item. Then the estimates of σ_O^2, ρ_S, and ρ_I are given by the expressions:

$$S_O^2 = U / 2$$

$$r_S = 1 - \frac{L_S}{U}$$

$$r_I = 1 - \frac{L_I}{U}$$

For the scores in Table 8, all of the pairwise squared differences are presented in Table 10. From these we can calculate the average squared difference among independent pairs, pairs with a common subject, and pairs with a common item: U equals 9.778, L_S equals 4.333, and L_I equals 8.222. Accordingly the three estimates equal:

$$S_O^2 = 4.889$$

$$r_S = 0.557$$

$$r_I = 0.159$$

Note that the dependency due to subjects, r_S, is identical to the intraclass correlation treating items as a random factor that was computed previously. It tells us about the intercorrelation between the items. The dependency due to items, r_I, is the subject intraclass correlation, estimating the intercorrelation between subjects. Additionally, the values of the variance components, due to subjects, items, and error, can be directly calculated from the three values of U, L_S, and L_I:

$$S_S^2 = (U - L_S)/2 \qquad = (9.778 - 4.333)/2 \qquad = 2.722$$

$$S_I^2 = (U - L_I)/2 \qquad = (9.778 - 8.222)/2 \qquad = 0.778$$

$$S_E^2 = (L_S + L_I - U)/2 = (4.333 + 8.222 - 9.778)/2 = 1.389$$

The variance of the independent scores, S_O^2, equals the sum of these three components, as it should since scores that are independent of each other come from different subjects and different measures.

In sum, this approach to estimating dependencies is identical to the variance components approach outlined above. Its advantage comes from the fact that values of U, L_S, and L_I can be computed even with substantial amounts of missing data, when either mean squares or correlations among items could not be computed. Imagine, for instance, that each subject was missing one or even two scores on a random basis. Neither correlations between items nor sums of squares and mean squares could be computed readily. Yet values of U, L_S, and L_I could be computed, assuming that there were some pairs in all three categories (i.e., independent, from a common subject, from a common item). Simulations reported in Kenny and Judd (1996) reveal that the estimated intraclass correlation and variance components appear to be reasonable even with substantial missing data.

Convergent and Discriminant Validity

Almost all of what has been reviewed so far in this section of the chapter concerns the estimation of reliability, although under the variance components approach we did consider variation due to items as well as true score variation associated with subjects and error variation. We turn now to the treatment of systematic, rather than error, variation in our measures and procedures for discriminating between systematic variation due to the construct that we wish to be measuring and systematic variation due to constructs of disinterest. We will refer to this latter variation as systematic error variation.

In general, information about convergent and discriminant validity of a particular variable is contained in the set of covariances or correlations between that variable and other variables assessing both the same and different constructs. The basic principle underlying this statement is the realization that two variables ought to covary to the extent that they measure the same or related constructs. To the extent that they measure different and unrelated constructs, their covariance should be small.

Consider two variables, X_1 and X_2. We assume that each one measures, to some extent, three different latent constructs, η_1, η_2, and η_3. Let us assume that η_1 represents the construct of interest and the other two constructs are sources of systematic error. Additionally, each variable contains a certain amount of random error, ϵ_{1i} and ϵ_{2i}. For algebraic ease, we assume that all variables and constructs have expected values of zero and unit variances. Accordingly, the λ_{jk} loading coefficients indicate the extent to which latent construct k contributes to measured variable j. The following are the construct or latent variable equations that represent the components of the two variables:

$$X_{1i} = \lambda_{11}\eta_{1i} + \lambda_{12}\eta_{2i} + \lambda_{13}\eta_{3i} + \lambda_{1\epsilon}\epsilon_{1i}$$

$$X_{2i} = \lambda_{21}\eta_{1i} + \lambda_{22}\eta_{2i} + \lambda_{23}\eta_{3i} + \lambda_{2\epsilon}\epsilon_{2i}$$

TABLE 10
Squared Differences Between Pairs of Scores in Table 8

	A1	A2	A3	B1	B2	B3	C1	C2	C3	D1	D2	D3	E1	E2	E3	F1	F2	F3
A1																		
A2	1																	
A3	16	9																
B1	4	9	36															
B2	4	9	36	0														
B3	1	0	9	9	9													
C1	1	0	9	9	9	0												
C2	16	9	0	36	36	9	9											
C3	4	1	4	16	16	1	1	4										
D1	0	1	16	4	4	1	1	16	4									
D2	0	1	16	4	4	1	1	16	4	0								
D3	0	1	16	4	4	1	1	16	4	0	0							
E1	9	16	49	1	1	16	16	49	25	9	9	9						
E2	4	9	36	0	0	9	9	36	16	4	4	4	1					
E3	0	1	16	4	4	1	1	16	4	0	0	0	9	4				
F1	9	16	49	1	1	16	16	49	25	9	9	9	0	1	9			
F2	1	4	25	1	1	4	4	25	9	1	1	1	4	1	1	4		
F3	4	9	36	0	0	9	9	36	16	4	9	4	1	0	4	1	1	

Using the algebra of variances and covariances (Kenny, 1979), we can derive expectations for the variances of the two variables and for their correlation (ρ represents the expected correlation between two variables or constructs):

$$\sigma_{X_1}^2 = \lambda_{11}^2 + \lambda_{12}^2 + \lambda_{13}^2 + 2\lambda_{11}\lambda_{12}\rho_{\eta_1\eta_2} + 2\lambda_{11}\lambda_{13}\rho_{\eta_1\eta_3} + 2\lambda_{12}\lambda_{13}\rho_{\eta_2\eta_3} + \lambda_{1\epsilon}^2$$

$$\sigma_{X_2}^2 = \lambda_{21}^2 + \lambda_{22}^2 + \lambda_{23}^2 + 2\lambda_{21}\lambda_{22}\rho_{\eta_1\eta_2} + 2\lambda_{21}\lambda_{23}\rho_{\eta_1\eta_3} + 2\lambda_{22}\lambda_{23}\rho_{\eta_2\eta_3} + \lambda_{2\epsilon}^2$$

$$\rho_{X_1X_2} = \lambda_{11}\lambda_{21} + \lambda_{12}\lambda_{22} + \lambda_{13}\lambda_{23} + (\lambda_{11}\lambda_{22} + \lambda_{12}\lambda_{21})\rho_{\eta_1\eta_2} + (\lambda_{11}\lambda_{23} + \lambda_{13}\lambda_{21})\rho_{\eta_1\eta_3} + (\lambda_{12}\lambda_{23} + \lambda_{13}\lambda_{22})\rho_{\eta_2\eta_3}$$

According to these expressions, the variance of each measured variable is a function of the relative contributions of each latent construct to the variable, the correlations between the latent constructs, and random error. The correlation between the two measured variables is a complex function of the extent to which the same latent constructs contribute to both and the extent to which the latent constructs are themselves correlated. Examining the magnitude of this correlation is likely to be relatively uninformative about the construct validity of the two measured variables unless we can make certain assumptions about the makeup of the two variables. For instance, let us assume that the two constructs of disinterest are measure-specific, that is η_2 contributes only to X_1 and η_3 contributes only to X_2. In other words, we are assuming that λ_{13} and λ_{22} both equal zero. Then the expectation for the correlation between the two measured variables reduces to:

$$\rho_{X_1X_2} = \lambda_{11}\lambda_{21} + \lambda_{12}\lambda_{21}\rho_{\eta_1\eta_2} + \lambda_{11}\lambda_{23}\rho_{\eta_1\eta_3}$$

Thus, the correlation between the two measured variables is now affected solely by the extent to which they both measure the construct of interest ($\lambda_{11}\lambda_{21}$) and the extent to which the two sources of systematic error are in turn correlated with the construct of interest. Note, however, that all three terms in this equation have at least one loading coefficient of one of the measured variables on the construct of interest. As a result, the correlation between the two variables will tend to be large only if the two variables each tend to possess convergent validity. Additionally, as the correlations between the two sources of systematic error and the construct of interest approach zero, the equation reduces further:

$$\rho_{X_1 X_2} = \lambda_{11}\lambda_{21}$$

The correlation reflects only the extent to which the two variables both measure the construct of interest. In other words, if we can make these simplifying assumptions, the correlation between two variables is indicative of the variables' joint convergent validity.

These assumptions are, of course, highly restrictive. Nevertheless, they provide the justification for the reliance upon the "multiple operations" approach to construct validity (Campbell, 1960; Campbell & Fiske, 1959; Cook & Campbell, 1979; Cronbach & Meehl, 1955; Judd & Kenny, 1981; Webb et al., 1981). Multiple measures of the same construct should be highly related to each other if they in fact do jointly measure the construct of interest. But high intercorrelations are not a sufficient condition for claiming convergent validity. Additionally, one must have confidence that the multiple measures do not share other systematic sources of variation or constructs of disinterest. In other words, one needs multiple measures that are as dissimilar as possible in terms of their irrelevancies or sources of systematic error.

Although most social psychologists have learned the lesson that multiple operations are important, all too often we are content to use multiple measures whose irrelevancies may be highly redundant. Thus, we tend to use redundant questionnaire items and convince ourselves of their validity by showing that they are highly intercorrelated (i.e., a high coefficient alpha). But high internal consistency is not the same thing as convergent validity because high intercorrelations between items may simply mean that they are all successfully measuring something we would rather not be measuring, i.e., a construct of disinterest rather than the one of interest. Large intercorrelations between items are indicative of convergent validity only when we can be convinced that they do not share large components of systematic error.

Discriminant validity is demonstrated by showing that measures of the construct of interest intercorrelate more highly with each other than they do with measures that assess the construct of disinterest against which discriminant validity is sought. In its most stringent form, one would like evidence that measures of the construct of interest are uncorrelated with measures of the construct of disinterest. But such a situation should be expected only if the two constructs are themselves unrelated to each other. A more reasonable expectation is that measures of the construct of interest should be more highly correlated with each other than they are with measures of the construct of disinterest.

Multitrait-Multimethod Correlation Matrix   Evidence for simultaneous convergent and discriminant validity derives from the multitrait-multimethod correlation matrix, as outlined by Campell and Fiske (1959). Such a matrix involves multiple measures of two or more constructs, crossing alternative methods of measurement with constructs. For instance, a social psychologist interested in person perception might collect data measuring the sociability, creativity, and intelligence of a set of target individuals. Each of the three traits is measured in multiple ways: self-ratings provided by the target, ratings of the target provided by a close friend, and performance scores on inventories designed to measure the three constructs. The hypothetical correlation matrix of Table 11 results. Scores on each measure are assumed to be a function of three components: the relevant trait construct (sociable versus creative versus intelligent), systematic error due to method (self-rating versus friend ratings versus inventory), and random error. Following the logic summarized above when we derived the factors contributing to the correlation between two measured variables, the correlations in the present matrix are due to:

1. convergent validity between measures of the same trait using different methods;
2. shared systematic error variance due to measures using the same method;
3. correlations between the latent trait constructs; and
4. correlations between the latent method constructs.

In addition to providing evidence for convergent validity, the matrix provides evidence for two sorts of discriminant validity. First, it enables the researcher to examine the extent to which systematic error variance due to method contributes to the observed measures. Thus, it discriminates between true-score trait variance and method variance. Additionally, it permits the researcher to examine whether the latent trait constructs are discriminable.

Campbell and Fiske (1959) outlined an informal logic for the analysis of multitrait-multimethod matrices. This logic centers around the values of three sorts of correlations in the matrix:

1. correlations between measures of the same traits using different methods; Campbell and Fiske (1959) called these validity correlations (bold type in Table 11)
2. correlations between different traits using the same methods (italicized in Table 11)
3. correlations involving measures of different traits with different methods.

Campbell and Fiske (1959) argued that four criteria should be met if the correlation matrix shows evidence of convergent and discriminant validity:

1. correlations involving measures of the same trait with different methods (i.e., the validity correlations) should be substantially larger than zero
2. correlations involving measures of the same trait with different methods should be larger than correlations involving measures of different traits with different methods
3. correlations involving the same trait but different methods should be higher than correlations involving different traits and the same method
4. roughly the same pattern of correlations should be observed between measures of the different traits within each of the types of methods.

The first two criteria suggest convergent validity. The third argues that the contribution of trait construct variance to the measures is larger than method variance, thus suggesting discriminant validity against method constructs. And the fourth criteria suggests that the underlying trait constructs are consistently discriminable regardless of method.

At a later point in this section of the chapter, we will examine more formal procedures for analyzing multitrait-multimethod matrices. These analyses permit the researcher to estimate the contribution of trait variance, method variance, and error variance to each of the measures, as well as to estimate the correlations between the trait constructs and between the method constructs. In spite of these analytic advances, however, the informal criteria outlined by Campbell and Fiske (1959) continue to have great intuitive appeal and utility.

Variance Components and Generalizability Theory In our earlier discussion of reliability that focused on the estimation of intraclass correlations, we raised the possibility that variation due to measures or items might be considered to be an aspect of error variation depending on the

type of generalization that one sought to make. If, for instance, in an anticipated study, different individuals were to receive different items, then differences between items would constitute a component of unreliability and accordingly ought to be included in the denominator of the intraclass correlation. An alternative way to understand this result is to argue that an individual's score is in part due to his or her true standing on the construct of interest, in part due to the systematic error associated with a particular item, and in part random error. Thus, the earlier analysis that separated random error from systematic error due to item in fact was exploring issues of convergent and discriminant validation.

The variance components approach has been importantly extended by Lee Cronbach and others into what has become widely known as Generalizability Theory (Cronbach, Gleser, Nanda, & Rajaratnam, 1972; Cronbach, Rajaratnam, & Gleser, 1963; Fyans, 1983; Shavelson & Webb, 1991). The fundamental insight of this theory is that any score has potentially many factors that contribute to it: the person being measured, the measure being used, the experimenter administering the measure, the setting, the season of the year, the time of the day, etc. And all of these factors (or facets in the terms of Generalizability Theory) affect the magnitude of error in the score and the degree to which one can generalize from it. Thus, if generalization across measures is wanted, then variation due to measures needs to be included as a component of error. Similarly, if one wishes to generalize across experimenters or settings, then these too need to be considered as components of systematic error. The theory therefore takes issue with the assumption of classic test theory that there is a single error component. Rather, there are multiple facets that contribute to each score and whether these are considered a part of the true score variation or components of error depends on the situation to which one wishes to generalize. Accordingly,

TABLE 11
Multitrait-Multimethod Matrix: Three Traits by Three Methods

Method	Trait	S-S	S-C	S-I	F-S	F-C	F-I	I-S	I-C	I-I
Self	Sociable									
	Creative	*0.34*								
	Intelligent	*0.27*	*0.45*							
Friend	Sociable	**0.58**	0.18	0.20						
	Creative	0.14	**0.42**	0.09	*0.29*					
	Intelligent	0.19	0.12	**0.46**	*0.21*	*0.38*				
Inventory	Sociable	**0.53**	0.14	0.05	**0.60**	0.12	0.03			
	Creative	0.06	**0.31**	0.12	0.10	**0.34**	0.09	*0.18*		
	Intelligent	0.12	0.14	**0.47**	0.08	0.15	**0.43**	*0.14*	*0.24*	

there is no single index of reliability; rather there are alternative generalizability coefficients dependent on the generalization intended.

Analytically, the approach of Generalizability Theory is an experimental one in which variance components associated with multiple facets are estimated from the mean squares that one calculates through analysis of variance, just as we did above in the case of the design where subjects were crossed with items. This earlier design is considered to be a one-facet design, since facets are defined as systematic variation in components other than subjects. A two-facet design would be one in which both items and occasions varied, and so forth. The estimation of the relevant components of variance depends on whether facets are crossed with each other or nested and on whether their levels are considered to be fixed or random. As always, subjects are considered to be a random effect and are generally, although not always, crossed with facets. Most typically, facets are considered to be random, since we typically wish to generalize to situations involving other measures, occasions, experimenters, and so forth. The important point, however, is that the definition of the facets, whether they are considered to be random or fixed, and whether they are considered to be a component of error in calculating generalizability coefficients (or intraclass correlations) depends on the situation to which one would like to generalize.

General rules for deriving expected values for mean squares given a wide variety of designs are provided in books devoted to analysis of variance and experimental design (e.g., Kirk, 1982; Winer, Brown, & Michels, 1991). These generally follow the classic exposition on the subject set out by Cornfield and Tukey (1956). The expected mean squares are functions of the components of variance attributable to facets, subjects, and their interactions. One can derive estimates of the components by substituting the obtained mean squares for their expected values. We followed that procedure earlier in considering the design in which subjects were crossed with items. We illustrate it now with a two-facet design.

Suppose we wished to measure subjects' tendency to display prejudice towards outgroup members. We sample 100 majority group subjects and ask them to indicate their agreement with three alternative measures of outgroup derogation, directed towards three different outgroups. The three measures are:

1. "_____ are too pushy in insisting on their rights in our society."
2. "Affirmative action really isn't needed anymore to guarantee the fair treatment of _____ in our society."
3. "_____ don't appreciate the extent to which you have to work hard to make it in our society."

These items are given to subjects, referencing three different minority outgroups, substituting "Blacks," "Hispanics," and "Native Americans" in turn for the blanks in each item. In total then, each subject gives nine ratings.

From the resulting data, we estimate the sums of squares and mean squares due to subjects, items, outgroups, and their interactions. These values are given at the top of Table 12. Treating all three factors as random, the expected values of these mean squares are given in the middle panel of Table 12. Here n_S is the number of subjects and σ_S^2 is the variance component due to subjects. Other subscripts reference items (I) and groups (G). Variance components for interactions are indicated by products of the subscripts. The triple interaction is confounded in this design with residual error. Its variance component has an R subscript. From the expressions for the expected values of the mean squares and their actual computed value from the data, one can derive estimates of the variance components. These estimates are given at the bottom of Table 12.

The estimated variance components themselves are readily interpretable. The variance component due to subjects represents the variation between subjects in their habitual or average response regardless of the outgroup being rated or the measure used. In the present context, it can be interpreted as individual variation in generalized prejudice, regardless of the outgroup and the question asked. Similar interpretations can be made for the variance component due to groups or items. For instance, the variance component due to groups tells us about variation between groups in prejudice expressed towards them, collapsing across items and subjects.

The components associated with the subject by group and subject by items interactions are also of interest. The subject by group interaction estimates the extent to which subjects respond differently to the different outgroups. Higher values would indicate that individual differences in prejudice depend on the outgroup towards whom prejudice is expressed. The subject by item interaction represents variation in expressed prejudice as a function of the specific item used.

A variety of different generalizability coefficients (which are generalizations of the intraclass correlations computed earlier) can be computed from these variance components, depending on the nature of future research to which one would like to generalize. In general, the form of these coefficients is the ratio of the variance component(s) of interest to the variance of the observed score in the anticipated study. Thus, for instance, suppose we wanted to know the reliability of an individual's score in a future study where different subjects would be asked about different groups. The appropriate coefficient would then tell us about the ratio of the variance component due to subject to the sum of the variance components due to subject, group, subject by group, and residual:

$$\frac{S_S^2}{S_S^2 + S_G^2 + S_{SG}^2 + S_R^2} = \frac{7.80}{7.80 + 1.03 + 14.49 + 8.35} = 0.25$$

As is apparent from this calculation, one reason this coefficient is not very large is because there is substantial variation associated with the subject by group interaction (S_{SG}^2). The relative magnitude of this component tells us that expressed prejudices are relatively group specific. Equivalently, there seems to be a fair amount of discriminant validity among the prejudices towards individual groups. Hence, in an anticipated study where different subjects are asked about different groups, the reliability of responses suffers because group varies between subjects. On the other hand, if in a future study group was held constant, then we would expect greater reliability.

This discussion illustrates how the variance components inform us about convergent and discriminant validity in this two-facet design as well as about anticipated reliability. If prejudices are group specific, that is, if there exists discriminant validity between prejudice expressed towards one outgroup and that expressed towards another, then we should find the variance component due to the subject by group interaction to be large relative to the variance component due to subjects. Kenny (1994) shows that the average discriminant validity correlation between prejudices expressed towards different outgroups in this design equals

$$\frac{S_S^2}{S_S^2 + S_{SG}^2} = \frac{7.80}{7.80 + 14.49} = 0.35$$

In other words, over and above item differences, the correlation between expressed prejudice toward one outgroup in these data and another equals, on average, 0.35.

These components of variance tell us not only about discriminant validity between prejudice directed towards one outgroup versus another but also about whether different measures give discriminably different results. In this case, of course, we would like to argue against discriminant validity due to items, that is, we would like to argue that one gets the same answers regardless of which item is used. The parallel discriminant validity correlation for items is

$$\frac{S_S^2}{S_S^2 + S_{SI}^2} = \frac{7.80}{7.80 + 1.49} = 0.84$$

Over and above group differences, the correlation between expressed prejudice on one item and another equals on average 0.84.

Thus, these data and their associated variance components suggest that although there are stable individual differences in prejudice regardless of the outgroup against which prejudice is expressed, there is also substantial evidence for discriminant validity in the expressions of preju-

TABLE 12

Variance Components Analysis of a Two-Facet Randomized Design

Source Table from Data

Source	Sum of Squares	df	Mean Square
Subjects	12525.92	99	126.52
Items	28.86	2	14.43
Groups	722.41	2	361.21
Subjects X Items	2540.10	198	12.83
Subjects X Groups	10259.35	198	51.81
Items X Groups	37.33	4	9.33
Residual	3305.65	396	8.35

Expected Mean Squares **Estimated Variance Components**

$\text{EMS}_S = n_I n_G \sigma_S^2 + n_I \sigma_{SG}^2 + n_G \sigma_{SI}^2 + \sigma_R^2$ $S_S^2 = 7.80$

$\text{EMS}_I = n_S n_G \sigma_I^2 + n_S \sigma_{IG}^2 + n_G \sigma_{SI}^2 + \sigma_R^2$ $S_I^2 = 0.00$

$\text{EMS}_G = n_S n_I \sigma_G^2 + n_S \sigma_{IG}^2 + n_I \sigma_{SG}^2 + \sigma_R^2$ $S_G^2 = 1.03$

$\text{EMS}_{SI} = n_G \sigma_{SI}^2 + \sigma_R^2$ $S_{SI}^2 = 1.49$

$\text{EMS}_{SG} = n_I \sigma_{SG}^2 + \sigma_R^2$ $S_{SG}^2 = 14.49$

$\text{EMS}_{IG} = n_S \sigma_{IG}^2 + \sigma_R^2$ $S_{IG}^2 = 0.01$

$\text{EMS}_R = \sigma_R^2$ $S_R^2 = 8.35$

dice towards one outgroup as opposed to another. Additionally, these data suggest that method variance is not substantial and that expressions of prejudice from one item to another are hardly discriminable.

It probably has occurred to the reader by now that the data we have been using here to compute variance components and illustrate their utility are in form no different from the data that are used to construct a multitrait-multimethod matrix. If we assume that different outgroups constitute different traits and different methods are different items, then the correspondence is exact. In Table 13 we present the multitrait-multimethod correlation matrix computed from the same raw data that were used to conduct the analysis of variance reported in Table 12. Not only are these data parallel in form to data used to construct a multitrait-multimethod matrix, but also we have used the variance component approach to examine the issues of construct validity typically assessed by examining a multitrait-multimethod correlation matrix. Specifically, we have examined whether these data exhibit discriminant validity between traits (i.e., between outgroups) and whether there is substantial variation due to methods. Later in this section we will illustrate a more exact parallel between the analysis of variance or variance component approach to the multitrait-multimethod matrix and that based on examining the resulting correlations or covariances (following the lead of Kenny, 1994, also discussed in Cronbach et al., 1972).

We have only illustrated the variance components approach and Generalizability Theory in a relatively simple case. The theory has been extended to handle a variety of designs more complex than the one we have used as an illustration. Additionally, the theory takes into account the sort of decision to be made about subjects in future studies, for instance, whether one is solely interested in identifying the relative position of each subject compared to the others or whether one wishes to ascertain the absolute position of subjects on a measurement scale. Finally, the theory has been extended to the multivariate case. The point of our exposition is simply to familiarize social psychologists with this approach to systematic error. It is a very fruitful approach that is at present underutilized in the social psychological literature. While one encounters studies that estimate the reliability of judges or measures by reporting an intraclass correlation, following the procedures discussed earlier in this section, seldom does one encounter the sort of systematic variation of multiple facets that permits the generalization of measurement results outlined by Cronbach and his colleagues. We believe that more careful at-

TABLE 13

Means, Variances, and Correlations (Covariances) of Subjects by Groups by Items Data Reported in Table 12

(Variables Defined as Ratings of Specific Groups on Specific Items; Correlations Computed across Subjects; Means [Variances] Reported in Diagonal Cells)

Group	Item	G1I1	G1I2	G1I3	G2I1	G2I2	G2I3	G3I1	G3I2	G3I3
1	1	8.64 (24.40)								
1	2	0.66 (18.05)	9.37 (30.72)							
1	3	0.60 (15.77)	0.71 (20.78)	8.81 (28.17)						
2	1	0.35 (10.88)	0.34 (11.92)	0.22 (7.45)	9.63 (40.29)					
2	2	0.31 (9.34)	0.37 (12.77)	0.26 (8.55)	0.75 (29.38)	9.48 (38.15)				
2	3	0.16 (4.62)	0.18 (5.62)	0.14 (4.42)	0.69 (25.12)	0.72 (25.53)	10.01 (33.27)			
3	1	0.26 (7.06)	0.24 (7.53)	0.15 (4.56)	0.44 (15.62)	0.34 (11.62)	0.22 (6.99)	10.72 (31.08)		
3	2	0.12 (3.46)	0.20 (6.39)	0.19 (5.74)	0.34 (12.33)	0.27 (9.59)	0.12 (3.91)	0.69 (22.28)	11.26 (33.11)	
3	3	0.19 (5.22)	0.30 (9.19)	0.26 (7.45)	0.32 (11.22)	0.33 (11.19)	0.30 (9.49)	0.68 (20.62)	0.73 (23.09)	11.33 (30.02)

tention to multiple facets and their role in inducing systematic error variation is appropriate in social psychology. Additionally, we think the computation of estimated variance components and their comparison has much to recommend it. Particularly promising in this regard are advances that have been made in modeling multilevel data (see Kenny, Kashy, & Bolger, 1997, in this *Handbook*).

Construct Validation Through Confirmatory Factor Analysis

The distinct advantage of the variance components approach is that through experimental manipulation of multiple facets, one can directly estimate the contribution of various sources of systematic error to the measured variable(s). One would like to be able to do this also in situations where the components of error have not been manipulated systematically. Let us revisit the hypothetical construct equations for two variables, X_1 and X_2, presented earlier in this section:

$$X_{1i} = \lambda_{11}\eta_{1i} + \lambda_{12}\eta_{2i} + \lambda_{13}\eta_{3i} + \lambda_{1\epsilon}\epsilon_{1i}$$
$$X_{2i} = \lambda_{21}\eta_{1i} + \lambda_{22}\eta_{2i} + \lambda_{23}\eta_{3i} + \lambda_{2\epsilon}\epsilon_{2i}$$

It would be useful to estimate the loading coefficients in these construct equations, the λ_{jk}'s, as well as the correlations among the latent constructs, η_k, even if those latent constructs have not been systematically varied through facet manipulations. Direct estimation of these unknowns would provide maximal information relevant to the variables' construct validity.

Depending on the nature of the hypothesized latent construct model underlying each measured variable and on the number of measured variables, it is sometimes possible to accomplish this direct estimation through the use of confirmatory factor analysis. Confirmatory factor analysis is a general procedure for estimating the parameters of a certain class of structural equations models (Bentler, 1979; Jöreskog, 1981; Judd, Jessor, & Donovan, 1986; Kenny, 1979; Loehlin, 1992) in which one wishes to estimate the loading coefficients of observed variables on latent or hypothetical constructs and the variances and covariances of these latent constructs. Structural parameters linking the latent constructs to each other are not hypothesized in confirmatory factor analysis models although they are estimable in the more general class of structural equation models. As we will see, in addition to estimating the parameters of construct equations (the loadings and construct variances and covariances), confirmatory factor analysis can also in some cases test the consistency of the hypothesized construct model with the observed data. Thus, like the representational approaches to measurement, the use of confirmatory factor analysis in evaluating construct validity

provides the possibility of testing a hypothesized measurement model.

To provide an accessible introduction to confirmatory factor analysis and its utility in assessing construct validity, we initially will make the assumption that variables and constructs are standardized (expectations of zero and unit variances). We will later relax this assumption in the application of confirmatory factor analysis to particular models.

Consider a very simple construct model in which two observed variables (or indicators in the language commonly used in confirmatory factor analysis) are hypothesized to derive jointly from a single latent construct, with their residual variances being attributable to random error:

$$X_{1i} = \lambda_1\eta_i + \lambda_{1\epsilon}\epsilon_{1i}$$
$$X_{2i} = \lambda_2\eta_i + \lambda_{2\epsilon}\epsilon_{2i}$$

The expected value of a product of any two standardized variables is their correlation. Accordingly, the correlation between these two variables can be expressed as the expected value of the product of their two construct models:

$$r_{X_{1i}X_{2i}} = \mathbf{E}\{X_{1i}X_{2i}\} = \mathbf{E}\{(\lambda_1\eta_i + \lambda_{1\epsilon}\epsilon_{1i})(\lambda_2\eta_i + \lambda_{2\epsilon}\epsilon_{2i})\}$$

Since the errors in these variables are assumed to be random, the expected value of products involving ϵ_{1i} and ϵ_{2i} are all zero. Hence, this expression reduces to:

$$r_{X_{1i}X_{2i}} = \lambda_1\lambda_2\mathbf{E}\{\eta_i^2\} = \lambda_1\lambda_2$$

If we make the assumption that these two variables are equally valid indicators (i.e., $\lambda_1 = \lambda_2$), then their loading coefficients on the latent construct equal the square root of their correlation:

$$\lambda_1 = \lambda_2 = \sqrt{r_{X_{1i}X_{2i}}}$$

Note that this solution for the loading coefficients is equivalent to the estimation of the reliability of two variables, assuming that they are each "parallel forms," according to the classic test theory derivation given at the start of this section on psychometric measurement.

The procedure that we have just illustrated for this very simple two variable, single construct model can be generalized to much more complex models. In essence, the expected value of the product of two observed standardized variables equals their correlation and this correlation can be expressed as the expected value of the product of their two construct equations. One can then simplify this latter expected value so that the correlation between the observed variables equals a function of the loading coefficients (i.e., the λ's) and correlations between the latent constructs (i.e., the η's). One does this for all pairs of observed variables, with the result being a set of simultaneous equations in which the observed correlations are expressed as functions of the unknown parameters (i.e., loading coefficients and latent variable correlations). Given that the number of unknown parameters is less than or equal to the number of correlations between observed variables, one can then solve for the unknown loading coefficients and latent construct correlations. We illustrate this general approach with a few more simple examples borrowed from Kenny (1979) and other classic sources.

Suppose we had three indicators of a single latent construct. Thus, our three construct equations are:

$$X_{1i} = \lambda_1 \eta_i + \lambda_{1\epsilon}\epsilon_{1i}$$
$$X_{2i} = \lambda_2 \eta_i + \lambda_{2\epsilon}\epsilon_{2i}$$
$$X_{3i} = \lambda_3 \eta_i + \lambda_{3\epsilon}\epsilon_{3i}$$

We now have three correlations among observed variables and these are functions of the unknown loading coefficients:

$$r_{X_{1i}X_{2i}} = \lambda_1\lambda_2$$
$$r_{X_{1i}X_{3i}} = \lambda_1\lambda_3$$
$$r_{X_{2i}X_{3i}} = \lambda_2\lambda_3$$

Unlike the previous case with only two observed variables, we now have as many unknown parameters to be estimated as observed correlations. Hence we have an exact solution for the three unknown parameters without making the equality assumption we did in the two indicator case. The estimates of the unknown loadings are:

$$\lambda_1 = \sqrt{\frac{r_{X_{1i}X_{2i}}r_{X_{1i}X_{3i}}}{r_{X_{2i}X_{3i}}}}$$

$$\lambda_2 = \sqrt{\frac{r_{X_{1i}X_{2i}}r_{X_{2i}X_{3i}}}{r_{X_{1i}X_{3i}}}}$$

$$\lambda_3 = \sqrt{\frac{r_{X_{1i}X_{3i}}r_{X_{2i}X_{3i}}}{r_{X_{1i}X_{2i}}}}$$

Adding a fourth indicator to this single latent factor model gives us six equations with only four unknown loading coefficients:

$$r_{X_{1i}X_{2i}} = \lambda_1\lambda_2$$
$$r_{X_{1i}X_{3i}} = \lambda_1\lambda_3$$
$$r_{X_{1i}X_{4i}} = \lambda_1\lambda_4$$
$$r_{X_{2i}X_{3i}} = \lambda_2\lambda_3$$
$$r_{X_{2i}X_{4i}} = \lambda_2\lambda_4$$
$$r_{X_{3i}X_{4i}} = \lambda_3\lambda_4$$

These yield three estimates for each of the unknown parameters. For instance,

$$\lambda_1 = \sqrt{\frac{r_{X_{1i}X_{2i}}r_{X_{1i}X_{3i}}}{r_{X_{2i}X_{3i}}}} = \sqrt{\frac{r_{X_{1i}X_{2i}}r_{X_{1i}X_{4i}}}{r_{X_{2i}X_{4i}}}} = \sqrt{\frac{r_{X_{1i}X_{3i}}r_{X_{1i}X_{4i}}}{r_{X_{3i}X_{4i}}}}$$

These three estimates should be close to each other if the hypothesized single construct model is the appropriate one for the data at hand.

As a final illustration, consider a model in which two indicators load on one latent construct, two load on a second, and the two latent constructs are correlated:

$$X_{1i} = \lambda_{11} \eta_{1i} + \lambda_{1\epsilon}\epsilon_{1i}$$
$$X_{2i} = \lambda_{21} \eta_{1i} + \lambda_{2\epsilon}\epsilon_{2i}$$
$$X_{3i} = \lambda_{32} \eta_{2i} + \lambda_{3\epsilon}\epsilon_{3i}$$
$$X_{4i} = \lambda_{42} \eta_{2i} + \lambda_{4\epsilon}\epsilon_{4i}$$

The expressions for the six observed correlations are:

$$r_{X_{1i}X_{2i}} = \lambda_{11}\lambda_{21}$$
$$r_{X_{1i}X_{3i}} = \lambda_{11}\lambda_{32}\rho_{\eta_{1i}\eta_{2i}}$$
$$r_{X_{1i}X_{4i}} = \lambda_{11}\lambda_{42}\rho_{\eta_{1i}\eta_{2i}}$$
$$r_{X_{2i}X_{3i}} = \lambda_{21}\lambda_{32}\rho_{\eta_{1i}\eta_{2i}}$$
$$r_{X_{2i}X_{4i}} = \lambda_{21}\lambda_{42}\rho_{\eta_{1i}\eta_{2i}}$$
$$r_{X_{3i}X_{4i}} = \lambda_{32}\lambda_{42}$$

In these equations, $\rho_{\eta_{1i}\eta_{2i}}$ is the unknown correlation between the two latent constructs. Now we have five unknowns in six equations (one for each observed correlation) and again the solution is overdetermined. Each loading coefficient has two estimates, for instance:

$$\lambda_{11} = \sqrt{\frac{r_{X_{1i}X_{2i}}r_{X_{1i}X_{3i}}}{r_{X_{2i}X_{3i}}}} = \sqrt{\frac{r_{X_{1i}X_{2i}}r_{X_{1i}X_{4i}}}{r_{X_{2i}X_{4i}}}}$$

and the latent construct correlation also has two estimates:

$$\rho_{\eta_{1i}\eta_{2i}} = \sqrt{\frac{r_{X_{1i}X_{3i}}r_{X_{2i}X_{4i}}}{r_{X_{1i}X_{2i}}r_{X_{3i}X_{4i}}}} = \sqrt{\frac{r_{X_{1i}X_{4i}}r_{X_{2i}X_{3i}}}{r_{X_{1i}X_{2i}}r_{X_{3i}X_{4i}}}}$$

In the first case we examined, with a single correlation between two variables and two loading parameters of those variables on their single latent construct, we had insufficient information to solve for the loading coefficients unless we assumed that they were equivalent. In the last two examples, first with four indicators of a single latent construct and then with two indicators each of two correlated constructs, we had more equations than we needed to derive the unknown parameter estimates. The issue of whether there exists a solution for the unknown parameters or whether in fact multiple solutions are possible constitutes the issue of model identification. Models are underidentified when the number of unknown parameters to be estimated exceeds the number of known variances and covariances (correlations in the standardized case) and, as a result, no solution of the simultaneous equations is possible. Models in which the number of unknowns exactly equals the number of equations are said to be just identified. Models such as the last two we presented, with more equations than unknowns and hence multiple solutions, are overidentified.

The issue of identification is crucial, for only if a model is identified can we estimate the loading coefficients and construct correlations that can be used to examine the construct validity of measured variables. Kenny, Kashy, and Bolger (1998, in this *Handbook*) give a set of rules for determining whether a model is identified. In general, the simpler the construct theory or model that is hypothesized to underlie the measured variables, the greater the probability that the model will be identified. But one should certainly not posit an unrealistically simple model just to achieve identification. One needs to build an adequate measurement model for the variables at hand and then explore issues of identification. If the model is not identified, then constraints need to be placed on further data collection that permit identification. In fact, this is what generalizability theory is doing by orthogonally manipulating multiple facets or constructs. By doing this, the theory assures that the latent constructs are uncorrelated with each other, thus reducing the number of unknown parameters to be estimated.

When a model is overidentified, the presence of multiple simultaneous solutions provides a mechanism for examining the consistency of the hypothesized construct model with the data from which the model's parameters are estimated. For if the model is appropriate for the data at hand, then the multiple parameter solutions ought to give equivalent answers, within the limits of sampling error. In other words, the model implies that the alternative solutions for the unknown parameters should be equal to each other. If they are not, then we have evidence that the hypothesized construct model is inappropriate for the data at hand. In this sense, confirmatory factor analysis can provide a test of the adequacy of a construct theory, or a set of construct validity equations, given overidentification.

The general formulation for confirmatory factor analysis posits that observed variables are functions of latent constructs with unknown parameters of loading coefficients and construct variances and covariances (correlations in the standardized case). The construct model implies that the variances and covariances (again, correlations in the standardized case) among the observed variables can be expressed as functions of the unknown model parame-

ters. Given identification, one then estimates the unknowns by solving the system of simultaneous equations. An algebraically efficient approach to this solution, given a large number of such equations and overidentification (where multiple solutions exist) is an iterative approach in which arbitrary initial values of the unknown parameters are used to generate a predicted variance/covariance matrix among the observed variables and then those parameter values are adjusted across iterations such that the discrepancies between the predicted variance/covariance matrix and the one observed in the data are minimized. Typically a maximum likelihood discrepancy function is used. Software that accomplishes this estimation includes the LISREL program (Jöreskog & Sörbom, 1993), EQS (Bentler, 1993), PROC CALIS in SAS (SAS Institute, 1990), RAMONA (Browne & Mels, 1994), and AMOS (Arbuckle, 1995).

Given overidentification and the presence of sampling error, there will never be perfect convergence between the predicted matrix and the observed data matrix. Assuming multivariate normality, a maximum likelihood solution, and a sufficiently large sample, a function of the discrepancy is distributed as a chi-square statistic. This statistic can be used to test whether the predicted and observed variance/covariance matrices reliably differ from each other. If they do, then the model is revealed to be inconsistent with the data, since no solution exists that satisfies the multiple constraints resulting from overidentification. If the resulting chi-square is not significant, then the model is said to be consistent with the observed sample data.

This test of model consistency is unlike most traditional statistical inference tests, in that we wish to argue that a hypothesized construct model is consistent with the sample data, thereby wanting to verify the null hypothesis that discrepancies between the observed and predicted variance/covariance matrices are not significant. As a result, all we can conclude is that the model and the data are not inconsistent with each other. The model can never be verified since alternative construct theories or models might be equally or more consistent with the sample data. Additionally, considerations of statistical power run counter to normal notions about the value of large samples. Although adequate sample size is necessary to meet the assumption that the maximum likelihood statistic is in fact distributed as chi-square, an exceedingly large sample will lead to the rejection of all models since substantively trivial discrepancies between the predicted and observed variance/covariance matrices will emerge as significant. A variety of other goodness-of-fit statistics have been proposed to evaluate model consistency, given simulation results showing that the chi-square statistic is overly conservative, leading to inappropriate model rejections (Bentler, 1990; Bollen & Long, 1993, Jaccard & Wan, 1995). Many of these focus on the comparative fit of a given model with some alternative model, usually one in which the observed variables are assumed to be independent. As one example, Bentler's Comparative Fit Index (CFI; Bentler, 1990), which varies between 0 and 1, with reasonable models having CFI's of 0.90 or greater, seems to perform well in a variety of circumstances.

The final point to be made before illustrating the use of confirmatory factor analysis is that one can compare nested models to each other. Imagine that we had a model with four indicators all loading on a single latent construct. Initially we would estimate this model allowing the loadings to vary across the indicators. We then might want to compare this model to one in which the four indicators are assumed to have equal loadings. The second model is said to be nested under the first since relaxing the constraint of equality of loadings makes it the first model. We can test whether the additional constraints lead to a significant deterioration in the fit of the model by subtracting the chi-square of the less constrained model from that of the more constrained model. The difference is itself distributed as a chi-square, with degrees of freedom equal to the difference in the two original degrees of freedom. A significant chi-square indicates that the more constrained model is reliably less consistent with the sample data than the less constrained one.

Example 1: Measures of Attitudes Toward Deviance
Judd, Jessor, and Donovan (1986) used confirmatory factor analysis to explore the construct validity of nine measures designed to assess adolescents' attitudes toward deviant behaviors. We recapitulate a portion of their analysis here as our initial illustration.

The data were collected as part of a larger longitudinal study of social development from adolescence through young adulthood. Descriptions of the full sample and methods can be found in Jessor and Jessor (1977) and Jessor, Donovan, and Costa (1991). The data reported by Judd, Jessor, and Donovan (1986) and used here were gathered from 153 seventh-graders who were asked to indicate how "wrong" various deviant behaviors were. The exact questions are given in Table 14 along with the resulting correlation matrix.

Problem-behavior theory (Jessor & Jessor, 1977) predicts that there ought to be a general attitude toward deviant behavior and that all of these items should tap this single underlying construct. Accordingly, the construct theory is that each variable should load on a single latent construct with uncorrelated residual variation. The parameters of this model were estimated with SAS's PROC CALIS using a maximum likelihood criterion. The resulting standardized loadings of the measures on the single latent construct varied between 0.57 and 0.80 and are reported in Figure 1 of Judd, Jessor, and Donovan (1986). The magnitude of these loadings (which are estimates of the item correlations with the latent construct) indicates considerable

convergent validity, as all of the items seem to reflect substantial components of the shared general factor. However, the fit of this model was far from ideal. The resulting chi-square, with 27 degrees of freedom, equaled 156.49, a highly significant value. Additionally, the value of the Comparative Fit Index (Bentler, 1990) was only 0.78, indicating a relatively poor fit of model to the sample data.

A close inspection of the nine items plus an examination of the discrepancies between the correlation matrix predicted by the single factor model and the sample matrix suggested that the nine items might be better thought of as measuring four different, although related, constructs. The first two items seem to concern petty thievery; the next three dishonesty; items six and seven fighting; and the last two items vandalism. Presumably there might exist related but slightly different attitudes in the four domains. Accordingly, a four factor solution was estimated, with each measured variable loading on one of four latent constructs and these latent constructs allowed to correlate with each other. The maximum likelihood estimates of the loadings and construct intercorrelations are given in Figure 14, which is reproduced from Figure 3 of Judd, Jessor, and Donovan (1986). The fit of this four factor model was considerably better than that of the one factor model, $\chi^2(21) = 26.08$; $p > 0.20$; CFI = 0.99.

The single factor model is in fact nested under the four factor model, since the four factor model reduces to the single factor one if all six of the correlations among the factors are constrained to equal 1.0. Hence, we can ask not only about the fit of the four factor model in an absolute sense, but also about its comparative fit, relative to the single factor model. The chi-square difference between the two models equals 130.41 which is highly significant with 6 degrees of freedom.

In sum, this approach to the construct validity of these nine variables revealed that they are not consistent with a model in which the only thing they are assumed to have in common is a single underlying attitude towards deviant behavior. Rather, we must speak of a series of highly interrelated, although discriminable, attitudes, with the multiple measures of each one showing considerable convergent validity.

Example 2: Multitrait-Multimethod Matrix Specification As the second example of the utility of confirmatory factor analysis in assessing construct validity, let us return to the data that we used to illustrate Generalizability Theory. Recall that in these simulated data 100 subjects rated their agreement with three items assessing prejudice levels towards three outgroups. The sums of squares and mean squares for these data were given in Table 12. The resulting multitrait-multimethod correlation matrix was presented in Table 13. The nine variables that are correlated are subjects' responses to the three questions (methods) designed

TABLE 14
Attitude Towards Deviance Items from Judd, Jessor, and Donovan (1986)

ATD Items (Scale 0 = not wrong at all; 9 = very wrong)

1. How wrong is it to take little things that don't belong to you?
2. How wrong is it to take something from a store without paying for it?
3. How wrong is it to give your teacher a fake excuse for missing an exam or being absent?
4. How wrong is it to lie to your parents about where you have been or who you were with?
5. How wrong is it to lie about your age when applying for a license or a job?
6. How wrong is it to beat up another kid without much reason?
7. How wrong is it to get into fist fights with kids?
8. How wrong is it to damage public or private property that does not belong to you just for fun?
9. How wrong is it to damage school property on purpose—like library books, or musical instruments, or gym equipment?

Correlation Matrix

	ATD1	ATD2	ATD3	ATD4	ATD5	ATD6	ATD7	ATD8	ATD9
ATD1	1.00	.	.	.	.	.	.	.	.
ATD2	0.73	1.00	.	.	.	.	.	.	.
ATD3	0.54	0.52	1.00	.	.	.	.	.	.
ATD4	0.55	0.57	0.62	1.00	.	.	.	.	.
ATD5	0.43	0.52	0.54	0.53	1.00	.	.	.	.
ATD6	0.32	0.43	0.28	0.38	0.38	1.00	.	.	.
ATD7	0.31	0.41	0.26	0.36	0.35	0.67	1.00	.	.
ATD8	0.42	0.59	0.31	0.44	0.35	0.61	0.46	1.00	.
ATD9	0.43	0.54	0.43	0.41	0.38	0.61	0.51	0.69	1.00

to tap prejudice towards each of the three outgroups (traits).

The most complete construct theory for a multitrait-multimethod matrix is one in which both traits and methods are specified as latent constructs and each measured variable is allowed to load on its respective trait and method factors. These trait and method factors are assumed to correlate with each other to some extent. Finally, each measured variable is assumed to have some unique residual variance, uncorrelated with all other latent constructs.

More formally, the construct theory or equation for each measured variable is as follows:

$$X_{jki} = \lambda_j \eta_{ji} + \lambda_k \eta_{ki} + \epsilon_{jki} \qquad (1)$$

In this equation, X_{jki} is the ith subject's score on the measured variable expressing prejudice toward the jth outgroup using the kth question. Thus subscript j refers to trait and subscript k refers to method. η_{ji} and η_{ki} are latent trait and method factors that are allowed to be correlated with each

other. ϵ_{jki} is residual or error variance unique to the specific variable.

Although this model would seem to be the most appropriate for the construct validity of measures in a multitrait-multimethod matrix, considerable difficulty has been encountered in estimating its parameters across a wide variety of different matrices (Kenny & Kashy, 1992; Marsh, 1989). Kenny and Kashy (1992) attribute these estimation difficulties to potential identification problems in the model, given that a more restricted version of the full model, one with equal loading coefficients, can be shown to be underidentified. Kenny and Kashy (1992) recommend that a considerably more restrictive model be estimated, one in which each measure is assumed to load on a latent trait construct and these latent trait constructs are allowed to correlate. Additionally, the residual or error components of each measured variable are allowed to correlate with the residuals of other variables that share the same measurement method. They refer to this model as the "correlated uniqueness model."

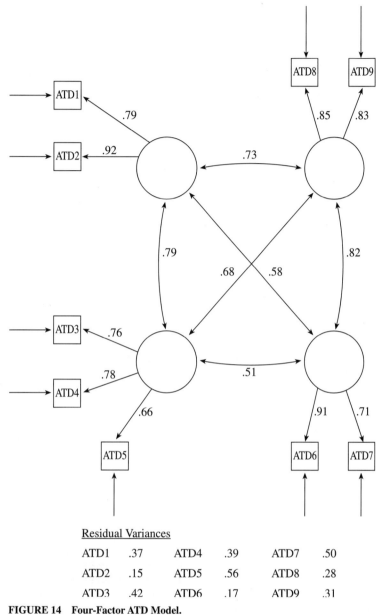

Residual Variances

ATD1	.37	ATD4	.39	ATD7	.50
ATD2	.15	ATD5	.56	ATD8	.28
ATD3	.42	ATD6	.17	ATD9	.31

FIGURE 14   Four-Factor ATD Model.
(*Source:* Judd, Jessor, & Donovan, 1986, Figure 3, p. 168.)

A model that is very close to the "correlated unique-ness" model but that still involves both trait and method factors is a variant on the full model with the restrictions that the method factors (the η_{ki}'s in equation 1) correlate neither with each other nor with the trait factors. Thus each measured variable loads on both trait and method factors, but each of the three method factors is assumed to be un-correlated with all other latent variables. It turns out that for many multitrait-multimethod matrices, including the present one, this restricted version of the full model is fully compatible with the data.

Using PROC CALIS in SAS, we estimated the parame-ters of this restricted model. The estimates from the result-ing standardized solution, using the maximum likelihood criterion, are given in Table 15. The model was found to be consistent with the data, $\chi^2(15) = 21.98$; $p > 0.10$; CFI =

TABLE 15
Restricted Multitrait-Multimethod Matrix Model for Data in Table 13

	Loadings						
	Trait Factors			**Method Factors**			
Variable	**Trait 1**	**Trait 2**	**Trait 3**	**Method 1**	**Method 2**	**Method 3**	**Residual**
G1I1	0.74	0	0	0.28	0	0	0.61
G1I2	0.88	0	0	0	0.21	0	0.59
G1I3	0.80	0	0	0	0	0.08	0.59
G2I1	0	0.86	0	0.25	0	0	0.45
G2I2	0	0.88	0	0	0.16	0	0.44
G2I3	0	0.79	0	0	0	0.30	0.53
G3I1	0	0	0.79	0.40	0	0	0.47
G3I2	0	0	0.88	0	−0.25	0	0.42
G3I3	0	0	0.87	0	0	0.42	0.28

	Factor Correlations					
	Trait 1	**Trait 2**	**Trait 3**	**Method 1**	**Method 2**	**Method 3**
Trait 1	1.00					
Trait 2	0.37	1.00				
Trait 3	0.40	0.33	1.00			
Method 1	0	0	0	1.00		
Method 2	0	0	0	0	1.00	
Method 3	0	0	0	0	0	1.00

0.99, and the estimates reveal considerable evidence of convergent and discriminant validity of these measures. First, all nine variables have large and highly significant loadings on their respective trait constructs. Thus, all nine variables show considerable convergent validity as measures of prejudice toward the specific outgroup referenced. Second, there is discriminant validity among the three trait constructs, since the inter-trait correlations, although substantial, are considerably less than 1.0. It thus appears that prejudice against one outgroup is moderately, although far from perfectly, correlated with prejudice against another outgroup. Finally, the measures show only mild influence deriving from the measurement method used. Only the loadings on the first method factor differ significantly from zero. Thus, there is evidence of discriminant validity against measurement method.

Earlier we examined the construct validity of these simulated data by estimating the variance components due to subjects, measures, groups, and their interactions. We promised then that we would show the equivalence of that variance components approach with the more general confirmatory factor analysis approach just presented. Our presentation here follows the insights of Kenny (1994), although we present a slightly different model specification than the one he presents for the confirmatory factor analysis model that is equivalent to the variance components approach.

The model whose parameter estimates are provided in Table 15 is already considerably constrained compared to the full multitrait-multimethod matrix model that seems most theoretically appropriate but has proven not to be estimable. Let us add some additional constraints, however. Specifically, we will additionally assume the following:

1. all loadings of observed variables on the three trait factors, λ_j, are equal to each other;
2. all three correlations among the three latent trait factors are equal to each other;
3. all loadings of observed variables on the three method factors, λ_k, are equal to each other; and

4. all of the observed variables' residual variances are equal to each other.

Obviously these are a very strong set of assumptions about the model. In fact, they are sufficiently strong that they are equivalent to assuming, among other things, that all of the observed variables have equal variances. In order to evaluate the merit of this assumption, one needs to estimate the model's parameters using the variance/covariance matrix among the observed variables rather than their standardized correlation matrix. The reason for this is that through standardization one already has forced equal variances. But with this new constrained model, the imposition for the equal variance assumption comes from the model itself and so we wish to estimate that model with the variables in their raw metric.

The estimation of an unstandardized model involves estimating the variances and covariances of the latent factors rather than their loadings. All loading coefficients are constrained to equal 1.0; the variances of the three trait factors are constrained to equal each other; the covariances among the three trait factors are constrained to equal each other; the variances of the three method factors are constrained to equal each other; and finally, the residual variances are all constrained to equal each other. In this highly constrained model, there are only four parameters that are estimated (maximum likelihood estimates from PROC CALIS of SAS are included in parentheses):

1. the variance of the latent trait factors (22.29);
2. the variance of the latent method factors (1.49);
3. the covariance of the latent trait factors (7.80); and
4. the residual variance to the observed variables (8.35).

These estimated values are equivalent to some of the estimated variance components computed from these same data in Table 12. Thus, the variance of the latent trait factors is equal to the estimated variance component due to subjects plus the estimated variance component due to the subject by group interaction ($S_S^2 + S_{SG}^2$). The variance of the latent method factors is exactly equal to the estimated variance component due to the subjects by measures interaction (S_{SM}^2). And the residual variance is equal to the residual variance component (S_R^2). Additionally, if we convert the covariance between the latent trait factors to a correlation, by dividing their covariance by the variance of the trait factors:

$$\frac{7.80}{22.29} = 0.35$$

we get the same value for the discriminant validity coefficient among the three latent trait factors that we computed in the variance component approach.

In sum, although the variance components approach to the analysis of this multitrait-multimethod matrix is certainly useful, it is identical to an extremely constrained confirmatory factor analysis model in which it is assumed that all observed variables have equal variance, the variances and covariances of all underlying trait constructs are equal, and method influences on measures are all equivalent. It seems reasonable to estimate the convergent and discriminant validity of observed variables in a multitrait-multimethod matrix initially in a form that doesn't make these strong assumptions. In this sense the confirmatory factor analysis approach is considerably more general.

Summary

The psychometric approach to measurement starts with the assumption that individual observed scores are heavily infected with errors of measurement. Accordingly it seeks to assess the validity of measured variables by aggregating observations and asking whether the observed variances and covariances are consistent with the theory about the underlying constructs. Generalizability theory and the use of confirmatory factor analysis represent very significant advances in the psychometric measurement tradition. These permit us to ask about systematic sources of error variation, significantly extending the classic psychometric model that presumed that what was not true score variation was simply random error. These advances now permit much more rigorous examination of measurement models, including the estimation of variance due to multiple facets or components and the testing of underlying construct theories.

LINKAGES BETWEEN REPRESENTATIONAL AND PSYCHOMETRIC APPROACHES

As we noted in the introduction, it is remarkable how infrequently and inadequately the two measurement traditions discussed in the previous two sections have communicated with each other. Indeed, it is a rare treatise on measurement that even discusses both of them within the same book or chapter. For example, one would expect that books titled *An Introduction to the Logic of Psychological Measurement* (Michell, 1990) and *Measurement Theory for the Behavioral Sciences* (Ghiselli, Campbell, & Zedeck, 1981) would be more or less directed to the same topic and to the same audience. However, there is absolutely no overlap; the first is representational and the second is psychometric. Exceptions, other than this chapter, that do include both perspectives are Dawes and Smith (1985) and Himmelfarb (1993). Both Cliff (1989) and Fischer (1995), among others, have directly examined implications of the representational approach for the psychometric approach. In this concluding section we identify some major differences between the two approaches and then explore areas in which the gap might be bridged or in which the approaches might inform each other.

Some Differences Between the Approaches

Focus of Relationships   The focus of the representational approach is the relationship between individual observations. For example, in the illustrations of Thurstonian and Fechnerian scaling above, the key was the empirical relationship of judging one item more or less liberal than another item. Representational models use observed empirical relationships to make predictions about specific observations (as in the case of transitivity, for example). In contrast, the focus of the psychometric approach is the relationship between variables. For example, in one of the illustrations of the psychometric approach above, the key was the covariance between items assessing prejudice in different ways. No individual observations are important; rather, the focus is the pattern of relationships among variables. Psychometric models make predictions about specific covariances or relationships between variables.

A by-product of the different foci is that reliability is almost never assessed for representational measures whereas it is of paramount importance for psychometric measures. In a later section we explore how this difference in focus might be partially bridged by considering how representational approaches might profitably examine covariances among representational measures.

Falsification versus Verification   Representational models make strong predictions about specific observations. As a consequence, such models are easily falsified. A single observation can falsify a model and foil the construction of a scale. For example, a clear failure of transitivity definitely rejects even an ordinal scale. No monotonic transformation (i.e., a differential stretching or shrinking of the scale), no change in assumptions about a probability distribution, and in general no changes about any assumptions can rescue the model. Such model rejections often identify powerful context effects that reveal the psychological processes underlying responses to social psychological stimuli. The disadvantage is that the ease of falsification makes representational models so fragile that it is often too difficult to construct scales to be used to make predictions about other psychological constructs. This problem is made all the more severe by the absence of a theory of response errors in the representational approach. The danger is that one might reject a representational model for a scale, not because it is fundamentally in error, but rather because of unreliability or noise in individual subject responses.

Psychometric models, on the other hand, are more difficult to falsify and relatively easy to verify. No single obser-

vation can possibly falsify a psychometric model, but there can be problematic items whose covariances with other items are not consistent. When such problematic items are encountered, it is common practice to discard them until a reasonable model results. Thus, it is usually possible to find a set of items for which the psychometric model is verified. Even if a confirmatory factor analysis revealed a bad fit, one would be left wondering if the rejection were due to an incorrect model or if it were perhaps due to non-linearities in the response scale, incorrect assumptions about a statistical distribution, etc. In other words, with the psychometric model, falsifications tend to be weak ones.

Difficulty of Respondent's Task   The construction of representational measures poses relatively simple tasks to respondents. Individuals simply indicate which alternative they prefer or which item they think has more of some specified property. The judgment tasks are almost always relative comparisons. In contrast, psychometric approaches typically require, sometimes implicitly, respondents to assign numbers—to do the measuring themselves—to represent their responses to items. Social psychology (along with some other areas of psychology) is one of the few scientific disciplines that expects the entities it studies, rather than the scientists doing the studying, to assign the numbers. Furthermore, the psychometric approach typically involves absolute judgments of individual items, rather than relative comparisons. In general, absolute judgments are more difficult psychologically than relative judgments.

The psychometric approach assumes that respondents are sophisticated users of rating scales and that they can maintain consistent use of the response scale across many items. As a consequence, the psychometric approach might best be used with a somewhat restricted set of respondents. In particular, it is difficult to use the psychometric approach with the very young or the very old, with people in cultures where exposure to rating scales is rare, and with animals. On the other hand, the relatively simpler comparison tasks of choice or "which has more" of the representational approach can be adapted to a much greater variety of respondents. For example, it is relatively easy to construct (or test for the existence of) an ordinal scale for a dog's preferences for treats by seeing which treats are eaten first from pairs of alternatives. With repeated trials, it is even easy to construct a Thurstonian or Fechnerian scale assuming that there isn't perfect dominance within pairs of treats.

There are, however, other issues which make the representational approach more difficult for respondents than the psychometric approach. While the simple, relative judgment tasks of representative measurement are in general easy, the sheer number of judgments required for all the internal consistency checks can sometimes be numbing to respondents. This is especially true if replications are used to assess reliability. Also, with more sophisticated representational models, the judgment tasks, even though they are relative, can be rather complex psychologically. For example, to test axioms for multidimensional scaling requires respondents to judge whether one pair of stimuli is more or less similar than another pair of stimuli. To do this task, the respondent must first determine which attributes are appropriate for judging similarity in this case, assess the locations of all four stimuli on those attributes, develop some rule for psychologically measuring the distance between the alternatives in terms of those attributes, and then report the greater (or lesser) distance for the two pairs of stimuli. For interesting social stimuli, this can be very difficult to do!

There is another subtle way in which the tasks used to construct representational measures can be difficult. Thurstonian and Fechnerian methods were derived from psychophysical methods that depend on confusions. Hence, attitude items used in these scaling methods must be close enough to be "confused" so that at least some people think, for example, that *a* is more liberal than *b*, while others think the reverse. If the items are too extreme, then such confusions or reversals are unlikely. Similarly, items are most useful in the unfolding model if their scale values fall between the ideal points of respondents. If there is a normal distribution of ideal points, then it is best to have a number of items fairly close together to each other in the middle of the scale in order to make discriminations among respondents. Although relative judgments are easier, making many relative judgments about items that are close together psychologically can be quite difficult. The psychometric approach, on the other hand, tends to favor extreme items that are very far apart. Deciding whether one agrees or disagrees with extreme items can often be easy, even though it is an absolute judgment.

As a further bridge between the two approaches we will explore in more detail the implications of the unfolding model for item covariances in the psychometric approach. As we will see, the results underline the difference between the two approaches in the utility of relatively extreme versus more confusable items.

Implications of an Unfolding Model for Item Covariances

One of the strengths of the representational approach to measurement is that it makes explicit a theoretical model for data (Coombs, 1964). In this section, we wish to start with a given theoretical model, namely, the unfolding model for preference data, and explore its implications for assessments of construct validity using the resulting pattern of item interrelationships and confirmatory factor analysis. The goal is to examine the implications of the unfolding model of preference data for the psychometric approach to assessing the construct validity of the items towards which preferences have been expressed. Our

approach bears resemblances to that of Coombs and Kao (1960; see also Coombs, 1964, Chapter 8).

Imagine that we have a set of ten attitude statements or items on each of two issues, say abortion rights and affirmative action. Imagine further that the ten items on each issue can be ordered from the most liberal viewpoint to the most conservative in the sentiments they express on the issue. We assume that the ten scale values of these statements on each issue are $-5, -4, -3, -2, -1, 1, 2, 3, 4$, and 5. These scale values represent the distance, in units of standard deviation, from the mean of the distribution of ideal points (which will be described shortly). If these two issues are orthogonal to one another, then in a two-dimensional space they are at right angles and all items for one issue have scale values of zero on the second. On the other hand, it is quite reasonable that these two issues are correlated, with statements or items that are liberal on one issue, implying liberal points of view on the other as well. For instance, if the correlation between the two issues was 0.40, then the appropriate two-dimensional representation of the items puts vectors for the two issues at an angle of approximately 66 degrees.

Assume that the population of individual ideal points has a bivariate normal distribution (standardized so that $\mu = 0$ and $\sigma = 1$ for both dimensions) with no intercorrelation. Each individual ideal point, then, has two coordinates that give the individual's ideal preferences or positions on the two dimensions. And an individual's expressed preference or (dis)agreement for each of the items is assumed to equal the Euclidean distance between the individual's ideal point in the two-dimensional space and the location of each item (ten items for each of two issues) in that space. The result is a set of expressed preferences or agreements of each individual with each of the twenty items in the space and an expected matrix of item correlations can be constructed from these. The correlation, across people, between the two issues is a function of the angle between the issue vectors in the two-dimensional space.

Based on this multidimensional unfolding model of item preferences, we can then select different scales (i.e., subsets of these twenty items) and examine the resulting correlation matrix among these items to assess the construct validity of scales for the two issues using confirmatory factor analytic procedures. According to the unfolding model, we know that the individual items can in fact be ordered along two vectors, that the preferences of the subjects for those items is a perfect function of their Euclidean distances from those items, and that the correlation between the two issue scales is known. The estimated confirmatory factor analysis model treats the items as indicators of two latent factors and both the indicator loadings and the factor correlation are estimated.

We conducted a series of simulations to examine the ability of confirmatory factor analysis to recover the two-dimensional preference unfolding model. In each trial of the simulations, we randomly sampled 150 individual ideal points from the full population of ideal points, computed preferences (Euclidean distances) of these individuals for all of the twenty items, computed correlations among those preferences, and then estimated the parameters of the two-factor confirmatory factor analysis model for subsets of the items. Two attributes varied between the simulation trials: the true correlation between the two issue vectors in the space (0, 0.2, 0.4, and 0.6) and the scale extremity of the subset of items included in the confirmatory factor analysis. On one set of simulations, the four items with scale values of +5, and −5 were included. Other simulations used sets of four items having scale values of +4 and −4, +3 and −3, +2 and −2, and +1 and −1. At each level of these two crossed attributes (true issue intercorrelation and extremity of items) 200 simulations were run, sampling anew 150 individual ideal points for each.[5]

Each cell of Table 16 presents the results from each set of 200 simulation trials, with the two varied attributes fixed at their row and column values. The four numbers that are included in each cell are medians across the 200 simulation

trials of the goodness of fit χ^2 value, the CFI (Bentler, 1990), the estimated correlation between the factors, and the percentage of simulation trials where convergence was achieved and standard errors of estimates computed. Medians are presented rather than means due to the positive skew in the distributions of the estimates.

If we assume that an unfolding model underlies preference judgments, then the results of these simulations are informative about the important role of item selection in the use of confirmatory factor analysis to uncover the latent structure of the items. As the extremity of the scale values of the items decreases, there is a dramatic decrease in the quality of the model's fit and its parameter estimates. The quality of fit of the models, examining both the χ^2 and the CFI, becomes quite unacceptable with items that have scale values less than 2 standard deviations away from the mean. Additionally, all items yield attenuated estimates of the factor intercorrelation, and this attenuation increases with less extreme items. Finally, there are considerable convergence problems with models with relatively nonextreme items. This is because such models, especially when the two dimensions are uncorrelated, tend to be unidenti-

TABLE 16

Simulation Results: Confirmatory Factor Analysis Given Indicators from a Two-Dimensional Unfolding Model

Scale Value of Item Indicators		Parameter Value of Correlation Between the Two Factors			
		0.0	**0.2**	**0.4**	**0.6**
−5, +5	χ^2	1.06	1.21	6.18	24.30
	CFI	1.00	1.00	0.99	0.97
	r	−0.03	0.19	0.38	0.58
	Converged	49.0%	85.5%	96.5%	88.5%
−4, +4	χ^2	1.17	1.67	8.64	28.57
	CFI	1.00	0.99	0.99	0.96
	r	−0.05	0.17	0.37	0.57
	Converged	38.5%	77.5%	93.0%	85.5%
−3, + 3	χ^2	1.73	3.73	15.41	39.46
	CFI	0.99	0.99	0.97	0.93
	r	−0.01	0.06	0.27	0.52
	Converged	19.5%	56.5%	76.5%	79.0%
−2, +2	χ^2	12.25	9.71	30.28	65.63
	CFI	0.96	0.97	0.92	0.85
	r	−0.01	0.02	0.03	0.04
	Converged	0%	2.5%	7.0%	18.0%
−1, +1	χ^2	76.32	49.41	92.17	140.42
	CFI	0.74	0.78	0.75	0.68
	r	−0.03	5.50	4.42	3.38
	Converged	0%	0%	0.5%	0.5%

fied empirically (Kenny, Kashy, & Bolger, 1997, in this *Handbook*). The lesson, then, is that if the Euclidean multidimensional unfolding model of preferences is an appropriate model, then confirmatory factor analyses of item interrelationships yield satisfactory results only in the case of items that have scale values considerably more extreme than the ideal points of typical respondents.

Conceptually, these results derive from the fact that the magnitude of disagreement with more moderate items fails to indicate the direction of an individual's ideal point. For example, imagine two individuals with unidimensional ideal point values of +2 and –2. Although they dramatically disagree with each other, they are in agreement about their preferences for an item having a scale value of 0. Only items that are more extreme than respondents permit an unambiguous assessment of directional preferences.

Of course this extremity criterion for item selection poses the additional dilemma of insuring adequate variance in the actual measurement of subjects' preferences. In our simulations, the preferences (Euclidean distances) are continuously measured. Hence, regardless of the extremity of an item, there remains variation in preferences. If quite extreme items are used in actual preference data collection, where subjects indicate preferences on rating scales, one needs to be confident that variation in preferences will be detected even with quite extreme items with which nearly all subjects disagree.

Examining Covariances among Representational Measures

The strengths of the representational approach to measurement derive from the explicit theoretical models that underlie measurement and the internal consistency checks that can be used to evaluate the appropriateness of those theoretical models. But a consequence of these internal consistency checks is that external criteria for evaluating the utility of a scale or variable have generally not been used. In other words, those who have advocated representational approaches to measurement in social psychology have seldom encouraged researchers to exploit the virtues of the psychometric approach in evaluating the predictive success of those measures. Useful and valid measures ideally should meet not only the representational criteria (i.e., have an explicit theory that is internally testable), but they also ought to correlate with other measures of similar and related constructs in predictable ways, following the insights of the psychometric approach. To our mind (and in agreement with Dawes, 1994), a significant shortcoming of the representational approach is that issues of predictability, reliability, and external validation have generally been ignored.

Suppose, for instance, that we asked subjects to rank order attitude statements on an issue, say abortion rights, and from these rank orders, we applied unidimensional unfolding procedures, revealing scale values for both the attitude statements and the subjects. And suppose further that the internal consistency checks of the unfolding approach were found to hold, so that we had confidence that a single attitude continuum was adequate to represent preferences in this domain. Would that be sufficient? What about the psychometric criteria for evaluating the reliability and construct validity of this measurement approach? Are these criteria irrelevant given that the internal consistency checks have been met?

We suggest that these psychometric criteria are perfectly appropriate and that one of the shortcomings of the representational approach to measurement is that it has ignored the potential informativeness of covariances at the aggregate level. It would certainly be informative to know, for instance, whether these subjects' scale values show evidence of reliability, stability over time, and convergent and discriminant validity with other measures of the same and different constructs. One could imagine, for instance, embedding these scale scores as one variable in a multitrait-multimethod study of different methods of measuring two or more attitudes and then using confirmatory factor analysis to evaluate the discriminant and convergent validity of the included measures. We suspect that the assurance from the unfolding model that there is in fact a single underlying dimension that is assessed ought to mean that these scale scores should show evidence of considerable construct validity when patterns of covariance are examined. But in fact, the empirical work to demonstrate this convergence has not been done.

CONCLUSION

We conclude by offering a few integrative comments that we hope will be provocative for future developments in measurement theory and practice.

In writing this chapter we have been struck by two facts. First, both of the measurement traditions in social psychology have distinct strengths. And these tend to be complementary, each tradition excelling in areas that are largely neglected by the other. Thus, the representational approach starts with a strong theoretical model and derives consistency tests from such a model in order to evaluate the adequacy of measurement at the level of the individual entity. On the other hand, the psychometric approach starts with the very reasonable assumption that individual responses are filled with error and noise. It therefore proceeds to assess measurement adequacy only at the aggregate level.

The second fact is one that we mentioned more than once: there is almost no literature in psychology where the two measurement traditions have spoken to each other. This is particularly unfortunate given the fact that their strengths are largely complementary and that each tradition could benefit from the lessons the other one has to teach.

Largely neglected within the representational approach is a theory about measurement error and how it influences individual entity responses and measurement model evaluation. As we have discussed at a number of points, this is largely responsible for the relative disuse of representational approaches among social psychologists. In the previous section we put forward some ideas about how the strengths of the psychometric approach, in assessing both random and systematic error variation in measurement, might be fruitfully explored by those working in the representational tradition.

Going the other way, the psychometric approach almost never makes explicit a theoretical measurement model that can be used to understand the responses of individual entities. As a result, the psychological processes through which those responses are generated are largely left unspecified. If one only worries about patterns of responses at the aggregate level, then an adequate measurement theory can afford to leave the individual respondent relatively unfathomed. Whether or not social psychology can afford this as a discipline is far less clear.

In the previous section we attempted to illustrate how the strengths of each approach might be used to advance measurement theory and practice in the other. Exploring these and other avenues of integration, we believe, will lead to measurement advances. And such advances have the potential of leading in turn to theoretical advances for the discipline. Our final thought is to encourage all of us as active researchers to spend a little more time reflecting on our theories and practices of measurement; the discipline of social psychology will benefit.

NOTES

1. This is similar to the well-known conundrum in factor analysis concerning the "correct" number of factors to extract and rotate. Exploratory factor analysis is routinely used both to provide evidence for a measurement theory and to examine relationships between multiple constructs (i.e., oblique factors). Two individuals can look at the same correlation matrix and factor solution and conclude very different things about the number of constructs underlying the individual measures.

2. An interval scale is one in which the ratio of intervals remains constant under any permissible change in the scale values. In this case,

$$\frac{H(93\%) - H(75\%)}{H(75\%) - H(51\%)} = 1$$

Clearly, adding (or subtracting) a constant from each value of $H()$ would not change this ratio and neither would multiplying each value of $H()$ by a positive constant. Hence, such manipulations are permissible for in-

terval scales. The additive constant determines (or is determined by the choice of) the origin and the multiplicative constant determines (or is determined by the choice of) the unit of measurement.

3. Note that if all values are positive, then the multiplicative model

$$f(a)g(p)$$

is noninteractive because taking logs (a monotonic transformation) yields the additive model:

$$\log[f(a)g(p)] = \log[f(a)] + \log[g(p)]$$

4. This formula can be used to calculate the number of items needed in an index or sum to achieve a given reliability of the sum, assuming a given average correlation between items. One solves the equation for k:

$$k = \frac{\rho_{SUM}(1 - \bar{r}_{ij})}{\bar{r}_{ij}(1 - \rho_{sum})}$$

5. The simulations were conducted using PROC CALIS in SAS. The code is available from the authors.

REFERENCES

Aguinis, H., Pierce, C. A., & Quigley, B. H. (1995). Enhancing the validity of self-reported alcohol and marijuana consumption using a bogus pipeline procedure: A meta-analytic review. *Basic and Applied Social Psychology, 16,* 515–534.

Anderson, N. H. (1981). *Foundations of information integration theory.* New York: Academic Press.

Anderson, N. H. (1982). *Methods of information integration theory.* New York: Academic Press.

Anderson, N. H., Ed. (1991). *Contributions to information integration theory* (Vols. 1–3). Hillsdale, NJ: Lawrence Erlbaum Associates.

American Psychological Association (1966). *Standards for educational and psychological tests and manuals.* Washington, D.C.: American Psychological Association.

Anastasi, A. (1961). *Psychological testing* (2nd ed.). New York: Macmillan.

Arbuckle, J. L. (1995). *AMOS for Windows: Analysis of moment structures* (Version 3.5). Chicago, IL: Smallwaters.

Armor, D. J. (1974). Theta reliability and factor scaling. In H. L. Costner (Ed.), *Sociological methodology, 1973–1974* (pp. 17–50). San Francisco: Jossey-Bass.

Arrow, K. J. (1951). *Social choice and individual values.* New York: Wiley.

Bennett, J. F., & Hays, W. L. (1960). Multidimensional unfolding: Determining the dimensionality of ranked preference data. *Psychometrika, 25,* 27–43.

Bentler, P. M. (1968). Alpha-maximized factor analysis and its relation to alpha and canonical factor analysis. *Psychometrika, 33,* 335–346.

Bentler, P. M. (1979). Multivariate analysis with latent variables: Causal modeling. *Annual Review of Psychology, 31,* 419–456.

Bentler, P. M. (1990). Comparative fit indices in structural models. *Psychological Bulletin, 107,* 238–246.

Bentler, P. M. (1993). *EQS program manual.* Los Angeles: BMD Statistical Software.

Bernieri, F. J., & Rosenthal, R. (1991). Interpersonal coordination: Behavior matching and interactional synchrony. In R. S. Felman and B. Rimé (Eds.), *Fundamentals of nonverbal behavior* (pp. 401–432). Cambridge: Cambridge University Press.

Bollen, K., & Long, S. (1993). *Testing structural equation models.* Newbury Park, CA: Sage.

Bradley, R. A., & Terry, M. E. (1952). Rank analysis of incomplete block designs: I. The method of paired comparisons. *Biometrika, 39,* 324–345.

Browne, M. W., & Mels, G. (1994). *RAMONA: User's Guide.* Ohio State University, Department of Psychology.

Burke, C. J., & Zinnes, J. L. (1965). A paired comparison of pair comparisons. *Journal of Mathematical Psychology, 2,* 53–76.

Cacioppo, J. T., & Petty, R. E. (1979). Attitudes and cognitive responses: An electrophysiological approach. *Journal of Personality and Social Psychology, 37,* 2181–2199.

Campbell, D. T. (1960). Recommendations for APA test standards regarding construct, trait, or discriminant validity. *American Psychologist, 15,* 546–553.

Campbell, D. T., & Fiske, D. W. (1959). Convergent and discriminant validation by the multitrait-multimethod matrix. *Psychological Bulletin, 56,* 81–105.

Chernoff, H. (1973). The use of faces to represent points in k-dimensional space graphically. *Journal of the American Statistical Association, 68,* 361–368.

Chernoff, H., & Rizvi, H. M. (1975). Effect on classification error of random permutations of features in representing multivariate data by faces. *Journal of the American Statistical Association, 70,* 548–554.

Clark, W. A. V. (1982). A revealed preference analysis of intraurban migration choices. In R. G. Golledge & J. N. Rayner (Eds.), *Proximity and preference: Problems in the multidimensional analysis of large data sets.* Minneapolis: University of Minnesota Press.

Cleveland, W. S. (1993a). A model for studying display methods of statistical graphics (with discussion). *Journal of Computational and Statistical Graphics, 2,* 323–343.

Cleveland, W. S. (1993b). *Visualizing data.* Summit, NJ: Hobart Press.

Cleveland, W. S., & McGill, R. (1987). Graphical perception: The visual decoding of quantitative information in graphical displays of data. *Journal of the Royal Statistical Society, Series A, 150,* 192–229.

Cliff, N. (1989). Ordinal consistency and ordinal true scores. *Psychometrika, 54,* 75–91.

Cliff, N. F. (1992). Abstract measurement theory and the revolution that never happened. *Psychological Science, 3,* 186–190.

Condorcet, M. (1785). *Essai sur l'application de l'analyse à la probabilité des decisions rendues à la pluralité des voix.* Paris: Impr. Royale. [reprinted New York: Chelsea Publishing Co., 1972].

Cook, S. W., & Selltiz, C. (1964). A multiple-indicator approach to attitude measurement. *Psychological Bulletin, 62,* 36–55.

Cook, T. D., & Campbell, D. T. (1979). *Quasi-experimentation: Design and analysis issues for field settings.* Boston: Houghton Mifflin.

Coombs, C. H. (1950). Psychological scaling without a unit of measurement. *Psychological Review, 57,* 145–158.

Coombs, C. H. (1964). *A theory of data.* New York: Wiley.

Coombs, C. H., & Avrunin, G. S. (1988). *The structure of conflict.* Hillsdale, NJ: Lawrence Erlbaum Associates.

Coombs, C. H., Coombs, L. C., & McClelland, G. H. (1975). Preference scales for number and sex of children. *Population Studies, 29,* 273–298.

Coombs, C. H., & Kao, R. C. (1960). On a connection between factor analysis and multidimensional unfolding. *Psychometrika, 25,* 219–231.

Coombs, L. C. (1974). The measurement of family size preferences and subsequent fertility. *Demography, 11,* 587–611.

Cornfield, J., & Tukey, J. W. (1956). Average values of mean squares in factorials. *Annals of Mathematical Statistics, 27,* 907–949.

Cronbach, L. J. (1951). Coefficient alpha and the internal structure of tests. *Psychometrika, 16,* 297–334.

Cronbach, L. J. (1960). *Essentials of psychological testing* (2nd ed.). New York: Harper.

Cronbach, L. J. (1984). *Essentials of psychological testing* (4th ed.). New York: Harper.

Cronbach, L. J., Gleser, G. C., Nanda, H., & Rajaratnam, N. (1972). *The dependability of behavioral measurements: Theory of generalizability for scores and profiles.* New York: Wiley.

Cronbach, L. J., & Meehl, P. E. (1955). Construct validity in psychological tests. *Psychological Bulletin, 52,* 281–302.

Cronbach, L. J., Rajaratnam, N., & Gleser, G. C. (1963). Theory of generalizability: A liberalization of reliability theory. *British Journal of Statistical Psychology, 16,* 137–163.

Dawes, R. M. (1994). Psychological measurement. *Psychological Review, 101,* 278–281.

Dawes, R. M., & Moore, M. (1979). Guttman scaling orthodox and randomized responses. In F. Peterman (Ed.), *Attitude Measurement* (pp. 117–133). Gottinger: Verlag für Psychologie.

Dawes, R. M., & Smith, T. L. (1985). Attitude and opinion

measurement. In G. Lindzey & E. Aronson (Eds.), *The handbook of social psychology* (3rd ed., Vol. 1, pp. 509–566). New York: Random House.

Dawkins, R. (1969). A threshold model of choice behavior. *Animal Behavior, 17,* 120–133.

de Leeuw, J., Young, F. W., & Takane, Y. (1976). Additive structure in qualitative data: An alternating least squares method with optimal scaling features. *Psychometrika, 41,* 471–503.

Dovidio, J. F., Evans, N., & Tyler, R. (1986). Racial stereotypes: The contents of their cognitive representations. *Journal of Experimental Social Psychology, 22,* 22–37.

Fazio, R. H., Sanbonmatsu, D. M., Powell, M. C., & Kardes, F. R. (1986). On the automatic activation of attitudes. *Journal of Personality and Social Psychology, 50,* 229–238.

Fischer, G. H. (1995). Some neglected problems in IRT. *Psychometrika, 60,* 459–487.

Fyans, L. J., Jr. (Ed.) (1983). *Generalizability theory: Inferences and practical applications.* San Francisco: Jossey-Bass.

Ghiselli, E. E., Campbell, J. P., & Zedeck, S. (1981). *Measurement theory for the behavioral sciences.* San Francisco: W. H. Freeman.

Green, B. F., Jr. (1977). Parameter sensitivity in multivariate methods. *Multivariate Behavioral Research, 12,* 263–288.

Green, P. E., & Srinivasan, V. (1990). Conjoint analysis in marketing: New developments with implications for research and practice. *Journal of Marketing, 54,* 3–19.

Greenberg, B. C., Abdula, A. L., Simmons, W. R., & Horvitz, D. G. (1969). The unrelated question in randomized response model, theoretical framework. *Journal of the American Statistical Association, 64,* 520–539.

Hambleton, R. K. (1989). Principles and selected applications of item response theory. In R. Linn (ed.), *Educational measurement* (3rd ed., pp. 147–200). New York: Macmillan.

Hambleton, R. K., & Swaminathan, H. (1985). *Item response theory: Principles and applications.* Boston: Kluwer Academic Publishers.

Hammond, K. R., McClelland, G. H., & Mumpower, J. (1980). *Human judgment and decision making.* New York: Hemisphere Publishing.

Hammond, K. R., Stewart, T. R., Brehmer, B., & Steinmann, D. (1975). Social judgment theory. In M. Kaplan & S. Schwartz (Eds.), *Human judgment and decision processes.* New York: Academic Press.

Hastie, T. J. (1992). Generalized additive models. In J. M. Chambers & T. J. Hastie (Eds.), *Statistical models in S.* Pacific Grove, CA: Wadsworth.

Hastie, T. J., & Tibshirani, R. (1990). *Generalized additive models.* London: Chapman & Hall.

Hays, W. L., & Bennett, J. F. (1961). Multidimensional unfolding: Determining configuration from complete rank order preference data. *Psychometrika, 26,* 221–238.

Himmelfarb, S. (1993). The measurement of attitudes. In A. H. Eagly & S. Chaiken (Eds.), *The psychology of attitudes* (pp. 23–88). Fort Worth, TX: Harcourt, Brace, Jovanovich.

Jaccard, J., & Wan, C. K. (1995). Measurement error in the analysis of interaction effects between continuous predictors using multiple regression: Multiple indicator and structural equation approaches. *Psychological Bulletin, 117,* 348–357.

Jessor, R., Donovan, J. E., & Costa, F. M. (1991). *Beyond adolescence: Problem behavior and young adult development.* New York: Cambridge University Press.

Jessor, R., & Jessor, S. L. (1977). *Problem behavior and psychosocial development: A longitudinal study of youth.* New York: Academic Press.

Jones, E. E., & Sigall, H. (1971). The bogus pipeline: A new paradigm for measuring affect and attitude. *Psychological Bulletin, 76,* 349–364.

Jöreskog, K. G. (1981). Analysis of covariance structures. *Scandinavian Journal of Statistics, 8,* 65–92.

Jöreskog, K. G., & Sörbom, D. (1993). *LISREL8: The SIMPLIS command language.* Chicago: Scientific Software.

Judd, C. M., Jessor, R., & Donovan, J. E. (1986). Structural equation models and personality research. *Journal of Personality, 54,* 149–198.

Judd, C. M., & Kenny, D. A. (1981). *Estimating the effects of social interventions.* New York: Cambridge University Press.

Kenny, D. A. (1979). *Correlation and causality.* New York: Wiley-Interscience.

Kenny, D. A. (1994). The multitrait-multimethod matrix: Design, analysis, and conceptual issues. In P. E. Shrout & S. T. Fiske (Eds.), *Personality, research methods, and theory* (pp. 111–124). Hillsdale, NJ: Erlbaum.

Kenny, D. A., & Judd, C. M. (1996). A general procedure for the estimation of interdependence. *Psychological Bulletin, 119,* 138–148.

Kenny, D. A., & Kashy, D. A. (1992). The analysis of the multitrait-multimethod matrix by confirmatory factor analysis. *Psychological Bulletin, 112,* 165–172.

Kenny, D. A., Kashy, D. A., & Bolger, N. (1998). Data analysis in social psychology. In D. Gilbert, S. T. Fiske, & G. Lindzey (Eds.), *The handbook of social psychology* (4th ed., Vol. 1, pp. 233–265). New York: McGraw-Hill.

Kirk, R. E. (1982). *Experimental design.* Belmont, CA: Brooks/Cole.

Kosslyn, S. M. (1989). Understanding charts and graphs. *Applied Cognitive Psychology, 3,* 185–226.

Krantz, D. H., Luce, R. D., Suppes, P., & Tversky, A. (1971). *Foundations of measurement: Vol. 1. Additive and polynomial representations.* New York: Academic Press.

Kruskal, J. B. (1965). Analysis of factorial experiments by estimating monotone transformations of the data. *Journal of the Royal Statistical Society,* Series B, *27,* 251–263.

Kruskal, J. B., & Wish, M. (1978). *Multidimensional scaling.* Beverly Hills & London: Sage.

Lehner, P. E., & Noma, E. (1980). A new solution to the problem of finding all numerical solutions to ordered metric structures. *Psychometrika, 45,* 135–137.

Lichtenstein, S., & Slovic, P. (1971). Reversals of preference between bids and choices in gambling decisions. *Journal of Experimental Psychology, 89,* 46–55.

Loehlin, J. C. (1992). *Latent variable models: An introduction to factor, path, and structural analysis.* Hillsdale, NJ: Erlbaum.

Lopes, L. L. (1995). Algebra and process in the modeling of risky choice. In J. Busemeyer, R. Hastie, & D. L. Medin (Eds.), *Decision making from a cognitive perspective. [The Psychology of Learning and Motivation, Vol. 32.]* San Diego: Academic Press.

Luce, R. D. (1959). *Individual choice behavior.* New York: Wiley.

Luce, R. D. (1995). Four tensions concerning mathematical modeling in psychology. *Annual Review of Psychology, 46,* 1–26.

Luce, R. D. (1996). The ongoing dialog between empirical science and measurement theory. *Journal of Mathematical Psychology, 40,* 78–98.

Luce, R. D., Krantz, D. H., Suppes, P., & Tversky, A. (1990). *Foundations of measurement: Vol. 3. Representation, axiomatization, and invariance.* New York: Academic Press.

Luce, R. D., & Tukey, J. W. (1964). Simultaneous conjoint measurement: A new type of fundamental measurement. *Journal of Mathematical Psychology, 1,* 1–27.

Luce, R. D., & von Winterfeldt, D. (1994). What common ground exists for descriptive, prescriptive and normative utility theories. *Management Science, 40,* 263–279.

Macrae, C. N., Bodenhausen, G. V., Milne, A. B., & Jetten, J. (1994). Out of mind but back in sight: Stereotypes on the rebound. *Journal of Personality and Social Psychology, 67,* 808–817.

Marley, A. A. J. (1992). Measurement, models, and autonomous agents. *Psychological Science, 3,* 93–96.

Marsh, H. W. (1989). Confirmatory factor analyses of multitrait-multimethod data: Many problems and a few solutions. *Applied Psychological Measurement, 13,* 335–361.

McClelland, G. H., & Coombs, C. H. (1975). ORDMET: A general algorithm for constructing all numerical solutions to ordered metric structure. *Psychometrika, 40,* 269–290.

McDonald, R. P. (1978). A simple comprehensive model for the analysis of covariance structures. *British Journal of Mathematical and Statistical Psychology, 31,* 59–72.

Messick, S. (1989). Validity. In R. L. Linn (Ed.), *Educational measurement* (pp. 13–102). New York: Macmillan Publishing Co.

Messick, S. (1995). Validation of psychological assessment: Validation of inferences from persons' responses and performances as scientific inquiry into score meaning. *American Psychologist, 50,* 741–749.

Michell, J. (1990). *An introduction to the logic of psychological measurement.* Hillsdale, NJ: Lawrence Erlbaum Associates.

Nickerson, C. A., McClelland, G. H., & Petersen, D. M. (1991). Measuring contraceptive values: An alternative approach. *Journal of Behavioral Medicine, 14,* 241–266.

Osgood, C. E., Suci, G. J., & Tannenbaum, P. H. (1957). *The measurement of meaning.* Urbana: University of Illinois Press.

Petty, R. E., & Cacioppo, J. T. (1983). The role of bodily responses in attitude measurement and change. In J. T. Cacioppo & R. E. Petty (Eds.), *Social psychophysiology: A sourcebook* (pp. 51–101). New York: Guilford Press.

Pfanzagl, J., in collaboration with V. Baumann & H. Huber. (1968). *Theory of measurement.* New York: Wiley.

Rankin, R. E., & Campbell, D. T. (1955). Galvanic skin response to Negro and white experimenters. *Journal of Abnormal and Social Psychology, 51,* 30–33.

Roskam, E. E. (1992). ORDMET3: An improved algorithm to find the maximin solution to a system of linear (in)equalities. *Methodika, 6,* 30–53.

SAS Institute. (1990). *SAS/STAT user's guide, Version 6, Fourth edition* (Vols. 1 & 2). Cary, NC: SAS Institute.

Shah, P., & Carpenter, P. A. (1995). Conceptual limitations in comprehending line graphs. *Journal of Experimental Psychology: General, 124,* 43–61.

Shavelson, R. J., & Webb, N. M. (1991). *Generalizability theory: A primer.* Newbury Park, CA: Sage.

Shrout, P. E., & Fleiss, J. L. (1979). Intraclass correlations: Uses in assessing rater reliability. *Psychological Bulletin, 86,* 420–428.

Simkin, D., & Hastie, R. (1987). An information-processing analysis of graph perception. *Journal of the American Statistical Association, 82,* 454–465.

Stevens, S. S. (1951). Mathematics, measurement, and psychophysics. In S. S. Stevens (Ed.), *Handbook of experimental psychology* (pp. 1–49). New York: Wiley.

Suppes, P., Krantz, D. H., Luce, R. D., & Tversky, A. (1989). *Foundations of measurement: Vol. 2. Geometrical, threshold, and probabilistic representations.* New York: Academic Press.

Suppes, P., & Zinnes, J. L. (1963). Basic measurement theory. In R. D. Luce, R. R. Bush, & E. Galanter (Eds.), *Handbook of mathematical psychology* (Vol. 1, pp. 1–76). New York: Wiley.

Thurstone, L. L. (1927). A law of comparative judgment. *Psychological Review, 34,* 373–386.

Torgerson, W. S. (1958). *Theory and methods of scaling.* New York: Wiley.

Tufte, E. R. (1990). *Envisioning information.* Cheshire, CT: Graphics Press.

Tversky, A. (1969). Intransitivity of preferences. *Psychological Review, 76,* 31–48.

Tversky, A., & Russo, J. E. (1969). Substitutability and similarity in binary choices. *Journal of Mathematical Psychology, 6,* 1–12.

Tversky, A., Sattath, S., & Slovic, P. (1988). Contingent weighting in judgment and choice. *Psychological Review, 95,* 371–384.

Tversky, B., & Schiano, D. J. (1989). Perceptual and conceptual factors in distortions in memory for graphs and maps. *Journal of Experimental Psychology: General, 118,* 387–398.

van der Ven, A. H. G. S. (1980). *Introduction to scaling.* New York: Wiley.

Wainer, H. (1976). Estimating coefficients in linear models: It don't make no nevermind. *Psychological Bulletin, 83,* 213–217.

Wainer, H., & Theissen, D. (1981). Graphical data analysis. *Annual Review of Psychology, 32,* 191–241.

Warner, S. L. (1965). Randomized response: A survey technique for eliminating evasive answer bias. *Journal of the American Statistical Association, 60,* 63–69.

Webb, E. J., Campbell, D. T., Schwartz, R. D., & Sechrest, L., Grove, J. B. (1981). *Nonreactive measures in the social sciences* (2nd ed.). Boston: Houghton-Mifflin.

Weiss, D. J., & Yoes, M. E. (1990). Item response theory. In R. K. Hambleton & J. N. Zaal (Eds.), *Advances in educational and psychological testing* (pp. 69–96). Boston: Kluwer Academic Publishers.

Winer, B. J., Brown, D. R., & Michels, K. M. (1991). *Statistical principles in experimental design.* New York: McGraw-Hill.

Wish, M. (1971). Individual differences in perceptions and preferences among nations. In C. W. King & D. Tigert (Eds.), *Attitude research reaches new heights.* Chicago: American Marketing Association.

Wittenbrink, B., Judd, C. M., & Park, B. (1997). Evidence for racial prejudice at the implicit level and its relationship with questionnaire measures. *Journal of Personality and Social Psychology, 72,* 262–274.

Wittink, D. R., & Cattin, P. (1989). Commercial use of conjoint analysis: An update. *Journal of Marketing, 53,* 91–96.

Woodmansee, J. J. (1970). The pupil response as a measure of social attitudes. In G. F. Summers (Ed.), *Attitude measurement* (pp. 514–533). Chicago: Rand McNally.

Yellott, J. I. (1977). The relationship between Luce's choice axiom, Thurstone's theory of comparative judgment, and the double exponential distribution. *Journal of Mathematical Psychology, 15,* 109–144.

Young, F. W. (1984). Scaling. *Annual Review of Psychology, 35,* 55–81.

CHAPTER SIX

DATA ANALYSIS IN SOCIAL PSYCHOLOGY

DAVID A. KENNY, *University of Connecticut*
DEBORAH A. KASHY, *Texas A & M University*
NIALL BOLGER, *New York University*

Since the state of data analysis in social psychology was last reviewed in the *Handbook of Social Psychology* (Kenny, 1985), there have been many important advances in data-analytic methods designed to address problems specific to the study of human social behavior. These new techniques are replacing the data-analytic approaches that were initially developed for agricultural research. Problems such as nonindependence of observations, measurement error, and generalizability of results from specific operations are being directly addressed.

Among these recent developments, meta-analysis represents one of the most important methodological advances in the social and behavioral sciences over the last 25 years. Its capacity to integrate rigorously the results of multiple studies has already proven invaluable in a myriad of substantive areas. Because several sources detailing the methods of meta-analysis already exist, we do not discuss this method in this chapter. We refer the interested reader to an excellent review by Cooper and Hedges (1994).[1]

Similarly, major strides have been made in the analysis of data in which persons interact with or rate multiple partners. For the analysis of nominal outcomes (e.g., sociometric judgments of liking), Wasserman and Faust (1994) provide an almost encyclopedic coverage. For the analysis of variables measured at the interval level of measurement, Kenny (1996a) details recent designs, models, and analysis techniques.

Despite advances such as these, the standard data-analytic tool for most social psychologists remains the analysis of variance (ANOVA). We use ANOVA so much in our thinking that we have wondered whether laypeople also use ANOVA to make sense of their world (Kelley, 1967). Recent developments in ANOVA are presented in review articles by Wilcox (1987) and Judd, McClelland, and Culhane (1995) and in texts by Judd and McClelland (1989), Maxwell and Delaney (1990), and Harris (1994). Moreover, Abelson (1995) has written a thoughtful book on statistics, much of which covers ANOVA issues. The first part of the chapter is an extended discussion of the analysis of data from group research, largely from an ANOVA framework. Nonindependence of observations is a serious issue that is often just ignored. We consider the consequences of using person or group as the unit of analysis on Type I and II errors.

With some reluctance, social psychologists have begun to recognize the limitations of ANOVA and are turning to more general methods of data analysis that overcome these limitations. In our chapter, we focus extensively on two such methods, structural equation modeling and multilevel modeling.

Structural equation modeling has been increasingly applied in social psychological research, most notably attitude structure. Although there is not a thorough and readable discussion of this method, Loehlin (1992) provides a general introduction and Hayduk (1987) and Byrne (1994) provide useful introductions to the computer programs of LISREL and EQS, respectively. Finally, Bollen's book (1989) serves as a beneficial technical resource. Although structural equation modeling has delivered fewer theoretical insights than were initially promised (though there are

This research was supported in part by grants from the National Science Foundation (DBS-9307949) and the National Institute of Mental Health (RO1-MH51964). Brian Lashley and Cynthia Mohr were helpful in preparing the chapter, and Charles Judd, Thomas Malloy, and Irene Elkin provided useful comments that helped us in revising the chapter. Robert Calsyn generously shared with us his data.

notable exceptions, e.g., Jussim, 1991), it has provided important clarifications in the conceptual meaning of measures (see Judd & McClelland, 1998, in this *Handbook*).

Despite the increasing use of this technique, there is still considerable confusion regarding two fundamental issues: (a) whether a given structural equation model can be estimated, a topic called identification; and (b) whether the results of a structural equation model indicate the existence of causal mediation. Determining whether a model is identified is, we feel, the least understood aspect of structural equation modeling among social psychologists. For this reason we treat it in detail.

Determining whether a structural equation model shows causal mediation is better understood by social psychologists, but there are nonetheless many instances in the literature where tests of mediation are carried out incorrectly. Therefore, we provide a detailed discussion of the estimation and testing of mediational models by expanding and clarifying the analysis proposed by Baron and Kenny (1986) and Judd and Kenny (1981).

In addition to structural equation modeling, multilevel modeling has also emerged as a competitor to ANOVA in the last decade. For social psychologists who work with repeated-measures data, this method is useful because it overcomes many limitations of repeated-measures ANOVA. It can handle situations where the between-subject and within-subject independent variables are continuous variables and where there are missing data on the repeated measure. For social psychologists who do small group research, it is useful because it can easily handle the nonindependence of persons within groups and does not require equal numbers of persons in each group. More generally, multilevel modeling can be used to analyze any data that involve at least two levels of analysis (e.g., persons with repeated measurements within each person and groups with multiple persons within each group). Because this method is likely to be unfamiliar to most social psychologists, we cover it extensively.

We begin the chapter by discussing nonindependence of observations in group research. After considering ANOVA solutions, we discuss how multilevel models can be used to estimate many forms of grouped data. Finally, we discuss identification in structural equation models and the problem of testing mediation.

UNIT OF ANALYSIS IN GROUP RESEARCH[2]

Researchers studying small groups, relationships, or organizations face the difficulty of choosing the unit of analysis. This problem arises because of the hierarchical structure of the data: individuals are nested within groups such that each person is a member of one and only one group. (Kenny [1996a] considers designs in which persons are members of more than one group.) Typically the choice of the unit of analysis is between person and group. If person

is used as the unit of analysis, the assumption of independent units is likely to be violated because persons within groups may influence one another (Kenny & Judd, 1986). Alternatively, if group (i.e., couple, team, or organization) is used as the unit of analysis, the power of the statistical tests is likely to be reduced because there are fewer degrees of freedom than there are in the analysis that uses person as the unit of analysis. In this section, we concentrate on categorical, not continuous, independent variables. In addition, we do not consider independent variables that are random and operate at the group level (Griffin & Gonzalez, 1995; Kenny & La Voie, 1985).

In discussing the ramifications of the two choices for the unit of analysis, an important distinction must be made among three types of independent variables (denoted as *A*): nested, crossed, and mixed. A nested independent variable occurs when groups are assigned to levels of the independent variable such that every member of a given group has the same score on *A* with some groups at one level of *A* and other groups at other levels of *A*. A crossed independent variable occurs when *A* varies within the group, with some group members in one level of *A* and other group members in the other level of *A*, but for all groups the group average for *A* is the same. A mixed independent variable shares characteristics of both nested and crossed independent variables in that it varies both between and within groups. When the independent variable is mixed, persons within the group may differ on *A* and group averages on *A* may differ from group to group.

Consider the case in which *A* is gender. Gender would be nested if all groups contained same-gender members; gender would be crossed if each group consisted of both women and men with the restriction that each group has the same gender ratio; and gender would be mixed if the gender ratio varied from group to group as when some groups are same-gender and some are mixed-gender. A mixed variable, which is likely to be a new concept to most social psychologists, can provide significant conceptual leverage but also presents data-analytic difficulties. The question of whether group or person should be the unit of analysis is considered separately for the three types of independent variables. Within this section of the chapter, it is assumed that there are an equal number of persons per group and that there are two levels of *A*. In the multilevel modeling section of the chapter, the assumption of equal group sizes is relaxed.

Nested Independent Variable

Imagine the following hypothetical study: a researcher investigates the effect of two types of problem-solving strategies on group-member motivation. The researcher forms twenty five-person groups, ten of which use strategy 1 and ten of which use strategy 2. The key features of this example are the 100 persons and twenty groups, the two treatment conditions, and each group being in only one level of the treatment.

These data can be analyzed within an ANOVA framework as presented in Table 1. There are three sources of variation in the nested design. There is variation due to the independent variable, strategy type, which is denoted as factor *A* in the table. One type of strategy may be more motivating on average than the other type of strategy. Second, within each level of *A* some groups may be more motivated than other groups (*G/A*). Finally, within the groups some persons may be more motivated than others (*S/G/A*).

Generally, the central question addressed in a study of this type is whether there is an effect of strategy type or *A*. There are three different choices of error term with which one can test the effect of factor *A*. These are group within *A* (*G/A*), person within group within *A* (*S/G/A*), and person within *A* ignoring group (*S/A*). The *S/A* error term (the pooling of the *S/G/A* and *G/A* sources) involves treating person as the unit of analysis and ignoring group. The pooled sum of squares is 108 + 160 or 268 and the pooled degrees of freedom are 18 + 80 or 98. So person within *A* (ignoring group) has a mean square of 2.735, and the resulting *F* test of the strategy main effect is 10.97 with 1 and 98 degrees of freedom. Note that this approach in which person is the unit of analysis (and group is ignored) is equivalent to treating the design as if it were a single-factor ANOVA design in which there are only two sources of variation, *A* and *S/A*.

If group is used as the unit of analysis, *G/A* is used as the error term, and the *F* test equals 5.00 with 18 degrees of freedom. If person is used as the unit but group effects are controlled, the error term is *S/G/A*, and the *F* test is 15.00 with 80 degrees of freedom. Thus these three different choices concerning the unit of analysis yield three different *F*s with three different degrees of freedom and three different error terms. The appropriate choice among these three analyses is dictated by the degree to which the data within the groups are related or nonindependent.

Measuring Nonindependence: The Intraclass Correlation When person is used as the unit of analysis for the data in Table 1, the *F* test is two to three times as large as it is when group is the unit of analysis. Although it is desirable to have a healthy *F* ratio, an assessment of group effects is needed before group can be ignored and *S/A* can be used as the error term. Group effects occur if the scores of individuals within a group are more similar to one another than are the scores of individuals who are in different groups. Because it seems reasonable to believe that individuals in some groups may be more motivated than those in other groups, the measurement and statistical evaluation of group effects are required.

The standard measure employed to assess group effects is the *intraclass correlation* which is denoted as ρ. The intraclass correlation measures the correlation between two persons' outcomes who are both in the same group. So an intraclass correlation of .25 means that the correlation between the motivations of two persons who are in the same group is .25. Alternatively, the intraclass correlation can be viewed as the amount of variance in the persons' scores that is due to the group, controlling for the effect of *A*.

The standard measure of the intraclass correlation uses the mean squares from the ANOVA. The ingredients to the formula are the mean square for groups within *A* (*G/A*), the mean square for persons within groups within *A* (*S/G/A*), and the number of persons per group (*n*; see Table 1). The intraclass correlation can alternatively be estimated using correlational methods instead of ANOVA (Griffin & Gonzalez, 1995).

The intraclass correlation is like a product-moment correlation in that its upper limit is one. However, its lower limit is not always minus one. In general, its lower limit is $-1/(n-1)$ where *n* is the number of persons per group. So if *n* is twenty, then the intraclass can be no smaller than $-.0526$. Note that if *n* is two as in dyadic analysis, the lower limit is minus one. An example of a negative intraclass correlation may occur with married couples if one member experiences positive outcomes from the treatment (*A*) but his or her spouse experiences negative outcomes. Although negative intraclass correlations are relatively rare, they generally should be given serious consideration.

After the intraclass correlation has been estimated, it is tested for statistical significance by an *F* test. To create the *F* ratio, one places the larger of the two mean squares ($MS_{G/A}$ and $MS_{S/G/A}$) on the numerator and the smaller mean square is placed on the denominator. The degrees of freedom for *F* are determined accordingly. The obtained *F* is compared to a critical value for which the *p* value is divided by two. The *p* value is divided by two because, unlike the typical *F* test in ANOVA, both tails of the *F* distrib-

TABLE 1

ANOVA Source Table for the Nested Design Example with Twenty Groups of Five Persons

Source	SS	df	MS
Between Groups			
Strategy (*A*)	30	1	30
Group (*G/A*)	108	18	6
Within Groups			
Person (*S/G/A*)	160	80	2

$$\rho = \frac{MS_{G/A} - MS_{S/G/A}}{MS_{G/A} + [n-1]MS_{S/G/A}}$$

(where *n* is the number of persons per group)

$$\rho = \frac{6-2}{6+[4]2} = .29$$

$$F(18,80) = \frac{MS_{G/A}}{MS_{S/G/A}} = 3.00, p < .001, \text{ two tailed}$$

ution are being used, as in the use of the F distribution to test for unequal variances. A significant F statistic implies that there is nonindependence of data within the groups.

Because the intraclass correlation is used in determining whether there is nonindependence in the data, it is essential that there be sufficient power in its test. If there were not enough power, the researcher might mistakenly conclude that the data are independent when they are not. Table 2 presents the power tables for the test of the intraclass correlation for an alpha of .05, two-tailed. We used a method described by Koele (1982) to estimate power. Three factors are varied in the table: group size, overall sample size, and the degree of nonindependence. It is assumed that there is a single nested independent variable with two levels.

Not surprisingly, power increases as the intraclass correlation and sample size increase. Generally, there is more power when group size is larger, unless there are very few groups ($N = 40$ and $n = 10$). We see that especially when the intraclass correlation is not large and total sample size and the group size are small, power is very low. For example, with twenty groups of five persons and an intraclass of .15, the probability of making a Type II error is .56. Because of this low power, it is advisable to raise alpha to .2 in the test of the intraclass correlation (Myers, 1979). We return to the issue of power in the test of the intraclass correlation in the "General Guidelines" section.

Effect of Nonindependence on Tests of the Independent Variable   To what degree does ignoring nonindependence bias tests used to determine whether the treatment (factor A) has a statistically significant effect? That is, if there are group effects but person (ignoring group) is used as the unit of analysis, does the p value associated with the obtained F statistic truly represent the likelihood of obtaining that F if the null hypothesis were true and there were no effects due to the independent variable?

To determine the effect of nonindependence on the effective alpha for the three types of independent variables, a three-step procedure developed by Kenny (1995) is used. First, the critical value for the F test with person as unit is determined for the degrees of freedom. That critical value is divided by a bias factor (denoted as B in Table 3) to produce an adjusted F that is then used to determine the adjusted critical value. The bias factor B depends on the type of independent variable (i.e., nested, crossed, or mixed) and the size of the intraclass correlation. Finally, the degrees of freedom for the adjusted F test are reduced given the type of design and the size of the intraclass (denoted as df' in Table 3). The p value associated with the adjusted F and the adjusted degrees of freedom gives the effective alpha for the test.

The first row of formulas in Table 3 presents the formulas for the bias factor and the corrected degrees of freedom for a nested independent variable. For instance, if the total sample size is 100, the nonindependent observations are pairs of observations ($n = 2$), and the intraclass correlation of ρ is .5, then the bias factor which divides F is 1.52, and the effective degrees of freedom are 78.08, not 98. So the F test is inflated by about 50 percent, and the real degrees of freedom are about 20 less. Formulas for other designs are also presented in Table 3 and are used later in this section.

Table 4, using the formulas contained in Table 3, presents the value of the effective alpha when person is used

TABLE 2

Power (Times 100) of the Test of the Intraclass Correlation (ρ) with Two-tailed Alpha of .05 for the Nested Design

As a Function of the Size of the Correlation, Group Size (n), and Total Sample Size (N)

	N								
	40			100			200		
	n			n			n		
ρ	2	5	10	2	5	10	2	5	10
−.05	5	5	5	6	9	15	8	16	37
.05	6	8	10	6	11	16	8	17	27
.15	10	21	25	18	44	57	32	72	85
.25	19	40	40	42	78	82	71	97	98
.35	33	60	54	71	94	94	95	100	100
.45	53	76	65	92	99	98	100	100	100

Note: There are two treatment groups.

TABLE 3
Corrections to the F test (B) and the Degrees of Freedom (df') for Error

Nested

$$B = \frac{1+\rho(n-1)}{1-\rho(n-1)/(N/2-1)}$$

$$df' = \frac{[N-2-2\rho(n-1)]^2}{N-2+\rho(n-1)\{\rho[N-2(n-1)]-4\}}$$

Crossed

$$B = \frac{1-\rho}{1-\rho(n-2)/(N-2)}$$

$$df' = \frac{[N-2-\rho(n-2)]^2}{N-2+\rho^2[n-2+(n-1)(N-n)]-2\rho(n-2)}$$

Crossed with Interaction

$$\rho_1 = \frac{\rho_G}{1+\rho_{GxA}/(1-\rho_{GxA})}$$

$$\rho_2 = \frac{\rho_{GxA}}{1+\rho_G/(1-\rho_G)}$$

$$B = \frac{(N-2)[1-\rho_1+\rho_2(n/2-1)]}{N-2-\rho_1(n-2)-\rho_2(n/2-1)/2}$$

$$a = (N-n)n/2$$
$$b = (n-2)(N-n+2)/2$$
$$c = 2(n-2)$$

$$df' = \frac{[N-2-\rho_1(n-2)-\rho_2(n/2-1)/2)]^2}{N-2+a\rho_1^2+b(\rho_1+\rho_2)^2-c(\rho_1+\rho_2)}$$

Mixed ($n = 2$)

$$B = 1+\frac{N\rho_x\rho_y}{N-(1+\rho_x)(1+\rho_y)}$$

$$df' = \frac{d}{e+f+g}$$

where

$$d = (N-2)[N-(1+\rho_y)(1+\rho_x)]^2$$
$$e = \rho_x^2+[\rho_y^2(N^2-3N+1)]$$
$$f = (N-1)[N-2(1+\rho_y+\rho_x)+1]$$
$$g = \rho_y\rho_x[\rho_y\rho_x(N+1)+2\rho_x-2\rho_y(N-1)-2(N-2)]$$

Note: N is the total number of observations in the study, n the group size (and so the number of groups is N/n), and ρ the degree of nonindependence. For the mixed design, n equals 2, ρ_x represents nonindependence of the independent variable, and ρ_y represents nonindependence of the dependent variable. For all cases, there are two treatment groups.

as the unit of analysis even though there are group effects. Varied in the table are the total sample size N, the degree of nonindependence as measured by the intraclass correlation ρ, and the number of persons per group n. In this table there are always two treatment conditions; the total sample size is 40, 100, or 200; and the group size is 2, 5, or 10. Note that the total number of groups in a study is the total sample size divided by the group size. If alpha is greater than .05, then the statistical test is said to be too *liberal* and the null hypothesis is rejected too often. If alpha is less than .05, the test is said to be too *conservative* and the test has artificially low power.

As seen in Table 4, the degree of distortion in alpha depends on several factors. Looking first at the total sample size, it appears that N has virtually no impact on alpha. Only with large intraclass correlations can any effect be seen; with the larger sample size, there is slightly less distortion in alpha. Because the number of groups equals N/n, that factor too has virtually no effect on alpha.

The intraclass correlation is an important factor in alpha distortion. If the intraclass correlation is negative, the test is too conservative. That is, the null hypothesis is not rejected as often as it should be. As the value of the intraclass correlation becomes more positive, however, the test becomes increasingly liberal. For large values of the intraclass correlation, the null hypothesis is rejected much more often than it should be. Group size is a second important factor in determining the bias. With larger group sizes and a fixed total sample size, the larger the group size, the greater the alpha distortion.

To summarize, alpha is affected by the size of the intraclass and the group size but not affected very much by the total sample size or the number of groups. In essence, when the intraclass correlation and group size are both large but person is used as unit, the p values are grossly inflated. Fortunately, it seems likely that as group size increases, the intraclass declines (see Latané, 1981). As shown in Table 2, the power of the test of the intraclass correlation is affected by N. A small N study would have very little power in the test of the intraclass correlation and the intraclass correlation may be fairly large but not significant. For such a study there might be substantial distortion in the effective alpha value.

When the intraclass correlation is small and there are few persons per group, the distortion in alpha is fairly small. For instance, when the intraclass correlation is .05 and there are just two persons per group, using person as the unit of analysis results in a slightly too liberal test, the alpha being only .06.

Power Clearly ignoring nontrivial levels of nonindependence can seriously distort alpha. What then are the consequences if, because of nonindependence, group instead of person is used as the unit of analysis when testing for differences in the effects of strategy type? The second part of

TABLE 4

Probability (Times 100) of Making a Type I Error (Alpha) for the Nested Design with Person the Unit of Analysis

As a Function of the Intraclass Correlation (ρ), Group Size (n), and Total Sample Size (N)

	N								
	40			**100**			**200**		
	n			*n*			*n*		
ρ	**2**	**5**	**10**	**2**	**5**	**10**	**2**	**5**	**10**
−.05	4	3	1	4	3	1	4	3	1
.05	6	7	11	6	7	10	6	7	10
.15	7	12	21	7	12	21	7	12	20
.25	8	17	30	8	17	29	8	17	28
.35	9	22	37	9	21	35	9	21	34
.45	11	26	44	10	25	40	10	25	39

Note: There are two treatment groups.

the dilemma comes into focus: there is a decrease in power in the F test of the independent variable. Recall that power is the probability of rejecting the null hypothesis when the null hypothesis is false. In this section, power loss due to using group as unit is determined.

To determine power when group is used as the unit of analysis, the value of Cohen's d (the mean difference divided by the within-condition standard deviation) or the effect size for the treatment, must be adjusted using a formula presented by Barcikowski (1981) among others. The value of d is multiplied by

$$\sqrt{\frac{n}{1+(n-1)\rho}}$$

where n is the number of persons per group and ρ is the intraclass correlation. An examination of the formula reveals some interesting results. When ρ is one, the most extreme case of nonindependence, the effect size does not change, but because treating group as the unit results in a loss of error degrees of freedom, there is a net loss of power. However, if ρ is zero yet group is mistakenly treated as the unit of analysis, the degrees of freedom are reduced but the effect size gets multiplied by the square root of n. So even though there is a loss of degrees of freedom by using group as the unit of analysis, whenever ρ is small the loss in power due to reduced degrees of freedom is offset by a larger effect size. In other words, the penalty in power for inappropriately using group as unit is small, whereas the penalty in too liberal alpha levels can be quite large when person is inappropriately used as unit.

Table 5 presents the estimates of power of the test of A for a hypothetical study in which group is treated as the unit of analysis using an approximation developed by Severo and Zelen (1960). In each case, there are 100 persons and two treatment groups. In the table, Cohen's d is used as the measure of effect size, and there are small (0.2), medium (0.5), and large (0.8) effect sizes. The number of persons per group, or n, also varies. This factor has been set to 1, 2, 5, and 10. When "group" size is one, nonindependence does not matter because each score is independent of all the other scores. The case in which there is one person per group serves as the baseline condition because it is the case in which person is the unit of analysis and there is independence in the data. The intraclass correlation can take on any value, and the power does not change. For the other group sizes, the intraclass correlation is set to five different values: .0, .1, .2, .3, and .4.

Consider first the case in which the intraclass correlation equals zero. In this case, the researcher inappropriately uses the group as the unit, when person should have been used. Quite surprisingly, power is only very slightly diminished when compared to the power for one person per group. The small decline is due to the increasing critical value needed to achieve significance. For instance, with degrees of freedom of 98 (the value for one person per group), the critical value for F is 3.94, but for degrees of freedom of 8 (the value for 10 persons per group), the critical value is 5.32, an increase of 35 percent, and this greater critical value makes it somewhat more difficult to obtain significant results.

However, if there are sufficient degrees of freedom for error when group is the unit, there is surprisingly little loss

TABLE 5
Power (Times 100) with Group as the Unit of Analysis for the Nested Design with Two Treatment Groups and 100 Persons

	n																
	1*		2					5					10				
	ρ_G		ρ_G					ρ_G					ρ_G				
ES†	—	.0	.1	.2	.3	.4	.0	.1	.2	.3	.4	.0	.1	.2	.3	.4
0.2	17	15	14	14	13	12	15	12	10	9	9	14	9	8	7	7
0.5	70	69	65	61	57	54	66	51	41	34	30	59	34	25	20	17
0.8	98	99	98	96	95	93	98	91	82	73	65	95	73	55	44	37

*Baseline condition; person as unit with independence.
†Effect size (Cohen's *d*).

in power. When group becomes the unit, sample size declines by a factor of *n* (the number of persons per group), but the adjusted effect size increases by that same factor. These two factors nearly exactly offset each other. Given a sufficient number of groups (about twenty or more groups for the entire study), power is virtually unaffected when group is the unit of analysis and the intraclass correlation is zero. Thus, mistakenly making group the unit of analysis (when person should be) has little effect on power, at least when there are a sufficient number of groups. If the intraclass correlation is negative, the power increases when group is used as the unit of analysis. However, as the intraclass correlation increases, power does decline, especially when there are many persons per group. So there is less power when group scores are not independent.

When a researcher is faced with low power in a group study, there are, in principle, two ways that power can be enhanced (assuming a positive ρ). Either the number of groups (*N/n*) can be increased or the number of persons per group (*n*) can be increased. The latter strategy is available when the groups are large in size (e.g., classrooms or organizations) and the researcher samples a larger subset of the members. Consider the following example: a researcher has two treatment groups, within each group there are five classrooms, and from each classroom five students are sampled. For a large effect size (*d* = 0.8) and an intraclass correlation of .25, the power of the test is .42. Power can be increased by doubling the number of students per classroom to ten, and now the power is .50. But if instead the total number of classrooms in the study is doubled from ten to twenty and each group still has five students, the power climbs to .76. Both studies have 100 students (one with ten groups or classrooms each with ten students and the other with twenty groups each with five persons), but the second has considerably more power. The lesson to be learned is that it is generally better to add more groups to the study than it is to increase group size when the intraclass correlation is nontrivial.

General Guidelines for Nested Independent Variables If there is nonindependence, then group not person must be used as the unit of analysis. So in principle, the researcher should first evaluate whether there is nonindependence. If there is nonindependence, then group may be the unit of analysis; and if there is independence, then person may be the unit of analysis. To determine if there is nonindependence, the intraclass correlation is estimated and tested for statistical significance. There is one major sticking point with this procedure: the test of nonindependence may be very low in power. The usual standard for "sufficient power" is having an 80 percent chance of rejecting the null hypothesis (Cohen, 1988).

Given nonindependence and using person as the unit of analysis, there is bias in the test of the treatment effect. What is a reasonable value for the largest possible bias that researchers would accept? Of course, we would wish that there was no bias in alpha, but we are willing to tolerate small distortions in alpha for trivial levels of nonindependence. Because it has become fairly routine to treat *p* values between .05 and .10 as marginally significant, it would seem that .10 is the largest possible bias that most social psychologists would be willing to tolerate. Therefore, we define *consequential nonindependence* as the level of the intraclass correlation that occurs when person is inappropriately treated as the unit of analysis, and, as a result, the test of the independent variable is biased such that the nominal value alpha of .05 actually corresponds to an alpha of .10.[3]

Table 6 presents the minimum number of groups needed to detect consequential nonindependence. The rows in this table are group sizes and the columns are the alphas used to test the intraclass. The first column uses the standard alpha of .05 for the test of the intraclass correlation, and the second column uses the more liberal value of alpha of .20 which has been recommended by some authors (Myers, 1979).[4]

We see in Table 6 that thirty-six dyads are required to

TABLE 6

Minimum Number of Groups Needed to Have at Least .80 Power to Detect Consequential, Positive Nonindependence (Effective Alpha of .10)

As Function of Group Size and the One-tailed Alpha Used to Test the Intraclass Correlation

Group Size (n)	Number of Groups (N/n) One-tailed Alpha to Test ρ	
	.05	.20
2	36	18
3	56	28
4	66	34
5	72	36
6	76	38
7	80	40
8	82	40
9	82	40
10	84	42

achieve the standard of 80 percent power. Thus, to have an 80 percent chance of detecting nonindependence that biases the test of the independent variable to an effective alpha of .10, a minimum of thirty-six dyads are required. For groups of size eight, eighty-two groups (656 persons!) would be needed. The large number of groups needed when group size is large results from the fact that for large-sized groups, a very small level of nonindependence can create serious distortion of p values (see Table 4). Fewer groups are needed if the test of the intraclass is made more liberal, but the number of groups required is still substantial for large groups.

The implication of Table 6 is that the general advice given above is practical for studies with dyads and maybe triads, but it is not useful for studies in which groups are composed of four or more group members. For these studies, there is ordinarily insufficient power to test for consequential nonindependence.

If there are not enough groups to have a powerful test of the intraclass, group should be the unit of analysis. Unless the experimental procedure or previous research strongly indicates that the data are independent, group research requires using group as the unit. Fortunately, as shown in Table 5, there is surprisingly little loss of power in using group as unit when there is nonindependence.

Some researchers may be unwilling to use group as unit, or in some cases there may be so few groups per condition that there may be too little power to make group the unit. If person is the unit (something we do not recom-

mend!), then $S/G/A$ should be used as the error term to test for the effect of the independent variable, and the group variance (G/A) should still be removed. This approach of treating person as the unit has the advantage of removing the group effect from the error term, but it has the disadvantage of limiting the conclusions to the specific groups studied. Effectively, group is treated as a fixed, not a random, factor.

It might be argued that group should be treated as a random factor only when the groups are randomly sampled from the population of groups. However, persons are hardly ever randomly sampled, yet researchers routinely treat them as if they were random. Although sampling considerations are important in statistical decision making, it does not seem justifiable to insist on random sampling of groups and not to insist on random sampling of persons.

If person is used as the unit and the test of the independent variable is statistically significant, the fail-safe correlation (Kenny, 1995) can be computed. This correlation estimates how large nonindependence would have to be to render what is a statistically significant result no longer significant. An approximation to the fail-safe r is the following:

$$\frac{F - F_c}{F_c(n-1) + F(n-1)/(m-1)}$$

where F is the test statistic for A, F_C is the critical value for that test, m is the number of persons at each level of the independent variable, and n is the number of persons per group. If the fail-safe r is implausibly high, then nonindependence is not a plausible rival explanation of a significant result. We should make it clear that we do not recommend using person as unit. But if the researcher does not follow this advice, computing a fail-safe r would be advisable.

Crossed Independent Variable

Nested independent variables are much more frequently used in group research than crossed independent variables. In a crossed design, some members of each group are in one treatment condition whereas other members of the same group are in the second treatment condition. Thus, in this design, condition and group are crossed.

Consider another hypothetical study: a researcher studies the effect of gender in group communication and forms twenty-five groups. In each group there are two men and two women, and the total sample size is 100. Table 7 presents the ANOVA table for the study. Included in this table is the main effect of the experimental factor, a person's gender, denoted as factor A. This effect measures whether men or women talk more. The second factor in the table is the main effect of Group (G) which measures the extent to

TABLE 7

ANOVA Source Table for the Crossed Design Example with Twenty-Five Groups of Four Persons

Source	SS	df	MS
Between Group			
Group (G)	120	24	5
Within Group			
Gender (A)	25	1	25
GxA	72	24	3
Person (S/GxA)	100	50	2

$$\rho_{GxA} = \frac{MS_{GxA} - MS_{S/GxA}}{MS_{GxA} + [n/q - 1]MS_{S/GxA}}$$

(where n is the number of persons per group and q the number of levels of A)

$$\rho = \frac{3 - 2}{3 + [4/2 - 1]2} = .20$$

$$F_{(24,50)} = \frac{MS_{GxA}}{MS_{S/GxA}} = 1.50, p = .226, \text{two-tailed}$$

which people in some groups talk more than people in other groups. The next source of variation is the interaction between group and gender (GxA) which measures the extent to which, in some groups, gender differences are larger than in other groups. The final source of variation is person within the group X gender interaction (S/GxA) which measures the extent to which some persons talk more than others controlling for both group and gender. In general, for a crossed variable, there are n persons in each group and n/q persons at each of q levels of the independent variable. Note that if the researcher had studied opposite-gender dyads (groups of size two), the person within group by gender term could not be estimated. That is, within each dyad there would be only one male and one female and so variation within gender cannot be computed.

One key advantage of the crossed design over the nested design is that the group main effect and the group X condition interaction can be separated. In the nested design the group and the group X condition interaction are combined in the G/A term, and variance due to both is contained in the mean square for treatment. However, in the crossed design the condition effect contains only the group X condition interaction variance and not the group main effect variance. Thus, in the crossed design the effect of the independent variable is, at least in principle, estimated with greater precision and therefore tested with greater power than in the nested design.

For the crossed design, treating group as the unit of analysis involves testing the effect of the independent vari-

able A, using the group X treatment interaction mean square or MS_{GxA}. For the fictitious study presented in Table 7, that test is $F_{(1,24)} = 8.33$. If person is the unit of analysis, there are three possible ways to test the A effect. First, S/GxA could be used as the error term such that $F_{(1,50)} = 12.50$. Alternatively, the group X treatment interaction (GxA) could be pooled with S/GxA to yield a pooled error term of 2.32 ([72 + 100]/[24 + 50]). With this error term, the test of A yields $F_{(1,74)} = 10.76$. Finally, both the effects of group and its interaction with gender can be pooled with $MS_{S/GxA}$, and the resulting mean square error would equal 2.98 ([120 + 72 + 100]/[24 + 24 + 50]). The test of the independent variable would be $F_{(1,98)} = 8.39$. In the crossed design there are four alternative error terms. In the example, the mean square error term ranges from 2.00 to 3.00, the degrees of freedom from 24 to 98, and the F from 8.33 to 12.50.

Measuring the Group Main Effect and the Condition by Group Intraclass Correlations If person is treated as the unit of analysis in the crossed design there are two potential sources of nonindependence in the data: the group main effect and the group X condition interaction. The presence of either of these sources of variance results in nonindependence and invalidates the use of person as the unit of analysis. The intraclass correlation on the outcome measure for the group effect, or ρ_G, can be measured and tested for statistical significance as before with the nested design. The ingredients are the mean square for group which equals 5 in the example (see Table 7), the mean square for person within the group X condition interaction, which equals 2, and the total number of persons per group or 4. The value of ρ_G for the hypothetical example is [5 − 2]/[5 + (4 − 1)2] = .27.

The bottom of Table 7 shows how the intraclass correlation for the interaction, or ρ_{GxA}, can be assessed. The ingredients for the formula are the mean square for the interaction, the mean square for persons within this interaction, and the number of persons within each group and condition, two for the example. Like the group intraclass correlation, the interaction intraclass correlation can be tested by an F test. The lower limit of ρ_{GxA} is $-1/[n/q - 1]$ where q is the number of conditions.[5]

If the intraclass correlation for the interaction is positive, it means that within a group, the two women's levels of talking are more similar to one another than to the two men's; and correspondingly, the two men's levels of talking are more similar to each other than to the women's. Alternatively, the correlation implies that the gender difference in talking varies from group to group.

As stated earlier, if the group size equals the number of levels of the independent variable, it is not possible to separate variation due to S/GxA from variation due to GxA. Thus the group X condition interaction (GxA) cannot be tested and the intraclass correlations for *GxA* cannot be estimated. It is still possible to estimate the value of ρ_G by substituting MS_{GxA} for $MS_{S/GxA}$.

There has been very little systematic investigation of the size of the *GxA* interaction. However, it seems reasonable to expect that variance due to this interaction is fairly small. Usually, the group X condition intraclass correlation is smaller than the group intraclass ($\rho_{GxA} < \rho_G$); however, there are certain to be exceptions to this rule.

The power of the test for ρ_G is comparable to that for the nested design (see Table 2). The power of the test of ρ_{GxA} is likely even lower than the test of ρ_G for two reasons. First, ρ_{GxA} is usually smaller than ρ_G (see above), and second, for ρ_{GxA} the effective sample size is not n but rather n/q and smaller group sizes result in lower power (see Table 2).

Effect of Nonindependence on Tests of the Independent Variable   What are the consequences of ignoring nonindependence by treating person as the unit of analysis in the crossed design? Consider an example in which there are 100 persons and two conditions. Assume first that the group X condition interaction ρ_{GxA} is zero. When the group intraclass correlation ρ_G is negative, the test of factor A is slightly too liberal. However, in the much more likely case of a positive intraclass, the test is too conservative and therefore artificially low in power.

When the intraclass correlation for group is positive, the design is akin to a repeated measures design in the sense that each group has persons in each condition. If group is treated as the unit of analysis, variance due to group is subtracted from the error term that is used to test the treatment effect. Thus, treating group as the unit increases power in the same way as a within-subjects design has more power than a between-subjects design.

What, then, is the effect of treating person as the unit of analysis when there is nonindependence due to both the group and the group X condition interaction? As can be seen in Table 8, for dyads ($n = 2$) the interaction intraclass correlation is irrelevant. If group size is greater than two, the test of factor A becomes somewhat more liberal as the intraclass correlation for the interaction increases and as the intraclass correlation for group decreases. Also, as the number of groups declines (and hence the number of persons per group increases) the alpha inflation increases. Interestingly, when there are four persons per group and the intraclass correlation for groups equals the intraclass correlation for interaction, the two sources of bias virtually cancel each other. In addition, note the parallel between the crossed design with interaction effects and weak group effects and the nested design with group effects. For both designs, as the degree of nonindependence increases, the value of the effective alpha also increases.

Power   The determination of power of the test of a crossed independent variable depends on the effect size,

the total sample size (N), the group size (n), the intraclass correlation for group, and the intraclass correlation for the group X condition interaction. Using the Severo and Zelen (1960) approximation, Table 9 presents the power for a moderate effect size ($d = 0.5$); total sample sizes of 40 and 80; groups of size 2, 4, and 10; and intraclass correlations of $-.10$, $.00$, $.20$, and $.40$. The values in the table are based on the assumption that group is treated as the unit of analysis and so the A effect is tested by the *GxA* interaction. As a reference point, the power with person as unit and independence is .34 for $N = 40$ and .60 for $N = 80$.

The first thing to note in the table is that power increases as the intraclass correlation for group or ρ_G increases. Because variance due to group is removed, power is increased. However, power declines as ρ_{GxA} increases if the group size is larger than two. So for groups larger than two, the increase in power due to removing group variance can be lost if the variance due to group X condition interaction is large. Also, increasing group size lowers power, but this loss of power is most pronounced as ρ_{GxA} increases.

General Guidelines for Crossed Independent Variables   The best general advice to give for a crossed independent variable is to treat group as the unit of analysis. This would be accomplished by evaluating the effect of the independent variable using the group X condition interaction as the error term. This approach results in the removal of the group main effect which generally increases the power of the test. There are several reasons for this advice. First, very often crossed group designs are dyadic and so each group has just one person in each condition. In this case, the group X condition interaction is the only available error term. Second, even when each group has more than one person in each condition, usually there is more power in the test of a crossed independent variable when group, not person, is the unit of analysis.

When each group has more than one person in each condition, the two-stage strategy discussed for nested independent variables is an option. First, one estimates and tests the group X condition interaction using the $MS_{S/GxA}$ as the error term. We recommend as before using a liberal alpha of .20. If the interaction is significant, then group must be treated as the unit of analysis if effects are to be generalized beyond the specific groups studied.

If the test of group X condition is not significant, then person can be treated as the unit of analysis. Using person as the unit involves pooling the group X condition sums of squares (SS_{GxA}) with the sum of squares for persons within the group X condition interaction ($SS_{S/GxA}$). Similarly, the degrees of freedom from these two effects should be pooled. Pooling these two sources of variation should provide a more powerful test of a crossed independent variable than would occur if the $MS_{S/GxA}$ alone were used as the error term.

The major drawback of this two-stage procedure is that

TABLE 8

Effect of Group (ρ_G) and Group by Treatment (ρ_{GxA}) Correlations and Group (n) Size on Alpha (Times 100) with Person as the Unit of Analysis

ρ_{GxA}	n															
	2					**4**					**10**				
	ρ_G					ρ_G					ρ_G				
	−.1	**.1**	**.2**	**.3**	**.4**	**−.1**	**.1**	**.2**	**.3**	**.4**	**−.1**	**.1**	**.2**	**.3**	**.4**
−.1	6	4	3	2	1	5	3	2	1	1	2	1	0	0	0
.1	6	4	3	2	1	7	5	4	3	2	11	9	8	7	6
.2	6	4	3	2	1	9	6	5	4	3	16	14	13	12	11
.3	6	4	3	2	1	10	7	6	5	4	20	18	17	17	16
.4	6	4	3	2	1	11	9	8	6	5	24	22	22	21	20

Note: There are 100 persons and two treatment groups. The number of groups varies from fifty, twenty-five, to ten groups. The intraclass correlations are adjusted as in Table 3.

the test of the group X condition interaction may often have very low power. Unless it can be established that there is sufficient power, we feel the safest course of action is to use the group X condition interaction as the error term in the test of the independent variable.

Sometimes because of poor design, there may be too few groups to make group the unit of analysis. In this instance, the researcher may be forced to treat group as a fixed effect and person as the unit of analysis. However, the conclusions from such an analysis would refer to the specific groups that were sampled resulting in little generalizability.

Mixed Independent Variable

A mixed variable varies both between and within groups. For example, if one were studying romantic relationships (so n equals 2) and included gay as well as heterosexual couples, gender would be a mixed variable. A second example of a mixed variable is intelligence level in a study in

TABLE 9

Power (Times 100) for the Crossed Design with a Medium Effect Size ($d = 0.5$)

N	ρ_{GxA}	n											
		2				**4**				**10**			
		ρ_G				ρ_G				ρ_G			
		−.1	**.0**	**.2**	**.4**	**−.1**	**.0**	**.2**	**.4**	**−.1**	**.0**	**.2**	**.4**
40	−.1	28	31	38	48	28	31	38	51	26	30	41	66
	.0	28	31	38	48	26	28	34	44	19	20	24	30
	.2	28	31	38	48	23	24	28	34	13	13	15	16
	.4	28	31	38	48	20	21	24	28	11	11	11	12
80	−.1	54	58	69	82	56	61	72	87	63	70	87	99
	.0	54	58	69	82	52	56	66	79	45	48	58	70
	.2	54	58	69	82	45	48	56	66	28	29	32	36
	.4	54	58	69	82	40	42	48	56	21	22	23	25

Note: There are either forty or eighty persons and two conditions. Group is the unit of analysis. The intraclass correlations are adjusted as in Table 3.

which persons are randomly assigned to groups of four persons. Intelligence is a mixed variable because within groups some persons would be more intelligent than others, and some groups would have a higher average intelligence than others.

One way to determine whether an independent variable is mixed, nested, or crossed is to compute its intraclass correlation. To compute that correlation for the independent variable, denoted as ρ_x in this section, the independent variable is treated as a dependent variable. If the independent variable is nested, the intraclass correlation equals one; if the independent variable is crossed, the intraclass equals its lower limit; and if the independent variable is mixed, the intraclass correlation is not at either limit. The intraclass correlation for the outcome variable is denoted as ρ_y.

In our discussion of mixed variables we focus on three issues. First, we consider the effect of using person, rather than group, as the unit of analysis thereby ignoring nonindependence. Second, we discuss how mixed designs, unlike nested or crossed designs, allow the estimation of partner effects: the degree to which a person's level of the independent variable affects the dependent variable scores of other group members. Third, we describe the statistical analysis of mixed independent variables.

Effect on *p* Values   As noted, a mixed variable's intraclass correlation is less than one and greater than $-1/(n-1)$ where n is the group size. When the independent variable is not a manipulated variable, it is often mixed. For instance, in an investigation of the effect of attraction toward the group on work performance in groups, it is likely that attraction varies both between persons (some persons are more positive about the group than others) and between groups (some groups on average are more positive than others). Thus, attraction is likely to be a mixed independent variable with an intraclass correlation that is positive, but not perfect.

Kenny (1995) presents the details on how to compute the intraclass correlation when a variable is assumed to be caused by a mixed variable. The bias to the F test is quite complicated for the mixed case. Fortunately, for dyads the bias to F is relatively simple (Kenny, 1995) and is presented in Table 3. However, the adjustment to the degrees of freedom is very complicated, even for dyads.

Table 10 presents the bias in the test of the effect of a mixed independent variable when group size is limited to dyads. In this table, there are assumed to be fifty dyads (100 persons). When ρ_x and ρ_y have the same sign, the F test is inflated and so the test is too liberal. Importantly, there is not as much bias in the test when the independent variable is mixed as when it is nested or crossed. Because a mixed variable is between a nested and a crossed variable and because the effect of nonindependence is the opposite for nested and crossed designs, mixed independent variables create relatively weak effects due to nonindepen-

TABLE 10
Effect on Alpha of the Intraclass Correlation of the Independent (ρ_x) and Dependent Variable (ρ_y) for the Mixed Design for 100 Persons and 50 Dyads

ρ_y	ρ_x						
	−.5	**−.3**	**−.1**	**.0**	**.1**	**.3**	**.5**
−.5	.080	.068	.056	.051	.045	.034	.024
−.3	.068	.061	.054	.051	.047	.041	.034
−.1	.056	.053	.051	.050	.049	.047	.044
.0	.050	.050	.050	.050	.050	.050	.050
.1	.044	.047	.049	.050	.051	.053	.056
.3	.034	.040	.047	.050	.054	.061	.068
.5	.024	.034	.045	.051	.056	.068	.080

Note: The tabled values are the actual p values when the test statistic has a nominal p value of 0.05.

dence. In fact, if ρ_x and ρ_y are less than or equal to .3, alpha never exceeds .061. Generally, for mixed independent variables there is less distortion of alpha than there is for nested or crossed variables.

To determine the approximate power for a mixed independent variable, we can extrapolate from the power analyses that were done when the independent variable is nested or crossed. If the product of the two intraclasses $\rho_x\rho_y$ is positive, power tends to decline when dyad, not person, is the unit of analysis. Alternatively, if $\rho_x\rho_y$ is negative, power is usually increased by using dyad as unit. If ρ_x is near zero, there is little effect on power. So for small values of ρ_x, both power and p values are not much affected.

Partner Effects   Nested, crossed, and mixed independent variables all allow for the examination of the degree to which a person's score on the independent variable affects that person's score on the response variable. With a mixed independent variable, however, it is possible to estimate a second effect that cannot be estimated with either a nested or a crossed independent variable. This second effect measures the degree to which one person's score on the independent variable affects the responses of the other persons in the group. To distinguish these two types of effects, the former is called an *actor* effect and the latter a *partner* effect (Kashy & Kenny, 1997; Kenny, 1996b). As an example, consider again the effect of attraction toward the group on productivity. The actor effect measures whether persons who are highly attracted to the group are more productive. The partner effect measures whether being in a group with a person who is highly attracted to the group results in the other group members being more productive. Kashy and Kenny (1997) present a detailed discussion of what they call the *Actor-Partner Interdependence Model.*

Although the sizes of actor and partner effects are in principle independent, there are two special cases that are particularly relevant to the study of group behavior in social psychology. In the first case, which we will call *group orientation,* the actor and partner effects are approximately equal. In the second case, called *social comparison,* the actor and partner effects are equal in magnitude but opposite in sign, such that the actor effect is usually positive and the partner effect is negative. To illustrate these two types of effects, consider the effect of physical attractiveness on outcomes. If the model is group orientation, then a person's physical attractiveness leads to positive outcomes for the person and his or her partners. If the model is social comparison, then physical attractiveness leads to better outcomes for the self but reduced outcomes for the partner. Tesser's (1988) self-evaluation maintenance model explicitly considers these two types of effects.

Although the concept of partner effects may seem to be new, it has been used extensively in work in social psychology, particularly in small group theory and game theory. Consider first its use in small group theory. Partner effects provide an empirical method of gauging whether the group is one in which people see others as part of self or as different from self. If there are group-norm effects, then the success of the other leads to feelings of happiness, as much happiness as one's own success; it really does not matter who succeeds. If there are social comparison effects, then the success of the other leads to unhappiness.

Partner effects can also be used to define the classic prisoner's dilemma (PD) game. In this game, two people are given two choices. Each of these outcomes depends on their joint choice. If behavior choice is the independent variable (cooperative versus competitive) and outcome the dependent variable, then the essence of PD is that the actor effect and partner effect have different signs: actions that lead to better outcomes for the self have negative consequences for the partner. In fact, the defining feature of PD is that partner effects are larger than actor effects: a person's choice affects the partner's outcome more than that person's. Kelley and Thibaut (1978) decompose outcomes in two-person games into actor and partner effects, but they use different terms for the two effects.

Statistical Analysis Perhaps the first explicit recognition of the analysis difficulties raised by a mixed design, as well as a realization that partner effects can be estimated, is work by Kraemer and Jacklin (1979). Their approach though ground-breaking is limited: the independent variable can be only a dichotomy; there can be no additional independent variables; and the tests are large sample tests. Kenny (1996b) has developed two generalizations of the Kraemer and Jacklin (1979) approach. The first generaliza-

tion involves computation of two regression equations. In one regression, the group average of the independent variable is used to predict the group average of the response variable. In the second regression, the deviations from the group mean for both the independent and dependent variables are used in a regression equation. The regression coefficients from these two analyses are then pooled (Kashy & Kenny, 1997; Kenny, 1996b) to estimate the actor and partner effects. The second generalization involves the use of structural equation modeling (e.g., LISREL) and is described in detail in Kenny (1996b). These generalizations presume that group sizes are equal. A more general procedure for analyzing mixed designs, one that does not presume equal group sizes, is discussed in the multilevel modeling section of this chapter.

General Guidelines for the Analysis of Mixed Variables
An examination of Table 10 indicates that the value of the intraclass correlations must be very large to have consequential effects on the significance testing of the independent variable. If the intraclass correlation is not larger than .5, it is safe to use person as the unit of analysis, at least for dyads. We need further study about the effect of nonindependence and mixed variables for groups. The more important issue with mixed variables is to estimate partner effects because partner effects capture the truly interpersonal nature of group interaction. The analysis of data from mixed designs poses special difficulties that cannot be handled within a traditional ANOVA framework.

Summary

Most group research contains not one independent variable but multiple independent variables. Likely, some variables are nested, others are crossed, and some are mixed. As we have seen, a given level of nonindependence has very different effects for the different types of independent variables. For instance, if the intraclass correlation of the outcome variable were .45 and person is the unit, for a nested variable the *F* test would be too large, for a crossed variable it would be too small, and for the mixed variable there may be little or no effect.

Generally the safest course of action is to make group the unit of analysis and so it is then necessary to collect data from a sufficient number of groups. Although there may be some loss of power (perhaps not nearly as much as might be thought), treating group as the unit avoids many of the problems detailed in this section.

MULTILEVEL MODELS

In the previous section, ANOVA provided the framework for analyzing data from nested and crossed independent variables. As noted, ANOVA models cannot be used to analyze data from mixed variables; these models are further limited by the assumptions that group sizes are equal and the independent variables are categorical. There is an alternative to the ANOVA approach that can be used with any of the three types of independent variables which allows both continuous independent variables and unequal group sizes. This data-analytic approach has many names: multilevel models, hierarchical linear models, mixed model ANOVA, and random regression estimation.

The defining feature of multilevel data is that there is a hierarchy of observations. The lower level is the level at which the outcome variable is measured and is nested or grouped within an upper-level unit. In group research, the lower-level unit is person, and the upper-level unit is group. Applications of multilevel modeling are not, however, limited to group research. Most especially, in repeated-measures research (e.g., diary studies), observation or time point can be treated as the lower-level unit, and person can be treated as the upper-level unit. There is no requirement that persons have the same number of data points, as there is in repeated-measures ANOVA.

The Basic Data Structure

As an example of the basic data structure, we consider a fictitious study examining the effects of leadership style, authoritarianism, and satisfaction of group members. The participants in this "study" are military recruits in twenty-three platoons. Platoons range in size from five members to fifteen members, and recruits are randomly assigned to platoons with either a democratic or an autocratic leader. At the beginning of the study, all the recruits are pretested on authoritarianism. After six weeks of boot camp, the recruits rate their level of satisfaction with their platoon.

This study can be used to investigate several questions concerning leadership style, authoritarianism, and group satisfaction. First, it can test whether recruits generally are more satisfied with autocratic or democratic leadership styles. This first question concerns the effects of a nested independent variable, and ANOVA could be used to analyze such data if the leadership effect were the sole question of interest. The second question that can be addressed by this study is whether authoritarianism predicts satisfaction. Authoritarianism is a mixed independent variable because some recruits in a platoon are more authoritarian than others and some platoons score higher on average in authoritarianism than others. The third question that this study can address, using a multilevel approach, is the interaction between leadership style and authoritarianism: are recruits who are higher in authoritarianism more satisfied with autocratic leaders?

In this example, recruit is the lower-level unit and platoon is the upper-level unit. Authoritarianism is a lower-level predictor variable which we symbolize as X. Note that X can be either continuous or categorical (categorical

Xs are dummy coded). When X is continuous, as is the case for authoritarianism, it should be centered (Aiken & West, 1991) so that the intercepts are more interpretable. To center the variable, we subtracted the grand mean of authoritarianism (i.e., 5.53) from each score in this artificial data set. Leadership style is an upper-level predictor variable and is denoted Z. Like X, Z can be either continuous or categorical. In the present example, leadership style is effect coded: $Z = -1$ for the democratic style and $Z = 1$ for the autocratic style. Again, if Z were continuous, it should be centered. Finally, the outcome variable, satisfaction with the platoon, is measured on a seven-point scale at the lower level (recruit) and is symbolized as Y. Table 11 presents selected observations from this fictitious example data set.

Note that we are not allowing for partner effects (see the discussion of mixed variables in the previous section). For the example, the partner effect would refer to the effect of the authoritarianism of the other platoon members on the recruit's satisfaction. Had we wished to allow for such effects, we would create an additional X variable: the mean authoritarianism of those in the platoon besides the recruit (Kenny, 1996a).

Consistent with the conclusions drawn in the unit of analysis section, in multilevel modeling the upper-level unit, platoon in the example, is treated as the fundamental unit of analysis. The basic analysis is a two-step procedure in which an analysis is performed within each upper-level unit (platoon) and then the results of all these analyses are pooled. That is, in the first step the relationship between X and Y is estimated for each upper-level unit. In the example data set, the first step of the analysis estimates the relationship between authoritarianism and satisfaction separately for each platoon. In the second step, the results from the step one analyses are pooled across the upper-level units and the effects of the upper-level predictor variable, leadership condition, are assessed.

Unweighted Regression

It is usually advisable to relate X and Y by a regression analysis. So for each upper-level unit, Y is regressed on X. In the example, for platoon i with recruit j, the model is Equation 1 where platoon i has its own intercept b_{0i} and slope b_{1i}:

$$Y_{ij} = b_{0i} + b_{1i}X_{ij} + e_{ij} \qquad (1)$$

This analysis approach presumes that there are at least three observations for each group and that both X and Y vary for each group. There are k groups, n_i observations for group i (so there are n_i recruits in platoon i), and N or Σn_i total observations. The number of observations per group need not be equal. These k regressions are called the *first-step* regressions.

TABLE 11
Selected Observations from the Leadership and Authoritarianism Hypothetical Data Set

Platoon Number	Leadership Condition	Recruit Number	Authoritarianism	Satisfaction
2	−1	7	−0.53	4
2	−1	8	−1.53	3
2	−1	9	−2.53	4
2	−1	10	2.47	5
2	−1	11	2.47	4
2	−1	12	0.47	3
2	−1	13	−0.53	6
4	1	22	0.47	6
4	1	23	1.47	4
4	1	24	1.47	5
4	1	25	3.47	6
4	1	26	2.47	5

For the second-step analysis, the regression coefficients estimated in the first-step regressions (see Equation 1) are assumed to be a function of the upper-level predictor variable Z:

$$b_{0i} = a_0 + a_1 Z_i + d_i \qquad (2)$$

$$b_{1i} = c_0 + c_1 Z_i + f_i \qquad (3)$$

There are two second-step regression equations, the first of which treats the first-step intercepts as a function of the Z variable and the second of which treats the first-step regression coefficients as a function of Z. The parameters in Equations 2 and 3 are as follows:

a_0: the response on Y for persons scoring zero on both X and Z

a_1: the effect of Z on the average response on Y

c_0: the effect of X on Y for groups scoring zero on Z

c_1: the effect of Z on the effect of X on Y.

For the intercepts (b_{0i}, a_0, and c_0) to be interpretable, both X and Z must be scaled so that either zero is meaningful or the mean of the variable is subtracted from each score. In the example used here, X is continuous and centered around its mean and Z is an effect-coded (−1, 1) categorical variable. With this coding scheme, zero can be thought of as an "average" across the two types of groups (democratic

and autocratic). The top of Table 12 gives the interpretation of these four parameters for our example.

To repeat, there are two steps in the estimation procedure. In the first step, the slope and the intercept, b_{1i} and b_{0i}, are estimated for each group. That is, for each group Y is regressed on X as in Equation 1 and the slope b_{1i}, and intercept b_{0i}, are estimated. In the second step these slopes and intercepts serve as criterion measures in two regression equations in which Z is the predictor variable.

This two-step analysis procedure, where regression slopes from the first step are dependent variables in the second step, may seem unfamiliar. In fact, this procedure is similar in important respects to a conventional regression analysis with interactions between the lower-level predictor X and the upper-level predictor Z. To see this clearly, we need to substitute the terms for b_{0i} and b_{1i} in Equations 2 and 3 into Equation 1. This results in the following combined equation:

$$Y_{ij} = a_0 + a_1 Z_i + c_0 X_{ij} + c_1 Z_i X_{ij} + d_i + f_i X_{ij} + e_{ij} \qquad (4)$$

If we ignore the terms d_i and $f_i X_{ij}$, we can see that this equation is identical to a conventional regression equation that specifies an interaction between X and Z; i.e., the effect of the lower-level predictor X depends on the upper-level predictor Z. A conventional regression model of this sort contains only one random effect, e_{ij}. However, the multilevel model specified in Equation 4 contains two additional random effects: d_i, a random intercept effect; and $f_i X_{ij}$, a random slope effect for X_{ij}. It is essential that these

TABLE 12
Definition of Effects and Variance Components for the Example

Effect Estimate

Constant: a_0
  Typical level of satisfaction across all recruits and platoons

Leadership Style (Z): a_1
  Degree to which recruits in the autocratic condition are more satisfied than recruits in the democratic condition

Authoritarianism (X): c_0
  Degree to which a recruit's authoritarianism relates to satisfaction, controlling for leadership style

X by Z: c_1
  Degree to which the effect of leadership style varies by authoritarianism

Variance

Platoon: s_d^2
  Platoon differences in the recruits' satisfaction, controlling for leadership style and level of authoritarianism

X by Platoon: s_f^2
  Platoon differences in the relationship between authoritarianism and satisfaction, controlling for leadership style

Error: s_e^2
  Within-platoon variation in satisfaction, controlling for authoritarianism

---

additional random effects be considered to draw correct inferences from multilevel data.

Table 13 presents the estimates from these second-step regressions for the fictitious platoon data set. They are presented under the column designated OLS (ordinary least squares). We see that the intercept is about four and a half units. The estimates in Table 13 indicate that recruits in groups with autocratic leaders say that they are more satisfied than recruits with democratic leaders by about two-thirds of a point. (Because of effect coding, the coefficient must be doubled.) Also, recruits high in authoritarianism are more satisfied than those low in authoritarianism, but the effect is only marginally significant. There was no significant evidence of a differential effect of authoritarianism on satisfaction for the two leadership conditions.

Weighted Regressions

The first-step regression coefficients are likely to differ in their precision. Some are estimated more precisely than others because they are based on more observations and because X varies more. It seems reasonable to weight the second-step equation by the precision of the first-step esti-

mates. That is, groups whose coefficients are better estimated should count more than groups whose coefficients are not well estimated.

Although weighting greatly complicates multilevel analysis, it provides two important dividends. First, when the second-step regressions are weighted, the estimates are more precise; i.e., they are, in principle, closer to the population values than the unweighted estimates. Second, because weighting corrects for sampling error, variances of effects can be estimated. For instance, it can be determined whether the effect of X on Y varies across upper-level units. In terms of the example, we can estimate the degree to which the relationship between authoritarianism and satisfaction varies across platoons. So weighting at step two provides important benefits. Two different weighting strategies are considered: weighted least squares (WLS) and maximum likelihood (ML).

WLS Weighting To determine the weight or the accuracy of each group's regression coefficient w_i, we use the sum of squares for X or SS_i. This weight depends on two factors: the number of observations for group i and the variance of X for group i. Note that the larger the value of w_i, the more precisely b_{1i} is estimated and the more it is weighted in the second-step regression equation.

To better understand the difference between OLS and WLS, Table 14 presents information concerning the relationship between authoritarianism and satisfaction for five of the twenty-three groups. Platoon nine's data should be weighted more heavily because that platoon has more recruits than platoon four. Note also that the weight of platoon eleven is larger than platoon nine's, despite the fact that platoon nine has more recruits than platoon eleven. The pattern in the weights happens because platoon nine has less variation in authoritarianism than platoon eleven and so platoon nine has a smaller weight.

Table 13 presents the WLS estimates which are somewhat similar to the OLS estimates. Platoons with autocratic leaders have more satisfied recruits, and recruits higher in authoritarianism are more satisfied. The interaction is now statistically significant. Recruits higher in authoritarianism are especially satisfied when they have autocratic leaders.

For the weighted solution, there are two variances of effects. First, there is variance in the intercepts of σ_d^2. (From Equation 2, d is the residual term in the second-step regression of the intercepts.) It measures the extent to which there are differences between upper-level units in their average scores on Y when X is zero, after removing variation due to Z. So σ_d^2 measures the degree to which platoons differ in average levels of satisfaction controlling for both the levels of authoritarianism in the platoon and leadership style. The interpretation of σ_d^2 depends on the meaning of zero for the X variable. Recall that the inter-

TABLE 13
Estimates and Tests of Coefficients and Variance Components
for the Example

	Coefficients					
	OLS		WLS		ML	
	b	*t*	*b*	*t*	*b*	*t*
Constant	4.645	37.63**	4.598	39.76**	4.604	41.79**
Leadership (*Z*)	0.352	2.85*	0.346	2.99**	0.318	2.88*
Author. (*X*)	0.162	1.94†	0.206	2.58*	0.162	2.03*
X by *Z*	0.141	1.69	0.158	1.97†	0.163	2.04†

	Variances			
	s^2	*F*	s^2	χ^2/df
Platoon (*G/Z* or *d*)	0.109	1.55†	0.085	1.54†
X by *G/Z* (*f*)	0.087	2.42**	0.087	2.44**
Error	1.470		1.481	

**p < .01
*p < .05
†p < .10

cept for group i is the predicted score when X is zero. Because authoritarianism is centered on its mean, the intercept is the level of satisfaction for a recruit who is average in authoritarianism.

Additionally, there is variance in the coefficients or σ_f^2 (see Equation 3). This variance measures the extent to which the relationship between X and Y varies across the upper-level units after removing variation due to Z. So for the example, this variance assesses the degree to which the relationship between satisfaction and authoritarianism varies across platoons, controlling for leadership style.

To summarize, there are two group effects that are represented by variances:[6]

σ_d^2: group or upper-level differences in the average response controlling for X and Z

σ_f^2: group or upper-level differences in the effect of X on Y controlling for Z.

The bottom of Table 12 presents the interpretation of these variances for the platoon example.

To test whether there is significant variance in the first-

TABLE 14
Five Selected Platoons from the Example

Platoon	Group Size	Variance in Authoritarianism	Effect of Authoritarianism	Weight*
4	5	1.30	0.115	5.20
9	9	2.44	0.341	19.56
11	8	5.56	0.608	38.88
15	13	2.42	−0.489	29.08
18	9	3.61	−0.212	28.89

*Weight equals the variance of authoritarianism times the group size less one.

step regression coefficients, one must first compute the following:

s_f^2: the error variance from the weighted second-step regression where b_{1i} was treated as the criterion variable

s_p^2: the pooled error variance or $\Sigma(df_i s_{ei}^2)/\Sigma df_i$

where s_{ei}^2 and df_i are the error variance in group i and its degree of freedom. By pooling the error variances, we are assuming that they are homogeneous across the upper-level units (groups). The test of whether the first-step regression coefficients vary significantly ($\sigma_f^2 = 0$) is $F(k - 2, N - 2k) = s_f^2/s_p^2$ where k equals the number of groups and N the total number of observations in the data set. The estimate of the variance of the coefficients or σ_f^2 is

$$\frac{s_f^2 - s_p^2}{q} \quad (5)$$

The value of q can be viewed as an average of the weights. When the weights do not vary, q equals that weight. But when the weights do change, q is a quite complicated average of weights (Kashy, 1991; Kenny, Bolger & Kashy, 1997).

In the bottom of Table 13, for the platoon example, the variances are presented. The standard deviation for the platoons is about 0.3 and is only marginally significant. However, the effect of authoritarianism on satisfaction does vary significantly from platoon to platoon. Assuming a normal distribution of slopes, the results indicate that about 68 percent of the platoons have authoritarianism slopes between 0.206 ± 0.295. So, although in most platoons recruits higher in authoritarianism are more satisfied, in some platoons recruits who are lower in authoritarianism are more satisfied.

The value of q for the example is 23.900 for the slopes and 7.371 for the intercepts. As has been stated, the value of q can be viewed as an average weight. This WLS estimation method can be implemented using the GLM procedure done within SAS (Kenny, Bolger & Kashy, 1997).

Maximum Likelihood (ML) Weighting　In multilevel modeling, WLS estimation is rarely used, the more common method being maximum likelihood. To explain the difference between ML and WLS weights, consider the simplest multilevel model, one with no X or Z variables. As an example, fifteen members of three platoons rate their satisfaction with the group.

The model is the familiar one-way ANOVA model with random effects. There is only one fixed effect in this model, the constant or typical level of satisfaction. At issue here is how to estimate that effect. There are two different approaches: the weighted mean (sum of all the observations divided by N) and the unweighted mean (sum of all the group means divided by k). The OLS estimate of the intercept is the unweighted mean whereas the WLS estimate is the weighted mean.

ML uses a compromise between these two means based on the ratio of the variation within each group's data and the variation between groups. Consider the two sets of data in Table 15. In both sets there are three platoons whose means are 6, 7, and 8. The unweighted mean for both data sets is 7.000 and the weighted mean is 6.733. The difference between the two data sets is that for data set A, there is no within-group variance (recruits from the same platoon agree) whereas for B there is considerable variation. The unweighted mean is the appropriate measure of the intercept for data set A. Because there is no variation within platoons, having more observations really does not increase the precision in the estimation. But for data set B, there is considerably more variation and so having more observations is meaningful. So for data set B, the ML estimate (using the computer program HLM; see below) of the intercept is 6.746, which is closer to the weighted mean than the unweighted mean. Thus, the ML estimate does not use either the weighted or unweighted mean but rather uses an appropriate compromise based on the data.

The ML weight used to estimate σ_d^2 is $s_d^2 + w_i s_p^2$ where w_i is the WLS weight for unit i, s_d^2 is the variance of the intercepts, and s_p^2 is the pooled error variance. Note that if there is no within-group variation ($s_p^2 = 0$), which is the case for the data set A of Table 15, then the weights are homogeneous and the unweighted mean is used. If, however, s_d^2 is near zero (its estimate for data set B is only 0.054), then the weighted mean is used.

Although there is an impressive statistical logic to ML weighting, it presents an estimation difficulty. To estimate σ_d^2 one must know s_d^2 beforehand because s_d^2 is used in the weighting. This is the fundamental computational difficulty with ML. It results in the following consequences: iterative solutions and approximate standard errors. For more extended descriptions of maximum likelihood estimation of multilevel models, the reader should consult Bryk and Raudenbush (1992); Hedeker, Gibbons, and Flay (1994); and Goldstein (1995).

There is now a wide array of specialized computer programs that calculate these maximum likelihood estimates: HLM/2L and HLM/3L (Bryk, Raudenbush, & Congdon,

TABLE 15
Illustration of Weighting

Group	Data Set A	Data Set B
1	6 6 6 6 6 6	3 4 5 6 7 8 9
2	7 7 7 7 7	4 6 7 8 10
3	8 8 8	6 8 10

Unweighted Mean = 7.000; Weighted Mean = 6.733.

1994), MIXREG (Hedeker, 1993), MLn (Goldstein, Rasbash, & Yang, 1994), as well as 5V within BMDP and PROC MIXED within SAS. It should be noted that these programs actually accomplish the estimation in one step (and then iterate) and do not take two steps as do the OLS or WLS approaches. Also, most programs implement a variety of estimation approaches, the most common being restricted maximum likelihood.

We used the computer program HLM (Bryk et al., 1994) to estimate the parameters for the example platoon data set. Both the OLS and WLS results are fairly similar to the ML estimates. HLM uses a chi square test to evaluate the statistical significance of the variances. To compare this value to the WLS F tests, we divided the chi square by its degrees of freedom. As with WLS, the test that the effect of authoritarianism varied across groups is statistically significant.

ML also provides a measure of the covariance between d_i and f_i, the degree to which group differences in the slopes and intercepts are correlated. (Although WLS does not estimate this term, WLS does not assume that it is zero.) For the example, the correlation between d and f is .338 which indicates that platoons with more satisfied recruits also had a more positive effect of authoritarianism on satisfaction.

Summary

There are three strategies for estimating models with group or upper-level as unit: OLS, WLS, and ML. An OLS solution is the simplest to accomplish, but least efficient, and there are no estimates of the variances of the effects. A WLS solution provides estimates of the variances, but it can be much less efficient than the ML method. The ML method is the most efficient and is the most computationally complex. However, multilevel software is becoming increasingly ac-

cessible. It seems certain that ML will become the method of choice for the estimation of multilevel models.

It is helpful to contrast multilevel modeling with ML estimation to ANOVA with least-squares estimation. The major differences between the two are presented in Table 16. Within multilevel modeling, variables are denoted as fixed or random. In ANOVA, such a distinction can be made, but it is usually not featured. There is typically only one random factor: person. However, in many settings there are multiple random variables. As has been extensively discussed in this chapter, in group research there are two random variables: person and group.

One potential benefit of the use of multilevel models in social psychology is that they are likely to promote greater awareness of the distinction between fixed and random effects. In particular, stimuli in social psychological experiments (e.g., targets, words, sentence-stems) should properly be treated as random effects, but instead they are treated as fixed. Strictly speaking, then, the results of such experiments do not generalize beyond the specific stimuli used. Persons, on the other hand, are always treated as random effects, and statistical theory permits generalization to the population from which they were drawn. It is ironic that we social psychologists, who theorize that the situation is more important than the person, use analysis methods that make the person more important than the situation.

Random factors are featured much more in multilevel modeling than are fixed factors. The analyst examines the variance due to the presumed random effects in the model. If such variances are near zero, the model would be reestimated with the term dropped. Also, fixed factors may interact with random factors.

Classically in ANOVA, designs are balanced. Equal sample sizes in each cell of the design, though not a requirement, are highly desirable. Although this assumption can sometimes be relaxed, ANOVA works best on designs that are balanced. Multilevel modeling can handle bal-

TABLE 16

Differences Between ANOVA and Multilevel Modeling Paradigms

Factor	Paradigm	
	ANOVA	**Multilevel modeling**
Random factors	One	More than one
Terms estimated	Effects	Effects and variances
Design	Balanced	Unbalanced
Missing data	None	Allowable
Estimation technique	Least squares	Maximum likelihood
Formulas for estimates	Yes	No

anced as well as unbalanced designs. Although multilevel models can handle unbalanced data, the principle of balance is important and researchers should strive for it when they design research. There is a comparable parallel in latent variable modeling. Although those models allow the researcher to analyze unreliable measures (see below), it is still desirable to have as reliable measures as possible.

A related feature of multilevel modeling is that it allows for missing data. Consider conventional repeated-measures designs. Within ANOVA, if there are missing data from a person on a repeated measure, that person would have to be dropped from the analysis or the missing data would have to be "imputed." Multilevel models are often able to analyze all the data. Another feature is the estimation method for multilevel models. ANOVA models are estimated by least squares and significance tests involve comparison of mean squares. Generally, multilevel modeling employs maximum likelihood estimation.

Within ANOVA one can use the raw data to estimate an effect, and very often the estimates are means. For many classic social psychological experiments, the entire study is captured by a 2×2 table of means. With multilevel modeling, very complicated algorithms are used and the estimates are so complicated that no formula can be used to provide an estimate. Instead an iterative algorithm is used to approximate an estimate. The estimates are not means but coefficients from a complicated two-level analysis. Thus, it is much more difficult to go from the raw data to the results from the statistical analysis.

Multilevel modeling is quite different from the standard ANOVA framework. It promises to allow for more efficient and more flexible estimation of models than ANOVA. Moreover, it is reasonable to expect that multilevel modeling will become easier to implement and to interpret. We return to these differences in the conclusion of the chapter.

IDENTIFICATION IN STRUCTURAL EQUATION MODELING

Contemporary research in social psychology routinely uses structural equation models (Breckler, 1990). These models employ latent constructs that are measured by imperfect indicators. The set of links between indicators and latent constructs is called the *measurement model* (see Judd & McClelland, 1998, in this *Handbook*), and the set of links between constructs (i.e., causal paths) is called the *structural model*.

Structural equation modeling involves four steps. In the first step, called *specification,* the researcher determines which indicators reflect which latent variable and what the causal relations between latent variables are. Specification not only involves stating what causes what, but also what does *not* cause what. Certainly all models are incorrectly specified. The goal is to specify a model that is not too

complex that it cannot be estimated (see below), but not too simple that it is trivial. Such a blend of "complex simplicity" can be difficult to achieve.

In the second step, called *identification,* the researcher determines whether there is enough information to estimate the model. For many investigators, this is the most mysterious step. The focus of this section is to provide guidance on this topic.

In the third step, called *estimation,* the parameters of the model are estimated. For some models without latent variables (called *path analysis models*), multiple regression is the estimation method. The estimation of models with latent variables requires specialized structural equation computer programs and, generally, maximum likelihood estimation is the estimation method. Because maximum likelihood estimation of structural equation models usually presumes a multivariate normal distribution, less restrictive estimation methods have also been developed.

The statistical theory on which structural equation modeling is based presumes that the models are estimated using the covariance matrix (a covariance between two variables equals their correlation times the product of their standard deviations). In practice, many models do not require that the covariance matrix be used for estimation (Cudeck, 1989), and a correlation matrix can be used instead. It is possible to reformulate the statistical theory and presume that the model is estimated from a correlation, not a covariance, matrix (Browne & Mels, 1994).

In the fourth step, the fit of the model is evaluated. If the fit is poor, the model can be respecified and so part of the evaluation of model fit is the determination of where the poor fit lies. Since the pioneering paper by Bentler and Bonett (1980), literally hundreds of measures of model fit have been developed (Bollen & Long, 1993). Although the choice of model fit depends on a host of factors, the Tucker-Lewis or nonnormed measure (Bentler & Bonett, 1980) is very often quite informative (Marsh, Balla, & McDonald, 1988).

After all four steps, the model is usually respecified based on the analysis of the data. In structural equation modeling, the researcher usually cycles through the steps of specification, identification, estimation, and model fit many times. Models that are respecified based on the data are exploratory and not confirmatory. Generally, the significance testing within structural equation modeling presumes that the model was specified without looking at the data. Capitalization on chance is a serious problem when models are substantially altered based on the analysis of the data (MacCallum, Roznowski, & Necowitz, 1992). Exclusive reliance on statistical and not theoretical criteria for respecification can lead to misleading models.

In the estimation step, the measured variables are correlated, and their correlations (or more generally covariances) are used for parameter estimation. However, sometimes the information available from the correlations is not sufficient to enable the researcher to estimate the parameters. For instance, for a model in which two variables indicate a single latent variable, there is a single correlation. With that one correlation, it is impossible to solve for the two factor loadings. The problem is a standard algebraic one of fewer equations than unknowns. In cases such as this, there is no unique mathematical solution for the model's parameters and the model is said to be *not identified*. An essential task in structural equation modeling is to establish whether the model is identified.

Traditionally, the determination of a model's identification status requires a formal mathematical analysis that is described in texts like Bollen's (1989). In practice, this analysis is too complex for most researchers, and so they rely on structural equation modeling software to determine whether a given model is identified (Hayduk, 1987). However, finding out that one's model is not identified at the data analysis stage means that the study has to be redesigned and rerun. Researchers need to know if their models are identified, in principle, *before* they collect the data. This section presents rules so that researchers can determine if their models are identified before they are estimated.

However, even models that are in principle identified may not be identified when they are actually estimated. Such models are said to be *empirically underidentified*. A simple example can illustrate this condition: if a causal variable does not vary in the sample, its effects cannot be empirically estimated. So a second purpose of this section is to assist researchers in the recognition of models that are not identified empirically.

The following set of rules can be used to check whether a given model is identified. What follows should be taken as a guide and not as gospel. The rules, by no means exhaustive, are nonetheless helpful in determining identification. What follows presumes some knowledge of structural equation modeling. If the reader lacks that knowledge, this section should be skipped.

If both the structural and the measurement models are identified, then the entire model is identified. For the entire model to be identified, the structural model must be identified. Occasionally, the measurement model alone is not but the entire model may be identified when certain paths in the structural model are set to zero (see Condition B3b).

Measurement Model Identification

In the measurement model, indicators are used to assess constructs or latent variables. For example, ratings by three friends of a target's friendliness might serve as indicators of target friendliness, and ratings of intelligence from the same three friends might be indicators of intelligence. Pairs of latent constructs may be correlated. That is, there may be a correlation between the constructs of friendliness and

intelligence. Variance in the indicators that is not due to the latent constructs is called measurement error, and the errors of two indicators may be correlated. For example, the ratings by the same friend of friendliness and intelligence are likely correlated due to a halo effect.

For the measurement model to be identified, five conditions labeled A through E must hold. Conditions A and B must be satisfied by each construct, Condition C refers to each pair of constructs, and Condition D refers to each measure or indicator. Condition E refers to indicators that load on two or more constructs.

These rules primarily concern models in which each measure loads on only one construct. Fortunately, most estimated models in social psychology are of this type. If a variable loads on more than one construct, that variable is set aside and is discussed under Condition E.

Condition A: Scaling the Latent Variable   Because a latent variable is unmeasured, its units of measurement must be fixed by the researcher. This condition concerns the manner in which the units of measurement are fixed. Each construct must have either:

1. one fixed nonzero loading (usually 1.0),
2. for causal or exogenous factors, fixed factor variance (usually 1.0), or for factors that are caused, fixed factor disturbance variance (usually 1.0), or
3. a fixed causal path (usually 1.0) leading into or out of the latent variable (see Kenny, 1979, pp. 180–182).

Some computer programs require that only strategy one be used, but the other two strategies are perfectly legitimate. For pure measurement model situations (no causation between latent variables) or confirmatory factor analysis, strategy two is often used, yielding the standard factor analysis model. Strategy three is hardly ever used.

Condition B: Sufficient Number of Indicators per Construct   For each construct in the model, at least one of the following three conditions must hold.

1. The construct has at least three indicators whose errors are uncorrelated with each other.
2. The construct has at least two indicators whose errors are uncorrelated and either
   a. both the indicators of the construct correlate with a third indicator of another construct but the two indicators' errors are uncorrelated with the error of that third indicator (i.e., the two constructs must be correlated), or
   b. the two indicators' loadings are set equal to each other.
3. The construct has one indicator and either:
   a. the indicator's error variance is fixed to zero or some other a priori value (e.g., the quantity one minus the reliability times the indicator's variance), or

b. there is another variable that can serve as an instrumental variable (see Rule C under "Identification of the Structural Model" below) in the structural model and the error in the indicator is not correlated with that instrumental variable.

Condition C: Construct Correlations
For every pair of constructs either

1. there are at least two indicators, one from each construct, that do not have correlated measurement error between them, or
2. the correlation between the pair of constructs is specified to be zero (or some other a priori value).

Condition D: Loading Estimation
For every indicator, there must be at least one other indicator (not necessarily of the same construct) with which it does not share correlated measurement error. If the three above conditions hold and Condition D does not, then drop from the model all indicators that do not meet this condition and the model is still identified.

Condition E: Estimation of Double Loadings
One important model in which *all* indicators have double loadings is the classic model for the multitrait-multimethod matrix (Campbell & Fiske, 1959). Each indicator loads on both a trait and method factor. Kenny and Kashy (1992) have shown that there are serious empirical identification difficulties with this model. All but the most adventurous researchers are well advised to avoid the estimation of such models. Alternative forms of multitrait-multimethod matrix models can be estimated (Kenny & Kashy, 1992; Millsap, 1995; Wothke, 1995).

However, a subset of indicators may load on two or more factors as long as Conditions A, B, and C are met for those constructs by including some indicators that load on only one construct. We refer to this as Condition E. Consider the indicator X_1 that loads on more than one construct. The errors of X_1 may be correlated with the errors of other indicators, but for each construct on which X_1 loads, there must be at least one singly-loading indicator that does not share any correlated error with X_1.

The rule in the previous paragraph is a sufficient condition for the identification of models with double-loading indicators. That is, some models that do not meet Condition E are identified in principle. However, in practice these models are often empirically under-identified.

Summary

For most measurement models, Condition E is not relevant, and it is usually very easy to verify that C and D are satis-

fied. Condition A can always be satisfied (but the researcher must make sure that it is), and so ordinarily the key condition to scrutinize carefully is B.

Constructs with a single error-free indicator (e.g., gender) are best handled by fixing their loading to one, forcing their error variance to zero, and leaving their variances free to be estimated. Of course, the assumption of zero error variance must be justified theoretically.

Empirical Identification of the Measurement Model
Some models that are identified in theory are not identified for a particular study. Following Kenny (1979), these models are called *empirically underidentified models*. Consider a simple one-factor model with three indicators, X_1, X_2, and X_3. It can be shown that the standardized loading of X_1 on the factor equals the square root of $r_{12}r_{13}/r_{23}$. Mathematically for there to be a solution r_{23} must not equal zero. If its value is near zero, then there is no well-defined solution and the model is said to be empirically underidentified.[7]

Condition B, the number of indicators per construct, is critical to the empirical identification of each construct. Condition B1 requires three indicators. For these three indicators, each of the three correlations between those indicators should be statistically significant and the product of the three correlations must be positive.

Condition B2a has three indicators, two of which load on the latent variable and the third loads on another factor. As with B1, the three indicators must correlate significantly with each other and their product must be positive. If the two indicators of one construct correlate with the one indicator of the other construct, then those two constructs must be correlated.

For two indicators that are assumed to have equal loadings (Condition B2b), the correlation between the two must be significantly positive. If the correlation is large but negative, given theoretical justification, the loadings can be forced to be equal but of opposite signs.

If there is a single indicator and instrumental variable (Condition B3b) estimation is used, the indicator must share unique variance with the instrument (see Rule C below).

If the latent variable is scaled by fixing a loading to one (Condition A1), the indicator with a loading of one must correlate with other indicators of the latent variable. If all of the loadings are free and the disturbance of residual variance is fixed, empirical identification problems can occur if all or nearly all of the variance of the latent variable is explained by the other latent variables in the model.

If an indicator loads on two constructs (Condition E), the correlation between these two constructs cannot be very large. If that correlation is too large, the resulting multicollinearity makes it difficult to determine the indicator's loadings on the two factors.

Illustrations Figure 1 contains a series of examples. The latent factors or constructs are denoted by circled Fs and Gs, the measures are denoted by Xs, and the errors by Es. The reader should decide whether each model is identified and then read the text that follows.

Models I through IV are single-factor models. So Conditions C and E do not apply. Condition A is met in each model because one path is fixed to one. The key condition for these models is Condition B, but D must also be checked.

Model I meets Condition B1 and so is identified. Model II does not meet Condition B and so is not identified. Model III, though very similar to Model II, is identified because it meets Condition B2. Model IV meets Condition B1 but indicator X_4 fails to meet Condition D. So to identify this model, indicator X_4 must be dropped from the model.

Models V through VIII are two-factor models. All the conditions need to be checked, but we concentrate on Condition B. Models V and VI are not identified because they fail to meet Condition B. Both models would be identified if the errors were not correlated. Model VII is identical to Model VI, but there are three indicators per factor instead of two. This model is identified because it meets both Conditions B1 and B2a. Model VIII is identified because it meets Condition B2a. However, Model IX is not identified because B2a is not met since X_1 and X_2 do not correlate with X_3 and X_4 given that the correlation between the constructs is zero. Finally, Model X is identified. Condition B2a is met for both factors and so under Condition E, X_3 can load on both latent variables.

Identification of the Structural Model

The structural model consists of a set of causal equations. Variables that serve only as causes in the model are called *exogenous variables*. Unexplained variation in the effect variable is referred to as *disturbance*.

Rule A: Minimum Condition of Identifiability Let k be the number of constructs in the structural model and q be equal to $k(k-1)/2$. The *minimum condition of identifiability* is that q must be greater than or equal to p where p equals the sum of:

a. the number of paths,
b. the number of correlations between exogenous variables,
c. the number of correlations between a disturbance and an exogenous variable, and
d. the number of correlations between disturbances.

In nearly all models, c is zero, and in many models d is zero. Theory places restrictions on a. Generally, b should

be set at the maximum value; that is, all pairs of exogenous variables should be correlated.

If a structural model satisfies this minimum condition, the model *may* be identified. If it does not, the model is not identified; however, some but not all of the parameters of the model may be identified.

Rule B: Apparent Necessary Condition All models that satisfy the following condition appear to be identified: if between any pair of constructs, X and Y, no more than one of the following is true:

X directly causes Y

Y directly causes X

X and Y have correlated disturbances or if either X or Y is exogenous, it is correlated with the other's disturbance

X and Y are correlated exogenous variables.

Models that can be estimated by multiple regression form an important special case of this rule. For such models, the structural equations can be ordered such that if a variable appears as a cause in a given equation, it never later appears as an effect. Although we know of no proof for Rule B, we know of no exception. It seems likely that the rule generally holds.

Rule C: Instrumental Variable Estimation This rule considers exceptions to the previous rule: models that fail to satisfy Rule B but are nonetheless identified. The material in this section is very dense and may have to be read more than once. Because of these complications, this estimation method has rarely been used in social psychology, however, there have been some important uses of the method (e.g., Felson, 1981; Smith, 1982).

The estimation method is called *instrumental variable estimation*. An instrumental variable is assumed not to cause directly the effect variable. The absence of a causal path is what permits the estimation of an otherwise not identified model.

Consider X as a causal variable and Y as an effect variable. Instrumental variable estimation can be applied to the three following conditions:

1. spuriousness: an unmeasured variable causes both X and Y,
2. reverse causation: Y causes X, and
3. measurement error: measurement error in X which has only a single indicator.

Notice that conditions 1 and 2 violate Rule B. For all three conditions, the path from X to Y cannot be estimated by traditional means.

These models can be identified by instrumental vari-

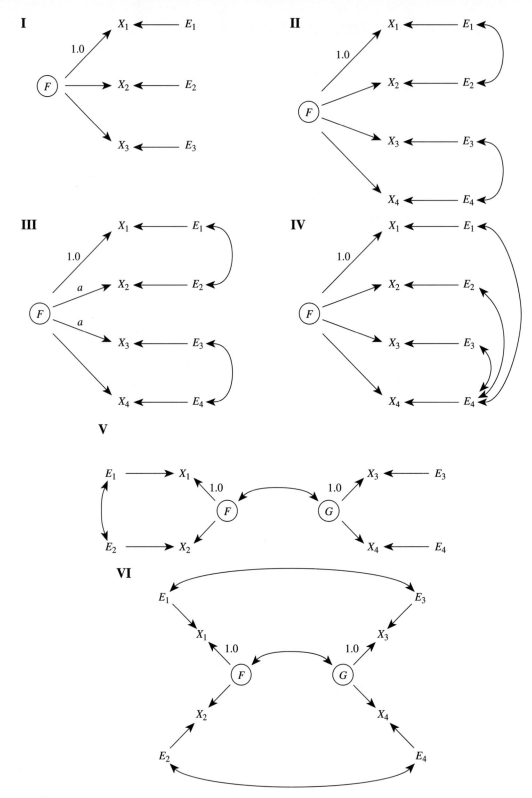

FIGURE 1 Measurement Model Identification Examples.
Latent constructs are denoted by circled *F*s and *G*s, measures by *X*s, and errors by *E*s.

256

VII

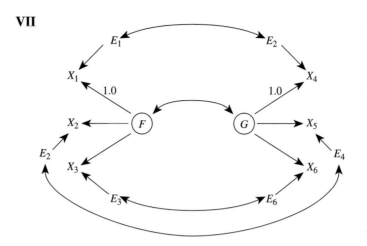

VIII

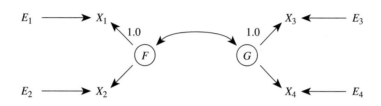

IX

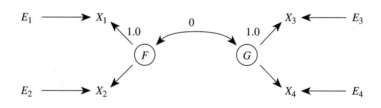

X

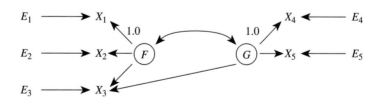

ables. Denote X as a causal variable that meets one of the three above conditions, Y as the effect variable, U as Y's disturbance, I as an instrumental variable, and Z as a causal variable not needing an instrumental variable. The defining feature of an instrumental variable is that I is assumed not to cause Y directly: the path from I to Y is zero. This zero path is used to identify the model, but it must be given by theory, not by empirical analysis.

The following conditions are necessary for a model with instrumental variables to be identified.

1. The variable I must not directly cause Y or be correlated with U.
2. There must be as many or more I variables as there are X variables.[8]

Empirical Identification of the Structural Model   If two variables that cause a third variable are strongly correlated, a condition called *multicollinearity,* the paths are not very precisely estimated. When there is perfect correlation between a pair of causal variables, the coefficients for those causal variables cannot be estimated at all.

For models with instrumental variables, the conditions for empirical identification are complicated. As before, let X be the variable that needs an instrumental variable, I be an instrumental variable, and Z be a causal variable that does not need an instrument. After the partialling out variance due to Z, the set of I variables must significantly correlate (i.e., have a large multiple correlation) with X. For there to be a correlation between I and X and for Rule C1 not to be violated, the following must hold for the appropriate use of instrumental variable estimation.

1. For spuriousness, X cannot cause I and I cannot be correlated with the omitted variable.
2. When X is measured with error, variable I cannot be correlated with the measurement error in X, however I itself may have measurement error. That part of X that contains error may cause I.
3. For a feedback relationship, X cannot cause I.

If there is more than one X variable (i.e., variables needing instruments) that cause Y, when each X is regressed on I and Z, the correlation between the predicted Xs should not be too large (see Kenny [1979] p. 91). Finally, in a feedback loop, the same variable cannot serve as the instrumental variable for both variables in the loop.[9]

Illustrations   Figure 2 contains six models containing four variables, and the question is whether the structural model is identified or not. Model I is not identified because it fails to satisfy Rule A, the minimum condition of identifiability. There are four variables and so there are six correlations. Because there are eight parameters to be estimated in

Model I, the minimum condition of identifiability has not been met. All the remaining models meet that condition.

The next three models are identified because they satisfy Rule B. Models II and III can be estimated by multiple regression, and a variant of Model III is presented in the section on mediation. Model IV contains a feedback cycle (X_1 causes X_2, X_2 causes X_3, X_3 causes X_4, and X_4 causes X_1), and it is identified.

Because Models V and VI do not meet Rule B, we need instrumental variables and Rule C to identify these models. Model V has a feedback loop between X_3 and X_4. The variable X_1 can serve as an instrumental variable in estimating the effect of X_4 on X_3, and X_2 can serve as instrumental variable in estimating the effect of X_3 on X_4. For Model VI, the path from X_2 to X_4 needs an instrumental variable, because X_2 is correlated with the disturbance in X_4. It would seem that X_3 could serve as an instrumental variable, but it cannot because X_2 causes X_3 making the instrument correlated with the disturbance in X_4. Given this correlation, X_3 cannot serve as an instrumental variable and so Model VI is not identified.

Conclusion

This section on identification is very dense, but it does address an important and neglected issue in causal modeling. To design intelligent measurement and the structural models, the researcher needs to know whether the models are identified. Waiting to find out that model is not identified during the estimation stage is too late. Issues of identification are particularly relevant for the testing of mediational models, the topic of the next section.

MEDIATIONAL ANALYSIS

Structural equation modeling greatly facilitates the estimation and testing of causal sequences, particularly those involving theoretical constructs rather than measured variables. One particular type of causal model, a model proposing a mediational process, occurs frequently in social psychology. Very often a phenomenon is discovered (e.g., social facilitation or group polarization), and researchers are eager to discover the process by which the phenomenon operates. As discussed by Taylor (1998, in this *Handbook*), much of what social psychologists do is attempt to understand how internal processes mediate the effect of the situation on behavior. When a mediational model involves latent constructs, structural equation modeling provides the basic data analysis strategy. If the mediational model involves only measured variables, the basic analytical approach is multiple regression. Regardless of which data-analytic method is used, the steps necessary for testing mediation are the same. In this section, we describe the analyses required for testing mediational hypotheses

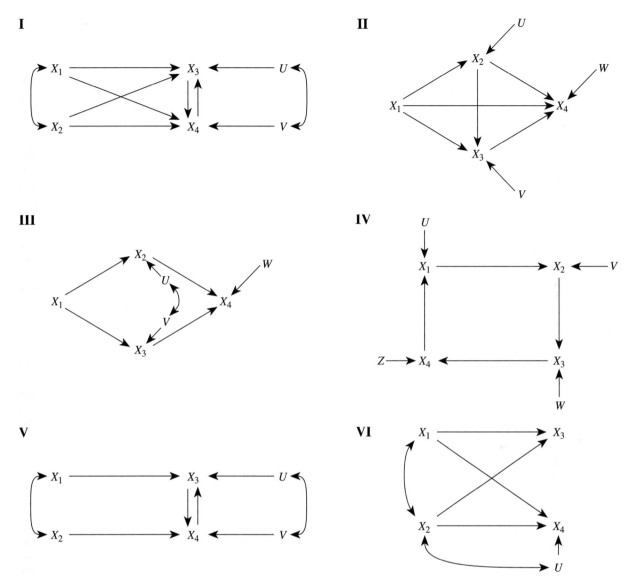

FIGURE 2   Structural Model Identification Examples, Each with Four Variables.

and we address several questions that such analyses have engendered.

Consider a variable X that is assumed to affect another variable Y. The variable X is called the *initial variable* and the variable that it causes or Y is called the *outcome*. In diagrammatic form, the unmediated model is presented in Figure 3(a). The effect of X on Y may be mediated by a process variable M, and the variable X may still affect Y. The mediated model is presented in diagrammatic form in Figure 3(b). The mediator has been called an *intervening* or *process* variable. *Complete mediation* is the case in which variable X no longer affects Y after M has been con-

trolled and so path c' in Figure 3(b) is zero. *Partial mediation* is the case in which the path from X to Y is reduced in *absolute* size but is still different from zero when the mediator is controlled.

Baron and Kenny (1986) and Judd and Kenny (1981) have discussed four steps in establishing mediation.

Step 1. Show that the initial variable is correlated with the outcome. Use Y as the criterion variable in a regression equation and X as a predictor—estimate and test path c in Figure 3(a). This step establishes that there is an effect that may be mediated.

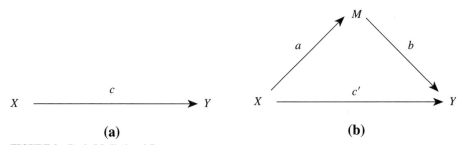

FIGURE 3   Basic Mediational Structure.
X is the initial variable, *Y* the outcome variable, and *M* the mediator.

Step 2. Show that the initial variable is correlated with the mediator. Use *M* as the criterion variable in the regression equation and *X* as a predictor—estimate and test path *a* in Figure 3(b). This step essentially involves treating the mediator as if it were an outcome variable.

Step 3. Show that the mediator affects the outcome variable. Use *Y* as the criterion variable in a regression equation and *X* and *M* as predictors—estimate and test path *b* in Figure 3(b). It is not sufficient just to correlate the mediator with the outcome; the mediator and the outcome may be correlated because they are both caused by the initial variable *X*. Thus, the initial variable must be controlled in establishing the effect of the mediator on the outcome.

Step 4. To establish that *M completely* mediates the *X-Y* relationship, the effect of *X* on *Y* controlling for *M* should be zero—estimate and test path *c′* in the Figure 3(b). The effects in both Steps 3 and 4 are estimated in the same regression equation.

If all four of these steps are met, then the data are consistent with the hypothesis that *M* completely mediates the *X-Y* relationship, and if the first three steps are met but Step 4 is not, then partial mediation is indicated. Meeting these steps does not, however, conclusively establish that mediation has occurred because there are other (perhaps less plausible) models that are consistent with the data (MacCallum, Wegener, Uchino, & Fabrigar, 1993). Some of these models are considered later in this section.

The amount of mediation is defined as the reduction of the effect of the initial variation on the outcome or *c − c′*. This difference in coefficients can be shown to equal exactly the product of the effect of *X* on *M* times the effect of *M* on *Y* or *ab* and so *ab = c − c′*. Note that the amount of reduction in the effect of *X* on *Y* is not equivalent to either the change in variance explained or the change in an inferential statistic such as *F* or a *p* value. It is possible for the *F* from the initial variable to the outcome to de-

crease dramatically even when the mediator has no effect on the outcome.

If Step 2 (the test of *a*) and Step 3 (the test of *b*) are met, it follows that there necessarily is a reduction in the effect of *X* on *Y*. An indirect and approximate test that *ab* = 0 is to test that both *a* and *b* are zero (Steps 2 and 3). Baron and Kenny (1986) provide a direct test of *ab* which is a modification of a test originally proposed by Sobel (1982). It requires the standard error of *a* or s_a (which equals a/t_a where t_a is the *t* test of coefficient *a*) and the standard error of *b* or s_b. The standard error of *ab* can be shown to equal approximately the square root of $s_a{}^2 s_b{}^2 + b^2 s_a{}^2 + a^2 s_b{}^2$ and so under the null hypothesis that *ab* equals zero, the following

$$\frac{ab}{\sqrt{s_a{}^2 s_b{}^2 + b^2 s_a{}^2 + a^2 s_b{}^2}}$$

is approximately distributed as *Z*. Measures and tests of indirect effects are also available within many structural equation modeling programs.

One might ask whether all of the steps have to be met for there to be mediation. Certainly, Step 4 does not have to be met unless the expectation is for complete mediation. Moreover, Step 1 is not required, but a path from the initial variable to the outcome is implied if Steps 2 and 3 are met.[10] So the essential steps in establishing mediation are Steps 2 and 3.

Example

Morse, Calsyn, Allen, and Kenny (1994) examined the effect of an intervention that was designed to reduce the number of days homeless. The participants in this research were 109 homeless adults in a large Midwestern city, and the intervention was an intensive case management program. A total of 46 persons was randomly assigned to the intervention and the remaining 63 were assigned to a comparison group. The intervention serves as the initial variable and is dummy coded such that 1 is treated and 0 is

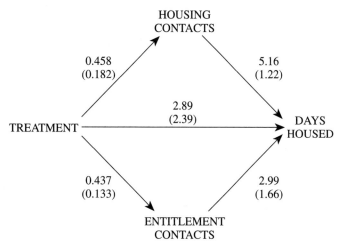

FIGURE 4 **Mediation of Intervention Effects on Homelessness by Housing and Entitlement Contacts.**

control. The outcome measure is the number of days housed per month during a period of 12 to 18 months after the intervention was initiated. For this illustration, two mediators are tested. The first mediator is the number of contacts per month about housing, and the second is the number of contacts per month about entitlements (money). Both mediators were measured for nine months after the intervention was initiated.

The total effect of the intervention on homelessness is 6.56 days, meaning that persons who received intensive case management were housed about one week more per month than those who did not. This effect is statistically significant ($p = .009$). So the Step 1 criterion is met.

Figure 4 presents the estimated coefficients and their standard errors in parentheses for this example. We see that the intervention resulted in both more housing and entitlement contacts. The effect for housing contacts is 0.458 ($p = .013$) and for entitlements it is 0.437 ($p < .001$). Both effects indicate that individuals in the treatment group received an average of about five more contacts per year than did control group members. Because both effects are statistically significant, the Step 2 criterion is met for both mediators.

Also presented in Figure 4 are the effects from the mediators to the outcome. This effect is 5.16 for housing ($p < .001$) and 2.99 for entitlements ($p = .07$, not significant). The effect for the housing contact mediator indicates that for every monthly housing contact, the person was housed about five more days. The Step 3 criterion is met for only the housing contact mediator.

Finally, Figure 4 presents the effect of the intervention on the outcome, controlling for the mediators. That effect is now 2.89 ($p = .23$). Thus, the Step 4 criterion is met. It can then be concluded that housing contacts mediates the effect of the intervention on the outcome.

Because the unmediated effect was 6.56, 56 percent of the total effect is explained. The total reduction in the effect is 2.36 due to housing (0.458 times 5.16) and 1.31 due to entitlements (0.437 times 2.99). The sum of these two effects exactly equals the reduction in the effect of the intervention when the mediators are introduced. Using the Baron and Kenny modification of the Sobel test, the reduction due to housing contacts is statistically significant ($Z = 2.12$, $p = .034$) and the reduction due to entitlements is not ($Z = 1.52$, $p = .13$).

Problems in Testing Mediation

There are several issues that complicate the analysis of mediation. They can be divided into design issues, specification issues, and multilevel data. These issues are considered in turn.

Design Issues

Distal and Proximal Mediation   To demonstrate mediation both paths *a* and *b* [see Figure 3(b)] need to be relatively large. Usually, the maximum size of the product *ab* is *c*, and so as *a* increases, *b* must decrease and vice versa.

The mediator can be too close in time or in the process to the initial variable and so *a* would be relatively large and *b* relatively small. An example of a *proximal* mediator is a manipulation check. The use of a proximal mediator may create multicollinearity which is discussed in the next part.

Alternatively, the mediator can be chosen too close to the outcome and with a *distal* mediator *b* is large and *a* is small. Ideally, standardized *a* and *b* should be comparable in size.

Multicollinearity   If M is a successful mediator, it is necessarily correlated with X due to path a. This correlation, called collinearity, affects the precision of the estimates of the last set of regression equations. If X explains all the variance in M, then there is no unique variance in M to explain Y. The power of the tests of the coefficients b and c' is compromised. The effective sample size for these tests is approximately $N(1 - r_{XM}^2)$ where N is the total sample size and r_{XM} is the correlation between the initial variable and the mediator. So if M is a strong mediator (path a is large), to achieve equivalent power the sample size would have to be larger than what it would be if M were a weak mediator.

Specification Errors

Reverse Causal Effects   The mediator may be caused by the outcome variable (Y would cause M in Figure 3). When the initial variable is a manipulated variable, it cannot be caused by either the mediator or the outcome. But because both mediator and the outcome variables are generally not manipulated variables, they may cause each other. Often if the mediator and the outcome variable were interchanged, the outcome would seem to "cause" the mediator.

Sometimes reverse causal effects can be ruled out theoretically. That is, a causal effect in one direction does not make sense. Design considerations may also weaken the plausibility of reverse causation. Ideally, the mediator should be measured before the outcome variable, as in the Morse et al. (1994) example.

If it can be assumed that c' is zero, then reverse causal effects can be estimated. (A review of the use of instrumental variables in the structural equation identification section may be helpful at this point.) That is, if it can be assumed that there is complete mediation (X does not directly cause Y), the mediator may cause the outcome and the outcome may cause the mediator.

Smith (1982) has developed another method for the estimation of reverse causal effects. Both the mediator and the outcome variables are treated as outcome variables, and they each may mediate the effect of the other. To be able to employ the Smith approach, for both the mediator and the outcome, there must be a different variable that is known to cause each of them but not the other. So a variable must be found that is known to cause the mediator but not the outcome and another variable that is known to cause the outcome but not the mediator. These variables are called *instrumental variables* (see the identification section).

Measurement Error in the Mediator   If the mediator is measured with less than perfect reliability, then the effects are likely biased. The effect of the mediator on the outcome (path b) is likely underestimated and the effect of the initial variable on the outcome (path c') is likely overestimated if ab is positive (which is typical). The overestima-

tion of c' is exacerbated to the extent to which the mediator is caused by the initial variable.

To remove the biasing effect of measurement error, multiple indicators of the mediator can be used to tap a latent variable. Alternatively, instrumental variable estimation can be used, but as before, it must be assumed that c' is zero. If neither of these approaches is used, the researcher needs to demonstrate that the reliability of the mediator is very high so that the bias is fairly minimal.

Omitted Variables   This is the most difficult specification error to solve. The variance that the mediator shares with the outcome may be due to another variable that causes both the mediator and the outcome. Although there has been some work on the omitted variable problem (Mauro, 1990), the only complete solution is to specify and measure such variables and control for their effects.

Sometimes the source of covariance between the mediator and the outcome is a common method effect. Ideally, efforts should be made to ensure that the two variables do not share method effects (e.g., both are self-reports from the same person).

Multilevel Data and Mediational Analyses   With multilevel data, there are two levels; for example, person may be the upper-level unit and time or day the lower-level unit. There are two types of mediation within multilevel models: the initial variable can be either an upper-level variable or a lower-level variable, but for both cases, the mediator and the outcome are lower-level variables. Before reading this part, the reader should have read the earlier section on multilevel modeling.

Upper-level Mediation   Consider the effect of stress on mood. On each day for two weeks, stress and mood are measured for each person. Imagine that half the sample is classified as high on neuroticism and the other half is not. So the mediational question is the extent to which stress mediates the effect of neuroticism on mood.

This data structure naturally lends itself to an investigation of both mediation and moderation (Baron & Kenny, 1986). First, there is the simple mediational hypothesis: those high on neuroticism experience more stress and that stress leads to negative moods. Second, there is the moderation hypothesis that those high on neuroticism may react to stress more than those who are not. So stress might moderate the effect of neuroticism on mood. Following Bolger and Schilling (1991), the total effect of neuroticism on mood can be partitioned into a mediation and a moderation piece.[11]

With multilevel modeling of over-time data, the general hypothesis that person interacts with a within-person variable can be tested. For the example, within levels of neuroticism, stress may have more or less of an effect on mood for some individuals than for others, i.e., some individuals react more to stress than do others. Multilevel modeling provides a method for determining whether processes vary by person.

Lower-level Mediation   We modify the example by making stress the initial variable and adding the lower-level variable, coping, that is assumed to mediate the stress-mood relationship, a model studied by Bolger and Zuckerman (1995). So coping, a lower-level variable, is triggered by stress and coping then elevates mood. It can be tested whether the mediational effects of coping vary across persons. First, the effect of stress could lead to coping for some persons and not for others. Second, coping may improve the mood of some but not others. In this way we can discern how the mediation of coping effects are moderated by individual differences.

Both mediational effects (the effect of stress on coping and the effect of coping on mood) can be treated as dependent variables, and measures of individual differences can be used to predict them. So, for example, it can be tested whether people who receive training in coping with stress do in fact use coping strategies when they experience stress and whether this coping is effective in raising mood. The training variable would serve as a moderator of the mediational process.

SUMMARY

Data analysis in social psychology all too often is a mindless exercise. Data are gathered using a standard design (a factorial experiment) and the same statistical analysis is performed (ANOVA followed by post hoc tests of means). An anthropologist might describe social psychological data analysis as a ritualistic exercise with Greek incantations mixed with practices developed in the early twentieth century to test the relative advantages of crop fertilizers.

Data analysis should be a more thoughtful process. Careful consideration should be given to the process that generated the data. Even with a factorial experiment, attention must be given to model assumptions. We have emphasized the assumption of independence in the first two sections of the chapter, but the other assumptions merit scrutiny (Judd et al., 1995; Wilcox, 1987).

We must learn to model a process not just to analyze data. Mediational analyses are likely to be helpful toward meeting this aim. Generally mediational analyses require structural equation modeling. This chapter has provided a detailed analysis of mediation, as well as provided advice concerning the difficult issue of identification. Moreover, we have discussed mediational analyses of multilevel data.

In the last twenty years we have witnessed a paradigm shift in the analysis of correlational data. Confirmatory factor analysis and structural equation modeling have replaced exploratory factor analysis and multiple regression as the standard methods. We are currently in the early stages of a paradigm shift in the analysis of experimental data. Multilevel modeling is replacing ANOVA. Certainly, ANOVA will remain a basic tool in social psychological research, but it can no longer be considered the only technique. Many models can be more efficiently estimated by multilevel modeling than by ANOVA. More importantly, many scientifically interesting hypotheses can be tested within multilevel modeling that cannot be easily addressed within an ANOVA framework.

Multilevel modeling is the wave of the future, and social psychology must begin to use it in research or other disciplines may lay claim to more of what is traditionally viewed as social psychology. Many traditional social psychological topics, such as group behavior and close relationships, are now being studied more by our colleagues in communications, family studies, and organizational behavior. If we continue to conceptualize social psychological research in terms of 2 × 2 designs and ANOVA, we will further narrow the scope of our field.

NOTES

1. Some meta-analysts are engaging in problematic practices. Occasionally, p values are reported as one-tailed tests when they should be two-tailed. Also very often large-sample theory is used (e.g., a Z test) when there is an available small-sample test (e.g., a t test). Finally, univariate tests (e.g., r or t tests of means) are used when multivariate tests (e.g., multiple regression) should be.

2. Some of the material in this section parallels the discussion of Crits-Christoph and Mintz (1991). Computations based on the formulas in Table 3 of this chapter were able to reproduce many of Crits-Christoph and Mintz's simulation results.

3. If a value of .10 seems too large, it should be realized that the effective alpha for the study would be only .06 because 80 percent of the time the nonindependence would be detected resulting in an alpha of .05 and 20 percent of the time the effective alpha would be .10.

4. Because only positive values of the intraclass correlation make the significance test of treatment effects too liberal (see Table 4), only positive values of the intraclass correlation are tested and so the tests in Table 6 are one-tailed.

5. The intraclass correlations, ρ_G and ρ_{GxA}, when computed using the formulas in Tables 1 and 4, are actually partial correlations. That is, the variance due to G is removed when ρ_{GxA} is computed, and the variance due to GxA is removed when ρ_G is computed. Sometimes the regular, nonpartial correlations are needed, and they are presented in Table 3 as ρ_1 and ρ_2.

6. Though not obvious, σ_d^2 takes on the role of ρ_G (discussed in the unit of analysis section) and σ_f^2 takes on the role of ρ_{GxA}.

7. Note that when r_{23} is zero, the estimate of the loading equals infinity. In physics, a black hole occurs when a particular equation has zero in its denominator. So empirical underidentification is causal modeling's equivalent of a black hole.

8. If an instrumental variable is needed because X has measurement error, then X need have an instrument in only one equation in which it is a causal variable. However, for both spuriousness and feedback, X needs to have an instrumental variable each time such conditions arise.

9. Alternatively one variable in the feedback loop need not have an instrument if the disturbances of the two variables in the loop are uncorrelated.

10. If c' is opposite in sign to ab, then it could be the case that Step 1 is not met, but there is still mediation. In this case the mediator acts like a suppressor variable.

11. Because of the differential weighting of estimators across groups that occurs in multilevel modeling, the total effect does not usually exactly equal the sum of the direct and the mediated or indirect effects.

REFERENCES

Abelson, R. P. (1995). *Statistics as principled argument.* Hillsdale, NJ: Erlbaum.

Aiken, L. S., & West, S. G. (1991). *Multiple regression: Testing and interpreting interactions.* Newbury Park, CA: Sage.

Barcikowski, R. S. (1981). Statistical power with group mean as the unit of analysis. *Journal of Educational Statistics, 6,* 267–285.

Baron, R. M., & Kenny, D. A. (1986). The moderator-mediator variable distinction in social psychological research: Conceptual, strategic and statistical considerations. *Journal of Personality and Social Psychology, 51,* 1173–1182.

Bentler, P. M., & Bonett, D. G. (1980). Significance tests and goodness of fit in the analysis of covariance structures. *Psychological Bulletin, 88,* 588–606.

Bolger, N., & Schilling, E. A. (1991). Personality and the problems of everyday life: The role of neuroticism in exposure and reactivity to daily stressors. [Special Issue: Personality and daily experience.] *Journal of Personality, 59,* 355–386.

Bolger, N., & Zuckerman, A. (1995). A framework for studying personality in the stress process. *Journal of Personality and Social Psychology, 69,* 890–902.

Bollen, K. A. (1989). *Structural equations with latent variables.* New York: Wiley.

Bollen, K. A., & Long, J. S. (Eds.) (1993). *Testing structural equation models.* Newbury Park, CA: Sage.

Breckler, S. J. (1990). Applications of covariance structure modeling in psychology: Cause for concern? *Psychological Bulletin, 107,* 260–273.

Browne, M. W., & Mels, G. (1994). *RAMONA: User's guide.* Ohio State University, Psychology Department.

Bryk, A. S., & Raudenbush, S. W. (1992). *Hierarchical linear models: Applications and data analysis methods.* Newbury Park, CA: Sage.

Bryk, A. S., Raudenbush, S. W., & Congdon, R. T. (1994). *Hierarchical linear modeling with the HLM/2L and HLM/3L programs.* Chicago, IL: Scientific Software International.

Byrne, B. M. (1994). *Structural equation modeling with EQS and EQS/Windows.* Newbury Park, CA: Sage.

Campbell, D. T., & Fiske, D. W. (1959). Convergent and discriminant validation by the multitrait-multimethod matrix. *Psychological Bulletin, 56,* 81–105.

Cohen, J. (1988). *Statistical power analysis for the behavioral sciences* (2nd ed.). Hillsdale, NJ: Erlbaum.

Cooper, H., & Hedges, L. V. (1994). *The handbook of research synthesis.* New York: Russell Sage Foundation.

Crits-Christoph, P., & Mintz, J. (1991). Implications of therapist effects for the design and analysis of comparative studies of pychotherapies. *Journal of Consulting and Clinical Psychology, 59,* 20–26.

Cudeck, R. (1989). Analysis of correlation matrices using covariance structure models. *Psychological Bulletin, 105,* 317–327.

Felson, R. B. (1981). Self- and reflected appraisal among football players: A test of the Meadian hypothesis. *Social Psychology Quarterly, 44,* 116–126.

Goldstein, H. (1995). *Multilevel statistical models.* New York: Halstead Press.

Goldstein, H., Rasbash, J., & Yang, M. (1994). *MLn: User's guide for Version 2.3.* London: Institute of Education, University of London.

Griffin, D., & Gonzalez, R. (1995). Correlational analysis of dyad-level data in the exchangeable case. *Psychological Bulletin, 118,* 430–439.

Harris, R. J. (1994). *ANOVA: An analysis of variance primer.* Itasca, IL: Peacock.

Hayduk, L. A. (1987). *Structural equation modeling with LISREL: Essentials and advances.* Baltimore: Johns Hopkins Press.

Hedeker, D. (1993). *MIXREG. A FORTRAN program for mixed-effects linear regression models.* Chicago, IL: University of Illinois.

Hedeker, D., Gibbons, R. D., & Flay, B. R. (1994). Random-effects regression models for clustered data with an example from smoking prevention research. *Journal of Consulting and Clinical Psychology, 62,* 757–765.

Judd, C. M., & Kenny, D. A. (1981). Process analysis: Estimating mediation in treatment evaluations. *Evaluation Review, 5,* 602–619.

Judd, C. M., & McClelland, G. H. (1989). *Data analysis: A model-comparison approach.* San Diego: Harcourt Brace Jovanovich.

Judd, C. M., & McClelland, G. H. (1998). Measurement. In D. Gilbert, S. T. Fiske, & G. Lindzey (Eds.), *The handbook of social psychology* (4th ed., Vol. 1, pp. 180–232). New York: McGraw-Hill.

Judd, C. M., McClelland, G. H., & Culhane, S. E. (1995). Data analysis: Continuing issues in the everyday analysis of psychological data. *Annual Review of Psychology, 46,* 433–465.

Jussim, L. (1991). Social perception and social reality: A reflection-construction model. *Psychological Review, 98,* 54–73.

Kashy, D. A. (1991). *Levels of analysis of social interaction diaries: Separating the effects of person, partner, day, and interaction* (Ph.D. dissertation, University of Connecticut).

Kashy, D. A., & Kenny, D. A. (1997). The analysis of data from dyads and groups. In H. Reis & C. M. Judd (Eds.), *Handbook of research methods in social psychology.* New York: Cambridge University Press.

Kelley, H. H. (1967). Attribution theory in social psychology. In D. Levine (Ed.), *Nebraska symposium on motivation* (Vol. 15, pp. 192–241). Lincoln: University of Nebraska.

Kelley, H. H., & Thibaut, J. W. (1978). *Interpersonal relations: A theory of independence.* New York: Wiley.

Kenny, D. A, (1979). *Correlation and causality.* New York: Wiley-Interscience.

Kenny, D. A. (1985). Quantitative methods for social psychology. In G. Lindzey & E. Aronson (Eds.), *Handbook of social psychology* (3rd ed., Vol. 1, pp. 487–508). New York: Random House.

Kenny, D. A. (1995). The effect of nonindependence on significance testing in dyadic research. *Personal Relationships, 2,* 67–75.

Kenny, D. A. (1996a). The design and analysis of social interaction research. *Annual Review of Psychology, 47,* 59–86.

Kenny, D. A. (1996b). Models of independence in dyadic research. *Journal of Social and Personal Relationships, 13,* 279–294.

Kenny, D. A., Bolger, N., & Kashy, D. A. (1997). *Estimation of multilevel models using weighted least squares.* Unpublished paper, University of Connecticut.

Kenny, D. A., & Judd, C. M. (1986). Consequences of violating the independence assumption in analysis of variance. *Psychological Bulletin, 99,* 422–431.

Kenny, D. A., & Kashy, D. A. (1992). Analysis of the multitrait-multimethod matrix by confirmatory factor analysis. *Psychological Bulletin, 112,* 165–172.

Kenny, D. A., & La Voie, L. (1985). Separating individual and group effects. *Journal of Personality and Social Psychology, 48,* 339–348.

Koele, P. (1982). Calculating power in analysis of variance. *Psychological Bulletin, 92,* 513–516.

Kraemer, H. C., & Jacklin, C. N. (1979). Statistical analysis of dyadic social behavior. *Psychological Bulletin, 86,* 217–224.

Latané, B. (1981). The psychology of social impact. *American Psychologist, 36,* 343–356.

Loehlin, J. C. (1992). *Latent variable models: An introduction to factor, path, and structural analysis.* Hillsdale, NJ: Erlbaum.

MacCallum, R. C., Roznowski, M., & Necowtiz, L. B. (1992). Model modifications in covariance structure analysis: The problem of capitalization of chance. *Psychological Bulletin, 111,* 490–504.

MacCallum, R. C., Wegener, D. T., Uchino, B. N., & Fabrigar, L. R. (1993). The problem of equivalent models in applications of covariance structure analysis. *Psychological Bulletin, 114,* 185–199.

Marsh, H. W., Balla, J. R., & McDonald, R. P. (1988). Goodness-of-fit indexes in confirmatory factor analysis: The effect of sample size. *Psychological Bulletin, 103,* 391–410.

Mauro, R. (1990). Understanding L.O.V.E. (left out variables error): A method for estimating the effects of omitted variables. *Psychological Bulletin, 108,* 314–329.

Maxwell, S. E., & Delaney, H. D. (1990). *Designing experiments and analyzing data: A model comparison perspective.* Belmont, CA: Wadsworth.

Millsap, R. E (1995). The statistical analysis of method effects in multitrait-multimethod data: A review. In P. E. Shrout & S. T. Fiske (Eds.), *Personality research, methods, and theory: A festschrift honoring Donald W. Fiske* (pp. 93–109). Hillsdale, NJ: Erlbaum.

Morse, G. A., Calsyn, R. J., Allen, G., & Kenny, D. A. (1994). Helping homeless mentally ill people: What variables mediate and moderate program effects? *American Journal of Community Psychology, 22,* 661–683.

Myers, J. L. (1979). *Fundamentals of experimental design* (3rd ed.). Boston: Allyn & Bacon.

Severo, N. C., & Zelen, M. (1960). Normal approximation to the chi-square and non-central *F* probability functions. *Biometrika, 47,* 411–416.

Smith, E. R. (1982). Beliefs, attributions, and evaluations: Nonhierarchical models of mediation in social cognition. *Journal of Personality and Social Psychology, 43,* 248–259.

Sobel, M. E. (1982). Asymptotic confidence intervals for indirect effects in structural models. In S. Leinhardt (Ed.), *Sociological methodology 1982* (pp. 290–312). San Francisco: Jossey-Bass.

Taylor, S. E. (1998). The Social Being in Social Psychology. In D. Gilbert, S. T. Fiske, & G. Lindzey (Eds.), *The handbook of social psychology* (4th ed., Vol. 1, pp. 58–95). New York: McGraw-Hill.

Tesser, A. (1988). Toward a self-evaluation maintenance model of social behavior. In L. Berkowitz (Ed.), *Advances in experimental social psychology* (Vol. 21, pp. 181–227). San Diego: Academic Press.

Wasserman, S., & Faust, K. (1994). *Social network analysis: Methods and applications.* Cambridge, England: Cambridge University Press.

Wilcox, R. R. (1987). New designs in analysis of variance. *Annual Review of Psychology, 38,* 29–60.

Wothke, W. (1995). Covariance components analysis of the multitrait-multimethod matrix. In P. E. Shrout & S. T. Fiske (Eds.), *Personality research, methods, and theory: A festschrift honoring Donald W. Fiske* (pp. 125–144). Hillsdale, NJ: Erlbaum.

PART THREE

INTRAPERSONAL PHENOMENA

CHAPTER SEVEN

ATTITUDE STRUCTURE AND FUNCTION

ALICE H. EAGLY, *Northwestern University*
SHELLY CHAIKEN, *New York University*

INTRODUCTION

Attitudes express passions and hates, attractions and repulsions, likes and dislikes. People have attitudes when they love or hate things or people and when they approve or disapprove of them. Because people express their likes and dislikes in many ways, all aspects of responding, including emotions, cognitions, and overt behavior, are infused with the evaluative meaning that attitudes impart. This chapter explicates the nature of attitudes by discussing their structure and the functions they serve for the people who hold them.

In formal terms, an attitude is a psychological tendency that is expressed by evaluating a particular entity with some degree of favor or disfavor. The idea that an attitude is a psychological tendency treats attitude as a state that is internal to the person and that lasts for a shorter or longer duration. As an internal state, an attitude is not directly observable but is inferred by psychologists from observable responses, as are other hypothetical constructs in psychology. These observable responses consist of evaluative responding that occurs in conjunction with the stimuli that denote the evaluated entity. That attitudes are inferred from observables and thus have the status of a hypothetical construct does not preclude localizing attitudinal processes in particular structures or processes of the brain or otherwise understanding the neural mechanisms underlying attitudinal processes.

An attitude is expressed by evaluative responses of some degree of favorability or unfavorability. A person is biased toward favorable responses if the attitude is positive and toward unfavorable responses if the attitude is negative. These evaluative responses can encompass a wide range of covert and overt responses. In general, evaluative responses are those that express approval or disapproval, approach or avoidance, and like or dislike.

Because the person directs these evaluative responses toward a particular entity, the stimuli that elicit the responses allow observers to identify this evaluated entity, which is termed the *attitude object* in attitude theory. For example, if an individual is verbally and nonverbally disparaging when interacting with or talking about members of a particular minority group, that individual can be described as holding a negative attitude toward this group of people. The negative attitude is an internal state inferred on the basis of this unfavorable responding to stimuli consisting of members of the minority group. In this instance, the group is the entity, or attitude object, that is evaluated.

An attitude object can be anything that is discriminated or held in mind by the individual. Attitude objects may be abstract (e.g., conservatism) or concrete (e.g., the Sears Tower) as well as individual (e.g., Monica Seles) or collective (e.g., professional athletes). The attitude objects that are commonly studied in attitude research include social policies, social groups, and individual persons, as well as behaviors and classes of behaviors. A researcher might thus investigate attitudes toward (a) social policies such as instituting a flat tax or allowing abortion, (b) social groups such as lawyers or Asian Americans, (c) individual persons such as Bill Clinton or one's dating partner, (d) behaviors such as obtaining a tetanus shot or eating tofu, and (e) classes of behaviors such as maintaining a healthy lifestyle or taking environmentally friendly actions.

We thank Blair Johnson, Neal Roese, Wendy Wood, Mark Zanna, and the editors for their helpful comments on earlier drafts.

Specialized terms are often applied to certain classes of attitudes. For example, attitudes toward minority groups are often called *prejudice,* especially if these attitudes are negative. Attitudes toward individual people are generally called *liking* or *interpersonal attraction.* Attitude toward one's self is generally termed *self-esteem.* Attitudes toward relatively abstract goals or end states of human existence (e.g., equality, freedom, salvation) are usually known as *values* (see Seligman, Olson, & Zanna, 1996). Finally, attitudes with implications for governmental policy or relations between social groups are sometimes called *social attitudes* or *political attitudes.*

The definition of attitudes in terms of people's evaluations of entities is consensual in psychology and the social sciences, although this consensus developed gradually as theorists' rather global definitions (e.g., G. W. Allport, 1935) were replaced by more precise definitions (e.g., Zanna & Rempel, 1988). Nonetheless, competing with the contemporary definition of attitudes as evaluative tendencies are narrower definitions in terms of particular evaluative processes, such as Fazio's (1989) definition of attitude as an association in memory between an attitude object and an evaluation. Such definitions, like earlier definitions in Hullian terms (e.g., Doob, 1947), use a specialized terminology that places the attitude concept within a particular theoretical tradition. These definitions are, however, compatible with the general definition of attitude as an evaluative tendency.

People may have predispositions to react positively or negatively to a novel attitude object. Some of these predispositions may reflect evolutionary adaptations, although most evidence on this issue is quite indirect (e.g., Buss & Schmitt, 1993). More direct evidence that attitudes may have biological substrates comes from behavior genetics estimates that some attitudes are substantially heritable (Tesser, 1993). Important as these predispositions to evaluate may be, they are not the same thing as attitudes because attitudes necessarily develop from evaluative responding to an attitude object. Thus, individuals do not have an attitude until they first encounter the attitude object (or information about it) and respond evaluatively to it on an affective, cognitive, or behavioral basis. For example, although humans are apparently predisposed to react negatively to sour tastes (e.g., Ganchrow, Streiner, & Daher, 1983), an individual would not have a negative attitude toward a sour-tasting fruit such as raw gooseberries until one was experienced in some fashion—for example, tasted and perceived to have a bad taste. Only after this first encounter would the individual have started to form a negative attitude toward raw gooseberries. The negativity of the attitude would be biologically influenced, but the formation of the attitude nonetheless requires direct or indirect experience with the attitude object.

Evaluative responding—whether it be covert or overt, implicit or explicit, automatic or deliberate—can thus produce a psychological tendency to respond with a particular degree of evaluation when subsequently encountering the attitude object. If this response tendency is established, the person can be said to have formed an attitude toward the object. Although it is certainly possible that a memory of one's overall evaluation (e.g., a dislike of gooseberries) may be stored and subsequently retrieved in future encounters with the attitude object, this type of conscious recollection of an abstract evaluation may be somewhat atypical of attitudinal responding (see Eiser, 1994). Instead, the tendency to evaluate may be carried forward to new situations by memories that are more episodic and less abstract (e.g., a fuzzy recollection of having tasted a sour gooseberry). Moreover, if asked to describe their evaluative state (e.g., to evaluate Clinton's program to reduce teenage smoking on an approve vs. disapprove scale), people may construct this evaluation on the spot from information that is temporarily accessible or situationally present (Wilson & Hodges, 1992). In addition, the mere presence of the attitude object can automatically produce a tendency to evaluate by preconscious processes not dependent on any conscious recollection of one's attitude or reflection on prior or current experience with the attitude object (Bargh, 1997). In agreement with the view that attitude can influence responding without conscious awareness, Greenwald and Banaji (1995) introduced the concept of *implicit attitudes,* which cannot be introspectively identified and consist of "traces of past experience" (p. 8) that then mediate evaluative responding. The attitude itself is the tendency to evaluate and is thus a mental representation in the form of a particular state (see E. R. Smith, 1998, in this *Handbook*)—that is, a state in which the individual engages in positive or negative evaluative responding in relation to the attitude object. The individual may be aware or unaware of this state.

The idea that attitudes develop on the basis of evaluative responding implies that an attitude in some fashion encompasses the direct and indirect experiences that an individual has with the attitude object. Understanding why certain types of experiences produce positive evaluative responses and other types produce negative responses—that is, understanding attitude formation—is beyond the scope of this chapter (see Brendl & Higgins, 1996; Petty & Wegener, 1998, in this *Handbook*). Insofar as these positive and negative experiences become attached to attitude objects in perceivers' minds, these perceivers would acquire mental associations linking the attitude object with relevant prior experience. These associations may have regularities that lead psychologists to ascribe various structural properties to them, and in this chapter the term *intra-attitudinal structure* refers to this aspect of attitudes. Also, because people form attitudes toward many different entities, attitudes may be interrelated in people's minds. These more global structures that encompass more than one attitude are termed *inter-attitudinal structure* in this chapter.

Intra-attitudinal and inter-attitudinal structure reflect contrasting ways that attitudes can be formed. One can form an attitude in an experiential way based on direct or indirect cognitive, affective, or behavioral responding to the attitude object. This intra-attitudinal mode of attitude formation entails storing the information produced by one's responses as associations between the attitude object and these responses. As evaluative meaning is abstracted from these associations, an attitude is formed as a generalization from more elementary associations.

Alternatively, one can form an attitude by forging linkages between the attitude object and other attitude objects. These linkages are stored, along with the target attitude itself. Often this mode of attitude formation entails an inference by which a new attitude is deduced from a more abstract or general attitude that has already been formed. Although the structure of most attitudes may have both intra-attitudinal and inter-attitudinal aspects, there would be considerable variation in the extent to which attitudes have been formed on one or the other of these bases.

The perspective that attitudes are tendencies that can be described as having various forms of structure does not assume that this structure is static. Consistent with the idea that attitude structure is an aspect of the mental state that constitutes attitude, the structure of an individual's attitude toward an object could be quite different at different points in time, even in the absence of new experience with the object. Helpful in understanding why the structure of a particular attitude can show this variability is the distinction between available and accessible structure (see Higgins, 1996). The *availability* of a structure is its storage in memory so that it can potentially be activated, whereas the *accessibility* of a structure is its activation potential—that is, its readiness to be activated at a particular point in time. Although an individual may thus have stored in memory an extensive set of associations concerning a social issue such as welfare reform, not all aspects of this structure would necessarily be accessible at any one point in time and therefore have the potential to influence responding. The accessibility of attitude structure would be a product of the demands of the perceiver's situation as well as a variety of other factors. An individual's attitude toward welfare reform might thus be activated on different occasions, accompanied by differing intra-attitudinal and inter-attitudinal associations or entirely devoid of such associations. It is the activated attitude and attitude structure that are most relevant to understanding attitudes' impact on information-processing and behavior.

This chapter starts out with the issue of attitudes' internal and external structure and ends with the motivational, or functional, issue of the goals that attitudes serve. The structural issue addresses the question of what attitudes are, and the motivational issue addresses the question of why people hold attitudes. After reviewing the classic tripartite cognitive-affective-behavioral analysis of attitudes and introducing the major approaches to understanding attitudes' internal and external structure, this chapter examines the important concept of attitude strength, which has been given a variety of definitions. The chapter proceeds by considering attitudinal selectivity at various stages of information processing—that is, the tendency to process information differentially depending on its consistency with one's attitudes. The next discussion pertains to the relation of attitudes to overt behaviors, one of the three response classes through which attitudes are expressed. The final section concerns the functional issue of how attitudes relate to people's general goals. For example, attitudes may enable people to maintain relationships with others, or they may allow them to express their personal values. As shown later in this chapter, understanding attitudes' functions should itself be considered a structural issue because the embedding of attitudes in molar structures of values, motives, and personal goals is the focus of theorizing in this tradition. Questions concerning attitudes' structure and function are thus closely intertwined.

COGNITIVE-AFFECTIVE-BEHAVIORAL ANALYSIS OF ATTITUDES

The responses elicited by attitude objects have often been described by psychologists as belonging to three classes—cognitive, affective, and behavioral (e.g., Breckler, 1984; D. Katz & Stotland, 1959; Rosenberg & Hovland, 1960). The cognitive category contains thoughts, the affective category consists of feelings or emotions, and the behavioral category encompasses actions and intentions to act. These thoughts, feelings, and behaviors are all directed to the entity that is the object of the attitude. Although factor analyses of attitudinal responding do not necessarily distinguish these three classes of responses as three dimensions or components of attitude (see Eagly & Chaiken, 1993), the tripartite cognitive-affective-behavioral terminology provides a convenient language for describing attitudinal phenomena. As several sections of this chapter demonstrate, the distinction between cognitive and affective aspects of attitudes has proven to be particularly helpful in understanding various attitudinal phenomena.

The cognitions or thoughts that are associated with attitudes are typically termed *beliefs* by attitude theorists. Beliefs are understood to be associations or linkages that people establish between the attitude object and various attributes that they ascribe to them (Fishbein & Ajzen, 1974). Beliefs express positive or negative evaluation of greater or lesser extremity and occasionally are exactly neutral in their evaluative content. Many beliefs are concrete, in the sense that they reflect specific images (e.g., one's image of Monica Seles being stabbed in the back). Often beliefs are more abstract, sometimes because they summarize many observations of similar events (e.g., Seles might be deemed to have a "powerful backhand").

Attitudes also encompass affective reactions that were elicited by the attitude object and therefore became associated with it. The affective aspect of attitude structure consists of feelings, moods, emotions, and sympathetic nervous-system activity that people have experienced in relation to an attitude object and subsequently associate with it (e.g., the pleasure elicited by hearing Dvořák's Cello Concerto). Like beliefs, these affects might reflect particular experiences or become more generalized by summarizing responses that occur on multiple occasions. Like cognitive responses, these affective responses also express positive or negative evaluation of greater or lesser extremity.

In contemporary usage affect is not isomorphic with evaluation, and the two terms should not be used interchangeably, as they were in some earlier treatments of attitude (Fishbein & Ajzen, 1975; Rosenberg, 1960) and even in some contemporary treatments (Markus & Zajonc, 1985). In recognition of the large body of research on affect and emotion, affect should refer distinctively to emotions and feelings, whereas evaluation refers to a state that is not necessarily rooted in affective experience. The definitions of evaluation and affect in attitude theory also clarify the undesirability of regarding affect as a general category that encompasses evaluation, as in Fiske and Taylor's (1991) definition of affect as "a generic term for a whole range of preferences, evaluations, moods, and emotions" (p. 410). Attitudes, understood as general evaluations of attitude objects, can stem from purely cognitive or behavioral responding and thus may have no affective aspect at all. To summarize, whereas evaluation is an intervening state that accounts for the covariation between classes of stimuli and the evaluative responses elicited by the stimuli, affect is only one of three general types of responding by which people form their attitudes and subsequently express them.

The behavioral aspect of intra-attitudinal structure refers to associations that encompass a person's overt actions toward the attitude object as well as intentions to act, which are not necessarily expressed in overt behavior. Although representations of particular behaviors become associated with attitude objects, behavioral representations may, like cognitions and affects, become generalized on the basis of repeated responding (e.g., attending concerts that feature pieces by Dvořák). Like cognitive and affective responses, behavioral responses also express positive or negative evaluation of greater or lesser extremity.

Consonant with the idea that there are three classes of attitudinal responses is attitude theorists' usual assumption that attitudes may have three different types of antecedents—cognitive, affective, and behavioral. Yet, different attitude theories have typically emphasized a particular mode of forming attitudes. Theories of message-based persuasion have often assumed a cognitive learning process whereby people gain information about the attitude object

that leads them to form beliefs about it. Changed attitudes are assumed to follow from recipients' derivation of their attitudes from the altered or new beliefs that they form from exposure to the information.

In contrast, an emphasis on affective or emotional experiences is inherent in a number of theories of attitude formation, especially the classical conditioning model of attitudes. At least from the perspective of early theoretical accounts of classical conditioning (e.g., Staats & Staats, 1958), attitude is a product of the pairing of an attitude object with a stimulus that elicits an affective response. As a result of repeated association, the attitude object comes to elicit this affective response, and an attitude is thereby formed. In developing another perspective that gives priority to affect, Zajonc (1980, 1984) argued that "preferences" (i.e., evaluations) are based primarily on affective responses, which are considered automatic insofar as they are quite immediate and unmediated by thinking.

The idea that attitudes derive from behavioral responses was clearly expressed in Bem's (1972) self-perception account of attitude formation. He argued that people tend to infer attitudes that are consistent with their prior behavior, at least if they do not think that external forces compelled them to engage in the behavior. In addition, learning theorists have described attitudes as deriving from behavioral responses. In the tradition of stimulus-response behavior theory, when overt behaviors (or covert cognitive responses) elicited by attitude objects are rewarded or punished, implicit evaluative responses occur (e.g., Doob, 1947; Hovland, Janis, & Kelley, 1953). Learning theorists regarded these implicit evaluative responses as synonymous with attitude.

Even though attitudes may be expressed through cognitive, affective, and behavioral responses and formed through responding of each of these types, attitudes do not necessarily have all three aspects, either at the point of their formation or at the point of attitudinal responding. Attitudes can be formed primarily or exclusively on the basis of any one of the three types of processes. Some attitudes are thus formed on the basis of acquiring beliefs about the attitude object, whereas others might be formed primarily by affective or behavioral processes. Especially when people directly encounter attitude objects, attitude formation probably occurs by all of these processes (see Zanna & Rempel, 1988). Just as attitudes can be formed through one or more of these types of processes, attitudes can be expressed through one or more response classes.

VARIETIES OF INTRA-ATTITUDINAL STRUCTURE

Traditionally attitudes have been measured along a bipolar dimension that runs from highly favorable to highly unfavorable to the attitude object. If theorists assume that attitude structure mirrors this operational definition, attitudes could not have anything but relatively simple structural properties. However, the great majority of attitude theories have been silent on the issue of whether a bipolar dimension can be an aspect of attitude structure and have instead described structure in terms of attitude objects' associations with beliefs, affects, and behaviors. Because these associations can themselves have a variety of structural properties and can relate to abstract evaluation in differing ways, understanding intra-attitudinal structure has emerged as central to modern attitude theory. The guiding assumption in this work is that attitudinal responding can be better predicted if attitudes' internal structure is taken into account along with the sheer favorableness versus unfavorableness of the overall attitude.

Dimensional Attitude Structure

Even though researchers typically assess individual differences in attitude by placing people on a bipolar evaluative continuum (see Himmelfarb, 1993), attitude theorists have not routinely assumed that attitude structure encompasses a continuum on which people locate their own attitudes. The issues of assessment and of psychological structure are not the same. Just as personality researchers who measure a trait on a high versus low dimension do not assume that this trait dimension exists in the minds of their respondents, attitude researchers who measure an attitude on a pro versus con dimension do not ordinarily assume that this attitudinal dimension exists in the minds of their respondents. That attitude theorists have typically treated attitudes as a point on a dimension at the level of individual psychological structure is a misconception found in the writing of some critics of attitude theory (e.g., Eiser, 1994; Ostrom, 1987). This misconception probably reflects their failure to distinguish between dimensional measurement, which *is* typically used by researchers, and dimensional attitudinal structure, which is *not* ordinarily posited by theorists. The assumption that people encode, store, and retrieve attitude-relevant information in terms of a *bipolar evaluative dimension* or *schema* is a specialized assumption that is not evident in most theories of attitudes but was given limited development primarily in two contexts—namely, in research on the processing of attitude-relevant information and in social judgment theory, a general theory of attitudes and attitude change.

It is no doubt true that, especially on widely debated social and political issues, people sometimes recognize that their own attitudes represent one side of a two-sided issue and therefore in this limited respect perceive their attitudes as existing on a dimension. In support of this viewpoint, Judd and Kulik (1980) argued that people conceptualize their own attitudes in terms of a bipolar continuum of knowledge, defined on one pole by attitude-relevant infor-

mation that they endorse and on the opposite pole by information that they reject but perceive that others endorse. The abortion issue probably fits this description in the minds of many citizens, who are aware of prolife and prochoice arguments and constituencies. Nonetheless, they endorse only one of these viewpoints and base their attitudes on information and other experience that is associated with one side of the issue. Judd and Kulik compared reactions to information that fits such a bipolar continuum, in the sense that the evaluative implications of the information are located at one or the other end of it, with reactions to information that fits it less well, because its evaluative implications are more neutral. They reasoned that information should be processed more easily to the extent that it fits the continuum. The evidence that these researchers obtained for this ease of processing consisted of somewhat faster responses and better memory for statements that were agreeable or disagreeable compared with more neutral statements.

Pratkanis (1989) enlarged this idea about dimensional structure by arguing that attitudes can have bipolar or unipolar structure—that is, people may represent knowledge on both sides of an attitudinal continuum or on only their own side (see also Feather, 1969). To the extent that people are unipolar and thereby possess mainly knowledge that is congruent with their own position, they may find it difficult to encode attitudinally uncongenial information. Conversely, to the extent that people are bipolar and thereby familiar with both supporting and opposing viewpoints, uncongenial information may be processed as easily as congenial information. Pratkanis's data suggested that bipolar structures may be common for controversial social issues like abortion, whereas unipolar structures may be common for a variety of other topics like sports and music, for which people have little sense of opposition to their own attitudes. He also produced some evidence that the bipolarity versus unipolarity of attitudinal structures affects the processing of attitude-relevant information (see subsequent discussion of attitudinal selectivity).

The idea that attitudes on controversial issues often have bipolar structures is inherent in Sherif and Sherif's social judgment theory (C. W. Sherif, Sherif, & Nebergall, 1965; M. Sherif & Hovland, 1961). The Sherifs assumed that people represent their attitudes in terms of a dimensional schema, which they termed a psychosocial scale or internal reference scale. They further proposed that people divide the evaluative continuum associated with an attitude into three ranges or latitudes, which are known as the latitudes of acceptance, rejection, and noncommitment. The latitude of acceptance contains information on an issue that a person finds acceptable, and the latitude of rejection contains unacceptable information. The latitude of noncommitment contains information found neither acceptable nor unacceptable. These researchers examined latitudes on social issues by presenting respondents with lists of statements that ranged from highly favorable to highly unfavorable toward a given attitude object (e.g., legalized abortion). Respondents would indicate which statements on such a list were acceptable and which were unacceptable; the remaining statements constituted the latitude of noncommitment. Although this three-latitude approach has proven quite durable in attitude research (e.g., B. T. Johnson et al., 1995), this division should be regarded as merely one version of a more general structural property of attitudinal dimensions, their *articulation*. This property was defined by Scott (1969, p. 263) as "the number of reliable distinctions" that an individual makes on a dimension. Recognizing that people differ in their articulation of attitudinal dimensions, the Sherifs hypothesized that people spontaneously group attitudinal positions on an issue into relatively few categories to the extent that they are highly involved in the issue (see C. W. Sherif, Sherif, & Nebergall, 1965).

Another consideration relevant to the dimensionality of attitudes is that on many social and political issues people who strongly agree with statements at one end of a conventional attitudinal continuum may be indifferent rather than truly opposed to statements at the other end. Consistent with this idea, Kerlinger (1984) showed that liberals, who generally favor ideas such as participatory social equality, were more indifferent than opposed to the values of the conservative agenda. Similarly, he showed that conservatives, who favored ideas such as the importance of business and industry in society, were more indifferent than opposed to the values of the liberal agenda. Kerlinger's research and that of several other researchers (e.g., Kristiansen & Zanna, 1988; Tourangeau, Rasinski, & D'Andrade, 1991; van der Pligt & Eiser, 1984) showed that people who hold presumably opposing attitudes base their attitudes on quite different considerations and may not clearly reject the beliefs held by people in the opposite camp. It may be mainly in the face of clear-cut social conflict on an issue that people's attitudes become bipolar in the sense that they divide their knowledge into clusters of congenial and uncongenial ideas, as suggested by the notion of latitudes of acceptance and rejection. Hot-button social issues such as abortion and affirmative action may thus commonly exist as bipolar dimensions in citizens' minds, whereas most other issues may not produce this structure.

Beliefs Associated with Attitudes

In attitude theory, beliefs are a basic building block of attitudes in the sense that attitudes are assumed to reflect the beliefs that people hold about attitude objects. In this approach, beliefs are understood as the associations that perceivers establish between the attitude object and various attributes. In forming attitudes, people abstract the evaluative meaning from these beliefs, although of course attitudes may be based on noncognitive experiences as well.

The beliefs that perceivers hold about social groups have been especially interesting to social psychologists, who refer to these beliefs as stereotypes. Ashmore and Del Boca's (1981, p. 16) frequently cited definition of stereotype as "a set of beliefs about the personal attributes of a group of people" makes explicit this treatment of stereotypes. Consistent with attitude theory's assumption that attitudes derive at least in part from the evaluative meaning of the beliefs associated with attitude objects, social psychologists treat stereotypes as a determinant of prejudice, when prejudice is understood as a negative attitude toward a group (Dovidio et al., 1996; Eagly & Mladinic, 1989).

Attitude theorists have classically represented beliefs in a propositional form that links an attitude object (e.g., abolishing capital punishment) to some other entity (e.g., violent crime) by means of a verb or other relational term expressing association or dissociation (e.g., would increase or would decrease) (e.g., Fishbein & Ajzen, 1975). The other entities to which attitude objects can be linked are diverse and frequently are expressed in adjectival form (e.g., humane, as in "Abolishing capital punishment would be humane"). This propositional mode of representing beliefs can be reconstrued in the associative network terms that have been popular for some years among cognitive psychologists (e.g., J. R. Anderson & Bower, 1974; Bower, 1981) and social psychologists (e.g., Wyler & Srull, 1989). Specifically, the attitude object and the entities with which it is associated can be regarded as linked nodes in a propositional network.[1] This associative network approach incorporates additional propositions, such as the idea that links between nodes are strengthened every time the nodes are simultaneously activated (see Higgins, 1989; Judd & Brauer, 1995; and subsequent discussion of balance theory).

Some of attitude theorists' interest in beliefs has been directed to the question of whether attitudes can be successfully predicted from beliefs' evaluative content. The most popular framework for answering this question is the expectancy-value model. Its central idea is that attitudes are a function of beliefs, when beliefs are rendered as the sum of the expected values of the attributes ascribed to an attitude object. These expected values have two components: the expectancy component of each attribute is the subjective probability that the attitude object has or is characterized by the attribute, and the value component is the subjective evaluation attached to the attribute. To predict an attitude, the expectancy and value terms associated with each attribute are multiplied together, and these products are added. Hence, the expectancy-value model of attitudes can be summarized as follows:

Attitude = Σ Expectancy × Value.   (1)

Although the expectancy-value approach to understanding relations of beliefs to attitudes was first proposed by a group of social psychologists at the University of Michigan (e.g., Peak, 1955; Rosenberg, 1956), Fishbein (1967a, 1967b) developed this approach substantially in the 1960s. Fishbein's form of the expectancy-value equation is the following:

$$A_o = \sum_{i=1}^{n} b_i e_i,$$ (2)

where A_o is the attitude toward the object, action, or event, o; b_i is the strength of the belief i about o (expressed as the subjective probability that o has attribute i); e_i is the evaluation of attribute i; and n is the number of attributes. The beliefs that are considered relevant to predicting attitude at a particular point in time are those that are activated and attended to at that time.

As initially shown by Fishbein (1967a, 1967b), attitudes are ordinarily positively correlated with their summed expectancy-value products. In studies in this tradition, attitudes were assessed by relatively direct measures such as the semantic differential or a single-item self-report of favorability toward the attitude object. To assess beliefs, investigators generally had respondents use rating scales to assign probabilities and evaluations to beliefs that pretesting had established were commonly held by members of the respondent population. Subsequently researchers raised questions about whether such evidence clearly indicates that beliefs causally determine attitudes, because the beliefs elicited by such techniques can serve merely as indicants of an attitude in the sense that they are determined by the attitude and constructed on the spot (see Eagly, Mladinic, & Otto, 1994). More convincing evidence that beliefs may determine attitudes follows from open-ended elicitation of respondents' idiosyncratic reports of those beliefs that are salient for them personally. Because this free-response method encourages respondents to list only the beliefs that they actually hold, it lessens the problem of attitude-to-belief inferences, which are invited by rating-scale methods that force respondents to rate an attitude object on attributes that they may never have considered ascribing to it. In studies using these free-response methods, which are less contaminated by attitude-to-belief inferences, correlations between expectancy-value products and attitudes are ordinarily positive, although not necessarily high (e.g., Eagly et al., 1994; Esses, Haddock, & Zanna, 1993).

Algebraic approaches such as N. H. Anderson's information integration theory (e.g., 1981a, 1981b) provide a wider range of mathematical models for representing beliefs' relations to attitudes. From this perspective, the expectancy-value model advances only one of several equations that might provide an adequate mathematical model of the relation between beliefs and attitudes. The broader information integration approach shares with the expectancy-value model the representation of each belief by a scale value on an evaluative scale and a weight that expresses the belief's importance as a determinant of attitude. However, in information integration theory, these weights can be coordinated to various features of beliefs—not necessarily to the strength of their association to the attitude object, which is the feature that expectancy-value models render as beliefs' subjective probability. For example, weights might be coordinated instead to beliefs' accessibility. Although these weighted beliefs might be averaged or added to produce the attitude, averaging models have proven to have wider applicability in attitude research (see Eagly & Chaiken, 1993). In contrast, the expectancy-value equation is strictly an adding model. Therefore, the expectancy-value model is properly considered one member of the family of stimulus combination rules that may provide appropriate algebraic models of beliefs' relations to attitudes.

Complexity of Beliefs

Among the various structural properties of the beliefs that are associated with attitudes, one of the most important is *complexity*, a property that has been given differing names, including cognitive complexity (Bieri, 1966), dimensionality (Scott, 1963), differentiation (Zajonc, 1960), and integrative complexity (Tetlock, 1989). Despite these different names and the wide variety of measurement instruments used to assess this structural property (see O'Keefe & Sypher, 1981; Scott, 1969), these various approaches share a definition of complexity as the dimensionality of the beliefs that a person holds about an attitude object, or, more formally, as the number of dimensions needed to describe the space utilized by the attributes ascribed to the attitude object. Consistent with this definition, complexity pertains, not to the evaluative meaning that people abstract from the attributes people ascribe to an attitude object, but to the degree to which these attributes tap distinctive dimensions of meaning. For example, two people may hold equally positive attitudes toward Nelson Mandela, but one person's beliefs may encompass only one attribute (e.g., that he is an effective leader) and the other person's beliefs may encompass multiple attributes (e.g., effective leadership, personal charisma, moral authority, and personal warmth). Multiple attributes confer complexity on the beliefs ascribed to an attitude object.

Understanding the relation between belief complexity and attitudinal extremity has been a major goal of attitude researchers' work on this structural variable. This issue is whether more complex beliefs would be found among people who have more extreme or more moderate attitudes (e.g., toward a social group such as the elderly). Linville (1982) established that greater complexity was associated with moderation of attitudes. However, other evidence had associated greater complexity with more extreme attitudes (e.g., Tesser & Leone, 1977). This apparent discrepancy in findings turns out to be explicable in terms of the extent to which the beliefs that researchers assessed were intercorrelated and therefore tended to be evaluatively redundant. Specifically, Judd and Lusk (1984) showed that complexity is associated with moderate attitudes when researchers (e.g., Linville) assess beliefs on uncorrelated (or orthogonal) dimensions, which tend to convey dissimilar evaluative meaning. Because the dissimilar evaluative meaning conveyed by these uncorrelated beliefs would tend to cancel when aggregated, attitudes would be relatively moderate. However, complexity is associated with extreme evaluations when beliefs are correlated and therefore somewhat evaluatively redundant. Because the similar evaluative meaning conveyed by these correlated beliefs would tend to cumulate when aggregated, attitudes would become relatively extreme (see also Lusk & Judd, 1988; Millar & Tesser, 1986b).

A specialized definition of the complexity of the beliefs underlying attitudes has been examined extensively in several investigators' research on *integrative complexity* (e.g., Schroder, Driver, & Streufert, 1967; Suedfeld & Ramirez, 1977; Tetlock, 1989). This version of the complexity variable encompasses, in addition to the dimensionality of beliefs, the extent to which the dimensions are perceived as linked to, or integrated with, one another by logical or causal bonds. With low integration, the various dimensions of a belief structure are perceived as relatively isolated properties of an attitude object, whereas with high integration, the dimensions are perceived to operate interactively and contingently. These features of belief structure are assessed by applying a coding system to verbal material that is elicited from participants or located in archival sources (see Tetlock, 1989).

Focusing on the relation between belief complexity and extremity of political attitudes on a liberal versus conservative dimension, Tetlock (1989) found that political extremists of both the left and the right in the United States and Great Britain were less integratively complex in their political reasoning than politicians closer to the middle of the political spectrum. These findings, mirroring those of Linville (1982), probably reflect the tendency for Tetlock's method of assessing beliefs' integrative complexity to treat beliefs as relatively independent of one another and therefore as evaluatively nonredundant.

The greater integrative complexity of attitudinally moderate individuals is explicated by Tetlock's *value pluralism model,* whose central tenet is that people who are integratively complex on an issue tend to endorse values that have conflicting evaluative implications for the issue (Tetlock, 1989; Tetlock, Peterson, & Lerner, 1996). For example,

people who are integratively complex on the issue of maintaining profitable trade relations with countries that deny basic civil liberties (and who therefore tend to hold relatively moderate attitudes) might perceive that this policy would enhance one of their values and diminish another. The enhanced value might be "maintaining a comfortable and prosperous life," and the diminished value might be "insuring that people have individual freedom." If, as in this illustration, one value fosters a positive attitude on an issue and the other value fosters a negative attitude, bringing both values to bear on the issue should induce complex thinking, at least to the extent that people who hold both values try to reconcile their conflicting implications (see Tetlock et al., 1996). In a particularly interesting demonstration of this point, Tetlock, Peterson, and Armor (1994) examined the slavery debate in antebellum America by coding historical texts (e.g., speeches, writings) for integrative complexity. They found that the beliefs of both abolitionists and slavery supporters were less complex than those of political figures who were more middle-of-the-road on the slavery issue. In addition, integrative complexity increased as politicians endorsed values that were regarded as in conflict in that historical period. In emphasizing the associations between attitudes and values, Tetlock raised a set of issues that are discussed in this chapter as aspects of inter-attitudinal structure.

Evaluative Consistency of Beliefs and Other Constituents of Attitude

In addition to the complexity of beliefs about attitude objects, their evaluative consistency, or coherence, is an important aspect of intra-attitudinal structure. The overall evaluation implied by a person's beliefs about an object may be more or less consistent with the person's abstract evaluation, or overall attitude. For example, a person may evaluate "doctors" very favorably yet hold beliefs about them that, on the average, imply a less positive evaluation or even a negative evaluation (e.g., "Doctors keep you waiting"; "Doctors charge a lot of money"). In addition, the evaluative implications of a person's beliefs may be more or less consistent with one another. This inconsistency within a set of beliefs could be manifested, for example, by a person holding some negative beliefs about doctors but also some positive beliefs (e.g., "Doctors help you get well").

These two structural properties, both of which take beliefs' consistency into account, do not exhaust the intra-attitudinal issue of evaluative consistency, because attitudes may be based on affective and behavioral experience with attitude objects as well as on cognitive experience. Therefore, in addition to consistency between attitudes and their constituent beliefs, it is important to consider consistency between attitudes and their constituent affects and behaviors. Attitudes can thus be more or less consistent with the overall evaluation implied by either affective associations or behavioral associations to the attitude object. And just as beliefs can vary in their evaluative consistency with one another, affects can be internally consistent or inconsistent, and so can behaviors. Moreover, evaluative consistency can also vary *across* response classes—for example, a person's beliefs about an attitude object could imply a different abstract evaluation of the object than the person's affective associations. Manifesting inconsistency across beliefs and affects, people who believe that doctors are helpful and caring could nonetheless feel anxious and fearful when interacting with them. The term *ambivalence* is often used to describe inconsistencies in evaluative responding that occur across response classes or within a response class, especially when this inconsistency is so marked that, as in the example, an individual could be described as holding two attitudes, one positive and one negative. These various forms of intra-attitudinal evaluative consistency are considered in this section.

Consistency between Attitudes and the Three Classes of Evaluative Responding There is good reason to expect overall consistency between attitudes and associated beliefs, affects, and behaviors. After all, an attitude is formed on the basis of cognitive, affective, and behavioral responding to an attitude object and, once the attitude is formed, it exerts an attitude-congruent bias on people's subsequent thoughts, feelings, and behavior related to the attitude object. In fact, as already explained in this chapter, quantitative models of the belief-attitude relation regard people as forming their attitudes by integrating the evaluative content of their beliefs. As such, these models assume an overall consistency between beliefs and attitudes. Although rarely done, these models could also be used to explore, in quantitative terms, the contribution of affective and behavioral information to attitudes (e.g., M. F. Kaplan, 1991). People may thus form (or update) their attitudes by integrating the evaluative meaning of their affective and behavioral responses to attitude objects. As in these models' treatment of the belief-attitude relation, such applications would assume an overall consistency between affect and attitudes and between behavior and attitudes. Nonetheless, the idea that attitudes are generally correlated with the evaluative implications of their associated beliefs, affects, and behaviors does not preclude thinking about such consistency as a variable property of attitude structure. In the discussion that follows, these properties are labeled *evaluative-cognitive* consistency, *evaluative-affective* consistency, and *evaluative-behavioral* consistency.

Evaluative-cognitive consistency refers to the degree of consistency between one's overall, abstract evaluation of an attitude object and the evaluative meaning of one's beliefs about the object. Although evaluative-cognitive consistency was discussed by several theorists as early as the 1950s (e.g., Abelson & Rosenberg, 1958; Festinger, 1957), it was Rosenberg (e.g., 1960, 1968) who first proposed this form of consistency as a variable property of attitude structure. He and subsequent investigators regarded evaluative-cognitive consistency, not as a general personality trait, but as an individual difference that is specific to a particular attitude or domain of attitude objects.

Most research on this structural property has used Rosenberg's (1960) label for it—*affective-cognitive consistency* (e.g., Norman, 1975). This label reflected Rosenberg's use of the term affect as a synonym for evaluation. In line with our admonition against using these two terms interchangeably and consistent with typical operationalizations of the variable that was known as affective-cognitive consistency, we have relabeled this property evaluative-cognitive consistency (Eagly & Chaiken, 1993). In fact, the older appellation is inappropriate because, in modern terms, it refers to an across-class type of evaluative consistency—that is, between affective responding and cognitive responding (see discussion below).

Rosenberg's (1956) early research on this structural property helped demonstrate the viability of the expectancy-value model of attitudes by showing that attitudes, operationalized as general evaluations, are generally consistent with the evaluative content of beliefs (see prior discussion of this model). However, his subsequent work emphasized the antecedents and consequences of the extent to which attitudes are consistent with beliefs. Most important, this work provided preliminary evidence that consistent attitudes, compared with inconsistent ones, are less likely to change in response to social influence attempts and more likely to persist over time. Subsequent research has replicated these effects and also shown that attitudes higher in consistency are more predictive of behavior (Norman, 1975) and more likely to polarize as a function of thinking about the attitude object (Chaiken & Yates, 1985; see Chaiken, Pomerantz, & Giner-Sorolla, 1995).

Although Rosenberg (1968) acknowledged that evaluative-cognitive inconsistency may occur because people hold beliefs that are truly discrepant from their attitudes, he preferred a second interpretation—namely, that such inconsistency indicates a "vacuous" attitude or, in Converse's (1970) terms, a *nonattitude*. More specifically, he argued that evaluative-cognitive inconsistency signals a lack of both genuine beliefs about the attitude object and a genuine attitude toward it. Persons who are inconsistent in this sense are uncertain about how to respond to attitude and belief questionnaires and so respond in an unreliable, top-of-the-head manner.

Rosenberg's (1968) reasoning predated the current view of attitudes as abstracted evaluation and thus did not appreciate that attitudes could be based on affective, behavioral, *or* cognitive input. This broader perspective allows a slight expansion of his vacuity interpretation—namely, that measured evaluations and beliefs could be inconsistent because the individual has little or no cognitive experience *or* affective and behavioral experience with the attitude object. The person would therefore lack an attitude altogether or might possess a weak attitude based on heuristic processing of attitude-relevant cues (Chaiken, Wood, & Eagly, 1996; Petty & Wegener, 1998, in this *Handbook*). In a more substantial departure from Rosenberg's logic, regarding affect and behavior as constituents of attitudes suggests that an attitude and its associated cognitions could easily be inconsistent even though the attitude is genuine, because the attitude is based primarily on affective or behavioral input whose evaluative implications are different from those carried by the beliefs held about the attitude object.

Although much of the literature on evaluative-cognitive consistency does suggest that low consistency attitudes could be considered nonattitudes, certain findings question it. If low consistency truly signaled a nonattitude, measures of consistency should be at least modestly correlated with other indicators of attitude strength, such as personal importance and accessibility. Such correlations, however, have typically been negligible (e.g., Krosnick et al., 1993). More direct evidence that high and low consistency attitudes differ more in structure than existence comes from research showing that high consistency participants exceeded low consistency participants in the extent to which their beliefs were homogeneous in evaluative content and their reactions to counterattitudinal information consisted of refutational thoughts (Chaiken & Baldwin, 1981; Chaiken & Yates, 1985). This work implies that attitudes high in evaluative-cognitive consistency are strong because they are accompanied by a highly organized set of supporting cognitions. Although attitudes low in evaluative-cognitive consistency may not be accompanied by such coherent cognitions, they should not unequivocally be dismissed as nonattitudes (Chaiken et al., 1995).

Both evaluative-affective consistency and evaluative-behavioral consistency also warrant consideration as structural variables. The logic of the view that attitudes' constituents can include affect and behavior, as well as cognition, implies that these two additional properties are also potentially important aspects of an attitude's internal structure. The first of these additional properties, evaluative-affective consistency, refers to the consistency between one's overall evaluation of an attitude object and the evaluative content of the emotions and feelings that one associates with that object. The limited amount of research carried out on this variable has suggested that evaluative-affective consistency is empirically distinguishable from evaluative-cognitive consistency. For example, researchers have shown that the two variables independently predict attitude stability as well as the extent to which a specific attitude is deduced from a more general attitude

(e.g., an attitude toward recycling is deduced from an attitude toward environmentalism) (Chaiken et al., 1995; Prislin, 1996; Prislin, Wood, & Pool, 1997). Moreover, whereas evaluative-cognitive consistency has been associated with better memory for attitudinally incongruent information, evaluative-affective consistency has been associated with better memory for congruent information (Chaiken et al., 1995; Zimmerman & Chaiken, 1996). Finally, other findings suggest that attitudes low in evaluative-cognitive consistency may aptly be described as vacuous only when they are also low in evaluative-affective consistency (Chaiken et al., 1995; Prislin et al., 1997). Consequently, when low evaluative-cognitive consistency is accompanied by high evaluative-affective consistency, it may signal genuine attitudes that are primarily grounded in affect.

Attitudes' consistency with affective and cognitive associations has also been implicated in research aiming to show that affect as well as cognition can inform attitude formation. For example, in research based on national surveys in the United States, Abelson, Kinder, Peters, and Fiske (1982) reported that affective reactions to a number of nationally prominent politicians were more consistent with overall evaluations of them than were cognitive reactions. Whether attitudes toward most politicians are grounded more in affect than in cognition is an intriguing question with obvious implications for practitioners of political persuasion. Studies that have examined attitudes toward various social categories (e.g., women, Republicans, homosexuals) and social policies (e.g., affirmative action) indicate that affective associations often do contribute uniquely to the prediction of overall attitudes, that is, over and above the contribution of cognitive associations (Eagly et al., 1994; Esses et al., 1993; Jackson et al., 1996; Stangor, Sullivan, & Ford, 1991). Yet, empirically based claims that affect is the primary basis for certain attitudes (e.g., toward out-groups; Stangor et al., 1991) should be viewed with caution pending greater attention to theory-relevant methodological issues such as whether affects and beliefs are assessed by closed-ended versus open-ended measures (Crites, Fabrigar, & Petty, 1994; Eagly et al., 1994) and whether available versus accessible aspects of attitude structure are assessed (e.g., Breckler & Wiggins, 1989; see Eagly & Chaiken, 1993).

Evaluative-behavioral consistency exists when the overall evaluation of an attitude object matches the evaluative content of behavioral experience with it. Obviously, the general question of whether attitudes *cause* people to behave in attitude-congruent ways is relevant to this structural property. The literature spawned by this question is reviewed later in this chapter. With regard to the reverse proposition, that behavior impacts on attitudes, this source of evaluative-behavioral consistency is the major theme of Bem's (1972) self-perception theory, which argues that people often infer their attitudes from the evaluation implied by their recent or salient behaviors. That people may, in addition, prefer such consistency is suggested by years of dissonance-inspired research on induced compliance: at least under certain conditions, inducing participants to engage in behavior whose valence runs opposite to their attitudes (thereby instigating evaluative-behavioral *inconsistency,* or "dissonance") causes these attitudes to change in a behavior-congruent direction that restores evaluative-behavioral consistency (see Eagly & Chaiken, 1993).

Also relevant to this structural property is research by Ross and colleagues (see Ross, 1989), who have shown that people tend to reconstruct their past behavior as relatively consistent with their current attitudes. Attitudes thus function as important cues when people recollect their behavior: people tend to believe that they have done things in the past that are consistent with their current attitudes, even when these current attitudes are newly revised. In fact, when attitudes change following receipt of a persuasive communication, such changes are more likely to persist if, just after the persuasion attempt, recipients have been asked to ponder their past behaviors (Lydon, Zanna, & Ross, 1988).

Other implications for evaluative-behavioral consistency are inherent in research on the relative impact of direct versus indirect behavioral experience. This research has shown that attitudes based on direct experience with an attitude object tend to be stronger in several senses (e.g., more predictive of subsequent behavior) than attitudes formed on the basis of indirect experience through, for example, exposure to persuasive appeals (see Fazio, 1989). Assuming that attitudes based on direct experience are high in evaluative-behavioral consistency, these findings cohere with findings indicating that evaluative-cognitive consistency and evaluative-affective consistency are also sources of attitude strength. Moreover, because interacting behaviorally with an attitude object generally yields emotional responses toward it as well as information about it (see Millar & Millar, 1996), direct experience may produce stronger attitudes not only by greater behavioral input but also by greater affective and cognitive input, especially to the extent that all three types of input are consistent with the overall attitude.

Finally, the body of findings on these three forms of evaluative consistency suggests a technology for exploring differences in the bases of attitude formation: specifically, the primary basis for an attitude may lie in the type of response—cognitive, affective, or behavioral—that produces the smallest evaluative discrepancy with the overall attitude. For example, affect may be the primary basis of a person's attitude toward "eating Japanese food" to the extent that evaluative-affective consistency is considerably higher for this attitude object than either evaluative-cognitive consistency or evaluative-behavioral consistency.

Consistency Within and Across Classes of Evaluative Responding: Varieties of Ambivalence Cognitions pertaining to an attitude object may be internally consistent in their evaluative implications but can also be mixed (e.g., Erber, Hodges, & Wilson, 1995), and so too may affective associations and behavioral associations. Moreover, consistency may vary across classes of responding. For example, the evaluation implied by one's beliefs about an object could range from highly consistent to highly inconsistent with the evaluation implied by one's emotions (e.g., Thompson, Zanna, & Griffin, 1995). As noted earlier, when the valence of evaluative responding is so discrepant within a class or across classes that the individual's attitude could be described as two attitudes—one positive and one negative—that individual's overall attitude (i.e., abstract evaluation) is considered to be ambivalent.

The concept of attitudinal ambivalence has its roots in psychoanalytic writings and other seminal analyses of psychological conflict (e.g., Lewin, 1951; N. E. Miller, 1944). Within mainstream attitude theory, the ambivalence concept was evident in theories of cognitive consistency, which emphasized that ambivalent (or inconsistent) structures are inherently unstable and therefore quite temporary because of perceivers' preference for consistent over inconsistent cognitive structure (see Abelson et al., 1968). Departing from this perspective, Scott (e.g., 1969) discussed ambivalence as a potentially more enduring structural property of attitudes, and K. J. Kaplan (1972) subsequently proposed an important technique for assessing this property.

Kaplan's (1972) contribution stemmed from a concern about the meaning of attitude scores falling at or near the midpoint of traditional bipolar measures of attitude. Are such respondents truly neutral in their attitudes, or do they harbor positive and negative beliefs (or feelings) that, when averaged, would merely make them appear indifferent? Kaplan demonstrated that at least some midscale-responders on traditional bipolar scales should indeed be considered ambivalent rather than merely neutral or indifferent in their attitudes. He did so by modifying the (bipolar) semantic differential technique to produce separate, *unipolar* assessments of the positivity and the negativity of respondents' attitudes. One set of scales assessed the degree to which respondents ascribed positive characteristics to the attitude object (e.g., beneficial, wise), and the other set assessed the degree to which they ascribed negative characteristics (e.g., harmful, foolish). Given these unipolar measures, Kaplan assessed ambivalence by means of a mathematical formula that was based on the assumptions that ambivalence increases as (a) the characteristics associated with an attitude object become more polarized (i.e., evaluatively extreme) and (b) the positive and negative associations become more equal in terms of the absolute value of the evaluative meaning they imply.

Subsequent investigators have generally agreed with Kaplan's (1972) conceptual definition and his unipolar technique of measuring ambivalence, although some have proposed alternative formulas for calculating ambivalence, in order to correct for deficiencies in Kaplan's formula (see Breckler, 1994; Priester & Petty, 1996; Thompson et al., 1995). In addition, the unipolar scales that have been used to assess ambivalence have been framed somewhat differently depending on the investigators' aims. One approach is to tap ambivalence at the overall level of abstract evaluation (e.g., How positive is your attitude toward X? How negative is your attitude toward X?). Another approach is to assess ambivalence within classes of evaluative responding (e.g., Considering only your beliefs about X, how positive is your attitude? Considering only your beliefs about X, how negative is your attitude?). Adding similar questions about emotions and feelings allows ambivalence to be assessed across classes of evaluative responding as well (see Thompson et al., 1995). Other approaches to assessing ambivalence follow from the assumptions that ambivalence is expressed through slower response times to attitude inquiries (Bargh et al., 1992; I. Katz, 1981) or manifested by lower correlations between unipolar measures of positive and negative responding to the attitude object (e.g., Cacioppo & Berntson, 1994). Self-report measures of experienced ambivalence have also been developed and consist of items such as "I find myself feeling 'torn' between two sides of the issue of X" (e.g., euthanasia) and "My mind and heart seem to be in disagreement on the issue of X" (see Jamieson, 1988, as cited in Thompson et al., 1995, p. 373). Such self-report measures have been shown to correlate at least moderately with other measures of ambivalence such as Kaplan's (Thompson, et al., 1995) and somewhat more highly with an empirically derived power function proposed by Priester and Petty (1996).

Research has documented that some persons are generally more ambivalent than others across a variety of attitude objects (Thompson & Zanna, 1995). For example, a chronic tendency to engage in and enjoy thinking (i.e., high need for cognition; Cacioppo et al., 1996) is associated with lower chronic ambivalence. Also, a chronic tendency to avoid errors in decision making (i.e., high personal fear of invalidity; Thompson, Naccarato, & Parker, 1989) is associated with higher chronic ambivalence. Most work, however, has treated ambivalence as an individual difference that is specific to particular attitude objects. This research has shown that extreme attitudes are generally less ambivalent than moderate attitudes, a result predictable from Kaplan's (1972) point that middling scores on bipolar attitude scales can represent ambivalence as well as indif-

ference. Other research suggests that lack of ambivalence is a form of attitude strength insofar as it predicts outcomes such as attitude stability and greater attitude-behavior correspondence (e.g., Erber et al., 1995; Moore, 1980). Moreover, ambivalence is correlated with attitude accessibility, the ease with which overall attitudes come to mind (Fazio, 1989); people are faster to respond to inquiries about attitudes that are relatively low in ambivalence (e.g., Bargh et al., 1992).

Some of the consequences of ambivalence do not necessarily follow from thinking about this structural property as reducing attitudes' strength. Most notably, Katz, Hass, and their colleagues (e.g., Hass et al., 1992) have shown that holding ambivalent attitudes toward minorities or other stigmatized social groups can amplify, or polarize, responses toward group members in a direction that is either positive or negative, depending on particulars of the judgmental context. According to Katz and Hass, this amplification tendency arises from the threat to the self-concept that ambivalence may induce. As noted in our subsequent discussion of inter-attitudinal structure, the ambivalence that Katz and Hass examined is between two sets of beliefs that are derived from broader values. One set implies a positive attitude toward minorities such as African Americans (e.g., "Many Whites show a real lack of understanding of the problems that Blacks face"), and the other set implies a negative attitude (e.g., "Many Black teenagers don't respect themselves or anyone else"; I. Katz & Hass, 1988, p. 905). Findings similar in spirit have been reported in a study by MacDonald and Zanna (1996) that compared participants whose attitudes toward "feminists" were equivalent in valence but either high or low in affective-cognitive ambivalence. Finally, Maio, Bell, and Esses (1996) have demonstrated the potentially motivating effect of ambivalence on the processing of persuasive communications. They found that Canadian participants whose overall evaluations of Hong Kong immigrants were more ambivalent processed a persuasive message more systematically (see Petty & Wegener, 1997, in this *Handbook*). This result was consistent with the authors' reasoning that ambivalent message recipients would attend more to message content because it might help resolve the conflict that accompanied their mixed attitudes on the issue of immigration.

As Cacioppo and Berntson (1994) noted, work on ambivalence does not necessarily imply that researchers should abandon their traditional bipolar method of assessing attitudes—in fact, correlations between respondents' actual bipolar attitude scores and their predicted bipolar scores, calculated as the difference between their positive and negative unipolar scale scores, are generally exceedingly high (e.g., K. J. Kaplan, 1972; Thompson et al., 1995). Therefore, in terms of assessing overall evaluation, bipolar and unipolar methods yield essentially identical information. What unipolar attitude scales and other measures assessing ambivalence add is insight into intra-attitudinal structure, potentially allowing greater understanding of various attitudinal phenomena.

In this regard, Cacioppo and Berntson (1994) suggested that separating positive from negative attitudinal responding to attitude objects could help illuminate a variety of attitudinal issues. Moreover, they argued that this separability of negative and positive evaluation is consistent, not only with psychometric evidence, but also with findings that positive and negative responding have different physiological correlates (e.g., differential facial muscular patterns; Cacioppo et al., 1986) and may be localized in the left and right frontal hemispheres, respectively (Davidson, 1992; see Tesser & Martin, 1996). In harmony with earlier analyses of conflict (e.g., N. E. Miller, 1944), Cacioppo and Berntson further argued that avoidance tendencies may typically produce stronger effects than approach tendencies. Thus, even though measured positivity and measured negativity toward an attitude object may be virtually equivalent in psychometric terms, the negative aspects of people's attitudes may ultimately exert stronger effects on their behavior than the positive aspects. More generally, a variety of attitudinal phenomena (e.g., attitudinal selectivity, resistance to persuasion) may be affected more strongly by negative aspects of people's attitudes. This thesis is bolstered by theoretical claims that physiological and psychological mechanisms are more likely to be engaged by negative than positive events (e.g., Taylor, 1991) and by empirical demonstrations that negative information is weighted more heavily in judgment than positive information (see Fiske & Taylor, 1991) and has a stronger impact on attitudes (Cacioppo, Gardner, & Berntson, 1997). Finally, ambivalence itself may be more closely associated with the activation of negativity than positivity (Cacioppo et al., 1997).

Regardless of the greater potency ascribed to negative evaluative responding, the heart of theory and research on ambivalence lies in the claim that unpacking the positive aspects of people's attitudes from the negative aspects has important implications for attitudinal responding. Ambivalent attitudes, those that signal mixed evaluations within or across classes of evaluative responding, do have different implications than unambivalent attitudes in relation to outcomes such as attitudinal stability, the predictability of behavior, and the processing of persuasive communications. Nonetheless, research on ambivalence has not fully taken into account the principle that attitudes' constituents include cognitive, affective, and behavioral experience with attitude objects. Thus, most research on ambivalence has construed ambivalence at the level of beliefs or at the level of overall attitude considered without regard to its cognitive, affective, or behavioral underpinnings. Although there have been some attempts to investigate ambivalence within noncognitive response classes (most notably, affect) and across response classes (most notably, cognitions vs. affects), this work remains sparse (e.g., Maio et al., 1996; Thompson et al., 1995). More research that takes into account the different types of evaluative responding that can underlie attitudes should prove informative. For example, although the positive or negative direction of behavior may be predictable from attitudes' affective or cognitive aspects, the magnitude, or strength, of behavior may be more predictable from affective associations (particularly, negative affects) because affective responses to attitude objects may be particularly motivating (Chaiken, Wood, & Eagly, 1996).

VARIETIES OF INTER-ATTITUDINAL STRUCTURE

Attitudes are ordinarily not isolated in people's minds but are linked to other attitudes in what can be considered more molar cognitive structures. For example, attitudes toward political issues such as decreasing the capital gains tax may be linked with attitudes toward prominent politicians who have taken positions on these issues. When an individual thinks about this tax, she may also think about, for example, Bob Dole's position on the issue. The structure and dynamics of such larger systems of attitudes have for several decades been conceptualized by many social psychologists in terms of balance theory. Also, using a quite different approach, psychologists have assumed that attitudes are linked to other attitudes in thematically consistent structures known as ideologies. For some citizens, for example, the capital gains tax issue may be linked with their conservative political ideology. Both of these approaches—balance theory and ideological analysis—have shed light on attitudes' relations to other attitudes.

Balance Theory

The most systematic and enduring approach to understanding attitudes' relations to one another is balance theory, whose origins lie in the innovative theoretical work of Fritz Heider (1946, 1958). This approach has been reformulated many times over and remains viable in contemporary research. Heider's balance theory emerged in perhaps roughly equal parts from Gestalt psychology, philosophical writing (especially Hume and Spinoza), and folk wisdom. By 1960, Heider's theory had become very popular among social psychologists, in large part because it fit within a more general intellectual movement in social psychology focusing on cognitive consistency as its governing principle (see Abelson et al., 1968).

Some of the appeal of balance theory derives from the symbolic language that Heider proposed for mapping the ways that people represent inter-attitudinal structure. This language comprises *elements,* which represent attitude objects, and *relations* between elements. In most applications, these relations represent the evaluations that a perceiver attaches to these attitude objects, which were named *sentiment relations* by Heider. Yet the language also allows for nonevaluative relations between elements, called *unit relations* (e.g., similarity, proximity, ownership, causality, possession).

As elements, Heider's language identifies the perceiver or reference person (p), the other person in the situation (o), and an impersonal entity or thing (x) toward which both p and o hold attitudes. Attitudes, represented as sentiment relations between elements, can be positive (liking) or negative (disliking). The perceiver's attitude toward another person is thus represented as a sentiment relation linking p and o, and p's attitude toward some issue or other nonperson entity is represented as a sentiment relation linking p and x. In turn, p's perception of o's attitude toward this x is represented as a sentiment relation between o and x. This relation is perceived rather than actual because all the elements and relations are mapped as they exist in the perceiver's mind. With this representation of three relations between p, o, and x, a simple inter-attitudinal structure emerges in the form of a triad (see Figure 1 for examples). Because this triad includes three attitudes—two of p's attitudes and p's perception of one of the other person's attitudes, balance theory posed important questions about inter-attitudinal structure. An even simpler inter-attitudinal structure that Heider discussed is the dyad, which comprises only two elements, p and o, and represents p's attitude toward o and p's perception of o's attitude toward p.

The p-o-x triads shown in Figure 1 were particularly of interest to Heider because they represent the interpersonal context of attitudes toward issues. In addition, Heider considered contexts involving p and two other people (o and q). Contexts not involving other persons were also analyzed by Heider and typically concerned the perceiver and two impersonal entities (x and y). These p-x-y triads allow the examination of consistency in structures consisting of interrelated attitudes toward issues.

In addressing the stability of inter-attitudinal structures, Heider proposed that there are two possible states in such a structure: a balanced state in which elements and relations are harmonious and stable, and an unbalanced state in which they are unharmonious and unstable. According to Heider, unbalanced structures tend to change into balanced ones. In defining balance, Heider (1946) noted that this state is achieved in a two-element structure if both relations have the same sign and in a three-element structure if

all three relations are positive or if two are negative and one positive. This principle was reformulated in more abstract terms by Cartwright and Harary (1956), who invoked the mathematics of graph theory to show that a structure is balanced if the multiplicative product of the signs of its relations is positive and imbalanced if this product is negative. This more abstract definition makes it possible to determine balance in structures with more than three elements.

Research inspired by balance theory took several directions. Following Jordan's (1953) seminal experiment in which participants role-playing p in hypothetical p-o-x triads rated these triads for their pleasantness, many experiments investigated judgments of the eight triads that are produced by varying the positive versus negative sign on each of the three relations of Heider's triad (see Figure 1). The balanced triads are *a, b, c,* and *d,* and the imbalanced triads are *e, f, g,* and *h.* The balanced triads could be said to represent agreement with a friend (*a* and *b*) and disagreement with an enemy (*c* and *d*), whereas the imbalanced triads could be said to represent disagreement with a friend (*e* and *f*) and agreement with an enemy (*g* and *h*).

In general, as reviews of Jordan-paradigm experiments have established (e.g., Insko, 1984), the two triads in which p has the same attitude toward x as a liked o does (triads *a* and *b* in Figure 1) were rated more positively than the other six triads, whereas according to a simple balance prediction, the four balanced triads (*a, b, c,* and *d*) should have been rated more positively than the four unbalanced triads (*e, f, g,* and *h*). Although Zajonc (1968) interpreted these findings as largely inconsistent with balance theory, Insko (1981, 1984) subsequently reconciled Jordan-paradigm findings with the theory by showing that participants infer other relations, which are not necessarily evaluative, from the information given in the three-relation balance scenarios. These inferred relations would be represented as additional relations in the p-o-x structure—for example, participants may infer they would interact with o in the future (a unit relation). When participants are thus assumed to hold in mind more complex inter-attitudinal structures than the classic three-relation triad, typical Jordan-paradigm findings become largely consistent with balance predictions.

Heider's balance principle may function as a schema or conceptual rule about how one's attitudes usually relate to another person's attitudes. People may thus hold a conceptual rule that they ordinarily agree with people they like and disagree with people they dislike. Consistent with this idea, research has established that information is more readily learned and retained to the extent that it fits this rule (Zajonc & Burnstein, 1965a, 1965b). Moreover, people process information about balanced triads considerably more efficiently than information about imbalanced triads (Sentis & Burnstein, 1979).

Other well-known applications of balance theory include Newcomb's (1961) field study evaluating the extent

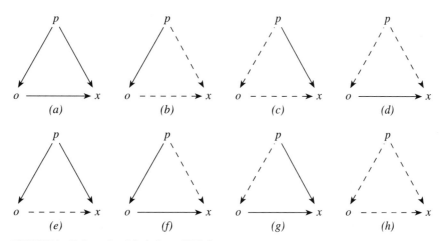

FIGURE 1   Balanced and Imbalanced Triads.
An unbroken arrow signifies a positive relation, and a broken arrow a negative relation.

to which students' attitudes toward issues and toward other members of their living group followed the predictions of balance theory. The theory has also been tested in studies of voters' perceptions of liked and disliked candidates' positions on political issues (e.g., Krosnick, 1990; Ottati, Fishbein, & Middlestadt, 1988). In addition, theorists and researchers have devoted considerable effort to predicting the responses by which people reduce imbalance, especially attitude change (Osgood & Tannenbaum, 1955; Tannenbaum, 1966), although a variety of more complex responses has also been explored (Abelson, 1959).

Newer work on balance theory has consisted of efforts to integrate the principles of balance theory with the more general cognitive principles inherent in associative network models of memory and connectionist models (see E. R. Smith, 1998, in this *Handbook*). Associative network interpretations of attitudes can easily accept balance principles into their propositions because this perspective represents attitude objects as nodes that are linked (e.g., Judd & Krosnick, 1989). To import balance theory into the associative network approach, these nodes are accorded positive or negative valence (to represent the perceiver's favorable or unfavorable attitude), and the nodes are linked by a positive or negative implicational relation that represents the perceived relation between attitude objects. According to the balance principle, pairs of linked attitudes are balanced if the signs of their evaluations times the sign of their relation is positive. Balanced associations between nodes should be stable, whereas imbalanced associations should produce change.

The gain from restating balance theory in associative network terms is that the broader theory that results incorporates propositions that are not part of balance theory. For example, some versions of associative network theory

(e.g., J. R. Anderson, 1983) accord nodes (i.e., attitudes) the property of strength. Strength reflects the frequency with which a node has been activated in the past. The more a person has thought about an attitude object, the stronger that node becomes. The link between nodes is stronger to the extent that the two nodes are themselves strong, the more often they have been thought about together, and the more similar they are semantically. The stronger the link is between two attitudinal nodes, the greater is the probability that these attitudes are brought simultaneously into awareness. As Judd and Krosnick (1989) reasoned, it would therefore be more likely that these attitudes would become evaluatively consistent by the balance principle. This prediction is not new, in view of, for example, Abelson and Rosenberg's (1958) much earlier claim that imbalance is resolved only to the extent that inconsistent elements become the object of thought. Nonetheless, the associative network rendition of this idea places it within a broader model that allows the balance principle to be integrated with other cognitive principles.

Other psychologists have applied an approach to cognitive modeling known as connectionism or parallel distributed processing to the domain of balance theory. These particular applications of connectionist models, called localist constraint-satisfaction networks (see E. R. Smith, 1998, in this *Handbook*; Read, Vanman, & Miller, 1997), can be similar to associative network models in representing attitudes as linked nodes. Attitudes may thus appear as nodes linked by positive or negative implicational relations that vary in intensity. Connectionist modelers attempt to map these attitudinal structures through assessment of perceivers' attitudes in a given domain. The processes of parallel constraint satisfaction allow each node to influence and be influenced by the other nodes to which it is connected, until the activations of these nodes settle into a state of overall coherence, or mathematical harmony.

In this type of localist connectionist approach, nodes may represent attitudinal propositions (e.g., Mary loves John), and strength of activation of a node is coordinated to degree of belief in the proposition (e.g., Read & Miller, 1994). Alternatively, nodes may represent attitude objects, and their positive or negative activation value then represents the strength of the favorable or unfavorable attitude (e.g., Spellman, Ullman, & Holyoak, 1993). In yet another approach, which allows for attitudinal ambivalence, each attitude or belief can be represented by the net activation of a pair of negatively connected units, one of which is positive and the other negative (Shultz & Lepper, 1996). Given any of these methods of representing attitudes, the positive or negative implicational relations between the nodes also have differing values, representing their intensity. Activation is assumed to spread around the network in parallel until it reaches a state of overall consistency. Each node receives activation from the nodes to which it is connected, and the amount of this activation depends on the strength and sign of the links and the activation of these linked nodes. This spreading activation is modeled by equations that are based on those introduced by J. L. McClelland and Rumelhart (1981; see also Thagard, 1989). Changes toward cognitive balance are thus a by-product of the general predictions of the model. Once the researcher specifies a network structure, a simulation is conducted that allows the model to "run" in iterative fashion until it produces mathematical harmony—that is, consistency.

By using this approach, a researcher can initially specify an attitudinal network, simulate attitude changes, and compare the results of the simulation to actual changes. For example, Spellman et al. (1993) applied such a model to simulate change over time in students' attitudes related to the Persian Gulf War. In this study, shifts in particular attitudes (e.g., toward Saddam Hussein) were correlated with shifts in other attitudes (e.g., the legitimacy of U.S. intervention), and the pattern of changes was successfully simulated by a computational model based on the equations of parallel constraint satisfaction. In a particularly interesting application of a constraint satisfaction model, Schultz and Lepper (1996) simulated the changes that should occur in classic dissonance paradigms (induced compliance and decision-making; see Eagly & Chaiken, 1993) and compared the results of these simulations to the findings of dissonance experiments. In general, the simulation results matched the findings of these experiments.

As illustrated by this incorporation of balance principles into associative networks and connectionist models, balance theory has been continually reinvented in tandem with the evolution of social psychologists' ideas about the structure of attitudes. In earlier and later research programs, balance theory has been pursued with considerable

rigor. Perhaps because the theory reflects basic principles of human logic (see Runkel & Peizer, 1968), it has proven to be a particularly enduring approach to understanding inter-attitudinal structure. Nonetheless, in contemporary developments, balance often does not function as a stand-alone theory but has been incorporated into more integrative cognitive models.

Ideological Context of Attitudes

One of the essential insights of theory about inter-attitudinal structure is that an attitude may be formed as an implication of or a deduction from a more general attitude that has already been formed. Perceivers may in top-down fashion deduce a novel attitude from a value that they endorse or from their attitude toward a much broader issue. In a particularly innovative demonstration of this point, Prislin et al. (1997) showed that some participants deduced their attitude toward a news item concerning sex discrimination from their existing evaluation on the general issue of equal rights for women. Similarly, Stern and his colleagues (e.g., Stern et al., 1995) argued that people derive their attitudes on specific environmental issues from their general values and internalized moral norms and presented correlational evidence in support of this view (see also Eagly & Kulesa, 1997). Regarding attitudes as deduced from relatively broad attitudes, including values, implies that attitudes may have a hierarchical structure that allows more concrete and specific attitudes to be derived from more abstract and general attitudes. More generally, as Feather (1996) argued, attitudes are often embedded in a complex network of relations between attitudes, beliefs, and values in which strongly held values are core, or central, elements in the sense that they are linked to many attitudes and beliefs as well as to other values.

Research on *ideologies* has consistently emphasized the hierarchical aspects of attitude structure (e.g., Converse, 1964; Kinder & Sears, 1985). Ideologies are construed as clusters of attitudes and beliefs that are interdependent in the sense that they are organized around a dominant societal theme such as liberalism and conservatism. The broader attitude in a structure of this type would have as its object liberalism or conservatism (or some other ideological theme). The beliefs associated with this general attitude may allow attitudes toward specific social issues to be derived. For example, people holding a conservative political ideology (i.e., a positive attitude toward conservatism) might consult, on a conscious or nonconscious basis, general principles of conservatism to develop a position on a specific issue that they newly encounter, such as the desirability of a constitutional amendment requiring a balanced federal budget.

Despite the plausibility of the assumption that people

organize their political attitudes around liberalism and conservatism, research suggests that often they do not derive attitudes consistent with these traditional ideological labels (e.g., Converse, 1964). Although these failures in accounting for political attitudes in terms of a general liberal versus conservative dimension may cause many people to appear nonideological, their attitudes may nonetheless be ideologically organized in terms of themes that are considerably narrower than liberalism and conservatism and sometimes quite idiosyncratic. Illustrating this principle, Conover and Feldman (1984) identified multiple liberal and conservative ideologies, defined at both a general level (e.g., "a philosophy of individualism") and at more specific levels pertaining to economics (e.g., "society's responsibility for economic inequities"), racial issues (e.g., "liberal integrationism"), and foreign affairs (e.g., "nonmilitaristic isolationism"). Moreover, they argued that these ideologies were hierarchically linked with one another and with attitudes on specific issues. For example, respondents whose basic political philosophy took a "Hobbesian-Freudian" form tended to adopt "free-market conservatism" as a general ideological principle, and they in turn stressed the "value of free enterprise" in the economic realm as well as "nationalism-ethnocentrism" in international affairs. Such hierarchically organized ideologies in turn related systematically to attitudes on specific issues such as school integration, marijuana use, and defense spending. Similarly, Hurwitz and Peffley (1987) argued that specific foreign policy attitudes on issues such as nuclear arms and international trade were derived from broader ideologies about foreign policy (e.g., "isolationism") and that these ideologies were in turn related to core values (e.g., "ethnocentrism"). In a related vein, Sears and Kinder (1985) contended that the political attitudes of U.S. citizens are often grounded in relatively vague attachments to certain groups and symbols as well as in general moral preferences and commitments to values. Indeed, other research suggests that the perceived relations of social policies to the attainment of values can be a more important source of inter-attitudinal organization than broader ideologies, especially among people who are not particularly knowledgeable about politics (Lavine, Thomsen, & Gonzales, 1997). With traditional liberal and conservative ideologies in considerable flux in recent years, it seems quite unlikely that most citizens would organize their thinking about political issues in terms of overarching ideological themes. Nonetheless, most people are able to make relatively easy judgments that assume knowledge of broad political ideologies—for example, respondents readily placed political parties and presidential candidates on a liberal-conservative continuum (Jacoby, 1995). In addition, political elites and citizens with considerable expertise about politics appear to achieve the type of broader organization of political attitudes that is reasonably consistent with traditional descriptions of liberal and conservative political ideologies (e.g., Judd & Krosnick, 1989; Lavine et al., 1997; Lusk & Judd, 1988).

Ideologies Related to Prejudice Toward Disadvantaged Social Groups Considerable attention has been directed to the ideologies that may constrain contemporary attitudes abut racial minorities, women, and other disadvantaged groups (see Brown's, 1995, review). In some of the research related to this theme, investigators maintained that many European Americans hold an ideology about African Americans, labeled *symbolic* or *modern racism,* that differs from earlier forms of more overt and hostile prejudice (e.g., McConahay, 1986; Sears, 1988). A key theme that organizes this ideology and thus affects racial attitudes is the endorsement of a Protestant ethic value that lauds work, individual achievement, and discipline or, in Kleugel and Smith's (1986) description of a *dominant ideology,* the endorsement of the idea that economic advancement follows from hard work. These work-ethic themes imply that people are responsible for their own economic fate and that the distribution of economic rewards is basically fair. This ideology promotes internal attributions for the social and economic problems faced by some minorities (e.g., lack of discipline and energy) and discourages external attributions (e.g., job discrimination). These attributions foster the denial of discrimination toward these minorities (e.g., African Americans), antagonism toward their demands, and resentment over special favors for them. As theorists of modern racism have maintained, an important consequence of this reasoning is opposition to specific social policies such as affirmative action and busing.

In another analysis of racism, Gaertner and Dovidio (1986; Dovidio & Gaertner, 1991) proposed the concept of *aversive racism* to describe the attitudes toward black Americans commonly held by white Americans who not only reject old-fashioned, blatant forms of racism but also are genuinely committed to tolerance. These Americans' liberal attitudes derive from their egalitarian value system, but their racism reflects the negative stereotypes and affect that they inevitably absorbed from the culture. These factors converge to produce attitudinal ambivalence, uncertainty and fear in interracial encounters, and, as demonstrated by these researchers, racist behavior that is manifested in indirect and subtle ways (e.g., whites failing to help blacks in situations in which helping is not normatively prescribed; see Dovidio & Gaertner, 1991).

A common thread in all these analyses of racism is that these attitudes' relations to values are critical to understanding their organization. This idea was given its most direct test in research by I. Katz and Hass (1988). These investigators showed that whites' racial attitudes are linked to two values: *individualism,* which corresponds to the Protestant ethic values emphasized in discussions of modern racism; and *communalism,* which emphasizes concern about community, equality, and the well-being of others. This dual-value perspective captures the ambivalence that many European Americans experience in relation to African Americans. Consistent with this chapter's prior discussion of ambivalence within classes of evaluative responding, ambivalent whites may thus hold both antiblack beliefs derived from the value of individualism and problack beliefs derived from the value of communalism. This approach to understanding whites' racial attitudes has much in common with Tetlock's (1989) research on value pluralism, which has shown that on a number of social issues people who are integratively complex link their attitudes to values that have conflicting implications for these attitudes.

Given these findings on racial attitudes, a broader question warranting attention is whether the ideological analyses applied to racism would apply to attitudes toward a wide range of minority groups. Suggestive of the utility of such analyses is Biernat, Vescio, Theno, and Crandall's (1996) evidence that attitudes toward homosexuals and overweight people were, like whites' attitudes toward blacks, predicted by I. Katz and Hass's (1988) individualism and communalism values. Yet, severely neglected in this research tradition is analysis of the values that may underlie the attitudes that members of minorities hold toward the majority group. For example, the structure of blacks' attitudes toward whites, including their value bases, awaits investigation, as does the structure of homosexuals' attitudes toward heterosexuals and overweight persons' attitudes toward normal weight persons.

Building on some of the themes of research on racial attitudes, several researchers have examined the ideological context of attitudes toward women and women's rights. Swim, Aikin, Hall, and Hunter (1995) delineated *modern sexism,* a contemporary ideology about gender that, like modern racism, can be distinguished from more overt and hostile forms of prejudice. Modern sexism fosters denial of continuing discrimination against women, antagonism toward women's demands, and resentment about special favors for women. A similar ideology, labeled *neosexism,* was examined by Tougas, Brown, Beaton, and Joly (1995). The idea that modern sexism may share some features with modern racism was supported by Glick and Fiske's (1996) examination of the ambivalence inherent in attitudes about women. These researchers defined two sets of beliefs about women, which they termed *hostile sexism* and *benevolent sexism.* The hostile dimension of sexism expresses a wide range of negative themes about women including distrust of feminism, whereas the benevolent dimension includes chivalrous beliefs and the endorsement of women's superior qualities in some domains. Just as European Americans' beliefs about African Americans can be organized in terms of antiblack and problack dimensions, beliefs about women can be organized in terms of an antiwoman dimension that expresses hostile sexism and a prowoman dimen-

sion that expresses benevolent sexism. Glick and Fiske's finding that both women and men showed this two-dimensional attitude structure is interesting in view of women's situation as the object of sexist attitudes.

Theory and research on ideology reveal an important aspect of attitudes' inter-attitudinal structure. Although these investigations are quite diverse, they share an emphasis on hierarchical structures in which social and political attitudes are formed at least partially in top-down fashion as generalizations from broader attitudes. On the surface, it may seem that treating attitudes in this fashion as associated in a broader ideology is quite different from treating them in the balance-theory mode as specific linked elements. However, as Feather (1996) argued, values may be treated as background factors that affect the strength and sign of the attitudes that are represented in conventional balance structures. For example, in his balance analysis of deservingness, Feather argued that general valuing of achievement and honesty would be translated into positive evaluations of specific achieving or honest actions and specific successes following such actions. In another reconciliation of the ideological and balance approaches, the attitudes and values implicated in ideologies could be rendered as cognitive elements (or nodes) and subjected to a balance analysis. Moreover, balance theory is fully compatible with the idea that attitudes may be formed in a top-down fashion through their associations with other attitudes. Most obviously, the classic *p-o-x* structure suggests that attitudes on issues may be derived from attitudes toward politicians who advocate positions on issues. Also, in *p-x-y* structures, attitudes toward *x* and *y* may differ in their generality, and one of these attitudes may be derivable from the other. Nonetheless, the contribution of ideological analysis is to highlight values and other overarching molar themes, whereas the contribution of the balance analysis is to highlight linkages between attitudes, regardless of the generality or abstractness of the attitudes.

ATTITUDE STRENGTH

Attitude strength has increasingly become a fundamental concept in attitude theory and research. This status stems from the importance accorded to the attitude construct itself: attitudes are viewed as preeminent causes of behavior and root causes of intergroup conflict, prejudice, and discrimination. Despite attitudes' presumed consequentiality, their impact on outcomes such as selective information processing and behavior has proven to be quite variable and sometimes negligible. Efforts to address this theoretical and empirical dilemma have taken many forms, as illustrated, for example, by several themes in research on the attitude-behavior relation (see subsequent section). The solution addressed in this section proposes that there is "something" over and above the positive versus negative character of an attitude that gives rise to its power to influence attitude-relevant responding. This property is called *attitude strength* and, in a slight refinement of traditional wisdom, investigators assume that strong attitudes are, in fact, consequential. As we will show, a variety of conceptions of attitude strength have been proposed, many of which are based on reasonable assumptions about the ways that attitude structure lends strength to attitudes. However, no one understanding of attitude strength dominates contemporary research. Contributing to this state of affairs is the tendency of most investigators of attitude strength to focus on only one indicator of strength. Although investigators usually provide good theoretical reasons for why their particular variable should index attitudes' strength, they have paid far less attention to explicating relations among various strength variables.

Investigators of attitude strength show consensus in identifying the presumed consequences of strength: strong attitudes lead to selective information processing and are resistant to change, persistent over time, and predictive of behavior. The danger in identifying effects without having achieved consensus on a conceptual definition of strength is that researchers might fall into a pragmatic definition (Petty & Krosnick, 1995)—namely, that any variable that happens to be correlated with strength's presumed effects has a legitimate claim on being considered an aspect of strength. Given the causal ambiguities of the correlational analyses that have provided the primary method of evaluating claims about attitude strength, this pragmatic approach would be unlikely to continue to yield much genuine scientific progress. More constructive definitions of strength derive from theory about the nature of attitudes and attitude structure. Consequently, the strength variables emphasized in this chapter derive from the framework presented in earlier sections.

In preparation for analyzing various forms of attitude strength, it is wise to dismiss attitudinal extremity as an appropriate definition of strength. Because bipolar measures of attitude convey two pieces of information about an attitude—its valence and its extremity, it may be tempting to equate extremity with strength. Would it not be true, for example, that a person whose attitude is "very favorable" rather than "somewhat favorable" toward Bill Clinton would be more likely to hold to this attitude throughout the 1996 presidential campaign, vote for Clinton, and selectively process information about him? Indeed, people holding more extreme attitudes are more likely to resist change in the face of social influence attempts, engage in attitude-congruent behavior, and make judgments and process information in a manner congenial to their attitudes (see Judd & Brauer, 1995).

Extremity would provide an economical definition of strength in a practical sense because strength would be assessed with the very same measure used to assess valence.

Extremity is thus the deviation of a respondent's score from the attitude scale's midpoint, or neutral value. Nonetheless, there are good reasons to avoid equating strength with extremity. As Fazio (1995) argued, the location of the attitude object on a scale of favorability versus unfavorability defines the attitude itself, not its strength. Attitude is thus an evaluative state that is characterized by extremity as well as valence. The extremity of this evaluative state is correlated with various structural characteristics that lend attitudes their strength (e.g., unambivalence of associated beliefs and affects) and often cause attitudes to be polarized. Consistent with Abelson's (1995) analysis of numerous social and individual processes that are associated with attitudinal extremification (e.g., polarization from group discussion of an issue), many experiences can produce the kinds of changes in attitude structure that cause attitudes to become more extreme. It is these structural changes that provide the most theoretically useful account of attitude strength.

Aside from extremity, researchers have proposed a large number of variables as forms of attitude strength. One group of strength variables are *structural* in the sense that they derive from an explicit model of attitude structure. Because most of these strength variables are defined in terms of intra-attitudinal or inter-attitudinal structure, they have already been described in this chapter and need only be reintroduced so that their implications for the presumed consequences of strength can be noted. A second important group of strength variables are not defined structurally and can be considered *experiential* because they are defined by subjective awareness of the strength of one's attitude—for example, by awareness that an attitude is important. Because these experiential strength variables are defined conceptually in terms of the phenomenology of the person who holds the attitude, they are defined operationally by subjective self-reports. Structural strength variables can also be assessed by self-reports, but these self-reports provide subjective impressions of structural features of attitudes rather than of attitudes' overall strength. For example, respondents can report how knowledgeable they are about an attitude object or introspect about the centrality of their attitudes to important values. Generally, however, structural strength variables are assessed by so-called direct or objective measures that elicit from respondents the presumed elements of their attitude structure; the investigator then combines these elements by a formula to produce a value that indexes the structural property. The formulas used to combine positive and negative reactions to an attitude object into an index of ambivalence illustrate these direct measures (see prior discussion).

In studies that have used both direct and subjective self-report measures, these two types of measures of the same structural property tend not to be highly correlated (Bassili, 1996; Krosnick et al., 1993; Priester & Petty, 1996). At the very least such findings show that measurement differences are not trivial and can cloud interpretation of results, particularly the findings of factor analytic investigations of various forms of strength (see below). Pursuing in depth the idea that strength has been assessed by different types of measures, Bassili (1996) made a conceptual distinction related to our distinction between direct measures and subjective self-reports. Thus, Bassili introduced the concept of *operative measures* and viewed them as linked to the judgment processes that produce attitudinal responding. For example, the latency of responding to an attitudinal inquiry is an operative index of attitude strength because it assesses the process of attitude activation. He also considered strength measures to be operative if they require the retrieval of information that is the product of attitudinal processes. To the extent that attitude itself (i.e., an overall evaluation of an attitude object) is stored in memory, it is the result of attitudinal processes, and measures that assess this overall evaluation also qualify as operative.

In contrast to such operative measures, Bassili (1996) considered measures *meta-attitudinal* to the extent that they require respondents to report on attitudinal properties that are not stored in memory and thus are not accessible to conscious scrutiny. Subjective self-reports of attitude strength (e.g., judging the importance of one's attitude) and attitude structure (e.g., judging the ambivalence of one's attitude) would be meta-attitudinal in terms of Bassili's distinction, because of the presumed unlikelihood that people store summary assessments of such attitudinal properties. As a consequence, according to Bassili's argument, meta-attitudinal measures of strength tend to be invalid and unreliable because they are vulnerable to contextual influences as respondents strive to describe attitudinal properties that are not stored in memory. Bassili's hypothesis about the superiority of operative measures is provocative and deserves exploration with a wider range of dependent variables that assess the consequences of attitude strength.

Structural Strength Variables

Intra-attitudinal Aspects of Strength   Attitudes have an internal structure that consists of associations between the attitude object and relevant prior experience. In general, to the extent that this intra-attitudinal structure is extensive and evaluatively coherent, an attitude possesses strength. The reason that intra-attitudinal structure confers strength is apparent from considering that the activation of an attitude by relevant cues tends also to activate its associated beliefs, affects, and (cognitions about) behaviors. In line with simple averaging models of attitudes (e.g., N. H. Anderson, 1981b), the persuasive impact of any new piece of information, be it cognitive, affective, or behavioral information, should be attenuated to the extent that intra-attitudinal associations are extensive and coherent (see Eagly &

Chaiken, 1995). An obvious consequence of this attenuation of change is that attitudes with extensive and coherent internal structure should also be more stable over time and, thus, presumably more predictive of behavior (Doll & Ajzen, 1992; Eagly & Chaiken, 1995). Another reason why such attitudes are likely to enhance resistance, stability, and attitude-behavior correspondence is that they may exert particularly marked effects on the processing of attitude-relevant information. For example, possessing an extensive and evaluatively coherent set of beliefs about an attitude object should enhance a person's ability to actively refute new counterattitudinal information and to elaborate favorably on new proattitudinal information (Chaiken et al., 1995; Wood et al., 1995). Similarly, possessing ample and coherent affective associations may increase ability to resist persuasive appeals, especially messages whose content is largely affective, and in addition may increase motivation to scrutinize and evaluate attitude-relevant information (Biek, Wood, & Chaiken, 1996).

As reviewed earlier in this chapter, there is ample evidence that attitudes high in evaluative-cognitive consistency are associated with the effects on attitudinal responding that strength is predicted to have. Although strength-oriented research on evaluative-affective consistency, evaluative-behavioral consistency, and ambivalence is sparse in comparison, existing research does suggest that these structural properties also represent distinctive aspects of attitude strength. As noted earlier, higher evaluative-affective consistency and lower ambivalence predict greater attitudinal stability, and ambivalence lessens attitude-behavior correspondence. In addition, experimental interventions that enhance or make salient the behavioral aspect of intra-attitudinal structure facilitate attitudinal resistance and persistence (e.g., Kiesler, Pallak, & Kanouse, 1968; Lydon et al., 1988; Ross et al., 1983). For example, *commitment* manipulations, by which people become pledged or bound to their behavioral acts, may have such impact by strengthening the associations between attitudes and the overt behaviors that support these attitudes (Kiesler, 1971). In summary, conferring strength on attitudes are intra-attitudinal variables that signal evaluative coherence, consisting of unambivalence and consistency of overall evaluation with associated cognitions, affects, and behaviors.

Over and above these forms of evaluative coherence, the extensiveness of intra-attitudinal associations is also a source of attitude strength. Providing people with information that adds beliefs to their intra-attitudinal structure confers resistance to persuasion (e.g., Himmelfarb & Youngblood, 1969). In addition, people high in *working knowledge*—those who are able to retrieve numerous attitude-relevant beliefs and behaviors from memory—exhibit greater attitudinal resistance and greater attitude-behavior correspondence (see Wood, Rhodes, & Biek, 1995). Extensiveness of intra-attitudinal associations may also underline the demonstrated consequentiality of attitudes based on direct experience with objects (see Fazio, 1989). Direct interactions may provide appreciably more associations, on a cognitive, affective, and behavioral basis, than do indirect interactions.

Inter-attitudinal Aspects of Strength Inter-attitudinal structure is also an important source of attitude strength. Earlier attitude theorists captured this aspect of strength in their concepts of *embeddedness* (Scott, 1968) and *centrality* (Rokeach, 1968), both of which refer to attitudes that are well connected to other attitudes. From a consistency theory perspective, an attitude that is linked to other attitudes in a molar structure may resist change for the simple reason that such change would create pressure for linked attitudes to change. Yet, thinking through the implications of change in one attitude for other, linked attitudes would require substantial mental effort, and this effort, if not justified in some fashion by the promise of positive outcomes, would tend to be avoided (Eagly & Chaiken, 1995; see also Fiske & Taylor's, 1991, discussion of perceivers as motivated tacticians). The more embedded the attitude is in a structure of related attitudes, the more mental effort would be required to think through the implications of change because the related attitudes would be numerous. Therefore, although change can reverberate through attitudinal structures, this change may often occur slowly, and inertial forces may tend to counter it (McGuire, 1981; McGuire & McGuire, 1991).

Most discussions of attitude-attitude linkages have featured the anchoring of attitudes to values. This emphasis implies that attitudes that are linked to more abstract attitudes (i.e., values) in a hierarchical structure may be particularly strong. If a lower-level attitude (e.g., recycling) is an implication of a more general attitude (e.g., environmental preservation), direct attack on the lower-level attitude, by, for example, pointing out the negative characteristics of the attitude object, would be ineffective because support of this lower-level attitude would derive from its relation to the higher-level attitude. Moreover, the higher-level attitude would have its own internal structure and typically would be linked by implication to additional lower-level attitudes as well. These features would also make change in the higher-level attitude unlikely. Although this analysis of the reasons why strong external structure should confer attitude strength pertains most directly to attitudes' resistance to change, this resistance should promote stability, which, in turn, should promote greater attitude-behavior correspondence (Doll & Ajzen, 1992). In addition, the embeddedness of an attitude in an extensive external structure may make the attitude more likely to be activated in a wide range of situations, where it may impact on behavior and provide a basis for deducing more specific attitudes on related issues (Prislin & Ouellette, 1996).

Exemplifying this emphasis on the hierarchical structure of attitudes is M. Sherif and Cantril's (1947) concept of *ego-involvement,* the linkage of attitudes to self-defining values and reference groups, although their discussion of ego-involvement's effects on outcomes such as resistance to persuasion stressed motivation (i.e., protection of the self-concept) more than structure per se. Subsequent investigators proposed similar concepts. In an explicitly structural account, for example, Ostrom and Brock (1968) advanced the idea that attitudes are strong or "involving" to the extent that they are linked to important values. In an experimental demonstration of this point, they showed that linking a target attitude to personally important values produced greater resistance to a counterattitudinal message. Other related concepts include *value-centrality* (Abelson & Prentice, 1989) and *value-relevant involvement* (B. T. Johnson & Eagly, 1989). Consistent with Ostrom and Brock's findings, Johnson and Eagly's (1989) meta-analysis of studies that examined the impact of involvement on persuasion confirmed that heightened value-relevant involvement generally increases resistance to persuasion. Also, as explained in the discussion of ideology earlier in this chapter, attitudes toward disadvantaged groups may tend to be linked to broader values and societal themes and therefore may be relatively strong.

Because values have traditionally been regarded as core aspects of the self-concept (e.g., Rokeach, 1968; Sherif & Cantril, 1947), it is not surprising that associations between attitudes and other aspects of the self have also received attention in discussions of attitude strength. Greenwald (1989), for example, has discussed linkages between attitudes and the private, public, and collective aspects of the self. Because beliefs about personal well-being are central to people's self-concepts, attitudes that express self-interest (or vested interest) should be strong; this form of strength has in fact been associated with a number of predicted outcomes of strength (e.g., Crano, 1995; Giner-Sorolla & Chaiken, 1997; Thomsen, Borgida, & Lavine, 1995).

Accessibility Definition of Strength Fazio (e.g., 1986, 1989, 1995) has provided evidence demonstrating the consequentiality of attitudes high in *accessibility*—attitudes that can be retrieved from memory quickly, in fact, automatically (Fazio et al., 1986). Although there is growing evidence that virtually all attitudes are capable of automatic activation (Bargh et al., 1992; Bargh et al., 1996; Chaiken & Bargh, 1993), Fazio (1993, 1995) maintained that this phenomenon occurs only to the extent that an attitude is relatively high in accessibility. Regardless of this controversy about automatic activation, Fazio and other investigators (e.g., Bassili, 1995, 1996) have shown that attitudes vary in their relative accessibility and that more accessible attitudes are more likely to be associated with outcomes such as stability, attitudinal resistance, selective judgment of attitude-relevant information, and attitude-behavior consistency (see Fazio, 1995).

Fazio (1989, 1995) described a structural model—specifically, a simple associative network model in which an attitude is represented as one node (e.g., "good") and the attitude object is represented as a second node (e.g., "Al Gore"). From this perspective, accessibility qualifies as a structural definition of attitude strength because it provides an index of the strength of the association in memory between an attitude object and its evaluation: the stronger the attitude, the stronger is its associative strength and, hence, the more easily it can be retrieved from memory. Consistent with this conceptual definition of accessibility in terms of speed of retrieval, some research has measured this construct by participants' response times to attitude inquiries, with faster responses implying higher accessibility. Alternatively, other research has increased accessibility experimentally by inducing participants to repeatedly express their attitudes, thus strengthening the object-evaluation association (see Fazio, 1995).

Research has established that accessibility is correlated with several features of intra-attitudinal or inter-attitudinal structure (e.g., unambivalence; Bargh et al., 1992; Fazio, 1995). This work suggests that the cause of variation in attitude accessibility could be variation in intra-attitudinal or inter-attitudinal structure, and that accessibility may therefore function as an indicator of the overall strength that these forms of structure confer on attitudes. Alternatively, accessibility could be a consequence of strength that is defined in intra- or inter-attitudinal terms. Just as attitude stability can be a consequence of these forms of attitude strength, so too might attitude accessibility.

Experiential Strength Variables

A number of other variables that have been investigated as forms of attitude strength are best viewed as metacognitions that people hold in relation to their attitudes insofar as these variables are conceptually defined as the subjective awareness that an attitude is strong. A prime example of this category is Krosnick's (e.g., 1988) concept of *attitude importance*. This construct is defined as the "subjective sense of the concern, caring and significance [a person] attaches to an attitude," and is typically assessed by research participants' self-reports of how personally important they consider the attitude object or issue to be (Boninger, Krosnick, & Berent, 1995, p. 62). A number of studies have shown that heightened attitude importance is associated with indicators of strength's pragmatic outcomes such as attitude-behavior correspondence, temporal stability, and resistance to change (see Boninger, Krosnick, Berent, & Fabrigar, 1995).

Other well-known examples of experiential strength variables include a subjective sense of *certainty* about one's attitude (or confidence; e.g., Gross, Holtz, & Miller, 1995) and *conviction* (or commitment; e.g., Abelson, 1988). These variables also have proven to be predictive of one or more of the outcomes expected of attitude strength (see Petty & Krosnick, 1995; Pomerantz, Chaiken, & Tordesillas, 1995).

Consideration should be given to the idea that the subjective sense that one's attitude is strong may merely be an indicant of its structural strength. From this perspective, features of intra-attitudinal or inter-attitudinal structure (e.g., evaluative coherence of associated beliefs and affects) may foster the perception that an attitude is strong, but it is underlying structure that is critical in producing strength's predicted outcomes. An alternate way of thinking about the role of experiential strength variables is that a subjective sense that an attitude is strong arises from certain conditions that may include strength-enhancing structural changes in attitudes; this subjective sense of strength then impacts on various processes (e.g., selectivity in information processing) and thereby produces the consequences expected of strong attitudes. Indeed, Krosnick and colleagues (e.g., Boninger, Krosnick, Berent, & Fabrigar, 1995) and other investigators have generally given this independent causal role to these phenomenologically defined forms of attitude strength.

Dimensionality of Attitude Strength

Although not all the strength variables reviewed in this chapter have been mapped onto all outcomes expected of strong attitudes, virtually all have been shown to predict one or more of these outcomes, especially attitude-behavior correspondence and resistance to influence. It may therefore be tempting to conclude that this plethora of indicators is reducible to a single construct that might be called attitude strength, and that, however assessed, strength has similar processing, judgmental, and behavioral consequences. However, the first of these conclusions is wrong, and the second is presently unwarranted and probably wrong.

Correlational studies of measures of attitude strength suggest that strength is multidimensional. Raden's (1985) study examining correlations among a large number of strength measures produced quite modest relations and led him to argue that strength is best viewed as multidimensional. Subsequent and more rigorous factor analytic investigations using a variety of attitudinal issues uniformly failed to yield a one-factor solution and thus proved consistent with Raden's conclusion (e.g., Abelson, 1988; Bassili, 1996; Erber et al., 1995; Krosnick et al., 1993; Pomerantz et al., 1995; Prislin, 1996; Tordesillas, Chaiken, & Zimmerman, 1994). Although one of the more sophisticated of these analyses failed to discern any clear factor structure among a large number of strength measures (Krosnick et al., 1993), these analyses face methodological challenges from Bassili's (1996) critique of meta-attitudinal measures. Also, the results of factor analyses fluctuate, depending on the particular set of variables included. Despite these concerns, there are some reasons to believe that attitude strength may eventually be understood in terms of fewer rather than many dimensions. In particular, a distinction between a relatively more cognitive dimension of attitude strength and a relatively more affective dimension follows from at least some of these factor analytic studies.

Abelson's (1988) factor analyses of various self-report measures of conviction yielded several item clusters that were relatively stable across eight political issues. In particular, one of these factors, *emotional commitment,* was defined by items such as "I can't imagine ever changing my mind" and "my beliefs about *X* express the real me," and a second factor, *cognitive elaboration,* was defined by items such as "it's easy to explain my views" and "several other issues could come up in a conversation about it" (Abelson, 1988, p. 273). Whereas the cognitive elaboration factor was composed primarily of items compatible with conceptions of strength as a cognitive variable, the emotional commitment factor was composed primarily of items more compatible with conceptions of strength as a more affective and motivational variable. Abelson's findings were thus suggestive of at least a partial separability of an affective and motivational dimension of strength from a cognitive dimension.

Lending support to a distinction between affective and cognitive aspects of strength was Pomerantz and colleagues' (1995) factor analysis of self-report strength measures, which yielded two clear factors across several different issues and participant samples. Loading highly on an *embeddedness* factor were participants' self-reports of the centrality of their attitudes to their self-concept and of the extent to which their attitudes were representative of their values. In contrast, loading highly on a *commitment* factor were participants' self-reports of certainty and the likelihood of changing their opinions. Consistent with Pomerantz and colleagues' (1995) interpretation of embeddedness as tapping cognitive aspects of strength and commitment as tapping affective aspects, Tordesillas and colleagues (1994) replicated this factor structure and showed further that embeddedness, but not commitment, was associated with prior exposure to issue-relevant information. Also confirming this separation between cognition and affect were the results of assessing ambivalence and evaluative extremity within participants' affective and cognitive associations: whereas affective unambivalence and affective extremity predicted commitment, cognitive extremity predicted embeddedness.

Also supporting a distinction between the affective and cognitive aspects of attitude strength are Pomerantz et al.'s (1995) findings concerning accessibility. The loading of this variable on their commitment factor and the affective nature of this factor suggest that accessibility might reflect a grounding of attitudes in affective experience. This interpretation coheres with Fazio's (1995) claim that attitudes based on emotion have stronger object-evaluation associations and are therefore more accessible. Bolstering this claim, Fazio and Powell (1992, reported in Fazio, 1995) showed that accessibility increases to the extent that respondents described their evaluations in terms of adjectives judged to convey emotional reactions.

Although several findings have thus suggested the utility of distinguishing cognitive from affective aspects of attitude strength, subsequent work may well yield other useful distinctions beyond, or within, these two broad dimensions. For example, Boninger, Krosnick, and Berent's (1995) finding that the importance of attitudes toward several social issues was predictable from measures of the extent to which these attitudes served concerns of value-expression, social identity, or self-interest suggests that strength's dimensionality may be organized around these or other functional themes. Whatever the dimensionality of strength, the issue of what constitutes strength per se versus strength's correlates, antecedents, and consequences requires greater attention. For example, attitude stability was sometimes regarded in past research as an indicator of strength (e.g., Raden, 1985), whereas more recent research has more appropriately treated this variable as a consequence of strength (e.g., Petty & Krosnick, 1995). The most theoretically productive approach is to define attitude strength by variables that illuminate the aspects of attitude structure that confer strength. Nonetheless, within this structural class of strength variables, some may prove antecedent to others. For example, extensive affective or cognitive associations may produce attitudes that are represented in memory as stronger object-evaluation associations and therefore are more accessible.

Subsequent research should go beyond the question of strength's dimensionality to the question of whether such distinctions matter. If all aspects of attitude strength produced the very same effects, the theoretical importance of distinguishing types of strength would be hollow. In this regard, it is noteworthy that the Pomerantz et al. (1995) research showed that their affective and cognitive strength factors differentially influenced variables such as selective cognitive elaboration and selective judgment and that the Biek et al. (1996) research found that their affective and cognitive strength factors differentially influenced selective judgment. Although these findings suggest that different aspects of attitude strength do indeed lead to different processing and judgmental outcomes, most existing studies have not addressed this issue because of their focus on a single strength variable in relation to a single consequence.

ATTITUDINAL SELECTIVITY

A major implication of the idea that attitudes are important psychological structures is the principle that they exert selective effects on information processing. This principle is fundamental to psychologists' understanding of attitudes. Attitudes' impact on information processing would be congruent with the functional claim, which we discuss later in this chapter, that attitudes organize and structure stimuli in an otherwise ambiguous informational environment. Moreover, because attitudes capture the evaluative meaning that is inherent in concepts, they inform people about the extent to which entities in their environment are likely to further or impede their progress toward their goals. That structures assumed to be motivationally important in this sense would affect information processing seemed obvious to early theorists and fit with their more general claims that perception and cognition are influenced by perceivers' expectancies, goals, moods, attitudes, and values (e.g., F. H. Allport, 1955; Asch, 1946; Lewin, 1935; M. Sherif, 1935).

The empirical literature on attitudinal selectivity features various versions of a single central proposition that attitudes bias information processing in favor of material that is congruent with one's attitudes—that is, in favor of proattitudinal information. The underlying rationale for this proposition is that people are motivated to defend their attitudes from information that would challenge them. Because this motivation was presumed to cause people to favor information that is proattitudinal—that is, attitudinally congenial—the predicted phenomena were labeled *congeniality effects* and were hypothesized to occur at all stages of information processing. Researchers thus expected to find selectivity that favors congenial information in exposure and attention, perception and judgment, and memory. Claiming support for these expectations, the President's Science Advisory Committee in 1962 recognized this type of attitudinal selectivity as one of the most basic principles established by behavioral research (Behavioral Science Subpanel, 1962). However, later in the 1960s reviewers of selectivity research maintained that strong and robust selectivity phenomena were often absent. Prominent attitude researchers promoted the view that, however reasonable it was to expect selectivity, it was not empirically validated (e.g., Freedman & Sears, 1965; McGuire, 1969). As this negative verdict has been gradually modified, a more complex view has emerged of the processes by which attitudes affect the acquisition and storage of information. As knowledge of these processes has improved, theorists have begun to develop a more differentiated view of the ways that selectivity is manifested and a more contingent view of the conditions under which attitudes affect information processing. Nonetheless, there is greater uncertainty about the empirical status of some forms of attitudinal selectivity than about most other attitudinal phenomena considered in this chapter.

Selective Exposure and Attention

The general idea that positive attitudes are expressed by approach behaviors and negative attitudes by avoidance behaviors suggests that attitudes would affect both exposure to information and attention paid to it. Although early theorists maintained that people approach and attend to information that upholds their attitudes and avoid and pay little attention to conflicting information (e.g., James, 1890/1952), Festinger (1957, 1964) was the first to discuss this idea in detail and subject it to empirical scrutiny. His cognitive dissonance theory predicted that, in order to reduce dissonance and ensure consonance, people would approach information that supports their attitudes and decisions and avoid information that challenges them.

Festinger (1957) became known for a somewhat narrower version of the selectivity principle than the idea that people favor information that agrees with their attitudes. Specifically, he emphasized the differences between information processing that preceded versus followed a decision. He maintained that people are willing to expose themselves to information in a relatively unbiased manner prior to committing themselves to a decision, whereas following commitment they are selective in the sense that they seek out information supportive of their decision and avoid nonsupportive information. Because people hold relatively positive attitudes toward whatever they have decided in favor of, this post-decisional selectivity is a form of attitudinal selectivity. Still, the broader selectivity principle that people favor information that is congenial with their attitudes is consistent with the general tenor of Festinger's discussion and certainly with other early discussions of selective exposure (e.g., Klapper, 1960).

Psychologists' belief in selective exposure and attention was challenged by the publication of Freedman and Sears' (1965) review of research in this area. These authors argued that there was in fact little evidence for attitudinal selectivity in exposure to information or attention to it when evidence was examined in experiments that controlled other causes of selectivity. According to Freedman and Sears, people tend to be exposed to a greater amount of supportive than nonsupportive information in their natural environments for reasons other than their attitudinal preferences. For example, supportive information may be more frequent in many settings or more useful under many circumstances.

It appeared to these reviewers that, once these causes of *de facto selectivity* were experimentally controlled, there remained neither a preference for supportive information nor an avoidance of nonsupportive information.

Even though Freedman and Sears' (1965) verdict and explicit directive for investigators to "turn away from" (p. 94) research on selective exposure dampened interest in the problem, a modest number of additional studies have accumulated in subsequent years. In fact, Festinger's (1964) second book on dissonance reported a program of research on selective exposure and promising support for several predictions derived from cognitive dissonance theory. According to Frey's (1986) narrative integration of selective exposure research, preference for attitudinally congenial information can be detected in a contingent pattern of effects that are in fact consistent with many of the hypotheses that Festinger put forth. For example, selectivity is more likely when people have freely chosen to perform an attitude-relevant behavior or have committed themselves to a particular attitude or course of action. Also, there appears to be no preference for supportive over nonsupportive information if both types of information are weak in the sense of being implausible or deriving from a low credibility source. When information is strong, the tendency to prefer supportive information is more robust. Frey and other reviewers (Wicklund & Brehm, 1976) have also maintained that evidence for selective avoidance of nonsupportive information is in general weaker than for selective approach of supportive information.

A crucial insight developed on the basis of experimental studies of selective exposure is that there are important tendencies other than attitudinal selectivity that also govern exposure and attention to attitude-relevant information. Especially strong is a tendency to prefer information that has high utility in relation to goal attainment or future decisions (e.g., Lowe & Steiner, 1968) and at least under some circumstances a tendency to prefer unfamiliar information (e.g., Brock, Albert, & Becker, 1970; Sears, 1965).

Although it is likely that selective exposure and attention would be more pronounced in relation to strong attitudes, many studies on selective exposure and attention examined relatively unimportant attitudes and behavioral commitments, and, moreover, measures of attitude strength have rarely been featured in this research. Suggesting that support for selectivity would have been more consistently obtained if strong attitudes had been challenged by highly credible events, Sweeney and Gruber (1984) obtained evidence for both selective approach of congenial information and selective avoidance of uncongenial information in a study that used survey research methods to examine interest in and attention to the Watergate scandal on the part of Nixon supporters, McGovern supporters, and undecided citizens. More research involving natural-setting events

that challenge important attitudes may clarify the prevalence of selective exposure.

Selective Perception and Judgment

Another form of the selectivity hypothesis is that attitudinally congenial information is perceived and evaluated more precisely than attitudinally uncongenial information. For example, Festinger (1957) emphasized that forced exposure to attitudinally uncongenial information would elicit biased perception and evaluation of the information, responses that he characterized as "quick defensive processes which prevent the new cognition from ever becoming firmly established" (p. 137). M. Sherif and Hovland (1961) argued that people's own attitudes serve as judgmental anchors and that, as a consequence, people assimilate or minimize the dissimilarity of information that is relatively close to their own attitudes whereas they contrast or exaggerate the dissimilarity of information that is relatively distant. Moreover, these perceptual distortions were assumed to influence judgment such that statements that are assimilated are evaluated relatively positively (e.g., as fair and unbiased), whereas those that are contrasted are evaluated relatively negatively (e.g., as unfair and biased). The central role of these selectivity postulates in attitude theory as well as the attention attracted by early demonstrations that attitudes apparently affect the perception of ambiguous information (e.g., Hastorf & Cantril, 1954) led investigators to believe that attitudes have strong and robust effects on the perception and judgment of information.

Experimental research has produced a number of findings consistent with the claims of selectivity theorists. For example, research on social judgment has shown that people contrast statements that differ substantially from their own position and (at least sometimes) assimilate statements that are close to their own position (e.g., Dawes, Singer, & Lemons, 1972; Hovland & Sherif, 1952; Manis, 1960). However, the status of assimilation and contrast as true perceptual effects was called into question by the suggestion that they merely reflect the impact of participants' own attitudes on their use of the response scale that they have available for rating attitudinal statements (e.g., Upshaw, 1969). However, subsequent work that took a variety of methodological issues into account suggested that assimilation and contrast are at least to some extent genuine perceptual phenomena in attitudinal contexts (e.g., Judd, Kenny, & Krosnick, 1983; Romer, 1983).

The proper theoretical understanding of assimilation and contrast effects remains a matter of some debate. The multiplicity of theories follows at least in part from the fact that numerous variables have been shown to moderate assimilation and contrast effects (see Eiser's, 1990, review). Although different theories have usually emphasized particular moderators, Schwarz and Bless (1992) proposed an especially integrative theory of assimilation and contrast effects in attitudinal and other judgments. This theory, known as the *inclusion/exclusion model,* emphasizes categorization processes that occur when people judge a target (e.g., a statement supporting a flat tax) in terms of context information that comes to mind (e.g., one's own attitude toward the flat tax). People form a category that encompasses the target (e.g., a Republican position on the flat tax), and either include or exclude from this target category the context information that comes to mind. Including this context information in the category is likely to produce assimilation of the target stimulus to this information, whereas exclusion of the context information from the category is likely to produce contrast of the target simulus away from this information. This theory has considerable power to explain, not only assimilation and contrast in attitudinal judgments, but also a variety of other phenomena, including context effects in responding to survey questions.

In contrast to the complexity of the debates about assimilation and contrast effects, the general principle that people unfavorably evaluate information that challenges their attitudes has received clear-cut support in several contexts. For example, people rate information that confirms their attitudes as more convincing and valid and as containing stronger arguments than information that disconfirms their attitudes (e.g., Lord, Ross, & Lepper, 1979), especially if their attitudes are strong (K. Edwards & Smith, 1966; Houston & Fazio, 1989; A. G. Miller et al., 1993; Pomerantz et al., 1995). Television viewers have been shown to bias their judgments of who won presidential debates in favor of the candidate they preferred prior to the debate (e.g., Bothwell & Brigham, 1983). The tendency for partisans on an issue to view the media as hostile to their views also shows that people's attitudes bias their evaluations of attitude-relevant information (e.g., Giner-Sorolla & Chaiken, 1994; Vallone, Ross, & Lepper, 1985). Demonstrating that the cognitive processes underlying this biased evaluation can be active and elaborative are studies showing that participants listed more counterarguments in response to messages that were attitudinally uncongenial compared with congenial and spent more time scrutinizing the uncongenial messages (e.g., Cacioppo & Petty, 1979; K. Edwards & Smith, 1996). In summary, selective evaluation is pervasive: ordinarily people do not like or enjoy attitudinally uncongenial information, they generally find such information to be relatively unconvincing and invalid, and they may work quite hard to refute such information. Yet, the consistency of such findings should hardly be surprising because the selective evaluation principle is merely the thoroughly commonsensical idea, easily rendered in balance-theory terms, that

people dislike information that is critical of things that they like.

Selective Memory

The hypothesis that proattitudinal information is more memorable than counterattitudinal information was popular in the earliest period of systematic research on attitudes. The first studies of attitudinal selectivity in memory generally yielded support for this congeniality bias (e.g., A. L. Edwards, 1941; Levine & Murphy, 1943; Postman & Murphy, 1943; Watson & Hartmann, 1939). Several conceptual replications of the congeniality effect were reported during the 1950s, although the findings were often weak and not entirely consistent within studies (e.g., Alper & Korchin, 1952; Doob, 1953). Notable among this second wave of experiments were demonstrations that the tendency for attitude-consistent information to be more memorable could be reversed in certain circumstances—for example, when uncongenial information would be useful in a subsequent counterarguing task (Jones & Aneshansel, 1956).

Several studies published during the 1960s failed to reveal any reliable effect of attitude on memory (e.g., Brigham & Cook, 1969; Fitzgerald & Ausubel, 1963; Greenwald & Sakumura, 1967; Waly & Cook, 1965). Several other experiments produced ambiguous data (e.g., Malpass, 1969; S. S. Smith & Jamieson, 1972). These null and ambiguous results fostered the perception that the effects produced in many early studies were at best fragile and may have been contaminated by a variety of methodological problems (see Greenwald, 1975; Greenwald & Sakumura, 1967). These events seemed to convince many 1970s investigators and textbook writers that people's attitudes exert little, if any, impact on their memory for attitude-relevant information. Despite the discouraging tone of some of the discussions of the impact of attitudes on memory, a moderate number of additional experiments have accumulated in the past 25 years (see Eagly & Chaiken, 1993). Although Roberts' (1985) quantitative review of a large number of experiments on selective memory concluded that the congeniality effect is a reliable phenomenon, findings in this research literature appear to be quite inconsistent, and many studies have produced convincingly null findings or reversals of the congeniality effect.

From a contemporary perspective, early researchers' logic for predicting attitudes' effects on memory seems overly simple—specifically, that people should screen out information that challenges their attitudes, in an effort to defend these attitudes. Given that many researchers studied highly controversial social issues and selected participants whose attitudes were known to be polarized, it is not unreasonable that these participants should be motivated to defend their attitudes. Yet, investigators typically assumed that perceivers would follow a defensive approach that can be deemed passive, whereby they would selectively screen out challenging information. In concentrating on passive defense against attitudinal attack, these researchers neglected to consider the possibility of the type of active defense that has been demonstrated in research on selective evaluation (e.g., K. Edwards & Smith, 1996). Thus, instead of passively screening out incongruent information, recipients who are active defenders would attend especially carefully to it and process it systematically, in order to refute it through counterarguing. Even though challenging information would become memorable, it would pose little threat to existing attitudes, to the extent that it was successfully counterargued.

Consistent with this logic, some studies have yielded preferences for attitudinally incongruent information, occasionally on an overall basis (e.g., Cacioppo & Petty, 1979), but more typically under certain circumstances or for certain types of people (e.g., J. T. Johnson & Judd, 1983; Jones & Aneshansel, 1956; Zimmerman & Chaiken, 1996). Other studies have yielded a preference for attitudinally extreme information (e.g., Judd & Kulik, 1980). Therefore, the central task remains to account for the complexity of these findings—that is, to delineate the conditions under which memory favors attitudinally congruent, incongruent, or extreme information.

In contemporary investigations of attitudes' effects on memory, understanding of findings' variability has begun to emerge from consideration of some of the structural features of people's knowledge in attitudinal domains. For example, Pratkanis (1989) drew attention to attitudes' bipolar or unipolar structure, a variable discussed earlier in this chapter. Pratkanis's argument is that, to the extent that people's attitudes are unipolar (i.e., they possess predominantly knowledge that is congruent with their own position), they may find it difficult to encode incongruent information or to counterargue it to the extent that they have encoded it. They may thus show the congeniality effect. Conversely, to the extent that people are bipolar (i.e., familiar with both supporting and opposing viewpoints), uncongenial information may be as strongly linked to stored knowledge as is congenial information. Under such circumstances, congenial and uncongenial information should be encoded equally well, and given sufficient motivation to defend attitudes, uncongenial information should be extensively counterargued and therefore recalled at least as well as congenial information.

The processes that mediate attitudinal selectivity in memory may operate more powerfully to the extent that perceivers' attitudes are strong. Following this logic, Eagly, Kulesa, Shaw-Barnes, Hutson-Comeux, and Brannon (1996) examined attitude strength's enhancement of the processes by which attitudes influence memory. Although these researchers found no evidence of congeniality or its opposite when comparing participants' memory for proattitudinal and counterattitudinal messages, they found evidence for contrasting attitudinally-driven processes, one that occurred with counterattitudinal message and the other with proattitudinal messages. Participants who received a counterattitudinal message counterargued it vigorously in order to defend their attitudes from attack; as a consequence, its arguments were well remembered. In contrast, participants who received a proattitudinal message showed general approval of the information and remembered it because its pleasing match to their prior beliefs facilitated retrieval that was not dependent on elaboration of the arguments. To the extent that participants' attitudes were strong, both of these processes operated more powerfully and thereby enhanced memory for the messages. More generally, progress should follow from greater understanding of the role of attitude structure and strength in moderating selectivity effects that occur at all stages of information processing. Because most selectivity research predated the contemporary work on strength and structure that is considered in this chapter, the implications of most of these developments for selectivity have yet to be explored.

This research thus illustrates that quite different processes may underlie attitudinal selectivity depending on the congeniality of the information that perceivers encounter. The possibility of active processes by which people enthusiastically engage attitudinally incongruent information, in order to counter its persuasive impact, needs further development in selectivity research. The possibility of active and passive defense is in harmony with contemporary dual-process theories of social judgment (e.g., Chaiken, 1980, 1987; Fiske & Neuberg, 1990; Petty & Cacioppo, 1986). Consistent with these theories, whether recipients of messages use a cognitively demanding, active approach or an avoidant, passive approach to defending their attitudes from attack would depend on their motivation and ability to use the more effortful, active approach. In the absence of motivation or ability, the easier, passive route to defense would be chosen; in the presence of both motivation and ability, the more effortful route of attacking counterattitudinal material would be more likely. These propositions deserve exploration in relation to selective exposure and attention as well as selective memory.

ATTITUDES AS PREDICTORS OF BEHAVIOR

Another very important structural issue is the relation of attitudes to behaviors. Highly relevant to this issue is one of the principles with which this chapter began—namely, that attitudes are expressed in overt behavior as well as in cognitions and affects. Inherent in this principle is the idea that attitudes cause people to behave in a manner that is evaluatively consistent with them. G. W. Allport's (1935) well-known statement that attitudes exert "a directive and dynamic influence upon the individual's response" (p. 810) hypothesized attitudes' causal impact on behavior in clear form. This claim that attitudes *cause* behaviors presents the attitude-behavior hypothesis in its strong form. In contrast, the claim that attitudes are merely *correlated with* behaviors presents the attitude-behavior hypothesis in its weaker form, devoid of the implication that the positive correlation necessarily arises from attitudes' causal impact on behavior. In fact, positive correlations between attitudes and behavior, although consistent with the hypothesis that attitudes cause behavior, are consistent as well with other hypotheses—in particular, with the hypothesis that behaviors cause attitudes. Although it may seem that the strong hypothesis is self-evident and that the weak hypothesis would be even more easily confirmed, adequately testing both forms of the hypothesis has proven to be challenging. This challenge became evident at an early point when some empirical studies produced weak attitude-behavior correlations (e.g., LaPiere, 1934). Many social scientists were surprised and became increasingly concerned about what they perceived as a rather bleak empirical picture (e.g., Blumer, 1955; Deutscher, 1966; Wicker, 1969). This escalation of concern, associated with increasing skepticism about attitudes' importance to behavior, produced a strong and constructive response among some attitude researchers, who collectively produced a body of theory and research that ultimately yielded considerable support for both the strong and the weak form of the attitude-behavior hypothesis.

Attitudes Toward Targets, Attitudes Toward Behaviors, and the Compatability of Attitudinal and Behavioral Measures

A fundamental insight is that understanding attitudes' predictive validity in relation to behavior requires distinguishing between two types of attitudes. From a psychometric perspective, predicting behavior is quite a different problem, depending on which type of attitude serves as a predictor. These two types, which are known as *attitudes toward behaviors* and *attitudes toward targets,* differ in their attitude object.[2] The object of the attitude is thus the behavior itself or the target of the behavior, which is the entity to which the behavior is directed. For example, if a citizen donates $100 to his senator's election campaign, the senator is the target of the behavior of donating, and this citizen probably holds a positive attitude toward this target. Simultaneously, this citizen probably also holds a positive attitude toward the behavior of giving money to the election campaign. However, for perhaps the majority of citizens, these two attitudes would not be equal in extremity or even in valence. It would be common that citizens would have a positive attitude toward their senator but a negative attitude toward donating money to the campaign, often because they believe that they cannot afford to donate. It is this latter type of attitude—namely, attitudes toward behaviors—that has proven to be particularly effective in predicting behavior. This predictive advantage stems from perceivers' tendency, when forming attitudes toward behaviors, to take into account considerations (e.g., barriers and limitations) that become salient in the situation of potential action.

In the early decades of attitude research, psychologists had confined their investigations to attitudes toward targets, most commonly social and political attitudes that people hold toward issues, institutions, and groups. Ordinarily, attitudes of this type show rather weak relations when used as predictors of single behaviors. The reason for these weak relations is obvious: a single behavior is typically influenced by a variety of factors in addition to an attitude toward a target. Whereas people take many of these other factors into account in forming their attitudes toward the behavior, they are not reflected in their attitudes toward the target. For example, as already argued, the act of donating money to a political candidate would be a function, not only of attitude toward the candidate, but also of whether a person can afford to donate, a consideration that would not influence the attitude toward the candidate. Because attitude toward the target is in this manner only a partial determinant of each behavior, in psychometric terms a single behavior would ordinarily provide a somewhat unreliable indicator of an attitude.

Fortunately, a reliable behavioral measure of an attitude toward a target can usually be produced by the simple device of aggregating each individual's responses across a number of different behaviors, each of which is partially influenced by the attitude. When an aggregated index of behaviors toward a given target is formed in this manner, the determinants of these behaviors other than the attitude in question tend to cancel one another. As Fishbein and Ajzen (1974) argued, by thus creating a reliable *multiple-act* behavioral criterion rather than relying on an unreliable *single-act* criterion, researchers produce attitude-behavior correlations of at least moderate size, provided that the attitude toward the target is reliably assessed (ordinarily by a set of questionnaire items). This *aggregation principle* has been supported by much empirical evidence, including Fishbein and Ajzen's (1974) questionnaire study predicting reported religious behaviors from attitudes toward religion and Weigel and Newman's (1976) field study predicting environmentally friendly behaviors from environmental attitudes.

If a researcher merely desires to achieve a moderately

high correlation between an attitude toward a target and behavior, the device of constructing an appropriate multiple-act behavioral criterion has much to recommend it. And of course the other device that will produce substantial attitude-behavior correlations is to predict a single behavior from the attitude toward the specific behavior that is predicted. These insights that attitudes toward targets successfully predict multiple-act criteria and that attitudes toward behaviors successfully predict single-act criteria were enlarged by Ajzen and Fishbein (1977) into a more comprehensive understanding of relations between different kinds of attitudes and behavioral criteria. They recognized that any single behavior or any broader or narrower set of behaviors can be predicted from an attitude if this attitude is appropriately formulated to be as broad or narrow as the behavioral criterion. This matching principle, known as the *principle of compatibility* (or *correspondence*), merely specifies that the critical features of the behavioral criterion should be incorporated into the attitude that is assessed to enable it to successfully predict the criterion.

Attitude-behavior correlations of at least moderate magnitude are virtually insured merely by following the principle of compatibility, as initially demonstrated by Ajzen and Fishbein's (1977) review of studies that differed in the compatibility of their measures and more recently by substantial evidence from quantitative syntheses of studies reporting attitude-behavior correlations. Kim and Hunter (1993) classified studies into high, medium, and low levels of compatibility of their measures of attitudes and behavior and found mean attitude-behavior correlations of .40, .64, and .86, respectively, after the correlations had been corrected for several sources of error that lowered their magnitude (e.g., measurement error). Other meta-analytic support for the compatibility principle was presented by Kraus (1995), who examined attitude-behavior correlations at different levels of correspondence in studies that manipulated this variable, and by Eckes and Six (1994), who classified studies by whether they had assessed attitudes toward behaviors or attitudes toward targets. Despite this overwhelming empirical support for the idea that compatible measures will produce substantial attitude-behavior correlations, high correlations are rarely as important a goal of research as understanding the psychological processes that account for these relationships. Therefore, the focus of attitude-behavior research quite appropriately moved from the compatibility principle to understanding attitudes' causal relations to behavior.

Causal Models of Attitudes' Impact on Behavior

Causal models of the attitude-behavior relation explore the psychological processes that intervene between the activation of an attitude and a behavioral response to the attitude object. Many such models have been proposed. To organize a presentation of the major approaches to causal models of the attitude-behavior relation, Figure 2 introduces a composite model of attitude-behavior relations, a model formulated for heuristic purposes to encompass the major variables that attitude researchers have incorporated into their causal theories (see Eagly & Chaiken, 1993). The terms of this model, reading from the right (or outcome) side of the model include (a) behavior, (b) intention to behave, (c) attitude toward the behavior, (d) habit, and (e) attitude toward the target of the behavior. As determinants of attitude toward the behavior, the model also includes the anticipated outcomes of the behavior, divided into three classes: (a) utilitarian outcomes (i.e., rewards and punishments), (b) normative outcomes (i.e., others' social approval and the pride and guilt that follow from internalized moral rules), and (c) self-identity outcomes (i.e., affirmations and repudiations of the self-concept). This model places attitudes within a network of other psychological variables that are relevant to behavior. Among its important features are the inclusion of the two distinct types of attitudes introduced in the prior section—attitudes toward behaviors and attitudes toward the targets of behavior.

Expectancy-value Models Many aspects of the composite model follow from expectancy-value models of behavior, especially from Fishbein and Ajzen's *theory of reasoned action* (Ajzen & Fishbein, 1980; Fishbein, 1980; Fishbein & Ajzen, 1975). In this theory, which is diagrammed in Figure 3, the proximal cause of behavior is not attitude, but an intention to engage in a behavior, which is a decision to act in a particular way; the composite model also allows that intention can play this important mediating role. The attitude that is featured in the theory of reasoned action is the attitude that is more proximal to behavior in the composite model—namely, attitude toward the behavior, which influences behavior through its impact on intention to engage in the behavior. Following the general principle of expectancy-value theories (see Feather, 1982), attitude toward the behavior is itself a function of the value one assigns to the perceived consequences of the behavior and the subjective probabilities one attaches to these consequences. Yet, in the theory of reasoned action the perceived consequences of behavior are divided into two classes: utilitarian consequences that consist of rewards and punishments that are directly experienced and normative consequences that consist of perceptions of others' approval or disapproval of one's behavior. Perceptions of these utilitarian consequences underlie *attitude toward the behavior,* which is one's evaluation of personally engaging in the behavior, and perceptions of these normative consequences underlie *subjective norm,* which is one's perception of the extent to which significant others think that one should en-

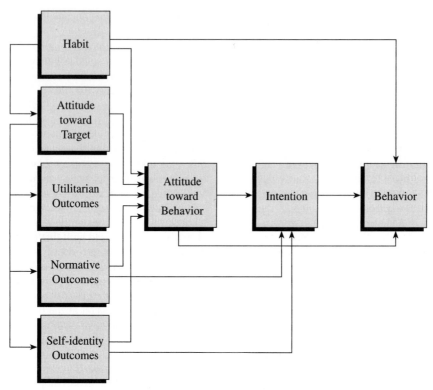

FIGURE 2   Representation of a Composite Attitude-Behavior Model.
For causal relations not discussed in the text, see Eagly and Chaiken (1993).

gage in the behavior. These two sets of perceived consequences then determine intention to engage in a behavior, which is the immediate antecedent of the behavior. The model is thus a statement of individual rationality or "reasoned action," defined in terms of behavior's consequences: to the extent that a behavior is expected to facilitate good outcomes and other people are thought to approve of the behavior, people intend to engage in the behavior, which then becomes more likely.

This seminal approach has stimulated many efforts to build expectancy-value models that have as their central feature the idea that people form attitudes toward behavioral acts by evaluating acts' likely consequences. In these models, attitudes then impact indirectly or directly on behavior. Some versions of the model differ in their treatment of anticipated consequences, with Fishbein and Ajzen (1975) dividing them into behavioral beliefs pertaining to directly experienced rewards and punishments, which in turn produce an overall attitude toward the behavior, and normative beliefs pertaining to others' approval and disapproval, which in turn produce an overall subjective norm. In some elaborations of the reasoned action model, other classes of consequences have been given priority. For example, some studies suggested that behavioral prediction

can be improved by taking into account self-identity outcomes, understood as the extent to which behaviors are expected to affirm one's self-concept (e.g., Biddle, Bank, & Slavings, 1987; Charng, Piliavin, & Callero, 1988). In order to highlight the various classes of anticipated outcomes that may influence behavior, the composite model includes utilitarian, normative, and self-identity outcomes.

The inclusion of various classes of outcomes in expectancy-value models of the attitude-behavior relation raises the question of whether beliefs from all these classes would necessarily be relevant to action. Consistent with empirical evidence and with the theory of reasoned action's differential weighting of its two classes of anticipated outcomes, the answer to this question is negative. There appear to be stable individual differences in the extent to which behaviors are under the control of different classes of outcomes (Trafimow & Finlay, 1996). Moreover, different types of perceived outcomes would become salient, depending on the nature of the behavior and situational cues. In harmony with this view, Ajzen (1996) has argued that the prediction of behavior from attitudes is more successful if the same beliefs are activated at the time of attitude assessment and the time of action. If a different set of beliefs is activated at the time of action, the attitude

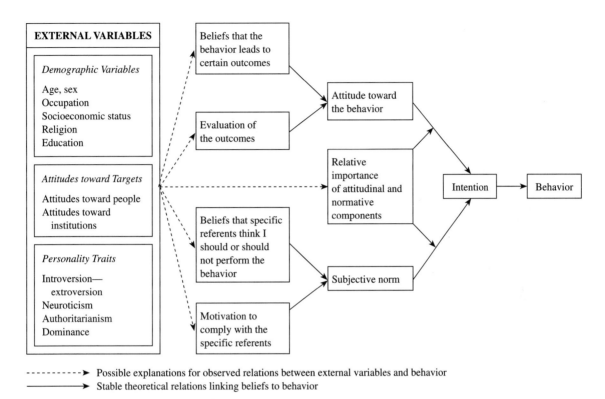

Possible explanations for observed relations between external variables and behavior
Stable theoretical relations linking beliefs to behavior

FIGURE 3   Representation of the Theory of Reasoned Action.
The term "external variables" refers to all variables not considered by the theory. (*Source:* Adapted from Ajzen
and Fishbein, 1980, Figure 7.1, p. 84.)

that actually influences behavior would be different from
the one that was assessed.

The emphasis of the theory of reasoned action on the
perceived consequences of behavior led it to be criticized
for its presumed assumption that people necessarily engage
in elaborate cogitation about consequences prior to taking
any action (e.g., Fazio, 1986; McGuire, 1985). However,
Ajzen and Fishbein (1980) emphasized that their theory
does not assume that people are buried in thought in the
sense that they scrutinize the determinants of their behavior prior to each and every behavioral act. Rather, their
view was merely that people have at some time formed
their attitudes toward behaviors by thinking about the consequences of their behavior. Once such an attitude is
formed, people need not review these consequences prior
to each and every behavioral opportunity. They may instead retrieve the attitude or perhaps only an intention, as a
prelude to behavior. Moreover, sometimes attitudes toward
behavior may produce behavioral acts that are not mediated by the formation of intentions to act (Bagozzi & Yi,
1989; Bentler & Speckart, 1979). Such relatively spontaneous behaviors can be treated in the expectancy-value tradition by linking attitudes toward behavior directly to be-

havior, a link included in the composite model. Acknowledging that intention is not a necessary precursor of behavior raises the important issue of when behavioral choices
are more spontaneous and when they are mediated by more
deliberative processes that may involve thinking about the
consequences of behavior or the attributes of attitude objects. Fazio and his colleagues addressed this issue in terms
of individuals having sufficient motivation and opportunity
to engage in the relatively effortful process of retrieving
and considering the beliefs that are associated with their attitudes (Fazio, 1990; Sanbonmatsu & Fazio, 1990).

Other theorists in the expectancy-value tradition explored the idea that some behaviors may not be volitional
at all because they are a product of well-learned predispositions to respond that might be termed *habits*. In contemporary terminology, the cognitive processing that controls
such responding can be termed automatic and thus is
quickly and easily performed, often in parallel with other
activities. These highly routinized behaviors can occur
without a conscious decision to act. Theorists such as
Bentler and Speckart (1979) acknowledged this possibility
by introducing past behavior as a predictor of behavior, in
addition to attitude and subject norm. Also, Triandis's

(1977, 1980) attitude-behavior model incorporated a habit term, which he defined as "situation-specific sequences that are or have become automatic, so that they occur without self-instruction" (Triandis, 1980, p. 204). Of course, habits and intentional behaviors are often intertwined, when, for example, a person consciously decides to drive to the grocery store and performs many habitual acts in the process of driving the car.

Ouellette and Wood's (1997) meta-analysis of studies that examined habit as a predictor of behavior or behavioral intention found that it was as effective a predictor as attitude and a particularly strong predictor of behaviors that have a high typical rate of occurrence in daily life (e.g., seatbelt usage). To recognize the importance of habit, understood as a tendency to repeat prior responses given constancies in the context of the behavior, the composite model includes a habit term that impacts directly on behavior (and on other terms of the model).

Another way to broaden the reasoned action model beyond purely volitional or voluntary acts is to consider more complex behaviors such as climbing a mountain, which often require planning, arranging for resources, and obtaining the cooperation of other people (see Liska, 1984). Moreover, attaining behavioral outcomes such as publishing a research article in a scientific journal or earning a high grade in a course requires that people coordinate sequences of behaviors by which they strive for goals. To predict complex behaviors and the attainment of behavioral outcomes, Ajzen's (1991, 1996) theory of planned behavior incorporated, as an additional predictor of intention and behavior, a construct closely related to Bandura's (1977) concept of self-efficacy. Ajzen named this construct *perceived behavior control* and defined it as people's perception of whether they can perform the behavior if they wish to do so. Consistent with Ajzen's reasoning, his model has yielded superior prediction of less controllable behaviors such as getting an A in a course (Madden, Ellen, & Ajzen, 1992) but not of more controllable behaviors such as attending meetings of groups devoted to political causes (e.g., Kelly & Breinlinger, 1995).[3] Nonetheless, the appropriate interpretation of this improved prediction is still open to some debate. Perhaps, as Ajzen maintained, the perception that one has little control weakens the intention to engage in a behavior; however, the perception that one has high control would seem to strengthen an intention only in the context of a positive attitude toward the behavior (see Eagly & Chaiken, 1993). Alternatively, as Manstead and Parker (1995) suggested, reporting low control over behaviors might merely serve to justify intentions that do not follow logically from attitudes toward behaviors and subjective norms.

In view of the various modifications that researchers have made to the theory of reasoned action, the approach is best considered a flexible family of expectancy-value models that give a causal role to attitudes toward behavioral acts in conjunction with several other hypothetical constructs. These models of behavior have been extremely popular in applied research since the 1970s. The unmodified theory of reasoned action has been used to predict many different behaviors, the majority of which are relatively simple and easily executed acts such as donating blood (Pomazal & Jaccard, 1976), voting (Fishbein, Middlestadt, & Chung, 1986), purchasing consumer products (Brinberg & Cummings, 1983), and brushing one's teeth (McCaul, O'Neill, & Glasgow, 1988). The model has also been used to predict gay men's intentions to perform AIDS-related sexual behaviors (Fishbein et al., 1992) and people's intentions to use contraceptive methods (Doll & Orth, 1993). In general, prediction on the basis of the model has been quite successful, as meta-analyses of this extensive research literature have shown (Sheppard, Hartwick, & Warshaw, 1988; Van den Putte, 1993). Moreover, variant models such as the theory of planned behavior have shown even more success in predicting behavior in the particular domains for which their added variables have been tailored (e.g., Madden et al., 1992).

In other attempts to predict behaviors that require planning and coordination, psychologists have examined the psychological processes relevant to planning and goal-oriented behavior (see Gollwitzer & Moskowitz, 1996). These models generally postulate that behavior is influenced by the feedback that follows from people's setting of standards (or goals) for their behavior, comparing their behavior with the standard, and attempting to reduce discrepancies between their behavior and the standard (e.g., Bandura, 1989; Scheier & Carver, 1988). The setting of goals is itself a process of considerable complexity. Planning theorists such as Vallacher and Wegner (1987) emphasized that goals may be identified by people at various levels ranging from a more abstract, comprehensive level (e.g., having a successful career in psychology) to a concrete, mechanistic level (e.g., finishing up a problem set for a statistics course). The level at which goals are formulated may shift over time and in particular become more concrete when actions are disrupted.

Also typical of planning theories is the delineation of stages representing the emergence of differing psychological processes as wishes and desires become translated into goals and action. Gollwitzer's (1996) model of these successive phrases stresses the *implementation intentions* that people form at the point when they become committed to plans. These intentions link situational cues to goal-directed behaviors (e.g., when I next go to the store, I'll buy paper plates for the picnic). The contingencies that are set up can lead to a relatively automatic control of behavior by environmental cues. These views are consistent with Bargh's (1990, 1997) auto-motive model. According to Bargh, goals can be activated by environmental cues without people making conscious choices or being aware that goals are activated, if these goals have been repeatedly and consistently paired with a particular situation in the past. These automatically activated goals then direct information-processing and behavior.

Although most planning theories do not explicitly invoke attitudes as determinants of behavior, they can be reformulated in attitudinal terms, because people can hold attitudes toward goals as well as toward goal-oriented behaviors. Along these lines, Bagozzi and Warshaw (1990) formulated a theory of goal pursuit that incorporates goals into an expectancy-value model. This theory treats goal attainment as the product of trying to attain the goal and gives important causal roles to attitudes toward trying and attitudes toward successful and unsuccessful goal attainment.

The importance that expectancy-value models accord to attitudes toward behaviors deflected attention from the possible causal impact of the kinds of social and political attitudes that were traditionally used as predictors of behavior, that is, attitudes toward targets. These broader attitudes have no formal place in the expectancy-value approach. Like other variables that are not included in the reasoned action model, they are consigned to the category of "external variables" (e.g., Ajzen & Fishbein, 1980; Fishbein, 1980), as shown in Figure 3. External variables can impact on behavior through their impact on the behavioral beliefs that determine attitudes toward behavior and on the normative beliefs that determine subjective norms; or they can impact on the relative importance of these attitudinal and normative determinants of behavior. Despite this very limited role that expectancy-value theories accord to attitudes toward targets as causes of behavior, other researchers maintained an interest, not just in predicting behavior from these broader attitudes, but in considering how they may function as causes of behavior.

Attitudinal Accessibility and the Automatic Activation Model In treating attitudes toward targets as predictors of behavior, Fazio (1986, 1995) evolved a theory of the attitude-behavior relation that emphasizes a particular aspect of attitude strength, namely, attitude accessibility, as the key to understanding when attitudes and behaviors will correspond (see earlier section on attitude strength). The initial stimulus for this theory was findings showing that direct behavioral experience with the target attitude object increases the consistency between an attitude and relevant behaviors (e.g., Regan & Fazio, 1977). Although there are a number of possible reasons why past experience has this moderating role (see Fazio & Zanna, 1981), Fazio and his colleagues argued that this effect is due to the greater accessibility from memory of attitudes based on direct experience (Fazio, 1986; Fazio et al., 1982). More accessible attitudes, defined operationally as those that are expressed more quickly, were presumed to be more powerful determinants of behavior because they are more likely to be activated upon exposure to the attitude object or cues related to it. Only if an attitude is activated can it influence behavior.

The importance Fazio (1986) accorded to accessibility followed from his definition of attitude as an association between the attitude object and an evaluation. As described earlier in the chapter, these associations vary in their strength: to the extent that the object-evaluation association is strong, the attitude is accessed easily and quickly in response to cues conveyed by the attitude object. In research designed to show that attitudes' associative strength moderates their relation to behavior, Fazio and his colleagues showed that direct experience produces more accessible attitudes (e.g., Fazio et al., 1982) and that more accessible attitudes are more highly correlated with behavior (e.g., Fazio & Williams, 1986). Moreover, other studies have shown that strengthening the association between the attitude object and one's evaluation of it by having people repeatedly express their attitudes produces greater accessibility of the attitude and higher consistency between the attitude and relevant behaviors (Fazio et al., 1982; Powell & Fazio, 1984).

Despite many findings showing that attitudes' accessibility is a plausible mediator of their influence on behaviors, the manipulations of direct experience and repeated expression that Fazio and his associates have used to make this point may function at least in part through aspects of attitudes that are not wholly a function of accessibility, although they may be correlated with it. For example, Doll and Ajzen (1992) showed that direct experience with an attitude object can increase the temporal stability of the attitude. Also, Downing, Judd, and Brauer (1992) showed that repeated expression of an attitude can increase its extremity, and Roese and Olson (1994) showed that it can increase attitude importance. Other research has shown that accessibility, as assessed by response latency, is correlated with many of the indicators of attitude strength discussed earlier in this chapter (e.g., extremity, lack of ambivalence; see Bargh et al., 1992; Bargh et al., 1996; Fazio, 1995). Therefore, research needs to examine more fully the role of accessibility in relation to other potential mediators of attitudes' relations to behavior.

Evidence that attitudes can be activated spontaneously and automatically (Fazio, Powell, & Herr, 1983; Fazio et al., 1986; see prior discussion) led Fazio to propose an automatic-processing model of the relation between attitudes and behaviors, a model that departs profoundly from expectancy-value models of the attitude-behavior relation. This model indicates that an attitude that is automatically accessed without active attention or conscious thought "biases perceptions of the object in the immediate situation, and behavior simply follows from these perceptions without any necessary conscious reasoning process" (Fazio, 1986, p. 237). Although this approach thus assumes that attitudinal selectivity (see preceding section of this chapter) is relevant to mediating the relation between attitudes and behavior, the approach does not take into account the more proximal determinants of action emphasized in expectancy-value models, namely, one's attitude toward the behavioral act and one's intention to engage in it. Instead, attitudes toward the targets of behavior impact relatively directly on behavior. Our composite model instead suggests that, at a minimum, the attitude toward the target would need to evoke a positive attitude toward the behavior that is elicited, although this attitude-attitude link could be automatic and neither attitude would necessarily be admitted to conscious awareness. This view is thus consistent with Fazio's (1990) claim that attitudes toward targets can impact on behaviors without necessarily evoking a conscious reasoning process.

Intra-attitudinal Structure and the Prediction of Behavior   Consistent with Ajzen's (1996) point that prediction is enhanced by having the same beliefs accessible at the time of attitude assessment and the time of action, Millar and Tesser (1986a) pointed out that the intra-attitudinal structure activated when an attitude is assessed is not necessarily the same structure that is activated when a person decides how to behave. According to Millar and Tesser, whether a measured attitude correlates with attitude-relevant behavior may depend on having the same aspect of intra-attitudinal structure activated at these two points in time—attitude assessment and actual behavior. For example, attitudes toward acquaintances can be based on beliefs about competence that produce respect or on affective reactions that produce sheer likability. Respect should predict favoring the person in a work-related situation, whereas likability should predict favoring the person in a purely social gathering.

In relevant research, Millar and Tesser (1986a) encouraged participants to focus on the cognitive or affective aspects of their attitudes by instructing them to introspect about their attitudes (toward puzzles that were presented as stimuli) from either a cognitive or an affective perspective. The participants either wrote down reasons for holding their attitudes, establishing a cognitive focus, or wrote down how the target attitude object made them feel, establishing an affective focus. Subsequently, they encouraged these same participants to focus on either the cognitive or the affective implications of their behavior (of playing with the puzzles). Attitude-behavior consistency was enhanced when the cognitive versus affective aspect of intra-attitudinal structure that was activated matched the cognitive versus affective behavioral focus that was induced. Millar and Tesser's innovative analysis thus illustrates the utility of taking attitude structure and the accessibility of structure into account when using attitudes toward targets to predict behavior.

Two Traditions of Attitude-Behavior Research   Research in social psychology has featured two traditions of theory concerning attitudes' relation to behavior. One tradition consists of a family of expectancy-value models that regard attitudes toward behavior as an important cause of behavior, albeit a causal influence that is ordinarily treated as mediated by behavioral intentions. In the alternative tradition, behavior is predicted from attitudes toward the targets toward which behavior is directed, with less specification of intermediary steps. A more complete understanding of attitudes as causes of behavior would emerge from joining these two traditions—in particular, from formulating causal sequences that take into account both attitudes toward behaviors and attitudes toward the entities or targets toward which behaviors are directed (see Eagly & Chaiken, 1993). Although attitudes toward targets may often come to mind automatically in the presence of attitude-relevant stimuli, such an attitude would not, in and of itself, prescribe any particular behavior. At least some of the components of expectancy-value models are needed to understand why people choose to engage in any one particular behavior. For example, one's attitude toward environmental preservation may come to mind when watching a television show on the logging of old growth forests in the Pacific Northwest. This attitude, however, does not dictate any one behavior: a person whose favorable environmental attitudes come to mind might complain to family members, write a letter to the editor of a local newspaper, contact a congressional representative, or do nothing at all. For action to occur in such a situation, an individual may have to perceive some link between the activated attitude and the behavioral possibility at hand (see Snyder, 1982). Although this link need not necessarily involve cogitation about the consequences of alternative courses of action, a thought of some sort may have to be formed or retrieved to activate behavior, as Ajzen and Fishbein's (1980) discussion implies. Yet, this attitude-behavior link may have been repeated often enough in the past that it will become automatically activated given activation of the attitude and the perception of certain environmental cues (Bargh, 1997). Even such a sequence may require that a positive attitude toward a behavioral act be activated, at least on a preconscious basis.

As shown by this section of this chapter, psychologists have been successfully filling the large theoretical gap that once existed between the activation of an attitude toward a target and the execution of a particular overt behavior. One symptom of this gap was the chronically low correlations obtained when attitudes toward targets predicted single behaviors. As the mediation of these attitude-behavior relations has been clarified, higher correlations have been obtained under theoretically meaningful circumstances (e.g., for highly accessible attitudes). Nonetheless, the psychometric lessons with which this section began remain valid: researchers can produce relatively high attitude-behavior correlations by following the advice that attitudinal and behavioral measures be made compatible. High correlations can thus reflect understanding of mediational processes or mere psychometric acumen.

FUNCTIONS OF ATTITUDES

The question of why people hold attitudes is the most far-reaching question that attitude theorists can raise. Like any extremely broad question, it can be answered on several levels. The assumption underlying all these answers is the usual functionalist assumption that attitudes enable individuals to adapt to their environment. The most profound sense in which attitudes help people adapt emerges readily from reflection on attitudes' definition in terms of evaluation. To evaluate—that is, to ascertain the degree of goodness versus badness inherent in features of one's world—is absolutely fundamental to the task of surviving in that world. If people were unable to identify as good those stimuli that enable their survival and enhance their well being and identify as bad those stimuli that threaten their survival and lessen their well being, they would quickly fail to thrive.

Consistent with this view, in seminal work on dimensions of semantic meaning Osgood, Suci, and Tannenbaum (1957) argued that evaluation is primary and offered as their main evidence numerous factor analyses of meaning in which an evaluative factor accounted for more variability than any other factor. The contention that evaluation is primary received further empirical support in experiments on automatic evaluation and evaluative primacy (e.g., Bargh et al., 1996; Bargh, 1997; Murphy, Monahan, & Zajonc, 1995). For example, Bargh, Litt, Pratto, and Spielman (1989) presented participants with trait words at exposure durations that were below participants' thresholds of conscious awareness. On each trial, participants were asked to indicate whether the subliminally presented trait word was good or bad *or* whether they thought another word was or was not a synonym of the subliminal trait word. Participants correctly answered the evaluative question, but not the synonym question, at better than chance levels, indicating that they had processed the evaluative meaning of the subliminally presented stimuli in the absence of access to its nonevaluative meaning (see also Bargh, Raymond, & Chaiken, reported in Bargh, 1997). Other research by Bargh and colleagues using the automatic attitude activation paradigm (e.g., Bargh et al., 1992; Fazio et al., 1986) has demonstrated that people immediately (i.e., within a fraction of a second) classify as good or as bad any stimulus object presented to them—regardless of whether the object is a word or a picture, regardless of the strength of one's stored evaluation of the object,

and even regardless of whether the object is familiar or novel (see Bargh, 1997). Contemporary research has thus supported earlier claims about the primacy of evaluation. However, there are stable individual differences in the extent to which people engage in evaluative responding, as Jarvis and Petty (1996) have shown: evaluation pervades the thoughts of some individuals more than other individuals.

Object-Appraisal Function

It is at this very general level of enabling people to identify the extent to which objects have favorable or unfavorable implications for them that attitudes are accorded the function that is inherent in their very definition. The earliest description of this function appeared in the writings of Smith and his colleagues (M. B. Smith, 1947; M. B. Smith, Bruner, & White, 1956), who identified attitudes' *object-appraisal* function, by which attitudes allow people to appraise stimuli in terms of their goals and concerns. Attitudes thus enable people to "classify for action the objects of the environment" and to make available "appropriate response tendencies" for relating to these objects (M. B. Smith et al., 1956, p. 41). This and other functions of attitudes emerged from Smith and his associates' qualitative research, which featured detailed clinical interviews that examined the attitudes toward Russia held by ten men.

Katz and his collaborators also produced a well-known analysis of the functions of attitudes (D. Katz, 1960; D. Katz & Stotland, 1959; Sarnoff & Katz, 1954). Whereas the Smith group apparently derived functions inductively from their case studies, the Katz group proceeded deductively by scrutinizing psychological theory for insights about essential motivational processes and then postulating that attitudes serve the goals assumed by these theories. This theory-driven strategy led Katz to partition Smith's object-appraisal function into two components, one that emphasized the cognitive function of facilitating people's ability to interpret and make sense of otherwise disorganized perceptions and another that emphasized the instrumental function of facilitating people's ability to maximize rewards and minimize punishments. Although this division may have resulted from the somewhat arbitrary separation that existed in psychology between cognitive theory (e.g., Bruner, Goodnow, & Austin, 1957) and learning theory (e.g., Hilgard, 1956), such a partition of function provides a reasonable analysis of the two major tasks involved in evaluating objects, people, and events. Specifically, to differentiate between the beneficial and harmful aspects of their world, people must do the cognitive work of forming concepts that organize stimuli in their minds, and they must do the instrumental work of determining the extent to which the categorized stimuli enhance or lessen their well being.

Appreciating the cognitive aspects of object appraisal, D. Katz (1960) labeled as attitudes' *knowledge* function their role in organizing and simplifying people's experiences. In serving this function, attitudes provide a schema for categorizing the stimuli that constitute the informational environment. An old idea in attitude theory, it was important in Allport's influential writing about attitudes: "To borrow a phrase from William James, [attitudes] 'engender meaning upon the world'; they draw lines about and segregate an otherwise chaotic environment; they are our methods for finding our way about in an ambiguous universe" (G. W. Allport, 1935, p. 806). Other attitude theorists had expressed this cognitive theme by describing attitudes as providing a *frame of reference* for interpreting the world (e.g., A. L. Edwards, 1941; M. Sherif, 1936). In this emphasis on attitudes' categorization of experience, early attitude theorists reflected early cognitive theorists' emerging understanding of the ways that concepts structure the stimulus environment (e.g., Bartlett, 1932; Bruner et al., 1957).

Acknowledging that the categorization of stimuli encompasses perceptions of reward and punishment, D. Katz (1960) also proposed an *instrumental* or *utilitarian* function by which attitudes enable people to maximize rewards in their environment and to minimize punishments. Whereas the heritage of the knowledge function is in cognitive theory's recognition that concepts or schemas organize stimuli, the heritage of the instrumental function is in learning theory's assumption that people develop favorable attitudes (or response tendencies) toward stimuli associated with rewards and unfavorable attitudes (or response tendencies) toward stimuli associated with punishments.

As these analyses demonstrate, object appraisal, which joins the knowledge and instrumental aspects of attitudes, is correctly regarded as attitudes' universal function. In agreement with this view, many contemporary discussions emphasize that attitudes allow people to categorize objects, persons, and events in their environment and to differentiate between things they should approach and things they should avoid. For example, Greenwald (1989) agreed that object appraisal is attitudes' primary function and defined object appraisal, as did M. B. Smith et al. (1956), as the development of representations of attitude objects' instrumentality for adjustment. Similarly, Fazio (1989) maintained that the object-appraisal function reveals the essential importance of holding attitudes.

Utilitarian Function

If object appraisal is construed as a universal function of attitudes, it implies a very general view of the kinds of rewards and punishments with which attitudes are associated. These positive and negative outcomes may reflect both narrow self-interest (money, access to opportunities) and more abstract benefits (affirmation of one's values or self-

concept). However, some theorists have promoted a more constrained interpretation of attitudes' utilitarian or instrumental function in terms of concrete rewards and punishments. This narrower definition is useful for contrast with a symbolic or expressive function of attitudes by which psychological benefits flow, not from the rewards or punishments that the attitude object provides directly, but from gains and losses (e.g., in self-esteem and social approval) that follow from holding or expressing an attitude (Abelson & Prentice, 1989; Herek, 1986; Prentice, 1987). For example, in discussions of *symbolic politics,* researchers have tried to determine whether people's attitudes toward political and social policies such as affirmative action are better predicted by narrow self-interest or by *symbolic beliefs,* a term that refers to the influence of internalized social values such as fairness and equality (e.g., Kinder & Sears, 1981). The majority of this research suggests that symbolic beliefs exert more influence than narrow self-interest on political attitudes (Sears & Funk, 1991).

Terminology with respect to attitudes' facilitation of rewarding outcomes has been somewhat in flux. To stabilize terminology, it would be helpful to confine the term *utilitarian function* to refer to attitudes' representation of narrow self-interest, consistent with usage in most contemporary research. In contrast, because inherent in the object-appraisal function is the idea that attitudes allow people to evaluate stimuli on any of a variety of bases, this function would encompass attitudes' representation of all classes of outcomes, including the gains of pride, self-esteem, and other types of self-reward and the losses of guilt, anxiety, and other types of self-punishment.

Other Important Functions

There are three additional functions of attitudes that have frequently been identified: *value expression, social adjustment,* and *ego defense.* Because these functions are *not* inherent in the nature of all attitudes, they, along with the utilitarian function, provide the portion of the functional analysis that leads to differential predictions about attitudinal responding. Attitudes thus may serve these more specific functions while they continue to serve their universal function of enabling people to evaluate and appraise stimuli in their environment. Each of these more specific functions may be important for some individuals, for some attitude objects, and under some circumstances. Each function implies that attitudes are structurally linked to certain classes of other attitudes and other psychological constructs. As subsequently discussed, identifying when attitudes serve these particular functions has become a key issue for researchers working in this tradition, and clarifying these functions' implications for attitude structure is a continuing concern for both theorists and researchers.

D. Katz (1960) proposed the value-expressive function by which attitudes provide a means for expressing personal values and other core aspects of the self-concept. Holding such attitudes is inherently rewarding because it satisfies people's needs to clarify and affirm their self-concepts. A person who draws self-esteem from being a feminist or an evangelical Christian, or who wishes to attain these identities, would be motivated to hold attitudinal positions that appropriately reflect these prized ideologies and their component values. This function encompasses Kinder and Sears' (1981) analysis of symbolic attitudes and echoes the theme of hierarchical structure considered earlier in this chapter in our discussion of attitudes' relation to ideology.

The social adjustive function proposed by M. B. Smith et al. (1956) considers the ways that attitudes mediate a person's relations with others. Attitudes that serve social adjustment may facilitate, maintain, and at times, disrupt social relationships. Expressing attitudes that are pleasing to others or that coincide with the norms and values of admired reference groups can facilitate entry into desired relationships and help maintain them, whereas expressing unacceptable attitudes can threaten such relationships and hasten their termination. Although the expression of some attitudes could thus merely be strategically intended to cement social relationships (or sometimes to damage them), Smith and his colleagues also implied that adopting the attitudes of reference groups can affirm those aspects of self-identity that stem from one's group memberships. This aspect of the social adjustment function thus echoes the theme of Katz's value-expressive function.

Given the substantial influence of psychoanalytic theory on social psychology in the 1950s, it is not surprising that one of its major themes defined another attitudinal function. D. Katz (1960) labeled this function ego-defensive, and M. B. Smith et al. (1956) labeled it externalization. In contrast to the value-expressive function, by which attitudes allow an important aspect of the self to be expressed, the ego-defensive function emphasizes that attitudes allow the self to be defended from potentially threatening events. Following the psychoanalytic principles that people use defense mechanisms such as denial, repression, and projection to protect their self-concepts against internal and external threats, these theorists noted that attitudes could enable people to cope with emotional conflicts and, more generally, to defend their self-concepts. In a research program in which Katz and his collaborators developed the implications of this psychoanalytic theme in relation to racial and ethnic prejudice, they argued that people may unconsciously project their own feelings of inferiority onto convenient racial, religious, and ethnic minority groups. By so doing, people can bolster their own egos by feeling superior to members of out-groups (D. Katz, 1960; Sarnoff, 1960; Sarnoff & Katz, 1954). This conception of prejudice as defensive stemmed in large part from the earlier work on the authoritarian personality, which was also psychoanalytic in orientation (Adorno, Frenkel-Brunswik, Levinson, & Sanford, 1950; see Fiske, 1998, in this *Handbook*). The main claim of the authoritarianism researchers was that prejudiced attitudes are grounded in ego defense rather than realistic perceptions of out-groups. Yet, as Katz argued, the ego-defensive function could also be served by attitudes in domains other than prejudice. For example, in the health domain, attitudes implying apathy or indifference to health threats like AIDS and breast cancer might reflect avoidance and denial mechanisms.

In a different rendition of the idea that attitudes serve an ego-defensive function, defense of the ego and self-esteem are viewed as acting to minimize the anxiety that stems from awareness of one's own mortality (see review by Solomon, Greenberg, & Pyszczynski, 1991). Greenberg, Pyszczynski, and their colleagues dubbed this broad perspective *terror management theory* and have argued that attitudinal responding can help people lessen anxieties that follow from fear of personal annihilation. Although in these authors' view, a wide range of social psychological phenomena have the function of protecting people from an existential fear of death, in experiments particularly interesting from an attitudinal perspective research participants who were reminded of their mortality became more intolerant of those who threatened their beliefs and more attracted to those who validated their beliefs (e.g., Greenberg et al., 1990).

Another useful direction for exploring attitudes' defensive function would enlarge the concept of defense to include defense of an extended self that encompasses one's societal in-group. Such a perspective would encompass a key principle of social identity theory (e.g., Tajfel, 1981). This principle is that attitudes toward societal out-groups and the beliefs (or stereotypes) that underlie these attitudes allow in-group members to differentiate themselves from out-group members and to justify their treatment of the out-group. From this perspective, prejudice toward societal groups defends a group-based or collective ego rather than the individual ego and allows group members to avoid recognizing the arbitrariness of their own group's status and privilege. Moreover, Jost and Banaji (1994) argued that stereotypes of societal groups contribute to the preservation of existing social arrangements by implying that groups, including one's own in-group, are destined for whatever is their social and economic position in society. In this sense, attitudes may justify the social system in which the individual is embedded. This enlarged sense of attitudes' defensive function is tailored to the analysis of intergroup prejudice and would encompass aspects of M.

B. Smith et al.'s (1956) discussion of the social adjustive function.

Structures Implied by Functions

The idea that attitudes may serve utilitarian, value-expressive, social adjustive, and ego-defensive functions has important implications for attitude structure because it implies that the networks of attitudes and other constructs in which attitudes are embedded differ substantially across attitudes. Indeed, because the structure and function of attitudes should be closely linked, the functional analysis quite properly reiterates some of the themes of our discussion of intra-attitudinal and inter-attitudinal structure.

To understand the implications of attitudes' function for their structure, let us first consider the object-appraisal function and acknowledge that this universal function has only very general implications for structure. The generality of these implications follows from this function's underlying premise that evaluation is integral to the categorization of stimuli. Although D. Katz's (1960) use of the term *knowledge* to refer to the cognitive aspects of object appraisal might connote that beliefs underlie attitudes, the general concept of object appraisal does not exclude the idea that attitudes can be formed from affects and behaviors. Similarly, although Katz's use of the term *instrumental* to refer to attitudes' representation of rewards and punishments might be taken to connote that expectancy-value representations of rewards and punishments underlie attitudes, the general idea of evaluation does not exclude more affective mechanisms for attaching evaluations to concepts (e.g., classical conditioning). Therefore, because object appraisal is inherent in attitude formation, this function has no implications for structure other than those developed at the beginning of this chapter in the general discussion of attitude structure.

When interest is confined to the utilitarian function of attitudes—that is, to their implications for the rewards and punishments that are delivered directly by the attitude object—some more specific structural implications can be discerned. Attitude objects would then be associated with representations of these rewards and punishments and with the positive and negative affects associated with such rewarding and punishing consequences. Although such a description of attitude structure would be consistent with our general depiction of intra-attitudinal structure, the range of positive and negative outcomes underlying an attitude would be constrained to those that follow from rather concrete rewards and punishments.

The value-expressive function implicates aspects of inter-attitudinal structure. This function of course implies that attitudes are linked to values in a hierarchical relation: by this function, people develop attitudes that are consistent with their values in order to express and act on those values. The value-expressive function is thus consistent with the research on ideology reviewed earlier in this chapter. That research suggested that in the political domain many citizens have somewhat organized attitudes that follow from principles of moderate generality such as free-market conservatism or at the least from attachments to political symbols and reference groups. Also, in thinking about disadvantaged and stigmatized social groups, people appear to have organized sets of attitudes that reflect their broader values.

The social adjustive function also implicates other aspects of inter-attitudinal structure. This function implies that people's attitudes toward issues are embedded in broader structures that represent their attitudes toward other people and reference groups. Balance theory of course captured this insight at at early point in Heider's (1958) emphasis on the *p-o-x* triad, which embedded *p*'s attitude toward an issue *x* in a structure that contained *p*'s attitude toward another person, *o*. In balance theory predictions, if both another person and an issue come to mind simultaneously, one's attitude toward the issue tends to become reconciled with one's attitude toward the person. Thus, the balance proposition that liking another person implies that the perceiver should hold the same attitude as this other person is congenial with the social adjustive function's assumption that attitudes can cement social relationships. Ideas harmonious with attitudes' social adjustive function were further developed in Kelman's (1961) concept of *identification,* a form of influence that occurs when a message recipient adopts an attitude endorsed by a communicator because this attitude helps establish or maintain a positive self-defining relationship with the communicator. The knowledge structures that regulate identification according to Kelman are those that represent the recipient's role relationship with the source of influence. Encompassing a secondary theme of the social adjustive function, Kelman's theory also acknowledged the possibility of *compliance* with a communicator, which consists of public agreement to gain a favorable reaction or forestall an unfavorable reaction. When people comply, the expression of an attitude is associated in their minds with gains or losses mediated by the communicator.

If the ego-defensive function is construed in classic psychoanalytic terms, its structural implications remain somewhat obscure because psychoanalytic theory fell from favor in social psychology shortly after the functional theorists gave this approach a starring role in their analysis. Freud's (1920/1953) concepts of id, ego, and superego now seem archaic and moreover do not lend themselves to attitudinal analysis. If indeed people sometimes hold an attitude because it protects them from their own unacceptable impulses, attitudes are linked to unconscious or repressed aspects of the self. As the notion of preconscious and unconscious processes are re-established in psychology and specifically in attitude theory (e.g., Bargh, 1997; Bornstein, 1989), the structural implications of the ego-defensive function may become better understood. If this function is construed more broadly in terms of defending one or more aspects of the self, including group-anchored social identities, a variety of structural implications could be developed (see Greenwald, 1989).

Mutability of Functions

Although the idea that functions imply structure might be taken to imply that attitudes' functions are fixed, this implication would be incorrect. Although attitudes may become linked to values and representations of social roles, these associations may be merely available in the sense that they are present in memory so that they could potentially be used for processing stimulus input. These aspects of attitude structure are not necessarily accessible in the sense that they would be ready to be used in information processing at a particular point in time. As emphasized earlier in this chapter, the accessibility of components of a structure would be a product of the demands of the perceiver's situation as well as a variety of other factors. Consistent with this reasoning, the mutability of attitudes' structure (and by implication the mutability of their functions) is a classic principle in attitude theory. For example, Zajonc (1960) introduced the concept of *cognitive tuning*—the idea that people activate cognitive structures that are instrumental for the task they face. Thus, if people face a task of social adjustment, the associations of attitudes with significant others and reference groups would presumably come to mind, whereas if they face a task of value expression, the associations of attitudes with their broader values and ideologies would come to mind. In the face of threats to their egos, associations of attitudes with forbidden impulses and disavowed aspects of the self would become important but perhaps not consciously accessible. This mutability of attitudes' functions thus suggests possibilities for attitude researchers to manipulate experimentally the importance of attitudes' functions.

Techniques for manipulating functions attempt to increase the accessibility of the structures that underlie a particular function. Researchers thus might make salient particular sets of reasons for holding an attitude—such as self-interest or expressing one's values. For example, Young, Thomsen, Borgida, Sullivan, and Aldrich (1991) primed the utilitarian function by having participants listen to a taped dialogue of two men discussing the importance of evaluating government policy in terms of personal needs and interests (and having other participants listen to a dialogue that did not refer to personal needs or interests). This priming of the utilitarian function caused participants to show greater consistency between their attitudes on a particular policy and their personal needs and interests. Using another priming approach, Maio and

Olson (1995) exposed participants to different versions of posters that concerned donating money to cancer research. In the condition in which the value-expressive function was primed, the poster affirmed altruistic values and associated altruism with donating. In the condition in which the utilitarian function was primed, the poster emphasized utilitarian reasons for donating to cancer research and associated donating with self-interest. In the value-expressive condition, participants exhibited stronger relations between their values and attitudes than they did in the utilitarian condition. Moreover, in this condition, values predicted intentions to donate to cancer research, even when the predictors of Ajzen's (1988) theory of planned behavior were taken into account. In addition, Murray, Haddock, and Zanna (1996) developed a three-part procedure for priming the value-expressive and social adjustive functions. Participants in this research read a description of the virtues of people whose attitudes serve the primed function, responded to a values questionnaire whose items were biased to encourage endorsement of one of the functions, and performed a bonding task that required them to think through the implications of the attitude for the function in question. These techniques, as well as those used by other researchers, have shown success in temporarily heightening the extent to which attitudes serve a particular function.

Although experimental manipulations of attitudes' functions have provided useful demonstrations of the mutability of attitudes' functions, earlier approaches emphasized individual differences in the extent to which attitudes fulfilled differing functions. For example, in research on changing the attitudes of prejudiced people, Katz and his colleagues (e.g., D. Katz, Sarnoff, & McClintock, 1956) sought to identify individuals for whom racial and ethnic attitudes served an ego-defensive function. Katz's method consisted of classifying people according to their presumed level of defensiveness, as assessed by personality measures such as the authoritarian personality researchers' F Scale (Adorno et al., 1950). The mixed success of this research program (see Eagly & Chaiken, 1993) may account for the long lag between these efforts and more contemporary efforts to use personality measures to differentiate between people for whom attitudes serve contrasting functions. Particularly successful is research using Snyder's (1974) self-monitoring construct to assess the extent to which people's attitudes are aligned with the social adjustive or value-expressive function. According to Snyder and DeBono's (1985) analysis, the attitudes of high self-monitoring individuals are more likely to serve the social adjustive function than the value-expressive function, whereas the attitudes of low self-monitoring individuals are more likely to serve the value-expressive function than the social adjustive function. In several studies, Snyder, DeBono, and their colleagues tested a form of functional theory's *matching hypothesis of persuasion* by which persuasive appeals are more successful if they are based on the function served by recipients' attitudes. Consistent with the hypothesis, high self-monitoring participants were persuaded more by messages that appealed to reference groups, whereas low self-monitoring participants were persuaded more by messages that appealed to values that they considered important (e.g., DeBono, 1987; Lavine & Snyder, 1996). In a different approach to individual differences, Prentice (1987) used multidimensional scaling procedures to assess the extent to which people view their material possessions (e.g., stereos, wallets, photographs) in utilitarian versus symbolic terms.

Researchers have also explored open-ended techniques that allow more direct assessments of attitudes' functions. For example, Herek (1987) had participants write essays about their attitudes toward homosexuality; these essays were then content-analyzed for their functional themes. Similarly, Shavitt (1990) used a thought-listing task to determine the functional basis of respondents' attitudes toward a number of consumer products that had been preselected for their potential to engage particular functions. Both Herek's essay procedure and Shavitt's thought-listing procedure appear to yield valid measures of the functions that attitudes serve. Moreover, Shavitt's work, and also Prentice's (1987), supported the ideas that different attitude objects tend to activate different functional concerns and that some attitude objects commonly serve multiple functions.

Sets of closed-ended items have also been used to assess functions. Herek (1987) developed a questionnaire measure of attitudes' functions that contains subsets of items pertaining to particular functions that may be served by attitudes toward social groups. Similarly, Clary, Snyder, Ridge, Miene, and Haugen (1994) developed a measure of the extent to which attitudes toward volunteering served each of several functions.

Although assessing functions through the content of people's thoughts or by self-report measures has demonstrated validity, an emphasis of early functional theory was that attitudes have latent, motivational significance that is not necessarily manifested directly in conscious thought. Consistent with this emphasis, researchers might consider coding thoughts about attitude objects by rules akin to those used in projective tests of general motives such as achievement, affiliation, and power (e.g., C. P. Smith et al., 1992). The assumption that attitudes' motivational bases may be expressed indirectly has much in common with some personality theorists' ideas about implicit motives (e.g., D. C. McClelland, Weinberger, & Koestner, 1989).

The multiplicity of methods that researchers have invented for studying attitudes' functions is thoroughly consistent with D. Katz's (1960) analysis, which implied that there should be variation in functions across persons, attitude objects, and situations. Although ingrained personality tendencies may predispose individuals' attitudes to serve particular functions, certain attitude objects may be inherently linked to particular functions, and situations may contain strong pressures toward aligning attitudes with certain functions. Moreover, viewing attitude functions from a cultural perspective suggests the possibility of very broad cultural variation in the functions that attitudes commonly serve.

Cultural variation in attitudes' functions might particularly be expected along the individualism-collectivism dimension that cross-cultural researchers have consistently identified as the most basic psychological dimension of cultural variability (e.g., Markus & Kitayama, 1991; Triandis, McCusker, & Hui, 1990). If in individualistic cultures, people tend to subordinate group goals to personal goals, attitudes may often serve the utilitarian function. If in collectivist cultures, people tend to subordinate personal goals to group goals, attitudes may often serve the social adjustive function. In support of this analysis, Han and Shavitt (1994) examined magazine advertisements in one individualistic culture, the United States, and one collectivist culture, Korea. In the United States advertisements tended to appeal to individual preferences and benefits, personal success, and independence, whereas in Korea advertisements tended to appeal to in-group benefits, harmony, and family integrity. Testing the matching hypothesis of persuasion, these investigators further showed that, compared with advertisements presented to participants in Korea, advertisements presented to participants in the United States were more persuasive when they emphasized individualistic benefits and less persuasive when they emphasized family or in-group benefits. This study thus provided another demonstration of D. Katz's (1960) proposition that the functional base of an attitude dictates the form that social influence takes.

Other Analyses with Functional Emphases

Given the ubiquity of the idea that attitudes help people cope with their environments, it is not surprising that functional themes appear in many attitude theories that do not fall under the rubric of functional theory. For example, a strong functional theme is evident in the basic assumption of expectancy-value models of the attitude-behavior relation—namely, that people are goal-oriented in the sense that they take the consequences of behavior into account in making behavioral choices. Moreover, mirroring functional theories' division of functions into types that reflect differing motivations, expectancy-value theories classify consequences in various ways (e.g., utilitarian outcomes, normative outcomes, self-identity outcomes; see prior discussion of these models).

Theorists of message-based persuasion use functional analysis when they focus on the motivations that may underlie attitude change. Although modern dual-process persuasion theories (see Petty & Wegener, 1998, in this *Handbook*) were once aligned with the object-appraisal function in their assumption that message recipients are motivated to attain valid opinions that are in line with the relevant facts, persuasion theorists have begun to take into account more specific motives that may also engage people's attitudes. Specifically, Chaiken and her colleagues (Chaiken, Giner-Sorolla, & Chen, 1996; Chaiken, Liberman, & Eagly, 1989; Chen, Shechter, & Chaiken, 1996) provided a multiple-motive version of the heuristic-systematic model in which *accuracy motivation,* a desire to align one's attitudes with the facts, is only one orientation that message recipients might adopt in a situation of potential social influence. Other motives that may be prepotent include *defense motivation,* the desire to form or to defend particular attitudinal positions, and *impression motivation,* the desire to express attitudes that are socially acceptable or that, more generally, facilitate self-presentation. Defense motivation is compatible with broader construals of the ego-defensive function, and impression motivation is aligned with the social adjustive function.

Other persuasion researchers have addressed functional concerns by invoking the concept of involvement, which appeared in the earlier section on attitude strength. Although this construct generally refers to a state of heightened motivation induced by an association between an attitude and some aspect of the self, the term has been used in differing ways by attitude theorists. In deconstructing these meanings, B. T. Johnson and Eagly (1989) proposed that the term had been used in three distinct senses: *value-relevant involvement,* which refers to the motivational state created by an association between an activated attitude and one's central and important values; *outcome-relevant involvement,* which refers to the motivational state created by an association between an activated attitude and one's ability to attain desirable outcomes; and *impression-relevant involvement,* which refers to the motivational state created by an association between an activated attitude and the public self, or the impression one makes on others. These three forms of involvement are conceptually related to three of the well-known functions of attitudes: value-relevance resembles the value-expressive function, outcome-relevance resembles the utilitarian function, and impression-relevance resembles the social adjustive function.

The prevalence of functional constructs in persuasion theory is not surprising in view of the emphasis that early functional theorists placed on attitude change. Indeed, D. Katz (1960) provided guidelines for changing attitudes that serve each of his functions. Similarly, Kelman's (1961) analysis of influence processes was organized by functional themes pertaining to the formation and maintenance of differing types of social relationships. These classic analyses, along with more contemporary efforts, have af-

firmed the general principle that social influence follows different rules when differing functions are engaged.

Further Development of Functional Theory

In the decades immediately following the introduction of functional theories by Smith (M. B. Smith et al., 1956), D. Katz (1960), and their colleagues, relatively little empirical work directly tested these theories. The barrier to effective empiricism may well have been the difficulty early researchers experienced in operationalizing the various attitude functions that the theories had delineated. The theories nonetheless continued to receive attention in textbooks and general discussions of attitudes, no doubt because of their breadth and unique focus on the motivational bases of attitudes and their expression. With greater methodological flexibility, contemporary researchers have devised several procedures for varying or assessing attitudes' functions. Awaiting development is a more complete understanding of the ways that attitudes serving different functions vary in their structural properties. Also inviting analysis is the issue of the multiple functions that attitudes often serve. Thus, a particular attitude—for example, a negative attitude toward affirmative action held by a politically conservative white man—might readily serve the value-expressive, social adjustive, and utilitarian functions simultaneously. If attitudes typically serve multiple functions, the problem for attitude researchers is to weight people's attitudes according to the extent to which they serve each function. Such a perspective would move the functional approach beyond exclusive emphasis on the ideal-type concepts that are embodied in each of attitudes' several functions. Developing techniques to address these issues will continue to challenge attitude researchers.

CONCLUSION

Analysis of attitudes' structure and functions has captured an increasing proportion of attitude researchers' energies. This emphasis reflects the emerging power of these analyses to contribute to the traditional missions of attitude theory. These missions have long included discovering the methods by which attitudes can be changed, predicting the conditions under which attitudes cause attitude-consistent behavior, and understanding the impact of attitudes on information processing. The majority of traditional approaches in these areas treated attitudes merely as abstract evaluations and thus included relatively little attention to attitudes' internal or external structure or to the broader functions that they serve. Detailed consideration of structure and function has enriched theoretical analyses in these domains, improved researchers' ability to predict attitudinal phenomena, and opened up new research questions.

In the study of persuasion, theorists regard influence

techniques as changing an attitude, when attitude is defined as an abstract evaluation of an object. Knowledge of attitude structure has enhanced this domain in two major ways. Most obviously, structural variables have been used as predictors of attitude change, when researchers proposed, for example, that various forms of attitude strength serve as moderators of change in the sense that certain persuasive techniques are more likely to be effective when attitudes have certain structural characteristics (Petty & Krosnick, 1995). For example, when attitudes are strong by any of several of the definitions of strength that we discussed, they are more stable and less vulnerable to influence. In fact, for strong attitudes the main analytical task becomes understanding the processes that enable resistance and the persuasive techniques by which resistance might be overcome.

A second way that knowledge of attitude structure furthers the analysis of persuasion is less obvious. Specifically, the goal of persuasive efforts could be viewed as changing attitude structure as well as changing abstract evaluations. A persuasive message might change aspects of structure even though it is not immediately successful in changing the overall attitude, or evaluation, of the attitude object. In other words, structural change might often precede change in overall attitudes. For example, weakening an attitude's external structure by decoupling it from a more abstract attitude or value to which it is hierarchically linked might render it more vulnerable to further persuasive attempts (see Eagly & Chaiken, 1995). Or, in the spirit of social judgment theory, influence inductions might expand the range of acceptable positions on an issue without necessarily changing a person's preferred position. This type of structural change could also pave the way for subsequent attitude change. Treating structural change as an outcome of persuasion may prove to be especially important when influencing agents desire to change strong attitudes, which often show relatively little change from single persuasive messages. With strong attitudes, attitude change may occur in stages in which structural change precedes change in abstract evaluation.

Knowledge of attitudes' functions has demonstrated value for studying attitude change. From the beginnings of functional theory in the 1950s, many researchers have tested the matching hypothesis by which effective influence inductions address the functional base of an attitude. As we noted earlier in this chapter, these tests have become more adequate and convincing as researchers developed better methods for determining which functions attitudes serve. Additional exploitation of the functional perspective for predicting attitude change awaits better understanding of the structural implications of functions.

The study of structure and function has also contributed to delineating the conditions under which attitudes impact on behavior. As Fazio (1986) argued, attitudes' accessibil-ity, a form of attitude strength, is a determinant of their activation and thus a moderator of the attitude-behavior relation. As we argued earlier in this chapter, the impact of accessibility may depend in turn on its structural correlates, given that more accessible attitudes are less ambivalent and more likely to be based on affect. Other researchers have given tantalizing evidence that attitudes' affective determinants contribute to behavior, above and beyond their cognitive determinants (e.g., Triandis, 1980); the relative importance of cognitive and affective aspects of attitude structure in influencing intentions and behavior deserves attention in attitude research.

Attitude structure and function have been explored less thoroughly in relation to attitudes' effects on information processing. This relative neglect reflects the slow progress of research in this area. Although attitudinal selectivity was an early focus of investigation, the complexity of the theoretical issues and the diversity of research findings that were obtained for most aspects of information processing discouraged further work in this area. Therefore, relatively little research has examined the implications of attitude structure for selectivity issues, and functional analyses have seen very little application in this area.

The history of psychologists' attention to attitude structure and function is intriguing because progress in this domain has not been continuous. Investigators of the 1960s had some interest in structure, as witnessed in particular by Scott's (1963, 1969) research and his *Handbook of Social Psychology* chapter on attitude measurement (Scott, 1968), which was devoted in large part to attitudes' structural properties. These and other efforts (e.g., Zajonc, 1968) seemed to lie dormant for many years, however, insofar as they impacted little on the majority of attitude research. Instead, investigators focused on understanding attitudes' impact on behavior, because the possibility that this relation might be inherently very weak threatened the entire enterprise of studying attitudes. Researchers also focused on developing more sophisticated models of attitude change, but these theories featured mediational processes (e.g., cognitive elaboration of message content) rather than attitude structure as their primary emphasis. Only relatively recently have structural variables come into their own as a major focus of attitude change research.

Functional theory also seemed to lie dormant for many years, after the initial flurry of interest in the 1950s and early 1960s. Problems in operationalizing the constructs suggested by these theories retarded development, as noted earlier in this chapter. In the resurgence of interest in the 1980s and 1990s, tests of functional theory have been rather narrowly focused on the matching hypothesis of persuasion, to the exclusion of other hypotheses. Further progress would require that attitudes' functions be more than ideal-type concepts that point to differing bases of attitudes: substantial progress will require a detailed understanding of the structures implied by functions. With the considerable gain in knowledge about attitude structure in recent years, these developments will no doubt follow relatively quickly.

NOTES

1. Alternatively, evaluation itself might be regarded as a linked node, as in Fazio's (e.g., 1986, 1989) definition of attitude as an association between an attitude object and an evaluation.

2. Traditionally attitudes toward targets were known as attitudes toward "objects" in order to distinguish them from attitudes toward behaviors (e.g., Fishbein & Ajzen, 1975). This terminology uses the term *object* to refer to a special class of attitude objects—namely, those attitude objects that are not behaviors but are targets of behavior. This terminology confuses matters because it imparts a narrower meaning to the term object while retaining its broader meaning in the general term *attitude object*. Therefore, a clearer terminology contrast attitudes toward targets and attitudes toward behaviors.

3. Although perceived behavior control does not appear as an explicit term in the composite model, we regard it as affecting the link between attitudes toward behaviors and intentions. This causal link is influenced by the individual's assessment of the constraints that he faces in the immediate situation. If an individual desires to engage in a behavior but perceives that he has little control, his intention to engage in the behavior would be weakened.

REFERENCES

Abelson, R. P. (1959). Modes of resolution of belief dilemmas. *Journal of Conflict Resolution, 3,* 343–352.

Abelson, R. P. (1988). Conviction. *American Psychologist, 43,* 267–275.

Abelson, R. P. (1995). Attitude extremity. In R. E. Petty & J. A. Krosnick (Eds.), *Attitude strength: Antecedents and consequences* (pp. 25–41). Mahwah, NJ: Erlbaum.

Abelson, R. P., Aronson, E., McGuire, W. J., Newcomb, T. M., Rosenberg, M. J., & Tannenbaum, P. H. (Eds.). (1968). *Theories of cognitive consistency: A sourcebook.* Chicago: Rand McNally.

Abelson, R. P., Kinder, D. R., Peters, M. D., & Fiske, S. T. (1982). Affective and semantic components in political person perception. *Journal of Personality and Social Psychology, 42,* 619–630.

Abelson, R. P., & Prentice, D. A. (1989). Beliefs as possessions: A functional perspective. In A. R. Pratkanis, S. J. Breckler, & A. G. Greenwald (Eds.), *Attitude structure and function* (pp. 361–381). Hillsdale, NJ: Erlbaum.

Abelson, R. P., & Rosenberg, M. J. (1958). Symbolic psychologic: A model of attitudinal cognition. *Behavioral Science, 3,* 1–13.

Adorno, T. W., Frenkel-Brunswik, E., Levinson, D. J., & Sanford, R. N. (1950). *The authoritarian personality.* New York: Harper & Row.

Ajzen, I. (1988). *Attitudes, personality, and behavior.* Chicago: Dorsey.

Ajzen, I. (1991). The theory of planned behavior. *Organizational Behavior and Human Decision Processes, 50,* 179–211.

Ajzen, I. (1996). The directive influence of attitudes on behavior. In P. M. Gollwitzer & J. A. Bargh (Eds.), *The psychology of action: Linking cognition and motivation to behavior* (pp. 385–403). New York: Guilford.

Ajzen, I., & Fishbein, M. (1977). Attitude-behavior relations: A theoretical analysis and review of empirical research. *Psychological Bulletin, 84,* 888–918.

Ajzen, I., & Fishbein, M. (1980). *Understanding attitudes and predicting social behavior.* Englewood Cliffs, NJ: Prentice-Hall.

Allport, F. H. (1955). *Theories of perception and the concept of structure.* New York: Wiley.

Allport, G. W. (1935). Attitudes. In C. Murchison (Ed.), *Handbook of social psychology* (pp. 798–844). Worcester, MA: Clark University Press.

Alper, T. G., & Korchin, S. J. (1952). Memory for socially relevant material. *Journal of Abnormal and Social Psychology, 47,* 25–37.

Anderson, J. R. (1983). *The architecture of cognition.* Cambridge, MA: Harvard University Press.

Anderson, J. R., & Bower, G. H. (1974). A propositional theory of recognition memory. *Memory and Cognition, 2,* 406–412.

Anderson, N. H. (1981a). *Foundations of information integration theory.* New York: Academic Press.

Anderson, N. H. (1981b). Integration theory applied to cognitive responses and attitudes. In R. E. Petty, T. M. Ostrom, & T. C. Brock (Eds.), *Cognitive responses in persuasion* (pp. 361–397). Hillsdale, NJ: Erlbaum.

Asch, S. E. (1946). Forming impressions of personality. *Journal of Abnormal and Social Psychology, 41,* 258–290.

Ashmore, R. D., & Del Boca, F. K. (1981). Conceptual approaches to stereotypes and stereotyping. In D. L. Hamilton (Ed.), *Cognitive processes in stereotyping and intergroup behavior* (pp. 1–35). Hillsdale, NJ: Erlbaum.

Bagozzi, R. P., & Warshaw, P. R. (1990). Trying to consume. *Journal of Consumer Research, 17,* 127–140.

Bagozzi R. P., & Yi, Y. (1989). The degree of intention formation moderator of the attitude-behavior relationship. *Social Psychology Quarterly, 52,* 266–279.

Bandura, A. (1977). Self-efficacy: Toward a unifying theory of behavioral change. *Psychological Review, 84,* 122–147.

Bandura, A. (1989). Self-regulation of motivation and action through internal standards and goal systems. In L. A. Pervin (Ed.), *Goal concepts in personality and social psychology* (pp. 19–85). Hillsdale, NJ: Erlbaum.

Bargh, J. A. (1990). Auto-motives: Preconscious determinants of social interaction. In E. T. Higgins & R. M. Sorrentino (Eds.), *Handbook of motivation and cognition* (Vol. 2, pp. 93–130). New York: Guilford.

Bargh, J. A. (1997). The automaticity of everyday life. In R. S. Wyer, Jr. (Ed.), *Advances in social cognition* (Vol. 10, pp. 1–61). Mahwah, NJ: Erlbaum.

Bargh, J. A., Chaiken, S., Govender, R., & Pratto, F. (1992). The generality of the automatic attitude activation effect. *Journal of Personality and Social Psychology, 62,* 893–912.

Bargh, J. A., Chaiken, S., Raymond, P., & Hymes, C. (1996). The automatic evaluation effect: Unconditional automatic attitude activation with a pronunciation task. *Journal of Experimental Social Psychology, 32,* 104–128.

Bargh, J. A., Litt, J., Pratto, F., & Spielman, L. A. (1989). On the preconscious evaluation of social stimuli. In A. F. Bennett & K. M. McConkey (Eds.), *Cognition in individual and social contexts: Proceedings of the 24th International Congress of Psychology* (Vol. 3, pp. 357–370). Amsterdam: Elsevier/North-Holland.

Bartlett, F. C. (1932). *Remembering: A study in experimental and social psychology.* Cambridge, England: Cambridge University Press.

Bassili, J. N. (1995). Response latency and the accessibility of voting intentions: What contributes to accessibility and how it affects vote choice. *Personality and Social Psychology Bulletin, 21,* 686–695.

Bassili, J. N. (1996). Meta-judgmental versus operative indexes of psychological attributes: The case of measures of attitude strength. *Journal of Personality and Social Psychology, 71,* 637–653.

Behavioral Science Subpanel of President's Science Advisory Committee. (1962). Strengthening the behavioral sciences. *Behavioral Science, 7,* 275–288.

Bem, D. J. (1972). Self-perception theory. In L. Berkowitz (Ed.), *Advances in experimental social psychology* (Vol. 6, pp. 1–62). New York: Academic Press.

Bentler, P. M., & Speckart, G. (1979). Models of attitude-behavior relations. *Psychological Review, 86,* 452–464.

Biddle, B. J., Bank, B. J., & Slavings, R. L. (1987). Norms, preferences, identities and retention decisions. *Social Psychology Quarterly, 50,* 322–337.

Biek, M., Wood, W., & Chaiken, S. (1996). Working knowledge, cognitive processing, and attitudes: On the inevitability of bias. *Personality and Social Psychology Bulletin, 22,* 547–556.

Bieri, J. (1966). Cognitive complexity and personality development. In O. J. Harvey (Ed.), *Experience, structure, & adaptability* (pp. 13–37). New York: Springer.

Biernat, M., Vescio, T. K., Theno, S. A., & Crandall, C. S.

(1996). Values and prejudice: Toward understanding the impact of American values on outgroup attitudes. In C. Seligman, J. M. Olson, & M. P. Zanna (Eds.), *The Ontario Symposium: The psychology of values* (Vol. 8, pp. 153–189). Mahwah, NJ: Erlbaum.

Blumer, H. (1955). Attitudes and the social act. *Social Problems, 3,* 59–65.

Boninger, D., Krosnick, J., & Berent, M. (1995). Origins of attitude importance: Self-interest, social identification, and value relevance. *Journal of Personality and Social Psychology, 68,* 61–80.

Boninger, D., Krosnick, J. A., Berent, M., & Fabrigar, L. R. (1995). The causes and consequences of attitude importance. In R. E. Petty & J. A. Krosnick (Eds.), *Attitude strength: Antecedents and consequences* (pp. 159–190). Mahwah, NJ: Erlbaum.

Bornstein, R. F. (1989). Subliminal techniques as propaganda tools: Review and critique. *Journal of Mind and Behavior, 10,* 231–262.

Bothwell, R. K., & Brigham, J. C. (1983). Selective evaluation and recall during the 1980 Reagan-Carter debate. *Journal of Applied Social Psychology, 13,* 427–442.

Bower, G. H. (1981). Mood and memory. *American Psychologist, 36,* 129–148.

Breckler, S. J. (1984). Empirical validation of affect, behavior, and cognition as distinct components of attitude. *Journal of Personality and Social Psychology, 47,* 1191–1205.

Breckler, S. J. (1994). A comparison of numerical indexes for measuring attitude ambivalence. *Educational and Psychological Measurement, 54,* 350–365.

Breckler, S. J., & Wiggins, E. C. (1989). Affect versus evaluation in the structure of attitudes. *Journal of Experimental Social Psychology, 25,* 253–271.

Brendl, C. M., & Higgins, E. T. (1996). Principles of judging valence: What makes events positive or negative? In M. P. Zanna (Ed.), *Advances in experimental social psychology* (Vol. 28, pp. 95–160). San Diego, CA: Academic Press.

Brigham, J. C., & Cook, S. W. (1969). The influence of attitude on the recall of controversial material: A failure to confirm. *Journal of Experimental Social Psychology, 5,* 240–243.

Brinberg, D., & Cummings, V. (1983). Purchasing generic prescription drugs: An analysis using two behavioral intention models. *Advances in Consumer Research, 11,* 229–234.

Brock, T. C., Albert, S. M., & Becker, L. A. (1970). Familiarity, utility, and supportiveness as determinants of information receptivity. *Journal of Personality and Social Psychology, 14,* 292–301.

Brown, R. (1995). *Prejudice: Its social psychology.* Cambridge, MA: Blackwell.

Bruner, J. S., Goodnow, J. J., & Austin, G. A. (1957). *A study of thinking.* New York: Wiley.

Buss, D. M., & Schmitt, D. F. (1993). Sexual strategies theory:

An evolutionary perspective on human mating. *Psychological Review, 100,* 204–232.

Cacioppo, J. T., & Berntson, G. G. (1994). Relationship between attitudes and evaluative space: A critical review, with emphasis on the separability of positive and negative substrates. *Psychological Bulletin, 115,* 401–423.

Cacioppo, J. T., Gardner, W. L., & Berntson, G. G. (1997). Beyond bipolar conceptualizations and measures: The case of attitudes and evaluative space. *Personality and Social Psychology Review, 1,* 3–25.

Cacioppo, J. T., & Petty, R. E. (1979). Effects of message repetition and position on cognitive response, recall, and persuasion. *Journal of Personality and Social Psychology, 37,* 97–109.

Cacioppo, J. T., Petty, R. E., Feinstein, J. A., & Jarvis, W. B. G. (1996). Dispositional differences in cognitive motivation: The life and times of individuals varying in need for cognition. *Psychological Bulletin, 119,* 197–253.

Cacioppo, J. T., Petty, R. E., Losch, M. E., & Kim, H. S. (1986). Electromyographic activity over facial muscle regions can differentiate the valence and intensity of affective reactions. *Journal of Personality and Social Psychology, 50,* 260–268.

Cartwright, D., & Harary, F. (1956). Structural balance: A generalization of Heider's theory. *Psychological Review, 63,* 277–293.

Chaiken, S. (1980). Heuristic versus systematic information processing and the use of source versus message cues in persuasion. *Journal of Personality and Social Psychology, 39,* 752–766.

Chaiken, S. (1987). The heuristic model of persuasion. In M. P. Zanna, J. M. Olson, & C. P. Herman (Eds.), *The Ontario Symposium: Social influence* (Vol. 5, pp. 3–39). Hillsdale, NJ: Erlbaum.

Chaiken, S., & Baldwin, M. W. (1981). Affective-cognitive consistency and the effect of salient behavioral information on the self-perception of attitudes. *Journal of Personality and Social Psychology, 41,* 1–12.

Chaiken, S., & Bargh, J. A. (1993). Occurrence versus moderation of the automatic attitude activation effect: Reply to Fazio. *Journal of Personality and Social Psychology, 64,* 759–765.

Chaiken, S., Giner-Sorolla, R., & Chen, S. (1996). Beyond accuracy: Defense and impression motives in heuristic and systematic information processing. In P. M. Gollwitzer & J. A. Bargh (Eds.), *The psychology of action: Linking cognition and motivation to behavior* (pp. 553–578). New York: Guilford Press.

Chaiken, S., Liberman, A., & Eagly, A. H. (1989). Heuristic and systematic processing within and beyond the persuasion context. In J. S. Uleman & J. A. Bargh (Eds.), *Unintended thought* (pp. 212–252). New York: Guilford Press.

Chaiken, S., Pomerantz, E. M., & Giner-Sorolla, R. (1995).

Structural consistency and attitude strength. In R. E. Petty & J. A. Krosnick (Eds.), *Attitude strength: Antecedents and consequences* (pp. 387–412). Hillsdale, NJ: Erlbaum.

Chaiken, S., Wood, W. L., & Eagly, A. H. (1996). Principles of persuasion. In E. T. Higgins & A. W. Kruglanski (Eds.), *Social psychology: Handbook of basic principles* (pp. 702–742). New York: Guilford Press.

Chaiken, S., & Yates, S. (1985). Affective-cognitive consistency and thought-induced attitude polarization. *Journal of Personality and Social Psychology, 49,* 1470–1481.

Charng, H., Piliavin, J. A., & Callero, P. L. (1988). Role identity and reasoned action in the prediction of repeated behavior. *Social Psychology Quarterly, 51,* 303–317.

Chen, S., Shechter, D., & Chaiken, S. (1996). Getting at the truth or getting along: Accuracy- versus impression-motivated heuristic and systematic processing. *Journal of Personality and Social Psychology, 71,* 262–275.

Clary, E. G., Snyder, M., Ridge, R. D., Miene, P. K., & Haugen, J. A. (1994). Matching messages to motives in persuasion: A functional approach to promoting volunteerism. *Journal of Applied Social Psychology, 24,* 1129–1149.

Conover, P. J., & Feldman, S. (1984). How people organize the political world: A schematic model. *American Journal of Political Science, 28,* 95–126.

Converse, P. E. (1964). The nature of belief systems in mass publics. In D. E. Apter (Ed.), *Ideology and discontent* (pp. 206–261). New York: Free Press.

Converse, P. E. (1970). Attitudes and non-attitudes: Continuation of a dialogue. In E. R. Tufte (Ed.), *The quantitative analysis of social problems* (pp. 168–189). Reading, MA: Addison-Wesley.

Crano, W. D. (1995). Attitude strength and vested interest. In R. E. Petty & J. A. Krosnick (Eds.), *Attitude strength: Antecedents and consequences* (pp. 131–157). Mahwah, N.J.: Erlbaum.

Crites, S. L., Jr., Fabrigar, L. R., & Petty, R. E. (1994). Measuring the affective and cognitive properties of attitudes: Conceptual and methodological issues. *Personality and Social Psychology Bulletin, 20,* 619–634.

Davidson, R. J. (1992). Emotion and affective style: Hemispheric substrates. *Psychological Science, 3,* 39–43.

Dawes, R. M., Singer, D., & Lemons, F. (1972). An experimental analysis of the contrast effect and its implications for intergroup communication and the indirect assessment of attitude. *Journal of Personality and Social Psychology, 21,* 281–295.

DeBono, K. G. (1987). Investigating the social-adjustive and value-expressive functions of attitudes: Implications for persuasion processes. *Journal of Personality and Social Psychology, 52,* 279–287.

Deutscher, I. (1966). Words and deeds: Social science and social policy. *Social Problems, 13,* 235–254.

Doll, J., & Ajzen, I. (1992). Accessibility and stability of predictors in the theory of planned behavior. *Journal of Personality and Social Psychology, 63,* 754–765.

Doll, J., & Orth, B. (1993). The Fishbein and Ajzen theory of reasoned action applied to contraceptive behavior: Model variants and meaningfulness. *Journal of Applied Social Psychology, 23,* 395–415.

Doob, L. W. (1947). The behavior of attitudes. *Psychological Review, 54,* 135–156.

Doob, L. W. (1953). Effects of initial serial position and attitude upon recall under conditions of low motivation. *Journal of Abnormal and Social Psychology, 48,* 199–205.

Dovidio, J. F., Brigham, J. C., Johnson, B. T., & Gaertner, S. L. (1996). Stereotyping, prejudice, and discrimination: Another look. In C. N. Macrae, C. Stangor, & M. Hewstone (Eds.), *Stereotypes and stereotyping* (pp. 276–319). New York: Guilford Press.

Dovidio, J. F., & Gaertner, S. L. (1991). Changes in the expression and assessment of racial prejudice. In H. J. Knopke, R. J. Norrell, & R. W. Rogers (Eds.), *Opening doors: Perspectives on race relations in contemporary America* (pp. 119–148). Tuscaloosa, AL: University of Alabama Press.

Downing, J. W., Judd, C. M., & Brauer, M. (1992). Effects of repeated expressions on attitude extremity. *Journal of Personality and Social Psychology, 63,* 17–29.

Eagly, A. H., & Chaiken, S. (1993). *The psychology of attitudes.* Fort Worth, TX: Harcourt Brace Jovanovich.

Eagly, A. H., & Chaiken, S. (1995). Attitude strength, attitude structure, and resistance to change. In R. E. Petty & J. A. Krosnick (Eds.), *Attitude strength: Antecedents and consequences* (pp. 413–432). Mahwah, NJ: Erlbaum.

Eagly, A. H., & Kulesa, P. (1997). Attitudes, attitude structure, and resistance to change: Implications for persuasion on environmental issues. In M. H. Bazerman, D. M. Messick, A. E. Tenbrunsel, & K. A. Wade-Benzoni (Eds.), *Environment, ethics, and behavior: The psychology of environmental valuation and degradation.* San Francisco: New Lexington Press.

Eagly, A. H., Kulesa, P., Shaw-Barnes, K., Hutson-Comeux, S., & Brannon, L. (1996). *Attitudes and attitude strength as determinants of memory for attitude-relevant information.* Unpublished manuscript.

Eagly, A. H., & Mladinic, A. (1989). Gender stereotypes and attitudes toward women and men. *Personality and Social Psychology Bulletin, 15,* 543–558.

Eagly, A. H., Mladinic, A., & Otto, S. (1994). Cognitive and affective bases of attitudes toward social groups and social policies. *Journal of Experimental Social Psychology, 30,* 113–137.

Eckes, T., & Six, B. (1994). Fakten und Fiktionen in der Einstellungs-Verhaltens-Forschung: Eine Meta-Analyse [Fact and fiction in research on the relationship between attitude and behavior: A meta-analysis]. *Zeitschrift fuer Sozialpsychologie, 25* 253–271.

Edwards, A. L. (1941). Rationalization in recognition as a result of a political frame of reference. *Journal of Abnormal and Social Psychology, 36,* 224–235.

Edwards, K., & Smith, E. E. (1996). A disconfirmation bias in the evaluation of arguments. *Journal of Personality and Social Psychology, 71,* 5–24.

Eiser, J. R. (1990). *Social judgment.* Pacific Grove, CA: Brooks/Cole.

Eiser, J. R. (1994). *Attitudes, chaos & the connectionist mind.* Cambridge, MA: Blackwell.

Erber, M. W., Hodges, S. D., & Wilson, T. D. (1995). Attitude strength, attitude stability, and the effects of analyzing reasons. In R. E. Petty & J. A. Krosnick (Eds.), *Attitude strength: Antecedents and consequences* (pp. 433–454). Mahwah, NJ: Erlbaum.

Esses, V. M., Haddock, G., & Zanna, M. P. (1993). Values, stereotypes, and emotions as determinants of intergroup attitudes. In D. M. Mackie & D. L. Hamilton (Eds.), *Affect, cognition, and stereotyping: Interactive processes in group perception* (pp. 137–166). San Diego, CA: Academic Press.

Fazio, R. H. (1986). How do attitudes guide behavior? In R. M. Sorrentino & E. T. Higgins (Eds.), *Handbook of motivation and cognition: Foundations of social behavior* (pp. 204–243). New York: Guilford Press.

Fazio, R. H. (1989). On the power and functionality of attitudes: The role of attitude accessibility. In A. R. Pratkanis, S. J. Breckler, & A. G. Greenwald (Eds.), *Attitude structure and function* (pp. 153–179). Hillsdale, NJ: Erlbaum.

Fazio, R. H. (1990). Multiple processes by which attitudes guide behavior: The MODE model as an integrative framework. In M. P. Zanna (Ed.), *Advances in experimental social psychology* (Vol. 23, pp. 75–109). New York: Academic Press.

Fazio, R. H. (1993). Variability in the likelihood of automatic attitude activation: Data reanalysis and commentary on Bargh, Chaiken, Govender, and Pratto (1992). *Journal of Personality and Social Psychology, 64,* 753–758.

Fazio, R. H. (1995). Attitudes as object-evaluation associations: Determinants, consequences, and correlates of attitude accessibility. In R. E. Petty & J. A. Krosnick (Eds.), *Attitude strength: Antecedents and consequences* (pp. 247–283). Mahwah, NJ: Erlbaum.

Fazio, R. H., Chen, J., McDonel, E. C., & Sherman, S. J. (1982). Attitude accessibility, attitude-behavior consistency, and the strength of the object-evaluation association. *Journal of Experimental Social Psychology, 18,* 339–357.

Fazio, R. H., Powell, M. C., & Herr, P. M. (1983). Toward a process model of the attitude-behavior relation: Accessing one's attitude upon mere observation of the attitude object. *Journal of Personality and Social Psychology, 44,* 723–735.

Fazio, R. H., Sanbonmatsu, D. M., Powell, M. C., & Kardes, F. R. (1986). On the automatic activation of attitudes. *Journal of Personality and Social Psychology, 50,* 229–238.

Fazio, R. H., & Williams, C. J. (1986). Attitude accessibility as a moderator of the attitude-perception and attitude-behavior relations: An investigation of the 1984 presidential election. *Journal of Personality and Social Psychology, 51,* 505–514.

Fazio, R. H., & Zanna, M. P. (1981). Direct experience and attitude-behavior consistency. In L. Berkowitz (Ed.), *Advances in experimental social psychology* (Vol. 14, pp. 161–202). San Diego, CA: Academic Press.

Feather, N. T. (1969). Attitudes and selective recall. *Journal of Personality and Social Psychology, 12,* 310–319.

Feather, N. T. (Ed.). (1982). *Expectations and actions: Expectancy-value models in psychology.* Hillsdale, NJ: Erlbaum.

Feather, N. T. (1996). Values, deservingness, and attitudes toward high achievers: Research on tall poppies. In C. Seligman, J. M. Olson, & M. P. Zanna (Eds.), *The Ontario Symposium: The psychology of values* (Vol. 8, pp. 215–251). Mahwah, NJ: Erlbaum.

Festinger, L. (1957). *A theory of cognitive dissonance.* Evanston, IL: Row, Peterson.

Festinger, L. (1964). *Conflict, decision, and dissonance.* Stanford, CA: Stanford University Press.

Fishbein, M. (1967a). A behavior theory approach to the relations between beliefs about an object and the attitude toward the object. In M. Fishbein (Ed.), *Readings in attitude theory and measurement* (pp. 389–400). New York: Wiley.

Fishbein, M. (1967b). A consideration of beliefs, and their role in attitude measurement. In M. Fishbein (Ed.), *Readings in attitude theory and measurement* (pp. 257–266). New York: Wiley.

Fishbein, M. (1980). A theory of reasoned action: Some applications and implications. In H. E. Howe, Jr. & M. M. Page (Eds.), *Nebraska Symposium on Motivation, 1979* (Vol. 27, pp. 65–116). Lincoln: University of Nebraska Press.

Fishbein, M., & Ajzen, I. (1974). Attitudes toward objects as predictors of single and multiple behavioral criteria. *Psychological Review, 81,* 59–74.

Fishbein, M., & Ajzen, I. (1975). *Belief, attitude, intention, and behavior: An introduction to theory and research.* Reading, MA: Addison-Wesley.

Fishbein, M., Chan, D. K., O'Reilly, K., Schnell, D., Wood, R., Beeker, C., & Cohn, D. (1992). Attitudinal and normative factors as determinants of gay men's intentions to perform AIDS-related sexual behaviors: A multisite analysis. *Journal of Applied Social Psychology, 22,* 999–1011.

Fishbein, M., Middlestadt, S. E., & Chung, J. (1986). Predicting participation and choice among first time voters in U.S. partisan elections. In S. Kraus & R. Perloff (Eds.), *Mass media and political thoughts: An information processing approach* (pp. 65–82). Beverly Hills, CA: Sage.

Fiske, S. T. (1998). Stereotypes, prejudice, and discrimination. In D. Gilbert, S. T. Fiske, & G. Lindzey (Eds.), *Handbook of social psychology* (4th ed., Vol. 2, pp. 357–411). New York: McGraw-Hill.

Fiske, S. T., & Neuberg, S. L. (1990). A continuum of impression formation, from category-based to individuating processes: Influences of information and motivation on attention and interpretation. In M. P. Zanna (Ed.), *Advances in experimental social psychology* (Vol. 23, pp. 1–74). San Diego, CA: Academic Press.

Fiske, S. T., & Taylor, S. E. (1991). *Social cognition* (2nd ed.). New York: McGraw-Hill.

Fitzgerald, D., & Ausubel, D. P. (1963). Cognitive versus affective factors in the learning and retention of controversial material. *Journal of Educational Psychology, 54,* 73–84.

Freedman, J. L., & Sears, D. O. (1965). Selective exposure. In L. Berkowitz (Ed.), *Advances in experimental social psychology* (Vol. 2, pp. 57–97). New York: Academic Press.

Freud, S. (1953). *A general introduction to psychoanalysis.* Garden City, NY: Permabooks. (Original work published 1920).

Frey, D. (1986). Recent research on selective exposure to information. In L. Berkowitz (Ed.), *Advances in experimental social psychology* (Vol. 19, pp. 41–80). New York: Academic Press.

Gaertner, S. L., & Dovidio, J. F. (1986). The aversive form of racism. In J. F. Dovidio & S. L. Gaertner (Eds.), *Prejudice, discrimination, and racism* (pp. 61–89). Orlando, FL: Academic Press.

Ganchrow, J. R., Streiner, J. E., & Daher, M. (1983). Neonatal facial expressions in response to different qualities and intensities of gustatory stimuli. *Infant Behavior and Development, 6,* 189–200.

Giner-Sorolla, R., & Chaiken, S. (1994). The causes of hostile media judgments. *Journal of Experimental Social Psychology, 30,* 165–180.

Giner-Sorolla, R., & Chaiken, S. (1997). Selective use of heuristic and systematic processing under defense motivation. *Personality and Social Psychology Bulletin, 23,* 84–97.

Glick, P., & Fiske, S. T. (1996). The Ambivalent Sexism Inventory: Differentiating hostile and benevolent sexism. *Journal of Personality and Social Psychology, 70,* 491–512.

Gollwitzer, P. M. (1996). The volitional benefits of planning. In P. M. Gollwitzer & J. A. Bargh (Eds.), *The psychology of action: Linking cognition and motivation to behavior* (pp. 287–312). New York: Guilford Press.

Gollwitzer, P. M., & Moskowitz, G. B. (1996). Goal effects on action and cognition. In E. T. Higgins & A. W. Kruglanski (Eds.), *Social psychology: Handbook of basic principles* (pp. 361–399). New York: Guilford Press.

Greenberg, J., Pyszczynski, T., Solomon, S., Rosenblatt, A., Veeder, M., Kirkland, S., & Lyon, D. (1990). Evidence for terror management theory II: The effects of mortality salience on reactions to those who threaten or bolster the cultural worldview. *Journal of Personality and Social Psychology, 58,* 308–318.

Greenwald, A. G. (1975). Consequences of prejudice against the null hypothesis. *Psychological Bulletin, 82,* 1–20.

Greenwald, A. G. (1989). Why attitudes are important: Defining attitude and attitude theory 20 years later. In A. R. Pratkanis, S. J. Breckler, & A. G. Greenwald (Eds.), *Attitude structure and function* (pp. 429–440). Hillsdale, NJ: Erlbaum.

Greenwald, A. G., & Banaji, M. R. (1995). Implicit social cognition: Attitudes, self-esteem, and stereotypes. *Psychological Review, 102,* 4–27.

Greenwald, A. G., & Sakumura, J. S. (1967). Attitude and selective learning: Where are the phenomena of yesteryear? *Journal of Personality and Social Psychology, 7,* 387–397.

Gross, S. R., Holtz, R., & Miller, N. (1995). Attitude certainty. In R. E. Petty & J. A. Krosnick (Eds.), *Attitude strength: Antecedents and consequences* (pp. 215–245). Mahwah, NJ: Erlbaum.

Han, S., & Shavitt, S. (1994). Persuasion and culture: Advertising appeals in individualistic and collectivistic societies. *Journal of Experimental Social Psychology, 30,* 326–350.

Hass, R. G., Katz, I., Rizzo, N., Bailey, J., & Moore, L. (1992). When racial ambivalence evokes negative affect: Using a disguised measure of mood. *Personality and Social Psychology Bulletin, 18,* 786–797.

Hastorf, A. H., & Cantril, H. (1954). They saw a game: A case study. *Journal of Abnormal and Social Psychology, 49,* 129–134.

Heider, F. (1946). Attitudes and cognitive organization. *Journal of Psychology, 21,* 107–112.

Heider, F. (1958). *The psychology of interpersonal relations.* New York: Wiley.

Herek, G. M. (1986). The instrumentality of attitudes: Toward a neofunctional theory. *Journal of Social Issues, 42*(2), 99–114.

Herek, G. M. (1987). Can functions be measured? A new perspective on the functional approach to attitudes. *Social Psychology Quarterly, 50,* 285–303.

Higgins, E. T. (1989). Knowledge accessibility and activation: Subjectivity and suffering from unconscious sources. In J. S. Uleman & J. A. Bargh (Eds.), *Unintended thought* (pp. 75–123). New York: Guilford Press.

Higgins, E. T. (1996). Knowledge activation: Accessibility, applicability, and salience. In E. T. Higgins & A. W. Kruglanski (Eds.), *Social psychology: Handbook of basic principles* (pp. 133–168). New York: Guilford Press.

Hilgard, E. R. (1956). *Theories of learning* (2nd ed.). New York: Appleton-Century-Crofts.

Himmelfarb, S. (1993). The measurement of attitudes. In A. H. Eagly & S. Chaiken, *The psychology of attitudes* (pp. 23–87). Fort Worth, TX: Harcourt Brace Jovanovich.

Himmelfarb, S., & Youngblood, J. (1969). Effects of factual information on creating resistance to emotional appeals. *Psychonomic Science, 14,* 267–270.

Houston, D. A., & Fazio, R. H. (1989). Biased processing as a function of attitude accessibility: Making objective judgments subjectively. *Social Cognition, 7,* 51–66.

Hovland, C. I., Janis, I. L., & Kelley, H. H. (1953). *Communication and persuasion: Psychological studies of opinion change.* New Haven, CT: Yale University Press.

Hovland, C. I., & Sherif, M. (1952). Judgmental phenomena and scales of attitude measurement: Item displacement in Thurstone scales. *Journal of Abnormal and Social Psychology, 47,* 822–832.

Hurwitz, J., & Peffley, M. (1987). How are foreign policy attitudes structured? A hierarchical model. *American Political Science Review, 81,* 1099–1120.

Insko, C. A. (1981). Balance theory and phenomenology. In R. E. Petty, T. M. Ostrom, & T. C. Brock (Eds.), *Cognitive responses in persuasion* (pp. 309–338). Hillsdale, NJ: Erlbaum.

Insko, C. A. (1984). Balance theory, the Jordan paradigm, and the Wiest tetrahedron. In L. Berkowitz (Ed.), *Advances in experimental social psychology* (Vol. 18, pp. 89–140). Orlando, FL: Academic Press.

Jackson, L. A., Hodge, C. N., Gerard, D. A., Ingram, J. M., Ervin, K. S., & Sheppard, L. A. (1996). Cognition, affect, and behavior in the prediction of group attitudes. *Personality and Social Psychology Bulletin, 22,* 306–316.

Jacoby, W. G. (1995). The structure of ideological thinking in the American electorate. *American Journal of Political Science, 39,* 314–335.

James, W. (1952). *The principles of psychology.* Chicago: Encyclopaedia Britannica. (Original work published 1890).

Jarvis, W. B. G., & Petty, R. E. (1996). The need to evaluate. *Journal of Personality and Social Psychology, 70,* 172–194.

Johnson, B. T., & Eagly, A. H. (1989). The effects of involvement on persuasion: A meta-analysis. *Psychological Bulletin, 106,* 290–314.

Johnson, B. T., Lin, H., Symons, C. S., Campbell, L. A., & Ekstein, G. (1995). Initial beliefs and attitudinal latitudes as factors in persuasion. *Personality and Social Psychology Bulletin, 21,* 502–511.

Johnson, J. T., & Judd, C. M. (1983). Overlooking the incongruent: Categorization biases in the identification of political statements. *Journal of Personality and Social Psychology, 45,* 978–996.

Jones, E. E., & Aneshansel, J. (1956). The learning and utilization of contravaluant material. *Journal of Abnormal and Social Psychology, 53,* 27–33.

Jordan, N. (1953). Behavioral forces that are a function of attitudes and of cognitive organization. *Human Relations, 6,* 273–287.

Jost, J. T., & Banaji, M. R. (1994). The role of stereotyping in system-justification and the production of false consciousness. *British Journal of Social Psychology, 33,* 1–27.

Judd, C. M., Kenny, D. A., & Krosnick, J. A. (1983). Judging the positions of political candidates. Models of assimilation and contrast. *Journal of Personality and Social Psychology, 44,* 952–963.

Judd, C. M., & Krosnick, J. A. (1989). The structural bases of consistency among political attitudes: Effects of political expertise and attitude importance. In A. R. Pratkanis, S. J. Breckler, & A. G. Greenwald (Eds.), *Attitude structure and function* (pp. 99–128). Hillsdale, NJ: Erlbaum.

Judd, C. M., & Kulik, J. A. (1980). Schematic effects of social attitudes on information processing and recall. *Journal of Personality and Social Psychology, 38,* 569–578.

Judd, C. M., & Lusk, C. M. (1984). Knowledge structures and evaluative judgments: Effects of structural variables on judgmental extremity. *Journal of Personality and Social Psychology, 46,* 1193–1207.

Judd, M., & Brauer, M. (1995). Repetition and evaluative extremity. In R. E. Petty & J. A. Krosnick (Eds.), *Attitude strength: Antecedents and consequences* (pp. 43–71). Mahwah, NJ: Erlbaum.

Kaplan, K. J. (1972). On the ambivalence-indifference problem in attitude theory and measurement: A suggested modification of the semantic differential technique. *Psychological Bulletin, 77,* 361–372.

Kaplan, M. F. (1991). The joint effects of cognition and affect on social judgment. In J. P. Forgas (Ed.), *Emotion and social judgments* (pp. 73–82). Oxford, England: Pergamon Press.

Katz, D. (1960). The functional approach to the study of attitudes. *Public Opinion Quarterly, 24,* 163–204.

Katz, D., Sarnoff, D., & McClintock, C. (1956). Ego-defense and attitude change. *Human Relations, 9,* 27–45.

Katz, D., & Stotland, E. (1959). A preliminary statement to a theory of attitude structure and change. In S. Koch (Ed.), *Psychology: A study of a science* (Vol. 3, pp. 423–475). New York: McGraw-Hill.

Katz, I. (1981). *Stigma: A social psychological analysis.* Hillsdale, NJ: Erlbaum.

Katz, I., & Hass, R. G. (1988). Racial ambivalence and American value conflict: Correlational and priming studies of dual cognitive structures. *Journal of Personality and Social Psychology, 55,* 893–905.

Kelly, C., & Breinlinger, S. (1995). Attitudes, intentions, and behavior: A study of women's participation in collective action. *Journal of Applied Social Psychology, 25,* 1430–1445.

Kelman, H. C. (1961). Processes of opinion change. *Public Opinion Quarterly, 25,* 57–78.

Kerlinger, F. N. (1984). *Liberalism and conservatism: The nature and structure of social attitudes.* Hillsdale, NJ: Erlbaum.

Kiesler, C. A. (1971). *The psychology of commitment: Experiments linking behavior to belief.* San Diego, CA: Academic Press.

Kiesler, C. A., Pallak, M. S., & Kanouse, D. E. (1968). Interactive effects of commitment and dissonance. *Journal of Personality and Social Psychology, 8,* 331–338.

Kim, M., & Hunter, J. E. (1993). Attitude-behavior relations: A meta-analysis of attitudinal relevance and topic. *Journal of Communication, 43,* 101–142.

Kinder, D. R., & Sears, D. O. (1981). Prejudice and politics: Symbolic racism versus racial threats to the good life. *Journal of Personality and Social Psychology, 40,* 414–431.

Kinder, D. R., & Sears, D. O. (1985). Public opinion and political action. In G. Lindzey & E. Aronson (Eds.), *Handbook of social psychology* (3rd ed., Vol. 2, pp. 659–741). New York: Random House.

Klapper, J. T. (1960). *The effects of mass communications.* New York: Free Press.

Kluegel, J. R., & Smith, E. R. (1986). *Beliefs about inequality: Americans' views of what is and what ought to be.* New York: Aldine de Gruyter.

Kraus, S. J. (1995). Attitudes and the prediction of behavior: A meta-analysis of the empirical literature. *Personality and Social Psychology Bulletin, 21,* 58–75.

Kristiansen, C. M., & Zanna, M. P. (1988). Justifying attitudes by appealing to values: A functional perspective. *British Journal of Social Psychology, 27,* 247–256.

Krosnick, J. A. (1988). Attitude importance and attitude change. *Journal of Experimental Social Psychology, 24,* 240–255.

Krosnick, J. A. (1990). Americans' perceptions of presidential candidates: A test of the projection hypothesis. *Journal of Social Issues, 46*(2), 159–182.

Krosnick, J. A., Boninger, D. S., Chuang, Y. C., Berent, M. K., & Carnot, C. G. (1993). Attitude strength: One construct or many related constructs? *Journal of Personality and Social Psychology, 65,* 1132–1151.

LaPiere, R. T. (1934). Attitudes vs. actions. *Social Forces, 13,* 230–237.

Lavine, H., Thomsen, C. J., & Gonzales, M. H. (1997). A shared consequences model of the development of inter-attitudinal consistency: The influence of values, attitude-relevant thought, and expertise. *Journal of Personality and Social Psychology, 72,* 735–749.

Lavine, H., & Snyder, M. (1996). Cognitive processing and the functional matching effect in persuasion: The mediating role of subjective perceptions of message quality. *Journal of Experimental Social Psychology, 32,* 580–604.

Levine, J. M., & Murphy, G. (1943). The learning and forgetting of controversial material. *Journal of Abnormal and Social Psychology, 38,* 507–517.

Lewin, K. (1935). *A dynamic theory of personality.* New York: McGraw-Hill.

Lewin, K. (1951). *Field theory in social science: Selected theoretical papers.* New York: Harper.

Linville, P. W. (1982). The complexity-extremity effect and age-based stereotyping. *Journal of Personality and Social Psychology, 42,* 193–211.

Liska, A. E. (1984). A critical examination of the causal structure of the Fishbein/Ajzen attitude-behavior model. *Social Psychology Quarterly, 47,* 61–74.

Lord, C. G., Ross, L., & Lepper, M. R. (1979). Biased assimilation and attitude polarization: The effects of prior theories on subsequently considered evidence. *Journal of Personality and Social Psychology, 37,* 2098–2109.

Lowe, R. H., & Steiner, I. D. (1968). Some effects of the reversibility and consequences on postdecision information preferences. *Journal of Personality and Social Psychology, 8,* 172–179.

Lusk, C. M., & Judd, C. M. (1988). Political expertise and the structural mediators of candidate evaluations. *Journal of Experimental Social Psychology, 24,* 105–126.

Lydon, J. E., Zanna, M. P., & Ross, M. (1988). Bolstering attitudes by autobiographical recall: Attitude persistence and selective memory. *Personality and Social Psychology Bulletin, 14,* 78–86.

MacDonald, T. K., & Zanna, M. P. (1996). *Ambivalence toward feminists: The behavioral implications of holding ambivalent attitudes toward social groups.* Manuscript submitted for publication.

Madden, T. J., Ellen, P. S., & Ajzen, I. (1992). A comparison of the theory of planned behavior and the theory of reasoned action. *Personality and Social Psychology Bulletin, 18,* 3–9.

Maio, G. R., Bell, D. W., & Esses, V. M. (1996). Ambivalence and persuasion: The processing of messages about immigrant groups. *Journal of Experimental Social Psychology, 32,* 513–536.

Maio, G. R., & Olson, J. M. (1995). Relations between values, attitudes, and behavioral intentions: The moderating role of attitude function. *Journal of Experimental Social Psychology, 31,* 266–285.

Malpass, R. S. (1969). Effects of attitude on learning and memory: The influence of instruction-induced sets. *Journal of Experimental Social Psychology, 5,* 441–453.

Manis, M. (1960). The interpretation of opinion statements as a function of recipient attitude. *Journal of Abnormal and Social Psychology, 60,* 340–344.

Manstead, A. S. R., & Parker, D. (1995). Evaluating and extending the theory of planned behaviour. In W. Stroebe & M. Hewstone (Eds.), *European review of social psychology* (Vol. 6, pp. 69–95). New York: Wiley.

Markus, H. R., & Kitayama, S. (1991). Culture and the self: Implications for cognition, emotion, and motivation. *Psychological Review, 98,* 224–253.

Markus, H., & Zajonc, R. B. (1985). The cognitive perspective in social psychology. In G. Lindzey & E. Aronson (Eds.), *Handbook of social psychology* (3rd ed., Vol. 1, pp. 137–230). New York: Random House.

McCaul, K. D., O'Neill, H. K., & Glasgow, R. E. (1988). Predicting the performance of dental hygiene behaviors: An examination of the Fishbein and Ajzen model and self-efficacy expectations. *Journal of Applied Social Psychology, 18,* 114–128.

McClelland, D. C., Weinberger, J., & Koestner, R. (1989). How do self-attributed and implicit motives differ? *Psychological Review, 96,* 690–702.

McClelland, J. L., & Rumelhart, D. E. (1981). An interactive activation model of context effects in letter perception: Part I. An account of basic findings. *Psychological Review, 88,* 375–407.

McConahay, J. B. (1986). Modern racism, ambivalence, and the Modern Racism Scale. In J. F. Dovidio & S. L. Gaertner (Eds.), *Prejudice, discrimination, and racism* (pp. 91–125). Orlando, FL: Academic Press.

McGuire, W. J. (1969). The nature of attitudes and attitude change. In G. Lindzey & E. Aronson (Eds.), *Handbook of social psychology* (2nd ed., Vol. 3, pp. 136–314). Reading, MA: Addison-Wesley.

McGuire, W. J. (1981). The probabilogical model of cognitive structure and attitude change. In R. E. Petty, T. M. Ostrom, & T. C. Brock (Eds.), *Cognitive responses in persuasion* (pp. 291–307). Hillsdale, NJ: Erlbaum.

McGuire, W. J. (1985). Attitudes and attitude change. In G. Lindzey & E. Aronson (Eds.), *Handbook of social psychology* (3rd ed., Vol. 2, pp. 233–246). New York: Random House.

McGuire, W. J., & McGuire, C. V. (1991). The content, structure, and operation of thought systems. In R. S. Wyer, Jr., & T. K. Srull (Eds.), *Advances in social cognition* (Vol. 4, pp. 1–78). Hillsdale, NJ: Erlbaum.

Millar, M. G., & Millar, K. U. (1996). The effects of direct and indirect experience on affective and cognitive responses and the attitude-behavior relation. *Journal of Experimental Social Psychology, 32,* 561–579.

Millar, M. G., & Tesser, A. (1986a). Effects of affective and cognitive focus on the attitude-behavior relation. *Journal of Personality and Social Psychology, 51,* 270–276.

Millar, M. G., & Tesser, A. (1986b). Thought-induced attitude change: The effects of schema structure and commitment. *Journal of Personality and Social Psychology, 51,* 259–269.

Miller, A. G., McHoskey, J. W., Bane, C., & Dowd, T. G. (1993). The attitude polarization phenomenon: Role of response measure, attitude extremity, and behavioral consequences of reported attitude change. *Journal of Personality and Social Psychology, 64,* 561–574.

Miller, N. E. (1944). Experimental studies in conflict. In J. M. Hunt (Ed.), *Personality and the behavior disorders: A handbook based on experimental and clinical research* (Vol. 1, pp. 431–465). New York: Ronald Press.

Moore, M. (1980). Validation of the Attitude Toward Any Practice Scale through the use of ambivalence as a moderator variable. *Educational and Psychological Measurement, 40,* 205–208.

Murphy, S. T., Monahan, J. L., & Zajonc, R. B. (1995). Additivity of nonconscious affect: Combined effects of priming and exposure. *Journal of Personality and Social Psychology, 69,* 589–602.

Murray, S. L., Haddock, G, & Zanna, M. P. (1996). On creating value-expressive attitudes: An experimental approach.

In C. Seligman, J. M. Olson, & M. P. Zanna (Eds.), *The Ontario Symposium: The psychology of values* (Vol. 8, pp. 107–133). Mahwah, NJ: Erlbaum.

Newcomb, T. M. (1961). *The acquaintance process.* New York: Holt, Rinehart and Winston.

Norman, R. (1975). Affective-cognitive consistency, attitudes, conformity, and behavior. *Journal of Personality and Social Psychology, 32,* 83–91.

O'Keefe, D. J., & Sypher, H. E. (1981). Cognitive complexity measures and the relationship of cognitive complexity to communication. *Human Communication Research, 8,* 72–92.

Osgood, C. E., Suci, G. S., & Tannenbaum, P. H. (1957). *The measurement of meaning.* Urbana: University of Illinois Press.

Osgood, C. E., & Tannenbaum, P. H. (1955). The principle of congruity in the prediction of attitude change. *Psychological Review, 62,* 42–55.

Ostrom, T. M. (1987). Bipolar survey items: An information processing perspective. In H.-J. Hippler, N. Schwarz, & S. Sudman (Eds.), *Social information processing and survey methodology* (pp. 71–85). New York: Springer-Verlag.

Ostrom, T. M., & Brock, T. C. (1968). A cognitive model of attitudinal involvement. In R. P. Abelson, E. Aronson, W. J. McGuire, T. M. Newcomb, M. J. Rosenberg, & P. H. Tannenbaum (Eds.), *Theories of cognitive consistency: A sourcebook* (pp. 373–383). Chicago: Rand McNally.

Ottati, V., Fishbein, M., & Middlestadt, S. E. (1988). Determinants of voters' beliefs about the candidates' stands on issues: The role of evaluative bias heuristics and the candidates' expressed message. *Journal of Personality and Social Psychology, 55,* 517–529.

Ouellette, J. A., & Wood, W. (1997). *Habit: Predicting frequently-occurring behaviors in constant contexts.* Manuscript submitted for publication.

Peak, H. (1955). Attitude and motivation. In M. R. Jones (Ed.), *Nebraska Symposium on Motivation* (Vol. 3, pp. 149–188). Lincoln: University of Nebraska Press.

Petty, R. E., & Cacioppo, J. T. (1986). *Communication and persuasion: Central and peripheral routes to attitude change.* New York: Springer-Verlag.

Petty, R. E., & Krosnick, J. A. (Eds.). (1995). *Attitude strength: Antecedents and consequences.* Mahwah, NJ: Erlbaum.

Petty, R. E., & Wegener, D. T. (1998). Attitude change: Multiple roles for persuasion variables. In D. Gilbert, S. T. Fiske, & G. Lindzey (Eds.), *Handbook of social psychology* (4th ed., Vol. 1, pp. 323–390). New York: McGraw-Hill.

Pomazal, R. J., & Jaccard, J. J. (1976). An informational approach to altruistic behavior. *Journal of Personality and Social Psychology, 33,* 317–326.

Pomerantz, E. M., Chaiken, S., & Tordesillas, R. (1995). Attitude strength and resistance processes. *Journal of Personality and Social Psychology, 69,* 408–419.

Postman, L., & Murphy, G. (1943). The factor of attitude in associative memory. *Journal of Experimental Psychology, 33,* 228–238.

Powell, M. C., & Fazio, R. H. (1984). Attitude accessibility as a function of repeated attitudinal expression. *Personality and Social Psychology Bulletin, 10,* 139–148.

Pratkanis, A. R. (1989). The cognitive representation of attitudes. In A. R. Pratkanis, S. J. Breckler, & A. G. Greenwald (Eds.), *Attitude structure and function* (pp. 71–98). Hillsdale, NJ: Erlbaum.

Prentice, D. A. (1987). Psychological correspondence of possessions, attitudes, and values. *Journal of Personality and Social Psychology, 53,* 993–1003.

Priester, J. R., & Petty, R. E. (1996). The gradual threshold model of ambivalence: Relating the positive and negative bases of attitudes to subjective ambivalence. *Journal of Personality and Social Psychology, 71,* 431–449.

Prislin, R. (1996). Attitude stability and attitude strength: One is enough to make it stable. *European Journal of Social Psychology, 26,* 447–477.

Prislin, R., & Ouellette, J. (1996). When it is embedded, it is potent: Effects of general attitude embeddedness on formation of specific attitudes and behavioral intentions. *Personaity and Social Psychology Bulletin, 22,* 845–861.

Prislin, R., Wood, W., & Pool, R. (1997). *Structural consistency and the deduction of novel from existing attitudes.* Manuscript submitted for publication.

Raden, D. (1985). Strength-related attitude dimensions. *Social Psychology Quarterly, 48,* 312–330.

Read, S. J., & Miller, L. C. (1994). Dissonance and balance in belief systems: The promise of parallel constraint satisfaction processes and connectionist modeling approaches. In R. D. Schank & E. Langer (Eds.), *Beliefs, reasoning and decision making: Psycho-logic in honor of Bob Abelson* (pp. 209–235). Hillsdale, NJ: Erlbaum.

Read, S. J., Vanman, E. J., & Miller, L. C. (1997). Connectionism, parallel constraint satisfaction processes, and Gestalt principles: (Re)introducing cognitive dynamics to social psychology. *Personality and Social Psychology Review, 1,* 26–53.

Regan, D. T., & Fazio, R. H. (1977). On the consistency between attitudes and behavior: Look to the method of attitude formation. *Journal of Experimental Social Psychology, 13,* 38–45.

Roberts, J. V. (1985). The attitude-memory relationship after 40 years: A meta-analysis of the literature. *Basic and Applied Social Psychology, 6,* 221–241.

Roese, N. J., & Olson, J. M. (1994). Attitude importance as a function of repeated attitude expression. *Journal of Experimental Social Psychology, 30,* 39–51.

Rokeach, M. (1968). *Beliefs, attitudes, and values: A theory of organization and change.* San Francisco: Jossey-Bass.

Romer, D. (1983). Effects of own attitude on polarization of judgment. *Journal of Personality and Social Psychology, 44,* 273–284.

Rosenberg, M. J. (1956). Cognitive structure and attitudinal affect. *Journal of Abnormal and Social Psychology, 53,* 367–372.

Rosenberg, M. J. (1960). An analysis of affective-cognitive consistency. In C. I. Hovland & M. J. Rosenberg (Eds.), *Attitude organization and change: An analysis of consistency among attitude components* (pp. 15–64). New Haven, CT: Yale University Press.

Rosenberg, M. J. (1968). Hedonism, inauthenticity, and other goads toward expansion of a consistency theory. In R. P. Abelson, E. Aronson, W. J. McGuire, T. M. Newcomb, M. J. Rosenberg, & P. H. Tannenbaum (Eds.), *Theories of cognitive consistency: A sourcebook* (pp. 73–111). Chicago: Rand McNally.

Rosenberg, M. J., & Hovland, C. I. (1960). Cognitive, affective, and behavioral components of attitudes. In C. I. Hovland & M. J. Rosenberg (Eds.), *Attitude organization and change: An analysis of consistency among attitude components* (pp. 1–14). New Haven, CT: Yale University Press.

Ross, M. (1989). Relation of implicit theories to the construction of personal histories. *Psychological Review, 96,* 341–357.

Ross, M., McFarland, C., Conway, M., & Zanna, M. P. (1983). Reciprocal relation between attitudes and behavior recall: Committing people to newly formed attitudes. *Journal of Personality and Social Psychology, 45,* 257–267.

Runkel, P. J., & Peizer, D. B. (1968). The two-valued orientation of current equilibrium theory. *Behavioral Science, 13,* 56–65.

Sanbonmatsu, D. M., & Fazio, R. H. (1990). The role of attitudes in memory-based decision making. *Journal of Personality and Social Psychology, 59,* 614–622.

Sarnoff, I. (1960). Psychoanalytic theory and social attitudes. *Public Opinion Quarterly, 24,* 251–279.

Sarnoff, I., & Katz, D. (1954). The motivational basis of attitude change. *Journal of Abnormal and Social Psychology, 49,* 115–124.

Scheier, M. F., & Carver, C. S. (1988). A model of behavioral self-regulation: Translating intention into action. In L. Berkowitz (Ed.), *Advances in experimental social psychology* (Vol. 21, pp. 303–346). San Diego, CA: Academic Press.

Schroder, H. M., Driver, M. J., & Streufert, S. (1967). *Human information processing: Individuals and groups functioning in complex social situations.* New York: Holt, Rinehart, & Winston.

Schwarz, N., & Bless, H. (1992). Constructing reality and its alternatives: An inclusion/exclusion model of assimilation and contrast effects in social judgment. In L. L. Martin & A. Tesser (Eds.), *The construction of social judgments* (pp. 217–245). Hillsdale, NJ: Erlbaum.

Scott, W. A. (1963). Conceptualizing and measuring structural properties of cognition. In O. J. Harvey (Ed.), *Motivation and social interaction: Cognitive determinants* (pp. 266–288). New York: Ronald Press.

Scott, W. A. (1968). Attitude measurement. In G. Lindzey & E. Aronson (Eds.), *Handbook of social psychology* (2nd ed., Vol. 2, pp. 204–273). Reading, MA: Addison-Wesley.

Scott, W. A. (1969). Structure of natural cognitions. *Journal of Personality and Social Psychology, 12,* 261–278.

Sears, D. O. (1965). Biased indoctrination and selectivity of exposure to new information. *Sociometry, 28,* 363–376.

Sears, D. O. (1988). Symbolic racism. In P. A. Katz & D. A. Taylor (Eds.), *Eliminating racism: Profiles in controversy* (pp. 53–84). New York: Plenum Press.

Sears, D. O., & Funk, C. L. (1991). The role of self-interest in social and political attitudes. In M. P. Zanna (Ed.), *Advances in experimental social psychology* (Vol. 24, pp. 2–91). San Diego, CA: Academic Press.

Sears, D. O., & Kinder, D. R. (1985). Whites' opposition to busing: On conceptualizing and operationalizing group conflict. *Journal of Personality and Social Psychology, 48,* 1141–1147.

Seligman, C., Olson, J. M., & Zanna, M. P. (Eds.). (1996). *The Ontario Symposium: The psychology of values* (Vol. 8). Mahwah, NJ: Erlbaum.

Sentis, K. P., & Burnstein, E. (1979). Remembering schema-consistent information: Effects of a balance schema on recognition memory. *Journal of Personality and Social Psychology, 37,* 2200–2211.

Shavitt, S. (1990). The role of attitude objects in attitude functions. *Journal of Experimental Social Psychology, 26,* 124–148.

Sheppard, B. H., Hartwick, J., & Warshaw, P. R. (1988). The theory of reasoned action: A meta-analysis of past research with recommendations for modifications and future research. *Journal of Consumer Research, 15,* 325–343.

Sherif, C. W., Sherif, M., & Nebergall, R. E. (1965). *Attitude and attitude change: The social judgment-involvement approach.* Philadelphia: Saunders.

Sherif, M. (1935). A study of some social factors in perception. *Archives of Psychology, 27,* 1–60.

Sherif, M. (1936). *The psychology of social norms.* New York: Harper.

Sherif, M., & Cantril, H. (1947). *The psychology of ego-involvements: Social attitudes and identifications.* New York: Wiley.

Sherif, M., & Hovland, C. I. (1961). *Social judgment: Assimilation and contrast effects in communication and attitude change.* New Haven, CT: Yale University Press.

Shultz, T. R., & Lepper, M. R. (1996). Cognitive dissonance reduction as constraint satisfaction. *Psychological Review, 103,* 219–240.

Smith, C. P., McClelland, D. C., Atkinson, J. W., & Veroff, J. (1992). *Motivation and personality: Handbook of thematic content analysis.* New York: Cambridge University Press.

Smith, E. R. (1998). Mental representation and memory. In D. Gilbert, S. T. Fiske, & G. Lindzey (Eds.), *Handbook of social psychology* (4th ed., Vol. 1, pp. 391–445). New York: McGraw-Hill.

Smith, M. B. (1947). The personal setting of public opinions: A study of attitudes toward Russia. *Public Opinion Quarterly, 11,* 507–523.

Smith, M. B., Bruner, J. S., & White, R. W. (1956). *Opinions and personality.* New York: Wiley.

Smith, S. S., & Jamieson, B. D. (1972). Effects of attitude and ego involvement on the learning and retention of controversial material. *Journal of Personality and Social Psychology, 22,* 303–310.

Snyder, M. (1974). Self-monitoring of expressive behavior. *Journal of Personality and Social Psychology, 30,* 526–537.

Snyder, M. (1982). When believing means doing: Creating links between attitudes and behavior. In M. P. Zanna, E. T. Higgins, & C. P. Herman (Eds.), *The Ontario Symposium: Consistency in social behavior* (Vol. 2, pp. 105–130). Hillsdale, NJ: Erlbaum.

Snyder, M., & DeBono, K. G. (1985). Appeals to images and claims about quality: Understanding the psychology of advertising. *Journal of Personality and Social Psychology, 49,* 586–597.

Solomon, S., Greenberg, J., & Pyszczynski, T. (1991). A terror management theory of social behavior: The psychological functions of self-esteem and cultural worldviews. In M. Zanna (Ed.), *Advances in experimental social psychology* (Vol. 24, pp. 93–159). San Diego, CA: Academic Press.

Spellman, B. A., Ullman, J. B., & Holyoak, K. J. (1993). A coherence model of cognitive consistency: Dynamics of attitude change during the Persian Gulf War. *Journal of Social Issues, 49*(4), 147–165.

Staats, A. W., & Staats, C. K. (1958). Attitudes established by classical conditioning. *Journal of Abnormal and Social Psychology, 57,* 37–40.

Stangor, C., Sullivan, L. A., & Ford, T. E. (1991). Affective and cognitive determinants of prejudice. *Social Cognition, 9,* 359–380.

Stern, P. C., Dietz, T., Kalof, L., & Guagnano, G. A. (1995). Values, beliefs, and proenvironmental action: Attitude formation toward emergent attitude objects. *Journal of Applied Social Psychology, 25,* 1611–1636.

Suedfeld, P., & Ramirez, C. (1977). War, peace, and integrative complexity: UN speeches on the Middle East problem, 1947–1976. *Journal of Conflict Resolution, 21,* 427–442.

Sweeney, P. D., & Gruber, K. L. (1984). Selective exposure: Voter information preferences and the Watergate affair. *Journal of Personality and Social Psychology, 46,* 1208–1221.

Swim, J. K., Aikin, K. J., Hall, W. S., & Hunter, B. A. (1995). Sexism and racism: Old-fashioned and modern prejudices. *Journal of Personality and Social Psychology, 68,* 199–214.

Tajfel, H. (1981). *Human groups and social categories: Studies in social psychology.* Cambridge, England: Cambridge University Press.

Tannenbaum, P. H. (1966). Mediated generalization of attitude change via the principle of congruity. *Journal of Personality and Social Psychology, 3,* 493–499.

Taylor, S. E. (1991). Asymmetrical effects of positive and negative events: The mobilization-minimization hypothesis. *Psychological Bulletin, 110,* 67–85.

Tesser, A. (1993). The importance of heritability in psychological research: The case of attitudes. *Psychological Review, 100,* 129–142.

Tesser, A., & Leone, C. (1977). Cognitive schemas and thought as determinants of attitude change. *Journal of Experimental Social Psychology, 13,* 340–356.

Tesser, A., & Martin, L. (1996). The psychology of evaluation. In E. T. Higgins & A. W. Kruglanski (Eds.), *Social psychology: Handbook of basic principles* (pp. 400–432). New York: Guilford Press.

Tetlock, P. E. (1989). Structure and function in political belief systems. In A. R. Pratkanis, S. J. Breckler, & A. G. Greenwald (Eds.), *Attitude structure and function* (pp. 129–151). Hillsdale, NJ: Erlbaum.

Tetlock, P. E., Peterson, R. S., & Armor, D. (1994). The slavery debate in antebellum America: Cognitive style, value conflict, and the limits of compromise. *Journal of Personality and Social Psychology, 66,* 115–126.

Tetlock, P. E., Peterson, R. S., & Lerner, J. S. (1996). Revising the value pluralism model: Incorporating social content and context postulates. In C. Seligman, J. M. Olson, & M. P. Zanna (Eds.), *The Ontario Symposium: The psychology of values* (Vol. 8, pp. 25–51). Mahwah, NJ: Erlbaum.

Thagard, P. (1989). Explanatory coherence. *Behavioral and Brain Sciences, 12,* 435–502.

Thompson, M. M., & Zanna, M. P. (1995). The conflicted individual: Personality-based and domain-specific antecedents of ambivalent social attitudes. *Journal of Personality, 63,* 259–288.

Thompson, M. M., Naccarato, M. E., & Parker, K. (June, 1989). *Measuring cognitive needs: The development and validation of the personal need for structure (PNS) and personal fear of invalidity (PFI) measures.* Paper presented at the annual meeting of the Canadian Psychological Association, Halifax.

Thompson, M. M., Zanna, M. P., & Griffin, D. W. (1995). Let's not be indifferent about (attitudinal) ambivalence. In R. E. Petty & J. A. Krosnick (Eds.), *Attitude strength: Antecedents and consequences* (pp. 361–386). Mahwah, NJ: Erlbaum.

Thomsen, C. J., Borgida, E., & Lavine, H. (1995). The causes and consequences of personal involvement. In R. E. Petty & J. A. Krosnick (Eds.), *Attitude strength: Antecedents and consequences* (pp. 191–214). Mahwah, NJ: Erlbaum.

Tordesillas, R. S., Chaiken, S., & Zimmerman, J. (1994, June). *Cognitive and affective determinants of attitude strength.*

Poster presented at the annual meetings of the American Psychological Society, Washington, DC.

Tougas, F., Brown, R., Beaton, A. M., & Joly, S. (1995). Neosexism: Plus ça change, plus c'est pareil. *Personality and Social Psychology Bulletin, 21,* 842–849.

Tourangeau, R., Rasinski, K. A., & D'Andrade, R. (1991). Attitude structure and belief accessibility. *Journal of Experimental Social Psychology, 27,* 48–75.

Trafimow, D., & Finlay, K. A. (1996). The importance of subjective norms for a minority of people: Between-subjects and within-subjects analyses. *Personality and Social Psychology Bulletin, 22,* 820–828.

Triandis, H. C. (1977). *Interpersonal behavior.* Monterey, CA: Brooks/Cole.

Triandis, H. C. (1980). Values, attitudes, and interpersonal behavior. In H. E. Howe, Jr. & M. M. Page (Eds.), *Nebraska Symposium on Motivation, 1979* (Vol. 27, pp. 195–259). Lincoln: University of Nebraska Press.

Triandis, H. C., McCusker, C., & Hui, C. H. (1990). Multimethod probes of individualism and collectivism. *Journal of Personality and Social Psychology, 59,* 1006–1020.

Upshaw, H. S. (1969). The personal reference scale: An approach to social judgment. In L. Berkowitz (Ed.), *Advances in experimental social psychology* (Vol. 4, pp. 315–371). New York: Academic Press.

Vallacher, R. R., & Wegner, D. M. (1987). What do people think they're doing? Action identification and human behavior. *Psychological Review, 94,* 3–15.

Vallone, R. P., Ross, L., & Lepper, M. R. (1985). The hostile media phenomenon: Biased perception and perceptions of media bias in coverage of the Beirut massacre. *Journal of Personality and Social Psychology, 49,* 577–585.

Van den Putte, B. (1993). *On the theory of reasoned action.* Unpublished doctoral dissertation, University of Amsterdam, The Netherlands.

van der Pligt, J., & Eiser, J. R. (1984). Dimensional salience, judgment, and attitudes. In J. R. Eiser (Ed.), *Attitudinal judgment* (pp. 161–177). New York: Springer-Verlag.

Waly, P., & Cook, S. W. (1965). Effect of attitude on judgments of plausibility. *Journal of Personality and Social Psychology, 2,* 745–749.

Watson, W. S., & Hartmann, G. W. (1939). The rigidity of a basic attitudinal frame. *Journal of Abnormal and Social Psychology, 34,* 314–335.

Weigel, R. H., & Newman, L. S. (1976). Increasing attitude-behavior correspondence by broadening the scope of the behavioral measure. *Journal of Personality and Social Psychology, 33,* 793–802.

Wicker, A. W. (1969). Attitude versus actions: The relationship of verbal and overt behavioral responses to attitude objects. *Journal of Social Issues, 25*(4), 41–78.

Wicklund, R. A., & Brehm, J. W. (1976). *Perspectives on cognitive dissonance.* Hillsdale, NJ: Erlbaum.

Wilson, T. D., & Hodges, S. D. (1992). Attitudes as temporary constructions. In L. L. Martin & A. Tesser (Eds.), *The construction of social judgments* (pp. 37–65). Hillsdale, NJ: Erlbaum.

Wood, W. L., Rhodes, N., & Biek, M. (1995). Working knowledge and attitude strength: An information-processing analysis. In R. E. Petty & J. A. Krosnick (Eds.), *Attitude strength: Antecedents and consequences* (pp. 283–313). Mahwah, NJ: Erlbaum.

Wyer, R. S., Jr., & Srull, T. K. (1989). *Memory and cognition in its social context.* Hillsdale, NJ: Erlbaum.

Young, J., Thomsen, C. J., Borgida, E., Sullivan, J. L., & Aldrich, J. H. (1991). When self-interest makes a difference: The role of construct accessibility in political reasoning. *Journal of Experimental Social Psychology, 27,* 271–296.

Zajonc, R. B. (1960). The process of cognitive tuning in communication. *Journal of Abnormal and Social Psychology, 61,* 159–167.

Zajonc, R. B. (1968). Cognitive theories in social psychology. In G. Lindzey & E. Aronson (Eds.), *Handbook of social psychology* (2nd ed., Vol. 1, pp. 320–411). Reading, MA: Addison-Wesley.

Zajonc, R. B. (1980). Feeling and thinking: Preferences need no inferences. *American Psychologist, 35,* 151–175.

Zajonc, R. B. (1984). On the primacy of affect. *American Psychologist, 39,* 117–123.

Zajonc, R. B., & Burnstein, E. (1965a). The learning of balanced and unbalanced social structures. *Journal of Personality, 33,* 153–163.

Zajonc, R. B., & Burnstein, E. (1965b). Structural balance, reciprocity, and positivity as sources of cognitive bias. *Journal of Personality, 33,* 570–583.

Zanna, M. P., & Rempel, J. K. (1988). Attitudes: A new look at an old concept. In D. Bar-Tal & A. W. Kruglanski (Eds.), *The social psychology of knowledge* (pp. 315–334). Cambridge, England: Cambridge University Press.

Zimmerman, J., & Chaiken, S. (1996). *Attitude structure, processing goals, and selective memory.* Manuscript submitted for publication.

CHAPTER EIGHT

ATTITUDE CHANGE: MULTIPLE ROLES FOR PERSUASION VARIABLES

RICHARD E. PETTY, *The Ohio State University*
DUANE T. WEGENER, *Purdue University*

OVERVIEW

The O. J. Simpson criminal "trial of the century" in the mid-1990s captured the attention of the American populace more than any other public spectacle since the kidnapping of the Lindberg baby in the 1930s. A prominent football player and popular sportscaster was charged with a gruesome double homicide. The attorneys for the prosecution and defense were of various races and genders. The evidence presented on each side was at times amazingly simple, visual, and emotional, and at times was verbal, abstract, and probably incomprehensible to jurors. The witnesses included individuals of diverse styles, demeanors and credibility. The jurors, the recipients of the messages from their various sources, were themselves a mixed group of people of diverse backgrounds, beliefs, and personal experiences who had to sift through the trial material and arrive at a decision as to whether the defendant had been proven guilty or not. The context in which all this took place was at times tense and sad, and at times filled with humor and positive feelings. Not surprisingly, no experiment has ever captured the extraordinary complexity inherent in this situation, yet almost all the variables present in the trial (and many not present) have been examined in the social psychological literature on attitude formation and change. This chapter provides an overview of research on these diverse variables and addresses the processes by which these variables are thought to result in influence.

Although it has become a cliché to say that the attitude construct is the most indispensable concept in contemporary social psychology, this statement appears as true today as when G. W. Allport (1935) initially wrote it in the first *Handbook of Social Psychology* (Murchison, 1935; see Allport, 1935, and Fleming, 1967, for historical reviews of the attitude concept). Attitudes remain important as we enter the twenty-first century because of the fundamental role that individuals' attitudes, both explicit and implicit (Greenwald & Banaji, 1995), play in the critical choices people make regarding their own health and security as well as those of their families, friends, and nations. From purchase decisions provoked by liking for a product to wars spurred by ethnic prejudices, attitudes help to determine a wide variety of potentially consequential outcomes.

Before turning to the relevant studies, it is useful to address some definitional issues. The term *attitude* is used to refer to a person's overall evaluation of persons (including oneself), objects, and issues. Thus, one's attitude refers to how favorably or unfavorably or how positively or negatively in general one views some object of judgment such as "the defendant," "capital punishment," or "ice cream." These global evaluations can vary in a large number of ways in addition to their extremity such as whether they are based on emotions (e.g., "seeing the defendant makes me anxious"), beliefs (e.g., "capital punishment does not deter crime"), or past experiences and behaviors (e.g., "the last time I ate ice cream I had an unpleasant allergic reaction"; see Breckler, 1984; Zanna & Rempel, 1988), and whether they are internally consistent (e.g., being associated largely with positive feelings, attributes, and behaviors) or ambivalent (e.g., composed of a combination of positive and negative attributes, e.g., Kaplan, 1972). Much research has assumed that evaluative processing of information is quite natural, pervasive, and fundamental (Markus & Zajonc, 1985; Osgood, Suci, & Tannenbaum, 1957) in large part because of the adaptive and functional purposes of holding attitudes (see Pratkanis, Breckler, & Greenwald, 1989;

Eagly & Chaiken, 1998, in this *Handbook,* for discussions of the structure and function of attitudes). Jarvis and Petty (1996) suggested, however, that just as there are situational factors that influence one's motivation to evaluate (e.g., the need to form an opinion about an upcoming decision), so too are there individual differences in this need. They observed that some people were higher in their "need to evaluate" than others and these individuals were more likely to engage in on-line evaluation of a variety of stimuli and were more likely to hold opinions on a diverse set of social issues than were those low in this need (see also Petty & Jarvis, 1996). Nevertheless, regardless of the overall level of one's propensity to evaluate, it is still the case that nearly everybody forms evaluations of most common stimuli in their environment at some point (e.g., Bargh, Chaiken, Raymond, & Hymes, 1996; Fazio, 1995; see Petty, Wegener, & Fabrigar, 1997, for additional discussion).

Given the power of attitudes to determine many actions, it is not surprising that billions of dollars, deutsche marks, and yen are spent annually in an attempt to influence and change people's evaluations of various objects, issues, and people. Attitude *change* simply means that a person's evaluation is modified from one value to another. Change is often assessed relative to the person's initial attitude. *Polarization* occurs when people move in the direction of their initial tendency (e.g., an initially favorable person becomes even more favorable), and *depolarization* occurs when they move in the direction of neutrality. In persuasion settings, change is typically examined with respect to the position advocated in a communication. These change outcomes fall on a continuum anchored at one end by maximal acceptance (e.g., changing the maximal amount in the direct of some target position even if the change exceeds the target) and at the other by maximal boomerang (changing the maximal amount in the direction away from the advocated position). It is important to distinguish these attitude change outcomes from the processes that produce them. Acceptance processes are those that tend to move people in the targeted direction, whereas rejection or resistance processes are those that help people resist change and perhaps even move them significantly away from the target view. For each acceptance process documented in the literature, there is typically a corresponding resistance process (e.g., pro versus counterarguing; positive versus negative affect).

A categorical distinction between attitude *formation* versus attitude *change* is not used because the accumulated research suggests that it is more useful to regard attitudes that are changed as falling along a continuum ranging from nonattitudes (see Converse, 1970) to strong attitudes (see Fazio, 1986). That is, the factors involved in moving an individual with no attitude to adopt a position favorable toward an advocacy are more similar to the factors involved in making a person with a weak but existent attitude become more favorable toward the advocacy than to the factors involved in making the same change in an individual

with a strong initial attitude (see Petty, Wegener, Fabrigar, Priester, & Cacioppo, 1993). The nonattitude/strong attitude continuum is indexed by features such as how accessible the attitude is (e.g., Fazio, 1995), how much knowledge an individual has about the attitude object (e.g., Wood, Rhodes, & Biek, 1995), and other factors (see Petty & Krosnick, 1995, for reviews of the dimensions of attitude strength). Although this chapter focuses on attitude change, the processes of change that are described and the general principles of change are also applicable to changing more specific evaluative judgments—such as whether the defendant in a trial is guilty or not. In fact, even though there are functional differences between evaluative and nonevaluative beliefs, many of the principles that are outlined for attitude change are also relevant to changing nonevaluative judgments. For example, many of the same processes have been shown to operate in changing perceptions of desirability, an evaluative judgment, and likelihood, a nonevaluative judgment. Thus, just as early research on role-playing indicated that merely thinking about why something might be good could enhance perceptions of its goodness because of a biased scanning of the evidence (Janis & Gilmore, 1965), more recent research has indicated that simply thinking about why something might occur increases perceptions of its likelihood (Ross, Lepper, Strack, & Steinmetz, 1977) for similar reasons (Koehler, 1991). Therefore, although the thrust of our chapter is on processes of attitude change, the term "belief change" would often be equally applicable.

Bringing about change in attitudes (or beliefs) by presenting facts and information in a relatively objective fashion can be called *education,* whereas bringing about change by slanting information and evidence is often referred to as *propaganda* (Zimbardo, Ebbesen, & Maslach, 1977). The latter term was popular in the earlier part of this century (e.g., Doob, 1935), but because of its pejorative connotations has been replaced by the more neutral terms, *persuasion* and *attitude change* (see Petty & Cacioppo, 1981). In the following sections, some historical foundations of contemporary work on attitude change are reviewed and, using the Elaboration Likelihood Model (ELM; Petty & Cacioppo, 1986a, 1986b) as a guide, the high- and low-effort processes that have been hypothesized to account for changes in attitudes are discussed. Then, using the multiple roles aspect of the ELM, work is reviewed on the effects of specific source, message, recipient, and context variables on attitude change.

Historical Foundations

The formal discussion of principles of attitude change can be traced to the ancient Greeks (see Aristotle's *Rhetoric* and *Topics*), but as McGuire (1969) documented, also flourished in Cicero's Roman Republic and during the Italian Renaissance (see Quintillian's *Institutio Oratoria*). It was not until the current century, however, that ideas about persuasion were linked to empirical observations. Early work ranged from content analyses of political propaganda in which the authors speculated about the attitudinal and behavioral consequences of propaganda messages (e.g., Lasswell, Casey, & Smith, 1935), to case studies of the ebb and flow of public opinion in which the authors speculated about the causes of observed shifts in attitudes (e.g., Lazarsfeld, Berelson, & Gaudet, 1944).

In reviewing the history of research on communication and persuasion, Delia (1987) noted that in contrast to the mostly correlational approaches adopted in sociology and political science, the social psychological approach (e.g., F. H. Allport, 1924) was largely experimental. That is, features of some influencing agent (e.g., a propaganda message) were manipulated and their effects on attitudes were observed. For example, in the 1930s, the Motion Picture Research Council conducted a series of studies to examine the impact of different movies on children's knowledge, attitudes, and behavior (e.g., Peterson & Thurstone, 1933). The results of these studies were rather complex and provided an early warning that attitude change effects would depend on a host of individual and situational factors. In addition to these large-scale field studies, researchers in the 1930s also conducted individual experiments with a more limited set of independent and dependent variables that have more in common with current research practices (e.g., Knower, 1935).

Although research on attitude change had a significant presence in the first half of the twentieth century, the pioneering efforts of Carl Hovland and the eminent investigators he assembled at Yale in the 1950s were instrumental in making the study of attitude change one of the central foci of social psychology. During World War II, Hovland directed the mass communication program within the Army's Information and Education Division. The research that emanated from this effort (e.g., Hovland, Lumsdaine, & Sheffield, 1949) as well as the investigations conducted when Hovland returned to Yale after the war continue to be highly influential. In many instances, the Yale group was the first to examine systematically the variables that continue to be of interest today such as source credibility (Hovland, Janis, & Kelley, 1953), individual differences (Hovland & Janis, 1959), attitude structure (Hovland & Rosenberg, 1960), message order effects (Hovland, 1957), ego-involvement (Sherif & Hovland, 1961), and many others.

If social psychological research on attitude change in the 1950s was dominated by the work of the Yale group, research in the 1960s was led by the consistency theorists—especially Leon Festinger (1957) and his students and colleagues (see Abelson, Aronson, McGuire, Newcomb, Rosenberg, & Tannenbaum, 1968). In contrast to the Hovland group, which explored a wide variety of external variables and explained the persuasion outcomes of these variables with a diversity of learning-type formulations, the consistency theorists were more focused conceptually—

emphasizing the internal tension that was thought to result when people engaged in actions that were inconsistent with their beliefs, attitudes, and values. The approaches taken by the Hovland and Festinger groups are still influential today (for a recent discussion of the divergent research styles of these groups, see McGuire, 1995a).

Contemporary Conceptualizations

By the 1970s, attitude change research had become so abundant that the whole enterprise was threatened with collapse due to an embarrassment of conflicting findings and theories. Reviewers of the literature noted that there were literally thousands of empirical efforts, but little conceptual coherence (e.g., Fishbein & Ajzen, 1972; Kiesler & Munson, 1975). Sherif (1977, p. 370) bluntly stated that there was "reigning confusion in the area" and a "scanty yield in spite of a tremendously thriving output." Fortunately, this state of affairs did not last long as new multiprocess frameworks developed that accounted for many of the apparently conflicting findings. The two most popular of these models, the Elaboration Likelihood Model (ELM) and the Heuristic-Systematic Model (HSM) originated in doctoral dissertations in the late 1970s (Chaiken, 1978; Petty, 1977) and were subsequently expanded into full persuasion theories (Chaiken, 1987; Chaiken, Liberman, & Eagly, 1989; Petty & Cacioppo, 1981, 1986a, 1986b). These models placed greater focus on the moderation and mediation of attitude change effects and explained how the same variable (e.g., source credibility, mood) could have different effects on attitude change in different situations, and how a given variable could produce the same persuasion outcome by different processes in different situations. A key idea in these new frameworks was that some processes of attitude change required relatively high amounts of mental effort, whereas other processes of persuasion required relatively little mental effort. Thus, Petty and Cacioppo (1981) reasoned that most of the major theories of persuasion were not necessarily competitors or contradictory, but operated in different circumstances. Later in this chapter, this notion is used to organize the major processes of persuasion. Although these models share many notions, the ELM and HSM had somewhat different conceptual parents. The ELM's high-effort central route was based on cognitive response theory (Greenwald, 1968; Brock, 1967) whereas the HSM's view of detailed (systematic) message processing, in some early treatments at least, was linked to "effort exerted in comprehending message content, not effort exerted in cognitive responding or thinking about message content" (p. 56, Eagly, Chaiken, & Wood, 1981). Today the models have more similarities than differences and can generally accommodate the same empirical results, though the explanatory language and sometimes the assumed mediating processes vary (addi-

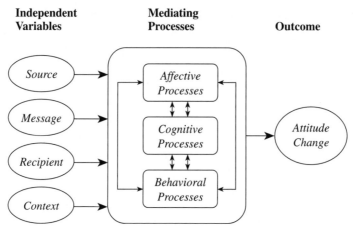

FIGURE 1   General Processes Mediating Effects of Independent Variables on Attitude Change

tional coverage of some differences between the models is presented later).

Before undertaking our review, it is useful to consider the generic mediational analysis of attitude change that has explicitly or implicitly guided most persuasion research in the twentieth century (see Figure 1). In this diagram, some independent variable has an impact on one's affect (emotions), cognitions, or behavior toward some object, and this in turn has an impact on one's attitude toward (overall evaluation of) that object. For example, a television commercial might induce pleasant feelings in connection with a political candidate. Associating these pleasant feelings with the candidate could produce favorable attitudes toward the candidate (i.e., commercial → positive mood → favorable attitude). Sometimes the hypothesized causal sequence is more complex. For example, in the dissonance paradigm, an individual is enticed to act (behavior) in a way that is inconsistent with his or her attitude, which induces an aversive state of tension (affect), which in turn leads to behaviorally supportive thoughts (cognition), which finally results in an attitude that is consistent with the behavior (Cooper & Fazio, 1984).

Almost every conceivable causal sequence of affect, cognition, and behavior has been proposed to account for attitudes in at least some circumstances. For example, in their two stage model of message repetition, Cacioppo and Petty (1980) argued that moderate repetition enhanced people's ability to cognitively respond to the message in a relatively objective manner (stage 1). However, as repetition becomes excessive (stage 2), negative affect sets in (i.e., the message becomes obnoxious and irritating) and this negative affect biases subsequent cognitive responses to the message. It is also possible for a variable to exert parallel effects on affect and cognition. For example, in his analysis of fear appeals, Leventhal (1970) postulated that fear induced both cognitive responses designed to protect

oneself from danger (such as accepting the advocacy) and emotional responses aimed at protecting oneself from aversive arousal (such as avoidance). Roselli, Skelly, and Mackie (1995) argued that persuasion in response to cognitive arguments was mediated by cognitive responses to the message, but persuasion in response to affective arguments was mediated by both cognitive and affective responses (see also Zuwerink & Devine, 1996). The accumulated literature makes it clear that although the affective, cognitive, and behavioral bases of attitudes can be independent (Zanna & Rempel, 1988), they are often inextricably interlinked as postulated by the consistency theorists. That is, if one's affect changes, one's cognitive responses and behavioral tendencies typically change as well (e.g., Rosenberg, 1960). To the extent that this does not occur, people remain in an ambivalent state that can itself be aversive (Cacioppo & Berntson, 1994; Priester & Petty, 1996; Thompson, Zanna, & Griffin, 1995).

Although much of the early work on attitude change dealt with relatively complex social issues (such as whether atomic submarines should or should not be built, Hovland & Mandell, 1957), tenets of contemporary theories have also been tested using simpler objects such as consumer products (e.g., Petty, Cacioppo, & Schumann, 1983; Snyder & DeBono, 1989). Thus, although many of the examples in this chapter use complex issues as attitude objects, these same attitude change processes are also generally applicable to the full range of possible attitude objects.

PROCESSES OF ATTITUDE CHANGE

As noted previously, contemporary persuasion theorists recognize that different processes can lead to attitude change in different circumstances. Some of these processes require diligent and effortful information processing activity whereas others proceed with relatively little mental effort. In this section, the Elaboration Likelihood Model of persuasion is described, and some prominent factors that determine whether people will tend to exert high or low amounts of mental effort in a persuasion situation are reviewed (the HSM is discussed subsequently). Next, the persuasion processes that tend to require relatively high amounts of mental effort are described in more detail. Following this, the persuasion processes that tend to require relatively low amounts of mental effort are described.

The Elaboration Likelihood Model of Persuasion

The Elaboration Likelihood Model (ELM) of persuasion (Petty & Cacioppo, 1981, 1986a) is a theory about the processes responsible for attitude change and the strength of the attitudes that result from those processes. A key construct in the ELM is the elaboration likelihood continuum. This continuum is defined by how motivated and able people are to assess the central merits of a person, issue, or position (i.e., the attitude object). The more motivated and able people are to assess the central merits of the attitude object, the more likely they are to effortfully scrutinize all available object-relevant information. Thus, when the elaboration likelihood is high, people will assess object-relevant information in relation to knowledge that they already possess, and arrive at a reasoned (though not necessarily unbiased) attitude that is well articulated and bolstered by supporting information (central route). When the elaboration likelihood is low, however, information scrutiny is reduced and attitude change can result from a number of less resource demanding processes that do not require effortful evaluation of the object-relevant information (peripheral route). Attitudes that are changed by low effort processes are postulated to be weaker than attitudes that are changed the same extent by high effort processes. The hypothesis of both high- and low-effort attitude change comes from recognizing that it is neither adaptive nor possible for people to exert considerable mental effort in thinking about all of the messages and attitude objects to which they are exposed. In order to function in life, people must sometimes act as "cognitive misers" (Taylor, 1981), but at other times it is more adaptive to be generous with one's cognitive resources.

The elaboration likelihood continuum incorporates both a quantitative and a qualitative distinction (see Petty, 1997). That is, as one goes higher on the elaboration continuum, central route processes increase in magnitude, and as one goes down the continuum, central route processes diminish in magnitude. This quantitative variation suggests that at high levels of elaboration, people's attitudes will be determined by their effortful examination of all relevant information, but at lower levels of elaboration, attitudes can be determined, for example, by less effortful (less careful) examination of the same information, or effortful examination of less information (e.g., the person critically examines just the first argument in a message, but not the remaining arguments). In addition, however, the ELM incorporates a qualitative distinction. For example, consider a person who is exposed to a message with ten arguments. The high elaboration (central route) processor would tend to think about most or all of the information. If motivation or ability to think was reduced, the recipient might think about each argument less carefully, or think about fewer arguments (quantitative difference). However, the ELM proposes that other (peripheral) mechanisms that do not involve thought about the substantive merits of the arguments could also influence attitudes when the elaboration likelihood is low. For example, a low elaboration processor might simply count the arguments and reason that "if there are ten reasons to favor it, it must be worthwhile" (see Petty & Cacioppo, 1984a). Note that this process is qualitatively different from the argument elaboration process in that this mechanism does not involve consideration of the merits of the arguments but instead involves reliance on a rule of thumb or heuristic that the person generates or retrieves from memory (see also Chaiken, 1987). Other relatively low-effort peripheral mechanisms that are capable of producing attitude change without processing the substantive merits of the information provided include: classical conditioning (Staats & Staats, 1958; Cacioppo, Marshall-Goodell, Tassinary, & Petty, 1992), identification with the source of the message (Kelman, 1958), misattribution of affect to the message (Petty & Cacioppo, 1983; Schwarz & Clore, 1983), and mere exposure effects (Bornstein, 1989; Zajonc, 1968).

Two ELM notions—the "tradeoff" hypothesis and the "multiple roles" hypothesis—have been the subject of some confusion in the literature (e.g., Eagly & Chaiken, 1993; Stiff, 1986a; see Petty & Wegener, in press-a for additional discussion). The first hypothesis postulates a tradeoff between the impact of central and peripheral processes on judgments along the elaboration likelihood continuum. That is, as the impact of central route processes on judgments increases, the impact of peripheral route processes on judgments decreases. Note that the tradeoff hypothesis is not about the *occurrence* of central and peripheral processes, but is about the impact of these processes on judgments. For example, the presence of one's friend might invoke the heuristic, "I agree with people I like" (Chaiken, 1980), but under high elaboration conditions, this heuristic would be subjected to careful scrutiny just as the arguments in a message are subjected to scrutiny (Petty & Cacioppo, 1986a; Petty, 1994). If the heuristic is found to lack merit as an argument for supporting the advocated view, then it would have little impact on one's summary judgment. On the other hand, if the heuristic was deemed cogent, then it would. This scrutiny of the heuristic for merit would be less likely under low elaboration conditions where the mere invocation of the heuristic would be sufficient for persuasion. It is important to note that the ELM tradeoff hypothesis implies a number of things. First, at most points along the continuum, central and peripheral processes would co-occur and jointly influence judgments (Petty, Kasmer, Haugtvedt, & Cacioppo, 1987). Second, however, movement in either direction along the continuum would tend to enhance the *relative* impact of one or the other *process* (e.g., effortful scrutiny for merit versus reliance on a heuristic) on judgments.

It is important to note that changing the relative impact of one *process* over another on attitudes does not imply that the impact of any given *variable* (e.g., source expertise, mood) on judgments must increase or decrease as one moves along the continuum. This is because of the multiple roles hypothesis. In essence, the multiple roles notion is that any given variable can influence attitudes by different processes at different points along the elaboration continuum (Petty & Cacioppo, 1986a). Thus, for example, consider whether a manipulation of "beautiful scenery" in an advertisement for a vacation location should increase or decrease in impact as the elaboration likelihood is increased. If a person was not thinking about the ad very much (low elaboration likelihood), then the beautiful scenery might have a positive impact simply due to its mere association with the target location much as it might have a similar positive impact on evaluations of a new car that was located in the scenery (peripheral route). But, as the elaboration likelihood is increased and the scenery is processed for its merits with respect to the product, then the impact of the scenery on attitudes could be increased in the ad for the vacation location due to its perceived relevance and merit (or have the same impact as under low processing conditions, but for a different reason). For the car ad, however, high processing of the scenery could lead to decreased impact due to its perceived irrelevance for this product (see also the later section on multiple roles for persuasion variables).[1]

Determinants and Dimensions of Elaboration   In sum, the ELM notes that attitude change can vary in the extent to which it is based on mental effort. Persuasion researchers have identified a number of ways to assess the extent to which persuasion is based on effortful consideration of information. Perhaps the most popular procedure has been to vary the quality of the arguments contained in a message and to gauge the extent of message processing by the size of the argument quality effect on attitudes (Petty, Wells, & Brock, 1976). Greater argument quality effects suggest greater argument scrutiny. Another procedure involves assessment of the number and profile of issue relevant thoughts generated (Petty, Ostrom, & Brock, 1981). High elaboration conditions are associated with more thoughts (e.g., Burnkrant & Howard, 1984) and thoughts that better reflect the quality of the arguments presented (e.g., Harkins & Petty, 1981a). Also, correlations between message-relevant thoughts and post-message attitudes tend

to be greater when argument scrutiny is high (e.g., Chaiken, 1980; Petty & Cacioppo, 1979b), and high message elaboration can produce longer reading or exposure times than more cursory analyses (e.g., Mackie & Worth, 1989; see Wegener, Downing, Krosnick, & Petty, 1995).

According to the ELM, in order for high-effort processes to influence attitudes, people must be both motivated to think (i.e., have the desire to exert a high level of mental effort) and have the ability to think (i.e., have the necessary skills and opportunity to engage in thought). There are many variables capable of affecting the elaboration likelihood and thereby influencing whether attitude change is likely to occur by the high- or low-effort processes that are described in more detail shortly. Some of these motivational and ability variables are part of the persuasion situation, whereas others are part of the individual. Some variables affect mostly the amount of information processing activity whereas others tend to influence the direction or valence of the thinking.

Perhaps the most important variable influencing a person's motivation to think is the perceived personal relevance or importance of the communication (see Petty & Cacioppo, 1979b, 1990; Johnson & Eagly, 1989). When personal relevance is high, people are more influenced by their processing of the substantive arguments in a message and are less impacted by peripheral processes (e.g., Petty, Cacioppo, & Goldman, 1981). Of course, variables other than relevance can modify a person's motivation to think about a message. For example, people are more motivated to scrutinize information when they believe that they are solely responsible for message evaluation (Petty, Harkins, & Williams, 1980), when they are individually accountable (Tetlock, 1983), when they recently have been deprived of control (Pittman, 1993), and when they expect to discuss the issue with a partner (Chaiken, 1980). Increasing the number of message sources can enhance information processing activity (e.g., Harkins & Petty, 1981a, b; Moore & Reardon, 1987), especially when the sources are viewed as providing independent assessments of the issue (Harkins & Petty, 1987). Messages that are moderately inconsistent with an existing attitude schema can enhance processing over schema-consistent messages presumably because the former could pose some threat that needs to be understood or some incongruity that needs to be resolved (Cacioppo & Petty, 1979b). Other incongruities can also increase information processing activity, such as when an expert source presents surprisingly weak arguments (Maheswaran & Chaiken, 1991), when the message does not present the information in a form that was expected (Smith & Petty, 1996), and when people feel ambivalent rather than certain about the issue (Maio, Bell, & Esses, 1996). In addition to factors associated with the persuasive message, issue, or the persuasion context, there are individual differences in people's motivation to think about persuasive communications. For example, people who enjoy thinking (i.e., those high in need for cognition; Cacioppo &

Petty, 1982) tend to follow the central rather than the periph-eral route to persuasion (see Cacioppo, Petty, Feinstein, & Jarvis, 1996, for a review).

Among the important variables influencing a person's ability to process issue-relevant arguments is message rep-etition. As noted previously, moderate message repetition provides more opportunities for argument scrutiny (e.g., Cacioppo & Petty, 1979b; Gorn & Goldberg, 1980), which will prove beneficial for processing as long as tedium is not induced (Cacioppo & Petty, 1989; Cox & Cox, 1988). External distractions (e.g., Petty, Wells, & Brock, 1976), fast presentations (Smith & Shaffer, 1995), external pacing of messages (such as those on radio or television rather than in print; Chaiken & Eagly, 1976; Wright, 1981), time pressures on processing (e.g., Kruglanski & Freund, 1983), enhancing recipients' physiological arousal via exercise (e.g., Sanbonmatsu & Kardes, 1988), placing recipients in an uncomfortable posture (Petty, Wells, Heesacker, Brock, & Cacioppo, 1983), and making the message complex or difficult to understand (e.g., Hafer, Reynolds, & Obertyn-ski, 1996) all decrease substantive message processing and should increase the impact of peripheral processes. Inter-estingly, even though a number of studies have examined differences in the actual ability of recipients to process a persuasion message, little work has examined differences in perceived ability to process. Thus, a message that ap-pears technical or overly quantitative (Yalch & Elmore-Yalch, 1984) may reduce processing not because it inter-feres with actual ability, but because it interferes with a person's perceived ability to process (e.g., "it's probably too complicated for me, so why bother").

Individual differences also exist in the ability of people to think about a persuasive communication. For example, as general knowledge about a topic increases, people can become more able (and perhaps more motivated) to think about issue-relevant information (Wood et al., 1995). Knowledge is only effective to the extent that it is accessi-ble, however (e.g., Brucks, Armstrong, & Goldberg, 1988). When knowledge is low or inaccessible, people are more reliant on simple cues (e.g., Wood & Kallgren, 1988). To date, researchers have not examined differences in per-ceived knowledge. It is reasonable that even if actual knowledge differences were constant, people with less per-ceived expertise might be less likely to process a complex message and be more influenced by peripheral processes.

Finally, it is important to note that in most communica-tion settings, a confluence of factors determines the nature of information processing rather than one variable acting in isolation. For example, ending arguments with rhetorical questions rather than statements can increase thinking about a persuasive message if the questions follow the arguments and motivation to think about the message would normally be low (Petty, Cacioppo, & Heesacker, 1981). On the other hand, if people are already motivated to think about the message, then the use of rhetoricals can actually disrupt the

normal processing that would have occurred (see Howard, 1990; Petty, Cacioppo, & Heesacker, 1981). Although the effects of many individual variables on information pro-cessing have been examined, there is a shortage of studies examining the potential interactions possible when multiple ability and motivational variables are combined.

Relatively Objective Versus Biased Information Pro-cessing The variables already discussed, such as distrac-tion or need for cognition, tend to influence information processing activity in a relatively objective manner. That is, all else being equal, distraction tends to disrupt whatever thoughts a person is thinking (Petty, Wells, and Brock, 1976). The distraction per se does not specifically target one type of thought (e.g., favorable or unfavorable) to im-pede. Similarly, individuals with high need for cognition are more motivated to think in general than people low in need for cognition (Cacioppo, Petty, & Morris, 1983). They are not more motivated to think certain kinds of thoughts over others. Some variables, however, are selec-tive in their effects on thinking. For example, people are fa-cilitated in thinking favorable thoughts and disrupted from thinking negative thoughts when they are instructed to move their heads in an up and down ("yes") manner. Mov-ing one's head in a side to side ("no") manner, appears to facilitate negative thinking and disrupt positive thinking (Wells & Petty, 1980; see also Förster & Strack, 1996).

Default Biases Before considering other variables, like head nodding, that induce specific biases in information processing, it is useful to consider the default biases that can influence judgment. Specifically, research has sug-gested that in the absence of contrary information, people tend to assume that what others say is true (Gilbert, 1991), and that unfamiliar objects and people in our environment are good. The latter has been called the leniency/positivity bias (Bruner & Tagiuri, 1954; Peeters & Czapinski, 1990) or the positivity offset (Cacioppo & Berntson, 1994). How-ever, if a source is known to be a liar, and this information is retrieved, statements from this source would not be as-sumed to be true even if no specific issue-relevant informa-tion to the contrary was available. Also, even though unfa-miliar objects and people are sometimes assumed to be good, people would not necessarily assume that an unfa-miliar insect was good even if no explicit negative informa-tion about the new insect was available (because the cate-gory *insect* contains many negative instances whereas the category *person* contains more positive instances). How-ever, a "new" insect might be seen as less negative than the generic category of existing insects.

Interestingly, research by Cacioppo, Gardner, and Berntson (1997) suggests that there may be a default posi-tive bias to evaluative processing. They demonstrated that when people were presented with six completely neutral statements about an unfamiliar insect, judgments were more positive than when this information was not available. This could be because of a default positive bias to evaluative processing as suggested by Cacioppo et al., or it might result from application of Gricean rules of conversation. Grice (1975) argued that people expect information from others to be informative and relevant. If the most relevant information the experimenter can provide about an insect is neutral, one might safely assume that there is little negative information to convey (e.g., the insect must not be poisonous or surely this would have been included). The Gricean interpretation would suggest that if the experimenter presented six neutral items about an unfamiliar vacation location, however, people might assume that if this is the most relevant information, there must be little positive information to convey and attitudes could be less positive than in the absence of any information.

Motivational and Ability Factors in Bias   The ELM accommodates both relatively objective and relatively biased information processing by pointing to the motivational and ability factors involved. Regarding motivation, the ELM holds that motivation is relatively objective when no a priori judgment is preferred and a person's implicit or explicit goal is to seek the truth "wherever it might lead" (Petty & Cacioppo, 1986b). In contrast, a motivated bias can occur whenever people implicitly or explicitly prefer one judgment over another. This is similar to what Kruglanski (1989) has called a "need for specific closure" (see also Kunda, 1990). A wide variety of motivations can determine which particular judgment is preferred in any given situation. For example, if the reactance motive (Brehm, 1966) is aroused, people will prefer to hold whatever judgment is forbidden. If balance motives (Heider, 1958) are operating, people would prefer to adopt the position of a liked source but distance themselves from a disliked source. If impression management motives (Tedeschi, Schlenker, & Bonoma, 1971) are operating, people would prefer to hold whatever position they think would be ingratiating. If self-affirmation motives (Steele, 1988) are high, people would prefer the position that would make them feel best about themselves, and so forth. Importantly, many of these biasing motives could have an impact on judgments by either high or low effort processes. For example, invocation of reactance could lead to simple rejection of the forbidden position without much thought, or to rejection because of intense counterarguing of the position. Which occurs (central or peripheral bias) would depend on other variables such as whether the person was motivated (e.g., high personal relevance) or able (e.g., low distraction) to think.

The ELM holds that biased processing can occur even if no specific judgment is preferred (i.e., if based on motivational factors alone, one would expect that processing would be relatively objective). This is because ability factors can also determine bias. For example, some people might simply possess a biased store of knowledge compared to other people. If so, their ability to process the message objectively can be compromised. Recipients with a biased store of knowledge typically will be better able to see the flaws in opposition arguments and the merits in their own side compared to recipients with a more balanced store of knowledge (cf., Lord, Ross, & Lepper, 1979). In addition, variables in the persuasion situation can bias retrieval of information even if what is stored is completely balanced and no motivational biases are operating. For example, a positive mood can increase access to positive material in memory (e.g., Bower, 1981). In general, biases in processing a persuasive message are fostered when the message contains information that is ambiguous or mixed rather than clearly strong or weak (Chaiken & Maheswaran, 1994).

Bias not only impacts judgments by influencing the nature of on-line information processing, but also can influence judgments by biasing the integration of information. For example, if people have an unbiased store of information in memory, and a balanced set of elaborations is generated, certain ideas might be given greater weight than others in forming a judgment (e.g., Anderson, 1981). In fact, considerable evidence exists for the proposition that negative information is often given more weight than equally extreme positive information (see Fiske, 1980; Kanouse & Hanson, 1971; but see Skowronski & Carlston, 1989). This might account for the finding that in order to move one's rating from the bad to the good side of a rating scale requires not 51 percent positive attributes associated with an object, but over 60 percent (Lefebvre, 1985). Although there are a number of ways to account for this negativity bias in information integration (see Cacioppo & Berntson, 1994; Peeters & Czapinski, 1990), one appealing explanation is that the negativity bias stems from the default tendency that was noted earlier for people to prefer and expect positive information. That is, if people expect positive information, then negative information would seem especially diagnostic and would be weighted more heavily. In addition, if positive information is expected and preferred, then negative information would be more surprising or threatening, either of which could enhance attention to the information and the processing of it (Baker & Petty, 1994). This suggests, however, that in situations in which negative information is expected or preferred, positive information should be perceived as more diagnostic or should be processed more (Smith & Petty, 1996).

Bias Correction   It is important to note that just because some motivational or ability factor results in biased information processing, this does not mean that a biased judgment will result. This is because people sometimes attempt to correct for factors they believe might have unduly biased their evaluations (e.g., Petty & Wegener, 1993; Wilson & Brekke, 1994). Initial discussions of such phenomena described these corrections as proceding only in one direction (i.e., a "partialling" process moved "corrected" assessments away from reactions activated by the biasing stimulus; e.g., Martin, Seta, & Crelia, 1990; Schwarz & Bless, 1992). More recent discussions have noted (and empirically shown) that corrections can proceed in different directions depending on recipients' theories of how the biasing event or stimulus (e.g., an attractive source) is likely to have influenced their views (e.g., Wegener & Petty, 1995). Specifically, according to the Flexible Correction Model (see Wegener & Petty, 1997), in order for corrections to occur, people should: (a) be motivated and able to identify potentially biasing factors, (b) possess or generate a naive theory about the magnitude and direction of the bias, and (c) be motivated and able to make the theory-based correction. In some cases, integrative processing of the information (e.g., Schul & Burnstein, 1985) could make it difficult for people to correct for the biasing effect of an individual piece of information that contributed to an overall evaluation. That is, even if motivated to be correct, people might not have the ability to do so. When people are motivated and able to correct, however, theory-based corrections can result in reversals of typical persuasion effects. For example, in one study, when people were made aware of possible biases due to the message source, an overcorrection led a disliked source to be more persuasive than a liked one (Petty, Wegener, & White, in press; see Wegener & Petty, 1997, for additional discussion of correction processes in persuasion and other settings).

High-Effort Processes

As outlined above, a number of factors influence the likelihood that people will allocate mental effort in persuasion situations. However, when people engage in high-effort processing, what do they do? Through the years, a number of high-effort processes have been proposed. Many of the theoretical positions discussed in this section were originally proposed—and some still hold them to be—general models of attitude change (e.g., see Fishbein & Middlestadt, 1995). As was noted previously, however, within the ELM, these high-effort processes are viewed as falling along a continuum such that these processes occur to a greater extent when ability and motivation to scrutinize the central merits of a position or object are relatively high.

A variety of relatively high-effort processes have been discussed over the years. These include message learning/reception processes, cognitive responses, probabilogical/expectancy-value processes, information integration, and at least in its original formulation, dissonance-produced reassessments of attitude-relevant thoughts and actions.

Message Learning/Reception Processes Our starting point in discussing contemporary high-effort information processing approaches is the Communication-Persuasion matrix model outlined by William McGuire in previous editions of this handbook (1969, 1985). McGuire began as a valuable contributor to the Hovland group and as an important consistency theorist (e.g., McGuire, 1960a). His matrix model and related work provided an essential bridge from the Yale/Hovland work to more contemporary information processing models (e.g., McGuire, 1964).

McGuire's analysis is generally compatible with the Hovland/Yale view that attitude change depends on a series of information processing stages described as: attention, comprehension, learning, acceptance, and retention of the message and its conclusion (Hovland et al., 1953). A person was assumed to engage in these "output" or "mediating" steps to the extent that the persuasive source, message, or context ("input" factors) provided incentives (i.e., rewards) for doing so. McGuire's (1968, 1989) model incorporates and significantly elaborates these ideas. At the same time, McGuire proposed an elegant simplification of the output factors by noting that persuasion is often most dependent upon factors related to the reception of message arguments and yielding to them. Thus, some variables might decrease the likelihood of attitude change by making reception more difficult (e.g., distraction from the message content by a secondary task), whereas others might decrease persuasion by making yielding less likely (e.g., a poorly reasoned message). From this perspective, some of the most interesting variables were those that might influence reception and yielding in opposite ways. For example, as the self-esteem or intelligence of message recipients increased, reception might increase (i.e., because higher levels of these characteristics would likely increase attention and comprehension) but yielding might decrease (e.g., because these people would likely have greater confidence in their initial opinions or would be more critical of new information; Eagly & Warren, 1976). For variables that have opposite effects on reception and yielding, persuasion should be maximal at a moderate level of the variable—the "compensation principle" (McGuire, 1968). This perspective provided considerable flexibility over the original message learning approach in that either reception or yielding could become more important in a given persuasion setting. For example, if a message consisted of complex but compelling arguments, factors affecting reception might be most related to persuasion outcomes (because most people would yield to compelling arguments), but if a message consisted of simple but somewhat weak arguments, factors related to yielding might take on greater importance (see McGuire, 1968).[2]

Although some studies have examined the curvilinear hypothesis from this model (see Rhodes & Wood, 1992, for a review), most of the attention devoted to the reception/yielding perspective has examined the notion that reception is a prerequisite to persuasion. Regarding comprehension of the arguments, research clearly suggests that if a message is gibberish, persuasion can be reduced when compared to a comprehensible message (Eagly, 1974), unless, perhaps, if the arguments in the message were very weak, and processing the intact message would have produced boomerang. Considerable attention has been paid to the issue of whether people must learn and remember the message arguments in order for persuasion to occur. Consequently, researchers have examined the extent to which argument learning (and retention), as assessed by message recall or recognition, is related to persuasion. Perhaps surprisingly, early research provided little evidence for a link between message recall and either initial persuasion or its persistence over time (see Eagly & Chaiken, 1993; McGuire, 1969, for reviews).

There are several possible reasons for low attitude change-argument memory relationships. Perhaps the most important is that a pure reception/learning model does not take into account the idiosyncratic evaluations individuals have of the arguments. That is, one person can find an argument very compelling and relevant, another only slightly convincing, and a third might find the same argument to be completely ridiculous and irrelevant (Petty, Ostrom, & Brock, 1981; see section on cognitive responses). Consistent with McGuire's (1968) suggestions, however, when recalled information is weighted by a person's idiosyncratic evaluation of it, attitude-recall relationships are increased (e.g., Chattopadhyay & Alba, 1988).

In some situations, however, there might be a substantial relation between memory for message arguments and attitude change. For example, if a judgment is to be made when no information has been presented on the topic for some time, or if people were distracted from careful on-line evaluation of the information when it was presented, then people are more likely to base attitudes or other judgments on the implications of the information that can be recalled if that information is perceived to be relevant at the time of judgment (Hastie & Park, 1986). However, because the messages in the persuasion studies showing significant recall-attitude correlations (e.g., Haugtvedt & Petty, 1992; Haugtvedt & Wegener, 1994; Mackie & Asuncion, 1990) contained reasonably strong arguments, it is not clear if the memory-recall relationships that were observed were due to the fact that people favorably evaluated the arguments they recalled at the time of judgment, or whether they simply made inferences of validity based on the mere number of arguments that they could recall (Petty & Cacioppo, 1984a). That is, attitude-memory correlations can stem from either central or peripheral routes to persuasion.

It is somewhat ironic that although the learning/reception perspective was originally formulated in a way that suggests a high-effort process, the circumstances in which

message recall relates most closely to attitudes might actually be those in which relatively little on-line evaluation of message arguments takes place (i.e., passive learning of arguments used as a cue or evaluated later rather than active on-line consideration of them). Specifically, current research suggests that the correlation between message recall and attitudes should be relatively high if: (a) the likelihood of elaborating the message arguments at the time of message exposure is relatively low, (b) an unexpected judgment is required following message exposure, and (c) no simple cues (e.g., source expertise, strong prior attitude) are available or attended to by the recipient that could produce an attitude at the time of judgment in the absence of on-line argument scrutiny. In such circumstances, in order to express an opinion, people would likely attempt to recall the information presented and base their judgment on what they can remember. This judgment could reflect either a mere quantity heuristic (the more information recalled, the more agreement), or a careful evaluation of the information that is recalled such that the attitude-memory correlation would be positive if the implications of the recalled arguments are favorable but negative if the implications are unfavorable. Which of these would occur would depend on the person's motivation and ability to process the recalled information at the time of judgment.

In sum, although the reception hypothesis has a long history, and some consider it to be proven (Chaiken, Wood, & Eagly, 1996), our view is that accurate understanding or learning of message arguments is not necessary for persuasion to occur. Rather, as emphasized by the cognitive response approach discussed shortly, a person's subjective perception of understanding the arguments is more important than actual understanding or learning of the information presented. A person can completely misperceive the message arguments (score zero on accurate reception) and nevertheless generate favorable responses to what was inaccurately perceived. In addition, peripheral processes (e.g., classical conditioning) can influence attitudes in the absence of reception of message arguments. Nevertheless, it is likely that the role of message reception is probably underestimated in the typical persuasion study, in part because the variance in reception is often too low to detect effects (Eagly & Chaiken, 1984, 1993).

Cognitive Responses

Thoughts in Response to Messages   In response to numerous findings of low attitude-recall correlations (which challenged the message learning view implied by the Yale approach of the 1950s), researchers—especially at Ohio State University—developed the cognitive response approach to persuasion (e.g., Brock, 1967; Greenwald, 1968; Petty, Ostrom, & Brock, 1981). For example, Greenwald (1968) proposed that it was not the specific arguments in a message that were associated with the message conclusion (or attitude object) in memory. Rather, a person's idiosyncratic cognitive responses or reactions to the message arguments were paired with the conclusion and were thus responsible for persuasion or resistance (see also Kelman, 1953; McGuire, 1964). The persistence of these cognitive responses was also postulated to be responsible for the persistence of attitude change (Love & Greenwald, 1978; Petty, 1977). Of course, at the most basic level, individuals can only cognitively *respond* to something that they have received. In the cognitive response analysis, however, a person's thoughts can be in response to incorrectly perceived arguments as well as correctly perceived arguments. In fact, the thoughts can be to the message conclusion in the absence of receipt of any arguments. The original cognitive response approach was also sufficiently general that it accommodated cognitive responses elicited by the tone of the message or by extra-message factors such as the source or context of the message (e.g., "experts are generally correct"). In any case, to the extent that a person's cognitive responses were favorable, persuasion was the postulated result, but to the extent that they were unfavorable (e.g., counterarguments, source derogations, negative emotional thoughts), resistance or even boomerang was possible.

The cognitive response approach has generated a considerable body of evidence consistent with the view that in certain situations people spontaneously produce thoughts during message presentation and the favorability of these thoughts is a good predictor of post-message attitudes and beliefs (see reviews by Eagly & Chaiken, 1993; Petty & Cacioppo, 1986a). In a typical cognitive response study, message recipients list or verbally report their thoughts either during or after the message. Studies in support of the cognitive response approach have shown that: (a) physiological activity indicative of information processing (e.g., facial EMG) is elevated when cognitive responding is presumed to occur (e.g., Cacioppo & Petty, 1979a); (b) thought profiles show the same pattern as the attitude measure in response to some manipulation (e.g., the manipulation produces increased persuasion and increased favorable thoughts and/or decreased unfavorable thoughts, e.g., Osterhouse & Brock, 1970); (c) the polarity of these thoughts (e.g., positive minus negative thoughts) is a good predictor of the post-message attitude (e.g., Mackie, 1987); and (d) removing the effect of some manipulation on thoughts eliminates its effect on attitudes, but controlling for attitudes does not eliminate the manipulation's effect on thoughts (e.g., Insko, Turnbull, & Yandell, 1974; see Cacioppo & Petty, 1981, for a review).

Although most studies simply categorize thoughts into the valence dimension of favorable, unfavorable, and neutral categories, other coding schemes are possible. For example, thoughts can be based mostly on affect or cognition (e.g., Ickes, Robertson, Tooke, & Teng, 1986) and can reiterate

the message content or include self-generated material (e.g., Greenwald, 1968). It is also possible to distinguish between cognitive responses that are based on message content (e.g., counterarguments) versus thoughts that are based on simple cues (e.g., source derogations). Consistent with the multiprocess models, it is the former type of cognitive response that best predicts attitudes when elaboration is high; the latter category of thoughts predicts attitudes best when elaboration is low (e.g., Chaiken, 1980; Petty & Cacioppo, 1979b, 1984a). Although considerable work has addressed factors that determine the extent of thinking and the content of thinking about a persuasive message at the time a message is presented, little work has addressed the recurrence of thinking in persuasion contexts (but see Lassiter, Pezzo, & Apple, 1993). That is, what factors determine whether people return to thinking about the message or issue at some point following a communication (see Martin & Tesser, 1996; Petty, Jarvis, & Evans, 1996, for discussion)?

Thoughts When No Message Is Present   Thoughts do not only determine the direction and extent of attitude change when a message is presented. The powerful and persisting effects of completely self-generated messages were shown in early research on "role-playing" (e.g., Janis & King, 1954; Watts, 1967). A consistent research finding is that active generation of a message is a successful strategy for producing attitude change (e.g., McGuire & McGuire, 1996). It doesn't seem to matter whether people generate the message because they are assigned a position to take, or they select a position based on a desire to communicate with another person. For example, people tend to tell others what they want to hear (Tesser & Rosen, 1975), and construction and delivery of such biased messages can produce attitude change in the transmitter (see Higgins, 1981). Change tends to be greater when people generate messages regarding attributes that a target possesses than attributes that a target lacks (McGuire & McGuire, 1996).

Furthermore, self-generated attitude changes tend to persist longer than changes based on passive exposure to a communication (e.g., Elms, 1966). Attitude changes that come about due to active generation of arguments might be more persistent because they are often based on more extensive processing of attitude-relevant information than are attitude changes due to passive receipt of messages (and argument generation might make the arguments more accessible than when they are passively received; Greenwald & Albert, 1968; Slamecka & Graf, 1978). Similarly, people who are asked to imagine hypothetical events come to believe that these events have a higher likelihood of occurring than before thinking about them (e.g., Sherman, Cialdini, Schwartzman, & Reynolds, 1985). Furthermore, self-generation of explanations has been shown to be a powerful way to establish or change beliefs, and beliefs based on the generated explanations are remarkably impervious to change (e.g., Anderson, Lepper, & Ross, 1980; Sherman, Zehner, Johnson, & Hirt, 1983).

Tesser (1978) and his colleagues have examined the effects of merely asking someone to think about an issue, object, or person. In one early study, Sadler and Tesser (1973) introduced research participants to a likable or dislikable partner (via a tape-recording). Some participants were instructed to think about the partner whereas others were distracted from doing so. The thinking manipulation polarized judgments of the partner. More recent research shows that the polarization effect requires that people have a well-integrated and consistent schema to guide processing and that they are motivated to utilize this issue-relevant knowledge (e.g., Chaiken & Yates, 1985). In the absence of these conditions, such as when motivation to think is low or when the issue-relevant information in memory is not highly interconnected (and consistent), mere thought is associated with attitude moderation (e.g., Judd & Lusk, 1984; see Tesser, Martin, & Mendolia, 1995, for a review of mere thought research).

In a variation of this mere thought procedure, Wilson and colleagues have examined the effects of asking people to think about why they hold the attitudes they do (e.g., why do you like strawberry ice-cream? see Wilson, Dunn, Kraft, & Lisle, 1989). The primary conclusion from a series of studies is that evaluations following a reasons analysis tend to be overinfluenced by cognitive factors and underinfluenced by affective factors. Thus, decisions following an analysis of reasons can be maladaptive because people consider only a subset of the real reasons they like or dislike something. In a similar vein, Levine, Halberstadt, and Goldstone (1996) demonstrated that when asked to analyze why they liked a target object prior to making judgments of a series of previously unfamiliar (and not very important) stimuli, people use different dimensions of judgment when judging the target on different occasions. Thus, when analyzing reasons, judgments of objectively similar objects were rated as less similar than when reasons were not analyzed prior to evaluating the objects.

Probabilogical and Expectancy/Value Processes   Although the probabilogical (e.g., McGuire, 1960b; Wyer, 1974) and expectancy/value (e.g., Fishbein & Ajzen, 1975; Rosenberg, 1956) models have largely been discussed in relation to the underlying structure of attitudes (see Eagly & Chaiken, 1998, in this *Handbook*; Petty, Priester, & Wegener, 1994), each is also applicable to thoughtful processes of attitude change. For example, the underlying structure of at least some attitudes might consist of two premises that lead to a conclusion:

Premise 1:   Candidate A favors tax reduction.
Premise 2:   Tax reduction is good for the country.

Conclusion: Candidate A is good for the country.

Therefore, one could change the attitude toward Candidate A by changing either of the premises, either in terms of the content of the premise (e.g., candidate A favors tax increases) or in terms of the likelihood that the premise is true (e.g., there is a 0.2 rather than a 0.9 probability that premise 1 is true; McGuire, 1960a, 1960b; Wyer, 1974). To the extent that the attitude has an extensive horizontal or vertical structure (McGuire, 1981), it might take change in a greater number of premises in order to effect noticeable changes in the target attitude. Such a view also indicates that one might find changes in attitudes that are not even mentioned in a persuasive message if the attitudes are logically related to claims in the message. Consistent with this view, research shows that a message about abortion can produce changes in people's attitudes toward the unmentioned issue of contraception (e.g., if abortion is viewed as especially bad, then avoiding abortion by using contraception might be viewed as more desirable than would otherwise be the case; see Mugny & Perez, 1991; Dillehay, Insko, & Smith, 1966). This "indirect change" might even occur if the "direct change" of the targeted attitude is not evidenced (e.g., if change in the targeted attitude is inhibited by social pressure such as a norm against agreeing with a minority source, but no such pressure is associated with the indirect conclusion; Mugny & Perez, 1991). In fact, simply responding to an attitude item on one issue can produce an attitude polarization effect on a related issue (Henninger & Wyer, 1976; Judd, Drake, Downing, & Krosnick, 1991), perhaps because of respondents perceiving links between the issues—links that dictate changes in the related opinion as a means of maintaining consistency among attitudes in the system.

Versions of the probabilogical model have addressed both the likelihood and desirability of premises of syllogisms like that presented above (McGuire, 1960a; McGuire & McGuire, 1991; Wyer, 1973). That is, researchers have examined the determinants of both the desirability and likelihood of various belief statements. For example, consider Premise 1 above that "Candidate A favors tax reduction." If this was an argument in a message advocating Candidate A for president, it would be effective to the extent that people found tax reduction to be desirable *and* they believed that it was true that Candidate A really favored tax reduction. A theme of this chapter is that desirability (evaluative) judgments can be made based on effortful or noneffortful analyses, but it is less commonly recognized that likelihood or truth judgments can also vary in the extent of effort required (as can other judgments). Some theorists, for example, have posited that likelihood judgments involve a relatively effortful consideration of the potential antecedents of the event (McGuire & McGuire, 1991). Other theorists, however, have argued that likelihood judgments can be based largely on perceptions of familiarity of the idea (Arkes, Boehm, & Xu, 1991; Wyer, 1991). As noted earlier, research suggests that propositions are initially assumed to be true unless contradictory information is retrieved which allows one to determine that the proposition is false (Gilbert, 1991). To the extent that this formulation is valid, people should be biased toward assuming truth when the elaboration likelihood is low (Gilbert, Tafarodi, & Malone, 1993). Similarly, as noted earlier, people might be biased toward assuming goodness when the elaboration likelihood is low (Cacioppo & Berntson, 1994; Peeters & Czapinski, 1990). Repetition under low elaboration conditions appears to enhance these default biases. That is, when the elaboration likelihood is low, repeated exposure to statements can make them seem more true (Arkes et al., 1991) and repeated exposure to objects can make them seem more good (Zajonc, 1968). As the elaboration likelihood increases, however, propositions and objects should be judged either true or false and good or bad, depending on the outcome of one's effortful processing.

Regardless of whether the likelihood and desirability of a proposition are determined effortfully or not, these parameters need to be combined. The most common approach to combining likelihood and desirability aspects of information comes from expectancy-value theories which analyze attitudes by focusing on the extent to which people believe that the attitude object is linked to important values or is associated with positive versus negative outcomes (e.g., Rosenberg, 1956; see Bagozzi, 1985, for review). In the most influential formulation, Fishbein and Ajzen (1975) hold that the desirability of each attribute associated with an object is weighted by the likelihood that the object possesses the attribute, and the products of the likelihood and desirability components are summed over all attributes. The major implication of expectancy-value theories for attitude change is that a persuasive message will be effective to the extent that it produces a change in either the likelihood or the desirability component of an attribute that is linked to the attitude object (see Fishbein & Ajzen, 1981; Petty & Wegener, 1991, for discussions). Given the wide applicability of the Fishbein and Ajzen model and the extensive number of studies documenting the link between attitudes and the likelihood and desirability components of beliefs, it is surprising that relatively little work on attitude *change* has been guided explicitly by this framework. Nevertheless, existing research supports the view that messages can influence attitudes by changing either the desirability or the likelihood component of beliefs (e.g., Lutz, 1975; MacKenzie, 1986). Although some advocates of this perspective assume that virtually all attitude change takes place through relatively effortful expectancy-value processes (e.g., Fishbein & Middlestadt, 1995), there are some indications that these processes account for more variance in attitudes when elaboration likelihood is high

(e.g., when message recipients are high in need for cognition, Wegener, Petty, & Klein, 1994; or have high levels of topic-relevant knowledge, Lutz, 1977).

Information Integration Regardless of whether one conceptualizes high elaboration processes as cognitive responses, assessments of likelihood and desirability of attributes of the attitude object, or as learning and retention of attitude-relevant information, these information units must be integrated in some manner to form an overall attitudinal reaction. Two combinatory rules have generated the bulk of research attention. Fishbein and Ajzen's expectancy-value formulation described earlier provides one such model (i.e., summation of the likelihood × desirability products for each unit of information). An alternative integration formula is provided by Anderson's (1971) information integration theory. In contrast to the additive rule specified by Fishbein and Ajzen, Anderson posits that the pieces of information in a communication (or one's cognitive responses; Anderson, 1981) are typically combined by a weighted averaging process. Specifically, the person's evaluation of the salient information is weighted by the importance of the information for the judgment and is averaged with the person's weighted initial attitude to form a new attitude.

Perhaps the biggest strength of the information integration model is simultaneously its greatest weakness, namely, the very flexible use of the weighting parameters (Eagly & Chaiken, 1984; Petty & Cacioppo, 1981). That is, the fact that the weighting parameter can take on either positive or negative values of different magnitudes across different situations gives the model a virtually unlimited domain of applicability. Unfortunately, the lack of a priori prediction concerning when and why the weighting parameter for certain variables changes magnitude or sign makes the model more useful as a descriptive rather than explanatory tool for understanding attitude changes.[3]

Cognitive Dissonance Theory Of the various theories proposing a motive to maintain cognitive consistency (e.g., Heider, 1958; Osgood & Tannenbaum, 1955), the most prominent is the theory of cognitive dissonance (Festinger, 1957, 1964). In Festinger's original formulation of the theory, two elements in a cognitive system (e.g., a belief and an attitude; an attitude and a behavior) were said to be *consonant* if one followed from the other. The elements were *dissonant* if one belief implied the opposite of the other. Of course, two elements could also be *irrelevant* to each other. Festinger proposed that the psychological state of dissonance was aversive and that people would be motivated to engage in cognitive activity in order to reduce it. Because people in a dissonant state are motivated to achieve a particular outcome, their effortful information processing activity is clearly biased (i.e., of two equally plausible interpretations, the interpretation most consistent with the other salient cognitive elements is preferred). The most obvious solution to dissonance is to engage in cognitive work to modify one of the dissonant elements (i.e., self-generated attitude change). Strategies other than changing the dissonant elements are also possible, however. For example the person could try to generate cognitions that make the dissonant elements consistent with each other (bolstering). Alternatively, the person could try to minimize the importance of one of the dissonant cognitions (i.e., trivializing; see Simon, Greenberg, & Brehm, 1995).

Perhaps the most studied dissonance situation involves inducing people to engage in some behavior that is inconsistent with their attitudes (Brehm & Cohen, 1962). For example, one common way of producing dissonance in the laboratory is by inducing a person to write an essay that is inconsistent with the person's attitude under high choice conditions and with little incentive (e.g., Zanna & Cooper, 1974). Because behavior is usually difficult to undo, dissonance can be reduced by changing beliefs and attitudes to bring them into line with the behavior (i.e., convincing oneself that the behavior reflects one's true position). In the most famous dissonance experiment, students at Stanford University engaged in the quite boring task of turning pegs on a board (Festinger & Carlsmith, 1959), and then were induced to tell a waiting participant that the task was interesting for either a sufficient ($20) or an insufficient ($1) incentive. When later asked how interesting they actually found the task to be, students reported that the task was more interesting the less they were paid.

A large number of studies have examined the novel reverse-incentive predictions of dissonance theory in a wide variety of situations. For example, dissonance theorists have discovered that people will come to like a group more the more unpleasant the initiation required to get into the group (Aronson & Mills, 1959). People were found to report liking an exotic food more the more dislikable the person who induced them to try the food (Zimbardo, Weisenberg, Firestone, & Levy, 1965). Also, it was found that people's evaluations of two objects were more discrepant some time after a choice between them than before the choice took place. Following a choice, biased cognitive activity renders the chosen option more favorable and the unchosen option less favorable (Brehm, 1966).

It is now clear that many of the situations described by Festinger as inducing dissonance produce the physiological changes and perceptions of unpleasantness predicted by the theory. Evidence for this proposition has been found both with self-report (Elliot & Devine, 1994) and physiological measures (e.g., Elkin & Leippe, 1986; Losch & Cacioppo, 1990). Furthermore, the accumulated research of dissonance theory suggests that the negative feelings associated with dissonance can be reduced not only directly by modifying one of the cognitions involved, but indirectly by

virtually any other means that would make a person feel less unpleasant. For example, one can reduce dissonance by misattributing the unpleasant feelings to a temporary source such as a pill one has taken or some other plausible cause (Fried & Aronson, 1995; Zanna & Cooper, 1974). Or, one can drown out the dissonance with alcohol (Steele, Southwick, & Critchlow, 1981), or watch a funny movie (Cooper, Fazio, & Rhodewaldt, 1978), or bolster some irrelevant aspects of oneself (Steele, 1988; Tesser & Cornell, 1991). Some research suggests that people will use whatever means of reducing dissonance is presented first (e.g., Aronson et al., 1995; Simon et al., 1995), but relatively little work has examined the consequences of giving people the choice of modes to reduce dissonance. In one study, when given the choice of direct or indirect ways to reduce dissonance, most choose the direct over the indirect (though the indirect was used if it was the only alternative; Stone, Wiegand, Cooper, & Aronson, 1997). It is not clear, however, if indirect ways to reduce dissonance only postpone dissonance reduction because the underlying conditions producing the unpleasant feelings have not been modified. In support of this view, Higgins, Rhodewaldt, and Zanna (1979) found that dissonance processes could be reinitiated two weeks after dissonance was apparently attenuated by misattribution.

It is also important to note that the mere performance of an inconsistent action does not always produce dissonance. One reason for this is that some people may not have a need for consistency (Cialdini, Trost, & Newsom, 1995). Alternatively, some theorists have questioned Festinger's view that inconsistency per se produces discomfort in people, and have suggested that it is necessary for people to believe that they have freely chosen to bring about some foreseeable negative consequence for themselves or other people (e.g., Cooper & Fazio, 1984). Thus, if telling a waiting research participant that a boring task is interesting (Festinger & Carlsmith, 1959) results in no harmful consequence (e.g., because the waiting participant doesn't believe you), there is no dissonance. But, if the harmful consequences are high (e.g., the waiting participant decides to stay and take part in the experiment rather than study for an exam), dissonance occurs and attitude change toward the task results (see Calder, Ross, & Insko, 1973). Other theorists argue that inconsistency is involved, but the inconsistency must involve a critical aspect of oneself or a threat to one's positive self-concept (e.g., Aronson, 1969; Greenwald & Ronis, 1978).

Interestingly, theorists from both camps have argued that proattitudinal advocacy (making a speech that is consistent with one's attitudes) can also produce dissonance under certain conditions (see also, Schlenker, 1982). Advocates of the negative consequences view argue that proattitudinal advocacy can induce dissonance if the proattitudinal advocacy ends up having negative consequences (Scher

& Cooper, 1989; but see Johnson, Kelly, & LaBlanc, 1995). Advocates of the self-inconsistency view also argue that proattitudinal advocacy can produce dissonance if, as a result of the advocacy, people feel hypocritical (which threatens self-esteem; Stone, Aronson, Craine, Winslow, & Fried, 1994).

Although research has supported both the negative consequences and the self-inconsistency predictions, disentangling these viewpoints has proven difficult. The reason for this is that each framework generally can accommodate the results generated by the other. The conceptual problem stems from the fact that freely choosing to bring about negative consequences is clearly inconsistent with most people's views of themselves as rational, caring individuals. That is, choosing to bring about negative consequences is inconsistent with one's positive self-view. However, it is also true that when people do something inconsistent with their positive self-views, the resulting feeling of guilt, shame, stupidity, or hypocrisy is an aversive consequence (Aronson, 1969). That is, by choosing to violate one's self-view, one has freely chosen to bring about an aversive outcome (see Petty, 1995).

A third viewpoint on the causes of dissonance is provided by self-affirmation theory (Steele, 1988). According to this framework, dissonance is not produced by inconsistency per se, being responsible for negative consequences, or the distress of self-inconsistency in particular, but rather stems from a violation of general self-integrity. According to this viewpoint, actions produce dissonance only when the behavior threatens one's "moral and adaptive adequacy" (see also Tesser & Cornell, 1991). The self-consistency and self-affirmation points of view have much in common, but they differ in their predictions of whether high or low self-esteem people should be more susceptible to dissonance effects. The self-consistency point of view argues that high self-esteem individuals would experience the most dissonance by engaging in esteem threatening behavior because such actions are most inconsistent with their favorable self-conceptions. The self-affirmation point of view suggests that low self-esteem individuals should show stronger dissonance effects because high self-esteem individuals can more easily restore self-integrity by thinking about the many positive traits they have. Unfortunately, the research evidence on this question is mixed with some studies showing greater dissonance effects for low self-esteem individuals (Steele, Spencer, & Lynch, 1993), and other studies showing greater dissonance effects for high self-esteem persons (Gerard, Blevans, & Malcolm, 1964).

In sum, it is not clear whether dissonance results from cognitive inconsistency per se, the production of aversive consequences, inconsistency in specific aspects of the self-concept, threats to general self-integrity, all of the above, or some other process. In fact, each of the postulated mechanisms might be responsible for dissonance, but in

different situations. One attempt at integration is Stone and Cooper's (1996) proposal that dissonance results whenever one's behavior violates some self-standard (see Higgins, 1989). That is, Stone and Cooper argue that dissonance can stem from failure to behave in a manner consistent with how a person thinks he or she wants to be (ideal-self) or how the person thinks he or she should be (ought-self), or how others want you to be or think you should be (i.e., normative standards). In this framework, depending on which self-standard is salient, any given act may or may not induce dissonance. Among the most important implications of this integration are that the self-consistency view of dissonance prevails whenever personal self-standards are salient and violated, but the negative consequences view holds whenever normative standards are salient and violated. In addition, this view holds that self-affirmation will only reduce dissonance when the affirmation is on dimensions irrelevant to the dissonant act. Relevant affirmations will serve to increase dissonance suggesting self-consistency motives remain at the core of dissonance theory.

Regardless of the exact motivational underpinnings of dissonance, the evidence clearly indicates that attitudinally discrepant actions can result in a reanalysis of the reasons why a person engaged in a certain behavior (or made a certain choice), and cause a person to rethink the merits of an attitude object. The end result of this effortful but generally biased cognitive activity can be a relatively enduring change in attitude toward the object.

Low Elaboration Processes

If the high-effort processes just outlined were the only ones that could produce attitude change, it would appear that changes typically require a diligent message recipient— one who is willing (at a minimum) to passively learn the information presented, and might also assess the likelihood and desirability of the attributes of the object, generate new information and implications of the information, and weigh and combine the information to form an overall judgment. If so, attitude change should become less likely as such processes are impaired. According to contemporary multiprocess perspectives, however, there are a variety of situations in which attitudes are formed or changed without a great deal of effortful attention or consideration of the substantive information. When this occurs, a number of "peripheral" mechanisms can be responsible for changing attitudes. In fact, a number of theories that were first proposed as general theories of attitude change were comprised of mechanisms that do not require much (if any) effortful scrutiny of the merits of attitude objects. Our discussion of relatively low-effort change processes begins with conditioning and priming mechanisms that associate affect with the attitude object, and concludes with a consideration of simple cognitive inference and other processes that can produce attitude change in the absence of learning or effortfully evaluating the substantive information or arguments presented. Although these peripheral mechanisms vary in the extent of mental effort they require, none requires the recipient to personally evaluate the relevant pieces of information for their central merits.

Associating Affect with the Attitude Object

Classical Conditioning One of the most primitive means of changing attitudes involves the direct association of "affect" with objects, issues, or people through classical conditioning. Considerable research has shown that attitudes can be modified by pairing initially neutral objects with stimuli about which people already feel positively or negatively. For example, people's evaluations of words (e.g., Staats & Staats, 1958), other people (e.g., Griffitt, 1970), political slogans (e.g., Razran, 1940), products (e.g., Gresham & Shimp, 1985), and persuasive communications (e.g., Janis, Kaye, & Kirschner, 1965) have been modified by pairing them with affect producing stimuli (e.g., unpleasant odors and temperatures, the onset and offset of electric shock, harsh sounds, pleasant pictures, and elating versus depressing films; e.g., Gouaux, 1971; Staats, Staats, & Crawford, 1962; Zanna, Kiesler, & Pilkonis, 1970). Contractions of muscles associated with positive or negative experiences (e.g., smiling versus frowning; Strack, Martin, & Stepper, 1988; or flexing arm muscles associated with moving objects toward rather than away from oneself; Cacioppo, Priester, & Berntson, 1993) can also influence evaluative responses. That is, when an initially unconditioned (neutral) stimulus (UCS) is encountered along with a conditioning stimulus that is already strongly associated with positive or negative experiences (CS), the initially neutral stimulus can come to elicit positive or negative reactions (the conditioned response).

Consistent with the view that conditioning effects can be obtained by nonthoughtful means, DeHouwer, Baeyens, and Eelen (1994) reported evidence of evaluative conditioning even when the unconditioned stimuli were presented subliminally. Also consistent with the notion that conditioning processes largely act as a peripheral means to establish or change attitudes, Cacioppo et al. (1992) showed that classical conditioning using electric shock had a greater impact on initially neutral nonwords (which, of course, were not associated with any preexisting meaning or knowledge) than on initially neutral words; see also Shimp, Stuart, & Engle, 1991). Similarly, isometric flexion versus extension of upper arm muscles (i.e., processes associated with approach and withdrawal, respectively) during evaluative processing has been shown to influence preferences for neutral nonwords more than for neutral words (Priester, Cacioppo, & Petty, 1996).

Affective Priming In a procedure similar to conditioning, people are presented with affect-inducing positive or negative material (e.g., pictures) just prior to receipt of the target stimulus. This "backward conditioning" or "affective priming" procedure has proven successful in modifying attitudes. For example, research participants who were exposed to subliminal positive photos (e.g., a group of smiling friends) subsequently rated a target person performing normal everyday activities more positively than participants exposed to negative photos (e.g., a bucket of snakes; Krosnick, Betz, Jussim, & Lynn, 1992). Murphy and Zajonc (1993) found that the effectiveness of this type of affective priming procedure may be dependent on presenting the primes outside of conscious awareness. That is, when positive and negative affective primes (smiling and frowning faces) were presented just prior to a target stimulus (a Chinese ideograph), attitudes toward the target were influenced when the primes were presented subliminally, but not when they were presented visibly (see also Murphy, Monahan, & Zajonc, 1995). One possible reason for such an effect might be that visibly presented priming stimuli are noticed as obviously irrelevant to perceptions of the targets. Therefore, this "blatant priming" might instigate an avoidance of the perceived effects of the emotional primes (Martin et al., 1990; Petty & Wegener, 1993).

In sum, studies of affect association (i.e., classical conditioning and affect priming) show that primitive affective processes are most likely to influence attitudes toward objects that have little meaning and for which people possess little or no knowledge, and when opportunities for processing are low (see also Zajonc, 1998, in this *Handbook*). This does not mean, however, that affect will have an impact on attitudes only when the likelihood of elaborating attitude-relevant information is low. As discussed in the section on multiple roles for persuasion variables, affect can also modify attitudes when the elaboration likelihood is quite high. In such cases, however, the processes that lead to those changes are different than those discussed here.

Inference-Based Approaches

Attribution Theory Although attributional processes can, themselves, vary in the amount of cognitive effort required (see Gilbert, 1998, in this *Handbook*), some attributional processes (e.g., inferring that a favorable view of an object is responsible for one's seeking of it) likely require somewhat less effort than the active scrutiny of attitude-relevant information. Because of this, such attributional inferences might be used at times as a short cut for assessing the validity of a stance toward an attitude object (perhaps so that effortful processing of information about the object can be foregone). The attributional approach has been applied to attributions about the attitude object itself, as well as to attributions about the source of information about an attitude object. Most generally, the attributional approach focuses on people inferring underlying characteristics about themselves and others from the behaviors that they observe and the perceived situational constraints that are imposed on those behaviors (e.g., Bem, 1965; Jones & Davis, 1965). Bem (1965) suggested that people sometimes have no special knowledge of their own internal states and therefore must infer their attitudes in a manner similar to that by which they infer the attitudes of others (i.e., from the observed behavior and context in which it occurred).

During much of the 1970s, Bem's *self-perception theory* was thought to provide an alternative account of dissonance effects (Bem, 1972). For example, in the classic Festinger and Carlsmith (1959) study described earlier, a person who observed an individual saying a task is interesting after being given only $1 might infer that this person liked the task more than a person who said it was interesting for $20. That is, the less money it takes to induce a person to say something, the more they must really believe it. If an external observer might make this reasonable inference, so too might the person him or herself, Bem argued. Subsequent research indicated, however, that self-perception processes could not account for all dissonance effects (e.g., Beauvois, Bungert, & Mariette, 1995). Rather, the two processes operate in different domains. In particular, the underlying internal discomfort mechanism of dissonance theory operates when a person engages in attitude-discrepant action that is disagreeable (e.g., advocating a discrepant position in one's latitude of rejection; Fazio, Zanna, & Cooper, 1977; performing self-deprecating behavior; Jones, Rhodewalt, Berglas, & Skelton, 1981), whereas self-perception processes are more likely when a person engages in attitude-discrepant but more agreeable behavior (e.g., advocating a discrepant position in one's latitude of acceptance; Fazio et al., 1977; performing a self-enhancing behavior; Jones et al., 1981). Also, self-perception processes do not require scrutiny of the central merits of an attitudinal position (i.e., "viewing" the behavior is all that is necessary), but dissonance reduction is conceived as a thorough (but biased) form of information processing (Festinger, 1957). Thus, in elaboration likelihood terms, one might expect self-perception processes to be more likely when elaboration likelihood is low, but dissonance processes to be more likely when elaboration likelihood is high (e.g., when the cognitions are very important or self-relevant; Petty & Cacioppo, 1986a). Of course, especially difficult or complex attributions might be less likely to occur under such low-effort settings.

Self-perception theory also accounted for some unique attitudinal phenomena. For example, the *overjustification effect* occurs when a person is provided with more than sufficient reward for engaging in an action that is already highly regarded (e.g., Lepper, Greene, & Nisbett, 1973). To the extent that the person comes to attribute the action to the external reward rather than to the intrinsic enjoyment of the behavior, attitudes toward the behavior will become less favorable (Deci, 1975). Thus, if people are provided with extrinsic rewards for advocating a position that they already like, they may come to devalue the position when the external rewards stop to the extent that they have come to view their attitude expression as caused by the rewards rather than by the true merits of the position (e.g., Scott & Yalch, 1978).

As noted earlier, according to the ELM, people should be more likely to rely on simple self-perception inferences when elaboration likelihood is low. Consistent with this notion, in one study, Taylor (1975) asked women to evaluate pictures of men who they believed they would actually meet (high personal relevance/elaboration) or not (low personal relevance/elaboration). Participants received false feedback about their "positive physiological responses" toward some of the men (Valins, 1966). The information about physiological reactions influenced the women's reported attitudes only when there was no expected meeting with the man in the picture but not when the consequences were high (see also, Chaiken & Baldwin, 1981; Wood, 1982, for conceptually similar findings).

The attributional approach has also been useful in understanding how inferences about message sources can influence attitudes. For example, Eagly, Chaiken, and Wood (1981) argued that people often approach a persuasion situation with some expectation regarding the position a communicator will take. They argued that, if the premessage expectation is confirmed by the communicator's presentation, the recipient attributes the message to the traits and pressures that generated the expectation rather than to the validity of the position espoused. Thus, in these cases, the person needs to process the message to determine its validity. However, when the premessage expectation is disconfirmed, the communicator is viewed as relatively trustworthy, and the message as veridical. Thus persuasion can occur without the need to process message arguments (e.g., Eagly, Wood, & Chaiken, 1978). The reduced processing of trustworthy sources is especially evident among people low in need for cognition (Priester & Petty, 1995). In addition, disconfirmation of a premessage expectancy only leads to perceiving the source as trustworthy when the disconfirmation entails the source violating his or her own self-interest. If disconfirmed expectancies occur in the absence of a self-interest violation, then the surprise of the disconfirmation enhances message processing (Harasty, Petty, & Priester, 1996).[4]

Heuristic/Systematic Model   Like the ELM, the heuristic/systematic model of persuasion (HSM) considers multiple processes of persuasion. Importantly, the HSM identified a unique peripheral persuasion process. Specifically,

Chaiken (1980, 1987; Chaiken et al., 1989) proposed that in contrast to "systematic" (or central route) processes, many source, message, and other cues are evaluated by means of simple cognitive heuristics that people have learned on the basis of past experience and observation. Unlike attributional inferences which can be novel and generated on-line, the use of heuristics was proposed to be dependent on their availability and accessibility in memory.

According to the HSM, the likelihood of systematic processing increases whenever confidence in one's attitude drops below the desired level of confidence (the "sufficiency threshold"). Whenever actual and desired confidence are equal, heuristic processing is more likely. For example, because of prior personal experience, people could base acceptance of a message on the expertise of the message source by retrieving the heuristic "experts are usually correct" (Chaiken, 1980; Petty, Cacioppo, & Goldman, 1981). Heuristics that are available in memory and accessible (activated from memory) are the most likely to be used. Furthermore, the HSM holds that as the motivation and ability to process increase, there is also an increased likelihood of heuristic processing. This is because any factor that increases the importance of assessing the validity of support for a position should also increase the salience (accessibility) of heuristics relevant to accomplishing that goal (Chaiken et al., 1989, p. 225). Although this enhancement of heuristic processing is hypothesized to occur, the increased scrutiny of the merits of the attitude object might provide information that contradicts accessible heuristics, and thus might attenuate the impact of heuristic cues (attenuation effect). As long as the two processing modes do not yield conflicting reactions, however, increases in the importance of assessing attitude validity should increase the impact of heuristics within this model (additivity effect).

The expanded HSM also deals with biased processing (Chaiken et al., 1989). According to this model, bias can occur in at least two ways. First, Chaiken et al. argue that in some circumstances, heuristic processing can bias systematic processing (e.g., accessing the heuristic that "experts are correct" can lead people to engage in favorable elaboration of a message). Second, in addition to postulating an "accuracy motive" that produces relatively objective information processing, two other motives (defense and impression management) operate to produce biased processing either through biasing systematic or heuristic processing. When defense motives are operating, for example, people are motivated to defend their existing attitudes but can do so either by biased systematic processing or selectively using heuristics (Chaiken, Wood, & Eagly, 1996).

Although considerable research supports the general predictions of the HSM (and typically the ELM as well), little research has addressed the defining feature of the HSM—the notion that people have learned and stored in memory various persuasion heuristics that are used to evaluate a message.

Some research has varied the accessibility (Roskos-Ewoldsen & Fazio, 1992) or vividness (Pallak, 1983) of the peripheral cues in a message—and presumably the accessibility of the associated heuristics—yet, relatively little evidence has been collected relating to the accessibility of the heuristics themselves. In perhaps the most pertinent research, Chaiken (1987) had people memorize eight phrases relevant to the length implies strength heuristic (e.g., "the more the merrier") or eight irrelevant phases. Memorizing the relevant phrases led to greater impact of a source claiming to have ten versus two reasons than memorizing the irrelevant phrases. This effect occurred only for people classified as low in need for cognition (Cacioppo & Petty, 1982) who would presumably be most likely to rely on a low-effort heuristic strategy. Cialdini (1987) analyzed several other heuristics that might be effective in influencing behavior (see Cialdini & Trost, 1998, in this *Handbook*). For example, although people might reason that the more people endorsing an object, the better it is, they can also reason that the object is better if relatively few rather than many are available (i.e., the "scarcity heuristic;" see Brock, 1968). Although many such cues have been shown to influence attitudes (mostly when the elaboration likelihood is low), it has not been clearly demonstrated that such cues operate primarily through stored heuristics rather than one of the other peripheral processes. Nevertheless, the heuristic notion has itself served as a very useful heuristic for guiding interesting persuasion research.

Although the HSM and ELM share many features (e.g., attitude change can result from both high- and low-effort mental processes which can be relatively objective or biased), a number of differences do exist regarding the impact of cues in high-thought situations and mechanisms hypothesized to account for biased processing outcomes. Recall that in the ELM, increased elaboration likelihood can lead to salient cues being evaluated for strength just as the message arguments are evaluated (Petty, 1994). Thus, if a potential cue such as an attractive source is scrutinized and found lacking (e.g., "attractiveness of the source is not a good reason to support the advocacy," or "it is biasing to go along just because the source is attractive"), then the attractive source could either have little impact on attitudes or even reduce persuasion (e.g., if an overcorrection for the perceived bias induced by the source occurs; Petty et al., in press; see Wegener & Petty, 1997). On the other hand, if source attractiveness is deemed relevant and informative when scrutinized, it would add to the impact of the other information. Note that in the ELM, this additive impact is not a result of a low-effort heuristic adding to the impact of high-effort central/systematic processing (cf., Maheswaran & Chaiken, 1991), but is due to the fact that the cue/heuristic is effortfully scrutinized as a potential argument along with all other information available.

Consider the notion of biased processing in the expanded HSM. In general, the idea that heuristic processing can bias systematic processing is similar to the ELM multiple roles notion (Petty & Cacioppo, 1986a) that variables that serve a cue (or heuristic) function when the elaboration likelihood is low, can bias information processing when the elaboration likelihood is high (though, in the ELM, the variable producing a bias need not do so by invoking a heuristic; e.g., positive mood can make positive thoughts more likely to come to mind even if a mood heuristic is not invoked). As noted previously, the ELM holds that objective processing occurs when people have no a priori position to favor and that motivated biased processing (via either the central or the peripheral route) can be produced when people prefer one position over another. Importantly, in the ELM, people can come to prefer one position over another for a variety of motivational reasons (e.g., consistency, reactance, self-esteem, etc.). Of most interest, accuracy motives can also result in biased processing if people are highly confident that their current view is correct and are motivated to defend it because of its presumed validity. If people are confident that their attitudes are correct, any increase in the motivation to be accurate would presumably increase motivation to defend their attitudes. Conversely, reducing the need to be accurate would free people to go along with others and abandon their presumably accurate views. Consider another way in which accuracy motives can produce biased processing. If the elaboration likelihood is high and people are confronted with an ambiguous argument, people may be more likely to elaborate it in a way that is favorable to the advocacy if the source is perceived to be an expert than if the source is not (Chaiken & Maheswaran, 1994). This favorable interpretation of the arguments could be motivated by wanting to have the most accurate interpretation of the evidence and the assumption that an expert source is more likely to hold accurate opinions than a nonexpert. Alternatively, it might be that people prefer to identify with the position of experts for reasons of self-esteem maintenance, or because of aversive feelings of imbalance or confusion if experts are wrong, and thus these motives rather than accuracy would account for the biased processing. In any case, within the ELM framework, accuracy motivation per se can bring about biased outcomes that look "defensive," and additional motivations other than defense or impression management can be responsible for biased outcomes (in addition to the ability factors discussed earlier).

Other Peripheral Processes

Mere Exposure   When objects are presented to an individual on repeated occasions, this mere exposure is capable of making the person's attitude toward the objects more positive (see Zajonc & Markus, 1982). An early explanation of the mere exposure effect was provided by Titchener (1910), who proposed that familiar objects led people to

experience a "glow of warmth, a sense of ownership, a feeling of intimacy" (p. 411). Work on this phenomenon has shown that simple repetition of objects can lead to more positive evaluations even when people do not consciously recognize that the objects are familiar. For example, Kunst-Wilson and Zajonc (1980) repeatedly presented polygon images under viewing conditions that resulted in chance reports of recognition. During a later session, pairs of polygons were presented under ideal viewing conditions. In each pair, one shape had been seen in the earlier session, but the other was new. When asked which shape they liked better and which one they had seen before, research participants were unable to recognize beyond chance which polygon was new and which was old, but they showed a signficant preference for the "old" shapes.

Just because people do not consciously recognize that a stimulus was presented many times previously, does not mean that people are not aware at some level that these repeated stimuli are easier to perceive and process. This *perceptual fluency* (Bornstein, 1989; Jacoby, Kelley, Brown, & Jasechko, 1989) might be attributed to or confused with the favorability of the stimulus, but might also be attributed to other stimulus dimensions (e.g., brightness, darkness, etc.), and account for why repeated exposure produces more extreme judgments of a variety of stimulus-relevant dimensions (Mandler, Nakamura, & Shebo Van Zandt, 1987). In fact, if people attribute a sense of familarity to the experimental procedure itself, the mere exposure effect is weakened (Bornstein & D'Agostino, 1994). Just as repeated *exposure* can influence a variety of judgments, Downing, Judd, and Brauer (1992) found that repeated *expression* of either evaluative or nonevaluative (i.e., color) responses can lead to more extreme judgments on the evaluative or nonevaluative dimensions respectively. Downing et al. (1992) reasoned that this occurred because of a link between the response and the object becoming stronger over repeated expressions.

Mere exposure effects (especially on the favorability dimension) have been shown using a variety of stimuli such as tones, nonsense syllables, Chinese ideographs, photographs of new faces, and foreign words (e.g., see Bornstein, 1989, for a review). It is important to note that all of these stimuli tend to be low in prior experience and meaning to the people receiving them and thus are relatively unlikely to elicit spontaneous elaboration. In fact, mere exposure appears to be especially successful in influencing attitudes when conscious processing of a repeated stimulus is minimal (see Harrison, 1977) or impossible (e.g., when the stimulis is presented subliminally, Bornstein & D'Agostino, 1992). Manipulations that increase thinking, such as evaluation apprehension, reduce mere exposure effects (Kruglanski, Freund, & Bar-Tal, 1996; for additional discussion, see Zajonc, 1998, in this *Handbook*).

When more meaningful stimuli are presented, the effect of such exposures is quite different from the mere exposure effect. That is, increased exposures of more meaningful stimuli enhance the dominant cognitive response to the stimuli (Brickman, Redfield, Harrison, & Crandall, 1971). Thus, attitudes toward negative words (e.g., "hate") and toward weak message arguments actually become more *unfavorable* with increased exposures, but attitudes toward positive words (e.g., "love") and toward strong arguments become more *favorable,* at least until the point of tedium (e.g., Cacioppo & Petty, 1989; Grush, 1976). Interestingly, some research has suggested that the initial likability of stimuli can moderate mere exposure effects even when simple stimuli are presented subliminally. Specifically, Klinger and Greenwald (1994) divided pictures of octagons into those that were initially liked and disliked and presented these to participants under conditions unfavorable to conscious recognition. Increased exposures increased preference for the initially liked octagons, but decreased preference for the initially disliked octagons. Consistent with the perceptual fluency idea noted earlier, they argue that subliminal mere exposure produces a feeling of familiarity (based largely on perceptual features of the stimulus) that can be misattributed to liking, disliking, or other attributes depending on the context at the time of judgment (see also Jacoby et al., 1989; Mandler et al., 1987).

Balance   Although cognitive imbalance can lead to effortful (though potentially biased) scrutiny of attitude-relevant information (Festinger, 1957), one can also conceive of less effortful means of addressing imbalance. For example, consider the relations among a person, his or her boss, and an object (the three of which make up a person-other-object triad). According to Heider (1958), balance occurs when people agree with people they like (or with whom they are strongly associated) or when people disagree with people they dislike (or are strongly dissociated). An imbalanced triad in which a person has a unit relationship with the other person (e.g., his or her boss), the person dislikes an object (e.g., a painting), but the boss likes the object, is likely to put the person in an uncomfortable state (see Heider, 1958). Because the unit relationship is likely difficult to change, the person might find that the easiest way to balance this triad is to change his or her view of the painting (see Rosenberg & Abelson, 1960). This can be done simply because it feels "harmonious" and not because the person has effortfully reconsidered the merits of the painting (as dissonance theory might suggest). In addition to preferences for "balanced" relations among entities and attitudes, people have also been shown to prefer "attraction" (i.e., positive sentiments between the two people in a triad) and "agreement" relations (i.e., when the two people agree in their attitudes toward the object regardless of their sentiments toward each other; see Miller & Norman, 1976). Importantly, such positivity preferences and any changes in attitudes that they might bring about could take place with little or no consideration of what the person perceives to be the central merits of the attitude object. One could also generate new relations among the elements in a triad by relating pairs of the elements to new elements, but such processes might also take place without consideration of the central merits of the attitude objects involved in the triad (see Insko, 1984; Newcomb, 1968, for further discussions).

Summary   Thus, a variety of attitude change processes have been discussed over the years, and these processes can generally be classified according to the overall mental effort necessary for them to affect attitudes and according to the role (or lack thereof) of scrutiny of the central merits of the attitude object (see Petty & Cacioppo, 1981). Although many of these processes were initially introduced as global models of attitude change, contemporary multi-process models emphasize the conditions under which the high- and low-effort processes are most likely to occur. In the following sections, the multiple role feature of the ELM is used to organize and review empirical work on persuasion variables. Incorporating traditional classifications of these variables, the presentation is organized into source, message, recipient, and context categories.

PERSUASION VARIABLES

From Lasswell's (1948) well-known question—Who says what to whom with what effect?—to Hovland et al.'s (1953) classic *Communication and Persuasion* volume, to McGuire's (1969, 1985) communication/persuasion matrix model (described earlier), variables having an impact on attitude change have traditionally been organized into source, message, recipient, and context categories. This organization scheme is not very conceptual, is to some extent arbitrary (e.g., mood can be considered a "recipient" variable when measured, but a "context" variable when manipulated), and breaks down as an organizational scheme when categories of variables interact (e.g., source × message). Nonetheless, this organization has provided a handy reference for those interested in selecting variables for applications of persuasion theory for over half a century. Thus, in this section an overview and updating of some of the most researched variables falling into these traditional categories is presented. First, however, it is useful to consider, in a general way at least, the variety of processes by which any given variable might have its impact on persuasion.

The earliest research on source, message, recipient, and context variables tended to assume that the particular variable under study (e.g., source credibility) had a unidirectional effect on attitude change (e.g., increasing credibility increased persuasion) and produced this effect by a particular process (e.g., increasing credibility fostered learning of the message arguments). Decades of research on attitude change clearly indicated that (unfortunately) these simple assumptions were untenable (Petty, 1997). The accumulated research indicated that even simple and seemingly obvious variables like source credibility were sometimes associated with increased influence (Kelman & Hovland, 1953) and sometimes with decreased influence (Sternthal, Dholakia, & Leavitt, 1978). One solution to this complexity was to suggest that each outcome was caused by a different psychological process. However, research on many variables indicated that the same process could sometimes lead to opposite outcomes, and the same outcome could be caused by different processes (Petty & Cacioppo, 1986a).

Thus, in order to understand source, message, recipient, and contextual variables, it is necessary to relate them to the underlying processes of persuasion. In the preceding sections of this chapter, processes that might be responsible for changes in attitudes when the mental effort allocated was particularly high or low were discussed. In addition, the factors of motivation and ability that determine whether the persuasion situation is characterized by high or low amounts of mental effort were highlighted. After reviewing the multiple processes by which variables can have an impact on attitude change, the existing literature on the effects of source, message, recipient, and context variables is examined, and the observed effects are related, when possible, to the multiple roles possible for persuasion variables.

Multiple Roles for Persuasion Variables

As previously noted, across situations, people, and objects, there are differences in the extent to which people are willing and able to put a high level of effort into arriving at their evaluations. To the extent that people are both motivated and able to put effort into forming or changing their views of an object, they are more likely to carefully scrutinize all information relevant to that object (i.e., they are likely to effortfully assess the "central merits" of the object in order to determine the extent to which the object is good or bad; see Petty & Cacioppo, 1979b, 1986a). Thus, when motivation and ability are high, one way for a variable to influence judgments is for it to be treated as an argument— a piece of information relevant to determining the merit of the object or issue. For example, if one wishes to assess the extent to which it would be good or bad to hire a particular person as a model for a cosmetic product, then the appearance of that person is likely a central dimension to be used in that assessment. Therefore, in such a case, variations in the attractiveness of the person could influence evaluations through effortful consideration of the person's attractiveness (along with considerations of all other information relevant to determining merit such as past modeling experience and so forth).[5]

As discussed earlier, another way for a variable to influence judgments when motivation and ability are high is to bias the processing of attitude-relevant information. That is, if multiple interpretations of information are possible, a variable might make one interpretation more likely than other equally plausible interpretations.[6] For example, it has been repeatedly shown that people assume that attractive people possess other positive traits (e.g., Cooper, 1981; Thorndike, 1920). This halo effect could bias processing of information from an attractive source by making positive interpretations of ambiguous information more likely than if the source were not attractive. In sum, when motivation and ability to process attitude-relevant information are high, variables can affect judgments by serving as arguments and/or by biasing interpretations of attitude-relevant information (especially when the information is ambiguous).

For some situations, people, or objects, however, either motivation or ability to process attitude-relevant information is lacking. When this is the case, people are more likely to use some kind of shortcut for determining what a reasonable view of the object might be (e.g., relying on one's first impression rather than scrutinizing all the information). That is, people low in motivation or ability are likely to form or change their views of the object on the basis of some factor that allows them to do so without engaging in the cognitive work needed to assess fully the central merits of the target object (e.g., Chaiken, 1980; Petty, Cacioppo, & Goldman, 1981). Thus, when either motivation or ability to process information is lacking, a variable can impact judgments if that variable can influence attitudes by one of the relatively low-effort peripheral route processes that were described previously. People are sometimes aware of the operation of these low-effort processes, and sometimes they are not. In either case, they arrive at a judgment of the object with relatively little mental effort expended.

Finally, some variables can affect attitudes by influencing one's motivation or ability to think carefully about judgment-relevant information. Of course, the likelihood of any given variable influencing the amount of scrutiny is constrained by all of the background variables also affecting the baseline level of scrutiny. If the baseline likelihood of elaboration is already quite low (e.g., because distraction is at a high level, Kiesler & Mathog, 1968; Petty et al., 1976) or quite high (e.g., because the attitude object is very important or personally relevant, Leippe & Elkin, 1987; Petty & Cacioppo, 1979b; or because the people receiving attitude-relevant information are very high in need for cognition, Cacioppo et al., 1983), then impact of a variable on attitudes is most likely to occur through the low- or high-elaboration roles outlined earlier. If background variables do not constrain elaboration to be particularly high or low, and especially if a person is not sure whether or not effortful scrutiny of information about the target is merited, however, then the variable might affect attitudes by helping to determine the level of thought given to the merits of the attitude object.

In sum, according to the ELM, variables can influence judgments (1) by serving as arguments relevant to determining the merits of an object or position, (2) by biasing processing of attitude-relevant information (both of which are most likely when motivation and ability to scrutinize attitude-relevant information are high), (3) by serving as a peripheral cue (when motivation or ability is low), and (4) by itself affecting the level of scrutiny given to attitude-relevant information (when elaboration likelihood is not constrained by other factors to be particularly high or low). Therefore, the ELM is a model of moderated mediation (see Petty, Wegener, Fabrigar, Priester, & Cacioppo, 1993, for further discussion). It is important to note, however, that the ELM is not aimed at predicting how every persuasion variable influences persuasion at each level of elaboration likelihood. Rather, the ELM provides an organizing framework that specifies which classes of processes operate under which levels of elaboration. Theoretical and empirical complements to the ELM framework specify the particular effects of most variables (e.g., whether and when positive moods enhance versus reduce processing of persuasive messages; e.g., Wegener & Petty, 1996).

In the following sections, the ELM notion of multiple roles for variables across the elaboration continuum is used to organize the work done on four broad classes of variables (i.e., source, message, recipient, and context). Each section begins with a brief definition, and then the kinds of effects and general principles that have been found within each class of variables are described.

Source Variables

Source variables refer to aspects of the person(s) or group(s) presenting the persuasive appeal. At times, the identity of a source might be made very explicit (e.g., when a candidate makes a speech on behalf of his or her candidacy), but at other times, the source is merely implied (e.g., when an unpictured narrator announces a new product, presumably on behalf of the company producing that product). Traditionally, source effects have been organized according to a taxonomy introduced by Kelman (1958) which separated source factors into effects of credibility, attractiveness, and power (see also McGuire, 1969). Kelman (1958) discussed credibility effects as due to *internalization,* which entailed acceptance of information and integration of that information into one's existing cognitive system, attractiveness effects as due to *identification,* which relied on salience of one's bond to or relationship with the message source, and power effects as due to *compliance,* which would occur only as long as the source maintained control over potential rewards and punishments. Although these classifications and principles have proven quite useful, recent research suggests, for instance, that credibility can also influence attitudes when relatively

little information scrutiny or internalization takes place, and that attractiveness has effects even when no bond or relationship between source and message recipient is possible. An alternative framework for organizing source effects focuses on the effects of sources across levels of elaboration likelihood, with an eye toward the multiple roles that sources can play in persuasion settings. A variety of characteristics related to source credibility, attractiveness, and power has been investigated.

Credibility   In one of the earliest investigations of source credibility, Hovland and Weiss (1951) presented students with a message on one of four topics and then told them the source of the message (with the source either being high or low in credibility). Although Hovland and Weiss (1951) focused on the overall effect of source credibility (collapsed across messages), the credibility effect was more pronounced for the two topics that were less likely to directly impact students (e.g., who to blame for a steel shortage) than for the two topics more likely to be relevant to students (e.g., will television decrease the number of movie theaters in operation). Thus, even early studies of source credibility provided some indications that variables such as source credibility might not operate in the same way (or to the same extent) in all circumstances. Although many studies of source credibility have used sources that vary in both knowledge (expertise) and presumed honesty (trustworthiness; e.g., Kelman & Hovland, 1953), a variety of studies have more directly studied the impact of differences in expertise or trustworthiness per se (see Petty & Cacioppo, 1981).

Expertise   Expertise generally refers to a source's presumed knowledge and ability to provide accurate information. Perhaps the most prevalent characterization of source expertise effects is as a peripheral cue. Consistent with the peripheral cue notion, highly expert sources have led to more persuasion than inexpert sources to a greater extent when a topic is presented as low rather than high in personal relevance (e.g., Petty, Cacioppo, & Goldman, 1981; Rhine & Severance, 1970). Similarly, source expertise effects have been moderated by other variables thought to influence the amount of scrutiny given to persuasive messages. For example, source expertise has a greater impact when distraction is high rather than low (e.g., Kiesler & Mathog, 1968), when topic relevant knowledge is low rather than high (Wood & Kallgren, 1988), and when messages are externally paced (i.e., taped) rather than self-paced (i.e., written; e.g., Andreoli & Worchel, 1978).

Although less commonly studied, source expertise has also been shown to relate to the amount of scrutiny given to persuasive messages when the elaboration likelihood is not constrained at a high or low level. Specifically, Heesacker, Petty, and Cacioppo (1983) found that field-dependent message recipients (see Witkin, Goodenough, & Oltman, 1979) engaged in greater message scrutiny (i.e., were more persuaded by strong than by weak arguments) when the message was presented by an expert rather than inexpert source. DeBono and Harnish (1988) found that individuals low in self-monitoring (Snyder, 1974) processed messages to a greater extent when they were presented by an expert rather than an attractive source (see additional discussion in recipient variable section). Moore, Hausknecht, and Thamodaran (1986) established three levels of elaboration likelihood by presenting an advertisement at a fast, moderately fast, or normal speech rate and manipulated source expertise and argument quality. When the ad was presented rapidly, recipients were influenced by source expertise, but not the quality of the arguments (peripheral cue effect). When the ad was presented at a normal pace, the impact of argument quality was increased and the source expertise effect decreased compared to the rapid pace. These effects replicate other research on the tradeoff between cue and argument effects across the elaboration continuum. Of greatest interest, when the ad was presented at a moderately fast pace such that processing was possible but challenging, expertise interacted with argument quality such that the message received greater scrutiny when presented by an expert than a nonexpert source.

Finally, the potential biasing impact of source expertise under high elaboration conditions was demonstrated by Chaiken and Maheswaran (1994). First, they showed that source expertise had a greater impact on attitudes when unambiguous strong or weak arguments were presented on an unimportant topic rather than an important topic (similar to Petty, Cacioppo, & Goldman, 1981). More importantly, Chaiken and Maheswaran (1994) also showed that an expert source was more persuasive than an inexpert source under both high and low importance conditions when the arguments were ambiguous (i.e., not clearly strong or weak). When the ambiguous arguments were presented on an important topic, expertise significantly affected the valence of message-relevant thinking (i.e., expertise biased message processing), but when the topic was unimportant, expertise did not affect message-relevant thoughts (i.e., expertise acted as a persuasion cue).

Trustworthiness Credible sources are not only knowledgeable (i.e., expert) and able to be accurate about the topic, but are also perceived as trustworthy (i.e., are motivated to tell the truth; see Hass, 1981; Petty & Cacioppo, 1981). In fact, trustworthiness per se has been shown to have effects on overall persuasion and on processing of persuasive messages. For example, as noted earlier, Eagly and her colleagues found that sources regarded as trustworthy or sincere (because of presenting a point of view that disagreed with the views of a message audience) were more persuasive than sources perceived as untrustworthy (e.g., Eagly, Wood, & Chaiken, 1978; Mills & Jellison, 1967). Trustworthiness is a clear cue to validity and if the message does not warrant processing for other reasons, it can simply

be accepted if the source is presumed to be knowledgeable and trustworthy. Priester and Petty (1995) found that people who do not enjoy thinking were especially likely to accept a message from a trustworthy source without scrutiny. When the source was untrustworthy (but knowledgeable), however, people low in need for cognition (Cacioppo & Petty, 1982) engaged in as much message processing as those high in need for cognition (because the untrustworthy character of the source left them uncertain whether or not the position of the message held merit or not).

Attractiveness/Likableness Although some manipulations of "attractiveness" have varied physical characteristics of the source (e.g., Snyder & Rothbart, 1971), many manipulations of this construct have also incorporated other likable versus dislikable features of the source (e.g., Petty et al., 1983; Zimbardo et al., 1965). In addition, when physical characteristics have been manipulated, the effects of physical attractiveness have appeared to be mediated by effects on liking of the communicator (see Chaiken, 1986).

As with other source characteristics, attractiveness or likableness has been studied primarily in relation to its role as a peripheral cue (see Chaiken, 1987; Cialdini 1987). Consistent with the cue notion, effects of source attractiveness/likableness have been greater when elaboration likelihood is low rather than high. That is, source attractiveness or liking has been observed to exert a greater impact when relevance of the topic is low rather than high (e.g., Chaiken, 1980; Petty et al., 1983), when attitude-relevant knowledge is low rather than high (e.g., Wood & Kallgren, 1988), and when messages are externally paced on audio- or videotapes rather than self-paced and written (e.g., Chaiken & Eagly, 1983). In each of these experiments, arguments that were unambiguously strong or weak have been used, but if ambiguous arguments had been used, one might also have found evidence of biased processing when elaboration was high.

In addition, the attractiveness of the source has been shown to influence the amount of message scrutiny that takes pace when elaboration likelihood is moderate or ambiguous. For example, Puckett, Petty, Cacioppo, and Fisher (1983) presented college students with a message advocating comprehensive exams as a graduation requirement, but the time frame for any consideration of the issue at their university was left unspecified (rendering the personal relevance ambiguous). Puckett et al. (1983) found that message recipients engaged in greater message scrutiny when the message was presented by a socially attractive rather than unattractive source. Also, DeBono and Harnish (1988) found that individuals high in self-monitoring (Snyder, 1974) processed messages to a greater extent when they were presented by an attractive rather than an expert source (see also discussion in the section on recipient variables).

In a study examining multiple roles for source attractiveness, Shavitt, Swan, Lowery, and Wänke (1994) manipulated the attractiveness of an endorser in an advertisement for a restaurant, the salient (central) features of the product (either unrelated to attractiveness—taste and aroma—or related to attractiveness—public image of the restaurant), and motivation to process the ad. When endorser attractiveness was unrelated to the central merits of the product (and the ELM would predict that any impact of attractiveness would be due to its impact as a peripheral cue), attractiveness had an impact on evaluations of the product under low but not high motivation (and had little impact on thoughts about the product). However, when endorser attractiveness was related to the central merits of the product (and thus could itself act as an argument), the same variation in attractiveness influenced evaluations of the product under high motivation (and under high motivation, influenced the favorability of cognitive responses to the ad).

Power Power of the source over a message recipient has been analyzed in terms of the extent to which the source is perceived as having control over positive or negative sanctions and has the ability to monitor whether or not the recipient accepts the source's position or not (see McGuire, 1969). These aspects of power have been shown to affect the persuasiveness of sources (with powerful sources persuading others more than weak sources; e.g., Festinger & Thibaut, 1951; Raven & French, 1958).[7] Yet, little work has investigated the information processing consequences of message presentation by a powerful versus weak source. In some instances, change to powerful sources undoubtedly reflects mere compliance rather than a true expression of opinion (Kelman, 1958). However, it is possible that as long as the power of the source is not obviously coercive, powerful sources could induce genuine change because of the operation of low-effort or high-effort processes.

One area of research with direct implications for these processes is the work on stereotyping of and by powerful people (e.g., Fiske, Morling, & Stevens, 1996). For example, when people depend on the actions of others to reap benefits, those people form more detailed, individuated impressions (as opposed to simple, category-based impressions—stereotypes) of the others (Fiske & Neuberg, 1990). This occurs not only in situations where people are mutually interdependent, but also when asymmetrical power exists over tangible rewards (i.e., one person depends on the other, but not vice versa). Interestingly, Fiske et al. (1996) suggest that persuasive messages presented by a source with power over task outcomes might receive greater scrutiny than the same messages presented by a powerless source (so long as the elaboration likelihood is not already constrained by other factors), but that messages from sources with power over evaluations might be more likely to be processed in a positively biased fashion, presumably because people want to convince themselves that the evaluator will be generous.

Each of the multiple roles outlined by the ELM would seem applicable to sources that vary in power. If processing is limited (e.g., by distraction), one might agree with a powerful source simply because it is generally good to agree with people who control one's fate. If the power of a source makes it appear more likely that a proposed policy will be enacted, it could be that people would be more likely to process information about that policy than if the source lacked the ability to institute the program. Also, if thinking is already extensive (e.g., because the topic is of great intrinsic interest or relevance), one might be disposed toward adopting interpretations of the information that agree with a powerful source. Or, if the powerful source induces reactance (e.g., from attempting overt coercion), motivation to counterargue (privately, at least) might be provoked.

Additional Source Factors Related to Credibility, Liking, and Power A number of source characteristics have been studied that appear at least somewhat related to perceptions of credibility, liking, or power. That is, sources belonging to different groups can speak at certain speeds, in certain styles, using certain forms of language, and message recipients often make inferences about the credibility, likableness, or power qualities of the source based on these variations. Thus, each of these "style" variables can potentially have an effect on message processing and persuasion at least in part because of their effects on perceptions of the source's credibility, likableness, power, or some combination of the three.

Speed of Speech Several studies of the rate (i.e., words per minute) with which speakers present their position have shown a relation between speech rate and judged credibility of the source (i.e., speaking quickly has been associated with greater perceived credibility; Miller, Maruyama, Beaber, & Valone, 1976). This effect has not been universal, however (see O'Keefe, 1990). One reason for the lack of consistency in relations between speech rate and judged credibility might be that speech rate has also been found to influence elaboration of persuasive messages. As noted earlier, Moore et al. (1986) found that rapidly presented radio ads led to a reduced effect of argument quality than when the same ads were presented at a more moderate speed. Smith and Shaffer (1995) found that persuasive effects of faster speech were mediated by perceptions of credibility when the message was low to moderate in personal relevance, but faster speech had no direct effect on credibility or persuasion for a message high in personal relevance (though faster speech rate did decrease processing of the messages when personal relevance was high—presumably because it was more difficult to process the message when it was presented quickly).[8]

Demographic Variables One can imagine a host of source demographic variables being related to perceptions of likableness, credibility, or power. Although many demographic characteristics have been studied (e.g., gender, age, and ethnicity), few of these studies have considered the possible simple versus elaborative nature of such effects. To the extent that effects of these variables occur because of inferences related to credibility, likableness, or power, demographic variables might serve the multiple roles outlined earlier for these variables.

For example, demonstrating a classic effect of source gender, Goldberg (1968) found that the scientific content of an article labeled as written by "John McKay" was rated more favorably than when the same article was attributed to "Joan McKay." Why did this occur? Depending on one's assumptions about the level of scrutiny given to the material in the article, there could be a variety of reasons (see Deaux & LaFrance, 1998, in this *Handbook*). If scrutiny was relatively low, the male or female label could have acted as a simple persuasion cue. The conceptual reason for this cue impact could be, for example, that men were viewed as more expert for the particular topic involved (i.e., science). Such a possibility would also account for situations in which an article written on a traditionally feminine topic is rated more favorably when attributed to a female rather than male author (e.g., Levenson, Burford, & Davis, 1975). If scrutiny of the information is high, the effects could be because of bias in favor of the author whose gender matches the topic or against the author whose gender mismatches the topic. It could also be, however, that gender of the source influenced how much the information in the article was processed (especially if background levels of elaboration were relatively moderate, and people were unsure whether the article merited much scrutiny). Although little empirical work has attempted to explicate the processes responsible for source gender effects, such effects might include each of the multiple roles outlined earlier. Paying greater attention to the factors determining elaboration likelihood in such studies might also help to account for the heterogeneity of effects across studies (see a recent meta-analysis by Swim, Borgida, Maruyama, & Myers, 1989).

People of different ages are also likely to be viewed as differing in expertise (or in trustworthiness, power, or likableness) on many topics, as would people of different ethnicities or socioeconomic status (e.g., consider the perceived self-interest of well-to-do members of congress arguing on behalf of tax breaks for the wealthiest segments of society). To the extent that these inferences take place, demographic variables such as age, ethnicity, or socioeconomic status of the source could assume the multiple roles taken on by the conceptual variables of credibility, likableness, or power described previously. Some work associating demographic characteristics with one or more of the multiple roles has taken place. For example, early work suggested a cue effect for source race (e.g., Whittler & DiMeo, 1991), but more recent work has studied race as it relates to processing of a persuasive message. White and

Harkins (1994) found that Caucasian message recipients process information presented by an African American source more than when the same information was presented by a Caucasian source. According to White and Harkins, this occurred because message recipients held a negative attitude toward the African American social group, but did not want to appear racist (see also Fazio, Jackson, Dunton, & Williams, 1995; Gaertner & Dovidio, 1986). Consistent with this notion, White and Harkins (1994) also found more extensive processing of messages presented by a member of another group toward which message recipients held a negative attitude (i.e., Hispanics) than for messages presented by sources from other equally novel groups toward which message recipients were not as negative (i.e., Asians and Native Americans). The multiple roles of source race and other demographic variables should receive attention in the future.

Majority/Minority Status   Like early work on many persuasion variables, initial studies of majority/minority source status tended to ask questions such as whether majorities or minorities had greater influence (e.g., Asch, 1956; Moscovici, Lage, & Naffrechoux, 1969). Over the years, the primary research question has changed to whether majorities and minorities produce influence through the same or different persuasion processes (Moscovici, 1980; Nemeth, 1986). It has also been acknowledged recently that the majority/minority status of a source can have various effects depending on the motivational and cognitive factors present (see Kruglanski & Mackie, 1990; Mugny & Perez, 1991; and Wood, Lundgren, Ouellette, Busceme, & Blackstone, 1994; for reviews of minority influence work).

Within the multiple roles perspective, when the elaboration likelihood is low, majority/minority source status is most likely to serve as a simple cue. Thus, whether a position is endorsed by a majority or a minority of others can provide message recipients with a simple decision rule as to whether they should agree with the message especially when people have no special interest or knowledge about the issue, or no message is even presented (Giner-Sorolla & Chaiken, 1997). These effects are presumably due to inferences about the presumed validity of the position or assumptions about the credibility, likableness, or power of the source associated with the majority or minority view. Source perceptions do not necessarily covary directly with majority/minority status (Kruglanski & Mackie, 1990), however. For example, consistency in a source's behavior can increase attributions of competence (e.g., Moscovici & Neve, 1973) or can increase attributions of rigidity (e.g., Levine, Saxe, & Harris, 1976; see Maass & Clark, 1984).

When people are unsure whether they should carefully scrutinize the message or not, majority/minority status can determine the amount of message scrutiny. Interestingly, some researchers have concluded that majority sources foster greater elaboration, but others have concluded that minority sources foster greater elaboration. For example, Mackie (1987) found that message recipients tended to recall more majority than minority arguments, and also generated more favorable cognitive responses to the majority message. Based on these findings, she concluded that majority sources induce greater message processing that is biased in a favorable direction. However, other researchers concluded that minorities foster higher levels of elaboration (e.g., Maass & Clark, 1983). More recent research has found that either majorities or minorities can induce greater message scrutiny depending upon other factors in the persuasion situation. For example, Baker and Petty (1994) found that people engaged in greater scrutiny of a counterattitudinal message when it was portrayed as the majority position, but more scrutiny of a proattitudinal message when it was portrayed as the minority position. They reasoned that if people receive a counterattitudinal message from a majority source, this implies that the message recipient is in the minority which can be surprising and perhaps even threatening, making scrutiny of what the majority has to say more likely. If a recipient encounters a proattitudinal message, however, the same reasoning predicts greater processing when the source is a minority because a proattitudinal message from a minority implies that the message recipient is also in the minority (which can be surprising or threatening). In a somewhat similar study, Giner-Sorolla and Chaiken (1997) presented students with poll results that either supported or opposed their recently stated vested interests (rather than their attitudes per se). In this study, enhanced message processing was evident when the poll was incongruent with students' vested interests over when the pool was congenial. Although the students did not report being surprised by the poll, they may well have been threatened by it.

Finally, when the motivation and ability to process an incoming message are high, majority/minority status should impact persuasion primarily by influencing the nature of thoughts that come to mind. For example, Mackie (1987) noted that in her research, biased processing might have produced the relatively greater proportion of positive cognitive responses generated for messages from the majority source. Trost, Maass, and Kenrick (1992) found that recipients for whom the message was highly relevant derogated the minority message more than the majority communication. Thus, biased information processing of majority and minority sources might be found primarily under conditions that foster elaboration.

Similarity to Receiver   A great deal of work suggests that people like other people with whom they share similar attitudes (e.g., Byrne & Griffitt, 1966) or ideology (Newcomb, 1956) and dislike those with whom they disagree (e.g., Rosenbaum, 1986). This source-receiver similarity has also been shown to increase persuasion (e.g., Brock, 1965).

Sometimes there are benefits of dissimilarity, however. For example, although agreement from similar sources induces greater confidence in one's judgment when the issue is perceived to be a subjective one, agreement with dissimilar sources induces greater confidence when the issue is perceived as objective (Goethals & Nelson, 1973; see also Crano & Hannula-Bral, 1994). Unfortunately, little work has investigated the mechanisms by which persuasive effects of similarity might occur. As with the other source variables, similarity could produce attitude change by acting as a simple persuasion cue when elaboration is low, by biasing processing when elaboration is high, or by affecting the amount of processing when background levels of elaboration likelihood are relatively moderate.

An exception to this dearth of process-level investigation relates to the effects of messages presented by an in-group versus out-group source (i.e., by a person who is similar to the message recipient by virtue of belonging to the same group as the recipient or is dissimilar by belonging to a different group). In one study, Mackie, Worth, and Asuncion (1990) presented University of California–Santa Barbara research participants with strong or weak messages on either a topic presumably irrelevant to them (i.e., acid raid in the northeast) or presumably relevant (i.e., oil drilling off the southwest coast of the United States). The messages were attributed to either a UCSB student (i.e., an in-group member) or to a student of the University of New Hampshire (i.e., an out-group member). When people received the message on the irrelevant topic, the in-group source was more persuasive than the out-group source, regardless of the quality of the arguments presented. That is, when the message was low in relevance, group membership of the source acted as a simple persuasion cue. When the message was on the more relevant topic, however, message recipients processed the messages presented by the in-group source more than when the same messages were presented by the out-group source. Thus, for the more group-relevant message, similarity based on group membership influenced the amount of processing of the persuasive messages (see Fleming & Petty, in press, for a review).[9]

Number of Sources   In addition to particular characteristics of sources, some research attention has been given to the sheer number of sources who present the arguments in a persuasive message. Although early work focused on conformity pressures (e.g., Asch, 1951) or on agreement based on a desire to appear correct (see Jellison & Arkin, 1977), additional evidence supports the view that multiple sources can influence scrutiny of message arguments. Harkins and Petty (1981a) hypothesized that when each argument in a message is presented by a different source, elaboration of the message content is enhanced (see also Moore & Reardon, 1987). In addition, this effect occurs if reception of the message is the person's only task, but is eliminated if recipients are distracted by a secondary task (e.g., Harkins & Petty, 1981b).

Why do people process information from multiple sources more than when the same information is presented by one source? It appears that this effect is due to perceptions that the sources represent independent perspectives (and thus, the converging view is more worthy of consideration). Evidence consistent with this notion was obtained by showing that the usual multiple source processing effect is attenuated when the sources are characterized as a committee that worked together to generate the arguments (Harkins & Petty, 1987). Importantly, this method of undermining the processing of a message presented by multiple sources is only effective if it is introduced before rather than after message presentation. Also, if multiple sources are described as being similar rather than dissimilar in background, the multiple source effect is reduced (Harkins & Petty, 1987).

These studies have been conducted without specifying the relevance of the communication for message recipients. If personal relevance of the topic were extremely low (or elaboration likelihood were constrained to be low by some factor such as distraction), the mere number of sources could influence persuasion by a low-effort peripheral process. It is also conceivable that the number of sources could bias the thoughts that people have when elaboration likelihood is high (especially for message recipients who care about agreeing with significant others, i.e., high self-monitors).

Message Variables

Message variables refer to aspects of the communication itself. At a minimal level, a persuasion situation contains some topic (e.g., capital punishment) or attitude object (e.g., ice cream) that is the focus of the influence attempt. Usually, the message has many more features, but sometimes the attitude object alone serves as the "message" when it is simply repeated (e.g., Zajonc, 1968) as described in our previous discussion of mere exposure effects. In addition to presenting the topic of the message, the message usually takes a particular position, includes some substantive reasons supporting the position taken, and can be organized in a variety of ways.

Message Topic, Position, and Style

Issue-Relevance/Importance   Perhaps the most investigated aspect of the message topic is its importance or relevance to the message recipient. This feature of a message has been referred to as issue-involvement (e.g., Zimbardo, 1960), personal involvement (Thomsen et al., 1995), personal and self-relevance (Petty, Cacioppo, & Haugtvedt, 1992), vested interest (Crano, 1995), attitude importance

(e.g., Boninger, Krosnick, Berent, & Fabrigar, 1995), and ego-involvement (Sherif, Sherif, & Nebergall, 1965). Although the terms are different, the basic notion is that there are some issues that people care about more than others. The primary determinant of how much a person cares about some issue is the extent to which the issue is relevant to some aspect of oneself (i.e., one's beliefs, possessions, values, groups, etc., Boninger et al., 1995; Petty et al., 1992). In this regard, issue importance can be considered a "recipient" variable, but because the influence agent can do things to the message to enhance its perceived personal relevance (e.g., using personal rather than impersonal pronouns; Burnkrant & Unnava, 1989), it is discussed here.

Early analyses of the relevance or importance of the topic were based on the social judgment theory notion that one's attitude served as a stronger judgmental anchor when the topic was ego-involving (Sherif et al., 1965). This meant that an involving *proattitudinal* message would be seen as closer to one's own position than an uninvolving one (i.e., involvement led to greater assimilation) and an involving *counterattitudinal* message would be seen as further away from one's own position than an uninvolving one (i.e., involvement led to greater contrast). According to social judgment theory, both judgmental distortions should reduce the likelihood of attitude change. This is because discrepancy was thought to foster attitude change for agreeable communications (and perceptions of discrepancy are decreased with assimilation) but discrepancy inhibited change for disagreeable communications (and discrepancy was perceived as greater with greater contrast; see subsequent discussion of message discrepancy).

In contrast to this view, Petty and Cacioppo (1979b) postulated that increased personal relevance or importance would enhance thinking about the communication which would increase persuasion if the arguments were strong, but decrease persuasion if the arguments were weak. In a meta-analytic review of research on issue-involvement, Johnson and Eagly (1989) concluded that this prediction was supported, but with qualifications. Specifically, they argued that when studies examined whether the issue concerned an important consequence for an individual or not ("outcome-relevant involvement"), involvement interacted with argument quality as predicted. However, when studies examined whether the issue concerned participants' cherished beliefs or not ("value-relevant involvement") two effects were observed. In addition to the interaction of involvement with argument quality, a main effect of involvement was observed such that increasing involvement led to less persuasion as predicted by social judgment theory. Petty and Cacioppo (1990) argued that because the latter studies tended to be correlational rather than experimental, involvement was likely to be confounded with a number of other variables. That is, participants classified as high in value relevance were likely to have more extreme initial attitudes, more knowledge supporting their attitudes, and so forth, than did participants who were classified as low in value relevance. Thus, the self-relevance per se would increase message processing (accounting for the interaction of involvement and argument quality), but the more polarized attitudes and greater attitude-congruent knowledge on high value-relevant issues would bias the processing in an attitude consistent direction (accounting for the main effect of involvement).

A similar argument can be made regarding recent work on attitude importance. As in the early work on social judgment theory, work on attitude importance tends to find that people are more likely to resist a message when they consider the topic to be high rather than low in importance (e.g., Zuwerink & Devine, 1996; see Boninger et al.,1995, for a review). Again, it seems likely that this resistance is not necessarily due to issue importance per se. That is, there is no reason to reject a message simply because the topic is personally important. Rather, just as in the social judgment research on ego-involvement, investigators interested in importance have measured this construct rather than manipulated it. Thus, importance is likely to be confounded with a number of other variables such as attitude extremity, knowledge, commitment, etc., and it is these constructs that could be responsible for the resistance. Consistent with this notion, when an unfamiliar issue is made more important by introducing it as likely to personally affect the message recipient, increases in objective processing of the message arguments are the most likely result (see Petty et al., 1992). That is, importance influences the extent of information processing, but it is the other variables (many of which are likely related to attitude strength) that produce both cognitive and affective biases in the ongoing processing activity (see also Wegener, Downing, Krosnick, & Petty, 1995, for discussions about manipulations and measures of this and other strength constructs).

In addition to these information processing consequences, there are other important implications of making salient a link between a position and the message recipient. For example, people tend to like things that are associated with themselves more than things that are associated with others. Thus, research on dissonance theory showed that an object tends to be seen as more valuable as soon as an individual chooses it (e.g., Brehm, 1956). In fact, objects are also seen as more valuable even if people are simply given the items and no choice is involved (Kahneman, Knetsch, & Thaler, 1991). People overvalue members of their ingroup (Tajfel, 1970) and have even shown preferences for the letters in their own names over other letters (Nuttin, 1985). Recall that one explanation for why active generation of arguments produces more persuasion than passive exposure to them is that people find their own arguments to be superior (Greenwald & Albert, 1968). This preference for things associated with the self has been called the

"ownness bias" (Perloff & Brock, 1980), the "mere ownership" effect (Nuttin, 1985), and the "instant endowment" effect (Kahneman et al., 1991). Thus, if a speaker presented a message about an object that a person just purchased, the person would presumably be especially motivated to see the merits of the object. If the object was sufficiently important, the self-linkage would presumably induce biased processing. If the object was unimportant or processing was impaired, people might simply reason that "if it's mine, it must be good." Research in which self-linkage produced greater processing rather than biased processing has tended to make salient the *potential* relevance of the object or issue to the self (e.g., you have the option of choosing this product; Petty et al., 1983) rather than the *certain* relevance (e.g., you will receive this product; see Petty & Cacioppo, 1990).

Position/Discrepancy   Perhaps the most salient initial feature of a message is whether it takes a position that the recipient generally finds to be agreeable (proattitudinal message) or disagreeable (counterattitudinal message). A number of investigators have proposed that attitude change should be an increasing function of message discrepancy (how far the message position is from one's own attitude; e.g., Anderson & Hovland, 1957; Hunter, Danes, & Cohen, 1984). Social judgment theorists (e.g., Sherif & Hovland, 1961) provided a more complex hypothesis. The prediction was that attitude change was an increasing function of discrepancy as long as the message took a position in the recipient's *latitude of acceptance* (i.e., the range of positions the person found agreeable), but was a decreasing function of discrepancy when the message took a position in the *latitude of rejection* (the range of positions the person found objectionable). Attitude change was proposed to reach a peak when the message took a position in the *latitude of noncommitment* (the range of positions between the latitudes of acceptance and rejection). Although many studies found an overall inverted-U pattern between message discrepancy and attitude change as expected by the theory (e.g., Hovland, Harvey, & Sherif, 1957)—especially when the source was of low credibility (e.g., Aronson, Turner, & Carlsmith, 1963)—careful analyses did not prove congenial to the view that recipients' latitudes moderated the effects as expected (e.g., Eagly & Telaak, 1972).

Alternatives to the social judgment theory analysis of message position have been sparse, though a few suggestions have been made. According to the ELM (Petty et al., 1992), for example, message discrepancy could serve in several roles. Specifically, when the elaboration likelihood is low, message position could serve as a simple cue. That is, agreeable sounding messages would be accepted but disagreeable sounding messages would be rejected with relatively little scrutiny. When the elaboration likelihood is moderate, the message position will determine, in part, the extent of message processing. For example, counterattitu-dinal messages (which threaten a person's views) might often receive greater scrutiny than proattitudinal messages (Cacioppo & Petty, 1979b; Edwards & Smith, 1996). When the elaboration likelihood is high, people will en-gage in negatively biased processing of counterattitudinal messages, but in positively biased processing of proattitu-dinal communications. Zanna (1993) further suggested that the bias will be greater for counter than for pro communi-cations. That is, biased processing need not be symmet-ric—people can be more biased in their assessment of mes-sages that disagree than those that agree with them.

Although the multiple roles for message position have not been examined in research, some evidence is consistent with the proposition that counterattitudinal messages re-ceive greater scrutiny than proattitudinal messages when other factors have not constrained the elaboration likeli-hood to be high or low. In one study, for example, recipi-ents generated a greater number of counterargument thoughts as the message became more counterattitudinal (Brock, 1967). In another study, students were presented with one set of arguments that were framed as supporting either a pro or a counterattitudinal position (Cacioppo & Petty, 1979b). Recipients recalled more of the arguments when they were used in support of the counterattitudinal advocacy suggesting that this framing induced greater at-tention to the message content (see also Worth & Mackie, 1987). In other research, students who were given an unfa-vorable medical diagnosis engaged in greater thought about it than did students who were given a favorable med-ical diagnosis (i.e., they generated more alternative expla-nations for the counterattitudinal than the proattitudinal in-formation; Ditto & Lopez, 1992). As might be expected if people scrutinize counterattitudinal information more than proattitudinal information, people take longer when pro-cessing the latter than the former (Edwards & Smith, 1996). Of course, as the issue becomes more important and emotionally involving, the enhanced processing of counter-attitudinal messages could also be biased in an unfavorable direction.

Conclusion Drawing   Another issue that has generated a small body of research is the question of whether the mes-sage should make its position explicit or whether the spe-cific point being advocated should be implicit. For exam-ple, a college president can provide arguments about the benefits of a tuition increase without ever explicitly stating the conclusion that tuition should be raised by 10 percent. A number of studies have suggested that it is preferable to make the message position explicit (e.g., Hovland et al., 1949), though other research suggests that if the recipient draws the conclusion on his or her own, this can be supe-rior (Fine, 1957). The problem seems to be that recipients are often either unable to draw the correct conclusion or

are unmotivated to do so (McGuire, 1969). However, when people are motivated and able to draw the conclusion for themselves, such as when the message is highly involving or the recipients are high in their propensity to think, then it can be better to leave the conclusion implicit (e.g., Stay-man & Kardes, 1992). Engaging in the work of self-gener-ation is also likely to make the conclusion more memo-rable (Slamecka & Graf, 1978).

Use of Rhetorical Questions   Although the most common form of presenting an argument is to make statements, message arguments can include rhetorical questions that ask whether the argument is true. For example, one could summarize an argument with a statement that "institution of comprehensive exams will aid students who are apply-ing to graduate schools," or one could ask "wouldn't insti-tution of comprehensive exams aid students applying to graduate schools?" (e.g., Petty, Cacioppo, & Heesacker, 1981). Some research suggests that inclusion of rhetorical questions makes the speaker appear more polite and likable (e.g., Bates, 1976). As such, use of rhetorical questions could function as a source cue when the elaboration likeli-hood is low, or bias processing when the elaboration likeli-hood is high. At times, however, rhetorical questions also make the speaker appear less confident (Newcombe & Arnkoff, 1979) which could operate as a negative rather than positive cue (or bias). In addition, Zillmann (1972) suggested that use of rhetorical questions becomes associ-ated through socialization with strength of arguments (i.e., people only tend to use rhetoricals when arguments are strong). Therefore, the presence of rhetorical questions could itself be used as a signal that the information is of high quality.

As noted earlier, Petty, Cacioppo, and Heesacker (1981) proposed that the use of rhetorical questions in a message could increase message processing if people were not ordi-narily inclined to think about the communication. Use of a rhetorical question literally requires the person to think about the argument just presented in order to address the question. A number of recent studies have supported this proposal. Specifically, when messages are audiotaped, it has been found that use of rhetorical questions enhances processing when baseline levels of elaboration are low, but use of rhetorical questions disrupts processing when base-line levels of elaboration are high (Petty, Cacioppo, & Hee-sacker, 1981). One possible reason for the latter effect is that the rhetoricals are distracting when people are ordinar-ily inclined to think about the message. Consistent with this distraction notion, the presence of rhetorical questions only disrupts processing when the message is externally paced. When the message is self-paced and when rhetorical questions precede rather than follow the arguments, rhetor-ical questions increase message processing (e.g., Burnkrant & Howard, 1984).

Message Content   Perhaps the most studied message feature is the substantive message content (i.e., the kind of information included in the message). Among the content variables that have been studied are the quality of the message arguments, the quantity of information presented, whether the information is focused on emotions or cognitions, and whether the message includes only content favorable to the advocated side or whether it includes content on the other side as well.

Argument Quality   One of the most manipulated variables in the contemporary literature is the quality or cogency of the message arguments. As documented earlier in our review, the list of variables that interact with argument quality in determining persuasion is now quite lengthy. However, despite the large number of studies, relatively little is known about what makes an argument persuasive. This is because following the initial use of it for this purpose (Petty et al., 1976), most studies have manipulated argument quality primarily as a methodological tool to examine whether some other variable increases or decreases message scrutiny, not to examine the determinants of argument cogency per se.

So, what makes an argument persuasive? Although arguments can take many logical forms (e.g., Fogelin, 1982), a typical argument presents some consequence that is likely to occur if the advocacy is adopted. Based on expectancy value notions (e.g., Fishbein & Ajzen, 1975), consequences that are maximally likely and desirable should be more compelling than those that are less likely or desirable (Areni & Lutz, 1988; Petty & Wegener, 1991). Of course, arguments can take other forms. For example, one could argue that a negative consequence can be avoided if the advocacy were adopted. In such cases, selecting consequences that are maximally likely and undesirable would be most persuasive (Petty & Wegener, 1991; but see later discussion of fear appeals). One particularly effective way to convince a person that a consequence is likely is to provide a causal explanation (Slusher & Anderson, 1996). Thus, a speaker arguing that "instituting comprehensive exams for college seniors will result in higher paying starting jobs" would be better off providing an explanation as to why this result occurs rather than simply citing statistical evidence that it will occur.

Some researchers have suggested that arguments will be perceived as better the more they match the way the recipient looks at the world. For example, people who think of themselves as religious will find arguments that appeal to religion to be more persuasive than arguments that are legalistic (Cacioppo, Petty, & Sidera, 1982), and people who chronically consider the future consequences of potential behaviors will be more persuaded by arguments that include such consequences than ones that do not (Strathman, Gleicher, Boninger, & Edwards, 1994). This point of view

is generally compatible with functional theories of attitudes (e.g., Smith, Bruner, & White, 1956; Katz, 1960) which hold that individuals and attitude objects can differ in the attributes that are most important, and cogent arguments would be those that related best to these important attributes (e.g., Shavitt, 1989; Snyder & DeBono, 1989). Thus, attribute importance might be added to desirability and likelihood in determining argument quality. For example, most students might agree that pretty flowers are very desirable, and that if tuition were raised, it is very likely that pretty flowers could be planted on campus. However, most students would probably not agree that having pretty flowers on campus is important. This would attenuate the cogency of the flowers argument.

An additional factor is the novelty of the consequences proposed. Burnstein and Vinokur (1975; Vinokur & Burnstein, 1974) have argued that all else being equal, an unfamiliar or unique argument has greater impact than a familiar one. After all, if a person has already considered an argument previously, it is unlikely to generate much in the way of new favorable (or unfavorable) responses that could lead to persuasion (or boomerang).

Whether it is necessary to add factors such as importance and novelty to the more traditional likelihood and desirability dimensions awaits further research. It may turn out that these factors are already considered when people think about the desirability of consequences. For example, the desirability of flowers may not be invariant, but may change with the situation. Thus, a student might reason that having pretty flowers is desirable in a fancy restaurant, but is not desirable on campus if it means raising tuition. If so, then perceived importance of the consequence might not contribute to overall persuasiveness above and beyond the perceived desirability of the consequence (cf., Hackman & Anderson, 1968; Wyer, 1970). Unfortunately, relatively few studies have examined what properties of arguments are the most critical in mediating persuasive influence. In one exception, Wegener, Petty, and Klein (1994) found that, for thoughtful individuals at least, happy and sad mood created differences in persuasion by influencing the perceived likelihoods (but not desirability) of the consequences mentioned in the message (see later discussion of mood effects).

Argument Quantity   Early research suggested that increasing the number of arguments included in a message enhanced persuasion (e.g., Calder, Insko, & Yandell, 1974; Leventhal & Niles, 1965). Even if people are not thinking about the arguments, they can reason that the more arguments, the better the position is, or the more knowledgeable the source is (see also Josephs, Giesler, & Silvera, 1994). In fact, when the elaboration likelihood is low, such as when the issue is low in personal relevance or people have little knowledge on the topic, increasing the number of arguments (Petty & Cacioppo, 1984a) or making each argument longer (Wood, Kallgren, & Preisler, 1985) increases persuasion regardless of the quality of those arguments. However, if the elaboration likelihood is high, then increasing the number of strong arguments enhances persuasion, but increasing the number of weak arguments reduces persuasion because people are thinking about the arguments (Petty & Cacioppo, 1984a). Furthermore, under high elaboration conditions, if weak arguments are added to strong arguments, persuasion can decrease when compared with presentation of the strong arguments alone (Friedrich, Fetherstonhaugh, Casey, & Gallagher, 1996).

Positive Versus Negative Framing of Arguments As noted previously, arguments can take several forms. For example, an argument against smoking can be stated in a negative manner such as, "If you don't stop smoking, you will die sooner," or in a positive manner such as "If you stop smoking, you will live longer." (Arguments could also be phrased as failing to take action making positive outcomes unlikely or as taking action making negative outcomes unlikely, see Petty & Wegener, 1991.) Some research has suggested that negatively framed messages have greater impact on attitudes than comparable positively framed ones (e.g., Meyerowitz & Chaiken, 1987). What would account for this? If, as noted earlier, negative information gets more weight in people's judgments, this might account for the advantage of negative framing. The enhanced impact of negatively framed arguments is larger when people are motivated to think about each of the pieces of information presented than when motivation is low (Maheswaran & Meyers-Levy, 1990; cf. Rothman, Salovey, Antone, Keough, & Martin, 1993). When people are not motivated to engage in careful message scrutiny, positively framed messages can be more impactful than negatively framed ones (Maheswaran & Meyers-Levy, 1990). In these low-effort situations, individuals may demonstrate a simple affinity for the more pleasant sounding communication (cf. Zajonc, 1968).

In the health domain, some researchers have made a distinction between behaviors aimed at preventing versus detecting disease, with positive (gain) frames being more effective for prevention, but negative (loss) frames being more effective for detection, behaviors (e.g., Rothman et al., 1993). The prevention versus detection categorization likely proxies for one or more conceptual variables such as the extent to which the disease or other positive versus negative aspects of the behavior are salient in that setting. This might be understood by focusing on the perceived likelihoods of aspects of the message arguments (e.g., Wegener et al., 1994). Specifically, if thinking about detection behaviors makes the negative aspects of the disease more salient, then the undesirable outcomes of failing to engage in the detection behavior might seem more likely (i.e., the impact of negatively framed arguments would be enhanced). If thinking about prevention behaviors makes the

positive aspects of not having the disease more salient, then the desirable outcomes of engaging in the prevention behavior might seem more likely (i.e., the impact of positively framed arguments would be enhanced; see Rothman & Salovey, 1997; Salovey, Rothman, & Rodin, 1998, in this *Handbook,* for additional discussion of message framing in health domains).

Individual differences can also be important in determining which framing is more effective. For example, Higgins's (1989) self-discrepancy theory notes that individuals who have a discrepancy between their actual-self (i.e., how one actually is) and their ideal-self (how the person wants to be) are oriented toward maximizing the presence of positive outcomes and minimizing their absence, whereas those with a discrepancy between their actual-self and their ought-self (how the person should be) are oriented toward minimizing the presence of negative outcomes and maximizing their absence. Based on this, Tykocinski, Higgins, and Chaiken (1994) hypothesized that a negatively framed message would "activate the vulnerability system" and cause distress for people with an actual-ought discrepancy. This distress was postulated to reduce persuasibility. For similar reasons, a positively framed message would reduce persuasion for individuals with an actual-ideal discrepancy. Consistent with this reasoning, actual-ideal discrepancy individuals were more influenced by a negatively than positively framed message, and actual-ought discrepancy individuals demonstrated the reverse. However, the mechanism by which distress reduced attitude change was not clear. Perhaps the distress reduced change by a low-effort peripheral process such as classical conditioning. Or, if the message arguments were strong, perhaps the distress inhibited persuasion by reducing processing of the message. Or, perhaps mismatching the message frame to one's chronic orientation increased the extent of message processing because a mismatched message was more surprising.

In an explicit attempt to link message framing to message processing, Smith and Petty (1996) demonstrated that either positive or negative framing could lead to more processing depending on which type of frame was expected. Recipients (especially those low in need for cognition) who were led to expect a positively framed message were more influenced by the quality of the arguments in a negatively framed than a positively framed message, but recipients who were led to expect a negatively framed message engaged in greater scrutiny of the arguments in the positively framed communication.

Fear/Threat Appeals When very strong negative consequences (e.g., failing an important course, denial of tenure, death) are implied if an advocacy is not adopted, a threat appeal is being used. These messages are often referred to as fear appeals since it is assumed that emotional reactions are often induced as well, though empirically this is not always the case.[10] On the surface, at least, it would appear that such appeals would be very effective because they depict extremely negative consequences as being likely to occur unless the recipient agrees with the message. Thus, in terms of an expectancy-value analysis of argument strength, threat appeals should be quite cogent. In fact, a meta-analysis of the fear appeals literature indicated that overall, increasing fear is associated with increased persuasion (Boster & Mongeau, 1984).

Yet, fear appeals are not invariably found to be more affective. In fact, one of the earliest studies on fear appeals suggested the opposite conclusion (Janis & Feshbach, 1953). There are several factors that work against the effectiveness of fear appeals. First, even if people view the threatened negative consequence as horrific, they are often motivated by self-protection to minimize the likelihood that some frightening consequence might befall them (e.g., Ditto, Jemmott, & Darley, 1988). Second, to the extent that the threat is so strong that it becomes physiologically arousing or distracting, message processing could be disrupted (Baron, Inman, Kao, & Logan, 1992; Jepson & Chaiken, 1990; cf. Baron, Logan, Lilly, Inman, & Brennan, 1994). This would reduce persuasion if the arguments were strong. Fear is especially likely to reduce message processing if recipients are assured that the recommendations are effective and the processing might undermine this assurance (Gleicher & Petty, 1992). It is important to note that when fear reduces message processing, this does not mean that use of fear will be ineffective in changing attitudes. Rather, it suggests that the effectiveness of some fear appeals could be due to disrupting processing of weak arguments, or increasing reliance on various peripheral cues (e.g., a reassuring expert).[11]

The dominant perspective in this literature is Rogers' (1983) protection motivation theory. Consistent with expectancy-value notions, this model holds that fear appeals will be effective to the extent that the message convinces the recipient that the consequences are severe (i.e., are very undesirable) and very likely to occur if the recommended action is not followed. Importantly, this theory also holds that effective fear messages should also convey that the negative consequences can be avoided if the recommended action is followed and that the recipient has the requisite skills to take the recommended action (see also Beck & Frankel, 1981; Sutton, 1982). Considerable evidence supports these predictions and has also shown that if people do not believe that they can cope effectively with the threat, then increasing threat tends to produce a boomerang effect presumably as a consequence of attempting to restore control or reduce fear (e.g., Mullis & Lippa, 1990; Rippetoe & Rogers, 1987). Interestingly, in young children both self-efficacy and threat produce main effects on evaluations rather than an interaction as these individuals may not yet have developed a defensive avoidance mechanism (Sturges & Rogers, 1996).

Note, however, that the protection motivation framework could be applied to virtually any negatively framed argument. In fact, with rewording, it could also apply to any positively framed argument (i.e., a promissory appeal will be effective to the extent that it conveys that the consequence is highly desirable, likely, the person has the skill to bring about the positive outcome, etc.). The emotional reaction of fear in this cognitive analysis plays relatively little role (see also Leventhal, 1970; Dillard, in press). However, fear might contribute to persuasion by leading thoughtful recipients to overestimate how bad the consequences are or how likely they are (Petty & Wegener, 1991; Rogers, 1983).

In sum, threat appeals can be analyzed just as any other message that conveys the likelihood of some positive or negative consequence occurring. To the extent that the threat appeal also induces an emotional reaction, however, this emotional reaction presumably can have an additional effect on message acceptance by serving as a simple cue, biasing message processing, or determining the extent of message scrutiny (see subsequent discussion of mood effects).

Emotion Versus Reason in Messages   Another issue that was of considerable early empirical interest, and has re-emerged, is the question of whether emotional (affective) appeals are more or less effective than appeals to reason and evidence (cognitive appeal). This issue has its roots in the distinction Aristotle drew in his *Rhetoric* between "pathos" and "logos" (McGuire, 1969). The initial work on this question either found no overall difference in effectiveness between the two types of appeals (e.g., Knower, 1935) or tended to favor affective over cognitive messages (e.g., Hartmann, 1936).

Current research suggests that which type of appeal is superior depends on the basis of the attitude under challenge. In a series of studies, Edwards (1990; Edwards & von Hippel, 1995) concluded that matching was best. That is, it is better to match the persuasive appeal to the basis of the attitude than to mismatch. For example, if the attitude is based primarily on emotion, then an emotional appeal is more effective than a cognitive appeal in changing the attitude. On the other hand, in a separate series of studies, Millar and Millar (1990) concluded that mismatching is best—if the attitude is based on affect, a cognitive challenge is more effective than an affective one. These studies used very different methods and materials in testing their hypotheses and thus it is difficult to pinpoint the reason for the different results obtained. One potentially important difference between the two sets of studies is that Edwards used attitude objects about which participants had relatively little information, whereas Millar and Millar used attitude objects for which participants had already established attitudes (Olson & Zanna, 1993). This could account for the different results because with well-formed attitudes, people may be better able to counterargue a direct attack on the underlying basis of their attitude (Millar & Millar, 1990). Alternatively, it may be that which effect occurs depends on the cogency of the attack. That is, if the attack is strong enough to undermine the basis of the attitude, then, matching is better, but if the attack is weak, then mismatching may be superior (Petty, Gleicher, & Baker, 1991). Future work will also likely develop and rely on more advanced methods for measuring the extent to which existing or experimentally created attitudes are based on affect or cognition (e.g., Crites, Fabrigar, & Petty, 1994).

One- Versus Two-Sided Messages   So far, only cases in which the content of a persuasive message presents just one side of the issue—the side being advocated—were considered. In contrast to these typical one-sided messages, several investigations have examined the consequences of including information on both sides of an issue. In an influential study, Lord et al. (1979) demonstrated that after examining equally strong evidence on both sides of an issue, people believed that the evidence on their side was more compelling than the evidence on the other side (called "biased assimilation"), and they came to believe that their own attitudes toward the issue had polarized. This is the expected result if one's attitude biases interpretation of the evidence. Consistent with this reasoning, Schuette and Fazio (1995) found that the biased assimilation effect was strongest when attitudes toward the topic were made highly accessible (see also Houston & Fazio, 1989) and recipients were not made apprehensive about being evaluated. The biased assimilation effect is also stronger when people are emotionally invested in their attitudes (Edwards & Smith, 1996). However, Miller, McHoskey, Bane, and Dowd (1993) noted that the Lord et al. study and subsequent replications did not demonstrate any actual attitude change as a result of biased assimilation because only perceived attitude change (polarization) and/or biased thinking were assessed. To rectify this, they conducted conceptual replications of the Lord et al. research and included measures of participants' attitudes toward the topic. Although they replicated the biased assimilation effect and self-reports of polarization on the issue of capital punishment, after reading essays on both sides of affirmative action, participants were about equally likely to perceive they had depolarized as polarized. It is important to note that on neither topic did actual attitude polarization occur. Miller et al. speculated that participants could have held ambivalent attitudes on these topics which prevented polarization from taking place.

In another relevant study, Pomerantz, Chaiken and Tordesillas (1995) found that polarization was only evident among individuals who were highly committed to their attitudes. Path analyses indicated that increased commitment led to attitude polarization both directly and as mediated by biased elaboration of the evidence. Finally, Giner-

Sorolla and Chaiken (1997) had people read a message presenting both sides of an issue after assessing their vested interests on the issue. Consistent with past research, participants engaged in a biased evaluation of the evidence, but attitude polarization was not found. Rather, attitudes came more in line with participants' own vested interests following the message. That is, people who initially held attitudes in conflict with their own interests moved in the direction of self-interest, but people who already held attitudes in line with their interests tended to depolarize. Thus, processing a message presenting both sides of an issue does not inevitably result in polarized attitudes as suggested by the Lord et al. research. Rather, a number of variables related to the strength of one's attitude appear to determine whether processing the message will result in polarization, depolarization, or no change.

In the research using the Lord et al. paradigm, the two-sided message is balanced in that it does not clearly favor one side over the other. In another line of research, however, two-sided messages are presented in which one side is clearly the position advocated, whereas the other side is not. Furthermore, the opposition side is usually presented with weaker arguments than the focal side, or is explicitly refuted. The effectiveness of these two-sided messages is compared with the effectiveness of a one-sided message in which the opposition side is not mentioned. The initial research on this suggested that one-sided messages were more effective for those who initially favored the advocated position, and for those who were relatively low in educational level, but that two-sided messages were more effective for those in opposition to the position and of higher educational attainment (Hovland et al., 1949).

As reasonable as these early findings appeared, a meta-analytic review of the accumulated literature failed to provide support (Allen, 1991). Specifically, across the accumulated literature, whether the recipients agreed or disagreed with the message did not moderate the results. It is possible that the original results were obtained not because of educational level or prior attitudes per se, but because people who oppose the message (or are of higher educational levels) are more likely to be aware that opposition arguments exist (and thus dealing with them directly presumably helps to undermine their implicit impact; Hass & Linder, 1972). Thus, future meta-analyses and primary research might measure the extent to which recipients are aware of the different sides of the issue in addition to the recipients' own attitudes. Allen's (1991) meta-analysis also discovered that it was important to distinguish two-sided messages that explicitly refuted the other side (two-sided refutational message) versus those that presented the other side but did not counter it (two-sided nonrefutational message). Across the relevant literature, refutational messages were more effective than one-sided communications, but nonrefutational messages were less effective than one-sided messages. This finding was confirmed in primary research using a diversity of topics and messages (Allen et al., 1990). In addition, Hale, Mongeau, and Thomas (1991) found that two-sided refutational messages produced more favorable cognitive responses than two-sided nonrefutational messages. Another possible benefit of two-sided refutational messages is that they can be more effective than one-sided communications in instilling resistance to counterattacks (Lumsdaine & Janis, 1953).

To date, only one study has examined the possible multiple roles that two-sided messages can play in producing attitude change. In this research, Pechmann and Estaban (1994) established three levels of motivation to process an advertisement using a combination of motivational instructions and situational distraction. Participants received an advertisement containing strong or weak arguments that favorably compared an unfamiliar product to a popular product (two-sided message) or did not mention the competing popular brand (one-sided message). Consistent with the ELM multiple roles notion, under low elaboration conditions, argument quality did not influence purchase intentions but the two-sided ad elicited more favorable reactions than the one-sided ad (cue effect). Because the two-sided message favorably compared an unknown brand to a highly liked brand (positive cue), a simple inference of quality could be responsible for the effect. Under high elaboration, however, only argument strength had an impact. Under moderate elaboration, the two-sided (comparative) ad elicited greater message scrutiny than the one-sided ad. The data further suggested that this enhanced scrutiny was biased in a favorable direction. Although research is sparse at present, it seems likely that two-sided messages would generally elicit greater scrutiny than one-sided messages (given the need to make comparisons, resolve discrepancies, etc.) as long as the elaboration likelihood was not constrained by other variables to be high or low. However, whether two-sided messages serve as positive or negative cues (or biasing agents) will likely depend on the nature of the two-sided appeal or the message recipients. For example, two-sided appeals can make the source seem more fair, but might also make the definitiveness of the position seem less clear.

Message Organization   A number of variables have been studied concerning how a message is organized including whether one should start or end with the strongest arguments (e.g., Sponberg, 1946) and whether the source should be presented before or after the substantive message arguments (e.g., Mills & Harvey, 1972; Pratkanis, Greenwald, Leippe, & Baumgardner, 1988; see subsequent discussion of the sleeper effect).

Perhaps the most researched variable, however, concerns the placement of competing messages on different sides of an issue. That is, all else being equal, is it to one's persuasive advantage to present one's side first or second?

In the most cited study on this phenomena, Miller and Campbell (1959) relied on learning theory to predict that primacy would be expected when the two messages are presented together in time but the attitude assessment is delayed. This is because proactive inhibition would prevent the second message from being learned as well as the first and the second would have a faster decay. On the other hand, a recency effect would occur if the second message was presented some time after the first (so that proactive inhibition was minimized) and the attitude measure was taken shortly after the second message (so there was little decay of the second message). These predictions were supported in the attitude data, but there was little evidence that memory for the message arguments was responsible for the effects (see also Insko, 1964). However, if memory for one's own favorable thoughts to the communications followed the learning and decay patterns predicted by Miller and Campbell, the same attitudinal results would be expected. In any case, one moderator of primary/recency effects is the temporal ordering of the messages and attitude measures.

In reviewing the primacy/recency literature, Haugtvedt and Wegener (1994) noted another possible moderating factor. Specifically, they noted that several of the studies finding primary effects tended to use controversial or familiar issues that likely instilled a high likelihood of elaboration, whereas several of those that produced recency effects likely instilled a low elaboration likelihood (see Lana, 1964, for an early review). Using the ELM, they argued that the greater the processing of the first message, the more likely that a strong attitude would be formed that would facilitate counterarguing of and resistance to the second message (Haugtvedt & Petty, 1992; Lund, 1925). In support of this hypothesis, Haugtvedt and Wegener (1994) found that when the personal relevance of the two messages was manipulated to be high, primacy effects were observed, but when the personal relevance of the two messages was manipulated to be low, recency was observed (see need for cognition section for additional discussion of effects of elaboration on primacy/recency effects).

Recipient Variables

Recipient variables refer to any aspects that the receiver of the influence attempt brings to the persuasion situation. That is, the "recipient" category generally refers to relatively enduring aspects of the individual such as the person's demographic category (e.g., gender, race), or personality and individual skills (e.g., self-esteem, intelligence). Characteristics of the issue-relevant attitude that the person holds before the persuasive appeal is presented are discussed first. These initial attitudes can be determined by a variety of previous experiences, of course, but are brought to the persuasion situation by the message recipient.

Attitudinal Variables Influence attempts can be presented to individuals who either have or do not have a prior attitude on the issue, and if the person has an attitude, this evaluation can be relatively strong or weak. A large literature now exists on the features that contribute to or are indicative of strong attitudes (Petty & Krosnick, 1995). In general, strong attitudes are more stable over time, resistant in the face of counterpressure, and have a larger impact on other judgments and behavior than weak attitudes (Krosnick & Petty, 1995). Attitudes can be strong for a wide variety of reasons. For example, the attitude can be based on a heritable component (Tesser, 1993), a consistent and organized belief structure (Chaiken et al., 1995), and so forth. Among the indicators of strong attitudes are their knowledge base (Wood et al., 1995), accessibility (e.g., Fazio, 1995), and confidence (Gross, Holtz, & Miller, 1995).

Attitude Accessibility What impact do these strength factors have on attitude change? In general, many attitude strength factors would serve in the same roles as other variables. For example, consider the accessibility of one's attitude. When the elaboration likelihood is high, then the more accessible the attitude, the more it will bias message processing in an attitude-consistent direction (Houston & Fazio, 1989). This, of course, would make movement toward counterattitudinal positions less likely. If the elaboration likelihood is constrained to be low, however, then the more accessible the attitude, the more likely the person will make snap decisions based on the salient attitude (i.e., the attitude serves as a peripheral cue; Jamieson & Zanna, 1989). Finally, if the elaboration likelihood is not constrained, increasing attitude accessibility increases the likelihood that people will scrutinize the message (Fabrigar, Priester, Petty, & Wegener, in press).

Issue-Relevant Knowledge One of the most studied characteristics of attitudes in persuasion contexts is the issue-relevant knowledge a person has about the attitude issue. Issue-relevant knowledge can vary in both amount and the extent to which it is consistent with the person's attitude. One can also examine the objective knowledge that a person has as well as perceptions of knowledge. Like other variables, recipient knowledge should be capable of serving in multiple roles. For example, one's perceived amount of knowledge could function as a peripheral cue (e.g., "I'm the expert so I can reject the disagreeable advocacy") especially when the elaboration likelihood is low. Alternatively, knowledge could serve to affect the extent of information processing through either motivational ("I've never heard of that, so I'm curious about it," or "I've heard so much about that, I'm bored with it"), or ability factors (providing sufficient background to be able to discern the merits of strong arguments and the flaws in weak ones). Or, knowledge can bias information processing by motivating or enabling pro or counterarguing depending on whether the message was compatible or incompatible with one's existing attitude and knowledge (Petty & Cacioppo, 1986a; Petty et al., 1994).

In one early study, Lewan and Stotland (1961) provided students with factual information about the unfamiliar country of Andorra or not, and then exposed them to an emotional message attacking the country. People with some prior knowledge about Andorra were less influenced by the attack than people who had no prior knowledge. It is not clear, however, if high knowledge recipients resisted because knowledge instilled greater confidence in their initial opinions, because the knowledge motivated them to process the arguments and the arguments were deemed weak, or because the prior knowledge motivated or enabled counterarguing of the attack.

More contemporary research has attempted to examine the processes by which knowledge has its impact, and has consistently demonstrated that people with high amounts of issue-relevant knowledge tend to engage in greater scrutiny of messages relevant to their knowledge than people with low amounts of issue-relevant knowledge, and are less reliant on peripheral cues (see Wood, Rhodes, & Biek, 1995, for a review). In addition, research suggests that people with high knowledge tend to resist influence on counterattitudinal issues more than people with low knowledge (e.g., Wood et al., 1985) but also tend to be more accepting of proattitudinal messages (Johnson, Lin, Symons, Campbell, & Ekstein, 1995; Wu & Shaffer, 1987). However, because most contemporary work on prior knowledge tends to measure knowledge rather than manipulate it, it is not surprising that high knowledge is associated with more attitude congenial outcomes. This is because measured knowledge is likely to be attitude congruent and confounded with other variables that would foster this bias (e.g., high levels of confidence, attitude extremity, etc.). If knowledge was more balanced and not confounded in this way, it would presumably be more likely to determine the extent of information processing activity with bias resulting from other motivational and ability factors (e.g., intense affect; see Biek, Wood, & Chaiken, 1996).

Demographic Variables

Gender Early research tended to show that women were more susceptible to influence than were men (e.g., Janis & Field, 1959; Knower, 1936). One explanation was based on culture. That is, society had greater conformity expectations for women (Hovland & Janis, 1959). Another explanation relied on the presumed greater message reception skills of women (McGuire, 1969). Early research also suggested that sometimes this effect was due to the gender of the influence agent—when this was controlled, the gender difference disappeared (Weitzenhoffer & Weitzenhoffer,

1958). McGuire (1968) also speculated that the effect might be due to the fact that the experimental materials in most studies of the time were constructed by men.

More recent analysts have concluded that a small gender difference exists and is exacerbated when the study is conducted by a male investigator or influence is assessed in a group-pressure situation (Cooper, 1979). For social reasons, males might be more effective in eliciting compliance from females than are other females, and women might be more interested in social harmony than are men (due in part to their early socialization or their expected social roles; Eagly, 1978; Eagly & Wood, 1991). For example, in some situations if one's gender is salient, and motivation or ability to carefully scrutinize the merits of the issue are reduced, a cultural norm might determine the extent of influence (e.g., "as a man, I shouldn't give in").

These explanations suggest that gender differences will persist as long as cultural factors remain similar. Cultural factors do not account for all of the variance in gender effects, however. Some of the effect can be attributed to the nature of the influence topic. For example, in some cases, the topic of the message might determine how much scrutiny is given to the message (e.g., "this message is relevant to all women, so I should think about it"). Or, if the topic is one on which men have stronger attitudes than women (e.g., due to greater attitude-supportive knowledge), then women might be more influenceable because they would be less motivated or able to defend their attitudes. If the attitude strength differences are reversed, however, then men would be more influenceable (Cacioppo & Petty, 1980; Sistrunk & McDavid, 1971). In addition, the message content can be critical even if the topic is held constant. For example, different arguments might appear stronger (on average) to each gender. One study, for instance, found that women were more susceptible to an appeal to sympathy than reciprocity (Fink, Rey, Johnson, Spenner, Morton, & Flores, 1975).

Age   Effects of age on influenceability have been of intense interest in the 1990s due to charges that prosecutors had subtly (and not so subtly) influenced young children to testify to events that did not occur in some high profile child molestation cases. Early research examined susceptibility to influence by exposing individuals of different ages to various suggestion and hypnotism tests. This research suggested that young children were quite open to suggestion (e.g., Messerschmidt, 1933), and more recent studies reinforce this conclusion (e.g., Ceci & Bruck, 1993). Another approach to examining age differences has been to compare the test-retest attitude correlations for individuals of different ages. In general, these studies have indicated greater stability in attitudes for older than younger individuals (e.g., Alwin, Cohen, & Newcomb, 1991).

A number of hypotheses have been put forth regarding the empirical relation between age and susceptibility to influence. Some investigators have argued that people generally become less susceptible to influence as they grow older (e.g., Glenn, 1980). Others have argued that the decrease in susceptibility is not gradual as one ages, but is rather abrupt as individuals leave their "impressionable" childhood and young adult years behind them (Mannheim, 1952). Still others have suggested a curvilinear relationship with younger and older individuals being most susceptible to change (e.g., Sears, 1981), though some evidence suggests that the increased susceptibility among the oldest individuals could be due to increased measurement error (Krosnick & Alwin, 1989).

Because of the general consensus that young people, at least, are more susceptible to persuasion than older adults, Sears (1986) argued that the typical laboratory study with college students overestimates the ease of attitude change in the general population. Of course, the goal of laboratory research is not typically to provide population estimates, but rather to examine some conceptual hypothesis. Furthermore, it seems unlikely that age per se relates to influenceability. Rather, a number of factors associated with age are probably responsible for any link between aging and attitude change and many of these factors could be studied within the population of college students (Petty & Cacioppo, 1996). For example, young people may appear to exhibit less stability in attitude surveys because they happen to be exposed to more challenges to their attitudes than are older individuals (Tyler & Schuller, 1991). Alternatively, as people grow older, their knowledge on many issues increases. As noted previously, attitude-congruent knowledge can help a person resist an incoming message. In addition, some people might hold beliefs (such as "older is wiser") that confer resistance even though other people of the same age do not hold such beliefs. In addition, individuals of different ages will likely find different topics of greater or lesser interest and different arguments as being of higher or lower quality. It is likely that each of these factors operates and accounts, at least in part, for observed age differences in different situations. Importantly, each of these conceptual questions can be studied within any given sample of individuals.

Personality/Skills   Although individual differences in the propensity to engage in evaluation and form attitudes have recently been uncovered (Jarvis & Petty, 1996), the search for a personality variable that captures a general susceptibility to persuasion across a wide variety of situations has met with little success (e.g., Hovland & Janis, 1959; see Eagly, 1981). Some early evidence indicated that individuals' responses to various suggestibility tests showed a small positive correlation (see Eysenck & Furneaux, 1945; Hilgard, 1965) as did responses to various conformity situations (e.g., Abelson & Lesser, 1959). More success in persuasion situations has come from research examining specific individual differences in skills and personality traits. In fact, a wide number of specific traits have been linked to persuasion outcomes including: uncertainty orientation (Sorrentino, Bobocel, Gitta, Olson, & Hewitt, 1988), internal-external locus of control (e.g., Sherman, 1973), public self-consciousness (Carver & Scheier, 1982), need for closure (Kruglanski, Webster, & Klein, 1993), and many others. Our focus is on the stable traits that have received the most research attention.

Intelligence   Primary studies have provided support for both positive (e.g., Cooper & Dinerman, 1951) and negative (see Crutchfield, 1955) relations between intelligence and influenceability. As noted previously, McGuire (1968) argued that which effect occurred should depend on whether reception or yielding processes were more important. For example, with a complex but cogent message, reception would be more important and thus intelligence would be positively related to persuasion. With a simple message, yielding would be more important, and intelligence would be negatively related to persuasion because highly intelligent people would be more resistant (see also Eagly & Warren, 1976). That is, intelligent individuals would likely have greater issue-relevant knowledge on many issues and thus have a greater ability to defend their current positions. However, their greater knowledge might also enable them to see the merits in complex arguments that would pass by less intelligent people.

A meta-analytic examination of the accumulated literature on intelligence and persuasion revealed that increased intelligence was generally associated with decreased persuasion (Rhodes & Wood, 1992). Given that intelligent people have a greater ability to scrutinize messages than people of less intelligence, this finding probably implies that most counterattitudinal messages used in experiments are not so cogent that intelligent people cannot counterargue them when they are motivated to think about them. Although it has not been studied explicitly, perceived intelligence could also serve as a peripheral cue when motivation to think is low. For example, someone might reason that "I'm probably more intelligent than the source, so why should I change *my* view?" This inference might be less likely if the message appeared to be very complex, thus making the source appear more competent.

Self-esteem   The overall regard that a person has for him or herself—self-esteem—has also been subjected to McGuire's reception/yielding analysis. As with intelligence, some research has demonstrated a positive relationship with persuasion (e.g., Berkowitz & Lundy, 1957) whereas other research has demonstrated a negative relationship (e.g., Janis, 1954). McGuire (1968) thus suggested that the relation between self-esteem and persuasion

should be positive when reception processes dominate, but negative when yielding processes dominate (see also Nisbett & Gordon, 1967). If both processes operate simultaneously, then one would expect a curvilinear relationship between self-esteem and persuasion. Although a meta-analysis of the literature revealed that this curvilinear relationship holds (Rhodes & Wood, 1992), it is not entirely clear that the reception/yielding model provides the best account of these data.

For example, Skolnick and Heslin (1971) examined previously published studies on self-esteem and persuasion and had the messages used in these studies rated for their overall persuasiveness and comprehensibility. Comprehensibility (a stand-in for reception) did not account for the relation between self-esteem and persuasion, but the rated quality of the arguments did. Specifically, when Skolnick and Heslin divided the accumulated studies into those finding a positive relationship between self-esteem and persuasion and those finding a negative relationship, they found that the positive relationship studies used more cogent arguments than the negative relationship studies. This finding is consistent with the view that argument quality was more important in determining the attitudes of high than low self-esteem individuals. Low self-esteem individuals might have little need to scrutinize the merits of a communication because they would believe that most people are more competent than they are and thus, the message can be accepted on faith. A high self-esteem person, however, would have the confidence to scrutinize the message. If situational factors inhibited message processing (e.g., high levels of distraction), then one might expect high self-esteem individuals to be generally more resistant than low self-esteem individuals because they would be more likely to reason that their own opinion was as good as or better than that of the source. High self-esteem individuals would presumably be more susceptible to the "ownness bias" (Perloff & Brock, 1980) that was described previously.

Self-monitoring   Snyder (1974) introduced the notion that some people—called high self-monitors—are very sensitive to cues that indicate socially appropriate behavior in a given situation, whereas other people—called low self-monitors—are more guided by their internal beliefs and values. High and low self-monitors have differed in a number of important ways. For example, because internal beliefs are more important to low self-monitors, they are more susceptible to dissonance effects (Snyder & Tanke, 1976). Most research on self-monitoring has examined the notion that attitudes serve different functions (see Katz, 1960; Smith et al., 1956) for people who are high versus low in self-monitoring, and that each group should be more persuaded by messages that matched (versus mismatched) the function served by their attitudes. More specifically, attitudes should serve a social-adjustive function for high self-monitors and thus they should be especially influenced by arguments that make claims about the social images one can attain by agreeing with the advocacy. In contrast, the attitudes of low self-monitors should serve a value-expressive function and thus these individuals should be especially influenced by arguments that make claims about the underlying merits or true qualities of the issue or object under consideration. Several tests of these ideas proved congenial. That is, high self-monitors were more influenced by appeals to image or status whereas low self-monitors were more influenced by messages that made appeals to values or quality (e.g., DeBono, 1987; Lavine & Snyder, 1996; Snyder & DeBono, 1989).

In contrast to the functional hypothesis that focuses on the overall effectiveness of messages that match an attitude's function, Petty and Wegener (in press) hypothesized that if the elaboration likelihood was not constrained to be high or low, people would engage in greater scrutiny of message content that matched the functional basis of their attitudes. This implies that when the message arguments are strong, functional matching will lead to enhanced persuasion (as postulated by the functional theorists), but when the message arguments are weak, functional matching can lead to reduced persuasion. Some suggestive evidence for this was provided by DeBono and Harnish (1988). This study found that high and low self-monitors engaged in greater scrutiny of a message when the message *source* matched the functional basis of the attitudes. That is, high self-monitors engaged in greater scrutiny of the arguments when they were presented by an attractive source (who might be expected to make an image appeal) than an expert source (who presumably would make a quality appeal), whereas low self-monitors demonstrated the reverse pattern. In this study, the actual content of the communications was the same, however. Thus, observed processing effects could be due to the messages *not* entirely matching the expectations associated with the sources of the messages. Also, in other settings, message sources that serve the needs of message recipients have led to less rather than more processing of the message content (e.g., DeBono & Klein, 1993). In order to examine whether individuals would engage in greater processing of messages when the substantive *content* of the message actually matched the function served by the attitude, Petty and Wegener (in press) had high and low self-monitors read image or quality appeals that contained strong or weak arguments. Consistent with the processing view, the cogency of the arguments had a larger effect on attitudes when the message matched rather than mismatched the functional basis of the attitude.

According to the ELM, functional matching should influence the extent of message scrutiny primarily when other factors in the persuasion setting have not already established the elaboration likelihood to be very high or very low. If circumstances constrained the overall likelihood of

elaboration as very low, a functional match could serve as a simple cue to enhance persuasion. For example, if a source simply asserted that his or her arguments were relevant to a person's values, a low self-monitor might be more inclined to agree than a high self-monitor by reasoning, "if it speaks to my values, it must be good." On the other hand, if circumstances rendered the likelihood of elaboration as high, matching the content of the message to the functional basis of the attitude might bias processing—especially if the messages are ambiguous in quality. For example, a high self-monitor would be more motivated to generate favorable thoughts to a message that made an appeal to image rather than an appeal to values (see Lavine & Snyder, 1996).

Need for Cognition   In deference to Cohen's (1957) pioneering work on scaling individual differences in cognitive motivation, Cacioppo and Petty (1982) called their scale measuring individual differences in the motivation to think, the need for cognition scale. Individuals who are high in need for cognition enjoy cognitive activities and engage in them when given the chance. Individuals who are low in need for cognition are cognitive misers who avoid effortful thinking unless situational demands require it (see Cacioppo et al., 1996, for a review).

Research has supported the ELM notion that people who are inclined to engage in effortful cognitive activity are more influenced by the substantive arguments in a persuasive message (e.g., Cacioppo et al., 1983) and are less influenced by simple peripheral cues (e.g., Haugtvedt et al., 1992) than are those who are less inclined to think. It is important to note two additional findings. First, the more extensive thinking of individuals high in need for cognition is not necessarily objective. In fact, two studies have provided evidence that moods can introduce a significant bias to the thought content of people high in need for cognition (Petty, Schumann, Richman, & Strathman, 1993; Wegener et al., 1994). Second, research indicates that even low need for cognition individuals can be motivated to scrutinize the message arguments and eschew reliance on cues if situational circumstances are motivating—such as when the message is of high personal relevance (Axsom et al., 1987), the source is potentially untrustworthy (Priester & Petty, 1995), or the message content is surprising (Smith & Petty, 1996).

Two empirical discrepancies have arisen regarding need for cognition and attitude change. The first involves the mere thought effect (in which thinking about one's attitude leads to a polarization of that attitude; see Tesser, 1978). Given the greater propensity of high need for cognition individuals to engage in thought, one might expect them to show greater attitude polarization following a period of reflection on their attitudes. Although one study supported this idea (Smith, Haugtvedt, & Petty, 1994), another found the opposite (Leone & Ensley, 1986). Research by Lassiter,

Apple, and Slaw (1996) suggests that this discrepancy might be resolved by considering the different instructions used in the two studies. Specifically, Lassiter et al. found that when participants were instructed to think about their attitudes (as in Leone & Ensley), low need for cognition individuals showed greater polarization than high need for cognition individuals. However, when no explicit instructions to think were provided (as in Smith et al., 1994), high need for cognition individuals showed greater polarization. This suggests that when thinking is instructed rather than spontaneous, high need for cognition individuals may consider all sides of the issue and thus show moderation rather than polarization.

The second discrepancy involves primacy and recency effects. Specifically, one study found that individuals high in need for cognition demonstrated greater primacy in judgment than individuals low in need for cognition (Kassin, Reddy, & Tulloch, 1990). This result is consistent with the view presented earlier that high amounts of thinking about early information can enhance counterarguing and rejection of later information (Haugtvedt & Petty, 1992; Haugtvedt & Wegener, 1994). However, another study found that low need for cognition individuals demonstrated greater primacy in judgments than individuals high in need for cognition (Ahlering & Parker, 1989). This result is consistent with the view that low amounts of thinking can cause individuals to freeze on the early information and ignore subsequent information (Kruglanski & Freund, 1983). Petty and Jarvis (1996) noted that this discrepancy might be resolved by considering the fact that in the studies finding greater primacy under high thinking conditions, the materials presented two clear sides to an issue (e.g., the prosecution and defense positions in a trial; Kassin et al., 1990; independent pro and con messages on an issue; Haugtvedt & Wegener, 1994), and participants first received information from one source on one side of the issue and then the other source on the other side. In contrast, studies finding greater primacy under low thinking conditions have not divided the information neatly into two sides. Rather the information came in a continuous stream (Ahlering & Parker, 1989). In the former procedure, thoughtful individuals would likely form a thoughtful opinion after the initial side and then be biased in processing the second side. When there are no clear sides, however, highly thoughtful individuals would be more likely to process all the information prior to rendering a judgment. This would attenuate any primacy effect.

Context Variables

Context refers to any factors related to the setting in which the communication is presented. This is a broad category of variables that includes such features as any distractions that are present in the setting, whether the message is repeated or not, whether the surroundings create a pleasant or unpleasant atmosphere, whether people are forewarned of the message content or not or expect to discuss the issue with others, and so forth. The impact of these variables on the processes of persuasion are discussed next.

Distraction   It is not uncommon for people to simultaneously encounter a persuasive message and engage in one or more other tasks, or have various kinds of distracting stimuli present that tax cognitive capacity. Festinger and Maccoby (1964) proposed that distraction could increase persuasion by interfering with counterarguing. Early research supported this proposition by showing that increases in distraction resulted in increases in persuasion when attention was focused on the message, but not on the distracting events (e.g., Insko, Turnbull, & Yandell, 1974) and that increases in distraction led to decreases in counterarguments measured in thought-listings (e.g., Osterhouse & Brock, 1970; see Baron, Baron, & Miller, 1973, for a dissonance interpretation). Petty et al. (1976) tested a more general thought-disruption view of distraction by crossing distraction with a manipulation of argument quality. According to the disruption of processing view, distraction should lead to decreases in whatever cognitions would normally have occurred. Thus, if the dominant cognitive responses would have been favorable when no distraction was present—as would be the case if the arguments were strong—then distraction should disrupt these favorable thoughts and reduce persuasion. However, if the dominant cognitive responses would have been unfavorable when no distraction was present—as would be the case if the arguments were weak—then distraction should disrupt these unfavorable thoughts and increase persuasion. The data supported this hypothesis and provided evidence for the view that distraction influences attitudes by disrupting one's thoughts.At the same time, this study provided strong support for the cognitive response model of persuasion.

Further support for an interpretation of distraction effects as due to disruption of ability to process the content of message arguments comes from studies in which manipulations of distraction have been crossed with manipulations of persuasion cues. For example, Kiesler and Mathog (1968) found that a high-credibility source led to more favorable attitudes than a low-credibility source to a greater extent when distraction was high rather than low (see also Miller & Baron, 1968, cited in Baron et al., 1973). One ironic effect of distraction is that it can lead people to favor positions they intend to disfavor. Specifically, in one study, students were asked to try not to believe in the conclusion of a message. When not distracted, those trying to disbelieve had no problem doing this. When distracted, however, the opposite resulted—those attempting not to believe came to favor the proposal more presumably because distraction prevented them from suppressing the unwanted belief (see Wegner, 1994, for discussion of this and other examples of thought suppression).

Audience Reactions   When a persuasive message is encountered, other recipients of the message might provide noticeable reactions to the message (i.e., of agreement or disagreement with the message). For example, Axsom et al. (1987) presented research participants with an audiotaped strong or weak message accompanied by taped audience reactions. The message advocacy (probation as an alternative to imprisonment) was introduced as being high in personal relevance (i.e., considered for the participants' own state) or low in personal relevance (i.e., considered for a distant state). In addition, research participants were classified as either high or low in need for cognition (Cacioppo & Petty, 1982). When elaboration likelihood was lowest (i.e., when personal relevance and need for cognition were both low), audience agreement reactions (i.e., taped applause that was consistent and enthusiastic) led to more favorable attitudes than audience disagreement (i.e., inconsistent and sparse applause). In contrast, when elaboration likelihood was high (i.e., when personal relevance, need for cognition, or both were high), audience reactions had no effect on favorability of attitudes. Instead, under such conditions, only message quality influenced attitudes. That is, when elaboration likelihood was low, audience applause acted as a persuasion cue, but when elaboration likelihood was high, the audience cue had little effect.

In this study, unambiguous strong or weak messages were used. If ambiguous messages were used, however, one might find evidence of biases in processing under high elaboration conditions (as people looked for reasons why other message recipients seem to agree with the ambiguous arguments). In one study relevant to potential biased processing instigated by audience reactions under high elaboration conditions, Petty and Brock (1976) investigated the effects of hecklers on persuasion. They found that when a speaker ignored hecklers or provided irrelevant responses, audience members expressed less agreement with the message than when no heckling occurred (perhaps because of negatively biased processing when others voiced their counterarguments to the message). When the source provided relevant responses to the hecklers (i.e., counterarguing the counterarguments), however, this reduced the deleterious effects of heckling.

Of course, other reactions of audiences could be studied, some of which might be likely to influence the amount of message processing if other factors do not constrain processing to be high or low. For example, one could imagine audience reactions that communicate to other message recipients that the message is interesting or important versus uninteresting or unimportant. If so, such reactions might be especially likely to affect how much other audience members process the message.

Forewarning   At times, people receive persuasive messages when they have already learned either the position to be advocated by the message or the intent of the provider(s) of the message to persuade. Some studies of forewarning have included both types of forewarning (e.g., Brock, 1967) though, as noted by Papageorgis (1968), the two types are conceptually distinct. In fact, most research has independently investigated the effects of each type of forewarning.

Forewarning of Position   McGuire and Papageorgis (1962) noted that warning of the position of a persuasive message might motivate people to consider information that supports their current opinion on the issue and counterargue opposing positions in anticipation of the message. If this is the case, one should find that whether or not there is time between the forewarning and the communication creates a difference in the resistance to the message (with time for preemptive counterarguing leading to greater resistance). Consistent with such a possibility, Freedman and Sears (1965) found that forewarning teenage students of a message opposing teenage driving led to little resistance to the message if the forewarning was provided immediately before the message but to significantly more resistance if provided 10 minutes prior to the message (see also Hass & Grady, 1975).

Petty and Cacioppo (1977) found additional support for the anticipatory counterargument position by showing that thought listings revealed significantly greater incidence of anticipatory counterargumentation when people were forewarned of counterattitudinal message content than when they listed thoughts but were not forewarned, and by showing increased physiological activity indicative of concentrated negative thought during the postwarning-premessage period (Cacioppo & Petty, 1979a). In addition, Petty and Cacioppo (1977) noted that it was not the forewarning per se that induced resistance to an attacking appeal, but rather the activation and consideration of attitude-relevant knowledge. That is, activation of attitude-relevant knowledge (accomplished by asking people to list thoughts on the topic without forewarning them of the content of the upcoming message) prior to receipt of an attacking message was sufficient to produce resistance to the appeal equal to that of forewarning.

Consistent with the idea that activation of attitude-relevant knowledge was responsible for resistance when people are forewarned of the message position, it has been shown that resistance only occurs to the extent that the message is on a topic that is personally important or involving to the message recipient (Apsler & Sears, 1968). Attesting to the importance of motivational and ability factors, Chen, Reardon, Rea, and Moore (1992) found that a forewarning of message position on a counterattitudinal issue led people to resist the message and generate unfavorable thoughts to both strong and weak arguments primarily when the issue was personally involving and they were not distracted (see also Freedman, Sears, & O'Connor, 1964; Romero, Agnew, & Insko, 1996).

Forewarning of Persuasive Intent   If a person does not even know what a communication is about, it seems unlikely that he or she could generate anticipatory counterarguments. Therefore, one must look to other mechanisms to account for the effects of forewarning of persuasive intent (see Cialdini & Petty, 1981). An empirical indication that forewarning of persuasive intent works differently than forewarning of message position is that forewarning of intent is equally effective, regardless of the amount of time between the forewarning and the message (e.g., Hass & Grady, 1975). It could be that intent to persuade is regarded as an intended restriction of freedom to think or act in some way. If so, recipients of such a forewarning might experience reactance (Brehm, 1966) that would instigate counterarguing once the persuasive appeal has begun (counterarguing cannot begin until the topic of the appeal is known; see Fukada, 1986, for differential self-reports of reactance by warned and unwarned message recipients). In order to investigate whether counterarguing during the message was responsible for the effects of forewarning of persuasive intent, Petty and Cacioppo (1979a) exposed research participants to a message arguing that senior comprehensive exams be instituted after the issue was described as either high or low in personal relevance and participants were either forewarned of persuasive intent or not. Results showed that forewarning led to less favorable opinions of the advocacy, but only significantly so when the topic was high in personal relevance. This suggested that forewarning was not acting as a simple rejection cue (which would have worked under low, rather than high, relevance), but was acting to bias the processing that occurred when personal relevance was high. That is, relevance increased processing and led to greater acceptance of the strong arguments in the message when no forewarning was present, but when a forewarning was present, then the relevance-inspired processing became negatively biased.

Additional evidence for the view that forewarning of persuasive intent biases processing of a message comes from research demonstrating that such warnings are effective in reducing persuasion when they are presented before rather than after the message (Kiesler & Kiesler, 1964) and produce resistance only when message recipients are not distracted during message presentation (Watts & Holt, 1979).

Anticipated Discussion or Interaction   A number of studies have examined how opinions are modified when people are asked to interact with or be accountable to some

other person or persons. Like other variables, anticipation of discussion or accountability to others has produced a number of effects. In general, when people feel they are accountable or might have to justify their stance to others, this engages concerns about one's social appearance (Cialdini et al., 1976; Leippe & Elkin, 1987; Tetlock, 1992). How one goes about maximizing a favorable impression, however, varies with the situation. Consider first the case in which a person expects to discuss or be held accountable for an issue that is not particularly important or is somewhat unfamiliar. In such cases, if the opinions of the audience (or person to whom one is accountable) are unknown, people tend to diligently think about any information presented on the issue in an attempt to adopt the best or most justifiable position (Chaiken, 1980; Petty et al., 1980; Tetlock, 1983). If no information is presented, however, and the audience's opinion is unknown, people tend to adopt a moderate and presumably defensible position in anticipation of interaction with the audience (Cialdini et al., 1976). When the audience's opinions are known, communications to these audiences tend to be biased in favor of the audience's opinions and people tend to shift their own opinions toward those expected to be held by the audience (e.g., Chen, Shechter, & Chaiken, 1996; Higgins & McCann, 1984; Tetlock, 1983).

When the issue is important or people have a previous commitment to a particular position, things change. Specifically, being held accountable or expecting to discuss the issue leads people to justify their initial positions (Lambert et al., 1996; Tetlock, Skitka, & Boettger, 1989) which can result in attitude polarization rather than moderation (Cialdini et al., 1976; see Cialdini & Petty, 1981; Tetlock, 1992, for additional discussion).

Channel (Message Modality)   Any given persuasive message can be presented in various ways, through various media. Although the messages presented in social psychological studies are often written (on paper or computer screen), audiotaped, or videotaped, one conceptual variable likely represented in these categories is a distinction between self-paced and externally-paced presentation. That is, a written message is typically self-paced (i.e., a reader can go back to read and reread anything that he or she likes, e.g., Chaiken & Eagly, 1976; for an exception, see Mackie & Worth, 1989). When a communication is audiotaped or videotaped, however, it is more likely to be controlled by someone other than the message recipient (e.g., Andreoli & Worchel, 1978; Chaiken & Eagly, 1976).

What persuasive effects are such differences likely to have? Although little basic research has investigated differences in communication modality, most of the relevant work suggests that some methods of presenting a message cause greater scrutiny than others. As might be expected, self-paced messages generally receive greater scrutiny than externally paced messages (perhaps because it is more difficult to thoroughly scrutinize the content of an externally-paced message, at least when it is reasonably complex in nature). Consistent with this idea, when Chaiken and Eagly (1976) presented research participants with a complex, cogent message, they found that the message led to greater persuasion and recall of message arguments when it was written (self-paced) than when the message was audiotaped or videotaped (externally-paced). This is to be expected assuming that the message arguments were strong.

In addition, it has been shown that peripheral persuasion cues such as communicator credibility or likableness tend to have a greater impact when the message is videotaped (i.e., externally-paced) rather than written (self-paced; e.g., Andreoli & Worchel, 1978; Chaiken & Eagly, 1983). These effects could be due to the difficulty of processing complex material when externally paced (as previously mentioned), but could also be due in part to the salience of source cues across the different versions of the message. Many visual aspects of the person or setting in which a source speaks could enhance perceptions of credibility or likableness, and these features of the person and setting can only truly affect message recipients when the person and setting are clearly pictured with the message (which can occur when a message is videotaped but not audiotaped). Finally, the modality of the message itself could serve as a cue or a determinant of biased processing in that some people might, for example, be more impressed with messages appearing in the print media (e.g., newspapers, books, magazines) than on television.

Mood   A variety of events or aspects of one's environment can change the way one feels. In empirical investigations of effects of mood on persuasion, this has generally been accomplished by providing people with written, audiotaped, or videotaped material that is generally very pleasant or unpleasant prior to message exposure, thus setting a persuasion context in which the recipient's mood is positive, negative, or neutral. Effects of positive and negative moods have been examined across the elaboration continuum.

According to the ELM, mood can serve in the same multiple roles as other variables (Petty et al., 1991). Thus, when the likelihood of issue-relevant thinking is low, a person's mood should impact attitudes by a peripheral process. Consistent with this view, early investigations of mood and persuasion were often guided by classical conditioning notions of a direct association between the attitude object and the person's affective state (e.g., Griffitt, 1970; Zanna et al., 1970). More recently, affective states have been postulated to influence attitudes by a simple inference process in which misattribution of the cause of the mood state to the persuasive message or to the attitude object occurs (e.g., I must feel good because I like or agree with the message advocacy; see Petty & Cacioppo, 1983; Schwarz, 1990). Importantly, these direct effects of mood on attitude seem to be more likely when elaboration likelihood is low than high (e.g., Gorn, 1982; Petty et al., 1993).

As the likelihood of elaboration increases, mood takes on different roles (see also Forgas, 1995). Specifically, when the elaboration likelihood is more moderate, mood has been shown to have an impact on the extent of argument elaboration. Competing theoretical positions have been put forward to explain effects of mood on message processing. The "cognitive capacity" and "feelings-as-information" views both predict that happy moods disrupt processing of message content (see Mackie & Worth, 1991; Schwarz, Bless, & Bohner, 1991). For the cognitive capacity view, this is because happy moods activate positive thoughts in memory which occupy a person's attentional capacity and render the message recipient less able to process incoming information (Mackie & Worth, 1989, 1991). In comparison, the feelings-as-information view states that negative moods signal that something is wrong in the environment and that some action is necessary, whereas positive moods indicate that no scrutiny of the environment is required (Schwarz, 1990). Because of this, negative states generally instigate active processing strategies in order to deal with problems in the environment, but positive states do not (although active processing can be done in positive states if other goals that necessitate such processing become salient; see Bless, Bohner, Schwarz, & Strack, 1990). Although these views have been used to account for a large number of studies, virtually all the persuasion experiments investigating the effects of mood on processing have used counterattitudinal or depressing messages (e.g., on topics such as acid rain, gun control, student tuition increases, etc.; see Wegener & Petty, 1996, for a review). Because of this, one might also account for deficits in message processing by happy people by considering the possibility that happy people pay more attention to the hedonic consequences of their actions than people in neutral or sad states. If this were the case, then happy people might be especially avoidant of activities perceived as likely to be depressing, but might especially engage in uplifting activities. Wegener and Petty (1994) developed this hedonic contingency idea by noting that hedonic rewards (i.e., feeling better rather than worse after engaging in an activity) are more contingent on the scrutiny of the hedonic consequences of action in happy than in sad states.

Empirical tests of the hedonic contingency possibility have been encouraging. Wegener, Petty, and Smith (1995, Experiment 1) found that use of a proattitudinal message led to greater message processing from happy than neutral people (which would not be predicted by either the "cognitive capacity" or "feelings-as-information" views). Wegener et al. (1995, Experiment 2) manipulated the introduction of messages so that the same arguments could be used to support either a proattitudinal (uplifting) position or a counterattitudinal (depressing) position and found that happy people processed the arguments more when they addressed an uplifting proposal than when they addressed a depressing proposal, whereas sad people processed the messages to the same extent, regardless of the uplifting or depressing introduction. Organized another way, this result showed that the hedonic contingency idea was capable of accounting for the past effects of mood on message processing. That is, when a depressing version of the topic was used (as in the past research, e.g., Bless et al., 1990; Mackie & Worth, 1989), happy people processed the messages less than sad people (replicating the past results). However, when an uplifting version of the topic was used, the same arguments were processed more by happy people than by sad people.

Thus, it appears that happy people do not universally process information less than neutral or sad people. Rather, happy people engage in cognitive tasks to the extent that the task is viewed as enabling the person to remain happy (or keep from feeling badly). This view might account for why happy moods have been found to enhance cognitive activities in some areas outside the persuasion domain (e.g., enhancement of creative problem solving, Isen, Daubman, & Nowicki, 1987; enhancement of generation of similarities and differences between pairs of targets, Murray, Sujan, Hirt, & Sujan, 1990). Of course, within the multiple roles framework, such effects on amount of cognitive processing should be most likely if background factors do not constrain elaboration likelihood to be extremely high or low.

When the elaboration likelihood is high and people are processing the message arguments already, the ELM holds that affective states can influence attitudes by influencing the nature of the thoughts that come to mind. Positive mood can facilitate the retrieval of positive or inhibit the retrieval of negative material from memory (e.g., see Blaney, 1986; Bower, 1981; Isen, 1987). Thus, a person's mood during message processing can be related to the favorability of the cognitive responses generated. Support for this possibility has been found in a number of studies (e.g., Breckler & Wiggins, 1991; Mathur & Chattopadhyay, 1991), some of which explicitly varied the elaboration likelihood. In two studies, Petty et al. (1993) found that positive mood had an impact on the favorability of thoughts of people high in elaboration likelihood (i.e., for people high in need for cognition or under high message relevance conditions), and these thoughts influenced attitudes. In contrast, when elaboration likelihood was low, mood did not influence thought valence, but rather influenced attitudes directly, presumably by a low effort peripheral process.

This is not to say that positive moods should always bias processing toward being more favorable toward the position advocated or that negative moods should invari-

ably render the message conclusion less acceptable. For example, negative moods have been shown to make negative events seem more likely than positive events (e.g., Johnson & Tversky, 1983) and positive events and behaviors are seen as more likely in positive as opposed to negative moods (e.g., Mayer, Gaschke, Braverman, & Evans, 1992). Thus, to the extent that message arguments include statements that a plan should be followed in order to avoid negative consequences, negative moods lead high elaboration recipients to view these arguments as more compelling and to be more persuaded by them (see Petty & Wegener, 1991; Wegener et al., 1994).

Repetition of the Message   Models of persuasion that viewed attitude change as acquisition of a new verbal habit (e.g., Hovland et al., 1953) suggested that repetition of a message would enhance persuasion. Work on this question has shown substantial variability in effects, however (see Grush, 1976), and the most common pattern of findings has been an initial increase in agreement with increased repetition, followed by a decrease in agreement with further repetition (e.g., Cacioppo & Petty, 1979b). As noted earlier, these effects can be accounted for by a two-stage model of increases in objective processing of message content, followed by increases in biased processing as tedium and irritation sets in with further repetitions (see Stewart & Pechmann, 1989, for a review).

That is, at low levels of repetition, increasing the number of times a person receives the message provides the person with greater opportunity to scrutinize the merits of the object or position. This would lead to increased persuasion if the arguments are strong (as in most of the research noted above), but would actually lead to decreased persuasion if the arguments are weak (Cacioppo & Petty, 1989). This increase in processing with increased repetitions should be most evident when the messages are relatively complex (and the number of repetitions necessary for tedium might be related to the amount of complexity in the messages).

Thought-listing studies have supported the biased-processing interpretation of the tedium effect obtained with high levels of message repetition. For example, Cacioppo and Petty (1979b) found that counterarguing of strong arguments decreased from one to three message repetitions (consistent with increases in relatively objective processing with moderate repetition), but increased from three to five repetitions of the same message (consistent with irritation or reactance setting in with high levels of repetition). Favorable thoughts showed the opposite quadratic pattern, and thoughts such as complaints of boredom increased with higher message repetition. Although increases in repetition led to increases in recall of message arguments (suggesting increased processing), it was favorability of thoughts rather than amount of recall that predicted agreement. Similar effects have been found in field settings. For example, Gorn and Goldberg (1980) found that children preferred an ice cream product most with moderate repetitions of an ad for the ice cream, and that expressions of displeasure (e.g., "not again!") increased with high levels of ad repetition. One way to reduce the tedium of increasing repetition and continue to enhance the effectiveness of the advocacy is to introduce variation in the messages. In two studies, Schumann, Petty, and Clemons (1990) found that cosmetic (peripheral) variations (e.g., new pictures in the ads) across repetitions played a greater role in reducing tedium effects when the likelihood of message processing was low rather than high, but substantive variation in the message arguments (i.e., adding new arguments) was more influential in enhancing persuasion with repetition when the likelihood of message processing was high rather than low.

Summary of Effects of Persuasion Variables

Although it is still the case that most studies have examined just one role for any given persuasion variable, each of the possible multiple roles for persuasion variables has been observed for one or more of the source, message, recipient, and context variables that were reviewed. For example, effects of source characteristics have been found across the entire elaboration continuum. Even though the most studied role of source factors is that of persuasion cue when the elaboration likelihood is low, source characteristics have also been shown to influence persuasion when elaboration likelihood is high, but this has occurred because source factors were processed as arguments (Petty & Cacioppo, 1984b) or biased the processing of the communication—especially when arguments in the message were ambiguous (Chaiken & Maheswaran, 1994). Finally, numerous source characteristics have been shown to influence the amount of processing of persuasive messages when background factors do not constrain elaboration to be extremely high or low (DeBono & Harnish, 1988). Similar multiple roles have been observed for message, recipient, and context factors. Of course, some variables have only been shown to operate in one role in existing research, and studies that examine all roles within the same study are quite rare. Future research will undoubtedly more fully explore the multiple roles by which variables can influence attitudes. In addition, use of the multiple roles framework might be used to generate unique hypotheses. For example, although distraction has been studied mostly in its role as a disrupter of processing, it is possible that mild distraction might also serve as a motivator of processing if people feel that because of the distraction they need to exert extra effort in attending to the message. If this effort is greater than is actually necessary to overcome the distraction, enhanced processing over no distraction conditions would be the result. In addition, some forms of distraction could also be

annoying, which could serve as a simple disagreement cue or serve to bias processing (much as annoying message repetition has been shown to bias processing).

CONSEQUENCES OF DIFFERENT PERSUASION PROCESSES

Understanding the processes by which source, message, recipient, and context variables have their impact on attitude change is important not only for the conceptual understanding it provides, but also because there are some very important consequences associated with the process by which attitudes are changed. In this final section, some of the important characteristics and consequences of attitudes that are changed by high- versus low-effort processes are reviewed briefly (see also Eagly & Chaiken, 1998, in this *Handbook*). In particular, the temporal persistence of attitude changes, the resistance of newly changed attitudes to counterpersuasion, and the ability of newly formed or changed attitudes to predict behavior (and behavioral intentions) are highlighted.

Over the past few decades, a number of studies have addressed these topics. A general conclusion is that attitude changes that are accompanied by high levels of issue-relevant cognitive activity about the dimensions central to the attitude object are stronger than changes that are accompanied by little issue-relevant thought, or considerable thought but along dimensions that are not central to the merits of the attitude object (see Petty, Haugtvedt, & Smith, 1995, for a review). High levels of issue-relevant cognitive activity are likely to require frequent accessing of the attitude and the corresponding knowledge structure. This activity should therefore tend to increase the number of linkages and strengthen the associations among the structural elements, making the attitude schema more internally consistent, accessible, and enduring (Crocker, Fiske, & Taylor, 1984; Fazio, Sanbonmatsu, Powell, & Kardes, 1986; McGuire, 1981). In comparison, attitude change that results from simple on-line inference or heuristic processes typically involve accessing the attitude structure only once in order to incorporate the affect or inference associated with a salient persuasion cue (Petty & Cacioppo, 1986a). In general then, these attitudes should be weaker.

In the ELM analysis, attitude changes are stronger the more they are based on issue-relevant thinking and it does not matter if this thinking occurs because the experimenter instructs the person to generate a message, if the thinking is inspired naturally by the personal importance of the issue or an impending discussion, and so forth. Similarly, it doesn't matter if the enhanced thinking is relatively objective or is biased by consistency, reactance, self-esteem, impression management, or other motives. It is important to note, however, that this consequences postulate does not imply that thoughtfully changed attitudes necessarily will be stronger than one's initial attitude. It simply means that a thoughtfully changed attitude will be stronger than an unthoughtfully changed attitude. When one's attitude toward some object is changed to a new position, the "old" attitude might still exist along with the new attitude, and if the new attitude is not as strong as the old one, the old attitude could still be accessed and guide thinking and behavior. This is particularly important in many applied domains in which one wants the new attitude rather than the old one to guide action. For example, based on a health education campaign, adolescents may develop new attitudes toward safe sex. However, even if these new attitudes are induced by the central route, people may still need to think before they act so that the new attitude rather than the old attitude or salient situational cues guide behavior (Petty, Gleicher, & Jarvis, 1993).

Persistence of Attitude Change

In an attitude change context, *persistence* refers to the extent to which the newly changed attitude endures over time. In a comprehensive review of the experimental work on the persistence of attitude change, Cook and Flay (1978) concluded quite pessimistically that most of the laboratory studies on attitude change tended to find very little persistence. In the years since this influential paper, it has become more clear when attitude changes will persist and when they will not.

Current research is compatible with the view that when attitude changes are based on extensive issue-relevant thinking, they tend to endure (e.g., Mackie, 1987; see Petty et al., 1995). That is, conditions that foster people's motivation and ability to engage in issue-relevant cognitive activity at the time of message exposure are associated with increased persistence of persuasion. Thus, research has shown that self-generation of arguments (e.g., Elms, 1966; Watts, 1967) and autobiographical instances relevant to an issue (Lydon, Zanna, & Ross, 1988), using interesting or involving communication topics (Ronis, Baumgardner, Leippe, Caciopp o, & Greenwald, 1977), providing increased time to think about a message (e.g., Mitnick & McGinnies, 1958), increasing message repetition (e.g., Johnson & Watkins, 1971), reducing distraction (e.g., Watts & Holt, 1979), and leading recipients to believe that they might have to explain or justify their attitudes to other people (e.g., Boninger, Brock, Cook, Gruder, & Romer, 1990; Chaiken, 1980) are all associated with increased persistence. Also, people who characteristically enjoy thinking (high need for cognition) show greater persistence of attitude change than people who do not (Haugtvedt & Petty, 1992; Verplanken, 1991). Interestingly, simple cues can become associated with persistent attitudes if the cues remain salient over time (though attitudes that persist for this reason might often be relatively easy to change when

challenged, see Haugtvedt, Schumann, Schneier, & Warren, 1994). Relative persistence can be accomplished by repeated pairings of the cue and attitude object so that the cue remains relatively accessible (e.g., Haugtvedt et al., 1994) or by reinstating the cue at the time of attitude assessment (e.g.. Kelman & Hovland, 1953).

The Yale group explicitly acknowledged the role of "peripheral cues" and their impact on attitude persistence in their work on the "sleeper effect." A sleeper effect is said to occur when a message that is accompanied initially by a negative cue (e.g., a noncredible source) increases in effectiveness over time (see Cook, Gruder, Hennigan, & Flay, 1979; Hovland et al., 1949). To account for this effect, Kelman and Hovland (1953) proposed that in addition to message arguments, various cues could have an impact on attitude change. These cues were thought to add to (or subtract from) the effects of the persuasive message. Importantly, the cues and message were viewed as *independent* and were postulated to have different decay functions. Given this formulation, a sleeper effect would be produced if a person was exposed to a message with a discounting cue and the following conditions were met: (a) the message alone had a strong positive impact, (b) the discounting cue was sufficiently negative to suppress the positive impact of the message, and (c) the message conclusion became dissociated from the discounting cue more quickly than it became dissociated from the message arguments (Cook et al., 1979). Thus, at a later point in time, it is possible for the positive residue of the message to outlast the negative effect of the cue, leading to increased agreement with the message conclusion (compared with a no-message control).

This analysis suggests that one key to producing a sleeper effect is to construct a situation in which both a strong negative cue *and* strong arguments have an initial impact. According to the multi-process models, however, this should be difficult either because of a tradeoff between the impact of central and peripheral processes (as argument impact increases, cue impact decreases; Petty, Cacioppo, & Goldman, 1981), or because of an attenuation effect (processing strong arguments should overpower the negative cue; Maheswaran & Chaiken, 1991; Petty, 1994), or an interaction between cues and arguments (e.g., people might ignore a message from a low credible source, overturning one of the critical conditions for the effect; Heesacker et al., 1983). A solution to this conceptual dilemma is to have recipients process the message arguments first so that the strength of the issue-relevant information is realized, and *following this* present a discounting cue that causes them to doubt the validity of the message (e.g., telling people the message was false). In fact, this is the procedure used in a number of successful sleeper effect studies (Cook et al., 1979; Kelman & Hovland, 1953). In a relevant series of experiments, Pratkanis et al. (1988) showed that presenting the discounting cue after the message was critical for obtaining a reliable sleeper effect (see also Petty, Wegener, Fabrigar, Priester, & Cacioppo, 1993).

Resistance to Counterpersuasion

Resistance refers to the extent to which an attitude change is capable of surviving an attack from contrary information. Attitudes are more resistant the less they change in the direction of contrary information when challenged. Although attitude persistence and resistance tend to co-occur, their potential independence is shown conclusively in McGuire's (1964) work on cultural truisms. Truisms such as "you should sleep eight hours each night," tend to be highly persistent in a vacuum, but very susceptible to influence when challenged. As McGuire notes, people have very little practice in defending these beliefs because they have never been attacked. These beliefs were likely formed with little issue-relevant thinking at a time during childhood when extensive thinking was relatively unlikely. Instead, the truisms were probably presented repeatedly by powerful, likable, and expert sources. As noted previously, the continual pairing of a belief with positive cues can produce a relatively persistent attitude, but these attitudes might not prove resistant when attacked (Haugtvedt et al., 1994).

The resistance of attitudes can be improved by bolstering them with relevant information (e.g., Lewan & Stotland, 1961). In his work on *inoculation theory,* McGuire (1964) demonstrated that two kinds of bolstering can be effective in inducing resistance. One form relies on providing individuals with a supportive defense of their attitudes or having them generate supportive information. For example, people whose initial attitudes were bolstered by recalling autobiographical instances relevant to the attitude showed greater resistance to an attacking message than people whose attitudes were followed by the generation of autobiographical instances that were irrelevant to the attitude issue (Ross, McFarland, Conway, & Zanna, 1983). A second type of defense relies on a biological analogy. That is, McGuire suggested that just as people can be made more resistant to a disease by giving them a mild form of the germ, people could be made more resistant to discrepant messages by inoculating their initial attitudes. The inoculation treatment consists of exposing people to a few pieces of counterattitudinal information prior to the threatening communication and showing them how to refute this information. This presumably produces subsequent resistance because the inoculation poses a threat that motivates and enables people to develop bolstering arguments for their somewhat weakened attitude (see also McGuire & Papageorgis, 1961; Pfau et al., 1990).

There is relatively little work on the specific qualities that render attitude changes resistant to attack. However, any treatment that links the new attitude to the various factors known to be associated with strength (e.g., confidence,

high knowledge, etc.; Petty & Krosnick, 1995; see Eagly & Chaiken, 1998, in this *Handbook*) should increase the resistance of the attitudes. The existing data support the view that attitudes are more resistant to attack when they are accessible (Bassili, 1996) and have resulted from considerable issue-relevant elaboration. For example, Haugtvedt and Petty (1992) provided people who were high or low in need for cognition with an initial message about the safety of a food additive. This initial message, containing strong arguments from an expert source, was followed by an opposite message containing rather weak arguments from a different expert source. Although both high and low need for cognition individuals were equally persuaded by the initial message, the attitudes of the high need for cognition individuals were more resistant to the attacking message. In addition, high need for cognition individuals engaged in greater counterarguing of the attacking message. Similarly, as noted previously, Haugtvedt and Wegener (1994) found that people who encountered an initial message under conditions of high personal relevance (and thus processed it extensively) were relatively uninfluenced by a subsequent opposing message. In comparison, people who received the same messages under conditions of low relevance were more influenced by the second communication. Furthermore, people in the high relevance conditions engaged in more counterarguing of the second (opposing) message.

A strong initial attitude should prove especially effective in resisting a subsequent message if that message is susceptible to counterarguing (i.e., presents a counterattitudinal position with weak or mixed arguments). Consistent with this reasoning, Wu and Shaffer (1987) varied attitude strength by manipulating whether the initial attitude toward a new consumer product was based on direct or indirect experience. They found that attitudes based on direct experiences were more resistant to a counterattitudinal appeal but more susceptible to a proattitudinal appeal than were attitudes based on indirect experience. Information gleaned from direct experience (e.g., the taste of the product) might be more accessible, held with greater confidence, and be linked more strongly to the attitude object allowing a person to more easily recognize the flaws in contrary information but the merits in congruent information. In addition, when initial attitudes were based on direct experience, attitudes were less influenced by the credibility of the source of the second message regardless of whether the message was pro or counterattitudinal. That is, strong attitudes were less susceptible to peripheral cues (see Petty et al., 1995, for a review).

Attitude-Behavior Consistency

Perhaps the most important quality of attitudes for those interested in applications of persuasion theory concerns the ability of attitudes to predict people's actions. One important consideration in this regard is the match between the attitude that is salient at the time of attitude measurement and the attitude that is salient at the time of behavioral measurement. Any factors that reduce this match will reduce attitude-behavior consistency. Thus, initial measurements of cue-based attitudes are generally low in their power to predict subsequent behavior because these attitudes are easily changed when the cue is forgotten or new information is encountered. However, even if no external cues or information are involved, different *internal* information may be salient at the behavioral opportunity than at the time of attitude measurement. For example, research indicates that when expressing attitudes toward individuals in various social categories (e.g., African-Americans, homosexuals, etc.), people may call to mind different exemplars of the category at different points in time (Sia, Lord, Lepper, Blessum, & Ratcliff, 1997). To the extent that these different exemplars are evaluated differently, attitude instability and reduced attitude-behavior consistency can result. In a similar vein, an extensive series of studies by Wilson and colleagues (see Wilson et al., 1989) has shown that thinking about the basis of one's attitude can temporarily modify the attitude expressed and reduce the ability of this attitude to predict behavior. For example, if the central merits of an attitude object (e.g., one's spouse) are affectively based, but thinking about the basis of the attitude makes cognitive rather than affective information salient prior to attitude expression, the attitude expressed after thought will be less predictive of behavior than an attitude expressed without thought—especially if the behavior is affectively based as well (see Millar & Tesser, 1992, for a review).

In addition to this attitude salience issue, a number of situational and dispositional factors have been shown to enhance the consistency of attitudes with behaviors (see Kraus, 1995, for a recent meta-analysis). For example, attitudes are more predictive of behavior when: (a) the persons tested are of a certain personality type (e.g., are low in "self-monitoring," Snyder & Swann, 1976; or high in "need for cognition," Cacioppo, Petty, Kao, & Rodriguez, 1986); (b) the attitudes in question are consistent with underlying beliefs (e.g., Norman, 1975); (c) the attitudes are based on high rather than low amounts of issue-relevant knowledge (e.g., Davidson, Yantis, Norwood, & Montano, 1985; Kallgren & Wood, 1986); (d) the attitudinal issues are on topics of high personal relevance (e.g., Petty et al., 1983; Verplanken, 1991); and (e) the attitudes are high rather than low in accessibility (e.g., Bassili, 1995; see Fazio, 1995). What these factors likely have in common is that each is associated with attitudes that are initially based on high amounts of issue-relevant thinking (see Petty et al., 1995, for a review).

Although much research has examined how methodological factors and existing characteristics of attitudes

(e.g., extent of knowledge), people (e.g., personality), and situations (e.g., time pressure) moderate attitude-behavior consistency, relatively few studies have examined whether different attitude formation or change processes are related to the ability of newly formed or changed attitudes to predict behavior. However, some research has shown that attitudes correlate to a greater extent with behavior when the attitudes were formed under high than under low personal relevance conditions (Leippe & Elkin, 1987; Sivacek & Crano, 1982). Fazio and his colleagues have examined attitudes that were formed as a result of direct or indirect experience with the object and have found that the former are more predictive of behavior (see Fazio & Zanna, 1981, for a review). A primary reason for this is that attitudes based on direct experience are more accessible and thus more able to color perception of the attitude object and guide behavior (Fazio, 1990, 1995; see Eagly & Chaiken, 1998, of this *Handbook,* for additional discussion). One possible reason why attitudes based on direct experience are more accessible is that direct experience might typically lead to greater thought relevant to the attitude object than passive exposure to a persuasive message.

CONCLUSIONS

Research on attitude change has come a long way from initial assumptions that variables have unidirectional effects on persuasion (e.g., source credibility is good for persuasion), or that variables have an impact on persuasion by a single process (e.g., source credibility facilitates learning of the message). It is now clear that the many source, message, recipient, and context variables that have been studied over the past century can have complex effects—increasing persuasion in some situations and decreasing it in others. These bidirectional effects have been the case even for variables that on the surface, at least, seemed to be "obviously" unidirectional. For example, what could be more obvious but that distraction would be detrimental to persuasion or that expert sources would be good for persuasion? Yet, contemporary research indicates that distraction can enhance persuasion if the arguments are weak because the distraction can disrupt the normal counterarguing that would take place and expertise can be bad for persuasion when it leads to enhanced thinking about weak arguments.

Just as this single effect assumption had to be abandoned, so too did the single process assumption that variables tend to have their impact on attitudes by just one mechanism. It is now clear that variables can produce attitude change by different processes in different situations. Thus, for example, a credible source or a positive mood can lead to more persuasion by invoking a simple heuristic in low-thought situations, by influencing the extent of message processing when people are unsure whether thought is merited or not, and by biasing the ongoing processing when thought is high. Furthermore, it is clear that the same outcome can be produced by different processes in different situations. Thus, a positive mood can increase persuasion under low elaboration conditions by a simple inference process, but can produce the same amount of persuasion under high elaboration conditions by biasing the content of one's elaborations of the message content.

Although there are multiple specific processes that can determine the extent and direction of attitude change, current research strongly indicates that it is useful to divide the theoretical processes responsible for modifying attitudes into those that emphasize effortful thinking about the central merits of the attitude object from those that do not. This framework allows understanding and prediction of *what variables will affect attitudes by what processes in what general situations and what the consequences of these attitudes are.* This framework also helps to place the various mini-theories of attitude change in their proper domain of operation. For example, high-effort processes and theories like cognitive responses and dissonance should account for attitude change in those contexts in which thinking is expected to be high, whereas lower effort processes and theories such as self-perception, balance or use of simple heuristics should be more likely to account for empirical effects in those contexts in which thinking is expected to be relatively low. Finally, recognition of an elaboration continuum permits understanding and prediction of the strength of attitudes changed by different processes. That is, attitudes that are changed as a result of considerable mental effort tend to be stronger than those changed with little thought and thus are more persistent, resistant to counterpersuasion, and predictive of behavior than attitudes that are changed by processes invoking little mental effort in assessing the central merits of the object.

As might be expected, contemporary persuasion theories and those that will dominate in the twenty-first century are considerably more complicated than those that reigned in earlier periods. These theories must accommodate multiple effects of individual variables and multiple processes by which these variables have their impact. Furthermore, these theories must specify the conditions under which the different processes operate, and any differential consequences of these processes. Attitude change researchers have made great strides over the past century in identifying the building blocks of such a multifaceted theory, though considerable work remains to be done.

NOTES

1. Discussions of the tradeoff hypothesis are not meant to imply that one could not construct situations in which information relevant to a given heuristic or peripheral process is complex or difficult to assess. In such a situation, one should find an impact of that peripheral process only if people think enough to assess that information.

2. McGuire (1995b) has recognized some limitations of this input-output matrix model. Among the most notable limitations he mentions are that many of the model's input factors have been shown to interact rather than having main effects on the output or mediating factors, and that the model "exaggerates the elaborateness with which audiences usually process persuasive communications (p. 235)."

3. Although these integration rules have generally been applied in attitude change settings to integration of arguments in a persuasive message, they can also be used to model the impact of variables such as source credibility (Birnbaum, Wong, & Wong, 1976) and multiple sources (Himmelfarb, 1972). Of course, the same issues regarding a priori specification of changes in the weighting parameter apply to these applications of the integration rules.

4. If attributional processes were used to evaluate the central merits of an attitudinal position rather than make a simple inference about characteristics of the source of the message, such processing would have more in common with the high-elaboration processes discussed in the earlier section of this chapter. For example, in some situations, consumers might make more effortful or complex attributions about why advertisers omit pieces of information that are noted by competitors (inferring that the product is inferior on that feature; see Kardes, 1994).

5. It is also possible that a variable is relevant to the central merits of the attitude object (e.g., the attractiveness of the model in the current example) but under certain circumstances influences persuasion through its operation as a simple cue—as described later in the text. For example, if a person receiving a communication about the potential model is distracted (and thus is unable to extensively think about the merits of the person), then the attractiveness of the person might influence the opinions of the message recipient through a peripheral process (even though the attractiveness of the person would have been considered more carefully as a central merit if the message recipient had been able to scrutinize the information).

6. Use of the word "bias" is not meant to imply a necessary inaccuracy or incorrectness. Rather, the term "bias" is used to denote a situation in which one of a number of possible interpretations is consistently chosen based on the presence or absence of some other variable.

7. Some researchers delineated a variety of types and sources of power. For example, French and Raven (1959) compared reward power and coercive power (stemming from the ability to deliver rewards and punishments, respectively), legitimate power (stemming from societal norms), referent power (stemming from identification with the

source), expert power (stemming from perceptions of the source's knowledge), and informational power (stemming from the strength of the arguments given by the source; see also Raven, 1993). The first five types of power related to perceptions of the source himself or herself, but the last form of power related purely to the information conveyed by the source. It has been more common to discuss the effects of norms, identification with sources, expertise of sources, and information presented by sources separate from the label of power (with discussions of power being limited primarily to the ability to regulate rewards and punishments (i.e., reward and coercive power; see Kelman, 1958). Our discussion in this section is limited to power with regard to control over positive and negative outcomes, with discussions of the other characteristics of sources occurring under the respective labels (e.g., source expertise).

8. Smith and Shaffer (1995) actually showed an effect of both speech rate and argument quality under low to moderate relevance, but only an effect of argument quality when relevance was high. This is consistent with the notion of a continuum of elaboration in which the impact of peripheral cue processes is maximal at the low-elaboration end of the continuum and decreases across the continuum (until the high-elaboration end is reached, when the impact of peripheral processes is minimal; see Petty & Cacioppo, 1986a; Petty et al., 1987).

9. It is also possible that these effects are due to differences in perceived knowledge or expertise of the in-group versus out-group source. The two topics used in the study were not rated by participants as differentially important, though participants rated the in-group sources as more qualified to speak to the oil drilling issue than the out-group source (but not differentially qualified for the acid rain issue).

10. In fact, in the literature on fear appeals, a number of operationalizations are used. In some, the high fear message may include a greater number of negative consequences, or negative consequences of greater severity than in the low fear message, or the same consequences may be implied but are depicted more vividly, or are repeated more times in the high than low fear message. In still other studies, the same message is given, but recipient reactions are assessed to determine fear. Or, combinations of these features may be used to create high and low fear messages. Because of this complexity and confounding, some fear studies are open to simple alternative interpretations (e.g., the high fear message was more persuasive because it included more or better arguments).

11. Some have argued that fear has opposite effects on some of the underlying processes of persuasion (e.g., reducing reception but enhancing yielding). If so, then an inverted-U relationship might be expected between fear and persuasion (e.g., Janis, 1967; McGuire, 1968). This has not generally been observed (Boster & Mongeau, 1984), but perhaps the high levels of fear needed to obtain it have not been present in the available research.

REFERENCES

Abelson, R. P., Aronson, E., McGuire, W. J., Newcomb, T. N., Rosenberg, M. J., & Tannenbaum, P. (1968). *Theories of cognitive consistency: A sourcebook.* Chicago, IL: Rand McNally.

Abelson, R. P., & Lesser, G. S. (1959). The measurement of persuasability in children. In C. I. Hovland & I. L. Janis (Eds.), *Personality and persuasibility* (pp. 141–166). New Haven, CT: Yale University Press.

Ahlering, R. F., & Parker, L. D. (1989). Need for cognition as a moderator of the primacy effect. *Journal of Research in Personality, 23,* 313–317.

Allen, M. (1991). Meta-analysis comparing the persuasiveness of one-sided and two-sided messages. *Western Journal of Speech Communication, 55,* 390–404.

Allen, M., Hale, J., Mongeau, P., Berkowits-Stafford, S., Stafford, S., Shanahan, W., Agee, P., Dillon, K., Jackson, R., & Ray, C. (1990). Testing a model of message sidedness: Three replications. *Communication Monographs, 57,* 274–291.

Allport, F. H. (1924). *Social psychology.* Boston: Houghton Mifflin.

Allport, G. W. (1935). Attitudes. In C. Murchison (Ed.), *Handbook of social psychology* (pp. 798–884). Worcester, MA: Clark University Press.

Alwin, D. F., Cohen, R. L., & Newcomb, T. M. (1991). *The women of Bennington: A study of political orientations over the life span.* Madison: University of Wisconsin Press.

Anderson, C. A., Lepper, M. R., & Ross, L. (1980). Perseverance of social theories: The role of explanation in the persistence of discredited information. *Journal of Personality and Social Psychology, 39,* 1037–1049.

Anderson, N. H. (1971). Integration theory and attitude change. *Psychological Review, 78,* 171–206.

Anderson, N. (1981). Integration theory applied to cognitive responses and attitudes. In R. Petty, T. Ostrom, & T. Brock (Eds.), *Cognitive responses in persuasion* (pp. 361–397). Hillsdale, NJ: Erlbaum.

Anderson, N. H., & Hovland, C. I. (1957). The representation of order effects in communication research (Appendix A). In C. I. Hovland (Ed.), *The order of presentation in persuasion* (pp. 158–169). New Haven, CT: Yale University Press.

Andreoli, V., & Worchel, S. (1978). Effects of media, communicator, and message position on attitude change. *Public Opinion Quarterly, 42,* 59–70.

Apsler, R., & Sears, D. O. (1968). Warning, personal involvement, and attitude change. *Journal of Personality and Social Psychology, 9,* 162–166.

Areni, C. S., & Lutz, R. J. (1988). The role of argument quality in the elaboration likelihood model. *Advances in Consumer Research, 15,* 197–203.

Arkes, H. R., Boehm, L. E., & Xu, G. (1991). Determinants of judged validity. *Journal of Experimental Social Psychology, 27,* 576–605.

Aronson, E. (1969). The theory of cognitive dissonance: A current perspective. In L. Berkowitz (Ed.), *Advances in experimental social psychology* (Vol. 4, pp. 1–34). San Diego, CA: Academic Press.

Aronson, E., & Mills, J. (1959). The effects of severity of initiation on liking for a group. *Journal of Abnormal and Social Psychology, 59,* 177–181.

Aronson, E., Turner, J., & Carlsmith, M. (1963). Communicator credibility and communicator discrepancy as determinants of opinion change. *Journal of Abnormal and Social Psychology, 67,* 31–36.

Aronson, J., Blanton, H., & Cooper, J. (1995). From dissonance to disidentification: Selectivity in the self-affirmation process. *Journal of Personality and Social Psychology, 68,* 986–996.

Asch, S. E. (1951). Effects of group pressure upon the modification and distortion of judgments. In H. Guetzkow (Ed.), *Groups, leadership, and men* (pp. 177–190). Pittsburgh, PA: Carnegie Press.

Asch, S. E. (1956). Studies of independence and conformity: I. A minority of one against a unanimous majority. *Psychological Monographs, 70* (9, Whole No. 416).

Axsom, D., Yates, S. M., & Chaiken, S. (1987). Audience response as a heuristic cue in persuasion. *Journal of Personality and Social Psychology, 53,* 30–40.

Bagozzi, R. P. (1985). Expectancy-value attitude models: An analysis of critical theoretical issues. *International Journal of Research in Marketing, 2,* 43–60.

Baker, S. M., & Petty, R. E. (1994). Majority and minority influence: Source-position imbalance as a determinant of message scrutiny. *Journal of Personality and Social Psychology, 67,* 5–19.

Bargh, J. A., Chaiken, S., Raymond, P., & Hymes, C. (1996). The automatic evaluation effect: Unconditional automatic attitude activation with a pronunciation task. *Journal of Experimental Social Psychology, 31,* 104–128.

Baron, R. S., Baron, P. H., & Miller, N. (1973). The relation between distraction and persuasion. *Psychological Bulletin, 80,* 310–323.

Baron, R. S., Inman, M., Kao, C., & Logan, H. (1992). Emotion and superficial social processing. *Motivation and Emotion, 16,* 323–345.

Baron, R. S., Logan, H., Lilly, J., Inman, M., & Brennan, M. (1994). Negative emotion and message processing. *Journal of Experimental Social Psychology, 30,* 181–201.

Bassili, J. N. (1995). Response latency and the accessibility of voting intentions: What contributes to accessibility and how it affects vote choice. *Personality and Social Psychology Bulletin, 21,* 686–695.

Bassili, J. N. (1996). Meta-judgmental versus operative indexes of psychological attributes: The case of measures of attitude strength. *Journal of Personality and Social Psychology, 71,* 637–653.

Bates, E. (1976). *Language and context: The acquisition of pragmatics.* New York: Academic Press.

Beauvois, J. L. Bungert, M., & Mariette, P. (1995). Forced compliance: Commitment to compliance and commitment to activity. *European Journal of Social Psychology, 25,* 17–26.

Beck, K. H., & Frankel, A. (1981). A conceptualization of threat communications and protective health behavior. *Social Psychology Quarterly, 44,* 204–217.

Bem, D. J. (1965). An experimental analysis of self-persuasion. *Journal of Experimental Social Psychology, 1,* 199–218.

Bem, D. J. (1972). Self-perception theory. In L. Berkowitz (Ed.), *Advances in experimental social psychology* (Vol. 6, pp. 1–62). New York: Academic Press.

Berkowitz, L., & Lundy, R. M. (1957). Personality characteristics related to susceptibility to influence by peers or authority figures. *Journal of Personality, 25,* 306–316.

Biek, M., Wood, W., & Chaiken, S. (1996). Working knowledge and cognitive processing: On the determinants of bias. *Personality and Social Psychology Bulletin, 22,* 547–556.

Birnbaum, M. H., Wong, R., & Wong, L. K. (1976). Combining information from sources that vary in credibility. *Memory and Cognition, 4,* 330–336.

Blaney, P. H. (1986). Affect and memory: A review. *Psychological Bulletin, 99,* 229–246.

Bless, H., Bohner, G. Schwarz, N., & Strack, F. (1990). Mood and persuasion: A cognitive response analysis. *Personality and Social Psychology Bulletin, 16,* 331–345.

Boninger, D. S., Brock, T. C., Cook, T. D., Gruder, C. L., & Romer, D. (1990). Discovery of reliable attitude change persistence resulting from a transmitter tuning set. *Psychological Science, 1,* 268–271.

Boninger, D., Krosnick, J. A., Berent, M. K., & Fabrigar, L. R. (1995). The causes and consequences of attitude importance. In R. E. Petty & J. A. Krosnick (Eds.), *Attitude strength: Antecedents and consequences* (pp. 159–189). Mahwah, NJ: Lawrence Erlbaum Associates.

Bornstein, R. F. (1989). Exposure and affect: Overview and meta-analysis of research, 1968–1987. *Psychological Bulletin, 106,* 265–289.

Bornstein, R. F., & D'Agostino, P. R. (1992). Stimulus recognition and the mere exposure effect. *Journal of Personality and Social Psychology, 63,* 545–552.

Bornstein, R. F., & D'Agostino, P. R. (1994). The attribution and discounting of perceptual fluency: Preliminary tests of a perceptual fluency/attributional model of the mere exposure effect. *Social Cognition, 12,* 103–128.

Boster, F. J., & Mongeau, P. (1984). Fear-arousing persuasive messages. In R. N. Bostrom (Ed.), *Communication yearbook* (Vol. 8, pp. 330–375). Beverly Hills, CA: Sage.

Bower, G. H. (1981). Mood and memory. *American Psychologist, 36,* 129–148.

Breckler, S. J. (1984). Empirical validation of affect, behavior, and cognition as distinct components of attitude. *Journal of Personality and Social Psychology, 47,* 1191–1205.

Breckler, S. J., & Wiggins, E. C. (1991). Cognitive responses in persuasion: Affective and evaluative determinants. *Journal of Experimental Social Psychology, 27,* 180–200.

Brehm, J. W. (1956). Postdecision changes in the desirability of alternatives. *Journal of Abnormal and Social Psychology, 52,* 384–389.

Brehm, J. W. (1966). *A theory of psychological reactance.* San Diego, CA: Academic Press.

Brehm, J. W., & Cohen, A. R. (1962). *Explorations in cognitive dissonance.* New York: Wiley.

Brickman, P., Redfield, J. Harrison, A. A., & Crandall, R. (1972). Drive and predisposition as factors in the attitudinal effects of mere exposure. *Journal of Experimental Social Psychology, 8,* 31–44.

Brock, T. C. (1965). Communicator-recipient similarity and decision change. *Journal of Personality and Social Psychology, 1,* 650–654.

Brock, T. C. (1967). Communication discrepancy and intent to persuade as determinants of counterargument production. *Journal of Experimental Social Psychology, 3,* 296–309.

Brock, T. C. (1968). Implications of commodity theory for value change. In A. G. Greenwald, T. C. Brock, & T. M. Ostrom (Eds.), *Psychological foundations of attitudes* (pp. 243–296). New York: Academic Press.

Brucks, M., Armstrong, G. M., & Goldberg, M. E. (1988). Children's use of cognitive defenses against television advertising: A cognitive response approach. *Journal of Consumer Research, 14,* 471–482.

Bruner, J. S., & Tagiuri, R. (1954). The perception of people. In G. Lindzey (Ed.) *Handbook of social psychology.* Cambridge, MA: Addison-Wesley.

Burnkrant, R. E., & Howard, D. J. (1984). Effects of the use of introductory rhetorical questions versus statements on information processing. *Journal of Personality and Social Psychology, 47,* 1218–1230.

Burnkrant, R. E., & Unnava, R. (1989). Self-referencing: A strategy for increasing processing of message content. *Personality and Social Psychology Bulletin, 15,* 628–638.

Burnstein, E., & Vinokur, A. (1975). What a person thinks upon learning he has chosen differently from others: Nice evidence for the persuasive-arguments explanation of choice shifts. *Journal of Experimental Social Psychology, 11,* 412–426.

Byrne, D., & Griffitt, W. (1966). A developmental investigation of the law of attraction. *Journal of Personality and Social Psychology, 4,* 699–702.

Cacioppo, J. T., & Berntson, G. G. (1994). Relationship between attitudes and evaluative space: A critical review with emphasis on the separability of positive and negative substrates. *Psychological Bulletin, 115,* 401–423.

Cacioppo, J. T., Gardner, W. L., & Berntson, G. G. (1997). Beyond bipolar conceptualizations and measures: The case of attitudes and evaluative space. *Personality and Social Psychology Review, 1,* 3–25.

Cacioppo, J. T., Marshall-Goodell, B. S., Tassinary, L. G., & Petty, R. E. (1992). Rudimentary determinants of attitudes: Classical conditioning is more effective when prior knowledge about the attitude stimulus is low than high. *Journal of Experimental Social Psychology, 28,* 207–233.

Cacioppo, J. T., & Petty, R. E. (1979a). Attitudes and cognitive response: An electro-physiological approach. *Journal of Personality and Social Psychology, 37,* 2181–2199.

Cacioppo, J. T., & Petty, R. E. (1979b). Effects of message repetition and position on cognitive responses, recall, and persuasion. *Journal of Personality and Social Psychology, 37,* 97–109.

Cacioppo, J. T., & Petty, R. E. (1980). Sex differences in influenceability: Toward specifying the underlying processes. *Personality and Social Psychology Bulletin, 6,* 651–656.

Cacioppo, J. T., & Petty, R. E. (1981). Social psychological procedures for cognitive response assessment: The thought listing technique. In T. Merluzzi, C. Glass, & M. Genest (Eds.), *Cognitive assessment* (pp. 309–342). New York: Guilford.

Cacioppo, J. T., & Petty, R. E. (1982). The need for cognition. *Journal of Personality and Social Psychology, 42,* 116–131.

Cacioppo, J. T., & Petty, R. E. (1989). Effects of message repetition on argument processing, recall, and persuasion. *Basic and Applied Social Psychology, 10,* 3–12.

Cacioppo, J. T., Petty, R. E., Feinstein, J., & Jarvis, B. (1996). Individual differences in cognitive motivation: The life and times of people varying in need for cognition. *Psychological Bulletin, 119,* 197–253.

Cacioppo, J. T., Petty, R. E., Kao, C. F., & Rodriguez, R. (1986). Central and peripheral routes to persuasion: An individual difference perspective. *Journal of Personality and Social Psychology, 51,* 1032–1043.

Cacioppo, J. T., Petty, R. E., & Morris, K. J. (1983). Effects of need for cognition on message evaluation, recall, and persuasion. *Journal of Personality and Social Psychology, 45,* 805–818.

Cacioppo, J. T., Petty, R. E., & Sidera, J. (1982). The effects of salient self-schema on the evaluation of proattitudinal editorials: Top-down versus bottom-up message processing. *Journal of Experimental Social Psychology, 18,* 324–338.

Cacioppo, J. T., Priester, J. R., & Berntson, G. G. (1993). Rudimentary determinants of attitudes II: Arm flexion and extension have differential effects on attitudes. *Journal of Personality and Social Psychology, 65,* 5–17.

Calder, B. J., Insko, C. A., & Yandell, B. (1974). The relation of cognition and memorial processes to persuasion in a simulated jury trial. *Journal of Applied Social Psychology, 4,* 62–93.

Calder, B. J., Ross, M., & Insko, C. A. (1973). Attitude change and attitude attribution: Effects of incentive, choice, and consequences. *Journal of Personality and Social Psychology, 25,* 84–99.

Carver, C. S., & Scheier, M. F. (1982). Outcome expectancy, locus of attribution for expectancy, and self-directed attention as determinants of evaluations and performance. *Journal of Experimental Social Psychology, 18,* 184–200.

Ceci, S. J., & Bruck, M. (1993). Suggestibility of the child witness: A historical review and synthesis. *Psychological Bulletin, 113,* 403–439.

Chaiken, S. (1978). *The use of source versus message cues in persuasion: An information processing analysis.* Unpublished doctoral dissertation. University of Massachusetts-Amherst.

Chaiken, S. (1980). Heuristic versus systematic information processing in the use of source versus message cues in persuasion. *Journal of Personality and Social Psychology, 39,* 752–766.

Chaiken, S. (1986). Physical appearance and social influence. In C. P. Herman, M. P. Zanna, & E. T. Higgins (Eds.), *Physical appearance, stigma and social behavior: The Ontario symposium* (Vol. 3). Hillsdale, NJ: Erlbaum.

Chaiken, S. (1987). The heuristic model of persuasion. In M. P. Zanna, J. M. Olson, & C. P. Herman (Eds.), *Social influence: The Ontario symposium* (Vol. 5, pp. 3–39). Hillsdale, NJ: Erlbaum.

Chaiken, S., & Baldwin, M. W. (1981). Affective-cognitive consistency and the effect of salient behavioral information on the self-perception of attitudes. *Journal of Personality and Social Psychology, 41,* 1–12.

Chaiken, S., & Eagly, A. H. (1976). Communication modality as a determinant of message persuasiveness and message comprehensibility. *Journal of Personality and Social Psychology, 34,* 605–614.

Chaiken, S., & Eagly, A. H. (1983). Communication modality as a determinant of persuasion: The role of communicator salience. *Journal of Personality and Social Psychology, 45,* 241–256.

Chaiken, S., Liberman, A., & Eagly, A. H. (1989). Heuristic and systematic processing within and beyond the persuasion context. In J. S. Uleman & J. A. Bargh (Eds.), *Unintended thought* (pp. 212–252). New York: Guilford Press.

Chaiken, S., & Maheswaran, D. (1994). Heuristic processing can bias systematic processing: Effects of source credibility, argument ambiguity, and task importance on attitude judgment. *Journal of Personality and Social Psychology, 66,* 460–473.

Chaiken, S., Pomerantz, E. M., & Giner-Sorolla, R. (1995). Structural consistency and attitude strength. In R. E. Petty and J. A. Krosnick (Eds.). *Attitude strength: Antecedents and consequences* (pp. 387–412). Mahwah, NJ: Erlbaum.

Chaiken, S., Wood, W., & Eagly, A. H. (1996). Principles of persuasion. In E. T. Higgins, & A. W. Kruglanski (Eds.), *Social psychology: Handbook of basic principles* (pp. 702–742). New York: Guilford Press.

Chaiken, S., & Yates, S. M. (1985). Affective-cognitive consistency and thought-induced attitude polarization. *Journal of Personality and Social Psychology, 49,* 1470–1481.

Chattopadhyay, A., & Alba, J. W. (1988). The situational importance of recall and inference in consumer decision making. *Journal of Consumer Research, 15,* 1–12.

Chen, H. C., Reardon, R., Rea, C., & Moore, D. J. (1992). Forewarning of content and involvement: Consequences for persuasion and resistance to persuasion. *Journal of Experimental Social Psychology, 28,* 523–541.

Chen, S., Shechter, D., & Chaiken, S. (1996). Getting at the truth or getting along: Accuracy- versus impression-motivated heuristic and systematic processing. *Journal of Personality and Social Psychology, 71,* 262–275.

Cialdini, R. B. (1987). Compliance principles of compliance professionals: Psychologists of necessity. In M. P. Zanna, J. M. Olson, & C. P. Herman (Eds.), *Social influence: The Ontario symposium* (Vol. 5, pp. 165–184). Hillsdale, NJ: Erlbaum.

Cialdini, R. B., Levy, A., Herman, C. P., Kozlowski, L. T., & Petty, R. E. (1976). Elastic shifts of opinion: Determinants of direction and durability. *Journal of Personality and Social Psychology, 34,* 633–672.

Cialdini, R. B., & Petty, R. E. (1981). Anticipatory opinion effects. In R. E. Petty, T. M. Ostrom, & T. C. Brock (Eds.), *Cognitive responses in persuasion* (pp. 217–235). Hillsdale, NJ: Erlbaum.

Cialdini, R. B., & Trost, M. R. (1998). Social influence: Social norms, conformity, and compliance. In D. Gilbert, S. Fiske, & G. Lindzey (Eds.), *Handbook of social psychology* (4th ed., Vol. 2, pp. 151–192). New York: McGraw-Hill.

Cialdini, R. B., Trost, M. R., & Newsom, J. T. (1995). Preference for consistency: The development of a valid measure and the discovery of surprising behavioral implications. *Journal of Personality and Social Psychology, 69,* 318–328.

Cohen, A. R. (1957). Need for cognition and order of communication as a determinant of opinion change. In C. I. Hovland (Ed.), *Order of presentation in persuasion* (pp. 79–97). New Haven, CT: Yale University Press.

Converse, P. E. (1970). Attitudes and non-attitudes: Continuation of a dialogue. In E. R. Tufte (Ed.), *The quantitative analysis of social problems* (pp. 168–189). Reading, MA: Addison-Wesley.

Cook, T. D., & Flay, B. R. (1978). The persistence of experimentally induced attitude change. In L. Berkowitz (Ed.), *Advances in experimental social psychology* (Vol. 11, pp. 1–57). New York: Academic Press.

Cook, T. D., Gruder, C. L., Hennigan, K. M., & Flay, B. R. (1979). History of the sleeper effect: Some logical pitfalls in accepting the null hypothesis. *Psychological Bulletin, 86,* 662–679.

Cooper, E., & Dinerman, H. (1951). Analysis of the film "Don't Be a Sucker": A study of communication. *Public Opinion Quarterly, 15,* 243–264.

Cooper, H. M. (1979). Statistically combining independent studies: Meta-analysis of sex differences in conformity research. *Journal of Personality and Social Psychology, 37,* 131–146.

Cooper, J., & Fazio, R. H. (1984). A new look at dissonance theory. In L. Berkowitz (Ed.), *Advances in experimental social psychology* (Vol. 17, pp. 229–266). New York: Academic Press.

Cooper, J., Fazio, R. H., & Rhodewalt, F. (1978). Dissonance and humor: Evidence for the undifferentiated nature of dissonance arousal. *Journal of Personality and Social Psychology, 36,* 280–285.

Cooper, W. H. (1981). Ubiquitous halo. *Psychological Bulletin, 90,* 218–224.

Cox, D. S., & Cox, A. D. (1988). What does familiarity breed: Complexity as a moderator of repetition effects in advertisement evaluation. *Journal of Consumer Research, 15,* 111–116.

Crano, W. D. (1995). Attitude strength and vested interest. In R. E. Petty & J. A. Krosnick (Eds.). *Attitude strength: Antecedents and consequences* (pp. 131–157). Mahwah, NJ: Erlbaum.

Crano, W. D., & Hannula-Bral, K. A. (1994). Context/categorization model of social influence: Minority and majority influence in the formation of a novel response norm. *Journal of Experimental Social Psychology, 30,* 247–276.

Crites, S. L., Jr., Fabrigar, L. R., & Petty, R. E. (1994). Measuring the affective and cognitive properties of attitudes: Conceptual and methodological issues. *Personality and Social Psychology Bulletin, 20,* 619–634.

Crocker, J., Fiske, S. T., & Taylor, S. E. (1984). Schematic bases of belief change. In R. Eiser (Ed.), *Attitudinal judgment.* New York: Springer-Verlag.

Crutchfield, R. S. (1955). Conformity and character. *American Psychologist, 10,* 191–198.

Davidson, A. R., Yantis, S., Norwood, M., & Montano, D. E. (1985). Amount of information about the attitude object and attitude-behavior consistency. *Journal of Personality and Social Psychology, 49,* 1184–1198.

Deaux, K., & LaFrance, M. (1998). Gender. In D. Gilbert, S. Fiske, & G. Lindzey (Eds.), *Handbook of social psychology* (4th ed., Vol. 1, pp. 788–827). New York: McGraw-Hill.

DeBono, K. G. (1987). Investigating the social-adjustive and value-expressive functions of attitudes: Implications for persuasion processes. *Journal of Personality and Social Psychology, 52,* 279–287.

DeBono, K. G., & Harnish, R. J. (1988). Source expertise, source attractiveness, and the processing of persuasive information: A functional approach. *Journal of Personality and Social Psychology, 55,* 541–546.

DeBono, K. G., & Klein, C. (1993). Source expertise and persuasion: The moderating role of recipient dogmatism. *Personality and Social Psychology Bulletin, 19,* 167–173.

De Houwer, J., Baeyens, F., & Eelen, P. (1994). Verbal evaluative conditioning with undetected US presentations. *Behavior Research and Therapy, 32,* 629–633.

Deci, E. L. (1975). *Intrinsic motivation.* New York: Plenum.

Delia, J. G. (1987). Communication research: A history. In C. R. Berger & S. H. Chaffee (Eds.), *Handbook of communication science* (pp. 20–98). Newbury Park, CA: Sage.

Dillard, J. P. (in press). Rethinking the study of fear appeals. *Communication Theory.*

Dillehay, R. C., Insko, C. A., & Smith, M. B. (1966). Logical consistency and attitude change. *Journal of Personality and Social Psychology, 3,* 646–654.

Ditto, P. H., Jemmott, J. B., & Darley, J. M. (1988). Appraising the threat of illness: A mental representational approach. *Health Psychology, 7,* 183–200.

Ditto, P. H., & Lopez, D. F. (1992). Motivated skepticism: Use of differential decision criteria for preferred and nonpreferred conclusions. *Journal of Personality and Social Psychology, 63,* 568–584.

Doob, L. W. (1935). *Propaganda.* New York: Holt, Rinehart & Winston.

Downing, J. W., Judd, C. M., & Brauer, M. (1992). Effects of repeated expressions on attitude extremity. *Journal of Personality and Social Psychology, 63,* 17–29.

Eagly, A. H. (1974). Comprehensibility of persuasive arguments as a determinant of opinion change. *Journal of Personality and Social Psychology, 29,* 758–773.

Eagly, A. H. (1978). Sex differences in influenceability. *Psychological Bulletin, 85,* 86–116.

Eagly, A. H. (1981). Recipient characteristics as determinants of responses to persuasion. In R. E. Petty, T. M. Ostrom, & T. C. Brock (Eds.), *Cognitive responses in persuasion* (pp. 173–195). Hillsdale, NJ: Erlbaum.

Eagly, A. H., & Chaiken, S. (1984). Cognitive theories of persuasion. In L. Berkowitz (Ed.), *Advances in experimental social psychology* (Vol. 17, pp. 268–361. New York: Academic Press.

Eagly, A. H., & Chaiken, S. (1993). *The psychology of attitudes.* Fort Worth, TX: Harcourt, Brace, Jovanovich.

Eagly, A. H., & Chaiken, S. (1998). Attitude structure and function. In D. Gilbert, S. Fiske, & G. Lindzey (Eds.), *Handbook of social psychology* (4th ed., Vol. 1, pp. 269–322). New York: McGraw-Hill.

Eagly, A. H., Chaiken, S., & Wood, W. (1981). An attribution analysis of persuasion. In J. H. Harvey, W. J. Ickes, & R. F. Kidd (Eds.), *New direction in attribution research* (Vol. 3, pp. 37–62). Hillsdale, NJ: Erlbaum.

Eagly, A. H., & Telaak, K. (1972). Width of the latitude of acceptance as a determinant of attitude change. *Journal of Personality and Social Psychology, 23,* 388–397.

Eagly, A. H., & Warren, R. (1976). Intelligence, comprehension, and opinion change. *Journal of Personality, 44,* 226–242.

Eagly, A. H., & Wood, W. (1991). Explaining sex differences in social behavior: A meta-analytic perspective. *Personality and Social Psychology Bulletin, 17,* 306–315.

Eagly, A. H., Wood, W., & Chaiken, S. (1978). Causal inferences about communicators and their effect on opinion change. *Journal of Personality and Social Psychology, 36,* 424–435.

Edwards, K. (1990). The interplay of affect and cognition in attitude formation and change. *Journal of Personality and Social Psychology, 59*, 202–216.

Edwards, K., & Smith, E. E. (1996). A disconfirmation bias in the evaluation of arguments. *Journal of Personality and Social Psychology, 71*, 5–24.

Edwards, K., & von Hippel, W. (1995). Hearts and minds. The priority of affective versus cognitive factors in person perception. *Personality and Social Psychology Bulletin, 21*, 996–1011.

Elkin, R. A., & Leippe, M. R. (1986). Physiological arousal, dissonance, and attitude change: Evidence for a dissonance-arousal link and a "Don't remind me" effect. *Journal of Personality and Social Psychology, 51*, 55–65.

Elliot, A. J., & Devine, P. G. (1994). On the motivational nature of cognitive dissonance: Dissonance as psychological discomfort. *Journal of Personality and Social Psychology, 67*, 382–394.

Elms, A. C. (1966). Influence of fantasy ability on attitude change through role-playing. *Journal of Personality and Social Psychology, 4*, 36–43.

Eysenck, H. J., & Furneaux (1945). Primary and secondary suggestibility: an experimental and statistical study. *Journal of Experimental Psychology, 35*, 485–503.

Fabrigar, L. R., Priester, J. R., Petty, R. E., & Wegener, D. T. (in press). The impact of attitude accessibility on elaboration of persuasive messages. *Personality and Social Psychology Bulletin.*

Fazio, R. H. (1986). How do attitudes guide behavior? In R. M. Sorrentino & E. T. Higgins (Eds.), *Handbook of motivation and cognition: Foundations of social behavior* (pp. 204–243). New York: Guilford Press.

Fazio, R. H. (1990). Multiple processes by which attitudes guide behavior: The MODE model as an integrative framework. In M. P. Zanna (Ed.), *Advances in experimental social psychology* (Vol. 23, pp. 75–109). San Diego, CA: Academic Press.

Fazio, R. H. (1995). Attitudes as object-evaluation associations: Determinants, consequences, and correlates of attitude accessibility. In R. E. Petty & J. A. Krosnick (Eds.), *Attitude strength: Antecedents and consequences* (pp. 247–282). Mahwah, NJ: Erlbaum.

Fazio, R. H., & Cooper, J. (1983). Arousal in the dissonance process. In J. T. Cacioppo & R. E. Petty (Eds.), *Social psychophysiology: A sourcebook* (pp. 122–152). New York: Guilford Press.

Fazio, R. H., Jackson, J. R., Dunton, B. C., & Williams, C. J. (1995). Variability in automatic activation as an unobtrusive measure of racial attitudes: A bona fide pipeline? *Journal of Personality and Social Psychology, 69*, 1013–1027.

Fazio, R. H., Sanbonmatsu, D. M., Powell, M. C., & Kardes, F. R. (1986). On the automatic activation of attitudes. *Journal of Personality and Social Psychology, 50*, 229–238.

Fazio, R. H., & Williams, C. J. (1986). Attitude accessibility as a moderator of the attitude-perception and attitude-behavior relations: An investigation of the 1984 presidential election. *Journal of Personality and Social Psychology, 51*, 505–514.

Fazio, R. H., & Zanna, M. P. (1981). Direct experience and attitude behavior consistency. In L. Berkowitz (Ed.), *Advances in experimental social psychology* (Vol. 14, pp. 161–202). New York: Academic Press.

Fazio, R. H., Zanna, M. P., & Cooper, J. (1977). Dissonance and self-perception: An integrative view of each theory's proper domain of application. *Journal of Experimental Social Psychology, 13*, 464–479.

Festinger, L. (1957). *A theory of cognitive dissonance.* Evanston, IL: Row, Peterson.

Festinger, L. (1964). *Conflict, decision, and dissonance.* Stanford, CA: Stanford University Press.

Festinger, L., & Carlsmith, J. M. (1959). Cognitive consequences of forced compliance. *Journal of Abnormal and Social Psychology, 58*, 203–210.

Festinger, L., & Maccoby, N. (1964). On resistance to persuasive communication. *Journal of Abnormal and Social Psychology, 68*, 359–366.

Festinger, L., & Thibaut, J. (1951). Interpersonal communication in small groups. *Journal of Abnormal and Social Psychology, 46*, 92–100.

Fine, B. J. (1957). Conclusion-drawing, communicator credibility, and anxiety as factors in opinion change. *Journal of Abnormal and Social Psychology, 54*, 369–374.

Fink, E. L., Rey, L. D., Johnson, K. W., Spenner, K., Morton, D. R., & Flores, E. T. (1975). The effects of family occupational type, sex, and appeal style on helping behavior. *Journal of Experimental Social Psychology, 11*, 43–52.

Fishbein, M., & Ajzen, I. (1972). Attitudes and opinions. *Annual Review of Psychology, 23*, 487–544.

Fishbein, M., & Ajzen, I. (1975). *Belief, attitude, intention, and behavior.* Reading, MA: Addison-Wesley.

Fishbein, M., & Ajzen, I. (1981). Acceptance, yielding and impact: Cognitive processes in persuasion. In R. E. Petty, T. M. Ostrom, & T. C. Brock (Eds.), *Cognitive responses in persuasion* (pp. 339–359). Hillsdale, NJ: Erlbaum.

Fishbein, M., & Middlestadt, S. (1995). Noncognitive effects on attitude formation and change: Fact or artifact? *Journal of Consumer Psychology, 4*, 181–202.

Fiske, S. T. (1980). Attention and weight in person perception: The impact of negative and extreme behavior. *Journal of Personality and Social Psychology, 38*, 889–906.

Fiske, S. T., Morling, B., & Stevens, L. E. (1996). Controlling self and others: A theory of anxiety, mental control, and social control. *Personality and Social Psychology Bulletin, 22*, 115–123.

Fiske, S. T., & Neuberg, S. L. (1990). A continuum of impression formation, from category-based to individuating processes: Influences of information and motivation on attention and interpretation. In M. P. Zanna (Ed.), *Advances in experimental social psychology* (Vol. 23, pp. 1–74). San Diego, CA: Academic Press.

Fleming, D. (1967). Attitude: History of a concept. *Perspectives in American History, 1,* 287–365.

Fleming, M. A., & Petty, R. E. (in press). Identity and persuasion: An elaboration likelihood approach. In D. Terry & M. Hogg (Eds.), *Attitudes, behavior, and social context: The role of norms and group membership.* Mahwah, NJ: Erlbaum.

Fogelin (1982). *Understanding arguments* (2nd ed.). New York: Harcourt, Brace, Jovanovich.

Forgas, J. P. (1995). Mood and judgment: The affect infusion model (AIM). *Psychological Bulletin, 117,* 39–66.

Förster, J., & Strack, F. (1996). Influence of overt head movements on memory for valenced words: A case of conceptual-motor compatibility. *Journal of Personality and Social Psychology, 71,* 421–430.

Freedman, J., & Sears, D. (1965). Warning, distraction, and resistance to influence. *Journal of Personality and Social Psychology, 1,* 262–266.

Freedman, J. L., Sears, D. O., & O'Connor, E. F. (1964). The effects of anticipated debate and commitment on the polarization of audience opinion. *Public Opinion Quarterly, 28,* 615–627.

French, J. R. P., & Raven, B. (1959). The bases of social power. In D. Cartwright (Ed.), *Studies in social power* (pp. 150–167). Ann Arbor, MI: University of Michigan.

Fried, C. B., & Aronson, E. (1995). Hypocrisy, misattribution, and dissonance reduction. *Personality and Social Psychology Bulletin, 21,* 925–933.

Friedrich, J., Fetherstonhaugh, D., Casey, S., & Gallagher, D. (1996). Argument integration and attitude change: Suppression effects in the integration of one-sided arguments that vary in persuasiveness. *Personality and Social Psychology Bulletin, 22,* 179–191.

Fukada, H. (1986). Psychological processes mediating the persuasion inhibiting effect of forewarning in fear arousing communication. *Psychological Reports, 58,* 87–90.

Gaertner, S. L., & Dovidio, J. F. (1986). The aversive form of racism. In J. F. Dovidio & S. L. Gaertner (Eds.), *Prejudice, discrimination, and racism* (pp. 61–89). Orlando, FL: Academic Press.

Gerard, H. B., Blevans, S. A., & Malcolm T. (1964). Self-evaluation and the evaluation of choice alternatives. *Journal of Personality, 32,* 395–410.

Gilbert, D. T. (1991). How mental systems believe. *American Psychologist, 46,* 107–119.

Gilbert, D. T. (1998). Ordinary personology. In D. Gilbert, S. Fiske, & G. Lindzey (Eds.). *Handbook of social psychology* (4th ed., Vol. 2, pp. 89–150). New York: McGraw-Hill.

Gilbert, D. T., Tafarodi, R. W., & Malone, P. S. (1993). You can't not believe everything you read. *Journal of Personality and Social Psychology, 65,* 221–233.

Giner-Sorolla, R., & Chaiken, S. (1997). Selective use of heuristic and systematic processing under defense motiva-tion. *Personality and Social Psychology Bulletin, 23,* 84–97.

Gleicher, G., & Petty, R. E. (1992). Expectations of reassurance influence the nature of fear-stimulated attitude change. *Journal of Experimental Social Psychology, 28,* 86–100.

Glenn, N. O. (1980). Values, attitudes, and beliefs. In O. G. O'Brim & J. Kagan (Eds.), *Constancy and change in human development.* Cambridge, MA: Harvard Press.

Goethals, G. R., & Nelson, R. E. (1973). Similarity in the influence process: The belief-value distinction. *Journal of Personality and Social Psychology, 25,* 117–122.

Goldberg, P. (1968). Are women prejudiced against women? *Transaction, 5,* 28–30.

Gorn, G. J. (1982). The effects of music in advertising on choice behavior: A classical conditioning approach. *Journal of Marketing, 46,* 94–101.

Gorn, G. J., & Goldberg, M. E. (1980). Children's responses to repetitive television commercials. *Journal of Consumer Research, 6,* 421–424.

Gouaux, C. (1971). Induced affective states and interpersonal attraction. *Journal of Personality and Social Psychology, 20,* 687–695.

Greenwald, A. G. (1968). Cognitive learning, cognitive response to persuasion, and attitude change. In A. G. Greenwald, T. C. Brock, & T. M. Ostrom (Eds.), *Psychological foundations of attitudes* (pp. 147–170). New York: Academic Press.

Greenwald, A. G., & Albert, R. D. (1968). Acceptance and recall of improvised arguments. *Journal of Personality and Social Psychology, 8,* 31–34.

Greenwald, A. G., & Banaji, M. R. (1995). Implicit social cognition: Attitudes, self-esteem, and stereotypes. *Psychological Review, 102,* 4–27.

Greenwald, A. G., & Ronis, D. L. (1978). Twenty years of cognitive dissonance: Case study of a theory. *Psychological Review, 85,* 53–57.

Gresham, L. G., & Shimp, T. A. (1985). Attitude toward the advertisement and brand attitude: A classical conditioning perspective. *Journal of Advertising, 14,* 10–17.

Grice, H. P. (1975). Logic and conversation. In P. Cole & J. L. Morgan (Eds.), *Syntax and semantics* (Vol. 3, pp. 41–58). New York: Academic Press.

Griffitt, W. B. (1970). Environmental effects on interpersonal affective behavior: Ambient effective temperature and attraction. *Journal of Personality and Social Psychology, 15,* 240–244.

Gross, S. Holtz, R., & Miller, N. (1995). Attitude certainty. In R. E. Petty & J. A. Krosnick (Eds.). *Attitude strength: Antecedents and consequences* (pp. 215–245). Mahwah, NJ: Erlbaum.

Grush, J. E. (1976). Attitude formation and mere exposure phenomena: A nonartificial explanation of empirical findings. *Journal of Personality and Social Psychology, 33,* 281–290.

Hackman, J. R., & Anderson, L. R. (1968). The strength, relevance, and sources of beliefs about an object in Fishbein's attitude theory. *Journal of Social Psychology, 76,* 55–67.

Hafer, C. L., Reynolds, K., & Obertynski, M. A. (1996). Message comprehensibility and persuasion: Effects of complex language in counter attitudinal appeals to laypeople. *Social Cognition, 14,* 317–337.

Hale, J. Mongeau, P. A., & Thomas, R. M. (1991). Cognitive processing of one- and two-sided persuasive messages. *Western Journal of Speech Communication, 55,* 380–389.

Harasty, A., Petty, R. E., & Priester, J. R. (1996). *Self-interest versus group-interest as bases for expecting what a source will advocate: Implications for message processing and persuasion.* Unpublished manuscript, Ohio State University, Columbus, OH.

Harkins, S. G., & Petty, R. E. (1981a). The effects of source magnification of cognitive effort on attitudes: An information processing view. *Journal of Personality and Social Psychology, 40,* 401–413.

Harkins, S. G., & Petty, R. E. (1981b). The multiple source effect in persuasion: The effects of distraction. *Personality and Social Psychology Bulletin, 7,* 627–635.

Harkins, S. G., & Petty, R. E. (1987). Information utility and the multiple source effect. *Journal of Personality and Social Psychology, 52,* 260–268.

Harrison, A. A. (1977). Mere exposure. In L. Berkowitz (Ed.), *Advances in experimental social psychology* (Vol. 10, pp. 39–83). New York: Academic Press.

Hartmann, G. W. (1936). A field experiment on the comparative effectiveness of 'emotional' and 'rational' political leaflets in determining election results. *Journal of Abnormal and Social Psychology, 31,* 99–114.

Hass, R. G. (1981). Effects of source characteristics on cognitive responses and persuasion. In R. E. Petty, T. M. Ostrom, & T. C. Brock (Eds.), *Cognitive responses in persuasion* (pp. 141–172). Hillsdale, NJ: Erlbaum.

Hass, R. G., & Grady, K. (1975). Temporal delay, type of forewarning, and resistance to influence. *Journal of Experimental Social Psychology, 11,* 459–469.

Hass, R. G., & Linder, D. E. (1972). Counterargument availability and the effects of message structure on persuasion. *Journal of Personality and Social Psychology, 23,* 219–233.

Hastie, R., & Park, B. (1986). The relationship between memory and judgment depends on whether the judgment task is memory-based or on-line. *Psychological Review, 93,* 258–268.

Haugtvedt, C. P., & Petty, R. E. (1992). Personality and persuasion: Need for cognition moderates the persistence and resistance of attitude changes. *Journal of Personality and Social Psychology, 63,* 308–319.

Haugtvedt, C. P., Petty, R. E., & Cacioppo, J. T. (1992). Need for cognition and advertising: Understanding the role of personality variables in consumer behavior. *Journal of Consumer Psychology, 1,* 239–260.

Haugtvedt, C. P., Schumann, D. W., Schneier, W. L., & Warren, W. L. (1994). Advertising repetition and variation strategies: Implications for understanding attitude strength. *Journal of Consumer Research, 21,* 176–204.

Haugtvedt, C. P., & Wegener, D. T. (1994). Message order effects in persuasion: An attitude strength perspective. *Journal of Consumer Research, 21,* 205–218.

Heesacker, M. H., Petty, R. E., & Cacioppo, J. T. (1983). Field dependence and attitude change: Source credibility can alter persuasion by affecting message-relevant thinking. *Journal of Personality, 51,* 653–666.

Heider, F. (1958). *The psychology of interpersonal relations.* New York: Wiley.

Henninger, M., & Wyer, R. S. (1976). The recognition and elimination of inconsistencies among syllogistically related beliefs: Some new light on the "Socratic effect." *Journal of Personality and Social Psychology, 34,* 680–693.

Higgins, E. T. (1981). The "communication game": Implications for social cognition and persuasion. In E. T. Higgins, C. P. Herman, and M. P. Zanna (Eds.). *Social cognition: The Ontario symposium* (Vol. 1, pp. 343–392). Hillsdale, NJ: Erlbaum.

Higgins, E. T. (1989). Self-discrepancy theory: What patterns of self-beliefs cause people to suffer? In L. Berkowitz (Ed.), *Advances in experimental social psychology* (Vol. 22, pp. 93–136). New York: Academic Press.

Higgins, E. T., & McCann, C. D. (1984). Social encoding and subsequent attitudes, impressions, and memory: "Context-driven" and motivational aspects of processing. *Journal of Personality and Social Psychology, 47,* 26–39.

Higgins, E. T., Rhodewalt, F., & Zanna, M. P. (1979). Dissonance motivation: Its nature, persistence and reinstatement. *Journal of Experimental Social Psychology, 15,* 16–34.

Hilgard, E. R. (1965). *Hypnotic susceptibility.* New York: Harcourt, Brace, and World.

Himmelfarb, S. (1972). Integration and attribution theories in personality impression formation. *Journal of Personality and Social Psychology, 23,* 309–313.

Houston, D. A., & Fazio, R. H. (1989). Biased processing as a function of attitude accessibility: Making objective judgments subjectively. *Social Cognition, 7,* 51–66.

Hovland, C. I. (1957). *Order of presentation in persuasion.* New Haven, CT: Yale University Press.

Hovland, C. I., Harvey, O. J., & Sherif, M. (1957). Assimilation and contrast in communication and attitude change. *Journal of Abnormal and Social Psychology, 55,* 242–252.

Hovland, C. I., & Janis, I. L. (1959). *Personality and persuasibility.* New Haven, CT: Yale University Press.

Hovland, C. I., Janis, I. L., & Kelley, H. H. (1953). *Communication and persuasion: Psychological studies of opinion change.* New Haven, CT: Yale University Press.

Hovland, C. I., Lumsdaine, A. A., & Sheffield, F. D. (1949). *Experiments on mass communication.* Princeton, NJ: Princeton University Press.

Hovland, C. I., & Mandell, W. (1957). Is there a 'law of primacy' in persuasion? In C. I. Hovland (Ed.), *The order of presentation in persuasion* (pp. 1–22). New Haven, CT: Yale University Press.

Hovland, C. I., & Rosenberg, M. J. (1960). *Attitude organization and change.* New Haven, CT: Yale University Press.

Hovland, C. I., & Weiss, W. (1951). The influence of source credibility on communication effectiveness. *Public Opinion Quarterly, 15,* 635–650.

Howard, D. J. (1990). Rhetorical question effects on message processing and persuasion: The role of information availability and the elicitation of judgment. *Journal of Experimental Social Psychology, 26,* 217–239.

Hunter, J. E., Danes, J. E., & Cohen, S. H. (1984). *Mathematical models of attitude change: Change in single attitudes and cognitive structure.* San Diego, CA: Academic Press.

Ickes, W., Robertson, E., Tooke, W., & Teng, G. (1986). Naturalistic social cognitions: Methodology, assessment, and validation. *Journal of Personality and Social Psychology, 51,* 66–82.

Insko, C. A. (1964). Primacy versus recency in persuasion as a function of the timing of arguments and measures. *Journal of Abnormal and Social Psychology, 69,* 381–391.

Insko, C. A., (1984). Balance theory, the Jordan paradigm, and the Wiest tetrahedron. In L. Berkowitz (Ed.), *Advances in experimental social psychology* (Vol. 18, pp. 89–140). San Diego, CA: Academic Press.

Insko, C. A., Turnbull, W., & Yandell, B. (1974). Facilitative and inhibiting effects of distraction on attitude change. *Sociometry, 37,* 508–528.

Isen, A. M. (1987). Positive affect, cognitive processes, and social behavior. In L. Berkowitz (Ed.), *Advances in experimental social psychology* (Vol. 20, pp. 203–253). San Diego, CA: Academic Press.

Isen, A. M., Daubman, K. A., & Nowicki, G. P. (1987). Positive affect facilitates creative problem solving. *Journal of Personality and Social Psychology, 52,* 1122–1131.

Jacoby, L. L., Kelley, C. M., Brown, J., & Jasechko, J. (1989). Becoming famous overnight: Limits on the ability to avoid unconscious influences of the past. *Journal of Personality and Social Psychology, 56,* 326–338.

Jamieson, D. W., & Zanna, M. P. (1989). Need for structure in attitude formation and expression. In A. R. Pratkanis, S. J. Breckler, & A. G. Greenwald (Eds.), *Attitude structure and function* (pp. 383–406). Hillsdale, NJ: Erlbaum.

Janis, I. L. (1954). Personality correlates of susceptibility to persuasion. *Journal of Personality, 22,* 504–518.

Janis, I. L. (1967). Effects of fear arousal on attitude change: Recent developments in theory and experimental research. In L. Berkowitz (Ed.), *Advances in experimental social psychology* (Vol. 3, pp. 166–224). San Diego, CA: Academic Press.

Janis, I. L., & Feshbach, S. (1953). Effects of fear-arousing communications. *Journal of Abnormal and Social Psychology, 48,* 78–92.

Janis, I. L., & Field, P. B. (1959). Sex differences and personality factors related to persuasibility. In C. I. Hovland & I. L. Janis (Eds.), *Personality and persuasibility* (pp. 55–68). New Haven, CT: Yale University Press.

Janis, I. L., & Gilmore, J. B. (1965). The influence of incentive conditions on the success of role playing in modifying attitudes. *Journal of Personality and Social Psychology, 1,* 17–27.

Janis, I. L., Kaye, D., & Kirschner, P. (1965). Facilitating effects of "eating while reading" on responsiveness to persuasive communications. *Journal of Personality and Social Psychology, 1,* 181–186.

Janis, I. L., & King, B. T. (1954). The influence of role playing on opinion change. *Journal of Abnormal and Social Psychology, 49,* 211–218.

Jarvis, W. B. G., & Petty, R. E. (1996). The need to evaluate. *Journal of Personality and Social Psychology, 70,* 172–194.

Jellison, J., & Arkin, R. (1977). Social comparison of abilities: A self-presentation approach to decision making in groups. In J. Suls & R. Miller (Eds.), *Social comparison processes: theoretical and empirical perspectives.* Washington, DC: Himisphere.

Jepson, C., & Chaiken, S. (1990). Chronic issue-specific fear inhibits systematic processing of persuasive communications. *Journal of Social Behavior and Personality, 5,* 61–84.

Johnson, B. T., & Eagly, A. H. (1989). Effects of involvement on persuasion: A meta-analysis. *Psychological Bulletin, 106,* 290–314.

Johnson, B. T., Lin, H. Y., Symons, C. S., Campbell, L., & Ekstein, G. (1995). Initial beliefs and attitude latitudes as factors in persuasion. *Personality and Social Psychology Bulletin, 21,* 502–511.

Johnson, E., & Tversky, A. (1983). Affect, generalization, and the perception of risk. *Journal of Personality and Social Psychology, 45,* 20–31.

Johnson, H. H., & Watkins, T. A. (1971). The effects of message repetition on immediate and delayed attitude change. *Psychonomic Science, 22,* 101–103.

Johnson, R. W., Kelly, R. J., & LeBlanc, B. A. (1995). Motivational basis of dissonance: Aversive consequences or inconsistency. *Personality and Social Psychology Bulletin, 21,* 502–511.

Jones, E. E., & Davis, K. E. (1965). From acts to dispositions: The attribution process in person perception. In L. Berkowitz (Ed.), *Advances in experimental social psychology* (Vol. 2, pp. 219–266). New York: Academic Press.

Jones, E. E., Rhodewalt, F., Berglas, S., & Skelton, J. A. (1981). Effects of strategic self-presentation on subsequent self-esteem. *Journal of Personality and Social Psychology, 41,* 407–421.

Josephs, R. A., Giesler, R. B., & Silvera, D. A. (1994). Judgment by quantity. *Journal of Experimental Psychology: General, 123,* 21–32.

Judd, C. M., Drake, R. A., Downing, J. W., & Krosnick, J. A.

(1991). Some dynamic properties of attitude structures: Context-induced response facilitation and polarization. *Journal of Personality and Social Psychology, 60,* 193–202.

Judd, C. M., & Lusk, C. M. (1984). Knowledge structures and evaluative judgments: Effects of structural variables on judgment extremity. *Journal of Personality and Social Psychology, 46,* 1193–1207.

Kahneman, D., Knetsch, J., & Thaler, R. (1991). The endowment effect, loss aversion, and status quo bias. *Journal of Economic Perspectives, 5,* 193–206.

Kallgren, C. A., & Wood, W. (1986). Access to attitude-relevant information in memory as a determinant of attitude-behavior consistency. *Journal of Experimental Social Psychology, 22,* 328–338.

Kanouse, D. E., & Hanson, L. R. (1971). Negativity in evaluations. In E. E. Jones et al., *Attribution: Perceiving the causes of behavior* (pp. 47–62). Morristown: General Learning Press.

Kaplan, K. J. (1972). On the ambivalence-indifference problem in attitude theory and measurement: A suggested modification of the semantic differential technique. *Psychological Bulletin, 77,* 361–372.

Kardes, F. R. (1994). Consumer judgment and decision processes. In R. S. Wyer and T. K. Srull (Eds.), *Handbook of social cognition* (2nd ed., Vol. 2, pp. 399–466). Hillsdale, NJ: Erlbaum.

Kassin, S. M., Reddy, M. E., & Tulloch, W. F. (1990). Juror interpretations of ambiguous evidence: The need for cognition, presentation order, and persuasion. *Law and Human Behavior, 14,* 43–55.

Katz, D. (1960). The functional approach to the study of attitudes. *Public Opinion Quarterly, 24,* 163–204.

Kelman, H. C. (1953). Attitude change as a function of response restriction. *Human Relations, 6,* 185–214.

Kelman, H. C. (1958). Compliance, identification, and internalization: Three processes of attitude change. *Journal of Conflict Resolution, 2,* 51–60.

Kelman, H. C., & Hovland, C. I. (1953). "Reinstatement" of the communicator in delayed measurement of opinion change. *Journal of Abnormal and Social Psychology, 48,* 327–335.

Kiesler, C. A., & Kiesler, S. B. (1964). Role of forewarning in persuasive communications. *Journal of Abnormal and Social Psychology, 68,* 547–549.

Kiesler, C. A., & Munson, P. A. (1975). Attitudes and opinions. *Annual Review of Psychology, 26,* 415–456.

Kiesler, S. B., & Mathog, R. (1968). The distraction hypothesis in attitude change. *Psychological Reports, 23,* 1123–1133.

Klinger, M. R., & Greenwald, A. G. (1994). Preferences need no inferences?: The cognitive basis of unconscious mere exposure effects. In P. M. Niedenthal & S. Kitayama (Eds.), *The heart's eye: Emotional influences in perception and attention* (pp. 67–85). San Diego: Academic Press.

Knower, F. H. (1935). Experimental studies of change in attitude: I. A study of the effect of oral arguments on changes of attitudes. *Journal of Social Psychology, 6,* 315–347.

Knower, F. H. (1936). Experimental studies of change in attitude: II. A study of the effect of printed argument on changes in attitude. *Journal of Abnormal and Social Psychology, 30,* 522–532.

Koehler, D. J. (1991). Hypothesis generation and confidence in judgment. *Journal of Experimental Psychology: Learning, Memory, and Cognition, 20,* 461–469.

Kraus, S. J. (1995). Attitudes and the prediction of behavior: A meta-analysis of the empirical literature. *Personality and Social Psychology Bulletin, 21,* 58–75.

Krosnick, J. A., & Alwin, D. F. (1989). Aging and susceptibility to attitude change. *Journal of Personality and Social Psychology, 57,* 416–425.

Krosnick, J. A., Betz, A. L., Jussim, L. J., & Lynn, A. R. (1992). Subliminal conditioning of attitudes. *Personality and Social Psychology Bulletin, 18,* 152–162.

Krosnick, J. A., & Petty, R. E. (1995). Attitude strength: An overview. In R. E. Petty & J. A. Krosnick (Eds.), *Attitude strength: Antecedents and consequences* (pp. 1–24). Mahwah, NJ: Erlbaum.

Kruglanski, A. W. (1989). *Lay epistemics and human knowledge: Cognitive and motivational bases.* New York: Plenum Press.

Kruglanski, A. W., & Freund, T. (1983). The freezing and unfreezing of lay-inferences: Effects of impressional primacy, ethnic stereotyping, and numerical anchoring. *Journal of Experimental Social Psychology, 19,* 448–468.

Kruglanski, A. W., Freund, T., & Bar-Tal, D. (1996). Motivational effects in the mere-exposure paradigm. *European Journal of Social Psychology, 26,* 479–499.

Kruglanski, A. W., & Mackie, D. M. (1990). Majority and minority influence: A judgmental process analysis. In W. Stroebe & M. Hewstone (Eds.), *European review of social psychology* (Vol. 1, pp. 229–262). New York: John Wiley.

Kruglanski, A. W., Webster, D. M., & Klem, A. (1993). Motivated resistance and openness to persuasion in the presence or absence of prior information. *Journal of Personality and Social Psychology, 66,* 861–876.

Kunda, Z. (1990). The case for motivated reasoning. *Psychological Bulletin, 108,* 480–498.

Kunst-Wilson, W. R., & Zajonc, R. B. (1980). Affective discrimination of stimuli that cannot be recognized. *Science, 207,* 557–558.

Lambert, A. J., Cronen, S., Chasten, A. L., & Lickel, B. (1996). Private vs. public expressions of racial prejudice. *Journal of Experimental Social Psychology, 32,* 437–459.

Lana, R. E. (1964). Three interpretations of order effects in persuasive communications. *Psychological Bulletin, 61,* 314–320.

Lassiter, G. D., Apple, K. J., & Slaw, R. D. (1996). Need for cognition and thought induced attitude polarization: Another look. *Journal of Social Behavior and Personality, 11*, 647–665.

Lassiter, G. D., Pezzo, M. V., & Apple, K. J. (1993). The transmitter-persistence effect: A confounded discovery? *Psychological Science, 4*, 208–210.

Lasswell, H. D. (1948). The structure and function of communication in society. In L. Bryson (Ed.), *The communication of ideas: Religion and civilization series* (pp. 37–51). New York: Harper & Row.

Lasswell, H. D., Casey, R. D., & Smith, B. L. (1935). *Propaganda and promotional activities.* Minneapolis: University of Minnesota Press.

Lavine, H., & Snyder, M. (1996). Cognitive processing and the functional matching effect in persuasion: The mediating role of subjective perceptions of message quality. *Journal of Experimental Social Psychology, 32*, 580–604.

Lazarsfeld, P. F., Berelson, B., & Gaudet, H. (1944). *The people's choice.* New York: Duell, Sloan, and Pearce.

Lefebvre, V. A. (1985). The golden section and an algebraic model of ethical cognition. *Journal of Mathematical Psychology, 29*, 289–310.

Leippe, M. R., & Elkin, R. A. (1987). When motives clash: Issue involvement and response involvement as determinants of persuasion. *Journal of Personality and Social Psychology, 52*, 269–278.

Leone, C., & Ensley, E. (1986). Self-generated attitude change: A person by situation analysis of attitude polarization and attenuation. *Journal of Research in Personality, 20*, 434–446.

Lepper, M. R., Greene, D., & Nisbett, R. E. (1973). Undermining children's intrinsic interest with extrinsic reward: A test of the "overjustification" hypothesis. *Journal of Personality and Social Psychology, 28*, 129–137.

Levenson, H., Burford, B., & Davis, L. (1975). Are women still prejudiced against women? A replication and extension of Goldberg's study. *Journal of Psychology, 89*, 67–71.

Leventhal, H. (1970). Findings and theory in the study of fear communications. In L. Berkowitz (Ed.), *Advances in experimental social psychology* (Vol. 5, pp. 119–186). San Diego, CA: Academic Press.

Leventhal, H., & Niles, P. (1965). Persistence of influence for varying durations of exposure to threat stimuli. *Psychological Reports, 16*, 223–233.

Levine, G. L., Halberstadt, J. B., & Goldstone, R. L. (1996). Reasoning and the weighting of attributes in attitude judgments. *Journal of Personality and Social Psychology, 70*, 230–240.

Levine, J. M., Saxe, L., & Harris, H. J. (1976). Reaction to opinion deviance: Impact of deviate's direction and distance of movement. *Sociometry, 39*, 97–107.

Lewan, P. C., & Stotland, E. (1961). The effects of prior information on susceptibility to an emotional appeal. *Journal of Abnormal and Social Psychology, 62*, 450–453.

Lord, C. G., Ross, L., & Lepper, M. R. (1979). Biased assimilation and attitude polarization: The effects of prior theories on subsequently considered evidence. *Journal of Personality and Social Psychology, 37*, 2098–2109.

Losch, M. E., & Cacioppo, J. T. (1990). Cognitive dissonance may enhance sympathetic tonus, but attitudes are changed to reduce negative affect rather than arousal. *Journal of Experimental Social Psychology, 26*, 289–304.

Love, R. E., & Greenwald, A. G. (1978). Cognitive responses to persuasion as mediators of opinion change. *Journal of Social Psychology, 104*, 231–241.

Lumsdaine, A. A., & Janis, I. L. (1953). Resistance to 'counterpropaganda' produced by one-sided and two-sided 'propaganda' presentations. *Public Opinion Quarterly, 17*, 311–318.

Lund, F. H. (1925). The psychology of belief: IV. The law of primacy in persuasion. *Journal of Abnormal and Social Psychology, 20*, 183–191.

Lutz, R. J. (1975). Changing brand attitudes through modification of cognitive structure. *Journal of Consumer Research, 1*, 49–59.

Lutz, R. J. (1977). An experimental investigation of causal relations among cognitions, affect, and behavioral intention. *Journal of Consumer Research, 3*, 197–208.

Lydon, J., Zanna, M. P., & Ross, M. (1988). Bolstering attitudes by autobiographical recall: Attitude persistence and selective memory. *Personality and Social Psychology Bulletin, 14*, 78–86.

Maass, A., & Clark, R. D. (1983). Internalization versus compliance: Differential responses underlying minority influence and conformity. *European Journal of Social Psychology, 13*, 197–215.

Maass, A., & Clark, R. D. (1984). Hidden impact of minorities: Fifteen years of minority influence research. *Psychological Bulletin, 95*, 428–450.

Maccoby, E. E., & Jacklin, C. N. (1974). *The psychology of sex differences.* Stanford, CA: Stanford University Press.

MacKenzie, S. B. (1986). The role of attention in mediating the effect of advertising on attribute importance. *Journal of Consumer Research, 13*, 174–195.

Mackie, D. M. (1987). Systematic and nonsystematic processing of majority and minority persuasive communications. *Journal of Personality and Social Psychology, 53*, 41–52.

Mackie, D. M., & Asuncion, A. G. (1990). On-line and memory-based modification of attitudes: Determinants of message recall-attitude change correspondence. *Journal of Personality and Social Psychology, 59*, 5–16.

Mackie, D. M., & Worth, L. T. (1989). Processing deficits and the mediation of positive affect in persuasion. *Journal of Personality and Social Psychology, 57*, 27–40.

Mackie, D. M., & Worth, L. T. (1991). Feeling good, but not thinking straight: The impact of positive mood on persuasion. In J. Forgas (Ed.), *Emotion and social judgment* (pp. 201–219). Oxford, England: Pergamon Press.

Mackie, D. M., Worth, L. T., & Asuncion, A. G. (1990). Processing of persuasive in-group messages. *Journal of Personality and Social Psychology, 58,* 812–822.

Maheswaran, D., & Chaiken, S. (1991). Promoting systematic processing in low-motivation settings: Effect of incongruent information on processing and judgment. *Journal of Personality and Social Psychology, 61,* 13–33.

Maheswaran, D., & Meyers-Levy, J. (1990). The influence of message framing and issue involvement. *Journal of Marketing Research, 27,* 361–367.

Maio, G. R., Bell, D. W., & Esses, V. M. (1996). Ambivalence and persuasion: The processing of messages about immigrant groups. *Journal of Experimental Social Psychology, 32,* 513–536.

Mandler, G., Nakamura, Y., & Shebo Van Zandt, B. J. (1987). Nonspecific effects of exposure on stimuli that cannot be recognized. *Journal of Experimental Psychology: Learning, Memory, and Cognition, 13,* 646–648.

Mannheim, K. (1952). The problem of generations. In P. Kecskemeti (Ed.), *Essays on the sociology of knowledge* (pp. 276–322). London: Routledge & Kegan Paul.

Markus, H., & Zajonc, R. B. (1985). The cognitive perspective in social psychology. In G. Lindzey & E. Aronson (Eds.), *Handbook of social psychology* (3rd ed., Vol. 1, pp. 137–230). New York: Random House.

Martin, L. L., Seta, J. J., & Crelia, R. A. (1990). Assimilation and contrast as a function of people's willingness and ability to expend effort in forming an impression. *Journal of Personality and Social Psychology, 59,* 27–37.

Martin, L. L., & Tesser, A. (1996). Ruminative thought. In R. S. Wyer (Ed.), *Advances in social cognition* (Vol. 9, pp. 1–47). Mahwah, NJ: Erlbaum.

Mathur, M., & Chattopadhyay, A. (1991). The impact of moods generated by television programs on responses to advertising. *Psychology and Marketing, 8,* 59–77.

Mayer, J. D., Gaschke, Y. N., Braverman, D. L., & Evans, T. W. (1992). Mood-congruent judgment is a general effect. *Journal of Personality and Social Psychology, 63,* 119–132.

McGuire, W. J. (1960a). Cognitive consistency and attitude change. *Journal of Abnormal and Social Psychology, 60,* 345–353.

McGuire, W. J. (1960b). A syllogistic analysis of cognitive relationships. In C. I. Hovland & M. J. Rosenberg (Eds.), *Attitude organization and change: An analysis of consistency among attitude components* (pp. 65–111). New Haven, CT: Yale University Press.

McGuire, W. J. (1964). Inducing resistance to persuasion: Some contemporary approaches. In L. Berkowitz (Ed.), *Advances in experimental social psychology* (Vol. 1, pp. 191–229). New York: Academic.

McGuire, W. J. (1968). Personality and attitude change: An information-processing theory. In A. G. Greenwald, T. C. Brock, & T. M. Ostrom (Eds.), *Psychological foundations of attitudes* (pp. 171–196). New York: Academic.

McGuire, W. J. (1969). The nature of attitudes and attitude change. In G. Lindzey & E. Aronson (Ed.), *Handbook of social psychology* (2nd ed., Vol. 3, pp. 136–314). Reading, MA: Addison-Wesley.

McGuire, W. J. (1981). The probabilogical model of cognitive structure and attitude change. In R. E. Petty, T. M. Ostrom, & T. C. Brock (Eds.), *Cognitive responses in persuasion* (pp. 291–307). Hillsdale, NJ: Erlbaum.

McGuire, W. J. (1985). Attitudes and attitude change. In G. Lindzey & E. Aronson (Eds.), *Handbook of social psychology* (3rd ed., Vol. 2, pp. 233–346). New York: Random House.

McGuire, W. J. (1989). Theoretical foundations of campaigns. In R. E. Rice, & C. K. Atkin (Ed.), *Public communication campaigns* (pp. 43–66). Newbury Park: Sage.

McGuire, W. J. (1995a). The communication and attitude change program at Yale in the 1950s. In E. E. Dennis & E. Wartella (Eds.), *American communication research: The remembered history* (pp. 39–59). Mahwah, NJ: Erlbaum.

McGuire, W. J. (1995b). Transferring research findings on persuasion to improve drug abuse prevention programs. In T. E. Backer, S. L. David, & G. Soucy (Eds.), *Reviewing the behavioral science knowledge base on technology transfer* (pp. 225–245). Rockville, MD: National Institute on Drug Abuse (NIH Publication No. 95-4035).

McGuire, W. J., & McGuire, C. V. (1991). The content, structure, and operation of thought systems. In R. S. Wyer, Jr., & T. Srull (Eds.), *Advances in social cognition* (Vol. 4, pp. 1–78). Hillsdale, NJ: Erlbaum.

McGuire, W. J., & McGuire, C. V. (1996). Enhancing self-esteem by directed-thinking tasks: Cognitive and affective positivity asymmetries. *Journal of Personality and Social Psychology, 70,* 1117–1125.

McGuire, W. J., & Papageorgis, D. (1961). The relative efficacy of various types of prior belief-defense in producing immunity against persuasion. *Journal of Abnormal and Social Psychology, 62,* 327–337.

McGuire, W. J., & Papageorgis, D. (1962). Effectiveness of forewarning in developing resistance to persuasion. *Public Opinion Quarterly, 26,* 24–34.

Messerschmidt, R. (1933). The suggestibility of boys and girls between the ages of six and sixteen years. *Journal of Genetic Psychology, 43,* 422–427.

Meyerowitz, B. E., & Chaiken, S. (1987). The effect of message framing on breast self-examination attitudes, intentions, and behavior. *Journal of Personality and Social Psychology, 52,* 500–510.

Millar, M. G., & Millar, K. U. (1990). Attitude change as a function of attitude type and argument type. *Journal of Personality and Social Psychology, 59,* 217–228.

Millar, M. G., & Tesser, A. (1992). The role of beliefs and feelings in guiding behavior: The mis-match model. In C. Martin & A. Tesser (Eds.), *Construction of social judgment* (pp. 277–300). Hillsdale, NJ: Erlbaum.

Miller, A. G., McHoskey, J. W., Bane, C. M., & Dowd, T. G. (1993). The attitude polarization phenomenon: Role of response measure, attitude extremity, and behavioral consequences of reported attitude change. *Journal of Personality and Social Psychology, 64,* 561–574.

Miller, N., & Baron, R. S. (1968). *Distraction, communicator credibility and attitude change.* Unpublished manuscript, University of Iowa, Iowa City, IA.

Miller, N., & Campbell, D. T. (1959). Recency and primacy in persuasion as a function of the timing of speeches and measurements. *Journal of Abnormal and Social Psychology, 59,* 1–9.

Miller, N., Maruyama, G., Beaber, R., & Valone, K. (1976). Speed of speech and persuasion. *Journal of Personality and Social Psychology, 34,* 615–625.

Miller, C. E., & Norman, R. M. G. (1976). Balance, agreement, and attraction in hypothetical social situations. *Journal of Experimental Social Psychology, 12,* 109–119.

Mills, J., & Harvey, J. H. (1972). Opinion change as a function of when information about the communicator is received and whether he is attractive or expert. *Journal of Personality and Social Psychology, 21,* 52–55.

Mills, J., & Jellison, J. M. (1967). Effect on opinion change of how desirable the communication is to the audience the communicator addressed. *Journal of Personality and Social Psychology, 6,* 98–101.

Mitnick, L., & McGinnies, E. (1958). Influencing ethnocentrism in small discussion groups through a film communication. *Journal of Abnormal and Social Psychology, 56,* 82–92.

Moore, D. L., Hausknecht, D., & Thamodaran, K. (1986). Time compression, response opportunity, and persuasion. *Journal of Consumer Research, 13,* 85–99.

Moore, D. L., & Reardon, R. (1987). Source magnification: The role of multiple sources in the processing of advertising appeals. *Journal of Marketing Research, 24,* 412–417.

Moscovici, S. (1980). Toward a theory of conversion behavior. In L. Berkowitz (Ed.), *Advances in experimental social psychology* (Vol. 13, pp. 209–239). New York: Academic Press.

Moscovici, S., Lage, E., & Naffrechoux, M. (1969). Influence of a consistent minority on the responses of a majority in a color perception task. *Sociometry, 32,* 365–380.

Moscovici, S., & Neve, P. (1973). Studies in social influence: II. Instrumental and symbolic influence. *European Journal of Social Psychology, 3,* 461–471.

Mugny, G., & Perez, J. A. (1991). *The social psychology of minority influence.* Translated by V. W. Lamongie. New York: Cambridge University Press.

Mullis, J. P., & Lippa, R. (1990). Behavioral change in earthquake preparedness due to negative threat appeals: A test of protection motivation theory. *Journal of Applied Social Psychology, 20,* 619–638.

Murchison, C. (1935). *A handbook of social psychology.* Worcester, MA: Clark University Press.

Murphy, S. T., Monahan, J. L., & Zajonc, R. B. (1995). Additivity of nonconscious affect: Combined effects of priming and exposure. *Journal of Personality and Social Psychology, 69,* 589–602.

Murphy, S. T., & Zajonc, R. B. (1993). Affect, cognition, and awareness: Affective priming with optimal and suboptimal exposures. *Journal of Personality and Social Psychology, 64,* 723–739.

Murray, N., Sujan, H., Hirt, E. R., & Sujan, M. (1990). The influence of mood categorization: A cognitive flexibility interpretation. *Journal of Personality and Social Psychology, 59,* 411–425.

Nemeth, C. J. (1986). Differential contributions of majority and minority influence. *Psychological Review, 93,* 10–20.

Newcomb, T. M. (1956). The prediction of interpersonal attraction. *American Psychologist, 11,* 575–586.

Newcomb, T. M. (1968). Interpersonal balance. In R. P. Abelson, E. Aronson, W. J. McGuire, T. M. Newcomb, M. J. Rosenberg, & P. H. Tannenbaum (Eds.), *Theories of cognitive consistency: A sourcebook* (pp. 28–51). Chicago, IL: Rand McNally.

Newcombe, N., & Arnkoff, D. B. (1979). Effects of speech style and sex of speaker on person perception. *Journal of Personality and Social Psychology, 37,* 1293–1303.

Nisbett, R. E., & Gordon, A. (1967). Self-esteem and susceptibility to social influence. *Journal of Personality and Social Psychology, 5,* 268–276.

Norman, R. (1975). Affective-cognitive consistency, attitudes, conformity, and behavior. *Journal of Personality and Social Psychology, 32,* 83–91.

Nuttin, J. M., Jr. (1985). Narcissism beyond Gestalt and awareness: The name letter effect. *European Journal of Social Psychology, 15,* 353–361.

O'Keefe, D. J. (1990). *Persuasion: Theory and research.* Newbury Park, CA: Sage.

Olson, J. M., & Zanna, M. P. (1993). Attitude and attitude change. *Annual Review of Psychology.*

Osgood, C. E., Suci, G. J., & Tannenbaum, P. H. (1957). *The measurement of meaning.* Urbana, IL: University of Illinois Press.

Osgood, C. E., & Tannenbaum, P. H. (1955). The principle of congruity in the prediction of attitude change. *Psychological Review, 62,* 42–55.

Osterhouse, R. A., & Brock, T. C. (1970). Distraction increases yielding to propaganda by inhibiting counterarguing. *Journal of Personality and Social Psychology, 15,* 344–358.

Pallak, S. R. (1983). Salience of a communicator's physical attractiveness and persuasion: A heuristic versus systematic processing interpretation. *Social Cognition, 2,* 158–170.

Papageorgis, D. (1968). Warning and persuasion. *Psychological Bulletin, 70,* 271–282.

Pechmann, C., & Estaban, G. (1994). Persuasion processes associated with direct comparative and noncomparative advertising and implications for advertising effectiveness. *Journal of Consumer Psychology, 2,* 403–432.

Pechmann, C., & Stewart, D. W. (1989). Advertising repetition: A critical review of wearin and wearout. *Current Issues and Research in Advertising, 11,* 285–330.

Peeters, G., & Czapinski, J. (1990). Positive-negative asymmetry in evaluations: The distinction between affective and informational negative effects. *European Review of Social Psychology, 1,* 33–60.

Perloff, R. M., & Brock, T. C. (1980). And thinking makes it so: Cognitive responses to persuasion. In M. Roloff & G. Miller (Eds.), *Persuasion: New directions in theory and research* (pp. 67–100). Beverly Hills, CA: Sage.

Peterson, R. C., & Thurstone, L. L. (1933). *The effect of motion pictures on the social attitudes of high school children.* Chicago: University of Chicago Press.

Petty, R. E., (1977). *A cognitive response analysis of the temporal persistence of attitude changes induced by persuasive communciations.* Unpublished doctoral dissertation, Ohio State University, Columbus, OH.

Petty, R. E. (1994). Two routes to persuasion: State of the art. In G. d'Ydewalle, P. Eelen, & P. Bertelson (Eds.), *International perspectives on psychological science* (Vol. 2, pp. 229–247). Hillsdale, NJ: Erlbaum.

Petty, R. E. (1995). Attitude change. In A. Tesser (Ed.), *Advanced social psychology* (pp. 195–255). New York: McGraw-Hill.

Petty, R. E. (1997). The evolution of theory and research in social psychology. From single to multiple effect and process models of persuasion. In C. McGarty & S. A. Haslam (Eds.), *The message of social psychology: Perspectives on mind in society* (pp. 268–290). Oxford, England: Basil Blackwell, Ltd.

Petty, R. E., & Brock, T. C. (1976). Effects of responding or not responding to hecklers on audience agreement with a speaker. *Journal of Applied Social Psychology, 6,* 1–17.

Petty, R. E., & Cacioppo, J. T. (1977). Forewarning, cognitive responding, and resistance to persuasion. *Journal of Personality and Social Psychology, 35,* 645–655.

Petty, R. E., & Cacioppo, J. T. (1979a). Effects of forewarning of persuasive intent and involvement on cognitive responses. *Personality and Social Psychology Bulletin, 5,* 173–176.

Petty, R. E., & Cacioppo, J. T. (1979b). Issue-involvement can increase or decrease persuasion by enhancing message-relevant cognitive responses. *Journal of Personality and Social Psychology, 37,* 1915–1926.

Petty, R. E., & Cacioppo, J. T. (1981). *Attitudes and persuasion: Classic and contemporary approaches.* Dubuque, IA: Wm. C. Brown.

Petty, R. E., & Cacioppo, J. T. (1983). The role of bodily responses in attitude measurement and change. In J. T. Cacioppo & R. E. Petty (Eds.), *Social psychophysiology: A sourcebook* (pp. 51–101). New York: Guilford.

Petty, R. E., & Cacioppo, J. T. (1984a). The effects of involvement on responses to argument quantity and quality: Central and peripheral routes to persuasion. *Journal of Personality and Social Psychology, 46,* 69–81.

Petty, R. E., & Cacioppo, J. T. (1984b). Source factors and the elaboration likelihood model of persuasion. *Advances in Consumer Research, 11,* 668–672.

Petty, R. E., & Cacioppo, J. T. (1986a). *Communication and persuasion: Central and peripheral routes to attitude change.* New York: Springer-Verlag.

Petty, R. E., & Cacioppo, J. T. (1986b). The Elaboration Likelihood Model of persuasion. In L. Berkowitz (Ed.), *Advances in experimental social psychology* (Vol. 19, pp. 123–205). New York: Academic Press.

Petty, R. E., & Cacioppo, J. T. (1990). Involvement and persuasion: Tradition versus integration. *Psychological Bulletin, 107,* 367–374.

Petty, R. E., & Cacioppo, J. T. (1996). Addressing disturbing and disturbed consumer behavior: Is it necessary to change the way we conduct behavioral science? *Journal of Marketing Research, 33,* 1–8.

Petty, R. E., Cacioppo, J. T., & Goldman, R. (1981). Personal involvement as a determinant of argument-based persuasion. *Journal of Personality and Social Psychology, 41,* 847–855.

Petty, R. E., Cacioppo, J. T., & Haugtvedt, C. (1992). Involvement and persuasion: An appreciative look at the Sherifs' contribution to the study of self-relevance and attitude change. In D. Granberg & G. Sarup (Eds.), *Social judgment and intergroup relations: Essays in honor of Muzifer Sherif* (pp. 147–175). New York: Springer-Verlag.

Petty, R. E., Cacioppo, J. T., & Heesacker, M. (1981). Effects of rhetorical questions on persuasion: A cognitive response analysis. *Journal of Personality and Social Psychology, 40,* 432–440.

Petty, R. E., Cacioppo, J. T., & Schumann, D. W. (1983). Central and peripheral routes to advertising effectiveness: The moderating role of involvement. *Journal of Consumer Research, 10,* 135–146.

Petty, R. E., Gleicher, F., & Baker, S. M. (1991). Multiple roles for affect in persuasion. In J. Forgas (Ed.), *Emotion and social judgments* (pp. 181–200). Oxford, England: Pergamon Press.

Petty, R. E., Gleicher, F., & Jarvis, W. B. G. (1993). Persuasion theory and AIDS prevention. In J. B. Pryor & G. D. Reeder (Eds.), *The social psychology of HIV infection* (pp. 155–182). Hillsdale, NJ: Erlbaum.

Petty, R. E., Harkins, S. G., & Williams, K. D. (1980). The effects of group diffusion of cognitive effort on attitudes. An information processing view. *Journal of Personality and Social Psychology, 38,* 81–92.

Petty, R. E., Haugtvedt, C. P., & Smith, S. M. (1995). Elaboration as a determinant of attitude strength. In R. E. Petty & J. A. Krosnick (Eds.), *Attitude strength: Antecedents and consequences* (pp. 93–130). Mahwah, NJ: Erlbaum.

Petty, R. E., & Jarvis, W. B. G. (1996). An individual differences perspective on assessing cognitive processes. In N. Schwarz & S. Sudman (Eds.), *Answering questions: Methodology for determining cognitive and communicative processes in survey research* (pp. 221–257). San Francisco: Jossey-Bass.

Petty, R. E., Jarvis, W. B. J., & Evans, L. M. (1996). Recurrent thought: Some implications for attitudes and persuasion. In R. S. Wyer (Ed.), *Advances in social cognition* (Vol. 9, pp. 145–164). Mahwah, NJ: Erlbaum.

Petty, R. E., Kasmer, J. A., Haugtvedt, C. P., & Cacioppo, J. T. (1987). A reply to Stiff and Boster. *Communication Monographs, 54,* 257–263.

Petty, R. E., & Krosnick, J. A. (Eds.) (1995). *Attitude strength: Antecedents and consequences.* Mahwah, NJ: Erlbaum.

Petty, R. E., Ostrom, T. M., & Brock, T. C. (Eds.) (1981). *Cognitive responses in persuasion.* Hillsdale, NJ: Erlbaum.

Petty, R. E., Priester, J. R., & Wegener, D. T. (1994). Cognitive processes in attitude change. In R. S. Wyer and T. K. Srull (Eds.), *Handbook of social cognition* (2nd ed., Vol. 2, pp. 69–142). Hillsdale, NJ: Erlbaum.

Petty, R. E., Schumann, D. W., Richman, S. A., & Strathman, A. J. (1993). Positive mood and persuasion: Different roles for affect under high- and low-elaboration conditions. *Journal of Personality and Social Psychology, 64,* 5–20.

Petty, R. E., & Wegener, D. T. (1991). Thought systems, argument quality, and persuasion. In R. S. Wyer, Jr., & T. K. Srull (Eds.), *Advances in social cognition* (Vol. 4, pp. 147–161). Hillsdale, NJ: Erlbaum.

Petty, R. E., & Wegener, D. T. (1993). Flexible correction processes in social judgment: Correcting for context induced contrast. *Journal of Experimental Social Psychology, 29,* 137–165.

Petty, R. E., & Wegener, D. T. (in press-a). The Elaboration Likelihood Model: Current status and controversies. In S. Chaiken & Y. Trope (Eds.), *Dual process theories in social psychology.* New York: Guilford Press.

Petty, R. E., & Wegener, D. T. (in press-b). Matching versus mismatching attitude functions: Implications for scrutiny of persuasive messages. *Personality and Social Psychology Bulletin.*

Petty, R. E., Wegener, D. T., & Fabrigar, L. R. (1997). Attitudes and attitude change. *Annual Review of Psychology, 48,* 609–647.

Petty, R. E., Wegener, D. T., Fabrigar, L. R., Priester, J. R., & Cacioppo, J. T. (1993). Conceptual and methodological issues in the elaboration likelihood model of persuasion: A reply to the Michigan State critics. *Communication Theory, 3,* 336–363.

Petty, R. E., Wegener, D. T., & White, P. H. (in press). Flexible correction processes: Implications for persuasion. *Social Cognition.*

Petty, R. E., Wells, G. L., & Brock, T. C. (1976). Distraction can enhance or reduce yielding to propaganda: Thought disruption versus effort justification. *Journal of Personality and Social Psychology, 34,* 874–884.

Petty, R. E., Wells, G. L., Heesacker, M., Brock, T. C., & Cacioppo, J. T. (1983). The effects of recipient posture on per-

suasion. A cognitive response analysis. *Personality and Social Psychology Bulletin, 9,* 209–222.

Pfau, M., Kenski, H. C., Nitz, M., & Sorenson, J. (1990). Efficacy of inoculation strategies in promoting resistance to political attack messages: Application to direct mail. *Communication Monographs, 57,* 25–43.

Pittman, T. S. (1993). Control motivation and attitude change. In G. Weary, F. Gleicher, & K. Marsh (Eds.), *Control motivation and social cognition* (pp. 157–175). New York: Springer-Verlag.

Pomerantz, E. M., Chaiken, S., & Tordesillas, R. S. (1995). Attitude strength and resistance processes. *Journal of Personality and Social Psychology, 69,* 408–419.

Pratkanis, A. R., Breckler, S. J., & Greenwald, A. G. (Eds.) (1989). *Attitude structure and function.* Hillsdale, NJ: Erlbaum.

Pratkanis, A. R., Greenwald, A. G., Leippe, M. R., & Baumgardner, M. H. (1988). In search of reliable persuasion effects: III. The sleeper effect is dead. Long live the sleeper effect. *Journal of Personality and Social Psychology, 54,* 203–218.

Priester, J. R., Cacioppo, J. T., & Petty, R. E. (1996). The influence of motor processes on attitudes toward novel versus familiar semantic stimuli. *Personality and Social Psychology Bulletin, 22,* 442–447.

Priester, J. R., & Petty, R. E. (1995). Source attributions and persuasion: Perceived honesty as a determinant of message scrutiny. *Personality and Social Psychology Bulletin, 21,* 637–654.

Priester, J. R., & Petty, R. E. (1996). The gradual threshold model of ambivalence: Relating the positive and negative bases of attitudes to subjective ambivalence. *Journal of Personality and Social Psychology, 71,* 431–449.

Puckett, J. M., Petty, R. E., Cacioppo, J. T., & Fisher, D. L. (1983). The relative impact of age and attractiveness stereotypes on persuasion. *Journal of Gerontology, 38,* 340–343.

Ratneshwar, S., & Chaiken, S. (1991). Comprehension's role in persuasion: The case of its moderating effect on the persuasive impact of source cues. *Journal of Consumer Psychology, 18,* 52–62.

Raven, B. H. (1993). The bases of power: Origins and recent developments. *Journal of Social Issues, 49,* 227–251.

Raven, B. H., & French, J. R. P. (1958). Legitimate power, coercive power, and observability in social influence. *Sociometry, 21,* 83–97.

Razran, G. H. S. (1940). Conditioned response changes in rating and appraising sociopolitical slogans. *Psychological Bulletin, 37,* 481.

Rhine, R., & Severance, L. (1970). Ego-involvement, discrepancy, source credibility, and attitude change. *Journal of Personality and Social Psychology, 16,* 175–190.

Rhodes, N., & Wood, W. (1992). Self-esteem and intelligence affect influenceability: The mediating role of message reception. *Psychological Bulletin, 111,* 156–171.

Rippetoe, P. A., & Rogers, R. W. (1987). Effects of components of protection-motivation theory on adaptive and maladaptive coping with a health threat. *Journal of Personality and Social Psychology, 52,* 596–604.

Rogers, R. W. (1975). A protection motivation theory of fear appeals and attitude change. *Journal of Psychology, 91,* 93–114.

Rogers, R. W. (1983). Cognitive and physiological processes in fear appeals and attitude change: A revised theory of protection motivation. In J. T. Cacioppo & R. E. Petty (Eds.), *Social psychophysiology: A sourcebook* (pp. 153–176). New York: Guilford.

Romero, A. A., Agnew, C. R., & Insko, C. A. (1996). The cognitive mediation hypothesis revisited: An empirical response to methodological and theoretical criticism. *Personality and Social Psychology Bulletin, 22,* 651–665.

Ronis, D. L., Baumgardner, M. H., Leippe, M. R., Cacioppo, J. T., & Greenwald, A. G. (1977). In search of reliable persuasion effects: I. A computer-controlled procedure for studying persuasion. *Journal of Personality and Social Psychology, 35,* 548–569.

Roselli, F., Skelly, J. J., & Mackie, D. M. (1995). Processing rational and emotional messages: The cognitive and affective mediation of persuasion. *Journal of Experimental Social Psychology, 31,* 163–190.

Rosenbaum, M. E. (1986). The repulsion hypothesis. On the nondevelopment of relationships. *Journal of Personality and Social Psychology, 51,* 1156–1166.

Rosenberg, M. J. (1956). Cognitive structure and attitudinal affect. *Journal of Abnormal and Social Psychology, 53,* 367–372.

Rosenberg, M. J. (1960). Cognitive reorganization in response to hypnotic reversal of attitudinal affect. *Journal of Personality, 28,* 39–63.

Rosenberg, M. J., & Abelson, R. P. (1960). An analysis of cognitive balancing. In C. I. Hovland & M. J. Rosenberg (Eds.), *Attitude organization and change: An analysis of consistency among attitude components* (pp. 112–163). New Haven, CT: Yale University Press.

Roskos-Ewoldsen, D. R., & Fazio, R. H. (1992). The accessibility of source likability as a determinant of persuasion. *Personality and Social Psychology Bulletin, 18,* 19–25.

Ross, L., Lepper, M. R., Strack, F., & Steinmetz, J. (1977). Social explanation and social expectation: Effects of real and hypothetical explanations of subjective likelihood. *Journal of Personality and Social Psychology, 35,* 817–829.

Ross, M., McFarland, C., Conway, M., & Zanna, M. P. (1983). Reciprocal relation between attitudes and behavior recall: Committing people to newly formed attitudes. *Journal of Personality and Social Psychology, 45,* 257–267.

Rothman, A. J., & Salovey, P. (1997). Shaping perceptions to motivate healthy behavior: The role of message framing. *Psychological Bulletin, 121,* 3–19.

Rothman, A. J., Salovey, P., Antone, C., Keough, K., & Martin, C. D. (1993). The influence of message framing on intentions to perform health behaviors. *Journal of Experimental Social Psychology, 29,* 408–433.

Sadler, O., & Tesser, A. (1973). Some effects of salience and time upon interpersonal hostility and attraction. *Sociometry, 36,* 99–112.

Salovey, P., Rothman, A. J., & Rodin, J. (1998). Health behavior. In D. Gilbert, S. Fiske, & G. Lindzey (Eds.), *Handbook of social psychology* (4th ed., Vol. 2, pp. 633–683). New York: McGraw-Hill.

Sanbonmatsu, D. M., & Kardes, F. R. (1988). The effects of physiological arousal on information processing and persuasion. *Journal of Consumer Research, 15,* 379–385.

Scher, S. J., & Cooper, J. (1989). Motivational basis of dissonance: The singular role of behavioral consequences. *Journal of Personality and Social Psychology, 56,* 899–906.

Schlenker, B. R. (1982). Translating actions into attitudes: An identity-analytic approach to the explanation of social conduct. In L. Berkowitz (Ed.), *Advances in experimental social psychology* (Vol. 15, pp. 193–247). San Diego, CA: Academic Press.

Schuette, R. A., & Fazio, R. H. (1995). Attitude accessibility and motivation as determinants of biased processing: A test of the MODE model. *Personality and Social Psychology Bulletin, 21,* 704–710.

Schul, Y., & Burnstein, E. (1985). When discounting fails: Conditions under which individuals use discredited information in making a judgment. *Journal of Personality and Social Psychology, 49,* 894–903.

Schumann, D. W., Petty, R. E., & Clemons, D. S. (1990). Predicting the effectiveness of different strategies of advertising variation. A test of the repetition-variation hypotheses. *Journal of Consumer Research, 17,* 192–201.

Schwarz, N. (1990). Feelings as information: Informational and motivational functions of affective states. In E. T. Higgins & R. M. Sorrentino (Eds.), *Handbook of motivation and cognition: Foundations of social behavior* (Vol. 2, pp. 527–561). New York: Guilford.

Schwarz, N., & Bless, H. (1992). Constructing reality and its alternatives: An inclusion/exclusion model of assimilation and contrast effects in social judgment. In L. L. Martin & A. Tesser (Eds.), *The construction of social judgments* (pp. 217–245). Hillsdale, NJ: Erlbaum.

Schwarz, N., Bless, H., & Bohner, G. (1991). Mood and persuasion: Affective states influence the processing of persuasive communications. In M. P. Zanna (Ed.), *Advances in experimental social psychology* (Vol. 24, pp. 161–201). San Diego: Academic Press.

Schwarz, N., & Clore, G. (1983). Mood, misattribution, and judgments of well-being: Informative and directive functions of affective states. *Journal of Personality and Social Psychology, 45,* 513–523.

Scott, C. A., & Yalch, R. J. (1978). A test of the self-perception explanation of the effects of rewards on intrinsic interest. *Journal of Experimental Social Psychology, 14,* 180–192.

Sears, D. O. (1981). Life stage effects on attitude change, especially among the elderly. In S. B. Kiesler, J. N. Morgan, & V. K. Oppenheimer (Eds.), *Aging: Social change* (pp. 183–204). San Diego, CA: Academic Press.

Sears, D. O. (1986). College students in the laboratory: Influences of a narrow data base on social psychology's view of human nature. *Journal of Personality and Social Psychology, 51,* 515–530.

Shavitt, S. (1989). Operationalizing functional theories of attitude. In A. R. Pratkanis, S. J. Breckler, & A. G. Greenwald, (Eds.), *Attitude structure and function* (pp. 311–338). Hillsdale, NJ: Erlbaum.

Shavitt, S., Swan, S., Lowery, T. M., & Wänke, M. (1994). The interaction of endorser attractiveness and involvement in persuasion depends on the goal that guides message processing. *Journal of Consumer Psychology, 3,* 137–162.

Sherif, C. W., Sherif, M., & Nebergall, R. E. (1965). *Attitude and attitude change: The social judgment–involvement approach.* Philadelphia: Saunders.

Sherif, M. (1977). Crisis in social psychology: Some remarks towards breaking through the crisis. *Personality and Social Psychology Bulletin, 3,* 368–382.

Sherif, M., & Hovland, C. I. (1961). *Social judgment: Assimilation and contrast effects in communication and attitude change.* New Haven, CT: Yale University Press.

Sherman, S. J. (1973). Internal-external control and its relationship to attitude change under different social influence techniques. *Journal of Personality and Social Psychology, 26,* 23–29.

Sherman, S. J., Cialdini, R. B., Schwartzman, D. F., & Reynolds, K. D. (1985). Imagining can heighten or lower the perceived likelihood of contracting a disease: The mediating effect of ease of imagery. *Personality and Social Psychology Bulletin, 11,* 118–127.

Sherman, S. J., Zehner, K. S., Johnson, J., & Hirt, E. R. (1983). Social explanation: The role of timing, set, and recall on subjective likelihood estimates. *Journal of Personality and Social Psychology, 44,* 1127–1143.

Shimp, T. A., Stuart, E. W., & Engle, R. W. (1991). A program of classical conditioning experiments testing variations in the conditioned stimulus and context. *Journal of Consumer Research, 18,* 1–12.

Sia, T. L., Lord, C. G., Lepper, M. R., Blessum, K. A., & Ratcliff, C. D. (1997). Is a rose always a rose? The role of social category exemplar change in attitude stability and attitude-behavior consistency. *Journal of Personality and Social Psychology, 72,* 501–514.

Simon, L., Greenberg, J., & Brehm, J. (1995). Trivialization: The forgotten mode of dissonance reduction. *Journal of Personality and Social Psychology, 68,* 247–260.

Sistrunk, F., & McDavid, J. W. (1971). Sex variable in conforming behavior. *Journal of Personality and Social Psychology, 17,* 200–207.

Sivacek, J., & Crano, W. D. (1982). Vested interest as a moderator of attitude-behavior consistency. *Journal of Personality and Social Psychology, 43,* 210–221.

Skolnick, P., & Heslin, R. (1971). Quality versus difficulty: Alternative interpretations of the relationship between self-esteem and persuasibility. *Journal of Personality, 39,* 242–251.

Skowronski, J. J., & Carlston, D. E. (1989). Negativity and extremity biases in impression formation: A review of explanations. *Psychological Bulletin, 105,* 131–142.

Slamecka, N. J., & Graf, P. (1978). The generation effect: Delineation of a phenomenon. *Journal of Experimental Psychology: Human Learning and Memory, 4,* 592–604.

Slusher, M. P., & Anderson, C. A. (1996). Using causal persuasive arguments to change beliefs and teach new information. The mediating role of explanation availability and evaluation bias in the acceptance of knowledge. *Journal of Educational Psychology, 88,* 110–122.

Smith, M. B., Bruner, J. S., & White, R. W. (1956). *Opinions and personality.* New York: Wiley.

Smith, S. M., Haugtvedt, C. P., & Petty, R. E. (1994). Need for cognition and the effects of repeated expression on attitude accessibility and extremity. *Advances in Consumer Research, 21,* 234–237.

Smith, S. M., & Petty, R. E. (1996). Message framing and persuasion: A message processing analysis. *Personality and Social Psychology Bulletin, 22,* 257–268.

Smith, S. M., & Shaffer, D. R. (1995). Speed of speech and persuasion: Evidence for multiple effects. *Personality and Social Psychology Bulletin, 21,* 1051–1060.

Snyder, M. (1974). The self-monitoring of expressive behavior. *Journal of Personality and Social Psychology, 30,* 526–537.

Snyder, M., & DeBono, K. G. (1989). Understanding the functions of attitudes: Lessons from personality and social behavior. In S. J. Pratkanis, S. J. Breckler, & A. G. Greenwald (Eds.), *Attitude structure and function* (pp. 339–359). Hillsdale, NJ: Erlbaum.

Snyder, M., & Rothbart, M. (1971). Communicator attractiveness and opinion change. *Canadian Journal of Behavioural Science, 3,* 377–387.

Snyder, M., & Swann, W. B. (1976). When actions reflect attitudes: The politics of impression management. *Journal of Personality and Social Psychology, 34,* 1034–1042.

Snyder, M., & Tanke, E. D. (1976). Behavior and attitude: Some people are more consistent than others. *Journal of Personality, 44,* 510–517.

Sorrentino, R. M., Bobocel, D. R., Gitta, M. Z., Olson, J. M., & Hewitt, E. C. (1988). Uncertainty orientation and persuasion: Individual differences in the effects of personal relevance on social judgments. *Journal of Personality and Social Psychology, 55,* 357–371.

Sponberg, H. (1946). A study of the relative effectiveness of climax and anti-climax order in an argumentative speech. *Speech Monographs, 13,* 35–44.

Staats, A. W., & Staats, C. K. (1958). Attitudes established by classical conditioning. *Journal of Abnormal and Social Psychology, 57,* 37–40.

Staats, A. W., Staats, C. K., & Crawford, H. L. (1962). First-order conditioning of meaning and the parallel condition-ing of a GSR. *Journal of General Psychology, 67,* 159–167.

Stayman, D. M., & Kardes, F. R. (1992). Spontaneous infer-ence processes in advertising: Effects of need for cognition and self-monitoring on inference generation and utilization. *Journal of Consumer Psychology, 1,* 125–142.

Steele, C. M. (1988). The psychology of self-affirmation: Sus-taining the integrity of the self. In L. Berkowitz (Ed.), *Ad-vances in experimental social psychology* (Vol. 21, pp. 261–302). New York: Academic Press.

Steele, C. M., Southwick, L. Critchlow, B. (1981). Dissonance and alcohol: Drinking your troubles away. *Journal of Per-sonality and Social Psychology, 41,* 831–846.

Steele, C. M., Spencer, S. J., & Lynch, M. (1993). Self-image resilience and dissonance: The role of affirmational re-sources. *Journal of Personality and Social Psychology, 64,* 885–896.

Sternthal, B., Dholakia, R., & Leavitt, C. (1978). The persua-sive effect of source credibility: A test of cognitive response analysis. *Journal of Consumer Research, 4,* 252–260.

Stiff, J. B. (1986). Cognitive processing of persuasive mes-sage cues: A meta-analytic review of the effects of support-ing information on attitudes. *Communication Monographs, 53,* 75–89.

Stone, J., Aronson, E., Craine, A. L., Winslow, M. P., & Fried, C. B. (1994). Inducing hypocrisy as a means of encourag-ing young adults to use condoms. *Personality and Social Psychology Bulletin, 20,* 116–128.

Stone, J., & Cooper, J. (1996). *A self-standards model of dis-sonance.* Unpublished manuscript. Princeton University, Princeton, NJ.

Stone, J., Wiegand, A. W., Cooper, J., & Aronson, E. (1997). When exemplification fails: Hypocrisy and the motive for self-integrity. *Journal of Personality and Social Psychol-ogy, 72,* 54–65.

Strack, F., Martin, L., & Stepper, S. (1988). Inhibiting and fa-cilitating conditions of the human smile: A nonobtrusive test of the facial feedback hypothesis. *Journal of Personal-ity and Social Psychology, 54,* 768–777.

Strathman, A. J., Gleicher, F., Boninger, D. S., & Edwards, C. S. (1994). The consideration of future consequences: Weighing immediate and distant outcomes of behavior. *Journal of Personality and Social Psychology, 66,* 742–752.

Stuart, E. W., Shimp, T. A., & Engle, R. W. (1987). Classical conditioning of consumer attitudes: Four experiments in an advertising context. *Journal of Consumer Research, 14,* 334–349.

Sturges, J. W., & Rogers, R. R. (1996). Preventive health psy-chology from a developmental perspective: An extension of protection motivation theory. *Health Psychology, 15,* 158–166.

Sutton, S. R. (1982). Fear-arousing communications: A criti-cal examination of theory and research. In J. R. Eiser (Ed.),

Social psychology and behavioral medicine (pp. 303–337). Chichester, England: Wiley.

Swim, J., Borgida, E., Maruyama, G., & Myers, D. G. (1989). Joan McKay versus John McKay: Do gender stereotypes bias evaluations? *Psychological Bulletin, 105,* 409–429.

Tajfel, H. (1970). Experiments in intergroup discrimination. *Scientific American, 223,* 96–102.

Taylor, S. E. (1975). On inferring one's attitude from one's be-havior: Some delimiting conditions. *Journal of Personality and Social Psychology, 31,* 126–131.

Taylor, S. E. (1981). The interface of cognitive and social psy-chology. In J. H. Harvey (Ed.), *Cognition, social behavior, and the environment* (pp. 189–211). Hillsdale, NJ: Erlbaum.

Tedeschi, J. T., Schlenker, B. R., & Bonoma, T. V. (1971). Cognitive dissonance: Private ratiocination or public spec-tacle? *American Psychologist, 26,* 685–695.

Tesser, A. (1978). Self-generated attitude change. In L. Berkowitz (Ed.), *Advances in experimental social psychol-ogy* (Vol. 11, pp. 289–338). New York: Academic Press.

Tesser, A. (1993). The importance of heritability in psycholog-ical research: The case of attitudes. *Psychological Review, 100,* 129–142.

Tesser, A., & Cornell, D. P. (1991). On the confluence of self processes. *Journal of Experimental Social Psychology, 27,* 501–526.

Tesser, A., Martin, L., & Mendolia, M. (1995). The impact of thought on attitude extremity and attitude-behavior consis-tency. In R. E. Petty & J. A. Krosnick (Eds.), *Attitude strength: Antecedents and consequences* (pp. 73–92). Mah-wah, NJ: Erlbaum.

Tesser, A., & Rosen, S. (1975). The reluctance to transmit bad news: The MUM effect. In L. Berkowitz (Ed.), *Advances in Experimental Social Psychology* (Vol. 8, pp. 199–232).

Tetlock, P. E. (1983). Accountability and the complexity of thought. *Journal of Personality and Social Psychology, 45,* 74–83.

Tetlock, P. E. (1992). The impact of accountability on judg-ment and choice: Toward a social contingency model. *Ad-vances in Experimental Social Psychology, 25,* 331–376.

Tetlock, P. E., Skitka, L., & Boettger, R. (1989). Social and cognitive strategies of coping with accountability: Confor-mity, complexity, and bolstering. *Journal of Personality and Social Psychology, 57,* 632–641.

Thibodeau, R., & Aronson, E. (1992). Taking a closer look: Re-asserting the role of the self-concept in dissonance theory. *Personality and Social Psychology Bulletin, 18,* 591–602.

Thompson, M. M., Zanna, M. P., & Griffin, D. W. (1995). Let's not be indifferent about (attitudinal) ambivalence. In R. E. Petty & J. A. Krosnick (Eds.), *Attitude strength: Antecedents and consequences* (pp. 361–386). Mahwah, NJ: Erlbaum.

Thomsen, C. J., Borgida, E., & Lavine, H. (1995). The causes and consequences of personal involvement. In R. E. Petty & J. A. Krosnick (Eds.), *Attitude strength: Antecedents and consequences* (pp. 191–214). Mahwah, NJ: Erlbaum.

Thorndike, E. L. (1920). A constant error in psychological ratings. *Journal of Applied Psychology, 4,* 25–29.

Titchener, E. B. (1910). *Textbook of psychology.* New York: Macmillan.

Trost, M. R., Maass, A., & Kenrick, D. T. (1992). Minority influence: Personal relevance biases cognitive processes and reverses private acceptance. *Journal of Experimental Social Psychology, 28,* 234–254.

Tykocinski, O., Higgins, E. T., & Chaiken, S. (1994). Message framing, self-discrepancies, and yielding to persuasive messages: The motivational significance of psychological situations. *Personality and Social Psychology Bulletin, 20,* 107–115.

Tyler, T. R., & Schuller, R. A. (1991). Aging and attitude change. *Journal of Personality and Social Psychology, 61,* 689–697.

Valins, S. (1966). Cognitive effects of false heart-rate feedback. *Journal of Personality and Social Psychology, 4,* 400–408.

Verplanken, B. (1991). Persuasive communication of risk information: A test of cue versus message processing effects in a field experiment. *Personality and Social Psychology Bulletin, 17,* 188–193.

Vinokur, A., & Burnstein, E. (1974). The effects of partially shared persuasive arguments on group-induced shift: A group problem solving approach. *Journal of Personality and Social Psychology, 29,* 305–315.

Watts, W. A. (1967). Relative persistence of opinion change induced by active compared to passive participation. *Journal of Personality and Social Psychology, 5,* 4–15.

Watts, W. A., & Holt, L. E. (1979). Persistence of opinion change induced under conditions of forewarning and distraction. *Journal of Personality and Social Psychology, 37,* 778–789.

Wegener, D. T., Downing, J., Krosnick, J. A. & Petty, R. E. (1995). Measures and manipulations of strength-related properties of attitudes: Current practice and future directions. In R. E. Petty and J. A. Krosnick (Eds.), *Attitude strength: Antecedents and consequences* (pp. 455–487). Mahwah, NJ: Erlbaum.

Wegener, D. T., & Petty, R. E. (1994). Mood-management across affective states: The hedonic contingency hypothesis. *Journal of Personality and Social Psychology, 66,* 1034–1048.

Wegener, D. T., & Petty, R. E. (1995). Flexible correction processes in social judgment: The role of naive theories in corrections for perceived bias. *Journal of Personality and Social Psychology, 68,* 36–51.

Wegener, D. T., & Petty, R. E. (1996). Effects of mood on persuasion processes: Enhancing, reducing, and biasing scrutiny of attitude-relevant information. In L. L. Martin & A. Tesser (Eds.), *Striving and feeling: Interactions between goals and affect* (pp. 329–362). Mahwah, NJ: Erlbaum.

Wegener, D. T., & Petty, R. E. (1997). The flexible correction model: The role of naive theories in bias correction. In M. P. Zanna (Ed.), *Advances in experimental social psychology* (Vol. 29, pp. 141–208). San Diego, CA: Academic Press.

Wegener, D. T., Petty, R. E., & Klein, D. J. (1994). Effects of mood on high elaboration attitude change: The mediating role of likelihood judgments. *European Journal of Social Psychology, 24,* 25–43.

Wegener, D. T., Petty, R. E., & Smith, S. M. (1995). Positive mood can increase or decrease message scrutiny: The hedonic contingency view of mood and message processing. *Journal of Personality and Social Psychology, 69,* 5–15.

Wegner, D. M. (1994). Ironic processes of mental control. *Psychological Review, 101,* 34–52.

Weitzenhoffer, A. M., & Weitzenhoffer, G. B. (1958). Sex, transference, and susceptibility to hypnosis. *American Journal of Clinical Hypnosis, 1,* 15–24.

Wells, G. L., & Petty, R. E. (1980). The effects of overt head movement on persuasion: Compatibility and incompatability of responses. *Basic and Applied Social Psychology, 1,* 219–230.

White, P. H., & Harkins, S. G. (1994). Race of source effects in the Elaboration Likelihood Model. *Journal of Personality and Social Psychology, 67,* 790–807.

Whittler, T., & DiMeo, J. (1991). Viewers' reactions to racial cues in advertising stimuli. *Journal of Advertising Research,* December, 37–46.

Wilson, T. D., & Brekke, N. (1994). Mental contamination and mental correction: Unwanted influences on judgments and evaluations. *Psychological Bulletin, 116,* 117–142.

Wilson, T. D., Dunn, D. S., Kraft, D., & Lisle, D. J. (1989). Introspection, attitude change, and attitude-behavior consistency: The disrupting effects of explaining why we feel the way we do. *Advances in Experimental Social Psychology, 22,* 287–343.

Witkin, H. A., Goodenough, D. R., & Oltman, P. K. (1979). Psychological differentiation: Current status. *Journal of Personality and Social Psychology, 37,* 1127–1145.

Wood, W. (1982). Retrieval of attitude-relevant information from memory: Effects on susceptibility to persuasion and on intrinsic motivation. *Journal of Personality and Social Psychology, 42,* 798–910.

Wood, W., & Kallgren, C. A. (1988). Communicator attributes and persuasion: Recipients access to attitude-relevant information in memory. *Personality and Social Psychology Bulletin, 14,* 172–182.

Wood, W., Kallgren, C. A., & Preisler, R. M. (1985). Access to attitude-relevant information in memory as a determinant of persuasion: The role of message attributes. *Journal of Experimental Social Psychology, 21,* 73–85.

Wood, W., Lundgren, S., Ouellette, J. A., Busceme, S., & Blackstone, T. (1994). Minority influence: A meta-analytic review of social influence processes. *Psychological Bulletin, 115,* 323–345.

Wood, W., Rhodes, N., & Biek, M. (1995). Working knowledge and attitude strength: An information processing analysis. In R. E. Petty & J. A. Krosnick (Eds.), *Attitude strength: Antecedents and consequences* (pp. 283–313). Mahwah, NJ: Erlbaum.

Worth, L. T., & Mackie, D. M. (1987). Cognitive mediation of positive affect in persuasion. *Social Cognition, 5,* 76–94.

Wright, P. L. (1981). Cognitive responses to mass media advocacy. In R. E. Petty, T. M. Ostrom, & T. C. Brock (Eds.), *Cognitive responses in persuasion* (pp. 263–282). Hillsdale, NJ: Erlbaum.

Wu, C., & Shaffer, D. R. (1987). Susceptibility to persuasive appeals as a function of source credibility and prior experience with the attitude object. *Journal of Personality and Social Psychology, 52,* 677–688.

Wyer, R. S., Jr. (1970). The prediction of evaluations of social role occupants as a function of the favorableness, relevance and probability associated with attributes of these occupants. *Sociometry, 33,* 79–96.

Wyer, R. S., Jr. (1973). Category ratings as "subjective expected values": Implications for attitude formation and change. *Psychological Review, 80,* 446–467.

Wyer, R. S., Jr. (1974). *Cognitive organization and change: An information-processing approach.* Hillsdale, NJ: Erlbaum.

Wyer, R. S., Jr. (1991). The construction and use of thought systems: Some theoretical ambiguities. In R. S. Wyer & T. K. Srull (Eds.), *Advances in social cognition* (Vol. 4, pp. 203–214). Hillsdale, NJ: Erlbaum.

Yalch, R. F., & Elmore-Yalch, R. (1984). The effect of numbers on the route to persuasion. *Journal of Consumer Research, 11,* 522–527.

Zajonc, R. B. (1968). Attitudinal effects of mere exposure. *Journal of Personality and Social Psychology Monograph Supplements, 9,* 1–27.

Zajonc, R. B. (1998). Emotions. In D. Gilbert, S. Fiske, & G. Lindzey (Eds.), *Handbook of social psychology* (4th ed., Vol. 1, pp. 591–632). New York: McGraw-Hill.

Zajonc, R. B., & Markus, H. (1982). Affective and cognitive factors in preferences. *Journal of Consumer Research, 9,* 123–131.

Zanna, M. P. (1993). Message receptivity: A new look at the old problem of open- versus closed-mindedness. In A. A. Mitchell (Ed.), *Advertising exposure, memory and choice* (pp. 141–162). Hillsdale, NJ: Erlbaum.

Zanna, M. P., & Cooper, J. (1974). Dissonance and the pill: An attribution approach to studying the arousal properties of dissonance. *Journal of Personality and Social Psychology, 29,* 703–709.

Zanna, M. P., Kiesler, C. A., & Pilkonis, P. A. (1970). Positive and negative attitudinal affect established by classical conditioning. *Journal of Personality and Social Psychology, 14,* 321–328.

Zanna, M. P., & Rempel, J. K. (1988). Attitudes: A new look at an old concept. In D. Bar-Tal & A. W. Kruglanski (Eds.), *The social psychology of knowledge* (pp. 315–334). Cambridge, England: Cambridge University Press.

Zillmann, D. (1972). Rhetorical elicitation of agreement in persuasion. *Journal of Personality and Social Psychology, 21,* 159–165.

Zimbardo, P. G. (1960). Involvement and communication discrepancy as determinants of opinion conformity. *Journal of Abnormal and Social Psychology, 60,* 86–94.

Zimbardo, P. G., Ebbesen, E., & Maslach, C. (1977). *Influencing attitudes and changing behavior.* Reading, MA: Addison-Wesley.

Zimbardo, P. G., Weisenberg, M., Firestone, I., & Levy, B. (1965). Communicator effectiveness in producing public conformity and private attitude change. *Journal of Personality, 33,* 233–255.

Zuwerink, J. R., & Devine, P. G. (1996). Attitude importance and resistance to persuasion: It's not just the thought that counts. *Journal of Personality and Social Psychology, 70,* 931–944.

CHAPTER NINE

MENTAL REPRESENTATION AND MEMORY

ELIOT R. SMITH, *Purdue University*

INTRODUCTION

Since its beginnings, social psychology has emphasized the role of mental representations and memory, as well as interpersonal and group interaction, in social behavior. Attitudes, which have been termed the "most distinctive and indispensable construct" of social psychology (Allport, 1935, p. 198), are mental representations. Lewin's (1951) life space is a mental representation. So are person impressions (Asch, 1946), stereotypes (Allport, 1954), and group norms (Sherif, 1936). Of course, these constructs do not exist *only* in individual minds; they all have social and interpersonal dimensions as well. The stock of mental representations that each individual uses to navigate the social world is the product of social construction as well as individual cognitive activity (Levine, Resnick, & Higgins, 1993). Other chapters in this *Handbook,* such as those on "The Cultural Matrix of Social Psychology," "Attitude Change," "Ordinary Personology," "Social Influence: Social Norms, Conformity, and Compliance," and "Small Groups," detail many of the interpersonal and social processes that participate in this construction. The topic of this chapter is the individual-level construction and use of mental representations.

This chapter takes a broad conceptual view. The term "memory" in the title is intended to cover not only the everyday use of the term (corresponding to explicit or intentional recall) but any effect of past experiences, mediated by mental representations, on perceptions or judgments. In exchange for this breadth, the chapter will review specific substantive areas of research selectively, mostly as examples of significant conceptual points, rather than in exhaustive detail. Thorough substantive reviews of research on issues that this chapter touches on can be found in chapters on "Attitude Structure and Function," "Ordinary Personology," "The Self," and "Stereotypes, Prejudice, and Discrimination," among others.

This chapter is organized around four major views of mental representation, two that underlie much current research in social psychology and two more that are newer but may become influential in the near future. The chapter describes each perspective's major assumptions and its applications to key empirical phenomena. Another section then examines relationships among the four viewpoints. The chapter ends with a brief section that summarizes the most important conclusions from this review.

Definitions

Representation   Psychologists generally define a *representation* as an encoding of some information, which an individual can construct, retain in memory, access, and use in various ways. Thus your impression of your Uncle Harry—your body of interrelated feelings about him and beliefs about what kind of person he is—is a mental representation on which you might draw to describe, evaluate, or make behavioral decisions about him. However, this definition allows for two somewhat different ways of thinking about representations.

The author gratefully acknowledges helpful comments and suggestions from John Bargh, Galen Bodenhausen, Reid Hastie, Bernadette Park, and especially Don Carlston and John Skowronski. Preparation of this chapter was facilitated by a research grant (R01 MH48640) and a Research Scientist Development Award (K02 MH01178) from the National Institutes of Mental Health.

First, a representation can be viewed as a *thing* (cf. Abelson & Prentice, 1989). Our familiar metaphors for memory involving storage, search, and retrieval invoke the idea of a storehouse filled with thing-like representations. Similarly, we say we *create* a representation, *have* it, *use* it, and sometimes *lose* (i.e., forget) it.

Second, a representation can also be viewed as a *state* (Gilbert, 1993; Clark, 1993). Holding a given set of beliefs or attitudes amounts to being in a particular state; adopting a new belief is changing one's state. Note that a state (unlike a thing) is intrinsically time-bound. Thus, while it is natural to think of things as being stored away and later retrieved unchanged, the ability to re-enter a previous state (i.e., to reactivate a representation) requires specific sorts of underlying mechanisms. A distinction needs to be maintained between a currently activated representation and a representation that is currently in abeyance but able to become active given the appropriate circumstances.

Why should we consider the more abstract idea of a state rather than sticking with the familiar metaphor of a representation as a thing? The reason is that different metaphors implicitly suggest different properties. For example:

1. If representations are things, then we must search for one to use, as when we look in the pantry for a can of beans to include in the soup. A representation that is not selected in the search makes no contribution to the dish being prepared. On the other hand, all representations are part of the person's overall state, so no representations remain unused or inert (Gilbert, 1993); any representation might influence current processing.
2. A thing can be stored away and later retrieved unchanged. The can of beans that was put on the shelf last week should still be there in exactly the same form today. In contrast, a state is intrinsically dynamic, influenced by the immediate context and whatever else is going on as well as by the content of a particular representation.
3. What can be done with a thing, like putting a can of beans on the shelf, can be undone. Once the can is taken down and used, it is no longer in the pantry. In contrast, if acquiring a belief changes the person's state it may not be possible to exactly reverse that change—to "unbelieve" what was once believed and return to the status quo ante.

Of course, no metaphor can capture all the diverse properties of mental representations. For this reason the very familiarity of the thing metaphor is dangerous, for it may blind us to properties of representations that are un-thing-like. Therefore thinking in terms of a different metaphor, such as mental states, may be productive and conceptually liberating. The first two viewpoints to be treated in this chapter consider representations as things, while the third and fourth conceptualize them as states.

Memory To clarify the use of the term *memory* in this chapter, consider that mental representations can affect thought, feelings, and behavior in two basic ways. First, people often have explicit "recollective" experiences, where they are consciously aware of accessing a representation of some past event or experience. In everyday language we use words like "I remember when . . ." to describe such experiences. This is the type of memory that we curse when we forget our appointments or fail to come up with someone's name moments after being introduced to them. This meaning of memory fits well with the thing metaphor, for memories are thought of as being consciously searched for and retrieved from storage to be used.

Less obviously but more pervasively, representations in memory influence all our perceptions and judgments. What we know influences the way we interpret the world around us, put our experiences in context, and plan our actions. In everyday language we say "I know . . ." or "I believe . . ." rather than "I remember" to describe these uses of memory. Yet the construction of attitudes, judgments, and perceptions—in fact, the construction of all our conscious experience—draws on knowledge represented in memory just as much as explicitly recollective experiences do. This meaning of memory resonates better with the state metaphor, for we can regard the person's current state (i.e., the total set of representations they possess) as influencing the way they process new information or make decisions.

To emphasize the common points between these uses of memory, we adopt the terms *explicit memory* and *implicit memory* (Schacter, 1987, 1994). Explicit memory refers to the conscious or intentional recollection of prior experiences, such as when we recall yesterday's argument when encountering a friend, or remember what we need to buy when wheeling the cart through the grocery store. Implicit memory refers to effects produced by prior experiences that do not require any current intentional or conscious awareness of those experiences. For example, one well-studied form of implicit memory, termed "repetition priming," is the facilitation of identifying or processing items that have been previously processed. Reading a word such as "elephant" can improve people's ability to complete the word if it is later presented in fragmented form (as E_E__A_T), in a manner that does not depend on conscious or intentional retrieval of the previous experience of reading the word (Tulving, Schacter, & Stark, 1982). But implicit memory is not limited to laboratory tasks; it is at work when yesterday's argument makes our attitude toward our friend less positive, even if the argument is not consciously remembered.

The explicit/implicit distinction is one between *tasks* or *ways in which memory has effects* rather than between "memory systems" such as semantic versus episodic memory (Tulving, 1972). It may be tempting to assume that semantic memory (general knowledge about the world) shows itself in implicit tasks while episodic memory (autobiographical memory for specific events located in time and place) affects explicit tasks. But this is wrong; a specific episode can influence implicit memory (as in the repetition priming effects just mentioned) and general knowledge can certainly influence explicit memories through reconstructive processes (Ross & Conway, 1986). The explicit/implicit distinction refers to *uses* of memory: the consciously recollective use of memory as an object or its use as a tool in performing some other task, without conscious awareness of memory per se (Jacoby & Kelley, 1987).

Chapter Overview

We turn now to reviewing two models of representation and memory that are currently prominent in social psychology (associative networks and schematic representations), and two that are currently being applied in other areas of psychology and seem likely to have an increasing impact in social psychology (exemplars and distributed representations). The chapter will assess how each of the four types of representation accounts for what is known about the explicit and implicit effects of mental representation. Table 1 summarizes the discussion and may be helpful to the reader as an organizational aid in reading this chapter.

The following sections review four types of theoretical *mechanisms* rather than *theories* within social psychology. The distinction is important, for a single theory can incorporate several specific mechanisms for distinct purposes, as Wyer and Srull's well-known model (1989) includes both associative networks and schemas. For this reason, statements that a particular type of representation (such as schemas) cannot account for certain findings are generally sounder and less controversial as applied to theoretical mechanisms rather than theories. A schematic theory might be elaborated with a separate mechanism to account for the problematic findings. Then even if it were true that schematic mechanisms could not account for the findings, it could be inaccurate or at best controversial to say that schema theories could not do so.

For each of the four types of mechanism, the chapter will first review basic assumptions regarding representation formation and use. The issue of representation change will receive less attention than formation and use, because it brings in many additional issues such as the function of the knowledge for the perceiver, and the possibility of motivated resistance to change. Theories of social influence and persuasion have been developed specifically to account for changes in beliefs, attitudes, and behavior, and they are reviewed in other chapters of this *Handbook*. Following the overview of basic assumptions, illustrative models and applications of the class of theoretical mechanisms to specific issues within social psychology will be described in some detail. Emphasis will be given to ways the mechanism can account for the phenomena of explicit memory, implicit memory, and patterns of dependence and dissociations among various effects.

Finally, a section on the relationships among the four mechanisms considers the extent to which they offer competing explanations for the same data patterns, complementary explanations for distinct and nonoverlapping bodies of results, or alternative viewpoints or ways of looking at the same phenomena.

ASSOCIATIVE NETWORKS

Associative network models of memory representation trace their origins directly to British philosophers (Locke, 1690/1979; Hume, 1739/1978). These thinkers held that concepts arise from the association of more basic elements such as sensations and perceptions that are repeatedly paired. More recently, Ebbinghaus (1885/1964) developed ways to experimentally test associationist ideas, and influential theories in nonsocial cognition, such as Collins and Quillian (1969), Collins and Loftus (1975), and Anderson and Bower (1973), embodied generally similar assumptions.

Fundamental Assumptions

Within social psychology, several recent reviews have laid out basic assumptions of associative network memory representations (Carlston & Smith, 1996; Ostrom, Skowronski, & Nowak, 1994; Fiske & Taylor, 1991; Wyer & Carlston, 1994). The assumptions are as follows:

1. *Fundamental representational assumption:* Representations are constructed from discrete "nodes" connected by "links" of different types.
2. *Interpretation of nodes:* Nodes stand for preexisting concepts or are newly constructed, in which case they take their meaning from their pattern of linkages to other nodes. For example, an attitude may be represented as a link from an existing node representing the attitude object to a node representing the person's evaluative reaction. Or to interpret the sentence "The teenager mowed the neighbor's lawn" one could construct a new proposition (sentence) node with a *subject* link to a node representing teenager, a *verb* link to a node for mowed, and an *object* link to a node for the lawn.
3. *Formation of links through contiguity:* Links are formed (or strengthened if they already exist) when the objects they link are experienced or thought about together.
4. *Link strength:* Links can vary in strength, a property that is considered to change only slowly with time.

5. *Activation of nodes:* Nodes have a property termed activation, which can vary rapidly over time.

6. *Activation in long-term memory:* Long-term memory is assumed to be a single large, interconnected associative structure. Short-term memory is the currently activated subset of this structure; that is, memory retrieval amounts to raising a node's activation level above some threshold.

7. *Spread of activation:* When a node is activated because it is perceptually present or is actively thought about, other nodes to which it is linked also become active to some extent, as activation spreads across the links. Some theories quantitatively model this process (e.g., Anderson, 1983, chap. 3), but social psychological theories usually dispense with quantitative detail, assuming only that more activation flows across stronger links.

8. *Links as pathways for retrieval in free recall:* Because of the spread of activation, recall can be thought of as following links. Retrieving (activating) one node may result in the spread of enough activation to a neighboring node to elicit its retrieval. As a direct implication, the more links connecting to a particular node, the greater its probability of retrieval.

Though they tend to share the above assumptions in some form, associative network models in social psychology also have some points of variation:

1. *Decay of activation:* Some theorists postulate that activation on a node, unless maintained by a flow of activation from other nodes, decays relatively rapidly (within seconds at most; Anderson, 1983; Ostrom et al., 1994, p. 225). Others assume that activation can last for much longer (hours or days) or make more complex assumptions, such as activation on different nodes decaying at different rates (Higgins, 1996).

2. *Retrieval modeled as link traversal or as spreading activation:* Retrieval is sometimes conceptualized as the result of activation spreading in parallel across links until some threshold level is reached (Anderson, 1983, chap. 3), and sometimes as an explicit process of following links sequentially from one node to another (Hastie, 1988). However, these alternatives may give rise to qualitatively similar predictions.

3. *Level of interpretation of nodes:* Theorists disagree concerning the conceptual level at which the nodes are interpreted (see Wyer & Carlston, 1994, p. 7). That is, a node could be a feature, a concept, or a whole body of knowledge ("schema").

4. *Labeling of links:* Theorists disagree as to whether the links are labeled (e.g., Fiske & Taylor, 1991, p. 297) or unlabeled (Wyer & Srull, 1989, chap. 7). Most associative network theories in nonsocial cognition assume that links are of distinct types, such as the "ISA" (class

inclusion) and "feature" links of Collins and Quillian (1969) and the "subject," "relation" (predicate), and "object" links of Anderson (1983). However, associative theories in social psychology often have not made this assumption (Carlston & Smith, 1996, p. 194), causing conceptual difficulties and severely limiting the representational power of associative structures. For example, if "subject" and "object" links are not distinguished, identical associative structures would be constructed to represent the propositions "Dog bites man" and "Man bites dog."

Illustrative Models and Applications

Memory for Expectation-Consistent and -Inconsistent Information

Recall   One of the fundamental insights of social psychology is that people do not approach situations as neutral observers or recording devices; instead, they bring their own wishes and expectations with them, potentially influencing what they notice and remember. An important body of research in social cognition has explored the effects of expectations on memory, beginning by testing the common-sense assumption that information consistent with a prior expectancy would be better recalled than irrelevant or inconsistent information. Studies by Rothbart, Evans, and Fulero (1979) and Cohen (1981), among others, found support for this view in specific conditions. However, common sense was challenged by the results obtained by Hastie and Kumar (1979). In their study, subjects were initially given an expectation about a target person (e.g., that he is friendly and likable) and then, under instructions to form an impression of the individual, learned about a number of the target's behaviors. Behaviors that were inconsistent with the expectation were better recalled subsequently than behaviors that were consistent. A recent meta-analysis of fifty-four experiments (Stangor & McMillan, 1992) confirmed the robustness of this recall advantage for inconsistent information. As we will see shortly, the increased recall is generally assumed to result from extra processing that people give to the inconsistent information, presumably to try to account for it.

The effect is subject to several theoretically important moderator variables. Higgins and Bargh (1987) suggested that it is stronger when people are initially forming impressions than when they are testing confidently held impressions. Meta-analysis confirmed this suggestion, finding that the inconsistency advantage in recall is diminished or reversed when expectations are strong. The effect is also weaker when the information to be processed is complex or processing time is limited, when subjects try to memorize the information rather than form a coherent impression, or when the information concerns a social group rather than a single individual (Stangor & McMillan, 1992; Fyock & Stangor, 1994). Stangor and McMillan noted that these moderator variables all relate to the perceiver's ability and/or motivation to give special processing to inconsistent information. Such processing should be less likely when ability is absent (e.g., when behaviors are presented rapidly, as in Bargh & Thein, 1985) or when motivation is lacking (e.g., when consistency is not expected because the behaviors were enacted by different members of a group rather than by a single individual, as in Rothbart et al., 1979).

Recognition Stangor and McMillan (1992) also meta-analyzed studies that examined recognition of information that was consistent or inconsistent with the subject's initial expectations. In interpreting recognition results, it is important to pay attention to the way the test was constructed and the data analyzed (see Srull, 1984; Murdock, 1982). Proper analysis of recognition data can separate two parameters, sensitivity and bias. A simple hit rate confounds the effects of accurate recognition and guessing bias and is rarely the appropriate measure for analysis. Various parametric and nonparametric measures of sensitivity are available, though the intuitive "correction for guessing" formula (hit rate minus false alarm rate) is appropriate only under restrictive circumstances (Srull, 1984). Here I use the term "uncorrected recognition" for raw hit rates and other scores that confound correct recognition and guessing, and "recognition sensitivity" for measures that attempt in any way to control for guessing.

As noted earlier, in Stangor and McMillan's (1992) analysis, free recall measures showed a weak overall advantage for impression-inconsistent information, though this general trend was moderated by several conceptually important variables. The same overall effect held in stronger form in the nine studies that used recognition sensitivity measures: expectation-inconsistent information was more accurately recognized than consistent information. Some moderating effects were also found. Variables such as the strength of the expectation and the goal with which the subjects processed the information significantly interacted with consistency. What is striking is that most of these variables had significant effects in *opposite* directions on free recall and on recognition sensitivity. For example, expectation-inconsistent information had a larger advantage in free recall when the expectation was experimentally created (rather than being preexisting and presumably stronger), but inconsistent information had a smaller advantage in recognition sensitivity under the same circumstance.

Uncorrected recognition measures, including simple hit rates, showed a quite different pattern in the Stangor and McMillan meta-analysis. There was a strong overall advantage for expectation-consistent information (the reverse of the pattern found with recall and recognition sensitivity

measures). Presumably this pattern is largely attributable to expectation-consistent guessing. With only one exception, most moderator-variable effects paralleled those found with free recall. Overall, these findings underline the fact that free recall and recognition are not interchangeable measures that tap the "same memory trace" with greater or lesser degrees of sensitivity. They also emphasize the importance of separating recognition sensitivity from response bias measures, which can show independent or even opposite patterns (as in this meta-analysis).

Explanation in Terms of Associative Networks Hastie (1980, 1988) and Srull (1981) proposed closely related associative models of the processing of inconsistent information that yields its advantage in recall. Similar assumptions are part of the general model of Wyer and Srull (1989, chap. 7). Items of information about the target person, including consistent and inconsistent behaviors, are assumed to be separately and independently associatively linked to the central person node. When subjects try to form a coherent impression, they engage in extra processing of inconsistent behaviors that results in the formation of additional behavior-to-behavior links, which connect the inconsistent behaviors to others (either consistent or inconsistent). One prediction of this model is that the overall density of links will be greatest for inconsistent, less for consistent, and least for expectation-irrelevant behaviors. The overall level of recall is predicted (and found) to follow this same order by conditions. A further prediction is that links between consistent behaviors will be rare compared to consistent-inconsistent and inconsistent-inconsistent links (see Figure 1a). When the sequential order of recall is examined, evidence for this pattern is found as well (Srull, 1981).

Though this explanation has much empirical support (e.g., Belmore & Hubbard, 1987; Srull, Lichtenstein, & Rothbart, 1985), it also has boundary conditions, many of which were apparent in the Stangor and McMillan meta-analysis. For example, when perceivers are unmotivated or unable to devote special thought to inconsistent behaviors, the effect weakens or disappears (e.g., Bargh & Thein, 1985). These exceptions can be explained under the associative account, for the formation of extra links should be less probable under these conditions. However, the associative explanation fails to account neatly for the patterns obtained with recognition sensitivity measures. Compared to free recall, recognition should be little influenced by the formation of associative links between items, so the superior recognition sensitivity for expectation-inconsistent items remains a puzzle under a purely associative account. Perhaps people mentally elaborate individual inconsistent behaviors (e.g., by thinking about the details of when and how they might be performed; cf. Klein & Loftus, 1990) as well as thinking about them together with other behaviors (the activity that produces associative links).

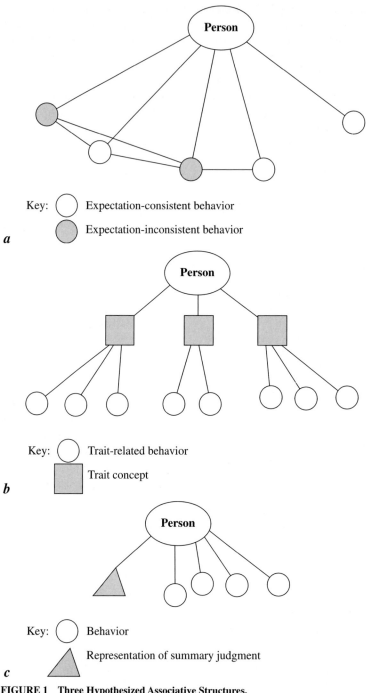

FIGURE 1   Three Hypothesized Associative Structures.

(*a*) Representation of Person Who Performed Expectation-Consistent and Inconsistent Behaviors.

(*b*) Representation of Person Who Performed Behaviors Related to Each of Several Traits.

(*c*) Representation of Person Incorporating Specific Behaviors and Separate Summary Judgment.

Recall of Person Information: Impact of Trait Organization   Another important line of research, like that on the effects of inconsistent information in impression formation, also deals with the impact on recall of perceiver goals and the structure of stimulus information. In a paradigm developed by Hamilton and his colleagues (Hamilton, 1981; Hamilton, Katz, & Leirer, 1980), subjects learn several items of information reflecting a few distinct trait themes about another person. For example, the perceiver might learn that the target person performed three intelligent behaviors as well as three honest behaviors. Hamilton and his colleagues also manipulated subjects' task instructions and measured free recall. They found that perceivers can recall more behaviors when instructed to form an impression of the target than when instructed to memorize the information, and that under impression instructions, recalled behaviors tend to be clustered by the traits they represent.

These effects have also been explained with associative network mechanisms. Hamilton and his associates (1980) proposed that when the target person's behaviors fall into trait categories, impression formation results in the formation of a hierarchically structured associative network. As the perceiver notes the categorical structure, he or she is presumed to connect the behaviors into trait-based clusters, with the traits in turn being linked directly to the person node (Figure 1b). Again, these extra links are predicted and found to lead to higher overall recall of the behaviors for an impression-formation instruction condition compared to a "memorize" instruction that presumably does not induce subjects to organize the behaviors. Further, as subjects traverse links in recalling the behaviors, several behaviors organized with the same trait are likely to be clustered together (recalled in sequence).

However, research by Klein and Loftus (1990) calls into question the idea that associative mechanisms (links forming behavior-trait clusters) are solely responsible for the increase in recall under impression instructions. In their study, an explicit category-sorting task, which forced organization of the behaviors, produced recall levels as high as impression formation and a much higher degree of clustering. Klein and Loftus proposed that superior recall under impression instructions is due not to the formation of associative links among behaviors but to semantic elaboration of individual behaviors in terms of related traits. Thus, for example, when a perceiver who is trying to form an impression encounters "enjoyed reading the philosophy book," ideas about the trait "intelligent" become linked to the mental representation of this behavior. According to this hypothesis, different behaviors are not associated in memory even if they reflect the same trait. The elaboration hypothesis predicts that elaboration should lead to improved recall even if every presented behavior represents a unique trait, so that clustering cannot occur. In contrast, inter-behavior links should improve recall only when several behaviors fall into a single trait cluster. Klein and Loftus (1990) set up a study to test this prediction and found support for the elaboration hypothesis. Thus, it appears that attempting to form an impression can trigger elaborative processing as well as the formation of inter-behavior associative links, and that either of these types of processing can produce representations that allow easier recall of the behaviors. Models involving *only* associative mechanisms (links connecting behaviors represented as distinct nodes) seem unable to fully account for these findings.

A General Associative Model of Person Impressions   Associated Systems Theory (Carlston, 1992, 1994) is a well-specified model postulating that person representations consist of associations among various forms of representations. Different forms of representation are hypothesized to relate differently to four basic mental systems, with the central features of each representational form deriving from the particular systems to which it is related. As summarized in Figure 2, appearance images are characterized as deriving from the visual system, traits from the verbal system, the perceiver's affective responses from the affective system, and behavioral responses from the action system. Other forms of representation derive from pairwise combinations of the four basic systems: categories from the visual and verbal systems, evaluations from the verbal and affective systems, orientations such as approach/avoid from the action and affective systems, and episodic memories of the target's behavior from the action and visual systems. Representations that relate to the same systems are hypothesized to have similar features and often to be associated with each other. The theory also describes the kinds of mental activities likely to lead to the generation of different representational forms, as well as the kinds of cognitive activities likely to be most affected by each form. Although aspects of Associated Systems Theory are controversial (see commentaries in Wyer, 1994), the theory does emphasize not only the diversity of forms in which social information can be represented, but also their patterns of associative connections and their implications for social judgment and behavior.

Semantic Priming   One effect of an experience—say, reading or thinking about a concept—is that semantically related stimuli can be processed more quickly for a brief time thereafter. This effect is termed *semantic priming*. Classic studies of semantic priming show that, for instance, people can more quickly identify the target word "nurse" if it is presented immediately following a prime like "doctor" than following an unrelated prime word like "tree" (Meyer & Schvaneveldt, 1971). Work by Neely (1977) and others shows that the effect can occur when the prime-target interval is too short for the perceiver to strategically generate an expectation about what type of word is coming next. It can

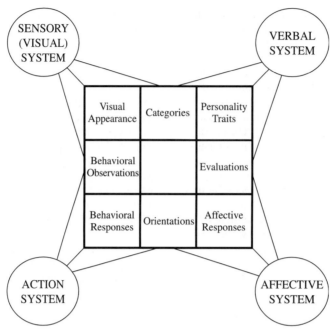

FIGURE 2   Types of Representation in Carlston's Associated Systems Theory.

also occur when the priming word is presented subliminally so that it cannot be consciously processed at all. Such evidence indicates that the effect is independent of any intentional use of the prime to facilitate task performance; i.e., it is a form of implicit memory by definition.

Within social psychology, important conceptual extensions of semantic priming have been studied. Gaertner and McLaughlin (1983) as well as Dovidio, Evans, and Tyler (1986) found that white subjects could respond more quickly to positive trait words following the prime "white" than following "black." Response times for negative words did not differ. The results are interpreted as indicating that "white" is semantically linked for positive concepts to a greater degree than is "black," and the authors suggest that this finding is relevant to racial stereotyping and prejudice. Another example is the effects of mood on judgment (Isen, 1984). A positive or negative mood appears to facilitate access to other concepts that are semantically or episodically linked to representations of the mood in memory, making those concepts more likely to be accessed and to influence judgments. A final example is evaluative priming (Fazio, Sanbonmatsu, Powell, & Kardes, 1986). Processing an evaluatively laden prime word (such as "cockroach") facilitates processing of an evaluatively congruent target ("death") while inhibiting the processing of an incongruent word ("beautiful"). The extent of these effects is controversial; some evidence suggests they occur for virtually all evaluatively nonneutral prime words and other evidence

that they are limited to words for which the person holds a relatively strong attitude (Bargh, Chaiken, Raymond, & Hymes, 1996; Fazio, 1993). Still, there is agreement on the robustness of the evaluative priming effect itself.

Empirically, semantic priming effects seem to be quite short-lived. They do not occur if the prime-target delay is more than a few seconds (unless the person rehearses the prime to keep its representation active), or if an unrelated word intervenes between the related prime and target (Masson, 1991; Ratcliff & McKoon, 1988).

Interpretation in Terms of Associations   Associative links are generally assumed to mediate semantic priming via a spreading activation mechanism. A concept that is activated in some way (for example by being perceptually present or the subject of conscious thought) is assumed to spread activation over links to its connected concept nodes. (e.g., Anderson, 1983, chap. 3). The result is that the excitation at these nodes approaches the threshold needed for activation, making them easier to activate by additional external (perceptual) inputs. Thus the word "nurse" is more quickly identified if it is presented following "doctor" than following an unrelated word because activation spreads over associative links from "doctor" to "nurse."

However, recent work has argued that nonassociative mechanisms may be responsible for semantic priming. As will be described later, Masson (1991) offers an explanation in terms of the overlap of distributed representational patterns for semantically related concepts. Also, Ratcliff and McKoon (1988) advanced a compound-cue explanation for semantic priming, arguing that the pair "doctor-nurse" serves as a better cue for information in memory that can be used to identify the target word "nurse" than does "tree-nurse." Some evidence supports the compound-cue explanation (Ratcliff & McKoon, 1988). This position remains controversial (see McKoon & Ratcliff, 1992; McNamara, 1992), but at least it should be noted that semantic priming effects may have other potential explanations besides associative mechanisms.

Dissociations Among Different Measures of Memory
A particular experience—say learning that Annette is honest—can have multiple effects. The perceiver may be able to recall or recognize that honesty is among Annette's characteristics later. The experience may temporarily increase the accessibility of the construct of honesty, possibly affecting the interpretation of later information. The person may be better able, for a time, to complete the word fragment H _ _ E _ T. A natural question then concerns the relationships among these various effects. Specifically, if they are all different manifestations of a single underlying memory representation, then one might expect dependence among them. That is, subjects who (because of individual differences or experimental conditions such as study task, delay, or available retrieval cues) are better able to recognize that Annette is honest should also be more apt to use the accessible concept of honesty in interpreting other information, better able to complete the word fragment, and so on. In fact, however, dissociations among different effects of an experience—such as explicit recall and effects on judgment—are common. Hastie and Park (1986) provided an influential review of this issue, which has been investigated in several specific areas within social psychology.

Recall and Judgmental Effects of Information   The intuitive expectation is that we will be able to recall mostly good things about people (or other objects) that we evaluate positively, and mostly bad things about people or objects we dislike. Though this relationship sometimes holds, more often it does not. In the classic study by Anderson and Hubert (1963), for example, people were given trait adjectives that described a target person. The effect of the traits on an overall evaluative judgment and the probability that they were recalled later showed reliably different patterns. This relative independence (or dissociation) between recall and judgment is probably the most typical pattern in the literature. Hastie and Park (1986) proposed several different processing models that could result in either a positive, negative, or no relationship between recall and judgment, and made specific predictions about when each pattern would be found.

A closely related literature has examined the relationship between people's overall attitudes toward an object

and their specific knowledge or beliefs about the object. Considerable variation exists across individuals and across attitudes in the degree of consistency, which has important correlates such as attitude certainty and extremity (Lusk & Judd, 1988; Judd & Krosnick, 1989). In cases where there is relatively little consistency between attitudes and beliefs, specific cues (such as the wording of the questions that are asked, the preceding content of the conversation or interview, and the general situational context) may strongly influence the attitude that is retrieved and overtly reported (e.g., Schuman & Presser, 1981; Tourangeau & Rasinski, 1988).

Self-traits and Behavioral Exemplars   Self-perception models (e.g., Bem, 1967) suggest that people form impressions of their own traits at least in part by inference from observations of their own behaviors. As in the case of summary judgments and judgment-relevant information, just reviewed, such theories lead to the intuitive expectation that trait self-impressions and autobiographical memory for trait-related behaviors should be strongly related. Research reviewed by Klein and Loftus (1993) challenges this assumption. Several studies demonstrate that questioning people about their traits (e.g., "are you sociable?") does not increase the speed with which they can then recall a specific behavioral instance of the trait. Nor does the reverse order of questions produce facilitation: retrieving a specific trait-related behavior does not speed judgments of one's general standing on the trait. Other studies show that when the task is changed slightly to certain types of trait judgments about another person, such facilitation is found—thus, the paradigm is sufficiently sensitive to show facilitation in some cases. For self-knowledge, however, Klein and Loftus's (1993) findings imply a clear dissociation between episodic memories of one's past behaviors and knowledge about one's general traits.

Recognition Memory, RT Facilitation, and Effects on Judgment   A study by Smith, Stewart, and Buttram (1992) had subjects make trait judgments about a variety of behaviors, some of which were repeated with varying lags. RT facilitation was found for judgments of repeated behaviors (relative to new ones) even at a seven-day lag. This facilitation was the same size for behaviors that the subjects could recognize as having been presented earlier and for unrecognized behaviors, demonstrating independence. Making a previous judgment about a behavior also influenced subjects' later evaluation of the behavior, and this effect was also independent of recognition of the behavior.

Recall, Word-fragment Completion, and Category Use   A study by Smith and Branscombe (1988) used three different dependent measures: free recall of trait words, completion of trait word fragments, and a "category accessibility" test in which subjects responded with a trait that they viewed as fitting a given ambiguous behavior. Subjects initially studied a number of traits under two conditions, either reading the trait word or generating the trait from a set of related behaviors plus the trait's initial letter. Results showed a clear pattern of dissociations: free recall was higher for generated than for read traits, as was category accessibility. In contrast, word-fragment completion was higher for traits that were read instead of generated.

Though category accessibility produced by "priming" and recall for the priming event showed a similar pattern of mean differences across conditions in this study, many other studies have found that these effects too can be dissociated. In fact, the typical pattern is a reverse association: priming effects are often found to be larger when subjects cannot recall the priming events and smaller or nil (sometimes even reversed) when recall is possible (Lombardi, Higgins, & Bargh, 1987; Martin, Seta, & Crelia, 1990).

Summary and Theoretical Interpretation   The extensive literature comparing different memory measures in nonsocial areas of cognition cannot be described in detail here. Influential reviews by Richardson-Klavehn and Bjork (1988) and Hintzman (1990) both find, in the words of the former

> although there are a number of clear dissociations between [explicit] and [implicit] tasks, there are at least as many examples of parallel effects, and of complex patterns in which the occurrence/nonoccurrence of dissociations varies systematically as a function of a critical variable. The complexity of the data pattern across [explicit] and [implicit] tests is complemented by an equally complex picture of dissociations and parallel effects within the [explicit] and [implicit] classes of test (Richardson-Klavehn & Bjork, 1988, p. 525).

As the above examples illustrate, these conclusions hold in the social domain as well (Hastie & Park, 1986). Dissociations among memory tasks are easy to find (e.g., Klein & Loftus, 1993; Anderson & Hubert, 1963). However, there are also examples of parallel effects (e.g., between recall and category accessibility; Smith & Branscombe, 1988) and positive dependencies among tasks.

Within the context of associative network mechanisms, theorists assume that the nature of the processing devoted to a stimulus determines the form of the representation that is constructed, and hence the effects of that experience (explicit or implicit) at a later time (Jacoby, 1983). This has been termed the "processing byproducts" principle (Carlston & Smith, 1996). For example, whether people devote extra processing to expectation-inconsistent behaviors determines whether they will be connected with extra links and therefore be better recallable later (Hastie & Kumar, 1979). Whether a person processes a word by thinking about it conceptually or by reading it can determine

whether conceptual or perceptual features of the word are emphasized in the representation that is constructed, and hence whether conceptual categorization or word-fragment completion performance benefits most at a later time (Smith & Branscombe, 1988).

The nature of processing can also determine whether different effects of the experience will covary or be dissociated from one another. Generally, if people form a single representation of a stimulus, so that different explicit or implicit measures draw on the common representation, performance on those measures will be expected to positively covary. For example, the person might simply store representations of a target person's behaviors, which would be accessed for recall and would also be retrieved and summarized to formulate trait judgments. This is termed "memory-based" processing by Hastie and Park (1986). In contrast, if people form two or more separate representations (such as a record of the details of the behaviors and also an overall summary judgment, such as a trait or evaluation; see Figure 1c), different tasks may access different representations. The retrieval of one representation (e.g., a trait-like summary judgment of the person) has no necessary implications for retrieval of others (e.g., trait-relevant behaviors), so the tasks may show dissociations. This is the case with "on-line" processing (Hastie & Park, 1986), which ordinarily leads to independence of recall and judgment. Thus, the principle of "processing byproducts" (Carlston & Smith, 1996), that the later effects of an experience will depend on the way it is processed, also influences whether the effects will be dissociated or will show positive dependence.

Associative Models of Stereotype Structure   Stereotypes have often been conceptualized as associative links between a node representing a social group and various traits and/or evaluations. The links allow for the spread of activation; thus, the process of semantic priming could make the stereotypic traits or evaluations active (and able to affect judgment and behavior) whenever a group member is encountered or thought about. Consistent with this hypothesis, as noted earlier, Gaertner and McLaughlin (1983) and others have found that white subjects respond more quickly to positive trait words following the prime "white" than following "black." These results have been interpreted as indicating a differential association of positive ideas to whites more than to blacks. Interestingly, high- and low-prejudice subjects responded identically.

In conceptually related work Devine (1989) assumed that all people have learned to associate social groups with consensually stereotypic attributes, though some nonprejudiced people do not personally endorse those stereotypes. She interpreted her findings as supporting these ideas. In her studies, subliminally priming subjects with words related to the African-American stereotype (but not including hostility or its direct synonyms) led people to interpret an ambiguous behavioral description as hostile. The effect is presumed to stem from the spread of activation from the stereotype to the associated concept of hostility; once the concept becomes active, it can influence the interpretation of input information. Importantly, the size of the priming effect was equal for subjects who scored high or low on an overt questionnaire measure of racial prejudice. However, conceptual questions arise about the underlying theory. In most associative models of stereotypes, the presence of an associative link between the group and a stereotypic attribute in the perceiver's cognitive structure represents the belief that the group possesses the attribute. In Devine's model, even low-prejudice subjects are presumed to share this associative structure, so it is unclear how a low-prejudice subject's presumed personal rejection of the belief is cognitively represented. The introduction of labeled links might help solve this problem.

Fazio's Associative Model of Attitudes In Fazio's (1986) model, an attribute is assumed to be represented by an associative link from the node corresponding to the attitude object to a node representing the object's evaluation. Such links are formed or strengthened by thinking about the object's evaluation, so in many of Fazio's studies, repeated attitude expression is used as a manipulation to strengthen the link. Link strength has important consequences, for a strong enough link results in the automatic activation of the attitude (by spreading activation) whenever the object is encountered or thought about. A number of studies have demonstrated that attitude activation in turn leads to evaluative priming effects, an increased likelihood of attending or remembering the object, and increased attitude-behavior consistency (see Fazio, 1986).

Associative Models of the Self A series of influential studies has found that information encoded with reference to the self benefits in a later recall test. Using an incidental memory paradigm, Rogers and his colleagues (e.g., Rogers, Kuiper, & Kirker, 1977) found that words for which subjects had made self-reference judgments ("Describes you?") were better recalled than words for which subjects had made other types of semantic judgments. Initial interpretations drew on the idea that the mental representation of the self had special properties, perhaps because of its evaluative implications or frequent use. However, later research, while generally replicating the self-reference effect itself, tended to downplay the notion of the self's special properties in favor of interpretations dealing with more general properties of memory (Klein & Kihlstrom, 1986; Klein & Loftus, 1988; Greenwald & Banaji, 1989; Klein, Loftus, & Burton, 1989) such as the formation of associative links. For example, self-reference may improve recall because linking a to-be-recalled item

to the self produces a reliable pathway that can be followed for later retrieval (Greenwald & Banaji, 1989).

Skowronski, Thompson, and their colleagues have assessed the impact of self-reference on recall using a daily diary technique. Over an extended period of time (usually many weeks) subjects keep a diary, recording descriptions and various ratings of an event that happened to them and an event involving another person each day. At a later time, a cued recall procedure is used: subjects are presented with the event descriptions and asked to give verbal reports on the events. Self-reference has a robust effect in this task, in that self-events are recalled better than other-events (Skowronski, Betz, Thompson, & Shannon, 1991; Thompson, Skowronski, Larsen, & Betz, 1996).

Associative network models of the self (Bower & Gilligan, 1979; Kihlstrom & Cantor, 1984; Linville & Carlston, 1994) assume that a central self node is linked to a variety of types of self-attributes (such as traits) or behavioral episodes. Some of these self-linked representations may also be interconnected; for example, a self-trait such as "honest" may be associated with a representation of a role such as "club treasurer" or with specific past behaviors that relate semantically or inferentially to that trait. Kihlstrom and Klein (1994, pp. 182–184) outline three specific versions of this general idea, differing in the patterns of linkages of behaviors and traits. They review evidence (e.g., Klein, Loftus, Trafton, & Fuhrman, 1992) suggesting that traits and behavioral episodes are independently linked to the self in a pattern like that portrayed in Figure 1c, rather than being interconnected in terms of their semantic relationships as in Figure 1b.

Affect and Recall Affect may influence recall in several different ways. For one thing, a match in affective valence between the perceiver's state at the time information is learned and at the time of retrieval has often been predicted to lead to enhanced recall. This phenomenon is termed state-dependent recall (Bower, Monteiro, & Gilligan, 1978). It has proven difficult to reliably empirically demonstrate, and recent reviews (Bower & Mayer, 1985; Clore, Schwarz, & Conway, 1994) seem doubtful of its robustness and generality. Another type of affective matching effect, conceptually though not always empirically separable from state-dependent recall, is termed mood-congruent recall. This is increased recall for information whose *valence* matches the state at the time of recall (e.g., Bower, 1981). Mood-congruent recall seems a relatively more robust phenomenon than state-dependent recall, though the effect seems to be stronger for positive moods than for negative moods (Singer & Salovey, 1988; Blaney, 1986).

These effects of affect on memory have been explained in the context of associative network models (e.g., Bower et al., 1978). An affect node (representing a concept such as happiness, sadness, or anger) is presumed to be associatively linked to nodes for information that is learned while in the relevant affective state. At a later time, therefore, if the perceiver is in a similar affective state activation may flow from the affect node to the nodes for the to-be-recalled information, increasing their likelihood of retrieval. These assumptions yield a prediction of state-dependent recall. They can also (with the added assumption that encountering valenced information activates a corresponding affect node) predict mood-congruent recall.

Finally, the affective quality of an event itself may influence recall, independent of the perceiver's state at the time of retrieval. For example, in the diary-based recall methodology used by Skowronski, Thompson, and their colleagues, the affective tone of an event (as rated by subjects at the time) influences its later recall. Results show both a positivity effect and an emotional extremity effect (Skowronski et al., 1991; Thompson et al., 1996). Positive events are recalled better than neutral or negative ones, but this effect holds only for self-events rather than other-events. Independently, events with relatively extreme pleasantness ratings (positive or negative) are recalled well, equally for self- and other-events. The explanation for these effects is less clear, but superior memory for positive self-events may be due to people's motivationally driven tendency to dwell on those events. The extremity effect may be an instance of the general superiority of memory for more distinctive events.

Summary

Associative network mechanisms have been used to explain a wide range of substantive findings within social psychology. The core assumption is that associative links bind together into a single representation different aspects of an object or concept, often together with related information such as the specific context in which the object was encountered. This binding occurs when the elements are thought about together, and it results in a unified representation that can be retrieved as a whole when activated by a part. For example, subjects might form an impression of a person who returned a lost wallet, has blond hair, and is inferred to be honest. These and other characteristics are associated into a single impression of the person (Carlston, 1994). At a later time, the associative structure serves as a retrieval mechanism that can reactivate all elements given the presence of a subset as cues.

We saw in several instances, though, that associative assumptions cannot fully account for empirical results (such as the recognition results summarized by Stangor & McMillan, 1992, or the findings of Klein & Loftus, 1990). In such cases associative explanations presumably need to be replaced or at least supplemented by other types of mechanism.

Another significant issue is that many, perhaps most, social psychological applications assume that associative links are unlabeled. Associative structures with unlabeled links have severely limited representational power (J. A. Anderson, 1995). They are unable (for example) to distinguish subject from object in a proposition and thus would represent "John kissed Mary" and "Mary kissed John" identically. Theorists in nonsocial cognition who use associative representational mechanisms, both historically (e.g., Collins & Quillian, 1969) and currently (e.g., J. R. Anderson, 1993) almost invariably specify that links are of distinct types, and social psychologists may find it useful to follow their example.

In summary, typical applications of associative representations in social psychology have the following characteristics:

1. The *formation* of an associative structure is explicitly modeled as the result of cognitive processes that occur when information is first encountered, as in most "person memory" theories (e.g., Hastie, 1980; Hamilton et al., 1980). The important principle that different processes at the time of study result in the formation of different structures is explicitly noted. Less frequently, an associative structure is assumed to exist as a result of pre-experimental learning, as in the research on associative models of stereotyping or the self.
2. The *effect of an associative structure on explicit memory retrieval* (almost always free recall) is modeled as a process of traversing associative links. The amount of information of different types (e.g., expectancy-consistent versus inconsistent) that can be recalled, and the sequence in which information is recalled, are often studied as dependent variables (e.g., Srull et al., 1985).
3. The *effect of an associative structure on implicit memory measures* (usually semantic priming) is modeled as a result of spreading activation. For example, Dovidio et al. (1986) and Fazio (1986) assume that when a given node is activated (a social group label or an attitude object), associative connections make linked nodes (representing stereotypic traits or evaluations) readily accessible, able to affect subsequent judgments or behaviors.
4. *Dissociations* among various effects such as recall and judgment are ordinarily modeled as due to accessing two separate structures (Hastie & Park, 1986).

SCHEMAS

Schematic and associationistic mechanisms are often presented as polar opposites (Brewer & Nakamura, 1984; Fiske & Taylor, 1991; Markus & Zajonc, 1985, p. 145). Associative mechanisms involve elementary nodes without internal structure; larger meanings are constructed "bottom up" by combining nodes. Schemas are larger-scale representations with significant internal structure. A single concept or observation could take on quite different meanings if incorporated within different schemas. The influence is mostly "top-down," with the whole psychological field (Gestalt) providing meaning to its constituent parts. However, as we shall see later, treating the models as opposites or even as competitors may be inappropriate.

Schematic models of memory trace their origins to the Gestalt psychologists (e.g., Koffka, 1935), whose influence was imported to North America by Kurt Lewin (1951) and others, and ultimately date back to German philosophers (e.g., Kant, 1781/1969). The most direct ancestors of schematic models in social psychology are Bartlett (1932), the "new look" movement in perception and particularly Bruner (1957), and a number of influential works in nonsocial cognition including Bransford and Franks (1971), Anderson and Pichert (1978), and Schank and Abelson (1977).

Fundamental Assumptions

Schematic mechanisms, as reviewed by Markus and Zajonc (1985), Carlston and Smith (1996), Fiske and Taylor (1991), and Wyer and Carlston (1994), generally share the following assumptions.

1. *Fundamental representational assumption:* A schema is a structured unit of general knowledge about some object or concept. In the words of Fiske and Taylor (1991, p. 98), "a schema may be defined as a cognitive structure that represents knowledge about a concept or type of stimulus . . . schemas are concerned with . . . abstract generic knowledge that holds across many particular instances." Or, from Markus and Zajonc (1985, p. 145), "for the most part social psychologists who have used the term *schemas* have viewed them as subjective 'theories' about how the social world operates. These 'theories' are derived from generalizing across one's experiences with the social world."
2. *Abstract knowledge:* As these definitions specifically note, schemas are assumed to represent general knowledge rather than episodes bound to particular times and contexts.
3. *Activation:* A schema can be activated by explicit thought about its topic or by an encounter with relevant information. Activation is all-or-none; that is, making the schema active renders readily accessible all the structured knowledge contained therein.
4. *Level of accessibility:* Even when a schema is below the threshold for activation, it can have a variable level of accessibility, which is influenced by recent or frequent use. A higher degree of accessibility means that the schema can more readily be activated and used.

5. *Independence of units:* Schemas are independent entities. Unlike nodes in an associative network model, they are not interlinked. Thus, if one schema becomes active this has no necessary implications for other, related schema.
6. *Interpretive function of schemas:* The primary function of an activated schema is to affect the interpretation of related information. The way ambiguous information is construed and the default values that are assumed for unavailable information are influenced by a schema. Through these interpretive processes, schemas will influence evaluations and other judgments about an object, and also behavior toward the object.
7. *Attentional function of schemas:* Another effect of an activated schema is to direct attention, sometimes to schema-consistent information and sometimes to unexpected or inconsistent information so that it can receive special processing.
8. *Retrieval cuing/reconstructive function of schemas:* Schemas can also influence memory retrieval and judgment. A schema can serve as a source of cues, generally facilitating retrieval of schema-consistent information. It can also serve as a guide for guessing and reconstruction when retrieval attempts fail or produce ambiguous results.
9. *Preconscious effects:* The effects of a schema are generally considered to occur at a preconscious level. That is, the perceiver generally believes that the result of schematic processing is what is "out there" and remains unaware of the contribution of his or her own knowledge structures to what is consciously perceived.

Schematic mechanisms as used by different theorists also differ in some respects, such as the following.

1. *Level of interpretation of schemas:* Typically schemas are assumed to represent detailed information about particular concepts, such as the rules of backgammon or the typical characteristics of a lawyer. However, in some cases schemas are assumed to be highly abstract and content-free, representing general rules of inference. An example is Heiderian balance, which could be viewed as a "schema" expressing the typical patterns of positive and negative links among a group of persons and objects.
2. *Conscious awareness:* Though (as noted above) schemas are typically assumed to have their effects below the level of conscious awareness, many researchers use verbal report as a method to assess the content of subjects' schemas.
3. *Models of accessibility:* Theorists have proposed several competing models of the effects of schema accessibility, including Storage Bins, battery, and synapse models (Wyer & Srull, 1989; Higgins, 1989).

Illustrative Models and Applications

Application of Knowledge to Interpret New Input
Since the 1930s, theorists such as Bartlett (1932), Bruner (1957), Minsky (1975), and Neisser (1976) have emphasized that perceivers do not take in and process new information in a neutral, unbiased fashion. Instead, prior knowledge serves as an organized framework that is used to interpret the new information—the perceiver plays an active rather than passive role in perception and cognition (Markus & Zajonc, 1985; Arbib, 1995). Prior knowledge has many effects in this interpretive process: it directs the perceiver's attention to particularly significant aspects of the information while allowing unimportant details to be ignored; it mediates inferences that permit the person to "go beyond the information given" (Bruner, 1957); it guides judgment and evaluation; and it fills in default or expected values for unobserved attributes. Most generally, it permits the construction of a stable, coherent picture of the world and the self out of fragmentary and complex perceptual input. All these processes are examples of implicit memory, because prior knowledge is brought to bear without any intentional or conscious recollection. We just "know" that someone's nasty remark means that he is a boorish person, rather than "remembering" this connection between a behavior and a trait.

These processes operate in a multitude of specific areas, and the relevant knowledge structures have various labels. Knowledge of typical sequences of social events used in comprehending everyday events or stories is termed a "script" (Schank & Abelson, 1977). Knowledge about the general characteristics of social groups is usually called a "stereotype," and knowledge of the typical characteristics of members of any category (such as vehicles or birds) a "prototype." In social psychology, the term *schema* is frequently used to refer to any of these types of generic prior knowledge that serve an interpretive function. In their predecessor to this chapter, Markus and Zajonc (1985, p. 145) wrote that the "primary research emphasis within social psychology has been on the functions that schemas serve in an individual's perceptual and memory system." This section will maintain this functional emphasis in reviewing the similar principles that underlie the use of prior knowledge across all these specific content areas to fill in unobserved aspects of new information, apply default values, make inferences, and direct attention. The review cannot be exhaustive but will focus on three areas of special interest to social psychological researchers: the use of knowledge about typical events to comprehend event sequences, the use of group stereotypes in person perception, and the inference of traits from behaviors.

Comprehension of Events   "John went to Bill's birthday party. Bill opened his presents. John ate the cake and left" is a boringly simple story that nevertheless illustrates an important function of knowledge in comprehension (Schank & Abelson, 1977, p. 39). To make sense of this story—for example, to know what the "presents" and the "cake" are, or to guess that Bill probably blew out candles—people must draw on their knowledge of the typical events that occur at a child's birthday party. Pioneering research by Bartlett (1932), as well as influential work by Bransford and his colleagues in the early 1970s (e.g., Bransford & Franks, 1971), have demonstrated that people's ability to remember stories and draw simple inferences depends on their ability to bring relevant knowledge structures to bear. For example, Bartlett showed that English subjects had great difficulty comprehending or reproducing a Native American folktale that involved several culturally unfamiliar concepts. Bransford and Franks (1971) gave subjects descriptions of common objects or events written in deliberately vague terms and found that they could not remember them well unless a label or picture gave them a clue to the correct schema.

In cases like these, an applicable schema allows the perceiver to link the story events to a general framework of knowledge, filling in gaps and inferring unstated events. Not only is memory for the overall gist of the material better when a schema is applied, but schema-relevant details are recalled better than irrelevant ones (e.g., Pichert & Anderson, 1977). This finding underlines the idea that one function of schematic knowledge is the direction of attention (in this case, toward relevant information and away from irrelevant material). Similarly, von Hippel, Jonides, Hilton, & Narayan (1993) found that people who are able to use schematic expectations pay less attention to irrelevant perceptual details of words they read.

When a schema is used to interpret input information, the result could be represented in memory in several different ways (Graesser, 1981; Brewer, 1988). At one extreme, the new object could be represented simply as a pointer to the existing schema, in effect, as "just another instance" of the schema. This notion predicts that schema-irrelevant information will be ignored and not encoded. Alternatively, a copy of the existing schema could be made (with changes whenever the current stimulus differs from the schematic assumptions). Finally, a schema pointer plus a separate list of exceptions or novel information could be stored. Studies by Schmidt and Sherman (1984) and Woll and Graesser (1982) supported the latter possibility, finding that events that are irrelevant to the schema (which would be separately stored under this model) are particularly accurately recognized.

Use of Stereotypic Knowledge in Person Perception   General knowledge about a group or type of person is often brought to bear as perceivers form impressions of individual members of the group (see Hamilton & Sherman, 1994; Hamilton & Trolier, 1986). Schematic representations of group characteristics may exist at the level of broad social categories (such as gender and ethnic groups) or more specific subgroups (such as "policewoman" or "white Midwestern small-town resident"). Categorizing an individual as a member of a group activates the representation of the group stereotype. As a result:

1. The individual's ambiguous behaviors may be interpreted as clearly confirming the stereotype (e.g., Duncan, 1976; Sagar & Schofield, 1980). For example, a child's ambiguous test performance (a mixture of correct and wrong answers) is interpreted as indicating a higher level of academic proficiency when the child is believed to come from an upper-middle-class home than when she comes from a poor background (Darley & Gross, 1983).

2. Expectations also shape attributions for behaviors, even if the behavior itself is unambiguous and not subject to reinterpretation. Stereotype-consistent behaviors are more likely to be attributed to the actor's stable personality characteristics, and inconsistent behaviors to luck, exceptional effort, or other unstable or situation-specific causes (Bodenhausen & Wyer, 1985; Deaux & Emswiller, 1974).

3. The individual may be inferred to possess stereotype-consistent attributes even when there is no concrete evidence for them at all; that is, the stereotype itself rather than the individual's characteristics is used as the basis for judgments (e.g., Fiske & Neuberg, 1990).

4. At a later time, stereotype-consistent observations may be falsely recalled or reconstructed (e.g., Fyock & Stangor, 1994). It might be predicted that perceivers should focus on and cognitively elaborate the individual's unexpected, stereotype-*inconsistent* characteristics, as they do in the process of forming an impression of an individual when they hold an initial trait-based expectancy (Hastie & Kumar, 1979). However, this pattern is rarely observed empirically (Stangor & McMillan, 1992). This is presumably because people do not expect the same type of tight consistency between a stereotype and every individual act of a group member, so they do not bother to think hard to resolve such inconsistencies.

These effects of stereotypes may not be inevitable. Despite debates over the extent to which stereotype application is "automatic" (Banaji & Greenwald, 1994; Devine, 1989; Gilbert & Hixon, 1991; see Bargh, 1994, for a review), it seems clear that when perceivers have time, motivation, and cognitive capacity, they can partially compensate for stereotype effects on person impressions and judgments (Bodenhausen, 1990; Macrae, Hewstone, & Griffiths, 1993).

Two prominent models have been advanced of the way

perceivers balance stereotype-driven and nonstereotypic processing (Brewer, 1988; Fiske & Neuberg, 1990). Both models share the assumption that stereotype-based processing is the default, performed unless some special motivating circumstances are present. Fiske and Neuberg (1990) assume that poor fit of the individual to the stereotype is one important factor; a person who does not seem to resemble the "typical" group member may be processed in a more individuated fashion, if motivation is present. Categorical or stereotypic processing and individuation (processing based on the person's specific behaviors or other idiosyncratic attributes) are regarded as two ends of a continuum. Brewer's (1988) model offers three discrete types of processing rather than a bipolar continuum. The target may be categorized (treated as an interchangeable member of the group), individuated (treated as a specific instance of the group, with one or more identifying attributes), or—if self-involvement provides sufficient motivation—personalized (treated as a unique individual). Brewer proposes that categorical and individuated representations differ in form, with the fomer being visual (or "pictoliteral") and the latter being verbal (or "propositional"). In contrast, Fiske and Neuberg argue that both categorical and individuated representations may have visual and verbal components. Both models agree that the type of processing performed (i.e., the relative attention devoted to category memberships versus unique personal attributes) depends on the stimulus configuration as well as the perceiver's goals. The relative diagnosticity of category membership versus available individuating information (Krueger & Rothbart, 1988) or the nature of the judgment required (Glick, Zion, & Nelson, 1988) may be important. Smith and Zárate (1992) discuss a number of related factors, including the immediate social context, cultural and normative factors, and the perceiver's own group membership.

Individuated processing is sometimes conceptualized as "data-driven," in contrast to the "theory-driven" processing said to be involved in schema-based categorization. However, this label reflects an oversimplification. First of all, as Smith and Zárate (1992) note, the distinction between a "category" and an "individuating attribute" is far from absolute. Occupation may be considered an individuating attribute of people who are categorized by race, but race may be an individuating attribute among, say, a group of professors. Thus it seems unlikely that *in general* categorical and individuating attributes are processed in very different ways. Second and more important, individuation rests on the perceiver's prior knowledge just as much as categorization does; the only difference is in the type of stimulus attributes that are focused on and used to access prior knowledge. For example, someone may be categorized as a woman and inferred to be relatively unassertive based on prior knowledge (a stereotype) that is retrieved based on her gender. Alternatively, individuating information such as the target's assertive actions may be used to draw an inference that the person is indeed assertive. But the perceiver''s knowledge (e.g., a trait representation, retrieved based on the observed behaviors) is involved in this case as well. No processing can ever be purely "data driven" and independent of the perceiver's prior knowledge.

Spontaneous Trait Inferences from Behavior As in the assertiveness example just given, people often make trait inferences from observed behaviors. One question that has excited a good deal of research attention is whether perceivers make such inferences spontaneously, or only in response to explicit task demands. To answer this question, researchers have coded attributional content in written materials or verbal communications (e.g., Harvey, Yarkin, Lightner, & Town, 1980). Methods borrowed from the cognitive lab have also been applied, including response-time measures (Smith & Miller, 1983), cued-recall tests (Winter & Uleman, 1984; Winter, Uleman, & Cunniff, 1985), recognition memory tests (Newman, 1991), and measures of savings in relearning (Carlston & Skowronski, 1994).

All together, these methodologically diverse studies lead to several important conclusions (see Smith, 1994a). First, spontaneous trait inferences are extremely sensitive to subjects' goals. Good evidence for trait inferences is usually found when subjects read sentences describing behaviors under instructions to form an impression of the actor. However, the evidence is much more mixed when subjects are told simply to memorize the sentences or when subjects are induced to treat the behavior sentences as distractor information whose content is unimportant. This goal-dependence suggests a hypothesis that Gilbert and Hixon (1991) and others have noted. If subjects expect experimenters' verbal communications (such as the behavior sentences) to follow conversational norms in being meaningful and informative (Grice, 1975), perhaps the use of written behavior descriptions in typical attribution studies implicitly gives subjects a goal of looking for trait inferences or other significant implications of the materials. This notion implies that subjects watching videotaped enactments of behaviors should be less likely to derive trait inferences than those who read sentences. And indeed, Carlston and Skowronski (1986) found no evidence that subjects spontaneously inferred traits when they visually observed trait-related behaviors.

A second conclusion that may be drawn from these studies is that there are several different types of attributional inferences that may follow different rules. Learning that Albert becomes confused by the television show, you may (a) infer the trait "unintelligent" as a categorization of the behavior, (b) infer that Albert is an unintelligent person, or (c) infer that Albert's unintelligence caused the behavior. Several studies demonstrate that a trait corresponding to a behavior can be activated or inferred (a or b) without a complete causal analysis (c) being performed (Bassili, 1989). For example, Smith and Miller (1979) found that people could infer traits much more rapidly than they could answer questions about causality. Uleman, Moskowitz, Roman, and Rhee (1993) find that the trait is more strongly linked to the behavior than to the sentence actor, suggesting that the trait does not constitute a dispositional inference (i.e., that people typically do a and not b or c). And Bassili (1989) found that an explicit causal judgment task did not lead to trait activation, while an impression formation task did—even when the available information suggested that the actor's trait characteristics did not cause the behavior. But whether a trait merely stands as an abstract summary of a specific behavior or is attached to an actor as a dispositional inference, its inference clearly draws on the perceiver's prior knowledge as much as on the details of the stimulus information. If a behavior is processed beyond a certain minimal level (and perhaps simply attempting to memorize a behavior sentence is not sufficient) its features may automatically cue a relevant trait schema. However, the evidence suggests that, unless the perceiver is explicitly attempting to form an impression, the schema is simply activated rather than being attached to the representation of the actor as a dispositional inference.

Other Effects of Prior Knowledge Judging by the amount of research attention, one would conclude that the primary function of existing knowledge is to serve as an interpretative framework to organize and make inferences about new stimulus input. Yet existing knowledge has other effects as well. In an earlier section, the effect of existing knowledge or expectations on guiding the processing of expectation-consistent and -inconsistent information was described. When the information pertains to an individual, expectation-inconsistent details receive extra processing and can be better recalled later (Hastie & Kumar, 1979). The creation of an associative structure in memory is usually regarded as responsible for these effects. In other circumstances, expectation-consistent information is favored in processing (e.g., Zadny & Gerard, 1974; Klatzky, Martin, & Kane, 1982; Rothbart et al., 1979).

Knowledge can also affect judgments, evaluations, or behavior toward a particular object not directly by influencing the person's interpretation of the object, but indirectly, by providing standards of comparison. No object or event can ever be judged or evaluated in a vacuum, but only against a background and context of related objects or events. Thus, people's behaviors and other attributes are often judged against group-specific standards and expectations (Biernat, Manis, & Nelson, 1991). So, for example, if general knowledge leads someone to expect that women are less assertive than men, a moderately assertive act performed by a woman might be seen as *more* assertive, relative to what is expected, than the identical act performed by a man.

Abstraction of Category Prototypes A prototype is defined as an abstracted representation of the central tendency, average, or typical attribute values of the members of a category (see E. E. Smith & Medin, 1981). In the 1970s, a series of interrelated empirical findings challenged the idea that people represent categories by a set of necessary and jointly sufficient features. For example, nonsocial categories like "furniture" or "bird" were often found to have unclear (nonconsensual) boundaries, and to have graded degrees of membership (e.g., people view a robin as a better member of the "bird" category than a chicken or penguin). In response to such observations, theorists postulated that people abstract category prototypes from a series of category members and then classify new exemplars on the basis of their relative similarity to the prototype. These theoretical models also accounted nicely for the observation that people can learn the prototype of a novel category without ever seeing it—simply through exposure to a series of category exemplars that are variations of the prototype (Posner & Keele, 1968; Reed, 1972).

Theorists in social psychology adopted these models, attracted by the intuitively appealing idea of economy of mental storage that results from the abstraction process (specific idiosyncracies of individual category members need not be represented or stored). For example, Cantor and Mischel (1977, 1979) proposed a prototype model of the representation of person types. Similar models were later elaborated to apply to representations of "person-in-situation" prototypes (such as "rabid fan at a football game") rather than simply person types (Cantor & Kihlstrom, 1987).

Conceptual distinctions can be drawn between prototypes and schemas. For example, a prototype representation is often considered to include all known attributes (e.g., the prototypic rabid fan has a particular hair color) while a schema would represent only category-relevant attributes. Further, a prototype is sometimes treated as an unorganized bundle of features, while a schematic representation is viewed as internally organized (Wyer & Gordon, 1984). Still, according to Fiske and Taylor (1991), the terms have often been used interchangeably by social psychologists, and the chief similarity—that both prototypes and schemas are abstract, general structures that represent a perceiver's knowledge about a category or concept—is more important for the purposes of this chapter.

Knowledge-based Reconstructive Processes in Memory The perceiver's knowledge may not only affect the way new information is *encoded* (e.g., Hastie & Kumar, 1979; Rogers et al., 1977), but also may serve as a source of *cues* to assist retrieval, or may be used to *reconstruct* aspects of the event that were not encoded or are not successfully retrieved. Often the cuing and reconstructive functions are empirically inseparable, though research designs can be devised to distinguish effects at the time of encoding from those that operate at the time of retrieval (e.g., Anderson & Pichert, 1978). Through these three mechanisms, effects of existing knowledge on recall are pervasive.

When existing knowledge serves as an organized source of retrieval cues (Greenwald & Banaji, 1989), it will generally lead to a recall advantage of expectation-consistent information or, in a recognition memory test, to a response bias in the same direction (e.g., Cantor & Mischel, 1977). Thus, for example, group stereotypes can bias memory as well as immediate perceptual interpretation. A recent meta-analysis shows that when people learn information about members of existing social groups that varies in its consistency with stereotypic expectations, people are more likely to recall consistent information at a later time (Fyock & Stangor, 1994).

A different effect of general knowledge on memory has been investigated by Michael Ross and others. Ross and Conway (1986) show that people's perceptions of themselves at the present time combine with their general expectations about personal stability or change to influence autobiographical memories. For example, someone whose attitudes toward smoking have become more negative over time may falsely recall that they were always about as antismoking as they are at present. Similarly, expectations about people in general may affect recall of information about other people as well as the self (McFarland & Ross, 1987; Hirt, 1990). These effects, which are typically interpreted as involving reconstruction at the time of retrieval, may also involve elements of knowledge-cued selective retrieval (Conway & Rubin, 1993). Related research shows that manipulated beliefs about the desirability of a trait influences subjects' recall of instances when they displayed that trait (Sanitioso, Kunda, & Fong, 1990), just as general beliefs about personal stability or change influence autobiographical recall or reconstruction.

A perceiver's general knowledge may influence what is recalled about any person or object—not just in the sphere of autobiographical memories. The change-of-standard effect (Clark, Martin, & Henry, 1993; Higgins & Lurie, 1983; Higgins & Stangor, 1988) is an instance of available knowledge influencing the interpretation of information in the course of memory retrieval. In studies demonstrating this effect, subjects receive information regarding the behavior of a particular person (the sentence decisions made by a judge) and the behavior of other individuals that set a standard or context (the sentencing decisions made by other judges). After some time, newly presented contextual information sets a new standard that influences subjects' recall of the judge's actions, as well as trait-like perceptions of the judge's harshness or leniency.

Priming and Accessibility One of the most fundamental observations about the effects of mental representations on perception, judgment, and behavior is that not all representations are equally likely to be used. Of course, the degree of fit or match between the current stimulus input and a given representation will influence the likelihood of the representation's being applied to the stimulus (see Higgins, 1989). But fit is not the only factor, as was emphasized by the "New Look" movement in perception a half-century ago. Bruner (1957) used the term *accessibility* to refer to the ease or speed with which a perceiver could apply a representation to a new input, and discussed factors such as the perceiver's current expectancies and motivational states that influenced accessibility. Schematically, the probability of using a given representation R to interpret input information I depends on:

$$p(\text{apply}(R, I)) = f(\text{fit}(R, I) * \text{accessibility}(R))$$

Much research in social psychology since the 1970s has confirmed that accessibility has this effect (see reviews by Higgins, 1989, 1996). For example, recently activated trait constructs influence the interpretation of ambiguous behavioral information. In one oft-replicated paradigm (Higgins, Rholes, & Jones, 1977), subjects are exposed to a set of trait-related words under a cover story. In a second, ostensibly unrelated study, they read a paragraph describing a target character's ambiguous behaviors. If the trait is applicable to the behaviors, subjects are more likely to use three "primed" trait schema to characterize the target person than are subjects in a control condition who did not see the trait-related priming words. This basic effect, an increased probability of using a schema that has been recently activated, can last for a surprisingly long time (e.g., 24 hours in Srull & Wyer, 1979). However, the effect does have limits. Under some circumstances, when the priming stimuli are blatant, extreme, or otherwise highly memorable, the effect disappears or even reverses (Lombardi et al., 1987; Martin, 1986).

Frequent use of a schema over a long period of time can also increase its accessibility in a more enduring fashion often termed "chronic accessibility" (Higgins, King, & Marvin, 1982). One study identified traits that subjects chronically used in thinking about others, by noting what traits were listed first in a number of free written descriptions of a variety of individuals. When these subjects were later given written behavioral descriptions, they were more likely to make inferences regarding, and to remember, information related to their chronically accessible traits than to other traits (Higgins et al., 1982). Many other studies

make similar points. For example, people for whom gender-related constructs are highly accessible interpret new information in terms of its implications for gender (Frable & Bem, 1985).

Models of Accessibility Effects of a schema's accessibility on the probability of its use have been the material for a wider range of competing models than has the nature of schema use itself (see Higgins, 1996). One prominent model by Wyer and Srull (1980, 1989) invokes Storage Bins as repositories for schemas. Schemas are presumed to be kept in order in Storage Bins, from which they are independently retrievable. Search of a Storage Bin for a schema that is applicable to some input proceeds from the top down, so a schema that is nearer the top is more likely to be used—that is, more accessible. The 1980 model assumed that a schema was returned to the top of the Storage Bin after use, providing the basis for predicting an effect of recent use on accessibility. Frequency of use (holding recency constant) is implied to have no effect, contrary to the data (e.g., Srull & Wyer, 1979). To fix this problem, the 1989 version of the model added the Copy Postulate: when a schema is withdrawn from the bin for use, it is left in the original location and a new copy is returned to the top of the bin. Thus, more frequently used schemas will be represented by more copies. Additionally, the top-down search is assumed to be probabilistic: an applicable schema is assumed to be used with probability $p < 1$, for otherwise extra copies below the top one would have no effect whatever.

Other prominent models of accessibility effects invoke a metaphor of a time-varying amount of "charge" or activation for each schema, rather than a one-dimensional ordering of schemas from top to bottom in a Storage Bin. Higgins, Bargh, and Lombardi (1985) present several variations of such models, concluding that the evidence favors what they term the "synapse model." In this model the use of a schema gives it a fixed amount of activation, which then decays over time; this property accounts for effects of recent priming. The rate of decay for a given schema, however, depends on its frequency of use: activation of more frequently used schemas decays at a slower rate. This accounts for the effects of frequency. With appropriate parameter values, this model can even account for a complex crossover pattern of empirical results. When one schema is primed several times and then another one a single time, an immediate test may show that the recently primed schema "wins," but after a delay the more frequently primed schema, decaying more slowly, can win.

In the nonsocial literature, J. R. Anderson's ACT-R theory (1993) also offers a model of knowledge accessibility as a function of recent and frequent use. The "base" accessibility B_i of any item of stored knowledge (i.e., its accessibility as an independent unit, disregarding any activation that may spread to it from other associated units) is

$$B_i = \log(\text{sum } (t_j^{-d})) + \text{constant}$$

Here t_j is the time since the jth use of the item, and the sum is over all uses; d is a power-function exponent between 0 and 1. In effect, each use of the knowledge item makes its own incremental contribution to accessibility, the separate contributions are summed, and each contribution decays independently though at the same rate. The accessibility B_i is proportional to the log-odds of the knowledge structure's use. This model's predictions are qualitatively identical to those of Higgins et al. (1985): decay of activation after a single use (governed by the power-function parameters d), and slower decay after multiple uses.

Effects of recent and frequent activation on accessibility have often been treated as equivalent (Higgins & King, 1981; Bargh, Lombardi, & Tota, 1986). However, as Carlston and Smith (1996, p. 198) note, the evidence in this direction is far from conclusive and there is also evidence that recent and frequent use can have somewhat distinctive effects (Bargh, Lombardi, & Higgins, 1988; Higgins et al., 1985; Smith & Branscombe, 1987). The synapse model implies that distinct mechanisms (i.e., short-term activation per se versus a long-lasting change in the rate of decay) are responsible for the effects of recent and frequent activation. The ACT-R model similarly has distinct mechanisms of power-function decay of each trace for recent activation and summation of many independently decaying traces for frequent activation. The idea that accessibility due to recent and frequent activation involves a single mechanism should not be considered firmly established.

Schemas as Unitized Representations Changes in accessibility apply to *all* the contents of a given schema, because a schema is assumed to be accessed and used in all-or-none fashion, as a single unit. This property has often been studied in the context of information-processing differences between experts and novices in a given domain. Experts process information in a given area more efficiently than less knowledgeable individuals, partly because they can organize or "chunk" more information into a schema that can then be treated as a single unit. For example, an influential early study (Chase & Simon, 1973) found that chess experts could cognitively represent a number of pieces and their locations on the board as a single unit, greatly improving their ability to recall and reconstruct game positions. Conceptually similar findings, resting on the theoretical idea that people vary in their expertise in conceptualizing and using particular social trait dimensions, have been obtained in social psychology (Sentis & Burnstein, 1979; Hayes-Roth, 1977; Fiske & Dyer, 1985). Someone who is an "expert" on depression, for instance, possessing a strong and well-articulated schema for that concept, may be able to organize several observations about another person (such as insomnia, negative moods, and loss of appetite) into a general concept that can be treated as a single cognitive unit. A nonexpert may have to treat these observations as separate and unrelated facts.

Dissociations Between Memory and Judgment Schematic mechanisms can account for the dissociations often observed between summary judgments (e.g., overall evaluations) and recall for specific information, by postulating that two or more separate schematic representations are formed based on the input information. For example, Wyer and Gordon (1984) argued that people interpret an individual's behaviors by forming both trait-based clusters and evaluative summaries, dumping each independently into the Storage Bin. Later, to make an evaluative judgment the evaluative cluster may be retrieved, while to recall the individual's behaviors the trait-based clusters would be used. Under this model, no necessary relationship would be expected between the content of the judgment and the evaluative implications of the behaviors that were recalled.

In some studies a reverse association is observed between the effects of an activated schema on judgment and the ability to recall the event that primed or activated it (Lombardi et al., 1987; Martin et al., 1990). That is, subjects who recall the priming events are less likely to assimilate new input to the primed schema than are subjects who fail to recall the events. Attributional processing seems to mediate this pattern. If people attribute their response (such as an interpretation of a stimulus) to something *other* than the intrinsic qualities of the stimulus, they may try to avoid bias by searching for an alternative but equally applicable concept. Of course, like any attributional judgment this one might be in error; social psychological researchers (e.g., Higgins et al., 1977) have become expert at activating concepts in people's minds without arousing suspicion or conscious attributions to the external priming events. In this case an applicable primed construct is usually applied without question. In general, this point illustrates the potential complexities raised by the interaction of automatic (nonconscious) processing and consciously controlled processing. It also suggests an important and general point, that conscious awareness allows increased *flexibility* in the way information is used or interpreted (Clark, 1993, chap. 4; Lombardi et al., 1987).

Schematic Models of the Self Several theorists (e.g., Markus, 1977; Rogers et al., 1977) have proposed that content domains that are particularly important to the self are cognitively represented as schemas. This model implies that self-knowledge about a given trait, represented as a unitized knowledge structure, is activated by thinking about the trait or by encountering trait-related concepts. The "schema" label emphasizes the idea that once it is active, structured self-knowledge can shape processing of further information. In the research that led to this conceptualization, specific characteristics (such as independent) were assumed to constitute a self-schema if they were important to the person and the person viewed himself or herself as extreme on the dimension. People are able to make self-reference judgments rapidly and accurately on such dimensions, compared to other dimensions (or to people who are not schematic on the given dimension). They also remember information related to their schematic dimensions quite well—such as examples of their past trait-relevant behavior. They make trait-consistent inferences and judgments quite readily, such as predictions that they will behave consistently with their chosen trait in the future. Finally, they resist and counterargue information that is inconsistent with their schematic self-conceptions (Markus, 1977; see review by Markus & Sentis, 1982). Effects of a self-schema for a particular dimension extend beyond self-perception and self-inference to include perceptions of other people (Markus & Smith, 1981). Consistent with the idea that having a particular trait as part of the self-schema implies being a sort of "expert" on that trait and its implications, people are ready to note the existence of such traits in other people (Fong & Markus, 1982). Note, though, that some of the early studies in this domain failed to distinguish the general chronic accessibility of a trait from the trait's status as part of the perceiver's self-schema.

More recently, studies by Higgins, van Hook, and Dorfman (1988) failed to find support for the hypothesis that the entire body of self-related information is represented as a unified self-schema. Presentation of a word that was self-related for a given subject (e.g., sincere) as a prime did not increase the activation level of a second self-related word (e.g., independent). This was true even when subjects' attention was self-focused, which should have rendered all self-knowledge readily accessible. Control conditions showed that in the same paradigm, an object word such as maple could prime a semantically related word like birch. Higgins et al. (1988) conclude that although (by definition) self-related concepts are all independently linked to a core self representation, there is no evidence that all self-related concepts are represented within a unified cognitive structure (schema) that is activated in all-or-none fashion. Independent support for the same conclusion comes from evidence, to be reviewed later, concerning the fluidity and context-sensitivity of the self-concept.

Summary

Schematic models have been the most popular conceptualization of mental representation within social psychology over the past two decades. The core domain of their application has been to the *interpretation* of new information based on existing knowledge, and effects of transient or chronic accessibility on those interpretative processes.

With rare exceptions (e.g., Higgins et al., 1988) researchers have not specified or tested detailed assumptions about the structure or content of the schemas they postulate. This typical vagueness regarding the use of a central theoretical term has often been decried in the literature (e.g., Fiske & Linville, 1980; Markus & Zajonc, 1985). In contrast, those who employ associative models have generally proposed a specific structure, at least in the form of a quick sketch of lines connecting nodes in a particular pattern (see Figure 1).

Still, it is possible to induce the following general points regarding schema theories within social psychology.

1. The *formation* of a schema is rarely explicitly considered; the vast majority of schema research in social psychology relies on subjects' pre-existing knowledge structures. When schema acquisition and development is considered (e.g., Fiske & Taylor, 1991, chap. 5), schemas are assumed to be learned from other people or formed by generalizing across a set of personal experiences.

2. The *effects of schemas on explicit memory* (almost always free recall) are seen as due to processes of schema-based interpretation and inference (at the time the stimulus information is learned) or schema-based retrieval cuing and reconstruction (at the time of recall).

3. The *effects of schemas on implicit memory* are of several types. Priming effects (e.g., Higgins et al., 1977) are regarded as effects of specific experiences that render schemas accessible, thereby influencing interpretation of later-presented information. Schemas also directly influence judgments, as when an object is evaluated based on information (such as an "affective tag") that is part of the schema rather than based on the object's directly available characteristics.

4. *Dissociations* among various effects such as recall and judgment are regarded as caused by recall and judgmental processes accessing separate schemas. For example, people might interpret an individual's behaviors by forming trait-based clusters representing the details of the behaviors as well as an overall evaluative summary, stored as a separate schema.

EXEMPLARS

Exemplar models of cognitive representation have a considerably shorter history than do associative and schematic models. They trace directly back only to the mid-1970s, and particularly to exemplar models of categorization such as the seminal work by Medin and Schaffer (1978). In contrast to then-prevailing abstractionist models of category representation (e.g., Posner & Keele, 1968), which hold that perceivers store and use information about the typical values or central tendency of a category, exemplar-based models postulate that people store more specific information, such as the details of particular category members (exemplars). These models found support in an important theoretical trend in the 1970s and 1980s that downplayed the role of abstractions and emphasized the role of specific experiences (in nonsocial cognition, see Brooks, 1978; Jacoby & Brooks, 1984; Whittlesea, 1987; in social psychology see Lewicki, 1985; Linville, Fisher, & Salovey, 1989; Smith, 1988, 1990).

Fundamental Assumptions

Exemplar mechanisms share the following core ideas.

1. *Fundamental representational assumption:* Representations record information about specific stimuli or experiences, rather than abstracted summaries or generalizations. Of course, these representations record what the person perceived and/or inferred, rather than veridical or objective stimulus information. Such a representation may be constructed on the basis of actually perceiving the stimulus object, imagining it, being told about it secondhand, etc.

2. *Representations record feature co-occurrences:* Schematic or prototype models often assume the abstraction and storage of information about the typical values of each feature, independently. For example, it might be learned that most members of the "bird" category are small and that most sing. A fundamental assumption of exemplar models is that representations of specific stimuli record patterns of feature co-occurrences, such as a thrush (a small, singing bird) and a gull (a large, nonsinging bird). Such representations support people's observed sensitivity to the correlations of features within categories (e.g., their knowledge that small birds are more likely to sing than large ones; Malt & Smith, 1984).

3. *Activation of exemplars by retrieval cues:* Retrieval cues (whether self-generated or external in origin) activate all exemplars in parallel, each exemplar to an extent depending on its similarity to the cues. Activation makes the exemplars available to influence judgments or impressions.

4. *Parallel on-line computation:* When a new stimulus is to be evaluated, judged, or categorized, it is compared in parallel to many activated exemplar traces. Similarly, when generalizations about a type of stimulus are required they can be computed by activating all exemplars of that type and summarizing them.

5. *Effects on interpretation, attention, and judgment:* The effects of an activated mass of exemplars are assumed to be the same as those attributed to schemas in schema theories: to influence interpretation, attention, retrieval, and reconstruction, at a preconscious level.

6. *Flexibility, context sensitivity:* In contrast to the all-or-none activation of a schema, different subsets of exemplar representations can be activated by different cues, contexts, etc. As a result, the effects of an activated set of exemplars may be strikingly specific and context sensitive. As Barsalou (1987) has illustrated, instead of accessing a monolithic and invariant "bird" concept, people construct quite different concepts of "bird" in the context of a barnyard (where chicken exemplars might be most central) versus a suburban backyard (in which case robin would be more similar to the concept than chicken).

7. *Independence of implicit and explicit memory:* Exemplar theorists assume that the differences in processes and in the cues supplied by judgment tasks (e.g., to categorize new exemplars) and explicit memory tasks (e.g., to recognize previously encountered exemplars) are sufficient to produce stochastic independence between tasks. That is, the exemplars that affect categorization and other judgments may or may not be those that are retrievable in an explicit memory test.

Exemplar mechanisms can also vary in significant ways.

1. *Level of exemplars:* Theorists' definitions of exemplars vary. In models of categorization an exemplar is most straightforwardly defined as a cognitive representation of a specific category member. However, the storage of exemplar information may be incomplete (Kruschke & Erickson, in press), leading to the possibility of what might be termed "subtype" representations. That is, if a category member is defined by three attributes (like "large blue cube") and only "large cube" is stored in memory, this can be viewed either as an incomplete representation of the particular stimulus or as a representation of a subtype (i.e., all large cubes of whatever color). In models of the representation of persons and groups, an exemplar is assumed to be a cognitive representation of a person (Smith & Zárate, 1992). The same argument regarding incomplete representations would allow for subtypes, a possibility emphasized by Linville and Fisher (1993) and Judd and Park (1988). Note that even if representations are always complete when stored, partial forgetting might mean that only an incomplete representation is accessible at a later time.

2. *Storage of abstractions as well as exemplars:* As will be discussed in more detail shortly, some theories assume that only exemplars are stored and used in judgment, while others assume that abstractions as well as exemplars can be used.

Illustrative Models and Applications

Exemplar-based Interpretation and Judgment The primary function of schemas, as reviewed above, is to summarize and organize past experiences into a representation that is useful for interpreting new input information, making judgments, and retrieving information from memory. Recent theoretical developments argue that exemplar-based mechanisms can serve the same functions.

An Exemplar-based Model of Social Judgment   Smith and Zárate (1992) proposed a general exemplar-based model of social judgment. The model's fundamental assumptions are reasonably typical of exemplar models in general, as the model builds on exemplar models of categorization (particularly Medin and Schaffer, 1978, and Nosofsky, 1986). The assumptions are extended to other types of evaluations and judgments (besides category membership) and to include effects of individual differences, motivation, and social context. In social psychology, important precursors of this model are the exemplar-based accounts of stereotyping provided by Rothbart and John (1985) and of group variability judgments provided by Linville et al. (1989).

Briefly, this model assumes (a) as the perceiver encounters or considers individual persons, cognitive representations of those persons (i.e., exemplars) are constructed and stored in memory. A representation of a "typical member of Group X" constructed on the basis of reflection about the group's general characteristics, a secondhand description of the group, or a joke or slur that implies the group possesses some stereotypical attribute, could also be stored as an exemplar. (b) When a judgment concerning a person or group is required, the known attributes of exemplars that are retrieved from memory by virtue of their similarity to the target form the basis of the judgment. (c) Similarity is modulated by the perceiver's attention to stimulus dimensions, as in Medin and Schaffer's (1978) context model. For example, if in evaluating a female lawyer the perceiver pays attention to gender, then other representations of females would be treated as most similar and would be most likely to be retrieved—resulting, presumably, in judgments that the target possesses gender-stereotypic attributes. In contrast, attention to occupation would result in the preferential retrieval of other lawyer exemplars and, presumably, judgments that the target shares their attributes. And if the perceiver pays attention to the person's unique individual characteristics (e.g., her manner of speaking), still other representations (e.g., representations of others who speak in a similar way) will be retrieved to influence judgments about her. (d) Social and motivational factors, including the current social situation, the perceiver's self-concept, and in-group/out-group dynamics, affect attention to stimulus dimensions and hence exemplar retrieval and judgment processes.

One characteristic of the Smith and Zárate (1992) model is that a single mechanism (similarity-based exemplar retrieval) is used to account for inferences about a new individual based on similarities to a specific person (Andersen

& Cole, 1990; Lewicki, 1985), and also for standard group stereotyping effects. The latter are interpreted as the massed effect of many representations of group members with stereotypical attributes, derived from social learning and/or personal encounters. The model emphasizes the powerful effects of the way the perceiver allocates attention at the time exemplars are initially processed and stored, and also at the time a new stimulus is encountered and similar exemplars are retrieved. What is stored is always the perceiver's interpretation, not the objective or veridical stimulus information (see Whittlesea & Dorken, 1993). Therefore directing attention to only group-typical attributes of a set of exemplars (e.g., to the verbal fluency and aggressiveness of a number of lawyers) results in the storage of a number of similar exemplar representations which, when retrieved, will mediate relatively stereotypic judgments about a newly encountered group member. But if attention focuses on each lawyer's idiosyncratic attributes (physical appearance, hobbies, personality traits) then retrieval of these exemplars to make judgments about a new lawyer is less likely to result in purely stereotypic perception.

In the exemplar-based model, stereotyping can pertain to an existing social category (e.g., women or African Americans) or to novel, never-before-considered groups (including groups newly emerged into most people's consciousness through media attention, such as "conservative talk-radio hosts," or conceptual combinations like "Brazilian lawyer"). The model also interprets certain implicit memory effects (such as the effect of mere exposure on liking) as products of exemplar retrieval and misattribution, as will be discussed below. The exemplar-based model thus suggests that exemplars contribute to a wide range of dependent variables involving judgment and memory, including the kinds of interpretive effects that are often attributed to schemas.

Norm Theory   Kahneman and Miller (1986) proposed "norm theory" as an account of the way perceivers interpret and evaluate objects and events in the context of relevant alternatives. Their key claim is that an experience elicits the retrieval of representations of similar past experiences (exemplars) or of counterfactual alternatives (constructed on-line on the basis of general knowledge). The elicited "norm" then serves as a context or standard that influences judgments of the experience's typicality or unusualness, comparative judgments, and affective reactions to the experience. The details of the experience itself influence the standard that is constructed and therefore the judgmental outcome. For example, if an automobile whizzes by and barely misses a bicycle rider, the rider is likely to construct counterfactual alternatives involving an actual collision and serious bodily injury. Feelings of relief may mingle with anger at the offending driver. Kahneman and Miller (1986, p. 136) emphasize that "each event brings its own frame of reference into being" by eliciting relevant exemplars from memory, in contrast to the typical view that events are judged with reference to static, precomputed expectancies.

Hintzman's MINERVA Model Applied to Social Psychological Phenomena Hintzman's MINERVA model (1986), a prominent exemplar model, successfully predicts a variety of explicit memory phenomena in nonsocial cognition. Most significantly, MINERVA can account for people's ability to learn to recognize the prototype or average of a series of patterns even when only the patterns (not the prototype itself) have been seen. Smith (1988, 1991) applied the same model to social psychological effects which had not been part of the original motivation for the development of the model. The model's processes of exemplar storage and retrieval, applied in a simulation of a typical "priming" paradigm, reproduced the standard results: ambiguous information is assimilated to the primed construct (Smith, 1988). The priming events are simply considered as additional experiences involving the use of the construct. When stored in memory, they in effect strengthen the mental representation of the general construct. This simulation calls into question the common assumption that priming effects must be mediated by changes in the accessibility of abstract construct representations; Hintzman's model reproduces those effects without even possessing any abstract representations.

Similarly, Smith (1991) showed that the same model could reproduce several aspects of typical "illusory correlation" results (Hamilton & Gifford, 1976; Hamilton & Sherman, 1989). In the illusory correlation paradigm, people judge a larger group more positively than a smaller group when members of each group are said to perform exactly the same ratio (say, 2:1) of positive to negative behaviors. The simulation works because MINERVA is sensitive to differences in *numbers* of positive and negative behaviors ascribed to the two groups, so if the larger group performs 8 positive and 4 negative its overall evaluation is proportional to +4, compared to the smaller group's +2 based on 4 positive, 2 negative behaviors. Though the model could not simulate all relevant findings in the literature (e.g., because MINERVA lacks a model of free recall), it nevertheless suggests an additional mechanism (besides the standard assumption of increased attention to the "distinctive" negative behaviors of the smaller group) that may contribute to illusory correlation effects. The success of these two applications suggests the possibility that pure-exemplar models might be able to account for additional empirical phenomena within social psychology (see Smith, 1990; Smith & Zárate, 1992).

Possible Role of Abstractions in Exemplar Models Models of memory representation and judgment may postulate the storage and use of only abstract (schematic) representa-

tions, only exemplar representations, or both. Many empirical tests have demonstrated that exemplar information is represented in memory and used in judgments (e.g., categorization judgments of new stimuli), ruling out the first type (*pure abstraction* models; Alba & Hasher, 1983; Smith, 1990). Definitive empirical tests between exemplar-only and exemplar-plus-abstraction models are more difficult to set up. Three positions can be distinguished.

1. The clear favorite within social psychology is the *dual-process exemplar-plus-abstraction* approach (e.g., Fiske & Neuberg, 1990; Hamilton & Sherman, 1994), which holds that perceivers maintain and can use both types of representations. The typical assumption is that when judgments are to be made abstractions have priority, and exemplars are used only as a last resort. For example, research on impression formation has frequently demonstrated dissociations between judgments about a target person and recall of the specific stimulus information (such as traits or behaviors; e.g., Anderson & Hubert, 1963). Such dissociations have traditionally been interpreted as evidence for dual storage: a specific, episodic representation of the original stimulus information is accessed for recall, and a relatively abstract evaluative representation is used for a judgment (Hastie & Park, 1986). Note, however, that such conclusions generally rest on comparisons of judgments with explicit memory measures (usually free recall). Research using implicit memory measure (e.g., Smith et al., 1992; see Schacter, 1987) demonstrates that representations of specific information may have an impact on judgment without being consciously accessible to recall or recognition. Thus, a dissociation between explicit memory and judgmental effects may not unequivocally point to the use of dual representations as is usually assumed.

2. A second possibility may be termed the *single-process exemplar-plus-abstraction* view; it is the idea that abstract as well as exemplar representations are stored, but that they are all retrieved and used in judgment through exactly the same mechanisms (Smith & Zárate, 1992). In this view, a perceiver who thinks about the "typical member of fraternity Alpha Beta Gamma," or who is told what such a person is like, is ipso facto constructing a cognitive representation of a person. This is an exemplar by definition, and it may be retained in memory and influence future categorizations or other judgments about group members. However, it is likely to be difficult to empirically discriminate the effects of this added abstraction from the massed effects of the individual group member representations to which it is presumably similar, so the predictions of this model may closely resemble those of a pure-exemplar view.

3. A *pure-exemplar* view holds that abstractions have not been demonstrated to be necessary. The massed effect of many similar exemplars is used to account for phenomena for which most theorists have turned to abstract representations, such as prototype learning (Hintzman, 1986).

Arguments favoring the first two types of models over the pure-exemplar view include the observation that information about a social group can be conveyed linguistically (abstractly) as well as learned through exposure to individual group members, and the idea that if people reflect on what a group is typically like, the result of summarizing many exemplar representations may be stored for efficient future retrieval (Hamilton & Mackie, 1990). Perhaps most important, social psychological researchers have emphasized processing flexibility and the role of the perceiver's goals and intentions in determining how information is represented and stored (Hastie & Park, 1986; Judd & Park, 1988). A number of studies suggest that abstraction is not automatic—that in the absence of special motivation, perceivers do not abstract typical properties of related stimuli (Medin, Dewey, & Murphy, 1983; Whittlesea, 1987; Whittlesea & Dorken, 1993) or interpret behaviors by abstracting traits to apply to the actor (Bassili, 1989; Klein et al., 1992). Still, when perceivers have the capacity and motivation, they are certainly able to abstract and summarize incoming information to form dual representations.

The most significant research questions at this point concern not whether but when people form abstractions, and how abstractions and exemplars independently or interactively affect various memory and judgmental tasks. Preliminary work (Schul & Burnstein, 1990; Smith & Zárate, 1990, 1992) suggests that a variety of factors such as the relative accessibility of abstract and exemplar representations (due to recency or frequency of use) and the perceiver's attention (which may be influenced by many cognitive, social, and situational factors) may tilt the balance toward the use of different types of representations in judgment.

Representation of Social Groups and Variability Though the issues just discussed about the respective roles of abstractions and exemplar representations are quite general, an important area of application has been the question of how information about social groups—particularly group variability—is represented in memory (Fiske & Taylor, 1991; Hamilton & Sherman, 1994). The four main theoretical contenders have been abstractionist models in which only the group prototype (i.e., its typical characteristics) is represented, abstractionist models representing the central tendency plus variability information, pure-exemplar models in which only representations of individual group members are used, and various mixture models in which both abstractions

and exemplars are represented. Prototype-only models can easily be ruled out on the basis of observations showing that perceivers retain and use information about group variability and about specific exemplars, as well as about a group's average characteristics (Linville et al.,1989; Smith & Zárate, 1990). It has proven more difficult to choose among the three remaining alternatives, particularly as applied to the well-known fact that people tend to view out-groups as less variable than in-groups (Judd & Park, 1988; Linville et al., 1989; Mackie, Sherman, & Worth, 1993; Park & Hastie, 1987; for a review, see Hamilton & Sherman, 1994, pp. 15–32). An emerging consensus (Hamilton & Sherman, 1994, p. 25; Leyens & Fiske, 1994, p. 53) appears to favor models using both abstractions and exemplars. One specific suggestion (Park & Judd, 1990; Park, Judd, & Ryan, 1991) is that people tend to form abstract prototype representations of both types of groups but also store information about specific exemplars of in-groups. However, such hybrid models—to a greater degree than more parsimonious exemplar-only models—raise complex and as yet empirically unresolved questions regarding which type of representation is formed and used when.

Repetition Priming This refers to the facilitation of processing of a stimulus when the same stimulus has been previously encountered. It is clearly distinguishable from semantic priming, reviewed earlier in this chapter, by its duration and in other ways. Of course, if reading "doctor" facilitates processing of the word "nurse" because it is semantically similar, it is trivially true that "nurse" will also prime "nurse" through the same mechanism. But that semantic priming effect should be short-lived, so if the effect lasts for hours, days, or months a distinctly different phenomenon must be involved. Repetition priming is by definition an implicit memory measure, for processing the item on the second encounter does not demand conscious or intentional recollection of the previous experience.

Word-fragment Completion As mentioned above, people are better able to complete a fragmented word such as _SS_SS__ for quite some time—even weeks or months—after they have read the word (assassin) on a list (Tulving et al., 1982; see Schacter, 1987, for a review). This is a form of repetition priming because reading the word (i.e., accessing the word's meaning from its visual appearance) facilitates reading the same word a second time, even in fragmented form. The facilitation is ordinarily found to be independent of subjects' ability to explicitly recognize that they have been exposed to the word in the experiment.

Social psychological researchers have adapted this finding to address the issue of spontaneous trait inference: do people infer a trait when they become aware that someone has performed a behavior in the absence of specific instructions to think about its trait implications? Bassili and

M. C. Smith (1986) showed that subjects were better able to complete fragmented trait words if they had previously read a behavioral sentence that implied the trait. They used this result to argue that subjects spontaneously inferred the traits from the behaviors. However, the interpretation of this finding is uncertain because others (Jacoby, 1983; Smith & Branscombe, 1988) have found no facilitation of word-fragment completion performance from tasks that involve the activation of a word through conceptually related cues—as when a trait word is accessed from trait-relevant behaviors. Perhaps special features of Bassili and Smith's study, such as the fact that the word-fragment test included *only* trait words from the previously studied sentences, encouraged subjects to use special intentional strategies to complete the word fragments.

Savings in Relearning Ebbinghaus (1885/1964) noted that information once learned and then forgotten could be more readily relearned than equivalent new information—another type of repetition priming. Carlston and Skowronski (1994; Carlston, Skowronski, & Sparks, 1995) used savings in relearning to address the question of spontaneous trait inference from behaviors. Their subjects saw photos of people paired with trait-implying behaviors. At a later time, they attempted to learn a series of photo-trait pairings. They were better able to learn a trait presented with a photo if it was implied by the behavior previously paired with the photo, compared to a new trait. This finding of savings in relearning implies that subjects had originally "learned" the photo-trait pairing in some form and hence that they had spontaneously inferred the trait implications of the behavior. Control tasks showed that the effect was not mediated by explicit memory for the original behavior.

Facilitation of Processing by Prior Experiences Facilitation of performance due to unintended (implicit) access to a memory trace of a prior experience can be measured not only by the level of performance on a word-fragment completion or savings test, but also by response time (RT) facilitation. In the nonsocial literature, long-lasting facilitation of responses to previously encountered stimuli has been demonstrated with diverse tasks, such as solving "alphabet arithmetic" problems (Logan, 1988), naming line drawings of common objects (Mitchell & Brown, 1988), and reading text in unfamiliar orientations (Kolers, 1976).

The same effect has been observed in a social judgment task. Smith, Stewart, and Buttram (1992) had subjects perform hundreds of trials of a behavior-to-trait inference task, responding "yes" or "no" as quickly as possible to indicate whether they thought a variety of behaviors were friendly or intelligent. Some of the behaviors were repeated within the series of trials, and others were repeated between experimental sessions separated by up to seven days. RTs for repeated behaviors were significantly shorter than for new ones, even across a week's delay. This RT facilitation, and also an effect of previous exposure on judgments of the behaviors, were independent of subjects' ability to recognize that a behavior had been previously presented.

These effects demand explanations that go beyond the idea that the recent use of a cognitive representation (such as a trait construct) may increase its general accessibility. Consider a comparison between two subjects who judge a given behavior on trial number 100, one subject who has not encountered this behavior before and a second subject who had judged the same behavior earlier in the sequence. Clearly, on trial 100 both the fit of the behavior to the trait and the overall accessibility of the trait representation are equal for these two subjects. Thus, some additional factor must be responsible for the item-specific facilitation of trial 100 in the second condition. One possibility is an increase in the accessibility of the representation of the stimulus item itself (i.e., the behavior) that facilitates some general, nontask-specific process (such as reading the item from the computer screen). However, control conditions in which subjects are asked to perform a *different* task on the second occurrence of a repeated stimulus demonstrate no facilitation (Smith, 1989). Facilitation is specific to the repetition of the same task, such as judging a behavior on a given trait. Such evidence shows that a third factor, the specific history of use of a general representation to interpret a specific input, must be added to the schematic equation governing the speed and ease of application of a mental representation R to input information I:

$$p(\text{apply}(R, I)) = f(\text{fit}(R, I) * \text{accessibility}(R) * \text{specific-history-of-use}(R, I))$$

Exemplar representations are the theoretical entities that are assumed to record the specific history of use of a general concept such as a trait to categorize or interpret a specific stimulus item. The representation of the item as it was processed or interpreted is stored (for example, a behavior together with the inferred trait). At a later time, reencountering the same behavior can trigger the retrieval of this exemplar representation and facilitate repetition of the same judgment (cf. Logan, 1988). Because of their abstract and general nature, schematic representations by definition cannot record details of specific episodes of schema use (Smith, 1990).

Process Specificity An exemplar representation records the properties of the stimulus *as it was processed,* so the latter effects of that representation will depend on how the stimulus was processed initially. Specifically, much research demonstrates that a match between the processing applied initially and the process engaged in at the time of retrieval results in the maximum amount of facilitation (Kolers & Roediger, 1984; Roediger & Blaxton, 1987). For example, Jacoby (1983) had subjects read target words (such as "cold") or generate them from their antonyms (hot–____). At a later time, they were given a recognition test or a word-fragment completion test for the target words. Recognition was better for words that subjects had generated rather than read, but subjects could better complete the word fragments for target words that had been read rather than generated. Von Hippel et al. (1993) similarly demonstrated that when people can bring a conceptually based expectation to bear as they read words they perform more poorly on a later word-fragment completion test, suggesting that they are less likely to attend to the perceptual details of the words.

These results contradict the idea that any encounter with a word or concept increases its accessibility in a way that facilitates all kinds of performance (whether explicit memory or fragment completion). Instead, different kinds of processing at the time of study facilitate specific types of performance later. This principle has been termed *transfer appropriate processing* (Morris, Bransford, & Franks, 1977). As applied to the Jacoby study, the principle holds that accessing the word from visual cues (in the read condition) or from conceptual cues (in the generate condition) creates distinct sorts of representations. When retrieved later, these facilitate distinct processes (respectively, fragment-completion and recognition—which is known to be sensitive to semantic or conceptual processing). In other words, facilitation of performance depends on the degree of overlap between the processes that were carried out originally on the stimulus and the processes that are required by the test (Roediger, Srinivas, & Weldon, 1989).

Similar findings have been obtained with social judgments. Smith and Branscombe (1988) designed an experiment conceptually patterned on Jacoby (1983), in which subjects studied trait words either by reading them or by generating them from a list of related behaviors plus the initial letter of the trait word. A later test assessed either subjects' free recall for the trait words, the ability to complete the trait words in fragmented form, or their use of the traits in categorizing ambiguously trait-related behaviors. The results showed that the pattern of performance on these three types of test depended on the study condition. Generating the trait word increased performance more than did reading on the free recall and category accessibility tests, while reading the word was more effective in strengthening fragment completion performance than was trait generation. Therefore, it is not the case that simply encountering trait-related information increases the accessibility of the trait construct independent of the process that is performed on the information. Instead, effects depend on the particular process that people performed at the time of study. Processing the trait word conceptually (in the generate condition) helped performance on tests that require conceptual processing, while reading the trait word helped performance on the word-fragment completion test.

In another area of social psychology, Fazio, Blascovich, and Driscoll (1992) exposed subjects to a series of novel abstract paintings, with instructions either to think about their attitude toward each painting or to name its predominant color. Only the intentional attitude access, not the simple exposure to the paintings, facilitated subjects' performance in a later task requiring them to evaluate the pictures. The principle of transfer appropriate processing organizes this and much other data in social and nonsocial cognition (Roediger et al., 1989). Processing a stimulus in a particular way creates a highly specific representation of that experience (an exemplar) whose retrieval can facilitate a later repetition of the same process on the same stimulus.

Misattribution of Exemplar Effects   When an effect of a prior experience on judgment or behavior occurs in the absence of conscious recollection of the prior experience— that is, when a dissociation between these two effects of memory exists—the door is open for the perceiver to misattribute the judgmental effect. For example, the judgment or action may be seen as due to intrinsic qualities of the stimulus, rather than being correctly attributed to the perceiver's prior encounter with that stimulus. There are a number of phenomena in the literature that may be seen as instances of such misattributions.

Liking Induced by Mere Exposure   One of the best-known effects in social psychology is the increase in liking that can be caused by "mere exposure" to previously neutral stimuli (Zajonc, 1968). The effect can occur even when the perceiver is unable to consciously remember the prior exposures (Mandler, Nakamura, & van Zandt, 1987; Seamon, Brody, & Kauff, 1983). Though some interpretations of this effect have emphasized the special nature of the affective system (Zajonc, 1980), it now appears that it is best viewed as a type of misattribution. The previous exposure changes the way the perceiver subjectively experiences the stimulus, producing a relatively vague feeling of familiarity. If the person is then asked how much he or she *likes* the stimulus, the vague feeling will be interpreted as liking. Consistent with this idea, Mandler et al. (1987) found that asking about other stimulus qualities (such as subjective brightness or darkness) also produced different responses for previously exposed stimuli. Evidently subjects are highly susceptible to subtle suggestions as to the particular stimulus qualities that might be taken as the *source* of their subjective experience.

Other Misattribution Effects   As the Mandler study shows, misattribution of effects produced by unrecognized previous exposures are not limited to affective judgments, and other research has illustrated a variety of effects. Jacoby, Kelley, Brown, and Jasechko (1989) exposed some subjects to nonfamous personal names during an initial pronunciation task, and then, after a delay, asked subjects to indicate how famous these and other names were. The names to which subjects had previously been exposed apparently were associated with feelings of familiarity, leading those names to "become famous overnight." However, when there was only a brief delay between the initial task and the fame judgment, subjects were presumably aware of the source of name familiarity, and the effect did not occur.

In another study (Jacoby, Allan, Collins, & Larwill, 1988) subjects listened to spoken sentences mixed with noise. Some of the sentences had also been heard on a previous occasion. The previously heard sentences could more readily be understood against the noise than could control sentences, but subjects did not attribute this perceptual fluency to the previous exposure. Instead, they said that the noise level was lower for some sentences (the old ones) than for others.

Similarly, one might suppose that an argument that one has previously heard might be rated as more persuasive because it can be easily comprehended and "feels" familiar, even (or perhaps especially) if one cannot recall the previous exposure. Consistent with this possibility, plausible general-knowledge statements that are familiar because of prior presentations are subjectively rated as more valid than comparable novel sentences (Begg, Armour, & Kerr, 1985; Hasher, Goldstein, & Toppino, 1977). Presumably subjects misattribute the familiarity, taking it as evidence that they have encountered the idea before outside the laboratory, and hence as evidence of its truth. In all these cases, prior exposure seems to have subjectively vague but perceptible effects on subjects' reactions to a stimulus. These effects can be misattributed by the subject, mistakenly ascribed to objective qualities of the stimulus rather than to the subject's history of exposure. Of course, such misattribution is more likely under circumstances where the subject cannot consciously recognize the occasion of prior exposure.

Flexible, Context-Sensitive Use of Concepts

Nonsocial Concepts   Knowledge representations are influenced by such transitory factors as the perceiver's momentary mood or goal state, the current situation, or the nature of the ongoing discourse or conversation—all intended to be captured in the general term "context." Even consensual knowledge about perfectly ordinary concepts has been found to be applied in a way that varies across people, contexts, and times. Barsalou (1987) conducted groundbreaking work on this topic using representations of nonsocial categories like "bird." In this work, the pattern of rated goodness of fit or centrality to the category of various exemplars is taken as the key indicator of the structure of a category representation. If the sentence or story context involved a barnyard, people's category-membership judgments indicated that "chicken" was a more central category member than "robin," while in a suburban backyard con-

text, the reverse was true. Similarly, Barsalou found that people showed distinct patterns of graded category membership for many "point-of-view" variants of a given concept, such as "bird" from the point of view of a French person, a Chinese person, or a sailor. Barsalou concluded that the use of even a basic, consensual concept like "bird" differed so much from one application to another that it could not be said to reflect a single context-free underlying representation. Instead, a concept is *a context-sensitive on-line construction* based on a substrate of stable, long-term representational resources.

Exemplar models interpret this flexibility as reflecting the on-line computation of a concept as an aggregate of a number of known exemplars, selected and weighted by their contextual relevance. Thus, the "barnyard" context makes chicken exemplars more readily retrievable than robin ones as the context-specific current version of the "bird" concept is computed. In fact, exemplar models predict that a completely novel concept (for which no pre-existing representation can exist) can be computed on the spot as a summary of relevant exemplars (cf. Kahneman & Miller, 1986). Barsalou (1987), for instance, has demonstrated that ad hoc concepts like "things that might fall on your head" or "ways to escape being killed by the Mafia" have the same structural properties as concepts that are represented more permanently. Similarly, it might be speculated that people can derive stereotypes (summaries of exemplars' typical characteristics) even for novel groups that they have not considered as groups before—Saturn owners, say, or "people who get to work before I do."

Social Concepts   In recent years, the theme of context-sensitivity and fluid variability has emerged in accounts of several types of social concepts. Markus and Wurf (1987) have advanced the notion of a "working self-concept," the contextually relevant set of self-attributes that are currently active. People's self-perceived traits as well as their motives and characteristic behaviors all vary by situation and social context, as contextually relevant information is activated while other information remains inaccessible (Linville & Carlston, 1994; see also Higgins et al., 1988). In fact, Turner, Oakes, Haslam, & McGarty (1994, p. 459) advance the radical suggestion that "the concept of the self as a separate mental structure does not seem necessary, because we can assume that any and all cognitive resources—long-term knowledge, implicit theories, . . . and so forth—are recruited, used, and deployed when necessary" to construct a situationally appropriate self-representation.

According to Wilson and Hodge (1992), attitudes too are constructed on the spot in a flexible and context-dependent manner rather than being retrieved from memory in invariant form every time they are accessed. For example, survey researchers have long realized that expressed attitudes can be strongly affected by the content of recently asked questions and the wordings of response alternatives (Strack & Martin, 1987; Tourangeau & Rasinski, 1988). Current mood and such seemingly innocuous manipulations as reflecting on the reasons behind one's attitude can also change the attitude (Schwarz & Clore, 1983; Wilson, 1990).

Stereotypes—though usually regarded as highly stable knowledge structures—are also sensitive to recent experiences, a point that has been strikingly illustrated by Bodenhausen and his colleagues (1995). These researchers asked subjects about well-liked African Americans (Oprah Winfrey or Michael Jordan) in the context of a task ostensibly concerning people's ability to estimate the height of various celebrities. This manipulation made subjects' attitudes toward African Americans in general more positive for a time, as indexed by more affirmative responses to a question regarding whether racial discrimination is still a problem in U.S. society, in an ostensibly unrelated questionnaire. This remarkable finding suggests first that subjects did not have a stable, preformed opinion on the prevalence of discrimination (which they could simply trot out in invariant fashion to answer the question). It also suggests that one's opinion concerning discrimination is a thinly disguised assessment of one's attitude toward blacks—which was in turn influenced by the recent exposure to a positively viewed exemplar. It seems likely that appropriate research designs will find that all types of cognitive representations are flexibly *reconstructed* in a context-sensitive way rather than *retrieved* from memory as they were stored—like items buried in a time capsule.

In summary, context can do more than raise or lower the overall accessibility of a representation (such as the self, or a given attitude). It also can tune and reshape the *content* of the representation in a fluid manner so that particular features are emphasized or de-emphasized in a particular situation. Exemplar models of mental representation appear well-suited to account for the variability and context sensitivity of representation use, by postulating that concepts are constructed on-line from a shifting array of exemplars whose accessibility can change depending on context. In contrast, schema models postulating fixed packages of knowledge, activated in all-or-none fashion, find these observations less congenial.

Summary

Theories involving exemplar representations have been more recently developed and have received less exploration to date than associative or schema representations. The domain of application of exemplar models overlaps greatly with that of schematic models (to which exemplars constitute, at least at the rhetorical level, a competing alternative). The key point is that, as Hintzman (1986) demonstrated in the nonsocial domain, under appropriate theoretical assumptions a large number of similar exemplars

processed in parallel can mimic the results of an abstracted summary (prototype or average) of those exemplars. Similarly, summaries of social exemplars have been argued to explain social stereotyping (Smith & Zárate, 1992). Exemplar mechanisms may thus be viewed as an extension of schematic mechanisms that include an account of how schematic knowledge is incrementally acquired (i.e., as the accumulation of exemplars).

Besides this overlap in schema and exemplar models' areas of applicability, exemplar mechanisms offer a natural account for certain additional phenomena that are much more difficult to explain using schematic mechanisms that emphasize abstract, generalized knowledge. These include repetition priming and other implicit effects of specific experiences on later performances (Roediger et al., 1989; Jacoby, 1983). Processes of exemplar retrieval and possibly misattribution appear to explain several types of social psychological effects including the effect of mere exposure on liking.

The most significant difference between exemplar mechanisms and the schematic and associative models already described, however, may be in their fundamental metaphorical approaches. Schemas and associative structures are regarded essentially as *things*. In particular, once constructed it is assumed that they can be stored away and retrieved again relatively unchanged at a later time. In contrast, in exemplar models mental representations are better considered as *states*. A representation is a temporary, online construction formed from currently activated exemplars, which will change over time and in different contexts (Barsalou, 1987). The underlying traces of specific exemplars may be considered as permanent "things" but in most exemplar models (e.g., Hintzman's MINERVA, 1986) these are not individually retrievable; only a temporary state-like summary of multiple activated exemplars can be accessed and used.

As we have seen in this section:

1. The *formation* of exemplar representations is assumed to reflect the way a particular stimulus is processed. This "processing byproducts" principle (Carlston & Smith, 1996) is also prominent in associative network theories (which assume that the way nodes are linked reflects the perceiver's processing goals and strategies) but is usually less emphasized in discussions of schematic processing.

2. The *effects of exemplar representations on explicit memory measures*—in the sense of the direct recollection of specific exemplars—are often not considered, as these theories tend to concentrate more on judgmental dependent variables and other forms of implicit memory. Of course, exemplar representations, by influencing the way information is interpreted and organized (just as schemas do), will thereby affect explicit memory such as recall.

3. The *effects of exemplar representations on implicit memory measures* are modeled by assuming that when prior exemplars are activated, they can influence many types of processing and judgment. For example, activated exemplars may affect judgments or evaluations of a current target stimulus (Kahneman & Miller, 1986; Smith & Zárate, 1992) or may facilitate the repetition of a judgment that was previously made (Smith et al., 1992).

4. *Dissociations* among various explicit and implicit effects are often assumed to be due to the different subsets of exemplars that are activated by the different types of cues offered by explicit and implicit memory tasks (Roediger & McDermott, 1993). In other models, dissociations may be attributed to explicit and implicit tasks accessing different types of cognitive representations (e.g., an abstracted summary for explicit recall, specific exemplars for judgments or other implicit tasks).

DISTRIBUTED MEMORY OR PDP MECHANISMS

The newest category of models of mental representation—the models variously labeled distributed memory, connectionist, or parallel distributed processing (PDP)—which have had virtually a revolutionary impact in several other areas of psychology and neuroscience, are only beginning to be applied in social psychology. However, history shows that theoretical advances from other areas of psychology (such as the "cognitive revolution" of the 1970s) eventually have a major impact within social psychology (see Devine, Hamilton, & Ostrom, 1994). Thus, it seems reasonable to predict that these new models too will become important over the coming years, making a review in this chapter appropriate. Space limitations preclude a full introductory treatment here; general introductions can be found in Churchland and Sejnowski (1992), Smolensky (1988), Rumelhart, McClelland, and others (1986), and McClelland, Rumelhart, and others (1986); a brief overview oriented toward social psychologists is Smith (1996).

Fundamental Assumptions

Distributed representation models generally embody these assumptions.

1. *Fundamental representational assumption:* A concept or object is represented by a *distributed representation,* a pattern of activation across a set of processing units in a module.[1] Distinct representations are different patterns across a *common* set of units. A useful analogy is the individual pixels on a television screen or computer monitor. No pixel has any specific meaning in itself, but by taking on different patterns of illumination, the entire array of pixels can constitute a large number of meaningful representations. Multiple modules may coexist, allowing the representation of multiple distinct patterns at the same time.

2. *Unity of representation and process:* Associative, schematic, and exemplar models of representation postulate that representations are static and require additional assumptions about processes that operate on representations. In contrast, a distributed representation is a single mechanism that processes as well as stores information.

3. *Computing with distributed representations:* Units are interconnected and send activation to each other across weighted connections. The activation sent by unit i to unit j is a function of the activation level of unit i and the weight on the connection from i to j. In turn, unit j's activation level is influenced by the total activation flowing in from other units (see Figure 3a). Thus, the pattern of activation—the representation—taken on by a given set of units is determined by the initial inputs to the network of units and the weights on the inter-unit connections.

4. *Positive or negative activation:* In most models, both the weights on inter-unit connections and the activation that flows between units can be either positive or negative. Negative activation decreases the activity level of the unit to which it flows; i.e., it has an inhibitory effect. This assumption contrasts with most associative-network models, in which "spreading activation" is always positive.

5. *Connection weights as long-term memory:* The weights on the connections are assumed to change only slowly, in contrast to the quickly changing activation values. Thus, the connection weights are the repository of the network's long-term memory.

6. *Pattern transformation:* A network like Figure 3a may have a set of input units on which patterns are imposed (by sensory inputs or by other networks). As activation flows over the connections, a distinct pattern will eventually appear on the network's output units. Such a network can serve to transform representations from one domain into another (J. A. Anderson, 1995). Examples are the transformation of input patterns representing behaviors into output patterns representing trait concepts, or inputs of letter sequences into output patterns representing a word's meaning or pronunciation.

7. *Pattern completion or memory:* Networks can also be built to do *pattern completion.* After the network learns a set of patterns, when the inputs constitute a subset or an approximation of one of those patterns, the network produces as output the entire pattern. Pattern completion can be viewed as a form of memory. However, the potential patterns are not explicitly "stored" anywhere. Instead, the network stores con-

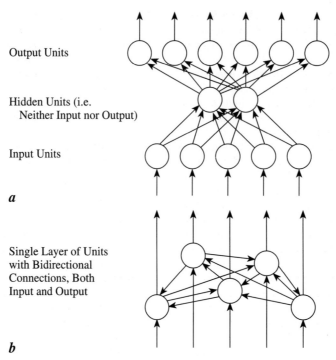

Output Units

Hidden Units (i.e.
    Neither Input nor Output)

Input Units

a

Single Layer of Units
with Bidirectional
Connections, Both
Input and Output

b

FIGURE 3   Two Types of Connectionist Network. (*a*) Feedforward
network. (*b*) Recurrent network.

nection strengths that allow many patterns to be reproduced given the right cues.

8. *Reconstruction, not retrieval:* When a network must
encode several patterns, the connection strengths are a
compromise. Hence, reproduction of any given pattern
from input cues will be imperfect and will be influenced by other related patterns encoded in the same
network. This contrasts with the assumption common
to most models of representation, that representations
are static, able to be stored and retrieved again in invariant form. It is better to think of a distributed representation as being *recreated* or *evoked* or *reconstructed* than as being *searched for* or *retrieved*
(McClelland, Rumelhart, & Hinton, 1986, p. 31).

9. *Parallel constraint satisfaction:* A network's output
pattern is determined by both the current input pattern
and the weights on the network's connections, which
encode its stored knowledge. In a network in which
feedback and bidirectional flows of activation between
units are possible (see Figure 3b), the network can be
thought of as converging on a final pattern of activation
that—as well as possible—simultaneously satisfies the
constraints represented by the current inputs (representing external stimuli) and the network weights (representing learned constraints) (Barnden, 1995a).

10. *"Fuzzy" or imprecise outputs:* A parallel-constraint-
satisfaction style of computation inherently treats constraints as "soft" rather than "hard" and absolute, because learned constraints and current inputs may
conflict and each can only be satisfied as well as possible. Thus, "fuzzy" or imprecise category boundaries
and other forms of approximate judgments are natural
outcomes.

11. *Learning:* The preceding paragraphs assumed that a
network's weights possessed special properties (e.g.,
to transform a series of input patterns into corresponding outputs). For many types of networks, learning algorithms exist that can incrementally modify a set of
initially random weights, to produce the desired final
properties. Thus, the weights need not be preset by the
theorist but can be shaped by a learning procedure as
the network processes many stimuli.

12. *Accessibility:* Because network learning rules alter the
weights *incrementally* as each pattern is processed, recently or frequently encountered patterns have larger
effects than do old and rare ones. Thus, the network
naturally embodies the principle of accessibility.

There are also many points on which different connectionist models differ.

1. *Level of interpretation of nodes:* Though the great majority of connectionist models to date have used distributed representations as described above, in which meaning is conveyed by patterns across many nodes, some models use localist representational schemes in which single nodes have meaningful interpretations (Thorpe, 1995). A node may be interpreted as a feature, an object or concept, or a whole proposition. A connection between nodes is interpreted as encoding a past experience of covariation between the nodes (if nodes represent features or objects) or logical constraints such as consistency or inconsistency between propositions (if nodes represent propositions). Such models lack most of the properties discussed above but retain the ability to satisfy in parallel multiple simultaneous constraints represented by connections among nodes (Kunda & Thagard, 1996; Read & Marcus-Newhall, 1993).

2. *Particular model assumptions:* In each of the three classes of exemplar, schematic, or associative network models considered to this point there are perhaps a handful of serious, well-specified competing models. In contrast, literally hundreds of distinct connectionist models have been proposed, with various network architectures (numbers and interconnection patterns of nodes), activation equations, and learning rules (see Hertz, Krogh, & Palmer, 1991). Properties of these diverse models are being actively explored in ongoing theoretical and simulation studies.

3. *Treatment of conscious thought:* Some connectionist theorists focus their modeling efforts on specific tasks (such as categorization or visual image processing) for which they can essentially ignore questions regarding conscious thought and strategic, controlled processing (see Touretzky, 1995; Barnden, 1995a). Other theorists have put forward broader proposals including ideas about the relation of consciousness to connectionist models, including Smolensky (1988), whose model will be described below.

Illustrative Models and Applications

Associative Linkages Facilitating Retrieval

Associative Versus Connectionist Models When people encounter or consider several items of information together, at a later time one of those items can facilitate recall of the others. This general finding has often been interpreted as due to the formation of associative linkages among the items of information, which then serve as pathways for retrieval (e.g., Hastie & Kumar, 1979). Connectionist networks using distributed representations can also account for these observations. Note first, however, that there is some potential for confusion between distributed representational models and the associative models described earlier (as well as the "S-R" behaviorist models out of which modern associative models developed). After all, both involve "nodes" connected by "links," and superficially Figure 3 looks like Figure 1. However, the differences are fundamental (see J. A. Anderson, 1995; Barnden, 1995a; Thorpe, 1995; Touretzky, 1995).

1. Associative networks are models of representational structure only, not process; additional processes must be postulated to construct and retrieve information (e.g, the productions of J. R. Anderson, 1983). In contrast, connectionist networks constitute the processor as well as the knowledge representation; flows of activation are the only processing mechanism.

2. Associative models use localist representations: a node represents a concept or proposition. In contrast, connectionist networks generally assume distributed representations in which a single node has no meaningful semantic interpretation; only a pattern of activation has any meaning.

3. Associative networks are assumed to be rapidly constructed and dynamically modified by interpretive processes. In contrast, connectionist networks are generally assumed to have a fixed topology, with the connection weights changing only slowly through learning.

4. In an associative network, positive activation is usually assumed to spread both ways over links (node A can spread activation to a connected node B, or B can activate A). In contrast, in a connectionist network activation can be excitatory or inhibitory and is ordinarily assumed to spread only one way (links are directional).

5. Links in associative networks are usually assumed to be labeled, while in contrast connectionist links are not of distinct types but simply conduct activation.

A summary of all of these points is that associative networks have been developed by theorists concerned to understand the representation and processing of linguistically encoded information, and they serve those purposes well (Barnden, 1995b). In contrast, connectionist networks have been developed with a greater concern for neural plausibility, though they still involve simplifications and idealizations rather than detailed matches to the properties of actual biological neurons.

It is important to note that localist constraint-satisfaction networks, which have recently been applied in social psychology (e.g., Kunda & Thagard, 1996; Miller & Read, 1991) actually share more important properties with associative mechanisms than with connectionist or distributed-memory mechanisms (see Barnden, 1995b). Specifically, these networks model structure only (not process). They use localist representations that are assumed to be rapidly constructed by interpretive processes. They spread activation both ways over links constructed to reflect positive or negative implicational relations among concepts; the links are not the results of a learning process. Such networks are obviously well-suited to representing certain types of information, and spreading-activation processes can be used to simultaneously satisfy a number of constraints represented by the links. However, their properties make them much more akin to associative networks than to connectionist models that use distributed representations (Thorpe, 1995; Touretzky, 1995).

Connectionist Accounts of Associative Recall Connectionist models of memory can account for the observation that when items of information are encountered or considered together, one can later facilitate recall of the others—in other words, they can record "associations" among the items (J. A. Anderson, 1995; Chappell & Humphreys, 1994; McClelland, McNaughton, & O'Reilly, 1995; Wiles & Humphreys, 1993). In general, they do this by combining the distributed patterns representing the several stimulus items into a single, larger pattern. The network learning rule then changes the weights on connections among units in a way that subserves the pattern-completion property. At a later time, then, representation of one or more of the "associated" stimulus items (a partial pattern), can lead to the completion of the pattern, as the remaining items (other parts of the pattern) are "retrieved."

One version of this general idea, accounting for the associative binding together of different aspects of everyday experiences (such as verbal names and visual, auditory, and tactile attributes of an object; see Damasio, 1989, or Carlston, 1994) has been described by Moll, Miikkulainen, and Abbey (1994). Once a pattern that binds together the different subpatterns is created and learned through connection weight changes, presentation of one aspect will lead to the reactivation of all. Thus the sight of a friend may reactivate her name, memories of her characteristic speech patterns, feelings about her, and other associated representations (Carlston, 1994). The authors demonstrate that the network architecture they propose has sufficient capacity (given the number of neurons estimated to exist in the appropriate brain regions) to store approximately 10^8 distinct associative memories, enough for several every minute over a human lifetime.

Explicit Memory The same pattern-completion mechanism that accounts for associative retrieval also underlies other forms of explicit memory access. An explicit memory is viewed as being reconstructed rather than retrieved (McClelland, Rumelhart, & Hinton, 1986, p. 31). Because all patterns encoding memories must be reconstructed by a common set of connection strengths, reproduction of any given pattern will be imperfect and will be influenced by other related patterns learned by the same network. This prediction fits much better than the standard assumption of invariant storage and retrieval with evidence showing that people's explicit memories are better viewed as reconstructed rather than retrieved exactly as they were stored (Ross & Conway, 1986; see Carlston & Smith, 1996, for a review).

Humphreys and his associates (Chappell & Humphreys, 1994; Humphreys, Bain, & Pike, 1989; Wiles & Humphreys, 1993) have extensively investigated the ability of a class of multiple-module connectionist models, schematically portrayed in Figure 4, to fit psychological findings regarding explicit memory retrieval. Recurrent network modules—in which connections run bidirectionally among units—serve to store central representations of knowledge via the pattern-completion property. Other networks perform input and output mappings (e.g., translating from visual features of letters into the central representation of a word's meaning). One version of this model (Chappell & Humphreys, 1994) fits many detailed data patterns from studies of recognition and cued recall. In this model, explicit memory depends on reactivation of representations in the central recurrent network memory, while some types of implicit memory (such as repetition priming) are due to weight changes in the input/output pattern associator networks, as will be discussed shortly.

These distributed models assume that a stimulus item is represented in memory as a pattern or vector of features. In fact, McClelland and Chappell (1995) observe that a large-scale transition or succession of generations is occurring in nonsocial memory models. The older models that best survived detailed tests against psychological data (e.g., J. R. Anderson, 1983, or the SAM model of Gillund & Shiffrin, 1984, and its relatives) used an associative language: an item in memory was conceptualized as a "node" with associative links (created by study) to other nodes and to the surrounding context. In contrast, the newer models (including Chappell & Humphreys, 1994; McClelland & Chappell, 1995; McClelland & Rumelhart, 1985) consider a memory item as a pattern of features, a conceptualization that maps very naturally onto a distributed representation as a pattern of activation across a set of units. This general transition has been driven by the recognition that the older associative models have great difficulty in accommodating certain newer findings such as the null list-strength effect (see McClelland & Chappell, 1995).

Semantic Priming Responding to a given stimulus facilitates a subsequent response to a semantically related stimulus; thus, people are faster to reply that "nurse" is a word after reading "doctor" than after reading an unrelated word

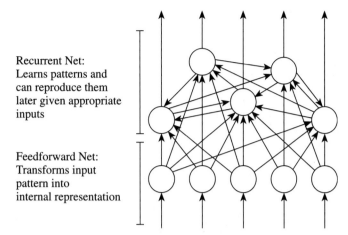

Recurrent Net:
Learns patterns and
can reproduce them
later given appropriate
inputs

Feedforward Net:
Transforms input
pattern into
internal representation

FIGURE 4 **A Multiple-Module Network.** Input feedforward net and central recurrent net.

(Meyer & Schvaneveldt, 1971). In a distributed memory model, this type of priming would not be explained as the result of activation spreading over links between nodes representing concepts, for concepts are not represented by single nodes. Instead, it could be explained in terms of pattern overlap (Masson, 1991). Distributed representations created by typical learning rules have the extremely useful property that related items have similar representations (Churchland & Sejnowski, 1992; van Gelder, 1991). The pattern of activation representing "nurse" is more similar to that for "doctor" than it is to "tree" (similarity, loosely, is the correlation of the vectors of activation values). Thus, if a given set of units is already in the "doctor" pattern, it takes less time and less definitive input information to change to the "nurse" pattern than it would from an unrelated starting pattern. This account of semantic priming, in contrast to the traditional spreading-activation account, predicts that priming should be abolished by a single unrelated intervening item. This prediction has been tested and confirmed (Masson, 1991).

Interpretation of Input Using Existing Knowledge An appropriate network architecture can perform pattern completion, as noted above. Given an input pattern that is a subset or an approximate version of a learned pattern, the network outputs the whole pattern. An input pattern that is a blend of two or more known patterns will elicit in the output either a blend or compromise between the patterns (in some types of connectionist models) or the single most similar pattern (in other types of models; Chappell & Humphreys, 1994). These can be viewed as ways in which the network interprets current input in light of its structured

prior knowledge. For example, a small sample of behaviors may be interpreted as an instance of a typical "extrovert" (assuming the network has learned that pattern by exposure to a number of examples), or a person may be seen as a member of a known social group with the group's typical characteristics.

This is the interpretive function usually attributed to a schema. The most important difference is that in a connectionist model a schema is not a "thing" that can be searched for or retrieved like a sheet of paper in a file cabinet. Instead, a schema is a state, one among many potential patterns that is implicit in a set of connection weights and can be elicited as a pattern of activation—given the appropriate input cues. As Rumelhart, Smolensky, McClelland, & Hinton (1986, p. 20) explain, in this model "there is no representational object which is a schema. Rather, schemata emerge at the moment they are needed from the interaction of large numbers of much simpler elements all working in concert with one another. Schemata are not explicit entities, but rather are implicit in our knowledge and are created by the very environment that they are trying to interpret." The same point was made earlier in the discussion of exemplar mechanisms: "schematic" effects, particularly interpretation of new input using past knowledge, need not force us to postulate the existence of "schemas" as things (explicit representations).

Repetition Priming This is the facilitation of processing of a stimulus when the same stimulus has been processed in the same way on a previous occasion. In sharp contrast to semantic priming, this is a long-lasting phenomenon (up to months; Sloman, Hayman, Ohta, Law, & Tulving,

1988). It generally does not require explicit memory for the initial experience (Schacter, 1987; Smith et al., 1992). Wiles and Humphreys (1993, pp. 157–163) have investigated the possible mediation of such effects in distributed memory models, and conclude that weight changes in networks that translate information from one representation to another (e.g., from letters to word meanings) are responsible. Learning changes weights incrementally after each individual pattern is processed. Because the changes are in the direction of more accurately and/or efficiently processing the given pattern, the pattern will have an advantage for a period of time after a single presentation. Similar suggestions have been made by Humphreys et al. (1989), Schacter (1994), and Moscovitch (1994). This theoretical idea locates repetition priming in separate networks (input/output pattern transformation networks) from those that subserve explicit memory (central recurrent or pattern-completion networks; see Figure 4). It thereby explains why these two forms of memory are often found to be independent of one another, both in normal subjects and in various forms of amnesia (see Schacter & Tulving, 1994).

Dissonance Reduction and Cognitive Dynamics Connectionist networks can function to find the optimal solution to a number of constraints in parallel fashion (Churchland & Sejnowski, 1992). Flows of activation and inhibition among units along connections whose weights have been shaped by learning can finally converge on a pattern that is affected by current input information as well as the regularities gleaned from past experiences (Barnden, 1995a; Hertz, 1995; Touretzky, 1995). As Shultz and Lepper (1996) have noted, this process has broad similarities to cognitive dissonance reduction (Festinger, 1957). It may therefore be a candidate for explaining several important classes of social psychological phenomena such as effects of counterattitudinal advocacy and insufficient justification. Shultz and Lepper (1996) made this case in the context of a localist model, which as noted earlier is better regarded as a type of associative model. However, the point holds equally well for distributed-representation models, which also perform parallel constraint satisfaction. The basic idea is that dissonance involves the postulation of numerous pairwise constraints (i.e., relations of consonance or dissonance) among cognitive elements such as beliefs and attitudes. The dissonance reduction process simultaneously satisfies such constraints by adjusting individual cognitions in the direction of better fit to the complete configuration (subject to the differential resistance to change of the individual cognitions).

Several conceptual issues related to this suggestion require clarification. Parallel constraint satisfaction (like other mental processes) can be considered to operate on several distinct levels. The preconscious schematic or inter-

pretive processing discussed earlier should not be identified with dissonance reduction, even though it also involves the simultaneous satisfaction of multiple constraints (stemming from input information and existing knowledge). Dissonance reduction itself is considered to be a more conscious, strategically controlled process—for example, it only occurs when people are motivated by experiencing arousal (Cooper & Fazio, 1984). In fact, modern dual-process models in social psychology (e.g., Chaiken, Liberman, & Eagly, 1989; Smith, 1994b) emphasize that people *cannot* be regarded as invariably and automatically satisfying all constraints, or systematically resolving all inconsistencies implicit in their knowledge. Such a process would mean that we never hold contradictory beliefs and are always aware of all the logical implications of what we know. Instead, resolving inconsistencies and satisfying constraints at the level of consciously accessible knowledge requires effort. As Gilbert (1993) notes, the specific outcome of this effortful processing is determined by the given input and the knowledge that is applied, but whether the outcome is generated at all depends on the perceiver's motivation and cognitive capacity (e.g., freedom from distractions). "A person may choose to do work or not to do work, but one cannot decide what the result of that work will be. The result is determined by the rules of the system in which the work is done" (Gilbert, 1993, p. 65). Framed in this way, dissonance reduction seems to be well-described as an optional and effortful constraint-satisfaction process.

More generally, beyond its speculative relationship to dissonance phenomena, the dynamic conception of cognition implicit in the notion of simultaneous constraint satisfaction using distributed representations has other implications for social psychology.

1. Heiderian balance and other general schemas or abstract expectations can be seen to play a role in processing as broad, nonspecific sources of constraint (which can, however, be overridden by more specific information).
2. Motives (such as self-esteem enhancement or mood regulation) can be viewed as additional constraints that, along with input information and learned expectations, affect processing. For example, a transient system state that fits current input well but has negative implications for self-esteem may change—as part of the simultaneous constraint satisfaction process—to one that fits the input slightly worse but has a much more positive implication for the self. Though fuller discussion goes beyond the scope of this chapter, this dynamic conceptualization offers the potential for an overall integration of cognition and motivation (see Dorman & Gaudiano, 1995).
3. Constraint satisfaction processes allow for multidirec-

tional causation among cognitive elements (beliefs, attitudes, behavioral intentions, etc.). Current theories in social psychology often presume a fixed causal ordering (e.g., attitudes cause behavioral intentions) and rarely reflect such complexities, though theorists sometimes pay lip service to the possibility of feedback and bidirectional causation. In a connectionist framework, mutual causation among a number of cognitions (beliefs, attitudes, goals) is an inevitable consequence of the process of mutual adjustment and constraint satisfaction in recurrent networks. All the cognitive elements are simultaneously adjusted so that all the constraints in the network as a whole (encoded in connections among units) are satisfied as well as possible. Once the system has reached such a state, changing any element may change all as the system adjusts to the perturbation—so any element can influence all the others.

4. Most fundamentally, this viewpoint presupposes that cognitive *representations* are not distinguished from cognitive *processes*. Both are encoded as connection weights through which activation flows. Instead of a picture of static representations that sit inertly until operated on by some active process, we can envision active and interactive representations that intrinsically influence all future processing (Gilbert, 1993). Such models promise to account for cognitive change as well as stasis. A general description of the advantages of such a dynamic account of human cognition can be found in Vallacher and Nowak (1994), though their treatment is at the highly abstract level of "dynamical systems theory" rather than being grounded specifically in the properties of connectionist networks.

Flexibility and Context Sensitivity   Another dynamic aspect of distributed representations is their flexibility and context sensitivity. In connectionist models, representations that are not currently active are not stored away until accessed by a retrieval process. Instead, flows of activation through connection weights that are shaped by learning reconstruct a representation as a distributed pattern of activation. In this process, any other patterns that may be concurrently active (e.g., patterns representing the person's mood, perceptually present objects, current concerns, goals, or objects of thought) will also serve as sources of activation that influence the resulting representation. For instance, thinking of an "extravert" in the context of a noisy party might activate a representation that includes "telling jokes" and "being the center of attention," while in the context of a used-car lot the resulting representation might include features like "pushy" and "impossible to discourage." Such thoroughgoing context sensitivity is an inherent property of state-like distributed representations. Clark (1993, especially chap. 2 and 5) summarizes his extensive discussion of the implications of this fact:

> The upshot is that there need be no context-independent, core representation for [a concept]. Instead, there could be a variety of states linked merely by a relation of family resemblance. . . . A single . . . [concept] will have a panoply of so-called subconceptual realizations [i.e., activation patterns], and which realization is actually present will make a difference to future processing. This feature (multiple, context-sensitive subconceptual realizations) makes for the vaunted fluidity of connectionist systems and introduces one sense in which such systems merely approximate their more classical cousins (Clark, 1993, pp. 24–25).

As reviewed earlier in the section on exemplar models, current thinking in many areas of social psychology (including the self, attitudes, and stereotypes) emphasizes the flexibility and context sensitivity of mental representations.

Relation to Conscious, Explicit Thought   In recent years many theorists have advanced dual-processing models in diverse areas of social psychology, particularly attitude change (e.g., Chaiken, 1980; Petty & Cacioppo, 1984; see Smith, 1994b, for a review). These models have in common a basic distinction between controlled (conscious, systematic) and automatic (nonconscious, heuristic) processing. The first type of process is assumed to occur only when adequate cognitive capacity and motivation are present, though individual models differ in their emphasis on these capacity and motivational factors. Most applications of connectionist models to date—for example, those involving repetition priming, preconscious interpretation of perceptual input, or semantic priming—involve processes that are independent of conscious awareness and explicit thought (Barnden, 1995a). Social psychologists in recent years have also emphasized the importance of preconscious and implicit processes (see Banaji & Greenwald, 1994; Bargh, 1994; Higgins, 1989), on the grounds that such processes determine our conscious experience and therefore direct our thoughts, feelings, and behavior. Only when we are specially motivated to look beneath the surface of things do we question the results of our preconscious processing (e.g., Martin et al., 1990). Thus, even if connectionist models prove to be useful in understanding *only* low-level, nonconscious mental processes they would still have great relevance to many issues of central concern to social psychologists.

Still, it is important to ask how and whether connectionist models can also account for the more conscious, thoughtful, systematic mode of processing, with its presumed heavy reliance on verbal, symbolic representations.

In attempts to answer this question, many connectionist theorists have proposed variants on a single theme. For example, Smolensky (1988) holds that people have two separate processors. The "top-level conscious processor" uses linguistically encoded and culturally transmitted knowledge as its "program"; this processor is responsible when people follow explicit step-by-step instructions or engage in conscious, effortful reasoning. The conscious processor works by manipulating linguistically encoded symbols. It is based on the same cognitive capacities that underlie public language use, such as grammatical abilities. Any system that can use language "will be able to encode linguistic expressions as patterns of activity; like all other patterns of activity, these can be stored in connectionist memories" (1988, pp. 12–14) and processed in connectionist networks. In this way, a connectionist system can build on its assumed linguistic capabilities to interpret and follow symbolically encoded rules. A variety of connectionist models of language use are under active investigation (see reviews by Elman, 1995, and Shastri, 1995). Because only one linguistically encoded pattern can be represented and operated on at a time, this mode of processing must initially be sequential and relatively slow. However, with extensive practice a series of operations can become directly encoded as activation flows in networks, as connection weights change.

In contrast, the "intuitive processor" directly rests on the properties of connectionist networks and mediates most human behavior (and all animal behavior), including perception, skilled motor behavior, and intuitive problem solving and pattern matching. The operation of this processor is (in broad terms) associative rather than rationally inferential like the symbol-manipulating conscious processor (Smolensky, 1988, p. 63). Descriptions of intuitive processing that are given in rational, symbolic terms will always be imprecise approximations.

This general architecture is by no means unique to Smolensky's model; Cohen, Servan-Schreiber, and McClelland (1992) and Sloman (1996) have made essentially similar proposals. The Cohen et al. paper advances simple connectionist models for the role of attention in cognitive processing and the interplay of automatic and controlled processes in Stroop interference. These models may be of great interest to social psychologists, for Stroop interference has often been both a topic of investigation and a tool for examining issues of automaticity in general within social psychology (e.g., Higgins et al., 1988; see Bargh, 1994). All these dual-process connectionist models are best viewed as programmatic sketches of appealing concepts rather than fully worked-out models at present. In particular, connectionist models of language processing are currently an extremely active and somewhat controversial research area (see Elman, 1995, and the commentaries following Smolensky, 1988). On the other hand, current dual-process models in social psychology can hardly make any better claim to offer fully detailed accounts of symbolic representations and processes.

The connectionist dual-process models contrast with those dual-process theories in social psychology that hold that the two types of processes are *fundamentally of the same sort*—described in terms of associative or schematic mechanisms—except for differences in efficiency and conscious accessibility. For example, some theories assume that all preconscious "perceptual" processes arise from processes that were originally conscious and controlled, through automatization with practice (see Smith, 1994b; Anderson, 1987; Bargh, 1994). This viewpoint makes it difficult to explain why our implicit or intuitive judgments and emotional reactions often seem to be "associative"—at the mercy of patterns repeatedly experienced in the past, only slowly adapting to new conditions—rather than cleverly inferential or "rational"—capable of one-shot learning (Bargh & Barndollar, in press; Carlston et al., 1995; Devine, 1989; Greenwald, 1992; Kirkpatrick & Epstein, 1992; Norman, 1981). For example, many of our emotional reactions or early-learned associations are difficult to overcome by intellectual discourse.

In summary, we humans often seem to be mentally divided creatures. At times our thought seems to nicely follow rational and logical inference rules—and so we sometimes do sensible things like maximizing subjective expected utility, analyzing arguments for their plausibility in light of our general knowledge, and the like. These descriptions seem to be most applicable in situations where we have extensive cognitive capacity and motivation. At other times such rules may be useful as approximate, global descriptions of the *results* of our cognitive processing yet without explicitly entering *into* processing. And at still other times the rules fail even as approximations (and then we say that our processing shows "biases"). This complete pattern seems to call for explanation in terms of dual processes, one more symbolically based (and hence more "logical") and more capacity-demanding, the other more contextually bound and driven by regularities in our past experiences.

Applications to Person Perception   Distributed representation models have recently been applied to several specific aspects of person perception and stereotyping.[2] Kashima and Kerekes (1994) presented a distributed connectionist model of the formation of an overall evaluation of a person based on a series of traits. Pairings between activation patterns representing the target person and the given trait information are computed and stored in a set of connection weights. It has long been known that overall evaluative judgments based on such trait presentations are well approximated by a weighted average of the evaluations of the items of input information (N. H. Anderson, 1981), and the Kashima and Kerekes model reproduces that pattern, as well as various details of order effects when the trait information is presented serially.

Smith and DeCoster (in press) applied the "schema" model of McClelland and Rumelhart (1985) to various aspects of person perception. They showed that the model could process many patterns and extract information about covariations among attributes to learn an "implicit personality theory." This was then used to make inferences about a new person presented as a cue. Stereotyping was also demonstrated; the model was given a number of patterns representing individual group members and it abstracted the group stereotype, then made stereotypic inferences about a new member of the group. Effects of frequency and recency on accessibility were found: the network was given many or few instances of a particular pattern, located early or late in a larger number of random patterns. Later presentation of cues tested how well the specific pattern was reconstructed, and results followed the principles of accessibility. Finally, the model was able to combine or blend multiple stereotypes. It even produced new "emergent" attributes—not part of either stereotype A or B, but considered to describe a person who was a member of both groups A and B. Investigations of this model and more sophisticated ones will continue, but general similarities between the model's output and human performance in such areas as these are encouraging.

Summary

Distributed memory models are the newest of the four classes described here; social psychological applications are only beginning to appear. Yet they appear to hold much promise, for they offer integrative accounts for disparate phenomena that have previously appeared to call for diverse and conflicting mechanisms. As reviewed above, connectionist networks using distributed representations can perform functions that can be characterized (at least approximately) as associatively binding discrete items of information together and using such associations for retrieval; learning general regularities about the world and using that knowledge to interpret new input; simultaneously satisfying multiple constraints arising from current inputs and past learning; and storing representations of specific experiences in ways that affect future repetitions of the same processing.

Despite their ability to account for many of the same phenomena as the mechanisms described earlier in this chapter, distributed representation models also present some strikingly contrasting properties. Associative and schematic theories postulate discrete and separate representations that, like "things," can be stored and accessed as independent units (like sheets of paper in a file cabinet). In contrast, distributed representations are states, transitory patterns of activation that are not *stored* anywhere but can

be approximately reconstructed given appropriate input cues. Other models assume that representations of mental content are distinct from process, so that unless acted on by some process, representations are static and unchanging. Distributed models assume that content and process are one, both being encoded in the same set of connection weights, so that every representation *necessarily* influences the course of future processing (i.e., the flow of activation). Other models assume a distinction between top-down (knowledge-driven) and bottom-up (stimulus-driven) processing; distributed models assume that these are inseparable because all processing is performed by flows of activation (ultimately arising from perceptual input) through connections (which encode existing knowledge).

In typical applications of distributed representation models:

1. The *formation* of knowledge representations is explicitly modeled, as the change in connection weights with learning. The principle of accessibility—increased impact of recent and frequent experiences—is inherent in the learning process.
2. *Explicit memory performance* is modeled by the input of retrieval cues to a network and the use of resulting output (e.g., Chappell & Humphreys, 1994). The fact that explicit memories are reconstructed in context-sensitive fashion rather than statically retrieved in unchanged form stems from the fundamental assumptions of distributed representations.
3. *Implicit memory performances* are modeled in various ways. Short-lived semantic priming can be regarded as due to the overlap among similar patterns representing meaningfully similar concepts (Masson, 1991). Repetition priming is due to the change in weights in pattern transformation networks (Wiles & Humphreys, 1993). Schematic interpretation of input information in light of existing knowledge is a consequence of processing that implements parallel constraint satisfaction (McClelland & Rumelhart, 1985).
4. *Dissociations* among various types of memory such as recognition and judgment can be interpreted as stemming from their reliance on distinct underlying representations (Wiles & Humphreys, 1993). Alternatively, the use of different cues in different memory tasks to address a common network representation may give rise to independence (Humphreys et al., 1989).

RELATIONS AMONG MEMORY MECHANISMS

Table 1 summarizes the major empirical phenomena discussed in this chapter, as well as their explanations under associative, schematic, exemplar, and distributed representation models.

TABLE 1

Summary of Key Phenomena and Their Explanations with Four Types of Theoretical Mechanisms

Phenomenon	Explanation with associative networks	Explanation with schemas	Explanation with exemplars	Explanation with distributed representations
Linking together of attributes of a single object and its context so that one attribute can serve as retrieval cue for others	Construction of associative links connecting nodes			Binding together of attributes and context into a single composite pattern
Reconstructive nature of explicit memory		Memory trace includes pointer to schema, which is accessed and used at the time of retrieval	Effect of mass of similar exemplars is similar to postulated effect of schema	All knowledge is stored in common set of connection weights, so related patterns inevitably affect reconstruction of a given pattern from cues
Semantic priming (facilitated response to target item after processing a related prime)	Spread of activation from prime node to related target node			Prime and target are represented by overlapping patterns
Repetition priming (facilitated response to an item that has been previously processed)			Activation and use of memory trace of that item (exemplar)	First encounter incrementally changes weights of connections in network, improving later performance on that and similar items
Interpretation of input cues using existing knowledge (filling in defaults, clarifying ambiguities, etc.)	Activation of knowledge makes strongly linked knowledge accessible for use in interpretation	Activation and use of schema containing the existing knowledge	Activation and use of mass of similar exemplars (with effects similar to schema) *or* activation and use of particular recent or frequent exemplar	Flows of activation perform pattern completion, creating as output existing pattern (or blend of patterns) that best fits input cues
Accessibility (greater influence of frequently or recently used constructs)	*Recency:* Residual activation of nodes *Frequency:* Greater strength of frequently accessed links between nodes	Changes in properties of schemas with use (either position and number of copies in Storage Bin or charge in schema's "battery")	More recent or frequent exemplar traces means more effect of this construct when all are massed together	Learning involves incremental changes of connection weights; more recently or frequently processed patterns have an advantage

(continued)

TABLE 1   (*continued*)

Summary of Key Phenomena and Their Explanations with Four Types of Theoretical Mechanisms

Phenomenon	Explanation with associative networks	Explanation with schemas	Explanation with exemplars	Explanation with distributed representations
Fluidity, context sensitivity of conceptual knowledge and judgment	Many separate representations are independently associated with core concept node; different subsets can be activated depending on context		Many exemplars are stored; different subsets can be activated depending on context	All representations are on-line reconstructions based on current input cues (including context) flowing through weights representing more stable long-term knowledge
Dissociations of recall and judgment	Recall and judgment mediated by separate representations which are independently associated with core concept node	Recall and judgment mediated by separate schemas, independently accessed	Different subsets of exemplar representations are accessed by the cues provided by recall and judgment tasks	Recall and judgment mediated by separate memory systems (connectionist modules) *or* distinct types of cues for the two tasks lead to dissociations even when both tasks rely on the same underlying representations

In this chapter to this point, as in many other recent reviews of theories of representation and memory within social psychology (Fiske & Taylor, 1991; Carlston & Smith, 1996; Wyer & Carlston, 1994), the associative, schematic, exemplar, and distributed mechanisms have implicitly been treated as competitors. Such a treatment seems natural, for theorists usually like to frame their views as opposing some existing theoretical conventional wisdom, and empirical researchers often describe their studies as testing between theoretical alternatives. Yet the relations among these theoretical mechanisms are more subtle than that. In this section I will discuss first the relations between associative and schematic mechanisms, then schematic and exemplar mechanisms, then exemplar and PDP mechanisms. Finally I will address the respective places of all four mechanisms as complementary rather than competing—as having distinct (though occasionally overlapping) domains of applicability. Though this conclusion may seem blandly ecumenical, it actually entails some fairly radical revisions of the way we think about these models.

Associative and Schematic Mechanisms

Associative and schematic mechanisms are commonly treated as conceptual alternatives, even as directly opposed

philosophically (Fiske & Taylor, 1991). It is true that early associative models descended from behavioristic "S-R" formulations and inherited severe representational and computational limitations (stemming, for instance, from the use of unlabeled links). Schema models—particularly the very earliest ones (e.g., Bartlett, 1932)—constituted a genuinely radical alternative to these viewpoints. However, modern associative models are well able to account for the types of observations that are usually viewed as supportive of schematic models (see Alba & Hasher, 1983; Anderson, 1983, pp. 36–40 and pp. 209–214; Reder & Anderson, 1980). A schema can be viewed as a small chunk of associative network within which the nodes are particularly strongly linked, so that activation of one tends to activate all the rest. With appropriate processing assumptions, such a model can mimic the effects of a schema. Within social psychology, Ostrom et al. (1994, p. 221) equated the two types of models, writing that the "schematic approach adopted a minimalist view of associative networks. The network terminology of nodes and pathways provided a basis for describing which beliefs were strongly associated and which were weakly associated. . . ." In addition, Wyer and Srull's (1989) well-known theory can be viewed as a hybrid, incorporating both associative and schematic assumptions (see Carlston & Smith, 1996). All these considerations suggest the possibility that at least in social psychology, "schema" is the name given to an interpretive *function* mediated by a body of tightly inter-associated knowledge.

However, we must also consider a significant distinction between typical applications of associative and schematic mechanisms. Associative networks are generally used to describe the organization of newly constructed knowledge (for example, information about a fictitious character in person memory studies, or a newly constructed person impression in Carlston's AST theory, 1994), and the use of that knowledge to generate recall or make judgments. Research and theory almost always consider the acquisition of the information and the creation of associative structures as well as its retrieval and use. Loosely, we may call this area *episodic memory*. In contrast, schematic mechanisms are usually invoked to explain how people use their existing (pre-experimentally acquired) general knowledge to interpret new input information, direct attention, and guide judgment. Little research deals with the acquisition or construction of schemas, in contrast to the great amount dealing with schema activation and use. These functions clearly pertain to *semantic memory*.

In fact, there is not only a distinction but a strong contrast between these two functions of memory. The ability to form new representations that record the details of specific events demands rapid, one-shot learning. In contrast, forming "schemas" that summarize the general statistical structure of the environment requires learning to be slow so the happenstance details of any particular recent event do not acquire too much weight. Many memory theorists have acknowledged this functional incompatibility between the demands of rapid episodic learning and of slow statistical or semantic learning, and concluded that they point to the existence of independent memory systems (Hirst, 1989; Humphreys et al., 1989; MacLeod & Bassili, 1989; Masson, 1989; Moscovitch, 1994; Schacter, 1994; Squire, 1994). Neurophysiological evidence from humans and nonhuman animals supports this distinction, suggesting that rapid episodic learning is mediated by the hippocampus and related structures, while slow semantic learning does not require the hippocampus but depends on cortical structures (Squire, 1994).

This whole complex of related observations has been modeled in a connectionist framework by McClelland, McNaughton, and O'Reilly (1995). They postulate a module analogous to the hippocampal system, which rapidly learns new information. Then this module serves as a "teacher" for another module analogous to the neocortex, repeatedly presenting the new information so that slow weight changes can integrate this new information into the structure of existing knowledge without catastrophic interference. This process of transferring new knowledge from one system into another is identified with the psychological

process termed "consolidation," which takes a long time (up to years) in humans and other animals.

What do these proposals of independent fast- and slow-learning systems mean for us in social psychology? One implication is that people have *separate* mechanisms that perform the functions usually attributed to associative networks and schemas. The schematic function of interpreting input information in terms of general world knowledge (e.g., Markus & Zajonc, 1985, p. 145) seems to be performed by neocortical systems that learn slowly, extracting regularities in the environment and using them in the course of processing further inputs. Though the learning is slow, specific recent or frequently repeated experiences may leave traces that have observable effects such as repetition priming or implicit memory (Schacter, 1994). In contrast, the associative function of rapidly binding together information about different aspects of an object or experience in its context (Wiles & Humphreys, 1993) seems to be served by hippocampal systems that exhibit one-shot learning and mediate conscious, explicit recollection. A consequence is that people's verbal reports about what they know may well rest on different representations than those they use in preconscious schematic interpretation, and so as a methodological principle it may not be wise to rely on verbal reports to assess the contents of people's "schemas."

In addition to these differences in learning speed and conscious accessibility, these two systems must differ in the type of information to which they attend. Schematic learning is chiefly concerned with regularities, so it records primarily what is typical and expected. In contrast, episodic memories should record the details of events that are novel and interesting: in other words, this system should attend more to the unexpected and unpredicted. Recall that, as reviewed earlier, social psychological studies (e.g., Hastie & Kumar, 1979) show that people attend to and recall mostly expectancy-inconsistent information when forming a new impression, but mostly expectation-consistent information when working with a well-formed and solid expectation (Higgins & Bargh, 1987). This empirical distinction may be a reflection of the more basic differences between two underlying memory systems: one that learns quickly and emphasizes novelty and one that slowly accumulates information and emphasizes regularities.

The independence of these two systems implies that the explicit episodic memories that are our conscious link to our autobiographical past are not the only residue that the past has left in us. Implicit learning in nonconscious systems also affects the way we see and interpret the world. This view may offer theoretical leverage for interpreting many seemingly puzzling observations. For example, "intuitive" emotional reactions such as a fear of flying are often stubbornly independent of our conscious knowledge (Kirkpatrick & Epstein, 1992), and associations of social groups with stereotypic traits may endure even in people who consciously and sincerely reject those stereotypes (Devine, 1989). A common-sense assumption is embodied in many social psychological theories: that all our knowledge and beliefs are represented in a single memory system—so that, for example, the beliefs we can consciously access and verbally report are the same ones that guide our preconscious interpretation of our experiences and reconstruction of our explicit memories. This assumption now seems highly questionable in light of converging evidence of many types (McClelland et al., 1995; Schacter & Tulving, 1994).

From this viewpoint, associative and schematic mechanisms are not competing alternatives. Instead, both describe functions that are part of our repertoire, but may be mediated by separate memory systems.

Schematic and Exemplar Mechanisms

As noted above, the flexibility and goal-directed nature of human cognitive processing makes it certain that people *can* abstract and summarize their specific experiences (such as knowledge of individual group members) to derive general truths (such as typical characteristics of the group). The real question is when this process occurs and what its effects are, and the very same flexibility means that universally applicable answers are unlikely to be forthcoming.

It might be productive, however, to bypass questions about the strategic processes of exemplar abstraction and use, and consider a mechanism that could automatically integrate exemplars and schemas within a preconscious interpretive system. Imagine a system that can learn about a series of exemplars and automatically extract communalities while glossing over their unique idiosyncracies. If a number of randomly selected variations on a theme are encountered, for instance, the underlying regularity of the theme itself will be recorded. However, the details of any particular variation or exemplar that is frequently or recently encountered may also be preserved. The system can be addressed and its knowledge tapped by a new cue. A cue that is similar to an abstracted theme will elicit that as a response, while one that is similar to an oft-repeated variation will elicit *that*. Note that no explicit process of summarizing is invoked in this picture, so we avoid difficult questions like "at what point in the accumulation of knowledge do people switch from storing exemplars to abstracting a more parsimonious summary representation?"

Connectionist networks can perform exactly this function. Both the generalization or abstraction function emphasized by discussions of schema mechanisms and the preservation of unique details (provided they are represented frequently or recently) thus stem from a single

mechanism (Churchland & Sejnowski, 1992; McClelland & Rumelhart, 1985). In a related vein, many have argued that one of the more promising features of connectionist models is that they can learn and represent in a single system both abstracted general knowledge (including general rules) and specific exemplars that constitute exceptions to the rules. "Imagine that it is 15 years ago and I propose to you that there is a type of knowledge representation that encodes both rule-governed cases and exceptions to the rules. Given the stock of theoretical ideas available at that time, my proposal could only be taken as vacuous. Yet encoding both types of knowledge is what some kinds of connectionist networks do. . . . Here is something that is not a wave and not a particle, but acts like both" (Seidenberg, 1993, p. 234). This property proves important in language processing, in which a number of transformations (e.g., from English spelling to pronunciation) are generally rule-governed but also involve numerous exceptions. It is also important in accounting for world knowledge (e.g., knowledge about social events, or about persons and groups) which is also characterized by some general regularities but also numerous exceptions and specific circumstances that must be represented independently (Plaut, McClelland, Seidenberg, & Patterson, 1996).

In summary, exemplars and schematic mechanisms are not necessarily competing alternatives. A single connectionist mechanism can now be described that fulfills the functions usually ascribed to both.

Exemplar and PDP Mechanisms

A particularly simple relation may hold between exemplars and PDP mechanisms: an "exemplar representation" may be identified with the set of changes in connection weights produced by the learning mechanism during the processing of a particular stimulus. For example, as a pattern-transformation network like that in Figure 3a operates on an input pattern representing a behavior to produce an output pattern representing a corresponding trait, the connection weights will change incrementally. Note the following implications of this speculative proposal:

1. *Repetition priming:* The set of weight changes—i.e., the "exemplar trace"—has the effect of facilitating the later processing of the same or a similar stimulus in the same way (see Wiles & Humphreys, 1993, pp. 158–163). This is because connectionist learning rules produce weight changes that tend to optimize processing of the given stimulus pattern.

2. *Accessibility:* As other stimuli are processed so that further learning modifies the weights, the effect of the exemplar trace will fade over time in a way that is sensitive to the recency and frequency of processing the particular stimulus pattern. Specifically, the accessibil-

ity law provided by ACT-R (Anderson, 1993) reviewed above, seems to describe the expected pattern
well. That law assumes that each exemplar trace
makes its own incremental contribution to accessibility, and the separate contributions (separate increments that move the weights in the same direction) are
summed. Finally, each contribution decays independently at the same rate (as the weight changes are
overwritten and muddied by changes produced by processing other, unrelated stimuli).

3. *Schema effects as massed effects of similar exemplars:*
If many similar patterns are processed (e.g., patterns
that are all instances of a given prototype plus random
variation), the network will in effect learn the prototype pattern (see Clark, 1993). This occurs because the
communalities are reinforced (certain weights are consistently changed in the same direction with every
such pattern) while the random variations are canceled
out by unsystematic weight changes. This idea parallels the account of schematic processing in exemplar
models (e.g., Hintzman, 1986).

4. *Independence of implicit and explicit memory:* Exemplar traces of the sort described here have implicit effects on future processing (such as repetition priming)
but will not mediate explicit memory retrieval. Only if
a record of a particular experience and its time and
place (context) is recorded by separate associative
memory systems will autobiographical recollection of
the episode be available.

Thus, many of the properties of exemplars seem to be
neatly explained in this framework. Exemplar theories may
be a higher-level language for approximately describing
the effects of the changes in connectionist networks produced by learning. However, the term "exemplar representation" may unfortunately connote an *explicit* representation that is consciously accessible and usable in many
types of process. Changes in weights in a network that performs a certain task, such as behavior-to-trait inference,
will in general affect only future performances of the same
task and are not more generally usable or verbally reportable (see Clark, 1993, chap. 4, for a general discussion
of the distinctions between implicit and explicit representations). Consistent with this observation, exemplar theorists
(e.g., Hintzman, 1986; Kahneman & Miller, 1986; Smith &
Zárate, 1992) have generally postulated that exemplars
may influence judgments or behaviors without being consciously retrievable.

Most important, exemplar and distributed representation models share the insight that explicit representations
are states rather than things. They are constructed on-line
from an underlying stock of more stable resources (i.e., exemplar traces or connection weights) rather than being

stored and retrieved in static form (Barsalou, 1987). This
permits the sort of context-sensitivity and flexibility that is
evident in people's use of representations.

Summary: Relations Among the Four Classes of Mechanisms

An Integrative View of Four Types of Theory   The perspective adopted in this chapter leads to a speculative proposal about the interrelations of all four classes of mechanisms reviewed here. First, the first three classes of
theories appear fundamentally different from the fourth.
Associative networks, schemas, and exemplar theories are
all *phenomenon-centered and functional*. The theories
were developed on a largely *inductive* basis: they started
with empirical observations and proceeded to assume that
unobserved structures corresponding to the empirical phenomena must exist inside the mind to account for the observations. For example, if two concepts are observed to be
associated, we assume that the nodes representing the concepts inside the head are connected by a link. If people use
a body of existing knowledge to interpret some input, we
assume that the body of knowledge is represented as a
schema in the head. As these examples illustrate, assumptions about underlying mechanisms in these three classes
of theories tend to maintain a one-to-one correspondence
with functional, observable properties. Therefore deriva-
tions of hypotheses from such theories are usually straightforward. Few questions arise about whether and how the
postulated mechanisms actually account for the access of
knowledge from related knowledge, the use of knowledge
to interpret new inputs, and so on.

In sharp contrast to all three of these, connectionist or
PDP theories have as their most fundamental principles
postulates about underlying representational structure and
process, rather than psychological observations.[3] The application of these theories takes a *deductive* rather than inductive form. The starting point is not a body of psychological observations but the postulation of an allowable set
of processing elements (i.e., simple, richly interconnected
units that can send and receive activation). Theoretical development then involves choosing from that allowed set
and seeing what functional, observable properties can be
produced by an appropriate network architecture. Because
the direction of development is deductive rather than inductive, questions exist about whether and how PDP models can reproduce specific psychological observations.
Many such questions are intensely active research areas at
present, but at a minimum it can be said that connectionist
models can qualitatively reproduce many psychological
observations concerning learning, implicit and explicit
memory, and many types of dissociation among dependent

measures, as well as making new predictions (see Chappell & Humphreys, 1994; McClelland & Rumelhart, 1985; Wiles & Humphreys, 1993).

It may be suggested, then, that all four types of theories have distinct and important places in guiding future empirical work and theoretical development. PDP models give an account of the underlying structures and processes that causally account for observable phenomena—the distinct functions that are summarized by the general principles of the other three theories. This idea that all four theories have roles to play rather than being zero-sum competitors may sound like a thoroughly wishy-washy conclusion. In actuality, however, its implications are somewhat radical, contradicting the familiar idea that the three "classic" types of theories in social psychology truly concern underlying representation structures and processes and not only functional properties. From the current perspective, it is a mistake to reify functional constructs such as schemas, associative networks, or exemplar representations and assume that they are actual entities in the mind. It may be more productive to assume that schemas, associations, and exemplar effects emerge as functional properties from the interaction of other more fundamental mechanisms and structures rather than being structures themselves.

Levels of Theory   A final question may be raised at this point: might it be reasonable for social psychologists—who are not, after all, cognitive psychologists or neuroscientists—to ignore the lowest level and focus *only* on functional properties as summarized by the three "classic" lines of theory? The short answer is "no." Of course, some theoretical progress can be made at the functional level. However, ultimately the properties of underlying representation and process must be relevant for core social psychological phenomena. Here are three arguments for this point.

First, *structure constrains function.* As social cognition researchers have long assumed, modeling the details of memory representations and cognitive processes will help shed light on social thoughts, feelings, and actions (e.g., Hastie & Kumar, 1979; Wyer & Srull, 1989). Progress may be made for a time with theories that pertain only to observable variables, as with early attitude-change theories that restricted themselves to predicting rating-scale responses as dependent variables. But such theories have long since been supplanted by more integrative theories that put attitudes and persuasion in the context of information processing in general and address cognitive processes, memory structures, and accessibility issues as well as rating-scale responses (e.g., Petty & Cacioppo, 1984; Chaiken et al., 1989). The "low-level" details of how mental representations are formed and used necessarily constrain such theories, and a theorist who fails to take advantage of such constraints is not only unnecessarily crippling

his or her own theory but is failing to participate in an integrative and cumulative science.

Second, *new theoretical mechanisms will display new properties.* The properties of connectionist networks are quite different from those that have been assumed to characterize other types of theoretical entities. As Hinton, McClelland, and Rumelhart (1986) and Rumelhart and McClelland (1986) have noted, theorists working with connectionist mechanisms have at their disposal powerful new operations to use as building blocks in constructing accounts of higher-level processes. Such operations might include "Find the globally optimal interpretation of the current situation in light of stored knowledge," "Apply many rules simultaneously to the current representation, weighting each rule to the extent that it is relevant," or "Retrieve the representation in memory that best matches the current input, while using other knowledge to plausibly reconstruct unavailable details." Theories regarding schematic processing (for instance) may serve as useful approximations to such properties of connectionist mechanisms, but they are only global approximations and may be expected to break down rather than yield fine-grained predictions.

As an example of particular relevance to social psychologists, the "schema" that emerges from a recurrent network is not the same kind of static object that schema theories have typically assumed. Here are some of the differences:

1. A connectionist network can simultaneously draw on *multiple* sources of constraint. That is, it may seamlessly combine elements of several "knowledge structures" in interpreting an input pattern. In contrast, existing schema theories emphasize the selection of *one* schema to use and are typically silent on such questions as how people interpret inputs that require more than one independent knowledge structure, such as a "birthday party on a boat" story or a "Hispanic carpenter" stereotype.

2. Connectionist networks can use specific instances to which they have been recently or frequently exposed, as well as abstracted general knowledge, to interpret new input. Schema theories, in contrast, emphasize only the use of general knowledge and must be supplemented with additional mechanisms (nonschematic by definition) to draw on specific knowledge.

3. Connectionist network models generally predict that the knowledge used by preconscious interpretive processes is distinct from the episodic knowledge that is consciously accessible and verbally reportable. Schema theories tend to assume that all knowledge is represented in the same format (i.e., schemas) and therefore do not predict this type of dissociation.

4. Connectionist networks, with their picture of representations as context-sensitive, on-line constructions, can

account for the flexibility and context-sensitivity of our conceptual knowledge, whereas schemas are fixed packages of knowledge that are activated and used in rather inflexible, all-or-none style.

As these examples show, while some of the properties of connectionist mechanisms may be approximately captured by higher-level constructs such as schema or associationist theories, other properties are quite distinct. Interestingly, in these and other ways the properties of connectionist networks are actually more in tune with empirical findings in social psychology than are the properties of the older types of theoretical mechanism. Similarly, as McClelland and Chappell (1995) note, cognitive psychologists have recently been turning away from the older models that conceptualized memory in terms of associative links among nodes (e.g., Gillund & Shiffrin, 1984) in favor of models that consider memories to be represented as patterns or features distributed across a number of units. This shift is not coming about because of theorists' vague desire for up-to-dateness or sudden hankering after neural plausibility, but is being forced by hard empirical results obtained in relatively mundane experiments on recognition memory.

Third, *modeling at a more fundamental level yields greater theoretical generality.* Traditionally, theories in social psychology have been aimed more at fitting empirical observations than at other desiderata such as parsimony, generality, and integrative potential. In accordance with this goal, most theories have been fine-tuned to account for the details of experimental results within a single substantive domain, and often within a single methodological paradigm as well. For example, theories of attribution aimed to spell out empirically valid laws or regularities that could describe people's judgments of causation. The result of this traditional strategy is a profusion of incommensurable domain-specific mini-theories, as many in our field have pointed out (e.g., Wyer & Srull, 1989). One benefit of the social cognition movement has been an increase in theoretical generality, as common principles were assumed to underlie processing in multiple domains; attitudes, attributions, and person impressions, for instance, would all be assumed to be represented and processed in similar ways (see Devine et al., 1994; Sherman, Judd, & Park, 1989). However, each theory still tends to adopt either an associative, schematic, or exemplar-based conceptual vocabulary, limiting its generality. Connectionist mechanisms offer greater potential generality, spanning the types of episodic phenomena for which theorists have typically turned to associative binding models as well as the uses of semantic knowledge for which theorists have invoked schemas or exemplars. Connectionist models also offer the potential for still broader integration across all of psychology, as they are increasingly being adopted by scientists modeling cognitive and perceptual processes such as memory and

language use, and also by neuroscientists concerned with the structure and function of the nervous system.

CONCLUSIONS

In the cognitive sciences and neurosciences in general, conceptions of representation are turning from the familiar but inadequate "thing" metaphor to the newer idea of a representation as a "state." Chief among the implications is that representations are active and interactive, flexibly constructed moment by moment in a manner that is intrinsically influenced by the context and the content of other knowledge, rather than being statically "stored," "searched for," and "retrieved" unchanged.

This general trend has important historical resonances within social psychology, for it brings back the idea of "cognitive dynamics." In this chapter's predecessor, Markus and Zajonc wrote in 1985:

> The corresponding chapter in the second edition of the *Handbook* (Lindzey and Aronson, 1968, p. 391) ended with the expectation that the emphasis on cognitive *dynamics* prevalent during the sixties, with its particular focus on cognitive dissonance and balance, would soon be combined with the earlier descriptive approaches that focused on the *structural* and substantive properties of cognitions. This expectation for an integrated approach to social cognition was definitely not realized. Not only have the seventies and the early eighties failed to achieve a synthesis of the dynamic and descriptive approaches, but for the most part they have abandoned cognitive dynamics altogether. Today's cognitive approaches in social psychology show little concern with the dynamic properties of cognitions—those that posit forces and interdependence among cognitions and produce changes over time (1985, p. 139).

As this quotation suggests, social psychological researchers have long observed important dynamic phenomena within the cognitive system. However, existing classes of theories have not readily accounted for such observations despite occasional vague, generally unelaborated claims (for example, the idea that schemas may include "processing elements" as well as knowledge structures).

Today we can fulfill the expectation of over a quarter-century ago, and bring dynamics back into our conceptions of mental representation. With connectionist models using distributed representations (and to a lesser extent with exemplar theories as well), we now have classes of theories that promise to yield more adequate accounts of social psychological findings. Achieving this goal will require focused theoretical and empirical development over the coming years. It may also impose the cost of giving up familiar and therefore appealing ideas, such as the notion that all representations are symbolic in nature, explicit encodings assembled from elements representing concepts—constituting almost a language of thought (Bickhard & Terveen, 1995; Clark, 1993).

The newer classes of theories overturn these familiar assumptions in favor of the idea that cognition and behavior emerge from the interaction of many simple underlying units (Smolensky, 1988). This idea provides an integrative theoretical language that may ultimately unify psychology and neuroscience, allowing researchers to draw on many new types of findings against which to test and validate theoretical ideas (e.g., McClelland et al., 1995; Sharkey & Sharkey, 1995). Perhaps more important for us, these new ideas, as argued here, may offer a unified account of many types of phenomena for which social psychological theorists have traditionally turned to apparently distinct associative, schematic, and exemplar mechanisms. The idea of someday understanding how social behavior arises from the mind—and how the mind arises from the brain—is a tantalizing promise indeed.

NOTES

1. Some models that may be regarded as connectionist depart from this assumption of distributed representations. These "localist" connectionist models will be discussed in this chapter, along with other assumptions that vary among models.
2. In addition, Miller and Read (1991) applied a localist constraint-satisfaction model of explanation to the issue of how perceivers make attributions for social behavior. Though they characterize the model as connectionist, in actuality it shares more features with associative representational models, as noted above (see Touretzky, 1995, and Barnden, 1995b).
3. Of course, present-day PDP models are also at a functional level rather than a fundamentally causal level, relative to the underlying properties of neurons, axons, synapses, neurotransmitters, and genes (see Sharkey & Sharkey, 1995). PDP models are intended as computationally tractable idealizations of actual neural computations, though PDP modelers are increasingly taking account of neuropsychological findings to constrain their models (Churchland & Sejnowski, 1992; McClelland, McNaughton, & O'Reilly, 1995). The point is simply that *relative to functional properties at the behaviorally observable level,* PDP models postulate lower-level underlying causal mechanisms.

REFERENCES

Abelson, R. P., & Prentice, D. A. (1989). Beliefs as possessions: A functional perspective. In A. R. Pratkanis, S. J. Breckler, & A. G. Greenwald (Eds.), *Attitude structure and function* (pp. 361–382). Hillsdale, NJ: Lawrence Erlbaum Associates.

Alba, J., & Hasher, L. (1983). Is memory schematic? *Psychological Bulletin, 93,* 203–231.

Allport, G. W. (1935). Attitudes. In C. Murchison (Ed.), *Handbook of social psychology* (pp. 798–844). Worcester, MA: Clark University Press.

Allport, G. W. (1954). *The nature of prejudice.* Cambridge, MA: Addison-Wesley.

Andersen, S. M., & Cole, S. W. (1990). "Do I know you?": The role of significant others in general social perception. *Journal of Personality and Social Psychology, 59,* 384–399.

Anderson, J. A. (1995). Associative networks. In M. A. Arbib (Ed.), *Handbook of brain theory and neural networks* (pp. 102–107). Cambridge, MA: MIT Press.

Anderson, J. R. (1983). *The architecture of cognition.* Cambridge, MA: Harvard University Press.

Anderson, J. R. (1987). Skill acquisition: Compilation of weak-method problem solutions. *Psychological Review, 94,* 192–210.

Anderson, J. R. (Ed.) (1993). *Rules of the mind.* Hillsdale, NJ: Lawrence Erlbaum Associates.

Anderson, J. R., & Bower, G. H. (1973). *Human associative memory.* Washington, DC: Winston & Sons.

Anderson, N. H. (1981). *Foundations of information integration theory.* New York: Academic Press.

Anderson, N. H., & Hubert, S. (1963). Effects of concomitant verbal recall on order effects in personality impression formation. *Journal of Verbal Learning and Verbal Behavior, 2,* 379–391.

Anderson, R. C., & Pichert, J. W. (1978). Recall of previously unrecallable information following a shift in perspective. *Journal of Verbal Learning and Verbal Behavior, 17,* 1–12.

Arbib, M. A. (1995). Schema theory. In M. A. Arbib (Ed.), *Handbook of brain theory and neural networks* (pp. 830–834). Cambridge, MA: MIT Press.

Asch, S. (1946). Forming impressions of personality. *Journal of Abnormal and Social Psychology, 41,* 258–290.

Banaji, M. R., & Greenwald, A. G. (1994). Implicit stereotyping and prejudice. In M. P. Zanna & J. M. Olson (Eds.), *The psychology of prejudice: The Ontario Symposium* (Vol. 7, pp. 55–76). Hillsdale, NJ: Lawrence Erlbaum Associates.

Bargh, J. A. (1994). The four horsemen of automaticity: Awareness, intention, efficiency, and control in social cognition. In R. S. Wyer & T. K. Srull (Eds.), *Handbook of social cognition* (2nd ed., Vol. 1, pp. 1–40). Hillsdale, NJ: Lawrence Erlbaum Associates.

Bargh, J. A., & Barndollar, K. (in press). Automaticity in action: The unconscious as repository of chronic goals and motives. To appear in P. M. Gollwitzer & J. A. Bargh (Eds.), *The psychology of action.* New York: Guilford Press.

Bargh, J. A., Chaiken, S., Raymond, P., & Hymes, C. (1996). The automatic evaluation effect: Unconditional automatic attitude activation with a pronunciation task. *Journal of Experimental Social Psychology, 32,* 104–128.

Bargh, J. A., Lombardi, W. J., & Higgins, E. T. (1988). Automaticity of chronically accessible constructs in person X situation effects on person perception: It's just a matter of time. *Journal of Personality and Social Psychology, 55,* 599–605.

Bargh, J. A., Lombardi, W. J., & Tota, M. E. (1986). The additive nature of chronic and temporary sources of construct accessibility. *Journal of Personality and Social Psychology, 50,* 869–879.

Bargh, J. A., & Thein, R. D. (1985). Individual construct accessibility, person memory, and the recall-judgment link: The case of information overload. *Journal of Personality and Social Psychology, 49,* 1129–1146.

Barnden, J. A. (1995a). Artificial intelligence and neural networks. In M. A. Arbib (Ed.), *Handbook of brain theory and neural networks* (pp. 98–102). Cambridge, MA: MIT Press.

Barnden, J. A. (1995b). Semantic networks. In M. A. Arbib (Ed.), *Handbook of brain theory and neural networks* (pp. 854–857). Cambridge, MA: MIT Press.

Barsalou, L. (1987). The instability of graded structure: Implications for the nature of concepts. In U. Neisser (Ed.), *Concepts and conceptual development* (pp. 101–140). Cambridge, England: Cambridge University Press.

Bartlett, F. C. (1932). *Remembering.* Cambridge, England: Cambridge University Press.

Bassili, J. N. (1989). Traits as action categories versus traits as person attributes in social cognition. In J. N. Bassili (Ed.), *On-line cognition in person perception* (pp. 61–89). Hillsdale, NJ: Erlbaum.

Bassili, J. N., & Smith, M. C. (1986). On the spontaneity of trait attributions: Converging evidence for the role of cognitive strategy. *Journal of Personality and Social Psychology, 50,* 239–245.

Begg, I., Armour, V., & Kerr, T. (1985). On believing what we remember. *Canadian Journal of Behavioral Science, 17,* 199–214.

Belmore, S. M., & Hubbard, M. L. (1987). The role of advance expectancies in person memory. *Journal of Personality and Social Psychology, 53,* 61–70.

Bem, D. J. (1967). Self-perception: An alternative interpretation of cognitive dissonance phenomena. *Psychological Review, 74,* 183–200.

Bickhard, M. H., & Terveen, L. (1995). *Foundational issues in artificial intelligence and cognitive science: Impasse and solution.* Amsterdam: Elsevier Scientific.

Biernat, M., Manis, M., & Nelson, T. F. (1991). Stereotypes and standards of judgment. *Journal of Personality and Social Psychology, 60,* 485–499.

Blaney, P. H. (1986). Affect and memory: A review. *Psychological Bulletin, 99,* 229–246.

Bodenhausen, G. V. (1990). Stereotypes as judgmental heuristics: Evidence of circadian variations in discrimination. *Psychological Science, 1,* 319–322.

Bodenhausen, G. V., Schwarz, N., Bless, H., & Wanke, M. (1995). Effects of atypical exemplars on racial beliefs: Enlightened racism or generalized appraisals? *Journal of Experimental Social Psychology, 31,* 48–63.

Bodenhausen, G. V., & Wyer, R. S. (1985). Effects of stereotypes on decision making and information processing strategies. *Journal of Personality and Social Psychology, 48,* 267–282.

Bower, G. H. (1981). Emotional mood and memory. *American Psychologist, 36,* 129–148.

Bower, G. H., & Gilligan, S. G. (1979). Remembering information related to one's self. *Journal of Research in Personality, 13,* 404–419.

Bower, G. H., & Mayer, J. D. (1985). Failure to replicate mood-dependent retrieval. *Bulletin of the Psychonomic Society, 23,* 39–42.

Bower, G. H., Monteiro, K. P., & Gilligan, S. G. (1978). Emotional mood as a context for learning and recall. *Journal of Verbal Learning and Verbal Behavior, 17,* 573–585.

Bransford, J. D., & Franks, J. J. (1971). The abstraction of linguistic ideas. *Cognitive Psychology, 2,* 331–350.

Brewer, M. B. (1988). A dual process model of impression formation. In T. Srull & R. Wyer (Eds.), *Advances in Social Cognition* (Vol. 1, pp. 177–183). Hillsdale, NJ: Erlbaum.

Brewer, W. F., & Nakamura, G. V. (1984). The nature and functions of schemas. In R. S. Wyer & T. K. Srull (Eds.), *Handbook of social cognition* (Vol. 1, pp. 119–160). Hillsdale, NJ: Lawrence Erlbaum Associates.

Brooks, L. (1978). Nonanalytic concept formation and memory for instances. In E. Rosch & B. B. Lloyd (Eds.), *Cognition and categorization* (pp. 169–211). Hillsdale, NJ: Lawrence Erlbaum Associates.

Bruner, J. S. (1957). Going beyond the information given. In H. Gruber, G. Terrell, & M. Wertheimer (Eds.), *Contemporary approaches to cognition.* Cambridge, MA: Harvard University Press.

Cantor, N., & Kihlstrom, J. F. (1987). *Personality and social intelligence.* Englewood Cliffs, NJ: Prentice-Hall.

Cantor, N., & Mischel, W. (1977). Traits as prototypes: Effects on recognition memory. *Journal of Personality and Social Psychology, 35,* 38–48.

Cantor, N., & Mischel, W. (1979). Prototypes in person perception. In L. Berkowitz (Ed.), *Advances in experimental social psychology* (Vol. 12, pp. 3–52). New York: Academic Press.

Carlston, D. E. (1992). Impression formation and the modular mind: The Associated Systems Theory. In L. L. Martin & A. Tesser (Eds.), *The construction of social judgments* (pp. 301–341). Hillsdale, NJ: Lawrence Erlbaum Associates.

Carlston, D. E. (1994). Associated systems theory: A systematic approach to cognitive representations of persons. In T. K. Srull & R. S. Wyer (Eds.), *Advances in social cognition: A dual process model of impression formation* (Vol. 7, pp. 1–78). Hillsdale, NJ: Lawrence Erlbaum Associates.

Carlston, D. E., & Skowronski, J. J. (1986). Trait memory and behavior memory: The effects of alternative pathways on impression judgment response times. *Journal of Personality and Social Psychology, 50,* 5–13.

Carlston, D. E., & Skowronski, J. J. (1994). Savings in the relearning of trait information as evidence for spontaneous inference generation. *Journal of Personality and Social Psychology, 66,* 840–856.

Carlston, D. E., Skowronski, J. J., & Sparks, C. (1995). Savings in relearning: II. On the formation of behavior-based trait associations and inferences. *Journal of Personality and Social Psychology, 69,* 420–436.

Carlston, D. E., & Smith, E. R. (1996). Principles of mental representation. To appear in E. T. Higgins & A. Kruglanski (Eds.), *Social psychology: Handbook of basic principles* (pp. 184–210). New York: Guilford Press.

Chaiken, S. (1980). Heuristic versus systematic information processing and the use of source versus message cues in persuasion. *Journal of Personality and Social Psychology, 39,* 752–766.

Chaiken, S., Lieberman, A., & Eagly, A. H. (1989). Heuristic and systematic information processing: Within and beyond the persuasion context. In J. S. Uleman & J. A. Bargh (Eds.), *Unintended thought: Limits of awareness, intention, and control* (pp. 212–252). New York: Guilford.

Chappell, M., & Humphreys, M. S. (1994). An auto-associative neural network for sparse representations: Analysis and application to models of recognition and cued recall. *Psychological Review, 101,* 103–128.

Chase, W. G., & Simon, H. A. (1973). The mind's eye in chess. In W. G. Chase (Ed.), *Visual information processing* (pp. 215–281). New York: Academic Press.

Churchland, P. S., & Sejnowski, T. J. (1992). *The computational brain.* Cambridge, MA: MIT Press.

Clark, A. (1993). *Associative engines: Connectionism, concepts, and representational change.* Cambridge, MA: MIT Press.

Clark, L. F., Martin, L. L., & Henry, S. M. (1993). Instantiation, interference, and the change of standard effect: Context functions in reconstructive memory. *Journal of Personality and Social Psychology, 64,* 336–346.

Clore, G. L., Schwarz, N., & Conway, M. (1994). Affective causes and consequences of social information processing. In R. S. Wyer & T. K. Srull (Eds.), *Handbook of social cognition* (2nd ed., Vol. 1, pp. 323–418). Hillsdale, NJ: Lawrence Erlbaum Associates.

Cohen, C. E. (1981). Person categories and social perception: Testing some boundaries of the processing effects of prior knowledge. *Journal of Personality and Social Psychology, 40,* 441–452.

Cohen, J. D., Servan-Schreiber, D., & McClelland, J. L. (1992). A parallel distributed processing approach to automaticity. *American Journal of Psychology, 105,* 239–269.

Collins, A., & Loftus, E. F. (1975). A spreading activation theory of semantic memory. *Journal of Verbal Learning and Verbal Behavior, 8,* 240–247.

Collins, A. M., & Quillian, M. R. (1969). Retrieval time from semantic memory. *Journal of Verbal Learning and Verbal Behavior, 8,* 240–247.

Conway, M. A., & Rubin, D. C. (1993). The structure of autobiographical memory. In A. F. Collins, S. E. Gathercole, M. A. Conway, & P. E. Morris (Eds.), *Theories of memory* (pp. 103–137). Hove, England: Lawrence Erlbaum Associates.

Cooper, J., & Fazio, R. H. (1984). A new look at dissonance theory. In L. Berkowitz (Ed.), *Advances in experimental social psychology* (Vol. 17, pp. 229–266). New York: Academic Press.

Damasio, A. R. (1989). Multiregional activation: A systems level model for some neural substrates of cognition. *Cognition, 33,* 25–62.

Darley, J. M., & Gross, P. H. (1983). A hypothesis-confirming bias in labelling effects. *Journal of Personality and Social Psychology, 44,* 20–33.

Deaux, K., & Emswiller, T. (1974). Explanations of successful performance on sex-linked tasks: What is skill for the male is luck for the female. *Journal of Personality and Social Psychology, 29,* 80–85.

Devine, P. G. (1989). Stereotypes and prejudice: Their automatic and controlled components. *Journal of Personality and Social Psychology, 56,* 5–18.

Devine, P. G., Hamilton, D. L., & Ostrom, T. M. (Eds.). (1994). *Social cognition: Impact on social psychology.* Orlando, FL: Academic Press.

Dorman, C., & Gaudiano, P. (1995). Motivation. In M. A. Arbib (Ed.), *Handbook of brain theory and neural networks* (pp. 591–594). Cambridge, MA: MIT Press.

Dovidio, J. F., Evans, N., & Tyler, R. B. (1986). Racial stereotypes: The content of their cognitive representations. *Journal of Experimental Social Psychology, 22,* 22–37.

Duncan, B. L. (1976). Differential social perception and attribution of intergroup violence: Testing the lower limits of stereotyping of blacks. *Journal of Personality and Social Psychology, 34,* 590–598.

Ebbinghaus, H. (1964). *Memory: A contribution to experimental psychology* (trans. H. A. Ruger & C. E. Bussenius). New York: Dover. (Original publication, 1885).

Elman, J. L. (1995). Language processing. In M. A. Arbib (Ed.), *Handbook of brain theory and neural networks* (pp. 508–513). Cambridge, MA: MIT Press.

Fazio, R. H. (1986). How do attitudes guide behavior? In R. M. Sorrentino & E. T. Higgins (Eds.), *Handbook of motivation and cognition* (pp. 204–243). New York: Guilford Press.

Fazio, R. H. (1993). Variability in the likelihood of automatic attitude activation: Data reanalysis and commentary on Bargh, Chaiken, Govender, and Pratto (1992). *Journal of Personality and Social Psychology, 64,* 753–758.

Fazio, R. H., Blascovich, J., & Driscoll, D. M. (1992). On the functional value of attitudes: The influence of accessible attitudes on the ease and quality of decision making. *Personality and Social Psychology Bulletin, 18,* 388–401.

Fazio, R. H., Sanbonmatsu, D. M., Powell, M. C., & Kardes,

F. R. (1986). On the automatic activation of attitudes. *Journal of Personality and Social Psychology, 50,* 229–238.

Festinger, L. (1957). *A theory of cognitive dissonance.* Stanford, CA: Stanford University Press.

Fiske, S. T., & Dyer, L. M. (1985). Structure and development of social schemata: Evidence from positive and negative transfer effects. *Journal of Personality and Social Psychology, 48,* 839–852.

Fiske, S. T., & Linville, P. W. (1980). What does the schema concept buy us? *Personality and Social Psychology Bulletin, 6,* 543–557.

Fiske, S. T., & Neuberg, S. L. (1990). A continuum of impression formation, from category-based to individuating processes: Influences of information and motivation on attention and interpretation. In M. P. Zanna (Ed.), *Advances in experimental social psychology* (Vol. 23, pp. 1–74). New York: Academic Press.

Fiske, S. T., & Taylor, S. E. (1991). *Social cognition* (2nd ed.). New York: McGraw-Hill.

Fong, G. T., & Markus, H. (1982). Self-schemas and judgments about others. *Social Cognition, 1,* 191–205.

Frable, D. E. S., & Bem, S. L. (1985). If you are gender schematic, all members of the opposite sex look alike. *Journal of Personality and Social Psychology, 49,* 459–468.

Fyock, J., & Stangor, C. (1994). The role of memory biases in stereotype maintenance. *British Journal of Social Psychology, 33,* 331–343.

Gaertner, S. L., & McLaughlin, J. P. (1983). Racial stereotypes: Associations and ascriptions of positive and negative characteristics. *Social Psychology Quarterly, 46,* 23–40.

Gilbert, D. T. (1993). The assent of man: Mental representation and the control of belief. In D. M. Wegner & J. W. Pennebaker (Eds.), *Handbook of mental control* (pp. 57–87). Englewood Cliffs, NJ: Prentice-Hall.

Gilbert, D. T., & Hixon, J. G. (1991). The trouble of thinking: Activation and application of stereotypic beliefs. *Journal of Personality and Social Psychology, 60,* 509–517.

Gillund, G., & Shiffrin, R. (1984). A retrieval model for both recognition and recall. *Psychological Review, 91,* 1–67.

Glick, P., Zion, C., & Nelson, C. (1988). What mediates sex discrimination in hiring decisions? *Journal of Personality and Social Psychology, 55,* 178–186.

Graesser, A. C. (1981). *Prose comprehension beyond the word.* New York: Springer-Verlag.

Greenwald, A. G. (1992). New Look 3: Unconscious cognition reclaimed. *American Psychologist, 47,* 766–779.

Greenwald, A. G., & Banaji, M. R. (1989). The self as a memory system: Powerful, but ordinary. *Journal of Personality and Social Psychology, 57,* 41–54.

Grice, H. P. (1975). Logic and conversation. In P. Cole & J. L. Morgan (Eds.), *Syntax and semantics 3: Speech acts* (pp. 41–58). New York: Academic Press.

Hamilton, D. L. (1981). Cognitive representations of persons. In E. T. Higgins, C. P. Herman, & M. P. Zanna (Eds.), *So-cial cognition: The Ontario Symposium* (Vol. 1, pp. 135–160). Hillsdale, NJ: Lawrence Erlbaum Associates.

Hamilton, D. L., & Gifford, R. K. (1976). Illusory correlation in interpersonal perception: A cognitive basis for stereotypic judgments. *Journal of Experimental Social Psychology, 12,* 392–407.

Hamilton, D. L., Katz, L. B., & Leirer, V. (1980). Organizational processes in impression formation. In R. Hastie, T. M. Ostrom, E. B. Ebbesen, R. S. Wyer, D. Hamilton, & D. E. Carlston (Eds.), *Person memory.* Hillsdale, NJ: Lawrence Erlbaum Associates.

Hamilton, D. L., & Mackie, D. M. (1990). Specificity and generality in the nature and use of stereotypes. In T. K. Srull & R. S. Wyer (Eds.), *Advances in social cognition* (Vol. 3, pp. 99–110). Hillsdale, NJ: Lawrence Erlbaum Associates.

Hamilton, D. L., & Sherman, J. W. (1994). Stereotypes. In R. S. Wyer & T. K. Srull (Eds.), *Handbook of social cognition* (2nd ed., Vol. 2, pp. 1–68). Hillsdale, NJ: Lawrence Erlbaum Associates.

Hamilton, D. L., & Sherman, S. J. (1989). Illusory correlations: Implications for stereotype theory and research. In D. Bar-Tal, C. F. Graumann, A. W. Kruglanski, & W. Stroebe (Eds.), *Stereotypes and prejudice: Changing conceptions* (pp. 59–82). New York: Springer-Verlag.

Hamilton, D. L., & Trolier, T. K. (1986). Stereotypes and stereotyping: An overview of the cognitive approach. In J. F. Dovidio & S. L. Gaertner (Eds.), *Prejudice, discrimination, and racism* (pp. 127–163). Orlando, FL: Academic Press.

Harvey, J. H., Yarkin, K. L., Lightner, J. M., & Town, J. P. (1980). Unsolicited interpretation and recall of interpersonal events. *Journal of Personality and Social Psychology, 38,* 551–568.

Hasher, L., Goldstein, D., & Toppino, T. (1977). Frequency and the conference of referential validity. *Journal of Verbal Learning and Verbal Behavior, 16,* 107–112.

Hastie, R. (1980). Memory for information which confirms or contradicts a general impression. In R. Hastie, T. M. Ostrom, E. B. Ebbesen, R. S. Wyer, D. Hamilton, & D. E. Carlston (Eds.), *Person memory* (pp. 155–177). Hillsdale, NJ: Lawrence Erlbaum Associates.

Hastie, R. (1988). A computer simulation model of person memory. *Journal of Experimental Social Psychology, 24,* 423–447.

Hastie, R., & Kumar, P. A. (1979). Person memory: Personality traits as organizing principles in memory for behaviors. *Journal of Personality and Social Psychology, 37,* 25–38.

Hastie, R., & Park, B. (1986). The relationship between memory and judgment depends on whether the judgment task is memory-based or on-line. *Psychological Review, 93,* 258–268.

Hayes-Roth, B. (1977). Evolution of cognitive structure and processes. *Psychological Review, 84,* 260–278.

Hertz, J. (1995). Computing with attractors. In M. A. Arbib

(Ed.), *Handbook of brain theory and neural networks* (pp. 230–234). Cambridge, MA: MIT Press.

Hertz, J., Krogh, A., & Palmer, R. G. (1991). *Introduction to the theory of neural computation.* Redwood City, CA: Addison-Wesley.

Higgins, E. T. (1989). Knowledge accessibility and activation: Subjectivity and suffering from unconscious sources. In J. S. Uleman & J. A. Bargh (Eds.), *Unintended thought: The limits of awareness, intention, and control* (pp. 75–123). New York: Guilford Press.

Higgins, E. T. (1996). Knowledge activation: Accessibility, applicability, and salience. In E. T. Higgins & A. W. Kruglanski (Eds.), *Social psychology: Handbook of basic principles* (pp. 133–168). New York: Guilford.

Higgins, E. T., & Bargh, J. A. (1987). Social cognition and social perception. *Annual Review of Psychology, 38,* 369–426.

Higgins, E. T., Bargh, J. A., & Lombardi, W. (1985). Nature of priming effect on categorization. *Journal of Experimental Psychology: Learning, Memory and Cognition, 11,* 59–69.

Higgins, E. T., & King, G. A. (1981). Accessibility of social constructs: Information-processing consequences of individual and contextual variability. In N. Cantor & J. F. Kihlstrom (Eds.). *Personality, cognition, and social interaction* (pp. 69–112). Hillsdale, NJ: Lawrence Erlbaum Associates.

Higgins, E. T., King, G. A., & Mavin, G. H. (1982). Individual construct accessibility and subjective impressions and recall. *Journal of Personality and Social Psychology, 43,* 35–47.

Higgins, E. T., & Lurie, L. (1983). Context, categorization, and memory: The "change-of-standard" effect. *Cognitive Psychology, 15,* 525–547.

Higgins, E. T., Rholes, W. S., & Jones, C. R. (1977). Category accessibility and impression formation. *Journal of Experimental Social Psychology, 13,* 141–154.

Higgins, E. T., & Stangor, C. (1988). A "change-of-standard" perspective on the relations among context, judgment, and memory. *Journal of Personality and Social Psychology, 54,* 181–192.

Higgins, E. T., van Hook, E., & Dorfman, D. (1988). Do self-attributes form a cognitive structure? *Social Cognition, 6,* 177–207.

Hinton, G. E., McClelland, J. L., & Rumelhart, D. E. (1986). Distributed representations. In D. E. Rumelhart, J. L. McClelland, et al. (Eds.), *Parallel distributed processing* (Vol. 1, pp. 77–109). Cambridge, MA: MIT Press.

Hintzman, D. L. (1986). "Schema abstraction" in a multiple-trace memory model. *Psychological Review, 93,* 411–428.

Hintzman, D. L. (1990). Human learning and memory: Connections and dissociations. *Annual Review of Psychology, 41,* 109–140.

Hirst, W. (1989). On consciousness, recall, recognition, and the architecture of memory. In S. Lewandowsky, J. C. Dunn, & K. Kirsner (Eds.), *Implicit memory: Theoretical issues* (pp. 33–46). Hillsdale, NJ: Lawrence Erlbaum Associates.

Hirt, E. R. (1990). Do I see only what I expect? Evidence for an expectancy-guided retrieval process. *Journal of Personality and Social Psychology, 58,* 937–951.

Hume, D. (1978). *A treatise on human nature being an attempt to introduce the experimental method of reasoning into moral subjects.* Fair Lawn, NJ: Oxford University Press. (Original publication 1739).

Humphreys, M. S., Bain, J. D., & Pike, R. (1989). Different ways to cue a coherent memory system: A theory for episodic, semantic, and procedural tasks. *Psychological Review, 96,* 208–233.

Isen, A. M. (1984). Toward understanding the role of affect in cognition. In R. S. Wyer & T. K. Srull (Eds.), *Handbook of social cognition* (Vol. 3, pp. 179–236). Hillsdale, NJ: Lawrence Erlbaum Associates.

Jacoby, L. L. (1983). Perceptual enhancement: Persistent effects of an experience. *Journal of Experimental Psychology: Learning, Memory, and Cognition, 9,* 21–38.

Jacoby, L. L., Allan, L. G., Collins, J. C., & Larwill, L. K. (1988). Memory influences subjective experience: Noise judgments. *Journal of Experimental Psychology: Learning, Memory, and Cognition, 14,* 240–247.

Jacoby, L. L., & Brooks, L. R. (1984). Nonanalytic cognition: Memory, perception and concept learning. In G. Bower (Ed.), *The psychology of learning and motivation: Advances in research and theory* (Vol. 18). New York: Academic Press.

Jacoby, L. L., & Kelley, C. M. (1987). Unconscious influences of memory for a prior event. *Personality and Social Psychology Bulletin, 13,* 314–336.

Jacoby, L. L., Kelley, C. M., Brown, J., & Jasechko, J. (1989). Becoming famous overnight: Limits on the ability to avoid unconscious influences of the past. *Journal of Personality and Social Psychology, 56,* 326–338.

Judd, C. M., & Krosnick, J. A. (1989). The structural bases of consistency among political attitudes: Effects of political expertise and attitude importance. In A. R. Pratkanis, S. J. Breckler, & A. G. Greenwald (Eds.), *Attitude structure and function* (pp. 99–128). Hillsdale, NJ: Lawrence Erlbaum Associates.

Judd, C. M., & Park, B. (1988). Out-group homogeneity: Judgments of variability at the individual and group levels. *Journal of Personality and Social Psychology, 54,* 778–788.

Kahneman, D., & Miller, D. T. (1986). Norm theory: Comparing reality to its alternatives. *Psychological Review, 93,* 136–153.

Kant, I. (1969). *Critique of pure reason.* New York: St. Martin's Press. (Originally published 1781).

Kashima, Y., & Kerekes, A. R. Z. (1994). A distributed memory model of averaging phenomena in person impression formation. *Journal of Experimental Social Psychology, 30,* 407–455.

Kihlstrom, J. F., & Cantor, N. (1984). Mental representations of the self. In L. Berkowitz (Ed.), *Advances in experimen-*

tal social psychology (Vol. 17, pp. 2–48). New York: Academic Press.

Kihlstrom, J. F., & Klein, S. B. (1994). The self as a knowledge structure. In R. S. Wyer & T. K. Srull (Eds.), *Handbook of social cognition* (2nd ed., Vol. 1, pp. 153–208). Hillsdale, NJ: Lawrence Erlbaum Associates.

Kirkpatrick, L. A., & Epstein, S. (1992). Cognitive-experiential self-theory and subjective probability: Further evidence for two conceptual systems. *Journal of Personality and Social Psychology, 63,* 534–544.

Klatzky, R. L., Martin, G. L., & Kane, R. A. (1982). Influence of social-category activation on processing of visual information. *Social Cognition, 1,* 95–109.

Klein, S. B., & Kihlstrom, J. F. (1986). Elaboration, organization, and the self-reference effect in memory. *Journal of Experimental Psychology: General, 115,* 26–38.

Klein, S. B., & Loftus, J. (1988). The nature of self-referent encoding: The contributions of elaborative and organizational processes. *Journal of Personality and Social Psychology, 55,* 5–11.

Klein, S. B., & Loftus, J. (1990). Rethinking the role of organization in person memory: An independent trace storage model. *Journal of Personality and Social Psychology, 59,* 400–410.

Klein, S. B., & Loftus, J. (1993). The mental representation of trait and autobiographical knowledge about the self. In T. K. Srull & R. S. Wyer (Eds.), *Advances in social cognition* (Vol. 5, pp. 1–50). Hillsdale, NJ: Lawrence Erlbaum Associates.

Klein, S. B., Loftus, J., & Burton, H. A. (1989). Two self-reference effects: The importance of distinguishing between self-descriptiveness judgments and autobiographical retrieval in self-referent encoding. *Journal of Personality and Social Psychology, 56,* 853–865.

Klein, S. B., Loftus, J., Trafton, J. G., & Fuhrman, R. W. (1992). Use of exemplars and abstractions in trait judgments: A model of trait knowledge about the self and others. *Journal of Personality and Social Psychology, 63,* 739–753.

Koffka, K. (1935). *Principles of Gestalt psychology.* New York: Harcourt, Brace, & World.

Kolers, P. A. (1976). Reading a year later. *Journal of Experimental Psychology: Human Learning and Memory, 2,* 554–565.

Kolers, P. A., & Roediger, H. L. (1984). Procedures of mind. *Journal of Verbal Learning and Verbal Behavior, 23,* 425–449.

Krueger, J., & Rothbart, M. (1988). The use of categorical and individuating information in making inferences about personality. *Journal of Personality and Social Psychology, 55,* 187–195.

Kruschke, J. K., & Erickson, M. A. (in press). Five principles for models of category learning. To appear in Z. Dienes (Ed.), *Connectionism and human learning.* Oxford University Press.

Kunda, Z., & Thagard, P. (1996). Forming impressions from stereotypes, traits and behaviors: Parallel constraint satisfaction theory. *Psychological Review, 103,* 284–308.

Levine, J. M., Resnick, L. B., & Higgins, E. T. (1993). Social foundations of cognition. *Annual Review of Psychology, 44,* 585–612.

Lewicki, P. (1985). Nonconscious biasing effects of single instances of subsequent judgments. *Journal of Personality and Social Psychology, 48,* 563–574.

Lewin, K. (1951). *Field theory in social science: Selected theoretical papers.* New York: Harper.

Leyens, J.-P., & Fiske, S. T. (1994). Impression formation: From recitals to symphonie fantastique. In P. G. Devine, T. M. Ostrom, & D. L. Hamilton (Eds.), *Social cognition: Impact on social psychology* (pp. 39–75). Orlando, FL: Academic Press.

Linville, P. W., & Carlston, D. E. (1994). Social cognition of the self. In P. G. Devine, T. M. Ostrom, & D. L. Hamilton (Eds.), *Social cognition: Impact on social psychology* (pp. 143–193). Orlando, FL: Academic Press.

Linville, P. W., & Fischer, G. W. (1993). Exemplar and abstraction models of perceived group variability and stereotypicality. *Social Cognition, 11,* 92–125.

Linville, P. W., Fischer, G. W., & Salovey, P. (1989). Perceived distributions of the characteristics of in-group and out-group members: Empirical evidence and a computer simulation. *Journal of Personality and Social Psychology, 57,* 165–188.

Locke, J. (1979). *Essay concerning human understanding.* New York: Oxford University Press. (Original publication 1690).

Logan, G. D. (1988). Toward an instance theory of automatization. *Psychological Review, 95,* 492–527.

Lombardi, W. J., Higgins, E. T., & Bargh, J. A. (1987). The role of consciousness in priming effects on categorization: Assimilation versus contrast as a function of awareness of the priming task. *Personality and Social Psychology Bulletin, 13,* 411–429.

Lusk, C. M., & Judd, C. M. (1988). Political expertise and the structural mediators of candidate evaluations. *Journal of Experimental Social Psychology, 24,* 105–126.

Mackie, D. M., Sherman, J. W., & Worth, L. T. (1993). On-line and memory-based processes in group variability judgments. *Social Cognition, 11,* 44–69.

MacLeod, C. M., & Bassili, J. N. (1989). Are implicit and explicit tests differentially sensitive to item-specific vs. relational information? In S. Lewandowsky, J. C. Dunn, & K. Kirsner (Eds.), *Implicit memory: Theoretical issues* (pp. 159–172). Hillsdale, NJ: Lawrence Erlbaum Associates.

Macrae, C. N., Hewstone, M., & Griffiths, R. J. (1993). Processing load and memory for stereotype-based information. *European Journal of Social Psychology, 23,* 77–87.

Malt, B. C., & Smith, E. E. (1984). Correlated properties in natural categories. *Journal of Verbal Learning and Verbal Behavior, 23,* 250–269.

Mandler, G., Nakamura, Y., & van Zandt, B. J. (1987). Nonspecific effects of exposure on stimuli that cannot be recognized. *Journal of Experimental Psychology: Learning, Memory and Cognition, 13,* 646–648.

Markus, H. (1977). Self-schemata and processing information about the self. *Journal of Personality and Social Psychology, 35,* 63–78.

Markus, H., & Sentis, K. P. (1982). The self in social information processing. In J. Suls (Ed.), *Psychological perspectives on the self* (Vol. 1, pp. 41–70). Hillsdale, NJ: Lawrence Erlbaum Associates.

Markus, H., & Smith, J. (1981). The influence of self-schemas on the perception of others. In N. Cantor & J. F. Kihlstrom (Eds.), *Personality, cognition, and social interaction* (pp. 233–262). Hillsdale, NJ: Lawrence Erlbaum Associates.

Markus, H., & Wurf, E. (1987). The dynamic self-concept: A social psychological perspective. *Annual Review of Psychology, 38,* 299–337.

Markus, H., & Zajonc, R. B. (1985). The cognitive perspective in social psychology. In G. Lindzey & E. Aronson (Eds.), *Handbook of social psychology* (3rd ed., Vol. 1, pp. 137–230). New York: Random House.

Martin, L. L. (1986). Set/reset: Use and disuse of concepts in impression formation. *Journal of Personality and Social Psychology, 51,* 493–504.

Martin, L. L., Seta, J. J., & Crelia, R. A. (1990). Assimilation and contrast as a function of people's willingness and ability to expend effort in forming an impression. *Journal of Personality and Social Psychology, 59,* 38–49.

Masson, M. E. J. (1989). Fluent reprocessing as an implicit expression of memory for experience. In S. Lewandowsky, J. C. Dunn, & K. Kirsner (Eds.), *Implicit memory: Theoretical issues* (pp. 123–138). Hillsdale, NJ: Lawrence Erlbaum Associates.

Masson, M. E. J. (1991). A distributed memory model of context effects in word identification. In D. Besner & G. W. Humphreys (Eds.), *Basic processes in reading: Visual word recognition* (pp. 233–263). Hillsdale, NJ: Lawrence Erlbaum Associates.

McClelland, J. L., & Chappell, M. (1995). Familiarity breeds differentiation: A Bayesian approach to the effects of experience in recognition memory. Unpublished paper, Carnegie-Mellon University.

McClelland, J. L., McNaughton, B. L., & O'Reilly, R. C. (1995). Why there are complementary learning systems in the hippocampus and neocortex: Insights from the successes and failures of connectionist models of learning and memory. *Psychological Review, 102,* 419–457.

McClelland, J. L., & Rumelhart, D. E. (1985). Distributed memory and the representation of general and specific information. *Journal of Experimental Psychology: General, 114,* 159–188.

McClelland, J. L., Rumelhart, D. E., & Hinton, G. E. (1986). The appeal of parallel distributed processing. In D. E. Rumelhart, J. L. McClelland, et al. (Eds.), *Parallel distributed processing* (Vol. 1, pp. 3–44). Cambridge, MA: MIT Press.

McClelland, J. L., Rumelhart, D. E., and the PDP Research Group (Eds.). (1986). *Parallel distributed processing* (Vol. 2). Cambridge, MA: MIT Press.

McFarland, C., & Ross, M. (1987). The relation between current impressions and memories of self and dating partners. *Personality and Social Psychology Bulletin, 13,* 228–238.

McKoon, G., & Ratcliff, R. (1992). Spreading activation versus compound cue accounts of priming: Mediated priming revisited. *Journal of Experimental Psychology: Learning, Memory and Cognition, 18,* 1155–1172.

McNamara, T. P. (1992). Theories of priming: I. Associative distance and lag. *Journal of Experimental Psychology: Learning, Memory and Cognition, 18,* 1173–1190.

Medin, D. L., Dewey, G. I., & Murphy, T. D. (1983). Relations between item and category learning: Evidence that abstraction is not automatic. *Journal of Experimental Psychology: Learning, Memory, and Cognition, 9,* 607–625.

Medin, D. L., & Schaffer, M. M. (1978). Context theory of classification learning. *Psychological Review, 85,* 207–238.

Meyer, D. E., & Schvaneveldt, R. W. (1971). Facilitation in recognizing pairs of words: Evidence of a dependence between retrieval operations. *Journal of Experimental Psychology, 90,* 227–234.

Miller, L. C., & Read, S. J. (1991). On the coherence of mental models of persons and relationships: A knowledge structure approach. In G. J. O. Fletcher & F. Fincham (Eds.), *Cognition in close relationships* (pp. 69–99). Hillsdale, NJ: Lawrence Erlbaum Associates.

Minsky, M. (1975). A framework for representing knowledge. In P. H. Winston (Ed.), *The psychology of computer vision.* New York: McGraw-Hill.

Mitchell, D. B., & Brown, A. S. (1988). Persistent repetition priming in picture naming and its dissociation from recognition memory. *Journal of Experimental Psychology: Learning, Memory, and Cognition, 14,* 213–222.

Moll, M., Miikkulainen, R., & Abbey, J. (1994). The capacity of convergence-zone episodic memory. *Proceedings of the Twelfth National Conference on Artificial Intelligence.*

Morris, C. D., Bransford, J. D., & Franks, J. J. (1977). Levels of processing versus transfer appropriate processing. *Journal of Verbal Learning and Verbal Behavior, 16,* 519–533.

Moscovitch, M. (1994). Memory and working with memory: Evaluation of a component process model and comparisons with other models. In D. L. Schacter & E. Tulving (Eds.), *Memory systems 1994* (pp. 269–310). Cambridge, MA: MIT Press.

Murdock, B. B. (1982). Recognition memory. In C. R. Puff (Ed.), *Handbook of research methods in human memory and cognition.* New York: Academic Press.

Neely, J. H. (1977). Semantic priming and retrieval from lexical memory: Roles of inhibitionless spreading activation and limited-capacity attention. *Journal of Experimental Psychology: General, 1,* 226–254.

Neisser, U. (1976). *Cognition and reality*. San Francisco: Freeman.

Newman, L. S. (1991). Why are traits inferred spontaneously? A developmental approach. *Social Cognition, 9*, 221–253.

Norman, D. A. (1981). Categorization of action slips. *Psychological Review, 88*, 1–15.

Nosofsky, R. M. (1986). Attention, similarity, and the identification-categorization relationship. *Journal of Experimental Psychology: General, 115*, 39–57.

Ostrom, T. M., Skowronski, J. J., & Nowak, A. (1994). The cognitive foundation of attitudes: It's a wonderful construct. In P. G. Devine, T. M. Ostrom, & D. L. Hamilton (Eds.), *Social cognition: Impact on social psychology* (pp. 195–257). Orlando, FL: Academic Press.

Park, B., & Hastie, R. (1987). Perception of variability in category development: Instance versus abstraction-based stereotypes. *Journal of Personality and Social Psychology, 53*, 621–635.

Park, B., & Judd, C. M. (1990). Measures and models of perceived group variability. *Journal of Personality and Social Psychology, 59*, 173–191.

Park, B., Judd, C. M., & Ryan, C. M. (1991). Social categorization and the representation of variability information. In W. Stroebe & M. Hewstone (Eds.), *European review of social psychology* (Vol. 2, pp. 211–245). Chichester, England: Wiley.

Petty, R. E., & Cacioppo, J. T. (1984). The effects of involvement on responses to argument quantity and quality: Central and peripheral routes to persuasion. *Journal of Personality and Social Psychology, 46*, 69–81.

Pichert, J. W., & Anderson, R. C. (1977). Taking different perspectives on a story. *Journal of Educational Psychology, 69*, 309–315.

Plaut, D. C., McClelland, J. L., Seidenberg, M. S., Patterson, K. E. (1996). Understanding normal and impaired word reading: Computational principles in quasi-regular domains. *Psychological Review, 103*, 56–115.

Posner, M. I., & Keele, S. W. (1968). On the genesis of abstract ideas. *Journal of Experimental Psychology, 77*, 353–363.

Ratcliff, R., & McKoon, G. (1988). A retrieval theory of priming in memory. *Psychological Review, 95*, 385–408.

Read, S. J., & Marcus-Newhall, A. (1993). Explanatory coherence in social explanations: A parallel distributed processing account. *Journal of Personality and Social Psychology, 65*, 429–447.

Reder, L. M., & Anderson, J. R. (1980). A partial resolution of the paradox of interference: The role of integrating knowledge. *Cognitive Psychology, 12*, 447–472.

Reed, S. K. (1972). Pattern recognition and categorization. *Cognitive Psychology, 3*, 382–407.

Richardson-Klavehn, A., & Bjork, R. A. (1988). Measures of memory. *Annual Review of Psychology, 39*, 475–544.

Roediger, H. L., & Blaxton, T. A. (1987). Retrieval modes produce dissociations in memory for surface information. In D.

S. Gorfein & R. R. Hoffman (Eds.), *Memory and cognitive processes: The Ebbinghaus Centennial Conference* (pp. 349–379). Hillsdale, NJ: Lawrence Erlbaum Associates.

Roediger, H. L., & McDermott, K. B. (1993). Implicit memory in normal human subjects. In F. Boller & J. Erafman (Eds.), *Handbook of neuropsychology* (Vol. 8, pp. 63–131). Amsterdam: Elsevier.

Roediger, H. L., Srinivas, K., & Weldon, M. S. (1989). Dissociations between implicit measures of retention. In S. Lewandowsky, J. C. Dunn, & K. Kirsner (Eds.). *Implicit memory: Theoretical issues*. Hillsdale, NJ: Lawrence Erlbaum Associates.

Rogers, T. B., Kuiper, N. A., & Kirker, W. S. (1977). Self reference and the encoding of personal information. *Journal of Personality and Social Psychology, 35*, 677–688.

Ross, M., & Conway, M. (1986). Remembering one's own past: The construction of personal histories. In R. M. Sorrentino & E. T. Higgins (Eds.), *Handbook of motivation and cognition* (pp. 122–144). New York: Guilford Press.

Rothbart, M., Evans, M., & Fulero, S. (1979). Recall for confirming events: Memory processes and the maintenance of social stereotyping. *Journal of Experimental Social Psychology, 15*, 343–355.

Rothbart, M., & John, O. P. (1985). Social categorization and behavioral episodes: A cognitive analysis of the effects of intergroup contact. *Journal of Social Issues, 41*(3), 81–104.

Rumelhart, D. E., & McClelland, J. L. (1986). PDP models and general issues in cognitive science. In D. E. Rumelhart, J. L. McClelland, & the PDP Research Group (Eds.), *Parallel distributed processing* (Vol. 1, pp. 110–146). Cambridge, MA: MIT Press.

Rumelhart, D. E., McClelland, J. L., & the PDP Research Group (Eds.). (1986). *Parallel distributed processing* (Vol. 1). Cambridge, MA: MIT Press.

Rumelhart, D. E., Smolensky, P., McClelland, J. L., & Hinton, G. E. (1986). Schemata and sequential thought processes in PDP models. In J. L. McClelland & D. E. Rumelhart (Eds.), *Parallel distributed processing: Explorations in the microstructure of cognition* (Vol. 2, pp. 7–57). Cambridge, MA: MIT Press.

Sagar, H. A., & Schofield, J. W. (1980). Racial and behavioral cues in black and white children's perceptions of ambiguously aggressive acts. *Journal of Personality and Social Psychology, 39*, 590–598.

Sanitioso, R., Kunda, Z., & Fong, G. T. (1990). Motivated recruitment of autobiographical memories. *Journal of Personality and Social Psychology, 59*, 229–241.

Schacter, D. L. (1987). Implicit memory: History and current status. *Journal of Experimental Psychology: Learning, Memory, and Cognition, 13*, 501–518.

Schacter, D. L. (1994). Priming and multiple memory systems: Perceptual mechanisms of implicit memory. In D. L. Schacter & E. Tulving (Eds.), *Memory systems 1994* (pp. 233–268). Cambridge, MA: MIT Press.

Schacter, D. L., & Tulving, E. (Eds.). (1994). *Memory systems 1994.* Cambridge, MA: MIT Press.

Schank, R., & Abelson, R. P. (1977). *Scripts, plans, goals, and understanding.* Hillsdale, NJ: Lawrence Erlbaum Associates.

Schmidt, D. F., & Sherman, R. C. (1984). Memory for persuasive messages: A test of a schema-copy-plus-tag model. *Journal of Personality and Social Psychology, 47,* 17–25.

Schul, Y., & Burnstein, E. (1990). Judging the typicality of an instance: Should the category be accessed first? *Journal of Personality and Social Psychology, 58,* 964–974.

Schuman, H., & Presser, S. (1981). *Questions and answers in attitude surveys: Experiments on question form, wording, and context.* San Diego, CA: Academic Press.

Schwarz, N., & Clore, G. L. (1983). Mood, misattribution, and judgments of well-being: Informative and directive functions of affective states. *Journal of Personality and Social Psychology, 45,* 513–523.

Seamon, J. G., Brody, N., & Kauff, D. M. (1983). Affective discrimination of stimuli that are not recognized: Effects of shadowing, masking, and cerebral laterality. *Journal of Experimental Psychology: Learning, Memory, and Cognition, 9,* 544–555.

Seidenberg, M. S. (1993). Connectionist models and cognitive theory. *Psychological Science, 4,* 228–235.

Sentis, K. P., & Burnstein, E. (1979). Remembering schema consistent information: Effects of a balance schema on recognition memory. *Journal of Personality and Social Psychology, 37,* 2200–2211.

Sharkey, A. J. C., & Sharkey, N. E. (1995). Cognitive modeling: Psychology and connectionism. In M. A. Arbib (Ed.), *Handbook of brain theory and neural networks* (pp. 200–203). Cambridge, MA: MIT Press.

Shastri, L. (1995). Structured connectionist models. In M. A. Arbib (Ed.), *Handbook of brain theory and neural networks* (pp. 949–952). Cambridge, MA: MIT Press.

Sherif, M. (1936). *The psychology of social norms.* New York: Harper.

Sherman, S. J., Judd, C. M., & Park, B. (1989). Social cognition. *Annual Review of Psychology, 40,* 281–326.

Shultz, T. R., & Lepper, M. R. (1996). *Cognitive dissonance reduction as constraint satisfaction. Psychological Review 103,* 219–240.

Singer, J. A., & Salovey, P. (1988). Mood and memory: Evaluating the network theory of affect. *Clinical Psychology Review, 8,* 211–251.

Skowronski, J. J., Betz, A. L., Thompson, C. P., Shannon, L. (1991). Social memory in everyday life: Recall of self-events and other-events. *Journal of Personality and Social Psychology, 60,* 831–843.

Sloman, S. A. (1996). The empirical case for two systems of reasoning. *Psychological Bulletin, 119,* 3–22.

Sloman, S. A., Hayman, C. A. G., Ohta, N., Law, J., & Tulving, E. (1988). Forgetting in primed fragment completion. *Journal of Experimental Psychology: Learning, Memory, and Cognition, 14,* 223–239.

Smith, E. E., & Medin, D. L. (1981). *Categories and concepts.* Cambridge, MA: Harvard University Press.

Smith, E. R. (1988). Category accessibility effects in a simulated exemplar-only memory. *Journal of Experimental Social Psychology, 24,* 448–463.

Smith, E. R. (1989). Procedural efficiency: General and specific components and effects on social judgment. *Journal of Experimental Social Psychology, 25,* 500–523.

Smith, E. R. (1990). Content and process specificity in the effects of prior experiences. Target Article in T. K. Srull & R. S. Wyer (Eds.), *Advances in social cognition* (Vol. 3, pp. 1–60). Hillsdale, NJ: Lawrence Erlbaum Associates.

Smith, E. R. (1991). Illusory correlation in a simulated exemplar-based memory. *Journal of Experimental Social Psychology, 27,* 107–123.

Smith, E. R. (1994a). Attribution theory and research: Returning to Heider's conceptions. In P. G. Devine, D. L. Hamilton, & T. M. Ostrom (Eds.), *Social cognition: Impact on social psychology* (pp. 77–108). Orlando, FL: Academic Press.

Smith, E. R. (1994b). Procedural knowledge and processing strategies in social cognition. In R. S. Wyer & T. K. Srull (Eds.), *Handbook of social cognition* (2nd ed., Vol. 1, pp. 99–151). Hillsdale, NJ: Lawrence Erlbaum Associates.

Smith, E. R. (1996). What do connectionism and social psychology offer each other? *Journal of Personality and Social Psychology, 70,* 893–912.

Smith, E. R., & Branscombe, N. R. (1987). Procedurally mediated social inferences: The case of category accessibility effects. *Journal of Experimental Social Psychology, 23,* 361–382.

Smith, E. R., & Branscombe, N. R. (1988). Category accessibility as implicit memory. *Journal of Experimental Social Psychology, 24,* 490–504.

Smith, E. R., & DeCoster, J. (in press). Knowledge acquisition, accessibility, and use in person perception and stereotyping: Simulation with a recurrent connectionist network. *Journal of Personality and Social Psychology.*

Smith, E. R., & Miller, F. D. (1979). Attributional information processing: A response time model of causal subtraction. *Journal of Personality and Social Psychology, 37,* 1723–1731.

Smith, E. R., & Miller, F. D. (1983). Mediation among attributional inferences and comprehension processes: Initial findings and a general method. *Journal of Personality and Social Psychology, 44,* 492–505.

Smith, E. R., Stewart, T. L., & Buttram, R. T. (1992). Inferring a trait from a behavior has long-term, highly specific effects. *Journal of Personality and Social Psychology, 62,* 753–759.

Smith, E. R., & Zárate, M. A. (1990). Exemplar and prototype use in social categorization. *Social Cognition, 8,* 243–262.

Smith, E. R., & Zárate, M. A. (1992). Exemplar-based model of social judgment. *Psychological Review, 99,* 3–21.

Smolensky, P. (1988). On the proper treatment of connectionism. *Behavioral and Brain Sciences, 11,* 1–74.

Squire, L. R. (1994). Declarative and nondeclarative memory: Multiple brain systems supporting learning and memory. In D. L. Schacter & E. Tulving (Eds.), *Memory systems 1994* (pp. 203–232). Cambridge, MA: MIT Press.

Srull, T. K. (1981). Person memory: Some tests of associative storage and retrieval models. *Journal of Experimental Psychology: Human Learning and Memory, 7,* 440–463.

Srull, T. K. (1984). Methodological techniques for the study of person memory and social cognition. In R. S. Wyer & T. K. Srull (Eds.), *Handbook of social cognition* (Vol. 2, pp. 1–72). Hillsdale, NJ: Lawrence Erlbaum Associates.

Srull, T. K., Lichtenstein, M., & Rothbart, M. (1985). Associative storage and retrieval processes in person memory. *Journal of Experimental Psychology: Learning, Memory, and Cognition, 11,* 316–345.

Srull, T. K., & Wyer, R. S. (1979). The role of category accessibility in the interpretation of information about persons: Some determinants and implications. *Journal of Personality and Social Psychology, 37,* 1660–1672.

Stangor, C., & McMillan, D. (1992). Memory for expectancy-congruent and expectancy-incongruent information: A review of the social and social developmental literatures. *Psychological Bulletin, 111,* 42–61.

Strack, F., & Martin, L. L. (1987). Thinking, judging, and communicating: A process account of context effects in attitude surveys. In H.-J. Hippler, N. Schwarz, & S. Sudman (Eds.), *Social information processing and survey methodology* (pp. 123–148). New York: Springer-Verlag.

Thompson, C. P., Skowronski, J. J., Larsen, S. F., & Betz, A. L. (1996). *Autobiographical memory: Remembering what and remembering when.* Hillsdale, NJ: Lawrence Erlbaum Associates.

Thorpe, S. (1995). Localized and distributed representations. In M. A. Arbib (Ed.), *Handbook of brain theory and neural networks* (pp. 549–552). Cambridge, MA: MIT Press.

Tourangeau, R., & Rasinski, K. A. (1988). Cognitive processes underlying context effects in attitude measurement. *Psychological Bulletin, 103,* 299–314.

Touretzky, D. S. (1995). Connectionist and symbolic representation. In M. A. Arbib (Ed.), *Handbook of brain theory and neural networks* (pp. 243–247). Cambridge, MA: MIT Press.

Tulving, E. (1972). Episodic and semantic memory. In E. Tulving & W. Donaldson (Eds.), *Organization of memory.* New York: Academic.

Tulving, E., Schacter, D. L., & Stark, H. (1982). Priming effects in word-fragment completion are independent of recognition memory. *Journal of Experimental Psychology: Learning, Memory, and Cognition, 8,* 336–342.

Turner, J. C., Oakes, P. J., Haslam, S. A., & McGarty, C. (1994). Self and collective: Cognition and social context. *Personality and Social Psychology Bulletin, 20,* 454–463.

Uleman, J. S., Moskowitz, G. B., Roman, R. J., & Rhee, E. (1993). Tacit, manifest, and intentional reference: How spontaneous trait inferences refer to persons. *Social Cognition, 11,* 321–351.

Vallacher, R. R., & Nowak, A. (1994). *Dynamical systems in social psychology.* Orlando, FL: Academic Press.

van Gelder, T. (1991). What is the "D" in "PDP"? A survey of the concept of distribution. In W. Ramsey, S. P. Stitch, & D. E. Rumelhart (Eds.), *Philosophy and connectionist theory* (pp. 33–60). Hillsdale, NJ: Lawrence Erlbaum Associates.

von Hippel, W., Jonides, J., Hilton, J. L., & Narayan, S. (1993). Inhibitory effect of schematic processing on perceptual encoding. *Journal of Personality and Social Psychology, 64,* 921–935.

Whittlesea, B. W. A. (1987). Preservation of specific experiences in the representation of general knowledge. *Journal of Experimental Psychology: Learning, Memory, and Cognition, 13,* 3–17.

Whittlesea, B. W. A., & Dorken, M. D. (1993). Incidentally, things in general are particularly determined: An episodic-processing account of implicit learning. *Journal of Experimental Psychology: General, 122,* 227–248.

Wiles, J., & Humphreys, M. S. (1993). Using artificial neural nets to model implicit and explicit memory test performance. In P. Graf & M. E. J. Masson (Eds.), *Implicit memory: New directions in cognition, development, and neuropsychology* (pp. 141–165). Hillsdale, NJ: Lawrence Erlbaum Associates.

Wilson, T. D. (1990). Self-persuasion via self-reflection. In J. M. Olson & M. P. Zanna (Eds.), *Self-inference processes: The Ontario Symposium* (Vol. 6, pp. 43–68). Hillsdale, NJ: Lawrence Erlbaum Associates.

Wilson, T. D., & Hodges, S. D. (1992). Attitudes as temporary constructions. In L. L. Martin & A. Tesser (Eds.), *The construction of social judgments* (pp. 37–65). Hillsdale, NJ: Lawrence Erlbaum Associates.

Winter, L., & Uleman, J. S. (1984). When are social judgments made? Evidence for the spontaneousness of trait inferences. *Journal of Personality and Social Psychology, 47,* 237–252.

Winter, L., Uleman, J. S., & Cunniff, C. (1985). How automatic are social judgments? *Journal of Personality and Social Psychology, 49,* 904–917.

Woll, S. B., & Graesser, A. C. (1982). Memory discrimination for information typical or atypical of person schemata. *Social Cognition, 1,* 287–310.

Wyer, R. S. (Ed.) (1994). *Associated systems theory: A systematic approach to cognitive representations of persons.* Hillsdale, NJ: Lawrence Erlbaum Associates.

Wyer, R. S., & Carlston, D. E. (1994). The cognitive representation of persons and events. In R. S. Wyer & T. K. Srull (Eds.), *Handbook of Social Cognition* (2nd ed., pp. 41–98). Hillsdale, NJ: Lawrence Erlbaum Associates.

Wyer, R. S., & Gordon, S. E. (1984). The cognitive representation of social information. In R. S. Wyer & T. K. Srull (Eds.), *Handbook of social cognition* (Vol. 2, pp. 73–150). Hillsdale, NJ: Lawrence Erlbaum Associates.

Wyer, R. S., & Srull, T. K. (1980). The processing of social stimulus information: A conceptual integration. In R. Hastie, T. M. Ostrom, E. B. Ebbesen, R. S. Wyer, D. Hamilton, & D. E. Carlston (Eds.), *Person memory* (pp. 227–300). Hillsdale, NJ: Lawrence Erlbaum Associates.

Wyer, R. S., & Srull, T. K. (1989). *Memory and cognition in its social context.* Hillsdale, NJ: Lawrence Erlbaum Associates.

Zadny, J., & Gerard, H. B. (1974). Attributed intentions and information selectivity. *Journal of Experimental Social Psychology, 10,* 34–52.

Zajonc, R. B. (1968). Attitudinal effects of mere exposure. *Journal of Personality and Social Psychology, 9,* Monograph Suppl. No. 2, part 2.

Zajonc, R. B. (1980). Feeling and thinking: Preferences need no inferences. *American Psychologist, 35,* 151–175.

CHAPTER TEN

CONTROL AND AUTOMATICITY IN SOCIAL LIFE

DANIEL M. WEGNER, *University of Virginia*
JOHN A. BARGH, *New York University*

Topics come and go in social psychology, and this is one that is coming. This is the first *Handbook of Social Psychology* with a chapter devoted to the role of control and automaticity in social life. *Handbooks* have varied somewhat over the years in how they subdivide the field, acting as barometers to measure the relative importance of topics over time—so we are happy to note that this time around control and automaticity have surfaced as key concepts in the way social psychology is being understood.

These are not, however, flash-in-the-pan ideas. The distinction between automaticity and control of behavior has been with us at least since David Hartley remarked in *Observations on Man* (1749) that "The *Motions* of the body are of two kinds, *automatic* and *voluntary*." Notions of control and automaticity have far earlier pedigrees than this, however, in the philosophical study of free will and determinism, and have resurfaced in psychology as fundamental themes in the debates earlier in this century between the cognitivists and behaviorists. Perhaps as a reflection of these foundations, and also for contemporary reasons we examine in this chapter, it now turns out that control and automaticity have developed into mature and important organizing ideas for the understanding of social behavior. The tricky questions of when and how people control their behavior, and the related but not identical questions of when and how behavior occurs automatically, have arrived in scientific social psychology with a bang. In this chapter, we ask these questions and review what is currently known or surmised about their answers.

As a first step in this analysis, we consider the classic studies of the field with a view toward exploring how concerns about control or automaticity of behavior have been historically central to the field. The middle sections of the chapter serve to define the concepts of control and automaticity in greater detail, first by looking at the nature of each idea and then by considering how they are interrelated. The final major section treats the social psychological literature on a series of topics for which issues of control and automaticity have special relevance. These include attitudes, social cognition, emotion, and expressive behavior.

THEMES OF CONTROL AND AUTOMATICITY IN THE CLASSIC EXPERIMENTS

Even with the capricious comings and goings of topics in social psychology considered over time, there is considerable unanimity in what social psychologists currently see as the core ideas of the field. We make this claim on the basis of a small and decidedly nonrandom sample of social psychologists we recently asked to help us identify the field's classic experiments. As it happens, they seem to settle on the same list almost every time.

The studies nominated for this honor usually include Milgram's (1963) obedience experiments, Asch's (1952) conformity studies, Schachter and Singer's (1962) emotion

Work on this chapter was supported in part by the National Institute of Mental Health Grant MH 49127 and a fellowship from the Center for Advanced Study in the Behavioral Sciences to Wegner and by the National Science Foundation Grant SBR-9409448 to Bargh. Our thanks to Serena Chen, Bella DePaulo, Ap Dijksterhuis, Jonathan Haidt, Neil Macrae, Leonard Newman, Jim Uleman, Robin Vallacher, and Cheryl Witt for their help and comments.

experiments, Festinger and Carlsmith's (1959) cognitive dissonance study, the Darley and Latané (1968) helping experiments, and the Haney, Banks, and Zimbardo (1973) prison simulation. There are other extremely classic and wonderful ones, of course, and this particular selection is certainly influenced by our personal taste and age and sex and politics and other shortcomings. We nonetheless suggest it here because these studies are ones that most students of our field will know in some detail, and they serve as useful points of departure for an analysis of control and automaticity in the field as it now stands.

What do these classic studies have in common? This question by itself could occupy an entire seminar on social psychology, as there are many intriguing resemblances and themes. Perhaps the most obvious theme, though, is the emphasis on the situational causation of behavior. As Ross and Nisbett (1991) have reminded us so well, social psychology is the study of situational determinants of thought, emotion, and behavior, and its best-known findings highlight the power and insidiousness of situational forces. These classic studies share a focus on what the individual does when he or she has to decide or respond in difficult circumstances, under extreme duress, unusually quickly, or in an otherwise stressful, uncomfortable position. As a rule, people in these powerful situations don't acquit themselves very well, as they succumb to pressures that make them do things ranging from merely uncharitable to frighteningly robotic.

Classic social psychology, in other words, makes people appear to be automatons. The situational influences on behavior investigated in these studies often were (a) *unintended* on the part of the individual, (b) not something of which the person was *aware,* (c) a response to the situation occurring before the individual had a chance to reflect on what to do (i.e., *efficient*), or (d) *difficult to control or inhibit* even when the person was cognizant of the influence. As it happens, these are characteristics of automatic psychological processes, not of conscious control, and comprise a handy working definition of automaticity (Bargh, 1994). Let's take a quick look at the classics to see how one or more of these features surface in each case.

The Classic Experiments

Consider first the Festinger and Carlsmith (1959) study, in which a participant is asked to mislead another person into believing that a boring task is interesting. Participants themselves come to believe that the boring task is fun as a result, but only when they are paid just a dollar for their deception. Those paid $20 do not change their attitudes. Many later studies showed that such attitude change occurs only when the participant believes he or she has free choice in lying to the other person (Brehm & Cohen, 1962; Wicklund & Brehm, 1976). Thus, it would not have been possible to obtain the original cognitive dissonance findings if the participants in Festinger and Carlsmith (1959) had been *aware* of the power of the experimenter's request in instigating their behavior. Action occurring without awareness was the starting point for this classic finding.

The same issue seems to have come up in Asch's investigations of conformity to group pressure. In fact, Asch (1952) was expressly interested in whether his participants were aware of the sources of their own conformity. He conducted variations of the basic line-judgment paradigm to see if people knew that the majority influence had made them conform, and to see whether they had deliberately or unintentionally abandoned their own private opinions. On the basis of these studies, Asch (1952, p. 182) concluded: "Of significance is the fact that the members lacked awareness that they drew their strength from the majority, and that their reactions would change drastically if they faced the dissenter individually." Thus, in the Asch conformity paradigm, participants also show a *lack of awareness* of the influence that the situation has in determining their behavior.

As part of his obedience research, Milgram (1963, 1974) focused on a different aspect of automaticity. He attempted to document the *counter-intentional* nature of his participants' behavior. For example, he gave a sample of 100 psychiatrists, college students, and middle-class adults a description of the experimental procedure and asked them to predict what they would do in the experimental session, were they to take the part of the "teacher" participant instructed by the experimenter to shock the "learning" participant. All these respondents said that they would stop before 300 volts, and most said that they would stop giving shocks much earlier than that, regardless of the experimenter's requests and demands that they continue. The actual results were quite different, of course; very few of the actual participants in any variation of the experiment disobeyed the experimenter before 300 volts had ostensibly been delivered to the victim. Participants did things, then, that opposed the best estimates of their likely intentions.

The Milgram studies also illustrate the *efficiency* of the processes that lead people to obey. People in these studies obeyed pretty much "on the spot," without a lot of time to reflect on their behavior. When people are given time to reflect, and so can turn over in their minds what they will be doing and what its consequences may be, more effortful and less efficient processes can take over. The effect of this is that people decide to behave differently, and the degree of obedience is actually reduced (Sherman, 1980). Again, then, a classic study illustrates a form of human automatic behavior rather than control.

This is also true of Schachter and Singer's (1962) research on emotion. In their model, a state of physiological arousal produced by situational events becomes experienced as an emotion by virtue of the person's cognitive interpretation of the situational meaning of the arousal. For their research, arousal was manipulated through an administration of adrenaline to some participants but not others, but only some of the participants in each condition were informed of the possible excitatory side effects of this "learning drug." During the experiment, a confederate reacted visibly to the assigned task either with euphoria or anger, and this influenced the mood of the uninformed but not the informed participants. That is, participants lacked awareness of the cause of their emotional experience, and if not supplied with a cause by the experimenter, used the confederate's emotional expression as a cue as to how they themselves felt.

Although neither Schachter and Singer (1962) nor Schachter (1964) remark on the awareness or intentionality of this interpretive process, the tenor of their analysis is that people are actively and intentionally looking at the situation and its features and using these to construct the meaning of the physiological state that they are experiencing. However, Schachter and Singer (1962) did not ascribe to people any great degree of accuracy or sensitivity in detecting the true source of the emotional reaction. (Indeed, Schachter's [1964, p. 79] discussion of the source of emotion labels closely followed Skinner's [1953, chap. 17] analysis concerning one's lack of access to the cause of private, internal events.) If people were generally *aware* of the true reasons for their emotional state, it would not have been possible for Schachter and Singer (1962) to move the reported subjective experience around by virtue of how the experimental confederate reacted to the same situation.

Were participants in the Darley and Latané (1968) experiments on bystander intervention aware of the effect that the number of people present had on their likelihood to help? The authors addressed this question by asking all participants whether the presence (or absence) of others had affected their decision to help or not to help. Although all participants reported being aware of the presence of others, they nonetheless did not feel that it made any difference to their behavior (Darley & Latané, 1968, p. 381). In fact, this very *lack of awareness* was taken as a sign of hope by the authors that things could be different, as they ended their article on this optimistic note: "If people understand the situational forces that can make them hesitate to intervene, they may better overcome them" (p. 383). In these studies, it is also clear that participants were behaving in a rushed, impromptu fashion, and thus needed to rely on *efficient* rather than time-consuming judgment processes.

The final classic study we consider is the Haney, Banks, and Zimbardo (1973) prison simulation study, in which the basement of the Stanford psychology building was turned into a mock prison that nevertheless became quite real for its occupants. Randomly assigned to the role of guard or prisoner, participants were so *unable to control or inhibit*

the powerful effect of their assigned role that they seemed to forget that it was only an experiment that they could leave at any time. When told they were eligible for parole, 60 percent of the prisoner participants said they would forfeit all money earned for participation in order to be released, oblivious to the fact that as participants in an experiment they could have left at any time if they were willing to forego payment. This study is known for its demonstration of the transforming power of the guard and prisoner roles on the personalities of the participants, turning them into sadistic or servile creatures, respectively—behavior that ran *counter to the participant's intentions* as to how to behave in that situation, as assessed by self-report personality inventories and the participants' responses during the lengthy debriefing process. The participants reported regretting their inability to inhibit the responses to the situation, both as guards and as prisoners.

The classic experiments all seem to highlight a basic conflict between the automaticity of behavior and the desire to control it. In each case, we find people behaving in ways they do not seem to control, but which are at the same time so morally reprehensible or just plain blockheaded that they cry out for control. Participants in these studies believe their own hypocritical lies, make patently dishonest judgments in order to conform, obey instructions to hurt others, blindly mimic others' emotions, ignore the plight of people in distress, or adhere slavishly to assigned roles. They seem to be led almost casually out of control. Each classic experiment is a morality play in which Everyperson is led astray by his or her unwitting susceptibility to social influence, lapsing into unaware automaticity at the precise juncture when conscious control seems so important. The haunting suspicion that people should "know better" appears everywhere in the classics, and it is this fundamental observation that fuels much of the social psychological interest in the nature of control and automaticity.

The Experimental Control of Personal Control

In a way, this had to happen. An emphasis on automaticity is a natural result of the social psychological desire to observe *genuine* behavior. Researchers don't want to be fooled by a participant's self-presentations or deceptive motivations, and in the pursuit of genuineness, they restrict the focus of the experiment's microscope to items that the person couldn't control or even be interested in controlling. Behavior that occurs without an individual's awareness, or that occurs quickly, unintentionally, or uncontrollably, after all, seems to have a stamp of genuineness on it—it is the *real* response to the situation, not just something the person has devised for the experimenter's amusement or misdirection. In the attempt to rule out these strategic explanations, experimental social psychology's special brand of "principled argumentation'' (Abelson, 1995) emphasizes automaticity with little room for control.

In fact, research specifically attempting to rule out control or strategic activity of any kind must often create unusual and extreme behavior settings to make sure control is not happening. Studies attempt to rule out control by blocking participants' awareness entirely (e.g., by subliminal stimulation), for instance, or by seriously crippling the participants' expenditure of effort on inefficient mental processes (e.g., by imposing mental load or time pressure). Researchers have tried to ensure that the behavior they observe in participants is so unwanted that it couldn't possibly be intentional, and they delight in producing situations that have such profound influence on participants that the participants cannot inhibit the behavior even when they deeply desire to do so. Only when stringent experimental controls of personal control are imposed, in other words, do participants show behaviors that can be classified as truly automatic (Bargh, 1989; Wegner & Pennebaker, 1993).

In one sense, these observations suggest that contemporary social psychology is a science of automaticity, not control (Bargh, 1997; Howard & Conway, 1986). The evidence accrued in the classic experiments and their progeny points regularly to situational causes of behavior that participants had no ability or opportunity to control, and that therefore seems irrelevant to the nature of control processes. In another sense, though, this massive scientific effort aimed at the prevention of control processes in the pursuit of forms of automatic behavior suggests that control processes themselves must be profoundly powerful indeed. The entire edifice of social psychological experimental method strains to extinguish the gleam of control in even the most tightly shuttered experimental closet, and still control shines through here and there.

Control also shines through in the classics. After all, it is not the case that the behaviors people performed in these studies were all done with perfect automaticity. The behaviors were certainly not *all* performed without any awareness, while at the same time occurring efficiently, unintentionally, and beyond inhibition. Rather, one or the other of these aspects of automaticity was created in the experiment for a time, and this disabling of control was enough to allow the experimenters to conclude that the observed behavior was a genuine response to the situation. In all likelihood, people in these studies were quite in control of *some* behavior in the experiment, just not the one of interest to the experimenter. Participants in a conformity experiment may have been trying desperately not to look silly to the other participants in the room, for example, whereas those in an obedience study may have been working hard consciously to control their emotions as they dealt with the conflicting pressures they were feeling.

Control processes were evident in the classic experiments when participants accepted instructions on what to do—and then did what they were told. This seems a pedestrian observation indeed, but its apparent subtlety masks its considerable importance. The fact is, people participating in the classic experiments were almost always conscious of an intention, following a plan, putting forth effort in thinking about some aspect of their activity, and inhibiting or controlling certain behaviors. Social psychological research has long depended on the ability of people to do many different things in response to instruction, even though it is only recently that the person's instructed performance has come to be understood as a key focus in the study of control processes (Wegner & Pennebaker, 1993).

What this means is that control is not absent in the world at large just because researchers are interested in aspects of behavior that are automatic in experiments. Instead, it makes sense to understand human behavior in experiments and elsewhere as consisting of elements of both automaticity and control. As we shall see, the broader part of behavior in social situations is governed by a welter of automatic processes, many of which do end up yielding exactly the kinds of mindless gestures recorded in the classic experiments. Against this backdrop of automaticity, however, there is also an important, powerful thread of conscious control. Psychological processes that are simultaneously open to awareness, intentional, inefficient, and able to be inhibited do exist, and are linked together into the chain of our waking social lives.

The nature and interplay of these control and automatic sources of behavior are matters of continuing discovery in our field. Because experimental social research has dug the idea of control into something of a hole, we begin our excavations in the analyses that follow by considering control first. As we shall see, it turns out that the idea of control is down in that hole because it is the foundation concept on which an understanding of automaticity stands.

THE NATURE OF CONTROL

Psychological control is a mental process that produces behavior. We begin in this section by considering first the scientific status of control. Then, we turn to the key elements of control in human and other systems. Next, we explore the larger problem of locating control processes in conscious life and considering how it is that consciousness can be said to control behavior. We then examine the *sense* of control to distinguish it from control per se and to review its separate psychological consequences.

Science and Control: From the Ghost to the Machine

The control of behavior strikes some people as mysterious, like ESP or crop circles. This is because behavior that is controlled is frequently understood to be the opposite of behavior that is determined. In this view, control is what is left over once the scientific analysis of behavior is completed. As we have seen, the strategy of classic research in social psychology has often been to limit or circumvent the operation of voluntary or control processes with a view toward discovering those automatic forces that determine behavior. In this way of thinking, it seems that the best role left over for a concept of control is as some kind of homunculus—an agent, spirit, or magical entity that has the special property of *being able to do things that are not caused.*

Consternation over this kind of control has troubled psychologists and philosophers alike, and the whole study of goal-oriented activity on the part of humans has carried on under something of a cloud as a result (Wegner & Vallacher, 1987). The philosopher Gilbert Ryle (1949) referred to conscious control as "the ghost in the machine," for example, and dismissed the theory of psychological control as inconsistent with the causal determinism of behavior. He reasoned that the ghost is unnecessary if all it does is haunt the machine that actually churns out everything the person does. And even if the ghost could have an influence on the machine, Dennett (1984) has observed that this hardly provides a kind of free will worth wanting. A controller whose primary activity in life is doing things that are not caused by prior events seems no more than a capricious imp one would not trust with a water balloon.

Why then retain the concept of psychological control? For one thing, most people have an unshakeably insistent sense that they control their behavior in accord with their conscious thoughts and attitudes, and this should not be ignored as long as we hope to continue to stay on speaking terms with the human race. More important, though, is the realization that control is not the opposite of determinism. The way in which people control their behavior is no less determined than the way in which their automatic behavior occurs. Control is merely one conduit by which the determinants of behavior express their influence. Far from the ghost in the machine, then, the process of control is a particularly interesting *machine* in the machine.

This approach may strip away the mystery of control too completely, leaving it naked and squinting in the light. The sense that we humans cause our actions is indeed compelling, and any analysis that offends this sense runs the risk of prompt rejection. We believe that this sense or feeling of control is not good evidence that the ghostly form of control exists, however, as there are people who sense that they control the rotation of the earth and that certainly doesn't mean they do. The sense of control is itself an intriguing property of humans that can be conceptualized as an effect and as a cause of deterministic processes. As we shall see, there is much to be gained by viewing psychological control simply as a process that produces behavior, a process that has certain fundamental characteristics no

matter whether the behavior issues from humans, animals, plants, or machines. (Ghosts, however, need not apply.)

The initial discovery that control in humans could be studied in this way is widely attributed to Norbert Wiener's (1948) *Cybernetics,* a book that introduced a computational approach to the problems of control—although glimmerings of the idea are also found in Craik (1948). The use of self-guiding mechanisms had swept the field of engineering in the years just before and after World War II, and it was a natural next step to consider how such control systems might model human thought and behavior (Heims, 1991). Simple mechanical gadgets such as the thermostat, the engine governor, and the logic circuit could be given goals (e.g., 72 Fahrenheit, 2400 RPM, "True"), and they could then regulate the behavior of systems such that those goals could be met. Although it seems perfectly natural now to describe humans as intelligent machines containing control systems, this was a revolutionary idea at the time, as it broke down many of Ryle's and other behaviorists' objections to the study of a "ghost" that behaved in accord with unobservable purposes and goals. Eventually, this breakthrough produced a large literature on control in humans, and it is to the elements of such control that we turn next.

Elements of Control

At the most basic level, to control something is just to influence it in a certain direction. A hat controls hair, for instance, and a person holding a leash controls a dog. We don't usually call influence "control" when its direction is random or unknown. So, for example, we wouldn't say that a tropical windstorm controls hair or that a roomful of humpable knees controls a dog.

These intuitions about the everyday meaning of control coincide well with formal analyses of the elements of control, as such analyses typically begin by distinguishing two features of control—a *control action* (the influence) and a *control criterion* (the direction). Control involves acting upon something until a certain criterion is reached. In the case of the hat, the control action is rather static, as the criterion involves simply keeping the hair from escaping. The case of walking a dog on a leash illustrates dynamic control, in turn, as the criterion might be to get the dog moving toward the park and the action might involve pulling at the leash while the dog leans hard toward something that smells interesting.

Control theories also make a general distinction between the input and output of a control process. The *input* to a control process is information from outside the control system that sets the criterion. The desire to "keep my hair down" might be thought of as the input when a person puts on a hat, whereas the person's desire to "walk the dog to the park" might be thought of as the input in the case of the person walking the dog on the leash. What the hair or the dog does, in turn, is commonly called the control system's *output*. The output is the behavior of the target of control.

There is a distinction between open-loop and closed-loop control in engineering that is particularly important for psychology. An *open-loop* control system (also sometimes called a *feedforward* system) is one in which the control action is independent of the system's output. So, for instance, a timed microwave oven is an open-loop system because the action (microwaving) is set to a criterion (say, 4 minutes for microwave popcorn) and doesn't change as a result of the system's output (the temperature or doneness of the popcorn). A *closed-loop* control system (also called a *feedback* system) is one in which the control action is somehow dependent on the system's output. Some ovens come with an attached meat thermometer, for example, that can be inserted in a roast and that will turn off the oven when the meat reaches a preset temperature.

Although a meat thermometer may not quite capture the excitement we were hoping to create here ("C'mere, everybody! Look what they're writing about now!"), we wish to emphasize that closed-loop control is important for conceptualizing human self-control of behavior. This is largely because closed-loop control is more effective than open-loop control in any circumstance in which there is variability—and life throws lots of variability our way. Microwave oven popcorn is notoriously variable, too, for instance, so it is no wonder that when we only get to set the cooking time (an open loop) we end up sometimes with unpopped kernels and others with a bag of cinders. Occasionally the instructions on the bag will tell us to listen for the number of pops per second late in the time interval, and this adds a measure of closed-loop control to the system that can up our hit rate on decent popcorn. But really, it would be nice to have a microwave with a popcorn doneness sensor and enjoy closed-loop control all the time.

Open-loop control can be thought of as control that begins with a very specific plan, and then sticks to it. This kind of control involves starting off with the control criterion already set, and then not checking again to see if the control criterion is being met. Open-loop control is what we humans do when we must behave very quickly or when there's no chance for adjustment, and it probably also corresponds to the starting point of many of our behaviors. When we set out to do something, after all, we don't just begin blindly doing anything at all and then check to see whether that random act got us any closer to the control criterion (Carver & Scheier, 1990). We begin with a launch plan of sorts. Open-loop control, in this sense, is more characteristic of an automatic process than a control process, and there are many automatic processes that function just to "launch" behavior in this way, with no further steering or guidance. What this means is that the *essence of control is the closing of the loop*, the connection between

the system's control action and its prior output. In contrast to automaticity, control involves making adjustments to the output through further control action when prior outputs haven't met the control criterion.

The idea that controlled human behavior stems from closed-loop control systems has appeared in a variety of psychological theories. Perhaps the best-known feedback theory in psychology is the test-operate-test-exit or TOTE unit introduced by Miller, Galanter, and Pribram (1960; see Figure 1). These theorists proposed that the influence of plans on human behavior could be modeled by a control system that exerts control actions to reduce the incongruity between a behavioral output and a control criterion. The TOTE sequence (1) tests for the degree to which the output is consistent with a control criterion, (2) operates a control action to increase congruity with the criterion, and (3) tests again for the degree to which output matches the control criterion. If it doesn't match, the control action is initiated again (2), but if it matches, then (4) the loop is exited. A TOTE unit of this kind provides a general way of understanding how people might control behaviors all the way from hammering a nail into a board through getting a Nobel Prize. In essence, every such behavior involves multiple iterations of two events: doing something and checking to see whether what was done achieved the goal.

Although we commonly think of control in terms of the "operate" function—after all, that's the part of control that actually supplies influence—the "test" function of the TOTE unit reminds us of the other important element of control: the *comparator* or *monitor* (Powers, 1973). For successful feedback, some comparison must be made between the control system's output and the control criterion. If one is trying to impress the boss by stamping out the answers to math problems with one's foot, for example, it would be nice to know whether one is in fact making a good impression. A monitoring or comparing process must somehow be built into any control system such that the control action will occur whenever there is a discrepancy. The monitor learns of the discrepancy and "feeds back" by initiating the control action.

Control has been described in a different way by Newell and Simon (1972) in terms of what they call production systems—control systems that operate through a series of conditional or if-then statements. One could write a computer program to get a robot down the street, for example, with statements in it such as "if the traffic light is red, then stop," "if the traffic light is green, then go," "if going and right foot on pavement, then step with left foot," and "if going and left foot on pavement, then step with right foot." A list of such statements could be reviewed repeatedly such that when any "if" turns out to be true, the associated "then" is produced. The program's repeated review of these conditional statements is continually "watching" for each of the conditions, monitoring the relation of the robot

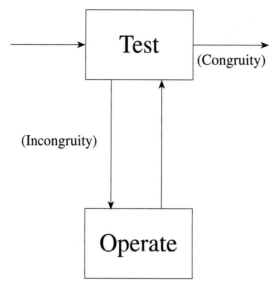

FIGURE 1   A TOTE Unit.

to the environment to determine whether each control action should be taken. The production system is monitoring the robot's progress.

In a sense, then, control involves constant or repeated vigilance, a kind of self-consciousness or self-knowledge that is wired into the control system. The test process is more than a mere error-checker, in this light—it is the critical element that creates the "loop" whereby the system is influenced by its own past actions. Any system that is reflexive in this way has special properties that make it fundamentally more adaptive (and unpredictable) than systems that do not (Hofstadter, 1979). The scientific study of nonlinear dynamical systems and chaos (Gleick, 1987; Vallacher & Nowak, 1994) involves the mathematical description and understanding of just such reflexive systems.

It may have been the resemblance of this reflexive feature of control to the self-awareness people feel in social situations (Duval & Wicklund, 1972; Wicklund, 1975) that inspired Carver and Scheier (1981, 1990) to introduce a general theory focused on the role of self-awareness in the control process. This theory suggests that the adjustments people make in their social behavior arise because self-attention prompts people to reduce discrepancies between their actual behavior and standards of correctness. Noticing that one is not being as helpful as one would like to be (Duval, Duval, & Neely, 1979), for example, or as aggressive as one would hope (Carver, 1975) or as unprejudiced as one would prefer (Macrae, Bodenhausen, & Milne, 1995), all involve monitoring how discrepant one's behavior is from a control criterion. Experimentally increasing self-focused attention beyond its natural levels enhances

control in each of these cases, and this points to the crucial role of the monitoring process in the occurrence of control.

A final important element of control processes is the setting of the control criterion—how the control system's input is achieved. When we set a thermostat to a particular temperature and let it control the furnace, for example, we provide the input to the system by giving the thermostat a control criterion. The question of how criteria are set for human control is sometimes just this simple; our commanding officer in the military may set us to "march" or to "shoot" and we may accept that input without question (Milgram, 1974). Miller et al. (1960) suggest, too, that this is how hypnosis operates. The control criterion is set by the hypnotist and the hypnotic subject then acts as a control system seeking that criterion. Environmental reminders can suggest control criteria to us when we are not hypnotized, of course, and so set us toward the purposes they suggest (Bargh & Barndollar, 1996; Bargh & Gollwitzer, 1994).

Sometimes people set their control criteria themselves. When we choose without any obvious external urging to go to college or to take up selling drugs, for example, it could be said that we have set our own control criteria. Carver and Scheier (1981) and Powers (1973) have suggested that the setting of such criteria is the output of a prior control system, and that it is thus possible to imagine a hierarchy of control systems in which the outputs of those above provide inputs for those below. The development of conscious plans to behave, in this light, is the output of a control system that selects from among different alternative actions, perhaps in accord with broader principles or values. The person who chooses college over selling drugs may do so because of a higher-order control system with a control criterion set to "be good."

Choosing states of mind may follow this pattern as well. Wegner and Wenzlaff (1996) propose that such *mental control* involves a *mental state selection process* that functions to set us in pursuit of particular mental states. So, for instance, when we get it in our heads that we want to avoid thinking about an old flame, that we want to fall asleep, or that we want to stop being angry, these goals are often set for us by a higher-level process that decides that a certain mental state would be good in our particular situation. Although we may experience a variety of mental states just because they are elicited automatically by our environments, we can also intentionally control them when control criteria are set that institute mental states as goals.

Knowing whether an input to a control system comes from inside or outside the person may ultimately be less important than knowing simply what it is. As it turns out, inputs to control systems can occur *under different descriptions,* and this turns out to be particularly crucial for understanding how actions are launched and how they are then monitored. Actions can be identified at various levels, stretching from low-level details to higher-level purposes or effects (Vallacher & Wegner, 1985, 1987; Wegner & Vallacher, 1986). Someone who "shoots a person," for example, can also be said to have done what might be identified at lower levels as "moving a finger" or "pulling a trigger." The act might also admit to higher-level identities such as "protecting oneself" or "getting into trouble" or "committing a crime." Clearly, unless control processes for action are incredibly complex and somehow anticipate the many ways in which an act can be identified, the input to such a process is likely to be just one of these act identities, not all. In this sense, any control process is rather single-minded, focusing on the production of only a very circumscribed effect.

In summary, the elements of control in psychological theory center on the description of the closed-loop control or feedback system. Such a control system changes something (produces output) by performing an operation (a control action) whenever it is discovered (by a monitoring process) that there is a discrepancy between the system's output and a desired state (a control criterion). The system's input sets the control criterion, and this can come from many possible sources including the environment and other control systems.

Conscious Control

The control processes we have encountered thus far don't really distinguish our mental operations from those of a very elaborate household appliance. To go to the next level and become really human, we need to add another feature that is at once immense, confusing, exciting, wondrous, and, to some commentators anyway, possibly useless—consciousness. Intuitively, after all, most people think of control in humans as conscious control, so much so that the term "unconscious control" doesn't seem right at all. To begin understanding the role of consciousness in control we need to examine consciousness itself.

Consciousness   A useful way to approach the analysis of consciousness is to distinguish conscious mental states from other mental states. A mental state may be said to be conscious when it is accompanied by a roughly simultaneous but higher-order thought *about* that very mental state (Armstrong, 1980; Rosenthal, 1993). So, for example, the conscious experience of pain involves more than the simple registering of a painful sensation in the mind. It includes a parallel realization that one is having this sensation, a thought that "I am feeling pain." Some commentators even describe this distinction in terms of separate parts of the brain, one of which is focused on some item of mental content, and the other of which is focused on the fact that the first is focused on that item (e.g., Gazzaniga, 1988; Jaynes, 1976). Others suggest that the important characteristic of consciousness is that the self becomes involved; sensations and actions come to have an author, the "I" (Dennett, 1991; Kihlstrom & Tobias, 1991).

The main idea here is captured with a distinction between two sorts of consciousness. The more rudimentary sort is what Armstrong (1980) calls *minimal consciousness*—just what distinguishes mental activity from mental passivity. A person is minimally conscious if the mind accepts inputs such as sensations and produces outputs such as behavior—in other words, it is not unconscious. One can infer that even a sleeping person is minimally conscious when, say, one prods the person in mid-snore and the person turns over. It is easy to think of animals as having this sort of consciousness, and this is probably the kind of consciousness many of us enjoy for much of what we do on a daily basis. Although such "reactivity" (Jaynes, 1976) is no more sophisticated than what plants do when they turn toward the sun, it is a beginning. We are plugged in to the world, a big step above comatose. But this is not full consciousness.

In *full consciousness,* a stream of higher-order thoughts carries on in parallel with one's (minimally conscious) mental or physical activities. As one thinks in turn of, say, one's fingers moving at a computer keyboard and then the music playing in the distance, there is the parallel presence of a higher-order thought of the fact that one is minimally conscious of each of these things ("I was typing along and then I heard the lilting strains of yonder flugelhorn"). This is something that the garden-variety houseplant can never enjoy, no matter how vigorously it turns toward the sun each day. Full consciousness introduces thoughts *about* what we are thinking and doing. Such higher-order thought is not always present. One's finger could move at the keyboard and one could respond to the music (perhaps by baying softly), quite without full consciousness, as the mind normally carries on many such activities without making us think of the fact that it is doing them. When full consciousness does occur, however, the mind is occupied not only with the keyboard and music, but simultaneously carries on a stream of thought about the fact that it has each of these occupations in turn.

The observation that full consciousness can come and go, visiting some of our minimally conscious activities and skipping past others, has long been appreciated by psychologists. Jastrow (1906) remarked on the common experience of performing some routinized action and finding one's mind wandering away from the act, only then to "come to" and realize that for some time one has been unaware of what one was doing (see also Carpenter, 1874). Such a return of full consciousness can also occur on purpose, and this corresponds to "introspective" consciousness (Rosenthal, 1993). Like full consciousness, introspection involves higher-order thoughts about one's acts of minimal consciousness (Nisbett & Wilson, 1977). In introspection, however, the higher-order thoughts are intended, whereas in normal full consciousness the occurrence of the higher-order train of thought seems unintended.

Full consciousness also seems to have a special connection with language. We don't normally talk about or describe mental events of which we are minimally conscious. The mental events that are fully conscious, on the other hand, are quite readily narrated in language—so readily that it seems that such narration may somehow be a fundamental part of the way in which we become fully conscious (Dennett, 1978). Although we may sometimes have trouble putting our fully conscious contents into the *right* words, we are never doubtful of the possibility that we can put them into *some* words. Part of what happens when we reach the higher-level thoughts about our minimally-conscious contents may involve the translation of the experience into a sequential form that allows it to be rendered in language. In this vein, Dennett (1969) made a distinction much like the one between full and minimal consciousness in which he suggested that being **aware₁** (a verbalizable awareness) is not the same as being **aware₂** (a mere connection with stimulation that causes behavior). Speaking yet more broadly, it may be that the role of consciousness in translating the parallel, time-unbound workings of the mind to the demands of a serial, sequential outside world transcends language per se. Serialization is a property imposed on all responses to the environment (such as actions) which must take place one at a time (see Bargh, 1997; Lashley, 1951; Shallice, 1972; Vallacher & Wegner, 1985), and this seems to be an important part of what full consciousness does.

The leap from minimal to full consciousness has been explained in another related way among developmental psychologists studying the child's "theory of mind" (Astington, Harris, & Olson, 1988; Leslie, 1987; Gopnik, 1993). Researchers in this tradition have observed that children experience a transition during the ages of three to four in which they become capable of thinking about their own mental states and those of others. Before this, a child might report after discovering that a candy box contained pencils, for example, that he or she had always thought it contained pencils and had never held the mistaken belief that it held candy—even though this was clearly the case. Similarly, the child might attribute knowledge of the pencil contents to another child being shown the closed candy box for the first time. This apparent extension of what the child knows now into answers about what the child knew before or about what other uninformed children know now suggests an inability to represent mental contents as independent of reality. This basic ability would seem to be necessary for the operation of the higher-order thinking associated with full consciousness. In this light, full consciousness is something we gain when we develop the capacity not just to have mental states, but to think and talk about them.

With this understanding of consciousness, we can now turn to the question of conscious control. Our analysis of consciousness into two forms suggests that some proportion of a person's control processes may carry on with only minimal consciousness, whereas the remaining control processes have full consciousness. In what follows, we will use the term "conscious control" to refer only to the case of full consciousness.

To examine conscious control, we must be careful to specify *when* the consciousness of interest is occurring. Conscious processes can occur (1) well in advance of behavior as we think, plan, or deliberate about what we will do, (2) in the form of conscious intention that appears in mind just before the behavior occurs, and (3) during a behavior as we consciously notice aspects of the enactment. To keep these epochs of consciousness straight, let us call them *conscious planning, conscious intention,* and *conscious monitoring.* Each of these points of conscious contact with control is worth considering separately.

Conscious Planning   There seems to be little doubt that work done in the mind, and of which we are fully conscious, can contribute importantly to subsequent control of behavior. Although full consciousness of goal selection and behavior planning may not be a necessary requirement for cognitive control of behavior (Bargh & Gollwitzer, 1994), it is often sufficient. Conceptualizations of conscious planning usually divide it into two kinds of processes (Miller et al., 1960; Vallacher & Wegner, 1985), each of which has attracted considerable research attention. One set of conscious processes deliberates among multiple possible goals of action (e.g., Carver & Scheier,

1990; Higgins, 1987; Markus & Nurius, 1986; Mischel, Cantor, & Feldman, 1996; Powers, 1973; Vallacher & Wegner, 1985). Another set of conscious processes creates or retrieves courses of action to achieve a given goal (e.g., Abelson, 1981; Bower, Black, & Turner, 1979; Gollwitzer, 1993; Graesser, 1978; Schank & Abelson, 1977). In terms of control process language, these two emphases focus, respectively, on the control criterion (what to do) and the control action (how to do it).

These conscious planning processes appear to build the pathways for future action, but they do not seem to compel the action to occur. A person may well have thought through several potential goals and selected just the right one, for instance, and then have considered in detail how to behave so as to achieve that goal, but still just not do it. In this sense, conscious planning is preparatory rather than inevitably effective in producing controlled activity. This remarkable wobbliness in the causal linkage from planning to acting is clear to anyone who has lain in a cozy bed too long in the morning, uselessly resolving again and again to get up—a fact observed early on by James (1890, Vol. 2, p. 524). Much of the research on conscious planning has focused on this tenuous link (see Baumeister, Heatherton, & Tice, 1995; Fiske, 1989; Gollwitzer, 1993; Mischel et al., 1996), as this seems to be the central impediment in the path to self-control. It has been learned, for example, that conscious planning is more likely to compel action when it is detailed and includes reasons for action (Ajzen, 1991), when planned identifications of what will be done match the person's ability to act (Vallacher & Wegner, 1987), when the initiation of plans is linked to specific future environmental events (Bargh & Gollwitzer, 1994; Gollwitzer, 1993), and when conscious images of the action have been formed (Anderson & Godfrey, 1987; Feltz & Landers, 1983). Still, the specific moment of the transition from conscious plan to action remains somehow outside of conscious control. As we shall see, this seems to occur because conscious intentions are not the causes of action we had always hoped them to be.

Conscious Intention   After planning, the next point at which consciousness parallels control processes is in the conscious intention to behave. An interesting approach to the role of conscious intention is suggested by the work of Libet (1985). His studies have focused on the prior finding that a "readiness potential" (RP), a scalp-recorded slow negative shift in electrical potential generated by the brain, begins up to a second or more before a self-paced, apparently voluntary motor act (Gilden, Vaughan, & Costa, 1966; Kornhuber & Deecke, 1965). In studies of spontaneous, intentional finger movement (e.g., "Please move your finger voluntarily and intentionally at some point in the next few minutes"), Libet found this RP preceded the occurrence of finger flexion (measured electromyographically) by a minimum of about 550 milliseconds. This find-

ing by itself suggests simply that some sort of brain activity reliably precedes the onset of voluntary action.

The twist that Libet added here was to attempt to measure the point in time at which the person has conscious awareness of the intention to act. He asked participants whose RPs were being measured to recall the spatial clock position of a revolving spot at the time of their initial awareness of intending or wanting to move their finger. It was found that the awareness of intentionally acting *followed* the RP by about 350–400 milliseconds. So, although the conscious intention regularly preceded the actual finger movement, it occurred well after whatever (unconscious) brain events were signaled by the RP. He was careful, too, to subtract the time it took people to monitor the clock—so it appears that conscious intention to act follows the RP and precedes the finger movement.

The implication here is that consciousness is somehow sweeping up after (or at best during) the parade, not setting it all in motion. The consciousness of voluntarily acting appears to occur after brain events that cause the action. This finding remains controversial, as reflected in a variety of commentaries published with the Libet (1985) paper. However, at some level Libet's findings are exactly what we should expect. If conscious intentions popped into mind without any prior brain activity, nothing but a ghost-in-machine theory could predict when we would perform voluntary actions. Consciousness occurring before any brain event would be spooky indeed. If, however, conscious awareness of intention follows brain events in this way, the mechanistic determinism of voluntary action is preserved.

This sequence of events also suggests why we perceive that our conscious intentions cause our actions. The brain events associated with the RP probably produce *both* the conscious intention and the observable action in sequence (see Figure 2). Because we become consciously aware of anything at all in this sequence for the first time just when the conscious intention occurs, and this intention is then typically followed by the action, it makes good sense that we would develop the strong impression that the conscious intention was *causing* the action. This impression could lead us, then, to suppose that we are agents who knowingly cause our acts. The sense of conscious control of action could arise because both conscious intent to act and the action itself are reliably produced, in that order, by unconscious prior brain events.

This analysis should not be read to say that conscious thought plays no part in the voluntary control of action. To the contrary, it is clear that Libet's participants were verbally instructed to move their fingers "at some time," and so were already fully conscious of the plan to move in advance of the moment at which the spontaneous intent to move "now" came to mind. Participants in Libet's experiments were consciously aware in a general sense of what they were going to do in the situation, and were merely waiting for a conscious intention to act to come to mind. In

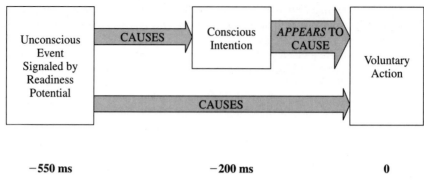

−550 ms   −200 ms   0

FIGURE 2   Real and Apparent Paths of Action Causation.

a sense, they had intended to intend. Conscious control, then, may involve considerable influence by prior consciousness (in the form of planning and anticipating when actions should be done), but apparently little influence by immediately-prior conscious intention. Consciousness indicates the direction in which voluntary action is being launched, but the momentary conscious intention does not participate in the actual launching.

The key question for this analysis is, of course, why one would want such a system (cf. Harnad, 1982). Why would it be useful to have a control system that can be prepared for action by prior consciousness, but that produces momentary conscious intentions to act that are not necessarily themselves causal of the act? There are at least two suggestions of functions such conscious intention may serve. For handy reference, we can call them the *responsibility hypothesis* and the *criterion hypothesis.*

The responsibility hypothesis has been long suggested by both social scientists (Mead, 1934) and moral philosophers (Hart, 1948/1949; Feinberg, 1970), and appears as well in current social psychology (Fiske, 1989; Uleman, 1989). The idea here is that we become conscious of our intentions so that the social rewards and costs for our actions can be calculated, both by ourselves and others. This notion hinges on the observation that responsibility is allocated in social life on the basis of our intentional social actions, and that our sense that we "could have done otherwise" allows the distribution of social outcomes for what we did do. We humans develop self-conceptions as agents based on the actions we knowingly and intentionally perform, and then expect and receive social recognition for what we have done and the selves these acts represent. This explanation suggests, in short, that conscious intentions are the currency by which we compute who's been bad and good. This social function presumably has become so pressing that it has created the mental processes that report our intentions to consciousness. This is an evolutionary hypothesis, then, that suggests a long process of development of the human ability to foresee our actions.

A second explanation for why we have conscious intentions is the criterion hypothesis. This is the suggestion that intentions alert consciousness to what we are going to do so that the conscious monitoring of our actions and their outcomes can occur. If we didn't know what we were intending, after all, we wouldn't be able to know whether our intention had been successfully achieved. Vallacher and Wegner (1985, 1987) and Wegner and Vallacher (1986) spelled out this idea in the theory of action identification, suggesting that each person has a specific, verbalizable notion of what he or she is doing available for report during any moment of full consciousness. In other words, the question "What are you doing?" posed to a conscious person always has an answer.

In this view, the intentions that arise in mind as we act inform us consciously of what to watch for in our behavior—and so of what can be counted as completion of the action. When we find ourselves waving a hand in a restaurant, for example, it would be good to know whether we are "signaling the waiter" or "cooling off our fingers." This allows us consciously to observe when the action is finished and whether it is successful, and so to discern what to do next (or whether to do it over). When intentions are understood consciously in advance of action, they allow a constant conscious representation of action to accompany the action and serve as a guide to its proper construction. Conscious intention thus allows conscious monitoring (our next topic) and provides for updates of conscious planning—so to allow action to unfold with the benefit of feedback processes.

To summarize, we should note first that our conclusions about conscious intention in this section are preliminary ones. Libet's research, in particular, has not been followed up by enough other researchers to allow us to draw strong conclusions. But at this point, the implication is that conscious intentions signal the direction of action—but without causing the action. Although the trajectory of controlled action is specified in advance by conscious planning, it appears that the precise brain events that trigger the action may precede conscious intention. The role of conscious intentions, then, may be to serve as signals of what we will do. These conscious intentions may serve as socially-driven indicators of our responsibility for what we do, or may function as criteria for what we are doing that allow us to adjust our action as it unfolds.

Conscious Monitoring   Consciousness can occur during behavior, and though it can certainly be directed elsewhere at the time (witness the often-unconscious behaviors of yawning or scratching), it may often be directed toward the behavior continuously or occasionally as it unfolds. What role does such conscious monitoring play in the control process? As a rule, consciousness is attracted to action primarily when the action is faulty. This can happen in two ways. When action is strongly expected to be faulty or error-prone, we may direct conscious attention to it all along. Such premeditated monitoring does not accompany all action, but it does seem to happen regularly when we are especially concerned about our ability to control a particular action. The second kind of conscious monitoring occurs when consciousness is drawn to action by the occurrence of unexpected turns or errors in the action. We can refer to these different conscious monitoring processes as *deliberate monitoring* and *event-driven monitoring.*

Deliberate monitoring plays an important part in the construction of difficult action sequences. The beginning pianist, for example, will struggle through almost every new piece deliberately monitoring the action at many levels ("Did I play an *F*? Why does it sound wrong? Is it supposed to be a sharp?"). Such chronic consciousness of action, although one of the most painful and anxiety-producing aspects of being inexpert at an action (Baumeister, 1984; Kirschenbaum & Tomarken, 1982; Wine, 1971), seems necessary for piecing together the elements of complex action sequences. Consciousness of what is or is not being done allows verbal and other symbolic systems (e.g., musical notes) to set control criteria for parts of complex action sequences that may not even be considered when the person begins the action as a whole (Bargh & Barndollar, 1996; Norman & Shallice, 1986; Sudnow, 1978; Vallacher & Kaufman, 1996; Vallacher & Wegner, 1985).

Event-driven monitoring, on the other hand, seems to happen when actions that are expected to go well instead somehow get off track. The act of driving a car down the street, for example, can suddenly become conscious when the tire strays over the yellow line, when the steering wheel jiggles unexpectedly, or when any of a variety of other potential discrepancies occur. Because consciousness is not focused on the action until the error happens, it must be the case that there are unconscious error-monitoring processes that can thrust their findings into consciousness. Wegner (1994) has suggested that every consciously planned control process invokes such an unconscious error-monitoring process, and that such error monitors function to alert con-

sciousness to the failure of control and reinstate the conscious planning (or re-planning) of action. From this perspective, the incidental conscious monitoring of action, like conscious intention more generally, is itself produced by unconscious processes.

The consequence of this error-monitoring system is usually, then, that errors of control are noticed and attempts are made to repair them by instituting new control criteria. The person who fails to keep the car in the proper lane notices this and consciously plans to steer back into position. According to the theory of ironic processes of mental control (Wegner, 1994), however, the unconscious error-monitoring process has its own influence on mind and behavior that can act ironically to produce the very errors that are being monitored. Someone who consciously plans to keep the car in the lane, for example, institutes at the same time an ironic monitoring process that searches for lane-violating behaviors and may even subtly produce them.

Examples of the operation of ironic monitoring processes usually crop up when the person's conscious control processes are overwhelmed by distractions or stress. So, for example, people who are trying to suppress a thought may have difficulty generally (Wegner, Schneider, Carter, & White, 1987; Wegner, Shortt, Blake, & Page, 1990), but while they hold a number in mind at the same time, they find that the thought becomes even more likely to intrude (Wegner & Erber, 1992). People who are trying to be happy find that under cognitive load, their efforts make them sad—while those who are trying to be sad find that such loads make them happy (Wegner, Erber, & Zanakos, 1993). Similar ironic effects have been found in the control of relaxation (Wegner, Broome, & Blumberg, 1997), sleep (Ansfield, Wegner, & Bowser, 1996), and simple movement (Wegner, Ansfield, & Pilloff, 1996), as well as in the control of the expression of sexist thoughts (Wegner, Erber, Bowman, & Shelton, 1996). People under cognitive load who try to do these things may find themselves—respectively—agitated, awake, moving, or saying just the sexist things they were hoping to avoid (Wegner, 1994, 1996). It seems that imposing conscious control and not allowing it the luxury of plenty of mental work space is a fine way to prompt ironic errors.

In short, although conscious monitoring is helpful in the processes whereby action is corrected as it is ongoing, it seems that monitoring also produces its own family of problems. Deliberate monitoring yields control-repair processes but also prompts obsessive and anxiety-producing overconsciousness of potential errors. Event-driven monitoring, in turn, is involved in most fix-ups of faulty action, but also may produce many instances of counter-control—actions precisely in opposition to what was planned. Although monitoring is an essential element of control that distinguishes it from automatic processes, it is not without its disadvantages.

The Sense of Control

People may sense that they control something when they do not. A disconcerting example of this occurred to one of the authors, for instance, when he was intently operating the controls of a video game for some time, only to find the words "Insert Coin" appearing on the screen—to indicate that the game action was being demonstrated by the machine without any influence from him at all. People may also sense that they do not control something when they actually do. The seemingly magical movement of a Ouija Board pointer is an example of this. Although the sense of control does seem to coincide rather well with actual control in many instances, there are enough divergences to remind us that they are clearly different phenomena (Alloy & Tabachnik, 1984; Ansfield & Wegner, 1996; Langer, 1975).

The sense of control has been far more widely studied and celebrated in social psychology than has actual control. Without much concern about whether the sense of control corresponds with actual control or not, theorists and researchers have examined variations in the sense of control all by itself—usually with the hypothesis in mind that a sense of control is always good. It is difficult to tell exactly where this hypothesis began—as it seems in some ways to resemble the idea (also so popular as to be untraceable) that high self-esteem is a uniformly desirable state (Baumeister, Smart, & Boden, 1996)—and it may be more a North American cultural world view than a derivation from a specific theory. The rise of the idea in modern psychology, however, is often ascribed to White's (1959) theory of effectance motivation.

White held that organisms have an innate desire to have an effect on their environments and gave examples indicating that this desire surfaces in lots of seemingly capricious little expressions of control. Mice who are given a button to push that changes the illumination in their cages, for instance, soon arrive at a preferred level and return the lights to that level if humans attempt to adjust it. The reactions of these testy mice represent, for White, expressions of a general motive for effectance that drives the behavior of all organisms. This need for mastery and autonomy is satisfied not only by actual control over the environment, but also by circumstances that produce illusions of such control.

The largest share of the theory and research on the sense of control has focused on the analysis of individual differences in perceived control, although there has also been interest in situational variations (see Baumeister, 1998, in this *Handbook*; Pittman, 1998, in this *Handbook*). The number of theoretical constructs proposed in the last 30 years either to represent perceived control generally or to express various facets of the idea is truly staggering. An incomplete list would include locus of control (Rotter, 1966; Weiner, 1974), self-efficacy (Bandura, 1977), and intrinsic motivation (Deci, 1975), to be sure, and then embrace constructs including personal causation (DeCharms,

1968), perceived control (Glass & Singer, 1972), attributional style (Peterson, Maier, & Seligman, 1993), illusion of control (Langer, 1975), personal control (Folkman, 1984), optimism (Scheier & Carver, 1985), psychological reactance (Brehm, 1966), personal agency (Vallacher & Wegner, 1989), positive illusions (Taylor & Brown, 1988), and control motivation (Weary, Gleicher, & Marsh, 1993)—to name a few (see reviews by Haidt & Rodin, 1995; Skinner, 1995).

The indications in this voluminous literature that it is psychologically beneficial to perceive control are simply overwhelming. And indeed, this is an important message that has come to be useful in attempts to increase the effectiveness of therapies and interventions of many kinds (e.g., Baltes & Baltes, 1986; S. S. Brehm, 1976). It has come to the point, though, that further demonstrations of perceived control effects are becoming increasingly uninformative. Far too many renamings of the dimension have come and gone, and analyses of the limitations of this broad effect are themselves beginning to gather interest (Colvin & Block, 1994; Burger, 1989; Taylor & Brown, 1994; Thompson, Cheek, & Graham, 1988). Although it is useful to pursue the benefits of perceived control for those individuals to whom real control is by fate impossible, the analysis of perceived control must eventually be integrated with the study of processes of real control if significant scientific progress is to be made.

For our purposes, this literature serves as an important reminder that control must be understood not only as a psychological process but as a *feeling,* an experience one has of controlling or being in control. Control requires effort, and this effort as it is expended yields a continuous sense that one is doing something, not just allowing something to happen. Both the actual expenditure of cognitive effort, and the phenomenal experience of effortfulness, appear to be at a maximum during conscious control.

Summary of Control

This review of the nature of control in social psychology suggests that the concept has both a larger and a smaller meaning. Control in the larger sense is a multifarious psychological process that operates according to control theory. In this sense, "control" incorporates a wide array of the mechanisms and features that seem necessary in the psychological engine that runs a human being. Such control is not opposed to automatic processes and instead can be said to include them as an important special case. But control also has a more limited meaning, one that becomes particularly evident when we consider it in comparison to automaticity. The more limited definition of control includes key properties such as consciousness, and the "closed loop" ability to monitor our behavior so as to vary it flexibly in response to feedback. We turn now to focus on automaticity, so to put the broad theory of control into this important perspective.

THE NATURE OF AUTOMATICITY

People have always understood that there are functions of their bodies that they can't control, even if they want to. The beating of the heart, workings of the intestines, functioning of the internal organs, and breathing all go on whether we want them to or not. If we try to exert control, such as by holding our breath, the bodily function eventually wins out over our attempt, even if it has to knock us unconscious to do so. Hartley's (1749) early mention of the term "automatic," for instance, was in reference to bodily functions, and not anything psychological such as perception, reasoning, or behavior. Only with the birth of psychology as a science—that is, only for the past 100 years of intellectual history—has the mind been considered and analyzed as an internal bodily organ, instead of a soul or spiritual essence. Along with this demotion of the mind to the physical realm came, among other things, the possibility that the mind, like other bodily organs, could also have some of its operations occurring outside of the individual's control (see Carpenter, 1874; Jastrow, 1906).

Historical Overview

In this section, we trace the concept of automaticity through the history of psychology, beginning with its dual origins in William James's notion of habit and Freud's concept of hidden, motivated influences on thought. From these two sources developed separate research traditions: *skill acquisition* on the one hand, and *preconscious processing* on the other (i.e., the "New Look"; Bruner, 1957). Although these domains of research have very different historical roots, both are considered today as focusing on the *automaticity* of mental life, because they are both concerned with forms of thought that differ in important ways from conscious control—ones that can operate and run to completion without conscious guidance, just like breathing.

Skill Acquisition   Automatic cognitive processes are mental habits. Although William James (1890) did not have much truck with the nonconscious, considering this theoretical concept to be "a tumbling ground for whimsies" (p. 163), he nonetheless believed in the importance of habit in daily life. James advised young people to develop good habits of social and ethical behavior, and a disciplined attitude toward their work life as well, so that these could be carried on throughout life rather effortlessly and without much thought. These habits were to be ingrained by consistent and diligent practice on a daily basis. Bad habits, he noted, were very hard to break, and to do so re-

quired the utmost vigilance against the unwanted behavior, and no lapses or backsliding.

So while James (1890) expressed skepticism about the importance of nonconscious thought processes, he also held to a model of automaticity very similar to that of present-day psychology: one in which activities frequently and consistently engaged in require less and less conscious effort over time. These patterns become the deep grooves into which behavior falls when not consciously attended, as in James' famous example of the husband being sent up to dress for dinner by his wife because of unexpected dinner guests. With his mind on the tribulations of his day at work, the husband fails consciously to monitor what he is doing and is found upon the arrival of the guests to be in his nightclothes and asleep in bed.

In this example, James anticipated contemporary models of the interaction of conscious and automatic mental processes, in which the role of conscious or effortful processes is to support strategic deviations from the routine, for which there are no preestablished pathways (e.g., Posner & Snyder, 1975). When conscious effort is not forthcoming to support the temporary thought or behavior strategy, the only recourse is the well-worn grooves usually followed in that situation (resulting in absent-minded action slips; Norman, 1981; Reason, 1979).

Whereas James shied away from the idea of nonconscious cognition, Jastrow (1906) explicitly applied the concept of habit to mental life. He proposed a *subconscious* stratum of thought. Routine, unchanging modes of perception and reasoning were held to recede from awareness, and to operate outside of consciousness. In this way the subconscious consisted of the residue of extensive, routine conscious activities, as opposed to a distinct, unconscious mental organ. Jastrow (1906, p. 11) contended that people were designed to be aware of only what they need to be aware of, and not to be aware of those workings of the body—such as the liver or intestine—about which they can do nothing anyway. He called this the "principle of utility" and related it to the operation of the mind as well as the body:

> The principle involved is easily formulated. At the outset each step of the performance is separately and distinctly the object of attention and effort; and as practice proceeds and expertness is gained . . . the separate portions thereof become fused into larger units, which in turn make a constantly diminishing demand upon consciousness (p. 42).

Another important point drawn by Jastrow (1906, p. 45) was the linkage between awareness and intentionality. When habitual thought and behavior patterns eventually drop out of conscious awareness and become subconscious, they also can become subvoluntary. Jastrow thus recognized both the awareness and the intentionality qualities of consciousness.

During the rest of the twentieth century, skill acquisition research (see J. R. Anderson, 1982; Newell & Rosenbloom, 1981; Shiffrin & Schneider, 1977; Smith, 1984, 1998, in this *Handbook*) proceeded to deal with the development of mental expertise or "procedural knowledge," and particularly with the ability of some cognitive processes to operate with a minimum of conscious attention. This is the form of automaticity that Bryan and Harter (1899) and Jastrow (1906) had discussed as mental habits, the delegation to the subconscious over time of routine conscious tasks. In line with Anderson's (1982) more recent notion of compilation of mental skills, Bryan and Harter (1899) held that expertise consists of the automatization of units successively higher in a hierarchy of habits—a buildup of ever larger units or "chunks" of knowledge that operate autonomously once activated (see also Hayes-Roth, 1977; Simon, 1974; Vallacher & Wegner, 1987). For present purposes, a critical guiding assumption of skill acquisition research has been that these processes were put into motion by an act of conscious will. That is, driving and typing and searching for a target in a rapidly changing display were described as becoming automatic after practice, but in all cases the individual knowingly and intentionally engaged in the activity.

Research on attentional information processing soon showed it to be relatively time-consuming in completing its assigned task, limited in scope at any given moment, and serial in nature (Miller, 1956; Sternberg, 1966). Because of these limitations, it became clear to attention researchers "that normal human behavior could not take place if all activity had to be governed by attentive processes operating in such a limited fashion" (Shiffrin, 1988, p. 740). There had to be a different, nonattentional, very fast form of processing operating as well.

This logical analysis led to research by Shiffrin and Schneider (1977) and others designed to search for and demonstrate the existence of this other, *automatic* form of information processing. In the Shiffrin and Schneider (1977) studies, participants were given considerable practice in searching for a target stimulus among an array of other, distracter stimuli. Whereas the time participants took to find a target stimulus in a rapidly changing display began as a function of how many distracters were presented along with the target (i.e., set-size), over many trials this set-size variable ceased to matter: participants were just as fast to find the target in a display of sixteen stimuli as in a display of four or nine. This kind of attentional search therefore had to be parallel in nature, able to scan many targets simultaneously, otherwise the time taken to find the target would be an increasing function of the number of stimuli to scan.

Preconscious Processing   A second tradition of research bears on our contemporary understanding of automaticity.

Unlike research on skill acquisition, however, this line of research did not assume that the individual's consent or even knowledge of the process was a necessary condition for the obtained effects. Instead, it focused on the initial perceptual analysis of the environment that occurred prior to conscious awareness and participation in the processing—that is, *preconscious* information processing. This research was inspired by Freudian thinking but was not guided much by psychoanalytic theory per se.

The "New Look" in perception (see reviews in Allport, 1955; Bruner, 1957; Dixon, 1981; Erdelyi, 1974) was the seminal line of this research, as it focused on motivational and personality determinants of conscious perceptual thresholds. (For early theoretical arguments in support of preconscious influences on perception, also see Helmholtz [1867/1968].) The notion of *perceptual defense*—in which thresholds are higher for emotionally threatening stimuli—was controversial at the time because it required perceptual analysis to occur prior to the percept reaching conscious awareness. This violated the then firmly held assumption that conscious perception was entirely determined by qualities of the stimulus (see Stevens, 1951) and so emotional and other experiential reactions to the stimulus had to be both in conscious awareness and post-perceptual. There was great resistance as a result to the idea of preconscious perceptual analysis, and so the New Look research findings were largely discredited and treated with skepticism (Erdelyi, 1974). The rehabilitation of the New Look ideas took place only after advances in cognitive theory and research had diminished the importance of consciousness in perceptual analysis (Neisser, 1967; Shiffrin, 1988).

A major reason for the reduced importance given to conscious, intentional processes in perceptual interpretation was a separate research thread on selective attention, which grew out of Broadbent's (1958) work. Broadbent's theory was that selective attention is driven by an early internal gating of incoming information, based on its physical features. Sources of information to which attention is not directed are simply not picked up. Quickly, however, it became apparent that some information did get through this attentional barrier, being processed despite the fact that conscious attention is directed elsewhere. Treisman (1960) found that narration presented to the unattended ear in a dichotic listening task sometimes drew attention if it was related to the meaning of the content presented to the attended ear (although this effect occurred relatively infrequently). This could only occur if the material presented to the unattended ear was analyzed for meaning at least to some extent.

Following Treisman's (1960) finding, there was considerable debate between so-called early-selection and late-selection theorists. Broadbent and Treisman were among those who believed there is only a limited amount of nonattentional analysis of informational input for meaning;

Neisser (1967) made this position the mainstream within cognitive psychology. Others, such as Deutsch and Deutsch (1963; also Erdelyi, 1974; Marcel, 1983) posited a full and complete preconscious analysis of all sensed information for meaning and importance, with entry into consciousness determined by the relevance of the activated meanings for the goals of the individual.

Although theorists today continue to stake out different positions as to the extent of preconscious analysis for meaning, the dominant contemporary view continues to be that expressed by Neisser (1967) and Normal (1968). Building on research in the Gestalt tradition on the development of percepts, which traced the stages of perception from sensation to pattern recognition to figural synthesis of the final, consciously perceived object (Flavell & Draguns, 1957; Werner, 1956), Neisser (1967) persuasively argued that all perception had to involve a process of construction. The final percept that feels phenomenally immediate to us—the house or tree or person—is actually the result of considerable precognitive processing. However, the extent of this preconscious analysis, according to Norman (1968), was not the same for every stimulus event. His model of selective attention emphasized the match between the strength or diagnosticity of external information and the readiness or accessibility of memory representations relevant to that information. These sources of activation jointly determined which external information entered conscious awareness and attention.

But this is only what the New Look theorists had been arguing during the previous quarter century. Norman's (1968) interactive model echoed Postman's (1951; and later, Bruner's, 1957) view of perception as a hypothesis-testing activity, with the outcome of perception being a joint function of the diagnosticity or degree of match between stimulus features and an internal representation of that stimulus event on the one hand, and the internal readiness or accessibility of those internal representations on the other. The readiness to perceive related to the individual's preconceptions or expectations about what was going to happen, as well as internal goals and need states (i.e., what the individual is looking for in the environment).

Thus, in the long run, the essence of the New Look argument about perception won the day. Perception is now widely understood to be an interactive function of internal states—including motivations, values, physiological and emotional state, expectations, and relevant knowledge—and the information available in the environment.

Summary Two basic forms of automatic processes have been studied in psychological research. One concerns the initial perceptual analysis and attentional screening of the environment, prior to and in the absence of conscious involvement. The other concerns efficient attentional and behavioral skills that are started in motion consciously and

attentionally. Note that although these have been distinct research traditions, they have always shared a concern with dimensions or qualities that differentiate mental processes. The New Look and selective attention research threads have identified unintentional influences on perception that occur outside of awareness, in contrast to conscious processes that are intended and in awareness. The skill acquisition thread has identified efficient processes that run in parallel once instigated by an act of will (i.e., intention), in contrast to attention-demanding and serial conscious processes.

These research traditions agree as to the nature of the *conscious* processing to which they contrast with their form of automatic processing. There has always been a degree of consensus that conscious processes are those of which the individual is aware, are demanding of limited attentional resources, are intentional, and are serial in that they focus on one object or concept at a time. It was with this consensual view of conscious processes—but with no complementary consensus as to the nature of nonconscious or automatic processes—that contemporary dual-process models of cognition began. The lack of consensus as to the qualities of the nonconscious process—because two different varieties had been studied—was to create some conceptual and interpretational confusion in subsequent years.

Contemporary Views

Psychologists were forced early on to concede that it was impossible for such a slow and resource-consuming form of processing as consciousness to take care of all mental business (Shiffrin, 1988). When contemporary research on automatic processing began, therefore, automaticity was defined as having all the opposite qualities of conscious processing (Posner & Snyder, 1975; Shiffrin & Schneider, 1977); thus, automatic processes were said to be those that were *unintentional,* occurred *outside of awareness, efficient* in that they consumed little if any attentional capacity (enabling them to operate in *parallel* with other processes), and *uncontrollable* (not able to be stopped once started). Hence, early cognitive models of conscious versus automatic processes proposed a dichotomy: a process was either conscious and controlled or it was automatic, with all the defining features of one type but none of the other.

The Posner-Snyder Model Because automatic processes operated concurrently with conscious processes, an important question was how the two forms of processing interacted, especially when their outcomes were contradictory. Posner and Snyder (1975) addressed the interaction of these two forms of processing. In their model, automatic processes at encoding were triggered directly by the presence of the relevant stimulus—that is, without conscious intention—and did not consume attentional resources.

These processes also occurred quickly, within 200 or 300 milliseconds. (Because they were concerned with processes occurring at the time of the original perceptual encoding of the stimulus, the Posner-Snyder theory and research was in the tradition of the New Look and other studies of preconscious perceptual analysis.)

Conscious processes take longer to develop—at least 500 or 600 milliseconds—and require considerable attentional resources, but they are flexible and can be suited to meet strategic processing goals. As for the interaction of these two processes, Posner and Snyder (1975) held that if given enough time to develop, strategic conscious processes can override automatic ones if the responses suggested by the two are incompatible, but if there is insufficient time or attentional resources to support the conscious process the automatic one would prevail.

Empirical support for this model was quick to come. Neely (1977), using a lexical decision task, had participants indicate as quickly as possible whether each of a series of target stimuli was a word or nonword. Prior to the presentation of each target a prime word was presented. Target words were members of the category BODY (i.e., parts of the body such as *heart* or *leg*) or the category FURNITURE (e.g., *chair, table*). The prime stimulus was either the word BODY or the word FURNITURE. A key element of Neely's (1977) design was to vary the delay between prime and target presentation. With brief delays (e.g., 250 milliseconds), only automatic effects should be able to occur; thus, the prime BODY should facilitate (speed up) responses to names of parts of the body (and likewise for FURNITURE and names of pieces of furniture) because strong, automatic connections are assumed to exist between these target concepts and their higher-order category concept. Only with longer delays (e.g., 750 milliseconds) should strategic conscious expectations be able to influence responses.

In the critical experimental condition, participants had a conscious expectancy for the *opposite* of the semantically consistent prime-target combination. In other words, they expected the BODY prime to be followed by names of pieces of furniture and for FURNITURE to be followed by names of body parts. However, the automatic effect would remain the same as always, as it reflects long-term associations and cannot flexibly adapt to temporarily altered circumstances. In support of the Posner-Snyder model, Neely (1977) found that under these conditions, category-name primes continued to facilitate responses to members of that category under the short prime-target delay conditions—even though the usual pairing in the experiment was for the prime to be followed by members of the other category. And under the longer prime-target delay, category-name primes facilitated responses to members of the alternative category, despite the automatic activation of same-category members.

This research confirmed several important features of automatic processing and its interaction with conscious processing. First, automatic processes are a mapping of the long-term regularities of the environment and do not change or adapt to short-term fluctuations in those regularities. Conscious control processes, on the other hand, are flexible and can be tuned to map the local circumstances when they differ from the usual. Second, when automatic and conscious control processes suggest competing responses, the conscious process dominates the automatic. This would seem quite a functional arrangement in that it allows adaptation to those times when "what one knows is wrong." Indeed, for it to be the other way around and have the automatic process dominate would make the flexible conscious or strategic processing entirely superfluous. Implicit in this second point is that the interaction of the two modes of processing nonetheless produces a single response instead of an attempt to make both (or many, given the parallel nature of automatic processing). For the conscious process to "win out" over the automatic response in the critical opposed-responses condition of the Neely (1977) study, it must inhibit the automatic response.

This points to a third difference between automatic and conscious processes—the controlling or inhibitory nature of conscious processes and the inhibitionless nature of automaticity (see also Shallice, 1972). Although such inhibition does not come without a cost of attentional effort and thus time (resulting in longer response times, as in the Stroop color-word effect; see Logan, 1980), it nonetheless enables a single, nonhabitual response to the environment.

Fourth, and finally, automatic processes—at least during perceptual encoding—do not require the person's intention that they occur and in fact are not controllable; clearly in the Neely (1977) study the participants were trying to control the automatic response when it was known to be incorrect, as they did so when they had enough time to accrue the attentional resources to do so (i.e., in the long prime-target delay condition).

The Shiffrin-Schneider Research   Whereas the Posner-Snyder theory and related research were in the tradition of preconscious automaticity research, Shiffrin and Schneider's (1977) research grew out of the skill acquisition tradition. Shiffrin and Schneider (1977) demonstrated the development of automatic attention responses to target stimuli over time, with such attentional skills depending on frequent and consistent mapping of a given target or set of targets to the detection goal. In other words, if a given stimulus (e.g., the letter "G") was the target to be detected on some trials (by pressing a button as quickly as possible after it was presented) within a display of items (the others being distracters), but was on other trials a distractor item (with some other letter as the target), automatic detection capabilities did not develop. When a given stimulus was consistently the target across trials, the participant became able to detect it more and more quickly in the display, moving from a process in which each item in the display had to be searched serially (so that response times were an increasing linear function of the number of items in the display) to a process in which the display could be searched in parallel (with response times not a function of the size of the search-set).

The qualities of automatic processes evidenced by Shiffrin and Schneider's (1977) results were as follows. Automatic processes develop out of frequent and consistent experience with the environment; they operate in parallel and are very efficient in their use of attentional resources. As the participant's goal was to find the assigned target on each experimental trial, these automatic attention processes were intentionally put into motion—just as the attentional and motor skills involved in driving or typing require the intention to drive or type (see Logan & Cowan, 1984). But given the overarching intention to find a consistently mapped target in the Shiffrin-Schneider paradigm, the process required no further conscious guidance; the act of intention or will effectively delegated the task to subconscious processes (see Jastrow, 1906, pp. 16–17).

Summary of Automaticity

What is the essence of automaticity that emerges from these historical and modern considerations? In all cases, the process is autonomous in that, once started, it runs by itself and does not need conscious guidance or monitoring. In all cases, the process is very fast and efficient in that it uses only minimal attentional capacity. It also appears that all automatic processes—both in perceptual categorization and in skill acquisition—develop out of frequent and consistent experience in an environmental domain. (However, affective influences in perception as studied by the New Look investigators as well as contemporary researchers may be an exception to this general principle.)

The major difference between the two forms of automaticity lies in the conditions needed to start them in motion. Long ago, Jastrow (1906, p. 45) had differentiated these two varieties, noting that some subconscious processes "require merely the initial start," whereas others require even less, just "the familiar succession of slight stimuli, to run themselves off the reel." Thus some automatic processes are goal-dependent while others are goal-independent, being driven by the stimulus environment itself, prior to any conscious involvement in their processing (see Bargh, 1989).

Automatic processes grow out of one's frequent and consistent experience, so that they represent the regularities of that experience. Routine conscious processes, whether they are concerned with perceptual or behavioral responses to the environment, become subsumed by effi-

cient automatic processes that operate without the need for conscious guidance, attention, or awareness. Automatic processes vary as to the conditions needed to set them into operation; some require just the mere presence of the relevant stimuli in the environment (as in the activation of perceptual categories) while others require an act of conscious will (as in the engagement of well-practiced attentional or motor skills).

RELATIONSHIPS BETWEEN CONTROL AND AUTOMATICITY

We have discussed the concepts of control and automaticity largely in isolation to this point because the literatures surrounding these concepts, despite their obvious definitional interdependence, have grown up quite independently. Consequently, sensible stories about them can be told with little reference to each other. Now, however, it is time to take explicit stock of the relationships between control and automatic processes. We begin with a brief overview of the distinction between these processes to review the discussion so far, and then we posit seven distinct relationships between control and automatic processes that seem to capture much of what is known about how the two kinds of processes interact.

Control and Automaticity Compared

The definitions of control and automaticity do not stand on equal footing. Although there seems to be substantial intuitive and theoretical agreement as to the defining qualities of a conscious control process, the nature of automaticity has been a matter of frequent discussion and refinement. As detailed in the previous section, for some time it seemed perfectly reasonable to define an automatic process simply as having qualities polar opposite to those of conscious control (Posner & Snyder, 1975), but this approach has proven problematic. Unlike the properties of conscious control, those of automatic processes do not hang together in an all-or-none fashion (Bargh 1984, 1989; Neumann, 1984; Shiffrin, 1988).

There are several features which must be jointly present in a psychological process for it to count as an instance of conscious control. As we have seen, conscious control occurs with a conscious intention of what the control will accomplish, a sense or feeling of control, an expenditure of effort in the control action, and a (closed-loop) monitoring of the control output. Automatic processes do not necessarily lack *all* these features, and in this sense they are not complete polar opposites of conscious control. Rather, automaticity is used to refer to a family of processes which share only the lack of some one or a subset of these features. Automaticity, then, is a negatively defined concept—an absence of at least one key quality of conscious control.

This means that automatic processes often seem very much like conscious control processes and function in many of the same circumstances. The process that determines whether we say "hello" to someone we pass on the street can vary in seemingly minor ways, and move dramatically as a result from a conscious control process to automatic or back the other way. Automatic and conscious control processes have many of the same kinds of behavioral consequences and may respond to many of the same kinds of environmental inputs. In essence, although they may differ at a fundamental level, they both fall broadly under the rubric of psychological control processes. With this in mind, we can now consider the relationships that exist between control and automatic processes.

Control and Automaticity Together: Their Basic Relations

The complicated interplay of control and automatic processes in everyday life can be parsed into a relatively small set of basic relations. In what follows, we enumerate these with a view toward capturing what we see to be the fundamental ways in which these processes combine and interact in psychological functioning.

1. Multitasking: Control and Automatic Processes Can Run in Parallel   The flow of thought and behavior pieces together an array of processes. At any one time, one process is probably consciously controlled (Shallice, 1972). A very limited number of others can be consciously controlled if they can claim enough attention (Neisser, 1976). By and large, however, because of their lower attentional requirements, automatic processes can run in parallel, not only with control processes but also with each other (Bargh, 1997). It is not clear what limits there might be to the number of parallel automatic processes (Shiffrin, 1988).

In a social interaction, for example, we may well respond rather automatically or "mindlessly" (Langer, 1978, 1989) to the conversation of one person that has long since ceased to interest us, but at the same time effortfully plan a witty remark in order to impress another person standing nearby. Are we interacting automatically here, or consciously? If we think of the entire interaction as a single process no clear answer can be given to that question, but if we analyze the interaction into its components, then the matter is much clearer. Both automatic and control processes are operating; even when we are "on automatic" about one aspect of our environment, the conscious attentional capacity that is freed up is able to be deployed in the pursuit of other important goals we have. Ultimately, both kinds of processes are responsible for the successful negotiation of the social world.

2. Delegation: A Control Process Can Launch an Automatic Process   In social psychology many studies have shown that dispositional attribution, social judgment, and stereotyping processes are so efficient as to be capable of operating in the absence of conscious attention. Yet in all these studies, participants were explicitly instructed to engage in social perception or judgment tasks (see Bargh, 1989, 1994, for reviews). Thus the processing was under intentional control, while at the same time being very efficient and autonomous. These are examples of automatic processes that are instigated by a control process.

3. Orienting: An Automatic Process Can Launch a Control Process   Orienting happens when a distinctive, salient event automatically attracts our attention and control processing. Something out of the ordinary happens, a friend does something totally out of character, or we see something really unusual—and control processes are instigated in order to understand and fit this new piece of information into what we already think we know. The literature discussed in this chapter on attention effects documents this case of orienting, when control processes are automatically triggered by environmental events or stimuli.

4. Intrusion: An Automatic Process Can Override a Control Process   Automatic processes have been held suspect as the causes of errors that get in the way of consciously controlled behavior for many years, certainly since Freud (but see Bargh, 1997; Bargh & Barndollar, 1996). Research on ironic processes of mental control (Wegner, 1994) illustrates a variety of cases in which counterintentional automatic processes are produced that inhibit conscious control, not just randomly but as a direct result of their inherence in conscious control. When we try to suppress a thought while we are under mental load and find it coming back more often, we suffer from an automatic process that intrudes upon and inhibits conscious control.

5. Regulation: A Control Process Can Override an Automatic Process   When control processes have access to enough attentional capacity, they can inhibit automatic processes (Bargh, 1989). As Devine (1989) has pointed out, for example, stereotyping consists of the automatic activation of the stereotypic representation of the social group, and the use of the information stored within that representation in making judgments about an individual. Her research showed the first, activation component process to be uncontrollable given stimuli related to the stereotyped group (African Americans) but the second, application component process to be controllable for individuals motivated to engage in that act of control. Control processes are commonly marshaled in service of just such inhibition (see also Fiske, 1989).

6. Automatization: A Control Process Can Be Transformed into an Automatic Process When a control process is repeated often enough, it can become automatic (e.g., Bargh, 1984; Jastrow, 1906; Shiffrin & Schneider, 1977). This may entail reduced monitoring, increased efficiency, reduced flexibility, losses in the sense of control, and a variety of other consequences. Although this observation may seem too obvious to mention, it is worth noting that this principle suggests there is a constant flux in the status of the conscious control of any given process throughout daily life (Vallacher & Wegner, 1985, 1987). Processes called upon to deal with new environmental stimuli may be consciously controlled at first, only to recede from conscious control in one or another way as habits grow.

7. Disruption: An Automatic Process Can Be Transformed into a Control Process Given the often only slight difference between automaticity and control, it may take no more than a bit of conscious reminding about a process before it occurs, for example, or a touch of monitoring of it afterwards, to turn it from automatic into consciously controlled. We all have had the experience of finding our conscious attention drawn to a previously automatic act, for instance, when the act occurs ineffectively or conspicuously. Although this is commonly understood as a disruptive event (Baumeister, 1984; Wegner, 1994), it is also the source of renewed flexibility and potential adaptation of the action (Vallacher & Wegner, 1985, 1987).

These seven basic relations between control and automatic processes are useful in describing and accounting for the operation of mind across a wide range of social behavior. In the next section, these terms serve as a shorthand to capture many of the theoretical and research themes of the field.

DOMAINS OF CONTROL AND AUTOMATICITY RESEARCH

There are several areas of social psychological research for which issues of control and automaticity have special relevance. We consider here the topics of attitudes, social cognition, emotion experience, and expressive behavior. These topics all bring issues of control and automaticity to the fore because they share, along with the classic studies in the field, a concern with the genuineness of social behavior. Does the person genuinely hold this attitude, really believe in that stereotype, actually experience a given emotion, or privately experience the state signified by the publicly expressed behavior? When it comes to "crunch time," where do a person's loyalties and inclinations lie? The rule of thumb here has been that if a behavior can be attributed to automatic processes, it is more genuine than one that reflects conscious control. We believe that this is because people recognize that strategic editing of one's

opinions and beliefs, and shaping of one's behavior towards what others expect and wish to see, require control and do not happen automatically.

This is not necessarily a safe universal assumption, as there are exceptions—indeed, sometimes the behaviors we perform automatically occur only because we consciously do not want to do them (Wegner, 1994), or because of passive effects of perception on behavior (Bargh, Chen, & Burrows, 1996). As we shall see, though, the issue of genuineness retains its interest value across topics and has given rise to informative scientific literatures addressing the control and automaticity of a range of social behaviors.

Attitudes and Beliefs

Issues of automaticity and control have long been a theme of attitude research, in all areas: the control one has over the formation of one's attitudes in the first place, over changing those attitudes in response to persuasive influences, and in the role those attitudes play in guiding one's behavior toward the objects of the attitudes.

Attitude Formation Attitudes that form just because the person is exposed to the novel attitude object repeatedly over time (Zajonc, 1968) can be considered to have developed automatically. This mere exposure effect appears to be due to a buildup in strength of the representation of the novel object with repeated exposure to it that increases the ease of perceiving the object (Gordon & Holyoak, 1983; see also Jacoby, Kelley, Brown, & Jasechko, 1989). Such perceptual fluency produces a positively valenced feeling of familiarity associated with the attitude object.

Because the individual did not intend to evaluate the object, the increasingly positive attitude that results from repeatedly encountering it did not require any conscious involvement in the process (such as consideration of how the object relates to important self-goals). That the mere exposure effect does not require conscious involvement to occur is indicated by the often replicated finding by Kunst-Wilson and Zajonc (1980) that the effect occurs even with repeated subliminal presentation of novel stimuli (see review by Bornstein, 1989). (In the case of subliminally presented novel stimuli the positive affect due to fluency is misattributed in the test phase to observable qualities of the stimulus, because the participant has no conscious recollection or experience of ever having seen it.) In terms of the seven relations between control and automatic processing, such automatic attitude formation is an instance of *multitasking,* because it occurs while the person is dealing with the attitude object simultaneously with a nonevaluative control process. (Even in the case of subliminal stimulus presentation, the participant has some kind of ongoing control processing task.)

Another automatic source of attitude formation is via

classical conditioning: the association of the novel attitude object with another object or event that already has a positive or negative valence. The original studies that attempted to demonstrate classical conditioning of attitudes (e.g., Staats & Staats, 1958) were open to alternative interpretations, the most problematic being demand effects (see review in Eagly & Chaiken, 1993, pp. 399–412). However, a study by Krosnick, Betz, Jussim, Lynn, and Stephens (1992) used subliminal presentation of the unconditioned stimulus (UCS)—faces with either positive or negative emotional expressions—in order to eliminate such objections. Novel attitude object stimuli were paired with subliminal emotional facial expressions, and subsequently expressed attitudes toward these novel objects were in line with the valence of the UCS (facial expressions) associated with them during the study phase of the experiment. A similar interpretation could be made of the finding by Niedenthal (1990) that subliminally presenting an emotional (human) face just before a target cartoon face affected whether the cartoon character was perceived as being sad or happy. Although Niedenthal (1990) interpreted the effect in terms of affective priming, in light of Krosnick et al.'s (1992) results, it could also be that the valence of the subliminal facial expression conditioned the participants' attitudes toward the cartoon characters.

A form of automatic attitude formation appears in the finding of Cacioppo, Priester, and Berntson (1993) that muscular feedback influences attitude formation. When an individual's arm was flexed (bent with hand near shoulder), he or she tended to form favorable attitudes toward novel stimuli; when the arm was extended straight out, the individual tended to form negative attitudes. Presumably, arm flexion is associated with approach motivations (see Lewin, 1935), in that the arm is in the position of pulling something in toward the body. Arm extension is associated with avoidance motivations, as the arm is pushing away from the body. Because people are motivated to approach those objects that they positively evaluate, and to avoid those they negatively evaluate, the muscular feedback associated with approach and avoidance reactions was apparently associated with the novel stimuli, producing another type of classical conditioning of attitudes. Again, this effect on attitude formation is preconsciously automatic (and a case of *multitasking*) because the participants in the experiment were not aware of any relation between their arm positions and their feelings about the novel attitude objects.

There appear to be immediate, automatic processes operating in belief formation as well as in attitude formation. In an analysis of the dynamics of belief formation, Gilbert (1991, 1993) contrasted the Cartesian model, in which an idea is first represented in the mind and then (consciously and deliberately) assessed for its truth value, with the argument by Spinoza that ideas are by default (i.e., automatically) accepted as true—that is, they are believed—and

only then tested for falsity (via a conscious and deliberate process). In terms of the various relations between automatic and control processes, Descartes' position on belief formation is clearly one of control *regulation* of the automatic belief representation, whereas that of Spinoza is one of *multitasking* as automatic belief happens independently of concurrent control processing.

As with Gilbert's (1989; Gilbert & Malone, 1995) related work on default attribution processes, the importance of positing an initial automatic belief stage is that if the second, conscious stage of checking the initial belief for veracity is prevented for some reason—a common one being a momentary lack of attentional resources to support the conscious process—then the idea will be accepted and believed when it otherwise might not have been.

Gilbert, Tafarodi, and Malone (1993) tested the Spinozan against the Cartesian model of belief formation by having participants allegedly learn a new language. They saw statements of the form "An X is a Y" with either the word true or the word false coming on the screen after each statement. On some trials, the task was interrupted prior to the appearance of true or false and participants instead were confronted with a reaction time task. The effect of this manipulation was to prevent the second stage of truth assessment. If ideas were merely represented initially without being automatically accepted as true, then statements presented on these interruption trials should be no more likely to be accepted as true as other statements. However, in line with Spinoza's claims, participants were more likely to misidentify these interruption-trial statements as true when they were in fact false than false items on noninterruption trials. And also consistent with Spinoza's model, the interruption manipulation had no effect on the subsequent correct identification of true statements. In another experiment, Gilbert et al. (1993) showed the real-life importance of automatic initial acceptance of information. In a jury trial simulation, false information about a defendant was nevertheless believed by participants and affected their sentencing decisions if participants' attentional resources were diverted by a secondary task. Without the conscious processing resources to correct or check the veracity of incoming information, then, we tend by default to believe it to be true.

Models of Attitude Change The road to attitude change may sometimes lead through a reasoned, effortful consideration of message content and other features of the communication—or it may happen automatically and without much conscious thought at all. Models of persuasion taking into account such dual processes bear some similarity to the distinction between control and automatic processes but also differ from it in important ways.

One such model is Chaiken's (1980) heuristic-systematic model (HSM), a distinction between *heuristic* and *sys-*

tematic processing of persuasive messages. Systematic processing corresponds to an effortful consideration of the quality of the arguments, including consideration of relevant nonmessage information such as the expertise of the source. Heuristic processing, on the other hand, makes use of simple decision rules (e.g., "length equals strength" of an argument) which enable decisions to be made as to whether to accept or reject the persuasive attempt without effortful consideration and weighing of the arguments themselves.

The heuristic-systematic distinction resembles but is not identical to the automatic-control process dichotomy. Both heuristic and systematic consideration of persuasive messages can involve intentional processing, because to engage in one processing strategy versus the other is a choice made by the individual. The different strategies are really a choice between features of the communication situation to which one will attend, with this choice driven by the importance of the issue for the individual as well as other motivations he or she might currently have. These different possible motivations also affect the *nature* of the processing the information receives. As in models of automatic and conscious processing (e.g., Posner & Snyder, 1975; Logan, 1980), the HSM holds a multitasking assumption, in that the heuristic mode can influence processing even when systematic consideration of the message is underway. Indeed, the outcome of the systematic processing of the message may be influenced by the ongoing heuristic processing of it.

The Elaboration-Likelihood Model (ELM) of persuasive message processing (Petty & Cacioppo, 1984) also distinguishes between two routes to persuasion; a "central" route in which the quality and logic of the arguments themselves are the basis for the attitude change, and a "peripheral" route in which other features of the persuasion situation are the basis. Examples of such message-external features are the expertise or credentials of the source, or the extent to which the source is seen as objective versus having a vested interest in the matter. Factors that move the individual from one route to the other when presented with a persuasive message are the importance and relevance of the issue to the individual's goals and concerns. Thus, the ELM characterizes the interplay between automatic and control processes more in terms of *regulation* than *multitasking.*

When motivation to engage in effortful (systematic or central-route) processing is low, or attentional capacity to be able to engage in it (even when motivated) is in short supply, or both, one would expect a greater reliance on the less effortful modes of processing. It appears to be a general rule throughout attitude and social cognition research that conscious, deliberate forms of processing information about attitude issues as well as about people are not used unless the individual has both the attention and the inten-

tion to give the matter full consideration (Bargh, 1989; Bargh & Thein, 1985); in their stead, stereotypic and heuristic shortcuts are taken.

Both the HSM and ELM dual-process models bear some similarity to the automatic-control process distinction, in terms of the differential amounts of effort needed to reach an attitude position required by the two processes. However, within both models, even the less effortful mode of message processing is to some extent intentional and strategic on the part of the individual. Moreover, in neither model do the respective theorists contend that the heuristic or the peripheral route processing is autonomous once instigated, not requiring any conscious guidance.

Automatic Attitude Activation A more direct application to attitude research of the Posner and Snyder (1975) model of automatic and control processing was made by Fazio (1986, 1990), specifically apropos of the attitude-behavior relation. To the extent one's attitude toward a person, event, or object becomes active only when one consciously retrieves it, the attitude might not play any role in behavior toward the attitude object if such conscious retrieval is prevented. If the person is paying attention to other things at the time, for example, he or she might not stop to think about feelings toward the object before dealing with it. But attitudes that become active *automatically* upon the presence of the attitude object, on the other hand, would not be so restricted by the current demands on control processing, and would thus be able to exert a more consistent influence on behavior across situations.

Therefore, Fazio, Chen, McDonel, and Sherman (1982) proposed a model of *attitude accessibility.* This model, which combined Fiske's (1982) notion of *category-based affect* with Higgins and King's (1981) work on the determinants of knowledge accessibility in memory, defined an attitude as an evaluative tag associated with the representation of its corresponding attitude object. The key principle of this model was that the probability of an attitude influencing behavior was a function of its likelihood of becoming active in the mere presence of the attitude object (i.e., without the need of intentional or control processing to active it), and that this likelihood was in turn a function of the strength of the associative connection between the object representation and the attitude.

Early studies of this idea (Fazio et al., 1982) increased the accessibility of attitudes temporarily via a repeated-expression manipulation and found increased accessibility resulting in behavior more consistent with the expressed attitude. But it was important for this model of the attitude-behavior relation to be able to show that preconscious automatic activation of attitudes occurred, and not just postconscious automatic activation due to recent use and activation. To support the proposed account of why some attitudes but not others consistently affect behaviors, it had to be shown that the mere presence of the attitude object was all that was needed to activate the associated attitude.

Several tests of this hypothesis were provided by Fazio, Sanbonmatsu, Powell, and Kardes (1986). In a conceptual replication of the Neely (1977) experiment, the names of attitude objects were presented as prime words, followed by a target adjective to which participants responded. In all three experiments, a trial consisted of one attitude object name appearing as a prime, and then an adjective as a target, and participants were to press a button (either one labeled "good" or one labeled "bad") as quickly as they could to report whether the adjective was positive or negative in meaning. On the critical trials, following Neely's (1977) procedure, the delay between prime and target was too brief (ca. 250 milliseconds) for any conscious, strategic processing of the attitude object prime. Thus, if the name of the attitude object automatically activated its associated attitude in memory—with *attitude* defined by Fazio et al. (1986) as the evaluation of the object as good or bad—then participants should be predisposed to make that response (i.e., "good" or "bad") to the target adjective that followed. This would facilitate or speed up responses to adjectives of the same valence as the attitude object prime (i.e., good-good or bad-bad trials), and also cause responses to adjectives of the opposite valence to be slowed down (i.e., good-bad or bad-good trials) because of the need to inhibit the automatically activated incorrect response (see Logan, 1980).

Fazio et al. (1986) predicted such an automatic activation effect only for the participant's strongest attitudes, not for all attitudes. In line with the *automatization* relation between control and automatic processes, Fazio et al. (1986) held that attitudes become automatic through frequent and consistent controlled evaluation of the object. The strength of an attitude was defined operationally in terms of how quickly participants evaluated each of the attitude object stimuli as quickly as they could after its name was presented on the computer screen. The attitude objects corresponding to the four fastest "good" and "bad" responses, and to the four slowest "good" and "bad" responses, were selected to serve as the attitude object primes for the experimental phase of the study.

Results confirmed that the automaticity effect occurred for the participants' strongest but not weakest attitudes; in two experiments, only the names of the participants' "strong" attitude objects facilitated responding to adjective targets of the same valence, compared to when the targets were of the opposite valence. Given the brief time between prime and target (stimulus onset asynchrony, or SOA) on those trials, too short for a conscious expectancy to develop regarding the valence nature of the target word, such an effect could only occur if the strongly held attitudes had become activated automatically. Under conditions in which the SOA was longer (1000 milliseconds), control regulation of the automatic process did occur.

Subsequent research by Bargh, Chaiken, and their colleagues (Bargh, Chaiken, Govender, & Pratto, 1992; Bargh, Chaiken, Raymond, & Hymes, 1996; Chaiken & Bargh, 1993) centered on two issues. First, given that the effect occurred for the strongest but not the weakest of the participants' attitudes, what about the great majority of the participants' attitudes across the middle of the strength distribution? Was automatic attitude activation a rare or a common event? Second, was the effect truly automatic in that it would occur if—unlike in the original paradigm—participants were not explicitly instructed to evaluate the target words and had not just given their evaluations of the prime words? Did attitudes spring to mind automatically in real world situations, in which one has not recently thought about one's likes and dislikes?

The answer to the first question turned out to be related to the answer to the second question. When these problematic aspects of the Fazio et al. (1986) procedure were removed—when a two-day delay was interposed between the attitude assessment phase and the automaticity task, for instance, and when participants pronounced instead of explicitly evaluated the target stimuli—the effect was obtained for all attitude objects studied, and with no moderation by attitude strength (Bargh et al., 1996; Chaiken and Bargh, 1993). That is, when intentional, control evaluative processing aspects of the paradigm were removed in order to test for their contributing role in producing the effect, not only did the effect continue to occur (strongly demonstrating its automaticity), but it occurred more generally, across a wide range of attitude strengths, and was not moderated by differences in strength.

As it turns out, Kihlstrom (1987) had presaged this exact pattern of results a decade ago. Specifically, he argued that deliberate, control processing of a given stimulus could restrict or interfere with implicit and nonconscious affective reactions to that stimulus. It is important to note that over the same ten-year period, research programs in several other domains have produced the same conclusion. In a meta-analytic review of the mere exposure effect, Bornstein (1989) concluded that subliminal presentations of the novel stimuli produced stronger effects than did supraliminal presentations. Research on the "affective primacy" hypothesis has experimentally demonstrated that subliminal presentation of affect-laden stimuli results in stronger and more pervasive affective priming effects than supraliminal presentation of the same primes (Murphy, Monahan, & Zajonc, 1995; Murphy & Zajonc, 1993). And there are suggestions in the ongoing research on automatic stereotype activation (see below) that passive processing of stereotype-relevant features results in a more pervasive stereotype activation effect than do experimental conditions involving more active, control processing of the stereotypic features (see Bargh, Chen, & Burrows, 1996; Devine, 1989; Fazio, Jackson, Dunton, & Williams, 1995).

It appears, then, that the automatic activation of evaluations or attitudes by the mere presence of the attitude object in the environment is a ubiquitous phenomenon, similar to the activation of semantic meaning by the presence of a word during reading, or to Gilbert's (1993) demonstration of default, preconscious belief processes. Activation of its evaluation by an environmental stimulus thus is a default, preconscious reaction, occurring as part and parcel of the perception of that object. The most important consequence of this is that variations in the automatic attitude activation effect per se cannot explain variations in the attitude-behavior relation, because all attitude objects activate their evaluation upon their mere presence in the environment. That is, the reason why some attitudes affect behavior more consistently than do other attitudes cannot be because the mere presence of some attitude objects in the environment activates the associated attitude, while the mere presence of other objects does not.

The evidence is that it takes more than the mere presence of the attitude object to produce variations in attitude activation according to attitude strength. When a person is currently or has just engaged in conscious evaluative thinking, then and only then does the accessibility of the attitude (technically speaking, the strength of the object-evaluation association in memory; see Fazio, 1986; Fazio et al., 1982) seem to moderate the subsequently observed automatic attitude effect. In other words, the evidence to date suggests that attitude strength does play a moderating role in the activation of the attitude to the extent the object is being given conscious scrutiny (i.e., when it is the current focus of the person's goals); otherwise, any and all attitudes become activated automatically.

In summary, automatic processing is involved in all aspects of attitude functioning, from formation to change processes to the effect of attitude on behavior. The growing body of evidence of automaticity in these areas is conceptually related to the growing evidence of automaticity in affective information processing more generally, especially for models of attitudes that focus particularly on their evaluative dimension.

Social Judgment, Attribution, and Stereotyping

Attaining an understanding of a person is a seriously important activity in social life. Control processes and automatic processes are both involved in this enterprise, but the general trend in this area of research has been to examine the degree to which social cognition proceeds automatically—against the background assumption that the balance of the processes involved include the exercise of conscious control. In what follows, we trace these automatic effects of the social environment as they proceed ever further inside the mind. We start with automatic determinants of perceptual selection and attention to social information—what types of information catch one's eyes and ears with regularity?

Once social information is noticed in the first place, it can of course be processed according to current goals and purposes, but automatic effects can also continue on to reach higher levels of analysis—that is, to the activation of more abstract representations of the information such as concepts, categories, and schemas. However, objects and events in the social environment can be categorized in a great many different ways, and so we review the evidence as to which types of categorizations tend to occur naturally, stimulated by the presence of the relevant information alone. The forms of such automatic categorization that have received the lion's share of research attention have been the categorization of social behaviors in terms of trait concepts, and the pigeonholing of individual members of distinctive social groups in terms of that group's stereotype.

The last steps in social perception involve understanding what people are like and why they do what they do. Do automatic effects of the environment extend so far as to influence the formation of impressions and causal attributions? This has been a central question in social cognition for the past two decades, and we end this section with an answer based on a survey of the relevant evidence.

Initial Screening of the Environment Some forms of information are more likely than others to be selected for attention and consideration out of the great amount of available stimulation, because they automatically grab one's attention. Automatic attention responses take two forms, goal-dependent and preconscious. Goal-dependent automatic attention occurs when, once a goal is in place and operating, objects and events relevant to that goal seem to "pop out" from the background. Preconscious automatic attention occurs when social information attracts our attention regardless of our current goal.

Attention is often if not usually goal-directed. What we look at and the way in which we think about it are mainly determined and regulated by the goal we have at the time. When we walk down a busy street, we see the people, bicycles, cars, and also puddles that we need to avoid in pursuing our goal of safely and dryly navigating to our destination. And we have done this often enough not to have to intend or try to seek out these obstacles so as to avoid them: our currently active goal causes them to jump out at us because they are relevant to that goal (see Bruner, 1957).

But if we see the same people in another context, for example at a restaurant or a classroom, we no longer focus automatically on their speed and trajectories, but on other features, such as whether we know them or not, or if they are wearing something interesting, or if they seem to be enjoying their meal (and if so, what did they order?). So not only *what* we pay attention to but also *which* of its aspects we pay attention is largely determined by our current purposes, and in such a way that we do not need to control the direction of our attention. The important pieces of information related to those goals will jump out at us automatically (i.e., the *orienting* relation), at least if we have engaged in that goal often enough (such as walking down a street safely). When we are driving a car, for example, the red light or stop sign automatically grabs our attention and we respond accordingly, our foot moving toward the brake pedal without our need to intentionally decide to do so. But if we are just walking down the street, or looking out our office window at it, the red light or stop sign has no such effect (see Bargh, 1992b). The automatic attention response is dependent on which intentional control process is currently operating.

Therefore, as Jones and Thibaut (1958) first noted, the information that is picked up in a social interaction is heavily dependent on the person's current conscious purpose, or operating control processes (see Bargh, 1990; Gollwitzer & Moskowitz, 1996; Read & Miller, 1989; Wyer & Srull, 1989, for reviews). It is very much as if the conscious operating goal *delegates* to automatic processes the job of detecting and alerting the system to the presence of goal-relevant information. These goals are not only the one most frequently studied in social cognition experiments, however—the goal of impression formation. Often if not usually one has other important goals to pursue during the interaction. One's pickup of information when interacting with people is largely determined by their utility for achieving that goal (Wicklund & Steins, 1996) rather than by their personal characteristics. If an individual is trying to ingratiate or impress another person, for example, information concerning whether that person is reacting favorably or not is gobbled up voraciously, whereas one cares much less about such evaluative feedback if the other is a subordinate to whom one is giving instructions (see Fiske, 1993; Kipnis, 1976).

"Most Favored Information" Status: Privileged Access to the Judgment Process

In addition to information relevant to our current goals, there are forms that seem to gain access to our minds independently of these goals—and thus serve as a chronic and consistent source of influence on our judgments. There are four such privileged types of information that we should note: information related to the *self;* information that is *frequently experienced;* information about *negatively valued* social behavior; and *social category* information.

Self-relevant information chronically attracts our attention and intrudes on our ongoing control processing, the most famous example being our own name—a phenomenon known as the "cocktail party effect" (Cherry, 1953). We may have no idea what a cluster of people at a party are talking about, engaged as we are in our own conversation with others, but if someone in that other group says our name, suddenly our ears zero in on their conversation. It is as if we have sensitive antennae that pick up self-relevant information even when we are not intending to pick it up;

such information is often able to break through the attentional barrier set up by our current goals and purposes.

Other research has shown that we are similarly sensitive to any information directly relevant to the self, not just to our name. In an important early study, Postman, Bruner, and McGinnies (1948) found that people had lower recognition thresholds to words related to their idiosyncratically important values (e.g., religiosity, justice); they saw and reported these words at briefer presentation times than words related to values not as personally important to them.

We are also generally more sensitive to information related to our self-concepts. In one study (Bargh, 1982), participants engaged in a dichotic listening task in which they shadowed or repeated aloud each of a series of words presented to one ear, and tried to ignore words presented concurrently to the opposite ear. On one block of trials, the words presented to the unattended ear were related to the trait of independence. For participants for whom the trait was an important part of their self-concept (see Markus, 1977), the presence of those independence-related words distracted attentional resources from the controlled shadowing task (as measured by a probe reaction time task), indicating that they were detected and processed automatically, outside of awareness (though the control task was able to regulate the automatic process from usurping awareness). In another study that made use of the dichotic listening task, Nielsen and Sarason (1981) showed that participants made more shadowing errors (i.e., were distracted to a greater extent) when words related to their anxieties (i.e., dating, school) were presented to the unattended channel (see also Geller & Shaver, 1976; Hull & Levy, 1979).

Bargh and Tota (1988) used the Markus (1977) adjective endorsement task to assess the efficiency with which the self-concept becomes active. In one condition of the experiment, participants were to judge the self-descriptiveness of each of a series of positive and negative trait adjectives, by saying yes or no as quickly as they could. Half of the participants performed this task by itself, but the remaining participants had to hold a six-digit number (different each trial) in memory while making each judgment, so that the degree to which the two types of judgments required attentional resources could be assessed. To the extent the judgment could be made automatically, response latencies should be unaffected by the concurrent attentional load. Results showed that participants think about themselves automatically in positive trait terms, such that they were just as fast to make those judgments with a concurrent memory task as without it. With negative trait judgments, however, the attentional load manipulation slowed responses, showing that these traits did not become active automatically.

Other research has shown that the effect of attentional load is to make the self-concept more favorable (Paulhus, Graf, & Van Selst, 1989). Thus, if one can use what comes to mind automatically, when control processes are prevented, as a "truer" measure of what people really believe, then it would seem that people in general have pretty high opinions of themselves. Tice, Butler, Muraven, and Stillwell (1995) have found, however, that we become pretty good at regulating or hiding these smug feelings, at least from friends. They found that one's self-presentations to friends were more modest than to strangers. Moreover, the automaticity of these self-presentational strategies was shown by the fact that when participants were instructed to engage in self-enhancement with friends or modesty with strangers, compared to their natural tendencies to be modest with friends and self-enhance with strangers, their ability to recall the interaction was poorer. Engaging in the opposite self-presentational strategies apparently required more attention, taking it away from external environmental events and resulting in poorer memory for them.

Research by Andersen and her colleagues (e.g., Andersen & Cole, 1990; Andersen, Glassman, Chen, & Cole, 1995) is relevant to the self research, in that it obtains similar effects for the other significant people in one's life (e.g., parents, romantic partners). When we encounter people whose features resemble significant others in some important way, the representation of that significant other becomes activated without the perceiver's awareness by the presence of those features, and that activated representation becomes used to anticipate and interpret the behavior of the new acquaintance. In several studies, if the new stimulus person resembled a participant's significant other, the participant assumed that the target would possess additional characteristics of the significant other as well.

The self may have a quite different effect on the automatic activation of trait information when self-conceptions are unwanted. Newman, Duff, and Baumeister (1997) have found that when people suppress thoughts about their own characteristics, they become more inclined to pick up information about those characteristics in others. This effect appears both when people suppress thoughts about their traits in response to instruction, and when they do so as a result of their own dispositional repressive tendencies.

Such findings put a new spin on the Freudian notion of defensive projection—and suggest its possible roots in ironic monitoring processes underlying the control of thoughts about the self. The person who is most worried and nonplussed about a property of self may be monitoring it so intently as to make it hyperaccessible in perceptions of others (cf. Wegner & Erber, 1992). Perhaps the same set of chronically accessible trait constructs, both positive and negative, may be operating in both self and other perception (Bargh & Tota, 1988; Higgins & Bargh, 1987), but with the addition of a regulatory, self-protective stage of rationalization operating to defend against negative trait construals of the self (e.g., Steele, 1988; Tesser, Martin, & Cornell, 1996).

This latter possibility points to the fact that automatic attention responses are not limited to the self; they occur in response to any form of information that is frequently attended. Frequently attended information is the second kind of "most favored information" for social judgment. Higgins, King, and Mavin (1982) found that in reading about the behaviors of another person, people attended to and later remembered certain kinds of behavior more than others. There were individual differences in terms of which behaviors a person would attend to and remember, predicted by which trait dimensions they listed first in a free response questionnaire about the types of people they encountered in their daily lives. Presumably, those that came to mind first, without prompting by semantic or other associative relations with other dimensions, were those that the individual used very frequently in thinking about other people (see also Wegner, 1977). Higgins et al. (1982) termed these *chronically accessible* trait constructs, in that they led to the pickup of relevant behavioral information without priming or recent use.

Bargh and Pratto (1986) applied the Stroop color-word paradigm to this issue. Participants were to name the color in which each of a series of words was presented as quickly as possible, with the meaning of the word irrelevant (and a distracter) to this task. It was found that participants were more distracted by words related to their chronically accessible constructs than those related to their inaccessible constructs. Because the participant's goal was merely to name the word color, and not to form impressions of anyone, we can conclude from this that automatic attention responses exist for behaviors relevant to a person's chronically accessible personality constructs. Such automatic attention effects have also been extended to the domain of attitudes. Roskos-Ewoldsen and Fazio (1992) obtained the same Stroop-like uncontrollable orientation effect for the names of attitude objects, when the attitudes associated with these objects in memory were made temporarily more accessible by repeated expression.

Thus, it appears that for aspects of one's life one *frequently thinks about*—values, important dimensions of one's self concept and of the behavior of others, and attitudes—the presence of information related to those aspects automatically attracts our attention. These forms of information, then, are more likely than others to be noticed, thought about, and remembered, even if our control processing currently lies with other aspects of the environment.

A third general source of automatic attention responses or "most favored information" is *negative* social behavior, including negative emotional expressions (Fiske, 1980; Hansen & Hansen, 1988; Pratto & John, 1991). People seem to be especially vigilant about negative or potentially threatening social information (Wegner & Vallacher, 1977). In one study, Fiske (1980) instructed participants to form an impression of each of several target persons whose behavior was conveyed by means of photographs. Participants were allowed to advance at their own pace the slide projector displaying the photographs, and Fiske (1980) surreptitiously measured how long the participant looked at each one as an indication of relative attention. In general, negative behaviors were looked at longer and subsequently were given more weight in the participant's impressions of the targets, than were positive behaviors.

In a related finding, Pratto and John (1991) had participants name the colors in which a variety of personality trait terms were presented (i.e., the Stroop task) and obtained longer naming latencies for undesirable than desirable trait terms. This finding confirms that the greater attention given to the negative social behaviors, as in Fiske's (1980) experiment, is due to an automatic attention response, because participants in the Pratto and John (1991) study could not control the attention-demanding nature of the negative personality information. Pratto (1994) reported further studies demonstrating the strong tendency to orient toward negative social information, in which the greater attention allocation occurred even after participants were told about the effect and encouraged to overcome it if they could.

Features that signal a person's *social category membership* represent a fourth kind of "most favored information" that has privileged access to the mind. Easily discriminable *personal features*—especially the "big three" of gender, race, and age—tend to activate preconsciously the categories or stereotypes associated with them (e.g., Bargh, 1994; Brewer, 1988; Fiske & Neuberg, 1990; Macrae, Stangor, & Milne, 1994), with these stereotypes consisting in part of collections of personality trait constructs (Hamilton & Sherman, 1994; Stangor & Lange, 1994). These features tend to be easily encoded and detectable, such as skin color, and age-related and gender-related characteristics. They are not limited to visual features, however; regional (e.g., Southern United States) and national (e.g., German, Chinese) stereotypes can be triggered by speech accents and dialects as well (especially over the telephone when no visual features are present). Also, the mere presence of features associated with a particular role in society (e.g., a waiter's or police officer's uniform) can also trigger stereotypes associated with that role (see Cohen & Ebbesen, 1979; Taylor, 1981).

To a certain extent, categorizing and pigeonholing people quickly and efficiently in terms of their group membership is adaptive and defensible in that we cannot possibly attend and individuate everyone we encounter. Macrae, Milne, and Bodenhausen (1993; see also Macrae, Bodenhausen, et al., 1994) have found that stereotypes do allow for more efficient processing of information about people, in that less attentional capacity is needed and can thus be devoted to other, goal-relevant tasks. Dijksterhuis and van Knippenberg (1996a) provide evidence suggesting that stereotype activation also inhibits stereotype-inconsistent information from gaining access to control processes. Thinking accurately and completely about anything—including people and attitude issues—takes effort, and unless an individual is especially motivated to engage in this effort, control over the default automatic process is usually not taken (Devine, 1989; Fiske & Neuberg, 1990). And, if the person is not aware that a stereotype has been activated and is influencing his or her judgment, no control is possible anyway (Bargh, 1989; Strack & Hannover, 1996).

Is Stereotyping Inevitable? The automaticity of the pickup of stereotype-relevant information makes one wonder whether stereotyping is indeed obligatory in social judgment. This remains, however, an open question. The evidence to date suggests that automatic stereotype activation depends on the strength of the association between the representation of the group (including distinguishing group features) and the representation of the group stereotype in memory. While for many stereotypes this connection may be so frequently used by most people that it becomes automatic for the average person, for other stereotypes that are less implicitly assumed by members of the culture, this connection may be more tenuous.

Devine (1989) has found that white Americans' stereotype of African Americans becomes active when verbal stimuli related to that stereotype are presented subliminally; thus stereotypes can become activated without the individual being aware of it and consequently, unintentionally, given the presence of group features in the environment. Pratto and Bargh (1991) found that gender stereotypes become active to influence judgments about a target person even under information overload conditions; that is, efficiently (see also Macrae et al., 1993). But Gilbert and Hixon (1991) did not find an influence of the mere presence of an Asian-American in a videotape on stereotypic completions of word fragments (e.g., S_Y as SHY instead of SPY) when participants' attentional capacity was loaded by a secondary task (whereas the stereotypic influence did occur in the nonoverload condition). It appears, therefore, that stereotypes may vary in their ease or automaticity of activation. Those that are activated more consistently upon the presence of a member of the stereotyped group will be more likely subsequently to become activated unintentionally and efficiently.

One might expect this connection between representation of a group and its stereotypic trait concepts to vary in strength as a function of the prejudice level of the individual. That is, the more prejudiced a person, the more likely he or she activates those stereotypic trait concepts when encountering a member of that group. Devine (1989), however, found that the probability of automatic activation of the African-American stereotype did not fluctuate as a function of scores on the Modern Racism Scale (McConahay, Hardee, & Batts, 1981). The subliminal presentation of stimuli related to the stereotype (e.g., musical, lazy, welfare, ghetto) activated the entire stereotype, including content not presented as priming stimuli such as "hostile," for all participants regardless of their responses on the racism scale. Stereotype activation was evidenced by more hostile ratings of a target person in a subsequent impression formation task by those participants exposed to the stereotype-relevant stimuli. Bargh, Chen, and Burrows (1996, Experiment 3) recently found that subliminal presentation of African-American faces to white male participants resulted in increases in the participant's own hostile behavior—a behavioral effect of automatic stereotype activation—and again this effect was not moderated by participants' Modern Racism scores.

In contrast to this, Fazio et al. (1995) have observed individual variations in prejudicial behavior as a function of stereotype strength. They presented participants with the faces of African Americans and whites as part of an explicit memory task; participants were instructed to attend to each of the faces because they would be asked to remember them later (they could, later, at better than chance levels). Following each (brief) face presentation a target adjective appeared that participants were to classify quickly as either good or bad in meaning. Following the logic of the Fazio et al. (1986) study on automatic attitude activation, the authors argued that attitudes toward African Americans could be measured in terms of whether the presence of black faces facilitated responses to negative adjective targets and slowed responses to positive targets, as would be expected if the presence of a black face automatically activated a negative evaluation (i.e., a prejudicial response).

For each participant the degree of such automatic evaluation was calculated. It was found that this score did in fact predict the positivity of the participant's behavior to an African-American experimenter, who during debriefing at the end of the session had coded the participant's friendliness. Thus, variations in the automaticity of the white participants' stereotypic conception of African Americans did appear to exist, and parlayed into behavioral differences with the black experimenter. Modern Racism scores did not correlate significantly with this behavioral measure, though they did with other questionnaire indicants of prejudice (i.e., the perceived fairness of the acquittal of the four police officers in the Rodney King case).

It seems then that individual differences do exist in the automatic activation of stereotypes upon the mere presence of stereotyped-group features, and that the more prejudiced an individual, the greater the likelihood of automatic stereotyping (see also Lepore & Brown, 1997). In part, the discovery of this possibility has been complicated by the use of the Modern Racism Scale in this research, as it has proven somewhat problematic as a measure of these individual differences (see Fazio et al., 1995). At the same time, however, moderation of stereotyping by degree of racism may be limited to situations in which the individual is processing information about the target person in a deliberate and goal-directed way. Just as in the automatic attitude activation literature, the results to date suggest that the greater the degree of control processing of the stereotype-relevant stimuli, the greater the likelihood of obtaining moderation of stereotyping effects by strength of stereotyped beliefs.

Automatic stereotype activation has effects beyond impressions and judgments of stereotype group members. Because of the passive, spreading effects that social perception tends to have on social behavior (cf. Berkowitz, 1984), the perceiver may behave toward the stereotyped-group member in line with the content of the activated stereotype without realizing he or she is doing so. Bargh, Chen, and Burrows (1996; Experiment 2) found that nonconscious activation of the elderly stereotype caused their experimental participants to walk more slowly down the hall (i.e., in line with the "weak" and "slow" features of the stereotype) when leaving the experimental session, and that subliminal activation of the African-American stereotype caused participants to react with greater hostility to the experimenter. In related work, Dijksterhuis and van Knippenberg (1996b) found that participants primed with the "professor" stereotype subsequently scored higher in a game of Trivial Pursuit than did participants primed with the "soccer hooligan" stereotype.

Such evidence raises the spectre of a most insidious way in which stereotypes have influence and can be perpetuated: on being primed with the stereotype of a target, the perceiver produces the very behavior expected from the target. As the perceiver does not intend to behave in this way, and so has no memory of any intention of doing so, any reciprocal behavior prompted from the target is likely to be attributed to the target and not the perceiver. This is particularly problematic in the case of negative stereotypes and behavior. An experiment by Chen and Bargh (1997) has verified this *automatic* "behavioral confirmation" effect (cf. Snyder & Swann, 1978): subliminal priming of the African-American stereotype in one participant caused his or her interaction partner's behavior to be rated as more hostile both by blind coders and by the stereotype-primed participant.

Ironic Effects of Control of Stereotyping It turns out that the control of stereotype-based judgments is not only difficult at times, but may in fact yield exactly the stereotype inferences that one is attempting to control. It is not only, then, that control processes may suffer *intrusion* by automatic stereotype inferences, but that the control processes may themselves *create* such inferences. This is not a simple matter of the *delegation* of a control task to an automatic process that serves the same purpose as the control process. Rather, the production of such ironic inferences appears to occur as a result of the creation of automatic monitoring processes in the service of conscious control—one which serves a purpose opposite the control process (Wegner, 1994). Part of the mind looks automatically for the stereotypic thought the conscious mind is trying to control.

In their studies of the instructed suppression of a stereotype, Macrae, Bodenhausen, Milne, and Jetten (1994) have found that instructed control of prejudice can be problematic in just this way. These researchers asked participants to suppress stereotype thoughts in imagining the life of a target person belonging to a stereotyped group (a "skinhead"), and then later gave these participants the opportunity to write their impressions of another person of this group. As compared to the impressions of participants who did not first suppress stereotyping, these participants formed more stereotypical impressions of the second target. In another study in this series, Macrae, Bodenhausen et al. (1994) examined the effects of this manipulation on participants' choices of how close to sit to a target just after having controlled their stereotypes of the target in an earlier impression-formation session. As compared to participants who were not instructed to suppress, these participants indeed had created less stereotypical imaginings about the target. However, also as compared to these uninstructed participants, the stereotype suppressors subsequently chose to sit at a greater distance from the target.

According to the theory of ironic processes of mental control (Wegner, 1994), to suppress a prejudiced state of mind is to introduce operating and monitoring processes and their inevitable potential for the production of ironic thoughts and actions. Macrae, Bodenhausen et al. (1994) provided evidence for this in their third study. They examined the effect of stereotype suppression on participants' lexical decision latencies. Participants suppressing the stereotype of a skinhead indeed wrote less stereotypical impressions of him, but at the same time were faster in making correct decisions about stereotype-related words. So, although they were successful in controlling their overall impressions, they appeared to be influenced by an ironic monitoring process that enhanced the automatic activation of stereotype inferences.

A similar eventuality has been tested in research by Wegner, Erber, Bowman, and Shelton (1996) on the mental control of sexism. Participants for one study were given the task of completing sentences that prompted sexist responses (e.g., "Women who go out with lots of men are ___," either under time pressure (mental load) or without such pressure. Some participants were instructed not to be sexist in their completions, whereas others were given no particular instruction. Ratings were made by observers of the degree of sexism in each sentence comple-

tion. It was found that without the imposition of time pressure, participants indeed made fewer sexist responses when they were trying not to be sexist. However, with time pressure imposed, participants made more sexist responses when they were trying not to be sexist than when they were not attempting any mental control at all. The desire to control sexist responding, under the conditions of diminished cognitive resources produced by time pressure, created the ironic tendency instead to blurt out sexist remarks.

This ironic tendency was observed in a second experiment that called for participants to respond rapidly to sexist and nonsexist statements by judging them true or false (Wegner, Erber et al., 1996). When participants were specifically instructed not to be sexist, they made unwanted judgments (calling a sexist statement true or an egalitarian statement false) more quickly than desired judgments (calling sexist statements false or egalitarian statements true). Without the instruction not to be sexist, these judgments were all made with similar latencies. In both of these experiments, the ironic effect was similar for both males and females—and was no more pronounced for people of either sex who were high in dispositional sexism. This suggests that extreme underlying attitudes may not increase the likelihood of ironic monitoring errors

Behavior Categorization Effects   We have been concerned thus far with automaticity and control primarily in the pickup of social information. A next step in social judgment is connecting social information to more abstract conceptions of personality. Now as it happens, social behaviors, once perceived, tend automatically to activate personality trait constructs to which they unambiguously correspond (Carlston & Skowronski, 1994; Moskowitz & Roman, 1992; Srull & Wyer, 1979; Winter & Uleman, 1984).

In initially proposing this idea, Smith and Miller (1979) suggested that such trait categorization is a pervasive response we make to any and all behaviors, even when we aren't trying to form impressions of the actor. To the extent the features of the behavior match closely with the features of the trait representation—that is, if the behavior is unambiguous and clearly diagnostic of that trait—the trait category is activated as part of perceiving the behavior. But if the behavior is vague or ambiguous, open to more than one interpretation, then which category is used to interpret it becomes a matter of the relative accessibilities—or ease of activation—of the various relevant categories in memory (Bruner, 1957; Higgins, Rholes, & Jones, 1977). It is important, conceptually, to separate this categorization of the behavior in trait terms from any subsequent attributional processing in search of the cause of the behavior (e.g., Trope, 1986).

Several lines of research document the automaticity of this categorization process. Srull and Wyer (1979) primed the trait concepts of hostility or kindness in their participants by exposing them to scrambled versions of hostile or kind behavior descriptions ("the kick shoe dog") as part of an alleged test of linguistic ability. That these behaviors unintentionally activated the corresponding trait concepts was shown subsequently by more extreme ratings of a target person along that trait dimension. This effect was replicated by Moskowitz and Roman (1992), who produced similar priming effects through having participants memorize trait-relevant behavior descriptions. Although in these studies the participant's control processing task had nothing to do with personality or social judgment, the behavior descriptions nonetheless activated the relevant trait concepts.

The studies reviewed in the previous section provided participants with behaviors that were clearly diagnostic of a given personality trait. In such cases, as long as the person has sufficient experience in encoding that behavior and similar behaviors as instances of the trait in question, the mere occurrence of the behavior activates the trait concept in memory. This is a data-driven or "bottom-up" effect of the environmental information on categorization. Knowledge is activated to the extent it is *applicable* to the environmental event (e.g., Higgins, 1989, 1996). However, often social behaviors are ambiguous, open to more than one interpretation (Bruner, 1958). Was the person whom we saw running down the street late for something important, rushing to help a family member in trouble, trying to escape after committing a crime, or just trying to get some exercise?

When behaviors are not clearly diagnostic of a personality trait, two things can happen. One is that the perceiver engages in a "search after meaning" (Postman, 1951): a controlled consideration of the features of the behavior and its match with stored features of various relevant trait concepts and other knowledge structures. For example, let's say that our street-runner was dressed in a business suit. That doesn't fit our schema for someone out for some exercise, so we can move on to other, more likely reasons. The second thing that can happen in the case of ambiguity is that one of the relevant trait concepts may be accessible enough in memory that it captures the behavior (Bruner, 1957; Higgins & King, 1981), producing by its top-down effect the same categorization as would have been produced if the behavior itself was more diagnostic.

Trait concepts can become more accessible—and thus likely to capture relevant though ambiguous behaviors—either through long-term frequency or recency of use. Those concepts that are applied again and again by the person in the controlled perceiving and judging of self and others eventually become *automatized* and capable of activation by the mere presence of the relevant behavior in the environment, regardless of the current focus of controlled at-

tentional processing (Bargh, 1984; Bargh & Pratto, 1986; Bargh & Thein, 1985; Higgins, King, & Mavin, 1982). As proposed by Smith and Branscombe (1988), these chronically accessible trait constructs correspond to very efficient behavior-to-trait encoding pathways. Thus, even when attention is overloaded, these constructs detect and process relevant behaviors (Bargh & Thein, 1985). And chronically accessible constructs also capture and encode behaviors that are ambiguously relevant to that trait, so that the perceiver considers them diagnostic of that trait (and so influencing the impression of the target on that trait dimension) when other perceivers—who don't have that construct chronically accessible—would not (Bargh, Bond, Lombardi, & Tota, 1986; Bargh, Lombardi, & Higgins, 1988).

Trait constructs also can become temporarily more accessible than other relevant ones if they have been used recently (i.e., "primed"). Higgins, Rholes, and Jones (1977) showed that if participants had been exposed to a trait term (e.g., adventurous, brave) recently as part of a task having nothing to do with personality or social perception, they were more likely to interpret a subsequently presented ambiguous behavior (e.g., "he sailed alone across the Atlantic") in terms of that trait instead of other potentially relevant trait concepts (e.g., reckless, completely nuts). Subsequent studies have replicated this finding and explored its parameters (e.g., Bargh & Pietromonaco, 1982; Erdley & D'Agostino, 1987; Srull & Wyer, 1979).

What is important about trait construct accessibility is that it produces automatic behavior-to-trait encodings just as if the behavior was not ambiguous but instead clearly diagnostic. The individual is not aware of the influence of accessibility on the ease or fluency of the perceptual process, just that the behavior seemed clearly relevant to that trait and that no effortful search after meaning was necessary. People may use the felt ease of categorization as a cue to its validity, and trust perceptions that require little or no effort more than those that do.

For example, Sherman, Mackie, and Driscoll (1990) had participants evaluate the effectiveness of politicians. Information about the politician's abilities in both foreign affairs and in domestic affairs (e.g., managing the economy) was presented. Participants had been primed beforehand, however, on dimensions relevant to one or the other ability domain. Results showed that the primed dimension was subsequently given more weight in the participant's overall evaluations, consistent with the hypothesis that the participant would attribute the greater processing ease or fluency caused by the priming to the diagnosticity of the information itself.

What the priming literature shows is that people are typically not aware of the impact that their internal perceptual readinesses play in their interpretations of the social environment and will misattribute the apparent clarity of the perceptual interpretation produced by that readiness or accessibility to the clarity and unambiguity of the information itself. This is both good news and bad news. Taking the bad news first, priming and other accessibility influences operate as nonconscious biases, and if a person is not aware of a source of bias, he or she cannot adjust or control for it (Bargh, 1989). The good news is that the "bias" may be less of an error than a reflection of the individual's frequent or recent experience; in a way, then, accessibility influences add in "priors" or base-rates of behavioral probabilities into the interpretation equation (see Higgins & Bargh, 1987; also Anderson, 1990).

Assumed in this discussion is that priming results in the assimilation of the ambiguous behavioral information into the accessible category; that is, the behavior is seen as an instance of that trait. This is the passive or automatic effect of priming. However, if the person is aware of possibly having been influenced by the priming events, *regulation* occurs and control is exerted over that influence. Herr, Sherman, and Fazio (1984) showed that when extreme examples of a trait-type are used as primes (e.g., Dracula as a prime of the trait of hostility), the outcome is contrast away from, rather than assimilation into, the category. The observation "Donald demands his money back at a store" pales somewhat as an instance of hostility compared to the practice of sucking the blood out of countless victims. One possible reason for the contrast effect (instead of assimilation) is that extreme primes are especially memorable, and so are likely to still be in consciousness later on when judging the ambiguous target behaviors. This is consistent with the principle that for control over a social judgment to be exerted, the individual must be aware of the (potential) influence.

Additional support for this interpretation comes from several subsequent studies (Lombardi, Higgins, & Bargh, 1987; Newman & Uleman, 1990; see Strack & Hannover, 1996) in which awareness of the priming events at the time of the later impression formation task resulted in contrast effects, while a lack of residual awareness resulted in assimilation effects. Awareness was assessed by seeing if participants could still recall any of the earlier priming events. Another manipulation likely to increase the chances that the priming events will still be in consciousness later at the time of the impression task—a more effortful processing of the priming stimuli by participants (Martin, Seta, & Crelia, 1990)—also results in contrast instead of assimilation effects.

Intriguingly, there seems to be something automatic about this control process, because all that was required to produce contrast in the Lombardi et al. (1987) study was that the priming stimuli were still in consciousness enough to be recalled; participants were not aware of how they were being influenced by those priming stimuli, which had been presented (as is usual) as part of a separate, earlier experiment.

Control over a priming effect need not always result in contrast effects, however. Wegener and Petty (1995) have shown that it depends on that participant's theory of how he or she might have been influenced by the prime. If the theory is that the effect should be one of contrast, such as judging the desirability of Salt Lake City as a vacation destination after being primed with names such as Bermuda and San Francisco, then the control process results in assimilation, not contrast, to the primed categories.

Finally, it appears to be possible for control over priming effects to be exerted even before the primes have been presented. Thompson, Roman, Moskowitz, Chaiken, and Bargh (1994) informed some participants that they would have to justify and defend their judgments to others later on. This "accountability" manipulation (Tetlock, 1985) prevented subsequently presented priming stimuli from influencing impressions for these participants, while participants not made to feel accountable showed the usual assimilative priming effect. Apparently, motivations to be accurate can protect even against priming influences on judgments.

Are Social Judgments Made Automatically?   Once social information is detected and comprehended—and has activated trait categories, stereotypes, and other stored information in memory—are there automatic ways in which these sources of information are subsequently used? Research on the automaticity of social judgments has shown, for the most part, that impressions and other judgments are not made unless the individual has both the *intention* and the *attention* (i.e., enough processing capacity) to make them (Bargh, 1989, 1990). Bargh and Thein (1985), for example, gave participants explicit instructions to form an impression of a target person, but those for whom attentional resources were in short supply (due to rapid presentation of the relevant information) were not able to do so while the target information was being presented.

What if the participant had the attention but not the intention? Chartrand and Bargh (1996) presented to participants the same information as in the Bargh and Thein (1985) study, giving them plenty of time to read and consider each behavior, but with no explicit instructions other than to read them in order to answer questions about them later. Participants in the control condition showed no signs of having formed an impression about the target person. (The impression-formation goal was primed subliminally for other participants in the experiment, and they *did* form an on-line impression of the target.) Thus, it appears that both the intention to form an impression and the attentional capacity to do so are necessary ingredients if judgments are to be made.

Research on the *spontaneous trait inference* effect (Lupfer, Clark, & Hutchison, 1990; Newman & Uleman, 1989; Winter & Uleman, 1984; Winter, Uleman, & Cunniff, 1985) also typically asks participants to memorize behavior descriptions that are clearly diagnostic of a certain trait (e.g., "The plumber took the orphans to the circus"). After the study phase of the experiment, a cued recall test is given in which participants try to remember each of the sentences. Different types of cues are given, some related to the actor of the sentence (e.g., "pipes"), some to the gist of the sentence (e.g., "enjoyable outing"), and some corresponding to the trait implications of the behavior (e.g., "kind"). To the extent that participants had spontaneously—unintentionally and in the course of memorizing the sentence—encoded it in terms of a personality trait, this trait cue should produce the highest recall. In an often-replicated finding, the trait cue does increase the retrievability of the behavioral portion of the sentence, again confirming that behaviors are unintentionally encoded in terms of trait concepts.

An important issue in this line of research is whether the encoding of behaviors in trait terms stops with trait categorization, or continues on to the encoding of the target person—the actor—in terms of that trait concept as well. This would be tantamount to automatic dispositional attributions, going directly from the perception of a social behavior to an encoding of the actor as having the personality trait exemplified by that behavior.

The evidence for such preconscious dispositional attribution is mixed. Although Winter and Uleman (1984) obtained superior recall of the behavioral portion of the sentence stimuli with trait cues, recall of the sentence actor was not facilitated, as would be expected if participants had been attributing that trait automatically to the actor. Bassili and Smith (1986) and Lupfer et al. (1990) replicated these findings using the original paradigm, in which participants were not trying to form an impression of the actor; but in experimental conditions in which participants did have the conscious impression goal, the trait cue did later facilitate recall of the sentence actor (Bassili & Smith, 1986; Moskowitz & Uleman, 1994; D'Agostino, 1991). It would seem from these studies that the preconscious effect is limited to trait categorization of the behavior, but that causal attribution for the behavior in terms of the actor's personality is a goal-dependent consequence of trying to form an impression of him or her.

In line with this conclusion, Gilbert and his colleagues have found that when participants have the intention of forming an impression of a person, they do go directly from the target's behavior to an attribution of the cause of the behaviors to the target's personality or disposition (e.g., Gilbert, 1989, 1998, in this *Handbook*; Gilbert & Krull, 1988; Gilbert & Malone, 1995; Gilbert & Osborne, 1989; Gilbert, Pelham, & Krull, 1988). Given that the individual is motivated to form an accurate, detailed impression of the target person (see Fiske & Neuberg, 1990), he or she will typically examine the situational context in which behavior

takes place when developing an attribution for its cause. What Gilbert's research has shown is that the first step in this attribution process—given the goal to form an impression—is an automatic attribution of the cause to the target's personality. He has demonstrated this by preventing the control process, which requires attentional capacity, from operating by distracting participants with a second task. When attentional capacity is not loaded through this cognitive busyness manipulation, participants are influenced by clear situational constraints on a target person's behavior—such as a person looking anxious and embarrassed when asked publicly to describe her sexual fantasies. But when instructed to report each of a series of numbers scrolling by on the videotape monitor on which they are watching the target person, participants disregard the situational constraints and conclude the target is dispositionally anxious (Gilbert et al., 1988).

The spontaneous trait inference and cognitive busyness research combine to show that behaviors are unintentionally encoded in terms of personality trait constructs, and, especially if the goal of forming an impression is operative, the person who performed those behaviors may also be automatically encoded as possessing those traits. However, going from behaviors to traits is not an innate cognitive function. We must first learn what behavioral features stand for each trait, and only when we engage in this encoding procedure sufficiently often does the associative pathway between behavioral features and trait constructs become automatized.

Newman (1991), for example, examined the development of spontaneous trait inference propensities; first-graders rarely made even intentional trait inferences, but the tendency to use trait concepts to understand behavior blossomed in fifth-grade students (in fact, fifth-graders were more likely to infer traits spontaneously than were adults). Smith (e.g., Smith, Branscombe, & Bormann, 1988; Smith & Lerner, 1986; Smith, Stewart, & Buttram, 1992; for reviews see Smith, 1994, 1998, in this *Handbook*) has found that the efficiency (speed) with which behaviors are encoded in terms of traits increases with practice. Bassili (1993) found too that prior practice in making trait inferences from behaviors increased the probability of participants' spontaneously making them later. Newman (1993; Uleman, Newman, & Moskowitz, 1996) reported both cross-cultural and individual differences in the occurrence of spontaneous trait inferences.

Taken together, the lesson of these findings is that behaviors are encoded spontaneously and unintentionally in terms of the trait constructs for which they are relevant, at least for the more frequently used trait dimensions, and when there is sufficient processing capacity to make the inferences. Efficiency in trait categorization, on the other hand, comes with practice in applying that category (e.g., Bargh & Thein, 1985).

Automatic Activation of Judgment Standards   There are other aspects of the judgment process besides informational input that can exert unintended, automatic influences. Judgments involve a comparison of the observed behavioral event to a comparison standard (e.g., Helson, 1964; Biernat, Manis, & Nelson, 1991), with the event being either assimilated to or contrasted against that standard. Higgins and Stangor (1988) found in a *change of standard* effect that if one keeps the informational input the same, but changes the judgment standard, the judgment is changed as well. This accounts for why it may seem to us that it snowed more when we were kids than now as adults, because back then it frequently came all the way up to our knees.

Because judgments involve a comparison of input to a standard, automatic activation of standards can exert an unseen influence on judgments just as can automatic informational input. Several studies have now demonstrated such effects. Baldwin, Carrell, and Lopez (1990; see also Baldwin & Holmes, 1987) subliminally primed participants with the faces of significant others in their lives and showed an effect of these primed standards on participants' self-evaluations. Strauman and Higgins (1987) presented participants with stimuli related to either their self-standard for how they ought to be or to their self-standard for who they ideally want to be. These stimuli automatically produced physiological reactions in line with the emotions associated with these standards (i.e., anxiety/higher arousal to the activated ought standard, dejection/lower arousal to the activated ideal standards), as predicted from the fact that participants' opinion of the actual self was significantly discrepant from these standards.

Summary   In general, informational input to social judgment as well as behavioral response processes can be furnished either through automatic or control process means. The preconscious automatic processing of certain features of people and their behavior occurs, by definition, regardless of the current focus of control processing (i.e., *multitasking*). If there is no current control process operating to pick up information relevant to it, then subsequent social judgment processes will, by default, be based largely on automatically furnished sources of input (Bargh, 1989). Current purposes add into the mix the forms of information relevant to those purposes; for example, if one is motivated to form an accurate, fleshed-out impression of an individual, the control process will attend to and pick up individuating details about that person, so that the impression will not be based only on the automatically supplied input (largely stereotypic assumptions based on easily observable features; see Fiske & Neuberg, 1990).

There are a variety of internal representations that become activated automatically in the course of social life, such as attitudes, representations of social groups, anything to do with one's sense of self, and whatever is relevant to achieving one's current goals. Not only do these activated representations then play a major role in one's impressions and judgments about the situation, they also directly and nonconsciously affect one's behavior in it. All these automatic effects—from attitude activation to stereotype activation to behavior categorization—appear to be more pervasive and general when the environmental event is not currently the focus of control processing, and to vary in probability as a function of one's frequency of experience with the event when it is the current focus of deliberate processing.

Emotion Experience

In the traditional philosophy of emotions, the passions arise in us only to be overcome by reason. Emotional states happen to us automatically, in other words, and then we may try to stop them through the implementation of some control process (Clark & Isen, 1982; Gilligan & Bower, 1984; Öhman, 1993). So, for example, we automatically get angry when we are provoked by a bad driver and then we try to control this anger, ideally before we get out of the car and bite someone. As it happens, though, automatic starting and controlled stopping are not the only processes governing emotional experience. There are times when it is useful to think of controlled starting of emotions (as when our conscious thought processes help us to understand what emotion we should be feeling in an ambiguous situation), and there are also instances when automatic stopping becomes evident (as when we anticipate fear or sadness and immediately try not to think about it). In this section, we consider separately the cases of emotion-relevant processing suggested by the fourfold table of automaticity versus control and starting versus stopping.

Automatic Starting   The automaticity of emotion onset seems almost definitional of the concept of emotion. Emotions typically interrupt our activities, reorienting us toward something we had not been considering (Simon, 1967). We may have the conscious goal of emptying the wastebasket, for example, and be interrupted by an emotional reaction when we see something disgusting at the bottom. Mandler (1984) points out, though, that emotional interruptions do not invoke irrelevant or bizarre concerns. Rather, they reorient us toward items that we may not have currently been considering in consciousness, but that are background concerns that always matter in some sense, and that probably should be considered consciously *at this time*. In this sense, the processes that produce emotions may be said to yield unconscious vigilance for items of potential significance to us.

The idea that emotion onset is automatic comes from a

variety of literatures, most of which point to the "basic-ness" of emotional expression and behavior. Emotion seems basic in view of the similarity of human emotional behavior to animal emotional behavior (Andrew, 1963), the early development of emotional responses (Emde, 1984) and processes of emotion imitation (Haviland & Lelwica, 1987), the evolutionary primitiveness of some of the brain centers that govern emotion (MacLean, 1993), and the cross-cultural similarity of emotion expressions (Ekman, 1992). These observations point to an evolutionarily funda-mental behavior production system. It is unlikely that be-haviors emanating from such an apparently innate system (Frijda, 1986) would not be automatic in several important senses. Analyses and reviews of research on the automatic-ity of emotional responses (Clark & Isen, 1982; Gilligan & Bower, 1984; Hansen & Hansen, 1994; Öhman, 1993; Pratto, 1994) point to the wide range of contemporary cog-nitive and social research that is consistent with this gen-eral hypothesis.

Research has assessed automaticity directly, for exam-ple, by establishing that emotional behavior and experience can occur without awareness or cognitive effort. Corteen and Wood (1972) performed an important study suggesting this possibility, in which participants attended to a prose passage presented to one ear while repeating it aloud. At the same time, a list of city names was presented to the nonattended ear. Participants who had previously experi-enced mild electric shocks linked with some of the city names showed higher skin conductance level (SCL; a mea-sure of autonomic nervous system arousal) during the pre-sentation of those names as compared with others, whereas participants without such prior experience did not show this response. This result was replicated by Corteen and Dunn (1974) when additional checks were made to ensure participants' lack of awareness of the city names that were presented.

A different approach to the automaticity of emotional responses was initiated by Zajonc (1980) with the theory of affective primacy, as mentioned earlier. The affective pri-macy theory has received a different sort of test in more re-cent research by Murphy and Zajonc (1993). These studies examined participants' affective responses to Chinese ideo-graphs that were presented following either extremely brief presentations or longer presentations of smiling or frown-ing faces. The briefly presented faces generated shifts in participants' preferences for the ideographs, whereas the faces presented at longer durations did not. This interesting finding suggests that emotional priming may be more ef-fective when it occurs without consciousness than when it occurs with consciousness.

It makes sense that emotions are more compelling and intense when they intrude upon our consciousness as the result of automatic processes than when they are brought into consciousness as the result of conscious intention.

This idea is reflected in Proust's *Law of Intermittence,* that "emotion-laden stimuli that leave one cold when sought out or turned to in thought may move one strongly when stumbled upon" (Frijda, 1986, pp. 427–428). Wegner and Gold (1995) suggested that this effect might explain why the suppression of emotional thoughts enhances subse-quent emotional reactions to those thoughts (cf. Wegner, 1992; Wegner et al., 1990). The intrusive, automatic return of emotional thoughts stirs emotional experience following suppression more than the controlled appearance of such thoughts that occurs when we intend to entertain them. Wegner and Gold found marked emotional reactions (i.e., increased SCL) in participants who had just finished trying to suppress the emotional thought of a still-desired old flame. The *intrusion* relation between control and auto-maticity may thus have relevance for the experience of emotion.

Controlled Starting The initiation of emotional experi-ence through control processes represents an interesting counterpoint to the literature on automatic initiation. The idea that people might, under certain circumstances, con-sciously or effortfully participate in the creation of their own emotions has surfaced only sporadically in the litera-ture, usually just in the form of the hypothesis that people try to be happy (Clark & Isen, 1982; Klinger, 1982; Zill-mann, 1988). Although this is an important observation, there are reasons to believe that control processes may par-ticipate in the production of a far wider range of emotional experience. As Ekman, Friesen, and Simons (1985) have suggested, some degree of conscious regulation may even be inherent in all emotional experience, differentiating it from simple reflexes such as the startle response.

One line of thinking in this regard is suggested by Schachter and Singer's (1962) analysis of the role of "epistemic search" processes in the production of emo-tion. Their theory proposed that the effect of an emotional stimulus is to initiate a generalized form of autonomic arousal, and that, to the extent such arousal is unexplained or not easily attributed to an emotional stimulus, the fur-ther effect is the creation of a cognitive search for emotion-relevant information. Although Schachter and Singer did not specify whether this search process is likely to be auto-matic or controlled, subsequent research has suggested that it could require monitoring—at least one harbinger of a control process. In particular, Wegner and Giuliano (1980, 1983) found that arousal created conditions of self-focused attention, in that participants who had exercised were sub-sequently more inclined to select first-person singular pro-nouns to complete ambiguous sentences. The related find-ings that experimentally enhanced self-focused attention tends to intensify emotion experience (Scheier & Carver, 1977) while decreasing susceptibility to emotion misattri-bution (Gibbons, Carver, Scheier, & Hormuth, 1979) suggest that the operation of this monitoring process does function to instigate effective labeling of emotional states.

The notion that control processes are involved in emotion appraisal brings with it the implication that emotional situations and the emotions themselves may differ in their reliance on automatic versus control processes. Certain broad or important emotional meanings (in particular, the positive-negative dimension) might exert their influences on the person quite automatically, whereas other meanings might require significant cognitive effort and conscious reflection to appreciate (see Leventhal, 1979; Scherer, 1984; Zajonc, 1980). Many emotional states, then, might be "fine points" placed on our automatic responses, in the sense that they require the operation of conscious processes even for the emotion to be felt. The specific emotion one feels in a grocery store upon having someone push a cart over one's foot, for example, might begin automatically with some global negative feeling, and then resolve over time with a conscious review of the circumstances into a specific feeling of anger or annoyance.

Controlled Stopping   The role of control processes in emotional experience is, as we mentioned previously, usually understood as an inhibitory one. The prototypical emotion control processes are, after all, the defense mechanisms, and their role in protecting the individual from unwanted negative emotions is widely celebrated in Freudian psychology. The operation of defense mechanisms has not been empirically verified in a satisfying way by psychoanalysis proper, but the reconceptualization of such processes in terms of emotion control has occurred in many quarters (e.g., Lazarus, 1966, 1975; Meichenbaum, 1977) and has produced a rush of research and discovery.

The basic theme in this research is that people often desire to avoid certain emotional experiences, and they therefore perform significant mental and behavioral work in the attempt to prevent or terminate them. Research has indicated, for instance, that people attempt (with variable success) to control sad moods (Clark & Isen, 1982; Morris & Reilly, 1987; Salovey, Hsee, & Mayer, 1993), depression or sorrow (Nolen-Hoeksema, 1993; Pennebaker, 1989; Tait & Silver, 1989; Wenzlaff, 1993), anxiety and worry (Roemer & Borkovec, 1993), pain (Cioffi, 1993), and anger (Tice & Baumeister, 1993). On occasion, even positive emotions are controlled when they become unwanted (Erber, Wegner, & Therriault, 1996; Parrott, 1993). These control processes include behavioral attempts to avoid situations that would evoke the emotions, as well as processes that are more specifically targeted at the suppression of mental contents and behavioral expressions associated with the emotion (cf. Schneider, 1993; Wegner, 1989).

Emotion control processes vary in their effectiveness for two key reasons: *strategy choice* and *control expertise* (Wegner, 1994). Like any form of mental control, emotion control depends on how it is done and how well it is done. Strategy choice is a key element of emotion control because many strategies can simply be faulty, not up to the job. The person who tries to overcome social anxiety by envisioning the awkwardness and weirdness that could happen in an upcoming social encounter, for example, is not likely to enjoy much control over this emotion. Strategies vary dramatically in their effectiveness for emotion control, as clinical research clearly documents (e.g., Klinger, 1993), and quite different strategies are needed, too, for the control of different emotions (Frijda, 1986). The most nettlesome problem in strategy choice, though, occurs because people do not seem naturally to appreciate the fact that simple suppression strategies usually backfire. There is now a considerable body of evidence to indicate that while thoughts themselves might subside for a time (e.g., Kelly & Kahn, 1994; Wegner & Gold, 1995), emotions are often intensified by our attempts to suppress thoughts about them (Foa & Kozak, 1986; Pennebaker, 1990; Rachman, 1980; Wegner et al., 1990; Wegner & Gold, 1995; Wegner et al., 1993). Strategies involving distraction or reinterpretation that differ from suppression only subtly may, nevertheless, be quite helpful (Nolen-Hoeksema, 1993; Wegner & Wenzlaff, 1996), and for this reason the complexities of strategy choice can be challenging indeed.

The second general factor in the effectiveness of emotion control is the individual's level of expertise in controlling the emotion. Often, this just comes down to practice. The depressed person has frequently pushed sadness from mind, for example, and so becomes somewhat adept at doing this under certain conditions (Wegner & Zanakos, 1994). So, while emotion control may be conscious and intentional, it can benefit from the kinds of automatization processes that occur with frequent use. Still, the automaticity of emotion control that is achieved by a depressed person who repeatedly tries not to entertain sad thoughts, or the anxious person who attempts recurrently to avoid thoughts of the anxiety-producing situation, is likely to be fragile. One typical emotion control strategy in depression, for example, is to focus constantly on the future in a fierce attempt to find a way out of the current situation; usually these repeated attempts fail and the individual is left with a chronic and negative set of beliefs about the future (Andersen, Spielman, & Bargh, 1992). Moreover, because attempts to control emotion frequently call for strategies that can instigate ironic processes, even practiced control processes can occasionally introduce ironic monitoring that reinstates the unwanted emotion intrusively and repeatedly. It may be only when emotion control processes become so skilled as to be deployed without conscious intent that they can quell emotion without inadvertently creating it.

This line of thinking suggests that a range of emotional

sensitivities usually ascribed to automatic emotion starting might rather be considered in terms of the ironic effects of controlled emotion stopping. What has come to be known as the emotional Stroop effect, for example, is often considered a unique sensitivity to emotional stimuli held by people suffering from emotional disorders. Watts, McKenna, Sharrock, and Trezise (1986) found that individuals with anxiety disorders are likely to take longer to name the color of a word when that word is relevant to their anxiety stimulus, and this effect has been observed now for depression and several other emotions (Dalgleish & Watts, 1990). The related effect observed by Pratto and John (1991), and also by McKenna and Sharma (1995), is interference with color naming for negative emotion words even among normal participants. This kind of sensitivity might be traced either to automatic emotion starting processes (such as those mentioned previously in the discussion of automatic attitude activation), or to the ironic, automatic effects of conscious stopping processes (Wegner, Erber, & Zanakos, 1993). If conscious stopping can have such undesirable ironic effects, it may be that stopping might better be carried out without conscious direction at all. This possibility is the focus of the next section.

Automatic Stopping   There are cases when the desire to avoid emotion may be itself uncontrollable, unintentional, unconscious, or relatively effortless. Frijda (1988) has proposed such "involuntary emotion control," remarking that "one cannot at will shed restraint, as little as one can at will shed anxiety or timidity" (p. 355). The automatic inhibition of emotion makes sense as a way to understand the contemporary literature on emotion repression (Erdelyi & Goldberg, 1979; Weinberger, Schwartz, & Davidson, 1979). Inhibitory processes may occur prior to or during emotional response, and these need not be initiated through conscious control.

Indeed, it often seems that the desire to avoid emotional states in certain forms of psychopathology is as deeply and insistently experienced as the emotion itself. Reiss, Peterson, Gursky, and McNally (1986), for example, find that the sensitivity to anxiety has dispositional properties. Wegner and Zanakos (1994) reported that the tendencies to suppress thoughts in general and to avoid sad thoughts in particular are also reliable dispositions. The compulsion people feel to avoid their unwanted emotions is remarkable, and some people seem to feel this compulsion more than others. Curiously, though, when people do report conscious interest in suppressing emotion, they seem to be particularly awful at it. Conscious preoccupation with the avoidance of anxiety or depression, in contrast to the trait of defensive repression signaled by reports of low anxiety and high social desirability (as in Weinberger et al., 1979), is associated with chronic high levels of the very emotion that is unwanted (Wegner & Zanakos, 1994).

Unfortunately, most of the current evidence on differences between conscious and automatic emotion stopping comes from individual-difference findings that do not allow the clear analysis of psychological process. This evidence suggests, though, that it may be useful to pursue the hypothesis that the effectiveness of emotion stopping turns on its consciousness. Emotion inhibition may work quite effectively as long as the person is unaware of its operation. When automatic processes that inhibit emotion are overridden by conscious intention, however, ironic processes surface to increase the accessibility of the very emotional thoughts and sensations that are being inhibited, and the result is the intrusion of emotions (Wegner, 1994). Just as one may carry a brimfull cup of coffee across the room without a lurch as long as one is not thinking about it, only to spill at the very moment one tries consciously not to spill, emotion inhibition processes that come into consciousness may activate the unwanted emotions.

Expressive Behavior

Some social behaviors occur more or less naturally and spontaneously, expressing responses to situations or internal states. Others appears to be generated on purpose to create an impression. These observations have long been important in the study of nonverbal behavior and self-presentation. The distinction between involuntary and voluntary expressions was made early in the study of facial expression (Darwin, 1872; Duchenne de Boulogne, 1862/1990), and related distinctions between expressive behavior that is spontaneous, genuine, or natural as opposed to intentional, posed, or deceptive are made in the study of self-presentation and nonverbal communication more generally (DePaulo, 1992; Ekman & Friesen, 1975; Goffman, 1959; Jones & Pittman, 1982; Paulhus, 1993; Schlenker, 1980).

These literatures are reviewed elsewhere in this *Handbook* (Baumeister, 1998; DePaulo & Friedman, 1998), but we wish to consider three key topics of this area here: the anatomical substrate of control and automaticity, the difficulty of control, and the social perception of control and automaticity.

Anatomy of Control and Automaticity   The literature on expressive behavior reveals that the distinction between automatic and conscious control of behavior in some cases can be drawn not just psychologically, but anatomically. Genuine and posed facial expressions, it seems, differ both in the muscles and nerves involved. In the case of muscles, for example, whereas muscles around the mouth are enervated in posed smiles, those surrounding the eyes become involved in spontaneous or "Duchenne" smiles (Duchenne de Boulogne, 1862/1990; Ekman, Davidson, & Friesen,

1990). And more generally, the muscles in the lower half of the face are more open to voluntary control than those in the upper half (Ekman & Friesen, 1975). It is interesting that the most "voluntary" parts of the face are also those involved in talking.

The differing neural pathways of voluntary and spontaneous facial expressions have been traced in detail. According to Rinn's (1984) comprehensive review, volitionally induced movements of the face arise in the cortical motor strip and course to the face through the pyramidal (cortical) tract. Impulses for spontaneous emotional facial expressions, in turn, arise from a phylogenetically older motor system known as the extrapyramidal motor system. Just as the cortex produces intelligent and flexible behavior in general, while subcortical processes yield heartbeats, sneezes, and yawns, it appears that the more flexible forms of facial expression arise cortically whereas the less flexible forms arise subcortically.

These differing pathways are particularly clear in the double dissociation of the voluntary and spontaneous facial expression systems found in clinical cases (Rinn, 1984). Some patients show "mimetic facial paralysis" in which the facial muscles can be moved voluntarily, but all spontaneous movement is lost. Other patients, in turn, show involuntary laughing and/or weeping (with only slight or no provocation), but with an inability to inhibit these responses voluntarily. In the case of facial expression, then, automaticity and control appear to be highly differentiated anatomically. Although it may not be the case that such distinct systems produce automatic versus controlled behavior of other kinds, the possibility of such partitioning may be worthy of further study.

Difficulty of Control   Perhaps the most emphatic theme in the literature on expressive behavior is the difficulty of expressive control. The control of nonverbal behavior for self-presentational purposes often sets control processes against automatic processes, after all, and this *regulation conflict* is often won by automaticity—so to result in *intrusion.* Ekman and Friesen (1969) dubbed this phenomenon "nonverbal leakage," the occurrence of uncontrolled expressive behavior reflecting the person's genuine emotions or attitudes even in the face of attempts at the conscious control of social impressions. We all know what it is like to plan to be nice to someone we dislike, for example, only to encounter the person and have our intended smile twist into a demented grimace.

The central problem of the control of expressive behavior is that there seems to be so much to control. To create a positive impression on a potential employer in an hour-long interview, for example, one might potentially try to control one's words, of course, but also facial expressions, gestures, postures, leanings, sighs, and vocal intonations. This is not to mention the control of coughs, yawns, eye-rolling, sneezes, blushes, itches, hooting, and all the other little horrors of interview hell. The accumulated literature on nonverbal communication shows that the failure to control almost any of these little acts can yield an unwanted interpretation (e.g., DePaulo, 1992; Ekman, 1985), and the prospect of trying to control all of this, or even just some tiny part of it, seems not just daunting but preposterous. How does a person ever fool anyone in everyday life?

One avenue to successful control is *automatization.* The repeated practice of self-presentational strategies may result in fluid and well-integrated performances that can be deployed at will (DePaulo, 1902; Jones & Pittman, 1982; Paulhus, 1993). Expressive actions that were once deliberate can take on the appearance of genuineness when they flow so well that they no longer require conscious control. The added benefit of automatization is that individual expressive acts become linked together such that each one need not be thought about or controlled individually, and instead the entire sequence becomes performable as one piece. Vallacher and Wegner (1985, 1987) have suggested that this integration allows the person to control the action through higher-level action descriptions. So, for example, someone who is practiced in impressing others can simply intend to make a good impression, and so will not need to identify all the components of this act separately and control them one by one (e.g., smile, shake hands, don't sweat, don't undress immediately, etc.). People who have not practiced a particular self-presentation will not benefit by such an integrative understanding, however, and may even be hurt by trying to control the overall impression they make. Their performance could be hurt by the *disruption* of automaticity by conscious control.

Several studies have tested this *optimal identification level* hypothesis. Experimental participants in such studies are given a self-presentational task that is easy or difficult for them; they are told that a person they are meeting is easy or difficult to impress (Vallacher, Wegner, McMahan, Cotter, & Larsen, 1992), or that an audience is easy or difficult to convince (Vallacher, Wegner, & Somoza, 1989). Ritts and Patterson (1996) manipulated such difficulty by testing socially anxious people (for whom self-presentation was assumed to be more difficult) and comparing them to the nonanxious. Participants are then given either big self-presentation tasks to perform (e.g., make a good impression), or small ones (e.g., remember to smile). The finding of these studies is that people who identify their act of control at the level appropriate for the difficulty of the task perform most successfully and feel best about their performance. So, when the task is easy and likely to be automatic, one can jump right in and try to "make a good impression." When the task is difficult and likely to require control of many details, however, it is better to focus on some one detail (e.g., smiling) and attempt to control that alone.

A different way to secure the control of expressive behavior is the creation of genuine change. Quite simply, if one's inner state changes in the appropriate way, expressive behavior can then issue directly from the expression of that state and will not need to be controlled. This is the approach of the method actor (Stanislavski, 1965; see also Hodges & Wegner, 1997). Of course, there are yet new dark rooms filled with stumbling blocks in the area of the mental control of inner states (Wegner, 1994), but the goal of effortless control of expressive behavior might often promote just such attempts at inner control. Wegner and Erber (1993) suggested that the control of internal states for self-presentational purposes in fact requires three varieties of mental control: the suppression of one's natural state of mind, concentration on one's preferred state of mind, and suppression of any performance-related states (e.g., anxiety, concerns about the success of control, etc.). This seems like a lot to remember. However, all this might come quite naturally with just the right mental control strategy. A good strong image of one's own death in a plane crash, for example, might motivate the perfect state of mind for the effective presentation to the flight attendant of one's desire for another alcoholic beverage. Appropriate concentration on the right state of mind seems to carry along with it an auxiliary ability to suppress the wrong state as well as the worries about one's state.

Tampering with inner states in the pursuit of self-presentation can be dangerous, however, as one is not likely to remember to put those inner states back the way one found them when the self-presentation gambit is no longer needed (Wegner & Wenzlaff, 1966) The person who tries to act tough and threatening in a job as prison guard, for example, may find that the self-generated anger bleeds over inappropriately into interactions with family and friends. Self-presentations erected for passing social pressures can stay in place when mental control is used to help them along, after all, and the result may be permanent inner changes that are not permanently desired (cf. Jones, 1990; Tice, 1994). And even on a short-term basis, self-presentational goals are like other goals in that they stay active following their intentional use and can thus operate for a time unintentionally, in a fashion similar to primed trait concepts (see Bargh & Green, 1997; Gollwitzer, Heckhausen, & Steller, 1990).

Another danger of the self-presentational control of both expressive behavior and inner states is that too much control can be exerted. With sufficient motivation, a person might try to quell every wrong behavior, and the result of this is a kind of general social paralysis (Greene, O'Hair, Cody, & Yen, 1985). At the extreme, control can also yield ironic effects, such that people find themselves performing the very expressive behaviors that are most unwanted (Wegner, 1994). Experimental participants who are highly motivated to deceive are often most inclined to "freeze"

and leak nonverbal evidence of their deceit to observers in just this way (DePaulo, Lanier, & Davis, 1983).

Perceptions of Control and Automaticity In most domains of control and automaticity research, the issue of whether a behavior, thought, or emotion is controlled or automatic is pretty much a matter of what is going on inside the person. With expressive behavior, however, this concern becomes fully public and, in fact, a matter of greater importance to others. Perceivers become very curious about the actor's use of conscious control when they expect that they might be deceived. The question "does he love me or is this a line?" comes up in many guises. Control and automaticity are, in this sense, person perception problems.

It is important to remember, though, that conscious control of behavior does not on its face necessarily signify deceit, nor does automaticity imply genuineness. If conscious control leads a person to help someone in need, for example, who is to say that this act is not genuine? Similarly, if a person makes an unintentional and automatic error, does this mean that it says something genuine about the person's inner states or propensities? As a rule, the inference of deceit versus genuineness requires something beyond evidence on the control or automaticity of behavior per se: there must be the intention to deceive. Conscious control of behavior is deceptive when the control is intended to deceive others; automatic behavior is genuine, in turn, when it occurs in the context of conscious control that has been initiated in the intent to deceive.

Given this caveat, it is interesting to examine just how well the control and automaticity of expressive behaviors are discerned by perceivers. It turns out that when there is no intent to deceive, the discrimination of posed versus spontaneous expressive behavior is not very easy. Hess and Kleck (1994) found, for instance, that coders were generally poor at discriminating posed from spontaneous facial expressions. There are some cues, however, and the general trend seems to be for spontaneous movements to be more ambiguous and often less extreme than intended or controlled movements (e.g., Motley & Camden, 1988). Posed facial expressions tend also to differ from spontaneous ones in their timing, duration, and symmetry (Ekman, 1985). When deception is specifically intended, perceivers seem to be able to pick up on these cues and make fairly good judgments of whether the target is trying to deceive (DePaulo, 1992).

The literature on expressive behavior reminds us, in sum, of several key observations about control and automaticity that do not surface in the other literature on these concepts. This approach emphasizes that control and automaticity are not just different psychological processes but also can have different neuropsychological substrates. Looking at expressive behavior also illustrates the sheer difficulty of control in many social settings. And, this line of inquiry leads to an appreciation of the fact that control and automaticity are not only functions within the person, but are themselves perceived and studied by others in the conduct of social interaction.

CONCLUSION

Are people in control of their behavior in interactions with other people, the opinions they form of those others, their emotional reactions to events of the day? To what extent are people aware of the important determinants of their judgments, emotions, and actions, such as the powerful effects of authority and conformity and the presence of others? These are questions that the classic studies in social psychology were designed to address. These are issues that lie at the heart of most social psychological phenomena we study today.

We have seen in this chapter that the classic studies highlight automatic forms of human responding. Like much of social psychology, these studies take the conscious control of behavior as a kind of backdrop, a taken-for-granted assumption that makes interesting news when it is shown to be in error. And in fact, this is a theme that has served social psychology well and no doubt will continue to do so as we march forward in our continued quest to test science against any and all sacred cows. As it turns out, however, this chapter has also revealed that the larger portion of mental processes, including those involved in social life, are characterized by mixtures, transformations, and relations between control and automaticity. We have attempted to classify the forms of these interactions, such as when a behavior is governed by a control versus an automatic process, and what consequences this has for the phenomenon in question. The field is learning, as have we, that there is a fundamental interplay between these processes in social life. The mere observation that people don't have control here or don't have control there may no longer be sufficient to create "classic" social psychological investigation.

We have also emphasized that control and automaticity both can be described broadly in terms of control theories. That is, both kinds of processes operate in the service of the individual's goals and purposes. Automatic processes furnish a massive amount of information to control judgment and decision processes, more efficiently than would be possible with the slower and energy-demanding control processes alone. They transform complex patterns of stimulation and produce simplifying categorizations on which the slower and more limited control processes can then operate. Conscious control processes can then consider this input in a flexible and creative fashion should that serve the current purpose of the person—such as when it matters to be accurate and complete in one's opinion or decision. Moreover, the control process is capable of regulating the habitual or automatic process, again given the motivational impetus to exert this control.

We have also discovered, in our reviews of the classic and contemporary research in the field, that control and automatic processing are not merely interesting topics for cognitive psychologists to research. They parlay into very serious consequences for a person's phenomenal experience (such as to the degree to which one has control over one's emotions) and for one's relations with others (such as whether one's opinions and treatment of them is biased). They relate to the way in which attitudes form and change, to the way in which inner states are expressed to others, and by implication, to one's degree of free will in obeying authority, conforming to others, and reacting to people in need of help.

The distinction between control and automatic mental processes is of critical importance in social psychology precisely because it is the dividing line between what we purport to know about ourselves and what we do not. While the classic experiments in our field have shown us to be largely ignorant of the powerful effects that authority figures and majority opinion have on our behavior, at the same time they demonstrate our rather automatic ability to get along with others and function smoothly in a social organization, instead of as individuals acting in the service of our separate goals. Automatic processes constitute a broad undercurrent of life that keeps us connected to the world and behaving effectively on many planes in response to a welter of environmental and internal stimulation. Yet at the same time a thin thread of conscious control organizes these automatic processes and relates them to our goals and concerns. The moment-to-moment interaction between control and automatic processes is therefore the place where human goals and mental processes meet, and where the daily tasks of survival become infused with larger purposes and direction.

REFERENCES

Abelson, R. P. (1976). Social psychology's rational man. In S. I. Benn & G. W. Mortimore (Eds.), *Rationality and the social sciences* (pp. 58–89). London: Routledge.

Abelson, R. P. (1981). Psychological status of the script concept. *American Psychologist, 36,* 715–729.

Abelson, R. P. (1995). *Statistics as principled argument.* Hillsdale, NJ: Erlbaum.

Ajzen, I. (1991). The theory of planned behavior. *Organizational Behavior and Human Decision Processes, 50,* 179–211.

Alloy, L. B., & Tabachnik, N. (1984). The assessment of covariation by humans and animals: The joint influence of prior expectations and current situational information. *Psychological Review, 91,* 112–149.

Allport, F. H. (1955). *Theories of perception and the concept of structure.* New York: Wiley.

Andersen, S. M., & Cole, S. W. (1990). "Do I know you?": The role of significant others in general social perception. *Journal of Personality and Social Psychology, 59,* 384–399.

Andersen, S. M., Glassman, N. S., Chen, S., & Cole, S. W. (1995). Transference in social perception: The role of chronic accessibility in significant other representations. *Journal of Personality and Social Psychology, 69,* 41–57.

Andersen, S. M., Spielman, L. A., & Bargh, J. A. (1992). Future-event schemas and certainty about the future: Automaticity in depressives' future-event predictions. *Journal of Personality and Social Psychology, 63,* 711–723.

Anderson, C. A., & Godfrey, S. S. (1987). Thoughts about actions: The effects of specificity and availability of imagined behavioral scripts on expectations about oneself and others. *Social Cognition, 5,* 238–258.

Anderson, J. R. (1982). Acquisition of cognitive skill. *Psychological Review, 89,* 369–406.

Anderson, J. R. (1987). Skill acquisition: Compilation of weak-method problem solutions. *Psychological Review, 94,* 192–210.

Anderson, J. R. (1990). *The adaptive nature of thought.* Hillsdale, NJ: Erlbaum.

Andrew, R. J. (1963). The origin and evolution of the calls and facial expressions of the primates. *Behavior, 20,* 1–109.

Ansfield, M. E., & Wegner, D. M. (1996). The feeling of doing. In P. M. Gollwitzer & J. A. Bargh (Eds.), *The psychology of action: Linking cognition and motivation to behavior* (pp. 482–506). New York: Guilford.

Ansfield, M., Wegner, D. M., & Bowser, R. (1996). Ironic effects of sleep urgency. *Behaviour Research and Therapy, 34,* 523–531.

Armstrong, D. M. (1980). *The nature of mind.* Ithaca, NY: Cornell University Press.

Asch, S. E. (1952). Effects of group pressure on the modification and distortion of judgments. In G. E. Swanson, T. M. Newcomb, & E. L. Hartley (Eds.), *Readings in social psychology* (2nd ed., pp. 2–11). New York: Holt.

Astington, J. W., Harris, P. L., & Olson, D. R. (1988). *Developing theories of mind.* Cambridge, England: Cambridge University Press.

Baldwin, M. W., Carrell, S. E., & Lopez, D. F. (1990). My advisor and the Pope are watching me from the back of my mind. *Journal of Experimental Social Psychology, 26,* 435–454.

Baldwin, M. W., & Holmes, J. G. (1987). Salient private audiences and awareness of the self. *Journal of Personality and Social Psychology, 53,* 1087–1098.

Baltes, M. M., & Baltes, P. B. (1986). *The psychology of control and aging.* Hillsdale, NJ: Erlbaum.

Bandura, A. (1977). Self-efficacy: Toward a unifying theory of behavioral change. *Psychological Review, 84,* 191–215.

Bargh, J. A. (1982). Attention and automaticity in the processing of self-relevant information. *Journal of Personality and Social Psychology, 43,* 425–436.

Bargh, J. A. (1984). Automatic and conscious processing of social information. In R. S. Wyer, Jr., & T. K. Srull (Eds.), *Handbook of social cognition* (Vol. 3, pp. 1–43). Hillsdale, NJ: Erlbaum.

Bargh, J. A. (1989). Conditional automaticity: Varieties of automatic influence in social perception and cognition. In J. S. Uleman & J. A. Bargh (Eds.), *Unintended thought* (pp. 3–51). New York: Guilford.

Bargh, J. A. (1990). Auto-motives: Preconscious determinants of social interaction. In E. T. Higgins & R. M. Sorrentino (Eds.), *Handbook of motivation and cognition* (Vol. 2, pp. 93–130). New York: Guilford Press.

Bargh, J. A. (1992a). Being unaware of the stimulus versus unaware of its interpretation: Why subliminality per se does not matter to social psychology. In R. Bornstein & T. Pittman (Eds.), *Perception without awareness* (pp. 236–255). New York: Guilford.

Bargh, J. A. (1992b). The ecology of automaticity: Toward establishing the conditions needed to produce automatic processing effects. *American Journal of Psychology, 105,* 181–199.

Bargh, J. A. (1994). The four horsemen of automaticity: Awareness, intention, efficiency, and control in social cognition. In R. S. Wyer & T. K. Srull (Eds.), *Handbook of social cognition* (2nd ed., Vol. 1). Hillsdale, NJ: Erlbaum.

Bargh, J. A. (1997). The automaticity of everyday life. In R. S. Wyer (Ed.), *The automaticity of everyday life: Advances in social cognition* (Vol. 10, pp. 1–61). Mahwah, NJ: Erlbaum.

Bargh, J. A., & Barndollar, K. (1996). Automaticity in action: The unconscious as a repository of chronic goals and motives. In P. M. Gollwitzer & J. A. Bargh (Eds.), *The psychology of action* (pp. 457–481). New York: Guilford.

Bargh, J. A., Bond, R. N., Lombardi, W. J., & Tota, M. E. (1986). The additive nature of chronic and temporary sources of construct accessibility. *Journal of Personality and Social Psychology, 50,* 869–878.

Bargh, J. A., Chaiken, S., Govender, R., & Pratto, F. (1992). The generality of the automatic attitude activation effect. *Journal of Personality and Social Psychology, 62,* 893–912.

Bargh, J. A., Chaiken, S., Raymond, P., & Hymes, C. (1996). The automatic evaluation effect: Unconditionally automatic attitude activation with a pronunciation task. *Journal of Experimental Social Psychology, 32,* 185–210.

Bargh, J. A., Chen, M., & Burrows, L. (1996). Automaticity of social behavior: Direct effects of trait construct and stereotype activation on action. *Journal of Personality and Social Psychology, 71,* 230–244.

Bargh, J. A., & Green, M. (1997). *Unintended consequences of intentional processes.* Manuscript submitted for publication, New York University.

Bargh, J. A., & Gollwitzer, P. M. (1994). Environmental control of goal-directed action: Automatic and strategic contingencies between situations and behavior. *Nebraska Symposium on Motivation, 41,* 71–124.

Bargh, J. A., Lombardi, W. J., & Higgins, E. T. (1988). Automaticity of Person x Situation effects on impression formation: It's just a matter of time. *Journal of Personality and Social Psychology, 55,* 599–605.

Bargh, J. A., & Pietromonaco, P. (1982). Automatic information processing and social perception: The influence of trait information presented outside of conscious awareness on impression formation. *Journal of Personality and Social Psychology, 43,* 437–449.

Bargh, J. A., & Pratto, F. (1986). Individual construct accessibility and perceptual selection. *Journal of Experimental Social Psychology, 22,* 293–311.

Bargh, J. A., & Thein, R. D. (1985). Individual construct accessibility, person memory, and the recall-judgment link: The case of information overload. *Journal of Personality and Social Psychology, 49,* 1129–1146.

Bargh, J. A., & Tota, M. E. (1988). Context-dependent automatic processing in depression: Accessibility of negative constructs with regard to self but not others. *Journal of Personality and Social Psychology, 54,* 925–939.

Bassili, J. N. (1993). Procedural efficiency and the spontaneity of trait inference. *Personality and Social Psychology Bulletin, 19,* 200–205.

Bassili, J. N., & Smith, M. C. (1986). On the spontaneity of trait attribution: Converging evidence for the role of cognitive strategy. *Journal of Personality and Social Psychology, 50,* 239–245.

Baumeister, R. F. (1984). Choking under pressure: Self-consciousness and the paradoxical effects of incentives on skilled performance. *Journal of Personality and Social Psychology, 46,* 610–620.

Baumeister, R. F. (1998). The self. In D. Gilbert, S. T. Fiske, & G. Lindzey (Eds.), *Handbook of social psychology* (4th ed., Vol. 1, pp. 680–740). New York: McGraw-Hill.

Baumeister, R. F., Heatherton, T. F., & Tice, D. M. (1995). *Losing control.* San Diego, CA: Academic Press.

Baumeister, R. F., Smart, L., & Boden, J. M. (1996). Relation of threatened egotism to violence and aggression: The dark side of high self-esteem. *Psychological Review, 103,* 5–33.

Belmore, S. M., & Hubbard, M. L. (1987). The role of advance expectancies in person memory. *Journal of Personality and Social Psychology, 53,* 61–70.

Berkowitz, L. (1984). Some effects of thoughts on anti- and prosocial influences of media events: A cognitive-neoassociation analysis. *Psychological Bulletin, 95,* 410–427.

Biernat, M., Manis, M., & Nelson, T. E. (1991). Stereotypes and standards of judgments. *Journal of Personality and Social Psychology, 60,* 485–499.

Bornstein, R. F. (1989). Exposure and affect: Overview and meta-analysis of research, 1968–1987. *Psychological Bulletin, 106,* 265–289.

Bower, G. H., Black, J., & Turner, T. (1979). Scripts in text comprehension and memory. *Cognitive Psychology, 11,* 177–220.

Brehm, J. W. (1966). *A theory of psychological reactance.* New York: Academic Press.

Brehm, J. W., & Cohen, A. R. (1962). *Explorations in cognitive dissonance.* New York: Wiley.

Brehm, S. S. (1976). *The application of social psychology to clinical practice.* New York: Wiley.

Brewer, M. B. (1988). A dual process model of impression formation. In T. K. Srull & R. S. Wyer, Jr. (Eds.), *Advances in social cognition* (Vol. 1, pp. 1–36). Hillsdale, NJ: Erlbaum.

Brewer, W. F., & Dupree, D. A. (1983). Use of plan schemata in the recall and recognition of goal-directed actions. *Journal of Experimental Psychology: Learning, Memory, and Cognition, 9,* 117–129.

Broadbent, D. E. (1958). *Perception and communication.* London: Pergamon.

Bruner, J. S. (1957). On perceptual readiness. *Psychological Review, 64,* 123–152.

Bruner, J. S. (1958). Social psychology and perception. In E. E. Maccoby, T. M. Newcomb, & E. L. Hartley (Eds.), *Readings in social psychology* (3rd ed., pp. 85–93). New York: Holt Rinehart Winston.

Bryan, W. L., & Harter, L. (1899). Studies on the telegraphic language: The acquisition of a hierarchy of habits. *Psychological Review, 6,* 345–378.

Burger, J. M. (1989). Negative reactions to increases in perceived personal control. *Journal of Personality and Social Psychology, 56,* 246–256.

Cacioppo, J. T., Priester, J. R., & Berntson, G. G. (1993). Rudimentary determinants of attitudes: II: Arm flexion and extension have differential effects on attitudes. *Journal of Personality and Social Psychology, 65,* 5–17.

Carlston, D. E., & Skowronski, J. J. (1994). Savings in the relearning of trait information as evidence for spontaneous inference generation. *Journal of Personality and Social Psychology, 66,* 840–856.

Carpenter, W. B. (1874). *Principles of mental physiology, with their applications to the training and discipline of the mind and the study of its morbid conditions.* New York: Appleton.

Carver, C. S. (1975). Physical aggression as a function of objective self awareness and attitudes toward punishment. *Journal of Experimental Social Psychology, 11,* 510–519.

Carver, C. S., & Scheier, M. F. (1981). *Attention and self-regulation: A control-theory approach to human behavior.* New York: Springer-Verlag.

Carver, C. S., & Scheier, M. F. (1990). Principles of self-regulation. In E. T. Higgins & R. N. Sorrentino (Eds.), *Handbook of motivation and cognition* (Vol. 2, pp. 3–52). New York: Guilford.

Chaiken, S. (1980). Heuristic versus systematic information processing and the use of source versus message cues in persuasion. *Journal of Personality and Social Psychology, 39,* 752–766.

Chaiken, S., & Bargh, J. A. (1993). Occurrence versus moderation of the automatic attitude activation effect: Reply to Fazio. *Journal of Personality and Social Psychology, 64,* 759–765.

Chartrand, T. L., & Bargh, J. A. (1996). Automatic activation of impression formation and memorization goals: Nonconscious goal priming reproduces effects of explicit task instructions. *Journal of Personality and Social Psychology, 71,* 464–478.

Chen, M., & Bargh, J. A. (1997). On the automaticity of self-fulfilling prophecies: The nonconscious effects of stereotype activation on social interaction. *Journal of Experimental Social Psychology.*

Cherry, E. C. (1953). Some experiments on the recognition of speech, with one and with two ears. *Journal of the Acoustical Society of America, 25,* 975–979.

Cioffi, D. (1993). Sensate body, directive mind: Physical sensations and mental control. In D. M. Wegner & J. W. Pennebaker (Eds.), *Handbook of mental control* (pp. 410–442). Englewood Cliffs, NJ: Prentice-Hall.

Clark, M. S., & Isen, A. M. (1982). Toward understanding the relationship between feeling states and social behavior. In A. H. Hastorf & A. M. Isen (Eds.), *Cognitive social psychology* (pp. 73–108). New York: Elsevier/North-Holland.

Cohen, C. E., & Ebbesen, E. B. (1979). Observational goals and schema activation: A theoretical framework for behavior perception. *Journal of Experimental Social Psychology, 15,* 305–329.

Colvin, C. R., & Block, J. (1994). Do positive illusions foster mental health? An examination of the Taylor and Brown formulation. *Psychological Bulletin, 116,* 3–20.

Corteen, R. S., & Dunn, D. (1974). Shock-associated words in a non-attended message: A test for momentary awareness. *Journal of Experimental Psychology, 102,* 1143–1144.

Corteen, R. S., & Wood, B. (1972). Autonomic responses to shock-associated words in an unattended channel. *Journal of Experimental Psychology, 94,* 308–313.

Craik, K. J. W. (1948). Theory of the human operator in control systems: II. Man as an element in a control system. *British Journal of Psychology, 38,* 142–148.

D'Agostino, P. R. (1991). Spontaneous trait inferences: Effects of recognition instructions and subliminal priming on recognition performance. *Personality and Social Psychology Bulletin, 17,* 70–77.

D'Agostino, P. R., & Beegle, W. (in press). A re-evaluation of the evidence for spontaneous trait inferences. *Journal of Experimental Social Psychology.*

Dalgleish, T., & Watts, F. N. (1990). Biases of attention and memory in disorders of anxiety and depression. *Clinical Psychology Review, 10,* 589–604.

Darley, J. M., & Batson, C. D. (1973). "From Jerusalem to Jericho": A study of situational and dispositional variables in helping behavior. *Journal of Personality and Social Psychology, 27,* 100–108.

Darley, J. M., & Latané, B. (1968). Bystander intervention in emergencies: Diffusion of responsibility. *Journal of Personality and Social Psychology, 8,* 377–383.

Darwin, C. (1872). The expression of the emotions in man and animals. New York: Appleton.

Deaux, K., & Lewis, L. L. (1984). Structure of gender stereotypes: Interrelations among components and gender label.

Journal of Personality and Social Psychology, 46, 991–1004.

DeCharms, R. (1968). *Personal causation.* New York: Academic Press.

Deci, E. L. (1975). *Intrinsic motivation.* New York: Plenum Press.

Dennett, D. (1969). *Content and consciousness.* London: Routledge & Kegan Paul.

Dennett, D. (1978). Toward a cognitive theory of consciousness. In H. Feigl & G. Maxwell (Eds.), *Minnesota studies in the philosophy of science* (Vol. 9, pp. 201–228). Minneapolis, MN: University of Minnesota Press.

Dennett, D. (1984). *Elbow room: The varieties of free will worth wanting.* Cambridge, MA: MIT Press.

Dennett, D. (1991). *Consciousness explained.* New York: Basic Books.

DePaulo, B. (1992). Nonverbal behavior and self-presentation. *Psychological Bulletin, 111,* 203–243.

DaPaulo, B. M., & Friedman, H. S. (1998). Nonverbal communication. In D. Gilbert, S. T. Fiske, & G. Lindzey (Eds.), *Handbook of social psychology* (4th ed., Vol. 2, pp. 3–40). New York: McGraw-Hill.

DePaulo, B., Lanier, K., & Davis, T. (1983). Detecting the deceit of the motivated liar. *Journal of Personality and Social Psychology, 45,* 1096–1103.

Deutsch, J. A., & Deutsch, D. (1963). Attention: Some theoretical considerations. *Psychological Review, 70,* 80–90.

Devine, P. G. (1989). Stereotypes and prejudice: Their automatic and controlled components. *Journal of Personality and Social Psychology, 56,* 680–690.

Dijksterhuis, A., & van Knippenberg, A. (1996a). The knife that cuts both ways: Facilitated and inhibited access to traits as a result of stereotype activation. *Journal of Experimental Social Psychology, 32,* 271–288.

Dijksterhuis, A., & van Knippenberg, A. (1996b). *Automatic behavior, or how to win a game of Trivial Pursuit.* Manuscript submitted for publication, University of Nijmegen.

Dixon, N. F. (1981). *Preconscious processing.* New York: Wiley.

Duchenne de Boulogne, G. B. (1990). *The mechanism of human facial expression.* (R. A. Cutherbertson, Trans.). Cambridge: Cambridge University Press. (Original work published 1862.)

Duval, S., & Wicklund, R. (1972). *A theory of objective self-awareness.* New York: Academic Press.

Duval, S., Duval, V. H., & Neely, R. (1979). Self-focus, felt responsibility, and helping behavior. *Journal of Personality and Social Psychology, 37,* 1769–1778.

Eagly, A. H., & Chaiken, S. (1993). *The psychology of attitudes.* New York: Harcourt Brace Jovanovich.

Ekman, P. (1985). *Telling lies.* New York: Norton.

Ekman, P. (1992). An argument for basic emotions. *Cognition and Emotion, 6,* 169–200.

Ekman, P., Davidson, R. J., & Friesen, W. V. (1990). The

Duchenne smile: Emotional and brain physiology II. *Journal of Personality and Social Psychology, 58,* 342–353.

Ekman, P., & Friesen, W. V. (1969). Nonverbal leakage and clues to deception. *Psychiatry, 32,* 88–106.

Ekman, P., & Friesen, W. V. (1975). *Unmasking the face.* Englewood Cliffs, NJ: Prentice-Hall.

Ekman, P., Friesen, W. V., & Simons, R. C. (1985). Is the startle reaction an emotion? *Journal of Personality and Social Psychology, 49,* 1416–1426.

Emde, R. N. (1984). Levels of meaning for infant emotions: A biosocial view. In K. R. Scherer & P. Ekman (Eds.), *Approaches to emotion* (pp. 77–107). Hillsdale, NJ: Erlbaum.

Erber, R., Wegner, D. M., & Therriault, N. (1996). On being cool and collected: Mood regulation in anticipation of social interaction. *Journal of Personality and Social Psychology, 70,* 757–766.

Erdelyi, M. H. (1974). A new look at the New Look: Perceptual defense and vigilance. *Psychological Review, 81,* 1–25.

Erdelyi, M. H., & Goldberg, B. (1979). Let's not sweep repression under the rug: Toward a cognitive psychology of repression. In J. F. Kihlstrom & F. J. Evans (Eds.), *Functional disorders of memory* (pp. 355–402). Hillsdale, NJ: Erlbaum.

Erdley, C. A., & D'Agostino, P. R. (1987). Cognitive and affective components of automatic priming effects. *Journal of Personality and Social Psychology, 54,* 741–747.

Fazio, R. H. (1986). How do attitudes guide behavior? In R. M. Sorrentino & E. T. Higgins (Eds.), *Handbook of motivation and cognition* (Vol. 1, pp. 204–243). New York: Guilford.

Fazio, R. H. (1990). Multiple processes by which attitudes guide behavior: The MODE model as an integrative framework. In M. P. Zanna (Ed.), *Advances in experimental social psychology* (Vol. 23, pp. 75–109). San Diego, CA: Academic Press.

Fazio, R. H., Chen, J., McDonel, E. C., & Sherman, S. J. (1982). Attitude accessibility, attitude-behavior consistency, and the strength of the object-evaluation association. *Journal of Experimental Social Psychology, 18,* 339–357.

Fazio, R. H., Jackson, J. R., Dunton, B. C., & Williams, C. J. (1995). Variability in automatic activation as an unobtrusive measure of racial attitudes: A bona fide pipeline? *Journal of Personality and Social Psychology, 69,* 1013–1027.

Fazio, R. H., Sanbonmatsu, D. M., Powell, M. C., & Kardes, F. R. (1986). On the automatic activation of attitudes. *Journal of Personality and Social Psychology, 50,* 229–238.

Feinberg, J. (1970). *Doing and deserving.* Princeton, NJ: Princeton University Press.

Feltz, D. L., & Landers, D. M. (1983). The effects of mental practice on motor skill learning and performance: A meta-analysis. *Journal of Sport Psychology, 5,* 25–57.

Festinger, L., & Carlsmith, J. M. (1959). Cognitive consequences of forced compliance. *Journal of Abnormal and Social Psychology, 58,* 203–210.

Fiske, S. T. (1980). Attention and weight in person perception: The impact of negative and extreme behavior. *Journal of Personality and Social Psychology, 38,* 889–906.

Fiske, S. T. (1982). Schema-triggered affect. In M. S. Clark & S. T. Fiske (Eds.), *Affect and cognition: The seventeenth annual Carnegie symposium on cognition.* Hillsdale, NJ: Erlbaum.

Fiske, S. T. (1989). Examining the role of intent: Toward understanding its role in stereotyping and prejudice. In J. S. Uleman & J. A. Bargh (Eds.), *Unintended thought.* New York: Guilford.

Fiske, S. T. (1993). Controlling other people: The impact of power on stereotyping. *American Psychologist, 48,* 621–628.

Fiske, S. T., & Neuberg, S. E. (1990). A continuum of impression formation, from category-based to individuating processes: Influences of information and motivation on attention and interpretation. In M. P. Zanna (Ed.), *Advances in experimental social psychology* (Vol. 23, pp. 1–74). San Diego: Academic Press.

Flavell, J. H., & Draguns, J. (1957). A microgenetic approach to perception and thought. *Psychological Bulletin, 54,* 197–217.

Foa, E. B., & Kozak, M. J. (1986). Emotional processing of fear: Exposure to corrective information. *Psychological Bulletin, 99,* 20–35.

Folkman, S. (1984). Personal control and stress and coping processes: A theoretical analysis. *Journal of Personality and Social Psychology, 46,* 839–852.

Frijda, N. H. (1986). *The emotions.* Cambridge, England: Cambridge University Press.

Frijda, N. H. (1988). The laws of emotion. *American Psychologist, 43,* 349–358.

Gazzaniga, M. S. (1988). Brain modularity: Towards a philosophy of conscious experience. In A. J. Marcel & E. Bisiach (Eds.), *Consciousness in contemporary science* (pp. 218–238). Oxford, England: Clarendon Press.

Geller, V., & Shaver, P. (1976). Cognitive consequences of self-awareness. *Journal of Experimental Social Psychology, 12,* 99–108.

Gibbons, F. X., Carver, C. S., Scheier, M. F., & Hormuth, S. E. (1979). Self-focused attention and the placebo effect: Fooling some of the people some of the time. *Journal of Experimental Social Psychology, 15,* 263–274.

Gilbert, D. T. (1989). Thinking lightly about others: Automatic components of the social inference process. In J. S. Uleman & J. A. Bargh (Eds.), *Unintended thought* (pp. 189–211). New York: Guilford.

Gilbert, D. T. (1991). How mental systems believe. *American Psychologist, 46,* 107–119.

Gilbert, D. T. (1993). The assent of man: Mental representation and the control of belief. In D. M. Wegner & J. W. Pennebaker (Eds.), *Handbook of mental control* (pp. 57–87). Englewood Cliffs, NJ: Prentice-Hall.

Gilbert, D. T. (1998). Ordinary personology. In D. Gilbert, S. T. Fiske, & G. Lindzey (Eds.), *Handbook of social psychology* (4th ed., Vol. 2, pp. 89–150). New York: McGraw-Hill.

Gilbert, D. T., & Hixon, J. G. (1991). The trouble of thinking: Activation and application of stereotypic beliefs. *Journal of Personality and Social Psychology, 60,* 509–517.

Gilbert, D. T., & Krull, D. S. (1988). Seeing less and knowing more: The benefits of perceptual ignorance. *Journal of Personality and Social Psychology, 54,* 193–202.

Gilbert, D. T., & Malone, P. S. (1995). The correspondence bias. *Psychological Bulletin, 117,* 21–38.

Gilbert, D. T., & Osborne, R. E. (1989). Thinking backward: Some curable and incurable consequences of cognitive busyness. *Journal of Personality and Social Psychology, 57,* 940–949.

Gilbert, D. T., Pelham, B. W., & Krull, D. S. (1988). On cognitive busyness: When persons perceivers meet persons perceived. *Journal of Personality and Social Psychology, 54,* 733–740.

Gilbert, D. T., Tafarodi, R. W., & Malone, P. S. (1993). You can't not believe everything you read. *Journal of Personality and Social Psychology, 65,* 221–233.

Gilden L., Vaughan, H. G., Jr., & Costa, L. D. (1966). Summated human EEG potentials with voluntary movement. *Electroencephalography and Clinical Neurophysiology, 20,* 433–438.

Gilligan, S. G., & Bower, G. H. (1984). Cognitive consequences of emotional arousal. In C. E. Izard, J. Kagan, & R. B. Zajonc (Eds.), *Emotions, cognition, and behavior* (pp. 547–588). New York: Cambridge University Press.

Glass, D. C., & Singer, J. E. (1972). *Urban stress.* New York: Academic Press.

Gleick, J. (1987). *Chaos: Making a new science.* New York: Viking.

Goffman, E. (1959). *The presentation of self in everyday life.* Garden City, NY: Doubleday/Anchor.

Gollwitzer, P. M. (1993). Goal achievement: The role of intentions. In W. Stroebe & M. Hewstone (Eds.), *European review of social psychology* (Vol. 4, pp. 141–185). London: Wiley.

Gollwitzer, P. M., Heckhausen, H., & Steller, B. (1990). Deliberative and implemental mind-sets: Cognitive tuning toward congruous thoughts and information. *Journal of Personality and Social Psychology, 59,* 1119–1127.

Gollwitzer, P. M., & Moskowitz, G. (1996). Goal effects on thought and behavior. In E. T. Higgins & A. Kruglanski (Eds.), *Social psychology: Handbook of basic principles.* New York: Guilford.

Gopnik A. (1993). How we know our minds: The illusion of first-person knowledge of intentionality. *Behavioral and Brain Sciences, 16,* 1–14.

Gordon, P. C., & Holyoak, K. J. (1983). Implicit learning and generalization of the "mere exposure" effect. *Journal of Personality and Social Psychology, 45,* 492–500.

Graesser, A. C. (1978). How to catch a fish: The representation and memory of common procedures. *Discourse Processes, 1,* 72–89.

Greene, J. O., O'Hair, H. D., Cody, M. J., & Yen, C. (1985). Planning and control of behavior during deception. *Human Communication Research, 11,* 335–364.

Greenwald, A. G., & Banaji, M. R. (1995). Implicit social cognition: Attitudes, self-esteem, and stereotypes. *Psychological Review, 102,* 4–27.

Hamilton, D. L., & Sherman, J. W. (1994). Stereotypes. In R. S. Wyer, Jr., & T. K. Srull (Eds.), *Handbook of social cognition* (2nd ed., Vol. 2, pp. 1–68). Hillsdale, NJ: Erlbaum.

Haidt, J., & Rodin, J. (1995). *Control and efficacy: An integrative review.* Unpublished manuscript, John D. and Catherine T. MacArthur Foundation.

Haney, C., Banks, C., & Zimbardo, P. G. (1973). Interpersonal dynamics in a simulated prison. *International Journal of Criminology and Penology, 1,* 69–97.

Hansen, C. H., & Hansen, R. D. (1988). Finding the face in the crowd: An anger superiority effect. *Journal of Personality and Social Psychology, 54,* 917–924.

Hansen, C. H., & Hansen, R. D. (1994). Automatic emotion: Attention and facial efference. In P. M. Niedenthal & S. Kitayama (Eds.), *The heart's eye: Emotional influences in perception and attention* (pp. 217–243). San Diego, CA: Academic Press.

Harnad, S. (1982). Consciousness: An afterthought. *Cognition and brain theory, 5,* 29–47.

Hart, H. L. A. (1948/1949). The ascription of responsibility and rights. *Proceedings of the Aristotelian Society, 49,* 171–194.

Hartley, D. (1749). *Observations on man, his frame, his duty, and his expectations.* London: S. Richardson.

Hastie, R. (1981). Schematic principles in human memory. In E. T. Higgins, C. P. Herman, & M. P. Zanna (Eds.), *Social cognition: The Ontario symposium* (Vol. 1, pp. 39–88). Hillsdale, NJ: Erlbaum.

Hastie, R., & Kumar, P. A. (1979). Person memory: The processing of consistent and inconsistent person information. *Journal of Personality and Social Psychology, 37,* 25–38.

Haviland, J. M., & Lelwica, M. (1987). The induced affect response: 10-week-old infants' response to three emotion expressions. *Developmental Psychology, 23,* 97–104.

Hayes-Roth, B. (1977). Evolution of cognitive structure and processes. *Psychological Review, 84,* 260–278.

Heider, F. (1958). *The psychology of interpersonal relations.* New York: Wiley.

Heims, S. J. (1991). *The cybernetics group.* Cambridge, MA: MIT Press.

Helmholtz, H. (1968). Concerning the perceptions in general. In W. Warren & R. Warren (Eds.), *Helmholtz on perception* (pp. 171–203). New York: Wiley. (Original work published 1867).

Helson, H. (1964). *Adaptation-level theory.* New York: Harper & Row.

Herr, P. M., Sherman, S. J., & Fazio, R. H. (1984). On the consequences of priming: Assimilation and contrast effects. *Journal of Experimental Social Psychology, 19,* 323–340.

Hess, U., & Kleck, R. E. (1994). The cues decoders use in attempting to differentiate emotion-elicited and posed facial expressions. *European Journal of Social Psychology, 24,* 367–381.

Higgins, E. T. (1987). Self-discrepancy: A theory relating self and affect. *Psychological Review, 94,* 319–340.

Higgins, E. T. (1989). Knowledge accessibility and activation: Subjectivity and suffering from unconscious sources. In J. S. Uleman & J. A. Bargh (Eds.), *Unintended thought* (pp. 75–123). New York: Guilford.

Higgins, E. T. (1996). Knowledge activation: Accessibility, applicability, and salience. In E. T. Higgins & A. Kruglanski (Eds.), *Social psychology: Handbook of basic principles* (pp. 133–168). New York: Guilford.

Higgins, E. T., & Bargh, J. A. (1987). Social perception and social cognition. *Annual Review of Psychology, 38,* 369–425.

Higgins, E. T., & King, G. A. (1981). Accessibility of social constructs: Information-processing consequences of individual and contextual variability. In N. Cantor & J. F. Kihlstrom (Eds.), *Personality, cognition, and social interaction* (pp. 69–122). Hillsdale, NJ: Erlbaum.

Higgins, E. T., King, G. A., & Mavin, G. H. (1982). Individual construct accessibility and subjective impressions and recall. *Journal of Personality and Social Psychology, 43,* 35–47.

Higgins, E. T., Rholes, W. S., & Jones, C. R. (1977). Category accessibility and impression formation. *Journal of Experimental Social Psychology, 13,* 141–154.

Higgins, E. T., & Stangor, C. (1988). A "change-of-standard" perspective on the relation among context, judgment, and memory. *Journal of Personality and Social Psychology, 54,* 181–192.

Hodges, S., & Wegner, D. M. (1997). Automatic and controlled empathy. In W. J. Ickes (Ed.), *Empathic accuracy* (pp. 311–339). New York: Guilford.

Hofstadter, D. R. (1979). *Gödel, Escher, Bach: An eternal golden braid.* New York: Viking Press.

Howard, G. S., & Conway, C. G. (1986). Can there be an empirical science of volitional action? *American Psychologist, 41,* 1241–1251.

Hull, J. G., & Levy, A. S. (1979). The organizational function of the self: An alternative to the Duval and Wicklund model of self-awareness. *Journal of Personality and Social Psychology, 37,* 756–768.

Jacoby, L. L., Kelley, C., Brown, J., & Jasechko, J. (1989). Becoming famous overnight: Limits on the ability to avoid unconscious influences of the past. *Journal of Personality and Social Psychology, 56,* 326–338.

James, W. (1890). *Principles of psychology.* New York: Holt.

Janis, I. L. (1972). *Victims of groupthink: A psychological study of foreign policy decisions and fiascoes.* Boston: Houghton-Mifflin, 1972.

Jastrow, J. (1906). *The subconscious.* Boston: MA: Houghton-Mifflin.

Jaynes, J. (1976). *The origin of consciousness in the breakdown of the bicameral mind.* London: Allen Lane.

Jones, E. E. (1990). *Interpersonal perception.* New York: W. H. Freeman.

Jones, E. E., & Pittman, T. S. (1982). Toward a general theory of strategic self-presentation. In J. Suls (Ed.), *Psychological perspectives on the self* (Vol. 1, pp. 231–262). Hillsdale, NJ: Erlbaum.

Jones, E. E., & Thibaut, J. W. (1958). Interaction goals as bases of inference in interpersonal perception. In R. Taguiri & L. Petrullo (Eds.), *Person perception and interpersonal behavior* (pp. 151–178). Stanford, CA: Stanford University Press.

Kelly, A. E., & Kahn, J. H. (1994). Effects of suppression of personal intrusive thoughts. *Journal of Personality and Social Psychology, 66,* 998–1006.

Kihlstrom, J. F. (1987). The cognitive unconscious. *Science, 237,* 1445–1452.

Kihlstrom, J. F., & Tobias, B. A. (1991). Anosognosia, consciousness, and the self. In G. P. Prigatano & D. L. Schachter (Eds.), *Awareness of deficit after brain injury* (pp. 198–222). New York: Oxford University Press.

Kipnis, D. (1976). *The powerholders.* Chicago: University of Chicago Press.

Kirschenbaum, D. S., & Tomarken, A. J. (1982). On facing the generalization problem: The study of self-regulatory failure. In P. C. Kendall (Ed.), *Advances in cognitive-behavioral research and therapy* (Vol. 1). New York: Academic Press.

Klinger, E. (1982). On the self-management of mood, affect, and attention. In P. Karoly & F. H. Kanfer (Eds.), *Self-management and behavior change* (pp. 129–164). New York: Pergamon.

Klinger, E. (1993). Clinical approaches to mood control. In D. M. Wegner & J. W. Pennebaker (Eds.), *Handbook of mental control* (pp. 344–369). Englewood Cliffs, NJ: Prentice-Hall.

Kornhuber, H. H., & Deecke, L. (1965). Hirnpotentialänderungen bei Wilkürbewegungen und passiv Bewegungen des Menschen: Bereitschaftspotential und reafferente Potentiale. *Pflügers Archiv für Gesamte Psychologie, 284,* 1–17.

Krosnick, J. A., Betz, A. L., Jussim, L. J., Lynn, A. R., & Stephens, L. (1992). Subliminal conditioning of attitudes. *Personality and Social Psychology Bulletin, 18,* 152–162.

Kunst-Wilson, W. R., & Zajonc, R. B. (1980). Affective discrimination of stimuli that cannot be recognized. *Science, 207,* 557–558.

Langer, E. J. (1975). The illusion of control. *Journal of Personality and Social Psychology, 32,* 311–328.

Langer, E. J. (1978). Rethinking the role of thought in social interaction. In J. H. Harvey, W. I. Ickes, & R. F. Kidd (Eds.), *New directions in attribution research* (Vol. 2, pp. 35–58). Hillsdale, NJ: Erlbaum.

Langer, E. J. (1989). *Mindfulness.* Reading, MA: Addison-Wesley.

Lashley, K. S. (1951). The problem of serial order in behavior. In L. A. Jeffress (Ed.), *Cerebral mechanisms in behavior: The Hixon symposium* (pp. 112–136). New York: Wiley & Sons.

Lazarus, R. S. (1966). *Psychological stress and the coping process.* New York: McGraw-Hill.

Lazarus, R. S. (1975). The self-regulation of emotion. In L. Levi (Ed.), *Emotions—Their parameters and measurement* (pp. 47–67). New York: Raven.

Lepore, L., & Brown, R. (1997). Category and stereotype activation: Is prejudice inevitable? *Journal of Personality and Social Psychology 72,* 275–287.

Leslie, A. M. (1987). Pretense and representation: The origins of "theory of mind." *Psychological Review, 94,* 412–426.

Leventhal, H. (1979). A perceptual-motor processing model of emotion. In P. Pliner, K. R. Blankstein, & I. M. Spigel (Eds.), *Perception of emotion in self and others* (pp. 1–46). New York: Plenum.

Lewin, K. (1935). *A dynamic theory of personality.* New York: McGraw-Hill.

Libet, B. (1985). Unconscious cerebral initiative and the role of conscious will in voluntary action. *Behavioral and Brain Sciences, 8,* 529–566.

Logan, G. D. (1980). Attention and automaticity in Stroop and priming tasks: Theory and data. *Cognitive Psychology, 12,* 523–553.

Logan, G. D. (1988). Toward an instance theory of automatization. *Psychological Review, 95,* 492–527.

Logan, G. D., & Cowan, W. B. (1984). On the ability to inhibit thought and action: A theory of an act of control. *Psychological Review, 91,* 295–327.

Lombardi, W. J., Higgins, E. T., & Bargh, J. A. (1987). The role of consciousness in priming effects on categorization. *Personality and Social Psychology Bulletin, 13,* 411–429.

Lupfer, M. B., Clark, L. F., & Hutchinson, H. W. (1990). Impact of context on spontaneous trait and situational attributions. *Journal of Personality and Social Psychology, 58,* 239–249.

MacLean, P. D. (1993). Cerebral evolution of emotion. In M. Lewis & J. M. Haviland (Eds.), *Handbook of emotions* (pp. 67–83). New York: Guilford.

Macrae, C. N., Bodenhausen, G. V., & Milne, A. B. (1995). *Saying no to unwanted thoughts: The role of self-awareness in the regulation of mental life.* Manuscript submitted for publication.

Macrae, C. N., Bodenhausen, G. V., Milne, A. B., & Jetten, J. (1994). Out of mind but back in sight: Stereotypes on the rebound. *Journal of Personality and Social Psychology, 67,* 808–817.

Macrae, C. N., Milne, A. B., & Bodenhausen, G. V. (1993). Stereotypes as energy-saving devices: A peek inside the cognitive toolbox. *Journal of Personality and Social Psychology, 66,* 37–47.

Macrae, C. N., Stangor, C., & Milne, A. B. (1994). Activating social stereotypes: A functional analysis. *Journal of Experimental Social Psychology, 30,* 370–389.

Mandler, G. (1984). *Mind and body: Psychology of emotion and stress.* New York: Norton.

Marcel, A. J. (1983). Conscious and unconscious perception: An approach to the relations between phenomenal experience and perceptual processes. *Cognitive Psychology, 15,* 238–300.

Markus, H. (1977). Self-schemata and processing information about the self. *Journal of Personality and Social Psychology, 35,* 63–78.

Markus, H., & Nurius, P. (1986). Possible selves. *American Psychologist, 41,* 954–969.

Martin, L. L., Seta, J. J., & Crelia, R. (1990). Assimilation and contrast as a function of people's willingness and ability to expend effort in forming an impression. *Journal of Personality and Social Psychology, 59,* 27–37.

McArthur, L. Z. (1981). What grabs you? The role of attention in impression formation and causal attribution. In E. T. Higgins, C. P. Herman, & M. P. Zanna (Eds.), *Social cognition: The Ontario symposium* (Vol. 1, pp. 201–246). Hillsdale, NJ: Erlbaum.

McConahay, J. B., Hardee, B. B., & Batts, V. (1981). Has racism declined? It depends upon who's asking and what is asked. *Journal of Conflict Resolution, 25,* 563–579.

McGuire, W. J., & Padawer-Singer, A. (1976). Trait salience in the spontaneous self-concept. *Journal of Personality and Social Psychology, 33,* 743–754.

McKenna, F. P., & Sharma, D. (1995). Intrusive cognitions: An investigation of the emotional Stroop task. *Journal of Experimental Psychology: Learning, Memory, and Cognition, 21,* 1595–1607.

Mead, G. H. (1934). *Mind, self, and society.* Chicago, IL: University of Chicago Press.

Meichenbaum, D. (1977). *Cognitive-behavior modification.* New York: Plenum.

Milgram, S. (1963). Behavioral study of obedience. *Journal of Abnormal and Social Psychology, 67,* 371–378.

Milgram, S. (1974). *Obedience to authority.* New York: Harper & Row.

Miller, G. A. (1956). The magical number seven, plus or minus two: Some limits on our capacity for processing information. *Psychological Review, 63,* 81–97.

Miller, G. A., Galanter, E., & Pribram, K. H. (1960). *Plans and the structure of behavior.* New York: Holt.

Mischel, W., Cantor, N., & Pribram, K. H. (1960). *Plans and the structure of behavior.* New York: Holt.

Mischel, W., Cantor, N., & Feldman, S. (1996). Goal-directed self-regulation. In E. T. Higgins & A. W. Kruglanski (Eds.),

Social psychology: Handbook of basic principles. New York: Guilford.

Moskowitz, G. B., & Roman, R. J. (1992). Spontaneous trait inferences and self-generated primes: Implications for conscious social judgment. *Journal of Personality and Social Psychology, 62,* 728–738.

Morris, W. N., & Reilly, N. P. (1987). Toward the self-regulation of mood: Theory and research. *Motivation and Emotion, 11,* 215–249.

Motley, M. T., & Camden, C. T. (1988). Facial expression of emotion: A comparison of posed expressions versus spontaneous expressions in an interpersonal communication setting. *Western Journal of Speech Communication, 52,* 1–22.

Murphy, S. T., Monahan, J. L., & Zajonc, R. B. (1995). Additivity of nonconscious affect: Combined effects of priming and exposure. *Journal of Personality and Social Psychology, 69,* 589–602.

Murphy, S. T., & Zajonc, R. B. (1993). Affect, cognition, and awareness: Affective priming with optimal and suboptimal stimulus exposures. *Journal of Personality and Social Psychology, 64,* 723–739.

Neely, J. H. (1977). Semantic priming and retrieval from lexical memory: Roles of inhibitionless spreading activation and limited-capacity attention. *Journal of Experimental Psychology: General, 106,* 226–254.

Neisser, U. (1967). *Cognitive psychology.* New York: Appleton-Century-Crofts.

Neisser, U. (1976). *Cognition and reality.* San Francisco: Freeman, 1976.

Neumann, O. (1984). Automatic processing: A review of recent findings and a plea for an old theory. In W. Prinz & A. F. Sanders (Eds.), *Cognition and motor processes* (pp. 255–293). Berlin: Springer-Verlag.

Newell, A., & Rosenbloom, P. S. (1981). Mechanisms of skill acquisition and the law of practice. In J. R. Anderson (Ed.), *Cognitive skills and their acquisition* (pp. 1–55). Hillsdale, NJ: Erlbaum.

Newell, A., & Simon, H. A. (1972). *Human problem solving.* Englewood Cliffs NJ: Prentice-Hall.

Newman, L. S. (1991). Why are traits inferred spontaneously? A developmental approach. *Social Cognition, 9,* 221–253.

Newman, L. S. (1993). How individualists interpret behavior: Idiocentrism and spontaneous trait inference. *Social Cognition, 9,* 221–253.

Newman, L. S., Duff, K. J., & Baumeister, R. F. (1997). A new look at defensive projection: Thought suppression, accessibility, and biased person perception. *Journal of Personality and Social Psychology, 72,* 980–1001.

Newman, L. S., & Uleman, J. S. (1989). Spontaneous trait inference. In J. S. Uleman & J. A. Bargh (Eds.), *Unintended thought* (pp. 155–188). New York: Guilford.

Newman, L. S., & Uleman, J. S. (1990). Assimilation and contrast effects in spontaneous trait inference. *Personality and Social Psychology Bulletin, 16,* 224–240.

Niedenthal, P. M. (1990). Implicit perception of affective information. *Journal of Experimental Social Psychology, 26,* 505–527.

Nielsen, S. L., & Sarason, I. G. (1981). Emotion, personality, and selective attention. *Journal of Personality and Social Psychology, 41,* 945–960.

Nisbett, R. E., & Wilson, T. D. (1977). Telling more than we can know: Verbal reports on mental processes. *Psychological Review, 84,* 231–259.

Nolen-Hoeksema, S. (1993). Sex differences in control of depression. In D. M. Wegner & J. W. Pennebaker (Eds.), *Handbook of mental control* (pp. 306–324). Englewood Cliffs, NJ: Prentice-Hall.

Norman, D. A. (1968). Toward a theory of memory and attention. *Psychological Review, 75,* 522–536.

Norman, D. A. (1981). Categorization of action slips. *Psychological Review, 88,* 1–15.

Norman, D. A., & Shallice, T. (1986). Attention to action: Willed and automatic control of behavior. In R. J. Davidson, G. E. Schwartz, & D. Shapiro (Eds.), *Consciousness and self-regulation* (Vol. 4, pp. 1–18). New York: Plenum.

Öhman, A. (1993). Fear and anxiety as emotional phenomena. In M. Lewis & J. M. Haviland (Eds.), *Handbook of emotions* (pp. 511–536). New York: Guilford.

Parrott, W. G. (1993). Beyond hedonism: Motives for inhibiting good moods and for maintaining bad moods. In D. M. Wegner & J. W. Pennebaker (Eds.), *Handbook of mental control* (pp. 278–305). Englewood Cliffs, NJ: Prentice-Hall.

Paulhus, D. L. (1993). Bypassing the will: The automatization of affirmations. In D. M. Wegner & J. W. Pennebaker (Eds.), *Handbook of mental control* (pp. 573–587). Englewood Cliffs, NJ: Prentice-Hall.

Paulhus, D. L., Graf, P., & Van Selst, M. (1989). Attentional load increases the positivity of self-presentation. *Social Cognition, 7,* 389–400.

Pennebaker, J. W. (1989). Confession, inhibition, and disease. In L. Berkowitz (Ed.), *Advances in experimental social psychology* (Vol. 22, pp. 211–244). Orlando, FL: Academic Press.

Pennebaker, J. W. (1990). *Opening up: The healing power of confiding in others.* New York: Morrow.

Peterson, C., Maier, S. F., & Seligman, M. E. P. (1993). *Learned helplessness.* New York: Oxford University Press.

Petty, R. E., & Cacioppo, J. T. (1984). The effects of involvement on responses to argument quantity and quality: Central and peripheral routes to persuasion. *Journal of Personality and Social Psychology, 46,* 69–81.

Pittman, T. S. (1998). Motivation. In D. Gilbert, S. T. Fiske, & G. Lindzey (Eds.), *Handbook of social psychology* (4th ed., Vol. 1, pp. 549–590). New York: McGraw-Hill.

Posner, M. I., & Snyder, C. R. R. (1975). Attention and cognitive control. In R. L. Solso (Ed.), *Information processing and cognition: The Loyola symposium* (pp. 55–85). Hillsdale, NJ: Erlbaum.

Postman, L. (1951). Toward a general theory of cognition. In

J. H. Rohrer & M. Sherif (Eds.), *Social psychology at the crossroads* (pp. 242–272). New York: Harper.

Postman, L., Bruner, J. S., & McGinnies, E. (1948). Personal values as selective factors in perception. *Journal of Abnormal and Social Psychology, 43,* 142–154.

Powers, W. T. (1973). *Behavior: The control of perception.* Chicago: Aldine.

Pratto, F. (1994). Consciousness and automatic evaluation. In P. M. Niedenthal & S. Kitayama (Eds.), *The heart's eye: Emotional influences in perception and attention* (pp. 115–143). San Diego, CA: Academic Press.

Pratto, F., & Bargh J. A. (1991). Stereotyping based on apparently individuating information: Trait and global components of sex stereotypes under attention overload. *Journal of Experimental Social Psychology, 27,* 26–47.

Pratto, F., & John, O. P. (1991). Automatic vigilance: The attention-grabbing power of negative social information. *Journal of Personality and Social Psychology, 61,* 380–391.

Rachman, S. (1980). Emotional processing. *Behaviour Research and Therapy, 18,* 51–60.

Read, S. J., & Miller, L. C. (1989). Inter-personalism: Toward a goal-based theory of persons in relationships. In L. Pervin (Ed.), *Goal concepts in personality and social psychology* (pp. 413–472). Hillsdale, NJ: Erlbaum.

Reason, J. (1979). Actions not as planned: The price of automatization. In G. Underwood & R. Stevens (Eds.), *Aspects of consciousness* (Vol. 1, pp. 67–89). New York: Academic Press.

Reiss, S., Peterson, R. A., Gursky, D. M., & McNally, R. J. (1986). Anxiety sensitivity, anxiety frequency, and the prediction of fearfulness. *Behavior Research and Theory, 24,* 1–8.

Rinn, W. E. (1984). The neuropsychology of facial expression: A review of the neurological and psychological mechanisms for producing facial expressions. *Psychological Bulletin, 95,* 52–77.

Ritts, V., & Patterson, M. L. (1996). Effects of social anxiety and action identification on impressions and thoughts in interaction. *Journal of Social and Clinical Psychology, 15,* 191–205.

Roemer, L., & Borkovec, T. D. (1993). Worry: Unwanted cognitive activity that controls unwanted somatic experience. In D. M. Wegner & J. W. Pennebaker (Eds.), *Handbook of mental control* (pp. 220–238). Englewood Cliffs, NJ: Prentice Hall.

Rosenthal, D. M. (1993). Thinking that one thinks. In M. Davies & G. W. Humphries (Eds.), *Consciousness: Psychological and philosophical essays* (pp. 197–223). Oxford, England: Blackwell.

Roskos-Ewoldsen, D. R., & Fazio, R. H. (1992). On the orienting value of attitudes: Attitude accessibility as a determinant of an object's attraction of visual attention. *Journal of Personality and Social Psychology, 63,* 198–211.

Ross, L., & Nisbett, R. E. (1991). *The person and the situation: Perspectives of social psychology.* New York: McGraw-Hill.

Rotter, J. B. (1966). Generalized expectancies for internal versus external control of reinforcement. *Psychological Monographs, 80* (1, Whole No. 609).

Ryle, G. (1949). *The concept of mind.* London: Hutchinson.

Salovey, P., Hsee, C. K., & Mayer, J. D. (1993). Emotional intelligence and the self-regulation of affect. In D. M. Wegner & J. W. Pennebaker (Eds.), *Handbook of mental control* (pp. 258–277). Englewood Cliffs, NJ: Prentice-Hall.

Schachter, S. (1964). The interaction of cognitive and physiological determinants of emotional state. In L. Berkowitz (Ed.), *Advances in experimental social psychology* (Vol. 1, pp. 49–80). New York: Academic Press.

Schachter, S., & Singer, J. (1962). Cognitive, social, and physiological determinants of emotional state. *Psychological Review, 69,* 379–399.

Schank, R. C., & Abelson, R. P. (1977). *Scripts, plans, goals, and understanding.* Hillsdale, NJ: Erlbaum.

Scheier, M. F., & Carver, C. S. (1977). Self-focused attention and the experience of emotion: Attraction, repulsion, elation, and depression. *Journal of Personality and Social Psychology, 37,* 1576–1588.

Scheier, M. F., & Carver, C. S. (1985). Optimism, coping, and health: Assessment and implications of generalized outcome expectancies. *Health Psychology, 4,* 219–247.

Scherer, K. R. (1984). Emotion as a multicomponent process: A model and some cross-cultural data. In P. Shaver (Ed.), *Review of personality and social psychology* (Vol. 5, pp. 37–63). Beverly Hills, CA: Sage.

Schlenker, B. R. (1980). *Impression management.* Monterey, CA: Brooks-Cole.

Schneider, D. J. (1993). Mental control: Lessons from our past. In D. M. Wegner & J. W. Pennebaker (Eds.), *Handbook of mental control* (pp. 13–35). Englewood Cliffs, NJ: Prentice-Hall.

Shallice, T. (1972). Dual functions of consciousness. *Psychological Review, 79,* 383–393.

Sherman, S. J. (1980). On the self-erasing nature of errors of prediction. *Journal of Personality and Social Psychology, 39,* 211–221.

Sherman, S. J., Mackie, D. M., & Driscoll, D. M. (1990). Priming and the differential use of dimensions in evaluation. *Personality and Social Psychology Bulletin, 16,* 405–418.

Shiffrin, R. M. (1988). Attention. In R. C. Atkinson, R. T. Herrnstein, G. Lindzey. & R. D. Luce (Eds.), *Steven's Handbook of Experimental Psychology,* (2nd ed., Vol. 2, pp. 739–811). New York: Wiley.

Shiffrin, R. M., & Schneider, W. (1977). Controlled and automatic human information processing: II. Perceptual learning, automatic attending, and a general theory. *Psychological Review, 84,* 127–190.

Simon, H. A. (1967). Motivational and emotional controls of cognition. *Psychological Review, 74,* 29–39.

Simon, H. A. (1974). How big is a chunk? *Science, 83,* 482–488.

Skinner, B. F. (1953). *Science and human behavior.* New York: Free Press.

Skinner, E. (1995). *Perceived control, motivation, and coping.* Thousand Oaks, CA: Sage.

Smith, E. R. (1984). Model of social inference processes. *Psychological Review, 91,* 392–413.

Smith, E. R. (1994). Procedural knowledge and processing strategies in social cognition. In R. S. Wyer & T. K. Srull (Eds.), *Handbook of social cognition* (2nd ed., Vol. 1, pp. 99–152). Hillsdale, NJ: Erlbaum.

Smith, E. R. (1998). Mental representation and memory. In D. Gilbert, S. T. Fiske, & G. Lindzey (Eds.), *Handbook of social psychology* (4th ed., Vol. 1, pp. 391–445). New York: McGraw-Hill.

Smith, E. R., & Branscombe, N. (1988). Category accessibility as implicit memory. *Journal of Experimental Social Psychology, 24,* 490–504.

Smith, E. R., Branscombe, N., & Bormann, C. (1988). Generality of the effects of practice on social judgment tasks. *Journal of Personality and Social Psychology, 54,* 385–395.

Smith, E. R., & Lerner, M. (1986). Development of automatism of social judgments. *Journal of Personality and Social Psychology, 50,* 246–259.

Smith, E. R., & Miller, F. D. (1979). Salience and the cognitive mediation of attribution. *Journal of Personality and Social Psychology, 37,* 2240–2252.

Smith, E. R., Stewart, T. L., & Buttram, R. T. (1992). Inferring a trait from a behavior has long-term, highly specific effects. *Journal of Personality and Social Psychology, 62,* 753–759.

Snyder, M., & Swann, W. B., Jr. (1978). Behavioral confirmation in social interaction: From social perception to social reality. *Journal of Experimental Social Psychology, 14,* 148–162.

Srull, T. K., & Wyer, R. S., Jr. (1979). The role of category accessibility in the interpretation of information about persons: Some determinants and implications. *Journal of Personality and Social Psychology, 37,* 1660–1672.

Srull, T. K., & Wyer, R. S., Jr. (1989). Person memory and judgment. *Psychological Review, 96,* 58–83.

Srull, T. K., Lichtenstein, M., & Rothbart, M. (1985). Associated storage and retrieval processes in person memory. *Journal of Experimental Psychology: Learning, Memory, and Cognition, 11,* 316–345.

Staats, A. W., & Staats, C. K. (1958). Attitudes established by classical conditioning. *Journal of Abnormal and Social Psychology, 57,* 37–40.

Stangor, C., & Lange, J. E. (1994). Mental representations of social groups: Advances in understanding stereotypes and stereotyping. In M. P. Zanna (Ed.), *Advances in experimental social psychology* (Vol. 26, pp. 357–416). San Diego, CA: Academic Press.

Stanislavski, C. (1965). *An actor prepares.* New York: Theater Arts Books. (Original work published 1948.)

Steele, C. M. (1988). The psychology of self-affirmation: Sustaining the integrity of self. In L. Berkowitz (Ed.), *Ad-*

vances in experimental social psychology* (Vol. 21, pp. 261–302). New York: Academic Press.

Sternberg, S. (1966). High-speed scanning in human memory. *Science, 153,* 652–654.

Stevens, S. S. (1951). *Handbook of experimental psychology.* New York: Wiley.

Strack, F., & Hannover, B. (1996). Awareness of influence as a precondition for implementing correctional goals. In P. M. Gollwitzer & J. A. Bargh (Eds.), *The psychology of action.* New York: Guilford.

Strauman, T. J., & Higgins, E. T. (1987). Automatic activation of self-discrepancies and emotional syndromes: When cognitive structures influence affect. *Journal of Personality and Social Psychology, 53,* 1004–1014.

Sudnow, D. (1978). *Ways of the hand.* New York: Harper & Row.

Tait, R., & Silver, R. (1989). Coming to terms with major negative life events. In J. S. Uleman & J. A. Bargh (Eds.), *Unintended thought* (pp. 351–382). New York: Guilford Press.

Taylor, S. E. (1981). A categorization approach to stereotyping. In D. L. Hamilton (Ed.), *Cognitive processes in stereotyping and intergroup behavior* (pp. 88–114). Hillsdale, NJ: Erlbaum.

Taylor, S. E., & Brown, J. D. (1988). Illusion and well-being: A social psychological perspective on mental health. *Psychological Bulletin, 103,* 193–210.

Taylor, S. E., & Brown, J. D. (1994). Positive illusions and well-being revisited: Separating fact from fiction. *Psychological Bulletin, 116,* 21–27.

Taylor, S. E., & Fiske, S. T. (1978). Salience, attention, and attribution: Top of the head phenomena. In L. Berkowitz (Ed.), *Advances in experimental social psychology* (Vol. 11, pp. 249–288). New York: Academic Press.

Taylor, S. E., Fiske, S. T., Etcoff, N. L., & Ruderman, A. (1978). Categorical bases of person memory and stereotyping. *Journal of Personality and Social Psychology, 36,* 778–793.

Tesser, A., Martin, L. L., & Cornell, D. P. (1996). On the substitutability of self-protective mechanisms. In P. M. Gollwitzer & J. A. Bargh (Eds.), *The psychology of action* (pp. 48–68). New York: Guilford.

Tetlock, P. E. (1985). Accountability: A social check on the fundamental attribution error. *Social Psychology Quarterly, 48,* 227–236.

Thompson, E. P., Roman, R. J., Moskowitz, G. B., Chaiken, S., & Bargh, J. A. (1994). Accuracy motivation attenuates covert priming: The systematic reprocessing of social information. *Journal of Personality and Social Psychology, 66,* 474–489.

Thompson, S. C., Cheek, P. R., & Graham, M. A. (1988). The other side of perceived control: Disadvantages and negative effects. In S. Spacapan & S. Oskamp (Eds.), *The social psychology of health* (pp. 69–93). Beverly Hills, CA: Sage.

Tice, D. M. (1994). Pathways to internalization: When does

overt behavior change the self-concept? In T. M. Brinthaupt & R. P. Lipka (Eds.), *Changing the self: Philosophies, techniques, and experiences* (pp. 229–250). Albany, NY: State University of New York Press.

Tice, D. M., Butler, J. L., Muraven, M. B., & Stillwell, A. M. (1995). When modesty prevails: Differential favorability of self-presentation to friends and strangers. *Journal of Personality and Social Psychology, 69,* 1120–1138.

Tice, D. M., & Baumeister, R. F. (1993). Controlling anger: Self-induced emotion change. In D. M. Wegner & J. W. Pennebaker (Eds.), *Handbook of mental control* (pp. 393–409). Englewood Cliffs, NJ: Prentice-Hall.

Treisman, A. (1960). Contextual cues in selective listening. *Quarterly Journal of Experimental Psychology, 52,* 347–353.

Trope, T. (1986). Identification and inferential processes in dispositional attribution. *Psychological Review, 93,* 239–257.

Trzebinski, J., & Richards, K. (1986). The role of goal categories in person impression. *Journal of Personality and Social Psychology, 22,* 216–227.

Uleman, J. S. (1989). A framework for thinking intentionally about unintended thoughts. In J. S. Uleman & J. A. Bargh (Eds.), *Unintended thought* (pp. 425–449). New York: Guilford.

Uleman, J. S., & Moskowitz, G. B. (1994). Unintended effects of goals on unintended inferences. *Journal of Personality and Social Psychology, 66,* 490–501.

Uleman, J. S., Newman, L., & Moskowitz, G. B. (1996). People as spontaneous interpreters: Evidence and issues from spontaneous trait inference. In M. Zanna (Ed.), *Advances in experimental social psychology* (Vol. 28). San Diego, CA: Academic Press.

Uleman, J. S., Newman, L., & Winter, L. (1992). Can personality traits be inferred automatically? Spontaneous inferences require cognitive capacity at encoding. *Consciousness and Cognition, 1,* 77–90.

Vallacher, R. R., & Kaufman, J. (1996). Dynamics of action identification. In P. M. Gollwitzer & J. A. Bargh (Eds.), *The psychology of action* (pp. 260–282). New York: Guilford.

Vallacher, R. R., & Nowak, A. (1994). *Dynamical systems in social psychology.* San Diego, CA: Academic Press.

Vallacher, R. R., & Wegner, D. M. (1985). *A theory of action identification.* Hillsdale, NJ: Erlbaum.

Vallacher, R. R., & Wegner, D. M. (1987). What do people think they're doing? Action identification and human behavior. *Psychological Review, 94,* 3–15.

Vallacher, R. R., & Wegner, D. M. (1989). Levels of personal agency: Individual variation in action identification. *Journal of Personality and Social Psychology, 57,* 600–671.

Vallacher, R. R., Wegner, D. M., McMahan, S. C., Cotter, J., & Larsen, K. A. (1992). On winning friends and influencing people: Action identification and self-presentation success. *Social Cognition, 10,* 335–355.

Vallacher, R. R., Wegner, D. M., & Somoza, M. P. (1989).

That's easy for you to say: Action identification and speech fluency. *Journal of Personality and Social Psychology, 56,* 199–208.

Watts, F. N., McKenna, F. P., Sharrock, R., & Trezise, L. (1986). Color naming of phobia-related words. *British Journal of Psychology, 77,* 97–108.

Weary, G., Gleicher, F., and Marsh, K. (1993). *Control motivation and social cognition.* New York: Springer-Verlag.

Wegener, D. T., & Petty, R. E. (1995). Flexible correlation processes in social judgment: The role of naive theories in corrections for perceived bias. *Journal of Personality and Social Psychology, 68,* 36–51.

Wegner, D. M. (1977). Attribute generality: The development and articulation of attributes in person perception. *Journal of Research in Personality, 11,* 329–339.

Wegner, D. M. (1989). *White bears and other unwanted thoughts.* New York: Viking/Penguin.

Wegner, D. M. (1992). You can't always think what you want: Problems in the suppression of unwanted thoughts. In M. Zanna (Ed.), *Advances in experimental social psychology* (Vol. 25, pp. 193–225). San Diego, CA: Academic Press.

Wegner, D. M. (1994). Ironic processes of mental control. *Psychological Review, 101,* 34–52.

Wegner, D. M. (1996). Why the mind wanders. In J. D. Cohen & J. W. Schooler (Eds.), *Scientific approaches to the question of consciousness* (pp. 295–315). Mahwah, NJ: Erlbaum.

Wegner, D. M., Ansfield, M., & Pilloff, D. (1996). *The putt and the pendulum: Ironies of motor control.* Manuscript submitted for publication.

Wegner, D. M., Broome, A., & Blumberg, S. (1997). Ironic effects of trying to relax under stress. *Behaviour Research and Therapy, 35,* 11–21.

Wegner, D. M., & Erber, R. (1992). The hyperaccessibility of suppressed thoughts. *Journal of Personality and Social Psychology, 63,* 903–912.

Wegner, D. M., & Erber, R. (1993). Social foundations of mental control. In D. M. Wegner & J. W. Pennebaker (Eds.), *Handbook of mental control* (pp. 36–56). Englewood Cliffs, NJ: Prentice-Hall.

Wegner, D. M., Erber, R., Bowman, R., & Shelton, J. N. (1996). *On trying not to be sexist.* Unpublished manuscript.

Wegner, D. M., Erber, R., & Zanakos, S. (1993). Ironic processes in the mental control of mood and mood-related thought. *Journal of Personality and Social Psychology, 65,* 1093–1104.

Wegner, D. M., & Giuliano, T. (1980). Arousal-induced attention to self. *Journal of Personality and Social Psychology, 38,* 719–726.

Wegner, D. M., & Giuliano, T. (1983). On sending artifact in search of artifact: A reply to MacDonald, Harris, and Maher. *Journal of Personality and Social Psychology, 44,* 290–293.

Wegner, D. M., & Gold, D. B. (1995). Fanning old flames: Emotional and cognitive effects of suppressing thoughts of a past relationship. *Journal of Personality and Social Psychology, 68,* 782–792.

Wegner, D. M., & Pennebaker, J. W. (1993). Changing our minds: An introduction to mental control. In D. M. Wegner & J. W. Pennebaker (Eds.), *Handbook of mental control* (pp. 1–12). Englewood Cliffs, NJ: Prentice-Hall.

Wegner, D. M., & Schaefer, D. (1978). The concentration of responsibility: An objective self awareness analysis of group size effects in helping situations. *Journal of Personality and Social Psychology, 36,* 147–155.

Wegner, D. M., Schneider, D. J., Carter, S., & White, T. (1987). Paradoxical effects of thought suppression. *Journal of Personality and Social Psychology, 53,* 5–13.

Wegner, D. M., Shortt, J. W., Blake, A. W., & Page, M. S. (1990). The suppression of exciting thoughts. *Journal of Personality and Social Psychology, 58,* 409–418.

Wegner, D. M., & Vallacher, R. R. (1977). *Implicit psychology: An introduction to social cognition.* New York: Oxford University Press.

Wegner, D. M., & Vallacher, R. R. (1986). Action identification. In E. T. Higgins & R. Sorrentino (Eds.), *Handbook of motivation and cognition* (pp. 550–582). New York: Guilford.

Wegner, D. M., & Vallacher, R. R. (1987). The trouble with action. *Social Cognition, 5,* 179–190.

Wegner, D. M., & Wenzlaff, R. M. (1996). Mental control. In E. T. Higgins & A. W. Kruglanski (Eds.), *Social psychology: Handbook of basic principles* (pp. 466–492). New York: Guilford.

Wegner, D. M., & Zanakos, S. (1994). Chronic thought suppression. *Journal of Personality, 62,* 615–640.

Weinberger, D. A., Schwartz, G. E., & Davidson, J. R. (1979). Low-anxious, high-anxious, and repressive coping styles: Psychometric patterns and behavioral and physiological responses to stress. *Journal of Abnormal Psychology, 88,* 369–380.

Weiner, B. (1974). *Achievement motivation and attribution theory.* Morristown, NJ: General Learning Press.

Wenzlaff, R. M. (1993). The mental control of depression: Psychological obstacles to emotional well-being. In D. M. Wegner & J. W. Pennebaker (Eds.), *Handbook of mental control* (pp. 239–257). Englewood Cliffs, NJ: Prentice-Hall.

Werner, H. (1956). Microgenesis and aphasia. *Journal of Abnormal and Social Psychology, 52,* 347–353.

White, R. B. (1959). Motivation reconsidered: The concept of competence. *Psychological Review, 66,* 297–333.

White, J. D., & Carlston, D. E. (1983). Consequences of schemata for attention, impressions, and recall in complex social interactions. *Journal of Personality and Social Psychology, 45,* 538–549.

Wicklund, R. (1975). Objective self-awareness. In L. Berkowitz (Ed.), *Advances in experimental social psychology* (Vol. 8). New York: Academic Press.

Wicklund, R. A., & Brehm, J. W. (1976). *Perspectives on cognitive dissonance.* Hillsdale, NJ: Erlbaum.

Wicklund, R. A., & Steins, G. (1996). Person perception under pressure: When motivation brings about egocentrism. In P. M. Gollwitzer & J. A. Bargh (Eds.), *The psychology of action* (pp. 511–528). New York: Guilford.

Wiener, N. (1948). *Cybernetics.* New York: Wiley.

Wilson, T. D., & Brekke, N. (1994). Mental contamination and mental correction: Unwanted influences on judgments and evaluations. *Psychological Bulletin, 116,* 117–142.

Wine, J. D. (1971). Test anxiety and the direction of attention. *Psychological Bulletin, 76,* 92–104.

Winter, L., & Uleman, J. S. (1984). When are social judgments made? Evidence for the spontaneousness of trait inferences. *Journal of Personality and Social Psychology, 47,* 237–252.

Winter, L., Uleman, J. S., & Cunniff, C. (1985). How automatic are social judgments? *Journal of Personality and Social Psychology, 49,* 904–917.

Wyer, R. S., Jr., & Srull, T. K. (1989). *Memory and cognition in its social context.* Hillsdale, NJ: Erlbaum.

Zajonc, R. B. (1968). Attitudinal effects of mere exposure. *Journal of Personality and Social Psychology, 9* (Supplement No. 2, Part 2).

Zajonc, R. B. (1980). Feeling and thinking: Preferences need no inferences. *American Psychologist, 35,* 151–175.

Zillmann, D. (1988). Mood management: Using entertainment to full advantage. In L. Donohew, H. E. Sypher, & E. T. Higgins (Eds.), *Communication, social cognition, and affect* (pp. 147–171). Hillsdale, NJ: Erlbaum.

CHAPTER ELEVEN

BEHAVIORAL DECISION MAKING AND JUDGMENT

ROBYN M. DAWES, *Carnegie Mellon University*

Behavioral decision making is now a recognized area in psychology. This chapter is the second that describes behavioral decision making in this *Handbook*. Since the last edition (Abelson & Levi, 1985), a number of extensive literature reviews, textbooks, and books integrating the authors' work with other work in "the field" have been published. Some of the more notable (in chronological order) are Hogarth (1987), Dawes (1988), Yates (1990), Plous (1993), Payne, Bettman, and Johnson (1993), and Camerer (1995). In addition, many areas of applied decision making have begun to rely on principles of behavioral decision making; see, for example, Faust's (1986) or Bersoff's (1992) scathing reviews of expert psychological testimony in our courts.

Basically, behavioral decision making is the field that studies how people make decisions. Because all types of people are making all sorts of decisions all the time, the field is potentially very broad. What has characterized the field both historically and theoretically is the comparison of actual decision making with certain principles of rationality in decision making—for example, that increasing the number of options available to a decision maker should not increase the probability that a particular option from the more restricted set is chosen, or that the way in which iden-

tical choices are described ("framed") should not affect choice. When actual decisions violate such principles *systematically* (not just as a result of unreliability or "error"), this deviation is termed an *anomaly*—if the people who violate these principles simultaneously accept them as ones that they believe *should* govern their decision making.

An informal analysis of the commonly versus less commonly referenced work indicates that the former is primarily about these anomalies of decision making, while the latter involves applications in particular areas of interest to the authors. While much of the current author's own work involves application (even two chapters in a single book of applications; see Dawes, 1994b, 1994c), an emphasis on a common concern with anomalies rather than a diverse set of applications will form the core of this chapter. I do not mean to downgrade applications; in fact, as will be indicated in one section of this chapter, the area has grown to a large extent as a result of interest in applied decision making. It is, however, an interest that stems from the observation that while people often "muddle through" in either their day-to-day or expert decision making, they do so in ways that lead to predictable biases and departures from "rationality" (broadly defined—not in terms of selfishness of goals, or even in terms of the likelihood of means to achieve these goals, but in terms of avoiding outright contradictions in the policies or thought processes leading to choice). Thus, an understanding of the anomalous characteristics of decision making—that can (not necessarily do) arise when people are not self-consciously aware of their existence or potential impact—forms a basis for both the core work in behavioral decision making and its applications.

As people become more systematic in their decision making, they tend to evaluate both the desirability ("util-

This work was supported in part by NIAAA Grant # AA 09198-01. I would like to thank Daniel Kahneman and the late Amos Tversky for examining the penultimate draft of this chapter for possible errors and possible ways to shorten it. I am also particularly grateful to Provost Paul Christiano of Carnegie Mellon University for providing me with a half-time secretary. Most of all, I want to acknowledge my extraordinary luck in subsequently hiring a superb person for that job, Nan Krushinski.

ity") of outcomes and the probabilities of these outcomes in an explicit manner. Even if outcomes are considered certain (as in choosing between one new automobile versus another with no cost), their desirability is not. Hence, it is very important to understand not just how people (we) regard options, but to understand their (our) probability judgments as well.

In the area of probabilistic judgment, anomalies occur because subjects systematically violate implications of Bayes Theorem while simultaneously endorsing the rules ("axioms," "principles") of probability theory from which it is derived (in two steps). For example, an individual can endorse the definition of conditional probability yet confuse the probability of a disease given a positive test result with the probability of the positive test result given the disease—without simultaneously believing that the "base rates" of disease and positive test results are the same.

Again, were these anomalies to occur in an ad hoc manner, they would be of little interest. But they are in fact systematic (Dawes, 1983) and highly replicable in experimental settings. It is, of course, possible to weaken (or strengthen!) the magnitude of their effect or the probability they occur through various experimental manipulations, but that does not question their existence (Gigerenzer, Hell, & Blank, 1988; Gigerenzer & Hoffrage, 1995). As Camerer (1995, p. 674) writes: "*Destructive* tests, often motivated by skepticism, are designed to check whether apparent anomalies are replicable, robust across settings, or might be due to flaws in experimental design. My opinion is that *some* occasional tests of this sort are essential, but too much energy has been devoted to destructive test with very little payoff. Not a single major recent (post-1970) anomaly has been 'destroyed' by hostile replication of this sort" (italics in original).

Manipulations involving the extent (strength or frequency) of an anomaly are, however, extraordinarily important in providing insight into the nature of the decision making process that leads to it. In particular, as will be noted throughout this chapter, anomalies can arise because subjects are systematically solving some problem other than the one they might wish to solve on further consideration (and hence avoid the anomaly). This perspective is summarized by Fischhoff (1983, p. 135) in the following statement:

> Two overriding presumptions underlie this [behavioral decision making] analysis (and most research into judgment and decision making). The first is that, to a first approximation, the thought processes of most uninstitutionalized adults are quite similar. The content of those thoughts may be quite different. . . . The similarities lie in how they deal with those contents when appraising their validity, combining them in order to reach summary judgments, revising them in the light of subse-

quent experience, and storing or retrieving them from memory. Although it seems unlikely to hold up under detailed scrutiny, this presumption seems to be a useful rule. . . .

> The second metaprinciple is that there is some good reason for most things that people do (March, 1978; Newell, 1981). That is, even when people seem to be behaving irrationally or unreasonably, it is worthwhile assuming that they are honestly trying to solve some problem with the best resources at their disposal. . . . Such obstacles may be *internal,* aspects of people's psychology that restrict their performance (e.g., failure to realize the limitations of judgmental strategies that are usually valid). Or, they may be *external,* constraints imposed by their world (e.g., limited access to necessary information).

The only proviso to this statement is that it applies not only to "most uninstitutionalized adults" but to most institutionalized as well—most of the time (see Brown, 1973).

This chapter will focus on anomalies (as opposed, for example, to providing a listing of applications in social psychology). This focus is meant to convey the basic ideas and theoretical concerns of behavioral decision making. These theories and concerns are not just "relevant" to social psychology, but central to it—because much of social psychology is decision making, and many if not most important decisions are social. The outline of the chapter is simple. The first two sections illustrate two anomalies—one of which is quite clear and one of which is more ambiguous. Then, a third section will discuss some methodological problems prior to proceeding to anomalies at the heart of decision making, which will be found in subsequent sections. These discussions will be followed by a section outlining expected utility theory, and one devoted to questions of how decisions may be improved. The section on decision making will conclude with a brief statement of the author's own suggestions for productive areas of future research.

The second main part of this chapter will concern probabilistic judgment. After an introductory section indicating how anomalies of probabilistic inference can be framed in terms of Bayes Theorem, separate sections will discuss particular anomalies. Finally, again, there will be a concluding section that suggests productive future directions in judgment research. Thus, the organization of both the decision making and judgment sections of this chapter centers around anomalies—their specifications and what they imply for both the thinking process of the decision maker and how decisions can be improved. Examples are primarily from social psychology.

Before proceeding, it is important to note that some writers make a distinction between "riskless" versus "risky" choice. That distinction is not made here, but rather all choice is viewed as risky (and judgment—at least of the type discussed in this chapter—as involving uncertainty of risk). The philosophy is that stated by MacCrimmon, Stanbury, and Wehrung (1980, p. 155): "All decisions involve risk taking. A decision is risky to the extent that it involves uncertain outcomes and possible losses. So, even in minor situations, such as weekly grocery shopping, one runs risks, such as getting spoiled merchandise, missing bargains at another store, and so forth. In major situations, risk pervades the decision process."

In fact, some decisions that are most apt to be considered "riskless" actually involve the most risk. These are decisions where an individual knows exactly what it is that can be obtained, or traded, as the result of various decisions, but does not know how these alternatives will affect him or her—or others. For example, it is possible to know exactly how much money might be traded for one car versus another, thereby balancing the amount left in a checking account (or debt) against possessing one particular physical object or another, but the importance of these physical objects resides in their use, and that is extraordinarily uncertain (as, incidentally, are the effects of having a certain amount of money in the bank or a certain amount of debt). In the automobile example, these results could even involve life and death.

I. DECISION MAKING

A. A Clear Anomaly: Violation of the Sure Thing Principle

If I prefer one option to another no matter what happens—or has happened—then I should prefer that option without knowing what happens, or has happened. The preferred option *dominates* the other. Because it is preferred "no matter what," it is not necessary to know "what " in order to prefer it.

L. J. Savage (1954) has enunciated this principle in its simplest form. Suppose that option *x* is preferred to option *y* if an event occurs *and* it is preferred to *y* if the event does not occur. Then *x* is preferred to *y*. Savage termed this condition the *Sure Thing Principle.*

A striking example of violating the sure thing principle was developed by Tversky and Shafir (1992). Subjects were asked to consider a gamble with a 50-50 chance of winning $200 or losing $100. In general, only about a third of subjects offered that gamble hypothetically accepted it.

What Tversky and Shafir did was to ask subjects to imagine that they had already played it, and they were now being offered the opportunity to play it a second time. In one condition, subjects were asked to imagine that they had won the gamble the first time; 69 percent indicated a desire to play a second time. In another condition, the subjects were told to imagine that they had lost the first time

they had played this gamble; 59 percent expressed a desire to play it a second time. In the third condition, however, subjects were told to "imagine that the coin had already been tossed, but you do not know whether you have won $200 or lost $100 until you make your decision concerning the second, identical gamble." In that third condition, only 36 percent of their subjects wished to play the gamble a second time.

It is easy to hypothesize why subjects in the first two conditions wished to play the gamble again. Those who had hypothetically won faced a hypothetical choice between a 50-50 chance of ending up with either $400 or $100 if they played a second time—versus a certainty of ending up with $200 if they refused. Given "nothing to lose," the choice of the second gamble is compelling. It is also easy to understand why people will play a second time if they had lost. If they play again, they have at least a 50 percent chance of ending up winning overall (first losing $100 and then gaining $200), while if they refuse the chance, they have lost $100 for sure—an aversive outcome.

The authors present two basic explanations for why subjects might refuse to play a second time if they do not know whether they have won or lost. One involves what is termed *prospect theory* (Kahneman & Tversky, 1979b). The basic idea here is that people *choose as if* they are evaluating outcomes relative to a status quo or zero-point—where the value of gains and losses has the form of Figure 1 (taken from Tversky & Kahneman 1986, p. S259).

The value of a gamble of the type studied is equal to the probability of winning times the value of the gain plus the probability of losing times the (negative) value of the loss. The value function for gains is not as steep as it is for losses; both functions have a "diminishing marginal re-

FIGURE 1   A Typical Value Function.

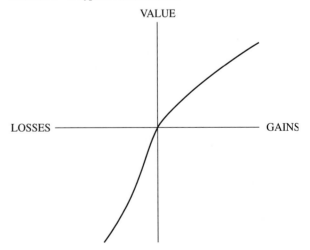

turns" shape. (That is, the function is "convex in gains and concave in losses.") This shape represents the behavior in the three conditions in the Tversky and Shafir study. When subjects have won, the average of the value of $100 and $400 may well be greater than the value of the $200 they already won—despite the concavity of the value function for gains. When the subjects have lost, the (negative) value for –$100 is less than the average of that value for –$200 and for +$100. (The shape of this function both above and below the zero-point guarantees that.) When, however, people do not know whether they have won or lost, they act as if they were making the choice anew from a zero-point. Here, the gamble does not appear very attractive. This interpretation is consistent with the finding that an almost identical proportion of subjects choose to play the game for the first time as choose to play the game a second time when they do not know the outcome of the first play.

What have we learned about the limitations of subjects? One interpretation is that subjects find it extraordinarily difficult to integrate the results of their past decisions—or rather the possible results of these decisions—into their current thinking about a present decision, especially when they do not know those results with certainty. In fact, the whole idea of looking at decisions from a status quo or zero-point was proposed some years ago by Markowitz (1952) to describe decisions even in situations where people understand exactly the results of their past decisions. In contrast, expected utility theory—which will be described in a later section in this chapter—assumes that peoples' choice among options involving uncertainty (such as the 50-50 gamble) is explained in terms of their final wealth position; for example, if an individual's assets were worth $150,000, then the 50-50 gamble for +$200 versus –$100 presents that individual with a 50-50 chance of having a final asset position of $150,200 or $149,900. Moreover, an initial asset position takes into account (at least implicitly) the possible results of all previous financial decisions and their probabilities. Doing so explicitly would require cognitive operations well beyond those available to most of us when making simple decisions, but not doing so implicitly can easily lead to a violation of the sure thing principle.

Tversky and Shafir (1992)—and later Shafir, Osherson, and Smith (1993)—offer another explanation as well. People often wish to have "good reasons" for what it is they do. (Previously Pennington & Hastie, 1988, and subsequently Gigerenzer & Goldstein, 1996, have made the same argument about reason-based choice in other contexts.) In the case of accepting the gamble for a second play, the fact that if they have won the first time and hence have "nothing to lose" presents a good reason for playing the second time. If they have lost the first time, the idea of "not quitting when behind" provides a good reason for playing a second time. When, however, they do not know whether they have won or lost, no such reason is com-

pelling—or rather the reasons that might be considered (nothing to lose and not quitting while behind) are contradictory. Thus, in the face of no good reason for taking the chance, people prefer the status quo of not playing.

Let us return to the basic proposition enunciated by Fischhoff. What problem are people solving? What are their limitations? By responding to uncertain proposition in terms of gains or losses, they are adopting an approach that is readily understandable and based on their own limited ability to understand everything in terms of effect on their final asset positions, especially when these positions involve the outcomes of choices whose outcomes are yet unknown. By adopting a "rule-of-thumb" that decisions should be made for good reasons, and not in the absence of such reasons, people are protecting themselves from stupidity. The problem is that by solving the problems presented in a way that "satisfices" (Simon, 1955) in terms of good reasons and in terms of avoiding computational complexity, however, people are simultaneously violating the sure thing principle—which is a very difficult principle to dispute. It may appear generally prudent to make decisions that can be justified to others—perhaps even to an imagined other who would hold one "accountable" (Tetlock, 1991). In fact, it may be intelligent to engage in a dialogue with a hypothetical "impartial spectator," as proposed by Adam Smith (1960); it may even be reasonable to be worried that someone will suddenly demand justification—just as H. L. Mencken suggests that conscience is "the inner voice which warns us that someone may be looking" (Cooke, 1955, p. 231). But, once again, it is also difficult to justify a violation of the sure thing principle.

In fact, when Tversky and Shafir make the sure thing principle *transparent,* their subjects do not violate it. They make the principle clear by having subjects decide whether to play the gamble a second time without knowing the outcome of the first play only after deciding whether to play it a second time if they have won *or* if they have lost; then the subjects choose in accord with the principle. "Only 6% of the subjects in the concurrent presentation exhibited the pattern 'accept after win, accept after lost, but reject when uncertain' . . ." (pp. 308–309). Previously, when the same subjects had made the choices with and without knowledge of previous results a week apart, 27 percent exhibited this pattern.

B. An Ambiguous Anomaly: Attending to Sunk Costs

The two of you are halfway to the resort. The weekend to be spent there is something that you have both looked forward to for a number of weeks; you were also happy to purchase an inexpensive package for the weekend by paying the nonrefundable fee in advance.

The only problem is that you both don't want to go. The

weather is terrible, you both feel slightly ill and "out of sorts," and there is no question that both of you would prefer to spend the weekend in town. It is not "unlikely" that you would enjoy the time at the resort more; it is quite certain you would not. Nevertheless, if you do not continue to the resort now, you will have "wasted" the nonrefundable weekend fee. You press on.

Is that rational? You have already paid the money. When you did, your total wealth was diminished by the amount of the fee. You have whatever wealth you have. Is the fact that you would have more wealth had you not paid the fee a sufficient justification for spending the weekend at a place you do not wish to spend it as opposed to a place you do? Suppose, for example, that your total wealth had diminished by the same amount of the fee on the same day you had paid that fee—but for some other reason, such as buying two new tires for your car. Would that have justified going to the resort rather than staying home? If not, what is the difference between the two situations? In both cases, the money is gone, and you're faced with the choice between doing what you want to do versus doing what you don't want to do.

Or suppose that you could have the fee returned. Would you then turn around and go back home? If so, what you are deciding is that if your wealth can be increased by a certain amount (the amount of the returned fee), then you will do what you prefer doing—while if your total wealth cannot be increased by this amount, you will not. Does such a decision appear at all rational? Or suppose that you had been awarded the weekend at the resort as a result of a random drawing conducted as a promotional activity.

The nonrefundable money already paid to the resort is termed a *sunk cost*. It is gone. You already paid for the trip in the past, and you have no control over the money anymore. What you will do on the next two days is in the future—and you are able to control it. There appears to be no rational argument to behave in the future in a way that you find undesirable in the interest of *honoring* the sunk cost. Doing so is anomalous.

Do people often honor sunk cost? The answer is clearly yes, often with a rationale that they do not wish to be wasteful. However, it is not possible to change the past. In fact, allowing one's "ill-spent money" to affect choice by honoring it in future behavior, creating unhappiness rather than happiness, is doubly irrational. Simply letting these costs affect present behavior at all is in itself anomalous.

On the day the Gulf War started (1/16/91), the *San Francisco Chronicle* featured a story titled "Troops Know the Day Has Come" on its front page. . . . "'Finally, the day has finally come,' he (Sergeant Robby Felton) said. 'You've got to think *logically* and *realistically*. Too much money's been spent, too many troops are over here, too many people had too many hard times to not kick somebody's ass' " (italics added).

Yes, people do honor sunk costs. The work of Arkes and Blumer (1985) and Staw (1982; Staw & Ross, 1989) attempts both to demonstrate the phenomenon and to investigate circumstances that encourage or discourage such anomalous behavior. There are, however, a number of essential ambiguities.

First, it is often not clear whether honoring the sunk costs is a rationale or a rationalization for the behavior, the determinants of which lie elsewhere. Consider, for example, the soldier quoted the day the Gulf War started. He was about to risk his life anyway, with very little choice about the matter. Why not think of a "logical and realistic" reason for doing so—even if the reason itself will not withstand logical scrutiny? As another example, consider the statement of the senators from Tennessee in favor of continuing the Tennessee-Tombigbee Project that had been initiated *even though the value of the completed project was less than the amount yet to be spent to complete it.* These statements were (Dawes, 1988, p. 23) " 'To terminate a project in which $1.1 billion has been invested represents an unconscionable mishandling of taxpayers' dollars'— Senator Jeremiah Denton, November 4, 1981. 'Completing Tennessee-Tombigbee is not a waste of taxpayers' dollars. Terminating the project at this late stage of development would, however, represent a serious waste of funds already invested'—Senator James Sasser, November 4, 1981."

Perhaps these senators were motivated mainly by desire to keep government funding for these projects, in order to provide employment in their state. So perhaps they were not "really" honoring sunk costs. The problem with this explanation, however, is that it fails to explain why it is they thought that others would find the sunk costs reasoning persuasive—just as labeling Sergeant Robby Felton's reasoning a rationalization rather than a rationale fails to explain why he finds it persuasive.

A second problem with interpreting a decision as honoring sunk cost is that there are often many other factors simultaneously affecting the decision, whether the reasoning is considered either a rationale or a rationalization. It is, for example, almost impossible to separate the decision to honor the cost from the factors that led to the initial decision that the cost was a good one to incur.

Another problem with the interpretation that a choice is honoring a sunk cost is that the individual may be simply protecting a reputation for "being decisive" or "not being wasteful"—even though the individual knows that the *particular* choice involved is irrational. The future cost in having a bad reputation may be more negative than the cost of honoring the initial investment without expecting an outcome worth the continued investment. There is a real problem here in that if others believe and honor sunk costs, then someone who behaves "rationally" might be derogated by these others. Moreover, these examples and analyses of sunk costs are often in organizational settings where someone will be held "responsible" when the final costs are calculated. In such a situation, an individual who initiated the cost may well decide that even though it is extraordinarily improbable that honoring it will result in a positive outcome, the sure loss involved in admitting it is there and ceasing to honor it is intolerable. (There is also the possibility in an organizational setting—as pointed out by Rob Austin [personal communication, 1989]—that if enough time intervenes between the initiation of the cost and the decision to stop honoring it, other members of the organization may have forgotten who was responsible for its initiation.)

Avoiding a sure loss is the standard explanation of honoring sunk costs, whether avoiding the loss itself or not letting others appreciate the decision maker's responsibility for a sure loss (Thaler, 1985). Such avoidance is consistent with prospect theory, as outlined in the previous section. What must be added, however, is that the individual who makes the commitment—or the observer—must consider the status quo as the situation *prior* to the initiation of the cost. In contrast, the explanation for refusing to play the second bet without knowing the outcome of the first in the previous section involves looking at a *fresh* status quo of zero when presented with the opportunity to play the bet again. Thus, the prospect theory explanation of honoring sunk costs involves a "sticky" status quo, while the prospect theory interpretation of violating the sure thing principle involves a rapidly changing one. That raises the interesting research question of when the status quo will change, which is an important question in both behavioral decision making and social psychology—one which may or may not yield to a general answer. The point here, however, is that the prospect theory interpretation not only provides a framework for studying the anomaly but can be used as a way of overcoming it. When, for example, faced with an argument that failing to honor sunk costs results in a sure loss, we can reinterpret the situation as one in which the status quo is already changed and we "do not wish to send good money after bad." Thus, just as a sticky status quo may provide a motive to honor sunk costs, a rapid change in the status quo may provide a way of rationalizing a decision not to honor the sunk costs.

Finally, people occasionally propose invalid examples of honoring sunk costs. Consider, for example, waiting for a bus. The longer one has been waiting, the greater the expectation that the bus will arrive, which results in a greater willingness to continue waiting, rather than to consider other means of transportation.

C. Some Methodological Concerns

As will be clear throughout this chapter, the field of behavioral decision making and judgment relies on observations and data analyses conducted in particular contexts—some

involving critical decisions in applied areas, some involving decisions with clear financial incentives in controlled settings, and some involving hypothetical decisions. The decisions studied are both of experts in applied fields and of subjects (often college sophomores or MBA students) who need to satisfy requirements of being in experiments. (These requirements are of course for their own educational benefit, rather than for the benefit of the researchers who have no funds to pay their subjects.) Research papers often involve some combination of observation and experiment, where the observation is made to illustrate a "theory" and the experiment is designed to "test" it. The results can be described, variously, as "carefully controlled hypothetico-deductive analyses of theoretically specified hypotheses" or as "cleverly collected and contrived anecdotes meant to illustrate a point." These somewhat opposite descriptions point to a number of methodological concerns in much of the research in this area, concerns that will be discussed in this section.

The previous two sections emphasize one paper by Tversky and Shafir and one by Arkes and Blumer. These papers have something in common. First, both refer to illustration of the phenomenon that occurs outside the studies themselves. For example, there is a remarkable footnote in the Tversky and Shafir paper noting that "even" experienced academics can violate the sure thing principle: "We first noticed this pattern in the context of a hiring decision. Having made a job offer to one candidate, the committee was considering another candidate for a second position. Members of the committee were intent on making the second offer if the first were declined; they were also intent, for somewhat different reasons, on making it if the first were accepted. However, they were not prepared to make the second offer without knowing whether the first was accepted or declined" (p. 306). Note that the committee was actually risking the loss of the second candidate to some other university, perhaps a more serious consequence of violating the sure thing principle than could be constructed ethically in behavioral decision making experiment. In the Arkes and Blumer study as well, the authors mention "real-world" examples of honoring sunk costs and then proceeded to "test" subjects to determine if they in fact would honor these costs in hypothetical situations, and to determine what factors would encourage or discourage such behavior.

The first methodological point to be made here is that the questions posed to the subjects in the experiments do not arise in isolation; they are not simply "verbal tricks" that the researchers have devised. The whole point of constructing the questions is to "capture" the phenomenon observed outside the laboratory in a way that does in fact duplicate it inside. If, then, by "ecological validity" is meant "the extent to which the causal mechanisms under study are illuminated by the study's setting" Ceci (1991, p. 4), these questions are devised in order to have such validity. If, however, what is meant by that term is a "representative sampling" of decisions made outside the laboratory, then these experiments clearly do not possess it. How often, for example, do people make choices between ski trips they have inadvertently scheduled for the same weekend? How often, for example, do people make decisions about gambles involving hundreds of dollars?

If all that were desired were statistical generalizations, these experiments would be of little value. What is involved, instead, however, is an attempt to "test" particular propositions about decision making and judgment outside the experiment. In order to conduct such tests, it is necessary that there is some plausibility that the experiments will turn out opposite the direction found—that is, opposite the direction predicted by the researchers (Dawes, 1992a). Thus, for example, prior to investigation, it is perfectly reasonable to hypothesize that people do not violate the sure thing principle, or that if they do so automatically, making the violation "transparent" will not reduce its magnitude. It is reasonable that people would not honor sunk cost in contexts other than those in which they must justify their behavior to someone else. Neither of these results were found. One limitation, however, is that the hypotheses testing involved direction, not magnitude; many of the theories tested may be termed "weak." The other problem is that they can be tested only in a number of contexts in any particular experiment, and that only particular types of people are available to be subjects in any particular experiment.

Seeking consistency—qualitative consistency—across a number of observational experimental contexts (Dawes, 1992b) does involve some methodological problems. Consider, for example, the use of statistics *within* each experiment. The standard model of statistical inference involves random sampling from a *well-specified* population, in order to estimate quantities, test hypotheses, compare hypotheses, or predict the effect of various interventions. For example, we might sample from a well-defined population of people intending to vote on election day and asked about their voting intentions. On the assumption that they can accurately report their intentions, we can make some prediction about the outcome of the vote. Even if we do not wish to assume anything about the relationship between what they tell us and what they will do, we can generalize from our sample to what we would be told about intentions. Or, consider randomized trials in medicine (Nowak, 1994).

In contrast, in experiments in behavioral decision making, statistics are computed *as if* the subjects have been randomly selected from a well-specified population of "people" about whom we wish to generalize. But have they been? The statements are about cognitive capacities and behaviors of "people," while the subjects are always chosen according to some constraint of convenience—such as being physically available in a classroom and being re-

quired as an "educational experience" to participate. Moreover, when experts in applied areas are used as subjects, it is not clear exactly what it is that is being sampled. What is the definition of "an expert"? And even if we could decide on that, how could we conceivably randomly sample from people we have now decided are experts? Nevertheless, the experimenters compute chi-squares, estimate correlation coefficients, and provide tests of statistical significance. (These last tests specify the probability that if in fact nothing is there, we have sampled this or a more extreme value of the nothing.) Then there is a further problem of sampling the questions. Hammond, Hamm, and Grassia (1986) have suggested that not just people but "items" and even tasks should be sampled in order to achieve "external validity." But exactly what is this population of questions from which we can randomly sample? Where is a population of "decision making" or of "probabilistic judgment" tasks from which we can sample? We at least have some idea about the population of people to whom we wish to generalize—and we know we are not sampling randomly from it—when we do these experiments, but the problem of justifying the sampling of tasks is even more daunting.

The justification for the research cannot be found in the type of statistical model used for population sampling or testing medical or psychological procedures. It is found, rather, in the consistency of the results across types of subjects and across samplings of tasks. It is found, moreover, by testing critics' claims that with different subjects or with different tasks the results would have been different—and finding they are not. For example, Fischhoff (1988, p. 178) discusses studies that have attempted to show that two judgmental biases (overconfidence and the hindsight effect) have been found only when the wrong subjects were used, or when the tasks were "unfair" due to ambiguity in the instructions, trivial consequences of not doing them well, restricted response modes, and so on. He finds *no* evidence that any of these hypothesized "unfair task factors" account for the findings. As he writes later: "If this pattern of results were sustained by additional studies considering other biases, the burden of proof might shift to the critics and situations in which neither they nor the defenders of the biases have any specific data" (p. 178).

There is another important aspect of these studies. When discussing anomalies, we are referring to inconsistencies that occur *within* individuals. Often, in contrast, we can only test different people with different questions and *infer* contradictions within people. An example may be found in work by Hershey, Kunreuther, and Schoemaker (1982). These experimenters asked subjects whether they preferred to take a 0.001 chance of losing $5000 or lose $5 for sure. They also asked the subjects whether they would pay for a $5 "insurance policy" to insure against a 0.001 chance of losing $5000. When the $5 loss was framed as insurance, 62 percent of subjects accepted it, whereas when it was framed as a gamble only 51 percent did. That 11 percent discrepancy meant that there were at least 11 percent of subjects who were inconsistent. In fact, because these experimenters asked subjects to make both choices, it is possible to check the exact percentage of inconsistent subjects, which turned out to be 15 percent. The 11 percent figure is obtained by subtracting the 2 percent who were inconsistent in the direction opposite the majority choice from the 13 percent who were inconsistent in the direction of the majority trend.

A final methodological consideration is that many of the questions in experiments involve gambles. The point is not that people are particularly used to gambles or that subjects gamble often in their lives outside the experiments. In fact, people who gamble a lot often have quite different attitudes towards gambling than do people who do not (Wagenaar, 1988). For example, veteran gamblers distinguish between "chance" versus "luck," while investigators in behavioral decision making experiments wish the subjects to pay strict attention to the probability without ascribing random variation either to factors external to themselves (the gamblers' "chance") or internal to themselves (the gamblers' "luck"). The reason that gambles are used so extensively is that it is possible to evaluate choice among gambles, and the coherence, rationality, and wisdom of choice among gambles—without depending on their outcomes. For example, it is irrational to be willing to bet even money that snake-eyes will occur as a result of rolling fair dice, even though if we actually did roll the dice, one time in 36 we would obtain snake-eyes.

Of course there are other contexts in which gambles are not used, for example, the context involving sunk costs. Here, once again, the experimenters devise and phrase the questions in order to test ideas beyond the experiments themselves. For example, the Emperor Hirohito at the end of the second world war did *not* honor the sunk costs involved in pursing that war earlier, but in fact surrendered ("Enduring the unendurable . . ."). Charles DeGaulle withdrew France from Algeria, after being placed in power by a coup engineered by people who chose him in part because they believed that his military expertise would allow France to defeat the Algerian nationalists. John F. Kennedy was rarely more popular than after he withdrew from the Bay of Pigs, and Ronald Reagan was rarely more popular than when he withdrew from Lebanon. How did these people manage to avoid honoring sunk costs? That is exactly the type of question that future experiments will be designed to answer. In fact, the experimental work in behavioral decision making is intertwined with applied work, and in fact many behavioral decision making researchers do engage in applied work, sometimes applied research and sometimes consulting. The alternation of experiment with field work with application is an intrinsic part of the field.

Finally, it is important to note that many studies use "think aloud" techniques (Ericsson & Simon, 1993). Subjects talk as thoughts occur to them while making a decision. Subjects are not to censor what they're thinking about, and in particular they are not to "explain" their decision—especially not on a retrospective basis once it is made. Rather, they are to talk as they are making it without constraining what comes to mind. (Ironically, there is a communality with Freudian free association here in that subjects are encouraged to be verbally spontaneous without censoring their words. Freud's followers, however, virtually gave up the technique of free association while retaining some of the speculations of Freud and others based on the free associations of clients. In "think aloud" protocols in contrast, experimenters are attempting to "trace"—perhaps in order to simulate with the computer program—the thinking processes of subjects reaching decisions, and they use the words the subjects emit as cues in that process.)

While there is some concern that think aloud constructions can change behavior, the context in which this has been found to occur is somewhat limited—for example, evaluating the taste qualities of jams (Wilson and Schooler, 1991). There are other findings that people have *claimed* cast doubt on the think aloud technique, but upon closer examination they do not. For example, people might not be able in some circumstances to explain *why* they have made particular decisions (e.g., a preference for commodities placed to the right of others, Nisbett and Wilson, 1977), but careful think aloud protocol instructions do not ask people to explain "why." In addition, there is some evidence that images created by instructions to describe things verbally can interfere with visual images (specifically an eyewitness identification, Schooler & Engstler-Schooler, 1990), but once again subjects are not asked to describe their decision making processes, but rather talk about what comes to mind as they are engaged in them.

D. Violations

1. Violation of Regularity   This section and the next involve violations of very simple principles that are implied by the existence of a "value system"—or even "values"—on the part of the decision maker. The idea is that the decision maker values certain options or alternatives or "things" more than others. In these sections we are not concerned with why the decision maker would value something more than something else, or with how certain values might imply others, or with how a decision maker should react in the face of uncertainty—effects of how choices are framed, or effects of how preference is expressed. The anomalies in these two sections demonstrate that decision making can be inconsistent with simple values.

Before proceeding, it must be pointed out that there is reason to believe that people do not make value-based choices. First, people may be quite inconsistent; as March (1978, pp. 595–596) points out, "tastes [read 'values'] are not necessarily absolute, relevant, stable, consistent, precise, or 'exogenous' " (meaning unchanged by the person herself or himself during the decision making process). In fact, as March goes on, sometimes behavior just does not make sense, even to the person engaged in it. It may even be "perverse," although that particular characteristic (with the exception of sexual perversity) has not been investigated either as a characteristic of behavior *per se* or as a characteristic on which people differ.

Second, the very act of making decisions can elicit—or construct—values that did not exist prior to the decision making process. In fact, Langer (1997), Montgomery (1983), and Svenson (1992) all suggest that values can arise in response to the necessity of reaching a decision, and that they are modified to justify a decision as "clear"—justifiable both to the decision maker and to a real or hypothetical individual who might question the decision maker (Tetlock, 1991). (Of course, these theorists not only "propose" that the necessity of reaching a decision may create values, they present evidence that in certain circumstances that process occurs.)

Now let us return to the idea that people make value-based choices. One immediate implication is termed *regularity*. This condition is that the probability a particular option is chosen from a set of possibilities cannot be increased by adding additional possibilities to that set. The rationale is very simple. Adding additional possibilities can only enhance the overall attractiveness—or value—of the *other* alternatives considered as a group. Thus, for example, if a subject has a tendency to pick alternative *x* when the choice is between *x* and *y,* this tendency cannot be enhanced by allowing the choice to be between *x, y,* and *z.* At the very least, *z* might have no effect on the choice—in which case the *x, y* choice would involve the value of *x* versus the value of *y,* while if *z* might be chosen, then the value of *x* in comparison with those of *y and z* would be less than its value in comparison to that of *y* alone.

But regularity can be violated. There are two simple ways to accomplish the violation and hence create the anomaly. One is to increase the set of alternatives by introducing one that is clearly inferior to a given alternative, thereby making this alternative "appear good," and hence increasing the probability of choosing it. For example, (Tversky & Simonson, 1993): "In another study, subjects received descriptions and pictures of microwave ovens taken from the Best catalogue. One group (*n* = 60) was asked to choose between an Emerson priced at $110 and a Panasonic priced at $180. Both items were on sale, a third off the regular price. Here, 57 percent chose the Emerson and 43 percent chose the Panasonic. A second group was presented with these options along with a $200 Panasonic at a 10 percent discount. Because the two Panasonics were

quite similar, the one with the lower discount appeared inferior to the other Panasonic but it was not clearly inferior to the Emerson. Indeed, only 13 percent of the subjects chose the more expensive Panasonic, but its presence increased the percentage of subjects who chose the less expensive Panasonic from 43 percent to 60 percent, contrary to regularity" (p. 1182).

This method—termed the "asymmetric domination method"—had previously been introduced by Huber, Payne, and Puto (1982). It is particularly striking that the asymmetrically dominated alternative itself is almost never chosen; thus, we have managed to enhance the probability that one item is chosen by introducing an additional item into the choice set that itself is generally not chosen. Moreover, it appears to be the introduction of the asymmetrical dominated alternative itself, rather than any effect it has on how subjects "weight" dimensions or on how they believe options are distributed on these dimensions that creates the effect (Wedell, 1991).

Is that a true anomaly? Yes. The problem is that we can enlarge the choice set of *x* and *y either* by introducing a third alternative that is dominated by *x or* by introducing a third alternative that is dominated by *y.* Even if these alternatives themselves are not chosen, the first will enhance the probability that *x* is chosen, while the second will enhance the probability that *y* is chosen. The introduction may be either inadvertent or manipulative. Yes, it is true that looking at the asymmetric domination, subjects may have "good reasons" for now choosing the dominating option, but the result is a choice that has no relation to any "value system."

There are other ways of violating regularity. For example, introducing a new alternative that makes a particular alternative look "moderate" may enhance the tendency to choose this now "moderate" alternative: ". . . an alternative's choice probability increases when it becomes a compromise or middle alternative, even if there is no superiority relationship" (Simonson, 1989, p. 161).

2. Violating Independence from Irrelevant Alternatives

A violation of regularity is a special case of violation of independence from irrelevant alternatives. The idea here is that the *relative* choice of *x* or *y* should not be affected by the introduction of a third alternative *z* (or other alternatives). Clearly, a violation of regularity is a violation of independence of irrelevant alternatives, but there are other situations in which the relative preference for *x* and *y* can be manipulated by a third alternative without violating regularity, that is, without increasing the probability an alternative is chosen *overall.*

Again, it is possible to make an alternative appear attractive or valuable by the introduction of a new one that is neither dominated by that alternative nor makes that alternative moderate. Huber and Puto (1983), for example, provided subjects with hypothetical choices between calculator batteries that differ in the number of hours they work and on price. One battery lasts 22 hours and costs $1.80, while the second lasts 28 hours and costs $2.10. The investigators then introduced one of two different "decoys." The first decoy lasts 14 hours and costs $1.50. While the battery that lasts 22 hours and costs $1.80 does not actually dominate that first decoy, it looks quite good in comparison—many more hours for just a small price increase. When given a choice between the two original batteries and this decoy as well, the 22 hour/$1.80 battery is preferred to the 28 hour/$2.10 battery by a 10:6 ratio, but a different decoy lasting 32 hours and costing $2.70 reversed that choice.

It is possible to have a violation of independence from irrelevant alternatives even when the choice is just between two items themselves—by having subjects concentrate on different "reference points" from which to make the choice. Kahneman, Knetsch, and Thaler (1991) present an example concerning hypothetical jobs. The choice is between job *A* which has "limited contact with others and involves a 20-minute commute" versus job *D* which is "moderately sociable but involves a 60-minute commute." When individuals making hypothetical choices between jobs *A* and *D* are told that their "present job" involves being isolated for long stretches and a 10-minute commute, they have a tendency to prefer job *A* (70 percent); the commuting time of *A* is only slightly worse than that of their present job, while the sociability factor is clearly superior. When subjects are told, however, that they should consider their present jobs as involving much pleasant social interaction and an 80-minute daily commute, they tended to choose job *D* (66 percent); the sociability factor appeared only slightly worse for job *D* while the sociability factor appeared a lot worse in job *A*. The authors concluded: "Subjects are more sensitive to the dimension in which they are losing relative to the reference point" (p. 201). The situation is presented schematically in Figure 2. Job *A* seems more desirable than job *D* when evaluated from point *A'*, while job *D* appears more valuable than job *A* when evaluated from point *D'*.

The problem with this choice is, however, that if jobs *A* and *D* have particular values to the choosers, these values should not be dependent on the "present job" as a reference point—given that the chooser will in any case no longer have that job once the choice of the new job is made. Here, we have a clear instance of violating independence from irrelevant alternatives even without introducing new ones.

One objection to the conclusion that this choice involves an anomaly is that subjects may *experience* the new job differently depending on the reference point provided by their current jobs. That is, the actual value of the job may depend on *trajectory* from current status. Here, we face an argument quite analogous to that involving sunk costs—that is,

Multiple reference points for the choice between *A* and *D*

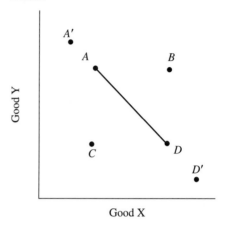

Job	Contact with others	Commute time
Present job	Isolated for long stretches	10 min.
Job A	Limited contact with others	20 min.
Job D	Moderately sociable	60 min.

FIGURE 2   An Illustration of Multiple Reference Points.

that people simply don't evaluate the future in terms of isolation from a past they cannot escape and make decisions in accord only with projected future consequences and experiences. People may have some value for the connection between future and past even though "the past is gone and only the future remains." This trajectory idea will appear again in other contexts, such as in violations of dominance and in anomalies of intertemporal choice.

In the last example, we can infer—as before—from the between subject analysis that if the same subjects were presented with both choices, the proportion who would be inconsistent in the predicted direction minus a proportion inconsistent in the unpredicted direction would have been 37 percent (70 percent − 33 percent). It is, however, possible to regard value-based choices as those in which the value of an alternative is related to just such a probability. The idea is its value leads to what is termed a *simple scalability* of the alternative; that is, a scale value for the individual for that alternative such that the *within subject* probability that the alternative is chosen in a context involving it and others is a positive function of its scale value and a negative function of the scale values of the others in the set— the larger its value and/or the smaller the sum of the other values, the more likely it is to be chosen (see Tversky & Russo, 1969).

The simplest model of such simple scalability was presented by Luce in a famous book in 1959. The model is that the probability a particular alternative is chosen from a choice set is equal to the scale value of the alternative divided by the scale value of all the alternatives (including it) in the set. That model has also been proposed by Bradley and Terry (1952). What Luce demonstrated in his book was that the existence of such scale values could be inferred from several simple conditions, the most crucial of which was termed the *constant ratio rule*. This condition stated that the probability an alternative *x* is chosen out of a set divided by the probability an alternative *y* is chosen out of the same set (which must include both *x* and *y*) is a constant independent of the other alternatives in the set.

It is immediately clear how the constant ratio rule implies regularity within people. Thus, a violation of regularity implies a violation of the constant ratio rule. The converse inference cannot be made, however, because regularity is a purely qualitative condition, while the ratio rule is a quantitative one. (It should be noted in passing that simple scalability implies both the ratio rule and hence regularity, while certain "technical" conditions must be added to the ratio rule to obtain simple scalability.) It is also true that individuals can satisfy simple scalability while averaging across them violates it. In contrast, if each individual satisfies regularity, amalgamation across individuals will as well.

What all the material in this section converges on is that value-based choice must be independent of context, and that context often matters; it can lead to violations of regularity, of independence of irrelevant alternatives, and of simple scalability. This insight is not new, although understanding its impact in many areas is an important part of behavioral decision making as an ongoing enterprise. In fact, some of the people most interested in behavioral decision making years back noted that strong stochastic transitivity (hence simple scalability, hence value-based choice) would be routinely violated by almost any three alternatives *x*, *y*, and *y* + $1 when *x* and *y* were substantial and roughly equivalent. (The choice of *y* + $1 over *y* would be certain, but the other two choices not.)

This example of *y* + $1 leads to a general principle, which can be found in probabilistic choice within an individual as well. Mellers and Biagini (1994) enunciate this principle for which they find strong experimental support: "There was a systematic pattern in the strong transitivity violations. Violations of strong transitivity were more likely to occur with triplets that included one or more similar pairs and at least one dissimilar pair than with triplets consisting of three dissimilar pairs" (p. 511).

3. Violation of Transitivity   However it is that alternatives are evaluated, if alternative *x* is preferred to alternative *y* and alternative *y* is preferred to alternative *z*, then *any* value-based decision procedure (not just one resulting in simple scalability) requires that alternative *x* is preferred to alternative *z*. Moreover, suppose that was not true—and that an individual really did have a preference for *x* over *y*

and *y* over *z* but *z* over *x*. Such an individual should be willing to sacrifice *something* to be able to choose the alternative she or he desires. So let us give that individual alternative *z* and then ask if that individual prefers *y*. The answer would be "yes" and that individual should be willing to "pay" at least something to switch from *z* to *y*—let's assume at least five cents. Now we present the individual with a choice between *y* and *x*. The individual now prefers *x*, and let us again suppose that the ability to switch is worth at least five cents. Now we have collected ten cents from the individual, and the individual has alternative *x* available. But the individual prefers *z* to *x*. We now allow the individual to switch back to *z* for a five cent fee; we have collected fifteen cents, and the individual has ended up exactly where he or she started. That individual has become what is technically termed a *money pump*. Anyone whose decisions deviate from value-based choice to yield intransitivities is susceptible to becoming a money pump—at least in theory.

Intransitivity may arise either as a result of fluctuations in value and choice or as a result of systematic factors. It is the systematic factors that are important to behavioral decision making; two will be covered in this section.

The first involves dimensional change. When options are evaluated in terms of their dimensions, it is possible that differences in some dimensions are more salient than differences in others, with the result that pairs of options may appear to be virtually identical on some dimensions—perhaps because these differences do not span a "just noticeable difference"—while the cumulative effect of these dimensions in comparing alternatives with more extreme values on them may be quite striking. That phenomenon can be best illustrated by considering the alternatives used by Tversky (1969), who first illustrated it. These alternatives were gambles consisting of a probability *p* of winning a particular amount of money, otherwise receiving nothing. Subjects chose among five such gambles, which are presented in Table 1.

The probabilities of winning were presented as sectors of a disk with a spinner, while the amount to be won was displayed as a numerical value. Subjects were told that they would receive the amount specified if the spinner

TABLE 1
The Gambles Employed in Experiment 1

Gamble	Probability of winning	Payoff (in $)	Expected value (in $)
a	7/24	5.00	1.46
b	8/24	4.75	1.58
c	9/24	4.50	1.69
d	10/24	4.25	1.77
e	11/24	4.00	1.83

ended up in the white area. These areas, as shown in the table, ranged from 7/24 to 11/24 of the complete circle. The smaller the area, the larger the payoff, but the smaller the expected value. Tversky hypothesized that the differences in the areas (probabilities) of winning as the areas decrease slightly would not be as noticeable to the subjects as the 25 cent differences in amount to be won. Thus, Tversky hypothesized that gamble *d* would be preferred to gamble *e, c* to *d,* and so on with finally *a* preferred to *b.* But in a comparison of *a* with *e,* the difference in the probability of winning (and perhaps the expected value) would be quite clear to subjects, with the results that they would choose *e* over *a.* The hypothesis was confirmed.

The point is not that subjects are necessarily insensitive to small differences in probability of winning, or necessarily less sensitive to such probabilities than to the amount to be won, or insensitive to expected value. The point is the way alternatives are presented to the subjects; they found some differences to be more salient than others, so they differentially weighted these differences—until they found that the cumulative effect of the other differences was more important. In fact, Leland (1994) has been able to replicate the results of Tversky but reversing the roles of probability and potential amount won by simply reversing the ways in which these two characteristics of these gambles are displayed (i.e., probability of winning numerically and amount to be won visually, rather than *vice versa*). The overall point is that subjects may be "seduced" by differences, which appear inconsequential in comparison to others, into making judgments one at a time that they would not make were they to consider everything at once. That clearly is a possibility outside of choice among gambles. For example, Allen (1984) discusses the effectiveness of the Nazi "*Coup d'état* by installments" (Konrad Heiden's words, p. 298) in the town of Northeim during the year after Hitler became chancellor of Germany. Changes were very gradual, almost unnoticeable—until it suddenly turned out that the town of Northeim (and in fact the rest of Germany) had been radically changed without many peoples' awareness that the small steps had cumulated into remarkable differences. First this, and then that small social or political function was taken over by the Nazi party itself; then slightly larger units were taken over by the Nazi party, and so on. Thus, for example, the school children of Northeim were one day "surprised" to find that none of their Jewish friends were there (after avoiding singing the "Horst Wessel Song" to avoid offending them), but in retrospect their absence "made sense" in terms of what had happened immediately before, which made sense in terms of what went on before that, and so on. The "final solution" followed the same principle. First only Nazi party members were supposed to boycott Jewish businesses; then there was a one-day boycott of all businesses except those of a respected banker; then there were longer boycotts in

which everyone was to participate; then there was *Kristallnacht.* It is reasonable to speculate that many of the citizens of Germany had they been presented immediately with the choice between the status quo and the more extreme measures (which kept getting more extreme) would have immediately rejected these measures in favor of the status quo. The structure of "gradualism" that can lead to intransitivity was, however, quite effective in promoting acceptance of the Nazi program.

Another way in which intransitivity may occur is through *regret* (Bell, 1982; Fishburn, 1982; Loomes, Starmer, & Sugden, 1991; Loomes & Sugden, 1982). Here, choices are based not just on what can occur as a result, but also on what *could have occurred but didn't*. How such "regret" can lead to intransitivities is illustrated in Table 2, which involves payoffs for three options depending on whether a red, white, or blue chip is chosen from a book bag containing an equal number of each color of chip (so that the probability of choosing any particular color equals exactly one third).

Consider the choice between alternatives one and two in Table 2. They appear to be identical except for which color leads to the $5,000, $10,000, or $15,000 payoff. But now consider how much we would "regret" having chosen alternative one if a red, blue, or white chip is chosen. We would be $5,000 better off with alternative one if a red or blue chip is chosen, but $10,000 better off with alternative two if a white chip is chosen. Thus, in order to "minimize regret" we might choose alternative two over alternative one. Similarly, we would be $5,000 better off having chosen alternative two than alternative three if a red or white chip were chosen, but $10,000 better off having chosen alternative three if a blue chip were chosen; potential regret could now lead to choice of alternative three over alternative two. When comparing alternatives one and three, however, we achieve the intransitivity because we would have $10,000 worth of regret for choosing alternative three were red chosen, but a maximum of $5,000 of regret for having chosen alternative one (were blue or white drawn). Thus, concern with minimizing maximum regret could lead to an intransitivity. Alternative two is preferred to one, three is preferred to two, but one preferred to three.

Of course, we might note that while minimizing maximum regret can lead to intransitivity, minimizing the probability of regret (i.e., of being at all unhappy we have chosen

TABLE 2
Chip

	Red	White	Blue
Option 1	$15,000	$ 5,000	$10,000
Option 2	$10,000	$15,000	$ 5,000
Option 3	$ 5,000	$10,000	$15,000

one alternative rather than another) could lead to the exact opposite type of intransitivity. In the actual development of "regret theory" Loomes and Sugden argue that regret tends to be an "escalating" function of "what might have been," since the former type of intransitivity is more likely than the latter. The point is not to elaborate the whole theory here but to note that regret can lead to intransitivity.

But does such irrationality rule out the potential importance of regret in decision making? Loomes and Sugden (1982) argue that ruling out consideration of *rejoicing* or *regret* that results from comparing what happens to what could have happened means ignoring important emotions people experience as a result of their decisions—and hence can anticipate they will experience. These authors write: "A choice may be rational or irrational, but an experience is just an experience . . . if an individual does experience such feelings [as rejoicing or regret], we cannot see how we can be deemed irrational for consistently taking [anticipation of] those feelings into account" (p. 820).

4. Violations of Dominance Violations of regularity, independence from irrelevant alternatives, and transitivity all involved considering alternatives as a whole. The reasons for the violations may result from characteristics of alternatives, but the violations themselves are defined in terms of choice of alternatives rather than in terms of the alternatives' characteristics. In the following two sections, in contrast, violations are defined in terms of the component—or characteristics—of the alternatives.

The first is violation of *dominance*. The basic idea is if one alternative is superior to another in all respects, then this alternative must be chosen in preference to the other. (Some authors refer to that as the "sure thing principle," but in the present chapter I will limit that phrase to refer to the outcome of probabilistic events.)

The simplest violation of dominance of all arises when two alternatives consist of clearly comparable characteristics, one is superior to the other on every one of these, yet the other is chosen. Such a choice would appear to be extraordinarily foolish, but there may in fact be good reasons for making this type of choice in particular contexts.

Hsee, Abelson, and Salovey (1991) present a rather compelling example of such a choice. Subjects are asked to choose between two jobs that are comparable in all respects except salary, which varies over a four-year period. The first job pays $18,000 the first year, $17,000 the second, $16,000 the third, and $15,000 the fourth; in contrast, the second job pays $12,000 the first, $13,000 the second, $14,000 the third, and $15,000 the fourth. Thus, the first job pays more than the second for the first three years and the same amount for the fourth year. Yet, most subjects (hypothetically!) preferred the second job. The reason appears to be that it has a "positive trajectory," while the decreasing salary over the years of the first job is in and of it-

self a negative characteristic. These authors argue in this article and elsewhere that the *direction of change* in life is indeed an important variable determining satisfaction, and hence decision. The problem, of course, is that such concern with change can lead to what appears to many of us to be flat-out irrationality, in this case choosing less money every single year (except the fourth, which is tied) to more money and identical circumstances. (Even people who are fearful that more money "than needed" can yield temptation to engage in behavior they consider undesirable can avoid this temptation by giving the money away.)

Other violations of dominance can arise because people simply do not understand that various combinations of decision yield anomalous results. For example, Tversky and Kahneman (1981, p. 454) ask people to make two choices—one between favorable prospects and one between unfavorable ones—where it is assumed that the two selected prospects would be played independently. The first was a choice between a sure gain of $240 versus a 25 percent chance to gain $1000 and a 75 percent to gain nothing. The second was a choice between a sure loss of $750 versus a 75 percent chance to lose a $1000 and a 25 percent chance to lose nothing. People are attracted to sure gains and repelled by sure losses—and hence of 150 subjects presented with these two choices "simultaneously," 84 percent chose the sure gain of $240 while 87 percent chose the 75 percent chance to lose $1000 in preference to the sure loss of $750. What happens, however, when we combine these two choices? The result is a 75 percent chance of losing $760 and a 25 percent chance of gaining $240. In contrast, combining the two options that subjects don't choose (the 25 percent chance to gain $1000 with a sure loss of $750) yields a 75 percent chance to lose $750 with a 25 percent chance to gain $250. Clearly, the second pair of alternatives is dominating. But the majority choosing in a way violating dominance is so overwhelming that we can make the usual between to within subjects inference; the difference between those who made a dominated pair of choices versus those who made a dominating one is at least 61 percent.

5. Violations of Independence The condition generally termed *independence* is an absolutely critical one in decision making (one that must be distinguished from "independence from irrelevant alternatives"). Because the concept of independence is more technical than its name might imply, it might best be understood by first considering a condition termed *betweenness*.

Suppose a decision maker prefers an alternative *A* to an alternative *B*. Now construct a new alternative in which the decision maker receives alternative *A* with probability *p* and alternative *B* with probability $1 - p$. These alternatives may be anything, even probabilistic combinations of other alternatives. The betweenness condition states that if alternative *A* is preferred to alternative *B,* then alternative *A* must be preferred to this combination of *A* and *B,* which in turn must be preferred to alternative *B.* The combination is typically termed a "probability mixture."

To justify this betweenness condition, consider the alternative *A* alone to be the alternative *A* that occurs with probability *p* and *A* again that occurs with probability 1 – *p*; similarly we consider the alternative *B* to be the alternative *B* with probability *p* and the alternative *B* with again probability 1 – *p*. Then, betweenness follows from dominance. The reason is that *A* with probability *p* is the same in both the alternative *A* and the probability mixture, while by dominance the alternative *A* with probability 1 – *p* is preferred to alternative *B* with probability 1 – *p*; hence, by dominance *A* is preferred to the probability mixture; by the same reasoning, the mixture is preferred to *B.* The only step from dominance to betweenness is in considering this probability mixture of *A* and *B* as a unit rather than thinking separately of each component. This step is termed *reduction.*

Does choice always satisfy betweenness? Consider, for example, the following choice discussed by Camerer and Ho (1994, p. 171). *A* is a 0.34 chance of receiving $20,000 (otherwise nothing). *B* is a 0.17 chance of receiving $30,000 (otherwise nothing) while *C* is a 0.01 chance of receiving $30,000, a 0.32 chance of receiving $20,000, and a 0.67 chance of receiving nothing. Most people prefer *C* to both *A* and *B* even though it is equivalent to a probability mixture of *A* with probability 16/17 and *B* with probability 1/17.

The independence condition is more complicated than the betweenness one because it involves three alternatives rather than two. The idea is, however, analogous. If some alternative *A* is preferred to an alternative *B,* then a probability mixture consisting of *C* with probability *p* and *A* with probability 1 – *p* must be preferred to the probability mixture consisting of *C* with probability *p* and *B* with probability of 1 – *p*. In fact, the relationship is "if and only if."

This independence condition may appear innocuous until an example of its violation is examined. Consider, a choice between a probability of 0.90 of receiving $3,000 (otherwise nothing) and a probability of 0.45 of receiving $6,000 (otherwise nothing); now consider a choice of 0.002 of receiving the same $3,000 (otherwise nothing) and a choice of 0.001 of receiving $6,000 (otherwise nothing). In the first choice, people tend to prefer the 0.90 chance of $3,000 over the 0.45 chance of $6,000, while given the latter choice people tend to prefer the 0.001 chance of $6,000 over the 0.002 chance of $3,000. But that pattern of choices does in fact violate independence. Label choice of 0.90 of $3,000 (otherwise nothing) as *A* and the choice of 0.45 of $6,000 (otherwise nothing) as *B*. *A* is preferred to *B*. Now let *C* consist of receiving nothing at all. *C* with probability 0.9978 and *A* with probability 0.0022 is exactly the chance of receiving the $3,000 with probability 0.002 (otherwise nothing), while *C* with that same proba-

bility of 0.9978 and *B* with probability 0.0022 consists of receiving the $6,000 with probability 0.001 (otherwise nothing). The difference between a 0.002 and a 0.001 probability (both of which are considered "near impossibilities") is just not discriminable to the subjects, while the difference between a 0.90 probability and a 0.45 one is quite discriminable (see, for example, Leland, 1994).

The famous "Allais paradox" is another example of violation of independence (Allais, 1952/1979). Most people would prefer $20,000 for sure to a 0.89 chance of $20,000, a 0.10 chance of $100,000, and a 0.01 chance of nothing. (Being economists, the original people who discussed this paradox used figures of one and five million, but here I used numbers whose impact is available to the imaginations of at least some readers.) But these same people prefer an option of $100,000 with probability 0.10 (otherwise nothing) to one of $20,000 with probability 0.11 (otherwise nothing).

How does this pattern of choices violate the independence axiom? Let *C* consist of the option of receiving $20,000, *B* consist of the option of receiving $20,000, and *A* consist of the option of receiving $100,000 with probability 10/11 and otherwise nothing. The first choice states that receiving *C* with probability 0.89 and *B* with 0.11 is preferred to receiving *C* with probability 0.89 and *A* with probability 0.11. (Work it out.) But the if and only if condition of independence means that this choice implies that *B* is preferred to *A*. Now, let *C'* consist of receiving nothing at all. Then, by applying the independence condition again, *C'* with probability 0.89 and *B* with probability 0.11 must be preferred to *C'* with probability 0.89 and *A* with probability 0.11, that is, $20,000 with probability 0.11 (otherwise nothing) must be preferred to a 0.11 chance of $100,000 with probability 10/11 (otherwise nothing), which is equivalent to a 0.10 chance of $100,000.

In this chapter, independence is considered to result from dominance combined with reduction. In effect, decisions are considered in terms of implicit choices between potentially complex alternatives—where these implicit choices must satisfy dominance and be consistent with the choice made. Figure 3 illustrates the two violations of independence viewed in this manner. In both cases, the violation occurs because "one arm" of the decision making process diagram contains identical outcomes in the two cases. In the first instance, the probability of this arm is manipulated while in the second the payoff associated with this arm is changed. In either case, since the outcomes are identical with this one arm, it should be "irrelevant" from a rational perspective. When people violate independence, it is not.

This diagrammatic presentation of the violation of independence illustrates it. Roughly speaking, a decision will satisfy the independence condition when viewed in terms of implicit sequential choice ("extensive form") *if*

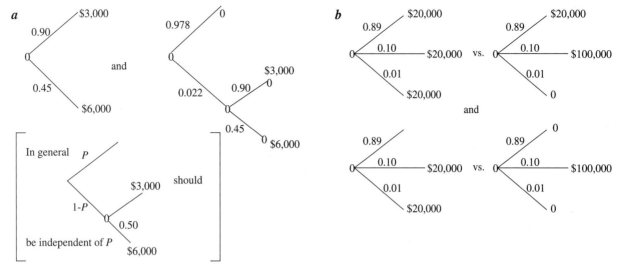

FIGURE 3   A Graphical Representation of Independence.

and only if it is *path independent.* Consider, for example, the top part of the figure. We should make the same choice between the options involving $6,000 with some probability and $3,000 with twice the probability if we *happen* to face that choice, no matter how it is the choice came about. In the Allais paradox, we again may be faced with the choice between a probability of 10/11 of $100,000 (otherwise nothing) versus a sure $20,000. It doesn't matter that with probability 0.89 in one case we receive nothing, whereas with probability 0.89 in the other case we receive $20,000. We are at what is termed technically a "node" of a choice procedure where we are required to make a choice, and how we arrived at the node is really not relevant to the question of what choice should be made once we are at it.

Finally, it should be pointed out that it is not necessary to analyze independence in terms of sequential implicit choice. The condition can stand on its own as an intuitively compelling one, and even as a necessary and important one for implying a type of expected utility theory that deals only with final states but not sequences. Here, however, I propose a principle of consistency between choice viewed in terms of implicit sequences and choice viewed in terms of final outcomes. That principle is analogous to one in game theory that would require "normal" and "extensive" forms to be equivalent, but with one important difference. A game considered in extensive form may involve actual sequential choices of those playing it—so that even without knowing exactly what another player chooses, a player may be affected by knowing that a choice has in fact been made. In contrast, the position here is that a decision maker shall *not* be affected by internal deliberations about how a simple choice could be restructured as a sequential one where only

the final end points of the sequence specify consequences.

Do people satisfy the independence condition? There are many reasons not to—ranging from difficulty in discriminating probabilities to sheer confusion. For example, Luce (1992) notes how complex satisfying the condition can be: "If one considers a lottery that consists of three stages [for example], which itself may result in a third lottery that determines a positive payoff, is the probability over final outcomes actually clear to most decision makers? Or, in an example familiar to all of us, when purchasing home and auto insurance, how many of us work out the full probability distributions of the several consequences, including that of the car being in the house when the latter burns? The ability to know that distribution is exactly what one (explicitly) postulates by assuming that all monetary gambles, including compound ones, are random variables" (p. 6).

Some people—notably Machina—have suggested that a completely rational and self-consistent theory of decision making can be constructed without the independence axiom (Machina, 1982, 1987, 1989). But as he himself describes it (1987, p. 121) the independence condition can be very compelling. Paraphrasing Samuelson (without referencing him) Machina describes this condition as being "the same as being offered a coin [which yields one particular payoff if it lands tails but with varying probabilities] and being asked before the coin is flipped whether you would rather have $P*$ or P in the event of a head. Now either the coin will land tails, in which case your choice won't have mattered, or else it will land heads, in which case you are in effect back to a choice between $P*$ or P, and it's only 'rational' to make the same choice as you would before [i.e., between $P*$ and P had no coin been flipped]." Some readers find that description of the independence condition more compelling than Machina's subsequent reasons for abandoning it.

While the Allais paradox and the examples of violations following it have the characteristic that the higher payoff with lower probability options become more attractive as the probability of winning itself is reduced, that is not a necessary characteristic of violations of the independence axiom. In "evidence of a new violation of the independence axiom" (Loomes, 1991), Loomes allows subjects to distribute amounts of money $A and ($20 – $A), where the subject either receives A with probability 0.6 and the remainder with probability 0.4 or receives A with probability 0.3, the remainder ($20 – $A) with probability 0.2 and nothing with probability 0.5. To be consistent with the $30/$45 example, the subjects should choose a higher amount for A in the latter situation (i.e., when the probability of receiving anything at all is reduced). In fact, for twenty-two of twenty-four subjects who consistently indicate a preference, the amount of A is *smaller* in the situation where the subjects receive nothing at all with probability 0.50. Apparently, when distributing money rather than making a choice from options provided by the experimenter, subjects wish to get "at least something good." That does appear to be a contradiction not only of the independence axiom but of the increased preference for the greater amount (e.g., the $6,000 versus the $3,000) as probability of getting anything diminishes.

Not surprisingly, Loomes interprets this new violation in terms of avoiding anticipated regret. In fact, the most compelling example given by Machina (at least compelling to this author) also involves regret—that is, feeling differently about watching a movie with one's favorite star after having potentially lost an opportunity to be with her or him than seeing that movie were there no possibility of interaction.

6. Anomalies Due to the Framing of Alternatives With the exception of one of the examples involving stochastic dominance, the ways in which the alternatives were presented to the subjects were not critical in eliciting self-contradictory choice. Alternatives were generally described in a single way, and people were asked to pick one from a set of possible alternative courses of action, often from a set of two. The current section, in contrast, will consider inconsistencies that arise from the way alternatives are presented, which is technically termed their *framing*. It turns out that when alternatives are presented in different ways, people often make different choices, even though the alternatives themselves remain unchanged. That violates the "consequentialist" position—which will be discussed later—that alternatives should be chosen in terms of their probable consequences and the probable (or at least possible) effects of these consequences on the decision maker and others. In fact, it violates any type of value-based choice approach. If x is preferred to y when the two alter-

natives are presented one way but y is preferred to x when the two alternatives are presented another way, then the choice of x versus y cannot be based on the values of the decision maker.

Consider, first, categorization. We all are urged to "budget" our money, for example, to decide how much to spend on an automobile and how much to spend on entertainment. Thaler (1980, 1985) notes that we also have *psychic budgets,* and the apparent desirability of an alternative is often determined to a large extent by the "budget" in which it is placed. Consider, for example, a CD player in a new automobile. Unless the individual who considers buying the car is limited to rather inexpensive varieties, the cost of this CD player may not be considered to be great when it is regarded as part of the "car budget." In contrast, its cost may be considered even prohibitive if it is regarded as part of the decision maker's entertainment budget. The costs and benefits of *any* alternative may be affected quite strongly by the category ("budget") in which it is placed. As Thaler points out, a man who is considering buying an expensive sweater he does not need for himself may well consider it to be in the category of "luxury," or "frivolous expense." But suppose that it is a gift from his wife or girlfriend. Then, it is in a different category, and even if he and she have a joint bank account—so that the net effect of buying the sweater is exactly the same whether he buys it for himself or she buys it as a gift for him—its presence in this gift category may provide a much better rationale for purchasing it than would its presence in a clothes category.

Placement of an alternative in a category can have a number of different effects depending on the alternative and the category. As Thaler points out, however, there is one general effect concerning costs. We tend to think of costs proportionately (and raises in salary tend to be proportionate as well, although it is not clear that there is any good individual or social rationale for such proportionality). Thus, for example, the CD is—for most people—a much smaller proportion of their automobile budget than of their entertainment budget, while an unneeded purchase tends to be a much higher proportion of our "luxury for self" budget than of our "gift for others" budget, and so on. This proportionality can be exploited by clever salespeople, for example, by marking up unneeded items that appear inexpensive in the context of buying a car. It is possible to defend oneself against such exploitation by asking questions such as: "If I already owned this car, would I be willing to pay for that overpriced, low fidelity CD system to put inside it?"

Categorization can also lead to contradictory choices involving the gain of money as well as its loss. For example, consider buying a car and being told that an identical one is available across town for $25 less; saving $25 does not appear to be much of an incentive to travel across town in that context. Now consider buying a vacuum cleaner for $75 and being told that there is an identical one across town for

$25 less; the savings of 33 percent do appear to many people to be a sufficient incentive to leave and go across town. In the first case, the decision maker is indicating that a trip across town is not worth $25, while in the second case that same decision maker is indicating that it is.

Another type of monetary categorization that can be extraordinarily important is that of "house money" versus "mine." The prototype example involves winning in a gambling house. Continuing to play with the money won and subsequently losing it (with almost certain probability) does not appear to involve the same sort of "waste" as playing with and losing the same amount of money that had been obtained in some other way.

Two other important ways in which alternatives may be framed are as constituting part of a status quo versus a change from it or as taking action versus refraining from taking action. When alternatives are framed as part of a status quo, especially if they are a "default" option, they usually are more likely to be endorsed or chosen than when they are framed as constituting a change. For example, people who take their children to pediatricians who administer vaccinations are likely to think of such vaccinations as "normal," or not to think about them at all, whereas a decision not to have the child vaccinated (for example one based on comparing the probabilities of suffering ill-effects as a result of the vaccination with the probabilities of suffering the ill-effects of the disease if not vaccinated) would involve "making a choice." For example (an example discussed at length later), being given an object and the opportunity to sell it makes retention of it the status quo and exchanging it for money an action.

Finally, individuals may favor the status quo because they do not even realize that it is possible to make a choice deviating from it, or because they may be simply "cautious" about doing so—even when there is evidence that departing from the status quo could be beneficial. For example, when the State of New Jersey instituted "limited tort" liability insurance in its automotive plans, people were provided with this option unless they specifically requested to be switched to a "full tort" plan (Austin, 1995). (The difference involved how much people could sue for pain and suffering and inconvenience in the event of accidents without injury.) In contrast, when the State of Pennsylvania initiated the same plan, people had to request "limited tort" or the previous full tort insurance was continued. Not surprisingly, a much higher proportion of car owners in New Jersey (77 percent) than in Pennsylvania (47 percent) "chose" limited tort.

It might appear that the distinction between an alternative that involves action versus one involving inaction is completely equivalent to the distinction between an alternative constituting the status quo versus one involving change. As Ritov and Baron (1992) note, however, these distinctions can be different. They present subjects with the following scenario: "Henry owns shares in a company A.

During the past year his investment manager asked him whether he would object to switching to stock in company B. Henry objected and got to keep his shares in company A" (p. 53). In this example, Henry must take action (objecting) to retain the status quo. The authors found that people were unhappier with the decisions in retrospect when these decisions involved action rather than inaction *and* when these decisions involved departing from the status quo rather than sticking with it.

In general, of course, inaction is confounded with retaining the status quo and action with changing it. In general, both these factors are also confounded with the third one, which is whether the action must be taken at a particular point in time, or involve a repeated decision to "do nothing" (perhaps "go with the flow"). For example, in discussing the finding that nonactions are generally judged more leniently than our actions, Teigen (1994) points out that: "the problem is that they [actions and nonactions] rarely are comparable. For one thing . . . commissions usually take place at a definite point in time, whereas omissions are more difficult to pinpoint. I can regret not having vaccinated my child, but should I regret not having done it this week, or the week before, or last month?" (p. 30). (The situation is even more complicated than Teigen makes it out to be. He is assuming that vaccinating is an action and not vaccinating is an inaction. Suppose, however, that the parents are seeing a pediatrician for whom vaccinations are routine.) Of course, this noncomparability problem does not always occur. Consider an example of Thaler's involving people's (hypothetical) reaction to a probability of 0.001 of developing an inevitably fatal disease. If they are told that they have no chance at all of contracting this disease and are asked how much money they would demand in order to have a probability of 0.001 of contracting it, they demand on the average $10,000. If, in contrast, they are told that they already have a probability of 0.001 of contracting it, they on the average would pay only $200 for a vaccine to reduce that probability to zero. Here, they are presented with a particular choice at a particular time (receive the money for taking a shot that yields a 0.001 probability of getting the disease, pay the money for a vaccine that eliminates that probability).

There is one rather important effect that is common to all categorical framing. Something is in a category if and only if its negation is not in the category. That principle is true of alternatives, outcomes, or anything else. (For our present purposes, we may accept Aristotle's "law of the excluded middle.") Both actions and consequences can therefore be framed in one of two ways—involving categories or their negations; or that the choice of a frame may have a profound influence on the choice of behavior, or the explanation for it. For example, rather than "giving orders," many doctors believe that they should make the probabilistic consequences of various courses of action clear to their patients and let the patients be the ultimate decision makers about which course to take. In some states, such consultation is mandated. In addition to raising the problem of how probable a positive or negative consequence must be in order for the physician to discuss its possibility with the patient, this policy raises the important problem of whether physicians should discuss procedures in terms of their positive consequences or of their negative ones—health versus continued disease. The most clear contrary framing involves life versus death. For example, a statement that a patient of a particular type has a 90 percent chance of being alive a month after a certain operation is equivalent to a statement that such a patient has a 10 percent chance of being dead. And while the probability of life is simply one minus the probability of death (and vice versa), subjects may not view these probabilities in light of that equivalence. For example, a 10 percent chance of death may appear to someone to be a much more serious threat than "only" a 90 percent chance of survival. McNeil, Pauker, Saks, and Tversky (1982) have discovered just that effect in framing alternative treatments in terms of living versus dying. Material about possible treatments for lung cancer was presented in terms of the probability of living versus dying—immediately after an operation or the initiation of radiation, one year hence, and five years hence. The actual *mortality* rate for surgery is 10 percent during treatment, 32 percent by the end of the first year, and 66 percent by the end of five years; these translate into survival probabilities of 90 percent, 68 percent, and 34 percent. In contrast, the mortality figures for radiation are 0 percent immediate, 23 percent by the end of the first year, and 78 percent by the end of five years; those are survival probabilities of 100 percent, 77 percent, and 22 percent. On a between-subject basis, mortality ratios differentially favor radiation (the difference between 78 percent and 66 percent at the end of five years not being as salient as the difference in the earlier percentages), which was chosen 42 percent of the time, while survival ratios strongly favored surgery (radiation being chosen only 25 percent of the time).

In addition to studying framing effects involving categorizations of alternatives and consequences, behavioral decision researchers have extensively investigated framing effects in which alternatives and consequences are compared to specific points that are psychologically salient—for example, a zero point, a status quo, an aspiration level, a "security level," a "breakeven point," or even a "survival point." A particular outcome may be viewed much differently depending on whether it is below or above such a point, and hence alternative courses of action can be evaluated differently depending on what point is introduced when they are being considered. The framing effects leading to contradictions occur because the same alternatives may be considered with respect to different points.

The clearest framing problem involves the zero point. Consider, for example, the following choice (Kahneman & Tversky, 1979a). Would you prefer $15,000 for sure or a 50/50 chance of $10,000 or $20,000? Most people pick the $15,000 for sure. Now suppose that instead you had been given the $20,000, and you must immediately make another choice. Give back $5,000, or accept a 50/50 chance of giving back nothing or $10,000. Most people choose the latter option. The problem is that receiving $20,000 and taking a 50/50 chance of giving back $10,000 or nothing is exactly equivalent to a 50/50 chance of receiving $10,000 or $20,000, while giving back $5,000 for sure is exactly equivalent to receiving $15,000 with certainty—which was preferred. This pair of choices is flat out contradictory.

How does the contradiction arise? The idea, which goes back to Markowitz (1952), is that people are evaluating these options relative to a zero-point. When thinking about $15,000 for sure versus a 50/50 chance of $10,000 or $20,000, people are thinking of gains, in particular the sure gain of $15,000. In contrast, when thinking about giving back $5,000 versus taking a 50/50 chance of giving back zero or $10,000, people are thinking in terms of losses. If, as indicated by prospect theory, sure gains are desirable and sure losses are to be avoided, then $15,000 is chosen for sure while giving back $5,000 is eschewed. The readers should refer to Figure 1 in this chapter, which represents the type of choice just hypothesized—*provided* subjects are framing the choices in terms of gains or losses from a zero-point. (What is important here is that the choices are *identical, not* that the alternatives in each choice [$15,000 versus a 50/50 chance of $10,000 or $20,000] have equal expected value.)

This type of framing contradiction is not limited to pairs of choices involving money. In a classic pair of (hypothetical) questions concerning life and death, Tversky and Kahneman find exactly the same effect. These pairs are presented as problems 5 and 6 in their 1986 article (p. S260), although they were first discussed in their 1981 article. (The percentages after each option indicate the percentage of subjects who chose it.)

> Problem 5 (N = 152): Imagine that the U.S. is preparing for the outbreak of an unusual Asian disease, which is expected to kill 600 people. Two alternative programs to combat the disease have been proposed. Assume that the exact scientific estimates of the consequences of the programs are as follows:
>
> If Program A is adopted, 200 people will be saved [72%].
>
> If Program B is adopted, there is a 1/3 probability that 600 people will be saved, and a 2/3 probability that no people will be saved [28%].

In problem 5 the outcomes are stated in positive terms (lives saved), and the majority choice is accordingly risk averse. The prospect of certainly saving 200 lives is more attractive than a risky prospect of equal expected value. A second group of respondents was given the same cover story with the following descriptions of the alternative programs.

Problem 6 (N = 155):

If Program C is adopted 400 people will die [22%].

If Program D is adopted there is a 1/3 probability that nobody will die, and 2/3 probability that 600 people will die [78%].

Again, the important contradiction arises because the choices are identical, not because the two alternatives in each have equal expected value in terms of lives saved and lost. A contradiction arises because "the first life saved is the most important" while that same principle is also applied to lives lost. The result can again be represented by the gain or loss functions of prospect theory, which embodies the general "certainty effect"—that sure gains are sought and sure losses avoided.

Another example that can be represented by these functions and again captures the effect is termed *pseudocertainty*. The effect occurs when a purely probabilistic set of alternatives is broken down into components when some outcomes are *framed* as certain—just "provided" other events occur. The effect—which may occur in personal life, medicine, business, and other contexts—can be obtained when an original choice is considered in terms of subsequent choices *if* certain contingencies arise, where some of these subsequent choices yield desirable or undesirable outcomes with certainty.

A classic prototype is to decompose the choice of receiving $45 with probability 0.20 versus receiving $30 with probability 0.25 into a *two-stage* problem. Subjects are told that they have a 0.75 probability of receiving nothing at the end of stage one and a 0.25 probability of facing a choice between a certainty of $30 versus a 0.80 probability of $45 at the end of that stage. They are asked to choose, prior to learning the outcome of the first stage, whether they would prefer the $30 or the 0.80 chance of $45. The point is that picking the 0.80 chance of $45 is identical to choosing the 0.20 chance of $45 in preference to the 0.25 chance of $30. Yet, those very same subjects who prefer 0.20 of $45 to 0.25 of $30 are quite apt to pick $30 for sure rather than a 0.80 chance of $45 when the choice is presented in this two-stage manner. The problem is presented in Figure 4. Again, the "path independence" property of independence is critical.

The question arises: zero with respect to what? In the examples discussed, zero had a pretty clear meaning—hence positive and negative were well-defined. But a zero point can also involve the past; that is, people may believe that they have gained if they end up better than in the past and lost otherwise. For example, Thaler and Johnson (1990) ask us to "consider the case of a manager's diversion that lost $10 million under her administration and who

must choose between two projects. Project A will earn a sure $5 million. Project B will earn $20 million with the probability 0.5 and lose $5 million with probability 0.5. Does this past history influence the decision? Suppose instead that these projects were described using final asset positions: A produces a sure loss of $5 million and B yields a 50 percent chance to lose $15 million and a 50 percent chance to earn $10 million. Does this change in description make a difference?" (p. 643). The point here is that the administrator may either consider the decision with the status quo point for zero and may then well opt for the sure $5 million. On the other hand, the administrator may consider the zero point to be the beginning of her administration, in which case she may well opt for the risky alternative. The point is that neither location of zero point is demanded by the problem itself; yet choice may be strongly influenced by where it is located.

In addition to being influenced by the decision frame that leads to the location of the zero point or status quo, decision making can be influenced by other points as well. For example, both people and organizations often have "aspiration levels." ("We will be doing well if we can crack the 8 percent profit barrier," "I will be doing well if I have managed to save $5,000 a year for my childrens' education," etc.); while having an outcome slightly above a level versus slightly below it may appear trivial, the exact value of this aspiration may in fact have a profound effect on decision making. For example, one way of "satisficing" for an individual or an organization with an aspiration level is to search through alternatives until finding one that appears to satisfy it, and then choose that alternative and stop the search (Simon, 1955, 1956). When such a sequential search occurs, there may be better alternatives that are not even considered, because the decision maker or decision making organization has already "satisfied the aspirations."

There are other points as well. For example, Lopes (1987) suggests that in many situations people choose in order to maximize a probability of achieving some "security level"—and presents evidence that they do. Thus, when considering positive outcomes, people may prefer positively to negatively skewed distributions because the latter have more "poor" outcomes than the former. (Of course the problem is rather complicated by the actual values of the outcome and the degree to which the subject looks at probabilities versus values; for example, people who ignore the possibility of "bad luck" may in fact feel more secure with negatively skewed distributions of outcomes, because they believe the actual result will not be in that undesirable tail of the distribution.)

A point closely allied to the security level that business people talk about (March & Shapira, 1987) is the "downside risk" amount to be lost in a business venture. That refers to the actual amount, not the probability. Executives wish to minimize its likelihood or its amount, and interestingly appear to attend primarily to the amount because they

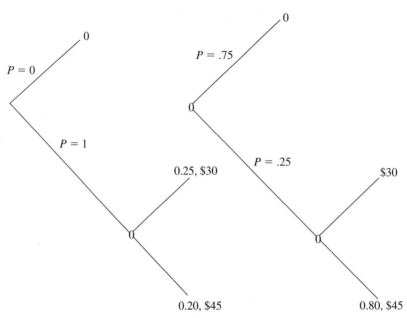

FIGURE 4   Two Different Framings of the Same Choice.

believe they can generally "control" the chance factors that would lead to unacceptable amounts below it. March and Shapira also find that executives and others consider not just downside risk but "breakeven points," aspiration levels, and "survival" points (the amounts necessary to continue in business) as well. It is unfortunately easy to hypothesize an aspiration level post hoc in order to account for results. Nevertheless, the aspiration to get something from the potential $20 could well explain the unusual violation of independence at the end of the previous section that Loomes documents, as it could the behavior of some quiz show contestants (Gertner, 1993). Often, choice is *not* a matter of considering possible consequences in and of themselves so much as it is considering these possible consequences in relation to these various "anchors." There are even points that may define whether a decision maker is or is not "disappointed" (Gul, 1991).

Theorists interested in building formal models of decision making relative to single or multiple focal points have developed an approach termed "rank and sign dependent" utility theory. The actual details lie beyond the scope of this chapter, and they could not be presented anyway until the more simple expected utility theory is covered. The reader should know, however, that the development of this theory can be found in Luce (1991), Luce and Fishburn (1991), and Tversky and Kahneman (1992).

7. Violations of Response Invariance   While the previous section dealt with (some of) the multiple ways in which alternatives may be framed to influence choice, the actual choice itself remained rather simple. Subjects were asked to pick or choose. In contrast, the present section deals with how choice can be influenced by the method—often termed "procedure"—by which decision makers express their preferences and choices. A very simple difference, for example, is between choosing one object or another versus willingness to pay for one or another of those objects. Naively, we might expect no inconsistency (and in this respect, neoclassical economists may be considered naive), but in point of fact, investigators studying behavioral decision making have found that the procedure used for expressing preference may have a profound effect.

Let me begin with a rather striking example presented by Irwin, Slovic, Lichtenstein, and McClelland (1993). People are asked whether they would prefer a particular environmental improvement or a certain electronic gadget for their own use. They are asked both to choose directly and to state how much they would be willing to pay for the improvement or the gadget. In the first study these researchers conducted, while people tended to choose the environmental improvement when asked to make a direct choice, they were willing to pay *relatively* more for the gadget. There was an overall effect in favor of environmental improvement. Consequently, in a second study, the quality of the electronic gadget was enhanced from a simple television to a television/VCR combination. In that study, an absolute reversal was found. People were willing to pay more for the gadget than for the improvement, but preferred the improvement when making a direct choice. Those two studies looked at choice and willingness to pay on a between-subject basis (i.e., different subjects were asked to make the choice and about their willingness to pay). In a final study, the experimenters used a within-subject design. Out of seventy-one subjects, twenty-nine indicated a direct choice for the environmental improvement while being able to pay more for the electronic gadget, while *none* were inconsistent in the opposite direction.

There is a problem with this study, were it to be considered in isolation. Apparently because the experimenters believed it would be very awkward to ask subjects to generate an actual amount of money they would be willing to pay for an environmental improvement, subjects in the first two experiments were asked "which would your household be willing to pay MORE for?"—while in the third experiment they were asked "which *difference* in value is greater for you?" In this context, "value" clearly refers to the money. That procedure does bypass the problem that some people object to paying out of pocket for environmental improvement, as opposed to legislating for a collective payment or fines to those who degrade the environment (Fischhoff et al., 1993). Moreover, it does get around the "put your money where your mouth is" problem where subjects may either feel an experimental demand to proffer an amount consistent with their choices (to be consistent with this oft violated maxim) or conversely feel free (as the maxim implies many people are) to make a socially desirable statement in favor of the environment while not "paying for" the preference. As will become clear later, however, this type of reversal involving valuing something with money versus making a simple choice is quite common.

Before proceeding to that type of reversal, however, this chapter will discuss the simplest type of violation of procedural invariance—found when people are asked to accept alternatives versus reject them. This type of inconsistency was found in the late 1970s by Coombs, Donnell, and Kirk (1978) who were investigating another matter. Subjects were asked to order alternatives by picking one from a set of three or by rejecting one from that same set of three. The ordering of the alternatives devised by these two methods was basically the same, but subjects were a great deal more consistent when asked to reject one of three than when asked to pick one of three. Apparently, at least in the context of the alternatives Coombs and his colleagues considered, subjects knew what they didn't want better than they knew what they wanted.

A particular theory for deciding *which alternatives* are likely to be chosen or rejected has been developed by Shafir (1993), applicable to multiattribute alternatives that have both good and bad characteristics. Shafir argues that a "choose" orientation leads subjects to search for good qualities of options, while a "reject" orientation leads subjects to search for bad ones. Now consider two alternatives

both of which have good and bad characteristics. If Shafir is correct, then the *same* alternative may be both picked and rejected if it contains both more positive characteristics *and* more negative characteristics than the other one. But of course, when deciding between two alternatives, picking one is logically equivalent to rejecting the other. This basic idea of a match between the problem response (choosing versus rejecting) and the stimulus characteristics (positive versus negative) can be found in much earlier work on "stimulus-response compatibility" in human performance (Fitts & Posner, 1967).

A particularly striking example involves (hypothetical) awarding custody. (The percentages included again indicate the percentage choosing each parent in the "award" versus the "deny" conditions.) "Problem 1 (N = 170). Imagine that you serve on the jury of an only-child sole-custody case following a relatively messy divorce. The facts of the case are complicated by ambiguous economic, social, and emotional considerations, and you decide to base your decision entirely on the following few observations. [To which parent would you award sole custody of the child?/ Which parent would you deny sole custody of the child?] (p. 549)."

Parent A	Award	Deny
Average income	36%	45%
Average health		
Average working hours		
Reasonable rapport with child		
Relatively stable social life		

Parent B	Award	Deny
Above-average income	64%	55%
Very close relationship with the child		
Extremely active social life		
Lots of work-related travel		
Minor health problems		

Shafir explains the results in terms of constructing preferences for good reasons, just as Tversky and Shafir explained the violation of the sure thing principle this way. Another possible explanation is that people become confused when attempting to weight dimensions in multiattribute choice problems (as will be detailed in a subsequent section of this chapter) and thus develop a heuristic of searching for salient values, or eliminating alternatives in terms of their good or bad characteristics (Tversky, 1972). Whether salience or elimination is based on positive or negative values can be influenced by whether the choice is to accept or reject.

Shafir (1993) ends his paper by noting that "whether we end up choosing or rejecting often seems an accident of fate" (pp. 534–554). That is a rather distressing observation to many of us. In fact, Dawes (1988) discusses at some length that contradictions due to framing and procedure are among those we are *least* happy to acknowledge, because (unlike, for example, violations of transitivity or independence from irrelevant alternatives) they tend to be based on absolutely trivial aspects of the choice situation, rather than on the characteristics of the choice alternatives themselves. Yet, as was clear in the last section and will be clear in this, these anomalies are among the strongest found within the area of behavioral decision making.

The type of violation of procedural invariance most studied by behavioral decision makers has been preference reversal—defined as choosing one alternative in preference to another but placing a higher monetary value on this other—as illustrated in the Irwin, Slovic, Lichtenstein, and McClelland (1993) article. The original stimuli used to elicit such reversals were two outcome gambles consisting of a probability p (often illustrated with a spinner) to win a certain amount of money and a probability of $1 - p$ to win zero. When presented with a pair of bets where one had a high probability of winning a small amount and the other a low probability of winning a large amount, people who were inconsistent tended to choose the bet with the high probability of winning but placed a higher monetary value on the bet with the higher payoff. Of course, not all subjects were inconsistent in their choices versus pricing of all pairs of bets; when they were, however, their inconsistency was overwhelmingly in the direction of preferring the high probability one and valuing the high payoff one more.

Lichenstein and Slovic (1971) were the discoverers of this type of preference reversal and the first people to examine it in some detail. Considering it as an example of the well-established principle of stimulus-response compatibility in human performance, these authors did not elaborate at great lengths about implications of such a reversal for the foundations of economic theory, or for "rationality" *per se*. They were, however, delighted to have the opportunity to extend their work in the Four Queens Casino in Las Vegas, where people would both choose among gambles and pay or sell monetary equivalence of these gambles for substantial amounts of money (Lichtenstein & Slovic, 1973). The reversal effect was every bit as strong in Las Vegas as it was among college students making hypothetical choices. They were also able to extend the finding from the simple gambles they first used to more complicated ones, such as "duplex gambles" where there is one probability to win a certain amount of money (otherwise nothing) and another to lose a certain amount of money (otherwise nothing). What Lichtenstein and Slovic did not anticipate was that the stability of their result and the explanation for it would become a major focus of behavioral decision making research, including even an entire conference (Santa Barbara, 1986) devoted to studying and explaining it.

Almost all the work on preference reversals predates the

Shafir accept/reject work, so there is little that investigates rejection rather than acceptance. But how is it possible to determine subjects' monetary value of gambles? One simple method is to ask them, and hope that they can estimate in the same sense that they can estimate the prices of various commodities they might buy and the monetary value of these commodities to them. Another method is to ask them for their *minimal selling price.* Subjects may be told that they "own" a gamble of positive expected value and be asked how much they would be willing to accept in cash to give it up. The minimal amount that they would accept in place of the gamble is then interpreted as a measure of its monetary value to them. Another method is to ask subjects for their *maximal buying price.* "How much would you pay to play this gamble?" (Think only of gambles with positive outcomes to understand these pricing mechanisms; they can also be used for gambles that people value negatively, but then selling prices and buying prices become themselves negative—in effect reversed.) Both the minimal buying price and the maximal selling price are termed *reservation prices* in standard economic theory—a maximal buying price being the reservation price of a buyer, while the minimal selling price is that of the seller.

Becker, DeGroot, and Marshak (1964) devised a method for obtaining monetary value that gets around these problems. This method, termed the Becker-DeGroot-Marshak (BDM) mechanism, has been used in many studies. The BDM mechanism involves a spinner that chooses a number from one clearly worth less than the gamble is worth to one clearly worth more. The person is asked to "price" the gamble. Subsequently, the spinner is spun. If the spinner ends on an amount greater than the value assigned to the gamble, then the individual is given that amount of money. When it ends on an amount less than the value assigned, the individual plays the gamble. It works very simply. Suppose, for example, the respondent suggests an amount less than her or his true value. If the spinner falls below that amount, the gamble is played—just as if a higher amount had been specified. If, however, the spinner falls between the amount specified and the actual value for the subject, then the subject receives the amount indicated by the spinner—whereas the subject would rather play the gamble. So there is no motive to underestimate the monetary value. Conversely, suppose the respondent overestimates the value. If the spinner indicates an amount greater than the overestimation, the subject is given that amount—just as the subject would be given that amount had the subject stated her or his true value. If, however, the spinner ends in a place between the true value and the stated value, the subject ends up playing the gamble when the subject would actually prefer the amount of money indicated by the spinner. So there is no motive to overestimate the value either.

Because this simple but "elegant" mechanism provides

a greater justification than buying or selling price for believing the number generated by subjects to be their "true monetary worth" for the gamble, it has been used extensively in the research summarized here. It turns out it does not matter much whether the BDM mechanism is used, whether the subject is simply asked to state a number, or whether the subject is asked to state a minimal selling or maximal buying price. The results are the same. (One consequence is that the results do not *follow from* use of the BDM mechanism.)

The research on the preference reversals of gambles received substantial impetus from an article by Grether and Plott (1979), who pointed out that the result poses a substantial challenge to standard economic theory, and concluded that it "should" therefore be artifactual. But they then presented substantial evidence that it was not. Why the challenge? Standard theory is based on the idea that two people will trade goods if and only if both would benefit from the trade. That is, person A will trade *a* for *b* possessed by person B, only if person A values *b* higher than she or he values *a*. B will agree to the trade only if she or he values *a* more than *b* (*a* and *b* may be commodities, options, effort, opportunities, money, or whatever.) Thus, creating a society in which trade is freely and easily available to everybody is a universal good. The problem with direct barter, however, is that it can become very complicated. If, for example, I grow apples, while a second person grows peaches, a third herds sheep, and a fourth produces clothing, making trades separately in all six pairs becomes time consuming, and almost impossible when we have thousands of people or organizations specializing in producing thousands of products. The solution is money, a universal commodity that can be traded for other commodities. Thus, I pay the person herding sheep for mutton, who in turn satisfies her or his needs by taking the money to pay for other things. If this system, however, is to make any sense, people must be willing to pay more for one commodity than another only if they value it more. If I trade *a* for *b* while I am simultaneously willing to accept less money for *b* than I paid for *a,* when I subsequently trade *b* for its monetary equivalent (or perhaps even a little more), I have less than I started with which I used to purchase *a.* Because I should prefer more money to less, my trading has resulted in a net, *dominating,* loss for me. But trade should benefit everyone willing to trade according to the theoretical justification for allowing people to trade whenever they wish. That justification has now been violated. (It is possible to think of the problem either in terms of violating dominance or in terms of intransitivity where one component involves money, hence in terms of a "money pump"; the conclusion is the same.)

Being economists and believing in its standard theory, Grether and Plott set out to find an artifactual explanation for the previous findings of Lichtenstein and Slovic. They listed an impressive number of what they considered to be problems in the original research—ranging from the hypothetical nature of the stakes to the fact that the experimenters were psychologists and hence would be mistrusted by subjects with any sophistication. Accounting for every problem that they thought *might* plague the earlier work, Grether and Plott replicated it. They concluded that the phenomenon was indeed a robust one that should be of substantial concern to economists.

Many other investigators have replicated the effect (again using many different response measures for eliciting monetary values). The question is why. The answer is, of course, that different "expressions" of preference can result in different orders of alternatives (Goldstein & Einhorn, 1987). In fact, labeling the bet with the higher probability of payoff as the P-bet and the one with the high monetary value as the $-bet, the relative preference of the $-bet is strongest for selling prices, weaker in choice or "strength of preference" ratings, and weakest of all in attractiveness ratings (Fisher & Hawkins, 1993; Mellers, Chang, Birnbaum, & Ordonez, 1992; Mellers, Ordonez, & Birnbaum, 1992). There are two explanations for the finding—both of which may be true, but specify different factors that operate simultaneously. The first is that when people are asked to make an actual choice or decide which of two things is more attractive, they often have little difficulty if one dominates the other. In the present context, if one bet had a higher probability of winning more than another, there would be no problem at all. But when having to make a choice between alternatives that vary in conflicting dimensions, people tend to make it primarily in terms of the more important dimension, even if that means giving it more weight than it would be assigned in a pricing or matching task (Tversky, Sattath, & Slovic, 1988). That is termed the *prominence effect.* That effect is found in context outside preference reversals as well. People *must* make a choice. It is more easily justified in terms of the important rather than the unimportant dimension when there is a conflict, or in terms of most important dimension when there are three or more. The *constructivist* approach to choice discussed earlier of Tversky and Shafir and Shafir, Simonson, Langer, Montgomery, and Svenson—among others—can explain the result. People are actively constructing a rationale for choosing; the more prominent dimensions provide one. In gambles, the prominent dimension is whether the gamble will be won or lost.

Another explanation concerns "scale compatibility." That was the original "stimulus-response compatibility" explanation considered by Lichtenstein and Slovic. The payoffs of the gambles are in terms of dollars, and the subject pricing the gamble (in one of the many ways that leads to reversal results) must do so in terms of money. Hence, the subject may focus on the dollar amount as an "anchor" and "adjust downward" in terms of the probability of winning. In the simplest case of a gamble that has a positive payoff with probability p and a zero payoff with probability $1 - p$, the adjustment is "downward" in light of the value of $1 - p$. As has been determined in many contexts (see Dawes, 1988, chap. 6), when people engage in an anchoring or adjustment process, there is a general bias not to adjust sufficiently. (Again, the direction is that there is more of a tendency for insufficient adjustment than for oversufficient adjustment, although the latter occurs on occasion.)

Insufficient anchoring and adjustment would result in *overpricing* the $-bet. Tversky, Slovic, and Kahneman (1990) provide evidence that such overpricing occurs. They ask people either to choose between pairs of gambles or to provide minimal selling prices, the latter in a rather interesting context. Subjects are told that the way the minimum selling prices will be used is that when a few pairs of gambles are chosen after the experiment for actual play, they will play the one for which they indicated the higher minimal selling price. A few other pairs of gambles will be chosen, and they will play the one for which they indicated a preference. Thus, *all the minimal selling prices are doing is indicating an implicit preference between two gambles by using money as an indicator.* Nowhere is there either a real or a hypothetical exchange of money for gambles or *vice versa.* Nevertheless, the experimenters obtain the effect. Thus, not only does the effect defy rationality, but the method of obtaining it does as well, because the monetary value generated is simply a way other than direct comparison of indicating which of two gambles is preferred.

The authors demonstrate that the $-bet is overvalued by noting the selling price generated and then later requiring the subject to choose between playing the gamble versus receiving an amount of money that is slightly *lower* than this amount. When subjects choose the money, it is clear that they have overpriced the gamble. The experimenters also investigated other possible patterns of choices that would have indicated that the P-bet was underpriced, or that the subject was simply intransitive, and they did not find these patterns.

So which is more important, the prominence effect or scale compatibility? The most reasonable answer is undoubtedly sometimes one and sometimes the other—depending on the situation (just as sometimes floods and sometimes winds destroy more forest). It is important to note, however, that even an article demonstrating the primary importance of the prominence effect in a particular context (Fisher & Hawkins, 1993) *also* finds a scale compatibility effect.

The final type of violation of response to be discussed in this section concerns the discrepancy between peoples' *willingness to pay* (WTP) to obtain a commodity or possibility versus their *willingness to accept* (WTA) money in place of that same alternative or commodity. The bottom line is that when people possess a commodity, they require a higher amount to depart with it (WTA) than they are willing to pay in order to obtain it (WTP). (In what follows, we will ignore "income effects," that is, problems arising because people cannot afford the transfer; the clearest situations involving large amounts of money can be found in markets, those involving small amounts may be found in everyday consumer choices of the type of experiments reported here.) As Hoffman and Spitzer (1993) note: "This prediction—that whenever ownership does not determine value and final distribution of rights is independent of the initial assignment—is known as the Coase Theorem [named after R. H. Coase, see 1960], and serves as a basis for many normative arguments" (p. 63). A difference between WTP and WTA violates the Coase Theorem, and it consequently violates principles of "market equilibrium."

That the WTA/WTP discrepancy cannot be explained in strategic terms can be demonstrated in experiments in which some people are randomly "endowed" with an object and others not. Then, subjects are given the opportunity to trade: objects for money or *vice versa.* Exactly half the objects should be traded. The way to understand this prediction is to note that if two people are chosen at random, one is going to value the object more than the other—assuming that these objects have value to each in a way that is independent of whether they are to be kept or bought. The probability that the person who values it more has been endowed with it is exactly one half. Thus, in the half of the cases where the person who values it more does not possess it, that person should be willing to pay an amount in order to obtain it that is greater than its value to the person possessing it. In fact, as Kahneman, Knetsch, and Thaler (1991) report, many fewer than half of the objects in such situations are sold. The reason is that the people possessing them would accept only more money than they are offered.

The rationales can also be considered in terms of the entire group; according to standard economic theory, the supply and demand functions should converge with half the objects trading hands; again, according to the Coase Theorem, it does not matter which people possess the objects at the outset; the objects should end up in the hands of the people who value them most (which—if they are originally distributed at random to half the people—implies that half of them should change hands). Objects typically used in experiments demonstrating this effect are coffee mugs, pen and pencil sets, or lottery tickets (Knetsch & Sinden, 1984).

Two main approaches explain this discrepancy. The first involves the insights of prospect theory. Again referring back to Figure 1, note that the value functions in that theory represent a greater sensitivity to loss than to gain. Moreover, maintaining something in one's possession involves a certainty, as does the money in one's pocket, while the object that could be obtained possesses uncertain attributes even though it is in the individual's view ("to rather bear those ills we have than fly to others that we know not of''). Of course, that claim of certainty to describe possessed objects may be a bit overstated; after all, it is the *use* of an object or the meaning to the possessor that determines its value, and neither future use or future meaning can be assessed with certainty (see the introduction of this chapter).

Another interpretation of this "greener grass on my side" effect is pure familiarity. Repeated exposure to stimuli (often even including people—for example one's own children) tends to enhance their subjective value (Zajonc, 1980). Thus, for example, our house may appear more attractive to us after we have lived in it than it would to us when we consider buying it, simply because we have lived in it for a period of time, not necessarily because it is "we" who own it or because we wish to "get a good deal" by demanding a lot of money for it. In fact, Zajonc has conducted an eloquent series of experiments demonstrating that while other factors may be relevant in some contexts, mere exposure itself is sufficient to enhance liking. The one qualification is that the stimulus must be positive or neutral at the outset and not take on negative characteristics during the exposure. Familiarity can breed contempt—for example for people who are contemptible—but generally breeds liking.

E. Expected Utility Analysis

We now move from anomalies to the standard normative model of expected utility, which—if followed—yields none of these anomalies. Consider the 50/50 chance of winning $200 or losing $100. The expected value of this gamble is 0.50 (+$200) + 0.50 (–$100) = +$50. Even though this expectation does not correspond to either outcome, it is the best estimate of what we expected from a single play at the gamble; and, as John Bournouili proved, the *average* payoff in multiple plays of the gamble will *converge* on $50 as we play it often enough. (In contrast, the sum payoff of n plays does *not* converge on n x $50, but in fact diverges, because the variance of the sum of independent variables is the sum of the variance.)[1]

Casinos win money because the games that they provide to their clients have a positive expected value for the house. In fact, in Nevada it is illegal to provide a game that does *not* have a positive value for the casino, because such a game would reduce tax revenues. While the house depends on the total amount of money exchanging hands (and hence the expected value of the sum) rather than the average, this expectation is sufficiently positive for the house that there is a virtual certainty of making money.

A single individual, unlike the casino, may not respond positively to a gamble with positive expected value. (The question of whether a rational individual would respond differently to playing such a gamble once versus playing it a large number of times—somewhat analogous to the situation of the casino—is a fascinating one; see Samuelson [1963, 1977], Lopes [1982, 1987], and Tversky and Bar-Hillel [1983]. While playing the gamble multiple times may be considered simply to be a *different gamble* than playing it once, the general conclusion is that if a potential pattern of wins and losses does not change the decision maker's financial asset position enough to affect choices considered singly, then this person should play the gamble once if and only if the person is willing to play it any finite number of times.)

One reason for declining to play the gamble with equal chances of winning $200 or losing $100 is that the positive subjective value of the $200 gain to the decision maker may not be as great as the negative subjective value of the $100 loss. Perhaps, for example, a $100 loss would be very painful—while a $200 gain is an unanticipated windfall that will not have much of an effect on the individual's life. This possibility is captured in an expected utility theory through the *utilities* of the money for the individual making the decision. That is, we associate a utility with the $200 gain and another with the $100 loss. These utilities are generally symbolized as u(+$200) and u(–$100). According to this expected utility theory, the gamble should be attractive if and only if it has positive *utility* to the individual, in this case if $0.50u$(+$200) + $0.50u$(–$100) is greater than zero. Moreover, standard utility theory assumes that these utilities involve the total consequences of the outcomes, which means they incorporate all the other "assets" (economic, psychological, social, etc.) in the individual decision maker's life as well as the particular outcome that can occur as a result of the gamble (i.e., probabilistic choice). In what follows we will simply assume that all these other factors are incorporated, but it must be kept in mind that when we are referring to the utility of a particular outcome we are referring to the utility of that outcome added to everything else in the decision maker's life—that is, the utility of the decision maker's life incremented (or decremented) by that outcome—as opposed to the utility of a particular outcome considered in isolation from everything else.

If we could assign utilities to outcomes and make choices in terms of expected utilities, none of the anomalies discussed in this chapter would be possible. Utilities are, for example, scale values, which rules out violation of regularity or other forms of independence from irrelevant alternatives; scale values also rule out intransitivity. The utility analysis cannot honor sunk costs, because the incor-

---

[1] Let V be the variance of the outcome of a single play of a gamble. The variance of the outcome if n independent plays is nV. But the variance of a times a variable is a^2 times the original variance. Since the average is $1/n$ times the sum, its variance is $(1/n)^2$ times that of the sum or $(1/n)^2 nV = V/n$.

poration of everything else in the decision maker's life including the outcome involves having paid the cost in the past no matter what occurs in the future, and so on. Critically, an expected utility analysis satisfies the independence axiom, because $pu(C) + (1 - p)u(A)$ will be greater than or equal to $pu(C) + (1 - p)u(B)$ if and only if $u(A)$ is greater than $u(B)$ (since utilities are numbers). Moreover, a utility analysis cannot violate framing invariance, because the utilities are associated with consequences *per se*. Finally, decisions made in accord with expected utility analysis cannot violate procedural invariance—first because the utilities are associated with consequences, and second because (being numbers) utilities involving different procedures are automatically comparable and well-ordered.

The preceding paragraphs have discussed utilities as numbers that represent subjective values. The question is where these numbers come from. The answer is that we can hypothesize that utilities might exist and then show that if they satisfy certain conditions we can create a *numerical representation* of them—that is, provide actual real numbers that can be termed utilities that satisfy these conditions. This procedure was first followed in a famous appendix to von Neumann and Morgenstern's book entitled *The Theory of Games and Economic Decisions* (1944). Because the current chapter is not one of mathematics, the proof will be neither introduced nor even sketched, but rather discussed. The first step is to hypothesize the possibility that choices are "well-ordered," which means that for any two alternatives, one is preferred to the other or they are equally preferred, and which means that a transitive ordering results from such comparisons. These orders must also satisfy the dominance and independence conditions discussed earlier (noting that dominance and reduction together imply independence), and they must satisfy one other critical condition termed *solvability*. That condition is:

> If an alternative A is preferred to B that in turn is preferred to C, then there exists a probability such that the decision maker is indifferent to receiving B versus a probability mixture of A received with probability p and C received with probability $1 - p$.

This solvability condition incorporates two ideas. The first is that no alternatives are so bad or good that including them in some probability mixture makes them incomparable to others, as would occur if A is so desirable that a decision maker would always pick a probability mixture containing it, or that C is so undesirable that a decision maker would always avoid any mixture containing it. The other basic idea is contained in the name of this condition, that is, that there is a *solution*—when we wish to devise a probability mixture of the best and worst of the three alternatives to be equal in utility to that of the alternative in the middle. (Note that it is trivial for three numbers $A > B > C$ there exists a $p < 1$ such that $B = pA + (1 - p)C$; p simply

equals $(B - C)/(A - C)$; the point here is that the solvability condition as applied to *alternatives* allows us to infer *numbers,* which by definition are their "utilities.")

It turns out that the numbers assigned are not totally unique, but that any two *sets* of numbers assigned to describe a decision making situation or situations must be related to each other in a *linear* manner. This concept of linearity might be familiar to the reader trained in psychology: it means that given one set of utilities—symbolized by u—that describe the decision process and another set of utilities—symbolized by u'—then for any alternative X, $u(X) = a + b\,u'(X)$, where b is positive.

Because utilities are unique only up to a linear transformation, it is possible to use the solvability axiom to assign them to alternatives. When the alternatives are ordered such that $u(A) > u(B) > u(C)$, we can arbitrarily assign the value 1 to $u(A)$ and 0 to $u(B)$. That yields a value of p for $u(B)$. So, for example, if an individual is indifferent between $100 for sure versus a 0.30 chance of $500 and otherwise nothing, we can state that relative to the assignment of 0 to nothing and 1 to $500, the utility for $100 is 0.30. In other words, the utility of $100 is 30 percent of the way from the utility from zero to the utility of $500. That proportion would remain after any linear transformation of the numbers involved. (The reader may wish to work out the simple algebra in order to "get a feel" of what is involved with utility assignment.)

Finally, it should be noted that the solvability condition is an *existence* one involving *actual manipulation and creation,* as opposed to most of the other conditions, which concern choice among alternatives already formed. (For example, that they can be ordered, that they satisfy the independence condition, and so on.)

Expected utility theory is used in one of two major ways: *analytically* or *synthetically* (see Dawes, 1988, chap. 8). In its analytic use, choices are studied, and if they correspond to the conditions necessary to infer utility, these utilities are specified. Usually, individuals are studied, although groups and even whole societies are studied as well in order to analyze their *implied* utilities. What can be concluded is that the choosing individual or unit is behaving *as if* the inferred utilities are the ones that the particular individual or unit has for the consequences of the alternatives analyzed. Except for the rule that more must be preferred to less by domination (because more can always be transferred to less by discarding the excess), there are no rules to govern the "taste" the utilities represent. Actual choice is interpreted as *revealing* preference; this approach is referred to as the "revealed preference" one. As Schoemaker (1982, p. 539) comments on the problems with the revealed preference approach, "Many economist has acknowledged the postdictive perspective in economics, some with sorrow and some with pride." While basically agreeing with Schoemaker, Lopes (1987) writes that "in the modern [analytic] view, utility does not precede and cause preferences; it is instead merely a convenient fiction that can be used by the practitioner to summarize the preferences of those who, by choice or chance, follow the dictates of the von Neumann and Morgenstern axiom system" (p. 286). And, I would add, it is a convenient "fiction" to summarize the preferences of those who, by choice or chance, violate those dictates but might wish to reconsider.

The revealed preference approach is not totally vacuous, as indicated by the anomalies discussed in this chapter. In order for choice and decision to be *represented* by expected utility theory, subjects cannot violate any of the conditions that they violate. In addition, expected utility theory has certain implications concerning probabilities that go even beyond the anomalies. For example, Viscusi, Margat, and Huber (1987) find that the amount that people are willing to pay to reduce the rate of poisoning or injuries from fifteen per 10,000 uses to ten per 10,000 is less than the *additional* amount they are willing to pay to reduce from ten per 10,000 to five per 10,000, and than they are willing to pay a much larger amount to reduce risks from five per 10,000 to zero per 10,000. But an expected utility analysis implies that people should value the latter change less.

Finally, a revealed preference approach might be justified on the basis of *what* is revealed. In addition to his work on familiarity and liking, Zajonc (1980) has done extensive work on comparing emotional reactions to cognitive ones, and he has concluded that in many contexts we do not respond emotionally to people, alternatives, or situations on the basis of evaluating their characteristics and then combining our evaluations to reach an overall judgment—but rather reach these evaluations directly and rapidly (often only subsequently understanding them on a cognitive basis). Zajonc has demonstrated that we can sometimes more quickly and reliably indicate whether we have been exposed to a stimulus on the basis of our emotional reaction to it—the greater the exposure the more positive the reaction—than on the basis of a judgment about whether we have in fact been exposed. The problems with such immediately revealed preferences are, however, that they may be contradictory (as in loving the sin but not the sinner).

Conversely, expected utility theory may be used *synthetically*. People may be asked to make explicit judgments about their utilities and probabilities, and then these component judgments may be combined to indicate what the expected utility theory would imply. In fact, people often do behave in this sequence, trying to figure out first what is likely to happen and what it is they want to happen and only subsequently figuring out what to do. As Tversky and Kahneman (1974) point out, we often try to figure out what it is that we want and what it is that is likely to happen in order to reach a decision, as opposed to trying to figure out on the basis of a decision reached what it is we want and what it is we think is likely to happen. Thus, while the analytic use of expected utility theory may strike

us as intellectually interesting, even challenging, its important use for us is generally synthetic. There are some contexts, such as psychotherapy, in which we may be interested in trying to figure out what it is our own behavior implies about our own utilities and beliefs, but they tend to be rare ones. The problem in this approach is, however, the very anomalies described here that make the elicitation of even simple utilities difficult (see Hershey, Kunreuther, & Schoemaker, 1982).

Also, utility theory can be used in a *normative* manner, or in a *descriptive* one. (Again, see chap. 8 of Dawes, 1988, for a fuller discussion of this normative versus descriptive distinction.) Often, behavioral decision theorists will argue that there is a distinct difference between normative use of expected utility theory (indicating how people *should* decide) versus a descriptive view (indicating how people *do* decide). For example, Edwards (1992) noted that researchers often believe in one but not the other. (In what follows, the abbreviation SEU refers to *subjective* expected utility, which is similar to expected utility except that subjective probabilities are used in place of "objective" ones, a distinction that may or may not make sense depending on one's philosophy about what justifies probability statements.)

Edwards opened a recent conference ("Utility: Theories, Measurements, and Applications," Santa Cruz, California, June 11–15, 1989) by asking "for a show of hands on the following question: Do you consider SEU maximization to be an appropriate normative rule for decision making under risk or uncertainty? Every hand went up! Scarcely believing my good fortune, I decided to press it hard. So I asked for a show of hands on a second question: Do you feel the experimental and observational evidence has established as a fact the assertion that people do not maximize SEU; that is, that SEU maximization is not defensible as a descriptive model of the behavior of unaided decision makers? Again, every hand went up, including my own!" (Edwards, 1992, pp. 254–255).

A distinction between normative versus descriptive uses of expected utility theory can, however, obscure a rather important point—which is that most of us *want* to make *good* decisions and believe that being logically coherent is important. That is, without being naive Platonists, most of us believe that we should avoid contradictions in our thinking, because contradictions indicate what cannot exist, and what cannot exist does not exist. When our reasoning leads us to a contradiction, we believe that there is something wrong with it. We do not just say, "Oh, well, here's a contradiction" in the same sense that in commenting on a particularly warm day in the middle of winter we might say, "Oh well, here's unusual weather this day."

For example, in his book *Image Theory,* Beach (1990) first notes that people often feel committed to principles in decision making, and that such principles—in contrast to things that are "merely" liked or disliked—are in part normative. After referencing Zander (1985) to support that distinction, Beach writes: "As Christensen-Szalanski (1978) has pointed out, decision makers want to make the correct decision (decision theorists want them to make the decision correctly, which is quite a different matter); the essence to decision making is an effort to do the right thing, it has no other purpose" (p. 59). Yes, the decision making principles discussed in this chapter are involved with *how* people make decisions, but that cannot be completely separated from the question of whether they make correct decisions. It might be "quite a different matter," but it is hardly an unrelated one.

Philosophically, the distinction between normative versus descriptive sounds easy, but it is not. Consider, for example, the story of the three umpires. The first one says, "I call 'm like they are." That sounds like a purely normative statement. The second one says, "I call them like I see them." That appears to be a statement about attempting to reach a "correct" call, a statement that leads to all sorts of intriguing and as yet unanswered questions about the relation between perception and the world perceived. The third one says, "They ain't nothin' 'til I call 'm." Here, the third one appears to be a philosopher who ignores the normative—much as "emotivism" in ethics does. But then the first one says to the third, "Oh yeah? Then why do you bother to look?" People do make decisions, and they consider the content of their decisions, because they wish to make the *right* decisions. We consider both the content of our decisions and the ways in which we go about making them. Even the philosophically sophisticated umpire bothers to look.

Turning from general principles to specifics, a good argument can be made for accepting the normative virtues of expected utility, and hence allowing it to *become* descriptively valid, once it is presented in a forceful and persuasive manner. For example, Sarin (1992) writes,

> To illustrate the principle of optimality, consider an example of a joint innovation marketing decision. Suppose an entrepreneur is working on an innovation. The entrepreneur realizes a lottery *H* if the innovation is unsuccessful. If, however, the innovation is successful, she could either sell it to a marketing firm or produce the product herself. The marketing firm offers her a fixed sum *F* to buy the rights to produce and market the product. If she produces and markets the product herself she would realize a lottery *G*. Should her choice between *F* and *G* depend on the likelihood (*a*) that she would be successful in developing the product or for that matter her payoffs if the innovation fails? We think not (p. 141).

Many of us find such arguments persuasive.

Finally, there are two other characteristics that are usually associated with expected utility theory which should be mentioned here. The first is *consequentialism*. The whole idea of utility theory is to evaluate decisions in terms of their potential consequences; for example, only by combining in terms of consequences can we be sure that probability mixtures of alternatives satisfy the independence condition. But what exactly *are* the "consequences" of such a choice?

Consider, for example, Abelson's (1995) example of "the doter's paradox." A man wishes to visit his grown children in order to "dote" on a particular grandchild who he thinks is just wonderful. He knows that his doting will not help her achieve anything much in life (could even conceivably get in the way), and that although he expects her to be an absolutely remarkable individual as an adult, he will not even be around to witness that outcome. So what does "doting" accomplish? Is it "nonconsequential"? Well, the problem of deciding it does not create consequences is that it in and of itself might be considered to be a consequence (e.g., of visiting his children).

Or consider fairness. Kahneman, Knetsch, and Thaler (1986) interviewed people to determine whether they approved of certain commercial actions—all of which were based on the standard economic "law" of supply and demand. According to that law, there is no such thing as "a reasonable profit" or "price gouging." The market price is determined by a willingness of sellers to sell for a profit and the demand of potential buyers. We construct a "supply curve" and a "demand curve," and the market price is the point at which these two curves intersect. That "law" can be derived from a principle of unrestricted trade. Now, subjects were asked whether they approved of the owner of a hardware store who raised the price of a snow shovel either (1) because his wholesale price for the same shovel had been increased, or (2) because there had been a bad snow storm and there was great demand for the shovel. According to the standard economic theory, the former factor should not determine the price of the shovel, while the latter should. But the respondents on the survey indicated that they thought the raised price was perfectly appropriate when the wholesale price went up but horribly inappropriate, unfair—if not immoral—when it resulted from increased demand brought about by the snow storm. Responses to other similar questions followed exactly the same pattern. For example, respondents thought it would be fine for an owner or organization during a depression to hire new workers at a wage less than that of a worker who had been previously hired, but not to reduce the wages of workers already employed. Again, according to standard economic theory, an employer or organization should pay employees the least amount of money necessary to prevent their going elsewhere, that is, pay them their "market value."

Another way in which fairness is judged is by a comparison of self to varying people in the same circumstances—particularly a comparison of one's self to others.

For example, when two people have a symmetric relationship, they expect to be treated equally. In a series of experiments concerning such equality, Loewenstein, Thompson, and Bazerman (1989) asked subjects to evaluate their satisfaction with a distribution of benefits of cost resulting from joint action. When the relationship between the individual subject and the hypothetical other was either neutral or positive, and when both hypothetically contributed the same to a product or were equally responsible for an expense, subjects preferred total equality of payment or cost—even preferring that to being "one up" on the other person. But subjects indicated an intense dislike for payoffs yielding "disadvantageous inequality," where they were "one down." Moreover, beliefs about fairness may be affected by institutions (Frey & Bohnet, 1995). Could not even procedural fairness (Tyler, 1990) be considered a "consequence" of a decision making method?

Should such fairness or unfairness be considered *part* of the consequences of action? I do not have any clear answer to that question. For example, consider the situation where people are willing to forego additional assets for everyone to equalize outcomes. Arkes asked (1994, p. 11): "Are such people failing to follow the consequentialist norm? His answer is: "I believe so" (p. 12). In contrast, commenting on the same article advocating "consequentialism," Katz (1994) asked: "Why can't even respecting rights count as a goal in the consequentialist system," and Sen (1982) suggests: "To show such goals to be mistaken, some more substantively normative criticism than that allowed by . . . instrumentally justified norms or prescriptions based on other goals would be needed—if we were not to debate the question by playing favorites between goals" (p. 22).

Or consider cooperating in social dilemma situations with anonymity and no repetition (hence no concern for reciprocal altruism or reputation). Here, by definition, the dominating strategy (hence the one an expected utility analysis favors) is *not* to cooperate. But people do—apparently out of a sense of fairness if they cannot communicate with others or a desire to help the group if they can (Dawes, 1991; Caporael, Dawes, Orbell, & van de Kragt, 1989). Should their motives be incorporated in a utility analysis? Or considered a departure from it?

Or consider punishment as retribution. Baron and Ritov (1993) have demonstrated that at least the subjects they questioned do not support the criminal justice punishment policies based on deterrence or their personal utilitarian consequences.

Or consider the act of voting, which from a naive consequentialist position makes no sense, because except in the very smallest of communities the probability that an outcome is determined by a single vote is virtually zero. Why vote? It has been discussed by a number of people— including Meehl (1977b) and Simon (1985). Voting is very difficult to explain in regular consequentialist terms, especially when people claim that they are voting because they care about the outcome. It can become, however, explained in "socio-tropic" terms or in terms of expressing a preference. So is "doing one's duty," "expressing a preference," or "feeling good about yourself" not a legitimate consequence of voting? The general problem is that *if we answer such questions in the affirmative, then there seem to be very few restraints that arise from a consequentialist perspective. If, however, we answer in the negative, we may be ignoring the very consequences that are most important to people.*

Whether used analytically or synthetically, expected utility theory itself does not constrain what it is decision makers value, that is, what their utilities are inferred to be or what they themselves believe them to be. Typically, however, two assumptions are made along with the theory. The first is that decision makers tend to be selfish. As has been discussed at some length in the previous section, this assumption is not an automatic consequence of "consequentialism." There is, for example, nothing to preclude altruism as "an argument" in someone's utility function— even though many theorists might restrict such concerns to what Andreoni (1990) terms *impure* altruism (i.e., the type of altruism that leads the altruistic individual to feel good about herself or himself, as opposed to that which focuses on the benefit for the recipient of the altruistic act).

When, however, the utility of money is considered, theorists tend to agree that there is a "marginally decreasing" utility function. That is, more is better, but the impact of the given increase decreases as a function of the original amount; for example, increasing total wealth ("asset position") by $10,000 has a lesser impact if the original amount is one million dollars than if the original amount is $5,000. Mathematically, such a utility function can be described as one whose first derivative is positive (more is better) but whose second derivative is negative (more is better, but at a decreasing rate); logarithmic functions and power functions with exponents less than one are typical of those having these two properties. In fact, many theorists and experimentalists often approximate the utility function for money with a power function (with an exponent of about 0.75). This type of utility function, described on the right side of Figure 1, illustrates the prospect theory value function from a status quo of zero.

Many of us hold a "decreasing marginal returns" intuition about the utility for other good things in life besides money. More is better, but at a decreasing rate. These good things can involve such diverse alternatives as sex or observing a mountain view on a camping trip. The problem with this intuition is that there are clear units of money over which to plot a function, but units elude us in many other contexts; even if we were to count occurrences (e.g., glances at the mountain view), such counting may strike us as somewhat arbitrary, having only a loose relationship to what we really mean by *amount* of these good things. And ironically, the more important they are, the more arbitrary simply counting instances may appear to be. Nevertheless, the intuition that "good things satiate" is a strong one.

In fact, this intuition combined with the one that "bad things escalate" can serve as a rationale for concluding that we have a "single-peaked utility function" over quantities of things and activities—whose good and bad characteristics both increase with magnitude. For example, the longer the vacation the more it is potentially enjoyed, while at the same time the greater the demands for "catch up" upon returning from it. For a very simple example, consider food.

This intuition about "good versus bad things" has led to a general conception by Coombs and Avrunin (1988) of social conflict explained in terms of different "ideal points" yielding single-peaked utility functions over quantities. That extends the earlier work of Coombs (1964) on such single-peaked functions as representing individual choice. In fact, it is not necessary to postulate "escalation" for negative consequences of amount in order to obtain a single-peaked function—just that the rate of increment for the negative consequences is greater than the rate for the positive one (i.e., that the second derivative is greater, but need not be actually positive rather than negative). The problem remains, however, that it is necessary to have some metric in order to make these ideas precise, while the intuition remains in the absence of the metric. Coombs (1964) has devised methods for developing numerical scales that represent not just orders but orders of differences (e.g., "ordered metric scales"), but these still do not have units.

Another common assumption added to utility theory concerns the timing of consuming good things in life. Here, as with money, there are very clear units involved, for example, minutes, hours, days, months, years. (In fact, many theorists may have added assumptions about utility for money and utility across time in part *because* both money and time are easily broken down into units.) The general assumption is that the sooner we experience good outcomes the better. This assumption is often formalized in terms of a "discount function," where the utility of something is "discounted" by a constant fraction depending on the length of time until it is experienced.

One important difference between the added assumptions concerning "marginal decreasing utility for money" versus "temporal discounting" is that people often behave in ways consistent with the former but not with the latter. For example, the standard discounting assumption concerning the future implies that we should not only prefer good outcomes sooner rather than later, but that when we have two good outcomes of different magnitudes, we should prefer the one with greater utility first. That does not happen. For example, Loewenstein and Prelac (1993) find that while most of their subjects do in fact prefer a French meal to an Italian one when allowed to choose either for free, they prefer to have the Italian one first if they

are to have both. That preference involves "savoring." It also involves a preference for increasing utility across time, which is quite opposed to the standard discounting assumption. The most striking example is that people prefer to have increasing incomes across time, even though in terms of total income they would be best off to have the most the soonest (because they could always invest any excess). Researchers (Loewenstein & Thaler, 1989) have even found a "crossover effect" in choices involving a conflict between good outcomes soon versus better ones later. For example, we might prefer receiving $5,000 right now to $7,500 two years from now, but if asked whether we would prefer $5,000 in 10 years or $7,500 in 12 years, we may opt for the larger payoff with the greater delay. There is absolutely no way to predict such a crossover effect from the standard idea of expected utility combined with the standard idea of temporal discounting. But there is no way to predict a preference for increasing income either; yet as pointed out earlier, this preference could be so strong that it leads to a violation of dominance (see Hsee, Abelson, & Salovey, 1991).

Finally, many people distinguish between expected utility versus subjective expected utility, as does Edwards in the passage quoted earlier. The main distinction is whether probabilities are "objective" or "subjective." Because this distinction is based primarily on *interpretation* of what *probabilities mean* it tends to be critical here only when considering probabilities for single events, or considering the "reduction" of complicated lotteries into simple ones. The latter consideration is the more important for this chapter. Recall that the rather critical independence condition can be considered to be a combination of dominance and reduction. That holds only if probabilities can be manipulated in the standard way. Most "subjectivists'" interpretations of probability theory imply that they can—because these manipulations result from a necessity that probabilities, however they are interpreted, satisfy certain constraints (the "axioms of probability theory"). It is possible, however, to claim that we have subjective probabilities for certain events considered singly that need not satisfy these conditions, or at least to claim that we often act as if they do not.

What should be pointed out here, however, is that we can make the same distinction between analytic versus synthetic with use of the theory concerning probabilities ("subjective" or not) that we have previously made about utilities. Probabilities can either be inferred from choice, or can be elicited independent of choice and then become determinants of choice. As Tversky and Kahneman (1974) point out, the latter (synthetic) use is more common: "It should perhaps be noted that, while subjective probabilities can sometimes be inferred from preferences among bets, they are normally not formed in this fashion. The person bets on team *A* rather than on team *B* because he believes that team *A* is more likely to win; he does not infer this belief from his betting preferences. Thus, in reality, subjective probability determine preferences among bets and are not derived from them . . ." (p. 1130).

F. Improving Decision Making

Anomalies create conflicts. We want to make good decisions, and—once again—we do not have to be naive Platonists to believe that decisions that violate principles of rationality we accept will tend not to be good ones. That which can't happen doesn't happen. So the question is how can decisions be improved, and this question has led to an entire field of "prescriptive decision making" populated by people who claim that they can help others make "good" decisions, or at least improve the process by which they go about making these decisions (see, for example, Raiffa, 1968, 1982).

One method is simply to apply expected utility analysis in a synthetic, self-conscious manner. For example, Pauker (1976) uses utility theory in a synthetic, prescriptive manner to make recommendations about when to use coronary bypass surgery and when not to. The expected utility theory analysis yields a recommendation in each specific case. This analysis included "patient preference" and "attitudes" as well as physical variables (p. 8).

But even if the theory is not used explicitly, decisions consistent with certain characteristics of the theory may be superior to decisions made on an ad hoc basis. Specifically, the theory tends to make each decision on a "policy" basis, involving probabilities and utilities that are applicable not just to the particular decision making problem being considered, but applicable to others as well that the decision maker *might* face (but doesn't actually face). The actual problem is viewed as an instance of possible problems, a view which Inhelder and Piaget (1958) believed to be the basis of logical thinking. This imbedding within general principles of utility theory yields an "outside" view as opposed to an "inside" one; with an outside view, the scope of the problem is actually enhanced, so that a general principle rather than an intuitively satisfactory solution to the decision problem is sought. Kahneman and Lovallo (1993) not only distinguish between this outside versus inside view, but present evidence that the outside view is in fact superior—at least in terms of predicting what is likely to happen in particular circumstances. As Dawes (1988) points out, the outside view is also "Kantian" in that each decision is viewed as a realization of a decision policy that is to be universally applied. Dawes argues that the worst decisions are made either when they are viewed in isolation or in terms of a policy with the proviso that "ordinarily I wouldn't do this but. . . ."

The virtues of policy—as opposed to case-by-base decision making—can be found in the literature comparing clinical with "statistical" (i.e., actuarial) prediction of im-

portant human outcomes. Such outcomes include: response to types of psychological treatment, success or failure on parole or in business or academic programs (e.g., graduate school), likelihood of behaving violently (always less than 0.50, but varying from person to person), and even the longevity of people with a fatal disease. Here, clinical predictions are made by an expert in a field relevant to the prediction (e.g., a parole or personnel officer, a psychologist, the "world's expert" in treating the fatal condition), while the statistical prediction is made by an actuarial model based on the relevant input (usually a linear—i.e., "weighted average"—model, or a Bayesian one involving classification with or without specification of differential cost for differential types of error). In virtually all instances in which comparisons have been made empirically, the information on which the model is based is available to the clinical experts who are also making the predictions.

Paul Meehl's 1954 book *Clinical Versus Statistical Predictions: A Theoretical Analysis and Review of the Evidence* presented about twenty empirical studies in which the two methods of prediction were compared. The book created quite a "controversy" in the field of psychology because in no comparison was the clinical prediction superior. At that time, the field itself was beginning its remarkable expansion into a professional practice based on the assumption that training and experience would lead to superior "clinical judgment" (as the result of "scientific" training). But the results of the studies summarized by Meehl implied that superior prediction of important human outcomes could best be obtained by ignoring trained clinicians, that is, bypassing them altogether in favor of establishing simple relationships between input and result, worse yet input of which clinicians were aware.

Meehl insisted that in the studies he summarized the clinical prediction and the statistical prediction be based on the same predictive variables. One possible problem, then, is that such comparison unfairly derogates clinical judgment *in its entirety,* because such judgment may allow the clinician to appreciate and assess variables that do not appear in the simple predictive equations of the statistical (actuarial) models. Or perhaps clinicians are able to appreciate *Gestalt* patterns—such as those in a chess game—that could not be simply analyzed and "quantified" in the statistical models. Those questions were addressed in a review twelve years later by Sawyer (1966). Sawyer included not just the twenty or so studies Meehl did in which the two predictions were based on the same variables, but also included studies in which the variables used in a statistical model were a *proper subset* of those available to the clinician. For example, the clinician might have access to past records and test scores *and* clinical interview impressions, while the model was based only on the summaries of past behavior and the test scores. Again, there were no instances of superiority of clinical prediction. Moreover, Sawyer considered the question of how to *amalgamate* clinical and statistical prediction, for example, how to combine the two types of predictions when they are different. One method, for example, would be to present the predictions of the statistical models to the clinician and allow the clinician to use "judgment" in integrating this prediction with her or his beliefs in order to reach a final prediction. That type of amalgamation is intuitively appealing to people and is in fact often used in contexts such as personnel selection (including selection for Graduate Fellowship Recipients, see McCauley, 1991). The converse method is to use the clinical prediction as just another predictor variable in a statistical model. The latter type of amalgamation turns out to be superior. Moreover, twenty-three years of subsequent research did not invalidate any of these conclusions, but rather garnered more and more evidence for them. Dawes, Faust, and Meehl (1989) were able to conclude that at least the question of how best to combine information to reach a prediction about an important human outcome should no longer be in doubt—or at least that in any new context someone claiming that clinical prediction might be superior should shoulder a very heavy burden of proof. As Meehl (1986) wrote a few years earlier: "There is no controversy in social science which shows such a large body of qualitatively diverse studies coming out so uniformly in the same direction as this one. When you are pushing ninety investigations [in 1986], predicting everything from the outcome of football games to the diagnosis of liver disease and when you can hardly come up with a half dozen studies showing even a weak tendency in favor of the clinician, it is time to draw a practical conclusion" (pp. 372–373).

By 1995 roughly 150 studies have pointed in the same direction (Grove & Meehl, 1996). One possibility is that these results are due to the *optimizing* nature of statistical predictive model. Alternatively, it might be that it is the *decomposition* strategy and *generality* of the statistical models that have led to their success. The variables are combined explicitly, and the combination rule is a *policy* one, the epitome of an "outside" view of the problem.

Dawes and Corrigan (1974) provided both an empirical and theoretical analysis of the data available at that time indicating that the latter alternative was the one that explained the success of the models. What they did was to consider linear models whose weights were randomly chosen (from normal or uniform distributions) except for sign. They then demonstrated that the output of these provided better predictions than the output of clinical judgment. The reason that the authors considered only weights with the correct positive or negative sign was that in the prediction context they were interested in, people should have at least some idea of the *direction* of the relationship between predictor and criterion. Moreover, many predictors are specifically constructed or chosen on the basis of their direction

(for example, a test score, a measure of the "success" of past behavior, the number of past criminal convictions). The argument was that since the *random linear models* outperformed the clinical judges, then the optimization characteristics of the models could not be the important ones for this differential finding. Rather, it was the consistency of the models and the generality that accounted for it. As Einhorn (1986) argued later, the point of the statistical model was that it provided a *general* predictive framework that *accepted* error—because it would certainly not make a wonderful prediction for every single instance—but accepted error in order "to make less error."

Before moving from this topic, a few observations are important. First, people may have faith in their clinical judgment because the judgment itself biases subsequent information (Einhorn & Hogarth, 1978); for example, having decided that a given student is worthy of a great deal of investment, this investment itself may lead the student to do well, thereby "validating" the judgment; for example, deciding that somebody is hopelessly violent and then assigning that person to a crowded and harsh prison situation may in fact encourage violence, thereby "validating" the judgment that the violent criminal was "irredeemable."

Another problem that arises is that both predictions tend to be rather low. The fact that in general neither statistical nor clinical prediction is very good leads to what Dawes (1979, 1994a) has termed "arguing from a vacuum." While the statistical prediction may be superior to the clinical one, it is usually not very impressive—i.e. as good as desired or believed possible; therefore, some other type of prediction may do better than the statistical one; therefore—according to the unjustified inference—some other type *will* do better; most people believe that the statistical prediction cannot be improved (although it can be—often easily), but the clinical one *could* be. Simply postulating the potential superiority of some other clinical prediction, however, does not indicate that it is there. And in fact attempts to find such superior clinical prediction have failed, while at least some attempts to improve statistical prediction by using research results to devise new—better—models have succeeded (see Knaus, Wagner, & Lynn, 1991). One problem is that we may not understand exactly how difficult it is to predict important human outcomes because we confuse the ability to find statistical contingency on a retrospective basis with that of using such contingency in a predictive manner (Dawes, 1993). Another problem arises from our need for the world to be "just" (Lerner, 1987). An unpredictable world cannot be a just one; hence, a need for a just world implies a need for a predictable one. Finally, it should be pointed out that despite the literature about clinical versus statistical prediction, there is a great reluctance to use statistical prediction; in fact there is a great reluctance to consider an individual as a member of a group, even in a medical context where the individual has no characteristics different from those defining group membership (Redelmeier & Tversky, 1990).

It should, in ending this section, be pointed out that those few exceptions of the clinical versus statistical prediction are found in either business or medicine where the clinician has access to more information than is used in the model (but *not* when studying the predictions of psychologists, who are perhaps still suffering hangovers from naive acceptance of psychoanalytic theory).

Regarding all specific decisions as policy ones is one way to improve them—at least improve them *in general.* There are other methods as well. As suggested by Dawes (1988, chap. 8), analyzing a decision problem explicitly in terms of expected utility need not commit the decision maker in advance to whatever outcome is judged to have the highest expected utility but is unlikely to hurt, at least as an adjunct procedure for reaching the decision. The expected utility model avoids all the anomalies discussed earlier, and if the decision maker rejects the model, making the model explicit will at the very least make clear which anomalies are being embraced. Even though it may be again somewhat circular, Fischhoff (1977, p. 194) concludes (perhaps a bit "tongue-in-cheek") that "I believe that the benefits of cost-benefit analysis can substantially outweigh the cost." Other such beliefs are that we should follow a "divide and conquer strategy of multiattribute utility theory" when faced with a complex problem (again Fischhoff, 1977, p. 187) or that (Kahneman & Tversky, 1984, p. 344) "It is therefore good practice to test the robustness of preferences by deliberate attempts to frame a decision problem in more than one way. . . ." In addition, we may wish to practice some of the rather simple visual interpretations of probabilities and utilities that applied decision theorists use when they act as advisors to those making difficult decisions, for example, making certain axioms "transparent" by the use of balls or graphs (Keller, 1985).

G. Quo Vadis?

Observing all the systematic violations of rational decision making, some authors have asked (Hastie, 1991, p. 131): "will the field ever escape the oppressive yoke of normative 'rational' models?" One answer to this question is that (Hastie, 1991, p. 138): "The good news is, 'yes.' The expected utility model is too simple and it is an invalid description of decision processes in most situations." Yes, as shown in this chapter, it is "invalid" as a descriptor of how people often go about making decisions—when they do *not* use expected utility theory, when they do *not* think of individual decisions as instances of general principles, when they do *not* attempt to make principles transparent by

requiring themselves to do such things as consider multiple frames of the same problem.

But people do want to make good decisions, which is a constant across these situations. In contrast, the types of limitations that become apparent when we studied the anomalies in particular decisions tend to be "situated" (i.e., specific to the situation). Thus, even some rather "heroic" attempts to develop theories that are orthogonal to theories of rational choice are often quite limited. For example, Mellers and her colleagues (Mellers, Chang, Birnbaum, & Ordonez, 1992; Mellers, Ordonez, & Birnbaum, 1992) have developed a type of scaling procedure that leads not to a "simple scalability" value for each alternative, but rather to value which is then modified differently depending upon the decision making task involved. But even these modifications tend to be quite specific to the task, and it is not clear that if we face a new situation in which a preference may be expressed in a new way exactly how we should modify the scale values. Or, in another example, Simonson and Tversky (1992) have "developed in this article a context-dependent model that explains the observed findings in terms of two component processes: a contingent weighting model that represents the effect of background context, and a binary comparison model that describes the effect of the local context" (p. 1187). But: "Like other descriptive models of choice, the present account is at best approximate and incomplete. In particular, it does not address the various heuristics of choice and editing operations . . . that are commonly employed to simplify the representation and the evaluation of options. We made no attempt to capture these complexities; we sought a simple mathematical model that is consistent with trade off contrast and extremeness aversion. The present model, however, is considerably more complicated than the standard theory of value maximization." The particular model, thus, captures the reality of context effects, whose reality was never in doubt to most social psychologists, but does so in a rather complicated way that is once again "situated."

Alternatively, it is possible to view decision makers as attempting to behave rationally, but being limited in doing so. That raises a number of fascinating social-psychological questions. How, for example, can simple principles be made "transparent" when they tend to be ignored when people focus on particular decisions? Moreover, even after they are made transparent (recall the original work of Tversky and Shafir on the "sure thing principle"), exactly what are the cognitive processes involved in "understanding" such transparency? That is, while in a particular context we might be able to encourage its existence, the process itself remains somewhat mysterious. Exactly, for example, what is going on "in the heads" of the subjects who appreciate the "sure thing principle" (when asked what would happen in either eventuality) as opposed to what is going on for the subjects for whom the sure thing principle still remains opaque? An honest answer is that we do not know.

Another important problem that must be faced if we are to attempt to make decisions rationally is how to evaluate reaction to probable consequences. How, exactly, do we decide what their "utility" for us will be—that is, how we will value them? We have recent evidence (e.g., Kahneman, 1994) that we do not evaluate our reactions very well—and that there are systematic biases in "predicting future tastes," and biases of memory that lead even to violations of dominance in predicting these tastes—but as yet we have no *general* theory of how these predictions are made. (People recall an extreme pain of a particular duration followed by a slightly lesser pain as constituting overall a *less* painful experience than the same severe pain of the same duration followed by nothing.)

At an even more basic level, how do we evaluate potential alternatives? That is, how do we even decide which aspects of a problem are relevant or irrelevant, which consequences are important to evaluate, before we even begin to decide which alternatives to choose? Again, there is some intriguing early work on this question (Gettys, Plisky, Manning, & Casey, 1987; Keeney, von Winterfeldt, & Eppel, 1990; Keller & Ho, 1988), but again a clear general theory has yet to be developed. Beach's (1990) "image" analysis is important here; in fact, apparent conflicts between it and more "traditional" behavioral decision theory may stem in part from a difference in which aspect part of the overall decision making process is emphasized—constructing alternatives or choosing between them.

Finally, how do we even decide that there is a "decision to be made"? This decision about whether to reach a decision as opposed to responding "automatically" to a situation—in terms of what William James termed "habit"—may be in fact the single most important type of decision that we ever make.

Examples abound—from the seemingly trivial to the profound. Consider, for example, the question of how to travel somewhere. As Verplanken, Aarts, van Knippenberg, and van Knippenberg point out (1994, p. 286–287): "We rarely consider travel mode for a particular journey for the first time. First, in a more specific sense, we often make exactly the same journey under the same circumstances in the same way time and again. In any subsequent journey, we then need not deliberate on travel mode choice at all. . . . In other words, on such occasions, travel mode choice is a matter of habit, rather than reasoned action. Habits are relatively stable behavioral patterns, which have been reinforced in the past. Habits are executed without deliberate consideration, and result from automatic processes, as opposed to controlled processes like consciously made decisions (cf. Shiffrin & Schneider, 1977.)"

Or consider the "decision" to bomb for the eighty-seventh time a previously neutral village in South Vietnam be-cause it was in the control of the Viet Cong at night. Was it even considered to be a "decision"? (In contrast, "loss aversion"—in this case of "Vietnam" [which many of us never knew we possessed] appears to have been a considerable influence in the overall policy decision in the summer of 1965 to escalate our involvement; see Berman, 1982.)

II. PROBABILISTIC JUDGMENT

The topic of probabilistic inference *per se* could fill a major portion of a handbook of cognition, or—especially after the "cognitive revolution in psychology"—one of social psychology. Here, I will limit discussion to inference about probabilities, specifically inferences about the probability that a particular prediction or hypothesis is true given certain evidence. As pointed out in the Tversky and Kahneman quote in the section on Improving Decision Making, people often base their decisions in large part on such probability estimates. Thus, principles about how these judgments are made are critical to behavioral decision making.

Many authors make the distinction between risk, uncertainty, and ignorance. Virtually all agree that risk is an appropriate term for a decision made when probabilities are known or estimated; hence an appropriate term for a probability estimate is a "judgment of risk." Authors also agree to use the term ignorance (Hogarth & Kunreuther, 1995) when no probability estimates are involved, although many of us find it very difficult to conceive of a situation where people face choices that involve uncertain outcomes but know *absolutely nothing* about the probabilities. The term uncertainty has been used much more ambiguously; for example, I (Dawes, 1988) use it in a book title to refer to situations in which probabilities are estimated. The problem with the term risk is that it appears awkward when discussing such things as diagnoses, or likelihoods of certain outcomes. For example, "What is the risk that this person is an extrovert as opposed to an introvert?" Here, I will use the term uncertainty, with the proviso that what I am discussing is probability estimation, while some other authors may use the term uncertainty to be synonymous with what I have here termed ignorance.

The approach in discussing probabilistic inference will be exactly that used in discussing decision making. This chapter will concentrate on anomalies. There is one important difference, however. The first anomalies of decision making discussed were those involving violations of very broad principles of rationality (e.g., regularity), and then the discussion progressed to increasingly specific principles—ending with the principles of expected utility theory. In contrast, the anomalies of inference can be categorized and discussed in terms of violation of a particular rule of inference—Bayes Theorem. Here, I followed the lead of Fischhoff and Beyth-Marom (1983). The reason is that Bayes Theorem follows from the simplest possible rules (or "axioms") of probability theory. The theorem is not something that requires assumptions beyond these very simple rules (which in fact are sometimes cited as constituting the *definition* of probability); nor is it necessary to appeal to broad intuitions to justify these rules—as it was, for example, to justify principles of dominance or transitivity. A violation of Bayes Theorem involves a violation of the very notion of probability; hence inference that violates the theorem is incoherent, irrational.

Consider, for example, the relationship between a symptom *S* and a disease *D*. We are often interested in the probability of the disease given the symptom, while "criterion group validation" yields an estimate of the probability of the symptom given the disease. (In such validation, what we do is to form a group of people who are known to have the conditions and observe the probability of various symptoms or characteristics.) Bayes Theorem involving symptoms and disease can be expressed very simply as

$$P(D/S) = \frac{P(S/D)P(D)}{P(S)} \tag{1}$$

This equation has some rather profound implications for behavioral decision making. First, the probability of the disease given the symptom is equal to the probability of the symptom given the disease if and only if the probability of the symptom equals the probability of the disease. These simple probabilities are often termed "base rates." What has been discovered, however, in behavioral contexts involving the diagnosis of disease is that people tend to confuse these two conditional probabilities. (For a striking example, see Eddy, 1982.) For example, a claim that a test for HIV is "95 percent accurate" may be based on the observation that 95 percent of the people actually infected test positive (and 95 percent of those not infected test negative); the inference that therefore someone who tests positive has a 0.95 probability of being infected is compelling to many people, but it is just not true. The latter probability involves that of the *disease given the* ("symptom" of a) *positive test result,* while the 95 percent figure refers to the probability of that *symptom given the disease* (the "inverse" probability).

The use of Bayes Theorem to understand the relationship between symptoms and disease leads naturally to its use in this section—which concerns the general relationship between hypotheses and evidence. Let *e* refer to some bit of evidence about whether a hypothesis (*h*) is or is not true; for example, a symptom may be regarded as a bit of evidence, and having a particular disease a hypothesis; or a hypothesis may concern who was going to win the elections in the United States in the year 2000 and a particular bit of evidence may be the margin of victory or defeat of a potential candidate in a more local election. Bayes Theorem expressed in terms of evidence and hypotheses is presented as

$$P(h/e) = \frac{P(e/h)P(h)}{P(e)} \tag{2}$$

Now this form of Bayes Theorem, while true, often

leads to complications in trying to evaluate the probability of hypotheses given evidence. There is, however, a way of avoiding having to estimate the probability of the evidence. What we can do is to consider *odds* that the hypothesis is true. These odds are the probability the hypothesis is true given the evidence divided by the probability that this hypothesis is false given the evidence—that is, by the ratio $P(h/e)/P(-h/e)$. Once we know the odds, it is trivial to compute the probability. The advantage of considering odds is that the denominator in Bayes Theorem cancels out when we compute these odds. That is,

$$\frac{P(h/e)}{P(-h/e)} = \frac{P(e/h)\ P(h)}{P(e/-h)\ P(-h)} \tag{3}$$

Let us consider our example in light of this *odds version* of Bayes Theorem. Due to space limitations, we will consider only the possibility that the individual tests positive, again an individual whom we estimated prior to testing to have a probability of 0.10 of being infected. Then, $P(e/h) = 0.95$, $P(h) = 0.10$, $P(e/-h) = 0.05$, and $P(-h) = 0.90$. The result is that the ratio equals 2.11. Odds of 2.11 correspond to a probability of 0.68, because odds equal $p/(1 - p)$ (hence *p* is equal to the odds divided by 1 plus the odds).

Before specifying exactly how this form of Bayes Theorem is related to behavioral decision making, we must first expand our discussion to include multiple hypotheses and multiple bits of evidence. The multiple hypothesis situation is simplest; suppose, for example, we are comparing two hypotheses h_1 versus h_2. Then, the odds form of Bayes Theorem becomes:

$$\frac{P(h_1/e)}{P(h_2/e_1)} = \frac{P(e/h_1)\ P(h_1)}{P(e/h_2)\ P(h_2)} \tag{4}$$

In fact, equation (2) may be considered a special case of equation (4) in which the second hypothesis is simply the negation of the first.

Considering multiple bits of evidence is a bit more complicated, because it involves a principle that could be termed "chaining." This principle can be illustrated by two bits of evidence that will be labeled e_1 and e_2. Let us consider, moreover, how these two bits of evidence may be used to distinguish between two hypotheses h_1 and h_2. Thus,

$$\frac{P(h_1/e_1 \text{ and } e_2)}{P(h_2/e_1 \text{ and } e_2)} = \frac{P(e_1 \text{ and } e_2 \text{ and } h_1)}{P(e_1 \text{ and } e_2 \text{ and } h_2)} \tag{5}$$

The first characteristic of equation (5) to note is that the order of the two bits of evidence is *not important*. We can "chain" them by simply expanding our very first principle of probability expressed in equation (1). Just as $P(a \text{ and } b) = P(a/b)P(b)$, $P(a \text{ and } b \text{ and } c) = P(a/b \text{ and } c)P(b/c)P(c)$ where we can consider this chaining in any order. Thus, for example, $P(e_1 \text{ and } e_2 \text{ and } h_1) = P(e_2/e_1 \text{ and } h_1)P(e_1/h_1)P(h_1)$ and $P(e_1 \text{ and } e_2 \text{ and } h_2) = P(e_2/e_1 \text{ and } h_2)P(e_1/h_2)P(h_2)$— and again, since the order of e_1 and e_2 is not important, they can be interchanged in these chains. Thus,

$$\frac{P(h_1/e_1 \text{ and } e_2)}{P(h_2/e_1 \text{ and } e_2)} = \frac{P(e_2/e_1 \text{ and } h_1)P(e_1/h_1)P(h_1)}{P(e_2/e_1 \text{ and } h_2)P(e_1/h_2)P(h_2)}$$

or   (6)

$$\frac{P(h_1/e_1 \text{ and } e_2)}{P(h_2/e_1 \text{ and } e_2)} = \frac{P(e_1/e_2 \text{ and } h_1)P(e_2/h_1)P(h_1)}{P(e_1/e_2 \text{ and } h_2)P(e_2/h_2)P(h_2)}$$

Often, we are concerned with the special case of *independence* of the evidence. In the case of evidence, what we mean by *conditional independence* of e_1 and e_2 is that for the hypotheses we are interested in (which here will be symbolized simply as h):

$$P(e_2/e_1 \text{ and } h) = P(e_2/h) \qquad (7)$$

That is, *everything* remains conditional on h, but given that broad dependence, the probability of e_2 given e_1 is simply equal to the probability of e_2. Again, as noted, everything is symmetric once independence is satisfied. Thus, in the special case of independence, equation (6) becomes:

$$\frac{P(h_1/e_1 \text{ and } e_2)}{P(h_2/e_1 \text{ and } e_2)} = \frac{P(e_2/h_1)P(e_1/h_1)P(h_1)}{P(e_2/h_2)P(e_1/h_2)P(h_2)} \qquad (8)$$

We now have all the available tools for understanding anomalies of inferring hypotheses from evidence. Following Fischhoff and Beyth-Marom, the standard biases are very simply stated.

Pseudodiagnosticity refers to making an inference about the validity of a hypothesis h on the basis of evidence e without considering alternative hypotheses, in particular, without considering the hypothesis $-h$. Another way of stating pseudodiagnosticity is that it involves considering only the numerator in equation (5). People do that when they state that a bit of evidence is "consistent with" or "typical of" some hypothesis without concerning themselves about alternative hypotheses, or in particular the negation of the hypothesis. For example, after the William Kennedy Smith rape trial, a number of "experts" on a talk show expressed the opinion that they wished they could have testified in order to inform judge and jury of "what a rape victim was like." These experts who work in such places as women's shelters in fact had a great deal of experience with rape victims. What none had, however, was experience with women who claimed they were raped when they were not. But the whole point of the trial was to make a judgment about whether the person claiming was actually raped or not. Thus, all the experience in the world with actual rape victims can simply yield some estimate of the probability of particular types of evidence given that person was a rape victim. But using that probability alone yields a "pseudodiagnostic" inference, because no comparison is made.

Another type of anomaly is making inferences on the basis of *representativeness*. Such inferences involve considering the probability of the evidence given the hypothesis or hypotheses without looking at the second terms in equation (3), that is, the prior odds. The reason that these

odds are important is that—as indicated by equation (4)—they yield the *extent* of the evidence and hypotheses considered. For example, being a poor speller may be evidence of dyslexia in the sense that it has a very high probability given dyslexia. However, in order to diagnose dyslexia on the basis of poor spelling we have to know something about the base rates of poor spelling and the base rates of dyslexia in the population from which the person whom we wish to diagnose was chosen. Sometimes representativeness involves pseudodiagnosticity, when only the numerator of the likelihood ratios is considered. But often the entire likelihood ratio may be considered (e.g., the probability of being a poor speller given one is dyslexic may be compared to that probability given one is not dyslexic), but still the neglect of the prior odds yields to neglecting the extent of the hypotheses [and hence of the hypotheses *and the evidence*—which is really the critical event, as illustrated in equation (6)].

Dilution effects occur when evidence that does not distinguish between hypotheses in fact influences people to change their mind. The point is similar to that found in pseudodiagnosticity in that people do not realize that evidence that is not very likely given the hypothesis may be equally unlikely given alternative hypotheses, or, again, the negation of that hypothesis, but may in fact believe a hypothesis less as a result of collecting evidence that is unlikely if it is true. Dilution is simply the converse of pseudodiagnosticity.

Finally, it is possible to categorize *availability* biases in terms of lack of independence, often lack of conditional independence. People believe that they are sampling evidence given the hypothesis, when in fact they are sampling this evidence given the hypothesis *combined with* the manner in which they are sampling. For example, when clinical psychologists claim that they are sampling characteristics of people who fall in a certain diagnostic category on the basis of their experience, what they are really sampling is people who fall in that category *and who come to them*. For example, when we sample our beliefs about "what drug addicts are like," most of us are sampling on the basis of how the media presents drug addicts—both in "news" programs and in dramatizations (Dawes 1994b). Or, in contrast, doctors often sample on the basis of their contact with addicts when these addicts are ill, perhaps gravely so, while police are often sampling on the basis of their experience with these same addicts during arrests and other types of confrontations. Is it surprising, then, that doctors are in favor of a "medical" approach to drug addiction including such policies as sterile needle exchanges, while police are in favor of much more punitive policies? Both are sampling evidence given addiction *and* their exposure to it. The result is that the very first bit of evidence may not be really evidence given the hypothesis but evidence given a hypothesis *and* a biased sampling procedure—while the chain of evidence in the multiple evidence context may be anything but conditionally independent. The anomaly occurs when people treat conditionally dependent evidence as if it were independent or unbiased; it is often very difficult to understand the biases in our own experience, even those we create by our own behavior (e.g., acting nasty with people whom we expect to be nasty—and then discovering they are nasty).

All these anomalies have been demonstrated experimentally, and they will be discussed in turn in brief sections here. Again, however, it is important to point out that the investigation of these anomalies did not spring simply from understanding Bayes Theorem and then from creating very clever experimental situations in which people systematically violate it when making inferences. Again, the motive to study these anomalies of judgment arises from having observed them on a more informal basis outside the experimental setting—and trying to construct an experimental setting, which yields a greater measure of control, that will allow them to be investigated in a coherent manner. The readers is referred, for example, to the essay of Meehl (1977a) or the book of Dawes (1994a) for descriptions of these biases in the clinical judgment of professional psychologists and psychiatrists who rely on their own "experience" rather than (dry, impersonal) "scientific" principles for diagnosis and treatment.

A. Pseudodiagnosticity

The main problem here is that hypotheses are not compared; instead, single hypotheses are evaluated in terms of the degree to which evidence is "consistent with" them; in addition, evidence is often *sought* in terms of its consistency with or inconsistency with "favorite hypotheses"—rather than in terms of its ability to distinguish *between* hypotheses. This type of pseudodiagnosticity has even made its way into the legal system, where experts are allowed to testify that a child's recanting of a report of sexual abuse is "consistent with" the "child sexual abuse accommodation syndrome" (Summit, 1983). The finding is that many children who are *known* to have been sexually abused deny the abuse later (recant); therefore, the probability of the evidence (the child recants) given the hypothesis (actual abuse) is not as low as might be naively assumed; therefore, recanting is "consistent with" having been abused (i.e., can be considered part of a "syndrome" of accommodation to abuse).

The problem with this pseudodiagnostic reasoning is that it compares the probability of the evidence given the hypothesis to the probability of the *negation of the evidence* given the hypothesis, whereas a rational comparison is of the probability of the evidence given the hypothesis to the probability of the evidence given the *negation of the hypothesis*. When considering this latter comparison, we understand immediately that the recanting would be diagnostic of actual abuse only if the probability of recanting

given actual abuse were higher than the probability of recanting given such abuse had not occurred—a highly implausible (not to mention paradoxical) conclusion.

Such pseudodiagnostic reasoning is involved in other disasters as well, for example, the Challenger explosion. When considering the possibility that cold temperatures might cause the O-rings to malfunction, "the worried engineers were asked to graph the temperatures at launch time for the flights in which problems have occurred" (Russo & Schoemaker, 1989, p. 197). Thus, these engineers attempted to evaluate the hypothesis that there would be O-ring problems by asking what the probability of the temperature was given the existence of these problems. As indicated in the top half of Figure 5 (figure 6 in Russo & Schoemaker, p. 198), there appeared to be no relationship. When, however, the temperature of launches in which there were *no* problems were considered, a very clear relationship between problems and temperature is evident (see the bottom part of Figure 5, from Russo and Schoemaker, Figure 7, p. 198.)

Moreover, people actively seek evidence compatible or incompatible with a hypothesis rather than evidence which distinguishes between hypotheses, as has been extensively studied by Doherty and his colleagues (see for example Doherty, Mynatt, Tweney, & Schiavo, 1979). Consider, for example, subjects who are asked to play the role of medical student (and actual medical students prior to specific training, see Wolf, Gruppen, & Billi, 1985) to determine whether patients have one of two conditions. The conditions are explained, and subjects are told that a patient has two symptoms (i.e., bits of evidence for having either). The judges are then presented with the conditional probability of one of these symptoms given one of the diseases (e.g., that it is very likely that the patient has a high fever given the patient has meningitis). They can then choose to find out the probability of the other symptom given the same disease, the probability of the first symptom given the second disease, or the probability of the second symptom given the second disease. While virtually no subjects choose a different symptom and a different disease, the majority choose to find the probability of the *second* symptom given the first disease (the "one that is focal" as a result of being told the first symptom). But for all these subjects know, of course, the first symptom may be more or less typical of the *alternative disease,* as may the second symptom. Finding out that the probability of these two symptoms given only one disease in no way helps to distinguish between that disease and some other. (Of course, in real medical settings doctors may have prior knowledge of these other disease/symptom relationships, but because the diseases are not even identified in the current setting, such knowledge would be of no help.)

Occasionally, pseudodiagnosticity has been confused with what has been termed a "confirmation bias"—that is, a desire to search for evidence that is very probable given a

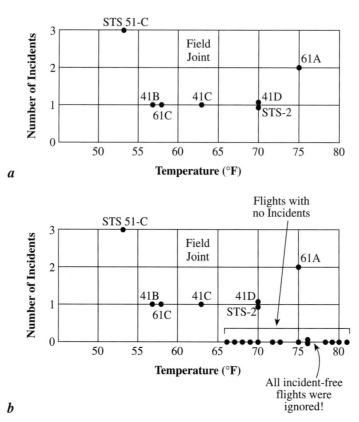

FIGURE 5   Partial and Total Analyses of the Relationship between (*a*) Data reviewed prior to launch. (*b*) The full story from past flights. (*Source:* Russo & Schoemaker, 1989, pp. 197–198.)

focal hypothesis. As both Fischhoff and Beyth-Marom (1983), Trope and Bassok (1982), and Skov and Sherman (1986) point out, however, such a search does not necessarily imply pseudodiagnosticity (or any other particular irrationality), because it may be possible that the evidence is *not* found—that is, that instead of finding the anticipated evidence, the diagnostician finds its negation. In fact, Skov and Sherman (1986) demonstrate that in searching for evidence—at least in their experimental context—subjects often became quite rational *when they are informed of the conditional probabilities.* The irrationality occurs in the search for which probabilities to seek, and in the "jumping" to a conclusion on the basis of only one probability (i.e., on the basis of the first term in the numerator in the odds form of Bayes Theorem).

The cognitive explanation is simple. People often think by association; in fact, whole computer programs have been built to simulate human judgment on the basis of "matching" characteristics for schemas. The point of pseudodiagnosticity is that only one "schema" (i.e., hypothe-

sis) is considered, whereas *coherent diagnostic judgment is always comparative.*

B. Judgment Based on the Representativeness Heuristic

As in the last section, let us begin with an example from outside the laboratory; this example is of a decision making process of a college admissions committee:

The next morning, the admissions committee scans applications from a small rural high school in the Southwest. It is searching for prized specimens known as neat small-town kids. Amy is near the top of her class, with mid-500 verbals, high-600 math and science. She is also poor, white, and geo—she would add to the geographic and economic diversity that saves Brown from becoming a postgraduate New England prep school. While just over 20% of the New York State applicants will get in, almost 40% will be admitted from Region

7—Oklahoma, Texas, Arkansas, and Louisiana. Amy's high school loves her, and she wants to study engineering. Brown needs engineering students: unfortunately, Amy spells engineering wrong. 'Dyslexia,' says Jimmy Wrenn, a linguistics professor. After some debate, the committee puts her on the waiting list (*Time,* April 9, 1979, p. 73).

The inference of "dyslexia" is not supported rationally. First, misspelling a single word does not imply that the individual misspelling it is poor at spelling overall; second, being poor at spelling overall does not imply dyslexia. Yes, the inferences in the opposite direction *are valid in terms of likelihood,* but not in terms of Bayes Theorem, which includes an additional term for "prior odds," or probability. That is, the evidence that somebody misspells a single word is more likely given the person's a poor speller than given the person is not (*h* versus *–h*), and the inference that someone who is dyslexic is more likely to be a poor speller than someone who is not is valid as well. But those two inferences yield likelihoods. What we are interested in, however—when considering the odds form of Bayes Theorem—are posterior odds, not likelihoods. Posterior odds are equal to the likelihood ratio multiplied by the prior odds, not just the likelihood ratio itself. The problem is that this likelihood ratio in and of itself represents the *degree of association* between the evidence and the hypotheses involved. When the prior odds are included as well, however, they incorporate the *extent* of the evidence and of the hypotheses under consideration, a critical extent. For example, the problem with the inference from poor spelling to dyslexia is that there are many more people who are poor spellers who *aren't* dyslexic than who are, that is, the extent of the class "poor speller" is much greater than the extent of the class "dyslexic"—even though poor spelling may be "diagnostic of" dyslexia by virtue of the relation that the class of dyslexics is almost entirely included in the class of poor spellers.

The heuristic was originally defined by Kahneman and Tversky (1972, p. 431): "A person who follows this heuristic evaluates the probability of an uncertain event, or a sample, by the degree to which it is (i) similar in essential properties to its parent population and (ii) reflects the salient features of the process by which it is generated." Clearly, the heuristic is broader than this definition; it refers to matching a characteristic to a category, or one category to another, and then evaluating probability in terms of the degree of match.

A pseudodiagnostic judgment is one based on representativeness, but not necessarily *vice versa.* Consider the misspelling example. Misspelling the single word engineering is *not* highly likely given the hypothesis that someone is a poor speller or dyslexic; in fact, misspelling a particular word is not at all likely; it is, however, much more likely given the hypothesis that someone is a poor speller or dyslexic than given the hypothesis that someone is not a poor speller. Thus, using the Fischhhoff and Beyth-Marom structure, the denominator as well as the numerator of the odds form of Bayes Theorem is considered; it's just the prior odds that are neglected. Of course, other matching judgments may be made without reference to hypotheses other than that being considered, in particular its negation.

As indicated by the example at the beginning of this section, making inferences according to the representativeness heuristic is found outside the laboratory. In fact, much of the interest in thinking according to representativeness heuristic was spurred by a "classic" paper of Meehl and Rosen from forty years ago (1955) documenting the degree to which psychiatric diagnoses made in staff meetings ignored prior odds; for example, someone could be diagnosed as schizophrenic on the basis of a "typical" schizophrenic response without any concern about prior probability that the person being diagnosed was schizophrenic. (Compare that diagnosis to the diagnosis of "dyslexia" based on misspelling a single word.)

In order to study the phenomena within the laboratory, investigators have developed certain "standard problems." The first is the "cab problem" of Kahneman and Tversky (1972). Bar-Hillel (1980, pp. 211–212) states it as follows:

Problem 1: Two cab companies operate in a given city, the Blue and the Green (according to the color of cab they run). Eighty-five percent of the cabs in the city are Blue and the remaining 15% are Green. A cab was involved in a hit-and-run accident at night. A witness later identified the cab as a Green cab. The court tested the witness' ability to distinguish between Blue and Green cabs under nighttime visibility conditions. It found that the witness was able to identify each color correctly about 80% of the time, but confused it with the other color about 20% of the time. What do you think are the chances that the errant cab was indeed Green, as the witness claimed?

Generally, people claim that the probability is 0.80, when it is in fact 0.41. (The likelihood ratio is 0.80/0.20, but the prior odds are 0.15/0.85.) One could object that somehow the witness might be taking account of the prior odds so that the "accuracy" figure incorporates them—even though this figure was specifically stated to be conditioned on the actual color of the cab, but that explanation for this particular example does not explain all the other examples that yield the same result (Bar-Hillel, 1980; Bar-Hillel, 1990; Doherty et al., 1979). Nor does it explain the observations of Meehl and Rosen or the type of reasoning of the admissions committee at Brown. What is of more interest are variables that affect whether or not base rates are incorporated into judgment.

One of particular importance to social psychologists involves whether the base rate is a "personal" one as opposed to one involving "dry statistics." This difference can, however, either enhance or diminish accuracy. For example, in a doctoral dissertation, Roy (1991) presented a problem identical to the cab one involving light bulbs either marked defective or not marked as defective. Eighty percent of those actually defective are marked as defective, while 20 percent of those not defective are marked as defective by mistake. Subjects are told that 15 percent of the light bulbs are defective and are asked to judge the probability that one marked defective is actually defective. Subjects tend to make the same type of judgment they do in the cab problem, which has an identical structure. (Note that here there can be no "excuse" involving the incorporation of the base rates in the statement of the probability of the evidence given the hypothesis.) But when the identical problem is presented in terms of red and blue balls that either have a star stuck on them or not, subjects are quite accurate.

In contrast, Wells (1992) finds that "naked statistical evidence of liability" is not incorporated in judgments of liability—while human judgment having parallel probabilities of classification are. For example, consider the distinction between a judgment that the probability a cab is blue is 0.90 (after incorporating relevant base rates) based on the testimony of a witness—as opposed to a "naked" base rate 0.90 because 90 percent of cabs in the area are blue. The former type of evidence yields a judgment that the blue cab company is liable. The latter does not. Here, it is the "personalized" evidence that leads to a judgment consistent with probability theory, while the impersonal one does not—quite the opposite of Roy's result. Wells speculates that people are willing to use the fallible human judgment on the grounds that it might "even out" over the long run—so that the mistaken liability judgments are equally likely to be biased toward or against the blue cab company—while the "naked base rate" judgment will always be against the blue cab company, and hence when in error will always hurt it.

What is not ambiguous is the role of an implicit "causal" model in getting people to attend to base rates (Ajzen, 1977). When the statement that 85 percent of the accidents are *due to* the blue cab company is substituted for the statement that 85 percent of the cabs are blue, then people attend to that base rate. In fact, one way of conceptualizing the problem—as proposed by Bar-Hillel (1990)—is whether people incorporate base rates into their prior probabilities (or odds), rather than whether people attend to or ignore these prior probabilities (odds). The problem with this conceptualization, however, is that we can only judge such incorporation (i.e., whether the base rates are considered "relevant") on the basis of the judgment itself.

Another possibility is that unless base rates achieve some special salience they tend not to be incorporated— just as other information tends not to be incorporated in probability judgments. This type of "conservatism" has been proposed and demonstrated by Melone et al. (1992); it is consistent with earlier results of Edwards (1968) that in a standard problem involving drawing poker chips from a book bag—ones quite similar to that discussed earlier— people do not change their judgments about the proportions of colored chips in the book bag as radically as they should according to Bayes Theorem.

Another possibility discussed by Bar-Hillel (1990) is that people incorporate base rates when they think of them as applicable to each member of a set "to some degree," but not when they think of them as specifying a particular subset of the set under consideration. This distinction is reminiscent of that of Wells. A cab is or is not blue, so the proportion of blue cabs may not be important, but witnesses are accurate to some degree, a degree which might be used to characterize all their judgments (while the proportion of blue cabs certainly does not characterize all cabs).

Finally, people have proposed that base rate neglect is found when the probability judgments involving different base rates are made by different people, but not when the same person makes different judgments when supplied with different base rates. This argument (Birnbaum & Mellers, 1983; Mellers, 1990) is followed by an assertion that we should attend only to the results within subjects, because after all judgment itself occurs only within subjects. The problem with this argument is that when the subjects in experiments are supplied with different base rates, they might well believe that they *should* attend to them—to avoid appearing stupid, to please the experimenter, and so on. In fact, Fischhoff and Bar-Hillel (1984) have demonstrated that subjects' judgments will vary as a function of being supplied with *irrelevant* base rates (e.g., being informed of a base rate of blue cabs in the entire city after being informed of the base rate of blue cabs in the area that the accident occurred). Dawes, Mirels, Gold, and Donahue (1993) have demonstrated that base rate neglect can be found within subjects quite as strongly as between subjects when the subjects themselves supply their own base rates, thus not responding to any "experimental demands" to incorporate them. In fact, in the original observations of Meehl and Rosen (1955), it was their own base rates of various psychiatric conditions that the clinical psychologists and psychiatrists ignored in making diagnoses.

Other types of incoherence that involve judgment according to the representativeness heuristic are: (1) judging probability according to similarity and consequently ignoring regression effects (Kahneman & Tversky, 1972), (2) expecting too much alternation in chance events (Gilovich, Vallone, & Tversky, 1985; Pickett, 1962), (3) ignoring sample size (Tversky & Kahneman, 1974), (4) confusing the probability of a positive test result given a medical condition with the probability of a medical condition given the positive test result (in mammography results; Eddy, 1982), and (5) confusing the probability of a past antecedent given a present consequence with the probability of the present consequence given the past antecedent (Dawes, 1993).

C. Dilution Effects

An examination of the odds form of Bayes Theorem indicates that evidence that does not favor any particular hypothesis under consideration should not have any effect on opinion. That is, when considering h_1 versus h_2 or h_1 versus $-h_1$, any evidence e that is equally probable given either alternative is irrelevant for distinguishing between them and hence should be ignored. Only it is not. What happens is that such "nondiagnostic" evidence tends to reduce confidence in *all* hypotheses, hence inappropriately biasing the odds form of Bayes Theorem toward one. Consider, for example, drawing the red versus blue chips from the book bag that has either 75 percent red chips in it or 75 percent blue chips in it. Given random draws and independence between draws (i.e., "drawing with replacement"), the odds form of Bayes Theorem implies that it is *the difference* between the number of red chips drawn versus the number of blue chips drawn that should determine our judgment about which bag we are drawing from. Nevertheless, people are more confident they are drawing from the 75 percent red bag when four red chips are drawn than when twelve red chips and eight blue chips are drawn. In a situation of twelve red and eight blue, we have eight *pairs* consisting of one red and one blue chip where each such pair is uninformative. What happens is that the existence of these pairs "dilutes" the judgment.

This dilution effect has been studied by Nisbett, Zukier, and Lemley (1981), who contrast judgment to that based on the type of "cognitive algebra" developed by Anderson (1968). These investigators find strong evidence for a dilution effect. When, for example, people are asked to make judgments about whether somebody else has a particular characteristic (e.g., aggressiveness) or problem, their judgments are more extreme when they are presented with information particularly relevant to that characteristic than when they are presented with the very same information plus a lot of information that implies neither that characteristic nor its negation. The point is that rationally this nondiagnostic information should be ignored, because it is equally likely if the characteristic is present or absent. Such information is not, however, ignored—any more than the pairs of red and blue chips are ignored in drawing from the urn with unknown proportions. Tetlock and Boettger (1989) find that the dilution effect is enhanced when judges are made "accountable" to others for their inferences. In fact, these authors find that accountability improves judgments only in the absence of dilution, or in the

presence of contradiction (in which case judgment *should* be moderated).

The dilution effect, while quite consistent with the original evidence for "conservatism" found by Edwards (1968), has not been studied as extensively as have other biases of judgment. It may, however, be very important in social context—particularly in context where people wish to manipulate others' judgment. Someone who has a strong opinion based on very clear evidence may be influenced to "moderate" this opinion by exposure to a flurry of uninformative information (which I am hesitant to call "evidence"). A barrage of nondiagnostic information may be even more effective (e.g., thirty-seven e-mail messages a day concerning a topic about which the recipient originally had an opinion). It is important to note that such information need be neither false nor misleading, and in fact may be very probable or improbable given a particular hypothesis, but just not relevant for *distinguishing between* hypotheses.

D. Availability Biases

Naturally, we make judgments on the basis of the information available to us. For example, if we wish to make some estimate of the number of psychologists in academic departments who are labeled "full" professors we may look for certain statistical sources, we may "scan" our memories, or we may even walk through hallways and code each person we meet or occupant of each office we walk by as either a full professor or not. These methods may yield different estimates. When we reach a probabilistic conclusion, we must sample in some way. This necessity is neither controversial nor in itself a reason for "bias." What happens, however, is that we often make a judgment about the thing we are sampling without realizing that our particular method of sampling has in and of itself a profound effect—or a profound effect when combined with the target of our sampling. When the sampling procedure yields a systematic bias of which we are unaware, we refer to the resulting conclusion as due to an *availability bias*. For example, when sampling from memory, we tend to sample instances which are particularly vivid, or experiences in which we have taken an active role, and so on. In many contexts, these tendencies provide systematic bias.

Consider, for example, the relationship between ideological commitment and self-interest. Most of us observe that these tend to be compatible. It turns out, however, that the compatibility is illusory, because we tend to observe mainly people who *act* on the basis of their ideological commitments, and it is true that among people who believe in certain policies or ideologies, those who have a self-interest *as well* tend to be those who are most active. Self-interest energizes (Green & Cowden, 1992). When, however, we have simply surveyed people to determine what they believe, their ideological commitments tend to be unrelated to their own interests (Green, 1992) (A lack of correlation, of course, implies that there are discrepancies; some people ascribe such discrepancies to "false consciousness" when they find an ideology opposed to self-interest; others ascribe such a discrepancy to the failure of the "selfish, rational person" model to characterize human beings; see Green & Shapiro, 1994.)

Let me illustrate an availability bias involving an active role we ourselves play from my own experience as president of the Oregon Psychological Association during the year in which licensing of professional psychologists was "sunsetted"; it was then necessary to recommend licensing laws to the state legislature—as if psychologists were being licensed for the first time. We had to decide on a recommendation for reporting suspected child abuse. The laws then current stated that confidentiality between client and therapist should be broken if the therapist suspected that a child was being abused and that continued abuse was possible. Thus, professional psychologists were not required or encouraged to make a judgment about whether or not someone would continue, but at the same time they were not to break confidentiality if there were no possibility of continuation. For example, they might learn of abuse that had occurred years earlier and there was no longer any contact between the client and the child, or the child might have been physically removed to a situation where contact with the abusive client was no longer possible. During many of the 1984 board meetings of the Oregon Psychological Association over which I presided, members would propose that the child abuse reporting laws be changed so that *all* suspected child abuse be reported—whether or not there was a current child in danger—because "one thing we know about child abusers is that they never stop on their own without therapy." This assertion of knowledge generally led to assent around the table. When I asked how "we" "knew" that, the response was that several clinicians present had had extensive contact with child abusers. How did that contact come about? The abusers were mandated by the court to be in treatment with the professionals who knew what they were like. I then pointed out that the reason these particular abusers came to the attention of the professionals was that they had *not* stopped on their own; moreover, it was logically impossible for the professionals to observe that these people could stop without psychotherapy, because in fact they saw these people only in psychotherapy. The general reaction to my comments was that I "had a point," but then the very next meeting the same argument about knowing that "they never stop on their own" was raised again—although sometimes with the proviso that I had expressed some hesitation about this generalization, together with a request that I please repeat the reason for this hesitation. The availability bias of my colleagues arose as a result of their own social role; it is similar to the availability bias about the nature of drug addicts

of a physician, who sees these people primarily when they are quite ill, versus the bias of a policeman or policewoman, who sees these addicts in contexts of arrests and violence.

Other availability biases are brought about not just by our role but by our own behavior; for example, a waiter who believes that well-dressed people give better tips than others may give better service to well-dressed people and believe his judgment to be "validated" when receiving better tips from them (Einhorn & Hogarth, 1978). Another example is a professor or executive who believes that a particular applicant shows great "promise" and may put a great deal of effort into training that applicant, and again feel that the judgment of potential is validated when the applicant does well.

Other availability biases have absolutely nothing to do with the individual's own behavior but result from selective exposure to information and from common biases of memory. For example, Christensen-Szalanski, Beck, Christensen-Szalanski, and Koepsell (1983) asked physicians and students to estimate the number of deaths per hundred thousand people that were due to each of forty-two diseases. "Both physicians and students were asked to indicate the number of people they had seen suffering from each disease during the past 12 months" (p. 279)—which is *not* the number of people that they know who had *died* of the disease in that period. The availability measure for the physicians was the "number of column inches given by the NEJM [New England Journal of Medicine] to each disease for the six month period preceding the test date (October 1, 1980–March 31, 1981)" (p. 279).

The rankings were fairly accurate, but the overestimation was wild—for both physicians and students—and it was strongly related to both sources of availability (personal notice for both students and physicians, number of lines for physicians). The finding is quite consistent with that of Fischhoff, Lichtenstein, Slovic, Derby, and Keeney (1981), who obtained estimates for all causes of death (not just diseases), and with that of Combs and Slovic (1979), who related these latter estimates to number of inches of newspaper coverage from two different towns. The last study was somewhat remarkable in that the subjects' *average* estimates across forty-one causes of death could be predicted with a multiple R of 0.94 from a linear combination (with close to equally weighted standard scores) of actual frequency and newspaper coverage, a major reason for the high prediction being that these two sources of influence were virtually uncorrelated ($r = .13$). All these studies show that particularly "dramatic" causes of death tend to be overestimated (e.g., leukemia, murder) while more mundane causes (e.g., diabetes, skin cancer) tend if anything to be underestimated (the latter by physicians, but not by students—who overestimate everything by several orders of magnitude). Even tornadoes, being more dramatic than floods, are estimated as being more lethal, when floods cause twice as many deaths per year.

The examples concerning death involve newspaper articles and other sources in the media that report "news." Naturally, such sources are biased to report interesting, exciting, and vivid events rather than mundane events, and there are other more subtle biases as well. For example, the local Pittsburgh television stations and papers report the murder of *anyone* in the area, while they report the suicide only of famous people. There is, moreover, another source of bias in the media that may be an important source of biased availability, but which has not been—to my knowledge—studied quite as extensively. That is fiction. Consider, for example, the views of people who do not interact with drug addicts about what drug addicts are like. (For a fuller discussion, see Dawes, 1994b.) Many of us have seen portrayals of people addicted to drugs in movies, television specials, or even standard television shows (as we have seen portrayals of people addicted to alcohol—while interestingly an addiction to tobacco does not form the basis of a dramatic presentation). These portrayals involve drama, and the basis of drama is personality and personality change—even though it may be brought about in response to external circumstances; thus, for example, Hamlet is viewed as a play about suffering excessively from doubt and indecision, rather than as a play about somebody presented "out-of-the-blue" with the absolutely impossible choice of trying to decide whether an apparition he sees is really his dead father's soul or the devil trying to condemn his immortal soul to hell for regicide. (For an alternative view, see Orbell, 1993.) We have a natural availability bias to ascribe the actions of others to their (personal) characteristics, because they are the focus of our attention when we observe them. This "fundamental attribution error" (Jones & Nisbett, 1972; Nisbett & Ross, 1980) is exaggerated by any fictional account that focuses on personality and personality change, in particular "internal struggle." Thus, it follows that people believe in dramatic change, often accompanied by such things as religious conversion, an entirely new outlook on life, or some special help from a special sort of other person (psychotherapist, priest, cop capable of tough love). Gradual change tends to be derogated because it is not dramatic (literally), although gradual change may be one of the most important types of change in human life—and in society (for example, the "coup d' état" by installments that the Nazis initiated after Hitler was appointed chancellor, as described in Allen, 1984).

Another area of availability bias important for social psychologists is the one involving personal vulnerability. People are believed to "suffer" from "illusions of invulnerability," because when we (adults as well as adolescents) are asked to compare our own risk of certain negative outcomes with that of other people, we believe ourselves to be less vulnerable (Weinstein, 1980). But this relative invulnerability could be due either to an underestimation of how vulnerable we are, an exaggeration of how vulnerable others are, or a combination of these two biases. Work by Whitley and Hearn (1991) indicates that at least in the area of vulnerability to unwanted pregnancy, this relative invulnerability is due to an exaggeration of others' vulnerability, rather than to an underestimation of our own vulnerability. As nearly as it was possible to determine, college women rated their own vulnerability to unwanted pregnancy quite accurately—when taking account of their own sexual behavior and the precautions they took to avoid pregnancy. But they grossly exaggerated the vulnerability of their classmates and exaggerated the vulnerability of women in general even more. The availability bias explanation is that they know about the precautions they themselves take but have no access to the precautions others take. And in addition, like tornadoes, unwanted pregnancies are quite vivid and for many people frightening.

Finally, people can be unaware of availability biases that result from social roles. For example, professors who question students get to make up the questions, and it is only natural that they can appear more knowledgeable than the students who cannot always answer these questions (unless the professors have been completely brainwashed by Skinnerian philosophy or are looking for an excuse to curry favor by giving all A's). Interestingly, professors in contrast to students have access to the processes by which questions are developed and may not be as subject to this availability bias as are the students—but other professors who observe what is going on (e.g., in oral examinations) may be. That general result was found by Ross, Amabile, and Steinmetz (1977) who randomly assigned roles of contestants and questioners to people where the questioners were asked to make up "trivia" questions that were "difficult but not impossible to answer." Both the contestants (who generally were unable to answer over half of the questions correctly) and the observers thought that the questioners were more knowledgeable than the contestants, but the questioners themselves were not as subject to this illusion. In a nonexperimental context, Ross and Sicoly (1979) and Thompson and Kelley (1981) have discovered that people in close relationships tend to exaggerate their "contribution" to the relationship—or at least that when two such people are asked to estimate the "proportion" they contribute, these two proportions sum to greater than 1.00. People are more knowledgeable of what they do, of the sacrifices they make, and of the effort that they might put forth "silently" (e.g., trying to figure out how to pay the bills when listening to music on the radio) than they are of the other's contribution. What is interesting in these studies is that these estimates of proportion contribution are *not* based on specific recall, but on general impressions. ("It is clear that contrary to our expectations, specific instances are only rarely cited as forming the basis of the responsibility judgment" [Thompson & Kelley, 1981, p. 475.]) This finding is consistent with that of Shedler and Manis (1986) that the effect of vividness on judgment (which presumably results from the availability bias to memory that vividness provides) was *not* mediated by memory of specific information. Availability due to biased memory—as in the social relationship examples—often results from the *judgment of* the "ease of recall," rather than from recall of specific material itself. The Shedler and Manis result is consistent with that of Hastie and Park (1986) indicating that judgment made "on-line" reflects input without being based on memory.

It should be pointed out that people are not always unaware of their availability biases. For example, our actions are often based on a number of situational factors, and hence we tend to ascribe our actions to these more than an observer does—given that the observer is not as aware of them as we are. (While it may be extraordinarily difficult to "see ourselves as others see us," it is even more difficult to see the environment as someone else does.) But, as Krueger, Ham, and Linford (1996) discovered, we could also understand that observers will not be aware of these situational (environmental) factors, and hence we can correctly infer that observers will give much more weight to our personality than to these factors in explaining our behavior; in other words, we are aware of the observers' availability bias, because we can construct it by "subtracting out" information that is available to us. In contrast, we are not aware of our own availability bias *as observers,* because as observers we do not have access to this information.

Finally, it should be pointed out that even important social policy can be based on availability biases of the simplest type (i.e., those that are "obvious" when pointed out, but highly effective until pointed out). For example, as this chapter is being written, the United States Congress is considering severe limits on malpractice suits—presumably because so many are exaggerated or totally without foundation, and consequently clog our court system unnecessarily, resulting in income for lawyers for "nonproductive" activity. Do most malpractice lawsuits lack a firm foundation? Saks (1993) reports an extensive study of approximately 31,000 patients treated in fifty-one New York hospitals during 1984 and concludes that the answer is yes. These patients were studied by independent panels of physicians who made a judgment about whether there was any "negligent adverse event" involved in their treatment. Of forty-seven claims filed, only eight (17 percent) were judged to involve such negligence. But when there was such negligence, how many claims were filed? In the opinion of the impartial experts, there were *280* "negligent adverse events," and—again—only eight (2.8 percent) filings. It turned out, then, that the *major* finding of the study that Saks reviewed was that such a tiny proportion of neg-

ligence actually led to lawsuits, while it was nevertheless true that most (83 percent) of the lawsuits were without basis. (I am happy to report that there were 28,802 instances in which no negligent adverse event was found and no claim was filed. Readers can fill in the 2×2 table for themselves from the information I have given here; they might also be interested in computing the phi coefficient between negligence and filing a claim, which is an unimpressive 0.07.)

Finally, availability to the imagination is important. Sometimes the imagination is based on pure memory, as when people are asked to judge whether the letter *r* is found more often in the first or third position of words three letters or longer (Tversky & Kahneman, 1973). At other times the bias involves imagination independent of memory, as when people are asked to judge how many subcommittees of two people can be formed out of a committee of eight people as opposed to subcommittees of six people. The answer, of course, is that an equal number of such committees can be formed—because each time a unique subcommittee of two is formed a unique subcommittee of six remains. Most subjects, however, believe that more subcommittees of two can be formed, because it is easier to imagine generating such subcommittees, availability's again being a matter of judgment of ease rather than actual generation. People also judge that there are more words beginning with *r* than having *r* in the third position, because it is easier to generate words knowing their first letter than their third. (In fact, *r* appears more often in the third position.) Another example involves asking people whether they believe there will be more six letter words in a particular text ending in *-ing* or six letter words having the letter *n* in the fifth position. The answer is the latter, because every six letter word ending in *-ing* has *n* in the fifth position, but not necessarily *vice versa*. But it is easier to generate the former.

This last example is of a conjunction (often termed *extension*) fallacy, which basically results from availability to the imagination, often combined with an influence of representativeness. This fallacy is the belief that a conjunction of two events (*A* and *B*) can be more probable than one of them alone. As pointed out by the very first equation in this section, that is impossible. The probability of *A* and *B* is equal to the probability of *B* times the probability of *A* given *B*; hence, the probability of *A* and *B* can be at most equal to the probability of *B*, but it is strictly less than that if the probability of *A* given *B* is less than 1.00. The reader wishing to verify this principle intuitively might also draw a Venn diagram.

This fallacy is particularly prone to occur when a subject is given information that makes one of the components of the combination quite likely but the other unlikely; then, the combination is often seen as more likely than the unlikely component. For example, physicians know that someone suffering from a blood clot in the lung is likely to be short of breath, but that dizziness is a symptom not associated with having such a blood clot (Tversky & Kahneman, 1983). Physicians actually surveyed state that it is more likely for a patient to suffer from both dizziness and shortness of breath than to suffer from dizziness alone. Sometimes, it is not even necessary that one member of the combination be "representative" and the other not; for example, running a four-minute mile *and* running the last half mile in less than two minutes might be judged as more likely than running the four-minute mile—even though there is no necessity of "rescuing" an unlikely component of the combination (running the four-minute mile) by a more likely one (the two-minute half mile being perhaps even more unlikely). Yes, the world's number one tennis player may be perceived to be more likely to lose the first set and win the match than to lose the first set alone, but this player also may be seen to be more likely to have a remarkable comeback after losing the first set than to have a remarkable comeback alone, even though by definition "remarkable" is unrepresentative.

What is especially striking in this conjunction fallacy is that we need not always infer it from combining judgments of different subjects. In fact, "transparent" as it may appear to be once it is understood (like the malpractice example!), even subjects who rate both the conjunction and its components may fall prey to the fallacy. In a problem that has now become classic "Linda" is described as "31 years old, single, outspoken, and very bright. She majored in philosophy. As a student, she was deeply concerned with issues of discrimination and social justice, and also participated in antinuclear demonstrations" (p. 297). People then are asked to rank various possibilities for what she is doing, and these include being a bank teller and being a bank teller *and* active in the feminist movement. Most subjects rate the latter alternative as more likely than the former; roughly half do so even when the bank teller alternative is expressed as "Linda is a bank teller whether or not she is active in the feminist movement" (p. 299).

The researchers investigating this fallacy have been criticized (for example, Dulany & Hilton, 1991) on the grounds that asking whether an alternative *A* or a combination of alternative *A* and *B* is more likely is a very unusual question, and that the subjects asked it may not interpret these possibilities as involving the "extensional" characteristics of probability theory, but, rather as indicating the knowledge of the person asserting either *A* alone or *A* and *B*. That is, we have conversational norms of "politeness" (Grice, 1975) that involve telling people not just what we know, but everything we know (as in "The truth, the whole truth, and nothing but the truth"). Thus, someone who tells us two things about somebody may be more knowledge-

able about that person than someone who tells only one of these things, hence more believable; subsequently, we may assign a higher *epistemic* probability to this conjunction than to the single statement.

When, however, people are asked post hoc how they interpret these statements involved in the Linda problem and in similar ones, roughly half those who interpret the problem in terms of "extension" as opposed to "epistemic probability" still commit the fallacy (roughly the same proportion who do so when in the "whether or not" condition). Moreover, the "epistemic probability" explanation could at least for some of these subjects be a rationalization when they realize that otherwise they have made an incoherent judgment (as, for example, the medical subjects realize when it is pointed out to them that two symptoms cannot be more probable than one of them alone—no matter how improbable this single symptom is given the condition). Finally, the criticism of the word problems ignores the establishment of the conjunction fallacy in other contexts, such as medical diagnoses and gambling.

E. Again, Quo Vadis?

Again, we face the problem of whether we wish to develop separate theories about how people "actually make judgments" or to develop ideas about how it is they are more or less encouraged to make them rationally. Again, I believe that while there is some legitimate debate, the latter alternative is preferable. It is true, for example, that people on juries are undoubtedly influenced by the order of the information presented to them, which they should not be according to Bayes Theorem. Moreover, their final judgment is influenced by the degree to which prosecution and defense can create "a good story" by manipulating order (Pennington & Hastie, 1988). It may also be true that framing problems in terms that make evolutionary "social sense" can in fact facilitate solving them correctly (Cosmides & Tooby, 1994); for example, logic problems are solved better when they are phrased in terms of paying a price in order to achieve a benefit (e.g., having to have a first-class stamp on an envelope in order to seal it) than when phrased abstractly (e.g., having an even number printed on one side of an index card when there is a vowel printed on the other). Perhaps the transparency of the problem in the cost/benefit frame can be related to an evolutionary need to "spot cheaters." (But on the other hand, rather complicated problems of logical or statistical inference are often solved better by drawing Venn diagrams than by attending to the content of the problem.) It is also true that making the probabilistic nature and questions explicit tends to reduce the frequency of the anomalies discussed here (Gigerenzer, 1991; Gigerenzer, Hell, & Blank, 1988). But even the most explicit language or manipulation does not lead to the disappearance of the anomalies; in fact, these manipulations themselves may be helpful in making the problems *"transparent"* so that subjects can make coherent judgments, i.e., judgments consistent with Bayes Theorem (as opposed to judgments consistent with "some other model of judgment").

When we are called to jury duty, do we really want our judgments to be influenced by the order in which information is presented? Again, we are of "two minds," just as we are when an anomaly of decision making has been made transparent to us. Generally, believing that what cannot be is not, we opt for coherence when presented with such a conflict. Moreover, despite all the evidence for the lack of generalized rationality presented in this chapter, and the speculations that what rationality there is may be highly specific to particular types of problems (e.g., those that "make evolutionary sense"), people can and do often reason according to general rules (see Smith, Langston, & Nisbett, 1992). The future of research in inference may be devoted to finding what encourages or discourages the use of such rules, rather than to searching for alternatives to them.

REFERENCES

Abelson, R. P. (1995). The secret existence of expressive behavior. *Critical Review, 9,* 21–36.

Abelson, R. P., & Levi, A. (1985). Decision making and decision theory. In G. Lindzey & E. Aronson (Eds.), *Handbook of social psychology* (3rd ed., pp. 231–309). New York: Random House.

Ajzen, I. (1977). Intuitive theories of events and the effects of base rate information on prediction. *Journal of Personality and Social Psychology, 35,* 303–314.

Allais, M. (1979). The foundations of a positive theory of choice involving risk and a criticism of the postulates and axioms of the American School. In M. Allais & O. Hagen (Eds.), *Expected utility hypotheses and the Allais paradox* (pp. 27–145). Dordrecht: Reidel (original work published 1952).

Allen, W. S. (1984). *The Nazi seizure of power: The experience of a single German town, 1922–1945* (Rev. ed.). New York: Franklin Watts.

Anderson, N. H. (1968). A simple model for information integration. In R. P. Abelson et al. (Eds.), *Theories of cognitive consistency: A source book.* Chicago: Rand McNally.

Andreoni, J. (1990). Impure altruism and donations to public goods: A theory of warm glow giving. *Economic Journal, 100,* 464–477.

Arkes, H. R. (1994). Three reservations about consequentialism. *Behavioral and Brain Sciences, 17,* 11–12.

Arkes, H. R., & Blumer, C. (1985). The psychology of sunk cost. *Organizational Behavior and Human Decision Processes, 35,* 124–140.

Austin, L. C. (1995). Consumers' insurance decision models:

An empirical study. Doctoral Dissertation, Department of Social and Decision Sciences, Carnegie Mellon University, Pittsburgh, PA.

Bar-Hillel, M. (1980). The base-rate fallacy in probability judgments. *Acta Psychologica, 44,* 211–233.

Bar-Hillel, M. (1990). Back to base-rates. In R. M. Hogarth (Ed.), *Insights in decision making: A tribute to Hillel J. Einhorn.* Chicago: University of Chicago Press.

Baron, J., & Ritov, I. (1993). Intuitions about penalties and compensation in the context of tort law. *Journal of Risk and Uncertainty, 7,* 17–33.

Beach, L. R. (1990). *Image theory: Decision making in personal and organizational contexts.* Chichester: Wiley.

Becker, G. M., DeGroot, M. H., & Marshak, J. (1964). Measuring utility by a single-response sequential method. *Behavioral Science, 9,* 226–232.

Bell, D. E. (1982). Regret in decision making under uncertainty. *Operations Research, 30,* 961–981.

Berman, L. (1982). *Planning a tragedy.* New York: W. W. Norton.

Bersoff, D. N. (1992). Judicial deference to nonlegal decision making: Imposing simplistic solutions on problems of cognitive complexity in mental disability law. *Southern Methodist University Law Review, 46,* 329–372.

Birnbaum, M. H., & Mellers, B. A. (1983). Bayesian inference: Combining base rates with opinions of sources who vary in credibility. *Journal of Personality and Social Psychology, 45,* 792–804.

Bradley, R. A., & Terry, M. E. (1952). Rank analysis of incomplete block designs: I. The method of paired comparisons. *Biometrika, 39,* 324–345.

Brown, R. (1973). Schizophrenia, language and reality. *American Psychologist, 28,* 395–403.

Camerer, C. F. (1995). Individual decision making. In J. H. Kagel & A. E. Roth (Eds.), *The handbook of experimental economics* (pp. 587–703). Princeton, NJ: Princeton University Press.

Camerer, C. F., & Ho, T. H. (1994). Violations of the betweenness axiom and nonlinearity in probability. *Journal of Risk and Uncertainty, 8,* 167–196.

Caporael, L., Dawes, R. M., Orbell, J. M., & van de Kragt, A. J. C. (1989). Selfishness examined: Cooperation in the absence of egoistic incentives. *Behavioral and Brain Sciences, 12,* 683–699.

Ceci, S. J. (1991). Some overarching issues in the children's suggestibility debate. In J. Doris (Ed.), *The suggestibility of children's recollections* (pp. 1–9). Washington, DC: American Psychological Association.

Christensen-Szalanski, J. J. J. (1978). Problem-solving strategies: A selection mechanism, some implications, and some data. *Organizational Behavior and Human Preference, 22,* 307–323.

Christensen-Szalanski, J. J. J., Beck, D. E., Christensen-Szalanski, C. M., & Koepsell, T. D. (1983). Effects of expertise and experience on risk judgments. *Journal of Applied Psychology, 68,* 278–284.

Coase, R. H. (1960). The problem of social cost. *Journal of Law and Economics, 3,* 1–44.

Combs, B., & Slovic, P. (1979). Newspaper coverage of causes of death. *Journalism Quarterly, 56,* 837–843, 849.

Cooke, A. (Ed.) (1955). *The vintage Mencken.* New York: Vintage Books.

Coombs, C. H. (1964). *A theory of data.* New York: John Wiley.

Coombs, C. H., & Avrunin, G. S. (1988). *The structure of conflict.* Hillsdale, NJ: Erlbaum.

Coombs, C. H., Donnell, M. L., & Kirk, D. B. (1978). An experimental study of risk preferences in lotteries. *Journal of Experimental Psychology: Human Perception and Performance, 4,* 497–512.

Cosmides, L., & Tooby, J. (1994). Better than rational: Evolutionary psychology and the invisible hand. *AEA Papers and Proceedings, 84,* 327–332.

Dawes, R. M. (1979). The robust beauty of improper linear models. *American Psychologist, 34,* 571–582.

Dawes, R. M. (1983). Is irrationality systematic? Comment on Cohen. *Behavioral and Brain Sciences, 6,* 491–492.

Dawes, R. M. (1988). *Rational choice in an uncertain world.* San Diego, CA: Harcourt, Brace, Jovanovich.

Dawes, R. M. (1991). Social dilemmas, economic self-interest, and evolutionary theory. In D. R. Brown & J. E. K. Smith (Eds.), *Recent research in psychology: Frontiers of mathematical psychology: Essays in honor of Clyde Coombs* (pp. 53–79). New York: Springer-Verlag. (Reprinted in R. M. Coughlin [Ed.], *Morality, rationality, and efficiency: New perspectives in socio-economics* [pp. 17–40]. New York: Sharpe.)

Dawes, R. M. (1992a). The importance of alternative hypotheses—and hypothetical counterfactuals in general—in social science. Division One William James Book Award Address on August 16, 1991. *The General Psychologist, 28,* no. 1, Spring, 1992, 2–7.

Dawes, R. M. (1992b). Quandary: Correlation coefficients and contexts. In L. Montada, S. H. Filipp, & M. J. Lerner (Eds.), *Life crises and experiences of loss in adulthood.* Hillsdale, NJ: Erlbaum.

Dawes, R. M. (1993). The prediction of the future versus an understanding of the past: A basic asymmetry. *American Journal of Psychology, 106,* 1–24.

Dawes, R. M. (1994a). *House of cards: Psychology and psychotherapy built on myth.* New York: Free Press.

Dawes, R. M. (1994b). AIDS, sterile needles, and ethnocentrism. In L. Heath, R. S. Tindale, J. Edwards, E. Posavac, F. B. Bryant, E. Henderson-King, Y. Suarez-Balcazar, & J. Myers (Eds.), *Social psychological applications to social issues, III: Applications of heuristics and biases to social issues* (pp. 31–44). New York: Plenum Press.

Dawes, R. M. (1994c). Affirmative action programs: Discontinuities between thoughts about individuals and thoughts about groups. In L. Heath, R. S. Tindale, J. Edwards, E. Posavac, F. B. Bryant, E. Henderson-King, Y. Suarez-Balcazar, & J. Myers (Eds.), *Social psychological applications to social issues, III: Applications of heuristics and biases to social issues* (pp. 225–239). New York: Plenum Press.

Dawes, R. M., & Corrigan, B. (1974). Linear models in decision making. *Psychological Bulletin, 81,* 95–106.

Dawes, R. M., Faust, D., & Meehl, P. E. (1989). Clinical versus actuarial judgment. *Science, 243,* 1668–1674.

Dawes, R. M., Mirels, H. L., Gold, E., & Donahue, E. (1993). Equating inverse probabilities in implicit personality judgments. *Psychological Science, 6,* 396–400.

Doherty, M. E., Mynatt, C. R., Tweney, R. D., & Schiavo, M. D. (1979). Pseudodiagnosticity. *Acta Psychologica, 43,* 111–121.

Dulany, D. L., & Hilton, D. J. (1991). Conversational implicature, conscious representation, and the conjunction fallacy. *Social Cognition, 9,* 85–110.

Eddy, D. M. (1982). Probabilistic reasoning in clinical medicine: Problems and opportunities. In D. Kahneman, P. Slovic, & A. Tversky (Eds.), *Judgment under uncertainty: Heuristics and biases* (pp. 249–267). New York: Cambridge University Press.

Edwards, W. (1968). Conservatism in human information processing. In B. Kleinmuntz (Ed.), *Formal representation of human judgment.* New York: Wiley, 17–52.

Edwards, W. (1992). Toward the demise of economic man and woman: Bottom lines from Santa Cruz. In W. Edwards (Ed.), *Utility theories: Measurements and applications* (pp. 253–267). Boston: Kluwer Academic Publishers.

Einhorn, H. J. (1986). Accepting error to make less error. *Journal of Personality Assessment, 50,* 387–395.

Einhorn, H. J., & Hogarth, R. M. (1978). Confidence in judgment: Persistence of the illusion of validity. *Psychological Review, 85,* 395–416.

Ericsson, K. A., & Simon, H. A. (1993). *Protocol analysis: Verbal reports as data.* Cambridge, MA: MIT Press.

Faust, D. (1986). Declarations versus investigations: The case for the special reasoning abilities and capabilities of the expert witness in psychology/psychiatry. *The Journal of Psychiatry and Law, 13,* 33–59.

Fischhoff, B. (1977). Cost benefit analysis and the art of motorcycle maintenance. *Policy Sciences, 8,* 177–202.

Fischhoff, B. (1983). Strategic policy preferences: A behavioral decision theory perspective. *Journal of Social Issues, 39,* 133–160.

Fischhoff, B., & Bar-Hillel, M. (1984). Diagnosticity and the base-rate effect. *Memory and Cognition, 12,* 402–410.

Fischhoff, B., & Beyth-Marom, R. (1983). Hypothesis evaluation from a Bayesian perspective. *Psychological Review, 90,* 239–260.

Fischhoff, B., Jacobs-Quadrel, M., Kamlet, M., Loewenstein,

G., Dawes, R. M., Fischbeck, P., Klepper, S., Leland, J., & Stroh, P. (1993). Embedding effects: stimulus representation and response mode. *Journal of Risk and Uncertainty, 6,* 211–234.

Fischhoff, B., Lichtenstein, S., Slovic, O., Derby, S. L., & Keeney, R. L. (1981). *Acceptable risk.* Cambridge: Cambridge University Press.

Fishburn, P. C. (1982). Nontransitive measurable utility. *Journal of Mathematical Psychology, 26,* 31–67.

Fisher, G. W., & Hawkins, S. A. (1993). Strategy compatibility, scale compatibility, and the prominence effect. *Journal of Experimental Psychology: Human Perception and Performance, 19,* 580–597.

Fitts, P. M., & Posner, M. I. (1967). *Human performance.* Belmont, CA: Brooks/Cole.

Frey, B. S., & Bohnet, I. (1995). Institutions affect fairness: Experimental investigations. *Journal of Theoretical Economics, 151,* 286–303.

Funder, D. C. (1987). Errors and mistakes: Evaluating the accuracy of social judgment. *Psychological Bulletin, 101,* 75–90.

Gertner, R. (1993). Game shows and economic behavior: Risk-taking on "Card Sharks." *Quarterly Journal of Economics,* May, 507–521.

Gettys, C. F., Plisky, R. M., Manning, C., & Casey, J. T. (1987). An evaluation of human act generation performance. *Organizational Behavior and Human Decision Processes, 39,* 23–51.

Gigerenzer, G. (1991). From tools to theories: A heuristic of discovery in cognitive psychology. *Psychological Review, 98,* 254–267.

Gigerenzer, G., & Goldstein, D. G. (1996). Reasoning the fast and frugal way: Models of bounded rationality. *Psychological Review, 103,* 650–664.

Gigerenzer, G., Hell, W., & Blank, H. (1988). Presentation and content: The use of base rates as a continuous variable. *Journal of Experimental Psychology: Human Perception and Performance, 14,* 513–525.

Gigerenzer, G., & Hoffrage, U. (1995). How to improve Bayesian reasoning without instruction: Frequency formats. *Psychological Review, 102,* 684–704.

Gilovich, T., Vallone, R., & Tversky, A. (1985). The hot hand in basketball: On the misperception of random sequences. *Journal of Personality and Social Psychology, 17,* 295–314.

Goldstein, W. M., & Einhorn, H. J. (1987). Expression theory and the preference reversal phenomena. *Psychological Review, 94,* 236–254.

Green, D. P. (1992). The price elasticity of mass preferences. *American Political Science Review, 86,* 128–148.

Green, D. P., & Cowden, J. A. (1992). Who protests: Self-interest and white opposition to busing. *The Journal of Politics, 54,* 471–496.

Green, D. P., & Shapiro, I. (1994). *Pathologies of rational choice theory: A critique of applications in political science.* New Haven, CT: Yale University Press.

Grether, D. M., & Plott, C. R. (1979). Economic theory of choice and the preference reversal phenomenon. *American Economic Review, 69,* 623–638.

Grice, H. P. (1975). Logic in conversation. In P. Cole and J. L. Morgan (Eds.), *Syntax and Semantics: 3. Speech Acts* (pp. 41–58). New York: Academic Press.

Grove, W. M., & Meehl, P. E. (1996). Comparative efficiency of formal (mechanical, algorithmic) and informal (subjective, expressionistic) prediction procedures. *Psychology, Public Policy, and Law, 2,* 293–323.

Gul, F. (1991). A theory of disappointment aversion. *Econometrica, 59,* 667–686.

Hammond, K. R., Hamm, R. M., & Grassia, J. (1986). Generalizing over conditions by combining the multitrait-multimethod matrix and the representative design of experiments. *Psychological Bulletin, 100,* 257–269.

Hastie, R. (1991). A review from a high place: The field of judgment and decision making as revealed in its current textbooks. *Psychological Science, 2,* 135–141.

Hastie, R., & Park, B. (1986). The relationship between memory and judgment depends on whether the judgment task is memory-based or on-line. *Psychological Review, 93,* 258–268.

Hershey, J. C., Kunreuther, H. C., & Schoemaker, P. J. H. (1982). Sources of bias in assessment procedures for utility functions. *Management Science, 28,* 936–954.

Hoffman, E., & Spitzer, M. L. (1993). Willingness to pay versus willingness to accept: Legal and economic implications. *Washington University Law Quarterly, 71,* 59–114.

Hogarth, R. (1987). *Judgment and Choice* (2nd ed.). New York: Wiley.

Hogarth, R. M., & Kunreuther, H. (1995). Decision making under ignorance: Arguing with yourself. *Journal of Risk and Uncertainty, 10,* 15–36.

Hsee, C. K., Abelson, R. P., & Salovey, P. (1991). The relative weighting of position and velocity in satisfaction. *Psychological Science, 2,* 263–266.

Huber, J., Payne, J. W., & Puto, C. (1982). Adding asymmetrically dominated alternatives: Violations of regularity and the similarity hypothesis. *Journal of Consumer Research, 9,* 90–98.

Huber, J., & Puto, C. (1983). Market boundaries and product choice: Illustrating attraction and substitution effects. *Journal of Consumer Research, 10,* 31–44.

Inhelder, B., & Piaget, J. (1958). *The growth of logical thinking from childhood to adolescence.* New York: Basic Books.

Irwin, J. R., Slovic, P., Lichtenstein, S., & McClelland, G. H. (1993). Preference reversals and the measurement of environmental values. *Journal of Risk and Uncertainty, 6,* 5–18.

Jones, E. E., & Nisbett, R. E. (1971). The actor and the observer: Divergent perceptions of the causes of behavior. In E. E. Jones, D. E. Kanouse, H. H. Kelley, R. E. Nisbett, S. Valins, & B. Weiner (Eds.), *Attribution: Perceiving the causes of behavior.* Morristown, NJ: General Learning Press.

Kahneman, D. (1994). New challenges to the rationality of assumptions. *Journal of International and Theoretical Economics, 150,* 18–36.

Kahneman, D., Knetsch, J. L., & Thaler, R. H. (1986). Fairness as a constraint on profit seeking: Entitlements in the market. *The American Economic Review, September,* 728–741.

Kahneman, D., Knetsch, J. L., & Thaler, R. H. (1991). Anomalies: The endowment effect, loss aversion and status quo bias. *Journal of Economic Perspectives, 5,* 193–206.

Kahneman, D., & Lovallo, D. (1993). Timid choices and bold forecasts: A cognitive perspective on risk taking. *Management Science, 38,* 17–31.

Kahneman, D., & Tversky, A. (1972). Subjective probability: A judgment of representativeness. *Cognitive Psychology, 3,* 430–454.

Kahneman, D., & Tversky, A. (1973). On the psychology of prediction. *Psychological Review, 80,* 237–251.

Kahneman, D., & Tversky, A. (1979a). Intuitive prediction: Biases and corrective procedures. *TIMS Studies in Management Science, 12,* 313–327.

Kahneman, D., & Tversky, A. (1979b). Prospect theory: An analysis of decision under risk. *Econometrica, 47,* 263–291.

Kahneman, D., & Tversky, A. (1984). Choices, values, and frames. *American Psychologist, 39,* 341–350.

Kahneman, D., & Tversky, A. (1995). Conflict resolution: A cognitive perspective. In K. Arrow, R. H. Mnookin, L. Ross, A. Tversky, & R. Wilson (Eds.), *Barriers to conflict resolution.* New York: W. W. Norton.

Katz, L. D. (1994). On begging the question when naturalizing norms. *Behavioral and Brain Sciences, 17,* 21–22.

Keeney, R. L., von Winterfeldt, D., & Eppel, T. (1990). Eliciting public values for complex policy decisions. *Management Science, 36,* 1011–1030.

Keller, L. R. (1985). The effects of problem representation on the sure-thing and substitution principles. *Management Science, 31,* 738–751.

Keller, L. R., & Ho, J. L. (1988). Decision problem structuring: Generating options. *IEEE Transactions on Systems, Man, and Cybernetics, 18,* 715–728.

Knaus, W. A., Wagner, D. P., & Lynn, J. (1991). Short-term mortality predictions for critically ill hospitalized adults: Science and ethics. *Science, 254,* 389–394.

Knetsch, J. L., & Sinden, J. A. (1984). Willingness to pay and compensation demanded: Experimental evidence of an unexpected disparity in measures of value. *Quarterly Journal of Economics, 99,* 507–521.

Krueger, J., Ham, J. J., & Linford, K. M. (1996) Perceptions of behavioral consistency: Are people aware of the actor-observer effect? *Psychological Science, 7,* 259–264.

Langer, E. (1994). The illusion of calculated decisions. In R. Schank & E. Langer (Eds.), *Beliefs, reasoning and decision making: Psycho-logic in honor of Bob Abelson.* Hillsdale, NJ: Erlbaum.

Leland, J. W. (1994). Generalized similarity judgments: An alternative explanation for choice anomalies. *Journal of Risk and Uncertainty, 9,* 151–172.

Lerner, M. J. (1987). Integrating social and psychological rules of entitlements. The basic task of each actor and fundamental problem for the social sciences. *Social Justice Research, 1,* 107–125.

Levi, J. S. (1992). Prospect theory and international relations: Theoretical applications and analytical problems. *Political Psychology, 13,* 283–310.

Lichtenstein, S., & Slovic, P. (1971). Reversals of preference between bids and choices in gambling decisions. *Journal of Experimental Psychology, 89,* 46–55.

Lichtenstein, S., & Slovic, P. (1973). Response-induced reversals of preference in gambling: An extended replication in Las Vegas. *Journal of Experimental Psychology, 101,* 16–20.

Loewenstein, G. F., & Prelac, D. (1993). Preferences for sequences of outcomes. *Psychological Review, 100,* 91–108.

Loewenstein, G. F., & Thaler, R. (1989a). Anomalies: Intertemporal choice. *Journal of Economic Perspectives, 3,* 181–193.

Loewenstein, G. F., Thompson, L., & Bazerman, M. H. (1989). Social utility and decision making in interpersonal contexts. *Journal of Personality and Social Psychology, 57,* 426–441.

Loomes, G. (1991). Evidence of a new violation of the independence axiom. *Journal of Risk and Uncertainty, 4,* 91–108.

Loomes, G., Starmer, C., & Sugden, R. (1991). Observing violations of transitivity by experimental methods. *Econometrica, 59,* 425–439.

Loomes, G., & Sugden, R. (1982). Regret theory: An alternative theory of rational choice under uncertainty. *Economic Journal, 92,* 805–824.

Lopes, L. (1982). Decision making in the short run. *Journal of Experimental Psychology: Human Learning and Memory, 7,* 377–385.

Lopes, L. (1987). Between hope and fear: The psychology of risk. In L. Berkowitz (Ed.), *Advances in experimental social psychology* (Vol. 20, pp. 255–295). New York: Academic Press.

Luce, R. D. (1959). *Individual choice behavior.* New York: John Wiley.

Luce, R. D. (1991). Rank- and sign-dependent linear utility models for binary gambles. *Journal of Economic Theory, 53,* 75–100.

Luce, R. D. (1992). Where does subjective expected utility fail descriptively? *Journal of Risk and Uncertainty, 5,* 5–27.

Luce, R. D., & Fishburn, P. (1991). Rank- and sign-dependent linear utility models for finite first-order gambles. *Journal of Risk and Uncertainty, 4,* 29–59.

MacCrimmon, K. R., Stanbury, W. T., & Wehrung, D. A. (1980). Real money lotteries: A study of ideal risk, context effects, and simple processes. In T. S. Wallsten (Ed.), *Cognitive processes in choice and decision behavior* (pp. 155–177). Hillsdale, NJ: Erlbaum.

Machina, M. J. (1982). "Expected utility" analysis without the independence axiom. *Econometrica, 50,* 277–323.

Machina, M. J. (1987). Choice under uncertainty: Problems solved and unsolved. *Economic Perspectives, 1,* 121–154.

Machina, M. J. (1989). Dynamic consistency and non-expected utility models of choice under uncertainty. *Journal of Economic Literature, 27,* 1622–1668.

March, J. G. (1978). Bounded rationality, ambiguity, and the engineering of choice. *Bell Journal of Economics, 9,* 586–608.

March, J. G., & Shapira, Z. (1987). Managerial perspectives on risk and risk taking. *Management Science, 33,* 1404–1418.

Markowitz, H. (1952). The utility of wealth. *Journal of Political Economy, 60,* 151–158.

McCauley, C. (1991). Selection of National Science Foundation fellows: A case study of psychologists failing to apply what they know about decision making. *American Psychologist, 46,* 1287–1291.

McNeil, B. J., Pauker, S. G., Saks, H. C., Jr., & Tversky, A. (1982). On the elicitation of preferences for alternative therapies. *New England Journal of Medicine, 306,* 1259–1262.

Meehl, P. E. (1954). *Clinical versus statistical predictions: A theoretical analysis and review of the evidence.* Minneapolis: University of Minnesota Press.

Meehl, P. E. (1977a). Why I do not attend case conferences. In P. E. Meehl (Ed.), *Psychodiagnosis: Selected papers* (pp. 225–302). New York: W. W. Norton.

Meehl, P. E. (1977b). The selfish voter paradox and the thrown-away vote argument. *American Political Science Review, 71,* 11–30.

Meehl, P. E. (1986). Causes and effects of my disturbing little book. *Journal of Personality Assessment, 50,* 370–375.

Meehl, P. E., & Rosen, A. (1955). Antecedent probability in the efficiency of psychometric signs, patterns, or cutting scores. *Psychological Bulletin, 52,* 194–216.

Mellers, B. (1990). Book review on R. M. Dawes' *Rational choice in an uncertain world. Journal of Mathematical Psychology, 34,* 332–335.

Mellers, B. A., & Biagini, K. (1994). Similarity and choice. *Psychological Review, 101,* 505–518.

Mellers, B. A., Chang, S., Birnbaum, M. H., & Ordonez, L. D. (1992). Preferences, prices, and ratings in risky decision making. *Journal of Experimental Psychology: Human Perception and Performance, 18,* 347–361.

Mellers, B. A., Ordonez, L. D., & Birnbaum, M. H. (1992). A change-of-process theory for contextual effects and preference reversals in risky decision making. *Organizational Behavior and Human Decision Processes, 52,* 331–369.

Melone, N. P., McGuire, T. W., Blazer, M., Erdner, D., Gerwing, T., McGuire, M. J., & Roy, M. C. (1992). Global conservatism in probability judgments: The base rate fallacy revisited. Working paper #1992-34. Graduate School of Industrial Administration, Carnegie Mellon University, Pittsburgh, PA.

Montgomery, H. (1983). Decision rules in the search for a dominance structure: Toward a process model of decision making. In P. C. Humphreys, O. Svenson, & A. Vari (Eds.), *Analyzing and aiding decision processes* (pp. 343–369). Amsterdam: North Holland.

Newell, A. (1981). The knowledge level. *AI Magazine, Summer,* 1–20.

Nisbett, R. E., & Ross, L. (1980). *Human inference: Strategies and shortcomings of social judgment.* Englewood Cliffs, NJ: Prentice-Hall.

Nisbett, R. E., & Wilson, T. D. (1977). Telling more than we can know: Verbal reports on mental processes. *Psychological Review, 84,* 231–259.

Nisbett, R. E., Zukier, H., & Lemley, R. E. (1981). The dilution effect: Nondiagnostic information weakens the implications of diagnostic information. *Cognitive Psychology, 13,* 248–277.

Nowak, R. (1994). Problems in clinical trials go far beyond misconduct. *Science, 264,* 1538–1541.

Orbell, J. (1993). *Hamlet* and the psychology of rational choice under uncertainty. *Rationality and Psychology, 5,* 127–140.

Orbell, J. M., van de Kragt, A. J. C., & Dawes, R. M. (1988). Explaining discussion-induced cooperation. *Journal of Personality and Social Psychology, 54,* 811–819.

Pauker, S. G. (1976). Coronary artery surgery: The use of decision analysis. *Annals of Internal Medicine, 85,* 8–18.

Payne, J. W., Bettman, J. R., & Johnson, E. J. (1993). *The adaptive decision maker.* Cambridge, MA: Cambridge University Press.

Pennington, N., & Hastie, R. (1988). Explanation-based decision making: Effects of memory structure on judgment. *Journal of Experimental Psychology: Learning, Memory, and Cognition, 14,* 521–533.

Pickett, R. M. (1962). Discrimination of constrained and random visual texture. Doctoral dissertation, University of Michigan, Ann Arbor, MI.

Plous, S. (1993). *The psychology of judgment and decision making.* New York: McGraw-Hill.

Quattrone, G. A., & Tversky, A. (1988). Contrasting rational and psychological analyses of political choice. *American Political Science Review, 82,* 719–736.

Raiffa, H. (1968). *Decision analysis: Introductory lectures on choices under uncertainty.* Reading, MA: Addison-Wesley.

Raiffa, H. (1982). *The art and science of negotiation.* Cambridge, MA: Harvard University Press.

Redelmeier, D. A., & Tversky, A. (1990). Discrepancy between medical decisions for individual patients and for groups. *New England Journal of Medicine, 322,* 1162–1164.

Ritov, I., & Baron, J. (1992). Status-quo and omission biases. *Journal of Risk and Uncertainty, 5,* 49–61.

Ross, L. D., Amabile, T. M., & Steinmetz, J. L. (1977). Social roles, social control, and biases in social-perception processes. *Journal of Personality and Social Psychology, 35,* 485–494.

Ross, M., & Sicoly, F. (1979). Egocentric biases and availability in attribution. *Journal of Personality and Social Psychology, 37,* 322–336.

Roy, M. C. (1991). The impact of causality on the use of base rates. Doctoral dissertation, Carnegie Mellon University, Pittsburgh, PA.

Russo, J. E., & Schoemaker, P. J. H. (1989). *Decision traps: Ten barriers to brilliant decision making and how to overcome them.* New York: Simon & Schuster.

Saks, M. J. (1994). Facing real problems and finding real solutions. A review of P. C. Weiler et al. (Eds.), *A measure of malpractice medical injury, malpractice litigation, and patient compensation. William and Mary Review, 35,* 693–723.

Samuelson, P. A. (1963). Risk and uncertainty: A fallacy of large numbers. *Scientia, 98,* 108–113.

Samuelson, P. A. (1977). The St. Petersburg paradox: Defanged, dissected, and historically described. *Journal of Economic Literature, 15,* 24–55.

Sarin, R. K. (1992). What now for generalized utility theory? In W. Edwards (Ed.), *Utility theories: Measurements and applications.* Boston: Kluwer Academic Publishers.

Savage, L. J. (1954). *The foundations of statistics.* New York: Wiley.

Sawyer, J. (1966). Measurement and prediction, clinical and statistical. *Psychological Bulletin, 66,* 178–200.

Schoemaker, P. J. H. (1982). The expected utility model: Its variants, purposes, evidence, and limitations. *Journal of Economic Literature, 20,* 529–563.

Schooler, J. W., & Engstler-Schooler, T. Y. (1990). Verbal overshadowing of visual memories: Some things are better left unsaid. *Cognitive Psychology, 22,* 36–71.

Sen, A. K. (1977). Rational fools: A critique of the behavioral foundations of economic theory. *Philosophy and Public Affairs, 6,* 317–344.

Sen, A. K. (1982). Rights and agency. *Philosophy and Public Affairs, 11,* 3–39.

Shafir, E. (1993). Choosing versus rejecting: Why some options are both better and worse than others. *Memory & Cognition, 21,* 546–556.

Shafir, E. B., Osherson, D. N., & Smith, E. E. (1993). The advantage model: A comparative theory of evaluation and choice under risk. *Organizational Behavior and Human Decision Processes, 55,* 325–378.

Shedler, J., & Manis, M. (1986). Can the availability heuristic explain vividness effects? *Journal of Personality and Social Psychology, 51,* 26–36.

Shiffrin, R. M., & Schneider, W. (1977). Controlled and automatic human information processing: II. Perceptual learning, automatic attending, and a general theory. *Psychological Review, 84,* 127–190.

Simon, H. A. (1955). A behavioral model of rational choice. *Quarterly Journal of Economics, 69,* 99–118.

Simon, H. A. (1956). Rational choice and the structure of the environment. *Psychological Review, 63,* 129–138.

Simon, H. A. (1985). Human nature in politics: The dialogue of psychology with political science. *American Political Science Review, 79,* 293–304.

Simonson, I. (1989). Choice based on reasons: The case of attraction and compromise effects. *Journal of Consumer Research, 16,* 158–174.

Simonson, I., & Tversky, A. (1992). Choice in context: Trade-off contrast and extremeness aversion. *Journal of Marketing Research, 29,* 231–295.

Skov, R. B., & Sherman, S. J. (1986). Information-gathering processes: Diagnosticity, hypothesis-confirmatory strategies, and perceived hypothesis confirmation. *Journal of Experimental Social Psychology, 22,* 93–121.

Smith, A. (1976). *The theory of moral sentiments.* Indianapolis: Liberty Classics.

Smith, E. E., Langston, C., & Nisbett, R. E. (1992). The case for rules in reasoning. *Cognitive Science, 16,* 1–40.

Staw, B. M. (1982). Counterforces to change. In P. S. Goodman (Ed.), *Changes in organizations* (pp. 87–121). San Francisco: Jossey-Bass.

Staw, B. M., & Ross, J. (1989). Understanding behavior in escalation situations. *Science, 246,* 216–220.

Summit, R. C. (1983). The child sexual abuse accommodation syndrome. *Child Abuse and Neglect, 7,* 177–193.

Svenson, O. (1992). Differentiation and Consolidation Theory of human decision making: A frame of reference for the study of pre- and post-decision processes. *Acta Psychologica, 80,* 143–168.

Teigen, K. H. (1994). Actions, inactions and the temporal dimension. *Behavioral and Brain Sciences, 17,* 30–31.

Tetlock, P. E. (1991). An alternative metaphor in the study of judgment and choice: People as politicians. *Theory and Psychology, 1,* 451–475.

Tetlock, P. E., & Boettger, R. (1989). Accountability: A social magnifier of the dilution effect. *Journal of Personality and Social Psychology, 57,* 388–398.

Thaler, R. (1980). Toward a positive theory of consumer choice. *Journal of Economic Behavior and Organization, 1,* 39–60.

Thaler, R. H., & Johnson, E. J. (1990). Gambling with the house money and trying to break even: The effects of prior outcomes on risky choice. *Management Science, 36,* 643–660.

Thompson, S. C., & Kelley, H. H. (1981). Judgments of responsibility for activities in close relationships. *Journal of Personality and Social Psychology, 41,* 469–477.

Trope, Y., & Bassok, M. (1982). Confirmatory and diagnosing strategies in social information gathering. *Journal of Personality and Social Psychology, 43,* 22–34.

Tversky, A. (1969). Intransitivity of preferences. *Psychological Review, 76,* 31–48.

Tversky, A. (1972). Elimination by aspects: A theory of choice. *Psychological Review, 79,* 281–299.

Tversky, A., & Bar-Hillel, M. (1983). Risk: The long and the short. *Journal of Experimental Psychology: Learning, Memory, and Cognition, 9,* 713–717.

Tversky, A., & Kahneman, D. (1973). Availability: A heuristic for judging frequency and probability. *Cognitive Psychology, 5,* 207–232.

Tversky, A., & Kahneman, D. (1974). Judgment under uncertainty: Heuristics and biases. *Science, 185,* 1124–1130.

Tversky, A., & Kahneman, D. (1981). The framing of decisions and the psychology of choice. *Science, 211,* 453–458.

Tversky, A., & Kahneman, D. (1983). Extensional versus intuitive reasoning: The conjunction fallacy in probability judgment. *Psychological Review, 90,* 293–315.

Tversky, A., & Kahneman, D. (1986). Rational choice and the framing of decisions. *Journal of Business, 59,* S251–S278.

Tversky, A., & Kahneman, D. (1991). Loss aversion and riskless choice: A reference dependent model. *Quarterly Journal of Economics, 106,* 1039–1061.

Tversky, A., & Kahneman, D. (1992). Advances in prospect theory: Cumulative representation of uncertainty. *Journal of Risk and Uncertainty, 5,* 297–323.

Tversky, A., & Russo, J. E. (1969). Substitutability and similarity in binary choices. *Journal of Mathematical Psychology, 6,* 1–12.

Tversky, A., Sattath, S., & Slovic, P. (1988). Contingent weighting in judgment and choice. *Psychological Review, 95,* 371–384.

Tversky, A., & Shafir, E. (1992). The disjunction effect in choice under uncertainty. *Psychological Science, 3,* 305–309.

Tversky, A., & Simonson, I. (1993). Context-dependent preferences. *Management Science, 39,* 1179–1189.

Tversky, A., Slovic, P., & Kahneman, D. (1990). The causes of preference reversal. *American Economic Review, 80,* 204–217.

Tyler, T. (1990). Justice, self-interest, and the legitimacy of legal and political authority. In J. J. Mansbridge (Ed.), *Beyond self-interest* (pp. 171–179). Chicago: University of Chicago Press.

Verplanken, B., Aarts, H., van Knippenberg, A., & van Knippenberg, C. (1994). Attitude versus general habit: Antecedents of travel mode choice. *Journal of Applied Social Psychology, 24,* 285–300.

Viscusi, W. K., Margat, W. A., & Huber, J. (1987). An investigation of the rationality of consumer valuations of multiple health risks. *RAND Journal of Economics, 18,* 465–479.

von Neumann, J., & Morgenstern, O. (1944/1947). *The theory of games and economic behavior* (2nd ed.). Princeton, NJ: Princeton University Press.

Wagenaar, W. A. (1988). *Paradoxes of Gambling Behavior.* Hillsdale, NJ: Erlbaum.

Wedell, D. H. (1991). Distinguishing among models of contextually induced preference reversals. *Journal of Experimental Psychology: Learning, Memory, and Cognition, 17,* 767–778.

Weinstein, N. D. (1980). Unrealistic optimism about future life events. *Journal of Personality and Social Psychology, 39,* 806–820.

Wells, G. L. (1992). Naked statistical evidence of liability: Is subjective probability enough? *Journal of Personality and Social Psychology, 62,* 739–752.

Whitley, B. E., Jr., & Hern, A. L. (1991). Perceptions of vulnerability to pregnancy and the use of effective contraception. *Personality and Social Psychology Bulletin, 17,* 104–110.

Wilson, T. D., & Schooler, J. W. (1991). Thinking too much: Introspection can reduce the quality of preferences and decisions. *Journal of Personality and Social Psychology, 60,* 181–192.

Wolf, F. M., Gruppen, L. D., & Billi, J. E. (1985). Differential diagnosis and the competing hypothesis heuristic—a practical approach to judgment under uncertainty and Bayesian probability. *Journal of the American Medical Association, 253,* 2858–2862.

Yates, J. F. (1990). *Judgment and decision making.* Englewood Cliffs, NJ: Prentice-Hall.

Zajonc, R. B. (1980). Feeling and thinking: Preferences need no inferences. *American Psychologist, 35,* 151–175.

Zander, A. (1985). *The purposes of groups and organizations.* San Francisco: Jossey-Bass.

CHAPTER TWELVE

MOTIVATION

THANE S. PITTMAN, *Gettysburg College*

In his chapter on major developments in social psychology for the third edition of the *Handbook of Social Psychology,* Jones (1985) discussed the waxing and waning of research interests. As he and others have noted, motivational analyses were definitely on the wane in the 1970s and 80s, beginning with the advent of attribution theories in the late 1960s and continuing with the subsequent growth of interest in the application of cognitive theories and paradigms to questions about social cognition. Consistent with this observation, if only symbolically, chapters on social motivation were part of the first and second editions of the *Handbook of Social Psychology* (Murphy, 1954; Berkowitz, 1969), but the third edition (1985) did not contain a chapter explicitly focused on motivation. Of course motivational research did not stop in 1969, but there has been a strong resurgence of interest in motivational thinking in the last decade; many of the new issues and approaches covered in this chapter have been introduced since my last contribution to a selective review of research on motivation in social psychology (Pittman & Heller, 1987). Motivational theories of the underpinnings of cognitive analysis and the construction of reality, the control and meaning of behavior, and of the functioning of self and coping with the knowledge of the end of self are currently generating insight, controversy, interest, and an increasing amount of research. Motivation is back.

I thank John Darley for his comments on an early draft of this chapter, Toni Wein for her editorial assistance on several drafts, Danielle Mikesell for her assistance with reference searchers, and Robert Bornstein, Paul D'Agostino, Tory Higgins, and Gifford Weary for their constructive comments.

It would not be feasible to cover everything motivational that has happened since 1969 in one chapter. In its broadest sense, motivation is part of a great many analyses, and even alluding to every project with a motivational aspect would not be possible here. But there are a more limited number of research projects in which the motivational assumptions that are made refer to broad or basic motives, more fundamental to the nature of human desire than particular specific motives that are the result of relatively unique or specific current conditions. These projects are the primary subject of this chapter.

THE NATURE OF MOTIVATIONAL APPROACHES

What is a motivational approach? An informal survey of general texts on motivation revealed no single agreed-upon definition. However, Young's (1961) specification of the roles of energizing and directing behavior (p. 24) is representative and serviceable for social psychological analyses if "behavior" includes the processing of information and the development of cognitive structures as well as more overt actions. Motivation, the activation of internal desires, needs, and concerns, energizes behavior and sends the organism in a particular direction aimed at satisfaction of the motivational issues that gave rise to the increased energy. However, one of the things that social psychologists quickly discovered about human motivation is that the connections between the energizing and direction functions are not always simple and straightforward (e.g., Schachter & Singer, 1962).

Focusing on motivation implies a particular preference for answers to scientific questions on the part of the researcher or theorist. All basic research is after the answers to *why* questions, but there are individual differences among social psychologists in the kinds of answers that seem to be interesting or satisfying. When trying to answer the question "Why did that behavior occur?" some find interest and satisfaction in an answer that specifies aspects of the stimulus field, or in an explanation of the nature of reinforcement contingencies, while others might prefer answers couched in terms of the organism's developmental history. Some look for regularities that will apply to all, while others prefer to concentrate on the things that make each of us different. Perhaps an answer that specifies only cognitive processes will strike some as entirely satisfactory.

Motivationally oriented psychologists like to look inside the person for desires: what is wanted, what is strived for, what will feel satisfying or unsatisfying to the actor? A basic characteristic of motivational analyses is the assumption that one salient feature of behavior in situations is that the person is an active participant, an originating striving source with needs, desires, hopes, and fears, and not simply a wet computer through which information enters, is processed, and is emitted as behavior. If a computer analogy must be used, then for one interested in motivation it has to be a motivated computer, a computer with an attitude, with a heart as well as a mind.

The kind of answer to a "why" question that one will take as satisfactory at any given time is a combination of scientific tactical decisions and personal preferences. The waxing and waning of interest, now in motivation, now in cognition, is a natural and good aspect of scientific cycles of concentration. There is no doubt that the recent focus on social cognition has greatly increased our knowledge of cognitive processes, and as motivational analyses begin their return perhaps the time is ripe for a fruitful new integration of these two approaches that have of course always been intertwined in social psychological theory.

Organizational Plan

This review is divided into three general areas: the construction of understanding, acting on and in the world, and coming to terms with self and the end of self. These distinctions are of course somewhat arbitrary and overlapping, but they capture much of the current motivational thinking in social psychology. The largest area of research, consonant with the recent focus on cognition, has been concerned with how motivation affects the *construction of understanding,* or mental representations of reality. Issues of accuracy and illusion are covered in this section. Another substantial part of this review focuses on how motivation affects overt action, or *acting on and in the world.* The general areas of research reviewed in this section include

work on intrinsic and extrinsic motivational orientations, and on issues of motivational arousal, effort expenditure, and task persistence. The final, and less extensive, section contains a selective review of motivational thinking in the research on *coming to terms with self and the end of self.*

Several topics that could have been included in this review are the subject of other chapters in this handbook and are covered lightly or not at all here. These topics include altruism (see Batson, 1998, in this *Handbook*), aggression (see Geen, 1998, in this *Handbook*), emotion (see Zajonc, 1998, in this *Handbook*), evolution (see Buss & Kenrick, 1998, in this *Handbook*), and the issue of self-regulation (see Wegner & Bargh, 1998, in this *Handbook*, and Baumeister, 1998, in this *Handbook*). Because of its centrality to a number of recent motivational theories, some aspects of the research of the self are covered, but for a more complete review see the chapter on the self (Baumeister, 1998, in this *Handbook*).

THE CONSTRUCTION OF UNDERSTANDING

One fundamental problem, an unavoidable project that presents itself to the unformed person and that remains an ongoing issue throughout life, is the task of making sense out of and acting in a world that is extremely complex and at best only partly open to understanding and influence. Creating useful and coherent mental representations of this environment is clearly a major aspect of development and functioning. In trying to understand how people proceed with this life-long activity of creating abstract systems for understanding and action, most current social psychological theories frame their assumptions from a stance that views the person as an active, generative source in interaction with external influences.[1] The task of making sense and operating effectively is embraced with gusto. The construction of interesting and even entertaining explanations can be satisfying in its own right and gives pleasure when things are working well—when the environment seems understandable and open to influence. However, it is also clear that things do not always hold together; inconsistencies arise, plans fail, expectations can be disconfirmed, and desired outcomes may not be attained or may be attained in ways that seem unpredictable and capricious. Sometimes the world seems to hang together just as expected, but sometimes it reveals a capricious and viciously chaotic aspect that is seriously troubling. Much of the recent work on motivation in social psychology addresses these twin issues of the construction of understanding, and dealing with an unresponsive, confusing, and sometimes frightening and hostile environment.

Because one clear goal is to generate accurate representations that can be used for effective prediction and explanation of events, and for making good action decisions designed to influence events and to achieve desired outcomes, much of the recent work on motivation has been directed toward understanding when and why accuracy motives are engaged. However, at other times the goal may be to construct and maintain favored or comforting conceptions of reality. When human desires enter to alter or bias the kinds of inferences, predictions, and explanations that are made, our understandings may be more illusory than accurate. This is the other main focus of work on motivation and making sense of the world, targeted on understanding the interplay between accuracy and illusion. Therefore, this section on the construction of understanding first considers research targeted on accuracy, and then reviews research targeted on illusion.

Accuracy

Why do people construct explanatory systems? That such explanatory systems are constructed is obvious, but why are they constructed? What do people hope to gain by developing these systems of understanding, what purpose do they serve? The answer seems obvious: without such systems of understanding there would be little hope of continuing to exist. For example, one has to learn what qualifies as food, where it is, and how to get it, or starvation will ensue. In the social realm, things are more complex, but still one needs to learn at least some of the rudiments of effective social interaction to get a job, attract a companion, or be invited to the next party.

From a motivational perspective, the key is to understand that making sense of reality doesn't happen automatically. It takes an energized and directed person to go out and explore, to seek, to make, to plan, to reflect, to err and learn from errors, and to generate, test, and revise hypotheses. But these activities are neither constant nor random. The motivational question is what gets these thoughts and actions going? When and why does desire energize and direct the active construction of reality?

In the realm of social understanding, much of the research on explanatory systems has been guided or informed by theories of attribution (see Gilbert, 1998, in this *Handbook*). Attribution theorists have assumed that inferences and attributions about the social world are made in the service of rendering that world predictable and, to some degree, potentially controllable (Jones & Davis, 1965; Kelley, 1967, 1971). This motive to render the world predictable and controllable is assumed to be a fundamental aspect of human nature, a basic motive that waxes and wanes but that is the underpinning of our attempts to make sense of things. If the world remained incomprehensible and unpredictable, sensible actions could not be taken, and indeed learning could not occur since learning is in essence discovering regularities in the environment. The desire to render order and sense out of chaos can be assumed to be a fundamental human motive, one that leads to pleasure and

confidence when satisfied and that leads to anxiety and confusion when thwarted (see Weary, Gleicher, & Marsh, 1993, for a variety of perspectives on this viewpoint).

Motivations related to control concerns have long been recognized. The desire to exert control over one's environment was a central theme in White's (1959) analysis of effectance, and the experience of competence and self-determination became a central part of theories of intrinsic motivation (e.g., Csikzenmihalyi, 1975; deCharmes, 1968; Deci, 1975; Deci & Ryan, 1985). Evidence that deprivation of the ability to control outcomes can have negative consequences was perhaps best represented by the research on learned helplessness (e.g., Abramson, Metalsky, & Alloy, 1989; Abramson, Seligman, & Teasdale, 1978; Seligman, 1975). In a different vein, research inspired by reactance theory (Brehm, 1966; S. Brehm & Brehm, 1981; Wicklund, 1974) suggested that when a specific behavioral freedom is threatened, that freedom becomes more attractive and attempts to reassert the freedom are initiated (see Brehm, 1993, for a discussion of reactance and control).

An early approach to the question of when attributional activity was likely to occur varied characteristics of the stimuli that were presented, characteristics that could be expected to differ in the extent to which they would incite effortful information processing. Findings indicating that some informational characteristics—such as unexpectedness or expectancy violation (e.g. Bargh & Thein, 1985; Clary & Tesser, 1983; Hastie, 1984; Hilton, Klein, & von Hippel, 1991; Lau & Russell, 1980; Pyszczynski & Greenberg, 1981; White & Carlston, 1983; Wong & Weiner, 1981) or unusual degrees of negativity (e.g., Harvey, Yarkin, Lightner, & Town, 1980; Wong & Weiner, 1981)—lead to increased information processing can now be understood from the perspective of a control motivation analysis. These informational characteristics are likely to act as cues that activate control motivation and accuracy concerns because they imply rather directly that something not yet understood or potentially threatening has transpired.

I will review several ways that an increase or decrease in the motivation to develop an accurate understanding has been varied more directly in recent research. One approach is to compare subjects who already differ in their current generalized concern with achieving an accurate conceptualization. This has been done either through a manipulated prior experience designed to enhance control motivation, or by utilizing naturally occurring individual differences in depression that are thought to have arisen at least in part due to experiences with lack of control. A second general approach involves placing subjects into situations that vary systematically in the extent to which they are likely to arouse control concerns, including variations in expectations of future interaction, outcome dependency, accountability for judgments, or the importance of judgments.

Changes in accuracy motivation have been measured in

several ways as well. Increased interest in and utilization of available information, the nature and complexity of inferences that are drawn from available information, and the amount of effort and time devoted to information analysis have all been measured. In other studies, interest in obtaining information about interaction partners, and sensitivity to such information, has been the focus. Another measure of interest has been in the effects of changes in accuracy motivation on errors and biases that frequently occur.

The effects of accuracy motivation have been studied directly in experiments in which attempts to be accurate have been varied by instruction, that is, the experimenter tells some of the subjects to form accurate impressions or judgments while giving different instructions to other subjects. Neuberg and Fiske (1987) found that explicit accuracy instructions (Experiment 3) led subjects to base their impressions on the actual information given rather than on category-based expectations. Neuberg (1989) gave subjects who were acting as interviewers either a negative expectancy or no expectancy, and either instructions to form an accurate impression or no such instructions. He found that the accuracy instructions counteracted the typical effects of a negative expectation. Accuracy instruction subjects formed less negative impressions of the target in the negative expectancy conditions and, generally, behaved in ways unlikely to elicit self-fulfilling prophecies from interviewees. Thompson, Roman, Moskowitz, Chaiken, and Bargh (1994) have shown that explicit accuracy instructions have the effect of attenuating the usual effects of covert priming of traits on impression formation, indicating that when accuracy motivation is increased, judgments become less susceptible to bias, even bias tendencies that occur without the subject's awareness (see also Pittman, 1992, for a discussion of related issues). Ford and Kruglanski (1995) also showed that accuracy instructions resulted in a decreased influence for primed traits when forming impressions, and in a second study showed that subjects chronically low in need for closure exhibited similar effects. There is ample evidence concerning the effects of direct instructions to be accurate, and in the research reviewed next these same sorts of dependent measures have been used to detect changes in accuracy concerns.

Differences in Prior Motivational State

Deprivation of Control   The proposal that control motivation underlies attributional analysis has been tested by varying the nature of a prior experience with deprivation of control, and then looking for heightened attributional activity in subsequent unrelated settings. If the motivation to render the social environment predictable and potentially controllable is the fundamental reason for engaging in attributional analysis, then deprivation of control in one setting should lead to an increased general level of control

motivation and therefore more effortful and careful attributional processing in the next setting. To test this prediction, Pittman and N. Pittman (1980) first gave subjects one of three different levels of control deprivation (high, moderate, or none; see N. Pittman & Pittman, 1979), and then a second experimenter in an ostensibly unrelated second experiment provided subjects with attributional materials containing an attribution-relevant informational variation that had already been shown to be sensitive to changes in level of motivation (Pittman, Scherrer, & Wright, 1977). As predicted, subjects did show increased utilization of the available information when responding to a variety of questions concerning the motivation and underlying attitudes of the communicator portrayed in the stimulus materials in the second part of the experiment. This result has been replicated using the same manipulations and materials (Liu & Steele, 1986), and also conceptually replicated by Burger and Hemans (1988) using a closely related individual difference variable—desire for control (Burger & Cooper, 1979).

Pittman and D'Agostino (1985, 1989) reported a further series of studies in which control-deprived subjects were found to be more likely to make and carefully store inferences from textual materials, and that this effect was due to differences in on-line as opposed to memory-based processing. Other studies found control-deprived subjects more willing to exert effort to obtain information (D'Agostino & Pittman, 1982), and more interested in and sensitive to diagnostic information about an interaction partner (Swann, Stephenson, & Pittman, 1981).

Pittman and D'Agostino (1985, 1989) argued that an experience with control deprivation (in a setting in which control was expected and desired) calls into question the general adequacy of one's understanding of the way things work, leading to a change in the mode of information processing likely to be employed. In an effort to ensure that controllability is reestablished, the person now processes new information in a careful and deliberate fashion (which could be described as bottom-up, data driven, or systematic) designed to generate accurate analyses that will be more likely to lead to understanding and control.

One implication of this analysis is that recently control-deprived subjects, because of the increased care and effort they will put into the construction of representations of new situations, may sometimes prove to be more accurate in their judgments and inferences and less likely to show errors or biases in situations where increased care and effort would be likely to lead to increased accuracy. This prediction was tested using the correspondence bias paradigm (Gilbert, 1998, in this *Handbook;* Jones, 1979; Jones & Harris, 1967). Correspondence bias refers to the "tendency to assume that a given action can be explained by reference to a correspondent disposition when actually people with a variety of different dispositions would have behaved in a similar way" (Jones, 1986, p. 44). In the attitude attribution paradigm (Jones & Harris, 1967), correspondence bias is evident when subjects assume that communicators believe what they say even when the communicators were given no choice about what position they would take in their speeches or essays.

Pittman, Quattrone, and Jones (1985; see also Pittman, 1993) predicted that control-deprived subjects would be less likely to show correspondence bias in this paradigm, particularly at higher levels of inferential generality (Cantor, Pittman, & Jones, 1982; Gilbert & Jones, 1986; Gilbert, Jones, and Pelham, 1987), because of the greater effort they would put into an attempt to construct an accurate representation. Given the underlying two-step correction process that has been identified as a major source of this bias (i.e., making the person attribution and then correcting for situational constraints) and the role that effort might play in the correction step (Gilbert, 1989; Gilbert, Pelham, & Krull, 1988; Quattrone, 1982; Trope, 1986a), the correspondence bias seemed a likely candidate for yielding to increased accuracy motivation. The results of the Pittman, Quattrone, and Jones study did show that control-deprived subjects were less likely to show the correspondence bias, particularly at higher levels of inferential generality.

The increased care in processing information by control-deprived subjects was also demonstrated in an attitude change paradigm. Using materials developed by Maheswaran and Chaiken (1991), Pittman (1993) found that control-deprived subjects were more likely than baseline subjects to rely on systematic rather than heuristic information processing (Chaiken, 1980) when forming their attitudes. A similar finding was obtained by Pittman and Worth (1990) using the Desire for Control scale developed by Burger and Cooper (1979) to identify persons high and low in chronic desire for control.

Depression and Control Motivation There are close parallels between the effects of experimentally induced control deprivation and naturally occurring mild to moderate depression on social information processing. Beck's (1967, 1974) model of depression and several versions of learned helplessness theory (Abramson, Metalsky, & Alloy, 1989; Abramson, Seligman, & Teasdale, 1978; Seligman, 1975) both assume that experience with inability to control one's environment is a precursor to depression. In these formulations a person's beliefs and expectations about uncontrollability are important mediators of depressive reactions. Weary, Marsh, Gleicher, & Edwards (1993) argued that experiences with lack of control lead to uncertainty about the true nature of the social environment. Such uncertainty can in turn lead to the kinds of careful and effortful processing that has been shown to result from laboratory manipulations of control deprivation, and to symptoms of mild to moderate depression.

There are several lines of converging evidence in support of this view. Experimental exposure to high levels of temporary control deprivation has been shown to produce the symptoms associated with depression (Burger & Arkin, 1980; Pittman & N. Pittman, 1980), suggesting at least a short-term link. In longitudinal studies expectations of uncontrollability have been shown to predict subsequent depression (Brown & Siegel, 1988; Lewinsohn, Hoberman, & Rosenbaum, 1988; Lewinsohn, Steinmetz, Larson, & Franklin, 1981; Pagel, Becker, & Coppel, 1985). In a different area of inquiry, studies of the overt task performance of moderately helpless subjects show that their performance declines only when the tasks are seen as having the potential for further loss of control (Pittman & D'Agostino, 1989; Snyder, Stephan, & Rosenfield, 1978). When the tasks are relatively simple and have no clear criteria for correct or incorrect judgments, or are otherwise not taken as diagnostic of underlying ability, then deprivation of control leads to improved performance (see the section on Illusion for an explanation of these findings). Putting these lines of evidence together, Weary et al. (1993) argued that because social judgment tasks are indeed ones in which there is no objective standard of correct or incorrect inference and impressions, and because depression is associated with feelings of lack of control and uncertainty, moderately depressed subjects should also show enhanced performance on social judgment tasks in the form of more careful and effortful processing of available information.

Several studies show that mild to moderate depression has effects on information processing similar to those found in studies in which prior control deprivation was manipulated. McCaul (1983) found that depressed subjects were more sensitive to information regarding the causes of another's behavior than nondepressed subjects—mirroring with the same attribution materials Pittman and N. Pittman's (1980) findings with manipulated deprivation of control. Marsh and Weary (1989) found that depressed subjects had higher attributional complexity scores than nondepressed subjects, and Flett, Pliner, and Blankstein (1989) found a similar relationship. Gleicher and Weary (1991) also showed that depressed subjects engage in more attributional activity than nondepressed subjects. Edwards and Weary (1993) found that depressed observers used individually-based information more than nondepressed subjects even when they had categorical information available, a result similar to the findings in research on outcome dependency (see the discussion below).

In the realm of information processing in the context of social interaction, Hildebrand-Saints and Weary (1989) found that depressed subjects showed the same increased interest in diagnostic information about an interaction partner as did control-deprived subjects in the Swann, Stephenson, and Pittman (1981) study. In a setting in which social information processing was measured, Weary, Jordan, and Hill (1985) found that depressed subjects were more sensitive to another's violation of a social norm, and similar findings were obtained by Marsh and Weary (1994). These findings of increased interest in information about others are complemented by Coyne, Aldwin, and Lazarus' (1981) finding that mildly depressed subjects were more interested in obtaining social comparison information following negative feedback than were nondepressed subjects.

Finally, Yost and Weary (1996) showed that depressed subjects were less likely to show the correspondence bias, a finding parallel to that of Pittman, Quattrone, and Jones (1985). In addition, Yost and Weary demonstrated that this effect was eliminated when a cognitive load was added, indicating that depressed subjects were indeed reducing the correspondence bias by relying on capacity-dependent additional information processing.

Despite some evidence to the contrary (e.g., Sullivan & Conway, 1989), the bulk of the research shows that mild to moderate depression leads to increased cognitive activity in the service of accuracy. Whether these same effects would be obtained with more severely depressed populations is still an open issue.

Manipulations of Situational Characteristics   Another approach to the study of motivational influences on the construction of understanding has been to vary some feature of the situation that could be expected to engage motivational concerns about the accuracy of inferences.

Expectation of Future Interaction   Early evidence for the efficacy of this approach was provided by Berscheid, Graziano, Monson, and Dermer (1976), who showed that when subjects expected to interact with (i.e., date) another person they paid more attention to that person's characteristics than when they had no such expectation. Monson, Keel, Stephens, and Genung (1982) also found that expectation of future interaction led to more elaborate and extreme attributions about the target. Feldman and Ruble (1988) found a compatible result in a study investigating whether young children would be more likely to use psychological terms in their descriptions of others if their motivation to understand others was increased through expectation of future interaction. Children ages five to six and nine to ten were shown videotapes of target children with whom they either did or did not expect to interact. For both age ranges, expectation of future interaction increased the use of central or psychological traits as opposed to peripheral or merely descriptive statements in the free descriptions the subjects gave of videotaped targets.

The expectation of interaction with another person raises the possibility that the partner's behavior will be important to interpret in order to understand and influence the coming interaction and its outcomes. So it makes sense that

attentional and cognitive resources would be mustered in an attempt to develop an accurate understanding on which to base the interaction. This interpretation has been given a more direct test in the studies on outcome dependency.

Outcome Dependency   Not only the fact of an anticipated interaction, but the nature of that interaction would be expected to affect the extent to which a person would be motivated to attempt to develop an accurate impression. In the research on outcome dependency, the extent to which one is dependent on an interaction partner for important outcomes has been varied to see if this variable moderates the extent of motivational arousal and the subsequent nature of social information processing (see Fiske, 1998, in this *Handbook*).

Fiske and Neuberg (1990) made a distinction between category-based and individuating or attribute-based methods of forming impressions. This distinction refers to the likelihood of using pre-existing structures such as stereotypes (heuristic or peripheral processing, top-down or theory-driven processing) versus constructing an impression from the raw data that is available about the target person (systematic or central processing, bottom-up or data-driven processing). Based on the evidence provided by the research on the effects of control deprivation on similar changes in information processing strategy, Fiske and Neuberg (1990) argued that outcome dependency typically motivates the person to construct impressions in a careful and deliberate fashion, relying less on stereotypes and more on individuating information, so as to have an accurate impression upon which to base control-relevant interaction decisions.

Neuberg and Fiske (1987) tested this prediction in several experiments in which subjects were or were not anticipating being dependent on another for a $20 prize. Information about the other was provided, including information that normally activates a stereotype and leads to category-based impression formation, as well as individuating information that by itself would lead to a different impression. The results across these studies indicated that subjects were more likely to engage in attribute-based processing and less likely to show the effects of category-based processing when they were outcome dependent on the other. These effects appear to be mediated by an increased concern with accuracy in the outcome-dependent conditions.

Erber and Fiske (1984) created outcome dependency and an expectation of competence, and then provided some subjects with information that was inconsistent with the expectation. They found that outcome-dependent subjects paid more attention to inconsistent information, and thought more about it, than did non-outcome-dependent subjects. With consistent information there were no such differences in attention and processing, suggesting that outcome-dependent subjects are particularly vigilant for information that suggests an expectation may be erroneous. This finding fits with the earlier research on expectation violation that found increased attention and deeper processing when information was unexpected (Clary & Tesser, 1983; Hastie, 1984; Pyszczynski & Greenberg, 1981; Wong & Weiner, 1981), and shows that this effect is related to or at least modulated by differences in situationally induced control motivation. Darley, Fleming, Hilton, and Swann (1988) also showed that when perceivers were dependent on each other, they sought more individuating information from their interaction partners.

These findings, when coordinated with the Neuberg and Fiske (1987) findings on time spent considering information about an interaction partner (time spent increases when outcome dependent—studies 1 and 2) and the parallel effects of accuracy instructions (study 3), and the Swann, Stephenson, and Pittman (1981) and the Hildebrand-Saints and Weary (1989) findings of increased interest in diagnostic information about an interaction partner due to prior deprivation of control or to depression, clearly suggest a [control motivation] → [interest in accuracy] → [change in information processing strategy] causal chain.

Fiske and her colleagues (Depret & Fiske, 1993; Fiske, 1993; Fiske, Morling, & Stevens, 1996) have extended the control motivation analysis to considerations of the effects of asymmetrical outcome dependency, or social power. Fiske (1993) proposed that the relatively powerless are likely to engage in the kind of careful and effortful processing of information about the relatively powerful which has been shown in the many studies on control deprivation and outcome dependence, but that the relatively powerful will not (because they do not need or care less to) expend such effort in forming impressions of the relatively powerless (see Depret & Fiske, 1993, and Fiske, Morling, & Stevens, 1996, for reviews of findings consistent with this analysis).

Personal Accountability　Another approach to situationally induced motivation has relied on making subjects accountable in some way for the conclusions or inferences they draw from a specified set of information. Similar to the effect of outcome dependency, this should create a concern with accuracy assuming that the subjects want their accounts to be judged reasonable. In fact this can be considered to be a different kind of outcome dependency, one in which the target of the inferences and the person on whom one is outcome dependent are separated.

With attitudes as the subject of information processing, Tetlock (1983a) found that when subjects were accountable, that is, they expected to have to justify their attitudinal positions to another person, their thoughts became more complex and less one-sided, particularly when the personal attitude of the person to whom the position would have to be justified was unknown. In the realm of impression formation, Tetlock and Kim (1987) varied whether subjects were told they would have to account for their personality inferences and predictions either before processing the available target personality information, after processing that information, or not at all. Consistent with the findings of Pittman and D'Agostino (1989), Tetlock and Kim found that more complex and accurate predictions were generated only when the accountability information was given before the information about the target was processed, indicating that the effect of accountability occurs as information is considered, as it does in the case of prior control deprivation. Weldon and Gargano (1988) also found that accountability reduced the usual effect of social loafing (Latané, Williams, & Harkins, 1979); on a task on which social loafing normally leads to less complex judgment strategies, accountability ameliorated the effect.

As with other sources of accuracy motivation, accountability has been shown to reduce the likelihood of primacy effects (Tetlock, 1983b) and correspondence bias (Tetlock, 1985). However, accountability does not *always* lead to more accurate judgments, because sometimes the willingness of accountable subjects to expend energy processing the available information and to generate more cognitively complex representations can lead to less optimum judgments. Tetlock and Boettger (1989) found that accountable subjects were more susceptible to the dilution effect (moderation of inferences caused by the addition of nondiagnostic information), presumably due to their willingness to try to use all the available information (also see Pelham & Neter, 1995). This is an important qualification to the general finding that increased accuracy motivation leads to more accurate inferences. Such improvements in accuracy will only be the case for those judgment tasks on which more careful and effortful processing is likely to increase the accuracy of judgments (see Pittman & D'Agostino, 1985).

Importance of the Task　Another way of inducing an accuracy set is to make the task seem important in some way, presumably motivating the person to come up with the best or most accurate judgment. Kassin and Hochreich (1977) found that when subjects were told that the task was important either because it was a reflection of social intelligence, or because it was important to the experimenter's doctoral research, subjects made more complex use of attribution-relevant information. Kruglanski and Freund (1983) manipulated "fear of invalidity" with instructions emphasizing the importance of the accuracy of the decision, as well as need for structure with a time deadline. They found that importance decreased the biasing effects of primacy, stereotyping, and numerical anchoring. Freund, Kruglanski, and Shpitzajzen (1985) also replicated the reduction of primacy effects using two different manipulations of the importance of forming an accurate impression.

Individual Difference Measures   There are a number of individual difference measures that have been developed to assess chronic preferences for engaging or not engaging in the kind of effortful and careful cognitive processing that is characteristic of control-oriented persons. These measures include: desire for control (Burger & Cooper, 1979; see Burger, 1993), which measures chronic desire for control; need for closure, which measures an individual's desire to attain or avoid closure on cognitive tasks (Webster & Kruglanski, 1994; see Kruglanski & Webster, 1996); personal need for structure, which measures chronic desire for simple cognitive structures (Neuberg & Newsome, 1993; see Moskowitz, 1993); need for cognition, which measures an individual's tendency to engage in and enjoy effortful cognitive activity (Cacioppo & Petty, 1982; see D'Agostino & Fincher-Kiefer, 1992); uncertainty orientation (Sorrentino & Short, 1986; see Driscoll, Hamilton, & Sorrentino, 1991), which measures individual differences in the tendency to approach and attend to, or avoid and ignore, uncertainty; and tolerance for ambiguity (Norton, 1974; see Andersen & Schwartz, 1992), which measures a person's tolerance or intolerance for ambiguous information and settings.

In each case, there is evidence that persons varying along these dimensions show the expected differences in cognitive activity and final conclusions that would be expected given the body of research reviewed here, and some of that evidence has already been reviewed. These measures clearly have at least some overlap, and the variety of supporting data certainly indicates similar effects on attention to and processing of information, but although a full review and comparison is no doubt in order, it is not within the scope of this chapter.

Summary   Taken together, the research on the effects of control deprivation and on the effects of mild to moderate depression establish fairly clearly that when experiences with lack of control undermine the sense that the world is understandable, the response is often to make attempts to develop more accurate conceptions in subsequent settings by devoting increased attention, effort, and care to the task of making sense. Very similar findings have been obtained with several different manipulations of situationally-induced accuracy motivation. Overall, this research can be organized under the general view that when prior motivational states, characteristics of the situation, characteristics of the stimulus, or individual difference preferences and habits activate control concerns, ensuing accuracy motivation results in more careful and effortful processing of information that will tend to produce more accurate conceptualizations when the information-processing task is amenable to more accurate analysis through increased attention and effort.

Illusion

Although it is clear that people are sometimes motivated to form accurate depictions of reality, it is equally clear that sometimes our motives are satisfied by or show themselves through distortions in those depictions. This tendency for motivation to distort conceptualization has been studied most intensely in the research inspired by cognitive dissonance theory, and in social psychology it was here that the concept of humans as rationalizers most clearly clashed with the traditional concept of "rational man" (see Taylor, 1998, in this *Handbook*). The very notion of a consistency principle would seem to imply a form of rational governor, and yet cognitive dissonance theory turned it into an engine of self-deception.

Control motivation, shown to lead to more careful and, often, more accurate information processing, has also been shown to produce a variety of biases and distortions. How can control motivation be conceptualized in a way that allows us to understand why, how, and when it leads to accuracy or to illusion? More generally, once a motive has been aroused, how does one manage to come to the conclusions that are desired without being aware of having done so? And what about the apparent self-destructive aspects of illusions? How can people operate effectively when they see the world through the distorted lens of illusory conceptualizations? These questions are addressed in this section on illusion.

The Motivation to Be Consistent   One key property of an understanding of the way things work, either in general or for a specific setting or set of events, is internal coherence of the explanatory system. Part of making sense of things is that perceptions, explanations, and beliefs hang together; do not contradict one another; or follow from one another within the assumptions of the framework of understanding. Likewise, expectations and events should show a reasonable degree of correspondence. When expectations are violated the person is likely to gear up the available analytical mechanisms in an effort to restore understanding. Putting things together in consistent ways, to form a coherent whole, was a basic tenet of gestalt psychology, a heritage brought to social psychology by Lewin (1951) and Heider (1958). Piaget's analysis of cognitive development also emphasized the construction of coherent schema, via the processes of accommodation and assimilation (Inhelder & Piaget, 1958; Piaget, 1965), that would make sense out of the physical world within the constraints of the child's current model.

The idea that consistent structures are sought and preferred was a basic assumption of the early theories of cognitive consistency (Abelson et al., 1968; Heider, 1946; Newcomb, 1961). Some of the early empirical work demonstrated that missing bonds are completed to form balanced structures (Burdick & Burnes, 1958; Morissette, 1958), that consistent relationships are easier to learn and remember than inconsistent ones (Picek, Sherman, & Shiffrin, 1975; Zajonc & Burnstein, 1965), and that balanced structures are preferred over imbalanced structures (Burdick & Burnes, 1958; Jordan, 1953).

Inconsistency and Cognitive Dissonance Theory But, of course, things are not so simple as a model of rational consistency might imply. There will always be some inconsistencies, some unexpected or unexplained events, since most models of the way things work are not going to be perfect (often, they are far from perfect). Some slippage would have to be tolerated, some degree of puzzlement that stays below the threshold for doing something about it, or else all of one's time and energy would be consumed tracking down and making sense of every tiny anomaly. And if inconsistency does reach the threshold of irritation or concern, perhaps there will be a temptation to ignore or do away with the inconsistency rather than admit that basic assumptions about how things work are wrong. Particularly when current conceptions have been in use for a while, have been working reasonably well, and have no clear alternative that would be easy to embrace, then the desire for consistency could be expected to lead to resistance and distortion, and therein lies one of the recurring puzzles in social psychological research. On the one hand, accuracy is obviously desirable; after all, inaccurate conceptions are inherently dangerous since they provide an erroneous launching pad for excursions into reality. On the other hand, inconsistency can be upsetting, troublesome, and difficult to understand, and some inconsistency is inevitable in any case, so ignoring or explaining away will sometimes seem like good ideas. Piaget suggested something like this: the child sticks with a current conception, even in the face of mounting evidence that it doesn't work, until reality and development allow a move to a better system of understanding. A compatible popular philosophical reference, suggesting that just these kinds of processes operate in the conduct of science, is Kuhn's (1962) suggestion that theories are not displaced by inconsistent evidence, since a good deal of inconsistent evidence is typically not enough to lead to the abandonment of a dominant paradigm until a better or more appealing approach becomes available.

If people like their explanations to have consistency, they should also dislike inconsistencies and should be motivated to resolve any obvious inconsistencies that arise. This was the basic assumption of Festinger's (1957) theory of cognitive dissonance. Cognitive dissonance research, once a dominant interest, waned in the late 1970s and 1980s, and this decline in interest has been the subject of several recent commentaries (see Aronson, 1992; Berkowitz, 1992; Berkowitz & Devine, 1989). However, along with the return of interest in motivation has come an unexpected significant other: like Lazarus or Dracula (depending on your sentiments), cognitive dissonance research is also back!

Cognitive Dissonance Theory Festinger (1957) proposed that when cognitive elements are in an inconsistent relationship they will create negative psychological tension, motivating the person to resolve the inconsistency so as to reduce the tension (see Eagly & Chaiken, 1998, in this *Handbook,* and Petty & Wegener, 1998, in this *Handbook,* for additional coverage of this topic). While most of the research was based on a simple two-cognitive-element version of the theory, Festinger also proposed that the total amount of negative psychological tension aroused would be determined by the proportion of relevant, weighted elements that are involved in dissonant relationships—where "relevant" means that only those elements that are consistent or inconsistent (i.e., not irrelevant) are included in the calculation, and weighting is done by considering the importance of each element. Dissonance reduction is achieved when changes in the cognitive structure bring the total amount of negative psychological tension down to the threshold of acceptability. Changing cognitive elements to make them more consistent or adding new consonant elements to reduce the proportion of dissonant relationships are the two modes of dissonance reduction that were studied in the early research.

Dissonance theory quickly generated a great deal of research (see Wicklund & Brehm, 1976, and Cooper & Fazio, 1984, for reviews) and a great deal of controversy. One implication of this early research is that people may often act in ways that are not entirely rational in the service of inconsistency reduction. They will change their beliefs to bring them into agreement with their behavior, blame their inconsistent behavior on situational constraints, embrace any available justification, convince themselves that their choices are much better than they thought they were before they made them, and selectively avoid new information that might imply inconsistency. In other words, people in these experiments seemed to be more interested in the illusion of consistency than in consistency itself. These findings were not easily accepted as presented and resulted in a number of alternative explanations for dissonance phenomenon.

The initial controversy, sparked by the reverse reinforcement effect obtained in the Festinger and Carlsmith (1959) experiment (i.e., the finding that participants paid only $1 to endorse an attitude-inconsistent position were more likely to adopt that position than were participants who were paid $20), was over whether this novel finding was simply an artifact of the experimental procedures. For example, Rosenberg (1965) argued that the Festinger and Carlsmith (1959) findings were the result of *evaluative apprehension* induced by using a single experimenter, suggesting that if the participants' concerns about how they appeared to the experimenter were eliminated the "reverse incentive" effect would also disappear. This controversy was resolved when Linder, Cooper, and Jones (1967) demonstrated that dissonance effects would be obtained only when the participants perceived that they had a choice to engage in counterattitudinal behavior, while reinforcement effects could be obtained under conditions of low perceived choice.

Another proposed alternative interpretation, *self-perception theory* (Bem, 1965, 1967), argued that participants in dissonance experiments were not experiencing negative psychological tension due to inconsistency but rather were simply inferring from their behavior, and the conditions under which it occurred, what attitudes they must hold through a self-attributional process essentially similar to that used for making attributions about others. One result of this argument was a series of studies designed to look for evidence of an increase in arousal after dissonance inductions. Several early studies obtained results indicating that participants were indeed experiencing the arousal that might be expected following the instantiation of an inconsistency (Kiesler & Pallak, 1976; Pallak & Pittman, 1972). This evidence for the presence of arousal was not consistent with the processes specified by self-perception theory. But it also became clear that the way in which arousal was involved in the dissonance reduction process did involve a form of self-attribution, one more similar to that described by Schachter and his colleagues (Schachter & Singer, 1962). Several investigators demonstrated that if arousal was misattributed to a dissonance-irrelevant source of arousal, then no evidence of dissonance reduction was obtained (Pittman, 1975; Zanna & Cooper, 1974, 1976). These findings suggested that the attribution of arousal to a dissonance-relevant source was a crucial mediating step in the dissonance arousal–dissonance reduction process.

The technique of misattribution of arousal was also used to establish some boundary conditions for the areas of applicability for cognitive dissonance and self-perception theories. Fazio, Zanna, and Cooper (1977) argued that with small discrepancies between attitude and behavior, defined as those within the subject's latitude of acceptance (C. Sherif, M. Sherif, & Nebergall, 1965; M. Sherif & Hovland, 1961), self-perception processes are likely to occur, but with larger discrepancies (those that fall in the subject's latitude of rejection), dissonance processes are more likely to predominate. By leading participants to misattribute arousal to an irrelevant source, Fazio et al. showed that such misattribution of arousal eliminated attitude change when the discrepancy was in the latitude of rejection, consistent with dissonance theory, but not when the discrepancy was within the latitude of acceptance, consistent with self-perception theory. This result seemed to put the dissonance versus self-perception controversy to rest.

The idea that cognitive dissonance results were simply an example of external *self-presentation,* not of internal changes in attitudes, was suggested as another kind of alternative (Tedeschi, Schlenker, & Bonoma, 1971). The research on this topic seems not to have come to as neat an end. Given the evidence on both sides, there seems again to be both self-presentational phenomena and dissonance results that cannot easily be explained in self-presentational terms (Baumeister & Tice, 1984; see Cooper & Fazio, 1984, for a review of research on the self-perception and self-presentation controversies).

Since the late 1970s and during the 1980s research on cognitive dissonance theory proceeded at a much slower pace but did not stop entirely. Research continued on applications of dissonance techniques in psychotherapy (Axsom, 1989; Axsom & Cooper, 1985; Cooper, 1980) and, more recently, prejudice reduction (Leippe & Eisenstadt, 1994). Some new findings on selective exposure to information as a result of cognitive dissonance were reported (Frey, 1986). One area of research that did continue, however, was the work targeted on the role of arousal in the dissonance reduction process.

Dissonance as Negative Psychological Tension   While the earlier work on arousal produced by cognitive dissonance was indirect, in their second experiment Croyle and Cooper (1983) found clear physiological evidence of dissonance arousal, although they were not able to reproduce the typical attitude change findings in this study. Subsequently Elkin and Leippe (1986) were able to demonstrate both arousal increases (GSR) and attitude change following a dissonance induction, but they also obtained an intriguing additional result: attitude change did not lead to a reduction in arousal, but participants who were not given an attitude posttest (not given an "opportunity" to reduce dissonance) did show decreases in arousal. Elkin and Leippe also failed to find significant within-cell correlations between attitude change and arousal. They speculated that perhaps, in natural settings, dissonance is simply ignored or tolerated for some time until it dissipates. Losch and Cacioppo (1990) attempted to assess the separate contributions of arousal and negative affect to the dissonance reduction process. Their results, using a neutral source dissonance-irrelevant misattribution cue described as producing either positive or negative affect, suggest that it is the negative affect, and not arousal per se, that mediates attitude change in the forced compliance paradigm. They found that participants in both of their high choice conditions were more aroused (GSR) than participants in the low choice condition, but those high choice participants who had been given a positive misattribution cue (and who therefore would be unlikely to misattribute their arousal, if as dissonance theory suggests the arousal produced by inconsistency is negatively toned) showed increased attitude change compared to the high choice participants who had been given a negative misattribution cue. There were also no positive within-cell correlations between arousal and attitude change in this study. Losch and Cacioppo concluded that it is negative affect, not simply arousal, that mediates dissonance reduction, but their evidence for negative affect was indirect since affective tone was not measured.

A study by Elliot and Devine (1994) does provide direct evidence concerning the role of negative affect. These investigators remind us that in the original statement of cognitive dissonance theory, Festinger (1957) specified *negative psychological tension* as the motivating result of cognitive inconsistency. This has been taken to include actual physiological arousal, and there is now ample evidence that such arousal is produced, but the active aspect of the changes produced by inconsistency may be negative affect rather than arousal itself. Higgins, Rhodewalt, and Zanna's (1979) work on the patterns of attribution and misattribution of arousal was consistent with this position. Elliot and Devine measured self-reported affect and found that participants given high choice to write a counterattitudinal essay reported more negative affect after agreeing to write the essay than did low choice participants. They also found that high choice participants exhibited more attitude change than did low choice participants, and that after attitude change high and low choice participants did not differ in reported negative affect. Across the two reported experiments, a modest but significant negative correlation also was obtained between amount of attitude change and final level of discomfort.

Taken together, the research on arousal indicates that cognitive dissonance does lead to an increase in arousal and negative affect, and at this point it appears that it is the negative affective tone that most clearly mediates dissonance reduction, although the definitive study in which both arousal and affect are tracked across the dissonance arousal and reduction period remains to be done.

New Controversies: Is Inconsistency Really Necessary?
The other recent source of cognitive dissonance research, perhaps not surprisingly given the history of the theory, stems from a new set of proposed alternative explanations for dissonance phenomena. Cooper and Fazio (1984) and Steele (1988; see also Schlenker, 1982) have proposed two different alternative formulations that reject the original theory's assumption that cognitive inconsistency leads to the arousal of negative psychological tension, while Aronson (1968, 1992) has revived his proposed emphasis on inconsistency with the self as crucial to the arousal of cogni-

tive dissonance, and the controversy resulting from these alternative formulations has spurred a new set of studies.

Cooper and Fazio (1984) have proposed a *"new look" alternative* to cognitive dissonance theory, reviewing a number of studies that suggest that the results predicted by cognitive dissonance theory in the forced compliance paradigm only occur when counterattitudinal behavior has consequences that are aversive (Cooper & Worchel, 1970; Cooper, Zanna, & Goethals, 1974; Goethals & Cooper, 1975; Nel, Helmreich, & Aronson, 1969) and foreseeable (Cooper & Goethals, 1974; Goethals, Cooper, & Naficy, 1979). Because these studies typically included conditions in which inconsistency without aversive or foreseeable consequences did not produce the attitude change predicted by cognitive dissonance theory, Cooper and Fazio concluded that inconsistency was not an important part of the mediating process in these studies. Their new look theory eliminates the entire line of reasoning based on the relations among consonant, dissonant, and irrelevant cognitions that formed the basis of cognitive dissonance theory, and instead argues that foreseeable unwanted events produce arousal which, if labeled negatively and as relevant to the behavior in question, will lead the person to reinterpret the event so that it is no longer unwanted.[2] In support of this position, a recent study reported by Sher and Cooper (1989) varied independently whether a speech was consistent or inconsistent with their participants' attitudes, and whether or not it entailed aversive consequences. Their finding was that aversive consequences, and not the inconsistency of the speech with attitudes, determined attitude change.

The new look position has been challenged by Aronson (1992) and his colleagues. Earlier Aronson had proposed a revision of dissonance theory, suggesting that cognitive dissonance theory makes predictions most clearly when the inconsistency in question involves an aspect of self (Aronson, 1968, 1969; Aronson, Chase, Helmreich, & Ruhnke, 1974). This modification, unlike the new look position, retained the original core assumptions about consistency and inconsistency. Aronson argues that all the aversive consequences experiments can be recast in terms of an inconsistency involving the self. For example, in the Sher and Cooper (1989) study, participants who made an attitude-consistent speech but who expected that it might "boomerang" and convince a committee to make the opposite decision showed the sort of attitude change typically predicted by dissonance theory. Because the attitude was not inconsistent with the position in the speech, Sher and Cooper reasoned that it was the aversive consequences of producing a boomerang effect with the committee, and not inconsistency, that was important. But this finding could be reinterpreted to argue that when participants knew that their speech might produce an unwanted effect, whether or not the speech itself was objectively consistent with their attitudes, they experienced an inconsistency between their behavior (I behaved in a way that produced an expected bad result) and their self-concept (I am a good person; see Thibodeau & Aronson, 1992).

This reinterpretation of the aversive consequences literature has been tested using a new dissonance-induction paradigm. In the "hypocrisy" paradigm, participants make attitude-consonant statements and then are reminded of past behavior that was not consistent with their currently expressed view. For example, Fried and Aronson (1995) had participants make a proattitudinal speech on the importance of recyling. When participants were asked to think about their own past behaviors after making the speech, they showed evidence of dissonance reduction when given an opportunity to volunteer for recycling-related behavior, compared to participants who in addition were given information that would allow them to misattribute dissonance to an irrelevant source. Since this procedure involves no aversive consequences from the current behavior, Fried and Aronson argued that these and other hypocrisy results could not be interpreted within the confines of the new look theory (Aronson, Fried, & Stone, 1991; Dickerson, Thibodeau, Aronson, & Miller (1992); Stone, Aronson, Crain, Winslow, & Fried, 1994).

In another study casting doubt on the new look position, Johnson, Kelly, and LeBlanc (1995) found that attitude change only occurred when inconsistency *and* aversive consequences were present, suggesting inconsistency is a necessary feature of dissonance-producing manipulations. Harmon-Jones, Brehm, Greenberg, Simon, and Nelson (1996) have also shown that the production of aversive consequences is not necessary for dissonance to occur. In their first study, participants who chose to drink an unpleasant tasting beverage showed dissonance reduction effects even though it is hard to argue that this behavior has any aversive consequences beyond the taste itself. In a second study, participants engaged in a counterattitudinal behavior that was private, and still showed attitude change. Their third study showed that the procedure used in the second study did indeed produce dissonance, by providing evidence of arousal in the high choice condition.

In another alternative formulation that rejects inconsistency as an important aspect of dissonance-producing situations, Steele (1988; Liu & Steele, 1986) proposed *self-affirmation theory*. Consistent with Aronson's proposed reformulation, Steele assumed that individuals are motivated to maintain a conception of self as effectively and morally good. When behavior suggests otherwise, such as in the forced compliance paradigm, it motivates a desire for self-affirmation. This may be accomplished by, for example, bringing one's attitude in line with one's behavior, or it may be done by any other means of self-affirmation, such as reasserting a valued aspect of self even if it is irrelevant to the original source of discomfort. Threat to self-esteem, not consistency, is assumed to be the impetus for this process.

Steele and Liu (1981, 1983) found that if participants were given an opportunity to affirm an important value, then dissonance reduction on an issue not related to the self-affirmed value was eliminated. Consistent with this theoretical perspective, Steele, Spencer, and Lynch (1993) again found that positive self-feedback eliminated the usual attitude change effects in the forced compliance paradigm, and also found that participants with high self-esteem (either measured or manipulated) also did not show dissonance effects even in the face of negative feedback, presumably because they (but not low self-esteem participants) had sufficient self-affirmational resources to absorb or defend against the implications of the self-discrepant behavior.

However, two different recent investigations cast doubt on Steele's rejection of inconsistency as a crucial element in studies of cognitive dissonance. J. Aronson, Blanton, and Cooper (1995) were able to demonstrate that participants who had been through a standard dissonance-induction treatment shied away from the self-affirmation opportunities most relevant to the source of dissonance in favor of dissonance-irrelevant self-affirmation opportunities. This demonstration of disidentification (Steele, 1990, 1992) is most interesting in its own right, but it is another finding in these studies that is most relevant to the current discussion. In these studies the dissonance induction led to attitude change even when opportunities for self-affirmation were supplied, in contradiction to the predictions of self-affirmation as an alternative to dissonance theory.

Perhaps even more directly challenging to the self-affirmation position, Simon, Greenberg, and Brehm (1995) have introduced yet another new dissonance paradigm, one that provides a dissonance-based alternative explanation for Steele's typical findings. Arguing that a mode of dissonance reduction open in the original theory, that is, changing the importance of an inconsistent cognition, has been neglected, Simon et al. (1995) presented another new dissonance paradigm, *trivialization*. Their suggestion is that dissonance reduction can be achieved by providing the opportunity for participants to reduce the importance of, or trivialize, an inconsistency. They argue that the self-affirmation procedures employed in Steele's research do just that. In the context of a self-affirmation that reaffirms the fundamental integrity and importance of a valued aspect of self, inconsistencies that might otherwise be bothersome are made to seem relatively unimportant. In a series of studies, Simon et al. showed that when participants were given trivialization opportunities, they eschewed other means of dissonance reduction, and they also demonstrated that self-affirmation opportunities do indeed lead to the trivialization of inconsistencies.

Perhaps the best way to view this recent set of proposed alternative explanations and their apparent rebuttal in some studies is to accept Berkowitz's (1992) suggestion that the attempt to specify or add on "necessary conditions" (e.g., relevance to self, or aversive consequences, or threat to self as effective and moral) may be misleading. It may be more sensible to view these conditions as moderating variables that enhance or diminish the basic dissonance processes rather than as absolutely necessary antecedent conditions.

Summary: The Return of Cognitive Dissonance Theory
One thing is clearly illustrated by the latest burst of research interest: cognitive dissonance theory is resilient. Having survived early alternative formulations based on evaluation apprehension, self-perception, and self-presentation, the most recent research suggests that the theory is also up to the task of rebutting the more recent alternative explanations based on the suggested primacy of aversive consequences or self-affirmation processes. It also appears that cognitive dissonance theory is still capable of generating interesting questions, and even new paradigms such as those based on hypocrisy and trivialization. New explorations into areas such as dissonance and humor (Hobden & Olson, 1994), dissonance and regret (Gilovich, Medvec, & Chen, 1995), and dissonance and inaction inertia (Tykocinski, Pittman & Tuttle, 1995) continue to arise, and Schultz and Lepper (1996) have proposed that cognitive dissonance reduction can be viewed as parallel constraint satisfaction.

One interesting implication of some of the recent research is that a preferred, and perhaps *the* preferred, mode of dissonance reduction may be simply to ignore inconsistency until it fades away. Elkin and Leippe (1986) found that arousal was most likely to fade away if participants were *not* given a dissonance reduction opportunity. In the hypocrisy paradigm (e.g., Aronson et al., 1991), evidence of dissonance-spurred activity was obtained only when prior inconsistent behaviors *and* a currently held attitude were both made salient; otherwise the rather obvious latent inconsistency was ignored. It is easy to imagine that a rather large number of such inconsistencies could be evoked for most people, suggesting that potential inconsistency is often ignored. Even when dissonance is aroused and dissonance reduction opportunities are present, they may not be taken. One example of a mechanism that might ultimately result in ignoring dissonance was suggested by Elliot and Devine's (1994) finding that participants did not immediately make use of an attitude change opportunity, suggesting that some plausibility constraints (Kunda, 1990; Pyszczynski & Greenberg, 1987; see the discussion of this below) may inhibit the immediate use of dissonance reduction strategies in favor of a slow dissipation as the dissonance-provoking incident is left behind in the stream of behavior (Barker, 1963). In this way, only the most pressing or salient inconsistencies need to be addressed in more energy-consuming fashion.

The status of inconsistency as a source of motivation has clearly been questioned from a variety of perspectives, and research on this basic issue is likely to continue. One

general question still to be resolved, if indeed inconsistency is a source of motivational arousal, concerns the origins of this motive. Is it an inherent property of cognitive systems, a distinct motivation on its own? Or is it a motive that develops in the service of more basic motivational issues of concern with understanding, control, and effective commerce with the environment, or is it an acquired concern generated by socially-defined expectations and norms for consistency?

Pan-motivational Analyses of Illusion   Recently several theoretical analyses of the cognitive processes through which motivational desires lead to distorted or illusionary conclusions have been proposed. The term "pan-motivational" is suggested because these analyses are targeted on what transpires after motivational desires have been aroused, without including in the formal analysis any restriction on what those motives might be, or how or when they might arise. For example, in their analysis of biased hypothesis testing (reviewed directly below), Pyszczynski and Greenberg (1987) specify the cognitive steps that might be taken so as to come to a desired conclusion, but the actual motivational concerns that would produce such desires could come from any of a wide variety of motivational sources, including ". . . needs for self-esteem, faith in the cultural world-view, ethnocentrism, control, cognitive consistency, equity, and a belief in a just world . . ." (p. 315). As such, these pan-motivational theories are about the *consequences* of motivational arousal, rather than about motivational arousal itself.[3]

After reviewing several of these analyses, using them in part to illustrate some of the sorts of motivated illusions that have been demonstrated in the literature, the discussion will return to control motivation to illustrate how the analysis of a specific motivation (control motivation) has been taken all the way through the process of studying how illusions can be generated.

Biased Hypothesis Testing   Building on previous work on biased hypothesis testing (e.g., Snyder & Gangsted, 1981), Pyszczynski and Greenberg (1987) reviewed the research on the self-serving bias, one of the sources of illusions that has been studied most intensively, showing that the tendency to take more credit than one deserves for success and less than one deserves for failure clearly involves a motivational impetus (as opposed to a purely cognitive explanation—see Miller & Ross, 1975; Nisbett & Ross, 1980; Zuckerman, 1979). They identified three categories of findings that implicate the presence of motivational influences. First, the sorts of affective reactions one would expect if participants in such experiments were motivated to make particular attributions are indeed present (McFarland & Ross, 1982; Mehlman & Snyder, 1985; Pyszczynski & Greenberg, 1985). Second, when these affective reactions are subjected to misattribution of arousal manipulations, the pattern of self-serving biases changes as expected (Stephan & Gollwitzer, 1981; Fries & Frey, 1980; Gollwitzer, Earl, & Stephan, 1982). Finally, the research on self-handicapping, because it shows that people will take action to place obstacles in their path in order to create excuses for failure, is cited as obvious evidence that people desire particular explanations for success or failure and are sufficiently motivated at times to create the necessary attributional conditions to be able to come to desired conclusions (e.g., Berglas & Jones, 1978; Jones & Berglas, 1978; Riggs, 1992).

Pyszczynski and Greenberg suggest that when perceivers are processing information they engage in hypothesis testing that may be more or less extensive, and more or less affected by motivational desires, but that the conclusions that perceivers will find acceptable operate within certain *plausibility constraints,* that is, the conclusions must be seen as sensible from at least some point of view (see Darley & Gross, 1983). When the hypothesis generation and testing process is actually biased by motivational desires, the resulting inferences still must have at least the illusion of objectivity.

Motivated Reasoning   Kunda (1990) has made an argument similar to that of Pyszczynski and Greenberg. She argues that motives can bias reasoning and inferences by subtly influencing the sorts of reasoning processes that are used, so that when a particular conclusion is desirable because of the arousal of a motivational state it is more likely to be reached, and plausibly reached, because cognitive processes and strategies are selected so as to make that outcome more likely. This is done so that the reasoner believes that the process was unbiased. This does mean that there are limits, or plausibility constraints (Pyszczynski & Greenberg, 1987), to the extent that bias can occur.

Particular motivations may have biasing effects through selective memory search and construction. Sanitioso, Kunda, and Fong (1990) found that participants who believed that a particular trait (introversion or extroversion) was more conducive to success biased their own self-characterizations in the favorable direction, but this bias occurred within the constraint of keeping the same overall self-view (i.e., participants moderated or made more extreme their introverted or extroverted status without actually changing that status). Evidence for an underlying biased memory search was suggested by the finding that participants tended first to generate memories in line with the purported valued characteristic, so that if introversion was considered conducive to success, participants tended to generate first autobiographical memories consistent with introversion.

There are a number of studies showing that people have self-serving personal theories of success (Dunning &

Cohen, 1992; Dunning & McElwee, 1995; Dunning, Perie, & Story, 1991; Kunda, 1987). A series of studies reported by Dunning, Leuenberger, and Sherman (1995) shows how the motivated inference bias identified by Kunda (1990) can lead to self-serving theories of success by using manipulations that in other settings have been shown to evoke an accuracy motive. In their first study, Dunning et al. (1995) compared participants who were to act as a therapist in front of an audience to participants who expected merely to observe such a performance. This manipulation should have made a good performance as a therapist more important to the actual performance participants, and indeed they proceeded to claim that the characteristics they believed they actually possessed were the ones associated with being a successful therapist. In the second and third studies, participants who were given success or failure feedback on a test of intellectual abilities were compared. The failure treatment would be expected to arouse control concerns and lead to accuracy motivation, as has been demonstrated in numerous other studies reviewed earlier. However, participants in these studies showed self-serving bias: failure participants were more likely than success participants to exhibit self-serving theories about the characteristics required for a successful marriage (Study 2) and to give more favorable evaluations to similar than to dissimilar others (Study 3). These results suggest that when the self is involved and the judgments are self-relevant, ostensibly objective processing can in fact led to self-serving conclusions. One general problem for future research is to identify the crossover point. When will participants actually seek accuracy, and when will they instead bias their apparent accuracy-seeking behaviors so as to come to a preferred conclusion?

There is also evidence that the employment of statistical heuristics can be altered to serve motivational desire. For example, although base rate information is often ignored, leading to erroneous conclusions that are presumably not the result of motivational desire (Kahneman, Slovic, & Tversky, 1982), it may sometimes be employed if a desired conclusion can only be reached through its use. In a most interesting study, Ginossar and Trope (1987, Experiment 4) gave participants a classic problem that has been used to show that participants typically ignore base rate information (Kahneman & Tversky, 1972). They found that participants did indeed use base rate information, but only when they were playing the role of a person who wished to come to a conclusion that could only be reached through the use of base rate information.

Another area of study in which biases have been shown to intrude is in the evaluation of research results. For example, Pyszczynski, Greenberg, and Holt (1985) found that participants who received positive feedback on a personality test agreed more with a study that suggested that the test was of high validity—and agreed less with a study that suggested that the test had low validity—when compared with participants who received negative feedback on the test.

These and other examples illustrate Kunda's (1990) basic contention, that the proposed mechanism behind many illusions is the construction of desired justifications that make use of a biased subset of all potentially available information and information analysis rules.

Need for Closure   Kruglanski and Webster (1996) have recently reviewed the research on need for closure. Need for closure refers to a person's current desire either to come to a nonambiguous conclusion on some problem, or to avoid coming to such a conclusion. As such it refers to what persons do after they have been previously motivated, as do the other pan-motivational theories. In the need for closure formulation, the source and nature of that prior motivation is what will determine where the person will be along the need-for-closure continuum. Variables that prompt haste in coming to a conclusion should lead to rather minimal processing, reliance on heuristics, and the construction of less complex explanations, all conditions that should be conducive to illusions and biases. Further, when pressure to achieve closure is high, participants may "freeze" on a solution early and stick with it. Thus manipulations such as time pressure, or indications that coming to a quick conclusion is desirable or indicates desirable traits, have been shown to lessen the amount of time and energy devoted to coming up with an accurate conception (e.g., Mayseless & Kruglanski, 1987, forming unambiguous, clear-cut opinions implies intelligence; Kruglanski & Mayseless, 1988, time pressure). On the other hand, variables that induce strong accuracy motives, such as an emphasis on having the correct answer or making important outcomes contingent on the answer, should lead to a desire to avoid premature closure and be characterized by more extensive and effortful information processing (see the previous section on accuracy in this chapter). As an example, Ford and Kruglanski (1995) showed that participants under an increased cognitive load were more likely to be affected by primed traits when forming impressions; they also showed that participants high in the dispositional need for closure exhibited similar effects.

Control and the Illusion of Control

Control Deprivation and Effort Withdrawal   Control motivation does not always lead to enhanced accuracy motivation (as reviewed in the earlier section on accuracy) or to improved performance. In fact, in the Pittman and N. Pittman (1980) study that first showed control deprivation leading to increased attributional activity, the same participants also showed decreased performance on an anagram solution task as has often been found in the learned helplessness literature. Pittman and D'Agostino (1985, 1989;

see also Pittman, 1993) have suggested that an experience with deprivation of control has two effects; it increases the desire to regain understanding and potential control, and also increases the desire to avoid the negative implications of any further loss of control. The person will thus be responsive to features of the situation that signal possible control restoration or that signal the danger of further experience of lack of control. If the situation is one in which increased effort, attention, and thought seem unlikely to fail, then accuracy motivation will predominate. However, if the situation appears to be one in which such attempts are likely only to lead to another experience with lack of control, then instead the person will initiate ego-protective measures. Such measures are seen in the literature on self-handicapping (Jones & Berglas, 1978; Riggs, 1992), where participants engage in effort withdrawal to fend off any personal negative implications of an unwanted performance. Such defensive measures can have the effect of maintaining an illusion of controllability ("I could have done it if I wanted to") although they are in fact more likely to guarantee that the situation will not be controlled or accurately understood.

When the "task" is a judgment task that seems to have no clear right or wrong answers, and when the behavior required is simply to pay attention and think, that is, no overt performance is called for, then the risks of a diagnostic failure are slim and accuracy motivation should prevail, as has already been shown in a number of studies reviewed earlier. But when the task calls for overt performance and looks like one on which attempts to exert control may fail as miserably as they just have on the previous task, then ego-protective effort withdrawal would seem a more likely outcome. Pittman and D'Agostino (1989, Experiment 3) tested this analysis by introducing a set of conditions that would have the effect of increasing the salience of self-protective concerns to see if that would reverse the enhanced information-processing effects found in their previous research. Ego-protective concerns were made salient by telling participants that the text-processing task on which they would be tested was highly diagnostic of ability (Frankel & Snyder, 1978). When this information about diagnosticity was not given until after the text had already been processed, control-deprived participants still showed better recognition of facts and inferences than did baseline participants, as in previous studies. But when these instructions were given before the text was read, control-deprived participants spent less time reading the text and performed more poorly than baseline participants when asked to recognize facts and inferences from the text, as would be expected when ego-protective concerns become ascendant.

Riggs and Pittman (1991), taking an opposite tack, showed that when the motivation to acquire control was increased the performance decrements usually found on anagram solution tasks were reversed. Following a control-deprivation procedure, half the participants were told that the better they did on the first part (the anagram solution task), the more control they would have in the second part. The other participants were not given this information. The performance decrements usually shown by control-deprived participants on the anagram solution task were obtained when participants were not led to expect anagram solution to increase control over the next task, but control-deprived participants performed better than baseline participants on the anagram task when they expected control enhancement through anagram solution.

One implication of these findings is that when the reaction to deprivation of control is ego protective and effort is withdrawn, or other defensive measures are employed, the person will become less accurate and more subject to falling prey to illusions and biases; part of the price of defensive behavior.

The Illusion of Control   The control motive can also lead directly to illusions of control. Because control is strongly desired, in ambiguous situations where the amount of control is difficult to ascertain, people might be expected to err on the side of believing that they have it. In this way, the control motive can show itself directly.

In an influential series of studies, Langer (Langer, 1975; Langer & Roth, 1975) demonstrated that people are indeed subject to illusions of control. She demonstrated that, on a variety of tasks in which outcomes are obviously determined by chance or random factors, participants are susceptible to the illusion of control. Langer argued that superficial control-related aspects of these settings, aspects that are often present in tasks where skill actually does play a role in obtaining desired outcomes, are responsible for the development of the illusion of control. This prediction has been confirmed in a variety of recent studies (Bouts & Van Avermaet, 1992; Burger, 1986; Dunn & Wilson, 1990; Fleming & Darley, 1990; Gilovich & Douglas, 1986). Biner, Angle, Park, Meltinger, & Barber (1995) reported findings that indicate that the person's need state increases the likelihood of the illusion of control; they also found support for the contention that these illusions of control are mediated by increased estimates of the role of skill in determining these chance outcomes. In one study, they found that the participants' degree of hunger affected both their confidence in winning a hamburger and their estimates of the amount of skill involved in the (chance) card drawing task that would determine whether the hamburger was obtained. Hungry participants thought they were more likely to win the hamburger and that more skill was involved in the card-drawing task compared to satiated participants. In a field study, Biner et al. (1995) showed a similar effect on state lottery games, finding that income level (presumably related to need for money) was negatively correlated with expectations of winning, and that the path

to these estimates went through estimates of the extent to which skill played a role in winning. Since Burger and his colleagues (Burger, 1986; Burger & Schnerring, 1982) have shown that participants high in dispositional desire for control are more likely to exhibit illusion of control effects, it can be argued that need state led to higher desire for control, which in turn led to greater susceptibility to the illusion of control.

The desire for control may also be related to the nature of thoughts about things that never occurred. Counterfactual thinking (Kahneman & Tversky, 1982) refers to imagining alternative worlds, events that might have happened but in fact did not occur. Counterfactual thinking is more likely to be generated by surprising or unexpected aspects of an event (Kahneman & Miller, 1986; Kahneman & Tversky, 1982) and by actions taken rather than actions not taken (Kahneman & Miller, 1986; Landman, 1987). These findings suggest some role for control concerns in the generation of counterfactuals.

Markman, Gavanski, Sherman, & McMullen (1995) investigated the role of perceived control on the generation of upward (imagining a better world) and downward (imagining a worse world) counterfactual thoughts. In a modified computer-generated "wheel of fortune" game, participants experienced either a near big win or a near big loss, and had been given control either over where the spin of their wheel would start, or which of two wheels would be theirs. The results showed that participants generated counterfactual thoughts about the dimension of control relevant to the choice they had (their wheel in the case of spin choice, the other wheel in the case of wheel choice), and affectively toned (upward or downward) based on the outcome associated with the wheel on which they focused. This finding suggests a strong role for control in the generation of thoughts about what might have been.

Taylor and Brown (1988, 1994), in their review of illusions and well-being, document three related positive illusions that appear to be common: unrealistically positive self-evaluations (e.g., Greenwald, 1980), exaggerated perceptions of control or mastery, and unrealistic optimism. For example, people generally believe they are more likely to experience positive outcomes (Weinstein, 1980) and less likely to experience negative outcomes (Kuiper, MacDonald, & Derry, 1983; Perloff & Fetzer, 1986; Robertson, 1977) than are other people. Taylor and Brown reviewed a variety of evidence suggesting that such positive illusions are associated with positive mental health outcomes. But since accuracy would seem to be required for effective action, how can illusions be good? Two pan-motivational models that make a distinction between thinking about acting and acting may provide at least part of the answer.

One of these models about how motivation can bias conclusions and create illusions in a positive way has been suggested by Hilton and Darley (1991). The general perspective taken in the interaction goals approach (Jones & Thibaut, 1958) is that the perceiver is a goal-driven, motivated actor, with limited resources *and* specific intended outcomes (e.g., Bargh, 1989; Fiske & Neuberg, 1990; Hilton, Darley, & Fleming, 1989; Miller & Turnbull, 1986; Srull & Wyer, 1986; Swann, 1984).

The interaction goals analysis, stemming from Jones and Thibaut (1958), specifies a range of interaction goals, from relatively permanent or basic goals to transient goals initiated by the specifics of the situation (see Gilbert, 1998, in this *Handbook*). These goals are subject to correction and modification as an interaction progresses (see also Bargh, 1990). How might one categorize the wide variety of possible goals? Jones and Thibaut (1958) made a distinction among causal-genetic sets (what caused an actor to behave in a particular way), value-maintenance sets (the approach and avoid-relevant aspects of an interaction partner), and situation-matching sets (finding the appropriate social norms for the current situation). However, Hilton and Darley (1991) suggest a different classification, distinguishing between *assessment sets* and *action sets*. When they are in assessment sets, perceivers are trying to generate correct impressions by carefully processing available information (see the review of accuracy earlier in this chapter). In action sets, however, participants are actively working toward some more concrete goal, and impressions are formed only to the extent that they are relevant in that context. Impressions in action sets would tend to be less rich, more stereotypical or category-based, and perhaps more automatic and less "corrected."

Action sets, which Hilton and Darley suspect are by far more common because people are usually doing and perceiving (not perceiving and doing), are more variable than assessment sets. Often it is not necessary to spend (waste) much time and effort on forming impressions because they are not really needed in order to act. For example, many interactions are so constrained by social norms that one need not pay attention to the particular actor fulfilling that role. Also, social interaction is often a process of negotiation in which actors make it clear what they want from their partners, thereby "creating" rather than finding the desired interaction partner characteristics. Consistent with this analysis, Hilton, Klein, & von Hippel (1991) found that expectancy effects were more robust when perceivers were using action sets rather than assessment sets.

A conceptually compatible analysis has also been provided in Gollwitzer's (Gollwitzer, 1990; Gollwitzer, Heckhausen, & Steller, 1990; Gollwitzer & Kinney, 1989) applications of Heckhausen's (1986) Rubicon model of action. Heckhausen made a distinction between behavior before a decision is made and behavior after a decision is made. Predecisional behavior is characterized by a *deliberative mind-set,* essentially the sort of accuracy-motivated style of information processing demonstrated in many of the stud-

ies reviewed earlier. Postdecisional behavior, however, is characterized by an *implemental mind-set,* where the concern shifts from attempts to figure out what to do to a concern with getting the job done. In an implemental mind-set, for example, thoughts such as "I can do this" and information coordinated to that point of view are more helpful since the decision to try has already been made. In the studies reported by Langer and others, participants are usually in the process of doing something. When asked to assess their degree of control, or to make decisions that would reflect their implicit assumptions about controllability, participants are probably in an action or implemental mind-set, and so may be making errors they would be less likely to make in assessment or deliberative sets (i.e., when accuracy motivation is ascendant).

Gollwitzer and Kinney (1989) tested the prediction that the illusion of control might be most likely, and even useful, when the person was already in a postdecisional implemental mind-set. They also predicted that the illusion of control would be less likely when the person was in a predecisional deliberative mind-set. In two experiments they found that deliberative mind-set participants were more accurate in their judgments of control than were participants in an implemental mind-set. This finding is quite compatible with other findings of reduction or elimination of bias when participants are accuracy-motivated, and suggests that the optimism associated with the illusion of control is most likely (and perhaps most useful) once the person is in an action or implemental mind-set.

The distinction between an assessment or deliberative set, and an action or implemental set made by Hilton and Darley (1991) and by Gollwitzer and Kinney (1989) may make sense of the illusion of control and mental health findings. Taylor and Gollwitzer (1995), using the deliberative-implemental analysis, argued that such illusions are less likely when persons are in a deliberative or pre-action phase, and more likely when persons are in an implemental or postdecisional phase. In three studies a deliberative mind-set was induced by asking participants to think about an unresolved personal problem, one for which the person had not decided whether to act or how to act, while an implemental mind-set was induced by asking participants to think about a project they had decided to start or had already started. The results indicated that participants in a deliberative mind-set were indeed less likely to show positive illusions than implemental mind-set participants, with baseline participants generally falling between these two groups.

The deliberative mind-set is presumably one in which the person has an accuracy goal, wanting to make the correct decision about whether to act, and if so how to act. The implemental mind-set, however, as Hilton and Darley (1991) have suggested, is more a case of doing and thinking than of thinking and doing, since the decision to act has already been made. It makes sense that in an implemental mind-set, resources are targeted on success or control rather than an evaluation of the situation since such an evaluation has either already been made, or is not considered to be necessary.

Summary   Overall the research on illusions shows clearly that sometimes motivation can intrude to bias beliefs, interpretations, and conclusions. In the research on cognitive dissonance theory, the motive to reduce the negative psychological tension produced by inconsistency can lead to attitude change, the addition of justifications, and changes in the perceived importance of attitudes and behaviors (but as we have seen, this interpretation has been and continues to be the subject of controversy). More generally, the activation of a variety of specific motivational sources can lead to subtle distortions in the reasoning process that have the effect of producing motivationally compatible conclusions. The work on control and the illusion of control, and on mind-sets, suggest two different ways of understanding when accuracy or comforting illusions will predominate. In the control motivation research, the relative salience of the opportunity to regain feelings of understanding and control versus the threat of further experience with inability to understand and control has been shown to determine whether accuracy motivation will predominate. The work on mind sets points to the importance of distinguishing the nature of the person's general goal or action state. Accuracy motivation is likely to predominate when a person is in the process of deciding what to do, while motivationally compatible illusions are more likely when the person has decided to act and is in the process of acting or about to act.

ACTING ON AND IN THE WORLD

The work on accuracy and illusion is primarily about cognitive representations, about the motivations that underlie and influence the construction and alteration of understanding. But this research (with some exceptions, of course) generally tends not to focus on meaningful overt behavior. Rather, it is designed to examine what happens to understanding either independently of overt action, before some often unspecified action might occur, or, as in the case of cognitive dissonance theory, after action has occurred. The dependent variables commonly used in this research are, appropriately, those most closely tied to and likely to reveal information about cognitive activity. But people are doers as well as thinkers, makers and destroyers of physical constructions both magnificent and trivial. The distinctions made by Hilton and Darley (1991), who assert that people are probably more often doing and thinking (action sets) rather than thinking and doing (assessment sets), and by Taylor and Gollwitzer (1995), who underline the differ-

ences between deliberative and implemental sets, point us in the direction of considering other aspects of behavior.

Understanding how motivation exerts its influence on overt behavior is a topic that can be considered in its own right. Identifying the motivational systems and preferences that underlie behavior is one major research enterprise. Sometimes attention is focused on the aspects of activities that are inherently satisfying, while at other times the focus is instead on more distant goals, and current actions are treated as steps along the way to those ends. The kinds of preferences and actions associated with these two different motivational orientations have been the subject of a considerable amount of research, reviewed in the next section.

Another fundamental aspect of taking action concerns choices about effort exertion. People do make calculations about the wisdom and usefulness of action. They do not always expend maximum effort, or engage in all of the possible behaviors that are open to them. How motivation affects the likelihood of behavior and the nature of behavior is the other area of motivational research on overt actions that is reviewed below.

Intrinsic and Extrinsic Motivational Orientations

When a person engages in an activity he or she may take either an intrinsic or an extrinsic motivational orientation (Pittman, Boggiano, & Ruble, 1983). This distinction concerns whether the reason for engaging in the activity is seen to be inherent in the activity, or instead is seen to be mediated by the activity. When a person adopts an *intrinsic motivational orientation,* the primary focus is on rewards inherent in engagement with the activity; the activity is approached as an "end in itself" (Kruglanski, 1975). Features such as novelty, entertainment value, satisfaction of curiosity, and opportunities for the experience of effectance and the attainment of mastery typically characterize the kinds of rewards sought from engagement in an activity when an intrinsic motivational orientation is taken. When a person adopts an *extrinsic motivational orientation,* the primary focus is on rewards that are mediated by but not part of the target activity. The activity is approached as a "means to an end" (Kruglanski, 1975), either motivated by or a step along the way to something else. Features associated with an expedient approach, such as predictability, simplicity, and ease of completion are typically preferred when an extrinsic motivational orientation is taken.

The initial research on the consequences of shifting from an intrinsic to an extrinsic motivational orientation documented the existence of an *overjustification effect* (Lepper, Greene, & Nisbett, 1973). When participants are given rewards for engaging in an activity that is initially intrinsically interesting, they show a decrease in interest during subsequent free choice periods (that is, they are less likely to choose to engage in the activity) compared to participants who engaged in the activity without being given rewards (Deci, 1971). This effect has been replicated with a wide variety of activities, rewards, and populations, and the general phenomenon of a decrease in free choice interest has also been demonstrated with a variety of external constraints other than reward, such as lack of choice, surveillance, and deadlines (for reviews see Deci, 1975; Lepper & Greene, 1978; Deci & Ryan, 1985; Pittman & Heller, 1987; Boggiano & Pittman, 1992). In general, the overjustification phenomenon can be thought of as occurring because the addition of contingent reward causes a shift from an intrinsic to an extrinsic motivational orientation (Pittman, Boggiano, & Ruble, 1983). Once an activity is categorized as one associated with an extrinsic orientation, it is less likely to be chosen in a free choice period because the reason for engaging in the activity (an external contingency or constraint) is no longer available and because it is less likely to be seen as the sort of thing one does in one's free time.

Cognitive Evaluation Theory   Deci (1975; Deci & Ryan, 1985) has argued that intrinsic motivation is based on feelings of competence and self-determination, feelings that are often influenced by external constraints. These constraints, such as contingent reward, have two aspects: informational and controlling. The informational aspect of events can provide information about competence, so that positive competence information can support or enhance intrinsic motivation. But external events can also exert control over behavior, and when the external controlling aspect of an event is salient it can undermine feelings of self-determination and resulting intrinsic motivation. When a person is extrinsically motivated, it is the controlling aspect of external events that is predominant. These basic tenets of cognitive evaluation theory have received substantial empirical support (see Deci, 1975; Lepper & Greene, 1978; Deci & Ryan, 1985; Pittman & Heller, 1987; Boggiano & Pittman, 1992, for reviews of this literature).

Motivational Orientations and Information Processing
Although the main thrust of research on intrinsic and extrinsic motivational orientations is behavioral, there are several studies that demonstrate a connection between motivational orientations and information processing effects, providing a point of contact between the previous general section on The Construction of Understanding and research on motivational orientations.

Boggiano and Main (1986) showed in a series of studies that if two activities are put into an "if you do A, then you can do B" relationship, the second activity becomes preferred over the first (Lepper, Sagotsky, Dafoe, & Greene, 1982). This effect presumably occurs because the first ac-

tivity is seen as a means to an end, leading to the adoption of an extrinsic motivational orientation, while the second activity becomes an end in itself, generating an intrinsic motivational orientation. In an interesting study that can be interpreted in that light, Webster (1993) told participants that they would be participating in two different tasks and varied whether the second task was more or less attractive than the first (while holding the first constant). When the second task was more interesting, participants could be expected to adopt an extrinsic motivational orientation toward the first task and would therefore be likely to adopt an expedient approach to the task (e.g., "let's get this over with"). When the first task was more attractive, however, participants might be expected to savor it (intrinsic motivational orientation) before going on to the comparative drudgery of the second task. The first task was actually a version of the Jones and Harris (1967) attitude attribution paradigm in which correspondence bias is typically demonstrated. Webster found that the correspondence bias was significantly reduced when it was the result of the more attractive task, presumably because in savoring the task participants engaged in the kind of extensive processing that accuracy-motivated participants have been shown to use (see the previous section on accuracy). Webster was able to produce the same sort of result when the first task was modified to produce overattribution to the situation (Quattrone, 1982). In another study, Webster found that participants who scored high in chronic need for closure (Webster & Kruglanski, 1994) were more likely to show the correspondence bias than participants who were high in the need to avoid closure, again suggesting that those who are intrinsically motivated to savor the process of making sense are more likely to show the kind of information processing characteristic of accuracy-motivated persons.

D'Agostino and Fincher-Kiefer (1992) reported a compatible finding: participants high in the need for cognition (Cacioppo & Petty, 1982), who could be said to be intrinsically motivated to think about things, were less likely than those low in need for cognition to show the correspondence bias. D'Agostino and Fincher-Kiefer also showed that the addition of a cognitive load produced the correspondence bias even among those high in need for cognition, implicating additional processing as the means by which participants high in the desire for cognition typically avoid correspondence bias.

These results suggest that the nature of a person's motivational orientation toward an activity may have a great influence on the kinds of information processing in which the person will engage. There are also indications that these effects are related to control motivation. Thompson, Chaiken, and Hazlewood (1993) gave participants either an extrinsic reward or no reward for engaging in a brainstorming task, and then assessed their participants' subsequent free choice interest in more brainstorming problems. In addition, they were able to divide the participants into groups on the basis of two individual difference measures: need for cognition (Cacioppo & Petty, 1982) and desire for control (Burger & Cooper, 1979). The results indicated that participants high in need for cognition were more likely to engage in additional brainstorming, but that this tendency was undermined by extrinsic reward. The same relationship was obtained with participants high in the desire for control, and in fact the desire for control scores were the strongest predictors of this effect: adding need for cognition into a regression equation after entering desire for control accounted for no additional variance. This finding suggests that desire for control is related to both need for cognition and to the undermining effects of extrinsic reward, and indicates that further exploration of the relationships between control motivation and intrinsic motivational orientations would be useful.

Competence and Competence Valuation   Feelings of competence and self-determination play a central role in maintaining and enhancing intrinsic motivation in cognitive evaluation theory, and therefore much of the recent research has been directly targeted on these mediating variables. One interesting outcome of this research is that an additional variable, *competence valuation* (the person's investment in doing well or performing competently on an activity), has been identified by Harackiewicz and her colleagues (Epstein & Harackiewicz, 1992; Harackiewicz, Manderlink, & Sansone, 1992; Harackiewicz, Sansone, & Manderlink, 1985) as an important mediator of the effects of various contextual manipulations on intrinsic motivation. For example, Elliot and Harackiewicz (1994) compared the effects of mastery-focused (emphasizing personal improvement) and performance-focused (emphasizing specific externally determined performance targets) goals in interaction with the participants' chronic level of achievement motivation (Atkinson & Raynor, 1974; Mc-Clelland, Atkinson, Clark, & Lowell, 1953). Overall, mastery goals were found to have a more positive influence on intrinsic motivation than performance goals (see Boggiano & Ruble, 1978). As in previous work (e.g., Harackiewicz et al., 1992), however, level of achievement motivation moderated these effects. For participants high in achievement motivation, performance goals did not undermine intrinsic motivation, while for participants low in achievement motivation, mastery goals were particularly effective in enhancing intrinsic motivation measured by free choice engagement. In both cases, degree of task involvement and competence valuation were shown to be important mediators of intrinsic motivation.

In a related area of research, some previous studies have found that competition undermines intrinsic motivation (Amabile, 1982; Deci, Bentley, Kahle, Abrams, & Porac,

1981), but others have found that competition can increase intrinsic motivation (e.g., Epstein & Harackiewicz, 1992; Reeve, Olson, & Cole, 1985, 1987; Vallerand & Reid, 1984). For example, research reported by Reeve and Deci (1996) indicates that competition can lead to enhanced intrinsic motivation, but only if the person wins in a setting that is not controlling. Reeve and Deci compared a no competition condition to four variants of competition (no feedback about the outcome, lose feedback, win feedback, and win feedback accompanied by pressure to win). Winning tended to increase subsequent intrinsic motivation, while pressure tended to decrease intrinsic motivation. Path analyses indicated that intrinsic motivation was enhanced through increased feelings of competence when winning, and decreased by decreased feelings of self-determination when pressured, while competence valuation enhanced intrinsic motivation both directly and through feelings of competence and self-determination.

The mastery versus performance or ego-involved distinction can be extended to research on self-esteem. Waschull and Kernis (1996) suggested that self-esteem can be characterized by its day-to-day variability. High variability implies that self-esteem is closely related to and affected by current events, while low variability implies some disconnection or insulation of self-esteem from daily events. This variable might be associated with differences in motivational orientation. Those who are ego-involved in daily tasks, or performance oriented and thus vulnerable to fluctuations in feedback, likely take an extrinsic orientation toward many activities and thus would be likely to behave in less intrinsically oriented fashion than those with stable self-esteem (Deci & Ryan, 1992; Ryan & Deci, 1989). Waschull and Kernis (1996) found that those with unstable self-esteem tended to prefer easy tasks over more challenging ones (see Boggiano, Ruble, & Pittman, 1982; Pittman, Emery, & Boggiano, 1982) and were more concerned with external evaluations such as grades and pleasing the teacher. Jenkins (1996) reported an interesting finding consistent with these results. She found that women with a self-defining personality style, as opposed to those with a socially defined identity, were more likely to show autonomy in personal relationships and to take more social-system initiatives.

Increasing Intrinsic Motivation   Most of the early research on intrinsic and extrinsic motivational orientations involved examination of the conditions under which intrinsic motivation was undermined, or changed to an extrinsic orientation.[4] Having become experts at ruining intrinsic motivation, more recently investigators have turned to the problem of creating or enhancing intrinsic motivational orientations.

One area where motivational orientations has been shown to be important is represented in Amabile's work on creativity (Amabile, 1983a, 1983b; Amabile & Hennesey, 1992). External constraints have been shown to reduce artistic creativity through external evaluation (Amabile, 1979) and competition (Amabile, 1982), and motivational orientation has been shown to underly creativity in creative writers (Amabile, 1985). Conti, Amabile, and Pollak (1995) have recently presented a technique for enhancing a creative, intrinsic orientation toward new learning. Participants were given a pretreatment that either consisted of a creative pretask related to the learning topic, or an equivalent-in-content noncreative version of the same pretask. Participants then engaged with the main learning task under one of three conditions: task focus (an emphasis on why the task is interesting), test focus (an emphasis on test performance), or a mix of task and test focus. The results indicated that overall those who were given the creative pretask showed greater long-term retention of the material. In addition, creativity with the new material was enhanced by the creative pretask, but only in the context of a task focus.

One line of research with obviously important applied implications has been targeted on the behavior of teachers. In several studies, it has been shown that teachers who are constrained in ways likely to reduce their own intrinsic motivation to teach behave in more controlling ways and in turn are less effective in teaching their students (Flink, Boggiano, & Barrett, 1990; Garbarino, 1975). It has also been shown that students find learning more enjoyable when their teachers use autonomy-enhancing as opposed to controlling teaching styles (Grolnick & Ryan, 1987; Ryan & Grolnick, 1986). Wild, Enzle, and Hawkins (1992) tested an intriguing hypothesis, namely, that the mere perception of the teacher as externally motivated might be enough to produce differences in student motivation, without any actual differences in teacher behavior. In a setting in which teachers were giving piano lessons, the students were led to believe either that the teacher was being paid for the session or was an unpaid volunteer (the teacher was blind to this manipulation). The results indicated that students who believed their teacher was a volunteer reported more interest in and enjoyment of the lesson. In a free play period, students who had believed their teacher to be a volunteer were significantly more likely to try new tunes rather than simply repeat what they had been taught. This latter result is consistent with other findings indicating that externally motivated participants are less likely to chose relatively challenging activities than are those who are intrinsically motivated (Pittman, Emery, & Boggiano, 1982). These results point to the students' perception of the teacher's motivation as an important but previously neglected variable. If the teacher is perceived to be intrinsically motivated, the students are more likely to be intrinsically motivated as well.

Perhaps the most obvious way to increase the likelihood of taking an intrinsic motivational orientation toward an activity is to give or add to the activity properties conducive to the satisfaction of the motivational underpinnings of intrinsic motivation. Adding the elements of mental stimulation, arousal and satisfaction of curiosity, and experiences of effectance and control should all facilitate attempts to enhance intrinsic motivation toward an activity. Lepper and his colleagues (Lepper & Cordova, 1992; Lepper & Malone, 1987; Malone & Lepper, 1987; Parker & Lepper, 1992) have studied these aspects of intrinsic motivation. Malone and Lepper (1987) identified four components of intrinsic motivation: challenge, control, curiosity, and fantasy.

Lepper and Cordova (1992) and Parker and Lepper (1992) studied the effects of the addition of fantasy to learning tasks (cf. Fein, 1981; Singer, 1977). Lepper and Malone (1987) observed that in order for the addition of fantasy to increase effective motivational involvement with a learning task the engagement in fantasy must be compatible with the learning objectives. If it is not, increasing interest in a distracting manner could actually interfere with learning. Parker and Lepper (1992) examined the effects of adding several different types of learning-compatible fantasy to the task of learning a basic computer-programming language. In their first study, they found that the addition of fantasy elements significantly increased interest in the activity, and in their second study they found striking evidence of increased performance on both immediate and delayed tests of learning and retention (see Lepper & Cordova, 1992, for similar findings).

Motivational Orientations and Interpersonal Interactions The intrinsic versus extrinsic motivational orientation analysis has also been applied to approaches to interpersonal interactions. An interaction with another person can be approached as an end in itself or as a means to an end. There are several studies in the literature consistent with this viewpoint. Garbarino (1975) found that tutors who were paid treated their students in a more demanding and critical way than did unpaid tutors. Seligman, Fazio, and Zanna (1980) emphasized either intrinsic or extrinsic characteristics of interpersonal relations for heterosexual couples; they found that less love was reported by partners when extrinsic compared to intrinsic aspects had been made salient. Rempel, Holmes, and Zanna (1985) also found a positive relationship in couples between the extent to which the partner is trusted and the partner's perceived degree of intrinsic motivation for the relationship. Kunda and Schwartz (1983) found lower reported feelings of moral obligation for helping another on the part of participants who previously had been paid for engaging in a moral act compared to those who had not been paid.

The research on activities such as games and puzzles suggests a number of predictions that can be made for effects within interpersonal interactions. Pittman, Boggiano, and Main (1992) reviewed several studies more explicitly targeted on the effects of shifts in motivational orientation on the nature of interpersonal interactions. For example, in one set of conditions Pittman (1982) demonstrated the overjustification effect in a context in which college students were either paid or not paid for talking with each other. In a free choice period, students who had been paid were less likely to converse with their former partners than were students who had not initially been paid. Similarly, in the third experiment of the Boggiano and Main (1986) report, when the activity of playing with another child was presented last in an "if you do this, then you can do that" series of activities, interest in playing with the other child was enhanced compared to the condition in which playing with the other child was the first activity.

Extending this analysis to what is known about the development of person perception, Pittman and Dool (1985) predicted that six-year-olds would react favorably to another child offering a bribe (a cookie) for playing with him or her because at that age children see friends and playmates in terms of external characteristics. However, nine-year-olds were expected to show an overjustification effect to the same offer, because they have more adult-like conceptions of friendship in which bribes or external inducements are seen as incompatible with intrinsic motivation. As expected, nine-year-olds reacted to the offer of a cookie by showing decreased interest in continued interaction with the peer, while six-year-olds showed no such decrease in interest.

Clark and Mills (1979, 1993) have made a distinction between types of relationships based on the norms for exchange of benefits that characterize the relationship. In *exchange relationships* (such as business transactions), benefits are exchanged within a norm of equity in which the expectation is that benefits will be returned in kind, or paid back, and that the ledger of benefits given and received will be kept in a balanced state. In contrast, in *communal relationships* (such as friendships or romantic partnerships) benefits are given in response to the other person's perceived need, and no repayment is expected nor is an explicit accounting of who has received what maintained.

The initial research on communal and exchange relationships has yielded results consistent with this analysis. For example, when participants desire or have a communal relationship, they are less happy with immediate repayment of a favor (Clark & Mills, 1979) less likely to keep track of who has contributed what (Clark, 1984; Clark, Mills, & Corcoran, 1989), and more likely to attend to the other person's needs (Clark, Mills, & Powell, 1986; Clark, Mills, & Corcoran, 1989) than are participants who either desire or have an exchange relationship. Participants desiring a communal relationship also react with more favorable affect to an opportunity or a requirement to help (Williamson & Clark, 1992) and with more negative affect to

their own refusal to help (Williamson, Clark, Pegalis, & Behan, 1996).

These differences in preferences for and reactions to the exchange of benefits can be seen in the light of the research on intrinsic and extrinsic motivational orientations. For example, if one desires a communal relationship, one presumably hopes that both partners will be focused on the relationship as an end in itself and not as a means to an end. Given this desire, benefit exchange that has the character of tit-for-tat would be undesirable because it both signals and actually promotes an extrinsic motivational orientation in which the relationship seems to or does exist as a means to an end. In other words, at least one function of following communal norms is to prevent the occurrence of overjustification effects, avoiding the shift to an extrinsic orientation that would lead to an exchange relationship.

Some of the findings reviewed earlier are consistent with this view of communal exchange norms as acting at least in part as devices for maintaining intrinsic motivational orientations. The relation in couples between the salience of intrinsic concerns and reported love (Seligman et al., 1980) and between trust and perceived intrinsic orientation (Rempel et al., 1985) suggests a link between such norms and intrinsic orientations. In the Pittman and Dool (1985) study, older children reacted to payment for interpersonal interaction with the overjustification effect, i.e., they were less interested in continued interaction in a free choice period. By adopting a norm that obfuscates the relation between exchange of benefits and the reasons for being in the relationship, such losses in intrinsic motivational orientation can be avoided. This analysis raises the more general question of what knowledge or meta-theories people have about the existence of differences in motivational orientations, and to what extent they have developed tactics to promote and maintain desired motivational orientations.

There is some evidence that these differences in motivational orientation and in reactions to benefits given and received are governed by more general cultural norms. For example, Miller and Bersoff (1994) found that reactions to helping under various instigating conditions differed strongly between countries having generally individualistic versus duty-based moral codes (United States versus India). The nature of intrinsic and extrinsic motivational orientations, and the conditions under which either is promoted or weakened, may also be sensitive to cultural practices and norms.

Motivational Arousal, Effort Expenditure, and Task Persistence

People do not always engage or attempt to engage in the behaviors available to them. Understanding what determines when behavior will and will not occur, and how much energy will be expended if behavior does occur, are fundamental motivational questions. The research on intrinsic and extrinsic motivational orientations points to several determinants of the likelihood of engaging in actions when the person has a "free choice," and highlighting the differences between the two kinds of motivational orientations also points to differences in the vigor with which activities will be approached, and the nature of those approaches.

Expectancy X Value Analyses Another very widely used analysis for understanding when overt behavior will occur is the expectancy-value approach. In this view, the likelihood of behaving and the amount of motivation aroused is thought to be a multiplicative function of the current value placed on behavioral outcomes, and expectations regarding the likelihood of actually obtaining those outcomes (for recent reviews, see Kuhl, 1986; Feather, 1990). Analyses of this general type have been widely applied, but perhaps are best known in the work on achievement motivation (e.g., Atkinson & Feather, 1966; Atkinson & Raynor, 1974; Weiner, 1986).

Although a general review of this voluminous literature is beyond the scope of this chapter, some interesting interconnections between expectancy-value analyses and the intrinsic-extrinsic motivational orientation analysis, and, in particular, two developments related to expectancy-value theory are addressed in the next two sections.

One implication of the intrinsic-extrinsic motivational orientation research is that the expectancy-value equation for the same activity will be very different depending on the motivational orientation taken. For example, the important potential behavioral outcomes in the expectancy-value equation would be those inherent task qualities most closely related to the goals of mastery (such as challenge and entertainment) when an intrinsic orientation is taken. But a switch to an extrinsic orientation shifts the person's focus to value instead the outcomes contingent on engagement in the activity rather than characteristics of the activity itself.

Energization Theory One recent development related to the general expectancy-value approach is energization theory (cf. Wright & Brehm, 1989). Brehm and Self (1989) have directed our attention to the importance of task difficulty in determining actual motivational arousal. They proposed making a distinction between potential motivation and actual motivational arousal. In their analysis, potential motivation is determined by the variables traditionally included in expectancy-value analyses, but actual motivational arousal, designed to energize the desired behavior, is a function of the perceived difficulty of the task. If the task is seen to require little effort, then little actual motivational arousal will be seen. In this view, a general principle of energy conservation serves to govern the arousal of motiva-

tion so that actual motivational arousal does not exceed the minimum amount of arousal required to perform the desired behavior. If the task calls for behaviors of low difficulty, very little actual motivational arousal is needed, even when the behavioral outcomes are highly desirable. However, if the task is seen as impossible, then Brehm and Self argue that motivational arousal will drop to zero no matter how desirable the outcomes.

In a series of investigations, these predictions about motivational arousal and perceived difficulty have been confirmed using measures of cardiovascular arousal showing that task difficulty and actual arousal are indeed coordinated (e.g., Wright, Brehm, & Bushman, 1988). The energization analysis also predicts that goal attractiveness should be a function of the amount of actual motivational arousal. Because motivational arousal is a function of task difficulty, increasing task difficulty should correspond to increasing goal attractiveness (up to the point at which difficulty begins to exceed the person's ability or willingness to perform the behavior). These predictions have also received empirical support (e.g., Brehm, Wright, Solomon, Silka, & Greenberg, 1983).

There may be a number of interesting intersections between the energization analysis and the intrinsic-extrinsic distinction. For example, the energy minimization assumption may be particularly relevant to extrinsic motivational orientations, where an expedient approach, looking for the path of least resistance to the goal, is characteristic. It may be less relevant to activities in which the person becomes absorbed in the flow (cf. Csikzenmihalyi, 1990) of the activity and where involvement with challenge or entertainment may lead to energy mobilization beyond what might be thought of as minimally adequate. On a related dimension, the optimal level of desired task difficulty tends to be quite different depending on motivational orientation, with intrinsic orientations likely to elicit interest in tasks of greater difficulty than those preferred when an extrinsic orientation is taken. Study of the conditions under which enhanced pleasure in energy mobilization, and changes in preferred levels of challenge, could be related to the energization model may provide one approach to integrating intrinsic-extrinsic and expectancy-value analyses.

Self-efficacy Theory One determinant of perceived task difficulty is the person's belief in her or his own abilities in the relevant behavioral domain. Bandura (1977, 1986) has argued that personal beliefs about self-efficacy (one's belief in one's ability to exercise control over events) are crucial determinants of action. Other elements of the expectancy-value equation being equal, self-efficacy beliefs can determine whether one is willing to act, and with what energy and persistence such actions will be characterized. These beliefs about one's ability to control or exercise mastery over events have been shown to be crucial mediators in a large number of empirical investigations (see Bandura, 1986).

In relation to energization theory, self-efficacy beliefs are clearly relevant to the assessment of personal task difficulty, and one would therefore expect an earlier down-turn in energy expenditure in those with lower self-efficacy beliefs (see Brehm & Self, 1989, for a review of research confirming this prediction). These control-related beliefs are also relevant to the work on task persistence and helplessness (see below). One interesting finding from the intrinsic-extrinsic motivation research relevant to self-efficacy beliefs is the finding that a focus on evaluating one's level of self-efficacy can in itself be an instigation for changing motivational orientation from intrinsic to extrinsic.

Task Persistence: Mastery Orientation and Learned Helplessness   The likelihood of behavioral persistence versus quitting or giving up in a task setting has been the focus of a great deal of research. Learned helplessness theory (Seligman, 1975; Abramson, Seligman, & Teasdale, 1978; Abramson, Metalsky, & Alloy, 1989) has inspired a large number of studies in which lack of control leads to effort withdrawal. The current learned helplessness analysis proposes an attributional mediator, so that the way in which the inability to exert control is explained is the key to subsequent decreases in motivational arousal. Recent research from a social-developmental perspective provides some insight into the conditions that lead to a helpless or a motivated state.

In her research with children, Dweck and her colleagues have found clear individual differences in response to challenge and failure, patterns of "helpless" and "mastery" orientations, of giving up versus persistence, and improving versus declining performance (Diener & Dweck, 1978; Dweck, 1975; Dweck & Leggett, 1988; Dweck & Reppucci, 1973). Elliot and Dweck (1988) proposed that the goals that individual children pursue tend to lead to these differences in performance and persistence. They distinguished between performance goals, where the salient task goal is to evaluate one's own performance in the hope of maintaining or enhancing ability evaluations, and learning goals, where the salient task goal is to increase one's ability or learn new skills. In the former case, the focus on evaluating ability could make one vulnerable to inferences of lack of ability following failure, while a learning goal orientation should lead one to take failure as information that would allow one to learn how to do better the next time. In this scenario, people with performance goals would be likely to infer lack of ability and give up, while people with learning goals would be likely to persist. The findings reported by Elliot and Dweck, consistent with earlier findings, were in line with this analysis. In older children, these differences in orientation appear to be associated with differences in the children's theories of intelligence. Cain and Dweck (1995) found that third- and fifth-grade children who showed the helpless reaction to failure also held the belief that intelligence is fixed, while those children who showed the mastery response to failure tended to see intelligence as something that could change with effort. As a precursor to these beliefs about intelligence, first-grade children did not show these differences in implicit theories of intelligence, but those who showed the helpless pattern gave explanations in terms of outcomes, while those who showed the mastery pattern gave explanations oriented toward learning processes.

Several other investigators have reported data consistent with this general sort of analysis (Ames, 1984; Nicholls, 1984). Butler (1992), for example, using a similar performance versus learning goal analysis, found differences in the preferred kinds of social comparisons: children given performance goals showed greater interest in comparisons related to ability assessment, while children given mastery goals showed more interest in comparisons relevant to learning about the task.

A similar mastery versus performance analysis has been studied in the intrinsic-extrinsic motivational orientations literature. In that literature, although participants generally succeed rather than fail, mastery goals promoting a task focus tended to lead to enhanced or maintained intrinsic motivation, but performance goals tended to interfere with intrinsic motivation (Boggiano & Ruble, 1978; Elliot & Harackiewicz, 1994). Putting the research on intrinsic-extrinsic motivational orientations and the work on learned helplessness together, Boggiano et al. (1992) proposed a diathesis-stress model of the development of a helpless behavioral style. They proposed that children who typically take an extrinsic orientation toward school tasks, in which performance and ability evaluation is a central concern, are particularly likely to quit and withdraw effort in the face of evaluative or controlling instructional techniques. In other words, the conditions that generally lead to a shift to an extrinsic orientation may in children who are already predisposed to take an extrinsic orientation lead to the performance and emotional decreases seen in the learned helplessness literature (Boggiano & Barrett, 1985).

Considering the Links between Cognition and Action
When it comes to action, and the impetus for action, the role of cognition becomes problematic. Some of the theorizing on the determinants of behavior assumes that cognition precedes action, essentially a rational analysis. The expectancy-value set of theories implies, for example, that calculations are made of the relative attractiveness of potential outcomes and the likelihood of achieving those outcomes, and then behavioral decisions are made accordingly. While these calculations may not always be made consciously or with a great deal of intentional deliberation, they may often be made in just that fashion. In contrast, the

influential paper by Nisbett and Wilson (1977; see also Bem, 1967, for a position on the epiphenomenal status of cognition) showed that people sometimes have absolutely no idea why they have behaved in a particular way. There are extensive literatures on automaticity in its various forms (see Wegner & Bargh, 1998, in this *Handbook*) and on perception without awareness (cf. Bornstein & Pittman, 1992), both illustrating that action is not always the result of conscious or rational decisions. There are, therefore, ample illustrations of occasions when behavior control can occur without conscious access to its determinants.

One way of coming to a resolution on how to view cognition and behavior is to accept that sometimes conscious decision making, or at least decisions based on information available to conscious scrutiny either before or after behavior, does occur and does account for our actions. But at other times, the determinants of behavior are essentially unavailable to conscious scrutiny. The task then is to treat the extent and nature of cognitive control as a variable, and this view has been represented in several theoretical analyses.

The distinction made by Duval and Wicklund (1972) between objective and subjective self-awareness has the flavor of such an approach. When a person is objectively self-aware, the self is an object of conscious analysis and evaluation, and behavior is compared to the person's standards. In this state, behavior is more likely to be influenced by considerations about one's attitudes, values, and beliefs, and behavioral choices should be affected most clearly by conscious analysis. When a person is subjectively self-aware, the focus is on what is happening outside and the self is not taken as an object. It would seem more likely that the person would follow inclinations, whims, and gut feelings in this state and might therefore be less able (or inclined) to think and talk about reasons for behavior. Csikzenmihalyi's (1975, 1990) analysis of the experience of flow, of complete absorption in the ongoing feel of a current task or experience, might be thought of as a strong example of subjective self-awareness, as is Zimbardo's (1970) analysis of deindividuation, or Langer's (1989) of mindlessness. More recently, McClelland, Koestner, and Weinberger (1989) have made a distinction between implicit and explicit (or self-attributed) motivation. Implicit motives are those that find expression directly in behavior, particularly over the long term, without the person necessarily having conscious access to them. These motives are revealed only indirectly, through methods such as projective techniques (McClelland, 1980). Explicit or self-attributed motives are those that are accessible to the person, particularly for current specific behaviors, and can be measured through techniques that amount to direct questioning. Woike (1995) found, for example, that implicit motives are most closely related to the affective experiences that are most memorable. Explicit motives, however, were most closely related to the routine self-relevant experiences that are most likely to be remembered. Understanding more

about the connections between cognition and overt action is clearly on the agenda for future research.

COMING TO TERMS WITH SELF AND THE END OF SELF

Motivation in Theories of the Self

One extremely important and characteristic feature of human development is the emergence of a sense of self. As a person comes to realize that he or she exists separately from the rest of reality, the desire to achieve a sense of personal coherence and strength becomes a major theme and aspect of life. Recognizing that this is a crucial part of human nature, it is not surprising that the self has taken center stage in many recent theoretical analyses of human motivation. The way the self develops, the way it is shaped and maintained, how it copes with threats and personal disasters, how it grows, and how it influences and is influenced by our actions and emotions are issues that have been addressed in the research generated by these theories.

Research on the self is reviewed extensively by Baumeister (1998, in this *Handbook*). But because motivation does appear prominently in research on the self, a brief review is included here to show how basic motivational analyses and issues have been or might be integrated into theories of the self. This very selective discussion is focused on five theories of self-functioning: self-assessment theory (Trope, 1986b), self-verification theory (Swann, 1983), self-discrepancy theory (Higgins, 1989), self-evaluation maintenance theory (Tesser, 1988), and self-affirmation theory (Steele, 1988). All these theories assume that the maintenance or enhancement of self-esteem is a fundamental motive, but they differ in the other motives that are given central consideration and their domains of applicability are disparate as well. For the purpose of this brief discussion, these analyses are considered in the context of the main categories of organization of this chapter (the construction of understanding, and acting on and in the world). Interestingly, most of the work inspired by these theories has to do with the maintenance of self-conceptions and, therefore, is related to the previously reviewed work on accuracy and illusions in the construction of understanding.

The Construction of Understanding: Accuracy and Illusion

The research reviewed previously shows that the motive for cognitive control can often lead to enhanced accuracy concerns, causing a shift to more effortful and careful information processing designed to produce accurate conceptualizations of new situations. However, at times cognitive control concerns can also lead to motivated illusions and distortions. The work on cognitive consistency has focused primarily on illusion and distortion, in the form of rationalizations designed to reduce or eliminate cognitive dissonance. Among the theories of self considered here, illusion, avoidance, distortion, and reassurance are clearly the dominant themes. Only Trope's (1986b) analysis of self-enhancement and self-assessment is explicitly oriented toward gaining an accurate conception of one's self.

Accuracy   Gaining veridical information about oneself, about capabilities, areas of weakness, likes, and dislikes, would seem to be required in order to function effectively and to make wise decisions. Acquiring such information requires that one gain diagnostic information about the self. Learning about one's areas of competence, for example, requires tasks that are capable of giving diagnostic information. The commonly noted preference for tasks of intermediate complexity presumably reflects avoidance of unreasonably easy or difficult tasks because they are not informative about competence, i.e., success on too easy a task or failure on too difficult a task implies little about one's ability. Trope (1986b) therefore argues that diagnostic tasks should be preferred when people are interested in learning about their capabilities, when they wish to make a self-assessment. Such diagnostic assessments come, however, with the potential cost of learning that one has less than a desirable level of competence at a particular activity, so the long-term goal of accurate self-knowledge may come at the cost of short-term discomfort.

This analysis of the nature of accurate self-assessment clearly connects to the research reviewed earlier on the motivation to come to accurate conceptualizations. A variety of motivational instigations, primarily creating concerns about cognitive control, have been shown to elicit more careful and accurate processing of incoming information. Similarly, it would be expected that information indicating some deficiency in understanding of self might increase the desire for diagnostic information. Swann, Stephenson, and Pittman (1981) found that control-deprived persons showed increased interest in obtaining diagnostic information about an interaction partner, and it might also be expected that such motivational instigations would enhance interest in gaining diagnostic information about the self. Although such a program of research has not been done, one could imagine a series of investigations designed to see if the kinds of motivational enhancements of accuracy motivation demonstrated when the target of understanding is a situation or another person would produce similar effects on interest in self-diagnostic information.

However, Trope also assumed that self-enhancement (maintaining and enhancing a positive view of self) was a general underlying motive, and recognized that to some extent the concerns with self-enhancement and self-assessment are naturally at odds. He argued that the tradeoff was of the form of potential short-term cost in self-esteem for long-term gain in self-knowledge. The motivational question yet to be addressed comprehensively is when the person will be more concerned with assessment or enhancement.

Illusion   Most of the research on motivation and the self has focused on illusion or illusion-related effects. The motive for cognitive consistency has featured prominently in these models. Self-verification theory adopts the general idea of mental construction of reality, that people strive to construct coherent and stable world views. Once such views are well-established, there may be a strong desire to maintain those views, and to defend or protect them from disconfirmation. Self-verification theory (Swann, 1983, 1987, 1990) parallels in the realm of the self the findings of cognitive dissonance research. The theory assumes that persons are motivated to verify their self-conceptions, and the research on self-verification has shown that inconsistent information or evaluations will be ignored, rejected, distorted, or avoided if possible. Most interestingly, self-verification theory makes this prediction regardless of the valence of the self-concept that has been embraced, so that negative self-conceptions will elicit the desire to ignore, reject, distort, and avoid *positive* information about the self. The motivation to have a positive self-conception is thus pitted against consistency motivation. Swann, Stein-Seroussi, and Geisler (1992) argue that information that implies one's conception of self is erroneous constitutes a fundamental threat to a sense of cognitive control because failing to understand one's self implies a very basic misconception of reality (if I do not understand myself, do I really understand anything?). The theory thus includes the assumption that cognitive control underlies the self-consistency motive. Some of the research generated by self-verification theory has explicitly pitted consistency and control motivation against self-esteem motivation. In two studies Swann et al. (1992) found an apparent priority for cognitive control through consistency over the desire for self-enhancement. Recently Swann and his colleagues (DeLaRonde & Swann, 1993; Swann, Griffin, Predmore & Gaines, 1987; Swann, Hixon, Stein-Seroussi, & Gilbert, 1990) have suggested a two-step enhancement-verification process in which self-enhancing reactions are seen to be affective and relatively automatic, while self-verification processes are primarily cognitive and require processing time and effort, so that the addition of a cognitive load interferes with self-enhancement. However, when sufficient time and resources are available, self-verification appears to override self-enhancement concerns when the two are in conflict (Swann & Schroeder, 1995).

One interesting difference between the self-verification research and much of the cognitive dissonance research is that self-verification inconsistencies are typically not between cognitions and behaviors, but rather between cognitions and other cognitions. When confronted with an inconsistency between a self-concept and incoming information, participants in the self-verification experiments work to bring new information into line with old information. With reference to the dissonance versus new look controversy reviewed earlier, this research seems to suggest most clearly that dissonance-reduction processes can be fully activated without the introduction of any aversive consequences other than inconsistency itself.

Self-discrepancy theory (Higgins, 1987, 1989) also features inconsistency as a fundamental principle. In this case, the theoretically relevant source of inconsistency is deviation from a self-standard, either one's own or another's ideal or ought self. One unique aspect of self-discrepancy theory is that it predicts different kinds of negative affective reactions to discrepancy depending upon the particular self-guide involved in the inconsistency. Failure to resolve an inconsistency, a form of lack of cognitive control, leads to specific negative emotional reactions that depend on whether the discrepancy involves the absence of positive outcomes (dejection-related emotions) or the presence of negative outcomes (agitation-related emotions). The entire pattern of self-guide discrepancies can be used to make specific predictions about the psychological meaning of and emotional reactions to particular self-discrepancies (Higgins, Vookles, & Tykocinski, 1992). In contrast with the emphases of other self-theories, self-discrepancy theory emphasizes the action-oriented or self-regulatory functions of the various self-guides.

Whether and to what extent discrepancies lead to negative emotions is predicted to depend on the extent to which the particular discrepancy is cognitively accessible. This prediction also relates to findings from the recent cognitive dissonance literature. Just as it appears that a major tactic for dealing with attitude-behavior inconsistency is by ignoring such discrepancies, so too it seems that the potential negative effects of self-discrepancies may be avoided primarily by ignoring the discrepancy. That is, by showing in the reported research that these emotional reactions are provoked by "activating" discrepancy (through priming, reminding, making salient), the research on self-discrepancy also suggests that these emotions probably are typically avoided by ignoring the discrepancies that do exist. This raises interesting questions about how one might actually go about making a discrepancy *inaccessible.* This argument is similar to the Duval and Wicklund (1972) assertion that the state of objective self-awareness is typically unpleasant (because self-focus usually reveals ways in which the self does not come up to some standard) and therefore is avoided precisely because it is likely that self-discrepancy will be activated. In self-awareness terms, the way to avoid objective self-awareness is by adopting an outward focus, becoming engaged in external tasks and events so that self-awareness is subjective.

Self-esteem has been the central focus of several recent theories of self. Self-evaluation maintenance (SEM) theory (Tesser, 1986, 1988) posits the motive to maintain a positive self-evaluation as its central assumption. SEM theory is unique in its focus on social comparison processes as a means of maintaining self-esteem. By analyzing whether a comparison other is closely associated with self, the quality of the other's performance, and the importance of the dimension of performance to self, SEM theory can be used to make predictions about whether social comparisons will be characterized by comparison (comparing one's own performance with that of another) or reflection (identifying with the performance of another). The theory predicts that comparison processes will be biased so as to maintain positive self-esteem.

Self-affirmation theory (Steele, 1988), considered earlier as a proposed alternative to cognitive dissonance theory, suggests that positive aspects of self can be used to blunt or obviate the need to confront directly events or information that imply something less than the desired level of adaptive and moral adequacy of self. Steele argues that threats to self based on experiences that suggest less cognitive control or cognitive consistency than desired (but see the earlier discussion of self-affirmation theory for issues concerning consistency) can either be dealt with on a dimension connected to the specific source of concern, as in cognitive dissonance (Steele & Liu, 1983) or control motivation research (Liu & Steele, 1986), or alternatively by simply reaffirming some valued aspect of self. The assumption is that self-affirmation is typically higher in the hierarchy of motive importance than either cognitive consistency or cognitive control motivation, so that satisfaction about the adaptive and moral adequacy of self at any level, while again perhaps not particularly rational ("I'm OK here, so I'll ignore those problems over there") should relieve the need to do any further work.

There have been a number of attempts to pit these various self-motives (assessment, consistency and control, and esteem maintenance or enhancement) against each other, either to establish whether they are indeed important aspects of self-functioning, to find some order of precedence or connection among the various motives, or to determine the circumstances under which a particular motive is likely to be important. For example, Sedikides (1993) found evidence for the predominance of self-enhancement, some evidence for self-verification, and little or no evidence for a desire for self-assessment in one set of studies. However, the recent research suggests that indeed all these motives are important at times, so that the task is to understand when a particular motive will be active. In addition to Swann's work on self-verification and self-enhancement reviewed above, Jussim, Yen, and Aiello (1995) found evidence that affective reactions are dominated by self-enhancement concerns, that attributions and perceptions of feedback accuracy are most related to self-consistency, and that expectations and self-evaluations are affected both by consistency and accuracy concerns. Dunning (1995) found that self-enhancement concerns predominated when task feedback was related to an ability described as unchangeable, while self-assessment concerns predominated when ability was described as malleable (see the previous review of Dweck's work for related findings). Tesser and Cornell (1991) found that SEM, self-affirmation, and cognitive dissonance are all possibly connected to the same underlying motive (affect or arousal is their suggested candidate). Taylor, Neter, and Wayment (1995) added self-improvement to the list of self-motives (along with self-assessment, self-enhancement, and self-verification) and argued that what may activate all four motives is a situation of past threat or failure, or anticipation of some important future threat or challenge. Further work on when particular self-motives will be ascendant can be expected in the near future.

Action While the main focus of these theories of motivation and the self has been on the construction and maintenance of the cognitive construction of self, and associated emotional reactions to inconsistencies and discrepancies, some of this research clearly implicates these emotions in action choices. For example, Swann et al. (1992) suggest that people will choose their interaction partners, or more generally construct their environments, so that self-verifying information is much more likely than self-inconsistent information. Similarly, the self-evaluation maintenance model suggests that particular kinds of interaction partners will be chosen based on the person's desires for social comparison of a particular kind. Self-discrepancy theory views the self as a guide for action in the pursuit of valued goals. All these theories suggest that individuals will at times be likely to seek out or avoid certain kinds of information and environmental settings, but the specific nature of those seeking and avoiding behaviors would depend on the specific self-motive that had been activated. There is still room for much more work on the action implications of these sources of self-motivation.

Self-preservation and Mortality: Terror Management Theory

There is another development that characterizes human existence. Along with a young person's immersion in the joys and setbacks of life, constructing larger world views and achieving new behavioral competencies, finding and keeping an understanding of self, comes some extremely bad news—life ends. This fact, perhaps uniquely clear to human beings, by its inevitability and apparently inexorable negation of all of life's projects, is an aspect of reality that must be addressed in some way.

The issue of mortality suggests an examination of the more general and fundamental motive to survive, presum-ably a rather basic source of motivation. In their recent summary of terror management theory, Pyszczynski, Greenberg, and Solomon (in press; see also Solomon, Greenberg, & Pyszczynski, 1991) argue that because survival is the basic, or "master" motive, knowledge of the inevitability of mortality has to be kept at bay. They proposed that the survival motive and the knowledge of mortality lead to (among other things) symbolic defensive behaviors, in the form of embracing a shared cultural world view that suggests a sense of symbolic if not literal immortality (Greenberg, Pyszczynski, Solomon, Simon, & Breus, 1994; Greenberg, Simon, Pyszczynski, Solomon, & Chatel, 1992), and experiencing positive self-esteem, i.e., a sense of personal value (Greenberg et al., 1992). These symbolic defenses are thought to provide a buffer against the otherwise terror-evoking fact of mortality.

In support of these proposals, two sets of data have been reported. In support of the proposed _anxiety-buffering function_ of self-esteem, several studies show that increases in self-esteem lead to decreases in anxiety caused by death-related stimuli and decreases in defensive responses to re-minders of mortality. In support of the _mortality salience hypothesis_ (that as the salience of mortality increases, so does the need for symbolic structures that provide protection against death-related anxiety), participants who are re-minded of their mortality show a variety of positive reactions to and assumptions about those who confirm their world views, and correspondingly negative reactions to those who challenge or violate those views (see Pyszczynski, Greenberg, & Solomon, in press, for a review of the empirical research).

The proposal that self-esteem serves an anxiety-buffering function is compatible with self-affirmation theory (Steele, 1988), in which self-esteem is also seen as a reassurance against a variety of threats, and with self-evaluation maintenance theory (Tesser, 1988), in which the maintenance of self-esteem is seen as a motive in itself. It would seem to be at odds with the motives of accuracy and self-assessment (Trope, 1986b) and self-verification (Swann, 1983) theories, in which negative information about the self may be sought, and with self-discrepancy theory, which specifies a different set of affective reactions depending on the particular nature of the self-discrepancy. However, if terror management is only one function of self-esteem, and particularly if concerns with control are seen as aspects of a survival motive, then terror management theory gives us one more example of the need for discovering the circumstances under which a particular self-motive will be most (and least) influential.

CONCLUSION

Consistent with the recent emphasis on cognition, much of the recent motivational research has been focused on how motivation affects cognition, both to promote accuracy and to create illusion. Less effort has been devoted to how motivation affects action and emotion, and these links will presumably be the subject of more intense scrutiny in the near future. The separate investigations of cognition, motivation, and emotion that have recently characterized research approaches may have matured sufficiently for theorists to consider new attempts at developing more fully integrated conceptualizations of reactions to external stimuli, inner psychological experience, and overt behavior.

As research on motivation continues, there will surely be motives in addition to the ones featured in this chapter. For example, motives for self-improvement or growth have been suggested as targets for research (Taylor et al., 1995; Pyszczynski et al., in press). A need to belong, or a social motive, has also been suggested recently (Stevens & Fiske, 1995; Baumeister, in press; Baumeister & Leary, 1995; Pittman, in press) as a fundamental source of human motivation (see Batson, 1998, in this *Handbook,* for related discussions of altruism). Whether these additional motives will turn out to have heuristic value for new research ideas remains to be seen, but putting them forward does raise some larger issues. These proposals, the disagreements about the role and nature of self-esteem, the work reviewed earlier that attempted to pit the various self theories against one another, and the work on basic motives related to accuracy and illusion and to overt action raise more general issues about the relative hierarchical status of the various motives that have been proposed. Perhaps it will be profitable to view all the various motives as stemming from a few most basic sources of desire, or perhaps such reduction will prove to be unprofitable. But consideration of these larger issues may presage a new movement away from small, highly constrained analyses in favor of a return to more sweeping attempts to understand human nature.

NOTES

1. One can focus on how an understanding of a specific event or situation is constructed, or move to higher levels of generality that might include overall world views (cf., Wegner & Vallacher, 1986). Unless specified, the general "understanding" language is meant to encompass the whole range of explanations.
2. Although Cooper & Fazio still call their position cognitive dissonance theory, clearly it is something entirely different from conventional cognitive dissonance theory, though focused on the same data base. The term "new look" is therefore used here.
3. These analyses might also be referred to as secondary rather than primary theories of motivation, but since the term secondary may carry some evaluative connotation I did not wish to convey, I use the term pan-motivational to indicate the nonspecific nature of the motivational inputs to these models.

4. One exception to this emphasis on undermining intrinsic motivation is the research on the effects of verbal rewards, or praise. From the earliest studies of the undermining effects of reward (Deci, 1971), it was clear that verbal rewards tend to enhance intrinsic interest, presumably because they directly support and encourage feelings of competence or mastery (Anderson, Manoogian, & Reznick, 1976; Deci, 1972; Swann & Pittman, 1977). However, even verbal rewards can reduce intrinsic motivation when delivered in a controlling manner in a controlling context (Pittman, Davey, Alafat, Wetherill, & Kramer, 1980).

REFERENCES

Abelson, R. P., Aronson, E., McGuire, W. J., Newcomb, T. M., Rosenberg, M. J., & Tannenbaum, T. M. (1968). *Theories of cognitive consistency: A sourcebook.* Skokie, IL: Rand McNally.

Abramson, L. Y, Metalsky, G. I., & Alloy, L. B. (1989). Hopelessness depression: A theory-based subtype of depression. *Psychological Review, 96,* 358–372.

Abramson, L. Y., Seligman, M. E., & Teasdale, J. D. (1978). Learned helplessness in humans: Critique and reformulation. *Journal of Abnormal Psychology, 87,* 49–74.

Amabile, T. M. (1979). Effects of external evaluation on artistic creativity. *Journal of Personality and Social Psychology, 37,* 221–233.

Amabile, T. M. (1982). Children's artistic creativity: Detrimental effects of competition in a field study. *Personality and Social Psychology Bulletin, 8,* 573–578.

Amabile, T. M. (1983a). *The social psychology of creativity.* New York: Springer-Verlag.

Amabile, T. M. (1983b). The social psychology of creativity: A componential conceptualization. *Journal of Personality and Social Psychology, 49,* 357–376.

Amabile, T. M. (1985). Motivation and creativity: Effects of motivational orientation on creative writers. *Journal of Personality and Social Psychology, 49,* 393–397.

Amabile, T. M., & Hennessey, B. A. (1992). The motivation for creativity in children. In A. Boggiano & T. Pittman (Eds.), *Achievement and motivation: a social-developmental perspective* (pp. 54–74). New York: Cambridge University Press.

Ames, C. (1984). Achievement attributions and self-instructions under competitive and individualistic goal structures. *Journal of Educational Psychology, 76,* 478–487.

Anderson, R., Manoogian, S., & Reznick, J. (1976). The undermining and enhancing of intrinsic motivation in preschool children. *Journal of Personality and Social Psychology, 34,* 915–922.

Aronson, E. (1968). Dissonance theory: Progress and problems. In J. Abelson, E. Aronson, W. J. McGuire, T. M. Newcomb, M. J. Rosenberg, & P. H. Tannenbaum (Eds.),

Theories of cognitive consistency: A sourcebook (pp. 5–27). Skokie, IL: Rand McNally.

Aronson, E. (1969). The theory of cognitive dissonance: A current perspective. In L. Berkowitz (Ed.), *Advances in experimental social psychology* (Vol. 4, pp. 1–34). New York: Academic Press.

Aronson, E. (1992). The return of the repressed: Dissonance theory makes a comeback. *Psychological Inquiry, 3,* 303–311.

Aronson, E., Chase, T., Helmreike, R., & Ruhnke, R. (1974). A two-factor theory of dissonance reduction: The effect of feeling stupid and feeling awful. *International Journal for Research and Communication, 3,* 59–74.

Aronson, E., Fried, C. B., & Stone, J. (1991). Overcoming denial and increasing the intention to use condoms through the induction of hypocrisy. *American Journal of Public Health, 81,* 1636–1637.

Aronson, J., Blanton, H., & Cooper, J. (1995). From dissonance to disidentification: Selectivity in the self-affirmation process. *Journal of Personality and Social Psychology, 68,* 986–996.

Atkinson, J. W., & Feather, N. T. (1966). *A theory of achievement motivation.* New York: Wiley.

Atkinson, J. W., & Raynor, O. J. (1974). *Motivation and achievement.* Washington, DC: Winston.

Axsom, D. (1989). Cognitive dissonance and behavior change in psychotherapy. *Journal of Experimental Social Psychology, 25,* 234–252.

Axsom, D., & Cooper, J. (1985). Cognitive dissonance and psychotherapy: The role of effort justification in inducing weight loss. *Journal of Experimental Social Psychology, 21,* 149–160.

Axsom, D., & Lawless, W. L. (1992). Subsequent behavior can erase evidence of dissonance-induced attitude change. *Journal of Experimental Social Psychology, 28,* 387–400.

Bandura, A. (1977). Self-efficacy: Toward a unifying theory of behavioral change. *Psychological Review, 84,* 191–215.

Bandura, A. (1986). *Social foundations of thought and action: A social cognitive theory.* Englewood Cliffs, NJ: Prentice-Hall.

Bargh, J. A. (1989). Conditional automaticity: Varieties of automatic influence in social perception and cognition. In J. Uleman & J. Bargh (Eds.), *Unintended thought.* New York: Guilford.

Bargh, J. A. (1990). Auto-motives: Preconscious determinants of social interaction. In E. Higgins & R. Sorrentino (Eds.), *Handbook of motivation and cognition* (Vol. 2). New York: Guilford.

Bargh, J. A., & Thein, R. D. (1985). Individual construct accessibility, person memory, and the recall-judgment link: The case of information overload. *Journal of Personality and Social Psychology, 49,* 1129–1146.

Barker, R. G. (Ed.). (1963). *The stream of behavior.* New York: Appleton-Century-Croft.

Batson, C. D. (1998). Altruism and prosocial behavior. In D. Gilbert, S. T. Fiske, & G. Lindzey (Eds.), *Handbook of social psychology* (4th ed., Vol. 2, pp. 282–316). New York: McGraw-Hill.

Baumeister, R. F. (1998). The self. In D. Gilbert, S. T. Fiske, & G. Lindzey (Eds.), *Handbook of social psychology* (4th ed., Vol. 1, pp. 680–740). New York: McGraw-Hill.

Baumeister, R. F. (in press). Intrapsychic and interpersonal processes. In J. Cooper & J. M. Darley (Eds.), *The legacy of Edward E. Jones.* Washington, DC: American Psychological Association.

Baumeister, R. F., & Leary, M. R. (1995). The need to belong: Desire for interpersonal attachments as a fundamental human motivation. *Psychological Bulletin, 117,* 497–529.

Baumeister, R. F., & Scher, S. J. (1988). Self-defeating patterns among normal individuals: Review and analysis of common self-destructive tendencies. *Psychological Bulletin, 104,* 3–22.

Baumeister, R. F., & Tice, D. M. (1984). Role of self-presentation and choice in cognitive dissonance under forced compliance: Necessary or sufficient causes? *Journal of Personality and Social Psychology, 46,* 5–13.

Beck, A. T. (1967). *Depression: Clinical, experimental, and theoretical aspects.* New York: Hoeber.

Beck, A. T. (1974). The development of depression: A cognitive model. In T. Friedman & M. Katz (Eds.), *The psychology of depression: Contemporary theory and research.* Washington, DC: V. H. Winston.

Bem, D. J. (1965). An experimental analysis of self-persuasion. *Journal of Experimental Social Psychology, 1,* 199–218.

Bem, D. J. (1967). Self-perception: An alternative interpretation of cognitive dissonance phenomena. *Psychological Review, 74,* 183–200.

Berglas, S., & Jones, E. E. (1978). Drug choice as a self-handicapping strategy in response to noncontingent success. *Journal of Personality and Social Psychology, 36,* 405–417.

Berkowitz, L. (1969). Social motivation. In G. Lindzey & E. Aronson (Eds.), *The handbook of social psychology* (2nd ed., Vol. 3, pp. 50–135). Reading, MA: Addison-Wesley.

Berkowitz, L. (1992). Even more synthesis. *Psychological Inquiry, 3,* 312–314.

Berkowitz, L., & Devine, P. G. (1989). Research tradition, analysis, and synthesis in social psychological theories: The case of dissonance theory. *Personality and Social Psychology Bulletin, 15,* 493–507.

Berlyne, D. D. (1960). *Conflict, arousal, and curiosity.* New York: McGraw-Hill.

Bersheid, E., Graziano, W., Monson, T., & Dermer, M. (1976). Outcome dependency: Attention, attribution, and attraction. *Journal of Personality and Social Psychology, 34,* 978–989.

Biner, P. M., Angle, S. T., Park, J. H., Mellinger, A. E., & Barber, B. C. (1995). Need state and the illusion of control. *Personality and Social Psychology Bulletin, 21,* 899–907.

Boggiano, A. K., & Barrett, M. (1985). Performance and motivational deficits of helplessness: The role of motivational orientations. *Journal of Personality and Social Psychology, 49,* 1753–1761.

Boggiano, A. K., & Main, D. S. (1986). Enhancing children's interest in activities used as rewards: The bonus effect. *Journal of Personality and Social Psychology, 51,* 1116–1126.

Boggiano, A. K., & Pittman, T. S. (1992). *Achievement and motivation: A social-developmental perspective.* New York: Cambridge University Press.

Boggiano, A. K., & Ruble, D. N. (1978). Competence and the overjustification effect. *Journal of Personality and Social Psychology, 37,* 1462–1468.

Boggiano, A. K., Ruble, D. N., & Pittman, T. S. (1982). The mastery hypothesis and the overjustification effect. *Social Cognition, 1,* 38–49.

Boggiano, A. K., Shields, A., Barnett, M., Kellam, T., Thompson, E., Simons, J., & Katz, P. (1992). Helplessness deficits in students: The role of motivational orientation. *Motivation and Emotion, 16,* 271–296.

Bornstein, R. F., & Pittman, T. S. (1992). *Perception without awareness: Cognitive, clinical, and social perspectives.* New York: Guilford.

Bouts, P., & Van Avermaet, E. (1992). Drawing familiar or unfamiliar cards: Stimulus familiarity, chance orientation, and the illusion of control. *Personality and Social Psychology Bulletin, 18,* 331–335.

Brehm, J. W. (1966). *A theory of psychological reactance.* New York: Academic Press.

Brehm, J. W. (1993). Control, its loss, and psychological reactance. In G. Weary, F. Gleicher, & K. Marsh (Eds.), *Control motivation and social cognition* (pp. 3–30). New York: Springer-Verlag.

Brehm, J. W. (1992). An unidentified theoretical object. *Psychological Inquiry, 3,* 314–315.

Brehm, J. W., & Self, E. A. (1989). The intensity of motivation. *Annual Review of Psychology, 40,* 109–131.

Brehm, J. W., Wright, R. A., Solomon, S., Silka, L., & Greenberg, J. (1983). Perceived difficulty, energization, and the magnitude of goal valence. *Journal of Experimental Social Psychology, 19,* 21–48.

Brehm, S. S., & Brehm, J. W. (1981). *Psychological reactance: A theory of freedom and control.* New York: Academic Press.

Brody, N. (1983). *Human motivation: Commentary on goal-directed action.* New York: Academic Press.

Brown, J. D., & Siegel, J. M. (1988). Attributions for negative life events and depression: The role of perceived control. *Journal of Personality and Social Psychology, 54,* 316–322.

Burdick, H. A., & Burnes, A. J. (1958). A test of "strain toward symmetry" theories. *Journal of Abnormal and Social Psychology, 57,* 367–369.

Burger, J. M. (1986). Desire for control and the illusion of control: The effects of familiarity and sequence of outcomes. *Journal of Research in Personality, 20,* 66–76.

Burger, J. M. (1993). Individual differences in control motivation and social information processing. In G. Weary, F. Gleicher, & K. Marsh (Eds.), *Control motivation and social cognition* (pp. 203–219). New York: Springer-Verlag.

Burger, J. M., & Arkin, R. (1980). Desire for control and the use of attributional processes. *Journal of Personality, 56,* 531–546.

Burger, J. M., & Cooper, H. M. (1979). The desirability of control. *Motivation and Emotion, 3,* 381–393.

Burger, J. M., & Hemans, L. T. (1988). Desire for control and the use of attribution processes. *Journal of Personality, 56,* 531–546.

Burger, J. M., & Schnerring, D. A. (1982). The effects of desire for control and extrinsic rewards on the illusion of control and gambling. *Motivation and Emotion, 6,* 329–335.

Buss, D. M., & Kenrick, D. T. (1998). Evolutionary social psychology. In D. Gilbert, S. T. Fiske, & G. Lindzey (Eds.), *Handbook of social psychology* (4th ed., Vol. 2, pp. 982–1026). New York: McGraw-Hill.

Butler, R. (1992). What young people want to know when: Effects of mastery and ability goals on interest in different kinds of social comparisons. *Journal of Personality and Social Psychology, 62,* 934–943.

Cacioppo, J. T., & Petty, R. E. (1982). The need for cognition. *Journal of Personality and Social Psychology, 42,* 116–131.

Cain, K. M., & Dweck, C. S. (1995). The relation between motivational patterns and achievement cognitions through the elementary school years. *Merrill-Palmer Quarterly, 41,* 25–52.

Cantor, N. E., Pittman, T. S., & Jones, E. E. (1982). Choice and attitude attributions: The influence of constraint information on attributions across levels of inferential generality. *Social Cognition, 1,* 1–20.

Chaiken, S. (1980). Heuristic versus systematic information processing and the use of source versus message cues in persuasion. *Journal of Personality and Social Psychology, 39,* 752–766.

Clark, M. S. (1984). Record keeping in two types of relationships. *Journal of Personality and Social Psychology, 47,* 549–557.

Clark, M. S., & Mills, J. (1979). Interpersonal attraction in communal and exchange relationships. *Journal of Personality and Social Psychology, 37,* 12–24.

Clark, M. S., & Mills, J. (1993). The difference between communal and exchange relationships: What it is and is not. *Personality and Social Psychology Bulletin, 19,* 684–691.

Clark, M. S., Mills, J., & Corcoran, D. M. (1989). Keeping track of needs and inputs of friends and strangers. *Personality and Social Psychology Bulletin, 15,* 533–542.

Clark, M. S., Mills, J., & Powell, M. C. (1986). Keeping track of needs in communal and exchange relationships. *Journal of Personality and Social Psychology, 51,* 333–338.

Clary, E. G., & Tesser, A. (1983). Reactions to unexpected events: The naive scientist and interpretive activity. *Personality and Social Psychology Bulletin, 9,* 609–620.

Collins, B. E. (1992). Texts and subtexts. *Psychological Inquiry, 3,* 315–320.

Conti, R., Amabile, T. M., & Pollak, S. (1995). The positive impact of creative activity: Effects of creative task engagement and motivational focus on college students' learning. *Personality and Social Psychology Bulletin, 21,* 1107–1116.

Cooper, J. (1980). Reducing fears and increasing assertiveness: The role of dissonance reduction. *Journal of Experimental Social Psychology, 16,* 199–213.

Cooper, J., & Fazio, R. H. (1984). A new look at dissonance theory. In L. Berkowitz (Ed.), *Advances in experimental social psychology* (Vol. 17, pp. 229–266). Orlando, FL: Academic Press.

Cooper, J., & Goethals, G. R. (1974). Unforeseen events and the elimination of cognitive dissonance. *Journal of Personality and Social Psychology, 29,* 441–445.

Cooper, J., & Worchel, S. (1970). Role of undesired consequences in arousing cognitive dissonance. *Journal of Personality and Social Psychology, 16,* 199–206.

Cooper, J., Zanna, M. P., & Goethals, G. R. (1974). Mistreatment of an esteemed other as a consequence affecting dissonance reduction. *Journal of Experimental Social Psychology, 10,* 224–233.

Coyne, J. C., Aldwin, C., & Lazarus, R. S. (1981). Depression and coping in stressful episodes. *Journal of Abnormal Psychology, 90,* 439–447.

Croyle, R. T., & Cooper, J. (1983). Dissonance arousal: Physiological evidence. *Journal of Personality and Social Psychology, 45,* 782–791.

Csikzenmihalyi, M. (1975). *Beyond boredom and anxiety.* San Francisco: Jossey-Bass.

Csikzenmihalyi, M. (1990). *Flow: The psychology of optimal experience.* New York: Harper & Row.

D'Agostino, P. R., & Fincher-Kiefer, R. (1992). Need for cognition and the correspondence bias. *Social Cognition, 10,* 151–163.

D'Agostino, P. R., & Pittman, T. S. (1982). Effort expenditure following control deprivation. *Bulletin of the Psychonomic Society, 19,* 282–283.

Darley, J. M., Fleming, J. H., Hilton, J. L., & Swann, W. B. (1988). Dispelling negative expectancies: The impact of interaction goals and target characteristics on the expectancy confirmation process. *Journal of Experimental Social Psychology, 24,* 19–36.

Darley, J. M., & Gross, P. H. (1983). A hypothesis confirming bias in labeling effects. *Journal of Personality and Social Psychology, 44,* 20–33.

deCharmes, R. (1968). *Personal causation.* New York: Academic Press.

Deci, E. L. (1971). Effects of externally mediated rewards on intrinsic motivation. *Journal of Personality and Social Psychology, 18,* 105–115.

Deci, E. L. (1972). Intrinsic motivation, extrinsic reinforcement and inequity. *Journal of Personality and Social Psychology, 22,* 113–120.

Deci, E. L. (1975). *Intrinsic motivation.* New York: Plenum.

Deci, E. L., Betley, G., Kahle, J., Abrams, L., & Porac, J. (1981). When trying to win: Competition and intrinsic motivation. *Personality and Social Psychology Bulletin, 7,* 79–83.

Deci, E. L., & Ryan, R. M. (1985). *Intrinsic motivation and self-determination in human behavior.* New York: Plenum.

Deci, E. L., & Ryan, R. M. (1992). The initiation and regulation of intrinsically motivated learning and achievement. In A. K. Boggiano & T. S. Pittman (Eds.), *Achievement and motivation: A social-developmental perspective.* New York: Cambridge University Press.

DeLaRonde, C., & Swann, W. B., Jr. (1993). Caught in the crossfire: Positivity and self-verification strivings among people with low self-esteem. In R. Baumeister (Ed.), *Self-esteem: The puzzle of low self-regard.* New York: Plenum.

Depret, E., & Fiske, S. T. (1993). Social cognition and power: Some cognitive consequences of social structure as a source of control deprivation. In G. Weary, F. Gleicher, & K. Marsh (Eds.), *Control motivation and social cognition* (pp. 176–202). New York: Springer-Verlag.

Dickerson, C., Thibodeau, R., Aronson, E., & Miller, D. (1992). Using cognitive dissonance to encourage water conservation. *Journal of Applied Social Psychology, 22,* 841–854.

Diener, C. I., & Dweck, C. S. (1978). An analysis of learned helplessness: Continuous changes in performance, strategy, and achievement cognitions following failure. *Journal of Personality and Social Psychology, 36,* 451–462.

Driscoll, D. M., Hamilton, D. L., & Sorrentino, R. M. (1991). Uncertainty orientation and recall of person-descriptive information. *Personality and Social Psychology Bulletin, 17,* 494–500.

Dunn, D. S., & Wilson, T. D. (1990). When the stakes are high: A limit to the illusion-of-control effect. *Social Cognition, 8,* 305–323.

Dunning, D. (1995). Trait importance and modifiability as factors influencing self-assessment and self-enhancement motives. *Personality and Social Psychology Bulletin, 21,* 1297–1306.

Dunning, D, & Cohen, G. L. (1992). Egocentric definitions of traits and abilities in social judgment. *Journal of Personality and Social Psychology, 63,* 341–355.

Dunning, D., Leuenberger, A., & Sherman, D. A. (1995). A new look at motivated inference: Are self-serving theories of success a product of motivational forces? *Journal of Personality and Social Psychology, 69,* 58–68.

Dunning, D., & McElwee, R. O. (1995). Idiosyncratic trait prototypes and self-description: Implications for self and social judgment. *Journal of Personality and Social Psychology, 68*, 936–946.

Dunning, D., Perie, M., & Story, A. L. (1991). Self-serving prototypes of social categories. *Journal of Personality and Social Psychology, 61*, 957–968.

Duval, S., & Wicklund, R. A. (1972). *A theory of objective self-awareness*. New York: Academic Press.

Dweck, C. S. (1975). The role of expectations and attributions in the alleviation of learned helplessness. *Journal of Personality and Social Psychology, 31*, 674–685.

Dweck, C. S., & Leggett, E. L. (1988). A social-cognition approach to motivation and personality. *Psychological Review, 95*, 256–273.

Dweck, C. S., & Reppucci, N. D. (1973). Learned helplessness and reinforcement responsibility in children. *Journal of Personality and Social Psychology, 25*, 109–116.

Eagly, A. H., & Chaiken, S. (1998). Attitude structure and function. In D. T. Gilbert, S. T. Fiske, & G. Lindzey (Eds.), *The handbook of social psychology* (4th ed., Vol. 1, pp. 269–322). New York: McGraw-Hill.

Edwards, J. A., & Weary, G. (1993). Depression and the impression formation continuum: Piecemeal processing despite the availability of category information. *Journal of Personality and Social Psychology, 64*, 636–645.

Elkin, R., & Leippe, M. (1986). Physiological arousal, dissonance, and attitude change: Evidence for a dissonance-arousal link and a "don't remind me" effect. *Journal of Personality and Social Psychology, 51*, 55–65.

Elliot, A. J., & Devine, P. G. (1994). On the motivational nature of cognitive dissonance: Dissonance as psychological discomfort. *Journal of Personality and Social Psychology, 67*, 382–394.

Elliot, A. J., & Harackiewicz, J. M. (1994). Goal setting, achievement orientation, and intrinsic motivation: A mediational analysis. *Journal of Personality and Social Psychology, 66*, 968–980.

Elliott, E. S., & Dweck, C. S. (1988). Goals: An approach to motivation and achievement. *Journal of Personality and Social Psychology, 54*, 5–12.

Enzle, M. E., & Schopflocher, D. (1978). Instigation of attribution processes by attribution questions. *Personality and Social Psychology Bulletin, 4*, 595–599.

Epstein, J. A., & Harackiewicz, J. M. (1992). Winning is not enough: The effects of competition and achievement orientation on intrinsic interest. *Personality and Social Psychology Bulletin, 18*, 128–138.

Erber, R., & Fiske, S. T. (1984). Outcome dependency and attention to inconsistent information. *Journal of Personality and Social Psychology, 47*, 709–726.

Fazio, R. H., Zanna, M. P., & Cooper, J. (1977). Dissonance and self-perception: An integrative view of each theory's proper domain of application. *Journal of Experimental Social Psychology, 13*, 464–479.

Feather, N. T. (1990). Bridging the gap between values and ac-
tions. In E. Higgins & R. Sorrentino (Eds.), *Handbook of motivation and cognition* (Vol. 2, pp. 151–192). New York: Guilford.

Fein, G. G. (1981). Pretend play in childhood: An integrative review. *Child Development, 52*, 1095–1118.

Feldman, N. S., & Ruble, D. N. (1988). The effect of personal relevance on psychological inference: A developmental analysis. *Child Development, 59*, 1339–1352.

Festinger, L. (1957). *A theory of cognitive dissonance*. Evanston, IL: Row, Peterson.

Festinger, L., & Carlsmith, J. M. (1959). Cognitive consequences of forced compliance. *Journal of Abnormal and Social Psychology, 58*, 203–210.

Fiske, S. T. (1993). Controlling other people: The impact of power on stereotyping. *American Psychologist, 48*, 621–628.

Fiske, S. T. (1998). Stereotypes, prejudice, and discrimination. In D. Gilbert, S. T. Fiske, & G. Lindzey (Eds.), *Handbook of social psychology* (4th ed., Vol. 2, pp. 357–411). New York: McGraw-Hill.

Fiske, S. T., Morling, B., & Stevens, L. E. (1996). Controlling self and others: A theory of anxiety, mental control, and social control. *Personality and Social Psychology Bulletin, 22*, 115–123.

Fiske, S. T., & Neuberg, S. L. (1990). A continuum of impression formation, from category-based to individuating processes: Influences of information and motivation on attention and interpretation. In M. Zanna (Ed.), *Advances in experimental social psychology* (Vol. 23, pp. 1–74). San Diego, CA: Academic Press.

Fiske, S. T., Neuberg, S. L., Beattie, A. E., & Milberg, S. J. (1987). Category-based and attribute-based reactions to others: Some informational conditions of stereotyping and individuating processes. *Journal of Experimental Social Psychology, 23*, 300–427.

Fleming, J. H., & Darley, J. M. (1990). The purposeful-action sequence and the illusion of control: The effects of foreknowledge and target involvement on observers' judgments of others' control of random events. *Personality and Social Psychology Bulletin, 16*, 346–357.

Flett, G. L., Pliner, P., & Blankstein, K. R. (1989). Depression and components of attributional complexity. *Journal of Personality and Social Psychology, 56*, 757–764.

Flink, C., Boggiano, A. K., & Barrett, M. (1990). *Journal of Personality and Social Psychology, 59*, 916–924.

Ford, T. E., & Kruglanski, A. W. (1995). Effects of epistemic motivations on the use of accessible constructs in social judgment. *Personality and Social Psychology Bulletin, 21*, 950–962.

Frankel, A., & Snyder, M. L. (1978). Poor performance following unsolvable problems: Learned helplessness or egotism? *Journal of Personality and Social Psychology, 36*, 1415–1423.

Freund, T., Kruglanski, A. W., & Shpitzajzen, A. (1985). The freezing and unfreezing of impressional primacy: Effects of the need for structure and the fear of invalidity. *Personality and Social Psychology Bulletin, 11,* 479–487.

Frey, D. (1986). Recent research on selective exposure to information. In L. Berkowitz (Ed.), *Advances in experimental social psychology* (Vol. 19, pp. 41–80). San Diego, CA: Academic Press.

Fried, C. B., & Aronson, E. (1995). Hypocrisy, misattribution, and dissonance reduction. *Personality and Social Psychology Bulletin, 21,* 925–933.

Fries, A., & Frey, D. (1980). Misattribution of arousal and the effects of self-threatening information. *Journal of Experimental Social Psychology, 16,* 405–416.

Garbarino, J. (1975). The impact of anticipated reward upon cross-aged tutoring. *Journal of Personality and Social Psychology, 32,* 421–428.

Geen, R. G. (1998). Aggression and antisocial behavior. In D. Gilbert, S. T. Fiske, & G. Lindzey (Eds.), *Handbook of social psychology* (4th ed., Vol. 2, pp. 317–356). New York: McGraw-Hill.

Gilbert, D. T. (1989). Thinking lightly about others: Automatic components of the social inference process. In J. S. Uleman & J. A. Bargh (Eds.), *Unintended thought* (pp. 189–211). New York: Guilford.

Gilbert, D. T. (1998). Ordinary personology. In D. Gilbert, S. T. Fiske, & G. Lindzey (Eds.), *Handbook of social psychology* (4th ed., Vol. 2, pp. 89–150). New York: McGraw-Hill.

Gilbert, D. T., & Jones, E. E. (1986). Perceiver-induced constraint: Interpretations of self-generated reality. *Journal of Personality and Social Psychology, 50,* 269–280.

Gilbert, D. T., Jones, E. E., & Pelham, B. W. (1987). Influence and inference: What the active perceiver overlooks. *Journal of Personality and Social Psychology, 52,* 861–870.

Gilbert, D. T., Pelham, B. W., & Krull, D. S. (1988). On cognitive busyness: When person perceivers meet persons perceived. *Journal of Personality and Social Psychology, 54,* 733–740.

Gilovich, T., & Douglas, C. (1986). Biased evaluations of randomly determined gambling outcomes. *Journal of Experimental Social Psychology, 22,* 228–241.

Gilovich, T., Medvec, V. H., & Chen, S. (1995). Commission, omission, and dissonance reduction: Coping with regret in the "Monty Hall" problem. *Personality and Social Psychology Bulletin, 21,* 182–190.

Ginossar, Z., & Trope, Y. (1987). Problem solving in judgment under uncertainty. *Journal of Personality and Social Psychology, 52,* 464–474.

Gleicher, F., & Weary, G. (1991). The effect of depression on the quantity and quality of social inferences. *Journal of Personality and Social Psychology, 61,* 105–114.

Goethals, G. R., & Cooper, J. (1975). When dissonance is reduced: The timing of self-justificatory attitude change. *Journal of Personality and Social Psychology, 32,* 361–367.

Goethals, G. R., Cooper, J., & Naficy, A. (1979). Role of fore-seen, foreseeable, and unforeseeable behavioral consequences in the arousal of cognitive dissonance. *Journal of Personality and Social Psychology, 37,* 1179–1185.

Gollwitzer, P. M. (1990). Action phases and mind-sets. In E. Higgins & R. Sorrentino (Eds.), *Handbook of motivation and cognition: Foundations of social behavior* (Vol. 2, pp. 53–92). New York: Guilford Press.

Gollwitzer, P. M., Earle, W. B., & Stephan, W. G. (1982). Affect as a determinant of egotism: Residual excitation and performance attributions. *Journal of Personality and Social Psychology, 61,* 702–709.

Gollwitzer, P. M., Heckhausen, H., & Steller, B. (1990). Deliberative versus implemental mind-sets: Cognitive tuning toward congruous thoughts and information. *Journal of Personality and Social Psychology, 59,* 1119–1127.

Gollwitzer, P. M., & Kinney, R. F. (1989). Effects of deliberative and implemental mind-sets on illusion of control. *Journal of Personality and Social Psychology, 56,* 531–542.

Greenberg, J., Pyszczynski, T., Solomon, S., Simon, L., & Breus, M. (1994). Role of consciousness and accessibility of death-related thoughts in mortality salience effects. *Journal of Personality and Social Psychology, 67,* 627–637.

Greenberg, J., Simon, L., Pyszczynski, T., Solomon, S., & Chatel, D. (1992). Terror management and tolerance: Does mortality salience always intensify negative reactions to others who threaten one's worldview? *Journal of Personality and Social Psychology, 63,* 212–220.

Greenberg, J., Solomon, S., Pyszczynski, T., Rosenblatt, A., Burling, J., Lyon, D., Simon, L., & Pinel, E. (1992). Why do people need self-esteem? Converging evidence that self-esteem serves an anxiety-buffering function. *Journal of Personality and Social Psychology, 63,* 913–922.

Greenwald, A. G. (1980). The totalitarian ego: Fabrication and revision of personal history. *American Psychologist, 35,* 603–618.

Greenwald, A. G., & Ronis, D. L. (1978). Twenty years of cognitive dissonance: Case study of the evolution of a theory. *Psychological Review, 85,* 53–57.

Grolnick, W. S., & Ryan, R. M. (1987). Autonomy in children's learning: An experimental and individual difference investigation. *Journal of Personality and Social Psychology, 52,* 890–898.

Harackiewicz, J. M., Manderlink, G., & Sansone, C. (1992). Competence processes and achievement motivation: Implications for intrinsic motivation. In A. K. Boggiano & T. S. Pittman (Eds.), *Achievement and motivation: A social-developmental analysis* (pp. 115–137). New York: Cambridge University Press.

Harackiewicz, J. M., Sansone, C., & Manderlink, G. (1985). Competence, achievement orientation, and intrinsic motivation. *Journal of Personality and Social Psychology, 48,* 493–508.

Harkness, A. R., DeBono, K. G., & Borgida, E. (1985). Personal involvement and strategies for making contingency judgments: A stake in the dating game makes a difference. *Journal of Personality and Social Psychology, 49,* 22–32.

Harmon-Jones, E., Brehm, J. W., Greenberg, J. Simon, L., & Nelson, D. E. (1996). Evidence that the production of aversive consequences is not necessary to create cognitive dissonance. *Journal of Personality and Social Psychology, 70,* 5–16.

Harvey, J. H., Yarkin, K. L., Lightner, J. M., & Town, J. P. (1980). Unsolicited attribution and recall of interpersonal events. *Journal of Personality and Social Psychology, 38,* 551–568.

Hastie, R. (1984). Causes and effects of causal attribution. *Journal of Personality and Social Psychology, 46,* 44–56.

Heckhausen, H. (1986). Why some time out might benefit achievement motivation research. In J. van den Bercken, T. Bergen, & E. De Bruyn (Eds.), *Achievement and task motivation* (pp. 7–39). Lisse, The Netherlands: Swets & Seitlinger.

Heider, F. (1946). Attitudes and cognitive organizations. *Journal of Psychology, 21,* 107–112.

Heider, F. (1958). *The psychology of interpersonal relations.* New York: Wiley.

Higgins, E. T. (1987). Self-discrepancy: A theory relating self and affect. *Psychological Review, 94,* 319–340.

Higgins, E. T. (1989). Self-discrepancy theory: What patterns of self-beliefs cause people to suffer? In L. Berkowitz (Ed.), *Advances in experimental social psychology* (Vol. 22, pp. 93–136). San Diego, CA: Academic Press.

Higgins, E. T., Rhodewalt, F., & Zanna, M. P. (1979). Dissonance motivation: Its nature, persistence, and reinstatement. *Journal of Experimental Social Psychology, 15,* 16–34.

Higgins, E. T., Vookles, J., & Tykocinski, O. (1992). Self and health: How "patterns" of self-beliefs predict types of emotional and physical problems. *Social Cognition, 10,* 125–150.

Hildebrand-Saints, L., & Weary, G. (1989). Depression and social information gathering. *Personality and Social Psychology Bulletin, 15,* 150–160.

Hilton, J. L., & Darley, J. M. (1991). The effects of interaction goals on person perception. In M. Zanna (Ed.), *Advances in experimental social psychology* (Vol. 24, pp. 236–267). New York: Academic Press.

Hilton, J. L., Darley, J. M., & Fleming, J. H. (1989). Self-fulfilling prophecies and self-defeating behavior. In R. Curtis (Ed.), *Self-defeating behaviors: Experimental research and practical implications* (pp. 41–65). New York: Plenum.

Hilton, J. L., Klein, J. G., & von Hippel, W. (1991). Attention allocation and impression formation. *Personality and Social Psychology Bulletin, 17,* 548–559.

Hobden, K. L., & Olson, J. M. (1994). From jest to antipathy: Disparagement humor as a source of dissonance-motivated attitude change. *Basic and Applied Social Psychology, 15,* 239–249.

Hunt, J. M. (1965). Intrinsic motivation and its role in psycho-

logical development. *Nebraska Symposium on Motivation, 13,* 189–282.

Inhelder, B., & Piaget, J. (1958). *The growth of logical thinking from childhood to adolescence.* New York: Basic.

Jenkins, S. R. (1996). Self-definition in thought, action, and life path choices. *Personality and Social Psychology Bulletin, 22,* 99–111.

Johnson, R. W., Kelly, R. J., & LeBlanc, B. A. (1995). Motivational basis of dissonance: Aversive consequences or inconsistency. *Personality and Social Psychology Bulletin, 21,* 850–855.

Jones, E. E. (1979). The rocky road from acts to dispositions. *American Psychologist, 34,* 107–117.

Jones, E. E. (1985). Major developments in social psychology during the past five decades. In G. Lindzey & E. Aronson (Eds.), *Handbook of social psychology* (3rd ed., Vol. 1, pp. 47–108). New York: Random House.

Jones, E. E. (1986). Interpreting interpersonal behavior: The effects of expectancies. *Science, 234,* 41–46.

Jones E. E., & Berglas, S. (1978). Control of attributions about the self through self-handicapping strategies: The appeal of alcohol and the role of underachievement. *Personality and Social Psychology Bulletin, 4,* 200–206.

Jones, E. E., & Davis, K. E. (1965). From acts to dispositions: The attribution process in person perception. In L. Berkowitz (Ed.), *Advances in experimental social psychology* (Vol. 2, pp. 220–266). New York: Academic Press.

Jones, E. E., & Harris, V. A. (1967). The attribution of attitudes. *Journal of Experimental Social Psychology, 3,* 1–24.

Jones, E. E., & Thibaut, J. (1958). Interaction goals as bases of inference in interpersonal perception. In R. Tagiuri & L. Petrullo (Eds.), *Person perception and interpersonal behavior.* Stanford, CA: Stanford University Press.

Jordan, N. (1953). Behavioral forces that are a function of attitudes and of cognitive organization. *Human Relations, 6,* 273–287.

Jussim, L., Yen, H., & Aiello, J. R. (1995). Self-consistency, self-enhancement, and accuracy in reactions to feedback. *Journal of Experimental Social Psychology, 31,* 322–356.

Kahneman, D., & Miller, D. T. (1986). Norm theory: Comparing reality to its alternatives. *Psychological Review, 93,* 136–153.

Kahneman, D., Slovic, P., & Tversky, A. (Eds.). (1982). *Judgment under uncertainty: Heuristics and biases.* New York: Cambridge University Press.

Kahneman, D., & Tversky, A. (1972). On prediction and judgment. *ORI Research Monograph, 12*(4).

Kahneman, D., & Tversky, A. (1982). The simulation heuristic. In D. Kahneman, P. Slovic, & A. Tversky (Eds.), *Judgment under uncertainty: Heuristics and biases* (pp. 201–208). New York: Cambridge University Press.

Kassin, S. M., & Hochreich, D. J. (1977). Instructional set: A neglected variable in attribution research. *Personality and Social Psychology Bulletin, 3,* 620–623.

Kelley, H. H. (1967). Attribution theory in social psychology. In D. Levine (Ed.), *Nebraska symposium on motivation* (Vol. 15, pp. 192–238). Lincoln, NE: University of Nebraska Press.

Kelley, H. H. (1971). Attribution theory in social interaction. In E. E. Jones et al. (Eds.), *Attribution: Perceiving the causes of behavior.* New York: General Learning Press.

Kiesler, C. A., & Pallak, M. S. (1976). Arousal properties of dissonance manipulations. *Psychological Bulletin, 83,* 1014–1025.

Kruglanski, A. W. (1975). The endogenous-exogenous partition in attribution theory. *Psychological Review, 83,* 387–406.

Kruglanski, A. W., & Freund, T. (1983). The freezing and unfreezing of lay inferences: Effects on impressional primacy, ethnic stereotyping, and numerical anchoring. *Journal of Experimental Social Psychology, 19,* 448–468.

Kruglanski, A. W., & Mayseless, O. (1988). Contextual effects in hypothesis testing: The role of competing alternatives and epistemic motivations. *Social Cognition, 6,* 1–21.

Kruglanski, A. W., & Webster, D. M. (1996). Motivated closing of the mind: "Seizing" and "freezing." *Psychological Review, 103,* 263–283.

Kuhl, J. (1986). Motivation and information processing: A new look at decision making, dynamic change, and action control. In R. M. Sorrentino & E. T. Higgins (Eds.), *Handbook of motivation and cognition: Foundations of social behavior* (Vol. 1, pp. 404–434). New York: Guilford Press.

Kuhn, T. S. (1962). *The structure of scientific revolutions.* Chicago: University of Chicago Press.

Kuiper, N. A., MacDonald, M. R., & Derry, P. A. (1983). Parameters of a depressive self-schema. In J. Suls & A. Greenwald (Eds.), *Psychological perspectives on the self* (Vol. 2, pp. 191–217). Hillsdale, NJ: Erlbaum.

Kunda, Z. (1987). Motivated inference: Self-serving generation and evaluation of causal theories. *Journal of Personality and Social Psychology, 53,* 37–54.

Kunda, Z. (1990). The case for motivated reasoning. *Psychological Bulletin, 108,* 480–498.

Kunda, Z., & Schwartz, S. H. (1983). Undermining intrinsic moral motivation: External reward and self-presentation. *Journal of Personality and Social Psychology, 45,* 763–771.

Landman, J. (1987). Regret and elation following action and inaction: Affective responses to positive and negative outcomes. *Personality and Social Psychology Bulletin, 13,* 524–536.

Langer, E. J. (1975). The illusion of control. *Journal of Personality and Social Psychology, 32,* 311–328.

Langer, E. J. (1989). *Mindfulness.* Reading, MA: Addison-Wesley.

Langer, E. J., & Roth, J. (1975). Heads I win, tails it's chance: The illusion of control as a function of the sequence of outcomes in a purely chance task. *Journal of Personality and Social Psychology, 32,* 951–955.

Latané, B., Williams, K., & Harkins, S. (1979). Many hands make light the work: The cause and consequences of social loafing. *Journal of Personality and Social Psychology, 37,* 822–832.

Lau, R. R., & Russell, D. (1980). Attributions in the sports pages. *Journal of Personality and Social Psychology, 39,* 29–38.

Leippe, M. R., & Eisenstadt, D. (1994). Generalization of dissonance reduction: Decreasing prejudice through induced compliance. *Journal of Personality and Social Psychology, 67,* 395–413.

Lepper, M. R., & Cordova, D. I. (1992). A desire to be taught: Instructional consequences of intrinsic motivation. *Motivation and Emotion, 16,* 187–208.

Lepper, M. R., & Greene, D. (1978). *The hidden costs of reward.* Hillsdale, NJ: Erlbaum.

Lepper, M. R., Greene, D., & Nisbett, R. E. (1973). Undermining children's intrinsic interest with extrinsic reward: A test of the overjustification hypothesis. *Journal of Personality and Social Psychology, 28,* 129–137.

Lepper, M. R., & Malone, T. W. (1987). Intrinsic motivation and instructional effectiveness in computer-based education. In R. E. Snow & M. J. Farr (Eds.), *Aptitude, learning, and instruction: III. Conative and affective process analyses* (pp. 255–296). Hillsdale, NJ: Erlbaum.

Lepper, M. R., Sagotsky, G., Dafoe, J. L., & Greene, D. (1982). Consequences of superfluous social constraints: Effects on young children's social inferences and subsequent intrinsic interest. *Journal of Personality and Social Psychology, 42,* 51–65.

Lewin, K. (1951). *Field theory in social science.* New York: Harper.

Lewinsohn, P. M., Hoberman, H. M., & Rosenbaum, M. A. (1988). Prospective study of risk factors for unipolar depression. *Journal of Abnormal Psychology, 97,* 251–264.

Lewinsohn, P. M., Steinmetz, J. L., Larson, D. W., & Franklin, J. (1981). Depression-related cognitions: Antecedents or consequence? *Journal of Abnormal Psychology, 90,* 213–219.

Linder, D. E., Cooper, J., & Jones, E. E. (1967). Decision freedom as a determinant of the role of incentive magnitude in attitude change. *Journal of Personality and Social Psychology, 6,* 245–254.

Liu, T. J., & Steele, C. M. (1986). Attribution analysis as self affirmation. *Journal of Personality and Social Psychology, 51,* 531–540.

Losch, M., & Cacioppo, J. (1990). Cognitive dissonance may enhance sympothetic tonis, but attitudes are changed to reduce negative affect rather than arousal. *Journal of Experimental Social Psychology, 26,* 289–304.

Maheswaran, D., & Chaiken, S. (1991). Promoting systematic processing in low-motivation settings: Effect of incongruent information on processing and judgment. *Journal of Personality and Social Psychology, 61,* 13–25.

Malone, T. W., & Lepper, M. R. (1987). Making learning fun: A taxonomy of intrinsic motivations for learning. In R. E. Snow & M. J. Farr (Eds.), *Aptitude, learning, and instruction: III. Conative and affective process analyses* (pp. 255–296). Hillsdale, NJ: Erlbaum.

Markman, K. D., Gavanski, I., Sherman, S. J., & McMullen, M. N. (1995). The impact of perceived control on the imagination of better and worse possible worlds. *Personality and Social Psychology Bulletin, 21,* 588–595.

Marsh, K. L., & Weary, G. (1989). Depression and attributional complexity. *Personality and Social Psychology Bulletin, 15,* 325–336.

Marsh, K. L., & Weary, G. (1994). Severity of depression and responsiveness to attributional information. *Journal of Social and Clinical Psychology, 13,* 15–32.

Mayseless, O., & Kruglanski, A. W. (1987). What makes you so sure? Effects of epistemic motivations on judgmental confidence. *Organizational Behavior and Human Decision Processes, 3,* 162–183.

McCaul, K. D. (1983). Observer attributions of depressed students. *Personality and Social Psychology Bulletin, 9,* 74–82.

McClelland, D. C. (1980). Motive dispositions: The merits of operant and respondent measures. In L. Wheeler (Ed.), *Review of personality and social psychology* (Vol. 1, pp. 10–41). Beverly Hills, CA: Sage.

McClelland, D. C., Atkinson, J. W., Clark, R. A., & Lowell, E. L. (1953). *The achievement motive.* New York: Appleton-Century-Crofts.

McClelland, D. C., Koestner, R., & Weinberger, J. (1989). How do self-attributed and implicit motives differ? *Psychological Review, 96,* 690–702.

McFarland, C., & Ross, M. (1982). Impact of causal attributions on affective reactions to success and failure. *Journal of Personality and Social Psychology, 43,* 937–946.

Mehlman, R. C., & Snyder, C. R. (1985). Excuse theory: A test of the self-protective role of attributions. *Journal of Personality and Social Psychology, 49,* 994–1001.

Miller, D. T., Norman, S. A., & Wright, E. (1978). Distortion in person perception as a consequence of the need for effective control. *Journal of Personality and Social Psychology, 36,* 598–607.

Miller, D. T., & Ross, M. (1975). Self-serving biases in the attribution of causality: Fact or fiction? *Psychological Bulletin, 82,* 213–225.

Miller, D. T., & Turnbull, W. (1986). Expectancies and interpersonal processes. In M. Rosenzweig & L. Porter (Eds.), *Annual review of psychology* (Vol. 37, pp. 233–256). Palo Alto, CA: Annual Reviews.

Miller, J. G., & Bersoff, D. M. (1994). Cultural influences on the moral status of reciprocity and the discounting of endogenous motivation. *Personality and Social Psychology Bulletin, 20,* 592–602.

Monson, T. C., Keel, R., Stephens, D., & Genung, V. (1982). Trait attributions: Relative validity, covariation with behavior, and prospect of interaction. *Journal of Personality and Social Psychology, 42,* 1014–1024.

Morrissette, J. O. (1958). An experimental study of the theory of structural balance. *Human Relations, 11,* 239–254.

Moskowitz, G. B. (1993). Individual differences in social categorization: The influence of personal need for structure on spontaneous trait inferences. *Journal of Personality and Social Psychology, 65,* 132–142.

Murphy, G. (1954). Social motivation. In G. Lindzey (Ed.), *Handbook of Social Psychology* (Vol. 2, pp. 601–633). Cambridge, MA: Addison-Wesley.

Nel, E., Helmreich, R., & Aronson, E. (1969). Opinion change in the advocate as a function of the persuasibility of his audience: A clarification of the meaning of dissonance. *Journal of Personality and Social Psychology, 12,* 117–124.

Neuberg, S. L. (1989). The goal of forming accurate impressions during social interactions: Attenuating the impact of negative expectancies. *Journal of Personality and Social Psychology, 56,* 374–386.

Neuberg, S. L., & Fiske, S. T. (1987). Motivational influences on impression formation: Outcome dependency, accuracy-driven attention and individuating processes. *Journal of Personality and Social Psychology, 53,* 431–444.

Neuberg, S. L., & Newsom, J. T. (1993). Personal need for structure: Individual differences in the desire for simple structure. *Journal of Personality and Social Psychology, 65,* 113–131.

Newcomb, T. M. (1961). *The acquaintance process.* New York: Holt, Rinehart & Winston.

Nicholls, J. G. (1984). Achievement motivation: Conceptions of ability, subjective experience, task choice, and performance. *Psychological Review, 91,* 328–346.

Nisbett, R. E., & Ross, L. (1980). *Human inferences: Strategies and shortcomings of social judgments.* Englewood Cliffs, NJ: Prentice-Hall.

Nisbett, R. E., & Wilson, T. D. (1977). Telling more than we can know: Verbal reports on mental processes. *Psychological Review, 84,* 231–259.

Pagel, M. D., Becker, J., & Coppel, D. B. (1985). Loss of control, self-blame, and depression: An investigation of spouse caregivers of Alzheimer's disease. *Journal of Abnormal Psychology, 94,* 169–182.

Pallak, M. S., & Pittman, T. S. (1972). General motivational effects of dissonance arousal. *Journal of Personality and Social Psychology, 21,* 349–358.

Parker, L. E., & Lepper, M. R. (1992). Effects of fantasy contexts on children's learning and motivation: Making learning more fun. *Journal of Personality and Social Psychology, 62,* 625–633.

Pelham, B. W., & Neter, E. (1995). The effect of motivation of judgment depends on the difficulty of the judgment. *Journal of Personality and Social Psychology, 68,* 581–594.

Perloff, L. S., & Fetzer, B. K. (1986). Self-other judgments and perceived vulnerability of victimization. *Journal of Personality and Social Psychology, 50,* 502–510.

Petty, R. E., & Cacioppo, J. T. (1986). In L. Berkowitz (Ed.), *Advances in experimental social psychology* (Vol. 19, pp. 123–205). Orlando, FL: Academic Press.

Petty, R. E., & Wegener, D. T. (1998). Attitude change: Multiple roles for persuasion variables. In D. Gilbert, S. T. Fiske, & G. Lindzey (Eds.), *Handbook of social psychology* (4th ed., Vol. 1, pp. 323–390). New York: McGraw-Hill.

Piaget, J. (1965). *The child's conception of the world.* Paterson, NJ: Littlefield, Adams.

Picek, J. S., Sherman, S. J., & Shiffrin, R. M. (1975). Cognitive organization and coding of social structures. *Journal of Personality and Social Psychology, 31,* 758–768.

Pittman, N. L., & Pittman, T. S. (1979). Effects of amount of helplessness training and internal-external locus of control on mood and performance. *Journal of Personality and Social Psychology, 37,* 39–47.

Pittman, T. S. (1975). Attribution of arousal as a mediator in dissonance reduction. *Journal of Experimental Social Psychology, 11,* 53–63.

Pittman, T. S. (1982). *Intrinsic and extrinsic motivational orientations toward others.* Paper presented at the 90th meeting of the American Psychological Association, Washington, DC.

Pittman, T. S. (1992). Perception without awareness in the stream of behavior: Processes that produce and limit nonconscious biasing effects. In R. Bornstein & T. Pittman (Eds.), *Perception without awareness: Cognitive, social, and clinical perspectives* (pp. 277–296). New York: Guilford.

Pittman, T. S. (1993). Control motivation and attitude change. In G. Weary, F. Gleicher, & K. Marsh (Eds.), *Control motivation and social cognition* (pp. 157–175). New York: Springer-Verlag.

Pittman, T. S. (in press). Intrapsychic and interpersonal processes: Cognition, emotion, and self as adaptations to other people or to reality? In J. Cooper & J. M. Darley (Eds.), *The legacy of Edward E. Jones.* Washington, DC: American Psychological Association.

Pittman, T. S., Boggiano, A. K., & Main, D. S. (1992). Intrinsic and extrinsic motivational orientations in peer interactions. In A. K. Boggiano & T. S. Pittman (Eds.), *Achievement and motivation: A social-developmental analysis* (pp. 37–53). New York: Cambridge University Press.

Pittman, T. S., Boggiano, A. K., & Ruble, D. N. (1983). Intrinsic and extrinsic motivational orientations: Limiting conditions on the undermining and enhancing effects of reward on intrinsic motivation. In J. Levine & M. Wang (Eds.), *Teacher and student perceptions: Implications for learning.* Hillsdale, NJ: Erlbaum.

Pittman, T. S., & D'Agostino, P. R. (1985). Motivation and attribution: The effects of control deprivation on subsequent information processing. In J. Harvey & G. Weary (Eds.), *Current perspectives on attribution research* (Vol. 1). New York: Academic Press.

Pittman, T. S., & D'Agostino, P. R. (1989). Motivation and cognition: Control deprivation and the nature of subsequent information processing. *Journal of Experimental Social Psychology, 25,* 465–480.

Pittman, T. S. Davey, M. E., Alafat, K. A., Wetherill, K. V., & Kramer, N. A. (1990). Informational versus controlling verbal rewards. *Personality and Social Psychology Bulletin, 6,* 228–233.

Pittman, T. S., & Dool, C. (1985). *Age, source of reward, and intrinsic motivation in peer interaction.* Paper presented to the Society for Research in Child Development, Toronto.

Pittman, T. S., Emery, J., & Boggiano, A. K. (1982). Intrinsic and extrinsic motivational orientations: Reward-induced changes in preference for complexity. *Journal of Personality and Social Psychology, 42,* 789–797.

Pittman, T. S., & Heller, J. F. (1987). Social motivation. In M. Rosenzweig & L. Porter (Eds.), *Annual Review of Psychology* (Vol. 38). Palo Alto, CA: Annual Reviews.

Pittman, T. S., & Pittman, N. L. (1980). Deprivation of control and the attribution process. *Journal of Personality and Social Psychology, 39,* 377–389.

Pittman, T. S., Quattrone, G., & Jones, E. E. (1985). *Control deprivation and the accuracy of attributional inferences.* Paper presented at the meeting of the Eastern Psychological Association, Boston.

Pittman, T. S., Scherrer, F. W., & Wright, J. B. (1977). The effect of commitment on information utilization in the attribution process. *Personality and Social Psychology Bulletin, 3,* 276–279.

Pittman, T. S., & Worth, L. T. (1990). *Desire for control and the processing of persuasive communications.* Paper presented at the meeting of the Eastern Psychological Association, Philadelphia, PA.

Pyszczynski, T. A., & Greenberg, J. (1981). Role of disconfirmed expectancies in the instigation of attributional processing. *Journal of Personality and Social Psychology, 40,* 31–38.

Pyszczynski, T. A., & Greenberg, J. (1985). Depression and preference for self-focusing stimuli following success and failure. *Journal of Personality and Social Psychology, 49,* 1066–1075.

Pyszczynski, T., & Greenberg, J. (1987). Toward an integration of cognitive and motivational perspectives on social inference: A biased hypothesis-testing model. In L. Berkowitz (Ed.), *Advances in experimental social psychology* (Vol. 20, pp. 297–340). San Diego, CA: Academic Press.

Pyszczynski, T. A., Greenberg, J., & Holt, K. (1985). Maintaining consistency between self-serving beliefs and available data: A bias in information evaluation. *Personality and Social Psychology Bulletin, 11,* 179–190.

Pyszczynski, T. A., Greenberg, J., & Solomon, S. (1997). Why do we need what we need? A terror management perspective on the roots of human social motivation. *Psychological Inquiry, 8,* 1–20.

Quattrone, G. A. (1982). Overattribution and unit formation: When behavior engulfs the person. *Journal of Personality and Social Psychology, 42,* 593–607.

Quattrone, G. A. (1985). On the congruity between internal states and action. *Psychological Bulletin, 98,* 3–40.

Reeve, J., & Deci, E. L. (1996). Elements of the competitive situation that affect intrinsic motivation. *Personality and Social Psychology Bulletin, 22,* 24–33.

Reeve, J., Olson, B. C., & Cole, S. G. (1985). Motivation and performance: Two consequences of winning and losing in competition. *Motivation and Emotion, 9,* 291–298.

Reeve, J., Olson, B. C., & Cole, S. G. (1987). Intrinsic motivation in competition: The intervening role of four individual differences following objective competence information. *Journal of Research in Personality, 21,* 148–170.

Rempel, J. K., Holmes, J. G., & Zanna, M. P. (1985). Trust in close relationships. *Journal of Personality and Social Psychology, 49,* 95–112.

Riggs, J. M. (1992). Self-handicapping and achievement. In A. K. Boggiano & T. S. Pittman (Eds.), *Achievement and motivation: A social-developmental perspective* (pp. 244–267). New York: Cambridge University Press.

Riggs, J. M., & Pittman, T. S. (1991). *Control deprivation and performance: The effect of perceived opportunity to regain control.* Paper presented at the meeting of the Eastern Psychological Association, New York.

Robertson, L. S. (1977). Car crashes: Perceived vulnerability and willingness to pay for crash protection. *Journal of Community Health, 3,* 136–141.

Rosenberg, M. J. (1965). When dissonance fails: On eliminating evaluation apprehension from attitude measurement. *Journal of Personality and Social Psychology, 1,* 28–42.

Ross, L. (1977). The intuitive psychologist and his shortcomings: Distortions in the attribution process. *Advances in Experimental Social Psychology, 10,* 174–220.

Ross, L., & Nisbett, R. E. (1991). *The person and the situation.* New York: McGraw-Hill.

Ryan, R. M., & Deci, E. L. (1989). Bridging the research traditions of task/ego-involvement and intrinsic/extrinsic motivation: Comment on Butler (1987). *Journal of Educational Psychology, 81,* 265–268.

Ryan, R. M., & Grolnick, W. S. (1986). Origins and pawns in the classroom: Self-report and projective assessments of individual differences in children's perceptions. *Journal of Personality and Social Psychology, 50,* 550–558.

Sanitioso, R., Kunda, Z., & Fong, G. T. (1990). Motivated re-cruitment of autobiographical memory. *Journal of Personality and Social Psychology, 59,* 229–241.

Schachter, S., & Singer, J. E. (1962). Cognitive, social, and physiological determinants of emotional state. *Psychological Review, 69,* 379–399.

Scheier, M. F., & Carver, C. S. (1988). A model of behavioral self-regulation: Translating intention into action. In L. Berkowitz (Ed.), *Advances in experimental social psychology* (Vol. 21, pp. 303–346). San Diego, CA: Academic Press.

Scher, S. J., & Cooper, J. (1989). Motivational basis of dissonance: The singular role of behavioral consequences. *Journal of Personality and Social Psychology, 56,* 899–906.

Schlenker, B. R. (1982). Translating actions into attitudes: An identity-analytic approach to the explanation of social conduct. In L. Berkowitz (Ed.), *Advances in experimental social psychology* (Vol. 15, pp. 193–247). New York: Academic Press.

Schlenker, B. R., & Weingold, M. F. (1989). Goals and the self-identification process: Constructing desired identities. In L. Pervin (Ed.), *Goal concepts in personality and social psychology* (pp. 243–290). Hillsdale, NJ: Erlbaum.

Sedikides, C. (1993). Assessment, enhancement, and verification determinants of the self-evaluation process. *Journal of Personality and Social Psychology, 65,* 317–338.

Seligman, C., Fazio, R. H., & Zanna, M. P. (1980). Effects of salience of extrinsic rewards on liking and loving. *Journal of Personality and Social Psychology, 38,* 453–460.

Seligman, M. E. P. (1975). *Helplessness: On depression, development, and death.* San Francisco: Freeman.

Sherif, C. W., Sherif, M., & Nebergall, R. E. (1965). *Attitude and attitude change: The social judgment-involvement approach.* Philadelphia: W. B. Saunders.

Sherif, M., & Hovland, C. I. (1961). *Social judgment: Assimilation and contrast effects in communication and attitude change.* New Haven, CT: Yale University Press.

Shultz, T. R., & Lepper, M. R. (1996). Cognitive dissonance reduction as constraint satisfaction. *Psychological Review, 103,* 219–240.

Simon, L., Greenberg, J., & Brehm, J. (1995). Trivialization: The forgotten mode of dissonance reduction. *Journal of Personality and Social Psychology, 68,* 247–260.

Singer, J. L. (1977). Imagination and make-believe play in early childhood: Some educational implications. *Journal of Mental Imagery, 1,* 127–144.

Snyder, M., & Gangsted, S. (1981). Hypothesis-testing processes. In J. W. Harvey, W. J. Ickes, & R. F. Kidd (Eds.), *New directions in attribution research* (Vol. 3). Hillsdale, NJ: Erlbaum.

Snyder, M. L., Stephan, W. G., & Rosenfeld, D. (1978). Attributional egotism. In J. Harvey, W. Ickes, & R. Kidd (Eds.), *New directions in attribution research* (Vol. 2, pp. 91–120). Hillsdale, NJ: Erlbaum.

Solomon, S., Greenberg, J., & Pyszczynski, T. (1991). A

terror management theory of social behavior: The psychological functions of self-esteem and cultural worldviews. In M. Zanna (Ed.), *Advances in experimental social psychology* (Vol. 24, pp. 93–159). New York: Academic Press.

Sorrentino, R. M., & Short, J. C. (1986). Uncertainty orientation, motivation and cognition. In R. Sorrentino & E. Higgins (Eds.), *Handbook of motivation and cognition: Social foundations of behavior* (pp. 379–403). New York: Guilford Press.

Srull, T. K., & Wyer, R. S., Jr. (1986). The role of chronic and temporary goals in social information processing. In R. M. Sorrentino & E. T. Higgins (Eds.), *Handbook of motivation and cognition: Foundations of social behavior* (pp. 503–549). New York: Guilford Press.

Steele, C. M. (1988). The psychology of self-affirmation: Sustaining the integrity of the self. In L. Berkowitz (Ed.), *Advances in experimental social psychology* (Vol. 21, pp. 261–302). San Diego, CA: Academic Press.

Steele, C. M. (1990). *Protecting the self: Implications for social psychology and minority achievement.* Paper presented at the annual meeting of the American Psychological Association, Boston, MA.

Steele, C. M. (1992). Race and the schooling of Black Americans. *Atlantic, 269,* 68–78.

Steele, C. M., & Liu, T. J. (1981). Making the dissonant act unreflective of the self: Dissonance avoidance and the expectancy of a value-affirming response. *Personality and Social Psychology Bulletin, 7,* 393–397.

Steele, C. M., & Liu, T. J. (1983). Dissonance processes as self-affirmation. *Journal of Personality and Social Psychology, 45,* 5–19.

Steele, C. M., & Spencer, S. J. (1992). The primacy of self-integrity. *Psychological Inquiry, 3,* 345–346.

Steele, C. M., Spencer, S. J., & Lynch, M. (1993). Self-image resilience and dissonance: The role of affirmational resources. *Journal of Personality and Social Psychology, 64,* 885–896.

Stephan, W. E., & Gollwitzer, P. (1981). Affect as a mediator of attributional egotism. *Journal of Experimental Social Psychology, 17,* 443–458.

Stevens, L. E., & Fiske, S. T. (1995). Motivation and cognition in social life: A social survival perspective. *Social Cognition, 13,* 189–214.

Stone, J., Aronson, E., Crain, A. L., Winslow, M. P., & Fried, C. B. (1994). Inducing hypocrisy as a means for encouraging young adults to use condoms. *Personality and Social Psychology Bulletin, 20,* 116–128.

Sullivan, M. J. L., & Conway, M. (1989). Negative affect leads to low-effort cognition: Attributional processing for observed social behavior. *Social Cognition, 7,* 315–337.

Swann, W. B., Jr. (1983). Self-verification: Bringing social reality into harmony with the self. In J. Suls & A. G. Green-wald (Eds.), *Social psychological perspectives on the self* (Vol. 2, pp. 33–66). Hillsdale, NJ: Erlbaum.

Swann, W. B., Jr. (1984). Quest for accuracy in person perception: A matter of pragmatics. *Psychological Review, 91,* 457–477.

Swann, W. B., Jr. (1987). Identity negotiation: Where two roads meet. *Journal of Personality and Social Psychology, 53,* 1038–1051.

Swann, W. B., Jr. (1990). To be adored or to be known? The interplay of self-enhancement and self-verification. In E. T. Higgins & R. M. Sorrentino (Eds.), *Handbook of motivation and cognition: Foundations of social behavior* (Vol. 2, pp. 408–448). New York: Guilford Press.

Swann, W. B., Jr., Griffin, J. J., Predmore, S., & Gaines, B. (1987). The cognitive-affective crossfire: When self-consistency confronts self-enhancement. *Journal of Personality and Social Psychology, 52,* 881–889.

Swann, W. B., Jr., Hixon, J. G., Stein-Seroussi, A., & Gilbert, D. T. (1990). The fleeting gleam of praise: Behavioral reactions to self-relevant feedback. *Journal of Personality and Social Psychology, 59,* 17–26.

Swann, W. B., Jr., & Pittman, T. S. (1977). Initiating play activity of children: The moderating influence of verbal cues on intrinsic motivation. *Child Development, 48,* 1128–1132.

Swann, W. B., Jr., Stein-Seroussi, A., & Geisler, R. B. (1992). Why people self-verify. *Journal of Personality and Social Psychology, 62,* 392–401.

Swann, W. B., Jr., & Schroeder, D. G. (1995). The search for beauty and truth: A framework for understanding reactions to evaluations. *Personality and Social Psychology Bulletin, 21,* 1307–1318.

Swann, W. B., Jr., Stephenson, B., & Pittman, T. S. (1981). Curiosity and control: On the determinants of the search for social knowledge. *Journal of Personality and Social Psychology, 40,* 635–642.

Taylor, S. E. (1998). The social being in social psychology. In D. Gilbert, S. T. Fiske, & G. Lindzey (Eds.), *Handbook of social psychology* (4th ed., Vol. 1, pp. 58–95). New York: McGraw-Hill.

Taylor, S. E., & Brown, J. D. (1988). Illusion and well-being: A social psychological perspective on mental health. *Psychological Bulletin, 103,* 193–210.

Taylor, S. E., & Brown, J. D. (1994). Illusion and well-being revisited: Separating fact from fiction. *Psychological Bulletin, 116,* 21–27.

Taylor, S. E., & Gollwitzer, P. M. (1995). Effects of mindset on positive illusions. *Journal of Personality and Social Psychology, 69,* 213–226.

Taylor, S. E., Neter, E., & Wayment, H. A. (1995). Self-evaluation processes. *Personality and Social Psychology Bulletin, 21,* 1278–1287.

Tedeschi, J. T., Schlenker, B. R., & Bonoma, T. V. (1971).

Cognitive dissonance: Private ratiocination or public spectacle? *American Psychologist, 26,* 685–695.

Tesser, A. (1986). Some effects of self-evaluation maintenance on cognition and action. In R. M. Sorentino & E. T. Higgins (Eds.), *Handbook of motivation and cognition* (Vol. 1, pp. 435–464). New York: Guilford.

Tesser, A. (1988). Toward a self-evaluation maintenance model of social behavior. In L. Berkowitz (Ed.), *Advances in experimental social psychology* (Vol. 21, pp. 181–227). San Diego, CA: Academic Press.

Tesser, A., & Cornell, D. P. (1991). On the confluence of self processes. *Journal of Experimental Social Psychology, 27,* 501–526.

Tetlock, P. E. (1983a). Accountability and complexity of thought. *Journal of Personality and Social Psychology, 45,* 74–83.

Tetlock, P. E. (1983b). Accountability and the perseverance of first impressions. *Social Psychology Quarterly, 46,* 285–292.

Tetlock, P. E. (1985). Accountability: A social check on the fundamental attribution error. *Social Psychology Quarterly, 48,* 227–236.

Tetlock, P. E., & Boettger, R. (1989). Accountability: A social magnifier of the dilution effect. *Journal of Personality and Social Psychology, 57,* 388–398.

Tetlock, P. E., & Kim, J. L. (1987). Accountability and judgment processes in a personality prediction task. *Journal of Personality and Social Psychology, 52,* 700–709.

Thibodeau, R., & Aronson, E. (1992). Taking a closer look: Reasserting the role of the self-concept in dissonance theory. *Personality and Social Psychology Bulletin, 18,* 591–602.

Thompson, E. P., Chaiken, S., & Hazlewood, J. D. (1993). Need for cognition and desire for control as moderators of extrinsic reward effects: A person X situation approach to the study of intrinsic motivation. *Journal of Personality and Social Psychology, 65,* 987–999.

Thompson, E. P., Roman, R. J., Moskowitz, G. B., Chaiken, S., & Bargh, J. A. (1994). Accuracy motivation attenuates covert priming: The systematic *r*eprocessing of social information. *Journal of Personality and Social Psychology, 66,* 474–489.

Toates, F. (1986). *Motivational systems.* Cambridge, England: Cambridge University Press.

Trope, Y. (1986a). Identification and inference processes in dispositional attribution. *Psychological Review, 93,* 239–257.

Trope, Y. (1986b). Self enhancement and self-assessment in achievement behavior. In R. M. Sorrentino & E. T. Higgins (Eds.), *Handbook of motivation and cognition* (Vol. 1, pp. 350–378). New York: Guilford.

Tykocinski, O. E., Pittman, T. S., & Tuttle, E. E. (1995). Inaction inertia: Foregoing future benefits as a result of illusory loss. *Journal of Personality and Social Psychology, 68,* 793–803.

Vallacher, R. R. (1992). Mental calibration: Forging a working relationship between mind and action. In D. M. Wegner & J. W. Pennebaker (Eds.), *Handbook of mental control.* Englewood Cliffs, NJ: Prentice-Hall.

Vallacher, R. R., & Wegner, D. M. (1985). *A theory of action identification.* Hillsdale, NJ: Erlbaum.

Vallacher, R. R., & Wegner, D. M. (1987). What do people think they're doing? Action identification and human behavior. *Psychological Review, 94,* 3–15.

Vallacher, R. R., & Wegner, D. M. (1989). Levels of personal agency: Individual variation in action identification. *Journal of Personality and Social Psychology, 57,* 660–671.

Vallerand, R. J., & Reid, G. (1984). On the causal effects of perceived competence on intrinsic motivation: A test of cognitive evaluation theory. *Journal of Sport Psychology, 6,* 94–102.

Waschull, S. B., & Kernis, M. H. (1996). Level and stability of self-esteem as predictors of children's intrinsic motivation and reasons for anger. *Personality and Social Psychology Bulletin, 22,* 4–13.

Weary, G., Gleicher, F., & Marsh, K. (1993). *Control motivation and social cognition.* New York: Springer-Verlag.

Weary, G., Jordan, J. S., & Hill, M. G. (1985). The attributional norm of internality and depressive sensitivity to social information. *Journal of Personality and Social Psychology, 49,* 1283–1293.

Weary, G., Marsh, K. L., Gleicher, F., & Edwards, J. A. (1993). Depression, control motivation, and the processing of information about others. In G. Weary, F. Gleicher, & K. Marsh (Eds.), *Control motivation and social cognition* (pp. 255–287). New York: Springer-Verlag.

Webster, D. M. (1993). Motivated augmentation and reduction of the overattribution bias. *Journal of Personality and Social Psychology, 65,* 261–271.

Webster, D. M., & Kruglanski, A. W. (1994). Individual differences in need for cognitive closure. *Journal of Personality and Social Psychology, 67,* 1049–1062.

Wegner, D. M., & Bargh, J. A. (1998). Control and automaticity in social life. In D. Gilbert, S. T. Fiske, & G. Lindzey (Eds.), *Handbook of social psychology* (4th ed., Vol. 1, pp. 446–496). New York: McGraw-Hill.

Wegner, D. M., & Vallacher, R. R. (1986). Action identification. In R. M. Sorrentino & E. T. Higgins (Eds.), *Handbook of motivation and cognition* (Vol. 1, pp. 550–582). New York: Guilford.

Weiner, B. (1985). "Spontaneous" causal thinking. *Psychological Bulletin, 97,* 74–84.

Weiner, B. (1986). *An attributional theory of motivation and emotion.* New York: Springer-Verlag.

Weinstein, N. D. (1980). Unrealistic optimism about future life events. *Journal of Personality and Social Psychology, 39,* 806–820.

Weldon, E., & Gargano, G. M. (1988). Cognitive loafing: The effects of accountability and shared responsibility on cognitive effort. *Journal of Personality and Social Psychology, 52,* 159–171.

White, J. D., & Carlston, D. E. (1983). Consequences of schemata for attention, impressions, and recall in complex social interactions. *Journal of Personality and Social Psychology, 45,* 538–549.

White, R. W. (1959). Motivation reconsidered: The concept of competence. *Psychological Review, 66,* 297–333.

Wicklund, R. A. (1974). *Freedom and reactance.* Hillsdale, NJ: Erlbaum.

Wicklund, R. A., & Brehm, J. W. (1976). *Perspectives on cognitive dissonance.* Hillsdale, NJ: Erlbaum.

Wicklund, R. A., & Gollwitzer, P. M. (1982). *Symbolic self-completion.* Hillsdale, NJ: Erlbaum.

Wild, T. C., Enzle, M. E., & Hawkins, W. L. (1992). Effects of perceived extrinsic versus intrinsic teacher motivation on student reactions to skill acquisition. *Personality and Social Psychology Bulletin, 18,* 245–251.

Williamson, G. M., & Clark, M. S. (1992). Impact of desired relationship type on affective reactions to choosing and being required to help. *Personality and Social Psychology Bulletin, 18,* 10–18.

Williamson, G. M., Clark, M. S., Pegalis, L. J., & Behan, A. (1996). Affective consequences of refusing to help in communal and exchange relationships. *Personality and Social Psychology Bulletin, 22,* 34–47.

Woike, B. A. (1995). Most-memorable experiences: Evidence for a link between implicit and explicit motives and social cognitive processes in everyday life. *Journal of Personality and Social Psychology, 68,* 1081–1091.

Wong, P. T. P., & Weiner, B. (1981). When people ask "why" questions, and the heuristics of attributional search. *Journal of Personality and Social Psychology, 40,* 650–663.

Wright, R. A., & Brehm, J. W. (1989). Energization and goal attractiveness. In L. Pervin (Ed.), *Goal concepts in personality and social psychology* (pp. 168–210). Hillsdale, NJ: Erlbaum.

Wright, R. A., Brehm, J. W., & Bushman, B. J. (1988). Cardiovascular responses to threat: Effects of the difficulty and availability of a cognitive avoidant task. *Basic and Applied Social Psychology, 10,* 161–171.

Yost, J. H., & Weary, G. (1996). Depression and the correspondent inference bias: Evidence for more effortful cognitive processing. *Personality and Social Psychology Bulletin, 22,* 192–200.

Young, P. T. (1961). *Motivation and emotion: A survey of the determinants of human and animal activity.* New York: Wiley.

Zajonc, R. B. (1998). Emotions. In D. Gilbert, S. T. Fiske, & G. Lindzey (Eds.), *Handbook of social psychology* (4th ed., Vol. 1, pp. 591–632). New York: McGraw-Hill.

Zajonc, R. B., & Burnstein, E. (1965). The learning of balanced and unbalanced social structures. *Journal of Personality, 33,* 153–163.

Zanna, M., & Cooper, J. (1974). Dissonance and the pill: An attribution approach to studying the arousal properties of dissonance. *Journal of Personality and Social Psychology, 29,* 703–709.

Zanna, M., & Cooper, J. (1976). Dissonance and the attribution process. In J. Harvey, W. Ickes, and R. Kidd (Eds.), *New directions in attribution research* (pp. 199–217). Hillsdale, NJ: Erlbaum.

Zimbardo, P. G. (1970). The human choice: Individuation, reason, and order versus deindividuation, impulse, and chaos. In W. J. Arnold & D. Levine (Eds.), *Nebraska Symposium on Motivation: 1969* (Vol. 17, pp. 237–307). Lincoln: University of Nebraska Press.

Zuckerman, M. (1979). Attribution of success and failure revisited, or: The motivational bias is still alive and well. *Journal of Personality, 47,* 245–287.

CHAPTER THIRTEEN

EMOTIONS

ROBERT B. ZAJONC, *Stanford University*

This is the first time a chapter on emotions appears in the *Handbook of Social Psychology*. Among the chapters in the previous editions, the topic of emotions received little attention. Yet emotional phenomena enter into almost every aspect of social life, and in themselves, emotions are distinctly social processes. Most of our happiness comes from events in the interpersonal realm. Our anger is directed to others in our social environment who cause us harm and grief. We are sad about the failures and illnesses of our friends or relatives. And we are disgusted with the opposing political party.

In fact, it can be readily argued that of all major psychological processes, emotions are of prime importance. For a world bereft of emotions cannot exist or be imagined. Could there be affiliation, could there be friendship, or art, or mating, or reproduction, or for that matter, could there be life? Take classical conditioning. In order for conditioning to occur a response must previously be succeeded by a reinforcing event. And an event is reinforcing only if the organism can discriminate it as a positive or a negative event. No learning and performance could emerge or be sustained because there would be no incentives, for incentives exist only by virtue of their positive or negative consequences. Rolls (1995), in fact, defined emotions as "states produced by instrumental conditioning stimuli" (p. 1091). An organism that could not discriminate between positive and negative consequences of its actions could not acquire stable response dispositions and could therefore not survive. This broad conception of emotions is commensurate with the growing state of our knowledge about these processes. Being strict and precise with a definition that specifically includes all phenomena that the term is meant to subsume and exclude all that it is not, runs into a host of overlapping and borderline phenomena which different authors sought to arbitrarily count as "emotion" and others not. For example, Izard (1978) considers interest to be among the basic emotions whereas Ekman (1973) does not. The best heuristic for defining emotion is by distinguishing it from the highly related and interacting process of cognition (see pp. 596–597). For our initial purposes consider emotions as responding to the approach/avoidance distinction and cognition as responding to the true/false distinction. This comparison sets the two processes to be distinct albeit in many ways the two processes share elements in common. A complete and coherent definition of emotion is equivalent to this entire chapter including the content of its references.

What about cognition? Couldn't the organism assign events to categories that subsume positive or negative consequences and modulate its actions accordingly? No. Because categories could not be formed without the ability to make hedonic discriminations. On the one hand, an individual could not learn categories if there was no way of differentially reinforcing correct and incorrect categorizing responses. On the other hand, a culture would not develop categories because there would be no incentives for its members to acquire them and maintain them. Categories do not exist because differences exist among objects and events. There are no categories for different contents of used Kleenex. Categories exist because some objects and some events *matter* and others not. Emotions, then, are primary, as I have argued elsewhere (Zajonc, 1980). And in his recent volume on the neuroscience of emotion and cognition, Damasio (1994) argued that the primary and fundamental reaction to external stimuli is not a perceptual or a cognitive reaction, but an emotional reaction modulated by what he called *somatic markers,* essentially "gut feelings" directed toward objects and events occurring at the onset of an encounter and essentially determining the subsequent sequence of the individual's reactions, including cognitive processes.

Given that behavior is highly selective, and given further that the environment at each instant of time confronts the organism with a vast number of alternatives as objects to be selectively attended to, and once selected, as instigations for an enormous variety of responses and reactions if processed fully, the decision time for the very first choice would exceed the individual's lifetime. The alternatives, also, must be compared on some criteria, and these inevitably involve the individual's needs, fears, hopes, and wishes. So the essential cuts in the selection process must be made with criteria that have affect as their primary element. Culture is an institution that provides its members with criteria for selection and these criteria are meant to elicit affective reactions from the individual. We are taught and told about things that are "good," things that are "bad," "dangerous," "harmful," or "foreign." We learn what actions are "polite," "heroic," or "despicable." And within the culturally determined categories of objects, events, experiences, and persons, we are individually selective based on the incentive value or "utilities" present at the given moment and appropriate to the individual's condition at that time. If we are hungry, therefore, a vast proportion of possible alternatives within the elements of the environment and the aspects of our action can be immediately ignored and eliminated, reducing the choice to a more reasonable proportion.

Emotions are pervasive among living species, present in humans in their most complex forms, in less elaborate forms in animals, and perhaps even in plants (Attenborough, 1995). It can hardly be doubted that emotions have a phylogenetic priority over cognitions. It must also be the case that the earliest evolutionary achievement was an approach/avoidance discrimination capacity. The emergence of more complex emotional potentials was slow and probably only in the advanced stages of evolution (MacLean, 1990). Complex behavioral patterns, such as aggression, flight, anger, diverse fears, surprise, sadness, joy, must be differentiations and elaborations of those very primitive and simple approach/avoidance discriminations. It is those that may have evolved driven by inclusive fitness or kin selection (Wilson, 1975). But many other processes, including cultural coevolution, must have taken part in promoting the emergence of more complex and uniquely human emotions.

There have been a number of serious critiques of the general validity of the concept of inclusive fitness and of the reproductive success motive as driving adaptive behavior (Gould, 1980; Midgley, 1978). Midgley (1979), for example, took Dawkins' (1989) idea about the *selfish gene* to task, disputing the claim that "the emotional nature of man

is exclusively self-interested" (p. 439) or that "calculating prudence[1] is the root of all social behavior" (p. 442).

I will define the capacity for emotional reaction in more general terms, making no commitment for the time being to the manner of their evolution. The capacity for emotional reaction, thus, is *the capacity to discriminate between and to respond adaptively to present and anticipated conditions that are likely to be harmful or beneficial to the individual or his/her community.* This definition is explicit in positing response potentials that are sensitive to reinforcement contingencies and to individual and social outcomes. They are responses that are flexible and plastic in their function. The definition views the organism not as a passive, blind, and shortsighted reactive entity but as a dynamic actor capable of discriminating among alternative environmental conditions, not only those currently prevalent but also ones that can be anticipated and evaluated for their individual and collective future consequences. This definition emphasizes the instrumental and reinforcing factors in emotions, as does Rolls (1990), rather than capacities that maximize reproductive potential or inclusive fitness. I have quite purposefully limited myself to defining emotional *reaction,* and avoided defining *emotion* which is much more of a challenge. Emotions are complex systems that implicate psychological, interpersonal, social, and cultural constraints and affordances; involve neurophysiological, neuroanatomic, and neurochemical processes; engage cognition and motivation; and no doubt are present in all facets of behavior. That, of course, is not a definition of the emotions. It is the acknowledgment of their important place and role in psychology.

Given the above definition, emotions are phenomena of remarkable breadth and richness, characterizing organisms from one end of the living spectrum to the other. At a superficial level, it may seem that the definition of emotional reactions is so broad as to include nonliving feedback systems as well. For it could be argued that such machines as, for example, the thermostat are included in the definition. The thermostat is indeed capable of discriminating air of varying temperatures, and adjusts the furnace accordingly to keep it in a specified range. Nonliving systems, however, and artifacts, cannot be included among the emotions as defined above for a number of reasons. I rely on the useful distinctions between living and not living systems made by Jacques Monod (1971) who postulated three necessary and sufficient attributes that separate animate and inanimate entities. The three attributes of living systems are *teleonomy, autonomous morphogenesis,* and *invariant reproduction.* Teleonomy is "one of the fundamental characteristics common to all living beings without exception: that of being *objects endowed with a purpose or project,* which . . . they exhibit in their structure and carry out through their performances . . ." (p. 9). Autonomous morphogenesis is the capacity of living systems to emerge as structures on the strength of their internal resources. DNA information provides all organs with directions for the form and function they will develop. Invariant reproduction, on the other hand, is the property of living systems to reproduce isomorphic "offspring." Human offspring grows to be much more like its parents than like those of any other species. Hammers, coat hangers, computers, harvesters, and gallows are objects that exhibit teleonomy but are not living systems. These objects are produced neither by virtue of *autonomous morphogenesis* nor are they products of *invariant reproduction.* Note that not only are living entities endowed with a purpose, their purpose is reflected in their structure. Thus, for example, the eye is constructed so as to allow for vision, and in that sense it is a model for the camera. All visual systems, natural and artificial, must allow the capture of reflected light. But a camera, while it exhibits teleonomy, has neither the property of autonomous morphogenesis nor invariant reproduction. Within the context of the three necessary and sufficient properties of living systems, emotions emerge as a crucial process that guides the growth of the living system and its organs in ways commensurate with the project and purpose.

Unlike cognitions, some qualitative distinctions have been made for emotions, treating some as *basic.* It is not entirely clear what makes an emotion basic (Mesquita & Frijda, 1992, Mesquita, Frijda, & Scherer, 1996). For Darwin (1904) it was the universality of facial expressions, a principle followed by others (e.g., Ekman, 1973) although disputed for its validity (Russell, 1994). For Descartes (1647) and Spinoza (1677) it was the fact that some emotions are composites of others and those that aren't are the basic ones. For example, shyness is the fear of humiliation, but fear is basic because it cannot be reduced to more primitive elements. This principle has also been followed in the linguistic analysis of emotions (see Johnson-Laird & Oatley, 1989). One could add that Ekman (1993) conjectured that basic emotions are controlled by specifically dedicated neural structures and mechanisms, whereas the same apparently cannot be said for the more complex compound emotions, such as disappointment. Thus far only scattered evidence has been obtained for the conjecture. LeDoux (1995) localized fear structures, the hypothalamus has been identified with anger and aggression, whereas sadness and depression have been related to the release of serotonin. But we are not certain whether the "fear" structures serve fear alone; we know that the hypothalamus controls not only aggression, but sex, eating, and thermoregulation, and that serotonin is not uniquely active in depression and has been found in association with other functions.

The pervasive nature of the emotions is clearly reflected in all spheres of life. One needs only to open the daily newspaper, turn on the television or the radio, or walk the streets of a city, and one is assaulted by messages and appeals designed to play on our emotions. And many of these emotional appeals are appeals to partake of emotional experiences—they are promises of a happier and better life, of excitement, of success, of entertainment, of pleasure. And if not that, then they are promises of reduction of pain and suffering, or at least inconvenience. Emotion captures a gigantic share of the market and public discourse—more so in the United States than in any other country, I believe. Nowhere else is the volume of marketing and advertising as large, no other country produces and consumes as many entertainment commodities—music, film, pulp fiction—as the United States. And these products flood the world markets and have virtually no competition abroad. In no other country, also, is the popularity of antidepressant drugs and methods as high. The yearly population of depressive disorder patients has exceeded 11 million, according to the latest figures.

This is not to say that there is no eager market for information. But information can become a commodity only if it is of value—which means nothing else than that it can touch our emotions. In short, I would venture a guess that commodities whose principal value is in producing emotion have the bigger share of the overall market than commodities whose principal value is offering or generating information.

As civilization has made its way from the nineteenth to the twentieth century, the public discourse in various domains—art, law, politics, business, science, journalism, literature, music, education—has moved from an emphasis on intellectual qualities—on reason—to an emphasis on emotional reactions. This is particularly obvious in the news media which signal the importance of an item by leads and headlines that shock and agitate. And in many instances, what appears to be an offering of information has a powerful emotional component that may in many instances obscure the information being offered. Thus, for example, the political situation in Sudan in 1993 was brought into dramatic focus by the Pulitzer Prize-winning photograph of a starving girl collapsed only a few feet from what appears to be a vulture waiting for her demise.[2] The picture had probably much more influence on U.S. foreign policy decisions and the general political response than any information or intelligence reports about the ethnic strife or political conflict in Sudan, and today more people remember the picture even though they know little about the specific political issues in that African country.

What is the prime subject of ordinary discourse and conversation? More often than not, interpersonal communication is a reciprocation of emotions—a dance of emotions—than an exchange of information (Kurasawa, 1994). In a recent attempt at reconceptualizing emotions, Parkinson (1995) makes the proposal to treat emotions as *interpersonal* rather than *intrapsychic phenomena.*

Every field of psychology has contributed to the study of the emotions, and the study of the emotions has played an important role in the conceptual development of all fields as well. Social psychology was among the early contributors to the understanding of emotion in the work of Schachter and Singer (1962), but it has been underused as an explanatory concept. Clinical psychologists are most interested in the role of emotion in pathology and treatment (e.g., Lazarus & Folkman, 1984). Developmental psychology seeks to understand the participation of emotional phenomena in the management of behavior and socialization (e.g., Izard, 1978). Personality theory recruits theories of emotion focusing on habitual ways of emotional reactions as a way toward a more precise personality taxonomy (Pervin, 1993). Cultural psychology seeks to specify culturally based differences in emotional reactions and expression to gain insight into the interface between mind and society (Markus & Kitayama, 1994). Cognitive psychology has less contact with the emotions; its most recent and most visible joint participation is in the study of mood and memory (Bower, 1981) and of recovered memories (Loftus & Ketcham, 1994). As a consequence, theories of emotion come from many fields of psychology, and these theories start with different perspectives, make different assumptions, and seek to accomplish different goals. A global view of research and theory in the field of emotion does not offer a coherent picture. And this chapter, I am afraid, reflects this incoherence in its organization.

Given the primacy and importance of emotional processes, it is difficult to understand why the topic was neglected for decades and why in fact it did not become the phenomenon to be studied first thus laying ground for the analysis of those processes that depend on it, including cognitive processes. Why did problems in the areas of cognition receive so much more attention and receive it so much earlier and much more systematically and extensively? It is indeed remarkable that the progress of psychology invested so much of its intellectual resources in a process that is not only a derivative of the emotions but fairly opaque. In mathematics, we solve equations by seeking to reduce the number of unknowns. The fewer the unknowns the more likely that the problem will be solved, theorem will be proven, or formulation understood. The same in science, except that here the unknowns are those variables and processes that we cannot observe. They are the unknowns in our scientific theories and we are obliged to make assumptions—sometimes unverifiable—about them. Now, emotion has many *directly* observable features. We can examine the instigating conditions, we can see the individual's emotional expressions following these instigations, we can measure physiological responses in the autonomic nervous system, we can look up MRIs, EEGs, or EMGs, we can inquire about the individual's subjective feeling (if it is a human individual), we can register instrumental responses, and we can manipulate all of these experimentally. But this is more difficult in cognition. Most

of the processes implicated in cognition—storage, access, representation, trace—are hidden from us and cannot be observed and measured directly. Traditionally, inferences about cognition have been based on linguistic utterances and while language is informative of cognitive processes and cognitive processes are informative about language, the concepts and processes identified in linguistics are incommensurate with concepts and processes explicating cognition. The word "chair" is a semantic representation of a class of objects in reality. But what can this knowledge tell us about what is the representation of the class "chair" in the mind or in the brain?

HISTORICAL BACKGROUND

Because emotion is a relative newcomer as an integral domain of psychological inquiry, it is useful to consider its historical antecedents. The attention given to cognition in preference to emotion dates to the notions of these processes developed in antiquity. Perhaps the earliest attempt to specify emotional processes is found in the fifth century BC in the writings of Empedocles (Battistini, 1968). This Ionian philosopher sought to reduce the infinite diversity of observable phenomena to a few elementary and unique substances and qualities. There were four elementary qualities lying on the orthogonal axes of warm/cold and dry/wet. At the extremes of the axes the qualities opposed each other, and at the diagonals they cohered, giving rise to the four basic elements: fire (warm and dry), water (cold and wet), air (warm and wet), and earth (cold and dry). The principles of cohesion and repulsion were fundamental: cohesion of elements giving rise to joy, repulsion to sadness, pain, destruction of tissues, injury, and disease.

The two basic forces of behavior, according to Plato (Fortenbaugh, 1975), are pleasure (*hêdonê*) and pain (*lupê*) and are called "foolish counsellors." They may misdirect wise action if one overreacts to them, as in *phobos* (fear)—the expectation of pain which, when excessive, results in maladaptive habitual risk aversion. In *Philebus* Plato compares pleasure and wisdom for their capacity to make life blessed. And Socrates gives nod to wisdom over pleasure, thus legitmizing the paradigm whereby passions are the animal-like impulses, and reason is the means of controlling them—a consequence that renders the individual mature and the society stable.

The earliest analysis of emotions takes place in the context of ethics. Most explicit are Aristotle's (trans. 1980) discussions of the role of emotions in Nicomachean Ethics which mainly deals with virtues and vices. Virtues and vices are acquired (*sic!*) dispositions to a variety of attributes, but mostly to emotions. Courage is a virtue because it is a predisposition to disregard fear. Cowardice is a vice because it succumbs to fear. Lechery is vice because it submits to sexual desire, gluttony to excessive appetite.

Virtues and vices, according to Aristotle, are *characteristics* of people and they themselves are not passions or emotions:

> Now neither the virtues nor the vices are *passions,* because we are not called good or bad on the ground of our passions, but on the ground of our virtues and our vices, and because we are neither praised or blamed for our passions (for the man who feels fear or anger is not praised, nor is the man who simply feels anger blamed, but the man who feels it in a certain way) (Roberts, 1989, 1105b).

Aristotle's ethics appeal to the virtue of moderation, treating passions as vices in their own right when excessive:

> Both fear and confidence and appetite and anger and pity and in general pleasure and pain may be felt too much and too little, and in both cases not well; but to feel them at the right times, with reference to the right objects, toward the right people, with the right motive, and in the right way, is what is both intermediate and best, and this is characteristic of virtue (Roberts, 1989, p. 1106b).

Anger is not a vice if it is expressed in outrage of injustice, and generally character, that is, the configuration of vices and virtues, is not immutable because both virtues and vices are *acquired* dispositions that are modifiable. For Aristotle, emotions derive from the alogical, biological sphere of antecedents of action and intellect. They were more imbedded in sensation whereas *reasoned reflection* was rooted in logic and the rational process. Emotions could, therefore, be sources of misjudgment and bias:

> For things do not seem the same to those who love and those who hate, nor to those who are angry and those who are calm, but either altogether different or different in magnitude. For the friend, the man about whom he is giving judgment seems either to have committed no offense or a minor one, while for the enemy it is the opposite. And to the man who is enthusiastic and optimistic, if what is to come should be pleased, it seems to be both likely to come and likely to be good, while to the indifferent or depressed man it seems the opposite. . . . Emotions are those things by the alteration of which men differ with regard to those judgments which pain and pleasure accompany, such as anger, pity, fear, and all other such and their opposites (Aristotle, trans. 1991, p. 141).

Thus the beginnings of inquiry into the emotion/cognition (*pathos/logos*) interface date to Aristotle and are especially clear in his *Rhetoric* which served as a manual of ef-

fective persuasion, oratory, and intellectual influence. Note that in psychology, the nature of emotion/cognition interaction preserved much of its antique form. The control of emotions by cognition in the form of cognitive appraisal is a standard view in personality and clinical psychology (e.g., Lazarus, 1991). But in *social* psychology cognitions were recruited to deal with discomfort produced, for example, by dissonance (Festinger, 1957), or to reduce ambiguity of nonspecific arousal (Schachter & Singer, 1962).

Cognition and Emotion

The early treatments of mental functions had no difficulty separating emotional and cognitive processes. Passions were the tendencies that made individuals alike, reason and intellect were functions that distinguished among them. Passions were forces to be controlled and reason was the means of controlling them. The earliest exponent of the cognitive appraisal theory was Aristotle. Fear, according to his view, was a complex phenomenon involving possible pain and the thought of impending danger, and shame was the thought of impending disgrace. Anger could be aroused when a person was treated so as to suffer pain, but if the treatment was justified then the person could not become angry (Fortenbaugh, 1975). In this formulation, emotional reactions could be viewed to be intelligent and vulnerable to reasoned persuasion.

A conception of emotions where cognitive processes are featured as the prime instruments of control, modulation, and management should be attributed to Descartes (1647). For it is Descartes who by positing the infallible certainty and mental supremacy of *cogito* undertook in his very last work, *Passions of the Soul,* to understand the emotions and thereby to discover the means of controlling them—means that were above all deriving from man's cognitive capacities. And for Descartes, *to understand* means to apply the powers of the rational process, *La méthode.* Passions were viewed as afflictions of the soul, causing untold grief and pain. They obscured thought and decision and led otherwise intelligent people into serious errors of judgment. In 1645, perhaps under the urging of his friend Princess Elisabeth of Bohemia who suffered from severe depression, he promised to produce a treatise that would employ the finest instruments of *La méthode* to mastering of the passions. For it was the challenge of all philosophy—a task that has now been appropriated by tabloid psychology—to discover the secret of eternal happiness. And for Descartes that secret was not to be found in piety, virtue, fate, or chance, but in reason.

In a recent critique of Descartes that makes careful use of new sources including the philosopher's letters, Kambouchner (1996) shows that Decartes assigned a more significant role to the passions than was previously believed. While emotions could well cause error and poor judgment, they are, in fact, indispensable. For they are the sources of energy for action that reason alone cannot generate. It is the passions that direct the will and move the organism to action, it is the passions that act as the most important selective factor in attention, a factor without which the soul could not possibly be the way it is. This new view makes Descartes' "error" much less serious than Damasio (1994) would have it, and in fact, if attention and will, both products of the passions, direct and precede cognition, then Damasio's own concept of "somatic markers" (as mentioned) belongs in the same theoretical class of inferences.

The most severe criticism of Descartes was directed to his mind-body dualism, a philosophical problem yet to be fully resolved (despite claims such as those of Dennett [1991] that the matter is finally laid to rest). The most troubling premise of the mind-body dualism is the assumption that mental matters are somehow materially independent of bodily tissue which, in the extreme, leads to the conclusion that there can be thoughts outside of the body, without meat, so to speak. That premise made thought, imagination, memory, and feeling rather ethereal and invulnerable to scientific analysis. But it is probably the case that Descartes' conception of the mind-body interface was more a capitulation to the church than a strong scientific conviction.

In spite of all the critique, the mind-body dualism appears as a serious implicit assumption in a number of treatments of the emotions. Clearly, the Schachter-Singer conception, by positing a bodily state that seeks explanation, is phrased in uncertain mind-body language. The ideas of "coping with emotions" and of "cognitive appraisal" implicitly assume a mind-body separation.[3] That early view does not differ in its superficial features from that of Arnold (1960), Mandler (1975), or Lazarus and Folkman (1984). But in the more recent years the emotion/cognition distinction became blurred. Thus, Abelson (1963) introduced the concept of "hot cognitions" which were essentially cognitive responses of evaluative and affective nature, and Schwarz and Clore (1983; see also Clore, Schwarz, & Conway, 1994) focused on the role of affect as a conveyer of information.

In general, dualism is a more troubling principle for philosophy than for psychology. It is only if we wish to fathom the "true" essence of the mind and require a precise answer to the "hard" question of how is it that the interactions of elementary particles reveal themselves as sonnets, mathematical proofs, or jokes, that we encounter difficulties. But for practical and empirical purposes, and for the time being, psychologists can make substantial progress without having a precise answer to this question. For, at some level, it is not at all confusing to assume that mind and body are distinct, and that some connection, yet to be fully specified, exists between mental and bodily processes. In disagreement with Dennett (1991), not all forms of dualism are "to be avoided at *all costs*" (p. 37).

Bertrand Russell saw no difficulty in some forms of dualism, finding it eminently acceptable, for example, for a father also to be a policeman. Similarly, a person may be a chief executive officer and at the same time be taller than average or have high testosterone level. But Russell finesses the mind-body problem using a false analogy by positing an irrelevant form of dualism. After all, being a father is neither a necessary nor a sufficient condition for being a policeman, or vice versa—a feature without which there wouldn't be any difficulties. It is only when we insist on a strictly deterministic explanation and aren't satisfied unless we pinpoint unique causes, that the problem is troublesome. It is only when we need to know how, for example, a particular collection of particles is transformed, step by step, into Fermat's Last Theorem or Picasso's *La Guernica,* where in the brain is my telephone number, or what patterns of ions distinguish between anger and indignation, that we confront mysteries.

But the mind-body problem need not be reduced to the level of elementary particles. We do not need that degree of resolution to explain, say, the Müller-Lyer illusion. And, in fact, that level of resolution would turn out much too cumbersome for it would overload us with unmanageable masses of information. All "causation" can be viewed from multiple perspectives and at multiple levels. In a sense, the sides of a right triangle completely "determine" the hypotenuse and its two angles. This sort of determinism is not dynamic in the sense that no energy is expended. No material elements make contact with each other, and there is no change in one as a *physical* function of the other. The "causes" are *formal,* as they are in logic or mathematics, and the causal structure of the mental processes can be analyzed to a substantial level of detail by assuming no more than formal causality (see p. 598). Moreover, the Pythagorean law can be verified empirically as well. The same goes for mental processes. I take it as an act of faith that, if the mind-body problem is ever resolved, it most likely will be resolved in the domain of the emotions, for they offer us phenomena where the mind-body interaction is most readily observable and manipulable.

Differences between Affect and Cognition

It is of value, therefore, to identify some features that distinguish emotion from cognition.

1. There is an infinite number of distinct cognitions. The number of distinct emotions is limited.
2. There are plausible assumptions about the existence of *basic* irreducible emotions. But what might be basic cognitions?
3. Emotions are readily classified into two categories—positive/negative, attraction/aversion, approach/avoidance. While there is disagreement about other categories, the polarity categorization is universally

accepted. Cognitions, too, can be classified into two large categories: true and false. There is, however, an important difference. The dual categorization of emotions refers to internal reactions, and to two states that have strikingly different consequences for behavior. However, the dual categorization of cognitions has an external standard of validity. Moreover, a false cognition will influence individual's behavior in the same way as a true cognition.

4. Cognitions can be evaluated for their correctness. Individuals can be asked to compare the heights of the Eiffel Tower and the Washington Monument and we can evaluate their accuracy. And we can ask the same individuals which of the two structures they prefer. But their preferences cannot be judged for accuracy or validity. Protarchus claimed 2,400 years ago that reasoned thought can be wrong but passions cannot.

5. Cognitions are always *about* something. They have a referent, an address, they stand *for* something. Emotions, too, are directed to objects, but they are neither about something nor stand for something else outside of themselves. Moreover, there exist emotions that have no referent. There is free-floating anxiety, for example, but there is no such thing as a free-floating cognition.

6. Emotions may carry an intrinsic instigation to action, sometimes very drastic and dangerous action. Anger will evoke agonistic reactions, fear will instigate flight, and millions lay buried as victims of anger or pride. But unless they first elicit an emotion, cognitions of themselves are incapable of triggering instrumental process. When someone tells us that our "article filled many necessary gaps," we will first process the communication to see if it was an insult or a compliment, and we may reciprocate in kind or simply sulk.

7. At the basic level, we share emotions with lower animals. Except for trivial features, cognitions are probably uniquely human.

8. Emotions are readily communicated by their expressions and for the most part there is little ambiguity in detecting them. Cognitions are for the most part covert, and we never know whether a person who starts with the sentence "I think that . . ." actually thought "that. . . ."

9. Emotions and emotional expressions are fairly universal across cultures. Cognitions, and certainly their means of broadcast—languages, are not.

10. In reacting to a stimulus, the affective features of a reaction seem to be primary. At least, the onset features of a reaction coordinate themselves to the valence of the stimulus object or event before the identity of the object or event is established. Cognitive reactions require more precise and more specific information input. There is a direct pathway from the visual system to the thalamus and then to the amygdala, bypassing the visual cortex. Hence an emotional reaction is possible without the participation of a cognitive appraisal (see pp. 598; 607).

11. All responses can be analyzed for their emotional antecedents, and all responses can be analyzed for their emotional qualities. But not all responses can be analyzed either for their cognitive antecedents or for their cognitive qualities. A person may prefer blue to green, and consistently choose that hue over the other, but this preference may have no detectable or specifiable cognitive antecedents or be attributed to specific properties of the particular hue, for the origin of preferences is in the experience of the person not in the quality of the object. Perhaps it goes back to having a blue blanket as a baby.

12. There are "cognitive virtuosos"—mathematical prodigies, mnemonists, geniuses—but there are no "emotional prodigies." We can speak of an "intellectual giant" but an "emotional giant" is an absurdity. It is only recently that attention had been drawn to the critical functions that emotions play in an efficient adaptation to our lives of growing complexity (Cantor & Kihlstrom, 1987; Goleman, 1995b; Mayer & Salovey, 1995). Of course, there are people who can manage their emotions better than others. There are good "smilers" and miserable "smilers," and one wouldn't be surprised if the former marry better and have higher incomes. But there is nothing in the domain of emotions that would make us say something like "Look, the young Gauss was able to prove complex theorems at age 6, and Pascal did the conic sections as a teenager."

13. Attention plays a more important and pervasive role in cognition than in affect. Many affective influences occur outside of awareness and direct attention.

14. There is perhaps a greater correspondence between an emotion and its motor representations (or somatic trace) than between a cognition and its motor representation.

Contemporary Theories of Emotion and Their Conceptual Elements

It is fair to say that while there are several theoretical treatments that consider the various facets of the emotion process separately, no one general theory systematically relates all these facets to each other. Thus, there are theories of emotional expression (Darwin, 1904; Ekman, 1973; Fridlund, 1994; Gratiolet, 1865; Izard, 1977; Piderit, 1867; Zajonc, 1985; etc.), the autonomic system underlying emotion (James, 1884; Lacy & Lacy, 1978; Levenson, Ekman, & Friesen, 1990; Leventhal, 1980), the neural substrate of emotional reactions (Damasio, 1994; Gray, 1987; LeDoux, 1987; Panksepp, 1982; Rolls, 1990), the role of cognitive factors such as appraisal (Ellsworth, 1991; Frijda, 1986; Lazarus, 1991; Schachter & Singer, 1962), its linguistic categories (Johnson-Laird & Oatley, 1989; Ortony & Clore, 1989; Wierzbicka, 1992), emotional development (Izard & Malatesta, 1987), affective elements in personality (Pervin, 1993; Larsen & Ketelaar, 1991; Plutchik, 1962), affective disorders (Beck, 1976), cultural influences on personality (Lutz, 1988; Markus & Kitayama, 1991; Mesquita & Frijda, 1992; Shweder, 1993), and perhaps some other theories. The crucial impediment to theoretical progress in the field of emotions is that these approaches, being oriented to diverse goals, bringing expertise from diverse specializations, and drawing on different and often conflicting assumptions, make little contact with each other. By default, the organization of this chapter follows these conceptual elements of emotions in detail.

Several of the above domains of research may well constitute segments in the emotional episode, and for some pairs a chronological order might be assumed. Thus, for example, most autonomic responses take about five seconds to develop and they would therefore have to appear after the early onset of expression or even instrumental behavior. That, however, does not automatically place instrumental behavior as the cause of the autonomic reaction for both could well be and are caused by an early neurophysiological response, except that the one takes somewhat longer to show itself as an observable manifestation. In the case of emotions, Aristotle's distinction among the four types of causes (Aristotle, trans. 1991) comes fairly close to the diverse domains of emotion research. *Causa materialis* (material cause) referred to the physical matter of which an object or event consisted. In the case of sculpture, it was the marble. In the case of anger it was the boiling blood around the heart. *Causa efficiens* (efficient cause) referred to the forces that set an event in motion. In the case of the sculpture it was the sculptor. In the case of anger it was the conspicuous slight or frustration. *Causa formalis* (formal cause) was the shape that the sculptor gave to the sculpture. In the case of anger it was the emotional expression, bearing one's teeth, for example, evoked in reaction to the instigation of anger. And *causa finalis* (final cause) was the ultimate function, purpose, or end of the action or event. A sculpture was to serve as an ornament or a monument. In the case of anger, the final cause was seeking of revenge. Thus, Aristotle subsumed the autonomic and neurochemical process in the material causes, emotional expression in formal causes, instigating events and cognitive appraisal in efficient causes, and instrumental motivated action in final causes.

Neuroanatomical Emotional Structures and Neurochemical Processes

The central subcortical structure implicated in emotional process is the amygdaloid complex (Amaral, Price, Pitkänen, & Carmichael, 1992; Weiskrantz, 1956). It is today quite firmly established that the amygdalae are responsive to the affective valence of sensory stimulation (Blanchard & Blanchard, 1972; Cohen, 1980; Davis, 1992; Fonberg, 1972; Goddard, 1964; Jones & Mishkin, 1972; Kapp, Frysinger, Gallagher, & Haselton, 1979; LeDoux, 1995; Nishijo, Ono, & Nishino, 1988; Rolls, 1981). Most research, however, dealt with fear arousal or response to novel stimuli (Nishijo, Ono, & Nishino, 1988). Hence, the role of the amygdala in other emotions is not clearly known. Recall that Cannon (1927) proposed that the affective valence of sensory input is processed by the hypothalamus. Amygdalae can respond to the affective significance of stimulation in all sensory modalities because they receive afferent inputs from all the sensory areas of the cortex (gustatory, visual, auditory, somatosensory, and olfactory). The amygdalae also receive afferent inputs from the hippocampus, a structure that is recognized today as the major site for the cognitive participation in the emotions. LeDoux (1989) suggests that although the hippocampus receives inputs from the sensory cortex, "the sensory inputs are integrated across sensory modalities in complex association cortex before reaching the hippocampus. As a result of the additional pre-processing, the hippocampus is slower to respond to sensory inputs than the amygdalae, but the information it receives is far more complex" (LeDoux, 1989, p. 276). The importance of these neural configurations becomes significant in the debate over affective primacy. The existing structures allow affective response to be made before stimulus identification or recognition takes place (Zajonc, 1980). Recent work comparing the functions of the hippocampus and the amygdala (Zola-Morgan, Squire, Alvarez-Royo, & Clower, 1991) strongly suggests the independence of affect from cognition. These authors, using monkeys, lesioned either the amygdalae, or the hippocampi, or both and measured emotional responsiveness (such as fear reactions, or responses to aversive stimuli) and cognitive functions (such as matching objects to sample), and found that the removal of the amygdalae leaves cognitive functions intact but damages emotional responsiveness, while the perfect opposite occurs when the hippocampi are removed. Adolphs, Tranel, Damasio, and Damasio (1994) found a patient (a thirty-year-old woman with nearly complete destruction of the amygdalae) who was unable to process emotion from photographs of emotional faces, and specifically, could not recognize fear in these faces but was able to recognize the identity of nineteen out of nineteen people's photographs. Thus, the patient retained full recognition memory (her hippocampus was intact) but lost emotional responsiveness. It is to be noted, however, that the amygdala is not the only brain structure that evaluates affective valence (Panksepp, 1982). The limbic frontal lobe has also been clearly implicated in emotional reactivity (Damasio & VanHoesen, 1983).

The analysis of neurochemical and neurophysiological processes in the context of emotion research has seen a growing enthusiasm, especially with the technological advances in the field of neuroimaging (Cohen & Bookheimer, 1994; Druckman & Lacey, 1989; Gur & Gur, 1991; Petersen, Fietz, & Corbetta, 1992; Raichle, 1994; Zülch, 1976). Whereas the work on hemispheric asymmetry (Davidson, 1993) using the EEG has sought mainly to establish differences between positive and negative emotions, there are much more ambitious goals and claims emerging in neuroscience today.

Sarter, Berntson, and Cacioppo (1996) have recently provided a cogent analysis of the unrealistic aspirations voiced by those engaging in imaging research. The size of the units in the brain examined has been steadily decreasing and the specificity of functions presumably served by these units has been steadily increasing. Thus, extremely specific brain sectors, involving at times very small brain units (often single neurons, Squire, 1987), and very specific functions such as individual chess moves (Blakeslee, 1994) have been examined for their causal relationship. There certainly has been a spectacular progress in the neuroscience of emotions, and there certainly are findings relating single neurons to specific functions (e.g., responses of the monkey's neuron in the temporal sulcus to faces, discovered by Perrett, Rolls, & Caan, 1982). Yet it is unrealistic to believe that complex behavior such as involved in emotion can be effectively analyzed at the single-neuron level. Adding the fact of the enormous plasticity of the brain, and the functional autonomy of diverse brain processes, the answer is probably more likely to be found in conventional behavioral research methods.

The structure-function debate in neuroscience is further complicated by a very simple but solid fact: causal bidirectionality. An event such as emotional instigation may be followed by a series of neurochemical and autonomic effects, but one can also obtain a variety of emotional consequences by manipulating the neurochemistry of the brain. For example, cooling of the hypothalamus can result in the rise of hedonic quality of behavior (Berridge & Zajonc, 1991). But induction of positive affect will result in a cooler brain (Zajonc, Murphy, & Inglehart, 1989). Changing the dominant status of an African cichlid fish (*Haplochromis burtoni*) changes the neurons that contain hormones that release gonadotropin. When the animal loses status these cells shrink (Francis, Soma, & Fernald, 1993). The same bidirectionality holds for testosterone and aggression (Sapolsky, 1997). Injections of testosterone increase aggression. But aggression shows increased testosterone levels. Work from Dabbs' laboratory in Georgia State University (Fielden, Lutter, & Dabbs, 1995) found a meaningful relationship between changes in testosterone level for individuals "basking in the reflected glory" of their favorite sports team. Male Brazilian and Italian soccer fans gave saliva samples for testosterone assay during the 1994 Brazil-Italy World Cup soccer match. The testosterone level of the Brazilian fans increased 27.6 percent whereas that of the Italian fans, who watched their team go down to defeat, dropped by 26.7 percent. Conversely, Yeh, Fricke, and Edwards (1996) discovered in crayfish a neuron (LG or lateral giant) that responds to serotonin in quite different ways depending on the hierarchical status of the individual animal. In those of higher rank, serotonin enhances the firing of the LG neuron to sensory stimuli, whereas it inhibits the neuron among low-status animals. The neuron controls the tailflip response of the crayfish—a response intimately implicated in status competition and aggressive behavior. Noradrenaline and cortisol level were found to change during the Chinese fitness exercise, Tai Chi (Jin, 1989). There are thousands of drugs having emotional effects—epinephrine, Prozac, propranolol, meprobamate, benzodiazopines, adrenaline. Recall in this context the classical Schachter-Singer (1962) experiment in which either epinephrine or a placebo was injected into unknowing subjects. Subjects who were not informed of the drug's effects nevertheless experienced arousal which they interpreted differently depending on the social cues with which they were confronted, the "happy" cues inducing positive affect, the "angry" cues inducing anger. What is important here is that the injection succeeded in changing the subjects' emotional state.

The bidirectional causality of these effects presents a serious problem for interpretation of the role of neurochemistry in emotion, not far removed from the Cannon/Sherrington attack on William James (see pp. 600–601 for details). Among the criticisms of the James position was the observation that the autonomic system is too sluggish to play a causal role in the elicitation of the subjective state. But the release of serotonin, for example, is a considerably faster process. Nevertheless, there are three possibilities: (1) Emotional behavioral responses (including efference, instrumental activity, and subjective feeling) are triggered by appropriate stimuli (in the form of conditioned or unconditioned responses), while the neurophysiological and neurochemical activity follows them. (2) The instigating stimuli, be they first processed by the neocortex or directly by the thalamus (LeDoux, 1987), induce neurochemical process that elicits emotion-appropriate behavior and subjective feelings. (3) Both (1) and (2) are possible.

Consider, however, that if the autonomic system is indeed one that mobilizes the organism's energy for action, then it needs to be there early. The process can, within some limits, function efficiently if there are sufficient reserves for immediate vigorous action (say, flight) that are replenished as soon as the autonomic system is turned on. A theoretical picture that emerges might be one akin to Bower's associative network (Bower, 1981) where the various elements of emotion (subjective state, labels, autonomic reactions, central process, instrumental action) form a cluster such that the activation of any one makes all the other units potentially active as well.

A structure of this sort, where attention; perceptual identification; hedonic evaluation; autonomic arousal; activity in the thalamus, amygdalae, the hippocampi, and the hypothalamus; activation of the motor cortex; deployment of skeletal responses, etc., constitute integrated systems, different for each emotion, whose components are ready to fire whenever any one of them is activated is difficult to contemplate. Take, for example, the autonomic system and the amygdalae. The brain stem autonomic nuclei receive impulses either from the hypothalamus or from the amygdalae and the orbitofrontal cortex. Could the autonomic nuclei be activated *without* the participation of the hypothalamus and of the amygdalae which would join in eventually into a simultaneous discharge with the other elements of the emotional process? Given the plasticity of the brain and the brain/behavior interface, the possibility cannot be excluded, but it is probably too clumsy an arrangement to have evolved. Recall that monkeys whose amygdalae had been bilaterally removed suffer an almost full deterioration of appropriate emotional responsiveness. They seem tame and limp, they might eat food that they previously found aversive, but are unable to benefit from learning under both positive reinforcement (Aggleton, 1993; Gaffan, 1992; Jones & Mishkin, 1972) and punishment (Weiskrantz, 1956).

If it turns out that the only structure that evaluates stimuli and events for their emotional significance is indeed the amygdaloid complex, then nothing much else in the emotion process could take place without the early participation of these neutral networks. This conjecture is cast in doubt by numerous examples of functions persisting or being obliterated by the same damage to the brain. The loss of verbal functions, for example, need not be accompanied by amusia (the loss of musical functions). Shebalin, the Russian composer, suffered a severe stroke in 1953 and another one in 1959 in the left temporal lobe, resulting in Wernicke's aphasia (caused by lesions in the posterior section of the superior temporal convolution). Yet he continued composing (Sergent, 1993). Benjamin Britten suffered a cerebral embolism but showed no impairment of his musical performance, appreciation, or composition (Henson, 1988). In any event, there is today no simple way to the understanding of the brain-behavior interaction in emotion, given the strong indication of a functional autonomy among the various mental processes that are often believed to be uniquely served by specific structures.

The Autonomic System

The implication of the autonomic nervous system (ANS) in emotion was observed by Hippocrates, and Aristotle spoke extensively about the displacement of blood and its changed temperature in the case of anger. Two seventeenth-century physiologists, William Harvey and Thomas Wright, played an important role in connecting emotions to the circulatory system (Rather, 1965). Harvey noted that in the case of emotional agitation there is a considerable disturbance of blood circulation. The face changes color, it may become quite pale or flushed with blood, the eyes redden in anger, and the pupils constrict. Harvey believed blood to be capable of expansion which was a force that allowed blood to circulate throughout the body. In diastole heart was said to distend because blood would swell by acquiring heat. Hypertension, he thought, derived from suppressed aggression. Hence the heart was the dominant organ for the emotions since it controlled the movements of the blood through the body.

Wright focused more on the humors (blood, phlegm, black and yellow bile) and hence connected emotions to temperament. He distinguished four types, sanguine, phlegmatic, melancholic, and choleric, respectively. He, too, observed the thermal variations in blood and connected them to the emotions. There were, according to Wright, six coveting appetites: love, desire, delight, hatred, abomination, and sadness. There were also five invading appetites: hope, despair, fear, audacity, and ire. The coveting appetites were revealed in enlargement or dilation of the heart, whereas the invading appetites in its constriction. Love was hot, fear was cold. Temperature of the body, in fact, was of the essence. *"Animi mores corporis temperaturam sequantur."* (The manners of the soul follow the temperature of the body). However he interpreted the above "law" to mean that humors and passions can cause each other: "passions engender humors and humors breed passions" (p. 64).

Autonomic reactions (changes in heart, blood pressure, breathing rate, etc.) are mobilized when there is requirement for action. Blood rushes to the skeletal muscles to prepare the organism to flee and remove itself from danger. These reactions are controlled by the brainstem autonomic nuclei, structures connected to the hypothalamus, which in turn receives pathways from the amygdala and the orbitofrontal cortex. There is also, on the instigation of an emotion-eliciting stimulus, an endocrine response in the form, for example, of the release of adrenaline. The configuration of these pathways constitutes the main connections between subcortical and autonomic systems that are active in emotion episodes (Gray, 1987; Rolls, 1990, 1995).

The autonomic system played an important role in Sherrington's (1900) and Cannon's (1927) attack on James (1884), who proposed a reversal of the conventionally assumed emotional sequence. It was commonly taken for granted that the emotional episode terminated with the instrumental response (e.g., running away) that was motivated by a prior fear reaction. We do not run away from a bear because we are afraid, we are afraid because we run, James said (1890). Instead, he offered a theory of four successive segments that constituted the sequence generating the subjective feeling in emotion. The episode begins with an instigating sensory stimulus (external or internal) that is transmitted to the cortex. Reflexive impulses are thereby evoked and they travel to the muscles, skin, and the viscera. In turn, these events are transmitted via afferent pathways back to the brain where the activation of the muscles and the viscera is combined with the original stimulus perception that gives the subjective feeling of an "emotional object." Sherrington criticized James on the grounds that visceral feedback could not possibly determine emotion because if afferent pathways of the autonomic system of a dog are destroyed from the shoulders down, thus preventing feedback from the viscera, dogs still react to emotional stimuli with typical facial efference, that is, head and fore-leg movements, barking, and growling. Cannon argued that the autonomic system reacts uniformly and globally to a variety of emotional states and could therefore not be used to discriminate locally among the various emotions, that the viscera are quite insensitive to stimulation, and that they are much slower than any observable emotional reaction.

Social psychologist Floyd Allport (1924) came to James' defense arguing that even though the autonomic system might not be exquisitely sensitive, yet it might be capable of approach-avoidance discrimination. In fact, the correlations between the autonomic reactions and other facets of emotion, even though claimed to be fairly high (Ekman, Levenson, & Friesen, 1983; Levenson, Carstensen, Friesen, & Ekman, 1991; Levenson, Ekman, & Friesen, 1990) are disappointingly low (Zajonc & McIntosh, 1992). On some thought, this should not be surprising. First, these autonomic reactions are generally collected under various manipulations of emotion. In some cases, there is the standard manipulation of facial muscles by instruction and in others the subject is asked to imagine and recall an emotional episode. Zajonc, Murphy, and Inglehart (1989) noted that responses arise not uniquely under emotional instigation, but in pain, as result of effort, or in response to intense stimulation. And a subject who imagines a fear situation that involves James' charging bear will recruit a different ANS pattern than a subject who fears a low grade in her course. Those two fears are not the same and will recruit very different instrumental resources. And even the same aversive or threatening stimulus may evoke different instrumental actions. Some organisms on some occasions flee from the predator, whereas others freeze. Since ANS prepares the organism for prompt action, a freezing response in the case of fear will show itself in a strikingly different ANS pattern than a fleeing response. Most important, none of the studies that measured ANS responses ever allowed the subject actually to engage in instrumental action. The subjects were, for the most part, remaining in their chairs while imaginations of emotional episodes ran through their minds. And the possibility cannot be excluded that ANS data obtained from a subject strapped for physiological tests and instructed to fashion his facial muscles one at a time in a previously unpracticed way, who is set to imagine anger might be, for all we know, reflecting nothing but frustration or irritation. Studies in which the emo-

tional episode did not include or allow an opportunity for an instrumental response cannot hope to obtain reliable information about consistent patterns of ANS reactions. If ANS has as its major function to get the organism set for a vigorous action, one would not expect an ANS output when the subjects are sitting in comfortable chairs and arrange their facial muscles so as to produce something which the experimenter would accept as an expression of fear. However, in agreement with Allport's (1924) expectations, although the autonomic responses did not discriminate *among* the negative emotions, they did in some studies discriminate between positive and negative emotions.

The interpretation of the differences obtained in the ANS must take into account the basic instrumental difference between positive and negative emotions; fear, anger, and disgust are emotions that terminate in a vigorous instrumental act of flight, fight, or explusion. But positive emotions are the consequences of an instrumental act that took place earlier. The pleasure of reaping an award in a violin competition comes from endless previous hours of training. And generally, the instrumental activity implicated in positive emotions occupies an early position in the emotion process and is therefore *proactive*. In negative emotions the instrumental act occupies the terminal position and is therefore *reactive*. Given this difference and given that in neither case is the subject allowed to engage in instrumental action, the significance of the autonomic reactions obtained in psychophysiological research on emotion is not altogether clear. Only when the ANS measures are taken from organisms allowed to complete a full emotional sequence, including instrumental action, will ANS data be more informative about its role.

Expression of Emotions

The earliest conceptions relating bodily manifestations to mental states, including passions, was offered by Aristotle (trans. 1980). Mental character was, according to him, "conditioned by the state of the body; and contrariwise the body is influenced by the affections of the soul. An alteration in the state of the soul produces an alteration in the form of the body, and contrariwise an alteration in bodily form produces an alteration in the state of the soul. Every modification of the one involves a modification of the other." Thus, his dualist position allowed reciprocal influences between emotional expressions and internal subjective states, a view that was under dispute on repeated occasions. His view was so broad as to include the expression of acute and short-lived emotional reactions, such as fear as well as more durable emotional dispositions, such as melancholia. Aristotle supported his argument on the grounds that experts on dogs and horses are able to judge their character and temperament by their bodily form. He looked at general animal traits and related them to their general bodily features. Thus, coarseness of hair which is characteristic of the lion is a mark of courage, whereas the silky and gentle hair of the lamb betrays cowardice and timidity. The noted French painter, Charles LeBrun (1648), took up the Aristotelian position quite literally in his drawings (see Figure 1).

The anatomy-temperament link was repeatedly invoked, for example, by Kretchmer (1922) and Sheldon (1942) whose position was quite conservative. They did not consider temperament mutable for a change in temperament would need to involve bodily change. They derive their position from that of the Swiss physiognomist Lavater (1853) who claimed that "to force a man to think like me, is equal to forcing him to have my exact forehead and nose." But Aristotle, recall, in spite of his appeal to horse and dog breeding, was considerably more flexible speaking of virtues and vices as acquired and modifiable dispositions (Roberts, 1989).

Two nineteenth-century physiologists (Gratiolet, 1865; Piderit, 1867) based their theory of emotional expression on the assumption that facial movements in emotion were generalizations of the peripheral muscular action elicited in the course of the sensory and perceptual processes. For example, we squint when there is too much light entering the pupil, we frown when we want to get a clearer or more focused image of an object at a distance, and we spit out a substance that has a vile taste. Both Piderit and Gratiolet pointed out that peripheral facial movements can be elicited not only in the service of these sensory processes but occur from imagination as well. Thus, ocular accommodation and convergence show correlated changes when we simply imagine a ship on the horizon or imagine threading a needle. For Gratiolet, *sentiment* was closely related to *sensation*. Both were responses to mental states, except that the former was a response to internal states whereas the latter was a response to external stimuli. Sentiments' internal origin, he traced to the term *sens intime,* an experience that originates within the organism and as such constitutes the basic element of emotion.

> No sensation, image, or thought . . . can occur without evoking a correlated sentiment which translates itself directly . . . into all spheres of external organs.

And conversely,

> The movements of bodily attitudes even if they arise from fortuitous causes, evoke correlated sentiments, which in turn influence imagination, feeling and thought.

Note, therefore, that both Piderit and Gratiolet believed that a smile could change a person's mood, a position somewhat akin to that of James and later substantiated empirically (Strack, Martin, & Stepper, 1988; Zajonc, 1985). Gratiolet distinguished between symbolic and metaphoric movements, illustrating the first by the bowlers or golfers who twist their bodies in the hope of influencing the trajectory of the ball, and the second by an expelling lower lip movement (perhaps more common among French nonverbal gestures) in response to a stupid idea which parallels the physical experience of disgust in response to a vile morsel.

Piderit (1867) claims he was first to propose a sensory theory of emotional expression, suggesting fairly directly that Gratiolet did not give him credit. In fact, Piderit presented his ideas at an 1859 meeting of the Biological Society in Paris of which Gratiolet was a member receiving the society's journal *Gazette Médicale* which published Piderit's presentation preceding Gratiolet's book by six years.

Darwin (1904), in his turn, did not take either Piderit or Gratiolet seriously, and when Piderit sent Darwin his book Darwin replied:

> I have a copy and know of your work on Mimic etc. which I have found very useful and often quote. But I am a poor German scholar and your style . . . I find very difficult to understand.

It is not surprising that Darwin could find little of interest in the work of the two physiologists who preceded him because his own work had as its main goal proving in a new domain—behavior—the theory of natural selection. As such, he concentrated on the communication function of emotional expressions. By virtue of displaying their internal states animals in communities can benefit from each other such that the fear reaction of one could prompt others to remove themselves from danger. He was thus most interested in the universality of expression across cultures and species.

In relative terms, emotional expressions indeed show a great deal of physical similarity across cultures (Ekman & Friesen, 1971), in some cases yielding as much as 100 percent agreement among judgments. The term "relative" is stressed because another means of expression of internal states—language, for example—displays a vastly greater diversity (but see the DePaulo & Friedman [1998] chapter on nonverbal communication in this *Handbook*).

The descriptive methods of Ekman and Friesen (1976) or Izard, Dougherty, and Hembree (1983) specify distinct muscular movements for each of the distinct emotional types, assuming that for each emotion (of the six or seven presumably "basic" types) there exists a hardwired program connecting subjective state, autonomic response, neurochemical and neurophysiological process, and instrumental behavior. The fact that nearly 100 percent agreement was observed in judging a smiling face as "expressing" joy and happiness (in a number of cultures) is taken to support the argument of universality, the discrete nature of emotional physiological programs, and the validity of the method. Matters, however, are much less clear or definitive than they may appear (Zajonc & McIntosh, 1992), and the

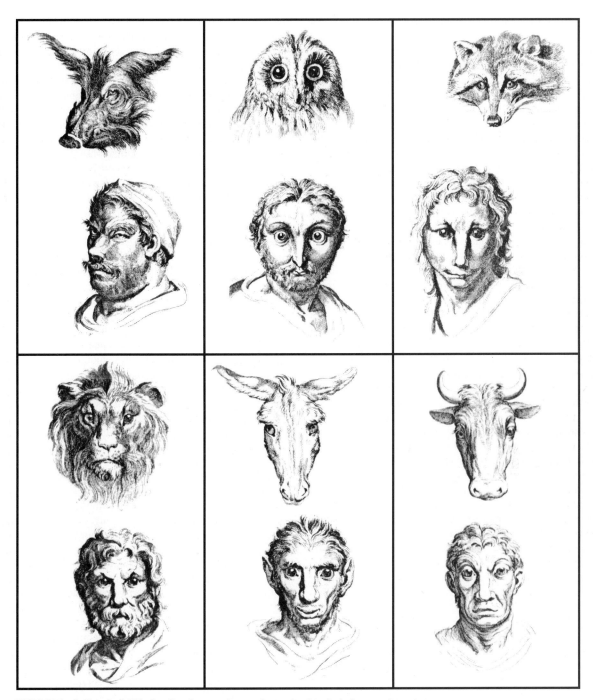

FIGURE 1 LeBrun's (1648) sketches that sought to reflect animal traits in human character.

"signatures" of discrete emotions taken from any taxonomy based on still photographs of posed or spontaneous expressions are fraught with difficulties. Probably the most serious problem with the posed displays is that subjects (in addition to the myogenically induced emotion) may feel mainly annoyance and irritation. Imagine a person in an experiment using the Facial Action Coding System (Ekman & Friesen, 1978), placed in a chair and ready to comply with whatever instructions are given by the prestigeful experimenter who controls his or her contribution to the partial course requirement earned through experimental participation. Seated in a chair, and ready to be diligent as expected, the subject is now asked first to narrow eyelids, which is a simple enough accomplishment. While holding his eyelids partly closed, the person is asked to raise his or her cheeks, which can with some effort be accomplished, adding it to the previous grimace. Now the experimenter asks to pull the cheeks apart, show teeth, without losing any of the other muscular contractions. The subject tries to comply. But "No, No, No!!!" says the experimenter, "This is not right, you opened your eyelids. Please keep them partly shut." So chagrined by failure the subject tries once more. And the experimenter shows again dismay saying "Well, you did close your eyelids, but you also covered your teeth. You must try to do all those things together!" The trials continue until the experimenter, usually quite demanding, is satisfied that the many component muscular twitches are appropriately frozen for several seconds on the subject's face. If a GSR (Galvanic Skin Response) is obtained under these circumstances it must be highly contaminated by reactions other than those intended to be generated by the particular facial muscular configurations that are presumed to express particular emotions.

Emotional expressions, elicited by emotion-inducing surrogate stimuli (such as slides of objects and events having emotional impact), or by the imagination or recall of the person's own emotional experiences, are also subject to questions of validity. For in these situations the instrumental response—a critical element in the emotion episode—is disallowed. The subject is viewing a film, and experiencing a number of emotions, some congruent with the action, others far removed from the context (see Frijda's [1986] discussion of dependence of emotional experience on "reality-level," p. 206). Of course, the posed expression method is not free from this shortcoming either. And the observation of naturally occurring emotions (such as at funerals, sports events, weddings, etc.) does not lend itself to the administration of other measures, for example, the autonomic response, subjective report, etc. Studies carried out in naturalistic settings (Kraut & Johnston, 1979; Fernández-Dols & Ruiz-Belda, 1995), however, do find that situations that we would normally consider generating joy or happiness (e.g., successful sports achievements of one's own or of one's favorite team) do not elicit smiles. One could not from the faces of the observed persons infer that their internal states were those of happiness, as is the case in the judgments of posed facial expressions. Smiles did occur, however, but only when the subject was in conversation with others who themselves were smiling. As Fridlund (1994) suggested, because of their communication function, expressions of internal states depend on the social context.

The naturalistic method, because it includes the social context, is very useful if used in combination with other methods. The posed expression and the surrogate process, however, both suffer from the absence of social constraints and affordances. Emotions are above all social (Bellelli, 1994; Rimé, 1994; Russell, Fernández-Dols, Manstead, & Wellenkamp, 1994). If expressions have an adaptive value because they broadcast internal states among conspecifics, then the presence of conspecifics must have at least a modulating effect on all aspects of the emotion process. And to the extent that emotions involve some form of arousal, the mere presence of others should, other things equal, have an augmenting effect (Zajonc, 1965).

The role of the face in behavior has been vastly underestimated and only recently research interest has begun to grow. The face is readily recognized and well stored, better that many other perceptual objects. It readily elicits approach or avoidance reactions. A 150 millisecond exposure suffices for a reliable judgment of attractiveness. Specialized cells have been found in the human and monkey temporal sulcus that respond to faces and nothing but faces (Perrett et al., 1982). But much remains to be understood about the role of the face in the emotional process. For instance, it is not clear which parts of the face dominate emotional expression. There has been some suspicion that the left side of the face communicates emotion better than the right side. Research by Davidson (1993) supports his idea that emotional process can be localized in the entire anterior lobe, with the positive emotions on the left and the negative emotions on the right. Robinson, Kubos, Starr, Rao, & Price (1984) have shown that patients who suffer post-stroke depression are mainly those who suffered the trauma in their left hemisphere.

And there are only guesses about what parts of the face dominate the reading of emotional expression. St. Jerome wrote in the fourth century AD that "the face is the mirror of the mind, and eyes without speaking, confess the secrets of the heart." But Dunlap (1927) has shown that this is not always the case. If photographs of a person are taken of a smiling and frowning face and the lower halves of the face are interchanged, the lower half of the face emerges as the dominant part (Figure 2). And Bassili (1979) found that different regions of the face are differentially informative for different emotions.

The repeated efforts to seek clues about disposition, temperament, and personality in the facial features and expressions has hovered between the extremes of innate and acquired positions. Lavater (1853), Sheldon (1942), and Kretchmer (1922) were all on the side of genetically fixed features. Lavater defended the hypothesis that because the body expresses the underlying features of personality, the various bodily elements must be consistent and congruent with each other. If one has a laughing mouth, the eyes must be laughing too.

Sheldon distinguished between *endomorphs, mesomorphs,* and *ectomorphs.* Endomorphs have round and soft bodies, mesomorphs have hard and firm bodies, strong and

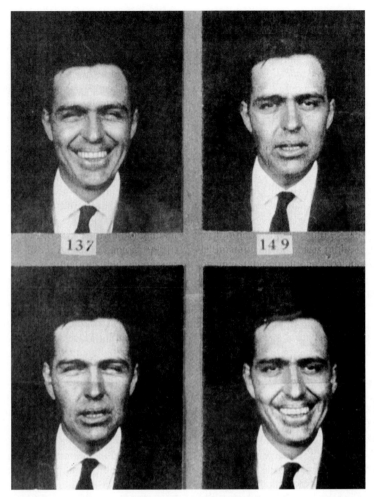

FIGURE 2   Dunlap's (1927) demonstration that the lower part of the face and not the eyes better conveys underlying emotion. The upper photographs show the intact face expressing pleasure and sadness. The lower photomontages have interchanged the lower halves of the face.

rectangular. Ectomorphs are fragile, linear, and slender. Temperament types are said to go hand in hand with bodily forms. Endomorphs tend to be *viscerotonic.* They love comfort, sociability, and conviviality. Mesomorphs tend to be *somatotonic.* They are agentic, assertive, and insensitive to others. Finally, ectomorphs are *cerebrotonic; that is,* they are attentive and inhibitory. Sheldon claims a correlation of 0.81 between the elements of physique and of temperment.[4] These claims, however, have been successfully challenged by D. Fiske (1942).

Some aspects of the body do change as a result of exercise or lack of it, diet, and even repeated mimicry. Dimberg (1990) has shown smiling and frowning photographs to subjects while recording their electromyographic responses from the zygomatic and corregator muscles. There was a clear mimicry effect. The question arises if when a person mimics another consistently, and for a long period of time, will the two faces converge in appearance. That seems to be the case according to Zajonc, Adelman, Murphy, and Niedenthal (1987). When photographs are taken at weddings and 25 years later, the judged similarity of the couples is higher at the later reading. Moreover, those judged more similar to each other after 25 years of marriage declare better marriages.

Should we assume, therefore, that there is a close relationship between expressivity and the ability to read the emotion of others? Some theories of emotion do relate the consistency and precision of the expressive output to the decoding ability of the individual (Fernández-Dols & Ruiz-Belda, 1995; Frijda, 1986; Plutchik, 1980; Tomkins, 1982). This supposition is contradicted, however, by data on the Gilles de la Tourette syndrome. Patients suffering from the syndrome have, in addition to symptoms such as inappropriate verbal and emotional outbursts and coprolalia (a tendency toward uncontrolled profanity and obscenity), a severely impaired emotional expression (Robertson, 1989). Yet, in a carefully controlled study, patients with Tourette syndrome were able to decode nonverbal emotional expressions at least as well and sometimes better than normal subjects (Davinsky, Bear, Moya, & Benowitz, 1993).

VISCERAL THEORY OF EMOTIONAL EFFERENCE (VTEE)

The term "emotional expression" has been taken for granted as a standard concept in the theory of emotions. Yet the concept is *preemptive.* It is preemptive because it implies a ready-made theory of the emotions without the theory having been even partially substantiated. The term implies that (1) a distinct internal state can be identified for each emotion; (2) these distinct internal states seek externalization of a distinct form; (3) there is a one-to-one correspondence between the internal state and its outward manifestation; (4) there exists a neural process that triggers the externalization of the internal state; and (5) the internal process is endowed with energy pressing toward externalization, but under some circumstances and with some opposing energy, the externalization may be suppressed (Terwogt & Stegge, 1994). For these reasons, I have used the term "emotional efference" instead of "emotional expression" and will observe this convention henceforth.

VTEE has an unusual origin. Its precursor was an idea about physiognomy offered at the turn of the century by a French physician, Israel Waynbaum (1907). Waynbaum's main insight was to seek the primary function of emotional efference, especially facial efference, in processes other than communication, as Darwin suggested. Without denying that facial efference is an important channel of communication, and that it can serve to display one organism's internal state to another, he explored the possibility that facial efference may above all have an internal function, namely, the partial influence over the vascular system of the head. He was struck by the fact that the main carotid artery splits into two branches, one supplying the brain and the other supplyng the skull. It was a configuration that did not make much sense at first glance because brain being such an important organ would be expected to draw on its own independent blood supply, rather than sharing it with other organs. Waynbaum offered the novel hypothesis that the vascular branching was in fact dedicated to a safer and a more efficient supply of blood to the brain because it provided a "safety valve" for the internal artery supplying the brain. Since the brain requires a very steady and virtually invariant blood supply, the external (facial) artery could take up surplus when too much blood was passing through the main carotid, or if there was not enough, it could add to blood flow in the internal carotid. How would such a process be accomplished? Muscles pressing against the bony structure of the face or relaxing their pressure at particular points, that is facial efference, are able to control blood volume in the arteries of the face, modulating total blood flow to the brain. And the muscular action present in what we call "emotional expression" is actually deployed to control vascular flow of the face and head. Waynbaum added a hedonic element: brain hyperaemia is experienced as a positive subjecive state whereas anemia is felt as discomfort.

Of course, much of the theory relied on nineteenth-century vascular physiology and was wrong. Because arteries have their own vasodilators and vasoconstrictors, it is unlikely that muscle pressure was needed to regulate arterial flow. In fact, it was not. However, venous flow is not regulated by vasoconstrictors and vasodilators, and it can be enhanced and impeded by muscular action of the face. Modifying Waynbaum's insights, VTEE placed focus on venous flow and relied on brain temperature as the explanatory process leading to subjective emotional changes (Zajonc, 1985). Instead of equating anemia and hyperaemia to distress and euphoria, respectively, VTEE suggests the possibility that changes in brain temperature and in particular, in hypothalamic temperature, might gate the release and synthesis of emotion-linked neurotransmitters and neurohormones, thus producing changes in subjective states.

Cooling of the hypothalamus is achieved by cooling the arterial blood as it enters the brain. A venous structure, the cavernous sinus, enveloping the internal carotid artery, receives blood from the nasal airways and is thereby able to lower the temperature of arterial blood at that point (Baker, 1972; Baker & Hayward, 1967; Caputa, Kadziela, & Narebski, 1976; Dean, 1988). Kluger and D'Alecy (1975) have shown that if a rabbit is prevented from breathing through the nose by means of a tracheal bypass, its hypothalamic temperature rises, showing absence of cooling by the cavernous sinus. Cooling of the cavernous sinus is accomplished by breathing patterns and facial muscular action on the facial veins that allow for heat exchange in the nasal airways. Both are capable of modulating nasal airflow. There is at present little evidence to show that the release of emotion-related neurotransmitters and neurohormones is modulated by hypothalamic temperature, mainly because most of the experiments with these neurochemicals are done at a constant 37°C. But the immune system reacts to temperature changes with extremely fine sensitivity (Miller & Clem, 1984).

Zajonc, Murphy, and Inglehart (1989) have shown in a number of experiments that facial efference can have a simultaneous influence over brain temperature and subjective feeling, low temperature being correlated with positive hedonic states. Berridge and Zajonc (1991) cooled the hypothalamus of the rat directly and obtained a substantial increment in behavior symptomatic of positive hedonic state.

Note that the hypothalamus not only regulates brain and body temperature, it also has control over eating, sexual behavior, aggression, and many other emotional reactions as well. VTEE is thus a theory that assembles a number of emotional correlates and relates them to each other. It considers in its analysis blood temperature and breathing as parts of the autonomic system, it makes a connection to hypothalamus, and thus makes contact with the neurobiology of the emotions. It relates facial efference (emotional expression) to these processes and examines changes in subjective feeling states. Moreover, it postulates a process that allows emotional reactions to emerge without the participation of cognitive appraisal (Lazarus, 1982), thus lending support to the hypothesis of affective primacy and affect/cognition independence, converging neuroanatomical evidence on the independence of emotions from cognition has been found (Zajonc, 1980). The conventional supposition about the emotion pathways has been that once the stimulus is registered, the sensory apparatus sends inputs to the thalamus, wherefrom the sensory areas of the neocortex take them and extract meaning and emotional significance. But there are shortcuts. There is apparently a direct pathway between the thalamus and the amygdala that is just one synapse long (Iwata, Chida, & LeDoux, 1987; Iwata, LeDoux, Meeley, Arneric, & Reis, 1986; LeDoux, 1986, 1987, 1990; LeDoux, Iwata, Cicchetti, Reis, 1988). Hence the amygdala can respond faster (by about 40 milliseconds) to an emotional stimulus than the hippocampus, which might mean that we can like or fear something without knowing what it is.

COGNITIVE CORRELATES OF EMOTION

While it is now well established that affective reactions can occur without the participation of cognitive processes (LeDoux, 1989, 1996; Zajonc, 1980), cognitive factors can and do play an important, indeed, major role in forming the emotional episode. Consider an experiment by Carroll and Russell (1996). Subjects are read a story describing a situation likely to elicit a particular emotion, such as anger, for example. Photographs of classical facial expressions claimed to be universal (such as taken by Ekman and Friesen, 1978) are then shown to them. The story might be incompatible with the expression, thus, for example, a fear expression is paired with a story about a woman who had to wait for a table in a restaurant for a very long time, being delayed and displaced several times (i.e., provoked anger). The subjects are asked "What emotion is this woman feeling, happiness, surprise, fear, anger, disgust, or sadness?" The results in a number of such studies clearly show that the story dominated the expression. Fear expression was rated as anger when the story implied an angry reaction, or disgust when the story implied disgust. Note, however, that when the emotional effects of prosody are evaluated, they dominate verbal content. The inflection of vocal utterance can be easily coded for emotional content even if we listen to a language we don't know. We are able to decode the feelings that are being communicated. And Argyle, Salter, Nicholson, Williams, and Burgess (1970), who observed typical live interactions, demonstrated dominance of prosody (voice parameters, such as inflection, energy, frequency range, rhythm, etc.) over content quite convincingly. The conclusions drawn by Carroll and Russell (1996) are therefore perhaps too strong, given their procedure. If the subjects were asked about the reliability of the two sources of information, the story and the photograph, they would assign higher reliability to the former. Clearly, the story contained very good and informative grounds for making inferences about what kind of reaction would follow, and the choices were always pretty obvious. In contrast, the photograph of the emotion, because it was a static 1/100 second sample of an emotional efference, could not receive a great deal of credibility.

A totally different emotional reaction, therefore, can be elicited depending on what meaning is attached to the eliciting stimulus situation, to the internal states, to the way events are construed, and to the possible consequences of one's own reaction. Already in the early days of social psychology the theory of frustration and its effects on aggression (Dollard, Doob, Miller, Mowrer, & Sears, 1938) assumed quite specifically that aggression motivated by frustration would be inhibited to the extent that aggression might be followed by punishment. And getting $1,000 from an insurance company for a loss may cause joy if one expected nothing, but it can cause chagrin if one expected to be awarded $100,000.

There is rich literature seeking to discover the dimensions of appraisal and cognitive interpretation assigned to various emotional episodes (for example, Ellsworth & Smith, 1988; Roseman, 1984; Scherer, 1984; Smith & Ellsworth, 1985, 1987; Stein & Levine, 1989). This literature separates itself from the view of emotions as a set of distinct categories (Ekman & Friesen, 1971; Izard, 1977; Tomkins, 1962, 1963). Yet, any categorial system for the taxonomy of emotions is vulnerable to dimensional analysis. For example, in seeking to find a systematic representation of the emotions, they are often assumed to resemble the color wheel with each emotion having its *opposite,* for example, joy being the opposite of sadness (Plutchik, 1980). But, necessarily, if there are categories that can be said to be opposite to each other, then they must represent endpoints on some dimension between which lie other points, ordered and, at the limit, continuous. Hence, there is a dimension. Neither the universality of emotion terms nor the structure of their interrelationships, similar to those found for color (Berlin & Kay, 1969; Rosch, 1975), however, have been documented, and in all probability emotion terms are not amenable to a systematic analysis found useful for color terms. It is difficult, for, example, to conceive of the opposite of anger, and most emotions when dimensionally calibrated do not go from +1, through 0, to –1, but from +1 or –1 to zero.

The discovery of emotional dimensions was first undertaken by Schlosberg (1941) who had subjects scale facial expressions. In analyzing these results and comparing them to the more recent approach based on the subjective feeling states (Averill, 1975; Block, 1957; Davitz, 1969; Izard, 1972; Russell, 1980; Russell & Mehrabian, 1977), Smith and Ellsworth (1985) found that the two approaches generated similar factor structures, with valence being one dimension and intensity another. More recently, Lang (1995) using a set of carefully standardized emotion-evoking photographs was able to map a variety of emotions in a two-dimensional space with *arousal* and *pleasure* as the two coordinates. Thus, sadness was in the quadrant of low arousal and low pleasure, whereas the position of joy was in the quadrant of high pleasure and high arousal. Interestingly, in the Smith-Ellsworth analysis, the dimension of *attentional activity* also emerged as a significant factor, but only for the studies based on facial expressions. Among the dimensions of emotional episodes found in the Smith-Ellsworth theory, using both Principal Component Analysis and multidimensional scaling, above all was *pleasantness,* which accounted for about one-quarter of the total variance. It would indeed be surprising if the valence dimension did not dominate the dimensional structure of emotion. To the extent that emotions serve the adaptive function and allow the individual to draw on the resources of the environment and protect the individual from its dangers, the approach-avoidance dichotomy is all-important. In fact, all studies, regardless of their basis, for example, facial expression or subjective feeling, also found valence as the dominant dimension, with intensity a close second.

Other dimensions discriminate among the positive and among the negative emotions. For instance, *anticipated effort* was found by Smith and Ellsworth to distinguish between challenge (high effort) and happiness (low effort). Certainty, on the other hand, discriminated between fear, hope, and surprise.

Among dimensions significant for social psychology is *agency* because it distinguishes outcomes caused by situational factors, the person himself or herself, or another person. As such, the sociopsychological research on the fundamental attribution error (Ross, 1977) intersects with the attribution of agency in the emotion. The focus of research, however, has been not so much on the properties of the emotional episodes, and the paradigm contributed little to a better understanding of emotional processes that are imbedded in social cognition. The actor-observer paradigm

(Jones & Nisbett, 1972) also intersects with the agency feature of situational construction of emotions. The most conspicuous finding in this domain is that actors attribute failure to situational causes while observers attribute to their abilities the failure of those they observe. The question then arises about the attribution of emotions and the actor-observer difference. Would an observer attribute his or her own emotions to his situational pressures and the emotions of others to their dispositional antecedents? Probably not and probably diverse findings would be obtained, depending on the eliciting conditions, the type of emotion (positive or negative), and the resulting instrumental action.

A useful taxonomy of the appraisal components of emotional excitation is offered by Frijda (1986). He distinguishes three types of components of the situational meaning of the emotions: core, context, and object components. The core components are those features of the situational meaning that make the instigating circumstances emotional or not. Among the core components are *objectivity, relevance, reality level, difficulty, urgency, seriousness, valence, demand character, clarity,* and *multiplicity.* When the situation imposes its meaning on the person, who remains passive and submits to it, such as the presence of a snake, the meaning is imbued with *objectivity,* says Frijda. *Relevance* is a property that accepts emotional significance, and classifies it in terms of its applicability to the person at the moment, as one worth reacting to or not, etc. *Reality level* distinguishes between emotions experienced in cases that call for an instrumental reaction, such as an approaching gunman, versus those that are imaginary such as we see in the movies, where the approaching gunman is nothing more than a pattern of light on a large screen. Some emotional instigation has a degree of ambiguity and is difficult to analyze for its antecedents and possible consequences. That component is Frijda's *difficulty. Urgency* refers to the time constraints within which a response is required. An approaching gunman requires an immediate and urgent response, a slowly declining stock needs attention but the response may or may not be immediate. The components of *seriousness, valence, clarity,* and *multiplicity* mean, more or less, what the terms imply. *Demand character,* however, is a more complex component. It relates the emotion instigation to such higher order tendencies as desire, interest, and curiosity. Desire, claims Frijda, because it "can be pleasurable as well as painful is the main reason to consider it hedonically neutral by itself" (1986, p. 207).

The *context components* include, among others, the property of *presence and absence.* This property, cross tabulated with *valence,* allows Frijda to distinguish among contentment, suffering, and desire. The presence of an object with positive valence leads to contentment and enjoyment, its absence is the hallmark of desire, however. The presence of a situation with negative valence leads to suffering, whereas its absence leads to contentment and safety. Among other context components are *certainty* and uncertainty of the effects to come or anticipated, *change* (i.e., the difference observed in comparison to a previous state, such as we see in grieving over a loss, or elation over an unexpected windfall), *openness-closedness* (i.e., the situation is characterized by closedness if there are no escape routes), and *intentionality* (i.e., an event caused by a friend can be intentional or not, however, an earthquake destroying the person's house cannot have that property). Among the important object components, the constituent of experience present in guilt, remorse, or shame is the ego. In shame, says Frijda, "the subject perceives himself, or one of his acts; in addition he perceives others perceiving him; imputes condemnation of his acts to those others; and shares their condemnation" (1986, p. 215).

In much more general terms, G. H. Mead (1934) argued that nearly all social acts are subject to influences of the social context of other participants, past, present, and future, and that they are very sensitive to the collective representations of the central elements of the social situation.

> If a given individual is to develop a self in the fullest sense, it is not sufficient for him merely to take the attitudes of other human individuals toward himself and toward one another within the human social process, and to bring that social process as a whole into his individual experience . . . he must also . . . take their attitudes toward the various phases or aspects of the common social activity or set of social undertakings in which, as members of an organized society, they are all engaged . . . It is in the form of the generalized other that the social process influences behavior of the individuals involved in it and carrying it on, i.e., that the community exercises control over the conduct of its individual members; for it is in this form that social process or community enters as a determining factor into the individual's thinking. . . . [O]nly by taking the attitude of the generalized other toward himself . . . can [the individual] think at all; for only thus can thinking—or the internalized conversation of gestures which constitutes thinking—occur (p. 154–156).

THE SEMANTICS OF EMOTIONS

The study of emotion depends on the particular perspective from which the questions emerge. Darwin (1904) took as his major focus facial efference. Ekman (1973) and Izard (1977), spurred on by Tomkins (1962, 1963) followed his path. James (1884) thought the autonomic process to be crucial. LeDoux (1989), Panksepp (1982), Gray (1987), Rolls (1995), Damasio (1994), Davidson (1993) and others focus on the brain regions and structures active during the emotional episode. Frijda (1986), Smith and Ellsworth (1985), Arnold (1960), Mandler (1975), Lazarus (1982),

Schachter and Singer (1962) and others zero in on what gives meaning to emotion. A central element of meaning-making is of course language, although William James (1890, p. 485) had very little faith in emotion labels, or language in general, doubting that they could provide significant clues for a coherent emotion theory.

Johnson-Laird and Oatley (1989) offer the view that there exists a close relationship between emotional experiences and the language by which they are labeled. ". . . [L]anguage and its underlying conceptual apparatus is intimately related to the real nature of emotions, and the meanings of emotional terms are neither arbitrary nor unanalyzable but do indeed relate to experience" (p. 105). In this vein, these authors proposed that "emotion can be set up by a cognitive evaluation" (p. 85) and that the "evaluation can set the processing modules into one of only a small number of emotional modes" (p. 85). These modes, *happiness, sadness, anger, fear,* and *disgust,* are the fundamental elements "out of which all subjective experiences of emotion are constructed." The assertion that "language . . . is intimately related to the *real* nature of emotions" (italics mine) begs the question of whether we can trust far enough the assumed isomorphism between the two for language alone to be reliably informative of reality. In the extreme, absurd consequences follow from the assertion because we can apply the same argument to ghosts, phantoms, cherubim, angels, devils, and leprechauns, and on the basis of such a semantic classification we could, as is the case with emotions, isolate the attributes that distinguish one class of angels, for example, from another. But our search for the referents of these semantic categories in nature would not reach beyond art and literature.

From a number of sources Johnson-Laird and Oatley collected 590 English emotion words. Their analysis generated seven semantic categories:

0. Generic emotions, for example, "emotions" and "feelings"
1. Basic emotions, for example, "happiness" and "elation"
2. Emotional relations, for example, "love" and "hate"
3. Caused emotions, for example, "gladness" and "horror"
4. Causatives, for example, "irritate" and "reassure"
5. Emotional goals, for example, "desire" and "avarice"
6. Complex emotions, for example, "embarrassment" and "pity."

When we speak of "basic terms" we usually mean terms that are the axiomatic primitives—undefined terms that cannot and need not be reduced to yet more fundamental terms. However, Johnson-Laird and Oatley do not employ that meaning in their "basic" category. Instead they speak of "words [that] should accordingly denote emotions that can be experienced without the experiencer knowing their cause" (p. 96). There are 109 words selected from their 590 word sample that denote basic emotions. These words like *carefree, high, euphoric,* and *ecstatic* for HAPPINESS; *depressed, gloomy,* etc. for SADNESS; *timid, tense,* and *anxious* for FEAR; *touchy, angry,* and *grouchy* for ANGER; and *queasy* for DISGUST. Words denoting emotional relations, on the other hand, are *like, adore,* and *love* in the HAPPINESS category, *afraid of* and *dread* in the FEAR category, etc. The major difference between the basic words and the relational words is that the latter category has an object. "Jack loves Jill" is an example of a relational word, whereas "Jack is light-hearted" is an example of the basic category. Words that denote emotional goals are of interest because they encompass the emotional episode with an emphasis on instrumental goals. Among the 42 such words are *greed, lust,* and *desire.* For example, the word *amorous* implies the desire to maintain proximity to the loved objects. But the word *disgusting* is not listed among the category of emotional words, even though it implies the desire to maintain distance.

It is not clear why the Johnson-Laird/Oatley theory posits only five emotion terms since by another popular convention six have been identified and distinguished as unique in terms of facial expression (Ekman, Friesen, & Ellsworth, 1972). In fact the missing "basic" emotion, "surprise," was one that generated the highest agreement among American, Brazilian, Chilean, and Argentinean subjects. For Japanese subjects there was 100 percent agreement that the face posing surprise was expressing surprise. Fear, on the other hand, produced the lowest agreement—as low as 54 percent among Argentineans.

Prosody and Emotion

The above analysis refers to written language. Spoken language, however, goes beyond the lexical limits for it includes important prosodic qualities that mark the emotional state of the speaker, transmit significant information, and are readily encoded. It is remarkable that speakers are much less aware of the prosodic features of their own verbal output than listeners. People are often surprised how they sound in a recording of their voice. Prosody, however, broadcasts the emotional tone of the utterance and it can readily change a generally positive meaning into a derogation. "You are a prince" can be uttered expressing gratitude or contempt with only a minor change of inflection. Argyle et al. (1970) have found that speech prosody carries much more affective impact and status reference than the semantic and lexical domain.

If prosody is a more intimate derivative of the emotional system, we would expect it to be more common with lower species and more universal than language (Marler, 1978; Pittam & Scherer, 1993). Generally, a distress signal

is characterized by a rising frequency whereas a contentment call displays a falling frequency (e.g., Hoffman, 1968; Zajonc, Markus, & Wilson, 1974). In nearly all countries, the auditory warning signals, say fire truck, ambulance, and police sirens are characterized by rising frequencies. And in two independent studies, Dutch and German subjects agreed to a remarkable degree in distinguishing among five vocal emotional signals (Pittam & Scherer, 1993, p. 190). At the same time, and in seeming contradiction, researchers found it quite difficult to distinguish among vocal cues for emotions on the basis of their acoustic parameters (Scherer, 1986).

There is simply too little empirical evidence to speak firmly about the universality of the prosodic qualities of speech. Only a handful of languages have been explored. The conjecture, however, that there is a greater universality in prosody than in the lexicon or semantics is probably defensible on theoretical grounds. The presence of prosody (if it can be called that, for animal vocalizations do not overlay language and are meaningful in their own right) among lower animal species is quite obvious. Most research on intonation and prosody in humans is concerned with semantics and grammar. And there is a great deal of universality here. *Shall we eat, mother? (On mange, maman?)* changes to a "cannibal attitude" when we change the pitch to *Shall we eat mother? (On mange maman?)* both in English and in French (Delattre, 1972). Questions differ from declarative statements by a terminal rise in frequency, compared to a fall in fundamental frequency (Hadding & Studdert-Kennedy, 1964). However, in those languages that have been studied for forms of intonation, it appears that of all speech parameters, frequency range is typically extended in heightened emotion. Universal features have been postulated for prosody quite frequently (Bolinger, 1972, p. 313–364; Hockett, 1963; Monrad-Krohn, 1963; Scherer, Koivumaki, & Rosenthal, 1972). "When we are excited our voice extends its pitch upward," says Bolinger (1975, p. 48). And it is assumed that the phenomenon holds true for all languages. There are, however, some distinct differences in the semantic load that is carried by the prosodic parameters of speech, and that load is ambiguous because one cannot always isolate prosody from phonetic output. A rising pitch in English, which communicates excitement and affect, represents a form of meaning in Chinese.

Emotions and Language Universals

Johnson-Laird and Oatley claim that "there is a set of basic emotion modes that correspond to internal signals that can impinge on consciousness. These modes—happiness, sadness, anger, fear, disgust—should be *universally* (italic mine) accepted as discriminable categories of direct experience" (1989, p. 90). There is at least one strong opposition to this view. In a number of papers, Wierzbicka (1990, 1992, 1994) takes these authors (and others who rely principally on English sources) to task. The challenge is that we cannot pretend that the whole world is Anglo-Saxon. She cites Ekman's (1973) assertion "facial behavior is associated with the same emotion for all people. . . . Regardless of the language, of whether the culture is Western or Eastern, industrialized or preliterate, these facial expressions are labeled with the same emotion terms: happiness, sadness, anger, fear, disgust, and surprise" (p. 219–220). Wierzbicka (1994) argues that "[C]ross-cultural lexical research undertaken by linguists and anthropologists demonstrates that concepts such as happy or angry are not universal, but constitute cultural artifacts of Anglo culture reflected in, and continually reinforced by, the English language" (pp. 134–135). The emotion communicated by the English word *sad* can be neither basic nor universal because the Australian Aboriginal language Pintupi has the following words for *sad:*

wtjilpa: preoccupation with thoughts of country and relatives. When one experiences this feeling one becomes sick with worry about them. Other people may try to assuage the worry, and even a doctor may be called in to help.

wurrkulinu: excessive concern or worry about land relatives.

viluruyiluru: dejection caused by worrying too much for absent relatives, for example, if they are in hospital.

vulatjarra: sympathy or sorrow for sick or deceased relatives.

Wierzbicka cites a large number of other counterexamples to the assumed linguistic universality of emotion terms. The Ilongot language spoken in some parts of the Philippines, or the Ifaluk language of Micronesia, have no words that correspond to the English word *anger.* And there is a word in Ilongot—*liget*—for which there is no corresponding word in English (Rosaldo, 1980). Nor is there an English word that corresponds to the Ifaluk meaning of *song* (Lutz, 1987).

How then do we translate (or find equivalents) for words that do not exist in our or related language? Wierzbicka (1972) offers a system of *semantic primitives* and *lexical universals.* Some words, she claims, are indeed universal in meaning. But a large number are culture-specific. Thus *nerd, cool,* and *screwball* are culture specific. But *say, want, good, think, something, feel,* are among those that Wierzbicka considers primitive and universal. And she claims that all meanings can in principle be expressed with the handful of the universals she proposes. Thus, for example, *sad* can be defined as follows:

X is sad:

X feels something

Sometimes people think something like this:

    something bad happened

    I would want it didn't happen

    because of this, if I could, I would want to do something

    I can't do anything.

In contrast, *angry* is:

X feels something

Sometimes people think something like this (of someone):

    this person did something bad

    I don't want this

    because of this, I want to do something

    I would want to do something bad to this person

because of this, they feel something bad

X thinks something like this

because of this, X feels something like this.

But the Ilongot parallel of *liget* has strikingly different connotations. It includes intimations about a desire to prove oneself, to show that one is not inferior, it has something to do with ambition and envy, etc.:

X feels something

Sometimes people think something like this:

    other people can do something

    they could think that I can't do it

    I don't want this, I want to do something

    I can do it

because of this, they feel something.

The Ilongot term *song* has been equated with the English "justifiable anger" or "righteous indignation," and as such it is claimed that the concept and the emotion that it represents is recognizable in other cultures and in other languages (Lutz, 1988). Wierzbicka (1995), however, failed to confirm the correspondence, such that *"song* is no more a 'variety of anger' than *anger* is 'a variety of *song*'" (p. 29). The argument that complete universality of linguistic terms cannot be asserted is well founded. But one can also see a considerable uniformity even among unrelated languages. Even if there was no universality of emotion terms, there still could be a uniformity of emotions themselves. Thus, Ortony and Clore (1989) accept the fact that it is difficult and perhaps impossible to match emotion terms across languages. One could say in English "I would be happy to meet you at 5:00 PM tomorrow." But it would not work in a host of other languages to employ the term *happy* in this context. One is not *heureux, glücklich,* or *szczesliwy* on an occasion of this sort. One might be perhaps, in these languages *content, satisfied,* or *glad*—but *happy* is patently excessive. Wierzbicka (1992) aptly observes that "emotions such as *bonheur, Glück, felicità,* or *sc˘ast'e* fill a human being to overflowing, leaving no room for any further desires or wishes" (p. 299). The English equivalent *happy* is considerably weaker. Or take another example. The conventional Italian translation of *anger* is *rabbia.* But *rabbia* is much more intense, and Wierzbicka (1995) observes that it "is not only intense, it is also uncontrolled (and almost uncontrollable), it is short term, it is irrational, it is hot, it is explosive, it is overtly expressed" (p. 32). Moreover, its second meaning is *rabies,* and hence the expression *schiumere di rabbia*—"to foam with rage." We simply don't know at the present how much is lost (or gained) in translation of emotion terms. And for a cogent account of everyday cross-language miscommunication, Hoffman (1989) offers a most insightful set of examples.

The proof of linguistic universality for emotion terms aside, one might still argue that the emotions themselves (or their crucial correlates, such as expression, subjective states, autonomic reactions, subcortical activity, instrumental response) are universal. But the argument would be contradicted in a number of ways. For some of these correlates, especially the instrumental response, universality is unlikely, given that there are diverse cultures with diverse inhibitions of violence, anger, or despair, etc. The Balinese avoid sadness and grief is highly ritualized (Frijda & Mesquita, 1994; Wikan, 1989).

Is there at least a *partial* correspondence between langauge and the emotional experience? Ortony and Clore (1989) offer a theory that is based on language but it is a theory of language *about* emotions. Language is merely a vehicle leading us to the explication of the underlying emotional experience. Thus, the meaning of *anger* requires two eliciting conditions: (1) "disapproving of someone's blameworthy action (reproach)" and (2) "(being) displeased about an undesirable event (distress)." The condition that satisfies the definition of emotion, according to Ortony and Clore, is that its "feelings must signify the results of an appraisal of some kind" (p. 127). Emotions are mental states that are valenced. If a term is an emotion then subjects can accept being in that state and "feeling" that state. Thus, one can be "sorry" and "feel sorry." Moreover, emotion is basic if it can be both understood for its reasons and not understood. It is acceptable to *"be happy"* without knowing why and it is possible *"to be happy"* and know why. But it is not possible to be *grateful* without knowing why or to whom.

The problem of correspondence between lexical types and emotional experience is partly the same as that of color and vision and color terms (Kay & McDaniel, 1978). In fact, it is a more difficult problem because in the case of color there is both a known physical reality and a well-known neuroanatomic and peripheral system. Yet both are subject to similar controversy and need to be resolved. Even fuzzy correspondence cannot be expected for all features of the emotional experience. To begin with, there is no consensus on whether emotions are a set of discrete categories or continuous distributions of a multidimensional nature. If they are discrete categories, then we need to find "signatures" for each of the emotion categories, be they six, three, or eight. The correlations among ANS measures, subjective reports, facial expression, etc. are seldom higher than 0.2 (Ellsworth, 1995; Rimé, Philippot, & Cisamolo, 1990; Tassinary, Cacioppo, & Geen, 1989) and generally, physiological measures fail to discriminate reliably among the emotions (Zajonc & McIntosh, 1992). More important, not all appraisals are fully oriented to reality such that language-reality or thought-reality correspondence can be assumed. Some appraisals are in fact illusory and nevertheless beneficial, especially under conditions of illness (Taylor, 1989). Taylor, Aspinwall, and Giuliano (1994) point out that "the payoffs of striving after difficult goals may be months, years, and even decades away. In contrast, the impact that positive illusions have on happiness or contentment occurs instantly, and it may be these immediate, positive effects that help to produce the long-term impact on caring for others, intellective functioning, motivation, and persistence" (p. 233).

The Independent Nature of Affective Experience

All psychologists are interested in the effects of experience. We all want to know what traces experiences leave on people. How do these experiences affect them? What sort of changes, temporary or permanent, in behavior are we to expect as a result of these experiences? This universal interest is fully reflected in our fundamental experimental paradigm. We present some stimuli and we record responses. Or we take it for granted that the individual had been somehow exposed to some stimuli in the past. These stimuli might be words, pictures, objects, smells, tastes, nonsense syllables, figures, stories, life events—all sorts of things. Sometimes we show these stimuli once, sometimes more than once. And we require the subject to make particular responses that are constrained in particular ways.

But not all psychologists observe and record the same outcomes. In cognitive psychology, for example, the major outcomes are recall, recognition, lexical decision, cognitive judgment, etc. The measures of these outcomes are mostly reaction time and accuracy. The major interest is in cognitive representations. How do they form, change, and are retrieved? The methods of contemporary *social* cognition do not differ a great deal from those of cognitive psychologists. But there used to be another paradigm. The traditional social psychologist also began by presenting some stimulus, sometimes once, sometimes more often. The focus, however, was not on recall or recognition alone.

There was less curiosity about the individuals' cognitive representations and more about their affective dispositions, their liking, their preferences, their attitudes. In short, the two paradigms of psychology differ in the focal dependent measures, and they differ in their scientific goals. Cognitive studies are about the ways we represent the world. Affective studies are about the ways we relate to the world.

Some significant implications follow from this distinction. And they are not so obvious. One may not care what happens to the subjects' affective disposition to the given word, picture, or story that had been presented. But whether the subjects are asked about these preferences and dispositions or not—the affective dispositions, changed or unchanged, are there. Subjects do not restrict their behavior to suit the experimenter's convenience. They do not confine their reactions to the experimental paradigms that we inflict on them. They change their cognitive representations with experience and *at the very same time, and as a result of the very same procedures,* they also change their affective dispositions. When we bombard the subjects with some experimental manipulation, they respond with all they have to respond with. Whether we record it or not.

And it is quite obvious that the affective disposition of a person to a particular stimulus is quite different when that stimulus had been presented but once before. When the individual sees an object, a person, indeed anything, for the second time, it is no longer the same thing. It has changed because the individual and the individual's experience with that object had changed—cognitively and affectively. We cannot step in the same river twice not because the water is different, but because *we* are now different. Significant increments in the liking for novel stimuli were obtained when they were presented just once and for only 4 milliseconds—a condition of exposure that did not allow for any recognition memory (Murphy, Monahan, & Zajonc, 1995). The field is beginning to realize that affective dispositions are at least as significant and informative as psychophysical reactions. And in fact, the access to the individual's mental state is wasted if we ignore one of its important constituent components—affect.

Affective Primacy

The terms "affect" and "cognition" (together with the term "conation") were regarded at the turn of the century to represent distinct and independent processes. In fact, they were referred to as "faculties." The distinctions between the terms became blurred over the decades. "Conation," which denoted behavior or action guided by will, that is, striving, came into disuse altogether, while cognition assumed dominant role, subsuming affects and emotions which at the point of the classical Schachter-Singer (1962) paper became diffuse excitations without meaning that achieve form and content only by cognitive appraisal. The

idea, however, that unexplained arousal seeks cognitive clarity, thus forming an emotional experience, was questioned by Reisenzein (1983) who found no support for the hypothesis that people *search* for an emotional explanation given some peripheral arousal. Twenty years later, it became clear that affects and emotions might possibly act without the participation of cognitive processes and could therefore, in themselves, deserve a closer scrutiny (Zajonc, 1980). In fact, one can today easily defend a position of *primacy* for affect on several grounds.

In an earlier paper, I offered the hypothesis that within the temporal segments of a response trajectory, the very first engagement following a sensory input could well be affective (Zajonc, 1980, p. 170). The conjecture was subsequently confirmed by an impressive number of neuroanatomical studies. Thus, LeDoux (1986, 1987, 1990, 1997) and his collaborators (e.g., LeDoux et al., 1988) have shown that there exists a direct pathway between the thalamus and the amygdalae, and while sensory input can pass through the thalamus and be directed to the cortex, it need not take that route and can activate the amygdalae directly to provoke an avoidance response (see p. 598).

The independence of affect from cognition can also be supported by a variety of other features.

1. Many affective reactions are difficult to verbalize and much of affect is transmitted through nonverbal channels—prosody, facial expression, posture, dress, make-up, etc. Moreover, we have very improverished access to the emotional manifestations of our reactions.

2. In designing the semantic differential, Osgood (1962) expected to obtain the sensory representation of reality. He hoped that the dimensions that would emerge would reflect the features of the physical space-time manifold—intensity, extension, etc. Instead, the factors that emerged—*evaluation, potency,* and *activity*—reflected the subjective reactions of the raters rather than the attributes of the objects and meanings they rated. Moreover, the evaluative dimensions accounted for about half of the entire variance. Osgood attributes this result to the evolutionary significance of affective discriminations. For when we are attacked by a wild animal, it is much more important to know whether it is dangerous than what particular breed or species it might be.

3. Affective reactions, for example, preferences, are not readily predictable from cognitive judgments. Thus, the multidimensional space generated by the psychophysical judgments of soft drinks has little to do with the order of preferences for these drinks (Cooper, 1973). Therefore, to the extent that the physical or objective properties of stimuli do not predict our affective dispositions to these stimuli, it is probable that there must be some form—not yet understood—of an

interaction between our own historically established dispositions—perhaps quite different in different individuals—and the objective features of the stimuli that account for our preferences. I called these dispositions *preferenda,*[5] distinguishing them from *discriminanda,* that is, properties of stimuli that allow us to make purely psychophysical judgments (Zajonc, 1980, p. 159).

The main body of evidence for the affective primacy hypothesis and for the independence of affect from cognition comes from work on the so-called "mere exposure" phenomenon (Zajonc, 1968). There is now solid evidence that if an individual is given perceptual or cognitive access to a novel (previously not encountered) stimulus, the liking for the stimulus will grow with repeated exposures and it will grow logarithmically. The "mere" in mere exposure means that the individual's experience with the stimulus is not constrained by requiring any sort of response on the part of the individual, nor is there any reward or reinforcement (positive or negative) associated with the exposure. Mere exposure effects were obtained in a variety of contexts, using a wide assortment of stimuli, populations, and procedures. Exposure effects were found for geometric figures, random polygons, Chinese and Japanese ideographs, photographs of faces, numbers, letters of the alphabet, letters of one's own name, random sequences of tones, food, odors, flavors, colors, actual persons, stimuli that were initially liked (Swap, 1977), and initially disliked stimuli (Litvak, 1969). Exposure effects were also found in conditions associated with aversive consequences and in conditions associated with pleasant consequences (Harrison, 1977; Saegert, Swap, & Zajonc, 1973). Found responsive to exposure effects were American undergraduates, nationals of dozens of different countries, sons of alcoholics, amnesics, dieters, chicks, ducklings, goslings, and many other species (Bornstein, 1989; Hill, 1978). And exposure effects were also found *prenatally* in fetuses (Rajecki, 1972). In fact, Smith and Bond (1993) claim that the mere exposure is the one solid sociopsychological effect that is found without exceptions across various cultures.

Perhaps the first formal inquiry into the effects of repeated exposure was undertaken by Maslow at the suggestion of E. L. Thorndike (Maslow, 1937). Fifteen Barnard college students participated over a period of ten days in seventeen experiments including familiarization to paintings, foreign names, rubber bands, paper clips, seating choices, blotters, 3×5 cards, cookies, etc. In each case the subjects were given a choice between a familiar and unfamiliar object or experience, and in the majority of cases they chose the familiar object even though at times it was the less convenient or less objectively "superior" item. Thus, for example, the subjects rated a set of unfamiliar paintings more beautiful than ones they had seen before,

but they liked the familiar paintings three times as much. Yet the overall results were mixed, perhaps because of insufficient controls and the absence of any sort of counterbalancing.

The typical experiments that followed the mere exposure paradigm were as simple as the phenomenon itself. A set of novel stimuli, generally of the same category, such as Chinese ideographs or photographs of faces, are exposed to subjects, varying frequency of exposure across the stimuli. The exposures are typically between 0 and 25, but as many as 81 (Zajonc, Swap, Harrison, & Roberts, 1971) and 243 (Zajonc, Crandall, & Kail, 1974) were at times employed. After the exposure phase the subjects are asked to rate the stimuli on some liking, attractiveness, or desirability scale. The pattern of results shows that preference for stimuli grows with the logarithm of the frequency of exposure. The logarithmic form of the relationship is such that the strongest increments are obtained early in the series which is why novel stimuli are normally employed. In order to effect an increment in attractiveness of a stimulus that is already quite familiar, one needs to add a considerable number of exposures, whereas for stimuli previously not encountered one exposure is often sufficient (Murphy et al., 1995).

An interesting application of the exposure phenomenon was reported by Mita, Dermer, and Knight (1997) who asked subjects which of two photographic prints of their faces they liked better—a normal or an inverted print. The inverted prints portray people as they see themselves in the mirror, whereas the normal prints portray people as other people see them. Predictably, the subjects preferred the inverted print of themselves but the normal print of their friends.

A variety of extensions and applications of the mere exposure phenomenon exist although not all of them are featured as instances of the mere exposure phenomenon. The following news item appeared in the *New York Times,* on July 17, 1969:

FOOT POWDER PRODUCES
HEADACHES IN ECUADOR

Quito, Ecuador, July 17 (Reuters). Controversy is raging here because a foot powder called Pulvapies was elected mayor of a town of 4,000 people. A company that manufactures a foot deodorant decided during the recent campaigns for municipal offices to use the slogan: 'Vote for any candidate, but if you want well-being and hygiene, vote for Pulvapies.' On the eve of the election, the company distributed a leaflet the same size and color as official voting paper saying: 'For Mayor, Honorable Pulvapies.' When the votes were counted, the coastal town of Picoaza had elected Pulvapies by a clear majority.

And the entire area of animal imprinting research has a

very close relationship to the mere exposure phenomenon and, in fact, it might be no more than a special case of the mere exposure effect. Thus, for example, Taylor and Sluckin (1964) allowed newly hatched chicks to live alone, with another chick, or with a matchbox. When tested for maintenance of proximity, the subjects raised with a chick did prefer to remain near another (however, not previously encountered) chick, while those raised with a matchbox preferred a matchbox to a live conspecific. Day-old chicks raised with others whose feathers were prenatally tinted green prefer green to untinted chicks, and they preferred red-tinted chicks if they were raised with red-tinted chicks (Zajonc, Wilson, & Rajecki, 1975). Birds of a feather do not always flock together. And rats reared to the sounds of Mozart favor Mozart over Schoenberg (Cross, Holcomb, & Matter, 1967). These and similar experiments that were carried in the context of imprinting research all show the exposure effect. The popular theory of imprinting features imprinting effects as contingent on the so-called critical period (e.g., Moltz & Stettner, 1961). However, it appears that what is considered to be a critical period is a phase during which precocial birds find attachments to other objects that interfere with imprinting on the target stimulus. If the bird is anesthetized, imprinting can be obtained even after four days (MacDonald, 1968), which is well past the twelve to fifteen hours that had been considered the peak period. And it was mentioned above that preference for stimuli can be induced prenatally (Rajecki, 1972).

Exposure effects are also supported by correlational evidence. In particular, any category of words, when examined for its frequency of occurrence (e.g., Thorndike & Lorge, 1944) will yield a substantial positive correlation with their evaluative meaning. Thus, for example, when fruit is rated for desirability a correlation of 0.81 with word frequency is found for the ten items

Fruit	Frequency*	Rated Preference
Apple	220	5.13
Cherry	167	5.00
Strawberry	121	4.83
Pear	62	4.38
Grapefruit	33	4.00
Cantaloupe	1.5	3.75
Avocado	16	2.71
Pomegranate	8	2.63
Gooseberry	5	2.63
Mango	2	2.38

*Frequency per 4,500,000 from the Thorndike-Lorge count.

For other word categories (nouns, verbs, adjectives, and adverbs if they can be ordered for preference), preference

order also correlates with the frequency of occurrence in language. Numerals and letters of the alphabet, too, show this pattern: *4* is preferred to *19* and *B* is preferred to *Q*. And even prepositions (which incidentally can also be evaluative for positivity of meaning) exhibit this relationship. For example, *on* is preferred to *off* and it is much more frequent in language. And the same holds for *in* and *out*. Now, one could argue that in the case of items such as fruit words or vegetable words, the correlation reflects a reversed causation. That is, we like apples therefore the production of apples is quite high, and so is the consumption. For the same reason, the word *apple* is a very frequent occurrence in our language. While this argument may hold for apples, it can hardly hold for a number,[6] say *4*, or a letter, say *B*, or the preposition *on* (Zajonc, 1968).

The letters of one's own name, too, have been found to be preferred to letters not in one's own name (Hoorens, 1990; Hoorens, Nuttin, Herman, & Pavakanun, 1990; Hoorens & Nuttin, 1993). Nuttin (1987) who discovered the phenomenon, however, does not attribute the results to mere exposure but to "mere ownership," that is, the particular positive affective disposition to items related to the self, such as one's material possessions, and also experiences. While the "mere ownership" hypothesis is certainly consistent with the data, and other results support the positive affect associated with the things we own (Abelson, 1986; Prentice, 1987); the mere exposure explanation is not thereby ruled out. When children learn the alphabet, among the very first words they learn to write, and then incessantly practice, is their own name. And they continue to see it on their notebooks, their desks, their books, labels, etc. In all probability, both "mere ownership" and "mere exposure" are phenomena each sufficient to enhance affective disposition to objects, and therefore, they are not mutually exclusive. Note that the "mere ownership" hypothesis is quite similar to Titchener's (1910) idea that familiarity and recognition induce in the individual a "glow of warmth, a sense of ownership, a feeling of intimacy" (p. 411).

There is no satisfactory explanation for the exposure effect. All explanations leave some anomalous findings unexplained. For instance, Matlin (1970) proposed the theory of response competition according to which novel stimuli tend to evoke a variety of responses that are in some competition with each other. The competition for emission derives from the fact that no stimulus is so novel as to evoke no response, at least partially. On the contrary, all stimuli including novel stimuli are similar to number of familiar stimuli and as such evoke at a weak level responses associated with these similar stimuli. Unlike well-known stimuli, however, they do not evoke one or a few dominant responses and hence the responses that they do evoke are in competition with each other. This competition is reduced over repeated exposures because some responses drop out and others are strengthened, and the discomfort disappears.

The response competition theory, therefore, views the growth in affect as a reduction of an aversion and a form of habituation. Observe that no positive affect could ever develop just because there is no response competition. But observing subjects in an imprinting experiment and their desperate efforts to maintain proximity to the focal objects, it is evident that exposure can indeed generate affect that is quite positive. Harmon-Jones and Allen (1996) have indeed documented a rise in positive affect (as will be discussed).

The same applies to a theory based on the orienting reflex (Sokolov, 1963). The orienting response occurs nearly universally in all species on encountering a novel stimulus. Its features are the sudden activation of the autonomic system, symptomatic of the organism placing its resources on alert, and a readiness for rapid action, usually flight or fight. However, if the organism suffers no harm from the intruder, the subsequent encounter with that stimulus engenders a weaker autonomic reaction, and after a few such encounters that are not accompanied by aversive consequences, the orienting reflex habituates. Thus, the orienting reflex theory also paints a picture of an initially aversive, or at least guarded, reaction that eventually reaches a neutral level after several exposures. Moreover, it is much more reasonable to apply the orienting reflex to a monkey confronted with a cobra than to an undergraduate confronted with a novel Chinese ideograph. The autonomic reaction in the latter would be considerably weaker, although quite clearly present. When skin conductance data are collected on a series of random stimulus exposures in which some stimuli are presented often and others less often, the measures show a clear drop in conductance with the logarithm of exposure frequency (Zajonc, 1968, pp. 20–21).

But skin conductance data and most other measures of the autonomic system do not discriminate the polarity of the reaction—we don't know whether the reaction is one of approach or one of avoidance. We only know from these measures that there is an increase in the level of excitation. Only three psychophysiological measures are able to discriminate between positive and negative polarity of affective reaction: temperature, facial EMG, and EEG. Recent studies have shown that when an organism experiences a positive emotional experience, his brain (and in particular, hypothalamic) temperature can drop as much as 0.3°C. Conversely, negative affect is associated with a comparable rise in temperature (Berridge & Zajonc, 1991; McIntosh, Zajonc, Vig, & Emerick, 1996; Zajonc et al., 1989). Thus far, no studies examined temperature changes as a function of exposure, although one is being carried out now in our laboratory. The second method of verifying if repeated exposure results in positive affect relies on the EEG records. It derives from the research of Davidson and his colleagues (Davidson, 1984, 1988, 1993; Tomarken, Davidson, & Henriques, 1990). It is based on the finding that affective reactions are associated with activity in the anterior regions of the brain, and that positive affect shows activation in the left hemisphere, whereas negative affect and avoidance or escape reactions are associated with activity in the right anterior regions. A recent study by Harmon-Jones and Allen (1996) took EEG measures and found EEG changes consistent with the hypothesis that exposure generates positive affect. The third measure, facial electromyography, has also been successfully employed by Harmon-Jones and Allen (1996). There was a significant increase from baseline in zygomatic activity when subjects were exposed to familiar stimuli but none when they were exposed to unfamiliar stimuli. Dimberg (1982) obtained pronounced activity in the zygomatic and corrugator muscles, respectively, when subjects were viewing photographs of smiling and frowning faces. Other research, too, has found very consistent patterns of this type (Cacioppo, Klein, Berntson, & Hatfield, 1993). Also, there was in the Harmon-Jones/Allen study a correlation between the familiar/unfamiliar difference in zygomatic activity and the familiar/unfamiliar liking ratings of the stimuli. The EMG data that show only a rise in positive affective response to familiarized stimuli and essentially no evidence of negative affect to unfamiliar stimuli might question the application of the orienting reflex theory, which predicts negative affect to novel stimuli, to explain the exposure effect.

The Nature of Unappraised Affect

Titchener's (1910) theory because it was the most obvious one was for decades the traditional explanation of the exposure effect. His idea of "sense of ownership," which became a basis for explaining the name-letter effect (Nuttin, 1987), was offered as one factor contributing to the growth of positive affect with familiarization. But the glow and *frisson* of recognition was another. Titchener took as a prototype of the phenomenon our experience of listening to a familiar piece of music. When the piece is familiar we can correctly anticipate phrases to follow, hum with the music, predict development of the next several bars, and generally "feel one" with it. While the subjective familiarity hypothesis holds high plausibility, there is very little evidence to support it. For example, Matlin (1970) carried out a typical exposure experiment, but in addition to collecting liking ratings she also collected recognition judgments. Independently of subjective familiarity, liking varied with the objective history of the individuals' experience and not with their subjective feelings of familiarity. This result was replicated several times (Kunst-Wilson & Zajonc, 1980; Moreland & Zajonc, 1977, 1979; Murphy et al., 1995; Wilson, 1979).

In most of the studies examining the mediating role of recognition, the stimuli were presented at optimal viewing conditions. However, Kunst-Wilson and Zajonc (1980) sought to reduce the contribution of recognition by experimental methods and they presented exposure stimuli well below subject's recognition threshold. The recognition memory measure showed chance performance. However, in the absence of any recognition, liking ratings disclosed clear dependence on previous exposures. Thus, preference ratings were a more reliable indicator of the effects of past experience than recognition memory.[7] Since the original study, several replications and variants of the design were published (Barchas & Perlaki, 1986; Bonnano & Stilling, 1986; Bornstein, Leone, & Galley, 1987; Mandler, Nakamura, & VanZandt, 1987; Seamon, Brody, & Kauff, 1983a, 1983b; Seamon, Marsh, & Brody, 1989). To come back to the question raised earlier about psychologists ignoring affective consequences of exposure when dealing with cognitive problems, I cannot refrain from noting that in these experiments the affective reaction was a better index of recognition (and as such, of a cognitive process) than was the recognition memory measure.

It has been contended that the exposure effect, especially when obtained under degraded stimulus presentations, is mediated by a subjective feeling of perceptual fluency (Jacoby, Kelley, & Dywan, 1989; Whittlesea, Jacoby, & Girard, 1990). Mandler, Nakamura, and VanZandt (1987) also argued that the effect is not specific. The perceptual fluency theory holds essentially that the liking measure is a proxy for recognition memory and it is an instance of implicit memory. Indeed, when the visual clarity of the stimuli is manipulated, the results do suggest a perceptual fluency mediation. It is in all probability the case that some form of perceptual process does participate in the exposure effect, but the extent or importance of this participation is probably minimal.

Theoretical considerations and several empirical findings cast doubt on the perceptual fluency hypothesis as a significant factor in the growth of affective reactions with repeated exposures. Above all, the mere exposure effect is a process of enormous adaptive significance. It is a fundamental adaptive mechanism that is probably hardwired (e.g., Porges, 1995). It is the basis of attachment, affiliation, and attraction (Zajonc, 1971). It allows for an efficient categorization of the environment, social and nonsocial, into those elements that are safe, approachable, and beneficent and others that are dangerous and threatening. By virtue of achieving such a categorization through the mere repeated exposure, the organism not only gains a cognitive differentiation, but simultaneously its affective dispositions toward the various aspects of the environment become superbly adaptive. No social bonds, or stable communities, could evolve or be maintained if nature did not equip organisms with a means of discriminating between objects that can be approached, in whose proximity the organism can remain without worry, and those to which a response must be infused with caution. And such a discrimination is acquired by an extremely simple and primi-

tive process that has powerful cognitive, affective, and behavioral consequences. It is equally present in lower animals. For these reasons one would not expect that an emotional consequence of this significance would be simply a proxy for perceptual fluency whose adaptive contribution is marginal.

Empirical data also speak against perceptual fluency as an important factor in exposure effects. First, when the exposure effect is obtained under optimal conditions the results are very much the same as they are in the case of degraded stimuli. In both cases, also, recognition measures have no relationship to liking, in the sense that recognition does not depend on liking nor does liking depend on recognition. And there is no relationship between subjective confidence in one's own recognition judgments and liking effects in repeated exposure designs. Moreland and Zajonc (1977, 1979) using structural equation models, analyzed the causal process of the exposure effects including such measures as familiarity, recognition, recognition confidence, recognition accuracy, and liking. They found that the strongest determinant of liking was the objective history of stimulus exposure, whereas subjective recognition, familiarity, recognition confidence, or accuracy did not contribute significantly to liking. Second, when exposures are varied *between* subjects, and subjects cannot, therefore, experience differences in perceptual fluency that are correlated with frequency of exposure, the exposure effect is nevertheless obtained (Moreland & Zajonc, 1976). Third, we would not expect perceptual fluency to activate the zygomatic muscles under repeated exposure, indicating the growth of positive affect, such as found by Harmon-Jones and Allen (1996). Also, Bentin, Moscovitch, and Heth (1992) obtained elevated scalp ERPs (Evoked Response Potentials) to previously shown words independently of subjects' recognition accuracy. These P300 measures were also found to depend on the recency of the prior exposure of the words. Fourth, we would not expect perceptual fluency to generalize to other stimuli in that category, an effect reported by Gordon and Holyoak (1983) and confirmed by Monahan, Murphy, and Zajonc (under review) or be sufficiently diffuse to transfer onto another irrelevant stimulus category documented also by Monahan, Murphy, and Zajonc.

In general, efforts to impose a cognitive explanation on the exposure effect are in the family of arguments on the relative primacy of cognitive and affective processes, which given the current state of evidence, should be laid to rest. These arguments must avail themselves of assumptions not justified by past empirical results, must view the subject as doggedly "repressing" an awareness of recognition, and deny the obvious and straightforward possibility that we do become attached to things with which we had considerable experience.[8]

What sort of affect could have been generated by an experience consisting of an almost totally degraded stimulus exposure? The subliminal presentations, to be sure, generated weak effects. The preference for the exposed stimuli exceeded novel stimuli by a little more than 10 percent. While the argument for affective primacy can be made on the strength of these data, the nature of affect that precedes cognitive processing and occurs without its participation, must have a character quite different from affect generated through cognitive appraisal and full access to information about its origin, target, and context. Above all it must be primitive, diffuse, and gross. While it differentially confers valence onto familiarized and novel stimuli, its direct link with the object is neither strong nor distinct. It must, therefore, be able to generalize to other similar stimuli, and even be capable of attaching itself to irrelevant contiguous targets. It is contagious or communicable and able to spread over new targets. The procedure of semantic priming examines the process where aspects of meaning are communicated or spread among targets. Spreading activation (Collins & Loftus, 1975) is a concept that suggests a semantic process that recruits associated meanings. The "contagion" of meanings is illustrated by the differences in meanings attributed to PATIENT when it follows DOCTOR and when it follows WAITING. Thus, IMPATIENT would be an association recruited by WAITING but not by DOCTOR.

The concept of *affective priming* represents a similar process for the emotions and moods, and perhaps more so for the latter. The contagion of affects is the principal feature of contiguity theory in conditioning and association learning. Its application to the study of nonconscious affect affords the possibility of learning something about affect and something about consciousness. While semantic priming is a cognitive process that depends on the semantic content of the targets and of primes, affective priming may have very diffuse spread, indiscriminate with respect to the semantic content of the target. The typical procedure is to choose photographs of smiling and frowning faces, present them very briefly (say for 4 milliseconds) prior to the presentation of the target stimulus (which could be a random polygon, Chinese ideograph, or any item whatsoever), and record the affective reaction of the subject to that target stimulus (Murphy, 1990; Murphy & Zajonc, 1987, 1988, 1993; Murphy et al., 1995). In these experiments targets preceded by smiling faces presented for only 4 milliseconds were judged more positively than targets preceded by frowning faces.

If nonconscious affect is diffuse and capable of spreading over contiguous targets, then nonconscious affect from different sources should combine to produce joint effects. Moreover, these joint effects should be additive. Affects deriving from distinct origins should not influence each other's contributions. Murphy, Monahan, and Zajonc (1995) have recently shown that indeed when the effects of repeated exposure are joined by the effects of affective priming, that is, if the Kunst-Wilson/Zajonc procedure is combined with the Murphy/Zajonc procedure, the two effects fuse in an additive manner, showing no interaction. In a recent study, deGroot (1996) found clear evidence of EMG activity produced by unconscious affective priming, using the same procedure as in the Murphy-Zajonc experiments. Zillmann (1991), too, found additive affective reactions for excitations of which the subject was not aware. A current stimulus produced excitation that was added onto a previously instigated arousal, in the so-called excitation-transfer paradigm. It should not be overlooked in this context that the study of consciousness which has recently become the subject of very active interest in cognitive science, neuroscience, artificial intelligence, philosophy, and computer science may well benefit by shifting from a focus on nonconscious cognitions to a focus on nonconscious emotions. The above research on subliminal affective priming provides, for example, a series of methods and approaches revealing properties of consciousness thus far not understood or appreciated.

AFFECT/COGNITION INTERFACE

Once it is established that cognition and emotion are two independent processes that are in constant interaction, where each influences the other, the proposition immediately begs the question of *where* and *how* contact is made between the two processes such that an influence of one over the other can in fact take place. The answer to this question would above all depend on one's perspective on the nature of emotions and the focus of one's interest. Those theories that assume a heavy participation of cognitive functions in the experience and in the elicitation of emotions (Lazarus, 1982; Mandler, 1975; Schachter & Singer, 1962) do not specify the nature of the participation of the two processes nor the properties of each process that are the arena of the contact. For Bower (1981), the affective and cognitive units are joined in an associative network of nodes, each with full capability of unspecified access to all others. Forgas (1995), on the other hand, proposed the Affect Infusion Model in which he distinguished among those judgments readily influenced by mood and other emotional factors and those that are not. For example, judgments that he considers to be "heuristic," that is, those that rely on only partial, habitual, and quick search strategies or those information processing strategies that involve extensive search are readily influenced by affect infusion. In contrast, judgments that are based on direct access to memory or those strongly under motivational control are less likely to be infused with affect. Hence, such effects as founded by Schwarz (1990) on misattribution of affective judgments (see above) should be obtained for heuristic and substantive processing but not for direct and motivated processing.

Most research on the interface of cognition and emotion, however, addresses the interaction not between cognition and emotion but between cognition of some event (say instigation, or appraisal) and the cognition *about* emotion. Here the problem of how and where the interaction takes place is easily resolved because it is relegated entirely to the domain of cognitive representations of both the particular eliciting event and of the experienced emotion. But is the only possible contact between emotion and cognition one that relies on cognitive representations? This is not a trivial problem for it is the one that has plagued philosophy of consciousness for 350 years—the mind-body problem that Descartes thought he had solved by postulating that the contact is made in the pineal gland. In an important paper on reductionism, Suppes (1991) has clarified the theoretical difficulties besetting the presumed connection between "hardware" and "software" even in computers. He argued that "the distinction is not as sharp as it might seem, for in some sense the software program must become a part of the hardware, i.e., part of the physical organization of the computer. Where, it might be asked, does hardware stop and software begin? Once the software is embodied in the computer, as it is in a different way in the brain, this is not an easy question to answer from purely physical considerations in the case of the computer or physiological ones in the case of the brain" (p. 196).

An approach was offered by Zajonc and Markus (1984) that does not fall prey to the mind-body duality nor to cognitive imperialism. It appeals to the concept of the *hard* interface. Undeniably, feelings, moods, and emotions have their cognitive and subjective correlates. But a host of other manifestations also are fairly well-correlated with these subjective states. There are the responses of the visceral system, there is facial expression, there are clenched fists, red faces, and pounding hearts. There is a typical posture and if the individual engages in instrumental action, there is a great deal of motor activity. Now, each of these manifestations can in its own right be considered a representation of the emotion—to be sure, it is a motor or somatic representation, yet representation nevertheless. For we need not mean anything else by "representation" than some reaction in the organism that *stands for* a particular referent, internal or external. An alarm call and freezing posture is a representation of the fear of emotion experienced by the subject, and a smile is a representation of a felt joy or pleasure.

But cognition, too, has its somatic representations. The kinesthetic pressure, the orientation of one's back, the position of his/her knees, and the constrains of the backrest against his/her spine, one feels while sitting in a chair and typing are very much parts of his/her representation of that chair. And it is not an accident that in problem solving a great deal of motor engagement can be observed. Problem solvers scratch their heads, furrow their eyebrows, rub their chins and foreheads. When you ask a person to imagine threading a needle, her convergence and accommodation will show a change corresponding to the image—quite different from that of people imagining a ship on the horizon. There have been some attempts to examine the role of the somatic system in information processing and memory (Smith, 1969), but the knowledge in this area of study is scant.

Almost sixty years ago, Max (1937) recorded EMG responses from the fingers of deaf and hearing subjects. Eighty-four percent of the deaf subjects showed significant responses in listening to spoken text. Only 31 percent of the hearing subjects generated responses of any sort and they were much weaker (means of 0.08 versus 3.41 microvolts). And on the guise of testing the performance of earphones, Wells and Petty (1980) asked subjects to move their heads laterally or vertically while listening to opinion and attitude statements. Those moving heads horizontally were more likely to disagree with the issue than those moving their heads in the approving gesture. Consistent with these are data reported on facial expression by Strack et al. (1988) who were able to influence affective judgments by altering the subjects' contractions of the zygomatic muscles.

Scripture (1891) describes an arithmetical prodigy, Truman Henry Safford, who always manifested an exceptionally rich motor participation when solving problems. When asked to multiply 365,365,365,365,365 by 365,365, 365,365,365,365 he "flew around the room like a top, pulled his pantaloons over the top of his boots, bit his hand, rolled his eyes in their sockets, sometimes smiling and talking, then seeming to be in agony, until no more than one minute, said he, 133,491,850,208,566,925,016, 658,299,941,583,225!" We don't think of such action as impression formation, or face recognition, as tasks that involve the motor system in a significant way and seldom inquire into the contribution that the motor system can make to speed and accuracy of the outcome measures. Yet, when subjects are shown a long series of photographs for a subsequent recognition memory test, those subjects who are asked to try to imitate the emotional expression of the faces have considerably higher accuracy than subjects for whom an interference with the participation of the motor system (by having them chew gum) was introduced (Pietromonaco, Zajonc, & Bargh, 1981; Zajonc, Pietromonaco, & Bargh, 1982).

SOCIETY, CULTURE, AND EMOTIONS

Emotions, even though their hallmark is the internal state of the individual—the viscera, the gut—are above all social phenomena. They are the basis of social interaction, they are the products of social interaction, their origins, and their currency (Fiske, Kitayama, Markus, & Nisbett, 1998, in this *Handbook*). The society and its culture establish institutional controls over the emotions, give them their meaning, constrain their expression, influence their subjective experience, influence their neurophysiological correlates, and most importantly they regulate the instrumental behavior that ensues from emotion-motivated antecedents. Socialization processes are directed toward the forming and framing of emotional experiences and emotional reactions, transferring the sources of behavioral control from external to internal. They are the roots of conscience (Kochánska, 1993) that, as Aristotle noted, direct which emotional proclivities we can allow ourselves and which we must resist, which will turn into virtues, and which into vices. And this is so because emotions are the individual sources of energy that society exploits for its own maintenance.

The position of a person in society, the person's role and hierarchical status, occupation, background, and connections to others, are very important factors allowing and demanding for certain emotions. For instance, among the Wolof in Senegal—a group numbering two to three million urban and rural people—emotional dispositions are directly associated with status (Irvine, 1995). Thus, nobility is solid, "heavy," lethargic, bland, and controlled. The lower-caste people are "light-weight," volatile, and excitable. And these are not stereotypes but normative emotional dispositions, seen in everyday behavior. Irvine (1995) offers the observation that "the contrast is sometimes described in terms of weight, sometimes in terms of differences in the viscosity of body fluids, and sometimes in terms of the elements—earth, air, fire, and water—as if the various castes consisted of these, or resembled these, in different degrees, balances, or emphases" (p. 253). The Wolof have two kinds of speech—*waxu géér* (noble speech) and *waxu gewel* (low-caste speech) that, corresponding to the emotional and temperamental dispositions of the two castes, differ in prosody, phonology, morphology, syntax, lexicon, and conversational norms (such as taking turns). The nobles speak slowly, laconically, low-pitch, in incomplete sentences. The low-castes are loud, rapid, with conspicuous gestures, high-pitched, repetitive, with a vivid vocabulary, and many intensifiers.

One can imagine a society that consists of 80 percent psychopaths and 20 percent sociopaths. It is a society in which no institutional and social constraints over emotions are present. Such a society, of course, could not exist for very long. The fact that psychopaths and sociopaths are exceptional and anomalous indicates the existence of feeling rules and constraints on emotion deriving from the social and cultural processes imposed on the interaction and interrelations among members of a society and community. As such, then, it is possible to imagine that similar constraints are probably present in animal societies as well, for there are limits on response to frustration, there are proper ways of courting and mating, there are selective forms of association, and there are conventional responses to threat among conspecifics—all these also exist in human societies and the only difference is that the subjective, linguistic, and ideological overlay, of course, is not present among animal societies, and presumably neither is guilt, shame, or indignation.

Culture must, of course, enter into an emotional experience with considerable force. To the extent that emotions entail a cognitive appraisal, the standards and norms of these appraisals must be under considerable cultural influence. We have to learn from our culture the difference between an insult and a slight, between courage and cowardice. Ellsworth (1991) notes that if there are cultures in which, for example, it is the general belief that people's behavior is ruled by demons, then interpersonal anger deriving from an injury caused by a fellow citizen is not a likely occurrence. And to the extent that a culture defines its vices and virtues, and to the extent that vices and virtues are but modulators of emotions and emotional responses, culture is deeply implicated in emotions. But here again, nearly all research on the culture/emotion interface is based on some form of lexical procedure, which must necessarily suffer shortcomings This is not to say that we somehow miss the crucial aspect of emotions. For as White (1993) observed, it is fairly well accepted today that "all language entails culturally specific modes of thought and action, which not only express but *create* the realities they represent. While the argument that language creates (and influences) social reality can be well defended, the specific details of the process, its parameters, methods of analysis are at a very early stage of development."

Perhaps the clearest evidence of cultural influences on emotions might be obtained by the studies of microcultures, such as in business organizations, symphony orchestras, prisons, sports teams, theater groups, dance troupes, small private schools, hospitals, circuses, etc. There must have been enormous differences in the control of anger reactions between the concentration and gulag inmates and their guards. In these camps grief and sadness had to be suppressed or habituated. There exist, in fact, institutional means with elaborate social controls for the suppression of some negative emotions, such as grief and sadness, for example, in Bali (Wikan, 1989). The shortcoming of the study of microculture effects, however, lies in the selective nature of the particular populations. Prison inmates do not constitute a representative sample of the population from which they are recruited, and they differ from that population in important physiological parameters (see Dabbs, Carr, Frady, & Riad, 1995, for example).[9] While "culture" in these isolated populations might be different, so might be the underlying neuroanatomical structures and neurochemical processes implicated in the emotional experiences that occur in these settings.

Markus and Kitayama (1994) argue that "a cultural

group's ways of feeling are shaped by the group's habitual and normative social behavior, and in turn, these ways of feeling influence the nature of this social behavior" (p. 91). Hence, a complete analysis of emotional meanings requires the understanding of the emotional reactions that accompany the various actions within a community together with the normative and institutional and cultural frames of the given community. Members' engagement in a culture builds their selves which respond in particular ways to the demands, constraints, and affordances of their own social environment. Cultural norms prescribe feeling rules (Hochschild, 1979) such that one knows how to behave upon the death of a loved one or the success of an enemy. In Japan, the most common negative emotion, according to surveys of students and adults, is the feeling that one has been a burden to someone, and the most frequently mentioned positive emotion is relief that things are just okay, that events are harmonious (Markus & Kitayama, 1994). In contrast, Americans asked to name frequent positive emotion, list feeling good about oneself, a sense of pride, a sense of affirmation of one's self-worth and self-esteem. The most frequent negative American emotion, on the other hand, is anger. These differences reflect the collective interdependent culture of the Japanese and the individualistic independent culture of the Western world. Stephan, Stephan, and DeVargas (1996) also found greater reluctance to express negative emotions in Costa Rica (a more collectivist culture) than in the United States. The most frequently mentioned emotion word in the Netherlands is *angst* (fear) and the least frequent is *liefde* (love). In Turkey *sevgi* (love) is the most frequently mentioned emotion, and *korku* (fear) is very low on the list (Frijda, Markam, Sato, & Wiers, 1995). In Belgium, the Netherlands' nearest neighbor, *joie* (joy) is the most frequently listed emotion, and in Surinam it is *sari* (sadness) (Mesquita, 1993). In Bali, one does not mourn the death of a lover because these expressions would be contagious and pollute the social environment (Wikan, 1990).

Recall that Aristotle was keen to draw the connection between emotions, virtues, and vices, hence between emotions and morality. Certainly, a large proportion of variations among the various elements of the emotional experience must be due to the moral structure of the given culture. Shweder, Much, Mahapatra, and Park (1996) distinguish among three forms of morality, one based on *autonomy,* another based on *community,* and a third centering on *divinity.*

The "ethics of autonomy" relies on regulative concepts such as "harm," "rights" and "justice" and aims to protect the zone of discretionary choice of "individuals" and to promote the exercise of individual will in the pursuit of personal preferences. This is the kind of ethic that is usually the official ethic of societies where "individualism" is an ideal. The "ethics of community" in contrast relies on regulative concepts such as "duty," "status," "hierarchy" and "interdependency." It aims to protect the moral integrity of the various stations or roles that constitute a "society" or a "community," where "society" or "community" is conceived of as a corporate entity with an identity, standing history, and reputation of its own. Finally, the "ethics of divinity" relies heavily on regulative concepts such as "sacred order," "natural order," "sin," "sanctity" and "pollution." It aims to protect the soul, the spirit, the spiritual aspects of the human agent and "nature" from degradation.

These ethical frames would afford some emotions and emotional experiences and prevent others. If the pursuit of personal preferences and the exercise of individual choice are topmost values of a culture, then interpersonal frustration would generate anger and anger would be a justifiable emotion. If duty is a high value, then there would be little fear in offering oneself in sacrifice for common good, and cooperation would be frequent and easy. In the community ethics, a failure to help is more distressing than a failure to achieve—which is suffered more severely in an autonomous culture. If sin is a major part of social control, then guilt and shame would be frequent emotional reactions.

Among basic concepts of culture are values. Acculturation and socialization—the basic process that impart values over generations—take place by means of social control which is exercised through institutions (police, schools, justice system, etc.) and through informal social interaction that include above all child-rearing practices (Saarni, 1993). For sociologists (e.g., Scheff, 1990), the major vehicles of social control are, in fact, the emotions of pride and shame. I suppose that in diverse societies social control might be exercised by different emotions, say guilt or fear. But the sorts of categories of values that have been enumerated (e.g., Rokeach, 1968) are not directly or even easily connected to emotions. What emotions, for example, do we connect to EQUALITY or FREEDOM? Yet at some more primitive level, emotional universality must exist— and not only a universality among cultures—but among species, as well, for the positive/negative distinction imposes itself on emotion research with an indisputable consistency. Whatever scaling, typology, or taxonomy is constructed, the hedonic polarity always emerges (White, 1994). And this should not be be surprising if emotions function to facilitate the organism's adaptation to an environment that is sometimes hostile and sometimes benign. How else would an organism or a species maintain its reproductive potential if it could not distinguish in its instrumental responses between hostile and benign events?

One value, regarded as crucial in some communities and cultures, is honor. It is only recently that laws prohibiting dueling have been passed. Nisbett and Cohen (1996) advanced the interesting hypothesis that differences ob-

TABLE 1
Murder Rates for French Polynesia

Year	Total Population	Murders
1900	28,960	0
1910	31,770	0
1920	34,910	0
1930	39,480	4
1940	49,770	0
1950	61,270	2
1953	67,280	0
1956	73,201	0
1959	Approx. 80,000	5

served in violence between the southern and northern United States can be attributed to the South's "culture of honor," that is, a culture in which the individual is willing to protect his (I say "his," because the culture of honor applies more to men than to women) reputation by resort to violence. According to Nisbett and Cohen, the culture of honor evolved in the context of cattle and sheepherding. This sort of economy lacks lawful protection and theft of heads of cattle is frequent, difficult to prosecute, and most often is punished by personal and direct methods. "Herdsmen the world over tend to be capable of great aggressiveness and violence because of their vulnerability to losing their primary resources, their animals." Hence, the citizens of these regions took upon themselves to create and maintain order. Between 1865 and 1915, the homicide rate in the Cumberland Mountains was 130 per 100,000, which is twice as in the most violent American large cities. Observe, in contrast, the murder rates for French Polynesia (Levy, 1973) as shown in Table 1.

LAST WORD

It is now obvious that there are many more questions about emotions and affect than there are answers or even ideas. In every domain of the emotion research unanswered empirical questions wait for a study to address them. And the interface among the various domains that this chapter examined is begging for answers even more urgently. Each new problem solved reveals several new ones. Progress in method, in theory, and in application allows us to learn more about emotions—a task that cannot be delayed for no understanding of behavior will ever be achieved without a better understanding of the emotions.

All fields of psychology will benefit from a better understanding of the emotions. Since they are integral components of all behavior, and since all branches of psychol-

ogy have in one way or another included emotional processes in many of their explanatory theories and findings, all will advance more rapidly and will be better able to verify their assumptions about the emotions when emotion theory is better specified and the findings that support it are better substantiated.

NOTES

1. Self-interest is seen as ultimately reflected in behavior that maximizes reproductive success (Wilson, 1975), or is otherwise motivated by reciprocal altruism (Trivers, 1971). But there is actually no need to postulate an "instinct" or "mechanism" driving individuals to maximize their reproductive success. It is entirely conceivable that altruism is self-reinforcing. By virtue of empathy, the pleasure and joy of the recipient of our altruistic act, seen or imagined, might act as a sufficient reinforcer of future altruistic acts.

2. *The New York Times,* 26 March 1993. It is of no minor significance that the photographer, Kevin Carter, committed suicide at the age of thirty-three having written at one point that he was "haunted by the memories of killings and corpses and anger and pain . . . of starving or wounded children, of trigger-happy madmen, often police, of killer executioners" (MacLeod, Scott, "The life and death of Kevin Carter," *Time,* 12 September 1994, 70–73).

3. But not all two-factor theories must implicate the dualism. Thus, for example, the theory of affective primacy and independence draws evidence from behavior and from the separate neural structures whereby the amygdalae dominate emotional responses and the hippocampus cognitive responses. Hence, both are bodily processes.

4. Sheldon's data were taken from the Ivy League colleges posture-photo policy. These schools, eager to assure that the offspring entrusted to them would grow up with fine mind and fine posture, took to the habit of photographing them in the nude. Thus, there would be no sloping shoulders or a sunken chest among the men and women of Harvard, Yale, Mt. Holyoke, Wellesley, Smith, Vassar, and Princeton. Among those photographed were Meryl Streep, Hilary Rodham Clinton, Diane Sawyer, George Bush, Bob Woodward, George Pataki, and many others of today's celebrities (Rosenbaum, 1995). Many of the photographs were destroyed but some apparently are still to be found in the National Museum of Natural History.

5. When the focus is not on the individual but on the stimulus, the concept of *collative variables,* first introduced by Berlyne (1965), specifies a similar aspect of subject-stimulus interaction. Here, stimulus properties such as novelty, surprisingness, complexity, ambiguity, etc., represent both some aspect of the stimulus and some aspect of the subject's experience. The clearest example of a collative variable is *novelty,* which depends on the subject's past

experience with the stimulus, and, of course, is reduced and completely eliminated after the original encounter as a function of the person's subsequent experience with the stimulus.

6. It is of some interest that the frequency of the digits 1 to 9 represents a definite order with the lower numbers having greater frequency as first digits in the logarithmic tables. The physicist, Frank Brandford, has shown in 1938, in fact, that the probability that a random decimal begins with the digit p is equal to $\log(p + 1) - \log p$ (Raimi, 1969). The formula predicts the actual count quite accurately, showing, for example, that the digit 1 has more than six times the probability than the digit 9 in such collections of tables as the *Handbook of Chemistry and Physics* and *The World Almanac*.

7. This result is not entirely unprecedented. The psychophysical phenomenon of discrimination in the absence of detection was reported by Nachmias and Sansbury (1974) and by Rollman and Nachmias (1972). Here subjects are presented randomly with red and blue lights, or trials in which no light at all is flashed. The task is to guess whether there was a light or not, and independently of the first response, what color it was. It turns out that even in the absence of detection, that is, when subjects report that there was no light flashing, the discrimination between red and blue is better than chance.

8. A similar example where the purely cognitive approach proved to be misleading is offered by Eich (1995) who has shown that what was thought to be the place-dependent memory effect proved to be affect-dependent memory.

9. The Nazi concentration camp and the gulag, or the ordinary prison, cannot be compared because in the latter most of the inmates have a history of some crime or transgression. This is certainly true in ordinary prisons. And if prisons are populated by individuals with emotional tendencies that distinguish them from the remaining population, then the question of cultural influence on emotion must be studied in prison as a special case. For example, many studies have shown an increased testosterone level among prison inmates, and a strong association between testosterone level and unruly behavior while in prison (Dabbs, Carr, Frady, & Riad, 1995; Dabbs & Morris, 1990; Dabbs, Ruback, Frady, Hopper, & Sgoutas, 1988; Ehrenkranz, Bliss, & Sheard, 1974; Kreuz & Rose, 1972).

REFERENCES

Abelson, R. P. (1963). Computer simulation of "hot cognitions." In S. Tomkins & S. Mednick (Eds.), *Computer simulation of personality*. New York: Wiley.

Abelson, R. P. (1986). Beliefs are like possessions. *Journal for the Theory of Social Behaviour, 16*, 223–250.

Adolphs, R., Tranel, D., Damasio, H., & Damasio, A. (1994). Impaired recognition of emotion in facial expressions following bilateral damage to the human amygdala. *Nature, 372*, 669–672.

Aggleton, J. P. (1993). The contribution of the amygdala to normal and abnormal emotional states. *Trends in Neuroscience, 16*, 328–333.

Allport, F. H. (1924). *Social psychology*. Chicago: Houghton Mifflin.

Amaral, D. G. (1987). Memory: anatomical organization of candidate brain regions. In F. Plum (Ed.), *Handbook of physiology. Section 1. The nervous system: Vol. V. Higher functions of the brain* (pp. 211–294). Bethesda, MD: American Physiological Society.

Amaral, D. G., Price, J. L., Pitkänen, A., & Carmichael, S. T. (1992). Anatomical organization of the primate amygdaloid complex. In J. P. Aggleton (Ed.), *The amygdala: Neurobiological aspects of emotion, memory, and mental dysfunction.* (pp. 1–66). New York: Wiley-Liss.

Argyle, M., Salter, V., Nicholson, H., Williams, M., & Burgess, P. (1970). The communication of inferior and superior attitudes by verbal and nonverbal signals. *British Journal of Social and Clinical Psychology, 9*, 222–231.

Aristotle. (1980). *Nicomachean ethics* (D. Ross, Trans.). Oxford: Oxford University Press.

Aristotle. (1991). *The art of rhetoric.* (H. C. Lawson-Tancred, Trans.). London: Penguin.

Arnold, M. B. (1960). *Emotions and personality.* New York: Columbia University Press.

Attenborough, D. (1995). *The private life of plants: A natural history of plant behavior.* Princeton: Princeton University Press.

Averill, J. R. (1975). A semantic atlas of emotional concepts. *JSAS Catalogue of Selected Documents in Psychology, 5*, 330 (Ms. No. 421).

Baker, M. A. (1972). Influence of the carotid rete on brain temperature in cats exposed to hot environments. *Journal of Physiology, 220*, 711–728.

Baker, M. A., & Hayward, J. N. (1967). Carotid rete and brain temperature in cat. *Nature, 216*, 139–141.

Battistini, Y. (1968). *Trois présocratiques.* Paris: Gallimard.

Barchas, P. R., & Perlaki, K. M. (1986). Processing preconsciously acquired information measured in hemispheric asymmetry and selection accuracy. *Behavioral Neuroscience, 100*, 343–349.

Bassili, J. N. (1979). Emotion recognition: The role of facial movement and the relative importance of upper and lower areas of the face. *Journal of Personality and Social Psychology, 37*, 2049–2058.

Beck, A. T. (1976). *Cognitive therapy and the emotional disorders.* New York: Guilford.

Bellelli, G. (1994). Knowing and labeling emotions: The role of social sharing. In J. A. Russell, J.-M. Fernández-Dols, A. S. R. Manstead, & J. C. Wellenkamp (Eds.), *Everyday conceptions of emotion: An introduction to the psychology, anthropology and linguistics of emotion* (pp. 121–143). Dordrecht, The Netherlands: Kluwer Academic Publishers.

Bentin, S., Moscovitch, M., & Heth, I. (1992). Memory with and without awareness: Performance and electrophysiological evidence of savings. *Journal of Experimental Psychology: Learning, Memory, & Cognition, 18,* 1270–1283.

Berlin, B., & Kay, P. (1969). *Basic color terms: Their universality and evolution.* Berkeley, CA: University of California Press.

Berlyne, D. E. (1965). *Structure and direction in thinking.* New York: Wiley.

Berridge, K. C., & Zajonc, R. B. (1991). Hypothalamic cooling elicits eating: Differential effects on motivation and pleasure. *Psychological Science, 2,* 184–189.

Blakeslee, S. (1994, May 24). Old accident points to brain's moral center. *The New York Times,* p. B.1.

Blanchard, D. C., & Blanchard, R. J. (1972). Innate and conditioned reactions to threat in rats with amygdaloid lesions. *Journal of Comparative Physiology and Psychology, 81,* 281–290.

Block, J. (1957). Studies in phenomenology of emotions. *Journal of Abnormal and Social Psychology, 54,* 358–363.

Bolinger, D. (Ed.). (1972). *Intonation.* Middlesex, England: Penguin Books.

Bolinger, D. (1975). *Aspects of language* (2nd ed.). New York: Harcourt Brace Jovanovich.

Bonnano, G. A., & Stilling, N. A. (1986). Preference, familiarity, and recognition after repeated brief exposure to random geometric shapes. *American Journal of Psychology, 99,* 403–415.

Bornstein, R. F. (1989). Exposure and affect: Overview and meta-analysis of research, 1968–1987. *Psychology Bulletin, 106,* 265–289.

Bornstein, R. F., Leone, D. R., & Galley, D. J. (1987). The generalizability of subliminal mere exposure effects: Influence of stimuli perceived without awareness on social behavior. *Journal of Personality and Social Behavior, 53,* 1070–1079.

Bower, G. H. (1981). Mood and memory. *American Psychologist, 36,* 129–148.

Cacioppo, J. T., Klein, D. J., Berntson, G. G., & Hatfield, E. (1993). The psychophysiology of emotion. In M. Lewis & J. M. Haviland (Eds.), *Handbook of emotions* (pp. 119–142). New York: Guilford.

Cannon, W. B. (1927). The James-Lange theory of emotions: A critical examination and an alternative theory. *American Journal of Psychology, 39,* 106–112.

Cantor, N., & Kihlstrom, J. F. (1987). *Personality and social intelligence.* Englewood Cliffs, NJ: Prentice Hall.

Caputa, M., Kadziela, W., & Narebski, J. (1976). Significance of cranial circulation for brain homeothermia in rabbits (2). The role of the cranial venous lakes in the defense against hyperthermia. *Acta Neeurobiologica Exoperimentalis, 36,* 625–638.

Carroll, J. M., & Russell, J. A. (1996). Do facial expressions signal specific emotions? Judging emotions from the face

in context. *Journal of Personality and Social Psychology, 70,* 205–218.

Clore, G. L., Schwarz, N., & Conway, M. (1994). Affective causes and consequences of social information processing. In R. S. Wyer & T. K. Srull (Eds.), *Handbook of social cognition* (2nd ed., Vol. 1). Hillsdale, NJ: Erlbaum.

Cohen, D. H. (1980). The functional neuroanatomy of a conditioned response. In R. F. Thompson, L. H. Hicks, & B. Shvyrkov (Eds.), *Neural mechanisms of goal-directed behavior* (pp. 283–302). New York: Academic Press.

Cohen, M. S., & Bookheimer S. Y. (1994). Localization of brain function using magnetic resonance imaging. *Trends in Neurosciences, 17,* 268–277.

Collins, A. M., & Loftus, E. F. (1975). A spreading activation theory of semantic processing. *Psychological Review, 82,* 407–428.

Cooper, L. G. (1973). A multivariate investigation of preferences. *Multivariate Behavioral Research, 8,* 253–272.

Cross, H., Holcomb, A., & Matter, C. G. (1967). Imprinting or exposure learning in rats given early auditory stimulation. *Psychonomic Science, 7,* 233–234.

Dabbs, J. M., Jr., Carr, T. S., Frady, R. L., Riad, J. J. (1995). Testosterone, crime, and misbehavior among 692 male prison inmates. *Personality and Individual Differences, 18,* 627–633.

Dabbs, J. M., Jr., & Morris, R. (1990). Testosterone, social class, and antisocial behavior in a sample of 4,462 men. *Psychological Science, 1,* 209–212.

Dabbs, J. M., Jr., Ruback, R. B., Frady, R. L., Hopper, C. H., & Sgoutas, D. S. (1988). Saliva testosterone and criminal violence among women. *Personality and Individual Differences, 9,* 269–275.

Damasio, A. R. (1994). *Descartes' error: Emotion, reason, and the human brain.* New York: Putnam.

Damasio, A. R., & VanHoesen, G. (1983). Emotional disturbances associated with focal lesions of the limbic frontal lobe. In K. M. Heilman & P. Saltz (Eds.), *Neuropsychology of human emotion* (pp. 85–110). New York: Guilford.

Darwin, C. (1904). *The expression of emotions in man and animals.* London: John Murray. (Original work published 1872.)

Davidson, R. J. (1984). Affect, cognition, and hemisphere specialization. In C. E. Izard, J. Kagan, & R. B. Zajonc (Eds.), *Emotions, cognition, and behavior* (pp. 320–365). Cambridge: Cambridge University Press.

Davidson, R. J. (1988). EEG measures of cerebral asymmetry: Conceptual and methodological issues. *International Journal of Neuroscience, 39,* 71–89.

Davidson, R. J. (1993). The neuropsychology of emotion and affective style. In M. Lewis and J. M. Haviland (Eds.), *Handbook of emotions* (pp. 143–154). New York: Guilford.

Davis, M. (1992). The role of the amygdala in conditioned fear. In J. P. Aggleton (Ed.), *The amygdala* (pp. 255–305). New York: Wiley-Liss.

Davitz, J. R. (1969). *The language of emotions.* New York: McGraw-Hill.

Dawkins, R. (1989). *The selfish gene.* Oxford: Oxford University Press.

Dean, M. C. (1988). Another look at the nose and the functional significance of the face and nasal mucous membrane for cooling the brain in fossil hominids. *Journal of Human Evolution, 17,* 715–718.

deGroot, P. (1966). Facial EMG and nonconscious affective priming. Masters Dissertation, University of Amsterdam.

Delattre, P. (1972). The distinctive function of intonation. In D. Bolinger (Ed.), *Intonation* (pp. 159–174). Middlesex, England: Penguin Books.

Dennett, D. C. (1969). *Content and consciousness.* London: Routledge & Kegan Paul.

Dennett, D. C. (1991). *Consciousness explained.* Boston: Little, Brown, and Co.

DePaulo, B. M., & Friedman, H. S. (1998). Nonverbal communication. In D. Gilbert, S. T. Fiske, & G. Lindzey (Eds.), *Handbook of social psychology* (4th ed., Vol. 2, pp. 3–40). New York: McGraw-Hill.

Descartes, R. (1647). *Les passions de l'âme.* Paris: Vrin.

Devinsky, O., Bear, D., Moya, K., & Benowitz, L. (1993). Perception of emotion in patients with Tourette's syndrome. *Neuropsychiatry, Neuropsychology, and Behavioral Neurology, 6,* 166–169.

Dimberg, U. (1982). Facial reactions to facial expressions. *Psychophysiology, 19,* 643–647.

Dimberg, U. (1990). Facial electromyography and emotional reactions. *Psychophysiology, 27,* 481–494.

Dollard, J., Doob, L. W., Miller, N. E., Mowrer, O. H., & Sears, R. R. (1938). *Frustration and aggression.* New Haven, CT: Yale University Press.

Druckman, D., & Lacey, J. I. (1989). *Brain and cognition. Some new technologies.* Washington, DC: National Academy Press.

Dunlap, K. (1927). The role of eye muscles and mouth muscles in the expression of emotions. *Genetic Psychology Monographs, 2,* 199–233.

Ehrenkranz, J., Bliss, E., & Sheard, M. H. (1974). Plasma testosterone: Correlation with aggressive behavior and social dominance in man. *Psychosomatic Medicine, 36,* 469–475.

Eich, E. (1995). Mood as a mediator of place dependent memory. *Journal of Experimental Psychology: General, 124,* 293–308.

Ekman, P. (1973). Cross-cultural studies of facial expressions. In P. Ekman (Ed.), *Darwin and facial expression: A century of research in review* (pp. 169–229). New York: Academic Press.

Ekman, P., & Friesen, W. V. (1971). Constants across cultures in the face of emotion. *Journal of Personality and Social Psychology, 17,* 124–129.

Ekman, P., & Friesen, W. V. (1978). *Facial Action Coding System: A technique for the measurement of facial movement.* Palo Alto, CA: Consulting Psychologists Press.

Ekman, P., Friesen, W. V., & Ellsworth, P. (1972). What emotion categories or dimensions can observers judge from facial behavior? In P. Ekman (Ed.), *Emotion in the human face* (pp. 39–55). New York: Cambridge University Press.

Ekman, P., Levenson, R. W., & Friesen, W. V. (1983). Autonomic system activity distinguishes among emotions. *Science, 221,* 1208–1210.

Ellsworth, P. C. (1991). Some implications of cognitive appraisal theories of emotion. In K. T. Strongman (Ed.), *International Review of Studies on Emotion* (Vol. I, pp. 143–161). New York: Wiley.

Ellsworth, P. C. (1995). The right way to study emotions. *Psychological Inquiry, 6,* 213–216.

Ellsworth, P. C., & Smith, C. A. (1988). From appraisal to emotion: Differences among unpleasant feelings. *Motivation and Emotion, 12,* 271–302.

Fernández-Dols, J.-M., & Ruiz-Belda, M.-A. (1995). Are smiles a sign of happiness? Gold medal winners at the Olympic Games. *Journal of Personality and Social Psychology, 69,* 1113–1119.

Festinger, L. (1957). *A theory of cognitive dissonance.* Stanford, CA: Stanford University Press.

Fielden, J. A., Lutter, C. D., & Dabbs, J. M. (1995). Basking in glory: Testosterone changes in World Cup Soccer fans. Unpublished.

Fiske, A. P., Kitayama, S., Markus, H. R., & Nisbett, R. E. (1998). The cultural matrix of social psychology. In D. Gilbert, S. T. Fiske, & G. Lindzey (Eds.), *Handbook of social psychology* (4th ed., Vol. 2, pp. 915–981). New York: McGraw-Hill.

Fiske, D. (1944). A study of relationships to somatotype. *Journal of Applied Psychology, 28,* 504–519.

Fonberg, E. (1972). Control of emotional behavior through the hypothalamus and amygdaloid complex. In D. Hill (Ed.), *Physiology, emotion, and psychosomatic illness* (pp. 131–162). Amsterdam: Elsevier.

Forgas, J. P. (1995). Mood and judgment: The affect infusion model (AIM). *Psychological Bulletin, 117,* 39–66.

Fortenbaugh, W. W. (1975). *Aristotle on emotions.* New York: Barnes and Noble.

Francis, R. C., Soma, K., & Fernald, R. D. (1993, August). Social regulation of the brain-pituitary-gonadal axis. *Proceedings of the National Academy of Sciences, USA, 90,* 7794–7798.

Fridlund, A. J. (1994). *Human facial expression: An evolutionary view.* San Diego, CA: Academic Press.

Frijda, N. H. (1986). *The emotions.* Cambridge: Cambridge University Press.

Frijda, N. H., Markam, S., Sato, K., & Wiers, R. (1995). In J. A. Russell, J.-M. Fernández-Dols, A. S. R. Manstead, & J. C. Wellenkamp (Eds.), *Everyday conceptions of emotion: An introduction to the psychology, anthropology, and linguistics of emotion* (pp. 121–143). Dordrecht, The Netherlands: Kluwer Academic Publishers.

Frijda, N. H., & Mesquita, B. (1994). The social roles and functions of emotions. In S. Kitayama & H. Markus (Eds.), *Emotion and culture: Empirical studies of mutual influence.* Washington, DC: American Psychological Association.

Gaffan, D. (1992). Amygdala and the memory of reward. In J. P. Aggleton (Ed.), *The amygdala* (pp. 471–483). New York: Wiley.

George, M. S., Ketter, T. A., Parekh, P. I., Horowitz, B., Herscovitch, P., & Post, R. M. (1995). Brain activity during transient sadness and happiness in healthy women. *American Journal of Psychiatry, 152,* 341–351.

Goddard, G. (1964). Functions of the amygdala. *Psychological Review, 62,* 89–109.

Goleman, D. (1995a, March 28). The brain manages happiness and sadness in different centers. *The New York Times,* pp. B9–B10.

Goleman, D. (1995b). *Emotional intelligence.* New York: Bantam Books.

Gordon, P., & Holyoak, K. (1983). Implicit learning and generalization of the "mere exposure" effect. *Journal of Personality and Social Psychology, 3,* 492–500.

Gould, S. J. (1980). *The panda's thumb.* New York: W. W. Norton.

Gratiolet, P. (1865). *De la physionomie et des mouvements d'expression.* Paris: Hetzel.

Gray, J. A. (1987). *The psychology of fear and stress* (2nd ed.). Cambridge: Cambridge University Press.

Gur, R. C., & Gur, R. E. (1991). The impact of neuroimaging on human neuropsychology. In R. G. Lister & H. J. Weingartner (Eds.), *Perspectives on cognitive neuroscience* (pp. 417–435). New York: Oxford University Press.

Hadding, K., & Studdert-Kennedy, M. (1964). An experimental study of some intonation contours. *Phonetica, 11,* 175–185.

Harmon-Jones, E., & Allen J. J. B. (1996). Anterior EEG asymmetry and facial EMG as evidence that affect is involved in the mere exposure effect. *Psychophysiology, 33,* 544 (Abstract).

Harrison, A. A. (1977). Mere exposure. In L. Berkowitz (Ed.), *Advances in experimental social psychology* (Vol. 10). New York: Academic Press.

Henson, R. A. (1988). *British Medical Journal, 296,* 1585–1588.

Hill, W. F. (1978). Effects of mere exposure on preferences in nonhuman animals. *Psychological Bulletin, 85,* 1177–1198.

Hochschild, A. R. (1979). Emotion work, feeling rules, and social structure. *American Journal of Sociology, 85,* 551–575.

Hockett, C. F. (1963). *Universals in language.* Cambridge, MA: Harvard University Press.

Hoffman, E. (1989). *Lost in translation.* New York: Dutton.

Hoffman, H. S. (1968). The control of distress vocalizations by imprinted stimulus. *Behaviour, 30,* 175–191.

Hoorens, V. (1990). Nuttin's affective self-particles hypothesis and the name letter effect. A review. *Psychologia Belgica, 20,* 23–48.

Hoorens, V., & Nuttin, J. M. (1993). Overvaluation of own attributes: Mere ownership or subjective frequency? *Social Cognition, 11,* 177–200.

Hoorens, V., Nuttin, J. M., Herman, I., & Pavakanun, U. (1990). Mastery pleasure versus mere ownership: A quasi-experimental cross-cultural and cross-alphabetical test of the name letter effect. *European Journal of Social Psychology, 20,* 181–205.

Irvine, J. T. (1995). A sociolinguistic approach to emotion concepts in a Senegalese community. In J. A. Russell, J.-M. Fernández-Dols, A. S. R. Manstead, & J. C. Wellenkamp (Eds.), *Everyday conceptions of emotion: An introduction to the psychology, anthropology and linguistics of emotion* (pp. 251–265). Dordrecht, The Netherlands: Kluwer Academic Publishers.

Iwata, J., Chida, K., & LeDoux, J. E. (1987). Cardiovascular responses elicited by stimulation of neurons in the central amygdaloid nucleus in awake but not anesthetized rats resemble conditoned emotional responses. *Brain Research, 418,* 183–188.

Iwata, J., LeDoux, J. E., Meeley, M. P., Arneric, S., & Reis, D. J. (1986). Intrinsic neurons in the amygdaloid field projected to by the medial geniculate body mediate emotional responses conditioned to acoustic stimuli. *Brain Research, 383,* 195–214.

Izard, C. E. (1972). *Patterns of emotion.* New York: Academic Press.

Izard, C. E. (1977). *Human emotions.* New York: Plenum.

Izard, C. E. (1978). On the development of emotions and emotion-cognition relationship in infancy. In M. Lewis & L. Rosenblum (Eds.), *The development of affect.* New York: Plenum.

Izard, C. E., Dougherty, L. M., & Hembree, E. A. (1983). *A system for identifying affect experiences by holistic judgments (Affex).* Newark: University of Delaware, Office of Instructional Technology.

Izard, C. E., & Malatesta, C. Z. (1987). Perspectives on emotional development. I: Differential emotions, theory of early emotional development. In J. D. Osofsky (Ed.), *Handbook of infant development* (2nd ed.), pp. 494–454). New York: Wiley.

Jacoby, L. L., Kelley, C. M., & Dywan, J. (1989). Memory attributions. In H. L. Roediger & F. I. M. Craik (Eds.), *Varieties of memory and consciousness: Essays in honour of Endel Tulving* (pp. 391–422). Hillsdale, NJ: Erlbaum.

James, W. (1884). What is an emotion? *Mind, 9,* 188–205.

James, W. (1890). *Principles of psychology.* New York: Holt.

Jin, P. (1989). Changes in heart rate, noradrenaline, cortisol and mood during Tai Chi. *Journal of Psychosomatic Research, 33,* 197–206.

Johnson-Laird, P. N., & Oatley, K. (1989). The language of emotions: An analysis of a semantic field. *Cognition and Emotion, 3,* 81–123.

Jones, B., & Mishkin, M. (1972). Limbic lesions and the problem of stimulus-reinforcement associations. *Experimental Neurology, 36,* 362–377.

Jones, E. E., & Nisbett, R. E. (1972). The actor and the observer: Divergent perceptions of the causes of behavior. In E. E. Jones, D. E. Kanouse, H. H. Kelley, R. E. Nisbett, S. Valins, & B. Weiner (Eds.), *Attribution: Perceiving the causes of behavior* (pp. 79–94). Morristown, NJ: General Learning Press.

Kambouchner, D. (1996). *L'homme des passions: Commentaires sur Descartes.* (Vol. I [Analitique], Vol. II [Canonique]). Paris: Albin Michel.

Kapp, B. S., Frysinger, R. C., Gallagher, M., & Haselton, J. (1979). Amygdala central nucleus lesions: Effects on heart rate conditioning in the rabbit. *Physiology and Behavior, 23,* 1109–1117.

Kay, P., & McDaniel, C. (1978). The linguistic significance of basic color terms. *Language, 54,* 610–646.

Kluger, M. J., & D'Alecy, L. G. (1975). Brain temperature during reversible upper respiratory bypass. *Journal of Applied Physiology, 38,* 268–271.

Kochańska, G. (1993). Toward a synthesis of parental socialization and child temperament in early development of conscience. *Child Development, 64,* 325–347.

Kraut, R. E., & Johnston, R. E. (1979). Social and emotional messages of smiling: An ethological approach. *Journal of Personality and Social Psychology, 37,* 1539–1553.

Kretschmer, E. (1922). *Körperbau und Charakter.* Berlin: Springer.

Kreuz, L. E., & Rose, R. M. (1972). Assessment of aggressive behavior and plasma testosterone in a young criminal population. *Psychosomatic Medicine, 34,* 321–332.

Kunst-Wilson, W. R., & Zajonc, R. B. (1980). Affective discrimination of stimuli that cannot be recognized. *Science, 207,* 557–558.

Kurasawa, M. (1994). Intersubjective emotions and the theory of mind research: A critique. In J. A. Russell, J.-M. Fernández-Dols, A. S. R. Manstead, & J. C. Wellenkamp (Eds.), *Everyday conceptions of emotion: An introduction to the psychology, anthropology and linguistics of emotion* (pp. 121–143). Dordrecht, The Netherlands: Kluwer Academic Publishers.

Lacy, B. C., & Lacy, J. I. (1978). Two-way communication between the heart and the brain. *American Psychologist, 33,* 99–113.

Lang, P. J. (1995). The emotion probe: Studies of motivation and attention. *American Psychologist, 50,* 372–385.

Larsen, R. J., & Ketelaar, T. (1991). Personality and susceptibility to positive and negative emotional states. *Journal of Personality and Social Psychology, 61,* 132–140.

Lavater, J. C. (1853). *Essays on physiognomy* (8th ed.). London: W. Tegg & Co.

Lazarus, R. S. (1982). Thoughts on the relations between emotion and cognition. *American Psychologist, 37,* 1019–1024.

Lazarus, R. S. (1991). Cognition and motivation in emotion. *American Psychologist, 46,* 352–367.

Lazarus, R. S., & Folkman, S. (1984). *Stress, appraisal, and coping.* New York: Springer.

LeBrun, C. (1648). *Effigies et repraesentatio affectionum animi.* Paris.

LeDoux, J. E. (1986). Sensory systems and emotion. *Integrative Psychiatry, 4,* 237–248.

LeDoux, J. E. (1987). Emotion. In F. Plum (Ed.), *Handbook of physiology. 1: The nervous system: Volume V: Higher functions of the brain* (pp. 419–460). Bethesda, MD: American Physiological Society.

LeDoux, J. E. (1989). Cognitive-emotional interactions in the brain. *Cognition and Emotion, 3,* 267–289.

LeDoux, J. E. (1990). Information flow for sensation to emotion: Plasticity in the neural computation of stimulus values. In M. Gabriel & J. Moore (Eds.), *Neurocomputation and learning: Foundation and adaptive networks* (pp. 3–52). Cambridge, MA: MIT Press.

LeDoux, J. E. (1995). Emotions: Clues from the brain. *Annual Review of Psychology, 46,* 209–235.

LeDoux, J. E. (1996). *The emotional brain.* New York: Simon and Schuster.

LeDoux, J. E., Iwata, J., Cicchetti, P., & Reis, D. J. (1988). Different projections of the central amygdaloid nucleus mediate autonomic and behavioral correlates of conditioned fear. *Journal of Neuroscience, 8,* 2517–2529.

Levenson, R. W., Carstensen, L. L., Friesen, W. V., & Ekman, P. (1991). Emotion, physiology, and expression in old age. *Psychology and Aging, 6,* 28–35.

Levenson, R. W., Ekman, P., & Friesen, W. V. (1990). Voluntary facial action generates emotion-specific autonomic nervous system activity. *Psychophysiology, 27,* 363–384.

Leventhal, H. (1980). Toward a comprehensive theory of emotion. In L. Berkowitz (Ed.), *Advances in Experimental Social Psychology, 13* (pp. 139–207). New York: Academic Press.

Levy, R. I. (1973). *Tahitians: Mind and experience in the Society Islands.* Chicago: University of Chicago Press.

Litvak, S. B. (1969). Attitude change by stimulus exposure. *Psychological Reports, 25,* 391–396.

Loftus, E. F., & Ketcham, K. (1994). *The myth of repressed memory: False memories and allegations of sexual abuse.* New York: St. Martin Press.

Lutz, C. (1987). Goals, events and understanding in Ifaluk emotion theory. In D. Holland & N. Quinn (Eds.), *Cultural models in language and thought* (pp. 290–312). Cambridge: Cambridge University Press.

Lutz, C. (1988). *Unnatural emotions: Everyday sentiments on a Micronesian atoll and their challenge to Western theory.* Chicago: University of Chicago Press.

MacLean, P. D. (1990). *The triune brain evolution: Role in paleocerebral functions.* New York: Plenum Press.

MacDonald, G. E. (1968). Imprinting: Drug-produced isolation and the sensitive period. *Nature, 217,* 1158–1159.

Mandler, G. (1975). *Mind and emotion.* New York: Wiley.

Mandler, G., Nakamura, Y., & VanZandt, B. J. S. (1987). Nonspecific effects of exposure on stimuli that cannot be recognized. *Journal of Experimental Psychology: Learning, Memory, and Cognition, 13,* 646–648.

Markus, H. R., & Kitayama, S. (1991). Culture and the self: Implications for cognition, emotion and motivation. *Psychological Review, 98,* 224–253.

Markus, H. R., & Kitayama, S. (1994). The cultural construction of self and emotion: Implications for social behavior. In S. Kitayama & H. R. Markus (Eds.), *Emotion and culture: Empirical studies of mutual influence,* (pp. 89–130). Washington, DC: American Psychological Association.

Marler, P. (1978). Affective and symbolic meaning: Some zoosemiotic speculations. In T. A. Sebeok (Ed.), *Sight, sound, and sense.* Bloomington, IN: Indiana University Press.

Maslow, A. H. (1937). The influence of familiarization on preference. *Journal of Experimental Psychology, 21,* 162–180.

Max, L. W. (1937). Experimental study of the motor theory of consciousness: IV. Action-current responses in the deaf during awakening, kinesthetic imagery and abstract thinking. *Journal of Comparative Psychology, 21,* 301–349.

Matlin, M. W. (1970). Response competition as a mediating factor in the frequency-affect relationship. *Journal of Personality and Social Psychology, 16,* 536–552.

Mayer, J. D., & Salovey, P. (1995). Emotional intelligence and the construction and regulation of feelings. *Applied and Preventive Psychology, 4,* 197–208.

McIntosh, D. N., Zajonc, R. B., Vig, P. S., & Emerick, S. W. (1997). Facial movement, breathing, temperature, and affect: Implications of the Vascular Theory of Emotional Efference. *Cognition and Emotion. 11,* 171–195.

Mead, G. H. (1934). *Mind, self, and society.* (Posthumous, C. M. Morris, Ed.). Chicago: University of Chicago Press.

Mesquita, B. (1993). *Cultural variations in emotions.* PhD Thesis, University of Amsterdam.

Mesquita, B., & Frijda, N. H. (1992). Cultural variations in emotions: A review. *Psychological Bulletin, 112,* 179–204.

Mesquita, B., Frijda, N. H., & Scherer, K. R. (1997). *Culture and emotion.* In J. W. Berry, P. R. Dasen, & T. S. Sarswathi (Eds.). *Handbook of cross-cultural psychology: Basic processes and human development.* (Vol. 2, pp. 255–297). Boston: Allyn and Bacon.

Midgley, M. (1979). Gene juggling. *Philosophy, 54,* 439–458.

Miller, N. W., & Clem, L. W. (1984). Temperature-mediated processes in teleost immunity: Differential effects of temperature on catfish in vitro antibody responses to thymus-dependent and thymus-independent antigens. *Journal of Immunology, 133,* 2356–2359.

Mita, T. H., Dermer, M., & Knight, J. (1997). Reversed facial images and the mere exposure hypothesis. *Journal of Personality and Social Psychology, 35,* 597–601.

Moltz, H., & Stettner, L. J. (1961). The influence of patterned-light deprivation on the critical period for imprinting. *Journal of Comparative Physiology and Psychology, 54,* 279–283.

Monod, J. (1971). *Chance and necessity: An essay on the natural philosophy of modern biology.* New York: Knopf.

Monrad-Krohn, G. H. (1963). The third element of speech: Prosody and its disorders. In L. Halpern (Ed.), *Problems of dynamic neurology* (pp. 107–117). Jerusalem: Hebrew University Press.

Moreland, R. L., & Zajonc, R. B. (1976). A strong test of exposure effects. *Journal of Experimental Social Psychology, 12,* 170–179.

Moreland, R. L., & Zajonc, R. B. (1977). Is stimulus recognition a necessary condition for the occurrence of exposure effects? *Journal of Personality and Social Psychology, 35,* 191–199.

Moreland, R. L., & Zajonc, R. B. (1979). Exposure effects may not depend on stimulus recognition. *Journal of Personality and Social Psychology, 37,* 1085–1089.

Murphy, S. T. (1990). *The primacy of affect: Evidence and extension.* Unpublished doctoral dissertation. University of Michigan, Ann Arbor.

Murphy, S. T., Monahan, J. L., & Zajonc, R. B. (1995). Additivity of nonconscious affect: Combined effects of priming and exposure. *Journal of Personality and Social Psychology, 69,* 589–602.

Murphy, S. T., & Zajonc, R. B. (1987, August-September). *Affect and awareness: Comparisons of subliminal and supraliminal affective priming.* Paper presented at the 95th Annual Convention of the American Psychological Association, New York, NY.

Murphy, S. T., & Zajonc, R. B. (1988, August). *Nonconscious influence of affective and cognitive processes.* Paper presented at the 96th Annual Convention of the American Psychological Association, Atlanta, GA.

Murphy, S. T., & Zajonc, R. B. (1993). Affect, cognition, and awareness: Affective priming with suboptimal and optimal stimulus. *Journal of Personality and Social Psychology, 64,* 723–739.

Nachmias, J., & Sansbury, (1974). Grating contrast: Discrimination may be better than detection. *Vision Research, 14,* 1039–1042.

Nisbett, R. E., & Cohen, D. (1996). *Culture of honor: The psychology of violence in the South.* Boulder, CO: Westview Press.

Nishijo, H., Ono, T., & Nishino, H. (1988). Single neuron responses in amygdala of alert monkey during complex sensory stimulation with affective significance. *Journal of Neuroscience, 8,* 3570–3583.

Nuttin, J. M. (1987). Affective consequences of mere ownership: The name letter effect in twelve European languages. *European Journal of Social Psychology, 17,* 381–402.

Ortony, A., & Clore, G. L. (1989). Emotions, moods, and conscious awareness. *Cognition and Emotion, 3,* 125–137.

Osgood, C. E. (1962). Studies on the generality of effective meaning systems. *American Psychologist, 17,* 10–28.

Panksepp, J. (1982). Toward a general psychobiological theory of emotions. *Behavioral and Brain Sciences, 5,* 407–468.

Parkinson, B. (1995). *Ideas and realities of emotion.* London: Routledge.

Perrett, D. I., Rolls, E. T., & Caan, W. (1982). Visual neurons responsive to faces in the monkey temporal cortex. *Experimental Brain Research, 47,* 329–342.

Pervin, L. A. (1993). Affect and personality. In M. Lewis & J. M. Haviland (Eds.), *Handbook of emotions* (pp. 301–311). New York: Guilford.

Petersen, S. E., Fietz, J. A., & Corbetta, M. (1992). Neuroimaging. *Current Opinion in Neurobiology, 2,* 217–222.

Piderit, T. (1867). *Mimik und Physiognomik.* Detmold, Germany: Meyer.

Pietromonaco, P., Zajonc, R. B., & Bargh, J. (1981). *The role of motor cues in recognition memory for faces.* Paper presented at the Annual Convention of the American Psychological Association, Los Angeles.

Pittam, J., & Scherer, K. R. (1993). Vocal expression and communication of emotion. In M. Lewis & J. M. Haviland (Eds.), *Handbook of emotions* (pp. 185–197). New York: Guilford.

Plutchik, R. (1962). *The emotions: Facts, theories and a new model.* New York: Random House.

Plutchik, R. (1980). *Emotion: A psychoevolutionary synthesis.* New York: Harper & Row.

Porges, S. W. (1995). Orienting in a defensive world: Mammalian modfications of our evolutionary heritage: A Polyvagal Theory. *Psychophysiology, 32,* 301–318.

Prentice, D. (1987). Psychological correspondence of possessions, attitudes, and values. Integrating personality and social psychology [Special issue]. *Journal of Personality and Social Psychology, 53,* 993–1003.

Raichle, M. E. (1994). Images of the mind: Studies with modern imaging techniques. *Annual Review of Psychology, 45,* 333–356.

Raimi, R. A. (1969). The peculiar distribution of first digits. *Scientific American, 221,* 109–115.

Rajecki, D. W. (1972). Effects of prenatal exposure to auditory and visual stimuli on social responses in chicks. Unpublished doctoral dissertation. University of Michigan.

Rather, L. J. (1965). *Mind and body in eighteenth century medicine.* Berkeley: University of California Press.

Reisenzein, R. (1983). The Schachter theory of emotion: Two decades later. *Psychological Bulletin, 94,* 239–264.

Rimé, B. (1994). The social sharing of emotion as a source for the social knowledge of emotion. In J. A. Russell, J.-M. Fernández-Dols, A. S. R. Manstead, & J. C. Wellenkamp (Eds.), *Everyday conceptions of emotion: An introduction to the psychology, anthropology and linguistics of emotion* (pp. 121–143). Dordrecht, The Netherlands: Kluwer Academic Publishers.

Rimé, B., Philippot, P., & Cisamolo, D. (1990). Social schemata of peripheral changes in emotion. *Journal of Personality and Social Psychology, 59,* 38–49.

Roberts, R. C. (1989). Aristotle on virtues and emotions. *Philosophical Studies, 56,* 293–306.

Robertson, M. M. (1989). The Gilles de la Tourette syndrome: the current status. *British Journal of Psychiatry, 154,* 147–169.

Robinson, R. G., Kubos, K. L., Starr, L. B., Rao, K., & Price, T. R. (1984). Mood disorders in stroke patients: Importance of location of lesion. *Brain, 107,* 81–93.

Rokeach, M. (1968). *Beliefs, attitudes and values.* San Francisco: Jossey-Bass.

Rollman, G. B., & Nachmias, J. (1972). Simultaneous detection and recognition of chromatic flashes. *Perception and Psychophysics, 12,* 309–314.

Rolls, E. T. (1981). Responses of amygdala neurons in the primate. In Y. Ben-Ari (Ed.), *The amygdaloid complex* (pp. 383–393). Amsterdam: Elsevier.

Rolls, E. T. (1990). A theory of emotion, and its application to understanding the neural basis of emotion. *Cognition and Emotion, 4,* 161–190.

Rolls, E. T. (1995). A theory of emotion and consciousness, and its application to understanding the neural basis of emotion. In M. S. Gazzaniga (Ed.), *The cognitive neurosciences* (pp. 1091–1106). Cambridge, MA: MIT Press.

Rosch, E. (1975). The nature of mental codes for color categories. *Journal of Experimental Psychology: Human Perception and Performance, 1,* 303–322.

Rosaldo, M. (1980). *Knowledge and passion: Ilongot notions of self and social life.* Cambridge: Cambridge University Press.

Roseman, I. (1984). Cognitive determinants of emotion: A structural theory. In P. Shaver (Ed.), *Review of personality and social psychology. Vol. 5: Emotions, relationships, and health* (pp. 11–36). Beverly Hills, CA: Sage.

Rosenbaum, R. (1995, January 15). *New York Times.*

Ross, L. (1977). The intuitive psychologist and his shortcomings: Distortions in the attribution process. In L. Berkowitz (Ed.), *Advances in experimental social psychology.* New York: Academic Press.

Russell, J. A. (1980). A circumplex model of affect. *Journal of Personality and Social Psychology, 39,* 1161–1178.

Russell, J. A. (1994). Is there universal recognition of emotion from facial expression? A review of cross-cultural studies. *Psychological Bulletin, 115,* 102–141.

Russell, J. A., Fernández-Dols, J.-M., Manstead, A. S. R., &

Wellenkamp, J. C. (Eds.). (1994). *Everyday conceptions of emotion: An introduction to the psychology, anthropology and linguistics of emotion* (pp. 121–143). Dordrecht, The Netherlands: Kluwer Academic Publishers.

Russell, J. A., & Mehrabian, A. (1977). Evidence for a three-factor theory of emotions. *Journal of Research in Personality, 11,* 273–294.

Ryle, G. (1949). *Concept of mind.* New York: Barnes & Noble.

Saarni, C. (1993). Socialization of emotion. In M. Lewis & J. M. Haviland (Eds.), *Handbook of emotions* (pp. 435–446). New York: Guilford.

Saegert, S. C., Swap, W. C., & Zajonc, R. B. (1973). Exposure, context, and interpersonal attraction. *Journal of Personality and Social Psychology, 25,* 234–242.

Sarter, M., Berntson, G. C., & Cacioppo, J. T. (1996). Brain imaging and cognitive neuroscience: Toward strong inference in attributing function to structure. *American Psychologist, 51,* 13–21.

Schachter, S., & Singer, J. E. (1962). Cognitive, social, and physiological determinants of emotional state. *Psychological Review, 69,* 379–399.

Scheff, T. (1990). *Microsociology: Discourse, emotion, and social structure.* Chicago: University of Chicago Press.

Scherer, K. R. (1984). On the nature and function of emotions: A component process approach. In K. R. Sherer & P. Ekman (Eds.), *Approaches to emotion* (pp. 293–317). Hillsdale, NJ: Erlbaum.

Scherer, K. R. (1986). Vocal affect expression: A review and a model for future research. *Psychological Bulletin, 99,* 143–165.

Scherer, K. R., Koivumaki, J., & Rosenthal, R. (1972). Minimal cues in the vocal communication of affect: Judging emotions from content-masked speech. *Journal of Psycholinguistic Research, 1,* 269–285.

Schlosberg, H. (1941). A scale of the judgment of facial expressions. *Journal of Experimental Psychology, 29,* 497–510.

Schwarz, N. (1990). Feeling as information: Informational and motivational functions of affective states. In E. T. Higgins & R. M. Sorrentino, *Handbook of motivation and cognition.* New York: Guilford Press.

Schwarz, N., & Clore, G. L. (1983). Mood, misattribution, and judgments of well-being: Informative and directive functions of affective states. *Journal of Personality and Social Psychology, 45,* 513–523.

Scripture, E. E. (1891). Arithmetical prodigies. *American Journal of Psychology, 4,* 1–59.

Seamon, J. G., Brody, N., & Kauff, D. M. (1983a). Affective discrimination of stimuli that are not recognized: Effects of shadowing, masking, and cerebral laterality. *Journal of Experimental Psychology: Learning, Memory, and Cognition, 9,* 544–555.

Seamon, J. G., Brody, N., & Kauff, D. M. (1983b). Affective discrimination of stimuli that are not recognized: II. Effect

of delay between study and test. *Bulletin of Psychonomic Society, 21,* 187–189.

Seamon, J. G., Marsh, R. L., & Brody, N. (1989). Critical importance of exposure duration for affective discrimination of stimuli that cannot be recognized. *Journal of Experimental Psychology, Learning, Memory, and Cognition, 10,* 465–469.

Sergent, J. (1993). Music, the brain and Ravel. *Trends in Neuroscience, 15,* 168–171.

Sheldon, W. H. (1942). *The varieties of temperament.* New York: Harper.

Sherrington, C. S. (1900). Experiments on the value of vascular and visceral factors for the genesis of emotion. *Proceedings of the Royal Society, London, 56,* 390–403.

Shweder, R. A. (1993). The cultural psychology of emotions. In M. Lewis & J. M. Haviland (Eds.), *Handbook of emotions* (pp. 417–431). New York: Guilford.

Shweder. R. A., Much, N. C., Mahapatra, M., & Park, L. (1996). The "big three" of morality (autonomy, community, divinity) and the "big three" explanations of suffering. In A. Brandt & P. Rozin (Eds.), *Morality and health.* Stanford, CA: Stanford University Press.

Smith, M. O. (1969). History of the motor theories of attention. *Journal of General Psychology, 80,* 243–257.

Smith, C. A., & Ellsworth, P. C. (1985). Patterns of cognitive appraisal and emotional response related to taking an exam. *Journal of Personality and Social Psychology, 52,* 475–488.

Smith, P. B., & Bond, M. B. (1993). *Social psychology across cultures.* New York: Harvester Wheatsheaf.

Sokolov, J. N. (1963). *Perception and the conditioned reflex.* Oxford: Pergamon Press.

Spinoza, B. (1677). *Ethics.*

Squire, L. (1987). Memory: Neural organization and behavior. In V. Mountcastle, F. Plum, & S. R. Geiger (Eds.), *Handbook of Physiology. The nervous system* (Vol. 5, pp. 295–371). Bethesda, MD: American Physiological Society.

Stein, N., & Levine, L. L. (1989). Thinking about feelings: The development and organization of emotional knowledge. In R. E. Snow & M. Farr (Eds.), *Aptitude, learning, and instruction: Cognition, conation, and affect* (Vol. 3, pp. 165–198). Hillsdale, NJ: Erlbaum.

Stein, N., & Levine, L. L. (1990). Making sense out of emotion: The representation and use of goal-structural knowledge. In N. L. Stein, B. Leventhal, & T. Trabasso (Eds.), *Psychological and biological approaches to emotion* (pp. 45–73). Hillsdale, NJ: Erlbaum.

Stephan, W. G., Stephan, C. W., & DeVargas, M. C. (1996). Emotional expression in Costa Rica and the United States. *Journal of Cross-Cultural Psychology, 27,* 147–160.

Strack, F., Martin, L. L., & Stepper, S. (1988). Inhibiting and facilitating conditions of facial expressions: A non-obtrusive test of the facial feedback hypothesis. *Journal of Personality and Social Psychology, 54,* 768–777.

Suppes, P. (1991). Can psychological software be reduced to

physiological hardware? In E. Agazzi (Ed.), *The problem of reductionism in science* (pp. 183–198). Amsterdam: Kluver Academic Publishers.

Swap, W. C. (1977). Interpersonal attraction and repeated exposure to rewarders and punishers. *Personality and Social Psychology Bulletin, 3,* 248–251.

Tassinary, L. G., Cacioppo, J. T., & Geen, T. R. (1989). A psychometric study of surface electrode placements for facial electromyographic recording: I. The brow and cheek muscle regions. *Psychophysiology, 26,* R943–R954.

Taylor, K. F., & Sluckin, W. (1964). Flocking in domestic chicks. *Nature, 201,* 108–109.

Taylor, S. E. (1989). *Positive illusions: Creative self-deception and the healthy mind.* New York: Basic Books.

Taylor, S. E., Aspinwall, L. G., & Giuliano, T. A. (1994). Emotions as psychological achievements. In S. H. M. Van Goozen, N. E. Van de Poll, & J. A. Sergeant (Eds.), *Emotions: Essays on emotion theory* (pp. 219–239). Hillsdale, NJ: Erlbaum.

Terwogt, M. M., & Stegge, H. (1994). Children's understanding of the strategic control of negative emotions. In J. A. Russell, J.-M. Fernández-Dols, A. S. R. Manstead, & J. C. Wellenkamp (Eds.), *Everyday conceptions of emotion: An introduction to the psychology, anthropology and linguistics of emotion* (pp. 121–143). Dordrecht, The Netherlands: Kluwer Academic Publishers.

Thorndike, E. L., & Lorge, I. (1944). *Teacher's wordbook of 30,000 words.* New York: Teachers College, Columbia University.

Titchener, E. B. (1910). *A textbook of psychology.* New York: Macmillan.

Tomarken, A. J., Davidson, R. J., & Henriques, J. B. (1990). Resting frontal brain asymmetry predicts affective responses to film. *Journal of Personality and Social Psychology, 59,* 791–801.

Tomkins, S. S. (1962). *Affect, imagery, and consciousness: Vol. 1. The positive affects.* New York: Springer.

Tomkins, S. S. (1963). *Affect, imagery, and consciousness: Vol. 2. The negative affects.* New York: Springer.

Tomkins, S. S. (1982). Affect theory. In P. Ekman (Ed.), *Emotion in the human face* (2nd ed., pp. 353–395). New York: Cambridge University Press.

Trivers, R. L. (1971). The evolution of reciprocal altruism. *Quarterly Review of Biology, 46,* 35–57.

Waynbaum, I. (1907). *La physionomie humaine: Son mécanisme et son rôle social.* Paris: Alcan.

Weiskrantz, L. (1956). Behavioral changes associated with ablation of the amygdaloid complex in monkeys. *Journal of Comparative Physiology and Psychology, 49,* 381–391.

Wells, G. L., & Petty, R. E. (1980). The effects of overt head movement on persuasion: Compatability and incompatibility of responses. *Basic and Applied Social Psychology, 1,* 219–230.

White, G. M. (1993). Emotions inside out: The anthropology of affect. In M. Lewis & J. M. Haviland (Eds.), *Handbook of emotions* (pp. 29–39). New York: Guilford.

White, G. M. (1994). Affecting culture: Emotion and morality in everyday life. In S. Kitayama & H. R. Markus (Eds.), *Emotion and culture: Empirical studies of mutual influence* (pp. 219–239). Washington, DC: American Psychological Association.

Whittlesea, B. W. A., Jacoby, L. L., & Girard, K. (1990). Illusions of immediate memory: Evidence of an attributional bias for feelings of familiarity and perceptual quality. *Journal of Memory and Language, 29,* 716–732.

Wierzbicka, A. (1972). *Semantic primitives.* Frankfurt: Athenäum.

Wierzbicka, A. (1990). The semantics of emotions: Fear and its relatives in English. *Australian Journal of Linguistics, 10,* 359–375.

Wierzbicka, A. (1992). *Semantics, culture, and cognition: Universal human concepts in culture-specific configurations.* New York: Oxford University Press.

Wierzbicka, A. (1994). Emotion, language, and cultural scripts. In S. Kitayama & H. R. Markus (Eds.), *Emotion and culture: Empircal studies of mutual influence.* Washington, DC: American Psychological Association.

Wierzbicka, A. (1995). Everyday conceptions of emotion: A semantic perspective. In J. A. Russell, J.-M. Fernández-Dols, A. S. R. Manstead, & J. C. Wellenkamp (Eds.), *Everyday conceptions of emotion: An introduction to the psychology, anthropology and linguistics of emotion* (pp. 17–47). Dordrecht, The Netherlands: Kluwer Academic Publishers.

Wikan, U. (1989). Illness from fright or soul loss: A North Balinese culture-bound syndrome? *Culture, Medicine, and Psychiatry, 13,* 25–50.

Wikan, U. (1990). *Managing turbulent hearts: A Balinese formula for living.* Chicago: University of Chicago Press.

Wilson, E. O. (1975). *Sociobiology: The new synthesis.* Cambridge, MA: Harvard University Press.

Wilson, W. R. (1979). Feeling more than we can know: Exposure effects without learning. *Journal of Personality and Social Psychology, 37,* 811–821.

Yeh, S.-R., Fricke, R. A., & Edwards, D. H. (1996). The effect of social experience on serotonergic modulation of the escape circuit of crayfish. *Science, 271,* 366–369.

Zajonc, R. B. (1965). Social facilitation. *Science, 149,* 269–274.

Zajonc, R. B. (1968). Attitudinal effects of mere exposure. *Journal of Personality and Social Psychology* [Monograph], *9,* 1–27.

Zajonc, R. B. (1971). Attraction, affiliation, and attachment. In J. E. Eisenberg & W. S. Dillon (Eds.), *Man and beast: Comparative social behavior* (pp. 141–179). Washington, DC: Smithsonian Institution Press.

Zajonc, R. B. (1980). Feeling and thinking: Preferences need no inferences. *American Psychologist, 35,* 151–175.

Zajonc, R. B. (1985). Emotion and facial efference: A theory reclaimed. *Science, 228,* 15–21.

Zajonc, R. B., Adelman, K. A., Murphy, S. T., & Niedenthal, P. M. (1987). Convergence in the physical appearance of spouses. *Motivation and Emotion, 11,* 335–346.

Zajonc, R. B., Crandall, R., & Kail, R. V., Jr. (1974). Effect of extreme exposure frequencies on different affective ratings of stimuli. *Perceptual and Motor Skills, 38,* 667–678.

Zajonc, R. B., & Markus, H. (1984). Affect and cognition: The hard interface. In C. Izard, J. Kagan, & R. B. Zajonc (Eds.) *Emotion, cognition, and behavior* (pp. 73–102). Cambridge: Cambridge University Press.

Zajonc, R. B., Markus, H., & Wilson, W. R. (1974). Exposure, object preference, and distress in the domestic chick. *Journal of Comparative and Physiological Psychology, 86,* 581–585.

Zajonc, R. B., & McIntosh, D. N. (1992). Emotion research: Some promising questions and some questionable promises. *Psychological Science, 3,* 70–74.

Zajonc, R. B., Murphy, S. T., & Inglehart, M. (1989). Feeling and facial efference: Implications of the vascular theory of emotions. *Psychological Review, 96,* 395–416.

Zajonc, R. B., Pietromonaco, P., & Bargh, J. (1982). Independence and interaction of affect and cognition. In M. S. Clark & S. T. Fiske (Eds.), *Affect and cognition: The seventeenth annual Carnegie symposium on cognition* (pp. 211–227). Hillsdale, NJ: Erlbaum.

Zajonc, R. B., Swap, W. C., Harrison, A. A., & Roberts, P. (1971). *Journal of Personality and Social Psychology, 18,* 384–391.

Zajonc, R. B., Wilson, W. R., & Rajecki, D. W. (1975). Affiliation and social discrimination produced by brief exposure in day-old domestic chicks. *Animal Behavior, 23,* 131–138.

Zillmann, D. (1991). Television viewing and physiological arousal. In J. Bryant & D. Zillmann (Eds.), *Responding to the screen: Reception and reaction processes* (pp. 103–133). Hillsdale, NJ: Erlbaum.

Zola-Morgan, S., Squire, L. R., Alvarez-Royo, P., & Clower, R. P. (1991). Independence of memory functions and emotional behavior: Separate contributions of the hippocampal formation and the amygdala. *Hippocampus, 1,* 207–220.

Zülch, K. J. (1976). A critical appraisal of "Lokalisationslehre" in the brain. *Die Naturwissenschaften, 63,* 255–265.

PART FOUR

PERSONAL PHENOMENA

CHAPTER FOURTEEN

UNDERSTANDING PERSONALITY AND SOCIAL BEHAVIOR: A FUNCTIONALIST STRATEGY

MARK SNYDER, *University of Minnesota*
NANCY CANTOR, *University of Michigan*

INTRODUCTION

Why is there a chapter on personality and social behavior in the *Handbook of Social Psychology?* That the *Handbook of Social Psychology* includes a chapter on the topic of personality and social behavior reflects, at a minimum, the belief that an understanding of personality has some implications for understanding social behavior. Beyond that belief, though, are the propositions that there are some fundamentally important overlapping concerns between personality and social psychology, and that these shared concerns are made particularly evident by (and can be discussed productively in the context of) considerations of personality and social behavior. Ultimately, perhaps, the inclusion of a chapter on personality and social behavior in the *Handbook* reflects the belief that, just as considerations of personality can tell us something important about social psychology, so too may social psychology provide some perspective on the nature of personality.

Any discussion of personality and social behavior begins with the premise that there is such a thing as "personality," that there is such a thing as "social behavior," and that the two are somehow linked with each other. That is, if there is such a thing as personality, then we can say what it is and what it does, including what it does to determine social behavior. And, if there is a category of behaviors that are "social" behaviors, then it should be possible to specify the defining properties of social behavior, to say what social behavior is and to identify what it can tell us about personality.

In accord with these premises, this chapter reflects the faith that there is such a thing as personality (loosely defined in terms of regularities in feeling, thought, and action that are characteristic of an individual), that there is such a thing as social behavior (referring to those domains of thought, feeling, and action concerned with people and events in their social worlds), and that the two are linked, both in theory and in practice, such that personality can tell us something important about social behavior, and that social behavior can tell us something important about personality. Thus, any discussion of "personality and social behavior" is both a discussion of the role that personality plays in determining social behavior and a discussion of the role that social behavior plays in determining personality.

To be sure, this is not the first *Handbook* chapter on the topic of personality and social behavior. There was a chapter entitled "Personality and Social Interaction" in the second edition of the *Handbook*. In that chapter, Marlowe and Gergen (1969) documented linkages between diverse attributes of personality (conceptualized and identified as individual differences along dimensions such as cognitive complexity, locus of control, anxiety, ego strength, Machiavellianism, dominance, self-esteem, and need for approval) and a whole host of phenomena of concern to social psychologists, with special and detailed attention to studies of personality and social conformity and of personality and interpersonal attraction. The third edition of the

This chapter was prepared with the support of a grant from the National Institute of Mental Health (MH 47673) to Mark Snyder.

Correspondence with the authors should be addressed to Mark Snyder, Department of Psychology, University of Minnesota, 75 East River Road, Minneapolis, MN 55455-0344 (e-mail: msnyder@ maroon.tc.umn.edu) or to Nancy Cantor, Horace H. Rackham School of Graduate Studies, University of Michigan, 915 East Washington Street—Room 1006, Ann Arbor, MI 48109-1070 (e-mail: necantor@ umich.edu).

Handbook also featured a chapter on "Personality and Social Behavior," contributed by Snyder and Ickes (1985). In their chapter, Snyder and Ickes (1985) took as their primary task the defining of *strategies* for the study of personality and social behavior. They defined and traced the historical and intellectual evolution of three such strategies—the dispositional strategy, the interactional strategy, and the situational strategy—and assessed the assets and liabilities of each strategy in the context of representative and illustrative examples of research reflecting each strategy in action.

We consider it our great and good fortune to follow in the footsteps, and to continue in the traditions, of these previous statements about personality and social behavior. Accordingly, in this chapter on personality and social behavior for the fourth edition of the *Handbook*, we do not seek to reinvent the wheel, so to speak, but rather to build on these previous efforts in the spirit of cumulative intellectual inquiry. So, at this point, the reader is advised to take a break from our chapter and to read (or to reread) the previous chapters on personality and social behavior, because we begin where they leave off.

In this regard, the chapter on personality and social behavior in the third edition of the *Handbook* provides an ideal point of departure for our considerations of personality and social behavior. That chapter leaves off with Snyder and Ickes (1985) pointing (hopefully, wishfully, and optimistically) toward the emergence of a hybrid discipline of personality and social behavior, residing at the interface of personality and social psychology. In fact, over the years there has been the emergence of the hybrid discipline of personality and social behavior, operating at the interface of both, drawing on the characteristic investigative orientations of both, and constituting the work of investigators adopting a social psychological perspective on personality and a personological perspective on social psychology. Whereas once the boundary line between personality and social psychology was a distinct one, and investigators working at the interface could be construed as crossing back and forth across that boundary, at times wearing their hats as personality psychologists and at times as social psychologists, this boundary has grown rather indistinct, such that investigators may become aware that they have moved from personality into social psychology, or vice versa, but not know exactly when the boundary line was crossed.

Just how much the times have been changing is readily apparent in looking back at the progression of the goals set by the authors of the successive treatments of personality and social behavior in successive editions of the *Handbook*. In the 1960s, at the time of the preparation of the second edition, Marlowe and Gergen (1969) took as their task the documenting of instances of associations between personality and social behavior. Presumably, they did so because it was then necessary to point out such associations to those who might not otherwise notice them; this was, after all, a time of considerable skepticism about the existence of stable traits and enduring dispositions and a time of doubt about whether measures of personal attributes (whether in the form of personality traits or as social attitudes) ever would or even could possibly account for much of the variance in actual behavior (e.g., Mischel, 1968; Wicker, 1969).

In the early 1980s, at the time of the preparation of the third edition of the *Handbook*, Snyder and Ickes (1985) no longer felt that they needed to convince others that personality was involved in social behavior. Rather, building on the premise that the meaningful regularities and consistencies that are thought to constitute personality do reside in social behavior, they took as their task the laying out of strategies for conceptualizing and investigating the dispositional and situational origins of these regularities and consistencies in the behaviors of individuals in social context—strategies that could and would guide research and theorizing at the interface of personality and social psychology. In accord with Lewin's (1936) assertion that "Every psychological event depends on the state of the person and at the same time on the environment, although their relative importance is different in different cases" (p. 12), they defined three investigative strategies that differed among themselves in their relative emphasis on dispositional and situational properties in studying personality and social behavior:

1. *The dispositional strategy:* The dispositional strategy for the study of personality and social behavior seeks to understand consistencies in social behavior in terms of relatively stable traits, enduring dispositions and other properties that are thought to reside "within" individuals. In particular, the dispositional strategy seeks to identify those domains of social behavior within which it is possible to identify individuals who characteristically manifest the regularities and consistencies in social behavior that might reflect the influence of underlying dispositional features.

2. *The interactional strategy:* The interactional strategy for the study of personality and social behavior seeks to understand regularities and consistencies in social behavior in terms of the interactive influence of dispositional and situational features. In particular, the interactional strategy seeks to identify those categories of traits, of behaviors, of individuals, and of situations within which such regularities and consistencies typically are to be found.

3. *The situational strategy:* The . . . situational strategy for the study of personality and social behavior seeks to understand consistencies in social behavior in terms of the features of social situations. In particular, the situational strategy seeks to identify the personal antecedents and the

social consequences of regularities and consistencies in the settings and contexts within which individuals live their lives (Snyder & Ickes, 1985, p. 884).

In articulating these three strategies, Snyder and Ickes (1985) not only gave explicit recognition to the variety of lenses, some more person-focused and some more situation-focused, through which regularities and consistencies in personality and social behavior can be viewed, they also captured significant variation in perspectives on the relative independence or interdependence of persons and situations in the construction of social behavior. The dispositional strategy, exemplified, for example, in the long-standing program of research of Costa and McCrae on the Five-Factor Model of personality (e.g., Costa & McCrae, 1980; McCrae & Costa, 1985a; McCrae & John, 1992), strives as much as is possible to separate person-centered, dispositionally derived consistencies in social behavior from the contextual stage on which they are performed. The interactional strategy, exemplified, for example, by the lock-and-key metaphor in Baron and Boudreau's (1987) ecological model, provides for a stable or "mechanistic" interaction of persons and situations in which situational affordances unlock dispositional regularities in social behavior and dispositions selectively and regularly prepare individuals to make the most of particular situational opportunities (e.g., Cantor & Kihlstrom, 1982, on statistical versus dynamic interactionism). The situational strategy, exemplified, for example, in Snyder's (1981) model of individuals constructing (that is, choosing and influencing) the social contexts of their lives and Buss's (1987) model of selection, evocation, and manipulation, endorses a "dynamic" interdependence between persons and situations, albeit one that emphasizes persons and their personalities shaping situations somewhat more than situations shaping persons and their personalities.

Now, in the mid-1990s, as we take our tour of the horizon of activity in personality and social behavior, it appears to us that the messages of the previous *Handbook* chapters on personality and social behavior have reached their intended audiences, who have embraced their messages and have heeded their recommendations to take seriously the roles of personality in social behavior and social behavior in personality and to systematically incorporate considerations of personality and social behavior into their strategies of scholarly inquiry.

In fact, it often seems to us that just about everyone is doing personality and social behavior these days. In the tripartite *Journal of Personality and Social Psychology*, one whole section is devoted to personality processes and individual differences. Yet, the pages of the other two sections of that journal (the section on attitudes and social cognition and the section on interpersonal relations and group processes) as well as the pages of the other major outlets for empirical work in personality and social psychology are well stocked with reports of research reflecting the tenets of the dispositional, interactional, and situational strategies for the study of personality and social behavior—reports of the development of inventories to assess social phenomena (reflecting the dispositional strategy), reports of research involving measures of personality processes and constructs as moderator variables (reflecting the interactional strategy), and reports of research on choosing and influencing situations (reflecting the situational strategy).

Gone are the days, it would seem, when one was greeted with skepticism, polite or otherwise, for working to understand the nature of personality or to chart the linkages between personality and social behavior. Even in this, the fourth edition of the *Handbook*, considerations of personality are not confined to this chapter on personality and social behavior. One example is the chapter on social psychology and health behavior, which includes a large section on "personality and health" (Salovey, Rothman, & Rodin, 1998); other examples are to be found in the chapters on "personal relationships" (Berscheid & Reis, 1998) and on "culture" (Fiske, Kitayama, Markus, & Nisbett, 1998), to mention only a few of those that consider the relevance of personality differences and processes for aspects of social behavior.

Clearly, then, we believe that the previous *Handbook* chapters on personality and social behavior have done their jobs well, and this chapter can move on to do a somewhat different job. What is not needed is a chapter on why social psychologists must pay attention to personality and why the theories and methods of personality can contribute meaningfully to the social psychological enterprise. Marlowe and Gergen (1969) delivered that message effectively in the second edition of the *Handbook*, and that message has been echoed many times since in pleas for integrating and synthesizing the concerns and activities of personality and social psychology (e.g., Blass, 1984; Carlson, 1984; Kenrick, 1986; Kihlstrom, 1987; Ross & Nisbett, 1991; Snyder, 1987b).

Moreover, our survey of the literature in personality and social behavior convinces us that the three investigative strategies articulated by Snyder and Ickes (1985) in the third edition of the *Handbook* remain viable ones and, in point of fact, have generated, and continue to generate, considerable amounts of research. Without any pretense of providing an exhaustive review, let us attempt a sampling to illustrate some of the ways in which the dispositional, interactional, and situational strategies have been emphasized in research on personality and social behavior reported in the past dozen or so years (that is, research reports that appeared after the third edition of the *Handbook* went to press).

Reflecting the *dispositional strategy* described by Snyder and Ickes (1985), there have been numerous reports of the development of inventories to assess social phenomena, for example, measures of interpersonal orientation (Swap & Rubin, 1983), loneliness in diverse relationships (Schmidt & Sermat, 1983), propensities to initiate and elicit intimate self-disclosure (Miller, Berg, & Archer, 1983), cognitive orientations toward certainty and uncertainty (Sorrentino & Hewitt, 1984), cognitive and behavioral strategies for coping with stress (Miller, 1987), social dominance orientation (Pratto, Sidanius, Stallworth, & Malle, 1994), sexism (Glick & Fiske, 1996), need for cognitive closure (Webster & Kruglanski, 1994), preference for consistency (Cialdini, Trost, & Newsom, 1995), need to evaluate (Jarvis & Petty, 1996), ego-resiliency (Klohnen, 1996), proneness to shame and guilt (Tangney, 1990), social awareness (Sheldon, 1996), styles of thinking (Epstein, Pacini, Denes-Raj, & Heier, 1996), well-being (Diener, Emmons, Larsen, & Griffin, 1985; Scheier & Carver, 1985; Watson, Clark, & Tellegen 1988), and hope (Snyder et al., 1991), to cite but a few representative examples.

The *interactional strategy,* as articulated by Snyder and Ickes (1985), sought to identify the traits, behaviors, persons, and situations particularly predictive of the regularities and consistencies associated with personality. Examples of research using measures of personality processes and constructs as moderator variables have proliferated, including work on the interaction of dispositional and situational predictors of behavior in such social domains as prosocial behavior (e.g., Carlo, Eisenberg, Troyer, Switzer, & Speer, 1991; Knight, Johnson, Carlo, & Eisenberg, 1994; Romer, Gruder, & Lizzadro, 1986; Tice & Baumeister, 1985); small group behaviors including dominance, conformity, and dissent (e.g., Aries, Gold, & Weigel, 1983; Maslach, Santee, & Wade, 1987); intergroup anxiety (e.g., Britt, Boniecki, Vescio, Biernat, & Brown, 1996); reactions to stressors (e.g., Cook, 1985; Davis & Matthews, 1996); alcohol consumption (e.g., Hull & Young, 1983); motivations to control outcomes (e.g., Schorr & Rodin, 1984); intrinsic motivation and responses to extrinsic rewards (e.g., Thompson, Chaiken, & Hazlewood, 1993); self and social behavior (e.g., Brown & Smart, 1991; Swann & Ely, 1984); perceptions of social support (e.g., Lakey et al., 1996); intimacy and self-disclosure (e.g., Shaffer, Ogden, & Wu, 1987); obedience to authority (e.g., Blass, 1991); resistance to persuasion (e.g., Zuwerink & Devine, 1996); repression (e.g., Mendolia, Moore, & Tesser, 1996); as well as general considerations of the potential and the performance of the moderator variable strategy for personality and prediction (e.g., Chaplin, 1991; Funder & Colvin, 1991; Hull, Tedlie, & Lehn, 1992; Murtha, Kanfer, & Ackerman, 1996; Paunonen, 1988; Shoda, Mischel, & Wright, 1993, 1994; West, Aiken, & Krull, 1996; Zuckerman et al., 1988).

The *situational strategy* for the study of personality and

social behavior, as articulated by Snyder and Ickes (1985), jointly emphasizes (1) the proposition that regularities and consistencies in social situations can give rise to the behavioral regularities and consistencies thought of as personality and (2) the proposition that some of these regularities and consistencies in social situations reflect the role that individuals play in choosing and influencing the social situations in which they operate. In accord with the first proposition, there have been attempts to quantify the impact of situations on behavior and to demonstrate that their impact is comparable to that of dispositions (e.g., Funder & Ozer, 1983), as well as to search for predictable social settings associated with more or less behavioral variance (e.g., Schutte, Kenrick, & Sadalla, 1985). With respect to the second proposition, there have been theoretical and empirical attempts to specify alternative (although not necessarily competing) models (e.g., ecological, biological, developmental, evolutionary) of the mechanisms by which persons "choose" situations and situations "choose" persons such that a congruence or matching emerges between persons and environments (e.g., Baron & Boudreau, 1987; Buss, 1987; Caspi, Bem, & Elder, 1989; Emmons, Diener, & Larsen, 1986; Snyder, 1981). Moreover, a considerable body of literature has accumulated on choices of situations, two examples of which are studies of identity and studies of relationships. In the domains of identity and self-evaluation, there has been research on the influence of environments on features of identity (e.g., Adams & Fitch, 1983), on the role of selection of situations in features of identity negotiation such as self-verification and self-enhancement (e.g., McNulty & Swann, 1994; Swann, 1987; Swann, Stein-Seroussi, & Giesler, 1992), and on the role of choice of situation in social comparison (e.g., Wood, Giordano-Beech, Taylor, Michela, & Gaus, 1994) and seeking social support (e.g., Harlow & Cantor, 1995). In the domains of friendship and social relationships, there have been studies of the role of choosing situations in understanding the selection of friends as activity partners (e.g., Snyder, Gangestad, & Simpson, 1983), the evaluation of prospective dating partners (e.g., Snyder, Berscheid, & Glick, 1985), sensitivity to rejection in romantic relationships (e.g., Downey & Feldman, 1996), the seeking of sexual partners (e.g., Snyder, Simpson, & Gangestad, 1986), and choosing mates and spouses (e.g., Buss, 1984; Caspi & Herbener, 1990). Moreover, in more applied domains, there have been studies of determinants of choices of situations such as the decision to seek medical treatment (e.g., Matthews, Siegal, Kuller, Thompson, & Varat, 1983), the influence of interpersonal orientations on choices of social networks as decision-making resources in organizational contexts (e.g., Kilduff, 1992), the influence of gender-linked differences in support for group inequality on selection of occupational roles (e.g., Pratto, Stallworth, Sidanius, & Siers, 1997), as well as the influence of features of self-concept on choice of therapist (Niedenthal & Mordkoff, 1991). Finally, a particularly ambitious application of the notion of choosing situations explores the long-term implications of choices of situations for developmental trajectories (e.g., Caspi et al., 1989; Waller, Benet, & Farney, 1994).

Clearly, the dispositional, interactional, and situational strategies have been conspicuously present in research on personality and social behavior. Clearly, too, the task of reviewing all, or even most, of the exemplars of each strategy that have been reported in the interval between editions of the *Handbook* would be a daunting task, for it would fill not a chapter, but a full volume. Thus, we set a different task for ourselves, and chart a different course for this chapter on personality and social behavior. We begin by acknowledging that the case for the importance of research and theorizing at the interface of personality and social psychology has been made, that work at this interface is an active and a productive enterprise, and that all three investigative strategies articulated by Snyder and Ickes (1985) are viable ones for the study of personality and social behavior (see also Blass, 1984; Kihlstrom, 1987).

Taking these investigative strategies as our point of departure, however, we wish to focus particularly closely on the situational strategy for the study of personality and social behavior. We do so for several reasons. First, as Snyder and Ickes (1985) noted, it was, at the time that they were writing their chapter on personality and social behavior, a newly emerging strategy, one that would no doubt, given the evolutionary quality of the strategies for the study of personality and social behavior, come into its own after the publication of their chapter. Indeed, it would appear that, in the interval between editions of the *Handbook*, the situational strategy has been, if not predominant, certainly extremely generative of empirical inquiry (for a review of research on how individuals choose and influence social situations, see Ickes, Snyder, & Garcia, 1997).

Our second reason for focusing on the situational strategy as the springboard for our current considerations of personality and social behavior emerges from this evolutionary quality of the strategies. For, something has emerged in the course of this evolution that sets the situational strategy apart from dispositional and interactional strategies and helps to build a bridge toward (what we see as) the next generation of strategies for understanding personality and social behavior. As conceptualized by Snyder and Ickes (1985), all three strategies concern the *sources* of the regularities and consistencies in social behavior that are thought of as personality, with the strategies differing in their *relative emphasis* on dispositional and situational sources of these regularities and consistencies. Over the course of their evolution, these strategies have moved from an emphasis on understanding consistencies in social behavior in terms of stable traits and enduring dispositions (the dispositional strategy) to an attempt to enhance the ability to identify these regularities and consistencies by considering the interactive influence of dispositional and

situational predictors of social behavior from such traits and dispositions (the interactional strategy) to a recognition that regularities and consistencies in social situations themselves can be sources of regularities and consistencies in social behavior (the situational strategy).

But, in addition to this evolution in emphasis on sources of regularities and consistencies in social behavior, the three strategies can be characterized by an evolution in the *mechanisms* of these regularities and consistencies in social behavior—from the dispositional strategy which, other than proposing that we look to dispositions to explain behavior, was silent on the mechanisms by which dispositions led to behavior, to the interactional strategy which implied that something was integrating dispositional and situational determinants of behavior in a mechanistic or statistical interactionist form, to the situational strategy which, in addition to placing its emphasis on regularities and consistencies in situations as sources of regularities and consistencies also proposed one mechanism by which these regularities and consistencies in situations came about, namely, the active choosing and influencing of situations by individuals. As such, the situational strategy sets itself apart from the strategies earlier in the evolutionary sequence by having something explicit to say about the mechanisms that generate regularities and consistencies in social behavior. In fact, we believe that much of the credit for the generativity of this strategy for studying personality and social behavior can be traced to its "dynamic interactionist" themes—with its emphasis on the reciprocal interplay and mutual influence of persons and situations, with persons choosing, influencing, and changing the situations in which they function and, in turn, being guided, directed, and changed by the opportunities and specifications provided by those situations.

Increasingly, it appears to us that these dynamic interactionist themes have come to define the hybrid discipline of personality and social behavior. In addition to offering hypotheses about the mechanisms of personality and social behavior, we suggest that these themes capture the shared intellectual concerns of personality and social psychology with the purposes, directions, and consequences of social behavior, and provide opportunities for productively integrating and synthesizing the characteristic investigative strategies of personality and social psychology. They do this, in large measure, we wish to argue, precisely because they focus on shared concerns with *motivation*. And, as we shall argue, they lay the foundation for the next generation of strategies for conceptualizing and investigating personality and social behavior.

SHARED MOTIVATIONAL CONCERNS OF PERSONALITY AND SOCIAL PSYCHOLOGY

In keeping with the root meaning of the term "motivation" is the idea of "movement" (see Hilgard, 1987, for one analysis of the historical evolution of motivation as a psychological concept); the shared motivational concerns of personality and social psychology reflect shared concerns with "movement," movement *of* individuals and movement *by* individuals. The metaphor of movement is inherent in the concept of motivation; and indeed, the metaphor of movement shows up in the classic theories of personality and social psychology that serve as forerunners to much active research today. Of course, the Lewinian idea of "locomotion" and movement through the life space (Lewin, 1936) is familiar to all students of personality and social psychology, but the theories of Murray (1938) and Freud (1938) also are amenable to interpretation in the context of a movement metaphor (especially in light of Murray's emphasis on *press* and Freud's on *libidinal drives*). So too is the "teleonomic" theory of Floyd Allport which stressed the importance of trying to understand what a person "is trying to do" in his or her life (F. Allport, 1937, p. 204). From a slightly different but complementary perspective, Erikson (1950, 1959) framed personality development as a progressive journey through life stages, a movement from one set of social rituals and age-graded tasks to the next.

One common cause, thus, that these classic theorists all championed is the concern with movement—with what people want to do in their lives, with where they are encouraged to head in their lives, and with the directions that their lives actually take. Let us elaborate, therefore, on just what we mean by these shared concerns with how people are moved, or influenced, by determining forces, and with how people move, or influence, their worlds.

How People Are Moved from Within and Without

First, let us consider how people are moved by determining forces, both from within and from outside themselves. Most, if not all, definitions of social psychology are variations on a theme articulated by G. Allport: "With few exceptions, social psychologists regard their discipline as an attempt to understand and explain how the thought, feeling, and behavior of individuals are influenced by the actual, imagined, or implied presence of others" (1968, p. 3). Definitions of social psychology emphasize the psychology of how people are influenced by situational considerations, that is, how they are "moved" by the opportunities selectively afforded to individuals by social forces—be they cultures, groups, or dyadic partnerships.

By the same token, definitions of personality psychology typically include references to the quest for an understanding of how the actions of individuals reflect stable and enduring traits, needs, and other attributes thought to reside within them; thus, in G. Allport's words, "personality is the dynamic organization within the individual of those psychophysical systems that determine his unique adjustments to his environment" (1937, p. 48). That is, a defining concern of personality psychology is how people are "moved" to action by dispositional forces. In other words, both social psychology and personality work with a metaphor of movement, namely, movement of individuals by forces in their surrounding situations and by forces within themselves.

From this perspective on the shared concerns, it would seem that personality and social psychology are fundamentally *motivational* in their defining and characteristic orientations. We should emphasize that we believe this to have been true even in those periods of time when intellectual historians would characterize these fields as being dominated by concerns with cognition. For, so many of the treatments of cognitive phenomena and processes offered by personality and social psychologists represent rather motivational views of cognition. The very notion, which underlies so much cognitive and attributional theorizing in social psychology and personality, that people engage in cognitive activity in the service of gaining stable and predictable images of the world that they can and do use to help guide them through their lives is ultimately a motivational idea. That is, this notion places cognitive activity in a clearly and explicitly goal-directed context, one which emphasizes that, as it has been characterized in pragmatic terms, "thinking is for doing" (Cantor, 1990; Fiske, 1992).

How People Move Their Worlds

But, increasingly, in keeping with the dynamic interactionist themes associated with, and emerging from, the situational strategy for the study of personality and social behavior (Snyder & Ickes, 1985), theorizing and research in social psychology and personality have also become concerned with the complementary influences exerted by individuals in the choice of the situations in which they operate and in their influence on those situations, that is, with how, through their actions, people "move" and construct their social worlds. Within social psychology, much of this emphasis has grown out of research on the ways that individuals use the beliefs and expectations that they hold about other people to guide their social interactions in ways that, to some degree, constrain others to fulfill those expectations, a phenomenon known variously as the self-fulfilling prophecy, expectancy confirmation, and behavioral confirmation (Darley & Fazio, 1980; Rosenthal, Baratz, & Hall, 1974; Snyder, 1984). Demonstrations of behavioral confirmation, such as occurred in the "noise-weapon" study of Snyder and Swann (1978) in which individuals who believed that they were dealing with others disposed to be hostile actually elicited hostility from them, serve as powerful reminders of how individuals move their social worlds. In that case, for example, the "hostile" perceiver creates a hostile environment simply by virtue of his or her behavior toward an unsuspecting target and reaps the consequences in return. To the extent that the behaviors of those with whom people interact are very much a part of their social situations, such research represents a clear example of the guiding and constraining influence of individuals' social expectations on their social situations and, more generally, on the social worlds within which they live.

In personality psychology, much of the emphasis on the influence of individuals on situations has grown out of theorizing and research on the ways that people select and shape situations conducive to their personal traits and dispositions, thereby constructing social worlds that facilitate the expression of their personalities and may even bolster those tendencies or proclivities. A substantial part of this influence occurs in the everyday choices that individuals make of: activities to do (e.g., Emmons, Diener, & Larsen, 1986; Zirkel & Cantor, 1990); people to date and to marry (e.g., Caspi & Herbener, 1990; Sanderson & Cantor, 1995; Snyder et al., 1985); places in which to live (e.g., Niedenthal, Cantor, & Kihlstrom, 1985); therapists to see (e.g., Niedenthal & Mordkoff, 1991); jobs to seek (e.g., Snyder, 1987a); and forms of volunteer service to pursue (e.g., Snyder & Omoto, 1992). The influence of individuals on situations also emerges strongly and importantly in the different ways in which individuals take on normative roles and tasks across the life course (Cantor & Fleeson, 1994; Caspi, 1987).

The influence of individuals on situations is also readily evident in relatively unstructured social interactions. When Thorne (1987), for example, asked introverts and extroverts to interact in a typically freewheeling "getting to know each other conversation," she found that quite quickly into the conversation the introverts assumed a secondary role, actively moving the focus of attention away from themselves and on to their extroverted partner by taking on a kind of "interviewer" stance. Thus, even dispositional tendencies characterized by behavioral inhibition exert an interpersonal press which systematically shapes the nature and outcomes of social interactions.

And, in the same vein of individuals choosing and influencing their situations, personal and social motivations also exert a guiding hand in leading people toward roles and opportunities for them to act on their motivations. For example, in their research with AIDS volunteers, Snyder and Omoto (1992) have noted that volunteer motivations guide people into volunteer roles, with those gravitating toward direct, face-to-face service with persons living with AIDS motivated by concern for others, compassion, empathy, and a desire to learn, and those volunteers gravitating toward opportunities that do not involve direct contact with persons living with AIDS being motivated by considerations of esteem enhancement and cravings for social recognition. What appears to be going on here is that, in accord with the general theme that people actively seek out life situations conducive to their own personalities, volunteers systematically gravitate toward volunteer roles that fulfill their personal motivations.

What we have, then, are two complementary propositions about the reciprocal motivational influences that operate between individuals and their social worlds. On the one hand, individuals are influenced and guided in their actions by situational and interpersonal and cultural considerations and by personal and dispositional forces that "move" them to action in ways that reflect those social and personal motivational forces. On the other hand, through their actions, individuals "move" the worlds around them; that is, through their choices of interaction partners, through their choices of roles, through their choices of interaction contexts, and through their shaping influences on all of these things, whether these actions are guided by situational considerations (e.g., interpersonal and cultural expectations, roles, norms, and prescriptions) or dispositional properties (e.g., traits, attitudes, identities, and other personal attributes), individuals "move" the social worlds in which they operate.

It would seem, then, that the case can be made that dynamic interactionist themes are so important to considerations of personality and social behavior precisely because they capture the defining concerns of personality and of social psychology and precisely because they make salient the shared, defining concerns of social psychology and personality with motivation as movement. We certainly believe this to be true. Yet, we wish to emphasize that there is an additional way in which the dynamic interactionism of the situational strategy has become a springboard recently for the study of personality and social behavior. In considering the personal and social forces that "move" people and the selective ways in which people "move" their social worlds, more and more thought has been given to the purposes of that movement, to understanding *how, why, and to what end do people act*—that is, to the setting of personal and social agendas and the pursuing of ends and goals. This concern with purpose has been applied to both sides of the movement equation.

When looking, for example, at the social and personal forces that "move" people, social psychologists have considered the question of *to what end and for what purposes* do: cultures structure life collectively rather than individualistically (e.g., Markus & Kitayama, 1991, 1994; Singelis & Brown, 1995; Triandis, 1989, 1993; Triandis, McCusker, & Hui, 1990); subcultures exact conformity to behavioral norms (e.g., Crandall, 1988); and groups allocate power selectively (e.g., Bargh, Raymond, Pryor, & Strack, 1995; S. T. Fiske, 1993; Rudman & Borgida, 1995). Similarly, personality psychologists have enriched the analysis of dispositional forces by asking *to what end and for what purposes* do: affectively reactive individuals experience mood swings (e.g., Larsen, 1987; Larsen & Kasimatis, 1990; Watson, 1988); individuals high in self-uncertainty seek social affirmation (e.g., Campbell, 1990; Campbell & Fairey, 1986; Campbell, Tesser, & Fairey, 1986); and those high in goal conflict inhibit their goal pursuits (e.g., Emmons & King, 1988).

In the same vein, when looking at the ways in which individuals selectively "move" their social worlds, both social psychologists and personality psychologists uncover complexities introduced by motivational dynamics. For example, increasingly today, the literature on behavioral confirmation recognizes that the outcome of the interaction between partners depends critically on the sometimes diverging purposes of the participants, forcing a more explicit attunement to the potential for countervailing forces rather than the inevitability of a (one-sided) confirmation scenario (e.g., Snyder & Haugen, 1994, 1995). Similarly, although individuals do much to accentuate over time their own dispositional proclivities by their behavior in situations (e.g., Caspi et. al., 1989), this process is marked in significant ways by the purposive agendas of cultures. Weisz, Rothbaum, and Blackburn (1984), for example, have demonstrated the pervasive influence of these cultural agendas in their analysis of the social norms of "standing out" and "standing in" that permeate the lives of American and Japanese children, respectively, and therein change their ways of being dominant or compliant, respectively.

In all of these cases, recognition of the purposes for which, and the processes through which, influence is reciprocally exerted adds complexity to the picture. Nonetheless, it also takes us further from the mechanistic assumptions of some earlier interactionist models and closer to a model of personality and social behavior as it dynamically unfolds in real time and in real places (McAdams, 1993). In large measure, these dynamic motivational themes are the intellectual and investigative legacies of the situational strategy for the study of personality and social behavior. That is, they take as a starting point the *active* and *selective* processes of personal and social influence elucidated by the situational strategy, and consider, then, the ways in which those processes hook on to the agendas that people deliberately set for themselves, that they planfully pursue in the course of their lives, and that characterize their functioning in diverse domains.

We should offer one disclaimer, though, to accompany this description of an evolution in investigative strategies for studying personality and social behavior. The fact that emphasis has been placed, and increasingly so, on the dynamic motivational themes associated with, and emerging from, the situational strategy does not mean that the intent behind either the dispositional or the interactionist strategies (that is, to elucidate the stability of personality as a force in social behavior or the moderating influence of those personal stabilities in unlocking situational affordances) are necessarily being left behind. Rather, as we shall ultimately argue, they come back to life with new meaning and their full potential can be realized by being integrated into a dynamic, motivational perspective guided by, what

we will be calling, the *functionalist strategy* for understanding personality and social behavior.

THE FUNCTIONALIST STRATEGY FOR PERSONALITY AND SOCIAL BEHAVIOR

Before tackling the ways in which the situationist strategy has evolved into a functionalist strategy, and the ways in which this functionalist strategy can guide us in conceptualizing and investigating personality and social behavior, it is perhaps worthwhile for us to take a moment for some stage setting, both conceptual and historical in content. First, we need to ask what it is that we mean when we refer to a "functionalist" strategy for studying personality and social behavior. The word "functional" is amenable to many interpretations, both in its dictionary definitions and in its usage in the psychological lexicon. By one definition, the one with which we work in our theorizing, a functionalist strategy is concerned with the reasons and the purposes, the need and the goals, the plans and the motives that underlie and generate psychological phenomena; that is, such a strategy is concerned with the motivational foundations of people's actions, and with the agendas that they set for themselves and that they act out in pursuit of their goals. By necessity and importantly, this perspective puts a premium on understanding the dynamics of agenda-setting and pursuit since individuals' agendas can be continuously updated in the face of experience, as the personal and social forces that afford and constrain them change. Additionally, special attention is placed in a functionalist analysis on the ends or outcomes of human social behavior, that is, not only on what people do in pursuing agendas but also on how well they do it and to what ends their strivings bring them.

Of course, this kind of functionalist theorizing about human motivation and adjustment has a long and a distinguished history in psychology, and so part of our stage setting is to ask about the traditions from which it derives. Psychology today owes much to the nineteenth-to-twentieth century shift away from *structuralist* attempts (such as those of Wundt and Tichener) to describe and classify mental events. In contrast, the *functionalist* theorists (such as Angell, Dewey, and James) argued that psychology should concern itself with mental and behavioral functions and, in so doing, understand the adaptation of organisms to their environments. If structuralism was the descriptive psychology of "is," then functionalism was the purposive psychology of "is for." From its beginnings in concerns with the gratification of basic physiological needs, functionalism spread rapidly in American psychology, leading to the emergence and development of many areas of basic and applied psychology. Functionalist themes pervade psychological perspectives as diverse as psychoanalysis, behaviorism, psychobiology, and evolutionary psychology—each of which emphasizes, in its own way, the adaptive and purposive pursuit of ends and goals.

Within personality and social psychology, the themes of functionalism currently popular derive in part from those long-standing concerns of Allport, Murray, Erikson, and others, with the active and purposeful strivings of human beings toward personal and social ends. For example, Little (1983) drew inspiration in his analysis of *personal projects* from Murray's theories, particularly the construct of *serials* in individuals' lives; Emmons (1986) gave central emphasis to F. Allport's *teleonomic trends* in his theory of *personal strivings*; and Cantor and Kihlstrom (1987) took as a starting point the cultural anthropology of Havighurst and the developmental theory of Erikson in focusing on individuals' *life tasks*. Looking more broadly, as summarized for example in Pervin's (1989) edited volume on *Goal Concepts in Personality and Social Psychology,* functionalist themes are evident throughout the literature on goals (see Austin & Vancouver, 1996), striking a resonant note with the defining concerns of personality and social psychology, especially personality psychology's concern with how people are motivated from within by their own traits and dispositions and social psychology's concern with how people are motivated from without by the social and interpersonal forces that surround them.

Structure and Function in Personality and Social Psychology

Moreover, as in years past, rather than turning entirely away from a concern with structure to a concern with function, today's functionalist theorizing builds dynamically upon assumptions about the structure of personality and of social environments as inputs to individuals' agendas (e.g., Cantor, 1994; Snyder, 1993). Specifically, if we look at what has been going on structurally, the most salient example is personality psychology's search for basic structural units of personality, embodied most prominently in the Five-Factor Model (Costa & McCrae, 1980; McCrae & Costa, 1987). In recent years, there has been a dramatic and an enthusiastic resurgence of interest in traits as building blocks of personality, and a striking (although not a unanimous) convergence on the "Big Five" as a basic structure for personality, one in which most traits can be understood in terms of, and placed in the structural context defined by, the basic dimensions of neuroticism, extraversion, openness, agreeableness, and conscientiousness (for a collection of articles about the Five-Factor Model, see the special issue of the *Journal of Personality* edited by Mc-Crae, 1992).

Viewed from the perspective of the structural goal of inquiry in psychology, the Big Five clearly constitutes one candidate—and, for many personality psychologists, the leading candidate—for a basic structure for personality.

The evidence in support of the Big Five is substantial and, even if not totally overwhelming (Pervin, 1994), certainly sufficient to warrant consideration by psychologists of all stripes. As a structural model, the Big Five has the potential to tell us much about what personality is, how it is organized, and how it might be assessed. Whether or not one accepts the Big Five as the final word on these matters, one must admit that it clearly tackles the fundamental goal of understanding the structure of personality.

Structuralist movements are perhaps not as overtly or centrally evident in social psychology. To be sure, there are recurring attempts to construct catalogues or taxonomies of interaction goals and self-presentational needs (e.g., Jones & Pittman, 1982), to discover the basic dimensions for categorizing situations (e.g., Eckes, 1995; Frederiksen, 1976; Magnusson, 1971), to look at the basic units of person perception (e.g., Andersen & Klatzky, 1987; Miller & Read, 1991), to define schemas and prototypes for conceptions of people and of situations (e.g., Cantor & Mischel, 1979; Cantor, Mischel, & Schwartz, 1982). Yet, it is a common observation that the language of situations is not nearly as well articulated as the language of persons (at least not as extensive as the language of traits), and that the attempt to define fundamental dimensions and basic units of situations has not been nearly as generative an enterprise as that of defining fundamental dimensions and basic units of personality (Frederiksen, 1976; Murtha, Kanfer, & Ackerman, 1996). Perhaps it is a matter of the level of analysis which has proven useful for traits and dispositions not being quite right for social situations and social behaviors. For example, one could well argue that the evergrowing fascination of social psychologists with cultural and social organizations structured along collectivist or individualist lines (e.g., A. Fiske, 1993; Markus & Kitayama, 1991, 1994; Sampson, 1995; Triandis, 1989) represents a comparably generative, consensually adopted structuralist position in social psychology quite on par with the Big Five movement in personality psychology.

Therefore, even if analyses of features of social situations do not lend themselves to an emphasis on a basic structure comparable to the basic structures offered for personality, it still seems that, at a more global level of consideration, contemporary social psychological analyses of culture, gender, ethnicity, and class constitute structural analyses, with their emphases on cultures as structural forces that constrain the agendas of persons operating within the culture and on gender and ethnicity as forces that constrain the opportunities available to persons in the course of their lives. Thus such analyses emphasize socially mediated *organizing frameworks* that guide and direct opportunities and behaviors, that represent situational affordances specifying rules, norms, and other constraints to human action.

Thus, culture, ethnicity, and class can be seen as relatively stable and enduring situational affordances that move people toward particular courses of action. In fact, when seen in this light, it is evident that structure and function are intimately intertwined, since this proposition tells us something both about structure (what culture, ethnicity, and class *are*—they are organizing frameworks) and about function (what culture, ethnicity, and class *do*—they guide and direct opportunities for behavior). This same approach can be applied to other properties of situations, permitting us to see roles, interaction partners, and immediate social settings in terms of the situational affordances and constraints of opportunity that they represent (that is, as structural features) and in terms of the guiding and directing influences that these affordances exert on action (that is, as functional processes). Of course, and as we shall see, it is important to recognize the differences in abstraction and generality that are being applied when thinking about relatively global, stable, and enduring properties of situations such as culture and ethnicity, and properties of situations that are more immediate, shifting, and transitory, such as the press of immediate circumstances.

The same arguments about the intertwining of structure and function can be made, and have been made, for features of personality as well, with part of the answer to the question of the functions of personality being provided by knowing the structure for personality, that is, the traits of the Big Five, or any other structural organizing framework for personality dispositions being seen as providing opportunities and constraints that guide and direct behavior, that move people toward particular agendas with particular consequences. And, just as we were able to apply the same considerations to a great diversity of features of situations (contrasting the stable and enduring influences of culture, class, and ethnicity with the more context dependent and shifting influences such as immediate social settings, interaction partners, and task requirements), we can apply the same considerations to features of persons, where it must be recognized that just as there are units of personality thought to be stable across situations and enduring over time (such as the Big Five dimensions) so too are there many units of personality not entirely enduring and/or stable, such as conditional trait units, tasks, projects, and remembered selves.

In this sense, there is a parallelism between structural and functional considerations in personality and in social psychology. Just as personality traits and dispositions can be seen as relatively stable and enduring dispositional propensities that move people toward particular agendas and courses of action, so too can features of situations be seen as affording and constraining opportunities for agendas and actions, whether in a stable and enduring sense, such as global traits and dispositions and the forces of culture and class, or not, as in the pressures of immediate social situations or the influences of conditional trait units

and personal projects. That is, we can see properties of persons and properties of situations as organizing frameworks that provide inputs to the agendas that guide and direct actions, whether these inputs are in the form of dispositional propensities or situational affordances. From a structural perspective, these considerations answer questions of what is the nature of the personal and situational forces that move people to action. If this analysis doesn't quite provide a common structural language for features of persons and of situation, it at least provides a common perspective or analytic strategy, one that facilitates integrating both sets of features into the larger framework of the functionalist strategy for personality and social behavior.

That these considerations of structure lead so inevitably to considerations of function suggests that there is a need to go beyond structural considerations to functional considerations. This evolution is similar in both form and content to the move from mechanistic interactional models associated with the interactional strategy for the study of personality and social behavior to the reciprocal interplay and the dynamic interactionism associated with the situationist strategy, as noted earlier. That is, we need to consider how features of personality and features of social situations work dynamically and interdependently to guide and direct human functioning in diverse life domains.

Building this bridge from structure to function, we ask: If features of persons and features of situations can be seen in terms of the opportunities they afford and the constraints that they provide, then what happens to those opportunities and constraints and what is made of them as people are "moved to action" in their purposeful strivings toward ends and goals? The implication, quite clearly, of thinking in terms of opportunities afforded and constraints provided by features of persons and situations is that we should think in terms of what people do with those opportunities and constraints, how and why and to what end they take advantage of them, and how opportunities and constraints get translated or not translated into courses of action.

That is, having tackled questions of structure, of what personality is and what social situations are, we must move on to considering how to understand what personality does and what social situations do, in particular to address what it is that they do to determine the course of people's lives, to understand *what* people are trying to do in their lives, *how* they are trying to do it, and *why* they are trying to do it. To do so, we take as our central analytical concept the idea of *agendas* constructed and enacted by individuals in a social context.

Agendas for Action

In the functionalist strategy for studying personality and social behavior, agendas play an *integrating role,* thus highlighting the reciprocal and interdependent influences of personal and social forces. Agendas, in keeping with the purposeful goal-oriented nature of our functionalist theorizing, are thought to be carried out in pursuit of *outcomes*. These outcomes may be specific to the individual actor, such as his or her individual happiness and well-being. Or, these outcomes may be pursued in the context of dyadic relationships, such as facilitating the course of an ongoing interaction or maximizing the satisfaction to be derived from that interaction. Or, these outcomes may be pursued in the larger context of groups and organizations, or even society itself, such as outcomes that may come from joining an organization and pursuing its goals, or engaging in social and political activism on behalf of societally important causes with the intent of making the world a better place to live.

In conceptualizing these integrating agendas, we find it of particular heuristic value to consider the ways that agendas can and do vary in how many people other than the individual actor may be involved in their pursuit or affected by their outcomes. Specifically, we conceptualize agendas at the *individual, interpersonal, relationship,* and *group* levels of analysis (recognizing that these are not necessarily discrete categories, and may in fact represent partially overlapping levels of analysis).

Individual Level Agendas   These are agendas that typically can be defined with reference to the person alone. They are directed at outcomes for and about the individual. Exemplifying this level of agenda are the problems and tasks associated with self and identity, including the defining of one's social identity (e.g., Brewer, 1991; Deaux, 1993), the articulating of one's values and beliefs (e.g., Bilsky & Schwartz, 1994; Schwartz, 1992), the operation of self-serving motivational biases in self-perception (e.g., Klein & Kunda, 1993; Kunda & Sanitioso, 1989), the constructing of personal narratives (e.g., McAdams, 1988), and the setting up of personal projects (e.g., Little, 1983). Although these agendas may be defined with reference to the individual alone, their pursuit very well may involve other people as sources of input and influence, and may have consequences for other people as well.

Interpersonal Level Agendas   These are agendas that must involve an interaction partner, someone whom one is getting to know, trying to get along with, presenting an image to, and exerting a social influence on (e.g., Jones & Pittman, 1982). Defining these dyadic agendas may require specifying the interaction goals, the strategies and tactics, the guiding beliefs and assumptions of the parties involved (Chen, Shechter, & Chaiken, 1996; Copeland & Snyder, 1995; Darley, Fleming, Hilton, & Swann, 1988; Hilton & Darley, 1985; Neuberg, 1989, 1994; Neuberg & Fiske,

1987; Neuberg, Judice, Virdin, & Carrillo, 1993; Pelletier & Vallerand, 1996; Snyder & Haugen, 1995). Because of their dyadic context, these are agendas whose outcomes may include the construction of public appearances (e.g., self-presentation and impression management) and the confirmation of social expectations (e.g., self-fulfilling prophecies and behavioral confirmation outcomes).

Relationship Level Agendas   These agendas represent the unfolding of relationships that may grow from the interaction agendas referred to above, but which are typically more enduring, more extended in time, and involve greater bonds of attachment, closeness, emotion, and commitment (e.g., Clark & Reis, 1988; Kelley, 1979; Kelley et al., 1983). Defining these agendas may require knowing about personal orientations toward relationships (e.g., strivings for closeness [Kelley et al., 1983; McAdams, 1980], attachment styles [Bowlby, 1969, 1973, 1980; Hazan & Shaver, 1987], etc.) and the unfolding stages of relationship development and evolution.

Group Level Agendas   These agendas involve the person in larger group, organizational, and societal contexts. They involve membership in organizations, communities, participation in the affairs of society, and collective action and social activism (e.g., Snyder, 1993; Wuthnow, 1994). We should note that, although we may appear to be covering quite a bit of territory in terms of size of groups here, from small groups to society, the fact of the matter is that, often the participation in societal level action is undertaken in the context of much smaller groups, such as a political campaign for a local office or a community action group of the "think globally, act locally" variety. Moreover, it is almost inevitable that individuals' participation in these groups serves individual as well as group level agendas.

Although we have tended to define these levels by exemplar, we can specify that, with respect to understanding what these "levels" refer to, these levels are graded by, foremost among other considerations, the number of actors or players involved and the focus of the agenda and its intended outcomes on some continuum from self-focused to group-focused. Even so, the other actors and players may be only symbolically present and distantly in focus, as in people's symbolic relations with others, people's imagined dealing with others, their sense of community, and their affiliation with society. And the focus of the outcome may readily draw in agendas with outcomes at other levels, as when an agenda for self-development implicates interpersonal agendas (e.g., adolescents learning to be independent from family by cultivating strong friendship networks; Zirkel & Cantor, 1990). Further, although we do not regard the levels as graded in any sense of better or worse, desirable or undesirable, important or trivial, agendas are intimately linked to outcomes, some that do turn out better and some worse.

Outcomes of Agendas

Our emphasis on outcomes is an important reminder that, in the functionalist approach to personality and social behavior, conceptual and empirical activity does not end with behavior, but rather must look also to outcomes of individuals' pursuit of agendas, such as the "quality of life" that they may seek and that they may or may not succeed in creating for themselves. And, by extension, the levels of analysis which can be used to characterize agendas can also be used for conceptualizing their outcomes. That is, the outcomes being pursued by individuals can also be specified at the individual, interpersonal, relationship, and group levels. Thus, it is possible to theorize about and to investigate, for example, features of well-being or well-functioning at the personal or *individual* level (e.g., mood), at the dyadic interaction or *interpersonal* level (e.g., smoothly flowing interactions), at the *relationship* level (e.g., relationship satisfaction and endurance), and at the *group* level (e.g., productive groups and organization, organizational climates) as outcomes, in the pursuit of which people construct and enact their agendas.

Actually, we expect that there is likely to be substantial *matching* between levels of agendas and levels of outcomes because people, in setting an agenda, are likely to be doing so with some notion of the outcome to be pursued. Similarly, in identifying outcomes to be pursued, people also will likely be thinking of the agenda that leads them to it. It may be that people don't really distinguish between the outcome and the process. For example, for many people, in their psyches and in their lives, the goal of physical fitness and the agenda for its pursuit may be one and the same thing, namely, going to the athletic club each day and doing their minutes or hours on the stairmaster, even though the psychological observer can readily recognize and discriminate between the goal being sought and the agenda for pursuing it (as well as the personal and social inputs to that agenda). So, it may not really be possible to easily and cleanly separate the defining of outcomes and the setting of agendas. Both may be instantiated in the tasks that people engage in when they are in the pursuit of their agendas and outcomes.

Another complexity, but an intriguing one, to the functionalist analysis is the prevalence of *multiple* agenda-outcome pairings, varying in levels and contributing at the same time to a person's actions. For example, consider a person who is intent on maximizing self-esteem. Such an individual may well seek personal pleasure by pursuing both individual and interpersonal or even group-level agendas and outcomes, as when individuals gain self-esteem enhancement by volunteering in community service orga-

nizations (e.g., Omoto & Snyder, 1995). To the extent that this volunteer work is aimed at (and successfully fulfills) both individual, interpersonal, and group goals, such as when a volunteer assists a person living with AIDS and not only helps that person but feels good himself or herself and simultaneously enhances the visibility of the volunteer organization, then multiple levels of agendas-outcomes have been addressed at the same time or in the same action. Thus, it becomes useful sometimes to unpack the relevant levels (of agendas-outcomes) within a single example.

Personal and Social Contexts for Agenda-Setting

If these are the levels of agendas and outcomes that people pursue, what then are the *inputs* that people draw on in setting their agendas and pursuing their outcomes? Our analysis of previously articulated strategies for personality and social behavior (i.e., the dispositional, interactional, and situational strategies discussed by Snyder & Ickes, 1985) and our considerations of structure and function have already foreshadowed, to some degree, our answer to this question. Our characterization of the dispositional, interactional, and situational strategies as being concerned with the sources of the regularities and consistencies of personality and social behavior—in particular with the relative emphasis accorded to dispositional and situational sources—suggests that it is features of persons and features of situations that serve as sources of inputs to agendas for action in the functionalist strategy for personality and social behavior. And, our view of features of persons and features of situations as inputs to agendas for action regards these features as sources of opportunities afforded to and constraints imposed on individuals in their pursuit of agendas, and that these agendas are constructed and enacted in the pursuit of ends and goals. A graphic representation of this functionalist model is presented in Figure 1, with personal contexts and situational contexts serving as inputs to agendas carried out in pursuit of outcomes.

In applying a functionalist strategy, such features of persons as their traits, motives, biological temperament, values and attitudes, and self-narratives establish a *personal context* and such features of social environments as culture, gender, evolutionary history, ethnicity, and immediate social situations establish a *social context*. These contexts serve as *inputs* which get integrated and played out in agendas. And just as it was heuristically useful to think of agendas for action as varying in their levels, we also find it useful to think of these personal and social inputs to agendas as varying in their levels, although here the dimension underlying this variation in level is perhaps better viewed as one of globality/specificity, with features of persons and of social environments conceptualized at varying levels of breadth or abstractness (e.g., having a high-strung temperament versus possessing a self-schema as an anxious per-

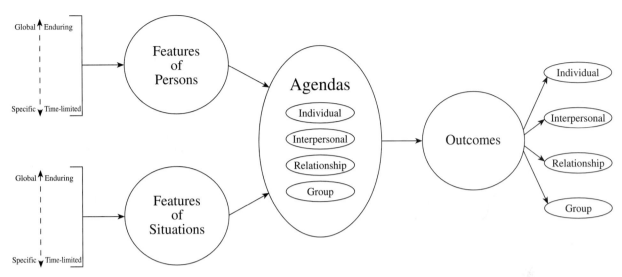

FIGURE 1   The Functionalist Strategy for Personality and Social Behavior.

son) and relative permanence or enduringness (e.g., cultural frameworks change more slowly than do situational prescriptions). Here, we consider first features of persons in varying degrees of globality/specificity that serve as input to agendas-outcomes at all levels and then features of social contexts that also vary in globality/specificity and serve as inputs to all levels of agendas-outcomes.

Inputs: Features of Persons

Features of persons that serve as input to agendas vary rather strikingly in their globality or specificity, both in the expanse of situations to which they apply and in their presumed stability as characteristics of the person (Buss & Cantor, 1989; McAdams & Emmons, 1995). Some of these features of persons can be thought of in relatively broad-gauged terms as decontextualized inputs, such as those implied in the Big Five model, in various temperament models, in classic motive taxonomies, and in many theories of personal value systems (Caspi & Bem, 1990; Schwartz, 1992). Others, by contrast, are more explicitly linked to places and times in a person's life, such as is often true of self-conceptions, conditional traits, significant-other schemas, and identity narratives (Andersen & Cole, 1990; A. Aron, E. N. Aron, & Smollan, 1992; Banaji & Prentice, 1994; Gordon, 1968; McAdams, 1992, 1995; Ogilvie & Ashmore, 1991; Sande, Goethals, & Radloff, 1988; Wright & Mischel, 1987).

Regardless of how global or specific, enduring or transitory, features of persons serve as input to agendas at multiple levels. As such, one can consider as inputs to *individual* agendas of self-development, for example, a variety of per-

son features from internalized value systems of a culture to highly specific remembered selves (Cousins, 1989; Markus & Kitayama, 1991; Singer & Salovey, 1988). Inputs to *interpersonal agendas* might come from rather global characteristic orientations toward social stimulation (e.g., openness to experience, affective reactivity or extraversion [McCrae, 1996; McCrae & Costa, 1985b; Eysenck, 1973]) or, instead, from styles of interacting with specific others (e.g., authority figures, members of the opposite sex [Leary & Kowalski, 1990]). Those features of persons that provide inputs to *relationship* agendas might well include rather global and enduring orientations, such as attachment styles (Baldwin, Fehr, Keedian, Seidal, & Thomson, 1993; Feeney & Noller, 1990; Hazan & Shaver, 1987), relationship closeness (Berscheid, Snyder, & Omoto, 1989a, 1989b; Kelley et al., 1983), communal versus exchange orientations (Fiske, 1991; Markus & Kitayama, 1991), or they may again represent more delimited attitudes, habits of interaction (Christenson & Heavey, 1990; Filsinger & Thoma, 1988), and affective reactions to particular significant others in a person's life (Berscheid, 1983). And *group* level agendas will draw their inputs from features of persons that encourage or discourage membership, involvement, and group participation, ranging in globality from a person's level of political consciousness (Verba, Schlozman, & Brady, 1995), to their specific desire to fit in with a currently fashionable group (Snyder, 1987a).

Of course, it is easiest to think (as we did in the examples in the preceding paragraph) in terms of features of persons that somehow "match" in content the level of agenda, such as attachment styles for relationship agendas and political consciousness for group participation agendas. However, it is important to also consider that all kinds of features of persons, at varying levels, can and will serve as inputs to agendas at all levels. In this regard, for example, individual differences in affective reactivity (e.g., Larsen, 1987; Watson & Clark, 1984) may be as relevant to relationship agendas as are personal attachment styles (e.g., Hazan & Shaver, 1987), even though the latter has a more face valid connection to the relationship level of analysis. Or, attachment styles may well serve as personal constraints on group level agendas for participation even though they are typically derived from a close dyadic relationship (e.g., insecure attachment may make for less than easy involvement in a group [Simpson, 1992]). In other words, the personal inputs to agendas and outcomes are likely to vary not only in terms of the breadth and enduringness of the opportunities and constraints that they represent in agenda-setting and outcome pursuit, but also in the directness of the link to the ostensible focus of the agenda, whether at the individual, interpersonal, relationship, or group level of analysis.

Inputs: Features of Social Contexts

Features of social contexts that serve as inputs to agendas also vary in their globality/specificity and in their enduringness. On one hand, there are all manner of rules, roles, and norms that prescribe very specifically how individuals should act in particular places and at particular times (Deutsch & Gerard, 1955; Sherif, 1936). These prescriptions provide highly elaborate and time-delimited input to agendas. Consider, for example, the variety of specific behaviors viewed as appropriate or not appropriate for a girl or a boy to perform, as a function of the situation (e.g., boys can wear makeup in the theater, but not typically in other public settings). Yet these situationally specific social context inputs are also often mirrored in broader, more enduring societal structures such as those associated with class, race, gender, and geographical region, that also serve as input to agendas, and that are less likely to change rapidly (Argyle & Henderson, 1985; Eagly, 1987; Williams & Best, 1990; Zanna & Pack, 1975). In this regard, whereas the specific norms for gender-appropriate behavior may have loosened up in recent years (e.g., women as wine connoisseurs), national debates over the best ways to regulate the relations between the sexes at a more global or pervasive level still rage on (e.g., women in combat duty). In between, in terms of level of globality and enduringness, come the inputs provided by such features of social context as family structure, social network, work, and recreation (Veroff, 1983).

As described above for the personal contexts, inputs from social contexts have a sort of natural pairing with levels of agendas, at least when it comes to the relative ease of thinking of examples of inputs to agendas, even though this pairing may really be somewhat artificial in light of the multiple affordances and constraints on every agenda. As such, at the *individual* level, features of social context that can and do serve as inputs to agendas for action include role specifications and prescriptions of situationally "appropriate" or mandated behaviors associated with gender, age, ethnicity, and related roles. Clearly, these inputs overlap with the internalization of these constraints referred to as personal context inputs, suggesting that some inputs to agendas may have counterparts operating as both personal and social sources of opportunity and constraint. For example, a man striving to develop his self-image as a "feminist" may well be influenced in the moment both by his own internalized gender schema suggesting what is appropriate for all people, male or female, to be able to do, and by the evolving social norms modeled by his friends and by the media as appropriate for "liberated" men (e.g., Bem, 1981, 1984).

At the *interpersonal* level, features of social context that one naturally thinks of as providing inputs to agendas include the interaction contexts of one's social networks. Examples of these properties of interaction context are the status and resource differences that mark the participants to an interaction and that constitute sources of social power and influence (and ultimately control) of the agenda (Erber & Fiske, 1984; Fiske & Neuberg, 1990); as well as the social support and evaluative contexts provided by parties to social interaction (Schachter, 1959). Again, these features of context can and do vary greatly in breadth and enduringness. Consider, for example, how status and resource differences are structured on the one hand by very specific features of the context of an interaction, such as the placement of chairs in front of or behind a desk in an interview (Bargh & Gollwitzer, 1994) and on the other hand by more enduring structural constraints such as those associated with the relative position in a status hierarchy (Fiske, 1993).

At the *relationship* level, features of social context that provide sources of opportunity and constraint to individuals as they define and pursue agendas include the relatively long-lasting structuring influence of enduring roles such as parent, child, spouse, family member, as well as the somewhat more transitory and specific impact of roles such as date or coach or student. Similarly, at the *group* level, social contextual inputs to agendas for action can come from the specific roles available locally in a group, such as those offered by a teacher to students in a classroom (e.g., teachers encouraging collaborative group work [Aronson, Blaney, Stephan, Sikes, & Snapp, 1978; Slavin, 1985]) or from the broader frameworks for group participation set up at a more systemic level, such as that of the educational philosophy of a school system (e.g., the American educational system is organized along an individualist model [Hess et al., 1986]). Related, but at an even broader, *societal* level are political climate, societal structure, and cultural structure.

Despite this natural pairing of input and agenda, once again as noted above for personal contextual inputs, the opportunities and constraints afforded by the social environment have relevance for agenda-setting and pursuit at all levels. This state of affairs is illustrated clearly in findings emerging today in the field of cultural psychology which demonstrate the ways in which broad cultural frameworks for societal organization, such as the collectivist or individualist organization (Markus & Kitayama, 1991; Triandis, 1989, 1993), have impact not only in the expected way on group or societal level agendas (e.g., corporate climate and organization), but also shape agendas for self, social partnerships, and relationships (see Fiske, Kitayama, Markus, & Nisbett, 1998, in this *Handbook*).

Varying and Matching Levels of Analysis

In specifying features of persons and features of social contexts that can and do serve as inputs to all kinds of agendas for action, we have tried to show how it is important to look for inputs that vary in globality and enduringness. Several productive benefits accrue from taking this perspective.

First, with respect to features of persons and features of social contexts, it should be apparent that our functionalist strategy is applicable not just with the "big units" of personality and not just with the "big units" of social contexts. That is, ours is not just an analysis about the opportunities and constraints provided at the "big unit" level of culture, gender, and ethnicity on the social context side of the equation and at the "big unit" level of global, highly generalized dispositions or super-traits of personality on the personal context side of the equation.

Moreover, there is a clear and evident parallelism between levels (defined here with regard to globality) on the person side and on the situation side. For example, the Big Five dimensions of personality and features of culture and societal structure reside at a similar, global level of abstraction, and conditional trait units and situationally specific role requirements occupy a similar, lower level of abstraction. One benefit of this parallelism is that it can and does sensitize us to gaps in theorizing and in assessment of features of persons and of situations, that is, to places where a relative lack of attention to matters of theory or assessment either of persons or of situations provide an opportunity to engage in new theorizing and new assessment efforts.

For example, it seems to us that recently there has been a substantial move forward in considering the personal and situational contexts that afford or constrain agendas regulating the display of power in interpersonal interactions. Personal inputs such as those deriving from relatively global individual differences in need for power or in communal-exchange orientations have been examined in social contexts organized rather broadly along lines of outcome dependence or status hierarchies (e.g., Bargh et al., 1995; S. T. Fiske, 1993; Pryor, Giedd, & Williams, 1995). Seeing the value of parallelism in these investigations, it now becomes more likely that researchers will also move in parallel to a more "middle level" of analysis (Kelley, 1992). This level of analysis might involve, for example, considering the particular ways in which the agendas of interpersonal power are pursued differently in different life spheres, such as in intimate relationships rather than in work settings. Personal inputs might well implicate domain-specific personal orientations toward negotiating with romantic versus work partners (e.g., Stewart & Healy, 1989), and social inputs might involve the presence of different situational norms in the home or in the workplace, norms that encourage or discourage agendas for power (e.g., Veroff, 1983).

Thus, whereas it is useful to think of agendas and outcomes as varying in consort along a dimension from rather self-focused to group-focused, it is also important to allow for both personal and social contexts varying in globality and enduringness to provide input to all levels of agendas-outcomes. For example, in pursuit of outcomes related to individual happiness and well-being, individuals are likely to engage self-regulatory agendas, such as those implicated in mood regulation (e.g., Larsen, 1987; Larsen & Ketelaar, 1991; Nolen-Hoeksema, 1991; Rusting & Larsen, 1995). Such agendas primarily focus at the individual level even if they also ultimately involve other people in the process (e.g., telling others of one's achievements to make the most of a good mood; e.g., Langston, 1994).

Moreover, even when agendas and outcomes "reside" at the same level, the personal and social inputs to them may well vary in both content and globality. For example, in the case of the above-mentioned hedonist, possessing an acute sense of interpersonal empathy might well shape the form that pursuit of this rather self-oriented agenda takes (e.g., the hedonist might engage in false modesty in the face of a personal achievement, thereby preserving interpersonal face while still focusing the mind's eye on a good event [Goffman, 1959; Leary & Kowalski, 1990]). Similarly, on the social context side, one can easily imagine a level of input as broad as the organizational climate of a cooperative work team, that would constrain the individual level agendas of the hedonist. Hence, as far as inputs to the agenda-setting and agenda-pursuing processes go, there is likely to be much variety of levels of inputs from both the social and personal sides of the equation.

In fact, a distinct advantage of applying a functionalist strategy is that these layers of input to agendas for action become more obvious precisely because agendas serve to integrate personal and social inputs of differing degrees of globality. For example, think about relationship level agendas for forming and sustaining romantic attachments and the inputs on which they might draw. Such agendas might draw on (and, in fact, have been investigated in terms of) personal contexts of specific relevance to relationships, such as working models of attachment (Baldwin et al., 1993; Bowlby, 1982; Hazan & Shaver, 1987), and social contexts of similarly specific relevance to relationships, such as family structure (Lee & Stone, 1980). But, such agendas have *also* been found to implicate somewhat more global personal and social contextual inputs, such as generalized individual differences in intimacy motives and sociocultural structures that constrain the form that all public relationships will take (e.g., regulation of women's public behavior in Muslim countries). Although these layers of inputs complicate the picture that forms of the agenda-setting and agenda-pursuit process, they also provide a snapshot of social behavior that is far more textured, and thereby undoubtedly more realistic, than that obtained through analyses focused more narrowly on one or other level of analysis.

THE FUNCTIONALIST STRATEGY IN ACTION: THREE CASE EXAMPLES

At this point, it may be useful to illustrate the application of the functionalist approach as an investigative strategy for studying personality and social behavior. A functionalist analysis of personality and social behavior takes as its charge the examination of social behavior from many different angles, integrating the traditional concerns of psychologists from different corners of the field—personologists focusing on characteristics of individuals, social psychologists on characteristics of situations, organizational psychologists on organizations, and cultural psychologists on cultures, as well as clinicians concerned with human adjustment and biopsychologists investigating human evolution.

As we have suggested, the building blocks of the functionalist approach to inquiry in personality and social behavior are personal and social inputs, the agendas that integrate these inputs, and the outcomes in pursuit of which people set and follow agendas. We have further suggested that inputs, agendas, and outcomes can be defined at multiple levels of analysis. However, we have also argued that there will tend to be a matching between levels of agendas and levels of outcomes, such that people most likely will define their agendas in terms of outcomes to be pursued, with these agendas and outcomes varying in tandem along a dimension from rather self-focused to rather group-focused, and then shape agendas that will help them progress toward these outcomes, and do so by drawing on and integrating features of themselves and of their social worlds from diverse levels of these inputs, with these inputs varying in their globality and enduringness.

Thus, a functionalist strategy takes as its "food for thought" agendas and outcomes that vary across levels of analysis that all too often have been examined in isolation,

and conceptualizes personal and social contexts in ways that naturally cross the boundaries of our subdisciplines. This integrating role is perhaps easiest to see when a functionalist strategy is applied to characterize social behavior in terms of the problems that most concern individuals as social actors. For this purpose, we will consider as illustrative problem areas, three examples chosen to systematically sample the domains of thinking, feeling, and acting that have traditionally covered much of psychological inquiry. In particular, we will consider people's attempts: *to know and to understand themselves, to feel social connectedness and to stave off loneliness, to participate in society and thereby counter alienation and inaction.*

Taking this problem-focused approach occurs naturally in a functionalist strategy because, as a strategy of inquiry, it focuses empirical and conceptual attention on people's agendas and the outcomes for which they strive in pursuit of those agendas. It is also in the application of this strategy in a problem-focused way that the boundaries between basic and practical research are crossed most easily, as we consider the benefits and the costs for individuals of setting particular agendas and pursuing relevant outcomes in particular ways as they strive to address these common human problems.

In illustrating the functionalist strategy with these problem-focused examples of thinking, feeling, and acting, we will first try to show how this strategy of inquiry provides a layered view of social behavior as deriving from multiple and varying agendas, which draw on and integrate diverse features of persons and of situations as inputs, and with diverse outcomes, some good and some bad for individuals, dyads, relationships, and groups. We chose these particular problem areas because, having each pursued a functionalist approach in them, we are personally familiar with literature that takes such a perspective on individuals' quests to understand the self, to belong, and to participate in society (e.g., Cantor, 1994; Snyder, 1993). However, although we will be sampling from large literatures in each case example, we fully anticipate that there will be gaps in the existing literature revealed by this exercise. But, these gaps really should come as no surprise, given that even in these areas the existing literatures were not necessarily generated with a functionalist strategy in mind. To the contrary, the gaps revealed by this approach can and will serve as signals of new research agendas to be charted and new inquiries to be conducted. Moreover, although we have at times found it convenient to illustrate this functionalist approach in areas in which we have pursued empirical research (research, not incidentally, guided by functionalist perspectives), it is our hope that readers will be motivated by this exercise to consider applying a functionalist strategy in their own familiar domains of inquiry about personality and social behavior.

Ultimately, and in the spirit of cumulative inquiry building on the foundations provided by previous treatments of personality and social behavior, we also hope to illustrate how the concerns of the three strategies for studying personality and social behavior outlined earlier by Snyder and Ickes (1985) are addressed in the functionalist strategy's analysis of personal and social inputs to people's agendas and in their pursuit of relevant outcomes. That is, in keeping with our previous focus on the dispositional, interactional, and situational strategies as concerned with the sources of regularities and consistencies in social behavior, we will argue that the focus of the *dispositional strategy* is represented largely in the personal context for agendas and outcomes, that the emphasis of the *situational strategy* on regularities in the features of situations that attract individuals is given form in the situational context for agendas, and finally that the agenda integrates these features of persons and features of situations, much as the lock-and-key metaphor of the *interactional strategy* suggests. We strive to convince readers, therefore, that not only are these long-standing investigative traditions and concerns well-represented here, but that they are given explicit form in this functionalist strategy in ways that highlight the interdependence of persons and situations and the movement back and forth between personal and social inputs in the construction of social behavior.

In fact, as an approach built upon the successes of the dispositional, interactional, and situational strategies for revealing regularities in the relations between personality and social behavior, the functionalist strategy holds out the hope of improving our ability to predict systematic patterns of interdependence of personal and social inputs in the construction of social behavior. It does so by following several prescriptions integral to examining personality and social behavior with a functionalist strategy. First, this strategy asks problem-focused or task-focused questions about personality and social behavior—*what is the person trying to do, how does he or she do it, and to what end are these efforts taken.* Therefore, as we shall see in the following examples, the strategy considers personal and social inputs as they interactively serve as *affordances* (both positive and negative) for individuals' agendas. Second, recognizing that there are multiple levels of agendas and outcomes that an individual might be pursuing, and that the pursuit process has an extended time course in which agendas and outcomes evolve and change, the functionalist strategy looks for the personal and social inputs most likely to map the functionally relevant agendas of a person at a particular time in a given social context. Third, since agendas are pursued with outcomes in mind, the analysis should not end with behavior; instead, behavior should be examined as a conduit that moves a person closer to or farther away from desired outcomes. Accordingly, the objective of the functionalist strategy is to explicate the systematic associations between salient agendas, relevant inputs, and

desired outcomes, as they interact to guide the construction of more or less functional social behavior.

Knowing the Self and the Search for Identity

Typically, matters of self-knowledge and identity are thought of as intrapsychic phenomena, operating and functioning within individuals (Baumeister, 1987; Greenwald & Pratkanis, 1984; James, 1890/1968). In accord with this intrapsychic perspective on the self, researchers have generated a considerable body of theoretical and empirical literature to document the largely cognitive processes of self-reflection (Dixon & Swann, 1993; Duval & Wicklund, 1972), self-inference, self-perception (Bem, 1972; Chaiken & Baldwin, 1981; Fazio, 1987; Miller, Brickman, & Bolen, 1975; Schlenker & Trudeau, 1990), and self-attribution (Bradley, 1978) that are involved in knowing the self and forming an identity (e.g., Kihlstrom & Cantor, 1984; Klein & Loftus, 1993). However, it is becoming clearer, with the cumulative products of generations of research and theorizing, that matters of self-knowledge and individual identity are very much affected by social considerations, that personal identity emerges in the context of the individual's involvement in a social world, one involving social interactions, social roles (Bem, 1984; Goffman, 1959), social relationships (A. Aron, E. N. Aron, Tudor, & Nelson, 1991; Baldwin, 1992; Baldwin, Carrell, & Lopez, 1990), social structures (Tajfel, 1982), and social group memberships (e.g., Banaji & Prentice, 1994). This idea of the social nature of self-knowledge is one, of course, that surfaces historically in classic symbolic interactionist views of the looking glass self (Cooley, 1902/1964; Mead, 1934). More recently, it surfaces in contemporary concerns with the interpersonal origins of inferential judgments about one's own personal attributes and identity (e.g., Neisser, 1993; Tomasello, 1993) and with the representation of social group identities within the self-system (e.g., Deaux, 1993; Turner, Oakes, Haslam, & McGarty, 1994). It is an idea that surfaces in the growing realization that there is a cultural context for self and identity as well, with self and identity reflecting such cultural considerations as collectivism versus individualism and interdependence versus independence (Cousins, 1989; Markus & Kitayama, 1991, 1994; Miller, 1988; Triandis, 1989, 1993). And, as we shall see, it is an idea that meshes well with the functionalist strategy of considering multiple levels of agendas for action.

From the perspective of the functionalist strategy for personality and social behavior, the foregoing considerations suggest the benefits of considering multiple levels of agendas associated with the tasks of knowing the self and forming an identity, and with systematically looking at features of persons and features of situations as inputs that provide interacting opportunity structures for the setting of agendas in pursuit of diverse outcomes. Let us first look at multiple levels of agendas for self and identity and the desired outcomes of pursuing them, and then at the inputs to these agendas. In doing so, we draw selectively for illustration on the existing literature, with an attempt to organize it guided by the schematic representation of the functionalist strategy which we presented earlier in Figure 1.

What, then, from the functionalist perspective, are the *agendas* for self and identity? At the individual level of agendas for self and identity are the activities of self-inference, self-perception, self-attribution, self-narration, and self-memory that have been the targets of intense theoretical and empirical investigation in personality and social psychology (e.g., Cantor & Kihlstrom, 1987; McAdams, 1993; Singer & Salovey, 1993). Agendas for knowing the self and forming an identity at the interpersonal level are revealed in research on how social interaction provides opportunities for reflected appraisal and social comparison to contribute to individuals' identities (Arkin, 1980; Leary & Kowalski, 1990), for individuals to use strategies and tactics of self-presentation to create images in the eyes of their beholders and thereby socially fashion self-identities (Arkin, 1980; Jones & Pittman, 1982; Leary & Kowalski, 1990; Schlenker, 1980; Schlenker & Weigold, 1992; Tedeschi & Norman, 1985), and for self-verification and self-affirmation processes to be used to bolster and shore up identities (Steele, 1988; Swann, 1984). In the context of ongoing and longer term relationships, considerable research reveals how the processes of entering into and maintaining relationships that help create, support, and sustain identities constitute relationship level agendas for self and identity (e.g., A. Aron et al., 1991; Baldwin, 1992). Finally, individuals' agendas for self and identity often concern the social or collective identity obtained through membership in social categories and involvement in social groups (e.g., Brewer, 1991; Brewer & Gardner, 1996; Deaux, 1993).

In accord with our functionalist theorizing, not only are there multiple levels of agendas involved in the quest for self and identity, but these agendas can be graded on a dimension of the number of other actors involved in the pursuit of these agendas, from the solitary pursuit of individual level agendas (e.g., self-reflection is a solitary activity), to the involvement of single other actors in dyadic interaction in interpersonal level agendas, to the involvement of others in sustained, deeper relationships at the relationship level of agendas, and to the involvement of multiple other actors in groups and organizations at the group level of agendas.

Following the functionalist strategy's emphasis on agendas as in pursuit of outcomes, it is critical next to consider the nature of the *outcomes* typically associated with pursuing agendas for self and identity at these different levels. First, of course, are the personal narratives, the elaborated self-concepts, the remembered selves, that come, hopefully, as a consequence of the search for self-understanding and self-clarity at the individual level (Gregg,

1995; McAdams, 1995; Singer, 1995). In this regard, the desired outcome is to see the self through a coherent, well-integrated, and clear story, script, or schema (Campbell & Lavellee, 1993; Donahue, Robins, Roberts, & John, 1993; Gregg, 1995). By contrast, an individual pursuing self and identity at an interpersonal level, one that implicates agendas for social comparison and social self-presentation, may well be more focused on enhancing the self and distancing from the undesired self (Ogilvie, 1987) through favorable comparisons (e.g., Taylor & Lobel, 1989; Wood, 1989) and flexible self-presentation (e.g., Snyder, 1979; Jones & Pittman, 1982), than on obtaining accurate feedback (e.g., Sedikides, 1993). At the relationship level of agenda pursuit, self-understanding may not come from gaining insight into the "real" self or from comparing the self favorably to others, but rather from seeing the self as connected to and belonging with another (Baumeister & Leary, 1995) and finding solidarity and interdependence (e.g., Markus & Cross, 1990), if not codependence. Finally, this self-through-other connection is extended further at the group level of agenda for self and identity, when the self takes its definition and its strength from the ties that bind individuals with the collective, promising desired outcomes such as collective esteem (e.g., Crocker, Luhtanen, Blaine, & Broadnax, 1994), value affirmation (e.g., Lyndon & Zanna, 1990), commitment rather than alienation and anomie (Brickman, 1987), and an optimum degree of identification with and differentiation from the group (Brewer, 1991).

Considering these multiple levels of agendas for self and identity, and the quite different outcomes for which one strives in trying to understand the self at each level, allows us then to organize the analysis of personal and social inputs in terms of the features of persons and features of situations most likely to afford the setting of agendas and the pursuing of outcomes at a given level. These features, varying in globality, enduringness, and abstractness, serve as opportunity structures, residing in the person or in the situations, but coordinated as they interactively shape individuals' agendas for self and identity.

With respect to *features of persons,* there are those likely to afford the setting of individual level agendas (from relatively global, enduring features such as the traits of self-certainty and need for closure to more specific and probably time-limited ones such as personal projects to define one's true beliefs [Emmons, 1986; Little, 1989; Pelham, 1991; Sorrentino & Hewitt, 1984; Webster & Kruglanski, 1994; Zirkel & Cantor, 1990]). Other features of persons are more likely to guide the formation of interpersonal level agendas for identity (e.g., the need for power, self-monitoring [Fleeson, 1992; Snyder, 1979; Winter, 1973]), or relationship level agendas (varying again from relatively enduring qualities such as an insecure attachment style or a heightened need for connectedness to more particularistic features associated with the relationship schemas that individuals hold with and about significant others in their lives [Andersen & Cole, 1990; Collins & Read, 1994; Hazan & Shaver, 1987]). Yet other features may be more conducive to understanding the self through groups and collectives (e.g., being marked by a specific personal stigma or disability; minority status; internalizations of global cultural and societal prescriptions [Crocker & Major, 1989; Frable, 1993; Markus & Kitayama, 1991; Markus & Oyzerman, 1989]).

With regard to *features of situations* that serve as sources of opportunity and constraint in agendas for identity, a tour of the literature suggests that these features too can be viewed and categorized along a continuum, starting with those most readily thought of as affordances for personal level agendas (e.g., age-graded norms that encourage adolescents to self-reflect and to strive for individualism [Higgins & Eccles-Parsons, 1983; Zirkel & Cantor, 1990]), and moving to those features of situations that encourage individuals to define themselves in terms of their dyadic or interpersonal contexts (including the influence of one's interaction partners as sources of reflected appraisal, self-verification, self-affirmation, and behavioral confirmation [Snyder, 1992; Steele, 1988; Swann, 1987]). Then, moving on to those features of situations most readily thought of as conducive to thinking of oneself as being defined through one's relationships with other people (including the influence of ongoing relationships and roles, and the opportunities they provide, such as those of parents and children and the construction of identities through dialogue and questioning [Miller, Potts, Fung, Hoogstra, & Mintz, 1990]; as well as the press of age-graded norms for connectedness and generativity [McAdams, 1993; Stewart & Healy, 1992; Zirkel, 1992]). And, finally coming to these features of situations best seen as affording group level agendas (including the relatively specific and time-bounded demographic composition of classrooms and workplaces that influence the spontaneous self-concepts that emerge in their members [McGuire & McGuire, 1981]; the somewhat less transient social categories identified by social identity theory as riveting the individual's attention on social aspects of self [Turner et al., 1994]; and the relatively more long-lasting affordances represented in the collectivistic or individualistic structure of societies and cultures [Sampson, 1988; Shweder & Bourne, 1991]).

A central tenet of the functionalist perspective on personality and social behavior is the intimate interplay between and among these inputs, agendas, and outcomes. For example, many of the features of persons and features of situations listed above constitute matching affordances for agendas about the self and identity (e.g., attachment styles and parent-child relationship roles). As such, the lock-and-key metaphor of the interactionist strategy is given concrete form in the functionalist analysis. However, there is also room for the asymmetric interaction of these personal

and social inputs, tipping the balance either toward the features of persons as in the dispositional strategy (e.g., low self-monitoring individuals may be unlikely to let even the most powerful of interpersonal situations define the self) or the features of situations as in the situationist strategy (e.g., high self-monitoring individuals may become who they are in accord with the social affordances of the interpersonal situations in which they choose to live). What is important in this strategy, however, is the assumption that agenda-setting is a dynamic process, one in which individuals' agendas change, and accordingly so too does the relative influence of and relationship between personal and social inputs. For example, low self-monitors may come to be as much defined by their interpersonal interactions as are high self-monitors to the extent that they selectively associate with others who affirm their self-values (Snyder, 1987a). Ultimately, the emphasis in the functionalist strategy is not on any static equation or balance of power, but rather on the ways in which individuals work with and within the opportunity structures of their dispositions and their situations to pursue their agendas.

Furthermore, the dynamic is made more complex by the multiple levels of agendas implicated in any given process. For example, even an individual intent on private self-reflection and self-examination, such as a prototypical low self-monitor who wants to be true to him- or herself, may well set interpersonal level agendas for self and identity, in the service of moving toward the individual level outcome of self-clarity. Those who study personal narratives write frequently of the centrality of the dialogic self, one defined through private self-reflection but of a very interactive, interpersonal sort (Hermans, 1992). Consequently, it becomes even more critical than ever to ask not just about a static slice of behavior, but instead to focus on the agendas and outcomes at the heart of the episode. The low self-monitor may use private dialogues and private audiences (Baldwin & Holmes, 1987) to move closer to a "real" self, whereas the high self-monitor may be more likely to look for social affirmation and to stay more rooted therefore to the interpersonal level of agenda for self and identity. In other words, a trademark of this strategy is the focus on behavior as a means to an end, and the questioning of just how successful an individual is at moving closer to that end, even if it often forms an everchanging target.

Seeking Connectedness and Avoiding Loneliness

As our second problem-focused example of viewing existing theory and research, and charting new research agendas from the perspective of the functionalist strategy for personality and social behavior, we sample from the domain of "feelings" or functioning in the affective domain, looking at a problem that concerns many, if not most, people as social actors, namely, the interrelated tasks of seeking feelings of belongingness and avoiding feelings of loneliness (e.g., Baumeister & Leary, 1995). Many theorists, writing from the diverse perspectives of evolutionary psychology (e.g., Caporael, Dawes, Orbell, & van de Kragt, 1989), social psychology (Myers & Diener, 1995), health psychology (Ryff, 1989), and clinical psychology (Brickman & Coates, 1987), emphasize these strivings for social connectedness as fundamental sources of affective well-being and social adjustment. Of course, although much of the personality and social psychology literature on this topic has focused on the need for intimacy and human attachment as fulfilled in close friendships and intimate relationships (see, e.g., Hazan & Shaver, 1987; McAdams, Healy, & Krause, 1984; Reis & Patrick, 1996), social connectedness can come in many forms, from the solitary reminiscences of self-with-other (Baldwin, 1992) to the feelings of belonging that can accompany participation in social groups and communities (Egan, 1984). Hence, it is a particularly fertile arena of human social behavior within which to examine the diverse agendas that individuals set and the outcomes they seek differentially in the common pursuit of feelings of belongingness (Baumeister & Leary, 1995).

As we did with our example about self and identity, we begin with the schematic representation of the functionalist strategy for personality and social behavior. Its focus is on the integrating role of agendas, into which features of persons and features of situations serve as inputs, and from which flow diverse outcomes. We then systematically work our way through the multiple levels of agendas, outcomes, and inputs (see Figure 1).

Although it might be an exaggeration to characterize the extensive literature on intimacy and loneliness as being particularly concerned with the states and traits of individuals and their friendships and close relationships, or the lack thereof, the functionalist strategy for personality and social behavior suggests that rather than, or at least in addition to, trying to understand when and why and to what extent people feel lonely or experience intimacy in their relationships, we examine the *agendas* that people construct and pursue to stave off loneliness and to fulfill a broader need to belong (for a related perspective, see Rook, 1984, 1988). Thus, and in keeping with the integrating role of agendas in the functionalist strategy, we first work our way through the levels at which agendas for seeking connection and avoiding loneliness can be pursued by individuals and can be conceptualized and investigated by researchers.

When we think of individual level agendas in this domain, it is perhaps easiest to begin with a focus on what individuals try to do by and for themselves to feel connected to others and to forestall feelings of isolation and loneliness. Indeed, there have been attempts to catalog the specific strategies that individuals can and do use to avoid loneliness (e.g., Revenson, 1981). And recent writings on relational schemas and working models of relationships

(e.g., Baldwin, 1992; Hazan & Shaver, 1987; Collins & Read, 1994) suggest that the richly relational world of self and social knowledge provides a basis for self-focused strategies for seeking social belongingness and avoiding loneliness. In fact, many people's agendas in their day-to-day friendships may be distinctly self-focused (such as when friends and acquaintances provide an understanding of the way the world is and what the people who make up the world are like or when individuals seek out others of different or complementary attitudes and personality, thus providing a counterpoint to their own attributes and inclinations, as well as grist for self-exploration). Although these agendas may not seem on the surface to reflect a striving for connection and an avoidance of loneliness, theorists have long argued that the tasks of individuation and attachment are inextricably linked in human development (Bowlby, 1969; Erikson, 1950; Guisinger & Blatt, 1994), and therefore it would be strange if many of the agendas that individuals set for fulfilling a need to belong did not include a strong component of self-focused exploration (Epstein, 1994; Sanderson & Cantor, 1995). Relatedly, as House and Kahn (1985) argued persuasively, people often seek ostensibly *social* support for decidedly *personal* reasons, including obtaining instrumental help to reach their own goals of self-improvement and emotional reassurance to bolster flagging self-confidence (e.g., Harlow & Cantor, 1995).

Of course, avoiding loneliness and seeking belongingness can most readily be seen as agendas at the interpersonal and relationship levels of analysis, since agendas at these levels by definition involve other actors in their pursuit, and involvements with other people clearly have the potential to solve the problems of loneliness and connection. In fact, and perhaps not surprisingly, intimacy motivation is negatively related to wanting to be alone (McAdams & Constantian, 1983), which would suggest that intimacy motivation will propel people into social circumstances that would provide opportunities to pursue interpersonal and relationship level agendas.

At the interpersonal level of agendas, individuals may seek out friends and social interactions that serve to fulfill a general need to belong but that explicitly connect the self to others in particular ways. Typically, research on friendship has asked questions of the form, "Who is friends with whom?", seeking, often in somewhat mechanistic form, to identify such properties of potential or actual friends as their similarity ("birds of a feather flock together") and their complementarity ("opposites attract," "two halves of the same coin") to understand impersonal attraction and the formation of friendships. From the functionalist perspective on personality and social behavior, we suggest that it is helpful to move a step beyond such relatively static conceptions of friendship and attraction, to ask questions about the diverse initiating interpersonal agendas served by friendships—that is, to ask and answer questions about what specific forms of interpersonal connectedness people are seeking when they enter into friendships, what they are trying to do in their friendships, and what specific outcomes they are pursuing in the course of their friendships. For example, several different motivational agendas have been discussed in the relationship literature as likely to dispose people to seek particular kinds of friends (e.g., Snyder, 1992). Some people may choose friends with similar tastes and preferences because they can most easily feel connectedness with persons with whom they identify and with whom they can be themselves (e.g., Snyder, 1987a). Others may pursue more "asymmetric" friendships because they can best belong by controlling and "standing out," rather than merging and "standing in" (as in the case of insecure people in positions of authority surrounding themselves with deferential "yes-types" who flatter their sense of power and control; Jones & Pittman, 1982). Still others may enter friendships with persons who can most easily smooth the course of social interaction in particular life contexts (as in the case of individuals whose own social anxieties inhibit their experience of connectedness if they can not be with those skilled in facilitating the flow of the interaction [Thorne, 1987]).

This emphasis on the diverse interpersonal agendas served by friendships, in contrast to a focus on the properties of friendships, has an additional benefit; that benefit is the facilitation of consideration of the dynamic time course or evolution of individuals' agendas in friendships. Friendships represent the interaction of potentially divergent interpersonal agendas, as one partner looks for one outcome and the other perhaps seeks a different form of social connectedness, and so it is both important and informative to consider friendship as a social *process,* subject to the clashes and the convergences typical of such dynamic interactions (Hilton, 1997; Jones & Thibaut, 1958; Snyder, 1992, 1997; Snyder & Haugen, 1995). Moreover, knowing the interpersonal agendas of the interacting partners in a friendship may help substantially in foreshadowing events later on, such as predicting the kinds of activities that will characterize the friendship (e.g., Cantor, Mackie, & Lord, 1983-84; Setterlund & Niedenthal, 1993; Snyder, Gangestad, & Simpson, 1983) and the types of events that will likely disrupt the friendship and threaten its survival (Snyder & Simpson, 1984).

At the level of sustained, ongoing, and close relationships, investigators can examine the extent to which the prototypical relationship agenda to achieve belongingness and to avoid loneliness by seeking intimacy and interdependence serves as the primary "cement" that bonds partners together and sustains a relationship, and may even perpetuate it in the face of other threats to the survival of the relationship (Kelley et al., 1983; McAdams, 1989; Reis & Shaver, 1988). There is, in fact, a large literature cen-

tered on the processes surrounding the creation of intimacy in close relationships (see Reis & Patrick, 1996). Relationships built on such agendas are those most likely to include intense, regular, and reciprocal self-disclosure and social support between partners (although both self-disclosure and social support can serve other more self-focused agendas, e.g., Miller & Read, 1987). Moreover, those who pursue intimacy of this sort may well turn ordinary friendships into close relationships by virtue of their commitment to this agenda. In this regard, there is evidence that individuals high in intimacy motivation are more likely to pursue friendships involving higher levels of self-disclosure and more concern for the well-being of their friends, both of which are plausible mechanisms for reducing loneliness and increasing intimacy through relationships (e.g., McAdams, Healy, & Krause, 1984).

Although the primary thrust of relationship level agendas for securing social connectedness and avoiding loneliness may well reflect strivings for intimacy, individuals surely enter and sustain close relationships with other purposes in mind as well. Some of these purposes are probably best thought of as individual level agendas even though they may be played out in close relationships, for example, those of self-exploration noted earlier (e.g., Sanderson & Cantor, 1995); or perhaps those of understanding and validation, identified by Reis and Patrick (1996) as key goals of intimate social exchange. However, we suspect that there are other more strictly relationship level agendas that have received less attention because of the relative predominance of an intimacy model in the literature on close relationships. For example, the literature in evolutionary psychology suggests alternative agendas implicated in human mating and sexual relationships (Buss, 1989; Buss & Schmitt, 1993; Gangestad & Simpson, 1990); and the growing clinical literature on codependence suggests yet other relationship agendas. Understanding the diverse ways in which individuals define their own need to belong through close relationships seems to us to be an as yet not fully explored area of an otherwise rich research literature (Baumeister & Leary, 1995).

Finally, when taking the perspective of group level agendas, the functionalist strategy suggests that there may be productive gains from examining the ways that individuals use membership in groups and organizations—and their participation in the affairs of their communities, states, and nations—as strategies to find social connectedness and thereby avoid loneliness and alienation (Brickman, 1987; Durkheim, 1933). In this regard, a stock in trade of the "Dear ——" advice columns in the newspaper to those who write in search of advice for how to shed their loneliness is to join a club or an organization where they can meet others of like interests, and perhaps even contribute to a worthy cause at the same time. In fact, research on the motivations that prompt people to serve as volunteers reveals that, among the diverse motivations that dispose people to engage in this form of prosocial action, are motivations associated with meeting new people, making new friends, and (presumably) feeling less lonely (e.g., Clary et al., in press; Omoto & Snyder, 1995). Similarly, research on the determinants of civic participation has revealed that such participation is associated with, and perhaps motivated by, desires for the social gratifications and feelings of connectedness with others (and, by inference, lesser feelings of loneliness) associated with participation in civic groups, organizations, and social movements (e.g., Verba, Schlozman, & Brady, 1995). And, approaching from the other direction, individuals sometimes choose their friendships specifically for their strategic value in helping to gain entry into important reference groups, as well as to fit in and to get along with those in these groups. In fact, recent writings in evolutionary psychology have begun to place more stock than in prior literature on these group level manifestations of sociality, positing cooperativeness, group loyalty, and adherence to group norms as significant assets in social life (e.g., Caporael et al., 1989; Caporael & Brewer, 1991).

What, then, are the *inputs* to these different agendas for seeking social connectedness and avoiding loneliness and social isolation? A wide array of *features of persons* can serve as inputs to these agendas, helping to identify those individuals who will be likely to construct agendas for belongingness primarily at the individual, interpersonal, relationship, or group levels. Some of these features of persons are relatively global and presumably enduring aspects of an individual's orientation toward the social world. For example, in considering the prototypical relationship level agendas for intimacy, motivational styles, such as the need for intimacy (e.g., McAdams, 1989), and attachment styles developed at a young age but presumed to endure for some time (e.g., Bartholomew & Horowitz, 1991; Brennan & Shaver, 1995; Collins & Read, 1990; Hazen & Shaver, 1987), would certainly inform both the intensity and content of intimacy strivings; as would gender, which seems to influence preferences rather than capacities for intimacy (e.g., Reis, Senchak, & Solomon, 1985) and the setting of intimacy goals (e.g., Buss, 1989; Buss & Schmitt, 1993; Langan-Fox, 1991) in ways that might lead toward different kinds of relationship level agendas for men and women; and developmental capacities for intimacy (e.g., Levitz-Jones & Orlofsky, 1985). Yet other dispositional features of persons might be more likely to suggest individual level agendas (for example, those high in need for cognition may seek social contact with an agenda of better understanding the world; those with low self-esteem or low self-certainty may strive to verify and/or bolster the self via social interactions and acquaintanceships; Swann, Pelham, & Krull, 1989); whereas other dispositions may encourage striving for connectedness at the interpersonal level (for example, high self-monitors seem to choose friends on the basis of their ability to facilitate the enactment of particular

social roles; Snyder, 1987a). In the same vein, some relatively enduring features of persons may incline individuals toward social connectedness at the group level, such as the cluster of dispositions concerned with social and group approval (e.g., need for approval, fear of negative evaluation, authoritarianism).

It is tempting to think of the features of persons that contribute to agendas for social connectedness as primarily enduring properties of persons, such as those in the above examples, that make individuals more or less permanently suitable as partners in certain kinds of relationships and participants in certain social contexts or groups. In fact, much of the literature on, for example, friendships and relationships, takes such an approach. However, the functionalist strategy suggests an additional look at some of the relatively less enduring features of persons, such as particular relational schemas or current personal projects or newly articulated possible selves, that may serve in the moment as affordances for pursuing social relations with individual, interpersonal, relationship, or group level agendas in mind. Expanding the analysis to include these more mutable features of persons is particularly appropriate in this domain because strivings for social connectedness are carried out over time, typically in an interpersonal context, and are thereby subject to the pressures of the social dynamic (Reis & Shaver, 1988; Snyder, 1992). Even those engaged in close relationships may evolve different agendas, some more self-focused and others more likely to encourage interdependence and intimacy, over the course of time as a function of their own and their partners' current concerns (e.g., Cantor & Malley, 1991).

Similarly, when it comes to *features of situations* as inputs to agendas, it is productive to examine them along a continuum from the relatively enduring contexts (such as the macro-contexts of culture and community that differentially encourage relatively more individual or collective agendas for social connectedness [Sampson, 1988]) to the more time-bound features of life environments (such as age-graded norms that encourage adolescents to move slowly from group to relationship pursuits and older adults to move from the intimate relationships of adulthood to the group participation of old age; Harlow & Cantor, 1996; Ryff, 1987; Sanderson & Cantor, 1995). In between, we have the opportunity structures provided by people's social networks and social contacts (such as the opportunities for interaction and the choices of interaction partners afforded by one's current social environment, including the matching of intimacy potential of situations with the intimacy motives of the individual [e.g., Woike, 1994; Woike & Aronoff, 1992]; and the matching of styles of disclosure between interactional partners [e.g., Miller & Kenny, 1986]), and by their set of significant relationships (such as the opportunities and constraints provided by existing and ongoing relationships to seek intimacy and avoid loneliness, including differences in the psychological closeness of relationships [e.g., Berscheid et al., 1989a, b]; and in the intimacy goals of partners in a close relationship [e.g., Sanderson & Cantor, 1997]).

Once again, these features of situations are best construed as affordances that encourage or constrain the setting of diverse agendas for social connectedness, and their differential enduringness is then best seen as suggesting a time-line for the influence of the affordance. For example, two features that differ in enduringness may still conspire to influence the setting of the same agenda for social connection, as when a sudden absence from a parent or caregiver induces a young child to retreat to a defensive, self-protective agenda similar to that induced by a more enduring and persistent regime of inadequate or unreliable parenting or caregiving (Bowlby, 1969, 1982; Hazen & Shaver, 1987). However, the time-line of influence will be critically shaped by the relative mutability of the situational context within which the person continues to pursue social connections across the life course (e.g., Sroufe, 1996).

And, finally, if it is the case that agendas for social connnection can take these many forms, especially over the life course, and in line with changing personal and situational inputs, then it is also the case that we must look carefully for the different *outcomes* as a function of pursuing those diverse agendas. Some of these outcomes are rather straightforwardly connected to the general need to belong (Baumeister & Leary, 1995). For example, intimacy motivation, as it is typically played out in close, sustained relationships and in intimate friendships, is correspondingly likely to produce positive affect (e.g., warmth, friendliness, trust, happiness) and closeness to others. Among the outcomes that accrue to individuals motivated to seek intimacy are more interpersonal thoughts and positive affect experienced in social situations (e.g., McAdams & Constantian, 1983). Moreover, the quest for intimacy seems to bring with it greater feelings of happiness and gratification in women and a lack of feelings of strain and uncertainty in men (McAdams & Bryant, 1987). In the longer terms these effects may accumulate to produce lasting consequences; indeed, Zeldow, Daugherty, and McAdams (1988) have found that, over the course of the college years, individuals high in intimacy motivation (and correspondingly low on power motives) had the highest levels of well-being and, over an even longer slice of the life course, McAdams and Vaillant (1982) have found that, among men at least, high intimacy motivation at age 30 was predictive of better social and emotional adjustment 17 years later.

Other outcomes associated with agendas for social connection, however, may not be as transparently derived from the general motivation to find closeness and interdependence. For example, when an individual pursues connection with many different people in the service of exploring the self, then the desired outcomes may be those that affirm

a distinct rather than a merged self (e.g., Sanderson & Cantor, 1995). And even when the agenda is one that draws the self closer to others, the outcomes may not be subsumed always under the rubric of intimacy or interdependence (Acitelli & Duck, 1987). At the interpersonal level, those who seek social connection with partners especially skillful and good at keeping an interaction flowing smoothly may themselves become particularly adept at being sensitive, responsive, and conforming to the interpersonal expectations of their interaction partners (e.g., Snyder & Haugen, 1995). Whereas, for those whose friendships confirm asymmetric power relationships, their interpersonal agendas may hone the skill for "staying on top" (e.g., S. T. Fiske, 1993). By contrast, the outcomes most pleasurably associated with group level agendas for belongingness may be those that affirm (free of conflict or even intense emotion) one's secure place in the group, which may be far less observable as individuals stand in with, rather than stand out against, others in the collective.

In other words, in line with the diverse agendas of sociality come diverse aspects of social well-being. When the agenda is to understand how the world works, then *sustaining* a relationship may not matter; when it is to find intimacy then *relationship duration* becomes of paramount concern. When the agenda is to gain *interpersonal control* then the social connectedness that comes from *fitting in* (being a cog in the group's wheel) will not satisfy. The same can be said of the *undesired* outcomes associated with different agendas for social connectedness. When the quest is for smoothly flowing interactions, then *conflict* may be more disruptive than when it is for interpersonal control. When people desire to be "one with the collective" they may be less comfortable with *intense* emotionality than when intimacy with a close other is the strived for outcome. As we have noted several times already, and as these examples serve to underscore, the functionalist strategy forces a close examination of the many ends to which people with different agendas (want to and do not want to) come; asking, in this case, not just whether a person finds connection and avoids loneliness, but *how* this is accomplished and *to what ends*. In fact, we see as a distinct benefit of this strategy, greater attention being paid in the future to a finely tuned collection of measures, those that reveal the multiple channels on which social well-being can be played.

Participating in Society and Solving the Problem of Inaction

As our third and final problem-focused example, we turn to the domain of "action" or functioning in the behavioral domain, and look at issues associated with individuals participating in society, either on their own or as members of groups and organizations, to address some of the problems that confront individuals and society. As we have done with our examples in the domains of thinking and feeling, we will be guided in our considerations by our schematic representation of the functionalist strategy for understanding personality and social behavior to examine agendas for action, their associated outcomes, and the inputs to these agendas (see Figure 1).

We begin with the challenge of citizen participation and the accompanying problem of inaction. It has been argued that citizen participation—people learning the habits of recycling to help protect and preserve the environment, neighbors watching out for each other to reduce crime, activists organizing for civil and human rights, voters going to the polls so that their voices will be heard in elections, volunteers offering their services to help others in need—are essential to solving many of the world's problems, many of which are fundamentally human problems, problems caused by the actions of humans and problems that will require the actions of humans to solve them (Boyte, 1991). But, if citizen participation is part of the human solution to human problems, then the accompanying *problem of inaction* must be recognized and solved.

What is the problem of inaction? Although we live in a country that was founded on the premise that inherent in the concept of freedom was the freedom to participate in the public realm (in the affairs of community, state, and nation), the facts are that rates of participation are low, whether participation is indexed by voting (surely one of the least effortful ways of participating in the affairs of society, yet barely half of eligible voters cast their ballots in presidential elections, and that rate has been declining steadily), joining civic and community organizations (a declining rate of participation symbolized by Putnam as the phenomenon of "bowling alone," with the decline in participation in organized bowling leagues as an indicator of declining membership in community groups and civic organizations), acting in the collective interests of society (even though more than 75 percent of Americans identify themselves as environmentalists, less than half even claim to participate in neighborhood recycling programs ["Household Waste," 1988; Kohut & Shriver, 1989]; and, even though at least three out of every four of us supports the idea of a nuclear freeze, the typical response to the threat of nuclear war is to do nothing at all [Fiske, 1987; Fiske, Pratto, & Pavelchak, 1983]).

What can be done to solve the problem of inaction? Some clues to answer this question are provided by the example set by people serving as volunteers, helping others in need by, for example, volunteering to be a tutor to an illiterate child or to assist a shut-in elderly person with household chores. Volunteer service, after all, is one way that people can help solve some of society's problems, including the problem of inaction. In fact, the values of volunteerism are widely shared (by margins of three to one, people believe that people should volunteer some of their

time to help other people) and practiced (in the United States, some 98.4 million adults engaged in volunteer work in 1989 with some 25.6 million adults devoting five or more hours each week to their volunteer service [Independent Sector, 1990]).

Even though when one first thinks of volunteerism, one tends to think at the societal level, with examples of millions of people giving their time and energy to address the problems of society, the fact is that, as much as volunteerism is a phenomenon of collective action, it is clearly also very much an individual phenomenon, with individuals identifying and acting on their own motivations to volunteer, seeking out and pursuing opportunities to volunteer that provide experiences that fulfill their motivations. That is, volunteerism as a form of civic participation is readily conceptualized in terms of agendas that individuals construct, drawing on the impetus provided by their own motivations and the opportunities to volunteer afforded them, and pursue in the course of the sustained ongoing helping behavior and prosocial action that is volunteerism.

As before, applying a functionalist strategy to the analysis of a problem area, in this case to the questions of why, how, and to what end do individuals volunteer and thereby overcome societal inaction, reveals possibilities for multiple levels of agendas. In fact, although theory and research on volunteerism has typically focused on sustained prosocial action in an interpersonal, relationship, or group context (for reviews, see Clary & Snyder, 1991; Omoto, Snyder & Berghuis, 1993; Piliavin & Charng, 1990), recent analyses have revealed a rich source of volunteerism in the individual level motivations for helping (e.g., Clary et al., in press; Omoto & Snyder, 1995). That is, since volunteerism is an activity often actively sought out, rather than being pressed into service by circumstance or by fate, volunteers may deliberate long and hard about the decision to get involved, about the degree of their involvement, and about the degree to which different volunteer opportunities suit them and their personal motivations. At the level of *individual agendas,* volunteers may be intent on affirming their personal values, on personally understanding the world, and on boosting self-esteem or sharpening their skills, and these "self-interested" agendas may well inform their choice of volunteer activity more so than might the desire to help another person or to improve or change society. Of course, much of the helping and prosocial action of volunteers is conducted in dyadic contexts, involving individual volunteers being of help and service to individual recipients of their services (e.g., a volunteer tutoring a child, offering companionship to an elderly person, etc.), and these volunteers may possess largely *interpersonal level agendas* associated with working out the dynamics of these interactions, involving the perspectives both of the volunteer and the recipient. Moreover, since many forms of volunteerism involve ongoing commitments that may extend over considerable periods of time and that involve the development of close and meaningful relationships with those that they help (relationships that truly begin at "point zero" since volunteers typically do not know those that they help in advance, often being matched with the recipients of their helping by volunteer service organizations), agendas associated with the development of *relationships* are particularly relevant to an understanding of volunteerism. And, since much volunteerism occurs in the context of groups and organizations that have been formed to recruit, train, and place volunteers in service opportunities, *agendas at the group level* associated with intentions to improve society are critically relevant to understanding volunteerism.

When it comes to the outcomes of pursuing agendas for participation, clearly many of these will be at the level of the individual (such as the increases to self-esteem, affirmation of values, and new skills that may accrue to those who serve as volunteers), others will be of a more interpersonal nature (such as the new people one meets, the new friends one makes, and the new patterns of socializing that will develop), still others will affect one's relationships (such as changes in patterns of social support, impact of participation on one's existing relationships), and still others will affect groups, organizations, and society (such as volunteer organizations meeting their goals through the service of volunteers, or nations becoming "kinder and gentler" through the good works of individual volunteers). In keeping with this multilayered view of the outcomes of participation, in their attempts to understand individuals who had become active in civic and political causes, Verba, Schlozman, and Brady (1995) have identified four categories of benefits derived from civic participation: selective material benefits (e.g., furthering one's own career), selective social gratifications (e.g., being with other people), selective civic gratification (e.g., making the community or nation a better place), and collective outcomes (e.g., influencing government policy), which clearly span a continuum from outcomes of relatively specific benefit to individual activists to outcomes that benefit larger collectives of individuals in communities, states, and nations.

If the agendas for, and the outcomes of, voluntary action are multiple—and can be construed at the individual, interpersonal, relationship, and group levels of analysis—what are the *inputs* to these agendas? In keeping with the functionalist strategy, we consider features of persons and features of situations that serve as sources of opportunity and constraint to individuals as they set and pursue agendas for voluntary action. With respect to *features of persons,* we can imagine some that would likely promote individual level agendas for participation in which the focus is on strengthening, affirming, or expressing the self through volunteerism (e.g., the low self-monitor desiring to affirm personal values [Snyder, 1987a]; the individual low in

self-clarity desiring to establish the self through commitment to a cause). By contrast, other features, including the traditionally studied traits of the "altruistic personality" (Penner, Fritzche, Craiger, & Freifeld, 1995) or the "helping personality" (Clary et al., in press; Omoto & Snyder, 1995), might more likely incline an individual to volunteer with interpersonal or relationship level agendas in mind. For example, features of persons likely to afford interpersonal agendas are those personal attributes that are defined with reference to other people (e.g., need for social recognition as a potential impetus to help others, need for affiliation as a potential motivator of helping others). Some features of persons that can serve as inputs to agendas for voluntary helping are more relationship oriented, such as the influence of communal versus exchange orientations to relationships and attachment styles as potential inputs to relationship level agendas for participation (Clark & Mills, 1979; Hazan & Shaver, 1987). Finally, shared meanings associated with gender, ethnicity, and race may serve as inputs to agendas for participation (e.g., Cole & Stewart, 1996); so too, the internalization of individualistic versus collectivistic cultural orientations may serve as highly generalized inputs that may dispose or constrain people from entering into voluntary helping with group level agendas in mind.

Among the sources of opportunity and constraint to participation provided by *features of situations* are those likely to influence the setting of individual level agendas (such as the salient models in one's environment that exemplify strength of character through participation; Erikson, 1950), and those that operate to encourage interpersonal agendas for helping (such as the influences of norms for women to be nurturant or older persons to participate socially; Havighurst, 1972). There are also features of situations likely to encourage or discourage service as a relationship building process (such as the facilitating or inhibiting effect of one's preexisting personal relationships, which can serve as sources of support and encouragement to serve and to buffer the stresses associated with sustained helpfulness, but which can also serve as barriers to involvement if and when conflicts develop between the allocation of time, energy, and psychological investment to one's preexisting relationships and to one's voluntary service relationships). Finally, there are those that operate to facilitate group level agendas for participation (such as the volunteer service organizations that make available opportunities for service, the religious and social groups that encourage participation as a form of group solidarity, the societal programs that provide opportunities for service such as Americorps or Elder-Volunteers, and the larger societal ideologies that promote or discourage service as a way of bettering society).

Thus, volunteering is a phenomenon that is meaningfully looked at from the perspective of multiple levels of analysis, with personal and situational affordances encouraging participation for different purposes and in different ways. However, as diverse as the agendas pursued by volunteers are, we would suggest that they all share the potential to solve the problem of inaction, a problem identified at least as long ago as Alexis de Tocqueville's nineteenth-century tour of America, after which he struggled with the problem of how to link actions for the public good with the private interests of individuals (de Tocqueville, 1969). That linking is, of course, precisely what many volunteers succeed in doing, when they fulfill their own diverse agendas for volunteering through some action that more or less directly benefits others and thereby serves society. That is, agendas for volunteerism are ones that link benefits to the self (attaining the outcomes that fulfill one's motivations, whatever form they take) into benefits for society (the help to others that addresses some of society's problems), thereby creating a "win-win" situation in which both self and society gain. More generally, the solution to the problem of inaction may be found in constructing and playing out agendas for action in the service of diverse societal needs that, rather than pitting individualism and social responsibility against each other, bring together—in much the same way that volunteers do—benefits to self and to society (e.g., Snyder, 1993).

Viewed from this perspective, the functionalist analysis of volunteerism reveals the interweaving and interdependence of agendas at multiple levels, allowing us to go beyond the limits of traditional antagonisms between theoretical and philosophical perspectives in the helping behavior literature (e.g., Batson, 1991). Just as applying the strategy to the problem of self-understanding revealed an extended portrait from individual intrapsychic strivings to thoroughly socially-situated searches for collective self-identity, so too did we see here how prosocial behavior can serve personal interests. However, while reaping the benefits of analysis at multiple levels, the strategy also encourages us to consider carefully the implications of individuals volunteering for different purposes, guided as they are to a preferred level of agenda by personal and situational affordances. For example, as Omoto and Snyder (1995) have demonstrated in their longitudinal studies of individuals volunteering in AIDS service organizations, some volunteer roles may serve some agendas and not others, with implications for how well and how long a person will sustain their participation. Individuals high in need for social recognition, pursuing their volunteer service with interpersonal agendas, may not last long or find satisfaction in a relatively solitary post as budget director for a fledgling service group. In fact, Omoto and Snyder (1995) found that the traits of the traditional "helping personality" were most effective in predicting outcomes relevant to interpersonal helping agendas (e.g., how integrated a volunteer feels in the service group), whereas focusing on those with more self-interested motivations enabled prediction of the

duration of participation in self-relevant volunteer roles. In this case, the functionalist strategy's emphasis on behavior in the service of multiple possible agendas suggests a reason for differential predictive utility of these different features of persons. Individuals with strong self-focused agendas for service may be sustained in their participation by the belief that they can personally work to obtain their desired rewards, impervious, for example, to the comings and goings of other volunteers in the organization. By contrast, those looking for interpersonal rewards seek outcomes less directly under their personal control, more dependent on the particularities of the interpersonal context in which service is performed. For those latter volunteers, persistence in the volunteer role may not be a very sensitive measure of their commitment to helping, instead their agenda may be better reflected in the intensity, however short-lived, of their satisfaction with the relationships they form or the people with whom they interact in the group.

In other words, by centering the analysis around the operative agendas for participants, the functionalist strategy holds the promise of improved behavior prediction, that is, of finding systematic associations between the particular features of persons and situations as inputs most likely to guide particular kinds of behaviors in the service of particular kinds of outcomes. In this regard, the functionalist strategy serves the mandate of prior dispositionist, interactionist, and situationist strategies, though it does so by emphasizing the agenda as an integrating unit of analysis rather than by partialling variance to persons, situations, or their interaction.

Lessons Learned from These Case Examples

In considering the "value-added" by applying the functionalist strategy to problem areas of human concern such as those described here, we are struck by the many complexities of personality and social behavior revealed in the process. The agendas that individuals set as they face these problems are not always those that come first to mind. For example, agendas for self-understanding are not always at the intrapsychic level; agendas for social connectedness are not always at the relationship level; and those serving to combat inaction are not always at the group level. In turn, the outcomes for which individuals strive in these domains are multiple, not always derivable directly from the desire to fulfill a basic or commonly defined need. As we have seen, some individuals strive for self-definition against others and other strive to merge the self with others; some people find connectedness through multiple, short-lived interactions whereas others desire long-lasting closeness to only one other or at most a few persons; for some volunteers the group is paramount, but for other, also fervently committed volunteers, the chance to fulfill personal values, even on one's own, is sufficient motivation for service. And, in a similar vein, whereas some personal and social inputs serve as matching affordances for agenda-setting, as when an individual high in need for approval is encouraged by a tight-knit family structure to find social connectedness in familiar social groups, others may clash, as when strivings for self-renewal and self-clarification meet head-on with mid-life prescriptions for relationship intimacy and loyalty.

We began our presentation of these case examples with the forewarning that, even though we would be sampling from large literatures, there very well might be gaps in the existing literatures revealed by this exercise. And, in fact, true to this expectation, our exercise in applying the functional strategy has oversampled from research domains where there are already indications of emerging functionalist perspectives. In fact, our very choice of problems of identity, connectedness, and participation reflects the presence of functionalist themes in the existing literatures on agendas associated with these problems. Moreover, our examples of inputs to these agendas have clearly oversampled features of persons (e.g., various features of self) and situations (e.g., aspects of culture) where research has already taken on a functionalist flavor. But, even in areas where our examples involve undersampling, the very same functionalist logic that we have used can be applied productively, we suggest. For example, even though we may have undersampled aspects of the Big Five as personal inputs to the agendas in our case examples, it is quite possible to think of these units of personality from a functionalist perspective, as our earlier discussion of structure and function in personality and social behavior has indicated.

We fully recognize that it is complexities such as the foregoing ones that may make the functionalist strategy one that may not automatically appeal to those whose appetites are wet by parsimony and simplicity. On the other hand, as we hope that these case examples do reveal, the functionalist strategy is well-suited to capturing the dynamics of personality and social behavior precisely because it recognizes the multiplicity of individuals' agendas and how they can change over time, and the various ways in which personal and social inputs interact as affordances for the pursuit of these agendas. As well, it emphasizes and underscores the diversity of ends to which people strive, and sensitizes to the consequences of individuals pursuit of agendas and outcomes for diverse aspects of their well-being, as well as that of their social and interpersonal worlds. In a related vein, the functionalist perspective recognizes that individuals want different things at different times in their lives (as when an adolescent wants to self-reflect and an adult wants to teach others); that some outcomes seem less appealing in reality than in the imagination (as when the intimacy of a close relationship becomes constraining rather than freeing); that some personal and situational affordances are hard to ignore or to change, whereas other ones provide truly time-limited inputs (as when the constraints of gender and gender roles loosen for men and women in their later years).

Hence, the functionalist analysis, while looking for regularities in social behavior, does not take a steady-state for granted, considering instead the *process* through which individuals travel enroute to their desired outcomes. Further, it assumes that along the way, the dynamics may well change because the agendas of others will impinge, and those desired outcomes may turn out to be less pleasant than expected. As such, and as illustrated (we hope) in our case examples, the search for *self-understanding, social connectedness, and societal participation* are evolving searches, and they need to be analyzed with strategies that do not presume a fixed equation of either one-sided or matching personal or situational forces. We believe that the functionalist strategy is especially well-suited to this task, and that our beliefs will come to be shared by others who will apply functionalist strategies in their own preferred domains of inquiry. Thus, to facilitate its growth and development as an investigative strategy for personality and social behavior, we now turn to a consideration of the defining features and "meta-features" of the functionalist strategy of inquiry.

FEATURES AND META-FEATURES OF THE FUNCTIONALIST STRATEGY

Having laid out a functionalist strategy for personality and social behavior and illustrated it in the context of specific research problems, we can now articulate some of the defining features and "meta-features" of this investigative strategy, which will help place it in the context of other investigative strategies for personality and social behavior, both those that have previously been articulated and those that are yet to emerge.

It Is Not Just about Persons, or Situations, or Behavior

Historically, treatments of personality and social behavior have drawn on notions of persons and situations and behavior. And, even though almost all analyses of personality and social behavior have subscribed to some variation of the Lewinian article of faith that "behavior is a function of the person and the situation," individual treatments of personality and social behavior have tended to emphasize one or the other, in effect giving either persons or situations a "first among equals" status. In fact, the chapter on personality and social behavior by Snyder and Ickes (1985) in the third edition of the *Handbook* explicitly used the relative emphasis given features of situations and features of persons as a way of categorizing and analyzing strategies for the study of personality and social behavior.

In this context, therefore, we wish to underscore an important and fundamental aspect of this strategy for investigating personality and social behavior, one which is already a recurring theme in this essay. Our analysis is not just about features of behavior, and not just about features of persons and features of situations that influence behavior. But rather, our analysis is about the ways in which features of persons and features of situations are incorporated into the agendas that people construct in pursuit of outcomes.

It Avoids One-Sided Characterizations of Persons and Situations

With its emphasis on the agenda as the central unit of analysis, the functionalist approach to personality and social behavior that we are advocating avoids the potential pitfalls of being a one-sided characterization, emphasizing either person or situation. Throughout this essay, we have stressed the guiding influences both of person and of situation features as inputs (that is, sources of opportunity and constraint) in the setting of agendas and in the pursuit of outcomes by individuals in important domains of their lives. Of course, we recognize that previous attempts to develop interactionist strategies for the study of personality and social behavior have attempted to include both persons and situations as determinants of social behavior. However, to the extent that most of these previous interactionist approaches have been ''mechanistic'' interactionist approaches, designed to parcel out and apportion the variation in social behavior to variation in person features and to variation in situation features, these previous approaches have, in effect, given a ''separate, but equal'' status to features of persons and features of situations. However, the present approach, with its dynamic interactionist stance, stands in contrast to prior, nonfunctionalist interactionist approaches in emphasizing the reciprocal interplay and mutual influence of persons and situations as inputs and sources of opportunities for agendas, which constitute the central point of the functionalist strategy for personality and social behavior.

It Affords a Comparable Richness for Situations and for Persons

Moreover, not only is it important to emphasize that the functionalist strategy for personality and social behavior avoids the problems associated with taking an ''either-or'' or a ''separate but equal'' stance toward persons or situations, but also it is important to reiterate and to emphasize that this approach gives comparable richness to situations and to persons. We have already noted that the psychology of personality has long provided a considerably richer vocabulary and set of theoretical concepts for defining and assessing features of persons than social psychology has provided for conceptualizing and measuring features of situations. In fact, calls for more work to bolster the analysis of situations are a commonplace, a stock in trade of previous treatments of situations (e.g., Frederiksen, 1976; Murtha et al., 1996.) Heeding those calls, the functionalist strategy for personality and social behavior takes the same perspective on understanding features of persons and features of situations as inputs to agendas for action, namely, viewing features of persons and features of situations as affordances, or sources of opportunity and constraint, which can be systematically examined at multiple levels of generality and globality. And, as we have seen in working through representative examples of programs of inquiry into phenomena, problems, and processes in the social psychological domains of thought, feeling, and action, it is possible to identify as rich a set of features of situations as features of persons that can and do function as inputs to agendas for action.

In addition to emphasizing the ways that the functionalist strategy for personality and social behavior responds to calls for added richness to the conceptualization and assessment of situations, it is also important to note that the functionalist strategy for personality and social behavior also meets oft-expressed calls for much needed articulation of conceptualizations of features of persons. We, and others (e.g., Pervin, 1994), have noted that structural models of personality, such as the Big Five factor models of personality often seem to be presenting dimensions of personality in ways that are all but abstracted from any context in which they might operate. The functionalist strategy for personality and social behavior offers one solution to this nagging problem. Its solution to this problem comes from the context that it gives for the units of personality, by linking them to agendas that people pursue in the course of their lives and the outcomes that flow from those agendas. Not only does this approach provide a context for thinking about dimensions of personality, but it also provides a way of thinking about the units of personality in terms of the agendas that flow from them. That is, as we emphasized in our discussion of the importance of recognizing and pursuing the intellectual goals of structure and function, our approach stresses the importance of defining personality not just in terms of what it is, but also in terms of what it does. The importance of thinking of personality in terms of what it does is, of course, made particularly salient in considerations of personality and social behavior, since what it is that personality does can be seen as the bridge that links personality to social behavior.

It Never Ends with Behavior Itself

Further, the emphasis on the purposeful pursuit of agendas and outcomes serves to underscore another meta-feature of the functionalist strategy for studying personality and social behavior: It never ends with the behavior itself. For example, the familiar dictum that "behavior is a function of the person and of the situation," as true as it is, and as important a lesson in interactionist approaches to prediction and causality as it teaches, also has the effect of offering a rather static view of human nature, one that lacks the dynamic qualities of the functionalist strategy's emphasis on movement toward ends and goals. Moreover, not only does the functionalist strategy go beyond asking questions about the determinants of behavior to ask questions about process (in its consideration of the active pursuit of agendas), but also it goes even further to ask questions about "to what end" is behavior performed and "to what end" are agendas pursued. That is, it readily incorporates such notions as "well-being" and "quality of life" as the ends that these agendas are in pursuit of ultimately, and applies these notions to evaluate the outcomes of individual, interpersonal, relationship, and group level agendas.

Thus, in comparison with approaches to understanding personality and social behavior that are focused on characterizing either the person or the situation, and even in contrast to mechanistic interactionist approaches that seek to quantify the amounts of influence to be apportioned to persons and to situations as determinants of behavior, the functionalist approach is a dynamic interactionist one that takes as its integrating focus the agenda and its actual and implied outcomes. That is, our approach to understanding personality and social behavior is a dynamic, process-oriented one that emphasizes movement and context.

It Is a Dynamic Approach, Emphasizing Movement and Context

Our emphasis on the active and purposeful setting of agendas and pursuing of outcomes reveals another "meta-feature" of the functionalist strategy, namely, that it provides a "process" model in the sense of process meaning movement, as in how people move through their lives, how they get from point A to point B in their pursuit of ends and goals. The movement, of course, can be real or symbolic (as in imagined courses of action that one might take, that one might have taken, that one fears, that one regrets, or that one hopes for). Essential to this emphasis on movement is the notion that movement takes place in space and in time. Therefore, the emphasis on explicating processes that move people is another reminder that the functionalist strategy for examining personality and social behavior takes seriously the temporal span of life and the spatial context of life. It is therefore a truly contextual and contextualized approach.

With respect to *temporal contexts,* as we have seen in our discussion of inputs as sources of opportunity and constraint for the pursuit of agendas, one of the ways in which

these inputs differ is in their historical time line of influence (e.g., culture is the accumulation of generations of influences, whereas a one-time request for brief help is highly time limited; similarly, enduring traits and dispositions can be expected to exert their influences in somewhat more reliable and stable form over time than, say, more circumscribed personal projects or life tasks).

Moreover, by their very definition, the pursuit of agendas is a process that unfolds over time, one that may vary considerably in temporal context (for example, the pursuit of the agenda of asking for a favor may occupy a fairly short time course, that of making a new friendship a somewhat longer time course, that of developing and maintaining a marriage or other life partnership an even longer time course). Agendas also take form in a temporal context defined by their positioning and sequencing in the life course of individuals (e.g., Helson & Moane, 1987, and Helson, Mitchell, & Moane, 1984, on social clock projects; Caspi, 1987, and Ryff, 1987, on roles across the life course; Stewart & Healy, 1992, on the influence of the timing of historical events on personality development).

And, in turn, agendas are defined in terms of outcomes that themselves vary in their temporal extension (for example, an agenda to articulate one's core self-defining values can be expected to have long-lasting impact, whereas the pursuit of a dating partner frequently may be directed at a less permanent outcome). Outcomes are also marked temporally by the extent of their focus on the past, the present, or the future (for example, the adult who wants to come to terms with a far distant childhood relationship may pursue an agenda of self-analysis very differently than might the adult intent on forgetting the past and taking hold of the future). The functionalist strategy places considerable importance, therefore, on the temporal context for and the temporally defined features of the pursuit of agendas.

With respect to *spatial contexts,* it is important to recognize that agendas are played out in particular locations which provide environmental and ecological contexts for their pursuit. It is, of course, easy to see the linkages between features of social contexts and spatial contexts, since situations are often defined in geographical spatial terms; for example, one may pursue a work-related agenda in the office, a health and fitness agenda at the athletic club, and a parenting agenda in the home. In addition, with respect to social contexts, there are clear linkages between spatial contexts and the agendas being pursued in them; for example, one pursues friends and relationship partners in different locations than one seeks to advance one's career, and these spatial contexts can and do differ in the opportunities and resources that they provide to facilitate the enactment of agendas.

With respect to features of persons, the links to spatial context may be a little less evident; yet, a few moments reflection will reveal that many, if not most, dispositions call for particular spatial contexts for those dispositions to be translated into behavior. For example, acting on the disposition of extraversion calls for parties or other sociable situations or, at the very least, the presence of at least one other person. In fact, several recent treatments of traits explicitly define them with respect to conditional *if-then* relationships that associate patterns of behavior with spatial and interpersonal contexts (e.g., Thorne, 1987; Wright & Mischel, 1987).

Further, a functionalist extension of the situationist investigative strategy places a priority on understanding what a person is trying to do by arranging the spatial and activity contexts within which he or she lives (e.g., Emmons et al., 1986). And it is almost always the case that even if those personal strivings can be articulated in situation-free terms, such as becoming a happy person or finding intimacy, nevertheless, the agendas for action that follow from those strivings are highly contextualized in spatial as well as in temporal terms (e.g., having a more laid-back reaction to my disagreeable roommate; e.g., Buss & Cantor, 1989; Caspi & Bem, 1990; Emmons, 1991). Moreover, the outcomes that follow from agendas in daily life are evaluated as better or worse largely in light of their providing a reasonable "solution" to the "problems" of living in specific spatial contexts, be they those defined by the opportunity for certain activity, the presence of certain partners, or the norms of a group. In the simplest of terms, life is lived in context, and so success at living is a relative matter that depends on where and when you are living.

Finally, considerations of matters of temporal and spatial contexts provide ready links to other, and even larger, considerations of context. By extension to longer and longer periods of time, the temporal context becomes the developmental context, ultimately requiring a consideration of the life phase and the stages of life as critical contexts for defining personal and social agendas. Moreover, the shifting spatial contexts that characterize movement through the stages of life represent further extensions of the role of spatial context in understanding the progression of agendas pursued over the course of a life. And, taken in even larger context, the spatial context becomes the larger ecological and environmental and cultural contexts of human functioning (that is, the pursuit of agendas occurs in, and influences, environmental and ecological and cultural contexts) and the temporal context becomes the evolutionary context within which agendas are set and pursued.

It Readily Incorporates Levels of Analysis

Finally, we emphasize that the functionalist strategy is one that readily incorporates levels of analysis, both in the agendas and outcomes that people pursue in their lives and in the features of persons and features of situations that serve as sources of opportunity and constraint for those agendas and outcomes. As we have taken care to explicate, the levels of analysis are defined somewhat differently for inputs than for agendas and outcomes. Nevertheless, as we have worked our way through case examples of problems of social thought, feeling, and action as seen through the lens of the functionalist research agenda, there are considerable benefits from systematically considering multiple levels of inputs, agendas, and outcomes, both in terms of organizing existing literature and in charting the course of new empirical and theoretical inquiries.

The ready affinity of the functionalist strategy for levels of analysis makes it an approach that sensitizes us to the possibilities that, even though we may "naturally" think first about a phenomena at one level of analysis, there very well may be other informative levels. These levels of analysis also add considerable potential for building bridges between the psychological sciences and other social, behavioral, and biological sciences. Thus, for example, systematic considerations of culture as a social input afford the possibility of a bridge to anthropology; similarly, considerations of the features of society as social inputs readily permit a bridge to sociology; and, considerations of evolutionary and genetic contexts as personal inputs permit bridge-building opportunities with the biological sciences.

THE FUNCTIONALIST STRATEGY IN CONTEXT

As much as we have argued for the benefits of the functionalist strategy, we by no means wish to claim that it is the only approach to personality and social behavior. To the contrary, we believe that it should be seen in the context of other strategies for inquiry into personality and social behavior, and for that matter that other strategies for the study of personality and social behavior can be viewed in the context of the functionalist strategy. For this reason, in articulating the functionalist strategy for personality and social behavior, we have tried to build systematically on the three investigative strategies articulated by Snyder and Ickes (1985)—the dispositional strategy, the interactional strategy, and the situational strategy—and to contribute to the conceptual and historical evolution to strategies for the study of personality and social behavior.

It Embraces Previously Articulated Strategies

In that spirit, we wish to emphasize that one way the functionalist strategy continues the conceptual and historical evolution is by embracing and incorporating elements of each of the previously articulated strategies for personality and social behavior. As we have indicated, part of the conceptual evolution from the dispositional to the interactional to the situational strategy has been in the growing emergence of a concern with—in addition to identifying *sources* of regularities and consistencies in social behavior (the calling cards of "personality" as it is manifested in social behavior)—specifying the *mechanisms* of such regularities and consistencies (with the dispositional strategy being essentially mute on the issue of mechanism, with the interactional strategy implying some mechanistic calculation of the relative emphasis of situational and dispositions sources, and with the situational strategy explicitly proposing that individuals' dispositionally guided choices of and influences on situations constitute one mechanism of consistency in social behavior).

The functionalist strategy continues this evolutionary pattern of growth and development, explicitly recognizing the importance of identifying sources of the regularities and consistencies associated with personality and social behavior. Its approach to the matter of sources is to be found in its treatment of features of persons and features of situations as inputs to agendas for action; by preserving attention to both features, it continues the long tradition in treatments of personality and social behavior associated with the Lewinian "behavior is a function of the person and the situation" dictum and readily permits their relative emphases to vary. Thus, at a minimum, our treatment of personality and social behavior, with its concern with features of persons and features of situations as inputs to agendas, or sources of opportunity and constraint as individuals set agendas and pursue outcomes, readily incorporates those features of the previously articulated dispositional, interactional, and situational strategies that are concerned with sources of regularities and consistencies in social behavior. Moreover, emphasizing affordances as both sources of opportunity and as sources of constraint reminds us that the very same forces that move people to action may also block, restrain, impede, and otherwise constrain action.

It Enhances Previously Articulated Strategies

Yet, much as the functionalist strategy for personality and social behavior embraces and incorporates features of the dispositional, interactional, and situational strategies, we do not mean to imply that these previously articulated strategies no longer have any intrinsic value or inherent utility as strategies of inquiry. To the contrary, we believe that the newly emerging functionalist strategy for personality and social behavior gives new life and adds vitality to the dispositional, the interactional, and situational strategies for inquiry in personality and social behavior. We believe that research guided by each of these strategies can benefit by explicit attention both to sources of regularities

and consistencies in social behavior and to the mechanisms of the linkages between personality and behavior.

For example, we fully expect that investigators will continue to be concerned with dispositional orientations in diverse domains of social behavior. When viewed from the functionalist perspective, practitioners of the dispositional strategy might consider how those dispositional orientations get translated into corresponding patterns of action and, when developing measures of those dispositional orientations, consider those that may be revealing not only of individual differences in the dispositional orientations themselves but in the mechanisms that link those dispositions to behavior.

Similarly, we fully expect that, in accord with the interactional strategy for personality and social behavior, researchers will continue in their quest to maximize their ability to predict social behavior from personality, reaping the benefits of identifying just the right mix of dispositional and situational predictors and just the right array of moderator variables. Reflecting the joint concerns with the sources and the mechanisms of linkages between personality and social behavior emphasized in the functionalist approach, we expect that the search for the perfect recipe for prediction can be guided by considerations of the mechanisms that link personality and social behavior and that the most effective moderator variables will be ones that tap into the actual mediators and mechanisms of personality and social behavior linkages. In this regard, we would encourage investigators searching for these recipes for prediction to examine properties of the agendas being pursued by individuals as potential moderator variables in their prediction equations.

Finally, we fully expect that the situational strategy will continue to be an active and a productive one, but one that very well can benefit from the functional perspective. Thus, we would encourage practitioners of the situational strategy to pay explicit attention to the possibilities that the situations that individuals choose may actually function as sources of constraint on their behavioral options as well as sources of opportunities, that individuals' choices of situations may include avoiding situations that place constraints on them as well as approaching situations that present them with opportunities, and that individuals' attempts to influence their situations may at times be directed at reducing or even eliminating the constraints imposed by situations. Moreover, we would alert practitioners of the situational strategy to the possibility that the very activities of choosing and influencing situations may themselves be subject to constraints in the opportunities actually available to individuals. That is, one can only choose among those situations actually available for the choosing, and there very well may be limits on the influences that can be exerted on those situations. For example, individuals' choices of situations may be constrained by, among other things, race, gender, social class, economic status, and geography; similarly, their influence on those situations may be limited by their abilities, aptitudes, and other resources.

But, It Stands Apart from Other Strategies

As much as the functionalist strategy builds on, and incorporates and integrates features of, previously articulated strategies for the study of personality and social behavior, there are, it should be recognized and emphasized, some aspects that set it apart from other approaches to conceptualizing and investigating personality and social behavior. One feature that sets this approach apart from previously articulated strategies for personality and social behavior is that the "up-front" questions with which it begins are "process" questions about movement in time and space, about pursuing agendas, about striving toward outcomes, and the quest for well-being, rather than being questions just about behavior itself.

This is not to say that it is an unproductive enterprise to begin with questions about behavior itself. To the contrary, previous *Handbook* chapters on personality and social behavior began very explicitly with asking questions about behavior, specifically about whether there were any indications of personality in social behavior and about the origins of the regularities and consistencies in social behavior that are thought to reflect personality. However, since an avowed goal of this *Handbook* chapter is to build on the accomplishments of the chapters on personality and social behavior that have preceded it, and to contribute to the continuing evolution, growth, and development of strategies for intellectual inquiries concerning personality and social behavior, it is only fitting that our up-front question moves beyond the question of behavior to a question about process that can represent a further evolution beyond the previously articulated strategies for studying personality and social behavior. It is for these reasons that a recurring theme in the functionalist treatment of personality and social behavior has been dynamic processes of movement, movement through space and time as people actively construct and pursue agendas that move them toward the life outcomes that they are seeking.

This *dynamic* approach to understanding personality and social behavior can and should be contrasted with a *static* framework for life, in at least two significant ways. First, with its explicit concern with providing solid contexts, both temporal and spatial, for features of persons and features of situations as inputs to agendas for action (which themselves are played out in spatial and temporal contexts), this approach to personality and social behavior not only continues long-standing concerns with disposi-

tional and situational determinants of behavior, but provides temporal and spatial contexts for their reciprocal interplay, their active back and forth mutual influence in dynamic interrelationships.

Moreover, by focusing on the setting of agendas and the pursuing of outcomes, this approach provides a dynamic perspective that represents somewhat more of a departure from theorizing of a more static nature. Indeed, it is the emphasis on the outcomes that accrue to individuals—those that they succeed in attaining and those that they don't, those that are intended and those that aren't, those that are welcome and those that are not—that helps the functionalist strategy take the evolution of strategies for understanding personality and social behavior forward. In this regard, the functionalist strategy's emphasis on outcomes provides a new perspective on matters of individuals' well-being, with the costs and benefits associated with their pursuing of agendas. It is an approach that naturally leads to asking and answering questions of the form "How well is it going?" "Are the benefits outweighing the costs?" and "How is the individual progressing?" That is, there is an "applied" benefit of the dynamic, functionalist approach to personality and social behavior that simply may not be as readily evident in more mechanistic approaches to accounting for behavior.

FINAL THOUGHTS ON PERSONALITY AND SOCIAL BEHAVIOR

We end where we started, by coming back full circle to where we began this chapter, and reflecting on what a functionalist strategy for personality and social behavior says about the shared intellectual concerns of personality and of social psychology. In our attempt to articulate the next generation of strategies for understanding personality and social behavior, we have built systematically on the foundations provided by personality and social psychology's shared concerns with the metaphor of movement (individuals "moved" by dispositions and "moved" by situations, individuals "moving" their social worlds) and built on these shared motivational themes to articulate strategies for understanding personality and social behavior that are true to the purposeful, goal-seeking nature of both personality and social psychology.

Incorporating these shared motivational themes, and speaking to the defining concerns of both social psychology and personality, we believe that the functionalist strategy has the potential to move us forward toward a meaningful integration of personality and social psychology, with one unified, integrated, shared disciplinary perspective emphasizing individuals in active and purposeful pursuit of agendas that draw on and integrate features of persons and of situations and that carry people toward their goals and bring outcomes to them.

At the outset, we noted that ours is not the first *Handbook* chapter to deal with issues of personality and social behavior. In fact, we have more than once expressed our pride at being able to stand on the shoulders of the authors of these previous chapters—to build on their efforts, to pick up where they left off, and to carry on the work that they began. Moreover, we have noted that the goals of the successive chapters on personality and social behavior have evolved over the course of the successive editions of the *Handbook*. Now, we find ourselves in the position of having to acknowledge that, with continued growth and development, a chapter on "personality and social behavior" in the *Handbook* could itself eventually evolve out of existence.

For, if the intellectual evolution that we envision actually comes to pass, and there does come a time when there is the unified and integrated discipline of personality and social psychology that we envision, a time when matters of personality and social behavior so permeate all inquiries into human nature, then we very well may see a *Handbook of Social Psychology* in which considerations of personality and social behavior will be woven seamlessly into each and every one of the substantive and methodological domains defined by its chapters. If this scenario comes to pass, then the answer to the question with which we introduced this chapter, "Why is there a chapter on personality and social behavior in the *Handbook of Social Psychology*?", eventually may be that there is no longer a need for a distinct chapter on personality and social behavior in the *Handbook*.

REFERENCES

Acitelli, L. K., & Duck, S. W. (1987). Intimacy as the proverbial elephant. In D. Perlman & S. W. Duck (Eds.), *Intimate relationships: Development, dynamics, and deterioration* (pp. 297–308). Newbury Park, CA: Sage.

Adams, G. R., & Fitch, S. A. (1983). Psychological environments of university departments: Effects on college students' identity status and ego stage development. *Journal of Personality and Social Psychology, 44*(6), 1266–1275.

Allport, F. H. (1937). Teleonomic description in the study of personality. *Character and Personality, 5,* 202–214.

Allport, G. (1937). *Personality: A psychological interpretation.* New York: Holt.

Allport, G. (1968). The historical background of modern social psychology. In G. Lindzey & E. Aronson (Eds.), *The handbook of social psychology: Vol. 1. Historical introduction and systematic positions* (2nd ed., pp. 1–80). Reading, MA: Addison-Wesley.

Andersen, S. M., & Cole, S. W. (1990). "Do I know you?": The role of significant others in general social perception. *Journal of Personality and Social Psychology, 59,* 384–399.

Andersen, S. M., & Klatzky, R. L. (1987). Traits and social stereotypes: Levels of categorization in person perception. *Journal of Personality and Social Psychology, 53,* 235–246.

Argyle, M., & Henderson, M. (1985). *The anatomy of relationships.* London: Heinemann.

Aries, E. J., Gold, C., & Weigel, R. H. (1983). Dispositional and situational influences on dominance behavior in small groups. *Journal of Personality and Social Psychology, 44*(4), 779–786.

Arkin, R. M. (1980). Self-presentation. In D. M. Wegner & R. R. Vallacher (Eds.), *The self in social psychology.* New York: Oxford University Press.

Aron, A., Aron, E. N., & Smollan, D. (1992). Inclusion of the other in the self scale and the structure of interpersonal closeness. *Journal of Personality and Social Psychology, 63,* 596–612.

Aron, A., Aron, E. N., Tudor, M., & Nelson, G. (1991). Close relationships as including the other in self. *Journal of Personality and Social Psychology, 60,* 241–253.

Aronson, E., Blaney, N., Stephan, C., Sikes, J., & Snapp, M. (1978). *The jigsaw classroom.* Beverly Hills, CA: Sage Publications.

Austin, J. T., & Vancouver, J. B. (1996). Goal constructs in psychology: Structure, process, and content. *Psychological Bulletin, 120,* 338–375.

Baldwin, M. W. (1992). Relational schemas and the processing of social information. *Psychological Bulletin, 112,* 461–484.

Baldwin, M. W., Carrell, S. E., & Lopez, D. F. (1990). Priming relationship schemas: My advisor and the pope are watching me from the back of my mind. *Journal of Experimental Social Psychology, 26,* 435–454.

Baldwin, M. W., Fehr, B., Keedian, E., Seidal, M., & Thomson, D. W. (1993). An exploration of the relational schema underlying attachment styles: Self-report and the lexical decision approaches. *Personality and Social Psychology Bulletin, 19,* 746–754.

Baldwin, M. W., & Holmes, J. G. (1987). Salient private audiences and awareness of the self. *Journal of Personality and Social Psychology, 52,* 1087–1098.

Banaji, M. R., & Prentice, D. A. (1994). The self in social contexts. *Annual Review of Psychology, 45,* 297–332.

Bargh, J. A., & Gollwitzer, P. M. (1994). Environmental control of goal-directed action: Automatic and strategic contingencies between situations and behavior. In W. Spaulding (Ed.), *Nebraska symposium on motivation* (Vol. 41, pp. 71–124). Lincoln: University of Nebraska Press.

Bargh, J. A., Raymond, P., Pryor, J. B., & Strack, F. (1995). Attractiveness of the underling: An automatic power × sex association and its consequences for sexual harassment and aggression. *Journal of Personality and Social Psychology, 68,* 768–781.

Baron, R. M., & Boudreau, L. A. (1987). An ecological perspective on integrating personality and social psychology. *Journal of Personality and Social Psychology, 53*(6), 1222–1228.

Batholomew, K., & Horowitz, L. M. (1991). Attachment styles among young adults: A test of a four-category model. *Journal of Personality and Social Psychology, 61,* 226–244.

Batson, C. D. (1991). *The altruism question: Toward a social psychological answer.* Hillsdale, NJ: Erlbaum.

Baumeister, R. F. (1987). How the self became a problem: A psychological review of historical research. *Journal of Personality and Social Psychology, 52,* 163–176.

Baumeister, R. F., & Leary, M. R. (1995). The need to belong: Desire for interpersonal attachments as a fundamental human motivation. *Psychological Bulletin, 117,* 497–529.

Bem, D. J. (1972). Self-perception theory. In L. Berkowitz (Ed.), *Advances in experimental social psychology* (Vol. 6, pp. 2–61). New York: Academic Press.

Bem, S. L. (1981). Gender schema theory: A cognitive account of sex typing. *Psychological Review, 88,* 354–364.

Bem, S. L. (1984). Androgyny and gender-schema theory: A conceptual and empirical integration. In *Nebraska symposium on motivation: Psychology and gender* (pp. 179–226). Lincoln: University of Nebraska Press.

Berscheid, E. (1983). Emotion. In H. H. Kelley, E. Berscheid, A. Christensen, J. H. Harvey, T. L. Huston, G. Levinger, E. McClintock, L. A. Peplau, & D. R. Peterson (Eds.), *Close relationships* (pp. 110–168). New York: Freeman.

Berscheid, E. (1994). Interpersonal relationships. *Annual Review of Psychology, 45,* 79–129.

Berscheid, E., & Reis, H. (1998). Attraction and close relationships. In D. Gilbert, S. T. Fiske, & G. Lindzey (Eds.), *The handbook of social psychology* (4th ed., Vol. 2, pp. 193–281). New York: McGraw-Hill.

Berscheid, E., Snyder, M., & Omoto, A. M. (1989a). Issues in studying close relationships: Conceptualizing and measuring closeness. In C. Hendrick (Ed.), *Close relationships: Review of personality and social psychology* (Vol. 10, pp. 63–91). Newbury Park, CA: Sage.

Berscheid, E., Snyder, M., & Omoto, A. M. (1989b). The relationship closeness inventory: Assessing the closeness of interpersonal relationships. *Journal of Personality and Social Psychology, 57,* 792–807.

Bilsky, W., & Schwartz, S. H. (1994). Values and personality. *European Journal of Personality, 8*(3), 163–181.

Blass, T. (1984). Social psychology and personality: Toward a convergence. *Journal of Personality and Social Psychology, 47*(5), 1013–1027.

Blass, T. (1991). Understanding behavior in the Milgram obedience experiment: The role of personality, situations, and their interactions. *Journal of Personality and Social Psychology, 60*(3), 398–413.

Bowlby, J. (1969). *Attachment and loss: Attachment.* New York: Basic Books.

Bowlby, J. (1973). *Attachment and loss: Separation, anxiety, and anger.* New York: Basic Books.

Bowlby, J. (1980). *Attachment and loss: Sadness and depression.* New York: Basic Books.

Bowlby, J. (1982). Attachment and loss: Retrospect and prospect. *American Journal of Orthopsychiatry, 52,* 664–678.

Boyte, H. C. (1991). Civic and community participation. In C. F. Bahmueller (Ed.), *Civitas: A curriculum framework for civic education.* Calabasas, CA: Center for Civic Education.

Bradley, G. W. (1978). Self-serving biases in the attribution process: A reexamination of the fact or fiction question. *Journal of Personality and Social Psychology, 36,* 56–71.

Brehm, S. S. (1992). *Intimate relationships.* New York: McGraw-Hill.

Brennan, K. A., & Shaver, P. R. (1995). Dimensions of adult attachment, affect regulation, and romantic relationship functioning. *Personality and Social Psychology Bulletin, 21,* 267–283.

Brewer, M. B. (1991). The social self: On being the same and different at the same time. *Personality and Social Psychology Bulletin, 17*(5), 475–482.

Brewer, M. B., & Gardner, W. (1996). Who is this "we"? Levels of corrective identity and self-representations. *Journal of Personality and Social Psychology, 71,* 83–93.

Brickman, P. (1987). Commitment. In C. B. Wortman & R. Sorrentino (Eds.), *Commitment, conflict, and caring* (pp. 1–18). Englewood Cliffs, NJ: Prentice-Hall.

Brickman, P., & Coates, D. (1987). Commitment and mental health. In C. B. Wortman & R. Sorrentino (Eds.), *Commitment, conflict, and caring* (pp. 222–309). Englewood Cliffs, NJ: Prentice-Hall.

Britt, T. W., Boniecki, K. A., Vescio, T. K., Biernat, M., & Brown, L. M. (1996). Intergroup anxiety: A person × situation approach. *Personality and Social Psychology Bulletin, 22,* 1177–1188.

Brown, J. D., & Smart, S. A. (1991). The self and social conduct: Linking self-representations to prosocial behavior. *Journal of Personality and Social Psychology, 60*(3), 368–375.

Buss, D. M. (1984). Toward a psychology of person-environment (PE) correlation: The role of spouse selection. *Journal of Personality and Social Psychology, 47*(2), 361–377.

Buss, D. M. (1987). Selection, evocation, and manipulation. *Journal of Personality and Social Psychology, 53*(6), 1214–1221.

Buss, D. M. (1989). Sex differences in human mate preferences: Evolutionary hypotheses tested in 37 cultures. *Behavioral & Brain Sciences, 12,* 1–49.

Buss, D. M., & Cantor, N. (1989). Introduction. In D. M. Buss & N. Cantor (Eds.), *Personality psychology: Recent trends and emerging directions* (pp. 1–12). New York: Springer-Verlag.

Buss, D. M., & Schmitt, D. P. (1993). Sexual strategies theory: An evolutionary perspective on human mating. *Psychological Review, 100,* 204–232.

Byrne, D. (1971). *The attraction paradigm.* New York: Academic Press.

Cacioppo, J. T., & Petty, R. E. (1982). The need for cognition. *Journal of Personality and Social Psychology, 42,* 116–131.

Campbell, J. D. (1990). Self-esteem and the clarity of the self-concept. *Journal of Personality and Social Psychology, 59*(3), 538–549.

Campbell, J. D., & Fairey, P. J. (1986). Better than me or better than thee? Reactions to intrapersonal and interpersonal performance feedback. *Journal of Personality, 54*(3), 479–493.

Campbell, J. D., & Lavellee, L. F. (1993). Who am I? The role of self-concept confusion in understanding the behavior of people with low self-esteem. In R. F. Baumeister (Ed.), *Self-esteem: The puzzle of low self-regard* (pp. 3–21). New York: Plenum Press.

Campbell, J. D., Tesser, A., & Fairey, P. J. (1986). Conformity and attention to the stimulus: Some temporal and contextual dynamics. *Journal of Personality and Social Psychology, 51*(2), 315–324.

Cantor, N. (1990). From thought to behavior: "Having" and "doing" in the study of personality and cognition. *American Psychologist, 45,* 735–750.

Cantor, N. (1994). Life task problem solving: Situational affordances and personal needs. *Personality and Social Psychology Bulletin, 20*(3), 235–243.

Cantor, N., & Fleeson, W. (1994). Social intelligence and intelligence goal pursuit: A cognitive slice of motivation. In W. D. Spaulding (Ed.), *Integrative views of motivation, cognition, and emotion. Nebraska symposium on motivation, Vol. 41* (pp. 125–179). Lincoln: University of Nebraska Press.

Cantor, N., & Kihlstrom, J. F. (1982). Cognitive and social processes in personality. In G. T. Wilson & C. M. Franks (Eds.), *Contemporary behavior therapy: Conceptual and empirical foundations* (pp. 142-201). New York: Guilford.

Cantor, N., & Kihlstrom, J. F. (1987). *Personality and social intelligence.* Englewood Cliffs, NJ: Prentice-Hall.

Cantor, N., Mackie, D., & Lord, C. (1983–84). Choosing partners and activities: The social perceiver decides to mix it up. *Social Cognition, 2,* 256–272.

Cantor, N., & Malley, J. (1991). Life tasks, personal needs, and close relationships. In G. J. O. Fletcher & F. D. Fincham (Eds.), *Cognition in close relationships.* Hillsdale, NJ: Erlbaum.

Cantor, N., & Mischel, W. (1979). Prototypicality and personality: Effects on free recall and personality impressions. *Journal of Research in Personality, 13*(2), 187–205.

Cantor, N., Mischel, W., & Schwartz, J. C. (1982). A prototype analysis of psychological situations. *Cognitive Psychology, 14*(1), 45–77.

Caporael, L. R., & Brewer, M. B. (1991). Reviving evolutionary psychology: Biology meets society. *Journal of Social Issues, 47,* 187–195.

Caporael, L. R., Dawes, R. M., Orbell, J. M., & van de Kragt, A. (1989). Selfishness examined: Cooperation in the absence of egoistic incentives. *Behavioral and Brain Sciences, 12,* 683–739.

Carlo, G., Eisenberg, N., Troyer, D., Switzer, G., & Speer, A. L. (1991). The altruistic personality: In what contexts is it apparent? *Journal of Personality and Social Psychology, 61*(3), 450–458.

Carlson, R. (1984). What's social about social psychology? Where's the person in personality research? *Journal of Personality and Social Psychology, 47*(6), 1304–1309.

Caspi, A. (1987). Personality in the life course. *Journal of Personality and Social Psychology, 53*(6), 1203–1213.

Caspi, A., & Bem, D. J. (1990). Personality continuity and change across the life course. In L. A. Pervin (Ed.), *Handbook of personality* (pp. 549–569). New York: Guilford.

Caspi, A., Bem, D. J., & Elder, G. H., Jr. (1989). Continuities and consequences of interactional styles across the life course. *Journal of Personality, 57*(2), 375–406.

Caspi, A., & Herbener, E. S. (1990). Continuity and change: Assortative marriage and the consistency of personality in adulthood. *Journal of Personality and Social Psychology, 58*(2), 250–258.

Chaiken, S., & Baldwin, M. W. (1981). Affective-cognitive consistency and the effect of salient behavioral information on the self-perception of attitudes. *Journal of Personality and Social Psychology, 41,* 1–12.

Chaplin, W. F. (1991). The next generation of moderator research in personality psychology. *Journal of Personality, 59*(2), 143–178.

Chen, S., Shechter, D., & Chaiken, S. (1996). Getting at the truth or getting along: Accuracy versus impression-motivated heuristic and systematic processing. *Journal of Personality and Social Psychology, 71,* 262–275.

Christenson, A., & Heavey, C. L. (1990). Gender and social structure in the demand/withdraw pattern of marital conflict. *Journal of Personality and Social Psychology, 59,* 73–81.

Cialdini, R. B., Trost, M. R., & Newsom, J. T. (1995). Preference for consistency: The development of a valid measure and the discovery of surprising behavioral implications. *Journal of Personality and Social Psychology, 69(2),* 318–328.

Clark, M. S., & Mills, J. (1979). Interpersonal attraction in exchange and communal relationships. *Journal of Personality and Social Psychology, 37,* 12–24.

Clark, M. S., & Reis, H. T. (1988). Interpersonal processes in close relationships. *Annual Review of Psychology, 39,* 609–672.

Clary, E. G., & Snyder, M. (1991). A functional analysis of altruism and prosocial behavior: The case of volunteerism. In

M. Clark (Ed.), *Prosocial behavior, review of personality and social psychology* (pp. 119–148). London/New Delhi: Sage Publications.

Clary, E. G., Snyder, M., Ridge, R. D., Copeland, J., Stukas, A. A., Haugen, J., & Miene, P. (in press). Understanding and assessing the motivations of volunteers: A functional approach. *Journal of Personality and Social Psychology.*

Clore, G. L., & Byrne, D. (1974). A reinforcement-affect model of attraction. In T. L. Huston (Ed.), *Foundations of interpersonal attraction* (pp. 143–170). New York: Academic Press.

Cole, E. R., & Stewart, A. J. (1996). Meanings of political participation among black and white women: Political identity and social responsibility. *Journal of Personality and Social Psychology, 71,* 130–140.

Collins, N. L., & Read, S. J. (1990). Adult attachment, working models, and relationship quality in dating couples. *Journal of Personality and Social Psychology, 58,* 644–663.

Collins, N. L., & Read, S. J. (1994). Cognitive representations of attachment: The content and function of working models. In K. Bartholomew & D. Perlman (Eds.), *Advances in personal relationships: Vol. 5* (pp. 53–90). London: Jessica Kingsley.

Cook, J. R. (1985). Repression-sensitization and approach-avoidance as predictors of response to a laboratory stressor. *Journal of Personality and Social Psychology, 49*(3), 759–773.

Cooley, C. H. (1902/1964). *Human nature and the social order.* New York: Schocken Books.

Copeland, J., & Snyder, M. (1995). When counselors confirm: A functional analysis. *Personality and Social Psychology Bulletin, 21*(11), 1210–1220.

Costa, P. T., & McCrae, R. R. (1980). Enduring dispositions in adult males. *Journal of Personality and Social Psychology, 38*(5), 793–800.

Cousins, S. D. (1989). Culture and self-perception in Japan and the United States. *Journal of Personality and Social Psychology, 56,* 124–131.

Crandall, C. S. (1988). Social contagion of binge eating. *Journal of Personality and Social Psychology, 55*(4), 588–598.

Crocker, J., Luhtanen, R., Blaine, B., & Broadnax, S. (1994). Collective self-esteem and psychological well-being among white, black, and Asian college students. *Personality and Social Psychology Bulletin, 20,* 503–513.

Crocker, J., & Major, B. (1989). Social stigma and self-esteem: The self-protective properties of stigma. *Psychological Review, 96,* 608–630.

Darley, J. M., & Fazio, R. H. (1980). Expectancy confirmation processes arising in the social interaction sequence. *American Psychologist, 35*(10), 867–881.

Darley, J. M., Fleming, J. H., Hilton, J. L., & Swann, W. B. (1988). Dispelling negative expectancies: The impact of interaction goals and target characteristics on the expectancy confirmation process. *Journal of Experimental Social Psychology, 24*(1), 19–36.

Davis, M. C., & Matthews, K. A. (1996). Do gender-relevant characteristics determine cardiovascular reactivity? Match versus mismatch of traits and situations. *Journal of Personality and Social Psychology, 71,* 527–535.

Deaux, K. (1993). Reconstructing social identity. *Personality and Social Psychology Bulletin, 19*(1), 4–12.

de Tocqueville, A. (1969). *Democracy in America* (G. Lawrence, Trans.; J. P. Meyer, Ed.). New York: Anchor Books, Doubleday. (Original work published 1835)

Deutsch, M., & Gerard, H. G. (1955). A study of normative and informational social influence upon individual judgment. *Journal of Abnormal and Social Psychology, 51,* 629–636.

Diener, E., Emmons, R. A., Larsen, R. J., & Griffin, S. (1985). The satisfaction with life scale. *Journal of Personality Assessment, 49,* 71–75.

Dixon, J. G., & Swan, W. B. (1993). When does introspection bear fruit? Self-reflection, self-insight, and interpersonal choices. *Journal of Personality and Social Psychology, 64,* 35–43.

Donahue, E. M., Robins, R. W., Roberts, B. W., & John, O. P. (1993). The divided self: Concurrent and longitudinal effects of psychological adjustment and social roles on self-concept differentiation. *Journal of Personality and Social Psychology, 64,* 834–846.

Downey, G., & Feldman, S. I. (1996). Implications of rejection sensitivity for intimate relationships. *Journal of Personality and Social Psychology, 70,* 1327–1343.

Durkheim, E. (1933). *On the division of labor in society.* (G. Simpson, Trans.). New York: Macmillan. (Original work published in 1912)

Duval, S., & Wicklund, R. A. (1972). *A theory of objective self-awareness.* New York: Academic Press.

Eagly, A. H. (1987). *Sex differences in social behavior: A social role interpretation.* Hillsdale, NJ: Erlbaum.

Eckes, T. (1995). Features of situations: A two-mode clustering study of situation prototypes. *Personality and Social Psychology Bulletin, 21*(4), 366–374.

Egan, G. (1984). People in systems: A comprehensive model for psychosocial education and training. In D. Larson (Ed.), *Teaching psychosocial skills* (pp. 21–48). Belmont, CA: Wadsworth.

Emmons, R. A. (1986). Personal strivings: An approach to personality and subjective well-being. *Journal of Personality and Social Psychology, 51*(5), 1058–1068.

Emmons, R. A. (1991). Personal strivings, daily life events, and psychological and physical well-being. *Journal of Personality, 59,* 453–472.

Emmons, R. A., Diener, E., & Larsen, R. J. (1986). Choice and avoidance of everyday situations and affect congruence: Two models of reciprocal interactionism. *Journal of Personality and Social Psychology, 51*(4), 815–826.

Emmons, R. A., & King, L. A. (1988). Conflict among personal strivings: Immediate and long-term implications for psychological and physical well-being. *Journal of Personality and Social Psychology, 54*(6), 1040–1048.

Epstein, S. (1994). Integration of the cognitive and psychodynamic unconscious. *American Psychologist, 49,* 709–724.

Epstein, S., Pacini, R., Denes-Raj, V., & Heier, H. (1996). Individual differences in intuitive-experiential and analytical-rational thinking styles. *Journal of Personality and Social Psychology, 71,* 390–405.

Erber, R., & Fiske, S. T. (1984). Outcome dependency and attention to inconsistent information. *Journal of Personality and Social Psychology, 47,* 709–726.

Erikson, E. (1950). *Childhood and society.* New York: Norton.

Erikson, E. (1959). Identity and the life cycle: Selected papers. *Psychological Issues, 1*(1), 5–165.

Eysenck, H. J. (1973). *Eysenck on extraversion.* New York: John Wiley and Sons.

Fazio, R. H. (1987). Self-perception theory: A current perspective. In M. P. Zanna, J. M. Olson, & C. P. Herman (Eds.), *Social influence: The Ontario Symposium* (Vol. 5, pp. 129–150). Hillsdale, NJ: Erlbaum.

Feeney, J. A., & Noller, P. (1990). Attachment style as a predictor of adult romantic relationships. *Journal of Personality and Social Psychology, 58,* 281–291.

Filsinger, E. E., & Thoma, S. J. (1988). Behavioral antecedents of relationship stability and adjustment: A five-year longitudinal study. *Journal of Marriage and the Family, 50,* 785–795.

Fiske, A. P. (1991). *Structures of social life.* New York: Free Press.

Fiske, A. P. (1993). Social errors in four cultures: Evidence about universal forms of social relations. *Journal of Cross-Cultural Psychology, 24*(4), 463–494.

Fiske, A. P., Kitayama, S., Markus, H., & Nisbett, R. (1998). The cultural matrix of social psychology. In D. Gilbert, S. T. Fiske, & G. Lindzey (Eds.), *Handbook of social psychology* (4th ed., Vol. 2, pp. 915–981). New York: McGraw-Hill.

Fiske, S. T. (1987). People's reactions to nuclear war: Implications for psychologists. *American Psychologist, 42,* 207–217.

Fiske, S. T. (1992). Thinking is for doing: Portraits of social cognition from daguerreotype to laserphoto. *Journal of Personality and Social Psychology, 63,* 877–889.

Fiske, S. T. (1993). Controlling other people: The impact of power on stereotyping. *American Psychologist, 48,* 621–628.

Fiske, S. T., & Neuberg, S. L. (1990). A continuum of impression formation, from category-based to individuating processes: Influences of information and motivation on attention and interpretation. *Advances in Experimental Social Psychology, 23,* 1–73.

Fiske, S. T., Pratto, F., & Pavelchak, M. (1983). Citizens' images of nuclear war. *Journal of Social Issues, 39,* 41–65.

Fleeson, W. W. (1992). *Life tasks, implicit motives, and self-regulation in daily life.* Unpublished doctoral dissertation, University of Michigan.

Fletcher, G. J. O., & Fincham, F. D. (1991). Attribution processes in close relationships. In G. J. O. Fletcher & F. D. Fincham (Eds.), *Cognition in close relationships* (pp. 7–35). Hillsdale, NJ: Erlbaum.

Fletcher, G. J. O., & Fincham, F. D. (Eds.). (1991). *Cognition in close relationships.* Hillsdale, NJ: Erlbaum.

Frable, D. E. (1993). Being and feeling unique: Statistical deviance and psychological marginality. *Journal of Personality, 61,* 85–110.

Frederiksen, N. (1976). Toward a taxonomy of situations. In N. S. Endler & D. Magnusson (Eds.), *Interactional psychology and personality* (pp. 487–502). Washington, DC: Hemisphere.

Freud, S. (1938). *The basic writings of Sigmund Freud.* New York: Modern Library.

Funder, D. C., & Colvin, C. R. (1991). Explorations in behavioral consistency: Properties of persons, situations, and behaviors. *Journal of Personality and Social Psychology, 60*(5), 773–794.

Funder, D. C., & Ozer, D. J. (1983). Behavior as a function of the situation. *Journal of Personality and Social Psychology, 44*(1), 107–112.

Gangestad, S., & Simpson, J. A. (1990). Toward an evolutionary history of female sociosexual variation. *Journal of Personality, 58,* 69–96.

Glick, P., & Fiske, S. T. (1996). The Ambivalent Sexism Inventory: Differentiating hostile and benevolent sexism. *Journal of Personality and Social Psychology, 70,* 491–512.

Goffman, E. (1959). *The presentation of self in everyday life.* Garden City: Doubleday.

Gordon, C. (1968). Self-conceptions: Configurations of content. In C. Gordon & K. J. Gergen (Eds.), *The self in social interaction* (Vol. 1, pp. 115–136). New York: Wiley & Sons.

Greenwald, A. G., & Pratkanis, A. R. (1984). The self. In R. S. Wyler & R. K. Srull (Eds.), *Handbook of social cognition.* Hillsdale, NJ: Erlbaum.

Gregg, G. S. (1995). Multiple identities and the integration of personality. *Journal of Personality, 63,* 617–641.

Guisinger, S., & Blatt, S. J. (1994). Individuality and relatedness: Evolution of a fundamental dialectic. *American Psychologist, 49,* 104–111.

Harlow, R. E., & Cantor, N. (1995). To whom do people turn when things go poorly? Task orientation and functional social contacts. *Journal of Personality and Social Psychology, 69*(2), 329–340.

Harlow, R. E., & Cantor, N. (1996). Still participating after all these years: A study of life task participation in later life. *Journal of Personality and Social Psychology, 71,* 1235–1249.

Havighurst, R. J. (1972). *Developmental tasks and education.* New York: Longman.

Hazan, C., & Shaver, P. (1987). Romantic love conceptualized as an attachment process. *Journal of Personality and Social Psychology, 52,* 511–524.

Helson, R., Mitchell, V., & Moane, G. (1984). Personality and patterns of adherence and nonadherence to the social clock. *Journal of Personality and Social Psychology, 46,* 1079–1096.

Helson, R., & Moane, G. (1987). Personality change in women from college to midlife. *Journal of Personality and Social Psychology, 53,* 176–186.

Hermans, H. J. M. (1992). Telling and retelling one's self-narrative: A contextual approach to life-span development. *Human Development, 35,* 361–375.

Hess, R., Azuma, H., Kashiwagi, K., Dickson, W. P., Nagano, S., Holloway, S., Miyake, K., Price, G., Hatano, G., & McDevitt, T. (1986). Family influences on school readiness and achievement in Japan and the United States: An overview of a longitudinal study. In H. Stevenson, H. Azuma, & K. Hakuta (Eds.), *Child development and education in Japan* (pp. 147–166). New York: Freeman.

Higgins, E. T., & Eccles-Parsons, J. E. (1983). Social cognition and the social life of the child: Stages and subcultures. In E. T. Higgins, D. N. Ruble, & W. W. Hartup (Eds.), *Social cognition and social development: A sociocultural perspective* (pp. 15–62). New York: Cambridge University Press.

Hilgard, E. R. (1987). *Psychology in America: A historical survey.* San Diego, CA: Harcourt Brace Jovanovich.

Hilton, J. L. (1997). Interaction goals and person perception. In J. Cooper and J. Darley (Eds.), *Attribution processes, person perception, and social interaction: The legacy of Ned Jones.* Washington, DC: American Psychological Association.

Hilton, J. L., & Darley, J. M. (1985). Constructing other persons: A limit on the effect. *Journal of Experimental Social Psychology, 21*(1), 1–18.

Hilton, J. L., & Darley, J. M. (1991). The effects of interaction goals on person perception. In M. P. Zanna (Ed.), *Advances in experimental social psychology* (Vol. 24, pp. 236–267). San Diego: Academic Press.

House, J. S., & Kahn, R. L. (1985). Measures and concepts of social support. In S. Cohen & S. L. Syme (Eds.), *Social support and health* (pp. 83–108). Orlando, FL: Academic Press.

Household waste threatening environment: Recycling helps ease disposal problem. (1988). *Gallup Report* (No. 280), pp. 30–34.

Hull, J. G., Tedlie, J. C., & Lehn, D. A. (1992). Moderator variables in personality research: The problem of controlling for plausible alternatives. *Personality and Social Psychology Bulletin, 18*(2), 115–117.

Hull, J. G., & Young, R. D. (1983). Self-consciousness, self-esteem, and success-failure as determinants of alcohol consumption in male social drinkers. *Journal of Personality and Social Psychology, 44*(6), 1097–1109.

Ickes, W., Snyder, M., & Garcia, S. (1997). Personality influ-

ences on the choice of situations. In R. Hogan, J. Johnson, & S. Briggs (Eds.), *Handbook of personality psychology.* New York: Academic Press.

Independent Sector. (1990). *Giving and volunteering in the United States.* Washington, DC: Gallup Organization for Independent Sector.

James, W. (1890/1968). The self. In C. Gordon & K. J. Gergen (Eds.), *The self in social interaction* (Vol. 1, pp. 41–49). New York: Wiley and Sons.

Jarvis, W. B. G., & Petty, R. E. (1996). The need to evaluate. *Journal of Personality and Social Psychology, 70*(1), 172–194.

Jones, E. E., & Pittman, T. S. (1982). Toward a general theory of strategic self-presentation. In J. Suls (Ed.), *Psychological perspectives on the self* (Vol. 1, pp. 231–262). Hillsdale, NJ: Erlbaum.

Jones, E. E., & Thibaut, J. (1958). Interaction goals as bases of inference in interpersonal perception. In R. Tagiuri & L. Petrullo (Eds.), *Person perception and interpersonal behavior.* Stanford, CA: Stanford University Press.

Kelley, H. H. (1979). *Personal relationships: Their structures and processes.* Hillsdale, NJ: Erlbaum.

Kelley, H. H. (1992). Common-sense psychology and scientific psychology. *Annual Review of Psychology, 43,* 1–23.

Kelley, H. H., Berscheid, E., Christensen, A., Harvey, J. H., Huston, T. L., Levinger, G., McClintock, E., Peplau, L. A., & Peterson, D. R. (Eds.). (1983). *Close relationships.* New York: Freeman.

Kendrick, D. T. (1986). How strong is the case against contemporary social and personality psychology? A response to Carlson, *Journal of Personality and Social Psychology, 50*(4), 839–844.

Kihlstrom, J. F. (1987). Introduction to the special issue: Integrating personality and social psychology. *Journal of Personality and Social Psychology, 53*(6), 989–992.

Kihlstrom, J. F., & Cantor, N. (1984). Mental representations of the self. In L. Berkowitz (Ed.), *Advances in experimental social psychology: Vol. 17* (pp. 2–40). New York: Academic Press.

Kilduff, M. (1992). The friendship network as a decision-making resource: Dispositional moderators of social influences on organizational choice. *Journal of Personality and Social Psychology, 62*(1), 168–180.

Klein, S. B., & Loftus, J. (1993). The mental representation of trait and autobiographical knowledge about the self. In T. K. Srull & R. S. Wyer (Eds.), *Advances in social cognition: Vol. 5.* Hillsdale, NJ: Erlbaum.

Klein, W. M., & Kunda, Z. (1993). Maintaining self-serving social comparisons: Biased reconstruction of one's past behaviors. *Personality and Social Psychology Bulletin, 19*(6), 732–739.

Klohnen, E. C. (1996). Conceptual analysts and measurement of the construct of ego-resiliency. *Journal of Personality and Social Psychology, 70,* 1067–1079.

Knight, G. P., Johnson, L. G., Carlo, G., & Eisenberg, N. (1994). A multiplicative model of the dispositional antecedents of a prosocial behavior: Predicting more of the people more of the time. *Journal of Personality and Social Psychology, 66*(1), 178–183.

Kohut, A., & Shriver, J. (1989). The environment. *Gallup Report* (No. 285), pp. 2–12.

Kunda, Z., & Sanitioso, R. (1989). Motivated changes in the self-concept. *Journal of Experimental Social Psychology, 25*(3), 272–285.

Lakey, B., McCabe, K. M., Fisicaro, S. A., & Drew, J. B. (1996). Environmental and personal determinants of support perceptions: Three generalizability studies. *Journal of Personality and Social Psychology, 70,* 1270–1280.

Langan-Fox, J. (1991). Motivation and the self concept: Persisting goals of young women and men. *International Journal of Psychology, 26,* 409–427.

Langston, C. A. (1994). Capitalizing on and coping with daily-life events: Expressive responses to positive events. *Journal of Personality and Social Psychology, 67,* 1112–1125.

Larsen, R. J. (1987). The stability of mood variables: A spectral analytic approach to daily mood assessments. *Journal of Personality and Social Psychology, 52,* 1195–1204.

Larsen, R. J., & Kasimatis, M. (1990). Individual differences in entrainment of mood to the weekly calendar. *Journal of Personality and Social Psychology, 58,* 164–171.

Larsen, R. J., & Ketelaar, T. (1991). Personality and susceptibility to positive and negative emotional states. *Journal of Personality and Social Psychology, 61,* 132–140.

Leary, M. R., & Kowalski, R. M. (1990). Impression management: A literature review and two-component model. *Psychological Bulletin, 107,* 34–47.

Lee, G. R., & Stone, L. H. (1980). Mate selection systems and criteria: Variation according to family structure. *Journal of Marriage and the Family, 42,* 319–326.

Lent, R. W., Brown, S. D., & Hackett, G. (1994). Toward a unifying social cognitive theory of career and academic interest, choice, and performance. *Journal of Vocational Behavior, 45,* 79–122.

Levitz-Jones, E. M., & Orlofsky, J. L. (1985). Separation-individuation and intimacy capacity in college women. *Journal of Personality and Social Psychology, 49,* 156–169.

Lewin, K. (1936). *A dynamic theory of personality.* New York. McGraw-Hill.

Little, B. R. (1983). Personal projects: A rationale and method for investigation. *Environment and Behavior, 15*(3), 273–309.

Little, B. R. (1989). Personal projects analysis: Trivial pursuits, magnificent obsessions, and the search for coherence. In D. M. Buss and N. Cantor (Eds.), *Personality psychology: Recent trends and emerging directions* (pp. 15–31). New York: Springer-Verlag.

Lott, A. J., & Lott, B. E. (1974). The role of reward in the formation of positive interpersonal attitudes. In T. L. Huston (Ed.), *Foundations of interpersonal attraction* (pp. 171–189). New York: Academic Press.

Lydon, J. E., & Zanna, M. P. (1990). Commitment in the face of adversity: A value-affirmation approach. *Journal of Personality and Social Psychology, 58,* 1040–1047.

Magnusson, D. (1971). An analysis of situational dimensions. *Perceptual and Motor Skills, 32,* 851–867.

Markus, H., & Cross, S. (1990). The interpersonal self. In L. A. Pervin (Ed.), *Handbook of personality: Theory and research* (pp. 576–608). New York: Guilford.

Markus, H., & Kitayama, S. (1991). Culture and the self: Implications for cognition, emotion, and motivation. *Psychological Review, 98*(2), 224–253.

Markus, H., & Kitayama, S. (1994). A collective fear of the collective: Implications for selves and theories of selves. *Personality and Social Psychology Bulletin, 20*(5), 568–579.

Markus, H. R., & Oyserman, D. (1989). Gender and thought: The role of the self-concept. In M. Crawford & M. Hamilton (Eds.), *Gender and thought* (pp. 100–127). New York: Springer-Verlag.

Marlowe, D., & Gergen, K. J. (1969). Personality and social interaction. In G. Lindzey & E. Aronson (Eds.), *Handbook of social psychology: Vol. 3. The individual in a social context* (2nd ed., pp. 590–665). Reading, MA: Addison-Wesley.

Maslach, C., Santee, R. T., & Wade, C. (1987). Individuation, gender role, and dissent: Personality mediators of situational forces. *Journal of Personality and Social Psychology, 53*(6), 1088–1093.

Matthews, K. A., Siegal, J. M., Kuller, L. H., Thompson, M., & Varat, M. (1983). Determinants of decisions to seek medical treatment by patients with acute myocardial infarction symptoms. *Journal of Personality and Social Psychology, 44*(6), 1144–1156.

McAdams, D. P. (1980). A thematic coding system for the intimacy motive. *Journal of Research in Personality, 14,* 413–432.

McAdams, D. P. (1988). Biography, narrative, and lives: An introduction. *Journal of Personality, 56,* 1–18.

McAdams, D. P. (1989). *Intimacy: The need to be close.* New York: Harper & Row.

McAdams, D. P. (1992). The five factor model in personality: A critical appraisal. Special issue: The five factor model: Issues and applications. *Journal of Personality, 60,* 329–361.

McAdams, D. P. (1993). *Stories we live by: Personal myths and the making of the self.* New York: William Morrow and Company.

McAdams, D. P. (1995). Personality, modernity, and the storied self: A contemporary framework for studying persons. *Psychological Inquiry, 7,* 295–321.

McAdams, D. P., & Bryant, F. B. (1987). Intimacy motivation and subjective mental health in a nationwide sample. *Journal of Personality, 55,* 395–413.

McAdams, D. P., & Constantian, C. A. (1983). Intimacy and affiliation motives in daily living: An experience sampling analysis. *Journal of Personality and Social Psychology, 45,* 851–861.

McAdams, D. P., & Emmons, R. A. (Eds.). (1995). Levels and domains in personality [Special issue]. *Journal of Personality, 63.*

McAdams, D. P., Healy, S., & Krause, S. (1984). Social motives and patterns of friendship. *Journal of Personality and Social Psychology, 47,* 828–838.

McAdams, D. P., Jackson, R. J., & Kirshnit, C. (1984). Looking, laughing, and smiling in dyads as a function of intimacy motivation and reciprocity. *Journal of Personality, 52,* 261–273.

McAdams, D. P., & Powers, J. (1981). Themes of intimacy in behavior and thought. *Journal of Personality and Social Psychology, 40,* 573–587.

McAdams, D. P., & Vaillant, G. E. (1982). Intimacy motivation and psychosocial adjustment: A longitudinal study. *Journal of Personality Assessment, 46,* 586–593.

McCrae, R. R. (Ed.). (1992). The five-factor model: Issues and applications [Special issue]. *Journal of Personality, 60*(2).

McCrae, R. R. (1996). Social consequences of experiential openness. *Psychological Bulletin, 120,* 323–337.

McCrae, R. R., & Costa, P. T., Jr. (1985a). Updating Norman's "adequate taxonomy": Intelligence and personality dimensions in natural language and in questionnaires. *Journal of Personality and Social Psychology, 49,* 710–721.

McCrae, R. R., & Costa, P. T., Jr. (1985b). Openness to experience. In R. Hogan and W. H. Jones (Eds.), *Perspectives on personality: Vol. 1* (pp. 145–172). Greenwich, CT: JAI Press.

McCrae, R. R., & Costa, P. T., Jr. (1987). Validation of the five-factor model of personality across instruments and observers. *Journal of Personality and Social Psychology, 52,* 81–90.

McCrae, R. R., & John, O. P. (1992). An introduction of the five-factor model and its applications. *Journal of Personality, 60,* 175–215.

McGuire, W. J. (1984). Search for the self: Going beyond self-esteem and the reactive self. In R. A. Zucker, J. Aronoff, & A. I. Rabin (Eds.), *Personality and the prediction of behavior* (pp. 73–120). New York: Academic Press.

McGuire, W. J., & McGuire, C. V. (1981). The spontaneous self-concept as affected by personal distinctiveness. In L. Lynch, D. Mervin, A. Norem-Hebeisen, & K. Gergen (Eds.), *Self-concept: Advances in theory and research* (pp. 147–171). New York: Ballinger.

McGuire, W. J., & McGuire, C. V. (1988). Content and process in the experience of self. *Advances in Experimental Social Psychology, 21,* 97–144.

McNulty, S. E., & Swann, W. B., Jr. (1994). Identity negotiation in roommate relationships: The self as architect and consequence of social reality. *Journal of Personality and Social Psychology, 67*(6), 1012–1023.

Mead, G. H. (1934). *Mind, self, and society.* Chicago: University of Chicago Press.

Mendolia, M., Moore, J., & Tesser, A. (1996). Dispositional and situational determinants of repression. *Journal of Personality and Social Psychology, 70*(4), 856–867

Mikulincer, M., & Nachson, O. (1991). Attachment styles and patterns of self-disclosure. *Journal of Personality and Social Psychology, 61,* 321–331.

Miller, J. G. (1988). Bridging the content-structure dichotomy: Culture and the self. In M. H. Bond (Ed.), *Cross cultural research and methodology series: Vol. 11* (pp. 266–281). Newbury Park, CA: Sage.

Miller, L. C., Berg, J. H., & Archer, R. L. (1983). Openers: Individuals who elicit intimate self-disclosure. *Journal of Personality and Social Psychology, 44*(6), 1234–1244.

Miller, L. C. & Kenny, D. A. (1986). Reciprocity of self-disclosure at the individual and dyadic levels: A social relations analysis. *Journal of Personality and Social Psychology, 50,* 713–719.

Miller, L. C., & Read, S. J. (1987). Why am I telling you this? Self-disclosure in a goal-based model of personality. In V. J. Derlega & J. H. Berg (Eds.), *Self-disclosure: Theory, research, and therapy* (pp. 35–58). New York: Plenum.

Miller, L. C., & Read, S. J. (1991). On the coherence of mental models of persons and relationships: A knowledge structure approach. In G. J. O. Fletcher & F. D. Fincham (Eds.), *Cognition in close relationships* (pp. 69–99). Hillsdale, NJ: Erlbaum.

Miller, P. J., Potts, R., Fung, H., Hoogstra, L., & Mintz, J. (1990). Narrative practices and the social construction of self in childhood. *American Ethnologist. 17,* 292–311.

Miller, R. L., Brickman, P., & Bolen, D. (1975). Attribution versus persuasion as a means for modifying behavior. *Journal of Personality and Social Psychology, 31,* 430–441.

Miller, S. (1987). Monitoring and blunting: Validation of a questionnaire to assess styles of information seeking under threat. *Journal of Personality and Social Psychology, 52*(2), 345–353.

Mischel, W. (1968). *Personality and assessment.* New York: Wiley.

Murray, H. A. (Ed.). (1938). *Explorations in personality.* New York: Oxford University Press.

Murtha, T. C., Kanfer, R., & Ackerman, P. L. (1996). Toward an interactionist taxonomy of personality and situations: An integrative situational-dispositional representation of personality traits. *Journal of Personality and Social Psychology, 71*(1), 193–207.

Myers, D. G., & Diener, E. (1995). Who is happy? *Psychological Science, 6,* 10–19.

Neisser, U. (Ed.). (1993). *The perceived self: Ecological and interpersonal sources of self-knowledge.* New York: Cambridge University Press.

Neuberg, S. L. (1989). The goal of forming accurate impressions during social interactions: Attenuating the impact of negative expectancies. *Journal of Personality and Social Psychology, 56*(3), 374–386.

Neuberg, S. L. (1994). Expectancy-confirmation processes in stereotype-tinged social encounters: The moderating role of social goals. In M. P. Zanna & J. M. Olson (Eds.), *The psychology of prejudice: The Ontario Symposium, Vol. 7* (pp. 103–130). Hillsdale, NJ: Erlbaum.

Neuberg, S. L., & Fiske, S. T. (1987). Motivational influences on impression formation: Outcome dependency, accuracy-driven attention, and individuating processes. *Journal of Personality and Social Psychology, 53*(3), 431–444.

Neuberg, S. L., Judice, T. N., Virdin, L. M., & Carrillo, M. A. (1993). Perceiver self-presentational goals as moderators of expectancy influences: Ingratiation and the disconfirmation of negative expectancies. *Journal of Personality and Social Psychology, 64*(3), 409–420.

Niedenthal, P., Cantor, N., & Kihlstrom, J. F. (1985). Prototype matching: A strategy for social decision making. *Journal of Personality and Social Psychology, 48*(3), 575–584.

Niedenthal, P., & Mordkoff, J. T. (1991). Prototype distancing: A strategy for choosing among threatening situations. *Personality and Social Psychology Bulletin, 17*(5), 483–493.

Nolen-Hoeksema, S. (1991). Responses to depression and their effects on the duration of depressive episodes. *Journal of Abnormal Psychology, 100,* 569–582.

Ogilvie, D. M. (1987). The undesired self: A neglected variable in personality research. *Journal of Personality and Social Psychology, 52,* 379–385.

Ogilvie, D. M., & Ashmore, R. (1991). Self-with-other representation as a unit of analysis in self-concept research. In R. C. Curtis (Ed.), *The relational self* (pp. 282–314). New York: Guilford.

Omoto, A. M., & Snyder, M. (1991). AIDS volunteers: Who are they and why do they volunteer. In V. Hodgkinson & R. D. Sumariwalla (Eds.), *Leadership and management.* Washington, DC: Independent Sector.

Omoto, A. M., & Snyder, M. (1995). Sustained helping without obligation: Motivation, longevity of service, and perceived attitude change among AIDS volunteers. *Journal of Personality and Social Psychology, 68,* 671–686.

Omoto, A. M., Snyder, M., & Berghuis, J. P. (1993). The psychology of volunteerism: A conceptual analysis and a program of action research. In J. B. Pryor & G. D. Reeder (Eds.), *The social psychology of HIV infection* (pp. 333–356). Hillsdale, NJ: Erlbaum.

Paunonen, S. V. (1988). Trait relevance and the differential predictability of behavior. *Journal of Personality, 56*(3), 599–619.

Pelham, B. W. (1991). On confidence and consequence: The certainty and importance of self-knowledge. *Journal of Personality and Social Psychology, 60,* 518–530.

Pelletier, L. G., & Vallerand, R. J. (1996). Supervisors' beliefs and subordinates' intrinsic motivation: A behavioral confirmation analysis. *Journal of Personality and Social Psychology, 71,* 331–340.

Penner, L. A., Fritzche, B. A., Craiger, J. P. Freifeld, T. S. (1995). Measuring the prosocial personality. In J. N. Butcher & C. D. Spielberger (Eds.), *Advances in personality assessment,* (Vol. 10, pp. 147–163). Hillsdale, NJ: Erlbaum.

Pervin, L. A. (Ed.). (1989). *Goal concepts in personality and social psychology.* Hillsdale, NJ: Erlbaum.

Pervin, L. A. (1994). A critical analysis of current trait theory. *Psychological Inquiry, 5*(2), 103–113.

Piliavin, J. A., & Charng, H. (1990). Altruism: A review of recent theory and research. *Annual Review of Sociology, 16,* 27–65.

Pratto, F., Sidanius, J., Stallworth, L. M., & Malle, B. F. (1994). Social dominance orientation: A personality variable predicting social and political attitudes. *Journal of Personality and Social Psychology, 67*(4), 741–763.

Pratto, F., Stallworth, L. M., Sidanius, J., & Siers, B. (1997). The gender gap in occupational role attainment: A social dominance approach. *Journal of Personality and Social Psychology, 72,* 37–53.

Pryor, J. B., Giedd, J. L., & Williams, K. B. (1995). A social psychological model for predicting sexual harassment. Special issue: Gender stereotyping, sexual harassment, and the law. *Journal of Social Issues, 51,* 69–84.

Reis, H. T., & Patrick, B. C. (1996). Attachment and intimacy: component processes. In E. T. Higgins & A. W. Kruglanski (Eds.), *Social psychology: Handbook of basic principles* (pp. 523–563). Hillsdale, NJ: Erlbaum.

Reis, H. T., Senchak, M., & Solomon, B. (1985). Sex differences in the intimacy of social interaction: Further examination of potential explanations. *Journal of Personality and Social Psychology, 48,* 1204–1217.

Reis, H. T., & Shaver, P. (1988). Intimacy as an interpersonal process. In S. W. Duck (Ed.), *Handbook of personal relationships* (pp. 367–389). Chichester, England: Wiley.

Revenson, T. A. (1981). Coping with loneliness: The impact of causal attributions. *Personality and Social Psychology Bulletin, 7,* 565–571.

Romer, D., Gruder, C. L., & Lizzaro, T. (1986). A person-situation approach to altruistic behavior. *Journal of Personality and Social Psychology, 51*(5), 1001–1012.

Rook, K. S. (1984). Promoting social bonding: Strategies for helping the lonely and socially isolated. *American Psychologist, 39,* 1389–1407.

Rook, K. S. (1988). Toward a more differentiated view of loneliness. In S. Duck, D. F. Hay, S. E. Hobfoll, W. Ickes, & B. M. Montgomery (Eds.), *Handbook of personal rela-*

tionships: Theory, research, and interventions (pp. 571–589). Chichester, England: John Wiley & Sons.

Rosenthal, R., Baratz, S. S., & Hall, C. M. (1974). Teacher behavior, teacher expectations, and gains in pupils' rated creativity. *Journal of Genetic Psychology, 124*(1), 115–121.

Ross, L., & Nisbett, R. E. (1991). *The person and the situation: Perspectives of social psychology.* New York: McGraw-Hill.

Rudman, L. A., & Borgida, E. (1995). The afterglow of construct accessibility: The behavioral consequences of priming men to view women as sexual objects. *Journal of Experimental Social Psychology, 31,* 493–517.

Rusting, C. L., & Larsen R. J. (1995). Moods as sources of stimulation: Relationship between personality and desired mood states. *Personality and Individual Differences, 18,* 321–329.

Ryff, C. D. (1987). The place of personality and social structure research in social psychology. *Journal of Personality and Social Psychology, 53,* 1192–1202.

Ryff, C. D. (1989). Happiness is everything, or is it? Explorations on the meaning of psychological well-being. *Journal of Personality and Social Psychology, 52,* 823–832.

Salovey, P., Rothman, A. J., & Rodin, J. (1998). Health behavior. In D. Gilbert, S. T. Fiske, & G. Lindzey (Eds.), *The handbook of social psychology* (4th ed., Vol. 2, pp. 633–683). New York: McGraw-Hill.

Sampson, E. E. (1988). The debate on individualism: Indigenous psychologies of the individual and their role in personal and social functioning. *American Psychologist, 43,* 15–22.

Sampson, E. E. (1995). The challenge of social change for psychology: Globalization and psychology's theory of the person. In N. R. Goldberger and J. B. Veroff (Eds.), *The culture and psychology reader* (pp. 417–434). New York: New York University Press.

Sande, G. N., Goethals, G. R., & Radloff, C. E. (1988). Perceiving one's own traits and others': The multifaceted self. *Journal of Personality and Social Psychology, 54,* 13–20.

Sanderson, C. A., & Cantor, N. (1995). Social dating goals in late adolescence: Implications for safer sexual activity. *Journal of Personality and Social Psychology, 68*(6), 1121–1134.

Sanderson, C. A., & Cantor, N. (1997). Creating satisfaction in steady dating relationships: The role of personal goals and situational affordances. *Journal of Personality and Social Psychology,* in press.

Schachter, S. (1959). *The psychology of affiliation: Experimental studies of the sources of gregariousness.* Stanford, CA: Stanford University Press.

Scheier, M. F,. & Carver, C. S. (1985). Optimism, coping, and health. Assessment and implications of generalized outcome expectancies. *Health Psychology, 4,* 219–247.

Schlenker, B. R. (1980). *Impression management: The self-concept, social identity, and interpersonal relations.* Malabar, FL: Robert E. Krieger.

Schlenker, B. R., & Trudeau, J. V. (1990). The impact of self-presentations on private self-beliefs: Effects of prior self-beliefs and misattribution. *Journal of Personality and Social Psychology, 58,* 22–32.

Schlenker, B. R., & Weigold, M. F. (1992). Interpersonal processes involving impression regulation and management. *Annual Review of Psychology, 43,* 133–168.

Schmidt, N., & Sermat, V. (1983). Measuring loneliness in different relationships. *Journal of Personality and Social Psychology, 44*(5), 1038–1047.

Schorr, D., & Rodin, J. (1984). Motivation to control one's environment in individuals with obsessive-compulsive, depressive, and normal personality traits. *Journal of Personality and Social Psychology, 46*(5), 1148–1161.

Schutte, N. S., Kenrick, D. T., & Sadalla, E. K. (1985). The search for predictable settings: Situational prototypes, constraint, and behavioral variation. *Journal of Personality and Social Psychology, 49*(1), 121–128.

Schwartz, S. H. (1992). Are there universal aspects in the structure and contents of human values? *Journals of Social Issues, 50*(4), 19–45.

Scott, C. K., Fuhrman, R. W., & Wyer, R. S., Jr. (1991). Information processing in close relationships. In G. J. O. Fletcher & F. D. Fincham (Eds.), *Cognition in close relationships* (pp. 36–67). Hillsdale, NJ: Erlbaum.

Sedikides, C. (1993). Assessment, enhancement, and verification determinants of the self-evaluation process. *Journal of Personality and Social Psychology, 65,* 317–338.

Setterlund, M. B., & Niedenthal, P. M. (1993). "Who am I? Why am I here?" Self-esteem, self-clarity, and prototype-matching. *Journal of Personality and Social Psychology, 65,* 769–780.

Shaffer, D. R., Ogden, J. K., & Wu, C. (1987). Effects of self-monitoring and prospect of future interaction on self-disclusure reciprocity during the acquaintance process. *Journal of Personality, 55*(1), 75–96.

Sheldon, K. M. (1996). The Social Awareness Inventory: Development and applications. *Personality and Social Psychology Bulletin, 22,* 620–634.

Sherif, M. (1936). *The psychology of social norms.* New York: Harper and Row.

Shoda, Y., Mischel, W., & Wright, J. C. (1993). The role of situational demands and congitive competencies in behavior organization and personality coherence. *Journal of Personality and Social Psychology, 65*(5), 1023–1035.

Shoda, Y., Mischel, W., & Wright, J. C. (1994). Intraindividual stability in the organization and patterning of behavior: Incorporating psychological situations into the idiographic analysis of personality. *Journal of Personality and Social Psychology, 67*(4), 674–687.

Shweder, R. A., & Bourne, E. J. (1991). *Thinking through cul-*

tures: Expeditions in cultural psychology. Cambridge, MA: Harvard University Press.

Simpson, J. A. (1992). Support seeking and support giving within couples in an anxiety-provoking situation: The role of attachment styles. *Journal of Personality and Social Psychology, 62,* 434–446.

Singelis, T. M., & Brown, W. J. (1995). Culture, self, and collectivist communication: Linking culture to individual behavior. *Human Communication Research, 21*(3), 354–389.

Singer, J. A. (1995). Seeing one's self: Locating narrative memory in a framework of personality. *Journal of Personality, 63,* 429–457.

Singer, J. A., & Salovey, P. (1988). Mood and memory: Evaluating the network theory of affect. *Clinical Psychology Review, 8,* 211–251.

Singer, J. A., & Salovey, P. (Eds.). (1993). *The remembered self: Emotion and memory in personality.* New York: Free Press.

Slavin, R. E. (1985). Cooperative learning: Applying contact theory in desegregated schools. *Journal of Social Issues, 41,* 45–62.

Snyder, C. R., Harris, C., Anderson, J. R., Holleran, S. A., Irving, L. M., Sigmon, S. T., Yoshinobu, L., Gibb, J., Langelle, C., & Harney, P. (1991). The will and the ways: Development and validation of an individual-differences measure of hope. *Journal of Personality and Social Psychology, 60*(4), 570–585.

Snyder, M. (1979). Self-monitoring processes. In L. Berkowitz (Ed.), *Advances in experimental social psychology: Vol. 12* (pp. 85–128). New York: Academic Press.

Snyder, M. (1981). On the influence of individuals on situations. In N. Cantor & J. F. Kihlstrom (Eds.), *Personality, cognition, and social interaction.* Hillsdale, NJ: Lawrence Erlbaum Associates.

Snyder, M. (1984). When belief creates reality. *Advances in Experimental Social Psychology, 18,* 247–305.

Snyder, M. (1987a). *Public appearances/Private realities: The psychology of self-monitoring.* New York: W. H. Freeman and Company.

Snyder, M. (1987b, August). The study of personality and psychological social psychology. Paper presented at the 95th Annual Convention of the American Psychological Association, New York, NY.

Snyder, M. (1992). Motivational foundations of behavioral confirmation. *Advances in Experimental Social Psychology, 25,* 67–114.

Snyder, M. (1993). Basic research and practical problems: The promise of a "functional" personality and social psychology. *Personality and Social Psychology Bulletin, 19*(3), 251–264.

Snyder, M. (1997). Interaction goals: Their structure and function. In J. Cooper & J. Darley (Eds.), *Attribution processes, person perception, and social interaction: The*

legacy of Ned Jones. Washington, DC: American Psychological Association.

Snyder, M., Berscheid, E., & Glick, P. (1985). Focusing on the exterior and the interior. Two investigations of the initiation of personal relationships. *Journal of Personality and Social Psychology, 48*(6), 1427–1439.

Snyder, M., Gangestad, S., & Simpson, J. A. (1983). Choosing friends as activity partners: The role of self-monitoring. *Journal of Personality and Social Psychology, 45*(5), 1061–1072.

Snyder, M., & Haugen, J. A. (1994). Why does behavioral confirmation occur? A functional perspective on the role of the perceiver. *Journal of Experimental Social Psychology, 30*(3), 218–246.

Snyder, M., & Haugen, J. A. (1995). Why does behavioral confirmation occur? A functional perspective on the role of the target. *Personality and Social Psychology Bulletin, 21*(9), 963–974.

Snyder, M., & Ickes, W. (1985). Personality and social behavior. In G. Lindzey & E. Aronson (Eds.), *Handbook of social psychology: Vol. 2. Special fields and applications* (3rd ed., pp. 883–948). New York: Random House.

Snyder, M., & Omoto, A. M. (1992). Volunteerism and society's response to the HIV epidemic. *Current Directions in Psychological Science, 1*(4), 113–116.

Snyder, M., & Simpson, J. A. (1984). Self-monitoring and dating relationships. *Journal of Personality and Social Psychology, 47,* 1281–1291.

Snyder, M., Simpson, J. A., & Gangestad, S. (1986). Personality and sexual relations. *Journal of Personality and Social Psychology, 51*(1), 181–190.

Snyder, M., & Swann, W. B. (1978). Behavioral confirmation in social interaction: From social perception to social reality. *Journal of Experimental Social Psychology, 14*(2), 148–162.

Sorrentino, R. M., & Hewitt, E. C. (1984). The uncertainty-reducing properties of achievement tasks revisited. *Journal of Personality and Social Psychology, 47*(4), 884–899.

Sroufe, L. A. (1996). *Emotional development: The organization of emotional life in the early years.* New York: Cambridge University Press.

Steele, C. M. (1988). The psychology of self-affirmation: Sustaining the integrity of the self. *Advances in Experimental Social Psychology, 21,* 261–301.

Stewart, A. J., & Healy, J. M. (1989). Linking individual development and social change. *American Psychologist, 44,* 30–42.

Stewart, A. J., & Healy, J. M., Jr. (1992). Assessing adaptation to life changes in terms of psychological stances toward the environment. In C. P. Smith, J. W. Atkinson, D. C. McClelland, & J. Veroff (Eds.), *Motivation and personality: Handbook of thematic content analysis* (pp. 440–450). New York: Cambridge University Press.

Swann, W. B., Jr. (1984). Self-verification: Bringing social reality into harmony with the self. In J. Suls & A. G. Greenwald (Eds.), *Psychological perspectives on the self* (Vol. 2, pp. 33–66). Hillsdale, NJ: Erlbaum.

Swann, W. B., Jr. (1987). Identity negotiation: Where two roads meet. *Journal of Personality and Social Psychology, 53*(6), 1038–1051.

Swann, W. B., Jr., & Ely, R. J. (1984). A battle of wills: Self-verification versus behavioral confirmation. *Journal of Personality and Social Psychology, 46*(6), 1287–1302.

Swann, W. B., Jr., Pelham, B. W., & Krull, D. S. (1989). Agreeable fancy or disagreeable truth? Reconciling self-enhancement and self-verification. *Journal of Personality and Social Psychology, 57,* 782–791.

Swann, W. B., Jr., Stein-Seroussi, A., & Giesler, R. B. (1992). Why people self-verify. *Journal of Personality and Social Psychology, 62*(3), 392–401.

Swap, W. C., & Rubin, J. Z. (1983). Measurement of interpersonal orientation. *Journal of Personality and Social Psychology, 44*(1), 208–219.

Tajfel, H. (Ed.). (1982). *Social identity and intergroup relations.* London: Cambridge University Press.

Tangney, J. P. (1990). Assessing individual differences in proneness to shame and guilt: Development of the self-conscious affect and attribution inventory. *Journal of Personality and Social Psychology, 59*(1), 102–111.

Taylor, S. E., & Lobel, M. (1989). Social comparison activity under threat: Downward evaluation and upward contacts. *Psychological Review, 96,* 569–575.

Tedeschi, J. T., & Norman, N. (1985). Social power, self-presentation, and the self. In B. R. Schlenker (Eds.), *The self and social life* (pp. 293–322). New York: McGraw-Hill.

Thompson, E. P., Chaiken, S., & Hazlewood, J. D. (1993). Need for cognition and desire for control as moderators of extrinsic reward effects: A person $\times$ situation approach to the study of intrinsic motivation. *Journal of Personality and Social Psychology, 64*(6), 987–999.

Thorne, A. (1987). The press of personality: A study of conversations between introverts and extraverts. *Journal of Personality and Social Psychology, 53*(4), 718–726.

Tice, D. M., & Baumeister, R. F. (1985). Masculinity inhibits helping in emergencies: Personality does predict the bystander effect. *Journal of Personality and Social Psychology, 49*(2), 420–428.

Tomasello, M. (1993). On the interpersonal origins of self concept. In U. Neisser (Ed.), *The perceived self: Ecological and interpersonal sources of self-knowledge* (pp. 174–184). New York: Cambridge University Press.

Triandis, H. C. (1989). The self and social behavior in differing cultural contexts. *Psychological Review, 96*(3), 506–520.

Triandis, H. C. (1993). Collectivism and individualism as cultural syndromes. *Cross-Cultural Research: The Journal of Comparative Social Science, 27*(3–4), 155–180.

Triandis, H. C., McCusker, C., & Hui, C. H. (1990). Multimethod probes of individualism and collectivism. *Journal of Personality and Social Psychology, 59*(5), 1006–1020.

Turner, J. C., Oakes, P. J., Haslem, S. A., & McGarty, C. (1994). Self and collective: Cognition and social context. *Personality and Social Psychology Bulletin, 20,* 454–463.

Verba, S., Schlozman, K. L., & Brady, H. E. (1995). *Voice and equality: Civic voluntarism in American politics.* Cambridge, MA: Harvard University Press.

Veroff, J. (1983). Contextual determinants of personality. *Personality and Social Psychology Bulletin, 9,* 331–343.

Waller, N. G., Benet, V., & Farney, D. L. (1994). Modeling person-situation correspondence over time: A study of 103 Evangelical disciple-makers. *Journal of Personality, 62*(2), 177–197.

Watson, D. (1988). Intraindividual and interindividual analyses of positive and negative affect: Their relation to health complaints, perceived stress, and daily activities. *Journal of Personality and Social Psychology, 54,* 1020–1030.

Watson, D., & Clark, L. A. (1984). Negative affectivity: The disposition to experience aversive emotional states. *Psychological Bulletin, 96,* 465–490.

Watson, D., Clark, L. A., & Tellegen, A. (1988). Development and validation of brief measures of positive and negative affect: The PANAS Scales. *Journal of Personality and Social Psychology, 54,* 1063–1070.

Webster, D. M., & Kruglanski, A. W. (1994). Individual differences in need for cognitive closure. *Journal of Personality and Social Psychology, 67*(6), 1049–1062.

Weisz, J. R., Rothbaum, F. M., & Blackburn, T. C. (1984). Standing out and standing in: The psychology of control in America and Japan. *American Psychologist, 39*(9), 955–969.

West, S. G., Aiken, L. S., & Krull, J. L. (1996). Experimental personality designs: Analyzing categorical by continuous variable interactions. *Journal of Personality, 64,* 1–48.

Wicker, A. W. (1969). Attitudes versus actions: The relationship of verbal and overt behavioral responses to attitude objects. *Journal of Social Issues, 25,* 41–78.

Williams, K. D., & Best, D. L. (1990). *Sex and psyche: Gender and self viewed cross-culturally.* Newbury Park, CA: Sage.

Winter, D. G. (1973). *The power motive.* New York: Free Press.

Woike, B. A. (1994). The use of differentiation and integration processes: Empirical studies of "separate" and "connected" ways of thinking. *Journal of Personality and Social Psychology, 67,* 142–150.

Woike, B. A., & Aronoff, J. (1992). Antecedent of complex social cognitions. *Journal of Personality and Social Psychology, 63,* 97–104.

Wood, J. V. (1989). Theory and research concerning social comparisons of personal attributes. *Psychological Bulletin, 106,* 231–248.

Wood, J. V., Giordano-Beech, M., Taylor, K. L., Michela, J.

L., & Gaus, V. (1994). Strategies of social comparison among people with low self-esteem: Self-protection and self-enhancement. *Journal of Personality and Social Psychology, 67*(4), 713–731.

Wright, J. C., & Mischel, W. (1987). A conditional approach to dispositional constructs: The local predictability of social behavior. *Journal of Personality and Social Psychology, 53,* 1159–1177.

Wuthnow, R. (1994). *Sharing the journey: Support groups and America's new quest for community.* New York: Free Press.

Zanna, M. P., & Pack, S. J. (1975). On the self-fulfilling nature of apparent sex differences in behavior. *Journal of Experimental Social Psychology, 11,* 584–591.

Zeldow, P. B., Daugherty, S. R., & McAdams, D. P. (1988). Intimacy, power, and psychological well-being in medical students. *Journal of Nervous and Mental Disease, 176,* 182–187.

Zirkel, S. (1992). Developing independence in a life transition: Investing the self in the concerns of the day. *Journal of Personality and Social Psychology, 61,* 506–521.

Zirkel S., & Cantor, N. (1990). Personal construal of life tasks: Those who struggle for independence. *Journal of Personality and Social Psychology, 58*(1), 172–185.

Zuckerman, M., Koestner, R., DeBoy, T., Garcia, T., Maresca, B. C., & Sartoris, J. M. (1988). To predict some of the people some of the time: A reexamination of the moderator variable approach in personality theory. *Journal of Personality and Social Psychology, 54*(6), 1006–1019.

Zuwerink, J. R., & Devine, P. G. (1996). Attitude importance and resistance to persuasion: It's not just the thought that counts. *Journal of Personality and Social Psychology, 70,* 931–944.

CHAPTER FIFTEEN

THE SELF

ROY F. BAUMEISTER, *Case Western Reserve University*

INTRODUCTION

What is the self? In some ways, the thousands of journal articles dealing with the self have seemed to make the answer to that fundamental question more elusive rather than clearer. Even finding a way to sort and group that mass of information is intimidating. This overview of the social psychology of self begins with the proposition that there are three important roots of selfhood. These are powerful, prototypical patterns of experience in which people grasp the basic meaning of self.

The first is the experience of reflexive consciousness, that is, conscious attention turning back toward its own source and gradually constructing a concept of oneself. When you lie awake in bed late at night, thinking about your failures and inadequacies, or glorying in your triumphs; when you look in the mirror or step on the scale or read your resume; when after hearing about someone else's heroic or heinous action, you pause to wonder whether you are the sort of person who could ever do such a thing; when you contemplate your future or your spiritual center or your dwindling resources; or when you try to answer some questions honestly about your opinions, traits, habits, qualifications, and past experiences—these are the sort of experiences that involve reflexive consciousness. Without them, self would have no meaning or value and would hardly exist at all. Self begins when awareness turns around in a circle, so to speak.

The second root is the interpersonal aspect of selfhood. When someone looks into your eyes and smiles a little and says your name, and you have a feeling of warm gladness; or the same happens and you feel anxious terror; when you join a group, or quit it; when you have drinks and sex to celebrate an anniversary; when you try to make a good impression on someone or live up to that person's expectations; when you discover that someone has been watching you and you blush; when you keep a promise to a friend; when you attend your child's graduation; when you feel humiliated and jealous upon learning that your beloved has had romantic contact with someone else; when you exult after defeating a major rival in an important competition, or despair after losing same—these and similar experiences reveal the interpersonal aspect of self. Selfhood is almost unthinkable outside a social context, and selves are vital for making interpersonal relationships and interactions possible. Selves are handles and tools for relating to other people.

The third is the executive function, the agent, the controller, the origin. When you make a resolution or vow; when you drag yourself out of bed too early on a cold morning; when you decide what it is that you really want to buy or work on or become; when you stop yourself from acting on an impulse, such as to eat or drink or smoke, or to hit someone, or to sleep with the wrong person; when you vote, or when you take out a bank loan; when you resist fatigue and temptation and make yourself put forth the maximum effort, beyond the normal call of duty—these experiences involve the executive function of self as an active agent and decision-maker. Without this aspect, the self would be a mere helpless spectator of events, of minimal use or importance.

I thank NIMH Grant 51482 for support, Steve Hastings and Brenda Wilson for research assistance, and Todd Heatherton, Kristin Sommer, Dianne Tice, and social seminar members for comments on a draft.

These three types of experience are what constitute self-hood. These three things are what bodies do, and they comprise the major experiences of selfhood. At present they seem adequate to encompass social psychology's wide assortment of contributions to the psychology of self, and this chapter will group the research findings according to these three basic facets of self.

The present chapter is decidedly not trying to coin new terms or propose new concepts. These terms (reflexive consciousness, interpersonal being, and executive function) are standard, generic terms borrowed from prior usage. They have the advantage of being broad and precise, and they are not linked to or based on any of the particular current theories about the self.

If one could understand all the ways that these three aspects of self are interrelated, one would attain to a deep and full understanding of the nature of selfhood, but that is at least several decades away. For the present, there is sufficient challenge in merely fleshing out the three categories, while scarcely beginning to address the questions of integration. This sounds as if a full understanding of the self is a long way off, and it is, but that does not detract from the fact that social psychology has made enormous progress.

Background

In 1943, a leading and influential social psychologist wrote that "we may safely predict that ego-psychology will flourish increasingly" (Allport, 1943). The subsequent half-century has abundantly confirmed that prediction. Indeed, although Allport himself once proposed that the attitude is the most important concept in social psychology, self has equal claim. A recent survey of articles in psychology found 31,550 abstracts dealing with *self* during the two decades 1974–1993, which is roughly the same tally found for *attitude* (Ashmore & Jussim, in press). It is clear that the study of self has preoccupied social psychologists and their colleagues, as indicated by a steady flow of special conferences, special issues of journals, and edited books, as well as the ordinary flow of scientific publications. Trying to keep abreast of the research on self is like trying to get a drink from a fire hose.

The difficulty in compiling a comprehensive overview of the social psychology of self has multiple sources, beyond the sheer volume of information. One source of difficulty is that self is not really a single topic at all, but rather an aggregate of loosely related subtopics. Indeed, if one were to list all the terms used by social psychologists that start with the prefix *self*, one would have a long list that would begin to show the diversity and heterogeneity of self as a topic of study. A partial list of such subtopics would include self-affirmation, self-appraisal, self-as-target effect, self-awareness, self-concept, self-construal, self-deception, self-defeating behavior, self-enhancement, self-esteem,

self-evaluation maintenance, self-interest, self-monitoring, self-perception, self-presentation, self-protection, self-reference, self-regulation, self-serving bias, self-verification.

Providing a comprehensive overview of the research literature on self is further complicated by the fact that the research community has repeatedly shifted its interests and emphases among the many subtopics. In the 1970s, research on self-perception, identity crisis, self-monitoring, and self-concept flourished, while self-presentation and self-schema received only sporadic interest. The latter two topics came into their own in the early 1980s, but interest had diminished by the end of that decade, when self-regulation was instead attracting heavy interest from multiple perspectives. Meanwhile, interest in self-awareness and self-esteem has been perennial, but the concepts, methods, and theories have changed, in some cases radically. Looking ahead to the turn of the century, it seems safe to predict that the self will continue to be in the center of social psychology, but it is much more hazardous to guess which subtopics will capture the interest and efforts of the leading researchers.

Definitions

Although the word *self* is probably spoken by nearly everyone every day, especially if one includes part-word usages (e.g., *yourself*), it is quite difficult to define. Probably the term is rooted in such widespread common experience and basic linguistic, communicative needs that linguistic definitions may often fail to do it justice. Even dictionaries are quite unhelpful for defining *self*. It is a word that everyone uses but no one defines. The present treatment assumes that everyone is familiar with colloquial usages of the word *self*, and the word here is used in the same meaning that it has in such everyday speech.

A particular source of confusion in social psychology is the occasional use of *self* and *self-concept* as if the two terms were interchangeable. A self-concept is an idea about something; the entity to which the self-concept refers is the self. As we shall see, there are important reasons for confusing the two, beyond mere conceptual sloppiness or laziness, because part of the nature of selfhood involves cognitive construction. Yet it is easy to see the fallacy: If the self were only a concept, how could it make decisions or carry on relationships to people?

A well-known paper by Epstein (1973) criticized the notion of a self-concept and said that it may be more appropriate to speak of a self-theory. That is, people have ideas about the nature of the self, about the world, and about the interactions between the two. This view effectively distinguishes the self from the self-concept (a.k.a. self-theory), as well as placing self-knowledge in an appropriately pragmatic context.

Unity versus Multiple Selves   Although most theories of self and identity have emphasized unity as a defining criterion, several treatments in social psychology have discussed multiple selves. But the concept of self loses its meaning if a person has multiple selves, and the discussions of multiplicity should be regarded as heuristics or metaphors. The essence of self involves integration of diverse experiences into a unity. As Loevinger (1969) wrote, "to integrate . . . experience is not one ego function among many but the essence of the ego" (p. 85).

In a famous, often-quoted passage, William James wrote, "A man has as many social selves as there are individuals who recognize him and carry an image of him in their mind" (1892, p. 179). Taken literally, the sentence is plainly absurd. If each person who knew the man knew a different self, his acquaintances could not even talk about him as the same person. More likely, they know the same self and disagree about some of his attributes. Even such disagreements will tend to be small, if only because of cognitive convenience. As Tesser and Moore (1986) pointed out, it is extremely difficult to maintain very many different impressions in different acquaintances. James himself began backing off from that dramatic assertion immediately, by saying that it would be more correct to propose that there are as many social selves as *groups* of individuals who know him, and that changes in behavior with different audiences resulted in "practically" a division into different selves. The multiplicity of selfhood is a metaphor. The unity of selfhood is its defining fact.

The attributes, therefore, cannot be mistaken for the being of the self. This point was made cleverly long before James. David Hume (1739) wrote that if the self is understood to be the totality of thoughts, feelings, and perceptions, then as soon as one learns or forgets anything— thereby altering the sum totality—one has a new self. A similar argument refutes the notion that memory constitutes the self. Instead, memory seems to presuppose self. As Shoemaker (1963) explained, without presupposing selfhood, a man could not remember that *he* broke the front window last week; he could only remember that *someone* broke the front window last week.

More recently, Singer and Salovey (1993) have explored how the self constructs memory. Seemingly minor events may become focal, important memories because they embody important motivational themes of the self. Such self-defining events can continue to evoke emotional responses long after the fact, simply because of their continuing relevance to the self's goals.

This issue of unity versus multiplicity has not been fully resolved. Most people would say that being a wife or a lawyer is part of someone's identity. Yet if the person gets a divorce or changes jobs, is she now someone else? Similar misunderstandings have produced differing interpretations of Markus and Nurius's (1986) widely cited concept of "possible selves." They explained that people have multiple concepts of how they might turn out, such as the overweight self, the slender self, the successful self, the self in prison, the self as parent, and so forth. Again, though, these are all conceptions of the same self in different circumstances (and with different attributes).

In short, unity is one of the defining features of selfhood and identity. Concepts of multiple selfhood may be dramatic metaphors for discussing some phenomena, not to mention their usefulness in science fiction, but they do risk undermining the basic concept of self. Different people have different perspectives on the same self, and so there may be variations among the cognitive representations of the self (e.g., Higgins, 1987), but it is the same self.

Nature of Selfhood   Thus, what is constant in terms of the meaning of self? Ideally there would be one single core phenomenon that would be constant across cultures and societies, and one could point to that as the basic root of selfhood. Instead of one, however, it seems necessary to propose several, because not all usages of self refer to the same basic phenomenon. Three basic root phenomena of selfhood will be emphasized here, and they will serve as the organizing scheme for this chapter. These are the three categories of self-experience with which this chapter began. Let us briefly offer definitions to accompany the examples given earlier.

First, the experience of reflexive consciousness appears to be common to all normal human beings and is central to the nature of selfhood. By reflexive consciousness is meant the experience in which the person is aware of self. (The term *reflexive* is used here in its linguistic sense of referring back to self, and it has nothing to do with reflexes.) Reflexive consciousness is what enables identical twins to tell themselves apart. In a seemingly miraculous fashion, the information-processing capacity that makes people aware of their environments can be turned around to become aware of self. Without this capacity, selfhood would be absent or meaningless.

Second, the self is an interpersonal being. Selves do not develop and flourish as atomistic units in isolation. Existentialists were once fond of remarking that a person enters (and leaves) the world alone, but that assertion is empirically false: People are always born in the presence of others, and they only survive to adulthood by virtue of extensive social contact. Furthermore, people learn who and what they are from other people, and they always have identities as members of social groups. By the same token, close personal relationships are potent and probably crucial to the development of selfhood. A human being who spent his or her entire life in social isolation would almost certainly have a stunted and deficient self.

Third, the self is an entity that makes choices and decisions, initiates action, and takes responsibility. It has an executive function, so to speak. It has become conventional to label this aspect of selfhood as that of being an *agent*, but that usage is slightly misleading. In ordinary speech, being an agent is a matter of acting for someone else (e.g., an insurance agent or FBI agent), whereas for self theory the essence of agency involves acting on one's own. Selves make choices and are defined in turn by the choices that they make. For this reason, the term *executive function* will be used here to refer to the aspect of self that makes choices and initiates actions.

A particularly important aspect of the executive function involves how the self acts upon itself, often altering or overriding its initial responses. The capacity for self-regulation exists to a limited extent in many living creatures, but it is far more extensively developed among human beings than among other species. Indeed, it can be regarded as the sovereign or master function that is involved in nearly all the self's activities (Higgins, 1996; see also Baumeister, Heatherton, & Tice, 1994; Carver & Scheier, 1981). A full understanding of selfhood is impossible without an appreciation of self-regulation.

In sum, the psychological self may be understood as the totality of these three types of activities and experiences. Self begins with the human body and involves the construction of a definition that entails unity and temporal continuity. Self is an entity marked by reflexive consciousness, interpersonal roles and reputation, and executive function.

Plan of Chapter   In the following sections, social psychology's major research findings on self will be presented, organized according to the three experiential roots of selfhood. This organization will allow seemingly disparate areas to be presented together if they share common assumptions about what the self is or what aspect of self is to be studied. Historical and cultural variations in selfhood will then be covered in a final section.

Although a great deal of information will be covered in the following pages, it is inevitable that a great deal is also left out. The effort to be broadly inclusive in the available space also entails that many topics will receive shorter shrift than their most enthusiastic adherents will think appropriate. Priority has been given to main findings, core ideas, issues needing further study, and especially material that has broad implications for the nature of self. This chapter seeks to illuminate the nature of self by an integrative, interpretive reading of social psychology's research findings. It is not, therefore, an exhaustive presentation of everything social psychologists have had to say about the self.

REFLEXIVE CONSCIOUSNESS

The capacity of the human organism to be conscious of itself is a distinguishing feature and is vital to selfhood.

Without it, people would not be able to grasp the meaning of self. This does not imply that all aspects of self are conscious. But a conscious experience is central to selfhood. In particular, all cognitive representations of self invoke this reflexive consciousness, at least to the extent of providing the entity (the self) to which they refer.

In psychology, a famous and influential formulation by William James (1892) distinguished between the "I" and the "me" as the two main parts of the self. The "I" referred to the knower, in the sense of being the active perceiver; the "me" referred to the known aspect of selfhood, as in the self-concept. Reflexive consciousness is in these terms a matter of the "I" perceiving the "me." Both the "I" and the "me" will be covered in this section.

Yet speaking in terms of the "I" and the "me" can be misleading. There is no single or simple object that is the "me" that can be directly perceived. This fact has plagued self-awareness theory from the start. Thus, in social psychology, the original and seminal formulation by Duval and Wicklund (1972) proposed that attention can be directed either outward or inward, that is, to the stimulus environment or to the self, as if the two were on a par. The problem with that simple and elegant formulation is it is too simple: there is no one entity that is the object of such awareness, as if you could be aware of self in the same way you are aware of a table or a painting. David Hume raised this problem two centuries ago. He said that whenever he sought to attend to his self, he found instead some act of perceiving something else: "I can never catch *myself* at any time without a perception, and never can observe any thing but the perception" (1739, p. 534).

Instead, it seems more appropriate to propose that self-awareness is superimposed on other awareness; the self is caught in the act, so to speak, of doing something else in interaction with the world. This is an idea that has been put forward occasionally, less often than the simple-object theories, but perhaps less often because it is more complicated. It does have some impressive supporters. Probably the first and in some ways still the best formulation was in a key passage of Kant's (1787/1956) *Critique of Pure Reason*. Kant said (agreeing with Hume) you cannot perceive yourself directly. However, the act of perceiving something in the world can itself become perceived. So you perceive the act of perceiving (hence the term *apperception*, perception of a perception), and get some information about the self that way, although it has to be distilled. The self is not perceived, but some activity of the self is perceived, and one can learn about the self from that.

There are important implications that accompany Kant's point. The self is not perceived directly, but always inferred or deduced. The self can only be perceived in relation to the world. One can notice or imagine oneself doing various things and being in various places, but one cannot perceive or imagine oneself completely separate from all social context or situations. The self is always situated. You can be aware of self riding a bicycle or losing an argument or asking for a date or paying bills or sitting alone, but you cannot be directly aware of the self without some such situation.

The self that transcends situations is therefore always a construction, which is to say a product of abstraction, inference, and deduction, rather than something known directly. Only one's experiences are known directly. Consider what is involved in knowing that you are shy. You notice that you always get nervous in the presence of others, and you prefer to avoid large social gatherings and meeting new people; these observations permit the conclusion that you are shy, in the sense that your self-concept acquires the trans-situational schema of shyness. But you cannot perceive your shyness directly, in the absence of encounters with the world and the absence of behavioral and emotional responses.

A similar conclusion emerges from recent cognitive work. In particular, Higgins (1996) argues persuasively that self-knowledge is not primarily sought in isolation or for its own sake. He says that people construct a "self digest" that contains useful information about the self, and the driving question behind the construction of the self digest is not "Who am I?" but rather "What is my relation to the world?" In this view, self-knowledge is pursued for the sake of adaptive benefits of improving person-environment fit. Knowing the self is a means, not an end in itself, and the nature of the self-knowledge reflects this pragmatic, interactive focus.

The implication is that the "me"—the conceptions of self that the person has, and that others have of him or her—is a construct, the result of cognitive processes, rather than a real entity that exists in the world. These constructions are tentative inferences, hypotheses, conclusions based on observations, so they are unlikely to be a precise fit to what the person will actually do, although close. Moreover, after a body of knowledge about the self is built up, the person can reflect on it, and in that sense one can be self-aware of an abstract, disembodied self. But self-awareness does not yield a direct, decontextualized perception of self. *Self-knowledge* is therefore more accurate than *self-perception* as a term to refer to the "me." One does not perceive the self directly, but rather one builds up knowledge about the self, and so one can use and think about this knowledge base.

The notion that the self is just an object to be perceived like any other retains its appeal, however. It is implicit in the modern Western conception of the inner or hidden self that can be discovered. Indeed, many of today's leading researchers on self grew up amid the hippies of the 1960s who could speak with a straight face of "finding yourself" and "being yourself" and of seeking optimal attunement to "inner vibes." The popular idea of self as buried treasure or submerged wonderland probably reflects some belief that

perceiving the self directly is hampered by various obstacles, rather than being inherently impossible.

Self-Reference

Well before the cognitive revolution, social psychologists noticed that information pertaining to the self was processed in special ways. In an important early study of how people would predict future performance from recent performance feedback, Jones, Rock, Shaver, Goethals, and Ward (1968) found opposite patterns for self as opposed to others. Specifically, feedback about other people showed a clear primacy effect, whereas feedback about the self showed a recency effect. Apparently, people make up their minds about others rather quickly but remain open-minded to revising self-appraisals, especially when upward revisions are implied. Later, the distinction between the self-attributions and other-attributions became one of the cornerstones of attribution theory in the actor-observer bias (Jones & Nisbett, 1971), which again asserted that people will often draw firm dispositional inferences about others while refusing to do so about themselves.

An early contribution to social cognition was the *self-reference effect* (Rogers, Kuiper, & Kirker, 1977): information bearing on the self is processed more thoroughly and deeply, and hence remembered better, than other information. Subjects in Rogers et al.'s studies were presented with a series of words and asked to make a judgment about each one. When the judgment was *does this word describe you?*, people recalled the word much better than if the judgment did not involve the self. This effect applied even for words that the person decided did not pertain to the self. Apparently, thinking about the word in relation to the self was sufficient to create a stronger memory trace, as compared to thinking about the word in some other connection.

This is not to say that the self is unique or extraordinary as a memory organizer. Greenwald and Banaji (1989) likewise found self-reference effects, in the sense that words cued by self-generated names were remembered better than words cued by other-generated names. Still, they concluded that the mnemonic benefits of self are due to "the self's being a highly familiar and well-organized body of evaluatively polarized knowledge" (p. 50). Other memory hooks with similar properties may confer similar advantages. Higgins and Bargh (1987) likewise concluded that self-reference is neither necessary nor sufficient for facilitation of memory, and that the effects of the self on memory are not unique. Still, the self is one powerful memory system, and things generated by the self do leave especially strong memory traces.

The self-reference effect may account for a variety of other findings. Langer (1975) showed that when people chose their own lottery ticket, they requested a higher price to resell it (before the lottery) than did people who were simply assigned a particular ticket. Choice thus seems to invoke self-reference: the fact that people had chosen something made it more valuable to them, even though all lottery tickets were of the same value and each had precisely the same chance of winning.

Events that bear on the self are treated differently. Staw (1976) studied irrational persistence in an unsuccessful course of action. He found that persistence was greater if the initial decision was one's own, as opposed to someone else's. Beggan (1994) showed that people will construct a more positive cognitive frame for loan repayment if it is their own debt rather than someone else's that is to be repaid.

Ownership may be an important form of self-reference. Ownership consists of a special bond between the self and some object, and so the existence of a self is presupposed. Beggan (1992) found that attitudes toward objects (cold drink insulators) were affected by ownership: people liked them better when they owned them, even when the gift had been apparently random and when they had not used them or become familiar with them. Kahneman, Knetsch, and Thaler (1990) showed that things seem to gain in value merely by being owned, in the sense that people demand a higher price to sell something than they would give to buy it. Thus, merely owning something—attaching it to the self—apparently endows it with special, increased value.

The ownership effect extends even to seemingly trivial things. Nuttin (1985, 1987) has shown that people prefer letters from their own name over other letters of the alphabet. It is hard to argue that there is any rational or pragmatic basis for such a bias. It suggests the power of the self to endow things with value and affection.

Self-Awareness

Awareness of self seems to be the very essence of reflexive consciousness, although the simple experience of attending to oneself does not exhaust all the research efforts done under the rubric of self-awareness. Self-awareness theory was introduced into social psychology in 1972 in a book by Duval and Wicklund that was clearly ahead of its time. Experiments based on measuring behavioral changes caused by seating subjects in front of mirrors were initially dismissed by some psychologists as frivolous, but self-awareness theory has continued to evolve and add new methods and concepts, to the point at which it has become one of the most steadily productive spheres of self theory throughout the last three decades. Undoubtedly the wide range and variety of work in self-awareness indicate not only the enduring creativity of the original researchers but also the fertility and importance of the topic.

As the work developed, the terms proliferated. Most researchers follow the conventions proposed by Carver and Scheier (1981): *self-awareness* refers to the state, *self-*

consciousness refers to the personality trait, and *self-attention* and *self-focus* refer to either or both.

Basic Theory The original theory proposed by Duval and Wicklund (1972) said that self-awareness was "binary" in the sense that it can be directed either inward or outward. Some features of the original theory, such as a distinction between different kinds of self-awareness (objective and subjective), have failed to have any meaningful impact in the subsequent empirical work and therefore been largely forgotten, but others have been quite influential. In particular, Duval and Wicklund proposed that awareness of self typically invokes a comparison to some standard. Sheila does not merely notice the fact that she has a certain height and weight; rather, she compares them to standards such as an ideal height and weight. Duval and Wicklund also observed that plenty of emotion can accompany these comparisons with standards. Sheila gets upset if she thinks she weighs too much. Duval and Wicklund went so far as to propose that self-awareness will generally be an aversive state, because people will usually fall short of the standards against which they measure themselves.

Comparison to standards has been perhaps the most enduring and influential aspect of self-awareness theory. Apparently, the simple human phenomenon of reflexive consciousness does not remain simple for long. Self-attention is therefore highly evaluative and motivational. People start wanting to change themselves so as to approach their standards, or to escape from awareness of self when change is not possible (Steenbarger & Aderman, 1979).

The initial notion that self-awareness is generally unpleasant has been changed. Carver and Scheier (1981) reported some of their own studies to the effect that people enjoy self-awareness under some circumstances, which certainly fits ample everyday observations that many people enjoy talking and thinking about themselves and looking in mirrors. The choice of standard may make a huge difference. When people compare themselves to their ideals, they may often feel upset or dejected because they fall short (e.g., Higgins, 1987). But people typically believe that they are superior to the average person or to various other targets, and so when they compare themselves to other people (or an abstract average) they often feel quite good about themselves (e.g., Brown & Dutton, 1995; Taylor, 1989; Taylor & Brown, 1988).

The motivational aspect of self-awareness theory has evolved in parallel fashion. Duval and Wicklund (1972) pointed out that people feel bad when they fall short of their standards, and so they are motivated to do either of two things: improve so as to meet the standard, or escape from the aversive state of self-awareness. Their theory was confirmed by research findings (see Wicklund, 1975), but it needed to be modified to accommodate the pleasant side of self-awareness that accompanies feeling that one is surpassing certain standards. Following success or other favorable comparisons, people may enjoy and seek out self-awareness.

A study by Greenberg and Musham (1981) persuasively demonstrated the two sides of self-awareness. When people had recently performed counterattitudinal behavior that was designed to make them feel bad about themselves, they tended to avoid seats that faced toward a row of mirrors. This occurred because the mirrors would make them self-aware, which would be unpleasant in view of their recent acts. In contrast, when people acted in ways that exemplified their values, they preferred seats facing toward mirrors. Thus, people seek out cues to increase self-awareness when they have reason to feel good about themselves.

The notion that self-awareness can motivate self-change led Carver and Scheier (1981, 1982) to propose an elaborate theory of self-awareness as a form of self-regulation, which will be covered later (in the section on self-regulation), and Higgins (1987, 1996) has likewise argued that self-awareness is fundamentally oriented toward self-regulation. Still, early work was sufficient to demonstrate the motivational effect. Self-awareness was shown to increase the effort people put into performing well at laboratory tasks (Wicklund & Duval, 1971). Unfortunately, some tasks depend more on skill than on effort, and self-awareness appears to be detrimental to skilled performance (Baumeister, 1984). Thus, self-attention may either improve or hamper task performance, depending on the type of task.

When basic values are involved, self-awareness seems to increase people's tendency to live up to their positive attitudes. People showed stronger cognitive dissonance effects in front of mirrors than when not made self-aware, which suggests that self-attention increases the tendency to be consistent (Wicklund & Duval, 1971). More important, perhaps, is that moral and virtuous behavior seems to be increased by self-awareness. A mirror manipulation of self-awareness led to a reduction in cheating on a test by college students (Diener & Wallbom, 1976). A mild form of stealing—taking extra candy during a Halloween visit—was significantly reduced among children who were made self-aware (Beaman, Klentz, Diener, & Svanum, 1979). Sexual morals are likewise intensified, or at least activated, by self-awareness: Gibbons (1978) found that people with high levels of sexual guilt and shame were more negative toward erotic stimuli when they were made self-aware. The same goes for aggression: men's inhibitions against attacking women are intensified by self-awareness, resulting in lower levels of aggression (Scheier, Fenigstein, & Buss, 1974). The latter authors cited other (unpublished) evidence showing that when aggression is presented in a positive light, self-awareness increases aggression. Even inner restraints that do not involve morality are intensified by self-aware-

ness. Thus, Heatherton, Polivy, Herman, & Baumeister (1993) showed that a failure experience led to increased eating of ice cream, but high self-awareness prevented this response—yet this pattern was only found among dieters, who have strong inner restraints against eating.

In these views, self-awareness serves a highly adaptive, beneficial function, even though it may sometimes be unpleasant. Yet the other side of the coin is apparent: Ingram (1990) reviewed considerable evidence that high states of self-awareness are associated with major forms of psychopathology, including depression, anxiety, schizophrenia, and alcoholism. Self-awareness is thus at best a mixed blessing.

Escaping Self-Awareness In the original form, self-awareness theory said that self-awareness is nearly always aversive, and so people would often want to escape from it. Later the theory acknowledged that it can be very pleasant too, but it is nonetheless often aversive, and so escaping it can be quite important. Early studies showed that people try to avoid unpleasant states of self-awareness, and efforts to escape were often measured simply in terms of avoidance of mirrors or other self-focusing stimuli (Gibbons & Wicklund, 1976; Greenberg & Musham, 1981; Steenbarger & Aderman, 1979). In everyday life, however, avoidance of mirrors is often not the issue and not sufficient to terminate a miserable spell of reflecting on one's failures and inadequacies. How do people escape self-awareness?

One method that has withstood the test of time is to consume alcohol. Hull (1981) proposed that one of the main effects of alcohol is to reduce self-awareness (by impairing the complex information processing that often accompanies self-attention). When people feel bad about themselves, therefore, they may wish to become intoxicated as a way of escaping from this aversive state. Sure enough, alcohol consumption increases when people are self-focused after a failure experience (Hull, Levenson, Young, & Sher, 1983; Hull & Young, 1983). In fact, alcoholics relapse most quickly and thoroughly when they have high self-consciousness and experience aversive or negative life events (Hull, Young, & Jouriles, 1986), which suggests that they use alcohol to escape the unpleasant state.

Alcohol may operate directly on brain physiology, but other techniques can accomplish the same result of escaping from unpleasant self-awareness. These often operate on attention: they focus attention narrowly on relatively concrete, unemotional stimuli (see Steele & Josephs, 1990), and in particular they replace the meaningful (and hence troubling) aspects of self-awareness with a minimal, here-and-now focus on simple movement and sensation. Such shifts effectively *deconstruct* the self, in the sense that they undo the elaborate and meaningful construction of identity and leave only the bare bones of self-awareness, which are least subject to evaluative standards and hence least likely to evoke unpleasant emotion. Put another way, the phenomenal self is shrunk to a minimum (Baumeister, 1991a).

Some widely different behavioral patterns have been linked to such efforts to escape self-awareness. Binge eating involves just such a restriction of focus to the physical sensations of chewing, tasting, and swallowing, thus temporarily blotting out the broader issues of selfhood (Heatherton & Baumeister, 1991). Sexual masochism involves the use of pain, loss of control, and embarrassment to make the ordinary identity impossible to sustain and hence to transform the person temporarily into someone else (Baumeister, 1988, 1989a). Meditation disciplines the mind to restrict its focus to a minimal self-awareness, such as attending to one's breathing, in order to overcome the concerns and motives of selfhood for the sake of spiritual advancement (Baumeister, 1991a). Suicidal behavior is often an effort to terminate highly aversive self-awareness into oblivion (Baumeister, 1990). Spurious memories about being abducted into flying saucers likewise appear to be driven by the motivation to escape self-awareness, and indeed they have important parallels to the fantasies of sexual masochists (Newman & Baumeister, 1996).

In fact, failure to escape self-awareness can be quite maladaptive. Greenberg and Pyszczynski (1986) proposed that depression is centrally linked to perseverating in an aversive self-aware state. They showed that failure tends to make everyone self-aware for a while, which may be helpful in that it prompts people to examine what went wrong and how they failed. Nondepressed people soon come out of this state, however. Depressed people tend to stay in it much longer, perseverating in their distress-filled thoughts about their failures and inadequacies. The authors argued that remaining indefinitely in the self-aware state is not helpful or useful and serves merely to prolong the distress.

Cognitive Consequences of Self-Awareness   Other researchers have examined the cognitive consequences of self-awareness. One important view is that self-attention should improve introspection. After all, people should know what is going on in their own psyches if they are attending to it.

Several signs indicate that self-awareness does improve introspection. A pair of studies of attitude-behavior consistency by Pryor, Gibbons, Wicklund, Fazio, and Hood (1977) found that self-awareness increased such consistency. More precisely, self-ratings filled out in the presence of a mirror predicted subsequent behavior better than self-ratings filled out with no mirror.

Similarly, self-awareness seems to intensify emotional reactions, or at least make them more salient. Scheier and Carver (1977) showed that both state and trait self-focus were associated with higher (i.e., more intense) ratings of emotional responses to erotic pictures and mood-inducing statements. The means by which self-awareness has this

effect are unclear, but one plausible explanation is simply that self-awareness makes people more aware of their inner states.

Hull and Levy (1979) proposed that self-awareness should be understood as a pattern of information processing. Thus, their theory presents self-awareness as a cognitive process. Specifically, it involves processing information in relation to the self, including heightened sensitivity to implications of events for the self. They provided evidence, for example, that self-awareness increased the self-reference effect. Highly self-aware people were especially likely to remember words that they had processed in relation to the self.

One of the most interesting cognitive consequences of self-awareness, which seemingly follows directly from the Hull and Levy view, is that it makes people overestimate the degree to which external events are directed at them. This *self-as-target* phenomenon (Fenigstein, 1984) may form one basis of paranoid thinking among normal people. A memorable study by Fenigstein used the occasion of handing back midterm exams. In his study, the instructor held up one exam before passing them back and gave a little speech about how this exam was one of the worst (or, in another condition, one of the best) he had ever seen. Fenigstein found that highly self-conscious students were most likely to think the exam was theirs. Paranoid thinking is in an important sense merely the high end of the self-reference effect.

Self-Concept, Self-Knowledge

The self is therefore not a simple object but rather a construct. It is not directly perceived or known; instead, the person (with the help of others) builds up a body of beliefs about it (Higgins, 1996). The accumulation of this set of beliefs is, in essence, the construction of the self, and it has been a major concern of social psychology. For many years, psychology studied "the" self-concept, as if it were a single and unified entity. Gradually, however, it became clear that people have a great deal of information about themselves that is stored in a very loose fashion. It is therefore more appropriate to think about an aggregate of self-schemas than about a single conception of self.

One definitional point is necessary. Dictionaries and philosophers use the term *knowledge* to refer to beliefs that are correct: "You can't know what ain't so," as philosophy instructors chant in seminars. It is quite clear that people have many beliefs about themselves that are far from definitely correct, and that they have some that are definitely wrong. Conventional usage in social psychology accepts the term *self-knowledge* even for false beliefs about the self, although informally some have acknowledged the need for a term that would be restricted to correct beliefs.

In this chapter, *self-knowledge* includes all beliefs about the self, whether true or false.

Phenomenal Self   An important corollary is that only a small part of self-knowledge can be present in awareness at any given time. In a sense, the very term "self-awareness" is unrealistic, because a person could not possibly cram the full stock of self-knowledge into awareness at once. Many have adopted the term "phenomenal self" (from Jones & Gerard, 1967) to refer to the part of self-knowledge that is present in awareness at any given time. Other terms used for the same purpose include the *spontaneous self-concept* (McGuire, McGuire, Child, & Fujioka, 1978; McGuire, McGuire, & Winton, 1979), and the *working self-concept* (Markus & Kunda, 1986). To use the ever popular analogy of the computer, the full stock of self-knowledge might be compared to the disk full of information, and the phenomenal self would be compared to the small part of it that is displayed on the screen at one time.

The distinction between the phenomenal self and the full stock of self-knowledge is quite important. It means that different beliefs about the self can coexist even if they might be inconsistent. Only the phenomenal self would be under pressure to be internally consistent; the person could otherwise hold widely discrepant and even contradictory views about self. As long as these did not become activated simultaneously, the person might never notice the contradiction.

Such discrepancies help explain things such as the "P. T. Barnum Effect" (Meehl, 1956), which refers to the layperson's willingness to accept an arbitrary, ambiguous statement by an expert as pertaining accurately to the individual layperson. Social psychologists have used this effect in many procedures: they administer a personality test and then give each subject an identical, bogus personality evaluation, but most people believe it is indeed an individual summary of their personalities (e.g., Aronson & Mettee, 1968). Of course, social psychologists are not alone in their usage of the Barnum effect. The Barnum effect has probably enabled astrologers, fortune tellers, and the like to stay in business despite the lack of any valid basis for offering people accurate, individual self-knowledge. Even social psychologists like to read their fortune cookies.

The malleability and diversity of self-knowledge received even more dramatic support from studies such as those by Fazio, Effrein, and Falender, 1981. Biased questions asked people to furnish self-knowledge fitting broad patterns of either extraversion or introversion (by random assignment). Responding to these questions required the activation of one particular type of self-knowledge, which then predominated in the phenomenal self. Sure enough, the subjects who furnished self-reports of extraverted acts and tendencies later rated themselves as more extraverted than subjects who had been asked to furnish self-reports of introverted acts. In fact, they even acted in a more extraverted fashion in a subsequent situation. The point of the study is as follows: people have self-knowledge that makes them seem introverted and other self-knowledge that makes them seem extraverted, and either one can be activated so as to take over the phenomenal self (temporarily). When it does, self-descriptions and even behavior will fit the pattern that has been activated.

Apart from inconsistent self-knowledge, there are certain beliefs about the self that may become either salient and central or may remain neglected and overlooked. Studies by McGuire and his colleagues have shown that the social composition of one's current situation can bring out different features of the self-concept. It appears that people become quite sensitive to factors that distinguish them from other people around them. Being the lone male in an otherwise female environment makes maleness quite central, and one is much more likely to list maleness as a prominent and important feature of one's self-concept, as compared with being male in a heavily male environment (McGuire et al., 1979).

The same applies to race and ethnicity (McGuire et al., 1978). If your racial or ethnic group is a minority, you are likely to be quite aware of that aspect of your identity. In contrast, when you are with people mainly like yourselves, that aspect of identity may drop out of your phenomenal self. It is common for members of majority groups to complain that minority members seem obsessed with their ethnic, racial, or gender identity, but that seems to be partly a simple consequence of minority status. Those same majority group members would likewise become acutely conscious of their race or ethnicity if they one day found themselves alone among people from a different group.

It is important to avoid assuming that all self-appraisals are on a dichotomy or continuum. Markus (1977) introduced a crucial concept of being *aschematic*. For example, one person may regard himself as independent or dependent, but another person may simply lack any view of herself as one or the other.

Three Main Motives   It is readily apparent that self-knowledge does not emerge simply out of a dispassionate operation of cognitive processes. Beliefs about the self are almost always subject to motivational forces. Few people can remain indifferent to important implications or facts about themselves. The motivations surrounding self-knowledge can be grouped into three main types.

The first of these is the simple desire to learn about oneself, which can be called the *appraisal* motive. In a sense, this reflects a mere healthy curiosity about the self. People like to learn how others appraise them, what the stars might have to say about them, what computerized personality tests might produce, and so forth, even if they harbor doubts about the validity of such methods. It is particularly a preference for *accurate* feedback. People seek to appraise their abilities, opinions, and traits. The simple wish for feedback is undeniable (Trope, 1983, 1986).

A second motivation is the wish for favorable information about the self, which is typically called the *self-enhancement* motive. Although a person may simply want to learn about the self, usually he or she has strong preferences as to what that information will be, and the most common preference is to learn that one is good: competent, likable, morally good, attractive, and so forth.

Third, people wish to confirm what they already believe about themselves, which can be called the *consistency* motive. Once people have formed an opinion about themselves, it is typically quite resistant to change. They will tend to seek out evidence that confirms it, and they distrust, criticize, and often reject contrary evidence (Swann, 1985, 1987).

Thus, there are three different types of information about the self that people seek. They desire accurate information, favorable information, or information that confirms their existing beliefs. Assuming that people develop beliefs about the self because these are useful, helpful, and otherwise adaptive, it seems fairly easy to rank the three motives in terms of their usefulness. It seems fairly clear that accurate self-knowledge would be the most useful, because false beliefs about the self leave one vulnerable to making poorly founded decisions. Consistency would seem helpful although not as helpful as accurate knowledge. People do have a strong desire for a stable, predictable environment, and so people should also want self-knowledge to be stable. (This argument parallels the reasoning that pertains to people's views about other people, in which there seems to be a strong preference for consistency, even to the point of minimizing inconsistent or contrary information; see Jones & Nisbett, 1971.) Meanwhile, favorable knowledge about the self would probably be the least useful or adaptive, especially when it consists of inflated or false beliefs about the self, such as delusions of grandeur.

On an a priori basis, therefore, one might predict that self-appraisal would be the strongest motivation, followed by consistency, with enhancement the weakest. Empirical tests by Sedikides (1993) concluded, however, that people's motivations actually have the opposite ranking. He showed that self-enhancement is the strongest motive, followed by consistency, with the appraisal motive being the weakest. In other words, people are most strongly driven to discover and hear favorable, flattering things about themselves. As a distant second, they desire information that confirms what they already believe about themselves. The wish to learn new, accurate information about the self is the weakest (although it is nonetheless real). Converging evidence by Paulhus and Levitt (1987) showed that when people are distracted or aroused, they tend to fall back on automatic responses that are exceptionally favorable about the self. (There may however be an automatic modesty response when one is among close friends; see Tice, Butler, Muraven, & Stillwell, 1995). Thus, the response of "automatic egotism" again indicates a basic, deeply rooted orientation toward self-enhancement. Why should self-enhancement tendencies be so strong?

Benefits of Self-Enhancement The most likely explanation is that the simple analysis presented above of the usefulness and adaptiveness of different types of self-knowledge is wrong. Possibly self-enhancing beliefs, even if unfounded, have strong benefits. For example, confidence may breed persistence, which may be helpful for achieving many forms of success (Taylor, 1989). Thus, a false but favorable belief about the self may lead to persistence which in the end may produce genuine success.

Along the same lines, favorable views of self may form a valuable resource for coping with stresses and setbacks. Steele (1988) has proposed that high self-esteem is a kind of resource that enables people to continue functioning well in the face of failures and other problems. In this view, people who think well of themselves have more of a resource than people who think poorly of themselves. The greater resource may help them in times of trouble.

The term *positive illusions* was coined by Taylor and Brown (1988) to refer to beliefs about the self that are not necessarily true. They provided evidence that these illusions are associated with good adjustment and mental health, and they concluded that seeing oneself in a highly favorable light helps to promote health and adjustment. Realistic (and thus relatively negative) views of self are linked to maladjustment, depression, and other problems (see also Alloy & Abramson, 1979; cf. Colvin & Block, 1994). They proposed that positive illusions promote happiness, improve interpersonal relations, boost intellectual functioning, and facilitate motivation and persistence, although they noted that the evidence was sparse except for motivation and persistence.

Such benefits might seemingly be outweighed by the dangers of illusions. After all, overconfidence might breed fruitless persistence, overcommitment, and dangerous risk-taking. Pelham (1993) described a study showing the people with high self-esteem were more likely than others to ride motorcycles without wearing helmets, for example. The common theme among these dangers is that false beliefs (such as inflated views of the self) constitute an unsuitable basis for making decisions.

There are two hypotheses as to how people avoid these pitfalls of positive illusions. One is that they keep their illusions relatively small, so that they can enjoy the benefits without having their decision-making process warped by major inaccuracies (Baumeister, 1989b). The other is that people manage to turn off their illusions when they have an important decision to make. Gollwitzer and Kinney (1989) showed that people seem to become quite accurate and realistic when they are in the frame of mind associated with making decisions; once the decision is made, they return to a frame of mind suited to implementing it, and this latter state is accompanied by positive illusions.

Self-Deception Processes   Given the powerful motivation to think well of oneself, it is necessary to ask how people manage to maintain such self-flattering views in the face of mixed and even contrary evidence. Social psychologists have in fact devoted considerable time and effort to the study of such processes. Insofar as these constitute ways of supporting an inflated view of self, they may be called *self-deception*. It must be acknowledged, however, that this is a very loose definition of self-deception. More traditional and rigorous views of self-deception require proof that the person simultaneously knows and does not know the same information, in order to fill both the roles of deceiver and deceived (Gur & Sackeim, 1979; Sackeim & Gur, 1979; Sartre, 1953). Very little work has satisfied these stringent criteria, leading Gur and Sackeim (1979) to label self-deception "a concept in search of a phenomenon."

Yet the evidence is clear that people do end up with inflated views of themselves. Self-esteem scores typically run from the high end to the middle of possible scores, but there are very few at the low end (Baumeister, Tice, & Hutton, 1989), suggesting that self-esteem is generally somewhat inflated across the population. A survey of high school seniors found that only 2 percent rated themselves as below average in leadership ability and none rated themselves as below average on ability to get along with others (whereas 25 percent rated themselves as being in the top 1 percent on the latter dimension!) (College Board, 1976–1977; see Gilovich, 1991). Svenson (1981) found that 90 percent of an adult sample rated themselves as above average drivers. Cross (1977) showed that 94 percent of college professors rated themselves as better than their average colleague at their jobs.

A classic paper by Greenwald (1980) compared the self to a totalitarian regime: it distorts the past and manipulates the present. Whatever makes it look good is exaggerated. Whatever makes it look bad is downplayed, discredited, and denied. Taylor and Brown (1988) outlined three main patterns of positive illusion (see also Goleman, 1985). People have unrealistically positive views of their abilities and good traits. They also exaggerate their control over events. And they are excessively optimistic about their own future.

Given the fact that self-deception occurs right at the interface between motivation and cognition, which are two enduring and fundamental concerns of most psychologists, considerable research has been devoted to the multiple processes and tricks that sustain these favorable views of self. The major ones are as follows.

First, people show a *self-serving bias* in interpreting outcomes. The self-serving bias essentially means making internal attributions for success and external attributions for failure. Hence the self gets credit when things go well but dodges the blame when things go badly. Zuckerman (1979) reviewed thirty-eight studies and found that, in most of them, failure led to an increase in external attributions. Recent evidence points to parallel patterns with moral transgressions: people tend to minimize their misdeeds and transgressions by citing external causes and mitigating circumstances (Baumeister, Stillwell, & Wotman, 1990; Gonzales, Pederson, Manning, & Wetter, 1990).

Second, people discover flaws in evidence that depicts them in an unflattering light. They are not so critical, however, about evidence that portrays them in a good light. Thus, in several studies, people have been critical of the validity of tests on which they had failed (Pyszczynski, Greenberg, & Holt, 1985; Wyer & Frey, 1983; see also Kunda, 1990). As most instructors know, students who get top grades tend to think the test was fair and reasonable, whereas those who do poorly are more inclined to see bias and unfairness.

Third, people minimize the amount of time they spend processing critical feedback, at least when it is practical to do so (Baumeister & Cairns, 1992). A person may linger over praise or success feedback, exploring all the nuances and implications, but criticism does not generally receive the same thorough reception (except perhaps when one is searching for reasons to refute it). Bad feedback is therefore less likely to be encoded into memory.

Fourth, and possibly as a result of the reduced encoding time, people selectively forget failure feedback while recalling positive information about themselves very well. Crary (1966) showed that people boosted their self-esteem by not remembering failures. Kuiper and Derry (1982) found that nondepressed people recalled favorable adjectives better than unfavorable ones, when these were processed in relation to the self. Mischel, Ebbesen, and Zeiss (1976) showed a memory bias toward recalling feedback about one's good traits better than feedback about one's faults and shortcomings.

Fifth, people compare themselves against targets that can make them look good (Wills, 1981). Crocker and Major (1989) proposed that even though women and some minority groups may earn less money and achieve less success than white men, they can maintain high self-esteem by not comparing themselves against white men. Instead, they compare themselves against others in their group, which makes them look good. Indeed, ego threats seem to increase the tendency to compare oneself against less successful others, as well as the tendency to derogate and devalue others (Wills, 1981), which makes the defensive nature of this form of self-deception especially apparent.

Sixth, in response to immediate demands, people sort

through their memory in a very biased way to find evidence that they have desirable traits. When people are led to believe that introversion is desirable and is associated with success, they recall more of their own actions as introverted, and they are quicker to come up with introverted memories, than when they are told that extraversion is associated with success (Sanitioso, Kunda, & Fong, 1990). These biased memory searches help people shift their self-ratings in the desired direction (Kunda & Sanitioso, 1989). Murray and Holmes (1993, 1994) provided a memorable demonstration of this in the field of relationship perceptions, which has recently converged with self-perceptions to the extent that people try to convince themselves of the superior quality of their close relationships just as they convince themselves of the high quality of their personal attributes. When subjects were asked about conflict in their dating relationships, most subjects indicated very little conflict, consistent with their assumption that conflict was a sign of a troubled or inferior relationship. Other subjects, however, were given bogus evidence that supposedly showed that some conflict is a healthy sign of a good relationship. These subjects abruptly began to recall quite a bit of conflict in their relationships.

Seventh, people tend to think that their good traits are unusual, while their faults and flaws are common (Campbell, 1986; Marks, 1984; Suls & Wan, 1987). In particular, people distort their perception of others differently with regard to opinions and abilities. With opinions, people overestimate how many people are similar to them, which presumably helps furnish the sense that one's views are correct. With abilities, however, people underestimate how many others are similar to them, which helps furnish a sense that one's abilities are special or unique (Marks, 1984). These patterns are especially strong among people with high self-esteem (Campbell, 1986). These patterns are also especially strong for one's best abilities and on those most relevant to one's self-concept (Campbell, 1986; Marks, 1984).

Eighth, people shift the meaning of ambiguous traits so as to maximize the payoff for themselves (Dunning, Meyerowitz, & Holzberg, 1989). For example, nearly everyone wants to be a good parent, but the precise criteria of good parenthood may be quite variable. Some may claim to be good parents on the basis of never punishing the child, while others may claim to be a good parent because of being careful and stern disciplinarians. Some may claim to be good parents because they stayed home with the child much of the time, while others who spent little time may say they were good parents because they were good role models for hard work and because they provided material goods. Gilovich (1991) provided a memorable illustration of this effect by pointing out that every kid can have the best dog on the block, simply by choosing a different criterion of canine excellence.

Ninth, people sometimes dismiss criticism as motivated by prejudice or other factors that discredit it (Crocker & Major, 1989). Crocker, Voelkl, Testa, and Major (1991) showed that the state self-esteem of black subjects was unaffected by derogatory feedback from white subjects, as long as the blacks were able to assume that prejudice might have influenced the evaluation. Only when they were told that the white evaluators did not know their race did the black subjects show a drop in self-esteem as a result of those evaluations.

Thus, people have many ways of creating a favorable bias in the way they process information about themselves. The multiplicity of self-deceptive processes is an important indication of the power of the self-enhancement motive. People want to resist loss of esteem at all costs. By engaging in one or more of these strategies, people can maintain favorable views of themselves and even make their self-images more favorable, even when objective reality does not quite cooperate in furnishing a steady stream of flattering indications.

Maintaining Consistency The previous section argued that self-deception is common and pervasive. There is however an important qualification to the conclusion that people are relentlessly concerned with raising their self-esteem. Although a self-enhancement motive would certainly predict a great deal and variety of self-deception, a self-consistency motive would make many of the same predictions. After all, people already think well of themselves, perhaps better than reality should allow. Perhaps they engage in self-deception simply to maintain this consistent belief in their good qualities and traits.

Although consistency has certainly been the most-studied motive in the social psychology of attitudes, it has not enjoyed equal prominence in the study of the self. Yet it cannot be denied that people try to maintain consistent views about themselves. Sullivan (1953) proposed that once a child (or older person) forms some concept about the self, he or she is very reluctant to change it. Most other writers about the self have agreed with this assertion (e.g., Greenwald, 1980).

The self-consistency motive in social psychology has figured prominently in the work of Swann (e.g., 1985, 1987). In an early study, Swann and Hill (1982) noted the seeming contradiction that many social psychologists regarded self-concepts as pliable and malleable, whereas clinical psychologists (who are in the business of trying to change people) often found it discouragingly difficult to effect such changes. They proposed that social psychologists may have maintained this view of self-concept malleability by choosing ambiguous traits about which people may lack definite self-conceptions, and by denying people the opportunity to resist or refute efforts to change them. In their study, they provided people with feedback that was discrepant from their self-conceptions. They found that people generally rejected that feedback and reasserted their prior beliefs about themselves. Only when people were unable to make such contrary assertions did they show any malleability of self-concept.

Swann (1985, 1987) went on to coin the term *self-verification* to describe people's quest for feedback that would confirm their views about themselves. In Swann's view, people desire stable predictability above all else, and changes to one's self-concept are therefore unwelcome— even including changes toward a more positive view of self. He contended that people seek out confirmatory feedback, especially with regard to self-schemas about which they are certain. When people do not have clear and definite views about themselves, they may be receptive to discrepant (and favorable) information.

The consistency motive overlaps with the enhancement motive in many cases. As already noted, most people think well of themselves, and so the widespread preference for favorable feedback—like the common tendencies to dismiss and discredit bad feedback—may serve both the enhancement and consistency motives. The two diverge, however, with regard to people who hold firm but unfavorable views about themselves. Do these people with low self-esteem prefer flattering or unflattering feedback? Do people desire to hear that they are better than they had thought, and if they do receive such information do they believe it? Different studies have provided different answers, but gradually some common conclusions have emerged.

One conclusion is that the consistency motive tends to dominate cognition, whereas the enhancement motive dominates affect. For example, suppose Ellen does not think she is beautiful, but Harry tells her that she is. She may feel good at hearing this, but she does not necessarily believe it; indeed, after receiving such a compliment, she may like Harry more than she trusts him. Maybe he is just preparing to ask to borrow some money from her. A literature review by Shrauger (1975) found that most of the studies favoring enhancement motives had used affective measures, whereas most of the ones yielding consistency effects had used cognitive ones. Swann, Griffin, Predmore, and Gaines (1987) proposed that these discrepant responses produce a "cognitive-affective crossfire" for people who receive feedback telling them they are better than they thought (see also Jussim, Yen, & Aiello, 1995; McFarlin & Blascovich, 1981). The heart says yes, while the brain says no.

A later paper proposed that the self-enhancement response is automatic, whereas the self-verification one is controlled (Swann, Hixon, Stein-Seroussi, & Gilbert, 1990). Consistency effects therefore are slower and require more cognitive processing than enhancement effects. People quickly and easily feel good when they receive highly favorable feedback. To begin questioning it takes some time and thought, however. In a sense, the self-verification response requires the person to override the initial, favorable reaction to the praise. For this reason, self-consistency effects may be less obvious and common than self-enhancement effects. In the long run, however, they may sometimes prove to be the more powerful and decisive ones.

Self-Perception versus Introspection   Thus far the discussion has emphasized how self-knowledge is modified, shaped, and maintained, which have indeed been the major concerns of social psychologists. But how does self-knowledge begin? One broad and counterintuitive theory on the formation of self-knowledge was offered by Bem (1965, 1972) under the title of *self-perception theory*. (Bem's theory was originally proposed as an alternative explanation for research findings on cognitive dissonance, and as such it will be covered elsewhere in this *Handbook*. For present purposes, the issue is simply how well self-perception can serve as a model for the construction of self-knowledge.)

The essence of self-perception theory is that people learn about themselves in much the same way they learn about other people: they observe behavior and make inferences. What is radical about self-perception theory is that it minimizes the reliance on introspection and concepts of privileged access (e.g., that you can know your own mind better than anyone else can know it). Although most people do believe in special knowledge and privileged access, social psychology has repeatedly questioned such beliefs and at least shown that introspection is far less capable and accurate than people assume (Nisbett & Wilson, 1977). It treats self-perception as merely another case of person perception, subject to the same attributional principles and inference processes.

It must be acknowledged that the term *self-perception* is somewhat misleading. As already noted, the self cannot be perceived directly. Rather, one observes the self in its activities and in interaction with the environment, and one draws inferences about the self based on those observations. *Self-observation* would therefore be a more precise and apt title for the theory than *self-perception*, although it is admittedly easy and somewhat unfair to criticize someone's selection of terminology three decades after the fact. It is also worth noting that the process outlined in self-perception theory is an especially clear and vivid demonstration of the sort of process Kant outlined for the basis of self-knowledge, given that the self cannot be perceived directly but merely constructed from observations of acts.

The self-perception processes as described by Bem (1972) are fundamentally correct in that they do happen. Research on attitudes has shown that people do sometimes infer their opinions from their actions, especially when drastic changes to the self-concept are not involved (Fazio, Zanna, & Cooper, 1977; Taylor, 1975). Likewise, people seem often to infer their motivations from observing their actions rather than from directly knowing what they like and dislike (Lepper, Greene, & Nisbett, 1973). Thus, there are cases in which people can be fooled about themselves: if they are induced to act in certain ways, they will draw distorted or even false conclusions about themselves.

On the other hand, self-perception appears to be just one of several processes by which self-knowledge is formed and maintained. To say that self-perception processes occur when no major self-views are at stake and the inferences lie within the person's latitude of acceptance (i.e., within the range of what the person is willing to believe about self; Fazio et al., 1977) is to say that self-perception processes are not the major causes of important changes in beliefs about the self. Taylor (1975) concluded that self-perception processes seem limited to cases in which the issues are relatively unimportant and inconsequential. When even moderately important consequences were involved (in her study, choosing a member of the opposite sex as an interaction partner), people did not succumb to illusions of self-perception and instead paused to consider all available information carefully.

The importance of inner phenomena to self-knowledge was shown by Andersen (1984; Andersen & Ross, 1984). Andersen and Ross (1984) noted that research had not properly appreciated Bem's (1965, 1972) own caveats regarding self-perception processes. In particular, Bem had said that self-perception based on making inferences from one's behavior would occur mainly when internal cues (such as thoughts and emotions) were weak or ambiguous. Thus, Bem was not making the radical proposal that all self-knowledge derived from the self-perception processes he outlined. He merely said that people fall back on such processes when they have nothing else to use.

In any case, Andersen and Ross (1984) showed the importance of inner, private phenomena. They showed that thoughts and feelings are regarded as providing a much better guide to what someone is really like than mere overt behavior. In one study, subjects reported that another person would learn more about them from knowing their thoughts and feelings for one day than from observing their overt behavior for several months. Both actors and observers believed that thoughts and feelings reveal more about the self than actions. In another study, Andersen (1984) showed that hearing about someone's thoughts and feelings permits one to make more accurate inferences about that person than hearing about the person's behavior. (Accuracy was measured by degree of agreement between the observer's ratings and both the target's self-ratings and ratings by the target's close friends.)

In this connection, it is useful to recall that one of the most stimulating debates in social psychology has concerned the extent and validity of introspection. A classic work by Nisbett and Wilson (1977) argued that introspec-

tion is overrated: people do not use it when they think they do, and it is often inaccurate. They proposed that even when people try to introspect and give an honest explanation for their acts, they are often merely reciting a priori theories and standard explanations. Critical responses to their article have objected that their experimental tests made unreasonable demands on the introspective capacity and were excessively negative in their conclusions (e.g., Sabini & Silver, 1981; Smith & Miller, 1978).

Probably the best integration of this work is to note that people generally do know the contents of their minds but may generally be unable to know the process by which these emerged. Introspection may be quite valid and accurate when people are asked to report what they are thinking and feeling. It may however be quite inaccurate when people seek to analyze how they arrived at these thoughts and feelings (see Wilson, Dunn, Bybee, Hyman, & Rotondo, 1984).

The most appropriate conclusion appears to be that self-knowledge is derived from several sources of information. There is a widespread and at least somewhat valid belief that thoughts and feelings form a very good basis for learning about the self. When such information is not readily available, merely observing behavior and making inferences is a useful alternative source.

Organization of Self-Knowledge Social psychology has only begun to explore how self-knowledge is organized in memory. It is clear that the organization is fairly loose, especially insofar as the phenomenal self can bring up quite different images of self and seemingly inconsistent self-views can coexist (e.g., Jones, Rhodewalt, Berglas, & Skelton, 1981; Tetlock, 1986). The general organization corresponds to what Fiske and Taylor (1991) described as a schema, in the sense that there are nodes with attributes loosely attached to the nodes but not necessarily attached to each other.

Of particular interest in this connection is a study by Higgins, Van Hook, and Dorfman (1988). They used a modified Stroop color-naming task to look for evidence that various parts of the self-concept (i.e., various traits that people had used to describe themselves) would prime each other. They found no effects to suggest that different pieces of self-knowledge are interconnected. They were not ready to conclude that self-knowledge is thoroughly disconnected, but their findings suggest that interconnections among pieces of self-knowledge can often be weak and distant at best.

Probably the most thoroughly studied aspect of the organization of self-knowledge is Higgins's (1987; see also Higgins, Klein, & Strauman, 1987) theory that people have different *self-guides*. The main ones are the ideal self (containing mainly positive ideas about the person one would like to be) and the ought self (involving various moral and other obligations about what one should try to be). Higgins's full theory has added that people actually have to grapple with occasional differences between what they themselves think they ought to be and what someone else (e.g., a parent) thinks they ought to be. Different situations can activate either the ought self or the ideal self.

A particularly important aspect of Higgins's theorizing is that different emotions are implicated as a function of which self-guide is operating. When people believe they are falling short of their ideal selves—that is, when they perceive a discrepancy between their actual self and their ideal self—they tend to feel aversive emotions with low arousal levels, such as sadness, dejection, and depressed mood. In contrast, a discrepancy between actual self and ought self leads to aversive but high arousal emotions, such as anxiety and guilt.

The notion that people vary in the organization of self-knowledge was introduced by Linville (1985, 1987). She proposed that some people have simple organizations of self-knowledge, which means that different features of the self-concept are interrelated. In contrast, other people have complex organizations, in which the different facets are largely unrelated. Linville developed a method for assessing these differences, although some researchers have suggested that the particular method does not do justice to Linville's conceptions (Buder Shapiro, 1995).

Perhaps the most intriguing consequence that accompanies these differences in self-complexity is in the impact of stress or other aversive events. The complex self has an advantage under stress because it can compartmentalize the threatening implications. Thus, for example, if Phyllis has a simple self in which her identities as mother and painter overlap, then she is fully vulnerable: any failure as a mother will also spill over into her painter identity. If she maintains a complex self and the two identities are largely unrelated, she may still be upset if her teenage daughter dyes her hair purple and starts sleeping with scores of rock musicians, but it will have less impact on her painting.

Another pattern of individual differences in the organization of self-knowledge was proposed by Hansen and Hansen (1988). In their view, repressors manage to maintain a happy, untroubled attitude by using a variation on the Freudian defense mechanism of isolation. Specifically, they prevent associations from forming between unpleasant experiences or thoughts. For many people, one upsetting thought will remind them of another, resulting in an associative chain of misery. Hansen and Hansen found that repressors got just as upset as other people in terms of their primary response to something unpleasant, but among repressors the first bad memory did not set off other bad feelings and thoughts.

Compartmentalization of good and bad aspects of self-knowledge was studied by Showers (1992). Like Hansen and Hansen, she proposed that keeping undesirable information about the self isolated in memory can be a defensive way to minimize its impact. Although the strategy broke down when the unfavorable aspects of self were highly important, compartmentalization was linked to high self-esteem and the absence of depression.

Self-Esteem

Self-esteem may be defined as the positivity of the person's evaluation of self. Thus, self-esteem is the evaluative aspect of reflexive consciousness: it makes a value judgment based on self-knowledge. In an important sense, self-reference makes self-awareness possible, which makes self-knowledge possible, which in turn makes self-esteem possible. Amid the social psychology research community's extensive shifts of interest among the various subtopics pertaining to self, self-esteem has been quite consistent and durable. Every decade has seen important contributions. Apparently the topic of self-esteem has a deeply rooted or multifaceted appeal to researchers.

Interest in self-esteem is not confined to the research community, of course. The American general public has gradually come to appreciate (some would say overestimate; see Dawes, 1994) the importance of self-esteem in ordinary human functioning. Politicians, educators, social workers, and others have come to hope that self-esteem may hold the key to understanding and even solving many social problems (see California Task Force, 1990). In particular, parents and schools seem now widely concerned with ensuring that children have high self-esteem.

The reality of the effects of self-esteem is far more limited and prosaic than these optimistic assessments might suggest. Self-esteem is linked to some advantages and positive outcomes, yet even with these it is not entirely clear which direction the causal arrow points. Thus, for example, people with high self-esteem are generally more persistent in the face of failure than people with low self-esteem (e.g., Shrauger & Rosenberg, 1970; Shrauger & Sorman, 1977). It seems likely that high self-esteem causes greater persistence, but it is difficult to rule out the hypothesis that higher persistence may contribute to higher self-esteem. Meanwhile, even this advantage is mixed: people with high self-esteem persist longer than others even when persistence is counterproductive, so sometimes they end up wasting time, effort, and other resources on lost causes (McFarlin, Baumeister, & Blascovich, 1984).

Some basic disagreements remain about how to approach the topic of self-esteem. As an evaluation, self-esteem would seem to have both cognitive and affective components. (As will shortly be shown, both affective and cognitive aspects of self-esteem have been shown, consistent with the view that self-esteem involves both.) The relative importance of these two is subject to controversy. Although most researchers have recently emphasized the cognitive (i.e., self-knowledge) aspect of self-esteem, Brown (1993b) has contended that self-esteem should be understood as primarily an affective response: a global liking for oneself or, in the case of low self-esteem, a muted liking (or in extreme cases, dislike). Brown (1994) compared self-esteem to a parent's esteem for his or her child: the affective response seems to appear strongly and immediately, without waiting for detailed cognitive appraisals.

Another perennial debate is whether to emphasize global self-esteem or specific dimensions. John may think he sings poorly but plays tennis well, while Ann thinks she sings beautifully and can scarcely make contact with a bouncing ball. Attempts to predict these two individuals' responses to the upcoming choir tryouts from their global self-esteem may be misguided. On the other hand, measures of global self-esteem have been used far more widely and produced far more significant results than measures of domain-specific self-esteem. Some may say, though, that the global measures do well because they generally emphasize broad issues of competence, aptitude, and ability to get along with others, which are important to nearly everyone.

One tentative resolution of the global versus specific debate uses a hierarchical model (Fleming & Courtney, 1984). In this view, people do have various domain-specific self-appraisals, but they also have a global evaluation. It may also be that there is a general or global self-esteem factor which is strongly related to most of the domain-specific self-appraisals. If so, self-esteem would resemble intelligence, in which there are multiple distinct abilities but also a global (*g*) factor that is correlated with all of them. In the foreseeable future, it seems likely that basic researchers will continue to rely mainly on measures of global self-esteem, but they may maintain some awareness of domain-specific variations. Global self-esteem has the greatest theoretical importance, but applied research may favor the domain-specific measures. When seeking to predict responses confined to a specific sphere, in particular, it may be useful and advantageous to shift to the appropriate domain-specific measure.

A last area of controversy concerns whether to regard self-esteem as a state or a trait. Although trait measures of self-esteem have dominated the research (e.g., Janis & Field, 1959), some researchers have sought to manipulate self-esteem states, such as by giving bogus feedback (e.g., Aronson & Mettee, 1968; Sigall & Gould, 1977). Such manipulations are subject to alternative explanations involving affect and self-presentational concerns, so they have generally dropped out of fashion as a preferred way of studying self-esteem. Still, recent work has provided evidence of state fluctuations in self-esteem (e.g., Kernis, 1993), and a reliable measure of state self-esteem is available (Heatherton & Polivy, 1991). The state measure appears to be strongly correlated with the trait measures. The implication seems to be that most people have a rather stable and clear

baseline of self-esteem, and their current self-appraisals fluctuate (to varying degrees) around that baseline.

Motivation: Why Care about Self-Esteem? Whatever the optimal approach to measuring self-esteem may be, and whatever the practical benefits may or may not turn out to be, it is clear that self-esteem is quite important to people. Changes in self-esteem level are often accompanied by strong emotional responses. A great deal of the research in social psychology relies on the assumption that people are motivated to protect and enhance their self-esteem, as indeed the discussion on self-deception earlier in this chapter showed.

But why is it important? Contrary to popular impression, self-esteem does not have a broad range of direct consequences. It is difficult to argue that nature has instilled a strong self-esteem motive, because the evolutionary benefits of self-esteem (in terms of increasing survival or reproduction) seem negligible. Indeed, one might invoke an evolutionary argument that self-esteem should be counterproductive, insofar as overconfidence could lead to dangerous risk-taking. Furthermore, as we shall see shortly, there is a serious lack of evidence for beneficial or adaptive consequences of self-esteem, which suggests that there is very little pragmatic reason for people to want it.

Several answers have been proposed regarding the roots of concern with self-esteem. Greenberg, Pyszczynski, and Solomon (1986; see also Pyszczynski et al., 1997) have proposed that people are fundamentally motivated by the fear of death and that self-esteem is a way of conquering that fear. They have adapted Becker's (1973) view that people are driven by death anxiety to identify with cultural groups and values, and that self-esteem consists of seeing oneself as a valued member of such a group, which somehow helps to minimize the existential terror of mortality.[1]

To support their "terror management" views about self-esteem, these researchers showed that high levels of self-esteem reduced self-reported anxiety and physiological arousal in response to cues designed to evoke thoughts of death and pain (Greenberg, Solomon et al., 1992). They also cite Paulhus and Levitt's (1987) finding that people described themselves more positively when distracted by stimulus words connected with death (e.g., *coffin*). Unfortunately, these may reflect broad affective patterns rather than being specific to death. Paulhus and Levitt found similar patterns for emotionally laden words that were not death-related (e.g., *penis*). An attempt to find direct links

---

[1]This seems illogical. Self-esteem should exacerbate rather than attenuate the fear of death. The greater the value placed on the self—that is, the higher the self-esteem—the greater the calamity one's death is. Low self-esteem would seem to be the best way to deal with fear of death, because it minimizes the value of what dies.

between death anxiety and self-esteem failed to show any correlations (Leary, Saltzman, & Bednarski, 1995; Leary & Schreindorfer, 1997).

Another theory that may be relevant to the concern with self-esteem is Steele's (1988) self-affirmation theory (see also Spencer, Josephs, & Steele, 1993). In this view, positive opinions about the self are a valuable affective resource to aid in coping. Failure, misfortune, ego threats, and other sources of stress may be debilitating to people with low self-esteem, but people with high self-esteem can persist and endure better.

The self-affirmation view has the advantage that it fits nicely with the few advantages that have been associated with high self-esteem, specifically persistence in the face of failure. To provide further support, self-affirmation researchers have shown that people with high self-esteem are less upset by failures and other forms of bad feedback, in part because they have plenty of positive traits to think about even if they do fail in some particular domain. In contrast, people with low self-esteem are more likely to be discouraged and dejected by failures, because they do not have a large stock of other good points with which to console themselves (Spencer et al., 1993).

The self-affirmation explanation has the added advantage that it emphasizes the emotional benefits, which seem to be the main ones. As already noted, self-esteem does not have strong pragmatic or material consequences, and yet people go to great lengths to preserve and protect it. Why would they try so hard to gain and preserve something that is worth little? A likely answer is that self-esteem makes one feel good, regardless of objective consequences. Indeed, there is a strong negative correlation between self-esteem and depression, although the causal interpretation is highly unclear (see Tennen & Affleck, 1993). The main drawback of the self-affirmation theory is that it is somewhat circular as an explanation of the desire for self-esteem. Yes, self-esteem does help one cope with threats to self-esteem—but why are threats to self-esteem so problematic in the first place? Why is there so much affect surrounding self-esteem?

A third view is that self-esteem is important because it serves as an aid in the basic human project of getting along with others. Leary, Tambor, Terdal, and Downs (1995) proposed that self-esteem is a *sociometer*, that is, an internal measure of how one is succeeding at social inclusion. They provided evidence that self-esteem rises when one is accepted or liked by others, while social rejection and exclusion tends to bring about a decline in self-esteem.

The sociometer theory has much to recommend it. In the first place, there is abundant evidence that people are pervasively concerned with the need to form and maintain interpersonal connections (Baumeister & Leary, 1995), and such a drive would have clear evolutionary benefits. The sociometer view can also readily explain why so much emotion is linked to self-esteem, because strong emotional responses are generally associated with interpersonal relationships. Self-esteem as an internal mechanism to serve that need would be highly plausible. Furthermore, it is apparent that self-esteem is based on the same traits that make one appealing to others: competence, likability, and attractiveness. Meanwhile, whereas death anxiety showed negligible correlations with self-esteem, social anxiety is strongly correlated. A review of multiple studies concluded that the average correlation between social anxiety and self-esteem is about -0.50 (Leary & Kowalski, 1995).

There are several possible objections to the sociometer view. It does seem that people can have high self-esteem without having any close relationship at that moment, that self-esteem seems more stable than social inclusion status, and that the link between one's immediate social status and self-esteem is not just a direct and simple link. To elucidate those issues is the current challenge for sociometer theory.

Thus, at present there are several competing views about the source of the concern with self-esteem. Although it is common to treat them as rival theories, they are in many respects compatible, and it may turn out that all have some validity. It is clear that self-esteem is important to most people, even despite its apparent lack of pragmatic or objective benefits.

Cognitive and Affective Aspects An influential study by McFarlin and Blascovich (1981) resolved some basic questions about how people with low self-esteem understand and approach task performance. They showed that people with low self-esteem want to succeed just as much as people with high self-esteem, but they are less prone to expect that they will. Thus, in a sense, the motivations and desires are similar, but the cognitive expectations are different. Initial failure causes people with low self-esteem to lower their expectations about future performance, whereas people with high self-esteem ironically raise their expectations. The latter pattern seems irrational—how can initial failure increase one's expectation of success?—unless one assumes that high self-esteem makes people believe that failure is an unacceptable, exceptional occurrence that is unlikely to be repeated. Subsequent work suggested that people with high self-esteem prefer to avoid tasks following initial failure if they have the option, whereas low self-esteem makes people turn their attention to their deficiencies and failures in order to bring themselves up to an adequate level (Baumeister & Tice, 1985). The common thread is that people with high self-esteem are determined to avoid repeating a failure. The conclusion is that people with high self-esteem expect and aspire to be outstanding, and they are not very interested in remedying deficiencies. In contrast, people with low self-esteem focus on remedying their deficiencies rather than cultivating their most promising traits, because they are mainly concerned with avoiding failures.

The cognitive processes associated with self-esteem have been decisively illuminated in recent work by Campbell (1990; Campbell & Lavallee, 1993). These studies provided strong and extensive evidence of a series of cognitive and affective differences that are correlated with self-esteem. The general conclusion is that high self-esteem is associated with more thorough, accurate, and extensive self-knowledge than low self-esteem. These findings, taken from Campbell (1990) except as otherwise noted, can be summarized as follows.

First, people with high self-esteem give themselves more extreme self-ratings than people with low self-esteem. People with low self-esteem tend to give themselves intermediate, noncommittal ratings (even on nonevaluative dimensions), consistent with the view that they do not have definite self-knowledge. Further relevant evidence was provided by Greenwald, Bellezza, and Banaji (1988), who showed that people with high self-esteem can furnish longer lists than people with low self-esteem of liked and disliked activities, group memberships, and similar open-ended self-reports, suggesting that high self-esteem is associated with more extensive self-knowledge.

Second, people with high self-esteem have higher certainty about their self-knowledge. When people are asked to rate themselves on various trait scales and to say how certain or confident they are that their self-ratings are correct, self-esteem is correlated with certainty. Likewise, it takes people with low self-esteem longer to respond to questions about themselves. Campbell's (1990) conclusions received support from another investigation by Baumgardner (1990), who found that people with low self-esteem were slower to answer questions about themselves and furnished broader (i.e., less precise and specific) confidence intervals for those answers.

Third, the self-ratings of people with high self-esteem fluctuate less over time than those of people with low self-esteem. Campbell found this in a simple test-retest procedure. She also found that prior self-ratings were more strongly correlated with ratings of how one had acted in a specific interpersonal encounter among people with high than low self-esteem. Thus, low self-esteem is associated with fluctuations in ideas about oneself, as well as with inconsistency between initial, global self-ratings and specific responses. Self-knowledge is apparently more consistent across time among people with high self-esteem.

Fourth, the self-knowledge of people with high self-esteem is more internally consistent than that of people with low self-esteem. In one study Campbell obtained self-ratings on a long measure that contained several sets of synonyms and antonyms. People with high self-esteem tended to give the same answers regardless of the precise word that was used. People with low self-esteem were

more likely to give answers that contradicted what they had already said about themselves.

Fifth, people with high self-esteem show more self-serving biases in their responses to feedback and other events. A review by Blaine and Crocker (1993) showed several patterns. High self-esteem is associated with a tendency to take credit for success and deny blame for failure, as well as with memory biases that exaggerate successes and minimize failures, and with a tendency to exaggerate one's control over events (especially ones that turn out well). They found that people with low self-esteem and depressed people do not seem to have those self-serving biases. In some studies, these people are relatively even-handed (e.g., taking equal credit for success and failure), and in some studies they show self-deprecating biases (e.g., blaming oneself for failure but rejecting credit for success).

It must be noted that there are both cognitive and motivational explanations for the biases documented by Blaine and Crocker (1993), as they were careful to explain. People with high self-esteem may have higher and clearer expectations about how life will treat them, and these expectations may cause them to attend to and encode different information than what someone lacking self-esteem would. They concluded that high and low self-esteem people have similar motivations, especially insofar as they both would like to have successes and other positive outcomes, but people with low self-esteem are less likely to act on the basis of these self-enhancing motives.

Sixth, there are important emotional differences. In a longitudinal diary study, Campbell, Chew, and Scratchley (1991) examined how people respond emotionally to the events of their daily lives. They found that people with low self-esteem generally had less pleasant and less positive moods than people with high self-esteem. They also found that people with low self-esteem had greater emotional variability. They provided some evidence that the events experienced by their subjects did not vary as a function of self-esteem; that is, it was not the case that people with low self-esteem had more extreme or more unpleasant things happen to them. They simply reacted to similar events with wider and wilder mood swings. The implication is that high self-esteem operates as a kind of emotional anchor, producing affective stability in the face of events.

These patterns provide a consistent and compelling picture of the cognitive and emotional aspects of self-esteem. Apparently self-knowledge is more thorough and precise (which is not necessarily to say more accurate) among people with high self-esteem. Put another way, people with low self-esteem suffer from what Campbell and Lavallee (1993) call "self-concept confusion," insofar as their ideas about themselves are uncertain, contradictory, and unstable. The lack of firm self-knowledge may well be what leaves those people at the mercy of daily events, and this vulnerability is reflected in their high emotional reactivity. People with high self-esteem have firm and favorable views of themselves, which they seem to protect vigorously by processing information in biased, self-serving ways, and which keep them on an even emotional keel amid the slings and arrows of daily life.

Social and Interpersonal Patterns   Self-esteem is also associated with different patterns of social behavior, apart from the cognitive and affective differences. (In principle these belong in the next part of this chapter, along with interpersonal patterns, but for the reader's convenience these are presented here with the rest of the self-esteem material.) Indeed, such differences were one of the original sources of research interest in self-esteem. Janis (1954) began to study self-esteem in connection with persuasion, pursuing the hypothesis that people with low self-esteem are more easily persuaded than people with high self-esteem. One of the most influential and popular measures of self-esteem was developed specifically for use in studies of attitude change (Janis & Field, 1959).

The view that low self-esteem is associated with greater persuasibility was supported in those early studies, and subsequent work built upon that start to link low self-esteem to a broad range of susceptibility to influence and manipulation. An influential review by Brockner (1984) concluded that low self-esteem is marked by what he called "behavioral plasticity"—that is, people with low self-esteem are broadly malleable. A broad variety of experimental manipulations, ranging from anxiety-provoking stimuli to expectancy and self-focus inductions, seems to produce stronger and more reliable effects on people with low than with high self-esteem.

Another broad interpersonal pattern concerns the relative strength of self-enhancement versus self-protection motives. Many studies have found self-esteem differences more strongly or only in public (i.e., interpersonal) situations, and self-esteem may be fundamentally tied toward self-presentational patterns (see Baumeister, Tice, & Hutton, 1989, for review). More precisely, it appears that people with high self-esteem are generally oriented toward self-enhancement, whereas people with low self-esteem are associated with self-protection. High self-esteem is associated with wanting to capitalize on one's strengths and virtues and being willing to take chances in order to stand out in a positive way. Low self-esteem is associated with wanting to remedy one's deficiencies and seeking to avoid standing out in a bad way.

The evidence reviewed thus far does not paint an entirely consistent picture of people with low self-esteem. On the one hand, they seem to desire success, acceptance, and approval, but on the other hand they seem skeptical about it and less willing to pursue it openly. Brown's (e.g., 1993a) work has addressed this conflict directly by proposing that

people with low self-esteem suffer from a motivational conflict. Brown and McGill (1989) found that positive, pleasant life events had adverse effects on the physical health of people with low self-esteem. In contrast to people with high self-esteem, who seem healthier when life treats them well, low self-esteem seemed to lead to sickness when too many good things happened. It may be that positive events exceed the expectations of people with low self-esteem and pressure them to revise their self-concepts in a positive direction, and such revisions are sufficiently stressful that they become ill.

Is High Self-Esteem Always Good?   To place the findings about self-esteem in perspective, it is useful to ask how important and beneficial high self-esteem is. In modern America there is a widespread view that it is extremely beneficial. Moreover, the strong belief in its benefits is one major reason for high and enduring interest in it, which has among other things produced close to seven thousand books and articles (Mruk, 1995).

The belief that high self-esteem is a vital aspect of mental health and good adjustment is strong and widespread (e.g., Bednar, Wells, & Peterson, 1989; Mruk, 1995; Taylor & Brown, 1988). In many studies, in fact, self-esteem is measured as an index of good adjustment, so even the operational definition of healthy functioning involves self-esteem (e.g., Heilbrun, 1981; Kahle, Kulka, & Klingel, 1980; Whitley, 1983).

In support of the presumed link between self-esteem and mental health, there are important correlations. As already noted, self-esteem is negatively correlated with depression (Tennen & Affleck, 1993) and social anxiety (Leary & Kowalski, 1995). The causal direction is unclear, but nonetheless people with high self-esteem do seem to be healthier and happier than lows. Presumed links between self-esteem and other social pathologies have encouraged many to hope that raising self-esteem will cure social problems. The California Task Force to Promote Self-Esteem and Personal and Social Responsibility (1990) asserted that self-esteem is a "social vaccine" that could prevent assorted problems ranging from drug abuse to teen pregnancy. Across the country, many schools, parents, and others began to place a high priority on ensuring that children were all encouraged to have high self-esteem. Criticism was muted, standards were diluted, and awards proliferated. Thus, instead of reserving trophies for the competitive champions, most children's sport leagues now give trophies to everyone who shows up (Adler, 1992).

On the other hand, the enthusiasm for self-esteem never did find a strong empirical basis. The report of the California Task Force was accompanied by an edited volume discussing the empirical links between self-esteem and the personal and social ills it was supposed to cure. The editors of the volume summarized the findings thus: "The news most consistently reported, however, is that the associations between self-esteem and its expected consequences are mixed, insignificant, or absent" (Mecca, Smelser, & Vasconcellos, 1989, p. 15). Dawes (1994) has likewise criticized what he calls the "myth" that self-esteem is beneficial.

Researchers have been slower, however, to link bad outcomes to high self-esteem. One reason may be that researchers' bias in favor of self-esteem has influenced the wording of scale items. When researchers study favorable self-appraisal under other names, such as narcissism or egotism, it is easier to find problematic or undesirable links (e.g., Raskin, Novacek, & Hogan, 1991; Wink, 1991).

One noteworthy pattern is that it is high rather than low self-esteem that seems conducive to interpersonal violence (Baumeister, Smart, & Boden, 1996). Aggression seems to be most common among people who think well of themselves but encounter someone who disputes their favorable self-appraisal. In particular, inflated, unrealistic, or fluctuating forms of high self-esteem are conducive to violence, probably because they are most vulnerable to ego threats (e.g., Kernis, Granneman, & Barclay, 1989, Kernis et al., 1993). People appear to lash out at others who criticize or disrespect them as a way of avoiding any downward revision of their self-esteem and the accompanying affect (especially shame; see Tangney, Wagner, Fletcher, & Gramzow, 1992).

The violence pattern involves an apparently potent combination of self-esteem and ego threat. Blaine and Crocker (1993) and others have noted that people with high self-esteem seem to change their behavior drastically when confronted with ego threats. Normally people with high self-esteem do not seem defensive, but that may be because they go through life thinking well of themselves and expecting to succeed at most things. When they do fail or are rejected, to their surprise, they may respond dramatically.

The defensive and occasionally self-destructive nature of responses to ego threats was examined by Baumeister, Heatherton, and Tice (1993). Subjects performed a task for a long time and then were asked to bet any amount on their final performance. To earn the most money, one had to bet high and perform well, but one could also keep some money by making a low bet, especially if one did not expect to perform well on the final trial. Thus accurate self-knowledge and self-prediction would be very useful. Under favorable conditions, people with high self-esteem did very well, making appropriate bets and earning good rewards. Following an ego threat, however, they tended to make extremely optimistic predictions and then perform poorly, thereby losing their money. Thus, self-esteem seems to be linked to accurate self-knowledge and making appropriate commitments under favorable conditions, but an ego threat undermines all that and produces costly, destructive responses.

Another approach is to look at inflated self-esteem. Colvin, Block, and Funder (1995) contrasted self-descriptions with acquaintance descriptions as a means of identifying people who regard themselves more favorably than their friends regard them. Such self-enhancing patterns were linked to poor social skills and psychological maladjustment in longitudinal data. In a laboratory study, these people with inflated self-esteem were observed to interrupt others, be socially awkward, express hostility, irritate others, talk at instead of talking with partners, and perform a variety of other negatively evaluated behaviors. The composite picture is one of a self-centered, conceited person who lacks genuine regard for others. Such a picture is quite consistent with the literal meaning of high self-esteem, even if it does not fit the most popular stereotype.

Based on the currently available evidence, the consequences of self-esteem can be summarized as follows. First, high self-esteem is linked to various positive outcomes and low self-esteem to bad outcomes, but often the self-esteem is the result rather than the cause. Second, high self-esteem does seem to make people feel better, and so it is subjectively pleasant. Third, high self-esteem has a small number of practical, material benefits, such as greater persistence in the face of failure. Fourth, most social and personal problems are not caused by a lack of self-esteem, so raising self-esteem is unlikely to solve them. Fifth, high self-esteem, especially when not grounded in actual accomplishments, may breed interpersonal violence and other possible undesirable consequences. Sixth, the combination of high self-esteem and an ego threat seems to be an especially potent source of problematic responses that can be destructive to both self and others.

Summary and Implications

Self-knowledge begins when attention turns around toward its source, a phenomenon commonly called reflexive consciousness. Social psychology has made great progress with studying how the self knows itself. The broad outlines have become clear, even though many specific questions remain, and some subtopics are controversial or poorly understood. The self cannot be known directly or observed in quiescent isolation, but one can form elaborate knowledge about the self based on observing it in action and knowing its thoughts and feelings. Information bearing on the self is processed in special ways, including more thorough, extensive cognition and stronger affect. Most people seem to feel a quick and special affection for whatever is linked to the self, including possessions and symbols.

Self-awareness begins with the basic phenomenon of reflexive consciousness, but it typically adds the evaluative comparison to abstract standards. Its effects are extensive and complex. Thus, self-awareness can improve task performance by increasing the motivation to measure up to standards, but it can impair performance by undermining skill. It can increase inhibitions (such as by making standards more salient), and it can decrease impulsive generosity—or impulsive violence. It can be pleasant or unpleasant, depending on which standards are used and how the self compares. Aversive self-awareness has been linked to various pathological patterns, and the effort to escape from self-awareness produces a broad range of strange and seemingly paradoxical behavior.

The accumulation of self-knowledge is guided by three main motives: people want accurate self-knowledge, they want confirmation of what they believe, and they want favorable feedback. Among these, the self-enhancement motive (for favorable information) seems strongest and is most directly tied to emotional responses. The accuracy and consistency motives may have greater influence over cognitive responses, such as whether to agree with an evaluation one receives.

The interface between motivation and cognition can be seen in the ways people maneuver to sustain favorable or inflated views of self, and these maneuvers form the main thrust of self-deception. People avoid bad feedback, selectively forget it, actively discredit it, judge themselves by biased and self-serving criteria, and selectively compare themselves against inferior targets or weak standards. The assortment of self-deceptive techniques presumably reflects both the difficulty and the widespread desirability of convincing yourself that you are better than objective reality might warrant.

Social psychology's early efforts to study self-knowledge were strongly influenced by behaviorist and black-box views, but these have largely given way to cognitive and even introspectionist approaches, although the biases and limits of introspection have been well documented. Still, people do identify with their thoughts and feelings more than with mere behaviors. Self-perception processes, which propose that self-knowledge (like knowledge about others) is formed by observing behavior, are important but operate mainly in the absence of other sources of self-knowledge. More common, perhaps, are processes in which situations and behavior activate some parts of self-knowledge, making them more salient than others. The relation between the focal portion of self-knowledge (the phenomenal self) and the far more extensive but tacit domain of self-knowledge is far from fully understood.

Likewise, social psychology has only begun to understand the organization of self-knowledge. Most findings pertain to defensive responses that isolate some parts of self-knowledge from others, so as to minimize vulnerability to unfavorable feedback or the self's deficiencies. Whether there are other theoretically interesting issues regarding the organization of self-knowledge remains to be seen.

Self-esteem involves a global value judgment about the self. People are powerfully and pervasively driven to achieve and maintain high self-esteem, and American society currently places great hopes and emphasis on increasing self-esteem. Yet the clear benefits of self-esteem seem confined to being an affective resource for coping with misfortune, such as persisting in the face of failure or feeling better after setbacks. Researchers have begun to grow more critical of high self-esteem, especially inflated views of self, as studies link such views to violence, dangerous risk-taking, and maladjustment. Most of the negative findings involve high but threatened self-esteem, which seems to elicit irrational and dangerous responses, and so it appears that ego threats (interacting with high self-esteem) warrant special attention from further research. Meanwhile, there are several competing theories about why people care so much about self-esteem, and none is entirely satisfactory.

Individual differences in self-esteem have been studied extensively. Low self-esteem is accompanied by problems and deficits in self-knowledge, including its being less certain, less consistent, and less stable. People with low self-esteem show greater emotional reactivity, greater malleability in response to external influence, and greater orientations toward self-protection, than others.

INTERPERSONAL BEING

In principle, a full-fledged self might require nothing more than a body and reflexive consciousness. In practice, however, selves always develop amid frequent, ongoing interpersonal relations, and probably those are indispensable to proper, successful development of selfhood. Self is not only a consequence but an active participant in those social relationships.

Thus, a second crucial aspect of selfhood is that the self is essentially an interpersonal tool. One reason we have selves is in order to facilitate interactions and relationships with others. Anyone who has ever tried to go out on a first date during an identity crisis, for example, probably knows how difficult it is to relate to another person without a firm understanding of self. Such observations are probably what prompted Erik Erikson (1950, 1968) to make his famous assertion that identity is a prerequisite for intimacy, in the sense that people must settle the problems of identity before they are developmentally ready for intimate relations. The sequence may not be that simple, because identity and intimacy seem to develop together, but the link between the two is hard to deny (Orlofksy, Marcia, & Lesser, 1973; Tesch & Whitbourne, 1982).

The social identity is also constructed extensively out of social roles. An elaborate series of cluster analyses by Deaux, Reid, Mizrahi, and Ethier (1995) revealed five main types of social identities: relationships (lover, sibling), vocational or avocational role (gardener, teacher), political affiliation (Republican, feminist), stigmatized identity (homeless person, fat), and religion or ethnicity (Christian, Hispanic). As products of the culture and society, roles again reveal the interpersonal dimension of selfhood. To be a mother, a policeman, a philanthropist, or an athlete is to make the self fit a script that is collectively defined. Each person may interpret a given role in a slightly different way, but the role is nonetheless understood by the social group and is a way of relating to others.

Indeed, reflexive consciousness itself may depend partly on interpersonal contact. Sartre's (1956) famous analysis of consciousness emphasized what he called "the look," that is, the subjective experience of looking at someone else and knowing that that person is looking at you. The rise in adolescent self-consciousness and social awkwardness is in part a result of the increased cognitive ability to understand how one appears to others.

How Are Self-Views Affected By Others?

One important set of processes concerns how interpersonal relations shape and alter the self. The *tabula rasa* view of human nature that is occasionally popular holds that selves are the products of interpersonal relations. Although such views are elegant and sometimes politically appealing, they may suggest too passive or simple a role of the self.

The broader issue is how selfhood is maintained in an interpersonal environment. It seems essential to postulate that part of the self exists in other people's minds—or, at least, other people form an important repository for knowledge about the self. Selfhood cannot be achieved or constructed in solitude. Indeed, we have already seen evidence that self-esteem is centrally concerned with social acceptance (Leary, Tambor et al., 1995).

Reflected Appraisals Undoubtedly much information about the self is gleaned through interactions with other people. Often information about the self is only meaningful in relation to others, as social comparison theory emphasizes: being tall or short, smart or stupid, fast or slow, friendly or grumpy are not absolute properties but are relative to other people. In such cases, self-knowledge can only be obtained through interpersonal processes and indeed implicitly involves other people.

Meanwhile, other people are important sources of social feedback. For example, Sullivan's (1953) interpersonal theory of personality described how one close friendship during preadolescence often serves a crucial developmental function by simply giving the young person feedback about how he or she is perceived by others, in many specific instances.

Symbolic interactionism provided a systematic view of the social bases of self-knowledge (e.g., Mead, 1934). In this view, very little originates inside the individual; rather,

most of what is known about the self is derived from others. One learns about oneself from others. The process of reflected appraisals (i.e., how other people's appraisals of you shape your self-understanding) is often described with Cooley's (1902) term the *looking-glass self.*

An influential literature review by Shrauger and Schoeneman (1979) sought to compile the evidence to see whether the symbolic interactionist view was correct, at least with regard to the basic prediction that how people perceive themselves should be essentially similar to how they are perceived by others. They found, however, that the correlations tended to be rather low. Self-concepts do not closely resemble the way those same people are perceived by others who know them. Subsequent studies have managed to find some positive correlations, although these generally remain small (Edwards & Klockars, 1981; Felson, 1981; Funder, 1980; Kenrick & Stringfield, 1980; Koestner, Bernieri, & Zuckerman, 1989; Malloy & Albright, 1990), and even some of these weak links can be questioned on methodological grounds, as noted by Felson (1989).

On the other hand, Shrauger and Shoeneman found (and subsequent work has replicated) that self-concepts were highly correlated with how people *believed* that others perceived them. There was a link after all (although the causal direction is unclear and probably bidirectional) between self-perceptions and other-perceptions. The discrepancy arises between how people actually perceive Fred and how Fred thinks other people perceive him. But his view of himself is quite similar to how he thinks others see him.

There seem to be two major causes that contribute to the discrepancy between how people believe others regard them and how the others actually regard them (see Felson, 1989). The first is that people do not generally tell someone precisely what they think of him or her (Jones & Wortman, 1973). The exchange of interpersonal evaluations is highly distorted by such factors as the desire to make a good impression on others and to win the liking of others, as well as the desire to avoid hostile or distressed responses. When refusing a date, for example, people tend to give false and misleading explanations, often resulting in their being unable to discourage further invitations from the same person (e.g., Folkes, 1982). Even when people are engaging in deliberate self-presentation, they are not very accurate at estimating the impression they actually make on another person (e.g., DePaulo, Kenny, Hoover, Webb, & Oliver, 1987). Given that people do not tell a person precisely what they think of him or her, it is no surprise that the person's self-concept remains blissfully unaffected by those concealed opinions and appraisals.

The other source of distortion is self-deception. As explained earlier in this chapter, people do not accept information directly into their views of themselves. Instead, they filter it, bias it, and adapt it to fit in with what they already believe and what they prefer to believe. Hence even if others do tell Fred exactly what they think of him, he may discount or ignore the unwelcome parts of the message.

Influence of Others' Expectancies   If people do not simply internalize what others think of them, perhaps they cooperate in shaping themselves according to the guidelines and expectations of other people. It has long been established that people are influenced by the expectancies of others. Rosenthal and Jacobson (1968) showed that teachers' initially false expectancies about their students led to changes in the performances of the students that confirmed those expectancies.

Do self-concepts change in response to others' expectancies? Darley and Fazio (1980) noted that there are three different outcomes that can all be labeled a self-fulfilling prophecy: the perceiver's expectancy can be confirmed by the perceiver's final belief, by the target's actual behavior, or by the target's self-appraisal. The evidence for the last of these was the weakest, however. Thus, perceivers may often believe that their expectancies are confirmed, and their actions may sometimes cause the target to respond behaviorally to confirm the expectancies, but it is rarer for the target to come to share the perceiver's initially false belief about him or her.

For example, one of the most widely cited studies of self-fulfilling prophecies was done by Snyder, Tanke, and Berscheid (1977). In their study, male subjects were given bogus photos of female interaction partners and then had telephone conversations. The males' expectancies regarding the attractiveness and social charm of their interaction partners were confirmed in the males' beliefs and in the behavioral responses of the female partners. The women did not however accept the way the men treated them when it was unfavorable. When the man thought the woman was unattractive and treated her accordingly, she tended to reject and discount (as inaccurate) his view of her.

A subsequent study by Snyder and Swann (1978) induced expectancies that one's interaction partner was hostile. The subsequent interaction, featuring a noise weapon, showed confirmation of these expectancies in both the perceivers' views and in the targets' responses. The crucial question was however whether the target would then go on to act in a hostile manner with a new interaction partner, which would suggest some degree of generalization and possible internalization. Snyder and Swann only found such carry-over effects in a condition in which the targets were induced to make dispositional attributions about the way they had acted during the first interaction. In other words, an experimental manipulation was necessary in order to help them see their actions as reflecting their traits. Otherwise the hostile behavior did not carry over into the next interaction. These results again suggest that it is not easy to alter another person's self-appraisal.

Altering the Self   How do self-conceptions change? This question has considerable theoretical and practical importance. Answers have been slow in coming, partly because of the difficulty of measuring self-concept change, and partly because some self-concept changes would be unethical to induce. Still, some conclusions have taken shape, and many of them point to the importance of interpersonal factors.

The stability of self-conceptions is dependent to some degree on interpersonal relations. Brainwashing, for example, is a deliberate attempt to change another person's views extensively. A common feature among the more successful brainwashing programs is that the person is separated from all those who knew him or her. When social contacts continue with one's older acquaintances (e.g., prisoners who spend the day under indoctrination but then return to their fellow prisoners in the evening), brainwashing tends to fail (see Baumeister, 1986, for review).

When people try to change themselves, their interpersonal involvements are again extremely potent determinants of success or failure. Heatherton and Nichols (1994) compared two samples of accounts: one in which people had changed in an important way, and another in which people had tried but failed to change. There was ample evidence of involvement by others. Successful change was often instigated by others (e.g., pressure from one's spouse to quit smoking). Sometimes the motivation to change was stimulated by observing someone else change (and these occurrences were associated with successful rather than unsuccessful changes). Lastly, people who succeeded reported considerable help and support from other people, much more than people who failed to change.

These findings emphasize actual, behavioral change. There is also reason to consider changes in the self-concept that may occur independent of real change. After all, one way to change the self-concept is to make yourself a different person and then change your self-concept to match. Another, presumably easier route is simply to revise your self-concept without having to change your behavior.

In any case, evidence points to the importance of the social environment for self-concept change too. Several studies by Harter (1993) have provided evidence about change in self-esteem. Self-esteem is most likely to change at points in life where there is a substantial change in one's social environment. When one graduates from high school and begins college, for example, it often happens that one reduces interactions with many family members and prior friends and instead begins interacting with a new set of peers at college. Self-esteem change is much more common at such times than during periods when one continues to interact with the same people. These findings are consistent with the implication of the brainwashing studies: the self becomes much more malleable when deprived of contact with the people that know it well. Another way to describe this pattern is to suggest that other people, especially stable relationship partners, may inhibit change, possibly because people expect each other to remain the same and put pressure on each other to be consistent.

Internalization of Behavior One of the most compelling routes to self-concept change is through internalization of behavior. Self-perception theory and other theories have provided ample reason to think that if people can be induced to act in a certain way, they may gradually see themselves as being the sort of person who acts that way. Self-concept change may therefore derive from behavioral change, by some process of internalization.

One likely mechanism has to do with the multifaceted nature of the self. A certain behavior pattern may access relevant knowledge about the self, and so that knowledge will weigh most heavily in subsequent judgments about the self. Research by Fazio et al. (1981) provided important preliminary evidence of such changes. Subjects responded to loaded questions designed to make them regard themselves as introverted or extraverted. Accessing relevant self-knowledge (in order to answer the loaded questions) apparently had at least a temporary effect, in that people later rated themselves as being the sort of person the questions had implied. Thus, people who had to describe how they would liven up a dull party were more likely to describe themselves as extraverts than people who had been asked what they dislike about crowded settings. Fazio et al. (1981) also showed behavioral changes: those who had responded to the questions biased in favor of extraversion were more likely to strike up a conversation with a confederate later on, in an ostensibly unrelated setting.

The pattern of findings reported by Fazio et al. (1981) was elaborated into a *biased scanning* theory of self-concept change by Jones et al. (1981). They proposed that when people reflect on themselves, they scan all the available information about themselves—but recent experiences can bias this scan so that they are more likely to think of certain kinds of information. In their studies, subjects were induced to present themselves in certain ways, and they later rated their self-concepts as consistent with the ways they had presented themselves.

The biased scanning and accessibility theories essentially describe intrapsychic processes of self-concept change: the person observes his or her behavior, thinks of relevant information about the self, and that information then takes center stage the next time the person is asked about self-conceptions. More recent work, however, has shifted the emphasis from intrapsychic to interpersonal processes—or, more precisely, it has shown that the intrapsychic processes are heavily dependent on interpersonal ones. Self-concept change thus appears to be one

version of the interplay between interpersonal and intrapsychic processes (Tetlock & Manstead, 1985).

Tice (1992) noted that despite the intrapsychic thrust of biased scanning theory, the experimental procedures had been interpersonal, and she hypothesized that the interpersonal dimension was decisive. In her studies, people only showed the self-concept (and behavioral) changes if their actions had been observed by others. The same behaviors done in a private or confidential context failed to alter self-concept. Thus, one tends to internalize actions mainly when those actions gain social reality from being observed by others; apparently other people have an important capacity to magnify the self-perception process.

The role of other people's awareness was confirmed by Schlenker, Dlugolecki, and Doherty (1994), who then went on to challenge the biased scanning view. These researchers included several conditions in which biased scanning was induced but the interpersonal behavior did not occur (e.g., people prepared for a certain interaction which was canceled at the last minute), and yet no self-concept change was found. In a final study, they had people present themselves one way and then engage in biased scanning for the opposite view (e.g., present yourself as an extravert, and then scan your memory for introverted acts). The scanning appeared to have little or no effect on self-concept change. Only the interpersonal actions were internalized.

In retrospect, resistance to self-concept change may have the same interpersonal dimension. Swann and Hill (1982) showed that self-ratings changed if people passively received discrepant feedback, but if they were allowed to respond (and dispute the feedback), they did not change. It may well have been the public assertion of the self-view that enabled it to resist pressure to change.

At present, then, the precise mechanism of internalization and self-concept change needs further study. Tice interpreted her internalization findings as fitting a biased scanning view, with the important addition that interpersonal interaction seems important for causing the scanning to take place. Schlenker et al. (1994) found, as Tice did, that self-concept change occurred in public but not in private circumstances, yet they doubt that the biased scanning mechanism is a correct description of the process. In any case, the importance of the social, interpersonal context seems more clearly established than the precise intrapsychic mechanism that mediates its effects.

Self-Presentation

Undoubtedly the most obvious and proactive way that the self participates in social life is through self-presentation, which is defined as people's attempts to convey information about or images of themselves to others. Part of the self exists outside, in the minds of others: one does not have an identity unless it is validated by others, which means that others must recognize and acknowledge one's self.

Concern over self-presentation is extremely pervasive. Baumeister (1982) showed that many of social psychology's effects only were obtained as a result of self-presentation: that is, people only showed many of the effects when others were watching. Cognitive and intrapsychic theories that explained many effects seemed to be missing something, because the effects depended on interpersonal contexts. Thus, helping, attitude change, emotion, aggression, attributional patterns, and other responses seemed to change when the individual's acts would be seen by others. Leary (1995) has furnished an even longer and more impressive list, showing effects of self-presentation in contexts ranging from sports teams to business meetings to the beach to mental hospitals.

Hence it was necessary to reappraise how social the person was. Unfortunately, some of the early efforts were carried out in a hostile, antagonistic fashion, such as the famous assertion that cognitive dissonance did not actually produce attitude change but merely reflected a superficial tendency of people to pretend they were changing in order to make a good impression (Tedeschi, Schlenker, & Bonoma, 1971). Later work however adopted a more moderate tone and concluded that actual attitude change does occur as a result of self-presentational factors, and indeed that some dissonance can occur without self-presentational motivations, although self-presentation is quite a fundamental and potent cause of dissonance (Schlenker, 1982; also Baumeister & Tice, 1984; Paulhus, 1982).

The dissonance debate provided a model for subsequent debates about the role of self-presentation. Self-presentation often appeared as an alternative explanation for intrapsychic theories, and often a series of experiments were done to contrast whether people "really" had the intrapsychic responses originally proposed or were instead merely superficially reporting such responses out of self-presentational concerns. In an influential paper, Tetlock and Manstead (1985) proposed that such debates were likely to remain unresolved and that it was often a theoretical dead end to pit intrapsychic and interpersonal processes against each other. They proposed instead that researchers seek to develop theories that would integrate self-presentational and intrapsychic processes. This is a crucial and important suggestion, because as we shall see there is substantial and bidirectional influence between interpersonal and intrapsychic processes.

Self-Presentational Motives   Two main kinds of motivations for self-presentation are important. One is largely instrumental, aimed at influencing others as a means toward gaining practical and material rewards. The other is expressive, aimed at constructing a certain image of self and claiming an identity for oneself. A full understanding of the empirical evidence of self-presentational patterns requires both (Baumeister, 1982).

The instrumental uses of self-presentation have long been apparent to researchers (e.g., Jones, 1964). People are heavily and extensively dependent on others, and making a favorable impression on someone is often a useful way to help secure the rewards that others control. Whether the reward at stake is a major promotion or merely an extra napkin, the person who comes across as disagreeable and incompetent is less likely to secure the willing cooperation of others.

These instrumental forms of self-presentation can be described as *strategic self-presentation*, insofar as the task of impressing others is a strategy for achieving ulterior goals. Jones and Pittman (1982) proposed a taxonomy of instrumental goals that one can pursue with various types of impression management, as follows. *Ingratiation* involves convincing others that you have appealing traits, as a way of getting them to like you. *Intimidation* refers to making others fear you, usually by convincing them that you have the dangerous potential to harm them and are willing to use it. *Self-promotion* is a matter of showing one's competence and aptitude, in order to get others to respect you. *Exemplification* refers to convincing people that you are a good person, in the sense of having admirable moral virtues. Last, *supplication* involves convincing others that you are needy, dependent, and deserving, in order to induce them to give you aid and other benefits.

The purpose of these strategies is frankly and explicitly to manipulate others. If people like you, for example, they will generally reward you and refrain from punishing you, because to punish you would cause them to feel bad. If they respect your competence, they will hire and promote you, give you rewards that accompany merit and achievement. If they fear you, they will desist from interfering with what you want to do. If they feel sorry for you, they will try to help you. And if they respect your moral virtue, they will refrain from criticizing your acts, and you can remain a respected member of the community.

The situational importance of such strategic self-presentation was nicely demonstrated by Kowalski and Leary (1990). Subjects were asked to describe themselves for a supervisor, who did or did not have the power to assign them tasks later (and these included one unpleasant task). People altered their self-presentations only when the supervisor had power. Apparently, they were only willing to exert themselves self-presentationally when there was some advantage to be had by manipulating the audience.

The other form of self-presentational motive is expressive: constructing the self. Sometimes people want to make an impression on others in order to claim an identity. Hence people sometimes present themselves in ways contrary to what others will like and approve. One example of this kind of self-presentation is in studies on reactance. Research has shown that people will assert their freedom against those who have sought to curtail it. Clearly, such rebellious self-assertion is not designed to please the person against whom the rebellion is directed. But it often may seem vitally important to people to convey to precisely that person that they are not giving in to his or her demands. A confidential assertion of one's freedom is not enough (Baer, Hinkle, Smith, & Fenton, 1980; Heilman & Toffler, 1976).

An intriguing program of research on this expressive form of self-presentation was conducted by Wicklund and Gollwitzer (1982). They too provided evidence that people will sometimes engage in self-presentation that is contrary to what the intended audience will like or approve. In a memorable study, male subjects got to meet a confederate named Debbie, who had already made it clear that she preferred confident and self-enhancing people—or, in the other condition, modest and self-deprecating people. This information would seemingly make it easy for the subject to gain her approval, simply by conforming to the norms that she had implicitly set. Yet if the subjects had been led to feel insecure about their claims to their most important identity, they were unable to follow the norm to be modest. These subjects had taken a bogus personality test, supposedly in another context, and they received feedback that they were not the sort of person who was likely to be successful in their chosen field. They were unable to conform to the modesty norm. Even though Debbie had shown that she disliked boastful, self-enhancing people, they insisted on presenting themselves very positively with regard to their chosen field. (In contrast, people who had received reassuring feedback about their identity claims were less driven to make positive claims to Debbie, and so they were willing to be modest and self-deprecating with her when appropriate.)

The responses to Debbie thus capture the seemingly paradoxical nature of expressive self-presentation: one presents oneself in a way that the other person will likely dislike and disapprove, as long as this is consistent with one's own private image of one's desired identity. Self-presentation is thus sometimes driven by the values and ideals of the self rather than those of the audience to whom one is communicating. Needless to say, the opposite is true of the other (instrumental) form of self-presentation: if the goal is to secure rewards from the other person, then one tries to present oneself as closely as possible to the other person's values and preferences.

The broader point is that people use self-presentation to construct an identity for themselves. Most people have a certain ideal image of the person they would like to be. It is not enough merely to act like that person or to convince oneself that one resembles that person. Identity requires social validation. The common assumption seems to be that you are not really a great artist, or an attractive lover,

or a trustworthy partner, or a success in your job unless other people perceive you as such. Self-esteem, self-deception, and similar intrapsychic processes may be fine as far as they go, but they are inadequate for identity.

Thus, self-presentation often occurs in the tension of opposing forces: Should one present oneself consistent with one's own values and ideals, or with those of the intended audience? Fortunately the two motives probably agree in many cases, especially insofar as people interact with friends and others who share the same values. Still, there are cases in which people must choose between two opposing forces: conforming their self-presentations to what the interaction partner would like best versus being true to their own identity aspirations.

Favorability of Self-Presentation   A general tendency toward favorable self-presentations is not without exceptions. For example, people do on occasion "play dumb" in order to please someone who may like that better (Leary, 1995). There is some validity to the stereotype of women feigning intellectual inferiority when interacting with men, but in other contexts men are more likely to play dumb, and overall there does not appear to be a sex difference in frequency of playing dumb (Dean, Braito, Powers, & Britton, 1975).

Still, in general, people want to present themselves favorably. In terms of seeking feedback for one's self-concept, I noted earlier that people are often torn between the conflicting motives of consistency and self-enhancement. A similar distinction applies to self-presentation, with some interesting twists due to the interpersonal constraints. The basic question is this: How favorably should one present oneself? People's answers appear to depend on several factors. In Schlenker's (1980, 1986) terms, self-presentation is often the result of a tradeoff between the opposing forces of favorability and plausibility. On the one hand, people want to make a good impression, and they often believe that making positive and favorable claims is the best way to accomplish this. On the other hand, excessively positive claims about the self may not be believed, and they run the additional risk of being discredited. Moreover, having one's favorable self-assertions shown to be false can be humiliating, and the net resulting impression may often be quite poor.

Accordingly, the self-presenter must strike a balance between favorability and plausibility. A particularly important constraint on plausibility is whether the intended audience is likely to gain independent verification of one's claims. After all, it is easy to claim to be a great swimmer or an accomplished pianist when chatting with someone on a ski lift, because there is little chance of having to back up such assertions with performance. To make similar claims when lounging by a pool or a piano (respectively) is another matter, however.

In one of the earliest and most cited experiments on self-presentation, Schlenker (1975) gave subjects feedback about their abilities on a novel task prior to a group performance session. Then they were asked to describe themselves to the group members. Schlenker wanted to see whether subjects would describe themselves consistent with the (sometimes negative) feedback or in more positive, favorable terms. He found that the answer depended on whether the upcoming group performance was expected to be public or private. If it was to be private, so that no one would know one's performance, then subjects presented themselves in rather favorable terms. But if they thought other people would be able to see how well they did, they refrained from boasting. Thus, people seemed to present themselves as favorably as they could get away with: they boasted when it was safe to do so but remained modest and circumspect when it seemed likely that the truth would be found out.

The possibility of future disconfirmation is not the only interpersonal constraint on self-presentational favorability. Another is rooted in the past: one's prior actions or other socially available information about the self form the point of departure for any subsequent self-presentations to people who know you. After all, people do not simply form a wholly new impression of someone with every single interaction. New information is added to old information. The self-presenter must anticipate this and know that whatever he or she does now will be combined, in the observer's mind, with what the observer already knows.

An initial study of the constraining effects of prior knowledge on self-presentation was conducted by Baumeister and Jones (1978). Subjects were told that their interaction partner would read their personality profile, based on a previous test. As in Schlenker's (1975) study, people felt constrained to be consistent with what the independent information said: in this case, they conformed their self-presentations to the randomly assigned feedback, even depicting themselves unfavorably if that was what their test results said. Yet they did not leave the matter at that: they sought to compensate for the unfavorable image of themselves by presenting themselves extra favorably on other, unrelated dimensions. Thus, they were indeed constrained to be consistent with what the observer already knew about them, but they could make up for a bad impression by bringing in unrelated, highly favorable information about themselves.

The general thrust toward favorable self-presentation may therefore have severe limits. An additional and quite important limit was recently identified by Tice, Butler, Muraven, and Stillwell (1995). These authors noted the irony that nearly all self-presentation research had been done on first meetings between strangers, whereas the vast majority of actual social interactions take place between people who already know each other. They showed that people tend to be positive and self-enhancing when interacting with strangers—but they turn modest and neutral when presenting themselves to friends.

Why? Strangers know nothing about you, and so it is necessary to convey one's good traits in order to make a favorable impression on them; moreover, they will not have any basis for disputing an overly favorable self-presentation. In contrast, friends already have substantial information about you, and so it is not necessary to tell them about one's good traits that they already know. Meanwhile, friends will know when you are exaggerating, and even if you are correct in touting your good points, they may dislike the immodesty of such statements.

Cognition and Self-Presentation   Despite the widely noted exhortation by Tetlock and Manstead to integrate intrapsychic and self-presentational theorizing, relatively little work has examined the cognitive processes in self-presentation. The methodological difficulties of doing such research are probably one factor.

One basic question is how accurately people can judge their success at self-presentation: that is, do people know what impressions they convey to others? DePaulo, Kenny, Hoover, Webb, and Oliver (1987) investigated that question by having subjects conduct a round-robin interaction pattern. Each subject interacted with three others, one at a time, in interactions that were structured around different tasks (e.g., a teaching task and a competition). After each interaction, both subjects rated their impression of the partner and the impression they thought they had made on the partner. By seeing how well those ratings matched up, the researchers could assess how well people could estimate the impressions they made.

The answers were mixed. There was indeed significant accuracy, although most of the correlations were rather low. People could tell in a general way how the other person's impression of them changed over time. They were not however very effective at inferring which partner liked them the most or perceived them as most competent. In other words, you probably cannot form a very accurate guess of which person you made the best impression on.

Another large gap between perceived and real impressions is that people tended to think they made roughly the same impression on everyone, whereas in fact different partners formed quite different impressions of the same person. People seem to overestimate the consistency of the image they project to different persons.

Cognitive processes that occur during self-presentation were studied by Baumeister, Hutton, and Tice (1989). Subjects in that study were interviewed in pairs, and one member of each pair had been taken aside and given special instructions to self-present in either a modest or self-enhancing fashion. After the interview, subjects were given a surprise recall test for both their own and their partner's self-presentations, as well as for impressions of the partner. Subjects who had been instructed to be modest and self-effacing showed impaired memory for the interaction. Apparently, modesty (which is an unusual way to act when presenting oneself to strangers) consumes cognitive resources and thus interferes with one's encoding of the interaction. Another finding was that subjects seemed unaware of the effect they had on the other person (see Gilbert & Jones, 1986). Thus, for example, if Bob presents himself by saying highly favorable things about himself, Harry may also start to say highly favorable things about himself—which will lead Bob to conclude that Harry must be rather conceited or at least have high self-esteem. In fact, though, Harry's self-promotion was merely a response to Bob's.

The fact that deliberate self-presentation seems to consume cognitive resources and thereby interferes with other information processing may help explain some of the findings of DePaulo et al. (1987). When people are concentrating on trying to make a certain impression, they may not be fully able to attend to how the other person is responding. After a series of interactions, what may be salient in their own memory is that they tried to make roughly the same good impression on each interaction partner, rather than the fact that the partners did not all seem to respond in quite the same way.

These findings suggest that the consequences of self-presentation may often be driven primarily by the inner and cognitive processes that accompany it. People seem to be affected by the impression they are trying to make, to a greater extent than by the actual interpersonal responses and consequences, and indeed the cognitive work that accompanies a difficult self-presentation may often reduce their ability to discern those interpersonal responses and consequences.

Harmful Aspects of Self-Presentation A series of health risks associated with self-presentation was documented by Leary, Tchividjian, and Kraxberger (1994). Concern over how one is seen by others can lead people to engage in various risky and harmful behaviors. These indicate that the drive to impress others can take precedence even over rational and self-preservation motives.

Skin cancer provides one relevant sphere. People believe that a suntan makes them look attractive, but in recent years warnings of the carcinogenic and other harmful effects of sun exposure have proliferated. Leary and Jones (1993) showed that the risky behaviors of sunbathing were mainly linked to concern about how one is viewed by others, especially one's physical appearance, rather than concern (or lack of concern) about health. People sunbathe to make themselves attractive, often ignoring the physical danger involved.

Risky sexual behavior is also influenced by self-presen-tation. Condoms are generally regarded as the safest method for having intercourse outside of stable, monogamous relationships, but many people do not use them. Reasons for not taking these precautions are often self-presentational, including embarrassment over buying them and fear of what store clerks and patrons will think, as well as fear that having a condom and wanting to use it will make a bad impression on one's anticipated sexual partner (Leary, 1995).

Other risks reviewed by Leary et al. (1994) include hazardous dieting and eating patterns, use of alcohol and illegal drugs, cigarette smoking, steroid use, accidental injury and even death (e.g., not wearing safety equipment), and complications from cosmetic surgery. Taken together, these provide strong evidence that self-presentational concerns often take precedence over the concerns with maintaining health and even protecting life.

Interpersonal Consequences of Self-Views

It is clear that the nature of the self exerts some influence over interpersonal relations. One of the best-known findings in social psychology is the link between similarity and attraction (Byrne, 1971; Schiller, 1932; Smeaton, Byrne, & Murnen, 1989), which means that in some sense people seek out and like partners who resemble them. (Or, at least, they avoid and dislike people who are different from them; Rosenbaum, 1986.) Similarities on important, heritable traits are especially potent bases for liking and disliking others (Crelia & Tesser, 1996; Tesser, 1993).

Although the preference for others similar to oneself is well established, it is not safe to conclude that specific views about the self lead invariably to effects on interpersonal relations. This section will examine what is known about how self-views shape such relations, including perceptions of other people and the formation of relationship patterns. (The interpersonal consequences of self-esteem were covered earlier.)

Self-Views Alter Person Perception Does the self-concept operate as an important anchor or filter that shapes how people understand others? The operation of self-schemas in person perception was studied by Markus, Smith, and Moreland (1985; see also Fong & Markus, 1982). They proposed that having a self-schema in a particular domain makes one act like an expert in that domain. More precisely, such schematic people will be quicker than others to spot information relevant to their domain, better able to integrate it with previously acquired information, better able to make up the gaps in new information, and better able to integrate the details of actions with the big picture. In their research, people who were schematic for masculinity tended to form larger units in the masculinity-relevant behavior of a stimulus person, and they saw the stimulus person as more masculine and more like themselves than did aschematic individuals. When attending to detail was important, the schematics shifted more than other subjects toward greater processing of details.

Thus, aspects of self-concept can influence the perception of others (although it is conceivable that some prior interest in the area leads to the expertise and the self-perception). The key point appears to be that a particularly well developed aspect of self-knowledge makes one act like an expert in that sphere. If your view of yourself emphasizes loyalty, for example, you will likely be extra sensitive to loyalty or disloyalty in others, and you may move more readily between specific details of loyalty (or disloyalty) and the broader patterns and issues than would someone else.

The *self-image bias* is one mechanism by which people's self-concepts bias the way they perceive others (Lewicki, 1983, 1984). According to this bias, people tend to judge others according to the traits on which they themselves look good. The self-image bias shows a correlation between how favorably the person rates himself or herself on some dimension and the centrality of that dimension in the person's perceptions of others (Lewicki, 1983). (Centrality refers to the number of other dimensions correlated with it.) For example, students who did well in a computer science course tended to place more emphasis on computer skills in perceiving others than did the other, less successful students (Hill, Smith, & Lewicki, 1989). Lewicki (1984) showed that the self-image bias serves a defensive function: When people receive critical, upsetting feedback, the effect of self-image bias on perception of others is increased.

Another link between self-concepts and perception of other people involves the way people define the crucial traits. Dunning, Perie, and Story (1991) found that people construct prototypes of social categories such as intelligence, creativity, and leadership in ways that emphasize their own traits. Thus, inquisitive people think inquisitiveness is a valuable aid to creativity, but noninquisitive people disagree. These prototypes then influence how people evaluate others.

Most research has emphasized how people's views of themselves affect person perception, but it may be that defensive processes (such as rejecting a view of self) can exert an effect too. Newman, Duff, and Baumeister (1997) put forward a new model of the Freudian defense mechanism of *projection*, which in essence means seeing one's faults in other people rather than in oneself. Newman et al. built on evidence that when people try not to think about something, that something tends to become highly accessible in memory (Wegner & Erber, 1992; Wegner, Schneider, Carter, & White, 1987). They also found that certain people tend to deny their bad traits and yet see other people as having those same traits. A laboratory experiment showed that when people tried to suppress thoughts about some

bad trait that had been imputed to them, they ended up interpreting other people's behavior as reflecting that bad trait. Thus, person perception can be shaped by the traits you are trying to deny in yourself, just as much as by the traits that you do see in yourself.

Accessibility appears to be the common theme among all these effects. The attributes the self emphasizes, and those the self seeks to deny, operate as highly accessible categories for interpreting others' behavior (Higgins, King, & Mavin, 1982). Social perception thus tends to be self-centered and self-biased. Still, these effects appear to be specific and limited, and one should not assume that all interpersonal perception is wildly distorted by self-appraisals. In particular, these effects seem to be limited to cases in which information about the target person is ambiguous (Lambert & Wedell, 1991; Sedikides & Skowronski, 1993).

Self-Evaluation Maintenance   Several important links between the quest for self-esteem and interpersonal relations have been elaborated in Tesser's (1988) self-evaluation maintenance theory. Among other consequences, this theory explains how people may draw closer to or draw away from relationship partners as a result of pressures to maintain self-esteem.

Two main processes link self-views to interpersonal outcomes, according to Tesser. The first of these is a *reflection* process, by which one gains esteem and credit from being linked to successful others. People seem to gain a boost in esteem simply because their cousin won a national golf tournament, because they slept with a rock artist or Congressman, because their child was valedictorian, or because they once shared a taxi with a movie star. Cialdini and his colleagues have shown how people bask in reflected glory of institutions, such as by wearing school colors more frequently following a team victory than following a defeat (Cialdini et al., 1976; Cialdini & Richardson, 1980).

The other process is one of *comparison* (see Festinger, 1954; Wills, 1981), and it can yield the opposite result. People may compare themselves with others close to them— and feel bad if the other person is outperforming them. If your sibling gets better grades than you, if your dimwit brother-in-law earns double your salary, or if your wife knows more about cars than you do, you may lose esteem.

Thus, the reflection and comparison processes produce opposite results in terms of how one's esteem is affected by the achievements of close others. Tesser's work has therefore gone on to look for factors that determine which process will predominate. One such factor is the *relevance* of the ability to one's own self-concept. Thus, your cousin's golf tournament victory may bring you esteem as the reflection process predicts—but only if golf is not highly relevant to your own self-esteem. If you entered the same tournament and lost ignominiously, your cousin's success would make you look that much worse by comparison. Sometimes people prefer to see strangers succeed rather than close friends, because the stranger's success invokes a less salient comparison and is less humiliating. Tesser and Smith (1980) showed that people will do more to help a stranger than a friend to succeed at a task that is relevant to their own self-esteem.

Meanwhile, the closer the bond, the stronger the outcome. You gain (or lose) more esteem if your spouse wins a major award than if your former neighbor wins it. Close relationships may therefore be especially vulnerable to disruption through the comparison process. If a romantic partner succeeds on something irrelevant to one's own self-esteem, one may pull closer to that person, but if the success is in something relevant to one's own strivings then one may feel jealous or threatened, and the intimate relationship may be damaged (Beach, 1992). When the comparison process makes you look bad, the only way to limit the damage may be to reduce closeness. Pleban and Tesser (1981) showed that people may distance themselves from someone who performs too well on something that is highly relevant to their self-concepts.

Self-Monitoring An early and influential theory about individual differences in how the self structures interpersonal processes was proposed by Snyder (1974, 1987). Snyder began with an interest in cross-situational consistency, stimulated by Bem and Allen's (1974) suggestion that some people have more traited consistency than others. He distinguished between high self-monitors, who attend to the situation and the behavior of others for cues as to how to behave and modify their own actions accordingly, and low self-monitors, who do not try to alter their behavior to suit each situational nuance. For example, Snyder and Swann (1976) showed high attitude-behavior consistency for people with low self-monitoring: Their attitudes predicted their verdicts in a simulated jury case. In contrast, high self-monitors' attitudes did not predict their behavior well at all, presumably because they modified their statements on the case to fit the immediate situational demands and cues. Snyder (1987) explained that high self-monitors do not see any necessary relation between their private beliefs and their public actions, and so discrepancies do not bother them.

Thus, there is a basic difference in how these two types of people see themselves. Low self-monitors regard themselves as having strong principles and as consistently upholding them. High self-monitors see themselves as pragmatic and flexible rather than principled. They respond to the situation and do what they regard as appropriate, which often includes altering their own self-presentations.

Subsequent work elaborated the different interaction patterns that accompany the different levels of self-monitoring. For low self-monitors, friendship is based on the emotional bond, and they prefer to spend most of their time with the people they like best. High self-monitors, however, see friendship in terms of shared activities, and so they spend time with whoever is best suited to the relevant activity. Thus, for example, the low self-monitor would prefer to play tennis with his best friend, regardless of how well the friend plays. The high self-monitor would rather play tennis with the best tennis player among her acquaintances (or the one best matched to her own abilities). As a result, the social worlds of high self-monitors are well compartmentalized, with different friends and partners linked to specific activities. Those of low self-monitors are relatively undifferentiated by activities, and people are chosen instead based on the emotional bonds.

The interpersonal patterns carry over into romantic activities too (Snyder, 1987; Snyder & Simpson, 1984). High self-monitoring males choose dating patterns based mainly on physical appearance, whereas low self-monitors look for personality and other inner qualities. High self-monitors tend to have more romantic and sexual partners than lows. When it comes to marriage, high self-monitors again look for shared activities and interests, whereas low self-monitors emphasize mainly the pleasures and satisfactions of simply being together.

Partner Views of Self A simpler theory about how interpersonal relationships are shaped by self-views was put forward by Swann (1992) as an extension of self-verification theory. In his view, people prefer a romantic partner who sees them as they see themselves. Several important theoretical issues are relevant. As the earlier discussion of motivations surrounding self-concepts made clear, people are sometimes torn between a desire to see themselves favorably and a desire to confirm what they already think of themselves. Moreover, love is widely regarded as distorting interpersonal appraisal, so that someone in love may tend to see the beloved partner in an idealized fashion. Would that be helpful or harmful?

Swann and his colleagues (1992; Swann, Hixon, & De La Ronde, 1992) have examined such dilemmas in various relationships, ranging from roommates to spouses. On a variety of measures, they have found support for consistency effects. People choose, like, and retain partners who see them accurately (or at least who see them consistently with their self-views, which are not necessarily accurate). In this view, the idealizing effects of love would be downright dangerous and harmful to the relationship. Apparently people want their friends and lovers to see all their faults.

A large independent investigation failed to replicate those patterns, however. Murray, Holmes, and Griffin (1996) found that favorable views of one's partner were associated with better relationships. Idealization was associated with greater satisfaction and happiness about the relationship, and in an as yet unpublished follow-up study it also predicted greater stability and durability of the relationship. In this view, then, there is good reason for love to be blind (or at least nearsighted enough to wear rose-colored glasses when looking at one's beloved). Idealization and positive illusions about one's partner seem to strengthen the relationship, making it more pleasant and more likely to last. Seeing the real you beneath the facade is not always the beginning of real intimacy: sometimes it is the beginning of the end.

These somewhat discrepant results do at least agree that it is quite important for people to believe that their friends and lovers appreciate their good points. Whether they want their partners to see their faults and flaws too is less clear. One possible moderator is that most of the self-consistency work has emphasized traits about which the person is highly certain of and committed to having, whereas the enhancement effects tend to emphasize a broader spectrum of less central and less certain traits. Possibly people want their close relationship partners to recognize one or two favorite faults but otherwise maintain a highly favorable view of them.

There is also intriguing but preliminary evidence that relationship partners can help sustain consistency. Swann and Predmore (1985) gave people feedback that was discrepant from their self-concepts and watched how they and their romantic partners responded. When the partner saw the subject as the subject saw himself or herself, the pair tended to join forces to reject the feedback: they discussed its flaws and decided how best to refute or dismiss it. In contrast, when the partner's view of the subject differed from the subject's self-concept, the discrepant feedback led to further disagreements within the couple. Although this study's sample was small and the emotionally potent distinction between positive (idealizing) and negative (disparaging) discrepancies was glossed over, the implications are important and worthy of further study. It may be that one vital function of close relationship partners is to help maintain and defend one's self-concept against the attacks of the outer world.

Emotionality of Interpersonal Self

Emotion is undoubtedly linked to interpersonal relations. In a review of evidence about the motive to form and maintain close attachments, Baumeister and Leary (1995) provided evidence that a broad assortment of negative affects result from threat or damage to relationships, whereas increasing attachment generally brings positive affect. One function of emotion is apparently to alert the self to changes in its interpersonal relations.

Emotions often reflect value judgments relevant to the self. Recent work has increasingly emphasized interpersonal determinants and processes of emotion. Thus, it appears that the interpersonal self is prominently involved in

emotion. Tangney and Fischer (1995) have compiled a collection of works on *The Self-Conscious Emotions*, and although self-consciousness might seem to connote simple reflexive awareness of self, the interpersonal concerns and processes figure prominently in many of the chapters.

Shame and Guilt   Undoubtedly there is a straightforward element of shame and guilt in self-evaluation, but both emotions seem to have strong interpersonal components. The difference between the two appears to be the globality of self-reference: guilt condemns a specific action by the self, whereas shame condemns the entire self (Lewis, 1971; Tangney, 1992, 1995).

Shame is regarded as the more destructive of the two emotions. Because shame signifies that the entire self is bad, simple reparations or constructive responses seem meaningless. Shame is therefore linked to pathological outcomes (Tangney, Burggraf, & Wagner, 1995). Shame also seems to produce socially undesirable outcomes. The immediate impact of shame seems to be social withdrawal: when one feels ashamed, one wants to hide and avoid others. Other people however respond to shame with anger (Tangney et al., 1992). The shift from shame into anger may be a defensive effort to repudiate the global negative evaluation implicit in shame, and there is some evidence that it can lead to violent outbursts (Baumeister, Smart, & Boden, 1996). Kitayama, Markus, and Matsumoto (1995) have proposed that the movement from shame to anger reflects the independent selfhood model common to Western cultures and may not occur in cultures that emphasize more interdependent selves.

Guilt, in contrast, is more manageable and less socially disruptive than shame. Considerable evidence of the interpersonal and prosocial functions of guilt was reviewed by Baumeister, Stillwell, and Heatherton (1994). Because guilt is focused on a specific transgression, the direct consequence is often a wish to repair the damage and make amends. Guilt also seems to arise most commonly in close and communal relationships (Baumeister, Stillwell, & Heatherton, 1994, 1995; Jones, Kugler, & Adams, 1995). Identical transgressions may produce greater guilt when the victim is a relationship partner than a stranger.

Embarrassment   Like shame and guilt, embarrassment seems to be a mixture of self-evaluation and interpersonal concerns. Modigliani (1971) linked embarrassment to the public self by showing that the best predictor of embarrassment was a situational, perceived loss of others' esteem. Edelmann (1985) made a similar point by showing that embarrassability correlates more highly with public self-consciousness than with private self-consciousness.

Two theoretical perspectives on embarrassment have predominated in recent years, as indicated in an authoritative overview by Miller (1995). One emphasizes concern over how one is being evaluated by others. Embarrassment thus requires concern over the other people and specifically with how they evaluate oneself. The alternative view invokes simply the difficulty and unpleasantness of awkward social interactions. Parrott, Sabini, and Silver (1988) provided support for this view using a hypothetical scenario in which the subject asks someone for a date and is refused. Subjects reported they would feel less embarrassed if the rejector used a transparent excuse that they knew to be a lie than if the rejector bluntly rebuffed them, even though the implicit evaluation by the other person was presumably the same. Miller (1995) however reported other evidence that making an excuse may itself convey a positive evaluation, such as concern for the rejected person's feelings. In reviewing the available evidence, he concluded that both perspectives have some validity, but the concern over social evaluation appears to be the stronger and more common cause of embarrassment.

Blushing is one common sign of embarrassment, yet sometimes people blush even when no clear social evaluation is being made. Leary, Britt, Cutlip, and Templeton (1992) concluded that the main cause of blushing is unwanted social attention. Still, the interpersonal processes of attention are complex. Leary (1995) offered this seemingly paradoxical pattern. In an informal survey, most subjects reported that they would not feel embarrassed over undressing with either their spouse or their same-sex parent in the same room. They would however feel embarrassed over undressing with both the spouse and the same-sex parent present.

Still, their functional analyses of blushing and embarrassment tend to focus on dealing with unfavorable evaluations by others. Leary et al. (1992) suggest that blushing is related to other appeasement behaviors, by which an individual can minimize punishment for transgressing or for violating social norms. Embarrassment does seem to mitigate bad evaluations from others: Semin and Manstead (1982) showed that a stimulus person who transgressed accidentally (by knocking over a display in a grocery store) was liked better if he responded with evident embarrassment than if he merely rebuilt the display without seeming embarrassed.

Social Anxiety   Schlenker and Leary (1982) explicitly linked social anxiety to self-presentation. In their view, social anxiety arises when the person wants to make a particular, desired impression but fears that he or she will fail to do so. As Leary and Kowalski (1995) put it, social anxiety is at its core a concern about controlling one's public impressions. Making a particular impression is a vital means of achieving two of the main, possibly innate social goals, namely, inclusion and status. Given the importance of being perceived in certain ways by others, it is hardly surprising that some people become extremely concerned and anxious.

Disclosing Emotion   Alongside the question of when do people feel emotions is the question of when they reveal them, and indeed such revelations may be central to the interpersonal operation of emotions. Clark, Pataki, and Carver (1995) have proposed some intriguing answers and provided experimental support. People selectively reveal their happiness when they want others to like them. They show anger to other people in order to encourage the others to go along with their preferences and wishes. And they express their sadness to get others to see them as helpless and dependent, as a way of eliciting help from others. These correspond to the self-presentational tactics of ingratiation, intimidation, and supplication (Jones & Pittman, 1982).

Another manipulative self-presentation of emotion was found by Baumeister, Stillwell, and Heatherton (1995): people sometimes exaggerate how hurt or upset they are by another person's actions, in order to make that person guilty. The guilt makes the other person more willing to comply with the inducer's wishes.

A more general statement was provided by DePaulo (1992). People have moderate success at both exaggerating and suppressing the nonverbal expression of emotion, in order to serve their self-presentational goals. That is, sometimes it is best to pretend to be having a strong emotional reaction, and other times it is advantageous to conceal one's emotions. DePaulo found, however, that the more strongly motivated people are to deceive others, the less successful they are at it.

Summary and Implications

Although the self is formed through extensive social interactions, it is far from a passive receptacle of external influences. Rather, it actively transforms and incorporates what it receives from the interpersonal world. Selves are shaped by the expectations and feedback of others, but mainly insofar as they choose to be and actively accept that input. People do not simply internalize what others think or expect of them: they are not robots programmed by society, culture, or mass media.

Interpersonally, the self is a receiver but also a sender. In self-presentation, people try to construct particular images in the eyes of others, sometimes even engaging in risky and dangerous activities to make a good impression. These images are often finely tailored to the situation, reflecting the high motivation and extensive cognitive processing that go on behind self-presentational activity. Thus, the favorability of self-presentation is a balance between the desire to make a favorable impression, the various constraints posed by the other person's knowledge, and the limits of plausibility. There is also an assortment of self-presentational tactics aimed at making a specific impression on others for the sake of manipulating them in useful ways (e.g., to be afraid of you and hence do what you want).

Aspects of self influence social relations in other ways than self-presentation. Self-conceptions shape person perception, mainly by making some categories more accessible than others. Several motivational aspects of self-conceptions (such as a desire to see one's positive traits as important, and a desire to believe one does not have particular undesired traits) seem to draw attention to certain kinds of traits which are then influential in interpreting ambiguous behavior of other people. The desire to maintain favorable self-evaluations makes people sensitive to processes of reflected glory and social comparison, and as a result people may pull closer to or away from particular others.

The link between close relationships and self has begun to be explored. Some processes of self-deception and self-enhancement have parallels in the way people think about their relationships. Norms and behavioral patterns change, such as the fact that people present themselves favorably toward strangers but modestly toward friends. Intimates can serve as a buffer that stabilizes the self-concept against external feedback. Some emotions, such as guilt and jealousy, seem to function mainly to regulate the self's close relationships. High self-monitors choose partners to suit their activities, whereas lows prefer the same partners for all activities. People remain longest and happiest in relationships with partners who share their inflated views of themselves.

The self exhibits several intriguing processes that construct the self by means of influencing other people. Thus, people require others to validate their identity claims, and so the construction of self requires one to influence or persuade others. Self-concept change is not simply the internalization of one's own behavior through self-observation but rather depends on involving other people to lend social reality to the pivotal actions. People seem to choose to enter or avoid various interpersonal encounters and possibly even close relationships based partly on the chances to protect, confirm, or enhance their views of themselves.

The interplay between cognitive processes, emotional processes, and interpersonal behavior looms as a major challenge for the coming generation of research. At present, it appears that people disclose or conceal (or possibly exaggerate) certain emotions for self-presentational reasons, and self-presentational activities seem to create a cognitive load that impairs the processing of information about the other person (but intensifies internalization processes). Such findings hint at far more extensive and complex links.

EXECUTIVE FUNCTION

The third major aspect of the self is its executive function: the self makes decisions, initiates actions, and in other

ways exerts control over both self and environment. Common terms *agency, choice, control,* and *decision-making* refer to this aspect of self. Without this active function, the self would be merely a passive spectator, aware of itself and related to others, but unable to do anything except perceive and interpret the flow of events (and experience emotions). Such a theory would be deficient, because selves do more than interpret and belong. Indeed, the motive for control is one of the most fundamental and pervasive features of human selfhood. Self-regulation is in many ways the self's most remarkable capacity.

Action, especially moral or responsible action, presupposes (and defines) a self. Indeed, one of the differences between action and mere behavior involves the unity of self. An eyeblink, a drool, or a wiggling of toes may qualify as behavior, and no self is required to initiate such responses. Action, however, refers to behavior that is done by the person acting as a unity. Marrying, placing a bet, taking a vow, or voting, for example, are actions by whole persons, not just by a certain body parts, and they have implications for the entire self. The entire self does not blink, but the entire self does marry. By the same token, concepts of responsibility invoke the entire person, in the sense that the consequences and implications of actions pertain to the full self. If one's irresponsible actions lead to bankruptcy, divorce, or arrest, it is the entire self that is affected, as a unit.

Social psychology has been slower to study this executive function of the self than to study the interpersonal being or the cognitive construction of self. Several reasons may be suggested for this, but among them is certainly the tendency to treat laboratory participants as objects rather than subjects. One can readily arrange a certain situation for the experimental participant and measure his or her response; it is much more difficult to study how people may arrange their own situations and initiate actions that are outside a certain menu preselected by the experimenter. Still, this indifference to agency is vanishing, partly under the influence of the large body of research on self-regulation.

Another possible reason that the executive function of self has received less attention is that many decisions are not dramatic. The rational pursuit of self-interest is a guiding theme in the actions of most people most of the time. This is unfortunately so obvious that psychologists cannot advance their careers by demonstrating it. The facts that people will generally choose the more attractive job offer, or prefer to date the more attractive partner, or will try to get the best price for their house or car, or will select the foods they most like to eat, are unsurprising.

Therefore there has been something of a premium put on finding ways in which people act contrary to their rational self-interest. This very search presupposes the pervasiveness of self-interested rationality, insofar as exceptions almost automatically are seen as interesting. Social psychologists have therefore become interested in the few cases when people choose the worst offer, accept a poor deal, or spurn what they would most like, even though these make up only a small percentage of the total variance in human decisions. They reveal flaws in the executive function and are therefore important indications about how it operates.

Interest in the executive function may also get a boost from the burgeoning interest in automatic versus controlled processes (e.g., Bargh, 1982, 1994). The self is the controller of controlled processes. The executive function of the self, in other words, is what makes controlled responses possible.

To Choose—Or Not?

There seems to be little doubt but that people desire control. A broad variety of behavior patterns reflect the quest for control. People identify much better with circumstances or acts they have chosen than those assigned to them (Linder, Cooper, & Jones, 1967). When deprived of control, they respond in negative ways, such as trying to do what is forbidden or aggressing against the person who took away their control (Brehm, 1966). Curiosity, skilled play, exploration, and similar patterns are pervasive and suggest a quest for control. Stressful experiences become much more harmful and traumatic when the person lacks control (e.g., Glass & Singer, 1972; Seligman, 1975). And even when people do not have control, they prefer to develop illusions of control (Langer, 1975), which seem to be beneficial despite the lack of pragmatic usefulness (Taylor, 1983).

Thus, it seems clear that the desire for control is one of the main motivations of the self. Actually, control motivation is not limited to human selfhood and may in fact flourish among other species without requiring much in the way of selfhood. Nonetheless, the self evolves in an organism that is fundamentally motivated to seek control, and the self therefore takes on the orientation toward control.

Broadly speaking, control and esteem are probably the two most important motivations of the self. People almost universally react badly to any major loss of either esteem or control, and they generally seem to desire and enjoy opportunities to gain either esteem or control. Both are strongly linked to happiness (Campbell, 1981; Campbell, Converse, & Rogers, 1976), and people will often augment their substantive esteem and control with inflated, exaggerated self-perceptions.

On the other hand, there do seem to be instances in which control is avoided or relinquished. Several patterns of such exceptions were listed by Burger (1989). People sometimes dislike control when it involves being responsible for possible bad outcomes. They also will give up control when it is in their best interest to do so (e.g., letting someone else drive if that person is a better driver or sober). Also, sometimes control can focus attention on bad outcomes, and that focus increases anxiety. They may also avoid control when control will not guarantee any improvement in their material outcomes (Skowronski & Carlston, 1982). Still, by and large, it is safe to say that people desire, seek, and prefer control.

One crucial point is that not all behavior involves choices or initiative. Some theories (e.g., Sartre, 1943/1956) have contended that people are "condemned to be free" and that everything a person does reflects free choice, insofar as the person could conceivably have done something else. While such a view may make an appealing doctrine in politics or religion, it is poor psychology. Clearly people perform a great deal of behavior without making any sort of deliberate choice, and they may often ignore alternatives that others might see. A married woman could, in principle, sleep with a different man on any given night, but it is misleading to say that therefore one must conclude that she freely chooses each night to sleep with her husband. It is more accurate to say that she decided long ago that she would sleep with one particular man regularly, and she married him. She probably does not go through an actual choice process each evening.

The implication is that one does not need to invoke the self's executive function to explain every single behavior. Most likely, active choice and initiative by the self are involved in a minority, although a very important minority, of behaviors. Most behaviors may occur without being directed or initiated by the executive function. Still, the executive function is very important just based on the cases in which it does take action.

Steering may serve as a useful analogy. To steer properly, you do not have to be exerting control at all times. The person who is steering merely intervenes from time to time, such as to make a turn and then straighten out again. But even though you are not actively steering most of the time, you would not reach your destination without those few very important moments.

Control, Self-Efficacy, Autonomy

A long tradition of psychological theory has asserted that people are fundamentally motivated to seek control. Although Freud's thinking neglected control in favor of sexual, aggressive, and self-preservation drives, Adler's theories (e.g., 1927; based on Nietzsche, 1887/1964) emphasized the need for power as the main motivation, and power can be regarded as one form of control. More precise assertions of control motivation date back at least to Murray (1938), who asserted achievement and autonomy as important psychological needs. Perhaps the most influential and best-known formulation was White's (1959) expression of effectance motivation. He rejected the then-popular drive theories of motivation as inadequate, because they fail to explain exploratory behavior and the urge to be competent at environmental mastery for its own sake.

Since then, psychologists have continued to emphasize

control motivations. DeCharms (1968) distinguished between being an origin and being a pawn, and he said that people are motivated to have some personal causation (i.e., to be an origin sometimes). Burger and Cooper (1979) have delineated individual differences in control motivation. Deci and Ryan (1991) have developed a theory about the need for autonomy, to which we will return shortly.

An important advance to theory of control motivations was furnished by Rothbaum, Weisz, and Snyder (1982), who distinguished between primary and secondary control. They proposed that primary control consists of attempts to change the environment to suit the self. Secondary control consists of changing the self to fit the environment. They reviewed a broad assortment of experimental findings showing that people systematically seek out both forms of control. Subsequent work has shown that both aspects of control predict success and adjustment, in somewhat different spheres. In highly controllable settings such as school performance, primary control is important, whereas in adjusting to many other circumstances secondary control is more important (Band & Weisz, 1988; Shaw, 1992; Weisz, McCabe, & Dennig, 1994).

What happens when people lack control? Research with animals suggested that deprivation of control leads quickly to a condition of learned helplessness, in which the animal gives up trying to control and fails to learn new contingencies (Seligman, 1975). With human beings, however, the first studies quickly showed that there is often the opposite pattern: When people are deprived of control, they try harder to reassert it, and it takes an impactful pattern of repeated failures to make them give up (Roth & Bootzin, 1974; Roth & Kubal, 1975).

The notion that people systematically resist losses of control was elaborated into a broad theory by Brehm (1966), who called such resistance *reactance*. According to Brehm, when people feel that their freedom is threatened in some way, they seek to reassert what is being taken away from them. In other cases, they may respond by aggressing toward the person or agent who has restricted their freedom. Although as noted above some reactance responses are due to self-presentational concerns, there are others that do not seem to depend on maintaining a particular public image (see Wright & Brehm, 1982).

Another very interesting response to the deprivation of control is to develop illusions of control. In other words, when the self cannot actually control its environment, sometimes it satisfies itself with convincing oneself that it can. Langer's (1975) seminal article on the illusion of control showed several ways in which people cultivate and maintain false beliefs in their control. In particular, people who are taking part in a lottery seem to become more confident of winning as the time for drawing approaches, and they become more confident as they think more about the lottery (and presumably about winning it). In some cases

they treat chance events as if these involved skill, thereby falsely thinking that they may be able to exert control.

A compelling demonstration of the illusion of control was furnished by Alloy and Abramson (1979), who specifically asked subjects to estimate their degree of control over the situation. They found that nondepressed people systematically overestimated how much control they had over positive outcomes. (Depressed people were more even-handed and more accurate in judging how much control they have.)

The findings about illusions of control underscore the importance of the self. One does not merely want to believe that control exists in the world someplace; rather, one cultivates the belief that oneself in particular has control. It might be argued that selfhood is not a prerequisite for control motivations, and indeed one may find evidence of control motivations in other species who have minimal sense of selfhood. But such animals do not presumably cultivate illusions of control. The linking of control with the sense of self is indicated by the illusions of control.

There is of course something of a paradox here. Actually having control would be quite useful and adaptive, because it enables you to make the world suit you better. On the other hand, illusions of control would not seem to be useful. Indeed it might be downright dangerous to think you are in control when you are not. Why are people so motivated to believe they are in control?

One broad and general answer is suggested by Bandura's (1977) research on self-efficacy. Bandura has proposed that when people believe they can exert control, in the sense of having confidence that they can make the desired response, they are better able to actually make that response. As in learned helplessness, a belief that one cannot make the requisite response (i.e., a deficit in self-efficacy) may prevent the person from acting in a way that can produce desired outcomes. A rich series of studies (see Bandura, 1982, 1986, 1989, for reviews) has confirmed various advantages of self-efficacy beliefs.

The implication is that even illusions of control may be sought because of the generally helpful nature of believing one has control. More precisely, if one is to err—and it is unlikely that one will always make the correct appraisal of situational contingencies—it is better to assume control when it is objectively lacking than to assume an absence of control when one could have had it.

Another thoughtful and detailed statement of the benefits of perceived control was furnished by Taylor (1983), who noted that there are important affective and other benefits for coping. She found that trauma victims seemed to benefit from such illusions of control. Thus, women with breast cancer seemed to derive affective and other benefits from medically unfounded beliefs about how they could control the spread of cancer or prevent its recurrence. If nothing else, illusions of control help life seem less random and thereby support the optimism that one can eventually help some things turn out well.

Self-Determination   A novel and important approach to this agentic aspect of the self has been taken by Deci and Ryan (e.g., 1995). They have articulated the importance of looking at the self as an agent who initiates acts, as opposed to merely responding to events. Their emphasis on agency has been accompanied by a strong focus on the motivational rather than the cognitive features of selfhood.

The roots of self-determination theory lie in Deci's pioneering work in intrinsic motivation (e.g., Deci, 1971). The basic distinction was that extrinsic motivation involved doing something for the sake of external rewards and benefits, whereas intrinsic motivation led to doing it for the sake of the activity itself. Research studied these two patterns of motives, particularly with respect to how extrinsic motives would come to dominate and undermine intrinsic motivation (e.g., Lepper, Greene, & Nisbett, 1973). Subsequent work showed, however, that under some circumstances rewards and external reinforcers can sustain or even strengthen intrinsic motivation, such as if they convey symbolic affirmations of competence (Rosenfeld, Folger, & Adelman, 1980) or as a function of interpersonal context and communication (Ryan, 1982; Ryan, Mims, & Koestner, 1983). Such findings gradually complicated the picture and led Deci and Ryan to propose that theory should move beyond the simple intrinsic/extrinsic distinction.

In their current thinking, Deci and Ryan (1991, 1995) propose that self-determination involves activities initiated by the self in pursuit of its three main intrinsic motives. These motives are as follows. First, a need for competence involves learning to control the environment and experience oneself as capable and effective, as opposed to feeling helpless or incompetent. Second, a need for autonomy involves the experience of an internal locus of causality for one's actions—that is, feeling that one's acts originate from within the self, as opposed to being controlled or directed by external forces. Third, the need for relatedness involves the construction and maintenance of satisfying involvements in the world of other people, including knowing and caring for other people as well as believing that they care about oneself.

The theoretical issue that lies at the core of self-determination theory is that some of one's actions must reflect the independent, autonomous pursuit of these goals, as opposed to being driven by external forces. In particular, Deci and Ryan emphasize that it is not enough that the self consider and deliberately, intentionally initiate some actions. They have provided a thoughtful critique of Bandura's (1989) and similar positions that in their view gloss over this important distinction between deliberately responding to another's influence and deliberately acting from within

the self. True autonomy does not involve behaving thoughtfully in service of someone else's directives.

As a vivid example, Hawk (1985) found records of self-criticism sessions held for Cambodian torturers during the Khmer Rouge regime (see also Becker, 1986). The self-criticism process (which was standard in many Communist organizations) presumably led to thoughtful and effective action in service of the regime and its ideology, although it was certainly quite well focused. Hawk found, for example, that there were ample instances of self-criticism for not keeping proper records, for letting the prisoner die too early in the process, and even for failing to keep pencils sharpened, but there was little sign of reproaching oneself for participating in inhumane acts, such as inflicting gruesome pain and death on innocent fellow citizens. Deci and Ryan would say that these self-reflective torturers were acting intentionally but not really pursuing the self's intrinsic goals.

Closer to home, Deci and Ryan have sorted some of the major goals and motives that drive people into the intrinsic and extrinsic varieties and to look at some of the consequences. Thus, Kasser and Ryan (1993, 1996) considered personal growth, meaningful relationships, and community contributions to be among the main intrinsic motivations listed among the aspirations of a large sample of college students. These goals were regarded as being ends in themselves and fostering the intrinsic motives of competence, autonomy, and relatedness. In contrast, they labeled the pursuit of financial success, fame, and physical attractiveness as extrinsic aspirations, because they are largely instrumental means toward other ends and because they embody external controls on one's actions (e.g., needing to do jobs for others to gain money).

Kasser and Ryan then looked at how the relative emphasis among these intrinsic and extrinsic aspirations was associated with various measures of subjective well-being and ill-being, including mental health, adjustment, and happiness. The more emphasis people placed on wanting to be rich, famous, and physically attractive, the less well off they were in terms of anxiety, depression, social functioning, vitality, self-actualization, and other measures. In contrast, placing emphasis on the intrinsic aspirations such as growth and meaningful relationships was positively linked to good adjustment and well-being.

On the basis of such findings, Deci and Ryan (1995) have criticized self-esteem research for simplistically ignoring the same distinction between self-determined and merely intentional acts. The successful pursuit of externally controlled rewards, such as money or fame (or the approval of the torture supervisor) may furnish high self-esteem, but this is not the same as self-esteem that is based on self-determined behaviors. Deci and Ryan consider only the latter to be *true self-esteem*, insofar as it is based on autonomous, integrated aspects of the self.

Active versus Passive Responses An underused but promising way to study the executive function is differences between active and passive responses. The executive function is by nature active, and so one would expect active responses to have different consequences than passive responses. (As the next section will make plain, however, inaction is not always passive, because an active internal response may sometimes be required to prevent oneself from doing something.)

There is some evidence of asymmetry between active and passive responses. Fazio, Sherman, and Herr (1982) had subjects judge the funniness of various cartoons with a procedure that either required them to press a button if it was funny but do nothing if it was not funny, or vice versa. Active responses led to more extreme subsequent ratings than passive ones. Allison and Messick (1988) had subjects express attitudes by marking a box versus doing nothing, and they too found that active responses led to stronger subsequent attitudes as well as an increased false consensus effect.

Cioffi and Garner (1996) showed behavioral consequences of active versus passive responses, and once again the active ones were more potent. Even when passive responses were made unambiguous, active ones were more likely to lead to behavioral follow-through: specifically, people were induced to volunteer either actively or passively to help with an AIDS project, and those who did so actively were more likely to show up. Also, subjects who responded actively (in either direction) gave more reasons for their decision than did those who responded passively, suggesting that active responses involve more extensive internal processing than passive ones—consistent with the notion that it activates the executive function of the self.

Most of these researchers have treated the active-passive differences as merely being a curious anomaly within self-perception theory: that is, even though active and passive responses might seem equally meaningful in principle, people draw stronger inferences from active than passive ones. The implications of these findings may be far more profound than that, however, if considered in the context of the executive function of the self. Active responses use the executive function and perhaps therefore have stronger and more dramatic consequences than passive responses, which scarcely invoke the self.

Self-Regulation

The capacity of the self to change itself is one of the most important, useful, and adaptive aspects of the executive function. Indeed, Higgins (1996) has emphasized what he calls *the sovereignty of self-regulation* to refer to its centrality for understanding the nature of the self. Unlike other aspects of the self, self-regulation only became widely appreciated by social psychologists during the 1980s. Al-

though the distinction between automatic and controlled processes was found increasingly useful in social psychology's theorizing (e.g., Bargh, 1982), the field was slower to recognize that being the controller of the controlled processes was a crucial aspect of selfhood.

Behavior can occur without much in the way of self. Other species have minimal selves but ample behavior. (To be sure, one does probably need a body in order to behave, but not much more than that.) Thus, the self—the constructed psychological self—is not a prerequisite for behavior. The self can become quite important, however, by intervening in the ongoing sequence of behavior to change it. A useful analogy would involve an actress changing her lines in the middle of a performance. She has a script to follow and could simply follow along in the normal sequence. But the executive function of the self would be vitally involved if she decided to deviate from the script and speak new, different lines. The influence of the executive function on behavior should perhaps be understood in terms of changing and steering the course of action rather than initiating it from a state of inaction.

The term *self-regulation* seems to have originated with the attempt to make learning theory more flexible and sophisticated so as to encompass a greater portion of human behavior. Laboratory rats may simply respond to the experimenter's presentation of reward and punishment contingencies, but people sometimes set their own contingencies, such as by promising yourself a reward of ice cream if you can get an A on the chemistry test or finish weeding the garden. By establishing contingencies and then rewarding or punishing themselves, people regulate themselves. More recent notions emphasize the controlling of thoughts, feelings, impulses, actions, and performances, as well as the general effort to change the self to make it conform to its own goals—what Banaji and Prentice (1994) referred to as self-improvement motivation, that is, "the desire to bring oneself closer to what one should or would ideally like to be" (p. 299).

Of particular importance is the matter of steering behavior toward distal goals. Most animals are capable of responding to immediate stimuli, and indeed stimulus-response theory proved reasonably adequate when psychological theorizing was confined to animal models. People can however resist the pressures and temptations of immediate stimuli in order to pursue goals that are in some cases years or decades in the future.

Perhaps the most important empirical root of the study of self-regulation has been the studies of delay of gratification, such as by Mischel and his colleagues (see Mischel, 1974, 1996, for reviews). In these studies, typically, the person must choose between taking an immediate but small reward or a larger but delayed one. Obviously, the capacity to delay gratification is crucial to the project of getting an education or building a career. Successful delay of gratification requires the individual to transcend the immediate situation, in the sense that one must see beyond it to appreciate the more valuable but more remote goal.

More recent work has emphasized a broad spectrum of restraining impulsive behavior. Spurred by societal interest in impulse problems, from dieting to sex to violence to addiction, psychologists have examined how people succeed (and why they fail) at self-control. Other work has examined how people control their thoughts and their emotions, as well as their performances.

Another useful context for understanding self-regulation is the distinction between primary and secondary control (described earlier). The concept of self-regulation overlaps extensively with that of secondary control, defined as changing oneself to fit the environment. The better able one is to change and adapt oneself, the easier it is to be happy and healthy in a wide range of circumstances.

The long-term stability and adaptive value of self-regulation for the individual personality have been best demonstrated by Mischel and his colleagues. Mischel, Shoda, and Peake (1988) assessed children's ability to delay gratification when they were four and five years old. Those who performed best in self-control at that age were significantly better off a decade later, in terms of school performance, social competence, and coping effectively with frustration and stress. A follow-up found that those same self-controlled children at age four and five had higher SAT scores in college (Shoda, Mischel, and Peake, 1990). These results suggest that some aspects of self-control take shape early in life and continue to yield benefits for many years.

Is self-control always good? The present state of the literature suggests that the answer is yes, or very nearly. There is almost no evidence of instances in which self-control is systematically disadvantageous to the person. Meanwhile, there is abundant evidence of its benefits. In this it is somewhat different from self-esteem, which as noted previously has relatively few benefits (other than feeling good) and some significant costs and drawbacks. Self-control can be put in service of bad ends, such as if self-discipline enables one to become an expert mass murderer or a highly successful torturer. But such cases seem to involve blaming the tool for what it builds. Weakening self-control would not really solve the problem. A high capacity for self-regulation appears to be an unmitigated good in that it improves one's chances for success in nearly every endeavor to which it is relevant.

Feedback Loops Self-regulation theory received a boost from important work by Carver and Scheier (1981, 1982), who combined Powers' (1973) elaboration of cybernetic theory with Duval and Wicklund's (1972) self-awareness theory. They proposed that self-awareness is often a matter of assessing how one is doing vis-à-vis one's goals and ideals (and other standards). It is not merely an idle curiosity, however, but part of a process of changing the self to bring it up to meet those standards.

The core idea they took from cybernetic theory was the feedback loop, summarized by the acronym TOTE (for test, operate, test, exit). The self-appraisal of how one is doing is the first test. If one finds oneself falling short of the standard (e.g., one is not keeping one's room clean enough), one proceeds to operate on the self to effect change (one cleans up the room). Soon one conducts another test to see whether one has reached the standard. If not, one resumes or continues the operation of changing. If so, then the control process is ended, and one can exit the loop (think about something else, or get a beer).

A second important idea in Carver and Scheier's work is that there is a hierarchy of feedback loops. Higher levels refer to broader units of behavior, whereas lower ones refer to smaller units. The lower levels are thus often means toward the goals of the higher ones (see also Vallacher & Wegner, 1985, 1987). When one is blocked in one's efforts to reach a goal at one level, self-awareness often shifts down to a lower level, in order to find and solve the problem. For example, perhaps you cannot seem to get your room clean enough because you keep leaving half your clothes on the floor, and so it may be necessary to buy another chest of drawers.

The role of emotion in service of self-control was elaborated in a later work (Carver & Scheier, 1990). Early self-awareness theory said, quite plausibly, that people feel upset when they conclude that they are falling short of their goals (Duval & Wicklund, 1972). Carver and Scheier observed however that people are always falling short of some goals and yet are not always feeling bad, even when they are self-aware and reflecting on these goals. They proposed therefore that emotion is often a response to the first derivative (over time) of one's standing vis-à-vis these goals. That is, one feels good when one is moving toward one's goals, and one feels bad when one is moving away from them (or moving toward them too slowly). In other words, the speed of improvement sets off emotional responses.

Much of social psychology's thinking about self-regulation has been heavily influenced by Carver and Scheier's work and the feedback-loop model. Issues of comparing oneself to standards have exerted considerable influence on self-awareness and self-regulation research. The hierarchy concept has received less research attention, partly because of the difficulty of operationalizing the main ideas, but in view of the concept's importance it seems only a matter of time before some creative researchers devise effective methods for testing and developing this aspect of the theory. Indeed, that very hierarchy of goals is quite central to the self and broadly directs the executive function most of the time.

One further and useful implication of the feedback-loop model is that it specifies several of the key ingredients of self-regulation, and so researchers interested in self-regulation failure can look for breakdowns in any area. Successful self-regulation apparently requires clear and viable standards, effective monitoring of self, and some potent means of operating on the self. Sure enough, self-regulation failure is often due to confused or conflicting standards, poor monitoring, and lack of strength or other capacity to produce change (Baumeister, Heatherton, & Tice, 1994).

Although research has emphasized the concept of bringing oneself closer to desired standards, there are also what Carver and Scheier (1981) have called *positive feedback loops* in which the goal is to increase the discrepancy of self from some negative standard, such as by maximizing the difference between oneself and a prejudiced or dishonest self. Often the motivation to change oneself away from something is more powerful than the motivation to change toward something (Ogilvie, 1987). Recent work by Higgins (1996) has been particularly aimed at showing that discrepancy-reducing and discrepancy-increasing processes differ in many ways and that self-regulation theory must encompass both. Roney, Higgins, and Shah (1995) have shown that the same task can sometimes be framed in either term (e.g., succeeding versus not failing), with very different results, such as that a focus on succeeding increases effort and confidence whereas a focus on not failing increases anxiety.

Monitoring and Ironic Processes   Wegner (1994) has proposed a somewhat different and less idealized view of self-regulation processes (or, in his preferred term, *mental control* processes; Wegner & Pennebaker, 1993). He shares with earlier theorists the view that effective monitoring is essential to successful self-regulation, but he has also indicated how monitoring can backfire and undermine self-regulation.

Wegner's work in this area began with studies that asked subjects to try not to think about a white bear (Wegner, Schneider, Carter, & White, 1987; Wegner, 1989). These studies found that thought suppression efforts were only partly successful. Moreover, once the suppression exercise ended, subjects often experienced a resurgence of the forbidden thought, which the researchers dubbed the *rebound effect*. These unwanted side effects of thought suppression proved a fertile topic for research, yielding such findings as the fact that suppressing thoughts about sex sometimes created more arousal than thinking about sex (Wegner, Shortt, Blake, & Page, 1990), that romantic contacts or relationships seem to gain a special allure when they have to be kept secret (Wegner, Lane, & Dimitri, 1994), and that depressed people (unlike others) seem to distract themselves from upsetting thoughts by thinking of other things that are also depressing, resulting in a change of thought content but not a change of mood (Wenzlaff, Wegner, & Roper, 1988).

Subsequent work led to a more elaborate and provocative theory of *ironic processes* (Wegner, 1994). Successful self-regulation requires both a monitoring process and an operating process: the monitoring process, which is automatic, searches for signs of the forbidden or proscribed activity, and the (controlled) operating process overrides the resulting impulses or thoughts. A dieter, for example, will automatically monitor the environment for food cues. When one is spotted, the operating process springs into action to resist the temptation, such as by making oneself close the refrigerator.

A problem may arise, however, because automatic processes continue to function even when one is too tired or taxed to invoke the operating process. After all, one main advantage of automatic processes is that they require far less cognitive resources than controlled ones (e.g., Bargh, 1982). When the dieter is under stress, for example, she may continue to watch for food cues but then not have the wherewithal to resist them. As a result, she may paradoxically eat more than she would if she were not dieting in the first place. Smart and Wegner (1996) have labeled this pattern "the evil monitor" because the automatic monitoring process switches easily from serving the self-regulation process to undermining it. Thus, the same mechanism that helps people achieve their self-regulatory goals most of the time can undermine them when people are distracted or stressed (Wegner, 1994).

Strength and Exertion   Several sources have recently argued that self-regulation conforms to a pattern of strength, consistent with traditional concepts of willpower (Mischel, 1996; also Baumeister & Heatherton, 1996; Baumeister, Heatherton, & Tice, 1994). In this view, impulses have a certain strength or intensity, and overcoming them would therefore require a corresponding form of strength. Such views differ from views of self-regulation as a skill or as a schema.

Consistent with a strength view, evidence suggests that self-regulation often requires mental and physical exertion. Pennebaker and Chew (1985) required subjects to tell one lie amid a series of truthful answers in a "guilty knowledge" paradigm. They found that the lie was associated with a reduction (presumably an inhibition) of nonverbal behavior as well as an increase in physiological arousal. Notarius, Wemple, Ingraham, Burns, and Kollar (1982) likewise found that inhibiting facial expressions of emotion was accompanied by increased arousal. The implication is that people must exert themselves (hence the arousal) to inhibit behaviors.

That self-regulation consumes cognitive resources was elegantly demonstrated by Gilbert, Krull, and Pelham (1988). Subjects watched a videotape depicting a social interaction but containing an irrelevant stream of meaningless stimuli at the bottom of the screen. They were quite able to form a thoughtful impression of the people on the tape, undistracted by the irrelevant stimuli. In another condition, however, subjects were instructed to ignore the irrelevant stimuli, and so they had to mobilize some cognitive resources to do what everyone else was doing anyway. Their impressions of the stimulus persons were relatively superficial and incomplete, presumably because the effort of ignoring the irrelevant information detracted from the attentional resources they could devote to processing the interaction. In short, cognitive capacity is apparently reduced by self-regulatory efforts, even if these are only devoted to doing what one would do anyway.

Evidence about naturally occurring failures in self-regulation seem consistent with a strength and depletion model. Impulsive crimes, addictive relapses, dietary failures (eating binges), inappropriate emotional outbursts, and other breakdowns in self-control are more common when people are tired or under stress (e.g., Gottfredson & Hirschi, 1990; see Baumeister, Heatherton, & Tice, 1994).

In addition, some laboratory evidence has indicated that self-regulatory exertions are followed by a subsequent reduction in self-regulatory performance. A well-known series of studies by Glass and Singer (1972; see also Glass, Singer, & Friedman, 1969) showed that having to cope with unpredictable, stressful noise led to a "psychic cost" in terms of poorer *subsequent* tolerance for frustration. Muraven, Tice, and Baumeister (in press) showed that self-regulatory exertions such as trying to suppress white bear thoughts or trying to alter one's emotional response were followed by poor performance on unrelated self-regulatory tasks.

Thus, the basic question of how self-regulatory operations work has begun to be answered in terms of a strength model, which is to say that people have a limited and depletable (but renewable) capacity to control themselves. The effort to control multiple things at once (such as when one makes several New Year's resolutions) may be ill-advised, and the imposition of new self-regulatory demands (such as stress, work pressures, or adapting to new circumstances) may undermine self-control in other spheres. A convenient and effective measure of individual differences in self-regulatory capacity would likely provide a powerful boost to research in this area, and new methods for studying the dynamics of strength (e.g., increasing it through exercise) are needed as well.

The strength model might help explain another seeming paradox, which concerns the role of emotion in self-regulation. As already noted, Carver and Scheier (1990) have provided an elegant theory about how emotion may aid self-regulation, and certain emotions such as guilt seem to contribute to regulatory success (e.g., Baumeister, Reis, & Delespaul, 1995). Yet a large body of evidence has repeatedly implicated emotional distress as a cause of self-regulatory failure (e.g., Heatherton & Baumeister, 1991; Heatherton, Herman, & Polivy, 1991; Heatherton & Polivy,

1992; Kirschenbaum, 1987). How can the apparently harmful effects of emotional distress be reconciled with the theorizing that depicts them as helpful?

One possible answer (among others) is that emotional distress is itself often a drain on regulatory strength, insofar as people try to cope with and escape from the bad feelings. These efforts leave less strength left to use for task persistence, resisting temptation, and the like. Still, this is only a tentative answer. Clarifying the relations between emotional distress and regulatory success and failure will be one of the most theoretically interesting challenges of the coming years.

Acquiescence   A controversial and theoretically consequential issue is whether (or to what extent) self-regulation failure involves the acquiescence of the individual. Thus, are people passively overwhelmed by irresistible impulses, or do they simply decide to give in to temptation? Clearly the implications for understanding the self's executive function are important.

Both views have their advocates. Western culture has a long tradition of emphasizing personal and individual responsibility. Concepts of sin hold people responsible for what they do; indeed, five of the "seven deadly sins" of medieval Christian thought involved self-regulation failure (i.e., actions based on greed or avarice, lust, gluttony, sloth or laziness, and wrath). In contrast, medical models, defense lawyers, and addict support groups have spearheaded a modern movement to view many impulses as irresistible and to regard people who fail at self-regulation as relatively innocent victims.

Recent years have seen several attacks on and critiques of the irresistible impulse view. Reed (1985) found that the accounts of compulsions and obsessions rarely indicated overwhelmingly powerful impulses but often emphasized weakness or inability to control the self. Rachman and Hodgson (1980) cited evidence that people with obsessive/compulsive disorder are more vulnerable than other subjects to experimentally created obsessions.

Perhaps the most strident voice against the irresistible impulse view in social psychology is that of Peele (1989). He reviewed multiple studies questioning the prevailing theories about addiction as an overwhelming impulse or compulsion. For example, American soldiers who were addicted to heroin in Vietnam often recovered immediately and without treatment from the addiction upon returning home, and some even used heroin in the United States without a resumption of their addiction! Likewise, the spiraling drinking binges among alcoholics appear to be due more to beliefs and expectations (as indicated by placebo effects) rather than the actual physiological dependency and effects of initial consumption of alcohol (Marlatt, Demming, & Reid, 1973). Peele also cited cultural differences, such as the fact that American Jews often drink but rarely become alcoholic, presumably because their cultural emphasis on personal responsibility does not exempt drinkers.

A recent review of the literature on self-control has yielded a conclusion that self-control failure involves *mitigated acquiescence* (Baumeister & Heatherton, 1996; Baumeister, Heatherton, & Tice, 1994). That is, people do not simply and freely choose (in most cases) to abandon self-control, but there is abundant evidence that they do go along and participate actively in the abandonment, especially after they start. For example, one cannot simply lie back and let forbidden activities of eating, drinking, or smoking happen—one must at least use hands and mouth to ingest the forbidden substances. Meanwhile, the arguments in favor of irresistible impulses seem too often disingenuous and self-serving (e.g., by defense lawyers). Perhaps it is most accurate at present to say that self-regulation is often a difficult and unpleasant task, especially when resisting a favorite pleasure, and it requires ongoing exertions—and so when people decide in a moment of weakness to break down, they avoid reconsidering the decision and instead participate actively in pursuing the forbidden activity. Shapiro (1996) has pointed out that self-deception may often be centrally involved in patterns of self-regulation failure, such as when people justify their indulgences (or indeed cite irresistible impulses). In any case, more research is needed on the causes, patterns, justifications, and degrees of acquiescence in self-regulatory failure.

One of the most interesting possibilities regarding acquiescence combines the hierarchy model of Carver and Scheier (1981) with the active/passive distinction. A dieter or reformed alcoholic may decide that it is too difficult to resist temptation, give in, and then actively take part in procuring and ingesting the forbidden delights. Thus, passivity at a high level is combined with active participation at a lower level. Even though the executive function ceases to function at a high level it is still able to operate at the lower one.

Self-Defeating Behavior

Self-defeating behavior has held a perennial fascination for psychologists because of its fundamental and paradoxical nature. The pursuit of enlightened self-interest is widely regarded as the essence of rationality. Therefore, to act in contrary ways is the essence of irrationality. Why do people do things that bring them suffering, failure, and other misfortunes?

The study of self-defeating actions promises to reveal much about the executive function of the self. When people act rationally to pursue material advantages, there is little need for elaborate theories about volition, choice, control, and initiative, and some would say that simple reinforcement theories are sufficient. In contrast, when people

thwart their own best interests, the need for explanation is greater, and these explanations seem likely to shed considerable light on how people make decisions and initiate actions. This approach can be compared to the study of errors by perception and cognitive psychologists, the interest in brain damage and lesions among physiological psychologists, and even the Freudian project of understanding normal functioning by studying neurosis. In a similar way, perhaps, self-defeating behavior can shed light on how the executive function operates. Let us now examine several of these patterns.

Self-Handicapping   In principle, people would always want to perform up to the best of their ability, and they would manage their affairs and arrange their performances so as to maximize their chances for success. Yet a contrary pattern was first proposed by Jones and Berglas (1978): sometimes people create obstacles to their own performance. These obstacles may include underachievement and withholding effort, abusing alcohol, and inadequate preparation. The pattern is called *self-handicapping*.

The first experimental demonstration (Berglas & Jones, 1978) involved taking drugs that were presented as likely to impair intellectual performance, just prior to an intelligence test. All subjects took an initial test and then were offered a choice between a drug that would allegedly make them temporarily smarter and one that would impair their performance. They were told that they would take a second test after the drug had entered their systems. The experimenters made a fuss over how remarkably well the subject had supposedly performed on the first test.

Actually the first test had been rigged. For some, the experimenter simply administered solvable problems and said that the number the subject had gotten right was far above average. For others, however, the problems were unsolvable, and the subject had to make a guess (according to the multiple-choice format). The experimenter repeatedly told the subject that his or her guess was correct. It was these latter (noncontingent success) subjects who chose the performance-impairing drug. The reason: at some level, they presumably knew that their ostensible success was merely a series of lucky guesses, and they feared that on the second test they would not live up to the newly inflated expectations of the experimenters. To avoid a humiliating failure, they chose the drug that would give them an excuse for performing poorly on the second test. That way, if they did fail on the follow-up, it would be taken as a sign of the power of the drug, rather than a disproof of their newly famous intellectual brilliance.

Self-handicapping captured the interest of a wide segment of the social psychology research community, in part because its implications spill over into many parts of the field (e.g., Higgins, Snyder, & Berglas, 1990). It has clear cognitive implications, especially regarding attributions:

by self-handicapping, one can forestall the drawing of unflattering attributions about oneself. Self-handicapping makes failure meaningless, and so if people already think that you are intelligent, the upcoming test cannot change that impression.

There is also a strong motivational aspect to self-handicapping. People want to preserve favorable views of themselves, and indeed they may want to enhance their reputations. The beauty of the self-handicapping strategy is that it offers both benefits, namely, protection against failure and enhancement of success. As Jones and Berglas (1978) pointed out, the student who does poorly in school after not trying hard is protected against the implication of being stupid, because the lack of effort is seen as the main explanation for poor performance. Meanwhile, though, the student who does well in school after not trying hard is perceived as especially gifted, because the success cannot be attributed to high effort and so must reflect high ability.

Which motive predominates? Tice (1991) created situations in which only success or only failure would be meaningful (the other being ambiguous), in order to see which would elicit self-handicapping. The response depended on self-esteem. People with high self-esteem self-handicapped to enhance their successes, and they seemed largely unconcerned about protecting themselves against possible failure. (Presumably they do not think they are going to fail anyway.) People with low self-esteem, however, engaged in self-handicapping in order to protect themselves against possible failure. Thus, both motives lead to self-handicapping, depending on the person and the situation.

There is also a strong interpersonal aspect to self-handicapping. Kolditz and Arkin (1982) manipulated whether several crucial aspects of the situation were public (i.e., known to others) or private (i.e., known only to the subject). Self-handicapping emerged mainly in the public conditions, that is, when the subject's handicap and subsequent performance would be known to others. Almost no self-handicapping was found when the experimenter would be unaware of the handicap (i.e., which drug the subject took). Apparently, self-handicapping is done mainly to control the way one is viewed by others, as a self-presentational strategy. People are less likely to self-handicap merely for the sake of protecting or enhancing their own private views about themselves.

Is self-handicapping self-destructive at all? One might argue that it seems a highly rational strategy, given that it both protects against failure and enhances one's credit for success. The cost, however, is that the actual quality of the performance suffers, as Tice and Baumeister (1990) showed. Failing to study for a test or getting drunk prior to an important presentation may have attributional benefits, but they do tend to prevent one from doing one's best. Self-handicapping thus sacrifices the quality of the performance in order to manipulate the meaning of the outcome.

Excessive Persistence   American culture extols the value of persistence, as indeed it should, because success often requires continuing to strive and try despite initial failures. On the other hand, there are undoubtedly cases in which persistence in a losing endeavor simply brings more losing, often with increased costs. The obstinate refusal to change wrong opinions, to cancel programs and policies that are failing, to stop investing money in fiscally unsound enterprises, or to treat people in ways that consistently backfire is hardly a sign of the virtues of persistence. Rather than praising all persistence, it may be more appropriate to praise *judicious* persistence, which involves both the capacity to keep trying and the ability to judge whether continued efforts are likely to lead to success or failure.

Research has examined what causes people to persist in costly failures. One crucial factor is the feeling of commitment generated by sunk costs. That is, people feel that they have already invested a certain amount of time, energy, care, or other resources into some endeavor, and if they quit now they will lose all they have put in. Rubin and Brockner (1975) gave subjects an initial monetary amount and offered them a series of choices between keeping what they had and investing it in the hope of earning more. The investments were rigged to do poorly, and people had to decide whether to keep putting in more, just as a gambler needs to keep coming up with more money in the hope of recouping losses and ending up ahead. Still, people continued to invest. In fact, nearly all of them continued to invest past the break-even point (at which even if they were to win they would still end up with less than what they had had at the start).

Thus, people seem to become psychologically entrapped in certain situations. They persist well beyond the point at which it would seem rational or desirable to continue. Sustained by the momentum and commitment of their initial investment, they feel unable to withdraw: "too much invested to quit" (Teger, 1980).

As with self-handicapping, research has shown that excessive persistence is mediated by cognitive, motivational, and interpersonal factors. Cognitive processes can increase or decrease destructive persistence. When people are encouraged to make careful and accurate calculations about their decisions and the relevant contingencies, they are less likely to persist beyond the rational point (Conlon & Wolf, 1980). Persistence thus may reflect a lack of thoughtful evaluation of the situation and its possibilities. If they have been told about the dangers of becoming entrapped in a persistence situation, they also seem better able to resist the self-defeating pattern (Nathanson et al., 1982). Witnessing another person come to grief through costly persistence, especially if the model says that persisting was a mistake, makes subjects less likely to repeat that mistake (Brockner et al., 1984).

Meanwhile, interpersonal motivations contribute to persistence. People become entrapped in persistence situations because of concern about how others will evaluate them. Sometimes people are reluctant to back out because they think others will think poorly of them. If they believe that the audience will think well of them for withdrawing, they are more willing to withdraw and hence can resist the persistence trap (Brockner, Rubin, & Lang, 1981).

The concern with others' perceptions of one's decision brings up an interpersonal aspect to the self's executive function. As noted earlier, action brings a sense of responsibility, which is often merely increased by the awareness of others. Staw (1976) showed that people are more prone to persist in a losing investment paradigm if the initial decision had been their own instead of someone else's, which shows the importance of feelings of personal responsibility. In particular, if the initial investment turned out badly, the person who made the initial decision will feel responsible for the bad outcome, which heightens the tendency to persist. Bazerman, Giuliano, and Appelman (1984) showed that such feelings of personal responsibility foster a sense of commitment, and the person may become determined to continue until eventual success, which the person refuses to doubt.

The interpersonal aspect of responsibility was highlighted by Fox and Staw (1979), who found that people were especially likely to persist if the initial decision had been made in the face of other people's objections. Apparently people are loath to expose themselves to the possibility of someone telling them that "I told you so." Teger (1980) noted that even when self-presentational or interpersonal concerns are largely irrelevant to the initial decision, persistence may come to be mediated by them later on, because losing face becomes increasingly salient as one's responsibility for bad outcomes increases.

For the purposes of understanding the role of the executive function of the self, one of the most relevant papers was by Brockner, Shaw, and Rubin (1979). Their experiment manipulated whether quitting or persisting was the passive option; that is, some subjects had to respond actively to quit but could continue by doing nothing (similar to letting one's stock investment ride), whereas others were in the reverse situation in which they had to make an active response to continue (akin to placing a new bet). The passive option was the more common response in both situations. Thus, destructive persistence was more common when it did not require the self to do anything. When the executive function of the self is mobilized, it seems to reduce some of the tendency toward excessive persistence.

The notion of the passive option shows that sometimes the involvement of the executive function is merely optional. The next generation of self researchers may begin to study the factors that determine whether the self adopts an active response or not. As this section has shown, active participation by the self is no guarantee of positive out-comes, for destructive persistence can occur either actively or passively, but it can make a difference.

Why Do People Self-Destruct?   Several cognitive and motivational causes of self-defeating behavior have been noted in connection with self-handicapping and destructive persistence (in the preceding sections). To appreciate the roots of self-defeating behavior, it is necessary to consider them in the context of other, parallel patterns. Such a review was attempted by Baumeister and Scher (1988), who on a priori grounds identified three levels of intentionality in self-defeating behavior and sought evidence for each of them. The three levels of intentionality implicate the executive function of the self in quite different ways.

The first and most obvious would be *deliberate self-destruction*, in which the person can presumably foresee the self-defeating consequences and chooses the course of action so as to cause them. In plain terms, the person wants to suffer or fail. There are hardly any empirical demonstrations of such patterns, and close examination of those few suggests that even in them the people did not really want the bad outcomes for their own sake. Although the view that people have self-destructive motives is a long-standing one in psychology (e.g., Menninger, 1938/1966), it does not appear to be correct, at least in the normal populations studied by social psychologists.

The second is the opposite extreme, in which the person neither foresees nor desires the self-defeating outcome. This category could be labeled *unintentional self-destruction*, insofar as people would prefer to avoid the bad outcomes they bring on themselves. These patterns involve counterproductive approaches, often based on misunderstanding of self and world. The person is typically trying for a positive outcome but goes about it in some way that produces a negative outcome. Although these are common, they do not really show the executive function of the self to be irrational—merely misinformed. In other cases, unintentional self-destruction results from misregulation of self, such as making oneself do something that backfires. The patterns of destructive persistence provide a good example of this form of self-defeat. Persisters are trying to achieve positive outcomes, yet they do so in ways that bring negative ones. Poor understanding of contingencies and misregulation of self bring about their counterproductive acts.

The third category lies in between the others. It involves *tradeoffs*—that is, circumstances in which positive and negative outcomes are linked. The bad outcome is perhaps foreseeable but is not desired. The person merely chooses an action for the sake of the positive outcome and accepts the negative one as an accompanying cost. Self-handicapping is a good illustration of the tradeoff pattern. Self-handicappers seek the positive outcomes of protection against humiliating failure and enhancement of credit for success. They accept the cost (of hampered performance) reluctantly, but it presumably seems worth it.

Tradeoffs are therefore the most useful and revealing form of self-defeating behavior for learning about the executive function of the self. People make choices with foreseeable bad consequences for themselves, and in the long run they often regret these choices—but they make them nonetheless. Why?

Several key factors that contribute to these self-defeating tradeoffs can be identified. First, self-defeating choices tend to involve immediate benefits but delayed costs (see also Loewenstein & Elster, 1992; Platt, 1973). Second, they tend to involve definite rewards but only probable, uncertain risks. Third, the situations that elicit them often seem to involve some high awareness of self. Fourth, these situations also tend to involve aversive emotional states, or at least the threat of them. It now appears that emotional distress fosters self-defeating behavior by creating a tendency to choose high-risk courses of action (Leith & Baumeister, 1996). Once again, self-handicapping illustrates these (except for the time delay factor): the attributional benefits are there either way, whereas the poorer performance outcome is not guaranteed. Concern over how the self is perceived leads to self-handicapping, as does evaluation anxiety or other negative affect.

Other Self-Defeating Patterns   Probably the most widespread form of self-harm involves substance abuse. Drinking alcohol, taking drugs, smoking cigarettes, and similar activities ring up a costly toll in terms of human misfortune. Still, these choices are tradeoffs, because people take these substances for the sake of pleasure and satisfaction rather than the harmful consequences. They provide a good example of immediate, definite rewards combined with uncertain, delayed costs, which is typical of self-defeating tradeoffs.

Another common pattern involves neglect of health, particularly in terms of failing to take medicine or comply with physicians' instructions. Noncompliance risks continued illness and even death, yet ironically people pay for health care and then fail to follow through (e.g., Dunbar & Stunkard, 1979). People especially fail to comply with medical regimens that are costly, inconvenient, or unpleasant.

Yet another tradeoff is the pursuit of revenge at cost to oneself. Brown (1968) showed that people are especially prone to accept costly means of getting even with someone if they have been embarrassed or humiliated. When the loss was merely financial, people would only seek revenge as long as it was profitable. Thus, interpersonal concerns over face-saving and negative affect (feeling humiliated) made people more willing to engage in this pattern.

There are also some findings suggesting that people will directly choose an unpleasant outcome. Although these initially seem to suggest deliberate self-destructive acts, on close inspection they resemble tradeoffs. On the basis of a just world (Lerner, Miller, & Holmes, 1976),

people sometimes seem to think that they will get a fixed amount of suffering, and so they may as well get it over with. When they believe (often irrationally) that present suffering will produce positive future outcomes or merely reduce future suffering, they will choose to suffer more in the present (Curtis, Rietdorf, & Ronell, 1980; Curtis, Smith, & Moore, 1984).

Also, in several studies, people are led to expect that they will be required to eat a worm or caterpillar. When offered a reprieve at the last minute, many will go ahead and choose to eat the worm anyway (Aronson, Carlsmith, & Darley, 1963; Foxman & Radtke, 1970; Walster, Aronson, & Brown, 1966). Comer and Laird (1975) showed that these choices were mediated by just-world beliefs (e.g., they deserved to suffer) and reinterpretation (e.g., the worm was not so bad). Although it is a stretch to call such choices self-defeating, the research findings do suggest an interesting pattern regarding the executive function of the self. Apparently what happens is that the person becomes focused on accommodating his or her reactions to the upcoming aversive event (i.e., secondary control). The last-minute option of backing out would require a shift of the executive function to primary control, by making a choice to change the situation, and apparently that is a difficult choice.

Lastly, people sometimes seek to fail when there are some attributional benefits or payoffs. Baumgardner and Brownlee (1987) found that people high in social anxiety may intentionally fail in order to escape the burden of other people's expectations for subsequent performance. Baumeister, Cooper, and Skib (1979) showed that people will fail when failure has been described as diagnostic of a desirable trait.

Implications for Executive Function   At the start of this section, it was suggested that one crucial justification for the study of self-defeating behavior (which, to be sure, is of interest in its own right) is that it may shed light on the executive function of the self. It is therefore important to consider the relevant implications briefly.

Nothing in the evidence about self-defeating behavior contradicts the notion that the pursuit of self-interest is the overriding, rational goal of the executive function. Self-defeating acts occur when people are misguided or mistaken, or when they fail to ascertain or pursue what would be best for them. They do not seem to desire failure, suffering, or other bad outcomes. When the executive function has a clear grasp of its best interest, it nearly always pursues it.

Self-defeating behavior therefore reflects some impairment or befuddlement of the executive function. Apparently people are prone to focus disproportionately on immediate and definite outcomes, to the (sometimes costly) neglect of long-term or merely possible consequences. The human executive function may be distinguished from that of other species by its exceptional capacity to appreciate long-term outcomes, but this capacity is underutilized.

People do respond strongly to immediate, salient pressures when making decisions. They are often sorry later.

Aversive emotional states seem to mediate many self-defeating acts. There is a long and dubious tradition in popular thinking of regarding emotions as irrational. The involvement of emotion in self-defeat lends some credence to that view. Just as emotion was apparently able to impair proper self-regulation, so it is also apparently capable of fostering self-defeating acts. Thus, broadly speaking, emotion appears to disturb the executive function. It seems that emotional distress leads to a highly risky pattern of decision-making, and so often the results will be catastrophic when people make important life decisions while they are angry or emotionally distraught. Beyond that, the relation between emotional distress (or emotion in general) and the executive function of the self is another high priority for further research.

Concern over self-esteem and especially over how one is perceived by others is another cause of several self-defeating processes. There is one particular combination of self-appraisals that is disaster-prone. That consists of a self-appraisal that is very favorable and a salient external appraisal that is bad, or at least substantially less favorable—in short, threatened egotism. People can remain rational after substantial material setbacks, but a blow to the ego tends to produce high order irrationality. Ego-threatened people tend to become both self-destructive and other-destructive. In terms of self-destruction, the cause seems to be a failure to use available knowledge, responding to superficial and misleading rather than adaptive situational cues (interpretations). In a sense it is a failure of self-control, such as making a decision based on short-term desires and impulses rather than properly appreciated long-term best interest. Meanwhile, with other-destructiveness, the mediation appears clearly to be premature abandonment of self-control. Thus, threatened egotism and the accompanying emotional distress seem often inimical to the executive function. They thwart its adaptive functioning.

Summary and Implications

The executive function of the self is a mechanism that initiates, alters, and directs behavior. It is not always "on," because many behaviors can occur without active intervention by the self, but its activities are quite important. Making choices, exerting control, and regulating the self are among its crucial functions, even if they only occur occasionally. Social psychology has not understood the executive function as well as the other two aspects of self covered in this chapter, but it seems fair to expect that at some point in the foreseeable future, the executive function will be the main focus of social psychology's research on the self, because it is starting to have the biggest unanswered questions, and because methods are becoming available.

The quest for control is one of the self's main concerns, both in terms of changing the environment to suit the self, and in terms of altering the self to fit in to the environment or measure up to standards. By improving the fit between person and environment, the executive function is a powerful tool to improve health, happiness, and adjustment. Control over the environment is widely, pervasively sought, is usually itself inherently pleasant, and produces a broad assortment of mostly positive outcomes. Similarly, control over the self is usually beneficial and produces many positive outcomes. When it is operating properly, the executive function is beneficial in many ways.

When people are deprived of control, they seek to regain control, and sometimes they cultivate illusions of control to compensate. If deprivation persists, people show distress such as frustration and depression, and they begin to exhibit various maladaptive patterns such as illness and aggression. Some degree of autonomy, which can be seen as a broad pattern of internal control at highly meaningful levels, may be important for health and happiness.

The executive function can be seen in active (rather than passive) and controlled (rather than automatic) responses. Such responses seem to require mental and physical effort. Active responses leave stronger internal (e.g., memory, attitudinal) traces than passive ones. Comparing active versus passive and controlled versus automatic responses may be a valuable research strategy for illuminating how the executive function operates.

The rational pursuit of self-interest is the guiding principle of the executive function, and so self-defeating and other irrational behavior patterns attract special interest. Many of these involve ignoring long-term contingencies in favor of immediate concerns. Emotional distress and other causes seem to heighten the short-term orientation that leads to destructive outcomes.

Self-regulation likewise seems to involve mental and physical effort, which raises the tantalizing possibility that decision-making and self-control draw on the same inner resource of selfhood. Feedback-loop models have provided considerable insight into how people try to conform to important standards. Yet many processes seem to cut both ways. Thus, emotional distress can increase the motivation to measure up to standards, but it can also undermine self-regulation. An automatic monitoring process may aid self-regulation under favorable circumstances but it can undermine it in times of stress, fatigue, or distraction. Meanwhile, misregulation of self can also contribute to self-defeating patterns, such as when people push themselves to persist in a doomed or losing endeavor.

The issue of acquiescence in self-regulation failure has both theoretical and practical importance. A hierarchy model of self-control may be helpful. At one level, people decide to give up and become passive, but then at a lower level they may actively participate in carrying out their impulses. Whether this reflects self-deception or a differential passivity (or difficulty) of different levels is a crucial issue for further research.

Emotion seems to activate the executive function, for better or worse. Emotional distress can either help or impair self-regulation, and likewise it can either help or impair control-seeking and decision-making. Thus, emotion per se is neither beneficial nor harmful to the executive function, but it is quite capable of altering its operation and outcome. At present, a reasonable guess would be that one main function of emotion is to alter or activate the executive function.

CULTURAL AND HISTORICAL VARIATIONS IN SELFHOOD

Most of the research covered thus far has been conducted at North American universities with samples of North American college students. Although much of value can be learned from these groups, one does wonder whether there are aspects of human selfhood that may be overlooked or underappreciated because of the empirical strategies that most social psychologists use. Given how extensively the self is a social construct, one would expect some cultural and historical variation. Before closing, therefore, it is useful to review briefly the current thinking about such variation.

Culture and Society

Interest in cultural determinants of selfhood has expanded in recent years. A seminal and influential article by Triandis (1989) integrated a large body of research to identify several key features of selfhood that vary across different cultures. In particular, cultures vary in the relative emphasis they place on each of the following. First, the *private self* refers to how people understand themselves. It involves self-regard, self-esteem, introspection, and individual decision-making. Second, the *public self* refers to how the individual is perceived by other people, thus including issues such as reputation, specific expectations of others, and impression management. Third, the *collective self* involves one's memberships in various social groups, from the family to an employing organization or an ethnic group. In Triandis's view, individualistic societies such as the United States tend to emphasize the private and public selves and downplay the collective self, whereas other (e.g., Asian) societies tend to emphasize the collective self while placing relatively little importance on the private self.

Indeed, Triandis (1989) proposed several important dimensions along which societies vary and which have important implications for the control and formation of self. One is individualism versus collectivism: individualistic societies support diversity, self-expression, and the rights of individuals, whereas collectivistic societies promote conformity and a sense of obligation to the group. Another

dimension is tightness, which refers to the degree of social pressure on individuals: tight societies put strong demands on individuals to conform to the group's values, role definitions, and norms, whereas loose ones allow people more flexibility to do what they want. (For that reason, tight societies tend to promote the public and collective selves, whereas loose ones allow more scope for the private self to flourish.)

A third dimension of cultural variation proposed by Triandis (1989) is the complexity of the society, which is defined in terms of the number of different relationships and groups to which an individual belongs. In a complex society, an individual tends to belong to many different groups, and so it is less imperative to stay on good terms with any of them. The collective self is therefore not so crucially important (although it may be highly developed in the simple sense that one belongs to many collectivities). Meanwhile, complex societies allow greater development of the private self (again because of the broad availability of many social relationships), and the public self is quite important because it is the common feature of all one's social relations. In contrast, in a simple society one belongs to relatively few groups, each of which is then quite important in defining the self. The collective self flourishes in adapting to these memberships, whereas the need to conform to the group tends to stifle the private self.

In a vivid and timely comparison, Triandis (1989) illustrated some of his central ideas by contrasting American and Japanese societies. Japan tends to be more collectivistic and tighter than the United States, and as a result there is much greater homogeneity: Japanese citizens tend to eat and dress similarly rather than allowing the private self to choose from a broad assortment as in the United States. Certain Asian traditions, such as having the oldest male order the same food for the entire table, would be unthinkable in American restaurants, where each individual's special preferences are elaborately cultivated.

Furthermore, Americans place a premium on sincerity, which can be approximately described as a congruency between public and private selves: one is supposed to say what one means and mean what one says. In Japan, in contrast, the public actions are what matter most, and private sentiments are less important. Triandis cited survey research using hypothetical dilemmas which included the option of thinking one thing and saying something quite different. Americans tended to object strongly to such an option, which they saw as hypocritical (e.g., privately objecting to an interracial romance for one's daughter but publicly supporting it). Japanese, however, tended to approve of such options.

Markus and Kitayama (1991) proposed that the basic difference in selfhood between Asian and Western cultures involves the dimension of independence versus interdependence. In their view, Western cultures emphasize the independent self: people are supposed to attend to themselves, to discover and express their unique attributes, and to try to stand out in important ways. In contrast, Asian cultures emphasize interdependence. Asians are expected to attend to others, to conform to group demands and role obligations, and to try to fit in to the group in important, harmonious ways. At bottom is a fundamental difference in the conception of selfhood: to the Western mind, the self is an autonomous unit which is essentially separate and unique, whereas the Asian view begins with an assumption of the basic and pervasive connectedness of people.

Multiple consequences can be linked to these differences between an independent and an interdependent view of self, as Markus and Kitayama reviewed. People from independent cultures tend to think of selves somewhat independent of context, focusing on the knowledge they have gleaned from multiple observations (e.g., he is stingy). In contrast, people from interdependent cultures tend to describe people more in terms of behaviors in particular contexts (e.g., "He behaves properly with guests but feels sorry if money is spent on them" p. 232). Pressures for cognitive consistency among private thoughts and feelings may be mainly associated with independent, self-contained selves, whereas such inner processes are of secondary concern in the interdependent view and may therefore not be seen as highly important. Politeness among independent selves involves giving the other person the maximum freedom to express and obtain unique, special, changing wishes. Politeness among interdependent selves involves anticipating what the other might want and showing appreciation for what the other does.

There are also emotional consequences, as Markus and Kitayama explain. In the West, the expression versus suppression of anger has long been a vexing point of controversy, because anger is socially disruptive yet helps assert the rights and needs of the self. In Asian cultures, however, there is no controversy, and anger is to be avoided at all costs.

The important implication is that many features of selfhood need to be examined for cultural relativity. The available body of empirical research findings on the self, like that on most psychological topics, has mainly been collected in the West, and as a result it may exaggerate the fundamental nature and pervasiveness of several features. Although certainly there are many important similarities among the concepts of selfhood in different cultures, there are important differences too.

Historical Evolution of Self

It is not necessary to visit multiple cultures to find variations in selfhood. There is often ample variation within a single culture. Indeed, our own culture's dominant ideas about selfhood have changed and evolved dramatically over the past few centuries (see Baumeister, 1986, 1987). Thus, the special nature of the modern Western form of

selfhood can be understood in a historical context just as well as a context of cross-cultural comparisons.

The burgeoning psychology of self is itself partly a reflection that the self confronts the modern Western individual as a problem and puzzle. The interest in finding oneself, knowing oneself, identity crisis, self-actualization, and the rest arises from this historically recent development. Medieval Westerners did not wonder who they were or have identity crises the way modern ones do.

One important source of change is that modern selves are based on changing rather than stable attributes. In earlier times, one's age, gender, and family were often decisive determinants of one's life, and so they defined identity in a simple and clear fashion. In contrast, modern societies have often made explicit efforts to reduce the impact of those factors (such as by banning sex discrimination), so their contribution to self is reduced. Instead, the course of one's life is left much more up to choice, ability, and perceived traits, and such determinants are much more flexible and fluid. The modern Western self is subject to negotiation and renegotiation to a much greater extent than the self of earlier eras.

The instability or openness of the society at large has also undermined the stability of selfhood. In the distant past, one lived among the same people for most of one's life, and there were clear and fixed rankings based on social status: aristocrats were superior to peasants, for example. Now, however, few people live in the same place or among the same associates for many decades, and there is no presumption that some people are innately superior to others. Indeed, although there is still some tendency to see the rich and famous as elite beings, it is common for people to rise from obscurity to that elite status, as well as to fall back into it. All this means that the self is a changing entity in a changing environment.

The greater freedom has also shifted the burden of defining the self onto the individual, which is alone sufficient reason for people to see the self as a compelling problem. To put it crudely, a rigid society told our ancestors who they were, and there was not much they could do about it. Today each individual can choose from a wide spectrum of possible identities, and this freedom brings with it the difficulty of finding ways to choose, as well as increasing the importance of knowing one's abilities and other traits so as to choose an appropriate career, mate, and so forth. The burden falls most heavily on adolescents, because adolescence ends with the formation of adult identity (e.g., Erikson, 1968). Hence in the twentieth century adolescence has become a period of indecision, uncertainty, experimentation, and identity crisis (see Baumeister & Tice, 1986).

A crucial step in the evolution of modern selfhood involved coming to see it as a hidden, inner reality. When you lived among the same people for decades, they knew you quite well, and even where strangers met (e.g., in cities) some identification was accomplished by often rather rigid dress codes. Hence the self was obvious. In contrast, the emergence of modern life multiplied contacts between strangers and reduced the visible markers of identity, enabling some people to pretend to be something they were not. The concern over the difference between inner and outer selves became acute in the sixteenth century, as was reflected in the literature, drama, philosophy, and other writings (e.g., Trilling, 1971). A hidden self is harder to know and define than a self that is explicit in one's acts and appearance. Inner selves are not known directly but are merely inferred.

The legacy of Puritanism, which is especially strong in America, diminished the certainty of self-knowledge by enhancing awareness of self-deception. Puritans believed that a vitally important aspect of the hidden self—specifically, whether one was destined to spend eternity in heaven or hell—was fixed and could be discerned by observing the self. Puritans therefore spent a relatively high amount of time and effort scrutinizing themselves for signs of whether they were among the Elect few or the damned many. Gradually they began to recognize that they, or at least their neighbors, were biasing these tests so as to boost their confidence in their eternal salvation. Self-knowledge had once been regarded as an especially secure form of knowledge, but its certainty gradually deteriorated as the pervasive possibility of self-deception rendered it increasingly suspect. The low point was perhaps in the twentieth century movement of psychoanalysis, which regarded self-knowledge as supremely difficult. Only after many expensive years of hard work and frequent consultations with a trained expert could someone even begin to approach self-knowledge.

A last facet of the modern dilemma of selfhood concerns values (see Baumeister, 1991b). Throughout most of history, moral values were inimical to selfhood: to act in a moral or virtuous way was the opposite of acting in a selfish way. Modernization and secularization of Western society created a value gap, however, in the sense that there was a shortage of firm, consensually recognized criteria of right and wrong. One response to the value gap has been to elevate the self into a major value. Modern Western individuals see it as a right and even a moral duty to learn about themselves, cultivate their talents, and generally pursue their own interests. There is some evidence that the self is elbowing other basic values aside. For example, if there was a conflict between what is best for the marriage and what is best for the self, earlier generations often placed the obligation to marriage as the supreme duty, but more recent ones have placed the self higher (see Zube, 1972). Likewise, this new value placed on selfhood has wrought fundamental changes in the way people understand their careers, their religion, their free time, and their mortality.

The use of the self as a basic value places a much greater burden on selfhood than it carried in previous eras. For a changing, uncertain, and partly metaphorical entity to fill the role of providing value to life is asking a great deal. In any case, it is hardly surprising that research on the self has flourished in the modern West, because the problematic nature is more acute and more pressing in this culture than in others.

CONCLUSION

This chapter has proposed that selfhood has three basic universal aspects (beyond the bare fact of a physical body), and that social psychology's contributions can be understood in relation to them. They are the experience of reflexive consciousness, interpersonal relatedness, and the executive function of choice and control (including self-control).

Selves everywhere have these three aspects. This is not to say that there are no cultural variations in selfhood, which would be patently false. Rather, these are the building blocks that cultures and societies can work on to shape distinctive forms of selfhood. Thus, all selves have an interpersonal dimension, but culture and society can have considerable influence on how selves belong, interact, and respond to other people.

The self area has a number of influential minitheories about important patterns or features of selfhood, such as self-esteem theory, self-monitoring theory, and self-evaluation maintenance theory. It is noteworthy that the major minitheories have gradually evolved to cover these three aspects of selfhood, even if the initial formulations neglected one or two. Future theorists of selfhood might benefit by treating the three aspects as one guideline for theory development. That is, even though one's theory may initially focus on interpersonal aspects of self, it may be worth considering what it could say to make contact with the large body of knowledge about the executive function.

Of the three areas, it seems clear that the executive function lags behind the other two in theoretical and methodological development. Given that researchers gravitate toward unsolved problems, it therefore seems likely that the executive function will be an important focus sometime soon. Rising interest in controlled processes and self-regulation patterns is one sign of that trend.

Once the broad outlines of the three aspects are understood, it will be time to understand how they are integrated. Indeed, already some subtopics have moved to connect them, such as the evolution of self-concept change research from a matter of reflexive self-understanding to one in which social reality is crucial.

It is fortunate that self researchers have largely moved beyond constraining distinctions between cognition, emotion, and motivation, for all are heavily interrelated when it comes to self. The interrelations among these three remain a fertile topic for study, such as in self-deception (i.e., motivated cognition) and self-defeating behavior (in which emotion biases cognition, often under the influence of conflicting motivations). At present, it seems that the cognitive features of self have been most successfully understood, although many issues remain. The cognitions in reflexive self-understanding have been well illuminated, but the interplay between cognition and interpersonal or executive processes has only begun to be understood.

There is also broad agreement about the major motivations associated with self, although an integrative paradigm for these is not yet in place. Moreover, a fuller understanding of how the self executes other motivations, especially with regard to the distinction between autonomous action versus carrying out externally motivated projects, remains for further work. Still, self researchers do not seem widely divided about what the self's motivations are, but only about how these various motivations compete and interact.

In contrast, the role of emotion in selfhood is not well understood, for the many scattered findings do not easily fit together into a coherent picture, and many basic, fascinating, important questions remain unanswered. Emotion clearly plays an important role in interpersonal relations, and just as clearly emotion exerts considerable influence over the executive function, but these two seem to suggest quite different views of what emotion is and how it is involved in selfhood.

The great surge of interest in self is probably driven in part by the culture's optimism that selfhood contains important answers to life's great questions and solutions to its problems. This positive, optimistic approach to the study of self has recently been compensated by a rather overdue skepticism about the virtues and values of selfhood. Evidence about the drawbacks of self-esteem, self-awareness, self-presentation, and other features has enabled a more balanced, evaluatively neutral (or ambivalent) view of self to begin to emerge. Probably this optimistic pattern has delayed the study of some topics on the more unsavory side of selfhood, such as self-pity, arrogance, and self-indulgence. These remain ripe for creative researchers to tackle.

The quest to know the nature of human selfhood has occupied eminent thinkers from many lands and eras, and it has retained its fascination even while the very nature of human selfhood has changed. The modern self is in some ways especially problematic and elusive, yet the methodological tools for studying it are also especially potent. Social psychologists deserve to be proud of the important and extensive contributions our discipline has made to understanding the self. It is to be hoped that that pride will help sustain the effort needed to continue and—dare we dream of it?—to finish the job.

REFERENCES

Adler, A. (1927). *Understanding human nature* (W. Wolfe, trans.). New York: Greenberg.

Adler, A. (1992, Feb. 17). Hey, I'm terrific. *Newsweek,* pp. 46–51.

Allison, S. T., & Messick, D. M. (1988). The feature-positive effect, attitude strength, and degree of perceived consensus. *Personality and Social Psychology Bulletin, 14,* 231–241.

Alloy, L. B., & Abramson, L. Y. (1979). Judgment of contingency in depressed and nondepressed students: Sadder but wiser? *Journal of Experimental Psychology: General, 108,* 441–485.

Allport, G. W. (1943). The ego in contemporary psychology. *Psychological Review, 50,* 451–478.

Andersen, S. M. (1984). Self-knowledge and social influence: II. The diagnosticity of cognitive/affective and behavioral data. *Journal of Personality and Social Psychology, 46,* 294–307.

Andersen, S. M., & Ross, L. (1984). Self-knowledge and social inference: I. The impact of cognitive/affective and behavioral data. *Journal of Personality and Social Psychology, 46,* 280–293.

Aronson, E., Carlsmith, J. M., & Darley, J. M. (1963). The effects of expectancy on volunteering for an unpleasant experience. *Journal of Abnormal Social Psychology, 66,* 220–224.

Aronson, E., & Mettee, D. (1968). Dishonest behavior as a function of differential levels of induced self-esteem. *Journal of Personality and Social Psychology, 9,* 121–127.

Ashmore, R. D., & Jussim, L. (in press). Toward a second century of the scientific analysis of self and identity. In R. Ashmore and L. Jussim (Eds.), *Self and identity: Fundamental issues.* New York: Oxford University Press.

Baer, R., Hinkle, S., Smith, K., & Fenton, M. (1980). Reactance as a function of actual versus projected autonomy. *Journal of Personality and Social Psychology, 38,* 416–422.

Banaji, M. R., & Prentice, D. A. (1994). The self in social contexts. In L. Porter & M. Rosenzweig (Eds.), *Annual Review of Psychology* (Vol. 45, pp. 297–332). Palo Alto, CA: Annual Reviews, Inc.

Band, E. B., & Weisz, J. R. (1988). How to feel better when it feels bad: Children's perspectives on coping with everyday stress. *Developmental Psychology, 24,* 247–253.

Bandura, A. (1977). Self-efficacy: Toward a unifying theory of behavior change. *Psychological Review, 84,* 191–215.

Bandura, A. (1982). Self-efficacy: Mechanism in human agency. *American Psychologist, 37,* 122–147.

Bandura, A. (1986). *Social foundations of thought and action.* Englewood Cliffs, NJ: Prentice-Hall.

Bandura, A. (1989). Human agency in social cognitive theory. *American Psychologist, 44,* 1175–1184.

Bargh, J. (1982). Attention and automaticity in the processing of self-relevant information. *Journal of Personality and Social Psychology, 43,* 425–436.

Bargh, J. A. (1994). The four horsemen of automaticity: Awareness, intention, efficiency, and control in social cognition. In R. S. Wyer, Jr., T. K. Srull (Eds.), *Handbook of social cognition* (pp. 1–40). Hillsdale, NJ: Lawrence Erlbaum Associates.

Baumeister, R. F. (1982). A self-presentational view of social phenomena. *Psychological Bulletin, 91,* 3–26.

Baumeister, R. F. (1984). Choking under pressure: Self-consciousness and paradoxical effects of incentives on skillful performance. *Journal of Personality and Social Psychology, 46,* 610–620.

Baumeister, R. F. (1986). *Identity: Cultural change and the struggle for self.* New York: Oxford University Press.

Baumeister, R. F. (1987). How the self became a problem: A psychological review of historical research. *Journal of Personality and Social Psychology, 52,* 163–176.

Baumeister, R. F. (1988). Masochism as escape from self. *Journal of Sex Research, 25,* 28–59.

Baumeister, R. F. (1989a). *Masochism and the self.* Hillsdale, NJ: Erlbaum.

Baumeister, R. F. (1989b). The optimal margin of illusion. *Journal of Social and Clinical Psychology, 8,* 176–189.

Baumeister, R. F. (1990). Suicide as escape from self. *Psychological Review, 97,* 90–113.

Baumeister, R. F. (1991a). *Escaping the self: Alcoholism, spirituality, masochism, and other flights from the burden of selfhood.* New York: Basic Books.

Baumeister, R. F. (1991b). *Meanings of life.* New York: Guilford Press.

Baumeister, R. F., & Cairns, K. J. (1992). Repression and self-presentation: When audiences interfere with self-deceptive strategies. *Journal of Personality and Social Psychology, 62,* 851–862.

Baumeister, R. F., Cooper, J., & Skib, B. A. (1979). Inferior performance as a selective response to expectancy: Taking a dive to make a point. *Journal of Personality and Social Psychology, 37,* 424–432.

Baumeister, R. F., & Heatherton, T. F. (1996). Self-regulation failure: An overview. *Psychological Inquiry, 7,* 1–15.

Baumeister, R. F., Heatherton, T. F., & Tice, D. M. (1993). When ego threats lead to self-regulation failure: Negative consequences of high self-esteem. *Journal of Personality and Social Psychology, 64,* 141–156.

Baumeister, R. F., Heatherton, T. F., & Tice, D. M. (1994). *Losing control: How and why people fail at self-regulation.* San Diego, CA: Academic Press.

Baumeister, R. F., Hutton, D. G., & Tice, D. M. (1989). Cognitive processes during deliberate self-presentation: How self-presenters alter and misinterpret the behavior of their interaction partners. *Journal of Experimental Social Psychology, 25,* 59–78.

Baumeister, R. F., & Jones, E. E. (1978). When self-presentation is constrained by the target's knowledge: Consistency and compensation. *Journal of Personality and Social Psychology, 36,* 608–618.

Baumeister, R. F., & Leary, M. R. (1995). The need to belong: Desire for interpersonal attachments as a fundamental human motivation. *Psychological Bulletin, 117,* 497–529.

Baumeister, R. F., Reis, H. T., & Delespaul, P. A. E. G. (1995). Subjective and experiential correlates of guilt in everyday life. *Personality and Social Psychology Bulletin, 21,* 1256–1268.

Baumeister, R. F., & Scher, S. J. (1988). Self-defeating behavior patterns among normal individuals: Review and analysis of common self-destructive tendencies. *Psychological Bulletin, 104,* 3–22.

Baumeister, R. F., Smart, L., & Boden, J. M. (1996). Relation of threatened egotism to violence and aggression: The dark side of high self-esteem. *Psychological Review, 103,* 5–33.

Baumeister, R. F., Stillwell, A. M., & Heatherton, T. F. (1994). Guilt: An interpersonal approach. *Psychological Bulletin, 115,* 243–267.

Baumeister, R. F., Stillwell, A. M., & Heatherton, T. F. (1995). Personal narratives about guilt: Role in action control and interpersonal relationships. *Basic and Applied Social Psychology, 17,* 173–198.

Baumeister, R. F., Stillwell, A., & Wotman, S. R. (1990). Victim and perpetrator accounts of interpersonal conflict: Autobiographical narratives about anger. *Journal of Personality and Social Psychology, 59,* 994–1005.

Baumeister, R. F., & Tice, D. M. (1984). Role of self-presentation and choice in cognitive dissonance under forced compliance: Necessary or sufficient causes? *Journal of Personality and Social Psychology, 46,* 5–13.

Baumeister, R. F., & Tice, D. M. (1985). Self-esteem and responses to success and failure: Subsequent performance and intrinsic motivation. *Journal of Personality, 53,* 450–467.

Baumeister, R. F., & Tice, D. M. (1986). How adolescence became the struggle for self: A historical transformation of psychological development. In J. Suls & A. G. Greenwald (Eds.), *Psychological Perspectives on the Self* (Vol. 3, pp. 183–201). Hillsdale, NJ: Erlbaum.

Baumeister, R. F., & Tice, D. M. (1990). Anxiety and social exclusion. *Journal of Social and Clinical Psychology, 9,* 165–195.

Baumeister, R. F., Tice, D. M., & Hutton, D. G. (1989). Self-presentational motivations and personality differences in self-esteem. *Journal of Personality, 57,* 547–579.

Baumgardner, A. H. (1990). To know oneself is to like oneself: Self-certainty and self-affect. *Journal of Personality and Social Psychology, 58,* 1062–1072.

Baumgardner, A. H., & Brownlee, E. A. (1987). Strategic failure in social interaction: Evidence for expectancy disconfirmation processes. *Journal of Personality and Social Psychology, 52,* 525–535.

Bazerman, M. H., Giuliano, T., & Appelman, A. (1984). Escalation of commitment in individual and group decision making. *Organizational Behavior and Human Performance, 33,* 141–152.

Beach, S. R. H. (1992, May). Self-evaluation maintenance and marital functioning. Presented at the conference of the Midwestern Psychological Association, Chicago, IL.

Beaman, A. L., Klentz, B., Diener, E., & Svanum, S. (1979). Self-awareness and transgression in children: Two field studies. *Journal of Personality and Social Psychology, 37,* 1835–1846.

Becker, E. (1973). *The denial of death.* New York: Free Press.

Becker, E. (1986). *When the war was over.* New York: Simon & Schuster.

Bednar, R., Wells, G., & Peterson, S. (1989). *Self-esteem: Paradoxes and innovations in clinical theory and practice.* Washington, DC: American Psychological Association.

Beggan, J. K. (1992). On the social nature of nonsocial perception: The mere ownership effect. *Journal of Personality and Social Psychology, 62,* 229–237.

Beggan, J. K. (1994). The preference for gain frames in consumer decision making. *Journal of Applied Social Psychology, 24,* 1407–1427.

Bem, D. J. (1965). An experimental analysis of self-persuasion. *Journal of Experimental Social Psychology, 1,* 199–218.

Bem, D. J. (1972). Self-perception theory. In L. Berkowitz (Ed.), *Advances in experimental social psychology* (Vol. 6, pp. 1–62). New York: Academic Press.

Bem, D. J., & Allen, A. (1974). On predicting some of the people some of the time: The search for cross-situational consistencies in behavior. *Psychological Review, 81,* 506–520.

Berglas, S., & Jones, E. E. (1978). Drug choice as a self-handicapping strategy in response to non-contingent success. *Journal of Personality and Social Psychology, 36,* 405–417.

Blaine, B., & Crocker, J. (1993). Self-esteem and self-serving biases in reactions to positive and negative events: An integrative review. In R. Baumeister (Ed.), *Self-esteem: The puzzle of low self-regard* (pp. 55–85). New York: Plenum.

Brehm, J. (1966). *A theory of psychological reactance.* New York: Academic Press.

Brockner, J. (1984). Low self-esteem and behavioral plasticity: Some implications for personality and social psychology. In L. Wheeler (Ed.), *Review of personality and social psychology* (Vol. 4, pp. 237–271). Beverly Hills, CA: Sage.

Brockner, J., Nathanson, S., Friend, A., Harbeck, J., Samuelson, C., Houser, R., Bazerman, M. H., & Rubin, J. Z. (1984). The role of modeling processes in the "knee deep in the big muddy" phenomenon. *Organizational Behavior and Human Performance, 33,* 77–99.

Brockner, J., Rubin, J. Z., & Lang, E. (1981). Face-saving and entrapment. *Journal of Experimental Social Psychology, 17,* 68–79.

Brockner, J., Shaw, M. C., & Rubin, J. Z. (1979). Factors affecting withdrawal from an escalating conflict: Quitting before it's too late. *Journal of Experimental Social Psychology, 15,* 492–503.

Brown, B. R. (1968). The effects of need to maintain face on interpersonal bargaining. *Journal of Experimental Social Psychology, 4,* 107–122.

Brown, J. D. (1986). Evaluations of self and others: Self-enhancement biases in social judgments. *Social Cognition, 4,* 353–376.

Brown, J. D. (1993a). Motivational conflict and the self: The double-bind of low self-esteem. In R. Baumeister (Ed.), *Self-esteem: The puzzle of low self-regard* (pp. 117–130). New York: Plenum.

Brown, J. D. (1993b). Self-esteem and self-evaluation: Feeling is believing. In J. Suls (Ed.), *Psychological perspectives on the self* (Vol. 4, pp. 27–58). Hillsdale, NJ: Erlbaum.

Brown, J. D. (1994, October). *Self-esteem: It's not what you think.* Paper presented to the Society for Experimental Social Psychology, Lake Tahoe, NV.

Brown, J. D., & Dutton, K. A. (1995). Truth and consequences: The costs and benefits of accurate self-knowledge. *Personality and Social Psychology Bulletin, 21,* 1288–1296.

Brown, J. D., & McGill, K. L. (1989) The cost of good fortune: When positive life events produce negative health consequences. *Journal of Personality and Social Psychology, 57,* 1103–1110.

Buder Shapiro, J. (1995, May). Self-complexity: More complex than it seems. Presented at Midwestern Psychological Association, Chicago, IL.

Burger, J. M. (1989). Negative reactions to increases in perceived personal control. *Journal of Personality and Social Psychology, 56,* 246–256.

Burger, J. M., & Cooper, H. M. (1979). The desirability of control. *Motivation and Emotion, 3,* 381–393.

Byrne, D. (1971). *The attraction paradigm.* New York: Academic Press.

Byrne, D., & Nelson, D. (1965). Attraction as a linear function of proportion of positive reinforcements. *Journal of Personality and Social Psychology, 1,* 659–663.

California Task Force to Promote Self-Esteem and Personal and Social Responsibility (1990). *Toward a state of self-esteem.* Sacramento, CA: California State Department of Education.

Campbell, A. (1981). *The sense of well-being in America.* New York: McGraw-Hill.

Campbell, A., Converse, P. E., & Rodgers, W. L. (1976). *The quality of American life: Perceptions, evaluations, and satisfactions.* New York: Russell Sage.

Campbell, J. D. (1986). Similarity and uniqueness: The effects of attribute type, relevance, and individual differences in self-esteem and depression. *Journal of Personality and Social Psychology, 50,* 281–294.

Campbell, J. D. (1990). Self-esteem and clarity of the self-concept. *Journal of Personality and Social Psychology, 59,* 538–549.

Campbell, J. D., Chew, B., & Scratchley, L. S. (1991). Cognitive and emotional reactions to daily events: The effects of self-esteem and self-complexity. *Journal of Personality, 59,* 473–505.

Campbell, J. D., & Lavallee, L. F. (1993). Who am I? The role of self-concept confusion in understanding the behavior of people with low self-esteem. In R. Baumeister (Ed.), *Self-esteem: The puzzle of low self-regard* (pp. 3–20). New York: Plenum.

Carver, C. S., & Scheier, M. F. (1981). *Attention and self-regulation: A control theory approach to human behavior.* New York: Springer-Verlag.

Carver, C. S., & Scheier, M. F. (1982). Control theory: A useful conceptual framework for personality-social, clinical and health psychology. *Psychological Bulletin, 92,* 111–135.

Carver, C. S., & Scheier, M. F. (1990). Origins and functions of positive and negative affect: A control-process view. *Psychological Review, 97,* 19–35.

Cash, T. F., & Pruzinsky, T. (1990). *Body images: Development, deviance, and change.* New York: Guilford.

Cialdini, R. B., Borden, R. J., Thorne, A., Walker, M. R., Freeman, S., & Sloan, L. R. (1976). Basking in reflected glory: Three (football) field studies. *Journal of Personality and Social Psychology, 34,* 366–375.

Cialdini, R. B., & Richardson, K. D. (1980). Two indirect tactics of image management: Basking and blasting. *Journal of Personality and Social Psychology, 39,* 406–415.

Cioffi, D., & Garner, R. (1996). On doing the decision: The effects of active vs. passive choice on commitment and self-perception. *Personality and Social Psychology Bulletin, 22,* 133–147.

Clark, M. S., Pataki, S. P., & Carver, V. H. (1995). Some thoughts on self-presentation of emotions in relationships. In G. Fletcher & J. Fitness (Eds.), *Knowledge structures in close relationships: A social psychological approach* (pp. 247–274). Hillsdale, NJ: Erlbaum.

College Board (1976–1977). *Student descriptive questionnaire.* Princeton, NJ: Educational Testing Service.

Colvin, C. R., & Block, J. (1994). Do positive illusions foster mental health? An examination of the Taylor and Brown formulation. *Psychological Bulletin, 116,* 3–20.

Colvin, C. R., Block, J., & Funder, D. C. (1995). Overly positive evaluations and personality: Negative implications for mental health. *Journal of Personality and Social Psychology, 68,* 1152–1162.

Comer, R., & Laird, J. D. (1975). Choosing to suffer as a consequence of expecting to suffer: Why do people do it? *Journal of Personality and Social Psychology, 32,* 92–101.

Conlon, E. J., & Wolf, G. (1980). The moderating effects of strategy, visibility, and involvement on allocation behavior. An extension of Staw's escalation paradigm. *Organizational Behavior and Human Performance, 26,* 172–192.

Cooley, C. H. (1902). *Human nature and the social order.* New York: Scribner's.

Crary, W. G. (1966). Reactions to incongruent self-experiences. *Journal of Consulting Psychology, 30,* 246–252.

Crelia, R. A., & Tesser, A. (1996). Attitude heritability and attitude reinforcement: A replication. *Personality and Individual Differences, 21,* 803–808.

Crocker, J., & Major, B. (1989). Social stigma and self-esteem: The self-protective properties of stigma. *Psychological Review, 96,* 608–630.

Crocker, J., Voelkl, K., Testa, M., & Major, B. (1991). Social stigma: The affective consequences of attributional ambiguity. *Journal of Personality and Social Psychology, 60,* 218–228.

Cross, P. (1977, Spring). Not can but will college teaching be improved? *New Directions for Higher Education, 17,* 1–15. Reported in D. G. Myers (1990), *Social psychology* (3rd ed.). New York: McGraw-Hill.

Curtis, R., Rietdorf, P., & Ronell, D. (1980). "Appeasing the gods?" Suffering to reduce probable future suffering. *Personality and Social Psychology Bulletin, 6,* 234–241.

Curtis, R., Smith, P., & Moore, R. (1984). Suffering to improve outcomes determined by both chance and skill. *Journal of Social and Clinical Psychology, 2,* 165–173.

Darley, J. M., & Fazio, R. H. (1980). Expectancy confirmation processes arising in the social interaction sequence. *American Psychologist, 35,* 867–881.

Dawes, R. M. (1994). *House of cards: Psychology and psychotherapy built on myth.* New York: Free Press.

Dean, D. G., Braito, R., Powers, E. A., & Britton, B. (1975). Cultural contradiction and sex roles revisited: A replication and a reassessment. *The Sociological Quarterly, 16,* 201–215.

Deaux, K., Reid, A., Mizrahi, K., & Ethier, K. A. (1995). Parameters of social identity. *Journal of Personality and Social Psychology, 68,* 280–291.

DeCharms, R. (1968). *Personal causation.* New York: Academic Press.

Deci, E. L. (1971). Effects of externally mediated rewards on intrinsic motivation. *Journal of Personality and Social Psychology, 18,* 105–115.

Deci, E. L., & Ryan, R. M. (1991). A motivational approach to self: Integration in personality. In R. Dienstbier (Ed.), *Nebraska symposium on motivation* (Vol. 38, pp. 237–288). Lincoln: University of Nebraska Press.

Deci, E. L., & Ryan, R. M. (1995). Human autonomy: The basis for true self-esteem. In M. Kernis (Ed.), *Efficacy, agency, and self-esteem* (pp. 31–49). New York: Plenum.

DePaulo, B. M. (1992). Nonverbal behavior and self-presentation. *Psychological Bulletin, 111,* 203–243.

DePaulo, B. M., Kenny, D. A., Hoover, C. W., Webb, W., & Oliver, P. V. (1987). Accuracy of person perception: Do people know what kinds of impressions they convey? *Journal of Personality and Social Psychology, 52*, 303–315.

Diener, E., & Wallbom, M. (1976). Effects of self-awareness on antinormative behavior. *Journal of Research in Personality, 10*, 107–111.

Dunbar, J. M., & Stunkard, A. J. (1979). Adherence to diet and drug regimen. In R. Levy, B. Rifkind, B. Dennis, & N. Ernst (Eds.), *Nutrition, lipids, and coronary heart disease* (pp. 391–423). New York: Raven Press.

Dunning, D., Meyerowitz, J. A., & Holzberg, A. (1989). Ambiguity and self-evaluation: The role of idiosyncratic trait definitions in self-serving assessments of ability. *Journal of Personality and Social Psychology, 57*, 1082–1090.

Dunning, D., Perie, M., & Story, A. L. (1991). Self-serving prototypes of social categories. *Journal of Personality and Social Psychology, 61*, 957–968.

Duval, S., & Wicklund, R. A. (1972). *A theory of objective self-awareness*. New York: Academic Press.

Edelmann, R. J. (1985). Individual differences in embarrassment: Self-consciousness, self-monitoring, and embarrassability. *Personality and Individual Differences, 6*, 223–230.

Edwards, A. L., & Klockars, A. J. (1981). Significant others and self-evaluation: Relationships between perceived and actual evaluations. *Personality and Social Psychology Bulletin, 7*, 244–251.

Epstein, S. (1973). The self-concept revisited: Or a theory of a theory. *American Psychologist, 28*, 404–416.

Erikson, E. H. (1950). *Childhood and society*. New York: Norton.

Erikson, E. H. (1968). *Identity: Youth and crisis*. New York: Norton.

Fazio, R. H., Effrein, E. A., & Falender, V. J. (1981). Self-perceptions following social interactions. *Journal of Personality and Social Psychology, 41*, 232–242.

Fazio, R. H., Sherman, S. J., & Herr, P. M. (1982). The feature-positive effect in the self-perception process: Does not doing matter as much as doing? *Journal of Personality and Social Psychology, 42*, 404–411.

Fazio, R. H., Zanna, M. P., & Cooper, J. (1977). Dissonance and self-perception: An integrative view of each theory's proper domain of application. *Journal of Experimental Social Psychology, 13*, 464–479.

Felson, R. B. (1981). Self and reflected appraisal among football players: A test of the Meadian hypothesis. *Social Psychology Quarterly, 44*, 116–126.

Felson, R. B. (1989). Parents and the reflected appraisal process: A longitudinal analysis. *Journal of Personality and Social Psychology, 56*, 965–971.

Fenigstein, A. (1984). Self-consciousness and the overperception of self as a target. *Journal of Personality and Social Psychology, 47*, 860–870.

Festinger, L. (1954). A theory of social comparison processes. *Human Relations, 7*, 117–140.

Fisher, S. (1986). *Development and structure of the body image*. Hillsdale, NJ: Erlbaum.

Fiske, S., & Taylor, S. E. (1991). *Social cognition* (2nd ed.). New York: McGraw-Hill.

Fleming, J. S., & Courtney, B. E. (1984). The dimensionality of self-esteem: II. Hierarchical facet model for revised measurement scales. *Journal of Personality and Social Psychology, 46*, 404–421.

Folkes, V. S. (1982). Communicating the reasons for social rejection. *Journal of Experimental Social Psychology, 18*, 235–252.

Fong, G. T., & Markus, H. (1982). Self-schemas and judgements about others. *Social Cognition, 1*, 191–204.

Fox, F. V., & Staw, B. M. (1979). The trapped administrator: Effects of insecurity and policy resistance upon commitment to a course of action. *Administrative Sciences Quarterly, 24*, 449–471.

Foxman, J., & Radtke, R. (1970). Negative expectancy and the choice of an aversive task. *Journal of Personality and Social Psychology, 15*, 253–257.

Funder, D. C. (1980). On seeing ourselves as others see us: Self-other agreement and discrepancy in personality ratings. *Journal of Personality, 48*, 473–493.

Gibbons, F. X. (1978). Sexual standards and reactions to pornography: Enhancing behavioral consistency through self-focused attention. *Journal of Personality and Social Psychology, 36*, 976–987.

Gibbons, F. X., & Wicklund, R. A. (1976). Selective exposure to self. *Journal of Research in Personality, 10*, 98–106.

Gilbert, D. T., & Jones, E. E. (1986). Perceiver-induced constraint: Interpretations of self-generated reality. *Journal of Personality and Social Psychology, 50*, 269–280.

Gilbert, D. T., Krull, D. S., & Pelham, B. W. (1988). Of thoughts unspoken: Social inference and the self-regulation of behavior. *Journal of Personality and Social Psychology, 55*, 685–694.

Gilovich, T. (1991). *How we know what isn't so*. New York: Free Press.

Glass, D. C., & Singer, J. E. (1972). *Urban stress: Experiments on noise and social stressors*. New York: Academic Press.

Glass, D. C., Singer, J. E., & Friedman, L. N. (1969). Psychic cost of adaptation to an environmental stressor. *Journal of Personality and Social Psychology, 12*, 200–210.

Goleman, D. (1985). *Vital lies, simple truths*. New York: Simon & Schuster.

Gollwitzer, P. M., & Kinney, R. F. (1989). Effects of deliberative and implemental mind-sets on illusion of control. *Journal of Personality and Social Psychology, 56*, 531–542.

Gonzales, M. H., Pederson, J. H., Manning, D. J., & Wetter, D. W. (1990). Pardon my gaffe: Effects of sex, status, and consequence severity on accounts. *Journal of Personality and Social Psychology, 58*, 610–621.

Gottfredson, M. R., & Hirschi, T. (1990). *A general theory of crime*. Stanford, CA: Stanford University Press.

Greenberg, J., & Musham, C. (1981). Avoiding and seeking self-focused attention. *Journal of Research in Personality, 15*, 191–200.

Greenberg, J., & Pyszczynski, J. (1985). Compensatory self-inflation: A response to the threat of self-regard of public failure. *Journal of Personality and Social Psychology, 49*, 273–280.

Greenberg, J., & Pyszczynski, J. (1986). Persistent high self-focus after failure and low self-focus after success: The depressive self-focusing style. *Journal of Personality and Social Psychology, 50*, 1039–1044.

Greenberg, J., Pyszczynski, T., & Solomon, S. (1986). The causes and consequences of self-esteem: A terror management theory. In R. Baumeister (Ed.), *Public self and private self*. New York: Springer-Verlag.

Greenberg, J., Solomon, S., Pyszczynski, T., Rosenblatt, A., Burling, J., Lyon, D., Simon, L., & Pinel, E. (1992). Why do people need self-esteem? Converging evidence that self-esteem serves an anxiety-buffering function. *Journal of Personality and Social Psychology, 63*, 913–922.

Greenwald, A. G. (1980). The totalitarian ego: Fabrication and revision of personal history. *American Psychologist, 35*, 603–618.

Greenwald, A. G., & Banaji, M. R. (1989). The self as a memory system: Powerful, but ordinary. *Journal of Personality and Social Psychology, 57*, 41–54.

Greenwald, A. G., Bellezza, F. S., & Banaji, M. R. (1988). Is self-esteem a central ingredient of the self-concept? *Personality and Social Psychology Bulletin, 14*, 34–45.

Gur, R. C., & Sackeim, H. A. (1979). Self-deception: A concept in search of a phenomenon. *Journal of Personality and Social Psychology, 37*, 147–169.

Hansen, R. D., & Hansen, C. H. (1988). Repression of emotionally tagged memories: The architecture of less complex emotions. *Journal of Personality and Social Psychology, 55*, 811–818.

Harter, S. (1993). Causes and consequences of low self-esteem in children and adolescents. In R. Baumeister (Ed.), *Self-esteem: The puzzle of low self-regard* (pp. 87–116). New York: Plenum.

Hawk, S. (1985). The Cambodian way of death, 1975–1979. In E. Stover & E. Nightingale (Eds.), *The breaking of bodies and minds* (p. 39). New York: Freeman.

Heatherton, T. F., & Baumeister, R. F. (1991). Binge eating as escape from self-awareness. *Psychological Bulletin, 110*, 86–108.

Heatherton, T. F., Herman, C. P., & Polivy, J. (1991). Effects of physical threat and ego threat on eating. *Journal of Personality and Social Psychology, 60*, 138–143.

Heatherton, T. F., & Nichols, P. A. (1994). Personal accounts of successful versus failed attempts at life change. *Personality and Social Psychology Bulletin, 20*, 664–675.

Heatherton, T. F., & Polivy, J. (1991). Development and vali-dation of a scale for measuring state self-esteem. *Journal of Personality and Social Psychology, 60*, 895–910.

Heatherton, T. F., & Polivy, J. (1992). Chronic dieting and eating disorders: A spiral model. In J. Crowther, S. Hobfall, M. Stephens, & D. Tennenbaum (Eds.), *The etiology of bulimia: The individual and familial context*. Washington, DC: Hemisphere.

Heatherton, T. F., Polivy, J., Herman, C. P., & Baumeister, R. F. (1993). Self-awareness, task failure, and disinhibition: How attentional focus affects eating. *Journal of Personality, 61*, 49–61.

Heilbrun, A. B. (1981). Gender differences in the functional linkage between androgyny, social congition, and competence. *Journal of Personality and Social Psychology, 41*, 1106–1118.

Heilman, M., & Toffler, B. (1976). Reacting to reactance: An interpersonal interpretation of the need for freedom. *Journal of Experimental Social Psychology, 12*, 519–529.

Higgins, E. T. (1987). Self-discrepancy: A theory relating self and affect. *Psychological Review, 94*, 319–340.

Higgins, E. T. (1996). The "self-digest": Self-knowledge serving self-regulatory functions. *Journal of Personality and Social Psychology, 71*, 1062–1083.

Higgins, E. T., & Bargh, J. A. (1987). Social cognition and social perception. *Annual Review of Psychology, 38*, 369–425.

Higgins, E. T., King, G. A., & Mavin, G. H. (1982). Individual construct accessibility and subjective impressions and recall. *Journal of Personality and Social Psychology, 43*, 35–47.

Higgins, E. T., Klein, R. L., & Strauman, T. J. (1987). Self-discrepancies: Distinguishing among self-states, self-state conflicts, and emotional vulnerabilities. In K. Yardley & T. Honess (Eds.), *Self and identity: Psychosocial perspectives* (pp. 173–186). Chichester, England: Wiley.

Higgins, E. T., Van Hook, E., & Dorfman, D. (1988). Do self-attributes form a cognitive structure? *Social Cognition, 6*, 177–207.

Higgins, R. L., Snyder, C. R., & Berglas, S. (1990). *Self-handicapping: The paradox that isn't*. New York: Plenum.

Hill, T., Smith, N., & Lewicki, P. (1989). The development of self-image bias: A real-world demonstration. *Personality and Social Psychology Bulletin, 15*, 205–211.

Hull, J. G. (1981). A self-awareness model of the causes and effects of alcohol consumption. *Journal of Abnormal Psychology, 90*, 586–600.

Hull, J. G., Levenson, R. W., Young, R. D., & Sher, K. J. (1983). Self-awareness-reducing effects of alcohol consumption. *Journal of Personality and Social Psychology, 44*, 461–473.

Hull, J. G., & Levy, A. S. (1979). The organizational functions of the self: An alternative to the Duval and Wicklund model of self-awareness. *Journal of Personality and Social Psychology, 37*, 756–768.

Hull, J. G., & Young, R. D. (1983). Self-consciousness, self-esteem, and success-failure as determinants of alcohol consumption in male social drinkers. *Journal of Personality and Social Psychology, 44,* 1097–1109.

Hull, J. G., Young, R. D., & Jouriles, E. (1986). Applications of the self-awareness model of alcohol consumption: Predicting patterns of use and abuse. *Journal of Personality and Social Psychology, 51,* 790–796.

Hume, D. (1739/1890). *A treatise of human nature.* Cleveland, OH: Langmans, Green, & Co.

Ingram, R. E. (1990). Self-focused attention in clinical disorders: Review and a conceptual model. *Psychological Bulletin, 107,* 156–176.

James, W. (1948/1892). *Psychology.* Cleveland, OH: World Publishing.

Janis, I. L. (1954). Personality correlates of susceptibility to persuasion. *Journal of Personality, 22,* 504–518.

Janis, I. L., & Field, P. (1959). Sex differences and personality factors related to persuasibility. In C. Hovland & I. Janis (Eds.), *Personality and persuasibility* (pp. 55–68 and 300–302). New Haven, CT: Yale University Press.

Jones, E. E. (1964). *Ingratiation.* New York: Irvington.

Jones, E. E., & Berglas, S. C. (1978). Control of attributions about the self through self-handicapping strategies: The appeal of alcohol and the role of underachievement. *Personality and Social Psychology Bulletin, 4,* 200–206.

Jones, E. E., & Gerard, H. B. (1967). *Foundations of social psychology.* New York: Wiley.

Jones, E. E., & Nisbett, R. E. (1971). *The actor and the observer: Divergent perceptions of the causes of behavior.* Morristown, NJ: General Learning Press.

Jones, E. E., & Pittman, T. S. (1982). Toward a general theory of strategic self-presentation. In J. Suls (Eds.), *Psychological perspectives on the self* (Vol. 1, pp. 231–262). Hillsdale, NJ: Erlbaum.

Jones, E. E., Rhodewalt, F., Berglas, S. C., & Skelton, A. (1981). Effects of strategic self-presentation on subsequent self-esteem. *Journal of Personality and Social Psychology, 41,* 407–421.

Jones, E. E., Rock, L., Shaver, K. G., Goethals, G. R., & Ward, L. M. (1968). Pattern of performance and ability attribution: An unexpected primacy effect. *Journal of Personality and Social Psychology, 10,* 317–340.

Jones, E. E., & Wortman, C. (1973). *Ingratiation: An attributional approach.* Morristown, NJ: General Learning Press.

Jones, W. H., Kugler, K., & Adams, P. (1995). You always hurt the one you love: Guilt and transgressions against relationship partners. In J. Tangney & K. Fischer (Eds.), *The self-conscious emotions* (pp. 301–321). New York: Guilford.

Jussim, L., Yen, H., & Aiello, J. R. (1995). Self-consistency, self-enhancement, and accuracy in reactions to feedback. *Journal of Experimental Social Psychology, 31,* 322–356.

Kahle, L. R., Kulka, R. A., & Klingel, D. M. (1980). Low adolescent self-esteem leads to multiple interpersonal problems: A test of social-adaptation theory. *Journal of Personality and Social Psychology, 39,* 496–502.

Kahneman, D., Knetsch, J. L., & Thaler, R. H. (1990). Experimental tests of the endowment effect and the Coase theorem. *Journal of Political Economy, 98,* 1325–1348.

Kant, I. (1956/original 1787). *Kritik der reinen Vernunft* [Critique of pure reason]. Frankfurt, Germany: Felix Meiner Verlag.

Kasser, T., & Ryan, R. M. (1993). A dark side of the American dream: Correlates of financial success as a central life aspiration. *Journal of Personality and Social Psychology, 65,* 410–422.

Kasser, T., & Ryan, R. M. (1996). Further examining the American dream: Differential correlates of intrinsic and extrinsic goals. *Personality and Social Psychology Bulletin, 22,* 280–287.

Kenrick, D. T., & Stringfield, D. O. (1980). Personality traits and the eye of the beholder: Crossing some traditional philosophical boundaries in the search for consistency in all of the people. *Psychological Review, 87,* 88–104.

Kernis, M. H. (1993). The roles of stability and level of self-esteem in psychological functioning. In R. Baumeister (Ed.), *Self-esteem: The puzzle of low self-regard* (pp. 167–182). New York: Plenum.

Kernis, M. H., Cornell, D. P., Sun, C. R., Berry, A., & Harlow, T. (1993). There's more to self-esteem than whether it's high or low: The importance of stability of self-esteem. *Journal of Personality and Social Psychology, 65,* 1190–1204.

Kernis, M. H., Granneman, B. D., & Barclay, L. C. (1989). Stability and level of self-esteem as predictors of anger arousal and hostility. *Journal of Personality and Social Psychology, 56,* 1013–1022.

Kirschenbaum, D. S. (1987). Self-regulatory failure: A review with clinical implications. *Clinical Psychology Reviews, 7,* 77–104.

Kitayama, S., Markus, H. R., & Matsumoto, H. (1995). Culture, self, and emotion: A cultural perspective on "self-conscious" emotions. In J. Tangney & K. Fischer (Eds.), *The self-conscious emotions* (pp. 439–464). New York: Guilford.

Koestner, B., Bernieri, F., & Zuckerman, M. (1989). Trait-specific versus person-specific moderators of cross-situational consistency. *Journal of Personality, 57,* 1–16.

Kolditz, T. A., & Arkin, R. M. (1982). An impression management interpretation of the self-handicapping strategy. *Journal of Personality and Social Psychology, 43,* 492–502.

Kowalski, R. M., & Leary, M. R. (1990). Strategic self-presentation and the avoidance of aversive events: Antecedents and consequences of self-enhancement and self-depreciation. *Journal of Experimental Social Psychology, 26,* 322–336.

Kuiper, N. A., & Derry, P. A. (1982). Depressed and nondepressed content self-reference in mild depression. *Journal of Personality, 50,* 67–79.

Kunda, Z. (1990). The case for motivated reasoning. *Psychological Bulletin, 108,* 480–498.

Kunda, Z., & Sanitioso, R. (1989). Motivated changes in the self-concept. *Journal of Experimental Social Psychology, 25,* 272–285.

Lambert, A. J., & Wedell, D. H. (1991). The self and social judgment: Effects of affective reaction and "own position" on judgments of unambiguous and ambiguous information about others. *Journal of Personality and Social Psychology, 61,* 884–897.

Langer, E. J. (1975). The illusion of control. *Journal of Personality and Social Psychology, 32,* 311–328.

Leary, M. R. (1995). *Self-presentation: Impression management and interpersonal behavior.* Madison, WI: Brown & Benchmark.

Leary, M. R., Britt, T. W., Cutlip, W. D., & Templeton, J. L. (1992). Social blushing. *Psychological Bulletin, 112,* 446–460.

Leary, M. R., & Jones, J. L. (1993). The social psychology of tanning and sunscreen use: Self-presentational motives as a predictor of health risk. *Journal of Applied Social Psychology, 23,* 1390–1406.

Leary, M. R., & Kowalski, R. (1995). *Social anxiety.* New York: Guilford.

Leary, M. R., Saltzman, J. L., & Bednarski, R. F. (1995). Does high self-esteem buffer people against fear of death? Unpublished manuscript/under editorial review, Wake Forest University, Winston-Salem, NC.

Leary, M. R., & Schreindorfer, L. S. (1997). Unresolved issues with terror management theory. *Psychological Inquiry, 8,* 26–29.

Leary, M. R., Tambor, E. S., Terdal, S. K., & Downs, D. L. (1995). Self-esteem as an interpersonal monitor: The sociometer hypothesis. *Journal of Personality and Social Psychology, 68,* 518–530.

Leary, M. R., Tchividjian, L. R., & Kraxberger, B. E. (1994). Self-presentation can be hazardous to your health: Impression management and health risk. *Health Psychology, 13,* 461–470.

Leith, K. P., & Baumeister, R. F. (1996). Why do bad moods increase self-defeating behavior? Emotion, Risk-taking, and self-regulation. *Journal of Personality and Social Psychology, 71,* 1250–1267.

Lepper, M. R., Greene, D., & Nisbett, R. E. (1973). Undermining children's intrinsic interest with extrinsic reward: A test of the "overjustification" hypothesis. *Journal of Personality and Social Psychology, 28,* 129–137.

Lerner, M. J., Miller, D. T., & Holmes, J. G. (1976). Deserving and the emergence of forms of justice. In L. Berkowitz & E. Walster (Eds.), *Advances in experimental social psychology* (Vol. 9, pp. 134–162). New York: Academic Press.

Lewicki, P. (1983). Self-image bias in person perception. *Journal of Personality and Social Psychology, 45,* 384–393.

Lewicki, P. (1984). Self-schema and social information processing. *Journal of Personality and Social Psychology, 47,* 1177–1190.

Lewis, H. B. (1971). *Shame and guilt in neurosis.* New York: International Universities Press.

Linder, D. E., Cooper, J., & Jones, E. E. (1967). Decision freedom as a determinant of the role of incentive magnitude in attitude change. *Journal of Personality and Social Psychology, 6,* 245–254.

Linville, P. W. (1985). Self-complexity and affective extremity: Don't put all your eggs in one cognitive basket. *Social Cognition, 3,* 94–120.

Linville, P. W. (1987). Self-complexity as a cognitive buffer against stress-related illness and depression. *Journal of Personality and Social Psychology, 52,* 663–676.

Loevinger, J. (1969). Theories of ego development. In L. Breger (Ed.), *Clinical-cognitive psychology: Models and integrations.* Englewood Cliffs, NJ: Prentice-Hall.

Loewenstein, G., & Elster, J. (Eds.). (1992). *Choice over time.* New York: Russell Sage. 1992.

Malloy, T. E., & Albright, L. (1990). Interpersonal perception in a social context. *Journal of Personality and Social Psychology, 58,* 419–428.

Marks, G. (1984). Thinking one's abilities are unique and one's opinions are common. *Personality and Social Psychology Bulletin, 10,* 203–208.

Markus, H., & Nurius, P. S. (1986). Possible selves. *American Psychologist, 41,* 954–969.

Markus, H., Smith, J., & Moreland, R. (1985). Role of the self-concept in the perception of others. *Journal of Personality and Social Psychology, 49,* 1494–1512.

Markus, H. R. (1977). Self-schemata and processing information about the self. *Journal of Personality and Social Psychology, 35,* 63–78.

Markus, H. R., & Kitayama, S. (1991). Culture and the self: Implications for cognition, emotion, and motivation. *Psychological Review, 98,* 224–253.

Markus, H. R., & Kunda, Z. (1986). Stability and malleability of the self-concept. *Journal of Personality and Social Psychology, 51,* 858–866.

Marlatt, G. A., Demming, B., & Reid, J. B. (1973). Loss of control drinking in alcoholics: An experimental analogue. *Journal of Abnormal Psychology, 82,* 223–241.

McFarlin, D. B., Baumeister, R. F., & Blascovich, J. (1984). On knowing when to quit: Task failure, self-esteem, advice, and nonproductive persistence. *Journal of Personality, 52,* 138–155.

McFarlin, D. B., & Blascovich, J. (1981). Effects of self-esteem and performance feedback on future affective preferences and cognitive expectations. *Journal of Personality and Social Psychology, 40,* 521–531.

McGuire, W. J., McGuire, C. V., Child, P., & Fujioka, T.

(1978). Salience of ethnicity in the spontaneous self-concept as a function of one's ethnic distinctiveness in the social environment. *Journal of Personality and Social Psychology, 36,* 511–520.

McGuire, W. J., McGuire, C. V., & Winton, W. (1979). Effects of household sex composition on the salience of one's gender in the spontaneous self-concept. *Journal of Experimental Social Psychology, 15,* 77–90.

Mead, G. H. (1934). *Mind, self, and society.* Chicago, IL: University of Chicago Press.

Mecca, A. M., Smelser, N. J., & Vasconcellos, J. (Eds.). (1989). *The social importance of self-esteem.* Berkeley: University of California Press.

Meehl, P. E. (1956). Wanted—a good cookbook. *American Psychologist, 11,* 263–272.

Menninger, K. (1938/1966). *Man against himself.* New York: Harcourt, Brace, & World.

Miller, R. S. (1995). Embarrassment and social behavior. In J. Tangney & K. Fischer (Eds.), *The self-conscious emotions* (pp. 322–339). New York: Guilford.

Mischel, W. (1974). Processes in delay of gratification. In L. Berkowitz (Ed.), *Advances in experimental social psychology* (Vol. 7, pp. 249–292). San Diego, CA: Academic Press.

Mischel, W. (1996). From good intentions to willpower. In P. Gollwitzer & J. Bargh (Eds.), *The psychology of action* (pp. 197–218). New York: Guilford.

Mischel, W., Ebbesen, E. B., & Zeiss, A. R. (1976). Determinants of selective memory about the self. *Journal of Consulting and Clinical Psychology, 44,* 92–103.

Mischel, W., Shoda, Y., & Peake, P. K. (1988). The nature of adolescent competencies predicted by preschool delay of gratification. *Journal of Personality and Social Psychology, 54,* 687–696.

Modigliani, A. (1971). Embarrassment, facework, and eye contact: Testing a theory of embarrassment. *Journal of Personality and Social Psychology, 17,* 15–24.

Mruk, C. (1995). *Self-esteem: Research, theory, and practice.* New York: Springer.

Muraven, M., Tice, D. M., & Baumeister, R. F. (in press). Self-control as limited resource: Regulatory depletion patterns. *Journal of Personality and Social Psychology.*

Murray, H. A. (1938). *Explorations in personality.* New York: Oxford University Press.

Murray, S. L., & Holmes, J. G. (1993). Seeing virtues in faults: Negativity and the transformation of interpersonal narratives in close relationships. *Journal of Personality and Social Psychology, 65,* 707–722.

Murray, S. L., & Holmes, J. G. (1994). Storytelling in close relationships: The construction of confidence. *Personality and Social Psychology Bulletin, 20,* 650–663.

Murray, S. L., Holmes, J. G., & Griffin, D. W. (1996). The benefits of positive illusions: Idealization and the construction of satisfaction in close relationships. *Journal of Personality and Social Psychology, 70,* 79–98.

Nathanson, S., Brockner, J., Brenner, D., Samuelson, C., Countryman, M., Lloyd, M., & Rubin, J. Z. (1982). Toward the reduction of entrapment. *Journal of Applied Social Psychology, 12,* 193–208.

Newman, L. S., & Baumeister, R. F. (1996). Toward an elaboration of the UFO abduction phenomenon: Hypnotic elaboration, extraterrestrial sadomasochism, and spurious memories. *Psychological Inquiry, 7,* 99–126.

Newman, L. S., Duff, K., & Baumeister, R. F. (1997). A new look at defensive projection: Suppression, accessibility, and biased person perception. *Journal of Personality and Social Psychology, 72,* 980–1001.

Nietzsche, F. (1887/1964). *Jenseits von Gut und Böse/Zur Genealogie der Moral* [Beyond good and evil/Genealogy of morals]. Stuttgart, Germany: Kröner.

Nisbett, R., & Wilson, T. D. (1977). Telling more than we can know: Verbal reports on mental processes. *Psychological Review, 84,* 231–259.

Notarius, C. I., Wemple, C., Ingraham, L. J., Burns, T. J., & Kollar, E. (1982). Multichannel responses to an interpersonal stressor: Interrelationships among facial display, heart rate, self-report of emotion, and threat appraisal. *Journal of Personality and Social Psychology, 43,* 400–408.

Nuttin, J. M. (1985). Narcissism beyond Gestalt and awareness: The name letter effect. *European Journal of Social Psychology, 15,* 353–361.

Nuttin, J. M. (1987). Affective consequences of mere ownership: The name letter effect in twelve European languages. *European Journal of Social Psychology, 17,* 381–402.

Ogilvie, D. M. (1987). The undesired self: A neglected variable in personality research. *Journal of Personality and Social Psychology, 52,* 379–385.

Orlofsky, J. L., Marcia, J. E., & Lesser, I. M. (1973). Ego identity status and the intimacy versus isolation crisis of young adulthood. *Journal of Personality and Social Psychology, 27,* 211–219.

Parrott, W. G., Sabini, J., & Silver, M. (1988). The roles of self-esteem and social interaction in embarrassment. *Personality and Social Psychology Bulletin, 14,* 191–202.

Paulhus, D. L. (1982). Individual differences, self-presentation, and cognitive dissonance: Their concurrent operation in forced compliance. *Journal of Personality and Social Psychology, 43,* 838–852.

Paulhus, D. L., & Levitt, K. (1987). Desirable responding triggered by affect: Automatic egotism? *Journal of Personality and Social Psychology, 52,* 245–259.

Peele, S. (1989). *The diseasing of America.* Boston, MA: Houghton Mifflin Co.

Pelham, B. W. (1993). On the highly positive thoughts of the highly depressed. In R. Baumeister (Ed.), *Self-esteem: The puzzle of low self-regard* (pp. 183–199). New York: Plenum.

Pennebaker, J. W., & Chew, C. H. (1985). Behavioral inhibition and electrodermal activity during deception. *Journal of Personality and Social Psychology, 49,* 1427–1433.

Platt, J. (1973). Social traps. *American Psychologist, 28,* 641–651.

Pleban, R., & Tesser, A. (1981). The effects of relevance and quality of another's performance on interpersonal closeness. *Social Psychology Quarterly, 44,* 278–285.

Powers, W. T. (1973). *Behavior: The control of perception.* Chicago, IL: Aldine.

Pruzinsky, T., & Cash, T. F. (1990). Integrative themes in body-image development, deviance, and change. In T. Cash & T. Pruzinsky (Eds.), *Body images: Development, deviance, and change* (pp. 337–349). New York: Guilford.

Pryor, J. B., Gibbons, F. X., Wicklund, R. A., Fazio, R. H., & Hood, R. (1977). Self-focused attention and self-report validity. *Journal of Personality, 45,* 514–527.

Pyszczynski, T., Greenberg, J., & Holt, K. (1985). Maintaining consistency between self-serving beliefs and available data: A bias in information processing. *Personality and Social Psychology Bulletin, 11,* 179–190.

Pyszczynski, T., Greenberg, J., & Solomon, S. (1997). Why do we need what we need? A terror management perspective on the roots of human social motivation. *Psychological Inquiry, 8,* 1–20.

Rachman, S. J., & Hodgson, R. J. (1980). *Obsessions and compulsions.* Englewood Cliffs, NJ: Prentice-Hall.

Raskin, R., Novacek, J., & Hogan, R. (1991). Narcissistic self-esteem management. *Journal of Personality and Social Psychology, 60,* 911–918.

Reed, G. F. (1985). *Obsessional experience and compulsive behavior: A cognitive-structural approach.* Orlando, FL: Academic Press.

Rogers, T. B., Kuiper, N. A., & Kirker, W. S. (1977). Self-reference and the encoding of personal information. *Journal of Personality and Social Psychology, 35,* 677–688.

Roney, C. J., Higgins, E. T., & Shah, J. (1995) Goals and framing: How outcome focus influences motivation and emotion. *Personality and Social Psychology Bulletin, 21,* 1151–1160.

Rosenbaum, M. E. (1986). The repulsion hypothesis: On the nondevelopment of relationships. *Journal of Personality and Social Psychology, 51,* 1156–1166.

Rosenfeld, D., Folger, R., & Adelman, H. F. (1980). When rewards reflect competence: A qualification of the overjustification effect. *Journal of Personality and Social Psychology, 39,* 368–376.

Rosenthal, R., & Jacobson, L. (1968). *Pygmalion in the classroom.* New York: Holt.

Roth, S., & Bootzin, R. R. (1974). Effects of experimentally induced expectancies of external control: An investigation of learned helplessness. *Journal of Personality and Social Psychology, 29,* 253–264.

Roth, S., & Kubal, L. (1975). Effects of noncontingent reinforcement on tasks of differing importance: Facilitation and learned helplessness. *Journal of Personality and Social Psychology, 32,* 680–691.

Rothbaum, F., Weisz, J. R., & Snyder, S. S. (1982). Changing the world and changing the self: A two-process model of perceived control. *Journal of Personality and Social Psychology, 42,* 5–37.

Rubin, J. Z., & Brockner, J. (1975). Factors affecting entrapment in waiting situations: The Rosencrantz and Guildenstern effect. *Journal of Personality and Social Psychology, 31,* 1054–1063.

Ryan, R. M. (1982). Control and information in the intrapersonal sphere: An extension of cognitive evaluation theory. *Journal of Personality and Social Psychology, 43,* 450–461.

Ryan, R. M., Mims, V., & Koestner, R. (1983). Relation of reward contingency and interpersonal context to intrinsic motivation: A review and test using cognitive evaluation theory. *Journal of Personality and Social Psychology, 45,* 736–750.

Sabini, J., & Silver, M. (1981). Introspection and causal accounts. *Journal of Personality and Social Psychology, 40,* 171–179.

Sackeim, H. A., & Gur, R. C. (1979). Self-deception, other-deception, and self-reported psychopathology. *Journal of Consulting and Clinical Psychology, 47,* 213–215.

Sanitioso, R., Kunda, Z., & Fong, G. T. (1990). Motivated recruitment of autobiographical memory. *Journal of Personality and Social Psychology, 59,* 229–241.

Sartre, J.-P. (1953). *The existential psychoanalysis.* (H. E. Barnes, trans.). New York: Philosophical Library.

Sartre, J.-P. (1956). *Being and nothingness.* (H. E. Barnes, trans.). Secaucus, NJ: Citadel Press. (Original work published in 1943)

Scheier, M. F., & Carver, C. S. (1977). Self-focused attention and the experience of emotion: Attraction, repulsion, elation, and depression. *Journal of Personality and Social Psychology, 35,* 625–636.

Scheier, M. F., Fenigstein, A., & Buss, A. H. (1974). Self-awareness and physical aggression. *Journal of Experimental Social Psychology, 10,* 264–273.

Schiller, B. (1932). A quantitative analysis of marriage selection in a small group. *Journal of Social Psychology, 3,* 297–319.

Schlenker, B. R. (1975). Self-presentation: Managing the impression of consistency when reality interferes with self-enhancement. *Journal of Personality and Social Psychology, 32,* 1030–1037.

Schlenker, B. R. (1980). *Impression management: The self-concept, social identity, and interpersonal relations.* Monterey, CA: Brooks/Cole.

Schlenker, B. R. (1982). Translating actions into attitudes: An identity-analytic approach to the explanation of social conduct. In L. Berkowitz (Ed.), *Advances in experimental social psychology* (Vol. 15, pp. 193–246). San Diego, CA: Academic Press.

Schlenker, B. R. (1986). Self-identification: Toward an integration of the private and public self. In R. Baumeister

(Ed.), *Public self and private self* (pp. 21–62). New York: Springer-Verlag.

Schlenker, B. R., Dlugolecki, D. W., & Doherty, K. (1994). The impact of self-presentations on self-appraisals and behavior: The roles of commitment and biased scanning. *Personality and Social Psychology Bulletin, 20,* 20–33.

Schlenker, B. R., & Leary, M. R. (1982). Social anxiety and self-presentation: A conceptualization and model. *Psychological Bulletin, 92,* 641–669.

Sedikides, C. (1993). Assessment, enhancement, and verification determinants of the self-evaluation process. *Journal of Personality and Social Psychology, 65,* 317–338.

Sedikides, C., & Skowronski, J. J. (1993). The self in impression formation: Trait centrality and social perception. *Journal of Experimental Social Psychology, 29,* 347–357.

Seligman, M. E. P. (1975). *Helplessness: On depression, development, and death.* San Francisco, CA: Freeman.

Semin, G. R., & Manstead, A. S. R. (1982). The social implications of embarrassment displays and restitution behavior. *European Journal of Social Psychology, 12,* 367–377.

Shapiro, D. (1996). The "self-control" muddle. *Psychological Inquiry, 7,* 76–79.

Shaw, R. J. (1992). Coping effectiveness in nursing home residents: The role of control. *Journal of Aging and Health, 4,* 551–563.

Shoda, Y., Mischel, W., & Peake, P. K. (1990). Predicting adolescent cognitive and self-regulatory competencies from preschool delay of gratification: Identifying diagnostic conditions. *Developmental Psychology, 26,* 978–986.

Shoemaker, S. (1963). *Self-knowledge and self-identity.* Ithaca, NY: Cornell University Press.

Showers, C. (1992). Compartmentalization of positive and negative self-knowledge: Keeping bad apples out of the bunch. *Journal of Personality and Social Psychology, 62,* 1036–1049.

Shrauger, J. S. (1975). Responses to evaluation as a function of initial self-perceptions. *Psychological Bulletin, 82,* 581–596.

Shrauger, J. S., & Rosenberg, S. E. (1970). Self-esteem and the effects of success and failure feedback on performance. *Journal of Personality, 38,* 404–417.

Shrauger, J. S., & Shoeneman, T. J. (1979). Symbolic interactionist view of self-concept: Through the looking glass darkly. *Psychological Bulletin, 86,* 549–573.

Shrauger, J. S., & Sorman, P. B. (1977). Self-evaluations, initial success and failure, and improvement as determinants of persistence. *Journal of Consulting and Clinical Psychology, 45,* 784–795.

Sigall, H., & Gould, R. (1977). The effects of self-esteem and evaluator demandingness on effort expenditure. *Journal of Personality and Social Psychology, 35,* 12–20.

Singer, J. A., & Salovey, P. (1993). *The remembered self: Emotion and memory in personality.* New York: Free Press.

Skowronski, J. J., & Carlston, D. E. (1982). Effects of previously experienced outcomes on the desire for choice. *Journal of Personality and Social Psychology, 43,* 689–701.

Smart, L., & Wegner, D. M. (1996). Strength of will. *Psychological Inquiry, 7,* 79–84.

Smeaton, G., Byrne, D., & Murnen, S. K. (1989). The repulsion hypothesis revisited: Similarity irrelevance or dissimilarity bias? *Journal of Personality and Social Psychology, 56,* 54–59.

Smith, E. R., & Miller, F. D. (1978). Limits on perception of cognitive processes: A reply to Nisbett and Wilson. *Psychological Review, 85,* 355–362.

Snyder, M. (1974). The self-monitoring of expressive behavior. *Journal of Personality and Social Psychology, 30,* 526–537.

Snyder, M. (1987). *Public appearances, private realities: The psychology of self-monitoring.* New York: Freeman.

Snyder, M., & Simpson, J. (1984). Self-monitoring and dating relationships. *Journal of Personality and Social Psychology, 47,* 1281–1291.

Snyder, M., & Swann, W. B. (1976). When actions reflect attitudes: The politics of impression management. *Journal of Personality and Social Psychology, 34,* 1034–1042.

Snyder, M., & Swann, W. B. (1978). Behavioral confirmation in social interaction: From social perception to social reality. *Journal of Experimental Social Psychology, 14,* 148–162.

Snyder, M., Tanke, E. D., & Berscheid, E. (1977). Social perception and interpersonal behavior: On the self-fulfilling nature of social stereotypes. *Journal of Personality and Social Psychology, 35,* 656–666.

Solomon, S., Greenberg, J., & Pyszczynski, T. (1991). A terror management theory of social behavior: The psychological functions of self-esteem and cultural worldviews. In M. P. Zanna (Ed.), *Advances in experimental social psychology* (Vol. 24, pp. 93–159). San Diego, CA: Academic Press.

Spencer, S. J., Josephs, R. A., & Steele, C. M. (1993). Low self-esteem: The uphill struggle for self-integrity. In R. Baumeister (Ed.), *Self-esteem: The puzzle of low self-regard* (pp. 21–36). New York: Plenum.

Staw, B. M. (1976). Knee-deep in the big muddy: A study of escalating commitment to a chosen course of action. *Organizational Behavior and Human Performance, 16,* 27–44.

Steele, C. M. (1988). The psychology of self-affirmation: Sustaining the integrity of the self. In L. Berkowitz (Ed.), *Advances in experimental social psychology* (Vol. 21, pp. 261–302). New York: Academic Press.

Steele, C. M., & Josephs, R. A. (1990). Alcohol myopia: Its prized and dangerous effects. *American Psychologist, 45,* 921–933.

Steenbarger, B. N., & Aderman, D. (1979). Objective self-awareness as a nonaversive state: Effect of anticipating discrepancy reduction. *Journal of Personality, 47,* 330–339.

Sullivan, H. S. (1953). *The interpersonal theory of psychiatry.* New York: Norton.

Suls, J., & Wan, C. K. (1987). In search of the false-uniqueness phenomenon: Fear and estimates of social consensus. *Journal of Personality and Social Psychology, 52,* 211–217.

Svenson, O. (1981). Are we all less risky and more skillful than our fellow drivers? *Acta Psychologica, 47,* 143–148.

Swann, W. B. (1985). The self as architect of social reality. In B. R. Schlenker (Ed.), *The self and social life* (pp. 100–125). New York: McGraw-Hill.

Swann, W. B. (1987). Identity negotiation: Where two roads meet. *Journal of Personality and Social Psychology, 53,* 1038–1051.

Swann, W. B. (1992). Seeking "truth," finding despair: Some unhappy consequences of a negative self-concept. *Current Directions in Psychological Science, 1,* 15–18.

Swann, W. B., Griffin, J. J., Predmore, S. C., & Gaines, B. (1987). The cognitive-affective crossfire: When self-consistency confronts self-enhancement. *Journal of Personality and Social Psychology, 52,* 881–889.

Swann, W. B., & Hill, C. A. (1982). When our identities are mistaken: Reaffirming self-conceptions through social interaction. *Journal of Personality and Social Psychology, 43,* 59–66.

Swann, W. B., Hixon, J. G., & De La Ronde, C. (1992). Embracing the bitter "truth": Negative self-concepts and marital commitment. *Psychological Science, 3,* 118–121.

Swann, W. B., Hixon, J. G., Stein-Seroussi, A., & Gilbert, D. T. (1990). The fleeting gleam of praise: Cognitive processes underlying behavioral reactions to self-relevant feedback. *Journal of Personality and Social Psychology, 59,* 17–26.

Swann, W. B., & Predmore, S. C. (1985). Intimates as agents of social support: Sources of consolation or despair? *Journal of Personality and Social Psychology, 49,* 1609–1617.

Tangney, J. P. (1992). Situational determinants of shame and guilt in young adulthood. *Personality and Social Psychology Bulletin, 18,* 199–206.

Tangney, J. P. (1995). Shame and guilt in interpersonal relationships. In J. Tangney & K. Fischer (Eds.), *The self-conscious emotions* (pp. 114–139). New York: Guilford.

Tangney, J. P., Burggraf, S. A., & Wagner, P. E. (1995). Shame-proneness, guilt-proneness, and psychological symptoms. In J. Tangney & K. Fischer (Eds.), *The self-conscious emotions* (pp. 343–367). New York: Guilford.

Tangney, J. P., & Fischer, K. W. (Eds.). (1995). *The self-conscious emotions: The psychology of shame, guilt, embarrassment, and pride.* New York: Guilford.

Tangney, J. P., Wagner, P. E., Fletcher, C., & Gramzow, R. (1992). Shamed into anger? The relation of shame and guilt to anger and self-reported aggression. *Journal of Personality and Social Psychology, 62,* 669–675.

Taylor, S. E. (1975). On inferring one's attitudes from one's behavior: Some delimiting conditions. *Journal of Personality and Social Psychology, 31,* 126–131.

Taylor, S. E. (1983). Adjustment to threatening events: A theory of cognitive adaptation. *American Psychologist, 38,* 1161–1173.

Taylor, S. E. (1989). *Positive illusions: Creative self-deception and the healthy mind.* New York: Basic Books.

Taylor, S. E., & Brown, J. D. (1988). Illusion and well-being: A social psychological perspective on mental health. *Psychological Bulletin, 103,* 193–210.

Tedeschi, J. T., Schlenker, B. R., & Bonoma, T. V. (1971). Cognitive dissonance: Private ratiocination or public spectacle? *American Psychologist, 26,* 685–695.

Teger, A. I. (1980). *Too much invested to quit.* New York: Pergamon.

Tennen, H., & Affleck, G. (1993). The puzzles of self-esteem: A clinical perspective. In R. Baumeister (Ed.), *Self-esteem: The puzzle of low self-regard* (pp. 241–262). New York: Plenum.

Tesch, S. A., & Whitbourne, S. K. (1982). Intimacy and identity status in young adults. *Journal of Personality and Social Psychology, 43,* 1041–1051.

Tesser, A. (1988). Toward a self-evaluation maintenance model of social behavior. In L. Berkowitz (Ed.), *Advances in experimental social psychology* (Vol. 21, pp. 181–227). San Diego, CA: Academic Press.

Tesser, A. (1993). The importance of heritability in psychological research: The case of attitudes. *Psychological Review, 100,* 129–142.

Tesser, A., & Moore, J. (1986). On the convergence of public and private aspects of self. In R. Baumeister (Ed.), *Public self and private self* (pp. 99–116). New York: Springer-Verlag.

Tesser, A., & Smith, J. (1980). Some effects of friendship and task relevance on helping: You don't always help the one you like. *Journal of Experimental Social Psychology, 16,* 582–590.

Tetlock, P. E. (1986). A value pluralism model of ideological reasoning. *Journal of Personality and Social Psychology, 50,* 819–827.

Tetlock, P. E., & Manstead, A. S. (1985). Impression management versus intrapsychic explanations in social psychology: A useful dichotomy? *Psychological Review, 92,* 59–77.

Tice, D. M. (1991). Esteem protection or enhancement? Self-handicapping motives and attributions differ by trait self-esteem. *Journal of Personality and Social Psychology, 60,* 711–725.

Tice, D. M. (1992). Self-presentation and self-concept change: The lookingglass self as magnifying glass. *Journal of Personality and Social Psychology, 63,* 435–451.

Tice, D. M., & Baumeister, R. F. (1990). Self-esteem, self-handicapping, and self-presentation: The strategy of inadequate practice. *Journal of Personality, 58,* 443–464.

Tice, D. M., Butler, J. L., Muraven, M. B., & Stillwell, A. M. (1995). When modesty prevails: Differential favorability of self-presentation to friends and strangers. *Journal of Personality and Social Psychology, 69,* 1120–1138.

Triandis, H. C. (1989). The self and social behavior in differing cultural contexts. *Psychological Review, 96,* 506–520.

Trilling, L. (1971). *Sincerity and authenticity.* Cambridge, MA: Harvard University Press.

Trope, Y. (1983). Self-assessment in achievement behavior. In J. Suls & A. Greenwald (Eds.), *Psychological perspectives on the self* (Vol. 2, pp. 93–121). Hillsdale, NJ: Erlbaum.

Trope, Y. (1986). Self-enhancement and self-assessment in achievement behavior. In R. Sorrentino & E. T. Higgins (Eds.), *Handbook of motivation and cognition* (Vol. 2, pp. 350–378). New York: Guilford.

Vallacher, R. R., & Wegner, D. M. (1985). *A theory of action identification.* Hillsdale, NJ: Erlbaum.

Vallacher, R. R., & Wegner, D. M. (1987). What do people think they're doing? Action identification and human behavior. *Psychological Review, 94,* 3–15.

Walster, E., Aronson, E., & Brown, Z. (1966). Choosing to suffer as a consequence of expecting to suffer: An unexpected finding. *Journal of Experimental Social Psychology, 2,* 400–406.

Wegner, D. M. (1989). *White bears and other unwanted thoughts.* New York: Vintage.

Wegner, D. M. (1994). Ironic processes of mental control. *Psychological Review, 101,* 34–52.

Wegner, D. M., & Erber, R. (1992). The hyperaccessibility of suppressed thoughts. *Journal of Personality and Social Psychology, 63,* 903–912.

Wegner, D. M., Lane, J. D., & Dimitri, S. (1994). The allure of secret relationships. *Journal of Personality and Social Psychology, 66,* 287–300.

Wegner, D. M., & Pennebaker, J. W. (Eds.). (1993). *Handbook of mental control.* Englewood Cliffs, NJ: Prentice-Hall.

Wegner, D. M., Schneider, D. J., Carter, S. R., & White, T. L. (1987). Paradoxical effects of thought suppression. *Journal of Personality and Social Psychology, 53,* 5–13.

Wegner, D. M., Shortt, J. W., Blake, A. W., & Page, M. S. (1990). The suppression of exciting thoughts. *Journal of Personality and Social Psychology, 58,* 409–418.

Weisz, J. R., McCabe, M. A., & Dennig, M. D. (1994). Primary and secondary control among children undergoing medical procedures: Adjustment as a function of coping style. *Journal of Consulting and Clinical Psychology, 62,* 324–332.

Wenzlaff, R. M., Wegner, D. M., & Roper, D. W. (1988). Depression and mental control: The resurgence of unwanted negative thoughts. *Journal of Personality and Social Psychology, 55,* 882–892.

White, R. (1959). Motivation reconsidered: The concept of competence. *Psychological Review, 66,* 297–333.

Whitley, B. E. (1983). Sex role orientation and self-esteem: A critical meta-analytic review. *Journal of Personality and Social Psychology, 44,* 765–778.

Wicklund, R. A. (1975). Objective self-awareness. In L. Berkowitz (Ed.), *Advances in experimental social psychology* (Vol. 8, pp. 233–275). New York: Academic Press.

Wicklund, R. A., & Duval, S. (1971). Opinion change and performance facilitation as a result of objective self-awareness. *Journal of Experimental Social Psychology, 7,* 319–342.

Wicklund, R. A., & Gollwitzer, P. M. (1982). *Symbolic self-completion.* Hillsdale, NJ: Erlbaum.

Wills, T. A. (1981). Downward comparison principles in social psychology. *Psychological Bulletin, 90,* 245–271.

Wilson, T. D., Dunn, D. S., Bybee, J. A., Hyman, D. B., & Rotondo, J. A. (1984). Effects of analyzing reasons on attitude-behavior consistency. *Journal of Personality and Social Psychology, 44,* 5–16.

Wink, P. (1991). Two faces of narcissism. *Journal of Personality and Social Psychology, 61,* 590–597.

Wright, R. A., & Brehm, S. S. (1982). Reactance as impression management: A critical review. *Journal of Personality and Social Psychology, 42,* 608–618.

Wyer, R. S., & Frey, D. (1983). The effects of feedback about self and others on the recall and judgments of feedback-relevant information. *Journal of Experimental Social Psychology, 19,* 540–559.

Zube, M. J. (1972). Changing concepts of morality: 1948–1969. *Social Forces, 50,* 385–393.

Zuckerman, M. (1979). Attribution of success and failure revisited, or: The motivational bias is alive and well in attribution theory. *Journal of Personality, 47,* 245–287.

CHAPTER SIXTEEN

SOCIAL DEVELOPMENT IN CHILDHOOD AND ADULTHOOD

DIANE N. RUBLE, *New York University*
JACQUELINE J. GOODNOW, *MacQuarie University*

Over the past twenty years, four reviews of research on social development have appeared in the *Annual Review of
Psychology* (Collins & Gunnar, 1990; Hartup & van
Lieshout, 1995; Hoffman, 1977; Parke & Asher, 1983). In
what ways will this review offer something new? First, we
have written the review with a double audience in mind: developmental psychologists and social psychologists. We
hope it will inform both and will break down the sense of
separate fields. That aim stems partly from the review being
written for the *Handbook of Social Psychology*. It stems also
from our conviction that the two fields are not completely
separate and can contribute to one another. Social psychologists may find no difficulty in regarding developmental studies as likely to benefit from the models and methods that social psychologists have brought to bear on topics such as
person perception or attitude change. We would argue that
there is equal benefit in asking what a developmental perspective would add to the way social psychologists view behavior and to the questions they might ask.

Second, we have strived to bring out the structure of developmental studies. Research in social development covers a wide range of topics and can present at first a picture
of almost endless diversity. We shall concentrate on clarifying the issues and the concepts that underlie the choice
of particular topics, designs, and populations. This concentration on the structure of the field, rather than on compiling results, helps differentiate among projects and illuminate the lines along which historical change has occurred.
It also makes developmental studies more intelligible to
anyone not immersed in the field. (It must be said, however, that we have also benefited from the exercise.)

Third, we have drawn from studies of development in
both childhood and adulthood. Past reviews have stopped
with young adults, and there has been little integration of
that material with what happens over the rest of the life
course. This is regrettable. It contributes to the misleading
view of developmental studies as being "all about children" (one more reason for social psychologists to feel that
developmental studies are not relevant to their interests). In
addition, reviewing both literatures—even selectively—
turns out to be a way of heightening our understanding of
what is happening at any one age. Overall, the larger share
of our examples comes from studies of childhood; the review of later phases of the life span is limited to asking
what such studies add to the picture.

The chapter is divided into four sections. The first covers some general features of developmental studies, together with points of overlap and difference between developmental and social psychological studies. The features
have to do with (a) the kinds of topics covered; (b) the
presence of a mixed research agenda; (c) the presence of a
wide age span; and (d) a pervasive concern with the nature
and the course of change. The second section concentrates
on approaches to the task of specifying the nature of social
development: what changes and the course that change follows. This section is organized around the dimensions that
differentiate among approaches, with each considered as it
appears in studies of childhood and then in studies of

We are grateful to Ann Boggiano, Philip Costanzo, William Green,
Eva Pomerantz, and Catherine Tamis-LeMonda for reading and commenting on an earlier draft and to Stephanie Aubry and Faith Greulich
for bibliographic assistance. Preparation of this chapter was supported
in part by a Research Scientist Award (MH01202) and a research grant
(MH37215) from NIMH.

adulthood. The same style of organization is followed in the third section, except that now we are considering approaches to the bases of change or variation and asking about the several contributions of external conditions, internal states, and their interconnections. With the nature of developmental studies now clarified, the final section explicitly takes up links between social and developmental psychology, by asking what changes in viewpoint and in research might follow if social psychologists adopted a developmental perspective.

DEVELOPMENTAL STUDIES: GENERAL FEATURES AND POINTS OF OVERLAP WITH SOCIAL PSYCHOLOGY

This is by no means the first paper to draw attention to the feasibility and the benefits of combining studies from developmental and social psychology (e.g., Brehm, Kassin, & Gibbons, 1981; Durkin, 1995; Eisenberg, 1995; Flavell and Ross, 1981; Goodnow, 1988; Higgins, Ruble, & Hartup, 1983). To make that point, and to expand upon previous ventures, we begin by laying out several general features of social developmental studies, noting as we proceed some specific points of overlap and divergence with social psychology. The first two features (the substantive topics covered and the presence of a mixed research agenda) will be covered relatively briefly, leaving the major space for the second pair (the nature of the age-range covered and the nature of the concern with change). It is the latter pair that provoke the stronger sense of difference between disciplines and call for the closer analysis of reasons for particular approaches.

The Topics Covered

In essence, the adjective "social" signals that the qualities, skills, or forms of processing being considered are particularly relevant to our lives with others. It involves such tasks as establishing relationships, understanding the emotions and intentions of others, gaining a sense of one's place in a group, and finding some comfortable balance between meeting the expectations of others and exercising some degree of choice. For both developmental and social psychologists, then, interest focuses on topics such as the quality and understanding of relationships, person perception, impression management, self-evaluation, aggressive or prosocial behavior, social roles, and prejudice, and the impact of others on one's self-perceptions, choices, and behaviors.

Also common to the two fields is a change over time in the degree of interest in particular topics. Referring to the four reviews of social development mentioned earlier, for instance, one finds an increase from Hoffman's (1977) review to the later reviews in the degree of attention to such

topics as the nature of relationships and emotions—a shift that social psychologists are likely to find familiar. They would also find familiar a continuing thread of interest in conditions that help establish or maintain behaviors that are of benefit to others or do not harm them. Across the four reviews, the label for that interest shows some changes (e.g., from "prosocial" behavior in the 1977 review to "social responsibility" in the review of 1995), but the underlying concern remains with behaviors that are both socially and morally desirable.

A Mixed Research Agenda

There is currently no single agenda within studies of social development. The focus may be on describing what happens in the course of development, on developing theories of how this comes about, on offering suggestions for improvement in the way people proceed or in the way social policies are framed, or on all of these combined. Historically, however, the "agenda of improvement" was originally dominant and at times stood alone.

Studies of social development in childhood and adolescence provide an example. As Sears (1975) notes in his historical account of the field, the universal draft in World War I produced a picture of American males as less than adequate for the tasks of war: "deadheads who could not fulfill the role of a fighter" (p. 20). As the public voiced their concern, President Wilson named 1919 as the Children's Year, and $12 million of Rockefeller money was dedicated to child development research (Sears, 1975). The agenda of improvement continued throughout a number of studies on the particular parental methods most strongly correlated with a variety of socially desirable qualities: competence, responsibility, ability to persist at a task, ability to get along with others or to keep aggression within reasonable bounds (see Maccoby & Martin, 1983, for one review).

Working out ways to improve the qualities of the young, however, was not the only agenda in sight. There was also considerable investment in studies devoted to laying out what usually appeared at various ages, especially during early childhood. These studies by and large paid little attention to parental methods or to individual differences except as departures from the norm. The research by Gesell and his colleagues (e.g., 1948; see Thelen & Adolph, 1992, for a review) is probably the best-known example. As the studies of parental methods and of apparently maturational patterns accumulated, however, the demand rose for closer attention to the processes that might account for observed effects and that might underlie either the emergence of modal changes or of variations from the mode. As Grusec and Lytton (1988) note, the end of the 1960s saw a major turn towards the development of theory, with social learning theory (e.g., Bandura, 1969) and ethological theory (e.g., Bowlby, 1969) occupying the most prominent spaces.

That same type of move toward theory is also found in studies concentrating on adolescence and adulthood. The improvement agenda, for instance, recurs in studies dealing with ways to promote involvement in school, to reduce the likelihood of pregnancy in adolescence or substance abuse at any age, to reduce prejudice at all ages, to promote healthy life styles as people grow older, to encourage sustained independence and a sense of well-being in late adulthood. In each age group, however, the historical shift takes the form of adding to the side of theoretical processes and moving towards combined rather than single agendas.

The turn towards theory in the social developmental literature is well exemplified in the four reviews we used earlier as a base for indicating historical continuities and shifts. The research that dominated the Hoffman (1977) review was primarily concerned with actions, and with a particular way of accounting for change and variations in those actions—namely, parent-child interactions. In addition, however, Hoffman described some research—by himself and by others—that asked more about the processes underlying correlations between parental methods and domains of social development. In this research, there was a strong emphasis on the impact of particular kinds of internal states, both affective in kind (the development of empathy attracted his particular attention) and cognitive in kind (primarily in the form of the ability to take the perspective of others). The 1983 review by Parke and Asher was marked by an explosion of interest in cognitive processes, as researchers extended the social-cognitive approach beyond role-taking to the growth of knowledge in domains such as achievement and person perception and the implications of such changes for personal and interpersonal behaviors. In addition, they extended the range of external conditions and processes considered. The impact of parent-child interactions and the importance of the individual's affective as well as cognitive states were still given explanatory prominence, but interpersonal interactions with siblings and peers were added, as were biological contributions (in the form of temperamental differences). By 1990 (Collins & Gunnar), affect had come to stand out as the internal state in particular need of attention, whereas in Hartup and van Lieshout's (1995) analysis, the focus was on the relation between temperament and social context in understanding continuity and change in individual's social behavior and personality.

This historical shift towards a theoretical process analysis provides a particular bridge to social psychology. Social psychologists would find familiar, for example, the original emphasis on cognitive processes, with a later rise of interest in the influence of affective processes. They would also find familiar some of the particular models used for cognitive and affective processes, such as attribution and information processing theories. There are nonetheless several points of difference in the particular kinds of internal states considered. Within developmental studies, for instance, the analysis of cognitive states contains a strong concern with age-related changes in the ability to make sense of events, a concern originally deriving from Piagetian theory. The analysis of affective states also contains a concern with some particular states, such as empathy (Dix, 1991; Hoffman, 1977) and with individual differences in temperament (essentially differences in reactivity, affective tone, and styles of regulation or inhibition). There are as well some similarities and differences in the kinds of external conditions that attract theoretical attention. The two disciplines share a common interest in the presence of conditions that fall into the broad category of "social support." Developmental studies, however, are somewhat more attentive to the reciprocal nature of the interactions between various external conditions and internal states over time—in ways that vary from mediating to moderating, cumulative, and "domino" effects (Hartup & van Lieshout, 1995).

A Wide Age Range with Divisions

The Nature of Divisions One of the major features associated with developmental studies is the degree of interest in making comparisons across age groups. In a later section, we ask what gives rise to the particular attention to age differences. In this section, however, we concentrate on the tendency to make age comparisons only within some particular age spans. Despite the frequent lip-service to life-span development, most studies—and most models—tend to focus on some particular age spans. To use our four reviews as a base, each of these tends to concentrate on a particular slice of the age span and none extends beyond early adulthood. In keeping with the heavy emphasis on disciplinary issues, the research Hoffman (1977) reviews focuses mainly on the preschool and early elementary school years. The exceptions are studies testing Kohlberg's (1964) theory of moral development and Horner's (1972) theory of fear of success, as well as studies including middle childhood as a point of comparison. Parke and Asher (1983) target a somewhat wider age range—infancy through preadolescence. Indeed, unlike the earlier review, they show a heavy emphasis on infancy, as part of their focus on biological determinants, temperament, and early affect. They explicitly refrained from examining studies of adolescence and adulthood, however, because other *Annual Review* chapters featured these periods. The period of research covered by Collins and Gunnar (1990) pays increasing attention to development after infancy, emphasizing middle childhood and adolescence. As before, however, their review shows little concern with social development after adolescence, except in terms of changes, such as divorce, that directly affect children. Finally, in the Hartup and van Lieshout (1995) review, the age span for developmental studies shows an expansion from the reviews in earlier years. Noted, for example, are studies asking about the extent to which aggressive or criminal behaviors during adolescence predict similar behaviors up to age 30 (e.g., Stattin & Magnusson, 1991), and about the extent to which shyness in middle childhood predicts the age of entry into paid work, the date of marriage, and the date of birth for a first child—in effect, the timing of a series of transitions during early adulthood (Caspi, Elder, & Bem, 1988). Beyond this age level, however, issues of stability or change are not pursued.

Studies emphasizing the earlier parts of life, however, are not the only ones to show particular concentrations on specific age groups. The same phenomenon appears in studies of adulthood. The initial focus was on middle adulthood (e.g., longitudinal studies that ranged up to age 60), followed by a rise of interest in later age groups (the "young-old" and the "old-old," with the latter starting at perhaps 75 or 80). Currently, the "old-old" appear to attract particular attention. This is in part because they represent a rapidly growing segment of the population in many countries, making it no longer reasonable to stop one's study of development at the ages of 65 or 70. More conceptually, the old-old raise again the possibility of rapid internal change (this time in the form of possible decline). Although this current keen interest in the old-old may weaken, the emphasis on life before 65, including the impact of anticipated or forced retirement, appears to have lost its previous dominance.

Reasons for Divisions   Why does a concentration on particular age periods occur? As a particular case, we ask why a division between studies targeting childhood and those targeting adulthood is so frequent. The problem is not the absence of models that cover both childhood and the several "seasons of adulthood" (Levinson, 1978). Erikson's model of normative "life-crises" covers this range (e.g., Erikson, 1959, 1982). Additional wide-span models have been offered by Loevinger for stages of "ego development" (e.g., Loevinger, 1976), and by Vaillant for "levels of defense mechanisms" (e.g., Vaillant, 1977). Nonetheless, most developmental accounts tend to concentrate on one side of the divide or another, separating childhood from adulthood.

One factor contributing to the division appears to be the nature of the empirical data sought or brought to bear on the conceptual models. The major part of the data used in connection with the Loevinger and the Vaillant models, for example, is drawn from adolescence or young adulthood on, although the models are not restricted to that range. Contributing also are some methodological concerns. Correlations across age tend to become more and more attenuated as the distance between any two ages increases. Also, as the age span spreads out, it becomes increasingly unclear as to whether measures assumed to assess the same construct (e.g., "shyness," "aggression") are actually

equivalent, a problem highlighted by Hartup and van Lieshout (1995). In addition, the relevance of a particular topic, or the problem it implies, may not be the same at one age as at another. Shyness, for example, is a topic that is more easily carried across the life span than, say, physical aggression. In a similar fashion, the effects of peer relationships are more easily pursued across the life span than are the effects of parent-child interactions.

The likelihood of finding variation is a further methodological concern. If, for example, analyzing the nature and bases of change is the primary research interest, there is little to be gained from choosing an age span where the dominant feature is likely to be one of continuity or inertia. Over and above these design-relevant factors, however, there appears to be a general bias towards dividing the field of developmental psychology by age groups. Journals are explicitly labeled as dealing with infancy, childhood, adolescence, adulthood, and aging. The very terms "life course" and "life-span development" are relatively recent incorporations into the vocabulary of most developmental psychologists, and for most the connotation is still a reference to studies of adulthood or even to studies of aging.

Implications of Divisions   Does it matter which age groups or which age span one chooses to work with, either within childhood or adulthood? One implication concerns the phenomena that stand out. One age, for example, may bring out distinctions in relationships that would be less salient at another age. The study of middle childhood, for example, brings out distinctions among varieties of friendship choices and patterns (Hartup, 1996; Newcomb & Bagwell, 1995) that may not be salient distinctions for friendships in late adolescence or adulthood. A second implication concerns the kinds of explanations for change or stability that are likely to arise. Childhood, for instance, is a time when there are major changes in cognitive capacity, together with a vulnerability to be controlled by others (at least, an image of amenability to control). Indeed, events that produce feelings of uncontrollability have been found to depend on the age of the child (Boggiano, Barrett, & Kellam, 1993). Adolescence is a time of possible further cognitive change, together with marked physical changes, and a shift in the degrees of control that others may exert. These age groups then are different from one another, and from most of adulthood, a period when cognitive skill, physical state, and vulnerability to control are relatively stable. In the study of adulthood, then, the nature of task demands and changing circumstances must pick up most of the burden of explanation for change. To use some familiar terms, the social timetable is now likely to matter more than the biological clock. It is only in late adulthood that we see a return of interest to the same set of possible contributors that marks childhood: physical change, a possible shift in cognitive capacity, and a possible increase in vulnerability to attempts by others to control one's life.

In short, some topics and issues invite a concentration on ages where a problem is marked, where change or variation is likely to be a feature, and where a particular type of contributing factor may be explored. At the same time, an age group—once chosen—leads us towards an awareness of some particular facets of development and some particular kinds of explanations.

Small wonder then that developmental psychologists, when they review research in social psychology, are likely to note that the target population of most social psychological studies—young adults—occupies a particular slot in the life span. As Sears (1986) carefully documents, although social psychologists in the 1940s and 1950s often conducted research with adults in natural settings, the 1960s ushered in a period of almost exclusive focus on college students that has continued into the present. This is a time of life, developmentalists would point out, where people have a particular set of concerns or tasks. In a freshman year at college, for example, there will be particular concerns with forming friendships or intimate relationships, establishing a life away from home, learning to swim in an academic environment that presents its incoming members with new comparison groups and probably with new definitions of ability. The data gathered from such populations, developmentalists would continue, must bear the marks of the age group that provides it; the interpretation of the data should surely keep in mind its base in a particular age or life phase. Indeed, Sears (1986) argues that conclusions in the social psychological literature that people readily change their attitudes and behave inconsistently with them may be heavily influenced by the reliance on adolescent populations with less-crystallized attitudes and a less well-formulated sense of self.

Concern with the Nature and Conditions of Change

This general concern is common to both developmental and social psychology. To bring out the features specific to developmental studies and to explain their bases, we break the general concern into three components.

The Nature of the Path Towards an End Point   The term "development" signals an interest in the way personal qualities, skills, or ways of processing change from one time to another, with particular attention given to change that appears to display some direction or course—to be following some kind of path or trajectory, to be moving towards some kind of end-state. This interest in the nature of the path does not assume that the end point is always defined in the same way. We may move towards more flexible processing, a deeper understanding of others, a stronger sense of self, or more differentiated categories than were previously used. The direction need not be towards some "better," more "mature," or more "desirable"

end state, although that direction is often wished for or implied. Even "terminal drop" (the changes that have been reported as occurring in the last few years before death) exhibits a directional quality.

The particular kind of concern social psychologists bring to occasions of change, clearly prominent in studies of social influence and of attitude change, is usually quite different. They are less likely to be interested in the extent to which there is a move towards or away from some particular end point. They do not tend to examine where any specific change fits into some general trajectory, forming part of a linear acceleration, an irregular decline, a plateau, a U-shaped curve, a move towards greater or lesser variability, or, in Robins and Rutter's (1990) phrase, providing "straight" versus "devious paths" from childhood to adulthood. They may, however, attach value judgments to the direction taken. For example, a drop in stereotyping on the basis of gender, race, or ethnicity may be regarded as a desirable change, or one way of acting or thinking may be described as more "basic" or more "primitive" than another (see Ruble & Dweck, 1995, for examples).

Concern with the Order and Sequence of Events   Both developmental and social psychological studies contain an interest in the order and sequence of events—an interest, for example, in the order with which particular ways of thinking, acting, or feeling appear on the scene in the course of working on a task or interacting with others. There are, nonetheless, differences in the way the issue is approached. In particular, there are differences in (a) the kinds of conceptual model likely to be used and (b) the kinds of conditions seen as influencing whether one particular way of acting, thinking, or feeling will appear before another.

Within developmental studies, the conceptual models that stand out stem primarily from a long-standing interest in the question: What happens to an old way of proceeding when a more "mature" way appears? Two broad kinds of answers have emerged. We shall label them as "lost-states" and "repertoire" models.

In the former, the old state is wiped out by the new. Once you understand, for instance, that a person wearing a change of clothes is still the same person, you cannot return to the assumption that a change in appearance creates a new identity. Once you have come to understand that a person can be both a parent and a physician, you cannot return to the earlier conviction that people can occupy only one identity or one social position at a time. This is the kind of model emphasized within most Piagetian approaches to development. It is one of the reasons for studies asking whether various ways of thinking on Piagetian tasks show the properties of a Guttman scale (e.g., Peel, 1959). It also underlies the use of particular Piagetian task procedures (e.g., the use of counter-suggestions or contrary evidence) to check whether traces of the old way of thinking are still present or whether "true conservation" can ever be "extinguished" (e.g., Smedslund, 1961). Moreover, lost states models provoke debates about the implications of findings that older adults may display forms of thinking that appear to be those of children, results that run counter to the expectation that regression does not occur (e.g., Hornblum & Overton, 1976; Labouvie-Vief, 1982).

In contrast, repertoire models allow the old and the new to coexist. By and large, repertoire models have been less prominent within developmental studies than have models implying stage-like shifts. They are, however, very much present. In some early critical comments on Piagetian theory, for example, Susan Isaacs (1929, 1930) proposed that no early state is really lost. We all remain capable of thinking and feeling in "childlike" ways, and we may do so either deliberately or when circumstances reduce our interest in, or our control over, more complex or demanding ways of proceeding.

Coexistence is also part of a distinction drawn, within research on memory, between strategies that are "accessible" (likely to be used on a first try, without prompting) and strategies that are "available" (these appear after some prompting or modeling, but without extensive training). The progression with age is then seen as a shift from a strategy being simply within the repertoire to its spontaneous use (Keniston & Flavell, 1979; Kobasigawa, 1974). Related proposals for coexistence have been offered for levels within the processing of perceptual information (Braine, 1978) and for levels of moral judgment (Colby, Kohlberg, Gibbs, & Liebermann, 1983). (Moral judgments also emerge as less scalable than are judgments in other content areas—Peel, 1959—raising the possibility that the appropriateness of the two models may vary from one content area to another.) On the contemporary scene, repertoire models are especially represented by Siegler's (1995) contrast between "step" models and "wave" models for cognitive strategies. In all these proposals, age is not seen as producing a permanent displacement of one way of proceeding by another but rather as raising one way to temporary dominance over another.

Why does it matter which model of sequence or order is considered? Clearly, the two models present different pictures of the shape that development takes. They also suggest different processes as underlying change. For our purposes, they also make a major difference in the kind of bridge that may exist between developmental and social psychology. The moment that multiple ways of acting, thinking, or feeling become acknowledged, for example, the question promptly arises: Given an available repertoire or bank, what gives rise to one way being accessed or drawn upon rather than another? That question will be instantly familiar to social psychologists. It underlies a variety of social psychological studies of, for example, differences in the accessibility of social constructs, shifts from

heuristic to systematic processing, the impact of overload or affect on the nature of processing, and the impact of priming on social perception.

The two fields, however, may still display differences from one another, even when the shared model is one of coexistence and attention turns to the forms and conditions of coexistence or "concurrence" (Flavell, 1977, p. 294). Developmental psychologists are more likely to look for the influencing conditions within the history of the individual, such as working models developed on the basis of past history, than to explore, say, the priming provided by recent experience or recent instructions. They are also more likely to see "developmental history" as encompassing predispositions present at birth (the wide interest in differences in temperament is an example), and as possibly related to the history of the species. We may at birth, for example, arrive with some individual predispositions toward particular levels of activity, irritability, impulsiveness, or shyness. We may also arrive on the scene with a predisposition to be responsive to social cues or to particular features of faces or particular kinds of speech—a general predisposition that is useful for the survival and health of the species (e.g., Emde, Biringer, Clyman, & Oppenheim, 1991). Recent arguments, however, have attempted to incorporate even these "core" developmental perspectives into social psychological analyses. Costanzo (1992), for example, documents the need to consider developmental histories as shaping the way events are monitored, interpreted, processed, acted upon, or remembered. In addition, the nature-nurture controversy—long a staple concern in developmental studies—is now the subject of considerable controversy in social psychology (e.g., Barkow, Cosmides, & Tooby, 1992; Buss, 1995; see Buss & Kenrick, 1998, in this *Handbook*).

Explaining Change: The Nature of the Concern with Age   As a way to investigate change, developmental psychologists are prone to making comparisons based on differences in age, either cross-sectionally or longitudinally. That inclination in itself may seem to be a feature that makes developmental studies unique. Age, however, is a shorthand variable, used with the understanding that it implies a shift in some underlying state: in the capacity to make sense of events, in the degree of experience, or in the kinds of demands that are being faced and the goals that are likely to be salient. The implication varies with the age of the population. For studies of children and the elderly, for example, the underlying state implied is most often one of capacity: capacity to think through a logical issue, to stay on task, to understand perspectives other than one's own, to regulate feelings and sustain a relatively even emotional keel. For studies of early and middle adulthood, the implication is usually one of changes in demands and opportunities, such as the demand to juggle both family and paid work, or the opportunity to explore a new direction. Conceptualizing age in this way facilitates the link to social psychology in that age-related changes may be seen as quite similar to changes in social context (Higgins & Parsons, 1983).

There are, we should point out, psychologists interested in social development who are unhappy when the analysis stops with comparisons based only on age differences, either cross-sectionally or longitudinally, and who argue for going beyond age as a variable. One way of doing so is to keep age relatively constant and to vary experience. This may be done by training studies or by manipulating the amount of information available. For example, Stangor and Ruble (1989) examined the implications for memory biases of different levels of schema development by varying the amount of schema-relevant knowledge made available to participants. The effects of different levels of experience have also been examined by taking advantage of naturally occurring variations. Parents with and without experience of the school system, for example, may be asked for their views about the capacities of children (e.g., Entwisle & Hayduk, 1978; Mugny & Carugati, 1985). A related type of design involves the study of school transitions, in which age is held constant but children or adolescents who have or have not made a transition are compared (e.g., Alfieri, Ruble, & Higgins, 1996; Seidman, Allen, Aber, Mitchell, & Feinman, 1994; Simmons & Blyth, 1987).

A further way of looking beyond age consists of turning toward variations in social position, a variation implicit in the studies we have just mentioned. An interest in social position is common to both social and developmental psychology, but there are again some points of difference. Social psychologists tend to frame their concern in terms of positions such as actor or observer, superior or subordinate, employer or employee, friend or acquaintance. Developmental psychologists frame their concern more in terms of variations in "developmental tasks," in age- or phase-related role expectations. They are then likely to turn to transitions that alter the nature of a demand, such as the transition from home to school, from primary to high school, from school to paid work, from being without children to being a parent, or from being fully engaged in parenting to returning to study or to paid work. Of course, such transitions also involve major changes in other aspects of the relation between the person and the social environment, shifts in position of the kind that social psychologists most often study (see Ruble & Seidman, 1996, for a review). To illustrate, the transition from primary to high school may move a student from being at the top of one social hierarchy to being at the bottom of another (Higgins & Parsons, 1983), and the transition from married couple to parents may involve disconfirmation of expectancies about joint tasks (Belsky, 1985; Hackel & Ruble, 1992). Developmentalists, however, are less likely to use

such shifts in social position as the starting point for choosing a particular transition than they are to use what they see as a change in the demand or the "developmental task."

Summary

Studies of social development are marked by some particular features that help define the field and that bring out some notable overlaps with studies within social psychology. We have described four such features. Two of them—the topics that are covered, and a mixed research agenda—show considerable overlap across social psychological and developmental approaches. The other two features—the study of a wide age range, and the nature and conditions of change—represent major points of distinction across the two disciplines. Yet, although age and change are not defining features of social psychology, we noted a number of interests among social psychologists that show a strong link to these basic developmental concerns. We by no means wish to imply that the two fields are identical. The overlaps are sufficient, however, to provide a first base for the argument that there are good grounds for social psychologists being interested in developmental studies.

APPROACHES TO THE NATURE OF CHANGE AND VARIATION

We now move further into the developmental field, describing in greater detail some of the major programs of research and issues that mark the field. To do so, we separate two themes: (a) what people seek to account for in the study of social development; and (b) the kinds of accounts they offer. Although these themes are inevitably related to one another, we need a sense of the phenomena that are of interest before we can adequately grasp the accounts of the conditions contributing to change and variation and the processes by which they do so.

We also aim at delineating the dimensions that give a structure to the history of research in this area and to the studies and debates that are appearing on the current scene. The apparent sprawl is not without coherence. We simply need ways of differentiating between one project or one approach and another, allowing us both to recognize some of the distinguishing features across projects or theories and to see the lines along which the field has changed.

Finally, within our coverage of each of the two major sections (what is to be accounted for in this section, and how that might be done in the next) we treat in sequence the "child" literature and the "adult" literature. (Studies that cover the age span after adolescence are placed in the latter group.) We trace the same issues through the two age groups, asking about the extent to which these issues appear in similar or different guises. Rather than flip from one literature to the other with each point, we have found that the material is more coherent, and easier to follow, if we first discuss what studies of childhood and adolescence have contributed and then ask what has been repeated, amended, or added by studies with adults.

We begin with approaches to the task of specifying the nature of change and variation. Developmental studies are differentiated along three dimensions, and landmark studies are noted in relation to each. A brief overview of these dimensions is offered first, followed by a closer look at what each of the selected three dimensions affords.

The first dimension has to do with whether, in any content area, the emphasis is on behavior, cognition, or affect. If we take Hartup and van Lieshout's (1995) "social responsibility" as an example of a content area, the emphasis may fall on the extent to which people behave responsibly, understand their obligations to others, or feel a sense of moral outrage and discomfort when the expected norms are violated. As we shall see, developmental studies often concentrate on one of the three aspects: actions, thoughts, or feelings. The research agenda may, for instance, be directed towards exploring only changes in understanding of obligations, the perspectives of others, or the intentions of others. Whatever, the starting point, however, interest inevitably develops in the interconnections among acting, thinking, and feeling—asking how one gives rise to or sustains the other.

The second dimension involves the extent to which designs and analyses are oriented toward the study of individual differences or normative patterns (Applebaum & McCall, 1983; Maccoby, 1984). Developmental studies sometimes emphasize individual differences and the extent to which they are stable over time. Do differences in reactivity (impulsiveness, shyness), in confidence, or in aggressiveness, for instance, persist from childhood through to later life? Alternatively, the emphasis may fall on normative patterns and the extent to which whole groups of people change as they shift from one age group or one social group to another, such as a move into puberty, into high school, into marriage, or in and out of paid work.

The third dimension involves what several commentators on the field have referred to as a fundamental distinction in the goals of social development (Costanzo, 1992; Damon, 1983). One goal is oriented toward establishing social connection: bringing the individual into the group, teaching conformity to the values and norms necessary to being a productive member of the society and interacting smoothly with others, as well as providing a sense of belonging. A second goal is individuation: developing a sense of oneself as clearly separate and distinct from others, and possessing a personal identity as an individual with a unique set of values, attitudes, and attributes, as well as an underlying essence that remains constant across diverse settings. Although most research topics cannot be categorized easily as addressing only one or the other goal, there

is usually a dominant emphasis, including sometimes an interest in the tension that exists between conforming to socialization pressures and being "one's own person."

Dimension 1: A Focus on Behavior, Cognition, and Affect

The degree of emphasis placed on each of these aspects is a feature that differentiates among projects on the current scene and reflects historical shifts. The historical portrait portrayed by the four *Annual Review* chapters, for example, suggests that between 1960 and the present, there was a relative shift from a focus on behavior, then cognition, and most recently, affect. More generally, the initial focus of studies of social development has usually been on behavior: the ability of a child to initiate friendships, for instance, or the extent to which the social contacts of an adult in late life showed a shrinkage over time. Subsequently, the research in an area tends to incorporate a concern with cognition (e.g., the understanding of authority, the kinds of social comparisons that are made, or with the meanings attributed to a change in health) and a concern with affect (e.g., the degree of satisfaction experienced with oneself or with the quality of one's life). Each of these concerns may be considered singly. Attention may be restricted, for example, to changes in the depth with which a social event is understood. Alternately, and increasingly over the course of social developmental studies, the emphasis falls on the way aspects are intercorrelated: on the extent, for example, to which cognitive changes are correlated with the regulation of emotion or the flexibility of action.

One advantage of examining social development in terms of these groupings is that it facilitates the observation of common courses of development, thereby providing insight about underlying process. For example, if certain kinds of social-cognitive realizations, such as gender constancy, racial constancy, or particular forms of theory of mind, tend to co-occur between ages four and six years, this signals the likely benefit of considering the common properties of these events for understanding the mechanisms of change. The absence of such connections is equally enlightening theoretically. For example, several early studies were guided by the hypothesis that a child's "identification" with a parent at five and six years of age underlies the development of several different actions. A boy closely identified with his father, for example, would exhibit highly masculine behavior and be able to resist temptation. These diverse aspects of behavior, however, turned out to be uncorrelated for the most part (see Maccoby, 1980, for a review), leading to considerable theoretical upheaval over the nature and significance of identification.

Within Studies of Childhood and Adolescence

Studies Focused on Changes in Behavior   In early research, the major behaviors of interest were closely related to the issues of family socialization and discipline. These included different aspects of moral behavior and self-regulation, such as resistance to temptation and reparation for wrongdoing (LaVoie, 1974), compliance (Minton, Kagan, & Levine, 1971), and delay of gratification (Mischel & Ebbesen, 1970). Basically, the questions at this time were how to shape children's behaviors to conform to societal standards and values. Depending upon theoretical orientations, researchers examined how parental practices (Sears, Rau, & Alpert, 1965), situational variations (Hartshorne & May, 1929), or modeling (Hoffman, 1970) affected these behaviors. Some influential conclusions, which were viewed with at least some surprise at the time, included: (a) that induction (reasoning) disciplinary techniques were often more effective than love withdrawal and physical punishment in producing more mature moral responses (Hoffman, 1970); (b) that a warning before an infraction occurred was more effective than discipline after (Aronfreed, 1968), and (c) that conditions that prompted distraction from thinking about a desirable object were most effective in promoting delay of gratification (Mischel & Ebbesen, 1970).

Subsequent research interests extended well beyond concerns of moral conduct and discipline during early childhood to examine broader issues of interpersonal functioning, such as aggression, friendship strategies and social competence, and prosocial behavior and altruism, as well as their manifestation in later childhood and adolescence. One of the most active areas of research during the past fifteen years has concerned the development of peer relationships: what behaviors distinguish accepted from rejected children, what kinds of acquaintance behaviors lead to friendships, and what kinds of behaviors represent competent social functioning (Collins & Gunnar, 1990; Parke & Asher, 1983). Contributing to this interest were findings from the clinical literature that peer rejection in childhood is a risk factor for mental illness in adolescence and adulthood (Kupersmidt, Coie, & Dodge, 1990; Parker & Asher, 1987).

Unlike most studies of interpersonal relationships among adults, much of the research with children provided detailed behavioral accounts of the development of relationships over time. For example, in an influential study, Gottman (1983) followed pairs of previously unacquainted children over time and described the nature of behavioral changes at both a macro and micro level in an attempt to understand why some pairs continued as friends and others did not. To illustrate, one key observation was that the establishment of "common ground" early in the relationship (i.e., behaviors that facilitated the identification of areas of common interest) tended to lead to a friendship. Other research has shown that aggression and disruptiveness are the characteristics most highly associated with peer rejection (Coie & Dodge, 1997). In addition, unpopular children tend to exhibit ineffective social strategies. For example, Putallaz and Gottman (1981) found that when attempting to enter a group of children already at play, unpopular children tended to exhibit behaviors that drew attention to the self rather than trying to blend into the activity presently engaging the group.

One question, of course, is whether ineffective social behavior produces the rejection or is an outcome of it (Parke & Asher, 1983). In some creative research, new groups have been formed in order to examine the emergence of social status and social behaviors. Such studies suggest that the actions of rejected children do indeed elicit rejection, because low social status tends to follow them even into a completely new group of peers (e.g., Coie & Kupersmidt, 1983). Moreover, other research suggests that some types of social skills training can change the social status of rejected children (Coie & Koeppl, 1990).

One limitation to much of the research on peer relationships, to date, is that it has tended to assume a kind of deficit model of interpersonal competence—that although more effective social behaviors can be taught, their lack is largely a matter of capacity or temperament. An additional possibility involves interpersonal goals and motivation (Parke & Asher, 1983; Ruble & Thompson, 1992). Like interest in achievement-related activities, motivation for interpersonal interaction may be undermined by conditions that promote feelings that one is engaging in the social behavior for extrinsic reasons (Pittman, Boggiano, & Main, 1992). For example, Boggiano, Klinger, and Main (1986) found that children's intrinsic interest in peer interaction was reduced when adults provided an extrinsic reason for the interaction (e.g., "because you can play with his new toys"). Interestingly, an awareness of the instrumental or strategic aspects of relationships appears to emerge after the early elementary school years (Thompson, Boggiano, Costanzo, Matter, & Ruble, 1995), suggesting perhaps that intrinsic interest in social relationships of younger children would be less affected by conditions highlighting extrinsic reasons for a relationship. Indeed, the effects reported above in the Boggiano et al. (1986) study held for nine-year-olds but not for children seven years and younger.

Studies of Cognitive Change   Traditionally, a distinction between "social" and "cognitive" development has always been a part of developmental psychology. The two could be kept neatly separate as long as one was regarded as dealing with logical skills and the other with social skills. That sharp division, however, became less sharp once it was recognized that social actions and social skills often depended on the way situations were understood and an area emerged with the label "social cognition"—broadly, cognition that is concerned with the ways in which we understand the nature of people (oneself or others), of relationships (the nature, for example, of friendships or family), and of social events or social structures (the understanding, for example, of options in the area of education or paid work).

There are two lines of interest in social cognition. One originates from Piagetian theory. It concentrates on changes in the level of understanding, on the capacity to combine disparate pieces of information into some coherent pattern. The two most prominent early examples are the extensive research programs on moral judgment and role taking. For example, Piaget's (1932) book on moral judgment led to a series of studies concerned with when and why young children make judgments about a social or moral violation more in terms of outcomes than in terms of underlying intentions. Much of this research has focused on revealing the limitations of Piaget's methodology, much like the extensive criticism of Piaget's theory in the domain of cognitive development (e.g., Gelman & Baillargeon, 1983). The results of several studies revealed that young children were able to detect variations in intentionality when proper designs were employed (Costanzo & Dix, 1983), and to use intentionality more when positive outcomes were being judged (Costanzo, Coie, Grumet, & Farnill, 1973) and when the order of presenting outcome and intentionality information was reversed (Feldman, Klosson, Parsons, Rholes, & Ruble, 1976), among other numerous situational variations. The basic conclusion from these studies was that children under seven years could base moral judgments on intentions as well as outcomes under certain circumstances. The question about whether they normally did so and how such judgments affected their daily interpersonal interactions, however, was left unresolved.

Since these early forays into the development of children's social knowledge in a few areas, interest in normative developmental changes in social understanding has increased enormously. Illustrative topics are knowledge about gender (e.g., Kohlberg, 1966), friendships (Youniss, 1980), social roles (Watson & Fisher, 1980), personal characteristics (Damon, 1977; Livesley & Bromley, 1973), achievement motivation and ability (Dweck, 1991; Nicholls, 1978), kinship networks (Jordan, 1980), economic needs (Siegal, 1981), and work (Bowes & Goodnow, 1996). The study of moral judgments also showed a number of shifts in emphasis and paradigm, first in the extensive study of Kohlberg's (1964) principles of moral reasoning as they extend into adulthood, and then into the separation of true moral judgments (e.g., about cheating and stealing) from judgments of social conventions (e.g., Turiel, 1983).

The second line of interest involves analyses of information processing. We take as an example the studies of aggressive behaviors among boys by Coie, Dodge, and their colleagues (see Coie & Dodge, 1997, for a review). The earlier landmark studies by Patterson concentrated on behaviors: the interwoven sequence of acts taken by a parent and a child, with particular attention to the points at which one responded to the other and to the presence of escalation (e.g., Patterson, 1982). In contrast, Dodge and

Coie looked at the way highly aggressive boys differed from their peers in the way they interpreted situations involving ambiguous provocations, perceiving them as occasions of hostility and reacting accordingly (e.g., Dodge, Coie, Pettit, & Prince, 1990). Recently, such analyses have been extended in a couple of interesting new directions: (a) aggressive-rejected children may be unaware of their social status because of self-protective biases in processing negative peer feedback (Zakriski & Coie, 1996); and (b) aggressiveness in boys is associated with differences in the way incoming information about an ambiguous aggressive act is organized, as assessed with a standard behavior segmentation procedure (Courtney & Cohen, 1996).

One interesting aspect about research on developmental social cognition is the unclear or uneasy relation between the social and cognitive aspects of the term. Are we studying cognitive aspects of social development or social aspects of cognitive development? Despite a few calls to take the social aspects of social-cognition seriously (e.g., Brehm et al., 1981; Higgins, Ruble, & Hartup, 1983), this area of research has generally been thought of as part of the cognitive domain. Both social-cognition chapters in the most recent editions of the *Handbook of Child Psychology* have been placed in the cognitive rather than the social volumes (Flavell, 1997; Shantz, 1983). Flavell (1977), for example, puts both physical and social cognition under the heading of cognitive change, but points out that the two differ in the conditions under which information is obtained. To take one point of difference, in contrast to rocks and other physical objects, people can influence a child's ability to recognize a distinction between appearance and reality by withholding or disguising information.

A recent infusion of sociocultural approaches to understanding cognition has brought out several alternative perspectives on the connection between what is "cognitive" and what is "social." This infusion is occurring both in the social psychological literature (e.g., Kitayama & Markus, 1994, see chapter on "The Cultural Perspective" in Vol. 1) and in the developmental literature (e.g., Cole, 1988; Goodnow, Miller, & Kessel, 1995; Rogoff, 1990; Wertsch, 1991). We single out two proposals. One is that social factors determine where we place any cognitive effort and the kind of effort we make. In the course of everyday life, for instance, we learn to distinguish between what is "trivial" and what is "significant," between what we need to learn and what we may treat as areas of "acceptable ignorance" (Goodnow, 1996). In addition, we learn when we should strive towards a conventional view of events and when some originality is tolerated or accepted. In most family situations, for instance, there is less parental pressure for conformity to the usual explanations of what rocks are made of than there is to understanding what it means to be honest or to be male or female (Goodnow, Knight, & Cashmore, 1985). The second proposal is broader. All thinking and all learning take place in a social context of some kind. We do not simply learn to read; we also learn what reading is "for" (Scribner & Cole, 1981). Even the experimental situations that appear to require thinking "by oneself" are socially structured. They are marked by implicit contracts indicating who should do what, how much help can be given, when we should speak up, and when a task may be ended. What may appear to be a change in logical capacity, then, may in fact be a change in the extent to which the implicit contract—the nature of what is expected—is understood (e.g., Perret-Clermont, Perret, & Bell, 1991).

Part of that "social" argument also points to the importance of specific expertise. It is accepted that one factor contributing to any kind of change may be some large-scale general changes in the capacity to put together various viewpoints or various pieces of information. That factor, however, is also influenced by variations in the knowledge base that people bring to various topics, a knowledge base that reflects social experience and social pressures as well as general cognitive development.

Studies Focused on Changes in Affect   As noted in the earlier comment on the four *Annual Review* pieces on social development, interest in affect and emotion has surged (Collins & Gunnar, 1990; Parke & Asher, 1983). Why has it gained prominence in recent years? What is its contribution? In part, it is seen as a form of social development in itself. Emotional expression and perception are fundamental aspects of connection to others, and there has been considerable interest in describing the natural course of emotional development and in analyzing the processes that influence it. Because one central issue has involved the relative influence of biological versus social construction processes, a large proportion of the research effort has focused on infants and young children (Collins & Gunnar, 1990). For example, Izard and Malatesta (1987) suggest that basic emotions have distinct neural circuits and that emotional state can be assessed from universal facial expressions. In contrast, constructivist accounts (Lewis & Michaelson, 1983; Sroufe, 1979) view biological factors as basic elements that then become emotional constructions as a result of early experiences and cognitive appraisals. In a recent review, Thompson (1993) argues that this focus on structure, or the ontogenesis of differentiated emotions, has given way to more functionalist accounts, in which emotions serve personal goals and motivations and regulate social behavior, such as interactions with parents, aggression, and altruism. The regulatory function can be seen in children's reactions to their own experiences of an emotion; anger or empathy, for example, affects their likelihood of engaging in prosocial or antisocial behavior (Eisenberg & Fabes, 1997). This function may also be seen in the impact of others' emotions on choices and behaviors. Through this "social referencing," children can use the emotional reac-

tions of others to decide whether to approach or avoid a novel situation or object (e.g., Klinnert, Emde, Butterfield, & Campos, 1986). In this sense, then, emotional development is important not only as an aspect of social experience in its own right, but also because it is seen as the engine that drives the rest—promoting action, or underlying continuity in thought or action.

One particularly noteworthy line of contemporary research is concerned with the development of emotion regulation capabilities and strategies (Thompson, 1993). This area of inquiry is linked to various early theoretical and empirical efforts to understand the emergence of self-control. Perhaps most familiar is psychoanalytic theorizing about how the development of the ego and superego gradually allow the child to gain some control over the primitive emotions that characterize the id. A pivotal empirical precursor is Mischel's analysis of conditions that promote children's abilities to delay gratification, to forego a small but immediate reward and wait for a delayed but larger one (e.g., Mischel & Ebbesen, 1970).

A continuing interest in self-regulation of emotion is not surprising, given the widely held view that strong emotions disrupt goal-oriented activities. A child who responds with overwhelming sadness to the distress of her friend, for example, may be too incapacitated to respond with needed assistance (Eisenberg & Fabes, 1997). Recent empirical and theoretical work has sought the strategies available to children to manage (primarily unwanted) emotions, and how these change with age (Kopp, 1989; Masters, 1991). Young infants can respond to over-arousal by gaze aversion whereas older infants can engage in self-soothing (Mangelsdorf, Shapiro, & Marzolf, 1995); toddlers and young children can utilize behavioral distraction—active engagement with alternative objects (Altshuler & Ruble, 1989; Grolnick, Bridges, & Connell, 1996); and older children may engage in cognitive distraction (Band & Weisz, 1988). Curiously, although a large number of strategies for managing emotions has been identified, the developmental research has made relatively little contact with the extensive social psychological literature on coping (e.g., Lazarus & Folkman, 1984; Taylor, 1983). This is unfortunate, in part because some of the distinctions in the literature, such as between controllable and uncontrollable stressors, may be essential to understanding developmental processes in how best to cope with negative emotions (Miller & Green, 1985). Moreover, a picture of developmental priorities may be enlightening to social psychological accounts by providing information about more primitive strategies that might be called into service under extreme conditions.

A final point of interest for the present concern with linking the child and adult literatures involves what might be called the flip side of emotion regulation—enhancing rather than minimizing arousal. As Thompson (1993) notes, the present emphasis on inhibition of emotional reactions may be partly due to the cultural emphasis on self-control, at least for North American researchers. Yet, there are times when knowing how to enhance an emotion, such as anger, may yield some benefit for social interaction in particular contexts. This idea of a strategic use of enhancing emotions also provides a nice bridge to recent work in social psychology concerned with anticipatory coping, knowing when, for example, one feels sufficiently strong emotionally to accept news that will have a negative emotional impact (Trope & Neter, 1994). Moreover, it is interesting to speculate that there may be points during the life span when emotional enhancement may be a goal in itself. This would seem especially likely during mid-life, when one's basic life goals have been realized, or at least as realized as they can be, and emotions are no longer a threat to goal attainment. At such times, one may allow intense emotion to continue rather than trying to control it in the service of action, even possibly accepting strong negative as well as positive emotions as enriching life's experiences. Middle-aged men, for instance, may feel the liberty to cry in public. Perhaps findings of a reduction in the number of interpersonal relationships among older individuals (Carstensen, 1995) may be interpreted in this context—i.e., as reflecting a desire for intensity rather than variety of emotional experiences.

Within Studies of Adulthood   What do studies of adulthood add to the picture generated by studies targeting children and adolescents? We shall again divide studies in terms of whether the primary focus is on behavior, cognition, or affect. Cutting across the three divisions, however, the reader will note a particular attention to some recurring themes: the extent to which change is general or varies from one content area to another; the extent to which a particular way of acting, thinking, or feeling is sustained over time; and, especially in late life, the use of ways of acting, thinking, and feeling as measures of "healthy" adjustment or of "successful aging" (a concern that, like the concern with whether changes are sustained over time, often springs from the underlying assumption that changes are more likely to be "losses" than "gains").

Studies Focused on Changes in Behavior   As in studies with younger populations, these studies cover a wide variety of topics. We select three as a base for bringing out what studies of adulthood add to the earlier picture. The three are prosocial behaviors, aggression, and involvement in interpersonal relationships.

Studies of prosocial behavior (see Batson, 1998, in this *Handbook*) are less prominent within research on adulthood than they are within studies of child development, unless one includes a body of work on the general nature of caring (e.g., Gilligan & Attanucci, 1988) and on the specific issue of caring for or about frail parents (e.g., Finch & Groves, 1983; Finch & Mason, 1993). One novel point to

emerge, however, is a sharp concern with the extent to which multiple measures yield the same patterns of relationships to age. Within studies of generosity, for example, the measure may be one of contributions to charitable organizations in the form of time (e.g., Hodgkinson & Weitzman, 1988) or in the form of money (e.g., Hodgkinson & Weitzman, 1988; Midlarsky & Hannah, 1989). The results do not point towards some simple trait of concern for others, cutting across all manifestations of concern. Contributions of time show a peak around the ages 35–44 years. Contributions of money, in relation to income, rise with age over a comparison of ages 15 to 75 plus, with a possible plateau in the 35–44 age group.

Studies of aggression (see Geen, 1998, in this *Handbook*) in relation to age also display a lower frequency than they do in analyses of childhood, perhaps because the incidence of all forms of acting-out deviance (e.g., drug use, theft, sexual promiscuity, drinking, fighting, in the list generated by Robins, 1978) declines over the course of adulthood. The topic is still very much present, however. It is, for instance, at the core of studies exploring the extent to which childhood behaviors and childhood experiences predict aggressive behaviors as a young adult (e.g., Caspi, Elder, & Bem, 1987; Eron, Huesmann, Dubow, Romanoff, & Yarmel, 1987). There is as well a marked interest in qualities such as assertiveness and concern for power, perhaps the adult equivalent of what is labeled "aggression" at younger ages. The novel feature to note is the degree of interest in the extent to which aggressive or assertive actions are negatively related over time to other kinds of actions. That concern is by no means unknown in studies with children. Dishion, Andrews, and Crosby (1995), for example, take up that issue when they ask whether aggressive boys are also isolates. (As it turns out, they are not friendless; their friendships, however, are with other aggressive boys). Within studies of adult change, however, there is a frequent concern with the extent to which common paths occur for interests in power and in affiliation, often linked to questions about the extent to which these paths are similar for males and for females. The cross-sectional studies by Veroff and his colleagues provide an example (Veroff, Reuman, & Feld, 1984). The data come from TAT stories, generated by people aged 21 to 55 plus, and scored for a variety of themes (e.g., affiliation, achievement, fear of weakness, hope for power). On themes of affiliation, men showed no differences across the age groups, whereas women showed a decline. On themes involving a hope for power, women showed no differences across age groups, whereas men showed a peak in the 35–44 age group, with a decline after that point. The specific patterns, one suspects, would vary with cultural subgroups and with cohorts.

Of the three topics, involvement in interpersonal relationships has attracted the widest attention. One reason for this is that studies of this topic highlight the issue of sustained action or sustained commitment. An example of particular interest is a study by Finch and Mason (1993), which asks who manages to sustain involvement in the care of elderly parents who need physical or emotional assistance. Individual differences on this score were marked (no particular normative pattern is proposed). Contributing strongly to the variations were several factors. One was the perception of action as a form of duty or as an expression of love (both may help sustain involvement but alter its form). Another was the perception of involvement as appropriate to one's gender (males were less likely, as a group, to sustain commitment to behaviors that are not within the conventional picture of male patterns of providing care). A third was the perception of alternatives. Contrary to what one might expect, Finch and Mason's (1993) study suggests that the perception of there being no alternatives (that is, no other family member with whom to share the work or provide a break from its demands) promotes reluctance to take on involvement rather than an acceptance of the task.

Involvement in interpersonal relationships is also at the heart of concern as to whether late-life brings with it an increasing restriction in the extent to which action is taken: a restriction sometimes referred to as "disengagement" (Cumming & Henry, 1961). Since the first introduction of the proposal, there has been considerable debate as to whether, when, and why "disengagement" occurs. Overall, the data suggest that "disengagement" may be too global a term. Instead, what is strongly indicated is a pattern of increasing selectivity, with people increasingly engaging only in interactions that they have reason to expect will be emotionally rewarding (Carstensen, 1993; Frederickson & Carstensen, 1990). This pattern, these researchers propose, is in line with a change in needs and goals over the life-course. Novelty, for instance, may be a goal in social interactions at a younger age but becomes less appealing as people grow older. The pattern is also in line with evidence of selectivity in other cognitive areas—for example, in the choice of which intellectual skills to maintain and which to let slide (Baltes, Dittmann-Kohli, & Dixon, 1984). In effect, a pattern of selective maximization and reduction may account for change in several areas, with the choice of what is maximized or reduced probably reflecting what is important or open to the individual.

Both selective and sustained action are of particular interest because of the potential link they offer to some social psychological analyses of behavior. Within social psychology, adults' actions are often regarded as organized around goals. Two approaches stand out. In one, the model of action is of a "vertical, hierarchical nature. . . . the individual advances from a concern with abstract, super-ordinate, higher-order goals to concrete, subordinate, lower-level goals" (Gollwitzer, 1990, p. 60). In the other, the model of action emphasizes "horizontal" or temporal phases of "de-

liberating, planning, acting and evaluating" (Gollwitzer, 1990, p. 60). In the particular temporal model known as the Rubicon model (e.g., Heckhausen & Gollwitzer, 1987), the metaphor of crossing the Rubicon is used to describe a point where deliberation with regard to pros and cons is put to rest and the individual displays commitment to a goal, making attempts to "conquer hindrances by spontaneously increasing effort, employing different means, taking more time to overcome hindrances, or trying to get around them by taking alternate routes" (Gollwitzer, 1990, p. 62). Commitment in this sense, Gollwitzer points out, is similar to conceptualizations of commitment and sustained action within analyses of relationships or ties to an organization. Some analysts of commitment to organizations would add some further phases to the model: phases involving the occurrence at some point of a reassessment of what crossing the Rubicon has involved, followed by either an affirmation of commitment or the decision to exit (e.g., Levine & Moreland, 1991). Either form of a temporally organized phase model of action, however, would offer a specific bridge between social and developmental studies of the forms that actions and changes in action may take.

Studies Focused on Changes in Cognition   In reviewing the literature on developmental changes in cognition, we again select some features that help bring out the structure of research in the area and that add to what has already been discussed regarding studies with younger populations. The first feature is an interest in the question: Is there a change in the content of what is thought about (as against a change in the way thinking proceeds)? Late-life, for instance, has been proposed as a time when there is an increase in the extent to which people engage in life review (e.g., Erikson, 1982) or a decrease in thinking about a possible future self, about the person that one might be (Ryff, 1991).

A second feature echoes one often found in studies with younger populations: Is change generalized or content-specific? That question in the adult research is usually asked, however, with decline rather than growth in mind. Is there a general slowing or a general loss of cognitive resources? Are there some areas of knowledge and skill that do not display this pattern? This issue underlies several comparisons of fluid with crystallized intelligence (e.g., Schaie, 1990) (fluid intelligence typically shows a decline in late life; crystallized intelligence is more likely to remain stable). It also underlies a particular search for areas where an increase may be found, providing evidence for adulthood as displaying a pattern of "gains and losses" (Heckhausen, Dixon, & Baltes, 1989). "Wisdom" has been one candidate for a possible increase (e.g., Staudinger, 1996). The capacity to plan a life course or to choose well between alternative life courses has been another (e.g., Smith, 1996). The ability to "read" the emotions of others has been a third (e.g., Malatesta, Izard, Culver, & Nicolich, 1987). The overall pattern of results takes the interesting form described by Pratt and Norris (1994, p. 92): "people of all ages are apparently 'better' at understanding the perspectives and qualities of their same age peers than those of other age groups." In effect, social understanding appears to be age-specific rather than cumulative.

There is, however, one relatively robust finding within the several searches for areas where older adults outperform younger adults. Older adults produce personal narratives (life stories) that are more likely to be rated as well-constructed and effective than are the stories produced by younger adults (Dittmann-Kohli, 1990; Kemper, Rash, Kynette, & Norman, 1990; Pratt & Robins, 1991). The performance of older adults, Dittmann-Kohli (1990) suggests, may reflect the wish to create order at a time of one's life when uncontrollable changes in physical states and the external environment are occurring.

Dittmann-Kohli's (1990) comment foreshadows the last special feature to studies of cognitive changes in adulthood. This is an interest in the extent to which people as they grow older use particular cognitive strategies in order to cope with events in their lives. In addition to arranging their life narratives into a better story form, older adults may stretch out the age range over which they see a variety of qualities—intellectual and personal—as open to change (Heckhausen et al., 1989). They may also change their ideas about the ages at which people are "young" or "old," with a bias towards perceiving as "young" either their own age group in general or themselves in relation to their peers (e.g., Montepare & Lachman, 1989). In short, what emerges in studies of adulthood is a picture of cognition that is close to the picture offered within social psychology of motivated cognition; people possess in their repertoire a variety of cognitive procedures and make choices among these "based on goals, motives, and needs" (Fiske & Taylor, 1991, p. 13).

Studies Focused on Changes in Affect   In the section on studies of affective changes during childhood, we noted one possibility that might cut across age periods. This is the possibility that, at various times in one's life, one may seek intensity in affect, even if the affect is potentially negative. What is avoided is blandness.

At this point, we know little about the conditions under which that aspect of affective life may occur. Evidence suggests that blandness does not characterize emotional expressiveness on the part of older adults. On the contrary, they emerge as more expressive than their younger counterparts (Malatesta-Magai, Jonas, Sheperd, & Culver, 1992).

Overall, there is a shortage of studies dealing with the ways in which particular emotions, or particular levels of emotion, are experienced or evaluated over the life course. In contrast, there are many studies asking whether age dur-

ing adult life brings with it changes in general satisfaction, subjective well-being, or distress. An occasional question is raised about the adequacy of global measures (e.g., Rook, 1987) but their attractiveness remains.

A frequent assumption in this area is that the loss of youth, the exposure to negative stereotypes of aging, and the expectable increase in health problems will inevitably bring a decline in happiness. Happiness in later life is then seen as a "paradox" (Baltes & Baltes, 1990), explained either in terms of the self-concept remaining essentially unchanged (e.g., Costa & McCrae, 1984) or in terms of revisions in expectations or self-image being made in the course of gradual and normative changes with age (e.g., Whitbourne, 1985). The assumption of loss and of the need for protection against loss and the threat that change presents is in fact so widespread that we single out a thread of research that argues for occasions of an increase in positive feeling over the course of adulthood. This thread has to do with people—women especially—who experience a change in life course, either by choice or as the result of losing a partner. Mixed in with the sense of difficulty and loss, it has been pointed out, are often feelings of renewal, and of "reclaimed powers" (Gutmann, 1987), and of pleasure over the acquisition of some new or forgotten forms of competence (e.g., Allen, 1989; Mathews, 1991; Silverman, 1987).

Before we conclude, however, that the expectation of inevitable loss reflects a youth-oriented society, it is worth noting that the expectation may not be unique to changes in adult age. At all ages, global measures of well-being are popular as measures of how well people cope with transitions of various types (Ruble & Seidman, 1996). The pervasive assumption appears to be that transitions are always crises; they are negative events to be overcome. It would be more effective, Ruble and Seidman (1996) propose, to regard transitions at any age as having the potential to produce positive affect or liberating attempts at restructuring one's life and identity rather than prompting only feelings of loss or disruption.

Dimension 2: Attention to Individual Differences versus Normative Variation

Developmental studies sometimes emphasize individual differences and ask about the extent to which these are stable over time. When and why, for example, do childhood differences in reactivity (impulsiveness, shyness), in confidence, in assertiveness, or in aggression arise? Do they persist into later life? Alternatively, the emphasis may fall on normative patterns and the extent to which whole groups of people change as they shift from one age group to another or from one life phase to another, as they move into puberty, into high school, into marriage, into parenting, or in and out of paid work. Partly because of its origins in practical concerns, most early social developmental research focused on questions about how to promote optimal functioning, and asked what processes lead to individual differences in aggression, moral behavior, or achievement motivation. The subsequent influences of ethological and cognitive development approaches, however, led to an increased emphasis on normative developmental changes, often in the same topics.

It may be misleading, however, to think of these directions of interest as aligned neatly with assumptions about the underlying bases of social development—that interest in individual differences is necessarily linked to variations in experiences and interest in normative patterns to the unfolding of some biological pattern. In fact, the alignment is more complex and more interesting. A focus on individual differences may accompany an interest in biologically based differences in temperament as well as in parental methods, for example. Similarly, in addition to ethological influences, a focus on normative patterns may be based on the view that the shift reflects a change in the nature of the social demands or situations that are being encountered, and would alter if these demands changed. In these broader senses, the normative versus individual difference perspective within social development nicely parallels the situation versus individual difference distinction within social-personality psychology.

Within Studies of Children and Adolescents   Attention to the distinction between normative and individual difference patterns has considerable heuristic value. Because studies of individual differences may focus on a relatively small proportion of the population, such as extremely shy or rejected children, whereas studies of normative change focus on averages, quite different conclusions may be drawn about the same topic from studies taking the different approaches. Let us illustrate this point with reference to research on the emergence of maladaptive (helpless) reactions to failure, such as self-denigration, negative affect, and performance impairment, and its relation to children's social perceptions.

Studies of normative development have emphasized age-related changes in children's perceptions of ability. The basic idea is that the emphasis of children's conceptions of people change between preschool and the middle elementary school years from concrete, external characteristics, such as appearance and behaviors, to more abstract, internal qualities, such as goals and traits (Livesley & Bromley, 1973; Rholes, Newman, & Ruble, 1990). The implication of this latter change is that children may not view ability as a stable characteristic until seven to nine years of age, and thus may not view their failures as having long-term repercussions. Consequently, according to this reasoning, children's maladaptive responses to failure should increase in conjunction with this change in social percep-

tion, because failure is now viewed as having much more significant consequences than before. Consistent with this reasoning, several studies have found that such helpless reactions to failure increase between five and ten years of age and are related to perceptions of people's behavior as stable (Boggiano et al., 1993; Miller, 1985; Rholes, Blackwell, Jordan, & Walters, 1980; Rholes, Jones, & Wade, 1988). This line of reasoning and associated set of findings has been interpreted as suggesting that young children do not see failure as reflecting fixed traits and are thus relatively invulnerable to failure experiences.

In contrast, an individual differences approach by Dweck and colleagues (Heyman, Dweck, & Cain, 1992; Smiley & Dweck, 1994) led to quite different conclusions. They have found clear indications of a helpless pattern in four- to five-year-olds. The pattern appears in a minority of the sample, but they do exhibit the same evidence of self-denigration and lack of persistence in response to failure or criticism that characterizes the helpless pattern found with older children (Dweck, 1991). In addition, these responses are linked to beliefs about the self. A focus on individual differences rather than average changes, therefore, led to a conclusion that the helpless pattern may be observed considerably earlier than previously thought. Moreover, it appears to be relatively stable and related to a particular set of social perceptions.

One way to look upon these different conclusions is to assume that one is right and one is wrong: either children begin to exhibit helpless responding during preschool or not until they have stable concepts of ability. Instead, we are suggesting that both approaches are needed to provide a complete picture, namely, that a relatively small number of children show the pattern at an early age but that age-related changes in social perceptions are likely to lead to increased maladaptive responses to failure. Indeed, recent evidence supports the idea that individual differences and conceptions of ability interact in influencing children's reactions to failure (Pomerantz & Ruble, in press). We would argue further than putting the two approaches side-by-side raises a number of issues not present by considering either one alone. Specifically, what is the process that governs maladaptive responding to failure? If young children do not perceive ability in stable terms, why would they respond maladaptively to failure? Is it possible that young children have more sophisticated perceptions than previously thought or that some other process underlies maladaptive responding?

Such issues were recently considered by Ruble and Dweck (1995), who examined the intersection of the normative and the individual difference approaches as part of a review of the literature on perceptions of stable traits and their consequences. Their proposal, still awaiting further empirical substantiation, was that preschool children do view people's characteristics in ways that may lead to extremely negative reactions to failure but that do not involve perceptions of stable traits. Specifically, whereas helpless reactions for older children are accompanied by conclusions that they are not smart, the concomitant conclusions for younger children involve a much more global, evaluative self-conception—that they are "bad." This focus on goodness is perhaps not surprising. Socializing agents are actively engaged in teaching preschoolers how to distinguish good and bad, right and wrong, and observations of young children indicate that they are highly concerned with being "good," conforming to what they perceive as the adult norms for proper behavior. When performance at a task is linked to being "good," therefore, young children may feel quite threatened by not meeting the adult standard provided.

Thus, a joint consideration of normative and individual difference approaches led to a recognition of seemingly contradictory conclusions about developmental changes in motivational processes. It also raised questions about the bases of helpless patterns in younger and older children and to a proposed resolution: that helplessness in young children is associated with a belief in a kind of stable characteristic, but one that relates to global goodness or badness, not intelligence. This suggestion, in turn, has implications for the literature on developmental changes in person perception. Specifically, it suggests that in apparent contrast to the conclusions of the normative approaches reported earlier (e.g., Rholes et al., 1990), preschool children may appear to show traitlike thinking for some behaviors: those that are global and evaluative in nature. Indeed, there is considerable evidence that young children make stable, traitlike predictions for behaviors that have a clear evaluative component, such as helpful or selfish, and that a high proportion of young children's open-ended descriptions of others are either global (nice) or conduct-relevant evaluations (messy) (Ruble & Dweck, 1995). Such findings may not reflect actual traitlike thinking, however, in the sense of perceiving the behavior in terms of enduring internal states that predispose individuals to behave in certain ways (Trope & Higgins, 1993). Instead, when young children exhibit signs of perceiving stability of behavior, it may reflect consistency in evaluations as good or bad (or even likability), instead of recognizing an internal state that drives behavior across situations.

Studies of Adulthood Social developmental studies of older samples also contain an interest in both normative patterns and in individual differences. What do these studies add to the kinds of points already made? Overall, what stands out is the frequent presence of reservations about normative patterns, accompanied by a concern that preoccupation with them may be deflecting attention from the presence of variability.

As an opening example, we may take proposals for the existence of a normative sequence in grief reactions after the death of a partner. On the one hand, there are proposals for stage-like steps, replacing one another in a predictable sequence (e.g., Bowlby, 1980; Sanders, 1989). On the other, there are proposals (1) that no "procrustean stages or schedules exist" (Feifel, 1990, p. 540), (2) that at any one point one may find a combination of responses (numbness and disbelief, depression and despair, anxiety over the future) with one of these likely to be more pronounced at one time than the others (Jacobs et al., 1987–1988, cited by Bee, 1992, p. 473), and (3) that no particular progression over time exists at all, with the interesting phenomenon being the presence of individual differences and the extent to which these may be stable over time (e.g., Wortman & Silver, 1989).

Although grief sequences refer to a possible order in time without any particular linkage to age, similar questions have been raised about the extent of age-related normative sequences. One frequent reservation has to do with the extent to which males and females show the same normative patterns: the same "seasons of life," the same kinds of crises or dilemmas at particular ages or life phases, or the same rises and falls in particular kinds of motivations or interests. There is certainly evidence of differences in age patterns as a function of being male or female. An example comes from the longitudinal Berkeley data, which covered both sexes over the ages of 17 to 50/60 years of age. Women displayed a rise in "assertiveness" between the 30s and 40s, and then a drop during the 50s and 60s. Men showed a rise already present during the 17 to 30 age span and a continued increase as they grew older (Haan, Millsap, & Hartka, 1986).

A stronger reservation still takes the form of asking whether the normative patterns we expect to find reflect stereotypes rather than firm data. That type of argument has been especially prominent in analyses of the hypothesis that late adulthood is accompanied by a decline in all aspects of cognition. The actual patterns may, in fact, be more complex. As discussed earlier, what appears to be decline may be more a matter of where one puts resources rather than of depleted reserves, a possibility explored in studies of the benefits of practice on a number of cognitive skills. With practice and the provision of useful strategies, late-age adults may reach or come close to the levels of performance displayed on cognitive tasks by younger adults (e.g., Kliegel, Smith, Herkhausen, & Baltes, 1987; Salthouse, 1990).

What appears to be normative change may also reflect the extent to which particular skills or forms of expertise are likely to be accessible at particular times. To illustrate, consider a study of "wisdom" that presented adults with vignettes describing dilemmas in social life (Smith & Baltes, 1990). Should this woman, for example, use saved money to cover some unexpected needs that have arisen for her adult son or should she pursue a path she had planned to take for herself? The dilemmas presented were chosen to represent dilemmas likely to occur at different ages, but the participants from various age groups worked through the complete set. The analyses focused on the complexity and richness of thought displayed in the course of thinking aloud about what might be done. The result of particular interest is that each age group is best when dealing with the dilemma that belongs to its own age group. At an earlier point, the "old" may have faced the dilemmas that mark earlier parts of the life span, but depth in processing was nonetheless largely reserved for the kind of dilemma that marks or could mark one's current life phase.

What then sustains the presence or the expectation of normative changes linked to age? One possibility is that normative patterns appear because experiences are structured by age. Most people, for example, become parents or retire during a particular age range. A further possibility is that we expect normative age changes because we are accustomed to dividing the life span into age brackets—the 40s, 50s, 60s, etc.—regardless of whether those age divisions map on to differences in experience. The language we use, for example, is replete with evaluations of change in relation to age-based expectations: people are said to marry late, retire early, die before their time, and so on. There are certainly cultures where this focus on chronological age is less marked than it is in Anglo-European groups. In the Indian community that Menon and Shweder (1994) describe, for instance, the divisions referred to when describing one's own life and that of others are predominantly changes in social position (e.g., before and after marriage, children, acquiring a house, becoming the senior woman in the house, becoming the head of the family). Such social transitions are also used in Anglo-European groups in order to provide "benchmarks" (Roth, 1963), but age grouping nonetheless appears to have a particular attraction and to drive an assumption of normative changes based on age despite evidence of marked individual differences.

Dimension 3: An Emphasis on Individuation versus Connectedness

We have been considering two dimensions that help bring out the structure of studies of social development in childhood and adulthood. The first of these has been the nature of attention to change in behavior, cognition, and affect. The second has been the attention given to individual differences as against normative variation. We now turn to a third and last dimension: the attention given to two possible goals in social development—individuation and connectedness.

These two goals—charting our own course versus acquiring the ways of acting, thinking, and feeling that are regarded as acceptable by the group to which we belong—

would appear to be inherently contradictory. Damon (1983) begins his textbook on social and personality development with the following observation: "Social development is a life process built upon a paradox. The paradox is that at the same time we are *both* social and individual beings, connected with others in a multitude of ways, as well as ultimately alone in the world. This dual condition of connectedness and separateness begins at the moment of birth and remains with us all through life" (p. 1). Similarly, Costanzo (1992) suggests that the "tasks of socialization . . . are directed at two seemingly oppositional goals—personal identity, or self-perceived distinctiveness from others, and social identity, or self-perceived connectedness to others" (p. 62).

Of course, the paradox is really more of an illusion. The two goals are complementary, and optimal social development involves a balance of the two. Social connection promotes cohesion, smooth interaction and organization among group members, while individuation promotes innovation, a sense of efficacy and self-determination (Costanzo, 1992). Indeed, most aspects of social development involve features of both. Developing interpersonal competence requires both an awareness of the norms of the group and of one's own unique skills and limitations. Similarly, the development of personal identity includes growing knowledge about the effectiveness of one's interpersonal behaviors.

Within Studies of Childhood and Adolescence

Individuation   A number of distinct topics emphasize the individuated aspect of social development. These include studies of early temperamental differences and their long-term consequences, the expression and regulation of emotion, and orientation toward achievement, including intrinsic motivation. Perhaps the most representative topic, however, is the study of the emergence of a sense of self and identity.

Much of developmental research on the development of the self has been based on James's (1890) distinction between the private self (the "I") and the public self (the "me"). The "I" represents the part of the self that is more like a subject or agent, acting upon the world; whereas the "me" is the part that is more like an object that may be reflected upon by oneself and others (Harter, 1983). Social developmental research has been concerned with how early either of these components of the self emerges and how they might be measured. Some research suggests, for example, that infants' discoveries that they can make things happen, such as making a mobile move by kicking their legs, indicate a sense of self as subject (e.g., Rovee-Collier, 1987).

One particularly interesting line of research examining such questions employs "self-recognition" paradigms

(Lewis & Brooks-Gunn, 1979). In one, mothers are asked to apply surreptitiously a spot of rouge on their baby's nose and then place them in front of the mirror. Self-recognition is shown when babies act differently when rouge is on their face than when it is not. For example, touching their own nose would appear to indicate a recognition that the rouge is on them, whereas touching the rouge on the mirror may indicate that they think it is on another baby. In another paradigm, babies watch television images that show either their own current behavior, their own previous behavior, or the behavior of another baby. On the basis of such findings, Lewis and Brooks-Gunn concluded that even during the first year, babies have a sense of the "I" self. That is, at this age babies respond most positively to live television images (i.e., their own current behavior), suggesting that they can recognize themselves from contingency cues. During the second year, however, they are increasingly able to distinguish themselves from others on the basis of physical features. It is not until approximately 18–24 months of age, for example, that babies frequently touch their nose when they see rouge on their face. Moreover, at about the same age, infants exhibit self-conscious behavior and begin to use personal pronouns (Kagan, 1981), suggesting that a significant shift in self-awareness is occurring.

Research on further developments of this latter "categorical" self has examined children's perceptions of themselves in terms of social categories, such as age (Stipek, Gralinski, & Kopp, 1990), sex (Thompson, 1975), and race (Aboud, 1988). Of particular interest is when and why children view themselves as possessing certain stable characteristics, similar to Piagetian notions of conversation—that is, that they will always be the same sex and race, regardless of superficial transformations in physical features or setting (Aboud & Ruble, 1987). As discussed in a later section, such social-cognitive changes are believed to have a number of consequences for children's perceptions of and interactions with their social world. With respect to the study of further development of the self as subject (the "I"), it is not so clear how to index this sense of self as an agent, since by definition it is less accessible to conscious awareness. The apparent awareness of contingency cues by infants, as represented in the Lewis and Brooks-Gunn (1979) research, is, at best, a very primitive and indirect aspect of this "existential" self. Shaffer (1994) suggests that recent research distinguishing the private from the public self may be one approach to this issue. For example, even three-year-olds are capable of making a distinction between what their private self knows and what their public self leads others to believe (Chandler, Fritz, & Hala, 1989).

Connectedness   Research concerned more with issues of social connectedness includes studies on interpersonal relationships and conflict, compliance with (internalization of) social norms, empathy and prosocial behavior, and

knowledge of social roles. Perhaps the most representative connectedness topic, however, is the study of attachment. According to Bowlby's (1969) pioneering evolutionary perspective, attachment between the infant and mother provides an essential foundation of security and protection from which safe exploration is possible. Interestingly, then, a sense of connectedness in the form of secure attachment may be viewed as promoting individuation.

The development of an empirical paradigm and identification of three core types of attachment styles (secure, avoidant, and ambivalent) by Ainsworth and her colleagues (e.g., Ainsworth, Blehar, Waters, & Wall, 1978) has generated voluminous research and considerable debate (Bretherton, 1992; Lamb, Thompson, Gardner, Charnov, & Estes, 1984; Waters, Vaughn, Posada, & Kondo-Ikemura, 1995). The idea most central and exciting is that early attachment provides a working model of relationships that governs the individual's approach to others throughout life and thereby contributes significantly to personal and interpersonal functioning (Costanzo, 1992). Indeed, recent work in social psychology has examined the utility of applying Ainsworth's basic categorization to the study of intimate adult relationships (e.g., Hazan & Shaver, 1987; Simpson, Rholes, & Nelligan, 1992).

Considerable research has suggested that children who are secure (versus avoidant or ambivalent) in their attachment to their mothers subsequently show higher levels of interpersonal competence, popularity, and even problem-solving and creativity (Bretherton, 1992). Although such findings are extremely important and promising, basic questions about the nature of the processes that link attachment to subsequent adjustment remain open. Most importantly, because of the correlational nature of the data, it is not clear whether attachment security "causes" subsequent adjustment or if instead both attachment and adjustment are themselves the results of other underlying processes, such as temperament (Goldsmith & Alansky, 1987) or stable family patterns. Indeed, "strange situation" behavior appears to predict subsequent behavior primarily when caretaking circumstances remain stable (Lamb et al., 1984). Because of the potential importance of this kind of "connectedness," research is needed to explore these various alternative explanations of observed relations between early attachment and later social functioning with longitudinal data on a variety of attachment behaviors and their presumed correlates assessed at multiple time points.

The Relation between Individuation and Connectedness
In an insightful analysis, Costanzo (1992) describes how the interplay between individuation and connection goals characterizes several central areas of development research. First, Harter's (1987) examination of the development of self-worth in children and adolescence is based on

the joint influence of two approaches to self-evaluation. One is based on James's (1890) view that evaluation is based on the ratio of one's successes to one's pretentions, a relatively more individuated approach. The other is based on Cooley's (1902) "looking-glass" vision of self-worth as based on the adoption of the evaluative attitude of the generalized other toward the self, an approach emphasizing more the importance of connection with others. In studies with eight- to fifteen-year-olds, Harter (1987) finds that success in areas of importance and the attitudes of significant others appear to be independent influences on a global sense of self-worth.

Second, Higgins refers to different kinds of self-standards that drive self-regulation, with the two most central standards in his research reflecting this dichotomy. The "individuation" standard is the discrepancy between "actual" and "ideal" self-concept—the extent to which one's perceptions of one's present attributes match a set of intrinsically determined goals. The "connection" standard is the discrepancy between "actual" and "ought" self-concept—the extent to which one's perceptions of one's present attributes match a set of externally determined goals, such as those held by parents. He finds, for example, that the different forms of discrepancy relate to different emotional consequences, with "ideal" discrepancies being more related to depressive affect and "ought" discrepancies being more related to anxiety.

Third, research exploring the developing impact of peers on children has found parallel trends in the emergence of changes in more individuated versus connection aspects. In terms of individuation processes, Ruble (1983, 1987) has argued that although young children engage in considerable social comparison, the use of such information to evaluate one's distinctive traits does not emerge until after eight years of age. In terms of connection, Costanzo and his colleagues (Costanzo, 1970; Costanzo & Shaw, 1966) have shown that peers become more salient sources of conformity pressures during this same period.

In short, the tradeoffs and interplay between individuated and connectedness processes appear to be integral to various domains of social development. They are also likely to be integral to recent cross-cultural analyses of socialization practices that promote ideologies of collectivism in some cultures (e.g., Japan) or individualism in others (e.g., United States). For example, Tamis-LeMonda, Bornstein, Cyphers, Toda, & Ogino (1992) have shown how such ideologies may be transmitted to the child through mother-child exchanges. The idea that individuated and connectedness processes are in constant interplay across development may help temper an inclination in some of this literature to suggest that cultures are either one or the other, rather than the more likely case: that they differ in the relative balance between these two goals of social development (Martin & Ruble, in press).

Within Studies of Adults   Studies of adulthood highlight two questions: (1) Are there normative patterns of change with age in the degree of interest in connectedness to others; and (2) Is there a tension between the two directions of interest—individuation and connectedness?

On the first score, several studies in the United States point to shifts in the degree of concern with friendships and with "independence." One example is Bray and Howard's (1983) longitudinal study of men, born between 1827 and 1936 and followed longitudinally over the ages of 25 to 50. Over time (especially the middle years), these men became "harder" (p. 30) in the sense of being less interested in making friends and in understanding others' motives, less ready to abide by regulations or conventions. For a sample of college-educated women, in a further longitudinal study, women also—over the middle years (27 to 43 years in this sample)—displayed an increase in "dominance" and "independence" (Helson, Mitchell, & Moane, 1984). Across studies, the data suggest that early adulthood is a peak time for being interested in making friends and in being open to the interest and feelings of a range of people. Once beyond early adulthood, the search for friendship may become less salient or less wide-ranging (fewer people are considered as possibilities), with women possibly showing the greater change (Veroff et al., 1984), perhaps because they start from a greater interest than men display.

The analysis of the second issue—the extent to which there is some tension or opposition between the two directions of interest—is more complex. On the one hand, there are general theories proposing that at various points in our lives we seek particular mixtures of "isolation and communion" (Bakan, 1966), of "union" and "independence" (Kegan, 1982). In Kegan's (1982) analysis, the degree of tension is fluctuating rather than constant, with each recurring bout of opposition giving rise to attempts at resolution and acting as spurs to development. At the same time, several questions have been raised. One takes the form of asking whether the sense of opposition is predominantly a feature of societies that emphasize individualism rather than interdependence (e.g., Bakan, 1966; Markus & Kitayama, 1991; Kitayama & Markus, 1994). In countries such as Japan, for example, the emphasis on interdependence may create a lesser degree of concern with how one maintains a sense of independence or uniqueness.

A further reservation has to do with the value often attached to connectedness. It is easy to assume that connectedness is equivalent to successful development. Involvement and identification with a group may also carry the risk of a degree of conformity, however, that limits change. What may be needed is some degree of "detribalization" (Levinson, 1978), some degree of distance from others that promotes "taking charge" of one's life rather than leaving its direction to others (Helson, Mitchell, & Moane, 1984). A questioning stance toward connectedness is contained also in Rook's (1987) concern with measuring connectedness by the amount of contact with other people. Behind policies advocating that people in late adulthood join groups such as seniors' clubs, she notes, there often lies the assumption that "more" is necessarily "better." In fact, some of these interactions may be aversive. They may involve occasions of unasked-for advice (Smith & Goodnow, 1995), or, especially for the old-old, the promotion of dependence (Baltes, 1986, 1995). The real goal may then be one of maintaining choice and control in one's interactions with others rather than maintaining a wide range of interactions or interconnections.

A similar opposition arises in social psychological analyses of social identity. Goals of individuation (to be perceived as distinct) need to be balanced against goals of connection and a positive social identity. Categorization into a low-status minority group provides a distinctive social identity but may make it more difficult to derive social value from that group membership (Tajfel, 1981). Thus, as Brewer (1991) notes, identities might be shifted in the hierarchy, depending upon relative needs for distinctiveness and the maintenance of positive self-esteem derived from connection (see Brewer & Brown, 1998, in this *Handbook*).

Summary

This section has focused on three dimensions that provide a framework for examining studies of social development: (a) a focus on behavior, cognition, and affect; (b) attention to individual differences versus normative variation; and (c) an emphasis on individuation versus connectedness. In reviewing some major research programs within each of these dimensions, we have tried to provide a sense of the ways in which various topics have been studied and of the particular features of development brought out by considering both children and adults. The next section shifts from a concern with *what* is changing to a concern with *how* change is conceptualized, again with emphases on how such explanations have shifted over time and how they recur or change as the target age group changes.

APPROACHES TO THE BASES OF CHANGE AND VARIATION

Historically, a line has always been drawn between accounts that are akin to Locke's emphasis on external conditions and guided learning, and Rousseau's emphasis on internal states and self-regulated activity (e.g., Crain, 1985; Kessen, 1965). In a broad sense, we shall honor that division. The first part of this section concentrates on approaches that start from a focus on external conditions of various kinds, whereas the latter part concentrates on accounts that start from a focus on internal conditions.

Those general starting points, however, are far from being the whole story. Accounts still differ in the kind of external condition or the kind of internal state they take as a starting point. In addition, all accounts—whatever the starting point—move towards giving some place to both external and internal factors and their interconnections. They differ, however, in the routes by which other factors are taken into account and in the kind of picture that emerges of such two-way effects.

We begin with approaches that start from an emphasis on external conditions, differentiating among them in terms of whether the account emphasizes an individual's direct or indirect experience (classical learning theory, for instance, emphasizes direct experience; social learning theory emphasizes as well the observation of what happens to various models rather than to oneself). Overall, the addition of internal states to an external conditions account is in terms of cognitive, motivational, or affective changes that are created by early experience with the external conditions. These new states may then be carried forward, influencing the impact of conditions experienced at a later point (the development of a sense of helplessness or a sense of mastery, for example).

The latter half of the section takes up approaches that begin from an emphasis on internal states of various kinds. The primary differentiation among these is in terms of the nature of the internal state. The emphasis may fall on: (1) cognitive states (the capacity, for instance, to coordinate two points of view, or the tendency to notice and interpret events in particular ways), (2) temperamental predispositions, (3) ethological heritage, or (4) motivational predispositions (e.g., a spontaneously arising desire for competence, for a positive self-image, or a sense of meaning and structure to one's life). External conditions are not irrelevant, of course, to the expression of internal states. Within the positions considered in this section, however, the internal conditions are the springboard from which the accounts of change begin.

Once again, within each section, we review first what has emerged from analyses of childhood and adolescence, and then ask how these points reappear or are added to by analyses of adulthood. The sharpest theoretical debates seem to grow out of analyses of the development and improvability of children. There are nonetheless several significant extensions and additions generated by studies of development throughout adult life.

Approaches Starting from an Emphasis on External Conditions

We mentioned Locke as a point of origin for many of these approaches, so let us begin there. Locke's core argument was that humans are born neither inherently good nor inherently evil. Instead, the infant is a blank slate, a tabula rasa. In Locke's account, infants are shaped through association, repetition, rewards, and punishments. The mixture of these events needed to be judicious. Rewards, for example, were to be used with caution, because they might encourage children to strive for money or food as the end goal rather than developing self-control. Whatever the external events, however, they had the power to create internal states and those internal states—the habit of self-control, for instance—could then be carried forward. As historians have pointed out (e.g., Crain, 1985; Kessen, 1965), Locke also recognized internal states in the form of temperamental differences among individuals. The primary reference to internal states, however, was to their being first an outcome of encounters with external events and then a way by which the effects of early encounters were maintained, with later events responded to on the basis of the states established at earlier times.

Historical accounts typically trace two lines of descent from Locke. Both are grouped under the broad heading of "learning theory" and qualified either as "behaviorist learning theory" or "social learning theory." We may distinguish between them in terms of the view taken of rewards and nonrewards. Both place a strong emphasis on the pattern of rewards, feedback, and other experiences presented by the situations that individuals encounter. In behaviorist learning theory, however, the emphasis is on direct experiences as a consequence of one's own actions. In social learning theory, these experiences also matter, but included as well is the experience of observing what happens to others—to people whom one sees as similar to oneself or to the person one would like to be, and who serve as "models." We begin with approaches that emphasize direct experience and trace the appearance of this kind of emphasis in analyses of development during childhood and then during adulthood.

Direct Experience of External Conditions

Studies of Childhood: Incorporating Internal States of the Child into Analyses of Socialization Practices From Locke, a line of descent is typically drawn to Watson and his insistence that the development of children depends almost entirely on the way they are trained (e.g., Watson, 1919; see Horowitz, 1992, for a review). The line typically includes as well efforts in the 1950s and 1960s to combine learning theory with psychoanalytic theory, primarily by way of an emphasis on experience as shaping a particular internal state: identification with a parent (see Grusec, 1992, for a review). The research agenda then became one of attempting to locate the particular parental methods that were associated with signs of identification, such as acquiring an appropriate sense of being male or female or compliance in the absence of surveillance (e.g., Sears, Maccoby, & Levin, 1957; Sears, Rau, & Alpert, 1965; Whiting & Child, 1953).

In time, references to the route of identification dropped

out. The process was felt to be too mysterious; the results often did not fit the predicted pattern; and explanations in terms of modeling turned out to be more parsimonious and to lead more easily to experimental demonstration of predicted effects (Maccoby, 1980, 1992). What remained, however, was a research agenda directed towards locating the particular parental methods, or the particular qualities of parental methods, that yielded specific forms of development. That agenda underlies, for instance, Hoffman's (1982) linking of particular forms of reasoning (drawing attention to the other person's state) to the development of empathy and compassion, Baldwin's (1955) associations of democratic versus autocratic home environments with children's functioning, and Baumrind's (1973) linking of particular styles of control (authoritarian, authoritative, and permissive) to the development of qualities such as confidence and social responsibility. More generally, analyses focused on how parental methods—regardless of their specific form—varied along certain dimensions, usually involving some aspect of restrictiveness/flexibility and of hostility/warmth (Maccoby & Martin, 1983, offer an effective summary).

Regardless of how these external events were described, however, the question remained: How do effects come about? The earliest answers tended to be in terms of simple changes in response strength. Early research, for example, showed that strong, consistent, and immediate punishments were most effective in promoting resistance to temptation in children (Parke, 1972). Many current lines of research implicitly assume this perspective as well, in that differential responsiveness to certain actions of children is assumed to affect the frequency of behaviors regardless of whether internal states mediate those responses. For example, considerable research on gender socialization has shown that parents and teachers provide different experiences and feedback to girls and boys, and that this differential treatment relates to later behavioral sex differences (see Ruble & Martin, 1997, for a review). Within much of this research, little attention may be given to whether the affective, motivational, or cognitive state of the child makes any difference in the nature or strength of the effects.

Other recent approaches examining how effects come about have considered mediators of the effects of external conditions on children in the form of various internal states: cognitive (e.g., understanding rules and standards), motivational (personal desires and interests), and affective (positive mood, guilt, or anxiety). An important reason for considering internal mediators is that they may help account for how it is that the same actions may have different effects at different times and in different settings. To illustrate, effecting child compliance depends upon the child recognizing that they have been requested to do something and that they have the capability to carry out the order (Grusec & Goodnow, 1994; Maccoby & Martin, 1983). More generally, children's reactions to the behaviors of socializing agents depend on their interpretation of those actions. Because interpretation depends upon the level of social-cognitive development of the child, the same actions by parents may have quite different effects at different ages. Considerable evidence concerning the development of children's abilities to engage in attributional reasoning, for example, suggests that kindergarten children are likely to respond more positively to some forms of controlling efforts by parents than fourth graders. It is not until children can associate external inducements (such as rewards for good behavior) with attempts to control that they may react negatively (Ruble & Thompson, 1992). Similarly, the meaning of external messages may vary in different social contexts, perhaps explaining in part findings of cultural differences in the impact of patterns of socialization. For example, authoritative parenting (based on Baumrind's classification system) is more strongly associated with achievement among European-American adolescents than among Asian- and African-American youngsters (e.g., Steinberg, Darling, & Fletcher, 1995). Such results are difficult to account for in terms of simple direct effects from parental methods or ethnicity. Mediating or moderating internal states, however, could account for the apparent discrepancy in results.

Various blends of cognitive and motivational states have been examined as potential mediators or moderators, and in some cases, such approaches have involved a productive blending of social psychological theory with socialization issues. For example, Grusec (1983) has shown that prosocial behavior is enhanced when socialization agents attribute the behavior to a quality of the child (e.g., kindness), relative to which they provide social reinforcement. Presumably, children are motivated to behave in ways consistent with their self-attribution of the characteristic they have been induced to believe they possess.

In an elegant related analysis, Lepper (1983) has described how attribution processes can explain when and why socialization practices involving control do or do not lead to internalized responding. According to his "minimal sufficiency principle," if children see themselves as engaging in particular behaviors (e.g., being kind, working hard in school, not lying or cheating) in order to avoid punishment or because they are being forced to by their parents or teachers, they will be less likely to perceive such behaviors as due to their own personal values and principles. The implication, then, is that internalization, the sense that behavior is self-generated and worth continuing, is most likely when socialization agents exert just barely sufficient control to induce compliance. External pressure that is too strong undermines children's perceptions that their behaviors are determined by their personal standards, beliefs, and values. Interestingly, parents and teachers appear to subscribe to a maximal operant as opposed to a minimal sufficiency principle. In direct contrast to Lepper's analy-

sis, research has shown that socializing agents believe that the larger the reward or punishment, the more likely they are to obtain a child's compliance. Even when presented with information to disconfirm this socialization strategy, adults continue to adhere to this belief (Boggiano, Barrett, Weiher, McClelland, & Lusk, 1987).

Another influential perspective has emphasized the importance of goals and beliefs as mediators of external conditions. For example, Dweck and Leggett (1988) have distinguished between children who are oriented toward learning versus performance goals in their approaches toward achievement situations. Performance goals involve the desire to demonstrate high competence and bolster esteem and are related to beliefs that intelligence is fixed and difficult to change. In contrast, learning goals involve the desire to increase competence and attain mastery and are associated with beliefs that intelligence is a more malleable quality. These goals and beliefs, in turn, help explain differential reactions to failure experiences. Children who exhibit a "helpless" response to failure (e.g., heightened anxiety, negative self-evaluation, decreased task performance) tend to have performance goals and beliefs in fixed ability, whereas children with a more mastery-oriented response to failure (e.g., plans for performance remediation, increased effort) tend to have learning goals and beliefs in malleable ability. These different goals and beliefs represent, in essence, internal states that develop out of experiences with external conditions assumed to involve personal criticism for poor performance. Indeed, as noted earlier, Dweck and her associates (Burhans & Dweck, 1995; Dweck, 1991) have found that children as young as preschoolers can be distinguished on the basis of their reactions to failure, and that this difference is associated both with beliefs about a fixed or stable characteristic, namely, being bad or good, and with perceptions of the responses of socializing agents. When asked to role-play parent and teacher reactions to their performance at puzzles, children who showed helpless reactions to failure role-played more punishment and criticism than children who showed more mastery-oriented reactions.

Other approaches to internal mediators have involved a mixture of affective and cognitive states, sometimes viewed as short-term and sometimes as long-term. A short-term affective state, for example, is part of Parpal and Maccoby's (1985) description of children as displaying "receptive compliance." When a parent accedes to a child's request on one occasion, the state is set—presumably by the generation of a positive mood—for the child's later acceding to the parent's request. In effect, one past event acts as an affective prime for the next event of the same kind. Longer term cognitive-affective states are at the core of proposals that noncontingent patterns of rewards or feedback promote a continuing sense of "learned helplessness" (e.g., Dweck, 1986; Seligman, 1975), an analysis not restricted to children. Long-term states are also at the core of proposals that what develops is an internal monitoring or self-regulatory system, a "self" that appraises the actions taken and issues approvals or disapprovals (Bussey & Bandura, 1992; Deci & Ryan, 1985).

Distinguishing among cognitive, motivational, and affective states is one way of differentiating among possible internal mediators. An alternative approach to differentiation asks where each state fits into a series of processing steps. A recently proposed multiple-step model provides an example (Grusec & Goodnow, 1994). The model has been offered for the effects of parents' disciplinary actions, but is extendable to other external events. It is marked by three features. First, the move towards internal states is broken into a series of processing steps. These steps include (a) the perception (accurate or inaccurate) of the actions or the intentions of the disciplining parent, (b) the acceptance or rejection of what is perceived as the course the child is expected to follow, and (c) the sense that this course, once accepted, is self-generated.

Second, each step is regarded as being influenced by both cognitive and affective factors, such as the perception that the punishment encountered is reasonable or unreasonable and the anxiety or receptiveness that are part of this and other encounters with the parent. The arousal of fear, for instance, may diminish the likelihood of an accurate understanding of what is needed or may incline the individual towards compliance but not acceptance, and may strongly lead away from the sense that this perspective is one's "own."

Third, each step is regarded as differentially influenced by particular factors. The clarity of a parent's message, for instance, and the child's ability to decode an ambiguous message, have particular ties to the accuracy of perception. The warmth of the parent-child relationship and the child's current mood have particular ties to the acceptance or rejection of the perceived message. The degree of perceived pressure has particular ties to the perception of a position as self-generated.

In short, contemporary approaches to the impact of external conditions on development have moved increasingly away from a notion of some global construct such as identification as a mediator toward an emphasis on multiple-step intervening processes. What is gained by differentiating among internal states in this way? For one thing, in the movement toward the analysis of process, the field of social development now shares a core ideology with social psychology, which should facilitate a link between developmental and social psychological analyses of action, affect, and cognition. The Grusec and Goodnow (1994) model, for example, is similar in type to the breakdown into steps offered by several social psychologists for the interplay of culture, emotion, and cognition (Ellsworth, 1994; Frijda & Mesquita, 1994; Posner, Rothbart, & Har-

man, 1994). Moreover, the specific processes now being emphasized in social developmental analyses—self-attributions, affective primes, personal goals, and motivations—are highly compatible with current social psychological models of social perception and behavior.

A further advantage to adding differentiated internal states to analyses that start from external conditions is that the addition encourages us to take a fresh look at some old topics. Consider, for instance, what happens when a parent issues a directive which the child may or may not follow. Events such as these have typically been analyzed in terms of only two kinds of behaviors: the parent has been seen as issuing a directive, and the child seen as complying or not complying. An orientation towards adding internal states, however, leads to the notion that what may be learned in the course of such encounters is not only a set of compliance behaviors but also an understanding of how to negotiate: how to say "no" acceptably or safely by strategies such as saying "later," offering an alternative, coming up with a good reason, agreeing but then not doing—in effect, by a variety of ways that avoid an outright "no" (e.g., Kuczynski & Kochanska, 1990; Leonard, 1993). What may develop also is an understanding of occasions and content areas that contain leeway and options as against those that are nonnegotiable (Goodnow, 1994, 1996). In turn, the awareness of this kind of processing leads back to a reanalysis of what the parent is doing. We may now perceive the parent, not as aiming at compliance but as teaching acceptable ways to negotiate (Kuczynski & Kochanska, 1990). We may also become alert to the occasions when parents indicate that "this is your choice," "this is up to you," rather than making the decision for the child (e.g., Nucci, 1994; Smetana, 1994), and to what happens when the child is slow to take up the option—slow, for instance, to choose what to wear or what to do (Nucci, 1994). In effect, the analysis now comes full circle: from a description of external conditions to an internal state, and from an internal state back to a second look at the original description of the external conditions.

Developmentalists have been slow in addressing these strategic elements of negotiation, apparently taking the difference in power and status in the parent-child interaction for granted and focusing primarily on when and why compliance occurs. Of course, similar blind spots may be present in social psychological analyses, as well. Adult subjects in social psychology experiments in many instances are participating in compliance requests involving unequal status and may similarly be assessing limits, ostensibly agreeing with a communication provided, but in a way that is tagged "not me" or "for now only." Such possibilities are reminiscent of Kelman's (1961) distinction between compliance, identification, and internalization in attitude change situations, but suggest the need to go further to assess how subjects perceive the actual negotiations involved and what impact this process may have on theoretical conclusions that are drawn.

Studies of Childhood: Alternative Approaches   Up to this point, we have been considering a variety of ways in which analyses of internal states have been added to studies that begin with a focus on external conditions, with the latter primarily in the form of strategies or practices that parents exhibit when they seek to encourage one behavior and discourage another. Before we turn to studies of adult development, some additional research directions emerging within childhood studies need to be noted. These are (1) experimental manipulations of external situations or events, rather than the study of natural variations in socialization contexts; (2) analyses that emphasize external events in terms of the ways in which the actions of two or more people are interwoven; and (3) the study of adults' actions towards children in relation to adults' internal states.

With respect to the first additional research direction, a long tradition of developmental research has manipulated situational variations in theorized process variables, much like the practice among experimental social psychologists. For example, several researchers have shown how manipulating children's mood can affect targeted socialization outcomes, such as performance (Masters, Barden, & Ford, 1979) and prosocial behavior (Cialdini, Kenrick, & Baumann, 1982). Interestingly, putting children into a sad mood can either increase or decrease prosocial behavior (Cialdini & Fultz, 1990). It is especially likely to increase helping for older children, perhaps because altruism becomes self-reinforcing with age, as children learn that they receive praise for such behaviors (Cialdini & Kenrick, 1976). In addition, whether or not the sadness is self- versus other-focused also seems to influence the results, with greater helping associated with other-focused sadness (Barnett, King, & Howard, 1979).

The second additional research direction, emphasizing the interwoven actions of two or more people, derives from some particular accounts of social or cultural contexts. We shall concentrate on the kinds of analysis of actions that these accounts have prompted, with minimal reference to the theoretical background. We shall also break the analyses into two sets.

One set uses as a base proposals from Vygotsky, drawing especially upon arguments that learning proceeds from a point of dependence on support from others to a point of being able to act with more independence (e.g., Vygotsky, 1978). The method often adopted then becomes one of analyzing teaching-learning situations in "microgenetic" fashion, observing the interplay of people with varying degrees of expertise. The facilitating parent, for example, helps a child to join a group of other children, maintaining a presence or a "way-in" for as long as needed but withdrawing as the child gains confidence or acceptance (e.g.,

Finnie & Russell, 1988). A variety of other examples, mostly concerned with shifts in support and responsibility on more "academic" occasions but extendable to more explicitly social events, is offered by Forman, Minick, and Stone (1993) and by Rogoff (1990). In all such situations, the child's experience may be described as one of "guided participation" (Rogoff, 1990). Internal states matter, but the internal states now emphasized belong primarily to the parent, in the form of appraisals related to the child's changing competence or interest. References to the child's appraisals of whether the adult has the right to make all the decisions or to set the pace are far less frequent (e.g., Verdonik, Flapan, Schmit, & Weinstock, 1988).

Another set of analyses that emphasizes interweaving looks less to variations in expertise and more to the extent to which participation in social events is shared with others who act in similar ways and has a routine, taken-for-granted quality to it. This kind of emphasis is contained within psychologists' analyses of "family rituals" (e.g., Fiese, 1992; Sameroff & Fiese, 1992) and in more anthropologically based analyses of "cultural practices" (e.g., Bourdieu, 1979, 1990). In essence, the argument common to these analyses is that the events that matter are those that are everyday routines—everyday ways, for example, of eating, speaking, sleeping, dressing, working, greeting each other at the end of the day, or celebrating birthdays. These routines then come to be experienced as part of a natural or moral order, an experience that—like the practice itself—is also shared with other members of the group. In the case of family rituals, the group is a family. In the case of cultural practices, the group is larger; the adjective "cultural" in fact signals that the practice in question is observed by all or most members of a social group.

Goodnow, Miller, and Kessel (1995) provide examples of developmental studies using cultural practice concepts. We limit our comments to noting two points. One is that assigning significance to what "most people" or "other families" do means that processes of social comparison (not as yet an explicit part) need to be incorporated into analyses of socialization (Harris, 1995; Ruble & Thompson, 1992). The other is that analyses in terms either of practices or routines highlight some particular outcomes in social development. One of these is the person's sense that the observance of a group's routines is part of belonging to the group. In Fiese's (1992) analysis of family rituals, for example, observing the rituals is part of feeling a sense of cohesion and identity with the family, just as taking oneself out of the rituals, for example, not joining in family outings, can be a mark on one's separate status (Miller, 1995). The other is that routines and practices lead away from any in-depth processing of events. The routines come to be seen as part of a natural order that calls for little reflection or questioning (e.g., Bourdieu, 1979; Miller & Goodnow, 1995).

The third and last additional research direction to be noted within analyses of external conditions during childhood concerns parents' internal states and their relation to children's experiences. This line of research has attracted interest since the late 1970s (for recent reviews and examples of specific studies, see Goodnow, 1996; McGillicuddy-DeLisi & Sigel, 1995; Smetana, 1994). The starting premise of this research is that children are not alone in interpreting, appraising, and responding with a variety of emotions to external conditions. Parents also engage in similar processes.

For our purposes, the main implications of this line of research have to do with suggestions, relevant to either adults or children, for the ways in which appraisals may emerge and for the ways in which actions, ideas, and emotions may be interwoven. The research underlines a *double path* to the emergence of appraisals. They may be constructed on the basis of the systematic processing of events directly experienced. They may also be taken over with little reflection from the set of ideas that are made available, and perhaps promoted, by others. Parents, for instance, may take over the "prepackaged" ideas about children that are available in their social group. Children may take over the ideas that their parents hold. Adolescents, to take one example, may reflect back the gender-stereotypic ideas of their parents with regard to success in such school subjects as English and mathematics (e.g., Eccles & Jacobs, 1986).

The research also underlines the presence of *complex paths* rather than simple linear ones (e.g., from ideas to actions). Any such path is likely to involve the presence of affect, influencing all steps along the way (e.g., Dix, 1991). Moreover, any such path will need to take account of the continuous interweaving of two sets of appraisals, feelings, and actions: one contributed by the parent, and one by the child. The task then is to untangle the constant interplay between the actions and internal states of two parties in a relationship rather than trace only the path within a single individual (e.g., Bugental & Goodnow, 1997). One recent line of research, for example, has begun to explore the interactions among the characteristics of both parents and children that affect value transmission in families (Rohan & Zanna, in press). To illustrate, greater similarity in parent-child values is found when parents are low in authoritarian beliefs, and this relation is mediated in part by children's perceptions of parental responsiveness.

Studies of Adulthood   We have been considering, within studies of children's social development, accounts of change that start from attention to external conditions and that subsequently often add attention to internal states—cognitive, motivational, or affective—as mediators or moderators. At this point, we ask, as in earlier sections, what studies of later ages add to the picture so far generated.

The additions we first single out are expansions on the concept of external conditions as presenting demands or expectations. One recurring theme in life-course analyses is the notion that shifts in age or status present us with changing tasks or changing demands. Erikson's (1959) view of shifting "crises" as we move from one age grouping to another is a prominent example. From one point in life to another, the argument runs, the nature of demands may change. They may range, for example, from "settling down" or "making a commitment" to "getting one's priorities straight" or "growing old gracefully." The demands may stem from changing physical states (puberty, pregnancy, middle-aged spread, the need to wear glasses, etc.) or from our own desires for change, for a new direction in life, a new challenge. Most of the demands, however, are seen as stemming from others: "Now that you've graduated, turned 30, become a parent, turned 50, retired, come to be divorced or widowed, etc." With each new role or transition point, others make it clear that particular ways of acting, thinking, and feeling are expected.

Studies with adult populations also add several useful ways of specifying the quality of a demand or expectation. The first of these has to do with whether the demand is "to do" or "to be" (Terkelsen, 1980). The demand to "go to college," for instance, is not the same as the demand to "grow up" or to "be a good father." Demands of the latter kind are less clear but for that very reason they also offer more scope for individual interpretation.

The second feature of demands highlighted by adult studies has to do with whether they are single or multiple. This quality of demand surfaces especially in analyses of timetables. It is possible to think of development as occurring along a single time line. The progression may be, for instance, from one general "season of adulthood" to another (Levinson, 1978) or one core dilemma to another (Erikson, 1959). The contrasting model proposes a series of progressions, each with its own time line. Changes occur, for example, in work roles, family roles, physical states, and the "personal" tasks one sets oneself (Perun & Bielby, 1980). In Perun and Bielby's model, each area has its own sequential pattern, but the lines may interlock at various points. When they do, the changes in one area may facilitate changes in another. Becoming a parent, for example, may facilitate change in the relationship to one's own parents. Interlocking may also give rise to what Neugarten (1979) has termed "a timetable crunch": the simultaneous demand, for example, to move into positions of responsibility in one's paid work at the same time as a change in housing or a shift into parenting is made.

Neugarten's proposal will be recognized as having some overlaps with concepts offered for the analysis of social development during earlier parts of life. There is, for instance, overlap with Higgins and Parsons' (1983) proposal that childhood be thought of not only in terms of a change in "ages" or "stages" but also in terms of life phases, varying in the demands they present. There is overlap as well with proposals to the effect that transitions during childhood can involve multiple stressors at one time. The transition to junior high school, for example, can involve at one and the same time a change in peer group, in school subjects, in status, in neighborhood, and in pubertal status (Ruble & Seidman, 1996).

The third and last feature of demands that is highlighted by adult studies has to do with their negotiability: the extent to which they allow for some degrees of leeway or flexibility. Again, this quality surfaces especially within analyses of social timetables. Erikson (1959), for instance, regarded young adulthood as a time when many societies granted a "moratorium," a period when deferring the resolution of one's identity was acceptable. Young adults, in this view, are allowed time to work out who they are or what they want to be. The negotiability of demands need not be linked to particular age periods. At any age, what may matter most is the extent to which one can present acceptable reasons for being "off-time": for being "slow to settle," for "marrying late" or "retiring early" (Neugarten, 1979). In both cases, the negotiations are seen as focused around the timing of expected transitions. The emphasis on negotiability in itself, however, offers a clear link back to the research on negotiations and occasions of acceptable divergence (e.g., when saying "no" to a parent is acceptable) that we noted earlier within analyses of childhood.

Up to this point, the emphasis has fallen on some added ways of specifying what may be involved when the individual faces a demand, an expectation or a developmental task. Where, one may ask, are the internal states that one would expect to see added to such analyses? Within studies of adulthood, these emerge predominantly in two forms. One consists again of cognitive states that give rise to particular interpretations of events, interpretations that may increase satisfaction with one's position or may at least soften the blow of some unexpected and unwanted change (e.g., Taylor & Lobel, 1989).

The other—the one that provides an emphasis less often seen in studies of childhood—has to do with internal states related to an active choice among alternative paths. Rather than focusing, for instance, on whether a society allows time out, the emphasis shifts to internal states that lead to the decision to take time out (Marcia, 1988). In effect, what was once an external condition—the objective feasibility of a moratorium—now is treated as if it were a form of individual differences. In related fashion, what is emphasized as a feature of later life is not the involuntary loss of cognition or perceptual resources—declining energy, a lessened ability to work fast for long periods, etc.—but the active decision to choose among possible paths or areas of involvement, discarding some and searching for ways to maintain or enrich others. This is, for example, the core of the proposal that age brings with it a process of "selective maximization with compensation" (Baltes & Baltes,

1990). Some such active choice (e.g., some active work in "getting one's priorities straight") may well occur at other times in life. Late adulthood, however, may be a time when this internal process is likely to be particularly relevant, perhaps because the shift in internal resources is no longer thought of as possibly temporary or perhaps because the demand to work out what to keep and what to give up now comes more from oneself than from others.

Making a choice, however, means that we now need to specify the nature of alternatives, either as they are perceived or as they exist. For an example, we turn again to the analysis of social timetables. Within U.S. society, it has been proposed, there are both "masculine" and "feminine" social clocks (Helson et al., 1984). The "masculine" clock, for instance, involves deferring commitments to marriage, parenting, or a long-term relationship until some progressions with regard to education or paid work are already in hand. For some women, this clock is not perceived as an available choice. It may not be economically feasible. It may seem out of line with their images of self. For others (college-educated women especially), the "masculine" clock is a choice seen as feasible and adopted. These women, however, do not have to construct a changed timetable *de novo*. Instead, they select an alternative that exists in their society but has not traditionally been the choice of their social group. Once again, attention to an internal state has an effect we noted as occurring within studies of childhood: researchers begin by focusing on external events that are directly experienced, add attention to internal states, and then circle back to a second look at the nature of external conditions.

Approaches Emphasizing Indirect Experience

Studies of Childhood   Without having to experience rewards or feedback for one's own actions, we may be strongly influenced by what we see happen to others. In fact, this basis of learning and of deciding whether to act or not may be the more frequent route. This seemingly simple and obvious proposal from Bandura and Walter's (1963) *Social Learning and Personality Development* created a revolution in its time. In addition to rejecting direct experience as the primary route to change, they argued that attempting to incorporate a psychoanalytic perspective into learning theory added unnecessary, unconscious baggage, and that simpler and more elegant accounts of social learning could be found by sticking to observable variables (Grusec, 1992; Maccoby, 1980). Thus, as discussed earlier, they dismissed the notion of identification as some internalized parent and replaced it with imitation. Accompanied by experiments demonstrating, for example, that the likelihood of a child's engaging in aggressive acts could be increased by his or her observing another act aggressively and not be punished, this proposal led to a series of studies that Hetherington and McIntyre (1975) described with less than complete enthusiasm:

> The topic in social development which continues to be the focus of the most research is that of modeling. Over 40 modeling studies were published in the last year . . . Children will imitate moral judgments . . . Whoopee! Children will imitate aggressive behavior . . . and self-reward . . . , and social interactions . . . and picture preferences, and button pressing . . . , and cognitive style, and Whoopee! Almost anything! (pp. 112–113)

Hetherington and McIntyre (1975) hasten to add that many of these studies have made important contributions. Their point was more that the field needed to move beyond simply demonstrating that imitation occurs. Indeed, the research at this time not only showed how central imitation and modeling were to children's social development, it also yielded a relatively clear-cut understanding of the factors (e.g., power and warmth) that facilitate such learning. Moreover, beyond this empirical contribution, social learning represented an important theoretical alternative to strict behavioristic accounts. This is because cognitive processes (attention, interpretation) must obviously be involved in such vicarious learning, especially when it occurs under conditions of delay or shows variation across differing eliciting conditions (e.g., selective imitation). As Maccoby (1980) points out, this view led to new directions in the socialization literature, as it became widely acknowledged that parents were not only agents of reward and punishment, but also were the most important models in the lives of young children.

This perspective continues today in many areas of social developmental research. Contemporary studies of gender development, for example, examine how variations in role modeling in the home, such as maternal employment or paternal involvement in child care, influence children's gender-related preferences and behaviors. To illustrate, several studies suggest that a more traditional division of labor in the home is associated with children's learning of gender distinctions at an earlier age (see Ruble & Martin, 1997, for a review). Interestingly, the impact of parental behaviors on gender-related concepts is not so clear at older ages, suggesting perhaps once again the importance of an internal state (in this case, an early script or schema about the nature of gender) that is created by external conditions, and that then affects the individual's response to subsequent external conditions.

Research on the process of observational learning has advanced in two general directions. One has concerned the elucidation of the processes linking the observations to the choices made or behaviors enacted. According to Bandura (1986), there are several steps along the way, involving attention, retention, and representation, and because of this emphasis on cognitive mediators, his theory was relabeled social cognitive theory (see Grusec, 1992, for a review). His answer to the question of how control over behavior shifts from external to internal sources was self-regulation. People develop personal standards of proper behavior from observing others that eventually are used to guide and evaluate their own choices and behaviors (Bussey & Bandura, 1992). Perhaps above all, what is carried forward to future events is a sense of self-efficacy: a belief that one can act effectively in a given situation (e.g., Bandura, Barbaranelli, Caprara, & Pastorelli, 1996). Exactly which standards are adopted depends partly on perceptions of self-efficacy in the particular domain of action and how that compares to the perceived competence of the model (Grusec, 1992).

A second general direction picks up the question of which sources are attended to or given the most weight in the face of a wide range of possible sources to observe. That question is prompted especially by the recognition that children pay attention to many models other than parents, including peers and characters portrayed in the mass media. Part of the answer to this question lies in the proposal that the significant sources are those seen as relevant to one's concept of self. The people who come to be effective models need to be seen as like oneself, either as one is or as one would like to be. The people with the least impact appear to be those who are perceived as unlike oneself or as examples to be avoided. Boys, for example, learn both to model themselves after other boys and also to avoid acting as girls (Bussey, 1983).

A further part of the answer lies in the number of people observed to act in particular ways. If several men and women are observed to act in stereotypic ways, then the likelihood is increased of children following a gender-differentiated pattern (Perry & Bussey, 1979). That type of finding is of particular interest for two reasons. First, it suggests that the appraisal process which accompanies observations involves the construction or use of social categories—for example, the notion that this is what "men" or "women" do rather than this is what "my mother" or "my father" does. Second, it suggests a way of linking analyses based on social learning theory to some theories of development that ask more explicitly about the impact of encountering the same "message" from a variety of sources (Harris, 1995). To take gender as an example, the message of gender differentiation is presented by a variety of sources, ranging from the ways in which people walk, speak, or dress to sayings such as "silence is a woman's crown," narratives such as *Sleeping Beauty,* or reading primers that begin with "Look, Jane, look; see Dick run." When information comes from sources that are so "multilayered" (Watson-Gegeo, 1992), people are likely to perceive what is observed as "natural" and as not open to question (Frijda & Mesquita, 1994; Miller & Goodnow, 1995).

Studies of Adulthood   Studies of observational learning in adults rarely refer to the same kinds of social learning theories that guide research with children. Instead, they come from different theoretical traditions. In social psychological research, studies of conformity (Asch, 1956) and social facilitation (Zajonc, 1965) have certainly been concerned with the impact of observing others, albeit as a short-term impact on an immediate behavior, but the process of modeling per se was not the main point of the research. Some recent interesting approaches to observational learning in the social psychological literature seem to have come to it almost inadvertently. For example, Taylor and Lobel (1989) invoked a related concept to help explain some apparent anomalies in social comparison processes observed among cancer victims. They found that many such individuals preferred to spend time with people who were doing better than they were rather than worse. Because of self-protective needs, this finding is difficult to interpret in terms of self-evaluation. Instead, the authors argued, cancer victims may engage in social comparison not to evaluate how well they are doing, but rather as a source of learning and inspiration as to how they themselves could do better.

Studies of the impact of observing others on longer term change in adults have generally been based on role theory perspectives, emphasizing roles demanded in the course of changes with age or status (Dion, 1985). The very concept of role enactment implies that there are many others who have faced the same demand and who are potentially available to serve as models or as points of comparison. There are, for instance, thousands of others who have moved into paid work, into committed relationships, into parenting, into retirement. We should not need to search far for someone who models the conventional performance of a role.

That very availability, however, means that the study of indirect socialization in adults has been less concerned with the impact of specific models per se than with other kinds of questions. To start with: how is it that people are not more alike than they are when they share a common age or a common status, and how is an individuated approach to a new role developed? Part of the answer must lie in the quality of demand that we have already emphasized—the fact that many or most roles offer some degree of leeway, some degree of choice or option in the way demands are met. For some roles, there may even be a social ethos that says "you have to learn how to do it your way; no one can really teach you." That ethos, Backett (1982) observed, was often referred to in comments on parenting by the sample of Scots parents she interviewed. Little could be learned, they thought, from manuals on parenting. Parents had to feel their way towards the best approaches to interactions between themselves and their children.

Phase models of role transitions (e.g., Levinson, 1978; Nicholson, 1990; Ruble, 1994) also suggest that there may be stages of high conformity in which attention is focused on the norms or prototypes of the new role, but these are subsequently passed as the individual begins to discern variability in the norms or to integrate them with personal needs or preferences. For example, according to Levinson (1978), each time that the pattern of external demands and inner needs changes, we proceed through a novice phase (a phase of trying out a new pattern), a mid-term phase (a point of review), and then a culminating phase (the pattern is brought to its smoothest point but again re-assessed, especially since by then needs or demands are likely to have altered or to be about to alter). Because we vary in what we need, in the ages at which we encounter particular demands, and in the way we pass through novice to end-phases, there is room for large individual differences, even though we may all experience some broad transitions from early to middle to late adulthood.

A related question, raised by the idea that there are different phases of role transitions, concerns when observational learning is likely to have the most impact. Suppose we take that concern to a specific study: a study of the extent to which women have acted on the view that combining a career and marriage was compatible or incompatible (Stewart & Healy, 1989). The sample is of women who were all in graduate school over the same time period (1945 to 1951), but who varied in their viewpoints and who came from different cohorts. The perception of marriage and career as compatible was strongest among those who were born between 1925 and 1929, and weakest among those born between 1906 and 1914. The latter group reached adulthood at a time when there was a strong ethos of one-worker-per-family. During the depression, they had learned the importance of being in work and being financially secure. They had also observed married women being in paid work during this time but that doing so was no point of pride. In contrast, the group who regarded marriage and career as compatible came into adulthood at a different historical time. Their observations of women in paid work took place during World War II, when wives and mothers were urged to enter paid work for positive reasons. The familist period after that war placed marriage and children again high on the list but at a time when these women had already experienced the presentation of paid work in a positive light. Role models, the study suggests, have particular effects at the time when one is first coming up to a possible new role and is open to what is happening and to the possibility of change.

Approaches Starting from an Emphasis on Internal Conditions

The previous section has considered accounts of change that start from an emphasis on external events and then moves towards the addition of internal states, both cognitive and affective in nature. We turn now to accounts that start with a focus on internal states. This section will be shorter than the section on external conditions, mainly because we have already given some attention to the nature of internal states as mediating or moderating the impact of external conditions.

Rousseau is often viewed as a point of origin of many of these approaches. In contrast to Locke, Rousseau felt the innate capacities of the child would unfold naturally in accordance with a stage-like growth of developmental skills, and that external instruction could only be damaging. This emphasis on nature is reflected most closely in ethological (e.g., Hinde, 1989) and maturational (e.g., Gesell, 1948) approaches. In addition, Rousseau viewed the child not as a receptive vessel, as Locke did, but rather as actively searching and constructing, a view later reflected in the cognitive-developmental theories of Piaget and Kohlberg. Such an extreme differentiation of Rousseau from Locke's position probably does not reflect well most current theories, which tend to represent more of a blend of external versus internal states. It does not even characterize Rousseau perfectly, in that he did not feel a child was best raised in solitary; the tutor played an important role by structuring the situation to meet the child's current needs and capacities. Nevertheless Rousseau's emphasis on the importance of internal states in driving development has remained a strong tradition in social developmental theory.

The relative dominance of theories emphasizing internal as opposed to external states has changed considerably since child development became a distinct field around the turn of the century. G. Stanley Hall (1844–1924) is often credited as the founder of developmental psychology (White, 1992). When he became the first president of Clark University in 1889, he promoted the child study movement, encouraging his students to develop questionnaires to understand children's thinking about a wide range of topics, including many that remain subjects of research in social development, such as play, emotions, and interests. Hall's approach was normative and descriptive, and as such was largely silent on issues of theoretical process. Implicitly, however, it can be conceptualized within an "internal states" approach, in part because it was influenced by Darwin, and in part because Hall's students, Gesell and Terman, were pioneers of the normative, maturational perspective. "In Gesell's hands, Rousseau's idea of an inner developmental force became the guiding principle behind extensive scholarship and research" (Crain, 1985, p. 23).

As described previously, most other early research efforts were to a large extent fueled by practical questions concerning how to promote child welfare, but results based on these external states approaches were for the most part disappointing. A number of alternatives emphasizing internal states emerged in the 1960s and 1970s, and these have had lasting influence. They may be distinguished in terms

of the nature of the internal state: (a) cognitive states, (b) temperamental predispositions, (c) ethological heritage, and (d) motivational predispositions.

Studies of Childhood

Cognitive States   A major internal states perspective concerns the constraints and personal orientations provided by the individual's level or type of cognitive understanding. One major source of this perspective was the work of Piaget, who viewed development in terms of qualitative changes in cognitive structures as the individual's existing structures were challenged by environmental demands. Although Piaget published extensively as early as the 1920s, his work received little attention in the United States until Flavell (1963) described and interpreted the findings for an English-speaking audience. Piaget's almost exclusive focus on intellectual development might make his work seem largely irrelevant to concerns of social development, but, in fact, his work has been enormously influential, for several reasons. First, one of his earliest publications reported a series of observations about children's understanding of morality (Piaget, 1932). As described earlier, initial conclusions about children's understanding of various aspects of moral behavior, such as intentionality, led to a series of challenges that resulted in a voluminous literature on moral judgments in the late 1970s (Costanzo & Dix, 1983).

Second, Kohlberg devoted his career to various implications of this developmental cognitive-structural approach for social development. Most of his energy focused on an alternative cognitive-developmental approach to moral development, in which changes in moral thinking were viewed as continuing in a stage-like fashion into adulthood (1964). This body of work has been extremely influential (see Rest, 1986, for a review), so much so that educational programs to promote advanced moral thinking have been designed for school systems based on his theory. In addition, Kohlberg described in considerable detail how a cognitive-developmental perspective would lead to alternative predictions about the nature of gender development (Kohlberg, 1966) and of socialization, more generally (Kohlberg, 1969).

Third, the incorporation of a cognitive perspective into the study of the social development of children intersected with a similar movement in social psychology, thereby promoting a growth in interest in social cognitive development (e.g., Brehm et al., 1981; Higgins et al., 1983). Fourth, approaches that started from an emphasis on cognitive states expanded perceptions of the part that they might play in social development. We have already seen that cognitive states may serve as critical mediating or moderating processes, such that the impact of the external socialization context depends on how the child processes and interprets it (Ruble, Higgins, & Hartup, 1983). Now, two further influences of cognitive states are considered: (a) that they are enabling, and (b) that they are motivating.

The first, again deriving originally from Piaget, proposes that the level of cognitive understanding in some domains may *enable* certain kinds of social functioning. The basic idea is that without a certain kind of knowledge, children will tend not to see opportunities for particular kinds of social behavior or find it difficult to enact certain social strategies.

This proposal is interesting, but the evidence is mixed. Consider, for example, the often examined role of perspective-taking in prosocial behavior and interpersonal relationships. Although such relations are often found, the findings from such studies have been quite mixed, and it is difficult to draw clear conclusions about how general cognitive changes relate to general social skills. One reason, perhaps, for the inconsistencies is that attempts to find relations may often be at too global a level. In many cases, it is not sufficiently clear why more mature social-cognitive skills would necessarily lead children to behave more positively; as Shantz (1983) notes, "social information and understanding, however derived . . . can be used for social good or ill" (p. 526).

Problems with mixed findings arise even when the proposed reason for the expected link is reasonably clear. For example, in the study of prosocial behavior, the assumption is that higher levels of perspective-taking skills allow children to understand others' needs, which fosters empathy and prosocial responding (Eisenberg, Shea, Carlo, & Knight, 1991; Hoffman, 1982). Although this relation has frequently been observed, it seems to depend upon other factors (see Eisenberg & Fabes, 1997, for a review). Children may require certain social skills, such as assertiveness, to put their understanding into effect (e.g., Denham & Couchoud, 1991). Also, the expected relation may depend on external conditions. It may be found only for situations that demand an understanding of others' needs to elicit prosocial behavior, for example, as opposed to one that compels such behaviors relatively automatically or for social desirability reasons (Eisenberg & Fabes, 1997). Finally, the type of reasoning being examined must be carefully calibrated in relation to age. For example, several studies have found a relation between spontaneous sharing and relatively advanced levels of prosocial moral reasoning for the age group—for example, for preschoolers, need-oriented as opposed to hedonistic (e.g., Eisenberg-Berg & Hand, 1979; Miller, Eisenberg, Fabes, & Shell, 1996).

A second approach views cognitive changes not only as enabling, but also as *motivating*. For example, Kohlberg (1966) proposed that children's growing understanding of their gender identity as constant over time and situation initiated a need to seek information relevant to gender norms and to organize their cognitions and behaviors in terms of gender. Although subsequent research has revealed that children are responsive to gender norms much

before they have attained a complete understanding of the constancy of gender, the stages of gender constancy are associated with a number of important aspects of children's gender-related behaviors, such as avoiding novel toys thought to belong to the other sex and making selections based on gender when more attractive options are available (see Ruble and Martin, 1997, for a review). This pattern of data has been interpreted as indicating that as children approach a complete understanding that they permanently belong to one sex category and not the other, they become motivated to consolidate their understanding of gender rules so that they do not behave incorrectly (Ruble, 1994). Similarly, Rholes et al. (1990) have proposed that changes in children's understanding of people's characteristics as stable and reflective of internal states contributes to new motivational orientations in various social arenas, such as interest in new aspects of interpersonal interactions or in different forms of evaluative feedback. For example, Camhy and Ruble (1994) found that seven- to eight-year-old children who perceived others' characteristics in stable terms were more likely to ask a newcomer questions about his or her internal characteristics and interests (e.g., "Do you like to play tricks") instead of external, peripheral characteristics (e.g., "How do you get to school") than were children who did not exhibit such an understanding.

Temperamental Predispositions   Another internal states approach emphasizes individual differences in temperament and personality, often assumed to be biologically based and present in infancy (Kagan & Moss, 1962; Thomas, Chess, Birch, Hertzig, & Korn, 1963). How do such attributes affect the processes and outcomes of socialization? According to the external states perspectives characterizing most early socialization research, the direction of causality was from the socializing agent to the child by means of reinforcement and modeling processes. A groundbreaking paper by Bell (1968) made the alternative case, however, that such influence processes are bidirectional. Variations in child temperament lead to different reactions such that, for example, persistently aggressive and strong-willed children may wear out their parents over time, leading them to become more permissive toward aggression at a later point. Thus, an association between parental permissiveness of aggression and aggressiveness in children may be due to the impact of the child on the parent, rather than the reverse. This point of view is currently represented in behavioral genetics research, suggesting that differences in exposure of children to various external states, including socialization practices and even mass media, are driven to a large extent by innate characteristics of the child (Plomin & Bergeman, 1991; Scarr, 1992), a view that has generated considerable controversy (Hoffman, 1991; Thelen, 1991).

This conceptual breakthrough that children influence parents as well as the reverse, which in retrospect seems obvious, has contributed to important advances in the field. One particularly interesting line of research is examining how temperamental characteristics of the child interact with features of the socialization environment to determine outcomes. For example, Kochanska (1995) has suggested that individual differences in children's tendency to experience anxiety associated with wrongdoing and in behavioral control (the ability to inhibit a prohibited action) determine, in part, how different disciplinary techniques influence the development of conscience in children. To illustrate, because some degree of arousal may facilitate attention to the parents' message but too much disrupt attention (Hoffman, 1977), highly fearful children may respond better to gentle rather than fear-arousing disciplinary strategies.

From perspectives beginning with temperamental internal states, then, the role of external states primarily involves (1) how different kinds of predispositions elicit certain kinds of external reactions, and (2) how the same external condition is responded to differently by children with different predispositions. In addition, external agents are not merely passive participants in socialization encounters. They have certain beliefs and expectations about temperamental characteristics and how they should respond to them, and these constructions also affect the nature of the interaction (Eder & Mangelsdorf, in press). For example, Caspi et al. (1988) have shown that shyness in girls does not have the same negative impact as shyness in boys, presumably because this attribute is perceived as less acceptable in boys than in girls.

Ethological Heritage　Another line of biological research, ethological approaches, borrowed some key notions from observations of animal behavior. It introduced the notion that the organism is biologically programmed to behave in functional, adaptive ways from birth, that children may be predisposed to learn some things more readily than others (that they are not really a tabula rasa). Moreover, the ethologists' observations of imprinting in animals (Lorenz, 1981) was influential in bringing attention to the differential effects of early experience and even the possibility that there may be critical periods in the development of children.

This perspective has led to a surge of interest in social developmental processes during infancy. By coding minute details of changes in behaviors, verbalizations, and affect, a number of researchers have documented that sometimes quite intricate "transactions" characterize interaction sequences between parent and child. For example, Tronick (1989) has shown that even young infants can control the nature of an interaction by innate signals, such as smiling and turning away when overstimulated. The observations suggest that periods of attention and inattention characterize infant behavior. Moreover, the effects of parental behaviors depend on how responsive parents are to the infant's state. As parents learn to recognize when their baby is receptive, smiling, and attentive, synchronized routines develop between infant and parent. Parents vary in how alert they are to their infants' states and how well they adapt their behavior to the infant's specific responses. This contingent responsiveness appears to be essential to establishing a pattern that communicates support and acceptance and is thought by some to be key to whether or not a strong reciprocal attachment develops (Isabella & Belsky, 1991).

Motivational Predispositions　One early internal states approach involved reconceptualizing the notion of drive. Theories attempting to reconcile learning and psychoanalytic perspectives had posited that the main motivation of human behavior was to satisfy primary needs (hunger, sex). Individual needs were seen to be at odds with those of the greater society. This portrait of human behavior and the function of society was unsatisfying to many, and within this context, proposals that human drives can be viewed in positive terms, as effectance motivation (White, 1959) or curiosity (Berlyne, 1960), were eagerly embraced. From these perspectives, socialization agents can support rather than fight with a child's primary needs. Such views contributed to the growth of contemporary theoretical orientations that portray individuals as mastery oriented (Harter, 1983), as engaging in self-determined behavior (Deci & Ryan, 1985), and as engaged in an active construction of their environment or "self-socialization" (Maccoby & Jacklin, 1974; Ruble, 1987).

These views of human behavior as guided by innate motives to understand and master the environment share many features of the perspective presented earlier involving indirect external states. Self-socialization by nature includes the acquisition of information about the social world through attention to models, narratives, and scripts. The main distinction is the presumed locus of the effect. From an external locus perspective, change occurs because individuals are exposed to particular models and scripts; internal states are involved through processes of attention and memory but the effect is driven externally not by inherent needs to search and construct. In contrast, from a self-socialization perspective, individuals actively search out information, strategically select relevant models, and construct narratives and scripts.

One contemporary line of research that represents the concept of internal positive motivation particularly well is Deci and Ryan's (1985) theory of intrinsic motivation, based on the idea that there are organismic needs to feel capable and effective in dealing with the environment and to experience one's actions as freely chosen and self-determined. According to this conceptualization, children do not need to be taught to strive for mastery but are naturally so inclined. Nevertheless, external conditions do play an important role: the environment may be structured in ways that either foster or undermine intrinsic motivation. Considerable social developmental research has examined what these conditions are and how they affect personal and interpersonal functioning. External conditions that foster a sense that one's actions are due to external pressures from parents or teachers, or that they are done as a means to an end rather than for their own sake, tend to undermine intrinsic motivation, increase maladaptive responses to failure, and negatively affect self-esteem (Boggiano & Pittman, 1992; Lepper, 1983).

Several studies support this conclusion. For example, teachers' orientations toward supporting students' autonomy versus controlling their behavior and the students' perceptions that the classroom climate supported self-determination have been related to students' intrinsic interest in school as well as their feelings of self-worth (Deci & Ryan, 1992). Similarly, use of controlling techniques by teachers (e.g., grades, rewards) were found to predict the development of extrinsic orientations which, in turn, predicted susceptibility to the performance and attributional deficits of helplessness, as well as low standardized test scores (Boggiano & Barrett, 1985; Boggiano et al., 1992). Even encouraging teachers to have their students perform "up to standards," thereby indirectly enhancing the probability of their use of controlling techniques, produces a performance decrement in students (Flink, Boggiano, & Barrett, 1990).

Of course, demonstrating that certain external conditions can undermine intrinsic motivation does not directly speak to the idea that it is a fundamental human need or that any effects begin from internal rather than external states. Indeed, most of the findings could be equally well interpreted from a perspective that begins with external conditions, that is, that socialization experiences may foster a set of beliefs and goals that contribute to an orientation toward mastery (e.g., Dweck, 1991), as discussed earlier.

It is noteworthy, therefore, that developmental analyses point to indications of mastery motivation in infancy. For example, very young infants appear to respond positively to indications of contingency, that their actions have a predictable effect on the environment (e.g., Bornstein & Tamis-LeMonda, 1989; Frodi, Bridges, & Grolnick, 1985). In addition, during their second year, children show joy or "mastery smiles" when they produce certain outcomes (e.g., Kagan, 1981). For example, as part of an in-depth study of toddlers and preschoolers' reactions to achievement-related outcomes, Stipek, Recchia, and McClintic (1992) found that even before 22 months of age, children show great pleasure when they master a challenge. Moreover, maternal praise is not required for such expressions of pleasure, and pleasure is especially likely when the task is self rather than mother-generated. Interestingly, intrinsic motivation for learning appears to decline as children progress through educational institutions (Harter, 1992), perhaps in response to structural factors that often lead children to feel pressured and controlled to do well. As Eccles and her colleagues have noted (e.g., Eccles & Midgley,

1989), it is ironic that the transition to junior high school is marked by a "tightening of the reins" and a concomitant decrease in intrinsic motivation, just as increased needs for autonomy and independence emerge.

Studies of Adulthood   Studies with adults again may start from a concern with several kinds of internal states: cognitive, temperamental, ethologically based, and motivational. This concern might be traced by considering each kind of state separately, asking for example how they respectively give rise to studies of perspective-taking, the understanding of relationships, ways of responding to infants, or the need for control and a sense of self-efficacy. Rather than go through each line of research, we have chosen instead to single out a theme that cuts across several lines of research, helps bring out what studies of adulthood add to studies of childhood, and highlights the possible ways in which external conditions and internal states may be interrelated. This theme has to do with the extent to which external conditions are needed in order to bring about or to sustain particular behaviors.

At one end of a spectrum are adult behaviors that appear to need minimal prompting or support from the outside world. As one example, across cultures adults display the same forms of vocal expressions towards infants (e.g., Papousek & Papousek, 1991), with little or no prompting. They adopt what has been called "infant-directed speech," exaggerating the contours of speech, even when asked to use a language other than their own (Fernald & Morikawa, 1993). They also appear to move spontaneously toward nurturant and engaging actions towards infants (e.g., Emde et al., 1991), although the incidence of neglect and abuse suggests that such actions may not be sustained in the face of aversive crying or the absence of some rewarding response from the child.

A second example of an internal state that appears to need little prompting or support in later life are the "working models" of relationships established in the course of one's own childhood. These are expected to persist into times when the individual becomes a parent (e.g., Main, Kaplan, & Cassidy, 1985). Change may then occur only in special circumstances. A supportive partner, for instance, can help undo a negative working model that would otherwise be carried over to one's own parenting.

In contrast, a number of other behaviors linked theoretically to an internal states perspective may persist into later life only if some particular circumstances occur. To remain in place, they may need (a) to be supported by general social approval, (b) to remain in line with the individual's needs, or (c) to be practiced by the individual.

The maintenance of certain temperamental characteristics is an example of the first kind of phenomenon. From adolescence to adulthood, for instance, shyness may have greater predictive value for women than for men because in "Anglo" cultures—at least in the cohorts studied to date—

shyness is a more acceptable quality in women than it is in men and consequently remains more stable over the life span (Caspi et al., 1988).

For an example of the second kind of basis to stability or change, we turn to reports that women become more assertive in mid-life than they are at earlier ages, while men become more nurturant. The basis for such changes, Labouvie-Vief (1994, 1996) proposes, does not lie within external conditions. It lies instead in the sense that the time has come to give rein to a so-far unfulfilled or incompletely expressed part of the self. External conditions may still enter the picture in the form of sanctioning change. The primary push, however, is seen as the internal wish for fulfillment, for the completion of the sense of self.

For examples of the last prop to stability (i.e., that stability depends on continued use), we turn to studies of perspective-taking. It might seem reasonable to expect that once an individual has achieved the cognitive capacity to "read" the intentions or viewpoints of others, this skill should stay in place. The evidence is not in line with this expectation, at least in later life. Beyond the age of 60, the individuals who maintain their skills in perspective-taking are those whose social life involves meeting new faces, anticipating differences of opinion, or having to cope with unexpected differences of opinion (as against those that are so familiar and expectable that they have ceased to be reflected upon). These are the people, for instance, who are executive officers for a club, rather than simply members of it. They are also the people who maintain contact with people outside their own age group and want to understand their positions or their actions (Cohen, Bearison, & Muller, 1987; Dolen & Bearison, 1982). The same phenomenon seems likely to be found also at younger ages.

In short, the general message from studies of adult change is that the stability of particular ways of viewing social events or of responding to them is neither to be taken for granted nor assumed to be unlikely. The critical questions then concern not the nature of the conditions—external or internal—that first spark a particular state, but the nature of the conditions that sustain, transform, reestablish, enhance, or diminish the richness or the accessibility of specific actions, understandings, or emotions.

Summary

The preceding general message from studies of adulthood may serve as a summary statement for this section on accounts of change that start from an emphasis on external conditions or on internal states and move, in both cases, towards ways of considering both. That move has led on the one hand towards many a second look at the nature of external conditions and the nature of internal states. It has led also to questions about the several ways in which external conditions and internal states are related to one another. External conditions emerge, for instance, as being inter-

preted, chosen, and searched for information: a process affected both by the individual's changing needs and by the availability or clarity of information or choices. Internal states, on the other hand, emerge as being to varying degrees supported, sustained, or undermined by external conditions (recall, for example, the extent to which intrinsic motivation is supported or undone by the provision of external rewards). Clearly no account of social development in either childhood or adulthood can concentrate exclusively on either external conditions or internal states. The challenge is to find both conceptual and methodological ways to combine the two.

WHAT IS SPECIAL ABOUT A DEVELOPMENTAL ANALYSIS OF SOCIAL PROCESSES?

The preceding discussion of what social developmentalists study and how they explain change and variation may lead many readers to the conclusion that the study of social development is quite similar to standard social psychological analyses, only conducted with different populations and with more of a focus on change. For example, the study of socialization processes may be viewed as a huge, complicated social psychology experiment of social influence. The exposure to the social influence message involves communicators who vary in numerous characteristics (power, clarity, personal/impersonal), using a variety of social influence strategies (coercion, reward, reciprocity, modeling), varying degrees of consensus, and a target whose ability to comprehend and whose knowledge and strength of attitudes about the message is changing over time.

Given that social psychological approaches can examine such issues using simpler paradigms and greater control, what is the benefit of a developmental perspective? Our response is that the process of development involves a number of "hidden" influences that affect behavior and can only be revealed by the study of change over time. There are several types of such hidden influences offered by a developmental perspective.

The most obvious implication from a developmental analysis is that a time course or life-span perspective necessitates a consideration of behavior in terms of its *dynamic or temporal qualities*. This can have several meanings. The first relates to points raised in the introductory section of this chapter. People's behaviors are situated in time and place, and observed reactions in any study are affected by the individual's place in history and ontogeny as they interact with his or her perceptions of the situation. The percentage of individuals who are "gender schematic," for example, will vary as a function of changes in cultural norms regarding gender, the age of the individual, and the salience of gender-related issues highlighted in the media over the preceding week.

A second temporal principle concerns the disproportionate weight accorded to the *effects of early experience*. Once a particular path is selected, it is more difficult to return to the starting point and select an alternative path. If little girls are given dolls and little boys are given trucks to play with, it is hardly surprising that differences in toy preferences would subsequently emerge because of the differential opportunity to explore the qualities of different activities. Moreover, experience with these different activities may foster the development of different skills—such as social versus mechanical.

One way this principle applies to social psychology is by questioning the almost exclusive focus on proximal relative to distal sources of influence on behavior (Costanzo, 1992). For example, many contemporary social psychologists emphasize the significance of automatic responding to proximal events on the basis of unconscious attitudes and habits (e.g., Bargh, 1996; Cialdini, 1988; Devine, 1989). Implicitly, such analyses acknowledge the legacy of developmental experiences, but the analysis typically stops short of a consideration of what those experiences might be and how they might influence current reactions. One exception is work by Costanzo and colleagues (e.g., Costanzo & Fraenkel, 1987) on the internalization of values. These studies suggest that in domains involving strongly socialized values, judgments may proceed rather automatically, often on the basis of the severity of outcomes, whereas in other domains, intentions and mitigating circumstances are likely to influence judgments. In terms of the present theoretical framework, external socialization experiences contribute to the formation of an internal state in the form of values. These values are accessible to contemporaneous measurement and influence what and how individuals respond to incoming social information.

A related notion is that there may be times of heightened sensitivity or even critical periods. One of the striking observations from the animal literature in the 1960s that had a large impact on the study of social develoment was the phenomenon of imprinting. Young chicks would adopt as their parent whomever or whatever was physically present at a particular point after their birth. More recently, both attachment or bonding (Bowlby, 1980) and gender identification (Money & Ehrhardt, 1972) have been associated with the notion of critical or sensitive periods. This notion is of obvious significance because it implies that the results of experiences occurring at a particular point in time are long-lasting and irrevocable. At the extreme, the principle would imply that mothers and infants will never be fully attached unless they have an opportunity to bond shortly after birth, and that a biological girl could identify herself as a boy if she receives male socialization until the age of five years or so, but not after that.

Although there are few true critical periods in the study of the social development of humans, the concept of periods of sensitivity is potentially relevant to a wide range of phenomena, and may well apply across the life span. Life transitions, such as becoming a parent or retiring, for example, are times of identity changes, and at these points individuals are likely to be particularly susceptible to social information relevant to the new identity. Moreover, once the new identity has stabilized, an individual is likely to be less influenced by incoming information, in part because they are no longer seeking it and in part because new cognitive structures associated with the new identity act as schema to affect the perception, interpretation, and memory of such information (Ruble, 1987, 1994). Thus, transitions throughout the life span may often function as sensitive periods, much like those associated with early childhood. The concept of sensitive periods may also prove useful in the study of social phenomena that have a distinct time line, such as the formation of close friendships and attitude formation and change.

A third temporal principle concerns the *pace and direction of change*. One reason researchers who study children may focus more on developmental processes than those who study adults is because it is a period of rapid growth. Similarly, developmental processes are a major focus among researchers who study late adulthood, in part because it is another period of rapid change, but this time in the other direction. What are the implications of studying social psychological processes during periods of rapid acceleration or deceleration? Although intuitively such changes would seem to exert a significant influence on observed behaviors, there has been little direct examination of this issue. A study of runners illustrates the kinds of differences one might expect to see (Frey & Ruble, 1990). More mature runners and those at any age whose performance was on the decline reported greater satisfaction when they evaluated their performance by means of social comparison than by temporal comparison. Younger runners and those at any age whose performance was improving showed the reverse pattern of greater satisfaction from evaluation based on temporal comparison. These findings are noteworthy in part because of the common assumption that social comparison should be avoided, that it frequently has negative implications for self-esteem, particularly in classroom situations where very few can be at the top. This assumption is derived primarily from research with children and young adults, however. In a later life sample, when resources and skills are declining, social comparison offers a very different perspective, a source of satisfaction that cannot often be gleaned from comparing one's current performance with the past.

A fourth temporal principle concerns the *course or trajectory of change*. Many forms of social knowledge may be viewed as a kind of linear accumulation of facts, but many others involve curves or bumps along the way. The concept of critical period, for example, suggests a pronounced curvilinear trend with development, as individuals show rapid growth during a very limited period of time and little further change. Other theories, such as Kohlberg's theory of moral development, implies a more step-like progression. Moreover, an incorporation of late-life perspectives reveals some limitations in implicit assumptions that there is an end point to the development of any area of social knowledge, that it reaches some final level and then stabilizes. In contrast, maintaining a high level may require constant use and practice, and the final stable line may instead represent a number of peaks and valleys. Even something as seemingly straightforward as internalized principles against cheating may lose ground during adulthood. Because of less attention to ethical ideals at this time than during adolescence and early adulthood, the structures underlying the principles may lose some supports or connections among them.

These developmental course perspectives have some potentially interesting implications for social psychology. Although the dependent variable of interest is often a change variable, social psychologists are rarely aware of the trajectory of change. After being presented with a prime or a persuasive message, for example, is the typical subjects' response linear or curvilinear in nature, and if the latter, is it U-shaped, or reverse U-shaped? For some paradigms, such knowledge could be key to determining whether or not an effect is found, because it provides a basis for determining when to take the dependent measure. Moreover, is the change one that is likely to stabilize and, if so, what processes are required for maintenance? Consider the possibility, for example, that differences in stereotyping across individuals, situations, or social categories reflect a developmental process, rather than personality (authoritarianism) or motivation (e.g., personal relevance), as they are typically conceptualized. The study noted earlier by D'Alessio (1977) illustrates this alternative interpretation. In this study, parents were asked to make judgments about five- and two-year-olds. Parents of two-year-olds did not make stereotyped judgments about two-year-olds, but the parents of five-year-olds did so. Even though they had had experience with two-year-olds, they were now past the point of daily experience, and their ideas appeared to have reverted to stereotyped forms. The results suggest both that the growth in understanding about two-year-olds resulting from personal experience may not be durable, and that differences in stereotyped responses to different social categories may reflect something about developmental processes, in this case, loss of expertise, rather than something about the social categories, per se.

Time course issues may affect social psychology studies in other ways. College students are likely to be at different points in the time course for different domains. For example, even though they may be quite advanced in terms of general cognitive operations, they may be quite immature in other social behaviors, such as entering and exiting intimate relationships, emotional expression, forms of coping, and so on. It may be obvious that one would not want to focus on this age group for the study of retirement plans and beliefs. Yet, without a clear understanding of the time course of values, goals, and social knowledge and experiences, the study of many topics at this age may lead to misleading conclusions. For example, Trope and Neter (1994) have found that individuals are better able to receive negative evaluative feedback after exposure to mood-enhancing information. Is this finding perhaps partly due to the importance of evaluative feedback among college students, the preferred mode of mood regulation, or some other developmental process not yet being considered?

Finally, a related temporal principle concerns time lags; the influence of a change at one point in time may not be seen immediately but rather later, sometimes considerably later. In one study, for example, the emergence of children's understanding of the functional features of social comparison did not affect actual social comparison behavior in the classroom until two years later (Pomerantz et al., 1995). Similarly, recent research has suggested that children's knowledge of gender stereotypes may affect their own gender-related preferences a year later even if there is no concurrent relation (Aubry, Ruble, & Silverman, 1997). Such lags may occur for many different reasons. For example, it may take time for the individual to recognize which behaviors are relevant to the new knowledge. Within social psychology, this principle is recognized as the "sleeper" effect. Although social psychologists devote considerable attention to mediating processes concerning *how* an effect occurs, it might be productive for both social and developmental psychologists to consider the processes influencing *when* an effect occurs.

Summary and Conclusions

This *Handbook* chapter differs from many others in that we have not tried to present a comprehensive, state-of-the-discipline portrait of everything we now know about social development. The field is too large and diverse to attempt such an endeavor. Instead, we have tried to address some fundamental questions about the goals of social developmental research and its past, present, and possible future in relation to social psychology. Three questions received particular attention.

First, in what ways can we extract a structure that might provide a kind of map to the main issues in the field? Although no doubt many structures are possible, we chose to highlight a few basic distinctions and dimensions. At the most general level, we distinguished between the topics that have been prominent within studies of social development and the kinds of accounts that have been offered for the occurrence of change and variation. Within each of these two broad sections, we reviewed major programs of past and current research as illustrations of some fundamental dimensions in the field, noting also some particular points of linkage with research within social psychology.

Some further subdivisions helped to bring out the shape of research on social development. With respect to the topics covered, three dimensions were examined: (1) emphasis on behavior, cognition, or affect; (2) emphasis on individual differences versus normative patterns; and (3) emphasis on individuation versus connectedness. With respect to explanations, we distinguished at the most general level between accounts that begin with an emphasis on external conditions—either direct (e.g., rewards) versus indirect (e.g., observation learning)—and those that begin with an emphasis on internal conditions, such as temperament or cognitive capacity. In spite of the necessity to make some distinctions, we also noted that all of these processes are intermingled during development. Thus, for example, external conditions influence development partly by means of fostering certain internal states—cognitions, emotions, motivation. Conversely, internal conditions influence development partly by means of fostering differentiated perception and selection of and reactions to external states.

A second question concerns in what ways the study of social development converges and diverges at early and later parts of the life span. In some cases, the topics and explanations were quite similar across the two age groups. Both age groups show a concern with certain key topics, such as prosocial behavior and perspective taking, and with certain explanations, such as observational learning. But there are many significant differences in issues and emphases that may be informative both about developmental process and about important gaps. For example, studies of childhood action are primarily concerned with age changes in the nature or frequency of particular actions, such as aggression and prosocial behavior, or in conditions that influence the likelihood of engaging or disengaging in particular actions. There is relatively little attention to how action is sustained in pursuit of a goal, as there is in the adulthood literature. Partly this may be because goal-oriented actions are more frequent or central to the social behavior of adults than of children. Alternatively, this gap in the childhood literature may reflect some fundamental assumptions about the nature of childhood—that actions are short-lived, are other- rather than self-directed, and that children are less influenced by goals—assumptions that may derive from historical theoretical traditions rather than the true nature of childhood.

The third question asks about the overlaps between social developmental and social psychological approaches and what the two fields might be able to contribute to each other. The nature of overlaps was examined in the introductory section of this chapter, and illustrations of possible contributions of a developmental approach to social psychology were offered in the final section. Overall, the overlap in topics and basic concern with change across the two disciplines is considerable. Considering the two perspectives together, however, also revealed why the question of the relation between the two fields continues to be asked.

In essence, each contains a "blind spot" that is central to the goals of the other. For social development, this omission has been the perseveration with age differences without fully coming to terms with what age stands for as a *process.* For social psychology, this omission is the neglect of time course as a variable governing observed relations, particularly as it applies to selection of samples. As we also noted in our review, however, such blind spots have been increasingly recognized among contemporary researchers, and we see considerable promise in the continuing convergence of the two fields.

REFERENCES

Aboud, F. E. (1988). *Children and Prejudice.* New York: Basil Blackwell.

Aboud, F. E., & Ruble, D. N. (1987). Identity constancy in children: Developmental processes and implications. In T. M. Honess & K. M. Yardley (Eds.), *Self and identity: Individual change in development* (pp. 95–107). London: Routledge and Kegan Paul.

Ainsworth, M. D. S. (1969). Object relations, dependency, and attachment: A theoretical review of the infant-mother relationship. *Child Development, 40,* 969–1025.

Ainsworth, M. D. S., Blehar, M. C., Waters, E., & Wall, S. (1978). *Patterns of attachment: A psychological study of the Strange Situation.* Hillsdale, NJ: Erlbaum.

Alfieri, T. J., Ruble, D. N., & Higgins, E. T. (1996). Gender stereotypes during adolescence: Developmental changes and the transition to Junior High School. *Developmental Psychology, 32,* 1129–1137.

Allen, K. R. (1989). *Single women/family ties: Life histories of older women.* Newbury Park, CA: Sage.

Altshuler, J. A., & Ruble, D. N. (1989). Developmental changes in children's awareness of strategies for coping with stress. *Child Develpment, 60,* 1337–1349.

Appelbaum, M. E., & McCall, R. B. (1983). Design and analysis in developmental psychology. In W. Kessen (Ed.), *Handbook of child psychology* (4th ed., Vol. 4, pp. 415–476). New York: Wiley.

Aronfreed, J. (1968). *Conduct and conscience: The socialization of internalized control over behavior.* New York: Academic.

Asch, S. E. (1956). Studies of independence and conformity: A minority of one against a unanimous majority. *Psychology Monographs, 70* (9, Whole No. 416).

Aubry, S., Ruble, D. N., & Silverman, L. (1997). The role of gender knowledge in children's gender-typed preferences. In C. Tamis-LeMonda & L. Balter (Eds.), *Child psychology: A handbook of contemporary issues.* New York: Garland (in preparation).

Backett, K. C. (1982). *Mothers and fathers.* London: Macmillan.

Bakan, D. (1966). *The duality of human existence: Isolation and communion in Western man.* Boston: Beacon.

Baldwin, A. L. (1955). *Behavior and development in childhood.* New York: Dryden Press.

Baltes, M. M. (1986). The etiology and maintenance of dependence in the elderly: Three phases of operant research. *Behavior Therapy, 19,* 301–319.

Baltes, M. M. (1995). Dependency in old age: Gains and losses. *Current Directions in Psychological Science, 4,* 14–19.

Baltes, P. B., & Baltes, M. M. (1990). Psychological perspectives on successful aging: The model of selective optimization with compensation. In P. B. Baltes & M. M. Baltes (Eds.), *Successful aging* (pp. 1–34). New York: Cambridge University Press.

Baltes, P. B., Dittmann-Kohli, F., & Dixon, R. A. (1984). New perspectives on the development of intelligence in adulthood: Toward a dual-process conception and a model of selective optimization with compensation. In P. B. Baltes & O. G. Brim, Jr. (Eds.), *Life-span development and behavior* (Vol. 6). New York: Academic Press.

Baltes, P. B., & Smith, J. (1990). Towards a psychology of wisdom and its ontogenesis. In R. J. Sternberg (Ed.), *Wisdom: Its nature, origins, and development.* New York: Cambridge University Press.

Band, E. B., & Weisz, J. R. (1988). How to feel better when it feels bad: Children's perspectives on coping with everyday stress. *Developmental Psychology, 24,* 247–253.

Bandura, A. (1969). Social-learning theory of identificatory processes. In D. A. Goslin (Ed.), *Handbook of socialization theory and research* (pp. 213–262). Chicago: Rand McNally.

Bandura, A. (1986). *Social foundations of thought and action: A social cognitive theory.* Englewood Cliffs, NJ: Prentice-Hall.

Bandura, A., Barbaranelli, C., Caprara, G. V., & Pastorelli, C. (1996). Multifaceted impact of self-efficacy beliefs on academic functioning. *Child Development, 67,* 1206–1222.

Bandura, A., & Walters, R. H. (1963). *Social learning and personality development.* New York: Holt, Rinehart & Winston.

Bargh, J. A. (1996). Automaticity in social psychology. In E. T. Higgins & A. Kruglanski (Eds.), *Social psychology: Handbook of basic principles.* New York: Guilford Press.

Barkow, J. H., Cosmides, L., & Tooby, J. (Eds.). (1992). *The adapted mind: Evolutionary psychology and the generation of culture.* New York: Oxford University Press.

Barnett, M. A., King, L. M., & Howard, J. A. (1979). Inducing affect about self or other: Effects on generosity in children. *Developmental Psychology, 15,* 164–167.

Batson, C. D. (1998). Altruism and prosocial behavior. In D. Gilbert, S. T. Fiske, & G. Lindzey (Eds.), *Handbook of social psychology* (4th ed., Vol. 2, pp. 282–316). New York: McGraw-Hill.

Baumrind, D. (1973). The development of instrumental competence through socialization. In A. D. Pick (Ed.), *Min-*

nesota Symposium on Child Psychology, Vol. 7. Minneapolis: University of Minnesota Press.

Bee, H. L. (1992). *The journey of adulthood.* New York: Macmillan.

Bell, R. Q. (1968). A reinterpretation of the direction of effects in studies of socialization. *Psychology Review, 75,* 81–95.

Belsky, J. (1985). Exploring individual differences in marital change across the transition to parenthood: The role of violated expectations. *Journal of Marriage and the Family, 47,* 1037–1044.

Benenson, J. F., & Dweck, C. S. (1986). The development of trait explanations and self-evaluations in the academic and social domains. *Child Development, 57,* 1179–1187.

Bengston, V. L., & Morgan, L. L. (1983). Ethnicity and aging: A comparison of three ethnic groups. In J. Sokolovsky (Ed.), *Growing old in different societies: Cross-cultural perspectives.* Belmont, CA: Wadsworth.

Berlyne, D. (1960). *Conflict, arousal, and curiosity.* New York: McGraw-Hill.

Boggiano, A. K., & Barrett, M. (1985). Performance and motivation deficits of helplessness: The role of motivation orientations. *Journal of Personality and Social Psychology, 49,* 1753–1761.

Boggiano, A. K., Barrett, M., & Kellam, T. (1993). Competing theoretical analyses of helplessness: A social-developmental analysis. Special Issue: Social contacts, social behaviors, and socialization. *Journal of Experimental & Child Psychology, 55*(2), 194–207.

Boggiano, A. K., Barrett, M., Weiher, A. W., McClelland, G. H., & Lusk, C. M. (1987). Use of the maximal operant procedure to motivate children's intrinsic interest. *Journal of Personality and Social Psychology, 53,* 866–879.

Boggiano, A. K., Klinger, C. A., & Main, D. S. (1986). Enhancing interest in peer interaction: A developmental analysis. *Child Development, 57,* 852–861.

Boggiano, A. K., & Pittman, T. S. (Eds.). (1992). *Achievement and motivation: A social-developmental perspective.* New York: Cambridge University Press.

Boggiano, A. K., Shields, A., Barrett, M., Kellam, T., Thompson, E., Simons, J., & Katz, P. (1992). Helplessness deficits in students: The role of motivational orientation. Special Issue: Perspectives on intrinsic motivation. *Motivation and Emotion, 16*(3), 271–296.

Bornstein, M. H., & Tamis-LeMonda, C. S. (1989). Maternal responsiveness and cognitive development in children. *New Directions for Child Development, 43,* 49–61.

Bourdieu, P. (1977). *Outline of a theory of practice.* Cambridge: Cambridge University Press.

Bourdieu, P. (1979). *Distinction: A social critique of the judgement of taste.* London: Routledge & Kegan Paul.

Bourdieu, P. (1990). *A logic of practice.* Stanford, CA: Stanford University Press.

Bowes, J. M., & Goodnow, J. J. (1996). Work for home, school, or labor force: The nature and sources of changes in understanding. *Psychological Bulletin, 119,* 300–321.

Bowlby, J. (1969). *Attachment.* New York: Basic Books.

Bowlby, J. (1980). *Attachment and loss: Vol. 3. Loss, sadness, and depression.* New York: Basic Books.

Braine, L. G. (1978). A new slant on orientation perception. *American Psychologist, 33,* 10–22.

Bray, D. W., & Howard, A. (1983). The AT&T longitudinal studies of managers. In K. W. Schaie (Ed.), *Longitudinal studies of adult psychological development* (pp. 266–312). New York: Guilford.

Brehm, S. S., Kassin, S. M., & Gibbons, F. X. (Eds.). (1981). *Developmental social psychology: Theory and research.* New York: Oxford University Press.

Bretherton, I. (1992). The origins of attachment theory: John Bowlby and Mary Ainsworth. *Developmental Psychology, 28,* 759–775.

Brewer, M. B. (1991). The social self: On being the same and different at the same time. *Personality and Social Psychology Bulletin, 17,* 475–482.

Brewer, M. B., & Brown, R. J. (1998). Intergroup relations. In D. Gilbert, S. T. Fiske, & G. Lindzey (Eds.), *Handbook of social psychology* (4th ed., Vol. 2, pp. 554–594). New York: McGraw-Hill.

Bugental, D. B., & Goodnow, J. (in press). *Socialization processes.* In W. Damon (Ed.), *Handbook of child psychology.* New York: Wiley.

Burhans, K., & Dweck, C. S. (1995). Helplessness in early childhood: The role of contingent worth. *Child Development, 66,* 1719–1738.

Buss, D. M. (1995). Evolutionary psychology: A new paradigm for psychological science. *Psychological Inquiry, 6,* 1–30.

Buss, D. M., & Kenrick, D. T. (1998). Evolutionary social psychology. In D. Gilbert, S. T. Fiske, & G. Lindzey (Eds.), *Handbook of Social Psychology,* (4th ed., Vo. 2, pp. 982–1026) New York: McGraw-Hill.

Bussey, K. (1983). A social-cognitive appraisal of sex-role development. *Australian Journal of Psychology, 35*(2), 135–143.

Bussey, K., & Bandura, A. (1992). Self-regulatory mechanisms governing gender development. *Child Development, 63,* 1236–1250.

Camhy, M., & Ruble, D. N. (1994). Information-seeking during acquaintanceship: Effects of level of social understanding and personal relevance. *Social Development, 3,* 89–107.

Carstensen, L. L. (1993). Social and emotional patterns in adulthood: Support for socioemotional selectivity theory. *Psychology and Aging, 7,* 331–338.

Carstensen, L. L. (1995). Evidence for a life-span theory of socioemotional selectivity. *Current Directions in Psychological Science, 4,* 151–156.

Caspi, A., Elder, G. H., & Bem, D. J. (1987). Moving against the world: Life-course patterns of explosive children. *Developmental Psychology, 23,* 308–313.

Caspi, A., Elder, G. H., & Bem, D. J. (1988). Moving away

from the world: Life-course patterns of shy children. *Developmental Psychology, 24,* 824–831.

Chandler, M., Frita, A. S., & Hala, S. (1989). Small-scale deceit: Deception as a marker of two, three and four year olds' early theories of mind. *Child Development, 60,* 1263–1277.

Cialdini, R. B. (1988). *Influences: Science and practice.* Glenview, IL: Scott-Foresman.

Cialdini, R. B., & Fultz, J. (1990). Interpreting the negative mood-helping literature via "mega" analysis: A contrary view. *Psychological Bulletin, 107,* 210–214.

Cialdini, R. B., & Kenrick, D. T. (1976). Altruism as hedonism: A social developmental perspective on the relationship of negative mood state and helping. *Journal of Personality and Social Psychology, 34,* 907–914.

Cialdini, R. B., Kenrick, D. T., & Baumann, D. J. (1982). Effects of mood on prosocial behavior in children and adults. In N. Eisenberg (Ed.), *The development of prosocial behavior* (pp. 339–359). New York: Academic Press.

Cohen, F., Bearison, D. J., & Muller, C. (1987). Interpersonal understanding in the elderly: The influence of age-integrated and age-segregated housing. *Research on Aging, 9,* 79–100.

Coie, J. D., & Dodge, K. A. (1997). Aggression and antisocial behavior. In W. Damon (Ed.), *Handbook of child psychology, Fifth edition.* [Vol. 3: Social, emotional, and personality development, N. Eisenberg (Ed.)]. New York: Wiley.

Coie, J. D., & Koeppl, G. K. (1990). Adapting intervention to the problems of aggressive and disruptive rejected children. In S. R. Asher & J. D. Coie (Eds.), *Peer rejection in childhood. Cambridge studies in social and emotional development* (pp. 309–337). New York: Cambridge University Press.

Coie, J. D., & Kupersmidt, J. B. (1983). A behavioral analysis of emerging social status in boys' groups. *Child Development, 54,* 1400–1416.

Colby, A., Kohlberg, L., Gibbs, J., & Liebermann, M. (1983). A longitudinal study of moral judgment. *Monographs of the Society for Research in Child Development, 48,* Serial No. 200.

Cole, M. (1988). Cross-cultural research in the socio-historical tradition. *Human Development, 31,* 137–152.

Collins, W. A., & Gunnar, M. R. (1990). Social and personality development. *Annual Review of Psychology, 41,* 387–416.

Cooley, C. H. (1902). *Human nature and the social order.* New York: Scribner's.

Costa, P. T., & McCrae, R. R. (1984). Personality as a lifelong determinant of well-being. In C. Z. Malatesta & C. E. Izard (Eds.), *Emotion in adult development* (pp. 141–155). Beverly Hills, CA: Sage.

Costanzo, P. R. (1970). Conformity development as a function of self-blame. *Journal of Personality and Social Psychology, 14,* 366–374.

Costanzo, P. R. (1992). External socialization and the development of adaptive individualism and social connection. In D. N. Ruble, P. E. Costanzo, & M. E. Oliveri (Eds.), *Social psychology and mental health.* New York: Guilford.

Costanzo, P. R., Coie, J. D., Grumet, J. F., & Farnill, D. (1973). A reexamination of the effects of intent and consequence on children's moral judgments. *Child Development, 44,* 154–161.

Costanzo, P. R., & Dix, T. H. (1983). Beyond the information processed: Socialization in the development of attributional processes. In E. T. Higgins, D. N. Ruble, & W. W. Hartup (Eds.), *Social cognition and social development: A sociocultural perspective.* Cambridge: Cambridge University Press.

Costanzo, P. R., & Fraenkel, P. (1987). Social influence, socialization, and the development of social cognition: The heart of the matter. In N. Eisenberg (Ed.), *Contemporary topics in developmental psychology.* New York: Wiley.

Costanzo, P. R., & Shaw, M. E. (1966). Conformity as a function of age level. *Child Development, 37,* 967–975.

Courtney, M. L., & Cohen, R. (1996). Behavior segmentation by boys as a function of aggressiveness and prior information. *Child Development, 67,* 1034–1047.

Crain, W. C. (1985). *Theories of development: Concepts and applications* (2nd ed.). Englewood Cliffs, NJ: Prentice-Hall.

Cumming, E., & Henry, W. (1961). *Growing old: The process of disengagement.* New York: Basic Books.

D'Alessio, M. (1977). Bambino generalizzato e bambino individualizzato nella stereotipia d'eta. In E. Ponzo (Ed.), *Il bambino simplificato e inesistente* (pp. 231–242). Rome: Bulzoni.

Damon, W. (1977). *The social world of the child.* San Francisco: Jossey-Bass.

Damon, W. (1983). *Social and personality development.* New York: Norton.

Deci, E. L., & Ryan, R. M. (1985). *Intrinsic motivation and self-determination in human behavior.* New York: Plenum.

Deci, E. L., & Ryan, R. M. (1992). The initiation and regulation of intrinsically motivated learning and achievement. In A. K. Boggiano & T. S. Pittman (Eds.), *Achievement and motivation: A social-developmental perspective.* New York: Cambridge University Press.

Deci, E. L., Schwartz, A. J., Sheinman, L., & Ryan, R. M. (1981). An instrument to assess adults' orientations toward control versus autonomy with children: Reflections on intrinsic motivation and perceived competence. *Journal of Educational Psychology, 73,* 642–650.

Denham, S. A., & Couchoud, E. A. (1991). Social-emotional predictors of preschoolers' responses to adult negative emotion. *Journal of Child Psychology and Psychiatry and Allied Disciplines, 32,* 595–608.

Devine, P. G. (1989). Stereotypes and prejudice: Their automatic and controlled components. *Journal of Personality and Social Psychology, 56,* 680–690.

Dion, K. K. (1985). Socialization in adulthood. In G. Lindzey

& E. Aronson (Eds.), *Handbook of social psychology* (Vol. 2, pp. 123–148). New York: Random House.

Dishion, T. J., Andrews, D. W., & Crosby, L. (1995). Antisocial boys and their friends in early adolescence: Relationship characteristics, quality, and interactional process. *Child Development, 66,* 139–151.

Dittmann-Kohli, F. (1990). The construction of meaning in old age: Possibilities and constraints. *Aging and Society, 10,* 270–291.

Dix, T. (1991). The affective organization of parenting: Adaptive and maladaptive processes. *Psychological Bulletin, 110,* 3–25.

Dodge, K. A., Coie, J. D., Pettit, G. S., & Prince, J. M. (1990). Peer status and aggression in boys' groups: Developmental and contextual analyses. *Child Development, 61,* 1289–1309.

Dolen, L. S., & Bearison, D. J. (1982). Social interaction and social cognition in aging: A contextual analysis. *Human Development, 25,* 430–442.

Durkin, K. (1995). *Developmental and social psychology: From infancy to old age.* Oxford, England: Blackwell Publishers, Inc.

Dweck, C. S. (1986). Motivational processes affecting learning. *American Psychologist, 41,* 1040–1048.

Dweck, C. S. (1991). Self-theories and goals: Their role in motivation, personality, and development. In R. Dienstbier (Ed.), *Nebraska symposium on motivation: Vol. 38, Perspective on motivation* (pp. 199–235). Lincoln: University of Nebraska Press.

Dweck, C. S., & Leggett, E. L. (1988). A social-cognitive approach to motivation and personality. *Psychological Review, 95,* 256–273.

Eagly, A. H., & Chaiken, S. (1993). *The psychology of attitudes.* New York: Harcourt Brace and Company.

Eccles, J. S. (1987). Adolescence: Gateway to gender-role transcendence. In D. B. Carter (Ed.), *Current conceptions of sex roles and sex typing: Theory and research* (pp. 225–241). New York: Praeger Publishers.

Eccles, J. S., & Jacobs, J. E. (1986). Social forces shape math attitudes and performance. *Signs, 11,* 367–380.

Eccles, J., & Midgley, C. (1989). Stage/environment fit: Developmentally appropriate classrooms for young adolescents. In R. E. Ames & C. Ames (Eds.), *Research on motivation in education* (Vol. 3, pp. 139–186). New York: Academic Press.

Eder, R. A., & Mangelsdorf, S. C. (in press). The emotional basis of early personality development: Implications for the emergent self-concept. In R. Hogan, J. Johnson, & S. Briggs (Eds.), *Handbook of personality psychology.* Orlando, FL: Academic Press.

Eisenberg, N. (Ed.). (1995). *Review of personality and social psychology: Social development* (Vol. 15). Thousand Oaks, CA: Sage.

Eisenberg, N., & Fabes, R. A. (in press). Prosocial development. In W. Damon (Ed.), *Handbook of child psychology* (5th ed.) [Vol. 3: Social, emotional and personality development, N. Eisenberg (Ed.)]. New York: Wiley.

Eisenberg, N., Shea, C. L., Carlo, G., & Knight, G. P. (1991). Empathy-related responding and cognition: A "chicken and the egg" dilemma. In W. M. Kurtines & J. L. Gewirtz (Eds.), *Handbook of moral behavior and development, Vol. 1: Theory. Vol. 2: Research. Vol. 3: Application* (pp. 63–88). Hillsdale, NJ: Lawrence Erlbaum Associates.

Eisenberg-Berg, N., & Hand, M. (1979). The relationship of preschoolers' reasoning about prosocial moral conflicts to prosocial behavior. *Child Development, 50,* 356–363.

Ellsworth, P. C. (1994). Sense, culture, and sensibility. In S. Kitayama & H. R. Markus (Eds.), *Emotion and culture* (pp. 23–50). Washington, DC: American Psychological Association.

Emde, R. N., Biringen, Z., Clyman, R. B., & Oppenheim, D. (1991). The moral self of infancy: Affective core and procedural knowledge. *Developmental Review, 11,* 251–270.

Entwisle, D. R., & Hayduk, L. A. (1978). *Too great expectations: The academic outlook of young children.* Baltimore: Johns Hopkins Press.

Erikson, E. H. (1959). *Identity and the life cycle.* New York: International Universities Press.

Erikson, E. H. (1968). *Identity: Youth and crisis.* New York: W. W. Norton.

Erikson, E. H. (1982). *The Life-cycle completed.* New York: Norton.

Eron, L. D., Huesmann, L. R., Dubow, E., Romanoff, R., & Yarmel, P. (1987). Aggression and its correlates over 22 years. In D. Crowell, I. Evans, & C. O'Donnell (Eds.), *Childhood aggression and violence* (pp. 249–262). New York: Plenum.

Feifel, H. (1990). Psychology and death: Meaningful rediscovery. *American Psychologist, 45,* 537–543.

Feldman, N. S., Klosson, E., Parsons, J. E., Rholes, W. S., & Ruble, D. N. (1976). Order of information presentation and children's moral judgements. *Child Development, 47,* 556–559.

Fernald, A., & Morikawa, H. (1993). Common themes and cultural variations in Japanese and American mothers' speech to infants. *Child Development, 64,* 637–656.

Fiese, B. H. (1992). Dimensions of family rituals across two generations: Relation to adolescent identity. *Family Process, 31,* 151–162.

Finch, J., & Groves, D. (Eds.). (1983). *A labour of love: Women, work, and caring.* London: Routledge.

Finch, J., & Mason, J. (1993). *Negotiating family responsibilities.* London: Routledge.

Finnie, V., & Russell, A. (1988). Preschool children's social status and their mothers' behavior and knowledge in the supervisory role. *Developmental Psychology, 24,* 789–801.

Fiske, S. T., & Taylor, S. E. (1991). *Social cognition* (2nd ed.). New York: McGraw-Hill.

Flavell, J. H. (1963). T*he developmental psychology of Jean Piaget.* New York: Van Nostrand.

Flavell, J. H. (1977). *Cognitive development.* Englewood Cliffs, NJ: Prentice-Hall.

Flavell, J. H. (1997). Social cognition. In W. Damon (Ed.), *Handbook of child psychology.* New York: Wiley.

Flavell, J. H., & Ross, L. (Eds.). (1981). *Social cognitive development: Frontiers and possible futures.* Cambridge: Cambridge University Press.

Flink, C., Boggiano, A. K., & Barrett, M. (1990). Controlling teaching strategies: Undermining children's self-determination and performance. *Journal of Personality and Social Psychology, 59,* 916–924.

Forman, E. A., Minick, N., & Stone, C. A. (1993). *Contexts of learning: Sociocultural dynamics in children's development.* New York: Oxford University Press.

Frederickson, B. L., & Carstensen, L. L. (1990). Choosing social partners: How old age and anticipated endings make people more selective. *Psychology and Aging, 5,* 335–347.

Frey, K. S., & Ruble, D. N. (1990). Strategies for comparative evaluation: Maintaining a sense of competence across the lifespan. In R. J. Sternberg & J. Kolligian (Eds.), *Perceptions of competence and incompetence across the lifespan.* New Haven, CT: Yale University Press.

Frijda, N. H., & Mesquita, B. (1994). The social roles and functions of emotions. In S. Kitayama & H. R. Markus (Eds.), *Emotion and culture: Empirical studies of mutual influence* (pp. 51–87). Washington, DC: American Psychological Association.

Frodi, A., Bridges, L., & Grolnick, W. (1985). Correlates of mastery-related behavior: A short-term longitudinal study of infants in their second year. *Child Development, 56,* 1291–1298.

Geen, R. G. (1998). Aggression and antisocial behavior. In D. Gilbert, S. T. Fiske, & G. Lindzey (Eds.), *Handbook of social psychology* (4th ed., Vol. 2, pp. 317–356). New York: McGraw-Hill.

Gelman, R., & Baillargeon, R. (1983). A review of Piagetian concepts. In J. H. Flavell & E. M. Markman (Eds.), *Handbook of child psychology. Vol. 3: Cognitive development.* New York: Wiley.

Gesell, A. (1948). *Studies in child development.* Westport, CT: Greenwood Press.

Gilligan, C., & Attanucci, J. (1988). Two moral orientations. In C. Gilligan, J. V. Ward, & J. M. Taylor (Eds.), *Mapping the moral domain* (pp. 73–87). Cambridge, MA: Harvard University Press.

Goldsmith, H. H., & Alansky, J. A. (1987). Maternal and infant temperamental predictors of attachment: A meta-analytic review. *Journal of Consulting and Clinical Psychology, 55,* 805–816.

Gollwitzer, P. M. (1990). Action phases and mind-sets. In E. T. Higgins and R. Sorrentino (Eds.), *Handbook of motivation and cognition: Foundations of social behavior* (Vol. 2, pp.

53–92). New York: Guilford.

Goodnow, J. J. (1988). Parents' ideas, actions and feelings: Models and methods from developmental and social psychology. *Child Development, 59,* 286–320.

Goodnow, J. J. (1994). Acceptable disagreement across generations. In J. G. Smetana (Ed.), *Beliefs about parenting* (pp. 51–64). San Francisco: Jossey-Bass.

Goodnow, J. J. (1995). Parents' knowledge and expectations. In M. Bornstein (Ed.), *Handbook of parenting* (Vol. 3, pp. 305–332). Mahwah, NJ: Erlbaum.

Goodnow, J. J. (1996). Acceptable ignorance, negotiable disagreement: An alternative view of learning. In D. Olson & N. Torrance (Eds.), *Handbook of education and human development* (pp. 345–368). Oxford: Blackwell.

Goodnow, J. J., Knight, R., & Cashmore, J. (1985). Adult social cognition: Implications of parents' ideas for approaches to development. In M. Perlmutter (Ed.), *Minnesota Symposium on Child Development* (Vol. 18, pp. 287–324). Hillsdale, NJ: Erlbaum.

Goodnow, J. J., Miller, P. J., & Kessel, F. (1995). *Cultural practices as contexts for development.* San Francisco: Jossey-Bass.

Goodnow, J. J., & Warton, P. M. (1992). Contexts and cognitions: Taking a pluralist view. In P. Light & G. Butterworth (Eds.), *Context and cognition* (pp. 85–112). London: Harvester Wheatsheaf.

Gottman, J. M. (1983). How children become friends. *Monographs of the Society for Research in Child Development, 48*(3), No. 201.

Grolnick, W. S., Bridges, L. J., & Connell, J. P. (1996). Emotion regulation in two-year-olds: Strategies and emotional expression in four contexts. *Child Development, 67,* 928–941.

Grusec, J. E. (1983). The internalization of altruistic dispositions: A cognitive analysis. In E. T. Higgins, D. N. Ruble, & W. W. Hartup (Eds.), *Social cognition and social development* (pp. 275–293). New York: Cambridge University Press.

Grusec, J. E. (1992). Social learning theory and developmental psychology: The legacies of Robert Sears and Albert Bandura. *Developmental Psychology, 28,* 776–786.

Grusec, J. E., & Goodnow, J. J. (1994). The impact of parental discipline methods on the child's internalization of values: A reconceptualization of current points of view. *Developmental Psychology, 30,* 4–19.

Grusec, J. E., Goodnow, J. J., & Cohen, L. (1996). Household work and the development of concern for others. *Developmental Psychology, 32,* 999–1007.

Grusec, J. E., & Lytton, H. (1988). *Social development: History, theory, and research.* New York: Springer-Verlag.

Guttmann, D. (1987). *Reclaimed powers: Towards a psychology of men and women in later life.* New York: Basic Books.

Haan, N., Millsap, R., & Hartka, E. (1986). As time goes by:

Change and stability in personality over fifty years. *Psychology and Aging, 1,* 220–232.

Hackel, L. S., & Ruble, D. N. (1992). Changes in the marital relationship after the first baby is born: Predicting the impact of expectancy disconfirmation. *Journal of Personality and Social Psychology, 62,* 944–957.

Harris, J. R. (1995). Where is the child's environment? A group socialization theory of development. *Psychological Review, 102,* 458–489.

Harter, S. (1983). Developmental perspectives on the self-systems. In E. M. Hetherington (Ed.), *Handbook of child psychology: Socialization personality and social development* (Vol. IV, pp. 103–196). New York: Wiley.

Harter, S. (1987). The determinants and mediational role of global self-worth in children. In N. Eisenberg (Ed.), *Contemporary topics in developmental psychology.* New York: Wiley.

Harter, S. (1992). The relationship between perceived competence, affect, and motivational orientation within the classroom: Processes and patterns of change. In A. K. Boggiano & T. S. Pittman (Eds.), *Achievement and motivation: A social-developmental perspective.* New York: Cambridge University Press.

Hartshorne, H., & May, M. S. (1929). *Studies in the nature of character. Vol. 1: Studies in self-control.* New York: Macmillan.

Hartup, W. W. (1996). The company they keep: Friendships and their developmental significance. *Child Development, 67,* 1–13.

Hartup, W. W., & van Lieshout, C. F. (1995). Personality development in social context. *Annual Review of Psychology, 46,* 655–687.

Hazan, C., & Shaver, P. (1987). Romantic love conceptualized as an attachment process. *Journal of Personality and Social Psychology, 52,* 511–524.

Heckhausen, H., & Gollwitzer, P. M. (1987). Thought contents and cognitive functioning in motivational versus volitional states of mind. *Motivation and Emotion, 11,* 101–120.

Heckhausen, J., Dixon, R. A., & Baltes, P. B. (1989). Gains and losses in development throughout adulthood as perceived by different age groups. *Developmental Psychology, 25,* 109–121.

Helson, R., Mitchell, V., & Moane, G. (1984). Personality and patterns of adherence and nonadherence to the social clock. *Journal of Personality and Social Psychology, 47,* 731–739.

Hess, E. H. (1959). The conditions limiting critical age of imprinting. *Journal of Comparative and Physiological Psychology, 52,* 515–518.

Hetherington, E. M., & McIntyre, C. W. (1975). Developmental psychology. *Annual Review of Psychology, 26,* 97–136.

Heyman, G. D., Dweck, C. S., & Cain, K. M. (1992). Young children's vulnerability to self-blame and helplessness: Relationship to beliefs about goodness. *Child Development, 63,* 401–415.

Higgins, E. T., & Parsons, J. E. (1983). Social cognition and the social life of the child: Stages as subcultures. In E. T. Higgins, D. N. Ruble, & W. W. Hartup (Eds.), *Social cognition and social development* (pp. 15–62). New York: Cambridge University Press.

Higgins, E. T., Ruble, D. N., & Hartup, W. W. (Eds.). (1983). *Social cognition and social development: A sociocultural perspective.* New York: Cambridge University Press.

Hinde, R. A. (1989). Ethological and relationships approaches. In R.Vasta (Ed.), *Annals of child development. Vol. 6: Theories of child development: Revised formulations and current issues.* New York: Appleton-Century-Crofts.

Hodgkinson, V., & Weitzman, M. (1988). *Giving and volunteering in the United States: 1988 edition.* Washington, DC: Gallup Organization, Inc.

Hoffman, L. W. (1991). The influence of the family environment on personality: Accounting for sibling differences. *Psychological Bulletin, 108,* 187–203.

Hoffman, M. L. (1970). Moral development. In P. H. Mussen (Ed.), *Carmichael's manual of child psychology.* New York: John Wiley.

Hoffman, M. L. (1977). Personality and social development. *Annual Review of Psychology, 28,* 295–321.

Hoffman, M. L. (1982). Development of prosocial motivation: Empathy and guilt. In N. Eisenberg (Ed.), *Development of prosocial behavior.* New York: Academic Press.

Hoffman, M. L. (1983). Affective and cognitive processes in moral internalization. In E. T. Higgins, D. N. Ruble, & W. W. Hartup (Eds.), *Social cognition and social development: A sociocultural perspective* (pp. 236–274). New York: Cambridge University Press.

Holden, G. W. (1995). Parental attitudes toward childrearing. In M. H. Bornstein (Ed.), *Handbook of parenting* (Vol. 3, pp. 305–332). Mahwah, NJ: Erlbaum.

Hornblum, J., & Overton, W. (1976). Area and volume conservation among the elderly: Assessment and training. *Developmental Psychology, 12,* 68–74.

Horner, M. S. (1972). Toward an understanding of achievement-related conflicts in women. *Journal of Social Issues, 28,* 157–175.

Horowitz, F. D. (1992). John B. Watson's legacy: Learning and environment. *Developmental Psychology, 28,* 360–367.

Isaacs, S. (1929). Critical notes: The child's conception of the world, by J. Piaget. *Mind, 38,* 506–513.

Isaacs, S. (1930). *Intellectual growth in young children.* New York: Harcourt Brace.

Isabella, R. A., & Belsky, J. (1991). Interactional synchrony and the origins of infant-mother attachment: A replication study. *Child Development, 62,* 373–384.

Izard, C. E., & Malatesta, C. Z. (1987). Perspectives on emotional development. I: Differential emotions theory of early emotional development. In J. D. Osofsky (Ed.), *Handbook of infant development* (2nd ed.). New York: Wiley.

James, W. (1890). *The principles of psychology* (2 volumes). New York: Dover.

Jordan, V. B. (1980). Conserving kinship concepts: A developmental study in social cognition. *Child Development, 51,* 146–155.

Kagan, J. (1981). *The second year: The emergence of self-awareness.* Cambridge, MA: Harvard University Press.

Kagan, J., & Moss, H. A. (1962). *Birth to maturity: A study in psychological development.* New York: John Wiley.

Kegan, R. (1982). *The evolving self.* Cambridge, MA: Harvard University Press.

Kelman, H. C. (1961). Processes of opinion change. *Public Opinion Quarterly, 25,* 57–58.

Kemper, S., Rash, S., Kynette, D., & Norman, S. (1990). Telling stories: The structure of adults' narratives. *European Journal of Cognitive Psychology, 2,* 205–228.

Keniston, A. H., & Flavell, J. H. (1979). A developmental study of intelligent retrieval. *Child Development, 50,* 1144–1152.

Kessen, W. (1965). *The child.* New York: Wiley.

Kitayama, S., & Markus, H. R. (1994). *Emotion and culture: Empirical studies of mutual influence.* Washington, DC: American Psychology Association.

Kliegel, R., Smith, J., Heckhausen, J., & Baltes, P. B. (1987). Minemonic training for the acquisition of skilled digit memory. *Cognition and Instruction, 4,* 203–223.

Klinnert, M. D., Emde, R. N., Butterfield, P., & Campos, J. J. (1986). Social referencing: The infant's use of emotional signals from a friendly adult with mother present. *Developmental Psychology, 22,* 427–432.

Kobasigawa, A. (1974). Utilization of retrieval cues by children in recall. *Child Development, 45,* 127–134.

Kochanska, G. (1995). Children's temperament, mothers' discipline, and security of attachment: Multiple pathways to emerging internalization. *Child Development, 66,* 597–615.

Kohlberg, L. (1964). Development of moral character and moral ideology. In L. W. Hoffman & M. L. Hoffman (Eds.), *Review of child development research* (Vol. 1). New York: Russell Sage Foundation.

Kohlberg, L. (1966). A cognitive-developmental analysis of children's sex-role concepts and attitudes. In E. E. Maccoby (Ed.), *The development of sex differences* (pp. 82–172). Stanford: Stanford University Press.

Kohlberg, L. (1969). Stage and sequence: The cognitive developmental approach to socialization. In D. A. Goslin (Ed.), *Handbook of socialization theory and research.* New York: Rand-McNally.

Kopp, C. B. (1989). Regulation of distress and negative emotions: A developmental view. *Developmental Psychology, 25,* 342–354.

Kuczynski, L., & Kochanska, G. (1990). Development of children's noncompliance strategies from toddlerhood to age 5. *Developmental Psychology, 26,* 398–408.

Kuczynski, L., Kochanska, G., Radke-Yarrow, M., & Girnius-Brown, O. (1987). A developmental interpretation of young children's noncompliance. *Developmental Psychology, 23,* 799–806.

Kupersmidt, J. B., Coie, J. D., & Dodge, K. A. (1990). The role of poor peer relationships in the development of disorder. In S. R. Asher & J. D. Coie (Eds.), *Peer rejection in childhood. Cambridge studies in social and emotional development* (pp. 274–305). New York: Cambridge University Press.

Labouvie-Vief, G. (1982). Discontinuities in development from childhood to adulthood: A cognitive-developmental view. In T. M. Field, A. Huston, H. C. Quay, L. Troll, & G. E. Finley (Eds.), *Review of human development* (pp. 447–455). New York: Wiley-Interscience.

Labouvie-Vief, G. (1994). *Psyche and Eros: Mind and gender in the life course.* New York: Cambridge University Press.

Labouvie-Vief, G. (1996). The social construction of women's development. In P. B. Baltes & U. Staudinger (Eds.), *Interactive minds: Life-span perspectives on the social foundation of cognition* (pp. 109–132). New York: Cambridge University Press.

Lamb, M. E., Thompson, R. A., Gardner, W. P., Charnov, E. L., & Estes, D. (1984). Security of infantile attachment as assessed in the "strange situation": Its study and biological interpretation. *The Behavioral and Brain Sciences, 7,* 127–171.

LaVoie, J. C. (1974). Type of punishment as a determinant of resistance to deviation. *Developmental Psychology, 10,* 181–189.

Lazarus, R. S., & Folkman, S. (1984). *Stress, appraisal, and coping.* New York: Springer.

Leonard, R. (1993). Mother-child disputes as arenas for fostering negotiation skills. *Early Development and Parenting, 2,* 157–167.

Lepper, M. R. (1983). Social-control processes and the internalization of social values: An attributional perspective. In E. T. Higgins, D. N. Ruble, & W. W. Hartup (Eds.), *Social cognition and social development: A sociocultural perspective* (pp. 294–330). New York: Cambridge University Press.

Levine, J. M., & Moreland, R. L. (1991). Culture and socialization in work groups. In L. B. Resnick, J. M. Levine, & S. D. Teasley (Eds.), *Perspectives on socially shared cognition* (pp. 257–279). Washington, DC: American Psychological Association.

Levinson, D. J. (1978). *The seasons of a man's life.* New York: Knopf.

Lewis, M., & Brooks-Gunn, J. (1979). *Social cognition and the acquisition of self.* New York: Plenum.

Lewis, M., Michaelson, L. (1983). *Children's emotions and moods: Developmental theory and measurement.* New York: Plenum.

Livesley, W., & Bromley, D. (1973). *Person perception in childhood and adolescence.* London: Wiley.

Loevinger, J. (1976). *Ego development.* San Francisco: Jossey-Bass.

Lorenz, K. Z. (1981). *The foundations of ethology.* New York: Springer-Verlag.

Maccoby, E. E. (1980). *Social development.* New York: Harcourt Brace Jovanovich.

Maccoby, E. E. (1984). Socialization and developmental change. *Child Development, 55,* 317–328.

Maccoby, E. E. (1992). The role of parents in the socialization of children: An historical overview. *Developmental Psychology, 28,* 1006–1017.

Maccoby, E. E., & Jacklin, C. N. (1974). *The psychology of sex differences.* Stanford: Stanford University Press.

Maccoby, E. E., & Martin, J. A. (1983). Socialization in the context of the family: Parent-child interaction. In E. M. Hetherington (Ed.), *Social development. Vol. III of Mussen's manual of child psychology* (4th ed.). New York: Wiley.

Main, M., Kaplan, N., & Cassidy, J. (1985). Security in infancy, childhood, and adulthood: A move to the level of representation. In I. Bretherton & E. Waters (Eds.), *Growing points in attachment theory and research* (Monographs of the Society for Research in Child Development, Vol. 50, No. 1–2, Serial No. 209, pp. 66–104). Chicago: University of Chicago Press.

Malatesta, C. Z., Izard, C. E., Culver, C., & Nicolich, M. (1987). Emotion communication skills in young, middle-aged, and older women. *Psychology and Aging, 2,* 193–203.

Malatesta-Magai, C. Z., Jonas, R., Shepard, B., & Culver, L. C. (1992). Type A behavior and emotion expression in younger and older adults. *Psychology and Aging, 7,* 555–561.

Mangelsdorf, S. C., Shapiro, J. R., & Marzolf, D. (1995). Developmental and temperamental differences in emotion regulation in infancy. *Child Development, 66,* 1817–1828.

Marcia, J. (1988). Identity, cognitive/moral development, and individuation. In D. K. Lapsley & F. C. Power (Eds.), *Self, ego, and identity: Integrative approaches* (pp. 211–225). New York: Springer-Verlag.

Markus, H. R., & Kitayama, S. (1991). Culture and the self: Implications for cognition, emotion, and motivation. *Psychological Review, 98,* 234–253.

Markus, H. R., & Kitayama, S. (1994). The cultural construction of self and emotion: Implications for social behavior. In S. Kitayama & H. R. Markus (Eds.), *Emotion and culture* (pp. 89–132). Washington, DC: American Psychological Association.

Masters, J. C. (1991). Strategies and mechanisms for the personal and social control of emotions. In J. Garber & K. A. Dodge (Eds.), *The development of emotional regulation and dysregulation* (pp. 182–207). New York: Cambridge University Press.

Masters, J., Barden, R. C., & Ford, M. (1979). Affective states, expressive behavior, and learning in children. *Journal of Personality and Social Psychology, 37,* 380–389.

Matthews, A. M. (1991). *Widowhood in later life.* Toronto: Butterworths.

McGillicuddy-DeLisi, A. V., & Sigel, I. (1995). Parental beliefs. In M. H. Bornstein (Ed.), *Handbook of parenting* (Vol. 3, pp. 333–358). Mahwah, NJ: Erlbaum.

Menon, U., & Shweder, R. A. (1994). Kali's tongue: Cultural psychology and the power of shame in Orissa, India. In S. Kitayama & H. R. Markus (Eds.), *Emotion and culture: Empirical studies of mutual influence* (pp. 241–282). Washington, DC: American Psychological Association.

Midlarsky, E., & Hannah, M. E. (1989). The generous elderly: Naturalistic studies of donations across the life span. *Psychology and Aging, 4,* 346–351.

Miller, A. (1985). A developmental study of the cognitive basis of performance impairment after failure. *Journal of Personality and Social Psychology, 49,* 529–538.

Miller, B. D. (1995). Precepts and practices: Researching identity formation among Indian Hindu adolescents in the United States. In J. J. Goodnow, P. J. Miller, & F. Kessel (Eds.), *Cultural practices as contexts for development* (pp. 71–86). San Francisco: Jossey-Bass.

Miller, P. A., Eisenberg, N., Fabes, R. A., & Shell, R. (1996). Relations of moral reasoning and vicarious emotion to young children's prosocial behavior toward peers and adults. *Developmental Psychology, 32,* 210–219.

Miller, P. J., & Goodnow, J. J. (1995). Cultural practices: Towards an integration of culture and development. In J. J. Goodnow, P. J. Miller, & F. Kessel (Eds.), *Cultural practices as contexts for development* (pp. 5–16). San Francisco: Jossey-Bass.

Miller, S. M., & Green, M. L. (1985). Coping with stress and frustration: Origins, nature, and development. In M. Lewis & C. Saarni (Eds.), *The socialization of emotions* (pp. 263–314). New York: Plenum.

Minton, C., Kagan, J., & Levine, J. A. (1971). Maternal control and obedience in the two-year-old. *Child Development, 42,* 1873–1894.

Mischel, W., & Ebbesen, E. B. (1970). Attention in delay of gratification. *Journal of Personality and Social Psychology, 16,* 329–337.

Money, J., & Ehrhardt, A. A. (1972). *Man & woman. Boy & girl.* Baltimore: Johns Hopkins University Press.

Montepare, J., & Lachman, M. (1989). "You're only as old as you feel": Self-perceptions of age, fears of aging, and life satisfaction from adolescence to old age. *Psychology and Aging, 4,* 73–78.

Mugny, G., & Carugati, F. (1985). *L'intelligence au pluriel: Les representations sociales de l'intelligence et de son developpement.* Cousset: Editions Delval (Published in English, 1989, under the title *Social representations of intelligence* by Cambridge University Press).

Neuberger, B. (1979). Time, age, and the life-cycle. *American Journal of Psychiatry, 136,* 887–894.

Neugarten, B. L. (1979). Time, age and the life cycle. *American Journal of Psychiatry, 136,* 887–894.

Newcomb, A. F., & Bagwell, C. L. (1995). Children's friendship relations: A meta-analytic review. *Psychological Bulletin, 117,* 306–347.

Nicholls, J. G. (1978). The development of the concepts of effort and stability, perception of academic attainment, and the understanding that difficult tasks require more ability. *Child Development, 49,* 800–814.

Nicholson, N. (1990). The transition cycle: Causes, outcomes, processes and forms. In S. Fisher & C. L. Cooper (Eds.), *On the move: The psychology of change and transition* (pp. 83–108). New York: Wiley.

Nucci, L. (1994). Mothers' beliefs regarding the personal domain of children. In J. G. Smetana (Ed.), *Beliefs about parenting* (pp. 88–89). San Francisco: Jossey-Bass.

Papousek, H., & Papousek, M. (1991). Innate and cultural guidance of infants' integrative competencies: China, the United States, and Germany. In M. H. Bornstein (Ed.), *Cultural approaches to parenting* (pp. 23–44). Hillsdale, NJ: Lawrence Erlbaum Associates.

Parke, R. D. (1972). Some effects of punishment on children's behavior. In W. W. Hartup (Ed.), *The young child* (Vol. 2). Washington, DC: National Association for the Education of Young Children.

Parke, R. D., & Asher, S. R. (1983). Social and personality development. *Annual Review of Psychology, 34,* 465–509.

Parker, J. G., & Asher, S. R. (1987). Peer relations and later personal adjustment: Are low-accepted children at risk? *Psychological Bulletin, 102,* 357–389.

Parpal, M., & Maccoby, E. E. (1985). Maternal response and subsequent child compliance. *Child Development, 56,* 1326–1334.

Patterson, G. R. (1982). *Coercive family process.* Eugene, OR: Castalia.

Peel, E. A. (1959). Experimental examination of some of Piaget's schemata concerning children's perception and thinking, and a discussion of their educational significance. *British Journal of Educational Psychology, 29,* 89–103.

Perret-Clermont, A.-N., Perret, J.-F., & Bell, N. (1991). The social construction of meaning and cognitive activity in elementary school children. In L. Resnick, J. M. Levine, & S. B. Teasley (Ed.), *Perspectives on socially shared cognition* (pp. 41–62). Washington, DC: American Psychological Association.

Perry, D. G., & Bussey, K. (1979). The social learning theory of sex differences: Imitation is alive and well. *Journal of Personality and Social Psychology, 37,* 1699–1712.

Perun, P. J., & Bielby, D. D. (1980). Structure and dynamics of the individual life course. In K. W. Back (Ed.), *Life course: Integrative theories and exemplary populations* (pp. 97–120). Boulder, CO: Westview Press.

Piaget, J. (1932). *The moral judgement of the child.* London: Kegan, Paul, Trench, & Trubner.

Pittman, T. S., Boggiano, A. K., & Main, D. S. (1992). In A. K. Boggiano & T. S. Pittman (Eds.), *Achievement and motivation: A social-developmental perspective.* New York: Cambridge University Press.

Plomin, R., & Bergeman, C. S. (1991). The nature of nurture: Genetic influences on "environmental" measures. *Behavioral and Brain Sciences, 14,* 373–427.

Pomerantz, E. M., & Ruble, D. N. (in press). Distinguishing multiple dimensions of conceptions of ability: Implications for self-evaluative processes. *Child Development.*

Pomerantz, E. M., Ruble, D. N., Frey, K.S., & Greulich, F. (1995). Meeting goals and confronting conflict: Children's changing perceptions of social comparison. *Child Development, 66,* 723–738.

Posner, M. I., Rothbart, M. K., & Harman, C. (1994). Cognitive science's contribution to culture and emotion. In S. Kitayama & H. R. Markus (Eds.), *Emotion and culture* (pp. 197–218). Washington, DC: American Psychological Association.

Pratt, M. W., & Norris, J. E. (1994). *The social psychology of aging.* Oxford: Blackwell.

Pratt, M. W., & Robins, S. (1991). That's the way it was: Age differences in the structure and quality of adults' personal narratives. *Discourse Process, 14,* 73–85.

Putallaz, M., & Gottman, J. M. (1981). An interactional model of children's entry into peer groups. *Child Development, 52,* 986–994.

Rest, J. R. (1986). *Moral development: Advances in research and theory.* New York: Praeger.

Rholes, W. S., Blackwell, J., Jordan, C., & Walters, C. (1980). A developmental study of learned helplessness. *Developmental Psychology, 16,* 616–624.

Rholes, W. S., Jones, M., & Wade, C. (1988). Children's understanding of personal dispositions and its relation to behavior. *Journal of Experimental Child Psychology, 45,* 1–17.

Rholes, W. S., Newman, L. S., & Ruble, D. N. (1990). Understanding self and other: Developmental and motivational aspects of perceiving people in terms of invariant dispositions. In E. T. Higgins and R. Sorrentino (Eds.), *Handbook of motivation and cognition: Foundations of Social Behavior* (Vol. II). New York: Guilford.

Robins, L. N. (1978). Sturdy childhood predictors of adult antisocial behavior: Replication from longitudinal studies. *Psychological Medicine, 8,* 611–622.

Rogoff, B. (1990). *Apprenticeship in thinking.* Oxford: Oxford University Press.

Rohan, M. J., & Zanna, M. P. (1996). Value transmission in families. In C. Seligman, J. M. Olson, & M. P. Zanna (Eds.), *The Ontario symposium: The psychology of values* (Vol. 8, 253–276). Hillsdale, NJ: Lawrence Erlbaum Associates.

Rook, K. S. (1987). Social support versus companionship: Effects on life stress, loneliness, and evaluations of others. *Journal of Personality and Social Psychology, 52,* 1132–1147.

Roth, J. A. (1963). *Timetables: Structuring the passage of time in hospital treatment and other careers.* Indianapolis: Bobbs-Merrill.

Rovee-Collier, C. (1987). Learning and memory in infancy. In J. D. Osofsky (Ed.), *Handbook of infant development* (2nd ed.). *Wiley series on personality processes* (pp. 98–148). New York: John Wiley & Sons.

Ruble, D. N. (1983). The development of social comparison processes and their role in achievement-related self-socialization. In E. T. Higgins, D. N. Ruble, & W. W. Hartup (Eds.), *Social cognition and social development: A sociocultural perspective* (pp. 134–157). New York: Cambridge University Press.

Ruble, D. N. (1987). The acquisition of self-knowledge: A self-socialization perspective. In N. Eisenberg (Ed.), *Contemporary topics in developmental psychology.* New York: Wiley.

Ruble, D. N. (1994). A phase model of transitions: Cognitive and motivational consequences. In M. Zanna (Ed.), *Advances in experimental social psychology, 26,* 163–214. New York: Academic Press.

Ruble, D. N., & Dweck, C. (1995). Self-conceptions, person conceptions, and their development. In N. Eisenberg (Ed.), *Review of personality and social psychology: Social Development* (Vol. 15, pp. 109–139). Thousand Oaks, CA: Sage.

Ruble, D. N., Higgins, E. T., & Hartup, W. W. (1983). What's social about social-cognitive development? In E. T. Higgins, D. N. Ruble, & W. W. Hartup (Eds.), *Social cognition and social development: A sociocultural perspective* (pp. 3–14). New York: Cambridge University Press.

Ruble, D. N., & Martin, C. (1997). Gender development. In W. Damon (Ed.), *Handbook of child psychology* (5th ed.). [Vol. 3: Personality and Social Development, N. Eisenberg (Ed.)]. New York: Wiley.

Ruble, D. N., & Seidman, E. (1996). Social transitions: Windows into social psychological processes. In E. T. Higgins and A. Kruglanski (Eds.), *Handbook of social processes.* New York: Guilford.

Ruble, D. N., & Thompson, E. P. (1992). The implications of research on social development for mental health: An internal socialization perspective. In D. N. Ruble, P. E. Constanzo, and M. E. Oliveri (Eds.), *Social psychology and mental health.* New York: Guilford.

Ryff, C. D. (1991). Possible selves in childhood and adulthood: A tale of shifting horizons. *Psychology and Aging, 6,* 286–295.

Salthouse, T. A. (1990). Influences of experience on age differences in cognitive functioning. *Human Factors, 32,* 551–569.

Sameroff, A. J., & Fiese, B. H. (1992). Family representations of development. In I. E. Siegel, A. V. McGillicuddy-DeLisi, & J. J. Goodnow (Eds.), *Parental belief systems: The psychological consequences for children* (2nd ed., pp. 347–369). Hillsdale, NJ: Lawrence Erlbaum Associates.

Sanders, C. M. (1989). Risk factors in bereavement outcome. *Journal of Social Issues, 44,* 97–111.

Scarr, S. (1992). Developmental theories for the 1990's: Development and individual differences. *Child Development, 63,* 1–19.

Schaie, K. W. (1990). Intellectual development in adulthood. In J. E. Birren & K. W. Schaie (Eds.), *Handbook of the psy-*

chology of aging (3rd ed., pp. 290–309). San Diego, CA: Academic Press.

Scribner, S., & Cole, M. (1981). *The psychology of literacy.* Cambridge, MA: Harvard University Press.

Sears, D. O. (1986). College sophomores in the laboratory: Influences of a narrow data base on social psychology's view of human nature. *Journal of Personality and Social Psychology, 51,* 513–530.

Sears, R. R. (1975). Your ancients revisited: A history of child development. In E. M. Hetherington (Ed.), *Review of child development research* (Vol. 5, pp. 1–73). Chicago: University of Chicago Press.

Sears, R. R., Maccoby, E. E., & Levin, H. (1957). *Patterns of child rearing.* Evanston, IL: Row-Peterson.

Sears, R. R., Rau, L., & Alpert, R. (1965). *Identification and child rearing.* Stanford, CA: Stanford University Press.

Seidman, E., Allen, L., Aber, J. L., Mitchell, C., & Feinman, J. (1994). The impact of school transitions in early adolescence on the self-esteem and perceived social context of poor urban youth. *Child Development, 65,* 507–522.

Seligman, M. E. P. (1975). *Helplessness: On depression, development, and death.* San Francisco: W. H. Freeman & Company Publishers.

Shaffer, D. R. (1994). *Social and personality development* (3rd ed.). Belmont, CA: Brooks/Cole.

Shantz, C. U. (1983). Social cognition. In E. M. Hetherington (Ed.), *Handbook of child psychology.* New York: Wiley.

Siegal, M. (1981). Children's perceptions of adult economic needs. *Child Development, 52,* 379–382.

Siegler, R. (1995). Children's thinking: How does change occur? In W. Schneider & F. Weinert (Eds.), *Memory performance and competencies: Issues in growth and development* (pp. 405–430). Hillsdale, NJ: Erlbaum.

Silverman, P. R. (1987). Widowhood as the next stage in the life course. In H. Z. Lopata (Ed.), *Widows* (Vol. 2, pp. 170–190). Durham, NC: Duke University Press.

Simmons, R. G., & Blyth, D. A. (1987). *Moving into adolescence: The impact of pubertal change and school context.* Hawthorn, NY: Aldine de Gruyler.

Simpson, J. A., Rholes, W. S., & Nelligan, J. S. (1992). Support seeking and support giving within couples in an anxiety-provoking situation. The role of attachment styles. *Journal of Personality and Social Psychology, 62,* 434–446.

Smedslund, J. (1961). The acquisition of conservation of substance and weight in children. III. Extinction of conservation of weight acquired "normally" and by means of empirical controls on a balance scale. *Scandinavian Journal of Psychology, 2,* 85–87.

Smetana, J. G. (1994). Parenting styles and beliefs about parental authority. In J. J. Goodnow, P. J. Miller, & F. Kessel (Eds.), *Cultural practices as contexts for development* (pp. 21–36). San Francisco: Jossey-Bass.

Smiley, P., & Dweck, C. S. (1994). Individual differences in achievement goals among young children. *Child Development, 65,* 1723–1743.

Smith, J. (1996). Planning about life: Toward a social-interactive perspective. In P. Baltes & U. Staudinger (Eds.), *Interactive minds: Life-span perspectives on the social foundation of cognition* (pp. 242–275). New York: Cambridge University Press.

Smith, J., & Baltes, P. B. (1990). Wisdom-related knowledge: Age/cohort differences in response to life-planning problems. *Developmental Psychology, 26,* 494–505.

Smith, J., & Goodnow, J. J. (November 1995). *Age and competence attributions in interactions of non-solicited support.* Unpublished paper presented at 48th Annual Scientific Meetings of the Gerontology Society of America, Los Angeles, CA.

Sroufe, L. A. (1979). The coherence of individual development: Early care, attachment, and subsequent development issues. *American Psychologist, 34,* 834–841.

Stangor, C., & Ruble, D. N. (1989). Strength of expectancies and memory for social information: What we remember depends on how much we know. *Journal of Experimental Social Psychology, 25,* 18–35.

Stattin, H., & Magnusson, D. (1991). Stability and change in criminal behavior up to age thirty. *British Journal of Criminology, 31,* 327–346.

Staudinger, U. (1996). Wisdom and the social-interactive foundation of the mind. In P. Baltes & U. Staudinger (Eds.), *Interactive minds: Life-span perspectives on the social foundation of cognition* (pp. 276–318). New York: Cambridge University Press.

Stinberg, L., Darling, N. E., & Fletcher, A. C. (1995). Authoritative parenting and adolescent adjustment: An ecological journey. In P. Moen, G. H. Elder, & K. Luscher (Eds.), *Examining lives in context: Perspectives on the ecology of human development* (pp. 423–466). Washington, DC: American Psychological Association.

Stewart, A. J., & Healy, J. M. (1989). Linking individual development and social changes. *American Psychologist, 44,* 30–42.

Stipek, D. J., Gralinski, J. H., & Kopp, C. B. (1990). Self-concept development in the toddler years. *Developmental Psychology, 26,* 972–977.

Stipek, D., Recchia, S., & McClintic, S. (1992). Self evaluation in young children. *Monographs of the Society for Research in Child Development, 57* (Serial No. 226).

Tajfel, H. (1981). *Human groups and social categories: Studies in social psychology.* New York: Cambridge University Press.

Tamis-LeMonda, C. S., Bornstein, M. H., Cyphers, L., Toda, S., & Ogino, M. (1992). Language and play at one year: A comparison of toddlers and mothers in the United States and Japan. *International Journal of Behavioral Development, 15*(1), 19–42.

Taylor, S. E. (1983). Adjustment to threatening events: A theory of cognitive adaptation. *American Psychologist, 38,* 1161–1173.

Taylor, S. E., & Lobel, M. (1989). Social comparison activity under threat: Downward evaluation and upward contacts. *Psychological Review, 96,* 569–576.

Terkelsen, K. G. (1980). Toward a theory of the family life cycle. In E. A. Carger & M. McGoldrick (Eds.), *The family life cycle.* New York: Gardner Press.

Thelen, E. (1991). Improvisations on the behavioral-genetics theme. *Behavioral and Brain Sciences, 14,* 409–410.

Thelen, E., & Adolph, K. E. (1992). Arnold L. Gesell: The paradox of nature and nurture. *Developmental Psychology, 28,* 368–380.

Thomas, A., Chess, S., Birch, H. G., Hertzig, M., & Korn, S. (1963). *Temperament and behavior disorders in children.* New York: New York University Press.

Thompson, E. P., Boggiano, A. K., Costanzo, P. E., Matter, J. A., & Ruble, D. N. (1995). Age-related changes in children's orientations toward strategic peer interactions : Implications for social perception and behavior. *Social Cognition, 13,* 71–104.

Thompson, R. A. (1993). Socioemotional development: Enduring issues and new challenges: Special issue: Setting a path for the coming decade: Some goals and challenges. *Developmental Review, 13,* 372–402.

Thompson, S. K. (1975). Gender labels and early sex role development. *Child Development, 46,* 339–347.

Tronick, E. Z. (1989). Emotions and emotional communication in infants. Special issue: Children and their development: Knowledge basics, research agenda and social policy application. *American Psychologist, 44,* 112–119.

Trope, Y., & Higgins, E. T. (1993). The what, when and how of dispositional inference: New answers and new questions. Special issue: On inferring personal dispositions from behavior. *Personality and Social Psychology, 19,* 493–500.

Trope, Y., & Neter, E. (1994). Reconciling competing motives in self-evaluation. *Journal of Personality and Social Psychology, 66,* 646–657.

Turiel, E. (1983). *The development of social knowledge: Morality and convention.* Cambridge, England: Cambridge University Press.

Vaillant, G. E. (1977). *Adaptation to life: How the best and brightest came of age.* Boston: Little, Brown.

Verdonik, F., Flapan, V., Schmit, C., & Weinstock, J. (1988). The role of power relationships in children's cognition: Its significance for research on cognitive development. *Quarterly Newsletter of the Laboratory of Comparative Human Cognition, 10,* 80–85.

Veroff, J., Reuman, D., & Feld, S. (1984). Motives in American men and women across the adult life span. *Developmental Psychology, 20,* 1142–1158.

Vygotsky, L. S. (1978). *Mind in society: The development of higher psychological processes.* Cambridge, MA: Harvard University Press.

Waters, E., Vaughn, B. E., Posada, G., & Kondo-Ikemura, K. (1995). Caregiving, cultural, and cognitive perspectives on secure-base behavior and working models: New growing points of attachment theory and research. *Monographs of the Society for Research in Child Development, 60* (Serial No. 244).

Watson, J. B. (1919). *Psychology from the standpoint of a behaviorist.* Philadelphia: Lippincott.

Watson, M. W., & Fischer, K. W. (1980). Development of social roles in elicited and spontaneous behavior during the preschool years. *Developmental Psychology, 16,* 483–494.

Watson-Gegeo, K. A. (1992). Thick explanation in the ethnographic study of child socialization: A longitudinal study of the problem of schooling for Kwara'ae (Solomon Islands) children. In W. A. Corsaro & P. J. Miller (Eds.), *Interpretive approaches to children's socialization. New directions for child development, No. 58: The Jossey-Bass education series* (pp. 51–66). San Francisco: Jossey-Bass.

Wertsch, J. (1991). *Voices of the mind.* Cambridge, MA: Harvard University Press.

Whitbourne, S. K. (1985). *The aging body: Physiological changes and psychological consequences.* New York: Springer-Verlag.

White, R. W. (1959). Motivation reconsidered: The concept of competence. *Psychological Review, 66,* 297–333.

White, S. H. (1992). G. Stanley Hall: From philosophy to developmental psychology. Special Section: APA Centennial series. *Developmental Psychology, 28,* 25–34.

Whiting, J. W., & Child, I. (1953). *Personality and child training.* New Haven, CT: Yale University Press.

Wortman, C. B., & Silver, R. C. (1989). The myths of coping with loss. *Journal of Consulting and Clinical Psychology, 57*(3), 349–357.

Youniss, J. (1980). *Parents and peers in social development.* Chicago: University of Chicago Press.

Zajonc, R. B. (1965). Social facilitation. *Science, 149,* 269–274.

Zakriski, A. L., & Coie, J. D. (1996). A comparison of aggressive-rejected and nonaggressive-rejected children's interpretations of self-directed and other-directed rejection. *Child Development, 67,* 1048–1070.

CHAPTER SEVENTEEN

GENDER

KAY DEAUX, *City University of New York*
MARIANNE LAFRANCE, *Boston College*

I. THE SOCIAL PSYCHOLOGY OF GENDER

Gender is a significant social psychological construct that, like social psychology in its most catholic conception, spans the range from individual beliefs and actions to the impact of societies and social systems. Gender is, for us as social animals, part of the "air we breathe," a reality that is ever part of our experience. Public debates about the nature of women and men are frequently in the spotlight, whether in media reports on the latest sex difference findings or in highly publicized legal cases involving single-sex educational institutions or sexual harassment. At the public level as well as in private conversations, gender is a salient, familiar, and personal topic, with the consequence that most people feel they have expertise on the issues. At the same time, like the air we breathe, the ubiquitous and subtle influence of gender is not always recognized or comprehended.

This chapter examines gender as a social psychological phenomenon. To accomplish this, a multidimensional, mul-tilevel, sometimes interdisciplinary perspective is adopted. Gender is considered a dynamic construct that draws on and impinges upon processes at the individual, interactional, group, institutional, and cultural levels. As such, the presented analysis is of gender-in-situated-action, an approach that is importantly and perhaps uniquely social psychological in its assumptions. At the core of this analysis is a framework for investigating gender as a context-dependent phenomenon first proposed by Deaux and Major (1987). To this earlier model, which focused primarily on dyadic interactions, additional considerations are raised. Social structures, social roles, power, status, and culture are factors and levels of analysis that must be considered for a fully-drawn picture of gender.

Underlying Assumptions

It is a truism of scientific research that the stance one takes affects the questions one asks, and in turn the answers that one's investigations yield. Within social psychology, testimony to this truism is abundant. As one example, European social psychologists at one point mounted a strong critique of the American work, noting the latter's emphasis on individuals over groups, of majority influence rather than minority action, of principles of equity over equality (Israel & Tajfel, 1972). More recently, critiques by feminists and other scholars outside the "mainstream" have pointed to lacunae and unexamined assumptions in the psychological project (Hare-Mustin & Marecek, 1990; Landrine, 1995; Morawski, 1994). Bem (1994) recently argued that psychology has followed the world at large in approaching questions of gender with three hidden assumptions, namely, gender polarization (mutually exclusive

The order of authors is alphabetical and their contributions are equivalent. The literature on gender and social psychology, even limiting it to that published in the ten to twelve years since the previous *Handbook* chapter, is enormous. In our need to be selective, we have omitted many important studies and discussions. To all of those who have contributed to our knowledge but whose work is not included here, we are grateful for your contributions and apologize for the omission.

We also thank Elizabeth Haines for her assistance in locating articles, and Monica Biernat, Mary Crawford, Cynthia Fuchs Epstein, Michelle Fine, Jill Morawski, Janet Taylor Spence, Janet Swim, Rhoda Unger, Jacqueline White, and the *Handbook* editors for their very helpful comments on an earlier version of this chapter.

scripts for being male and female), androcentrism (male experience as the neutral standard or norm), and biological essentialism (behaviors are the natural and inevitable consequence of intrinsic biological natures).

Accordingly, it is important to be explicit about the assumptions adopted in this review and interpretation of the social psychological work on gender. Our basic operating assumption is that any analysis of gender must recognize and incorporate the context in which women and men act and react. This position mirrors that of Epstein (1988) who argued that biased interpretation arises from "scientists' inability to capture the social context or their tendency to regard it as unnecessary to their inquiry" (p. 44). To truly capture context, social psychologists must be willing to push the conceptual boundaries of the field, looking to broader societal structures and cultural norms as well as to the immediate and micro features of experimental settings.

In short, this is *not* a chapter about sex differences. As Morawski (1994) observes, "Assumptions about differences, especially difference between men and women, are entrenched in the language, methods, and cognitive orientations of psychology" (p. 21). Certainly many investigators of gender have, over the years, taken this approach, producing innumerable reports about the superiority of one sex over the other on some specific trait or skill or task performance. As Shields (1975) pointed out, the focus on gender differences has been with psychology since its formal beginnings a little more than a century ago. Debates as to the strengths and weaknesses, validity and perils of this traditional approach are numerous (see *American Psychologist*, March 1995; Kitzinger, 1994).

From a social psychological perspective, a simple sex difference approach is necessarily incomplete. Questions about sex differences are often framed in such a way as to stress opposites rather than overlap, to emphasize the person rather than the setting, and to highlight biology or prior socialization rather than current assignment of women and men to different and unequal positions in the social structure. Further, analyses emerging from a sex differences framework typically feature stable dispositions rather than fluctuating patterns and pose overly simple rather than appropriately more complex explanations. A sex difference approach is, for our purposes of analyzing the *social psychology* of gender, a critically flawed model.

As an alternative, we adopt a gender-in-context model, with an emphasis on both the dynamic fluctuations of gender and the larger system in which gender is enacted. The resultant effort is not a catalogue of invariants (and indeed, the literature is too vast at this point to successfully compile such a catalogue, even if the intent were there). Rather, a compound framework is provided within which the significance of gender for social interaction can be understood.

Putting Gender into Context

Deaux and Major (1987) offered an interaction-based model that focuses on the proximal determinants of gender-related behaviors. The model assumes that gendered behaviors are highly flexible and influenced by context, and that events are often multiply determined. For convenience, this analysis assumes a perspective from one individual (termed the target or self) to another individual (termed the perceiver), although the reciprocality of social influence is clearly acknowledged. The various components of the model, as illustrated in Figure 1, can be summarized in terms of three basic clusters: first, the perceiver, who brings beliefs and expectations about gender into the interaction setting; second, the target individual himself or herself, who brings a set of self-conceptions and goals to the situation; and third, situational factors that can make gender more or less salient.

The first set of factors, related to a perceiver, highlights the beliefs that people have about gender and the ways in which those beliefs can be translated into action via the operation of expectancies. Gender belief systems, which include stereotypes, gender-role attitudes, and representations of one's own gender identity, serve as a filter through which individual women and men are perceived. These beliefs in turn influence the actions of people (perceivers) toward women and men, both as groups and as individuals. Hence gender exists not only in the minds of perceivers, but is acted out in specific contexts, ranging from the division of labor in a laboratory task (Skrypnek & Snyder, 1982) to sexual harassment in real world settings (Pryor, Giedd, & Williams, 1995). As considerable research has now shown, actions taken on the basis of beliefs can have self-fulfilling consequences (Snyder, Tanke, & Berscheid, 1977), thereby perpetuating the gender belief system.

In a dyadic interaction, both people participate. Thus the "target" brings to an interaction his or her own set of gender beliefs. Gender identity, like stereotypes and attitudes, is also a component of the gender belief system, as individuals define themselves, at least in part, in terms of broader social representations of gender. In addition to these belief systems, individuals engage in social interaction with a more specific set of goals, motives, and expectations that may be gendered as well. The source of these gendered beliefs is a frequent topic for debate, often defined in terms of an overstated opposition between forces of socialization versus biology. The concern here is less with these distal causal factors than with the more proximal influences and the actions taken in a given situation, giving expression to agendas that may be more or less gendered.

The third element of the Deaux–Major model concerns the situation, which makes gender more or less salient. When the proportion of women and men in a situation is highly skewed, for example, gender is more likely to be-

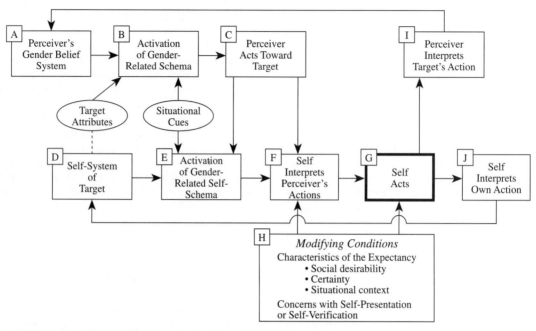

FIGURE 1   A Model of Social Interaction for Gender-Related Behavior.

come an issue. Particular settings, such as a professional football game, a Miss America pageant, a singles bar, or a fraternity-sorority mixer, can invoke gendered scripts for behavior that stress traditional male–female roles. But even less gender stereotypic situations can elicit gender congruent behavior through cues that subtly convey different performance expectations.

Although clearly specified as part of the Deaux–Major model, situational features were given less attention than were individual-level factors such as expectancies and motivational concerns. Yet as work on gender has progressed during the last decade, and as social psychologists have broadened their sampling of contexts beyond the traditional laboratory setting, it becomes apparent that examination of the "situation" must be extended and developed more fully to incorporate structural and systemic conditions that influence gender-related behaviors. There is also increasing recognition of the need to more sufficiently theorize the interaction between situation and person.

Enlarging the Frame of Analysis

The candidates for this enlarged analysis of gender-in-context are many and could include consideration of political systems and cultural traditions. Sociologists, anthropologists, and political scientists concerned with the ways in which gender is embedded in a culture provide many possible factors for an enlarged frame of reference. To keep the discussion manageable, however, as well as to maintain a social psychological voice, three variables that have engaged social psychologists in recent years are focused on here: social roles, status and expectation states, and power inequities.

Social Role Theory   Eagly's (1987) social role theory proposes that the division of labor within society along gender lines serves as the major influence on subsequent beliefs and behaviors about men and women. In contrast to those who rely on past cultural influences, such as childhood socialization practices, Eagly looks to current social arrangements as a key source of sex differences. Specifically, she argues that gender serves as a marker for critically different social roles that adults fill. The division of labor, in which men are more likely to be in paid occupational positions and women are more likely to be in the homemaker role, is said to affect two types of gender-related beliefs: (a) the expectations that people have for the traits and behaviors shown by women and men, and (b) the beliefs that women and men have about their own capacities and the skills that they could or should develop. These two sets of beliefs in turn shape the behaviors of women and men. The implications of this model are quite clear. If women and men typically operate in different domains in the society, for example, women in the home and men in the world of paid employment, then one would expect different patterns of behavior commensurate with the situation. These become unavoidably linked with a person's sex. With its stress on current structure rather than past socialization, Eagly's social role model implies that identical exposure to the same roles would result in equivalent gender patterns. Bem (1994) also argues that the sexual division of labor could itself produce two of the sexually differentiated behaviors that are frequently discussed in terms of biology, namely, physical aggression by males and maternal responsiveness by females.

Eagly and her colleagues present persuasive evidence for one of the links in this model, specifically the relationship between division of labor and behavioral expectations (Eagly & Steffen, 1984). They show that when people are asked to estimate the traits of either women or men who are homemakers versus full-time employees, the homemakers are judged to be more communal and less agentic than are full-time employees. Moskowitz, Suh, and Desaulniers (1994) adopted Eagly's role analysis as a frame for examining variations in agentic and communal behavior in a natural setting. Using event-sampling analysis, these investigators examined how women's and men's behavior varied as a function of their social role, specifically, whether they were a supervisor, coworker, or a person being supervised. Social role significantly influenced agentic and dominance behavior for both women and men: both were more dominant in a supervisory role and more submissive as a supervisee. It should be noted that these differences were within-subject findings. Thus, unlike the Eagly analysis that emphasizes the stable characteristics of occupational roles, the Moskowitz et al. (1994) data show people shifting from dominant to submissive behaviors as a function of the current interaction. In both cases, however, a structural variable is invoked to explain differences in individual behavior.

Social Status Status refers to the relative standing or evaluation of an individual or group within a particular group or community such that people high in status are perceived to be in some ways superior to those lower in status. The dimensions used to establish status hierarchies depend on the values of a society, and can vary across time and culture. Nonetheless, gender often covaries with status, such that women and activities associated with women are considered less valuable and less prestigious than men and the activities associated with them. The social roles that Eagly and her colleagues have studied are thus not equivalent: the role of employed "breadwinner" is viewed as being higher in status than the unemployed "homemaker."

Perceived status is the key variable for the expectation states theory (Berger, Rosenholtz, & Zelditch, 1980; Berger, Wagner, & Zelditch, 1985). According to this model, social interactions and performance expectations, particularly within a group setting, are based on the perceived status characteristics of the participants. Status

characteristics can be established on the basis of actual experience in a particular setting but are more often inferred on the basis of past information or belief. In the latter case, people differing in gender or race are described as having diffuse status characteristics. For instance, people of color and women are assumed to have less power and prestige, and hence their status in any particular situation will be lower. People's social expectations as to how different people will behave are seen to hinge on perceived relevant status characteristics. In the absence of information to the contrary, groups that are initially undifferentiated on other characteristics will assume that members with more valued states of the relevant status characteristic are more competent than those of lower status. These performance expectations, shared by all group members, affect the emergent power and prestige in the group.

Research supports the idea that gender is a status characteristic that elicits differential performance expectations. Not only are men expected to perform better than women, but because others hold higher expectations for performance from them, they get more opportunities to participate, initiate more actions, receive more positive reactions from others, and have more influence on decision making that takes place. This process of status generalization will occur even when the status characteristic is not specifically associated with ability to do the task at hand.

The use of gender as a basis for inferring status was shown by Wood and Karten (1986) in a study of small group interaction. With information only about the name and sex of other participants, members of experimentally formed groups believed that the male members were more competent than the female members. Ramifications of these beliefs included more talking by the men, particularly in the areas of giving information and offering opinions, and more positive social behaviors, such as agreement and acting friendly, by the women. In contrast, when specific and relevant status information not linked to gender was provided to participants, the previously observed sex differences disappeared, replaced by explicit status-based differences, that is, high-status people gave more opinions and low-status people were more supportive.

Lorenzi-Cioldi (1988) also analyzed the link between gender and status and hypothesized that high-status people are more likely to be seen as individuals, loosely associated in an aggregate, while people of lower status are viewed as interchangeable members of a more homogeneous group. This differential perception of groups varying in status was examined in a pair of studies by Lorenzi-Cioldi and his colleagues (Lorenzi-Cioldi & Deaux, 1997; Lorenzi-Cioldi, Eagly, & Stewart, 1995). When people are tested for their recall of information about a series of male or female targets, both women and men tend to homogenize women, that is, make errors that suggest a failure to differentiate among the various female targets. In contrast, respondents make fewer errors of this form in recalling information about male targets, suggesting that people individuate men to a greater extent (Lorenzi-Cioldi et al., 1995). That this difference in the perception of women and men is linked to status is supported by a subsequent study, in which status was explicitly controlled (a comparison of first-year students and seniors) or manipulated (minimal group paradigm). In two studies, members of both high status and low status groups were more likely to show a homogeneity effect when recalling information about the lower status group (Lorenzi-Cioldi & Deaux, 1997).

Power Although the terms status and power are often used interchangeably, some distinctions can be drawn. Whereas status refers primarily to *perceptions* of competence and superiority of one person or group of persons over another, power typically refers to the actual control that one person or group has over the resources and outcomes of another. Analyses of power relationships can occur at any one of several levels: societal, organizational, interpersonal, and individual (Ragins & Sundstrom, 1989; Yoder & Kahn, 1992), all of which are relevant to an analysis of gender.

At the societal level, sociologists and anthropologists have explored the ways in which patriarchal systems influence the economic and political positions of women and men in society. Within this context, the greater dependence of women on men, though sometimes conceptualized at the individual level, can be treated as a societal variable that is assessed by employment policies, existing wage gaps, and family politics (Baxter & Kane, 1995).

Within organizations, men typically have more power than women. Men are more highly placed in the organizational structure, are more likely to control financial resources, and typically supervise more people within the organization (Reskin & Padavic, 1994). Fiske and Glick (1995) catalogue a set of factors that predispose men to occupy the more powerful role in many occupational settings, including a preponderance of males in leadership positions, a history of men occupying key positions, and the recent entry of women to the setting, giving them a role of newcomer in an ongoing operation.

Interpersonal power differences between women and men are often documented within marital relationships. The economic dependence of wives on husbands is an important source of this power differential, which can then be generalized to the control of other resources (Baxter & Kane, 1995). Some of the correlates of asymmetrical power in a marital relationship can be subtle, as indexed by verbal and nonverbal communication patterns (Henley, 1977). Other correlates are more vivid, such as the association between a woman's lesser power and the husband's tendency toward violence and spouse abuse (Frieze & McHugh, 1992). More recently it has been suggested that

interpersonal interaction not only manifests power differences but it may be an important medium through which gender inequality is written into other developing forms of social organization (Ridgeway, 1992). In other words, gender relations played out in the relatively localized arena of interpersonal interaction may set the script for relations and roles at broader organizational and societal levels.

At the individual level, trait differences between women and men in dimensions such as a need for power or social dominance orientation have been proposed. Although findings indicate a widespread tendency for men to show significantly higher social dominance than women (Sidanius, Pratto, & Bobo, 1994), need for power does not show consistent sex differences in the strength of the power motive under neutral conditions (Winter, 1988). Individual-level differences, when observed, are undoubtedly multidetermined. Stewart and Winter (1976), for example, have shown that need for power can be aroused in women using the same procedures as those that raise need for power in men, namely, listening to excerpts of speeches by powerful men. Finally, in addition to the influence of societal, organizational, and interpersonal factors on how power interplays with gender, some theorists have suggested a biocultural or evolutionary basis as well (see Buss & Kenrick, 1998, in this *Handbook*).

Asymmetrical power, however it comes about, decidedly alters the nature of social interaction among unequals compared to equals. Recent evidence shows that those in power are much more likely to stereotype those who have less power (Fiske, 1993). People high in power pay less attention to the person with less power, but will increase their attention as the power of the other increases. For people who have less power, it is typically important to pay attention to those who do have power and exercise some degree of fate control. The powerful, in contrast, frequently believe themselves to be less contingent on their subordinates and hence have less need to pay attention to them.

Each of these factors—social roles, status and expectation states, and power—is critical to a comprehensive social psychological analysis of gender. Sometimes ignored, often implicit, these factors represent the various ways through which women and men are constrained by their situations. People also bring to situations internalized gender beliefs that predispose them to construct identities and behaviors that are consistent with them and congruent with the situation they find.

Preview of Coming Attractions

In this chapter, we consider a large body of literature on gender and social behavior, using gender-in-context as the guide. We begin with a review of research on the gender belief system, which includes work on stereotypes, gender-role attitudes, and gender identity. Next attention is turned to the role of gender in social interaction. From this very large domain, several areas are selected for particular attention: verbal and nonverbal communication, leadership and group processes, and social influence. The interplay of individual propensities and structural factors, and indeed the necessity for this form of multilevel analysis, is then applied to two social issues: occupational discrimination and sexual harassment. Finally, coverage concludes with a consideration of the questions and research strategies for future research on the social psychology of gender.

II. GENDER BELIEF SYSTEMS

Oh well, we say with a knowing lilt in our voice, that's a man for you. Or that's just the way women are. We accept, as a cosmic joke, the separate ways of men and women, their different levels of foolishness.
—CAROL SHIELDS, *The Stone Diaries*, 1994

The gender belief system is a mutlifaceted, all-encompassing set of ideas that people have about gender. Under this umbrella of gender beliefs, several separate components can be identified. These include the stereotypes that people have about the characteristics of women and men; the attitudes that they hold about the social roles occupied by women and men; and the views men and women themselves have about their own gender identity. Although highly related at face value, these components of gender beliefs are not synonymous, as many investigators, confronted with unexpectedly low correlations between seemingly related concepts, have discovered. Consideration of each component separately can, as is often the case in science, serve to isolate unique portions of the variance and gain a more finely tuned understanding of the various processes involved.

At the same time, the various phenomena involved in gender beliefs have common roots. At a sociocultural level, pervasive social representations of gender serve as a backdrop for individual beliefs about the characteristics, roles, and rights of women and men. At the individual level, stereotypes about characteristic traits can combine with beliefs about social roles to predict attitudes toward specific gender-related policies such as affirmative action for women.

A precise charting of the interrelationships among stereotypes, attitudes, and identity is not yet possible, although considerable progress has been made in recent years. Two factors contributing to this progress can be cited: (a) more sophisticated conceptual work has led to the development of important new measures; and (b) methodologies borrowed from cognitive psychology have allowed a better understanding of process. Signs of this progress are evident in the following coverage of stereotypes, gender-role attitudes, and gender identity.

Gender Stereotypes

Gender stereotypes consist of the set of specific beliefs about the characteristics that women and men are likely to possess (see Deaux & Kite, 1993, for a more extensive review of this area). Beyond these descriptive estimates, gender stereotypes frequently are prescriptive as well, reflecting beliefs as to how women and men *should* be (Fiske & Stevens, 1993). In a number of respects, stereotypes appear to be the most fundamental aspect of the gender belief system, both in terms of their durability over time and their pervasive influence on other aspects of the system.

Scope and Accuracy The scope of gender stereotypes is considerable, encompassing beliefs about physical characteristics, personality traits, role-related behaviors, occupational preferences, specific competencies, and emotional dispositions. Thus, for example, men are believed to be more assertive and independent than women, while women are expected to be more emotional and concerned with the welfare of others (Deaux & Lewis, 1984; Spence, Helmreich, & Stapp, 1975). In terms of emotions, women are thought to cry more often and to express anger less often than men (LaFrance & Banaji, 1992). People expect carpenters and pilots to be male and kindergarten teachers and social workers to be female (Glick, Wilk, & Perreault, 1995). Expectations for physical characteristics vary as well: men are expected to be taller, to have deeper voices, wider shoulders and shorter hair, as compared to women (Deaux & Lewis, 1984).

Fundamental to any discussion of stereotypes is the issue of accuracy: do gender stereotypes reflect the actual co-occurrence of gender categories with assigned characteristics? The question is deceptively simple, shrouding a host of complicated conceptual and methodological issues. One key issue is the potential disparity between an individual case and a group-based estimate. Thus, although women on the average may be both shorter and weaker than men, the pattern can be reversed for any particular man and woman. Because any assessed characteristic shows some degree of individual variation, often quite large and, in the case of women and men, often overlapping, the application of the average to a particular individual will often be in error.

At the group level, however, we can ask whether stereotyped traits map on to the actual distribution of that characteristic in the population. Swim (1994) addressed this question by first asking college students to estimate how women and men are distributed on several different characteristics and then comparing those estimates to results of meta-analytic studies. In a second study, she asked participants to make direct estimates of effect sizes of several sex differences. Her results showed a high degree of correspondence between people's estimates of sex differences and the magnitude of empirically obtained differences, suggesting that people have a reasonably accurate perception of differences between women and men. Underestimation was more common than overestimation, although the tendency toward minimization may have been influenced by demand characteristics, as participants were asked to make direct comparisons between women and men in a within-subjects design.

Further, it should be noted that assessing stereotype accuracy is not easy. Some beliefs about women and men can be checked with objective measures, such as average height or percentage of each sex in a particular occupation. Other gender stereotypes are more inferential, such as the level of emotionality or the degree of independence. When objective measures are not available, or when a question is framed in more subjective terms, judgments are made more complicated by what Biernat and Manis (1994) term "shifting standards." Thus, the subjective scale used to judge a woman's aggressiveness, for example, is different from that used to judge a man's aggressiveness. Because of the stereotype that men are more aggressive, people require a stronger display of aggression to consider a man aggressive; in contrast, because women are believed to be less aggressive, a less intense display will nonetheless seem above threshold and be judged as aggressive. The consequence of these shifting standards is that judgments of women and men may look fairly similar on subjective scales, while masking more discrepant stereotypic beliefs about actual behavior.

Stereotypes and Inference   As noted earlier, generalization from a group average to an individual case does not always yield successful prediction. A more troublesome aspect of stereotypes is that beliefs about group averages can bias evaluation as well. Biernat's work on estimates of height is a striking example of this bias (Biernat, 1993; Nelson, Biernat, & Manis, 1990). Among adults, men on the average are objectively taller than women. Biernat and her colleagues find that the reality of the advantage in men's average height biases people's judgments of photographs that match men and women in height, leading respondents to report that the presented men are taller than the women (Biernat, 1993; Nelson et al., 1990). Interestingly, this bias is significant only when people are judging adults, for whom the objective difference does favor men. In judgments of seventh graders, where girls on the average are taller than boys, people bias their judgments toward girls, and the bias is particularly strong among seventh graders themselves, who presumably have the most contact with the objective distribution. Thus, the reality of averages not only influences prediction but it can bias evaluation of the individual case as well.

The physical aspects of gender stereotypes are particularly interesting, both because they have immediate impact

and because other personality attributes covary in judgment with physical features. Deaux and Lewis (1984) found that among the set of gender stereotypic components, including traits, roles, occupations, and physical features, the latter carried the most weight in influencing people's inferences about other stereotypic components. Thus, a person described as deep voiced and broad shouldered was seen as far more likely to possess masculine traits and roles than a person described as having long hair and a slender build, or someone described in terms of a male-linked occupation.

In the case of height, a series of studies show psychological advantage for both children and adults who are taller. Eisenberg and her colleagues (Eisenberg, Roth, Bryniarski, & Murray, 1984; Villimez, Eisenberg, & Carroll, 1986) find biases favoring the taller child among both mothers and teachers in ratings of competence and independence. Similarly, taller adults, and in particular men, gain an advantage on judgments ranging from professional status to personal adjustment (Jackson & Ervin, 1992).

The link of gender stereotypic physical features to personal characteristics is also seen in the work of Friedman and Zebrowitz (1992) on baby-faced features. Being female and having baby-faced features (e.g., full cheeks, small jaw, large eyes) are both associated with greater warmth and lesser power. In nature, gender and facial maturity covary; experimentally, however, they can be varied independently through the systematic construction of facial stimuli. Taking this approach, Friedman and Zebrowitz (1992) found that males and females were judged to be equally warm and equally powerful when facial maturity was equivalent. In the natural confounded state of these two variables, however, facial maturity contributes to the strength of gender stereotypes.

Another example of the link between physical features and trait inference is the face-ism work of Archer and his colleagues (Archer, Iritani, Kimes, & Barrios, 1983). Over an impressive range of material, varying from news media and televised interviews to sixteenth-century art, men are represented with more emphasis on the head and face, while women are framed such that the face to body ratio is considerably lower. Although this visual representation is interesting in and of itself, its significance lies in the fact that people infer more intelligence and power to bodily representations that show greater face and head area. Experimental studies systematically varying face-ism proportion and sex of target show that inferences of competence are reliably associated with a high face-ism ratio.

The Automaticity of Gender Stereotypes   The persistent and pervasive character of gender stereotypes results in part from the fact that they are often processed automatically, operating at an implicit rather than explicit level of awareness (see Fiske, 1998, in this *Handbook*). As Devine (1989) and others have shown, overt attitudes do not necessarily correspond to underlying stereotypic beliefs. Thus, people who believe themselves to be free of gender bias may in fact hold stereotypic beliefs about gender at a nonconscious level—beliefs that can influence a range of biased judgments and behaviors.

The influence of implicit beliefs about gender is shown in the work of Banaji and her colleagues. In one set of studies (Banaji, Hardin, & Rothman, 1993), participants were initially exposed to either neutral information or information that primed images of aggression or dependency. Following neutral primes, participants showed no difference in their ratings of the dependence or aggression of male and female targets depicted in a brief story. In contrast, following gender-stereotypic primes for aggression or dependency, people were prone to rate the male character as more aggressive than the female, and the female character as more dependent than the male, thus implicating implicit gender stereotypes. In another series of studies, Banaji and Greenwald (1995) showed that recall of material can also be biased by gender beliefs. Judgments of the fame of names, familiar from an earlier experimental session, were greater for male than female names, implying an implicit association between fame and male-ness.

Similar subtleties emerge when people draw causal inferences from short descriptions of male–female interaction (LaFrance, Brownell, & Hahn, 1996). Reflecting inferred gender differences in power, people are more likely to attribute causality to an actor when the recipient of the action is female. Other investigators have shown that the presence of a stereotype can effectively block one's recognition of other variables that are relevant to an outcome but irrelevant to the stereotype. Thus, as an example, people attempting to explain a student's success or failure in a welding course ignored relevant information about course load and focused instead on experimentally irrelevant information about gender. In the authors' words, "stereotypes not only determine what people see but also determine what people do not see" (Sanbonmatsu, Akimoto, & Gibson, 1994, p. 79).

Agency, Communion, and Gender Polarization   The now-familiar distinction between agency and communion serves to organize many studies of gender stereotypes: men are characterized as independent, assertive, and initiating, while women are viewed as caring, emotionally expressive, and responsive to others (Ashmore, Del Boca, & Wohlers, 1986). Indeed, these two dimensions are so central to thinking about gender that they have often (but not without controversy) been considered the fundamental dimensions of masculinity and femininity (Bem, 1974).

Eagly and Mladinic (1989) report that perceived differences between women and men are particularly strong on the positive, communal traits. Although the "dark side" of gender stereotypes (Ashmore et al., 1986, p. 99) is less fre-

quently studied, measures developed by Spence and her collaborators (Spence, Helmreich, & Holahan, 1979) assess negative aspects of agency and communion as well as the positive. They find that men are more likely to be described as arrogant and unprincipled, while women are believed more likely to be servile and whiny.

Agency and communion have occupational connotations as well, a pattern that Eagly (1987) explores in her analysis of the origins of gender stereotypes. Thus, people described as employed workers are believed to be more agentic and people described as homemakers are believed to be more communal (Eagly & Steffen, 1984). For Eagly (1987), this division of labor is the antecedent for stereotypic beliefs about agency and communion. Because different societal roles are associated with different attributes, a gender-skewed distribution of women and men into social and occupational roles will shape both self and other beliefs about gender characteristics. This social role analysis was extended by Eagly and Kite (1987) to the case of national stereotypes. To the degree that men have higher status in a country and are more visible as players in national events, Eagly and Kite predicted that stereotypes of nationalities would more closely resemble the stereotype of men than of women within that country. By the same reasoning, in countries in which men and women occupy similar occupational and political roles, stereotypes of men and women should be relatively similar to each other and to the national stereotype. Their findings generally supported these predictions. U.S. college students viewed Iranians in general as very similar to Iranian men and very different from Iranian women, for example, while seeing no difference in the degree to which English women and English men resembled the national stereotype of the English. These patterns were particularly strong when respondents had a generally negative evaluation of the country under consideration.

Despite empirical evidence that agency and communion are conceptually independent, people tend to construe the differences between women and men in unidimensional, bipolar terms, a phenomenon that Bem (1993) calls gender polarization. Thus, ascribing agency to a person is typically accompanied by a de-emphasis of communality, and vice versa. One illustrative case of this tendency is seen in a study of stereotypes of gays and lesbians: Kite and Deaux (1987) found that people believe gay men have predominantly feminine characteristics and lesbians have primarily masculine traits.

Although some might argue that bipolar thinking is inherent to conceptions of gender, Biernat (1991) presents suggestive evidence that the perceived opposition between masculinity and femininity is learned. With research participants ranging from kindergarten-age to college students who described themselves in terms of gender-linked traits, roles, occupations, and physical characteristics, Biernat found that masculine and feminine components were positively related for the youngest children, became independent constructs in the middle childhood years, and only from tenth grade on were seen as opposite ends of a single dimension. Thus, as children become increasingly socialized into the culture and its belief system, their beliefs about gender take on a bipolarity that was not present initially.

Subtypes and Variations   Although stereotypes about women and men are pervasive and reflect considerable consensus, there are two important variations. First, different groups and societies can diverge in their stereotypes of women and men; and second, conceptions of women and men are often subdivided into more sharply defined subtypes.

Cross-national studies serve as one lens for looking at variations in gender stereotypes. In one of the most ambitious of such studies, covering thirty different countries, Williams and Best (1982) found that several aspects of gender stereotypes were shared across the majority of countries. Men in most countries were seen as more adventurous and independent, while women were viewed as more sentimental and submissive. Men were also consistently seen as stronger and more active than women. At the same time, there was considerable variation among countries, both in the degree to which women and men were seen as different from each other and in the assignment of particular features. Typically, these variations could also be linked to differences in religious tradition, for example, Catholic versus Protestant, underlining the importance of looking at systems as well as individuals when analyzing stereotypes. Stereotypes may also vary among subgroups within a culture. Although relatively little work has been done to explore these possible variations, preliminary evidence suggests that ethnic groups within the United States, for example, may have somewhat divergent gender stereotypes and be stereotyped differently as well (Landrine, 1985; Vickberg & Deaux, 1995).

The second important variation in gender stereotypes concerns the existence of stereotypic subtypes. People's gender stereotypes exist at varying levels of specificity and include beliefs about particular types of women and men, each with its own defining features. Several investigators have documented a variety of subtypes which, although varying somewhat from study to study, nonetheless attest to the existence of a set of specific visions of women and men (Clifton, McGrath, & Wick, 1976; Deaux, Winton, Crowley, & Lewis, 1985; Edwards, 1992; Noseworthy & Lott, 1984; Six & Eckes, 1991). Some of the commonly found stereotypic subtypes of women include housewife, career woman, sexy woman, and feminist. For men, the subtypes include athlete, blue-collar worker, businessman, and macho man. Although respondents are able to construct

subtypes of both women and men, several investigators have suggested that the boundary lines between subtypes are less clear and the degree of consensus less pronounced for male subtypes than for female subtypes (Deaux et al., 1985; Edwards, 1992; Six & Eckes, 1991). The reasons for such a difference are not yet clear: perhaps societal depictions of female roles are more extensive and more rigidly defined, resulting in a larger set of clearly articulated images. Alternatively, it may be that people resist typing higher status men, seeing them more as individuals rather than in terms of definable groups (Lorenzi-Cioldi, 1988).

Not only do types of women differ in the attributes assigned to them, but overall evaluations of the subtypes differ as well. In comparing evaluations of "housewives" and "feminist women," Haddock and Zanna (1994) report that college students rate housewives much more positively than they rate feminists. This effect was stronger for men than for women, and the devaluation of feminist women was particularly strong among men scoring high on a measure of right-wing authoritarianism. Other research shows implications of subtyping in the domain of sexual harassment (Burgess & Borgida, 1997). Respondents viewing women in nontraditional work settings are most likely to invoke an "iron woman" stereotype that emphasizes strength and invulnerability. A consequence of this view is that sexually harassing behaviors are taken less seriously than when a more traditional stereotype of women is invoked, presumably because the "iron woman" should be able to handle unwanted threats.

To summarize, stereotypes of gender are pervasive, durable, and influential, existing both at a general level of "women" and "men," as well as in the form of more specific subtypes. Because they operate at a nonconscious as well as a conscious level of awareness, their influence is often hard to recognize or detect. Further, the inferential net linked to these basic stereotypes is extensive. As a consequence, not only is the application of group stereotype to individual case problematic, but group inferences themselves may lose their actuarial base (e.g., when knowledge of average height differences leads to group-based judgments of competence). As noted earlier, the components of the gender belief system maintain some independence from one another. Nonetheless, stereotypes are in some respects the most basic element of that system, and they often influence other components.

Attitudes toward Gender Roles

Whereas gender stereotypes have remained quite constant over time, attitudes about the appropriate roles and responsibilities for women and men have shown considerable flexibility over time and place. In the previous edition of the *Handbook of Social Psychology*, Spence, Deaux, and Helmreich (1985) pointed to shifts that had occurred in attitudes between the mid-1960s and the mid-1970s. During this period, men and women in North America became increasingly liberal in their views of the appropriate roles and rights of women, with women consistently showing less conservatism than men. This increase has continued to 1992, with both men and women becoming more liberal in their attitudes toward women's roles (Spence & Hahn, 1995). In virtually all studies of attitudes toward gender roles, women report more egalitarian attitudes than do men.

As the endorsement of traditional attitudes about appropriate roles for women wane, however, several current studies suggest that new forms of sexist attitudes are developing. Swim and her colleagues (Swim, Aikin, Hall, & Hunter, 1995) contrast old-fashioned sexism with modern sexism, echoing a distinction made in the literature of racism. Old-fashioned sexism "is characterized by endorsement of traditional gender roles, differential treatment of women and men, and stereotypes about lesser female competence" (Swim et al., 1995, p. 199), attitudes that have been typically assessed by measures such as the Attitudes toward Woman scale (Spence & Helmreich, 1972). Modern sexism, while also rooted in negative feelings about the target group, incorporates concerns about contemporary practices. As characterized by Swim et al. (1995), the modern sexist may reject stereotypes of female inferiority, yet believe that discrimination is no longer a problem, feel negatively toward women who make political and economic demands, and think that the government and the media pay more attention to women than is appropriate. Tougas, Brown, Beaton, and Joly (1995) define "neo-sexism," conceptually similar to modern sexism, as a "manifestation of a conflict between egalitarian values and residual negative feelings toward women" (1995, p. 843).

Old-fashioned and modern sexism are not unrelated: Swim et al. (1995) report correlations of .42 to .30 in two studies of male and female U.S. college students; Tougas et al. report a correlation of .64 for Canadian male college students. Nonetheless, the two concepts predict different behaviors. Modern sexism, for example, predicts people's tendencies to overestimate the percentage of women in traditionally male occupations, consistent with the attitude that women no longer experience discrimination; the pattern was the opposite for old-fashioned sexism. When asked to explain sex segregation in the work force, people scoring high in modern sexism were more likely to invoke biological differences as a reason and less likely to use socialization or discrimination as explanations. Old-fashioned sexism was unrelated to these explanations. Tougas et al. (1995) show that neosexism but not old-fashioned sexism is predictive of men's negative attitudes toward affirmative action.

Glick and Fiske (1996) explore the ambivalence associated with attitudes toward women. Following the argu-

ments of Guttentag and Secord (1983), Glick and Fiske suggest that ambivalence is a product of the structural power that men have in most societies and the reproductive power than women have. Sexism, as a consequence, has both a hostile and a benevolent component. Hostile sexism focuses on competitive relations between women and men, heterosexual hostility, and the endorsement of dominant status for men. In contrast, benevolent sexism focuses on the presumed nicer qualities of women, while continuing to reflect beliefs in strong differences between women and men. An example of hostile sexism is the statement "Women exaggerate problems they have at work"; benevolent sexism is reflected in statements such as "A good woman should be set on a pedestal" and "Women have a superior moral sensibility." Extensive psychometric work shows that, although benevolent and hostile sexism are substantially correlated, they relate differently to other measures. Hostile sexism, for example, correlates significantly with the Swim et al. modern sexism scale, while benevolent sexism is unrelated to modern sexism when the influence of hostile sexism is controlled. The two measures also relate differently to ascriptions of positive and negative traits: hostile sexism predicts negative stereotypes of women while benevolent sexism is associated with positive stereotypic traits (the latter relationship true for men but not for women).

The distinction between hostile and benevolent sexist attitudes is important in understanding some recent and apparently anomalous findings reported by Eagly and Mladinic (1994). These authors find that women are evaluated more favorably than men on both semantic differential scales and free-response measures of gender stereotypes, a finding that they have designated the "women-are-wonderful" effect. When these general evaluations of women were related to more specific sexist attitudes, Glick and Fiske (1996) found that men who rate women favorably are likely to score low on hostile sexism but high on benevolent sexism. Interestingly, although Eagly and Mladinic (1994) report no sex of rater differences in evaluations of women, Glick and Fiske (1996) find significantly different (and less consistent) patterns of relationships for women between their separate measures of sexism and general evaluation. The reasons for these differences, though still speculative, may be a function of a different basis of sexism in women and men—motivationally based for men versus culturally learned for women (Glick and Fiske, 1996).

Complexity is also found among studies that evaluate the products and performances of women and men. It is not invariably true, as the early Goldberg (1968) study led many to believe, that women's performance will always be downgraded relative to men's. Meta-analyses suggest that the "main effect" difference, while consistent with the argument that women's performance is less valued, is nonetheless small (Eagly, Makhijani, & Klonsky, 1992;

Swim, Borgida, Maruyama, & Myers, 1989). The magnitude of the difference, however, is significantly linked to task characteristics. When the domain of judgment is one associated with women, differences in evaluated performance tend to disappear (though not, it might be noted, to favor the woman). In contrast, the more associated a domain is with men, whether by content, traditional occupancy, or gendered leadership style, the stronger is the tendency to devalue the performance of women relative to men (Eagly et al., 1992; Olian, Schwab, & Haberfeld, 1988; Swim et al., 1989).

Gendered characteristics of the task are critical in causal attributions for male and female performance as well, as a recent meta-analysis shows (Swim & Sanna, 1996). On masculine tasks, men's success is more likely attributed to ability than is women's success, while effort attributions are more likely to be used for women than for men. Differences in causal attributions are not evident when the task is either neutral or feminine (and again, the absence of a reversal on feminine tasks is worth noting). Thus, one can not conclude that women are always disadvantaged in performance judgments. Rather the disadvantages for women occur primarily in male domains. Moreover, women neither gain an advantage nor men suffer a disadvantage when the domain is one associated with women. To the extent that masculine domains are more valued by a society, or are more numerous, the disadvantages to women and the advantages to men are correspondingly greater.

Many other measures of attitudes toward women and men, their roles, responsibilities, and aptitudes, are available in the literature, and new measures continue to be developed (see Beere, 1990, for one compendium). Of necessity, only a few of these measures are discussed here. The basic criterion for selection is the estimated theoretical potential of the construct, in terms of linking gender-based attitudes to other social psychological processes. At the same time, it is important to note that many scales have been developed that tap very specific domains of gender beliefs, for example, rape mythology (Burt, 1980), the likelihood to rape (Malamuth, 1981), and the likelihood to sexually harass (Pryor, 1987; Pryor et al., 1995). In each case, they have shown substantial ability to predict behavior in targeted domains.

Gender and Self-Definition

At a very early age, children are aware of being male or female; as these categories gain a constancy, they also incorporate beliefs about what it means to be male or female in the society (Ruble & Martin, in press). These assessments of self, like descriptions of and evaluations of others, are shaped by the gender belief system. In important ways, a person's choice of activities, occupations, sexual relationships, and social networks are influenced by gender.

The term gender identity is often used to characterize those aspects of self that are relevant to gender. Yet, the term is both too simple and too general to be social psychologically useful. The most commonly used definition of gender identity is one's sense of being male or female. As such, it often refers specifically to a child's awareness and presumably correct labeling of his or her own sex. In analyzing gender development, however, psychologists have defined several components of children's awareness and incorporation of gender, including activities and interests, personality and social attributes, perceptions of social relationships, stylistic characteristics, and values (Huston, 1983; Ruble & Martin, in press). Each of these aspects has been heavily investigated, and each is part of the meaning that gender holds for the person, as a child and as an adult.

From the perspective of personality psychology, shaped by a tradition of individual differences (e.g., Terman & Miles, 1936), gender identity has slightly different connotations. Conventional definitions of masculinity and femininity were often seen as the manifestation of gender identity. More recently, Spence (1985) has offered a theoretical model of gender identity that emphasizes multidimensionality and individual variation. According to this perspective, gender identity is an idiosyncratic summation of characteristics that can be linked to gender. The sense of being male or female typically remains constant, but the traits and behaviors used to support or exemplify that gender identity are highly variable among people and across time.

A more social psychological approach considers gender as a category of group membership. Thus in claiming the identity of man or woman, one not only labels the self but also identifies with a group of people who share that category membership and, presumably, category-relevant characteristics as well. A variant of the categorical approach is to consider gender not as a single membership category but rather as a set of categories. From this latter perspective, the term gender identity would be replaced with a concept of gendered identities. Occupations, social roles such as parent, sexual orientation, and other forms of social identification each incorporate gender-related features, and each could be analyzed as a separate identity category.

Gender as a Social Category The process of social identification is one in which a person creates psychological links between the self and one or more other people (Deaux, 1996). An essential feature of this process is categorization, or the placing of oneself in a group that contains other people who share some critical characteristic—in this case, sex or gender. Social psychological theories differ in their treatment of the categorization process: categorization can be viewed as a relatively stable choice with long-term implications or as a more dynamic short-term reaction to specific circumstances (Deaux, 1996). Further, theories differ in their assumptions as to which conditions facilitate gender categorization.

Work on the "spontaneous self-concept" (Cota & Dion, 1986; McGuire, McGuire, & Winton, 1979), for example, assumes that aspects of self that are most distinctive in one's environment are most likely to be salient in the self-concept. In terms of stable environment, this model predicts and finds that girls and boys who are in a minority in their household are more likely, as a general tendency, to define themselves in terms of gender than are children whose sex is the majority within their household (McGuire & McGuire, 1981). The model predicts similar patterns for the short-term situation, and findings indicate that women who are a minority in a group setting are more likely to mention their gender than men who are the majority in that same group, and vice versa (Cota & Dion, 1986). A similar concern with the conditions that make gender salient is evident in the work on self-categorization theory (Oakes, 1987). According to this perspective, gender will be most salient and hence most likely be used as a basis of self-definition when it maximally distinguishes between group members. In a group of six women and six men, for example, gender would be most salient if the women all conveyed similar attitudes toward affirmative action and men all conveyed a different attitude. In contrast, if some women and some men favored affirmative action, and some women and some men opposed it, gender would, according to self-categorization theory, be less apt to be emphasized in self-definition. Note that although both the spontaneous self-concept perspective and self-categorization theory attend to sex composition of the group, their predictions are not necessarily congruent.

Social identity theory, a theory that predates self-categorization theory and that puts greater emphasis on intergroup relations, assumes that evaluation of one's ingroup typically involves comparison with an outgroup. Thus in the case of gender, women would compare their ingroup to men as the relevant outgroup, and vice versa (Skevington & Baker, 1989; Williams & Giles, 1978). If one assumes that men's status in society is higher than that of women, one would then expect to find men evaluating their ingroup more favorably than women would evaluate theirs. Research testing this general hypothesis has been mixed, however (Condor, 1986; Skevington & Baker, 1989). Mizrahi and Deaux (1997), for example, find that gender identification is associated with ingroup favoritism and outgroup bias only among men; among women, the strength of gender identification is reflected in increased feelings of collectivism with the ingroup but not with intergroup comparison. Because gender and power are frequently confounded, however, conclusions about the role of gender identity are frequently difficult to draw (Bourhis, 1993; Breakwell, 1979).

Social psychological accounts also need to address the multiplicity of gendered identities (Condor, 1986; Skevington & Baker, 1989). The ubiquity of gender in social relations means that gender is, perhaps inextricably, a part of other social identities. Thus to define the nature of parent, of nurse, or of Latina, as well as to predict the behavioral consequences that would flow from that identity state, it is necessary to address gender implications. Nor is the definition of woman, in and of itself, unambiguous. (In this case, the parallel research has not been done with men.) Gurin and Markus (1989), for example, compared the gender identity of women who were either traditional or nontraditional in their attitudes toward work and family. Gender was more central to the thinking of nontraditional women, and their sense of common fate with other women was significantly greater. Further, centrality of gender had different implications for the two groups of women: among traditional women, centrality was negatively related to a feminist consciousness, while it was positively associated with feminist consciousness for nontraditional women. Further research by Gurin and Townsend (1986) found that a sense of common fate with other women, defined by the authors as one key element of gender identity, was the strongest predictor of collective discontent, criticism of the legitimacy of gender disparities, and the advocacy of collective action for change (Gurin & Townsend, 1986).

Gender Identity as Masculinity and Femininity From the perspective of personality research, gender identity concerns not shared social categories but rather the meanings and traits that an individual associates with being male or female. Traditionally, personality models assumed that males typically can be characterized by a set of interrelated traits and behaviors that can be termed masculine, while females possess a set of associated characteristics that are termed feminine (Terman & Miles, 1936). Further, the assumption was made that masculinity and femininity were seen as opposite ends of a single bipolar dimension (Constantinople, 1973). In other words, one can be masculine *or* feminine, but not both. As noted earlier, people's stereotypic beliefs about women and men tend to reflect that assumption. So too are self-referent judgments of masculinity and femininity negatively correlated, when those specific, culturally loaded terms are used as self-descriptors (Spence, 1993). Also paralleling findings in the stereotype literature, the perceived negative correlation is learned. Young children do not initially put masculine and feminine attributes in opposition, but gradually learn to do so over time (Biernat, 1991).

The introduction of the concept of androgyny (Bem, 1974) challenged the bipolar assumption, proposing instead that masculinity and femininity are separate and orthogonal dimensions. Thus, people could be masculine, feminine, or androgynous, the latter combining both domains. (A fourth category of undifferentiated, consisting of people who score low on both masculinity and femininity, remains theoretically unclear.) While empirically separating masculinity and femininity, Bem's work continued to assume that each of these domains was in itself unidimensional (i.e., that various traits and behaviors considered masculine or feminine are highly interrelated), leading to lively and continuing debates in the literature. Probably the leading opponent of Bem's position is Spence (1985, 1993), who has argued that the commonly used measures, such as the Bem Sex Role Inventory (Bem, 1974) or the Personal Attributes Questionnaire (Spence, Helmreich, & Stapp, 1974) primarily tap dimensions of expressiveness and instrumentality and not other gender-related domains. Masculinity and femininity, Spence (1985, 1993; Spence & Buckner, 1995) argues, are each multidimensional concepts, the constituents of which are only loosely related. She suggests that the various factors contributing to gender identity (e.g., personality traits, physical attributes, abilities, recreational interests, occupational preferences, etc.) have different developmental histories and complex interactions. Further, people can selectively pick from the societal offerings those characteristics that they find compatible and ignore or dismiss other attributes that may typically be associated with masculinity and femininity. The terms masculine and feminine may trigger an agreed-upon set of social representations; but one's own masculinity and femininity can be defined in more variable and idiosyncratic terms.

The interplay between societal definitions and self-definitions has some interesting aspects. Endorsement of gender stereotypes about emotional expression, for example, is associated with people's own reported experience of emotions (Grossman & Wood, 1993). Women who believe that the intensity of emotional experience is greater for women than it is for men report personally experiencing more intense emotions; in contrast, men who endorse gender stereotypes, indicating that men are less emotional, self-report fewer emotional feelings. The sources of self-esteem may differ for women and men as well, reflecting cultural norms (Josephs, Markus, & Tafarodi, 1992). Overall, levels of self-esteem for women and men are approximately equivalent. Yet, cultures that endorse greater nurturance for women and greater independence for men, in both descriptive and prescriptive ways, affect bases for self-definition and self-evaluation. Following this line of reasoning, Josephs et al. (1992) found that among men but not women, high self-esteem is related to a tendency toward individualism. On the other hand, memory for information about other people was related to self-esteem among women but not men.

Other complex analyses of dispositional differences between women and men across cultures are reported by Kashima et al. (1995). Their investigation concerns several seemingly related dimensions on which women and men, as well as cultures, are often compared, namely, individualism, relatedness, and collectivism. On measures of individualism and collectivism, culture but not gender yielded differences, a finding consistent with the authors' contention that these dimensions reflect adaptations of a culture to specific social and natural environments that are present for both women and men. Relatedness, in contrast, did show sex differences (though the effect size was quite small), a pattern that can be linked to division of labor differences within a given society, as Eagly (1987) has argued.

Looking for Common Ground

Using the term gender belief systems reflects two underlying assumptions: (1) that beliefs are multifaceted, incorporating stereotypes, attitudes, and self-representations of gender, and (2) that beliefs about gender should not be conceptualized solely at the level of individual cognitions, but must also recognize social and structural factors in the creation and maintenance of belief systems. The first point was elaborated by the discussion of the various aspects of gender beliefs and the relationships among them. On the one hand, the multifaceted nature of gender beliefs, as well as variations in the sequence and conditions of learning those beliefs, results in a matrix of intercorrelations that is far from perfect (Spence, 1985, 1993). At the same time, components of the belief system are often related. Measures of ambivalent sexism relate in predictable ways to positive and negative gender stereotypes, for example (Glick & Fiske, 1996), and endorsement of gender stereotypes is connected to self-reported expression of emotion for both women and men (Grossman & Wood, 1993).

The second point, that gender beliefs do not exist independent of the social system, is one that both sociologists and European social psychologists have made often (Amancio, 1993; Durand-Delvigne, 1993; Epstein, 1970; Giele, 1988). The media serve as a major conduit for transmitting the beliefs of the society to its individual members (Moscovici, 1988), but members of the society can observe the consequences of gendered assumptions in many other facets of life as well. Eagly's (1987) social role theory emphasizes the social division of labor and occupational distributions as a source of gender-role expectations and sex-typed skills and beliefs. Lorenzi-Cioldi (1988) points to the asymmetry in conceptions of women and men, the result of differential power and status. Conditions such as these create a context in which gender beliefs are formed and in which they operate. At the same time, the system must be regarded as a dynamic, rather than a static one, in which the individual's own beliefs can be shaped by experience and vary from those of other individuals (Durand-Delvigne, 1993; Spence, 1993).

Accepting the position that gender operates dynamically at multiple levels, where does one enter the system?

How does the investigator or theorist decide on a starting point for analysis? Answers to these questions clearly differ, depending on one's frame of reference. For those following the tradition of individual differences, the point of embarkment is typically one of looking for sex differences in some trait or ability measure. From a more social psychological perspective, the investigator will consider the interaction context, simultaneously looking at the players and the setting. This latter strategy underlies the following section on gender and social interaction. In a more complex analysis, one can attempt to juggle several balls at once, trying to chart the interplay between persons, situations, and social structures. That strategy is represented in Section IV.

III. GENDER AND SOCIAL INTERACTION

Not everybody's life is what they make it. Some people's life is what other people make it.
—ALICE WALKER, *You Can't Keep a Good Woman Down*, 1981

Social interaction is not just marked by gender; it is actually in social encounters that gender gets materialized. A contextualist model of gender-related behavior holds that what appear at first pass to be basic sex differences are due less to the fact that women and men inhabit two different worlds than that people believe and expect gender to make a difference. Consider, for example, what happens when women and men are placed in same versus mixed-sex discussion groups. Women talk more in the former and listen more in the latter because they are responding to where they are and with whom they are rather than out of fixed blueprints (Fitzpatrick, Mulac, & Dindia, 1995). When a woman sits at the head of a table instead of a man or a woman interrupts a man rather than the reverse, others in attendance react with more irritation (LaFrance, 1992; Porter & Geis, 1981). If men believe that they are interacting with an attractive versus an unattractive woman not only do they respond more positively but their conversational partners become more social as well (Snyder, Tanke, & Berscheid, 1977). Consider the domain of social influence: women appear to succumb more than men but that difference dissipates when no group is present to exert pressure (Eagly, 1983).

The following sections show how gender processes are created and sustained by verbal and nonverbal behaviors and how social influence and group processes such as leadership and group interaction change when gender is added to the equation. Past research into interaction processes often began with questions about gender comparisons, that is, whether women and men adopt different behaviors. Now research has evolved to a point where the questions are less about who does what but rather about when the

presence of women and men elicit different possibilities. These sex-based expectations in turn are mediated by situational dynamics that differ in the degree to which social power is present, social roles are established, and competence or communality are needed.

A now classic study by Skrypnek and Snyder (1982) captured the dynamic and situated nature of gender effects. In that study, men and women undergraduates were assigned to different rooms and were instructed to use a signaling system to negotiate a division of labor on gender-typed tasks. Men who believed their partner was a woman assigned her more of the feminine tasks and were less yielding to her preferences than men who believed they were dealing with a man. Further, women whose partners knew they were women chose more feminine tasks for themselves than those whose partners believed they were men. Thus, gender-based expectations produce sex differences.

As noted earlier in the discussion of gender stereotypes, gender expectations and status expectancies for women and men are shared ideas about what *will* typically happen and prescriptions for what *should* happen in particular situations. For many social interactions, these constellations of expectancies produce gender-based interactional scripts, that is, hypothesized cognitive structures that organize how people comprehend events involving women and men as well as guiding their own performances (Abelson, 1981). For example, in heterosexual dating situations, men are expected to initiate, plan, pay, and be the sexual aggressor while women are supposed to be attractive, to have primary responsibility for facilitating conversation, and to limit sexual activity (Rose & Frieze, 1989).

Interpersonal conflicts also have scripted elements. In marital interaction, wives attempt to engage in more conflict talk than their husbands, while husbands are more likely to avoid conflict and be more conciliatory (Gottman & Levenson, 1988), resulting in what has been characterized as a "demand-withdraw" pattern. The demand and withdraw behaviors have been interpreted as sex differences, namely, as women's propensities to elicit emotional involvement and men's propensities to sidestep emotional situations. While not contesting that wives and husbands show different conflict-related behaviors, other investigators see them based less in sex and more in personality factors like gender identity and contextual factors like power differentials. Fitzpatrick (1991), for example, has noted that husband–wife conflict patterns are played out most conscientiously by women and men who subscribe to traditional gender roles. Noller (1993) argued that men are more likely to withdraw from marital conflict not because they have difficulty dealing with emotional arousal, nor even because they have been socialized to resist pressure from others, but because withdrawal is an effective way of exercising power. Later in this section, these various factors are considered again as explanations for other interactional patterns involving men and women.

Gender and Communication

Conversation is an exemplary domain in which to examine gender-related behavior, for verbal and nonverbal communication disclose a great deal about the nature of gender stereotypes and status expectations. Close examination of who talks and to whom and in what manner and about what is revelatory about how we expect women and men to behave in each other's company. As will become apparent, men tend to be given room to speak and women are more likely in the position of giving silent applause. The next sections review research in social psychology that has examined how gender impacts verbal and nonverbal communication. As this work has unfolded, the initial search for basic sex differences in communication has been superseded by a more complex understanding of the multidimensional nature of communication processes that, at the minimum, incorporates gender-expectancies, power asymmetries, and contextual constraints.

Language Use   The popular view of women's and men's communication patterns is that they speak different languages (Crawford, 1995; Tannen, 1990). Researchers operating with a similar premise have made sex comparisons in a myriad of verbal and nonverbal behaviors. Over twenty years ago, Thorne and Henley (1975) decried the fact that the cataloguing of sex differences in language was the primary task for many investigators. As a prime mover in that tradition, Lakoff (1973) observed that women's speech was weaker than men's by virtue of their greater use of intensifiers (so, really), hedges (sort of, kind of, you know), politeness (won't you please sit down), rising intonation, and tag questions (He was out at third, wasn't he?). More recently, researchers have taken a closer look and concluded that linguistic differences between the sexes are quite small (Ng & Bradac, 1993). Moreover, many linguistic behaviors take a number of forms, each of which has different functions and each of which is subject to the influences of both person and contextual influences.

When the category of tag questions was examined more closely, it was found to be both broader and narrower than initially supposed. Several subtypes emerged and when all categories are included, it became clear that both men and women use tag questions. Specific comparisons revealed that women tend to use forms that facilitate interaction and men tend to use forms that seek verification (Cameron, McAlinden, & Leary, 1988). Situational demands also emerged as a significant factor in affecting what subtype of tag questions would be in evidence. Specifically, anyone called upon to facilitate interaction is more likely to employ linguistic behaviors previously linked with women's

rather then men's behavior (Hochschild, 1983). Conversely, people in competitive or achievement situations are more likely to place greater emphasis on directness, thus eschewing tag questions, than when the context is more neutral (Clancy & Dollinger, 1993).

The fact that gender composition affects communicative behaviors shows that women and men are each more variable than the "two cultures" hypothesis implies. Tannen (1990) has become the foremost proponent of the idea that women and men typically engage in distinctive styles of communication with different behaviors, purposes, rules, and interpretations. However, data indicate considerable cross-situational variability in women's and men's communicative behavior. Specifically, both sexes use different modes when they are in same-sex than in mixed-sex encounters. For example, what appears to be a uniquely feminine linguistic style (e.g., questions, hedges, intensive adverbs) dissipates when women interact with men (Fitzpatrick et al., 1995). This appears to be the result of both women and men adjusting their behavior in order to accommodate the conversational partner, although women accommodate more than men. Accommodation also manifested itself in a study of how women described themselves to a male partner whose image of an ideal woman had previously been portrayed as either traditional or nontraditional. When the male partner was described as desirable, the women presented themselves more in terms of his ideal type regardless of their actual attitudes (Zanna & Pack, 1975).

Several theoretical perspectives implicate gender saliency as an important factor accounting for why sex composition affects men's and women's communicative behavior (Kanter, 1977; McGuire, 1984). As noted in the discussion of gender belief systems, a person's status as a minority heightens consciousness of being male or female (McGuire, 1984). According to Kanter (1977), when tokenism or numeric skewedness of one's group exists, the minority person experiences greater visibility, contrast (accentuation of perceived differences), and role encapsulation (pressure to produce gender-congruent behavior). As to the last of these, gender-congruent responses have been found to increase in mixed-sex decision-making groups (Johnson & Schulman, 1989). Specifically, men's task activity increased as their proportions decreased and lone women in a group of men had task-activity levels well below group averages. One's position as a minority, however, is insufficient to explain the propensity to show gender-congruent behavior. Additional situational factors like occupational inappropriateness, gender status, and occupational prestige also conspire to produce more gender-congruent behavior (Yoder, 1991; Zimmer, 1988).

Other linguistic behaviors show the effect of sex composition in dyadic interaction. For example, women use a more tentative communication style with men with whom they disagree than they do with other women in the same circumstances (Carli, 1990), and men interrupt the speech of women more frequently than the speech of men (Smith-Lovin & Brody, 1989). Tentative verbal style and interruptions in these situations may be more indicative of one's social standing than of concern about gender appropriateness (Johnson, 1994). In other words, the choice of one communication mode over another depends on whether the speaker and listener have equivalent power (O'Barr & Atkins, 1980).

Even in intimate relationships, power affects which partner attempts more conversational interruptions. In a study of heterosexual and homosexual couples, partners had to decide jointly how to resolve a hypothetical conflict about which they had been given differently slanted versions of the facts. In couples in which one partner was more powerful than the other in terms of relative influence over day-to-day decision making, the more powerful partner engaged in more interruptions regardless of gender (Kollock, Blumstein, & Schwartz, 1985). When the assumed lower status person is interruptive, such as when a woman interrupts a man, observers react with significantly more reproach than in other sex combinations (LaFrance, 1992).

Power and gender also combine to affect how people make verbal amends to someone they have wronged. In one study, people were induced to believe they had committed a gaffe with either mild or serious consequences and that the wronged other was either of higher or lower status. In the case of events with serious consequences, both men and women in both status conditions offered similar accounts even though women offered longer accounts, more concessions and reparations, and more explicit apologies than men. When the event was less serious, high status participants of both sexes were less likely to acknowledge responsibility and made less effort to provide an account (Gonzales, Pederson, Manning, & Wetter, 1990).

Finally, despite the stereotype that women are more talkative than men, evidence indicates the contrary to be true (Mulac, 1989). Again there are indications that power and gender identity moderate the effect of sex on talk-time. When explicit cues as to competence or power are unavailable, men out-talk women in mixed-sex groups but talk-times are equivalent in same-sex groups. When women become the majority in mixed-sex groups or when women are the experts in mixed-sex pairs, they talk more than their male partners (Bilous & Krauss, 1988; Leet-Pellegrini, 1980; Yamada, Tjosvold, & Draguns, 1983). Gender identity also affects talk-time. Hershey and Werner (1975) found that in discussions between husbands and wives, wives associated with feminist organizations spoke more than their husbands; wives not so affiliated spoke significantly less than their husbands. Husbands spoke the same amount of time in both contexts.

Nonverbal Interaction Research on nonverbal behavior has tended to follow the path set down by researchers ex-

ploring the gendered aspects of verbal behavior. Early work focused on whether women were nonverbally more expressive and more sensitive to the nonverbal cues coming from others than were men; findings have generally supported this hypothesis (Hall, 1984). Moreover, people at large believe that women are more nonverbally demonstrative and more nonverbally attuned than men (Briton & Hall, 1995).

Subsequent research has moved away from documenting sex differences toward an explicit examination of the factors that mediate or moderate the tendency for women to be nonverbally more immediate than men. Women were thought to be more expressive because they are more emotionally responsive than men. However, researchers who have examined the relationships among emotionality, expressivity, and sex have described a picture considerably more complex than simple sex differences in the tendency to be emotional (LaFrance & Banaji, 1992). For example, differences in degree of overt expressivity do not necessarily derive from differences in amount of felt emotion (Gallaher, 1992). While women are more expressive than men, they do not necessarily evidence more emotional responsivity (Buck, Miller, & Caul, 1974). Lay observers also believe that women and men differ more in the overt display of affect than in intensity of experienced affect (Fabes & Martin, 1991).

Beliefs that women are more demonstrative than men may contribute to the fact that the sexes are held to different standards of appropriate expressivity: women are to be expressive and men are to be composed (Hall, 1987; Riggio & Friedman, 1986). Stoppard and her colleagues, for example, have shown that women anticipate greater costs and fewer rewards than men if they fail to express positive emotion in response to someone else's good news (Stoppard & Gunn-Gruchy, 1993). Demands for nonverbal expressivity are not merely sex-based but are also role-based. For example, occupants of jobs that require interpersonal responsiveness, such as flight attendants, personal assistants, and day care workers (more often occupied by women than men), evidence greater expressivity than do those in jobs that are less interpersonally oriented (Hochschild, 1983).

Nonverbal expressivity like linguistic behavior has been linked with social power. According to a power perspective, women differ from men on a range of nonverbal behaviors because they have lower social status than men, and nonverbal behaviors like greater expressivity are required by people possessing lower status and power (Henley, 1977). Experimental support for this idea comes from studies on visual dominance, which is the ratio of time a person spends looking at a partner while speaking relative to the time spent looking while listening. Several studies report that high power people show more visual dominance than low power people (Ellyson, Dovidio, & Fehr, 1981).

When gender and power operate together, results indicate that women's nonverbal behavior is influenced by their having less power than men. Specifically, when the interactional context fails to provide explicit power cues or when women have uncertain as opposed to clear support in leadership positions, men express more visual dominance than women (Brown, Dovidio, & Ellyson, 1990). When people show more visual dominance (Ellyson, Dovidio, & Brown, 1992; Ellyson, Dovidio, & Fehr, 1981), they are perceived as more powerful.

A power-based explanation for women's greater skill at reading the nonverbal cues of other people has received mixed support (LaFrance & Henley, 1994). One meta-analysis indicated that power differences between men and women could not explain women's greater sensitivity (Hall, 1984). Rather, that analysis concluded that sex differences in social tension and affiliation were more responsible for moderating the sensitivity effect. At the same time some experimental evidence shows that when women and men are assigned to different power roles, low power people regardless of sex are better able to read their partner's cues (Snodgrass, 1985, 1992). In addition, those in people or service-oriented jobs decode others' emotions better than those whose jobs are less interpersonally oriented (Morgado, Cangemi, Miller, & O'Connor, 1993).

Group Processes

The definition of a group is that its members interact with one another and are influenced by one another (McGrath, 1984). The understanding of group dynamics is enhanced by taking into account how gender affects inter-member interactions. Theories of gender can be fleshed out by testing for specific effects in these multiperson interactional circumstances. The next sections address how gender influences the nature of leadership, the character of group processes, and how social influence operates.

Leadership Gender stereotypes and expectations filter people's assessment of women and men as leaders. A meta-analysis of the leadership evaluation literature found that in explicit leadership roles, women tend to be viewed less positively than men (Eagly et al., 1992). Subtle behavioral reactions by members to male versus female leaders mirror this differential evaluation. An experimental study found, for example, that group members direct more negative nonverbal behaviors toward women leaders than men leaders even when they offer the same suggestions and arguments (Butler & Geis, 1990).

The less than positive view of women as leaders may stem in part from the fact that the leadership schema is more compatible with the instrumental and dominant behavior associated more with men than with women (Cann & Siegfried, 1990). People who show more masculine-typed characteristics are more likely to be perceived as leaders (Kent & Moss, 1994). As a recent meta-analysis

showed, women are also evaluated less positively than men in leadership roles particularly when they occupy male-dominated roles and when leadership is carried out in an autocratic style (Eagly et al., 1992). In both cases, high expectations for assertive and forceful behaviors are more typically associated with men than with women.

Leadership emergence also shows the workings of gender-based expectations. Males are more likely to become leaders in initially leaderless groups in short-term situations and when the task does not require complex social interaction. In such situations, in which participants are either unfamiliar to each other or not taxed by situational demands, gender is more likely salient and hence gender stereotypes and expectation states most likely activated (Eagly & Karau, 1991). When gender is salient, sex as a general status characteristic is used to infer competence (Carli, 1991). However, when gender stereotypes are deliberately overridden, as by making the group task explicitly neutral, men and women are equally likely to emerge as leaders (Goktepe & Schneier, 1988).

A classic study on leader emergence showed, however, that both a person's sex and characteristic personality style affected who emerged as leader (Megargee, 1969). In that study, college students who had scored high or low on a measure of dispositional dominance were paired with the expectation that one should become the leader and the other the follower. As predicted, the more dominant personality was more likely to become the leader in same-sex pairings, indicating that when the focus is on leadership, dominant behavior weighs heavily in determining who becomes a leader. In contrast, gender-based expectations appear to have priority over personality in determining who becomes the leader in mixed-sex groups. When a high dominant woman was paired with a low dominant man, more often the man became the leader (Megargee, 1969; Nyquist & Spence, 1986). Even this effect is a complex one, appearing to result from the reluctance of women to assume the leadership role in that situation, and the assumption held even by low dominant men paired with high dominant women that men should lead.

The preceding section on differential evaluation and emergence of male and female leaders suggests that men are more likely to become leaders because they behave in a manner that more closely fits the image of what leaders do. What has not been addressed however is whether women and men actually adopt different ways of leading. In a stripped-down context, men may be evaluated more positively than women because evaluators have expectations for leaders; they also have sex-based expectations. In other words, evaluators expect leaders to be dominant and, all else being equal, men are assumed to be more dominant. In behaviorally richer situations, women and men can be observed to see whether they actually engage in different behaviors. If similar behavior by women and men as leaders results in differential evaluation, then sexist attitudes are responsible. If they actually do behave differently as leaders, then the evaluators' reliance on gender stereotypes recedes as the prime causal candidate and reasons for the behavioral differences need to be considered.

Do women behave differently than men as leaders? Women have been found to be more interpersonally oriented than men and men to be more task-oriented than women (Forsyth, Schlenker, Leary, & McCown, 1985). These gender-based stylistic differences are moderated by a number of important situational factors. One meta-analysis found that women are more interpersonally oriented than men (although no less task-oriented) in laboratory studies and in self-assessment situations (Eagly & Johnson, 1990). That same meta-analysis found no behavioral differences between women and men leaders in organizational settings. Presumably, in more complex organizational settings in contrast to laboratory contexts, existing structures and established roles are more critical in affecting leadership style. Self-appraisals also likely bring gender expectations to the forefront. For example, direct ratings of one's own leadership abilities adhere to gender-role stereotypes when women and men are randomly assigned to leadership positions (Forsyth et al., 1985). When more indirect self-report measures are used, self-assessed leadership of men and women is comparable (Eagly, Karau, Miner, & Johnson, 1994).

Group needs for both task leaders and social leaders and the association of these two functions with males and females respectively may make it more likely that women are maneuvered into a more interpersonal leadership style and men into a more task-oriented style in mixed-sex groups (Bales, 1950). Eagly and Karau's (1991) meta-analysis of leadership emergence supported this dual leadership model. They found a strong tendency for men to emerge as task leaders and general leaders and a weaker tendency for women to emerge as social leaders.

There is one dimension on which women and men do appear to lead differently. Results show that women tend to adopt a more democratic leadership style while men tend to adopt a more autocratic one (Eagly & Johnson, 1990). The difference between the two styles stems from the latter's emphasis on centralized authority and hierarchical intermember relations. The question is far from settled as to why this might be the case. Women might simply be more oriented toward a democratic style of leadership. For example, all-female groups are more likely than all-male groups to show equal participation and not to develop stable status hierarchies (Wood, 1987). Alternatively, gender per se may not be at the root of the observed difference; rather the choice of a democratic over an autocratic style by women may be a combination of expectations and context. This may work in the following way: particular types of women and men are recruited into leadership roles because of presumed sex differences in management style (Eagly & Johnson, 1990). When an organization needs a leader who is particularly assertive and authoritative, then the search might be restricted to male candidates. In contrast, when the situation calls for a more democratic manager, then expectations might induce a search for a woman to fill the role.

Second, women might adopt more democratic modes of leading, not across the board as a sex difference perspective would argue, but as a context specific response to the role conflict occasioned by leaders' perceptions of subordinates' reservations about the viability of a woman leader. Findings indicate that subordinates are more satisfied with leaders who behave in gender-stereotypic ways (Petty & Miles, 1976), suggesting that women have a better chance of succeeding as leaders if they are more communal in orientation. In other words, women leaders may deal with contradictory expectations by adopting a style that is aimed at winning over rather than bowling over subordinates (Leary, 1989). In fact, women leaders are evaluated more positively than men leaders when they demonstrate a leadership style based on consideration of members (Bartol & Butterfield, 1976).

Finally, power is implicated in why men and women respectively adopt autocratic and democratic leadership styles. Some evidence suggests that those in lower-level positions adopt a more democratic leadership style (Chusmir & Mills, 1989). Further research will need to determine how gender and hierarchical level separately or jointly affect democratic or autocratic styles of leading and managing others. More generally, the study of the relation between gender and leadership needs to be done on real groups as they operate over time in order to more clearly sort out when gender makes a difference.

Group Interaction   Analyses of group behavior more generally also show that women and men behave differently in group settings. Men make more task-oriented contributions to group activity; women are more socially oriented and make more contributions to the interpersonal aspects of group life (Wood, 1987). However, close attention to what gets labeled as task or social behaviors as well as where differences are and are not found reveals that gender plays a more complex role in groups than the mere unfolding of pre-established behavioral inclinations.

Although men emit more task-oriented behaviors than women, both groups devote the greatest proportion of their total group participation to the task at hand. For men, participation more often takes the form of proffering ideas, challenging the ideas of others, and directing the course of the conversation. Women's participation is characterized by greater receptivity to ideas, more showing of concern, and a stress on interpersonal relations. When the group goal is to accomplish a task, such as selecting a strategy for playing a trucking game or deciding how to invest money, the results are clear-cut: groups of men outperform groups of women. It is worth noting, however, that these outcome differences as well as the type of contribution made during the decision-making process are found more often in domains with which men have more experience. When a group's goal requires social rather than task activity, women outperform men (Wood, 1987). In short, participation in groups is affected by both the personal inclinations people bring to interactions and the particular situational characteristics they find there.

Evolutionary processes and sex role socialization no doubt help supply women and men with different behavioral propensities. The former perspective argues that women and men historically have faced different adaptive problems (Buss, 1996), while the latter perspective holds that the sexes in their own lifetimes have had systematically different access to and experience in various social domains. Maccoby (1990), for one, has argued that gender-marked behaviors derive from patterns initially set in children's same-sex play groups. Within these groups, each sex acquires culturally specific, gender-linked personality characteristics and learns gender-appropriate patterns of behavior. Children thus segregate themselves because they find same-sex play partners more compatible. However, others have been critical of the idea that men and women represent two different cultural groups, arguing that same-sex groups are the result of social processes that promote segregation and inequality (Caplan & Larkin, 1991; Meyer, Murphy, & Cascardi, 1991).

Gender differences in groups also result from concurrent situational pressures such as members treating each other with unequal performance expectations (Berger et al., 1985). Group members who are expected to perform well (e.g., men) are given and take more opportunities to contribute to the group's task (Cohen & Zhou, 1991). Males see themselves as more knowledgeable (Slevin & Aday, 1993). Several studies support the idea that contributions by boys more than girls in classrooms (LaFrance, 1991) and by men more than women in adult conversations are valued more and get more attention (Ridgeway, 1981). In short, men are perceived by themselves and by other group members to be more competent than women (Wood & Karten, 1986).

These performance-based expectation states appear to recede when other expectations are made salient. For example, the assumption that men are more competent than women can be altered if people are reminded about egalitarian gender-related beliefs (Porter, Geis, Cooper, & Newman, 1985). Initial gender-based expectations can also be overridden if participants are given explicit information about a woman's competence (Wood & Karten, 1986).

Interpersonal Influence

Gender has repeatedly been implicated in the processes by which people attempt to bring others around to their way of thinking, but the effects are not reducible to simple assertions that men are more persuasive than women. Both gender identity and power contribute to whether one is influential. As to the former, high masculinity rather than sex predicted who was more convincing in a dyadic situation (Sayers, Baucom, & Tierney, 1993). As to the latter, Eagly and Wood (1982) disentangled sex and status in an experiment that considered how people get others to do their bidding. Students were given scenarios describing a situation in which a man or a woman was trying to influence a person of the other sex. Some scenarios provided information regarding only the sex of the actors while other scenarios provided status information as well (e.g., bank vice president, bank teller). When status cues were provided, students used that information rather than sex to predict compliance, such that men and women of equal status were seen to have equal influence. When information about a person's sex was the only information provided, students inferred that the man held higher status and would be more successful in his influence attempts.

Another study also showed how gender operates as a diffuse status characteristic in influence situations. When men and women were described as having comparable expertise in task groups, both men and women selected more direct influence strategies than when they were described as having low expert power or when no information about their expertise was provided (Driskell, Olmstead, & Salas, 1993).

Gender as a diffuse status characteristic is evident not only in attempts to influence others in work contexts but also in intimate relationships (Bisanz & Rule, 1989; Sagrestano, 1992). Johnson (1976) argued that the observed variability in influence strategies used by men and women heterosexual American couples is due to the higher status and assumed greater expertise of men relative to women.

When power differences are explicitly measured in intimate couples, power better predicts choice of influence strategy than does sex. Among heterosexual, lesbian, and gay couples, individuals who perceived themselves as having less power than their partners report using more indirect and unilateral influence tactics to get their way (Falbo & Peplau, 1980). Similarly, individuals who have lower power in intimate same-sex and mixed-sex couples by virtue of having control of fewer resources than their partner (e.g., less income, more dependent on the relationship) are more likely to use indirect strategies such as manipulation and supplication than those who have more resources (Howard, Blumstein, & Schwartz, 1986). Although this latter study reported no main effect for sex in terms of who makes the influence attempt, a main effect for target sex was observed. Specifically, both men and women used less direct influence strategies when the person they were attempting to influence was a man versus a woman.

The fact that both men and women adopt more indirect strategies with a male partner not only shows how important sex composition is to a full understanding of the influence of gender on interaction processes, it also underlines that there is always another in a social interaction. When both men and women become more indirect in persuading a man, it is likely because people have different expectations of male than female targets. Such expectations may then become self-fulfilling, that is, men will prove harder to influence than women.

Besides using verbal influence strategies that vary in directness, influencers can also adopt nonverbal influence styles that vary in the degree to which they are dominant or submissive. The former would seem preferable, because people displaying submissive nonverbal behaviors are regarded as less competent and less influential (Ridgeway, 1987). But the problem of differential influence by women relative to men is not simply resolved by recommending that women adopt a more dominant style (Crawford, 1995). In the first place, a more dominant style by women might be perceived as a violation of both gender and status expectations which in turn could result in lowered ability to get things done. In the second place, the nonverbal cues associated with dominance are not necessarily the same ones associated with competence. Cues associated with dominance are direct eye contact, stern facial expressions, pointing gestures, and loud voice level. Competence or task-related nonverbal cues are moderate eye contact, rapid speech rate, upright posture, and modulated gestures. Competence cues would seem useful and appropriate while dominance cues may have the opposite effect, especially for women attempting to be influential. Influence is affected by nonverbal style but the effect is itself mediated by speaker sex and rater sex (Carli, LaFleur, & Loeber, 1995). Both male and female speakers are perceived to be more likable and more influential when they adopt a competent as opposed to a dominant nonverbal style, but male raters still found women who exhibited a competent style to be less likable, more threatening, and less influential than men exhibiting the same style. In addition, male raters were more inclined to like and be influenced by a competent woman when she was also social (Carli et al., 1995).

Turning to the sex of the person being persuaded, several meta-analyses document the finding that women are more easily persuaded than men (Becker, 1986; Eagly, 1987; Eagly & Carli, 1981). Each also notes that some situations and not others are associated with the finding that women are more easily influenced than men.

The sheer presence of others impacts women's and men's degree of compliance. In face-to-face situations, in group pressure conditions, and in laboratory studies, men are less easily persuaded than women (Cooper, 1979; Eagly, 1978). Women and men are equally influenced when participants are not observed, when no group pres-

sure is imposed, or when the task/topic is neutral rather than having a masculine cast (Becker, 1986; Eagly & Chrvala, 1986).

Conclusions

Gender clearly makes a difference in interaction but it takes layers of context to direct the route that it takes. When investigators first turned their attention to how women and men communicate and act in the company of others, they often found differences. Just as often they interpreted these differences as the result of distinct evolutionary-based mechanisms or different socialization histories or separate social roles. More recently, the separate spheres perspective has given way to the view that although social situations are impacted by these macro-level factors, they are also dynamic and affected by multiple micro-level processes. Social encounters take place in different settings with varied sex-composition, and they are enacted by individuals with particular styles and social skills. Women and men enter social situations with conceptions as to what constitutes appropriate behavior and about which people are more competent and more valued.

Some social psychologists have found power-based explanations wanting, arguing instead that sex differences in social behavior are better explained by different socialization and different social roles. Nonetheless, verbal and nonverbal interaction behaviors shown by men and women reflect not merely different modes but divergent statuses. In short, one's sex affects expectations about one's underlying attributes and likely worth. When gender is salient, women and men are expected to show different personalities, abilities, and preferences (Eagly, 1978); and they are also expected to show different levels of competence (Berger et al., 1985). In short, a person's gender is neither a simple nor a transparent stimulus. Rather it is a repository of possibilities from which situations select.

IV. THE MULTIPLE LEVELS OF GENDER: TWO CASE STUDIES

[Close cooperation between theoretical and applied psychology] can be accomplished . . . if the theorist does not look toward applied problems with highbrow aversion or with a fear of social problems, and if the applied psychologist realizes that there is nothing so practical as a good theory.
—LEWIN, 1951

The terrain of the preceding sections, including topics such as stereotypes, attitudes, communication, and social influence, is familiar to most readers. The focus on individual beliefs and on dyadic interactions, as they influence and are influenced by gender, reflects the level of analysis most common in contemporary social psychology. Although undoubtedly a productive approach, it is nonetheless incomplete when one moves to consider the social problems whose importance Lewin championed.

In this section, two "social problems" are selected for analysis: occupational discrimination and sexual harassment. Both of these areas are sometimes classified as applied or social problems, seemingly at some remove from basic social psychological theorizing. However, from a perspective that advocates multiple levels of analysis, ranging from individual differences to social structures, gendered social problems can be seen as fundamental social psychological phenomena.

When applied to social problems, the contextual model includes consideration of individual preferences and proclivities, interactions with relevant others, setting characteristics, and the social system in which the behaviors of interest occur. No single factor or level of analysis is adequate to explain the full range of gender-related social problems. Further, to understand how gender operates in conjunction with structural variables such as race or class, attention to macro-level variables is essential (Landrine, 1995; West & Fenstermaker, 1995; Wyche & Crosby, 1996). Thus, the dynamic interplay between factors at various levels of analysis is critical for understanding and, in the case of social action, for developing change strategies.

Occupational Choice and Gender Discrimination

Most members of industrialized societies, whatever their sex, ethnicity, or socioeconomic status, spend a major portion of their life in some form of paid employment. The near-universality of this life task, however, may sometimes mask how the specifics of gender, ethnicity, or socioeconomic status affect occupational choice. Consider the following data.

Over the past century, women's participation in the U.S. labor force has climbed steadily, from approximately 18 percent of all females in 1890 to 58 percent in 1992 (Reskin & Padavic, 1994). Internationally, these proportions vary considerably. Women's participation is typically lowest in the sex-segregated Muslim countries and in many developing countries; it is far higher, approaching parity with men, in Scandinavian countries as well as in many of the communist and formerly communist countries (Reskin & Padavic, 1994). Despite the equivalence of numbers, however, the specific jobs held by women and men continue to differ substantially. Men far outnumber women in managerial jobs and high-prestige professions; women are more heavily represented in clerical and low-status sales jobs (Giele, 1988). The ubiquity of the disparity is even greater than it first appears, as Bielby and Baron (1986) have documented. They report that fewer than 10 percent of U.S. workers occupy jobs that are not sex-segregated by task, by

location, or by shift. Thus, within the same occupational classification, separate tracks or specializations develop that are exclusively or primarily the province of women or of men. Similar segregation patterns are found when ethnicity is considered, although less extreme than for gender (Reskin & Padavic, 1994). Deaux and Ullman (1983), for example, found that women of color were far more likely to occupy janitorial positions in a steel mill than would be expected given their overall representation in the work force.

Salary figures also attest to the different experiences of women and men in the work force. Although the gap between average women's and men's earnings has decreased slightly over the past 20 years, 1991 figures show women earning only 70 percent of what men earn (Reskin & Padavic, 1994). Discrepancies are more apparent when ethnicity is also considered. Hispanic women employed full-time on the average earned only 78 percent of what white women earned, and African-American women earned 87 percent. Similarly, Black men earned less than 75 percent of the average white male earnings, and Hispanic men earned approximately two-thirds (Reskin & Padavic, 1994). Even when occupation is held constant, the earnings disparities persist.

The social psychological task is one of explaining why these strikingly different occupational patterns occur. At the most individual level of analysis, investigators look for sex differences in preferences for different kinds or conditions of work. In the hands of economists, this question became framed as human capital theory, considering sex differences in skills, experiences, and motivations. With the wider lens of a contextual model, the analysis of sex segregation in employment must also consider other factors and levels of analysis. These additional factors include the expectations and evaluations of others, opportunity structures, and societal norms regarding paid employment and family activities. Throughout the following analysis, which will necessarily be selective and illustrative rather than comprehensive and detailed, we will show how occupational outcomes are critically shaped by gender considerations at virtually all points in the process.

Individual Preferences and Choices Traditionally, the psychological literature on occupational choice emphasized the preferences or "tastes" of people for different types of jobs. Within this perspective, numerous differences between women and men were identified, suggesting, for example, that women were more likely to value pleasant co-workers while men placed more value on intrinsic job factors and organizational commitment (Lefkowitz, 1994). More recently, investigators have recognized that sex covaries with a number of important job-related variables, such as level of education, occupational level, and, especially, income. Controlling for these factors in the analysis leads one to conclude that men and women react very similarly to the world of work when job characteristics and reward systems are equivalent (Lefkowitz, 1994). While these results testify to the comparability of women's and men's attitudes, values, and preferences when situations are similar, they also underline the reality of gendered work environments.

For many years, Eccles and her colleagues have explored the complex social psychological matrix within which occupational and educational choices are made (Eccles, 1994; Eccles et al., 1983). In presenting her model, Eccles makes three key points. First, her model focuses on achievement-related choices that she believes are made as a continuous process, taking place at both conscious and nonconscious levels. Second, she stresses that choices are made in the context of a set of subjectively feasible choices—a set that is considerably smaller than the objective set that might exist in the person's environment. In analyzing gender, this point is particularly important, as the perceived options for women and men often differ considerably despite apparent equivalence of opportunities. Eccles' (1994) third point is that one needs to consider the choices *not* made as well as the choices made in order to fully understand achievement-related behaviors.

With these general principles as a base, Eccles and her colleagues have identified a set of factors that significantly influence achievement-related behavior. These factors, represented in Figure 2, include a person's expectations for success, sense of personal efficacy, the subjective value attached to each available option, gender roles, and other identity-relevant concerns. Fundamental to the choice that women and men make is a balancing of its attainment value, which includes a calculation of the fit between any particular choice and a person's basic goals, motivations, and self-definitions, with its perceived cost. None of these factors is gender-neutral, given existing patterns of socialization and societal expectations. Further, the development of many of these identity-relevant features begins quite early (Ruble & Martin, in press).

Preferences for work, and expectations for rewards once a person is employed, also show consistent gender-linked patterns. As Major (1994) and her colleagues have shown, women consistently reward themselves less and work longer for an equivalent payment, as compared to men. In her analysis of the antecedents of these differential outcomes, Major reveals a number of processes, each of which shows the sometimes subtle links between individual and structural variables. Most people, for example, rely on social comparison to evaluate their own standing vis-à-

FIGURE 2 **Theoretical Model of Achievement-Related Choices Developed by Eccles (Parsons), Adler, Futterman, Goff, Kaczala, Meece, and Midgley, 1983.**

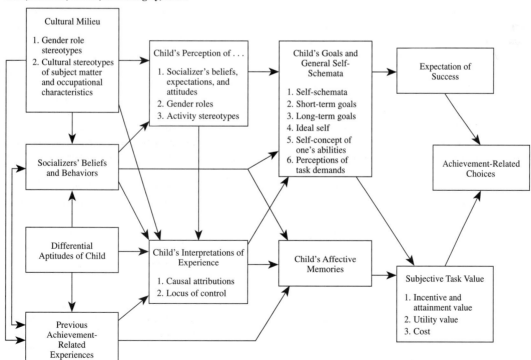

vis the prevailing norms. Yet because of the tendency for people to choose similar others with whom to compare, women often use other women as a reference point—a group that on average is underpaid relative to the overall wage-earning population. Thus, system-level realities have an influence on the particulars of individual-level processes. At the same time, these processes are not invariant, but rather can illustrate the flexibility and contextual variability of gendered behavior. Bylsma and Major (1992), for example, showed that when both comparison information and feedback are specific and equivalent for women and men, the reported sense of personal entitlement is equivalent as well.

Expectations and Evaluations of Others   Job preferences and occupational choice do not occur in a social vacuum. Other people, often people critical to the realization of individual goals, can clearly convey expectations for the preferences and performances of women and men. Children encounter these expectations early. In a large-scale study of mothers and their children, Jacobs and Eccles (1992) explored the influence of gender stereotypic beliefs on mothers' perceptions of their 11- and 12-year-old children's abilities, as well as on the self-perceptions of the children themselves. Their results showed that mothers with more strongly held gender stereotypes believed that their daughters had lower math ability and that their sons had higher math ability. Similar patterns were found for the mothers' estimates of their children's sports ability and, in the reverse direction, estimates of social abilities. These beliefs were further shown to influence the children's own assessments of their abilities, which reflected the biased views of the mothers. Thus gender stereotypes, mediated by the beliefs that mothers held about their own child's ability, affected the degree to which children believed they did or did not have ability in math and social domains.

The influences of others' expectations, the so-called self-fulfilling prophecy, are well established in the social psychological literature (Deaux & Major, 1987; Merton, 1968; Miller & Turnbull, 1986). Thus, to the extent that people hold different expectations for the performance of women and men, they will be likely to act on those expectations in such a way as to shape the opportunity structure available to the individual actor.

The impact of these different expectations could be exacerbated by women's tendency to put more credence in the evaluations of others, a phenomenon observed by Roberts and Nolen-Hoeksema (1994). In their studies, men and women performed a task, for example, giving a short speech to an audience of peers, and then were given feedback on their performance. Although women and men did not differ in their interpretation of the feedback, women's private self-evaluations reflected the external evaluation more, that is, they were more positive following favorable

feedback and more negative following unfavorable feedback. In pursuing the reasons for this difference, Roberts and Nolen-Hoeksema (1994) found that women were more likely to consider the feedback accurate and to take it seriously (unrelated to any differences in self-confidence)—in other words, feedback had more information value for women than for men. As applied to the job context, if negative stereotypes about women influence the judgment of an advisor or an employer, the consequent evaluation could have a significant negative impact on the woman's subsequent self-evaluations.

Workplace Environment   The workplace is not a gender-free environment, but rather one that is heavily segregated by sex and, to a slightly lesser degree, by race and ethnicity. Industries and corporations are uneven in their employment of women and men, occupations are segregated by sex, and tasks within occupational titles are differentially assigned by sex.

Reasons for the disparities are numerous. Some noted by Reskin and Padavic (1994) include efforts by dominant male groups to preserve their advantages, hiring policies of employers, and the attitudes and opposition of both coworkers and of customers. Whether formal policy or informal practice, factors such as these constrain the opportunity structure within which people make their choices.

Differential assignment of jobs in corporations can be subtle. Often the official job title suggests an equality that is far from the operating reality. In Deaux and Ullman's (1983) study of steel-mill workers, for example, women were more likely to be doing janitorial work while men were involved in the steel-making process itself, even though the formal job titles were the same. A consequence of the differential assignment was that women did not learn about making steel, and thus were unlikely to move up the job ladder. Similar findings were reported by Reskin and Padavic (1988) in a study of power-plant workers. Supervisors frequently shifted the assignments of women to jobs such as food preparation and plant cleaning, increasing the sex-segregation of the work force from its initial distribution.

Within prestigious legal firms, differential job assignment to women and men can also be seen (Epstein, 1993). In the past, for example, women were less likely than men to be assigned to high-visibility litigation work. In recent years, women have become more involved in litigation but are still treated differently from men in more subtle ways, for example, fewer travel assignments or opportunities for bringing in new business. A large-scale study of women and men in management (Reskin & Ross, 1992) found systematic differences in the job placements and assignments of women and men. Women managers were more likely to specialize in support services, while men were concentrated in positions that involved generating revenue. Examining the nature of managerial activities more carefully, these investigators found that men were responsible for making final decisions in significantly more areas than were women. The differences were apparent over a wide range of arenas, including setting goals for one's own unit, having responsibility for personnel decisions, having budget authority, and making links to other units in the organization.

Perhaps not surprisingly, given the data on job assignment, men and women view their work environments differently. Stokes, Riger, and Sullivan (1995) have developed a scale that assesses the degree to which a work environment is viewed as hostile or benign. Dimensions tapped by the scale include the perception of dual standards and opportunities, sexist attitudes and comments, informal socializing, sensitivity of the company to balancing work and personal obligations, and remediation practices. In a sample of employees at a large number of midwest U.S. companies, women rated their work environment significantly less favorable than did men. Further, independent of gender, people who intended to leave the company in two years or less were significantly less favorable than those who planned to stay longer.

Norms for Work and Family   As gender plays a role in the organization of occupational structure, so, too, is it implicated in societal norms regarding work and family life (Gilbert, 1994). In the United States, and in many other countries and cultures, both work and home life are structured on assumptions about gender roles. Until very recently, work policies assumed (and in many locations, continue to assume) that a married worker has someone at home to take care of house and children. Thus, work should not be interrupted or modified by the demands of domestic life; further, the demands of work were frequently based on an assumption that nonwork functions could and should adjust to the demands of work (e.g., job transfers, overtime assignments). These assumptions were both explicitly and implicitly linked to gender roles, specifically, a male worker and a female homemaker, with enormous consequence for women and men in both work and family life.

Challenges to these traditional assumptions, in the form of increased female employment, have elicited their own set of gendered hypotheses. Many have assumed, for example, that women will suffer more severe mental-health consequences than men when the demands of work and family conflict (Barnett, Raudenbush, Brennan, Pleck, & Marshall, 1995). From the perspective of work, these assumptions appear unfounded. In a longitudinal study of full-time employed dual-earner couples, Barnett et al. (1995) found that a change in job role quality was negatively associated with changes in psychological stress, and equally so for women and men. Differences did emerge, however, in the effects of changes in the quality of the marital role, which had a greater impact on women than on men.

These differences in the home arena are consistent with many studies showing that the household division of labor continues, with women spending far more hours in domestic work than men—what has been termed women's "second shift" (Hochschild, 1989). In virtually all tasks that require daily or semi-weekly involvement, for example, preparing meals, washing dishes, housecleaning, and shopping, full-time working women spend far more time than do men (Shelton, 1992). A number of factors moderate these patterns. African-American and Hispanic men, for example, spend more time on housework than do white men (Shelton & John, 1993, reported in Reskin & Padavic, 1994). Men's involvement in housework is also related to the income discrepancy between husband and wife: the less the discrepancy, the more likely men are to contribute to household chores (Deutsch, Lussier, & Servis, 1993). Interestingly, this same study showed clear differences in the determinants of husbands' involvement in housework versus child care. Men's feminist attitudes, for example, predicted their involvement in child care but were unrelated to housework activity. Relative power, in contrast, was more strongly implicated in housework allocations.

No single factor or level of analysis is sufficient to explain patterns of occupational choice and gender discrimination. Individual preferences, opportunities (both perceived and real), interactional influences, and social norms all contribute to the occupational choices that men and women make and the outcomes they experience. The social psychological task, as noted earlier, is to probe and interpret the interrelations among all these factors.

We turn now to a second gender-relevant social problem, namely, sexual harassment, to which the same contextual perspective is applied. As is the case with occupational preferences, sexual harassment is a complex phenomenon that must be analyzed by taking several levels of factors into account.

Sexual Harassment

Sexual harassment occurs when sexuality is in the foreground in a place where it is not relevant or appropriate, namely, where one works, studies, or prays. Sexual harassment is typically defined as unwelcome sexual behavior that has the potential and often the reality of thwarting or damaging a recipient's life and work. Harassment increases stress, lowers productivity and job satisfaction, adds to turnover and absenteeism, and enhances fear among victims that were they to complain, retribution would result (Lach & Gwartney-Gibbs, 1993).

This section focuses on sexual harassment as an example, albeit a pernicious one, of gender-related behavior. Although legal definitions of sexual harassment are not gender specific, in practice, sexual harassment is most often a problem experienced by women. In fact, the most common perpetuator of sexual harassment is male and the most common recipient is female (Fitzgerald & Shullman, 1993). Later in this section another kind of sexual harassment is broached, namely, that aimed at people who are perceived to be homosexual. In both cases, a person's gender is the defining feature. Although the focus here is on sexual harassment, there is heuristic value in conceiving of harassment as a subtype, namely, part of a larger category of aggression directed towards women by men with whom they are often acquainted or intimate. This larger category includes courtship violence, acquaintance rape, marital rape, and battering (White & Kowalski, in press).

As is the case with other matters having to do with gender, sexual harassment is multifaceted and multidetermined. As to the various forms it can take, sexual harassment can be primarily sexual or primarily hostile, that is, its goal could be to secure a sexual liaison or to make life uncomfortable for a woman or a person identified as homosexual. It may be linked to a single occurrence but more often sexual harassment gets identified when it consists of repeated actions. It can sometimes be ambiguous as is the case with behaviors that fall under the rubric of unwanted sexual attention, or unequivocally aggressive as is the case with sexual coercion. It may produce withdrawal or it may lead to legal action. In short, sexual harassment can be characterized on a number of dimensions.

From the perspective of a contextual model of gender-related behavior, sexual harassment results from a combination of characteristics of both perpetrator and target and both proximal and distal contextual factors. As to the particular people involved, evidence indicates that some men and not others enter situations with a propensity to sexually harass and that some women (and homosexuals) and not others are more likely to be the targets of harassing behaviors. As to the context, it is clear that some situations and organizations and not others are more likely to elicit sexually harassing behavior (Pryor et al., 1995). Although there are reliable individual differences in the tendency to sexually harass, situational factors represent the necessary conditions for such behaviors to occur repeatedly (Pryor & Whalen, 1996).

In the following sections, sexual harassment is viewed through the lens of a contextual model of gender behavior. The analysis begins with individual variation in the gender identity of both perpetrators and targets and goes on to consider situational factors linked with the likelihood of finding sexual harassment. Situational factors have also been linked to whether respondents label sexual advances or hostile behavior as sexual harassment. For example, sexual harassment is more likely to be mentioned when the perpetrator has higher status that the victim (Giuffre & Williams, 1994). It is important to keep in mind, however, that there are types and degrees of sexual harassment. Con-

sequently, the relevant individual dimensions and situational determinants also vary.

From a legal perspective, two kinds of sexually harassing behaviors are recognized and sanctionable: coerced sexual exchange and offensive sex-related behaviors that create a hostile work environment (U.S. EEOC, 1980). Social psychologists have made some additional distinctions. Sexually oriented harassment can consist on the one hand of unwanted sexual attention stemming from sexual attraction and on the other hand of sexual coercion or sexual exploitation (Fitzgerald, Gelfand, & Drasgow, 1995; Pryor & Whalen, 1996). Social psychological classification systems such as these also include other forms of gender-related hostile behavior that may not fit a strict legal definition of sexual harassment. These are included because they reflect the range of possible inhospitable behaviors elicited by notice of a person's gender. In similar fashion, while hostility directed towards homosexuals, short of assault, is not recognized legally, it has been identified within social psychology as an aggressive behavior rooted in hostility directed toward a person perceived to be a member of an outgroup (Pryor & Whalen, 1996).

Individual Differences in Propensity to Sexually Harass
Men differ in their likelihood to sexually harass. Some use their work situations to take advantage of coworkers for sexual ends. Others may be especially irritated by having members of the other sex or another sexual orientation as coworkers. Individual differences in the first type can be obtained via self reports. In one such measure, the Likelihood to Sexually Harass Scale, male respondents are asked to imagine themselves in a number of social situations in which they could sexually exploit women with relative impunity, a situation typically referred to as *quid pro quo* sexual harassment. Respondents are given the opportunity to indicate how likely it is that they would engage in sexually exploitative behavior. Some men reliably indicate that they think it likely that they would propose sexual favors in return for some job-related benefit (Pryor, 1987).

Men who score high on the Likelihood to Sexually Harass Scale have a gender schema that includes aggressive sexual behavior and traditional masculinity. They also are likely to score high on Rape Myth Acceptance (Burt, 1980) and Attraction to Sexual Aggression scales (Malamuth, 1989; Pryor, Giedd, & Williams, 1995). Men who show greater tolerance for sexual harassment see themselves as more masculine and they are also more likely to view friendly behavior of both sexes as sexy behavior and to believe that women display sexual interest by acting friendly (Stockdale, Dewey, & Saal, 1992, reported in Pryor, Gledd, & Williams, 1995). Furthermore, high scorers have a cognitive schema in which sexuality and power are closely linked. Specifically, a priming study found that among men who are likely to harass in contrast to those who are unlikely to do so, thoughts of power can trigger thoughts of sexuality and vice versa in a relatively automatic fashion (Bargh, Raymond, Pryor, & Strack, 1995).

Other individual differences among men have been linked to different categories of sexual harassment. Fiske and Glick (1995) suggest four types of harassers, distinguishable on the basis of their primary motivations. For one type, sexual intimacy is the primary motive; for another, domination is key; a third is characterized by ambivalence between feelings of paternalism and the desire for sexual intimacy; for the fourth, sexual intimacy is linked with the need to have strong distinctions between the sexes. In addition, evidence strongly suggests that sexually aggressive men do not so much misperceive women's responses as they doubt messages of any kind coming from women. In other words, it is not that they incorrectly interpret friendly messages as sexy messages but that they are inclined to distrust the truthfulness of any messages coming from women (Malamuth & Brown, 1994).

Target Characteristics and Likelihood of Being Sexually Harassed Women are more likely to be the victims of sexual harassment and are more likely than men to see the behaviors as sexually harassing. It appears that differences in interpretation by women and men of behaviors that might be construed as sexually harassing stem not from whether the behavior is sexual but rather from whether it is perceived to be unwanted. Men are more inclined than women to rate a range of behaviors as having sexual overtones; women are more inclined to label more of the same range as sexually harassing. The courts also have recognized this interpretative stance and have resolved it with the adoption of the "reasonable woman" standard (Gutek & O'Connor, 1995). In legal cases, the charge to jurors is to imagine whether a reasonable woman (not a reasonable person) would judge a particular situation as offensive. There are variations, however, among women in what gets labeled harassment. Those who believe that sexual harassment concerns power or male dominance are less likely to ignore or avoid reporting it than those who think that it is primarily sexual (Gruber & Smith, 1995).

Some data pertain to whether targets with particular attributes render them more susceptible to being sexually harassed. Being single or divorced and being between 20 and 44 years old have been identified as risk factors (Wyatt & Riederle, 1995). Data show that single black women are more likely than their white women cohort to be targets of sexually harassing behavior (Mansfield et al., 1991; Wyatt & Riederle, 1995). Other characteristics may also contribute to some targets being more personally vulnerable, such as being dependent on one's job (Fitzgerald & Shullman, 1993). Some women react to harassment with self

blame and embarrassment (Gruber & Smith, 1995), but personal vulnerability may be more a function of one's position than one's disposition. Women with lower organizational status are less likely to report sexual harassment with the attendant possibility that they are perceived to be more vulnerable by potential harassers (Gruber & Bjorn, 1986).

Situations that Prompt Sexually Harassing Behavior
Even among those who come to any situation with a proclivity to exploit others in a sexual way, harassing actions more often occur when the social context endorses or condones such behavior. Both perpetrators and targets look to others for indications of what behavior is promoted or permitted. From the target's (victim's) vantage point, her perceptions of whether her complaints will be taken seriously and whether the organization has an effective sanctioning procedure affect whether she protests the behavior to her supervisors (Baker, Terpstra, & Larntz, 1990). Perpetrators look to others for signs that this behavior is tolerated, perhaps even encouraged. Interestingly, groups of peers are as effective as authority figures in conveying to potential harassers that sexual harassing behaviors are legitimate (Pryor & Whalen, 1996). Men possessing the propensity to sexually harass take their lead from supportive contextual cues.

In what follows, several contextual factors that make gender salient and harassing behavior more likely are described. Some of these contexts are proximate such as the presence of sexually harassing models, the degree to which a particular work environment is sexualized, and the degree of power discrepancy between perpetrator and target, and some are more distal, such as the implicit and explicit rules in organizations or media portrayals that indicate that such behavior is normal and expected.

Sexual Exploitation and Sexualized Work Environments Environments, like people, can be highly sexualized. In highly sexualized work settings, flirtation is expected, sexual talk, including jokes and insults, is frequent, and personal appearance is important. In settings in which many kinds of sexual behavior are common, sexual harassment is also prevalent (Gutek, 1985). In short, in highly sexualized work environments, a sexual advance will be less likely to be interpreted as unwelcome (even if it is) and a friendly behavior will more likely be perceived in sexual terms (even if it isn't).

Some environments are more likely to become highly sexualized (Gutek, 1985). For example, women who have male rather than female supervisors are significantly more likely to report many kinds of social-sexual behaviors. In general, men have been found to be more preoccupied with sexual matters than women (Michael, Gagnon, Laumann, & Kolata, 1994). As a result, male-dominated workplaces tend to be more sexualized than female-dominated work environments. Consequently, when men are represented in greater numbers, their preferences become the operative climate.

Hostile Work Environment and Gender Harassment

Stereotypes about and attitudes toward women affect whether sexual harassment will tend to be sexually coercive or hostile. Women in traditional occupations are more likely to encounter *quid pro quo* harassment while women in nontraditional jobs encounter more hostile work environments (Lach & Gwartney-Gibbs, 1993). In the former, women fear losing their jobs if they do not comply with sexual requests; in the latter, they have to deal with threatening and demeaning work environments (e.g., taunts, hazing, sexual epithets, and public distribution of pornographic materials) presumably brought on by the incursion of women into previously male-dominated occupations.

Survey research has shown that the prevalence rates of sexual harassment are higher in workplaces and occupations where women have been traditionally underrepresented, particularly blue-collar occupations (Gutek, 1985). According to sex-role spillover theory, this happens because in those positions, female employees are more likely to be perceived in terms of their gender roles rather than their work roles. That is, stereotypes about women are carried over to the workplace where they are irrelevant, such as in expecting women to be more nurturing than men in the same occupation.

Nontraditionality of occupation for women is also associated with the finding that sexual harassment is less likely to be labeled as such. In one vignette study, participants read a series of scenarios depicting three types of sexual harassment in a male-dominated work setting in which the female target was employed either in a nontraditional occupation (e.g., steelworker) or in a traditional occupation (e.g., secretary). The results showed that when the type of harassment was sexual coercion and the woman was employed in the nontraditional occupation, participants were less likely to label the incident as having been a sexually harassing one and were less likely to endorse corrective measures (Burgess & Borgida, 1997).

Sexual harassment of the hostile variety is also more likely when women occupy nontraditional jobs or when they constitute a "threatening minority" (i.e., less than half, but more than a token few) (Gruber & Bjorn, 1986). Women in male-dominated jobs encounter hostility either because they are perceived to be a threat to men's jobs and/or because their behavior in those jobs (e.g., mining, fire fighting) is not stereotypically feminine. Attitudes toward women are highly situational, becoming more negative when women occupy jobs previously thought to be the province of males (Eagly & Mladinic, 1994). When small but significant numbers of women move into traditional male settings, they tend no longer to be perceived as individual females but rather as an outgroup whose presence represents a threat. According to Blalock (1967), the majority's reaction will be harshest when the minority is small.

Power and Sexual Harassment

Differences in power between perpetrator and target have often been cited as being at the center of sexual harassment. For example, women who occupy blue-collar jobs and possess less formal power are more likely to be harassed than women in white-collar occupations (Barak, Pitterman, & Yitzhaki, 1995). While it is true that individuals who are harassed by higher power persons are more likely to label the act as sexual harassment, evidence suggests that coworkers are more likely to actually engage in sexual harassment (Mazer & Percival, 1989). Even though sexual harassment from persons higher in power is more likely to be labeled as such, it is also less likely to be reported. Women are less likely to confront harassment if the perpetrator is a supervisor than a coworker and are more likely to quit the job in such a situation (Gruber & Smith, 1995).

Organizational Tolerance and Sexual Harassment

Gender harassment of all kinds is more likely when there is a general perception that the organization is tolerant of it (Pryor & Whalen, 1996). A stronger version of this theory argues that organizations create power differences based on gender. Men who have been allotted more power than women then use it for sexual gains (Collins, 1975). However, a study comparing women in kibbutz and women in urban settings found no difference in their experiences of sexual harassment (Barak et al., 1995). Theoretically, organizations with policies and practices favoring equality between men and women should have had lower rates of harassment. That was not the case. The authors surmised that although differing in some organizational respects both groups are exposed to the same cultural messages that condone sexual harassment. A similar conclusion was offered by researchers who found that neither organizational position nor gender composition could account for incidents of sexual harassment in a large study of U.S. federal employees (Fain & Anderton, 1987).

Organizations also differ in the degree to which members believe it is futile to report cases of sexual harassment. Studies of harassment victims consistently find that organizational inaction or retaliation is a major constraint on reporting the harassment (Fitzgerald, Swan, & Fischer, 1995). For example, one study found that victims who did not report sexually harassing experiences were more likely than those who did to believe that little positive was likely to come from it; that any benefits of reporting would be outweighed by the repercussions; that the complaint would be trivialized; and that reporting would exacerbate rather than relieve their situation (Rudman, Borgida, & Robertson, 1995).

Cultural Attitudes and Sexual Harassment The socio-cultural milieu is the most distal contextual factor impacting the presence of sexual harassment. Although more abstract and possibly more indirect in its influence on sexual harassment than proximate situational factors like gender ratios or the presence of harassing models, cultural factors nonetheless affect sexual harassment by suggesting typical or conceivable patterns of cross-gender and within-gender interaction.

The media constitute one source for beliefs about interaction between the sexes. Specifically, sexual violence in the media is cited as having an indirect effect on aggression toward women (Malamuth & Briere, 1986). Exposure to sexual violence in the media affects belief systems which in turn affect behavior. In other words, men exposed to media portrayals involving sexual aggression toward women develop attitudes that are more supportive of aggression towards women. Development of such attitudes increases the likelihood of acting on them if the situation permits.

From a related sociocultural perspective, sexual harassment derives from the efforts to exclude particular groups of people from certain spheres of activity. If women are discouraged from taking particular jobs or in working altogether, then beliefs about the proper place of women are easier to maintain (Tangri, Burt, & Johnson, 1982). In short, cultural attitudes foster sexual harassment via widely understood norms, values, and beliefs about what is typical or legitimate behavior for men to engage in vis à vis women. Cultural attitudes are also highly implicated in harassment towards those labeled as homosexual which is taken up in the next section.

Sexual Harassment toward Homosexuals

Harassing behavior directed at people because they are perceived to be homosexual is a clear example of hostile gender-related behavior. In a survey of public school students, no type of sexual harassment was thought more offensive than being called "gay" (American Association of University Women, 1993). Surveys typically find widespread rates of discrimination and harassment among lesbians and gay men whether this characteristic is disclosed or presumed (D'Augelli, 1989). Similar to other forms of harassment, men are more often the perpetrators (Herek & Berrill, 1992). Males generally experience greater levels of hostile sexual harassment, namely, threats, intimidation, and violence than lesbians, but the latter appear to encounter significantly more job discrimination (Berrill, 1990). Harassing behavior directed at gay people (or people labeled as such) is, however, not subject to the same legal sanctions as sexual harassment linked to gender-based discrimination under Federal Law. This exclusion not only reflects cultural proscriptions against gay people, it may also serve to legitimize them.

Like other forms of sexual harassment, harassment of people because of their presumed sexual orientation is a product of individual differences in targets and perpetrators as well as contexts that excuse or condone it. Herek (1990) has argued that gay people are stigmatized not only for their erotic behaviors but also for their perceived violation of gender norms. For instance, findings show that gay men who describe themselves as "feminine" are twice as likely as other gay men to have experienced gay bashing. Also, Klassen, Williams, and Levitt (1989) found that 70 percent of males and females in the general population "strongly agree" or "somewhat agree" that "homosexuals act like the opposite sex."

As evidence that harassment towards homosexuals shares a common base with harassment towards women, antihomosexual attitudes are shown to be linked to sexist attitudes: higher antigay prejudice is more prevalent among those who have more stereotyped notions of males and females (Dunbar, Brown, & Amoroso, 1973). Another important predictor of attitudes is whether respondents attribute choice to sexual orientation. People who believe that homosexuality is beyond an individual's control express significantly more favorable attitudes toward gay men and lesbians than people who regard homosexuality as a choice (Herek & Capitanio, 1995).

Most cultures have large stores available of negative views of lesbians and gay men for not following accepted gender and sexual roles. This likely stems from and contributes to the finding that media accounts of antigay violence are less specific and extreme (e.g., "incident" rather than "assault") than descriptions describing violence against nongays (Henley, Miller, Kaminsky, & Nguyen, 1996). Gay men and lesbians are also minorities and as such encounter reactions similar to that of other outgroups. For example, differences among gay men and lesbians are underemphasized and differences between heterosexuals and homosexuals are accentuated. However, interpersonal contact with homosexuals shrinks these tendencies.

Although little research has yet emerged on the contexts associated with homosexual harassment, a particular interactional situation has been linked with greater likelihood of antigay behavior. Evidence suggests that antihomosexual violence is more likely to occur when young men are in groups (Herek & Berrill, 1992). This may mirror sexual harassment directed at women when they become a threatening minority. In both cases, the harassment appears rooted in gender-based intergroup dynamics (Herek, 1990).

Summary

In sum, sexual harassment is a pernicious form of gender-related behavior. Like other forms of gender-related behavior, sexual harassment results from a confluence of individual differences and contextual factors, such that a combination better predicts sexual harassment than either factor alone. Like other forms of violence against women, sexual harassment is underwritten by cultural norms and social inequalities (White & Kowalski, in press). And like other forms of violence against women and homosexuals, sexual harassment is more likely to occur when individual proclivities to harass are sanctioned and supported by organizational and situational dynamics.

CONCLUSIONS

The perspective offered here for analyzing and understanding gender and its relevance to other social psychological phenomena is quite different from those offered in earlier volumes of the *Handbook*. In the first Murchison volume, gender was sex differences (Miles, 1935). Taking its place beside other demographic categories such as the Negro, the red man, the white man, and the yellow man, as well as insects, birds, and mammalian herds and packs, "Sex in social psychology" compared males and females in almost every conceivable domain. Absent from both the 1954 and 1967 editions of the *Handbook of Social Psychology*, gender reappeared in the 1985 *Handbook* in a chapter titled "Sex roles in contemporary American society" (Spence, Deaux, & Helmreich, 1985). Consistent with its title, that chapter focused on societally defined roles of women and men in the United States, with a particular emphasis on changes in vocational, social, and marital domains.

In concluding their chapter, Spence et al. (1985) noted that psychologists interested in gender "have had few theoretical concepts to inform their work, and coherent theoretical statements of any degree of breadth are undoubtedly some years away." Writing now, a decade later, we find an abundance of theoretical concepts guiding empirical work. Further, although a single and sovereign theory has not and is unlikely to emerge, several distinct theoretical positions have been articulated. From this possible set, we have chosen a gender-in-context perspective to frame the discussion in this chapter. In doing so, we have given short shrift to a number of alternative perspectives, each of which has advocates and arguments to support it. A brief discussion of some of these alternative positions may be useful in establishing the intellectual position of the present chapter, as well as to identify areas of overlap and points of discrepancy.

Sex Difference Perspective

The exploration and analysis of differences between women and men has a century-old record within psychology (see Morawski, 1996) and continues apace in this the last decade of the twentieth century. From the beginning, investigators sought to document areas of difference across the psychological spectrum. Many of these studies were and are atheoretical, with investigators content to catalogue differences in a wide range of mental and physical tasks. When explanations for such observed differences are found, they are often presented in a posthoc and untestable fashion. Indeed, many sex difference studies can still be classified as offering one of two typically oppositional explanations, namely, those that locate the differences in biological factors (nature) and those that implicate socialization conditions (nurture). For the most part, these two forms of explanation coexist as competing alternatives, with little effort to develop an inclusive theory (Morawski, 1996).

As noted earlier, the sex difference approach has many critics (see *American Psychologist*, March 1995; *Feminism & Psychology*, November 1994). Criticisms of this perspective point to the deterministic assumptions that are made, to the unsophisticated ideas of nature or nurture that are often invoked, and to the disregard of current social context, whether at the situational or system level, when interpreting differences. Critics have also pointed out that research into sex differences tends to treat women and men as global categories that possess no other salient social dimension, such as race, class, age, and sexuality. Further, findings of sex differences too often provide fodder for those who translate difference into deficit (Crawford, 1995). Finally, others have pointed out that the very enterprise of sex differences research is grounded in an unexamined readiness to see reality as carved naturally into polarized sex and gender categories (Bem, 1994). Indeed, debate has arisen regarding whether every study that uses people should test for sex differences (Baumeister, 1988; Eagly, 1987).

More recently, adherents of the sex differences perspective have enthusiastically adopted meta-analytic methods (Knight, Fabes, & Higgins, 1996). (See Hyde, 1994, and Hyde & Linn, 1986, for several examples of this approach.) This shift has resulted in two changes of consequence. First, meta-analysis is used to assess the size of sex differences and not merely whether they are statistically significant. Second, and more importantly, meta-analysis is used to examine what moderates differences that are found. For example, Eagly and Crowley's (1986) meta-analysis of sex differences in helping behavior found that overall men helped slightly more than women. More critically, however, they found that men are more likely to help when the situation is public and dangerous. In private, men are no more likely to help than women. Although reservations have recently been voiced about the limits of meta-analytic studies for establishing causality (Knight, Fabes, & Higgins, 1996), concern with variability and situational moderators has moved the sex differences perspective toward a more contextualized version of gender-related behavior.

Evolutionary Perspective

Whereas many discussions of sex differences are atheoretical, evolutionary psychology offers a strong theoretical perspective on gender. In pressing this position, Buss (1996) has posed evolutionary theory as a counter to gender role theories (Eagly, 1987), arguing that women and men are not passive recipients of roles, but rather the embodiment of active adaptive strategies. From an evolutionary perspective, sex differences are to be expected in those domains in which women and men have faced different adaptive problems over the course of evolutionary history; an absence of sex differences should be the case when adaptive problems have been the same (Buss, 1995; Buss & Kenrick, 1998, in this *Handbook*).

According to Buss (1995), mate choice and same-sex competition for access to mates are domains in which males and females face different adaptive problems. These are then linked to a variety of more specific empirical findings of difference, both social (e.g., mate selection preference, attitudes toward casual sex, sexual jealousy) and cognitive (e.g., spatial rotation, spatial location memory). For example, evolutionary psychologists have proposed that for males, a partner's physical attractiveness is appreciably more important to them than it is to females while for females, a partners' socioeconomic status and ambitiousness are more important to them than to males. These mate preferences are proposed as the result of women's heavy investment in protecting offspring and hence the need to be selective in their choice of partners, and men's "investment" in locating fertile women and hence their focus on sexual attractiveness. Indeed a recent meta-analysis found support for these mate preferences (Feingold, 1992).

The evolutionary approach is also not without its critics. Some have argued that the hunt for fundamental biological causes is based on a false understanding of biology (Fausto-Sterling, 1985), and that the dismissal of culture as an explanation for differences is unwarranted (Hinde, 1995). For example, with respect to the apparent differential parental investment by males and females described above, Caporael and Brewer (1995) argued that historically and culturally, there has been a wide variety of childrearing forms with most involving some type of collective parenting rather than the nuclear mother–father parenting envisioned by evolutionary psychologists. If so, then the theory linking mate selection to offspring survival is not as straightforward as proposed.

Moreover, while evolutionary theory does not argue that observed sex differences are due solely to biological factors, it has tended to underemphasize the role of ecologically valid situational cues, to say nothing of the beliefs, values, and norms that affect the presence and form of particular behaviors. As a consequence, the plasticity and variability of behavior tends on occasion to be overlooked.

Constructionist and Postmodern Perspectives

In contrast to sex difference and evolutionary perspectives, constructionist and postmodern perspectives on gender typically question the scientific assumptions on which the empirical exploration of gender rests (Harding, 1986; Morawski, 1996; Riger 1992). According to a constructionist perspective, gender is not a trait of individuals but a dynamic construct that characterizes social interactions. Whereas a sex differences approach to communication would focus on whether women and men use different verbal and nonverbal modes, and an evolutionary perspective would ask about the adaptive significance of behavioral differences, constructionists view communication as a set of strategies for negotiating the social landscape that for various reasons becomes gendered. Because women and men have different opportunity structures, communicative behaviors such as dominance and affiliativeness become gender-linked (Bohan, 1993). In short, one does not have a gender; one does gender (West & Zimmerman, 1987).

The central tenet of constructionist perspectives is that we have no way of knowing with certainty the nature of reality. Instead of assuming the possibility of establishing universal truths, constructionist critics allege that the position of the perceiver is critical in what questions are formulated and how answers are interpreted. By this reasoning, what is conceived to be the truth is a construction based on and inextricably linked with the contexts in which it is created. Gilligan's (1982) work on moral development is typically used to represent this position.

Methodological strategies are often questioned as well. Feminist methodology emphasizes several issues, including the relationship between investigator and informant, the utility of qualitative versus quantitative methods, and presumptions of investigator neutrality. (For points of entry to these discussions, see Fine, 1992; McGrath, Kelly, & Rhodes, 1993; Morawski, 1994; Riger, 1992; Worell & Etaugh, 1994).

Constructionist and postmodern perspectives both push the question of what one can know and reject the assumptions and the methods of empirical science. From these perspectives, all categories must be questioned and no truths are independent of the social-political system from which they emerge. In the specific case of gender, this perspective calls on one to question the basic status of categories such as male and female. Gender is an agreement that resides in social transactions; it is precisely what we agree it to be (Hare-Mustin & Marecek, 1990).

For many social psychologists, this relativistic stance is foreign and unnecessarily pessimistic about the possibility of empirical progress. Yet the perspective raises important conceptual questions that must be pondered when facing the subtle links and implicit assumptions associated with gender.

Gender-in-Context Perspective

In the gender-in-context analysis adopted here, the actions of women and men are conceptualized in dynamic and in-

terdependent terms. Without denying the influences of either biology or socialization, this approach emphasizes the
flexibility, variation, and contingency of gender-related behavior. Further, this perspective assumes that gender must
be considered at multiple levels of analysis, from individual through situational to larger systems and structures. As
noted above, the recent flurry of meta-analytic studies provides considerable empirical material for the gender-in-
context perspective: the question becomes not simply
whether a sex difference exists, but more fully, what the
moderators and mediators of gender-related behavior
might be.

Although clearly dependent on empirical findings, the
gender-in-context perspective is not necessarily positivist
in its roots (see also Unger, 1996). Consistent with the evolutionary epistemology offered by Campbell (1996), the
model relies on an accepted set of conventions for interpreting the likelihood of its premises. Yet consensus can
shift, forcing rethinking of the basic assumptions.

The change-oriented social psychologist, drawing
strength from the Lewinian tradition, also recognizes that
"as is" is not necessarily so. An analysis of gender's operation at multiple levels of a system can suggest multiple
entry points for change. Organizations, for example, can
effect any number of policies to counter the processes of
sex discrimination described earlier (Fiske et al., 1991;
Reskin & Padavic, 1994). Similarly, sexual harassment can
be combated more effectively when individual, situational,
and organizational influences are all taken into account.
When done this way, interventions complement the more
frequently considered individual change strategies of education or penalization.

The perspective offered here is not "neat." It's a
"messy" model, filled with concepts operating at different
levels, bidirectional causal paths, and as-yet unspecified relationships among concepts. Yet it is, we argue, the only
reasonable way to understand gender. Within this catholic
framework, individual investigators can and will address
individual components and single relationships. From an
empirical perspective, such a choice is both sensible and
valuable. At a conceptual level, that choice needs to be embedded in the broader framework in order to develop questions and interpret answers that will fairly represent the
complexity of gender.

REFERENCES

American Psychologist, (1995) Current issues, *50,* 145–171.

Abelson, R. P. (1981). Psychological status of the script concept. *American Psychologist, 36,* 715–729.

Amancio, L. (1993). Stereotypes as ideologies. The case of
gender categories. *Revista de Psicologia Social, 8,*
163–170.

American Association of University Women. (1993). *Hostile
hallways: The survey on sexual harassment in American
schools.* Annapolis, MD: AAUW.

Archer, D., Iritani, B., Kimes, D. D., & Barrios, M. (1983).
Face-ism: Five studies of sex differences in facial prominence. *Journal of Personality and Social Psychology, 45,*
725–735.

Ashmore, R. D., Del Boca, F. K., & Wohlers, A. J. (1986).
Gender stereotypes. In R. D. Ashmore & F. K. Del Boca
(Eds.), *The social psychology of female-male relations* (pp.
69–119). Orlando, FL: Academic Press.

Baker, D. D., Terpstra, D. E., & Larntz, K. (1990). The influence of individual characteristics and severity of harassing
behavior on reactions to sexual harassment. *Sex Roles, 22,*
305–325.

Bales, R. F. (1950). *Interaction process analysis: A method for
the study of small groups.* Reading, MA: Addison-Wesley.

Banaji, M. R., & Greenwald, A. G. (1995). Implicit gender
stereotyping in judgments of fame. *Journal of Personality
and Social Psychology, 68,* 181–198.

Banaji, M. R., Hardin, C., & Rothman, A. J. (1993). Implicit
stereotyping in person judgment. *Journal of Personality
and Social Psychology, 65,* 272–281.

Barak, A., Pitterman, Y., & Yitzhaki, R. (1995). An empirical
test of the role of power differential in originating sexual
harassment. *Basic and Applied Social Psychology, 17,*
497–517.

Bargh, J. A., Raymond, P., Pryor, J. B., & Strack, F. (1995).
The attractiveness of the underling: An automatic power →
sex association and its consequences for sexual harassment.
Journal of Personality and Social Psychology, 68, 768–781.

Barnett, R. C., Raudenbush, S. W., Brennan, R. T., Pleck, J.
H., & Marshall, N. L. (1995). Change in job and marital
experiences and change in psychological distress: A longitudinal study of dual-earner couples. *Journal of Personality
and Social Psychology, 69,* 839–850.

Bartol, K. M., & Butterfield, D. A. (1976). Sex effects in evaluating leaders. *Journal of Applied Psychology, 61,* 446–454.

Bartol, K. M., & Martin, D. C. (1986). Women and men in
task groups. In R. Ashmore & F. Del Boca (Eds.), *The social psychology of female-male relations* (pp. 259–310).
New York: Academic Press.

Baumeister, R. F. (1988). Should we stop studying sex differences altogether? *American Psychologist, 43,* 1092–1095.

Baxter, J., & Kane, E. W. (1995). Dependence and independence: A cross-national analysis of gender inequality and
gender attitudes. *Gender & Society, 9,* 193–215.

Becker, B. J. (1986). Influence again: Another look at gender
differences in social influence. In J. S. Hyde & M. C. Linn
(Eds.), *The psychology of gender: Advances through meta-
analysis* (pp. 178–209). Baltimore: Johns Hopkins University Press.

Beere, C. A. (1990). *Gender roles: A handbook of tests and
measurements.* New York: Greenwood Press.

Bem, S. L. (1974). The measurement of psychological androgyny. *Journal of Personality and Social Psychology, 42,* 155–162.

Bem, S. L. (1993). *The lenses of gender.* New Haven, CT: Yale University Press.

Berger, J., Rosenholtz, S. J., & Zelditch, M., Jr. (1980). Status organizing processes. *Annual Review of Sociology, 6,* 479–508.

Berger, J., Wagner, D. G., & Zelditch, M., Jr. (1985). Expectation states theory: Review and assessment. In J. Berger & M. Zelditch, Jr. (Eds.), *Status, rewards, and influence: How expectations organize behavior* (pp. 1–72). San Francisco: Jossey-Bass.

Berger, J. J., Fizek, H., Norman, R. Z., & Zelditch, M., Jr. (1977). *Status characteristics and social interaction.* New York: Elsevier.

Berrill, K. T. (1990). Anti-gay violence and victimization in the United States. *Journal of Interpersonal Violence, 5,* 274–294.

Bielby, W. T., & Baron, J. N. (1986). Men and women at work: Sex segregation and statistical discrimination. *American Journal of Sociology, 91,* 759–799.

Biernat, M. (1991). Gender stereotypes and the relationship between masculinity and femininity: A developmental analysis. *Journal of Personality and Social Psychology, 61,* 351–365.

Biernat, M. (1993). Gender and height: Developmental patterns in knowledge and use of an accurate stereotype. *Sex Roles, 29,* 691–713.

Biernat, M., & Manis, M. (1994). Shifting standards and stereotype-based judgments. *Journal of Personality and Social Psychology, 66,* 5–20.

Bilous, F. R., & Krauss, R. M. (1988). Dominance and accommodation in the conversational behavior of same- and mixed-sex dyads. *Journal of Language and Communication, 8,* 183–194.

Bisanz, G. L., & Rule, B. G. (1989). Gender and the persuasion schema: A search for cognitive invariants. *Personality and Social Psychology Bulletin, 15,* 4–18.

Blalock, H. (1967). *Toward a theory of minority group relations.* New York: Wiley.

Bohan, J. S. (1993). Regarding gender: Essentialism, constructionism, and feminist psychology. *Psychology of Women Quarterly, 17,* 5–21.

Borgida, E., & Fiske, S. T. (Eds.). (1995). Gender stereotyping, sexual harassment, and the law. *Journal of Social Issues, 51* (1).

Bourhis, R. Y. (1993). Power, gender, and intergroup discrimination: Some minimal group experiments. In M. Zanna & J. Olson (Eds.), *The psychology of prejudice: The Ontario symposium of personality and social psychology* (pp. 171–208). Hillsdale, NJ: Erlbaum.

Bradac, J. J., & Mulac, A. (1984). Attributional consequences of powerful and powerless speech styles in a crisis-intervention context. *Journal of Language and Social Psychology, 3,* 1–19.

Breakwell, G. M. (1979). Woman: Group and identity. *Women's Studies International Quarterly, 2,* 9–17.

Briton, N. J., & Hall, J. A. (1995). Beliefs about female and male nonverbal communication. *Sex Roles, 32,* 79–90.

Brown, C. E., Dovidio, J. F., & Ellyson, S. L. (1990). Reducing sex differences in visual displays of dominance: Knowledge is power. *Personality and Social Psychology Bulletin, 16,* 358–368.

Buck, R., Miller, R. E., & Caul, W. F. (1974). Sex, personality and physiological variables in the communication of affect via facial expression. *Journal of Personality and Social Psychology, 30,* 587–596.

Burgess, D., & Borgida, E. (1997). Sexual harassment: An experimental test of sex-role spillover theory. *Personality and Social Psychology Bulletin, 23,* 63–75.

Burt, M. (1980). Cultural myths and supports for rape. *Journal of Personality and Social Psychology, 38,* 217–230.

Buss, D. M. (1995). Psychological sex differences: Origins through sexual selection. *American Psychologist, 50,* 164–168.

Buss, D. M. (1996). The evolutionary psychology of human social strategies. In E. T. Higgins & A. W. Kruglanski (Eds.), *Social psychology: Handbook of basic principles* (pp. 3–38). New York: Guilford Press.

Buss, D. M., & Kenrick, D. T. (1998). Evolutionary social psychology. In D. Gilbert, S. T. Fiske, & G. Lindzey (Eds.), *Handbook of social psychology* (4th ed., Vol. 2, pp. 000–000). New York: McGraw-Hill.

Butler, D., & Geis, F. L. (1990). Nonverbal affect responses to male and female leaders: Implications for leadership evaluations. *Journal of Personality and Social Psychology, 58,* 48–59.

Bylsma, W. H., & Major, B. (1992). Two routes to eliminating gender differences in personal entitlement: Social comparisons and performance evaluations. *Psychology of Women Quarterly, 16,* 193–200.

Cameron, D., McAlinden, R., & Leary, K. (1988). Lakoff in contexts: The social and linguistic functions of tag questions. In J. Coates & D. Cameron (Eds.), *Women in their speech communities: New perspectives on language and sex* (pp. 74–93). London: Longman.

Campbell, D. T. (1996). *From evolutionary epistemology via selection theory to a sociology of scientific validity.* Unpublished manuscript, Lehigh University.

Cann, A., & Siegfried, W. D. (1990). Gender stereotypes and dimensions of effective leader behavior. *Sex Roles, 23,* 413–419.

Caplan, P., & Larkin, J. (1991). The anatomy of dominance and self-protection. *American Psychologist, 46,* 536.

Caporael, L. R., & Brewer, M. B. (1995). Hierarchical evolutionary theory: There is an alternative and it's not creationism. *Psychological Inquiry, 6,* 31–80.

Carli, L. L. (1990). Gender, language and influence. *Journal of Personality and Social Psychology, 59,* 941–951.

Carli, L. L. (1991). Gender, status and influence. In E. J. Lawler, B. Markovsky, C. Ridgeway, & H. A. Walker (Eds.), *Advances in group processes, 8,* pp. 89–113. JAI Press, Inc.

Carli, L. L., LaFleur, S. J., & Loeber, C. C. (1995). Nonverbal behavior, gender and influence. *Journal of Personality and Social Psychology, 68,* 1030–1041.

Chusmir, L. H., & Mills, J. (1989). Gender differences in conflict resolution styles of managers: At work and at home. *Sex Roles, 20,* 149–163.

Clancy, S. M., & Dollinger, S. J. (1993). Photographic depictions of the self: Gender and age differences in social connectedness. *Sex Roles, 29,* 477–495.

Clifton, A. K., McGrath, D., & Wick, B. (1976). Stereotypes of women: A single category? *Sex Roles, 2,* 135–148.

Cohen, B. P., & Zhou, X. (1991). Status processes in enduring work groups. *American Sociological Review, 56,* 179–188.

Collins, R. (1975). *Conflict sociology: Toward an explanatory science.* New York: Academic Press.

Condor, S. (1986). Sex role beliefs and "traditional" women: Feminist and intergroup perspectives. In S. Wilkinson (Ed.), *Feminist social psychology: Developing theory and practice* (pp. 97–118). Milton Keynes, England: Open University Press.

Constantinople, A. (1973). Masculinity-femininity: An exception to a famous dictum. *Psychological Bulletin, 80,* 389–407.

Cooper, H. M. (1979). Statistically combining independent studies: A meta-analysis of sex differences in conformity research. *Journal of Personality and Social Psychology, 37,* 131–146.

Cota, A. A., & Dion, K. L. (1986). Salience of gender and sex comparison of ad hoc groups: An experimental test of distinctiveness theory. *Journal of Personality and Social Psychology, 50,* 770–776.

Crawford, M. (1995). Talking difference: On gender and language. London: Sage.

D'Augelli, A. R. (1989). Lesbian's and gay men's experiences of discrimination and harassment in a university community. *American Journal of Community Psychology, 17,* 317–321.

Deaux, K. (1996). Social identification. In E. T. Higgins & A. Kruglanski (Eds.), *Social psychology: Handbook of basic principles* (pp. 777–798). New York: Guilford.

Deaux, K., & Kite, M. (1993). Gender stereotypes. In F. L. Denmark & M. A. Paludi (Eds.), *Psychology of women: A handbook of issues and theories* (pp. 107–139). Westport, CT: Greenwood Press.

Deaux, K., & Lewis, L. L. (1984). Structure of gender stereotypes: Interrelationships among components and gender label. *Journal of Personality and Social Psychology, 46,* 991–1004.

Deaux, K., & Major, B. (1987). Putting gender into context:

An interactive model of gender-related behavior. *Psychological Review, 94,* 369–389.

Deaux, K., & Ullman, J. C. (1983). *Women of steel: Female blue-collar workers in the basic steel industry.* New York: Praeger.

Deaux, K., Winton, W., Crowley, M., & Lewis, L. L. (1985). Level of categorization and content of gender stereotypes. *Social Cognition, 3,* 145–167.

Deutsch, F. M., Lussier, J. B., & Servis, L. J. (1993). Husbands at home: Predictors of paternal participation in childcare and housework. *Journal of Personality and Social Psychology, 65,* 1154–1166.

Devine, P. G. (1989). Stereotypes and prejudice: Their automatic and controlled components. *Journal of Personality and Social Psychology, 56,* 5–18.

Dion, K. L. (1985). Sex, gender, and groups: Selected issues. In V. O'Leary, R. K. Unger, & B. Strudler-Wallson (Eds.), *Women, gender, and social psychology* (pp. 293–347). Hillsdale, NJ: Erlbaum.

Dovidio, J. F., Ellyson, S. L., Keating, C. F., Heltman, K., & Brown, C. E. (1988). The relationship of social power to visual displays of dominance between men and women. *Journal of Personality and Social Psychology, 54,* 233–242.

Driskell, J. E., Olmstead, B., & Salas, E. (1993). Task cues, dominance cues, and influence in task groups. *Journal of Applied Psychology, 78,* 51–60.

Dunbar, J., Brown, M., & Amoroso, D. M. (1973). Some correlates of attitudes toward homosexuality. *Journal of Social Psychology, 89,* 271–279.

Durand-Delvigne, A. (1993). Self, others, and gender models of the person. In M.-F. Pichevin, M.-C. Hurtig, & M. Piolat (Eds.), *Studies on the self and social cognition* (pp. 15–31). Singapore: World Scientific.

Eagly, A. H. (1973). Sex differences in influenceability. *Psychological Bulletin, 85,* 86–116.

Eagly, A. H. (1983). Gender and social influence: A social psychological analysis. *American Psychologist, 38,* 971–981.

Eagly, A. H. (1987). *Sex differences in social behavior: A social role interpretation.* Hillsdale, NJ: Erlbaum.

Eagly, A. H., & Carli, L. L. (1981). Sex of researchers and sex-typed communications as determinants of sex differences in influenceability: A meta-analysis of social influence studies. *Psychological Bulletin, 90,* 1–20.

Eagly, A. H., & Chrvala, C. (1986). Sex differences in conformity: Status and gender role interpretations. *Psychology of Women Quarterly, 10,* 203–220.

Eagly, A. H., & Crowley, M. (1986). Gender and helping behavior: A meta-analytic review of the social psychological literature. *Psychological Bulletin, 100,* 283–308.

Eagly, A. H., & Johnson, B. T. (1990). Gender and leadership style: A meta-analysis. *Psychological Bulletin, 108,* 233–256.

Eagly, A. H., & Karau, S. J. (1991). Gender and the emergence of leaders: A meta-analysis. *Journal of Personality and Social Psychology, 60,* 685–710.

Eagly, A. H., Karau, S. J., Miner, J. B., & Johnson, B. T. (1994). Gender and motivation to manage in hierarchic organizations: A meta-analysis. *Leadership Quarterly, 5,* 135–159.

Eagly, A. H., & Kite, M. E. (1987). Are stereotypes of nationalities applied to both women and men? *Journal of Personality and Social Psychology, 53,* 451–462.

Eagly, A. H., Makhijani, M. G., & Klonsky, B. G. (1992). Gender and the evaluation of leaders: A meta-analysis. *Psychological Bulletin, 111,* 3–22.

Eagly, A. H., & Mladinic, A. (1989). Gender stereotypes and attitudes toward women and men. *Personality and Social Psychology Bulletin, 15,* 543–548.

Eagly, A. H., & Mladinic, A. (1994). Are people prejudiced against women? Some answers from research on attitudes, gender stereotypes, and judgements of competence. In W. Stroebe & M. Hewstone (Eds.), *European review of social psychology* (Vol. 5, pp. 1–35). Chichester, England: John Wiley.

Eagly, A. H., & Steffen, F. J. (1984). Gender stereotypes stem from the distribution of women and men into social roles. *Journal of Personality and Social Psychology, 46,* 735–754.

Eagly, A. H., & Wood, W. (1982). Inferred sex differences in status as a determinant of gender stereotypes about social influence. *Journal of Personality and Social Psychology, 43,* 915–928.

Eagly, A. H., & Wood, W. E. (1991). Explaining sex differences in social behavior: A meta-analytic perspective. Special issue: Meta-analysis in personality and social psychology. *Personality and Social Psychology Bulletin, 17,* 306–315.

Eccles, J. S. (1994). Understanding women's educational and occupational choices: Applying the Eccles et al. model of achievement-related choices. *Psychology of Women Quarterly, 18,* 585–609.

Eccles (Parsons), J., Adler, T. F., Futterman, R., Goff, S. B., Kaczala, C. M., Mese, J. L., & Midgley, C. (1983). Expectations, values and academic behaviors. In J. T. Spence (Ed.), *Perspective on achievement and achievement motivation* (pp. 75–146). San Francisco: W. H. Freeman.

Edwards, G. H. (1992). The structure and content of the male gender role stereotype: An exploration of subtypes. *Sex Roles, 27,* 533–551.

Eisenberg, N., Roth, K., Bryniarski, K. A., & Murray, E. (1984). Sex differences in the relationship of height to children's actual and attributed social and cognitive competencies. *Sex Roles, 7/8,* 719–734.

Ellyson, S. L., Dovidio, J. F., & Brown, C. (1992). The look of power: Gender differences and similarities in visual dominance behavior. In C. Ridgeway (Ed.), *Gender, interaction, and inequality* (pp. 50–80). New York: Springer-Verlag.

Ellyson, S. L., Dovidio, J. F., & Fehr, B. J. (1981). Visual behavior and dominance in women and men. In C. Mayo & N. M. Henley (Eds.), *Gender and nonverbal behavior* (pp. 63–79). New York: Springer.

Epstein, C. F. (1970). *Woman's place: Options and limits in professional careers.* Berkeley: University of California Press.

Epstein, C. F. (1988). *Deceptive distinctions: Sex, gender and the social order.* New Haven, CT: Yale University Press.

Epstein, C. F. (1993). *Women in law.* Urbana: University of Illinois Press.

Fabes, R. A., & Martin, C. L. (1991). Gender and age stereotypes of emotionality. *Personality and Social Psychology Bulletin, 17,* 532–540.

Fain, T. C., & Anderton, D. L. (1987). Sexual harassment: Organizational context and diffuse status. *Sex Roles, 22,* 291–311.

Falbo, T., & Peplau, L. A. (1980). Power strategies in intimate relationships. *Journal of Personality and Social Psychology, 38,* 618–628.

Fausto-Sterling, A. (1985). *Myths and gender: Biological theories about women and men.* New York: Basic Books.

Feingold, A. (1992). Gender differences in mate selection preferences: A test of the parental investment model. *Psychological Bulletin, 112,* 125–139.

Fine, M. (1992). *Disruptive voices: The possibilities of feminist research.* Ann Arbor: University of Michigan Press.

Fiske, S. T. (1993). Controlling other people: The impact of power on stereotyping. *American Psychologist, 48,* 621–628.

Fiske, S. T. (1998). Stereotypes, prejudice, and discrimination. In D. Gilbert, S. T. Fiske, & G. Lindzey (Eds.), *Handbook of social psychology* (4th ed., Vol. 2, pp. 357–411). New York: McGraw-Hill.

Fiske, S. T., Bersoff, D. N., Borgida, E., Deaux, K., & Heilman, M. E. (1991). Social science research on trial: Use of sex stereotyping research in Price Waterhouse v. Hopkins. *American Psychologist, 46,* 1049–1070.

Fiske, S. T., & Glick, P. (1995). Ambivalence and stereotypes cause sexual harassment: A theory with implications for organizational change. *Journal of Social Issues, 51,* 97–115.

Fiske, S. T., & Stevens, L. E. (1993). What's so special about sex? Gender stereotyping and discrimination. In S. Oskamp & M. Costanzo (Eds.), *Gender issues in contemporary society* (pp. 173–196). Newbury Park, CA: Sage.

Fitzgerald, L. F., Gelfand, M. J., & Drasgow, F. (1995). Measuring sexual harassment: Theoretical and psychometric analysis. *Basic and Applied Social Psychology, 17,* 425–445.

Fitzgerald, L. F., & Shullman, S. L. (1993). Sexual harassment: A research analysis and agenda for the 1990s. *Journal of Vocational Behavior, 42,* 5–27.

Fitzgerald, L. F., Swan, S., & Fischer, K. (1995). Why didn't she just report him? The psychological and legal implications of women's responses to sexual harassment. *Journal of Social Issues, 51,* 117–138.

Fitzpatrick, M. A. (1991). Sex differences in marital conflict: Social psychophysiological versus social cognitive explanations. *Texts, 11,* 341–364.

Fitzpatrick, M. A., Mulac, A., & Dindia, K. (1995). Gender preferential language use in spouse and stranger interaction. *Journal of Language and Social Psychology, 14*, 18–39.

Forsyth, D., Schlenker, B. R., Leary, M. R., & McCown, N. E. (1985). Self-presentational determinants of sex differences in leadership behavior. *Small Group Behavior, 16*, 197–210.

Friedman, H., & Zebrowitz, L. A. (1992). The contribution of typical sex differences in facial maturity to sex role stereotypes. *Personality and Social Psychology Bulletin, 18*, 430–438.

Frieze, I. H., & McHugh, M. C. (1992). Power and influence strategies in violent and nonviolent marriages. *Psychology of Women Quarterly, 16*, 449–465.

Gallaher, P. E. (1992). Individual differences in nonverbal behavior: Dimensions of style. *Journal of Personality and Social Psychology, 63*, 133–145.

Giele, J. Z. (1988). Gender and sex roles. In N. J. Smelser (Ed.), *Handbook of sociology* (pp. 291–323). Newbury Park, CA: Sage.

Gilbert, L. A. (1994). Reclaiming and returning gender to context: Examples from studies of heterosexual dual-earner families. *Psychology of Women Quarterly, 18*, 539–558.

Gilligan, C. (1982). *In a different voice*. Cambridge, MA: Harvard University Press.

Giuffre, P., & Williams, C. L. (1994). Boundary lines: Labeling sexual harassment in restaurants. *Gender and Society, 8*, 378–401.

Glick, P., & Fiske, S. T. (1996). The ambivalent sexism inventory: Differentiating hostile and benevolent sexism. *Journal of Personality and Social Psychology, 70*, 491–512.

Glick, P., Wilk, K., & Perreault, M. (1995). Images of occupations: Components of gender and status in occupational stereotypes. *Sex Roles, 32*, 565–582.

Goktepe, J. R., & Schneier, C. E. (1988). Sex and gender effects in evaluating emergent leaders in small groups. *Sex Roles, 19*, 29–36.

Goldberg, P. (1968). Are women prejudiced against women? *Transaction, 5*, 178–186.

Gonzales, M. H., Pederson, J. H., Manning, D. J., & Wetter, D. W. (1990). Pardon my gaffe: Effects of sex, status, and consequent severity on accounts. *Journal of Personality and Social Psychology, 58*, 610–621.

Gottman, J. M., & Levenson, R. W. (1988). The social psychophysiology of marriage. In P. Noller & M. A. Fitzpatrick (Eds.), *Perspectives on marital interaction* (pp. 182–200). Philadelphia: Multilingual Matters.

Grossman, M., & Wood, W. (1993). Sex differences in intensity of emotional experience: A social role interpretation. *Journal of Personality and Social Psychology, 65*, 1010–1022.

Gruber, J. E., & Bjorn, L. (1986). Women's responses to sexual harassment: An analysis of sociocultural, organizational, and personal resource models. *Social Science Quarterly, 67*, 814–825.

Gruber, J. E., & Smith, M. D. (1995). Women's responses to sexual harassment: A multivariate analysis. *Basic and Applied Social Psychology, 17*, 543–562.

Gurin, P., & Markus, H. (1989). Cognitive consequences of gender identity. In S. Skevington & D. Baker (Eds.), *The social identity of women* (pp. 152–172). London: Sage.

Gurin, P., & Townsend, A. (1986). Properties of gender identity and their implications for gender consciousness. *British Journal of Social Psychology, 25*, 139–148.

Gutek, B. (1985). *Sex and the workplace*. San Francisco: Jossey-Bass.

Gutek, B., & O'Connor, M. (1995). The empirical basis for the reasonable woman standard. *Journal of Social Issues, 51*, 151–166.

Guttentag, M., & Secord, P. (1983). *Too many women?* Beverly Hills, CA: Sage.

Haddock, G., & Zanna, M. P. (1994). Preferring "housewives" to "feminists": Categorization and the favorability of attitudes toward women. *Psychology of Women Quarterly, 18*, 25–52.

Hall, J. A. (1984). *Nonverbal sex differences: Communication accuracy and expressive style*. Baltimore: The Johns Hopkins University Press.

Hall, J. A. (1987). On explaining gender differences: The case of nonverbal communication. In P. Shaver & C. Hendrick (Eds.), *Sex and gender* (pp. 177–200). Newbury Park, CA: Sage.

Harding, S. (1986). *The science question in feminism*. Ithaca, NY: Cornell University Press.

Hare-Mustin, R. T., & Marecek, J. (1990). *Making a difference*. New Haven: Yale University Press.

Henley, N. M. (1977). Body politics: Power, sex, and nonverbal communication. Englewood Cliffs, NJ: Prentice-Hall.

Henley, N. M., Miller, M. D., Kaminsky, D., & Nguyen, D. N. (1996). *Newspapers use less violent terms in reporting violence against gays and straights*. Poster presented at the American Psychological Society, San Francisco: June.

Herek, G. M. (1990). The context of anti-gay violence: Notes on cultural and psychological heterosexism. *Journal of Interpersonal Violence, 5*, 316–333.

Herek, G. M., & Berrill, K. T. (1992). *Hate crimes: Confronting violence against lesbians and gay men*. Newbury Park, CA: Sage.

Herek, G. M., & Capitanio, J. P. (1995). Black heterosexuals' attitudes toward lesbians and gay men in the United States. *Journal of Sex Research, 32*, 95–105.

Hershey, S., & Werner, E. (1975). Dominance in marital decision making in women's liberation and non-women's liberation families. *Family Process, 14*, 223–233.

Hinde, R. A. (1995). The adaptionist approach has its limits. *Psychological Inquiry, 6*, 50–53.

Hochschild, A. (with A. Machung). (1989). *The second shift*. New York: Viking.

Hochschild, A. R. (1983). *The managed heart: Commercialization of human feeling*. Berkeley: University of California Press.

Howard, J. A., Blumstein, P., & Schwartz, P. (1986). Sex, power, and influence tactics in intimate relationships. *Journal of Personality and Social Psychology, 51*, 102–109.

Huston, A. C. (1983). Sex-typing. In E. M. Heatherington (Ed.), *Handbook of child psychology: Socialization, personality, and social development* (Vol. 4, pp. 388–467). New York: Wiley.

Hyde, J. S. (1994). Can meta-analysis make feminist transformations in psychology? *Psychology of Women Quarterly, 18*, 451–462.

Hyde, J. S., & Linn, M. C. (Eds.). (1986). *The psychology of gender: Advances through meta-analysis.* Baltimore: The Johns Hopkins University Press.

Israel, J., & Tajfel, H. (Eds.). (1972). *The context of social psychology: A critical assessment.* London: Academic Press.

Jackson, L., & Ervin, K. S. (1992). Height stereotypes of women and men: The liabilities of shortness for both sexes. *Journal of Social Psychology, 132*, 433–445.

Jacobs, J. E., & Eccles, J. S. (1992). The impact of mothers' gender-role stereotypic beliefs on mothers' and children's ability perceptions. *Journal of Personality and Social Psychology, 63*, 932–944.

Johnson, C. (1992). Gender, formal authority, and leadership. In C. Ridgeway (Ed.), *Gender, interaction, and inequality.* New York: Springer-Verlag.

Johnson, C. (1994). Gender, legitimate authority, and leader-subordinate conversations. *American Sociological Review, 59*, 122–135.

Johnson, P. (1976). Women and power: Toward a theory of effectiveness. *Journal of Social Issues, 32*, 99–109.

Johnson, R. A., & Schulman, G. I. (1989). Gender-role composition and role entrapment in decision-making groups. *Gender and Society, 3*, 355–372.

Josephs, R. A., Markus, H. R., & Tafarodi, R. W. (1992). Gender and self-esteem. *Journal of Personality and Social Psychology, 63*, 391–402.

Kanter, R. M. (1977). *Men and women of the corporation.* New York: Basic Books.

Kashima, Y., Yamaguchi, S., Kim, U., Choi, S.-C., Gelfand, M., & Yuki, M. (1995). Culture, gender, and self: A perspective from individualism-collectivism research. *Journal of Personality and Social Psychology, 69*, 925–937.

Kent, R. L., & Moss, S. E. (1994). Effects of sex and gender role on leader emergence. *Academy of Management Journal, 37*, 1335–1346.

Kite, M. E., & Deaux, K. (1987). Gender belief systems: Homosexuality and implicit inversion theory. *Psychology of Women Quarterly, 11*, 83–96.

Kitzinger, C. (Ed.). (1994). Should psychologists study sex differences? *Feminism & Psychology, 4*, 501–546.

Klassen, A. D., Williams, C. J., Levitt, E. E., & O'Gorman, H. J. (Eds.). (1989). *Sex and morality in the U.S.: An empirical enquiry under the auspices of The Kinsey Institute.* Middletown, CT: Wesleyan University Press.

Knight, G. P., Fabes, R. A., & Higgins, D. A. (1996). Concerns about drawing causal inferences from meta-analyses: An example in the study of gender differences in aggression. *Psychological Bulletin, 119*, 410–421.

Kollock, P., Blumstein, P., & Schwartz, P. (1985). Sex and power in interaction: Conversational privileges and duties. *American Sociological Review, 50*, 34–46.

Lach, D. H., & Gwartney-Gibbs, P. A. (1993). Sociological perspectives on sexual harassment and workplace dispute resolution. *Journal of Vocational Behavior, 42*, 102–115.

LaFrance, M. (1991). School for scandal: Different educational experiences for females and males. *Gender and Education, 3*, 3–13.

LaFrance, M. (1992). Gender and interruptions: Individual infraction or violation of the social order. *Psychology of Women Quarterly, 16*, 497–512.

LaFrance, M., & Banaji, M. (1992). Towards a reconsideration of the gender-emotion relationship. In M. S. Clark (Ed.), *Emotion and social behavior: Review of Personality and Social Psychology* (Vol. 14). Newbury Park, CA: Sage.

LaFrance, M., Brownell, H., & Hahn, E. (in press). Prerogatives to act and be acted upon: Interpersonal verbs, gender, and implicit causality. *Social Psychology Quarterly.*

LaFrance, M., & Henley, N. M. (1994). On oppressing hypotheses or sex differences in nonverbal sensitivity revisited. In L. Radtke & H. Stam (Eds.), *Power and gender.* London: Sage.

Lakoff, R. (1973). Language and women's place. *Language in Society, 2*, 45–80.

Landrine, H. (1985). Race × class stereotypes of women. *Sex Roles, 13*, 65–75.

Landrine, H. (Ed.). (1995). *Bringing cultural diversity to feminist psychology.* Washington, DC: American Psychological Association.

Leary, M. R. (1989). Self presentational processes in leadership. In R. A. Giacalone & P. Rosenfeld (Eds.), *Impression management in the organization.* Hillsdale, NJ: Lawrence Erlbaum Associates.

Leet-Pellegrini, H. M. (1980). Conversational dominance as a function of gender and expertise. In H. Giles, W. P. Robinson, & P. M. Smith (Eds.), *Language: Social psychological perspectives* (pp. 97–104). New York: Pergamon Press.

Lefkowitz, J. (1994). Sex-related differences in job attitudes and dispositional variables: Now you see them, ... *Academy of Management Journal, 37*, 323–349.

Lewin, K. (1951). *Field theory in social science.* New York: Harper.

Lorenzi-Cioldi, F. (1988). *Individus dominants et groupes dominés: Images masculines et feminines.* Grenoble: Presses Universitaires de Grenoble.

Lorenzi-Cioldi, F., & Deaux, K. (in preparation). *Group homogeneity as a function of relative social status and information processing goals.*

Lorenzi-Cioldi, F., Eagly, A. H., & Stewart, T. L. (1995). Homogeneity of gender groups in memory. *Journal of Experimental Social Psychology.*

Maccoby, E. E. (1990). Gender and relationships: A developmental account. *American Psychologist, 45*, 513–520.

Major, B. (1994). From social inequality to personal entitlement: The role of social comparisons, legitimacy appraisals, and group membership. *Advances in experimental social psychology, 26*, 293–355.

Malamuth, N. (1981). Rape proclivity among males. *Journal of Social Issues, 37*(4), 138–154.

Malamuth, N. M. (1989). The attraction to sexual aggression scale: Part one. *Journal of Sex Research, 26*, 26–49.

Malamuth, N. M., & Briere, J. (1986). Sexual violence in the media: Indirect effects on aggression against women. *Journal of Social Issues, 42*, 75–92.

Malamuth, N. M., & Brown, L. M. (1994). Sexually aggressive men's perceptions of women's communications: Testing three explanations. *Journal of Personality and Social Psychology, 67*, 699–712.

Mansfield, P. K., Koch, P. B., Henderson, J., Vicary, J. R., Cohn, M., & Young, E. W. (1991). The job climate for women in traditionally male blue-collar occupations. *Sex Roles, 25*, 63–79.

Martin, C. L., & Parker, S. (1995). Folk theories about sex and race differences. *Personality and Social Psychology Bulletin, 21*, 45–57.

Mazer, D. B., & Percival, E. F. (1989). Students' experience of sexual harassment at a small university. *Sex Roles, 20*, 1–22.

McGrath, J. E. (1984). *Groups: Interaction and performance*. Englewood Cliffs, NJ: Prentice-Hall.

McGrath, J. E., Kelly, J. R., & Rhodes, J. E. (1993). A feminist perspective on research methodology: Some metatheoretical issues, contrasts, and choices. In S. Oskamp & M. Costanzo (Eds.), *Gender issues in contemporary society* (pp. 19–37). Newbury Park, CA: Sage.

McGuire, W. J. (1984). Search for the self: Going beyond self-esteem and the reactive self. In R. A. Zucker, J. Arnoff, & A. I. Rabin (Eds.), *Personality and the prediction of behavior* (pp. 73–120). New York: Academic Press.

McGuire, W. J., & McGuire, C. V. (1981). The spontaneous self-concept as affected by personal distinctiveness. In M. D. Lynch, A. A. Norem-Hebeisen, & K. J. Gergen (Eds.), *Self-concept: Advances in theory and research*. Cambridge, MA: Ballinger.

McGuire, W. J., McGuire, C. V., & Winton, W. (1979). Effects of household sex composition on the salience of one's gender in the spontaneous self-concept. *Journal of Experimental Social Psychology, 15*, 77–90.

Megargee, E. (1969). Influence of sex roles on the manifestation of leadership. *Journal of Applied Psychology, 52*, 377–382.

Merton, R. K. (1968). *Social theory and social structure*. New York: Free Press.

Meyer, S. L., Murphy, C. M., & Cascardi, M. (1991). Gender and relationships: Beyond the peer group. *American Psychologist, 46*, 537.

Michael, R. T., Gagnon, J. H., Laumann, E. O., & Kolata, G. (1994). *Sex in America: A definitive survey*. Boston: Little, Brown.

Miles, C. C. (1935). Sex in social psychology. In C. Murchison (Ed.), *A handbook of social psychology* (Vol. 2, pp. 683–797). New York: Russell & Russell.

Miller, D. T., & Turnbull, W. (1986). Expectancies and interpersonal processes. *Annual Review of Psychology, 37*, 233–356.

Mizrahi, K., & Deaux, K. (1997). *Social identification and ingroup favoritism: The case of gender*. Manuscript submitted for publication.

Morawski, J. (1996). Gender theories. In S. I. Kutler (Ed.), *Encyclopedia of the United States in the twentieth century* (Vol. 2, pp. 899–915). New York: Charles Scribner's Sons.

Morawski, J. G. (1994). *Practicing feminisms, reconstructing psychology: Notes on a liminal science*. Ann Arbor: University of Michigan Press.

Morgado, I. A., Cangemi, J. P., Miller, R., & O'Connor, J. (1993). Accuracy of decoding facial expressions in those engaged in people-oriented activities vs. those engaged in non-people oriented activities. *Studia Psychologica, 35*, 73–80.

Moscovici, S. (1988). Notes towards a description of social representations. *European Journal of Social Psychology, 18*, 211–250.

Moskowitz, D. S., Suh, E. J., & Desaulniers, J. (1994). Situational influences on gender differences in agency and communion. *Journal of Personality and Social Psychology, 66*, 753–761.

Mulac, A. (1989). Men's and women's talk in same-gender and mixed-gender dyads. Power or polemic? *Journal of Language and Social Psychology, 8*, 249–270.

Nelson, T. E., Biernat, M., & Manis, M. (1990). Everyday base rates (sex stereotypes): Potent and resilient. *Journal of Personality and Social Psychology, 59*, 664–675.

Noller, P. (1993). Gender and emotion communication in marriage: Different cultures or differential social power? Special issue: Emotion communication, culture, and power. *Journal of Language and Social Psychology, 12*, 132–152.

Noseworthy, C. M., & Lott, A. J. (1984). The cognitive organization of gender-stereotypic categories. *Personality and Social Psychology Bulletin, 10*, 474–481.

Ng, S. H., & Bradac, J. J. (1993). *Power in language: Verbal communication and social influence*. Newbury Park, CA: Sage.

Nyquist, L. V., & Spence, J. T. (1986). Effects of dispositional dominance and sex-role expectations on leadership behaviors. *Journal of Personality and Social Psychology, 50*, 87–93.

Oakes, P. (1987). The salience of social categories. In J. Turner, M. Hogg, P. Oakes, S. Reicher, & M. Wetherell, *Rediscovering the social group: A self-categorization theory*. Oxford: Basil Blackwell.

O'Barr, W. M., & Atkins, S. (1980). "Women's language" or

"powerless language"? In S. McConnell-Ginet, R. Borker, & N. Fulman (Eds.), *Women and language in literature and society* (pp. 93–110). New York: Praeger.

Olian, J. D., Schwab, D. P., & Haberfeld, Y. (1988). The impact of applicant gender compared to qualifications on hiring recommendations: A meta-analysis of experimental studies. *Organizational Behavior and Human Decision Processes, 41*, 180–195.

Petty, M. M., & Miles, R. H. (1976). Leader sex-role stereotyping in a female dominated work culture. *Personnel Psychology, 29*, 393–404.

Porter, N., & Geis, F. L. (1981). Women and nonverbal leadership cues: When seeing is not believing. In C. Mayo & N. Henley (Eds.), *Gender and nonverbal behavior* (pp. 39–61). New York: Springer-Verlag.

Porter, N., Geis, F. L., Cooper, E., & Newman, E. (1985). Androgyny and leadership in mixed sex groups. *Journal of Personality and Social Psychology, 49*, 808–823.

Pryor, J. B. (1987). Sexual harassment proclivities in men. *Sex Roles, 17*, 269–290.

Pryor, J. B., Giedd, J. L., & Williams, K. B. (1995). A social psychological model for predicting sexual harassment. *Journal of Social Issues, 51*, 69–84.

Pryor, J. B., & Whalen, N. J. (1996). A typology of sexual harassment: Characteristics of harassers and social circumstances under which sexual harassment occurs. In W. O'Donohue (Ed.), *Sexual harassment: Theory, research, and treatment*. Needham Heights, MA: Allyn & Bacon.

Ragins, B. R., & Sundstrom, E. (1989). Gender and power in organizations: A longitudinal perspective. *Psychological Bulletin, 105*, 51–88.

Reskin, B. F., & Padavic, I. (1988). Supervisors as gatekeepers: Male supervisors' response to women's integration in plant jobs. *Social Problems, 35*, 536–550.

Reskin, B. F., & Padavic, I. (1994). *Women and men at work*. Thousand Oaks, CA: Pine Forge Press.

Reskin, B. F., & Ross, C. E. (1992). Jobs, authority, and earnings among managers. *Work and Occupations, 19*, 342–365.

Ridgeway, C. L. (1981). Nonconformity, competence, and influence in groups: A test of two theories. *American Sociological Review, 46*, 333–347.

Ridgeway, C. L. (1987). Nonverbal behavior, dominance, and the basis of status in task groups. *American Sociological Review, 52*, 683–694.

Ridgeway, C. L. (1992). Gender and the role of interaction in inequality. In C. L. Ridgeway (Ed.), *Gender, interaction, and inequality*. New York: Springer-Verlag.

Ridgeway, C. L., & Berger, J. (1986). Expectations, legitimation, and dominance behavior in task groups. *American Sociological Review, 51*, 603–617.

Riger, S. (1992). Epistemological debates, feminist voices: Science, social values, and the study of women. *American Psychologist, 47*, 730–740.

Riggio, R. E., & Friedman, H. (1986). Impression formation:

The role of expressive behavior. *Journal of Personality and Social Psychology, 50*, 421–427.

Roberts, T. A., & Nolen-Hoeksema, S. (1994). Gender comparisons in responsiveness to others' evaluations in achievement settings. *Psychology of Women Quarterly, 18*, 221–240.

Rose, S., & Frieze, I. H. (1989). Young singles' scripts for a first date. *Gender and Society, 3*, 258–268.

Rossi, A. S. (1964). Equality between the sexes: An immodest proposal. In R. J. Lifton (Ed.), *The woman in America* (pp. 98–143). Boston: Beacon.

Ruble, D. N., & Martin, C. L. (in press). Gender development. In W. Damon (Ed.), *Handbook of child psychology* (5th ed.) [Vol. 3: Social, emotional and personality development, N. Eisenberg (Ed.)].

Rudman, L. A., Borgida, E., & Robertson, B. A. (1995). Suffering in silence: Procedural justice versus gender socialization issues in university sexual harassment grievance procedures. *Basic and Applied Social Psychology, 17*, 519–541.

Sagrestano, L. M. (1992). The use of power and influence in a gendered world. Special issue: Women and power. *Psychology of Women Quarterly, 16*, 439–447.

Sanbonmatsu, D. M., Akimoto, S. A., & Gibson, B. D. (1994). Stereotype-based blocking in social explanation. *Personality and Social Psychology Bulletin, 20*, 71–81.

Sayers, S. L., Baucom, D. H., & Tierney, A. M. (1993). Sex roles, interpersonal control and depression: Who can get their way? *Journal of Research in Personality, 27*, 377–395.

Schulz, M. (1975). The semantic derogation of women. In B. Thorne & N. Henley (Eds.), *Language, gender and society*. Rowley, MA: Newbury House.

Sheilds, C. (1995). *The Stone diaries*. New York: Penguin. [Viking Penguin, 1994]

Shields, S. (1975). Functionalism, Darwinism, and the psychology of women: A study in social myth. *American Psychologist, 30*, 739–754.

Shelton, B. A. (1992). *Women, men, and time: Gender differences in paid work, housework, and leisure*. Westport, CT: Greenwood Press.

Sidanius, J., Pratto, F., & Bobo, L. (1994). Social dominance orientation and the political psychology of gender: A case of invariance? *Journal of Personality and Social Psychology, 67*, 998–1011.

Six, B., & Eckes, T. (1991). A closer look at the complex structure of gender stereotypes. *Sex Roles, 24*, 57–71.

Skevington, S., & Baker, D. (Eds.). (1989). *The social identity of women*. London: Sage.

Skrypnek, B. J., & Snyder, M. (1982). On the self-perpetuating nature of stereotypes about women and men. *Journal of Experimental Social Psychology, 18*, 277–291.

Slevin, K. F., & Aday, D. P., Jr. (1993). Gender differences in self-evaluations of information about current affairs. *Sex Roles, 29*, 11–12.

Smith-Lovin, L., & Brody, C. (1989). Interruptions in group

discussions: The effects of gender and group composition. *American Sociological Review, 54*, 424–435.

Snodgrass, S. E. (1985). Women's intuition: The effect of subordinate role on interpersonal sensitivity. *Journal of Personality and Social Psychology, 49*, 146–155.

Snodgrass, S. E. (1992). Further effects of role versus gender on interpersonal sensitivity. *Journal of Personality and Social Psychology, 62*, 154–158.

Snyder, M., Tanke, E. D., & Berscheid, E. (1977). Social perception and interpersonal behavior: On the self-fulfilling nature of social stereotypes. *Journal of Personality and Social Psychology, 35*, 656–666.

Spence, J. T. (1985). Gender identity and implications for concepts of masculinity and femininity. In T. B. Sondereggr (Ed.), *Nebraska symposium on motivation: Psychology and gender* (Vol. 32, pp. 59–96). Lincoln: University of Nebraska Press.

Spence, J. T. (1993). Gender-related traits and gender ideology: Evidence for a multifactor theory. *Journal of Personality and Social Psychology, 64*, 624–635.

Spence, J. T., & Buckner, C. (1995). The enigma of masculinity and femininity: Gender identity and its contribution to gender-differentiating phenomena. In P. Kalbfleish & M. Cody (Eds.), *Gender, power, and communication in human relationships* (pp. 105–138). Hillsdale, NJ: Erlbaum.

Spence, J. T., Deaux, K., & Helmreich, R. L. (1985). Sex roles in contemporary American society. In G. Lindzey & E. Aronson (Eds.), *The handbook of social psychology* (3rd. ed., pp. 149–178). New York: Random House.

Spence, J. T., & Hahn, E. D. (1997). The Attitudes toward Women Scale and attitude change in college students. *Psychology of Women Quarterly, 21*, 17–34.

Spence, J. T., & Helmreich, R. (1972). The Attitudes toward Women Scale. *JSAS Catalog of Selected Documents in Psychology, 2*, ms. #153.

Spence, J. T., Helmreich, R. L., & Holahan, C. K. (1979). Negative and positive components of psychological masculinity and femininity and their relationships to self-reports of neurotic and acting out behaviors. *Journal of Personality and Social Psychology, 37*, 1673–1682.

Spence, J. T., Helmreich, R. L., & Stapp, J. (1974). The Personal Attributes Questionnaire: A measure of sex-role stereotypes and masculinity and femininity. *JSAS: Catalog of Selected Documents in Psychology, 4*, 43–44.

Spence, J. T., Helmreich, R. L., & Stapp, J. (1975). Ratings of self and peers on sex role attributes and their relation to self-esteem and conceptions of masculinity and femininity. *Journal of Personality and Social Psychology, 32*, 29–39.

Steffen, V. J., & Eagly, A. H. (1985). Implicit theories about influence style: The effects of status and sex. *Personality and Social Psychology Bulletin, 11*, 191–205.

Stewart, A. J., & Winter, D. L. (1976). Arousal of the power motive in women. *Journal of Consulting and Clinical Psychology, 44*, 495–496.

Stokes, J., Riger, S., & Sullivan, M. (1995). *Measuring the working environment for women in corporate settings.* Manuscript under review.

Stoppard, J. M., & Gunn-Gruchy, C. D. (1993). Gender, context, and expression of positive emotion. *Personality and Social Psychology Bulletin, 19*, 143–150.

Swim, J., Borgida, E., Maruyama, G., & Myers, D. G. (1989). Joan McKay versus John McKay: Do gender stereotypes bias evaluations? *Psychological Bulletin, 105*, 409–429.

Swim, J. K. (1994). Perceived versus meta-analytic effect sizes: An assessment of the accuracy of gender stereotypes. *Journal of Personality and Social Psychology, 66*, 21–36.

Swim, J. K., Aikin, K. J., Hall, W. S., & Hunter, B. A. (1995). Sexism and racism: Old-fashioned and modern prejudices. *Journal of Personality and Social Psychology, 68*, 199–214.

Swim, J. K., & Sanna, L. J. (1996). He's skilled, she's lucky: A meta-analysis of observers' attributions for women's and men's successes and failures. *Personality and Social Psychology Bulletin, 22*, 507–519.

Tangri, S., Burt, M. R., & Johnson, L. B. (1982). Sexual harassment at work: Three explanatory models. *Journal of Social Issues, 38*, 33–54.

Tannen, D. (1990). *You just don't understand.* New York: Ballentine.

Terman, L., & Miles, C. C. (1936). *Sex and personality.* New York: McGraw-Hill.

Thorne, B., & Henley, N. M. (1975). *Language and sex: Difference and dominance.* Rowley, MA: Newbury House.

Thorne, B., Kramarae, C., & Henley, N. M. (Eds.). (1983). *Language, gender and society.* Rowley, MA: Newbury House.

Tougas, F., Brown, R., Beaton, A. M., & Joly, S. (1995). Neosexism: Plus ça change, plus c'est pareil. *Personality and Social Psychology Bulletin, 21*, 842–849.

Unger, R. (1996). Using the master's tools: Epistemology and empiricism. In S. Wilkinson (Ed.), *Feminist social psychologies: International perspectives* (pp. 165–181). Buckingham, England: Open University Press.

U.S. Equal Employment Opportunity Commission (1980). Guidelines on discrimination because of sex. *Federal Register, 45*, 74676–74677.

Vickberg, S. M. J., & Deaux, K. (1995). *Are all women white? Implicit assumptions of race in stereotypes about women.* Poster presented at American Psychological Society, June.

Villimez, C., Eisenberg, N., & Carroll, J. L. (1986). Sex differences in the relation of children's height and weight to academic performance and others' attributions of competence. *Sex Roles, 11/12*, 667–681.

West, C., & Fenstermaker, S. (1995). Doing difference. *Gender & Society, 9*, 8–37.

West, C., & Zimmerman, D. H. (1987). Doing gender. *Gender & Society, 1*, 125–151.

White, J. W., & Kowalski, R. M. (in press). Male violence toward women: An integrated perspective. In R. Geen & E. Donnerstein (Eds.), *Human aggression: Theories, research, and implications for policies.* New York: Academic Press.

Williams, J., & Giles, H. (1978). The changing status of women in society: An intergroup perspective. In H. Tajfel (Ed.), *Differentiation between social groups: Studies in the social psychology of intergroup relations*. London: Academic Press.

Williams, J. A. (1984). Gender and intergroup behaviour: Towards an integration. *British Journal of Social Psychology, 23*, 311–316.

Williams, J. E., & Best, D. L. (1982). *Measuring sex stereotypes: A thirty-nation study*. Newbury Park, CA: Sage.

Winter, D. G. (1988). The power motive in women—and men. *Journal of Personality and Social Psychology, 54*, 510–519.

Wood, W. (1987). Meta-analytic review of sex differences in group performance. *Psychological Bulletin, 102*, 53–71.

Wood, W., & Karten, J. (1986). Sex differences in interaction style as a product of inferred sex differences in competence. *Journal of Personality and Social Psychology, 50*, 341–347.

Wood, W., & Rhodes, N. (1992). Sex differences in interaction style in task groups. In C. Ridgeway (Ed.), *Gender, interaction and inequality* (pp. 97–121). New York: Springer-Verlag.

Worrell, J., & Etaugh, C. (1994). Transforming theory and research with women: Themes and variation. *Psychology of Women Quarterly, 18*, 443–450.

Wyatt, G. E., & Riederle, M. (1995). The prevalence and context of sexual harassment among African American and White American women. *Journal of Interpersonal Violence, 10*, 309–321.

Wyche, K. F., & Crosby, F. J. (1996). *Women's ethnicities: Journeys through psychology*. Boulder, CO: Westview Press.

Yamada, E. M., Tjosvold, D., & Draguns, J. G. (1983). Effects of sex-linked situations and sex composition on cooperation and styles of interaction. *Sex Roles, 9*, 541–553.

Yoder, J. D. (1991). Rethinking tokenism: Looking beyond the numbers. *Gender and Society, 5*, 178–192.

Yoder, J. D., & Kahn, A. S. (1992). Toward a feminist understanding of women and power. *Psychology of Women Quarterly, 16*, 381–388.

Zanna, M. P., & Pack, S. J. (1975). On the self-fulfilling nature of apparent sex differences in behavior. *Journal of Experimental Social Psychology, 11*, 583–591.

Zimmer, L. (1988). Tokenism and women in the workplace: The limits of gender-neutral theory. *Social Problems, 35*, 64–77.

NAME INDEX

SUBJECT INDEX